USA TODAY SPORTS

# RON SHANDLER'S 2019
# BASEBALL
# FORECASTER
## AND ENCYCLOPEDIA OF FANALYTICS

TRIUMPH
BOOKS

This book is available in quantity at special discounts for your group or organization. For further information, contact:

**Triumph Books LLC**
814 North Franklin Street
Chicago, Illinois 60610
(312) 337-0747
www.triumphbooks.com

Printed in U.S.A.
ISBN: 978-1-62937-613-4

Rotisserie League Baseball is a registered trademark of the Rotisserie League Baseball Association, Inc.

Statistics provided by Baseball Info Solutions

Cover design by Brent Hershey
Front cover photograph by Brad Mills-USA TODAY Sports
Author photograph by Kevin Hurley

## Ron Shandler's BASEBALL FORECASTER

### Editors
Ray Murphy
Brent Hershey

### Associate Editors
Brandon Kruse
Ryan Bloomfield

• • • • • •

### Tech/Data/Charts
Matt Cederholm
Mike Krebs
Rob Rosenfeld

### Graphic Design
Brent Hershey

### Player Commentaries
Ryan Bloomfield
Rob Carroll
Brant Chesser
Arik Florimonte
Brent Hershey
Brandon Kruse
Ray Murphy
Stephen Nickrand
Kristopher Olson
Greg Pyron
Brian Rudd
Brian Slack
Paul Sporer
Jock Thompson
Rod Truesdell

### Research and Articles
Matt Cederholm
Patrick Davitt
James Ferretti
Arik Florimonte
David Martin
Ray Murphy
Jeff Zimmerman
Fred Zinkie

### Prospects
Chris Blessing
Rob Gordon
Tom Mulhall

### Injury Chart
Rick Wilton

# Acknowledgments

Producing the *Baseball Forecaster* has been a team effort for a number of years now; the list of credits to the left is where the heavy lifting gets done. On behalf of Ron, Brent, and Ray, our most sincere thanks to each of those key contributors.

We are just as grateful to the rest of the BaseballHQ.com staff, who do the yeoman's work in populating the website with 12 months of incredible content: Dave Adler, Andy Andres, Matt Beagle, Dan Becker, Alex Beckey, Bob Berger, Derrick Boyd, Brian Brickley, Ed DeCaria, Doug Dennis, Matt Dodge, Alec Dopp, Greg Fishwick, Neil FitzGerald, Brandon Gavett, Sam Grant, Rick Green, Phil Hertz, Ed Hubbard, Tom Kephart, Brad Kullman, Chris Lee, Thomas McFeeley, Bill McKnight, Harold Nichols, Frank Noto, Josh Paley, Nick Richards, Peter Sheridan, Andy Smith, Tanner Smith, Skip Snow, Matthew St-Germain, Jeffrey Tomich, Nick Trojanowski, Michael Weddell and Mike Werner.

Thank you to all our industry colleagues, a truly impressive group. They are competitors, but they are also colleagues working to grow this industry, which is never a more evident than at our annual First Pitch Arizona gathering each November.

Thank you to Chris Pirrone, Ryan Bonini, and the team at USA Today Sports Media Group.

Thank you for all the support from the folks at Triumph Books and Action Printing.

And of course, thank *you*, readers, for your interest in what we all have to say. Your kind words, support and (respectful) criticism move us forward on the fanalytic continuum more than you know. We are grateful for your readership.

•

**From Brent Hershey**  For whatever reason, "sharing" has been on my mind lately. Maybe it's from the year-long work alongside all the shining *Baseball Forecaster* and BaseballHQ. com staff members. Or, from leading these projects with Ray, in a unique but fully transparent partnership that (we trust) extends Ron's inquisitive yet practical spirit. Perhaps it's from my lifestage, as daughters Dillon and Eden and wife Lorie each explore new worlds, only to return and re-live a portion with our family unit. Or it could be the anticipation of presenting a project like this with you, the reader. A heartfelt thanks to you all—whether you're the "share-er" or the "share-ee." Everyone benefits.

**From Ray Murphy**  It says "2019" on the cover of this book, which means that somehow 20 years have gone by since Ron first hired me. Ron still provides the DNA for this publication, and I remain as excited to work with him today as I was 20 years ago. Brent brings consistency, depth, and wisdom to our partnership, which is all the more impressive when you consider that the bulk of our interactions occur via Slack—he's even better in person. Our entire staff merits a 5555 AAA Mayberry rating; they are sharp analysts and terrific people. At home, my wife Jennifer raises the bar every year: this year, she's provided her usual full support of this project while resuming her own career. Her example is a daily reminder that what we do here barely qualifies as work. Teaching? Now that's *work*.

**From Ron Shandler**  As always, immense gratitude to Ray and Brent, the lead shepherds for this annual effort. Along with the dozens of talented BaseballHQ.com analysts, producing this bible has become a well-oiled machine.

Thank you for your support, whether this is your first year or 33rd. A lifetime of indebtedness for the career you've given me.

It's been four years since my last full family appreciation. For those keeping track: Darielle (27) still lives the NYC life as a stage manager and theatre techie. Justina (26) writes, performs and teaches songwriting at University of Miami… and to inmates at two penitentiaries. New addition Michele (28) is plotting out her "Less Pork, More Parsnips" career path. And if you come to Port St. Lucie for Mets spring training, say hi to Sue (and her bff Wilmer Flores) at the VIP Will Call window. I'll be in Section 105.

I dedicate #33 to Mart, who never really knew how big a role he had in all this.

# TABLE OF CONTENTS

# Losing

*by Ron Shandler*

In the seventh inning of the final game of the regular season, Marlins outfielder Lewis Brinson stepped in against Mets starter Noah Syndergaard. It was a meaningless at-bat in a meaningless game for two players who would probably be spending October at beer fests or fishing tournaments.

But Brinson took an 0-2 slider and lifted a flare into centerfield that dropped for a base hit. The stroke capped a forgettable rookie season in which he failed to get his batting average above the Mendoza Line. That final hit amidst a .232 September was not nearly enough to push him past .197 for the year.

But the innocuous flare elevated my fantasy team's aggregate batting average by .0003. That was enough to lift me one spot in the batting average standings. That one point propelled me up a full place in the overall standings, helping me achieve the goal I had set for myself in mid-season when it looked like I had a chance. It was my first taste of the Promised Land all year, and I finally reached it as the books closed on 2018.

Sweet success!

But it was less a revelry in glory than a wave of relief. That mid-season goal was to avoid finishing in last place, something I had never done in any league in 34 years of playing this game. Brinson's hit lifted me to 14th place, the Promised Land of Anywhere But Last.

The solace I felt in staving off that failure provided scant satisfaction. This was not the only league where I risked scraping bottom. In all, 2018 was my worst fantasy season ever. In my six leagues this past year, the results were arrrgh-inspiring:

| | | |
|---|---|---|
| Tout Wars | 15-team mixed redraft | 13th |
| XFL | 15-team mixed dynasty | 8th |
| NFBC AFL | 15-team, 50-player D&H | 12th |
| BABS Exhibition | 10-team, 50-player D&H | 8th |
| Private League 1 | 15-team mixed keeper | 14th |
| Private League 2 | 12-team H2H mixed | 1st[1] |

In all, 2018 was a really crappy year for me, in many ways, but it got me to thinking about the whole concept of winning. We spend so much time talking about it. What it takes to win. How to get an edge. Heck, even the promotional taglines for this book and BaseballHQ.com over the years have always been about winning:

*"For winners only, please"*

*"The winner's bible"*

*"Fantasy baseball intelligence for winners"*

*"More than three decades of winning"*

*"The fantasy baseball experts that know how to WIN"*

It's a downright obsession. But when it comes down to it, only one team in each league is going to win each year. The rest of us

are losers. Really, upwards of 93 percent of us are part of the Big Fat Fraternity of Failure. If elections were determined by fantasy league success, losers would run the world. (Wait a minute…)

Winners? You? You are the *real* One Percent. (Okay, 7-10 percent.) We revile you in your victory. How dare you set unrealistic expectations for the 93 percent of us who are destined to lose each year?

If we all go into each season with only a 7-10 percent chance of winning, *what kind of odds are those?* Yet we keep chasing those tiny odds, falling short and coming back to do it next year. And then again the following year. And then again the following year. Isn't that the definition of insanity?

We often soften the blow by awarding "money finishes" down to 4th or 5th place, but really, those are just participation trophies. Those shares of cash say, "I lost, but here's some coin to lure me back next year." However, once you're out of first place, it's over. As Dale Earnhardt once said, "Second place is the first loser." (Though at least you're first at something, I suppose.)

So yes, I was the torch-bearer for futility this past year. Did I make mistakes or was this just a correction for all those years of success? I could easily attribute it to random misfortune, I suppose. Jimmy Buffet probably best expresses my path to enlightenment:

*I know it's nobody's fault.*
*Hell, it could be my fault.*
*I know it's my own damn fault.*

Sadly, 2018 was not about a lack of "booze in the blender." I was fully complicit. After playing this game for so long, I have found myself drafting teams on auto-pilot. I have far surpassed the benchmark for "expert" based on the often-debunked "10,000 Hour Rule," but longevity and repetition often breed complacency. Admittedly, I got a bit cocky and careless last March, making some rookie mistakes because I was so confident I could succeed in spite of them.

Baseball's statistical environment was not kind either. The trends coming into 2018 were so sharp that I could not perceive of any direction other than regression. But some trends persisted while others pulled back. The fallout often produced shifts in the player pool that nobody could have predicted. How could anyone realistically project the game's seismic shifts? Clearly, I couldn't.

The smartest thing you can do when faced with failure is to try to learn from those mistakes. Well, boy did I learn. I learned about 379 lessons this past season. Reflecting on them won't necessarily increase my odds of rebounding to rejoice with the reviled, but at least I'll be more comfortable lodging with the laggards.

You can track the saga that weaves through the following lessons. Sadly, it's all 100 percent true.

**Lesson #1: All men(iscus tears) are not created equal.**

When bidding on J.D. Martinez surged into the early $30s, I was already looking ahead to the next player. Martinez was not only crossed off my list, he wasn't even on my list. Why would he be? After a career year in 2017 and two seasons of questionable

---

[1] Don't be fooled. This was a league in which half the owners had never played fantasy before. Had I lost this league, they would have had to take my name off the cover of this book. Still, even this team would not get through the season unscathed. I lost in the head-to-head finals. In a tie-breaker.

durability, this is the type of player whose risk outweighed his potential reward. He'd be way overpriced.

The Mayberry Method concurs, cautioning us to be wary of players with an injury history and to avoid them on Draft Day. Research confirms that the system works, especially for those players who are frequently hurt. By filtering out players with elevated health risk, we reduce the vastness of the player pool to more manageable levels. It's mostly sound advice.

But I discovered that it's a short walk from *educated* filtering to *maniacal* filtering. Given that fantasy leaguers tend to have obsessive personalities, it's easy to see how injury avoidance could make some of us OCD.

Okay, I'm just talking about myself.

I was so hell-bent on avoiding players with injury risk that I crossed off an All-Star team's worth of talent from my cheat sheet.

- J.D. Martinez? A good place to start.
- Trea Turner? Show me 500 AB first.
- Trevor Story? Not interested in a post-injury .239 BA.
- Aaron Nola? Even 170 IP seems elusive. Pass.
- Michael Brantley? Don't make me laugh.
- And there were more. So many more.

This is not to say that injury avoidance has no merit. The same exercise also warned against paying market price for players like Stephen Strasburg, Daniel Murphy, Danny Salazar, Yoenis Cespedes, Miguel Sano and many other players who likely went for $15 or more in most auctions.

In 2018, a full 60 percent of the Top 300 players ended up on the shelf for varying periods of time. That's the highest hit rate since I started compiling the stat in 2009.

But, if we are to avoid all players with some injury risk, the remaining pool will consist of three backup infielders, a mop-up reliever and Chris Davis.

As J.D's $41 season showed, even players who are frequently hurt can put up extraordinary seasons. History is littered with players who went through injury-prone stretches, only to become consistent first-rounders like Jose Reyes, and even Hall-of-Famers like Paul Molitor.

The question is one of extremes. It's easy to make decisions when we perceive things as absolutes. But nothing we do in this game is solely black or white. None of the research in this book provides a 100% percentage play. Every tactic, every piece of advice, every strategy has to be considered a shade of grey. We have to view all these tools as general tendencies that can shape our approach to building a team.

Which means rostering some injury risk is not only okay, it's necessary.

**Lesson #2: Too many youths spoil the broth.**

Last year, in this very space, I told you to eliminate the phrase, "no path to playing time" from your vocabulary. The skyrocketing use of the disabled list has accelerated the promotion of young talent, with every DL stint opening up new paths. The opportunity for even players buried on a depth chart to find at-bats or innings has become almost endless.

As we'd expect, the number of players making their major league debuts each year has been rising overall.

| Year | No. Debuts | 4-yr Avg |
|------|-----------|----------|
| 2003 | 182 | |
| 2004 | 208 | |
| 2005 | 206 | |
| 2006 | 220 | 204 |
| 2007 | 211 | |
| 2008 | 238 | |
| 2009 | 204 | |
| 2010 | 203 | 214 |
| 2011 | 239 | |
| 2012 | 206 | |
| 2013 | 230 | |
| 2014 | 234 | 227 |
| 2015 | 255 | |
| 2016 | 257 | |
| 2017 | 262 | |
| 2018 | 247 | 255 |

*(Source of all league chart data: Baseball-Reference.com)*

So, I saw this as an opportunity to target prospects with upside over risky veterans. Rather than settling for a Carlos Gomez or Mike Leake in the end game, I'd spend a few extra dollars to speculate that a higher skilled rookie would push his way onto a roster and into the lineup at some point.

And I did it at every opportunity.

I tossed away all the garbage veterans who used to clog up the bottom of my roster each year. I spent real draft dollars and draft picks on Michael Kopech, Victor Robles, Ryan McMahon, Kyle Tucker, Dustin Fowler, Brandon Woodruff and Lewis Brinson. During the season, I traded for Austin Meadows and Raimel Tapia. I spent $213 of precious FAAB on Franmil Reyes' first promotion (second highest bid was $0!). And if that masochism wasn't enough, I spent another $57 on him when he was called up again three months later. I'm nothing if not consistent. At least I got it right the second time.

The problem with unearthing new paths to playing time is that it only solves half the problem. It's one thing for a young player to get the at-bats and innings, but then he has to produce. Ahhh… right.

The only youngsters I hit on at the draft were Walker Buehler and Ryan Borucki. *Ryan Borucki?* Yes, I drafted Borucki on purpose, a player who missed the cut as a Top 10 Blue Jays prospect. In a league that drafts only 450 players, I made a conscious decision to draft a player outside of the Top 300 *prospects*. I'm sitting here typing this, thinking to myself, "What possessed me to do that?" and the only thing I can think of is, "He must have looked good last spring."

Borucki had a 9.39 ERA last spring. I'm clueless.

But I can't complain. His 3.87 ERA and 1.32 WHIP in half a season were better stats than Zack Godley gave me all year. So maybe I'm a genius. Of course, Borucki's support metrics were pretty pedestrian, so maybe I was just lucky.

Look, it was a good idea. I just took it to an unreasonable extreme, assuming an excessive amount of risk on too many young players.

And I picked the wrong players. A lot of them. One of the things you learn quickly in this game is, even if you have the best information, projections and strategy, you still have to pick the right players. But I'd do it again. Just not as much.

**Lesson #3: A switch in time saves the 9th.**

There is a pseudo-scientific process called "pasta-nalysis." This is where you toss a bunch of players against a wall to see who sticks. This is particularly prevalent in 50-player Draft & Hold (D&H) leagues where the preponderance of roster slots tends to encourage rampant speculation.

I employed my expert pasta-nalysis skills to building a bullpen in my two D&H leagues. I decided that saves were too risky to chase, so I'd grab a few cheap options at the draft and then back-fill with a trove of high-skilled closer wannabes. Problem was, I'd wanna, but they didn't.

So, how did that work out?

| Pitcher | Saves |
|---|---|
| Hector Neris | 11 |
| Andrew Miller | 2 |
| Kyle Barraclough | 10 |
| Carl Edwards, Jr. | 0 |
| Sam Dyson | 3 |
| Mychal Givens | 9 |
| Yusmeiro Petit | 0 |
| Brandon Kintzler | 2 |
| Joe Smith | 0 |
| Pedro Baez | 0 |

I finished 13th in saves.

Chasing saves in-season in 2018 standard leagues was a fool's quest. Nearly two-thirds of drafted closers went belly up, and the 20 relievers who replaced them experienced turnover as well. Four of the most expensive free agent acquisitions in the Tout Wars leagues—each costing their lucky owners more than $200 in precious FAAB dollars—were Keynan Middleton, Kyle Barraclough, Nate Jones and Jose Alvarado. Nearly $900 in FAAB was spent for a total of 29 saves.

The bullpen market has become highly fragmented and tough to value. You'll read Ray Murphy's essay later in this book that shows a version of these notable statistics:

| | Number of pitchers | | |
|---|---|---|---|
| Year | 30+ saves | 5+ saves | 1+ saves |
| 2013 | 19 | 41 | 131 |
| 2014 | 17 | 46 | 135 |
| 2015 | 19 | 44 | 146 |
| 2016 | 15 | 52 | 135 |
| 2017 | 10 | 51 | 163 |
| 2018 | 8 | 50 | 166 |

The top end of the pool is disappearing. Supply and demand dictates that you are going to be paying even more for potential 30-save closers in 2019 but with no less risk than before.

Given all this, I have to repeat my well-worn argument for replacing Saves with Saves-plus-Holds. Neither category is perfect —heck, they are both highly flawed—but Sv+Hld is a decent enough proxy for total bullpen contribution.

At minimum, Sv+Hld provides value to a greater number of pitchers, thereby spreading your saves dollars, and risk. Failed closers often move into roles that amass holds, and set-up men often back into 9th inning work, so there is less overall turnover and attrition. At the high end, the stat effectively doubles the number of pitchers that are worth some investment:

| | Number of pitchers | |
|---|---|---|
| Year | 20+ saves | 20+ holds |
| 2013 | 28 | 30 |
| 2014 | 25 | 30 |
| 2015 | 28 | 28 |
| 2016 | 22 | 33 |
| 2017 | 23 | 33 |
| 2018 | 20 | 28 |

You'll notice the drop in high-end output this past year. It could be an isolated outlier, but given how bullpen usage is evolving, I suspect that it's not. In a 15-team league, four clubs would have gone without even one 30-save closer last year. So if you think you can go into 2019 with an easy shot at two 30-save closers, you're deluding yourself.

Back in October, I polled the owners in the XFL (fantasyxperts.com) to see if they'd consider moving from Saves to Saves-plus-Holds and the proposal was defeated unanimously and vehemently. Similar polls in the past produced at least some support so I was surprised to see such a stark response. Maybe we are all exhausted from chasing *any* bullpen-based stat.

The fallout means we are just going to have to live within the skewed economics of the saves market. Here are the potential acquisition costs of rostering saves:

1. Overpay for them at the draft. Expect upwards of 60 percent odds of taking a loss.
2. Underpay for them at the draft. Expect the same 60 percent odds of loss, but the winners will be rostering mediocre or poor peripherals with their 1-2 dozen saves.
3. Throw low-cost or no-cost darts at random relievers at the draft and accept perhaps 10 percent odds of backing into an occasional bulls-eye.
4. Spend approximately 15-25 percent of your total FAAB budget, per player, for that day's flavor, who might only last a few weeks.
5. Trade for them.

*Trade for them?* Nah, who are we kidding? Nobody ever trades away stable saves sources, and if they do, you'll have to pay through the nose (which is a disturbing literal image).

Predicting which pitchers are going to fall into each category is an equally risky proposition. But there is one thing I can pretty much guarantee: Edwin Diaz will enter 2019 as one of the prime targets for potential saves, but the odds of him repeating anything close to his 57-save total is remote. History:

**40-save closers**

| | |
|---|---|
| 2018 | Edwin Diaz, Wade Davis, Craig Kimbrel |
| 2017 | Alex Colome, Greg Holland, Kenley Jansen |
| 2016 | Jeurys Familia, Zach Britton, Kenley Jansen, Mark Melancon, Franciso Rodriguez, A.J. Ramos |
| 2015 | Mark Melancon, Trevor Rosenthal, Jeurys Familia, Brad Boxberger, Huston Street |

Over the past four years, the 40-saves threshold has been reached 17 times by 14 different pitchers. For all anyone can predict, the 2019 saves leader could be Koda Glover. Or Brandon Woodruff.

**Lesson #4: Eight is (not) enough.**

Back in 2013, the Los Angeles Dodgers entered the season with eight legitimate starting pitchers on their roster. Behind Clayton Kershaw and Zack Greinke, it was anyone's guess who would end up slotting into the remaining three rotation spots on a regular basis. Josh Beckett? Hyun Jin-Ryu? Chris Capuano? Ricky Nolasco? Edinson Volquez? Ted Lilly?

However, the problem didn't last long, as injuries and ineffectiveness quickly weeded out the also-rans. Within weeks, the Dodgers found they were actually *short* of viable arms.

In D&H leagues, it's even more important to have enough arms since there is no access to free agents. You have to build that depth by the end of the draft. There are no second chances.

I have no idea what was going through my head when I thought it would be enough to draft just 10 starters in each of my D&H leagues. My starters in the 10-team league – where the pickings should have been more plentiful – looked like this mess:

| | |
|---|---|
| Carlos Martinez | 18 GS, 3.11 ERA, went to pen in August |
| Shohei Ohtani | 10 GS, 3.31 ERA, TJS |
| Jack Flaherty | 28 GS, 3.34 ERA |
| Zack Godley | 32 GS, 4.74 ERA |
| Brad Peacock | Was supposed to be a starter, dammit |
| Michael Kopech | 4 GS, 5.02 ERA, TJS |
| Alex Cobb | 28 GS, 4.90 ERA |
| Brent Suter | 18 GS, 4.44 ERA, TJS |
| Ty Blach | 13 GS, 4.25 ERA, went to pen in May |
| Chance Adams | 1 GS, 7.04 ERA |

Back in March, it didn't look this bad, I swear.

In most standard fantasy formats, this is not as big an issue as the free agent pool always has some depth of talent to draw from. At least that's how it used to be.

But we are now facing an even greater challenge – the sharp decline in the length of pitching starts. Innings per start were already tumbling before 2018, but with the additional variable of the new game "opener," now we can't be sure exactly what to expect. Innings, strikeouts and wins are all poised to take a hit in 2019.

This is interesting:

| Year | No. 100-pitch outings | % Change |
|---|---|---|
| 2014 | 2,114 | -0.4% |
| 2015 | 1,863 | -11.9% |
| 2016 | 1,737 | -6.8% |
| 2017 | 1,576 | -9.3% |
| 2018 | 1,225 | -22.3% |

It seems that 100 pitches is a good proxy for an outing we'd want counted for our fantasy teams. With the number of them in a steady, precipitous decline, we can expect that the cost of pitchers who provide this skill will spike. Supply and demand, again.

I was just offered a $34 Max Scherzer in the XFL. Over the past five years, he's posted 127 outings of 100 pitches or more, including 28 in 2018. A $34 price tag suddenly looks like an incredible bargain.

Last year, I advised that you would need to invest heavily in high-strikeout starting pitchers as they have become scarce. That trend has continued.

| Year | 200 IP | w/200+ K |
|---|---|---|
| 2013 | 36 | 10 |
| 2014 | 34 | 11 |
| 2015 | 28 | 14 |
| 2016 | 15 | 8 |
| 2017 | 15 | 10 |
| 2018 | 13 | 8 |

There are not enough stud 200/200 starters to go around in pretty much any standard league. If you want an anchor, you are going to have to pay up, big time.

**Lesson #5: We can't protect the environment when we don't understand the environment.**

Last year at this time, home runs and strikeouts were surging. Stolen bases were falling. We were drawing conclusions about juiced balls and still speculating about juiced players.

All of the bottom line stats were in the middle of multi-year trends with no let-up in sight. We expected at least some regression in 2018, but we said the same thing in 2017, and 2016, and we were wrong.

So, this happened:

| | | Players with | |
|---|---|---|---|
| Year | HR | 20+ HR | 30+ HR |
| 2011 | 4,552 | 68 | 23 |
| 2012 | 4,934 | 79 | 27 |
| 2013 | 4,661 | 70 | 14 |
| 2014 | 4,186 | 57 | 11 |
| 2015 | 4,909 | 64 | 20 |
| 2016 | 5,610 | 111 | 35 |
| 2017 | 6,105 | 118 | 41 |
| 2018 | 5,585 | 100 | 27 |

Homers tailed off after a three-year surge and nobody was talking about the baseballs anymore. These short news cycles are annoying to those of us who have attention spans longer than a housefly.

Was this power drop meaningful? The home run decline was 8.5 percent, which is not insignificant. Of course, if I claim that they just fixed the baseballs, I'll look like an idiot. So I'm betting on a number like 5,900 for 2019, which would normalize the trend to somewhere inside a more reasonable margin of error.

Then there was this:

| | | Players with | |
|---|---|---|---|
| Year | Tot SB | 20+ SB | 30+ SB |
| 2011 | 3,279 | 50 | 20 |
| 2012 | 3,229 | 48 | 23 |
| 2013 | 2,693 | 40 | 16 |
| 2014 | 2,764 | 39 | 15 |
| 2015 | 2,505 | 30 | 7 |
| 2016 | 2,537 | 28 | 14 |
| 2017 | 2,527 | 29 | 6 |
| 2018 | 2,474 | 28 | 11 |

Steals were down overall but the number of top speedsters saw an uptick. Last March, there were some who advised that you could still compete in the SB category even if you didn't draft elite wheels. Given the above data, I'm not so sure that was easy to do.

I fared pretty well in the SB category in some of my leagues. I finished first in the XFL thanks to Whit Merrifield and his 45 bags, backed by Manny Machado, Aaron Hicks, Travis Jankowski and the late surge by Amed Rosario. However, if Merrifield was only half as productive on the basepaths, I would have finished 7th in the category. That's the impact of an elite speedster.

And this:

| | | Pitchers with | |
|---|---|---|---|
| Year | Tot K | 150+ K | 200+ K |
| 2005 | 30,644 | 34 | 8 |
| 2006 | 31,655 | 39 | 6 |
| 2007 | 32,189 | 35 | 8 |
| 2008 | 32,884 | 43 | 10 |
| 2009 | 33,591 | 40 | 10 |
| 2010 | 34,306 | 49 | 15 |
| 2011 | 34,488 | 52 | 14 |
| 2012 | 36,426 | 53 | 13 |
| 2013 | 36,710 | 53 | 12 |
| 2014 | 37,441 | 56 | 13 |
| 2015 | 37,446 | 56 | 18 |
| 2016 | 38,982 | 54 | 12 |
| 2017 | 40,104 | 48 | 16 |
| 2018 | 41,207 | 60 | 18 |

Count 'em… strikeouts have now risen consistently for *13 consecutive years*, a nearly 35 percent increase during that time. That's an amazing statistic. The distribution of high-end K artists reversed itself after last year's lull, but we're still living in rarefied air. However, as noted earlier, that does not mean it is easier to draft stud starting pitchers who combine big innings with big strikeouts.

The fascinating part is that it's nearly impossible project the next data point. Regression and gravity may be the two strongest forces known to man, but they have been wrong for a dozen years.

A higher level look on the offense side:

| | | Three True Outcomes | | | |
|---|---|---|---|---|---|
| Year | Singles | HR | BB | K | Total |
| 2011 | 28,418 | 4,552 | 15,018 | 34,488 | 54,058 |
| 2012 | 27,941 | 4,934 | 14,709 | 36,426 | 56,069 |
| 2013 | 28,438 | 4,661 | 14,640 | 36,710 | 56,011 |
| 2014 | 28,423 | 4,186 | 14,020 | 37,441 | 55,647 |
| 2015 | 28,016 | 4,909 | 14,073 | 37,446 | 56,428 |
| 2016 | 27,539 | 5,610 | 15,088 | 38,982 | 59,680 |
| 2017 | 26,918 | 6,105 | 15,829 | 40,104 | 62,038 |
| 2018 | 26,322 | 5,585 | 15,686 | 41,207 | 62,478 |

So yes, home runs were down, but the three true outcomes continued to rise, with strikeouts the driving force. Singles were down 2.2 percent from 2017, but 7.4 percent from 2011.

This big question is, where is this all headed? Will these trends continue, or will some internal or external variable interrupt the trajectory?

I. Don't. Know.

The best we can do is play the game with what we know, and feel secure in the fact that everyone is facing the same uncertainties. Perhaps an owner might fortuitously structure his roster to take advantage of some unexpected trend reversal. But really, the odds of that are no different from the probability that these four players would all go in Round 29 of the Tout Wars mixed draft last year: German Marquez (pick #427), Walker Buehler (#430), Miguel Andujar (#433) and Adalberto Mondesi (#434).

Stuff happens. You react.

**Lesson #6: Despite assertions to the contrary, you *can* fall off the floor.**

Regression and gravity wait for no man. No matter what a player does in any given season, odds are about 70 percent that he will fare worse next year.

Still, we try to find players who have reasonable floors. There has to be a baseline level we can have some confidence in, right? Odds are Jose Altuve won't bat .250. Odds are Nolan Arenado won't hit 20 home runs. Odds are Max Scherzer won't have an ERA of 4.00. Right?

But those floors aren't always realistic. We used to be able to count on Adam Jones for 25 HRs. We used to be able to count on Felix Hernandez for a sub-4.00 ERA. And as bad as Chris Davis is, we never thought he'd get over 500 plate appearances with a batting average south of .170.

During last off-season, I keyed in on small isolated news items that positioned some mediocre players as safe targets. I saw them as having floors that would not kill me, but also a limited ceiling. I reasoned that it would be okay for a few roster slots.

At least that was what I thought.

However, a low ceiling and a high floor don't guarantee you anything. Any player can get hurt or slump, and those who are not established major leaguers have a higher risk of washing out.

So maybe I saw something in Randal Grichuk's move to Toronto. Maybe I saw some playing time opening up for JaCoby Jones and Mikie Mahtook. In the end, it was one boring summer having to watch this trio slog through their mediocrity. Grichuk did show some life in the second half, but by then, I was already arranging the deck chairs.

Their ceiling was low. Their floor was a mirage. But here is the real challenge going forward… as you scan the players in this book, you will find a lot of bad ones. Tons! The ceiling benchmarks are as sweet as ever, but those floors are dropping. There is a sharp stratification of the player pool—there are the Elite and there are the Dregs. *There is no middle class.* This puts a great deal of economic pressure on the marketplace.

How are you going to draft saves? Is .240 the new .270? Where are you going to find a roster-worthy catcher? (A scout at First Pitch Arizona said, "We are having trouble finding catchers at the MLB level so I can just imagine what you fantasy leaguers are going through.") The answer is: pay up for the elite or risk ending up with garbage.

This also means our tolerance for what we deem "roster-worthy" may have to drop. There are just so many elite players to go around. Once upon a time, you would never consider a .220 batter. Today, you can't completely discount him if he brings some other plus skill to the table.

Jones suddenly becomes almost palatable in that context. And Grichuk is damn near a star.

**Lesson #7: Don't draft Byron Buxton.**

Here are four steps to everlasting success:

1. Commit to believing that some player's nice second half has a bearing on what he is going to do the following year.
2. Hang on when he gets off to a bad start because "I know he is better than this."

3. Refuse to cash him in for a FAAB reclaim because "maybe he'll be back in the second half."

4. Keep him tucked away on your reserve all year because he is too expensive to cut.

As a 2018 Buxton owner, I successfully completed all of the above steps and can now report back that none of them worked. It's time to re-read the chapter in my economics textbook on "sunk costs."

There is always a Buxton every year. It could be Luke Voit. It could be Tommy Pham. It might even be Adalberto Mondesi *(Hey, don't say that!)*. I won't venture a real prediction. Just keep your eyes open.

**Lesson #8: They said there would be no math. There's *always* math.**

With my Tout Wars team floundering in last place, I shifted into desperation mode. On June 10, I posted the following to the league message board:

> *"Hello fellow Touts. I am in last place. I am not going to win. I am no threat to you. But I have a few really good players. I can finish in last place with the Vottos and Freemans and Carrascos, or without them. I have no particular affection for any of them. Not one sent me a birthday card this year.*
>
> *Look over my roster and make me an offer. Everyone is up for grabs, but the really good guys will require a 2-for-1 or 3-for-1 deal. So yes, you can own Zack Greinke or Walker Buehler. You can gain some nice position flexibility with Yangervis Solarte. Or you can even go down the rabbit hole with Byron Buxton. I hate them all. Maybe one of them will send you a birthday card.*
>
> *All reasonable offers considered. I'm not punting the season so don't offer me a bunch of scrubs. I'm offering an A for some Bs or Cs to replace some of my Ds and Fs."*

It is not always the case, but I did receive a bunch of legitimate offers. Two of the big names I dealt were Joey Votto and Freddie Freeman. At the time, I was in third place in OBP and figured I'd take a little hit, but it was worth it to bulk up in other areas.

However, I didn't do the math.

Within three weeks, I plummeted 12 spots to last place in OBP, effectively wiping out potential gains elsewhere. "Plummeted" is being modest. In my entire life, I have never seen an OBP dive into the abyss as quickly as this team's did. Picture a grand piano falling out of a 10th story window and crashing to the pavement, leaving a gaping crater that Edmund Hillary couldn't climb out of. I never saw a glimpse of OBP daylight after that.

Those ratio categories are tricky and a lot more volatile than we give them credit for. So you gotta do the math.

**Lesson #9: I'd gladly pay you Tuesday for a hamburger today.**

Seems like a fair deal. But when we make trades, we just don't know what the future holds. Maybe you'll get a hamburger. Maybe you'll get paid. Maybe you'll get a cookie (I don't know, why not?). And what kind of burger will you get? A McDonald's single or a LongHorn steakburger?

I thought I was trading for some juicy thickburgers this year, and ended up with a bunch of White Castle sliders[2]. In a few cases, Tuesday never came. Some were bad ideas. Some were bad luck.

During the off-season in a rebuilding year, I traded Justin Verlander for Michael Kopech. That helped hand a title to the eventual winner and has left me with nothing for 2019.

On July 2, I traded Carlos Carrasco, coming off a DL stint with a 4.24 ERA, for Kris Bryant, also coming off the DL. But after making the swap, Carrasco won nine games and struck out 135 with a 2.59 ERA while Bryant went back on the DL, only netting me 3 HRs and 14 RBI in 113 AB.

On July 19, in an attempt to bolster my pitching, I dealt Xander Bogaerts for Ross Stripling and Amed Rosario. Before the deal, Stripling was 8-2 with a 2.08 ERA. After the deal, he went 0-4 with a 6.41 ERA.

Did I mention that I lost a lot of leagues this year?

Okay, I just pulled off the deal for Max Scherzer. I dealt a $4 Kyle Tucker, a $22 Starling Marte and a future draft pick. Like Kershaw in years past, owning Scherzer can cover up a lot of flaws. And boy, does he have his work cut out for him.

But, who knows? I might have to wait until Tuesday to see my payday, or it could take weeks, or months. No matter how lopsided a trade seems at the time, especially in keeper leagues, it could take years for the winners and losers to shake out. Scherzer could turn into a pumpkin and Tucker could become the AL MVP. Marte could go 30-30 and that draft pick could become the next Mike Trout.

Geez, I hope not.

So I could say this lesson is to try to make better trades, but let's be realistic. You never know what's going to happen. I'm *still* waiting to find out the winner of the Michael Pineda for Jesus Montero deal. (Former Montero owner here.)

**Lesson #10: Love is a many splintered thing.**

I have been known to have the occasional man-crush on a player. I admit it. The phenomenon reaches beyond simple home-town allegiance. It's no surprise that I was a Tom Seaver fan growing up, or that I've followed David Wright's career intently. But those were not man-crushes. I was just being a fan.

A man-crush is when you keep drafting Dave Stieb because he once won you a title, even though he's barely draftable now. A man-crush is when you are all over Matt Capps' support metrics and keep hanging on to him even though Joe Nathan has already been named the closer. A man-crush is when you spend a whole season wishing for Ryan McMahon to find his playing time.

Yeah, I did that.

How can you not be drawn to a guy who went .355/.403/.583 in over 519 plate appearances in his last minor league season? How can you not salivate over those stats in Coors Field? Even when the Rockies signed Carlos Gonzalez in March, I kept saying to myself, "McMahon is just too good not to find his playing time."

There needs to be a certain space, some dispassion, between you and your players. Sure, you can grab a few favorites and have

---

[2] This is not intended as an insult; it's just a means of comparison. White Castle burgers are great! Especially at 3:00 a.m. on a Saturday night.

fun for awhile, but if you are serious about contending, there needs to come a time when you cut the non-performers.

McMahon was on my team all year. Even when he was demoted, I held on, watching the solid numbers he was still posting in Albuquerque. He'd be back, I told myself. And when he did come back but was getting less and less playing time each week, I still hung on every at bat. (Seriously, his weekly ABs after his recall were 17, 15, 10, 14, 10, 7, 5, 5, 3, 0.)

What's worse, because I have him at such a good price, I'll be protecting him into 2019. If I cut him, it's possible that I might be able to get him back in next year's draft, but why risk it?

Oh, Ryan. I wish I knew how to quit you.

Look, we know that young players will not all hit the ground running. Each prospect's progress is shaped by the context in which he plays, and for some, the path to major league productivity takes a little longer. However, if we can trust that their minor league performance gives us at least a hint at their potential, and that their skill will eventually help open up a path to playing time, shouldn't we take a chance that the 2018 strugglers are still protectable in keeper leagues?

This is either the pinnacle of prodigious perception or the depths of desperate denial. I am a flawed human being.

### Lesson #11: Keep making the same mistake until you are good at it.

Um… Ryan McMahon was on *three* of my teams. There, I said it.

Here are the other players who appeared on at least two of my teams in 2018: Zack Godley, Yangervis Solarte, Eric Thames, Tom Murphy, Brandon Crawford, Mike Zunino, Austin Hayes, Fernando Rodney, Hector Neris, Andrew Triggs, Chad Green and Brad Peacock.

What can I say? They all sent me birthday cards.

On one of my teams, through draft and trade, I somehow ended up with all three of Zack Greinke, Patrick Corbin and Zack Godley. That was actually a pretty fun ride… for about three months, and was particularly thrilling during the Diamondbacks' 8-19 September.

Sigh. I have become a cautionary tale.

> *"I guess if you keep making the same mistake long enough, it becomes your style."* —John Prine

> *"One should never learn from one's mistakes. Making the same mistakes, over and over again, is a source of unremitting pleasure."* —Peter York

> *"I never make the same mistake twice. I make it five or six times, just to be sure."* —Bill Murray

> *"We made too many wrong mistakes."* —Yogi Berra

Wait a minute…

Let's take a step back. Why did I fall into this trap? I should know not to draft too many of the same players on my teams. I should know not put an entire MLB team's rotation on my roster. Those are lessons from "Intro to Fantasy Baseball 101."

I think my behavior was the direct fallout from the stratification of the player pool. *There are fewer players who I like.* The great players are still great. The unwashed masses are still being filtered out. But the dearth of options in the middle forced me to focus

my draft efforts on a smaller pool of targets. And that led me to double and triple dip on too many players.

If the benchmarks we've been setting are producing fewer worthy players, we are going to be left with fewer options. Ten years ago, our target pool was Olympic-sized. Now we're hunting for rosterable rubber ducks in a kiddie pond.

Of course, we can lower our expectations, cast a wider net and dig a bigger pool. Actually, that's the only thing we can do. We still have to fill 23 roster spots and someone is going to have to draft Mike Zunino. So, close your eyes, hold your nose, and repeat after me: "Zunino is good. Zunino is good. Zunino is good."

Remember to breathe.

### My lessons, summarized

1. Avoid players with health issues, but a few speculations on talented hobblers won't kill you.

2. Speculate on a few upwardly mobile youngsters. The operable word there is "few."

3. Invest in your bullpen with the knowledge that you are going to be disappointed.

4. Spend up for the best pitchers and draft more arms than you think you'll need. You'll need them.

5. Don't obsess over trying to stay ahead of the statistical environment. You're going to be wrong, and everyone is going to be affected the same anyway.

6. You can't avoid drafting some bad players. Reset your definition of "bad."

7. Learn about sunk costs. There is a Byron Buxton every season.

8. As much as you hate to take the time, do the math.

9. The Red Sox never regretted trading away Jeff Bagwell for Larry Andersen. (Well, maybe they did.) Just trade and pray.

10. Stow your man-crushes if your team could be better without them.

11. Remember what mom always said: "Make good choices."

Finally, a bad year is just a bad year. It's a single data point. If this losing seeps into 2019 and beyond, then I might face the possibility of taking the Steve Carlton Path to Retirement. Otherwise, I'll just look at 2018 like Justin Verlander looks at 2008, or how Zack Greinke looks at 2016.

I intend to regress.

### Other Losses

Enough food, fun and frivolity. In 2018, there were some more important losses worth mentioning.

The baseball industry lost one of its pioneers when Steve Moyer died suddenly just days before the LABR experts draft last March. Steve helped found the Bill James Handbook, among many accomplishments, as well as being a leading analyst and writer for both baseball and music. His "Baseball Outsider" column, which he wrote for RotoWire for several years around the turn of the century, remains one of my favorite reads ever.

Steve's fantasy M.O. was to be the last person with open roster spots on draft day. If he had a half dozen $1 openings to fill, he was in his glory. While the rest of us were impatiently waiting for the post-draft after-party, Steve would be painstakingly pouring through his notes for the perfect, usually-obscure end-gamers. He won and lost as often as any of us in the experts leagues, but he carved his own unique path.

Coming into 2018, Steve was the defending champion in the XFL. The league has instituted an annual Seth Beer Award in Steve's honor to recognize the most obscure player drafted the previous year. It is named after Steve's first pick in the 2017 reserve draft. Fittingly, the first inductee is former Tigers prospect Steven Moya.

I also suffered a personal loss last year, when my younger brother Marty passed over the summer.

Back in April 1970, I was a 12-year-old nerdy math geek. My seven-year-old brother encouraged me to sit down to watch a Mets game on TV though I had no interest in sports. Marty pointed out the numbers on the bottom of the screen when Tommie Agee stepped up to the plate: Home Runs, RBI, Batting Average. I was enthralled. That was a moment that changed my life, and I have my brother to thank for that.

The rabbi at the funeral noted that Marty was one of the few people who was both a Mets fan and Yankees fan, an oddity in a city that revels in taking sides. But in the local interleague series each season, Marty would always root for "a ninth inning worth watching." During the 2000 Subway Series, Marty rooted for "Game 7."

Such pure enjoyment of the game means there are never any losers.

Life lesson.

# Welcome to the 33rd Edition

If you are new to the *Baseball Forecaster*, the sheer volume of information in this book may seem a bit daunting. We don't recommend you assessing its contents over a single commute to work, particularly if you drive. But do set aside some time this winter—instead of staring out the window, waiting for baseball to begin again, try immersing yourself in all the wisdom contained in this tome. There's a ton of it, and the payoff—Yoo-Hoo or otherwise—is worth it.

But where to begin?

The best place to start is with the Encyclopedia of Fanalytics, which provides the foundation concepts for everything else that appears in these pages. It's our research archive and collective memory, just as valuable for veterans as it is for rookies. Take a cursory read-through, lingering at any section that looks interesting. You'll keep coming back here frequently.

Then just jump in. Close your eyes, flip to a random page, and put your finger down anywhere. Oh, look—former MVP Andrew McCutchen, who is so obviously in decline. But wait ... his HctX rate is nearly 20% above league average, his xPX rebounded in 2018, he still stinging lots of line drives, and he recorded his best walk rate in years. Still just 32 years old (is that all?); there could be some life left here. See, you've learned something already!

## What's New in 2019?

*New contexts:* The times are a-changin', and the *Baseball Forecaster* helps you adapt. In a world of openers and bullpen games, of new-age bullpen usage, of not enough rosterable catchers, and of launch angle and Statcast, fantasy players must be flexible. Throughout this volume, we give tips and provide insight on the best ways to leverage the MLB reality for your fantasy success.

*Fastball Velocity:* The game is also about harder throwers—in the rotation, in the bullpen; everywhere. So for the first time in 2019, our pitcher boxes (starting on page 146) include average fastball velocity. So whether you want to know just *how* hard Josh Hader brought it from the left side in 2018 (that would be 94.5 mph), or whether Archie Bradley was privy to more giddyup since his move to a reliever role at the start of 2017 (that would be "yes"), you now have access to it, alongside other pitching metrics.

*Answers to questions,* such as: When do hitters get platooned? Is a larger sample size *always* more conclusive? Is fly ball "carry" a repeatable skill? How does a fantasy owner leverage all the team-given injury terminology? And much, much more.

## Updates

The *Baseball Forecaster* page at BaseballHQ.com is at www.baseballhq.com/bf2019. This is your headquarters for all information and updates regarding this book. Here you will find links to the following:

*Content Updates:* In a project of this magnitude, there are occasionally items that need clarification or correction. You can find them here.

*Free Projections Update:* As a buyer of this book, you get one free 2019 projections update. This is a set of Excel spreadsheet files that will be posted on or about March 1, 2019. Remember to keep the book handy when you visit as the access codes are hidden within these pages.

*Electronic book:* The complete PDF version of the *Forecaster*—plus Excel versions of most key charts—is available free to those who bought the book directly through the BaseballHQ.com website. These files will be available in January 2019 for most of you; those who have an annual standing order should have received the PDF just before Thanksgiving. Contact us if you do not receive information via e-mail about access. Information about the e-book version can be found at the above website.

If you purchased the book through an online vendor or bookstore, or would like these files earlier, you can purchase them from us for $9.95. Contact us at support@baseballhq.com for more information.

## Beyond the Forecaster

The *Baseball Forecaster* is just the beginning. The following companion products and services are described in more detail in the back of the book.

*BaseballHQ.com* is our home website. It provides regular updates to everything in this book, including daily updated statistics and projections. A subscription to BHQ gets you more than 1,000 articles over the course of a year updated daily from spring training through the end of the regular season, customized tools, access to data going back over a decade, plus much more. For a free peek, sign up for our BaseballHQFriday newsletter at www.baseballhq.com/friday.

*First Pitch Forums* are a series of conferences we run where you can meet top industry analysts and network with fellow fantasy leaguers in your area. We'll be in several cities in February and March. Our big annual symposium at the Arizona Fall League is the first weekend in November.

The 14th edition of the *Minor League Baseball Analyst* is the minor league companion to this book, with stat boxes for 1,000-plus prospects, essays on prospects, lists upon lists, and more. In an era where rookies matter, it is an essential resource. It is available in January.

*RotoLab* is the best draft software on the market and comes pre-loaded with our projections. Learn more at www.rotolab.com.

## Even further beyond the Forecaster

Visit us on *Facebook* at www.facebook.com/baseballhq. "Like" the BaseballHQ page for updates, photos from events and links to other important stuff.

Follow us on *Twitter*. Site updates are tweeted from @BaseballHQ and many of our writers share their insights from their own personal accounts. We even have a list to follow: www.twitter.com/BaseballHQ/lists/hq-staff.

But back to baseball. Your winter comfort awaits.

*—Brent Hershey and Ray Murphy*

# CONSUMER ADVISORY

## AN IMPORTANT MESSAGE FOR FANTASY LEAGUERS
## REGARDING PROPER USAGE OF THE *BASEBALL FORECASTER*

This document is provided in compliance with authorities to outline the prospective risks and hazards possible in the event that the Baseball Forecaster is used incorrectly. Please be aware of these potentially dangerous situations and avoid them. The publisher assumes no risk related to any financial loss or stress-induced illnesses caused by ignoring the items as described below.

1. The statistical projections in this book are intended as general guidelines, not as gospel. It is highly dangerous to use the projected statistics alone, and then live and die by them. That's like going to a ballgame, being given a choice of any seat in the park, and deliberately choosing the last row in the right field corner with an obstructed view. The projections are there, you can look at them, but there are so many better places to sit.

We have to publish those numbers, but they are stagnant, inert pieces of data. This book focuses on a live forecasting process that provides the tools so that you can understand the leading indicators and draw your own conclusions. If you at least attempt your own analyses of the data, and enhance them with the player commentaries, you can paint more robust, colorful pictures of the future.

In other words...

**If you bought this book purely for the projected statistics and do not intend to spend at least some time learning about the process, then you might as well just buy an $8 magazine.**

2. The player commentaries in this book are written by humans, just like you. These commentaries provide an overall evaluation of performance and likely future direction, but 60-word capsules cannot capture everything. Your greatest value will be to use these as a springboard to your own analysis of the data. Odds are, if you take the time, you'll find hidden indicators that we might have missed. Forecaster veterans say that this self-guided excursion is the best part of owning the book.

3. This book does not attempt to tackle playing time. Rather than making arbitrary decisions about how roles will shake out, the focus is on performance. The playing time projections presented here are merely to help you better evaluate each player's talent. Our online pre-season projections update provides more current AB and IP expectations based on how roles are being assigned.

4. The dollar values in this book are intended solely for player-to-player comparisons. They are not driven by a finite pool of playing time—which is required for valuation systems to work properly—so they cannot be used for bid values to be used in your own draft.

There are two reasons for this:

a. The finite pool of players that will generate the finite pool of playing time will not be determined until much closer to Opening Day. And, if we are to be brutally honest, there is really no such thing as a finite pool of players.

b. Your particular league's construction will drive the values; a $10 player in a 10-team mixed league will not be the same as a $10 player in a 12-team NL-only league.

**Note that book dollar values also cannot be compared to those published at BaseballHQ.com as the online values are generated by a more finite player pool.**

5. Do not pass judgment on the effectiveness of this book based on the performance of a few individual players. The test, rather, is on the collective predictive value of the book's methods. Are players with better base skills more likely to produce good results than bad ones? Years of research suggest that the answer is "yes." Does that mean that every high skilled player will do well? No. But many more of them will perform well than will the average low-skilled player. You should always side with the better percentage plays, but recognize that there are factors we cannot predict. Good decisions that beget bad outcomes do not invalidate the methods.

6. If your copy of this book is not marked up and dog-eared by Draft Day, you probably did not get as much value out of it as you might have.

7. This edition of the Forecaster is not intended to provide absorbency for spills of more than 7.5 ounces.

8. This edition is not intended to provide stabilizing weight for more than 18 sheets of 20 lb. paper in winds of more than 45 mph.

9. The pages of this book are not recommended for avian waste collection. In independent laboratory studies, 87% of migratory water fowl refused to excrete on interior pages, even when coaxed.

10. This book, when rolled into a cylindrical shape, is not intended to be used as a weapon for any purpose, including but not limited to insect extermination, canine training or to influence bidding behavior at a fantasy draft.

## For new readers...

Everything begins here. The information in the following pages represents the foundation that powers everything we do.

You'll learn about the underlying concepts for our unique mode of analysis. You'll find answers to long-asked questions, interesting insights into what makes players tick, and innovative applications for all this newfound knowledge.

This Encyclopedia is organized into several logical sections:

1. Fundamentals
2. Batters
3. Pitchers
4. Prospects
5. Gaming

Enough talking. Jump in.
Remember to breathe.

## For veteran readers...

As we do in each edition, this year's ever-expanding Encyclopedia includes relevant research results we've published over the past year. We've added some of the essays from the Research Abstracts and Gaming Abstracts sections in the 2018 *Forecaster* as well as some other essays from BaseballHQ.com.

And we continue to mold the content to best fit how fantasy leaguers use their information. Many readers consider this their fantasy information bible.

Okay, time to jump-start the analytical process for 2019. Remember to breathe—it's always good advice.

## Abbreviations

# Fundamentals

## What is Fanalytics?

Fanalytics is the scientific approach to fantasy baseball analysis. A contraction of "fantasy" and "analytics," fanalytic gaming might be considered a mode of play that requires a more strategic and quantitative approach to player analysis and game decisions.

The three key elements of fanalytics are:

1. Performance analysis
2. Performance forecasting
3. Gaming analysis

For performance analysis, we tap into the vast knowledge of the sabermetric community. Founded by Bill James, this area of study provides objective and progressive new ways to assess skill. What we do in this book is called "component skills analysis." We break down performance into its component parts, then reverse-engineer it back into the traditional measures with which we are more familiar.

Our forecasting methodology is one part science and one part art. We start with a computer-generated baseline for each player. We then make subjective adjustments based on a variety of factors, such as discrepancies in skills indicators and historical guidelines gleaned from more than 25 years of research. We don't rely on a rigid model; our method forces us to get our hands dirty.

You might say that our brand of forecasting is more about finding logical journeys than blind destinations.

Gaming analysis is an integrated approach designed to help us win our fantasy leagues. It takes the knowledge gleaned from the first two elements and adds the strategic and tactical aspect of each specific fantasy game format.

## Component Skills Analysis

Familiar gauges like HR and ERA have long been used to measure skill. In fact, these gauges only measure the outcome of an individual event, or series of events. They represent statistical output. They are "surface stats."

Raw skill is the talent beneath the stats. Players use these skills to create the individual events, or components, that are the building blocks of measures like HR and ERA. Our approach:

**1. It's not about batting average; it's about seeing the ball and making contact.** We target hitters based on elements such as their batting eye (walks to strikeouts ratio), how often they make contact and the type of contact they make. We then combine these components into an "expected batting average." By comparing each hitter's actual BA to how he should be performing, we can draw conclusions about the future.

**2. It's not about home runs; it's about power.** From the perspective of a round bat meeting a round ball, it may be only a fraction of an inch at the point of contact that makes the difference between a HR and a long foul ball. When a ball is hit safely, often it is only a few inches that separate a HR from a double. We tend to neglect these facts in our analyses, although the outcomes—the doubles, triples, long fly balls—may be no less a measure of that batter's raw power skill. We must incorporate all these components to paint a complete picture.

**3. It's not about ERA; it's about getting the ball over the plate and keeping it in the park.** Forget ERA. You want to draft pitchers who walk few batters (Control), strike out many (Dominance) and succeed at both in tandem (Command). You generally want pitchers who keep the ball on the ground (because home runs are bad), though some fly ball pitchers can succeed under the right conditions. All of this translates into an "expected ERA" that you can use to validate a pitcher's actual performance.

**4. It's never about wins.** For pitchers, winning ballgames is less about skill than it is about offensive support. As such, projecting wins is a very high-risk exercise and valuing hurlers based on their win history is dangerous. Target skill; wins will come.

**5. It's not about saves; it's about opportunity first and skills second.** While the highest-skilled pitchers have the best potential to succeed as closers, they still have to be given the ball with the game on the line in the 9th inning, and that is a decision left to others. Over the past 15 years, about 40% of relievers drafted for saves failed to hold the role for the entire season. The lesson: Don't take chances on draft day. There will always be saves in the free agent pool.

## Accounting for "luck"

Luck has been used as a catch-all term to describe random chance. When we use the term here, we're talking about unexplained variances that shape the statistics. While these variances may be random, they are also often measurable and projectable. To get a better read on "luck," we use formulas that capture the external variability of the data.

Through our research and the work of others, we have learned that when raw skill is separated from statistical output, what's remaining is often unexplained variance. The aggregate totals of many of these variances, for all players, is often a constant. For instance, while a pitcher's ERA might fluctuate, the rate at which his opposition's batted balls fall for hits will tend towards 30%. Large variances can be expected to regress towards 30%.

Why is all this important? Analysts complain about the lack of predictability of many traditional statistical metrics. The reason they find it difficult is that they are trying to project performance using metrics that are loaded with external noise. Raw skills metrics follow better-defined trends during a player's career. Then, as we get a better handle on the variances—explained and unexplained—we can construct a complete picture of what a player's statistics really mean.

## Baseball Forecasting

### Forecasting in perspective

The crystal ball aura of "predicting the future" conceals the fact it is a process. We might define it as "the systematic process of determining likely end results." At its core, it's scientific.

However, the *outcomes* of forecasted events are what is most closely scrutinized, and are used to judge the success or failure of the forecast. That said, as long as the process is sound, the forecast has done the best job it can do. *In the end, forecasting is about analysis, not prophecy.*

Baseball performance forecasting is inherently a high-risk exercise with a very modest accuracy rate. This is because the process involves not only statistics, but also unscientific elements, from random chance to human volatility. And even from within the statistical aspect there are multiple elements that need to be evaluated, from skill to playing time to a host of external variables.

Every system is comprised of the same core elements:

- Players will tend to perform within the framework of past history and/or trends.
- Skills will develop and decline according to age.
- Statistics will be shaped by a player's health, expected role and venue.

While all systems are built from these same elements, they also are constrained by the same limitations. We are all still trying to project a bunch of human beings, each one...

- with his own individual skill set
- with his own rate of growth and decline
- with his own ability to resist and recover from injury
- limited to opportunities determined by other people
- generating a group of statistics largely affected by external noise.

Research has shown that the best accuracy rate that can be attained by any system is about 70%. In fact, a simple system that uses three-year averages adjusted for age ("Marcel") can attain a success rate of 65%. This means all the advanced systems are fighting for occupation of the remaining 5%.

But there is a bigger question... *what exactly are we measuring?* When we search for accuracy, what does that mean? In fact, any quest for accuracy is going to run into a brick wall of paradoxes:

- If a slugging average projection is dead on, but the player hits 10 fewer HRs than expected (and likely, 20 more doubles), is that a success or a failure?
- If a projection of hits and walks allowed by a pitcher is on the mark, but the bullpen and defense implodes, and inflates his ERA by a run, is that a success or a failure?
- If the projection of a speedster's rate of stolen base success is perfect, but his team replaces the manager with one that doesn't run, and the player ends up with half as many SBs as expected, is that a success or a failure?
- If a batter is traded to a hitters' ballpark and all the touts project an increase in production, but he posts a statistical line exactly what would have been projected had he not been traded to that park, is that a success or a failure?
- If the projection for a bullpen closer's ERA, WHIP and peripheral numbers is perfect, but he saves 20 games instead of 40 because the GM decided to bring in a high-priced free agent at the trading deadline, is that a success or a failure?
- If a player is projected to hit .272 in 550 AB and only hits .249, is that a success or failure? Most will say "failure." But wait a minute! The real difference is only two hits per month. That shortfall of 23 points in batting average is because a fielder might have made a spectacular play, or a screaming liner might have been hit right at someone, or a long shot to the outfield might have been held up by the wind... once every 14 games. Does that constitute "failure"?

Even if we were to isolate a single statistic that measures "overall performance" and run our accuracy tests on it, the results will still be inconclusive.

According to OPS, these players are virtually identical:

| BATTER | HR | RBI | SB | BA | OBA | SLG | OPS |
|---|---|---|---|---|---|---|---|
| Smoak, J | 25 | 77 | 0 | .242 | .350 | .457 | .808 |
| Camargo, J | 19 | 76 | 1 | .272 | .349 | .457 | .806 |
| Merrifield, W | 12 | 60 | 45 | .304 | .367 | .438 | .806 |

If I projected Merrifield-caliber stats and ended up with Justin Smoak's numbers, I'd hardly call that an accurate projection, especially if my fantasy team was in dire need of stolen bases.

According to Roto dollars, these players are also dead-on:

| BATTER | HR | RBI | Runs | SB | BA | R$ |
|---|---|---|---|---|---|---|
| Carpenter, M | 36 | 81 | 111 | 4 | .257 | $21 |
| Albies, O | 24 | 72 | 105 | 14 | .261 | $21 |
| Smith, M | 2 | 40 | 65 | 40 | .296 | $21 |

It's not so simple for someone to claim they have accurate projections. And so, it is best to focus on the bigger picture, especially when it comes to winning at fantasy baseball.

More on this: "The Great Myths of Projective Accuracy"

http://www.baseballhq.com/great-myths-projective-accuracy

### *Baseball Forecaster*'s forecasting process

Our approach is to assemble component skills in such a way that they can be used to validate our observations, analyze their relevance and project a likely future direction.

In a perfect world, if a player's raw skills improve, then so should his surface stats. If his skills decline, then his stats should follow as well. But, sometimes a player's skill indicators increase while his surface stats decline. These variances may be due to a variety of factors.

Our forecasting process is based on the expectation that events tend to move towards universal order. Surface stats will eventually approach their skill levels. Unexplained variances will regress to a mean. And from this, we can identify players whose performance may potentially change.

For most of us, this process begins with the previous year's numbers. Last season provides us with a point of reference, so it's a natural way to begin the process of looking at the future. Component skills analysis allows us to validate those numbers. A batter with few HRs but elevated power metrics has a good probability of improving his future HR output. A pitcher whose ERA was poor while his pitching support metrics were solid might be a good bet for ERA improvement.

Of course, these leading indicators do not always follow the rules. There are more shades of grey than blacks and whites. When indicators are in conflict—for instance, a pitcher who is displaying both a rising strikeout rate and a rising walk rate—then we have to find ways to sort out what these indicators might be saying.

It is often helpful to look at leading indicators in a hierarchy. A rank of the most important pitching indicators might be: Command (k/bb), Dominance (k/9), Control (bb/9) and GB/FB rate. For batters, contact rate tops the list, followed by power, walk rate and speed.

## Assimilating additional research

Once we've painted the statistical picture of a player's potential, we then use additional criteria and research results to help us add some color to the analysis. These other criteria include the player's health, age, changes in role, ballpark and a variety of other factors. We also use the research results described in the following pages. This research looks at things like traditional periods of peak performance and breakout profiles.

The final element of the process is assimilating the news into the forecast. This is the element that many fantasy leaguers tend to rely on most since it is the most accessible. However, it is also the element that provides the most noise. Players, management and the media have absolute control over what we are allowed to know. Factors such as hidden injuries, messy divorces and clubhouse unrest are routinely kept from us, while we are fed red herrings and media spam. *We will never know the entire truth.*

Quite often, all you are reading is just other people's opinions... a manager who believes that a player has what it takes to be a regular or a team physician whose diagnosis is that a player is healthy enough to play. These words from experts have some element of truth, but cannot be wholly relied upon to provide an accurate expectation of future events. As such, it is often helpful to develop an appropriate cynicism for what you read.

For instance, if a player is struggling for no apparent reason and there are denials about health issues, don't dismiss the possibility that an injury does exist. There are often motives for such news to be withheld from the public.

And so, as long as we do not know all the facts, we cannot dismiss the possibility that any one fact is true, no matter how often the media assures it, deplores it, or ignores it. Don't believe everything you read; use your own judgment. If your observations conflict with what is being reported, that's powerful insight that should not be ignored.

Also remember that nothing lasts forever in major league baseball. *Reality is fluid.* One decision begets a series of events that lead to other decisions. Any reported action can easily be reversed based on subsequent events. My favorite examples are announcements of a team's new bullpen closer. Those are about the shortest realities known to man.

We need the media to provide us with context for our analyses, and the real news they provide is valuable intelligence. But separating the news from the noise is difficult. In most cases, the only thing you can trust is how that player actually performs.

## Embracing imprecision

Precision in baseball prognosticating is a fool's quest. There are far too many unexpected variables and noise that can render our projections useless. The truth is, the best we can ever hope for is to accurately forecast general tendencies and percentage plays.

However, even when you follow an 80% percentage play, for instance, you will still lose 20% of the time. That 20% is what skeptics use as justification to dismiss prognosticators; they conveniently ignore the more prevalent 80%. The paradox, of course, is that fantasy league titles are often won or lost by those exceptions. Still, long-term success dictates that you always chase the 80% and accept the fact that you will be wrong 20% of the time. Or, whatever that percentage play happens to be.

For fantasy purposes, playing the percentages can take on an even less precise spin. The best projections are often the ones that are just far enough away from the field of expectation to alter decision-making. In other words, it doesn't matter if I project Player X to bat .320 and he only bats .295; it matters that I project .320 and everyone else projects .280. Those who follow my less-accurate projection will go the extra dollar to acquire him in their draft.

Or, perhaps we should evaluate the projections based upon their intrinsic value. For instance, coming into 2018, would it have been more important for me to tell you that Paul Goldschmidt was going to hit 30 HRs or that Jesus Aguilar would hit 25 HRs (when all other touts predicted fewer)? By season's end, the Goldschmidt projection would have been more accurate, but the Aguilar projection—even though it was off by 10 HRs—would have been far more valuable. The Aguilar projection might have persuaded you to go an extra buck on Draft Day, yielding far more profit.

And that has to be enough. Any tout who projects a player's statistics dead-on will have just been lucky with his dart throws that day.

## Perpetuity

Forecasting is not an exercise that produces a single set of numbers. It is dynamic, cyclical and ongoing. Conditions are constantly changing and we must react to those changes by adjusting our expectations. A pre-season projection is just a snapshot in time. Once the first batter steps to the plate on Opening Day, that projection has become obsolete. Its value is merely to provide a starting point, a baseline for what is about to occur.

During the season, if a projection appears to have been invalidated by current performance, the process continues. It is then that we need to ask... What went wrong? What conditions have changed? In fact, has *anything* changed? We need to analyze the situation and revise our expectation, if necessary. This process must be ongoing.

## When good projections go bad

All we can control is the process. We simply can't control outcomes. However, one thing we *can* do is analyze the misses to see *why* they occurred. This is always a valuable exercise each year. It puts a proper focus on the variables that were out of our control as well as providing perspective on those players with whom we might have done a better job.

In general, we can organize these forecasting misses into several categories. To demonstrate, here are all the players whose 2018 Rotisserie earnings varied from projections by at least $10.

### The performances that exceeded expectation

**Development beyond the growth trend:** These are young players for whom we knew there was skill. Some of them were prized prospects in the past who have taken their time ascending the growth curve. Others were a surprise only because their performance spike arrived sooner than anyone anticipated... Miguel Andujar, Gleyber Torres, Adalberto Mondesi, Jose Peraza, Blake Snell, Mike Foltyniewicz, Jameson Taillon.

**Skilled players who just had big years:** We knew these guys were good too; we just didn't anticipate they'd be this good... Javier

Baez, Trevor Story, Francisco Lindor, Christian Yelich, Mookie Betts, Josh Hader, Aaron Nola, Jacob deGrom, Trevor Bauer.

**Unexpected health:** We knew these players had the goods; we just didn't know whether they'd be healthy or would stay healthy all year... Jurickson Profar, Michael Brantley.

**Unexpected playing time:** These players had the skills—and may have even displayed them at some time in the past—but had questionable playing time potential coming into this season. Some benefited from another player's injury, a rookie who didn't pan out or leveraged a short streak into a regular gig... Jesus Aguilar, Harrison Bader, Jack Flaherty, Eduardo Escobar.

**Unexpected role:** This category is reserved for players who played their way into, or backed into, a larger role than anticipated. For most, there was already some previously demonstrated skill: Jose Martinez, Ross Stripling, Kirby Yates.

**Unexpected discovery of the Fountain of Youth:** These players should have been done, or nearly done, or at least headed down the far side of the bell curve. That's what the trends were pointing to. The trends were wrong... Jed Lowrie, David Peralta, Ben Zobrist, Nick Markakis, Justin Verlander, Charlie Morton.

**Surprise, yes, but not as good as it looked:** These are players whose numbers were pretty, but unsupported by their skills metrics. Enjoy them now, but be wary of next year... Jhoulys Chacin, Edwin Diaz.

**Who the heck knows?** Maybe there are reasonable explanations, but this year was so far off the charts for... Max Muncy, Johan Camargo, Patrick Corbin.

### The performances that fell short of expectation

**The DL denizens:** These are players who got hurt, may not have returned fully healthy, or may have never been fully healthy (whether they'd admit it or not)... Corey Seager, Josh Donaldson, Yoenis Cespedes, Kris Bryant, Kevin Kiermeier, Miguel Cabrera, Elvis Andrus, Carlos Correa, Wil Myers, Jose Abreu, Steven Strasburg, Clayton Kershaw, Robbie Ray, Andrew Miller, Michael Fulmer, Garrett Richards, Johnny Cueto.

**Accelerated skills erosion:** These are players who we knew were on the downside of their careers or had soft peripherals but who we did not think would plummet so quickly. In some cases, there were injuries involved, but all in all, 2018 might be the beginning of the end for... Adrian Beltre, Josh Harrison, Ryan Zimmerman, Buster Posey, Gio Gonzalez, Alex Wood, Madison Bumgarner.

**Inflated expectations:** Here are players who we really should not have expected much more than what they produced. Some had short or spotty track records, others had soft peripherals coming into 2018, and still others were inflated by media hype. Yes, for some of these, it was "What the heck was I thinking?" For others, we've almost come to expect players to ascend the growth curve faster these days. (You're 23 and you haven't broken out yet? What's the problem??) The bottom line is that player performance trends simply don't progress or regress in a straight line; still, the skills trends were intriguing enough to take a leap of faith. We were wrong... Byron Buxton, Cody Bellinger, Mike Zunino, Justin Bour, Jonathan Gray, Carlos Martinez, Jose Quintana.

**Unexpected loss of role:** This category is reserved for players who ended up with a smaller role than expected, perhaps through a bad start, bad luck or bad timing... Kolten Wong, Adam Duvall, Cody Allen, Mark Melancon, Corey Knebel.

**Surprise, yes, but not as bad as it looked:** These are players whose numbers were ugly, but supported by better skills metrics. Diss them now, but keep an open mind for next year... Brian Dozier, Luis Castillo, Hector Neris, Chris Archer, Zach Godley

**Who the heck knows?** Maybe any one of these players could have been slotted into another category, but they still remain head-scratchers... Sonny Gray, Ken Giles.

### About fantasy baseball touts

As a group, there is a strong tendency for all pundits to provide numbers that are publicly palatable, often at the expense of potential accuracy. That's because committing to either end of the range of expectation poses a high risk. Few touts will put their credibility on the line like that, even though we all know that those outliers are inevitable. Among our projections, you will find no .350 hitters or 70-steal speedsters. *Someone* is going to post a sub-2.50 ERA next year, but damned if any of us will commit to that. So we take an easier road. We'll hedge our numbers or split the difference between two equally possible outcomes.

In the world of prognosticating, this is called the *comfort zone*. This represents the outer tolerances for the public acceptability of a set of numbers. In most circumstances, even if the evidence is outstanding, prognosticators will not stray from within the comfort zone.

As for this book, occasionally we do commit to outlying numbers when we feel the data support it. But on the whole, most of the numbers here can be nearly as cowardly as everyone else's. We get around this by providing "color" to the projections in the capsule commentaries, often listing UPside or DOWNside projections. That is where you will find the players whose projection has the best potential to stray beyond the limits of the comfort zone.

As analyst John Burnson once wrote: "The issue is not the success rate for one player, but the success rate for all players. No system is 100% reliable, and in trying to capture the outliers, you weaken the middle and thereby lose more predictive pull than you gain. At some level, everyone is an exception!"

## *Validating Performance*

### Performance validation criteria

The following is a set of support variables that helps determine whether a player's statistical output is an accurate reflection of his skills. From this we can validate or refute stats that vary from expectation, essentially asking, is this performance "fact or fluke?"

**1. Age:** Is the player at the stage of development when we might expect a change in performance?

**2. Health:** Is he coming off an injury, reconditioned and healthy for the first time in years, or a habitual resident of the disabled list?

**3. Minor league performance:** Has he shown the potential for greater things at some level of the minors? Or does his minor league history show a poor skill set that might indicate a lower ceiling?

**4. Historical trends:** Have his skill levels over time been on an upswing or downswing?

**5. Component skills indicators:** Looking beyond batting averages and ERAs, what do his support ratios look like?

**6. Ballpark, team, league:** Pitchers going to Colorado will see their ERA spike. Pitchers going to Oakland will see their ERA improve.

**7. Team performance:** Has a player's performance been affected by overall team chemistry or the environment fostered by a winning or losing club?

**8. Batting stance, pitching style/mastery:** Has a change in performance been due to a mechanical adjustment?

**9. Usage pattern, lineup position, role:** Has a change in RBI opportunities been a result of moving further up or down in the batting order? Has pitching effectiveness been impacted by moving from the bullpen to the rotation?

**10. Coaching effects:** Has the coaching staff changed the way a player approaches his conditioning, or how he approaches the game itself?

**11. Off-season activity:** Has the player spent the winter frequenting workout rooms or banquet tables?

**12. Personal factors:** Has the player undergone a family crisis? Experienced spiritual rebirth? Given up red meat? Taken up testosterone?

### Skills ownership

*Once a player displays a skill, he owns it.* That display could occur at any time—earlier in his career, back in the minors, or even in winter ball play. And while that skill may lie dormant after its initial display, the potential is always there for him to tap back into that skill at some point, barring injury or age. That dormant skill can reappear at any time given the right set of circumstances.

*Caveats:*

1. The initial display of skill must have occurred over an extended period of time. An isolated 1-hit shutout in Single-A ball amidst a 5.00 ERA season is not enough. The shorter the display of skill in the past, the more likely it can be attributed to random chance. The longer the display, the more likely that any reemergence is for real.

2. If a player has been suspected of using performance enhancing drugs at any time, all bets are off.

*Corollaries:*

1. Once a player displays a vulnerability or skills deficiency, he owns that as well. That vulnerability could be an old injury problem, an inability to hit breaking pitches, or just a tendency to go into prolonged slumps.

2. The probability of a player correcting a skills deficiency declines with each year that deficiency exists.

### Contract year performance *(Tom Mullooly)*

There is a contention that players step up their game when they are playing for a contract. Research looked at contract year players and their performance during that year as compared to career levels. Of the batters and pitchers studied, 53% of the batters performed as if they were on a salary drive, while only 15% of the pitchers exhibited some level of contract year behavior.

How do players fare *after* signing a large contract (minimum $4M per year)? Research from 2005-2008 revealed that only 30% of pitchers and 22% of hitters exhibited an increase of more than 15% in BPV after signing a large deal either with their new team, or re-signing with the previous team. But nearly half of the pitchers (49%) and nearly half of the hitters (47%) saw a drop in BPV of more than 15% in the year after signing.

## Risk Analysis

### Risk management and reliability grades

Forecasts are constructed with the best data available, but there are factors that can impact the variability. One way we manage this risk is to assign each player Reliability Grades. The more certainty we see in a data set, the higher the reliability grades assigned to that player. The following variables are evaluated:

*Health:* Players with a history of staying healthy and off the DL are valuable to own. Unfortunately, while the ability to stay healthy can be considered skill, it is not very projectable. We can track the number of days spent on the disabled list and draw rough conclusions. The grades in the player boxes also include an adjustment for older players, who have a higher likelihood of getting hurt. That is the only forward-looking element of the grade.

"A" level players would have accumulated fewer than 30 days on the major league DL over the past five years. "F" grades go to those who've spent more than 120 days on the DL. Recent DL stays are given a heavier weight in the calculation.

*Playing Time and Experience (PT/Exp):* The greater the pool of MLB history to draw from, the greater our ability to construct a viable forecast. Length of service—and consistent service—is important. So players who bounce up and down from the majors to the minors are higher risk players. And rookies are all high risk.

For batters, we simply track plate appearances. Major league PAs have greater weight than minor league PAs. "A" level players would have averaged at least 550 major league PAs per year over the past three years. "F" graded players averaged fewer than 250 major league PA per year.

For pitchers, workload can be a double-edged sword. On one hand, small IP samples are deceptive in providing a read on a pitcher's true potential. Even a consistent 65-inning reliever can be considered higher risk since it would take just one bad outing to skew an entire season's work.

On the flipside, high workload levels also need to be monitored, especially in the formative years of a pitcher's career. Exceeding those levels elevates the risk of injury, burnout, or breakdown. So, tracking workload must be done within a range of innings. The grades capture this.

*Consistency:* Consistent performers are easier to project and garner higher reliability grades. Players that mix mediocrity with occasional flashes of brilliance or badness generate higher risk projections. Even those who exhibit a consistent upward or downward trend cannot be considered truly consistent as we do not know whether those trends will continue. Typically, they don't. *(See next: Using 3-year trends as leading indicators)*

"A" level players are those whose runs created per game level (xERA for pitchers) has fluctuated by less than half a run during each of the past three years. "F" grades go to those whose RC/G or xERA has fluctuated by two runs or more.

Remember that these grades have nothing to do with quality of performance; they strictly refer to confidence in our expectations. So a grade of AAA for a poor player only means that there is a high probability he will perform as poorly as we've projected.

### Using 3-year trends as leading indicators *(Ed DeCaria)*
It is almost irresistibly tempting to look at three numbers moving in one direction and expect that the fourth will continue that progression. However, for both hitters and pitchers riding positive trends over any consecutive three-year period, not only do most players not continue their positive trend into a fourth year, their Year 4 performance usually regresses significantly. This is true for every metric tested (whether related to playing time, batting skills, pitching skills, running skills, luck indicators, or valuation). Negative trends show similar reversals, but tend to be more "sticky," meaning that rebounds are neither as frequent nor as strong as positive trend regressions.

### Reliability and age
Peak batting reliability occurs at ages 29 and 30, followed by a minor decline for four years. So, to draft the most reliable batters, and maximize the odds of returning at least par value on your investments, you should target the age range of 28-34.

The most reliable age range for pitchers is 29-34. While we are forever looking for "sleepers" and hot prospects, it is very risky to draft any pitcher under 27 or over 35.

### Evaluating Reliability *(Bill Macey)*
When you head into an upcoming auction or draft, consider the following with regard to risk and reliability:

- Reliability grades do help identify more stable investments: players with "B" grades in both Health and PT/Experience are more likely to return a higher percentage of their projected value.
- While top-end starting pitching may be more reliable than ever, the overall pool of pitchers is fraught with uncertainty and they represent a less reliable investment than batters.
- There does not appear to be a significant market premium for reliability, at least according to the criteria measured by BaseballHQ.com.
- There are only two types of players: risky and riskier. So while it may be worth going the extra buck for a more reliable player, be warned that even the most reliable player can falter—don't go overboard bidding up a AAA-rated player simply due to his Reliability grades.

### Normal production variance *(Patrick Davitt)*
Even if we have a perfectly accurate understanding of a player's "normal" performance level, his actual performance can and does vary widely over any particular 150-game span—including the 150-game span we call "a season." A .300 career hitter can perform in a range of .250-.350, a 40-HR hitter from 30-50, and a 3.70/1.15 pitcher from 2.60/0.95 to 6.00/1.55. And all of these results must be considered "normal."

## Health Analysis
### Disabled list statistics

| Year | #Players | 3yr Avg | DL Days | 3yr Avg |
|------|----------|---------|---------|---------|
| 2010 | 393 | 408 | 22,911 | 25,783 |
| 2011 | 422 | 408 | 25,610 | 24,924 |
| 2012 | 409 | 408 | 30,408 | 27,038 |
| 2013 | 442 | 419 | 29,551 | 28,523 |
| 2014 | 422 | 424 | 25,839 | 28,599 |
| 2015 | 454 | 439 | 28,982 | 28,124 |
| 2016 | 478 | 451 | 31,329 | 28,717 |
| 2017 | 533 | 488 | 30,913 | 30,408 |
| 2018 | 574 | 528 | 34,284 | 32,175 |

### DL days as a leading indicator *(Bill Macey)*
Players who are injured in one year are likely to be injured in a subsequent year:

| | |
|---|---|
| % DL batters in Year 1 who are also DL in year 2 | 38% |
| Under age 30 | 36% |
| Age 30 and older | 41% |
| % DL batters in Year 1 and 2 who are also DL in year 3 | 54% |
| % DL pitchers in Year 1 who are also DL in year 2 | 43% |
| Under age 30 | 45% |
| Age 30 and older | 41% |
| % DL pitchers in Yr 1 and 2 who are also DL in year 3 | 41% |

Previously injured players also tend to spend a longer time on the DL. The average number of days on the DL was 51 days for batters and 73 days for pitchers. For the subset of these players who get hurt again the following year, the average number of days on the DL was 58 days for batters and 88 days for pitchers.

### How a batter's age affects DL stays *(Jeff Zimmerman)*
Some players seem to get more than their fair share of injuries, but for those hitters with the "injury-prone" tag, it only takes one healthy season to make a difference. After breaking up hitters into three age groups (25 and younger; 26-29; 30 and older), a study examined length and frequency of DL stints. Among the findings:

1. If someone in the youngest group goes on the DL once, they aren't as likely to again the next season. The DL chance increase after two DL seasons is huge, however, going from 33% to 43%.
2. The best health is exhibited by the middle group. It seems this age is the sweet spot for avoiding hitter injuries. The hitters have shown they can hold up to a full season, but their bodies have not started to break down.
3. Not surprisingly, the oldest group takes longer to heal. The older player's DL-related stats hover above the league average, but the DL rate doesn't increase as a player racks up previous injuries.

As they age, a hitter's body breaks down more often and for longer periods of time, which may give them the appearance of being injury-prone. As a general overall rule, it's prudent to discount a hitter's injury history, especially those aged 26-29.

## Do overworked hitters wear down? *(Jeff Zimmerman)*

A study compared the first- and second-half statistics for batters who played the most games over the entire season from 2002-16. These players were continually run out on the field, and one figures that fatigue would show up in their statistics. But conversely, the numbers don't support the wear-down narrative. If anything, their output improves the more they play. Though this concept goes against conventional wisdom, it is true: If a hitter plays more, the more likely he is healthy and not wearing down.

## Spring training spin *(Dave Adler)*

Spring training sound bites raise expectations among fantasy leaguers, but how much of that "news" is really "noise"? Thanks to a summary listed at RotoAuthority.com, we were able to compile the stats for 2009. Verdict: Noise.

| BATTERS | No. | IMPROVED | DECLINED |
|---|---|---|---|
| Weight change | 30 | 33% | 30% |
| Fitness program | 3 | 0% | 67% |
| Eye surgery | 6 | 50% | 33% |
| Plans more SB | 6 | 17% | 33% |
| **PITCHERS** | **No.** | **IMPROVED** | **DECLINED** |
| Weight change | 18 | 44% | 44% |
| Fitness program | 4 | 50% | 50% |
| Eye surgery | 2 | 0% | 50% |
| New pitch | 5 | 60% | 40% |

## *In-Season Analysis*

### April performance as a leading indicator

We isolated all players who earned at least $10 more or $10 less than we had projected in March. Then we looked at the April stats of these players to see if we could have picked out the $10 outliers after just one month.

| | Identifiable in April |
|---|---|
| Earned $10+ more than projected | |
| BATTERS | 39% |
| PITCHERS | 44% |
| Earned -$10 less than projected | |
| BATTERS | 56% |
| PITCHERS | 74% |

Nearly three out of every four pitchers who earned at least $10 less than projected also struggled in April. For all the other surprises—batters or pitchers—April was not a strong leading indicator. Another look:

| | Pct. |
|---|---|
| Batters who finished +$25 | 45% |
| Pitchers who finished +$20 | 44% |
| Batters who finished under $0 | 60% |
| Pitchers who finished under -$5 | 78% |

April surgers are less than a 50/50 proposition to maintain that level all season. Those who finished April at the bottom of the roto rankings were more likely to continue struggling, especially pitchers. In fact, of those pitchers who finished April with a value *under -$10*, 91% finished the season in the red. Holes are tough to dig out of.

## The weight of early season numbers

Early season strugglers who surge later in the year often get little respect because they have to live with the weight of their early numbers all season long. Conversely, quick starters who fade late get far more accolades than they deserve.

For instance, take Odubel Herrera's month-by-month batting average. The perception is that his .255 BA was off his historical track record but not excessively so. Reality is different. The excellent .313 mark he posted through May 31 inflated his batting average for the rest of the year. From June 1 on, he batted only .222, and only .189 in August and September.

| Month | BA | Cum BA |
|---|---|---|
| Mar-Apr | .343 | .343 |
| May | .283 | .313 |
| June | .236 | .286 |
| July | .253 | .278 |
| August | .205 | .267 |
| Sept-Oct | .171 | .255 |

## Courtship period

Any time a player is put into a new situation, he enters into a courtship period. This period might occur when a player switches leagues, or switches teams. It could be the first few games when a minor leaguer is called up. It could occur when a reliever moves into the rotation, or when a lead-off hitter is moved to another spot in the lineup. There is a team-wide courtship period when a manager is replaced. Any external situation that could affect a player's performance sets off a new decision point in evaluating that performance.

During this period, it is difficult to get a true read on how a player is going to ultimately perform. He is adjusting to the new situation. Things could be volatile during this time. For instance, a role change that doesn't work could spur other moves. A rookie hurler might buy himself a few extra starts with a solid debut, even if he has questionable skills.

It is best not to make a decision on a player who is going through a courtship period. Wait until his stats stabilize. Don't cut a struggling pitcher in his first few starts after a managerial change. Don't pick up a hitter who smacks a pair of HRs in his first game after having been traded. Unless, of course, talent and track record say otherwise.

## Half-season fallacies

A popular exercise at the midpoint of each season is to analyze those players who are consistent first half to second half surgers or faders. There are several fallacies with this analytical approach.

**1. Half-season consistency is rare.** There are very few players who show consistent changes in performance from one half of the season to the other.

*Research results from a three-year study conducted in the late-1990s:* The test groups... batters with min. 300 AB full season, 150 AB first half, and pitchers with min. 100 IP full season, 50 IP first half. Of those groups (size noted):

| 3-year consistency in | BATTERS (98) | PITCHERS (42) |
|---|---|---|
| 1 stat category | 40% | 57% |
| 2 stat categories | 18% | 21% |
| 3 stat categories | 3% | 5% |

When the analysis was stretched to a fourth year, only 1% of all players showed consistency in even one category.

**2. Analysts often use false indicators.** Situational statistics provide us with tools that can be misused. Several sources offer up 3- and 5-year stats intended to paint a picture of a long-term performance. Some analysts look at a player's half-season swing over that multi-year period and conclude that he is demonstrating consistent performance.

The fallacy is that those multi-year scans may not show any consistency at all. They are not individual season performances but *aggregate* performances. A player whose 5-year batting average shows a 15-point rise in the 2nd half, for instance, may actually have experienced a BA decline in several of those years, a fact that might have been offset by a huge BA rise in one of the years.

**3. It's arbitrary.** The season's midpoint is an arbitrary delineator of performance swings. Some players are slow starters and might be more appropriately evaluated as pre-May 1 and post-May 1. Others bring their game up a notch with a pennant chase and might see a performance swing with August 15 as the cut-off. Each player has his own individual tendency, if, in fact, one exists at all. There's nothing magical about mid-season as the break point, and certainly not over a multi-year period.

### Half-season tendencies

Despite the above, it stands to reason logically that there might be some underlying tendencies on a more global scale, first half to second half. In fact, one would think that the player population as a whole might decline in performance as the season drones on. There are many variables that might contribute to a player wearing down—workload, weather, boredom—and the longer a player is on the field, the higher the likelihood that he is going to get hurt. A recent 5-year study uncovered the following tendencies:

**Batting**

Overall, batting skills held up pretty well, half to half. There was a 5% erosion of playing time, likely due, in part, to September roster expansion.

*Power:* First half power studs (20 HRs in 1H) saw a 10% drop-off in the second half. 34% of first half 20+ HR hitters hit 15 or fewer in the second half and only 27% were able to improve on their first half output.

*Speed:* Second half speed waned as well. About 26% of the 20+ SB speedsters stole *at least 10 fewer bases* in the second half. Only 26% increased their second half SB output at all.

*Batting average:* 60% of first half .300 hitters failed to hit .300 in the second half. Only 20% showed any second half improvement at all. As for 1H strugglers, managers tended to stick with their full-timers despite poor starts. Nearly one in five of the sub-.250 1H hitters managed to hit *more than* .300 in the second half.

**Pitching**

Overall, there was some slight erosion in innings and ERA despite marginal improvement in some peripherals.

*ERA:* For those who pitched at least 100 innings in the first half, ERAs rose an average of 0.40 runs in the 2H. Of those with first half ERAs less than 4.00, only 49% were able to maintain a sub-4.00 ERA in the second half.

*Wins:* Pitchers who won 18 or more games in a season tended to pitch *more* innings in the 2H and had slightly better peripherals.

*Saves:* Of those closers who saved 20 or more games in the first half, only 39% were able to post 20 or more saves in the 2H, and 26% posted fewer than 15 saves. Aggregate ERAs of these pitchers rose from 2.45 to 3.17, half to half.

### In-season trends in hitting and pitching *(Bob Berger)*

A study of monthly trends in traditional statistical categories found:

- Batting average, HR/game and RBI/game rise from April through August, then fall in September/October.
- Stolen bases decline in July and August before rebounding in September.
- ERA worsens in July/August and improves in September.
- WHIP gets worse in July/August.
- K/9 rate improves all season.

The statement that hitters perform better in warmer weather seems to be true broadly.

### Surprisingly Productive Years *(Ed DeCaria)*

When it comes to player valuation, drafters have always generally agreed on two basic points: 1) avoid players with negative projected values, and 2) ignore valuation once the season starts.

But sometimes we can gain an advantage by zigging when others zag. Here's a skills-based method of finding productive in-season roster additions:

1. Consider all batters projected for 50% or less playing time, all starting pitchers projected for 10% or less of his team's innings pitched (about 140 IP), and all relief pitchers projected for less than 4% of his team's innings pitched (about 50 IP)

2. Using each player's projected skills—not stats—in the form of his Mayberry scores, include only batters whose sum of three Mayberry skills (power, speed, and hitting) was 7 or higher (8 or higher for mixed leagues). For pitchers, only consider players whose sum of two Mayberry skills (xERA and strikeout rate) was 4 or higher (5 or higher for mixed leagues). For relievers, we also counted Mayberry's saves potential score, so we included only relievers whose sum of three scores was 7 or higher (8 or higher for mixed leagues).

3. Examine the specific situation of each player that met our first two criteria and assign a realistic playing time upside given his skills and injury, consistency, and forecast risk, and that of the player(s) ahead of him on his team's depth chart.

4. Calculate a single number that measured their "projected skill" over their "potential playing time" to arrive at their "potential value."

   a. For hitters, take his Mayberry sum and multiply it by his potential playing time (pPT). Then rank batters by this metric and subtract the minimum value of the group from all players, so that the least valuable batter had a marginal score (mSCORE) of zero. Then use mSCORE to calculate each player's "share" of the total, and multiply that by the league's total wasted dollars (using a 65/35 batter/pitcher split) to determine each batter's potential value (pR$).

b. Similarly for pitchers, take the Mayberry sum multiplied by potential innings percentage (pPT) and rank pitchers by this metric. Subtract the minimum value of the group from all pitchers, then use mSCORE to calculate each pitcher's "share" of the total, and multiply that by the league's total wasted dollars (using a 65/35 batter/pitcher split) to determine each pitcher's potential value (pR$).

Use these rankings to produce lists of players who are projected for far less than full playing time despite good or even great skills. A well-timed pick-up of any one of these players could be a boon to most teams' chances of winning their league. Another full exhibition of the exercise will appear at BaseballHQ.com in 2019.

## Teams

**Johnson Effect** *(Bryan Johnson)*: Teams whose actual won/loss record exceeds or falls short of their statistically projected record in one season will tend to revert to the level of their projection in the following season.

**Law of Competitive Balance** *(Bill James)*: The level at which a team (or player) will address its problems is inversely related to its current level of success. Low performers will tend to make changes to improve; high performers will not. This law explains the existence of the Plexiglass and Whirlpool Principles.

**Plexiglass Principle** *(Bill James)*: If a player or team improves markedly in one season, it will likely decline in the next. The opposite is true but not as often (because a poor performer gets fewer opportunities to rebound).

**Whirlpool Principle** *(Bill James)*: All team and player performances are forcefully drawn to the center. For teams, that center is a .500 record. For players, it represents their career average level of performance.

## Other Diamonds

### The Fanalytic Fundamentals

1. This is not a game of accuracy or precision. It is a game of human beings and tendencies.
2. This is not a game of projections. It is a game of market value versus real value.
3. Draft skills, not stats. Draft skills, not roles.
4. A player's ability to post acceptable stats despite lousy support metrics will eventually run out.
5. Once you display a skill, you own it.
6. Virtually every player is vulnerable to a month of aberrant performance. Or a year.
7. Exercise excruciating patience.

### Aging Axioms

1. Age is the only variable for which we can project a rising trend with 100% accuracy. (Or, age never regresses.)
2. The aging process slows down for those who maintain a firm grasp on the strike zone. Plate patience and pitching command can preserve any waning skill they have left.
3. Negatives tend to snowball as you age.

### Steve Avery List

Players who hang onto MLB rosters for six years searching for a skill level they only had for three.

### Bylaws of Badness

1. Some players are better than an open roster spot, but not by much.
2. Some players have bad years because they are unlucky. Others have *many* bad years because they are bad... and lucky.

### Christie Brinkley Law of Statistical Analysis

Never get married to the model.

### Employment Standards

1. If you are right-brain dominant, own a catcher's mitt and are under 40, you will always be gainfully employed.
2. Some teams believe that it is better to employ a player with any experience because it has to be better than the devil they don't know.
3. It's not so good to go *pffft* in a contract year.

### Brad Fullmer List

Players whose leading indicators indicate upside potential, year after year, but consistently fail to reach that full potential. Players like Byron Buxton and Lucas Giolito are on the list right now.

### Good Luck Truism

Good luck is rare and everyone has more of it than you do. That's the law.

### The Gravity Principles

1. It is easier to be crappy than it is to be good.
2. All performance starts at zero, ends at zero and can drop to zero at any time.
3. The odds of a good performer slumping are far greater than the odds of a poor performer surging.
4. Once a player is in a slump, it takes several 3-for-5 days to get out of it. Once he is on a streak, it takes a single 0-for-4 day to begin the downward spiral. *Corollary:* Once a player is in a slump, not only does it take several 3-for-5 days to get out of it, but he also has to get his name back on the lineup card.
5. Eventually all performance comes down to earth. It may take a week, or a month, or may not happen until he's 45, but eventually it's going to happen.

### Health Homilies

1. Staying healthy is a skill (and "DL Days" should be a Rotisserie category).
2. A $40 player can get hurt just as easily as a $5 player but is eight times tougher to replace.
3. Chronically injured players never suddenly get healthy.
4. There are two kinds of pitchers: those that are hurt and those that are not hurt... yet.
5. Players with back problems are always worth $10 less.
6. "Opting out of surgery" usually means it's coming anyway, just later.

### The Health Hush

Players get hurt and potentially have a lot to lose, so there is an incentive for them to hide injuries. HIPAA laws restrict the disclosure of health information. Team doctors and trainers have been instructed not to talk with the media. So, when it comes to information on a player's health status, we're all pretty much in the dark.

### The Livan Level

The point when a player's career Runs Above Replacement level has dropped so far below zero that he has effectively cancelled out any possible remaining future value. (Similarly, the Dontrelle Demarcation.)

### The Momentum Maxims

1. A player will post a pattern of positive results until the day you add him to your roster.
2. Patterns of negative results are more likely to snowball than correct.
3. When an unstoppable force meets an immovable object, the wall always wins.

### Noise

Irrelevant or meaningless pieces of information that can distort the results of an analysis. In news, this is opinion or rumor. In forecasting, this is random variance or irrelevant data. In ballparks, this is a screaming crowd cheering for a team down 12-3 with two outs and bases empty in the bottom of the ninth.

### Paradoxes and Conundrums

1. Is a player's improvement in performance from one year to the next a point in a growth trend, an isolated outlier or a complete anomaly?
2. A player can play through an injury, post rotten numbers and put his job at risk… or… he can admit that he can't play through an injury, allow himself to be taken out of the lineup/rotation, and put his job at risk.
3. Did irregular playing time take its toll on the player's performance or did poor performance force a reduction in his playing time?
4. Is a player only in the game versus right-handers because he has a true skills deficiency versus left-handers? Or is his poor performance versus left-handers because he's never given a chance to face them?
5. The problem with stockpiling bench players in the hope that one pans out is that you end up evaluating performance using data sets that are too small to be reliable.
6. There are players who could give you 20 stolen bases if they got 400 AB. But if they got 400 AB, they would likely be on a bad team that wouldn't let them steal.

### Paths to Retirement

1. **George Brett:** Get out while you're still putting up good numbers and the public perception of you is favorable. Like Chipper Jones, Mariano Rivera and David Ortiz.
2. **Steve Carlton:** Hang around the majors long enough for your numbers to become so wretched that people begin to forget your past successes. Current players who could be on a similar course include Bartolo Colon, Curtis Granderson and Matt Holliday.
3. **Johan Santana:** Stay on the disabled list for so long that nobody realizes you haven't officially retired until your

name shows up on a Hall of Fame ballot. Also: Cliff Lee. Perhaps: Carl Crawford.

### Process-Outcome Matrix *(Russo and Schoemaker)*

|  | Good Outcome | Bad Outcome |
|---|---|---|
| **Good Process** | Deserved Success | Bad Break |
| **Bad Process** | Dumb Luck | Poetic Justice |

### Quack!

An exclamation in response to the educated speculation that a player has used performance enhancing drugs. While it is rare to have absolute proof, there is often enough information to suggest that, "if it looks like a duck and quacks like a duck, then odds are it's a duck."

### Situation Dependent

An event that is affected by the context of team, ballpark, or other outside variables.

RBI: You can't drive in runs if there is nobody on base.

Runs: You can't score a run if no one drives you in.

Wins: You can't win a game unless your offense scores runs, no matter how well you pitch.

### Surface Stats

All those wonderful statistics we grew up with that those mean bean counters are telling us don't matter anymore. Home runs, RBIs, batting average, won-loss record. Let's go back to the 1960s and make baseball great again! [EDITOR: No.]

### Tenets of Optimal Timing

1. If a second half fader had put up his second half stats in the first half and his first half stats in the second half, then he probably wouldn't even have had a second half.
2. Fast starters can often buy six months of playing time out of one month of productivity.
3. Poor 2nd halves don't get recognized until it's too late.
4. "Baseball is like this. Have one good year and you can fool them for five more, because for five more years they expect you to have another good one." — Frankie Frisch

### The Three True Outcomes

1. Strikeouts
2. Walks
3. Home runs

### The Three True Handicaps

1. Has power but can't make contact.
2. Has speed but can't hit safely.
3. Has potential but is too old.

### Zombie

A player who is indestructible, continuing to get work, year-after-year, no matter how dead his skills metrics have become. Like Ryan Flaherty, Francisco Liriano, Tommy Milone and Colby Rasmus.

# Batters

## Batting Eye, Contact and Batting Average

### Batting average (BA, or Avg)

This is where it starts. BA is a grand old nugget that has long outgrown its usefulness. We revere .300 hitting superstars and scoff at .250 hitters, yet the difference between the two is one hit every five games. BA is a poor evaluator of performance in that it neglects the offensive value of the base on balls and assumes that all hits are created equal.

### Walk rate (bb%)

*(BB / (AB + BB))*

A measure of a batter's plate patience. **BENCHMARKS:** The best batters will have levels more than 10%. Those with poor plate patience will have levels of 5% or less.

### On base average (OB)

*(H + BB + HBP) / (AB + BB + HBP + Sac Flies)*

Addressing a key deficiency with BA, OB gives value to events that get batters on base, but are not hits. An OB of .350 can be read as "this batter gets on base 35% of the time." When a run is scored, there is no distinction made as to how that runner reached base. So, two-thirds of the time—about how often a batter comes to the plate with the bases empty—a walk really is as good as a hit. **BENCHMARKS:** We know what a .300 hitter is, but what represents "good" for OB? That comparable level would likely be .400, with .275 representing the comparable level of futility.

### Ground ball, line drive, fly ball percentages (G/L/F)

The percentage of all balls in play that are hit on the ground, as line drives and in the air. For batters, increased fly ball tendency may foretell a rise in power skills; increased line drive tendency may foretell an improvement in batting average. For a pitcher, the ability to keep the ball on the ground can contribute to his statistical output exceeding his demonstrated skill level.

| *BIP Type | Total% | Out% |
|---|---|---|
| Ground ball | 45% | 72% |
| Line drive | 20% | 28% |
| Fly ball | 35% | 85% |
| *TOTAL* | *100%* | *69%* |

*Data only includes fieldable balls and is net of HRs.

### Line drives and luck *(Patrick Davitt)*

Given that each individual batter's hit rate sets its own baseline, and that line drives (LD) are the most productive type of batted ball, a study looked at the relationship between the two. Among the findings were that hit rates on LDs are much higher than on FBs or GBs, with individual batters consistently falling into the 72-73% range. Ninety-five percent of all batters fall between the range of 60%-86%; batters outside this range regress very quickly, often within the season.

Note that batters' BAs did not always follow their LD% up or down, because some of them enjoyed higher hit rates on other batted balls, improved their contact rates, or both. Still, it's justifiable to bet that players hitting the ball with authority but getting fewer hits than they should will correct over time.

### Batting eye (Eye)

*(Walks / Strikeouts)*

A measure of a player's strike zone judgment. **BENCHMARKS:** The best hitters have Eye ratios more than 1.00 (indicating more walks than strikeouts) and are the most likely to be among a league's .300 hitters. Ratios less than 0.50 represent batters who likely also have lower BAs.

### Batting eye as a leading indicator

There is a correlation between strike zone judgment and batting average. However, research shows that this is more descriptive than predictive:

| | Batting Average | | | | |
|---|---|---|---|---|---|
| Batting Eye | 2014 | 2015 | 2016 | 2017 | 2018 |
| 0.00 - 0.25 | .238 | .243 | .248 | .245 | .232 |
| 0.26 - 0.50 | .253 | .257 | .255 | .255 | .252 |
| 0.51 - 0.75 | .268 | .267 | .271 | .270 | .259 |
| 0.76 - 1.00 | .270 | .280 | .286 | .269 | .287 |
| 1.01 and over | .304 | .293 | .255 | .295 | .271 |

We have been running the above chart for 19 years and the correlation at each successive cohort had always been perfect. But recently, some of the correlations have been breaking down because the sample sizes are too small. In 2018, for instance, there were only 17 players (min. 100 AB) in the "0.76-1.00" group and only five in the "1.01 and over" group.

We can create percentage plays for the different levels:

| For Eye | Pct who bat | |
|---|---|---|
| Levels of | .300+ | .250- |
| 0.00 - 0.25 | 7% | 39% |
| 0.26 - 0.50 | 14% | 26% |
| 0.51 - 0.75 | 18% | 17% |
| 0.76 - 1.00 | 32% | 14% |
| 1.01 - 1.50 | 51% | 9% |
| 1.51 + | 59% | 4% |

Any batter with an eye ratio more than 1.50 has about a 4% chance of hitting less than .250 over 500 at bats.

Of all .300 hitters, those with ratios of at least 1.00 have a 65% chance of repeating as .300 hitters. Those with ratios less than 1.00 have less than a 50% chance of repeating.

Only 4% of sub-.250 hitters with ratios less than 0.50 will mature into .300 hitters the following year.

In this study, only 37 batters hit .300-plus with a sub-0.50 eye ratio over at least 300 AB in a season. Of this group, 30% were able to accomplish this feat on a consistent basis. For the other 70%, this was a short-term aberration.

### Contact rate (ct%)

*((AB - K) / AB)*

Measures a batter's ability to get wood on the ball and hit it into the field of play. **BENCHMARKS:** Those batters with the best contact skill will have levels of 80% or better. The hackers will have levels of 70% or less.

## Contact rate as a leading indicator

The more often a batter makes contact with the ball, the higher the likelihood that he will hit safely.

| Contact Rate | Batting Average | | | | |
|---|---|---|---|---|---|
| | 2014 | 2015 | 2016 | 2017 | 2018 |
| 0% - 60% | .176 | .194 | .207 | .206 | .196 |
| 61% - 65% | .217 | .217 | .223 | .226 | .223 |
| 66% - 70% | .230 | .236 | .232 | .244 | .237 |
| 71% - 75% | .243 | .254 | .253 | .248 | .245 |
| 76% - 80% | .257 | .257 | .262 | .268 | .258 |
| 81% - 85% | .266 | .268 | .271 | .270 | .268 |
| 86% - 90% | .276 | .277 | .285 | .287 | .277 |
| Over 90% | .324 | .284 | .254 | .270 | .275 |

Here again, the dearth of players at the higher skill levels has broken the correlation. The "Over 90%" cohort had only one player with more than 100 AB in 2017—Ben Revere—and only two in 2018—Andrelton Simmons and Joe Panik. Pure contact hitters have become a dying breed.

## Contact rate and walk rate as leading indicators

A matrix of contact rates and walk rates can provide expectation benchmarks for a player's batting average:

| | | Walk rate (bb%) | | | |
|---|---|---|---|---|---|
| | | 0-5 | 6-10 | 11-15 | 16+ |
| Contact rate (ct%) | 65- | .179 | .195 | .229 | .237 |
| | 66-75 | .190 | .248 | .254 | .272 |
| | 76-85 | .265 | .267 | .276 | .283 |
| | 86+ | .269 | .279 | .301 | .309 |

A contact rate of 65% or lower offers virtually no chance for a player to hit even .250, no matter how high a walk rate he has. The .300 hitters most often come from the group with a minimum 86% contact and 11% walk rate.

## HCt and HctX  *(Patrick Davitt)*

*HCt= hard hit ball rate x contact rate*
*HctX= Player HCt divided by league average Hct, normalized to 100*
The combination of making contact and hitting the ball hard might be the most important skills for a batter. HctX correlates very strongly with BA, and at higher BA levels often does so with high accuracy. Its success with HR was somewhat limited, probably due to GB/FB differences. **BENCHMARKS:** The average major-leaguer in a given year has a HctX of 100. Elite batters have an HctX of 135 or above; weakest batters have HctX of 55 or below.

## Balls in play (BIP)

*(AB – K)*
The total number of batted balls that are hit fair, both hits and outs. An analysis of how these balls are hit—on the ground, in the air, hits, outs, etc.—can provide analytical insight, from player skill levels to the impact of luck on statistical output.

## Batting average on balls in play  *(Voros McCracken)*

*(H – HR) / (AB – HR – K)*
Or, BABIP. Also called hit rate (h%). The percent of balls hit into the field of play that fall for hits. **BENCHMARK:** Every hitter establishes his own individual hit rate that stabilizes over time. A batter whose seasonal hit rate varies significantly from the h% he has established over the preceding three seasons (variance of at least +/- 3%) is likely to improve or regress to his individual h% mean (with over-performer declines more likely and sharper than under-performer recoveries). Three-year h% levels strongly predict a player's h% the following year.

## Pitches/Plate Appearance as a leading indicator for BA  *(Paul Petera)*

The art of working the count has long been considered one of the more crucial aspects of good hitting. It is common knowledge that the more pitches seen, the greater opportunity he has to reach base safely.

| P/PA | OBA | BA |
|---|---|---|
| 4.00+ | .360 | .264 |
| 3.75-3.99 | .347 | .271 |
| 3.50-3.74 | .334 | .274 |
| Under 3.50 | .321 | .276 |

Generally speaking, the more pitches seen, the lower the BA, but the higher the OBA. But what about the outliers, those players that bucked the trend in year #1?

| | YEAR TWO | |
|---|---|---|
| | BA Improved | BA Declined |
| Low P/PA and Low BA | 77% | 23% |
| High P/PA and High BA | 21% | 79% |

In these scenarios, there was a strong tendency for performance to normalize in year #2.

## Expected batting average  *(John Burnson)*

$$xCT\% * [xH1\% + xH2\%]$$
where
$$xH1\% = GB\% \times [0.0004\ PX + 0.062\ ln(SX)]$$
$$+ LD\% \times [0.93 - 0.086\ ln(SX)]$$
$$+ FB\% \times 0.12$$
and
$$xH2\% = FB\% \times [0.0013\ PX - 0.0002\ SX - 0.057]$$
$$+ GB\% \times [0.0006\ PX]$$

A hitter's expected batting average as calculated by multiplying the percentage of balls put in play (contact rate) by the chance that a ball in play falls for a hit. The likelihood that a ball in play falls for a hit is a product of the speed of the ball and distance it is hit (PX), the speed of the batter (SX), and distribution of ground balls, fly balls, and line drives. We further split it out by non-homerun hit rate (xH1%) and homerun hit rate (xH2%). **BENCHMARKS:** In general, xBA should approximate batting average fairly closely. Those hitters who have large variances between the two gauges are candidates for further analysis. **LIMITATION:** xBA tends to understate a batter's true value if he is an extreme ground ball hitter (G/F ratio over 3.0) with a low PX. These players are not inherently weak, but choose to take safe singles rather than swing for the fences.

## Expected batting average variance

*xBA – BA*
The variance between a batter's BA and his xBA is a measure of over- or under-achievement. A positive variance indicates the potential for a batter's BA to rise. A negative variance indicates the

potential for BA to decline. BENCHMARK: Discount variances that are less than 20 points. Any variance more than 30 points is regarded as a strong indicator of future change.

## Power

### Slugging average (Slg)
*(Singles + (2 x Doubles) + (3 x Triples) + (4 x HR)) / AB*
A measure of the total number of bases accumulated (or the minimum number of runners' bases advanced) per at bat. It is a misnomer; it is not a true measure of a batter's slugging ability because it includes singles. Slg also assumes that each type of hit has proportionately increasing value (i.e. a double is twice as valuable as a single, etc.) which is not true. For instance, with the bases loaded, a HR always scores four runs, a triple always scores three, but a double could score two or three and a single could score one, or two, or even three. BENCHMARKS: Top batters will have levels over .500. The bottom batters will have levels less than .300.

### Fly ball tendency and power *(Mat Olkin)*
There is a proven connection between a hitter's ground ball/fly ball tendencies and his power production.

1. *Extreme ground ball hitters generally do not hit for much power.* It's almost impossible for a hitter with a ground/fly ratio over 1.80 to hit enough fly balls to produce even 25 HRs in a season. However, this does not mean that a low G/F ratio necessarily guarantees power production. Some players have no problem getting the ball into the air, but lack the strength to reach the fences consistently.

2. *Most batters' ground/fly ratios stay pretty steady over time.* Most year-to-year changes are small and random, as they are in any other statistical category. A large, sudden change in G/F, on the other hand, can signal a conscious change in plate approach. And so...

3. *If a player posts high G/F ratios in his first few years, he probably isn't ever going to hit for all that much power.*

4. *When a batter's power suddenly jumps, his G/F ratio often drops at the same time.*

5. *Every so often, a hitter's ratio will drop significantly even as his power production remains level.* In these rare cases, impending power development is likely, since the two factors almost always follow each other.

### Home runs to fly ball rate (hr/f)
The percent of fly balls that are hit for HRs.

### hr/f rate as a leading indicator *(Joshua Randall)*
Each batter establishes an individual home run to fly ball rate that stabilizes over rolling three-year periods; those levels strongly predict the hr/f in the subsequent year. A batter who varies significantly from his hr/f is likely to regress toward his individual hr/f mean, with over-performance decline more likely and more severe than under-performance recovery.

### Estimating HR rate for young hitters *(Matt Cederholm)*
Over time, hitters establish a baseline hr/f, but how do we measure the HR output of young hitters with little track record?

Since power is a key indicator of HR output, we can look at typical hr/f for various levels of power, as measures by xPX:

| xPX | hr/f percentiles | | | | |
|---|---|---|---|---|---|
| | 10 | 25 | 50 | 75 | 90 |
| <=70 | 0.9% | 2.0% | 3.8% | 5.5% | 7.4% |
| 71-80 | 3.3% | 5.1% | 6.4% | 8.1% | 10.0% |
| 81-90 | 3.8% | 5.4% | 7.4% | 9.0% | 11.0% |
| 91-100 | 4.7% | 6.6% | 8.9% | 11.3% | 13.0% |
| 101-110 | 6.6% | 8.3% | 10.9% | 13.0% | 16.2% |
| 111-120 | 7.4% | 9.8% | 11.9% | 14.7% | 17.1% |
| 121-130 | 8.5% | 10.9% | 12.8% | 15.5% | 17.4% |
| 131-140 | 9.7% | 11.9% | 14.6% | 17.1% | 20.4% |
| 141-160 | 11.3% | 13.1% | 16.5% | 19.2% | 21.5% |
| 161+ | 14.4% | 16.5% | 19.4% | 22.0% | 25.8% |

To predict changes in HR output, just look at a player and project his HR as if his hr/f was at the median for his xPX level. For example, if a player with a 125 xPX exceeds a 12.8% hr/f, we would expect a decline in the following season. The greater the deviation from the mean, the greater the probability of an increase or decline.

### Deserved home runs *(Arik Florimonte)*
This 2017 study created a model for expected home run rate given exit velocity (EV) and launch angle (LA) found in MLB's Statcast system. The model was applied to the entire database of batted balls over a two-year period to determine the likelihood that a particular batted ball "should" have been a home run, when adjusted for park effects. By comparing a hitter's actual home run total to deserved home runs (dHR) over a given year, we can estimate how much of that performance was earned or unearned, and adjust home run expectations for the following season.

### Hard-hit flies as a sustainable skill *(Patrick Davitt)*
A study of data from 2009-2011 found that we should seek batters with a high Hard-Hit Fly Ball percentage (HHFB%). Among the findings:

- Avoiding pop-ups and hitting HHFBs are sustainable core power skills.
- Consistent HHFB% performance marks batters with power potential.
- When looking for candidates to regress, we should look at individual past levels of HR/HHFB, perhaps using a three-year rolling average.

### Linear weighted power (LWPwr)
*((Doubles x .8) + (Triples x .8) + (HR x 1.4)) / (At bats- K) x 100*
A variation of Pete Palmer's linear weights formula that considers only events that are measures of a batter's pure power. BENCHMARKS: Top sluggers typically top the 17 mark. Weak hitters will have a LWPwr level of less than 10.

### Linear weighted power index (PX)
*(Batter's LWPwr / League LWPwr) x 100*
LWPwr is presented in this book in its normalized form to get a better read on a batter's accomplishment in each year. For instance, a 30-HR season today is much less of an accomplishment than 30 HRs hit in a lower offense year like 2014. BENCHMARKS: A

level of 100 equals league average power skills. Any player with a value more than 100 has above average power skills, and those more than 150 are the Slugging Elite.

### Expected LW power index (xPX) *(Bill Macey)*

*2.6 + 269\*HHLD% + 724\*HHFB%*

Previous research has shown that hard-hit balls are more likely to result in hits and hard-hit fly balls are more likely to end up as HRs. As such, we can use hard-hit ball data to calculate an expected skills-based power index. This metric starts with hard-hit ball data, which measures a player's fundamental skill of making solid contact, and then places it on the same scale as PX (xPX). In the above formula, HHLD% is calculated as the number of hard hit line-drives divided by the total number of balls put in play. HHFB% is similarly calculated for fly balls. The variance between PX and xPX can be viewed as a leading indicator for other power metrics.

### Pitches/Plate Appearance as a leading indicator for PX *(Paul Petera)*

Working the count has a positive effect on power.

| P/PA | PX |
|------|-----|
| 4.00+ | 123 |
| 3.75-3.99 | 108 |
| 3.50-3.74 | 96 |
| Under 3.50 | 84 |

As for the year #1 outliers:

| | YEAR TWO | |
|---|---|---|
| | PX Improved | PX Declined |
| Low P/PA and High PX | 11% | 89% |
| High P/PA and Low PX | 70% | 30% |

In these scenarios, there was a strong tendency for performance to normalize in year #2.

### Doubles as a leading indicator for home runs *(Bill Macey)*

There is little support for the theory that hitting many doubles in year x leads to an increase in HR in year x+1. However, it was shown that batters with high doubles rates (2B/AB) also tend to hit more HR/AB than the league average; oddly, they are unable to sustain the high 2B/AB rate but do sustain their higher HR/AB rates. Batters with high 2B/AB rates and low HR/AB rates are more likely to see HR gains in the following year, but those rates will still typically trail the league average. And, batters who experience a surge in 2B/AB typically give back most of those gains in the following year without any corresponding gain in HR.

### Opposite field home runs *(Ed DeCaria)*

Opposite field HRs serve as a strong indicator of overall home run power (AB/HR). Power hitters (smaller AB/HR rates) hit a far higher percentage of their HR to the opposite field or straight away (over 30%). Conversely, non-power hitters hit almost 90% of their home runs to their pull field.

| Performance in Y2-Y4 (% of Group) | | | |
|---|---|---|---|
| Y1 Trigger | <=30 AB/HR | 5.5+ RC/G | $16+ R$ |
| 2+ OppHR | 69% | 46% | 33% |
| <2 OppHR | 29% | 13% | 12% |

Players who hit just two or more OppHR in one season were 2-3 times as likely as those who hit zero or one OppHR to sustain

strong AB/HR rates, RC/G levels, or R$ values over the following three seasons.

| Y2-Y4 Breakout Performance (% Breakout by Group, Age <=26 Only) | | | |
|---|---|---|---|
| | AB/HR | RC/G | R$ |
| Y1 Trigger | >35 to <=30 | <4.5 to 5.5+ | <$8 to $16+ |
| 2+ OppHR | 32% | 21% | 30% |
| <2 OppHR | 23% | 12% | 10% |

Roughly one of every 3-4 batters age 26 or younger experiences a *sustained three-year breakout* in AB/HR, RC/G or R$ after a season in which they hit 2+ OppHR, far better odds than the one in 8-10 batters who experience a breakout without the 2+ OppHR trigger.

In fact, a 2015 Brad Kullman study that examined hard hit balls of all types (flies, liners, and grounders) by hitters with 100 or more plate appearances offered a broader conclusion. His research found that hitters who can effectively use the whole field are more productive in virtually every facet of hitting than those with an exclusively pull-oriented approach.

### Home runs in bunches *(Patrick Davitt)*

A study from HR data from 2010-2012 showed that batters hit HRs in a random manner, with game-gaps between HRs that correspond roughly to their average days per HR. Thus, the theory that batters hit HRs in "bunches" is a fallacy. It appears pointless to try to "time the market" by predicting the beginning or end of a drought or a bunch, or by assuming the end of one presages the beginning of the other, despite what the ex-player in the broadcast booth tells you.

### Power breakout profile

It is not easy to predict which batters will experience a power spike. We can categorize power breakouts to determine the likelihood of a player taking a step up or of a surprise performer repeating his feat. Possibilities:

- Increase in playing time
- History of power skills at some time in the past
- Redistribution of already demonstrated extra base hit power
- Normal skills growth
- Situational breakouts, particularly in hitter-friendly venues
- Increased fly ball tendency
- Use of illegal performance-enhancing substances
- Miscellaneous unexplained variables

## Speed

### Wasted talent on the base paths

We refer to some players as having "wasted talent," a high level skill that is negated by a deficiency in another skill. Among these types are players who have blazing speed that is negated by a sub-.300 on base average.

These players can have short-term value. However, their stolen base totals are tied so tightly to their "green light" that any change in managerial strategy could completely erase that value. A higher

OB mitigates that downside; the good news is that plate patience can be taught.

In the past, there were always a handful of players who had at least 20 SBs with an OBP less than .300, putting their future SBs at risk. . In 2018, there was Billy Hamilton (34 SB, .299 OBP), Dee Gordon (30, .288), Tim Anderson (26, .281), Michael Taylor (24, .287), Amed Rosario (24, .295) and Rajai Davis (21, .278).

### Speed score *(Bill James)*

A measure of the various elements that comprise a runner's speed skills. Although this formula (a variation of James' original version) may be used as a leading indicator for stolen base output, SB attempts are controlled by managerial strategy which makes speed score somewhat less valuable.

Speed score is calculated as the mean value of the following four elements:

1. Stolen base efficiency = $(((SB + 3)/(SB + CS + 7)) - .4) \times 20$

2. Stolen base freq. = $Square\ root\ of\ ((SB + CS)/(Singles + BB)) / .07$

3. Triples rating = $(3B / (AB - HR - K))$ and the result assigned a value based on the following chart:

| | | | |
|---|---|---|---|
| < 0.001 | 0 | 0.0105 | 6 |
| 0.001 | 1 | 0.013 | 7 |
| 0.0023 | 2 | 0.0158 | 8 |
| 0.0039 | 3 | 0.0189 | 9 |
| 0.0058 | 4 | 0.0223+ | 10 |
| 0.008 | 5 | | |

4. Runs scored as a percentage of times on base = $(((R - HR) / (H + BB - HR)) - .1) / .04$

### Speed score index (SX)

*(Batter's speed score / League speed score) x 100*

Normalized speed scores get a better read on a runner's accomplishment in context. A level of 100 equals league average speed skill. Values more than 100 indicate above average skill, more than 200 represent the Fleet of Feet Elite.

### Statistically scouted speed (Spd) *(Ed DeCaria)*

$(104 + \{[(Runs–HR+10*age\_wt)/(RBI-HR+10)]/lg\_av*100\} / 5$
$+ \{[(3B+5*age\_wt)/(2B+3B+5)]/lg\_av*100\} / 5$
$+ \{[(SoftMedGBhits+25*age\_wt)/(SoftMedGB+25)]/lg\_av*100\} / 2$
$- \{[Weight (Lbs)/Height (In)^2 * 703]/lg\_av*100\}$

A skills-based gauge that measures speed without relying on stolen bases. Its components are:

- *(Runs – HR) / (RBI – HR)*: This metric aims to minimize the influence of extra base hit power and team run-scoring rates on perceived speed.

- *3B / (2B + 3B)*: No one can deny that triples are a fast runner's stat; dividing them by 2B+3B instead of all balls in play dampens the power aspect of extra base hits.

- *(Soft + Medium Ground Ball Hits) / (Soft + Medium Ground Balls)*: Faster runners are more likely than slower runners to beat out routine grounders. Hard hit balls are excluded from numerator and denominator.

- *Body Mass Index (BMI)*: Calculated as *Weight (lbs) / Height (in)2 * 703*. All other factors considered, leaner players run faster than heavier ones.

In this book, the formula is scaled as an index with a midpoint of 100.

### Stolen base opportunity percent (SBO)

*(SB + CS) / (BB + Singles)*

A rough approximation of how often a baserunner attempts a stolen base. Provides a comparative measure for players on a given team and, as a team measure, the propensity of a manager to give a "green light" to his runners.

### Stolen base success rate (SB%)

*SB / (SB + CS)*

The rate at which baserunners are successful in their stolen base attempts. **BENCHMARK:** It is generally accepted that an 80% rate is the minimum required for a runner to be providing value to his team.

### Roto Speed (RSpd)

*(Spd x (SBO + SB%))*

An adjustment to the measure for raw speed that takes into account a runner's opportunities to steal and his success rate. This stat is intended to provide a more accurate predictive measure of stolen bases for the Mayberry Method.

### Stolen base breakout profile *(Bob Berger)*

To find stolen base breakouts (first 30+ steal season in the majors), look for players that:

- are between 22-27 years old
- have 3-7 years of professional (minors and MLB) experience
- have previous steals at the MLB level
- have averaged 20+ SB in previous three seasons (majors and minors combined)
- have at least one professional season of 30+ SB

## *Overall Performance Analysis*

### On base plus slugging average (OPS)

A simple sum of the two gauges, it is considered one of the better evaluators of overall performance. OPS combines the two basic elements of offensive production—the ability to get on base (OB) and the ability to advance baserunners (Slg). **BENCHMARKS:** The game's top batters will have OPS levels more than .900. The worst batters will have levels less than .600.

### Base Performance Value (BPV)

*(Walk rate - 5) x 2)*
*+ ((Contact rate - 75) x 4)*
*+ ((Power Index - 80) x 0.8)*
*+ ((Spd - 80) x 0.3)*

A single value that describes a player's overall raw skill level. This is more useful than traditional statistical gauges to track player performance trends and project future statistical output. This formula combines the individual raw skills of batting eye, contact rate, power and speed. **BENCHMARKS:** The best hitters will have a BPV of 50 or greater.

## Base Performance Index (BPX)

BPV scaled to league average to account for year-to-year fluctuations in league-wide statistical performance. It's a snapshot of a player's overall skills compared to an average player. **BENCHMARK:** A level of 100 means a player had a league-average BPV in that given season.

## Linear weights *(Pete Palmer)*

*((Singles x .46) + (Doubles x .8) + (Triples x 1.02)*
*+ (Home runs x 1.4) + (Walks x .33) + (Stolen Bases x .3)*
*- (Caught Stealing x .6) - ((At bats - Hits) x Normalizing Factor)*

(Also referred to as Batting Runs.) Formula whose premise is that all events in baseball are linear; that is, the output (runs) is directly proportional to the input (offensive events). Each of these events is then weighted according to its relative value in producing runs. Positive events—hits, walks, stolen bases—have positive values. Negative events—outs, caught stealing—have negative values.

The normalizing factor, representing the value of an out, is an offset to the level of offense in a given year. It changes every season, growing larger in high offense years and smaller in low offense years. The value is about .26 and varies by league.

LW is not included in the player forecast boxes, but the LW concept is used with the linear weighted power gauge.

## Runs above replacement (RAR)

An estimate of the number of runs a player contributes above a "replacement level" player. "Replacement" is defined as the level of performance at which another player can easily be found at little or no cost to a team. What constitutes replacement level is a topic that is hotly debated. There are a variety of formulas and rules of thumb used to determine this level for each position (replacement level for a catcher will be very different from replacement level for an outfielder). Our estimates appear below.

One of the major values of RAR for fantasy applications is that it can be used to assemble an integrated ranking of batters and pitchers for drafting purposes.

*To calculate RAR for batters:*
- Start with a batter's runs created per game (RC/G).
- Subtract his position's replacement level RC/G.
- Multiply by number of games played: (AB - H + CS) / 25.5.

Replacement levels used in this book:

| POS | NL | AL |
|-----|------|------|
| CA | 3.52 | 3.38 |
| 1B | 5.11 | 4.42 |
| 2B | 4.27 | 4.08 |
| 3B | 4.67 | 4.34 |
| SS | 3.82 | 4.10 |
| LF | 4.61 | 4.59 |
| CF | 4.24 | 4.04 |
| RF | 4.40 | 4.51 |
| DH | | 4.51 |

RAR can also be used to calculate rough projected team won-loss records. *(Roger Miller)* Total the RAR levels for all the players on a team, divide by 10 and add to 53 wins.

## Runs created *(Bill James)*

*(H + BB − CS) x (Total bases + (.55 x SB)) / (AB + BB)*

A formula that converts all offensive events into a total of runs scored. As calculated for individual teams, the result approximates a club's actual run total with great accuracy.

## Runs created per game (RC/G)

*Runs Created / ((AB - H + CS) / 25.5)*

RC expressed on a per-game basis might be considered the hypothetical ERA compiled against a particular batter. Another way to look at it: A batter with a RC/G of 7.00 would be expected to score 7 runs per game if he were cloned nine times and faced an average pitcher in every at bat. Cloning batters is not a practice we recommend. **BENCHMARKS:** Few players surpass the level of a 10.00 RC/G, but any level more than 7.50 can still be considered very good. At the bottom are levels less than 3.00.

## Plate Appearances as a leading indicator *(Patrick Davitt)*

While targeting players "age 26 with experience" as potential breakout candidates has become a commonly accepted concept, a study has found that cumulative plate appearances, especially during the first two years of a young player's career, can also have predictive value in assessing a coming spike in production. Three main conclusions:

- When projecting players, MLB experience is more important than age.
- Players who amass 800+ PAs in their first two seasons are highly likely to have double-digit Rotisserie dollar value in Year 3.
- Also target young players in the season where they attain 400 PAs, as they are twice as likely as other players to grow significantly in value.

## Skill-specific aging patterns for batters *(Ed DeCaria)*

Baseball forecasters obsess over "peak age" of player performance because we must understand player ascent toward and decline from that peak to predict future value. Most published aging analyses are done using composite estimates of value such as OPS or linear weights. By contrast, fantasy GMs are typically more concerned with category-specific player value (HR, SB, AVG, etc.). We can better forecast what matters most by analyzing peak age of individual baseball skills rather than overall player value.

For batters, recognized peak age for overall batting value is a player's late 20s. But individual skills do not peak uniformly at the same time:

*Contact rate (ct%):* Ascends modestly by about a half point of contact per year from age 22 to 26, then holds steady within a half point of peak until age 35, after which players lose a half point of contact per year.

*Walk rate (bb%):* Trends the opposite way with age compared to contact rate, as batters tend to peak at age 30 and largely remain there until they turn 38.

*Stolen Base Opportunity (SBO):* Typically, players maintain their SBO through age 27, but then reduce their attempts steadily in each remaining year of their careers.

*Stolen base success rate (SB%):* Aggressive runners (>14% SBO) tend to lose about 2 points per year as they age. However, less aggressive runners (<=14% SBO) actually improve their SB% by about 2 points per year until age 28, after which they reverse course and give back 1-2 pts every year as they age.

*GB%/LD%/FB%:* Both GB% and LD% peak at the start of a player's career and then decline as many hitters seemingly learn to elevate the ball more. But at about age 30, hitter GB% ascends toward a second late-career peak while LD% continues to plummet and FB% continues to rise through age 38.

*Hit rate (h%):* Declines linearly with age. This is a natural result of a loss of speed and change in batted ball trajectory.

*Isolated Power (ISO):* Typically peaks from age 24-26. Similarly, home runs per fly ball, opposite field HR %, and Hard Hit % all peak by age 25 and decline somewhat linearly from that point on.

### Catchers and late-career performance spikes *(Ed Spaulding)*
Many catchers—particularly second line catchers—have their best seasons late in their careers. Some possible reasons why:

1. Catchers, like shortstops, often get to the big leagues for defensive reasons and not their offensive skills. These skills take longer to develop.
2. The heavy emphasis on learning the catching/ defense/ pitching side of the game detracts from their time to learn about, and practice, hitting.
3. Injuries often curtail their ability to show offensive skills, though these injuries (typically jammed fingers, bruises on the arms, rib injuries from collisions) often don't lead to time on the disabled list.
4. The time spent behind the plate has to impact the ability to recognize, and eventually hit, all kinds of pitches.

### Spring training Slg as leading indicator *(John Dewan)*
A hitter's spring training Slg .200 or more above his lifetime Slg is a leading indicator for a better than normal season.

### Overall batting breakout profile *(Brandon Kruse)*
We define a breakout performance as one where a player posts a Roto value of $20+ after having never posted a value of $10. These criteria are used to validate an apparent breakout in the current season but may also be used carefully to project a potential upcoming breakout:

- Age 27 or younger
- An increase in at least two of: h%, PX or Spd
- Minimum league average PX or Spd (100)
- Minimum contact rate of 75%
- Minimum xBA of .270

## In-Season Analysis

### Batting order facts *(Ed DeCaria)*
Eighty-eight percent of today's leadoff hitters bat leadoff again in their next game, 78% still bat leadoff 10 games later, and 68% still bat leadoff 50 games later. Despite this level of turnover after 50 games, leadoff hitters have the best chance of retaining their role over time. After leadoff, #3 and #4 hitters are the next most likely to retain their lineup slots.

On a season-to-season basis, leadoff hitters are again the most stable, with 69% of last year's primary leadoff hitters retaining the #1 slot next year.

Plate appearances decline linearly by lineup slot. Leadoff batters receive 10-12% more PAs than when batting lower in the lineup. AL #9 batters and NL #8 batters get 9-10% fewer PAs. These results mirror play-by-play data showing a 15-20 PA drop by lineup slot over a full season.

Walk rate is largely unaffected by lineup slot in the AL. Beware strong walk rates by NL #8 hitters, as much of this "skill" will disappear if ever moved from the #8 slot.

Batting order has no discernable effect on contact rate.

Hit rate slopes gently upward as hitters are slotted deeper in the lineup.

As expected, the #3-4-5 slots are ideal for non-HR RBIs, at the expense of #6 hitters. RBIs are worst for players in the #1-2 slots. Batting atop the order sharply increases the probability of scoring runs, especially in the NL.

The leadoff slot easily has the highest stolen base attempt rate. #4-5-6 hitters attempt steals more often when batting out of those slots than they do batting elsewhere. The NL #8 hitter is a SB attempt sink hole. A change in batting order from #8 to #1 in the NL could nearly double a player's SB output due to lineup slot alone.

### DOMination and DISaster rates
Week-to-week consistency is measured using a batter's BPV compiled in each week. A player earns a DOMinant week if his BPV was greater or equal to 50 for that week. A player registers a DISaster if his BPV was less than 0 for that week. The percentage of Dominant weeks, DOM%, is simply calculated as the number of DOM weeks divided by the total number of weeks played.

### Is week-to-week consistency a repeatable skill? *(Bill Macey)*
To test whether consistent performance is a repeatable skill for batters, we examined how closely related a player's DOM% was from year to year.

| YR1 DOM% | AVG YR2 DOM% |
|---|---|
| < 35% | 37% |
| 35%–45% | 40% |
| 46%–55% | 45% |
| 56%+ | 56% |

### Quality/consistency score (QC)
*(DOM% – (2 x DIS%)) x 2*

Using the DOM/DIS percentages, this score measures both the quality of performance as well as week–to–week consistency.

### Projecting RBIs *(Patrick Davitt)*
Evaluating players in-season for RBI potential is a function of the interplay among four factors:

- Teammates' ability to reach base ahead of him and to run the bases efficiently
- His own ability to drive them in by hitting, especially XBH
- Number of Games Played

- Place in the batting order

**3-4-5 Hitters:**

*(0.69 x GP x TOB) + (0.30 x ITB) + (0.275 x HR) – (.191 x GP)*

**6-7-8 Hitters:**

*(0.63 x GP x TOB) + (0.27 x ITB) + (0.250 x HR) – (.191 x GP)*

**9-1-2 Hitters:**

*(0.57 x GP x TOB) + (0.24 x ITB) + (0.225 x HR) – (.191 x GP)*

*...where GP = games played, TOB = team on-base pct.* and *ITB = individual total bases (ITB).*

Apply this pRBI formula after 70 games played or so (to reduce the variation from small sample size) to find players more than 9 RBIs over or under their projected RBI. There could be a correction coming.

You should also consider other factors, like injury or trade (involving the player or a top-of-the-order speedster) or team SB philosophy and success rate.

Remember: the player himself has an impact on his TOB. When we first did this study, we excluded the player from his TOB and got better results. The formula overestimates projected RBI for players with high OBP who skew his teams' OBP but can't benefit in RBI from that effect.

**Ten-Game hitting streaks as a leading indicator** *(Bob Berger)*
Research of hitting streaks from 2011 and 2012 showed that a 10-game streak can reliably predict improved longer-term BA performance during the season. A player who has put together a hitting streak of at least 10 games will improve his BA for the remainder of the season about 60% of the time. This improvement can be significant, on average as much as .020 of BA.

**What can foul balls tell us?** *(Nick Trojanowski)*
Foul balls, because of their relatively meager influence on in-game outcomes, have been examined far less often than balls in play. Using 2008-17 data for every 500+ pitch season, we found that hitting and inducing foul balls is a skill, in that it's repeatable from year to year. Other findings:

1. Hitters who swing at more pitches, regardless of location, hit more foul balls, regardless of contact rate.
2. Pitchers who induce more swings at strikes allow more fouls, but pitchers who induce more chases do not.
3. Groundball pitchers tend to give up fewer foul balls than flyball pitchers.
4. For hitters, routinely fouling off pitches doesn't regularly lead to better outcomes, and in fact tends to make walks less likely.

## *Other Diamonds*

### It's a Busy World Shortcut
For marginal utility-type players, scan their PX and Spd history to see if there's anything to mine for. If you see triple digits anywhere, stop and look further. If not, move on.

### Chronology of the Classic Free-Swinger with Pop
1. Gets off to a good start.
2. Thinks he's in a groove.
3. Gets lax, careless.
4. Pitchers begin to catch on.
5. Fades down the stretch.

### Errant Gust of Wind
A unit of measure used to describe the difference between your home run projection and mine.

### Hannahan Concession
Players with a .218 BA rarely get 500 plate appearances, but when they do, it's usually once.

### Mendoza Line
Named for Mario Mendoza, it represents the benchmark for batting futility. Usually refers to a .200 batting average, but can also be used for low levels of other statistical categories. Note that Mendoza's lifetime batting average was actually a much more robust .215.

### Old Player Skills
Power, low batting average, no speed and usually good plate patience. Young players, often those with a larger frame, who possess these "old player skills" tend to decline faster than normal, often in their early 30s.

### Esix Snead List
Players with excellent speed and sub-.300 on base averages who get a lot of practice running down the line to first base, and then back to the dugout. Also used as an adjective, as in "Esix-Sneadian."

# Pitchers

## Strikeouts and Walks

### Fundamental skills

The contention that pitching performance is unreliable is a fallacy driven by the practice of attempting to project pitching stats using gauges that are poor evaluators of skill.

How can we better evaluate pitching skill? We can start with the statistical categories that are generally unaffected by external factors. These stats capture the outcome of an individual pitcher versus batter match-up without regard to supporting offense, defense or bullpen:

*Walks Allowed, Strikeouts and Ground/Fly Balls*

Even with only these stats to observe, there is a wealth of insight that these measures can provide.

### Control rate (Ctl, bb/9), or opposition walks per game
*BB allowed x 9 / IP*

Measures how many walks a pitcher allows per game equivalent. BENCHMARK: The best pitchers will have bb/9 of 2.5 or less.

### Dominance rate (Dom, k/9), or opposition strikeouts/game
*Strikeouts recorded x 9 / IP*

Measures how many strikeouts a pitcher allows per game equivalent. BENCHMARK: The best pitchers will have k/9 levels of 9.0 or higher.

### Command ratio (Cmd)
*(Strikeouts / Walks)*

A measure of a pitcher's ability to get the ball over the plate. There is no more fundamental a skill than this, and so it is used as a leading indicator to project future rises and falls in other gauges, such as ERA. BENCHMARKS: Baseball's best pitchers will have ratios in excess of 3.0. Pitchers with ratios less than 1.0—indicating that they walk more batters than they strike out—have virtually no potential for long-term success. If you make no other changes in your approach to drafting pitchers, limiting your focus to only pitchers with a command ratio of 2.5 or better will substantially improve your odds of success.

### Command ratio as a leading indicator

The ability to get the ball over the plate—command of the strike zone—is one of the best leading indicators for future performance. Command ratio (K/BB) can be used to project potential in ERA as well as other skills gauges.

*1. Research indicates that there is a high correlation between a pitcher's Cmd ratio and his ERA.*

| | Earned Run Average | | | | |
|---|---|---|---|---|---|
| Command | 2014 | 2015 | 2016 | 2017 | 2018 |
| 0.0 - 1.0 | 6.81 | 6.31 | 7.71 | 7.24 | 7.30 |
| 1.1 - 1.5 | 4.97 | 5.23 | 5.51 | 5.50 | 5.30 |
| 1.6 - 2.0 | 4.37 | 4.54 | 4.66 | 4.84 | 4.53 |
| 2.1 - 2.5 | 3.80 | 4.19 | 4.30 | 4.62 | 4.39 |
| 2.6 - 3.0 | 3.78 | 3.87 | 4.02 | 4.13 | 4.03 |
| 3.1 - 3.5 | 3.43 | 3.51 | 3.95 | 3.85 | 3.86 |
| 3.6 - 4.0 | 3.16 | 3.56 | 3.51 | 3.68 | 3.63 |
| 4.1+ | 2.92 | 3.07 | 3.30 | 3.20 | 3.17 |

We can create percentage plays for the different levels:

| For Cmd Levels of | % with ERA of | |
|---|---|---|
| | 3.50- | 4.50+ |
| 0.0 - 1.0 | 0% | 100% |
| 1.1 - 1.5 | 9% | 70% |
| 1.6 - 2.0 | 19% | 54% |
| 2.1 - 2.5 | 33% | 41% |
| 2.6 - 3.0 | 35% | 31% |
| 3.1 - 3.5 | 37% | 18% |
| 3.6 - 4.0 | 56% | 15% |
| 4.1 + | 61% | 11% |

Pitchers who maintain a Cmd over 2.5 have a high probability of long-term success. For fantasy drafting purposes, it is best to avoid pitchers with sub-2.0 ratios. Avoid bullpen closers if they have a ratio less than 3.5.

*2. A pitcher's Command in tandem with Dominance (strikeout rate) provides even greater predictive abilities.*

| | Earned Run Average | |
|---|---|---|
| Command | -5.6 Dom | 5.6+ Dom |
| 0.0-0.9 | 6.71 | n/a |
| 1.0-1.4 | 5.56 | n/a |
| 1.5-1.9 | 4.78 | 4.26 |
| 2.0-2.4 | 4.33 | 4.10 |
| 2.5-2.9 | 4.31 | 3.74 |
| 3.0-3.9 | 4.10 | 3.66 |
| 4.0+ | 3.79 | 3.09 |

This helps to highlight the limited upside potential of soft-tossers with pinpoint control. The extra dominance makes a huge difference.

### Swinging strike rate as leading indicator *(Stephen Nickrand)*
Swinging strike rate (SwK%) measures the percentage of total pitches against which a batter swings and misses. SwK% can help us validate and forecast a SP's Dominance (K/9) rate, which in turn allows us to identify surgers and faders with greater accuracy.

BENCHMARKS: SwK% baseline for all pitchers (SP and RP) is 11.1% in AL, 11.2% in NL; Expected Dom (xDom) can be estimated from SwK%; and a pitcher's individual SwK% does not regress to league norms.

The few starters per year who have a 12.0% or higher SwK% are near-locks to have a 9.0 Dom or greater. In contrast, starters with a 7.0% or lower SwK% have nearly no chance at posting even an average Dom. Finally, use an 9.5% SwK% as an acceptable threshold when searching for SP based on this metric; raise it to 10.5% to begin to find SwK% difference-makers.

### Fastball velocity and Dominance rate *(Stephen Nickrand)*
It is intuitive that an increase in fastball velocity for starting pitchers leads to more strikeouts. But how much?

Research shows that the vast majority of SP with significant fastball velocity gains

- experience a significant Dom gain during the same season.
- are likely to give back those gains during the following season.
- are likely to increase their Dom the following season, but the magnitude of the Dom increase usually is small.

The vast majority of SP with significant fastball velocity losses

- are likely to experience a significant Dom decrease during the same season.

Those SP with significant fastball velocity losses from one season to the next are just as likely to experience a fastball velocity or Dom increase as they are to experience a fastball or Dom decrease, and the amounts of the increase/decrease are nearly identical.

### First-pitch strike rate as leading indicator *(Stephen Nickrand)*

The measurement of a pitcher's rate of first-pitch strikes (FpK%) can help us validate and forecast a pitcher's Control (BB/9) rate. As first-pitch strike rate increases, walks are very likely to go down, and WHIP will follow. As it goes up, walks are likely to increase, as will WHIP. So if you're wondering if a pitcher's newfound good control is likely to hold, check out his FpK%.

The FpK% baseline is 60% for starting pitchers and does not vary significantly by league. Expected Ctl (xCtl) can be estimated from FpK%, and a starting pitcher's individual FpK% does not regress to league norms. BENCHMARKS: Elite pitchers will have a FpK% above 68% and most of them will have a Ctl below 2.0. Avoid pitchers with a FpK% below 55%, as they are likely to have a Ctl at or above 4.0.

### First-pitch strikes increase with age *(Ed DeCaria)*

On average, pitchers lose about 0.2 mph per season off their fastballs. Over time, this coincides with decreases in swinging strike rate (SwK%) and overall strikeout rate (K/PA)—the inevitable effects of aging. But one thing that pitchers can do to delay these effects is to throw more first pitch strikes.

Individual pitcher first pitch strike rates (FpK%) increase at a rate of 0.5% per year from age 22 to 26. Pitchers then typically add another 0.5-1.0% as they settle into their respective peak levels. Once pitchers reach their peaks, first pitch strike rate tends not to decline with age—it is a skill that pitchers own until retirement, even as their other physical skills deteriorate.

Younger pitchers (under age 26) with above average SwK% but below average FpK% make for great breakout targets.

### Power/contact rating

*(BB + K) / IP*

Measures the level by which a pitcher allows balls to be put into play. In general, extreme power pitchers can be successful even with poor defensive teams. Power pitchers tend to have greater longevity in the game. Contact pitchers with poor defenses behind them are high risks to have poor W-L records and ERA. BENCHMARKS: A level of 1.13+ describes pure throwers. A level of .93 or less describes high contact pitchers.

## Balls in Play

### Balls in play (BIP)

*(Batters faced – (BB + HBP + SAC)) + H – K*

The total number of batted balls that are hit fair, both hits and outs. An analysis of how these balls are hit—on the ground, in the air, hits, outs, etc.—can provide analytical insight, from player skill levels to the impact of luck on statistical output.

### Batting average on balls in play *(Voros McCracken)*

*(H – HR) / (Batters faced – (BB + HBP + SAC)) + H – K – HR*

Abbreviated as BABIP; also called hit rate (H%), this is the percent of balls hit into the field of play that fall for hits. In 2000, Voros McCracken published a study that concluded "there is little if any difference among major league pitchers in their ability to prevent hits on balls hit in the field of play." His assertion was that, while a Johan Santana would have a better ability to prevent a batter from getting wood on a ball, or perhaps keeping the ball in the park, once that ball was hit in the field of play, the probability of it falling for a hit was virtually no different than for any other pitcher.

Among the findings in his study were:

- There is little correlation between what a pitcher does one year in the stat and what he will do the next. This is not true with other significant stats (BB, K, HR).
- You can better predict a pitcher's hits per balls in play from the rate of the rest of the pitcher's team than from the pitcher's own rate.

This last point brings a team's defense into the picture. It begs the question, when a batter gets a hit, is it because the pitcher made a bad pitch, the batter took a good swing, or the defense was not positioned correctly?

### BABIP as a leading indicator *(Voros McCracken)*

The league average is 30%, which is also the level that individual performances will regress to on a year to year basis. Any +/- variance of 3% or more can affect a pitcher's ERA.

Pitchers will often post hit rates per balls-in-play that are far off from the league average, but then revert to the mean the following year. As such, we can use that mean to project the direction of a pitcher's ERA.

Subsequent research has shown that ground ball or fly ball propensity has some impact on this rate.

### Hit rate *(See Batting average on balls in play)*

### Opposition batting average (OBA)

*Hits allowed / (Batters faced – (BB + HBP + SAC))*

The batting average achieved by opposing batters against a pitcher. BENCHMARKS: The best pitchers will have levels less than .250; the worst pitchers levels more than .300.

### Opposition on base average (OOB)

*(Hits allowed + BB) / ((Batters faced – (BB + HBP + SAC)) + Hits allowed + BB)*

The on base average achieved by opposing batters against a pitcher. BENCHMARK: The best pitchers will have levels less than .300; the worst pitchers levels more than .375.

### Walks plus hits divided by innings pitched (WHIP)

Essentially the same measure as opposition on base average, but used for Rotisserie purposes. BENCHMARKS: A WHIP of less than 1.20 is considered top level; more than 1.50 indicative of poor performance. Levels less than 1.00—allowing fewer runners than IP—represent extraordinary performance and are rarely maintained over time.

### Ground ball, line drive, fly ball percentage (G/L/F)

The percentage of all balls-in-play that are hit on the ground, in the air and as line drives. For a pitcher, the ability to pitch to a ground ball or fly ball extreme can contribute to his statistical output exceeding his demonstrated skill level.

### Ground ball tendency as a leading indicator *(John Burnson)*

Ground ball pitchers tend to give up fewer HRs than do fly ball pitchers. There is also evidence that GB pitchers have higher hit rates. In other words, a ground ball has a higher chance of being a hit than does a fly ball that is not out of the park.

GB pitchers have lower strikeout rates. We should be more forgiving of a low strikeout rate if it belongs to an extreme ground ball pitcher.

GB pitchers have a lower ERA but a higher WHIP than do fly ball pitchers. On balance, GB pitchers come out ahead, even when considering strikeouts, because a lower ERA also leads to more wins.

### Groundball and strikeout tendencies as indicators

*(Mike Dranchak)*

Pitchers were assembled into 9 groups based on the following profiles (minimum 23 starts in 2005):

| Profile | Ground Ball Rate |
|---------|------------------|
| Ground Ball | higher than 47% |
| Neutral | 42% to 47% |
| Fly Ball | less than 42% |

| Profile | Strikeout Rate (k/9) |
|---------|----------------------|
| Strikeout | higher than 6.6 k/9 |
| Average | 5.4 to 6.6 k/9 |
| Soft-Tosser | less than 5.4 k/9 |

*Findings:* Pitchers with higher strikeout rates had better ERAs and WHIPs than pitchers with lower strikeout rates, regardless of ground ball profile. However, for pitchers with similar strikeout rates, those with higher ground ball rates had better ERAs and WHIPs than those with lower ground ball rates.

Pitchers with higher strikeout rates tended to strand more baserunners than those with lower K rates. Fly ball pitchers tended to strand fewer runners than their GB or neutral counterparts within their strikeout profile.

Ground ball pitchers (especially those who lacked high-dominance) yielded more home runs per fly ball than did fly ball pitchers. However, the ERA risk was mitigated by the fact that ground ball pitchers (by definition) gave up fewer fly balls to begin with.

### Extreme GB/FB pitchers *(Patrick Davitt)*

Among pitchers with normal strikeout levels, extreme GB pitchers (>3–7% of all batters faced) have ERAs about 0.4 runs lower than normal-GB% pitchers but only slight WHIP advantages. Extreme FB% pitchers (32% FB) show no ERA benefits.

Among High-K (>=24% of BF), however, extreme GBers have ERAs about 0.5 runs lower than normal-GB pitchers, and WHIPs about five points lower. Extreme FB% pitchers have ERAs about 0.2 runs lower than normal-FB pitchers, and WHIPs about 10 points lower.

### Revisiting flyballs *(Jason Collette)*

The increased emphasis on defensive positioning is often associated with infield shifting, but the same data also influences how outfielders are positioned. Some managers are positioning OFs more aggressively than just the customary few steps per a right- or left-handed swinging batter. Five of the top 10 defensive efficiency teams in 2013 —OAK, STL, MIA, LAA and KC—also had parks among the top 10 in HR suppression.

Before dismissing flyball pitchers as toxic assets, pay more attention to park factors and OF defensive talent. In particular, be a little more willing to roster fly ball pitchers who pitch both in front of good defensive OFs and in good pitchers' parks.

### Line drive percentage as a leading indicator *(Seth Samuels)*

The percentage of balls-in-play that are line drives is beyond a pitcher's control. Line drives do the most damage; from 1994-2003, here were the expected hit rates and number of total bases per type of BIP.

| | ├------- Type of BIP -------┤ | | |
|-------------|------|------|------|
| | GB | FB | LD |
| H% | 26% | 23% | 56% |
| Total bases | 0.29 | 0.57 | 0.80 |

Despite the damage done by LDs, pitchers do not have any innate skill to avoid them. There is little relationship between a pitcher's LD% one year and his rate the next year. All rates tend to regress towards a mean of 22.6%.

However, GB pitchers do have a slight ability to prevent LDs (21.7%) and extreme GB hurlers even moreso (18.5%). Extreme FB pitchers have a slight ability to prevent LDs (21.1%) as well.

### Home run to fly ball rate (hr/f)

*HR / FB*

The percent of fly balls that are hit for home runs.

### hr/f as a leading indicator *(John Burnson)*

McCracken's work focused on "balls in play," omitting home runs from the study. However, pitchers also do not have much control over the percentage of fly balls that turn into HR. Research shows that there is an underlying rate of HR as a percentage of fly balls of about 13%. A pitcher's HR/FB rate will vary each year but always tends to regress to that 13%. The element that pitchers do have control over is the number of fly balls they allow. That is the underlying skill or deficiency that controls their HR rate.

### "Just Enough" home runs as a leading indicator *(Brian Slack)*

Using ESPN's Home Run Tracker data, we analyzed year-to-year consistency of "Just Enough" home runs (those that clear the fence by less than 10 vertical feet or land less than one fence height past the fence). For the 528 starting pitchers who logged enough innings to qualify for the ERA title in consecutive years from 2006 through 2016 season, research showed:

- The percentage of Just Enough home runs that a pitcher gives up gravitates towards league average (32%) the following year.
- There is only a tenuous connection between a pitcher's ability to limit the percentage of Just Enough home runs and a pitcher's HR/FB rate. So we should avoid the

assumption that a pitcher with a high percentage of Just Enough home runs will necessarily improve his HR/FB rate (and presumably ERA) the following year, or vice versa.

- This means be careful not to over-draft a pitcher based solely on the idea of HR/FB improvement in the coming year. Conversely, one should not automatically avoid pitchers with perceived HR/FB downside.

### Opposition home runs per game (hr/9)

*(HR Allowed x 9 / IP)*

*Also, expected opposition HR rate = (FB x 0.10) x 9 / IP*

Measures how many HR a pitcher allows per game equivalent. Since FB tend to go yard at about a 10% rate, we can also estimate this rate off of fly balls. BENCHMARK: The best pitchers will have hr/9 levels of less than 1.0.

## *Runs*

### Expected earned run average (xERA)

Gill and Reeve version: *(.575 x H [per 9 IP]) + (.94 x HR [per 9 IP]) + (.28 x BB [per 9 IP]) − (.01 x K [per 9 IP]) − Normalizing Factor*

John Burnson version (used in this book):

*(xER x 9)/IP, where xER is defined as*

*xER% x (FB/10) + (1-xS%) x [0.3 x (BIP − FB/10) + BB]*

*where xER% = 0.96 − (0.0284 x (GB/FB))*

*and*

*xS% = (64.5 + (K/9 x 1.2) − (BB/9 x (BB/9 + 1)) / 20)*

*+ ((0.0012 x (GB%^2)) − (0.001 x GB%) - 2.4)*

xERA represents the an equivalent of what a pitcher's real ERA might be, calculated solely with skills-based measures. It is not influenced by situation-dependent factors.

### Expected ERA variance

*xERA − ERA*

The variance between a pitcher's ERA and his xERA is a measure of over or underachievement. A positive variance indicates the potential for a pitcher's ERA to rise. A negative variance indicates the potential for ERA improvement. BENCHMARK: Discount variances that are less than 0.50. Any variance more than 1.00 (one run per game) is regarded as a strong indicator of future change.

### Projected xERA or projected ERA?

Which should we be using to forecast a pitcher's ERA? Projected xERA is more accurate for looking ahead on a purely skills basis. Projected ERA includes *situation-dependent* events—bullpen support, park factors, etc.—which are reflected better by ERA. The optimal approach is to use both gauges as *a range of expectation* for forecasting purposes.

### Strand rate (S%)

*(H + BB − ER) / (H + BB − HR)*

Measures the percentage of allowed runners a pitcher strands (earned runs only), which incorporates both individual pitcher

skill and bullpen effectiveness. BENCHMARKS: The most adept at stranding runners will have S% levels over 75%. Those with rates over 80% will have artificially low ERAs which will be prone to relapse. Levels below 65% will inflate ERA but have a high probability of regression.

### Expected strand rate *(Michael Weddell)*

*73.935 + K/9 - 0.116 * (BB/9*(BB/9+1))*

*+ (0.0047 * GB%^2 - 0.3385 * GB%)*

*+ (MAX(2,MIN(4,IP/G))/2-1)*

*+ (0.82 if left-handed)*

This formula is based on three core skills: strikeouts per nine innings, walks per nine innings, and groundballs per balls in play, with adjustments for whether the pitcher is a starter or reliever (measured by IP/G), and his handedness.

### Strand rate as a leading indicator *(Ed DeCaria)*

Strand rate often regresses/rebounds toward past rates (usually 69-74%), resulting in Year 2 ERA changes:

| % of Pitchers with Year 2 Regression/Rebound | | | |
|---|---|---|---|
| Y1 S% | RP | SP | LR |
| <60% | 100% | 94% | 94% |
| 65 | 81% | 74% | 88% |
| 70 | 53% | 48% | 65% |
| 75 | 55% | 85% | 100% |
| 80 | 80% | 100% | 100% |
| 85 | 100% | 100% | 100% |

| Typical ERA Regression/Rebound in Year 2 | | | |
|---|---|---|---|
| Y1 S% | RP | SP | LR |
| <60% | -2.54 | -2.03 | -2.79 |
| 65 | -1.00 | -0.64 | -0.93 |
| 70 | -0.10 | -0.05 | -0.44 |
| 75 | 0.24 | 0.54 | 0.75 |
| 80 | 1.15 | 1.36 | 2.29 |
| 85 | 1.71 | 2.21 | n/a |

**Starting pitchers** (SP) have a narrower range of strand rate outcomes than do relievers (RP) or swingmen/long relievers (LR). **Relief pitchers** with Y1 strand rates of <=67% or >=78% are likely to experience a +/- ERA regression in Y2. **Starters and swingmen/long relievers** with Y1 strand rates of <=65% or >=75% are likely to experience a +/- ERA regression in Y2. Pitchers with strand rates that deviate more than a few points off of their individual expected strand rates are likely to experience some degree of ERA regression in Y2. Over-performing (or "lucky") pitchers are more likely than underperforming (or "unlucky") pitchers to see such a correction.

### Does it matter where runners are stranded? *(Nick Trojanowski)*

Leaving runners on base (S%) is more luck than skill, which holds true for stranding runners on a specific base as well. To confirm this, we created modified strand rates (mS%) for runners on first, second, and third base and found weak year-to-year correlations for all three. There isn't much evidence that stranding runners on a specific base is a skill, or that it's biased towards one type of pitcher (high-strikeout, high-groundball) or another.

# Wins

### Expected Wins (xW) *(Matt Cederholm)*

*[(Team runs per game)^1.8]/[(Pitcher ERA)^1.8 + (Team runs per game)^1.8] x 0.72 x GS*

Starting pitchers' win totals are often at odds with their ERA. Attempts to find a strictly skill-based analysis of this phenomenon haven't worked, but there is a powerful tool in the toolbox: Bill James' Pythagorean Theorem. While usually applied to team outcomes, recent research has shown that its validity holds up when applied to individual starting pitchers.

One key to applying the Pythagorean Theorem is factoring in no-decisions. Research shows that the average no-decision rate is 28% of starts, regardless of the type or quality of the pitcher or his team, with no correlation in ND% from one season to the next.

Overall, 70% of pitchers whose expected wins varied from actual wins showed regression in wins per start in the following year, making variation from Expected Wins a good leading indicator.

### Projecting/chasing wins

There are five events that need to occur in order for a pitcher to post a single win...

1. He must pitch well, allowing few runs.
2. The offense must score enough runs.
3. The defense must successfully field all batted balls.
4. The bullpen must hold the lead.
5. The manager must leave the pitcher in for 5 innings, and not remove him if the team is still behind.

Of these five events, only one is within the control of the pitcher. As such, projecting or chasing wins based on skills alone can be an exercise in futility.

### Home field advantage *(John Burnson)*

A 2006 study found that home starting pitchers get credited with a win in 38% of their outings. Visiting team starters are credited with a win in 33% of their outings.

# Usage

### Batters faced per game *(Craig Wright)*

*((Batters faced – (BB + HBP + SAC)) + H + BB) / G*

A measure of pitcher usage and one of the leading indicators for potential pitcher burnout.

### Workload

Research suggests that there is a finite number of innings in a pitcher's arm. This number varies by pitcher, by development cycle, and by pitching style and repertoire. We can measure a pitcher's potential for future arm problems and/or reduced effectiveness (burnout):

*Sharp increases in usage from one year to the next.* Common wisdom has suggested that pitchers who significantly increase their workload from one year to the next are candidates for burnout symptoms. This has often been called the Verducci Effect,

after writer Tom Verducci. BaseballHQ.com analyst Michael Weddell tested pitchers with sharp workload increases during the period 1988-2008 and found that no such effect exists.

*Starters' overuse.* Consistent "batters faced per game" (BF/G) levels of 28.0 or higher, combined with consistent seasonal IP totals of 200 or more may indicate burnout potential, especially with pitchers younger than 25. Within a season, a BF/G of more than 30.0 with a projected IP total of 200 may indicate a late season fade.

*Relievers' overuse.* Warning flags should be up for relievers who post in excess of 100 IP in a season, while averaging fewer than 2 IP per outing.

When focusing solely on minor league pitchers, research results are striking:

**Stamina:** Virtually every minor league pitcher who had a BF/G of 28.5 or more in one season experienced a drop-off in BF/G the following year. Many were unable to ever duplicate that previous level of durability.

**Performance:** Most pitchers experienced an associated drop-off in their BPVs in the years following the 28.5 BF/G season. Some were able to salvage their effectiveness later on by moving to the bullpen.

### Effects of short-term workloads on relief pitcher value *(Arik Florimonte)*

Using game logs from 2002-17, we studied the effects of recent workload on relief pitcher performance. After accounting for factors such as selection and usage bias—good pitchers get used on short rest more often—we discovered there is almost no measurable performance impact. Pitchers used heavily for several days, including the day before, show perhaps a 5-10% reduction in BPV.

Pitchers who have thrown often in the recent past are less likely to be used, which can significantly reduce their value, with a 36% reduction in saves and a 64% reduction in games pitched when "worn out".

In leagues with daily lineup changes, monitoring RP workloads can help owners decide to start rested closers of lesser quality, and therefore lower cost, over more expensive closers who may be worn out.

### Protecting young pitchers *(Craig Wright)*

There is a link between some degree of eventual arm trouble and a history of heavy workloads in a pitcher's formative years. Some recommendations from this research:

*Teenagers (A-ball):* No 200 IP seasons and no BF/G over 28.5 in any 150 IP span. No starts on three days rest.

*Ages 20-22:* Average no more than 105 pitches per start with a single game ceiling of 130 pitches.

*Ages 23-24:* Average no more than 110 pitches per start with a single game ceiling of 140 pitches.

When possible, a young starter should be introduced to the majors in long relief before he goes into the rotation.

## Overall Performance Analysis

### Base Performance Value (BPV)
*((Dominance Rate - 5.0) x 18)*
*+ ((4.0 - Walk Rate) x 27))*
*+ (Ground ball rate as a whole number - 40%)*

A single value that describes a player's overall raw skill level. The formula combines the individual raw skills of dominance, control and the ability to keep the ball down in the zone, all characteristics that are unaffected by most external factors. In tandem with a pitcher's strand rate, it provides a more complete picture of the elements that contribute to ERA, and therefore serves as an accurate tool to project likely changes in ERA. **BENCHMARKS:** A BPV of 50 is the minimum level required for long-term success. The elite of the bullpen aces will have BPVs in excess of 100 and it is rare for these stoppers to enjoy long term success with consistent levels under 75.

### Base Performance Index (BPX)
BPV scaled to league average to account for year-to-year fluctuations in league-wide statistical performance. It's a snapshot of a player's overall skills compared to an average player. **BENCHMARK:** A level of 100 means a player had a league-average BPV in that given season.

### Runs above replacement (RAR)
An estimate of the number of runs a player contributes above a "replacement level" player.

Batters create runs; pitchers save runs. But are batters and pitchers who have comparable RAR levels truly equal in value? Pitchers might be considered to have higher value. Saving an additional run is more important than producing an additional run. A pitcher who throws a shutout is guaranteed to win that game, whereas no matter how many runs a batter produces, his team can still lose given poor pitching support.

*To calculate RAR for pitchers:*
1. Start with the replacement level league ERA.
2. Subtract the pitcher's ERA. (To calculate projected RAR, use the pitcher's xERA.)
3. Multiply by number of games played, calculated as plate appearances (IP x 4.34) divided by 38.
4. Multiply the resulting RAR level by 1.08 to account for the variance between earned runs and total runs.

### Skill-specific aging patterns for pitchers *(Ed DeCaria)*
Baseball forecasters obsess over "peak age" of player performance because we must understand player ascent toward and decline from that peak to predict future value. Most published aging analyses are done using composite estimates of value such as OPS or linear weights. By contrast, fantasy GMs are typically more concerned with category-specific player value (K, ERA, WHIP, etc.). We can better forecast what matters most by analyzing peak age of individual baseball skills rather than overall player value.

For pitchers, prior research has shown that pitcher value peaks somewhere in the late 20s to early 30s. But how does aging affect each demonstrable pitching skill?

*Strikeout rate (k/9):* Declines fairly linearly beginning at age 25.

*Walk rate (bb/9):* Improves until age 25 and holds somewhat steady until age 29, at which point it begins to steadily worsen. Deteriorating k/9 and bb/9 rates result in inefficiency, as it requires far more pitches to get an out. For starting pitchers, this affects the ability to pitch deep into games.

*Innings Pitched per game (IP/G):* Among starters, it improves slightly until age 27, then tails off considerably with age, costing pitchers nearly one full IP/G by age 33 and one more by age 39.

*Hit rate (H%):* Among pitchers, H% appears to increase slowly but steadily as pitchers age, to the tune of .002-.003 points per year.

*Strand rate (S%):* Very similar to hit rate, except strand rate decreases with age rather than increasing. GB%/LD%/FB%: Line drives increase steadily from age 24 onward, and outfield flies increase beginning at age 31. Because 70%+ of line drives fall for hits, and 10%+ of fly balls become home runs, this spells trouble for aging pitchers.

*Home runs per fly ball (hr/f):* As each year passes, a higher percentage of a pitcher's fly balls become home runs allowed increases with age.

### Catchers' effect on pitching *(Thomas Hanrahan)*
A typical catcher handles a pitching staff better after having been with a club for a few years. Research has shown that there is an improvement in team ERA of approximately 0.37 runs from a catcher's rookie season to his prime years with a club. Expect a pitcher's ERA to be higher than expected if he is throwing to a rookie backstop.

### First productive season *(Michael Weddell)*
To find those starting pitchers who are about to post their first productive season in the majors (10 wins, 150 IP, ERA of 4.00 or less), look for:
- Pitchers entering their age 23-26 seasons, especially those about to pitch their age 25 season.
- Pitchers who already have good skills, shown by an xERA in the prior year of 4.25 or less.
- Pitchers coming off of at least a partial season in the majors without a major health problem.
- To the extent that one speculates on pitchers who are one skill away, look for pitchers who only need to improve their control (bb/9).

### Overall pitching breakout profile *(Brandon Kruse)*
A breakout performance is defined here as one where a player posts a Rotisserie value of $20 or higher after having never achieved $10 previously. These criteria are primarily used to validate an apparent breakout in the current season but may also be used carefully to project a potential breakout for an upcoming season.
- Age 27 or younger
- Minimum 5.6 Dom, 2.0 Cmd, 1.1 hr/9 and 50 BPV
- Maximum 30% hit rate
- Minimum 71% strand rate
- Starters should have a H% no greater than the previous year; relievers should show improved command
- Maximum xERA of 4.00

## Bounceback fallacy *(Patrick Davitt)*

It is conventional wisdom that a pitcher often follows a bad year (value decline of more than 50%) with a significant "bounceback" that offers profit opportunity for the canny owner. But research showed the owner is extremely unlikely to get a full bounceback, and in fact, is more likely to suffer a further decline or uselessly small recovery than even a partial bounceback. The safest bet is a $30+ pitcher who has a collapse—but even then, bid to only about half of the previous premium value.

## Pitchers crossing leagues *(Bob Berger)*

The AL has higher league-wide ERA and lower K/9 when compared to the NL. Fantasy owners should consider adjusting their ERA, WHIP, and K/9 expectations for pitchers moving to the "other" league. Pitchers moving to the NL may perform better than expected based on their recent career trends; pitchers moving to the AL may perform worse than expected.

# Closers

## Saves

There are six events that need to occur in order for a relief pitcher to post a single save:

1. The starting pitcher and middle relievers must pitch well.
2. The offense must score enough runs.
3. It must be a reasonably close game.
4. The manager must put the pitcher in for a save opportunity.
5. The pitcher must pitch well and hold the lead.
6. The manager must let him finish the game.

Of these six events, only one is within the control of the relief pitcher. As such, projecting saves for a reliever has less to do with skills than opportunity. However, pitchers with excellent skills may create opportunity for themselves.

## Saves conversion rate (Sv%)

*Saves / Save Opportunities*

The percentage of save opportunities that are successfully converted. **BENCHMARK:** We look for a minimum 80% for long-term success.

## Leverage index (LI) *(Tom Tango)*

Leverage index measures the amount of swing in the possible change in win probability indexed against an average value of 1.00. Thus, relievers who come into games in various situations create a composite score and if that average score is higher than 1.00, then their manager is showing enough confidence in them to try to win games with them. If the average score is below 1.00, then the manager is using them, but not showing nearly as much confidence that they can win games.

## Saves chances and wins *(Patrick Davitt)*

Some fantasy owners think that good teams get more saves because they generate more wins. Other owners think that poor teams get more saves because more of their wins are by narrow margins. The "good-team" side is probably on firmer ground,

though there are enough exceptions that we should be cautious about drawing broad inferences.

The 2014 study confirmed what Craig Neuman found years earlier: The argument "more wins leads to more saves" is generally correct. Over five studied seasons, the percentage of wins that were saved (Sv%W) was about 50%, and half of all team-seasons fell in the Sv%W range of 48%-56%. As a result, high-saves seasons were more common for high-win teams.

That wins-saves connection for individual team-seasons was much less solid, however, and we observed many outliers. Data for individual team-seasons showed wide ranges of both Sv%W and actual saves.

Finally, higher-win teams do indeed get more blowout wins, but while poorer teams had a higher percentage (73%) of close wins (three runs or fewer) than better teams (56%), good teams' higher number of wins meant they still had more close wins, more save opportunities and more saves, again with many outliers among individual team-seasons.

## Origin of closers

History has long maintained that ace closers are not easily recognizable early on in their careers, so that every season does see its share of the unexpected. Blake Treinen, Shane Greene, Keone Kela, Hunter Strickland, Seranthony Dominguez, Jose Leclerc, Robert Gsellman…who would have thought it a year ago?

Accepted facts, all of which have some element of truth:

- You cannot find major league closers from pitchers who were closers in the minors.
- Closers begin their careers as starters.
- Closers are converted set-up men.
- Closers are pitchers who were unable to develop a third effective pitch.

More simply, closers are a product of circumstance.

Are the minor leagues a place to look at all?

From 1990-2004, there were 280 twenty-save seasons in Double-A and Triple-A. Over that period, there were only 13 pitchers ever saved 20 games in the majors and only five who ever posted more than one 20-save season: John Wetteland, Mark Wohlers, Ricky Bottalico, Braden Looper and Francisco Cordero.

More recent data is even more pessimistic:

| Year | # with 20 Svs | MLB closers |
|------|---------------|-------------|
| 2006 | 25 | none |
| 2007 | 22 | none |
| 2008 | 19 | none |
| 2009 | 17 | none |
| 2010 | 14 | Craig Kimbrel |
| 2011 | 16 | none |
| 2012 | 16 | A.J. Ramos |
| 2013 | 16 | none |
| 2014 | 12 | none |
| 2015 | 17 | none |

That's 177 twenty-save seasons and only two major league closers.

One of the reasons that minor league closers rarely become major league closers is because, in general, they do not get enough innings in the minors to sufficiently develop their arms into big-league caliber.

In fact, organizations do not look at minor league closing performance seriously, assigning that role to pitchers who they do not see as legitimate prospects. The average age of minor league closers over the past decade has been 27.5.

### Elements of saves success

The task of finding future closing potential comes down to looking at two elements:

*Talent:* The raw skills to mow down hitters for short periods of time. Optimal BPVs over 100, but not under 75.

*Opportunity:* The more important element, yet the one that pitchers have no control over.

There are pitchers that have Talent, but not Opportunity. These pitchers are not given a chance to close for a variety of reasons (e.g. being blocked by a solid front-liner in the pen, being left-handed, etc.), but are good to own because they will not likely hurt your pitching staff. You just can't count on them for saves, at least not in the near term.

There are pitchers that have Opportunity, but not Talent. MLB managers decide who to give the ball to in the 9th inning based on their own perceptions about what skills are required to succeed, even if those perceived "skills" don't translate into acceptable metrics.

Those pitchers without the metrics may have some initial short-term success, but their long-term prognosis is poor and they are high risks to your roster. Classic examples of the short life span of these types of pitchers include Matt Karchner, Heath Slocumb, Ryan Kohlmeier, Dan Miceli, Joe Borowski and Danny Kolb. More recent examples include Brandon Kintzler, Sam Dyson, Brad Ziegler and Jeanmar Gomez.

### Closers' job retention *(Michael Weddell)*

Of pitchers with 20 or more saves in one year, only 67.5% of these closers earned 20 or more saves the following year. The variables that best predicted whether a closer would avoid this attrition:

- *Saves history:* Career saves was the most important factor.
- *Age:* Closers are most likely to keep their jobs at age 27. For long-time closers, their growing career saves totals more than offset the negative impact of their advanced ages. Older closers without a long history of racking up saves tend to be bad candidates for retaining their roles.
- *Performance:* Actual performance, measured by ERA+, was of only minor importance.
- *Being right-handed:* Increased the odds of retaining the closer's role by 9% over left-handers.

How well can we predict which closers will keep their jobs? Of the 10 best closers during 1989-2007, 90% saved at least 20 games during the following season. Of the 10 worst bets, only 20% saved at least 20 games the next year.

### Closer volatility history

| Year | Closers Drafted | Avg R$ | Closers Failed | Failure % | New Sources |
|------|------|------|------|------|------|
| 2008 | 32 | $17.78 | 10 | 31% | 11 |
| 2009 | 28 | $17.56 | 9 | 32% | 13 |
| 2010 | 28 | $16.96 | 7 | 25% | 13 |
| 2011 | 30 | $15.47 | 11 | 37% | 8 |
| 2012 | 29 | $15.28 | 19 | 66% | 18 |
| 2013 | 29 | $15.55 | 9 | 31% | 13 |
| 2014 | 28 | $15.54 | 11 | 39% | 15 |
| 2015 | 29 | $14.79 | 13 | 45% | 16 |
| 2016 | 33 | $13.30 | 19 | 58% | 17 |
| 2017 | 32 | $13.63 | 17 | 53% | 15 |
| 2018 | 27 | $13.22 | 17 | 63% | 20 |

*Drafted* refers to the number of saves sources purchased in both LABR and Tout Wars experts leagues each year. These only include relievers drafted specifically for saves speculation. *Avg R$* refers to the average purchase price of these pitchers in the AL-only and NL-only leagues. *Failed* is the number (and percentage) of saves sources drafted that did not return at least 50% of their value that year. The failures include those that lost their value due to ineffectiveness, injury or managerial decision. *New Sources* are arms that were drafted for less than $10 (if drafted at all) but finished with at least 10 saves.

The failed saves investments in 2018 were Archie Bradley, Chad Allen, Cam Bedrosian, Brad Brach, Alex Claudio, Alexander Colome, Ken Giles, Shane Greene, Kelvin Herrera, Kenley Jansen, Corey Knebel, Mark Melancon, Hector Neris, Roberto Osuna, Blake Parker, Fernando Rodney and Brad Ziegler. Some of these "failures" amassed significant saves totals but their ERA/WHIP did not justify their draft investments.

The new sources in 2018 were Kyle Barraclough, Brad Boxberger, Seranthony Dominguez, Robert Gsellman, Josh Hader, Jeremy Jeffress, Keone Kela, Jose Leclerc, A.J. Minter, Brandon Morrow, Bud Norris, Wily Peralta, Sergio Romo, Joakim Soria, Hunter Strickland, Pedro Strop, Aroldys Vizcaino, Will Smith and Kirby Yates. Note that many of these were temporary assignments and were subsequently replaced as well.

The erosion of fantasy bullpen value accelerated in 2018. Owners spent more than 40 cents less per pitcher, on average, than 2017, which was an all-time low. This is significant. In 2015, 17 percent of potential closers were drafted for less than $10, which used to be the standard floor value for saves speculation. In 2016, that percentage spiked to 30 percent. In 2017, the rate increased again to 34 percent. While the rate dropped to 30 percent in 2018, only 27 closers were drafted overall. Some MLB bullpens were in such disarray on Draft Day that the experts invested no more than token speculative bids on any reliever. The 20 new sources represents the highest churn since we began tracking these in 1999. Yet, of those 20, only four earned even $10 and another five returned $0 or less. As MLB managers continue to micro-manage their bullpens, investments in closers will likely continue to be depressed.

### Closers and multi-year performance *(Patrick Davitt)*

A team having an "established closer"—even a successful one—in a given year does not affect how many of that team's wins are saved in the next year. However, a top closer (40-plus saves) in a given year has a significantly greater chance to retain his role in the subsequent season.

Research of saves and wins data over several seasons found that the percentage of wins that are saved is consistently 50%-54%, irrespective of whether the saves were concentrated in the hands of a "top closer" or passed around to the dreaded "committee" of lesser closers. But it also found that about two-thirds of high-save closers reprised their roles the next season, while three-quarters of low-save closers did not. Moreover, closers who held the role for two or three straight seasons averaged 34 saves per season while closers new to the role averaged 27.

### BPV as a leading indicator *(Doug Dennis)*

Research has shown that base performance value (BPV) is an excellent indicator of long-term success as a closer. Here are 20-plus saves seasons, by year:

| Year | No. | BPV 100+ | BPV 75+ | BPV <75 |
|------|-----|------|-----|-----|
| 1999 | 26 | 27% | 54% | 46% |
| 2000 | 24 | 25% | 54% | 46% |
| 2001 | 25 | 56% | 80% | 20% |
| 2002 | 25 | 60% | 72% | 28% |
| 2003 | 25 | 36% | 64% | 36% |
| 2004 | 23 | 61% | 61% | 39% |
| 2005 | 25 | 36% | 64% | 36% |
| 2006 | 25 | 52% | 72% | 28% |
| 2007 | 23 | 52% | 74% | 26% |
| *MEAN* | *25* | *45%* | *66%* | *34%* |

Though 20-saves success with a 75+ BPV is only a 66% percentage play in any given year, the below-75 group is composed of closers who are rarely able to repeat the feat in the following season:

| Year | No. with BPV < 75 | No. who followed up 20+ saves <75 BPV |
|------|------|------|
| 1999 | 12 | 2 |
| 2000 | 11 | 2 |
| 2001 | 5 | 2 |
| 2002 | 7 | 3 |
| 2003 | 9 | 3 |
| 2004 | 9 | 2 |
| 2005 | 9 | 1 |
| 2006 | 7 | 3 |
| 2007 | 6 | 0 |

## Other Relievers

### Projecting holds *(Doug Dennis)*

Here are some general rules of thumb for identifying pitchers who might be in line to accumulate holds. The percentages represent the portion of 2003's top holds leaders who fell into the category noted.

1. Left-handed set-up men with excellent BPIs. (43%)

2. A "go-to" right-handed set-up man with excellent BPIs. This is the one set-up RHer that a manager turns to with a small lead in the 7th or 8th innings. These pitchers also tend to vulture wins. (43%, but 6 of the top 9)

3. Excellent BPIs, but not a firm role as the main LHed or RHed set-up man. Roles change during the season;

cream rises to the top. Relievers projected to post great BPIs often overtake lesser set-up men in-season. (14%)

### Reliever efficiency percent (REff%)

*(Wins + Saves + Holds) / (Wins + Losses + SaveOpps + Holds)*

This is a measure of how often a reliever contributes positively to the outcome of a game. A record of consistent, positive impact on game outcomes breeds managerial confidence, and that confidence could pave the way to save opportunities. For those pitchers suddenly thrust into a closer's role, this formula helps gauge their potential to succeed based on past successes in similar roles. BENCHMARK: Minimum of 80%.

### Vulture

A pitcher, typically a middle reliever, who accumulates an unusually high number of wins by preying on other pitchers' misfortunes. More accurately, this is a pitcher typically brought into a game after a starting pitcher has put his team behind, and then pitches well enough and long enough to allow his offense to take the lead, thereby "vulturing" a win from the starter.

## In-Season Analysis

### Pure Quality Starts

Pure Quality Starts (PQS) says that the smallest unit of measure should not be the "event" but instead be the "game." Within that game, we can accumulate all the strikeouts, hits and walks, and evaluate that outing as a whole. After all, when a pitcher takes the mound, he is either "on" or "off" his game; he is either dominant or struggling, or somewhere in between.

In PQS, we give a starting pitcher credit for exhibiting certain skills in each of his starts. Then by tracking his "PQS Score" over time, we can follow his progress. A starter earns one point for each of the following criteria:

1. The pitcher must go more than 6 innings (record at least one out in the 7th). This measures stamina.

2. He must allow fewer hits than innings pitched. This measures hit prevention.

3. His number of strikeouts must equal to or more than 5. This measures dominance.

4. He must strike out at least three times as many batters as he walks (or have a minimum of three strikeouts if he hasn't walked a batter). This measures command.

5. He must not allow a home run. This measures his ability to keep the ball in the park.

A perfect PQS score is 5. Any pitcher who averages 3 or more over the course of the season is probably performing admirably. The nice thing about PQS is it allows you to approach each start as more than an all-or-nothing event.

Note the absence of earned runs. No matter how many runs a pitcher allows, if he scores high on the PQS scale, he has hurled a good game in terms of his base skills. The number of runs allowed—a function of not only the pitcher's ability but that of his bullpen and defense—will tend to even out over time.

It doesn't matter if a few extra balls got through the infield, or the pitcher was given the hook in the fourth or sixth inning, or the bullpen was able to strand their inherited baserunners. When we look at performance in the aggregate, those events do matter, and will affect a pitcher's peripherals and ERA. But with PQS, the minutia is less relevant than the overall performance.

In the end, a dominating performance is a dominating performance, whether Max Scherzer is hurling a 2-hit shutout or giving up three runs while striking out 11 in 7 IP. And a disaster is still a disaster, whether Dylan Bundy gets pulled after allowing 7 runs on 5 hits without getting an out, or gets a 5th inning hook after giving up 7 runs on 11 hits.

### Skill versus consistency

Two pitchers have identical 4.50 ERAs and identical 3.0 PQS averages. Their PQS logs look like this:

```
PITCHER A:   3   3   3   3   3
PITCHER B:   5   0   5   0   5
```

Which pitcher would you rather have on your team? The risk-averse manager would choose Pitcher A as he represents the perfectly known commodity. Many fantasy leaguers might opt for Pitcher B because his occasional dominating starts show that there is an upside. His Achilles Heel is inconsistency—he is unable to sustain that high level. Is there any hope for Pitcher B?

- If a pitcher's inconsistency is characterized by more poor starts than good starts, his upside is limited.
- Pitchers with extreme inconsistency rarely get a full season of starts.
- However, inconsistency is neither chronic nor fatal.

The outlook for Pitcher A is actually worse. Disaster avoidance might buy these pitchers more starts, but history shows that the lack of dominating outings is more telling of future potential. In short, consistent mediocrity is bad.

### PQS DOMination and DISaster rates *(Gene McCaffrey)*

DOM% is the percentage of a starting pitcher's outings that rate as a PQS-4 or PQS-5. DIS% is the percentage that rate as a PQS-0 or PQS-1.

DOM/DIS percentages open up a new perspective, providing us with two separate scales of performance. In tandem, they measure consistency.

### Quality/consistency score (QC)

*(DOM% – (2 x DIS%)) x 2)*

Using PQS and DOM/DIS percentages, this score measures both the quality of performance as well as start-to-start consistency.

### The predictive value of PQS *(Arik Florimonte)*

Using data from 2010-2015, research showed that PQS values can be used to project future starts. A pitcher who even threw only one PQS-DOM start had a slightly better chance of throwing another DOM in his subsequent start. For a pitcher who posts two, three, or even four PQS-DOMs in a row, the streak does portend better results to come. The longer the streak, the better the results.

Fantasy owners best positioned to take advantage are those who can frequently choose from multiple similar SP options, such as in a DFS league, or streaming in traditional leagues. In either case, make your evaluations as you normally would (e.g. talent first, then matchups, ballpark or by using BaseballHQ.

com's Pitcher Matchups Tool)—and then give a value bump to the pitcher with the hot streak.

### PQS correlation with Quality Starts *(Paul Petera)*

| PQS | QS% |
| --- | --- |
| 0 | 8% |
| 1 | 18% |
| 2 | 38% |
| 3 | 63% |
| 4 | 87% |
| 5 | 99% |

### High pitch counts and PQS *(Paul Petera)*

A 2017 study found that high-scoring PQS starters who also ran up high pitch counts continued to thrive in their next start (and beyond). Taking three seasons of PQS and pitch-count data, starts were grouped by pitch count into five cohorts and averaged by PQS. The study then calculated the average PQS scores in the subsequent starts, and found that pitchers with higher pitch counts are safer bets to throw well in their next start (and beyond) than those who throw fewer pitches. Near-term fatigue or other negative symptoms do not appear to be worthy of concern; so do not shy away from these pitchers solely for that reason.

### In-season ERA/xERA variance as a leading indicator *(Matt Cederholm)*

Pitchers with large first-half ERA/xERA variances will see regression towards their xERA in the second half, if they are allowed (and are able) to finish out the season. Starters have a stronger regression tendency than relievers, which we would expect to see given the larger sample size. In addition, there is substantial attrition among all types of pitchers, but those who are "unlucky" have a much higher rate.

An important corollary: While a pitcher underperforming his xERA is very likely to rebound in the second half, such regression hinges on his ability to hold onto his job long enough to see that regression come to fruition. Healthy veteran pitchers with an established role are more likely to experience the second half boost than a rookie starter trying to make his mark.

### Pure Quality Relief *(Patrick Davitt)*

A system for evaluating reliever outings. The scoring :

1. Two points for the first out, and one point for each subsequent out, to a maximum of four points.
2. One point for having at least one strikeout for every four full outs (one K for 1-4 outs, two Ks for 5-8 outs, etc.).
3. One point for zero baserunners, minus one point for each baserunner, though allowing the pitcher one unpenalized runner for each three full outs (one baserunner for 3-5 outs, two for 6-8 outs, three for nine outs)
4. Minus one point for each earned run, though allowing one ER for 8– or 9-out appearances.
5. An automatic PQR-0 for allowing a home run.

### Avoiding relief disasters *(Ed DeCaria)*

Relief disasters (defined as ER>=3 and IP<=3), occur in 5%+ of all appearances. The chance of a disaster exceeds 13% in any 7-day period. To minimize the odds of a disaster, we created a model that produced the following list of factors, in order of influence:

1. Strength of opposing offense
2. Park factor of home stadium
3. BB/9 over latest 31 days (more walks is bad)
4. Pitch count over previous 7 days (more pitches is bad)
5. Latest 31 Days ERA>xERA (recent bad luck continues)

Daily league owners who can slot relievers by individual game should also pay attention to days of rest: pitching on less rest than one is accustomed to increases disaster risk.

### April ERA as a leading indicator *(Stephen Nickrand)*

A starting pitcher's April ERA can act as a leading indicator for how his ERA is likely to fare during the balance of the season. A study looked at extreme April ERA results to see what kind of in-season forecasting power they may have. From 2010-2012, 42 SP posted an ERA in April that was at least 2.00 ER better than their career ERA. The findings:

- Pitchers who come out of the gates quickly have an excellent chance at finishing the season with an ERA much better than their career ERA.
- While April ERA gems see their in-season ERA regresses towards their career ERA, their May-Sept ERA is still significantly better than their career ERA.
- Those who stumble out of the gates have a strong chance at posting an ERA worse than their career average, but their in-season ERA improves towards their career ERA.
- April ERA disasters tend to have a May-Sept ERA that closely resembles their career ERA.

### Using K–BB% to find SP buying opportunities *(Arik Florimonte)*

Research showed that finding pitchers who have seen an uptick in k–bb% over the past 30 days is one way to search for mid-season replacements from the waiver wire. Using 2014-2016 player-seasons and filtering for starting pitchers with ≥ 100 IP, the k–bb% mean is about 13%. The overall MLB mean is approximately 12%, and the top 50 SP tend to be 14% or higher.
The findings:

- Last 30 days k–bb% is useful as a gauge of next 30 days performance.
- Pitchers on the upswing are more likely to climb into the elite ranks than other pitchers of similar YTD numbers; pitchers with a larger uptick show a greater likelihood.
- Last-30 k–bb% surgers could be good mid-season pickups if they are being overlooked by other owners in your league.

### Second-half ERA reduction drivers *(Stephen Nickrand)*

It's easy to dismiss first-half-to-second-half improvement among starting pitchers as an unpredictable event. After all, the midpoint of the season is an arbitrary cutoff. Performance swings occur throughout the season.

A study of SP who experienced significant 1H-2H ERA improvement from 2010-2012 examined what indicators drove

second-half ERA improvement. Among the findings for those 79 SP with a > 1.00 ERA 1H-2H reduction:

- 97% saw their WHIP decrease, with an average decrease of 0.26
- 97% saw their strand (S%) rate improve, with an average increase of 9%
- 87% saw their BABIP (H%) improve, with an average reduction of 5%
- 75% saw their control (bb/9) rate improve, with an average reduction of 0.8
- 70% saw their HR/9 rate improve, with an average decrease of 0.5
- 68% saw their swinging strike (SwK%) rate improve, with an average increase of 1.4%
- 68% saw their BPV improve, with an average increase of 37
- 67% saw their HR per fly ball rate (hr/f) improve, with an average decrease of 4%
- 53% saw their ground ball (GB%) rate improve, with an average increase of 5%
- 52% saw their dominance (k/9) rate improve, with an average increase of 1.3

These findings highlight the power of H% and S% regression as it relates to ERA and WHIP improvement. In fact, H% and S% are more often correlated with ERA improvement than are improved skills. They also suggest that improved control has a bigger impact on ERA reduction than does increased strikeouts.

### Pitcher home/road splits *(Stephen Nickrand)*

One overlooked strategy in leagues that allow frequent transactions is to bench pitchers when they are on the road. Research reveals that several pitching stats and indicators are significantly and consistently worse on the road than at home.

Some home/road rules of thumb for SP:

- If you want to gain significant ground in ERA and WHIP, bench all your average or worse SP on the road.
- A pitcher's win percentage drops by 15% on the road, so don't bank on road starts as a means to catch up in wins.
- Control erodes by 10% on the road, so be especially careful with keeping wild SP in your active lineups when they are away from home.
- NL pitchers at home produce significantly more strikeouts than their AL counterparts and vs. all pitchers on the road.
- hr/9, groundball rate, hit rate, strand rate, and hr/f do not show significant home vs. road variances.

## *Other Diamonds*

### The Pitching Postulates

1. Never sign a soft-tosser to a long-term contract.
2. Right-brain dominance has a very long shelf life.
3. A fly ball pitcher who gives up many HRs is expected. A GB pitcher who gives up many HRs is making mistakes.
4. Never draft a contact fly ball pitcher who plays in a hitter's park.
5. Only bad teams ever have a need for an inning-eater.
6. Never chase wins.

### Dontrelle Willis List

Pitchers with peripherals so horrible that you have to wonder how they can possibly draw a major league paycheck year after year.

### Chaconian

Having the ability to post many saves despite sub-Mendoza peripherals and an ERA in the stratosphere.

### ERA Benchmark

A half run of ERA over 200 innings comes out to just one earned run every four starts.

### Gopheritis (also, Acute Gopheritis and Chronic Gopheritis)

The dreaded malady in which a pitcher is unable to keep the ball in the park. Pitchers with gopheritis have a FB rate of at least 40%. More severe cases have a FB% over 45%.

### The Knuckleballers Rule

Knuckleballers don't follow no stinkin' rules.

### Brad Lidge Lament

When a closer posts a 62% strand rate, he has nobody to blame but himself.

### Vin Mazzaro Vindication

Occasional nightmares (2.1 innings, 14 ER) are just a part of the game.

### The Five Saves Certainties

1. On every team, there will be save opportunities and someone will get them. At a bare minimum, there will be at least 30 saves to go around, and not unlikely more than 45.

2. Any pitcher could end up being the chief beneficiary. Bullpen management is a fickle endeavor.

3. Relief pitchers are often the ones that require the most time at the start of the season to find a groove. The weather is cold, the schedule is sparse and their usage is erratic.

4. Despite the talk about "bullpens by committee," managers prefer a go-to guy. It makes their job easier.

5. As many as 50% of the saves in any year will come from pitchers who are unselected at the end of Draft Day.

### Soft-tosser land

The place where feebler arms leave their fortunes in the hands of the defense, variable hit and strand rates, and park dimensions. It's a place where many live, but few survive.

# Prospects

## General

### Minor league prospecting in perspective

In our perpetual quest to be the genius who uncovers the next Mike Trout when he's still in high school, there is an obsessive fascination with minor league prospects. That's not to say that prospecting is not important. The issue is perspective:

1. During the 10 year period of 1996 to 2005, only 8% of players selected in the first round of the Major League Baseball First Year Player Draft went on to become stars.

2. Some prospects are going to hit the ground running (Ronald Acuna) and some are going to immediately struggle (Lucas Giolito), no matter what level of hype follows them.

3. Some prospects are going to start fast (since the league is unfamiliar with them) and then fade (as the league figures them out). Others will start slow (since they are unfamiliar with the opposition) and then improve (as they adjust to the competition). So if you make your free agent and roster decisions based on small early samples sizes, you are just as likely to be an idiot as a genius.

4. How any individual player will perform relative to his talent is largely unknown because there is a psychological element that is vastly unexplored. Some make the transition to the majors seamlessly, some not, completely regardless of how talented they are.

5. Still, talent is the best predictor of future success, so major league equivalent base performance indicators still have a valuable role in the process. As do scouting reports, carefully filtered.

6. Follow the player's path to the majors. Did he have to repeat certain levels? Was he allowed to stay at a level long enough to learn how to adjust to the level of competition? A player with only two great months at Double-A is a good bet to struggle if promoted directly to the majors because he was never fully tested at Double-A, let alone Triple-A.

7. Younger players holding their own against older competition is a good thing. Older players reaching their physical peak, regardless of their current address, can be a good thing too. The Max Muncys, Joe Wendles and Dereck Rodriguezes can have some very profitable years.

8. Remember team context. A prospect with superior potential often will not unseat a steady but unspectacular incumbent, especially one with a large contract.

9. Don't try to anticipate how a team is going to manage their talent, both at the major and minor league level. You might think it's time to promote Nick Senzel and give him an everyday role. You are not running the Reds .

10. Those who play in shallow, one-year leagues should have little cause to be looking at the minors at all. The risk versus reward is so skewed against you, and there is so much talent available with a track record, that taking a chance on an unproven commodity makes little sense.

11. Decide where your priorities really are. If your goal is to win, prospect analysis is just a *part* of the process, not the entire process.

### Factors affecting minor league stats *(Terry Linhart)*

1. Often, there is an exaggerated emphasis on short-term performance in an environment that is supposed to focus on the long-term. Two poor outings don't mean a 21-year-old pitcher is washed up.

2. Ballpark dimensions and altitude create hitters parks and pitchers parks, but a factor rarely mentioned is that many parks in the lower minors are inconsistent in their field quality. Minor league clubs have limited resources to maintain field conditions, and this can artificially depress defensive statistics while inflating stats like batting average.

3. Some players' skills are so superior to the competition at their level that you can't get a true picture of what they're going to do from their stats alone.

4. Many pitchers are told to work on secondary pitches in unorthodox situations just to gain confidence in the pitch. The result is an artificially increased number of walks.

5. The #3, #4, and #5 pitchers in the lower minors are truly longshots to make the majors. They often possess only two pitches and are unable to disguise the off-speed offerings. Hitters can see inflated statistics in these leagues.

### Minor league level versus age

When evaluating minor leaguers, look at the age of the prospect in relation to the median age of the league he is in:

| | |
|---|---|
| *Low level A* | *Between 19-20* |
| *Upper level A* | *Around 20* |
| *Double-A* | *21* |
| *Triple-A* | *22* |

These are the ideal ages for prospects at the particular level. If a prospect is younger than most and holds his own against older and more experienced players, elevate his status. If he is older than the median, reduce his status.

### Triple-A experience as a leading indicator

The probability that a minor leaguer will immediately succeed in the majors can vary depending upon the level of Triple-A experience he has amassed at the time of call-up.

| | BATTERS | | PITCHERS | |
|---|---|---|---|---|
| | < 1 Yr | Full | < 1 Yr | Full |
| Performed well | 57% | 56% | 16% | 56% |
| Performed poorly | 21% | 38% | 77% | 33% |
| 2nd half drop-off | 21% | 7% | 6% | 10% |

The odds of a batter achieving immediate MLB success was slightly more than 50-50. More than 80% of all pitchers promoted with less than a full year at Triple-A struggled in their first year in the majors. Those pitchers with a year in Triple-A succeeded at a level equal to that of batters.

## Major League Equivalency (MLE) *(Bill James)*

A formula that converts a player's minor or foreign league statistics into a comparable performance in the major leagues. These are not projections, but conversions of current performance. MLEs contain adjustments for the level of play in individual leagues and teams. They work best with Triple-A stats, not quite as well with Double-A stats, and hardly at all with the lower levels. Foreign conversions are still a work in process. James' original formula only addressed batting. Our research has devised conversion formulas for pitchers, however, their best use comes when looking at peripherals, not traditional stats.

## Adjusting to the competition

All players must "adjust to the competition" at every level of professional play. Players often get off to fast or slow starts. During their second tour at that level is when we get to see whether the slow starters have caught up or whether the league has figured out the fast starters. That second half "adjustment" period is a good baseline for projecting the subsequent season, in the majors or minors.

Premature major league call-ups often negate the ability for us to accurately evaluate a player due to the lack of this adjustment period. For instance, a hotshot Double-A player might open the season in Triple-A. After putting up solid numbers for a month, he gets a call to the bigs, and struggles. The fact is, we do not have enough evidence that the player has mastered the Triple-A level. We don't know whether the rest of the league would have caught up to him during his second tour of the league. But now he's labeled as an underperformer in the bigs when in fact he has never truly proven his skills at the lower levels.

## Bull Durham prospects

There is some potential talent in older players—age 26, 27 or higher—who, for many reasons (untimely injury, circumstance, bad luck, etc.), don't reach the majors until they have already been downgraded from prospect to suspect. Equating potential with age is an economic reality for major league clubs, but not necessarily a skills reality.

Skills growth and decline is universal, whether it occurs at the major league level or in the minors. So a high-skills journeyman in Triple-A is just as likely to peak at age 27 as a major leaguer of the same age. The question becomes one of opportunity—will the parent club see fit to reap the benefits of that peak performance?

Prospecting these players for your fantasy team is, admittedly, a high risk endeavor, though there are some criteria you can use. Look for a player who is/has:

- Optimally, age 27-28 for overall peak skills, age 30-31 for power skills, or age 28-31 for pitchers.
- At least two seasons of experience at Triple-A. Career Double-A players are generally not good picks.
- Solid base skills levels.
- Shallow organizational depth at their position.
- Notable winter league or spring training performance.

Players who meet these conditions are not typically draftable players, but worthwhile reserve or FAAB picks.

## A Deep-league prospecting primer *(Jock Thompson)*

There's no substitute for having a philosophy, objective, and plan for your fantasy farm system. Here's a personal checklist for the prospecting process:

*Commit to some prospecting time.* Sounds intuitive, but some owners either don't have the time or won't take the time to learn about their league's available prospects.

*Have a prospecting framework/philosophy.* Such as TINSTAPP—there is no such thing as a pitching prospect. The non-linear rise and development of prospects can be frustrating in general, but much more so with pitchers. Unlike with hitters, you're usually safe in forgoing low-minors pitching, and are better off speculating on near-ready pitching names.

*Have objectives.* Upside vs. MLB proximity is an ongoing dilemma, but rebuilders will always need to take on some far-away high-ceiling flyers.

*Devise a strategy and stick with it.* You'll need an idea as to how you'll 1) acquire available talent; and 2) upgrade your roster deficiencies. Above all, play out the year. Your team will improve by making good free agent assessments all season—not by taking off in August and September.

*Always account for defense.* A plus glove is a real advantage in finding MLB opportunity. Versatility and athleticism are even better, and often feed multi-position eligibility.

*Consider all the variables.* Things like age, opportunity, organization, venue, and club positional needs should all factor into your decisions.

*Exercise excruciating patience – with legit hitting prospects.* Even the most highly-regarded prospects do not grow to the moon in linear fashion.

*Speculate readily and be nimble with your in-season pitching moves.* If you see something that looks more promising than what you have, grab it fast. If you don't, someone else will.

*Pay attention and dig into in-season minor league developments.* All of these lights can flicker on and turn into big edges if you can identify them. For example: a plus hit tool guy suddenly begins tapping into power, a pitcher makes in-season mechanical changes, a hitter makes across-the-board improvement following a position change.

*Don't dismiss late bloomers with extended MLB opportunity.* Like the more publicized names, plenty of lesser prospects have playable talent, and are just late figuring out how to unlock it.

## Batters

### MLE PX as a leading indicator *(Bill Macey)*

Looking at minor league performance (as MLE) in one year and the corresponding MLB performance the subsequent year:

|  | Year 1 MLE | Year 2 MLB |
|---|---|---|
| Observations | 496 | 496 |
| Median PX | 95 | 96 |
| Percent PX > 100 | 43% | 46% |

In addition, 53% of the players had a MLB PX in year 2 that exceeded their MLE PX in year 1. A slight bias towards improved performance in year 2 is consistent with general career trajectories.

| Year 1 MLE PX | Year 2 MLB PX | Pct. Incr | Pct. MLB PX > 100 |
|---|---|---|---|
| <= 50 | 61 | 70.3% | 5.4% |
| 51-75 | 85 | 69.6% | 29.4% |
| 76-100 | 93 | 55.2% | 39.9% |
| 101-125 | 111 | 47.4% | 62.0% |
| 126-150 | 119 | 32.1% | 66.1% |
| > 150 | 142 | 28.6% | 76.2% |

Slicing the numbers by performance level, there is a good amount of regression to the mean.

Players rarely suddenly develop power at the MLB level if they didn't previously display that skill in the minors. However, the relatively large gap between the median MLE PX and MLB PX for these players, 125 to 110, confirms the notion that the best players continue to improve once they reach the major leagues.

### MLE contact rate as a leading indicator *(Bill Macey)*
There is a strong positive correlation (0.63) between a player's MLE ct% in Year 1 and his actual ct% at the MLB level in Year 2.

| MLE ct% | Year 1 MLE ct% | Year 2 MLB ct% |
|---|---|---|
| < 70% | 69% | 68% |
| 70% - 74% | 73% | 72% |
| 75% - 79% | 77% | 75% |
| 80% - 84% | 82% | 77% |
| 85% - 89% | 87% | 82% |
| 90% + | 91% | 86% |
| **TOTAL** | **84%** | **79%** |

There is very little difference between the median MLE BA in Year 1 and the median MLB BA in Year 2:

| MLE ct% | Year 1 MLE BA | Year 2 MLB BA |
|---|---|---|
| < 70% | .230 | .270 |
| 70% - 74% | .257 | .248 |
| 75% - 79% | .248 | .255 |
| 80% - 84% | .257 | .255 |
| 85% - 89% | .266 | .270 |
| 90% + | .282 | .273 |
| TOTAL | .261 | .262 |

Excluding the <70% cohort (which was a tiny sample size), there is a positive relationship between MLE ct% and MLB BA.

## Pitchers

### Skills metrics as a leading indicator for pitching success
The percentage of hurlers that were good investments in the year that they were called up varied by the level of their historical minor league peripherals prior to that year.

| Pitchers who had: | Fared well | Fared poorly |
|---|---|---|
| Good indicators | 79% | 21% |
| Marginal or poor indicators | 18% | 82% |

The data used here were MLE levels from the previous two years, not the season in which they were called up. The significance? Solid current performance is what merits a call-up, but this is not a good indicator of short-term MLB success, because a) the performance data set is too small, typically just a few month's worth of statistics, and b) for those putting up good numbers at a new minor league level, there has typically not been enough time for the scouting reports to make their rounds.

## Far East Baseball *(Tom Mulhall)*

### Comparing MLB and Japanese Baseball
The Japanese major leagues are generally considered to be equivalent to Triple-A ball and the pitching possibly better. However, statistics are difficult to compare due to differences in the way the game is played in Japan.

1. While strong on fundamentals, Japanese baseball's guiding philosophy is risk avoidance. Runners rarely take extra bases, batters focus on making contact rather than driving the ball, and managers play for one run at a time. Bunts are more common. As a result, offenses score fewer runs per number of hits, and pitching stats tend to look better.

2. Stadiums in Japan usually have shorter fences. This should mean more HRs, but given #1 above, it is the American players who make up the majority of Japan's power elite. No power hitters have yet made an equivalent transition to MLB.

3. There are more artificial turf fields, which increases the number of ground ball singles. A few still use all dirt infields.

4. Though improving, the quality of umpiring is questionable. Fewer errors are called, possibly reflecting a cultural philosophy of low tolerance for mistakes and the desire to avoid publicly embarrassing a player.

5. Teams have smaller pitching staffs and use a six-man rotation. Starters usually pitch once a week, typically on the same day since Monday is an off-day for the entire league. Some starters will also occasionally pitch in relief between starts. Managers push for complete games, no matter what the score or situation. Because of the style of offense, higher pitch counts are common. Despite superior conditioning, Japanese pitchers tend to burn out early due to overuse.

6. The ball is smaller and lighter, and the strike zone is closer to the batter. A new ball was introduced in 2011 with lower-elasticity rubber surrounding the cork, which limited offense and inflated pitching stats. A more hitter-friendly ball was used in 2013. But continue to exercise some skepticism when analyzing pitching stats.

7. If the score remains even after 12 innings, the game goes into the books as a tie.

8. There are fewer games in the Japanese schedule.

### Japanese players as fantasy farm selections
When evaluating the potential of Japanese League prospects, the key is not to just identify the best Japanese players—the key is to identify impact players who have the desire and opportunity to sign with a MLB team. Opportunity is crucial, since players must have nine years of professional experience in order to qualify for international free agency, or hope that their team "posts" them early through a bidding process. With the success of players like Ichiro, Darvish and Ohtani, it is easy to overestimate the value of drafting these players. Still, for owners who are allowed to carry a large reserve or farm team at reduced salaries, these players could be a real windfall, especially if your competitors do not do their homework.

### Korean players as fantasy farm selections

Korea also has a posting system which impedes free agency for seven professional seasons. Korean stadiums are notoriously hitter friendly. Jung-ho Kang had 40 HR the year before he joined the Pirates. When researching Korean players, note that the family name may be listed first, followed by the given name.

A list of Japanese and Korean League players who could jump to the majors appears in the Prospects section.

## *Other Diamonds*

### Age 26 Paradox

Age 26 is when a player begins to reach his peak skill, no matter what his address is. If circumstances have him celebrating that birthday in the majors, he is a breakout candidate. If circumstances have him celebrating that birthday in the minors, he is washed up.

### A-Rod 10-Step Path to Stardom

Not all well-hyped prospects hit the ground running. More often they follow an alternative path:

1. Prospect puts up phenomenal minor league numbers.
2. The media machine gets oiled up.
3. Prospect gets called up, but struggles, Year 1.
4. Prospect gets demoted.
5. Prospect tears it up in the minors, Year 2.
6. Prospect gets called up, but struggles, Year 2.
7. Prospect gets demoted.
8. The media turns their backs. Fantasy leaguers reduce their expectations.
9. Prospect tears it up in the minors, Year 3. The public shrugs its collective shoulders.
10. Prospect is promoted in Year 3 and explodes. Some lucky fantasy leaguer lands a franchise player for under $5.

Some players that are currently stuck at one of the interim steps, and may or may not ever reach Step 10, include Austin Meadows, Ryan McMahon and Raimel Tapia.

### Bull Durham Gardening Tip

Late bloomers have fewer flowering seasons.

### Developmental Dogmata

1. Defense is what gets a minor league prospect to the majors; offense is what keeps him there. *(Deric McKamey)*
2. The reason why rapidly promoted minor leaguers often fail is that they are never given the opportunity to master the skill of "adjusting to the competition."
3. Rookies who are promoted in-season often perform better than those that make the club out of spring training. Inferior March competition can inflate the latter group's perceived talent level.
4. Young players rarely lose their inherent skills. Pitchers may uncover weaknesses and the players may have difficulty adjusting. These are bumps along the growth curve, but they do not reflect a loss of skill.
5. Late bloomers have smaller windows of opportunity and much less chance for forgiveness.
6. The greatest risk in this game is to pay for performance that a player has never achieved.
7. Some outwardly talented prospects simply have a ceiling that's spelled "A-A-A."

### Rule 5 Reminder

Don't ignore the Rule 5 draft lest you ignore the possibility of players like Jose Bautista, Delino Deshields, Odubel Herrera, Hector Rondon, Johan Santana, Joakim Soria, and Jayson Werth. All were Rule 5 draftees.

### Trout Inflation

The tendency for rookies to go for exorbitant draft prices following a year when there was a very good rookie crop.

# Gaming

## *Standard Rules and Variations*

Rotisserie Baseball was invented as an elegant confluence of baseball and economics. Whether by design or accident, the result has lasted for more than three decades. But what would Rotisserie and fantasy have been like if the Founding Fathers knew then what we know now about statistical analysis and game design? You can be sure things would be different.

The world has changed since the original game was introduced yet many leagues use the same rules today. New technologies have opened up opportunities to improve elements of the game that might have been limited by the capabilities of the 1980s. New analytical approaches have revealed areas where the original game falls short.

As such, there are good reasons to tinker and experiment; to find ways to enhance the experience.

Following are the basic elements of fantasy competition, those that provide opportunities for alternative rules and experimentation. This is by no means an exhaustive list, but at minimum provides some interesting food-for-thought.

### Player pool

*Standard:* American League-only, National League-only or Mixed League.

AL/NL-only typically drafts 8-12 teams (pool penetration of 49% to 74%). Mixed leagues draft 10-18 teams (31% to 55% penetration), though 15 teams (46%) is a common number.

Drafting of reserve players will increase the penetration percentages. A 12-team AL/NL-only league adding six reserves onto 23-man rosters would draft 93% of the available pool of players on all teams' 25-man rosters.

The draft penetration level determines which fantasy management skills are most important to your league. The higher the penetration, the more important it is to draft a good team. The lower the penetration, the greater the availability of free agents and the more important in-season roster management becomes.

There is no generally-accepted optimal penetration level, but we have often suggested that 75% (including reserves) provides a good balance between the skills required for both draft prep and in-season management.

*Alternative pools:* There is a wide variety of options here. Certain leagues draft from within a small group of major league divisions or teams. Some competitions, like home run leagues, only draft batters.

*Bottom-tier pool:* Draft only players who posted a Rotisserie dollar value of $5 or less in the previous season. Intended as a test of an owner's ability to identify talent with upside. Best used as a pick-a-player contest with any number of teams participating.

### Positional structure

*Standard:* 23 players. One at each defensive position (though three outfielders may be from any of LF, CF or RF), plus one additional catcher, one middle infielder (2B or SS), one corner infielder (1B or 3B), two additional outfielders and a utility player/designated hitter (which often can be a batter who qualifies anywhere). Nine pitchers, typically holding any starting or relief role.

*Open:* 25 players. One at each defensive position (plus DH), 5-man starting rotation and two relief pitchers. Nine additional players at any position, which may be a part of the active roster or constitute a reserve list.

*40-man:* Standard 23 plus 17 reserves. Used in many keeper and dynasty leagues.

*Reapportioned:* In recent years, new obstacles are being faced by 12-team AL/NL-only leagues thanks to changes in the real game. The 14/9 split between batters and pitchers no longer reflects how MLB teams structure their rosters. Of the 30 teams, each with 25-man rosters, not one contains 14 batters for any length of time. In fact, many spend a good part of the season with only 12 batters, which means teams often have more pitchers than hitters.

For fantasy purposes in AL/NL-only leagues, that leaves a disproportionate draft penetration into the batter and pitcher pools:

|                    | BATTERS | PITCHERS |
|--------------------|---------|----------|
| On all MLB rosters | 195     | 180      |
| Players drafted    | 168     | 108      |
| Pct.               | 86%     | 60%      |

These drafts are depleting 26% more batters out of the pool than pitchers. Add in those leagues with reserve lists—perhaps an additional six players per team removing another 72 players—and post-draft free agent pools are very thin, especially on the batting side.

The impact is less in 15-team mixed leagues, though the FA pitching pool is still disproportionately deep.

|                | BATTERS | PITCHERS |
|----------------|---------|----------|
| On all rosters | 381     | 369      |
| Drafted        | 210     | 135      |
| Pct.           | 55%     | 37%      |

One solution is to reapportion the number of batters and pitchers that are rostered. Adding one pitcher slot and eliminating one batter slot may be enough to provide better balance. The batting slot most often removed is the second catcher, since it is the position with the least depth.

Beginning in the 2012 season, the Tout Wars AL/NL-only experts leagues opted to eliminate one of the outfield slots and replace it with a "swingman" position. This position could be any batter or pitcher, depending upon the owner's needs at any given time during the season.

### Selecting players

*Standard:* The three most prevalent methods for stocking fantasy rosters are:

**Snake/Straight/Serpentine draft:** Players are selected in order with seeds reversed in alternating rounds. This method has become the most popular due to its speed, ease of implementation and ease of automation.

In these drafts, the underlying assumption is that value can be ranked relative to a linear baseline. Pick #1 is better than pick #2, which is better than pick #3, and the difference between each pick is assumed to be somewhat equivalent. While a faulty assumption, we must believe in it to assume a level playing field.

**Auction:** Players are sold to the highest bidder from a fixed budget, typically $260. Auctions provide the team owner with more control over which players will be on his team, but can take twice as long as snake drafts.

The baseline is $0 at the beginning of each player put up for bid. The final purchase price for each player is shaped by many wildly variable factors, from roster need to geographic location of the draft. A $30 player can mean different things to different drafters.

One option that can help reduce the time commitment of auctions is to force minimum bids at each hour mark. You could mandate $15 openers in hour #1; $10 openers in hour #2, etc.

**Pick-a-player / Salary cap:** Players are assigned fixed dollar values and owners assemble their roster within a fixed cap. This type of roster-stocking is an individual exercise which results in teams typically having some of the same players.

In these leagues, the "value" decision is taken out of the hands of the owners. Each player has a fixed value, pre-assigned based on past season performance and/or future expectation.

*Hybrid snake-auction:* Each draft begins as an auction. Each team has to fill its first seven roster slots from a budget of $154. Opening bid for any player is $15. After each team has filled seven slots, it becomes a snake draft.

This method is intended to reduce draft time while still providing an economic component for selecting players.

## Stat categories

*Standard:* The standard statistical categories for Rotisserie leagues are:

**4x4:** HR, RBI, SB, BA, W, Sv, ERA, WHIP

**5x5:** HR, R, RBI, SB, BA, W, Sv, K, ERA, WHIP

**6x6:** Categories typically added are Holds and OPS.

**7x7, etc.:** Any number of categories may be added.

In general, the more categories you add, the more complicated it is to isolate individual performance and manage the categorical impact on your roster. There is also the danger of redundancy; with multiple categories measuring like stats, certain skills can get over-valued. For instance, home runs are double-counted when using the categories of both HR and slugging average. (Though note that HRs are actually already triple-counted in standard 5x5—HRs, runs, and RBIs)

If the goal is to have categories that create a more encompassing picture of player performance, it is actually possible to accomplish more with less:

*Modified 4x4:* HR, (R+RBI-HR), SB, OBA, (W+QS), (Sv+Hld), K, ERA

This provides a better balance between batting and pitching in that each has three counting categories and one ratio category. In fact, the balance is shown to be even more notable here:

| | BATTING | PITCHING |
|---|---|---|
| Pure skill counting stat | HR | K |
| Ratio category | OBA | ERA |
| Dependent upon managerial decision | SB | (Sv+Hold) |
| Dependent upon team support | (R+RBI-HR) | (W+QS) |

*Replacing saves:* The problem with the Saves statistic is that we have a scarce commodity that is centered on a small group of players, thereby creating inflated demand for those players. With the rising failure rate for closers these days, the incentive to pay full value for the commodity decreases. The higher the risk, the lower the prices.

We can increase the value of the commodity by reducing the risk. We might do this by increasing the number of players that contribute to that category, thereby spreading the risk around. One way we can accomplish this is by changing the category to Saves + Holds.

Holds are not perfect, but the typical argument about them being random and arbitrary can apply to saves these days as well. In fact, many of the pitchers who record holds are far more skilled and valuable than closers; they are often called to the mound in much higher leverage situations (a fact backed up by a scan of each pitcher's Leverage Index).

Neither stat is perfect, but together they form a reasonable proxy for overall bullpen performance.

In tandem, they effectively double the player pool of draftable relievers while also flattening the values allotted to those pitchers. The more players around which we spread the risk, the more control we have in managing our pitching staffs.

*Replacing wins:* Using reasons similar to replacing Saves with Saves + Holds, some have argued for replacing the Wins statistic with W + QS (quality starts). This method of scoring gives value to a starting pitcher who pitches well, but fails to receive the win due to his team's poor offense or poor luck. However, with the decline in the average length of starts, the number of QS outings has dropped sharply. W+QS was a good idea a few years ago; less so now.

## Keeping score

*Standard:* These are the most common scoring methods:

**Rotisserie:** Players are evaluated in several statistical categories. Totals of these statistics are ranked by team. The winner is the team with the highest cumulative ranking.

**Points:** Players receive points for events that they contribute to in each game. Points are totaled for each team and teams are then ranked.

**Head-to-Head (H2H):** Using Rotisserie or points scoring, teams are scheduled in daily or weekly matchups. The winner of each matchup is the team that finishes higher in more categories (Rotisserie) or scores the most points.

*Hybrid H2H-Rotisserie:* Rotisserie's category ranking system can be converted into a weekly won-loss record. Depending upon where your team finishes for that week's statistics determines how many games you win for that week. Each week, your team will play seven games.

| *Place | Record | *Place | Record |
|---|---|---|---|
| 1st | 7-0 | 7th | 3-4 |
| 2nd | 6-1 | 8th | 2-5 |
| 3rd | 6-1 | 9th | 2-5 |
| 4th | 5-2 | 10th | 1-6 |
| 5th | 5-2 | 11th | 1-6 |
| 6th | 4-3 | 12th | 0-7 |

*\* Based on overall Rotisserie category ranking for the week.*

At the end of each week, all the statistics revert to zero and you start over. You never dig a hole in any category that you can't climb out of, because all categories themselves are incidental to the standings.

The regular season lasts for 23 weeks, which equals 161 games. Weeks 24, 25 and 26 are for play-offs.

### Free agent acquisition

*Standard:* Three methods are the most common for acquiring free agent players during the season.

**First come first served:** Free agents are awarded to the first owner who claims them.

**Reverse order of standings:** Access to the free agent pool is typically in a snake draft fashion with the last place team getting the first pick, and each successive team higher in the standings picking afterwards.

**Free agent acquisition budget (FAAB):** Teams are given a set budget at the beginning of the season (typically, $100 or $1000) from which they bid on free agents in a closed auction process.

*Vickrey FAAB:* Research has shown that more than 50% of FAAB dollars are lost via overbid on an annual basis. Given that this is a scarce commodity, one would think that a system to better manage these dollars might be desirable. The Vickrey system conducts a closed auction in the same way as standard FAAB, but the price of the winning bid is set at the amount of the second highest bid, plus $1. In some cases, gross overbids (at least $10 over) are reduced to the second highest bid plus $5.

This method was designed by William Vickrey, a Professor of Economics at Columbia University. His theory was that this process reveals the true value of the commodity. For his work, Vickrey was awarded the Nobel Prize for Economics (and $1.2 million) in 1996.

*Double-Bid FAAB:* One of the inherent difficulties in the current FAAB system is that we have so many options for setting a bid amount. You can bid $47, or $51, or $23. You might agonize over whether to go $38 or $39. With a $100 budget, there are 100 decision points. And while you may come up with a rough guesstimate of the range in which your opponents might bid, the results for any individual player bidding are typically random within that range.

The first part of this process reduces the number of decision points. Owners must categorize their interest by bidding a fixed number of pre-set dollar amounts for each player. In a $100 FAAB league, for instance, those levels might be $1, $5, $10, $15, $20, $30, $40 and increasing $10 increments. All owners would set the general market value for free agents in these pre-set levels of interest.

The initial stage of the bidding process serves to screen out those who are not interested in a player at the appropriate market level. That leaves a high potential for tied owners, those who share the same level of interest.

The tied owners must then submit a second bid of equal or greater value than their first bid. These bids can be in $1 increments. The winning owner gets the player; if there is still a tie, then the player would go to the owner lower in the standings.

An advantage of this second bid is that it gives owners an opportunity to see who they are going up against, and adjust. If you are bidding against an owner close to you in the standings, you may need to be more aggressive in that second bid. If you see that the tied owner(s) wouldn't hurt you by acquiring that player, then maybe you resubmit the original bid and be content to potentially lose out on the player. If you're ahead in the standings, it's actually a way to potentially opt out on that player completely by resubmitting your original bid and forcing another owner to spend his FAAB.

Some leagues will balk at adding another layer to the weekly deadline process; it's a trade-off to having more control over managing your FAAB.

### The season

*Standard:* Leagues are played out during the course of the entire Major League Baseball season.

*Split-season:* Leagues are conducted from Opening Day through the All-Star break, then re-drafted to play from the All-Star break through the end of the season.

*50-game split-season:* Leagues are divided into three 50-game seasons with one-week break in between.

*Monthly:* Leagues are divided into six seasons or rolling four-week seasons.

The advantages of these shorter time frames:

- They can help to maintain interest. There would be fewer abandoned teams.
- There would be more shots at a title each year.
- Given that drafting is considered the most fun aspect of the game, these splits multiply the opportunities to participate in some type of draft. Leagues may choose to do complete re-drafts and treat the year as distinct mini-seasons. Or, leagues might allow teams to drop their five worst players and conduct a restocking draft at each break.

*Daily games:* Participants select a roster of players from one day's MLB schedule. Scoring is based on an aggregate points-based system rather than categories, with cash prizes awarded based on the day's results. The structure and distribution of that prize pool varies across different types of events, and those differences can affect roster construction strategies. Although scoring and prizes are based on one day's play, the season-long element of bankroll management provides a proxy for overall standings.

In terms of projecting outcomes, daily games are drastically different than full-season leagues. Playing time is one key element of any projection, and daily games offer near-100% accuracy in projecting playing time: you can check pre-game lineups to see exactly which players are in the lineup that night. The other key component of any projection is performance, but that is plagued by variance in daily competitions. Even if you roster a team full of the most advantageous matchups, even the best hitters will go 0-for-4 on a given night.

*Post-season league:* Some leagues re-draft teams from among the MLB post-season contenders and play out a separate competition. It is possible, however, to make a post-season competition that is an extension of the regular season.

Start by designating a set number of regular season finishers as qualifying for the post-season. The top four teams in a league is a good number.

These four teams would designate a fixed 23-man roster for all post-season games. First, they would freeze all of their currently-owned players who are on MLB post-season teams.

In order to fill the roster holes that will likely exist, these four teams would then pick players from their league's non-playoff teams (for the sake of the post-season only). This would be in the form of a snake draft done on the day following the end of the regular season. Draft order would be regular season finish, so the play-off team with the most regular season points would get first pick. Picks would continue until all four rosters are filled with 23 men.

Regular scoring would be used for all games during October. The team with the best play-off stats at the end of the World Series is the overall champ.

## Snake Drafting

### Snake draft first round history

The following tables record the comparison between pre-season projected player rankings (using Average Draft Position data from Mock Draft Central and National Fantasy Baseball Championship) and actual end-of-season results. The 15-year success rate of identifying each season's top talent is only 34%. Even if we extend the study to the top two rounds, the hit rate is only around 50%.

| 2011 | ADP | | ACTUAL = 6 |
|---|---|---|---|
| 1 | Albert Pujols | 1 | Matt Kemp |
| 2 | Hanley Ramirez | 2 | Jacoby Ellsbury |
| 3 | Miguel Cabrera | 3 | Ryan Braun (10) |
| 4 | Troy Tulowitzki | 4 | Justin Verlander |
| 5 | Evan Longoria | 5 | Clayton Kershaw |
| 6 | Carlos Gonzalez | 6 | Curtis Granderson |
| 7 | Joey Votto | 7 | Adrian Gonzalez (8) |
| 8 | Adrian Gonzalez | 8 | Miguel Cabrera (3) |
| 9 | Robinson Cano | 9 | Roy Halladay (15) |
| 10 | Ryan Braun | 10 | Cliff Lee |
| 11 | David Wright | 11 | Jose Bautista |
| 12 | Mark Teixeira | 12 | Dustin Pedroia |
| 13 | Carl Crawford | 13 | Jered Weaver |
| 14 | Josh Hamilton | 14 | Albert Pujols (1) |
| 15 | Roy Halladay | 15 | Robinson Cano (9) |

| 2012 | ADP | | ACTUAL = 4 |
|---|---|---|---|
| 1 | Matt Kemp | 1 | Mike Trout |
| 2 | Ryan Braun | 2 | Ryan Braun (2) |
| 3 | Albert Pujols | 3 | Miguel Cabrera (4) |
| 4 | Miguel Cabrera | 4 | Andrew McCutchen |
| 5 | Troy Tulowitzki | 5 | R.A. Dickey |
| 6 | Jose Bautista | 6 | Clayton Kershaw |
| 7 | Jacoby Ellsbury | 7 | Justin Verlander (8) |
| 8 | Justin Verlander | 8 | Josh Hamilton |
| 9 | Adrian Gonzalez | 9 | Fernando Rodney |
| 10 | Justin Upton | 10 | Adrian Beltre |
| 11 | Robinson Cano | 11 | Alex Rios |
| 12 | Joey Votto | 12 | David Price |
| 13 | Evan Longoria | 13 | Chase Headley |
| 14 | Carlos Gonzalez | 14 | Robinson Cano (11) |
| 15 | Prince Fielder | 15 | Edwin Encarnacion |

| 2013 | ADP | | ACTUAL = 5 |
|---|---|---|---|
| 1 | Ryan Braun | 1 | Miguel Cabrera (2) |
| 2 | Miguel Cabrera | 2 | Mike Trout (3) |
| 3 | Mike Trout | 3 | Clayton Kershaw (15) |
| 4 | Matt Kemp | 4 | Chris Davis |
| 5 | Andrew McCutchen | 5 | Paul Goldschmidt |
| 6 | Albert Pujols | 6 | Andrew McCutchen (5) |
| 7 | Robinson Cano | 7 | Adam Jones |
| 8 | Jose Bautista | 8 | Jacoby Ellsbury |
| 9 | Joey Votto | 9 | Max Scherzer |
| 10 | Carlos Gonzalez | 10 | Carlos Gomez |
| 11 | Buster Posey | 11 | Hunter Pence |
| 12 | Justin Upton | 12 | Robinson Cano (7) |
| 13 | Giancarlo Stanton | 13 | Alex Rios |
| 14 | Prince Fielder | 14 | Adrian Beltre |
| 15 | Clayton Kershaw | 15 | Matt Harvey |

| 2014 | ADP | | ACTUAL = 4 |
|---|---|---|---|
| 1 | Mike Trout | 1 | Jose Altuve |
| 2 | Miguel Cabrera | 2 | Clayton Kershaw (6) |
| 3 | Paul Goldschmidt | 3 | Michael Brantley |
| 4 | Andrew McCutchen | 4 | Mike Trout (1) |
| 5 | Carlos Gonzalez | 5 | Johnny Cueto |
| 6 | Clayton Kershaw | 6 | Felix Hernandez |
| 7 | Chris Davis | 7 | Victor Martinez |
| 8 | Ryan Braun | 8 | Jose Abreu |
| 9 | Adam Jones | 9 | Giancarlo Stanton |
| 10 | Bryce Harper | 10 | Andrew McCutchen (4) |
| 11 | Robinson Cano | 11 | Miguel Cabrera (2) |
| 12 | Hanley Ramirez | 12 | Carlos Gomez |
| 13 | Jacoby Ellsbury | 13 | Jose Bautista |
| 14 | Prince Fielder | 14 | Dee Gordon |
| 15 | Troy Tulowitzki | 15 | Anthony Rendon |

| 2015 | ADP | | ACTUAL = 4 |
|---|---|---|---|
| 1 | Mike Trout | 1 | Jake Arrieta |
| 2 | Andrew McCutchen | 2 | Zack Greinke |
| 3 | Clayton Kershaw | 3 | Clayton Kershaw (3) |
| 4 | Giancarlo Stanton | 4 | Paul Goldschmidt (5) |
| 5 | Paul Goldschmidt | 5 | A.J. Pollock |
| 6 | Miguel Cabrera | 6 | Dee Gordon |
| 7 | Jose Abreu | 7 | Bryce Harper |
| 8 | Carlos Gomez | 8 | Josh Donaldson |
| 9 | Jose Bautista | 9 | Jose Altuve (12) |
| 10 | Edwin Encarnacion | 10 | Mike Trout (1) |
| 11 | Felix Hernandez | 11 | Nolan Arenado |
| 12 | Jose Altuve | 12 | Manny Machado |
| 13 | Anthony Rizzo | 13 | Dallas Keuchel |
| 14 | Adam Jones | 14 | Max Scherzer |
| 15 | Troy Tulowitzki | 15 | Nelson Cruz |

| 2016 | ADP | | ACTUAL = 7 |
|---|---|---|---|
| 1 | Mike Trout | 1 | Mookie Betts |
| 2 | Paul Goldschmidt | 2 | Jose Altuve (11) |
| 3 | Bryce Harper | 3 | Mike Trout (1) |
| 4 | Clayton Kershaw | 4 | Jonathan Villar |
| 5 | Josh Donaldson | 5 | Jean Segura |
| 6 | Carlos Correa | 6 | Max Scherzer (15) |
| 7 | Nolan Arenado | 7 | Paul Goldschmidt (2) |
| 8 | Manny Machado | 8 | Charlie Blackmon |
| 9 | Anthony Rizzo | 9 | Clayton Kershaw (4) |
| 10 | Giancarlo Stanton | 10 | Nolan Arenado (7) |
| 11 | Jose Altuve | 11 | Daniel Murphy |
| 12 | Kris Bryant | 12 | Kris Bryant (12) |
| 13 | Miguel Cabrera | 13 | Joey Votto |
| 14 | Andrew McCutchen | 14 | Jon Lester |
| 15 | Max Scherzer | 15 | Madison Bumgarner |

| 2017 | ADP | | ACTUAL = 5 |
|---|---|---|---|
| 1 | Mike Trout | 1 | Charlie Blackmon |
| 2 | Mookie Betts | 2 | Jose Altuve (4) |
| 3 | Clayton Kershaw | 3 | Corey Kluber |
| 4 | Jose Altuve | 4 | Max Scherzer (12) |
| 5 | Kris Bryant | 5 | Paul Goldschmidt (7) |
| 6 | Nolan Arenado | 6 | Giancarlo Stanton |
| 7 | Paul Goldschmidt | 7 | Chris Sale |
| 8 | Manny Machado | 8 | Aaron Judge |
| 9 | Bryce Harper | 9 | Dee Gordon |
| 10 | Trea Turner | 10 | Clayton Kershaw (3) |
| 11 | Josh Donaldson | 11 | Nolan Arenado (6) |
| 12 | Max Scherzer | 12 | Jose Ramirez |
| 13 | Anthony Rizzo | 13 | Joey Votto |
| 14 | Madison Bumgarner | 14 | Marcell Ozuna |
| 15 | Carlos Correa | 15 | Elvis Andrus |

| 2018 | ADP | | ACTUAL = 3* |
|---|---|---|---|
| 1 | Mike Trout | 1 | Mookie Betts (7) |
| 2 | Jose Altuve | 2 | Christian Yelich |
| 3 | Nolan Arenado | 3 | J.D. Martinez |
| 4 | Trea Turner | 4 | Max Scherzer (11) |
| 5 | Clayton Kershaw | 5 | Jacob deGrom |
| 6 | Paul Goldschmidt | 6 | Jose Ramirez |
| 7 | Mookie Betts | 7 | Francisco Lindor |
| 8 | Giancarlo Stanton | 8 | Trevor Story |
| 9 | Charlie Blackmon | 9 | Justin Verlander |
| 10 | Bryce Harper | 10 | Mike Trout (1) |
| 11 | Max Scherzer | 11 | Blake Snell |
| 12 | Chris Sale | 12 | Javier Baez |
| 13 | Corey Kluber | 13 | Whit Merrifield |
| 14 | Carlos Correa | 14 | Aaron Nola |
| 15 | Kris Bryant | 15 | Manny Machado |

*Note that 2018 represents the lowest first round hit rate in the 15 years that we've been tracking ADPs. However, the next four players on the list would be:

| 16 | Trea Turner (4) |
|---|---|
| 17 | Chris Sale (12) |
| 18 | Nolan Arenado (3) |
| 19 | Corey Kluber (13) |

## ADP attrition

Why is our success rate so low in identifying what should be the most easy-to-project players each year? We rank and draft players based on the expectation that those ranked higher will return greater value in terms of productivity and playing time, as well as being the safest investments. However, there are many variables affecting where players finish.

Earlier, it was shown that players spend an inordinate number of days on the disabled list. In fact, of the players projected to finish in the top 300, the number who were disabled, demoted or designated for assignment has been extreme:

| Year | Pct. of top-ranked 300 players who lost PT |
|---|---|
| 2009 | 51% |
| 2010 | 44% |
| 2011 | 49% |
| 2012 | 45% |
| 2013 | 51% |
| 2014 | 53% |
| 2015 | 47% |
| 2016 | 47% |
| 2017 | 58% |
| 2018 | 60% |

When you consider that well over half of each season's very best players had fewer at-bats or innings pitched than we projected, it shows how tough it is to rank players each year.

The fallout? Consider: It is nearly a foregone conclusion that players like Christian Yelich and Javier Baez will be considerations for first round picks in 2019. This duo earned top 15 value for the first time last year after previously never finishing anywhere near the first round. The above data provide a strong argument against them returning first-round value in 2019. Yes, they are excellent players, in 2018 anyway. But the issue is not just their skills profiles. Since 2004:

- Two-thirds of players finishing in the Top 15 were not in the Top 15 the previous year. There is a great deal of turnover in the first round, year-to-year.
- Of those who were first-timers, only 14% repeated in the first round the following year.
- Established superstars who finished in the Top 15 were no guarantee to repeat.

As such, the odds are against Yelich or Baez repeating in the first round. In past years, sudden stars like Jonathan Villar, Carlos Gonzalez, Curtis Granderson and Dustin Pedroia have failed to repeat. Even 2017's top two players—Charlie Blackmon and Jose Altuve—finished 2018 ranked 23rd and 39th, respectively. These are not bad finishes, mind you, and a high-priced player returning 60-75 percent of his draft investment is not a total bust. The issue is context. As talented as these players were, it's not just about skill; it's also about skill relative to the rest of a volatile player pool.

### Importance of the early rounds *(Bill Macey)*

It's long been said that you can't win your league in the first round, but you can lose it there. An analysis of data from actual drafts reveals that this holds true—those who spend an early round pick on a player that severely under-performs expectations rarely win their league and seldom even finish in the top 3.

At the same time, drafting a player in the first round that actually returns first-round value is no guarantee of success. In fact, those that draft some of the best values still only win their league about a quarter of the time and finish in the top 3 less than half the time. Research also shows that drafting pitchers in the first round is a risky proposition. Even if the pitchers deliver first-round value, the opportunity cost of passing up on an elite batter makes you less likely to win your league.

### How a strong draft contributes to a winning season *(Todd Zola)*

The standings correlation based on draft-to-final results ranges from 0.42 to 0.94, with the mean around 0.73. The top hitting counting stat drafted is home runs; the fewest is stolen bases. The top pitching counting stat drafted is saves; the fewest is wins. More hitting is acquired at the draft or auction than pitching. The in-season influx of stats is greatest in Mixed Leagues, suggesting that owners should practice patience with in-season free agents in AL/NL formats while being cautiously aggressive in Mixed formats.

Top teams almost always improve ratio categories from their drafted rosters, despite available free agents sporting poorer aggregate ratios. This is most apropos if favoring improving pitching staff as the year progresses, but it's easier said than done.

Being top-three in saves is far more important in Mixed leagues than in AL/NL. Most Mixed champions draft the majority of saves while AL/NL winners often acquire saves in season.

### What is the best seed to draft from?

Most drafters like mid-round so they never have to wait too long for their next player. Some like the swing pick, suggesting that getting two players at 15 and 16 is better than a 1 and a 30. Many drafters assume that the swing pick means you'd be getting something like two $30 players instead of a $40 and $20.

Equivalent auction dollar values reveal the following facts about the first two snake draft rounds:

In an AL/NL-only league, the top seed would get a $44 player (at #1) and a $24 player (at #24) for a total of $68; the 12th seed would get two $29s (at #12 and #13) for $58.

In a mixed league, the top seed would get a $47 and a $24 ($71); the 15th seed would get two $28s ($56).

Since the talent level flattens out after the 2nd round, low seeds never get a chance to catch up:

| Dollar value difference between first player selected and last player selected | | |
|---|---|---|
| Round | 12-team | 15-team |
| 1 | $15 | $19 |
| 2 | $7 | $8 |
| 3 | $5 | $4 |
| 4 | $3 | $3 |
| 5 | $2 | $2 |
| 6 | $2 | $1 |
| 7-17 | $1 | $1 |
| 18-23 | $0 | $0 |

The total value each seed accumulates at the end of the draft is hardly equitable:

| Seed | Mixed | AL/NL-only |
|---|---|---|
| 1 | $266 | $273 |
| 2 | $264 | $269 |
| 3 | $263 | $261 |
| 4 | $262 | $262 |
| 5 | $259 | $260 |
| 6 | $261 | $260 |
| 7 | $260 | $260 |
| 8 | $261 | $260 |
| 9 | $261 | $258 |
| 10 | $257 | $260 |
| 11 | $257 | $257 |
| 12 | $258 | $257 |
| 13 | $254 | |
| 14 | $255 | |
| 15 | $256 | |

The counter-argument to this focuses on whether we can reasonably expect "accurate projections" at the top of the draft. Given the snake draft first round history, a case could be made that any seed might potentially do well. In fact, you might even consider the best draft position to be at the 15-16 wheel, which would essentially provide you with two picks from among the top 16 players.

### Using ADPs to determine when to select players *(Bill Macey)*

Although average draft position (ADP) data provides a good idea of where in the draft each player is selected, it can be misleading when trying to determine how early to target a player. This chart summarizes the percentage of players drafted within 15 picks of his ADP as well as the average standard deviation by grouping of players.

| ADP Rank | % within 15 picks | Standard Deviation |
|---|---|---|
| 1-25 | 100% | 2.5 |
| 26-50 | 97% | 6.1 |
| 51-100 | 87% | 9.6 |
| 100-150 | 72% | 14.0 |
| 150-200 | 61% | 17.4 |
| 200-250 | 53% | 20.9 |

As the draft progresses, the picks for each player become more widely dispersed and less clustered around the average. Most top 100 players will go within one round of their ADP-converted round. However, as you reach the mid-to-late rounds, there is much more uncertainty as to when a player will be selected. Pitchers have slightly smaller standard deviations than do batters (i.e. they tend to be drafted in a narrower range). This suggests that drafters may be more likely to reach for a batter than for a pitcher.

Using the ADP and corresponding standard deviation, we can to estimate the likelihood that a given player will be available at a certain draft pick. We estimate the predicted standard deviation for each player as follows:

$$Stdev = -0.42 + 0.42*(ADP - Earliest\ Pick)$$

*(That the figure 0.42 appears twice is pure coincidence; the numbers are not equal past two decimal points.)*

If we assume that the picks are normally distributed, we can use a player's ADP and estimated standard deviation to estimate the likelihood that the player is available with a certain pick (MS Excel formula):

$$=1-normdist(x,ADP,Standard\ Deviation,True)$$

*where «x» represents the pick number to be evaluated.*

We can use this information to prepare for a snake draft by determining how early we may need to reach in order to roster a player. Suppose you had the 8th pick in a 15-team league draft and your target was a player with an ADP of 128.9 and an earliest selection at pick 94. This would yield an estimated standard deviation of 14.2. You could have then entered these values into the formula above to estimate the likelihood that this player was still available at each of the following picks:

| Pick | Likelihood Available |
|---|---|
| 83 | 100% |
| 98 | 99% |
| 113 | 87% |
| 128 | 53% |
| 143 | 16% |
| 158 | 2% |

### ADPs and scarcity *(Bill Macey)*

Most players are selected within a round or two of their ADP with tight clustering around the average. But every draft is unique and every pick in the draft seemingly affects the ordering of subsequent picks. In fact, deviations from "expected" sequences can sometimes start a chain reaction at that position. This is most often seen in runs at scarce positions such as the closer; once the first one goes, the next seems sure to closely follow.

Research also suggests that within each position, there is a correlation within tiers of players. The sooner players within a generally accepted tier are selected, the sooner other players within the same tier will be taken. However, once that tier is exhausted, draft order reverts to normal.

How can we use this information? If you notice a reach pick, you can expect that other drafters may follow suit. If your draft plan is to get a similar player within that tier, you'll need to adjust your picks accordingly.

### Mapping ADPs to auction value *(Bill Macey)*

Reliable average auction values (AAV) are often tougher to come by than ADP data for snake drafts. However, we can estimate predicted auction prices as a function of ADP, arriving at the following equation:

**$y = -9.8\ln(x) + 57.8$**
*where ln(x) is the natural log function, x represents the actual ADP, and y represents the predicted AAV.*

This equation does an excellent job estimating auction prices (r2=0.93), though deviations are unavoidable. The asymptotic nature of the logarithmic function, however, causes the model to predict overly high prices for the top players. So be aware of that, and adjust.

### The value of mock drafts *(Todd Zola)*

Most assume the purpose of a mock draft is to get to know the market value of the player pool. But even more important, mock drafting is general preparation for the environment and process, thereby allowing the drafter to completely focus on the draft when it counts. Mock drafting is more about fine-tuning your strategy than player value. Here are some tips to maximize your mock drafting experience.

1. Make sure you can seamlessly use an on-line drafting room, draft software or your own lists to track your draft or auction. The less time you spend looking, adding and adjusting names, the more time you can spend on thinking about what player is best for your team. This also gives you the opportunity to make sure your draft lists are complete, and assures all the players are listed at the correct position(s).

2. Alter the draft slots from which you mock. The flow of each mock will be different, but if you do a few mocks with an early initial pick, a few in the middle and a few with a late first pick, you may learn you prefer one of the spots more than the others. If you're in a league where you can choose your draft spot, this helps you decide where to select. Once you know your spot, a few mocks from that spot will help you decide how to deal with positional runs.

3. Use non-typical strategies and consider players you rarely target. We all have our favorite players. Intentionally passing on those players not only gives you an idea when others may draft them but it also forces you to research players you normally don't consider. The more players you have researched, the more prepared you'll be for any series of events that occurs during your real draft.

### Draft preparation with a full-season mindset *(Matt Dodge)*

Each of the dimensions of your league setup—player pool, reserve list depth; type and frequency of transactions, scoring categories, etc.—should impact your draft day plan. But it may also be helpful to look at them in combination.

**Sources of additional stats after draft day**

| | League Player Pool | |
|---|---|---|
| Reserve List | Mixed 15 team | AL- or NL-only 12 team |
| Short | free agents | trades, free agents |
| Long | free agents, trades | trades |

Review the prior season's transactions for your league and analyze the successful teams' category contributions from trade acquisitions and free agent pickups. Trades are often necessary to add specific stats in AL/NL-only leagues as the player pool penetration is generally much deeper, and the size of a reserve roster further reduces the help possible from the free agent pool.

**Draft strategies related to in-season player acquisition**

| | Trade Activity | |
|---|---|---|
| FA Pool | Low | High |
| Shallow | solid foundation (STR) | tradable commodoties surplus counting stats |
| Deep | gamble on upside (S&S) | ultimate flexibility |

Trading activity is a function of multiple factors. Keeper leagues provide opportunities for owners to contend this year or play for next year. However, those increased opportunities are often controlled by rules to prevent "dump trading." Stratification of the standings in redraft leagues can cause lower ranked owners to lose interest, reducing the number of effective trading partners as the season goes on.

When deep rosters create a shallow free agent pool in a league with little trading, draft day success becomes paramount. In this case, a Spread the Risk strategy designed to accumulate at bats, innings, and saves is recommended. If the free agent pool is deep, the drafter can take more risks with a Stars and Scrubs approach, acquiring "lottery ticket" players with upside, knowing that replacements are readily available if the upside plays don't hit.

In leagues where trading is prevalent, a shallow free agent pool means you should acquire players on draft day with the intent of trading them. This could mean a traditional strategy of acquiring a category surplus (frequently saves and/or steals), and then trading them in-season to shore up other categories. In a keeper league, this includes grabbing a few bargains (to interest those who are rebuilding) or grabbing top performers to flip in trade (if you are already on "the two year plan").

**Draft Day Considerations for In-season Roster Management**

| Reserve List Txn Freq | 4 x 4 League Format | 5 x 5 League Format |
|---|---|---|
| Daily | careful SP management batting platoons positional flexibility | RP (K, ERA, WHIP) batting platoons positional flexibility |
| Weekly | SP (2 start weeks) cover risky starters | SP (2 start weeks) cover risky starters |

Owners must be careful with pitching, due to the negative impact potential of ERA and WHIP. Blindly streaming pitchers on a daily basis can be counter-productive, particularly in 4x4 leagues. In 5x5, the Strikeouts category can make a foundation of high Dom relievers a useful source of mitigation for the invariable starting pitching disappointments.

The degree that these recommendations can be implemented is also dependent on the depth of the reserve list. Those with more reserves can do more than those with fewer, obviously, but the key is deciding up front how you plan to use your reserves, and then tailoring your draft strategy toward that usage.

### Draft-day cheat sheet *(Patrick Davitt)*

1. Know what players are available, right to the bottom of the pool.
2. Know what every player is worth in your league format.
3. Know why you think each player is worth what you think he's worth.
4. Identify players you believe you value differently from the other owners.
5. Know each player's risks.
6. Know your opponents' patterns.
7. For sure, know the league rules and its history, and what it takes to win.

## Auction Value Analysis

### Auction values (R$) in perspective

R$ is the dollar value placed on a player's statistical performance in a Rotisserie league, and designed to measure the impact that player has on the standings.

There are several methods to calculate a player's value from his projected (or actual) statistics.

One method is Standings Gain Points, described in the book, *How to Value Players for Rotisserie Baseball*, by Art McGee. SGP converts a player's statistics in each Rotisserie category into the number of points those stats will allow you to gain in the standings. These are then converted back into dollars.

Another popular method is the Percentage Valuation Method. In PVM, a least valuable, or replacement performance level is set for each category (in a given league size) and then values are calculated representing the incremental improvement from that base. A player is then awarded value in direct proportion to the level he contributes to each category.

As much as these methods serve to attach a firm number to projected performance, the winning bid for any player is still highly variable depending upon many factors:

- the salary cap limit
- the number of teams in the league
- each team's roster size
- the impact of any protected players
- each team's positional demands at the time of bidding
- the statistical category demands at the time of bidding
- external factors, e.g. media inflation or deflation of value

In other words, a $30 player is only a $30 player if someone in your draft pays $30 for him.

### Roster slot valuation *(John Burnson)*

When you draft a player, what have you bought?

*"You have bought the stats generated by this player."*

No. You have bought the stats generated by his slot. Initially, the drafted player fills the slot, but he need not fill the slot for the season, and he need not contribute from Day One. If you trade the player during the season, then your bid on Draft Day paid for the stats of the original player plus the stats of the new player. If the player misses time due to injury or demotion, then you bought the stats of whoever fills the time while the drafted player is missing. At season's end, there will be more players providing positive value than there are roster slots.

Before the season, the number of players projected for positive value has to equal the total number of roster slots. However, the projected productivity should be adjusted by the potential to capture extra value in the slot. This is especially important for injury-rehab cases and late-season call-ups. For example, if we think that a player will miss half the season, then we would augment his projected stats with a half-year of stats from a replacement-level player at his position. Only then would we calculate prices. Essentially, we want to apportion $260 per team among the slots, not the players.

### Average player value by draft round

| Rd | AL/NL | Mxd |
|----|-------|-----|
| 1 | $34 | $34 |
| 2 | $26 | $26 |
| 3 | $23 | $23 |
| 4 | $20 | $20 |
| 5 | $18 | $18 |
| 6 | $17 | $16 |
| 7 | $16 | $15 |
| 8 | $15 | $13 |
| 9 | $13 | $12 |
| 10 | $12 | $11 |
| 11 | $11 | $10 |
| 12 | $10 | $9 |
| 13 | $9 | $8 |
| 14 | $8 | $8 |
| 15 | $7 | $7 |
| 16 | $6 | $6 |
| 17 | $5 | $5 |
| 18 | $4 | $4 |
| 19 | $3 | $3 |
| 20 | $2 | $2 |
| 21 | $1 | $2 |
| 22 | $1 | $1 |
| 23 | $1 | $1 |

Benchmarks for auction players:

- All $30 players will go in the first round.
- All $20-plus players will go in the first four rounds.
- Double-digit value ends pretty much after Round 11.
- The $1 end game starts at about Round 21.

### Dollar values: expected projective accuracy

There is a 65% chance that a player projected for a certain dollar value will finish the season with a value within plus-or-minus $5 of that projection. Therefore, if you value a player at $25, you only have about a 2-in-3 shot of him finishing between $20 and $30.

If you want to raise your odds to 80%, the range becomes +/- $9, so your $25 player has to finish somewhere between $16 and $34.

### Dollar values by lineup position *(Michael Roy)*
How much value is derived from batting order position?

| Pos | PA | R | RBI | R$ |
|-----|-----|-----|-----|--------|
| #1 | 747 | 107 | 72 | $18.75 |
| #2 | 728 | 102 | 84 | $19.00 |
| #3 | 715 | 95 | 100 | $19.45 |
| #4 | 698 | 93 | 104 | $19.36 |
| #5 | 682 | 86 | 94 | $18.18 |
| #6 | 665 | 85 | 82 | $17.19 |
| #7 | 645 | 81 | 80 | $16.60 |
| #8 | 623 | 78 | 80 | $16.19 |
| #9 | 600 | 78 | 73 | $15.50 |

So, a batter moving from the bottom of the order to the clean-up spot, with no change in performance, would gain nearly $4 in value from runs and RBIs alone.

### How likely is it that a $30 player will repeat? *(Matt Cederholm)*
From 2003-2008, there were 205 players who earned $30 or more (using single-league 5x5 values). Only 70 of them (34%) earned $30 or more in the next season.

In fact, the odds of repeating a $30 season aren't good. As seen below, the best odds during that period were 42%. And as we would expect, pitchers fare far worse than hitters.

| | Total>$30 | # Repeat | % Repeat |
|-----|-----|-----|-----|
| Hitters | 167 | 64 | 38% |
| Pitchers | 38 | 6 | 16% |
| Total | 205 | 70 | 34% |
| *High-Reliability\** | | | |
| Hitters | 42 | 16 | 38% |
| Pitchers | 7 | 0 | 0% |
| Total | 49 | 16 | 33% |
| *100+ BPV* | | | |
| Hitters | 60 | 25 | 42% |
| Pitchers | 31 | 6 | 19% |
| Total | 91 | 31 | 19% |
| *High-Reliability and 100+ BPV\** | | | |
| Hitters | 12 | 5 | 42% |
| Pitchers | 6 | 0 | 0% |
| Total | 18 | 5 | 28% |

*\*Reliability figures are from 2006-2008*

For players with multiple seasons of $30 or more, the numbers get better. Players with consecutive $30 seasons, 2003-2008:

| | Total>$30 | # Repeat | % Repeat |
|-----|-----|-----|-----|
| Two Years | 62 | 29 | 55% |
| Three+ Years | 29 | 19 | 66% |

Still, a player with two consecutive seasons at $30 in value is barely a 50/50 proposition. And three consecutive seasons is only a 2/3 shot. Small sample sizes aside, this does illustrate the nature of the beast. Even the most consistent, reliable players fail 1/3 of the time. Of course, this is true whether they are kept or drafted anew, so this alone shouldn't prevent you from keeping a player.

### Predicting player value from year 1 performance *(Patrick Davitt)*
Year-1 (Y1, first season >=100AB) batter results predict some—but not all—subsequent-year performance. About half of all Y1players have positive value. Players with higher Y1 value were likelier to get PT in subsequent seasons. Players with –$6 to –$10 in Y1 got more chances than players +$5 to –$5 and performed better. Batters with Y1 value of $16 or more are excellent bets to at least provide positive value in subsequent seasons, and those above $21 in Y1 value play in all subsequent seasons and return an average of $26. But even a $21 batter is only a 50-50 bet to do better in Y2.

### How well do elite pitchers retain their value? *(Michael Weddell)*
An elite pitcher (one who earns at least $24 in a season) on average keeps 80% of his R$ value from year 1 to year 2. This compares to the baseline case of only 52%.

Historically, 36% of elite pitchers improve, returning a greater R$ in the second year than they did the first year. That is an impressive performance considering they already were at an elite level. 17% collapse, returning less than a third of their R$ in the second year. The remaining 47% experience a middling outcome, keeping more than a third but less than all of their R$ from one year to the next.

### Valuing closers
Given the high risk associated with the closer's role, it is difficult to determine a fair draft value. Typically, those who have successfully held the role for several seasons will earn the highest draft price, but valuing less stable commodities is troublesome.

A rough rule of thumb is to start by paying $10 for the role alone. Any pitcher tagged the closer on draft day should merit at least $10. Those without a firm appointment may start at less than $10. Then add anywhere from $0 to $15 for support skills.

In this way, the top level talents will draw upwards of $20-$25. Those with moderate skill will draw $15-$20, and those with more questionable skill in the $10-$15 range.

### Profiling the end game
What types of players are typically the most profitable in the end-game? First, our overall track record on $1 picks:

| Avg Return | %Profitable | Avg Prof | Avg. Loss |
|-----|-----|-----|-----|
| $1.89 | 51% | $10.37 | ($7.17) |

On aggregate, the hundreds of players drafted in the end-game earned $1.89 on our $1 investments. While they were profitable overall, only 51% of them actually turned a profit. Those that did cleared more than $10 on average. Those that didn't—the other 49%—lost about $7 apiece.

| Pos | Pct.of tot | Avg Val | %Profit | Avg Prof | Avg Loss |
|-----|-----|-----|-----|-----|-----|
| CA | 12% | ($1.68) | 41% | $7.11 | ($7.77) |
| CO | 9% | $6.12 | 71% | $10.97 | ($3.80) |
| MI | 9% | $3.59 | 53% | $10.33 | ($4.84) |
| OF | 22% | $2.61 | 46% | $12.06 | ($5.90) |
| SP | 29% | $1.96 | 52% | $8.19 | ($7.06) |
| RP | 19% | $0.35 | 50% | $11.33 | ($10.10) |

These results bear out the danger of leaving catchers to the end; only catchers returned negative value. Corner infielder returns say leaving a 1B or 3B open until late.

| Age | Pct.of tot | Avg Val | %Profit | Avg Prof | Avg Loss |
|---|---|---|---|---|---|
| < 25 | 15% | ($0.88) | 33% | $8.25 | ($8.71) |
| 25-29 | 48% | $2.59 | 56% | $11.10 | ($8.38) |
| 30-35 | 28% | $2.06 | 44% | $10.39 | ($5.04) |
| 35+ | 9% | $2.15 | 41% | $8.86 | ($5.67) |

The practice of speculating on younger players—mostly rookies—in the end game was a washout. Part of the reason was that those that even made it to the end game were often the long-term or fringe type. Better prospects were typically drafted earlier.

| | Pct.of tot | Avg Val | %Profit | Avg Prof | Avg Loss |
|---|---|---|---|---|---|
| Injury rehabs | 20% | $3.63 | 36% | $15.07 | ($5.65) |

One in five end-gamers were players coming back from injury. While only 36% of them were profitable, the healthy ones returned a healthy profit. The group's losses were small, likely because they weren't healthy enough to play.

### Realistic expectations of $1 end-gamers *(Patrick Davitt)*

Many fantasy articles insist leagues are won or lost with $1 batters, because "that's where the profits are." But are they?

A 2011 analysis showed that when considering $1 players in deep leagues, managing $1 end-gamers should be more about minimizing losses than fishing for profit. In the cohort of batters projected $0 to -$5, 82% returned losses, based on a $1 bid. Two-thirds of the projected $1 cohort returned losses. In addition, when considering $1 players, speculate on speed.

## Advanced Draft Strategies

### Stars & Scrubs v. Spread the Risk

*Stars & Scrubs (S&S):* A Rotisserie auction strategy in which a roster is anchored by a core of high priced stars and the remaining positions filled with low-cost players.

*Spread the Risk (STR):* An auction strategy in which available dollars are spread evenly among all roster slots.

Both approaches have benefits and risks. An experiment was conducted in 2004 whereby a league was stocked with four teams assembled as S&S, four as STR and four as a control group. Rosters were then frozen for the season.

**The Stars & Scrubs teams won all three ratio categories.** Those deep investments ensured stability in the categories that are typically most difficult to manage. On the batting side, however, S&S teams amassed the least amount of playing time, which in turn led to bottom-rung finishes in HRs, RBIs and Runs.

One of the arguments for the S&S approach is that it is easier to replace end-game losers (which, in turn, may help resolve the playing time issues). Not only is this true, but the results of this experiment show that replacing those bottom players is critical to success.

**The Spread the Risk teams stockpiled playing time,** which led to strong finishes in many counting stats, including clear victories in RBIs, wins and strikeouts. This is a key tenet in drafting philosophy; we often say that the team that compiles the most ABs will be among the top teams in RBI and Runs.

The danger is on the pitching side. More innings did yield more wins and Ks, but also destroyed ERA/WHIP.

So, what approach makes the most sense? **The optimal strategy might be to STR on offense and go S&S with your pitching staff.**

STR buys more ABs, so you immediately position yourself well in four of the five batting categories. On pitching, it might be more advisable to roster a few core arms, though that immediately elevates your risk exposure. Admittedly, it's a balancing act, which is why we need to pay more attention to risk analysis.

### The LIMA Plan

The LIMA Plan is a strategy for Rotisserie leagues (though the underlying concept can be used in other formats) that allows you to target high skills pitchers at very low cost, thereby freeing up dollars for offense. LIMA is an acronym for Low Investment Mound Aces, and also pays tribute to Jose Lima, a $1 pitcher in 1998 who exemplified the power of the strategy. In a $260 league:

1. Budget a maximum of $60 for your pitching staff.
2. Allot no more than $30 of that budget for acquiring saves. In 5x5 leagues, it is reasonable to forego saves at the draft (and acquire them during the season) and re-allocate this $30 to starters ($20) and offense ($10).
3. Ignore ERA. Draft only pitchers with:
   - Command ratio (K/BB) of 2.5 or better.
   - Strikeout rate of 7.0 or better.
   - Expected home run rate of 1.0 or less.
4. Draft as few innings as your league rules will allow. This is intended to manage risk. For some game formats, this should be a secondary consideration.
5. Maximize your batting slots. Target batters with:
   - Contact rate of at least 80%
   - Walk rate of at least 10%
   - PX or Spd level of at least 100

Spend no more than $29 for any player and try to keep the $1 picks to a minimum.

The goal is to ace the batting categories and carefully pick your pitching staff so that it will finish in the upper third in ERA, WHIP and saves (and Ks in 5x5), and an upside of perhaps 9th in wins. In a competitive league, that should be enough to win, and definitely enough to finish in the money. Worst case, you should have an excess of offense available that you can deal for pitching.

The strategy works because it better allocates resources. Fantasy leaguers who spend a lot for pitching are not only paying for expected performance, they are also paying for better defined roles—#1 and #2 rotation starters, ace closers, etc.—which are expected to translate into more IP, wins and saves. But roles are highly variable. A pitcher's role will usually come down to his skill and performance; if he doesn't perform, he'll lose the role.

*The LIMA Plan says, let's invest in skill and let the roles fall where they may.* In the long run, better skills should translate into more innings, wins and saves. And as it turns out, pitching skill costs less than pitching roles do.

In *snake draft leagues,* you may be able to delay drafting starting pitchers until Round 10. In *shallow mixed leagues,* the LIMA Plan may not be necessary; just focus on the peripheral metrics. In *simulation leagues,* build your staff around those metrics.

### Variations on the LIMA Plan

*LIMA Extrema:* Limit your total pitching budget to only $30, or less. This can be particularly effective in shallow leagues where

LIMA-caliber starting pitcher free agents are plentiful during the season.

*SANTANA Plan:* Instead of spending $30 on saves, you spend it on a starting pitcher anchor. In 5x5 leagues where you can reasonably punt saves at the draft table, allocating those dollars to a high-end LIMA-caliber starting pitcher can work well as long as you pick the right anchor.

## Total Control Drafting (TCD)

On Draft Day, we make every effort to control as many elements as possible. In reality, the players that end up on our teams are largely controlled by the other owners. Their bidding affects your ability to roster the players you want. In a snake draft, the other owners control your roster even more. We are really only able to get the players we want within the limitations set by others.

However, an optimal roster can be constructed from a fanalytic assessment of skill and risk combined with more assertive draft day demeanor.

### Why this makes sense

*1. Our obsession with projected player values is holding us back.* If a player on your draft list is valued at $20 and you agonize when the bidding hits $23, odds are about two chances in three that he could really earn anywhere from $15 to $25. What this means is, in some cases, and within reason, you should just pay what it takes to get the players you want.

*2. There is no such thing as a bargain.* Most of us *don't* just pay what it takes because we are always on the lookout for players who go under value. But we really don't know which players will cost less than they will earn because prices are still driven by the draft table. The concept of "bargain" assumes that we even know what a player's true value is.

*3. "Control" is there for the taking.* Most owners are so focused on their own team that they really don't pay much attention to what you're doing. There are some exceptions, and bidding wars do happen, but in general, other owners will not provide that much resistance.

### How it's done

*1. Create your optimal draft pool.*

*2. Get those players.*

Start by identifying which players will be draftable based on the LIMA or Mayberry criteria. Then, at the draft, focus solely on your roster. When it's your bid opener, toss a player you need at about 50%-75% of your projected value. Bid aggressively and just pay what you need to pay. Of course, don't spend $40 for a player with $25 market value, but it's okay to exceed your projected value within reason.

From a tactical perspective, mix up the caliber of openers. Drop out early on some bids to prevent other owners from catching on to you.

In the end, it's okay to pay a slight premium to make sure you get the players with the highest potential to provide a good return on your investment. It's no different than the premium you might pay for a player with position flexibility or to get the last valuable shortstop. With TCD, you're just spending those extra dollars up front to ensure you are rostering your targets. As a side benefit, TCD almost assures that you don't leave money on the table.

## Mayberry Method

The foundation of the Mayberry Method (MM) is the assertion that we really can't project player performance with the level of precision that advanced metrics and modeling systems would like us to believe.

MM is named after the fictional TV village where life was simpler. MM evaluates skill by embracing the imprecision of the forecasting process and projecting performance in broad strokes rather than with hard statistics.

MM reduces every player to a 7-character code. The format of the code is 5555 AAA, where the first four characters describe elements of a player's skill on a scale of 0 to 5. These skills are indexed to the league average so that players are evaluated within the context of the level of offense or pitching in a given year.

The three alpha characters are our reliability grades (Health, Experience and Consistency) on the standard A-to-F scale. The skills numerics are forward-looking; the alpha characters grade reliability based on past history.

### Batting

The first character in the MM code measures a batter's power skills. It is assigned using the following table:

| Power Index | MM |
| --- | --- |
| 0 - 49 | 0 |
| 50 - 79 | 1 |
| 80 - 99 | 2 |
| 100 - 119 | 3 |
| 120 - 159 | 4 |
| 160+ | 5 |

The second character measures a batter's speed skills. RSpd takes our Statistically Scouted Speed metric (Spd) and adds the elements of opportunity and success rate, to construct the formula of $RSpd = Spd \times (SBO + SB\%)$.

| RSpd | MM |
| --- | --- |
| 0 - 39 | 0 |
| 40 - 59 | 1 |
| 60 - 79 | 2 |
| 80 - 99 | 3 |
| 100 - 119 | 4 |
| 120+ | 5 |

The third character measures expected batting average.

| xBA Index | MM |
| --- | --- |
| 0-87 | 0 |
| 88-92 | 1 |
| 93-97 | 2 |
| 98-102 | 3 |
| 103-107 | 4 |
| 108+ | 5 |

The fourth character measures playing time.

| Role | PA | MM |
| --- | --- | --- |
| Potential full-timers | 450+ | 5 |
| Mid-timers | 250-449 | 3 |
| Fringe/bench | 100-249 | 1 |
| Non-factors | 0-99 | 0 |

## Pitching

The first character in the pitching MM code measures xERA, which captures a pitcher's overall ability and is a proxy for ERA, and even WHIP.

| xERA Index | MM |
|---|---|
| 0-80 | 0 |
| 81-90 | 1 |
| 91-100 | 2 |
| 101-110 | 3 |
| 111-120 | 4 |
| 121+ | 5 |

The second character measures strikeout ability.

| K/9 Index | MM |
|---|---|
| 0-76 | 0 |
| 77-88 | 1 |
| 89-100 | 2 |
| 101-112 | 3 |
| 113-124 | 4 |
| 125+ | 5 |

The third character measures saves potential.

| Description | Saves est. | MM |
|---|---|---|
| No hope for saves; starting pitchers | 0 | 0 |
| Speculative closer | 1-9 | 1 |
| Closer in a pen with alternatives | 10-24 | 2 |
| Frontline closer with firm bullpen role | 25+ | 3 |

The fourth character measures **playing time**.

| Role | IP | MM |
|---|---|---|
| Potential #1-2 starters | 180+ | 5 |
| Potential #3-4 starters | 130-179 | 3 |
| #5 starters/swingmen | 70-129 | 1 |
| Relievers | 0-69 | 0 |

## Overall Mayberry Scores

The real value of Mayberry is to provide a skills profile on a player-by-player basis. I want to be able to see this…

| Player A | 4455 AAB |
|---|---|
| Player B | 5245 BBD |
| Player C | 5255 BAB |
| Player D | 5155 BAF |

…and make an objective, unbiased determination about these four players without being swayed by preconceived notions and baggage. But there is a calculation that provides a single, overall value for each player.

This is the calculation for the overall MM batting score:

### MM Score =

*(PX score + Spd score + xBA score + PA score)*
*x PA score*

An overall MM pitching score is calculated as:

### MM Score =

*((xERA score x 2) + K/9 score + Saves score + IP score)*
*x (IP score + Saves score)*

The highest score you can get for either is 100. That makes the result of the formula easy to assess.

BaseballHQ.com analyst Patrick Davitt did some great research about using Reliability Grades to adjust the Mayberry scores. His research showed that "higher-reliability players met their Mayberry targets more often than their lower-reliability counterparts, and players with all "D" or "F" reliability scores underperform Mayberry projections far more often. Those results can be reflected by multiplying a player's MM Score by each of three reliability bonuses or penalties:"

I've taken his work a minor step further and applied slightly different multipliers to each Reliability element.

| | Health | Experience | Consistency |
|---|---|---|---|
| A | x 1.10 | x 1.10 | x 1.10 |
| B | x 1.05 | x 1.05 | x 1.05 |
| C | x 1.00 | x 1.00 | x 1.00 |
| D | x 0.90 | x 0.95 | x 0.95 |
| F | x 0.80 | x 0.90 | x 0.90 |

So, let's perform the overall calculations for Player A above, using these Reliability adjustments.

### Player A: 4455 AAB
= (4+4+5+5) x 5
= 90 x 1.10 x 1.10 x 1.05
= **114.3**

## Portfolio3 Plan concepts

When it comes to profitability, all players are not created equal. Every player has a different role on your team by virtue of his skill set, dollar value/draft round, position and risk profile. When it comes to a strategy for how to approach a specific player, one size does not fit all.

*We need some players to return fair value more than others.* A $40/first round player going belly-up is going to hurt you far more than a $1/23rd round bust. End-gamers are easily replaceable.

*We rely on some players for profit more than others.* First-rounders do not provide the most profit potential; that comes from players further down the value rankings.

*We can afford to weather more risk with some players than with others.* Since high-priced early-rounders need to return at least fair value, we cannot afford to take on excessive risk. Our risk tolerance opens up with later-round/lower cost picks.

*Players have different risk profiles based solely on what roster spot they are going to fill.* Catchers are more injury prone. A closer's value is highly dependent on managerial decision. These types of players are high risk even if they have great skills. That needs to affect their draft price or draft round.

*For some players, the promise of providing a scarce skill, or productivity at a scarce position, may trump risk.* Not always, but sometimes. The determining factor is usually price.

Previously, we created a model that integrated these types of players into a roster planning tool, called the Portfolio3 Plan. However, over time, variables like baseball's changing statistical environment, the impact of the 10-day DL and the shifting MLB roster construction affected the utility of the model. The rigid player allocation framework of the tiers began to erode, and no fudging could retain the integrity of the model. So we have retired it. The Mayberry Method includes the relevant player evaluators that Portfolio3 used; you can rely on those to create your own roster plan that balances skill and risk.

### Consistency in Head-to-Head leagues *(Dylan Hedges)*

Few things are as valuable to H2H league success as filling your roster with players who can produce a solid baseline of stats, week in and week out. In traditional leagues, while consistency is not as important—all we care about are aggregate numbers—filling your team with consistent players can make roster management easier.

Consistent batters have good plate discipline, walk rates and on base percentages. These are foundation skills. Those who add power to the mix are obviously more valuable, however, the ability to hit home runs consistently is rare.

Consistent pitchers demonstrate similar skills in each outing; if they also produce similar results, they are even more valuable.

We can track consistency but predicting it is difficult. Many fantasy leaguers try to predict a batter's hot or cold streaks, or individual pitcher starts, but that is typically a fool's errand. The best we can do is find players who demonstrate seasonal consistency; in-season, we must manage players and consistency tactically.

### Building a consistent Head-to-Head team *(David Martin)*

Teams in head-to-head leagues need batters who are consistent. Focusing on certain metrics helps build consistency, which is the roster holy grail for H2H players. Our filters for such success are:

- Contact rate = minimum 80%
- xBA = minimum .280
- PX (or Spd) = minimum 120
- RC/G = minimum 5.00

### Ratio insulation in Head-to-Head leagues *(David Martin)*

On a week-to-week basis, inequities are inherent in the head-to-head game. One way to eliminate your competitor's advantage in the pure numbers game is to build your team's pitching foundation around the ratio categories.

One should normally insulate at the end of a draft, once your hitters are in place. To obtain several ratio insulators, target pitchers that have:

- Cmd greater than 3.0
- Dom greater than 7.5
- xERA less than 3.30

While adopting this strategy may compromise wins, research has shown that wins come at a cost to ERA and WHIP. Roster space permitting, adding two to four insulators to your team will improve your team's weekly ERA and WHIP.

### A Head-to-Head approach to the Mayberry Method *(David Martin)*

Though the Mayberry Method was designed for use in Rotisserie leagues, a skill set analysis about whether a player is head-to-head league material is built into each seven-digit Mayberry code. By "decoding" Mayberry and incorporating quality-consistency (QC) scores, one can assemble a team that has the characteristics of a successful H2H squad.

In reviewing the MM skills scores, we can correlate the power and contact skills as follows:

- PX > 4 or 5 = PX of 120 or higher
- xBA > 4 or 5 = xBA index of 103 or higher

Only full-time players will have an opportunity to produce the counting statistics required, so to create a top tier of players, we need to limit our search to those who earn a 5 for playing time. This top tier should be sorted by QC scores so that the more consistent players are ranked higher.

To create the second tier of players, lower the power index to 3, but keep all other skill requirements intact:

| PWR | SPD | BA | PT | HLTH |
|-----|-----|-----|-----|------|
| 3 | N/A | 4/5 | 5 | A/B |

The interplay between tiers is important; use Tier 2 in conjunction with Tier 1 and not simply after the top tier options are exhausted. For example, it might make sense to dip into Tier 2 if there is a player available with a higher QC score.

Additionally, while the H2H MM codes do not target players based on their speed skills, the second column of the MM codes contains this information. Though you are de-prioritizing the speed skill, you do not need to punt the steals category. You will typically find that the tiers nonetheless contain multiple players with a MM speed score of 3 or higher, so you can still be competitive in the steal category most weeks applying this approach.

### Consistency in points leagues *(Bill Macey)*

Previous research has demonstrated that week-to-week statistical consistency is important for Rotisserie-based head-to-head play. But one can use the same foundation in points-based games. A study showed that not only do players with better skills post more overall points in this format, but that the format caters to consistent performances on a week-to-week basis, even after accounting for differences in total points scored and playing-time.

Therefore, when drafting your batters in points-based head-to-head leagues, ct% and bb% make excellent tiebreakers if you are having trouble deciding between two players with similarly projected point totals. Likewise, when rostering pitchers, favor those who tend not to give up home runs.

## In-Season Analyses

### The efficacy of streaming *(John Burnson)*

In leagues that allow weekly or daily transactions, many owners flit from hot player to hot player. But published dollar values don't capture this traffic—they assume that players are owned from April to October. For many leagues, this may be unrealistic.

We decided to calculate these "investor returns." For each week, we identified the top players by one statistic—BA for hitters, ERA for pitchers—and took the top 100 hitters and top 50 pitchers. We then said that, at the end of the week, the #1 player was picked up (or already owned) by 100% of teams, the #2 player was picked up or owned by 99% of teams, and so on, down to the 100th player, who was on 1% of teams. (For pitchers, we stepped by 2%.) Last, we tracked each player's performance in the next week, when ownership matters.

We ran this process anew for every week of the season, tabulating each player's "investor returns" along the way. If a player was owned by 100% of teams, then we awarded him 100% of his performance. If the player was owned by half the teams, we gave him half his performance. If he was owned by no one (that is, he was not among the top players in the prior week), his performance

## Daily Fantasy Baseball

Daily Fantasy Sports (DFS) is an offshoot of traditional fantasy sports. Many of the same analytic methods that are integral to seasonal fantasy baseball are just as relevant for DFS.

### General Format

1. The overwhelming majority of DFS contests are pay-for-play where the winners are compensated a percentage of their entry fee, in accordance with the rules of that game.

2. DFS baseball contests are generally based on a single day's slate of games, or a subset of the day's games (i.e., all afternoon games or all evening games)

3. Most DFS formats are points-based salary cap games.

### Most Popular Contests

1. Cash Games: Three variants (50/50, Multipliers, and Head-to-Head) all pay out a flat prize to a portion of the entries.

2. GPP (Guaranteed prize pool) Tournaments: The overall winner earns the largest prize and prizes scale downward.

3. Survivor: A survivor contest is a multiple-slate format where a portion of the entries survives to play the following day.

4. Qualifiers/Satellites: Tournaments where the prize(s) consist of entry tickets to a larger tournament.

### DFS Analysis

1. Predicting single-day performance entails adjusting a baseline projection based on that day's match-up. This adjusted expectation is considered in context with a player's salary to determine his potential contributions relative to the other players.

2. Weighted on base average (wOBA) is a souped-up version of OBP, and is a favorite metric to help evaluate both hitters and pitchers. (For more useful DFS metrics, see next section)

3. Pitching: In DFS, innings and strikeouts are the two chief means of accruing points, so they need to be weighed heavily in pitching evaluation.

### Tips for Players New to DFS

1. Start slow and be prepared to lose: While cogent analysis can increase your chances of winning, the variance associated with a single day's worth of outcomes doesn't assure success. Short-term losing streaks are inevitable, so start with low cost cash games before embarking on tournament play.

2. Minimize the number of sites you play: The DFS space is dominated by two sites but there are other options. At the beginning, stick to one or two. Once you're comfortable, consider expanding to others.

3. Bankroll management: The recommended means to manage your bankroll is to risk no more than 10% on a given day. Within that portion, the suggested ratio is 80% cash games to 20% GPP tournament action.

4. General Strategies

   A. Cash Games: Conventional wisdom preaches to be conservative in cash games. Upper level starting pitchers make excellent cash game options. For hitters, it's best to spread your choices among several teams. In general, you're looking for players with a high floor rather than a high ceiling.

   B: GPP Tournaments: In tournaments (with a larger number of entrants), a common ploy is to select a lesser priced, though risky, pitcher with a favorable match-up. It's also very common to overload—or stack—several batters from the same team, hoping that squad scores a bunch of runs.

5. Miscellaneous Tips

   A. Pay extra attention to games threatened by weather, as well as players who are not a lock to be in the lineup.

   B. Avoid playing head-to-head against strangers until you're comfortable and have enjoyed some success.

   C. Stay disciplined. The worst thing you can do is eat up your bankroll quickly by entering into tournaments.

   D. Most importantly, have fun. Obviously, you want to win, but hopefully you're also in it for the challenge of mastering the unique skills intrinsic to DFS.

## Using BaseballHQ Tools in DFS

Here are some of the additional skill metrics to consider:

### Cash Game Metrics

bb%: This simple indicator may receive only a quick glance when building lineups, but it is imperative in providing insight on a batter's underlying approach and plate discipline. Walks also equal points in all DFS scoring structures.

ct%: Another byproduct of good plate discipline, reflecting the percentage of balls put in play. Players with strong contact rates tend to provide a higher floor, and less chance of a negative score from a free swinger with a high strikeout rate.

xBA: Measures a hitter's BA by multiplying his contact rate by the chance that a ball in play falls for a hit. Hitters whose BA is far below their xBA may be "due" for some hits.

### Tournament / GPP BPIs

PX / xPX: Home runs are the single greatest multi-point event. Using PX (power index) and xPX (expected power index) together can help identify underperformers who are due in the power category.

## Choosing Pitchers in DFS

The criteria for choosing a pitcher(s) may be more narrow than for full-season league, but the skills focus should remain.

### Major Considerations

• Overall skills. Look for the following minimums: 3.0 Ctl (bb/9), 9.0 Dom (k/9), 3.0 Cmd (k/bb), and max 1.0 HR/9.

• Home/Away. In 2018, MLB pitchers logged a 3.98 ERA, 8.6 Dom, 2.8 Cmd at home; 4.33 ERA, 8.4 Dom, 2.5 Cmd on the road.

• Is he pitching at Coors Field? (Even the best pitchers are a risky start there.)

### Moderate Considerations

• Recent performance. Examine Ks and BBs over last 4-5 starts.

• Strength of opponent. Refer to opposing team's OPS for the season, as well as more recent performance.

### Minor Considerations

• L/R issues. Does the pitcher/opponent have wide platoon splits?

• Park. Is the game at a hitter's/pitcher's/neutral park?

• Previous outings. Has he faced this team already this season? If so, how did he fare? (Skills; not just his ERA.)

You will hopefully be left with a tiered list of pitching options, ripe for comparing individual risk/reward level against their price point.

was ignored. A player's cumulative stats over the season was his investor return.

*The results...*

- 60% of pitchers had poorer investor returns, with an aggregate ERA 0.40 higher than their true ERA.
- 55% of batters had poorer investor returns, but with an aggregate batting average virtually identical to the true BA.

### Sitting stars and starting scrubs *(Ed DeCaria)*

In setting your pitching rotation, conventional wisdom suggests sticking with trusted stars despite difficult matchups. But does this hold up? And can you carefully start inferior pitchers against weaker opponents? Here are the ERAs posted by varying skilled pitchers facing a range of different strength offenses:

| | OPPOSING OFFENSE (RC/G) | | | | |
|---|---|---|---|---|---|
| Pitcher (ERA) | 5.25+ | 5.00 | 4.25 | 4.00 | <4.00 |
| 3.00- | 3.46 | 3.04 | 3.04 | 2.50 | 2.20 |
| 3.50 | 3.98 | 3.94 | 3.44 | 3.17 | 2.87 |
| 4.00 | 4.72 | 4.57 | 3.96 | 3.66 | 3.24 |
| 4.50 | 5.37 | 4.92 | 4.47 | 4.07 | 3.66 |
| 5.00+ | 6.02 | 5.41 | 5.15 | 4.94 | 4.42 |

Recommendations:

1. Never start below replacement-level pitchers.
2. Always start elite pitchers.
3. Other than that, never say never or always.

Playing matchups can pay off when the difference in opposing offense is severe.

### Two-start pitcher weeks *(Ed DeCaria)*

A two-start pitcher is a prized possession. But those starts can mean two DOMinant outings, two DISasters, or anything else in between, as shown by these results:

| PQS Pair | % Weeks | ERA | WHIP | Win/Wk | K/Wk |
|---|---|---|---|---|---|
| DOM-DOM | 20% | 2.53 | 1.02 | 1.1 | 12.0 |
| DOM-AVG | 28% | 3.60 | 1.25 | 0.8 | 9.2 |
| AVG-AVG | 14% | 4.44 | 1.45 | 0.7 | 6.8 |
| DOM-DIS | 15% | 5.24 | 1.48 | 0.6 | 7.9 |
| AVG-DIS | 17% | 6.58 | 1.74 | 0.5 | 5.7 |
| DIS-DIS | 6% | 8.85 | 2.07 | 0.3 | 5.0 |

Weeks that include even one DISaster start produce terrible results. Unfortunately, avoiding such disasters is much easier in hindsight. But what is the actual impact of this decision on the stat categories?

*ERA and WHIP:* When the difference between opponents is extreme, inferior pitchers can be a better percentage play. This is true both for 1-start pitchers and 2-start pitchers, and for choosing inferior one-start pitchers over superior two-start pitchers.

*Strikeouts per Week:* Unlike the two rate stats, there is a massive shift in the balance of power between one-start and two-start pitchers in the strikeout category. Even stars with easy one-start matchups can only barely keep pace with two-start replacement-level arms in strikeouts per week.

*Wins per week* are also dominated by the two-start pitchers. Even the very worst two-start pitchers will earn a half of a win on average, which is the same rate as the very best one-start pitchers.

The bottom line: If strikeouts and wins are the strategic priority, use as many two-start weeks as the rules allow, even if

it means using a replacement-level pitcher with two tough starts instead of a mid-level arm with a single easy start. But if ERA and/or WHIP management are the priority, two-start pitchers can be very powerful, as a single week might impact the standings by over 1.5 points in ERA/WHIP, positively or negatively.

### Six tips on category management *(Todd Zola)*

1. Disregard whether you are near the top or the bottom of a category; focus instead on the gaps directly above and below your squad.
2. Prorate the difference in stats between teams.
3. ERA tends to move towards WHIP.
4. As the season progresses, the number of AB/IF do not preclude a gain/loss in the ratio categories.
5. An opponent's point lost is your point gained.
6. *Most important!* Come crunch time, forget value, forget names, and forget reputation. It's all about stats and where you are situated within each category.

## *Other Diamonds*

### Cellar value

The dollar value at which a player cannot help but earn more than he costs. Always profit here.

### Crickets

The sound heard when someone's opening draft bid on a player is also the only bid.

### End-game wasteland

Home for players undraftable in the deepest of leagues, who stay in the free agent pool all year. It's the place where even crickets keep quiet when a name is called at the draft.

### FAAB Forewarnings

1. Spend early and often.
2. Emptying your budget for one prime league-crosser is a tactic that should be reserved for the desperate.
3. If you chase two rabbits, you will lose them both.

### Fantasy Economics 101

The market value for a player is based on the aura of past performance, not the promise of future potential. Your greatest advantage is to leverage the space between market value and real value.

### Fantasy Economics 102

The variance between market value and real value is far more important than the absolute accuracy of any individual player projection.

### Hope

A commodity that routinely goes for $5 over value at the draft table.

### Seasonal Assessment Standard

If you still have reason to be reading the boxscores during the last weekend of the season, then your year has to be considered a success.

### The Three Cardinal Rules for Winners

If you cherish this hobby, you will live by them or die by them...

1. Revel in your success; fame is fleeting.
2. Exercise excruciating humility.
3. 100% of winnings must be spent on significant others.

## Fly Ball Carry by Batter—Is it a Skill?

*by Arik Florimonte*

### Introduction

In previous years, we've introduced Deserved Home Runs (dHR), an estimate of the probability that a batted ball becomes a home run, calculated using Statcast data for Launch Angle (LA) and Exit Velocity (EV). We found that when park-adjusted, one year of dHR/FB data was as predictive as two years of HR/FB data. However, Statcast doesn't make public the data for spray angle of the ball nor the batted ball spin, so we lump all batted balls together without taking these other variables into account, and compare them to other batted balls with the same LA and EV.

In a May 2017 article on BaseballHQ.com, we estimated Carry: How much a fly ball travels compared to its projected distance based on LA and EV alone. In this article, we'll examine a batter's ability to impart Carry to their batted balls, and find that this skill is partially repeatable from year to year. We'll also examine whether prior Carry is a leading indicator for additional HR/FB.

### Methodology

Using Statcast batted ball data from 2015-2017, we include only balls traveling farther than 200 feet with an exit velocity greater than 60 mph, while removing any balls classified as ground balls. This leaves about 157,000 batted balls. We apply a least squares regression to fit the actual batted ball distance to a 2nd order polynomial combining LA, EV, EV*sin(LA), and EV*cos(LA). This batted ball distance model predicts the hit distance with an $R^2$ value of 0.85; i.e. 15% of the hit distance is attributable to something other than LA and EV. Carry is simply:

$$Carry = \frac{(Actual\ Batted\ Ball\ Distance)}{(Predicted\ Batted\ Ball\ Distance)}$$

To remove park and weather effects, we'll average the Carry for batted balls for a particular day in a particular park. Then we calculate the residual—how much more or less each baseball traveled than the average ball in that park on that day. We will credit the batter with the difference on that day, and then find the average Carry for each batter in each season.

### Carry by Batter

We calculate average Carry by batter within a year, using seasons with >50 fly balls that meet our criteria and weighting by number of batted balls. We find 17% correlation between average Carry and Undeserved HR (uHR) per fly ball. That is, batters with larger uHR/FB tended to have higher Carry, while those with lower uHR did so in part due to lower Carry.

(uHR = HR minus park-adjusted dHR. If uHR is positive, a batter was lucky; if negative, unlucky.)

### Year-to-Year Stickiness

If the Carry skill is consistent from year to year, it would tend to validate some of the home runs that we might have previously considered lucky, or "undeserved." Including only players with > 50 batted balls in both years, we find Carry is well-correlated, with Prior Year Carry explaining 47% of Current Year Carry. On average, a batter carries two-thirds of his prior year carry to the next year:

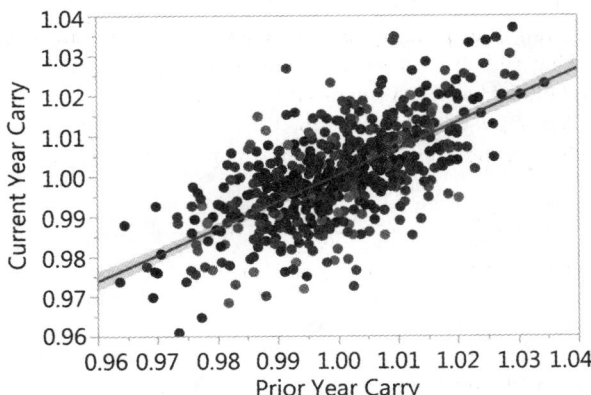

*(Shading indicates Weight, weighted by root mean square of fly ball count across both years)*

### Carry as a Leading Indicator

We divide the prior year's performance into quantiles, and look at the uHR/FB in the current year (normalized by league average HR):

| | | | Low* | Medium* | High* |
|---|---|---|---|---|---|
| **Home** | Unlucky | <25th percentile | -.023 | -.010 | +.012 |
| **Run** | Nominal | 25th-75th percentile | -.011 | +.007 | +.012 |
| **Luck** | Lucky | > 75th Percentile | +.007 | +.008 | +.010 |

*Low: <25th percentile; Medium: 25th-75th percentile; High: >75th percentile*

### Conclusions

- The ability to impart Carry to fly balls is a repeatable skill.
- On average, a batter will retain two-thirds of this fly ball Carry from year to year.
- Batters with unlucky HR totals in Year 0 tend to see an improvement in Year 1. Of those with High Carry in year 0, 88% will see improvement in uHR/FB, and the average gain is +0.059 (including non-gainers).
- Batters with High Carry in year 0 will on average add about 0.01 uHR/FB in year 1, regardless of uHR/FB in year 0.

We hope that as Statcast data accumulates, it will be possible to incorporate dHR (and uHR) with Carry into our models to further improve HR/FB projections.

## Sample-Size Studies for Pitchers and Batters

*by Arik Florimonte*

### Introduction

In baseball forecasting, it is widely understood that more data is better when trying to model future performance. Examining that assumption for both pitchers and batters, we determine when recent data becomes more significant than the historical data. We also find that occasionally, a smaller data set is actually more predictive than a larger one.

### Methodology

We will use logs from 2010-2017 only for pitcher seasons with ≥ 120 IP and pitcher months with ≥ 25 IP. We'll limit batter seasons to those with ≥ 350 PA, and batter months with ≥ 75 PA. Throughout this study, we'll use $R^2$ as a measure of correlation between data sets and consider a higher $R^2$ to indicate a more predictive relationship.

We will then create a linear model from past data to explain the next month's results, using data from the previous and current-year-to-date to find the point at which the current year-to-date results begin to weigh more than the previous year's results.

## PITCHERS

### Yearly versus Monthly

We compare correlations for several common pitching metrics and find the following:

$R^2$ values from year-year and month-month

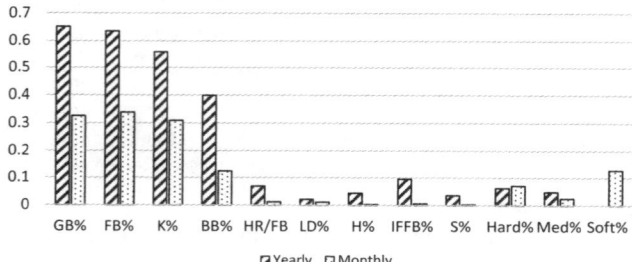

The most consistent year-to-year correlations are those we might expect: GB, FB%, K%, and BB%. And in each of those, the monthly correlations are also still pretty good despite having only 15-20% of the data sample. This suggests that there is some within-year correlation; if a year of data is just a bigger collection of monthly data, we'd expect the year-year correlation to be higher.

HR/FB, LD%, H%, IFFB%, and S% are all weakly correlated, both monthly and yearly. Longtime BaseballHQ.com subscribers will recall that these values for pitchers are generally considered non-predictive from year to year, and these low $R^2$ values bear that out.

The $R^2$ values for Hard, Medium, and Soft contact are also very low. Our truly surprising result is that for Hard% and Soft%, the month-to-month correlations are actually better than year-to-year correlations! What can we deduce from this?

- Pitchers do have some control over quality of contact.
- Inducing soft contact is not repeatable year to year—that's a zero $R^2$ for year-year for Soft%!
- The period over which a pitcher can continue to influence quality of contact (good or bad) is probably longer than 30 days but less than two years.

A 12% correlation in monthly soft contact rates is not earth-shattering, but it lends credence to the idea that some pitchers can succeed by suppressing quality contact. Do not expect any pitcher to repeat that the next year, though. Throw it away. Regress him to league average.

Furthermore, if a pitcher suppresses hard contact in one year, only a small portion of that carries over to the next year. This leads us to the final section. How should we weight the prior year and the current year data over the course of a season?

### Estimating the Coming Month

We created a simple linear model to evaluate the relative predictive value of last year's data and this year's data with respect to what happens in the coming month. The original article at BaseballHQ.com told this story with a ton of charts, but we'll summarize them here in a tidy table.

For each parameter, we are showing the coefficients for the linear model to predict each month's data. For example, for K% in May, the linear model is 59% Prior-Year_K%, 28% Year-to-Date_K% date results, and the remaining 13% a constant. The line below the coefficients shows the $R^2$ for that month's model – growing as the YTD data grows.

| | | Apr | May | Jun | Jul | Aug | Sep |
|---|---|---|---|---|---|---|---|
| **GB%** | PY | 0.74 | 0.74 | 0.51 | 0.44 | 0.36 | 0.44 |
| | YTD | 0.00 | 0.12 | 0.40 | 0.40 | 0.52 | 0.51 |
| | Noise/Regression | 0.26 | 0.14 | 0.09 | 0.16 | 0.12 | 0.05 |
| | $R^2$ | 0.40 | 0.43 | 0.47 | 0.42 | 0.48 | 0.49 |
| **FB%** | PY | 0.75 | 0.62 | 0.53 | 0.41 | 0.35 | 0.41 |
| | YTD | 0.00 | 0.28 | 0.36 | 0.38 | 0.51 | 0.56 |
| | Noise/Regression | 0.25 | 0.10 | 0.11 | 0.21 | 0.14 | 0.03 |
| | $R^2$ | 0.42 | 0.46 | 0.44 | 0.41 | 0.45 | 0.50 |
| **K%** | PY | 0.76 | 0.59 | 0.53 | 0.26 | 0.42 | 0.42 |
| | YTD | 0.00 | 0.28 | 0.41 | 0.59 | 0.53 | 0.54 |
| | Noise/Regression | 0.24 | 0.13 | 0.06 | 0.15 | 0.05 | 0.04 |
| | $R^2$ | 0.40 | 0.43 | 0.47 | 0.42 | 0.48 | 0.49 |
| **BB%** | PY | 0.70 | 0.54 | 0.33 | 0.35 | 0.33 | 0.38 |
| | YTD | 0.00 | 0.22 | 0.32 | 0.45 | 0.36 | 0.51 |
| | Noise/Regression | 0.30 | 0.24 | 0.35 | 0.20 | 0.31 | 0.11 |
| | $R^2$ | 0.23 | 0.26 | 0.22 | 0.24 | 0.23 | 0.26 |
| **Hard%** | PY | 0.44 | 0.16 | 0.08 | -0.10 | 0.10 | 0.02 |
| | YTD | 0.00 | 0.24 | 0.50 | 0.49 | 0.47 | 0.49 |
| | Noise/Regression | 0.56 | 0.60 | 0.42 | 0.61 | 0.43 | 0.49 |
| | $R^2$ | 0.07 | 0.08 | 0.17 | 0.14 | 0.15 | 0.14 |
| **Soft%** | PY | 0.12 | 0.07 | -0.02 | -0.05 | -0.06 | -0.17 |
| | YTD | 0.00 | 0.29 | 0.57 | 0.58 | 0.76 | 0.72 |
| | Noise/Regression | 0.88 | 0.65 | 0.45 | 0.47 | 0.30 | 0.45 |
| | $R^2$ | 0.01 | 0.09 | 0.23 | 0.20 | 0.31 | 0.29 |

## Conclusions—Pitchers

We found that the year-to-year correlations for soft- and hard-contact rates were extremely small, and that using only a month of current-year data is better than using a pitcher's previous season.

For the pitcher-influenced outcomes—K% and BB%, and GB% and FB%—we are better off waiting until June to rely on the year-to-date results than we are the previous season, but a combination of the two is even better.

Fanalytic owners can make use of this information as follows:

- Don't fully buy into a change in GB/FB mix or K/BB until June (although you may still want to speculate earlier if you can stash a player on reserve).
- Don't expect last year's hard and soft contact tendencies to continue into 2019.
- Pay some attention to the current year's Soft% and Hard%, but future outcomes are still largely noise and regression.

## BATTERS

### Yearly versus Monthly

We again start by comparing the year-to-year and month-to-month correlations:

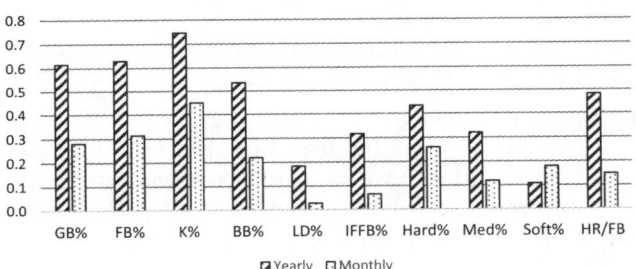

R² values from year-year and month-month

The yearly correlations are generally only twice as good as the monthly ones, despite containing five- to six-times as large a sample.

The metrics that we already regard as batter skills–namely, GB%, FB%, K%, and BB%–are again found to be sticky from year-to-year, with R² values above 0.5, but there is also a sizable month-to-month correlation of 20% or more.

Hard% & HR/FB are well-correlated year to year. This fits with our intuition: batters who hit the ball well tend to keep hitting the ball well. Soft% is the only parameter we studied that had a higher monthly correlation than yearly. This means that over the timescale of a year, Soft% highs and lows might average out, but from month to month there can be carryover.

### Estimating the Coming Month

As we did with pitchers, we created a simple linear model to evaluate the relative predictive value of last year's data and this year's data with respect to what happens in the coming month. The results are summarized:

|  |  | Apr | May | Jun | Jul | Aug | Sep |
|---|---|---|---|---|---|---|---|
| **GB%** | PY | 0.84 | 0.61 | 0.48 | 0.47 | 0.48 | 0.28 |
|  | YTD | 0.00 | 0.21 | 0.41 | 0.36 | 0.48 | 0.62 |
|  | Noise/Regression | 0.16 | 0.18 | 0.11 | 0.17 | 0.04 | 0.10 |
|  | $R^2$ | 0.40 | 0.41 | 0.46 | 0.40 | 0.43 | 0.45 |
| **FB%** | PY | 0.81 | 0.68 | 0.45 | 0.47 | 0.41 | 0.30 |
|  | YTD | 0.00 | 0.20 | 0.41 | 0.40 | 0.44 | 0.56 |
|  | Noise/Regression | 0.19 | 0.12 | 0.14 | 0.13 | 0.15 | 0.14 |
|  | $R^2$ | 0.40 | 0.47 | 0.46 | 0.44 | 0.44 | 0.43 |
| **K%** | PY | 0.85 | 0.65 | 0.61 | 0.53 | 0.39 | 0.34 |
|  | YTD | 0.00 | 0.26 | 0.32 | 0.42 | 0.59 | 0.63 |
|  | Noise/Regression | 0.15 | 0.09 | 0.07 | 0.05 | 0.02 | 0.03 |
|  | $R^2$ | 0.52 | 0.60 | 0.58 | 0.57 | 0.62 | 0.59 |
| **BB%** | PY | 0.75 | 0.59 | 0.57 | 0.45 | 0.33 | 0.46 |
|  | YTD | 0.00 | 0.21 | 0.29 | 0.41 | 0.51 | 0.53 |
|  | Noise/Regression | 0.25 | 0.20 | 0.14 | 0.14 | 0.16 | 0.01 |
|  | $R^2$ | 0.29 | 0.36 | 0.40 | 0.37 | 0.35 | 0.41 |
| **LD%** | PY | 0.47 | 0.42 | 0.36 | 0.35 | 0.21 | 0.34 |
|  | YTD | 0.00 | 0.09 | 0.15 | 0.15 | 0.32 | 0.33 |
|  | Noise/Regression | 0.53 | 0.49 | 0.49 | 0.50 | 0.47 | 0.33 |
|  | $R^2$ | 0.07 | 0.08 | 0.08 | 0.07 | 0.08 | 0.10 |
| **IFFB%** | PY | 0.60 | 0.46 | 0.42 | 0.39 | 0.48 | 0.41 |
|  | YTD | 0.00 | 0.13 | 0.24 | 0.27 | 0.17 | 0.35 |
|  | Noise/Regression | 0.40 | 0.41 | 0.34 | 0.34 | 0.35 | 0.24 |
|  | $R^2$ | 0.13 | 0.13 | 0.16 | 0.13 | 0.13 | 0.18 |
| **Hard%** | PY | 0.66 | 0.48 | 0.39 | 0.31 | 0.27 | 0.35 |
|  | YTD | 0.00 | 0.33 | 0.49 | 0.50 | 0.58 | 0.53 |
|  | Noise/Regression | 0.34 | 0.19 | 0.12 | 0.19 | 0.15 | 0.12 |
|  | $R^2$ | 0.24 | 0.35 | 0.40 | 0.35 | 0.41 | 0.40 |
| **Soft%** | PY | 0.35 | 0.22 | 0.16 | 0.16 | 0.05 | 0.09 |
|  | YTD | 0.00 | 0.33 | 0.52 | 0.61 | 0.70 | 0.68 |
|  | Noise/Regression | 0.65 | 0.45 | 0.32 | 0.23 | 0.25 | 0.23 |
|  | $R^2$ | 0.07 | 0.17 | 0.23 | 0.25 | 0.31 | 0.29 |
| **HR/FB** | PY | 0.73 | 0.63 | 0.51 | 0.39 | 0.41 | 0.38 |
|  | YTD | 0.00 | 0.14 | 0.27 | 0.44 | 0.42 | 0.43 |
|  | Noise/Regression | 0.27 | 0.23 | 0.22 | 0.17 | 0.17 | 0.19 |
|  | $R^2$ | 0.23 | 0.27 | 0.26 | 0.29 | 0.26 | 0.27 |

## Conclusions—Batters

The prior year results are a very good indicator of what to expect. As the year goes on, the additional data generally improves our understanding of the batter's ability and supplants the older data.

The exception was in Soft%, where we found that Prior Year results were nearly worthless in predicting the upcoming month's results and the Prior Month was more useful.

Contrary to the results for pitchers, where the year-to-date results tended to dominate mid-way through the year, for batters the YTD results didn't outweigh the Prior Year until August. That's nearly 110 games into the season!

Fanalytic owners can make use of this information as follows:

- Batters' base skills are a little more stable than pitchers' from year to year.
- Don't buy into early changes in batter skills until at least June.
- Don't expect 2018's Soft% to continue into 2019, but pay attention to the current year's Soft contact rates.
- Projections based on prior years' skills should remain your fallback position, but keep moving the needle toward the current year's results as the year goes on.

## What Does Mean Launch Angle Really Tell Us?

*by Arik Florimonte*

### Introduction

Statcast's Launch Angle (LA) has quickly become part of our baseball vernacular. It is understood that an increased launch angle is associated with more fly balls, which is associated with more home runs.

But how much does average launch angle tell us? What is the best average launch angle? As mean launch angle increases, does the proportion of good outcomes also increase? Are the answers the same for all types of hitters? Is launch angle consistent from year-to-year? And finally, if a batter's launch angle changes, do his results change with it?

To answer these questions, we used data from the "Statcast Era" (2015-2017) to calculate mean launch angle, standard deviation, and mean exit velocity for each batter-season.

We filter for batter-seasons with 200+ batted balls and use total bases per ball in play (TB/BIP) to compare the value of different batter profiles. For orientation purposes, here are the league-wide average values for TB/BIP by launch angle:

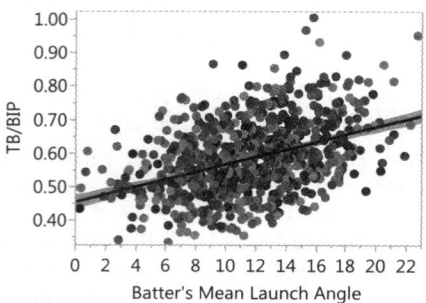

The sweet spot for batted ball launch angles ranges from 10 to 35 degrees, with the most productive fly balls between 20 and 30 degrees.

### Correlation Between Average Launch Angle and Production

When we plotted TB/BIP versus average launch angle, we found a noisy but significant correlation:

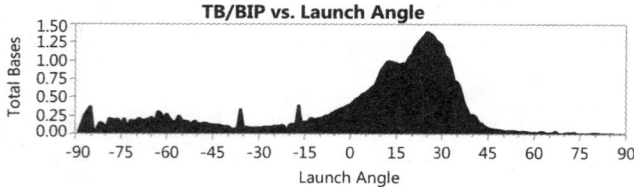

Darker shading reflects a larger number of balls in play. The resulting fit has an $R^2$ value of 0.17, which means that in general, as mean launch angle increases, batter output improves. We also observe that for the seasons represented in 2015-2017, there doesn't appear to be an upper limit of the best mean LA.

### Are the Results the Same for all Types of Hitters?

We know higher mean launch angle is good. Intuition tells us it is even better for someone who routinely creams the ball. To test that assumption, we divide our batters into tiers based on their average exit velocity for the season:

| Tier | Percentile | Values |
|------|-----------|--------|
| 1 | 0-15th | <86.0 mph |
| 2 | 15th-30th | 86.0-87.3 mph |
| 3 | 30th-70th | 87.3-89.8 mph |
| 4 | 70th-85th | 89.8-91.0 mph |
| 5 | 85th-100th | >91.0 mph |

We plot TB/BIP for each tier, and immediately we see that our intuition is correct:

**TB/BIP vs. Batter's Mean Launch Angle**

As mean launch angle increases, both the impact (slope) and relevance ($R^2$ value) are greater for higher exit velocity tiers. TB/BIP is essentially Slg/ct%, which means that in the top two EV tiers, a one-degree increase in LA is generally worth about 10 points of Slg (depending on contact rate).

### Launch Angle Variance

We also examined whether high variation in launch angle was good or bad for TB/BIP. We separated batters who were in either the lowest or highest ten percent in both launch angle and standard deviation of launch angle (LAv), and analyzed their season totals:

| Group | Launch Angle | LAv | GB% | FB% | Popup% | TB/BIP |
|-------|-------------|-----|-----|-----|--------|--------|
| A | < 10th PCTL | > 90th PCTL | 58% | 21% | 6% | 0.43 |
| B | > 90th PCTL | > 90th PCTL | 35% | 43% | 14% | 0.56 |
| C | < 10th PCTL | < 10th PCTL | 60% | 13% | 1% | 0.47 |
| D | > 90th PCTL | < 10th PCTL | 31% | 36% | 4% | 0.71 |

*(Note: league average TB/BIP for this period was 0.57)*

Group D batters coupled a high LA with a low LAv to produce 25% better TB/BIP than their high-LAv Group B counterparts, mainly by avoiding pop-ups. Of the poor LA batters, Group C with lower LAv also avoided pop-ups and produced about 10% better outcomes than group A.

### Year-to-Year Consistency and Effects of Changes

For batters with 200+ batted balls in both 2016 and 2017, we plotted next year's LA versus this year's and found a very strong correlation, with an $R^2$ value of 0.60. Launch angle variance had a year-to-year correlation of 0.36. For comparison, year-to-year Exit Velocity has an $R^2$ of 0.52.

We then considered individual batters who saw changes in LA or LAv from year-to-year to measure what happened to their TB/BIP. Hitters who had above-average exit velocity saw an average increase of 0.013 TB/BIP per degree of increase, with an $R^2$ value of 0.13. Batters who reduced their LAv saw an average increase of 0.018 TB/BIP, with an $R^2$ value of 0.12.

It's not a slam dunk that these changes in LA profile will yield great results, but they do generally help.

## Conclusions

We set out to validate or refute the idea that a batter's mean launch angle was a usable metric. Our key findings:

- Average launch angle by itself is somewhat useful, 17% correlated to TB/BIP.
- A batter's mean launch angle, launch angle variance, and exit velocity are fairly repeatable, with year-to-year correlations of 0.60, 0.36, and 0.52, respectively.
- A batter can improve TB/BIP by increasing launch angle, decreasing launch angle variance, or both.
- Batters with high mean Exit Velocity benefit most from changes to their launch angle profile.

Batters who increase mean launch angle have received much of the attention, but finding a consistent approach that reduces pop-ups and grounders appears just as important. We don't yet know how much control, if any, a batter has over his launch angle variance, but for now, take heed that a change in a batter's mean launch angle only tells a part of the story. If it comes with additional pop-ups or grounders, or without solid exit velocity, it may not be a transformation worth buying into.

## *When Do Hitters get Platooned?*

*by Jeff Zimmerman*

Since the 1800s, teams have been platooning opposite-handed batters compared to the pitcher to gain a production advantage. It's easier for hitters to see and hit a ball that isn't initially coming directly at their head. If a hitter happens to be put in a platoon, his fantasy value plummets from the lost plate appearances.

We're going to create a talent baseline to determine if a hitter can get platooned by examining historical examples. The extreme platoon advantages are isolated to just a few hitters, but it occurs league-wide. In 2017, right-handed hitters posted a .733 OPS against right-handed pitchers and a .775 OPS against lefties (42-point difference). On the other hand, left-handed hitters posted a .769 OPS against righties and a .683 OPS against lefties (86-point difference).

After looking over the data of 24 actual platoon situations, two distinct scenarios exist. The first is an extreme righty-lefty pair such as Cleveland had in 2017 with Lonnie Chisenhall and Brandon Guyer. Chisenhall hits RHP better with a career .752 OPS against them, but only a .697 OPS against LHP. Guyer, on the other hand, posts a .819 OPS against LHP and a .633 OPS against RHP. The other pairs one player with an extreme platoon split and someone without one.

We combined all the information and compared the hitter's projected OPS splits coming into the season. As we previously stated, some platoons involved players with little to no spreads, so we concentrated on the most extreme hitter of the pair.

### Spread: OPS Difference

- Max: .593
- Average: .238
- Median: .185
- Minimum: .082

Normally, a spread of ~200 points of OPS is needed to start a platoon. Looking through the data, in only two instances did a platoon happen with a projected split under 130 points.

The next benchmark is the upper OPS needed to start a platoon, as some bottom baseline needs to exist to be a major league hitter.

### Spread: The Pair's OPS Maximum

- Max: .942
- Average: .834
- Median: .832
- Minimum: .722

For most teams to implement a platoon, they need at least one player to have a projected platoon OPS around .830.

While these OPS values are the maximum ones, they help to set a minimum threshold for a platoon. A .722 projected OPS was the minimum, while all but two had an OPS over .775. Now, the minimum values:

### Spread: The Pair's OPS Minimum

- Max: .703
- Average: .587
- Median: .612
- Minimum: .218

These values could have been estimated using the two previous data sets. They set a minimum projected OPS in which teams begin using platoons. A player could have a 200-point spread, but if the low projected OPS is over .700, teams aren't likely to add another player to make up the difference.

The simple rule of an ".800-.600 OPS spread" works great for an average platoon benchmark. Owners may want to relax the values to snare a few more players with a .775-.625 OPS spread, or an ".800-.600 OPS spread with shrinkage".

## *Innovating Around the Catcher Pool*

*by Ray Murphy*

In 2018, The Great Fantasy Baseball Invitational (TGFBI) was a new entrant into the slate of industry competitions. Leagues like these have long been a testing ground for innovation in our game formats. TGFBI had one significant wrinkle in place for their inaugural season: It altered the traditional 14-man active hitting roster by taking the second catcher position and converting it into a second utility spot.

This is a change that other leagues should consider following.

### Not a new problem

We pulled 11 years' worth of data from BaseballHQ.com's Custom Draft Guide to put some actual numbers around the quality of the catcher pool. It's rather stunning to look at how bad this position has been, and for how long. Consider:

| | '18 | '17 | '16 | '15 | '14 | '13 | '12 | '11 | '10 | '09 | '08 |
|---|---|---|---|---|---|---|---|---|---|---|---|
| $1+ Cs | 12 | 9 | 13 | 14 | 19 | 19 | 19 | 17 | 14 | 14 | 15 |
| $5+ Cs | 5 | 6 | 6 | 9 | 11 | 13 | 11 | 9 | 7 | 10 | 7 |
| $10+ Cs | 1 | 4 | 4 | 1 | 5 | 8 | 7 | 7 | 4 | 4 | 5 |
| $15+ Cs | 0 | 1 | 1 | 1 | 2 | 2 | 3 | 2 | 2 | 2 | 2 |
| $20+ Cs | 0 | 0 | 0 | 1 | 1 | 0 | 1 | 2 | 0 | 1 | 0 |
| Total Val ($) | 88 | 87 | 104 | 104 | 158 | 182 | 180 | 150 | 103 | 132 | 123 |

- There has not been a $20 catcher in three years. Only once in the past decade have we seen two $20 catchers in a single season.

- 2018 did not produce a single $15 catcher for the first time in our sample. But only once in this period have we seen more than two of those in a single season.

- If your preferred standard is just "I'll take any positive value from the position", you have to go back four years to find a time where there were enough positive-valued catchers to put even one such catcher on every team in a 15-team mixed league.

- Not once in this 11-year sample have there been enough $5+ catchers to put one on every team in a 15-team league, let alone two of them.

- Even the relative "glory days" of 2012-15 were significantly skewed by just one player, as Buster Posey's values through those years ($25-$13-$23-$23) prop up the total values in that time period.

- As bad as it is in mixed leagues, it is so much worse in AL-only or NL-only formats.

All of this data really calls the question: "Why are we doing this to ourselves?" This isn't just a blip in the player development cycle. MLB organizations are clearly valuing non-fantasy skills (game-calling and pitch-framing) over offense from their backstops. Not only do we have a decade's worth of data to confirm this trend, but the industry trend line continues to point in the same direction.

For proof of this, look no further than the Cleveland Indians. They used Francisco Mejia, arguably the top backstop prospect in the game at the time, as a trade chip to get Brad Hand this summer. They did this because they were clearly disenchanted with Mejia's work behind the plate, and had trialed him at several other positions before deciding he didn't fit anywhere else, either.

Also this past summer, there was much rejoicing (and a mini-frenzy of FAAB activity) when TEX utility-man Isiah Kiner-Falefa (who ended the year 4-34-.264) appeared in his 10th game at catcher. This is what we're reduced to rooting for at this position? Why are we continuing to bang our heads against this wall?

Further, there are real merits to creating a 2nd utility spot:

- If you want to use that spot strategically to roster combinations of players you couldn't before (like, say, five corner infielders or seven outfielders), you can do that.

- It also reduces the penalty for rostering DH-only players. We don't have many of those anymore, but both Khris Davis and Kendrys Morales will start 2019 as DH-only (based on 20-game eligibility).

The bottom line: more flexibility, thus allowing more discretion and creativity in how we manage our teams, is something that should be encouraged. We encourage you to pitch this change to your rules committee this offseason: 1 catcher, 2 utility slots.

## When Do Top 100 Prospects Get Promoted?

*by Jeff Zimmerman*

For both hitters and pitchers, we've created a simple procedure to determine if—and when—a player will make it to the majors in the season after being ranked in BaseballHQ.com's HQ100 prospect list (2010 to 2017). It examines only the prospects who have not played in the majors.

**Position players**

*Step 1: Is the player 25 years old, foreign-born, and just signed by a major league team?*

If YES, the odds are quite good. Historically, 100% of these players debuted in the majors the following season.

If NO, move to Step 2.

*Step 2: Did the player end his previous season in Triple-A?*

If YES, then research shows that 93% debut in the majors the following season. In about every other non-debut instance, injury was the reason.

The higher the team winning percentage (at the end of the season), the sooner the HQ100 prospect who ended the previous season in Triple-A debuted. Here are the days into the season when these prospects got the call compared to team winning percentage:

| Team Win% | Days to Debut |
|---|---|
| 65% | 47 |
| 60% | 55 |
| 55% | 62 |
| 50% | 70 |
| 45% | 78 |
| 40% | 86 |
| 35% | 94 |

If the player did not end the previous season in Triple-A, move to Step 3.

*Step 3: Did the hitter end the season in Double-A?*

If YES, their major league chances drop to 53% the following season. Most of these players (95%) eventually debut in the majors. A Top 25 hitter has a two-in-three chance of making it to the majors, while it's closer to 50% for a hitter ranked 51-100:

| | |
|---|---|
| Avg Rank for Call Up | 43.0 |
| Median Rank for Call Up | 33.5 |
| Avg Rank for No Call Up | 50.5 |
| Median Rank for No Call up | 50.0 |

| Ranked in Top X | % Called Up |
|---|---|
| 10 | 63% |
| 16-25 | 74% |
| 26-50 | 57% |
| 51-100 | 53% |

While prospect ranking had no impact on the Triple-A players, the timing of the call up was significant for players in Double-A:

| Debut Day Range | Avg Rank |
|---|---|
| 1 to 30 | 36.4 |
| 31 to 60 | 31.5 |
| 61 to 90 | 39.0 |
| 91 to 120 | 47.1 |
| 121 to 150 | 47.4 |
| 151 to 180 | 52.3 |

If an owner is hoping for a prospect to get an early promotion from Double-A, they need to be looking at players in the top half of the ranking.

If the player did not end the season in either Triple-A or Double-A, move to Step 4.

*Step 4: Did the hitter end the previous season in any level of A-ball?*

Only 18% of these hitters make it to the majors the following season. Our rankers did a respectable job evaluating these prospects, as 95% eventually make the majors.

While hitters who were at least 22-years-old made up one-third of the entire group, they were 73% of the players promoted to the big leagues. Additionally, hitters who got promoted to the majors had an average ranking of 39, while the ones who didn't get promoted had an average ranking of 55. By subsetting out the 22-year-olds in the top half of the rankings, 53% of them get promoted.

If one of these prospects gets promoted, it will at least take a couple months, while not even half are promoted within four months:

| Debuted in season | Odds |
|---|---|
| 30 days or fewer | 0% |
| 60 days or fewer | 23% |
| 90 days or fewer | 46% |
| 120 days or fewer | 46% |
| 150 days or fewer | 69% |
| 180 days or fewer | 100% |

*Step 5: Was the hitter just drafted, in rookie ball, or in the Dominican league?*

None of these hitters have ever been promoted to the majors the same season they appeared on the HQ100.

### Pitchers

Because of major injuries that can cost pitchers entire seasons, the process was a bit more difficult.

*Step 1: Is the player foreign-born, and at least 23 years old?*

If YES, the odds of these guys making it to MLB has been 100%.
If NO, move to Step 2.

*Step 2: Did the pitcher end last season pitching in Triple-A?*

If YES: Like with hitters, the chances of making it to the majors are quite good—86% make the jump in the following season and 94% eventually debut in the majors. Here is when those pitchers will most likely get promoted:

| Debuted in season | Odds |
|---|---|
| 30 days or fewer | 38% |
| 60 days or fewer | 50% |
| 90 days or fewer | 74% |
| 120 days or fewer | 79% |
| 150 days or fewer | 88% |
| 180 days or fewer | 100% |

About half of the arms will be up within the first two months. With these pitchers, both team winning percentage and rank had

an impact on the call-up date. Unlike hitters, losing teams were more likely to bring up a pitcher.

If NO, move to Step 3.

*Step 3: Did the pitcher end the previous season in Double-A?*

If YES, the odds of making the majors in the following season drops to 50% for pitchers in Double-A, but 95% eventually make it to the majors. Like with hitters, ranking is important for these pitchers to be called up. Chances are good for a Top 20 prospect, but they drop to about one-in-three in the bottom 20:

| Rank | % Promoted |
|---|---|
| 1 to 20 | 75% |
| 21 to 40 | 50% |
| 41 to 60 | 65% |
| 61 to 80 | 50% |
| 81 to 100 | 33% |

Don't ignore those ranked between 21 and 80, as over half of them get called up. As for when they get called up, it's spread evenly over the entire season:

| Debuted in season | Odds |
|---|---|
| 30 days or fewer | 21% |
| 60 days or fewer | 39% |
| 90 days or fewer | 58% |
| 120 days or fewer | 67% |
| 150 days or fewer | 82% |
| 180 days or fewer | 100% |

With Double-A prospects, take the top arms and just hope they get the early call. If they didn't finish the prior season in Double-A or Triple-A, move to Step 4.

*Step 4: Did the pitcher end the season at A-ball?*

Of these pitchers, 21% get the call. While the prospects who get called up don't have a high ranking (avg. ranked 48th), the average rank is 57th for those who don't get called up. Unlike the hitters, age doesn't factor in with pitchers.

The average date on being called up is 107 days into the season, with the following distribution:

| Debuted in season | Odds |
|---|---|
| 30 days or fewer | 14% |
| 60 days or fewer | 21% |
| 90 days or fewer | 21% |
| 120 days or fewer | 64% |
| 150 days or fewer | 79% |
| 180 days or fewer | 100% |

*Step 5: Was the pitcher just drafted, in rookie ball, or in the Dominican league?*

None of these pitchers got called up in that season.

### Conclusion

The chances of a major league call-up for a healthy hitter or pitcher who last played:
- As a veteran in a foreign league: 100%
- In Triple-A: 90%
- In Double-A: 50%
- In A-ball: 20%
- Other: 0%

Additionally, to increase the odds, take the (1) higher ranked player; (2) the older player; and (3) the player on a contending team.

## The Fracturing Saves Market

*by Ray Murphy*

### The evolving closer role

Here's a 10-year scan of the MLB-wide saves distribution by pitcher:

|          | '18 | '17 | '16 | '15 | '14 | '13 | '12 | '11 | '10 | '09 | '08 |
|----------|-----|-----|-----|-----|-----|-----|-----|-----|-----|-----|-----|
| 6-10 Sv  | 10  | 15  | 11  | 9   | 8   | 5   | 10  | 10  | 10  | 10  | 9   |
| 10-20 Sv | 23  | 18  | 21  | 10  | 14  | 9   | 11  | 7   | 10  | 11  | 15  |
| 20-30 Sv | 9   | 13  | 7   | 9   | 8   | 9   | 12  | 10  | 16  | 13  | 10  |
| 30-40 Sv | 8   | 8   | 11  | 17  | 10  | 13  | 10  | 12  | 9   | 12  | 9   |
| 41+ Sv   | 1   | 3   | 5   | 4   | 7   | 6   | 5   | 7   | 5   | 4   | 6   |

Let's zoom in on the trend in the lower tier of saves sources:

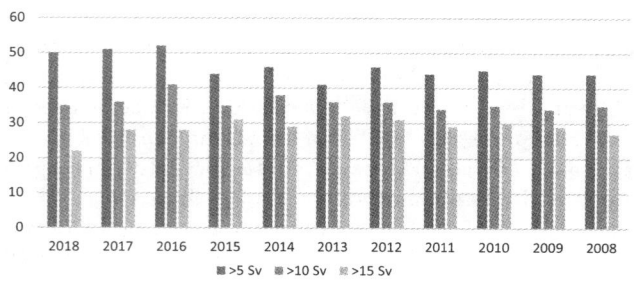

Sometimes Saves Sources, 2008-18

Clearly, the population of pitchers getting >5 and >10 saves is on the upswing. But keep in mind, this still includes the pool of full-time closers. Let's zoom in on that tier:

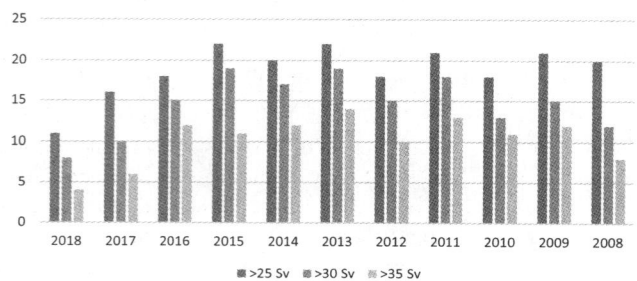

Full-time(ish) Saves Sources, 2008-18

The decline of the >25 and >30 save reliever is hard to deny from this view. League-wide saves aren't going down, so those missing saves have to get redistributed somewhere. Let's look at the saves distribution by tier of saves total, in a non-inclusive view (so now, the >10 Saves group doesn't include the >15 Saves group, etc.):

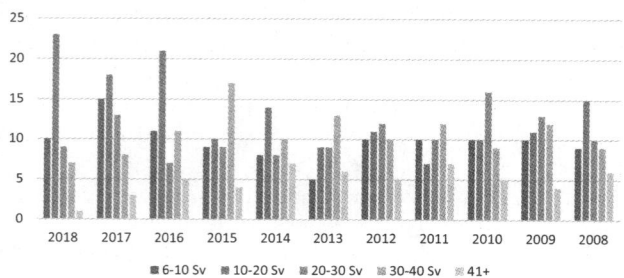

Saves distribution by tier, non-inclusive view

To digest this view, just look at the "lean" of each cluster. The recent ones (left side of the chart) are all "leaning" to the left: the first two bars (lowest saves totals) are the tallest. Toward the middle and right of the chart you see much less "lean" in the clusters: they are fairly well-balanced, even leaning to the right in a in a couple of cases (2013, 2015). What we're seeing in 2016-18 is very different from just a few years ago.

To be even more explicit, the main takeaway here is that we're seeing the emergence of a new class of reliever. In this age of "openers", etc., we're going to need a name for this guy. Let's call him the "par-closer":

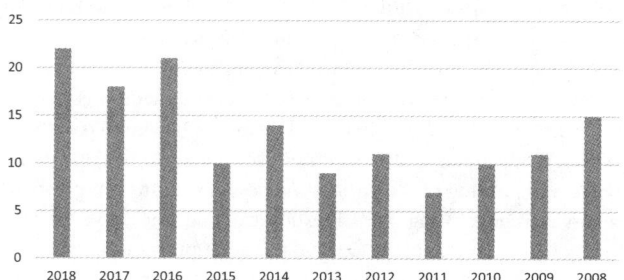

10-20 Sv

### Implications

There are any number of strategic implications for our games. In no particular order:

- The way we project saves needs an overhaul. There are no longer as many relievers getting 80%+ of their team's saves as we project every preseason, and it's time we steered into this skid and acknowledged that in our projections process. *[Ed. note: You see the beginnings of that change in this book.]*

- A more fractured talent pool for saves contributors should mean that it takes fewer saves to compete in the category, which in turn further opens the door for creative strategies to try and manage the category.

- The model for how we pay for saves needs to change to reflect this. If you are confident that a particular reliever is a 35+ saves guy, then you should be willing to pay even more for him, because of what he gives you relative to that category target/need. But if you don't believe in someone, there's less incentive than ever to pay for him just because he has the "closer label" in March.

- How do you plan your bench, and manage your FAAB, in terms of positioning your team to cycle through these par-closers as they emerge (and subsequently disappear) all season long?

- Looking at pitcher skills, overall bullpen composition, and managerial tendencies, can we do a better job of predicting in advance which relievers are going to work their way into this tier—both from above (projected closers) and below (projected non-closers)?

Re-calibrating how you manage the Saves category is a ripe area to gain an advantage in 2019, as your competitors may be slower to react to this shift.

## The Opener

*by Patrick Davitt*

OK, quick: Would you rather have Pitcher A, or Pitcher B?

|        | Pitcher A | Pitcher B |
|--------|-----------|-----------|
| ERA    | 2.71      | 5.80      |
| WHIP   | 1.16      | 1.48      |
| K/9    | 9.6       | 8.4       |
| K/BB   | 2.8       | 2.0       |
| OppOPS | .627      | .823      |
| Hard%  | 32%       | 40%       |
| Soft%  | 23%       | 17%       |

Clearly, you want Pitcher A. He has SP-2 skills and could be looking at a fat free-agent payday. Pitcher B will be lucky to avoid being sent to the minors.

But here's the kicker: They're the same pitcher.

Pitcher A is Jake Odorizzi (RHP, MIN), the first two times he pitches through the opposing batting order. Pitcher B is also Odorizzi, facing the order the third time.

Odorizzi isn't an outlier. Over the last two seasons, 76 starters faced at least 450 Batters Faced (BF) twice through the order and faced at least 150 a third time through. Of them, in that third time through the order:

- 84% got worse in ERA
- 75% got worse in Dominance (K/9)
- 64% got worse in Command Ratio (K/BB)

The pattern follows for every metric we use. And overall, almost half of these starters got worse in multiple metrics, often markedly.

Front offices and managers, urged by numbers people inside and outside the game, have been looking at this batting order split. Many now understand that if a pitcher is solid those first two times through the order but weak after that—an Odorizzi—they should limit him to those two times, and maximize the benefit by starting him lower down in the opposing order.

Earlier this season, one team put the theory into practice. On May 19, the Rays started closer Sergio Romo against the Angels.

The move made sense. In general, the first inning is the highest-scoring against starting pitchers. Moreover, the Rays wanted to start rookie Ryan Yarbrough, a southpaw, and the Angels 1-2-3 hitters would be RHBs Zack Cozart, Mike Trout, and Justin Upton. There was a good probability that Yarbrough could come out of the first behind in the score, up in pitch count, and shell-shocked.

But Romo had been a monster vs RHB, with a K% touching 30%. So the Rays thought he stood a better chance of getting through the first inning. They also thought Yarbrough would benefit from starting the second inning with a zero on the scoreboard and having avoided the Angels' top hitters. That's exactly what happened. The Rays adopted the scheme, avoiding borderline starters they believed would be cannon fodder by starting relievers who came to be called "openers" (a play on "closers").

This became a thing. Minnesota and Oakland started using openers, and MIN started applying it in their minor-league system, suggesting an organizational shift. And note that these three teams are not among MLB's big-revenue operations, so they recognize the financial benefits: capable short-stint and two-times-through pitchers are way easier to find—and therefore cheaper—than quality starters who get six-plus innings per start.

Of course, nobody knows if this opener experiment will work out over a longer test. Teams will have noticed that the Rays' winning percentage jumped from .500 to over .570 after they adopted openers, and that their runs allowed fell from 4.6 per game to 3.8. Wider adoption may now accelerate with some success with the concept in 2018's playoffs. When Kansas City won a World Series with strictly defined bullpen roles, many teams married that model.

So suppose Oakland had won the World Series using openers, and that more teams follow suit. How will fantasy be affected?

**Starters who can successfully pitch the third time through will become more valuable**—to their real teams and to fantasy owners. Of the 76 pitchers in the above-mentioned study, 12 actually improved in ERA, and 19 improved in K/9. Sometimes this is because their first- and second-times-through numbers were horrible, but some quality pitchers did get better later in the game. Corey Kluber and Max Scherzer are two of them.

**Used better, lower-value starters could see an uptick in value.** In first innings this year, Odorizzi logged a 5.40 ERA/1.30 WHIP with an OppOPS of almost .800. When we combine second, third, and fourth innings: 1.80/0.93, .527. Had MIN opened Odorizzi's games this season, he might have had far better results in the decimals and—as the pitcher of record in games with the lead—in wins.

**Leagues with minimum- and/or maximum-starts rules would have to change them.** Starts requirements are meant to require fantasy teams to roster a representative staff, including a fair number of "starting pitchers." But pitchers like Romo normally pitch every three days. With 182 days in a season, a fulltime "opener" could rack up 60+ "starts." Meanwhile, second-inning starters like Yarbrough would see their official starts disappear. Leagues would have some arguing to do about how to define pitcher roles, and maybe also define a category reward for a successful opener-type "start" beyond its effect on the decimals.

**Ditto for innings requirements.** We could see pitching staffs with only one or two true starters, and a bunch of other pitchers with workloads designed to get them 70-100 innings per season. When that happens, it might be nearly impossible to get 950 or 1,000 innings out of a nine-man roto pitching staff. Which also means...

**Leagues would have to reconsider their overall hitter-pitcher roster requirements.** The opener, if widely implemented, could mean a lot more pitchers on each MLB team's roster; maybe even more than we have now. That would mean shorter benches, more Marwin Gonzalez-type multi-utility guys, and fewer quality replacement hitters in the free-agent pool, especially in AL- and NL-only formats. Leagues would have to consider 11 hitters/12 pitchers or even 10/13.

There are probably other ramifications that haven't yet come to mind. One thing's for sure, though—it seems like when it comes to this particular show, we're only just seeing the "opening" act.

## Using Rotisserie Standings to Gain a H2H Edge

*by David Martin*

In the case of head-to-head fantasy baseball, analyzing your league's Rotisserie stats and standings can provide tremendous insight into performance. This information can be used to gain a competitive advantage on a variety of fronts, including in your weekly matchups, trades, and in analyzing your own team.

### The Standings

Below are examples of aggregate hitting and pitching statistics in a fictitious head-to-head league. This league has 12 teams and uses standard 5x5 categories. The snapshot below is from approximately six weeks into the season.

### Hitting

| Team | R | HR | RBI | SB | AVG |
|------|-----|----|-----|----|------|
| Team 1 | 242 | 77 | 247 | 21 | .280 |
| Team 2 | 240 | 66 | 226 | 24 | .266 |
| Team 3 | 237 | 69 | 215 | 27 | .257 |
| Team 4 | 235 | 58 | 225 | 35 | .272 |
| Team 5 | 229 | 70 | 213 | 18 | .252 |
| Team 6 | 226 | 61 | 226 | 39 | .285 |
| Team 7 | 200 | 56 | 177 | 31 | .258 |
| Team 8 | 199 | 57 | 209 | 25 | .250 |
| Team 9 | 194 | 58 | 187 | 27 | .238 |
| Team 10 | 192 | 53 | 166 | 31 | .253 |
| Team 11 | 186 | 54 | 193 | 24 | .269 |
| Team 12 | 179 | 64 | 227 | 20 | .240 |

### Pitching

| Team | SV | K | ERA | WHIP | W |
|------|----|-----|------|------|----|
| Team 8 | 35 | 455 | 3.74 | 1.20 | 21 |
| Team 11 | 33 | 439 | 3.05 | 1.09 | 21 |
| Team 2 | 29 | 527 | 3.28 | 1.14 | 27 |
| Team 6 | 29 | 444 | 3.97 | 1.14 | 21 |
| Team 9 | 20 | 368 | 4.19 | 1.35 | 18 |
| Team 12 | 20 | 410 | 3.64 | 1.25 | 23 |
| Team 5 | 20 | 456 | 3.71 | 1.26 | 25 |
| Team 7 | 19 | 444 | 3.74 | 1.27 | 35 |
| Team 3 | 18 | 489 | 3.61 | 1.19 | 24 |
| Team 1 | 15 | 433 | 3.45 | 1.21 | 27 |
| Team 10 | 13 | 582 | 4.30 | 1.33 | 40 |
| Team 4 | 13 | 406 | 4.08 | 1.33 | 27 |

### Matchup Analysis

The first way that this information is useful is as a weekly matchup tool. Prior to playing a team, assess its strengths and weaknesses. Try to get an understanding of what categories your team may win and lose in advance of a matchup.

Next, look for exploitable matchups. Let's say Team 2 is playing Team 1 this week. Team 2 has to decide who to start in its UTIL spot between Mallex Smith and Christian Villanueva. Team 2 notices that it has a slight edge in stolen bases (24-21) compared to Team 1. The smart play is go with Smith in an effort to try and win steals for the week. Smith may also help more in the runs category, where Team 1 and 2 have essentially even production on the season.

Third, analyze how a team is built. For instance, Team 10 leads the league in strikeouts and wins. However, these counting statistics have come at the expense of the team's ERA and WHIP, which are the worst in the league. When you play Team 10, expect to face an uphill battle in winning strikeouts and wins. But Team 10 is vulnerable in the pitching ratio categories. Rather than rolling the dice with your more inconsistent starting pitchers, bench those starters this week. Team 10 is also weak in saves. In the event that your team gets a comfortable lead in that category, it may make sense to bench a more volatile closer later in the week.

### Trade Analysis

Roto stats are also useful in determining both what your team could use via a trade and what a trade partner's team needs are. For instance, Team 2 knows that its lineup just falls short of Team 1 in most hitting categories. In a H2H playoff matchup, it could use a little more firepower. It makes sense for Team 2 to try and acquire a slugger to bridge the gap.

On the flip side, when engaging a team in trade talks, target a team that will have the ability to trade from a category of strength and improve a category of weakness. It is easier to convince someone to make a deal when you can say to them, "You're dominating the league in saves. You can afford to trade a closer to improve your HR production, where you are ranked 10th." The rotisserie standing stats provide an objective barometer that can be leveraged in a manner that comes across as fair and logical. Use these stats to highlight a potential trade partner's strengths and weaknesses.

Rotisserie stats can also be used to make your team more homogeneous. Determine which categories your team is competitive in, but not quite at the top of the standings. Typically, these will be categories where your team is ranked in the #4-6 range. If you're fourth in home runs, it makes sense to try and add a slugger to get closer to the top of the standings. It goes without saying that teams at the top of a given stat category will be more likely to win those categories. The goal is to solidify your team's dominance in those categories, which will lead to more consistent week-to-week production.

### Team Analysis

The final way that roto standings can be useful to H2H players is to perform a self-assessment of one's own team. Check to make sure that you're not sacrificing your ratio categories at the expense of counting statistics. That is frequently the downfall of teams built on free-swinging sluggers or pitchers with lackluster command (i.e., Team 10 above). If you are rostering too many hitters with low averages, figure out how to trade some of that power for hitters who make better contact.

Whether your team is over-performing or under-performing, there is also a component of luck involved with H2H play. Rotisserie standings can help you evaluate if your team has been lucky or unlucky. They eliminate the week-to-week snapshot and instead show year-to-date performance relative to other teams in the league, which can be reassuring during those weeks when you lose a close matchup.

### Conclusion

Rotisserie-style statistics and standings provide tremendous insight to head-to-head players. Savvy players should use this information to their advantage to make weekly roster decisions, leverage trades, and analyze their own team.

## The Perils of League Formatting

*by Matt Cederholm*

Many older, established leagues eventually confront the need to modernize their scoring format to account for the changes in MLB over the past 35 or so years. Major league teams now carry fewer hitters, while wins and saves are dispersed among more pitchers. But how do we modernize the roster and scoring formats?

The goals are rather simple: 1) More closely align league rosters with MLB, given the recent trend toward having more pitchers on the active roster, 2) Free up more hitters in the free-agent pool, 3) Recognize the value of middle relievers without significantly affecting the value of SP, and 4) Reduce the value of saves (or at least blur the line between closers and short relievers). But how would these changes affect player values as well as pitching values and budgets?

| Scoring | — 4x4 — | | — 5x5 — | | —4x4(S+H)— | | - 5x5 (S+H) - | |
|---|---|---|---|---|---|---|---|---|
| Hit/Pit Split | 14/9 | 13/10 | 14/9 | 13/10 | 14/9 | 13/10 | 14/9 | 13/10 |
| C. Yelich | $49 | $53 | $46 | $49 | $49 | $53 | $46 | $49 |
| N. Arenado | $31 | $33 | $31 | $33 | $31 | $33 | $31 | $33 |
| T. Turner | $39 | $43 | $37 | $40 | $39 | $43 | $37 | $40 |
| DJ Lemahieu | $16 | $17 | $18 | $19 | $16 | $17 | $18 | $19 |
| K. Jansen | $23 | $21 | $20 | $18 | $13 | $12 | $12 | $11 |
| B. Boxberger | $10 | $10 | $8 | $9 | $2 | $3 | $1 | $2 |
| R. Gsellman | $4 | $5 | $3 | $5 | $4 | $5 | $3 | $4 |
| M. Scherzer | $36 | $32 | $41 | $36 | $36 | $33 | $43 | $37 |
| J. Urena | $4 | $5 | $6 | $7 | $4 | $5 | $6 | $6 |
| S. Newcomb | $2 | $3 | $5 | $6 | $1 | $2 | $5 | $6 |

| Scoring | | — 4x4 — | | | — 5x5 — | | | —4x4(S+H)— | | | 5x5 (S+H) — | |
|---|---|---|---|---|---|---|---|---|---|---|---|---|---|
| | 14/9 | | 13/10 | | 14/9 | | 13/10 | | 14/9 | | 13/10 | | |
| P Tot | # | $ | # | $ | # | $ | # | $ | # | $ | # | $ | # $ |
| SP | 47 | 495 | 51 | 486 | 53 | 594 | 58 | 578 | 45 | 473 | 47 | 473 | 50 582 | 55 567 |
| MR | 57 | 382 | 72 | 411 | 50 | 307 | 60 | 338 | 62 | 474 | 67 | 478 | 54 381 | 62 400 |
| CL | 9 | 156 | 9 | 147 | 9 | 130 | 9 | 125 | 9 | 86 | 9 | 83 | 9 71 | 9 72 |

| % of P budget | | | | | | | | |
|---|---|---|---|---|---|---|---|---|
| SP | 48% | 47% | 58% | 56% | 46% | 46% | 56% | 55% |
| MR | 37% | 39% | 30% | 32% | 46% | 46% | 37% | 38% |
| CL | 15% | 11% | 13% | 12% | 8% | 8% | 7% | 7% |

*Dollar values were generated from BaseballHQ.com's Custom Draft Guide (CDG) for a 12-team, NL-only league. Note that the CDG uses the percent-value method of valuing players. When run using SGP, some of the changes were more dramatic.*

Going to a 13/10 hitter/pitcher split affected hitters more than pitchers (the table assumes no shift in draft dollars from hitting to pitching). Some pitching money shifts from starters and closers to middle relievers. Moving to standard 5x5 does reduce closer spending, but also hurts middle relievers, while giving starting pitchers a big boost in value. Going to Saves + Holds (S+H) shifts money from closers to middle relievers, while leaving starting pitching more or less unchanged.

What's the takeaway here? First, the game should be fun. We can only imitate baseball, not duplicate it. Second, know what you're getting into. Run your league's projections under various scenarios—the effects of a change will be different from league to league. Understand the effects of scoring and roster changes on draft-day values before you commit. Make sure your rule changes match with your goals. Leagues work best when owners have reasonable estimates of player value.

## Decimals

*by Patrick Davitt*

Many fantasy players think that later in the season, we can't move the decimals (BA, ERA, WHIP) because with the majority of at-bats or innings in the books, the ratio's large denominators make it hard to move the needle. While it's true we can't move as much late as early, we can still move enough to gain points.

We tested this idea at the two-thirds mark in the season. Using teams and stats in a 15-team mixed expert's league, we built spreadsheet tables to see how much an owner could gain in the decimals—first just by dropping a poor performer, and then by replacing a poor performer with a good performer.

**Batting Average**

The BA test projected a team to finish with a .257 BA (1,969 hits in 7,660 AB), 13th in the category. We first checked the effect of just dropping a hitter with 190 remaining projected AB (pAB) at various low BAs, without replacing him. Here's the result:

- Drop a .245 hitter: Team BA .25730, +.30, 11th place
- .235 hitter: .25756, 11th place
- .225 hitter: .25783, 10th place
- .215 hitter: .25810, 9th place

(If you're wondering, a team dropping Chris Davis and his .200 pBA would see a final team BA of .25850.)

Not huge gains, but most of us have played in leagues with much narrower BA margins. The gains are amplified when the poor hitter is replaced with a high-pBA hitter. Assuming both hitters have 190 AB, here are what those gains look like:

| pBA of Hitter Dropped | pBA of Hitter Added | | | | |
|---|---|---|---|---|---|
| | .305 | .295 | .285 | .275 | .265 |
| .215 | .25927 | .25901 | .25875 | .25849 | .25836 |
| .225 | .25901 | .25875 | .25849 | .25836 | .25809 |
| .235 | .25875 | .25849 | .25836 | .25809 | .25783 |
| .245 | .25849 | .25836 | .25809 | .25783 | .25757 |

In the top-left of the table, dropping a .215 pBA hitter and adding a .305 guy jumps team pBA by +.00227 over the .257 baseline, to .25927. That's a solid BA gain in many leagues, and in our test league it would gain the owner six places, from 13th up to seventh. Down in the lower-right corner, dropping a .245 and adding a .265 still gains 57 baseline points, good for two added points in the category.

**ERA**

Gains in the pitching decimals can be greater because the denominator is smaller than BA—around 1,200 innings instead of 7,600 at-bats. This part of the study used a team with a 4.00 final pERA in 1,325 IP; 10th place.

Let's start again by just dropping a poor performer with 55 pIP:

- Dropping a 4.25 pERA pitcher: Team ERA finished at 3.990, still 10th
- 4.50 pitcher: 3.976, 10th

- 4.75 pitcher: 3.969, 10th, but just thousandths short of ninth
- 5.00 pitcher: 3.954, ninth
- 5.25 pitcher: 3.947, ninth
- 5.50 pitcher: 3.933, eighth

And now, not only dropping a pitcher but adding a low-pERA replacement with the same 55 pIP:

| pERA of Pitcher Dropped | pERA of Pitcher Added | | | | | |
|---|---|---|---|---|---|---|
| | **2.75** | **3.00** | **3.25** | **3.50** | **3.75** | **4.00** |
| **5.50** | 3.885 | 3.892 | 3.906 | 3.912 | 3.926 | 3.933 |
| **5.25** | 3.899 | 3.906 | 3.919 | 3.926 | 3.940 | 3.946 |
| **5.00** | 3.906 | 3.912 | 3.926 | 3.933 | 3.946 | 3.953 |
| **4.75** | 3.919 | 3.926 | 3.940 | 3.946 | 3.960 | 3.967 |
| **4.50** | 3.926 | 3.933 | 3.946 | 3.953 | 3.967 | 3.974 |
| **4.25** | 3.940 | 3.946 | 3.960 | 3.967 | 3.980 | 3.987 |

In the upper-left corner of the table, we again see the best outcome. Dropping a 5.50 disaster for a 2.75 stud means a final pERA of 3.885, an improvement of .115 and a climb up into seventh in ERA. That's a move of three places in the model league. To the lower right, we see a more modest improvement, not enough to gain an ERA point, but moving the team closer to ninth.

### WHIP

Finally, we repeat the process for WHIP, with a baseline of a 1.257 WHIP in 1,325 pIP; 13th place. Again, let's start just by dropping a 55-pIP bad performer:

- Dropping a 1.30 pWHIP pitcher: 1.254 team pWHIP, improving by .003, and gaining three slots to 10th
- 1.35 pitcher: 1.253, ninth
- 1.40 pitcher: 1.250, ninth
- 1.45 pitcher: 1.248, eighth
- 1.50 pitcher: 1.246, eighth

Just dropping that 1.50-WHIP dud has jumped the team five points. And more significant gains come when dropping bad is paired with adding good:

| pWHIP of Pitcher Dropped | pWHIP of Pitcher Added | | | | |
|---|---|---|---|---|---|
| | **1.00** | **1.05** | **1.10** | **1.15** | **1.20** |
| **1.50** | 1.155 | 1.152 | 1.150 | 1.149 | 1.146 |
| **1.45** | 1.157 | 1.155 | 1.152 | 1.151 | 1.149 |
| **1.40** | 1.159 | 1.157 | 1.155 | 1.153 | 1.151 |
| **1.35** | 1.161 | 1.158 | 1.156 | 1.155 | 1.152 |
| **1.30** | 1.215 | 1.213 | 1.211 | 1.209 | 1.207 |

Similar to the ERA story above, we see a relatively gigantic move in the upper left, where the awful 1.50 guy is subbed by a 1.00 guy, creating a final pWHIP of 1.155. In the experts' league, that would vault this team into second, an 11-place jump. Down in the lower right, the result is muted, but even at that, it moves this sample team from 13th to fourth.

### Closing Thoughts

Needless to say, much depends on how each category is stratified in any league, but the main point is that we can make late

moves in the decimals. It's not easy—finding a 55-pIP guy with a 2.75/1.00 projected line means basically trading for Max Scherzer, and his owner might not want to give him up. But the tables also show there are useful gains even with lesser players, and of course there are gains just from dropping the guys who are killing us.

We have to make sure the gains in decimals aren't offset by losses in counting stats. Also, we must check the status of nearby competitors, who might have added bad decimals players in search of counting stats, and could help us by moving backwards in decimal categories. Aim where you and your opponents will be at the end, not where they are now.

## Trading Tips

*by Fred Zinkie*

We all need to make trades to win our leagues. And while every negotiation is unique, here are some quick tips that should make anyone more effective on the trade market.

*1. Learn how the other owner wishes to communicate.* Some owners prefer email, others like to get an offer via the league website, some prefer direct messaging on Twitter, and texting is often a desirable option in a local league. And there are even some folks who still want a phone call. The easy way to figure this out is to send your initial contact in multiple ways. Generally, the other owner's preferred communication tool is the one they use to send their initial reply.

*2. All negotiations start with an offer.* Don't beat around the bush—give the other owner something concrete to work with. You can start with your best deal or merely a respectable proposal, but you should get the ball rolling with a firm offer.

*3. Check your ego at the door.* You don't know everything about player analysis or fantasy strategy. Your opinions on player values and what makes sense for your opponent's roster are just your opinions. You should enter trade talks with low expectations and a willingness to accept a different point of view. The other owner is not necessarily wrong when they disagree with you.

*4. Be willing to unbalance your roster.* In general, owners who draft a balanced team and then only seek out deals that maintain that balance throughout the season are going to miss out on many buying opportunities. To improve your roster—especially during the first half of the season—you should be willing to have stretches with weak hitting, poor starting pitching, or a lack of saves sources. For those who are committed to wheeling and dealing, the goal is to acquire value. And sometimes the acquisition of more value means working with an unbalanced roster until you find the next deal. Of course, this means that your entire roster is available. Billy Hamilton may be your only steals source, but he will be off your roster in a heartbeat if you can get great value for him. You can later use your upgraded roster to acquire a speedster in a separate deal.

*5. Proofread.* You may only get one chance to present your case. Wise owners always take the extra minute to proofread their communication and ensure that their thoughts are clearly explained. Beyond looking for basic typos, you should be sure that all the players mentioned are the ones you intend to mention. You must also resist the urge to ramble. Keep your initial communication down to a couple sentences. And while additional replies may be longer, they should always be pared down to the essential points.

*6. Be prompt.* Trading is sometimes inconvenient, but an active trader makes time when the opportunity arises. You may have planned on going to bed early on Sunday, but you can operate on a little less sleep during Monday if a league-mate is willing to go back-and-forth on a deal later in the evening. I'm not suggesting that you get yourself fired or abandon your children in search of the perfect trade, but in general, you should be willing to work around your competitor's schedule.

*7. Send multiple offers.* Submitting multiple offers gives more power to the other owner, as you have put the ball in their court to pick the proposal they like best. If you don't want to take the time to send multiple offers via your league website, you can at least put in your communication that you would be willing to trade Player X, Y, or Z to get your desired return.

*8. Be clear about all the players who interest you on the other team.* An easy way to start negotiations is to mention all of the players who interest you on the other team during your initial communication. Again, this gives some control to the other owner, who can now tell you who among the players you seek is the most available.

*9. The message board is your last resort.* Posting trade messages usually makes you appear desperate. This is especially true if you are trying to unload a certain player. Like a house that sits on the real estate market, the asking price on your player tends to drop once a couple days have passed since you informed your entire league that he is available.

*10. Look for owners who may be desperate.* Because most owners seek to achieve balance on their rosters, you can often find opportunities to obtain value by helping those who have an immediate need. And you can always help an owner in need since you are the rare owner who is willing to unbalance their roster to obtain value. Start by looking at your standings, as owners who are low in a roto category are likely to trade away value in order to address their weakness. You can also look through the specific rosters to find teams who have subpar players at certain positions or are dealing with key injuries.

*11. Look for owners who have a surplus.* On the opposite end of the spectrum, owners are sometimes willing to make reasonable deals when they have a surplus of a certain position or skill. Checking your standings to find the owner who is running away with the steals category could get you a speedster at a reasonable price. And the owner who has found one of this year's emerging aces may be eager to trade away a stud starter.

*12. Have the guts to trade away overachievers.* This is one of the hardest tips to put into practice, but experience tells us that most players who have surprising stretches return to normal at some point. Christian Villanueva was one of nine players to hit 15 homers by the end of last May, and on the same date, Gio Gonzalez ranked sixth in the majors with a 2.10 ERA. If it sometimes seems too good to be true, it probably is.

## Reading Between the Lines: An Injury Primer
*by James C. Ferretti, DO*

*"An investment in knowledge pays the best interest."—Ben Franklin*

It used to be enough in fantasy baseball to have more and better information. Now, information—especially injury information—is everywhere, so one of the biggest advantages is having a better understanding of both injuries and the corresponding medical terms. Being able to better evaluate player injuries and terminology can give you a significant edge. First, we'll examine some anatomy and specific injuries, and then turn to common terms that team staff and media often use.

Here's a quick overview of the human musculoskeletal system; divided into five broad categories with their general function:

- *Bones:* The rigid support framework which is also a foundation for the other moving parts.
- *Cartilage:* Soft tissue that acts as a cushion and prevents wear—usually in areas where bones are close to each other.
- *Muscles:* Bundles of fibers that bend and stretch to perform work.
- *Tendons:* Bundles of (less bendy/stretchy) fibers that attach muscles to bones.
- *Ligaments:* Bundles of (even less bendy/stretchy) fibers that attach bones to other bones.

So what happens when the above are damaged/injured?

Injuries (even small or partial tears) to certain structures in a player's throwing arm will almost always require surgical repair and/or a long recovery. Examples include the ulnar collateral ligament (UCL or "Tommy John" ligament) in the elbow; the labrum (the cartilage ring in the shoulder joint); and the rotator cuff tendons in the shoulder. If your player is dealing with one of these injuries, it's probably prudent to initiate Plan B. With other common injury scenarios, you can gain a significant advantage by better understanding how injuries are reported/treated.

**Fractures**

A fracture is simply a break in a bone, which means it isn't able to act as a stabilizer or absorb/distribute forces. If a bone can't do that, then none of the other parts of the system around that bone can do their jobs well either. This is especially detrimental if that job includes catching, throwing, or swinging a bat.

How do you fix it? Line up the broken pieces, stabilize the area, and allow the bone to heal. Sometimes a cast is enough to accomplish this; sometimes surgery is needed to add plates, pins, rods, or screws.

Time to heal and/or long-term effects? Usually 4-6 weeks, though sometimes longer if surgery is needed. But once the new bone has matured, it's pretty much as good as new.

**Strains/Sprains**

These are tears of the fibers of muscles/tendons (strains) and ligaments (sprains). Most doctors categorize them on a Grade 1, 2, and 3 scale. Some characteristics:

- *Grade 1*—"Microtear": An injury to the fibers of the muscle, tendon or ligament that's not visible. An MRI will show abnormal appearance/signal at and around the site of injury, but this is where you often hear the term "no structural damage." This type of injury is less significant if it occurs in a large muscle (as opposed to a ligament/tendon) – as there are plenty of other intact fibers to pick up the slack for the injured portion.

- *Grade 2*—"Partial tear": An injury to some of the fibers visible on an MRI, but some of the fibers remain intact. These injuries can also be further broken down in severity as low, moderate or high-grade depending on the size of the tear. A low-grade partial tear only involves a few fibers, while high-grade suggests almost all of the fibers are torn.

- *Grade 3*—"Complete tear": Exactly what it sounds like—all of the fibers are torn. Importantly, a "grade 3 sprain/strain" sounds way more benign than "complete tear", but they both mean the same thing. When you hear/read "grade 3," you know it's severe.

How do you fix them? For lower grade injuries: rest. Higher grade injuries usually will require surgical repair (and then rest).

Time to heal and/or long-term effects? It can be tough to pin down an exact recovery timetable due to factors like player age, mechanism of injury or new vs. recurrent injury. A rough estimate for healing times is 2-4 weeks for a Grade 1, 4-8 weeks for a Grade 2, and at least 8 weeks for a Grade 3.

Unfortunately, there can be long-term effects. Whether the injury heals itself or requires the assistance of an orthopedic surgeon, the repaired areas contain fibrous ("scar") tissue, which is neither as strong nor as flexible as the original tissue. The injured area loses some functional strength and is more prone to re-injury after healing. The bigger the tear, the more scar tissue there is.

The fantasy takeaway is to pay attention when a reported injury timeline significantly deviates from the above estimates. For example, if your player has a Grade 2 injury, but is being reported to return "in 2-3 weeks," be skeptical.

### Inflammation

Inflammation is an irritation of the soft tissues, often from overuse or a repetitive motion and the structures affected get "angry." On an MRI, inflammation looks almost identical to a Grade 1 injury. Even though they may occur for different reasons, inflammation and a Grade 1 strain/sprain can behave similarly—and both can be extremely painful and keep a player out for weeks.

How do you fix it? Like a Grade 1 injury, inflammation requires rest so the soft tissue has enough time to time to heal.

Long-term effects? The injury/pain can recur, or even worsen without adequate time to heal. (So, maybe your player coming back a little early isn't such good news after all). In fact, consider holding on to a replacement player who's filling in admirably until you see your injured player demonstrate that he really is healthy.

The main takeaway is that when someone dismisses your player's injury as "just a little inflammation," don't just take it at face value. The player could still be looking at an extended absence.

With a quick anatomy lesson under our belts, let's look more closely at a few widely-used injury terms used by MLB clubs and/or media outlets. By knowing a bit more about these terms, you can gain an advantage by reading between the lines.

### "No structural damage"

We referenced this above, and while the diagnosis sounds reassuring, it's often misleading. When medical imagers unaffiliated with MLB clubs make an injury diagnosis, they might term it a fracture, dislocation, soft tissue tear, or inflammation; all of which are bad news. Or they may call it "normal," or "negative," which is good news. But rarely would they describe an injury in terms of "no structural damage."

Why? "No structural damage" is not an actual diagnosis. Rather, it's a way of saying that whatever body part being imaged is intact—there is no broken bone or soft tissue tear. But importantly, the term is not the same as a "normal" or "negative" diagnosis, because there can still be an injury present. When you hear "no structural damage" for one of your players, continue to keep a close eye on the situation, and maybe even line up that replacement player.

### "Day-to-Day"

We hear this often, and like "no structural damage," "day-to-day" sounds reassuring. Don't be fooled, as the term doesn't really tell you anything.

What a team doctor or media outlet is really saying: "We aren't sure how bad the injury is, or how long the player will be out." That's far more worrisome. Again, stay alert for further updates. You might be amazed at how often you can get the jump on grabbing a potential replacement by staying vigilant while a player is "day-to-day."

### "X-Rays are negative"

Imaging a player is usually prompted by a sudden or increasing onset of pain, or other suspicious symptoms: a "pop" or loss of range of motion, tightness or looseness in the joint, etc. An X-ray is usually ordered first.

The problem is that most baseball injuries are to soft tissue, which is never diagnosed with an X-ray alone. Unless there's suspicion of a broken bone or joint injury, the X-ray probably isn't going to tell you much. Despite this, we often see well-meaning writers and analysts take a "negative" X-ray report and use it to justify that the injury is "not believed to be serious."

In fact, X-rays are only one part of the diagnostic process. While a clean X-ray eliminates some possible outcomes, it rarely tells the whole story. Don't assume that just because an "X-ray was negative" that a player isn't seriously injured. Instead, take the time to line up a potential replacement for that player while you await the results of more definitive imaging/tests (like a CAT scan or MRI). Let other owners be lulled into a false sense of security from the "X-rays are negative" talk.

### Conclusion

Every player injury (and the associated recovery process) is unique and there is no shortage of information out there to sort through. Hopefully, this overview will assist you in gaining an advantage by reading between the lines and altering your approach —both before you draft, and as you manage your in-season roster.

## The New Normal (Maybe)

*by Matt Cederholm*

Over the past few years, home runs have jumped while stolen bases have declined. In addition, changes to the DL rules and how teams deploy bullpens have led to innings being spread across more pitchers. While trends in baseball often reverse course, these trends look more like a "new normal" (with one caveat at the end).

The increase in home runs (and offense in general) has been tied to changes in how baseballs are manufactured, beginning in mid-2015. In 2014, the top 220 fantasy hitters slugged 3,068 homers. In 2018, it was 4,167—a 36% increase. It's not due to more fly balls; the fly ball rate was right around 35% in both seasons. However, the league-wide hr/f jumped from 10% in 2014 to 13% in 2018. And it's not hitters swinging harder; exit velocities have not changed appreciably.

This has implications on both sides of your roster.

### Hitters

We'll start with a look at some aggregate hitting statistics.

**Hitter Comparison, Top 220 Hitters**

| | | HR | | | | SB | | | | AVG | | |
|---|---|---|---|---|---|---|---|---|---|---|---|---|
| | Total | SD | Top 10% | <$5 | Total | SD | Top 10% | <$5 | AVG | SD | Top 10% | <$5 |
| 2018 | 4,167 | 9.7 | 19% | 23% | 1,741 | 9.0 | 38% | 18% | .265 | 25.4 | .310 | .254 |
| 2014 | 3,068 | 8.5 | 22% | 23% | 2,106 | 11.0 | 37% | 20% | .270 | 27.1 | .320 | .252 |

Notes: SD=Standard Deviation; Top 10%=total/average for the top 10% of players in that category; <$5=% of cumulative stats from players valued at $5 or less

Even though MLB-wide HR output pulled back a bit in 2018, HR are still up by 36% for this population. But the overall increase is less important than the distribution. In the new normal, the top hitters have a lower share of the HR total. In fact, the top 10% of hitters have seen their home runs increase by 18%, while the middle two-thirds have seen a 46% jump. This makes intuitive sense if batted balls are traveling farther—the best hitters see many of their HR clear the fence by a wide margin, whereas the middle group has a lot more close calls.

Stolen bases have declined by about 17% (the bulk of the decrease is due to fewer singles and walks). There is also less dispersion among players—in 2014, four players stole 50+ bases (okay, Ben Revere had 49), while in 2018, only three players broke 40. However, the top 10% of base stealers did not decline as a percentage of total steals, suggesting that the decline is evenly distributed.

### Pitchers

**Pitcher Comparison, Top 175 Pitchers**

| | | W | | | | SV* | | | | K | | |
|---|---|---|---|---|---|---|---|---|---|---|---|---|
| | Total | SD | Top 10% | <$5 | Total | SD | Top 10% | <$5 | Total | SD | Top 10% | <$5 |
| 2018 | 1,336 | 4.7 | 22% | 45% | 983 | 13.3 | 60% | | 20,337 | 57.6 | 9% | 47% |
| 2014 | 1,469 | 5.0 | 21% | 44% | 1,060 | 15.8 | 65% | | 20,128 | 56.2 | 14% | 44% |

Notes: SD=Standard Deviation; Top 10%=total/average for the top 10% of players in that category; <$5=% of cumulative stats from players valued at $5 or less
*SD and Top 10% for saves was calculated using only players with at least one save

Total league wins can't really decline, so what we see here is that more wins are going to below-replacement pitchers outside the Top 175, mainly the result of changes in pitcher usage.

Saves among draft-worthy pitchers are down as well. The decline is mostly due to usage, similar to wins, where more below-replacement pitchers earned saves.

Not shown on the table: ERA is up slightly (3.27 in 2018 vs. 3.02 in 2014); WHIP is virtually unchanged. Elite starters are a little more elite in ERA (.90 runs below average ERA in 2014 vs. 1.18 in 2018), by about a third of a run.

The distribution of value has also shifted—the top 10% of pitchers are about 11% more valuable as a group in the current environment. These trends come down to one factor: there are far more innings going to lower-tier pitchers (see table in next section).

### The 10-Day DL

The 10-day DL has had a significant impact on roster management. Since the inception of the 10-day DL in 2017, the number of DL moves increased by 30%. That means less playing time for draftable players and more for replacements.

It turns out that the 10-day DL has had a negligible effect on hitters—there was virtually no change in the total AB accumulated among the top 220 hitters. On the pitching side, though, the total innings pitched (among the Top 175) declined by 11%.

**Number of Pitchers, Innings Threshold**

| | 30+ | 180+ | 200+ |
|---|---|---|---|
| 2018 | 467 | 32 | 13 |
| 2014 | 415 | 66 | 34 |

So now what?

While it's interesting to discover trends and see how the game has changed, the real question is how to adjust your draft strategy to account for these changes. Let's review what we've discovered:

- Home runs are up by more than 35%. The players most impacted are the early-to-middle-rounders.
- Steals are down, but aside from having fewer elite speed sources, the distribution hasn't changed much.
- Wins and saves among draftable players are down, so set your targets a bit lower.
- Strikeouts are about the same (a 2% difference isn't all that significant) and there's no clear change in how strikeouts are distributed.
- We're seeing fewer innings and starts from the draftable pitchers, though other than using reliability indicators, it's difficult to predict which pitchers will be impacted.

The bottom line: yes, you can wait on power. A little bit. But don't wait too long and don't forego too much power in the early rounds. Don't assume that there's power all over the place; there's not that much excess power relative to your opponents at the 2018 draft table.

You need less speed to compete. The elite SB sources are a tick more valuable, but just a tick. While speed is certainly more scarce, it's more scarce for everyone. Remember, it's the distribution that matters most, and that hasn't changed all that much.

Almost a third of the reliable pitchers (A or B Health) and almost half of the less reliable pitchers will hit the DL at some point. Wins are down, ERA is up, but the one relatively stable pitching stat is strikeouts, so target them.

With more players hitting the DL, roster management is a greater challenge. Focus on positional flexibility, and don't ignore pitching when building your reserve roster. As we've seen, pitchers are most affected by the change.

### The Caveat (Why "Maybe" is Included in the Title)

There is compelling evidence that the main driver in the home run surge is the baseball itself. Sure, hitters may be more aware of the plane of the bat and how it affects launch angle, but the sudden jump in home runs since 2015 is not consistent with a long-term trend (also, fly ball rates haven't changed). It is, however, consistent with changes in how the balls are manufactured.

A long-term trend usually doesn't reverse suddenly. A change in baseball manufacturing can. Just as quickly as the home runs appeared, they can go away. It doesn't seem likely that MLB wants that to happen but keep it in the back of your mind. We may be in a new normal, but that could be corrected at some point.

The following section contains player boxes for every batter who had significant playing time in 2018 and/or is expected to get fantasy roster-worthy plate appearances in 2019. You will find some prospects here, specifically the most impactful names who we project to play in 2019. For more complete prospect coverage, see our Prospects section.

## Snapshot Section

**The top band of each player box contains the following information:**

**Age** as of Opening Day 2019.

**Bats** shows which side of the plate he bats from—(L)eft, (R)ight or (B)oth.

**Positions:** Up to three defensive positions are listed and represent those for which he appeared a minimum of 20 games in 2018.

**Ht/Wt:** Each batter's height and weight.

**Reliability Grades** analyze each batter's forecast risk, on an A-F scale. High grades go to those who have accumulated few disabled list days (Health), have a history of substantial and regular major league playing time (PT/Exp) and have displayed consistent performance over the past three years, using RC/G (Consist).

**LIMA Plan Grade** evaluates how well a batter would fit into a team using the LIMA Plan draft strategy. Best grades go to batters who have excellent base skills, are expected to see regular playing time, and are in the $10-$30 Rotisserie dollar range. Lowest grades will go to poor skills, few AB and values less than $5 or more than $30.

**Random Variance Score (Rand Var)** measures the impact random variance had on the batter's 2018 stats and the probability that his 2019 performance will exceed or fall short of 2018. The variables tracked are those prone to regression—h%, hr/f and xBA to BA variance. Players are rated on a scale of –5 to +5 with positive scores indicating rebounds and negative scores indicating corrections. Note that this score is computer-generated and the projections will override it on occasion.

**Mayberry Method (MM)** acknowledges the imprecision of the forecasting process by projecting player performance in broad strokes. The four digits of MM each represent a fantasy-relevant skill—power, speed, batting average and playing time (PA)—and are all on a scale of 0 to 5.

**Commentaries** for each batter provide a brief analysis of his skills and the potential impact on performance in 2019. MLB statistics are listed first for those who played only a portion of 2018 at the major league level. Note that these commentaries generally look at performance related issues only. Role and playing time expectations may impact these analyses, so you will have to adjust accordingly. Upside (UP) and downside (DN) statistical potential appears for some players; these are less grounded in hard data and more speculative of skills potential.

## Player Stat Section

The past five years' statistics represent the total accumulated in the majors as well as in Triple-A, Double-A ball and various foreign leagues during each year. All non-major league stats have been converted to a major league equivalent (MLE) performance level. Minor league levels below Double-A are not included.

Nearly all baseball publications separate a player's statistical experiences in the major leagues from the minor leagues and outside leagues. While this may be appropriate for official record-keeping purposes, it is not an easy-to-analyze snapshot of a player's complete performance for a given year.

Bill James has proven that minor league statistics (converted to MLEs), at Double-A level or above, provide as accurate a record of a player's performance as major league statistics. Other researchers have also devised conversion factors for foreign leagues. Since these are adequate barometers, we include them in the pool of historical data for each year.

**Team designations:** An asterisk (*) appearing with a team name means that Triple-A and/or Double-A numbers are included in that year's stat line. Any stints of less than 20 AB are not included (to screen out most rehab appearances). A designation of "a/a" means the stats were accumulated at both AA and AAA levels that year. "for" represents a foreign or independent league. The designation "2TM" appears whenever a player was on more than one major league team, crossing leagues, in a season. "2AL" and "2NL" represent more than one team in the same league. Players who were cut during the season and finished 2018 as a free agent are designated as FAA (Free agent, AL) and FAN (Free agent, NL).

**Stats:** Descriptions of all the categories appear in the Encyclopedia.

- The leading decimal point has been suppressed on some categories to conserve space.
- Data for platoons (vL, vR), balls-in-play (G/L/F) and consistency (Wk#, DOM, DIS) are for major league performance only.
- Formulas that use BIP data, like xBA and xPX, only appear for years in which G/L/F data is available.

Batting average is presented alongside xBA. On base average and slugging average appear next, and the combined On Base Plus Slugging (OPS). OPS splits vs. left-handed and right-handed pitchers appear after the overall OPS column.

Batting eye and contact skill are measured with walk rate (bb%), contact rate (ct%). Eye is the ratio of walks to strikeouts.

Once the ball leaves the bat, it will either be a (G)round ball, (L)ine drive or (F)ly ball. Hit rate (h%), also referred to as batting average on balls-in-play (BABIP), measures how often a ball put into play results in a base hit. Hard contact index (HctX) measures the frequency of hard contact, compared to overall league levels. Looking at the ratio of fly balls is a good springboard to the Power gauges. Linear weighted power index (PX) measures a batter's skill at hitting extra base hits as compared to overall league levels. xPX measures power by assessing how hard the ball is being hit (rather than the outcomes of those hits). And the ratio of home runs to fly balls shows the results of those hits.

To assess speed, first look at on base average (does he get on base?), then Spd (is he fast enough to steal bases?), then SBO (how often is he attempting to steal bases?) and finally, SB% (when he attempts, what is his rate of success?).

In looking at consistency, we use weekly Base Performance Value (BPV) levels. Starting with the total number of weeks the batter accumulated stats (#Wk), the percentage of DOMinating weeks (BPV over 50) and DISaster weeks (BPV under 0) is shown. The larger the variance between DOM and DIS, the greater the consistency.

The final section includes several overall performance measures: runs created per game (RC/G), runs above replacement (RAR), Base performance value (BPV), Base performance index (BPX, which is BPV indexed to each year's league average) and the Rotisserie value (R$).

## 2019 Projections

Forecasts are computed from a player's trends over the past five years. Adjustments were made for leading indicators and variances between skill and statistical output. After reviewing the leading indicators, you might opt to make further adjustments.

Although each year's numbers include all playing time at the Double-A level or above, the 2019 forecast only represents potential playing time at the major league level, and again is highly preliminary.

Note that the projected Rotisserie values in this book will not necessarily align with each player's historical actuals. Since we currently have no idea who is going to play shortstop for the Orioles, or whether Victor Robles is going to break camp with the Nationals, it is impossible to create a finite pool of playing time, something which is required for valuation. So the projections are roughly based on a 12-team AL/NL league, and include an inflated number of plate appearances, league-wide. This serves to flatten the spread of values and depress individual player dollar

projections. In truth, a $25 player in this book might actually be worth $21, or $28. This level of precision is irrelevant in a process that is driven by market forces anyway. So, don't obsess over it.

Be aware of other sources that publish perfectly calibrated Rotisserie values over the winter. They are likely making arbitrary decisions as to where free agents are going to sign and who is going to land jobs in the spring. We do not make those leaps of faith here.

Bottom line… It is far too early to be making definitive projections for 2019, especially on playing time. Focus on the skill levels and trends, then consult BaseballHQ.com for playing time revisions as players change teams and roles become more defined. A free projections update will be available online in March.

## Do-it-yourself analysis

Here are some data points you can look at in doing your own player analysis:

- Variance between vLH and vRH OPS
- Growth or decline in walk rate (bb%)
- Growth or decline in contact rate (ct%)
- Growth or decline in G/L/F individually, or concurrent shifts
- Variance in 2018 hit rate (h%) to 2015-2017 three-year average
- Variance between Avg and xBA each year
- Growth or decline in HctX level
- Growth or decline in power index (PX) rate
- Variance between PX and xPX each year
- Variance in 2018 hr/f rate to 2015-2017 three-year average
- Growth or decline in statistically scouted speed (Spd) score
- Concurrent growth/decline of gauges like ct%, FB, PX, xPX, hr/f
- Concurrent growth/decline of gauges like OB, Spd, SBO, SB%
- Trends in DOM/DIS splits

## Abreu,Jose

| | | | |
|---|---|---|---|
| Age: 32 | Bats: R | Pos: 1B | |
| Ht: 6' 3" | Wt: 255 | | |
| Health | B | LIMA Plan | B |
| PT/Exp | A | Rand Var | +2 |
| Consist | C | MM | 4245 |

Aug surgery to "groin area," Sept thigh infection ended MLB-low performance. Career-low h% didn't help BA, but xBA questions full BA bounceback given earlier overachievement. GB% stroke and tepid xPX may cap his HR ceiling. An injury-related pass is tempting given track record, but penciling in another 30-100-.290 seems risky.

| Yr | Tm | AB | R | HR | RBI | SB | BA | xBA | OBP | SLG | OPS | vL | vR | bb% | ct% | Eye | G | L | F | h% | HctX | PX | xPX | hr/f | Spd | SBO | SB% | #Wk | DOM | DIS | RC/G | RAR | BPV | BPX | R$ |
|---|---|---|---|---|---|---|---|---|---|---|---|---|---|---|---|---|---|---|---|---|---|---|---|---|---|---|---|---|---|---|---|---|---|---|---|
| 14 | CHW | 556 | 80 | 36 | 107 | 3 | 317 | 307 | 383 | 581 | 964 | 1098 | 919 | 8 | 76 | 0.39 | 45 | 23 | 31 | 36 | 120 | 185 | 132 | 27% | 72 | 3% | 75% | 24 | 71% | 17% | 8.09 | 59.0 | 94 | 254 | $35 |
| 15 | CHW | 613 | 88 | 30 | 101 | 0 | 290 | 276 | 347 | 502 | 850 | 658 | 908 | 6 | 77 | 0.28 | 47 | 21 | 32 | 33 | 115 | 136 | 116 | 20% | 81 | 0% | 0% | 26 | 54% | 31% | 6.01 | 18.2 | 55 | 149 | $26 |
| 16 | CHW | 624 | 67 | 25 | 100 | 0 | 293 | 263 | 353 | 468 | 820 | 840 | 816 | 7 | 80 | 0.38 | 45 | 21 | 33 | 33 | 106 | 103 | 93 | 15% | 71 | 1% | 0% | 27 | 44% | 33% | 5.71 | 14.8 | 39 | 111 | $22 |
| 17 | CHW | 621 | 95 | 33 | 102 | 3 | 304 | 293 | 354 | 552 | 906 | 1033 | 866 | 5 | 81 | 0.29 | 45 | 18 | 36 | 33 | 133 | 134 | 123 | 18% | 99 | 2% | 100% | 27 | 59% | 22% | 6.95 | 26.5 | 73 | 221 | $28 |
| 18 | CHW | 499 | 68 | 22 | 78 | 2 | 265 | 276 | 325 | 473 | 798 | 915 | 769 | 7 | 78 | 0.34 | 44 | 21 | 35 | 30 | 109 | 127 | 103 | 16% | 69 | 2% | 100% | 24 | 46% | 25% | 5.19 | 11.1 | 50 | 167 | $16 |
| 1st Half | | 318 | 39 | 12 | 47 | 1 | 267 | 273 | 324 | 465 | 789 | 882 | 768 | 6 | 80 | 0.33 | 45 | 19 | 36 | 30 | 106 | 124 | 105 | 13% | 67 | 1% | 100% | 15 | 53% | 20% | 5.08 | 2.9 | 53 | 177 | $19 |
| 2nd Half | | 181 | 29 | 10 | 31 | 1 | 260 | 276 | 328 | 486 | 815 | 963 | 771 | 8 | 75 | 0.36 | 43 | 24 | 32 | 29 | 114 | 133 | 99 | 22% | 77 | 2% | 100% | 9 | 33% | 33% | 5.39 | 3.3 | 48 | 160 | $11 |
| **19** | **Proj** | **588** | **83** | **26** | **96** | **2** | **282** | **274** | **340** | **485** | **825** | **922** | **797** | **7** | **78** | **0.33** | **45** | **21** | **34** | **32** | **116** | **121** | **108** | **16%** | **81** | **2%** | **87%** | | | | **5.68** | **15.2** | **47** | **157** | **$22** |

## Acuna,Ronald

| | | | |
|---|---|---|---|
| Age: 21 | Bats: R | Pos: LF | |
| Ht: 6' 0" | Wt: 180 | | |
| Health | B | LIMA Plan | D+ |
| PT/Exp | D | Rand Var | -2 |
| Consist | B | MM | 4535 |

26-64-.293 with 16 SB in 433 AB at ATL. Late-April arrival, May knee sprain couldn't slow epic debut that came with tons of skill support: xPX says hr/f can stick; Spd, green light bolster SB floor; 2nd half BPV hints pitchers couldn't adjust. Contact issues might stunt BA growth for now, but this ride has already taken off.

| Yr | Tm | AB | R | HR | RBI | SB | BA | xBA | OBP | SLG | OPS | vL | vR | bb% | ct% | Eye | G | L | F | h% | HctX | PX | xPX | hr/f | Spd | SBO | SB% | #Wk | DOM | DIS | RC/G | RAR | BPV | BPX | R$ |
|---|---|---|---|---|---|---|---|---|---|---|---|---|---|---|---|---|---|---|---|---|---|---|---|---|---|---|---|---|---|---|---|---|---|---|---|
| 14 | | | | | | | | | | | | | | | | | | | | | | | | | | | | | | | | | | | |
| 15 | | | | | | | | | | | | | | | | | | | | | | | | | | | | | | | | | | | |
| 16 | | | | | | | | | | | | | | | | | | | | | | | | | | | | | | | | | | | |
| 17 | a/a | 442 | 63 | 17 | 59 | 28 | 331 | | 376 | 524 | 900 | | | 7 | 76 | 0.29 | | | | 41 | | 115 | | | 97 | 36% | 62% | | | | 6.81 | | 39 | 118 | $31 |
| 18 | ATL * | 523 | 86 | 27 | 67 | 20 | 276 | 252 | 344 | 499 | 843 | 992 | 890 | 9 | 71 | 0.36 | 42 | 18 | 39 | 34 | 117 | 139 | 140 | 21% | 139 | 19% | 77% | 21 | 52% | 33% | 6.01 | 26.7 | 59 | 197 | $27 |
| 1st Half | | 216 | 30 | 7 | 16 | 6 | 238 | 213 | 302 | 379 | 682 | 773 | 823 | 8 | 70 | 0.30 | 48 | 14 | 39 | 31 | 108 | 96 | 120 | 18% | 127 | 15% | 75% | 8 | 38% | 50% | 3.83 | -2.0 | 13 | 43 | $6 |
| 2nd Half | | 307 | 56 | 20 | 49 | 14 | 303 | 275 | 379 | 583 | 962 | 1106 | 914 | 10 | 73 | 0.40 | 40 | 20 | 40 | 36 | 121 | 168 | 148 | 22% | 140 | 21% | 78% | 13 | 62% | 23% | 7.88 | 32.0 | 89 | 297 | $42 |
| **19** | **Proj** | **579** | **90** | **31** | **73** | **21** | **281** | **259** | **345** | **510** | **855** | **902** | **837** | **8** | **72** | **0.32** | **41** | **19** | **39** | **34** | **116** | **143** | **137** | **19%** | **132** | **20%** | **71%** | | | | **6.01** | **23.6** | **55** | **185** | **$31** |

## Adames,Willy

| | | | |
|---|---|---|---|
| Age: 23 | Bats: R | Pos: SS | |
| Ht: 6' 0" | Wt: 200 | | |
| Health | A | LIMA Plan | B |
| PT/Exp | B | Rand Var | -5 |
| Consist | A | MM | 2405 |

10-34-.278 with 6 SB in 288 AB at TAM. Shiny debut from elite prospect on the surface, but we're not sold yet: too many GBs, not enough oomph (HctX/xPX) to sustain HR pace; bat-to-ball skills, xBA raise BA doubts; SB% says he hasn't figured out how to use plus wheels. Keeper star is bright, but take a rain check for now.

| Yr | Tm | AB | R | HR | RBI | SB | BA | xBA | OBP | SLG | OPS | vL | vR | bb% | ct% | Eye | G | L | F | h% | HctX | PX | xPX | hr/f | Spd | SBO | SB% | #Wk | DOM | DIS | RC/G | RAR | BPV | BPX | R$ |
|---|---|---|---|---|---|---|---|---|---|---|---|---|---|---|---|---|---|---|---|---|---|---|---|---|---|---|---|---|---|---|---|---|---|---|---|
| 14 | | | | | | | | | | | | | | | | | | | | | | | | | | | | | | | | | | | |
| 15 | | | | | | | | | | | | | | | | | | | | | | | | | | | | | | | | | | | |
| 16 | aa | 486 | 77 | 9 | 49 | 11 | 249 | | 338 | 382 | 720 | | | 12 | 72 | 0.48 | | | | 33 | | 93 | | | 113 | 12% | 63% | | | | 4.29 | | 22 | 63 | $11 |
| 17 | aaa | 506 | 69 | 9 | 58 | 10 | 258 | | 337 | 383 | 721 | | | 11 | 70 | 0.41 | | | | 35 | | 85 | | | 111 | 10% | 66% | | | | 4.38 | | 6 | 18 | $12 |
| 18 | TAM * | 533 | 74 | 13 | 63 | 9 | 268 | 212 | 335 | 386 | 722 | 675 | 786 | 9 | 68 | 0.32 | 52 | 18 | 30 | 37 | 87 | 77 | 89 | 17% | 164 | 10% | 51% | 17 | 24% | 65% | 4.33 | 3.5 | 2 | 7 | $17 |
| 1st Half | | 267 | 29 | 5 | 33 | 4 | 251 | 197 | 319 | 369 | 688 | 641 | 661 | 9 | 65 | 0.28 | 41 | 21 | 38 | 37 | 61 | 79 | 101 | 13% | 161 | 10% | 45% | 5 | 0% | 80% | 3.82 | -1.1 | -9 | -30 | $11 |
| 2nd Half | | 266 | 45 | 8 | 30 | 5 | 284 | 220 | 352 | 403 | 755 | 684 | 817 | 9 | 71 | 0.35 | 55 | 17 | 28 | 38 | 96 | 76 | 86 | 18% | 132 | 10% | 56% | 12 | 33% | 58% | 4.88 | 7.0 | 3 | 10 | $22 |
| **19** | **Proj** | **567** | **77** | **16** | **59** | **11** | **253** | **226** | **327** | **392** | **718** | **665** | **741** | **10** | **70** | **0.37** | **49** | **18** | **32** | **34** | **82** | **92** | **92** | **12%** | **156** | **11%** | **60%** | | | | **4.26** | **5.1** | **3** | **10** | **$17** |

## Adams,Matt

| | | | |
|---|---|---|---|
| Age: 30 | Bats: L | Pos: 1B | |
| Ht: 6' 3" | Wt: 245 | | |
| Health | C | LIMA Plan | C+ |
| PT/Exp | D | Rand Var | +2 |
| Consist | C | MM | 4033 |

Raised eyebrows with 9 HR in May, but June DL stint (finger), 2nd half h% sealed another "meh" season. Strong xPX history with FB% stroke build outstanding power foundation, while xBA and ct% uptick hint at mild BA rebound. His struggles vL make volume an issue, but if he ever finds 400 AB again... UP: 30 HR.

| Yr | Tm | AB | R | HR | RBI | SB | BA | xBA | OBP | SLG | OPS | vL | vR | bb% | ct% | Eye | G | L | F | h% | HctX | PX | xPX | hr/f | Spd | SBO | SB% | #Wk | DOM | DIS | RC/G | RAR | BPV | BPX | R$ |
|---|---|---|---|---|---|---|---|---|---|---|---|---|---|---|---|---|---|---|---|---|---|---|---|---|---|---|---|---|---|---|---|---|---|---|---|
| 14 | STL | 527 | 55 | 15 | 68 | 3 | 288 | 265 | 321 | 457 | 779 | 528 | 854 | 5 | 78 | 0.23 | 35 | 24 | 41 | 34 | 109 | 124 | 130 | 9% | 87 | 4% | 60% | 26 | 54% | 19% | 5.22 | 15.3 | 50 | 135 | $19 |
| 15 | STL | 175 | 14 | 5 | 24 | 1 | 240 | 237 | 280 | 377 | 657 | 499 | 683 | 5 | 77 | 0.24 | 41 | 20 | 39 | 29 | 125 | 95 | 120 | 10% | 57 | 3% | 100% | 13 | 38% | 31% | 3.59 | -9.2 | 12 | 32 | $1 |
| 16 | STL | 297 | 37 | 16 | 54 | 0 | 249 | 252 | 309 | 471 | 780 | 822 | 773 | 8 | 73 | 0.31 | 32 | 20 | 48 | 29 | 108 | 142 | 159 | 15% | 70 | 2% | 0% | 25 | 40% | 36% | 4.85 | -4.2 | 43 | 123 | $7 |
| 17 | 2 NL | 339 | 46 | 20 | 65 | 0 | 274 | 266 | 319 | 522 | 841 | 583 | 896 | 6 | 74 | 0.26 | 39 | 18 | 43 | 32 | 112 | 146 | 123 | 18% | 73 | 0% | 0% | 26 | 54% | 35% | 5.88 | -0.2 | 49 | 148 | $11 |
| 18 | 2 NL | 306 | 42 | 21 | 57 | 0 | 239 | 259 | 309 | 477 | 786 | 622 | 811 | 8 | 76 | 0.37 | 35 | 21 | 45 | 25 | 110 | 132 | 141 | 20% | 60 | 0% | 0% | 25 | 44% | 40% | 4.80 | -2.7 | 46 | 153 | $9 |
| 1st Half | | 153 | 24 | 13 | 36 | 0 | 275 | 291 | 351 | 575 | 926 | 670 | 978 | 9 | 76 | 0.43 | 35 | 23 | 41 | 28 | 125 | 169 | 156 | 27% | 52 | 0% | 0% | 13 | 54% | 23% | 6.94 | 9.5 | 75 | 250 | $14 |
| 2nd Half | | 153 | 18 | 8 | 21 | 0 | 203 | 226 | 265 | 379 | 644 | 533 | 656 | 7 | 76 | 0.31 | 34 | 18 | 48 | 21 | 94 | 96 | 126 | 14% | 83 | 0% | 0% | 12 | 33% | 58% | 3.10 | -7.9 | 23 | 77 | $4 |
| **19** | **Proj** | **325** | **42** | **19** | **57** | **0** | **254** | **254** | **311** | **479** | **790** | **634** | **817** | **7** | **75** | **0.31** | **36** | **20** | **45** | **28** | **109** | **131** | **136** | **17%** | **68** | **1%** | **45%** | | | | **5.02** | **2.4** | **32** | **107** | **$11** |

## Adrianza,Ehire

| | | | |
|---|---|---|---|
| Age: 29 | Bats: B | Pos: SS 3B | |
| Ht: 6' 1" | Wt: 170 | | |
| Health | F | LIMA Plan | C+ |
| PT/Exp | F | Rand Var | -2 |
| Consist | B | MM | 2323 |

Career utility man couldn't capitalize on early PT shot, but there are signs of life if you really squint. Efficient on basepaths despite 2018 red light, xPX hints at a few more HR, becoming slightly less futile vR. Multi-position eligible too, so while ct% slide, xBA say BA is maxed out, there are worse end game darts to throw.

| Yr | Tm | AB | R | HR | RBI | SB | BA | xBA | OBP | SLG | OPS | vL | vR | bb% | ct% | Eye | G | L | F | h% | HctX | PX | xPX | hr/f | Spd | SBO | SB% | #Wk | DOM | DIS | RC/G | RAR | BPV | BPX | R$ |
|---|---|---|---|---|---|---|---|---|---|---|---|---|---|---|---|---|---|---|---|---|---|---|---|---|---|---|---|---|---|---|---|---|---|---|---|
| 14 | SF | 97 | 10 | 0 | 5 | 1 | 237 | 226 | 279 | 299 | 578 | 499 | 605 | 5 | 77 | 0.23 | 36 | 25 | 39 | 31 | 60 | 63 | 71 | 0% | 108 | 9% | 50% | 15 | 27% | 47% | 2.66 | -1.4 | 3 | 8 | -$1 |
| 15 | SF * | 284 | 22 | 2 | 22 | 7 | 227 | 216 | 295 | 302 | 596 | 517 | 590 | 9 | 77 | 0.42 | 53 | 14 | 32 | 29 | 59 | 56 | 59 | 0% | 117 | 14% | 69% | 13 | 23% | 54% | 2.92 | -7.3 | 7 | 19 | $1 |
| 16 | SF * | 98 | 7 | 3 | 9 | 1 | 237 | 240 | 263 | 354 | 617 | 853 | 484 | 3 | 82 | 0.20 | 41 | 20 | 39 | 27 | 68 | 68 | 62 | 11% | 111 | 26% | 14% | 11 | 36% | 36% | 2.45 | -6.7 | 23 | 66 | -$1 |
| 17 | MIN * | 199 | 31 | 2 | 27 | 8 | 251 | 234 | 323 | 347 | 670 | 855 | 630 | 9 | 81 | 0.56 | 41 | 20 | 39 | 30 | 84 | 57 | 88 | 4% | 134 | 18% | 78% | 21 | 38% | 29% | 3.87 | -4.4 | 30 | 91 | $5 |
| 18 | MIN | 335 | 42 | 6 | 39 | 5 | 251 | 245 | 301 | 379 | 680 | 682 | 679 | 7 | 76 | 0.29 | 38 | 25 | 37 | 32 | 101 | 90 | 99 | 7% | 104 | 8% | 83% | 27 | 26% | 44% | 3.91 | -1.8 | 20 | 67 | $7 |
| 1st Half | | 187 | 24 | 4 | 19 | 4 | 262 | 251 | 315 | 412 | 727 | 782 | 705 | 7 | 73 | 0.28 | 36 | 27 | 36 | 34 | 96 | 106 | 102 | 8% | 120 | 9% | 100% | 15 | 33% | 47% | 4.59 | 3.4 | 30 | 100 | $8 |
| 2nd Half | | 148 | 18 | 2 | 20 | 1 | 236 | 237 | 283 | 338 | 621 | 536 | 649 | 6 | 78 | 0.31 | 39 | 23 | 38 | 29 | 108 | 71 | 94 | 5% | 91 | 6% | 50% | 12 | 17% | 42% | 3.15 | -3.6 | 12 | 40 | $5 |
| **19** | **Proj** | **392** | **47** | **9** | **45** | **8** | **247** | **244** | **300** | **378** | **678** | **743** | **646** | **7** | **78** | **0.33** | **40** | **22** | **38** | **30** | **89** | **83** | **86** | **8%** | **109** | **12%** | **71%** | | | | **3.77** | **-2.2** | **22** | **73** | **$11** |

## Aguilar,Jesus

| | | | |
|---|---|---|---|
| Age: 29 | Bats: R | Pos: 1B | |
| Ht: 6' 3" | Wt: 250 | | |
| Health | A | LIMA Plan | B |
| PT/Exp | C | Rand Var | -4 |
| Consist | C | MM | 4035 |

Example #972 of "draft skills, not roles," as he seized starting gig in April and blew past last year's "UP: 30 HR". Out over his skis a bit with 1st half h% spike, but power skills were sublime and he paired them with better plate approach. Mashed nearly equally vL/R too, so while BA is likely at peak, he'll keep thumping.

| Yr | Tm | AB | R | HR | RBI | SB | BA | xBA | OBP | SLG | OPS | vL | vR | bb% | ct% | Eye | G | L | F | h% | HctX | PX | xPX | hr/f | Spd | SBO | SB% | #Wk | DOM | DIS | RC/G | RAR | BPV | BPX | R$ |
|---|---|---|---|---|---|---|---|---|---|---|---|---|---|---|---|---|---|---|---|---|---|---|---|---|---|---|---|---|---|---|---|---|---|---|---|
| 14 | CLE * | 460 | 55 | 15 | 62 | 0 | 251 | 242 | 327 | 407 | 733 | 471 | 133 | 10 | 73 | 0.41 | 48 | 19 | 33 | 31 | 90 | 125 | 92 | 0% | 66 | 0% | 0% | 8 | 0% | 88% | 4.52 | 4.5 | 33 | 89 | $11 |
| 15 | CLE * | 529 | 48 | 16 | 81 | 0 | 244 | 281 | 296 | 394 | 690 | 583 | 818 | 7 | 75 | 0.29 | 42 | 33 | 25 | 30 | 215 | 107 | 171 | 0% | 58 | 0% | 0% | 4 | 0% | 50% | 3.93 | -22.5 | 17 | 46 | $9 |
| 16 | CLE * | 521 | 50 | 25 | 74 | 0 | 218 | 199 | 278 | 409 | 687 | 0 | 0 | 8 | 78 | 0.38 | 80 | 0 | 20 | 23 | 63 | 113 | 125 | 0% | 53 | 0% | 0% | 3 | 0% | 33% | 3.71 | -26.0 | 35 | 100 | $5 |
| 17 | MIL | 279 | 40 | 16 | 52 | 0 | 265 | 252 | 331 | 505 | 837 | 889 | 806 | 8 | 66 | 0.27 | 41 | 21 | 38 | 34 | 121 | 154 | 165 | 23% | 80 | 0% | 0% | 27 | 44% | 48% | 5.71 | -1.5 | 30 | 91 | $8 |
| 18 | MIL | 492 | 80 | 35 | 108 | 0 | 274 | 269 | 352 | 539 | 890 | 929 | 876 | 10 | 71 | 0.41 | 35 | 24 | 41 | 32 | 115 | 163 | 158 | 24% | 45 | 0% | 0% | 28 | 57% | 25% | 6.64 | 21.5 | 50 | 167 | $23 |
| 1st Half | | 220 | 41 | 19 | 54 | 0 | 309 | 288 | 368 | 627 | 995 | 1122 | 961 | 9 | 71 | 0.34 | 30 | 25 | 45 | 36 | 121 | 195 | 182 | 26% | 57 | 0% | 0% | 15 | 53% | 20% | 8.61 | 22.9 | 77 | 257 | $28 |
| 2nd Half | | 272 | 39 | 16 | 54 | 0 | 246 | 253 | 339 | 467 | 806 | 824 | 797 | 12 | 71 | 0.46 | 40 | 23 | 38 | 29 | 110 | 136 | 138 | 22% | 48 | 0% | 0% | 13 | 62% | 31% | 5.28 | 4.2 | 32 | 107 | $20 |
| **19** | **Proj** | **539** | **76** | **35** | **103** | **0** | **259** | **264** | **332** | **509** | **841** | **879** | **824** | **9** | **71** | **0.36** | **38** | **23** | **40** | **30** | **117** | **154** | **160** | **23%** | **56** | **0%** | **0%** | | | | **5.77** | **15.7** | **39** | **129** | **$22** |

## Ahmed,Nick

| | | | |
|---|---|---|---|
| Age: 29 | Bats: R | Pos: SS | |
| Ht: 6' 2" | Wt: 195 | | |
| Health | D | LIMA Plan | B+ |
| PT/Exp | D | Rand Var | +2 |
| Consist | B | MM | 3245 |

Elite leather helped him win SS job out of camp. Now the lumber is catching up, as he ditched GB% stroke, made harder contact, and didn't sacrifice plate skills to do so. Red light on basepaths should continue given SB% futility and he's vulnerable vR, but if xPX/HctX and new batted ball profile hold... UP: .270 BA, 20+ HR.

| Yr | Tm | AB | R | HR | RBI | SB | BA | xBA | OBP | SLG | OPS | vL | vR | bb% | ct% | Eye | G | L | F | h% | HctX | PX | xPX | hr/f | Spd | SBO | SB% | #Wk | DOM | DIS | RC/G | RAR | BPV | BPX | R$ |
|---|---|---|---|---|---|---|---|---|---|---|---|---|---|---|---|---|---|---|---|---|---|---|---|---|---|---|---|---|---|---|---|---|---|---|---|
| 14 | ARI * | 477 | 45 | 4 | 34 | 9 | 247 | 236 | 286 | 334 | 620 | 428 | 577 | 5 | 84 | 0.35 | 42 | 18 | 40 | 29 | 88 | 66 | 85 | 4% | 129 | 15% | 53% | 9 | 22% | 56% | 3.08 | -3.1 | 41 | 111 | $7 |
| 15 | ARI | 421 | 49 | 9 | 34 | 4 | 226 | 242 | 275 | 359 | 634 | 803 | 575 | 6 | 81 | 0.36 | 46 | 17 | 37 | 26 | 77 | 82 | 78 | 7% | 145 | 10% | 44% | 25 | 28% | 28% | 3.12 | -8.3 | 47 | 127 | $3 |
| 16 | ARI | 284 | 26 | 4 | 20 | 5 | 218 | 239 | 265 | 299 | 564 | 633 | 536 | 5 | 80 | 0.26 | 48 | 21 | 30 | 26 | 88 | 50 | 92 | 6% | 112 | 11% | 71% | 16 | 19% | 50% | 2.51 | -18.5 | 4 | 11 | $0 |
| 17 | ARI | 167 | 24 | 6 | 21 | 3 | 251 | 261 | 298 | 419 | 717 | 1078 | 568 | 6 | 77 | 0.26 | 48 | 20 | 32 | 30 | 99 | 96 | 91 | 15% | 124 | 19% | 43% | 13 | 38% | 46% | 3.84 | -3.3 | 34 | 103 | $3 |
| 18 | ARI | 516 | 61 | 16 | 70 | 5 | 234 | 270 | 290 | 411 | 700 | 769 | 664 | 7 | 79 | 0.37 | 41 | 24 | 35 | 27 | 114 | 107 | 124 | 11% | 96 | 8% | 56% | 28 | 46% | 29% | 3.88 | 0.9 | 46 | 153 | $11 |
| 1st Half | | 263 | 33 | 10 | 33 | 2 | 221 | 270 | 280 | 407 | 687 | 869 | 601 | 7 | 78 | 0.37 | 40 | 25 | 35 | 24 | 110 | 110 | 130 | 14% | 92 | 10% | 40% | 15 | 53% | 20% | 3.55 | -3.4 | 46 | 153 | $9 |
| 2nd Half | | 253 | 28 | 6 | 37 | 3 | 249 | 268 | 300 | 415 | 715 | 681 | 734 | 7 | 79 | 0.37 | 42 | 24 | 34 | 29 | 119 | 103 | 118 | 9% | 105 | 7% | 75% | 13 | 38% | 38% | 4.24 | 2.1 | 48 | 160 | $12 |
| **19** | **Proj** | **525** | **62** | **19** | **62** | **5** | **250** | **266** | **298** | **427** | **725** | **851** | **663** | **6** | **79** | **0.31** | **44** | **22** | **34** | **28** | **104** | **104** | **106** | **13%** | **115** | **9%** | **49%** | | | | **4.16** | **3.1** | **38** | **127** | **$14** |

RYAN BLOOMFIELD

## Albies,Ozzie

Age: 22 Bats: B Pos: 2B | Ht: 5' 8" Wt: 165
Health A | PT/Exp A | Consist B
LIMA Plan B+ | Rand Var +2 | MM 2525

Blazing April (.293, 9 HR, 20 RBI) turned heads, but 2nd half power collapse, PX in minors curb HR outlook. Steady bat-to-ball skills and xBA back BA repeat, but low bb% could limit SB opportunities despite prowess on basepaths. Even with fewer HR, his speed, age, and pedigree make for a solid investment.

| Yr | Tm | AB | R | HR | RBI | SB | BA | xBA | OBP | SLG | OPS | vL | vR | bb% | ct% | Eye | G | L | F | h% | HctX | PX | xPX | hr/f | Spd | SBO | SB% | #Wk | DOM | DIS | RC/G | RAR | BPV | BPX | R$ |
|---|---|---|---|---|---|---|---|---|---|---|---|---|---|---|---|---|---|---|---|---|---|---|---|---|---|---|---|---|---|---|---|---|---|---|---|
| 14 | | | | | | | | | | | | | | | | | | | | | | | | | | | | | | | | | | | |
| 15 | | | | | | | | | | | | | | | | | | | | | | | | | | | | | | | | | | | |
| 16 | a/a | 552 | 83 | 6 | 53 | 30 | 272 | | 338 | 372 | 710 | | | 9 | 81 | 0.52 | | | | 33 | | 59 | | | 135 | 26% | 69% | | | | 4.30 | | 31 | 89 | $23 |
| 17 | ATL * | 628 | 94 | 14 | 65 | 27 | 278 | 245 | 326 | 429 | 755 | 926 | 773 | 7 | 79 | 0.35 | 41 | 19 | 40 | 33 | 107 | 83 | 113 | 8% | 161 | 18% | 90% | 10 | 60% | 20% | 5.11 | 1.5 | 47 | 142 | $26 |
| 18 | ATL | 639 | 105 | 24 | 72 | 14 | 261 | 268 | 305 | 452 | 757 | 905 | 696 | 5 | 82 | 0.31 | 39 | 21 | 40 | 29 | 104 | 109 | 100 | 12% | 121 | 13% | 82% | 28 | 57% | 18% | 4.72 | 8.4 | 64 | 213 | $24 |
| 1st Half | | 349 | 64 | 17 | 48 | 7 | 275 | 288 | 316 | 510 | 826 | 891 | 600 | 5 | 82 | 0.29 | 38 | 22 | 40 | 29 | 115 | 135 | 116 | 15% | 112 | 15% | 70% | 15 | 80% | 7% | 5.48 | 13.1 | 81 | 270 | $32 |
| 2nd Half | | 290 | 41 | 7 | 24 | 7 | 245 | 245 | 290 | 383 | 673 | 922 | 569 | 6 | 82 | 0.34 | 40 | 20 | 40 | 28 | 90 | 78 | 81 | 8% | 133 | 11% | 100% | 13 | 31% | 31% | 3.86 | -2.7 | 43 | 143 | $14 |
| **19** | **Proj** | **589** | **91** | **16** | **61** | **18** | **267** | **251** | **318** | **427** | **746** | **892** | **691** | **6** | **81** | **0.36** | **40** | **20** | **40** | **31** | **103** | **92** | **103** | **9%** | **137** | **16%** | **81%** | | | | **4.71** | **9.1** | **54** | **180** | **$21** |

## Alfaro,Jorge

Age: 26 Bats: R Pos: CA | Ht: 6' 2" Wt: 225
Health A | PT/Exp D | Consist A
LIMA Plan C | Rand Var -5 | MM 3405

A breakout doesn't appear imminent for former top C prospect. Lack of contact, xBA are major roadblocks, and while LD%/h% combo prevented BA freefall in 2018, that's unlikely to happen again. 2nd half power spike hints at more HR to come, but now with three straight negative BPVs, he's best left for two-catcher leagues.

| Yr | Tm | AB | R | HR | RBI | SB | BA | xBA | OBP | SLG | OPS | vL | vR | bb% | ct% | Eye | G | L | F | h% | HctX | PX | xPX | hr/f | Spd | SBO | SB% | #Wk | DOM | DIS | RC/G | RAR | BPV | BPX | R$ |
|---|---|---|---|---|---|---|---|---|---|---|---|---|---|---|---|---|---|---|---|---|---|---|---|---|---|---|---|---|---|---|---|---|---|---|---|
| 14 | aa | 88 | 10 | 3 | 11 | 0 | 239 | | 280 | 393 | 673 | | | 5 | 72 | 0.20 | | | | 29 | | 116 | | | 91 | 0% | 0% | | | | 3.68 | | 21 | 57 | $0 |
| 15 | aa | 190 | 17 | 4 | 16 | 2 | 222 | | 251 | 369 | 621 | | | 4 | 66 | 0.11 | | | | 32 | | 124 | | | 100 | 9% | 59% | | | | 2.99 | | 1 | 3 | $0 |
| 16 | PHI * | 420 | 51 | 12 | 50 | 2 | 236 | 226 | 267 | 373 | 640 | 333 | 286 | 4 | 69 | 0.13 | 63 | 13 | 25 | 32 | 0 | 95 | -24 | 0% | 92 | 5% | 50% | 3 | 0% | 100% | 3.26 | -14.5 | -11 | -31 | $5 |
| 17 | PHI * | 431 | 41 | 12 | 51 | 1 | 240 | 200 | 269 | 369 | 637 | 500 | 1054 | 4 | 61 | 0.10 | 53 | 16 | 31 | 36 | 61 | 94 | 68 | 22% | 108 | 2% | 43% | 9 | 22% | 56% | 3.29 | -9.8 | -36 | -109 | $4 |
| 18 | PHI | 344 | 35 | 10 | 37 | 3 | 262 | 213 | 324 | 407 | 731 | 726 | 732 | 5 | 60 | 0.13 | 48 | 23 | 29 | 41 | 83 | 113 | 102 | 17% | 130 | 4% | 100% | 27 | 19% | 63% | 4.24 | 7.2 | -18 | -60 | $7 |
| 1st Half | | 199 | 18 | 5 | 16 | 0 | 251 | 211 | 297 | 387 | 684 | 642 | 701 | 5 | 59 | 0.12 | 51 | 24 | 25 | 40 | 69 | 111 | 71 | 17% | 136 | 0% | 0% | 15 | 13% | 67% | 3.78 | 2.0 | -24 | -80 | $4 |
| 2nd Half | | 145 | 17 | 5 | 21 | 3 | 276 | 213 | 358 | 434 | 792 | 878 | 770 | 5 | 61 | 0.14 | 43 | 22 | 34 | 42 | 103 | 116 | 142 | 16% | 109 | 8% | 100% | 12 | 25% | 58% | 4.93 | 6.1 | -17 | -57 | $11 |
| **19** | **Proj** | **435** | **45** | **15** | **50** | **4** | **243** | **219** | **306** | **402** | **708** | **581** | **755** | **4** | **62** | **0.12** | **49** | **20** | **31** | **35** | **78** | **116** | **95** | **18%** | **124** | **5%** | **82%** | | | | **3.76** | **4.0** | **-22** | **-73** | **$10** |

## Alford,Anthony

Age: 24 Bats: R Pos: LF | Ht: 6' 1" Wt: 215
Health B | PT/Exp F | Consist F
LIMA Plan D | Rand Var -1 | MM 2301

0-1-.105 with 1 SB in 19 AB at TOR. Speed-first OF struggled after March hamstring strain, which adds to lengthy injury history. Jump in whiffs says he now comes with more BA risk, and while value depends on his wheels, 2nd half SB% could limit SB upside. Weak power, poor contact say tough adjustment period lies ahead.

| Yr | Tm | AB | R | HR | RBI | SB | BA | xBA | OBP | SLG | OPS | vL | vR | bb% | ct% | Eye | G | L | F | h% | HctX | PX | xPX | hr/f | Spd | SBO | SB% | #Wk | DOM | DIS | RC/G | RAR | BPV | BPX | R$ |
|---|---|---|---|---|---|---|---|---|---|---|---|---|---|---|---|---|---|---|---|---|---|---|---|---|---|---|---|---|---|---|---|---|---|---|---|
| 14 | | | | | | | | | | | | | | | | | | | | | | | | | | | | | | | | | | | |
| 15 | | | | | | | | | | | | | | | | | | | | | | | | | | | | | | | | | | | |
| 16 | | | | | | | | | | | | | | | | | | | | | | | | | | | | | | | | | | | |
| 17 | TOR * | 265 | 38 | 5 | 22 | 16 | 292 | 275 | 369 | 405 | 775 | 0 | 750 | 11 | 80 | 0.61 | 60 | 20 | 20 | 35 | 65 | 73 | 124 | 0% | 86 | 22% | 83% | 2 | 50% | 50% | 5.57 | 6.1 | 27 | 82 | $12 |
| 18 | TOR * | 394 | 48 | 4 | 30 | 16 | 216 | 198 | 268 | 309 | 576 | 322 | 250 | 7 | 66 | 0.21 | 40 | 20 | 40 | 31 | 25 | 76 | -2 | 0% | 109 | 27% | 67% | 4 | 0% | 100% | 2.61 | -17.6 | -24 | -80 | $6 |
| 1st Half | | 192 | 26 | 3 | 15 | 10 | 202 | 196 | 272 | 293 | 565 | 384 | 400 | 9 | 64 | 0.27 | 38 | 25 | 38 | 30 | 30 | 71 | 4 | 0% | 125 | 26% | 81% | 2 | 0% | 100% | 2.64 | -9.1 | -29 | -97 | $6 |
| 2nd Half | | 202 | 22 | 2 | 15 | 6 | 229 | 167 | 263 | 324 | 587 | 0 | 0 | 4 | 69 | 0.15 | 50 | 0 | 50 | 33 | 0 | 81 | -27 | 0% | 87 | 29% | 52% | 2 | 0% | 100% | 2.57 | -9.9 | -24 | -80 | $7 |
| **19** | **Proj** | **129** | **17** | **2** | **10** | **5** | **231** | **226** | **293** | **349** | **642** | **642** | **642** | **8** | **72** | **0.31** | **44** | **20** | **36** | **30** | | **85** | | **7%** | **97** | **24%** | **69%** | | | | **3.33** | **-5.0** | **1** | **5** | **$4** |

## Allen,Greg

Age: 26 Bats: B Pos: CF | Ht: 6' 0" Wt: 175
Health A | PT/Exp F | Consist B
LIMA Plan C+ | Rand Var -2 | MM 1533

2-20-.257 with 21 SB in 265 AB at CLE. Green light in 2nd half drove value in speed-starved environment. MLB ct% (78% career) bodes well for BA, particularly if he can sustain that LD% stroke. HctX hints at possibility that he could be more than just a one-trick pony, but recent OBP remains a hurdle to full-time AB.

| Yr | Tm | AB | R | HR | RBI | SB | BA | xBA | OBP | SLG | OPS | vL | vR | bb% | ct% | Eye | G | L | F | h% | HctX | PX | xPX | hr/f | Spd | SBO | SB% | #Wk | DOM | DIS | RC/G | RAR | BPV | BPX | R$ |
|---|---|---|---|---|---|---|---|---|---|---|---|---|---|---|---|---|---|---|---|---|---|---|---|---|---|---|---|---|---|---|---|---|---|---|---|
| 14 | | | | | | | | | | | | | | | | | | | | | | | | | | | | | | | | | | | |
| 15 | | | | | | | | | | | | | | | | | | | | | | | | | | | | | | | | | | | |
| 16 | aa | 145 | 21 | 3 | 11 | 6 | 269 | | 342 | 398 | 740 | | | 10 | 82 | 0.60 | | | | 32 | | 76 | | | 122 | 28% | 47% | | | | 4.16 | | 46 | 131 | $4 |
| 17 | CLE * | 293 | 37 | 3 | 25 | 18 | 240 | 218 | 288 | 328 | 616 | 1300 | 345 | 6 | 76 | 0.29 | 58 | 8 | 35 | 31 | 99 | 62 | 31 | 11% | 113 | 29% | 89% | 6 | 17% | 33% | 3.37 | -12.1 | 4 | 12 | $8 |
| 18 | CLE * | 436 | 60 | 4 | 31 | 30 | 260 | 241 | 306 | 352 | 658 | 484 | 691 | 6 | 75 | 0.27 | 47 | 24 | 29 | 34 | 101 | 66 | 84 | 3% | 126 | 37% | 73% | 21 | 24% | 52% | 3.67 | -4.7 | 5 | 17 | $18 |
| 1st Half | | 229 | 30 | 2 | 9 | 11 | 247 | 226 | 296 | 347 | 643 | 476 | 567 | 6 | 71 | 0.24 | 41 | 26 | 33 | 34 | 95 | 76 | 90 | 5% | 151 | 28% | 70% | 9 | 22% | 78% | 3.42 | -5.0 | 3 | 10 | $10 |
| 2nd Half | | 207 | 30 | 2 | 22 | 19 | 274 | 254 | 316 | 357 | 673 | 489 | 765 | 6 | 80 | 0.31 | 50 | 24 | 26 | 33 | 107 | 56 | 81 | 3% | 107 | 45% | 75% | 12 | 25% | 33% | 3.96 | -1.1 | 11 | 37 | $26 |
| **19** | **Proj** | **327** | **44** | **5** | **26** | **21** | **256** | **254** | **322** | **374** | **696** | **502** | **738** | **7** | **77** | **0.31** | **46** | **24** | **29** | **32** | **102** | **77** | **85** | **7%** | **120** | **34%** | **77%** | | | | **3.94** | **-1.9** | **25** | **85** | **$15** |

## Almora,Albert

Age: 25 Bats: R Pos: CF | Ht: 6' 2" Wt: 190
Health A | PT/Exp C | Consist C
LIMA Plan C+ | Rand Var -3 | MM 1235

Early h% led to profit before 2nd half skills crashed. Lack of power and GB% stroke put pressure on BA to be his main source of value, as the red light on basepaths shut out SB. Youth says falling xBA, dip in hard contact may just be a blip, but without secondary skills, this currently looks like an -only league OF.

| Yr | Tm | AB | R | HR | RBI | SB | BA | xBA | OBP | SLG | OPS | vL | vR | bb% | ct% | Eye | G | L | F | h% | HctX | PX | xPX | hr/f | Spd | SBO | SB% | #Wk | DOM | DIS | RC/G | RAR | BPV | BPX | R$ |
|---|---|---|---|---|---|---|---|---|---|---|---|---|---|---|---|---|---|---|---|---|---|---|---|---|---|---|---|---|---|---|---|---|---|---|---|
| 14 | aa | 142 | 16 | 2 | 8 | 0 | 212 | | 220 | 312 | 532 | | | 1 | 83 | 0.07 | | | | 24 | | 72 | | | 117 | 5% | 0% | | | | 2.13 | | 30 | 81 | -$2 |
| 15 | aa | 405 | 56 | 5 | 37 | 7 | 248 | | 294 | 361 | 655 | | | 6 | 87 | 0.51 | | | | 27 | | 74 | | | 108 | 12% | 63% | | | | 3.52 | | 55 | 149 | $7 |
| 16 | CHC * | 432 | 50 | 6 | 47 | 8 | 268 | 280 | 288 | 383 | 672 | 827 | 724 | 3 | 84 | 0.17 | 43 | 28 | 29 | 31 | 96 | 72 | 92 | 12% | 113 | 12% | 70% | 12 | 42% | 17% | 3.81 | -10.5 | 34 | 97 | $10 |
| 17 | CHC | 299 | 39 | 8 | 46 | 1 | 298 | 273 | 338 | 445 | 782 | 898 | 711 | 6 | 82 | 0.36 | 49 | 21 | 30 | 34 | 98 | 85 | 69 | 11% | 111 | 1% | 100% | 27 | 37% | 33% | 5.51 | 3.7 | 44 | 133 | $9 |
| 18 | CHC | 444 | 62 | 5 | 41 | 1 | 286 | 246 | 323 | 378 | 701 | 742 | 684 | 5 | 81 | 0.29 | 51 | 20 | 29 | 34 | 82 | 61 | 47 | 5% | 122 | 3% | 25% | 28 | 25% | 39% | 4.25 | 0.1 | 23 | 77 | $11 |
| 1st Half | | 241 | 44 | 4 | 26 | 1 | 332 | 265 | 369 | 461 | 830 | 855 | 820 | 6 | 83 | 0.37 | 49 | 20 | 31 | 39 | 93 | 82 | 64 | 6% | 129 | 4% | 33% | 15 | 40% | 13% | 6.34 | 14.1 | 50 | 167 | $19 |
| 2nd Half | | 203 | 18 | 1 | 15 | 0 | 232 | 222 | 267 | 281 | 548 | 616 | 518 | 4 | 79 | 0.21 | 53 | 20 | 27 | 29 | 69 | 36 | 25 | 2% | 112 | 2% | 0% | 13 | 8% | 69% | 2.40 | -10.7 | -10 | -33 | $1 |
| **19** | **Proj** | **434** | **55** | **7** | **46** | **2** | **273** | **257** | **307** | **381** | **688** | **766** | **648** | **5** | **82** | **0.27** | **49** | **22** | **29** | **32** | **88** | **68** | **58** | **7%** | **122** | **4%** | **51%** | | | | **4.05** | **-1.1** | **14** | **48** | **$12** |

## Alonso,Peter

Age: 24 Bats: R Pos: 1B | Ht: 6'3" Wt: 245
Health A | PT/Exp F | Consist D
LIMA Plan D+ | Rand Var 0 | MM 4013

Took step foward with 36 HR across AA/AAA, though his 128 K suggests he sold out for it, which introduces some BA risk. Patient approach supports OBP foundation that could help extend the leash once he gets the call to NYM. While PX hints the power could play quickly, whiffs could create rocky MLB transition.

| Yr | Tm | AB | R | HR | RBI | SB | BA | xBA | OBP | SLG | OPS | vL | vR | bb% | ct% | Eye | G | L | F | h% | HctX | PX | xPX | hr/f | Spd | SBO | SB% | #Wk | DOM | DIS | RC/G | RAR | BPV | BPX | R$ |
|---|---|---|---|---|---|---|---|---|---|---|---|---|---|---|---|---|---|---|---|---|---|---|---|---|---|---|---|---|---|---|---|---|---|---|---|
| 14 | | | | | | | | | | | | | | | | | | | | | | | | | | | | | | | | | | | |
| 15 | | | | | | | | | | | | | | | | | | | | | | | | | | | | | | | | | | | |
| 16 | | | | | | | | | | | | | | | | | | | | | | | | | | | | | | | | | | | |
| 17 | aa | 45 | 7 | 2 | 5 | 0 | 291 | | 322 | 541 | 863 | | | 4 | 82 | 0.26 | | | | 32 | | 136 | | | 116 | 0% | 0% | | | | 6.26 | | 84 | 255 | $0 |
| 18 | a/a | 478 | 66 | 25 | 85 | 0 | 229 | | 311 | 443 | 754 | | | 11 | 68 | 0.37 | | | | 28 | | 142 | | | 82 | 3% | 0% | | | | 4.42 | | 33 | 110 | $12 |
| 1st Half | | 276 | 37 | 13 | 48 | 0 | 237 | | 334 | 419 | 752 | | | 13 | 70 | 0.48 | | | | 29 | | 117 | | | 84 | 4% | 0% | | | | 4.44 | | 26 | 87 | $14 |
| 2nd Half | | 202 | 28 | 13 | 37 | 0 | 219 | | 277 | 476 | 753 | | | 7 | 65 | 0.23 | | | | 27 | | 178 | | | 92 | 0% | 0% | | | | 4.31 | | 47 | 157 | $9 |
| **19** | **Proj** | **349** | **48** | **15** | **63** | **0** | **233** | **232** | **306** | **428** | **734** | **734** | **734** | **9** | **69** | **0.33** | **38** | **19** | **43** | **29** | | **131** | | **15%** | **91** | **2%** | **0%** | | | | **4.25** | **-5.5** | **14** | **46** | **$9** |

## Alonso,Yonder

Age: 32 Bats: L Pos: 1B | Ht: 6'1" Wt: 230
Health B | PT/Exp B | Consist F
LIMA Plan B | Rand Var 0 | MM 3135

Second year of high-launch approach not as fruitful as first. Fewer fly balls, xPX regression say there's only room for 20-ish HR, which gets lost in today's power-rich environment. His ct% hasn't recovered since 2016, which limits any BA upside, and his struggles vL carry platoon AB risk that move him down CI rankings.

| Yr | Tm | AB | R | HR | RBI | SB | BA | xBA | OBP | SLG | OPS | vL | vR | bb% | ct% | Eye | G | L | F | h% | HctX | PX | xPX | hr/f | Spd | SBO | SB% | #Wk | DOM | DIS | RC/G | RAR | BPV | BPX | R$ |
|---|---|---|---|---|---|---|---|---|---|---|---|---|---|---|---|---|---|---|---|---|---|---|---|---|---|---|---|---|---|---|---|---|---|---|---|
| 14 | SD | 267 | 27 | 7 | 27 | 6 | 240 | 279 | 285 | 397 | 682 | 607 | 699 | 6 | 87 | 0.47 | 43 | 19 | 38 | 25 | 120 | 110 | 121 | 8% | 69 | 13% | 86% | 16 | 44% | 13% | 3.85 | -2.3 | 68 | 184 | $5 |
| 15 | SD | 354 | 50 | 5 | 31 | 2 | 282 | 269 | 361 | 381 | 742 | 669 | 762 | 10 | 86 | 0.88 | 49 | 23 | 28 | 32 | 108 | 65 | 73 | 6% | 85 | 6% | 29% | 19 | 37% | 11% | 4.64 | -3.0 | 46 | 124 | $9 |
| 16 | OAK | 482 | 52 | 7 | 56 | 3 | 253 | 268 | 316 | 367 | 683 | 617 | 694 | 8 | 85 | 0.61 | 44 | 23 | 33 | 29 | 111 | 76 | 94 | 5% | 60 | 3% | 75% | 27 | 41% | 30% | 3.97 | -12.4 | 36 | 103 | $7 |
| 17 | 2 AL | 451 | 72 | 28 | 67 | 2 | 266 | 265 | 365 | 501 | 866 | 679 | 903 | 13 | 74 | 0.58 | 34 | 23 | 43 | 30 | 108 | 135 | 124 | 19% | 66 | 1% | 100% | 27 | 44% | 33% | 6.34 | 12.4 | 51 | 155 | $15 |
| 18 | CLE | 516 | 64 | 23 | 83 | 0 | 250 | 243 | 317 | 421 | 738 | 619 | 776 | 9 | 76 | 0.41 | 38 | 22 | 40 | 29 | 106 | 99 | 105 | 14% | 54 | 0% | 0% | 28 | 39% | 39% | 4.54 | 1.7 | 20 | 67 | $14 |
| 1st Half | | 255 | 33 | 12 | 43 | 0 | 247 | 246 | 318 | 435 | 753 | 621 | 797 | 9 | 77 | 0.44 | 38 | 19 | 42 | 28 | 111 | 111 | 109 | 14% | 53 | 0% | 0% | 15 | 47% | 40% | 4.67 | -0.7 | 33 | 110 | $14 |
| 2nd Half | | 261 | 31 | 11 | 40 | 0 | 253 | 241 | 316 | 406 | 722 | 617 | 756 | 9 | 75 | 0.39 | 38 | 24 | 38 | 30 | 101 | 88 | 101 | 14% | 64 | 0% | 0% | 13 | 31% | 38% | 4.41 | -2.7 | 11 | 37 | $14 |
| **19** | **Proj** | **473** | **61** | **19** | **68** | **2** | **256** | **252** | **329** | **426** | **755** | **630** | **787** | **10** | **78** | **0.49** | **39** | **22** | **39** | **29** | **108** | **100** | **107** | **14%** | **75** | **2%** | **74%** | | | | **4.80** | **0.5** | **26** | **85** | **$14** |

BRANT CHESSER

## Altherr,Aaron

| Age: 28 | Bats: R | Pos: RF | Health | D | LIMA Plan | D |
|---|---|---|---|---|---|---|
| Ht: 6' 5" | Wt: 215 | | PT/Exp | D | Rand Var | +2 |
| | | | Consist | F | MM | 4313 |

8-38-.181 with 3 SB in 243 AB at PHI. Unable to build off 2017 gains, as major ct% issues resurfaced, leading to July demotion. Power/speed metrics still hint at 20+ HR, double-digit SB, but that all hinges on full-time AB. Mounting strikeouts, recurring issues vR, and ongoing health concerns will make getting there an uphill battle.

| Yr | Tm | AB | R | HR | RBI | SB | BA | xBA | OBP | SLG | OPS | vL | vR | bb% | ct% | Eye | G | L | F | h% | HctX | PX | xPX | hr/f | Spd | SBO | SB% | #Wk | DOM | DIS | RC/G | RAR | BPV | BPX | R$ |
|---|---|---|---|---|---|---|---|---|---|---|---|---|---|---|---|---|---|---|---|---|---|---|---|---|---|---|---|---|---|---|---|---|---|---|---|
| 14 | PHI * | 454 | 41 | 12 | 43 | 9 | 201 | 172 | 235 | 337 | 572 | 0 | 0 | 4 | 71 | 0.16 | 33 | 0 | 67 | 25 | 103 | 110 | 235 | 0% | 97 | 21% | 58% | 2 | 0% | 50% | 2.40 | -24.5 | 14 | 38 | $3 |
| 15 | PHI * | 570 | 75 | 17 | 74 | 18 | 250 | 260 | 315 | 434 | 750 | 636 | 936 | 9 | 75 | 0.39 | 40 | 22 | 38 | 30 | 95 | 128 | 96 | 14% | 131 | 19% | 74% | 8 | 38% | 0% | 4.61 | -4.1 | 62 | 168 | $19 |
| 16 | PHI | 198 | 23 | 4 | 22 | 7 | 197 | 222 | 300 | 288 | 587 | 723 | 553 | 10 | 65 | 0.33 | 51 | 26 | 22 | 28 | 78 | 67 | 76 | 14% | 102 | 17% | 78% | 11 | 27% | 55% | 2.62 | -12.9 | -32 | -91 | $1 |
| 17 | PHI | 372 | 58 | 19 | 65 | 5 | 272 | 269 | 340 | 516 | 856 | 830 | 867 | 8 | 72 | 0.31 | 43 | 19 | 38 | 33 | 106 | 147 | 115 | 19% | 109 | 11% | 56% | 22 | 45% | 36% | 5.77 | 6.2 | 56 | 170 | $13 |
| 18 | PHI * | 362 | 40 | 10 | 47 | 6 | 187 | 200 | 280 | 314 | 594 | 696 | 595 | 11 | 62 | 0.34 | 47 | 18 | 34 | 27 | 84 | 97 | 111 | 15% | 110 | 9% | 75% | 22 | 32% | 55% | 2.77 | -18.8 | -16 | -53 | $2 |
| 1st Half | | 187 | 19 | 6 | 32 | 1 | 176 | 198 | 294 | 316 | 610 | 579 | 624 | 14 | 62 | 0.42 | 47 | 18 | 36 | 25 | 81 | 99 | 119 | 14% | 118 | 6% | 33% | 15 | 27% | 53% | 2.74 | -10.5 | -7 | -23 | $1 |
| 2nd Half | | 175 | 21 | 4 | 15 | 5 | 198 | 204 | 268 | 313 | 581 | 1019 | 488 | 9 | 62 | 0.25 | 50 | 19 | 31 | 30 | 95 | 94 | 84 | 18% | 106 | 13% | 100% | 7 | 43% | 57% | 2.81 | -9.1 | -26 | -87 | $4 |
| 19 | Proj | **253** | **31** | **10** | **33** | **5** | **215** | **231** | **306** | **395** | **700** | **796** | **656** | **10** | **66** | **0.31** | **45** | **20** | **35** | **28** | **92** | **123** | **99** | **17%** | **112** | **13%** | **73%** | | | | **3.70** | **-5.9** | **12** | **41** | **$4** |

## Altuve,Jose

| Age: 29 | Bats: R | Pos: 2B | Health | A | LIMA Plan | D+ |
|---|---|---|---|---|---|---|
| Ht: 5' 6" | Wt: 165 | | PT/Exp | A | Rand Var | -2 |
| | | | Consist | D | MM | 2555 |

A down year by his lofty standards. July knee soreness sent him to DL for first time in career; skills waned upon his return. Downward trending ct%, SBO indicate a full rebound is unlikely, but probably deserves a pass for 2nd half slide. As for the power, the metrics were never truly convinced he was a 20+ HR threat.

| Yr | Tm | AB | R | HR | RBI | SB | BA | xBA | OBP | SLG | OPS | vL | vR | bb% | ct% | Eye | G | L | F | h% | HctX | PX | xPX | hr/f | Spd | SBO | SB% | #Wk | DOM | DIS | RC/G | RAR | BPV | BPX | R$ |
|---|---|---|---|---|---|---|---|---|---|---|---|---|---|---|---|---|---|---|---|---|---|---|---|---|---|---|---|---|---|---|---|---|---|---|---|
| 14 | HOU | 660 | 85 | 7 | 59 | 56 | 341 | 296 | 377 | 453 | 830 | 1013 | 775 | 5 | 92 | 0.68 | 48 | 23 | 30 | 36 | 95 | 81 | 77 | 4% | 131 | 32% | 86% | 27 | 78% | 7% | 6.86 | 60.3 | 84 | 227 | $50 |
| 15 | HOU | 638 | 86 | 15 | 66 | 38 | 313 | 281 | 353 | 459 | 812 | 973 | 743 | 5 | 89 | 0.49 | 47 | 18 | 35 | 33 | 103 | 89 | 92 | 7% | 135 | 29% | 75% | 27 | 67% | 19% | 5.82 | 27.2 | 81 | 219 | $40 |
| 16 | HOU | 640 | 108 | 24 | 96 | 30 | 338 | 311 | 396 | 531 | 928 | 885 | 942 | 8 | 89 | 0.86 | 42 | 26 | 32 | 35 | 122 | 104 | 120 | 13% | 120 | 20% | 75% | 27 | 70% | 15% | 7.96 | 55.0 | 94 | 269 | $46 |
| 17 | HOU | 590 | 112 | 24 | 81 | 32 | 346 | 299 | 410 | 547 | 957 | 977 | 952 | 9 | 86 | 0.69 | 47 | 20 | 33 | 37 | 98 | 106 | 87 | 15% | 132 | 19% | 84% | 27 | 63% | 7% | 8.75 | 63.4 | 87 | 264 | $45 |
| 18 | HOU | 534 | 84 | 13 | 61 | 17 | 316 | 278 | 386 | 451 | 837 | 766 | 863 | 9 | 85 | 0.70 | 46 | 24 | 30 | 35 | 105 | 78 | 95 | 10% | 122 | 12% | 81% | 25 | 44% | 8% | 6.46 | 34.5 | 60 | 200 | $27 |
| 1st Half | | 333 | 55 | 7 | 41 | 12 | 342 | 284 | 407 | 483 | 890 | 746 | 946 | 10 | 86 | 0.76 | 42 | 26 | 32 | 38 | 122 | 83 | 117 | 8% | 125 | 12% | 86% | 15 | 53% | 0% | 7.72 | 30.8 | 70 | 233 | $37 |
| 2nd Half | | 201 | 29 | 6 | 20 | 5 | 274 | 266 | 351 | 398 | 749 | 801 | 732 | 9 | 84 | 0.61 | 52 | 21 | 27 | 30 | 77 | 69 | 58 | 14% | 110 | 11% | 71% | 10 | 30% | 20% | 4.71 | 3.1 | 43 | 143 | $12 |
| 19 | Proj | **576** | **96** | **18** | **73** | **24** | **326** | **286** | **390** | **485** | **875** | **873** | **875** | **9** | **86** | **0.68** | **47** | **23** | **31** | **35** | **100** | **88** | **89** | **12%** | **126** | **16%** | **80%** | | | | **7.08** | **44.9** | **67** | **225** | **$38** |

## Anderson,Brian

| Age: 26 | Bats: R | Pos: RF 3B | Health | A | LIMA Plan | B |
|---|---|---|---|---|---|---|
| Ht: 6' 3" | Wt: 185 | | PT/Exp | B | Rand Var | -3 |
| | | | Consist | B | MM | 1135 |

Lucky h% fueled 1st half success, but production eventually slipped, and crashed in Sept (.243 BA, 63% ct). Even when ct% was up, xBA wasn't buying BA improvement. Above average HctX doesn't do much for power when he's constantly hitting ground balls. Spd hints at hidden speed skills, if they only let him run.

| Yr | Tm | AB | R | HR | RBI | SB | BA | xBA | OBP | SLG | OPS | vL | vR | bb% | ct% | Eye | G | L | F | h% | HctX | PX | xPX | hr/f | Spd | SBO | SB% | #Wk | DOM | DIS | RC/G | RAR | BPV | BPX | R$ |
|---|---|---|---|---|---|---|---|---|---|---|---|---|---|---|---|---|---|---|---|---|---|---|---|---|---|---|---|---|---|---|---|---|---|---|---|
| 14 | | | | | | | | | | | | | | | | | | | | | | | | | | | | | | | | | | | |
| 15 | | | | | | | | | | | | | | | | | | | | | | | | | | | | | | | | | | | |
| 16 | aa | 301 | 34 | 7 | 36 | 0 | 216 | | 292 | 315 | 607 | | | 10 | 78 | 0.48 | | | | 26 | | 59 | | | 95 | 0% | 0% | | | | 2.99 | | 8 | 23 | $0 |
| 17 | MIA * | 513 | 77 | 18 | 81 | 1 | 246 | 273 | 317 | 415 | 733 | 543 | 787 | 9 | 73 | 0.38 | 49 | 28 | 23 | 30 | 88 | 103 | 83 | 0% | 122 | 2% | 28% | 6 | 17% | 67% | 4.38 | -12.2 | 30 | 91 | $10 |
| 18 | MIA | 590 | 87 | 11 | 65 | 2 | 273 | 252 | 357 | 400 | 757 | 751 | 759 | 9 | 78 | 0.48 | 52 | 20 | 29 | 33 | 110 | 82 | 78 | 8% | 124 | 3% | 33% | 27 | 48% | 33% | 4.69 | 4.9 | 36 | 120 | $16 |
| 1st Half | | 322 | 47 | 5 | 40 | 2 | 292 | 257 | 367 | 416 | 784 | 834 | 763 | 9 | 79 | 0.49 | 51 | 20 | 29 | 36 | 120 | 82 | 93 | 7% | 129 | 3% | 67% | 15 | 47% | 27% | 5.34 | 7.9 | 42 | 140 | $20 |
| 2nd Half | | 268 | 40 | 6 | 25 | 0 | 250 | 246 | 344 | 381 | 725 | 611 | 754 | 10 | 77 | 0.47 | 53 | 19 | 28 | 31 | 99 | 81 | 60 | 10% | 120 | 4% | 0% | 12 | 50% | 42% | 3.99 | -3.7 | 30 | 100 | $10 |
| 19 | Proj | **570** | **82** | **12** | **72** | **2** | **257** | **256** | **337** | **385** | **721** | **632** | **756** | **10** | **78** | **0.47** | **50** | **23** | **27** | **31** | **100** | **80** | **77** | **10%** | **121** | **3%** | **41%** | | | | **4.26** | **-3.3** | **17** | **55** | **$15** |

## Anderson,Tim

| Age: 26 | Bats: R | Pos: SS | Health | A | LIMA Plan | B |
|---|---|---|---|---|---|---|
| Ht: 6' 1" | Wt: 185 | | PT/Exp | A | Rand Var | +3 |
| | | | Consist | A | MM | 2525 |

SBO, bb%, and hr/f all surged during huge 1st half, but couldn't keep up the pace. Back to free-swinging ways in 2nd half, so sub-.300 OBP may be here to stay. Just 5 SB, 8 attempts post-ASB; HctX, xPX still well below average. Track record says h%, and in turn, BA should rebound, but expect fewer HR and SB.

| Yr | Tm | AB | R | HR | RBI | SB | BA | xBA | OBP | SLG | OPS | vL | vR | bb% | ct% | Eye | G | L | F | h% | HctX | PX | xPX | hr/f | Spd | SBO | SB% | #Wk | DOM | DIS | RC/G | RAR | BPV | BPX | R$ |
|---|---|---|---|---|---|---|---|---|---|---|---|---|---|---|---|---|---|---|---|---|---|---|---|---|---|---|---|---|---|---|---|---|---|---|---|
| 14 | aa | 44 | 5 | 1 | 5 | 0 | 326 | | 326 | 445 | 771 | | | 0 | 77 | 0.00 | | | | 41 | | 97 | | | 95 | 10% | 0% | | | | 4.88 | | 15 | 41 | $0 |
| 15 | aa | 513 | 70 | 5 | 41 | 43 | 287 | | 318 | 389 | 707 | | | 4 | 75 | 0.18 | | | | 38 | | 69 | | | 145 | 42% | 75% | | | | 4.37 | | 9 | 24 | $29 |
| 16 | CHW * | 657 | 89 | 12 | 46 | 19 | 279 | 248 | 300 | 407 | 707 | 797 | 721 | 3 | 72 | 0.11 | 54 | 21 | 25 | 37 | 94 | 86 | 86 | 12% | 176 | 17% | 75% | 18 | 28% | 50% | 4.28 | -0.5 | 17 | 49 | $22 |
| 17 | CHW | 587 | 72 | 17 | 56 | 15 | 257 | 248 | 276 | 402 | 679 | 811 | 629 | 2 | 72 | 0.08 | 53 | 19 | 28 | 33 | 83 | 89 | 68 | 14% | 143 | 14% | 94% | 27 | 15% | 59% | 3.87 | -12.9 | 10 | 30 | $15 |
| 18 | CHW | 567 | 77 | 20 | 64 | 26 | 240 | 248 | 281 | 406 | 687 | 788 | 649 | 5 | 74 | 0.20 | 47 | 20 | 33 | 29 | 82 | 104 | 83 | 14% | 122 | 30% | 76% | 27 | 41% | 44% | 3.76 | -5.9 | 27 | 90 | $21 |
| 1st Half | | 286 | 43 | 13 | 33 | 17 | 248 | 244 | 311 | 430 | 741 | 770 | 731 | 7 | 73 | 0.29 | 45 | 20 | 35 | 30 | 81 | 107 | 89 | 18% | 132 | 31% | 77% | 15 | 47% | 53% | 4.42 | 3.9 | 33 | 110 | $27 |
| 2nd Half | | 281 | 34 | 7 | 31 | 9 | 231 | 251 | 250 | 381 | 631 | 803 | 557 | 2 | 75 | 0.10 | 48 | 20 | 32 | 29 | 84 | 101 | 77 | 10% | 116 | 27% | 75% | 12 | 33% | 33% | 3.12 | -7.2 | 22 | 73 | $16 |
| 19 | Proj | **575** | **75** | **17** | **57** | **23** | **254** | **248** | **282** | **408** | **689** | **802** | **648** | **3** | **73** | **0.13** | **50** | **20** | **30** | **32** | **85** | **97** | **78** | **14%** | **143** | **26%** | **78%** | | | | **3.88** | **-1.3** | **21** | **69** | **$22** |

## Andreoli,John

| Age: 29 | Bats: R | Pos: LF | Health | A | LIMA Plan | F |
|---|---|---|---|---|---|---|
| Ht: 6' 1" | Wt: 210 | | PT/Exp | B | Rand Var | -4 |
| | | | Consist | A | MM | 1501 |

0-4-.230 with 2 SB in 61 AB at BAL/SEA. Speedster can draw walks, but the good news stops there. Way too many strikeouts and fly balls for this type of player, and success rate on bases has consistently been subpar. Converting wheels to bags is his only path to value, but not much reason to think it will happen.

| Yr | Tm | AB | R | HR | RBI | SB | BA | xBA | OBP | SLG | OPS | vL | vR | bb% | ct% | Eye | G | L | F | h% | HctX | PX | xPX | hr/f | Spd | SBO | SB% | #Wk | DOM | DIS | RC/G | RAR | BPV | BPX | R$ |
|---|---|---|---|---|---|---|---|---|---|---|---|---|---|---|---|---|---|---|---|---|---|---|---|---|---|---|---|---|---|---|---|---|---|---|---|
| 14 | aa | 209 | 27 | 0 | 6 | 20 | 177 | | 266 | 208 | 474 | | | 11 | 73 | 0.45 | | | | 24 | | 25 | | | 140 | 39% | 90% | | | | 2.05 | | -22 | -59 | $2 |
| 15 | aaa | 379 | 52 | 4 | 23 | 24 | 233 | | 308 | 331 | 639 | | | 10 | 70 | 0.35 | | | | 33 | | 77 | | | 131 | 32% | 72% | | | | 3.37 | | 1 | 3 | $11 |
| 16 | aaa | 507 | 68 | 8 | 43 | 30 | 205 | | 300 | 308 | 608 | | | 12 | 61 | 0.35 | | | | 32 | | 79 | | | 125 | 31% | 68% | | | | 2.90 | | -28 | -80 | $10 |
| 17 | aaa | 430 | 57 | 10 | 35 | 18 | 196 | | 276 | 338 | 614 | | | 10 | 61 | 0.29 | | | | 29 | | 102 | | | 136 | 31% | 60% | | | | 2.78 | | -10 | -30 | $4 |
| 18 | 2 AL * | 388 | 42 | 2 | 30 | 16 | 223 | 174 | 303 | 297 | 600 | 531 | 561 | 10 | 66 | 0.34 | 30 | 21 | 49 | 33 | 68 | 59 | 95 | 0% | 152 | 20% | 71% | 9 | 22% | 67% | 2.96 | -19.5 | -20 | -67 | $6 |
| 1st Half | | 224 | 28 | 2 | 17 | 10 | 215 | 247 | 290 | 314 | 604 | 0 | 833 | 10 | 67 | 0.32 | 0 | 67 | 33 | 31 | 0 | 75 | -27 | 0% | 127 | 26% | 66% | 2 | 50% | 50% | 2.88 | -12.1 | -14 | -47 | $7 |
| 2nd Half | | 164 | 14 | 0 | 13 | 6 | 235 | 152 | 321 | 274 | 595 | 531 | 526 | 11 | 65 | 0.36 | 33 | 18 | 50 | 36 | 72 | 35 | 104 | 0% | 135 | 13% | 82% | 7 | 14% | 71% | 3.04 | -7.8 | -47 | -157 | $5 |
| 19 | Proj | **188** | **22** | **3** | **14** | **9** | **214** | **189** | **294** | **320** | **613** | **609** | **619** | **11** | **64** | **0.33** | **39** | **20** | **42** | **32** | **65** | **78** | **94** | **6%** | **154** | **25%** | **71%** | | | | **3.07** | **-9.0** | **-21** | **-70** | **$4** |

## Andrus,Elvis

| Age: 30 | Bats: R | Pos: SS | Health | C | LIMA Plan | B |
|---|---|---|---|---|---|---|
| Ht: 6' 0" | Wt: 200 | | PT/Exp | B | Rand Var | +2 |
| | | | Consist | C | MM | 1445 |

Elbow fracture in April knocked him out for two months; likely played role in power regression. But what about the steals? Spd skill remains high, but has just 10 SB since July 2017. His green light dropped to 11% then and has never recovered. Hit rate should rebound, boosting BA, but we can't bank on return to 20+ SB.

| Yr | Tm | AB | R | HR | RBI | SB | BA | xBA | OBP | SLG | OPS | vL | vR | bb% | ct% | Eye | G | L | F | h% | HctX | PX | xPX | hr/f | Spd | SBO | SB% | #Wk | DOM | DIS | RC/G | RAR | BPV | BPX | R$ |
|---|---|---|---|---|---|---|---|---|---|---|---|---|---|---|---|---|---|---|---|---|---|---|---|---|---|---|---|---|---|---|---|---|---|---|---|
| 14 | TEX | 619 | 72 | 2 | 41 | 27 | 263 | 268 | 314 | 333 | 647 | 760 | 607 | 7 | 84 | 0.48 | 59 | 20 | 21 | 31 | 75 | 59 | 36 | 2% | 106 | 25% | 64% | 27 | 37% | 19% | 3.49 | 5.7 | 32 | 86 | $19 |
| 15 | TEX | 596 | 69 | 7 | 62 | 25 | 258 | 265 | 309 | 357 | 667 | 757 | 618 | 7 | 87 | 0.59 | 47 | 21 | 32 | 29 | 104 | 67 | 70 | 4% | 106 | 22% | 74% | 27 | 59% | 19% | 3.81 | -10.3 | 49 | 132 | $19 |
| 16 | TEX | 506 | 75 | 8 | 69 | 24 | 302 | 289 | 362 | 439 | 800 | 899 | 771 | 8 | 86 | 0.67 | 48 | 24 | 29 | 34 | 95 | 80 | 68 | 6% | 139 | 21% | 75% | 27 | 48% | 7% | 5.77 | 20.6 | 69 | 197 | $26 |
| 17 | TEX | 643 | 100 | 20 | 88 | 25 | 297 | 289 | 337 | 471 | 808 | 845 | 798 | 6 | 84 | 0.38 | 49 | 20 | 32 | 33 | 104 | 97 | 80 | 12% | 115 | 22% | 71% | 27 | 52% | 26% | 5.62 | 18.0 | 62 | 188 | $33 |
| 18 | TEX * | 419 | 54 | 6 | 33 | 5 | 243 | 252 | 294 | 348 | 641 | 725 | 653 | 7 | 83 | 0.43 | 50 | 19 | 31 | 28 | 104 | 63 | 59 | 6% | 131 | 9% | 54% | 19 | 42% | 37% | 3.35 | -9.4 | 38 | 127 | $6 |
| 1st Half | | 121 | 13 | 2 | 9 | 0 | 221 | 259 | 297 | 329 | 626 | 526 | 832 | 10 | 88 | 0.90 | 54 | 17 | 29 | 24 | 115 | 59 | 70 | 8% | 117 | 7% | 0% | 6 | 67% | 33% | 2.95 | -3.8 | 56 | 187 | -$7 |
| 2nd Half | | 298 | 41 | 4 | 24 | 5 | 252 | 248 | 293 | 356 | 649 | 776 | 586 | 5 | 82 | 0.31 | 48 | 20 | 32 | 30 | 100 | 65 | 55 | 5% | 130 | 10% | 71% | 13 | 31% | 38% | 3.52 | -3.9 | 30 | 100 | $12 |
| 19 | Proj | **555** | **75** | **10** | **57** | **15** | **271** | **268** | **323** | **397** | **721** | **743** | **713** | **7** | **85** | **0.47** | **50** | **20** | **30** | **31** | **102** | **74** | **66** | **7%** | **127** | **16%** | **67%** | | | | **4.37** | **6.6** | **46** | **152** | **$21** |

## Andujar,Miguel

| Age: 24 | Bats: R | Pos: 3B | Health | A | LIMA Plan | B+ |
|---|---|---|---|---|---|---|
| Ht: 6'0" | Wt: 215 | | PT/Exp | C | Rand Var | 0 |
| | | | Consist | C | MM | 4255 |

Injuries opened door for starting gig in April, and never looked back. BA was fully supported by xBA, a nice follow-up to 2017. Power spike has to be tempered bit by modest xPX. After pairing 87% ct% with 43% FB% over final 6 weeks, there could be more power to come. But he's young. Neither 25 HRs or 35 HRs would surprise.

| Yr | Tm | AB | R | HR | RBI | SB | BA | xBA | OBP | SLG | OPS | vL | vR | bb% | ct% | Eye | G | L | F | h% | HctX | PX | xPX | hr/f | Spd | SBO | SB% | #Wk | DOM | DIS | RC/G | RAR | BPV | BPX | R$ |
|---|---|---|---|---|---|---|---|---|---|---|---|---|---|---|---|---|---|---|---|---|---|---|---|---|---|---|---|---|---|---|---|---|---|---|---|
| 14 | | | | | | | | | | | | | | | | | | | | | | | | | | | | | | | | | | | |
| 15 | | | | | | | | | | | | | | | | | | | | | | | | | | | | | | | | | | | |
| 16 | aa | 282 | 27 | 2 | 40 | 2 | 255 | | 305 | 343 | 647 | | | 7 | 84 | 0.44 | | | | 30 | | 57 | | | 90 | 4% | 64% | | | | 3.55 | | 23 | 66 | $3 |
| 17 | NYY * | 488 | 62 | 18 | 81 | 6 | 303 | 283 | 342 | 489 | 831 | 1333 | 1600 | 6 | 84 | 0.36 | 57 | 14 | 29 | 33 | 97 | 103 | 81 | 0% | 73 | 7% | 64% | 5 | 40% | 40% | 6.03 | 15.8 | 53 | 161 | $20 |
| 18 | NYY | 573 | 83 | 27 | 92 | 2 | 297 | 295 | 328 | 527 | 855 | 822 | 869 | 4 | 83 | 0.26 | 44 | 20 | 36 | 32 | 110 | 133 | 99 | 16% | 93 | 3% | 67% | 27 | 59% | 15% | 6.21 | 29.6 | 77 | 257 | $25 |
| 1st Half | | 268 | 36 | 12 | 38 | 1 | 280 | 295 | 306 | 515 | 821 | 810 | 826 | 4 | 82 | 0.20 | 47 | 19 | 34 | 30 | 106 | 138 | 102 | 16% | 102 | 2% | 100% | 14 | 57% | 29% | 5.60 | 8.3 | 77 | 257 | $18 |
| 2nd Half | | 305 | 47 | 15 | 54 | 1 | 311 | 294 | 348 | 538 | 885 | 832 | 905 | 5 | 84 | 0.31 | 41 | 21 | 37 | 33 | 114 | 129 | 96 | 15% | 85 | 3% | 50% | 13 | 62% | 0% | 6.77 | 18.8 | 77 | 257 | $31 |
| 19 | Proj | **597** | **85** | **28** | **96** | **4** | **294** | **291** | **333** | **516** | **850** | **834** | **856** | **5** | **84** | **0.34** | **44** | **20** | **36** | **31** | **111** | **126** | **98** | **16%** | **101** | **5%** | **66%** | | | | **6.12** | **26.8** | **69** | **230** | **$28** |

BRIAN RUDD

## Arcia,Orlando

| | | | | | |
|---|---|---|---|---|---|
| Age: 24 | Bats: R | Pos: SS | Health | A | LIMA Plan D+ |
| Ht: 6' 0" | Wt: 165 | | PT/Exp | B | Rand Var 0 |
| | | | Consist | D | MM 1425 |

3-30-.236 with 7 SB in 348 AB at MIL. Even amid 2017's power/speed breakout, xPX and HctX thought this was a noodle bat, and SB% questioned the SB viability. Those concerns got borne out, leading to July exile to AAA. Post-demotion focus on LD% might be best path forward, but there's a lot to work on here.

| Yr | Tm | AB | R | HR | RBI | SB | BA | xBA | OBP | SLG | OPS | vL | vR | bb% | ct% | Eye | G | L | F | h% | HctX | PX | xPX | hr/f | Spd | SBO | SB% | #Wk | DOM | DIS | RC/G | RAR | BPV | BPX | R$ |
|---|---|---|---|---|---|---|---|---|---|---|---|---|---|---|---|---|---|---|---|---|---|---|---|---|---|---|---|---|---|---|---|---|---|---|---|
| 14 | | | | | | | | | | | | | | | | | | | | | | | | | | | | | | | | | | | |
| 15 | aa | 512 | 67 | 7 | 63 | 23 | 296 | | 332 | 432 | 764 | | | 5 | 85 | 0.36 | | | | 34 | | 90 | | | 105 | 24% | 73% | | | | 5.11 | | 55 | 149 | $25 |
| 16 | MIL * | 605 | 64 | 11 | 56 | 19 | 228 | 250 | 272 | 349 | 621 | 845 | 564 | 6 | 78 | 0.27 | 54 | 17 | 29 | 28 | 80 | 74 | 59 | 9% | 152 | 21% | 68% | 10 | 40% | 40% | 3.06 | -28.9 | 30 | 86 | $10 |
| 17 | MIL | 506 | 56 | 15 | 53 | 14 | 277 | 259 | 324 | 407 | 731 | 626 | 763 | 7 | 80 | 0.36 | 52 | 20 | 29 | 32 | 98 | 70 | 78 | 13% | 138 | 15% | 67% | 26 | 31% | 38% | 4.56 | 0.5 | 33 | 100 | $17 |
| 18 | MIL * | 433 | 43 | 4 | 35 | 8 | 244 | 232 | 280 | 325 | 606 | 596 | 570 | 5 | 76 | 0.21 | 56 | 19 | 25 | 31 | 71 | 58 | 54 | 5% | 120 | 13% | 62% | 25 | 16% | 56% | 3.00 | -10.6 | -2 | -7 | $6 |
| 1st Half | | 218 | 14 | 2 | 15 | 3 | 198 | 197 | 230 | 249 | 479 | 261 | 538 | 4 | 74 | 0.16 | 60 | 14 | 26 | 26 | 69 | 34 | 54 | 5% | 123 | 14% | 49% | 14 | 7% | 57% | 1.73 | -15.6 | -28 | -93 | -$2 |
| 2nd Half | | 215 | 29 | 2 | 20 | 5 | 292 | 264 | 331 | 403 | 734 | 931 | 618 | 6 | 77 | 0.26 | 49 | 26 | 25 | 37 | 74 | 80 | 54 | 4% | 116 | 13% | 73% | 11 | 27% | 55% | 4.77 | 4.9 | 20 | 67 | $15 |
| **19** | **Proj** | **463** | **51** | **7** | **43** | **10** | **254** | **250** | **296** | **356** | **652** | **702** | **636** | **6** | **78** | **0.27** | **51** | **22** | **27** | **31** | **82** | **66** | **63** | **7%** | **137** | **14%** | **62%** | | | | **3.50** | **-6.3** | **6** | **21** | **$9** |

## Arenado,Nolan

| | | | | | |
|---|---|---|---|---|---|
| Age: 28 | Bats: R | Pos: 3B | Health | A | LIMA Plan C |
| Ht: 6' 2" | Wt: 205 | | PT/Exp | A | Rand Var -1 |
| | | | Consist | B | MM 4155 |

As steady of an elite infield bat as you'll find. No obvious signs for worry, as both power foundation and plate skills are rock-solid. Just two things to monitor: 1) further erosion in FB rate will put near-40 HR at risk, 2) two-year production dip vR makes him elite vL only. For now, put this projection in stone.

| Yr | Tm | AB | R | HR | RBI | SB | BA | xBA | OBP | SLG | OPS | vL | vR | bb% | ct% | Eye | G | L | F | h% | HctX | PX | xPX | hr/f | Spd | SBO | SB% | #Wk | DOM | DIS | RC/G | RAR | BPV | BPX | R$ |
|---|---|---|---|---|---|---|---|---|---|---|---|---|---|---|---|---|---|---|---|---|---|---|---|---|---|---|---|---|---|---|---|---|---|---|---|
| 14 | COL | 432 | 58 | 18 | 61 | 2 | 287 | 300 | 328 | 500 | 828 | 973 | 776 | 5 | 87 | 0.43 | 38 | 21 | 42 | 30 | 127 | 142 | 134 | 11% | 97 | 3% | 67% | 20 | 80% | 10% | 5.80 | 25.3 | 102 | 276 | $18 |
| 15 | COL | 616 | 97 | 42 | 130 | 2 | 287 | 307 | 323 | 575 | 898 | 778 | 931 | 5 | 82 | 0.31 | 34 | 22 | 44 | 29 | 133 | 172 | 151 | 19% | 97 | 6% | 29% | 27 | 70% | 15% | 6.46 | 31.1 | 108 | 292 | $32 |
| 16 | COL | 618 | 116 | 41 | 133 | 2 | 294 | 290 | 362 | 570 | 932 | 875 | 951 | 10 | 83 | 0.66 | 35 | 18 | 47 | 30 | 128 | 146 | 148 | 17% | 118 | 3% | 40% | 27 | 81% | 11% | 7.38 | 41.4 | 107 | 306 | $32 |
| 17 | COL | 606 | 100 | 37 | 130 | 3 | 309 | 297 | 373 | 586 | 959 | 1313 | 843 | 9 | 83 | 0.58 | 34 | 21 | 45 | 32 | 123 | 145 | 149 | 16% | 118 | 3% | 60% | 27 | 74% | 7% | 7.99 | 44.2 | 102 | 309 | $32 |
| 18 | COL | 590 | 104 | 38 | 110 | 2 | 297 | 291 | 374 | 561 | 935 | 1199 | 822 | 11 | 79 | 0.60 | 40 | 21 | 39 | 32 | 126 | 150 | 138 | 21% | 89 | 2% | 50% | 28 | 71% | 11% | 7.54 | 46.8 | 88 | 293 | $31 |
| 1st Half | | 294 | 54 | 20 | 57 | 2 | 306 | 296 | 389 | 585 | 974 | 1374 | 765 | 13 | 78 | 0.65 | 37 | 25 | 38 | 33 | 124 | 158 | 134 | 23% | 99 | 3% | 67% | 15 | 80% | 7% | 8.39 | 31.3 | 95 | 317 | $34 |
| 2nd Half | | 296 | 50 | 18 | 53 | 0 | 287 | 281 | 357 | 537 | 895 | 960 | 872 | 9 | 81 | 0.54 | 43 | 18 | 40 | 30 | 127 | 142 | 141 | 19% | 83 | 1% | 0% | 13 | 62% | 15% | 6.73 | 18.5 | 83 | 277 | $28 |
| **19** | **Proj** | **601** | **103** | **38** | **118** | **2** | **297** | **291** | **364** | **563** | **928** | **1126** | **854** | **10** | **81** | **0.57** | **38** | **20** | **42** | **31** | **126** | **147** | **143** | **18%** | **102** | **3%** | **48%** | | | | **7.37** | **47.8** | **85** | **283** | **$33** |

## Astudillo,Williams

| | | | | | |
|---|---|---|---|---|---|
| Age: 27 | Bats: R | Pos: CA | Health | A | LIMA Plan D+ |
| Ht: 5' 9" | Wt: 225 | | PT/Exp | F | Rand Var +2 |
| | | | Consist | C | MM 1051 |

3-21-.355 in 93 AB at MIN. Quietly delivered top OPS and ct% of any CA-eligible bat in Sept. Was it a fluke? History of uber-elite contact says no, and even with likely regression of MLB 34% hit rate, xBA suggests a nice floor. Ability to play all over diamond helps AB potential too. UP: .300-10-50

| Yr | Tm | AB | R | HR | RBI | SB | BA | xBA | OBP | SLG | OPS | vL | vR | bb% | ct% | Eye | G | L | F | h% | HctX | PX | xPX | hr/f | Spd | SBO | SB% | #Wk | DOM | DIS | RC/G | RAR | BPV | BPX | R$ |
|---|---|---|---|---|---|---|---|---|---|---|---|---|---|---|---|---|---|---|---|---|---|---|---|---|---|---|---|---|---|---|---|---|---|---|---|
| 14 | | | | | | | | | | | | | | | | | | | | | | | | | | | | | | | | | | | |
| 15 | | | | | | | | | | | | | | | | | | | | | | | | | | | | | | | | | | | |
| 16 | aa | 322 | 23 | 3 | 28 | 1 | 235 | | 246 | 283 | 530 | | | 2 | 96 | 0.37 | | | | 24 | | 24 | | | 86 | 3% | 45% | | | | 2.30 | | 34 | 97 | $0 |
| 17 | aaa | 120 | 14 | 3 | 14 | 0 | 277 | | 292 | 442 | 734 | | | 2 | 95 | 0.41 | | | | 28 | | 92 | | | 86 | 6% | 0% | | | | 4.34 | | 85 | 258 | $1 |
| 18 | MIN * | 379 | 34 | 13 | 53 | 6 | 270 | 299 | 289 | 435 | 724 | 893 | 885 | 3 | 95 | 0.54 | 41 | 23 | 36 | 26 | 112 | 81 | 91 | 9% | 82 | 14% | 55% | 10 | 60% | 10% | 4.22 | 9.3 | 77 | 257 | $11 |
| 1st Half | | 182 | 15 | 7 | 23 | 5 | 256 | 238 | 273 | 437 | 710 | 2000 | 0 | 2 | 94 | 0.36 | 50 | 0 | 50 | 24 | 173 | 91 | 347 | 0% | 82 | 23% | 68% | 2 | 50% | 0% | 3.96 | 2.8 | 79 | 263 | $9 |
| 2nd Half | | 197 | 19 | 6 | 30 | 1 | 282 | 297 | 304 | 433 | 737 | 852 | 898 | 3 | 96 | 0.81 | 40 | 24 | 36 | 27 | 111 | 72 | 85 | 9% | 83 | 7% | 26% | 8 | 63% | 13% | 4.45 | 5.7 | 75 | 250 | $13 |
| **19** | **Proj** | **239** | **25** | **7** | **32** | **2** | **277** | **300** | **297** | **430** | **728** | **726** | **727** | **2** | **95** | **0.48** | **40** | **24** | **36** | **27** | **100** | **79** | **77** | **8%** | **73** | **8%** | **46%** | | | | **4.31** | **5.9** | **68** | **227** | **$8** |

## Asuaje,Carlos

| | | | | | |
|---|---|---|---|---|---|
| Age: 27 | Bats: L | Pos: 2B | Health | A | LIMA Plan D |
| Ht: 5' 9" | Wt: 158 | | PT/Exp | C | Rand Var 0 |
| | | | Consist | A | MM 1211 |

2-19-.196 in 189 AB at SD. Broke camp with everyday role, but lost it quickly and never recovered. Just doesn't do anything well enough to think he can stick as a full-time bat. Big warts vL carve potential part-time path, but hasn't hit RHers with any thump anyway. Not young enough to keep stashing either. Pass.

| Yr | Tm | AB | R | HR | RBI | SB | BA | xBA | OBP | SLG | OPS | vL | vR | bb% | ct% | Eye | G | L | F | h% | HctX | PX | xPX | hr/f | Spd | SBO | SB% | #Wk | DOM | DIS | RC/G | RAR | BPV | BPX | R$ |
|---|---|---|---|---|---|---|---|---|---|---|---|---|---|---|---|---|---|---|---|---|---|---|---|---|---|---|---|---|---|---|---|---|---|---|---|
| 14 | | | | | | | | | | | | | | | | | | | | | | | | | | | | | | | | | | | |
| 15 | aa | 495 | 47 | 6 | 48 | 7 | 226 | | 289 | 331 | 620 | | | 8 | 80 | 0.45 | | | | 27 | | 71 | | | 111 | 11% | 51% | | | | 3.04 | | 29 | 78 | $4 |
| 16 | SD * | 559 | 67 | 6 | 47 | 7 | 256 | 246 | 297 | 360 | 657 | 556 | 517 | 5 | 82 | 0.32 | 35 | 25 | 40 | 30 | 100 | 65 | 88 | 0% | 128 | 9% | 52% | 2 | 50% | 50% | 3.56 | -21.6 | 32 | 91 | $9 |
| 17 | SD * | 535 | 56 | 6 | 43 | 1 | 237 | 236 | 306 | 323 | 629 | 571 | 735 | 9 | 78 | 0.46 | 40 | 24 | 36 | 29 | 91 | 53 | 108 | 5% | 134 | 2% | 22% | 17 | 24% | 35% | 3.26 | -28.3 | 15 | 45 | $2 |
| 18 | SD * | 364 | 36 | 3 | 31 | 1 | 217 | 223 | 285 | 309 | 594 | 330 | 659 | 9 | 78 | 0.43 | 40 | 21 | 39 | 27 | 102 | 59 | 100 | 4% | 119 | 4% | 31% | 16 | 13% | 44% | 2.80 | -16.4 | 15 | 50 | $0 |
| 1st Half | | 239 | 22 | 3 | 23 | 0 | 230 | 226 | 283 | 327 | 610 | 368 | 616 | 7 | 81 | 0.39 | 44 | 18 | 38 | 27 | 118 | 58 | 117 | 6% | 129 | 4% | 0% | 9 | 11% | 11% | 2.94 | -9.0 | 25 | 83 | $1 |
| 2nd Half | | 125 | 15 | 1 | 9 | 1 | 194 | 213 | 288 | 275 | 563 | 269 | 709 | 12 | 73 | 0.49 | 33 | 25 | 42 | 26 | 77 | 60 | 73 | 0% | 110 | 3% | 100% | 7 | 14% | 86% | 2.55 | -6.4 | -1 | -3 | -$3 |
| **19** | **Proj** | **159** | **17** | **2** | **13** | **1** | **224** | **228** | **295** | **318** | **613** | **391** | **691** | **9** | **78** | **0.44** | **39** | **23** | **38** | **28** | **93** | **61** | **98** | **3%** | **120** | **5%** | **52%** | | | | **3.02** | **-5.7** | **3** | **10** | **$1** |

## Austin,Tyler

| | | | | | |
|---|---|---|---|---|---|
| Age: 27 | Bats: R | Pos: 1B DH | Health | C | LIMA Plan D+ |
| Ht: 6' 2" | Wt: 220 | | PT/Exp | D | Rand Var +2 |
| | | | Consist | B | MM 5123 |

17-47-.230 in 244 AB at MIN/NYY. Days of him being speculation-worthy are near an end. Holes in swing getting worse, never has shown power vR in majors for extended period, age no longer makes him a prospect. Theme alert: low-BA power sources like this will always be available if you need them.

| Yr | Tm | AB | R | HR | RBI | SB | BA | xBA | OBP | SLG | OPS | vL | vR | bb% | ct% | Eye | G | L | F | h% | HctX | PX | xPX | hr/f | Spd | SBO | SB% | #Wk | DOM | DIS | RC/G | RAR | BPV | BPX | R$ |
|---|---|---|---|---|---|---|---|---|---|---|---|---|---|---|---|---|---|---|---|---|---|---|---|---|---|---|---|---|---|---|---|---|---|---|---|
| 14 | aa | 396 | 45 | 8 | 37 | 2 | 243 | | 295 | 363 | 659 | | | 7 | 77 | 0.32 | | | | 30 | | 89 | | | 107 | 5% | 52% | | | | 3.56 | | 27 | 73 | $6 |
| 15 | a/a | 341 | 35 | 6 | 30 | 10 | 218 | | 280 | 312 | 592 | | | 8 | 68 | 0.27 | | | | 30 | | 73 | | | 101 | 15% | 74% | | | | 2.86 | | -22 | -59 | $3 |
| 16 | NYY * | 461 | 61 | 23 | 81 | 6 | 261 | 244 | 348 | 482 | 830 | 1097 | 621 | 12 | 66 | 0.39 | 43 | 17 | 40 | 35 | 91 | 160 | 135 | 26% | 76 | 6% | 85% | 9 | 33% | 67% | 5.82 | 12.9 | 40 | 114 | $15 |
| 17 | NYY * | 225 | 33 | 12 | 36 | 0 | 248 | 257 | 313 | 492 | 805 | 1258 | 429 | 9 | 64 | 0.26 | 28 | 32 | 40 | 33 | 104 | 165 | 154 | 20% | 93 | 0% | 0% | 9 | 22% | 56% | 5.22 | -0.9 | 35 | 106 | $4 |
| 18 | 2 AL * | 381 | 51 | 25 | 65 | 1 | 227 | 246 | 278 | 478 | 756 | 846 | 721 | 6 | 62 | 0.18 | 38 | 24 | 38 | 29 | 83 | 177 | 124 | 29% | 72 | 4% | 33% | 21 | 48% | 38% | 4.29 | -1.5 | 28 | 93 | $10 |
| 1st Half | | 156 | 22 | 11 | 31 | 1 | 223 | 238 | 272 | 488 | 760 | 826 | 691 | 6 | 56 | 0.15 | 39 | 25 | 36 | 32 | 74 | 212 | 125 | 32% | 67 | 8% | 50% | 12 | 42% | 42% | 4.26 | -2.4 | 27 | 90 | $8 |
| 2nd Half | | 225 | 29 | 14 | 35 | 0 | 230 | 250 | 281 | 472 | 753 | 876 | 743 | 7 | 67 | 0.22 | 37 | 23 | 40 | 28 | 89 | 156 | 123 | 27% | 89 | 2% | 0% | 9 | 56% | 33% | 4.31 | -3.1 | 35 | 117 | $12 |
| **19** | **Proj** | **290** | **39** | **18** | **47** | **1** | **238** | **247** | **300** | **486** | **786** | **957** | **702** | **8** | **64** | **0.24** | **40** | **21** | **39** | **30** | **86** | **171** | **128** | **24%** | **83** | **4%** | **58%** | | | | **4.82** | **0.5** | **32** | **106** | **$9** |

## Avila,Alex

| | | | | | |
|---|---|---|---|---|---|
| Age: 32 | Bats: L | Pos: CA | Health | C | LIMA Plan D |
| Ht: 5' 11" | Wt: 210 | | PT/Exp | D | Rand Var +3 |
| | | | Consist | F | MM 4001 |

Flashes of elite power continue to be washed away by maddening inconsistency. Blame it on being a hacker. Contact rate shows no signs that he'll change that profile, so the handful of homers he gives you will be accompanied by a near-.200 BA. Superb plate patience gives him marginal value in OBP leagues only.

| Yr | Tm | AB | R | HR | RBI | SB | BA | xBA | OBP | SLG | OPS | vL | vR | bb% | ct% | Eye | G | L | F | h% | HctX | PX | xPX | hr/f | Spd | SBO | SB% | #Wk | DOM | DIS | RC/G | RAR | BPV | BPX | R$ |
|---|---|---|---|---|---|---|---|---|---|---|---|---|---|---|---|---|---|---|---|---|---|---|---|---|---|---|---|---|---|---|---|---|---|---|---|
| 14 | DET | 390 | 44 | 11 | 47 | 0 | 218 | 222 | 327 | 359 | 686 | 589 | 720 | 13 | 61 | 0.40 | 45 | 25 | 30 | 32 | 105 | 136 | 147 | 15% | 63 | 3% | 0% | 27 | 37% | 44% | 3.68 | 2.6 | 2 | 5 | $3 |
| 15 | DET | 178 | 21 | 4 | 13 | 0 | 191 | 207 | 339 | 287 | 626 | 424 | 666 | 18 | 63 | 0.61 | 41 | 28 | 32 | 28 | 84 | 77 | 123 | 11% | 82 | 2% | 0% | 19 | 26% | 53% | 3.00 | -4.5 | -23 | -62 | -$3 |
| 16 | CHW * | 193 | 22 | 8 | 13 | 0 | 219 | 203 | 361 | 375 | 736 | 844 | 715 | 18 | 55 | 0.49 | 52 | 25 | 23 | 35 | 73 | 129 | 111 | 33% | 80 | 0% | 0% | 19 | 37% | 53% | 4.42 | 0.0 | -15 | -43 | $0 |
| 17 | 2 TM | 311 | 41 | 14 | 49 | 0 | 264 | 232 | 387 | 447 | 834 | 519 | 876 | 16 | 61 | 0.52 | 39 | 28 | 34 | 38 | 121 | 127 | 170 | 22% | 78 | 1% | 0% | 27 | 33% | 52% | 5.91 | 16.7 | 6 | 18 | $7 |
| 18 | ARI | 194 | 13 | 7 | 20 | 0 | 165 | 170 | 299 | 304 | 603 | 668 | 592 | 16 | 54 | 0.41 | 49 | 22 | 29 | 26 | 101 | 115 | 154 | 23% | 53 | 0% | 0% | 26 | 31% | 58% | 2.77 | -4.6 | -43 | -143 | -$3 |
| 1st Half | | 105 | 7 | 3 | 7 | 0 | 124 | 162 | 240 | 219 | 459 | 250 | 493 | 13 | 49 | 0.30 | 43 | 27 | 29 | 21 | 84 | 81 | 164 | 20% | 72 | 0% | 0% | 14 | 21% | 71% | 1.53 | -6.9 | -91 | -303 | -$7 |
| 2nd Half | | 89 | 6 | 4 | 13 | 0 | 213 | 177 | 363 | 404 | 767 | 1143 | 700 | 19 | 60 | 0.58 | 55 | 16 | 29 | 31 | 120 | 149 | 145 | 25% | 58 | 0% | 0% | 12 | 42% | 42% | 4.77 | 3.6 | 15 | 50 | $1 |
| **19** | **Proj** | **204** | **19** | **8** | **24** | **0** | **208** | **204** | **341** | **366** | **707** | **706** | **707** | **17** | **57** | **0.47** | **47** | **24** | **30** | **32** | **103** | **125** | **149** | **23%** | **63** | **0%** | **0%** | | | | **3.99** | **3.4** | **-30** | **-101** | **$2** |

## Bader,Harrison

| | | | | | |
|---|---|---|---|---|---|
| Age: 25 | Bats: R | Pos: CF RF | Health | A | LIMA Plan C+ |
| Ht: 6'0" | Wt: 195 | | PT/Exp | C | Rand Var -4 |
| | | | Consist | B | MM 2415 |

Sustained power/speed profile in first extended look in majors. Will it continue? Late bumps in HctX, xPX put 20 HR in cards. Problem is, waning rate of contact, friendly hit rate, xBA all suggest BA, OBP are headed south. Those warts put his steals at risk too. For now, more likely to regress than grow.

| Yr | Tm | AB | R | HR | RBI | SB | BA | xBA | OBP | SLG | OPS | vL | vR | bb% | ct% | Eye | G | L | F | h% | HctX | PX | xPX | hr/f | Spd | SBO | SB% | #Wk | DOM | DIS | RC/G | RAR | BPV | BPX | R$ |
|---|---|---|---|---|---|---|---|---|---|---|---|---|---|---|---|---|---|---|---|---|---|---|---|---|---|---|---|---|---|---|---|---|---|---|---|
| 14 | | | | | | | | | | | | | | | | | | | | | | | | | | | | | | | | | | | |
| 15 | | | | | | | | | | | | | | | | | | | | | | | | | | | | | | | | | | | |
| 16 | a/a | 465 | 57 | 15 | 47 | 11 | 242 | | 287 | 393 | 680 | | | 6 | 71 | 0.21 | | | | 31 | | 97 | | | 112 | 24% | 43% | | | | 3.38 | | 7 | 20 | $10 |
| 17 | STL * | 516 | 71 | 19 | 55 | 14 | 249 | 220 | 294 | 398 | 692 | 1200 | 496 | 6 | 70 | 0.21 | 44 | 16 | 39 | 32 | 97 | 91 | 109 | 13% | 111 | 21% | 57% | 8 | 13% | 50% | 3.73 | -20.6 | 2 | 6 | $14 |
| 18 | STL | 379 | 61 | 12 | 37 | 15 | 264 | 234 | 334 | 422 | 756 | 886 | 695 | 7 | 67 | 0.25 | 40 | 27 | 33 | 36 | 93 | 111 | 95 | 14% | 147 | 19% | 83% | 27 | 30% | 56% | 4.75 | 5.6 | 17 | 57 | $15 |
| 1st Half | | 161 | 26 | 5 | 12 | 7 | 267 | 244 | 337 | 398 | 735 | 859 | 671 | 8 | 70 | 0.29 | 46 | 29 | 25 | 35 | 84 | 80 | 59 | 18% | 156 | 19% | 78% | 14 | 29% | 57% | 4.53 | 1.9 | 10 | 33 | $9 |
| 2nd Half | | 218 | 35 | 7 | 25 | 8 | 261 | 229 | 332 | 440 | 772 | 909 | 712 | 7 | 65 | 0.22 | 35 | 25 | 40 | 37 | 100 | 136 | 123 | 12% | 132 | 18% | 89% | 13 | 31% | 54% | 4.91 | 4.9 | 24 | 80 | $19 |
| **19** | **Proj** | **490** | **69** | **15** | **53** | **14** | **241** | **227** | **303** | **388** | **691** | **952** | **588** | **7** | **69** | **0.23** | **43** | **22** | **35** | **32** | **95** | **100** | **101** | **13%** | **136** | **19%** | **64%** | | | | **3.68** | **-6.8** | **2** | **7** | **$16** |

STEPHEN NICKRAND

## Baez,Javier

| | | | | | |
|---|---|---|---|---|---|
| Age: 26 | Bats: R | Pos: 2B SS 3B | Health A | LIMA Plan B | |
| Ht: 6' 0" | Wt: 190 | | PT/Exp B | Rand Var -2 | |
| | | | Consist B | MM 4535 | |

Breakout into 5-category star fueled by uber-aggressive approach—at the plate and on basepaths. Can he sustain it? Big disparity in PX/xPX, just-okay HctX suggest some power give-back. And heck, they may just stop throwing him any strikes at all (2nd in MLB in chases outside zone). There's risk in a full bid.

| Yr | Tm | AB | R | HR | RBI | SB | BA | xBA | OBP | SLG | OPS | vL | vR | bb% | ct% | Eye | G | L | F | h% | HctX | PX | xPX | hr/f | Spd | SBO | SB% | #Wk | DOM | DIS | RC/G | RAR | BPV | BPX | R$ |
|---|---|---|---|---|---|---|---|---|---|---|---|---|---|---|---|---|---|---|---|---|---|---|---|---|---|---|---|---|---|---|---|---|---|---|---|
| 14 | CHC * | 601 | 74 | 26 | 81 | 17 | 209 | 213 | 260 | 393 | 654 | 569 | 546 | 6 | 60 | 0.17 | 41 | 14 | 45 | 30 | 81 | 166 | 120 | 17% | 97 | 24% | 64% | 9 | 33% | 67% | 3.17 | -4.2 | 17 | 46 | $15 |
| 15 | CHC * | 357 | 41 | 11 | 51 | 14 | 287 | 248 | 325 | 443 | 768 | 1082 | 617 | 5 | 69 | 0.18 | 37 | 31 | 31 | 39 | 103 | 117 | 121 | 6% | 115 | 21% | 72% | 6 | 33% | 67% | 5.06 | 9.1 | 16 | 43 | $16 |
| 16 | CHC | 421 | 50 | 14 | 59 | 12 | 273 | 241 | 314 | 423 | 737 | 850 | 689 | 3 | 74 | 0.14 | 44 | 20 | 36 | 34 | 88 | 95 | 89 | 13% | 116 | 16% | 80% | 26 | 27% | 38% | 4.44 | -5.1 | 17 | 49 | $15 |
| 17 | CHC | 469 | 75 | 23 | 75 | 10 | 273 | 247 | 317 | 480 | 796 | 934 | 747 | 6 | 69 | 0.21 | 49 | 15 | 36 | 35 | 91 | 129 | 104 | 20% | 118 | 12% | 77% | 27 | 44% | 41% | 5.31 | 3.9 | 30 | 91 | $19 |
| 18 | CHC | 606 | 101 | 34 | 111 | 21 | 290 | 283 | 326 | 554 | 881 | 933 | 865 | 4 | 72 | 0.17 | 46 | 22 | 32 | 35 | 96 | 163 | 110 | 24% | 154 | 25% | 70% | 28 | 61% | 29% | 6.23 | 33.7 | 77 | 257 | $37 |
| 1st Half | | 288 | 51 | 16 | 59 | 13 | 285 | 286 | 321 | 559 | 880 | 839 | 894 | 4 | 73 | 0.16 | 43 | 24 | 33 | 34 | 105 | 165 | 128 | 23% | 163 | 26% | 93% | 15 | 67% | 20% | 6.42 | 18.2 | 84 | 280 | $37 |
| 2nd Half | | 318 | 50 | 18 | 52 | 8 | 296 | 279 | 330 | 550 | 881 | 1033 | 841 | 5 | 72 | 0.19 | 48 | 20 | 31 | 36 | 87 | 160 | 93 | 25% | 136 | 23% | 50% | 13 | 54% | 38% | 6.06 | 17.2 | 68 | 227 | $36 |
| 19 | Proj | 566 | 86 | 28 | 93 | 17 | 280 | 261 | 319 | 503 | 821 | 923 | 788 | 5 | 71 | 0.18 | 46 | 20 | 34 | 35 | 92 | 141 | 105 | 20% | 139 | 20% | 70% | | | | 5.47 | 21.1 | 47 | 155 | $28 |

## Barnes,Austin

| | | | | | |
|---|---|---|---|---|---|
| Age: 29 | Bats: R | Pos: CA | Health A | LIMA Plan D | |
| Ht: 5' 10" | Wt: 190 | | PT/Exp D | Rand Var 0 | |
| | | | Consist F | MM 2321 | |

One wonders if spring elbow pain lingered, because this was a big disappointment. Maintained patient approach, but seemed to get more desperate as the year progressed. Power profile started to rebound some late, and it's unlikely he just forgot how to make contact. Expect at least a modest rebound, with... UP: 2017 redux.

| Yr | Tm | AB | R | HR | RBI | SB | BA | xBA | OBP | SLG | OPS | vL | vR | bb% | ct% | Eye | G | L | F | h% | HctX | PX | xPX | hr/f | Spd | SBO | SB% | #Wk | DOM | DIS | RC/G | RAR | BPV | BPX | R$ |
|---|---|---|---|---|---|---|---|---|---|---|---|---|---|---|---|---|---|---|---|---|---|---|---|---|---|---|---|---|---|---|---|---|---|---|---|
| 14 | aa | 284 | 41 | 7 | 32 | 6 | 245 | | 332 | 399 | 730 | | | 11 | 85 | 0.89 | | | | 26 | | 105 | | | 100 | 7% | 100% | | | | 4.60 | | 81 | 219 | $7 |
| 15 | LA * | 321 | 33 | 7 | 32 | 10 | 251 | 269 | 315 | 374 | 689 | 625 | 644 | 8 | 84 | 0.59 | 48 | 22 | 30 | 28 | 76 | 79 | 71 | 0% | 78 | 14% | 80% | 9 | 56% | 33% | 4.06 | 2.2 | 43 | 116 | $8 |
| 16 | LA * | 368 | 47 | 5 | 31 | 13 | 231 | 187 | 297 | 337 | 634 | 795 | 297 | 9 | 80 | 0.46 | 32 | 9 | 59 | 28 | 70 | 70 | 89 | 0% | 120 | 19% | 79% | 9 | 11% | 56% | 3.37 | -11.6 | 30 | 86 | $6 |
| 17 | LA | 218 | 35 | 8 | 38 | 4 | 289 | 295 | 408 | 486 | 895 | 886 | 902 | 15 | 80 | 0.91 | 45 | 26 | 29 | 33 | 100 | 112 | 94 | 16% | 114 | 6% | 80% | 27 | 56% | 26% | 6.95 | 17.7 | 77 | 233 | $8 |
| 18 | LA | 200 | 32 | 4 | 14 | 4 | 205 | 205 | 329 | 290 | 619 | 716 | 484 | 13 | 67 | 0.46 | 54 | 20 | 26 | 29 | 77 | 59 | 65 | 12% | 117 | 11% | 57% | 28 | 29% | 64% | 2.83 | -4.3 | -23 | -77 | $1 |
| 1st Half | | 126 | 22 | 1 | 5 | 2 | 214 | 224 | 340 | 270 | 610 | 709 | 509 | 13 | 72 | 0.54 | 57 | 22 | 21 | 29 | 67 | 42 | 39 | 5% | 125 | 5% | 100% | 15 | 20% | 73% | 2.87 | -2.2 | -12 | -40 | $0 |
| 2nd Half | | 74 | 10 | 3 | 9 | 2 | 189 | 175 | 310 | 324 | 635 | 725 | 417 | 14 | 57 | 0.38 | 46 | 15 | 38 | 28 | 92 | 98 | 126 | 20% | 101 | 23% | 40% | 13 | 38% | 54% | 2.72 | -1.8 | -34 | -113 | $2 |
| 19 | Proj | 214 | 31 | 7 | 24 | 5 | 231 | 240 | 343 | 376 | 719 | 769 | 655 | 13 | 72 | 0.52 | 49 | 21 | 30 | 29 | 89 | 92 | 91 | 15% | 116 | 13% | 61% | | | | 4.00 | 3.7 | 16 | 52 | $6 |

## Barnhart,Tucker

| | | | | | |
|---|---|---|---|---|---|
| Age: 28 | Bats: B | Pos: CA | Health A | LIMA Plan D+ | |
| Ht: 5' 11" | Wt: 192 | | PT/Exp C | Rand Var 0 | |
| | | | Consist B | MM 1035 | |

Was cruising along with a solid follow-up to 2017 until July hit. A small slump led to a loss of playing time, and it snowballed to a .179 month. Decent August tried to salvage his role but he slumped in Sept again. Still, his skills are largely stable and this all seems more like normal small sample size volatility.

| Yr | Tm | AB | R | HR | RBI | SB | BA | xBA | OBP | SLG | OPS | vL | vR | bb% | ct% | Eye | G | L | F | h% | HctX | PX | xPX | hr/f | Spd | SBO | SB% | #Wk | DOM | DIS | RC/G | RAR | BPV | BPX | R$ |
|---|---|---|---|---|---|---|---|---|---|---|---|---|---|---|---|---|---|---|---|---|---|---|---|---|---|---|---|---|---|---|---|---|---|---|---|
| 14 | CIN * | 310 | 16 | 2 | 21 | 0 | 202 | 189 | 259 | 258 | 517 | 167 | 568 | 7 | 84 | 0.48 | 60 | 7 | 33 | 24 | 79 | 39 | 38 | 7% | 105 | 1% | 0% | 9 | 22% | 44% | 2.10 | -13.2 | 14 | 38 | -$4 |
| 15 | CIN | 242 | 23 | 3 | 18 | 0 | 252 | 245 | 324 | 326 | 650 | 433 | 700 | 9 | 81 | 0.56 | 47 | 25 | 28 | 30 | 66 | 52 | 45 | 5% | 84 | 1% | 0% | 24 | 42% | 33% | 3.52 | -2.0 | 13 | 35 | $1 |
| 16 | CIN | 377 | 34 | 7 | 51 | 1 | 257 | 270 | 323 | 379 | 702 | 546 | 744 | 9 | 81 | 0.50 | 48 | 25 | 28 | 30 | 92 | 79 | 93 | 8% | 84 | 1% | 100% | 27 | 37% | 30% | 4.21 | -2.1 | 31 | 89 | $5 |
| 17 | CIN | 370 | 26 | 7 | 44 | 4 | 270 | 281 | 347 | 403 | 750 | 668 | 769 | 10 | 82 | 0.62 | 46 | 26 | 28 | 32 | 110 | 80 | 90 | 8% | 82 | 4% | 100% | 27 | 48% | 33% | 4.92 | 9.1 | 37 | 112 | $7 |
| 18 | CIN | 460 | 50 | 10 | 46 | 0 | 248 | 254 | 328 | 372 | 699 | 750 | 684 | 10 | 79 | 0.56 | 45 | 24 | 31 | 29 | 112 | 75 | 81 | 9% | 87 | 3% | 0% | 28 | 32% | 46% | 3.98 | 6.3 | 25 | 83 | $6 |
| 1st Half | | 246 | 28 | 5 | 27 | 0 | 268 | 262 | 346 | 386 | 733 | 1012 | 663 | 11 | 78 | 0.55 | 44 | 28 | 28 | 32 | 115 | 74 | 76 | 9% | 87 | 4% | 0% | 15 | 33% | 47% | 4.43 | 7.0 | 22 | 73 | $9 |
| 2nd Half | | 214 | 22 | 5 | 19 | 0 | 224 | 246 | 305 | 355 | 661 | 520 | 711 | 10 | 80 | 0.58 | 46 | 20 | 33 | 26 | 108 | 76 | 87 | 9% | 94 | 2% | 0% | 13 | 31% | 46% | 3.50 | 0.3 | 32 | 107 | $3 |
| 19 | Proj | 410 | 38 | 8 | 43 | 1 | 257 | 258 | 331 | 380 | 711 | 641 | 731 | 10 | 80 | 0.56 | 47 | 24 | 30 | 30 | 104 | 75 | 82 | 8% | 86 | 3% | 42% | | | | 4.25 | 9.7 | 18 | 60 | $8 |

## Barreto,Franklin

| | | | | | |
|---|---|---|---|---|---|
| Age: 23 | Bats: R | Pos: 2B | Health A | LIMA Plan C+ | |
| Ht: 5' 10" | Wt: 190 | | PT/Exp C | Rand Var -2 | |
| | | | Consist A | MM 4403 | |

5-16-.233 in 75 AB at OAK. Will 2019 be the year this perennial top prospect gets his shot? Dialed up the power numbers, including notable second-half step-up. Strikeouts an issue, but at 23, he's got time—and owns better contact skills in his past. May give some value back in BA, but if he lands a full-time role... UP: 30+ HR

| Yr | Tm | AB | R | HR | RBI | SB | BA | xBA | OBP | SLG | OPS | vL | vR | bb% | ct% | Eye | G | L | F | h% | HctX | PX | xPX | hr/f | Spd | SBO | SB% | #Wk | DOM | DIS | RC/G | RAR | BPV | BPX | R$ |
|---|---|---|---|---|---|---|---|---|---|---|---|---|---|---|---|---|---|---|---|---|---|---|---|---|---|---|---|---|---|---|---|---|---|---|---|
| 14 | | | | | | | | | | | | | | | | | | | | | | | | | | | | | | | | | | | |
| 15 | | | | | | | | | | | | | | | | | | | | | | | | | | | | | | | | | | | |
| 16 | a/a | 479 | 57 | 9 | 47 | 26 | 268 | | 313 | 390 | 702 | | | 6 | 80 | 0.32 | | | | 32 | | 76 | | | 105 | 36% | 59% | | | | 3.86 | | 26 | 74 | $19 |
| 17 | OAK * | 540 | 62 | 13 | 51 | 14 | 256 | 196 | 291 | 399 | 690 | 291 | 744 | 5 | 66 | 0.15 | 29 | 21 | 50 | 36 | 92 | 91 | 125 | 11% | 168 | 19% | 62% | 8 | 13% | 63% | 3.83 | -12.8 | 0 | 0 | $13 |
| 18 | OAK * | 355 | 55 | 19 | 54 | 4 | 231 | 201 | 296 | 449 | 744 | 684 | 781 | 8 | 60 | 0.23 | 35 | 9 | 56 | 33 | 90 | 163 | 159 | 21% | 121 | 8% | 65% | 14 | 21% | 71% | 4.35 | 2.6 | 25 | 83 | $10 |
| 1st Half | | 212 | 30 | 8 | 27 | 2 | 212 | 187 | 276 | 397 | 673 | 806 | 613 | 8 | 59 | 0.22 | 37 | 7 | 56 | 31 | 78 | 146 | 121 | 20% | 127 | 6% | 60% | 7 | 14% | 71% | 3.51 | -3.0 | 9 | 30 | $8 |
| 2nd Half | | 143 | 25 | 10 | 27 | 2 | 260 | 222 | 325 | 525 | 851 | 0 | 1056 | 9 | 61 | 0.25 | 31 | 13 | 56 | 35 | 113 | 188 | 222 | 22% | 95 | 11% | 69% | 7 | 29% | 71% | 5.80 | 7.7 | 43 | 143 | $13 |
| 19 | Proj | 359 | 50 | 18 | 47 | 7 | 250 | 220 | 309 | 461 | 770 | 766 | 772 | 7 | 65 | 0.21 | 37 | 16 | 47 | 33 | 84 | 143 | 123 | 16% | 147 | 16% | 59% | | | | 4.53 | 3.9 | 22 | 74 | $13 |

## Bauers,Jake

| | | | | | |
|---|---|---|---|---|---|
| Age: 23 | Bats: L | Pos: 1B | Health A | LIMA Plan B+ | |
| Ht: 6' 1" | Wt: 195 | | PT/Exp B | Rand Var +2 | |
| | | | Consist B | MM 3125 | |

11-48-.201 with 6 SB in 323 AB at TAM. Maybe he read his capsule in our 2018 book ("lack of HR punch caps upside"). Clearly opened up his swing going for said punch—and got it. Other numbers suffered some, but still owns past, much better ct%. Spd, SB% say not to count on SBs but at 23, a nice growth stock.

| Yr | Tm | AB | R | HR | RBI | SB | BA | xBA | OBP | SLG | OPS | vL | vR | bb% | ct% | Eye | G | L | F | h% | HctX | PX | xPX | hr/f | Spd | SBO | SB% | #Wk | DOM | DIS | RC/G | RAR | BPV | BPX | R$ |
|---|---|---|---|---|---|---|---|---|---|---|---|---|---|---|---|---|---|---|---|---|---|---|---|---|---|---|---|---|---|---|---|---|---|---|---|
| 14 | | | | | | | | | | | | | | | | | | | | | | | | | | | | | | | | | | | |
| 15 | aa | 257 | 30 | 4 | 30 | 5 | 249 | | 297 | 359 | 656 | | | 6 | 82 | 0.39 | | | | 29 | | 79 | | | 83 | 13% | 61% | | | | 3.52 | | 32 | 86 | $4 |
| 16 | aa | 493 | 69 | 12 | 68 | 9 | 249 | | 336 | 374 | 710 | | | 12 | 80 | 0.65 | | | | 29 | | 79 | | | 86 | 10% | 57% | | | | 4.15 | | 33 | 94 | $12 |
| 17 | aaa | 486 | 74 | 12 | 59 | 19 | 244 | | 343 | 379 | 722 | | | 13 | 74 | 0.57 | | | | 31 | | 88 | | | 92 | 15% | 85% | | | | 4.51 | | 22 | 67 | $15 |
| 18 | TAM * | 520 | 75 | 15 | 69 | 15 | 219 | 236 | 316 | 380 | 696 | 595 | 740 | 12 | 69 | 0.46 | 43 | 21 | 36 | 28 | 104 | 114 | 132 | 14% | 75 | 20% | 54% | 18 | 44% | 50% | 3.68 | -12.1 | 18 | 60 | $13 |
| 1st Half | | 272 | 39 | 6 | 28 | 10 | 252 | 270 | 344 | 406 | 750 | 1088 | 811 | 12 | 72 | 0.51 | 45 | 31 | 24 | 33 | 126 | 107 | 114 | 15% | 104 | 22% | 56% | 5 | 60% | 40% | 4.46 | -2.5 | 33 | 110 | $16 |
| 2nd Half | | 248 | 36 | 9 | 41 | 5 | 181 | 221 | 287 | 351 | 637 | 407 | 720 | 13 | 66 | 0.43 | 43 | 17 | 40 | 23 | 93 | 123 | 138 | 13% | 65 | 18% | 50% | 13 | 38% | 54% | 2.94 | -14.9 | 10 | 33 | $10 |
| 19 | Proj | 524 | 75 | 18 | 70 | 10 | 238 | 252 | 329 | 407 | 737 | 706 | 749 | 12 | 73 | 0.50 | 44 | 23 | 33 | 29 | 106 | 111 | 128 | 14% | 70 | 11% | 59% | | | | 4.37 | -6.2 | 30 | 99 | $16 |

## Bautista,Jose

| | | | | | |
|---|---|---|---|---|---|
| Age: 38 | Bats: R | Pos: RF 3B | Health B | LIMA Plan D | |
| Ht: 6' 0" | Wt: 205 | | PT/Exp B | Rand Var 0 | |
| | | | Consist C | MM 3101 | |

The biggest surprise here is that MLB folks decided he was worth 400 PA. Oh sure, he had that nice little run with PHI late. But overall skills were about the same as his awful 2017... which followed his so-so 2016. Get the drift? At 38, a solid career's end is drawing nigh—if it isn't here already. DN: 0 AB.

| Yr | Tm | AB | R | HR | RBI | SB | BA | xBA | OBP | SLG | OPS | vL | vR | bb% | ct% | Eye | G | L | F | h% | HctX | PX | xPX | hr/f | Spd | SBO | SB% | #Wk | DOM | DIS | RC/G | RAR | BPV | BPX | R$ |
|---|---|---|---|---|---|---|---|---|---|---|---|---|---|---|---|---|---|---|---|---|---|---|---|---|---|---|---|---|---|---|---|---|---|---|---|
| 14 | TOR | 553 | 101 | 35 | 103 | 6 | 286 | 290 | 403 | 524 | 928 | 1079 | 888 | 15 | 83 | 1.08 | 40 | 18 | 42 | 29 | 124 | 152 | 121 | 18% | 90 | 4% | 75% | 27 | 81% | 7% | 7.46 | 57.1 | 112 | 303 | $32 |
| 15 | TOR | 543 | 108 | 40 | 114 | 8 | 250 | 285 | 377 | 536 | 913 | 834 | 932 | 17 | 80 | 1.04 | 37 | 14 | 49 | 24 | 123 | 168 | 150 | 18% | 96 | 6% | 80% | 27 | 81% | 7% | 6.88 | 34.7 | 120 | 324 | $26 |
| 16 | TOR | 423 | 68 | 22 | 69 | 2 | 234 | 261 | 366 | 452 | 817 | 752 | 834 | 17 | 76 | 0.84 | 40 | 19 | 42 | 26 | 126 | 133 | 131 | 16% | 71 | 3% | 50% | 21 | 62% | 14% | 5.42 | 10.1 | 66 | 189 | $10 |
| 17 | TOR | 587 | 92 | 23 | 65 | 6 | 203 | 221 | 308 | 366 | 674 | 629 | 688 | 12 | 71 | 0.49 | 38 | 17 | 46 | 24 | 90 | 102 | 112 | 12% | 85 | 6% | 67% | 27 | 26% | 44% | 3.52 | -32.0 | 18 | 55 | $5 |
| 18 | 3 NL * | 361 | 56 | 14 | 52 | 5 | 202 | 215 | 333 | 368 | 702 | 700 | 738 | 16 | 66 | 0.59 | 34 | 20 | 46 | 26 | 97 | 117 | 128 | 13% | 66 | 8% | 52% | 23 | 43% | 30% | 3.83 | -8.9 | 14 | 47 | $6 |
| 1st Half | | 150 | 22 | 6 | 22 | 2 | 220 | 241 | 361 | 413 | 774 | 847 | 837 | 18 | 67 | 0.66 | 33 | 24 | 43 | 29 | 118 | 144 | 156 | 16% | 61 | 10% | 34% | 10 | 50% | 20% | 4.57 | -0.1 | 38 | 127 | $3 |
| 2nd Half | | 211 | 34 | 8 | 30 | 3 | 190 | 199 | 327 | 336 | 663 | 563 | 697 | 15 | 66 | 0.54 | 34 | 18 | 48 | 24 | 86 | 99 | 114 | 12% | 79 | 6% | 75% | 13 | 38% | 38% | 3.33 | -8.5 | 1 | 3 | $8 |
| 19 | Proj | 119 | 19 | 5 | 17 | 1 | 213 | 226 | 340 | 389 | 729 | 699 | 740 | 15 | 71 | 0.61 | 36 | 19 | 45 | 26 | 103 | 115 | 127 | 13% | 80 | 6% | 60% | | | | 4.15 | -1.1 | 23 | 78 | $3 |

## Beckham,Tim

| | | | | | |
|---|---|---|---|---|---|
| Age: 29 | Bats: R | Pos: SS 3B | Health D | LIMA Plan B | |
| Ht: 6'1" | Wt: 205 | | PT/Exp C | Rand Var +4 | |
| | | | Consist C | MM 3315 | |

Core muscle injury prematurely ended first half, and likely contributed to awful start. Showed signs of life late, with power skills rebounding to close to pre-injury levels in Aug/Sept. It's probably asking too much to expect a rebound to what was likely a career year in 2017. But 2018 second half is a reasonable baseline.

| Yr | Tm | AB | R | HR | RBI | SB | BA | xBA | OBP | SLG | OPS | vL | vR | bb% | ct% | Eye | G | L | F | h% | HctX | PX | xPX | hr/f | Spd | SBO | SB% | #Wk | DOM | DIS | RC/G | RAR | BPV | BPX | R$ |
|---|---|---|---|---|---|---|---|---|---|---|---|---|---|---|---|---|---|---|---|---|---|---|---|---|---|---|---|---|---|---|---|---|---|---|---|
| 14 | aaa | 62 | 7 | 0 | 3 | 0 | 225 | | 245 | 252 | 498 | | | 3 | 74 | 0.10 | | | | 30 | | 30 | | | 101 | 16% | 0% | | | | 1.66 | | -42 | -114 | -$2 |
| 15 | TAM * | 242 | 28 | 9 | 40 | 5 | 228 | 246 | 279 | 422 | 701 | 725 | 676 | 6 | 66 | 0.21 | 50 | 19 | 31 | 30 | 81 | 142 | 87 | 21% | 101 | 14% | 68% | 21 | 48% | 38% | 3.81 | -5.5 | 25 | 68 | $5 |
| 16 | TAM | 198 | 25 | 5 | 16 | 2 | 247 | 235 | 300 | 434 | 735 | 792 | 688 | 7 | 66 | 0.21 | 46 | 18 | 36 | 35 | 97 | 131 | 97 | 11% | 158 | 7% | 67% | 21 | 38% | 43% | 4.33 | -2.7 | 32 | 91 | $2 |
| 17 | 2 AL | 533 | 67 | 22 | 62 | 6 | 278 | 244 | 328 | 454 | 782 | 760 | 789 | 6 | 69 | 0.22 | 49 | 22 | 29 | 37 | 109 | 106 | 111 | 21% | 145 | 8% | 55% | 25 | 28% | 48% | 5.05 | 2.8 | 18 | 55 | $16 |
| 18 | BAL * | 392 | 46 | 12 | 35 | 2 | 223 | 233 | 276 | 360 | 636 | 715 | 640 | 7 | 73 | 0.27 | 46 | 20 | 33 | 27 | 82 | 89 | 84 | 13% | 86 | 4% | 46% | 20 | 35% | 60% | 3.21 | -13.5 | 5 | 17 | $4 |
| 1st Half | | 126 | 10 | 1 | 4 | 2 | 185 | 199 | 246 | 255 | 500 | 938 | 395 | 7 | 71 | 0.27 | 46 | 18 | 35 | 25 | 75 | 55 | 68 | 4% | 81 | 6% | 100% | 7 | 14% | 71% | 2.01 | -10.0 | -32 | -107 | -$10 |
| 2nd Half | | 266 | 36 | 11 | 31 | 0 | 241 | 247 | 298 | 410 | 707 | 633 | 737 | 7 | 74 | 0.28 | 46 | 21 | 32 | 28 | 85 | 104 | 90 | 17% | 93 | 3% | 0% | 13 | 46% | 38% | 3.87 | -5.1 | 23 | 77 | $11 |
| 19 | Proj | 523 | 62 | 18 | 52 | 5 | 248 | 237 | 301 | 410 | 712 | 774 | 682 | 7 | 70 | 0.24 | 47 | 20 | 33 | 32 | 90 | 106 | 92 | 15% | 122 | 7% | 61% | | | | 4.08 | 1.8 | 6 | 21 | $13 |

ROD TRUESDELL

## Bell,Josh

| Bell,Josh | | Health | A | LIMA Plan | B+ |
|---|---|---|---|---|---|
| Age: 26 | Bats: B Pos: 1B | PT/Exp | A | Rand Var | 0 |
| Ht: 6' 4" | Wt: 235 | Consist | A | MM | 3145 |

Missed two weeks in 2nd half (oblique). Significant sophomore pullback; hr/f regression exposed just how hard it is to clear fences when half of balls in play are GBs. And yet: controls the strike zone well; showed across-the-board gains in 2nd half. For now, a dull CI w/OBP utility. But if he gets the launch angle memo, look out.

| Yr | Tm | AB | R | HR | RBI | SB | BA | xBA | OBP | SLG | OPS | vL | vR | bb% | ct% | Eye | G | L | F | h% | HctX | PX | xPX | hr/f | Spd | SBO | SB% | #Wk | DOM | DIS | RC/G | RAR | BPV | BPX | R$ |
|---|---|---|---|---|---|---|---|---|---|---|---|---|---|---|---|---|---|---|---|---|---|---|---|---|---|---|---|---|---|---|---|---|---|---|---|
| 14 | aa | 94 | 10 | 0 | 5 | 3 | 249 | | 292 | 268 | 559 | | | 6 | 86 | 0.44 | | | | 29 | | 17 | | | 102 | 15% | 73% | | | | 2.67 | | 3 | 8 | $0 |
| 15 | a/a | 489 | 57 | 5 | 66 | 8 | 285 | | 356 | 390 | 747 | | | 10 | 86 | 0.77 | | | | 32 | | 65 | | | 116 | 8% | 63% | | | | 4.89 | | 52 | 141 | $15 |
| 16 | PIT * | 549 | 71 | 15 | 75 | 3 | 275 | 274 | 362 | 427 | 788 | 515 | 820 | 12 | 82 | 0.76 | 50 | 21 | 29 | 31 | 110 | 89 | 96 | 9% | 83 | 7% | 24% | 9 | 56% | 22% | 5.14 | -3.1 | 51 | 146 | $15 |
| 17 | PIT | 549 | 75 | 26 | 90 | 2 | 255 | 275 | 334 | 466 | 800 | 758 | 813 | 11 | 79 | 0.56 | 51 | 18 | 31 | 28 | 104 | 113 | 95 | 19% | 100 | 4% | 33% | 27 | 56% | 19% | 5.21 | -11.2 | 59 | 179 | $14 |
| 18 | PIT | 501 | 74 | 12 | 62 | 2 | 261 | 256 | 357 | 411 | 768 | 734 | 781 | 13 | 79 | 0.74 | 49 | 19 | 33 | 31 | 99 | 93 | 88 | 9% | 102 | 4% | 29% | 27 | 52% | 19% | 4.95 | -2.3 | 50 | 167 | $13 |
| 1st Half | | 283 | 40 | 5 | 41 | 0 | 251 | 248 | 330 | 385 | 715 | 784 | 693 | 11 | 79 | 0.60 | 49 | 19 | 33 | 30 | 83 | 85 | 74 | 7% | 106 | 2% | 0% | 15 | 40% | 27% | 4.28 | -4.1 | 40 | 133 | $12 |
| 2nd Half | | 218 | 34 | 7 | 21 | 2 | 275 | 266 | 390 | 445 | 835 | 684 | 904 | 16 | 80 | 0.93 | 48 | 20 | 32 | 32 | 120 | 103 | 105 | 13% | 99 | 6% | 40% | 12 | 67% | 8% | 5.88 | 7.0 | 65 | 217 | $13 |
| 19 | Proj | **522** | **73** | **18** | **67** | **4** | **264** | **265** | **352** | **438** | **789** | **713** | **814** | **12** | **80** | **0.71** | **49** | **19** | **32** | **30** | **106** | **101** | **94** | **13%** | **97** | **6%** | **39%** | | | | **5.20** | **6.6** | **48** | **160** | **$14** |

## Bellinger,Cody

| Bellinger,Cody | | Health | A | LIMA Plan | B+ |
|---|---|---|---|---|---|
| Age: 23 | Bats: L Pos: 1B CF | PT/Exp | B | Rand Var | -1 |
| Ht: 6' 4" | Wt: 210 | Consist | D | MM | 4525 |

His big splash from 1st half of 2017 (24 HR, 192 xPX, 31% hr/f) is fading from memory. Three subsequent halves look more mortal, culminating in swing-leveling adjustment in 2nd half of 2018. That yielded more ct% and LDs; could unlock 20-SB level. Power+speed make a nice value floor; just don't bid for 2017 1st half again.

| Yr | Tm | AB | R | HR | RBI | SB | BA | xBA | OBP | SLG | OPS | vL | vR | bb% | ct% | Eye | G | L | F | h% | HctX | PX | xPX | hr/f | Spd | SBO | SB% | #Wk | DOM | DIS | RC/G | RAR | BPV | BPX | R$ |
|---|---|---|---|---|---|---|---|---|---|---|---|---|---|---|---|---|---|---|---|---|---|---|---|---|---|---|---|---|---|---|---|---|---|---|---|
| 14 | | | | | | | | | | | | | | | | | | | | | | | | | | | | | | | | | | | |
| 15 | | | | | | | | | | | | | | | | | | | | | | | | | | | | | | | | | | | |
| 16 | a/a | 410 | 56 | 23 | 60 | 7 | 248 | | 325 | 458 | 784 | | | 10 | 75 | 0.45 | | | | 28 | | 124 | | | 86 | 8% | 76% | | | | 5.05 | | 47 | 134 | $12 |
| 17 | LA * | 547 | 99 | 43 | 109 | 16 | 272 | 266 | 356 | 578 | 934 | 903 | 948 | 11 | 69 | 0.42 | 35 | 18 | 47 | 32 | 120 | 183 | 178 | 25% | 122 | 13% | 84% | 23 | 70% | 17% | 7.25 | 21.0 | 83 | 252 | $29 |
| 18 | LA | 557 | 84 | 25 | 76 | 14 | 260 | 250 | 343 | 470 | 814 | 681 | 880 | 11 | 73 | 0.46 | 40 | 20 | 40 | 31 | 108 | 128 | 129 | 15% | 138 | 10% | 93% | 28 | 57% | 25% | 5.67 | 9.0 | 59 | 197 | $22 |
| 1st Half | | 292 | 49 | 16 | 40 | 5 | 240 | 249 | 323 | 483 | 806 | 797 | 810 | 11 | 71 | 0.43 | 37 | 18 | 45 | 28 | 104 | 149 | 158 | 17% | 132 | 7% | 100% | 15 | 60% | 13% | 5.34 | 5.0 | 68 | 227 | $22 |
| 2nd Half | | 265 | 35 | 9 | 36 | 9 | 283 | 250 | 365 | 457 | 822 | 552 | 955 | 11 | 75 | 0.49 | 43 | 22 | 35 | 35 | 112 | 105 | 100 | 13% | 139 | 12% | 90% | 13 | 54% | 38% | 6.04 | 9.5 | 49 | 163 | $23 |
| 19 | Proj | **529** | **83** | **27** | **85** | **16** | **266** | **248** | **347** | **487** | **835** | **730** | **886** | **11** | **72** | **0.44** | **38** | **19** | **42** | **32** | **113** | **136** | **146** | **17%** | **129** | **13%** | **84%** | | | | **5.93** | **17.9** | **57** | **190** | **$26** |

## Belt,Brandon

| Belt,Brandon | | Health | D | LIMA Plan | B |
|---|---|---|---|---|---|
| Age: 31 | Bats: L Pos: 1B | PT/Exp | B | Rand Var | 0 |
| Ht: 6' 4" | Wt: 235 | Consist | B | MM | 4225 |

Health is still the story. 2018 injury log: appendectomy in June, hyperextended knee in August, knee surgery in Sept. Relevant splits: Before appendectomy - .307/.403/.547 (11 HR) in 192 AB; afterwards - .203/.283/.290 (3 HR) in 207 AB. We'll stick with... UP: 30 HR if he can stay healthy for 500 AB. But that outlook is cloudy.

| Yr | Tm | AB | R | HR | RBI | SB | BA | xBA | OBP | SLG | OPS | vL | vR | bb% | ct% | Eye | G | L | F | h% | HctX | PX | xPX | hr/f | Spd | SBO | SB% | #Wk | DOM | DIS | RC/G | RAR | BPV | BPX | R$ |
|---|---|---|---|---|---|---|---|---|---|---|---|---|---|---|---|---|---|---|---|---|---|---|---|---|---|---|---|---|---|---|---|---|---|---|---|
| 14 | SF | 214 | 30 | 12 | 27 | 3 | 243 | 244 | 306 | 449 | 755 | 715 | 772 | 8 | 70 | 0.28 | 38 | 18 | 44 | 29 | 90 | 152 | 118 | 18% | 99 | 8% | 75% | 14 | 71% | 21% | 4.54 | 2.3 | 49 | 132 | $6 |
| 15 | SF | 492 | 73 | 18 | 68 | 9 | 280 | 257 | 356 | 478 | 834 | 802 | 845 | 10 | 70 | 0.38 | 33 | 29 | 38 | 37 | 123 | 145 | 156 | 14% | 89 | 9% | 75% | 24 | 46% | 33% | 5.97 | 8.5 | 45 | 122 | $20 |
| 16 | SF | 542 | 77 | 17 | 82 | 0 | 275 | 259 | 394 | 474 | 868 | 883 | 861 | 16 | 73 | 0.70 | 26 | 28 | 46 | 35 | 108 | 134 | 163 | 9% | 97 | 2% | 0% | 27 | 59% | 30% | 6.36 | 15.9 | 61 | 174 | $15 |
| 17 | SF | 382 | 63 | 18 | 51 | 3 | 241 | 258 | 355 | 469 | 823 | 713 | 879 | 15 | 73 | 0.63 | 30 | 23 | 47 | 28 | 113 | 140 | 154 | 14% | 86 | 5% | 60% | 18 | 61% | 28% | 5.49 | -4.7 | 60 | 182 | $8 |
| 18 | SF | 399 | 50 | 14 | 46 | 4 | 253 | 235 | 342 | 414 | 756 | 628 | 822 | 11 | 73 | 0.46 | 24 | 29 | 47 | 31 | 112 | 100 | 146 | 10% | 103 | 3% | 100% | 22 | 36% | 45% | 4.79 | -3.6 | 27 | 90 | $10 |
| 1st Half | | 244 | 38 | 13 | 37 | 2 | 291 | 263 | 384 | 512 | 896 | 724 | 992 | 12 | 75 | 0.56 | 24 | 29 | 47 | 34 | 125 | 132 | 177 | 15% | 92 | 3% | 100% | 14 | 50% | 29% | 7.02 | 15.3 | 60 | 200 | $19 |
| 2nd Half | | 155 | 12 | 1 | 9 | 2 | 194 | 193 | 273 | 258 | 531 | 451 | 568 | 9 | 70 | 0.33 | 24 | 28 | 48 | 27 | 90 | 47 | 94 | 2% | 113 | 5% | 100% | 8 | 13% | 75% | 2.22 | -12.5 | -27 | -90 | -$5 |
| 19 | Proj | **431** | **60** | **20** | **53** | **4** | **258** | **249** | **352** | **469** | **821** | **720** | **871** | **12** | **72** | **0.49** | **27** | **27** | **46** | **31** | **107** | **132** | **140** | **14%** | **100** | **4%** | **75%** | | | | **5.59** | **10.4** | **45** | **151** | **$15** |

## Beltre,Adrian

| Beltre,Adrian | | Health | C | LIMA Plan | C+ |
|---|---|---|---|---|---|
| Age: 40 | Bats: R Pos: 3B DH | PT/Exp | B | Rand Var | -1 |
| Ht: 5' 11" | Wt: 220 | Consist | D | MM | 2243 |

Second straight injury-ravaged season at tail end of a career marked by durability. It's hard to believe his epic 48-124-.334 season (2004, Dodgers) was nearly 15 years ago. Had an amazing late-career peak from 2010-16, with six of seven seasons in $24-$32 range. Whether or not this was the end, this journey ends in Cooperstown.

| Yr | Tm | AB | R | HR | RBI | SB | BA | xBA | OBP | SLG | OPS | vL | vR | bb% | ct% | Eye | G | L | F | h% | HctX | PX | xPX | hr/f | Spd | SBO | SB% | #Wk | DOM | DIS | RC/G | RAR | BPV | BPX | R$ |
|---|---|---|---|---|---|---|---|---|---|---|---|---|---|---|---|---|---|---|---|---|---|---|---|---|---|---|---|---|---|---|---|---|---|---|---|
| 14 | TEX | 549 | 79 | 19 | 77 | 1 | 324 | 286 | 388 | 492 | 879 | 984 | 845 | 9 | 87 | 0.77 | 42 | 22 | 36 | 35 | 125 | 111 | 122 | 11% | 86 | 1% | 50% | 26 | 73% | 12% | 7.16 | 50.9 | 81 | 219 | $28 |
| 15 | TEX | 567 | 83 | 18 | 83 | 1 | 287 | 288 | 334 | 453 | 788 | 929 | 715 | 7 | 89 | 0.63 | 42 | 23 | 36 | 30 | 130 | 97 | 109 | 10% | 96 | 1% | 100% | 25 | 60% | 16% | 5.45 | 14.0 | 76 | 205 | $21 |
| 16 | TEX | 583 | 89 | 32 | 104 | 1 | 300 | 287 | 358 | 521 | 879 | 1004 | 842 | 8 | 89 | 0.73 | 40 | 18 | 42 | 29 | 128 | 114 | 124 | 15% | 72 | 1% | 50% | 27 | 70% | 15% | 6.68 | 30.2 | 84 | 240 | $26 |
| 17 | TEX | 340 | 47 | 17 | 71 | 1 | 312 | 291 | 383 | 532 | 915 | 1124 | 862 | 10 | 85 | 0.75 | 43 | 20 | 37 | 33 | 124 | 116 | 119 | 16% | 62 | 1% | 100% | 18 | 61% | 39% | 7.57 | 24.9 | 72 | 218 | $15 |
| 18 | TEX | 433 | 49 | 15 | 65 | 1 | 273 | 261 | 328 | 434 | 763 | 700 | 790 | 7 | 78 | 0.35 | 38 | 26 | 36 | 32 | 121 | 98 | 112 | 12% | 72 | 1% | 100% | 26 | 50% | 42% | 4.97 | 7.8 | 27 | 90 | $12 |
| 1st Half | | 190 | 20 | 4 | 26 | 0 | 311 | 272 | 374 | 442 | 817 | 884 | 792 | 10 | 78 | 0.48 | 41 | 31 | 29 | 38 | 127 | 84 | 93 | 9% | 78 | 0% | 0% | 13 | 46% | 46% | 6.15 | 8.5 | 23 | 77 | $9 |
| 2nd Half | | 243 | 29 | 11 | 39 | 1 | 243 | 254 | 290 | 428 | 718 | 579 | 787 | 5 | 78 | 0.26 | 36 | 22 | 42 | 27 | 117 | 109 | 127 | 14% | 68 | 2% | 100% | 13 | 54% | 38% | 4.12 | -2.8 | 32 | 107 | $15 |
| 19 | Proj | **387** | **50** | **14** | **65** | **1** | **276** | **268** | **336** | **448** | **784** | **802** | **777** | **8** | **82** | **0.48** | **40** | **23** | **38** | **30** | **123** | **99** | **117** | **12%** | **73** | **1%** | **87%** | | | | **5.26** | **8.3** | **41** | **135** | **$14** |

## Benintendi,Andrew

| Benintendi,Andrew | | Health | A | LIMA Plan | B+ |
|---|---|---|---|---|---|
| Age: 24 | Bats: L Pos: LF CF | PT/Exp | B | Rand Var | -1 |
| Ht: 5' 10" | Wt: 170 | Consist | B | MM | 2445 |

According to BPX and R$, an all-around growth season. But there are warning signs: crashed after strong 1st half (as 1st half xPX foretold), and season-long drop in HctX is worrisome. Overall, a still-developing talent, and combo of plate skills, OBP and SB acumen form a nice foundation. But a return to 20 HR level is not assured.

| Yr | Tm | AB | R | HR | RBI | SB | BA | xBA | OBP | SLG | OPS | vL | vR | bb% | ct% | Eye | G | L | F | h% | HctX | PX | xPX | hr/f | Spd | SBO | SB% | #Wk | DOM | DIS | RC/G | RAR | BPV | BPX | R$ |
|---|---|---|---|---|---|---|---|---|---|---|---|---|---|---|---|---|---|---|---|---|---|---|---|---|---|---|---|---|---|---|---|---|---|---|---|
| 14 | | | | | | | | | | | | | | | | | | | | | | | | | | | | | | | | | | | |
| 15 | | | | | | | | | | | | | | | | | | | | | | | | | | | | | | | | | | | |
| 16 | BOS * | 342 | 48 | 8 | 50 | 7 | 289 | 288 | 345 | 481 | 826 | 429 | 984 | 8 | 84 | 0.53 | 36 | 25 | 39 | 33 | 112 | 117 | 116 | 6% | 116 | 19% | 47% | 8 | 50% | 25% | 5.51 | 12.1 | 81 | 231 | $13 |
| 17 | BOS | 573 | 84 | 20 | 90 | 20 | 271 | 257 | 352 | 424 | 776 | 622 | 813 | 11 | 80 | 0.63 | 40 | 21 | 38 | 31 | 112 | 85 | 100 | 11% | 111 | 14% | 80% | 26 | 46% | 23% | 5.24 | -3.4 | 46 | 139 | $24 |
| 18 | BOS | 579 | 103 | 16 | 87 | 21 | 290 | 274 | 366 | 465 | 830 | 694 | 877 | 11 | 82 | 0.67 | 41 | 24 | 35 | 33 | 84 | 104 | 81 | 9% | 115 | 14% | 88% | 27 | 59% | 4% | 6.27 | 27.4 | 68 | 227 | $30 |
| 1st Half | | 309 | 56 | 13 | 53 | 15 | 285 | 279 | 369 | 508 | 877 | 717 | 927 | 12 | 81 | 0.73 | 37 | 24 | 39 | 32 | 79 | 126 | 83 | 13% | 115 | 17% | 94% | 15 | 60% | 0% | 7.01 | 21.0 | 85 | 283 | $37 |
| 2nd Half | | 270 | 47 | 3 | 34 | 6 | 296 | 269 | 362 | 415 | 777 | 672 | 816 | 9 | 83 | 0.60 | 45 | 24 | 31 | 35 | 90 | 80 | 77 | 4% | 114 | 10% | 75% | 12 | 58% | 8% | 5.45 | 6.4 | 49 | 163 | $22 |
| 19 | Proj | **567** | **91** | **16** | **84** | **20** | **284** | **269** | **356** | **451** | **807** | **626** | **864** | **10** | **82** | **0.61** | **40** | **23** | **36** | **32** | **99** | **100** | **92** | **10%** | **115** | **15%** | **79%** | | | | **5.74** | **18.5** | **64** | **212** | **$29** |

## Betts,Mookie

| Betts,Mookie | | Health | A | LIMA Plan | C |
|---|---|---|---|---|---|
| Age: 26 | Bats: R Pos: RF | PT/Exp | A | Rand Var | -5 |
| Ht: 5' 9" | Wt: 180 | Consist | F | MM | 4555 |

An absolutely sterling season; just ponder that BPX for a moment. Repeatable? Rand Var has some quibbles: silly 2nd half h% and BA/xBA gap suggest we should use full-season xBA as our BA baseline. Even though xPX endorses the power, expect some pull back toward historical levels. But these are just minor blemishes on a diamond.

| Yr | Tm | AB | R | HR | RBI | SB | BA | xBA | OBP | SLG | OPS | vL | vR | bb% | ct% | Eye | G | L | F | h% | HctX | PX | xPX | hr/f | Spd | SBO | SB% | #Wk | DOM | DIS | RC/G | RAR | BPV | BPX | R$ |
|---|---|---|---|---|---|---|---|---|---|---|---|---|---|---|---|---|---|---|---|---|---|---|---|---|---|---|---|---|---|---|---|---|---|---|---|
| 14 | BOS * | 588 | 106 | 14 | 72 | 34 | 318 | 281 | 392 | 479 | 871 | 843 | 798 | 11 | 86 | 0.85 | 41 | 21 | 39 | 35 | 133 | 114 | 116 | 8% | 122 | 23% | 76% | 12 | 67% | 8% | 7.00 | 50.0 | 94 | 254 | $40 |
| 15 | BOS | 597 | 92 | 18 | 77 | 21 | 291 | 277 | 341 | 479 | 820 | 843 | 813 | 7 | 86 | 0.56 | 38 | 19 | 42 | 31 | 119 | 114 | 114 | 8% | 137 | 18% | 78% | 26 | 65% | 12% | 5.89 | 18.8 | 93 | 251 | $30 |
| 16 | BOS | 672 | 122 | 31 | 113 | 26 | 318 | 295 | 363 | 534 | 897 | 814 | 917 | 7 | 88 | 0.61 | 41 | 19 | 39 | 33 | 120 | 114 | 107 | 13% | 128 | 16% | 87% | 27 | 56% | 7% | 7.40 | 48.8 | 98 | 280 | $44 |
| 17 | BOS | 628 | 101 | 24 | 102 | 26 | 264 | 279 | 344 | 459 | 803 | 928 | 771 | 11 | 87 | 0.97 | 40 | 17 | 43 | 27 | 126 | 103 | 110 | 10% | 94 | 17% | 90% | 26 | 81% | 4% | 5.64 | 13.0 | 84 | 255 | $28 |
| 18 | BOS | 520 | 129 | 32 | 80 | 30 | 346 | 302 | 438 | 640 | 1078 | 1207 | 1037 | 13 | 83 | 0.89 | 34 | 21 | 45 | 37 | 135 | 166 | 151 | 16% | 140 | 20% | 83% | 26 | 77% | 8% | 10.93 | 87.0 | 133 | 443 | $46 |
| 1st Half | | 246 | 64 | 20 | 41 | 15 | 341 | 321 | 431 | 679 | 1110 | 1211 | 1074 | 13 | 85 | 1.03 | 32 | 22 | 46 | 34 | 139 | 179 | 157 | 20% | 128 | 22% | 88% | 13 | 92% | 0% | 11.46 | 45.0 | 151 | 503 | $46 |
| 2nd Half | | 274 | 65 | 12 | 39 | 15 | 350 | 286 | 444 | 606 | 1050 | 1200 | 1006 | 14 | 80 | 0.80 | 36 | 21 | 43 | 41 | 132 | 153 | 146 | 13% | 138 | 19% | 79% | 13 | 62% | 15% | 10.44 | 42.7 | 113 | 377 | $46 |
| 19 | Proj | **589** | **119** | **28** | **83** | **29** | **318** | **289** | **398** | **558** | **956** | **1054** | **927** | **11** | **85** | **0.84** | **37** | **20** | **43** | **34** | **130** | **134** | **130** | **13%** | **130** | **19%** | **84%** | | | | **8.35** | **62.2** | **110** | **366** | **$44** |

## Bichette,Bo

| Bichette,Bo | | Health | A | LIMA Plan | D+ |
|---|---|---|---|---|---|
| Age: 21 | Bats: R Pos: SS | PT/Exp | F | Rand Var | 0 |
| Ht: 6'0" | Wt: 200 | Consist | F | MM | 3441 |

One of top pure-hitting prospects in minors struggled in 1st half transition to Double-A. Then made significant progress in 2nd half, re-affirming his lofty status. Likely will need to repeat same cycle in Triple-A before he's ready for callup, but his bat (and legs) look to be impactful, and he's not far away.

| Yr | Tm | AB | R | HR | RBI | SB | BA | xBA | OBP | SLG | OPS | vL | vR | bb% | ct% | Eye | G | L | F | h% | HctX | PX | xPX | hr/f | Spd | SBO | SB% | #Wk | DOM | DIS | RC/G | RAR | BPV | BPX | R$ |
|---|---|---|---|---|---|---|---|---|---|---|---|---|---|---|---|---|---|---|---|---|---|---|---|---|---|---|---|---|---|---|---|---|---|---|---|
| 14 | | | | | | | | | | | | | | | | | | | | | | | | | | | | | | | | | | | |
| 15 | | | | | | | | | | | | | | | | | | | | | | | | | | | | | | | | | | | |
| 16 | | | | | | | | | | | | | | | | | | | | | | | | | | | | | | | | | | | |
| 17 | | | | | | | | | | | | | | | | | | | | | | | | | | | | | | | | | | | |
| 18 | aa | 539 | 84 | 10 | 66 | 28 | 281 | | 333 | 442 | 775 | | | 7 | 81 | 0.41 | | | | 33 | | 104 | | | 108 | 30% | 71% | | | | 5.09 | | 55 | 183 | $26 |
| 1st Half | | 322 | 53 | 7 | 39 | 23 | 268 | | 324 | 430 | 754 | | | 8 | 81 | 0.45 | | | | 31 | | 98 | | | 128 | 37% | 79% | | | | 4.88 | | 60 | 200 | $33 |
| 2nd Half | | 217 | 31 | 3 | 27 | 5 | 300 | | 348 | 460 | 807 | | | 7 | 80 | 0.36 | | | | 37 | | 113 | | | 103 | 20% | 51% | | | | 5.42 | | 55 | 183 | $16 |
| 19 | Proj | **162** | **25** | **4** | **20** | **6** | **287** | **270** | **339** | **476** | **815** | **815** | **815** | **7** | **80** | **0.41** | **40** | **20** | **40** | **34** | | **120** | | **8%** | **111** | **21%** | **71%** | | | | **5.64** | **5.3** | **70** | **235** | **$8** |

RAY MURPHY

## Bird,Gregory

| | | | | | |
|---|---|---|---|---|---|
| Age: 26 | Bats: L | Pos: 1B | Health | F | LIMA Plan D+ |
| Ht: 6' 4" | Wt: 220 | | PT/Exp | F | Rand Var +4 |
| | | | Consist | B | MM 4023 |

11-38-.199 in 272 AB with NYY. Right ankle surgery cost him the first two months, just latest in a long line of injuries. When he plays, the xPX and extreme FB% point to 30-HR upside. But poor ct%/h%/xBA are just as prevalent, and cap that upside as just another low-BA power source.

| Yr | Tm | AB | R | HR | RBI | SB | BA | xBA | OBP | SLG | OPS | vL | vR | bb% | ct% | Eye | G | L | F | h% | HctX | PX | xPX | hr/f | Spd | SBO | SB% | #Wk | DOM | DIS | RC/G | RAR | BPV | BPX | R$ |
|---|---|---|---|---|---|---|---|---|---|---|---|---|---|---|---|---|---|---|---|---|---|---|---|---|---|---|---|---|---|---|---|---|---|---|---|
| 14 | aa | 95 | 13 | 6 | 9 | 0 | 230 | | 334 | 504 | 838 | | | 13 | 69 | 0.50 | | | | 26 | | 218 | | | 95 | 0% | 0% | | | | 5.58 | | 106 | 286 | $1 |
| 15 | NYY * | 475 | 65 | 23 | 77 | 1 | 259 | 256 | 329 | 470 | 799 | 752 | 915 | 10 | 75 | 0.43 | 27 | 22 | 51 | 30 | 146 | 142 | 203 | 20% | 98 | 2% | 45% | 9 | 78% | 22% | 5.29 | 4.8 | 66 | 178 | $15 |
| 16 | | | | | | | | | | | | | | | | | | | | | | | | | | | | | | | | | | | |
| 17 | NYY * | 194 | 30 | 12 | 34 | 0 | 209 | 248 | 310 | 448 | 758 | 987 | 645 | 13 | 73 | 0.54 | 30 | 18 | 52 | 22 | 108 | 140 | 162 | 16% | 86 | 0% | 0% | 12 | 50% | 42% | 4.48 | -5.3 | 57 | 173 | $2 |
| 18 | NYY * | 303 | 29 | 14 | 43 | 0 | 196 | 225 | 280 | 392 | 672 | 764 | 647 | 10 | 71 | 0.40 | 34 | 16 | 49 | 23 | 104 | 126 | 143 | 11% | 66 | 0% | 0% | 20 | 45% | 25% | 3.48 | -8.9 | 26 | 87 | $1 |
| 1st Half | | 124 | 14 | 8 | 13 | 0 | 197 | 239 | 296 | 449 | 745 | 694 | 776 | 12 | 67 | 0.43 | 41 | 14 | 44 | 22 | 98 | 162 | 104 | 18% | 90 | 0% | 0% | 8 | 63% | 38% | 4.22 | -2.1 | 53 | 177 | -$1 |
| 2nd Half | | 179 | 15 | 6 | 30 | 0 | 196 | 216 | 271 | 352 | 623 | 783 | 576 | 9 | 73 | 0.38 | 31 | 18 | 52 | 23 | 108 | 103 | 161 | 9% | 67 | 0% | 0% | 12 | 33% | 17% | 3.00 | -10.0 | 16 | 53 | $3 |
| **19** | **Proj** | **311** | **38** | **17** | **46** | **0** | **228** | **239** | **319** | **451** | **770** | **889** | **738** | **11** | **72** | **0.44** | **32** | **18** | **50** | **26** | **112** | **140** | **156** | **15%** | **75** | **0%** | **50%** | | | | **4.66** | **-1.0** | **33** | **110** | **$5** |

## Blackmon,Charlie

| | | | | | |
|---|---|---|---|---|---|
| Age: 33 | Bats: L | Pos: CF | Health | A | LIMA Plan D+ |
| Ht: 6' 3" | Wt: 210 | | PT/Exp | A | Rand Var 0 |
| | | | Consist | D | MM 4455 |

Follow-up to MVP-caliber campaign fell short across the board. Plate skills held steady, but decline in hard contact and FB% drove HR and BA pullback. He's at an age where Spd tends to wane, but heightened selectivity on basepaths figures to keep him in double-digit SB. A return to .300 BA is more likely than 30 HR.

| Yr | Tm | AB | R | HR | RBI | SB | BA | xBA | OBP | SLG | OPS | vL | vR | bb% | ct% | Eye | G | L | F | h% | HctX | PX | xPX | hr/f | Spd | SBO | SB% | #Wk | DOM | DIS | RC/G | RAR | BPV | BPX | R$ |
|---|---|---|---|---|---|---|---|---|---|---|---|---|---|---|---|---|---|---|---|---|---|---|---|---|---|---|---|---|---|---|---|---|---|---|---|
| 14 | COL | 593 | 82 | 19 | 72 | 28 | 288 | 269 | 335 | 440 | 775 | 697 | 801 | 5 | 84 | 0.32 | 41 | 22 | 37 | 32 | 103 | 100 | 94 | 10% | 102 | 25% | 74% | 27 | 52% | 19% | 5.02 | 20.1 | 57 | 154 | $32 |
| 15 | COL | 614 | 93 | 17 | 58 | 43 | 287 | 266 | 347 | 450 | 797 | 709 | 828 | 7 | 82 | 0.41 | 38 | 25 | 37 | 33 | 117 | 100 | 119 | 9% | 137 | 34% | 77% | 27 | 59% | 22% | 5.37 | 18.7 | 64 | 173 | $36 |
| 16 | COL | 578 | 111 | 29 | 82 | 17 | 324 | 295 | 381 | 552 | 933 | 843 | 972 | 7 | 82 | 0.42 | 34 | 28 | 38 | 35 | 115 | 127 | 129 | 16% | 108 | 16% | 65% | 26 | 62% | 23% | 7.45 | 43.9 | 79 | 226 | $36 |
| 17 | COL | 644 | 137 | 37 | 104 | 14 | 331 | 294 | 399 | 601 | 1000 | 956 | 1023 | 9 | 79 | 0.48 | 41 | 22 | 37 | 37 | 125 | 141 | 141 | 20% | 165 | 13% | 58% | 27 | 56% | 7% | 8.63 | 61.7 | 98 | 297 | $42 |
| 18 | COL | 626 | 119 | 29 | 70 | 12 | 291 | 277 | 358 | 502 | 860 | 817 | 886 | 8 | 79 | 0.44 | 43 | 23 | 33 | 33 | 104 | 119 | 97 | 18% | 125 | 9% | 75% | 28 | 50% | 14% | 6.31 | 36.4 | 66 | 220 | $30 |
| 1st Half | | 314 | 60 | 14 | 35 | 5 | 271 | 265 | 348 | 459 | 806 | 772 | 828 | 10 | 79 | 0.51 | 45 | 22 | 33 | 30 | 96 | 99 | 81 | 17% | 135 | 9% | 63% | 15 | 47% | 7% | 5.35 | 11.0 | 58 | 193 | $26 |
| 2nd Half | | 312 | 59 | 15 | 35 | 7 | 311 | 289 | 369 | 545 | 914 | 862 | 946 | 8 | 78 | 0.38 | 42 | 25 | 33 | 36 | 111 | 139 | 114 | 19% | 113 | 10% | 88% | 13 | 54% | 23% | 7.41 | 27.7 | 74 | 247 | $34 |
| **19** | **Proj** | **604** | **114** | **28** | **78** | **13** | **302** | **283** | **367** | **524** | **892** | **838** | **920** | **8** | **80** | **0.44** | **42** | **24** | **34** | **34** | **112** | **124** | **116** | **17%** | **128** | **11%** | **71%** | | | | **6.80** | **44.5** | **74** | **247** | **$34** |

## Blandino,Alex

| | | | | | |
|---|---|---|---|---|---|
| Age: 26 | Bats: R | Pos: 2B | Health | C | LIMA Plan F |
| Ht: 6' 0" | Wt: 190 | | PT/Exp | D | Rand Var -5 |
| | | | Consist | C | MM 1101 |

Season-ending right knee surgery in late July casts doubt on spring availability. 2017 mechanical adjustments unlocked more pop, including twice as many doubles (36) as 2016, but results weren't there in MLB debut. Patient approach could spur growth in other areas, if opportunity finds him.

| Yr | Tm | AB | R | HR | RBI | SB | BA | xBA | OBP | SLG | OPS | vL | vR | bb% | ct% | Eye | G | L | F | h% | HctX | PX | xPX | hr/f | Spd | SBO | SB% | #Wk | DOM | DIS | RC/G | RAR | BPV | BPX | R$ |
|---|---|---|---|---|---|---|---|---|---|---|---|---|---|---|---|---|---|---|---|---|---|---|---|---|---|---|---|---|---|---|---|---|---|---|---|
| 14 | | | | | | | | | | | | | | | | | | | | | | | | | | | | | | | | | | | |
| 15 | aa | 115 | 13 | 3 | 15 | 2 | 214 | | 308 | 345 | 653 | | | 12 | 79 | 0.64 | | | | 25 | | 91 | | | 87 | 13% | 43% | | | | 3.26 | | 40 | 108 | $0 |
| 16 | aa | 401 | 47 | 8 | 34 | 13 | 215 | | 304 | 316 | 620 | | | 11 | 67 | 0.39 | | | | 30 | | 76 | | | 90 | 16% | 70% | | | | 3.11 | | -17 | -49 | $5 |
| 17 | a/a | 393 | 53 | 12 | 45 | 4 | 240 | | 337 | 416 | 753 | | | 13 | 74 | 0.57 | | | | 29 | | 117 | | | 88 | 11% | 31% | | | | 4.40 | | 45 | 136 | $6 |
| 18 | CIN | 128 | 14 | 1 | 8 | 0 | 234 | 194 | 324 | 289 | 613 | 627 | 607 | 9 | 68 | 0.32 | 45 | 23 | 32 | 34 | 84 | 43 | 73 | 4% | 114 | 0% | 0% | 15 | 7% | 73% | 2.94 | -5.0 | -39 | -130 | -$2 |
| 1st Half | | 115 | 12 | 1 | 6 | 0 | 217 | 186 | 308 | 270 | 577 | 607 | 563 | 9 | 68 | 0.32 | 47 | 21 | 32 | 31 | 84 | 40 | 69 | 4% | 114 | 0% | 0% | 13 | 8% | 77% | 2.56 | -5.7 | -42 | -140 | -$2 |
| 2nd Half | | 13 | 2 | 0 | 2 | 0 | 385 | 264 | 467 | 462 | 928 | 1000 | 916 | 7 | 69 | 0.25 | 22 | 44 | 33 | 56 | 85 | 73 | 112 | 0% | 113 | 0% | 0% | 2 | 0% | 50% | 8.20 | 1.3 | -15 | -50 | $0 |
| **19** | **Proj** | **156** | **18** | **3** | **14** | **1** | **221** | **221** | **321** | **321** | **642** | **633** | **644** | **11** | **71** | **0.42** | **45** | **23** | **32** | **30** | **86** | **73** | **62** | **8%** | **106** | **8%** | **45%** | | | | **3.11** | **-5.1** | **-20** | **-68** | **$2** |

## Bogaerts,Xander

| | | | | | |
|---|---|---|---|---|---|
| Age: 26 | Bats: R | Pos: SS | Health | A | LIMA Plan B+ |
| Ht: 6' 1" | Wt: 210 | | PT/Exp | A | Rand Var 0 |
| | | | Consist | C | MM 3455 |

Missed most of April with foot injury, which explains 1st half inactivity on bases. Mixed power metrics here: concurrent jumps in xPX and FB% bode well, while PX/xPX gap warns of possible hr/f pullback. Steady plate skills and HctX gains provide nice BA floor. Appealing skill set, but don't chase the next step forward.

| Yr | Tm | AB | R | HR | RBI | SB | BA | xBA | OBP | SLG | OPS | vL | vR | bb% | ct% | Eye | G | L | F | h% | HctX | PX | xPX | hr/f | Spd | SBO | SB% | #Wk | DOM | DIS | RC/G | RAR | BPV | BPX | R$ |
|---|---|---|---|---|---|---|---|---|---|---|---|---|---|---|---|---|---|---|---|---|---|---|---|---|---|---|---|---|---|---|---|---|---|---|---|
| 14 | BOS | 538 | 60 | 12 | 46 | 2 | 240 | 230 | 297 | 362 | 660 | 755 | 621 | 7 | 74 | 0.28 | 38 | 21 | 41 | 30 | 110 | 98 | 110 | 7% | 99 | 4% | 40% | 26 | 38% | 46% | 3.47 | 4.7 | 20 | 54 | $7 |
| 15 | BOS | 613 | 84 | 7 | 81 | 10 | 320 | 269 | 355 | 421 | 776 | 892 | 735 | 5 | 84 | 0.32 | 53 | 21 | 26 | 37 | 100 | 71 | 60 | 5% | 116 | 7% | 83% | 27 | 33% | 22% | 5.62 | 20.0 | 38 | 103 | $28 |
| 16 | BOS | 652 | 115 | 21 | 89 | 13 | 294 | 262 | 356 | 446 | 802 | 873 | 785 | 8 | 81 | 0.47 | 45 | 20 | 35 | 34 | 101 | 91 | 73 | 11% | 104 | 9% | 76% | 27 | 52% | 19% | 5.68 | 24.9 | 47 | 134 | $29 |
| 17 | BOS | 571 | 94 | 10 | 62 | 15 | 273 | 262 | 343 | 403 | 746 | 777 | 739 | 9 | 80 | 0.48 | 49 | 21 | 30 | 33 | 101 | 77 | 54 | 7% | 134 | 10% | 94% | 26 | 42% | 27% | 4.91 | 4.6 | 40 | 121 | $19 |
| 18 | BOS | 513 | 72 | 23 | 103 | 8 | 288 | 292 | 360 | 522 | 883 | 809 | 903 | 9 | 80 | 0.54 | 43 | 21 | 36 | 32 | 112 | 141 | 101 | 16% | 101 | 8% | 80% | 27 | 52% | 7% | 6.70 | 37.3 | 85 | 283 | $25 |
| 1st Half | | 263 | 36 | 12 | 44 | 2 | 278 | 287 | 338 | 502 | 840 | 746 | 868 | 7 | 80 | 0.40 | 44 | 20 | 35 | 31 | 115 | 137 | 101 | 16% | 92 | 5% | 67% | 14 | 50% | 0% | 5.82 | 13.9 | 75 | 250 | $20 |
| 2nd Half | | 250 | 36 | 11 | 59 | 6 | 300 | 296 | 383 | 544 | 927 | 885 | 938 | 12 | 80 | 0.68 | 42 | 22 | 36 | 34 | 108 | 146 | 101 | 15% | 109 | 10% | 86% | 13 | 54% | 15% | 7.68 | 25.6 | 96 | 320 | $29 |
| **19** | **Proj** | **573** | **86** | **22** | **93** | **11** | **286** | **279** | **353** | **484** | **837** | **825** | **840** | **9** | **80** | **0.49** | **45** | **21** | **34** | **33** | **106** | **118** | **83** | **14%** | **112** | **9%** | **84%** | | | | **6.09** | **34.3** | **66** | **220** | **$27** |

## Bonifacio,Jorge

| | | | | | |
|---|---|---|---|---|---|
| Age: 26 | Bats: R | Pos: RF | Health | A | LIMA Plan C+ |
| Ht: 6' 1" | Wt: 225 | | PT/Exp | C | Rand Var -3 |
| | | | Consist | B | MM 3123 |

4-23-.225 in 236 AB with KC. Suspended 80 games for PEDs and struggled upon return. xPX is his only plus skill (and just barely), so decision to hit more flyballs should help maximize value if he can get hr/f to cooperate. Shaky ct% and struggles vR mean he's just a bad-side platoon OF at this point.

| Yr | Tm | AB | R | HR | RBI | SB | BA | xBA | OBP | SLG | OPS | vL | vR | bb% | ct% | Eye | G | L | F | h% | HctX | PX | xPX | hr/f | Spd | SBO | SB% | #Wk | DOM | DIS | RC/G | RAR | BPV | BPX | R$ |
|---|---|---|---|---|---|---|---|---|---|---|---|---|---|---|---|---|---|---|---|---|---|---|---|---|---|---|---|---|---|---|---|---|---|---|---|
| 14 | aa | 505 | 40 | 3 | 42 | 7 | 212 | | 270 | 282 | 552 | | | 7 | 74 | 0.31 | | | | 28 | | 59 | | | 105 | 8% | 67% | | | | 2.45 | | -7 | -19 | $0 |
| 15 | aa | 483 | 49 | 13 | 52 | 2 | 218 | | 269 | 365 | 634 | | | 6 | 73 | 0.25 | | | | 27 | | 109 | | | 89 | 5% | 53% | | | | 3.16 | | 19 | 51 | $3 |
| 16 | aaa | 495 | 63 | 13 | 66 | 5 | 245 | | 299 | 389 | 689 | | | 7 | 72 | 0.27 | | | | 32 | | 93 | | | 110 | 6% | 67% | | | | 3.91 | | 10 | 29 | $9 |
| 17 | KC * | 435 | 60 | 19 | 49 | 1 | 258 | 252 | 320 | 443 | 763 | 713 | 768 | 8 | 71 | 0.31 | 39 | 26 | 35 | 32 | 92 | 109 | 98 | 18% | 99 | 2% | 50% | 25 | 24% | 40% | 4.84 | -1.0 | 19 | 58 | $9 |
| 18 | KC * | 287 | 40 | 4 | 30 | 0 | 247 | 226 | 327 | 381 | 709 | 777 | 629 | 11 | 71 | 0.41 | 34 | 23 | 43 | 34 | 93 | 100 | 111 | 6% | 96 | 1% | 0% | 15 | 27% | 53% | 4.17 | -2.8 | 14 | 47 | $3 |
| 1st Half | | 58 | 9 | 0 | 7 | 0 | 342 | 258 | 398 | 457 | 855 | 500 | 667 | 8 | 75 | 0.37 | 67 | 17 | 17 | 46 | 46 | 86 | -27 | 0% | 101 | 0% | 0% | 2 | 50% | 50% | 7.05 | 3.9 | 18 | 60 | -$4 |
| 2nd Half | | 229 | 31 | 4 | 23 | 0 | 223 | 223 | 313 | 362 | 675 | 794 | 629 | 11 | 69 | 0.41 | 33 | 24 | 44 | 30 | 93 | 103 | 116 | 6% | 96 | 2% | 0% | 13 | 23% | 54% | 3.62 | -5.9 | 13 | 43 | $5 |
| **19** | **Proj** | **383** | **51** | **12** | **43** | **1** | **258** | **242** | **326** | **430** | **756** | **803** | **738** | **9** | **72** | **0.34** | **35** | **25** | **40** | **33** | **93** | **113** | **109** | **11%** | **101** | **2%** | **50%** | | | | **4.74** | **3.2** | **21** | **69** | **$10** |

## Bote,David

| | | | | | |
|---|---|---|---|---|---|
| Age: 26 | Bats: R | Pos: 3B | Health | A | LIMA Plan D |
| Ht: 6' 1" | Wt: 210 | | PT/Exp | D | Rand Var +1 |
| | | | Consist | B | MM 2223 |

6-33-.239 in 184 AB with CHC. Has flashed glimpses of plus raw power since summer 2017 swing changes, but extreme GB% (both minors and MLB) and low ct% have dimmed it. Solving either problem would unlock some BA and HR upside. There's also enough speed to suggest a handful of precious SB. For deep speculators only.

| Yr | Tm | AB | R | HR | RBI | SB | BA | xBA | OBP | SLG | OPS | vL | vR | bb% | ct% | Eye | G | L | F | h% | HctX | PX | xPX | hr/f | Spd | SBO | SB% | #Wk | DOM | DIS | RC/G | RAR | BPV | BPX | R$ |
|---|---|---|---|---|---|---|---|---|---|---|---|---|---|---|---|---|---|---|---|---|---|---|---|---|---|---|---|---|---|---|---|---|---|---|---|
| 14 | | | | | | | | | | | | | | | | | | | | | | | | | | | | | | | | | | | |
| 15 | | | | | | | | | | | | | | | | | | | | | | | | | | | | | | | | | | | |
| 16 | a/a | 47 | 4 | 1 | 3 | 0 | 240 | | 289 | 290 | 580 | | | 6 | 73 | 0.26 | | | | 31 | | 27 | | | 105 | 0% | 0% | | | | 2.82 | | -38 | -109 | -$2 |
| 17 | aa | 470 | 58 | 13 | 53 | 4 | 249 | | 315 | 400 | 715 | | | 9 | 76 | 0.40 | | | | 30 | | 92 | | | 100 | 6% | 67% | | | | 4.24 | | 27 | 82 | $8 |
| 18 | CHC * | 419 | 48 | 15 | 63 | 5 | 230 | 242 | 295 | 399 | 693 | 871 | 668 | 8 | 68 | 0.29 | 57 | 18 | 24 | 30 | 97 | 111 | 101 | 19% | 119 | 11% | 50% | 19 | 32% | 42% | 3.74 | -11.8 | 16 | 53 | $9 |
| 1st Half | | 238 | 27 | 9 | 34 | 2 | 224 | 253 | 290 | 388 | 677 | 450 | 775 | 8 | 69 | 0.29 | 59 | 23 | 18 | 29 | 80 | 106 | 64 | 0% | 130 | 8% | 53% | 6 | 50% | 50% | 3.60 | -6.6 | 17 | 57 | $9 |
| 2nd Half | | 181 | 21 | 7 | 29 | 3 | 236 | 241 | 301 | 413 | 714 | 1029 | 655 | 8 | 67 | 0.28 | 57 | 17 | 26 | 31 | 99 | 117 | 108 | 22% | 111 | 13% | 48% | 13 | 23% | 38% | 3.94 | -3.1 | 15 | 50 | $9 |
| **19** | **Proj** | **257** | **30** | **7** | **35** | **3** | **242** | **248** | **309** | **393** | **702** | **698** | **704** | **8** | **71** | **0.31** | **54** | **21** | **25** | **31** | **91** | **99** | **90** | **16%** | **111** | **8%** | **54%** | | | | **3.94** | **-4.4** | **7** | **23** | **$7** |

## Bour,Justin

| | | | | | |
|---|---|---|---|---|---|
| Age: 31 | Bats: L | Pos: 1B | Health | D | LIMA Plan C+ |
| Ht: 6'3" | Wt: 265 | | PT/Exp | C | Rand Var +2 |
| | | | Consist | D | MM 3223 |

Failed to follow up on 2017 breakout despite extended opportunity. Saw more AB vL than ever before, and his immense struggles there reappeared. Overall, 2017 now looks like an outlier, but retains some value vs. RHers. His rate stats could rebound nicely if he finds a platoon role. Watch where he lands.

| Yr | Tm | AB | R | HR | RBI | SB | BA | xBA | OBP | SLG | OPS | vL | vR | bb% | ct% | Eye | G | L | F | h% | HctX | PX | xPX | hr/f | Spd | SBO | SB% | #Wk | DOM | DIS | RC/G | RAR | BPV | BPX | R$ |
|---|---|---|---|---|---|---|---|---|---|---|---|---|---|---|---|---|---|---|---|---|---|---|---|---|---|---|---|---|---|---|---|---|---|---|---|
| 14 | MIA * | 459 | 48 | 11 | 58 | 2 | 246 | 249 | 298 | 372 | 670 | 600 | 734 | 7 | 81 | 0.39 | 53 | 16 | 31 | 28 | 127 | 93 | 126 | 6% | 61 | 3% | 61% | 12 | 33% | 58% | 3.73 | -6.1 | 32 | 86 | $9 |
| 15 | MIA * | 460 | 48 | 24 | 77 | 1 | 258 | 254 | 321 | 458 | 779 | 573 | 845 | 8 | 77 | 0.40 | 48 | 17 | 35 | 29 | 112 | 128 | 110 | 21% | 46 | 1% | 100% | 25 | 48% | 28% | 5.06 | -4.1 | 41 | 111 | $14 |
| 16 | MIA | 280 | 35 | 15 | 51 | 0 | 264 | 276 | 349 | 475 | 824 | 533 | 857 | 12 | 80 | 0.68 | 43 | 22 | 35 | 28 | 114 | 117 | 107 | 19% | 55 | 0% | 0% | 18 | 61% | 28% | 5.80 | 3.7 | 56 | 160 | $8 |
| 17 | MIA | 377 | 52 | 25 | 83 | 1 | 289 | 279 | 366 | 536 | 902 | 809 | 929 | 11 | 75 | 0.49 | 43 | 23 | 34 | 33 | 118 | 138 | 127 | 26% | 41 | 1% | 100% | 22 | 41% | 36% | 7.09 | 12.4 | 46 | 139 | $16 |
| 18 | 2 NL | 423 | 49 | 20 | 59 | 2 | 227 | 231 | 341 | 404 | 746 | 570 | 819 | 15 | 71 | 0.59 | 45 | 19 | 36 | 27 | 97 | 108 | 109 | 18% | 57 | 1% | 100% | 27 | 37% | 41% | 4.57 | -6.8 | 17 | 57 | $8 |
| 1st Half | | 270 | 30 | 13 | 37 | 0 | 237 | 240 | 365 | 422 | 787 | 602 | 884 | 17 | 71 | 0.71 | 45 | 21 | 34 | 28 | 98 | 112 | 113 | 20% | 65 | 0% | 0% | 15 | 40% | 33% | 5.17 | 3.2 | 31 | 103 | $11 |
| 2nd Half | | 153 | 19 | 7 | 22 | 2 | 209 | 212 | 297 | 373 | 670 | 472 | 722 | 11 | 69 | 0.38 | 44 | 15 | 41 | 25 | 97 | 101 | 104 | 16% | 52 | 5% | 100% | 12 | 33% | 50% | 3.58 | -5.6 | -4 | -13 | $3 |
| **19** | **Proj** | **339** | **42** | **18** | **57** | **2** | **247** | **249** | **338** | **443** | **780** | **612** | **827** | **12** | **74** | **0.52** | **44** | **20** | **36** | **29** | **107** | **116** | **113** | **20%** | **78** | **2%** | **98%** | | | | **5.09** | **3.3** | **26** | **87** | **$11** |

GREG PYRON

## Bradley,Jackie

Age: 29 Bats: L Pos: CF | Ht: 5' 10" Wt: 200

Health A | PT/Exp A | Consist B | LIMA Plan B | Rand Var +2 | MM 3325

Sluggish start obscured a second half that looks a lot like 2015-16 (BPV). The difference? Two years of MLB experience, an unfortunate hr/f that effectively capped HR and ... manager Alex Cora (SBO). Contact and vL dives temper BA potential, but if xPX and baserunning opps continue ... UP: 20/20 season.

| Yr Tm | AB | R | HR | RBI | SB | BA | xBA | OBP | SLG | OPS | vL | vR | bb% | ct% | Eye | G | L | F | h% | HctX | PX | xPX | hr/f | Spd | SBO | SB% | #Wk | DOM | DIS | RC/G | RAR | BPV | BPX | R$ |
|---|---|---|---|---|---|---|---|---|---|---|---|---|---|---|---|---|---|---|---|---|---|---|---|---|---|---|---|---|---|---|---|---|---|---|
| 14 BOS * | 450 | 50 | 2 | 34 | 8 | 197 | 197 | 252 | 262 | 514 | 640 | 473 | 7 | 69 | 0.24 | 46 | 18 | 36 | 28 | 104 | 64 | 119 | 1% | 87 | 9% | 88% | 25 | 16% | 68% | 2.15 | -24.7 | -31 | -84 | -$1 |
| 15 BOS * | 503 | 75 | 17 | 68 | 6 | 267 | 264 | 337 | 460 | 796 | 918 | 791 | 9 | 76 | 0.44 | 48 | 16 | 36 | 32 | 106 | 132 | 133 | 18% | 98 | 8% | 59% | 15 | 53% | 47% | 5.27 | 11.2 | 61 | 165 | $17 |
| 16 BOS | 558 | 94 | 26 | 87 | 9 | 267 | 269 | 349 | 486 | 835 | 673 | 902 | 10 | 74 | 0.44 | 47 | 19 | 34 | 32 | 109 | 133 | 110 | 18% | 100 | 7% | 82% | 27 | 56% | 22% | 5.79 | 22.9 | 56 | 160 | $21 |
| 17 BOS | 482 | 58 | 17 | 63 | 8 | 245 | 246 | 323 | 402 | 726 | 766 | 713 | 9 | 74 | 0.39 | 49 | 18 | 33 | 30 | 100 | 91 | 89 | 15% | 96 | 9% | 73% | 26 | 31% | 38% | 4.24 | -7.2 | 19 | 58 | $10 |
| 18 BOS | 474 | 76 | 13 | 59 | 17 | 234 | 243 | 314 | 403 | 717 | 562 | 768 | 9 | 71 | 0.34 | 43 | 21 | 36 | 30 | 108 | 117 | 130 | 11% | 92 | 17% | 94% | 28 | 43% | 36% | 4.21 | 2.5 | 25 | 83 | $15 |
| 1st Half | 240 | 33 | 6 | 23 | 9 | 200 | 230 | 289 | 329 | 619 | 476 | 665 | 8 | 71 | 0.32 | 44 | 22 | 34 | 25 | 97 | 87 | 94 | 10% | 89 | 17% | 100% | 15 | 33% | 40% | 2.98 | -8.7 | 0 | 0 | $8 |
| 2nd Half | 234 | 43 | 7 | 36 | 8 | 269 | 258 | 340 | 479 | 818 | 650 | 875 | 9 | 71 | 0.35 | 42 | 19 | 39 | 35 | 118 | 148 | 167 | 11% | 97 | 16% | 89% | 13 | 54% | 31% | 5.75 | 10.9 | 52 | 173 | $22 |
| **19 Proj** | **479** | **72** | **15** | **63** | **14** | **245** | **247** | **321** | **421** | **742** | **662** | **770** | **9** | **73** | **0.35** | **46** | **19** | **35** | **31** | **107** | **115** | **120** | **13%** | **94** | **14%** | **88%** | | | | **4.53** | **5.5** | **40** | **133** | **$15** |

## Brantley,Michael

Age: 32 Bats: L Pos: LF | Ht: 6' 2" Wt: 200

Health F | PT/Exp D | Consist F | LIMA Plan B+ | Rand Var -2 | MM 2355

Season started off in a familar place—the DL (ankle surgery recovery). But after missing 6 games, health cooperated and reminded us of the value of elite ct%. Low FB% means <20 HR, production vL is waning, but success rate assures at least some SB. But when on the field, he's about one thing: Hard line drives. Lots of 'em.

| Yr Tm | AB | R | HR | RBI | SB | BA | xBA | OBP | SLG | OPS | vL | vR | bb% | ct% | Eye | G | L | F | h% | HctX | PX | xPX | hr/f | Spd | SBO | SB% | #Wk | DOM | DIS | RC/G | RAR | BPV | BPX | R$ |
|---|---|---|---|---|---|---|---|---|---|---|---|---|---|---|---|---|---|---|---|---|---|---|---|---|---|---|---|---|---|---|---|---|---|---|
| 14 CLE | 611 | 94 | 20 | 97 | 23 | 327 | 324 | 385 | 506 | 890 | 826 | 923 | 8 | 91 | 0.93 | 46 | 26 | 28 | 34 | 133 | 116 | 105 | 13% | 95 | 13% | 96% | 26 | 85% | 4% | 7.54 | 62.1 | 102 | 276 | $42 |
| 15 CLE | 529 | 68 | 15 | 84 | 15 | 310 | 308 | 379 | 480 | 859 | 785 | 908 | 10 | 90 | 1.18 | 46 | 23 | 32 | 32 | 121 | 107 | 88 | 10% | 77 | 10% | 94% | 26 | 77% | 0% | 6.92 | 36.1 | 92 | 249 | $28 |
| 16 CLE * | 67 | 7 | 0 | 8 | 1 | 197 | 258 | 255 | 253 | 508 | 821 | 504 | 7 | 88 | 0.64 | 44 | 24 | 32 | 22 | 115 | 43 | 108 | 0% | 103 | 7% | 100% | 3 | 33% | 67% | 2.11 | -4.5 | 32 | 91 | -$2 |
| 17 CLE | 338 | 47 | 9 | 52 | 11 | 299 | 288 | 357 | 444 | 801 | 696 | 857 | 8 | 85 | 0.62 | 49 | 22 | 28 | 33 | 117 | 81 | 74 | 11% | 97 | 12% | 92% | 20 | 50% | 10% | 5.94 | 4.5 | 53 | 161 | $15 |
| 18 CLE | 570 | 89 | 17 | 76 | 12 | 309 | 299 | 364 | 468 | 832 | 684 | 889 | 8 | 89 | 0.80 | 45 | 25 | 30 | 32 | 122 | 87 | 79 | 11% | 86 | 9% | 80% | 27 | 74% | 11% | 6.28 | 26.4 | 71 | 237 | $27 |
| 1st Half | 284 | 41 | 11 | 44 | 5 | 306 | 300 | 355 | 493 | 848 | 768 | 877 | 7 | 90 | 0.72 | 45 | 22 | 33 | 31 | 124 | 99 | 82 | 13% | 93 | 10% | 63% | 14 | 79% | 7% | 6.27 | 13.1 | 82 | 273 | $27 |
| 2nd Half | 286 | 48 | 6 | 32 | 7 | 311 | 300 | 373 | 444 | 817 | 608 | 901 | 9 | 89 | 0.87 | 45 | 28 | 28 | 33 | 120 | 76 | 76 | 8% | 83 | 8% | 100% | 13 | 69% | 15% | 6.28 | 13.0 | 62 | 207 | $28 |
| **19 Proj** | **513** | **76** | **14** | **73** | **12** | **301** | **298** | **361** | **456** | **817** | **700** | **872** | **8** | **89** | **0.81** | **46** | **24** | **30** | **32** | **122** | **87** | **81** | **11%** | **89** | **8%** | **94%** | | | | **6.12** | **21.4** | **72** | **241** | **$26** |

## Braun,Ryan

Age: 35 Bats: R Pos: LF | Ht: 6' 2" Wt: 205

Health C | PT/Exp B | Consist C | LIMA Plan B+ | Rand Var +4 | MM 4255

Missed games in each month due to injury, including two back-related DL stints. Though the time off affected totals, most skills continued to hold up. Elite-level HctX, solid Eye, more than enough power. If sub-30% FB% continues to be a thing, 20 HR will go by the wayside. Age and health raise the risk factor.

| Yr Tm | AB | R | HR | RBI | SB | BA | xBA | OBP | SLG | OPS | vL | vR | bb% | ct% | Eye | G | L | F | h% | HctX | PX | xPX | hr/f | Spd | SBO | SB% | #Wk | DOM | DIS | RC/G | RAR | BPV | BPX | R$ |
|---|---|---|---|---|---|---|---|---|---|---|---|---|---|---|---|---|---|---|---|---|---|---|---|---|---|---|---|---|---|---|---|---|---|---|
| 14 MIL | 530 | 68 | 19 | 81 | 11 | 266 | 278 | 324 | 453 | 777 | 823 | 760 | 7 | 79 | 0.36 | 47 | 20 | 33 | 31 | 115 | 131 | 124 | 14% | 119 | 13% | 69% | 25 | 56% | 24% | 4.94 | 17.7 | 71 | 192 | $21 |
| 15 MIL | 506 | 87 | 25 | 84 | 24 | 285 | 282 | 356 | 498 | 854 | 957 | 821 | 10 | 77 | 0.47 | 50 | 19 | 31 | 33 | 121 | 136 | 139 | 20% | 110 | 20% | 86% | 25 | 52% | 24% | 6.40 | 24.1 | 72 | 195 | $31 |
| 16 MIL | 511 | 80 | 30 | 91 | 16 | 305 | 303 | 365 | 538 | 903 | 1010 | 869 | 8 | 81 | 0.47 | 56 | 19 | 25 | 33 | 113 | 127 | 97 | 29% | 109 | 14% | 76% | 26 | 58% | 23% | 7.11 | 35.0 | 76 | 217 | $30 |
| 17 MIL | 380 | 58 | 17 | 52 | 12 | 268 | 291 | 336 | 487 | 823 | 872 | 808 | 9 | 80 | 0.50 | 49 | 19 | 32 | 30 | 126 | 124 | 122 | 17% | 95 | 17% | 75% | 21 | 62% | 24% | 5.64 | 4.2 | 68 | 206 | $15 |
| 18 MIL | 405 | 59 | 20 | 64 | 11 | 254 | 290 | 313 | 469 | 782 | 863 | 743 | 8 | 79 | 0.40 | 48 | 23 | 28 | 28 | 125 | 125 | 120 | 22% | 83 | 18% | 69% | 27 | 48% | 22% | 4.90 | 3.5 | 58 | 193 | $16 |
| 1st Half | 212 | 30 | 9 | 33 | 7 | 245 | 274 | 297 | 443 | 741 | 811 | 716 | 7 | 77 | 0.35 | 48 | 21 | 31 | 28 | 108 | 120 | 109 | 18% | 96 | 20% | 78% | 15 | 40% | 27% | 4.51 | -0.6 | 49 | 163 | $15 |
| 2nd Half | 193 | 29 | 11 | 31 | 4 | 264 | 307 | 330 | 497 | 828 | 897 | 780 | 8 | 81 | 0.47 | 49 | 25 | 26 | 27 | 145 | 131 | 132 | 28% | 72 | 16% | 57% | 12 | 58% | 17% | 5.35 | 4.3 | 70 | 233 | $17 |
| **19 Proj** | **418** | **63** | **21** | **65** | **10** | **269** | **292** | **330** | **491** | **822** | **893** | **792** | **8** | **80** | **0.43** | **50** | **21** | **29** | **29** | **125** | **128** | **120** | **22%** | **92** | **15%** | **68%** | | | | **5.50** | **11.0** | **67** | **222** | **$20** |

## Bregman,Alex

Age: 25 Bats: R Pos: 3B SS | Ht: 6' 0" Wt: 180

Health A | PT/Exp A | Consist B | LIMA Plan C | Rand Var +1 | MM 4355

The Perfect Growth Season? You laugh, but go column by column and note how many 2018 numbers represent improvement over 2017. (SPOILER: Almost all of 'em.) This is the exception to the "Prospect development is not linear" rule. Our minds (and research) say some regression is coming. But our hearts? UP: MVP

| Yr Tm | AB | R | HR | RBI | SB | BA | xBA | OBP | SLG | OPS | vL | vR | bb% | ct% | Eye | G | L | F | h% | HctX | PX | xPX | hr/f | Spd | SBO | SB% | #Wk | DOM | DIS | RC/G | RAR | BPV | BPX | R$ |
|---|---|---|---|---|---|---|---|---|---|---|---|---|---|---|---|---|---|---|---|---|---|---|---|---|---|---|---|---|---|---|---|---|---|---|
| 14 | | | | | | | | | | | | | | | | | | | | | | | | | | | | | | | | | | |
| 15 | | | | | | | | | | | | | | | | | | | | | | | | | | | | | | | | | | |
| 16 HOU * | 515 | 91 | 25 | 86 | 8 | 273 | 287 | 343 | 504 | 847 | 735 | 813 | 10 | 81 | 0.57 | 29 | 28 | 43 | 29 | 106 | 131 | 118 | 13% | 124 | 9% | 65% | 9 | 56% | 44% | 5.96 | 17.2 | 89 | 254 | $21 |
| 17 HOU | 556 | 88 | 19 | 71 | 17 | 284 | 276 | 352 | 475 | 827 | 974 | 776 | 9 | 83 | 0.57 | 38 | 22 | 40 | 32 | 110 | 106 | 102 | 10% | 124 | 15% | 77% | 27 | 56% | 26% | 5.89 | 16.2 | 72 | 218 | $24 |
| 18 HOU | 594 | 105 | 31 | 103 | 10 | 286 | 298 | 394 | 532 | 926 | 969 | 908 | 14 | 86 | 1.13 | 35 | 22 | 43 | 29 | 112 | 137 | 127 | 14% | 102 | 8% | 71% | 28 | 68% | 4% | 7.27 | 49.3 | 112 | 373 | $30 |
| 1st Half | 318 | 52 | 16 | 53 | 7 | 277 | 292 | 377 | 519 | 896 | 987 | 858 | 13 | 85 | 1.02 | 33 | 21 | 46 | 28 | 129 | 136 | 172 | 13% | 102 | 12% | 64% | 15 | 73% | 0% | 6.64 | 19.6 | 109 | 363 | $31 |
| 2nd Half | 276 | 53 | 15 | 50 | 3 | 297 | 307 | 413 | 547 | 960 | 950 | 965 | 15 | 86 | 1.26 | 36 | 23 | 41 | 30 | 91 | 139 | 75 | 15% | 103 | 3% | 100% | 13 | 62% | 8% | 8.05 | 27.0 | 119 | 397 | $30 |
| **19 Proj** | **588** | **101** | **28** | **93** | **12** | **285** | **290** | **374** | **516** | **890** | **948** | **868** | **12** | **84** | **0.82** | **35** | **23** | **42** | **30** | **108** | **130** | **110** | **14%** | **114** | **10%** | **75%** | | | | **6.75** | **37.3** | **95** | **316** | **$30** |

## Brinson,Lewis

Age: 25 Bats: R Pos: CF | Ht: 6' 3" Wt: 195

Health C | PT/Exp D | Consist D | LIMA Plan C+ | Rand Var +5 | MM 2525

11-42-.197 with 2 SB in 385 AB at MIA. The results were disastrous, but he posted solid power and speed metrics for a rookie. Hit rate has to improve, and better LD%, ct% and a green light would go a long way. It's a project for sure, but some pieces are in place. Channeling the patience of his team is one place to start.

| Yr Tm | AB | R | HR | RBI | SB | BA | xBA | OBP | SLG | OPS | vL | vR | bb% | ct% | Eye | G | L | F | h% | HctX | PX | xPX | hr/f | Spd | SBO | SB% | #Wk | DOM | DIS | RC/G | RAR | BPV | BPX | R$ |
|---|---|---|---|---|---|---|---|---|---|---|---|---|---|---|---|---|---|---|---|---|---|---|---|---|---|---|---|---|---|---|---|---|---|---|
| 14 | | | | | | | | | | | | | | | | | | | | | | | | | | | | | | | | | | |
| 15 a/a | 140 | 19 | 6 | 22 | 4 | 291 | | 343 | 482 | 825 | | | 7 | 74 | 0.30 | | | | 36 | | 131 | | | 96 | 14% | 79% | | | | 5.95 | | 46 | 124 | $6 |
| 16 a/a | 393 | 50 | 15 | 50 | 13 | 251 | | 280 | 441 | 721 | | | 4 | 76 | 0.17 | | | | 30 | | 115 | | | 108 | 26% | 66% | | | | 4.04 | | 39 | 111 | $12 |
| 17 MIL * | 346 | 49 | 12 | 37 | 9 | 261 | 267 | 319 | 445 | 764 | 933 | 314 | 8 | 74 | 0.33 | 57 | 17 | 27 | 32 | 100 | 109 | 99 | 25% | 121 | 17% | 61% | 5 | 40% | 40% | 4.71 | -4.8 | 38 | 115 | $10 |
| 18 MIA * | 432 | 32 | 12 | 45 | 3 | 194 | 218 | 228 | 327 | 556 | 637 | 555 | 4 | 69 | 0.15 | 52 | 17 | 31 | 25 | 99 | 82 | 109 | 13% | 159 | 5% | 74% | 21 | 24% | 71% | 2.36 | -27.9 | 1 | 3 | $0 |
| 1st Half | 277 | 21 | 10 | 30 | 1 | 188 | 218 | 231 | 347 | 577 | 656 | 541 | 4 | 67 | 0.13 | 50 | 17 | 33 | 24 | 100 | 97 | 124 | 16% | 157 | 5% | 50% | 15 | 27% | 73% | 2.37 | -18.5 | 4 | 13 | $2 |
| 2nd Half | 155 | 11 | 2 | 15 | 2 | 204 | 217 | 241 | 292 | 533 | 535 | 585 | 5 | 73 | 0.18 | 57 | 16 | 28 | 27 | 92 | 56 | 71 | 5% | 145 | 6% | 100% | 6 | 17% | 67% | 2.31 | -10.4 | -8 | -27 | -$2 |
| **19 Proj** | **463** | **48** | **13** | **52** | **9** | **232** | **241** | **278** | **384** | **662** | **697** | **651** | **6** | **73** | **0.22** | **54** | **16** | **30** | **29** | **95** | **94** | **92** | **13%** | **145** | **13%** | **70%** | | | | **3.46** | **-9.5** | **13** | **43** | **$10** |

## Broxton,Keon

Age: 29 Bats: R Pos: CF RF | Ht: 6' 3" Wt: 195

Health A | PT/Exp D | Consist C | LIMA Plan D | Rand Var 0 | MM 4501

4-11-.179 with 5 SB in 78 AB at MIL. Was one of the residuals of MIL's off-season OF makeover, but not at all surprising given his whifftastic history—though did reach 64% ct% in MLB. Still has the wheels for impact SB, and strength for power when he connects and lifts. But securing at-bats with those plate skills is a tall task.

| Yr Tm | AB | R | HR | RBI | SB | BA | xBA | OBP | SLG | OPS | vL | vR | bb% | ct% | Eye | G | L | F | h% | HctX | PX | xPX | hr/f | Spd | SBO | SB% | #Wk | DOM | DIS | RC/G | RAR | BPV | BPX | R$ |
|---|---|---|---|---|---|---|---|---|---|---|---|---|---|---|---|---|---|---|---|---|---|---|---|---|---|---|---|---|---|---|---|---|---|---|
| 14 aa | 407 | 48 | 9 | 37 | 18 | 226 | | 295 | 367 | 663 | | | 9 | 67 | 0.30 | | | | 32 | | 117 | | | 120 | 25% | 72% | | | | 3.53 | | 16 | 43 | $10 |
| 15 PIT * | 493 | 72 | 7 | 55 | 32 | 233 | 256 | 306 | 360 | 666 | 0 | 0 | 10 | 65 | 0.30 | 100 | 0 | 0 | 35 | 0 | 101 | -16 | 0% | 142 | 40% | 64% | 2 | 0% | 50% | 3.43 | -13.6 | 3 | 8 | $18 |
| 16 MIL * | 385 | 48 | 15 | 37 | 35 | 238 | 227 | 324 | 434 | 758 | 916 | 694 | 11 | 58 | 0.31 | 45 | 25 | 30 | 37 | 102 | 152 | 139 | 26% | 138 | 48% | 72% | 17 | 29% | 53% | 4.54 | -1.3 | 20 | 57 | $18 |
| 17 MIL * | 440 | 69 | 21 | 54 | 24 | 225 | 218 | 296 | 422 | 718 | 772 | 701 | 9 | 58 | 0.24 | 45 | 20 | 35 | 33 | 83 | 141 | 131 | 24% | 145 | 30% | 77% | 26 | 27% | 62% | 4.10 | -13.0 | 8 | 24 | $15 |
| 18 MIL * | 377 | 43 | 11 | 33 | 21 | 187 | 193 | 245 | 326 | 571 | 512 | 781 | 7 | 52 | 0.16 | 55 | 20 | 24 | 32 | 73 | 120 | 90 | 33% | 138 | 38% | 78% | 13 | 38% | 46% | 2.52 | -21.0 | -37 | -123 | $7 |
| 1st Half | 275 | 30 | 8 | 25 | 15 | 201 | 184 | 252 | 333 | 585 | 250 | 1455 | 6 | 50 | 0.14 | 70 | 10 | 20 | 37 | 92 | 120 | 148 | 100% | 119 | 37% | 75% | 2 | 50% | 50% | 2.67 | -13.0 | -54 | -180 | $11 |
| 2nd Half | 102 | 13 | 3 | 8 | 6 | 149 | 216 | 226 | 307 | 533 | 547 | 620 | 9 | 58 | 0.24 | 51 | 23 | 26 | 22 | 75 | 121 | 75 | 20% | 152 | 41% | 85% | 11 | 36% | 45% | 2.17 | -6.8 | -5 | -17 | -$2 |
| **19 Proj** | **192** | **25** | **8** | **19** | **10** | **204** | **217** | **277** | **389** | **665** | **712** | **640** | **9** | **57** | **0.22** | **47** | **23** | **30** | **31** | **88** | **141** | **115** | **23%** | **142** | **31%** | **79%** | | | | **3.44** | **-4.3** | **6** | **18** | **$6** |

## Bruce,Jay

Age: 32 Bats: L Pos: RF 1B | Ht: 6' 3" Wt: 225

Health C | PT/Exp B | Consist C | LIMA Plan B | Rand Var +3 | MM 4035

Early season foot/back issues may have affected numbers, but then a hip strain knocked out two full months. Was pretty much his old self upon return, with more patience and less hard contact. The body will need to cooperate, but there's still something left here. Like in 2016-17, a bucketful of HR could come cheap.

| Yr Tm | AB | R | HR | RBI | SB | BA | xBA | OBP | SLG | OPS | vL | vR | bb% | ct% | Eye | G | L | F | h% | HctX | PX | xPX | hr/f | Spd | SBO | SB% | #Wk | DOM | DIS | RC/G | RAR | BPV | BPX | R$ |
|---|---|---|---|---|---|---|---|---|---|---|---|---|---|---|---|---|---|---|---|---|---|---|---|---|---|---|---|---|---|---|---|---|---|---|
| 14 CIN | 493 | 71 | 18 | 66 | 12 | 217 | 240 | 281 | 373 | 654 | 556 | 685 | 8 | 70 | 0.30 | 45 | 21 | 34 | 27 | 99 | 122 | 109 | 15% | 88 | 14% | 80% | 26 | 35% | 46% | 3.44 | -9.9 | 21 | 57 | $12 |
| 15 CIN | 580 | 72 | 26 | 87 | 9 | 226 | 256 | 294 | 434 | 729 | 666 | 754 | 9 | 75 | 0.40 | 37 | 19 | 44 | 26 | 115 | 140 | 144 | 13% | 77 | 11% | 64% | 27 | 48% | 26% | 4.16 | -12.3 | 55 | 149 | $14 |
| 16 2 NL | 539 | 74 | 33 | 99 | 4 | 250 | 279 | 309 | 506 | 815 | 678 | 872 | 7 | 77 | 0.35 | 37 | 22 | 41 | 27 | 119 | 147 | 152 | 19% | 95 | 5% | 67% | 27 | 56% | 19% | 5.25 | 9.0 | 69 | 197 | $17 |
| 17 2 TM | 555 | 82 | 36 | 101 | 1 | 254 | 267 | 324 | 508 | 832 | 718 | 883 | 9 | 75 | 0.41 | 33 | 21 | 47 | 28 | 122 | 143 | 161 | 18% | 77 | 2% | 50% | 27 | 44% | 22% | 5.59 | 6.5 | 58 | 176 | $17 |
| 18 NYM | 319 | 31 | 9 | 37 | 2 | 223 | 236 | 310 | 370 | 680 | 660 | 688 | 11 | 76 | 0.55 | 28 | 24 | 48 | 26 | 94 | 94 | 126 | 8% | 74 | 6% | 40% | 20 | 30% | 35% | 3.66 | -7.2 | 28 | 93 | $3 |
| 1st Half | 212 | 17 | 3 | 17 | 2 | 212 | 226 | 292 | 321 | 613 | 501 | 656 | 10 | 77 | 0.50 | 31 | 23 | 45 | 26 | 93 | 73 | 111 | 4% | 85 | 6% | 67% | 13 | 15% | 38% | 3.02 | -9.5 | 16 | 53 | $1 |
| 2nd Half | 107 | 14 | 6 | 20 | 0 | 243 | 260 | 344 | 467 | 811 | 899 | 759 | 14 | 75 | 0.63 | 22 | 25 | 53 | 27 | 95 | 136 | 158 | 14% | 67 | 6% | 0% | 7 | 57% | 29% | 5.08 | 2.0 | 57 | 190 | $6 |
| **19 Proj** | **439** | **55** | **25** | **70** | **2** | **250** | **260** | **328** | **480** | **808** | **772** | **825** | **10** | **75** | **0.48** | **31** | **23** | **47** | **28** | **106** | **136** | **145** | **16%** | **74** | **5%** | **40%** | | | | **5.22** | **9.9** | **48** | **161** | **$15** |

BRENT HERSHEY

## Bryant,Kris

| Age: 27 | Bats: R | Pos: 3B | Health | B | LIMA Plan | B+ |
|---|---|---|---|---|---|---|
| Ht: 6' 5" | Wt: 230 | | PT/Exp | A | Rand Var | 0 |
| | | | Consist | C | MM | 4235 |

1st half looked sluggish on the surface, but xPX, HctX, Eye suggested all was well. Then shoulder woes cost two months and likely caused 2nd half fade. Drop in OPS vR and xBA are minor concerns, but he's young and talented enough to recover. With health, a return to 2017 production is plausible, only with fewer SB.

| Yr | Tm | AB | R | HR | RBI | SB | BA | xBA | OBP | SLG | OPS | vL | vR | bb% | ct% | Eye | G | L | F | h% | HctX | PX | xPX | hr/f | Spd | SBO | SB% | #Wk | DOM | DIS | RC/G | RAR | BPV | BPX | R$ |
|---|---|---|---|---|---|---|---|---|---|---|---|---|---|---|---|---|---|---|---|---|---|---|---|---|---|---|---|---|---|---|---|---|---|---|---|
| 14 | a/a | 492 | 91 | 33 | 85 | 12 | 290 | | 377 | 559 | 935 | | | 12 | 63 | 0.37 | | | | 40 | | 229 | | | 86 | 11% | 72% | | | | 7.48 | | 86 | 232 | $32 |
| 15 | CHC * | 587 | 92 | 28 | 107 | 15 | 276 | 233 | 361 | 492 | 854 | 797 | 875 | 12 | 64 | 0.38 | 34 | 21 | 45 | 38 | 104 | 165 | 148 | 16% | 129 | 11% | 78% | 26 | 50% | 35% | 6.28 | 26.8 | 53 | 143 | $29 |
| 16 | CHC | 603 | 121 | 39 | 102 | 8 | 292 | 273 | 385 | 554 | 939 | 1060 | 896 | 11 | 74 | 0.49 | 30 | 24 | 46 | 33 | 122 | 158 | 159 | 19% | 113 | 7% | 62% | 27 | 59% | 15% | 7.25 | 38.4 | 82 | 234 | $31 |
| 17 | CHC | 549 | 111 | 29 | 73 | 7 | 295 | 274 | 409 | 537 | 946 | 956 | 943 | 14 | 77 | 0.74 | 38 | 20 | 42 | 34 | 102 | 139 | 111 | 16% | 123 | 6% | 58% | 27 | 67% | 19% | 7.61 | 35.3 | 86 | 261 | $25 |
| 18 | CHC | 389 | 59 | 13 | 52 | 2 | 272 | 252 | 374 | 460 | 834 | 1138 | 749 | 11 | 72 | 0.45 | 34 | 25 | 41 | 35 | 83 | 125 | 119 | 11% | 120 | 5% | 33% | 22 | 45% | 36% | 5.49 | 9.2 | 49 | 163 | $12 |
| 1st Half | | 264 | 40 | 9 | 36 | 2 | 280 | 257 | 383 | 481 | 864 | 1235 | 775 | 11 | 75 | 0.52 | 33 | 24 | 44 | 34 | 101 | 129 | 146 | 10% | 129 | 8% | 33% | 13 | 46% | 38% | 5.88 | 10.4 | 67 | 223 | $17 |
| 2nd Half | | 125 | 19 | 4 | 16 | 0 | 256 | 245 | 356 | 416 | 772 | 995 | 687 | 10 | 67 | 0.34 | 36 | 29 | 34 | 35 | 47 | 117 | 55 | 14% | 96 | 0% | 0% | 9 | 44% | 33% | 4.72 | 0.8 | 13 | 43 | $2 |
| **19** | **Proj** | **526** | **91** | **25** | **75** | **5** | **281** | **255** | **381** | **502** | **883** | **1037** | **834** | **12** | **72** | **0.46** | **34** | **23** | **43** | **35** | **100** | **143** | **112** | **16%** | **117** | **6%** | **56%** | | | | **6.36** | **27.8** | **52** | **173** | **$21** |

## Buxton,Byron

| Age: 25 | Bats: R | Pos: CF | Health | C | LIMA Plan | C |
|---|---|---|---|---|---|---|
| Ht: 6' 2" | Wt: 190 | | PT/Exp | C | Rand Var | +4 |
| | | | Consist | C | MM | 3503 |

0-4-.156 in 94 AB at MIN. Lost 3 months to toe injury and wasn't recalled from AAA afterwards. Can't blame injury for terrible numbers, as poor plate skills consistent with history. Defense should earn MLB AB, but without more ct%, bb%, or GB% to exploit elite speed, he's on a Melvin Upton career path.

| Yr | Tm | AB | R | HR | RBI | SB | BA | xBA | OBP | SLG | OPS | vL | vR | bb% | ct% | Eye | G | L | F | h% | HctX | PX | xPX | hr/f | Spd | SBO | SB% | #Wk | DOM | DIS | RC/G | RAR | BPV | BPX | R$ |
|---|---|---|---|---|---|---|---|---|---|---|---|---|---|---|---|---|---|---|---|---|---|---|---|---|---|---|---|---|---|---|---|---|---|---|---|
| 14 | | | | | | | | | | | | | | | | | | | | | | | | | | | | | | | | | | | |
| 15 | MIN * | 421 | 61 | 8 | 43 | 20 | 261 | 220 | 310 | 411 | 721 | 318 | 704 | 7 | 74 | 0.27 | 43 | 14 | 43 | 34 | 88 | 96 | 104 | 6% | 189 | 24% | 79% | 10 | 20% | 70% | 4.43 | -0.9 | 45 | 122 | $16 |
| 16 | MIN * | 488 | 81 | 20 | 60 | 16 | 250 | 232 | 301 | 469 | 770 | 735 | 704 | 7 | 64 | 0.20 | 35 | 22 | 43 | 35 | 70 | 158 | 85 | 14% | 174 | 19% | 89% | 20 | 30% | 50% | 4.90 | 7.7 | 48 | 137 | $17 |
| 17 | MIN | 462 | 69 | 16 | 51 | 29 | 253 | 223 | 314 | 413 | 728 | 792 | 701 | 7 | 68 | 0.25 | 39 | 23 | 38 | 34 | 75 | 97 | 85 | 14% | 181 | 25% | 97% | 25 | 24% | 48% | 4.70 | -0.6 | 19 | 58 | $20 |
| 18 | MIN * | 226 | 27 | 4 | 16 | 9 | 212 | 222 | 248 | 330 | 578 | 222 | 422 | 5 | 67 | 0.14 | 43 | 23 | 33 | 30 | 75 | 92 | 48 | 0% | 122 | 24% | 88% | 7 | 14% | 86% | 2.74 | -9.0 | -9 | -30 | $2 |
| 1st Half | | 135 | 9 | 1 | 8 | 7 | 164 | 200 | 198 | 228 | 425 | 222 | 422 | 4 | 67 | 0.13 | 43 | 23 | 33 | 24 | 75 | 54 | 48 | 0% | 109 | 37% | 86% | 7 | 14% | 86% | 1.46 | -12.0 | -46 | -153 | -$1 |
| 2nd Half | | 91 | 18 | 3 | 8 | 2 | 282 | 250 | 321 | 482 | 803 | | | 5 | 67 | 0.17 | | | | 39 | | 149 | | | 129 | 9% | 100% | | | | 5.61 | | 40 | 133 | $8 |
| **19** | **Proj** | **363** | **54** | **8** | **34** | **15** | **245** | **219** | **292** | **392** | **684** | **646** | **699** | **6** | **67** | **0.19** | **39** | **21** | **39** | **34** | **75** | **104** | **77** | **8%** | **160** | **21%** | **92%** | | | | **3.99** | **-1.6** | **13** | **44** | **$13** |

## Cabrera,Asdrubal

| Age: 33 | Bats: B | Pos: 2B SS 3B | Health | B | LIMA Plan | B+ |
|---|---|---|---|---|---|---|
| Ht: 6' 0" | Wt: 205 | | PT/Exp | A | Rand Var | 0 |
| | | | Consist | A | MM | 3135 |

Another solid, unspectacular season. xPX and HctX remain strong and support 2018's HR output. xBA ticked down due to slight declines in plate skills, Spd. With playing time, another 20 HR within reason. Draft for: Reliable output (see A-grade Consistency) with roster flexibility. Don't draft for: draft room oohs and aahs.

| Yr | Tm | AB | R | HR | RBI | SB | BA | xBA | OBP | SLG | OPS | vL | vR | bb% | ct% | Eye | G | L | F | h% | HctX | PX | xPX | hr/f | Spd | SBO | SB% | #Wk | DOM | DIS | RC/G | RAR | BPV | BPX | R$ |
|---|---|---|---|---|---|---|---|---|---|---|---|---|---|---|---|---|---|---|---|---|---|---|---|---|---|---|---|---|---|---|---|---|---|---|---|
| 14 | 2 TM | 553 | 74 | 14 | 61 | 10 | 241 | 250 | 307 | 387 | 694 | 689 | 696 | 8 | 80 | 0.45 | 38 | 19 | 42 | 28 | 118 | 105 | 126 | 8% | 108 | 9% | 83% | 27 | 48% | 30% | 3.97 | 9.5 | 56 | 151 | $13 |
| 15 | TAM | 505 | 66 | 15 | 58 | 6 | 265 | 248 | 315 | 430 | 744 | 725 | 752 | 7 | 79 | 0.34 | 36 | 21 | 44 | 31 | 91 | 107 | 107 | 9% | 101 | 7% | 67% | 25 | 48% | 28% | 4.64 | 6.8 | 46 | 124 | $14 |
| 16 | NYM | 521 | 65 | 23 | 62 | 5 | 280 | 273 | 336 | 474 | 810 | 835 | 803 | 7 | 80 | 0.37 | 37 | 23 | 40 | 31 | 119 | 114 | 142 | 14% | 80 | 5% | 83% | 26 | 38% | 23% | 5.54 | 10.0 | 51 | 146 | $17 |
| 17 | NYM | 479 | 66 | 14 | 59 | 3 | 280 | 267 | 351 | 434 | 785 | 946 | 729 | 9 | 83 | 0.60 | 43 | 20 | 36 | 31 | 123 | 90 | 115 | 10% | 81 | 4% | 60% | 25 | 44% | 28% | 5.30 | 3.8 | 47 | 142 | $13 |
| 18 | 2 NL | 546 | 68 | 23 | 75 | 0 | 262 | 260 | 316 | 458 | 774 | 646 | 824 | 7 | 78 | 0.34 | 42 | 19 | 39 | 30 | 111 | 119 | 123 | 14% | 72 | 0% | 0% | 27 | 37% | 22% | 4.96 | 10.9 | 45 | 150 | $15 |
| 1st Half | | 308 | 36 | 13 | 44 | 0 | 279 | 265 | 321 | 471 | 792 | 732 | 818 | 6 | 80 | 0.30 | 43 | 21 | 37 | 31 | 123 | 112 | 133 | 15% | 90 | 0% | 0% | 15 | 47% | 13% | 5.35 | 10.2 | 48 | 160 | $19 |
| 2nd Half | | 238 | 32 | 10 | 31 | 0 | 239 | 252 | 309 | 441 | 750 | 516 | 832 | 8 | 76 | 0.39 | 41 | 17 | 42 | 27 | 94 | 128 | 109 | 13% | 56 | 0% | 0% | 12 | 25% | 33% | 4.49 | 2.3 | 44 | 147 | $10 |
| **19** | **Proj** | **517** | **67** | **20** | **66** | **2** | **265** | **261** | **325** | **448** | **773** | **731** | **788** | **8** | **80** | **0.40** | **41** | **20** | **39** | **30** | **112** | **111** | **121** | **12%** | **76** | **3%** | **71%** | | | | **4.98** | **12.0** | **41** | **138** | **$16** |

## Cabrera,Melky

| Age: 34 | Bats: B | Pos: RF | Health | A | LIMA Plan | D+ |
|---|---|---|---|---|---|---|
| Ht: 5' 10" | Wt: 210 | | PT/Exp | B | Rand Var | 0 |
| | | | Consist | B | MM | 2153 |

6-39-.280 in 250 AB at CLE. Split 1st half between AAA and unemployment before landing regular job in July. Good BA/OBP backed up by ct%, HctX; though those are his only assets. xPX and FB% trends agree power in decline, and it's unlikely to return at his age. If full-timer, BA floor gives him some value as a R/RBI accumulator.

| Yr | Tm | AB | R | HR | RBI | SB | BA | xBA | OBP | SLG | OPS | vL | vR | bb% | ct% | Eye | G | L | F | h% | HctX | PX | xPX | hr/f | Spd | SBO | SB% | #Wk | DOM | DIS | RC/G | RAR | BPV | BPX | R$ |
|---|---|---|---|---|---|---|---|---|---|---|---|---|---|---|---|---|---|---|---|---|---|---|---|---|---|---|---|---|---|---|---|---|---|---|---|
| 14 | TOR | 568 | 81 | 16 | 73 | 6 | 301 | 297 | 351 | 458 | 808 | 785 | 817 | 7 | 88 | 0.64 | 49 | 21 | 30 | 32 | 116 | 104 | 90 | 11% | 94 | 5% | 75% | 23 | 61% | 9% | 5.84 | 30.4 | 80 | 216 | $25 |
| 15 | CHW | 629 | 70 | 12 | 77 | 3 | 273 | 278 | 314 | 394 | 709 | 600 | 748 | 6 | 86 | 0.45 | 46 | 24 | 30 | 30 | 101 | 79 | 66 | 7% | 71 | 2% | 100% | 26 | 35% | 19% | 4.41 | -6.3 | 42 | 114 | $16 |
| 16 | CHW | 591 | 70 | 14 | 86 | 2 | 296 | 289 | 345 | 455 | 800 | 847 | 788 | 7 | 88 | 0.68 | 43 | 22 | 35 | 32 | 103 | 92 | 79 | 8% | 82 | 1% | 100% | 27 | 67% | 19% | 5.76 | 17.1 | 68 | 194 | $20 |
| 17 | 2 AL | 620 | 78 | 17 | 85 | 1 | 285 | 284 | 324 | 423 | 746 | 785 | 734 | 5 | 88 | 0.49 | 49 | 22 | 29 | 30 | 103 | 71 | 75 | 11% | 75 | 2% | 33% | 27 | 52% | 11% | 4.84 | -1.5 | 44 | 133 | $18 |
| 18 | CLE * | 328 | 33 | 6 | 45 | 2 | 275 | 291 | 319 | 401 | 720 | 841 | 722 | 6 | 85 | 0.42 | 45 | 29 | 26 | 31 | 122 | 79 | 70 | 11% | 54 | 4% | 70% | 16 | 38% | 25% | 4.48 | -0.2 | 32 | 107 | $7 |
| 1st Half | | 100 | 9 | 0 | 14 | 1 | 217 | 249 | 240 | 301 | 541 | 625 | 502 | 3 | 84 | 0.18 | 48 | 19 | 33 | 26 | 107 | 66 | 88 | 0% | 72 | 4% | 100% | 4 | 25% | 25% | 2.38 | -6.4 | 17 | 57 | -$6 |
| 2nd Half | | 228 | 24 | 6 | 31 | 2 | 300 | 305 | 352 | 444 | 797 | 905 | 791 | 7 | 85 | 0.54 | 45 | 32 | 24 | 33 | 127 | 84 | 64 | 15% | 53 | 4% | 63% | 12 | 42% | 25% | 5.65 | 7.5 | 40 | 133 | $13 |
| **19** | **Proj** | **297** | **33** | **7** | **41** | **2** | **278** | **286** | **319** | **419** | **738** | **792** | **719** | **6** | **86** | **0.45** | **46** | **24** | **29** | **30** | **112** | **82** | **75** | **9%** | **70** | **3%** | **73%** | | | | **4.73** | **2.3** | **43** | **144** | **$10** |

## Cabrera,Miguel

| Age: 36 | Bats: R | Pos: 1B | Health | F | LIMA Plan | C+ |
|---|---|---|---|---|---|---|
| Ht: 6' 4" | Wt: 249 | | PT/Exp | C | Rand Var | -1 |
| | | | Consist | F | MM | 3055 |

After litany of minor injuries since 2015, lost significant time in 2018, including season-ending surgery on a ruptured biceps. Underneath, he continued to display plus plate skills and elite HctX. Ignore xPX drop given injuries, small sample. Rebound depends on health, so don't pay for a full season to leave room for profit.

| Yr | Tm | AB | R | HR | RBI | SB | BA | xBA | OBP | SLG | OPS | vL | vR | bb% | ct% | Eye | G | L | F | h% | HctX | PX | xPX | hr/f | Spd | SBO | SB% | #Wk | DOM | DIS | RC/G | RAR | BPV | BPX | R$ |
|---|---|---|---|---|---|---|---|---|---|---|---|---|---|---|---|---|---|---|---|---|---|---|---|---|---|---|---|---|---|---|---|---|---|---|---|
| 14 | DET | 611 | 101 | 25 | 109 | 1 | 313 | 302 | 371 | 524 | 895 | 900 | 894 | 9 | 81 | 0.51 | 40 | 25 | 35 | 35 | 157 | 154 | 163 | 14% | 77 | 1% | 50% | 27 | 70% | 15% | 7.23 | 52.5 | 89 | 241 | $33 |
| 15 | DET | 429 | 64 | 18 | 76 | 1 | 338 | 290 | 440 | 534 | 974 | 1016 | 964 | 15 | 81 | 0.94 | 42 | 25 | 33 | 39 | 142 | 126 | 124 | 16% | 79 | 1% | 50% | 21 | 52% | 19% | 8.97 | 39.3 | 80 | 216 | $25 |
| 16 | DET | 595 | 92 | 38 | 108 | 0 | 316 | 293 | 393 | 563 | 956 | 926 | 966 | 11 | 81 | 0.65 | 42 | 23 | 36 | 34 | 134 | 137 | 144 | 22% | 73 | 0% | 0% | 27 | 52% | 22% | 8.24 | 43.7 | 78 | 223 | $31 |
| 17 | DET | 469 | 50 | 16 | 60 | 0 | 249 | 265 | 329 | 399 | 728 | 928 | 675 | 10 | 77 | 0.49 | 40 | 27 | 33 | 29 | 132 | 88 | 125 | 13% | 64 | 1% | 0% | 24 | 29% | 42% | 4.39 | -6.5 | 18 | 55 | $7 |
| 18 | DET | 134 | 17 | 3 | 22 | 0 | 299 | 279 | 395 | 448 | 843 | 756 | 876 | 14 | 80 | 0.81 | 55 | 25 | 20 | 36 | 136 | 100 | 59 | 14% | 51 | 0% | 0% | 9 | 44% | 44% | 6.47 | 7.2 | 45 | 150 | $2 |
| 1st Half | | 134 | 17 | 3 | 22 | 0 | 299 | 279 | 395 | 448 | 843 | 756 | 876 | 14 | 80 | 0.81 | 55 | 25 | 20 | 36 | 136 | 100 | 58 | 14% | 51 | 0% | 0% | 9 | 44% | 44% | 6.47 | 7.2 | 45 | 150 | $2 |
| 2nd Half | | | | | | | | | | | | | | | | | | | | | | | | | | | | | | | | | | | |
| **19** | **Proj** | **400** | **55** | **15** | **66** | **0** | **300** | **279** | **385** | **483** | **868** | **877** | **865** | **12** | **80** | **0.68** | **45** | **25** | **30** | **35** | **138** | **110** | **113** | **16%** | **64** | **0%** | **35%** | | | | **6.76** | **21.9** | **42** | **140** | **$18** |

## Cain,Lorenzo

| Age: 33 | Bats: R | Pos: CF | Health | B | LIMA Plan | D+ |
|---|---|---|---|---|---|---|
| Ht: 6' 2" | Wt: 205 | | PT/Exp | A | Rand Var | -3 |
| | | | Consist | B | MM | 1545 |

Surface stats held steady and fully supported by peripherals. Despite age, plate skills and HctX actually improved. Increased GB%, if it sticks, will cap HR output, but speed, SBO% makes that a worthwhile trade-off for owners given lack of SB producers. As low risk of a 33-year-old as you'll find.

| Yr | Tm | AB | R | HR | RBI | SB | BA | xBA | OBP | SLG | OPS | vL | vR | bb% | ct% | Eye | G | L | F | h% | HctX | PX | xPX | hr/f | Spd | SBO | SB% | #Wk | DOM | DIS | RC/G | RAR | BPV | BPX | R$ |
|---|---|---|---|---|---|---|---|---|---|---|---|---|---|---|---|---|---|---|---|---|---|---|---|---|---|---|---|---|---|---|---|---|---|---|---|
| 14 | KC | 471 | 55 | 5 | 53 | 28 | 301 | 260 | 339 | 412 | 751 | 827 | 720 | 5 | 77 | 0.22 | 51 | 23 | 26 | 38 | 72 | 90 | 68 | 5% | 130 | 26% | 85% | 25 | 28% | 28% | 5.20 | 17.9 | 31 | 84 | $25 |
| 15 | KC | 551 | 101 | 16 | 72 | 28 | 307 | 283 | 361 | 477 | 838 | 959 | 777 | 6 | 82 | 0.38 | 46 | 23 | 31 | 35 | 114 | 108 | 109 | 11% | 138 | 23% | 82% | 26 | 50% | 31% | 6.22 | 29.1 | 71 | 192 | $35 |
| 16 | KC | 397 | 56 | 9 | 56 | 14 | 287 | 257 | 339 | 408 | 747 | 1016 | 668 | 7 | 79 | 0.37 | 47 | 23 | 30 | 35 | 96 | 76 | 79 | 9% | 96 | 16% | 74% | 20 | 35% | 30% | 4.91 | 3.0 | 21 | 60 | $17 |
| 17 | KC | 584 | 86 | 15 | 49 | 26 | 300 | 269 | 363 | 440 | 803 | 824 | 797 | 8 | 83 | 0.54 | 44 | 23 | 33 | 34 | 104 | 76 | 84 | 9% | 150 | 15% | 93% | 27 | 37% | 22% | 5.99 | 15.0 | 56 | 170 | $28 |
| 18 | MIL | 539 | 90 | 10 | 38 | 30 | 308 | 273 | 395 | 417 | 813 | 979 | 753 | 11 | 83 | 0.76 | 55 | 22 | 23 | 36 | 116 | 66 | 72 | 10% | 143 | 19% | 81% | 26 | 31% | 27% | 6.11 | 27.9 | 51 | 170 | $29 |
| 1st Half | | 265 | 48 | 8 | 26 | 16 | 291 | 266 | 394 | 438 | 832 | 1178 | 749 | 14 | 80 | 0.81 | 53 | 19 | 28 | 34 | 108 | 90 | 80 | 13% | 111 | 20% | 84% | 13 | 38% | 15% | 6.33 | 16.4 | 55 | 183 | $30 |
| 2nd Half | | 274 | 42 | 2 | 12 | 14 | 325 | 279 | 396 | 398 | 794 | 865 | 759 | 9 | 85 | 0.68 | 56 | 25 | 18 | 38 | 125 | 44 | 65 | 5% | 163 | 17% | 78% | 13 | 23% | 38% | 5.89 | 13.0 | 45 | 150 | $29 |
| **19** | **Proj** | **540** | **84** | **10** | **47** | **27** | **304** | **267** | **373** | **419** | **793** | **922** | **748** | **9** | **82** | **0.56** | **50** | **23** | **27** | **36** | **109** | **69** | **77** | **9%** | **139** | **18%** | **83%** | | | | **5.78** | **24.6** | **39** | **131** | **$30** |

## Calhoun,Kole

| Age: 31 | Bats: L | Pos: RF | Health | B | LIMA Plan | B+ |
|---|---|---|---|---|---|---|
| Ht: 5'10" | Wt: 200 | | PT/Exp | A | Rand Var | +4 |
| | | | Consist | B | MM | 3225 |

Dreadful for 2 months, optioned to AAA, returned as a top-20 bat for 3 months. Seasonal totals suppressed by h%, but underneath he boosted HctX/xPX to best since rookie season, and in 2nd half traded contact to recover FB%. Defensive reputation should earn him AB. Expect 2017 but with lower BA, more power.

| Yr | Tm | AB | R | HR | RBI | SB | BA | xBA | OBP | SLG | OPS | vL | vR | bb% | ct% | Eye | G | L | F | h% | HctX | PX | xPX | hr/f | Spd | SBO | SB% | #Wk | DOM | DIS | RC/G | RAR | BPV | BPX | R$ |
|---|---|---|---|---|---|---|---|---|---|---|---|---|---|---|---|---|---|---|---|---|---|---|---|---|---|---|---|---|---|---|---|---|---|---|---|
| 14 | LAA * | 515 | 94 | 18 | 61 | 5 | 276 | 281 | 326 | 456 | 782 | 710 | 793 | 7 | 79 | 0.35 | 44 | 24 | 32 | 32 | 99 | 129 | 94 | 13% | 100 | 7% | 53% | 23 | 39% | 13% | 5.11 | 17.9 | 65 | 176 | $20 |
| 15 | LAA | 630 | 78 | 26 | 83 | 4 | 256 | 248 | 308 | 422 | 731 | 663 | 763 | 7 | 74 | 0.27 | 42 | 23 | 35 | 31 | 90 | 109 | 116 | 16% | 82 | 3% | 80% | 27 | 26% | 37% | 4.42 | -6.4 | 23 | 62 | $17 |
| 16 | LAA | 594 | 91 | 18 | 75 | 2 | 271 | 261 | 348 | 438 | 786 | 830 | 770 | 10 | 80 | 0.57 | 38 | 22 | 40 | 31 | 115 | 100 | 113 | 9% | 85 | 3% | 40% | 27 | 41% | 22% | 5.20 | 8.3 | 48 | 137 | $16 |
| 17 | LAA | 569 | 77 | 19 | 71 | 5 | 244 | 248 | 333 | 392 | 725 | 687 | 741 | 11 | 76 | 0.53 | 44 | 21 | 35 | 29 | 98 | 85 | 91 | 12% | 85 | 4% | 83% | 27 | 26% | 37% | 4.36 | -9.5 | 23 | 70 | $11 |
| 18 | LAA | 491 | 71 | 19 | 57 | 6 | 208 | 240 | 283 | 369 | 652 | 606 | 670 | 10 | 73 | 0.40 | 43 | 21 | 35 | 24 | 120 | 98 | 132 | 15% | 78 | 7% | 75% | 26 | 35% | 46% | 3.38 | -17.3 | 15 | 50 | $8 |
| 1st Half | | 210 | 20 | 3 | 15 | 4 | 162 | 209 | 216 | 224 | 440 | 338 | 463 | 7 | 76 | 0.29 | 52 | 17 | 30 | 20 | 104 | 34 | 83 | 6% | 93 | 12% | 80% | 13 | 23% | 54% | 1.51 | -20.4 | -27 | -90 | -$7 |
| 2nd Half | | 281 | 51 | 16 | 42 | 2 | 242 | 262 | 330 | 477 | 807 | 702 | 870 | 12 | 71 | 0.46 | 36 | 25 | 39 | 28 | 131 | 149 | 171 | 20% | 79 | 4% | 67% | 13 | 46% | 38% | 5.30 | 7.1 | 52 | 173 | $20 |
| **19** | **Proj** | **505** | **73** | **20** | **61** | **5** | **237** | **241** | **314** | **409** | **723** | **682** | **739** | **10** | **74** | **0.41** | **41** | **21** | **38** | **28** | **111** | **105** | **118** | **14%** | **83** | **5%** | **72%** | | | | **4.26** | **-3.0** | **25** | **84** | **$13** |

ARIK FLORIMONTE

## Calhoun,Willie

Age: 24 Bats: L Pos: LF | Ht: 5' 8" Wt: 187

Health A | PT/Exp B | Consist C | LIMA Plan D+ | Rand Var -1 | MM 2233

2-11-.222 in 99 AB at TEX. Expected ready prospect slogged through 1st half plagued by surprising HR dip. High ct% offers BA floor as we await the power return, but it should be at MLB level as he's conquered Triple-A (.858 OPS in 1004 PA). Bat should become an asset, but tough to expect that right away.

| Yr | Tm | AB | R | HR | RBI | SB | BA | xBA | OBP | SLG | OPS | vL | vR | bb% | ct% | Eye | G | L | F | h% | HctX | PX | xPX | hr/f | Spd | SBO | SB% | #Wk | DOM | DIS | RC/G | RAR | BPV | BPX | R$ |
|---|---|---|---|---|---|---|---|---|---|---|---|---|---|---|---|---|---|---|---|---|---|---|---|---|---|---|---|---|---|---|---|---|---|---|---|
| 14 | | | | | | | | | | | | | | | | | | | | | | | | | | | | | | | | | | | |
| 15 | | | | | | | | | | | | | | | | | | | | | | | | | | | | | | | | | | | |
| 16 | aa | 503 | 64 | 24 | 75 | 0 | 233 | | 284 | 425 | 709 | | | 7 | 86 | 0.50 | | | | 23 | | 103 | | | 82 | 0% | 0% | | | | 4.01 | | 65 | 186 | $8 |
| 17 | TEX * | 520 | 64 | 25 | 75 | 3 | 271 | 316 | 317 | 484 | 802 | 606 | 711 | 6 | 86 | 0.49 | 56 | 22 | 22 | 27 | 90 | 105 | 57 | 17% | 127 | 4% | 58% | 3 | 33% | 67% | 5.31 | -1.9 | 81 | 245 | $15 |
| 18 | TEX * | 531 | 57 | 9 | 46 | 3 | 252 | 248 | 293 | 366 | 660 | 445 | 670 | 6 | 86 | 0.41 | 39 | 19 | 42 | 28 | 78 | 72 | 77 | 6% | 87 | 2% | 100% | 10 | 30% | 40% | 3.69 | -13.8 | 40 | 133 | $8 |
| 1st Half | | 317 | 34 | 5 | 22 | 1 | 250 | 258 | 282 | 359 | 641 | | | 4 | 87 | 0.34 | | | | 28 | | 69 | | | 90 | 2% | 100% | | | | 3.46 | | 40 | 133 | $8 |
| 2nd Half | | 214 | 24 | 4 | 24 | 1 | 255 | 246 | 310 | 378 | 688 | 445 | 670 | 7 | 84 | 0.50 | 39 | 19 | 42 | 29 | 76 | 76 | 77 | 6% | 87 | 3% | 100% | 10 | 30% | 40% | 4.05 | -3.4 | 40 | 133 | $8 |
| 19 | Proj | 361 | 42 | 12 | 43 | 1 | 257 | 262 | 303 | 422 | 725 | 514 | 817 | 6 | 86 | 0.45 | 39 | 19 | 42 | 27 | 68 | 92 | 69 | 10% | 93 | 2% | 75% | | | | 4.38 | -2.3 | 48 | 159 | $7 |

## Camargo,Johan

Age: 25 Bats: B Pos: 3B | Ht: 6' 0" Wt: 195

Health B | PT/Exp C | Consist C | LIMA Plan B | Rand Var -1 | MM 3235

19-76-.272 in 464 AB at ATL. More selectivity (doubled bb%) and hr/f surge fueled HR boost as batted ball profile showed only marginal gains. Balanced L/R splits brought full-time 3B role, but could pull a 2018 Marwin Gonzalez if xPX, xBA, and 2nd half bb% losses continue. DN: 10 HR, sub-400 AB.

| Yr | Tm | AB | R | HR | RBI | SB | BA | xBA | OBP | SLG | OPS | vL | vR | bb% | ct% | Eye | G | L | F | h% | HctX | PX | xPX | hr/f | Spd | SBO | SB% | #Wk | DOM | DIS | RC/G | RAR | BPV | BPX | R$ |
|---|---|---|---|---|---|---|---|---|---|---|---|---|---|---|---|---|---|---|---|---|---|---|---|---|---|---|---|---|---|---|---|---|---|---|---|
| 14 | | | | | | | | | | | | | | | | | | | | | | | | | | | | | | | | | | | |
| 15 | | | | | | | | | | | | | | | | | | | | | | | | | | | | | | | | | | | |
| 16 | aa | 446 | 46 | 4 | 43 | 1 | 236 | | 277 | 320 | 597 | | | 5 | 79 | 0.26 | | | | 29 | | 52 | | | 119 | 3% | 31% | | | | 2.91 | | 4 | 11 | $2 |
| 17 | ATL * | 370 | 44 | 7 | 44 | 1 | 287 | 272 | 321 | 441 | 761 | 1129 | 636 | 5 | 80 | 0.24 | 48 | 21 | 31 | 34 | 92 | 96 | 64 | 7% | 103 | 1% | 100% | 18 | 33% | 33% | 5.07 | -2.4 | 37 | 112 | $9 |
| 18 | ATL * | 497 | 68 | 21 | 81 | 1 | 271 | 258 | 342 | 462 | 804 | 813 | 803 | 10 | 76 | 0.45 | 45 | 20 | 35 | 32 | 102 | 117 | 81 | 15% | 88 | 1% | 50% | 25 | 64% | 16% | 5.49 | 11.6 | 46 | 153 | $17 |
| 1st Half | | 222 | 30 | 9 | 40 | 0 | 255 | 261 | 347 | 449 | 796 | 763 | 802 | 12 | 79 | 0.66 | 46 | 18 | 36 | 29 | 117 | 114 | 89 | 13% | 91 | 2% | 0% | 12 | 75% | 8% | 5.24 | 4.8 | 60 | 200 | $12 |
| 2nd Half | | 275 | 38 | 12 | 41 | 1 | 284 | 254 | 343 | 473 | 816 | 854 | 801 | 7 | 74 | 0.31 | 44 | 21 | 35 | 34 | 90 | 119 | 75 | 17% | 90 | 1% | 100% | 13 | 54% | 23% | 5.69 | 9.2 | 36 | 120 | $21 |
| 19 | Proj | 456 | 57 | 14 | 62 | 1 | 272 | 258 | 326 | 437 | 762 | 897 | 704 | 7 | 78 | 0.33 | 46 | 20 | 34 | 32 | 98 | 102 | 74 | 12% | 98 | 2% | 60% | | | | 4.91 | 5.3 | 27 | 89 | $14 |

## Candelario,Jeimer

Age: 25 Bats: B Pos: 3B | Ht: 6' 1" Wt: 221

Health A | PT/Exp B | Consist B | LIMA Plan B+ | Rand Var 0 | MM 3125

Fast start (.894 OPS thru 2 months) fizzled into a mediocre season; left wrist tendinitis cost him 2 weeks in May and likely played a role (2nd half SLG). The ct% issues were new as he fanned just 17% of the time in the minors. Health and opportunity could bring mid-20s pop if career ct% and 1st half xPX return.

| Yr | Tm | AB | R | HR | RBI | SB | BA | xBA | OBP | SLG | OPS | vL | vR | bb% | ct% | Eye | G | L | F | h% | HctX | PX | xPX | hr/f | Spd | SBO | SB% | #Wk | DOM | DIS | RC/G | RAR | BPV | BPX | R$ |
|---|---|---|---|---|---|---|---|---|---|---|---|---|---|---|---|---|---|---|---|---|---|---|---|---|---|---|---|---|---|---|---|---|---|---|---|
| 14 | | | | | | | | | | | | | | | | | | | | | | | | | | | | | | | | | | | |
| 15 | aa | 158 | 17 | 4 | 20 | 0 | 264 | | 339 | 412 | 751 | | | 10 | 85 | 0.77 | | | | 29 | | 93 | | | 94 | 0% | 0% | | | | 4.84 | | 66 | 178 | $2 |
| 16 | CHC * | 485 | 58 | 10 | 61 | 0 | 242 | 215 | 325 | 389 | 714 | 500 | 350 | 11 | 76 | 0.50 | 67 | 0 | 33 | 30 | 154 | 101 | 100 | 0% | 83 | 2% | 0% | 1 | 0% | 100% | 4.17 | -11.6 | 32 | 91 | $6 |
| 17 | 2 TM * | 534 | 65 | 17 | 80 | 1 | 256 | 258 | 325 | 447 | 771 | 922 | 754 | 9 | 74 | 0.38 | 45 | 19 | 36 | 32 | 86 | 122 | 77 | 9% | 106 | 1% | 100% | 10 | 50% | 40% | 4.98 | 1.9 | 44 | 133 | $11 |
| 18 | DET | 539 | 78 | 19 | 54 | 3 | 224 | 228 | 317 | 393 | 710 | 842 | 661 | 11 | 70 | 0.41 | 42 | 18 | 41 | 28 | 91 | 112 | 88 | 12% | 94 | 4% | 60% | 27 | 33% | 37% | 3.97 | -6.0 | 22 | 73 | $9 |
| 1st Half | | 264 | 41 | 12 | 32 | 1 | 239 | 250 | 344 | 462 | 806 | 937 | 760 | 12 | 71 | 0.49 | 40 | 18 | 42 | 29 | 96 | 143 | 102 | 15% | 106 | 3% | 50% | 14 | 50% | 21% | 5.09 | 4.6 | 58 | 193 | $13 |
| 2nd Half | | 275 | 37 | 7 | 22 | 2 | 211 | 205 | 289 | 327 | 617 | 759 | 561 | 10 | 69 | 0.35 | 43 | 17 | 39 | 28 | 87 | 80 | 74 | 9% | 79 | 4% | 67% | 13 | 15% | 54% | 3.01 | -12.7 | -13 | -43 | $6 |
| 19 | Proj | 533 | 70 | 20 | 63 | 2 | 238 | 243 | 325 | 421 | 745 | 861 | 710 | 10 | 73 | 0.43 | 42 | 18 | 40 | 29 | 89 | 117 | 82 | 13% | 89 | 2% | 58% | | | | 4.44 | -1.1 | 31 | 102 | $12 |

## Canha,Mark

Age: 30 Bats: R Pos: CF LF | Ht: 6' 2" Wt: 210

Health C | PT/Exp D | Consist D | LIMA Plan D+ | Rand Var -1 | MM 3223

PRO: Added CF to defensive arsenal; crushed lefties; logged nearly 2x MLB AB as 2016-17 combined; ct% surged near previous best; xPX supported power growth. CON: A true short-side platoon option; better CF options in 2nd half cost him AB; HctX and xPX leveled off late. He's a deep league option at best.

| Yr | Tm | AB | R | HR | RBI | SB | BA | xBA | OBP | SLG | OPS | vL | vR | bb% | ct% | Eye | G | L | F | h% | HctX | PX | xPX | hr/f | Spd | SBO | SB% | #Wk | DOM | DIS | RC/G | RAR | BPV | BPX | R$ |
|---|---|---|---|---|---|---|---|---|---|---|---|---|---|---|---|---|---|---|---|---|---|---|---|---|---|---|---|---|---|---|---|---|---|---|---|
| 14 | aaa | 465 | 55 | 11 | 54 | 2 | 240 | | 297 | 373 | 671 | | | 7 | 72 | 0.29 | | | | 31 | | 107 | | | 94 | 3% | 62% | | | | 3.71 | | 18 | 49 | $8 |
| 15 | OAK | 441 | 61 | 16 | 70 | 7 | 254 | 252 | 315 | 426 | 742 | 587 | 821 | 7 | 78 | 0.34 | 42 | 18 | 40 | 29 | 107 | 111 | 114 | 11% | 106 | 9% | 78% | 27 | 56% | 37% | 4.46 | 0.8 | 49 | 132 | $14 |
| 16 | OAK | 41 | 4 | 3 | 6 | 0 | 122 | 190 | 140 | 341 | 481 | 632 | 352 | 0 | 51 | 0.00 | 36 | 18 | 45 | 11 | 81 | 167 | 157 | 30% | 84 | 50% | 0% | 6 | 17% | 67% | 0.94 | -4.7 | -33 | -94 | -$2 |
| 17 | OAK * | 445 | 53 | 13 | 50 | 5 | 218 | 234 | 269 | 397 | 666 | 581 | 689 | 6 | 70 | 0.24 | 33 | 20 | 47 | 28 | 80 | 120 | 75 | 9% | 98 | 6% | 100% | 16 | 38% | 56% | 3.54 | -26.0 | 22 | 67 | $3 |
| 18 | OAK | 365 | 60 | 17 | 52 | 1 | 249 | 259 | 328 | 449 | 778 | 941 | 665 | 8 | 76 | 0.39 | 38 | 22 | 40 | 28 | 104 | 123 | 114 | 15% | 98 | 3% | 33% | 26 | 50% | 27% | 4.69 | 1.1 | 50 | 167 | $10 |
| 1st Half | | 201 | 31 | 10 | 30 | 0 | 254 | 254 | 329 | 468 | 797 | 1031 | 642 | 9 | 74 | 0.40 | 38 | 20 | 42 | 30 | 111 | 136 | 134 | 16% | 100 | 0% | 0% | 13 | 54% | 15% | 5.18 | 3.4 | 54 | 180 | $11 |
| 2nd Half | | 164 | 29 | 7 | 22 | 1 | 244 | 265 | 328 | 427 | 755 | 838 | 694 | 7 | 79 | 0.37 | 38 | 24 | 38 | 27 | 96 | 108 | 92 | 14% | 96 | 8% | 33% | 13 | 46% | 38% | 4.11 | -2.4 | 46 | 153 | $9 |
| 19 | Proj | 292 | 43 | 11 | 39 | 2 | 251 | 248 | 323 | 436 | 759 | 789 | 738 | 7 | 75 | 0.31 | 37 | 21 | 42 | 30 | 95 | 116 | 98 | 12% | 104 | 5% | 62% | | | | 4.48 | 2.9 | 32 | 105 | $9 |

## Cano,Robinson

Age: 36 Bats: L Pos: 2B | Ht: 6' 0" Wt: 210

Health A | PT/Exp A | Consist C | LIMA Plan B | Rand Var -1 | MM 2155

Stunning PED suspension in mid-May lopped off half his season. Was himself upon return (.860 OPS) and base skills remain strong even in mid-30s. 2016 HR spike isn't returning, so buy the BA and durability. Rebound vL was h% regression. Suspension and age will likely drive the cost down and create a buying opportunity.

| Yr | Tm | AB | R | HR | RBI | SB | BA | xBA | OBP | SLG | OPS | vL | vR | bb% | ct% | Eye | G | L | F | h% | HctX | PX | xPX | hr/f | Spd | SBO | SB% | #Wk | DOM | DIS | RC/G | RAR | BPV | BPX | R$ |
|---|---|---|---|---|---|---|---|---|---|---|---|---|---|---|---|---|---|---|---|---|---|---|---|---|---|---|---|---|---|---|---|---|---|---|---|
| 14 | SEA | 595 | 77 | 14 | 82 | 10 | 314 | 301 | 382 | 454 | 836 | 746 | 891 | 9 | 89 | 0.90 | 53 | 23 | 25 | 34 | 109 | 95 | 81 | 11% | 81 | 7% | 77% | 27 | 59% | 11% | 6.38 | 48.2 | 75 | 203 | $29 |
| 15 | SEA | 624 | 82 | 21 | 79 | 2 | 287 | 285 | 334 | 446 | 779 | 715 | 815 | 6 | 83 | 0.40 | 50 | 24 | 25 | 32 | 118 | 100 | 107 | 16% | 74 | 5% | 25% | 27 | 52% | 11% | 5.11 | 14.7 | 48 | 130 | $22 |
| 16 | SEA | 655 | 107 | 39 | 103 | 0 | 298 | 290 | 350 | 533 | 882 | 770 | 955 | 7 | 85 | 0.47 | 46 | 18 | 36 | 30 | 122 | 124 | 96 | 19% | 75 | 1% | 0% | 27 | 59% | 7% | 6.63 | 34.3 | 76 | 217 | $29 |
| 17 | SEA | 592 | 79 | 23 | 97 | 1 | 280 | 281 | 338 | 453 | 791 | 557 | 891 | 8 | 86 | 0.58 | 50 | 19 | 31 | 30 | 128 | 91 | 111 | 15% | 66 | 1% | 100% | 26 | 54% | 27% | 5.39 | 12.7 | 52 | 158 | $19 |
| 18 | SEA | 310 | 44 | 10 | 50 | 0 | 303 | 284 | 374 | 471 | 845 | 893 | 818 | 9 | 85 | 0.68 | 48 | 23 | 29 | 33 | 130 | 99 | 110 | 13% | 74 | 0% | 0% | 15 | 47% | 0% | 6.35 | 19.3 | 61 | 203 | $11 |
| 1st Half | | 143 | 24 | 4 | 23 | 0 | 287 | 269 | 385 | 441 | 825 | 848 | 812 | 13 | 84 | 0.91 | 47 | 20 | 33 | 32 | 134 | 93 | 112 | 10% | 84 | 0% | 0% | 8 | 50% | 0% | 5.95 | 7.1 | 63 | 210 | $8 |
| 2nd Half | | 167 | 20 | 6 | 27 | 0 | 317 | 295 | 363 | 497 | 860 | 935 | 821 | 6 | 86 | 0.46 | 49 | 24 | 27 | 34 | 126 | 103 | 109 | 16% | 69 | 0% | 0% | 7 | 43% | 0% | 6.68 | 11.2 | 60 | 200 | $14 |
| 19 | Proj | 579 | 81 | 22 | 92 | 1 | 297 | 284 | 358 | 474 | 832 | 784 | 858 | 8 | 85 | 0.59 | 49 | 21 | 30 | 32 | 126 | 100 | 107 | 15% | 72 | 1% | 60% | | | | 6.08 | 30.5 | 50 | 166 | $25 |

## Caratini,Victor

Age: 25 Bats: B Pos: CA 1B | Ht: 6' 1" Wt: 215

Health A | PT/Exp D | Consist D | LIMA Plan D | Rand Var 0 | MM 1221

2-21-.232 in 181 AB with CHC. Couldn't sniff 0.65 Eye from MiLB, so wasn't able to tap into quality Triple-A skills (.334 BA, 14 HR in 407 AB). 2nd half h% killed his BA, even as xPX offered some hope. There's upside here, but he'll need consistent playing time to develop—something that could be hard to come by at MLB level.

| Yr | Tm | AB | R | HR | RBI | SB | BA | xBA | OBP | SLG | OPS | vL | vR | bb% | ct% | Eye | G | L | F | h% | HctX | PX | xPX | hr/f | Spd | SBO | SB% | #Wk | DOM | DIS | RC/G | RAR | BPV | BPX | R$ |
|---|---|---|---|---|---|---|---|---|---|---|---|---|---|---|---|---|---|---|---|---|---|---|---|---|---|---|---|---|---|---|---|---|---|---|---|
| 14 | | | | | | | | | | | | | | | | | | | | | | | | | | | | | | | | | | | |
| 15 | | | | | | | | | | | | | | | | | | | | | | | | | | | | | | | | | | | |
| 16 | aa | 412 | 47 | 5 | 39 | 2 | 259 | | 333 | 357 | 691 | | | 10 | 78 | 0.51 | | | | 32 | | 68 | | | 96 | 2% | 60% | | | | 4.08 | | 17 | 49 | $6 |
| 17 | CHC * | 351 | 44 | 9 | 49 | 1 | 288 | 282 | 336 | 452 | 788 | 1183 | 553 | 7 | 81 | 0.37 | 65 | 15 | 20 | 34 | 99 | 98 | 61 | 11% | 84 | 1% | 100% | 14 | 21% | 43% | 5.46 | 13.7 | 41 | 124 | $10 |
| 18 | CHC * | 296 | 31 | 5 | 37 | 0 | 243 | 236 | 303 | 336 | 640 | 446 | 647 | 8 | 76 | 0.36 | 53 | 23 | 24 | 30 | 79 | 63 | 62 | 6% | 89 | 0% | 0% | 23 | 9% | 65% | 3.44 | -0.6 | -1 | -3 | $3 |
| 1st Half | | 177 | 18 | 3 | 19 | 0 | 265 | 259 | 329 | 365 | 694 | 668 | 581 | 9 | 76 | 0.39 | 56 | 28 | 16 | 34 | 67 | 69 | 28 | 0% | 90 | 0% | 0% | 10 | 10% | 70% | 4.16 | 3.6 | 3 | 10 | $4 |
| 2nd Half | | 119 | 13 | 2 | 18 | 0 | 210 | 222 | 266 | 294 | 560 | 214 | 675 | 7 | 76 | 0.32 | 51 | 20 | 29 | 26 | 86 | 54 | 81 | 8% | 94 | 0% | 0% | 13 | 8% | 62% | 2.52 | -3.4 | -7 | -23 | $1 |
| 19 | Proj | 194 | 22 | 2 | 25 | 0 | 261 | 247 | 338 | 357 | 695 | 802 | 659 | 8 | 78 | 0.38 | 58 | 20 | 22 | 32 | 86 | 66 | 60 | 7% | 93 | 1% | 83% | | | | 3.93 | 2.7 | -3 | -12 | $4 |

## Carpenter,Matt

Age: 33 Bats: L Pos: 1B 3B | Ht: 6' 3" Wt: 205

Health A | PT/Exp A | Consist B | LIMA Plan B+ | Rand Var 0 | MM 4145

Off-season and spring questions about shoulder seemed prescient when he had a .558 OPS thru mid-May, but that confirmation bias might've cost you his explosive summer (.984 OPS, 33 HR in final 450 AB). Core skills remained firm throughout. xPX, Eye, and flyball lean point to continued success as a power/OBP stud.

| Yr | Tm | AB | R | HR | RBI | SB | BA | xBA | OBP | SLG | OPS | vL | vR | bb% | ct% | Eye | G | L | F | h% | HctX | PX | xPX | hr/f | Spd | SBO | SB% | #Wk | DOM | DIS | RC/G | RAR | BPV | BPX | R$ |
|---|---|---|---|---|---|---|---|---|---|---|---|---|---|---|---|---|---|---|---|---|---|---|---|---|---|---|---|---|---|---|---|---|---|---|---|
| 14 | STL | 595 | 99 | 8 | 59 | 5 | 272 | 253 | 375 | 375 | 750 | 722 | 762 | 13 | 81 | 0.86 | 41 | 24 | 35 | 32 | 117 | 80 | 97 | 5% | 114 | 4% | 63% | 26 | 50% | 27% | 4.86 | 19.6 | 53 | 143 | $17 |
| 15 | STL | 574 | 101 | 28 | 84 | 4 | 272 | 278 | 365 | 505 | 871 | 752 | 926 | 12 | 74 | 0.54 | 30 | 29 | 42 | 32 | 119 | 164 | 166 | 16% | 98 | 4% | 57% | 27 | 59% | 26% | 6.32 | 27.1 | 82 | 222 | $23 |
| 16 | STL | 473 | 81 | 21 | 68 | 0 | 271 | 282 | 380 | 505 | 885 | 809 | 920 | 14 | 77 | 0.75 | 31 | 26 | 43 | 31 | 131 | 144 | 174 | 13% | 88 | 3% | 0% | 24 | 63% | 21% | 6.46 | 20.3 | 81 | 231 | $15 |
| 17 | STL | 497 | 91 | 23 | 69 | 2 | 241 | 250 | 384 | 451 | 835 | 664 | 883 | 18 | 75 | 0.87 | 27 | 22 | 51 | 28 | 128 | 124 | 169 | 12% | 98 | 2% | 67% | 26 | 58% | 12% | 5.71 | 6.0 | 65 | 197 | $11 |
| 18 | STL | 564 | 111 | 36 | 81 | 4 | 257 | 273 | 374 | 523 | 897 | 817 | 930 | 15 | 72 | 0.65 | 26 | 27 | 47 | 29 | 130 | 170 | 189 | 19% | 77 | 3% | 80% | 28 | 54% | 25% | 6.67 | 32.8 | 79 | 263 | $23 |
| 1st Half | | 274 | 46 | 15 | 36 | 0 | 259 | 271 | 363 | 507 | 871 | 682 | 916 | 14 | 71 | 0.56 | 24 | 29 | 47 | 31 | 130 | 167 | 200 | 17% | 73 | 0% | 0% | 15 | 60% | 20% | 6.35 | 14.7 | 69 | 230 | $17 |
| 2nd Half | | 290 | 65 | 21 | 45 | 4 | 255 | 276 | 384 | 538 | 922 | 882 | 947 | 16 | 73 | 0.73 | 28 | 25 | 47 | 28 | 130 | 173 | 178 | 21% | 89 | 5% | 80% | 13 | 46% | 31% | 6.96 | 20.9 | 92 | 307 | $29 |
| 19 | Proj | 533 | 101 | 29 | 75 | 3 | 257 | 267 | 375 | 497 | 872 | 784 | 908 | 15 | 74 | 0.70 | 28 | 25 | 46 | 29 | 128 | 150 | 175 | 16% | 88 | 3% | 64% | | | | 6.29 | 23.8 | 70 | 235 | $21 |

PAUL SPORER

## Casali,Curtis

| Age: 30 | Bats: R | Pos: CA | Health | A | LIMA Plan | D |
|---|---|---|---|---|---|---|
| Ht: 6' 3" | Wt: 235 | | PT/Exp | F | Rand Var | 0 |
| | | | Consist | B | MM | 3013 |

4-16-.293 in 140 AB at CIN. Small sample career year or hints from a late bloomer? More ct% gains and uncharacteristic h%, LD% fueled BA surge as average power held firm. Historical inconsistency vR and so-so defense have held him back. A mixed bag, but cautiously watch-worthy in deep two-catcher formats.

| Yr | Tm | AB | R | HR | RBI | SB | BA | xBA | OBP | SLG | OPS | vL | vR | bb% | ct% | Eye | G | L | F | h% | HctX | PX | xPX | hr/f | Spd | SBO | SB% | #Wk | DOM | DIS | RC/G | RAR | BPV | BPX | R$ |
|---|---|---|---|---|---|---|---|---|---|---|---|---|---|---|---|---|---|---|---|---|---|---|---|---|---|---|---|---|---|---|---|---|---|---|---|
| 14 | TAM * | 298 | 24 | 3 | 25 | 0 | 202 | 201 | 303 | 282 | 585 | 521 | 460 | 13 | 65 | 0.42 | 44 | 23 | 33 | 30 | 50 | 82 | 69 | 0% | 70 | 0% | 0% | 11 | 9% | 73% | 2.73 | -6.7 | -24 | -65 | -$3 |
| 15 | TAM * | 213 | 24 | 13 | 28 | 1 | 199 | 228 | 271 | 425 | 696 | 864 | 911 | 9 | 67 | 0.30 | 43 | 12 | 46 | 23 | 93 | 161 | 116 | 32% | 71 | 2% | 100% | 12 | 75% | 25% | 3.69 | -0.8 | 38 | 103 | $1 |
| 16 | TAM * | 289 | 27 | 10 | 37 | 0 | 191 | 205 | 284 | 328 | 612 | 747 | 543 | 11 | 66 | 0.39 | 36 | 20 | 44 | 25 | 86 | 96 | 104 | 13% | 73 | 0% | 0% | 23 | 26% | 61% | 2.93 | -13.4 | -10 | -29 | -$2 |
| 17 | TAM * | 309 | 31 | 5 | 42 | 0 | 214 | 164 | 289 | 287 | 577 | 1100 | 1175 | 10 | 71 | 0.37 | 29 | 14 | 57 | 28 | 82 | 47 | 116 | 25% | 76 | 0% | 0% | 6 | 17% | 50% | 2.70 | -12.9 | -32 | -97 | -$1 |
| 18 | CIN * | 235 | 25 | 7 | 31 | 0 | 259 | 259 | 310 | 406 | 716 | 988 | 708 | 7 | 75 | 0.30 | 37 | 28 | 35 | 32 | 91 | 96 | 93 | 11% | 60 | 3% | 0% | 19 | 47% | 42% | 4.18 | 4.6 | 12 | 40 | $4 |
| 1st Half | | 123 | 15 | 4 | 17 | 0 | 252 | 234 | 293 | 402 | 696 | 1235 | 944 | 6 | 74 | 0.23 | 32 | 23 | 45 | 31 | 95 | 98 | 166 | 10% | 76 | 4% | 0% | 6 | 50% | 50% | 3.88 | 1.6 | 11 | 37 | $3 |
| 2nd Half | | 112 | 10 | 3 | 14 | 0 | 268 | 268 | 331 | 411 | 741 | 915 | 654 | 8 | 77 | 0.38 | 38 | 29 | 33 | 33 | 91 | 94 | 74 | 11% | 61 | 3% | 0% | 13 | 46% | 38% | 4.52 | 3.5 | 19 | 63 | $4 |
| 19 | Proj | **255** | **27** | **10** | **34** | **0** | **244** | **235** | **320** | **406** | **726** | **862** | **661** | **9** | **72** | **0.35** | **38** | **22** | **40** | **30** | **87** | **104** | **106** | **13%** | **65** | **2%** | **5%** | | | | **4.18** | **5.6** | **-2** | **-7** | **$3** |

## Castellanos,Nick

| Age: 27 | Bats: R | Pos: RF | Health | B | LIMA Plan | B |
|---|---|---|---|---|---|---|
| Ht: 6' 4" | Wt: 203 | | PT/Exp | A | Rand Var | -3 |
| | | | Consist | B | MM | 4245 |

1st half h% spike was responsible for most of the BA jump in an otherwise near-carbon copy of 2017. Disappointing HR production, sure. But stable peripherals with upticking bb%, LD% history and gobs of HctX set an attractive floor. 2nd half is the benchmark, but with a few more fly balls, still ... UP: 30+ HR.

| Yr | Tm | AB | R | HR | RBI | SB | BA | xBA | OBP | SLG | OPS | vL | vR | bb% | ct% | Eye | G | L | F | h% | HctX | PX | xPX | hr/f | Spd | SBO | SB% | #Wk | DOM | DIS | RC/G | RAR | BPV | BPX | R$ |
|---|---|---|---|---|---|---|---|---|---|---|---|---|---|---|---|---|---|---|---|---|---|---|---|---|---|---|---|---|---|---|---|---|---|---|---|
| 14 | DET | 533 | 50 | 11 | 66 | 2 | 259 | 252 | 306 | 394 | 700 | 693 | 702 | 6 | 74 | 0.26 | 35 | 29 | 37 | 33 | 108 | 108 | 135 | 8% | 108 | 3% | 50% | 27 | 33% | 37% | 4.10 | 3.1 | 28 | 76 | $11 |
| 15 | DET | 549 | 42 | 15 | 73 | 0 | 255 | 243 | 303 | 419 | 721 | 970 | 656 | 7 | 72 | 0.26 | 36 | 23 | 40 | 33 | 103 | 118 | 118 | 9% | 102 | 2% | 0% | 27 | 33% | 37% | 4.26 | -8.1 | 29 | 78 | $9 |
| 16 | DET | 411 | 54 | 18 | 58 | 1 | 285 | 260 | 331 | 496 | 827 | 656 | 894 | 6 | 73 | 0.25 | 31 | 26 | 43 | 35 | 106 | 135 | 166 | 14% | 131 | 2% | 50% | 20 | 50% | 30% | 5.80 | 12.6 | 54 | 154 | $13 |
| 17 | DET | 614 | 73 | 26 | 101 | 4 | 272 | 274 | 320 | 490 | 811 | 934 | 775 | 6 | 77 | 0.29 | 37 | 25 | 38 | 32 | 135 | 122 | 142 | 14% | 127 | 7% | 44% | 27 | 52% | 30% | 5.30 | 6.6 | 58 | 176 | $19 |
| 18 | DET | 620 | 88 | 23 | 89 | 2 | 298 | 276 | 354 | 500 | 854 | 1004 | 807 | 7 | 76 | 0.32 | 35 | 29 | 36 | 36 | 134 | 128 | 139 | 14% | 115 | 2% | 67% | 28 | 46% | 36% | 6.34 | 31.2 | 56 | 187 | $25 |
| 1st Half | | 327 | 42 | 12 | 49 | 1 | 309 | 280 | 356 | 517 | 873 | 1105 | 805 | 6 | 76 | 0.26 | 33 | 30 | 37 | 38 | 139 | 132 | 144 | 13% | 128 | 1% | 100% | 15 | 47% | 27% | 6.67 | 19.6 | 62 | 207 | $27 |
| 2nd Half | | 293 | 46 | 11 | 40 | 1 | 287 | 271 | 352 | 481 | 833 | 904 | 809 | 9 | 75 | 0.40 | 38 | 28 | 35 | 35 | 128 | 123 | 133 | 14% | 103 | 3% | 50% | 13 | 46% | 46% | 5.98 | 12.5 | 50 | 167 | $23 |
| 19 | Proj | **618** | **83** | **25** | **92** | **2** | **284** | **270** | **337** | **493** | **830** | **906** | **805** | **7** | **75** | **0.30** | **36** | **27** | **38** | **34** | **126** | **129** | **142** | **14%** | **120** | **3%** | **50%** | | | | **5.80** | **23.4** | **44** | **145** | **$25** |

## Castillo,Welington

| Age: 32 | Bats: R | Pos: CA | Health | B | LIMA Plan | D+ |
|---|---|---|---|---|---|---|
| Ht: 5' 10" | Wt: 220 | | PT/Exp | D | Rand Var | 0 |
| | | | Consist | D | MM | 3213 |

6-15-.259 in 170 AB at CHW. 80-game PED suspension shelved him until Sept, finished with a .571 OPS in final 54 AB. Historical xPX says power is still the attraction here, though hr/f history says this is shaky—as are the plate skills. Age, role add more uncertainty. Adjust your bidding accordingly.

| Yr | Tm | AB | R | HR | RBI | SB | BA | xBA | OBP | SLG | OPS | vL | vR | bb% | ct% | Eye | G | L | F | h% | HctX | PX | xPX | hr/f | Spd | SBO | SB% | #Wk | DOM | DIS | RC/G | RAR | BPV | BPX | R$ |
|---|---|---|---|---|---|---|---|---|---|---|---|---|---|---|---|---|---|---|---|---|---|---|---|---|---|---|---|---|---|---|---|---|---|---|---|
| 14 | CHC | 380 | 28 | 13 | 46 | 0 | 237 | 229 | 296 | 389 | 686 | 855 | 631 | 6 | 73 | 0.25 | 41 | 19 | 40 | 29 | 103 | 118 | 121 | 12% | 57 | 0% | 0% | 24 | 38% | 33% | 3.72 | 4.5 | 19 | 51 | $5 |
| 15 | 3 TM | 342 | 42 | 19 | 57 | 0 | 237 | 253 | 296 | 453 | 750 | 778 | 739 | 7 | 73 | 0.27 | 42 | 18 | 40 | 27 | 122 | 142 | 152 | 19% | 60 | 0% | 0% | 27 | 37% | 41% | 4.37 | 6.5 | 39 | 105 | $8 |
| 16 | ARI | 416 | 41 | 14 | 68 | 2 | 264 | 250 | 322 | 423 | 745 | 868 | 698 | 7 | 71 | 0.27 | 42 | 25 | 33 | 34 | 115 | 110 | 128 | 14% | 65 | 2% | 100% | 25 | 32% | 48% | 4.70 | 10.0 | 8 | 23 | $10 |
| 17 | BAL | 341 | 44 | 20 | 53 | 0 | 282 | 256 | 323 | 490 | 813 | 937 | 767 | 6 | 72 | 0.23 | 39 | 24 | 36 | 34 | 113 | 119 | 130 | 22% | 64 | 0% | 0% | 25 | 32% | 56% | 5.65 | 14.5 | 15 | 45 | $11 |
| 18 | CHW * | 207 | 18 | 6 | 17 | 1 | 238 | 217 | 277 | 362 | 640 | 748 | 694 | 5 | 71 | 0.19 | 41 | 21 | 38 | 31 | 97 | 82 | 102 | 13% | 68 | 2% | 100% | 14 | 14% | 57% | 3.39 | 0.1 | -18 | -60 | $1 |
| 1st Half | | 116 | 12 | 6 | 15 | 0 | 267 | 244 | 309 | 466 | 774 | 766 | 778 | 5 | 72 | 0.18 | 42 | 22 | 36 | 32 | 98 | 123 | 111 | 20% | 64 | 0% | 0% | 9 | 22% | 56% | 4.91 | 4.9 | 16 | 53 | $4 |
| 2nd Half | | 91 | 6 | 0 | 2 | 1 | 201 | 174 | 244 | 231 | 476 | 708 | 518 | 5 | 70 | 0.19 | 39 | 20 | 41 | 29 | 94 | 28 | 82 | 0% | 83 | 5% | 100% | 5 | 0% | 60% | 1.85 | -4.6 | -60 | -200 | -$3 |
| 19 | Proj | **304** | **30** | **12** | **33** | **1** | **247** | **233** | **296** | **410** | **705** | **803** | **668** | **6** | **71** | **0.21** | **40** | **22** | **38** | **31** | **105** | **103** | **112** | **15%** | **66** | **2%** | **100%** | | | | **4.04** | **5.3** | **-8** | **-28** | **$7** |

## Castro,Jason

| Age: 32 | Bats: L | Pos: CA | Health | F | LIMA Plan | D |
|---|---|---|---|---|---|---|
| Ht: 6' 3" | Wt: 215 | | PT/Exp | D | Rand Var | +5 |
| | | | Consist | D | MM | 3103 |

Season-ending knee surgery in May leave both role and future in doubt. If healthy, power/patience combo vR and superior glove-work will secure MLB AB for the time being. But HR have become fewer and farther between—and he'll always be a BA killer. R$ history suggests miniscule earnings even if things break right.

| Yr | Tm | AB | R | HR | RBI | SB | BA | xBA | OBP | SLG | OPS | vL | vR | bb% | ct% | Eye | G | L | F | h% | HctX | PX | xPX | hr/f | Spd | SBO | SB% | #Wk | DOM | DIS | RC/G | RAR | BPV | BPX | R$ |
|---|---|---|---|---|---|---|---|---|---|---|---|---|---|---|---|---|---|---|---|---|---|---|---|---|---|---|---|---|---|---|---|---|---|---|---|
| 14 | HOU | 465 | 43 | 14 | 56 | 1 | 222 | 225 | 286 | 366 | 651 | 619 | 662 | 7 | 68 | 0.23 | 45 | 20 | 36 | 30 | 87 | 119 | 110 | 12% | 98 | 1% | 100% | 26 | 35% | 58% | 3.30 | -0.3 | 10 | 27 | $5 |
| 15 | HOU | 337 | 38 | 11 | 31 | 0 | 211 | 229 | 283 | 365 | 648 | 512 | 707 | 9 | 66 | 0.29 | 37 | 24 | 38 | 28 | 90 | 124 | 121 | 13% | 77 | 0% | 0% | 25 | 32% | 44% | 3.31 | -4.3 | 5 | 14 | $0 |
| 16 | HOU | 329 | 41 | 11 | 32 | 2 | 210 | 222 | 307 | 377 | 684 | 478 | 757 | 12 | 63 | 0.37 | 46 | 20 | 34 | 30 | 90 | 124 | 102 | 16% | 103 | 4% | 67% | 26 | 31% | 46% | 3.69 | -1.7 | 7 | 20 | $1 |
| 17 | MIN | 356 | 49 | 10 | 47 | 0 | 242 | 242 | 333 | 388 | 720 | 737 | 714 | 11 | 70 | 0.42 | 42 | 25 | 33 | 32 | 102 | 101 | 112 | 12% | 79 | 0% | 0% | 26 | 38% | 50% | 4.26 | 1.2 | 7 | 21 | $4 |
| 18 | MIN | 63 | 4 | 1 | 3 | 0 | 143 | 194 | 257 | 238 | 495 | 375 | 501 | 12 | 59 | 0.35 | 42 | 26 | 32 | 22 | 80 | 84 | 111 | 8% | 83 | 0% | 0% | 6 | 33% | 67% | 1.77 | -3.3 | -46 | -153 | -$4 |
| 1st Half | | 63 | 4 | 1 | 3 | 0 | 143 | 194 | 257 | 238 | 495 | 375 | 501 | 13 | 59 | 0.35 | 42 | 26 | 32 | 22 | 80 | 84 | 111 | 8% | 83 | 0% | 0% | 6 | 33% | 67% | 1.77 | -3.5 | -46 | -153 | -$4 |
| 2nd Half | | | | | | | | | | | | | | | | | | | | | | | | | | | | | | | | | | | |
| 19 | Proj | **280** | **31** | **7** | **27** | **0** | **215** | **216** | **307** | **351** | **658** | **590** | **676** | **11** | **64** | **0.34** | **43** | **24** | **34** | **31** | **89** | **103** | **110** | **12%** | **84** | **1%** | **70%** | | | | **3.44** | **0.0** | **-23** | **-77** | **$3** |

## Castro,Starlin

| Age: 29 | Bats: R | Pos: 2B | Health | B | LIMA Plan | B |
|---|---|---|---|---|---|---|
| Ht: 6' 2" | Wt: 230 | | PT/Exp | B | Rand Var | -1 |
| | | | Consist | B | MM | 1235 |

Patience uptick, HctX were encouraging. Recent hr/f history says mild HR rebound might be lurking too. Regardless, it's a combo of unspectacular-but-stable hit tool, health and age that keep him in the lineup, particularly in an era of declining BAs. Unsexy profile, but handful of SBs add to sneaky profit potential.

| Yr | Tm | AB | R | HR | RBI | SB | BA | xBA | OBP | SLG | OPS | vL | vR | bb% | ct% | Eye | G | L | F | h% | HctX | PX | xPX | hr/f | Spd | SBO | SB% | #Wk | DOM | DIS | RC/G | RAR | BPV | BPX | R$ |
|---|---|---|---|---|---|---|---|---|---|---|---|---|---|---|---|---|---|---|---|---|---|---|---|---|---|---|---|---|---|---|---|---|---|---|---|
| 14 | CHC | 528 | 58 | 14 | 65 | 4 | 292 | 272 | 339 | 438 | 777 | 788 | 773 | 6 | 81 | 0.35 | 45 | 23 | 32 | 34 | 102 | 107 | 105 | 10% | 82 | 6% | 50% | 23 | 39% | 26% | 5.17 | 26.3 | 49 | 132 | $19 |
| 15 | CHC | 547 | 52 | 11 | 69 | 5 | 265 | 251 | 296 | 375 | 671 | 643 | 679 | 4 | 83 | 0.23 | 54 | 17 | 29 | 30 | 86 | 70 | 75 | 8% | 98 | 8% | 50% | 27 | 22% | 41% | 3.69 | -7.6 | 28 | 76 | $13 |
| 16 | NYY | 577 | 63 | 21 | 70 | 4 | 270 | 267 | 300 | 433 | 734 | 740 | 731 | 4 | 80 | 0.20 | 49 | 20 | 30 | 31 | 101 | 97 | 91 | 15% | 89 | 3% | 100% | 25 | 44% | 28% | 4.58 | -4.8 | 32 | 91 | $15 |
| 17 | NYY * | 474 | 69 | 17 | 65 | 2 | 299 | 263 | 332 | 450 | 783 | 836 | 778 | 5 | 79 | 0.24 | 52 | 20 | 28 | 35 | 93 | 84 | 69 | 16% | 100 | 2% | 100% | 22 | 41% | 32% | 5.47 | 5.9 | 24 | 73 | $17 |
| 18 | MIA | 593 | 76 | 12 | 54 | 6 | 278 | 253 | 329 | 400 | 729 | 773 | 715 | 7 | 79 | 0.39 | 51 | 20 | 29 | 33 | 109 | 77 | 87 | 9% | 108 | 6% | 60% | 28 | 32% | 39% | 4.62 | 6.0 | 27 | 90 | $17 |
| 1st Half | | 326 | 49 | 5 | 31 | 4 | 282 | 251 | 329 | 393 | 721 | 677 | 735 | 7 | 79 | 0.37 | 50 | 21 | 29 | 34 | 110 | 73 | 78 | 6% | 108 | 5% | 80% | 15 | 33% | 47% | 4.67 | 4.6 | 24 | 80 | $20 |
| 2nd Half | | 267 | 27 | 7 | 23 | 2 | 273 | 253 | 330 | 408 | 738 | 900 | 691 | 8 | 79 | 0.41 | 52 | 20 | 28 | 32 | 107 | 82 | 98 | 12% | 103 | 7% | 40% | 13 | 31% | 31% | 4.57 | 3.1 | 31 | 103 | $13 |
| 19 | Proj | **592** | **73** | **15** | **65** | **5** | **280** | **254** | **324** | **411** | **734** | **785** | **718** | **6** | **79** | **0.31** | **51** | **20** | **29** | **33** | **102** | **80** | **85** | **11%** | **102** | **5%** | **61%** | | | | **4.66** | **8.1** | **15** | **49** | **$19** |

## Cave,Jake

| Age: 26 | Bats: L | Pos: CF | Health | A | LIMA Plan | D+ |
|---|---|---|---|---|---|---|
| Ht: 6' 0" | Wt: 200 | | PT/Exp | C | Rand Var | -1 |
| | | | Consist | C | MM | 4223 |

13-45-.269 in 283 AB at MIN. Unheralded rookie took advantage of injuries, swung from the heels (18 BB / 102 K) and made it work. PX/xPX says newfound power is legit, sub-par plate skills and 2nd half h% says BA won't survive. Handedness and plus glove give him an outside shot at platoon role and 400 AB.

| Yr | Tm | AB | R | HR | RBI | SB | BA | xBA | OBP | SLG | OPS | vL | vR | bb% | ct% | Eye | G | L | F | h% | HctX | PX | xPX | hr/f | Spd | SBO | SB% | #Wk | DOM | DIS | RC/G | RAR | BPV | BPX | R$ |
|---|---|---|---|---|---|---|---|---|---|---|---|---|---|---|---|---|---|---|---|---|---|---|---|---|---|---|---|---|---|---|---|---|---|---|---|
| 14 | aa | 176 | 19 | 4 | 15 | 2 | 245 | | 304 | 393 | 697 | | | 8 | 72 | 0.30 | | | | 32 | | 114 | | | 122 | 12% | 33% | | | | 3.76 | | 34 | 92 | $2 |
| 15 | a/a | 529 | 64 | 2 | 35 | 15 | 256 | | 310 | 326 | 636 | | | 7 | 78 | 0.35 | | | | 33 | | 54 | | | 119 | 12% | 82% | | | | 3.53 | | 5 | 14 | $11 |
| 16 | a/a | 426 | 53 | 8 | 50 | 5 | 244 | | 298 | 388 | 685 | | | 7 | 72 | 0.27 | | | | 32 | | 97 | | | 114 | 13% | 41% | | | | 3.65 | | 15 | 43 | $7 |
| 17 | a/a | 406 | 58 | 21 | 49 | 2 | 276 | | 318 | 500 | 818 | | | 6 | 67 | 0.19 | | | | 36 | | 143 | | | 111 | 6% | 34% | | | | 5.42 | | 30 | 91 | $12 |
| 18 | MIN * | 499 | 76 | 18 | 69 | 5 | 257 | 242 | 312 | 428 | 740 | 642 | 844 | 7 | 67 | 0.24 | 44 | 26 | 31 | 35 | 93 | 118 | 130 | 23% | 96 | 7% | 62% | 19 | 37% | 42% | 4.51 | 6.9 | 9 | 30 | $15 |
| 1st Half | | 250 | 28 | 7 | 29 | 4 | 236 | 227 | 303 | 367 | 669 | 200 | 725 | 9 | 71 | 0.33 | 46 | 21 | 33 | 30 | 88 | 84 | 129 | 25% | 99 | 10% | 66% | 6 | 50% | 50% | 3.65 | -3.7 | 2 | 7 | $9 |
| 2nd Half | | 249 | 48 | 11 | 40 | 1 | 277 | 247 | 325 | 490 | 815 | 670 | 862 | 6 | 63 | 0.17 | 43 | 26 | 30 | 40 | 89 | 156 | 130 | 23% | 98 | 4% | 50% | 13 | 31% | 38% | 5.47 | 9.5 | 21 | 70 | $22 |
| 19 | Proj | **326** | **44** | **14** | **39** | **3** | **242** | **251** | **297** | **440** | **737** | **545** | **786** | **7** | **68** | **0.23** | **44** | **24** | **31** | **31** | **89** | **131** | **130** | **20%** | **102** | **8%** | **52%** | | | | **4.25** | **1.1** | **21** | **70** | **$9** |

## Cervelli,Francisco

| Age: 33 | Bats: R | Pos: CA | Health | F | LIMA Plan | D+ |
|---|---|---|---|---|---|---|
| Ht: 6' 1" | Wt: 210 | | PT/Exp | C | Rand Var | -1 |
| | | | Consist | B | MM | 2113 |

More OBP with a not-awful BA, again limited by DL stints. But it was improbable early season FB% spike and power burst (8 HR in April and May) that fueled most of his 2018 value, before the injuries set in. Age, history and second half warn not to expect a repeat performance. Better health would be a start.

| Yr | Tm | AB | R | HR | RBI | SB | BA | xBA | OBP | SLG | OPS | vL | vR | bb% | ct% | Eye | G | L | F | h% | HctX | PX | xPX | hr/f | Spd | SBO | SB% | #Wk | DOM | DIS | RC/G | RAR | BPV | BPX | R$ |
|---|---|---|---|---|---|---|---|---|---|---|---|---|---|---|---|---|---|---|---|---|---|---|---|---|---|---|---|---|---|---|---|---|---|---|---|
| 14 | NYY * | 172 | 19 | 2 | 13 | 1 | 274 | 247 | 328 | 384 | 712 | 735 | 830 | 7 | 73 | 0.30 | 44 | 26 | 30 | 36 | 112 | 97 | 126 | 6% | 96 | 2% | 100% | 17 | 47% | 35% | 4.46 | 4.9 | 16 | 43 | $2 |
| 15 | PIT | 451 | 56 | 7 | 43 | 1 | 295 | 249 | 370 | 401 | 771 | 856 | 747 | 9 | 79 | 0.49 | 52 | 21 | 27 | 36 | 106 | 69 | 100 | 7% | 128 | 1% | 50% | 27 | 22% | 41% | 5.20 | 17.2 | 30 | 81 | $13 |
| 16 | PIT | 326 | 42 | 1 | 33 | 6 | 264 | 236 | 377 | 322 | 699 | 888 | 663 | 14 | 78 | 0.78 | 56 | 20 | 24 | 34 | 86 | 44 | 59 | 2% | 98 | 6% | 75% | 21 | 24% | 43% | 4.18 | -2.1 | 7 | 20 | $6 |
| 17 | PIT | 265 | 31 | 5 | 31 | 0 | 249 | 246 | 342 | 370 | 712 | 677 | 722 | 11 | 75 | 0.49 | 52 | 21 | 27 | 31 | 100 | 75 | 101 | 9% | 105 | 3% | 0% | 20 | 35% | 40% | 4.02 | -0.2 | 17 | 52 | $2 |
| 18 | PIT | 332 | 39 | 12 | 57 | 2 | 259 | 237 | 378 | 431 | 809 | 803 | 811 | 13 | 75 | 0.61 | 39 | 19 | 42 | 31 | 93 | 103 | 110 | 11% | 117 | 5% | 40% | 24 | 42% | 38% | 5.16 | 16.1 | 44 | 147 | $9 |
| 1st Half | | 175 | 24 | 9 | 36 | 0 | 257 | 241 | 390 | 486 | 876 | 616 | 937 | 15 | 74 | 0.69 | 33 | 17 | 50 | 30 | 105 | 130 | 142 | 14% | 141 | 4% | 0% | 13 | 62% | 23% | 5.90 | 12.7 | 75 | 250 | $11 |
| 2nd Half | | 157 | 15 | 3 | 21 | 2 | 261 | 233 | 364 | 369 | 734 | 931 | 641 | 11 | 75 | 0.51 | 45 | 22 | 33 | 33 | 80 | 74 | 74 | 8% | 81 | 6% | 67% | 11 | 18% | 55% | 4.37 | 4.2 | 9 | 30 | $6 |
| 19 | Proj | **339** | **39** | **8** | **46** | **2** | **260** | **237** | **364** | **394** | **758** | **804** | **743** | **12** | **76** | **0.55** | **44** | **20** | **35** | **32** | **94** | **84** | **96** | **9%** | **107** | **4%** | **50%** | | | | **4.64** | **11.9** | **15** | **49** | **$9** |

JOCK THOMPSON

## Cespedes,Yoenis

Age: 33 Bats: R Pos: LF | Ht: 5' 10" Wt: 220
Health F | PT/Exp D | Consist B
LIMA Plan B+ | Rand Var -4 | MM 4233

It's the 157/217 split that's most troubling—Days Active/Disabled the past two years. Despite time lost (hip/foot/heel in 2018), power remains elite and FB bent gives it currency. Difficult to gauge impact of injuries on xBA and ct%. With age creeping into the equation, he's more like found money than a bankable asset.

| Yr | Tm | AB | R | HR | RBI | SB | BA | xBA | OBP | SLG | OPS | vL | vR | bb% | ct% | Eye | G | L | F | h% | HctX | PX | xPX | hr/f | Spd | SBO | SB% | #Wk | DOM | DIS | RC/G | RAR | BPV | BPX | R$ |
|---|---|---|---|---|---|---|---|---|---|---|---|---|---|---|---|---|---|---|---|---|---|---|---|---|---|---|---|---|---|---|---|---|---|---|---|
| 14 | 2 AL | 600 | 89 | 22 | 100 | 7 | 260 | 255 | 301 | 450 | 751 | 666 | 777 | 5 | 79 | 0.27 | 34 | 18 | 48 | 30 | 106 | 134 | 127 | 10% | 109 | 7% | 78% | 27 | 56% | 11% | 4.66 | 15.2 | 67 | 181 | $23 |
| 15 | 2 TM | 633 | 101 | 35 | 105 | 7 | 291 | 289 | 328 | 542 | 870 | 736 | 909 | 5 | 78 | 0.23 | 42 | 20 | 38 | 33 | 123 | 160 | 131 | 19% | 96 | 9% | 58% | 27 | 56% | 22% | 6.20 | 26.4 | 80 | 216 | $32 |
| 16 | NYM | 479 | 72 | 31 | 86 | 3 | 280 | 280 | 354 | 530 | 884 | 1081 | 839 | 9 | 77 | 0.47 | 37 | 21 | 41 | 30 | 123 | 145 | 137 | 20% | 73 | 3% | 75% | 24 | 58% | 17% | 6.54 | 25.9 | 68 | 194 | $20 |
| 17 | NYM | 291 | 46 | 17 | 42 | 0 | 292 | 264 | 352 | 540 | 892 | 906 | 886 | 8 | 79 | 0.43 | 34 | 16 | 50 | 32 | 135 | 134 | 159 | 15% | 93 | 1% | 0% | 16 | 63% | 19% | 6.71 | 11.8 | 70 | 212 | $10 |
| 18 | NYM | 141 | 20 | 9 | 29 | 3 | 262 | 223 | 325 | 496 | 821 | 624 | 875 | 8 | 65 | 0.26 | 30 | 17 | 53 | 34 | 79 | 157 | 128 | 18% | 74 | 9% | 100% | 9 | 67% | 22% | 5.70 | 4.5 | 25 | 83 | $5 |
| 1st Half | | 137 | 18 | 8 | 28 | 3 | 255 | 215 | 316 | 474 | 790 | 581 | 847 | 8 | 64 | 0.24 | 30 | 17 | 53 | 34 | 79 | 151 | 133 | 17% | 75 | 9% | 100% | 8 | 63% | 25% | 5.26 | 2.6 | 15 | 50 | $5 |
| 2nd Half | | 4 | 2 | 1 | 1 | 0 | 500 | 477 | 600 | 1250 | 1850 | 2000 | 1833 | 20 | 100 | 0.00 | 25 | 25 | 50 | 33 | 92 | 288 | 35 | 50% | 76 | 0% | 0% | 1 | 100% | 0% | 38.25 | 2.6 | 295 | 983 | -$8 |
| 19 | Proj | 401 | 59 | 23 | 71 | 4 | 275 | 252 | 332 | 510 | 842 | 796 | 855 | 8 | 74 | 0.32 | 35 | 19 | 47 | 32 | 111 | 142 | 138 | 17% | 89 | 6% | 80% | | | | 5.92 | 15.1 | 50 | 168 | $16 |

## Chapman,Matt

Age: 26 Bats: R Pos: 3B | Ht: 6' 0" Wt: 210
Health A | PT/Exp B | Consist C
LIMA Plan B+ | Rand Var -3 | MM 4125

Surprisingly solid production across the board. Wasn't a BA killer as was feared heading into 2018, with ct%, LD%, and HctX growth legitimizing xBA. Tanking FB% and PX/xPX discrepancy do highlight some downside risk in HR production, but he's still learning on the job. And he's definitely on the front end of the curve.

| Yr | Tm | AB | R | HR | RBI | SB | BA | xBA | OBP | SLG | OPS | vL | vR | bb% | ct% | Eye | G | L | F | h% | HctX | PX | xPX | hr/f | Spd | SBO | SB% | #Wk | DOM | DIS | RC/G | RAR | BPV | BPX | R$ |
|---|---|---|---|---|---|---|---|---|---|---|---|---|---|---|---|---|---|---|---|---|---|---|---|---|---|---|---|---|---|---|---|---|---|---|---|
| 14 | | | | | | | | | | | | | | | | | | | | | | | | | | | | | | | | | | | |
| 15 | | | | | | | | | | | | | | | | | | | | | | | | | | | | | | | | | | | |
| 16 | a/a | 514 | 77 | 27 | 80 | 6 | 210 | | 287 | 434 | 721 | | | 10 | 64 | 0.30 | | | | 27 | | 156 | | | 103 | 10% | 57% | | | | 3.92 | | 34 | 97 | $9 |
| 17 | OAK * | 465 | 63 | 26 | 64 | 4 | 229 | 234 | 305 | 472 | 777 | 786 | 785 | 10 | 65 | 0.32 | 34 | 16 | 51 | 29 | 95 | 161 | 134 | 14% | 114 | 11% | 34% | 16 | 56% | 25% | 4.49 | -5.3 | 45 | 136 | $8 |
| 18 | OAK | 547 | 100 | 24 | 68 | 1 | 278 | 266 | 356 | 508 | 864 | 810 | 886 | 9 | 73 | 0.40 | 40 | 20 | 39 | 34 | 117 | 148 | 114 | 15% | 118 | 2% | 33% | 26 | 50% | 23% | 6.15 | 28.2 | 68 | 227 | $20 |
| 1st Half | | 244 | 40 | 10 | 26 | 0 | 250 | 246 | 346 | 447 | 793 | 686 | 832 | 12 | 73 | 0.48 | 40 | 20 | 39 | 31 | 124 | 121 | 120 | 14% | 128 | 3% | 0% | 13 | 46% | 31% | 4.95 | 3.3 | 50 | 167 | $10 |
| 2nd Half | | 303 | 60 | 14 | 42 | 1 | 300 | 282 | 363 | 558 | 921 | 895 | 933 | 8 | 74 | 0.33 | 40 | 20 | 39 | 37 | 111 | 169 | 109 | 16% | 110 | 1% | 100% | 13 | 54% | 15% | 7.25 | 22.8 | 82 | 273 | $28 |
| 19 | Proj | 569 | 92 | 25 | 76 | 3 | 251 | 244 | 330 | 472 | 802 | 773 | 814 | 10 | 69 | 0.35 | 38 | 19 | 44 | 32 | 108 | 148 | 122 | 15% | 116 | 6% | 39% | | | | 5.05 | 9.3 | 43 | 142 | $18 |

## Chirinos,Robinson

Age: 35 Bats: R Pos: CA | Ht: 6' 1" Wt: 210
Health C | PT/Exp D | Consist D
LIMA Plan D+ | Rand Var -2 | MM 4203

Career-high games played yielded HR and RBI totals suitable for the lower rungs of primary backstops. The skills have been evident for a while now, as has the swing-and-miss that will continue to torpedo other facets of his production. But PX/xPX will play anywhere, so enjoy. Just don't expect too much else.

| Yr | Tm | AB | R | HR | RBI | SB | BA | xBA | OBP | SLG | OPS | vL | vR | bb% | ct% | Eye | G | L | F | h% | HctX | PX | xPX | hr/f | Spd | SBO | SB% | #Wk | DOM | DIS | RC/G | RAR | BPV | BPX | R$ |
|---|---|---|---|---|---|---|---|---|---|---|---|---|---|---|---|---|---|---|---|---|---|---|---|---|---|---|---|---|---|---|---|---|---|---|---|
| 14 | TEX | 306 | 36 | 13 | 40 | 0 | 239 | 259 | 290 | 415 | 705 | 759 | 682 | 5 | 77 | 0.24 | 42 | 21 | 37 | 27 | 100 | 126 | 129 | 15% | 73 | 2% | 0% | 26 | 35% | 38% | 3.81 | 4.5 | 42 | 114 | $6 |
| 15 | TEX | 233 | 33 | 10 | 34 | 0 | 232 | 253 | 325 | 438 | 762 | 845 | 717 | 10 | 73 | 0.45 | 35 | 19 | 45 | 27 | 89 | 145 | 133 | 13% | 86 | 0% | 0% | 19 | 53% | 26% | 4.57 | 5.8 | 58 | 157 | $3 |
| 16 | TEX * | 168 | 21 | 9 | 20 | 0 | 206 | 240 | 271 | 432 | 703 | 823 | 791 | 8 | 69 | 0.29 | 40 | 14 | 45 | 24 | 111 | 155 | 156 | 19% | 69 | 3% | 0% | 19 | 42% | 47% | 3.65 | -1.1 | 38 | 109 | $0 |
| 17 | TEX | 263 | 46 | 17 | 38 | 1 | 255 | 246 | 360 | 506 | 866 | 1113 | 775 | 11 | 70 | 0.43 | 40 | 14 | 46 | 30 | 100 | 150 | 124 | 20% | 103 | 1% | 100% | 26 | 50% | 38% | 5.91 | 13.6 | 55 | 167 | $7 |
| 18 | TEX | 360 | 48 | 18 | 65 | 2 | 222 | 210 | 338 | 419 | 757 | 760 | 756 | 11 | 61 | 0.32 | 30 | 21 | 49 | 31 | 99 | 142 | 151 | 17% | 91 | 2% | 100% | 27 | 37% | 44% | 4.28 | 9.9 | 9 | 30 | $8 |
| 1st Half | | 197 | 26 | 11 | 34 | 1 | 213 | 208 | 325 | 437 | 761 | 805 | 749 | 10 | 55 | 0.25 | 30 | 19 | 50 | 32 | 102 | 183 | 193 | 20% | 82 | 2% | 100% | 15 | 40% | 47% | 4.16 | 4.3 | 15 | 50 | $8 |
| 2nd Half | | 163 | 22 | 7 | 31 | 1 | 233 | 213 | 354 | 399 | 753 | 728 | 766 | 12 | 68 | 0.44 | 29 | 23 | 47 | 30 | 96 | 102 | 111 | 13% | 106 | 2% | 100% | 12 | 33% | 42% | 4.39 | 4.6 | 13 | 43 | $8 |
| 19 | Proj | 314 | 45 | 16 | 50 | 1 | 231 | 225 | 334 | 436 | 769 | 831 | 746 | 10 | 67 | 0.35 | 35 | 18 | 47 | 29 | 100 | 136 | 139 | 16% | 91 | 2% | 78% | | | | 4.48 | 9.8 | 17 | 57 | $9 |

## Chisenhall,Lonnie

Age: 30 Bats: L Pos: RF | Ht: 6' 2" Wt: 190
Health F | PT/Exp F | Consist B
LIMA Plan B | Rand Var -3 | MM 3433

1-9-.321 in 84 AB at CLE. Eight months missed between 2017-2018 and chronic calf injuries make the promise of 2014 seem like a lifetime ago. He's always had a nice LD stroke, and recent xPX figures have been tantalizing. But R$ history suggests more of a fine 4th/5th fantasy OF, if healthy. It's hard to bet on that "if."

| Yr | Tm | AB | R | HR | RBI | SB | BA | xBA | OBP | SLG | OPS | vL | vR | bb% | ct% | Eye | G | L | F | h% | HctX | PX | xPX | hr/f | Spd | SBO | SB% | #Wk | DOM | DIS | RC/G | RAR | BPV | BPX | R$ |
|---|---|---|---|---|---|---|---|---|---|---|---|---|---|---|---|---|---|---|---|---|---|---|---|---|---|---|---|---|---|---|---|---|---|---|---|
| 14 | CLE | 478 | 62 | 13 | 59 | 3 | 280 | 261 | 343 | 427 | 770 | 729 | 782 | 7 | 79 | 0.39 | 38 | 24 | 38 | 33 | 83 | 109 | 93 | 9% | 101 | 3% | 75% | 27 | 56% | 22% | 5.06 | 15.7 | 51 | 138 | $16 |
| 15 | CLE * | 490 | 53 | 9 | 61 | 5 | 245 | 239 | 291 | 371 | 662 | 624 | 676 | 6 | 78 | 0.29 | 41 | 20 | 40 | 30 | 80 | 92 | 74 | 7% | 93 | 5% | 83% | 21 | 38% | 43% | 3.67 | -15.9 | 26 | 70 | $8 |
| 16 | CLE * | 408 | 45 | 8 | 60 | 6 | 274 | 257 | 317 | 421 | 738 | 642 | 784 | 6 | 82 | 0.35 | 35 | 24 | 41 | 32 | 87 | 90 | 77 | 6% | 122 | 6% | 100% | 25 | 48% | 20% | 4.78 | 0.8 | 48 | 137 | $11 |
| 17 | CLE * | 279 | 38 | 13 | 56 | 3 | 279 | 252 | 340 | 490 | 830 | 967 | 857 | 8 | 76 | 0.38 | 39 | 16 | 46 | 33 | 103 | 126 | 145 | 14% | 105 | 7% | 58% | 18 | 28% | 28% | 5.79 | 6.8 | 54 | 164 | $10 |
| 18 | CLE * | 112 | 15 | 2 | 13 | 1 | 299 | 261 | 369 | 460 | 828 | 804 | 850 | 10 | 84 | 0.67 | 30 | 24 | 46 | 34 | 127 | 98 | 120 | 3% | 111 | 3% | 100% | 7 | 71% | 14% | 6.23 | 5.3 | 68 | 227 | $2 |
| 1st Half | | 107 | 14 | 2 | 11 | 1 | 285 | 249 | 359 | 434 | 793 | 804 | 799 | 10 | 84 | 0.71 | 30 | 22 | 48 | 32 | 123 | 87 | 114 | 3% | 117 | 3% | 100% | 7 | 71% | 14% | 5.63 | 3.5 | 63 | 210 | $2 |
| 2nd Half | | 5 | 1 | 0 | 2 | 0 | 600 | 442 | 600 | 1000 | 1600 | 0 | 1600 | 0 | 80 | 0.00 | 25 | 50 | 25 | 75 | 177 | 329 | 222 | | 101 | 0% | 0% | | | | 38.25 | 2.7 | 216 | 720 | -$3 |
| 19 | Proj | 323 | 43 | 12 | 48 | 3 | 276 | 259 | 339 | 462 | 801 | 780 | 805 | 8 | 80 | 0.43 | 35 | 21 | 44 | 31 | 100 | 110 | 103 | 10% | 113 | 5% | 85% | | | | 5.44 | 9.0 | 53 | 175 | $13 |

## Choi,Ji-Man

Age: 28 Bats: L Pos: DH | Ht: 6' 1" Wt: 230
Health A | PT/Exp D | Consist B
LIMA Plan C+ | Rand Var +1 | MM 4133

10-32-.263 in 190 AB at MIL/TAM. Had .877 OPS for TAM while inflicting nearly all of his damage vR. His resume is scant and he's limited defensively, so expectations have to be tempered. But he hasn't been deterred by contact challenges, and hard-hit metrics point to HR upside. Could be mini-steal on draft day.

| Yr | Tm | AB | R | HR | RBI | SB | BA | xBA | OBP | SLG | OPS | vL | vR | bb% | ct% | Eye | G | L | F | h% | HctX | PX | xPX | hr/f | Spd | SBO | SB% | #Wk | DOM | DIS | RC/G | RAR | BPV | BPX | R$ |
|---|---|---|---|---|---|---|---|---|---|---|---|---|---|---|---|---|---|---|---|---|---|---|---|---|---|---|---|---|---|---|---|---|---|---|---|
| 14 | a/a | 248 | 32 | 4 | 25 | 1 | 236 | | 314 | 324 | 638 | | | 10 | 79 | 0.55 | | | | 28 | | 62 | | | 106 | 5% | 39% | | | | 3.29 | | 21 | 57 | $2 |
| 15 | aaa | 57 | 5 | 1 | 11 | 0 | 239 | | 318 | 330 | 649 | | | 10 | 70 | 0.39 | | | | 33 | | 79 | | | 87 | 7% | 0% | | | | 3.23 | | -7 | -19 | -$1 |
| 16 | LAA * | 300 | 32 | 9 | 35 | 5 | 240 | 247 | 326 | 392 | 718 | 250 | 621 | 11 | 77 | 0.55 | 49 | 16 | 34 | 29 | 91 | 99 | 117 | 17% | 72 | 15% | 39% | 18 | 33% | 50% | 3.96 | -14.2 | 33 | 94 | $5 |
| 17 | NYY * | 303 | 37 | 17 | 63 | 3 | 252 | 229 | 329 | 493 | 822 | 0 | 1221 | 10 | 65 | 0.33 | 64 | 0 | 36 | 33 | 119 | 166 | 178 | 50% | 59 | 5% | 68% | 3 | 67% | 33% | 5.50 | 5.6 | 31 | 94 | $8 |
| 18 | 2 TM * | 393 | 46 | 15 | 61 | 3 | 250 | 245 | 349 | 434 | 784 | 513 | 908 | 13 | 70 | 0.51 | 43 | 21 | 35 | 32 | 113 | 125 | 116 | 21% | 67 | 2% | 100% | 17 | 65% | 24% | 5.20 | 8.0 | 29 | 97 | $10 |
| 1st Half | | 215 | 24 | 7 | 34 | 1 | 257 | 237 | 362 | 418 | 781 | 500 | 824 | 14 | 68 | 0.52 | 38 | 25 | 38 | 34 | 142 | 114 | 207 | 33% | 62 | 1% | 100% | 5 | 60% | 40% | 5.23 | 4.5 | 14 | 47 | $10 |
| 2nd Half | | 178 | 22 | 8 | 28 | 2 | 242 | 261 | 334 | 455 | 789 | 516 | 922 | 12 | 72 | 0.50 | 44 | 21 | 35 | 29 | 112 | 138 | 104 | 19% | 78 | 4% | 100% | 12 | 67% | 17% | 5.18 | 3.6 | 49 | 163 | $10 |
| 19 | Proj | 340 | 40 | 16 | 54 | 3 | 246 | 254 | 335 | 456 | 791 | 504 | 817 | 12 | 71 | 0.45 | 45 | 20 | 35 | 30 | 111 | 137 | 135 | 19% | 70 | 6% | 63% | | | | 5.09 | 5.9 | 36 | 120 | $11 |

## Choo,Shin-Soo

Age: 36 Bats: L Pos: DH RF LF | Ht: 5' 11" Wt: 210
Health C | PT/Exp B | Consist B
LIMA Plan B+ | Rand Var -1 | MM 3135

Save SB, his 2018 line reflects skills and production expected in a typical, healthy season. Plate discipline is unwavering, and while batted-ball outcomes aren't always sexy, play-him-and-forget him has tangible value. 2nd half fade may be of some concern at 36, but if anyone warrants a panoramic career view, it's him.

| Yr | Tm | AB | R | HR | RBI | SB | BA | xBA | OBP | SLG | OPS | vL | vR | bb% | ct% | Eye | G | L | F | h% | HctX | PX | xPX | hr/f | Spd | SBO | SB% | #Wk | DOM | DIS | RC/G | RAR | BPV | BPX | R$ |
|---|---|---|---|---|---|---|---|---|---|---|---|---|---|---|---|---|---|---|---|---|---|---|---|---|---|---|---|---|---|---|---|---|---|---|---|
| 14 | TEX | 455 | 58 | 13 | 40 | 3 | 242 | 236 | 340 | 374 | 714 | 673 | 732 | 11 | 71 | 0.44 | 50 | 20 | 30 | 31 | 113 | 104 | 109 | 13% | 89 | 5% | 43% | 21 | 33% | 43% | 4.01 | -0.5 | 19 | 51 | $8 |
| 15 | TEX | 555 | 94 | 22 | 82 | 4 | 276 | 267 | 375 | 463 | 838 | 708 | 917 | 12 | 74 | 0.52 | 51 | 21 | 28 | 34 | 105 | 130 | 122 | 19% | 85 | 3% | 67% | 27 | 48% | 33% | 5.89 | 6.9 | 49 | 132 | $21 |
| 16 | TEX * | 209 | 28 | 8 | 21 | 7 | 251 | 250 | 340 | 403 | 743 | 1016 | 665 | 11 | 74 | 0.51 | 47 | 22 | 31 | 31 | 129 | 96 | 127 | 18% | 73 | 19% | 55% | 13 | 23% | 62% | 4.38 | -7.0 | 19 | 54 | $6 |
| 17 | TEX | 544 | 96 | 22 | 78 | 12 | 261 | 268 | 357 | 423 | 780 | 752 | 787 | 12 | 75 | 0.57 | 49 | 25 | 26 | 31 | 110 | 92 | 107 | 20% | 80 | 9% | 80% | 26 | 35% | 38% | 5.18 | 4.9 | 25 | 76 | $19 |
| 18 | TEX | 560 | 83 | 21 | 62 | 6 | 264 | 254 | 377 | 434 | 810 | 638 | 892 | 14 | 72 | 0.59 | 50 | 22 | 28 | 33 | 112 | 110 | 124 | 19% | 83 | 4% | 86% | 28 | 39% | 39% | 5.57 | 17.3 | 31 | 103 | $18 |
| 1st Half | | 311 | 49 | 15 | 39 | 3 | 286 | 266 | 396 | 489 | 884 | 733 | 949 | 15 | 74 | 0.65 | 48 | 22 | 30 | 35 | 124 | 127 | 129 | 22% | 70 | 3% | 100% | 15 | 60% | 27% | 6.89 | 20.7 | 48 | 160 | $25 |
| 2nd Half | | 249 | 34 | 6 | 23 | 3 | 237 | 237 | 353 | 365 | 718 | 535 | 816 | 14 | 70 | 0.53 | 53 | 21 | 26 | 31 | 97 | 88 | 117 | 13% | 97 | 5% | 75% | 13 | 15% | 54% | 4.17 | -2.6 | 10 | 33 | $8 |
| 19 | Proj | 517 | 78 | 19 | 60 | 7 | 257 | 252 | 365 | 416 | 781 | 702 | 814 | 13 | 73 | 0.56 | 50 | 22 | 28 | 32 | 112 | 101 | 118 | 18% | 84 | 6% | 63% | | | | 5.00 | 7.5 | 21 | 71 | $17 |

## Ciuffo,Nick

Age: 24 Bats: L Pos: CA | Ht: 6' 1" Wt: 205
Health A | PT/Exp F | Consist A
LIMA Plan F | Rand Var -4 | MM 2301

1-5-.189 in 37 AB at TAM. 2013 first-rounder missed first two months of AAA season after failing a drug test (marijuana). In 1,550 minor league AB, hasn't displayed anything close to a major league hit tool, with a .250/.292/.340 line. At this point, he's a defense-only CA with a lot more work to put in everywhere else.

| Yr | Tm | AB | R | HR | RBI | SB | BA | xBA | OBP | SLG | OPS | vL | vR | bb% | ct% | Eye | G | L | F | h% | HctX | PX | xPX | hr/f | Spd | SBO | SB% | #Wk | DOM | DIS | RC/G | RAR | BPV | BPX | R$ |
|---|---|---|---|---|---|---|---|---|---|---|---|---|---|---|---|---|---|---|---|---|---|---|---|---|---|---|---|---|---|---|---|---|---|---|---|
| 14 | | | | | | | | | | | | | | | | | | | | | | | | | | | | | | | | | | | |
| 15 | | | | | | | | | | | | | | | | | | | | | | | | | | | | | | | | | | | |
| 16 | | | | | | | | | | | | | | | | | | | | | | | | | | | | | | | | | | | |
| 17 | aa | 371 | 37 | 6 | 37 | 2 | 220 | | 291 | 342 | 633 | | | 9 | 71 | 0.34 | | | | 30 | | 89 | | | 88 | 2% | 100% | | | | 3.28 | | 1 | 3 | $0 |
| 18 | TAM * | 258 | 25 | 5 | 29 | 0 | 226 | 177 | 266 | 327 | 594 | 500 | 575 | 5 | 67 | 0.17 | 46 | 13 | 42 | 32 | 53 | 74 | 35 | 10% | 88 | 0% | 0% | 5 | 0% | 40% | 2.87 | -3.8 | -32 | -107 | $1 |
| 1st Half | | 81 | 8 | 2 | 10 | 0 | 264 | 200 | 287 | 358 | 645 | | | 3 | 70 | 0.11 | | | | 36 | | 65 | | | 97 | 0% | 0% | | | | 3.56 | | -32 | -107 | -$3 |
| 2nd Half | | 177 | 18 | 4 | 20 | 0 | 209 | 178 | 257 | 313 | 571 | 500 | 575 | 6 | 66 | 0.19 | 46 | 13 | 42 | 29 | 52 | 79 | 35 | 10% | 90 | 0% | 0% | 5 | 0% | 40% | 2.60 | -4.7 | -30 | -100 | $2 |
| 19 | Proj | 164 | 16 | 4 | 18 | 0 | 226 | 199 | 286 | 359 | 645 | 603 | 657 | 6 | 69 | 0.22 | 46 | 13 | 42 | 30 | 47 | 95 | 32 | 9% | 91 | 1% | 100% | | | | 3.28 | -0.8 | -22 | -73 | $2 |

ROB CARROLL

## Conforto,Michael

Age: 26 Bats: L Pos: LF CF | Ht: 6' 1" Wt: 215

Health B | LIMA Plan B+ | PT/Exp B | Rand Var +1 | Consist F | MM 4135

Shaky 1st half suggests he probably rushed return from off-season shoulder surgery, though xPX shows power skills were mostly intact. Re-established elite hr/f level in 2nd half, and ended 2018 on a tear, with 9 HR, 79% ct%, .306 xBA in Sept. Even continued his vL growth. Age is still on his side, if health is too... UP: 40 HR

| Yr | Tm | AB | R | HR | RBI | SB | BA | xBA | OBP | SLG | OPS | vL | vR | bb% | ct% | Eye | G | L | F | h% | HctX | PX | xPX | hr/f | Spd | SBO | SB% | #Wk | DOM | DIS | RC/G | RAR | BPV | BPX | R$ |
|---|---|---|---|---|---|---|---|---|---|---|---|---|---|---|---|---|---|---|---|---|---|---|---|---|---|---|---|---|---|---|---|---|---|---|---|
| 14 | | | | | | | | | | | | | | | | | | | | | | | | | | | | | | | | | | | |
| 15 | NYM * | 347 | 48 | 13 | 48 | 1 | 277 | 274 | 346 | 479 | 825 | 481 | 872 | 10 | 77 | 0.47 | 39 | 23 | 39 | 32 | 137 | 137 | 157 | 17% | 95 | 2% | 46% | 12 | 83% | 17% | 5.80 | 14.7 | 69 | 186 | $11 |
| 16 | NYM * | 432 | 59 | 19 | 61 | 3 | 257 | 250 | 329 | 459 | 788 | 295 | 804 | 9 | 74 | 0.41 | 36 | 19 | 45 | 31 | 121 | 129 | 157 | 12% | 71 | 6% | 50% | 22 | 36% | 41% | 5.06 | 5.2 | 42 | 120 | $11 |
| 17 | NYM | 373 | 72 | 27 | 68 | 2 | 279 | 276 | 384 | 555 | 939 | 729 | 1012 | 13 | 70 | 0.50 | 38 | 24 | 38 | 33 | 117 | 166 | 141 | 27% | 86 | 2% | 100% | 20 | 50% | 20% | 7.39 | 24.5 | 65 | 197 | $16 |
| 18 | NYM | 543 | 78 | 28 | 82 | 3 | 243 | 245 | 350 | 448 | 797 | 803 | 794 | 13 | 71 | 0.53 | 44 | 20 | 37 | 29 | 93 | 128 | 130 | 20% | 85 | 4% | 43% | 27 | 41% | 33% | 5.08 | 13.7 | 39 | 130 | $16 |
| 1st Half | | 244 | 32 | 10 | 24 | 2 | 225 | 221 | 348 | 385 | 733 | 725 | 736 | 15 | 70 | 0.61 | 42 | 18 | 40 | 28 | 85 | 101 | 125 | 14% | 96 | 5% | 50% | 14 | 29% | 29% | 4.28 | 1.0 | 24 | 80 | $6 |
| 2nd Half | | 299 | 46 | 18 | 58 | 1 | 258 | 263 | 351 | 498 | 849 | 871 | 839 | 12 | 71 | 0.46 | 45 | 21 | 34 | 30 | 100 | 150 | 135 | 25% | 82 | 4% | 33% | 13 | 54% | 38% | 5.78 | 14.4 | 54 | 180 | $25 |
| 19 | Proj | **522** | **81** | **30** | **83** | **3** | **258** | **258** | **355** | **487** | **842** | **742** | **875** | **12** | **72** | **0.49** | **41** | **21** | **38** | **31** | **108** | **143** | **140** | **21%** | **84** | **4%** | **52%** | | | | **5.77** | **17.9** | **45** | **150** | **$18** |

## Contreras,Willson

Age: 27 Bats: R Pos: CA | Ht: 6' 1" Wt: 210

Health A | LIMA Plan B | PT/Exp C | Rand Var +2 | Consist B | MM 3235

Past skills indicated power regression was likely, just not to this degree. Career-high AB total, plus .564 OPS, 38 xPX, .207 xBA after 8/1—perhaps fatigue was an issue. Still owns those 2016-17 xPX, hr/f levels, but unless we learn there was an undisclosed injury, there's enough doubt here to knock him down a peg at CA.

| Yr | Tm | AB | R | HR | RBI | SB | BA | xBA | OBP | SLG | OPS | vL | vR | bb% | ct% | Eye | G | L | F | h% | HctX | PX | xPX | hr/f | Spd | SBO | SB% | #Wk | DOM | DIS | RC/G | RAR | BPV | BPX | R$ |
|---|---|---|---|---|---|---|---|---|---|---|---|---|---|---|---|---|---|---|---|---|---|---|---|---|---|---|---|---|---|---|---|---|---|---|---|
| 14 | | | | | | | | | | | | | | | | | | | | | | | | | | | | | | | | | | | |
| 15 | aa | 454 | 56 | 7 | 59 | 3 | 297 | | 361 | 422 | 784 | | | 9 | 84 | 0.65 | | | | 34 | | 85 | | | 94 | 5% | 41% | | | | 5.37 | | 54 | 146 | $15 |
| 16 | CHC * | 456 | 63 | 19 | 67 | 5 | 290 | 276 | 357 | 488 | 845 | 854 | 841 | 9 | 77 | 0.45 | 54 | 18 | 28 | 34 | 101 | 121 | 105 | 24% | 109 | 9% | 43% | 17 | 41% | 29% | 5.97 | 20.2 | 58 | 166 | $18 |
| 17 | CHC | 377 | 50 | 21 | 74 | 5 | 276 | 268 | 356 | 499 | 855 | 916 | 828 | 11 | 74 | 0.46 | 53 | 17 | 29 | 32 | 106 | 131 | 101 | 26% | 78 | 8% | 56% | 22 | 45% | 27% | 6.03 | 21.4 | 47 | 142 | $14 |
| 18 | CHC | 474 | 50 | 10 | 54 | 4 | 249 | 242 | 339 | 390 | 730 | 820 | 701 | 10 | 74 | 0.44 | 52 | 17 | 31 | 31 | 79 | 92 | 71 | 9% | 117 | 4% | 80% | 28 | 32% | 46% | 4.31 | 11.1 | 28 | 93 | $9 |
| 1st Half | | 260 | 28 | 6 | 30 | 3 | 269 | 251 | 356 | 435 | 790 | 864 | 767 | 10 | 78 | 0.48 | 48 | 16 | 36 | 33 | 88 | 103 | 85 | 8% | 123 | 6% | 75% | 15 | 33% | 33% | 5.16 | 12.8 | 51 | 170 | $12 |
| 2nd Half | | 214 | 22 | 4 | 24 | 1 | 224 | 230 | 320 | 336 | 656 | 767 | 621 | 10 | 71 | 0.40 | 58 | 19 | 23 | 30 | 69 | 78 | 52 | 12% | 103 | 2% | 100% | 13 | 31% | 62% | 3.40 | -0.3 | -2 | -7 | $4 |
| 19 | Proj | **473** | **56** | **16** | **67** | **4** | **263** | **256** | **346** | **435** | **781** | **857** | **753** | **10** | **75** | **0.45** | **54** | **18** | **29** | **32** | **91** | **107** | **84** | **16%** | **103** | **6%** | **59%** | | | | **4.99** | **21.2** | **30** | **101** | **$15** |

## Cooper,Garrett

Age: 28 Bats: R Pos: LF | Ht: 6' 6" Wt: 230

Health F | LIMA Plan D | PT/Exp D | Rand Var +3 | Consist F | MM 4031

0-2-.212 in 33 AB at MIA. HBP on right wrist in second game, reaggravated injury in July, had season-ending surgery in Aug. As he reaches prime age, we've got one great minor league season alongside questions about health and where he fits on defense. Go ahead and speculate on that 2017 line, just don't get carried away.

| Yr | Tm | AB | R | HR | RBI | SB | BA | xBA | OBP | SLG | OPS | vL | vR | bb% | ct% | Eye | G | L | F | h% | HctX | PX | xPX | hr/f | Spd | SBO | SB% | #Wk | DOM | DIS | RC/G | RAR | BPV | BPX | R$ |
|---|---|---|---|---|---|---|---|---|---|---|---|---|---|---|---|---|---|---|---|---|---|---|---|---|---|---|---|---|---|---|---|---|---|---|---|
| 14 | | | | | | | | | | | | | | | | | | | | | | | | | | | | | | | | | | | |
| 15 | aa | 29 | 3 | 0 | 4 | 0 | 504 | | 591 | 623 | 1214 | | | 17 | 92 | 2.65 | | | | 55 | | 71 | | | 112 | 0% | 0% | | | | 18.96 | | 95 | 257 | $1 |
| 16 | a/a | 428 | 34 | 8 | 54 | 2 | 248 | | 287 | 362 | 649 | | | 5 | 79 | 0.26 | | | | 30 | | 75 | | | 79 | 6% | 40% | | | | 3.42 | | 12 | 34 | $5 |
| 17 | NYY * | 349 | 61 | 18 | 77 | 0 | 313 | 324 | 370 | 556 | 927 | 979 | 697 | 8 | 77 | 0.40 | 34 | 38 | 28 | 36 | 117 | 144 | 60 | 0% | 91 | 0% | 0% | 5 | 60% | 40% | 7.65 | 16.4 | 71 | 215 | $17 |
| 18 | MIA * | 63 | 4 | 1 | 6 | 0 | 223 | 209 | 293 | 284 | 577 | 857 | 483 | 9 | 71 | 0.34 | 67 | 24 | 10 | 30 | 37 | 44 | -27 | 0% | 87 | 0% | 0% | 5 | 20% | 80% | 2.73 | -4.5 | -35 | -117 | -$2 |
| 1st Half | | 34 | 2 | 1 | 5 | 0 | 237 | 37 | 290 | 322 | 612 | 500 | 400 | 7 | 76 | 0.31 | 100 | 0 | 0 | 29 | 0 | 51 | -27 | 0% | 101 | 0% | 0% | 3 | 0% | 100% | 3.12 | -1.7 | -9 | -30 | -$3 |
| 2nd Half | | 29 | 2 | 0 | 1 | 0 | 207 | 211 | 297 | 241 | 539 | 1333 | 487 | 11 | 65 | 0.37 | 59 | 29 | 12 | 32 | 42 | 35 | -27 | 0% | 94 | 0% | 0% | 2 | 50% | 50% | 2.31 | -2.2 | -60 | -200 | -$2 |
| 19 | Proj | **163** | **22** | **7** | **30** | **0** | **256** | **261** | **308** | **455** | **763** | **1303** | **693** | **7** | **75** | **0.30** | **45** | **19** | **36** | **30** | **73** | **128** | | **15%** | **59** | **3%** | **33%** | | | | **4.74** | **0.7** | **34** | **114** | **$5** |

## Cordero,Franchy

Age: 24 Bats: L Pos: LF | Ht: 6' 3" Wt: 175

Health F | LIMA Plan C+ | PT/Exp D | Rand Var 0 | Consist A | MM 4523

7-19-.237 with 5 SB in 139 AB at SD. Made solid gains in bb% and xPX, hit 3 of 50 longest HR in MLB, posted 7th-best exit velocity... then June elbow surgery shut it all down. Poor ct%, struggles vL remain sizable obstacles, and xBAs are a red flag, but power/speed combo will likely lead to double-digit value anyway. Breakout potential.

| Yr | Tm | AB | R | HR | RBI | SB | BA | xBA | OBP | SLG | OPS | vL | vR | bb% | ct% | Eye | G | L | F | h% | HctX | PX | xPX | hr/f | Spd | SBO | SB% | #Wk | DOM | DIS | RC/G | RAR | BPV | BPX | R$ |
|---|---|---|---|---|---|---|---|---|---|---|---|---|---|---|---|---|---|---|---|---|---|---|---|---|---|---|---|---|---|---|---|---|---|---|---|
| 14 | | | | | | | | | | | | | | | | | | | | | | | | | | | | | | | | | | | |
| 15 | | | | | | | | | | | | | | | | | | | | | | | | | | | | | | | | | | | |
| 16 | a/a | 258 | 25 | 5 | 15 | 9 | 264 | | 305 | 387 | 693 | | | 6 | 70 | 0.20 | | | | 36 | | 76 | | | 147 | 24% | 59% | | | | 3.84 | | 0 | 0 | $6 |
| 17 | SD * | 482 | 62 | 14 | 53 | 11 | 262 | 226 | 295 | 454 | 748 | 610 | 718 | 4 | 62 | 0.12 | 48 | 19 | 33 | 39 | 97 | 127 | 125 | 19% | 192 | 17% | 67% | 7 | 29% | 57% | 4.50 | -10.6 | 18 | 55 | $13 |
| 18 | SD * | 165 | 21 | 8 | 20 | 7 | 234 | 227 | 305 | 421 | 725 | 586 | 816 | 9 | 60 | 0.25 | 46 | 25 | 29 | 34 | 107 | 134 | 144 | 29% | 123 | 22% | 78% | 8 | 25% | 63% | 4.27 | -1.6 | 5 | 17 | $4 |
| 1st Half | | 165 | 21 | 8 | 20 | 7 | 234 | 227 | 305 | 421 | 725 | 586 | 816 | 9 | 60 | 0.25 | 46 | 25 | 29 | 34 | 107 | 134 | 144 | 29% | 123 | 22% | 78% | 8 | 25% | 63% | 4.27 | -1.6 | 5 | 17 | $4 |
| 2nd Half | | | | | | | | | | | | | | | | | | | | | | | | | | | | | | | | | | | |
| 19 | Proj | **360** | **42** | **18** | **43** | **12** | **254** | **243** | **302** | **472** | **774** | **644** | **819** | **6** | **65** | **0.20** | **47** | **23** | **31** | **34** | **103** | **141** | **136** | **25%** | **149** | **24%** | **65%** | | | | **4.67** | **0.8** | **23** | **78** | **$15** |

## Correa,Carlos

Age: 24 Bats: R Pos: SS | Ht: 6' 4" Wt: 215

Health C | LIMA Plan B | PT/Exp B | Rand Var +3 | Consist F | MM 3335

June back stiffness that lingered through 2nd half dragged down his season. But even in stellar 2017, there were notable gaps between BA-xBA and PX-xPX. Overdrafted at ADP #6 in 2016 based on 387 MLB AB in 2015, and has yet to crack the top 50 in any season since. Skills still hint at upside; just don't overbid.

| Yr | Tm | AB | R | HR | RBI | SB | BA | xBA | OBP | SLG | OPS | vL | vR | bb% | ct% | Eye | G | L | F | h% | HctX | PX | xPX | hr/f | Spd | SBO | SB% | #Wk | DOM | DIS | RC/G | RAR | BPV | BPX | R$ |
|---|---|---|---|---|---|---|---|---|---|---|---|---|---|---|---|---|---|---|---|---|---|---|---|---|---|---|---|---|---|---|---|---|---|---|---|
| 14 | | | | | | | | | | | | | | | | | | | | | | | | | | | | | | | | | | | |
| 15 | HOU * | 602 | 85 | 30 | 101 | 28 | 287 | 302 | 352 | 517 | 869 | 899 | 836 | 9 | 80 | 0.50 | 49 | 22 | 29 | 32 | 115 | 146 | 103 | 24% | 91 | 21% | 84% | 18 | 67% | 6% | 6.59 | 37.4 | 83 | 224 | $36 |
| 16 | HOU | 577 | 76 | 20 | 96 | 13 | 274 | 275 | 361 | 451 | 811 | 730 | 839 | 11 | 76 | 0.54 | 50 | 22 | 27 | 33 | 115 | 113 | 100 | 17% | 109 | 9% | 81% | 26 | 46% | 31% | 5.69 | 22.9 | 51 | 146 | $22 |
| 17 | HOU * | 446 | 84 | 24 | 88 | 2 | 311 | 284 | 385 | 535 | 921 | 1077 | 906 | 11 | 78 | 0.55 | 48 | 20 | 32 | 35 | 125 | 125 | 108 | 23% | 94 | 2% | 67% | 20 | 60% | 20% | 7.61 | 36.0 | 64 | 194 | $23 |
| 18 | HOU | 402 | 60 | 15 | 65 | 3 | 239 | 241 | 323 | 405 | 728 | 798 | 705 | 11 | 72 | 0.48 | 44 | 20 | 36 | 29 | 77 | 107 | 83 | 14% | 95 | 3% | 100% | 22 | 41% | 36% | 4.49 | 4.7 | 28 | 93 | $10 |
| 1st Half | | 269 | 46 | 13 | 49 | 2 | 268 | 261 | 352 | 480 | 832 | 855 | 823 | 12 | 71 | 0.48 | 43 | 23 | 34 | 33 | 82 | 136 | 100 | 19% | 99 | 3% | 100% | 14 | 50% | 21% | 6.00 | 15.7 | 50 | 167 | $19 |
| 2nd Half | | 133 | 14 | 2 | 16 | 1 | 180 | 193 | 261 | 256 | 517 | 686 | 459 | 11 | 74 | 0.47 | 47 | 15 | 39 | 23 | 67 | 50 | 50 | 5% | 96 | 3% | 100% | 8 | 25% | 63% | 2.17 | -7.7 | -10 | -33 | -$7 |
| 19 | Proj | **530** | **78** | **24** | **87** | **5** | **265** | **259** | **342** | **458** | **800** | **872** | **776** | **11** | **75** | **0.50** | **47** | **20** | **33** | **31** | **97** | **116** | **87** | **18%** | **97** | **4%** | **81%** | | | | **5.50** | **23.5** | **40** | **133** | **$21** |

## Cozart,Zack

Age: 33 Bats: R Pos: 3B | Ht: 6' 0" Wt: 205

Health F | LIMA Plan B+ | PT/Exp C | Rand Var +5 | Consist F | MM 2335

Forearm tightness and labrum surgery ended season after two months, and h% swing killed his BA. Holding steady in HctX, FB%, and xPX bodes well for continued power, so it really comes down to the risk highlighted by Health grade and AB column. Given his age, expecting another career year is wishful thinking.

| Yr | Tm | AB | R | HR | RBI | SB | BA | xBA | OBP | SLG | OPS | vL | vR | bb% | ct% | Eye | G | L | F | h% | HctX | PX | xPX | hr/f | Spd | SBO | SB% | #Wk | DOM | DIS | RC/G | RAR | BPV | BPX | R$ |
|---|---|---|---|---|---|---|---|---|---|---|---|---|---|---|---|---|---|---|---|---|---|---|---|---|---|---|---|---|---|---|---|---|---|---|---|
| 14 | CIN | 506 | 48 | 4 | 38 | 7 | 221 | 231 | 268 | 300 | 568 | 702 | 532 | 5 | 84 | 0.32 | 45 | 18 | 38 | 26 | 84 | 55 | 77 | 3% | 134 | 6% | 100% | 27 | 26% | 33% | 2.60 | -16.4 | 33 | 89 | $2 |
| 15 | CIN | 194 | 28 | 9 | 28 | 3 | 258 | 276 | 310 | 459 | 769 | 931 | 718 | 7 | 85 | 0.48 | 39 | 19 | 42 | 26 | 98 | 117 | 118 | 13% | 94 | 14% | 50% | 10 | 60% | 10% | 4.61 | 0.2 | 77 | 208 | $5 |
| 16 | CIN | 464 | 67 | 16 | 50 | 4 | 252 | 266 | 308 | 425 | 732 | 737 | 731 | 7 | 82 | 0.44 | 39 | 21 | 40 | 28 | 104 | 102 | 106 | 10% | 90 | 5% | 80% | 23 | 43% | 26% | 4.46 | -4.6 | 53 | 151 | $10 |
| 17 | CIN | 438 | 80 | 24 | 63 | 3 | 297 | 285 | 385 | 548 | 933 | 1059 | 896 | 12 | 82 | 0.79 | 38 | 20 | 42 | 32 | 102 | 128 | 102 | 16% | 135 | 2% | 100% | 25 | 64% | 16% | 7.68 | 34.1 | 98 | 297 | $19 |
| 18 | LAA | 224 | 29 | 5 | 18 | 0 | 219 | 249 | 296 | 362 | 658 | 554 | 690 | 8 | 81 | 0.45 | 38 | 21 | 41 | 25 | 110 | 86 | 113 | 7% | 107 | 0% | 0% | 12 | 33% | 33% | 3.30 | -7.0 | 43 | 143 | $0 |
| 1st Half | | 224 | 29 | 5 | 18 | 0 | 219 | 249 | 296 | 362 | 658 | 554 | 690 | 8 | 81 | 0.45 | 38 | 21 | 41 | 25 | 110 | 86 | 113 | 7% | 107 | 0% | 0% | 12 | 33% | 33% | 3.30 | -8.3 | 44 | 147 | $0 |
| 2nd Half | | | | | | | | | | | | | | | | | | | | | | | | | | | | | | | | | | | |
| 19 | Proj | **418** | **60** | **14** | **46** | **3** | **251** | **260** | **318** | **423** | **742** | **772** | **732** | **8** | **82** | **0.50** | **39** | **20** | **41** | **28** | **103** | **97** | **106** | **10%** | **112** | **4%** | **72%** | | | | **4.48** | **-0.2** | **53** | **177** | **$11** |

## Crawford,Brandon

Age: 32 Bats: L Pos: SS | Ht: 6' 2" Wt: 227

Health A | LIMA Plan B+ | PT/Exp A | Rand Var 0 | Consist B | MM 2135

Tempting to blame 2nd half collapse on mid-August concussion, but 1st half was partly inflated by h%, and numbers were already down in July (.525 OPS, .223 xBA, -26 BPV). Overall though, last three years of xBA speak to consistency of his skill set, and 2017-18 R$ provides useful value baseline. How considerate of him.

| Yr | Tm | AB | R | HR | RBI | SB | BA | xBA | OBP | SLG | OPS | vL | vR | bb% | ct% | Eye | G | L | F | h% | HctX | PX | xPX | hr/f | Spd | SBO | SB% | #Wk | DOM | DIS | RC/G | RAR | BPV | BPX | R$ |
|---|---|---|---|---|---|---|---|---|---|---|---|---|---|---|---|---|---|---|---|---|---|---|---|---|---|---|---|---|---|---|---|---|---|---|---|
| 14 | SF | 491 | 54 | 10 | 69 | 5 | 246 | 229 | 324 | 389 | 713 | 879 | 637 | 10 | 74 | 0.46 | 38 | 20 | 42 | 32 | 91 | 103 | 125 | 6% | 123 | 6% | 63% | 27 | 48% | 37% | 4.26 | 14.1 | 37 | 100 | $11 |
| 15 | SF | 507 | 65 | 21 | 84 | 6 | 256 | 274 | 321 | 462 | 782 | 716 | 808 | 7 | 77 | 0.33 | 48 | 19 | 34 | 30 | 111 | 137 | 136 | 16% | 80 | 9% | 60% | 27 | 48% | 19% | 4.80 | 15.4 | 56 | 151 | $16 |
| 16 | SF | 553 | 67 | 12 | 84 | 7 | 275 | 257 | 342 | 430 | 772 | 713 | 801 | 9 | 79 | 0.50 | 43 | 21 | 36 | 33 | 113 | 92 | 114 | 8% | 117 | 4% | 100% | 27 | 37% | 30% | 5.27 | 10.2 | 46 | 131 | $16 |
| 17 | SF | 518 | 58 | 14 | 77 | 3 | 253 | 255 | 305 | 403 | 709 | 661 | 727 | 7 | 78 | 0.37 | 46 | 19 | 34 | 30 | 103 | 93 | 102 | 10% | 66 | 6% | 38% | 26 | 27% | 35% | 4.11 | -6.2 | 24 | 73 | $10 |
| 18 | SF | 531 | 63 | 14 | 54 | 4 | 254 | 258 | 325 | 394 | 719 | 765 | 693 | 8 | 77 | 0.41 | 44 | 25 | 31 | 31 | 103 | 88 | 91 | 11% | 77 | 6% | 44% | 28 | 29% | 54% | 4.16 | 5.3 | 20 | 67 | $11 |
| 1st Half | | 281 | 37 | 10 | 38 | 3 | 313 | 287 | 375 | 505 | 880 | 860 | 893 | 8 | 78 | 0.42 | 43 | 28 | 29 | 37 | 109 | 119 | 97 | 15% | 80 | 10% | 38% | 15 | 40% | 40% | 6.57 | 20.2 | 50 | 167 | $23 |
| 2nd Half | | 250 | 26 | 4 | 16 | 1 | 188 | 224 | 269 | 268 | 537 | 630 | 494 | 9 | 76 | 0.40 | 45 | 23 | 32 | 23 | 95 | 52 | 84 | 6% | 77 | 2% | 100% | 13 | 15% | 69% | 2.20 | -14.0 | -12 | -40 | -$1 |
| 19 | Proj | **545** | **63** | **13** | **66** | **4** | **249** | **253** | **315** | **388** | **702** | **720** | **694** | **8** | **77** | **0.40** | **44** | **23** | **32** | **30** | **103** | **87** | **100** | **10%** | **83** | **6%** | **54%** | | | | **4.03** | **1.1** | **20** | **67** | **$13** |

BRANDON KRUSE

## Crawford,J.P.

| Age: 24 | Bats: L | Pos: SS | Health | D | LIMA Plan | C |
|---|---|---|---|---|---|---|
| Ht: 6' 2" | Wt: 180 | | PT/Exp | C | Rand Var | -1 |
| | | | Consist | B | MM | 2425 |

3-12-.214 with 2 SB in 117 AB at PHI. Season stuck in neutral as hand/forearm/shoulder injuries limited pedigreed prospect to 49 games. Glove work should earn AB; PX/Spd give hope for potential power/speed asset. But waning ct% at advancing levels, lackluster HctX/xPX cast doubt that this'll be the year.

| Yr | Tm | AB | R | HR | RBI | SB | BA | xBA | OBP | SLG | OPS | vL | vR | bb% | ct% | Eye | G | L | F | h% | HctX | PX | xPX | hr/f | Spd | SBO | SB% | #Wk | DOM | DIS | RC/G | RAR | BPV | BPX | R$ |
|---|---|---|---|---|---|---|---|---|---|---|---|---|---|---|---|---|---|---|---|---|---|---|---|---|---|---|---|---|---|---|---|---|---|---|---|
| 14 | | | | | | | | | | | | | | | | | | | | | | | | | | | | | | | | | | | |
| 15 | aa | 351 | 43 | 5 | 27 | 6 | 240 | | 318 | 363 | 681 | | | 10 | 86 | 0.80 | | | | 27 | | 77 | | | 123 | 8% | 73% | | | | 3.87 | | 64 | 173 | $4 |
| 16 | a/a | 472 | 54 | 6 | 37 | 10 | 226 | | 315 | 306 | 621 | | | 12 | 81 | 0.68 | | | | 27 | | 51 | | | 97 | 12% | 58% | | | | 3.08 | | 19 | 54 | $5 |
| 17 | PHI * | 544 | 75 | 15 | 62 | 5 | 225 | 241 | 332 | 369 | 701 | 380 | 790 | 14 | 76 | 0.66 | 31 | 27 | 43 | 27 | 44 | 83 | 20 | 0% | 143 | 6% | 56% | 5 | 20% | 60% | 3.96 | -9.2 | 42 | 127 | $6 |
| 18 | PHI * | 175 | 22 | 4 | 18 | 3 | 220 | 220 | 289 | 374 | 664 | 495 | 749 | 9 | 68 | 0.30 | 38 | 23 | 39 | 30 | 64 | 102 | 74 | 10% | 136 | 7% | 100% | 12 | 33% | 50% | 3.62 | -1.0 | 12 | 40 | $1 |
| 1st Half | | 97 | 15 | 2 | 9 | 2 | 194 | 232 | 289 | 338 | 626 | 620 | 647 | 12 | 66 | 0.39 | 44 | 25 | 31 | 27 | 67 | 107 | 74 | 11% | 110 | 9% | 100% | 8 | 25% | 63% | 3.19 | -2.4 | 8 | 27 | -$1 |
| 2nd Half | | 78 | 7 | 2 | 9 | 1 | 251 | 180 | 290 | 420 | 711 | 0 | 1159 | 5 | 70 | 0.18 | 20 | 15 | 65 | 34 | 51 | 97 | 73 | 8% | 170 | 5% | 100% | 4 | 50% | 25% | 4.21 | 0.6 | 20 | 67 | $2 |
| **19** | **Proj** | **409** | **50** | **10** | **41** | **6** | **230** | **242** | **322** | **383** | **705** | **444** | **778** | **10** | **74** | **0.43** | **39** | **26** | **36** | **29** | **58** | **92** | **52** | **10%** | **122** | **8%** | **75%** | | | | **3.91** | **-0.7** | **26** | **85** | **$6** |

## Cron,C.J.

| Age: 29 | Bats: R | Pos: DH 1B | Health | B | LIMA Plan | C+ |
|---|---|---|---|---|---|---|
| Ht: 6' 4" | Wt: 235 | | PT/Exp | C | Rand Var | -1 |
| | | | Consist | C | MM | 4033 |

One of the season's quieter 30-HR performances, and PX/xPX gap warns he'll have trouble repeating. Unsustainable 40% h% vL says lefty-masher status not a given either. RAR and xBA history paint him as right around league average, so beware that more talented options could (again) push him to part-time role.

| Yr | Tm | AB | R | HR | RBI | SB | BA | xBA | OBP | SLG | OPS | vL | vR | bb% | ct% | Eye | G | L | F | h% | HctX | PX | xPX | hr/f | Spd | SBO | SB% | #Wk | DOM | DIS | RC/G | RAR | BPV | BPX | R$ |
|---|---|---|---|---|---|---|---|---|---|---|---|---|---|---|---|---|---|---|---|---|---|---|---|---|---|---|---|---|---|---|---|---|---|---|---|
| 14 | LAA * | 432 | 46 | 15 | 57 | 1 | 250 | 255 | 283 | 413 | 697 | 751 | 731 | 4 | 75 | 0.18 | 35 | 25 | 40 | 30 | 109 | 123 | 122 | 15% | 84 | 3% | 50% | 20 | 45% | 45% | 3.94 | -1.3 | 33 | 89 | $10 |
| 15 | LAA * | 471 | 47 | 20 | 66 | 3 | 260 | 263 | 290 | 448 | 738 | 672 | 774 | 4 | 79 | 0.20 | 45 | 18 | 37 | 29 | 96 | 120 | 107 | 14% | 79 | 4% | 75% | 25 | 44% | 32% | 4.47 | -13.4 | 45 | 122 | $13 |
| 16 | LAA | 407 | 51 | 16 | 69 | 2 | 278 | 270 | 325 | 467 | 792 | 674 | 827 | 5 | 82 | 0.32 | 41 | 20 | 39 | 31 | 107 | 111 | 106 | 12% | 85 | 5% | 40% | 22 | 41% | 32% | 5.10 | -4.5 | 54 | 154 | $13 |
| 17 | LAA * | 421 | 46 | 19 | 71 | 4 | 239 | 240 | 284 | 419 | 703 | 790 | 724 | 6 | 73 | 0.23 | 33 | 23 | 45 | 28 | 105 | 107 | 129 | 15% | 78 | 6% | 65% | 23 | 30% | 39% | 3.94 | -11.7 | 13 | 39 | $8 |
| 18 | TAM | 501 | 68 | 30 | 74 | 1 | 253 | 260 | 323 | 493 | 816 | 930 | 767 | 7 | 71 | 0.26 | 40 | 21 | 39 | 30 | 104 | 151 | 115 | 21% | 84 | 3% | 33% | 28 | 50% | 29% | 5.06 | 8.1 | 45 | 150 | $16 |
| 1st Half | | 292 | 40 | 16 | 38 | 1 | 233 | 232 | 310 | 435 | 745 | 819 | 713 | 6 | 69 | 0.22 | 44 | 17 | 39 | 28 | 90 | 128 | 107 | 20% | 93 | 3% | 50% | 15 | 40% | 47% | 4.03 | -4.2 | 21 | 70 | $16 |
| 2nd Half | | 209 | 28 | 14 | 36 | 0 | 282 | 297 | 342 | 574 | 916 | 1081 | 843 | 8 | 74 | 0.31 | 35 | 26 | 39 | 32 | 124 | 180 | 124 | 23% | 70 | 2% | 0% | 13 | 62% | 8% | 6.73 | 13.1 | 79 | 263 | $16 |
| **19** | **Proj** | **394** | **49** | **20** | **63** | **1** | **258** | **259** | **316** | **473** | **789** | **854** | **763** | **6** | **74** | **0.26** | **38** | **22** | **40** | **30** | **108** | **132** | **118** | **17%** | **81** | **3%** | **27%** | | | | **4.85** | **4.0** | **31** | **102** | **$13** |

## Cruz,Nelson

| Age: 39 | Bats: R | Pos: DH | Health | A | LIMA Plan | B+ |
|---|---|---|---|---|---|---|
| Ht: 6' 2" | Wt: 230 | | PT/Exp | A | Rand Var | +3 |
| | | | Consist | B | MM | 4135 |

Father Time is undefea— okay, wait. Sorry. That was a bit hasty. 2nd half BA/xBA dip is a concern, as are series of bumps and bruises (ankle, back, etc.) that limited him to lowest AB total since 2013. Yearly power metrics remain steady and ct% growth suggests decline will be gradual. One of these years though...

| Yr | Tm | AB | R | HR | RBI | SB | BA | xBA | OBP | SLG | OPS | vL | vR | bb% | ct% | Eye | G | L | F | h% | HctX | PX | xPX | hr/f | Spd | SBO | SB% | #Wk | DOM | DIS | RC/G | RAR | BPV | BPX | R$ |
|---|---|---|---|---|---|---|---|---|---|---|---|---|---|---|---|---|---|---|---|---|---|---|---|---|---|---|---|---|---|---|---|---|---|---|---|
| 14 | BAL | 613 | 87 | 40 | 108 | 4 | 271 | 285 | 333 | 525 | 859 | 977 | 823 | 8 | 77 | 0.39 | 42 | 17 | 41 | 29 | 119 | 173 | 131 | 20% | 91 | 6% | 44% | 27 | 63% | 15% | 5.91 | 33.0 | 92 | 249 | $30 |
| 15 | SEA | 590 | 90 | 44 | 93 | 3 | 302 | 277 | 369 | 566 | 936 | 1107 | 866 | 9 | 72 | 0.36 | 46 | 20 | 34 | 35 | 113 | 169 | 137 | 30% | 87 | 3% | 60% | 26 | 50% | 31% | 7.49 | 33.1 | 70 | 189 | $33 |
| 16 | SEA | 589 | 96 | 43 | 105 | 2 | 287 | 274 | 360 | 555 | 915 | 1020 | 864 | 9 | 73 | 0.39 | 44 | 18 | 38 | 33 | 108 | 160 | 134 | 26% | 87 | 1% | 100% | 26 | 62% | 23% | 7.07 | 25.8 | 67 | 191 | $27 |
| 17 | SEA | 556 | 91 | 39 | 119 | 1 | 288 | 268 | 375 | 549 | 924 | 834 | 950 | 11 | 75 | 0.50 | 40 | 18 | 42 | 32 | 123 | 146 | 150 | 22% | 60 | 1% | 50% | 27 | 52% | 26% | 7.18 | 36.0 | 58 | 176 | $25 |
| 18 | SEA | 519 | 70 | 37 | 97 | 1 | 256 | 266 | 342 | 509 | 850 | 936 | 817 | 9 | 76 | 0.45 | 44 | 18 | 39 | 27 | 119 | 139 | 123 | 24% | 54 | 1% | 100% | 27 | 52% | 37% | 5.72 | 18.4 | 54 | 180 | $20 |
| 1st Half | | 257 | 35 | 21 | 51 | 1 | 276 | 282 | 360 | 568 | 928 | 1151 | 847 | 9 | 79 | 0.45 | 40 | 17 | 42 | 27 | 124 | 154 | 115 | 24% | 71 | 2% | 100% | 14 | 57% | 29% | 6.79 | 16.7 | 81 | 270 | $25 |
| 2nd Half | | 262 | 35 | 16 | 46 | 0 | 237 | 244 | 324 | 450 | 775 | 745 | 787 | 11 | 74 | 0.45 | 48 | 18 | 34 | 26 | 114 | 123 | 132 | 24% | 45 | 0% | 0% | 13 | 46% | 46% | 4.78 | 2.1 | 30 | 100 | $16 |
| **19** | **Proj** | **504** | **74** | **31** | **85** | **1** | **260** | **256** | **344** | **486** | **830** | **874** | **813** | **10** | **75** | **0.45** | **44** | **18** | **39** | **29** | **118** | **130** | **134** | **21%** | **66** | **1%** | **69%** | | | | **5.59** | **15.8** | **40** | **133** | **$20** |

## Cuevas,Noel

| Age: 27 | Bats: R | Pos: RF | Health | A | LIMA Plan | D |
|---|---|---|---|---|---|---|
| Ht: 6' 2" | Wt: 210 | | PT/Exp | C | Rand Var | 0 |
| | | | Consist | B | MM | 1311 |

2-10-.233 in 146 AB with 1 SB at COL. Unheralded prospect got first taste of the majors in April, then shuttled back to PCL after rough June/July. Contact skills could help garner a longer audition, but lack of power and inability to take a walk will limit his role. Even in COL, far from an attractive target.

| Yr | Tm | AB | R | HR | RBI | SB | BA | xBA | OBP | SLG | OPS | vL | vR | bb% | ct% | Eye | G | L | F | h% | HctX | PX | xPX | hr/f | Spd | SBO | SB% | #Wk | DOM | DIS | RC/G | RAR | BPV | BPX | R$ |
|---|---|---|---|---|---|---|---|---|---|---|---|---|---|---|---|---|---|---|---|---|---|---|---|---|---|---|---|---|---|---|---|---|---|---|---|
| 14 | aa | 425 | 35 | 5 | 31 | 4 | 189 | | 227 | 272 | 498 | | | 5 | 75 | 0.20 | | | | 24 | | 59 | | | 127 | 9% | 56% | | | | 1.89 | | -2 | -5 | -$4 |
| 15 | aa | 406 | 37 | 3 | 40 | 24 | 246 | | 269 | 330 | 599 | | | 3 | 78 | 0.15 | | | | 31 | | 62 | | | 95 | 43% | 65% | | | | 2.79 | | 0 | 0 | $12 |
| 16 | a/a | 331 | 31 | 3 | 27 | 6 | 277 | | 300 | 387 | 687 | | | 3 | 83 | 0.19 | | | | 33 | | 66 | | | 121 | 17% | 47% | | | | 3.82 | | 29 | 83 | $7 |
| 17 | aaa | 493 | 53 | 11 | 53 | 11 | 274 | | 298 | 416 | 715 | | | 3 | 77 | 0.15 | | | | 34 | | 75 | | | 159 | 12% | 75% | | | | 4.34 | | 25 | 76 | $14 |
| 18 | COL * | 306 | 26 | 5 | 27 | 3 | 254 | 246 | 291 | 374 | 664 | 579 | 590 | 5 | 84 | 0.31 | 46 | 18 | 35 | 29 | 71 | 66 | 46 | 5% | 140 | 12% | 31% | 19 | 26% | 53% | 3.43 | -8.9 | 41 | 137 | $4 |
| 1st Half | | 172 | 16 | 2 | 13 | 1 | 265 | 251 | 306 | 383 | 688 | 625 | 634 | 6 | 83 | 0.34 | 45 | 21 | 34 | 31 | 68 | 64 | 46 | 3% | 157 | 11% | 25% | 11 | 45% | 36% | 3.73 | -3.7 | 43 | 143 | $3 |
| 2nd Half | | 134 | 10 | 3 | 15 | 2 | 240 | 225 | 271 | 362 | 633 | 485 | 286 | 4 | 84 | 0.27 | 50 | 10 | 40 | 27 | 78 | 69 | 48 | 8% | 104 | 14% | 40% | 8 | 0% | 75% | 3.06 | -5.7 | 33 | 110 | $4 |
| **19** | **Proj** | **101** | **9** | **2** | **10** | **2** | **257** | **235** | **290** | **384** | **674** | **640** | **755** | **4** | **81** | **0.23** | **48** | **15** | **37** | **30** | **74** | **71** | **47** | **6%** | **130** | **15%** | **52%** | | | | **3.59** | **-2.6** | **20** | **68** | **$3** |

## Culberson,Charlie

| Age: 30 | Bats: R | Pos: LF 3B SS | Health | A | LIMA Plan | D |
|---|---|---|---|---|---|---|
| Ht: 6' 0" | Wt: 200 | | PT/Exp | D | Rand Var | -5 |
| | | | Consist | F | MM | 2223 |

Well-traveled utility infielder worked his way into career-high AB and double-digit roto value. But a repeat? Unlikely. Hefty hr/f, especially in the 2nd half, is much to thank for power outburst, while FB%/xPX paint a more sober picture. Positional flexibility is nice, but only goes so far. You can do better.

| Yr | Tm | AB | R | HR | RBI | SB | BA | xBA | OBP | SLG | OPS | vL | vR | bb% | ct% | Eye | G | L | F | h% | HctX | PX | xPX | hr/f | Spd | SBO | SB% | #Wk | DOM | DIS | RC/G | RAR | BPV | BPX | R$ |
|---|---|---|---|---|---|---|---|---|---|---|---|---|---|---|---|---|---|---|---|---|---|---|---|---|---|---|---|---|---|---|---|---|---|---|---|
| 14 | COL | 210 | 17 | 3 | 24 | 2 | 195 | 207 | 253 | 290 | 544 | 505 | 559 | 5 | 70 | 0.19 | 52 | 14 | 34 | 26 | 73 | 76 | 71 | 6% | 124 | 10% | 50% | 26 | 19% | 65% | 2.13 | -8.4 | -7 | -19 | -$2 |
| 15 | | | | | | | | | | | | | | | | | | | | | | | | | | | | | | | | | | | |
| 16 | LA * | 332 | 30 | 4 | 32 | 5 | 228 | 226 | 257 | 323 | 581 | 784 | 474 | 4 | 73 | 0.15 | 45 | 21 | 34 | 30 | 83 | 70 | 70 | 6% | 110 | 17% | 47% | 14 | 14% | 43% | 2.57 | -23.5 | -7 | -20 | $2 |
| 17 | LA * | 397 | 27 | 3 | 24 | 5 | 194 | 203 | 232 | 256 | 489 | 429 | 542 | 5 | 77 | 0.22 | 56 | 11 | 33 | 24 | 70 | 39 | -26 | 0% | 107 | 11% | 58% | 5 | 20% | 20% | 1.84 | -40.3 | -15 | -45 | -$5 |
| 18 | ATL | 296 | 47 | 12 | 45 | 4 | 270 | 262 | 326 | 466 | 792 | 744 | 820 | 7 | 71 | 0.25 | 52 | 20 | 28 | 34 | 83 | 128 | 72 | 21% | 114 | 9% | 67% | 28 | 36% | 39% | 5.12 | 7.3 | 37 | 123 | $10 |
| 1st Half | | 138 | 25 | 4 | 19 | 3 | 268 | 252 | 322 | 435 | 757 | 766 | 750 | 7 | 74 | 0.28 | 55 | 16 | 29 | 34 | 83 | 103 | 43 | 14% | 140 | 12% | 75% | 15 | 33% | 40% | 4.79 | 2.5 | 36 | 120 | $8 |
| 2nd Half | | 158 | 22 | 8 | 26 | 1 | 272 | 268 | 329 | 494 | 823 | 718 | 871 | 7 | 69 | 0.22 | 49 | 24 | 27 | 35 | 83 | 151 | 98 | 28% | 85 | 6% | 50% | 13 | 38% | 38% | 5.42 | 5.6 | 37 | 123 | $12 |
| **19** | **Proj** | **264** | **31** | **7** | **31** | **3** | **249** | **239** | **299** | **390** | **688** | **703** | **675** | **6** | **73** | **0.23** | **49** | **20** | **31** | **32** | **82** | **92** | **73** | **12%** | **113** | **10%** | **57%** | | | | **3.77** | **-6.5** | **2** | **8** | **$7** |

## D Arnaud,Travis

| Age: 30 | Bats: R | Pos: CA | Health | F | LIMA Plan | D+ |
|---|---|---|---|---|---|---|
| Ht: 6' 2" | Wt: 210 | | PT/Exp | F | Rand Var | +5 |
| | | | Consist | C | MM | 2333 |

Oft-injured former prospect kept his yearly appointment with the DL—this time as Tommy John surgery shelved him for season after only four games. Contact skills and encouraging hard-contact trends from 2017 still hold true, however, and the catching pool isn't exactly awash with talent. Don't write him off just yet.

| Yr | Tm | AB | R | HR | RBI | SB | BA | xBA | OBP | SLG | OPS | vL | vR | bb% | ct% | Eye | G | L | F | h% | HctX | PX | xPX | hr/f | Spd | SBO | SB% | #Wk | DOM | DIS | RC/G | RAR | BPV | BPX | R$ |
|---|---|---|---|---|---|---|---|---|---|---|---|---|---|---|---|---|---|---|---|---|---|---|---|---|---|---|---|---|---|---|---|---|---|---|---|
| 14 | NYM * | 448 | 58 | 18 | 53 | 1 | 252 | 286 | 305 | 447 | 752 | 707 | 722 | 7 | 84 | 0.49 | 42 | 20 | 39 | 26 | 122 | 130 | 135 | 10% | 85 | 1% | 100% | 23 | 57% | 17% | 4.66 | 15.8 | 83 | 224 | $12 |
| 15 | NYM * | 267 | 33 | 12 | 42 | 0 | 260 | 269 | 319 | 461 | 780 | 1112 | 758 | 8 | 80 | 0.43 | 37 | 21 | 42 | 29 | 101 | 127 | 107 | 15% | 80 | 0% | 0% | 16 | 50% | 19% | 5.07 | 9.7 | 62 | 168 | $7 |
| 16 | NYM | 251 | 27 | 4 | 15 | 0 | 247 | 217 | 307 | 323 | 629 | 455 | 682 | 7 | 80 | 0.38 | 52 | 17 | 31 | 29 | 105 | 47 | 85 | 6% | 89 | 0% | 0% | 19 | 11% | 42% | 3.28 | -8.3 | 0 | 0 | $1 |
| 17 | NYM | 348 | 39 | 16 | 57 | 0 | 244 | 263 | 293 | 443 | 735 | 894 | 681 | 6 | 83 | 0.39 | 42 | 17 | 41 | 25 | 109 | 105 | 114 | 13% | 74 | 0% | 0% | 24 | 50% | 29% | 4.35 | 3.0 | 53 | 161 | $6 |
| 18 | NYM | 15 | 1 | 1 | 3 | 0 | 200 | 316 | 250 | 400 | 650 | 500 | 705 | 6 | 67 | 0.20 | 10 | 40 | 50 | 22 | 123 | 115 | 222 | 20% | 96 | 0% | 0% | 3 | 33% | 67% | 3.19 | -0.1 | 2 | 7 | -$3 |
| 1st Half | | 15 | 1 | 1 | 3 | 0 | 200 | 315 | 250 | 400 | 650 | 500 | 705 | 6 | 67 | 0.20 | 10 | 40 | 50 | 22 | 123 | 115 | 222 | 20% | 96 | 0% | 0% | 3 | 33% | 67% | 3.19 | -0.1 | 2 | 7 | -$3 |
| 2nd Half | | | | | | | | | | | | | | | | | | | | | | | | | | | | | | | | | | | |
| **19** | **Proj** | **293** | **35** | **11** | **39** | **0** | **252** | **256** | **310** | **426** | **736** | **829** | **708** | **7** | **82** | **0.41** | **42** | **19** | **39** | **28** | **107** | **99** | **109** | **12%** | **83** | **0%** | **100%** | | | | **4.43** | **8.4** | **34** | **114** | **$8** |

## Dahl,David

| Age: 25 | Bats: L | Pos: LF RF | Health | F | LIMA Plan | B |
|---|---|---|---|---|---|---|
| Ht: 6' 2" | Wt: 195 | | PT/Exp | D | Rand Var | -1 |
| | | | Consist | F | MM | 4445 |

16-48-.273 with 5 SB in 249 AB at COL. Broken foot cost him two months, but massive Sept (9 HR) and 2nd half ct%/PX spike will rekindle excitement about power/speed upside. Injury history hard to ignore, and Spd/SB% drop gives pause before slapping 20/20 label on him. Still, a growth stock that could pay off. UP: 20-20-.300

| Yr | Tm | AB | R | HR | RBI | SB | BA | xBA | OBP | SLG | OPS | vL | vR | bb% | ct% | Eye | G | L | F | h% | HctX | PX | xPX | hr/f | Spd | SBO | SB% | #Wk | DOM | DIS | RC/G | RAR | BPV | BPX | R$ |
|---|---|---|---|---|---|---|---|---|---|---|---|---|---|---|---|---|---|---|---|---|---|---|---|---|---|---|---|---|---|---|---|---|---|---|---|
| 14 | | | | | | | | | | | | | | | | | | | | | | | | | | | | | | | | | | | |
| 15 | aa | 288 | 38 | 5 | 20 | 18 | 274 | | 296 | 408 | 704 | | | 3 | 76 | 0.13 | | | | 34 | | 93 | | | 123 | 40% | 71% | | | | 4.07 | | 24 | 65 | $12 |
| 16 | COL * | 572 | 99 | 23 | 73 | 19 | 313 | 274 | 370 | 531 | 901 | 728 | 895 | 8 | 73 | 0.34 | 45 | 21 | 33 | 39 | 97 | 140 | 100 | 13% | 138 | 16% | 72% | 11 | 27% | 27% | 7.16 | 39.7 | 65 | 186 | $32 |
| 17 | aaa | 70 | 9 | 2 | 10 | 1 | 228 | | 251 | 377 | 629 | | | 3 | 75 | 0.12 | | | | 28 | | 78 | | | 142 | 14% | 39% | | | | 2.93 | | 14 | 42 | -$1 |
| 18 | COL * | 326 | 35 | 17 | 54 | 6 | 267 | 264 | 308 | 498 | 806 | 695 | 914 | 6 | 73 | 0.22 | 39 | 23 | 38 | 32 | 101 | 140 | 124 | 23% | 102 | 13% | 65% | 15 | 67% | 27% | 5.22 | 5.8 | 47 | 157 | $12 |
| 1st Half | | 117 | 9 | 4 | 16 | 3 | 257 | 232 | 282 | 435 | 717 | 393 | 964 | 3 | 69 | 0.11 | 44 | 20 | 36 | 34 | 91 | 112 | 129 | 17% | 132 | 16% | 72% | 6 | 50% | 50% | 4.16 | -1.5 | 13 | 43 | $0 |
| 2nd Half | | 209 | 27 | 13 | 38 | 3 | 272 | 282 | 323 | 533 | 856 | 925 | 888 | 7 | 75 | 0.30 | 37 | 24 | 39 | 30 | 107 | 154 | 122 | 26% | 85 | 11% | 60% | 9 | 78% | 11% | 5.87 | 7.7 | 65 | 217 | $18 |
| **19** | **Proj** | **460** | **62** | **23** | **68** | **12** | **284** | **267** | **327** | **511** | **838** | **673** | **891** | **6** | **73** | **0.24** | **42** | **22** | **36** | **34** | **99** | **139** | **115** | **19%** | **117** | **16%** | **72%** | | | | **5.85** | **16.5** | **53** | **178** | **$23** |

BRIAN SLACK

## Davidson,Matthew

| | | | |
|---|---|---|---|
| **Age:** 28 **Bats:** R **Pos:** DH 1B | **Health** C | **LIMA Plan** D+ | |
| **Ht:** 6' 3" **Wt:** 230 | **PT/Exp** C | **Rand Var** -3 | |
| | **Consist** A | **MM** 4003 | |

Hit 9 of his 20 HR by April 30. Did lingering May back injury cause ROS power outage? If so, HR could return, as skills otherwise sound. Gave back bb% gains in 2nd half, and struggles vR may continue to limit AB. Now wants to try to pitch? Well, he does know what a swing-and-miss looks like.

| Yr | Tm | AB | R | HR | RBI | SB | BA | xBA | OBP | SLG | OPS | vL | vR | bb% | ct% | Eye | G | L | F | h% | HctX | PX | xPX | hr/f | Spd | SBO | SB% | #Wk | DOM | DIS | RC/G | RAR | BPV | BPX | R$ |
|---|---|---|---|---|---|---|---|---|---|---|---|---|---|---|---|---|---|---|---|---|---|---|---|---|---|---|---|---|---|---|---|---|---|---|---|
| 14 | aaa | 478 | 39 | 15 | 37 | 0 | 163 | | 220 | 285 | 505 | | | 7 | 61 | 0.19 | | | | 23 | | 109 | | | 85 | 0% | 0% | | | | 1.91 | | -27 | -73 | -$6 |
| 15 | aaa | 528 | 51 | 20 | 60 | 1 | 175 | | 252 | 323 | 575 | | | 9 | 58 | 0.24 | | | | 26 | | 126 | | | 78 | 1% | 100% | | | | 2.52 | | -23 | -62 | -$3 |
| 16 | CHW * | 286 | 29 | 8 | 37 | 0 | 231 | 413 | 297 | 379 | 676 | 1000 | 0 | 9 | 63 | 0.26 | 0 | 100 | 0 | 33 | 0 | 118 | -24 | 0% | 73 | 0% | 0% | 1 | 0% | 100% | 3.73 | -9.2 | -9 | -26 | $2 |
| 17 | CHW | 414 | 43 | 26 | 68 | 0 | 220 | 218 | 260 | 452 | 711 | 759 | 693 | 4 | 60 | 0.12 | 36 | 17 | 46 | 29 | 93 | 158 | 147 | 22% | 79 | 1% | 0% | 25 | 32% | 48% | 3.70 | -14.6 | 1 | 3 | $5 |
| 18 | CHW | 434 | 51 | 20 | 62 | 0 | 228 | 214 | 319 | 419 | 738 | 882 | 687 | 10 | 62 | 0.32 | 41 | 19 | 40 | 32 | 90 | 142 | 120 | 18% | 82 | 0% | 0% | 27 | 30% | 48% | 4.30 | -0.3 | 9 | 30 | $8 |
| 1st Half | | 219 | 29 | 14 | 33 | 0 | 228 | 222 | 342 | 475 | 817 | 937 | 784 | 14 | 57 | 0.38 | 41 | 19 | 40 | 33 | 91 | 194 | 173 | 28% | 77 | 0% | 0% | 14 | 29% | 36% | 5.29 | 5.2 | 35 | 117 | $11 |
| 2nd Half | | 215 | 22 | 6 | 29 | 0 | 228 | 207 | 292 | 363 | 655 | 845 | 570 | 7 | 67 | 0.23 | 41 | 18 | 40 | 31 | 88 | 98 | 74 | 10% | 92 | 0% | 0% | 13 | 31% | 62% | 3.37 | -7.4 | -8 | -27 | $5 |
| 19 | Proj | 322 | 35 | 17 | 45 | 0 | 221 | 216 | 291 | 424 | 715 | 820 | 675 | 8 | 62 | 0.23 | 39 | 18 | 43 | 30 | 91 | 147 | 128 | 19% | 81 | 0% | 14% | | | | 3.92 | -5.8 | -8 | -28 | $4 |

## Davis,Chris

| | | | |
|---|---|---|---|
| **Age:** 33 **Bats:** L **Pos:** 1B | **Health** B | **LIMA Plan** D+ | |
| **Ht:** 6' 3" **Wt:** 230 | **PT/Exp** A | **Rand Var** +5 | |
| | **Consist** C | **MM** 4105 | |

How bad was it? Local bar offered free liquor shots for hits; he drove fans to drink... elsewhere. Never a contact specialist, but when ball met bat, far less happened than usual. Walk rate dipped, too. Was he pressing, or is ability to control strike zone gone for good? Four years left on contract says, "We'll find out." Yay?

| Yr | Tm | AB | R | HR | RBI | SB | BA | xBA | OBP | SLG | OPS | vL | vR | bb% | ct% | Eye | G | L | F | h% | HctX | PX | xPX | hr/f | Spd | SBO | SB% | #Wk | DOM | DIS | RC/G | RAR | BPV | BPX | R$ |
|---|---|---|---|---|---|---|---|---|---|---|---|---|---|---|---|---|---|---|---|---|---|---|---|---|---|---|---|---|---|---|---|---|---|---|---|
| 14 | BAL | 450 | 65 | 26 | 72 | 2 | 196 | 235 | 300 | 404 | 704 | 677 | 716 | 11 | 62 | 0.35 | 35 | 25 | 41 | 25 | 96 | 174 | 154 | 23% | 66 | 3% | 67% | 22 | 36% | 36% | 3.71 | -6.1 | 30 | 81 | $8 |
| 15 | BAL | 573 | 100 | 47 | 117 | 2 | 262 | 271 | 361 | 562 | 923 | 799 | 984 | 13 | 64 | 0.40 | 32 | 25 | 43 | 32 | 115 | 224 | 195 | 29% | 62 | 3% | 40% | 27 | 56% | 22% | 6.80 | 31.1 | 80 | 216 | $28 |
| 16 | BAL | 566 | 99 | 38 | 84 | 1 | 221 | 231 | 332 | 459 | 792 | 711 | 828 | 13 | 61 | 0.40 | 36 | 20 | 44 | 28 | 100 | 169 | 179 | 25% | 79 | 1% | 100% | 27 | 41% | 41% | 4.91 | 0.8 | 33 | 94 | $12 |
| 17 | BAL | 456 | 65 | 26 | 61 | 1 | 215 | 216 | 309 | 423 | 732 | 619 | 785 | 12 | 57 | 0.31 | 37 | 23 | 40 | 31 | 96 | 149 | 152 | 25% | 73 | 2% | 50% | 24 | 17% | 67% | 4.20 | -16.5 | -4 | -12 | $5 |
| 18 | BAL | 470 | 40 | 16 | 49 | 2 | 168 | 187 | 243 | 296 | 539 | 493 | 557 | 8 | 59 | 0.21 | 40 | 21 | 39 | 24 | 79 | 95 | 121 | 15% | 63 | 2% | 100% | 26 | 12% | 73% | 2.15 | -34.8 | -50 | -167 | -$2 |
| 1st Half | | 241 | 13 | 7 | 24 | 0 | 154 | 160 | 231 | 261 | 493 | 534 | 476 | 8 | 59 | 0.22 | 43 | 18 | 39 | 22 | 72 | 80 | 115 | 13% | 59 | 0% | 0% | 15 | 7% | 67% | 1.77 | -24.0 | -64 | -213 | -$7 |
| 2nd Half | | 229 | 27 | 9 | 25 | 2 | 183 | 201 | 256 | 332 | 588 | 447 | 640 | 8 | 59 | 0.20 | 36 | 25 | 39 | 26 | 86 | 110 | 127 | 17% | 80 | 4% | 100% | 11 | 18% | 82% | 2.59 | -16.0 | -33 | -110 | $4 |
| 19 | Proj | 441 | 55 | 21 | 56 | 2 | 207 | 206 | 293 | 383 | 677 | 601 | 709 | 10 | 59 | 0.28 | 37 | 22 | 40 | 29 | 90 | 129 | 143 | 20% | 70 | 2% | 81% | | | | 3.54 | -16.8 | -23 | -75 | $7 |

## Davis,J.D.

| | | | |
|---|---|---|---|
| **Age:** 26 **Bats:** R **Pos:** 3B | **Health** A | **LIMA Plan** D | |
| **Ht:** 6' 3" **Wt:** 225 | **PT/Exp** C | **Rand Var** 0 | |
| | **Consist** A | **MM** 3221 | |

1-5-.175 in 103 AB with HOU. Perils of a loaded organization: tearing up PCL (.989 OPS) guaranteed nothing. In part due to 23% MLB h%, couldn't sniff that OPS level in sporadic PT once up. Uptick in ct% offset by dip in HctX, PX/xPX, and GB tilt limits HR upside. Fantasy relevance may require change of scenery.

| Yr | Tm | AB | R | HR | RBI | SB | BA | xBA | OBP | SLG | OPS | vL | vR | bb% | ct% | Eye | G | L | F | h% | HctX | PX | xPX | hr/f | Spd | SBO | SB% | #Wk | DOM | DIS | RC/G | RAR | BPV | BPX | R$ |
|---|---|---|---|---|---|---|---|---|---|---|---|---|---|---|---|---|---|---|---|---|---|---|---|---|---|---|---|---|---|---|---|---|---|---|---|
| 14 | | | | | | | | | | | | | | | | | | | | | | | | | | | | | | | | | | | |
| 15 | | | | | | | | | | | | | | | | | | | | | | | | | | | | | | | | | | | |
| 16 | aa | 485 | 52 | 20 | 69 | 1 | 241 | | 296 | 432 | 727 | | | 7 | 66 | 0.23 | | | | 32 | | 140 | | | 80 | 4% | 20% | | | | 4.17 | | 15 | 43 | $8 |
| 17 | HOU * | 474 | 51 | 24 | 64 | 5 | 232 | 252 | 282 | 432 | 714 | 960 | 647 | 6 | 69 | 0.22 | 60 | 16 | 23 | 28 | 111 | 125 | 125 | 40% | 73 | 8% | 59% | 10 | 40% | 50% | 3.97 | -12.7 | 13 | 39 | $8 |
| 18 | HOU * | 436 | 48 | 13 | 61 | 2 | 250 | 248 | 304 | 396 | 700 | 568 | 413 | 7 | 74 | 0.30 | 50 | 22 | 28 | 31 | 89 | 94 | 71 | 5% | 85 | 2% | 100% | 15 | 0% | 60% | 4.12 | -2.7 | 13 | 43 | $9 |
| 1st Half | | 261 | 32 | 6 | 36 | 1 | 256 | 254 | 315 | 392 | 707 | 500 | 619 | 8 | 73 | 0.32 | 48 | 26 | 26 | 33 | 87 | 92 | 86 | 13% | 93 | 1% | 100% | 6 | 0% | 50% | 4.25 | -2.0 | 12 | 40 | $11 |
| 2nd Half | | 175 | 16 | 7 | 25 | 1 | 240 | 242 | 289 | 402 | 691 | 593 | 186 | 6 | 75 | 0.28 | 51 | 19 | 30 | 28 | 90 | 96 | 60 | 0% | 79 | 3% | 100% | 9 | 0% | 67% | 3.93 | -3.0 | 17 | 57 | $6 |
| 19 | Proj | 131 | 14 | 5 | 18 | 1 | 241 | 241 | 294 | 400 | 695 | 860 | 594 | 7 | 71 | 0.25 | 50 | 20 | 29 | 30 | 98 | 105 | 93 | 17% | 86 | 4% | 67% | | | | 3.90 | -2.3 | -1 | -5 | $3 |

## Davis,Khristopher

| | | | |
|---|---|---|---|
| **Age:** 31 **Bats:** R **Pos:** DH | **Health** A | **LIMA Plan** B+ | |
| **Ht:** 5' 10" **Wt:** 195 | **PT/Exp** A | **Rand Var** +2 | |
| | **Consist** A | **MM** 5235 | |

Doesn't take a Forecaster to tell you where his BA will end up, does it? Boost in FB% shows he knows his role, for which he is unquestionably qualified (see PX/xPX). Plenty of reasons to buy with confidence, including AAA reliability, lack of platoon splits, and age, which should provide another few years at this lofty plateau.

| Yr | Tm | AB | R | HR | RBI | SB | BA | xBA | OBP | SLG | OPS | vL | vR | bb% | ct% | Eye | G | L | F | h% | HctX | PX | xPX | hr/f | Spd | SBO | SB% | #Wk | DOM | DIS | RC/G | RAR | BPV | BPX | R$ |
|---|---|---|---|---|---|---|---|---|---|---|---|---|---|---|---|---|---|---|---|---|---|---|---|---|---|---|---|---|---|---|---|---|---|---|---|
| 14 | MIL | 501 | 70 | 22 | 69 | 4 | 244 | 278 | 299 | 457 | 756 | 777 | 749 | 6 | 76 | 0.26 | 39 | 21 | 40 | 28 | 132 | 161 | 157 | 14% | 85 | 5% | 80% | 26 | 54% | 27% | 4.45 | 6.0 | 70 | 189 | $15 |
| 15 | MIL | 392 | 54 | 27 | 66 | 6 | 247 | 259 | 323 | 505 | 828 | 729 | 864 | 10 | 69 | 0.36 | 42 | 17 | 40 | 29 | 105 | 174 | 169 | 25% | 87 | 8% | 75% | 22 | 64% | 18% | 5.25 | 0.7 | 63 | 170 | $15 |
| 16 | OAK | 555 | 85 | 42 | 102 | 1 | 247 | 266 | 307 | 524 | 831 | 881 | 815 | 7 | 70 | 0.25 | 43 | 17 | 40 | 27 | 111 | 171 | 145 | 27% | 85 | 3% | 33% | 26 | 54% | 38% | 5.25 | -4.0 | 58 | 166 | $18 |
| 17 | OAK | 566 | 91 | 43 | 110 | 4 | 247 | 257 | 336 | 528 | 864 | 786 | 886 | 11 | 66 | 0.37 | 38 | 19 | 42 | 30 | 112 | 177 | 174 | 27% | 75 | 3% | 100% | 27 | 56% | 26% | 6.01 | 19.0 | 51 | 155 | $19 |
| 18 | OAK | 576 | 98 | 48 | 123 | 0 | 247 | 261 | 326 | 549 | 874 | 811 | 897 | 9 | 70 | 0.34 | 35 | 16 | 49 | 27 | 116 | 185 | 171 | 24% | 72 | 0% | 0% | 28 | 50% | 14% | 5.88 | 23.3 | 68 | 227 | $25 |
| 1st Half | | 281 | 43 | 20 | 55 | 0 | 231 | 247 | 318 | 495 | 812 | 674 | 861 | 9 | 70 | 0.35 | 38 | 15 | 47 | 25 | 121 | 163 | 157 | 21% | 70 | 0% | 0% | 15 | 47% | 13% | 4.98 | 4.0 | 54 | 180 | $19 |
| 2nd Half | | 295 | 55 | 28 | 68 | 0 | 261 | 272 | 333 | 600 | 933 | 940 | 931 | 9 | 69 | 0.33 | 33 | 17 | 50 | 28 | 111 | 207 | 185 | 27% | 80 | 0% | 0% | 13 | 54% | 15% | 6.82 | 19.7 | 85 | 283 | $32 |
| 19 | Proj | 573 | 94 | 44 | 114 | 2 | 247 | 259 | 322 | 533 | 856 | 815 | 869 | 9 | 69 | 0.32 | 37 | 17 | 45 | 28 | 114 | 179 | 168 | 25% | 77 | 2% | 78% | | | | 5.70 | 20.2 | 58 | 193 | $24 |

## Davis,Rajai

| | | | |
|---|---|---|---|
| **Age:** 38 **Bats:** R **Pos:** CF LF | **Health** B | **LIMA Plan** D | |
| **Ht:** 5' 10" **Wt:** 195 | **PT/Exp** C | **Rand Var** 0 | |
| | **Consist** B | **MM** 1501 | |

Speed may be a skill of the young, but there's something to be said for manager's trust, too (see SBO). Still, ability to hang on to bench role in doubt, as days as valuable platoon bat vL seem done. Spd still robust, so maybe he gets late-summer call to be grizzled Terrance Gore. Compulsory retirement perhaps more likely.

| Yr | Tm | AB | R | HR | RBI | SB | BA | xBA | OBP | SLG | OPS | vL | vR | bb% | ct% | Eye | G | L | F | h% | HctX | PX | xPX | hr/f | Spd | SBO | SB% | #Wk | DOM | DIS | RC/G | RAR | BPV | BPX | R$ |
|---|---|---|---|---|---|---|---|---|---|---|---|---|---|---|---|---|---|---|---|---|---|---|---|---|---|---|---|---|---|---|---|---|---|---|---|
| 14 | DET | 461 | 64 | 8 | 51 | 36 | 282 | 269 | 320 | 401 | 721 | 939 | 617 | 4 | 84 | 0.29 | 50 | 19 | 31 | 32 | 74 | 88 | 58 | 7% | 109 | 41% | 77% | 26 | 46% | 19% | 4.46 | 7.6 | 49 | 132 | $26 |
| 15 | DET | 341 | 55 | 8 | 30 | 18 | 258 | 265 | 306 | 440 | 746 | 758 | 738 | 6 | 78 | 0.29 | 44 | 22 | 33 | 31 | 95 | 112 | 77 | 9% | 182 | 35% | 69% | 26 | 50% | 38% | 4.39 | -1.1 | 69 | 186 | $13 |
| 16 | CLE | 454 | 74 | 12 | 48 | 43 | 249 | 244 | 306 | 388 | 693 | 670 | 708 | 7 | 77 | 0.31 | 45 | 19 | 36 | 30 | 82 | 88 | 75 | 10% | 109 | 45% | 88% | 27 | 26% | 48% | 4.22 | -2.0 | 25 | 71 | $25 |
| 17 | 2 AL | 336 | 56 | 5 | 20 | 29 | 235 | 236 | 293 | 348 | 641 | 677 | 619 | 7 | 75 | 0.33 | 46 | 19 | 35 | 30 | 68 | 74 | 73 | 6% | 129 | 45% | 81% | 26 | 23% | 42% | 3.50 | -12.8 | 16 | 48 | $13 |
| 18 | CLE | 196 | 33 | 1 | 6 | 21 | 224 | 218 | 278 | 281 | 559 | 507 | 608 | 5 | 76 | 0.23 | 47 | 22 | 31 | 29 | 75 | 39 | 58 | 2% | 142 | 60% | 75% | 27 | 11% | 63% | 2.47 | -9.6 | -11 | -37 | $7 |
| 1st Half | | 126 | 23 | 1 | 6 | 16 | 246 | 229 | 304 | 294 | 598 | 505 | 688 | 7 | 79 | 0.33 | 47 | 24 | 29 | 31 | 82 | 32 | 68 | 3% | 115 | 53% | 84% | 15 | 13% | 60% | 3.27 | -3.4 | -10 | -33 | $11 |
| 2nd Half | | 70 | 10 | 0 | 0 | 5 | 186 | 198 | 230 | 257 | 487 | 508 | 468 | 3 | 70 | 0.10 | 47 | 17 | 36 | 27 | 61 | 54 | 37 | 0% | 127 | 82% | 56% | 12 | 8% | 67% | 1.33 | -6.7 | -31 | -103 | $0 |
| 19 | Proj | 165 | 26 | 2 | 8 | 13 | 222 | 225 | 275 | 316 | 592 | 583 | 598 | 6 | 75 | 0.24 | 46 | 20 | 34 | 28 | 72 | 63 | 61 | 4% | 131 | 47% | 75% | | | | 2.76 | -7.2 | 13 | 44 | $6 |

## Dean,Austin

| | | | |
|---|---|---|---|
| **Age:** 25 **Bats:** R **Pos:** LF | **Health** A | **LIMA Plan** D | |
| **Ht:** 6' 1" **Wt:** 190 | **PT/Exp** C | **Rand Var** -2 | |
| | **Consist** B | **MM** 2331 | |

4-14-.214 in 114 at MIA. Third time starting at AA proved to be charm (1.120 OPS in 88 PA), propelling rise to AAA, then majors in mid-August. Nothing he did thereafter suggests future as anything but reserve. Contact rate OK, but power lackluster for corner OF, and no inclination to run despite good Spd. You can do better.

| Yr | Tm | AB | R | HR | RBI | SB | BA | xBA | OBP | SLG | OPS | vL | vR | bb% | ct% | Eye | G | L | F | h% | HctX | PX | xPX | hr/f | Spd | SBO | SB% | #Wk | DOM | DIS | RC/G | RAR | BPV | BPX | R$ |
|---|---|---|---|---|---|---|---|---|---|---|---|---|---|---|---|---|---|---|---|---|---|---|---|---|---|---|---|---|---|---|---|---|---|---|---|
| 14 | | | | | | | | | | | | | | | | | | | | | | | | | | | | | | | | | | | |
| 15 | | | | | | | | | | | | | | | | | | | | | | | | | | | | | | | | | | | |
| 16 | aa | 480 | 53 | 9 | 60 | 1 | 212 | | 277 | 330 | 606 | | | 8 | 74 | 0.34 | | | | 27 | | 78 | | | 101 | 3% | 29% | | | | 2.90 | | 7 | 20 | $1 |
| 17 | aa | 234 | 28 | 4 | 29 | 3 | 257 | | 298 | 387 | 685 | | | 5 | 78 | 0.26 | | | | 32 | | 78 | | | 120 | 7% | 72% | | | | 3.94 | | 22 | 67 | $3 |
| 18 | MIA * | 510 | 74 | 13 | 70 | 3 | 277 | 249 | 329 | 410 | 738 | 448 | 692 | 7 | 82 | 0.44 | 42 | 21 | 37 | 31 | 97 | 74 | 91 | 12% | 123 | 3% | 53% | 7 | 43% | 14% | 4.69 | 1.1 | 42 | 140 | $16 |
| 1st Half | | 274 | 39 | 6 | 38 | 2 | 291 | 251 | 347 | 419 | 766 | | | 8 | 84 | 0.54 | | | | 33 | | 67 | | | 150 | 2% | 100% | | | | 5.28 | | 53 | 177 | $18 |
| 2nd Half | | 236 | 35 | 7 | 31 | 1 | 260 | 249 | 307 | 398 | 705 | 448 | 692 | 6 | 80 | 0.35 | 42 | 21 | 37 | 30 | 94 | 83 | 91 | 12% | 94 | 6% | 30% | 7 | 43% | 14% | 4.05 | -3.8 | 31 | 103 | $13 |
| 19 | Proj | 131 | 17 | 4 | 17 | 1 | 258 | 254 | 316 | 420 | 737 | 574 | 779 | 7 | 79 | 0.34 | 42 | 21 | 37 | 30 | 85 | 94 | 82 | 11% | 122 | 5% | 62% | | | | 4.37 | -0.9 | 34 | 113 | $4 |

## DeJong,Paul

| | | | |
|---|---|---|---|
| **Age:** 25 **Bats:** R **Pos:** SS | **Health** B | **LIMA Plan** B+ | |
| **Ht:** 6'1" **Wt:** 195 | **PT/Exp** B | **Rand Var** +1 | |
| | **Consist** D | **MM** 4125 | |

If not following closely, natural to conclude encore to smashing debut was a dud. But in reality, strong power display (17 HR in April, Aug/Sept) bookended fractured hand in May, gradual return to form. Yes, 2017 BA was a stretch, but ct%, bb% creeping in right direction. Plenty of FB, so if he can avoid injury... UP: 35 HR

| Yr | Tm | AB | R | HR | RBI | SB | BA | xBA | OBP | SLG | OPS | vL | vR | bb% | ct% | Eye | G | L | F | h% | HctX | PX | xPX | hr/f | Spd | SBO | SB% | #Wk | DOM | DIS | RC/G | RAR | BPV | BPX | R$ |
|---|---|---|---|---|---|---|---|---|---|---|---|---|---|---|---|---|---|---|---|---|---|---|---|---|---|---|---|---|---|---|---|---|---|---|---|
| 14 | | | | | | | | | | | | | | | | | | | | | | | | | | | | | | | | | | | |
| 15 | | | | | | | | | | | | | | | | | | | | | | | | | | | | | | | | | | | |
| 16 | aa | 496 | 52 | 18 | 61 | 3 | 235 | | 283 | 403 | 687 | | | 6 | 69 | 0.22 | | | | 30 | | 116 | | | 86 | 5% | 53% | | | | 3.76 | | 10 | 29 | $7 |
| 17 | STL * | 594 | 77 | 35 | 93 | 1 | 278 | 261 | 311 | 515 | 826 | 952 | 835 | 4 | 70 | 0.16 | 34 | 23 | 43 | 34 | 104 | 145 | 133 | 20% | 88 | 3% | 30% | 19 | 53% | 26% | 5.57 | 17.7 | 35 | 106 | $20 |
| 18 | STL | 436 | 68 | 19 | 68 | 1 | 241 | 245 | 313 | 433 | 746 | 651 | 777 | 7 | 72 | 0.29 | 32 | 24 | 44 | 29 | 102 | 125 | 134 | 14% | 107 | 2% | 50% | 22 | 50% | 45% | 4.32 | 6.5 | 36 | 120 | $11 |
| 1st Half | | 150 | 22 | 8 | 19 | 0 | 260 | 248 | 351 | 473 | 824 | 697 | 857 | 10 | 67 | 0.32 | 30 | 27 | 43 | 34 | 98 | 145 | 125 | 19% | 121 | 0% | 0% | 9 | 44% | 56% | 5.40 | 6.3 | 40 | 133 | $3 |
| 2nd Half | | 286 | 46 | 11 | 49 | 1 | 231 | 245 | 292 | 413 | 705 | 632 | 731 | 7 | 74 | 0.27 | 33 | 23 | 44 | 27 | 104 | 115 | 138 | 11% | 99 | 4% | 50% | 13 | 54% | 38% | 3.80 | -1.4 | 35 | 117 | $16 |
| 19 | Proj | 523 | 73 | 27 | 78 | 1 | 254 | 250 | 314 | 468 | 782 | 746 | 792 | 7 | 71 | 0.24 | 32 | 24 | 43 | 31 | 103 | 138 | 133 | 17% | 101 | 3% | 47% | | | | 4.80 | 12.9 | 24 | 81 | $17 |

KRISTOPHER OLSON

## Delmonico,Nick

| | | | | | |
|---|---|---|---|---|---|
| Age: 26 | Bats: L | Pos: LF | Health C | LIMA Plan C | |
| Ht: 6' 3" | Wt: 230 | | PT/Exp C | Rand Var 0 | |
| | | | Consist A | MM 3225 | |

8-25-.215 in 284 AB at CHW. Missed two months with hand fracture. Otherwise, apart from a couple of red-hot two-week stretches, took a step back. In truth, overall skills looked a lot like recent full-seasons' efforts. Still owns power upside, and still young enough to keep hoping. But stock is down from a year ago.

| Yr | Tm | AB | R | HR | RBI | SB | BA | xBA | OBP | SLG | OPS | vL | vR | bb% | ct% | Eye | G | L | F | h% | HctX | PX | xPX | hr/f | Spd | SBO | SB% | #Wk | DOM | DIS | RC/G | RAR | BPV | BPX | R$ |
|---|---|---|---|---|---|---|---|---|---|---|---|---|---|---|---|---|---|---|---|---|---|---|---|---|---|---|---|---|---|---|---|---|---|---|---|
| 14 | | | | | | | | | | | | | | | | | | | | | | | | | | | | | | | | | | | |
| 15 | aa | 223 | 23 | 3 | 23 | 2 | 210 | | 285 | 342 | 626 | | | 9 | 73 | 0.39 | | | | 28 | | 114 | | | 82 | 6% | 61% | | | | 3.11 | | 29 | 78 | -$1 |
| 16 | a/a | 402 | 45 | 14 | 48 | 2 | 243 | | 305 | 424 | 728 | | | 8 | 69 | 0.28 | | | | 32 | | 129 | | | 88 | 3% | 100% | | | | 4.38 | | 22 | 63 | $6 |
| 17 | CHW * | 519 | 68 | 19 | 58 | 5 | 231 | 250 | 311 | 386 | 697 | 894 | 844 | 10 | 77 | 0.51 | 40 | 22 | 37 | 26 | 91 | 86 | 104 | 23% | 107 | 5% | 69% | 8 | 38% | 25% | 3.96 | -23.3 | 32 | 97 | $7 |
| 18 | CHW * | 319 | 34 | 8 | 27 | 1 | 220 | 223 | 290 | 372 | 662 | 607 | 680 | 9 | 72 | 0.35 | 42 | 18 | 40 | 28 | 79 | 95 | 85 | 10% | 115 | 4% | 33% | 20 | 25% | 55% | 3.45 | -11.1 | 19 | 63 | $1 |
| 1st Half | | 116 | 10 | 1 | 7 | 1 | 224 | 205 | 333 | 302 | 635 | 521 | 653 | 12 | 79 | 0.67 | 39 | 17 | 43 | 27 | 73 | 48 | 60 | 3% | 113 | 6% | 50% | 8 | 25% | 38% | 3.09 | -5.4 | 16 | 53 | -$5 |
| 2nd Half | | 203 | 24 | 7 | 20 | 0 | 218 | 234 | 273 | 412 | 685 | 652 | 698 | 7 | 68 | 0.24 | 44 | 18 | 38 | 28 | 84 | 127 | 105 | 16% | 109 | 3% | 0% | 12 | 25% | 67% | 3.59 | -6.3 | 23 | 77 | $5 |
| **19** | **Proj** | **413** | **46** | **15** | **40** | **2** | **233** | **243** | **314** | **413** | **728** | **746** | **723** | **9** | **73** | **0.38** | **42** | **19** | **38** | **28** | **84** | **112** | **93** | **13%** | **102** | **4%** | **56%** | | | | **4.12** | **-6.0** | **26** | **87** | **$5** |

## Descalso,Daniel

| | | | | | |
|---|---|---|---|---|---|
| Age: 32 | Bats: L | Pos: 2B 3B | Health B | LIMA Plan D+ | |
| Ht: 5' 10" | Wt: 190 | | PT/Exp C | Rand Var -1 | |
| | | | Consist B | MM 3213 | |

Cemented 2017's FB spike and related power surge (see xPX in BOTH halves). It seems playing time will always be an issue, and he's a drag on BA. But now contributing solidly in HR and with walks keeping OBP decent, he's gone from a "mostly irrelevant" part-timer to "at least a somewhat relevant" part-timer.

| Yr | Tm | AB | R | HR | RBI | SB | BA | xBA | OBP | SLG | OPS | vL | vR | bb% | ct% | Eye | G | L | F | h% | HctX | PX | xPX | hr/f | Spd | SBO | SB% | #Wk | DOM | DIS | RC/G | RAR | BPV | BPX | R$ |
|---|---|---|---|---|---|---|---|---|---|---|---|---|---|---|---|---|---|---|---|---|---|---|---|---|---|---|---|---|---|---|---|---|---|---|---|
| 14 | STL | 161 | 20 | 0 | 10 | 1 | 242 | 220 | 333 | 311 | 644 | 899 | 575 | 11 | 80 | 0.61 | 43 | 17 | 39 | 30 | 72 | 68 | 50 | 0% | 97 | 8% | 25% | 26 | 27% | 42% | 3.19 | -0.4 | 25 | 68 | $0 |
| 15 | COL | 185 | 22 | 5 | 22 | 1 | 205 | 223 | 283 | 324 | 607 | 468 | 628 | 10 | 76 | 0.44 | 44 | 19 | 36 | 24 | 68 | 71 | 75 | 10% | 122 | 6% | 33% | 27 | 30% | 48% | 2.83 | -5.4 | 17 | 46 | -$1 |
| 16 | COL | 250 | 38 | 8 | 38 | 3 | 264 | 264 | 349 | 424 | 773 | 732 | 782 | 12 | 78 | 0.61 | 44 | 24 | 32 | 31 | 92 | 96 | 99 | 13% | 89 | 4% | 100% | 22 | 27% | 36% | 5.25 | 4.6 | 40 | 114 | $7 |
| 17 | ARI | 344 | 47 | 10 | 51 | 4 | 233 | 231 | 332 | 395 | 727 | 588 | 767 | 12 | 74 | 0.54 | 39 | 18 | 43 | 29 | 111 | 95 | 153 | 9% | 112 | 4% | 100% | 27 | 33% | 33% | 4.36 | -1.6 | 32 | 97 | $5 |
| 18 | ARI | 349 | 54 | 13 | 57 | 0 | 238 | 235 | 353 | 436 | 789 | 889 | 767 | 15 | 68 | 0.58 | 30 | 24 | 46 | 31 | 109 | 134 | 168 | 11% | 97 | 1% | 0% | 28 | 50% | 36% | 5.13 | 13.7 | 42 | 140 | $8 |
| 1st Half | | 205 | 28 | 9 | 42 | 0 | 254 | 242 | 352 | 488 | 840 | 830 | 841 | 14 | 69 | 0.52 | 31 | 20 | 49 | 32 | 111 | 152 | 172 | 12% | 91 | 2% | 0% | 15 | 60% | 33% | 5.84 | 11.4 | 56 | 187 | $12 |
| 2nd Half | | 144 | 26 | 4 | 15 | 0 | 215 | 232 | 354 | 361 | 715 | 976 | 668 | 18 | 67 | 0.66 | 29 | 29 | 42 | 29 | 105 | 108 | 161 | 10% | 105 | 0% | 0% | 13 | 38% | 38% | 4.16 | 0.9 | 25 | 83 | $2 |
| **19** | **Proj** | **361** | **54** | **12** | **51** | **2** | **235** | **235** | **343** | **411** | **754** | **788** | **746** | **14** | **72** | **0.58** | **35** | **22** | **43** | **29** | **102** | **113** | **142** | **11%** | **100** | **3%** | **68%** | | | | **4.68** | **5.5** | **34** | **112** | **$9** |

## DeShields Jr.,Delino

| | | | | | |
|---|---|---|---|---|---|
| Age: 26 | Bats: R | Pos: CF | Health B | LIMA Plan C | |
| Ht: 5' 9" | Wt: 200 | | PT/Exp C | Rand Var +3 | |
| | | | Consist D | MM 1503 | |

2-22-.216 with 20 SB in 334 AB at TEX. Toss out 2016 when he unwisely bulked up, and his first four MLB seasons tell a consistent story: He's the ultimate one-trick pony. Improved glove should keep him in the lineup at least part time, and age is still on his side. But weak stick likely caps SB totals. Bid for 20 bags, hope for more.

| Yr | Tm | AB | R | HR | RBI | SB | BA | xBA | OBP | SLG | OPS | vL | vR | bb% | ct% | Eye | G | L | F | h% | HctX | PX | xPX | hr/f | Spd | SBO | SB% | #Wk | DOM | DIS | RC/G | RAR | BPV | BPX | R$ |
|---|---|---|---|---|---|---|---|---|---|---|---|---|---|---|---|---|---|---|---|---|---|---|---|---|---|---|---|---|---|---|---|---|---|---|---|
| 14 | aa | 411 | 58 | 9 | 44 | 41 | 206 | | 288 | 309 | 598 | | | 10 | 69 | 0.38 | | | | 28 | | 81 | | | 105 | 51% | 73% | | | | 2.85 | | -3 | -8 | $17 |
| 15 | TEX * | 451 | 85 | 2 | 39 | 25 | 262 | 237 | 340 | 374 | 714 | 765 | 693 | 10 | 76 | 0.50 | 47 | 19 | 34 | 34 | 72 | 80 | 56 | 2% | 167 | 24% | 76% | 25 | 32% | 48% | 4.43 | -1.0 | 41 | 111 | $18 |
| 16 | TEX * | 389 | 64 | 6 | 26 | 24 | 218 | 218 | 295 | 307 | 602 | 541 | 614 | 10 | 69 | 0.35 | 55 | 17 | 28 | 30 | 57 | 66 | 51 | 12% | 105 | 33% | 69% | 18 | 22% | 50% | 2.90 | -18.1 | -17 | -49 | $10 |
| 17 | TEX | 376 | 75 | 6 | 22 | 29 | 269 | 218 | 347 | 367 | 714 | 751 | 696 | 10 | 71 | 0.40 | 45 | 20 | 35 | 36 | 69 | 65 | 68 | 7% | 168 | 30% | 78% | 27 | 22% | 52% | 4.52 | -2.4 | 8 | 24 | $19 |
| 18 | TEX * | 364 | 54 | 2 | 22 | 22 | 214 | 215 | 308 | 275 | 582 | 663 | 554 | 11 | 75 | 0.55 | 49 | 19 | 32 | 28 | 77 | 44 | 58 | 3% | 113 | 26% | 78% | 23 | 22% | 57% | 2.86 | -13.4 | -4 | -13 | $8 |
| 1st Half | | 235 | 42 | 2 | 16 | 16 | 237 | 228 | 327 | 309 | 636 | 828 | 554 | 12 | 77 | 0.57 | 51 | 20 | 30 | 30 | 82 | 49 | 58 | 4% | 119 | 24% | 89% | 12 | 25% | 58% | 3.66 | -3.4 | 7 | 23 | $14 |
| 2nd Half | | 129 | 12 | 0 | 6 | 6 | 173 | 190 | 272 | 212 | 485 | 416 | 554 | 12 | 73 | 0.51 | 46 | 17 | 37 | 24 | 66 | 35 | 58 | 0% | 94 | 30% | 59% | 11 | 18% | 55% | 1.72 | -10.5 | -26 | -87 | -$3 |
| **19** | **Proj** | **374** | **58** | **4** | **23** | **24** | **222** | **213** | **310** | **301** | **612** | **612** | **612** | **11** | **73** | **0.45** | **48** | **19** | **33** | **30** | **69** | **56** | **59** | **4%** | **131** | **30%** | **73%** | | | | **3.07** | **-12.5** | **-3** | **-11** | **$12** |

## Desmond,Ian

| | | | | | |
|---|---|---|---|---|---|
| Age: 33 | Bats: R | Pos: 1B | Health C | LIMA Plan C+ | |
| Ht: 6' 3" | Wt: 215 | | PT/Exp B | Rand Var +3 | |
| | | | Consist B | MM 2535 | |

Stayed healthy, and the numbers returned... with a little help from 1st half hr/f. The one that didn't return, BA, was suppressed by poor first-half h% fortune (see xBA). Power+speed drive his value; both are under pressure: power by the heavy GB%, speed by advancing age. Might not see either side of the 20/20 season repeated.

| Yr | Tm | AB | R | HR | RBI | SB | BA | xBA | OBP | SLG | OPS | vL | vR | bb% | ct% | Eye | G | L | F | h% | HctX | PX | xPX | hr/f | Spd | SBO | SB% | #Wk | DOM | DIS | RC/G | RAR | BPV | BPX | R$ |
|---|---|---|---|---|---|---|---|---|---|---|---|---|---|---|---|---|---|---|---|---|---|---|---|---|---|---|---|---|---|---|---|---|---|---|---|
| 14 | WAS | 593 | 73 | 24 | 91 | 24 | 255 | 247 | 313 | 430 | 743 | 771 | 734 | 7 | 69 | 0.25 | 50 | 18 | 32 | 33 | 97 | 136 | 107 | 18% | 107 | 20% | 83% | 27 | 41% | 37% | 4.60 | 14.2 | 34 | 92 | $26 |
| 15 | WAS | 583 | 69 | 19 | 62 | 13 | 233 | 229 | 290 | 384 | 674 | 757 | 653 | 7 | 68 | 0.24 | 53 | 16 | 31 | 31 | 83 | 113 | 91 | 15% | 113 | 14% | 72% | 27 | 26% | 48% | 3.65 | -18.8 | 12 | 32 | $13 |
| 16 | TEX | 625 | 107 | 22 | 86 | 21 | 285 | 264 | 335 | 446 | 782 | 880 | 753 | 6 | 74 | 0.28 | 53 | 21 | 26 | 35 | 92 | 101 | 81 | 18% | 118 | 16% | 78% | 26 | 46% | 38% | 5.28 | 11.6 | 29 | 83 | $30 |
| 17 | COL | 339 | 47 | 7 | 40 | 15 | 274 | 244 | 326 | 375 | 701 | 663 | 715 | 6 | 74 | 0.28 | 63 | 16 | 21 | 35 | 82 | 61 | 60 | 13% | 112 | 19% | 79% | 18 | 11% | 61% | 4.29 | -9.4 | -4 | -12 | $13 |
| 18 | COL | 555 | 82 | 22 | 88 | 20 | 236 | 269 | 307 | 422 | 729 | 840 | 678 | 9 | 74 | 0.36 | 62 | 16 | 22 | 28 | 93 | 109 | 87 | 25% | 140 | 20% | 77% | 28 | 39% | 32% | 4.25 | -5.9 | 43 | 143 | $21 |
| 1st Half | | 282 | 44 | 17 | 47 | 7 | 216 | 272 | 294 | 443 | 738 | 979 | 617 | 9 | 70 | 0.33 | 62 | 19 | 20 | 25 | 91 | 137 | 109 | 44% | 103 | 15% | 78% | 15 | 47% | 27% | 4.14 | -4.0 | 39 | 130 | $20 |
| 2nd Half | | 273 | 38 | 5 | 41 | 13 | 256 | 263 | 321 | 399 | 720 | 677 | 738 | 8 | 78 | 0.42 | 62 | 14 | 23 | 31 | 94 | 83 | 67 | 10% | 159 | 24% | 76% | 13 | 31% | 38% | 4.37 | -1.8 | 45 | 150 | $22 |
| **19** | **Proj** | **486** | **71** | **16** | **69** | **18** | **256** | **258** | **316** | **415** | **730** | **782** | **710** | **7** | **74** | **0.31** | **60** | **17** | **23** | **32** | **90** | **95** | **79** | **19%** | **133** | **19%** | **77%** | | | | **4.42** | **-4.9** | **28** | **93** | **$21** |

## Devers,Rafael

| | | | | | |
|---|---|---|---|---|---|
| Age: 22 | Bats: L | Pos: 3B | Health B | LIMA Plan B+ | |
| Ht: 6' 0" | Wt: 237 | | PT/Exp D | Rand Var 0 | |
| | | | Consist F | MM 4025 | |

21-66-.240 in 450 AB at BOS. PRO: Flashed plus power in first half; wasn't overwhelmed in first full season at age 21. CON: Nagging port-side injuries (shoulder, hammy), late GB spike, and poor ct% contributed to sub-par BA and 2nd half power dip. Just remember one key number: 22, as in years old. Future still shimmers.

| Yr | Tm | AB | R | HR | RBI | SB | BA | xBA | OBP | SLG | OPS | vL | vR | bb% | ct% | Eye | G | L | F | h% | HctX | PX | xPX | hr/f | Spd | SBO | SB% | #Wk | DOM | DIS | RC/G | RAR | BPV | BPX | R$ |
|---|---|---|---|---|---|---|---|---|---|---|---|---|---|---|---|---|---|---|---|---|---|---|---|---|---|---|---|---|---|---|---|---|---|---|---|
| 14 | | | | | | | | | | | | | | | | | | | | | | | | | | | | | | | | | | | |
| 15 | | | | | | | | | | | | | | | | | | | | | | | | | | | | | | | | | | | |
| 16 | | | | | | | | | | | | | | | | | | | | | | | | | | | | | | | | | | | |
| 17 | BOS * | 544 | 81 | 27 | 83 | 3 | 296 | 271 | 352 | 520 | 872 | 1074 | 743 | 8 | 78 | 0.39 | 49 | 15 | 36 | 34 | 109 | 127 | 98 | 17% | 82 | 5% | 42% | 11 | 27% | 18% | 6.47 | 24.4 | 55 | 167 | $22 |
| 18 | BOS * | 471 | 62 | 22 | 68 | 5 | 244 | 242 | 302 | 439 | 740 | 619 | 771 | 8 | 73 | 0.31 | 46 | 15 | 39 | 29 | 93 | 123 | 95 | 17% | 61 | 7% | 71% | 25 | 48% | 40% | 4.44 | 1.4 | 26 | 87 | $14 |
| 1st Half | | 311 | 39 | 14 | 46 | 5 | 251 | 245 | 294 | 447 | 741 | 624 | 787 | 6 | 73 | 0.24 | 43 | 17 | 40 | 30 | 100 | 126 | 106 | 15% | 66 | 9% | 83% | 15 | 53% | 33% | 4.53 | 0.2 | 26 | 87 | $19 |
| 2nd Half | | 160 | 23 | 8 | 22 | 0 | 231 | 230 | 312 | 423 | 735 | 599 | 737 | 11 | 73 | 0.44 | 52 | 12 | 36 | 27 | 76 | 118 | 69 | 19% | 66 | 2% | 0% | 10 | 40% | 50% | 4.26 | -1.2 | 29 | 97 | $3 |
| **19** | **Proj** | **512** | **72** | **25** | **75** | **3** | **252** | **251** | **316** | **458** | **773** | **808** | **762** | **9** | **75** | **0.37** | **49** | **14** | **37** | **29** | **95** | **126** | **90** | **18%** | **68** | **5%** | **51%** | | | | **4.85** | **5.2** | **37** | **124** | **$17** |

## Diaz,Aledmys

| | | | | | |
|---|---|---|---|---|---|
| Age: 28 | Bats: R | Pos: SS 3B | Health B | LIMA Plan B | |
| Ht: 6' 1" | Wt: 195 | | PT/Exp C | Rand Var 0 | |
| | | | Consist F | MM 2235 | |

Not a full rebound, but pretty close. And given that he outkicked his coverage some in 2016, this is probably as much as we could've hoped for. Solid contact rate sets reasonable BA floor, too. Nothing in peripherals suggests further big upside, but they do support 2018 level. Maybe he gets off the see-saw now?

| Yr | Tm | AB | R | HR | RBI | SB | BA | xBA | OBP | SLG | OPS | vL | vR | bb% | ct% | Eye | G | L | F | h% | HctX | PX | xPX | hr/f | Spd | SBO | SB% | #Wk | DOM | DIS | RC/G | RAR | BPV | BPX | R$ |
|---|---|---|---|---|---|---|---|---|---|---|---|---|---|---|---|---|---|---|---|---|---|---|---|---|---|---|---|---|---|---|---|---|---|---|---|
| 14 | aa | 117 | 11 | 2 | 14 | 5 | 251 | | 260 | 381 | 642 | | | 1 | 77 | 0.06 | | | | 31 | | 103 | | | 95 | 33% | 67% | | | | 3.22 | | 23 | 62 | $2 |
| 15 | a/a | 425 | 43 | 9 | 37 | 4 | 225 | | 269 | 349 | 618 | | | 6 | 80 | 0.31 | | | | 26 | | 85 | | | 91 | 13% | 38% | | | | 2.89 | | 31 | 84 | $3 |
| 16 | STL | 404 | 71 | 17 | 65 | 4 | 300 | 284 | 369 | 510 | 879 | 725 | 941 | 9 | 85 | 0.68 | 46 | 16 | 39 | 32 | 109 | 118 | 108 | 13% | 139 | 7% | 50% | 22 | 55% | 14% | 6.57 | 25.4 | 97 | 277 | $18 |
| 17 | STL * | 456 | 45 | 10 | 40 | 6 | 239 | 246 | 272 | 361 | 633 | 602 | 700 | 4 | 83 | 0.26 | 46 | 17 | 38 | 27 | 79 | 71 | 69 | 8% | 113 | 12% | 58% | 16 | 44% | 38% | 3.19 | -18.2 | 33 | 100 | $5 |
| 18 | TOR | 422 | 55 | 18 | 55 | 3 | 263 | 269 | 303 | 453 | 756 | 706 | 772 | 5 | 85 | 0.37 | 41 | 18 | 41 | 27 | 100 | 105 | 105 | 12% | 94 | 8% | 43% | 26 | 50% | 23% | 4.56 | 5.6 | 66 | 220 | $12 |
| 1st Half | | 195 | 26 | 7 | 19 | 1 | 248 | 255 | 285 | 400 | 685 | 466 | 767 | 4 | 85 | 0.30 | 42 | 19 | 40 | 26 | 107 | 85 | 104 | 11% | 113 | 7% | 33% | 13 | 46% | 15% | 3.62 | -2.0 | 51 | 170 | $6 |
| 2nd Half | | 227 | 29 | 11 | 36 | 2 | 278 | 282 | 318 | 498 | 816 | 959 | 775 | 6 | 86 | 0.44 | 40 | 18 | 42 | 28 | 94 | 122 | 106 | 13% | 84 | 8% | 50% | 13 | 54% | 31% | 5.45 | 9.7 | 80 | 267 | $18 |
| **19** | **Proj** | **464** | **58** | **16** | **57** | **5** | **269** | **262** | **310** | **441** | **751** | **691** | **770** | **5** | **84** | **0.36** | **43** | **17** | **40** | **29** | **94** | **98** | **93** | **11%** | **110** | **10%** | **51%** | | | | **4.60** | **8.5** | **48** | **159** | **$16** |

## Diaz,Elias

| | | | | | |
|---|---|---|---|---|---|
| Age: 28 | Bats: R | Pos: CA | Health C | LIMA Plan D+ | |
| Ht: 6'1" | Wt: 215 | | PT/Exp F | Rand Var -5 | |
| | | | Consist D | MM 2133 | |

Well, color us surprised. After years of lackluster performance, took things to a new level, especially vs LHP (though only 81 AB). It was all well supported by skills, too. Now, 250 AB isn't a huge sample size either, and he was a bit more pedestrian vR, so don't go overboard here. But if 2nd half LD/FB sticks... UP: 20 HR

| Yr | Tm | AB | R | HR | RBI | SB | BA | xBA | OBP | SLG | OPS | vL | vR | bb% | ct% | Eye | G | L | F | h% | HctX | PX | xPX | hr/f | Spd | SBO | SB% | #Wk | DOM | DIS | RC/G | RAR | BPV | BPX | R$ |
|---|---|---|---|---|---|---|---|---|---|---|---|---|---|---|---|---|---|---|---|---|---|---|---|---|---|---|---|---|---|---|---|---|---|---|---|
| 14 | a/a | 359 | 33 | 4 | 40 | 2 | 261 | | 305 | 343 | 648 | | | 6 | 82 | 0.36 | | | | 31 | | 66 | | | 79 | 6% | 39% | | | | 3.49 | | 20 | 54 | $6 |
| 15 | PIT * | 327 | 28 | 3 | 40 | 1 | 235 | 102 | 287 | 324 | 612 | 0 | 0 | 7 | 84 | 0.45 | 0 | 0 | 100 | 27 | 363 | 59 | 732 | 0% | 100 | 7% | 15% | 2 | 0% | 50% | 2.92 | -8.8 | 28 | 76 | $1 |
| 16 | PIT * | 105 | 3 | 0 | 10 | 1 | 224 | 249 | 248 | 249 | 497 | 0 | 0 | 3 | 80 | 0.16 | 33 | 33 | 33 | 28 | 0 | 21 | -24 | 0% | 82 | 3% | 100% | 1 | 0% | 100% | 2.07 | -7.4 | -30 | -86 | -$2 |
| 17 | PIT * | 406 | 34 | 3 | 41 | 3 | 225 | 238 | 260 | 300 | 560 | 646 | 557 | 4 | 80 | 0.24 | 52 | 18 | 30 | 27 | 84 | 53 | 70 | 2% | 67 | 4% | 100% | 15 | 27% | 53% | 2.60 | -17.9 | -4 | -12 | $0 |
| 18 | PIT | 252 | 33 | 10 | 34 | 0 | 286 | 263 | 339 | 452 | 792 | 925 | 730 | 8 | 84 | 0.53 | 45 | 20 | 35 | 31 | 112 | 92 | 104 | 13% | 84 | 1% | 0% | 25 | 48% | 36% | 5.41 | 13.4 | 52 | 173 | $7 |
| 1st Half | | 122 | 22 | 5 | 19 | 0 | 287 | 268 | 336 | 451 | 787 | 980 | 695 | 7 | 89 | 0.64 | 50 | 16 | 34 | 29 | 110 | 84 | 93 | 14% | 91 | 0% | 0% | 14 | 64% | 36% | 5.41 | 6.7 | 64 | 213 | $7 |
| 2nd Half | | 130 | 11 | 5 | 15 | 0 | 285 | 263 | 343 | 454 | 797 | 870 | 762 | 8 | 80 | 0.46 | 39 | 24 | 37 | 32 | 115 | 100 | 115 | 13% | 85 | 3% | 0% | 11 | 27% | 36% | 5.41 | 7.2 | 44 | 147 | $7 |
| **19** | **Proj** | **296** | **31** | **10** | **39** | **1** | **258** | **254** | **302** | **409** | **710** | **834** | **660** | **6** | **82** | **0.36** | **45** | **20** | **35** | **28** | **101** | **86** | **92** | **12%** | **86** | **3%** | **52%** | | | | **4.21** | **6.6** | **22** | **74** | **$8** |

ROD TRUESDELL

## Diaz,Yandy

Age: 27 Bats: R Pos: DH
Ht: 6' 2" Wt: 185

| Health | A | LIMA Plan | D+ |
|---|---|---|---|
| PT/Exp | C | Rand Var | -1 |
| Consist | B | MM | 1233 |

1-15-.312 in 109 AB at CLE. PRO: Line-drive stroke generates hard contact, which coupled with Spd gives BA potential; solid walk rate. CON: Dwindling ct% threatens to take down that BA; still pounds ball into ground. BA floor might help in some formats, but finding the AB may again be a challenge.

| Yr | Tm | AB | R | HR | RBI | SB | BA | xBA | OBP | SLG | OPS | vL | vR | bb% | ct% | Eye | G | L | F | h% | HctX | PX | xPX | hr/f | Spd | SBO | SB% | #Wk | DOM | DIS | RC/G | RAR | BPV | BPX | R$ |
|---|---|---|---|---|---|---|---|---|---|---|---|---|---|---|---|---|---|---|---|---|---|---|---|---|---|---|---|---|---|---|---|---|---|---|---|
| 14 | | | | | | | | | | | | | | | | | | | | | | | | | | | | | | | | | | | |
| 15 | a/a | 495 | 54 | 6 | 49 | 8 | 286 | | 371 | 368 | 739 | | | 12 | 85 | 0.89 | | | | 33 | | 51 | | | 112 | 9% | 50% | | | | 4.71 | | 39 | 105 | $14 |
| 16 | a/a | 444 | 53 | 8 | 47 | 9 | 287 | | 370 | 398 | 768 | | | 12 | 80 | 0.67 | | | | 34 | | 70 | | | 99 | 8% | 72% | | | | 5.25 | | 31 | 89 | $14 |
| 17 | CLE * | 465 | 69 | 4 | 39 | 3 | 293 | 260 | 385 | 378 | 763 | 727 | 648 | 13 | 78 | 0.69 | 59 | 22 | 19 | 37 | 104 | 57 | 60 | 0% | 121 | 3% | 54% | 11 | 27% | 55% | 5.20 | 4.3 | 23 | 70 | $12 |
| 18 | CLE * | 457 | 54 | 3 | 44 | 1 | 264 | 246 | 353 | 353 | 706 | 725 | 847 | 12 | 76 | 0.58 | 53 | 23 | 23 | 34 | 125 | 65 | 84 | 5% | 120 | 3% | 29% | 10 | 40% | 40% | 4.21 | -3.9 | 19 | 63 | $7 |
| 1st Half | | 230 | 23 | 1 | 16 | 1 | 248 | 211 | 361 | 325 | 686 | | | 15 | 73 | 0.66 | | | | 34 | | 66 | | | 105 | 5% | 17% | | | | 3.78 | | 8 | 27 | $2 |
| 2nd Half | | 227 | 30 | 2 | 28 | 1 | 280 | 260 | 344 | 381 | 726 | 725 | 847 | 9 | 79 | 0.48 | 53 | 23 | 23 | 34 | 130 | 65 | 84 | 5% | 134 | 1% | 100% | 10 | 40% | 40% | 4.68 | 1.1 | 30 | 100 | $12 |
| **19** | **Proj** | **308** | **39** | **3** | **30** | **3** | **279** | **256** | **365** | **371** | **736** | **704** | **757** | **12** | **79** | **0.63** | **56** | **23** | **22** | **35** | **120** | **63** | **74** | **6%** | **126** | **5%** | **54%** | | | | **4.71** | **1.8** | **10** | **33** | **$6** |

## Dickerson,Corey

Age: 30 Bats: L Pos: LF
Ht: 6' 1" Wt: 200

| Health | B | LIMA Plan | B+ |
|---|---|---|---|
| PT/Exp | A | Rand Var | 0 |
| Consist | B | MM | 3345 |

Made a conscious effort to trade power for contact, and it worked, to a degree. Massive ct% and LD spikes helped offset the HR dip. Skills found some middle ground in second half, which worked even better. Running more, too. This new approach suits him, though R$ says it's a wash. No reason to expect much of a regression.

| Yr | Tm | AB | R | HR | RBI | SB | BA | xBA | OBP | SLG | OPS | vL | vR | bb% | ct% | Eye | G | L | F | h% | HctX | PX | xPX | hr/f | Spd | SBO | SB% | #Wk | DOM | DIS | RC/G | RAR | BPV | BPX | R$ |
|---|---|---|---|---|---|---|---|---|---|---|---|---|---|---|---|---|---|---|---|---|---|---|---|---|---|---|---|---|---|---|---|---|---|---|---|
| 14 | COL | 436 | 74 | 24 | 76 | 8 | 312 | 298 | 364 | 567 | 931 | 724 | 985 | 8 | 77 | 0.37 | 37 | 27 | 36 | 36 | 123 | 176 | 135 | 20% | 122 | 13% | 53% | 25 | 60% | 24% | 7.33 | 42.6 | 102 | 276 | $28 |
| 15 | COL * | 252 | 32 | 11 | 33 | 0 | 296 | 293 | 325 | 514 | 839 | 662 | 938 | 4 | 76 | 0.18 | 38 | 30 | 32 | 35 | 123 | 149 | 135 | 19% | 118 | 2% | 0% | 16 | 44% | 25% | 5.94 | 8.5 | 69 | 186 | $9 |
| 16 | TAM | 510 | 57 | 24 | 70 | 0 | 245 | 256 | 293 | 469 | 761 | 589 | 807 | 6 | 74 | 0.25 | 38 | 17 | 45 | 29 | 95 | 144 | 119 | 14% | 90 | 2% | 0% | 27 | 52% | 33% | 4.52 | -1.5 | 51 | 146 | $10 |
| 17 | TAM | 588 | 84 | 27 | 62 | 4 | 282 | 265 | 325 | 490 | 815 | 820 | 813 | 6 | 74 | 0.23 | 42 | 22 | 36 | 34 | 101 | 122 | 106 | 17% | 117 | 5% | 57% | 27 | 37% | 37% | 5.53 | 4.6 | 42 | 127 | $19 |
| 18 | PIT | 504 | 65 | 13 | 55 | 8 | 300 | 284 | 330 | 474 | 804 | 735 | 827 | 4 | 84 | 0.26 | 38 | 27 | 35 | 34 | 106 | 100 | 101 | 9% | 128 | 9% | 73% | 27 | 44% | 30% | 5.61 | 14.0 | 65 | 217 | $19 |
| 1st Half | | 276 | 33 | 5 | 32 | 3 | 297 | 273 | 333 | 438 | 772 | 744 | 780 | 4 | 86 | 0.32 | 35 | 26 | 39 | 33 | 98 | 82 | 91 | 5% | 118 | 7% | 60% | 15 | 47% | 33% | 5.10 | 3.8 | 56 | 187 | $18 |
| 2nd Half | | 228 | 32 | 8 | 23 | 5 | 303 | 300 | 326 | 518 | 844 | 726 | 889 | 4 | 82 | 0.21 | 41 | 28 | 30 | 34 | 115 | 124 | 113 | 14% | 133 | 12% | 83% | 12 | 42% | 25% | 6.25 | 10.4 | 75 | 250 | $20 |
| **19** | **Proj** | **533** | **71** | **18** | **62** | **6** | **292** | **278** | **328** | **483** | **811** | **736** | **835** | **5** | **81** | **0.27** | **40** | **24** | **36** | **33** | **106** | **111** | **110** | **12%** | **120** | **7%** | **67%** | | | | **5.61** | **15.1** | **56** | **185** | **$22** |

## Dietrich,Derek

Age: 29 Bats: L Pos: LF 1B
Ht: 6' 0" Wt: 205

| Health | A | LIMA Plan | C+ |
|---|---|---|---|
| PT/Exp | B | Rand Var | -3 |
| Consist | A | MM | 2225 |

Mined some early value from counting stats and first-half h% fortune. That all ended with a second-half thud. He's managed a couple of two-month spurts in each of the last two seasons, but the end result keeps looking about the same. Heed Rand Var's tale; given xBA and xPX, there's no reason to expect any better.

| Yr | Tm | AB | R | HR | RBI | SB | BA | xBA | OBP | SLG | OPS | vL | vR | bb% | ct% | Eye | G | L | F | h% | HctX | PX | xPX | hr/f | Spd | SBO | SB% | #Wk | DOM | DIS | RC/G | RAR | BPV | BPX | R$ |
|---|---|---|---|---|---|---|---|---|---|---|---|---|---|---|---|---|---|---|---|---|---|---|---|---|---|---|---|---|---|---|---|---|---|---|---|
| 14 | MIA * | 240 | 41 | 9 | 28 | 2 | 235 | 246 | 281 | 399 | 680 | 372 | 762 | 6 | 75 | 0.26 | 43 | 19 | 38 | 28 | 99 | 114 | 100 | 11% | 105 | 3% | 100% | 12 | 42% | 42% | 3.78 | -2.9 | 38 | 103 | $5 |
| 15 | MIA * | 442 | 58 | 15 | 46 | 0 | 241 | 243 | 297 | 422 | 719 | 519 | 864 | 7 | 74 | 0.30 | 37 | 20 | 43 | 30 | 112 | 125 | 159 | 12% | 110 | 5% | 0% | 18 | 39% | 39% | 4.03 | -17.7 | 43 | 116 | $7 |
| 16 | MIA | 351 | 39 | 7 | 42 | 1 | 279 | 245 | 374 | 425 | 798 | 556 | 852 | 8 | 76 | 0.38 | 40 | 22 | 38 | 35 | 86 | 93 | 99 | 7% | 108 | 1% | 100% | 26 | 46% | 31% | 5.12 | -2.1 | 29 | 83 | $8 |
| 17 | MIA | 406 | 56 | 13 | 53 | 0 | 249 | 252 | 334 | 424 | 758 | 816 | 744 | 8 | 76 | 0.37 | 37 | 23 | 41 | 30 | 98 | 102 | 106 | 10% | 115 | 1% | 0% | 26 | 42% | 42% | 4.41 | -17.9 | 37 | 112 | $6 |
| 18 | MIA | 499 | 72 | 16 | 45 | 2 | 265 | 240 | 330 | 421 | 751 | 706 | 762 | 5 | 72 | 0.21 | 41 | 23 | 36 | 34 | 97 | 103 | 88 | 12% | 98 | 2% | 100% | 28 | 29% | 46% | 4.47 | -9.0 | 12 | 40 | $12 |
| 1st Half | | 284 | 41 | 11 | 30 | 1 | 292 | 257 | 350 | 472 | 822 | 751 | 841 | 5 | 73 | 0.20 | 39 | 26 | 35 | 37 | 101 | 115 | 92 | 15% | 99 | 1% | 100% | 15 | 40% | 47% | 5.59 | 6.5 | 27 | 90 | $19 |
| 2nd Half | | 215 | 31 | 5 | 15 | 1 | 228 | 218 | 304 | 353 | 658 | 629 | 664 | 6 | 70 | 0.22 | 43 | 20 | 38 | 30 | 92 | 86 | 83 | 9% | 97 | 2% | 100% | 13 | 15% | 46% | 3.24 | -10.0 | -7 | -23 | $4 |
| **19** | **Proj** | **458** | **63** | **13** | **47** | **1** | **255** | **239** | **332** | **411** | **743** | **678** | **757** | **7** | **74** | **0.27** | **40** | **22** | **38** | **32** | **96** | **100** | **98** | **10%** | **103** | **2%** | **73%** | | | | **4.26** | **-4.5** | **14** | **46** | **$11** |

## Difo,Wilmer

Age: 27 Bats: R Pos: 2B 3B
Ht: 5' 11" Wt: 200

| Health | A | LIMA Plan | B |
|---|---|---|---|
| PT/Exp | C | Rand Var | +2 |
| Consist | B | MM | 1535 |

PRO: Tremendous speed, improving walk rate still point to an untapped SB source; decent contact, xBA suggest BA upside. CON: That FB spike won't cut it with this weak contact; red light on bases plus weak OBP keeping putting the kibosh on the steals. Same as last year... UP: 25 SB if stars align.

| Yr | Tm | AB | R | HR | RBI | SB | BA | xBA | OBP | SLG | OPS | vL | vR | bb% | ct% | Eye | G | L | F | h% | HctX | PX | xPX | hr/f | Spd | SBO | SB% | #Wk | DOM | DIS | RC/G | RAR | BPV | BPX | R$ |
|---|---|---|---|---|---|---|---|---|---|---|---|---|---|---|---|---|---|---|---|---|---|---|---|---|---|---|---|---|---|---|---|---|---|---|---|
| 14 | | | | | | | | | | | | | | | | | | | | | | | | | | | | | | | | | | | |
| 15 | WAS * | 370 | 41 | 2 | 32 | 22 | 251 | 252 | 271 | 335 | 606 | 0 | 500 | 3 | 76 | 0.12 | 56 | 22 | 22 | 33 | 73 | 66 | 12 | 0% | 100 | 29% | 95% | 8 | 0% | 25% | 3.34 | -9.0 | -3 | -8 | $12 |
| 16 | WAS * | 473 | 66 | 6 | 43 | 28 | 240 | 266 | 297 | 324 | 621 | 774 | 725 | 8 | 83 | 0.48 | 59 | 20 | 22 | 28 | 95 | 51 | 52 | 10% | 113 | 32% | 69% | 10 | 40% | 50% | 3.16 | -24.8 | 24 | 69 | $15 |
| 17 | WAS * | 372 | 51 | 5 | 22 | 10 | 258 | 256 | 310 | 351 | 661 | 848 | 637 | 7 | 78 | 0.35 | 51 | 24 | 25 | 32 | 73 | 53 | 54 | 8% | 159 | 11% | 91% | 27 | 26% | 48% | 3.85 | -12.6 | 19 | 58 | $8 |
| 18 | WAS | 408 | 55 | 7 | 42 | 10 | 230 | 246 | 298 | 350 | 649 | 453 | 704 | 9 | 80 | 0.48 | 42 | 24 | 34 | 27 | 62 | 67 | 54 | 6% | 149 | 12% | 77% | 28 | 25% | 43% | 3.47 | -9.8 | 37 | 123 | $8 |
| 1st Half | | 244 | 33 | 3 | 22 | 5 | 246 | 250 | 298 | 348 | 646 | 548 | 683 | 7 | 80 | 0.38 | 42 | 27 | 31 | 30 | 59 | 58 | 39 | 5% | 147 | 11% | 71% | 15 | 13% | 47% | 3.49 | -5.0 | 27 | 90 | $9 |
| 2nd Half | | 164 | 22 | 4 | 20 | 5 | 207 | 242 | 298 | 354 | 652 | 179 | 730 | 11 | 79 | 0.62 | 43 | 19 | 38 | 24 | 66 | 81 | 75 | 8% | 136 | 14% | 83% | 13 | 38% | 38% | 3.45 | -3.7 | 47 | 157 | $6 |
| **19** | **Proj** | **484** | **65** | **9** | **44** | **17** | **245** | **252** | **304** | **362** | **666** | **631** | **677** | **8** | **80** | **0.41** | **48** | **23** | **30** | **29** | **71** | **67** | **57** | **8%** | **146** | **16%** | **81%** | | | | **3.78** | **-5.7** | **30** | **99** | **$15** |

## Dixon,Brandon

Age: 27 Bats: R Pos: 1B
Ht: 6' 2" Wt: 215

| Health | A | LIMA Plan | D |
|---|---|---|---|
| PT/Exp | C | Rand Var | -3 |
| Consist | B | MM | 4311 |

5-10-.178 in 118 AB at CIN. Sometimes the MLEs translate just right. Nothing of note has changed in these skills as he's ascended the minors. Horrific plate skills conspire against power potential to take a huge chunk out of overall productivity. And just 10-15 HR? That's not enough to justify the rest of it.

| Yr | Tm | AB | R | HR | RBI | SB | BA | xBA | OBP | SLG | OPS | vL | vR | bb% | ct% | Eye | G | L | F | h% | HctX | PX | xPX | hr/f | Spd | SBO | SB% | #Wk | DOM | DIS | RC/G | RAR | BPV | BPX | R$ |
|---|---|---|---|---|---|---|---|---|---|---|---|---|---|---|---|---|---|---|---|---|---|---|---|---|---|---|---|---|---|---|---|---|---|---|---|
| 14 | | | | | | | | | | | | | | | | | | | | | | | | | | | | | | | | | | | |
| 15 | aa | 336 | 29 | 7 | 34 | 14 | 221 | | 243 | 340 | 584 | | | 3 | 68 | 0.09 | | | | 30 | | 93 | | | 92 | 34% | 68% | | | | 2.61 | | -19 | -51 | $6 |
| 16 | aa | 419 | 55 | 16 | 59 | 14 | 242 | | 290 | 411 | 701 | | | 6 | 62 | 0.18 | | | | 35 | | 128 | | | 85 | 21% | 71% | | | | 3.94 | | -7 | -20 | $12 |
| 17 | aaa | 440 | 46 | 14 | 51 | 14 | 229 | | 278 | 395 | 673 | | | 6 | 66 | 0.20 | | | | 31 | | 116 | | | 92 | 27% | 61% | | | | 3.43 | | 0 | 0 | $9 |
| 18 | CIN * | 297 | 36 | 10 | 28 | 7 | 249 | 232 | 286 | 433 | 719 | 551 | 587 | 5 | 63 | 0.14 | 43 | 22 | 35 | 36 | 90 | 142 | 131 | 19% | 111 | 19% | 66% | 18 | 28% | 50% | 4.09 | -2.7 | 12 | 40 | $7 |
| 1st Half | | 158 | 17 | 4 | 13 | 6 | 270 | 249 | 310 | 434 | 745 | 368 | 915 | 5 | 66 | 0.17 | 60 | 20 | 20 | 39 | 92 | 125 | 60 | 25% | 103 | 28% | 64% | 7 | 29% | 57% | 4.47 | 0.1 | 6 | 20 | $8 |
| 2nd Half | | 139 | 18 | 6 | 15 | 1 | 224 | 228 | 258 | 431 | 689 | 625 | 495 | 4 | 61 | 0.12 | 37 | 22 | 41 | 32 | 87 | 163 | 158 | 18% | 112 | 4% | 100% | 11 | 27% | 45% | 3.69 | -3.3 | 17 | 57 | $6 |
| **19** | **Proj** | **199** | **23** | **6** | **22** | **5** | **237** | **227** | **275** | **397** | **673** | **585** | **730** | **5** | **64** | **0.15** | **46** | **21** | **33** | **34** | **89** | **122** | **119** | **14%** | **110** | **21%** | **65%** | | | | **3.54** | **-7.5** | **-3** | **-12** | **$6** |

## Donaldson,Josh

Age: 33 Bats: R Pos: 3B
Ht: 6' 1" Wt: 210

| Health | F | LIMA Plan | B+ |
|---|---|---|---|
| PT/Exp | B | Rand Var | +1 |
| Consist | C | MM | 4345 |

Those "nagging" injuries from 2017 did a lot more than nag him this go-round. Shoulder and (again) calf woes were the culprit, the latter costing him three months. Again came back strong late, and when healthy, he's still a top-flight hitter. But that's the tease. Once older players start to break down, they rarely get fully healthy again.

| Yr | Tm | AB | R | HR | RBI | SB | BA | xBA | OBP | SLG | OPS | vL | vR | bb% | ct% | Eye | G | L | F | h% | HctX | PX | xPX | hr/f | Spd | SBO | SB% | #Wk | DOM | DIS | RC/G | RAR | BPV | BPX | R$ |
|---|---|---|---|---|---|---|---|---|---|---|---|---|---|---|---|---|---|---|---|---|---|---|---|---|---|---|---|---|---|---|---|---|---|---|---|
| 14 | OAK | 608 | 93 | 29 | 98 | 8 | 255 | 264 | 342 | 456 | 798 | 1007 | 727 | 11 | 79 | 0.58 | 45 | 13 | 41 | 28 | 118 | 138 | 126 | 15% | 98 | 5% | 100% | 27 | 56% | 30% | 5.35 | 29.8 | 78 | 211 | $24 |
| 15 | TOR | 620 | 122 | 41 | 123 | 6 | 297 | 297 | 371 | 568 | 939 | 1024 | 919 | 10 | 79 | 0.55 | 45 | 17 | 38 | 32 | 129 | 170 | 140 | 22% | 91 | 3% | 100% | 27 | 74% | 19% | 7.71 | 53.6 | 100 | 270 | $37 |
| 16 | TOR | 577 | 122 | 37 | 99 | 7 | 284 | 289 | 404 | 549 | 953 | 932 | 960 | 16 | 79 | 0.92 | 38 | 21 | 41 | 30 | 130 | 148 | 135 | 20% | 110 | 4% | 88% | 27 | 74% | 11% | 7.84 | 49.3 | 102 | 291 | $29 |
| 17 | TOR | 415 | 65 | 33 | 78 | 2 | 270 | 272 | 385 | 559 | 944 | 1051 | 917 | 15 | 73 | 0.68 | 41 | 17 | 42 | 29 | 108 | 164 | 132 | 26% | 65 | 3% | 50% | 21 | 62% | 24% | 7.38 | 30.2 | 76 | 230 | $16 |
| 18 | 2 AL | 187 | 30 | 8 | 23 | 2 | 246 | 252 | 352 | 449 | 801 | 900 | 756 | 14 | 71 | 0.57 | 48 | 17 | 35 | 30 | 108 | 138 | 113 | 17% | 92 | 4% | 100% | 12 | 58% | 33% | 5.44 | 6.1 | 53 | 177 | $4 |
| 1st Half | | 137 | 22 | 5 | 16 | 2 | 234 | 247 | 333 | 423 | 757 | 809 | 733 | 13 | 68 | 0.48 | 48 | 19 | 33 | 31 | 93 | 140 | 98 | 16% | 81 | 5% | 100% | 8 | 38% | 50% | 4.81 | 1.3 | 36 | 120 | $5 |
| 2nd Half | | 50 | 8 | 3 | 7 | 0 | 280 | 256 | 400 | 520 | 920 | 1154 | 819 | 17 | 80 | 1.00 | 48 | 13 | 40 | 30 | 147 | 136 | 148 | 19% | 108 | 0% | 0% | 4 | 100% | 0% | 7.37 | 4.0 | 96 | 320 | $1 |
| **19** | **Proj** | **417** | **70** | **25** | **65** | **3** | **268** | **267** | **379** | **511** | **890** | **1005** | **849** | **15** | **76** | **0.72** | **44** | **17** | **39** | **30** | **122** | **145** | **131** | **20%** | **97** | **3%** | **83%** | | | | **6.74** | **26.8** | **69** | **229** | **$18** |

## Dozier,Brian

Age: 32 Bats: R Pos: 2B
Ht: 5'11" Wt: 200

| Health | A | LIMA Plan | B+ |
|---|---|---|---|
| PT/Exp | A | Rand Var | +4 |
| Consist | C | MM | 4325 |

A detective story. Most skills unchanged, but, hmm... those tell-tale dips in power and speed mean.... Sure enough, revealed in Sept. he was playing with a right-knee bone bruise. Here's betting he played through that injury, or another unrevealed one, most all year. With health, a decent bounce-back candidate. UP: 35 HR

| Yr | Tm | AB | R | HR | RBI | SB | BA | xBA | OBP | SLG | OPS | vL | vR | bb% | ct% | Eye | G | L | F | h% | HctX | PX | xPX | hr/f | Spd | SBO | SB% | #Wk | DOM | DIS | RC/G | RAR | BPV | BPX | R$ |
|---|---|---|---|---|---|---|---|---|---|---|---|---|---|---|---|---|---|---|---|---|---|---|---|---|---|---|---|---|---|---|---|---|---|---|---|
| 14 | MIN | 598 | 112 | 23 | 71 | 21 | 242 | 257 | 345 | 416 | 762 | 804 | 743 | 13 | 78 | 0.69 | 37 | 20 | 43 | 27 | 95 | 124 | 97 | 11% | 102 | 16% | 75% | 27 | 44% | 19% | 4.77 | 24.9 | 71 | 192 | $24 |
| 15 | MIN | 628 | 101 | 28 | 77 | 12 | 236 | 261 | 307 | 444 | 751 | 762 | 746 | 9 | 76 | 0.41 | 33 | 23 | 44 | 27 | 100 | 138 | 129 | 13% | 102 | 12% | 75% | 26 | 58% | 19% | 4.48 | 5.8 | 66 | 178 | $18 |
| 16 | MIN | 615 | 104 | 42 | 99 | 18 | 268 | 276 | 340 | 546 | 886 | 965 | 862 | 9 | 78 | 0.44 | 36 | 16 | 48 | 28 | 109 | 159 | 137 | 18% | 123 | 14% | 90% | 26 | 65% | 19% | 6.47 | 28.3 | 94 | 269 | $30 |
| 17 | MIN | 617 | 106 | 34 | 93 | 16 | 271 | 264 | 359 | 498 | 856 | 1057 | 794 | 11 | 77 | 0.55 | 38 | 19 | 43 | 30 | 106 | 124 | 138 | 17% | 116 | 13% | 70% | 27 | 63% | 22% | 6.03 | 18.2 | 67 | 203 | $27 |
| 18 | 2 TM | 553 | 81 | 21 | 72 | 12 | 215 | 240 | 305 | 391 | 696 | 643 | 718 | 11 | 77 | 0.54 | 39 | 17 | 44 | 24 | 105 | 107 | 112 | 11% | 93 | 11% | 80% | 28 | 43% | 29% | 3.88 | -6.6 | 44 | 147 | $13 |
| 1st Half | | 309 | 46 | 11 | 31 | 5 | 217 | 234 | 304 | 385 | 689 | 667 | 695 | 10 | 79 | 0.55 | 40 | 14 | 46 | 24 | 101 | 98 | 96 | 10% | 124 | 11% | 63% | 15 | 33% | 27% | 3.67 | -4.8 | 54 | 180 | $12 |
| 2nd Half | | 244 | 35 | 10 | 41 | 7 | 213 | 246 | 307 | 398 | 705 | 625 | 755 | 12 | 74 | 0.53 | 39 | 20 | 41 | 25 | 111 | 119 | 132 | 13% | 60 | 11% | 100% | 13 | 54% | 31% | 4.14 | -0.2 | 35 | 117 | $15 |
| **19** | **Proj** | **562** | **89** | **27** | **81** | **14** | **250** | **252** | **334** | **455** | **789** | **796** | **786** | **11** | **77** | **0.51** | **38** | **18** | **44** | **28** | **106** | **122** | **125** | **14%** | **100** | **12%** | **80%** | | | | **5.14** | **16.1** | **59** | **197** | **$23** |

ROD TRUESDELL

## Dozier,Hunter

Age: 27 Bats: R Pos: 1B 3B | Ht: 6' 4" Wt: 220
Health B | PT/Exp D | Consist C
LIMA Plan D+ | Rand Var -1 | MM 4205

11-34-.229 in 362 AB at KC. PRO: Strong PX/xPX; held his own vR; offered glimpse of more viable BA skills in Aug/Sept (74% ct, 132 HctX, .264 xBA). CON: History of poor ct%, unplayable BA/OBP; below average hr/f similar to rates in minors; BPV/BPX say he was a whole lot of nothing. More suspect than prospect at this point.

| Yr | Tm | AB | R | HR | RBI | SB | BA | xBA | OBP | SLG | OPS | vL | vR | bb% | ct% | Eye | G | L | F | h% | HctX | PX | xPX | hr/f | Spd | SBO | SB% | #Wk | DOM | DIS | RC/G | RAR | BPV | BPX | R$ |
|---|---|---|---|---|---|---|---|---|---|---|---|---|---|---|---|---|---|---|---|---|---|---|---|---|---|---|---|---|---|---|---|---|---|---|---|
| 14 | aa | 234 | 26 | 3 | 17 | 2 | 185 | | 262 | 271 | 533 | | | 9 | 68 | 0.33 | | | | 26 | | 80 | | | 93 | 9% | 52% | | | | 2.17 | | -13 | -35 | -$3 |
| 15 | aa | 475 | 50 | 9 | 41 | 5 | 183 | | 238 | 294 | 532 | | | 7 | 65 | 0.21 | | | | 26 | | 95 | | | 90 | 8% | 67% | | | | 2.17 | | -19 | -51 | -$3 |
| 16 | KC * | 505 | 67 | 17 | 61 | 6 | 259 | 255 | 319 | 448 | 767 | 550 | 545 | 8 | 71 | 0.31 | 45 | 18 | 36 | 33 | 53 | 136 | 44 | 0% | 92 | 6% | 83% | 3 | 0% | 100% | 4.94 | 2.1 | 40 | 114 | $13 |
| 17 | a/a | 100 | 12 | 3 | 9 | 1 | 200 | | 273 | 370 | 643 | | | 9 | 49 | 0.20 | | | | 37 | | 160 | | | 108 | 10% | 40% | | | | 3.09 | | -21 | -64 | -$2 |
| 18 | KC * | 480 | 49 | 12 | 42 | 3 | 225 | 221 | 287 | 367 | 654 | 601 | 704 | 8 | 67 | 0.26 | 41 | 22 | 37 | 31 | 111 | 102 | 132 | 12% | 107 | 7% | 45% | 20 | 30% | 35% | 3.37 | -14.2 | 0 | 0 | $5 |
| 1st Half | | 254 | 25 | 5 | 19 | 1 | 216 | 182 | 298 | 324 | 622 | 673 | 631 | 10 | 63 | 0.32 | 42 | 15 | 43 | 32 | 105 | 88 | 158 | 10% | 88 | 7% | 32% | 8 | 13% | 38% | 3.01 | -11.9 | -27 | -90 | $2 |
| 2nd Half | | 226 | 24 | 7 | 23 | 2 | 235 | 251 | 275 | 416 | 691 | 564 | 751 | 5 | 71 | 0.18 | 41 | 26 | 33 | 30 | 117 | 116 | 117 | 13% | 125 | 7% | 67% | 12 | 42% | 33% | 3.75 | -5.2 | 26 | 87 | $8 |
| 19 | Proj | **484** | **54** | **15** | **46** | **4** | **221** | **223** | **283** | **390** | **673** | **626** | **690** | **8** | **64** | **0.23** | **41** | **22** | **37** | **31** | **112** | **127** | **133** | **13%** | **103** | **8%** | **55%** | | | | **3.52** | **-18.6** | **0** | **1** | **$5** |

## Drury,Brandon

Age: 26 Bats: R Pos: 3B | Ht: 6' 2" Wt: 210
Health D | PT/Exp C | Consist B
LIMA Plan D | Rand Var 0 | MM 2023

1-10-.169 in 77 AB at NYY/TOR. Blurred vision, migraines got him Wally Pipp'd in NYY, fractured hand cut short time in TOR. In between was more taking, less raking—even promising 1st half xPX, hr/f were small MLB sample (26 AB) flukes. With career .915 OPS at Chase Field, .623 elsewhere, still seems like a desert mirage.

| Yr | Tm | AB | R | HR | RBI | SB | BA | xBA | OBP | SLG | OPS | vL | vR | bb% | ct% | Eye | G | L | F | h% | HctX | PX | xPX | hr/f | Spd | SBO | SB% | #Wk | DOM | DIS | RC/G | RAR | BPV | BPX | R$ |
|---|---|---|---|---|---|---|---|---|---|---|---|---|---|---|---|---|---|---|---|---|---|---|---|---|---|---|---|---|---|---|---|---|---|---|---|
| 14 | aa | 105 | 10 | 3 | 11 | 0 | 272 | | 309 | 435 | 744 | | | 5 | 80 | 0.27 | | | | 31 | | 119 | | | 87 | 0% | 0% | | | | 4.71 | | 55 | 149 | $1 |
| 15 | ARI * | 580 | 51 | 6 | 53 | 3 | 260 | 267 | 291 | 362 | 653 | 913 | 434 | 4 | 84 | 0.27 | 56 | 21 | 23 | 30 | 106 | 75 | 109 | 18% | 71 | 9% | 25% | 5 | 20% | 40% | 3.40 | -21.9 | 27 | 73 | $8 |
| 16 | ARI | 461 | 59 | 16 | 53 | 1 | 282 | 271 | 329 | 458 | 786 | 804 | 779 | 6 | 78 | 0.31 | 50 | 20 | 30 | 33 | 105 | 111 | 97 | 15% | 99 | 2% | 50% | 27 | 44% | 37% | 5.28 | 6.3 | 46 | 131 | $13 |
| 17 | ARI | 445 | 41 | 13 | 63 | 1 | 267 | 275 | 317 | 447 | 764 | 738 | 775 | 6 | 77 | 0.27 | 49 | 22 | 29 | 32 | 99 | 114 | 87 | 13% | 88 | 2% | 50% | 27 | 41% | 30% | 4.80 | -0.6 | 39 | 118 | $9 |
| 18 | 2 AL * | 295 | 32 | 7 | 36 | 2 | 226 | 212 | 312 | 347 | 659 | 476 | 541 | 11 | 65 | 0.36 | 42 | 23 | 35 | 32 | 64 | 91 | 91 | 5% | 81 | 4% | 67% | 8 | 13% | 38% | 3.56 | -6.9 | -16 | -53 | $3 |
| 1st Half | | 219 | 28 | 7 | 29 | 2 | 252 | 220 | 345 | 402 | 747 | 393 | 739 | 12 | 64 | 0.39 | 29 | 29 | 41 | 36 | 83 | 112 | 149 | 14% | 97 | 4% | 100% | 4 | 25% | 25% | 4.80 | 1.9 | 1 | 3 | $7 |
| 2nd Half | | 76 | 5 | 0 | 7 | 0 | 149 | 190 | 214 | 189 | 402 | 501 | 404 | 8 | 70 | 0.27 | 48 | 20 | 33 | 21 | 58 | 37 | 66 | 0% | 80 | 8% | 0% | 4 | 0% | 50% | 1.11 | -8.8 | -50 | -167 | -$10 |
| 19 | Proj | **259** | **25** | **6** | **30** | **1** | **249** | **240** | **317** | **385** | **702** | **686** | **710** | **8** | **73** | **0.31** | **45** | **22** | **32** | **32** | **85** | **94** | **97** | **10%** | **85** | **3%** | **35%** | | | | **3.93** | **-4.4** | **-3** | **-11** | **$5** |

## Duda,Lucas

Age: 33 Bats: L Pos: 1B DH | Ht: 6' 4" Wt: 255
Health F | PT/Exp D | Consist B
LIMA Plan D+ | Rand Var -2 | MM 4123

Negatives piling up: can't stay healthy; can't hit lefties; career-low HctX; lowest hr/f, BPX since 2012; 2nd half ct% slid into risky territory. And four cities in two years suggests teams are finding less and less use for his skills. Can't rule out another run at 25-30 HR, but "Hey, anything is possible" isn't a sound fantasy strategy.

| Yr | Tm | AB | R | HR | RBI | SB | BA | xBA | OBP | SLG | OPS | vL | vR | bb% | ct% | Eye | G | L | F | h% | HctX | PX | xPX | hr/f | Spd | SBO | SB% | #Wk | DOM | DIS | RC/G | RAR | BPV | BPX | R$ |
|---|---|---|---|---|---|---|---|---|---|---|---|---|---|---|---|---|---|---|---|---|---|---|---|---|---|---|---|---|---|---|---|---|---|---|---|
| 14 | NYM | 514 | 74 | 30 | 92 | 3 | 253 | 263 | 349 | 481 | 830 | 516 | 915 | 12 | 74 | 0.51 | 31 | 20 | 49 | 29 | 132 | 165 | 181 | 16% | 47 | 4% | 60% | 27 | 56% | 15% | 5.55 | 20.6 | 66 | 178 | $20 |
| 15 | NYM | 471 | 67 | 27 | 73 | 0 | 244 | 263 | 352 | 486 | 838 | 878 | 823 | 12 | 71 | 0.48 | 27 | 22 | 51 | 29 | 120 | 174 | 167 | 16% | 58 | 2% | 0% | 25 | 52% | 32% | 5.44 | 0.9 | 65 | 176 | $13 |
| 16 | NYM | 153 | 20 | 7 | 23 | 0 | 229 | 259 | 302 | 412 | 714 | 454 | 776 | 9 | 76 | 0.42 | 37 | 24 | 39 | 25 | 102 | 110 | 110 | 15% | 61 | 0% | 0% | 10 | 40% | 40% | 4.05 | -5.9 | 32 | 91 | $1 |
| 17 | 2 TM | 423 | 50 | 30 | 64 | 0 | 217 | 264 | 322 | 496 | 818 | 658 | 867 | 12 | 68 | 0.44 | 30 | 21 | 49 | 24 | 116 | 176 | 155 | 21% | 33 | 0% | 0% | 25 | 56% | 32% | 5.09 | -10.5 | 49 | 148 | $6 |
| 18 | 2 TM | 328 | 35 | 14 | 50 | 1 | 241 | 231 | 313 | 418 | 731 | 513 | 813 | 8 | 69 | 0.27 | 29 | 26 | 45 | 31 | 98 | 115 | 135 | 13% | 72 | 1% | 100% | 23 | 39% | 39% | 4.23 | -8.4 | 6 | 20 | $7 |
| 1st Half | | 152 | 14 | 5 | 22 | 0 | 243 | 241 | 310 | 388 | 698 | 431 | 822 | 6 | 73 | 0.24 | 29 | 27 | 44 | 30 | 103 | 93 | 138 | 10% | 63 | 0% | 0% | 11 | 27% | 36% | 3.80 | -4.4 | 0 | 0 | $3 |
| 2nd Half | | 176 | 21 | 9 | 28 | 1 | 239 | 227 | 317 | 443 | 760 | 609 | 806 | 9 | 65 | 0.30 | 28 | 25 | 47 | 31 | 93 | 136 | 133 | 16% | 84 | 2% | 100% | 12 | 50% | 42% | 4.62 | -0.8 | 16 | 53 | $10 |
| 19 | Proj | **254** | **30** | **13** | **39** | **1** | **234** | **244** | **316** | **443** | **759** | **565** | **822** | **9** | **70** | **0.35** | **30** | **24** | **46** | **28** | **105** | **134** | **140** | **16%** | **60** | **1%** | **83%** | | | | **4.52** | **-1.9** | **20** | **67** | **$6** |

## Duffy,Matt

Age: 28 Bats: R Pos: 3B | Ht: 6' 2" Wt: 170
Health F | PT/Exp D | Consist B
LIMA Plan C+ | Rand Var -3 | MM 1435

On the surface, looks like a bit of a dud, but in a BA/SB-scarce fantasy environment, he's a near-$20 dynamo. Problem is, xBA has never believed in him as a near-.300 hitter, and subpar SB% could turn his green light yellow at any time. And when you factor in the Health risk... DN: 300 AB, .260 BA, 6 SB

| Yr | Tm | AB | R | HR | RBI | SB | BA | xBA | OBP | SLG | OPS | vL | vR | bb% | ct% | Eye | G | L | F | h% | HctX | PX | xPX | hr/f | Spd | SBO | SB% | #Wk | DOM | DIS | RC/G | RAR | BPV | BPX | R$ |
|---|---|---|---|---|---|---|---|---|---|---|---|---|---|---|---|---|---|---|---|---|---|---|---|---|---|---|---|---|---|---|---|---|---|---|---|
| 14 | SF * | 427 | 48 | 2 | 59 | 16 | 291 | 267 | 347 | 379 | 726 | 888 | 300 | 8 | 79 | 0.41 | 41 | 33 | 26 | 36 | 80 | 72 | 56 | 0% | 123 | 17% | 75% | 11 | 18% | 55% | 4.74 | 12.4 | 29 | 78 | $17 |
| 15 | SF | 573 | 77 | 12 | 77 | 12 | 295 | 276 | 334 | 428 | 762 | 642 | 803 | 5 | 83 | 0.31 | 53 | 21 | 27 | 34 | 103 | 83 | 90 | 9% | 138 | 8% | 100% | 27 | 44% | 26% | 5.24 | 10.6 | 52 | 141 | $24 |
| 16 | 2 TM | 333 | 41 | 5 | 28 | 8 | 258 | 263 | 310 | 357 | 668 | 702 | 654 | 6 | 84 | 0.43 | 50 | 21 | 29 | 29 | 90 | 59 | 67 | 6% | 137 | 15% | 62% | 17 | 35% | 24% | 3.65 | -11.3 | 39 | 111 | $7 |
| 17 | | | | | | | | | | | | | | | | | | | | | | | | | | | | | | | | | | | |
| 18 | TAM | 503 | 59 | 4 | 44 | 12 | 294 | 264 | 361 | 366 | 727 | 718 | 731 | 8 | 82 | 0.51 | 54 | 25 | 20 | 35 | 93 | 48 | 44 | 5% | 121 | 11% | 67% | 27 | 26% | 37% | 4.63 | 4.1 | 19 | 63 | $16 |
| 1st Half | | 261 | 24 | 4 | 23 | 6 | 322 | 280 | 367 | 433 | 799 | 650 | 860 | 6 | 82 | 0.33 | 52 | 27 | 21 | 38 | 97 | 71 | 53 | 9% | 128 | 11% | 67% | 15 | 33% | 33% | 5.77 | 8.9 | 35 | 117 | $18 |
| 2nd Half | | 242 | 35 | 0 | 21 | 6 | 264 | 245 | 356 | 293 | 650 | 801 | 602 | 11 | 81 | 0.69 | 56 | 24 | 20 | 32 | 89 | 23 | 34 | 0% | 112 | 10% | 67% | 12 | 17% | 42% | 3.53 | -6.9 | 2 | 7 | $14 |
| 19 | Proj | **485** | **50** | **5** | **48** | **12** | **275** | **262** | **338** | **356** | **694** | **737** | **676** | **8** | **82** | **0.46** | **52** | **24** | **24** | **33** | **92** | **52** | **57** | **5%** | **126** | **12%** | **69%** | | | | **4.11** | **-5.5** | **14** | **46** | **$16** |

## Duggar,Steven

Age: 25 Bats: L Pos: CF | Ht: 6' 2" Wt: 189
Health B | PT/Exp F | Consist C
LIMA Plan C+ | Rand Var -1 | MM 2415

2-17-.255 with 5 SB in 141 AB at SF. With 2016's BA looking like h%-inflated fluke, and 2017's bb% a small sample illusion, 2018's contact loss is a troubling step toward becoming a BA/OBP liability. Speed is the value driver, and while SB% growth helps, downside risk is he'll be bench bound or plying his trade in AAA.

| Yr | Tm | AB | R | HR | RBI | SB | BA | xBA | OBP | SLG | OPS | vL | vR | bb% | ct% | Eye | G | L | F | h% | HctX | PX | xPX | hr/f | Spd | SBO | SB% | #Wk | DOM | DIS | RC/G | RAR | BPV | BPX | R$ |
|---|---|---|---|---|---|---|---|---|---|---|---|---|---|---|---|---|---|---|---|---|---|---|---|---|---|---|---|---|---|---|---|---|---|---|---|
| 14 | | | | | | | | | | | | | | | | | | | | | | | | | | | | | | | | | | | |
| 15 | | | | | | | | | | | | | | | | | | | | | | | | | | | | | | | | | | | |
| 16 | aa | 243 | 31 | 1 | 21 | 8 | 303 | | 369 | 412 | 781 | | | 9 | 77 | 0.45 | | | | 39 | | 75 | | | 122 | 20% | 51% | | | | 5.12 | | 25 | 71 | $9 |
| 17 | aaa | 46 | 6 | 1 | 5 | 2 | 223 | | 319 | 329 | 647 | | | 12 | 70 | 0.47 | | | | 29 | | 63 | | | 104 | 32% | 52% | | | | 3.03 | | -10 | -30 | -$1 |
| 18 | SF * | 457 | 56 | 4 | 32 | 13 | 232 | 215 | 290 | 352 | 642 | 846 | 627 | 8 | 64 | 0.23 | 43 | 23 | 34 | 35 | 70 | 102 | 72 | 6% | 136 | 18% | 69% | 8 | 25% | 50% | 3.34 | -12.4 | -4 | -13 | $7 |
| 1st Half | | 295 | 34 | 2 | 14 | 8 | 227 | 202 | 289 | 343 | 632 | | | 8 | 61 | 0.23 | | | | 36 | | 102 | | | 134 | 19% | 62% | | | | 3.17 | | -15 | -50 | $7 |
| 2nd Half | | 162 | 22 | 2 | 18 | 5 | 242 | 230 | 292 | 369 | 661 | 846 | 627 | 7 | 69 | 0.22 | 43 | 23 | 34 | 34 | 75 | 101 | 72 | 6% | 123 | 17% | 83% | 8 | 25% | 50% | 3.68 | -2.2 | 7 | 23 | $8 |
| 19 | Proj | **482** | **57** | **6** | **41** | **15** | **246** | **235** | **307** | **381** | **688** | **821** | **630** | **8** | **70** | **0.30** | **44** | **23** | **33** | **34** | **68** | **99** | **65** | **5%** | **141** | **21%** | **61%** | | | | **3.81** | **-4.8** | **14** | **47** | **$13** |

## Duvall,Adam

Age: 30 Bats: R Pos: LF | Ht: 6' 1" Wt: 215
Health A | PT/Exp B | Consist B
LIMA Plan D+ | Rand Var +5 | MM 4111

Disaster of a season was mostly due to simple skill regression, as PX leveled off and dragged BA/xBA down with it. Steady decline of hr/f, shift to subpar HctX, and age further diminish hope for a rebound. Always remember the Bull Durham Gardening Tip: "Late bloomers have fewer flowering seasons."

| Yr | Tm | AB | R | HR | RBI | SB | BA | xBA | OBP | SLG | OPS | vL | vR | bb% | ct% | Eye | G | L | F | h% | HctX | PX | xPX | hr/f | Spd | SBO | SB% | #Wk | DOM | DIS | RC/G | RAR | BPV | BPX | R$ |
|---|---|---|---|---|---|---|---|---|---|---|---|---|---|---|---|---|---|---|---|---|---|---|---|---|---|---|---|---|---|---|---|---|---|---|---|
| 14 | SF * | 432 | 51 | 18 | 63 | 1 | 219 | 243 | 258 | 395 | 653 | 525 | 629 | 5 | 72 | 0.19 | 38 | 21 | 42 | 26 | 105 | 132 | 155 | 14% | 81 | 2% | 100% | 11 | 27% | 45% | 3.34 | -5.8 | 29 | 78 | $7 |
| 15 | CIN * | 561 | 62 | 31 | 77 | 4 | 224 | 248 | 265 | 444 | 709 | 498 | 895 | 5 | 70 | 0.18 | 29 | 24 | 47 | 26 | 111 | 153 | 128 | 28% | 75 | 5% | 77% | 6 | 50% | 50% | 3.86 | -14.6 | 36 | 97 | $11 |
| 16 | CIN | 552 | 85 | 33 | 103 | 6 | 241 | 256 | 297 | 498 | 795 | 795 | 795 | 7 | 70 | 0.25 | 34 | 19 | 47 | 28 | 111 | 163 | 155 | 18% | 110 | 11% | 55% | 27 | 44% | 33% | 4.77 | 2.3 | 60 | 171 | $17 |
| 17 | CIN | 587 | 78 | 31 | 99 | 5 | 249 | 247 | 301 | 480 | 782 | 924 | 737 | 6 | 71 | 0.23 | 33 | 18 | 49 | 30 | 91 | 143 | 116 | 15% | 86 | 7% | 63% | 27 | 37% | 37% | 4.75 | -8.7 | 39 | 118 | $16 |
| 18 | 2 NL | 384 | 48 | 15 | 61 | 2 | 195 | 224 | 274 | 365 | 639 | 637 | 639 | 9 | 70 | 0.32 | 30 | 22 | 48 | 24 | 94 | 114 | 116 | 12% | 70 | 5% | 50% | 28 | 29% | 43% | 3.02 | -19.2 | 10 | 33 | $4 |
| 1st Half | | 253 | 27 | 12 | 49 | 2 | 206 | 238 | 286 | 399 | 685 | 855 | 617 | 10 | 70 | 0.37 | 32 | 22 | 45 | 24 | 101 | 126 | 116 | 15% | 64 | 7% | 50% | 15 | 40% | 40% | 3.56 | -8.3 | 23 | 77 | $9 |
| 2nd Half | | 131 | 21 | 3 | 12 | 0 | 176 | 197 | 250 | 298 | 548 | 241 | 682 | 6 | 68 | 0.21 | 26 | 21 | 53 | 23 | 79 | 91 | 116 | 6% | 95 | 0% | 0% | 13 | 15% | 46% | 2.10 | -10.6 | -12 | -40 | -$5 |
| 19 | Proj | **228** | **31** | **10** | **34** | **1** | **223** | **231** | **286** | **420** | **706** | **634** | **734** | **7** | **70** | **0.24** | **31** | **21** | **48** | **27** | **94** | **129** | **124** | **13%** | **89** | **5%** | **57%** | | | | **3.76** | **-5.9** | **20** | **67** | **$5** |

## Dyson,Jarrod

Age: 34 Bats: L Pos: CF | Ht: 5'10" Wt: 165
Health D | PT/Exp D | Consist C
LIMA Plan D | Rand Var +5 | MM 1531

Increased bb% is an interesting development, but OBP gains were offset on BA side by bad luck on h%, second year of too many wasted fly balls. Gradual Spd, SBO declines suggest age is eroding his best skill, which makes career-worst season especially bad timing. Reserve OFs in their mid-30s don't get a lot of second chances.

| Yr | Tm | AB | R | HR | RBI | SB | BA | xBA | OBP | SLG | OPS | vL | vR | bb% | ct% | Eye | G | L | F | h% | HctX | PX | xPX | hr/f | Spd | SBO | SB% | #Wk | DOM | DIS | RC/G | RAR | BPV | BPX | R$ |
|---|---|---|---|---|---|---|---|---|---|---|---|---|---|---|---|---|---|---|---|---|---|---|---|---|---|---|---|---|---|---|---|---|---|---|---|
| 14 | KC | 260 | 33 | 1 | 24 | 36 | 269 | 233 | 324 | 327 | 651 | 604 | 663 | 8 | 80 | 0.42 | 63 | 14 | 23 | 33 | 56 | 37 | 39 | 2% | 170 | 52% | 84% | 27 | 19% | 48% | 4.09 | 2.3 | 18 | 49 | $17 |
| 15 | KC | 200 | 31 | 2 | 18 | 26 | 250 | 278 | 311 | 380 | 691 | 578 | 715 | 6 | 82 | 0.38 | 54 | 23 | 23 | 30 | 68 | 77 | 28 | 6% | 169 | 60% | 90% | 26 | 42% | 38% | 4.29 | -2.5 | 53 | 143 | $12 |
| 16 | KC * | 321 | 51 | 1 | 26 | 33 | 275 | 280 | 335 | 378 | 713 | 1006 | 698 | 8 | 86 | 0.65 | 56 | 20 | 24 | 32 | 60 | 57 | 32 | 2% | 161 | 42% | 82% | 25 | 52% | 24% | 4.66 | 0.3 | 57 | 163 | $18 |
| 17 | SEA | 346 | 56 | 5 | 30 | 28 | 251 | 251 | 324 | 350 | 674 | 375 | 730 | 7 | 84 | 0.51 | 47 | 19 | 34 | 29 | 54 | 54 | 41 | 5% | 146 | 37% | 80% | 21 | 38% | 24% | 3.78 | -15.4 | 40 | 121 | $15 |
| 18 | ARI | 206 | 29 | 2 | 12 | 16 | 189 | 240 | 282 | 257 | 539 | 699 | 494 | 11 | 83 | 0.79 | 46 | 23 | 31 | 22 | 70 | 36 | 45 | 4% | 132 | 33% | 84% | 15 | 33% | 40% | 2.51 | -13.9 | 27 | 90 | $3 |
| 1st Half | | 200 | 28 | 2 | 10 | 14 | 185 | 239 | 274 | 255 | 529 | 644 | 499 | 11 | 84 | 0.76 | 47 | 22 | 31 | 21 | 70 | 37 | 45 | 4% | 135 | 31% | 82% | 15 | 33% | 40% | 2.36 | -14.5 | 28 | 93 | $4 |
| 2nd Half | | 6 | 1 | 0 | 2 | 2 | 333 | 285 | 500 | 333 | 833 | 1417 | 250 | 25 | 83 | 2.00 | 25 | 50 | 25 | 40 | 61 | 0 | 35 | 4% | 104 | 50% | 100% | | | | 9.88 | 0.8 | 17 | 57 | -$5 |
| 19 | Proj | **160** | **24** | **1** | **12** | **13** | **239** | **255** | **308** | **331** | **640** | **625** | **643** | **8** | **84** | **0.56** | **52** | **20** | **28** | **28** | **63** | **51** | **38** | **4%** | **128** | **38%** | **82%** | | | | **3.52** | **-3.0** | **43** | **143** | **$7** |

BRANDON KRUSE

## Eaton,Adam

| | | | |
|---|---|---|---|
| Age: 30 Bats: L Pos: RF | Health F | LIMA Plan B | |
| Ht: 5' 9" Wt: 176 | PT/Exp C | Rand Var -3 | |
| | Consist B | MM 2545 | |

Ankle injury and surgery derailed fast start and cost him two months. Sept AB were curtailed by achy left knee. Through it all, plate skills look rock-solid, running game good as ever despite limited SBO. Durability still key to tap into consistent playing time and previous pop. Still some upside here, but at 30, it's looking frayed.

| Yr | Tm | AB | R | HR | RBI | SB | BA | xBA | OBP | SLG | OPS | vL | vR | bb% | ct% | Eye | G | L | F | h% | HctX | PX | xPX | hr/f | Spd | SBO | SB% | #Wk | DOM | DIS | RC/G | RAR | BPV | BPX | R$ |
|---|---|---|---|---|---|---|---|---|---|---|---|---|---|---|---|---|---|---|---|---|---|---|---|---|---|---|---|---|---|---|---|---|---|---|---|
| 14 | CHW | 486 | 76 | 1 | 35 | 15 | 300 | 278 | 362 | 401 | 763 | 724 | 778 | 8 | 83 | 0.52 | 60 | 20 | 20 | 36 | 87 | 74 | 44 | 1% | 164 | 16% | 63% | 23 | 48% | 26% | 5.05 | 17.3 | 58 | 157 | $19 |
| 15 | CHW | 610 | 98 | 14 | 56 | 18 | 287 | 267 | 361 | 431 | 792 | 648 | 847 | 8 | 79 | 0.44 | 51 | 22 | 27 | 35 | 91 | 93 | 69 | 11% | 150 | 14% | 69% | 26 | 38% | 27% | 5.29 | 9.9 | 52 | 141 | $26 |
| 16 | CHW | 619 | 91 | 14 | 59 | 14 | 284 | 276 | 362 | 428 | 790 | 726 | 812 | 9 | 81 | 0.55 | 54 | 21 | 26 | 33 | 104 | 83 | 90 | 11% | 137 | 10% | 74% | 27 | 52% | 11% | 5.33 | 12.2 | 53 | 151 | $22 |
| 17 | WAS | 91 | 24 | 2 | 13 | 3 | 297 | 273 | 393 | 462 | 854 | 594 | 890 | 13 | 80 | 0.78 | 53 | 15 | 32 | 35 | 101 | 99 | 87 | 9% | 144 | 13% | 75% | 4 | 50% | 0% | 6.52 | 3.2 | 71 | 215 | $3 |
| 18 | WAS | 319 | 55 | 5 | 33 | 9 | 301 | 267 | 394 | 411 | 805 | 552 | 845 | 10 | 80 | 0.59 | 47 | 26 | 26 | 36 | 96 | 72 | 66 | 8% | 130 | 9% | 90% | 21 | 24% | 43% | 5.77 | 10.2 | 39 | 130 | $13 |
| 1st Half | | 84 | 18 | 2 | 8 | 0 | 298 | 270 | 372 | 417 | 789 | 369 | 881 | 8 | 82 | 0.47 | 49 | 25 | 26 | 34 | 132 | 71 | 105 | 11% | 112 | 4% | 0% | 9 | 22% | 44% | 5.07 | 1.1 | 36 | 120 | -$3 |
| 2nd Half | | 235 | 37 | 3 | 25 | 9 | 302 | 265 | 401 | 409 | 810 | 646 | 833 | 12 | 79 | 0.63 | 47 | 27 | 26 | 37 | 84 | 72 | 51 | 6% | 132 | 11% | 100% | 12 | 25% | 42% | 6.02 | 9.1 | 39 | 130 | $19 |
| 19 | Proj | **438** | **85** | **9** | **48** | **11** | **296** | **271** | **384** | **434** | **818** | **602** | **861** | **11** | **81** | **0.61** | **50** | **23** | **27** | **35** | **101** | **85** | **77** | **10%** | **144** | **10%** | **77%** | | | | **5.85** | **17.0** | **48** | **160** | **$19** |

## Ellsbury,Jacoby

| | | | |
|---|---|---|---|
| Age: 35 Bats: L Pos: DH | Health F | LIMA Plan D | |
| Ht: 6' 1" Wt: 195 | PT/Exp D | Rand Var 0 | |
| | Consist B | MM 1531 | |

Season was torpedoed out of the gate by multiple injuries; mid-summer surgery for torn hip labrum ended return hopes. Even past his prime, SBs and modest BA had remained roster-worthy. But lost season and these particular physical woes throw AB, running game and role into question at his age. He's now officially a flyer.

| Yr | Tm | AB | R | HR | RBI | SB | BA | xBA | OBP | SLG | OPS | vL | vR | bb% | ct% | Eye | G | L | F | h% | HctX | PX | xPX | hr/f | Spd | SBO | SB% | #Wk | DOM | DIS | RC/G | RAR | BPV | BPX | R$ |
|---|---|---|---|---|---|---|---|---|---|---|---|---|---|---|---|---|---|---|---|---|---|---|---|---|---|---|---|---|---|---|---|---|---|---|---|
| 14 | NYY | 575 | 71 | 16 | 70 | 39 | 271 | 276 | 328 | 419 | 747 | 828 | 711 | 8 | 84 | 0.53 | 42 | 25 | 34 | 30 | 103 | 98 | 87 | 10% | 109 | 28% | 89% | 25 | 60% | 16% | 5.06 | 19.4 | 64 | 173 | $31 |
| 15 | NYY | 452 | 66 | 7 | 33 | 21 | 257 | 248 | 318 | 345 | 663 | 652 | 669 | 7 | 81 | 0.41 | 45 | 24 | 31 | 30 | 79 | 58 | 56 | 6% | 131 | 24% | 70% | 21 | 19% | 43% | 3.61 | -12.1 | 26 | 70 | $15 |
| 16 | NYY | 551 | 71 | 9 | 56 | 20 | 263 | 267 | 330 | 374 | 703 | 618 | 744 | 9 | 85 | 0.64 | 46 | 23 | 31 | 30 | 91 | 64 | 67 | 6% | 113 | 17% | 71% | 27 | 30% | 22% | 4.22 | -2.3 | 44 | 126 | $17 |
| 17 | NYY | 356 | 65 | 7 | 39 | 22 | 264 | 273 | 348 | 402 | 750 | 637 | 795 | 10 | 82 | 0.65 | 46 | 23 | 31 | 30 | 87 | 78 | 62 | 8% | 126 | 24% | 88% | 22 | 59% | 23% | 4.96 | 2.2 | 52 | 158 | $16 |
| 18 | | | | | | | | | | | | | | | | | | | | | | | | | | | | | | | | | | | |
| 1st Half | | | | | | | | | | | | | | | | | | | | | | | | | | | | | | | | | | | |
| 2nd Half | | | | | | | | | | | | | | | | | | | | | | | | | | | | | | | | | | | |
| 19 | Proj | **192** | **29** | **4** | **19** | **10** | **262** | **260** | **330** | **378** | **708** | **666** | **728** | **8** | **83** | **0.53** | **45** | **24** | **31** | **30** | **87** | **68** | **65** | **7%** | **118** | **23%** | **79%** | | | | **4.31** | **-1.1** | **40** | **134** | **$9** |

## Encarnacion,Edwin

| | | | |
|---|---|---|---|
| Age: 36 Bats: R Pos: DH 1B | Health A | LIMA Plan B | |
| Ht: 6' 1" Wt: 230 | PT/Exp A | Rand Var 0 | |
| | Consist B | MM 4235 | |

Slow April start (.158 BA) and Sept power outage (85/76 PX/xPX, 3 HR) bookended another otherwise productive season. Power indices and HctX continue to hold up well. But age, ct% trend, Eye, performance vL all point to a gentle decline. And if the lapses accelerate... DN: Sub-30 HR, sub-100 RBI.

| Yr | Tm | AB | R | HR | RBI | SB | BA | xBA | OBP | SLG | OPS | vL | vR | bb% | ct% | Eye | G | L | F | h% | HctX | PX | xPX | hr/f | Spd | SBO | SB% | #Wk | DOM | DIS | RC/G | RAR | BPV | BPX | R$ |
|---|---|---|---|---|---|---|---|---|---|---|---|---|---|---|---|---|---|---|---|---|---|---|---|---|---|---|---|---|---|---|---|---|---|---|---|
| 14 | TOR | 477 | 75 | 34 | 98 | 2 | 268 | 300 | 354 | 547 | 901 | 870 | 909 | 11 | 83 | 0.76 | 36 | 16 | 47 | 26 | 137 | 176 | 153 | 18% | 76 | 2% | 100% | 22 | 68% | 14% | 6.75 | 36.9 | 120 | 324 | $24 |
| 15 | TOR | 528 | 94 | 39 | 111 | 3 | 277 | 297 | 372 | 557 | 929 | 836 | 950 | 12 | 81 | 0.79 | 36 | 19 | 45 | 27 | 129 | 166 | 142 | 20% | 54 | 3% | 60% | 27 | 81% | 4% | 7.17 | 25.9 | 101 | 273 | $28 |
| 16 | TOR | 601 | 99 | 42 | 127 | 2 | 263 | 284 | 357 | 529 | 886 | 902 | 881 | 12 | 77 | 0.63 | 38 | 20 | 41 | 28 | 118 | 155 | 137 | 22% | 55 | 1% | 100% | 27 | 78% | 7% | 6.54 | 18.1 | 75 | 214 | $24 |
| 17 | CLE | 554 | 96 | 38 | 107 | 2 | 258 | 269 | 377 | 504 | 881 | 857 | 891 | 16 | 76 | 0.78 | 37 | 21 | 42 | 27 | 116 | 131 | 136 | 21% | 61 | 1% | 100% | 27 | 52% | 19% | 6.52 | 26.7 | 60 | 182 | $20 |
| 18 | CLE | 500 | 74 | 32 | 107 | 3 | 246 | 250 | 336 | 474 | 810 | 739 | 831 | 11 | 74 | 0.48 | 36 | 20 | 44 | 27 | 115 | 130 | 142 | 20% | 63 | 2% | 100% | 27 | 48% | 33% | 5.33 | 12.2 | 41 | 137 | $20 |
| 1st Half | | 275 | 40 | 19 | 54 | 0 | 229 | 250 | 307 | 473 | 780 | 675 | 814 | 9 | 73 | 0.37 | 35 | 20 | 46 | 24 | 113 | 142 | 165 | 21% | 49 | 0% | 0% | 15 | 53% | 33% | 4.70 | 1.6 | 40 | 133 | $19 |
| 2nd Half | | 225 | 34 | 13 | 53 | 3 | 267 | 248 | 368 | 476 | 843 | 816 | 850 | 13 | 75 | 0.61 | 38 | 21 | 41 | 30 | 118 | 116 | 116 | 18% | 85 | 4% | 100% | 12 | 42% | 33% | 6.14 | 10.5 | 46 | 153 | $20 |
| 19 | Proj | **477** | **76** | **31** | **101** | **3** | **257** | **261** | **354** | **494** | **848** | **809** | **860** | **13** | **76** | **0.60** | **37** | **20** | **43** | **28** | **118** | **134** | **137** | **20%** | **64** | **2%** | **97%** | | | | **5.99** | **20.5** | **56** | **186** | **$21** |

## Engel,Adam

| | | | |
|---|---|---|---|
| Age: 27 Bats: R Pos: CF | Health A | LIMA Plan D | |
| Ht: 6' 2" Wt: 210 | PT/Exp C | Rand Var -5 | |
| | Consist B | MM 2503 | |

A year older, a year later and the profile hasn't changed. Lucked into early opportunity thanks to injuries, 1st half running game caught our attention, and 2nd half h% helped. But this combination of sub-par plate skills and power should not get 400+ AB again, even on a rebuilder. You can't possibly need the SBs that badly.

| Yr | Tm | AB | R | HR | RBI | SB | BA | xBA | OBP | SLG | OPS | vL | vR | bb% | ct% | Eye | G | L | F | h% | HctX | PX | xPX | hr/f | Spd | SBO | SB% | #Wk | DOM | DIS | RC/G | RAR | BPV | BPX | R$ |
|---|---|---|---|---|---|---|---|---|---|---|---|---|---|---|---|---|---|---|---|---|---|---|---|---|---|---|---|---|---|---|---|---|---|---|---|
| 14 | | | | | | | | | | | | | | | | | | | | | | | | | | | | | | | | | | | |
| 15 | | | | | | | | | | | | | | | | | | | | | | | | | | | | | | | | | | | |
| 16 | a/a | 455 | 58 | 6 | 32 | 30 | 215 | | 279 | 337 | 616 | | | 8 | 68 | 0.28 | | | | 30 | | 85 | | | 138 | 45% | 65% | | | | 2.86 | | 1 | 3 | $11 |
| 17 | CHW * | 466 | 49 | 12 | 35 | 11 | 171 | 191 | 227 | 314 | 541 | 647 | 467 | 7 | 62 | 0.19 | 41 | 14 | 45 | 24 | 64 | 103 | 98 | 8% | 136 | 20% | 71% | 19 | 11% | 79% | 2.17 | -39.5 | -14 | -42 | -$3 |
| 18 | CHW | 429 | 49 | 6 | 29 | 16 | 235 | 200 | 279 | 336 | 614 | 589 | 624 | 4 | 70 | 0.14 | 41 | 18 | 41 | 32 | 66 | 69 | 64 | 5% | 149 | 26% | 67% | 27 | 15% | 63% | 2.88 | -15.1 | -9 | -30 | $9 |
| 1st Half | | 216 | 24 | 2 | 17 | 10 | 218 | 197 | 280 | 306 | 585 | 523 | 606 | 6 | 72 | 0.21 | 39 | 18 | 43 | 29 | 68 | 62 | 71 | 3% | 129 | 26% | 83% | 15 | 13% | 67% | 2.70 | -9.6 | -11 | -37 | $7 |
| 2nd Half | | 213 | 25 | 4 | 12 | 6 | 254 | 204 | 277 | 366 | 643 | 647 | 642 | 2 | 68 | 0.07 | 43 | 18 | 38 | 35 | 64 | 77 | 56 | 7% | 156 | 27% | 50% | 12 | 17% | 58% | 3.05 | -7.0 | -13 | -43 | $11 |
| 19 | Proj | **265** | **30** | **5** | **18** | **10** | **212** | **196** | **268** | **329** | **597** | **640** | **581** | **5** | **67** | **0.17** | **41** | **16** | **42** | **30** | **65** | **83** | **77** | **6%** | **146** | **28%** | **65%** | | | | **2.60** | **-12.9** | **-15** | **-50** | **$5** |

## Ervin,Phillip

| | | | |
|---|---|---|---|
| Age: 26 Bats: R Pos: LF RF | Health A | LIMA Plan C+ | |
| Ht: 5' 10" Wt: 207 | PT/Exp C | Rand Var -1 | |
| | Consist B | MM 2323 | |

7-31-.252-6 SB in 218 AB at CIN. Former 1st round pick surged as season wore on, flashing skills that impressed scouts long ago. 2nd half MLB effort included .768 OPS, 5/1 SB/CS, 114 PX over 179 AB. Checkered minor league history keeps us guessing and ct% is a BA drag, but he's interesting again. UP: A 15/25 guy.

| Yr | Tm | AB | R | HR | RBI | SB | BA | xBA | OBP | SLG | OPS | vL | vR | bb% | ct% | Eye | G | L | F | h% | HctX | PX | xPX | hr/f | Spd | SBO | SB% | #Wk | DOM | DIS | RC/G | RAR | BPV | BPX | R$ |
|---|---|---|---|---|---|---|---|---|---|---|---|---|---|---|---|---|---|---|---|---|---|---|---|---|---|---|---|---|---|---|---|---|---|---|---|
| 14 | | | | | | | | | | | | | | | | | | | | | | | | | | | | | | | | | | | |
| 15 | aa | 51 | 6 | 2 | 7 | 3 | 216 | | 358 | 381 | 739 | | | 18 | 66 | 0.65 | | | | 29 | | 130 | | | 94 | 38% | 51% | | | | 3.83 | | 34 | 92 | $0 |
| 16 | aa | 419 | 65 | 13 | 41 | 33 | 221 | | 320 | 374 | 694 | | | 13 | 76 | 0.60 | | | | 26 | | 95 | | | 108 | 37% | 75% | | | | 3.93 | | 39 | 111 | $16 |
| 17 | CIN * | 421 | 45 | 9 | 42 | 22 | 226 | 207 | 284 | 344 | 628 | 944 | 689 | 7 | 73 | 0.30 | 33 | 19 | 49 | 29 | 67 | 76 | 107 | 14% | 103 | 30% | 74% | 10 | 30% | 30% | 3.20 | -26.9 | 1 | 3 | $10 |
| 18 | CIN * | 391 | 46 | 11 | 60 | 14 | 249 | 245 | 312 | 406 | 718 | 749 | 716 | 8 | 73 | 0.33 | 36 | 28 | 36 | 32 | 92 | 101 | 86 | 12% | 95 | 24% | 60% | 18 | 28% | 50% | 4.07 | -6.3 | 18 | 60 | $13 |
| 1st Half | | 161 | 19 | 2 | 19 | 7 | 217 | 242 | 288 | 320 | 608 | 900 | 500 | 9 | 70 | 0.33 | 33 | 37 | 30 | 30 | 57 | 76 | 1 | 0% | 92 | 33% | 56% | 6 | 0% | 67% | 2.74 | -9.6 | -12 | -40 | $3 |
| 2nd Half | | 230 | 27 | 10 | 41 | 7 | 271 | 258 | 329 | 467 | 796 | 739 | 786 | 8 | 74 | 0.34 | 37 | 26 | 37 | 33 | 101 | 118 | 103 | 14% | 99 | 17% | 65% | 12 | 42% | 42% | 5.21 | 4.1 | 39 | 130 | $20 |
| 19 | Proj | **320** | **38** | **10** | **40** | **15** | **240** | **239** | **317** | **395** | **712** | **850** | **658** | **9** | **73** | **0.36** | **34** | **26** | **40** | **30** | **76** | **100** | **79** | **11%** | **93** | **29%** | **67%** | | | | **3.91** | **-6.8** | **24** | **79** | **$13** |

## Escobar,Alcides

| | | | |
|---|---|---|---|
| Age: 32 Bats: R Pos: SS 3B | Health A | LIMA Plan C | |
| Ht: 6' 1" Wt: 205 | PT/Exp A | Rand Var +2 | |
| | Consist A | MM 1335 | |

Difference between awful 1st half and profitable 2nd half were h% and LD%, the full season of which ended closer to norms. Stable contact and SB% rebound suggest free agent could sniff another double digit R$ with increased SBO and some luck. But now past his prime, there's also... DN: Bench job.

| Yr | Tm | AB | R | HR | RBI | SB | BA | xBA | OBP | SLG | OPS | vL | vR | bb% | ct% | Eye | G | L | F | h% | HctX | PX | xPX | hr/f | Spd | SBO | SB% | #Wk | DOM | DIS | RC/G | RAR | BPV | BPX | R$ |
|---|---|---|---|---|---|---|---|---|---|---|---|---|---|---|---|---|---|---|---|---|---|---|---|---|---|---|---|---|---|---|---|---|---|---|---|
| 14 | KC | 579 | 74 | 3 | 50 | 31 | 285 | 265 | 317 | 377 | 694 | 784 | 663 | 4 | 86 | 0.28 | 44 | 24 | 32 | 33 | 82 | 70 | 62 | 2% | 129 | 25% | 84% | 27 | 37% | 22% | 4.31 | 10.6 | 47 | 127 | $25 |
| 15 | KC | 612 | 76 | 3 | 47 | 17 | 257 | 255 | 293 | 320 | 614 | 653 | 598 | 4 | 88 | 0.35 | 48 | 22 | 30 | 29 | 80 | 41 | 53 | 2% | 127 | 14% | 77% | 27 | 37% | 26% | 3.18 | -25.0 | 32 | 86 | $14 |
| 16 | KC | 637 | 57 | 7 | 55 | 17 | 261 | 256 | 292 | 350 | 642 | 584 | 660 | 4 | 85 | 0.28 | 50 | 20 | 30 | 30 | 77 | 52 | 49 | 4% | 126 | 13% | 81% | 27 | 41% | 48% | 3.55 | -23.2 | 29 | 83 | $14 |
| 17 | KC | 599 | 71 | 6 | 54 | 4 | 250 | 252 | 272 | 357 | 629 | 720 | 602 | 2 | 83 | 0.15 | 41 | 22 | 37 | 29 | 90 | 65 | 90 | 3% | 115 | 9% | 36% | 27 | 30% | 41% | 3.11 | -31.2 | 25 | 76 | $7 |
| 18 | KC | 485 | 54 | 4 | 34 | 8 | 231 | 250 | 279 | 313 | 593 | 636 | 576 | 5 | 85 | 0.39 | 46 | 22 | 32 | 27 | 95 | 51 | 67 | 3% | 115 | 9% | 80% | 28 | 43% | 32% | 2.88 | -21.4 | 27 | 90 | $5 |
| 1st Half | | 287 | 31 | 3 | 18 | 3 | 195 | 238 | 248 | 275 | 523 | 721 | 451 | 6 | 85 | 0.40 | 47 | 18 | 35 | 22 | 105 | 46 | 80 | 4% | 119 | 7% | 75% | 15 | 40% | 40% | 2.10 | -21.9 | 27 | 90 | $1 |
| 2nd Half | | 198 | 23 | 1 | 16 | 5 | 283 | 267 | 325 | 369 | 694 | 525 | 766 | 6 | 84 | 0.38 | 45 | 27 | 28 | 33 | 80 | 58 | 49 | 2% | 107 | 11% | 83% | 13 | 46% | 23% | 4.31 | -1.1 | 27 | 90 | $11 |
| 19 | Proj | **434** | **49** | **4** | **35** | **8** | **253** | **254** | **290** | **342** | **632** | **635** | **631** | **5** | **84** | **0.31** | **45** | **22** | **32** | **29** | **87** | **56** | **66** | **3%** | **117** | **11%** | **73%** | | | | **3.34** | **-8.0** | **25** | **82** | **$10** |

## Escobar,Eduardo

| | | | |
|---|---|---|---|
| Age: 30 Bats: B Pos: 3B SS | Health A | LIMA Plan B | |
| Ht: 5'10" Wt: 185 | PT/Exp B | Rand Var 0 | |
| | Consist C | MM 3145 | |

The pair of additional HRs looks AB-driven on the surface, but PX/xPX surge hints at more to come. Stable ct%, upticking bb% and another season-long HctX bump helped drive BA skills surge. The absence of the volatility that defined his 2017 is one more big plus. Some retrenchment likely but everything here says a repeat is doable.

| Yr | Tm | AB | R | HR | RBI | SB | BA | xBA | OBP | SLG | OPS | vL | vR | bb% | ct% | Eye | G | L | F | h% | HctX | PX | xPX | hr/f | Spd | SBO | SB% | #Wk | DOM | DIS | RC/G | RAR | BPV | BPX | R$ |
|---|---|---|---|---|---|---|---|---|---|---|---|---|---|---|---|---|---|---|---|---|---|---|---|---|---|---|---|---|---|---|---|---|---|---|---|
| 14 | MIN | 433 | 52 | 6 | 37 | 1 | 275 | 264 | 315 | 406 | 721 | 877 | 654 | 5 | 79 | 0.26 | 41 | 24 | 35 | 34 | 99 | 110 | 93 | 5% | 109 | 2% | 50% | 27 | 41% | 26% | 4.44 | 9.0 | 47 | 127 | $10 |
| 15 | MIN | 409 | 48 | 12 | 58 | 2 | 262 | 267 | 309 | 445 | 754 | 789 | 737 | 6 | 79 | 0.33 | 42 | 19 | 39 | 31 | 101 | 125 | 118 | 10% | 105 | 6% | 40% | 27 | 44% | 30% | 4.62 | -0.6 | 62 | 168 | $10 |
| 16 | MIN | 352 | 32 | 6 | 37 | 1 | 236 | 241 | 280 | 338 | 618 | 552 | 648 | 6 | 80 | 0.29 | 39 | 24 | 37 | 28 | 86 | 63 | 73 | 6% | 82 | 5% | 25% | 25 | 36% | 44% | 3.03 | -20.6 | 6 | 17 | $2 |
| 17 | MIN | 457 | 62 | 21 | 73 | 5 | 254 | 250 | 309 | 449 | 758 | 730 | 773 | 7 | 79 | 0.34 | 34 | 21 | 45 | 28 | 100 | 102 | 114 | 13% | 114 | 6% | 83% | 27 | 33% | 37% | 4.68 | -8.4 | 45 | 136 | $12 |
| 18 | 2 TM | 566 | 75 | 23 | 84 | 2 | 272 | 275 | 334 | 489 | 824 | 775 | 846 | 8 | 78 | 0.41 | 32 | 25 | 43 | 31 | 109 | 136 | 133 | 12% | 73 | 5% | 33% | 27 | 52% | 30% | 5.57 | 14.7 | 60 | 200 | $19 |
| 1st Half | | 290 | 36 | 12 | 49 | 1 | 276 | 282 | 332 | 528 | 860 | 657 | 955 | 8 | 75 | 0.33 | 29 | 25 | 47 | 33 | 110 | 170 | 142 | 12% | 70 | 5% | 33% | 15 | 53% | 40% | 6.00 | 12.4 | 74 | 247 | $21 |
| 2nd Half | | 276 | 39 | 11 | 35 | 1 | 268 | 269 | 337 | 449 | 786 | 893 | 732 | 9 | 81 | 0.53 | 36 | 25 | 39 | 30 | 108 | 104 | 124 | 12% | 86 | 4% | 33% | 12 | 50% | 17% | 5.12 | 4.9 | 53 | 177 | $17 |
| 19 | Proj | **481** | **61** | **19** | **67** | **3** | **270** | **267** | **332** | **465** | **798** | **784** | **804** | **8** | **80** | **0.45** | **33** | **24** | **43** | **30** | **102** | **115** | **116** | **12%** | **78** | **4%** | **47%** | | | | **5.27** | **10.6** | **49** | **163** | **$17** |

JOCK THOMPSON

## Fernandez,Jose M.

Age: 31 Bats: L Pos: 1B
Ht: 5' 10" Wt: 185

| Health | A | LIMA Plan | D |
|---|---|---|---|
| PT/Exp | F | Rand Var | +4 |
| Consist | A | MM | 0051 |

2-11-.267 in 116 AB at LAA. Line-drive machine with .931 OPS, 33/34 BB/K in Triple-A wasn't overmatched in MLB debut. But woeful glove and doubts about legitimacy of minor-league pop win him no love. Older Cuban import has limited window, but strong contact and xBA suggest... UP: 300+ AB, .280 BA, 10 HR.

| Yr | Tm | AB | R | HR | RBI | SB | BA | xBA | OBP | SLG | OPS | vL | vR | bb% | ct% | Eye | G | L | F | h% | HctX | PX | xPX | hr/f | Spd | SBO | SB% | #Wk | DOM | DIS | RC/G | RAR | BPV | BPX | R$ |
|---|---|---|---|---|---|---|---|---|---|---|---|---|---|---|---|---|---|---|---|---|---|---|---|---|---|---|---|---|---|---|---|---|---|---|---|
| 14 | | | | | | | | | | | | | | | | | | | | | | | | | | | | | | | | | | | |
| 15 | | | | | | | | | | | | | | | | | | | | | | | | | | | | | | | | | | | |
| 16 | | | | | | | | | | | | | | | | | | | | | | | | | | | | | | | | | | | |
| 17 | a/a | 343 | 35 | 12 | 47 | 0 | 239 | | 275 | 381 | 656 | | | 5 | 87 | 0.39 | | | | 24 | | 72 | | | 77 | 3% | 0% | | | | 3.38 | | 41 | 124 | $3 |
| 18 | LAA * | 473 | 46 | 12 | 44 | 2 | 239 | 289 | 276 | 359 | 635 | 579 | 719 | 5 | 87 | 0.39 | 44 | 29 | 28 | 25 | 114 | 67 | 54 | 7% | 78 | 5% | 44% | 11 | 36% | 27% | 3.26 | -16.5 | 36 | 120 | $6 |
| 1st Half | | 264 | 25 | 6 | 25 | 1 | 238 | 318 | 270 | 354 | 624 | 0 | 645 | 4 | 87 | 0.34 | 43 | 37 | 20 | 25 | 107 | 63 | 40 | 0% | 95 | 7% | 29% | 3 | 33% | 67% | 3.06 | -13.6 | 38 | 127 | $6 |
| 2nd Half | | 209 | 21 | 5 | 19 | 1 | 241 | 277 | 283 | 366 | 650 | 647 | 753 | 6 | 86 | 0.44 | 44 | 25 | 31 | 26 | 116 | 71 | 61 | 9% | 75 | 2% | 100% | 8 | 38% | 13% | 3.51 | -7.8 | 38 | 127 | $6 |
| 19 | Proj | 199 | 20 | 3 | 22 | 1 | 264 | 282 | 306 | 345 | 651 | 516 | 674 | 5 | 87 | 0.40 | 44 | 30 | 27 | 29 | 112 | 50 | 53 | 5% | 77 | 3% | 29% | | | | 3.51 | -7.3 | 10 | 34 | $2 |

## Field,Johnny

Age: 27 Bats: R Pos: LF RF
Ht: 5' 10" Wt: 180

| Health | A | LIMA Plan | D |
|---|---|---|---|
| PT/Exp | C | Rand Var | 0 |
| Consist | A | MM | 3311 |

9-21-.222 in 221 AB at TAM/MIN. Launch angle project in MLB debut, with small sample xPX bump offering hope. Needs more than this and a handful of SBs to compensate for sub-par BA and stagnant plate skills. Upside is as a bench player at best but inability to solve RHP makes it unlikely. Pass.

| Yr | Tm | AB | R | HR | RBI | SB | BA | xBA | OBP | SLG | OPS | vL | vR | bb% | ct% | Eye | G | L | F | h% | HctX | PX | xPX | hr/f | Spd | SBO | SB% | #Wk | DOM | DIS | RC/G | RAR | BPV | BPX | R$ |
|---|---|---|---|---|---|---|---|---|---|---|---|---|---|---|---|---|---|---|---|---|---|---|---|---|---|---|---|---|---|---|---|---|---|---|---|
| 14 | | | | | | | | | | | | | | | | | | | | | | | | | | | | | | | | | | | |
| 15 | aa | 432 | 54 | 11 | 52 | 14 | 218 | | 266 | 372 | 639 | | | 6 | 71 | 0.23 | | | | 28 | | 118 | | | 97 | 22% | 81% | | | | 3.26 | | 21 | 57 | $8 |
| 16 | a/a | 450 | 52 | 10 | 48 | 14 | 240 | | 282 | 391 | 673 | | | 6 | 72 | 0.21 | | | | 31 | | 104 | | | 102 | 25% | 60% | | | | 3.50 | | 16 | 46 | $10 |
| 17 | aaa | 445 | 55 | 10 | 50 | 11 | 227 | | 264 | 367 | 631 | | | 5 | 73 | 0.19 | | | | 29 | | 94 | | | 87 | 23% | 57% | | | | 3.02 | | 7 | 21 | $7 |
| 18 | 2 AL * | 310 | 40 | 10 | 29 | 6 | 224 | 226 | 259 | 379 | 639 | 757 | 590 | 4 | 70 | 0.16 | 39 | 19 | 41 | 29 | 91 | 108 | 122 | 15% | 95 | 12% | 83% | 20 | 40% | 60% | 3.26 | -12.5 | 7 | 23 | $5 |
| 1st Half | | 167 | 22 | 6 | 16 | 4 | 230 | 231 | 261 | 397 | 658 | 787 | 576 | 4 | 68 | 0.13 | 41 | 21 | 38 | 30 | 83 | 117 | 108 | 16% | 97 | 14% | 100% | 13 | 46% | 54% | 3.54 | -5.3 | 5 | 17 | $6 |
| 2nd Half | | 143 | 18 | 4 | 13 | 2 | 217 | 211 | 257 | 359 | 616 | 706 | 631 | 5 | 73 | 0.20 | 36 | 15 | 49 | 27 | 106 | 97 | 153 | 13% | 98 | 11% | 60% | 7 | 29% | 71% | 2.94 | -7.3 | 10 | 33 | $4 |
| 19 | Proj | 133 | 17 | 5 | 14 | 3 | 225 | 231 | 271 | 402 | 673 | 733 | 628 | 5 | 72 | 0.19 | 38 | 17 | 45 | 28 | 97 | 118 | 135 | 11% | 102 | 19% | 69% | | | | 3.42 | -4.8 | 22 | 73 | $3 |

## Fisher,Derek

Age: 25 Bats: L Pos: LF
Ht: 6' 3" Wt: 205

| Health | A | LIMA Plan | D |
|---|---|---|---|
| PT/Exp | C | Rand Var | +1 |
| Consist | B | MM | 3301 |

4-11-.165 in 79 AB at HOU. Legitimate power / speed prospect owns three 20+ HR seasons in the minors, with career .371 OBP and 103 SB. But he also owns a 57% ct% through 225 MLB AB with a power-suffocating 50% GB%. Pluses give him time for a career, but a limited one without some remedial bat-to-ball instruction.

| Yr | Tm | AB | R | HR | RBI | SB | BA | xBA | OBP | SLG | OPS | vL | vR | bb% | ct% | Eye | G | L | F | h% | HctX | PX | xPX | hr/f | Spd | SBO | SB% | #Wk | DOM | DIS | RC/G | RAR | BPV | BPX | R$ |
|---|---|---|---|---|---|---|---|---|---|---|---|---|---|---|---|---|---|---|---|---|---|---|---|---|---|---|---|---|---|---|---|---|---|---|---|
| 14 | | | | | | | | | | | | | | | | | | | | | | | | | | | | | | | | | | | |
| 15 | | | | | | | | | | | | | | | | | | | | | | | | | | | | | | | | | | | |
| 16 | a/a | 478 | 59 | 18 | 63 | 23 | 228 | | 323 | 394 | 717 | | | 12 | 63 | 0.38 | | | | 32 | | 120 | | | 105 | 23% | 75% | | | | 4.20 | | 4 | 11 | $15 |
| 17 | HOU * | 489 | 63 | 20 | 60 | 14 | 240 | 268 | 297 | 415 | 712 | 644 | 668 | 7 | 71 | 0.28 | 54 | 24 | 21 | 30 | 109 | 109 | 101 | 26% | 113 | 25% | 48% | 13 | 15% | 54% | 3.73 | -26.0 | 21 | 64 | $13 |
| 18 | HOU * | 318 | 43 | 11 | 34 | 9 | 188 | 201 | 260 | 344 | 604 | 937 | 527 | 9 | 55 | 0.21 | 50 | 21 | 29 | 30 | 83 | 125 | 144 | 36% | 115 | 16% | 89% | 10 | 30% | 60% | 2.89 | -17.1 | -26 | -87 | $4 |
| 1st Half | | 172 | 28 | 7 | 18 | 4 | 189 | 221 | 264 | 381 | 645 | 1175 | 543 | 9 | 58 | 0.24 | 50 | 21 | 29 | 28 | 87 | 145 | 144 | 36% | 127 | 12% | 100% | 8 | 38% | 50% | 3.27 | -7.2 | 5 | 17 | $5 |
| 2nd Half | | 146 | 15 | 4 | 15 | 5 | 188 | 167 | 255 | 301 | 556 | 0 | 0 | 8 | 52 | 0.19 | 44 | 20 | 36 | 33 | 0 | 98 | -27 | 0% | 100 | 20% | 82% | 2 | 0% | 100% | 2.47 | -10.0 | -67 | -223 | $3 |
| 19 | Proj | 160 | 18 | 6 | 16 | 5 | 218 | 222 | 287 | 376 | 663 | 892 | 614 | 9 | 61 | 0.24 | 52 | 22 | 26 | 32 | 96 | 116 | 127 | 22% | 111 | 20% | 68% | | | | 3.42 | -5.9 | -13 | -44 | $4 |

## Fletcher,David

Age: 25 Bats: R Pos: 2B 3B
Ht: 5' 10" Wt: 175

| Health | A | LIMA Plan | C+ |
|---|---|---|---|
| PT/Exp | D | Rand Var | 0 |
| Consist | D | MM | 1323 |

1-25-.275 with 3 SB in 284 AB at LAA. Prospect bumped contact into elite range, and his all-fields LD stroke produced .350 BA in hitter-friendly Triple-A environment. Held his own in MLB debut, base-running and glove are pluses. Has opportunity, but near-zero power and inability to draw walks keep role and upside tenuous.

| Yr | Tm | AB | R | HR | RBI | SB | BA | xBA | OBP | SLG | OPS | vL | vR | bb% | ct% | Eye | G | L | F | h% | HctX | PX | xPX | hr/f | Spd | SBO | SB% | #Wk | DOM | DIS | RC/G | RAR | BPV | BPX | R$ |
|---|---|---|---|---|---|---|---|---|---|---|---|---|---|---|---|---|---|---|---|---|---|---|---|---|---|---|---|---|---|---|---|---|---|---|---|
| 14 | | | | | | | | | | | | | | | | | | | | | | | | | | | | | | | | | | | |
| 15 | | | | | | | | | | | | | | | | | | | | | | | | | | | | | | | | | | | |
| 16 | aa | 80 | 10 | 0 | 6 | 1 | 284 | | 309 | 355 | 664 | | | 3 | 82 | 0.20 | | | | 35 | | 58 | | | 95 | 5% | 100% | | | | 3.99 | | 11 | 31 | $0 |
| 17 | a/a | 448 | 48 | 2 | 32 | 16 | 230 | | 265 | 290 | 555 | | | 5 | 86 | 0.34 | | | | 26 | | 37 | | | 104 | 22% | 71% | | | | 2.53 | | 16 | 48 | $6 |
| 18 | LAA * | 538 | 70 | 5 | 49 | 7 | 274 | 280 | 306 | 388 | 694 | 672 | 682 | 4 | 89 | 0.42 | 39 | 27 | 34 | 30 | 95 | 69 | 49 | 1% | 117 | 8% | 76% | 15 | 40% | 20% | 4.16 | 1.3 | 57 | 190 | $13 |
| 1st Half | | 288 | 36 | 4 | 29 | 5 | 279 | 233 | 308 | 415 | 723 | 862 | 745 | 4 | 90 | 0.40 | 33 | 13 | 53 | 30 | 77 | 78 | 64 | 0% | 133 | 12% | 69% | 4 | 25% | 50% | 4.46 | 2.3 | 71 | 237 | $16 |
| 2nd Half | | 250 | 34 | 1 | 20 | 2 | 268 | 280 | 307 | 356 | 663 | 645 | 674 | 5 | 88 | 0.43 | 40 | 29 | 31 | 30 | 97 | 59 | 46 | 1% | 106 | 3% | 100% | 11 | 45% | 9% | 3.82 | -2.5 | 43 | 143 | $10 |
| 19 | Proj | 367 | 47 | 1 | 32 | 8 | 266 | 245 | 309 | 343 | 652 | 656 | 650 | 5 | 88 | 0.38 | 38 | 22 | 40 | 30 | 89 | 51 | 53 | 1% | 111 | 12% | 73% | | | | 3.56 | -6.5 | 33 | 110 | $10 |

## Flores,Wilmer

Age: 27 Bats: R Pos: 1B
Ht: 6' 3" Wt: 205

| Health | B | LIMA Plan | C+ |
|---|---|---|---|
| PT/Exp | C | Rand Var | 0 |
| Consist | A | MM | 2133 |

Mixed signals from perennial tease. PRO: 1st half bb% spike; more gains vR; career-best ct% stayed intact for the duration. CON: Season-long struggles vL; BA the only survivor of poor 2nd half. Sept shut-down, diagnosis of early-onset arthritis in both knees casts some doubt on a power rebound.

| Yr | Tm | AB | R | HR | RBI | SB | BA | xBA | OBP | SLG | OPS | vL | vR | bb% | ct% | Eye | G | L | F | h% | HctX | PX | xPX | hr/f | Spd | SBO | SB% | #Wk | DOM | DIS | RC/G | RAR | BPV | BPX | R$ |
|---|---|---|---|---|---|---|---|---|---|---|---|---|---|---|---|---|---|---|---|---|---|---|---|---|---|---|---|---|---|---|---|---|---|---|---|
| 14 | NYM * | 479 | 54 | 14 | 64 | 1 | 250 | 257 | 283 | 393 | 676 | 382 | 749 | 4 | 84 | 0.28 | 40 | 20 | 40 | 27 | 101 | 95 | 103 | 7% | 110 | 3% | 30% | 20 | 40% | 35% | 3.71 | -6.8 | 54 | 146 | $11 |
| 15 | NYM | 483 | 55 | 16 | 59 | 0 | 263 | 267 | 295 | 408 | 703 | 955 | 637 | 4 | 87 | 0.30 | 42 | 21 | 37 | 27 | 109 | 86 | 95 | 10% | 92 | 1% | 0% | 26 | 46% | 23% | 4.06 | -18.2 | 54 | 146 | $11 |
| 16 | NYM | 307 | 38 | 16 | 49 | 1 | 267 | 274 | 319 | 469 | 788 | 1093 | 642 | 7 | 84 | 0.48 | 33 | 22 | 45 | 27 | 93 | 108 | 107 | 14% | 96 | 3% | 50% | 21 | 48% | 29% | 5.14 | -1.7 | 68 | 194 | $9 |
| 17 | NYM | 336 | 42 | 18 | 52 | 1 | 271 | 271 | 307 | 488 | 795 | 862 | 765 | 5 | 84 | 0.31 | 36 | 18 | 46 | 28 | 120 | 111 | 127 | 14% | 96 | 3% | 50% | 21 | 52% | 10% | 5.17 | -7.0 | 65 | 197 | $9 |
| 18 | NYM | 386 | 43 | 11 | 51 | 0 | 267 | 261 | 319 | 417 | 736 | 610 | 804 | 7 | 89 | 0.69 | 36 | 19 | 45 | 28 | 108 | 85 | 109 | 7% | 81 | 0% | 0% | 25 | 60% | 20% | 4.61 | -5.4 | 64 | 213 | $9 |
| 1st Half | | 162 | 17 | 6 | 26 | 0 | 259 | 255 | 322 | 444 | 767 | 610 | 882 | 9 | 88 | 0.84 | 34 | 16 | 50 | 26 | 117 | 103 | 127 | 8% | 76 | 0% | 0% | 14 | 64% | 14% | 4.99 | 1.0 | 78 | 260 | $6 |
| 2nd Half | | 224 | 26 | 5 | 25 | 0 | 272 | 264 | 317 | 397 | 714 | 610 | 758 | 5 | 90 | 0.57 | 37 | 22 | 41 | 29 | 101 | 71 | 95 | 6% | 94 | 0% | 0% | 11 | 55% | 27% | 4.35 | -2.7 | 57 | 190 | $11 |
| 19 | Proj | 362 | 42 | 14 | 51 | 0 | 267 | 263 | 312 | 437 | 749 | 742 | 752 | 6 | 87 | 0.47 | 36 | 20 | 44 | 28 | 108 | 93 | 112 | 10% | 91 | 1% | 46% | | | | 4.69 | -0.8 | 46 | 155 | $11 |

## Flowers,Tyler

Age: 33 Bats: R Pos: CA
Ht: 6' 4" Wt: 260

| Health | C | LIMA Plan | D+ |
|---|---|---|---|
| PT/Exp | D | Rand Var | +1 |
| Consist | B | MM | 2005 |

Lost April (and counting stats) to an oblique strain. Some BA regression had been expected, but 2nd half spiraled downward as ct% drifted and struggles vR took root. Age adds uncertainty coming off a down year. But continued HctX and bb% surge are bright spots—and xPX says double-digit HR, profit are still attainable.

| Yr | Tm | AB | R | HR | RBI | SB | BA | xBA | OBP | SLG | OPS | vL | vR | bb% | ct% | Eye | G | L | F | h% | HctX | PX | xPX | hr/f | Spd | SBO | SB% | #Wk | DOM | DIS | RC/G | RAR | BPV | BPX | R$ |
|---|---|---|---|---|---|---|---|---|---|---|---|---|---|---|---|---|---|---|---|---|---|---|---|---|---|---|---|---|---|---|---|---|---|---|---|
| 14 | CHW | 407 | 42 | 15 | 50 | 0 | 241 | 223 | 297 | 396 | 693 | 732 | 679 | 6 | 61 | 0.16 | 48 | 24 | 29 | 36 | 82 | 137 | 88 | 21% | 67 | 1% | 0% | 26 | 31% | 62% | 3.74 | 3.4 | -12 | -32 | $7 |
| 15 | CHW | 331 | 21 | 9 | 39 | 0 | 239 | 194 | 295 | 356 | 652 | 751 | 627 | 6 | 69 | 0.20 | 47 | 17 | 36 | 32 | 93 | 88 | 85 | 11% | 66 | 1% | 0% | 26 | 27% | 54% | 3.34 | -4.6 | -21 | -57 | $2 |
| 16 | ATL | 281 | 27 | 8 | 41 | 0 | 270 | 217 | 357 | 420 | 777 | 767 | 781 | 9 | 68 | 0.32 | 42 | 19 | 39 | 37 | 120 | 113 | 153 | 11% | 79 | 0% | 0% | 22 | 36% | 45% | 4.97 | 4.5 | 5 | 14 | $5 |
| 17 | ATL | 317 | 41 | 12 | 49 | 0 | 281 | 255 | 378 | 445 | 823 | 829 | 821 | 8 | 74 | 0.38 | 42 | 24 | 33 | 35 | 111 | 99 | 99 | 15% | 63 | 1% | 0% | 27 | 30% | 33% | 5.37 | 11.8 | 13 | 39 | $9 |
| 18 | ATL | 251 | 34 | 8 | 30 | 0 | 227 | 215 | 341 | 359 | 700 | 1117 | 540 | 12 | 70 | 0.46 | 41 | 21 | 38 | 29 | 126 | 86 | 132 | 12% | 70 | 0% | 0% | 24 | 29% | 54% | 3.81 | 2.2 | -5 | -17 | $2 |
| 1st Half | | 108 | 14 | 4 | 15 | 0 | 250 | 223 | 382 | 398 | 780 | 1348 | 516 | 14 | 73 | 0.59 | 38 | 20 | 42 | 31 | 140 | 92 | 156 | 12% | 74 | 0% | 0% | 12 | 25% | 58% | 4.77 | 4.2 | 17 | 57 | $1 |
| 2nd Half | | 143 | 20 | 4 | 15 | 0 | 210 | 210 | 309 | 329 | 638 | 886 | 555 | 11 | 67 | 0.38 | 44 | 22 | 34 | 28 | 115 | 82 | 112 | 12% | 70 | 0% | 0% | 12 | 33% | 50% | 3.16 | -1.3 | -20 | -67 | $3 |
| 19 | Proj | 409 | 50 | 13 | 54 | 0 | 248 | 224 | 346 | 390 | 736 | 956 | 661 | 10 | 70 | 0.37 | 43 | 21 | 36 | 32 | 117 | 95 | 121 | 13% | 70 | 0% | 0% | | | | 4.26 | 9.9 | -14 | -46 | $10 |

## Forsythe,Logan

Age: 32 Bats: R Pos: 2B
Ht: 6'1" Wt: 205

| Health | C | LIMA Plan | D |
|---|---|---|---|
| PT/Exp | B | Rand Var | +1 |
| Consist | B | MM | 1201 |

Shoulder woes stalled him in April, balky knee helped crush his Sept (.533 OPS in 87 AB), struggled uncharacteristically vL all season. But injuries alone don't explain the past 2 years. Plate skills still look playable, but power has fallen off a cliff—and suddenly that 2016 vR looks like an outlier. A big rebound isn't likely.

| Yr | Tm | AB | R | HR | RBI | SB | BA | xBA | OBP | SLG | OPS | vL | vR | bb% | ct% | Eye | G | L | F | h% | HctX | PX | xPX | hr/f | Spd | SBO | SB% | #Wk | DOM | DIS | RC/G | RAR | BPV | BPX | R$ |
|---|---|---|---|---|---|---|---|---|---|---|---|---|---|---|---|---|---|---|---|---|---|---|---|---|---|---|---|---|---|---|---|---|---|---|---|
| 14 | TAM | 301 | 32 | 6 | 26 | 2 | 223 | 224 | 287 | 329 | 616 | 708 | 536 | 7 | 76 | 0.35 | 41 | 19 | 40 | 27 | 83 | 80 | 100 | 6% | 103 | 3% | 100% | 27 | 30% | 59% | 3.08 | -2.8 | 17 | 46 | $2 |
| 15 | TAM | 540 | 69 | 17 | 68 | 9 | 281 | 255 | 359 | 444 | 804 | 972 | 728 | 9 | 79 | 0.50 | 40 | 20 | 41 | 33 | 108 | 109 | 105 | 10% | 106 | 8% | 69% | 26 | 46% | 27% | 5.44 | 17.8 | 57 | 154 | $20 |
| 16 | TAM | 511 | 76 | 20 | 52 | 6 | 264 | 259 | 333 | 444 | 778 | 775 | 778 | 8 | 75 | 0.36 | 42 | 23 | 35 | 32 | 110 | 110 | 115 | 15% | 122 | 9% | 50% | 24 | 50% | 25% | 4.83 | 1.5 | 43 | 123 | $14 |
| 17 | LA | 361 | 56 | 6 | 36 | 3 | 224 | 225 | 351 | 327 | 678 | 870 | 576 | 16 | 70 | 0.63 | 44 | 23 | 33 | 30 | 103 | 74 | 111 | 7% | 93 | 4% | 60% | 23 | 30% | 52% | 3.72 | -9.9 | 0 | 0 | $2 |
| 18 | 2 TM | 371 | 37 | 2 | 27 | 3 | 232 | 217 | 313 | 291 | 604 | 545 | 640 | 10 | 78 | 0.49 | 49 | 19 | 32 | 29 | 97 | 45 | 69 | 2% | 97 | 3% | 100% | 24 | 21% | 50% | 3.02 | -11.7 | -2 | -7 | $2 |
| 1st Half | | 157 | 11 | 2 | 11 | 2 | 204 | 232 | 254 | 306 | 560 | 526 | 580 | 7 | 83 | 0.41 | 44 | 17 | 40 | 23 | 100 | 68 | 97 | 4% | 85 | 6% | 100% | 11 | 45% | 27% | 2.56 | -7.9 | 26 | 87 | -$3 |
| 2nd Half | | 214 | 26 | 0 | 16 | 1 | 252 | 205 | 352 | 280 | 633 | 557 | 680 | 12 | 74 | 0.54 | 53 | 21 | 26 | 34 | 95 | 25 | 46 | 0% | 108 | 1% | 100% | 13 | 0% | 69% | 3.32 | -5.3 | -26 | -87 | $5 |
| 19 | Proj | 218 | 27 | 3 | 19 | 2 | 237 | 225 | 326 | 329 | 654 | 673 | 644 | 11 | 75 | 0.50 | 46 | 21 | 33 | 30 | 100 | 63 | 88 | 6% | 103 | 4% | 72% | | | | 3.53 | -4.2 | -7 | -24 | $4 |

JOCK THOMPSON

## Fowler,Dexter

| Age: 33 | Bats: B | Pos: RF | Health | D | LIMA Plan | C+ |
|---|---|---|---|---|---|---|
| Ht: 6' 5" | Wt: 195 | | PT/Exp | C | Rand Var | +5 |
| | | | Consist | D | MM | 2415 |

Broken foot ended season in early August; looks like a mercy-killing. Nothing wrong with his plate skills, suggesting some of this can be chalked off to an unfortunate h% that will rebound. But the simultaneous plunges in power, speed are less easily explained. Age suggests a big turnaround can't be banked upon.

| Yr | Tm | AB | R | HR | RBI | SB | BA | xBA | OBP | SLG | OPS | vL | vR | bb% | ct% | Eye | G | L | F | h% | HctX | PX | xPX | hr/f | Spd | SBO | SB% | #Wk | DOM | DIS | RC/G | RAR | BPV | BPX | R$ |
|---|---|---|---|---|---|---|---|---|---|---|---|---|---|---|---|---|---|---|---|---|---|---|---|---|---|---|---|---|---|---|---|---|---|---|---|
| 14 | HOU | 434 | 61 | 8 | 35 | 11 | 276 | 240 | 375 | 399 | 774 | 887 | 737 | 13 | 75 | 0.61 | 44 | 21 | 35 | 35 | 95 | 94 | 107 | 7% | 145 | 10% | 73% | 20 | 45% | 40% | 5.23 | 14.0 | 47 | 127 | $15 |
| 15 | CHC | 596 | 102 | 17 | 46 | 20 | 250 | 245 | 346 | 411 | 757 | 865 | 726 | 12 | 74 | 0.55 | 43 | 20 | 36 | 31 | 90 | 109 | 98 | 11% | 164 | 15% | 74% | 26 | 50% | 27% | 4.78 | -1.3 | 59 | 159 | $19 |
| 16 | CHC | 456 | 84 | 13 | 48 | 13 | 276 | 250 | 393 | 447 | 840 | 876 | 827 | 14 | 73 | 0.64 | 41 | 24 | 36 | 35 | 90 | 110 | 100 | 11% | 143 | 11% | 76% | 23 | 48% | 35% | 6.06 | 18.0 | 53 | 151 | $18 |
| 17 | STL | 420 | 68 | 18 | 64 | 7 | 264 | 269 | 363 | 488 | 851 | 754 | 883 | 13 | 76 | 0.62 | 39 | 22 | 38 | 31 | 117 | 124 | 150 | 15% | 147 | 8% | 70% | 24 | 54% | 38% | 6.04 | 10.4 | 75 | 227 | $14 |
| 18 | STL | 289 | 40 | 8 | 31 | 5 | 180 | 217 | 278 | 298 | 576 | 554 | 582 | 11 | 74 | 0.51 | 42 | 18 | 39 | 21 | 93 | 74 | 89 | 9% | 92 | 10% | 71% | 19 | 26% | 47% | 2.55 | -17.3 | 8 | 27 | $1 |
| 1st Half | | 216 | 30 | 5 | 20 | 3 | 171 | 214 | 276 | 278 | 554 | 303 | 606 | 12 | 75 | 0.54 | 38 | 20 | 42 | 20 | 98 | 68 | 95 | 7% | 95 | 9% | 60% | 15 | 27% | 47% | 2.27 | -15.5 | 9 | 30 | $1 |
| 2nd Half | | 73 | 10 | 3 | 11 | 2 | 205 | 225 | 286 | 356 | 642 | 933 | 492 | 11 | 71 | 0.43 | 54 | 15 | 31 | 24 | 78 | 92 | 70 | 18% | 98 | 11% | 100% | 4 | 25% | 50% | 3.49 | -2.2 | 12 | 40 | $1 |
| 19 | Proj | **399** | **61** | **13** | **50** | **9** | **250** | **237** | **343** | **405** | **748** | **826** | **721** | **12** | **74** | **0.54** | **44** | **20** | **36** | **31** | **95** | **95** | **103** | **12%** | **120** | **9%** | **79%** | | | | **4.74** | **3.4** | **30** | **99** | **$11** |

## Fowler,Dustin

| Age: 24 | Bats: L | Pos: CF | Health | C | LIMA Plan | C+ |
|---|---|---|---|---|---|---|
| Ht: 6' 0" | Wt: 195 | | PT/Exp | C | Rand Var | -2 |
| | | | Consist | C | MM | 2523 |

6-23-.224 with 6 SB in 192 AB at OAK. Owned Triple-A pitchers, teased MLB breakout with .294 BA, 4 HR 2 SB in June before crashing. Speed, handedness, average pop fueled minor league rise; HctX flashes hint at live bat. But awful Eye and .229 BA vR are MLB issues. DN: More inconsistency, AAA time.

| Yr | Tm | AB | R | HR | RBI | SB | BA | xBA | OBP | SLG | OPS | vL | vR | bb% | ct% | Eye | G | L | F | h% | HctX | PX | xPX | hr/f | Spd | SBO | SB% | #Wk | DOM | DIS | RC/G | RAR | BPV | BPX | R$ |
|---|---|---|---|---|---|---|---|---|---|---|---|---|---|---|---|---|---|---|---|---|---|---|---|---|---|---|---|---|---|---|---|---|---|---|---|
| 14 | | | | | | | | | | | | | | | | | | | | | | | | | | | | | | | | | | | |
| 15 | | | | | | | | | | | | | | | | | | | | | | | | | | | | | | | | | | | |
| 16 | aa | 541 | 63 | 13 | 83 | 24 | 268 | | 295 | 434 | 730 | | | 4 | 83 | 0.22 | | | | 30 | | 93 | | | 119 | 31% | 67% | | | | 4.26 | | 50 | 143 | $22 |
| 17 | a/a | 297 | 44 | 14 | 38 | 12 | 271 | | 303 | 504 | 807 | | | 4 | 76 | 0.19 | | | | 32 | | 129 | | | 135 | 29% | 68% | 1 | 0% | 100% | 5.12 | | 59 | 179 | $12 |
| 18 | OAK * | 421 | 48 | 9 | 44 | 16 | 266 | 237 | 292 | 410 | 701 | 297 | 633 | 3 | 78 | 0.16 | 41 | 20 | 39 | 32 | 113 | 83 | 88 | 10% | 129 | 25% | 72% | 17 | 18% | 59% | 4.07 | 0.4 | 26 | 87 | $14 |
| 1st Half | | 257 | 28 | 7 | 30 | 11 | 262 | 241 | 289 | 412 | 701 | 382 | 716 | 4 | 80 | 0.19 | 39 | 21 | 41 | 30 | 136 | 82 | 112 | 12% | 127 | 29% | 68% | 9 | 22% | 33% | 3.96 | -1.4 | 33 | 110 | $18 |
| 2nd Half | | 164 | 20 | 2 | 15 | 5 | 273 | 232 | 295 | 407 | 701 | 0 | 459 | 3 | 75 | 0.12 | 46 | 17 | 37 | 36 | 61 | 85 | 28 | 7% | 128 | 17% | 83% | 8 | 13% | 88% | 4.25 | 0.6 | 14 | 47 | $9 |
| 19 | Proj | **337** | **43** | **9** | **40** | **13** | **261** | **248** | **290** | **430** | **720** | **260** | **749** | **4** | **77** | **0.17** | **43** | **19** | **38** | **31** | **91** | **99** | **62** | **9%** | **125** | **26%** | **72%** | | | | **4.20** | **0.6** | **42** | **141** | **$14** |

## Franco,Maikel

| Age: 26 | Bats: R | Pos: 3B | Health | A | LIMA Plan | B+ |
|---|---|---|---|---|---|---|
| Ht: 6' 1" | Wt: 215 | | PT/Exp | A | Rand Var | 0 |
| | | | Consist | B | MM | 2245 |

BA rebounded, and more, along with h% and ct% boost. Despite AB drop-off, another 20+ HR season—fueled by hr/f uptick and 2nd half onslaught vR. Contact, age, health remain pluses; average power, sub-par patience remain warts; HctX skid, struggles vL leave questions. Think repeat, not growth.

| Yr | Tm | AB | R | HR | RBI | SB | BA | xBA | OBP | SLG | OPS | vL | vR | bb% | ct% | Eye | G | L | F | h% | HctX | PX | xPX | hr/f | Spd | SBO | SB% | #Wk | DOM | DIS | RC/G | RAR | BPV | BPX | R$ |
|---|---|---|---|---|---|---|---|---|---|---|---|---|---|---|---|---|---|---|---|---|---|---|---|---|---|---|---|---|---|---|---|---|---|---|---|
| 14 | PHI * | 577 | 55 | 14 | 65 | 2 | 222 | 240 | 253 | 358 | 611 | 277 | 573 | 4 | 82 | 0.23 | 49 | 12 | 40 | 25 | 32 | 97 | 26 | 0% | 104 | 3% | 68% | 5 | 0% | 60% | 2.96 | -13.3 | 46 | 124 | $6 |
| 15 | PHI * | 445 | 57 | 18 | 70 | 3 | 291 | 283 | 340 | 492 | 832 | 825 | 844 | 7 | 82 | 0.40 | 47 | 18 | 35 | 32 | 105 | 130 | 120 | 16% | 91 | 2% | 100% | 16 | 69% | 25% | 6.06 | 17.1 | 74 | 200 | $18 |
| 16 | PHI | 581 | 67 | 25 | 88 | 1 | 255 | 263 | 306 | 427 | 733 | 860 | 698 | 6 | 82 | 0.38 | 44 | 20 | 35 | 27 | 102 | 95 | 91 | 15% | 76 | 1% | 50% | 27 | 48% | 26% | 4.40 | -9.8 | 41 | 117 | $14 |
| 17 | PHI | 575 | 66 | 24 | 76 | 0 | 230 | 264 | 281 | 409 | 690 | 657 | 701 | 7 | 83 | 0.43 | 45 | 18 | 37 | 24 | 105 | 95 | 86 | 13% | 63 | 0% | 0% | 27 | 52% | 22% | 3.80 | -26.1 | 44 | 133 | $7 |
| 18 | PHI | 433 | 48 | 22 | 68 | 1 | 270 | 272 | 314 | 467 | 780 | 644 | 826 | 6 | 86 | 0.47 | 49 | 17 | 34 | 27 | 87 | 100 | 88 | 17% | 89 | 1% | 100% | 27 | 52% | 30% | 5.17 | 6.1 | 64 | 213 | $14 |
| 1st Half | | 233 | 25 | 10 | 38 | 0 | 258 | 262 | 302 | 442 | 744 | 737 | 747 | 6 | 85 | 0.44 | 53 | 15 | 32 | 27 | 83 | 98 | 85 | 16% | 93 | 0% | 0% | 15 | 53% | 33% | 4.63 | 0.9 | 59 | 197 | $13 |
| 2nd Half | | 200 | 23 | 12 | 30 | 1 | 285 | 279 | 329 | 495 | 824 | 492 | 909 | 6 | 87 | 0.50 | 45 | 20 | 36 | 28 | 92 | 102 | 90 | 19% | 87 | 2% | 100% | 12 | 50% | 25% | 5.83 | 7.5 | 70 | 233 | $16 |
| 19 | Proj | **506** | **57** | **23** | **74** | **1** | **258** | **267** | **304** | **442** | **746** | **632** | **786** | **6** | **84** | **0.42** | **47** | **18** | **35** | **27** | **93** | **98** | **86** | **15%** | **81** | **1%** | **87%** | | | | **4.63** | **1.8** | **43** | **145** | **$16** |

## Frazier,Adam

| Age: 27 | Bats: L | Pos: 2B | Health | A | LIMA Plan | B |
|---|---|---|---|---|---|---|
| Ht: 5' 10" | Wt: 180 | | PT/Exp | C | Rand Var | +2 |
| | | | Consist | A | MM | 2253 |

10-35-.277 in 318 AB at PIT. GB% spike, HctX plunge and unfortunate h% wrecked his 1st half. Looked like a different hitter afterward, and 2nd half xPX hints at more. Stable plate skills, speed offer solid foundation despite undeveloped running game. Has work to do vL but... UP: .280 BA, 15 HR, 10 SB.

| Yr | Tm | AB | R | HR | RBI | SB | BA | xBA | OBP | SLG | OPS | vL | vR | bb% | ct% | Eye | G | L | F | h% | HctX | PX | xPX | hr/f | Spd | SBO | SB% | #Wk | DOM | DIS | RC/G | RAR | BPV | BPX | R$ |
|---|---|---|---|---|---|---|---|---|---|---|---|---|---|---|---|---|---|---|---|---|---|---|---|---|---|---|---|---|---|---|---|---|---|---|---|
| 14 | | | | | | | | | | | | | | | | | | | | | | | | | | | | | | | | | | | |
| 15 | aa | 377 | 47 | 1 | 24 | 9 | 281 | | 328 | 356 | 684 | | | 7 | 88 | 0.57 | | | | 32 | | 51 | | | 115 | 15% | 52% | | | | 3.92 | | 41 | 111 | $10 |
| 16 | PIT * | 407 | 52 | 2 | 31 | 19 | 306 | 298 | 366 | 400 | 766 | 840 | 753 | 9 | 86 | 0.70 | 44 | 33 | 23 | 35 | 110 | 59 | 93 | 7% | 141 | 28% | 52% | 16 | 25% | 56% | 4.79 | 1.9 | 54 | 154 | $18 |
| 17 | PIT | 406 | 55 | 6 | 53 | 9 | 276 | 288 | 344 | 399 | 743 | 676 | 754 | 8 | 86 | 0.63 | 48 | 25 | 27 | 31 | 96 | 66 | 59 | 6% | 124 | 12% | 64% | 25 | 44% | 24% | 4.61 | -7.6 | 52 | 158 | $12 |
| 18 | PIT * | 439 | 59 | 10 | 48 | 2 | 251 | 266 | 309 | 397 | 706 | 586 | 853 | 8 | 83 | 0.49 | 49 | 20 | 31 | 28 | 106 | 87 | 79 | 12% | 107 | 8% | 21% | 22 | 59% | 14% | 3.93 | -8.9 | 50 | 167 | $8 |
| 1st Half | | 191 | 26 | 3 | 12 | 1 | 225 | 249 | 289 | 337 | 625 | 620 | 685 | 8 | 84 | 0.55 | 57 | 15 | 28 | 25 | 66 | 58 | 23 | 9% | 146 | 11% | 14% | 12 | 42% | 25% | 2.89 | -10.2 | 43 | 143 | $0 |
| 2nd Half | | 248 | 33 | 7 | 36 | 1 | 271 | 281 | 325 | 443 | 768 | 573 | 1015 | 7 | 82 | 0.44 | 43 | 23 | 34 | 31 | 137 | 110 | 123 | 14% | 91 | 5% | 31% | 10 | 80% | 0% | 4.87 | 1.9 | 60 | 200 | $15 |
| 19 | Proj | **407** | **54** | **9** | **43** | **7** | **269** | **282** | **331** | **413** | **743** | **615** | **772** | **8** | **85** | **0.53** | **48** | **24** | **29** | **30** | **104** | **83** | **76** | **9%** | **112** | **14%** | **48%** | | | | **4.42** | **2.9** | **49** | **165** | **$13** |

## Frazier,Clint

| Age: 24 | Bats: R | Pos: LF | Health | F | LIMA Plan | C+ |
|---|---|---|---|---|---|---|
| Ht: 6' 1" | Wt: 190 | | PT/Exp | D | Rand Var | -2 |
| | | | Consist | B | MM | 3403 |

0-1-.265 in 34 AB at NYY. Feb concussion delayed 2018 start, then lingered as migraines shelved him for good in July. Plus power, patience and speed are all intact, just needs sustained health and success vR to put it all together. This offseason might be your last buy-low opportunity on this one.

| Yr | Tm | AB | R | HR | RBI | SB | BA | xBA | OBP | SLG | OPS | vL | vR | bb% | ct% | Eye | G | L | F | h% | HctX | PX | xPX | hr/f | Spd | SBO | SB% | #Wk | DOM | DIS | RC/G | RAR | BPV | BPX | R$ |
|---|---|---|---|---|---|---|---|---|---|---|---|---|---|---|---|---|---|---|---|---|---|---|---|---|---|---|---|---|---|---|---|---|---|---|---|
| 14 | | | | | | | | | | | | | | | | | | | | | | | | | | | | | | | | | | | |
| 15 | | | | | | | | | | | | | | | | | | | | | | | | | | | | | | | | | | | |
| 16 | a/a | 463 | 70 | 18 | 51 | 12 | 253 | | 319 | 436 | 755 | | | 9 | 71 | 0.34 | | | | 32 | | 120 | | | 108 | 14% | 74% | | | | 4.72 | | 33 | 94 | $14 |
| 17 | NYY * | 407 | 57 | 16 | 54 | 9 | 235 | 242 | 304 | 447 | 751 | 771 | 695 | 9 | 71 | 0.34 | 38 | 17 | 45 | 29 | 115 | 132 | 158 | 10% | 122 | 13% | 80% | 11 | 36% | 36% | 4.55 | -11.0 | 44 | 133 | $9 |
| 18 | NYY * | 224 | 40 | 10 | 18 | 3 | 274 | 276 | 345 | 487 | 832 | 1145 | 530 | 10 | 67 | 0.33 | 52 | 29 | 19 | 37 | 106 | 147 | 139 | 0% | 128 | 9% | 59% | 7 | 14% | 71% | 5.76 | 7.6 | 47 | 157 | $6 |
| 1st Half | | 191 | 33 | 7 | 13 | 3 | 277 | 282 | 345 | 472 | 817 | 1225 | 690 | 9 | 68 | 0.32 | 53 | 33 | 13 | 38 | 116 | 136 | 106 | 0% | 136 | 11% | 59% | 5 | 20% | 60% | 5.59 | 5.4 | 41 | 137 | $8 |
| 2nd Half | | 33 | 7 | 3 | 5 | 0 | 256 | 271 | 345 | 572 | 917 | 933 | 348 | 12 | 65 | 0.39 | 50 | 17 | 33 | 30 | 80 | 208 | 222 | 0% | 107 | 0% | 0% | 2 | 0% | 100% | 6.77 | 2.1 | 86 | 287 | -$4 |
| 19 | Proj | **319** | **50** | **9** | **32** | **7** | **267** | **221** | **330** | **430** | **760** | **762** | **758** | **9** | **70** | **0.32** | **38** | **17** | **45** | **36** | **104** | **113** | **142** | **9%** | **128** | **11%** | **72%** | | | | **4.93** | **3.1** | **23** | **78** | **$12** |

## Frazier,Todd

| Age: 33 | Bats: R | Pos: 3B | Health | C | LIMA Plan | B |
|---|---|---|---|---|---|---|
| Ht: 6'3" | Wt: 220 | | PT/Exp | A | Rand Var | +1 |
| | | | Consist | A | MM | 3115 |

DL stints in May (hamstring) and July (rib-cage) cost him 8 weeks and cut into his production. Through it all, he remained the same low-h% / extreme-FB hitter as ever. Counting stats, hr/f should rebound with better health, with SBs as a bonus. But G/L/F, sub-par speed say BA is stuck on awful. Age adds to risk.

| Yr | Tm | AB | R | HR | RBI | SB | BA | xBA | OBP | SLG | OPS | vL | vR | bb% | ct% | Eye | G | L | F | h% | HctX | PX | xPX | hr/f | Spd | SBO | SB% | #Wk | DOM | DIS | RC/G | RAR | BPV | BPX | R$ |
|---|---|---|---|---|---|---|---|---|---|---|---|---|---|---|---|---|---|---|---|---|---|---|---|---|---|---|---|---|---|---|---|---|---|---|---|
| 14 | CIN | 597 | 88 | 29 | 80 | 20 | 273 | 263 | 336 | 459 | 795 | 750 | 807 | 8 | 77 | 0.37 | 41 | 22 | 37 | 31 | 114 | 127 | 123 | 17% | 92 | 17% | 71% | 27 | 48% | 19% | 5.24 | 26.5 | 54 | 146 | $30 |
| 15 | CIN | 619 | 82 | 35 | 89 | 13 | 255 | 273 | 309 | 498 | 806 | 908 | 773 | 6 | 78 | 0.32 | 33 | 19 | 48 | 28 | 125 | 157 | 155 | 15% | 79 | 17% | 62% | 27 | 63% | 30% | 5.01 | 6.1 | 76 | 205 | $24 |
| 16 | CHW | 590 | 89 | 40 | 98 | 15 | 225 | 245 | 302 | 464 | 767 | 803 | 758 | 10 | 72 | 0.39 | 36 | 16 | 49 | 24 | 92 | 142 | 111 | 19% | 70 | 15% | 75% | 27 | 44% | 30% | 4.57 | -7.3 | 45 | 129 | $19 |
| 17 | 2 AL | 474 | 74 | 27 | 76 | 4 | 213 | 243 | 344 | 428 | 772 | 883 | 736 | 14 | 74 | 0.66 | 34 | 18 | 47 | 23 | 96 | 122 | 122 | 16% | 76 | 5% | 57% | 27 | 44% | 33% | 4.52 | -11.5 | 46 | 139 | $8 |
| 18 | NYM | 408 | 54 | 18 | 59 | 9 | 213 | 228 | 303 | 390 | 693 | 534 | 752 | 10 | 73 | 0.43 | 36 | 19 | 46 | 25 | 109 | 110 | 132 | 13% | 81 | 13% | 69% | 23 | 39% | 39% | 3.70 | -12.3 | 25 | 83 | $10 |
| 1st Half | | 205 | 25 | 9 | 30 | 5 | 220 | 242 | 304 | 385 | 689 | 564 | 733 | 11 | 74 | 0.46 | 38 | 24 | 38 | 25 | 120 | 99 | 130 | 15% | 77 | 9% | 100% | 12 | 33% | 42% | 3.97 | -3.4 | 21 | 70 | $9 |
| 2nd Half | | 203 | 29 | 9 | 29 | 4 | 207 | 215 | 302 | 394 | 696 | 506 | 773 | 10 | 71 | 0.40 | 32 | 14 | 54 | 24 | 98 | 121 | 135 | 11% | 89 | 18% | 50% | 11 | 45% | 36% | 3.43 | -7.0 | 32 | 107 | $10 |
| 19 | Proj | **467** | **67** | **22** | **71** | **7** | **222** | **231** | **315** | **411** | **726** | **664** | **747** | **11** | **73** | **0.46** | **35** | **18** | **47** | **25** | **103** | **115** | **128** | **14%** | **80** | **10%** | **60%** | | | | **4.04** | **-6.8** | **30** | **99** | **$13** |

## Freeman,Freddie

| Age: 29 | Bats: L | Pos: 1B | Health | B | LIMA Plan | D+ |
|---|---|---|---|---|---|---|
| Ht: 6'5" | Wt: 220 | | PT/Exp | A | Rand Var | -1 |
| | | | Consist | B | MM | 4255 |

Launch angle in reverse? Power decline fueled by season-long FB slide; accelerated in 2nd half with hr/f, bb% plunges. At the same time, outstanding HctX / LD / ct% combination kept lofty h%, BA entrenched—and how 'bout that running game? Age, health, track record say he's still near-elite, with... UP: .320 BA.

| Yr | Tm | AB | R | HR | RBI | SB | BA | xBA | OBP | SLG | OPS | vL | vR | bb% | ct% | Eye | G | L | F | h% | HctX | PX | xPX | hr/f | Spd | SBO | SB% | #Wk | DOM | DIS | RC/G | RAR | BPV | BPX | R$ |
|---|---|---|---|---|---|---|---|---|---|---|---|---|---|---|---|---|---|---|---|---|---|---|---|---|---|---|---|---|---|---|---|---|---|---|---|
| 14 | ATL | 607 | 93 | 18 | 78 | 3 | 288 | 283 | 386 | 461 | 847 | 756 | 885 | 13 | 76 | 0.62 | 37 | 31 | 32 | 35 | 131 | 134 | 159 | 12% | 99 | 4% | 43% | 27 | 56% | 22% | 6.17 | 33.8 | 69 | 186 | $24 |
| 15 | ATL | 416 | 62 | 18 | 66 | 3 | 276 | 279 | 370 | 471 | 841 | 656 | 912 | 12 | 76 | 0.57 | 37 | 28 | 36 | 32 | 130 | 133 | 152 | 16% | 82 | 3% | 75% | 22 | 45% | 23% | 6.01 | 7.6 | 62 | 168 | $16 |
| 16 | ATL | 589 | 102 | 34 | 91 | 6 | 302 | 279 | 400 | 569 | 968 | 902 | 1001 | 13 | 71 | 0.52 | 30 | 29 | 41 | 38 | 125 | 173 | 177 | 20% | 110 | 4% | 86% | 27 | 59% | 15% | 8.21 | 46.4 | 83 | 237 | $29 |
| 17 | ATL | 440 | 84 | 28 | 71 | 8 | 307 | 300 | 403 | 586 | 989 | 880 | 1032 | 13 | 78 | 0.68 | 35 | 24 | 41 | 34 | 119 | 157 | 156 | 20% | 101 | 10% | 62% | 21 | 76% | 10% | 8.33 | 29.5 | 97 | 294 | $24 |
| 18 | ATL | 618 | 94 | 23 | 98 | 10 | 309 | 290 | 388 | 505 | 892 | 923 | 878 | 11 | 79 | 0.58 | 36 | 32 | 31 | 36 | 121 | 119 | 123 | 15% | 81 | 7% | 77% | 28 | 61% | 25% | 7.16 | 34.6 | 58 | 193 | $31 |
| 1st Half | | 313 | 52 | 15 | 54 | 6 | 316 | 290 | 408 | 540 | 948 | 1068 | 884 | 13 | 79 | 0.72 | 37 | 29 | 34 | 36 | 124 | 132 | 135 | 18% | 82 | 7% | 75% | 15 | 67% | 27% | 8.17 | 28.8 | 73 | 243 | $36 |
| 2nd Half | | 305 | 42 | 8 | 44 | 4 | 302 | 293 | 365 | 469 | 834 | 754 | 870 | 8 | 79 | 0.43 | 36 | 36 | 28 | 36 | 119 | 107 | 110 | 12% | 87 | 6% | 80% | 13 | 54% | 23% | 6.18 | 11.9 | 45 | 150 | $26 |
| 19 | Proj | **590** | **96** | **26** | **92** | **9** | **304** | **286** | **388** | **522** | **910** | **866** | **930** | **11** | **77** | **0.56** | **35** | **30** | **35** | **36** | **122** | **134** | **141** | **16%** | **101** | **7%** | **71%** | | | | **7.28** | **40.8** | **68** | **226** | **$31** |

JOCK THOMPSON

## Gallo,Joey

| | | | |
|---|---|---|---|
| Age: 25 Bats: L Pos: LF 1B | Health A | LIMA Plan A | |
| Ht: 6' 5" Wt: 235 | PT/Exp B | Rand Var +4 | |
| | Consist C | MM 5215 | |

You can bank on big HRs, along with gawd-awful contact and terrible BA. Age, xBA and ct% uptick hint at improvement, but otherwise stable skills advise not to count on it. Prototypical Three True Outcomes player; HR, BB, Ks were 56% of his 577 plate appearances, putting him among the elite.

| Yr | Tm | AB | R | HR | RBI | SB | BA | xBA | OBP | SLG | OPS | vL | vR | bb% | ct% | Eye | G | L | F | h% | HctX | PX | xPX | hr/f | Spd | SBO | SB% | #Wk | DOM | DIS | RC/G | RAR | BPV | BPX | R$ |
|---|---|---|---|---|---|---|---|---|---|---|---|---|---|---|---|---|---|---|---|---|---|---|---|---|---|---|---|---|---|---|---|---|---|---|---|
| 14 | aa | 250 | 36 | 17 | 46 | 2 | 211 | | 295 | 456 | 750 | | | 11 | 51 | 0.24 | | | | 32 | | 242 | | | 81 | 3% | 100% | | | | 4.38 | | 46 | 124 | $6 |
| 15 | TEX * | 429 | 49 | 24 | 64 | 5 | 210 | 217 | 303 | 433 | 736 | 477 | 836 | 12 | 52 | 0.28 | 35 | 27 | 37 | 33 | 115 | 206 | 185 | 32% | 80 | 5% | 100% | 10 | 40% | 50% | 4.29 | -1.4 | 23 | 62 | $7 |
| 16 | TEX * | 384 | 57 | 21 | 52 | 3 | 204 | 184 | 310 | 434 | 743 | 250 | 374 | 13 | 53 | 0.33 | 17 | 17 | 67 | 31 | 36 | 185 | 100 | 25% | 120 | 3% | 100% | 7 | 0% | 86% | 4.33 | 0.7 | 26 | 74 | $4 |
| 17 | TEX | 449 | 85 | 41 | 80 | 7 | 209 | 237 | 333 | 537 | 869 | 841 | 878 | 14 | 56 | 0.38 | 28 | 18 | 54 | 25 | 106 | 231 | 206 | 30% | 109 | 8% | 78% | 27 | 59% | 30% | 5.57 | 1.7 | 73 | 221 | $13 |
| 18 | TEX | 500 | 82 | 40 | 92 | 3 | 206 | 238 | 312 | 498 | 810 | 820 | 804 | 13 | 59 | 0.36 | 30 | 21 | 50 | 25 | 105 | 213 | 180 | 28% | 80 | 6% | 43% | 28 | 61% | 25% | 4.80 | 3.4 | 57 | 190 | $16 |
| 1st Half | | 279 | 43 | 20 | 44 | 3 | 194 | 219 | 297 | 452 | 748 | 660 | 783 | 12 | 58 | 0.33 | 29 | 17 | 53 | 24 | 106 | 190 | 187 | 23% | 74 | 8% | 60% | 15 | 60% | 40% | 4.07 | -4.7 | 34 | 113 | $15 |
| 2nd Half | | 221 | 39 | 20 | 48 | 0 | 222 | 260 | 331 | 557 | 887 | 989 | 832 | 14 | 59 | 0.40 | 30 | 25 | 45 | 26 | 103 | 243 | 173 | 34% | 94 | 4% | 0% | 13 | 62% | 8% | 5.82 | 8.4 | 88 | 293 | $17 |
| **19** | **Proj** | **516** | **86** | **43** | **92** | **4** | **209** | **237** | **319** | **515** | **834** | **803** | **846** | **13** | **57** | **0.35** | **30** | **21** | **49** | **26** | **106** | **228** | **189** | **30%** | **95** | **6%** | **61%** | | | | **5.14** | **8.8** | **63** | **209** | **$15** |

## Galvis,Freddy

| | | | |
|---|---|---|---|
| Age: 29 Bats: B Pos: SS | Health A | LIMA Plan B | |
| Ht: 5' 10" Wt: 185 | PT/Exp A | Rand Var -1 | |
| | Consist A | MM 2325 | |

Running game deteriorated notably; ct% slide didn't help BA. Salvaged season with more aggressive approach in 2nd half, turning more GB into LD, FB. HctX and xPX were impressive but outlier-ish. Glove fuels AB that fuels counting stats and value, but free agent needs a conducive new home. DN: 400 AB.

| Yr | Tm | AB | R | HR | RBI | SB | BA | xBA | OBP | SLG | OPS | vL | vR | bb% | ct% | Eye | G | L | F | h% | HctX | PX | xPX | hr/f | Spd | SBO | SB% | #Wk | DOM | DIS | RC/G | RAR | BPV | BPX | R$ |
|---|---|---|---|---|---|---|---|---|---|---|---|---|---|---|---|---|---|---|---|---|---|---|---|---|---|---|---|---|---|---|---|---|---|---|---|
| 14 | PHI * | 254 | 30 | 6 | 23 | 2 | 200 | 217 | 248 | 347 | 595 | 496 | 573 | 6 | 76 | 0.27 | 41 | 8 | 51 | 24 | 84 | 112 | 117 | 9% | 106 | 7% | 60% | 12 | 25% | 50% | 2.70 | -4.7 | 40 | 108 | $0 |
| 15 | PHI | 559 | 63 | 7 | 50 | 10 | 263 | 229 | 302 | 343 | 645 | 602 | 662 | 5 | 82 | 0.29 | 41 | 22 | 37 | 31 | 88 | 49 | 89 | 4% | 139 | 7% | 91% | 27 | 19% | 41% | 3.64 | -1.9 | 19 | 51 | $13 |
| 16 | PHI | 584 | 61 | 20 | 67 | 17 | 241 | 253 | 274 | 399 | 673 | 544 | 715 | 4 | 77 | 0.18 | 40 | 23 | 36 | 28 | 83 | 95 | 80 | 13% | 98 | 20% | 74% | 27 | 37% | 30% | 3.62 | -17.6 | 22 | 63 | $14 |
| 17 | PHI | 608 | 71 | 12 | 61 | 14 | 255 | 252 | 309 | 382 | 690 | 638 | 714 | 7 | 82 | 0.41 | 37 | 24 | 39 | 29 | 84 | 71 | 85 | 6% | 125 | 12% | 74% | 27 | 44% | 30% | 3.99 | -9.5 | 37 | 112 | $14 |
| 18 | SD | 602 | 62 | 13 | 67 | 8 | 248 | 239 | 299 | 380 | 680 | 778 | 635 | 7 | 76 | 0.31 | 41 | 22 | 37 | 31 | 112 | 85 | 118 | 8% | 105 | 10% | 57% | 28 | 43% | 43% | 3.77 | -0.9 | 17 | 57 | $13 |
| 1st Half | | 303 | 28 | 4 | 29 | 3 | 238 | 230 | 294 | 343 | 638 | 696 | 614 | 8 | 76 | 0.34 | 44 | 21 | 34 | 30 | 109 | 69 | 113 | 5% | 108 | 9% | 43% | 15 | 40% | 47% | 3.25 | -6.6 | 7 | 23 | $7 |
| 2nd Half | | 299 | 34 | 9 | 38 | 5 | 258 | 247 | 304 | 418 | 722 | 846 | 657 | 6 | 76 | 0.27 | 38 | 23 | 39 | 31 | 115 | 101 | 124 | 10% | 102 | 10% | 71% | 13 | 46% | 38% | 4.33 | 3.2 | 28 | 93 | $19 |
| **19** | **Proj** | **492** | **54** | **12** | **53** | **9** | **248** | **243** | **296** | **387** | **682** | **703** | **673** | **6** | **78** | **0.30** | **40** | **22** | **38** | **30** | **98** | **85** | **103** | **8%** | **110** | **12%** | **68%** | | | | **3.82** | **-2.2** | **22** | **75** | **$13** |

## Gamel,Benjamin

| | | | |
|---|---|---|---|
| Age: 27 Bats: L Pos: LF RF | Health A | LIMA Plan C+ | |
| Ht: 5' 11" Wt: 185 | PT/Exp C | Rand Var 0 | |
| | Consist A | MM 1423 | |

1-19-.272 with 7 SB in 257 AB at SEA. Hit rate again helped maintain AB vR early on; GB spike, LD freefall fueled 2nd half fade. Plate skills ticked up nicely; OBP and running game were pleasant surprises. But power is as anemic as ever, and HctX doesn't help. Part-timer outlook remains intact.

| Yr | Tm | AB | R | HR | RBI | SB | BA | xBA | OBP | SLG | OPS | vL | vR | bb% | ct% | Eye | G | L | F | h% | HctX | PX | xPX | hr/f | Spd | SBO | SB% | #Wk | DOM | DIS | RC/G | RAR | BPV | BPX | R$ |
|---|---|---|---|---|---|---|---|---|---|---|---|---|---|---|---|---|---|---|---|---|---|---|---|---|---|---|---|---|---|---|---|---|---|---|---|
| 14 | aa | 544 | 47 | 2 | 41 | 11 | 234 | | 273 | 301 | 574 | | | 5 | 82 | 0.30 | | | | 28 | | 57 | | | 93 | 13% | 66% | | | | 2.70 | | 14 | 38 | $5 |
| 15 | aaa | 500 | 68 | 10 | 56 | 11 | 276 | | 331 | 427 | 757 | | | 8 | 76 | 0.34 | | | | 35 | | 100 | | | 130 | 13% | 67% | | | | 4.89 | | 39 | 105 | $17 |
| 16 | 2 AL * | 531 | 81 | 7 | 51 | 17 | 273 | 237 | 330 | 375 | 705 | 1162 | 404 | 8 | 77 | 0.36 | 44 | 22 | 34 | 34 | 80 | 68 | 69 | 9% | 115 | 17% | 66% | 9 | 22% | 56% | 4.23 | -0.6 | 13 | 37 | $18 |
| 17 | SEA * | 569 | 73 | 12 | 65 | 5 | 273 | 247 | 327 | 404 | 731 | 699 | 746 | 7 | 76 | 0.34 | 45 | 22 | 33 | 34 | 91 | 79 | 80 | 8% | 123 | 4% | 69% | 24 | 29% | 38% | 4.61 | -13.7 | 22 | 67 | $14 |
| 18 | SEA * | 340 | 51 | 2 | 31 | 10 | 276 | 256 | 349 | 387 | 736 | 663 | 742 | 10 | 78 | 0.51 | 47 | 25 | 28 | 35 | 75 | 74 | 50 | 2% | 130 | 13% | 77% | 23 | 22% | 39% | 4.78 | 1.9 | 31 | 103 | $10 |
| 1st Half | | 175 | 25 | 1 | 12 | 5 | 292 | 272 | 358 | 399 | 757 | 519 | 842 | 9 | 80 | 0.50 | 42 | 32 | 26 | 36 | 75 | 69 | 39 | 3% | 136 | 13% | 71% | 12 | 25% | 42% | 5.10 | 2.5 | 35 | 117 | $9 |
| 2nd Half | | 165 | 26 | 1 | 19 | 5 | 259 | 234 | 341 | 374 | 715 | 880 | 588 | 11 | 75 | 0.51 | 56 | 13 | 32 | 34 | 77 | 79 | 70 | 0% | 118 | 12% | 83% | 11 | 18% | 36% | 4.47 | -0.6 | 25 | 83 | $11 |
| **19** | **Proj** | **319** | **45** | **3** | **32** | **8** | **268** | **245** | **336** | **381** | **717** | **725** | **715** | **9** | **77** | **0.42** | **48** | **21** | **31** | **34** | **82** | **74** | **66** | **4%** | **123** | **11%** | **74%** | | | | **4.40** | **-1.9** | **23** | **78** | **$10** |

## Garcia,Avisail

| | | | |
|---|---|---|---|
| Age: 28 Bats: R Pos: RF | Health D | LIMA Plan C+ | |
| Ht: 6' 4" Wt: 240 | PT/Exp C | Rand Var +2 | |
| | Consist F | MM 3325 | |

19-49-.236 in 381 AB at CHW. Expected h%, BA regression looks overdone. April hamstring strain cost him 2+ months and lingered all year; 2nd half knee woes required October surgery. Despite injuries and chronic GB%, both power and hr/f stepped up. Seemingly only more shelf time stops another $20+ year.

| Yr | Tm | AB | R | HR | RBI | SB | BA | xBA | OBP | SLG | OPS | vL | vR | bb% | ct% | Eye | G | L | F | h% | HctX | PX | xPX | hr/f | Spd | SBO | SB% | #Wk | DOM | DIS | RC/G | RAR | BPV | BPX | R$ |
|---|---|---|---|---|---|---|---|---|---|---|---|---|---|---|---|---|---|---|---|---|---|---|---|---|---|---|---|---|---|---|---|---|---|---|---|
| 14 | CHW * | 222 | 25 | 8 | 31 | 4 | 253 | 242 | 300 | 405 | 705 | 992 | 620 | 6 | 72 | 0.23 | 56 | 15 | 28 | 32 | 81 | 119 | 89 | 19% | 77 | 9% | 80% | 10 | 50% | 30% | 4.17 | 1.7 | 19 | 51 | $6 |
| 15 | CHW | 553 | 66 | 13 | 59 | 7 | 257 | 243 | 309 | 365 | 675 | 759 | 650 | 6 | 75 | 0.26 | 49 | 25 | 27 | 32 | 96 | 73 | 90 | 12% | 98 | 10% | 50% | 27 | 33% | 48% | 3.65 | -18.3 | 0 | 0 | $13 |
| 16 | CHW | 413 | 59 | 12 | 51 | 4 | 245 | 252 | 307 | 385 | 692 | 677 | 696 | 8 | 72 | 0.30 | 55 | 22 | 23 | 31 | 101 | 92 | 77 | 17% | 93 | 8% | 50% | 25 | 36% | 40% | 3.81 | -11.0 | 7 | 20 | $8 |
| 17 | CHW | 518 | 75 | 18 | 80 | 5 | 330 | 275 | 380 | 506 | 885 | 1030 | 837 | 6 | 79 | 0.30 | 52 | 20 | 27 | 39 | 112 | 98 | 89 | 16% | 135 | 5% | 63% | 25 | 48% | 44% | 7.04 | 28.9 | 47 | 142 | $26 |
| 18 | CHW * | 381 | 51 | 22 | 56 | 3 | 240 | 247 | 282 | 455 | 738 | 810 | 690 | 5 | 70 | 0.20 | 48 | 17 | 34 | 28 | 99 | 130 | 101 | 21% | 112 | 5% | 75% | 21 | 33% | 48% | 4.30 | -2.3 | 32 | 107 | $11 |
| 1st Half | | 135 | 15 | 7 | 16 | 0 | 256 | 248 | 269 | 455 | 724 | 667 | 654 | 2 | 71 | 0.06 | 52 | 18 | 30 | 31 | 104 | 122 | 87 | 16% | 120 | 4% | 0% | 8 | 38% | 38% | 4.03 | -1.7 | 23 | 77 | $1 |
| 2nd Half | | 246 | 36 | 15 | 40 | 3 | 232 | 247 | 290 | 455 | 746 | 862 | 706 | 8 | 70 | 0.27 | 47 | 17 | 36 | 27 | 97 | 135 | 108 | 23% | 102 | 6% | 100% | 13 | 31% | 54% | 4.44 | -0.1 | 35 | 117 | $17 |
| **19** | **Proj** | **559** | **76** | **23** | **79** | **5** | **266** | **249** | **316** | **440** | **756** | **856** | **723** | **6** | **73** | **0.24** | **51** | **19** | **30** | **33** | **102** | **106** | **93** | **18%** | **116** | **6%** | **63%** | | | | **4.68** | **3.6** | **16** | **54** | **$20** |

## Garcia,Leury

| | | | |
|---|---|---|---|
| Age: 28 Bats: B Pos: LF CF | Health F | LIMA Plan D+ | |
| Ht: 5' 8" Wt: 180 | PT/Exp D | Rand Var -3 | |
| | Consist A | MM 1423 | |

More DL time, first a month with a strained left knee, then most of Aug-Sept with a balky hamstring that cut into his running game. Even with HR regression, wheels and LD/GB stroke have overcome poor plate skills, soft contact to produce playable BA/SB combo—when he's healthy. Fragility curbs upside.

| Yr | Tm | AB | R | HR | RBI | SB | BA | xBA | OBP | SLG | OPS | vL | vR | bb% | ct% | Eye | G | L | F | h% | HctX | PX | xPX | hr/f | Spd | SBO | SB% | #Wk | DOM | DIS | RC/G | RAR | BPV | BPX | R$ |
|---|---|---|---|---|---|---|---|---|---|---|---|---|---|---|---|---|---|---|---|---|---|---|---|---|---|---|---|---|---|---|---|---|---|---|---|
| 14 | CHW | 145 | 13 | 1 | 6 | 11 | 166 | 190 | 192 | 207 | 399 | 368 | 421 | 3 | 67 | 0.10 | 62 | 14 | 24 | 24 | 57 | 38 | 25 | 4% | 90 | 48% | 92% | 26 | 12% | 73% | 1.41 | -10.8 | -66 | -178 | -$1 |
| 15 | CHW * | 363 | 47 | 3 | 27 | 26 | 257 | 266 | 293 | 336 | 629 | 533 | 444 | 5 | 77 | 0.22 | 100 | 0 | 0 | 33 | 95 | 60 | -16 | 0% | 119 | 43% | 65% | 9 | 0% | 67% | 3.15 | -13.8 | 1 | 3 | $14 |
| 16 | CHW * | 358 | 42 | 6 | 33 | 16 | 264 | 238 | 305 | 363 | 668 | 353 | 755 | 6 | 75 | 0.24 | 54 | 20 | 26 | 34 | 78 | 59 | 68 | 11% | 115 | 28% | 61% | 5 | 0% | 80% | 3.60 | -7.3 | -5 | -14 | $11 |
| 17 | CHW | 300 | 41 | 9 | 33 | 8 | 270 | 271 | 316 | 423 | 739 | 689 | 759 | 4 | 77 | 0.19 | 55 | 21 | 24 | 32 | 83 | 89 | 66 | 11% | 101 | 19% | 62% | 16 | 50% | 44% | 4.25 | -10.4 | 20 | 61 | $9 |
| 18 | CHW | 258 | 23 | 4 | 32 | 12 | 271 | 248 | 303 | 376 | 679 | 794 | 627 | 3 | 73 | 0.13 | 49 | 29 | 23 | 36 | 81 | 63 | 63 | 10% | 137 | 20% | 92% | 22 | 14% | 59% | 4.08 | -3.6 | -6 | -20 | $8 |
| 1st Half | | 149 | 13 | 2 | 15 | 9 | 275 | 256 | 312 | 369 | 681 | 883 | 605 | 3 | 77 | 0.15 | 54 | 25 | 21 | 35 | 91 | 54 | 60 | 9% | 129 | 24% | 100% | 12 | 17% | 50% | 4.23 | -1.6 | -1 | -3 | $9 |
| 2nd Half | | 109 | 10 | 2 | 17 | 3 | 266 | 237 | 289 | 385 | 675 | 700 | 661 | 4 | 68 | 0.11 | 40 | 34 | 26 | 38 | 67 | 76 | 69 | 11% | 128 | 15% | 75% | 10 | 10% | 70% | 3.89 | -2.2 | -20 | -67 | $7 |
| **19** | **Proj** | **269** | **29** | **5** | **31** | **11** | **263** | **247** | **300** | **379** | **679** | **685** | **676** | **4** | **73** | **0.16** | **51** | **25** | **24** | **34** | **76** | **71** | **60** | **11%** | **117** | **23%** | **75%** | | | | **3.82** | **-6.1** | **-1** | **-4** | **$10** |

## Gardner,Brett

| | | | |
|---|---|---|---|
| Age: 35 Bats: L Pos: LF CF | Health A | LIMA Plan B | |
| Ht: 5' 11" Wt: 195 | PT/Exp A | Rand Var +2 | |
| | Consist B | MM 2535 | |

Down year, start to finish. Early GB% surge impeded his production, hung on through July. Unfortunate h% drop killed 2nd half BA and while plate skills were stable, Spd says running game still elite. Age, free agency suggest big turnaround is unlikely. SBs, BA bounce look buyable, but... DN: 400 AB.

| Yr | Tm | AB | R | HR | RBI | SB | BA | xBA | OBP | SLG | OPS | vL | vR | bb% | ct% | Eye | G | L | F | h% | HctX | PX | xPX | hr/f | Spd | SBO | SB% | #Wk | DOM | DIS | RC/G | RAR | BPV | BPX | R$ |
|---|---|---|---|---|---|---|---|---|---|---|---|---|---|---|---|---|---|---|---|---|---|---|---|---|---|---|---|---|---|---|---|---|---|---|---|
| 14 | NYY | 555 | 87 | 17 | 58 | 21 | 256 | 254 | 327 | 422 | 749 | 687 | 775 | 9 | 76 | 0.42 | 42 | 22 | 37 | 31 | 95 | 117 | 91 | 11% | 140 | 18% | 81% | 27 | 48% | 30% | 4.73 | 17.0 | 59 | 159 | $22 |
| 15 | NYY | 571 | 94 | 16 | 66 | 20 | 259 | 247 | 343 | 399 | 742 | 761 | 734 | 10 | 76 | 0.50 | 45 | 21 | 34 | 31 | 88 | 94 | 87 | 11% | 115 | 15% | 80% | 27 | 37% | 48% | 4.70 | 5.1 | 38 | 103 | $22 |
| 16 | NYY | 547 | 80 | 7 | 41 | 16 | 261 | 257 | 351 | 362 | 713 | 645 | 745 | 11 | 81 | 0.66 | 52 | 21 | 27 | 31 | 84 | 61 | 43 | 6% | 128 | 11% | 80% | 27 | 30% | 37% | 4.38 | 1.6 | 34 | 97 | $15 |
| 17 | NYY | 594 | 96 | 21 | 63 | 23 | 264 | 266 | 350 | 428 | 778 | 590 | 840 | 11 | 79 | 0.59 | 44 | 22 | 33 | 30 | 92 | 89 | 79 | 13% | 123 | 16% | 82% | 26 | 38% | 46% | 5.17 | -4.7 | 49 | 148 | $23 |
| 18 | NYY | 530 | 95 | 12 | 45 | 16 | 236 | 247 | 322 | 368 | 690 | 628 | 712 | 11 | 80 | 0.61 | 49 | 18 | 33 | 27 | 81 | 75 | 58 | 8% | 154 | 12% | 89% | 28 | 36% | 61% | 4.03 | -8.7 | 49 | 163 | $15 |
| 1st Half | | 255 | 44 | 5 | 21 | 7 | 255 | 247 | 348 | 373 | 721 | 617 | 753 | 12 | 81 | 0.71 | 53 | 16 | 31 | 30 | 83 | 69 | 58 | 8% | 133 | 10% | 88% | 15 | 47% | 53% | 4.51 | -0.7 | 44 | 147 | $13 |
| 2nd Half | | 275 | 51 | 7 | 24 | 9 | 218 | 244 | 298 | 364 | 661 | 636 | 671 | 10 | 79 | 0.52 | 45 | 19 | 36 | 25 | 79 | 80 | 58 | 9% | 154 | 14% | 90% | 13 | 23% | 69% | 3.62 | -8.3 | 48 | 160 | $16 |
| **19** | **Proj** | **532** | **90** | **15** | **49** | **18** | **257** | **254** | **340** | **402** | **743** | **655** | **775** | **11** | **79** | **0.58** | **47** | **20** | **33** | **30** | **85** | **83** | **64** | **11%** | **141** | **13%** | **85%** | | | | **4.73** | **2.1** | **47** | **157** | **$20** |

## Garver,Mitch

| | | | |
|---|---|---|---|
| Age: 28 Bats: R Pos: CA | Health A | LIMA Plan C | |
| Ht: 6' 1" Wt: 220 | PT/Exp C | Rand Var -2 | |
| | Consist C | MM 3223 | |

Late-blooming rookie started slowly and spent half of Sept in MLB concussion protocol. But after June, HUGE across-the-board growth in BA/contact and power metrics, vL and vR. Late injury leaves questions, as does 2nd half sample size—and defense is a work-in-progress. But there are several paths to profit.

| Yr | Tm | AB | R | HR | RBI | SB | BA | xBA | OBP | SLG | OPS | vL | vR | bb% | ct% | Eye | G | L | F | h% | HctX | PX | xPX | hr/f | Spd | SBO | SB% | #Wk | DOM | DIS | RC/G | RAR | BPV | BPX | R$ |
|---|---|---|---|---|---|---|---|---|---|---|---|---|---|---|---|---|---|---|---|---|---|---|---|---|---|---|---|---|---|---|---|---|---|---|---|
| 14 | | | | | | | | | | | | | | | | | | | | | | | | | | | | | | | | | | | |
| 15 | | | | | | | | | | | | | | | | | | | | | | | | | | | | | | | | | | | |
| 16 | a/a | 434 | 42 | 10 | 62 | 1 | 241 | | 306 | 373 | 679 | | | 9 | 73 | 0.35 | | | | 31 | | 94 | | | 74 | 4% | 20% | | | | 3.71 | | 10 | 29 | $5 |
| 17 | MIN * | 366 | 55 | 16 | 43 | 2 | 256 | 254 | 346 | 477 | 822 | 762 | 530 | 12 | 70 | 0.46 | 45 | 16 | 39 | 32 | 91 | 143 | 95 | 0% | 106 | 2% | 100% | 8 | 13% | 50% | 5.68 | 16.4 | 52 | 158 | $8 |
| 18 | MIN | 302 | 38 | 7 | 45 | 0 | 268 | 246 | 335 | 414 | 749 | 629 | 806 | 9 | 76 | 0.40 | 40 | 23 | 38 | 33 | 114 | 95 | 122 | 8% | 107 | 0% | 0% | 26 | 46% | 46% | 4.79 | 12.3 | 32 | 107 | $7 |
| 1st Half | | 144 | 16 | 2 | 8 | 0 | 250 | 233 | 321 | 347 | 668 | 524 | 733 | 8 | 72 | 0.32 | 41 | 27 | 32 | 34 | 90 | 73 | 63 | 6% | 89 | 0% | 0% | 14 | 36% | 57% | 3.68 | 1.0 | -10 | -33 | -$1 |
| 2nd Half | | 158 | 22 | 5 | 37 | 0 | 285 | 260 | 349 | 475 | 823 | 720 | 874 | 9 | 80 | 0.52 | 39 | 19 | 42 | 33 | 135 | 113 | 170 | 9% | 123 | 0% | 0% | 12 | 58% | 33% | 5.93 | 11.0 | 69 | 230 | $13 |
| **19** | **Proj** | **379** | **50** | **9** | **55** | **1** | **261** | **242** | **336** | **410** | **746** | **634** | **799** | **10** | **74** | **0.42** | **40** | **22** | **38** | **33** | **117** | **102** | **127** | **8%** | **108** | **1%** | **69%** | | | | **4.72** | **14.0** | **18** | **62** | **$10** |

JOCK THOMPSON

## Gattis,Evan

| Age: 32 | Bats: R | Pos: DH | Health | B | LIMA Plan | D+ |
|---|---|---|---|---|---|---|
| Ht: 6' 4" | Wt: 270 | | PT/Exp | C | Rand Var | +3 |
| | | | Consist | B | MM | 4033 |

HR returned with hr/f rebound and FB% spike. But inconsistency reigns: ct% turned south again, 2nd half h%, HctX torpedoed BA. Logged 20 HR, .256 BA May thru July but 5 HR, .184 BA otherwise. Now eligible at DH only, his age and position-challenged volatility point to risky AB.

| Yr Tm | AB | R | HR | RBI | SB | BA | xBA | OBP | SLG | OPS | vL | vR | bb% | ct% | Eye | G | L | F | h% | HctX | PX | xPX | hr/f | Spd | SBO | SB% | #Wk | DOM | DIS | RC/G | RAR | BPV | BPX | R$ |
|---|---|---|---|---|---|---|---|---|---|---|---|---|---|---|---|---|---|---|---|---|---|---|---|---|---|---|---|---|---|---|---|---|---|---|
| 14 ATL | 369 | 41 | 22 | 52 | 0 | 263 | 259 | 317 | 493 | 810 | 970 | 773 | 5 | 74 | 0.23 | 39 | 17 | 45 | 30 | 123 | 163 | 165 | 18% | 68 | 0% | 0% | 24 | 50% | 25% | 5.19 | 12.2 | 59 | 159 | $13 |
| 15 HOU | 566 | 66 | 27 | 88 | 0 | 246 | 267 | 285 | 463 | 748 | 698 | 775 | 5 | 79 | 0.25 | 46 | 17 | 37 | 27 | 110 | 126 | 116 | 16% | 115 | 1% | 0% | 27 | 48% | 30% | 4.40 | -17.5 | 63 | 170 | $14 |
| 16 HOU * | 487 | 64 | 36 | 79 | 2 | 254 | 265 | 316 | 517 | 833 | 886 | 795 | 8 | 73 | 0.33 | 41 | 18 | 41 | 28 | 96 | 157 | 119 | 24% | 61 | 3% | 67% | 24 | 63% | 21% | 5.56 | 0.8 | 53 | 151 | $16 |
| 17 HOU | 300 | 41 | 12 | 55 | 0 | 263 | 277 | 311 | 457 | 767 | 728 | 783 | 6 | 83 | 0.36 | 37 | 21 | 42 | 28 | 113 | 109 | 82 | 11% | 50 | 2% | 0% | 23 | 61% | 22% | 4.75 | -0.9 | 49 | 148 | $7 |
| 18 HOU | 407 | 49 | 25 | 78 | 1 | 226 | 246 | 284 | 452 | 736 | 816 | 693 | 7 | 75 | 0.33 | 36 | 17 | 47 | 24 | 92 | 131 | 103 | 17% | 49 | 1% | 100% | 28 | 39% | 32% | 4.24 | -3.2 | 37 | 123 | $11 |
| 1st Half | 242 | 32 | 15 | 54 | 1 | 248 | 256 | 306 | 488 | 794 | 785 | 799 | 7 | 75 | 0.31 | 34 | 19 | 48 | 27 | 100 | 143 | 110 | 17% | 63 | 2% | 100% | 15 | 40% | 20% | 5.03 | 3.7 | 49 | 163 | $17 |
| 2nd Half | 165 | 17 | 10 | 24 | 0 | 194 | 223 | 251 | 400 | 651 | 872 | 553 | 8 | 76 | 0.35 | 40 | 14 | 46 | 19 | 80 | 113 | 93 | 17% | 47 | 0% | 0% | 13 | 38% | 46% | 3.25 | -6.6 | 25 | 83 | $1 |
| **19 Proj** | **358** | **44** | **20** | **62** | **1** | **237** | **252** | **291** | **456** | **747** | **814** | **716** | **7** | **77** | **0.32** | **38** | **18** | **44** | **25** | **98** | **125** | **102** | **17%** | **54** | **1%** | **54%** | | | | **4.40** | **-1.2** | **36** | **119** | **$8** |

## Gennett,Scooter

| Age: 29 | Bats: L | Pos: 2B | Health | A | LIMA Plan | B |
|---|---|---|---|---|---|---|
| Ht: 5' 10" | Wt: 185 | | PT/Exp | A | Rand Var | -5 |
| | | | Consist | B | MM | 3235 |

Strong encore to 2017, even with expected hr/f regression and power retrenchment. Continued to nudge plate skills and HctX upward, as elevated 1st half h% bumped him into the .300 club. That xBA points to some BA downside, but both age and Health say he'll be productive again.

| Yr Tm | AB | R | HR | RBI | SB | BA | xBA | OBP | SLG | OPS | vL | vR | bb% | ct% | Eye | G | L | F | h% | HctX | PX | xPX | hr/f | Spd | SBO | SB% | #Wk | DOM | DIS | RC/G | RAR | BPV | BPX | R$ |
|---|---|---|---|---|---|---|---|---|---|---|---|---|---|---|---|---|---|---|---|---|---|---|---|---|---|---|---|---|---|---|---|---|---|---|
| 14 MIL | 440 | 55 | 9 | 54 | 6 | 289 | 285 | 320 | 434 | 754 | 253 | 802 | 5 | 85 | 0.33 | 41 | 25 | 34 | 32 | 105 | 105 | 92 | 7% | 93 | 8% | 67% | 27 | 52% | 22% | 4.95 | 19.3 | 62 | 168 | $16 |
| 15 MIL * | 450 | 50 | 7 | 37 | 1 | 262 | 262 | 285 | 384 | 670 | 310 | 713 | 3 | 82 | 0.19 | 49 | 22 | 30 | 30 | 78 | 80 | 77 | 7% | 122 | 5% | 19% | 24 | 38% | 25% | 3.64 | -6.9 | 38 | 103 | $7 |
| 16 MIL | 498 | 58 | 14 | 56 | 8 | 263 | 256 | 317 | 412 | 728 | 708 | 733 | 7 | 77 | 0.33 | 44 | 22 | 35 | 32 | 91 | 97 | 90 | 11% | 87 | 7% | 89% | 26 | 42% | 38% | 4.55 | -4.5 | 28 | 80 | $13 |
| 17 CIN | 461 | 80 | 27 | 97 | 3 | 295 | 272 | 342 | 531 | 874 | 691 | 930 | 6 | 75 | 0.26 | 41 | 21 | 38 | 34 | 105 | 131 | 125 | 21% | 106 | 4% | 60% | 27 | 44% | 41% | 6.42 | 18.0 | 52 | 158 | $22 |
| 18 CIN | 584 | 86 | 23 | 92 | 4 | 310 | 264 | 357 | 490 | 847 | 774 | 882 | 7 | 79 | 0.34 | 40 | 24 | 36 | 36 | 112 | 105 | 113 | 14% | 96 | 4% | 67% | 27 | 41% | 30% | 6.41 | 33.9 | 42 | 140 | $27 |
| 1st Half | 304 | 48 | 13 | 54 | 2 | 332 | 277 | 372 | 526 | 898 | 958 | 874 | 6 | 79 | 0.31 | 38 | 26 | 36 | 39 | 116 | 117 | 105 | 15% | 88 | 2% | 100% | 15 | 47% | 33% | 7.56 | 26.9 | 50 | 167 | $33 |
| 2nd Half | 280 | 38 | 10 | 38 | 2 | 286 | 252 | 342 | 450 | 792 | 609 | 891 | 7 | 78 | 0.36 | 42 | 21 | 36 | 33 | 108 | 92 | 122 | 13% | 112 | 5% | 50% | 12 | 33% | 25% | 5.31 | 9.0 | 37 | 123 | $21 |
| **19 Proj** | **558** | **81** | **22** | **87** | **5** | **288** | **262** | **335** | **470** | **804** | **694** | **843** | **6** | **78** | **0.30** | **42** | **22** | **36** | **33** | **105** | **107** | **111** | **14%** | **100** | **5%** | **66%** | | | | **5.54** | **21.4** | **37** | **125** | **$24** |

## Goldschmidt,Paul

| Age: 31 | Bats: R | Pos: 1B | Health | A | LIMA Plan | D+ |
|---|---|---|---|---|---|---|
| Ht: 6' 3" | Wt: 225 | | PT/Exp | A | Rand Var | -1 |
| | | | Consist | B | MM | 4345 |

Paused for 19% h% in May (.144 BA) before resuming ongoing assault on h% norms and general overall excellence. Nothing wrong with 2nd half BA, plate skills remain stable, power on-point as ever. SBO% decline fueled SB slide, but rebound to double-digits seems doable. Still a stud.

| Yr Tm | AB | R | HR | RBI | SB | BA | xBA | OBP | SLG | OPS | vL | vR | bb% | ct% | Eye | G | L | F | h% | HctX | PX | xPX | hr/f | Spd | SBO | SB% | #Wk | DOM | DIS | RC/G | RAR | BPV | BPX | R$ |
|---|---|---|---|---|---|---|---|---|---|---|---|---|---|---|---|---|---|---|---|---|---|---|---|---|---|---|---|---|---|---|---|---|---|---|
| 14 ARI | 406 | 75 | 19 | 69 | 9 | 300 | 297 | 396 | 542 | 938 | 1115 | 894 | 13 | 73 | 0.58 | 45 | 22 | 33 | 37 | 139 | 194 | 173 | 19% | 105 | 9% | 75% | 19 | 58% | 16% | 7.78 | 40.4 | 107 | 289 | $24 |
| 15 ARI | 567 | 103 | 33 | 110 | 21 | 321 | 284 | 435 | 570 | 1005 | 1081 | 984 | 17 | 73 | 0.78 | 42 | 23 | 35 | 39 | 132 | 169 | 152 | 22% | 96 | 11% | 81% | 27 | 70% | 7% | 9.42 | 61.9 | 93 | 251 | $42 |
| 16 ARI | 579 | 106 | 24 | 95 | 32 | 297 | 274 | 411 | 489 | 899 | 1070 | 850 | 16 | 74 | 0.73 | 46 | 25 | 29 | 37 | 112 | 122 | 106 | 19% | 98 | 17% | 86% | 27 | 52% | 22% | 7.48 | 34.6 | 57 | 163 | $37 |
| 17 ARI | 558 | 117 | 36 | 120 | 18 | 297 | 284 | 404 | 563 | 966 | 1013 | 952 | 14 | 74 | 0.64 | 46 | 19 | 35 | 35 | 132 | 154 | 160 | 25% | 105 | 12% | 78% | 27 | 59% | 15% | 8.14 | 34.7 | 80 | 242 | $35 |
| 18 ARI | 593 | 95 | 33 | 83 | 7 | 290 | 268 | 389 | 533 | 922 | 966 | 904 | 13 | 71 | 0.52 | 39 | 25 | 36 | 36 | 121 | 153 | 139 | 22% | 117 | 6% | 64% | 28 | 54% | 29% | 7.25 | 35.7 | 69 | 230 | $28 |
| 1st Half | 303 | 56 | 17 | 42 | 2 | 264 | 261 | 374 | 515 | 888 | 1101 | 809 | 14 | 68 | 0.50 | 38 | 25 | 37 | 33 | 122 | 161 | 153 | 22% | 137 | 4% | 50% | 15 | 53% | 33% | 6.39 | 14.3 | 73 | 243 | $25 |
| 2nd Half | 290 | 39 | 16 | 41 | 5 | 317 | 274 | 405 | 552 | 957 | 842 | 1009 | 13 | 73 | 0.55 | 39 | 25 | 36 | 39 | 119 | 145 | 126 | 21% | 91 | 7% | 71% | 13 | 54% | 23% | 8.25 | 27.3 | 64 | 213 | $30 |
| **19 Proj** | **571** | **100** | **31** | **95** | **10** | **298** | **272** | **401** | **537** | **937** | **983** | **921** | **14** | **73** | **0.60** | **42** | **23** | **35** | **36** | **123** | **149** | **141** | **22%** | **108** | **7%** | **74%** | | | | **7.71** | **46.6** | **67** | **223** | **$32** |

## Gomes,Yan

| Age: 31 | Bats: R | Pos: CA | Health | C | LIMA Plan | D+ |
|---|---|---|---|---|---|---|
| Ht: 6' 2" | Wt: 215 | | PT/Exp | C | Rand Var | -4 |
| | | | Consist | C | MM | 3023 |

Performance, underlying metrics now mirror 2014 minus a few AB. Health is key; and he's avoided the DL for past 2 years. Plate skills hint at some BA regression, but ultra-aggressive 2nd half approach yielded ct%, HctX, LD% spikes that kept his value soaring. With continued durability, a worthy CA option.

| Yr Tm | AB | R | HR | RBI | SB | BA | xBA | OBP | SLG | OPS | vL | vR | bb% | ct% | Eye | G | L | F | h% | HctX | PX | xPX | hr/f | Spd | SBO | SB% | #Wk | DOM | DIS | RC/G | RAR | BPV | BPX | R$ |
|---|---|---|---|---|---|---|---|---|---|---|---|---|---|---|---|---|---|---|---|---|---|---|---|---|---|---|---|---|---|---|---|---|---|---|
| 14 CLE | 485 | 61 | 21 | 74 | 0 | 278 | 266 | 313 | 472 | 785 | 879 | 745 | 5 | 75 | 0.20 | 37 | 24 | 39 | 33 | 101 | 139 | 128 | 14% | 102 | 0% | 0% | 26 | 54% | 23% | 5.21 | 25.9 | 54 | 146 | $18 |
| 15 CLE | 363 | 38 | 12 | 45 | 0 | 231 | 248 | 267 | 391 | 659 | 545 | 702 | 3 | 71 | 0.13 | 34 | 26 | 40 | 29 | 86 | 120 | 102 | 11% | 63 | 0% | 0% | 20 | 40% | 40% | 3.35 | -4.2 | 9 | 24 | $4 |
| 16 CLE | 251 | 22 | 9 | 34 | 0 | 167 | 221 | 201 | 327 | 527 | 740 | 445 | 3 | 73 | 0.13 | 39 | 16 | 45 | 19 | 80 | 102 | 99 | 11% | 80 | 0% | 0% | 18 | 33% | 33% | 1.96 | -15.5 | 5 | 14 | -$4 |
| 17 CLE | 341 | 43 | 14 | 56 | 0 | 232 | 223 | 309 | 399 | 708 | 848 | 644 | 8 | 71 | 0.31 | 41 | 17 | 42 | 29 | 84 | 103 | 109 | 14% | 74 | 0% | 0% | 27 | 33% | 41% | 3.91 | -2.2 | 7 | 21 | $4 |
| 18 CLE | 403 | 52 | 16 | 48 | 0 | 266 | 251 | 313 | 449 | 762 | 840 | 731 | 5 | 70 | 0.18 | 32 | 27 | 41 | 34 | 112 | 125 | 142 | 14% | 95 | 0% | 0% | 27 | 44% | 44% | 4.71 | 15.5 | 22 | 73 | $10 |
| 1st Half | 205 | 26 | 9 | 24 | 0 | 249 | 231 | 314 | 449 | 763 | 1043 | 640 | 7 | 66 | 0.23 | 32 | 21 | 47 | 33 | 102 | 145 | 153 | 14% | 95 | 0% | 0% | 15 | 47% | 40% | 4.62 | 7.1 | 24 | 80 | $9 |
| 2nd Half | 198 | 26 | 7 | 24 | 0 | 283 | 273 | 311 | 449 | 760 | 584 | 820 | 2 | 75 | 0.10 | 32 | 32 | 36 | 35 | 123 | 107 | 132 | 13% | 94 | 0% | 0% | 12 | 42% | 50% | 4.80 | 7.5 | 22 | 73 | $12 |
| **19 Proj** | **399** | **48** | **15** | **54** | **0** | **248** | **241** | **295** | **421** | **716** | **799** | **683** | **5** | **72** | **0.18** | **35** | **23** | **41** | **31** | **100** | **114** | **124** | **13%** | **84** | **0%** | **0%** | | | | **4.07** | **7.4** | **0** | **0** | **$10** |

## Gomez,Carlos

| Age: 33 | Bats: R | Pos: RF | Health | C | LIMA Plan | D+ |
|---|---|---|---|---|---|---|
| Ht: 6' 3" | Wt: 220 | | PT/Exp | C | Rand Var | +3 |
| | | | Consist | D | MM | 3413 |

1st half train-wreck killed any 2nd half opportunity for potential 2019 suitors. Expected power flickered late, but power metrics in recent years are all over the place. Running game remains the one reliable piece of this profile, but age, mediocre plate skills leave his AB hanging by a thread.

| Yr Tm | AB | R | HR | RBI | SB | BA | xBA | OBP | SLG | OPS | vL | vR | bb% | ct% | Eye | G | L | F | h% | HctX | PX | xPX | hr/f | Spd | SBO | SB% | #Wk | DOM | DIS | RC/G | RAR | BPV | BPX | R$ |
|---|---|---|---|---|---|---|---|---|---|---|---|---|---|---|---|---|---|---|---|---|---|---|---|---|---|---|---|---|---|---|---|---|---|---|
| 14 MIL | 574 | 95 | 23 | 73 | 34 | 284 | 262 | 356 | 477 | 833 | 828 | 835 | 7 | 75 | 0.33 | 38 | 22 | 41 | 34 | 117 | 142 | 132 | 13% | 122 | 31% | 74% | 26 | 54% | 27% | 5.63 | 28.7 | 68 | 184 | $36 |
| 15 2 TM | 435 | 61 | 12 | 56 | 17 | 255 | 251 | 314 | 409 | 724 | 646 | 745 | 6 | 77 | 0.31 | 43 | 19 | 38 | 31 | 101 | 110 | 99 | 10% | 90 | 26% | 65% | 23 | 22% | 35% | 4.09 | -8.7 | 37 | 100 | $16 |
| 16 2 AL * | 444 | 48 | 14 | 55 | 18 | 230 | 227 | 285 | 383 | 668 | 636 | 699 | 7 | 66 | 0.23 | 44 | 21 | 35 | 32 | 81 | 110 | 87 | 14% | 109 | 25% | 74% | 25 | 20% | 52% | 3.58 | -15.3 | 2 | 6 | $11 |
| 17 TEX | 368 | 51 | 17 | 51 | 13 | 255 | 238 | 340 | 462 | 802 | 645 | 852 | 7 | 65 | 0.24 | 39 | 21 | 40 | 34 | 103 | 141 | 116 | 17% | 92 | 21% | 72% | 22 | 36% | 36% | 4.87 | -0.6 | 19 | 58 | $13 |
| 18 TAM | 360 | 42 | 9 | 32 | 12 | 208 | 209 | 298 | 336 | 634 | 580 | 662 | 6 | 71 | 0.24 | 33 | 21 | 46 | 27 | 80 | 84 | 89 | 8% | 105 | 20% | 80% | 27 | 22% | 63% | 2.85 | -18.7 | 0 | 0 | $5 |
| 1st Half | 238 | 25 | 7 | 17 | 4 | 197 | 205 | 274 | 332 | 606 | 636 | 593 | 6 | 71 | 0.23 | 32 | 21 | 47 | 25 | 78 | 83 | 82 | 9% | 116 | 15% | 57% | 15 | 20% | 60% | 2.52 | -14.7 | -2 | -7 | $4 |
| 2nd Half | 122 | 17 | 2 | 15 | 8 | 230 | 218 | 343 | 344 | 687 | 497 | 815 | 7 | 73 | 0.27 | 35 | 21 | 44 | 30 | 84 | 85 | 101 | 5% | 90 | 30% | 100% | 12 | 25% | 67% | 3.56 | -3.3 | 3 | 10 | $9 |
| **19 Proj** | **293** | **38** | **10** | **34** | **13** | **234** | **226** | **319** | **393** | **713** | **592** | **765** | **7** | **70** | **0.25** | **37** | **21** | **42** | **30** | **90** | **109** | **100** | **11%** | **100** | **24%** | **81%** | | | | **3.79** | **-6.0** | **16** | **53** | **$10** |

## Gonzalez,Carlos

| Age: 33 | Bats: L | Pos: RF | Health | B | LIMA Plan | B |
|---|---|---|---|---|---|---|
| Ht: 6' 1" | Wt: 220 | | PT/Exp | A | Rand Var | -1 |
| | | | Consist | B | MM | 4235 |

No longer mashing like 2015-16; age, recent hr/f suggest that's not coming back. Residual power, enduring plate skills offer value, particularly vR and at Coors Field—and therein lies the problem. As he seeks a new employer, he carries a career road OPS of .728. And a DN: 400 AB, 12 HR, .250 BA.

| Yr Tm | AB | R | HR | RBI | SB | BA | xBA | OBP | SLG | OPS | vL | vR | bb% | ct% | Eye | G | L | F | h% | HctX | PX | xPX | hr/f | Spd | SBO | SB% | #Wk | DOM | DIS | RC/G | RAR | BPV | BPX | R$ |
|---|---|---|---|---|---|---|---|---|---|---|---|---|---|---|---|---|---|---|---|---|---|---|---|---|---|---|---|---|---|---|---|---|---|---|
| 14 COL | 260 | 35 | 11 | 38 | 3 | 238 | 256 | 292 | 431 | 723 | 635 | 766 | 7 | 73 | 0.27 | 47 | 15 | 38 | 28 | 109 | 146 | 119 | 15% | 80 | 6% | 100% | 15 | 40% | 40% | 4.25 | 1.2 | 49 | 132 | $6 |
| 15 COL | 554 | 87 | 40 | 97 | 2 | 271 | 283 | 325 | 540 | 864 | 530 | 997 | 8 | 76 | 0.35 | 47 | 16 | 36 | 29 | 114 | 166 | 126 | 26% | 81 | 2% | 100% | 27 | 63% | 19% | 6.19 | 21.0 | 78 | 211 | $25 |
| 16 COL | 584 | 87 | 25 | 100 | 2 | 298 | 282 | 350 | 505 | 855 | 786 | 883 | 7 | 78 | 0.36 | 46 | 21 | 33 | 35 | 116 | 129 | 127 | 17% | 84 | 3% | 50% | 27 | 52% | 26% | 6.34 | 26.8 | 57 | 163 | $24 |
| 17 COL | 470 | 72 | 14 | 57 | 3 | 262 | 257 | 339 | 423 | 762 | 561 | 836 | 10 | 75 | 0.47 | 49 | 20 | 32 | 32 | 97 | 105 | 101 | 12% | 83 | 2% | 100% | 25 | 32% | 28% | 5.02 | -2.2 | 31 | 94 | $11 |
| 18 COL | 463 | 71 | 16 | 64 | 5 | 276 | 257 | 329 | 467 | 796 | 719 | 828 | 7 | 76 | 0.33 | 48 | 16 | 36 | 34 | 98 | 120 | 99 | 13% | 100 | 6% | 71% | 27 | 37% | 37% | 5.40 | 13.2 | 45 | 150 | $16 |
| 1st Half | 213 | 30 | 7 | 29 | 3 | 268 | 246 | 319 | 437 | 756 | 617 | 822 | 7 | 74 | 0.30 | 50 | 17 | 33 | 33 | 87 | 106 | 77 | 13% | 100 | 7% | 75% | 14 | 36% | 36% | 4.88 | 2.6 | 26 | 87 | $12 |
| 2nd Half | 250 | 41 | 9 | 35 | 2 | 284 | 266 | 338 | 492 | 830 | 822 | 833 | 7 | 77 | 0.35 | 46 | 16 | 38 | 34 | 107 | 132 | 116 | 12% | 98 | 5% | 67% | 13 | 38% | 38% | 5.86 | 9.9 | 61 | 203 | $20 |
| **19 Proj** | **419** | **64** | **15** | **59** | **3** | **262** | **260** | **320** | **453** | **773** | **662** | **818** | **8** | **76** | **0.35** | **48** | **18** | **35** | **31** | **102** | **121** | **107** | **14%** | **92** | **5%** | **75%** | | | | **5.01** | **6.7** | **43** | **143** | **$15** |

## Gonzalez,Erik

| Age: 27 | Bats: R | Pos: 2B 3B | Health | A | LIMA Plan | D |
|---|---|---|---|---|---|---|
| Ht: 6' 3" | Wt: 195 | | PT/Exp | F | Rand Var | 0 |
| | | | Consist | B | MM | 2431 |

Versatile bench utility owns good speed, has flashed pop, HctX in limited MLB experience. Historically elevated h% is a plus; so is 2nd half ct% surge even in a small sample. But any potential life in his bat is being suffocated by chronically poor plate patience and GB%. We'll pass until something changes.

| Yr Tm | AB | R | HR | RBI | SB | BA | xBA | OBP | SLG | OPS | vL | vR | bb% | ct% | Eye | G | L | F | h% | HctX | PX | xPX | hr/f | Spd | SBO | SB% | #Wk | DOM | DIS | RC/G | RAR | BPV | BPX | R$ |
|---|---|---|---|---|---|---|---|---|---|---|---|---|---|---|---|---|---|---|---|---|---|---|---|---|---|---|---|---|---|---|---|---|---|---|
| 14 aa | 129 | 17 | 1 | 13 | 5 | 314 | | 342 | 404 | 746 | | | 4 | 79 | 0.21 | | | | 39 | | 67 | | | 117 | 16% | 81% | | | | 5.20 | | 16 | 43 | $5 |
| 15 a/a | 549 | 61 | 8 | 60 | 16 | 237 | | 267 | 343 | 610 | | | 4 | 80 | 0.20 | | | | 28 | | 70 | | | 108 | 20% | 67% | | | | 2.99 | | 17 | 46 | $11 |
| 16 CLE * | 445 | 53 | 9 | 43 | 10 | 272 | 274 | 299 | 407 | 707 | 533 | 727 | 4 | 78 | 0.17 | 75 | 13 | 13 | 33 | 119 | 92 | 7 | 0% | 112 | 23% | 44% | 7 | 0% | 100% | 3.86 | -11.4 | 29 | 83 | $12 |
| 17 CLE * | 270 | 34 | 9 | 21 | 5 | 236 | 232 | 260 | 384 | 644 | 596 | 736 | 3 | 63 | 0.09 | 58 | 21 | 22 | 34 | 82 | 100 | 94 | 25% | 145 | 16% | 61% | 18 | 28% | 50% | 3.22 | -11.5 | -14 | -42 | $3 |
| 18 CLE | 136 | 17 | 1 | 16 | 3 | 265 | 257 | 301 | 375 | 676 | 566 | 755 | 3 | 75 | 0.15 | 55 | 22 | 23 | 35 | 108 | 82 | 77 | 4% | 113 | 10% | 100% | 26 | 23% | 50% | 3.90 | -0.6 | 9 | 30 | $1 |
| 1st Half | 75 | 8 | 1 | 13 | 1 | 293 | 263 | 338 | 453 | 791 | 779 | 799 | 5 | 71 | 0.18 | 47 | 26 | 26 | 40 | 108 | 121 | 95 | 7% | 107 | 6% | 100% | 14 | 21% | 50% | 5.47 | 2.7 | 24 | 80 | $2 |
| 2nd Half | 61 | 9 | 0 | 3 | 2 | 230 | 247 | 254 | 279 | 533 | 327 | 697 | 2 | 80 | 0.08 | 65 | 17 | 19 | 29 | 109 | 40 | 56 | 0% | 120 | 17% | 100% | 12 | 25% | 50% | 2.38 | -3.3 | -5 | -17 | $1 |
| **19 Proj** | **169** | **22** | **3** | **16** | **4** | **255** | **255** | **285** | **382** | **668** | **542** | **747** | **3** | **74** | **0.13** | **57** | **21** | **22** | **33** | **98** | **87** | **81** | **12%** | **123** | **15%** | **75%** | | | | **3.65** | **-2.6** | **5** | **17** | **$5** |

JOCK THOMPSON

## Gonzalez,Marwin

| | | | |
|---|---|---|---|
| Age: 30 Bats: B Pos: LF SS 2B | Health A | LIMA Plan B | |
| Ht: 6' 1" Wt: 205 | PT/Exp B | Rand Var +1 | |
| | Consist F | MM 3135 | |

2017 h% returned to earth and running game looks like a fleeting memory. But following slow start, post-May rebound is optimistic. 2nd half ct%, HctX spikes brought BA/xBA back to life and goosed hr/f; xPX hints at more to come. Not a .300 hitter, but versatile production still offers value.

| Yr Tm | AB | R | HR | RBI | SB | BA | xBA | OBP | SLG | OPS | vL | vR | bb% | ct% | Eye | G | L | F | h% | HctX | PX | xPX | hr/f | Spd | SBO | SB% | #Wk | DOM | DIS | RC/G | RAR | BPV | BPX | R$ |
|---|---|---|---|---|---|---|---|---|---|---|---|---|---|---|---|---|---|---|---|---|---|---|---|---|---|---|---|---|---|---|---|---|---|---|
| 14 HOU | 285 | 33 | 6 | 23 | 2 | 277 | 253 | 327 | 400 | 727 | 776 | 719 | 5 | 80 | 0.29 | 52 | 18 | 30 | 33 | 92 | 92 | 68 | 9% | 91 | 8% | 33% | 26 | 46% | 38% | 4.26 | 4.6 | 32 | 86 | $7 |
| 15 HOU | 344 | 44 | 12 | 34 | 4 | 279 | 265 | 317 | 442 | 759 | 843 | 701 | 4 | 78 | 0.22 | 44 | 23 | 33 | 33 | 109 | 107 | 100 | 14% | 94 | 11% | 44% | 27 | 48% | 44% | 4.62 | 2.2 | 38 | 103 | $11 |
| 16 HOU | 484 | 55 | 13 | 51 | 12 | 254 | 253 | 293 | 401 | 694 | 724 | 678 | 4 | 76 | 0.19 | 47 | 21 | 32 | 31 | 102 | 94 | 99 | 12% | 98 | 17% | 67% | 27 | 30% | 37% | 3.83 | -6.4 | 18 | 51 | $12 |
| 17 HOU | 455 | 67 | 23 | 90 | 8 | 303 | 283 | 377 | 530 | 907 | 789 | 946 | 10 | 78 | 0.49 | 44 | 20 | 36 | 35 | 104 | 132 | 94 | 18% | 82 | 8% | 73% | 27 | 56% | 30% | 7.14 | 21.2 | 64 | 194 | $23 |
| 18 HOU | 489 | 61 | 16 | 68 | 2 | 247 | 246 | 324 | 409 | 733 | 753 | 722 | 10 | 74 | 0.42 | 42 | 23 | 36 | 30 | 105 | 101 | 123 | 13% | 90 | 4% | 40% | 28 | 25% | 29% | 4.36 | -3.2 | 26 | 87 | $11 |
| 1st Half | 260 | 25 | 6 | 34 | 2 | 231 | 227 | 306 | 365 | 671 | 629 | 693 | 10 | 71 | 0.37 | 42 | 22 | 36 | 30 | 97 | 87 | 113 | 9% | 99 | 4% | 67% | 15 | 27% | 33% | 3.68 | -7.2 | 5 | 17 | $7 |
| 2nd Half | 229 | 36 | 10 | 34 | 0 | 266 | 267 | 344 | 459 | 802 | 904 | 754 | 10 | 78 | 0.49 | 41 | 23 | 36 | 30 | 115 | 116 | 134 | 16% | 85 | 3% | 0% | 13 | 23% | 23% | 5.21 | 4.1 | 51 | 170 | $15 |
| 19 Proj | 480 | 64 | 18 | 70 | 5 | 268 | 259 | 335 | 446 | 781 | 782 | 780 | 9 | 76 | 0.39 | 44 | 21 | 35 | 32 | 105 | 110 | 110 | 14% | 88 | 7% | 56% | | | | 5.02 | 5.9 | 33 | 111 | $15 |

## Goodrum,Niko

| | | | |
|---|---|---|---|
| Age: 27 Bats: B Pos: 2B 1B | Health A | LIMA Plan B | |
| Ht: 6' 3" Wt: 198 | PT/Exp C | Rand Var 0 | |
| | Consist B | MM 3425 | |

Older rookie with career .712 minor league OPS exceeded expectations. Running game was anticipated; power was not. 2nd half ct%, h%, LD% surges kept volatile BA at league average; xBA suggests growth potential. MLB sample leaves questions, but power/speed/versatility combo is intriguing.

| Yr Tm | AB | R | HR | RBI | SB | BA | xBA | OBP | SLG | OPS | vL | vR | bb% | ct% | Eye | G | L | F | h% | HctX | PX | xPX | hr/f | Spd | SBO | SB% | #Wk | DOM | DIS | RC/G | RAR | BPV | BPX | R$ |
|---|---|---|---|---|---|---|---|---|---|---|---|---|---|---|---|---|---|---|---|---|---|---|---|---|---|---|---|---|---|---|---|---|---|---|
| 14 | | | | | | | | | | | | | | | | | | | | | | | | | | | | | | | | | | |
| 15 aa | 209 | 25 | 4 | 14 | 13 | 214 | | 283 | 327 | 610 | | | 9 | 74 | 0.37 | | | | 27 | | 72 | | | 146 | 34% | 75% | | | | 3.01 | | 17 | 46 | $4 |
| 16 aa | 182 | 21 | 5 | 22 | 7 | 248 | | 315 | 398 | 713 | | | 9 | 69 | 0.31 | | | | 33 | | 104 | | | 102 | 19% | 75% | | | | 4.24 | | 10 | 29 | $4 |
| 17 MIN * | 478 | 66 | 12 | 60 | 10 | 241 | 225 | 283 | 386 | 669 | 167 | 167 | 6 | 71 | 0.20 | 71 | 0 | 29 | 32 | 123 | 92 | 81 | 0% | 127 | 17% | 56% | 6 | 0% | 83% | 3.49 | -16.4 | 8 | 24 | $10 |
| 18 DET | 444 | 55 | 16 | 53 | 12 | 245 | 252 | 315 | 432 | 747 | 783 | 732 | 9 | 70 | 0.32 | 44 | 23 | 33 | 31 | 95 | 126 | 102 | 16% | 114 | 16% | 75% | 27 | 41% | 33% | 4.52 | 5.9 | 35 | 117 | $13 |
| 1st Half | 191 | 24 | 7 | 25 | 6 | 220 | 240 | 304 | 414 | 718 | 731 | 710 | 10 | 68 | 0.36 | 45 | 17 | 38 | 28 | 93 | 138 | 115 | 14% | 106 | 17% | 86% | 14 | 50% | 29% | 4.14 | -0.2 | 37 | 123 | $8 |
| 2nd Half | 253 | 31 | 9 | 28 | 6 | 265 | 262 | 324 | 447 | 770 | 811 | 752 | 7 | 72 | 0.28 | 43 | 27 | 29 | 34 | 96 | 118 | 94 | 17% | 121 | 15% | 67% | 13 | 31% | 38% | 4.83 | 4.8 | 35 | 117 | $18 |
| 19 Proj | 420 | 53 | 12 | 49 | 10 | 242 | 243 | 305 | 405 | 710 | 770 | 688 | 8 | 71 | 0.28 | 44 | 23 | 33 | 31 | 95 | 108 | 102 | 13% | 123 | 14% | 70% | | | | 4.04 | -1.7 | 20 | 67 | $12 |

## Goodwin,Brian

| | | | |
|---|---|---|---|
| Age: 28 Bats: L Pos: CF | Health F | LIMA Plan C | |
| Ht: 6' 0" Wt: 200 | PT/Exp D | Rand Var -1 | |
| | Consist B | MM 4313 | |

6-25-.239 with 4 SB in 159 AB at WAS/KC. Mid-April wrist injury DL'd him for 6 weeks. Had opportunity and a pulse after July trade, before strained groin shelved him until September Power/speed skills were evident during injury-shortened 2017 (.807 OPS in 251 AB). But health—and ct%—remain obstacles.

| Yr Tm | AB | R | HR | RBI | SB | BA | xBA | OBP | SLG | OPS | vL | vR | bb% | ct% | Eye | G | L | F | h% | HctX | PX | xPX | hr/f | Spd | SBO | SB% | #Wk | DOM | DIS | RC/G | RAR | BPV | BPX | R$ |
|---|---|---|---|---|---|---|---|---|---|---|---|---|---|---|---|---|---|---|---|---|---|---|---|---|---|---|---|---|---|---|---|---|---|---|
| 14 aaa | 275 | 23 | 3 | 24 | 4 | 187 | | 282 | 266 | 547 | | | 12 | 62 | 0.35 | | | | 29 | | 73 | | | 111 | 12% | 49% | | | | 2.25 | | -33 | -89 | -$3 |
| 15 aa | 429 | 46 | 6 | 37 | 12 | 196 | | 250 | 282 | 532 | | | 7 | 76 | 0.29 | | | | 25 | | 62 | | | 103 | 22% | 60% | | | | 2.14 | | -1 | -3 | $1 |
| 16 WAS * | 478 | 46 | 12 | 64 | 13 | 250 | 241 | 312 | 388 | 700 | 750 | 746 | 8 | 71 | 0.32 | 59 | 15 | 26 | 33 | 114 | 96 | 105 | 0% | 97 | 14% | 79% | 7 | 14% | 43% | 4.15 | -7.1 | 10 | 29 | $12 |
| 17 WAS * | 341 | 48 | 15 | 38 | 8 | 241 | 245 | 303 | 446 | 749 | 1001 | 770 | 8 | 70 | 0.29 | 38 | 19 | 43 | 30 | 96 | 135 | 133 | 16% | 101 | 12% | 86% | 14 | 57% | 21% | 4.59 | -4.7 | 35 | 106 | $8 |
| 18 2 TM * | 214 | 27 | 8 | 34 | 5 | 223 | 224 | 293 | 379 | 672 | 643 | 717 | 9 | 66 | 0.29 | 43 | 23 | 34 | 30 | 81 | 110 | 83 | 17% | 92 | 13% | 70% | 20 | 30% | 50% | 3.61 | -2.7 | -1 | -3 | $4 |
| 1st Half | 67 | 9 | 3 | 13 | 4 | 169 | 188 | 279 | 304 | 583 | 429 | 619 | 13 | 60 | 0.38 | 47 | 17 | 37 | 23 | 65 | 92 | 89 | 18% | 87 | 27% | 79% | 11 | 36% | 55% | 2.69 | -3.2 | -31 | -103 | -$1 |
| 2nd Half | 147 | 18 | 5 | 21 | 1 | 247 | 241 | 299 | 414 | 713 | 686 | 771 | 7 | 68 | 0.23 | 42 | 25 | 33 | 33 | 89 | 118 | 80 | 17% | 104 | 6% | 50% | 9 | 22% | 44% | 4.11 | -0.1 | 13 | 43 | $7 |
| 19 Proj | 319 | 39 | 14 | 44 | 8 | 239 | 233 | 313 | 424 | 737 | 807 | 724 | 9 | 67 | 0.30 | 41 | 20 | 38 | 31 | 86 | 126 | 103 | 17% | 93 | 14% | 75% | | | | 4.34 | 1.9 | 15 | 48 | $11 |

## Gordon,Alex

| | | | |
|---|---|---|---|
| Age: 35 Bats: L Pos: LF | Health C | LIMA Plan C+ | |
| Ht: 6' 1" Wt: 225 | PT/Exp B | Rand Var 0 | |
| | Consist C | MM 2225 | |

Past-prime vet reversed 1st half GB spike, rode Aug/Sept HR/SB burst to 2nd half rebound. Average power looks healthier than a year ago. SB% says he's still picking spots despite sub-par speed. Nothing suggests upside from here; ongoing slide vL says AB are risky. Health, counting stats will determine value.

| Yr Tm | AB | R | HR | RBI | SB | BA | xBA | OBP | SLG | OPS | vL | vR | bb% | ct% | Eye | G | L | F | h% | HctX | PX | xPX | hr/f | Spd | SBO | SB% | #Wk | DOM | DIS | RC/G | RAR | BPV | BPX | R$ |
|---|---|---|---|---|---|---|---|---|---|---|---|---|---|---|---|---|---|---|---|---|---|---|---|---|---|---|---|---|---|---|---|---|---|---|
| 14 KC | 563 | 87 | 19 | 74 | 12 | 266 | 260 | 351 | 432 | 783 | 787 | 782 | 10 | 78 | 0.52 | 43 | 19 | 38 | 31 | 108 | 123 | 118 | 11% | 68 | 9% | 80% | 27 | 48% | 26% | 5.16 | 24.0 | 52 | 141 | $22 |
| 15 KC * | 382 | 44 | 14 | 52 | 2 | 276 | 250 | 367 | 435 | 802 | 817 | 805 | 12 | 74 | 0.55 | 38 | 25 | 38 | 34 | 107 | 111 | 125 | 13% | 73 | 6% | 29% | 20 | 45% | 35% | 5.39 | 10.9 | 33 | 89 | $12 |
| 16 KC * | 467 | 64 | 18 | 44 | 8 | 223 | 226 | 306 | 382 | 688 | 665 | 704 | 10 | 67 | 0.36 | 38 | 24 | 38 | 30 | 100 | 107 | 147 | 15% | 89 | 7% | 89% | 24 | 17% | 46% | 3.90 | -5.4 | 2 | 6 | $7 |
| 17 KC | 476 | 52 | 9 | 45 | 7 | 208 | 236 | 293 | 315 | 608 | 602 | 608 | 8 | 74 | 0.36 | 43 | 24 | 33 | 26 | 87 | 68 | 82 | 8% | 85 | 10% | 64% | 27 | 22% | 52% | 2.77 | -40.0 | -6 | -18 | $1 |
| 18 KC | 506 | 56 | 13 | 54 | 12 | 245 | 251 | 324 | 370 | 694 | 555 | 750 | 9 | 75 | 0.40 | 44 | 26 | 30 | 30 | 105 | 80 | 112 | 11% | 58 | 10% | 86% | 26 | 19% | 42% | 3.98 | -9.1 | 3 | 10 | $13 |
| 1st Half | 230 | 21 | 5 | 15 | 4 | 252 | 242 | 333 | 348 | 681 | 481 | 758 | 9 | 76 | 0.40 | 54 | 23 | 23 | 31 | 106 | 59 | 96 | 12% | 71 | 6% | 100% | 14 | 14% | 57% | 3.87 | -4.9 | -8 | -27 | $5 |
| 2nd Half | 276 | 35 | 8 | 39 | 8 | 239 | 257 | 316 | 388 | 704 | 613 | 743 | 9 | 75 | 0.41 | 35 | 29 | 36 | 29 | 105 | 99 | 126 | 11% | 55 | 14% | 80% | 12 | 25% | 25% | 4.06 | -4.5 | 16 | 53 | $19 |
| 19 Proj | 476 | 56 | 13 | 51 | 9 | 239 | 242 | 322 | 370 | 691 | 624 | 719 | 9 | 74 | 0.39 | 42 | 25 | 33 | 30 | 100 | 85 | 112 | 11% | 70 | 9% | 78% | | | | 3.85 | -10.6 | 8 | 26 | $12 |

## Gordon,Dee

| | | | |
|---|---|---|---|
| Age: 31 Bats: L Pos: 2B CF | Health B | LIMA Plan D+ | |
| Ht: 5' 11" Wt: 170 | PT/Exp B | Rand Var +1 | |
| | Consist C | MM 0545 | |

Nagging injuries—fractured toe, back/ankle/shoulder woes—took a toll, as 2nd half BA plunged and running game all but vanished. Increasingly abysmal bb% doesn't help. But volatile h% is still the BA/SB key—and all look due for a bounce. Age, health temper our expectations, but he's still elite on the bases.

| Yr Tm | AB | R | HR | RBI | SB | BA | xBA | OBP | SLG | OPS | vL | vR | bb% | ct% | Eye | G | L | F | h% | HctX | PX | xPX | hr/f | Spd | SBO | SB% | #Wk | DOM | DIS | RC/G | RAR | BPV | BPX | R$ |
|---|---|---|---|---|---|---|---|---|---|---|---|---|---|---|---|---|---|---|---|---|---|---|---|---|---|---|---|---|---|---|---|---|---|---|
| 14 LA | 609 | 92 | 2 | 34 | 64 | 289 | 274 | 326 | 378 | 704 | 719 | 699 | 5 | 82 | 0.29 | 60 | 21 | 19 | 35 | 62 | 62 | 27 | 2% | 190 | 49% | 77% | 27 | 37% | 19% | 4.39 | 8.9 | 48 | 130 | $38 |
| 15 MIA | 615 | 88 | 4 | 46 | 58 | 333 | 280 | 359 | 418 | 776 | 823 | 760 | 4 | 85 | 0.27 | 60 | 22 | 19 | 39 | 68 | 54 | 40 | 4% | 170 | 40% | 74% | 25 | 44% | 24% | 5.62 | 18.7 | 45 | 122 | $47 |
| 16 MIA * | 360 | 52 | 1 | 16 | 32 | 262 | 256 | 298 | 329 | 627 | 579 | 656 | 5 | 83 | 0.31 | 59 | 19 | 23 | 31 | 57 | 36 | 29 | 2% | 204 | 40% | 82% | 15 | 13% | 40% | 3.56 | -11.6 | 34 | 97 | $16 |
| 17 MIA | 653 | 114 | 2 | 33 | 60 | 308 | 281 | 341 | 375 | 716 | 648 | 744 | 4 | 86 | 0.27 | 58 | 23 | 20 | 36 | 56 | 37 | 20 | 2% | 198 | 39% | 79% | 27 | 22% | 22% | 4.69 | -1.0 | 41 | 124 | $43 |
| 18 SEA | 556 | 62 | 4 | 36 | 30 | 268 | 270 | 288 | 349 | 637 | 589 | 658 | 2 | 86 | 0.11 | 55 | 22 | 22 | 31 | 64 | 44 | 28 | 4% | 159 | 33% | 71% | 27 | 22% | 37% | 3.31 | -11.8 | 30 | 100 | $20 |
| 1st Half | 310 | 38 | 1 | 20 | 21 | 281 | 261 | 302 | 345 | 648 | 689 | 630 | 2 | 85 | 0.13 | 56 | 21 | 23 | 33 | 56 | 42 | 18 | 2% | 133 | 34% | 81% | 15 | 20% | 33% | 3.69 | -4.0 | 17 | 57 | $25 |
| 2nd Half | 246 | 24 | 3 | 16 | 9 | 252 | 281 | 271 | 354 | 624 | 459 | 693 | 1 | 87 | 0.09 | 55 | 24 | 21 | 28 | 75 | 47 | 40 | 7% | 177 | 31% | 56% | 12 | 25% | 42% | 2.86 | -9.6 | 43 | 143 | $13 |
| 19 Proj | 613 | 82 | 4 | 35 | 45 | 284 | 272 | 310 | 364 | 674 | 607 | 700 | 3 | 85 | 0.19 | 57 | 22 | 21 | 33 | 63 | 43 | 28 | 3% | 183 | 38% | 76% | | | | 3.91 | -4.7 | 32 | 105 | $32 |

## Grandal,Yasmani

| | | | |
|---|---|---|---|
| Age: 30 Bats: B Pos: CA | Health A | LIMA Plan B | |
| Ht: 6' 1" Wt: 235 | PT/Exp B | Rand Var 0 | |
| | Consist B | MM 4025 | |

Return of patient approach was the only big difference in near carbon-copy of 2017. 2nd half LD and h% spikes turned BA around, inexplicably as bb% soared and ct% dropped off. But BA, HR levels look entrenched and supported by stable contact and power metrics. Health suggests more of the same.

| Yr Tm | AB | R | HR | RBI | SB | BA | xBA | OBP | SLG | OPS | vL | vR | bb% | ct% | Eye | G | L | F | h% | HctX | PX | xPX | hr/f | Spd | SBO | SB% | #Wk | DOM | DIS | RC/G | RAR | BPV | BPX | R$ |
|---|---|---|---|---|---|---|---|---|---|---|---|---|---|---|---|---|---|---|---|---|---|---|---|---|---|---|---|---|---|---|---|---|---|---|
| 14 SD | 377 | 47 | 15 | 49 | 3 | 225 | 242 | 327 | 401 | 728 | 512 | 781 | 13 | 69 | 0.50 | 43 | 19 | 38 | 28 | 108 | 139 | 132 | 15% | 67 | 3% | 100% | 27 | 41% | 44% | 4.38 | 10.6 | 37 | 100 | $7 |
| 15 LA | 355 | 43 | 16 | 47 | 0 | 234 | 229 | 353 | 403 | 756 | 794 | 749 | 15 | 74 | 0.71 | 46 | 17 | 37 | 27 | 97 | 110 | 117 | 16% | 62 | 1% | 0% | 27 | 37% | 52% | 4.68 | 9.2 | 35 | 95 | $6 |
| 16 LA | 390 | 49 | 27 | 72 | 1 | 228 | 251 | 339 | 477 | 816 | 780 | 824 | 14 | 70 | 0.55 | 45 | 16 | 39 | 25 | 112 | 152 | 156 | 25% | 61 | 4% | 25% | 26 | 46% | 31% | 5.17 | 9.1 | 51 | 146 | $9 |
| 17 LA | 438 | 50 | 22 | 58 | 0 | 247 | 239 | 308 | 459 | 767 | 668 | 790 | 8 | 70 | 0.31 | 44 | 16 | 40 | 30 | 104 | 134 | 125 | 18% | 63 | 1% | 0% | 27 | 48% | 33% | 4.76 | 9.1 | 26 | 79 | $8 |
| 18 LA | 440 | 65 | 24 | 68 | 2 | 241 | 248 | 349 | 466 | 815 | 727 | 844 | 14 | 72 | 0.58 | 41 | 17 | 42 | 28 | 108 | 139 | 140 | 18% | 58 | 2% | 67% | 28 | 54% | 32% | 5.42 | 25.0 | 46 | 153 | $13 |
| 1st Half | 229 | 34 | 11 | 39 | 1 | 227 | 236 | 317 | 419 | 736 | 610 | 781 | 11 | 74 | 0.47 | 41 | 16 | 43 | 26 | 111 | 117 | 147 | 15% | 49 | 3% | 50% | 15 | 60% | 33% | 4.25 | 5.6 | 29 | 97 | $12 |
| 2nd Half | 211 | 31 | 13 | 29 | 1 | 256 | 260 | 383 | 517 | 899 | 873 | 907 | 17 | 69 | 0.68 | 41 | 19 | 40 | 31 | 104 | 166 | 132 | 22% | 75 | 1% | 100% | 13 | 46% | 31% | 6.84 | 20.9 | 69 | 230 | $14 |
| 19 Proj | 427 | 57 | 25 | 64 | 1 | 243 | 250 | 341 | 476 | 817 | 739 | 838 | 13 | 71 | 0.51 | 41 | 17 | 42 | 28 | 106 | 145 | 136 | 19% | 62 | 2% | 53% | | | | 5.43 | 25.2 | 42 | 139 | $13 |

## Granderson,Curtis

| | | | |
|---|---|---|---|
| Age: 38 Bats: L Pos: RF LF DH | Health A | LIMA Plan D+ | |
| Ht: 6' 1" Wt: 200 | PT/Exp B | Rand Var 0 | |
| | Consist A | MM 4231 | |

Gracefully aging part-timer impressed, as power / patience combo hung on, and h% rebound fueled a BA turnaround. But 2nd half reversal is a reminder that these late-career upticks are mere points in time, which waits for no one. Could offer more periodic flickers, but sustained production is history.

| Yr Tm | AB | R | HR | RBI | SB | BA | xBA | OBP | SLG | OPS | vL | vR | bb% | ct% | Eye | G | L | F | h% | HctX | PX | xPX | hr/f | Spd | SBO | SB% | #Wk | DOM | DIS | RC/G | RAR | BPV | BPX | R$ |
|---|---|---|---|---|---|---|---|---|---|---|---|---|---|---|---|---|---|---|---|---|---|---|---|---|---|---|---|---|---|---|---|---|---|---|
| 14 NYM | 564 | 73 | 20 | 66 | 8 | 227 | 236 | 326 | 388 | 714 | 742 | 703 | 12 | 75 | 0.56 | 34 | 19 | 47 | 27 | 105 | 119 | 132 | 10% | 93 | 6% | 80% | 27 | 56% | 26% | 4.15 | 6.2 | 49 | 132 | $12 |
| 15 NYM | 580 | 98 | 26 | 70 | 11 | 259 | 259 | 364 | 457 | 821 | 558 | 892 | 13 | 74 | 0.60 | 31 | 27 | 42 | 31 | 118 | 135 | 154 | 14% | 102 | 9% | 65% | 27 | 44% | 19% | 5.55 | 14.2 | 63 | 170 | $21 |
| 16 NYM | 545 | 88 | 30 | 59 | 4 | 237 | 265 | 335 | 464 | 799 | 723 | 826 | 12 | 76 | 0.57 | 36 | 22 | 42 | 26 | 114 | 131 | 127 | 17% | 98 | 4% | 67% | 27 | 48% | 22% | 5.06 | 7.0 | 64 | 183 | $12 |
| 17 2 NL | 449 | 74 | 26 | 64 | 6 | 212 | 250 | 323 | 452 | 775 | 668 | 806 | 13 | 73 | 0.58 | 33 | 19 | 49 | 23 | 104 | 140 | 154 | 16% | 111 | 7% | 75% | 26 | 50% | 31% | 4.66 | -8.3 | 65 | 197 | $8 |
| 18 2 TM | 343 | 60 | 13 | 38 | 2 | 242 | 253 | 351 | 431 | 782 | 557 | 798 | 13 | 69 | 0.51 | 32 | 31 | 37 | 31 | 95 | 130 | 133 | 15% | 85 | 3% | 67% | 28 | 43% | 29% | 4.99 | 3.9 | 35 | 117 | $8 |
| 1st Half | 187 | 29 | 9 | 26 | 1 | 251 | 248 | 361 | 465 | 826 | 426 | 866 | 14 | 64 | 0.44 | 33 | 31 | 36 | 35 | 97 | 153 | 157 | 21% | 81 | 4% | 50% | 15 | 40% | 33% | 5.55 | 5.2 | 31 | 103 | $10 |
| 2nd Half | 156 | 31 | 4 | 12 | 1 | 231 | 258 | 339 | 391 | 730 | 929 | 722 | 13 | 76 | 0.63 | 31 | 30 | 39 | 28 | 93 | 106 | 109 | 9% | 98 | 2% | 100% | 13 | 46% | 23% | 4.36 | -1.1 | 45 | 150 | $5 |
| 19 Proj | 213 | 36 | 9 | 24 | 2 | 232 | 253 | 338 | 437 | 774 | 672 | 792 | 13 | 72 | 0.55 | 33 | 26 | 42 | 28 | 102 | 129 | 136 | 15% | 96 | 5% | 73% | | | | 4.81 | 2.3 | 47 | 158 | $6 |

JOCK THOMPSON

## Gregorius,Didi

| | | | | |
|---|---|---|---|---|
| Age: 29 Bats: L Pos: SS | Health | B | LIMA Plan | B |
| Ht: 6' 3" Wt: 205 | PT/Exp | A | Rand Var | +1 |
| | Consist | A | MM | 3343 |

Legit: Mid-20s HR level finally backed by HctX, xPX; BA upside due to growth in bb% (including wackly 15% in April) and Eye. Not legit: Double-digit SB total stemmed from flukish 1st half SBO while unsightly SB% snickers. Truth: Playoff injury led to Tommy John surgery that will cost him multiple months in 2019. Plan accordingly.

| Yr Tm | AB | R | HR | RBI | SB | BA | xBA | OBP | SLG | OPS | vL | vR | bb% | ct% | Eye | G | L | F | h% | HctX | PX | xPX | hr/f | Spd | SBO | SB% | #Wk | DOM | DIS | RC/G | RAR | BPV | BPX | R$ |
|---|---|---|---|---|---|---|---|---|---|---|---|---|---|---|---|---|---|---|---|---|---|---|---|---|---|---|---|---|---|---|---|---|---|---|
| 14 ARI * | 496 | 62 | 8 | 43 | 5 | 239 | 241 | 292 | 362 | 654 | 424 | 706 | 7 | 83 | 0.45 | 37 | 20 | 43 | 27 | 101 | 82 | 106 | 6% | 135 | 4% | 100% | 19 | 42% | 26% | 3.59 | 4.4 | 55 | 149 | $7 |
| 15 NYY | 525 | 57 | 9 | 56 | 5 | 265 | 252 | 318 | 370 | 688 | 626 | 712 | 6 | 84 | 0.39 | 45 | 21 | 34 | 30 | 82 | 68 | 64 | 6% | 103 | 6% | 63% | 27 | 33% | 30% | 3.91 | -7.4 | 34 | 92 | $11 |
| 16 NYY | 562 | 68 | 20 | 70 | 7 | 276 | 271 | 304 | 447 | 751 | 834 | 721 | 3 | 85 | 0.23 | 40 | 20 | 40 | 29 | 85 | 96 | 78 | 10% | 102 | 7% | 88% | 27 | 56% | 19% | 4.74 | 6.9 | 58 | 166 | $18 |
| 17 NYY | 534 | 73 | 25 | 87 | 3 | 287 | 274 | 318 | 478 | 796 | 653 | 848 | 4 | 87 | 0.36 | 36 | 20 | 44 | 29 | 81 | 96 | 67 | 12% | 96 | 3% | 75% | 23 | 57% | 17% | 5.42 | 11.9 | 64 | 194 | $20 |
| 18 NYY | 504 | 89 | 27 | 86 | 10 | 268 | 282 | 335 | 494 | 829 | 764 | 854 | 8 | 86 | 0.70 | 39 | 20 | 42 | 26 | 114 | 114 | 100 | 15% | 109 | 13% | 63% | 26 | 54% | 15% | 5.55 | 21.3 | 88 | 293 | $23 |
| 1st Half | 290 | 48 | 15 | 43 | 9 | 255 | 270 | 324 | 469 | 793 | 647 | 854 | 9 | 85 | 0.68 | 37 | 19 | 44 | 26 | 115 | 110 | 110 | 14% | 101 | 19% | 64% | 15 | 53% | 20% | 5.03 | 9.3 | 78 | 260 | $26 |
| 2nd Half | 214 | 41 | 12 | 43 | 1 | 285 | 298 | 349 | 528 | 877 | 936 | 854 | 8 | 88 | 0.72 | 41 | 20 | 39 | 28 | 114 | 118 | 87 | 16% | 118 | 4% | 50% | 11 | 55% | 9% | 6.32 | 14.2 | 101 | 337 | $20 |
| **19 Proj** | **328** | **51** | **15** | **52** | **4** | **275** | **275** | **325** | **474** | **799** | **753** | **816** | **6** | **86** | **0.50** | **39** | **20** | **41** | **28** | **99** | **103** | **85** | **13%** | **109** | **7%** | **67%** | | | | **5.29** | **12.5** | **70** | **235** | **$12** |

## Greiner,Grayson

| | | | | |
|---|---|---|---|---|
| Age: 26 Bats: R Pos: CA | Health | A | LIMA Plan | F |
| Ht: 6' 6" Wt: 239 | PT/Exp | D | Rand Var | -2 |
| | Consist | A | MM | 1001 |

0-12-.219 in 96 AB at DET. Not a ton here outside of the bb%, but MiLB ct% suggests some BA upside. Career-long platoon also prevalent in short MLB sample. Offense-minded catching prospects are suspect gambles, but defensive-first ones who *might* be fringe second CAs like this barely register on the radar.

| Yr Tm | AB | R | HR | RBI | SB | BA | xBA | OBP | SLG | OPS | vL | vR | bb% | ct% | Eye | G | L | F | h% | HctX | PX | xPX | hr/f | Spd | SBO | SB% | #Wk | DOM | DIS | RC/G | RAR | BPV | BPX | R$ |
|---|---|---|---|---|---|---|---|---|---|---|---|---|---|---|---|---|---|---|---|---|---|---|---|---|---|---|---|---|---|---|---|---|---|---|
| 14 | | | | | | | | | | | | | | | | | | | | | | | | | | | | | | | | | | |
| 15 | | | | | | | | | | | | | | | | | | | | | | | | | | | | | | | | | | |
| 16 a/a | 212 | 16 | 6 | 24 | 1 | 251 | | 278 | 397 | 676 | | | 4 | 71 | 0.13 | | | | 33 | | 93 | | | 115 | 2% | 100% | | | | 3.78 | | 0 | 0 | $2 |
| 17 a/a | 342 | 29 | 12 | 37 | 0 | 210 | | 280 | 376 | 656 | | | 9 | 76 | 0.41 | | | | 24 | | 99 | | | 87 | 0% | 0% | | | | 3.40 | | 29 | 88 | -$1 |
| 18 DET * | 254 | 19 | 3 | 31 | 0 | 228 | 219 | 319 | 327 | 646 | 971 | 528 | 12 | 69 | 0.43 | 45 | 24 | 31 | 32 | 91 | 75 | 85 | 0% | 88 | 1% | 0% | 14 | 29% | 50% | 3.39 | 0.1 | -11 | -37 | $0 |
| 1st Half | 126 | 10 | 2 | 15 | 0 | 234 | 221 | 307 | 342 | 649 | 929 | 539 | 9 | 63 | 0.29 | 48 | 27 | 24 | 36 | 64 | 86 | 56 | 0% | 110 | 3% | 0% | 7 | 29% | 57% | 3.38 | -0.2 | -24 | -80 | -$1 |
| 2nd Half | 128 | 9 | 2 | 16 | 0 | 221 | 210 | 331 | 311 | 643 | 988 | 514 | 14 | 74 | 0.64 | 41 | 21 | 38 | 28 | 121 | 66 | 112 | 0% | 72 | 0% | 0% | 7 | 29% | 43% | 3.38 | -0.3 | 2 | 7 | $1 |
| **19 Proj** | **190** | **15** | **0** | **22** | **0** | **224** | **214** | **291** | **287** | **577** | **968** | **485** | **10** | **72** | **0.38** | **44** | **23** | **33** | **31** | **98** | **52** | **90** | **0%** | **91** | **1%** | **31%** | | | | **2.80** | **-3.7** | **-34** | **-114** | **$1** |

## Grichuk,Randal

| | | | | |
|---|---|---|---|---|
| Age: 27 Bats: R Pos: RF CF | Health | B | LIMA Plan | B |
| Ht: 6' 1" Wt: 205 | PT/Exp | C | Rand Var | +2 |
| | Consist | A | MM | 4225 |

Opened the first two months with awful April (.435 OPS) and month-long knee injury, but popped 23 HR in final 99 games. Skills nearly identical to 2016, though year-long HctX drop is a bit concerning. Returned to mashing lefties and managed to get that ct% back over 70%, but still is just a streaky OBP-challenged power source.

| Yr Tm | AB | R | HR | RBI | SB | BA | xBA | OBP | SLG | OPS | vL | vR | bb% | ct% | Eye | G | L | F | h% | HctX | PX | xPX | hr/f | Spd | SBO | SB% | #Wk | DOM | DIS | RC/G | RAR | BPV | BPX | R$ |
|---|---|---|---|---|---|---|---|---|---|---|---|---|---|---|---|---|---|---|---|---|---|---|---|---|---|---|---|---|---|---|---|---|---|---|
| 14 STL * | 546 | 63 | 20 | 59 | 6 | 224 | 231 | 257 | 392 | 649 | 689 | 662 | 4 | 72 | 0.16 | 39 | 15 | 46 | 27 | 141 | 127 | 162 | 8% | 104 | 14% | 43% | 11 | 27% | 45% | 3.13 | -16.4 | 33 | 89 | $10 |
| 15 STL | 323 | 49 | 17 | 47 | 4 | 276 | 265 | 329 | 548 | 877 | 819 | 907 | 6 | 66 | 0.20 | 38 | 21 | 42 | 37 | 107 | 202 | 139 | 19% | 138 | 9% | 67% | 22 | 55% | 14% | 6.12 | 12.5 | 81 | 219 | $13 |
| 16 STL * | 527 | 75 | 28 | 81 | 5 | 238 | 252 | 278 | 474 | 752 | 806 | 754 | 5 | 70 | 0.19 | 41 | 16 | 44 | 28 | 114 | 154 | 142 | 18% | 111 | 10% | 56% | 25 | 48% | 32% | 4.30 | -5.9 | 50 | 143 | $13 |
| 17 STL * | 479 | 63 | 27 | 69 | 6 | 236 | 249 | 279 | 477 | 756 | 662 | 788 | 6 | 67 | 0.18 | 36 | 21 | 43 | 29 | 109 | 154 | 152 | 18% | 109 | 8% | 86% | 24 | 29% | 29% | 4.46 | -10.5 | 37 | 112 | $11 |
| 18 TOR | 424 | 60 | 25 | 61 | 3 | 245 | 260 | 301 | 502 | 803 | 810 | 800 | 6 | 71 | 0.22 | 35 | 18 | 47 | 29 | 96 | 167 | 136 | 18% | 92 | 7% | 60% | 25 | 56% | 24% | 4.86 | 4.4 | 60 | 200 | $13 |
| 1st Half | 151 | 21 | 10 | 27 | 2 | 212 | 249 | 280 | 464 | 743 | 579 | 837 | 7 | 73 | 0.29 | 41 | 13 | 46 | 22 | 96 | 152 | 140 | 19% | 93 | 8% | 100% | 12 | 33% | 33% | 4.11 | -1.6 | 58 | 193 | $5 |
| 2nd Half | 273 | 39 | 15 | 34 | 1 | 264 | 266 | 313 | 524 | 837 | 964 | 781 | 5 | 70 | 0.19 | 32 | 22 | 47 | 32 | 95 | 176 | 133 | 17% | 92 | 6% | 33% | 13 | 77% | 15% | 5.32 | 6.9 | 62 | 207 | $18 |
| **19 Proj** | **463** | **64** | **25** | **67** | **4** | **241** | **251** | **290** | **482** | **773** | **752** | **782** | **6** | **70** | **0.20** | **37** | **18** | **45** | **29** | **104** | **158** | **142** | **17%** | **104** | **8%** | **66%** | | | | **4.54** | **1.1** | **45** | **149** | **$15** |

## Grossman,Robert

| | | | | |
|---|---|---|---|---|
| Age: 29 Bats: B Pos: RF DH LF | Health | A | LIMA Plan | D+ |
| Ht: 6' 0" Wt: 215 | PT/Exp | C | Rand Var | -2 |
| | Consist | A | MM | 2123 |

A h% jump was offset by another xPX loss. OBP driving league average output, but a drop in performance vR puts the AB count in danger with no other discernible skills. Gaudy 2nd half h% masked middling output as xBA and xPX show. No standout assets, no guarantees on AB relegates him to deep league fill-in.

| Yr Tm | AB | R | HR | RBI | SB | BA | xBA | OBP | SLG | OPS | vL | vR | bb% | ct% | Eye | G | L | F | h% | HctX | PX | xPX | hr/f | Spd | SBO | SB% | #Wk | DOM | DIS | RC/G | RAR | BPV | BPX | R$ |
|---|---|---|---|---|---|---|---|---|---|---|---|---|---|---|---|---|---|---|---|---|---|---|---|---|---|---|---|---|---|---|---|---|---|---|
| 14 HOU * | 535 | 63 | 9 | 47 | 16 | 247 | 231 | 334 | 355 | 689 | 566 | 703 | 12 | 72 | 0.46 | 41 | 24 | 35 | 33 | 63 | 92 | 76 | 7% | 85 | 17% | 56% | 21 | 19% | 43% | 3.82 | -1.0 | 11 | 30 | $13 |
| 15 HOU * | 396 | 42 | 5 | 29 | 9 | 191 | 176 | 267 | 266 | 534 | 345 | 567 | 9 | 69 | 0.34 | 55 | 6 | 39 | 26 | 47 | 61 | 56 | 8% | 84 | 19% | 49% | 6 | 33% | 50% | 2.09 | -31.2 | -28 | -76 | -$1 |
| 16 MIN * | 453 | 62 | 16 | 49 | 5 | 265 | 249 | 365 | 426 | 792 | 994 | 729 | 14 | 72 | 0.58 | 38 | 25 | 37 | 33 | 92 | 107 | 96 | 13% | 83 | 6% | 56% | 21 | 38% | 38% | 5.30 | 12.3 | 29 | 83 | $12 |
| 17 MIN | 382 | 62 | 9 | 45 | 3 | 246 | 262 | 361 | 380 | 741 | 696 | 762 | 15 | 79 | 0.85 | 41 | 25 | 34 | 29 | 99 | 81 | 83 | 9% | 90 | 3% | 75% | 25 | 36% | 36% | 4.61 | -1.5 | 40 | 121 | $6 |
| 18 MIN | 396 | 50 | 5 | 48 | 0 | 273 | 247 | 367 | 384 | 751 | 882 | 688 | 13 | 79 | 0.72 | 39 | 24 | 37 | 33 | 92 | 77 | 58 | 4% | 102 | 1% | 0% | 27 | 48% | 37% | 4.91 | 9.9 | 36 | 120 | $8 |
| 1st Half | 200 | 19 | 3 | 21 | 0 | 230 | 227 | 314 | 335 | 649 | 632 | 657 | 12 | 75 | 0.52 | 35 | 24 | 41 | 29 | 98 | 71 | 63 | 5% | 89 | 0% | 0% | 15 | 33% | 40% | 3.53 | -3.6 | 8 | 27 | $2 |
| 2nd Half | 196 | 31 | 2 | 27 | 0 | 316 | 268 | 419 | 434 | 852 | 1092 | 722 | 15 | 83 | 1.03 | 42 | 24 | 34 | 37 | 86 | 83 | 55 | 4% | 108 | 1% | 0% | 12 | 67% | 33% | 6.63 | 13.2 | 63 | 210 | $14 |
| **19 Proj** | **302** | **42** | **6** | **35** | **2** | **264** | **249** | **366** | **388** | **754** | **846** | **709** | **14** | **78** | **0.71** | **40** | **25** | **36** | **32** | **90** | **83** | **72** | **7%** | **95** | **4%** | **51%** | | | | **4.84** | **3.3** | **23** | **75** | **$8** |

## Guerrero Jr.,Vladimir

| | | | | |
|---|---|---|---|---|
| Age: 20 Bats: R Pos: 3B | Health | A | LIMA Plan | B+ |
| Ht: 6' 1" Wt: 200 | PT/Exp | F | Rand Var | 0 |
| | Consist | F | MM | 3155 |

Flawed service time rules will likely keep him in TOR minors until mid-April. Name isn't all he shares with dad as broad bat-to-ball skills giving him immediate BA and power upside. Incredible 1.08 MiLB Eye in 1030 AB offers rare floor for someone who has yet to step into an MLB batter's box. He could be special right away.

| Yr Tm | AB | R | HR | RBI | SB | BA | xBA | OBP | SLG | OPS | vL | vR | bb% | ct% | Eye | G | L | F | h% | HctX | PX | xPX | hr/f | Spd | SBO | SB% | #Wk | DOM | DIS | RC/G | RAR | BPV | BPX | R$ |
|---|---|---|---|---|---|---|---|---|---|---|---|---|---|---|---|---|---|---|---|---|---|---|---|---|---|---|---|---|---|---|---|---|---|---|
| 14 | | | | | | | | | | | | | | | | | | | | | | | | | | | | | | | | | | |
| 15 | | | | | | | | | | | | | | | | | | | | | | | | | | | | | | | | | | |
| 16 | | | | | | | | | | | | | | | | | | | | | | | | | | | | | | | | | | |
| 17 | | | | | | | | | | | | | | | | | | | | | | | | | | | | | | | | | | |
| 18 a/a | 344 | 59 | 19 | 71 | 3 | 383 | | 438 | 634 | 1072 | | | 9 | 89 | 0.89 | | | | 39 | | 133 | | | 86 | 5% | 48% | | | | 11.18 | | 108 | 360 | $25 |
| 1st Half | 205 | 40 | 10 | 50 | 3 | 411 | | 459 | 663 | 1122 | | | 8 | 90 | 0.85 | | | | 43 | | 137 | | | 91 | 8% | 47% | | | | 12.60 | | 114 | 380 | $34 |
| 2nd Half | 139 | 18 | 8 | 20 | 0 | 339 | | 402 | 582 | 984 | | | 10 | 88 | 0.91 | | | | 34 | | 125 | | | 89 | 0% | 0% | | | | 9.03 | | 101 | 337 | $12 |
| **19 Proj** | **413** | **49** | **17** | **54** | **2** | **294** | **290** | **359** | **497** | **856** | **856** | **856** | **9** | **84** | **0.64** | **40** | **23** | **37** | **32** | | **118** | | **13%** | **88** | **4%** | **50%** | | | | **6.35** | **21.2** | **65** | **217** | **$17** |

## Gurriel,Lourdes

| | | | | |
|---|---|---|---|---|
| Age: 25 Bats: R Pos: SS 2B | Health | B | LIMA Plan | B |
| Ht: 6' 2" Wt: 185 | PT/Exp | F | Rand Var | -3 |
| | Consist | C | MM | 2335 |

11-35-.281 in 249 AB at TOR. Put together blistering 17-game run (.423 AVG, 1.086 OPS) but demotion, injuries (concussion, hamstring), and mediocrity outside July (.623 OPS) resulted in uneven season. Strong history of contact, solid HctX/xPX, and Spd provides hope as an end-game gamble.

| Yr Tm | AB | R | HR | RBI | SB | BA | xBA | OBP | SLG | OPS | vL | vR | bb% | ct% | Eye | G | L | F | h% | HctX | PX | xPX | hr/f | Spd | SBO | SB% | #Wk | DOM | DIS | RC/G | RAR | BPV | BPX | R$ |
|---|---|---|---|---|---|---|---|---|---|---|---|---|---|---|---|---|---|---|---|---|---|---|---|---|---|---|---|---|---|---|---|---|---|---|
| 14 for | 221 | 35 | 5 | 41 | 6 | 287 | | 353 | 401 | 754 | | | 9 | 88 | 0.85 | | | | 31 | | 78 | | | 83 | 15% | 59% | | | | 4.85 | 10.2 | 60 | 162 | $10 |
| 15 for | 218 | 42 | 6 | 52 | 7 | 321 | | 370 | 480 | 850 | | | 7 | 90 | 0.78 | | | | 34 | | 100 | | | 79 | 16% | 68% | | | | 6.50 | 14.3 | 80 | 216 | $14 |
| 16 | | | | | | | | | | | | | | | | | | | | | | | | | | | | | | | | | | |
| 17 aa | 170 | 17 | 3 | 23 | 2 | 220 | | 256 | 337 | 593 | | | 5 | 81 | 0.25 | | | | 25 | | 72 | | | 83 | 5% | 100% | | | | 2.87 | | 16 | 48 | $0 |
| 18 TOR * | 455 | 52 | 17 | 71 | 4 | 276 | 253 | 299 | 432 | 730 | 826 | 727 | 3 | 77 | 0.14 | 43 | 24 | 33 | 33 | 86 | 92 | 92 | 17% | 115 | 9% | 44% | 15 | 33% | 47% | 4.35 | 3.2 | 23 | 77 | $15 |
| 1st Half | 256 | 27 | 8 | 40 | 4 | 255 | 242 | 275 | 401 | 676 | 327 | 771 | 3 | 76 | 0.11 | 43 | 21 | 36 | 31 | 101 | 89 | 133 | 16% | 116 | 17% | 49% | 6 | 50% | 50% | 3.54 | -3.2 | 18 | 60 | $15 |
| 2nd Half | 199 | 26 | 9 | 31 | 0 | 303 | 259 | 329 | 471 | 800 | 1129 | 711 | 4 | 77 | 0.17 | 43 | 25 | 32 | 36 | 81 | 96 | 77 | 18% | 112 | 2% | 0% | 9 | 22% | 44% | 5.54 | 8.7 | 28 | 93 | $16 |
| **19 Proj** | **466** | **59** | **16** | **63** | **6** | **262** | **259** | **301** | **419** | **720** | **728** | **716** | **5** | **78** | **0.24** | **43** | **23** | **34** | **30** | **89** | **95** | **99** | **13%** | **113** | **10%** | **62%** | | | | **4.22** | **3.6** | **22** | **72** | **$16** |

## Gurriel,Yulieski

| | | | | |
|---|---|---|---|---|
| Age: 35 Bats: R Pos: 1B 3B | Health | A | LIMA Plan | B+ |
| Ht: 6' 0" Wt: 190 | PT/Exp | C | Rand Var | -1 |
| | Consist | D | MM | 2345 |

13-85-.291 in 537 AB at HOU. Remains rare fantasy commodity: a late-round BA asset. Struggles vs RHP and a drop in hr/f affected HR total, though excellent ct% establishes floor. Dual eligibility (plus 2B in 15 G lgs) adds a smidge of value, while age will keep his price down. Can be a sneaky complementary roster piece.

| Yr Tm | AB | R | HR | RBI | SB | BA | xBA | OBP | SLG | OPS | vL | vR | bb% | ct% | Eye | G | L | F | h% | HctX | PX | xPX | hr/f | Spd | SBO | SB% | #Wk | DOM | DIS | RC/G | RAR | BPV | BPX | R$ |
|---|---|---|---|---|---|---|---|---|---|---|---|---|---|---|---|---|---|---|---|---|---|---|---|---|---|---|---|---|---|---|---|---|---|---|
| 14 for | 414 | 84 | 11 | 63 | 13 | 299 | | 352 | 480 | 833 | | | 8 | 87 | 0.62 | | | | 32 | | 131 | | | 92 | 14% | 85% | | | | 6.24 | 23.7 | 96 | 259 | $23 |
| 15 for | 175 | 39 | 4 | 34 | 10 | 320 | | 395 | 511 | 906 | | | 11 | 90 | 1.28 | | | | 34 | | 121 | | | 96 | 22% | 82% | | | | 7.64 | 11.8 | 111 | 300 | $12 |
| 16 HOU * | 165 | 15 | 4 | 19 | 1 | 234 | 250 | 262 | 348 | 611 | 537 | 739 | 4 | 85 | 0.25 | 42 | 20 | 38 | 26 | 98 | 68 | 74 | 7% | 84 | 6% | 50% | 6 | 67% | 0% | 2.98 | -9.3 | 28 | 80 | $0 |
| 17 HOU | 529 | 69 | 18 | 75 | 3 | 299 | 293 | 332 | 486 | 817 | 695 | 865 | 4 | 88 | 0.35 | 46 | 19 | 35 | 31 | 125 | 102 | 99 | 11% | 89 | 4% | 60% | 27 | 67% | 15% | 5.71 | 4.9 | 71 | 215 | $19 |
| 18 HOU * | 558 | 72 | 13 | 87 | 5 | 292 | 271 | 320 | 431 | 751 | 889 | 693 | 4 | 88 | 0.34 | 44 | 20 | 36 | 31 | 99 | 80 | 87 | 8% | 117 | 4% | 83% | 26 | 54% | 23% | 4.99 | 8.8 | 60 | 200 | $21 |
| 1st Half | 286 | 35 | 4 | 39 | 2 | 301 | 276 | 325 | 421 | 745 | 735 | 739 | 3 | 88 | 0.29 | 48 | 21 | 31 | 33 | 104 | 76 | 76 | 5% | 112 | 4% | 67% | 13 | 62% | 23% | 4.95 | 1.5 | 55 | 183 | $18 |
| 2nd Half | 272 | 37 | 9 | 48 | 3 | 283 | 267 | 323 | 441 | 764 | 1051 | 650 | 5 | 88 | 0.38 | 41 | 19 | 40 | 30 | 93 | 85 | 98 | 9% | 120 | 5% | 100% | 13 | 46% | 23% | 5.02 | 2.0 | 65 | 217 | $23 |
| **19 Proj** | **534** | **71** | **15** | **80** | **6** | **286** | **276** | **323** | **442** | **764** | **784** | **756** | **5** | **88** | **0.38** | **44** | **20** | **36** | **31** | **107** | **89** | **90** | **9%** | **105** | **6%** | **77%** | | | | **5.02** | **3.9** | **57** | **189** | **$22** |

PAUL SPORER

## Guzman,Ronald

| Age: 24 | Bats: L | Pos: 1B | Health | A | LIMA Plan | C |
|---|---|---|---|---|---|---|
| Ht: 6' 5" | Wt: 225 | | PT/Exp | B | Rand Var | 0 |
| | | | Consist | A | MM | 3225 |

Minor league profile said he didn't bring enough pop to stick as a 1Bman, so this PX spike was most welcome. xPX still casts doubt, though it started to warm in 2nd half. Platoon split poses another hurdle, but hope rules the day here: in-season jumps in BA, ct%, xPX, HctX, and his youth all buy him some time.

| Yr | Tm | AB | R | HR | RBI | SB | BA | xBA | OBP | SLG | OPS | vL | vR | bb% | ct% | Eye | G | L | F | h% | HctX | PX | xPX | hr/f | Spd | SBO | SB% | #Wk | DOM | DIS | RC/G | RAR | BPV | BPX | R$ |
|---|---|---|---|---|---|---|---|---|---|---|---|---|---|---|---|---|---|---|---|---|---|---|---|---|---|---|---|---|---|---|---|---|---|---|---|
| 14 | | | | | | | | | | | | | | | | | | | | | | | | | | | | | | | | | | | |
| 15 | | | | | | | | | | | | | | | | | | | | | | | | | | | | | | | | | | | |
| 16 | a/a | 463 | 50 | 14 | 56 | 2 | 256 | | 306 | 411 | 717 | | | 7 | 76 | 0.30 | | | | 31 | | 92 | | | 114 | 3% | 44% | | | | 4.24 | | 28 | 80 | $9 |
| 17 | aaa | 470 | 60 | 9 | 47 | 3 | 268 | | 323 | 382 | 705 | | | 7 | 81 | 0.41 | | | | 32 | | 66 | | | 106 | 3% | 73% | | | | 4.29 | | 24 | 73 | $9 |
| 18 | TEX | 387 | 46 | 16 | 58 | 1 | 235 | 235 | 306 | 416 | 722 | 572 | 774 | 8 | 69 | 0.27 | 41 | 22 | 37 | 30 | 83 | 119 | 81 | 16% | 91 | 1% | 100% | 26 | 27% | 46% | 4.11 | -3.6 | 15 | 50 | $8 |
| 1st Half | | 185 | 20 | 7 | 30 | 1 | 227 | 225 | 311 | 405 | 716 | 729 | 713 | 10 | 66 | 0.32 | 39 | 22 | 39 | 30 | 73 | 120 | 60 | 15% | 104 | 2% | 100% | 13 | 23% | 46% | 4.07 | -3.9 | 12 | 40 | $6 |
| 2nd Half | | 202 | 26 | 9 | 28 | 0 | 243 | 243 | 301 | 426 | 727 | 473 | 838 | 6 | 71 | 0.22 | 42 | 22 | 36 | 30 | 93 | 118 | 99 | 17% | 85 | 0% | 0% | 13 | 31% | 46% | 4.13 | -3.8 | 19 | 63 | $10 |
| 19 | Proj | **421** | **51** | **19** | **54** | **2** | **251** | **251** | **317** | **441** | **758** | **581** | **821** | **7** | **74** | **0.31** | **41** | **22** | **37** | **30** | **85** | **114** | **83** | **16%** | **95** | **2%** | **74%** | | | | **4.58** | **-2.2** | **25** | **83** | **$9** |

## Gyorko,Jedd

| Age: 30 | Bats: R | Pos: 3B | Health | B | LIMA Plan | B |
|---|---|---|---|---|---|---|
| Ht: 5' 10" | Wt: 215 | | PT/Exp | C | Rand Var | -1 |
| | | | Consist | B | MM | 3225 |

Injuries to hamstring (1st half) and groin (2nd half) limited him to career-low AB. When healthy, the news was good before contact (continuation of rising Eye trend) and bad after contact (xPX, hr/f, SBO%). 2nd half recovery didn't exactly save his season, but those plate skills give him another path to value even if xPX trend holds.

| Yr | Tm | AB | R | HR | RBI | SB | BA | xBA | OBP | SLG | OPS | vL | vR | bb% | ct% | Eye | G | L | F | h% | HctX | PX | xPX | hr/f | Spd | SBO | SB% | #Wk | DOM | DIS | RC/G | RAR | BPV | BPX | R$ |
|---|---|---|---|---|---|---|---|---|---|---|---|---|---|---|---|---|---|---|---|---|---|---|---|---|---|---|---|---|---|---|---|---|---|---|---|
| 14 | SD * | 424 | 41 | 11 | 54 | 3 | 210 | 239 | 275 | 333 | 608 | 669 | 594 | 8 | 75 | 0.36 | 44 | 22 | 35 | 25 | 95 | 93 | 115 | 10% | 64 | 5% | 60% | 20 | 30% | 40% | 2.93 | -10.3 | 13 | 35 | $3 |
| 15 | SD * | 482 | 39 | 19 | 63 | 0 | 242 | 231 | 289 | 391 | 679 | 803 | 654 | 6 | 75 | 0.26 | 42 | 21 | 37 | 29 | 113 | 96 | 129 | 14% | 58 | 2% | 0% | 25 | 20% | 56% | 3.72 | -13.8 | 8 | 22 | $8 |
| 16 | STL | 400 | 58 | 30 | 59 | 0 | 243 | 265 | 306 | 495 | 801 | 735 | 836 | 8 | 76 | 0.39 | 41 | 19 | 40 | 24 | 107 | 137 | 135 | 24% | 85 | 0% | 0% | 27 | 56% | 22% | 5.11 | 1.5 | 58 | 166 | $10 |
| 17 | STL | 426 | 52 | 20 | 67 | 6 | 272 | 257 | 341 | 472 | 813 | 975 | 763 | 10 | 75 | 0.45 | 41 | 20 | 39 | 32 | 94 | 114 | 114 | 16% | 78 | 7% | 75% | 24 | 38% | 33% | 5.68 | 4.6 | 38 | 115 | $14 |
| 18 | STL | 351 | 49 | 11 | 47 | 2 | 262 | 245 | 346 | 416 | 762 | 919 | 702 | 11 | 78 | 0.57 | 40 | 21 | 40 | 31 | 107 | 94 | 105 | 10% | 83 | 2% | 100% | 25 | 36% | 36% | 4.99 | 3.2 | 36 | 120 | $9 |
| 1st Half | | 165 | 13 | 5 | 21 | 1 | 236 | 215 | 289 | 376 | 665 | 993 | 554 | 7 | 73 | 0.27 | 40 | 17 | 43 | 30 | 108 | 92 | 122 | 10% | 66 | 3% | 100% | 14 | 29% | 43% | 3.65 | -4.2 | 0 | 0 | $2 |
| 2nd Half | | 186 | 36 | 6 | 26 | 1 | 285 | 270 | 392 | 452 | 844 | 864 | 835 | 15 | 83 | 1.00 | 40 | 23 | 37 | 32 | 106 | 96 | 91 | 10% | 97 | 1% | 100% | 11 | 45% | 27% | 6.32 | 9.5 | 68 | 227 | $15 |
| 19 | Proj | **408** | **55** | **17** | **58** | **3** | **260** | **250** | **337** | **438** | **774** | **874** | **736** | **10** | **77** | **0.50** | **40** | **20** | **39** | **30** | **103** | **105** | **113** | **14%** | **82** | **3%** | **81%** | | | | **5.08** | **6.8** | **35** | **115** | **$14** |

## Hamilton,Billy

| Age: 28 | Bats: B | Pos: CF | Health | B | LIMA Plan | C |
|---|---|---|---|---|---|---|
| Ht: 6' 0" | Wt: 160 | | PT/Exp | B | Rand Var | -1 |
| | | | Consist | A | MM | 1515 |

Ill-advised FB jump (seriously, you have one job!) conspired with third straight drop in SBO and four-year low in SB% to cut SB output by nearly half. Spd, 2nd half SBO rebound says this is still a 40+ SB profile, but will his perennially awful OPS cost him AB? You still know what you're buying, but now you do it less confidently.

| Yr | Tm | AB | R | HR | RBI | SB | BA | xBA | OBP | SLG | OPS | vL | vR | bb% | ct% | Eye | G | L | F | h% | HctX | PX | xPX | hr/f | Spd | SBO | SB% | #Wk | DOM | DIS | RC/G | RAR | BPV | BPX | R$ |
|---|---|---|---|---|---|---|---|---|---|---|---|---|---|---|---|---|---|---|---|---|---|---|---|---|---|---|---|---|---|---|---|---|---|---|---|
| 14 | CIN | 563 | 72 | 6 | 48 | 56 | 250 | 237 | 292 | 355 | 648 | 669 | 641 | 6 | 79 | 0.29 | 42 | 21 | 37 | 31 | 70 | 77 | 55 | 4% | 168 | 58% | 71% | 26 | 46% | 38% | 3.37 | -8.0 | 42 | 114 | $28 |
| 15 | CIN | 412 | 56 | 4 | 28 | 57 | 226 | 216 | 274 | 289 | 563 | 641 | 532 | 6 | 82 | 0.37 | 43 | 20 | 38 | 27 | 69 | 38 | 58 | 3% | 165 | 61% | 88% | 22 | 23% | 55% | 3.01 | -16.6 | 21 | 57 | $23 |
| 16 | CIN | 411 | 69 | 3 | 17 | 58 | 260 | 239 | 321 | 343 | 664 | 576 | 696 | 8 | 77 | 0.39 | 48 | 22 | 30 | 33 | 60 | 57 | 32 | 3% | 184 | 56% | 88% | 23 | 35% | 57% | 4.27 | -4.6 | 28 | 80 | $28 |
| 17 | CIN | 582 | 85 | 4 | 38 | 59 | 247 | 238 | 299 | 335 | 634 | 537 | 673 | 7 | 77 | 0.33 | 46 | 24 | 31 | 31 | 50 | 49 | 24 | 3% | 199 | 46% | 82% | 26 | 27% | 46% | 3.60 | -25.8 | 23 | 70 | $29 |
| 18 | CIN | 504 | 74 | 4 | 29 | 34 | 236 | 221 | 299 | 327 | 626 | 605 | 635 | 8 | 74 | 0.35 | 38 | 27 | 35 | 31 | 52 | 57 | 21 | 3% | 192 | 32% | 77% | 28 | 25% | 64% | 3.34 | -13.8 | 17 | 57 | $17 |
| 1st Half | | 251 | 42 | 3 | 18 | 15 | 215 | 211 | 299 | 303 | 602 | 570 | 614 | 11 | 69 | 0.38 | 39 | 28 | 32 | 30 | 60 | 54 | 29 | 6% | 183 | 25% | 83% | 15 | 13% | 73% | 3.10 | -8.2 | -3 | -10 | $14 |
| 2nd Half | | 253 | 32 | 1 | 11 | 19 | 257 | 231 | 299 | 352 | 651 | 642 | 654 | 6 | 79 | 0.30 | 37 | 26 | 38 | 32 | 44 | 59 | 14 | 1% | 179 | 41% | 73% | 13 | 38% | 54% | 3.58 | -4.3 | 30 | 100 | $20 |
| 19 | Proj | **486** | **71** | **4** | **28** | **41** | **241** | **229** | **297** | **331** | **628** | **588** | **644** | **7** | **76** | **0.34** | **42** | **25** | **34** | **31** | **54** | **56** | **26** | **3%** | **186** | **41%** | **79%** | | | | **3.42** | **-10.7** | **18** | **59** | **$22** |

## Hampson,Garrett

| Age: 24 | Bats: R | Pos: SS | Health | A | LIMA Plan | C+ |
|---|---|---|---|---|---|---|
| Ht: 5' 11" | Wt: 185 | | PT/Exp | F | Rand Var | -2 |
| | | | Consist | F | MM | 1523 |

0-4-.275 with 2 SB in 40 AB at COL. Speedster tore through Double-A and Triple-A with 36 SB, but never found his footing in three stilted call ups. Added some CF work to MI versatility this year. That makes his 0.75 Eye and 85% ct% in the minors a profile particularly enticing if he's given a full scale opportunity.

| Yr | Tm | AB | R | HR | RBI | SB | BA | xBA | OBP | SLG | OPS | vL | vR | bb% | ct% | Eye | G | L | F | h% | HctX | PX | xPX | hr/f | Spd | SBO | SB% | #Wk | DOM | DIS | RC/G | RAR | BPV | BPX | R$ |
|---|---|---|---|---|---|---|---|---|---|---|---|---|---|---|---|---|---|---|---|---|---|---|---|---|---|---|---|---|---|---|---|---|---|---|---|
| 14 | | | | | | | | | | | | | | | | | | | | | | | | | | | | | | | | | | | |
| 15 | | | | | | | | | | | | | | | | | | | | | | | | | | | | | | | | | | | |
| 16 | | | | | | | | | | | | | | | | | | | | | | | | | | | | | | | | | | | |
| 17 | | | | | | | | | | | | | | | | | | | | | | | | | | | | | | | | | | | |
| 18 | COL * | 484 | 60 | 8 | 32 | 27 | 281 | 249 | 341 | 411 | 751 | 1029 | 736 | 8 | 81 | 0.48 | 44 | 20 | 36 | 33 | 85 | 77 | 113 | 0% | 152 | 24% | 83% | 9 | 33% | 56% | 5.09 | 11.3 | 50 | 167 | $20 |
| 1st Half | | 302 | 41 | 6 | 23 | 22 | 282 | 257 | 344 | 417 | 761 | | | 9 | 83 | 0.56 | | | | 32 | | 79 | | | 134 | 31% | 79% | | | | 5.16 | | 56 | 187 | $28 |
| 2nd Half | | 182 | 18 | 2 | 9 | 5 | 281 | 237 | 335 | 401 | 736 | 1029 | 736 | 8 | 78 | 0.37 | 44 | 20 | 36 | 35 | 82 | 74 | 113 | 0% | 160 | 11% | 100% | 9 | 33% | 56% | 4.96 | 4.1 | 35 | 117 | $7 |
| 19 | Proj | **321** | **36** | **5** | **21** | **19** | **265** | **246** | **340** | **395** | **735** | **1078** | **655** | **8** | **80** | **0.46** | **44** | **20** | **36** | **32** | **74** | **78** | **102** | **5%** | **155** | **25%** | **84%** | | | | **4.62** | **6.2** | **43** | **144** | **$13** |

## Haniger,Mitch

| Age: 28 | Bats: R | Pos: RF CF | Health | B | LIMA Plan | B+ |
|---|---|---|---|---|---|---|
| Ht: 6' 2" | Wt: 215 | | PT/Exp | B | Rand Var | -2 |
| | | | Consist | A | MM | 4235 |

Showed flashes back in 2017 (1.054 OPS April, .987 Sept) and health cooperated for 600+ plate appearances, yielding a fully fledged breakout. Growth vL and a slight uptick in bb% stabilized the skills. xPX and xBA are calling for some pullback, but the foundation is a quality $20-something bat.

| Yr | Tm | AB | R | HR | RBI | SB | BA | xBA | OBP | SLG | OPS | vL | vR | bb% | ct% | Eye | G | L | F | h% | HctX | PX | xPX | hr/f | Spd | SBO | SB% | #Wk | DOM | DIS | RC/G | RAR | BPV | BPX | R$ |
|---|---|---|---|---|---|---|---|---|---|---|---|---|---|---|---|---|---|---|---|---|---|---|---|---|---|---|---|---|---|---|---|---|---|---|---|
| 14 | aa | 267 | 36 | 8 | 30 | 3 | 232 | | 277 | 366 | 643 | | | 6 | 81 | 0.33 | | | | 26 | | 89 | | | 99 | 5% | 100% | | | | 3.42 | | 39 | 105 | $4 |
| 15 | aa | 153 | 18 | 1 | 15 | 3 | 250 | | 307 | 340 | 648 | | | 8 | 76 | 0.35 | | | | 32 | | 73 | | | 100 | 20% | 41% | | | | 3.22 | | 10 | 27 | $1 |
| 16 | ARI * | 567 | 68 | 24 | 87 | 9 | 268 | 253 | 341 | 476 | 817 | 583 | 760 | 10 | 75 | 0.44 | 39 | 18 | 43 | 32 | 113 | 128 | 135 | 14% | 113 | 9% | 66% | 7 | 57% | 14% | 5.57 | 14.7 | 57 | 163 | $19 |
| 17 | SEA * | 408 | 63 | 18 | 52 | 5 | 275 | 267 | 334 | 484 | 818 | 734 | 877 | 8 | 76 | 0.37 | 44 | 19 | 37 | 32 | 106 | 124 | 120 | 16% | 101 | 9% | 56% | 19 | 53% | 32% | 5.53 | 7.1 | 50 | 152 | $13 |
| 18 | SEA | 596 | 90 | 26 | 93 | 8 | 285 | 265 | 366 | 493 | 859 | 889 | 847 | 10 | 75 | 0.47 | 42 | 21 | 36 | 34 | 103 | 128 | 109 | 16% | 105 | 6% | 80% | 27 | 56% | 26% | 6.35 | 30.9 | 57 | 190 | $26 |
| 1st Half | | 309 | 42 | 17 | 62 | 4 | 275 | 258 | 358 | 502 | 859 | 841 | 867 | 11 | 74 | 0.49 | 43 | 18 | 39 | 32 | 108 | 134 | 116 | 18% | 111 | 7% | 67% | 15 | 60% | 27% | 6.22 | 15.6 | 63 | 210 | $29 |
| 2nd Half | | 287 | 48 | 9 | 31 | 4 | 296 | 273 | 375 | 484 | 859 | 939 | 827 | 10 | 76 | 0.45 | 42 | 25 | 33 | 36 | 98 | 123 | 103 | 12% | 105 | 5% | 100% | 12 | 50% | 25% | 6.50 | 16.2 | 55 | 183 | $23 |
| 19 | Proj | **571** | **84** | **24** | **79** | **8** | **277** | **263** | **353** | **480** | **834** | **804** | **845** | **9** | **76** | **0.42** | **42** | **21** | **37** | **33** | **105** | **125** | **116** | **15%** | **106** | **8%** | **67%** | | | | **5.77** | **21.4** | **50** | **168** | **$24** |

## Hanson,Alen

| Age: 26 | Bats: B | Pos: 2B | Health | A | LIMA Plan | C+ |
|---|---|---|---|---|---|---|
| Ht: 6' 0" | Wt: 170 | | PT/Exp | D | Rand Var | -3 |
| | | | Consist | B | MM | 2523 |

8-39-.252 with 7 SB in 294 AB at SF. Opened with a flourish as PX, Spd, ct%, and HctX gelled to make him a popular waiver pickup. Only the Spd remained in the 2nd half as hitting skills cratered and he lost some playing time. 2nd half Eye and xPX are particularly alarming. Remains end game SB option at best.

| Yr | Tm | AB | R | HR | RBI | SB | BA | xBA | OBP | SLG | OPS | vL | vR | bb% | ct% | Eye | G | L | F | h% | HctX | PX | xPX | hr/f | Spd | SBO | SB% | #Wk | DOM | DIS | RC/G | RAR | BPV | BPX | R$ |
|---|---|---|---|---|---|---|---|---|---|---|---|---|---|---|---|---|---|---|---|---|---|---|---|---|---|---|---|---|---|---|---|---|---|---|---|
| 14 | aa | 482 | 48 | 7 | 43 | 19 | 241 | | 274 | 356 | 630 | | | 4 | 81 | 0.23 | | | | 29 | | 78 | | | 127 | 30% | 60% | | | | 3.06 | | 33 | 89 | $12 |
| 15 | aaa | 475 | 58 | 5 | 38 | 31 | 240 | | 288 | 342 | 630 | | | 6 | 80 | 0.33 | | | | 29 | | 63 | | | 148 | 38% | 70% | | | | 3.20 | | 28 | 76 | $16 |
| 16 | PIT * | 463 | 59 | 7 | 31 | 35 | 249 | 272 | 297 | 356 | 653 | 286 | 599 | 6 | 81 | 0.36 | 60 | 20 | 20 | 29 | 38 | 61 | -14 | 0% | 173 | 45% | 67% | 7 | 14% | 43% | 3.37 | -21.4 | 40 | 114 | $18 |
| 17 | 2 TM | 217 | 36 | 4 | 11 | 11 | 221 | 238 | 262 | 346 | 607 | 766 | 578 | 5 | 76 | 0.23 | 51 | 16 | 34 | 27 | 66 | 73 | 55 | 7% | 175 | 32% | 79% | 27 | 19% | 48% | 2.99 | -13.6 | 27 | 82 | $4 |
| 18 | SF * | 356 | 48 | 10 | 45 | 11 | 265 | 248 | 294 | 439 | 733 | 433 | 782 | 4 | 78 | 0.18 | 43 | 17 | 40 | 32 | 77 | 105 | 64 | 9% | 144 | 21% | 73% | 21 | 33% | 48% | 4.40 | 1.3 | 48 | 160 | $12 |
| 1st Half | | 177 | 32 | 7 | 27 | 8 | 295 | 278 | 339 | 533 | 872 | 426 | 1019 | 6 | 82 | 0.36 | 43 | 13 | 44 | 33 | 107 | 140 | 113 | 13% | 138 | 25% | 87% | 9 | 56% | 11% | 6.65 | 12.2 | 94 | 313 | $19 |
| 2nd Half | | 179 | 16 | 3 | 18 | 3 | 235 | 216 | 250 | 346 | 596 | 439 | 638 | 2 | 74 | 0.06 | 44 | 19 | 37 | 30 | 58 | 66 | 30 | 6% | 152 | 18% | 50% | 12 | 17% | 75% | 2.68 | -8.2 | -1 | -3 | $6 |
| 19 | Proj | **334** | **45** | **8** | **31** | **14** | **246** | **239** | **280** | **394** | **674** | **542** | **709** | **5** | **78** | **0.21** | **46** | **16** | **38** | **30** | **73** | **87** | **61** | **8%** | **155** | **29%** | **71%** | | | | **3.63** | **-5.5** | **35** | **118** | **$12** |

## Happ,Ian

| Age: 24 | Bats: B | Pos: OF 3B | Health | A | LIMA Plan | B |
|---|---|---|---|---|---|---|
| Ht: 6' 0" | Wt: 205 | | PT/Exp | C | Rand Var | -4 |
| | | | Consist | C | MM | 4215 |

Last year we preached caution while market pushed his price. Contact issues became debilitating, bb% jump could only help so much. Poor SB% puts SB contributions in doubt. Worthy xPX establishes HR floor, but can't counter meager xBA. Ceiling is capped without contact gains, but young enough to improve.

| Yr | Tm | AB | R | HR | RBI | SB | BA | xBA | OBP | SLG | OPS | vL | vR | bb% | ct% | Eye | G | L | F | h% | HctX | PX | xPX | hr/f | Spd | SBO | SB% | #Wk | DOM | DIS | RC/G | RAR | BPV | BPX | R$ |
|---|---|---|---|---|---|---|---|---|---|---|---|---|---|---|---|---|---|---|---|---|---|---|---|---|---|---|---|---|---|---|---|---|---|---|---|
| 14 | | | | | | | | | | | | | | | | | | | | | | | | | | | | | | | | | | | |
| 15 | | | | | | | | | | | | | | | | | | | | | | | | | | | | | | | | | | | |
| 16 | aa | 248 | 30 | 7 | 27 | 5 | 236 | | 286 | 369 | 655 | | | 7 | 73 | 0.26 | | | | 30 | | 90 | | | 86 | 13% | 70% | | | | 3.48 | | 5 | 14 | $4 |
| 17 | CHC * | 468 | 78 | 31 | 87 | 10 | 254 | 254 | 324 | 514 | 837 | 789 | 863 | 9 | 66 | 0.30 | 40 | 20 | 40 | 32 | 87 | 163 | 122 | 25% | 100 | 13% | 65% | 22 | 41% | 41% | 5.55 | 4.0 | 44 | 133 | $18 |
| 18 | CHC | 387 | 56 | 15 | 44 | 8 | 233 | 206 | 353 | 408 | 761 | 608 | 816 | 15 | 57 | 0.42 | 40 | 23 | 38 | 37 | 80 | 141 | 126 | 18% | 104 | 10% | 67% | 28 | 25% | 57% | 4.70 | 1.0 | 4 | 13 | $10 |
| 1st Half | | 202 | 30 | 9 | 22 | 4 | 248 | 202 | 369 | 441 | 810 | 707 | 850 | 16 | 55 | 0.42 | 34 | 23 | 43 | 40 | 89 | 159 | 144 | 19% | 113 | 7% | 80% | 15 | 20% | 60% | 5.51 | 5.5 | 14 | 47 | $11 |
| 2nd Half | | 185 | 26 | 6 | 22 | 4 | 216 | 211 | 335 | 373 | 708 | 486 | 780 | 15 | 59 | 0.42 | 45 | 23 | 32 | 33 | 70 | 124 | 108 | 17% | 97 | 13% | 57% | 13 | 31% | 54% | 3.90 | -4.0 | -4 | -13 | $8 |
| 19 | Proj | **401** | **59** | **20** | **56** | **8** | **239** | **229** | **333** | **445** | **778** | **664** | **820** | **12** | **63** | **0.36** | **40** | **22** | **38** | **33** | **82** | **147** | **123** | **21%** | **97** | **12%** | **66%** | | | | **4.83** | **8.4** | **22** | **73** | **$14** |

PAUL SPORER

## Harper,Bryce

| Age: 26 | Bats: L | Pos: RF CF | Health | B | LIMA Plan | B+ |
|---|---|---|---|---|---|---|
| Ht: 6' 3" | Wt: 220 | | PT/Exp | A | Rand Var | +2 |
| | | | Consist | F | MM | 4245 |

Volatility personified, randomly bouncing skills/output across the board. G/L/F, decent HctX look stable, but mercurial h%, sudden ct% plunge say another .300+ BA is a stretch. 25 HR floor seems like a lock; xPX, hr/f record points to risk. Only bb% is consistently elite. Tough to draft a sub-.250 BA in the 1st round, but someone will.

| Yr Tm | AB | R | HR | RBI | SB | BA | xBA | OBP | SLG | OPS | vL | vR | bb% | ct% | Eye | G | L | F | h% | HctX | PX | xPX | hr/f | Spd | SBO | SB% | #Wk | DOM | DIS | RC/G | RAR | BPV | BPX | R$ |
|---|---|---|---|---|---|---|---|---|---|---|---|---|---|---|---|---|---|---|---|---|---|---|---|---|---|---|---|---|---|---|---|---|---|---|
| 14 WAS | 352 | 41 | 13 | 32 | 2 | 273 | 234 | 344 | 423 | 768 | 765 | 769 | 10 | 70 | 0.37 | 44 | 22 | 35 | 35 | 92 | 110 | 115 | 15% | 129 | 4% | 50% | 18 | 44% | 39% | 5.02 | 9.3 | 30 | 81 | $10 |
| 15 WAS | 521 | 118 | 42 | 99 | 6 | 330 | 309 | 460 | 649 | 1109 | 986 | 1160 | 19 | 75 | 0.95 | 39 | 22 | 39 | 37 | 134 | 208 | 161 | 27% | 99 | 5% | 60% | 27 | 81% | 7% | 11.16 | 87.2 | 135 | 365 | $40 |
| 16 WAS | 506 | 84 | 24 | 86 | 21 | 243 | 252 | 373 | 441 | 814 | 764 | 833 | 17 | 77 | 0.92 | 40 | 17 | 42 | 27 | 106 | 117 | 111 | 14% | 89 | 17% | 68% | 26 | 54% | 31% | 5.48 | 12.3 | 64 | 183 | $21 |
| 17 WAS | 420 | 95 | 29 | 87 | 4 | 319 | 293 | 413 | 595 | 1008 | 802 | 1087 | 14 | 76 | 0.69 | 40 | 22 | 38 | 36 | 106 | 155 | 105 | 24% | 114 | 4% | 67% | 21 | 62% | 24% | 9.15 | 44.7 | 94 | 285 | $26 |
| 18 WAS | 550 | 103 | 34 | 100 | 13 | 249 | 262 | 393 | 496 | 889 | 857 | 904 | 19 | 69 | 0.77 | 40 | 22 | 38 | 30 | 108 | 161 | 148 | 23% | 82 | 8% | 81% | 28 | 61% | 25% | 6.67 | 37.0 | 70 | 233 | $26 |
| 1st Half | 278 | 47 | 20 | 49 | 6 | 219 | 266 | 366 | 482 | 848 | 774 | 885 | 19 | 71 | 0.79 | 39 | 22 | 39 | 23 | 108 | 161 | 150 | 26% | 76 | 9% | 75% | 15 | 60% | 27% | 5.78 | 11.4 | 73 | 243 | $22 |
| 2nd Half | 272 | 56 | 14 | 51 | 7 | 279 | 259 | 420 | 511 | 931 | 948 | 923 | 19 | 68 | 0.75 | 41 | 22 | 37 | 36 | 108 | 162 | 145 | 20% | 95 | 8% | 88% | 13 | 62% | 23% | 7.68 | 24.9 | 71 | 237 | $30 |
| 19 Proj | 523 | 102 | 31 | 96 | 11 | 265 | 267 | 389 | 507 | 896 | 823 | 927 | 17 | 72 | 0.74 | 40 | 21 | 38 | 31 | 108 | 152 | 130 | 21% | 96 | 8% | 74% | | | | 6.83 | 36.2 | 72 | 240 | $25 |

## Harrison,Josh

| Age: 31 | Bats: R | Pos: 2B | Health | C | LIMA Plan | C+ |
|---|---|---|---|---|---|---|
| Ht: 5' 8" | Wt: 185 | | PT/Exp | B | Rand Var | 0 |
| | | | Consist | B | MM | 1323 |

Fractured hand shelved him for 5 weeks in mid-April. Nagging 2nd half hamstring torpedoed running game, taking mid-tier value with it. Stagnant across-the-board BA skills are troubling, though profile isn't hopeless. With health, xPX, SB history suggest a 2019 uptick. But 2014 is a distant memory.

| Yr Tm | AB | R | HR | RBI | SB | BA | xBA | OBP | SLG | OPS | vL | vR | bb% | ct% | Eye | G | L | F | h% | HctX | PX | xPX | hr/f | Spd | SBO | SB% | #Wk | DOM | DIS | RC/G | RAR | BPV | BPX | R$ |
|---|---|---|---|---|---|---|---|---|---|---|---|---|---|---|---|---|---|---|---|---|---|---|---|---|---|---|---|---|---|---|---|---|---|---|
| 14 PIT | 520 | 77 | 13 | 52 | 18 | 315 | 284 | 347 | 490 | 837 | 856 | 832 | 4 | 84 | 0.27 | 37 | 24 | 39 | 35 | 116 | 121 | 117 | 8% | 131 | 20% | 72% | 27 | 52% | 15% | 6.15 | 39.2 | 84 | 227 | $29 |
| 15 PIT | 418 | 57 | 4 | 28 | 10 | 287 | 263 | 327 | 390 | 717 | 761 | 702 | 4 | 83 | 0.27 | 41 | 25 | 34 | 34 | 104 | 77 | 96 | 3% | 116 | 17% | 56% | 22 | 36% | 27% | 4.21 | 0.5 | 39 | 105 | $13 |
| 16 PIT | 487 | 57 | 4 | 59 | 19 | 283 | 250 | 311 | 388 | 699 | 810 | 674 | 3 | 84 | 0.24 | 44 | 19 | 36 | 33 | 95 | 63 | 99 | 3% | 147 | 19% | 83% | 23 | 35% | 35% | 4.34 | -7.3 | 41 | 117 | $18 |
| 17 PIT | 486 | 66 | 16 | 47 | 12 | 272 | 260 | 339 | 432 | 771 | 857 | 745 | 5 | 81 | 0.31 | 36 | 23 | 41 | 31 | 107 | 89 | 120 | 10% | 105 | 14% | 75% | 22 | 36% | 23% | 4.68 | -4.6 | 41 | 124 | $15 |
| 18 PIT | 344 | 41 | 8 | 37 | 3 | 250 | 245 | 293 | 363 | 656 | 678 | 648 | 5 | 80 | 0.26 | 38 | 25 | 37 | 29 | 97 | 67 | 114 | 8% | 100 | 4% | 100% | 22 | 27% | 32% | 3.60 | -6.7 | 16 | 53 | $6 |
| 1st Half | 195 | 27 | 4 | 20 | 2 | 267 | 254 | 303 | 369 | 673 | 661 | 676 | 4 | 85 | 0.27 | 34 | 28 | 38 | 30 | 105 | 56 | 125 | 6% | 117 | 4% | 100% | 11 | 18% | 27% | 3.85 | -1.8 | 28 | 93 | $8 |
| 2nd Half | 149 | 14 | 4 | 17 | 1 | 228 | 229 | 280 | 356 | 635 | 693 | 604 | 6 | 74 | 0.26 | 43 | 20 | 37 | 28 | 87 | 83 | 97 | 10% | 79 | 3% | 100% | 11 | 36% | 36% | 3.29 | -4.0 | 3 | 10 | $3 |
| 19 Proj | 400 | 49 | 9 | 42 | 8 | 262 | 248 | 308 | 391 | 700 | 747 | 684 | 5 | 81 | 0.26 | 39 | 23 | 38 | 30 | 99 | 77 | 110 | 8% | 108 | 10% | 79% | | | | 4.05 | -1.5 | 25 | 84 | $12 |

## Hays,Austin

| Age: 23 | Bats: R | Pos: OF | Health | A | LIMA Plan | D |
|---|---|---|---|---|---|---|
| Ht: 6' 1" | Wt: 195 | | PT/Exp | F | Rand Var | 0 |
| | | | Consist | F | MM | 1221 |

Off of .958 OPS at A+/AA in 2017, top prospect had been expected to resurface in BAL in 2018. But early struggles were followed by May ankle injury that lingered into Sept surgery and resulted in a lost season. Patience needs attention, but power, contact, opportunity keep him a defensible flyer and keeper league hold.

| Yr Tm | AB | R | HR | RBI | SB | BA | xBA | OBP | SLG | OPS | vL | vR | bb% | ct% | Eye | G | L | F | h% | HctX | PX | xPX | hr/f | Spd | SBO | SB% | #Wk | DOM | DIS | RC/G | RAR | BPV | BPX | R$ |
|---|---|---|---|---|---|---|---|---|---|---|---|---|---|---|---|---|---|---|---|---|---|---|---|---|---|---|---|---|---|---|---|---|---|---|
| 14 | | | | | | | | | | | | | | | | | | | | | | | | | | | | | | | | | | |
| 15 | | | | | | | | | | | | | | | | | | | | | | | | | | | | | | | | | | |
| 16 | | | | | | | | | | | | | | | | | | | | | | | | | | | | | | | | | | |
| 17 BAL * | 321 | 36 | 16 | 53 | 1 | 288 | 277 | 316 | 499 | 814 | 714 | 506 | 4 | 80 | 0.20 | 56 | 16 | 29 | 32 | 101 | 114 | 79 | 8% | 91 | 3% | 43% | 5 | 20% | 60% | 5.57 | 5.7 | 49 | 148 | $11 |
| 18 aa | 273 | 25 | 10 | 32 | 4 | 209 | | 234 | 363 | 597 | | | 3 | 77 | 0.14 | | | | 24 | | 89 | | | 99 | 17% | 57% | | | | 2.63 | | 16 | 53 | $2 |
| 1st Half | 174 | 16 | 5 | 13 | 4 | 194 | | 224 | 312 | 536 | | | 4 | 73 | 0.14 | | | | 24 | | 68 | | | 139 | 19% | 63% | | | | 2.13 | | -1 | -3 | $1 |
| 2nd Half | 99 | 9 | 5 | 19 | 1 | 236 | | 253 | 452 | 706 | | | 2 | 82 | 0.13 | | | | 24 | | 123 | | | 90 | 13% | 40% | | | | 3.64 | | 62 | 207 | $4 |
| 19 Proj | 237 | 24 | 4 | 36 | 2 | 267 | 240 | 287 | 379 | 665 | 847 | 609 | 3 | 79 | 0.16 | 56 | 16 | 29 | 32 | 91 | 71 | 71 | 8% | 93 | 8% | 58% | | | | 3.75 | | 2 | 6 | $7 |

## Healy,Ryon

| Age: 27 | Bats: R | Pos: 1B | Health | A | LIMA Plan | C+ |
|---|---|---|---|---|---|---|
| Ht: 6' 5" | Wt: 225 | | PT/Exp | B | Rand Var | +2 |
| | | | Consist | C | MM | 3025 |

Déjà vu 2017: Good start followed by collapse of 2nd-half FB%, hr/f, HctX that killed his power output. Big difference was season-long h% depression, uncharacteristically so vL. Mediocre Eye says BA expectation is more .250 than .270. Legit power when locked in; inconsistent, but young enough to adjust.

| Yr Tm | AB | R | HR | RBI | SB | BA | xBA | OBP | SLG | OPS | vL | vR | bb% | ct% | Eye | G | L | F | h% | HctX | PX | xPX | hr/f | Spd | SBO | SB% | #Wk | DOM | DIS | RC/G | RAR | BPV | BPX | R$ |
|---|---|---|---|---|---|---|---|---|---|---|---|---|---|---|---|---|---|---|---|---|---|---|---|---|---|---|---|---|---|---|---|---|---|---|
| 14 | | | | | | | | | | | | | | | | | | | | | | | | | | | | | | | | | | |
| 15 aa | 507 | 47 | 7 | 46 | 0 | 258 | | 290 | 357 | 646 | | | 4 | 82 | 0.25 | | | | 30 | | 70 | | | 85 | 1% | 0% | | | | 3.52 | | 21 | 57 | $6 |
| 16 OAK * | 606 | 85 | 23 | 90 | 1 | 296 | 268 | 336 | 499 | 835 | 886 | 853 | 6 | 77 | 0.26 | 42 | 20 | 39 | 35 | 93 | 130 | 102 | 16% | 103 | 1% | 42% | 13 | 54% | 15% | 6.03 | 19.7 | 55 | 157 | $22 |
| 17 OAK | 576 | 66 | 25 | 78 | 0 | 271 | 246 | 302 | 451 | 754 | 873 | 717 | 4 | 75 | 0.16 | 43 | 19 | 38 | 32 | 104 | 106 | 115 | 15% | 91 | 1% | 0% | 27 | 44% | 37% | 4.68 | -11.5 | 23 | 70 | $15 |
| 18 SEA | 493 | 51 | 24 | 73 | 0 | 235 | 240 | 277 | 412 | 688 | 631 | 715 | 5 | 77 | 0.24 | 44 | 19 | 37 | 26 | 97 | 99 | 100 | 17% | 73 | 0% | 0% | 26 | 19% | 35% | 3.78 | -9.5 | 22 | 73 | $10 |
| 1st Half | 255 | 32 | 16 | 40 | 0 | 251 | 253 | 284 | 471 | 754 | 709 | 771 | 4 | 76 | 0.18 | 40 | 19 | 41 | 27 | 108 | 121 | 133 | 20% | 79 | 0% | 0% | 13 | 23% | 31% | 4.52 | -1.9 | 37 | 123 | $16 |
| 2nd Half | 238 | 19 | 8 | 33 | 0 | 218 | 224 | 270 | 349 | 618 | 567 | 647 | 6 | 78 | 0.30 | 49 | 19 | 32 | 25 | 86 | 75 | 66 | 13% | 78 | 0% | 0% | 13 | 15% | 38% | 3.05 | -12.5 | 9 | 30 | $5 |
| 19 Proj | 500 | 54 | 22 | 69 | 0 | 254 | 248 | 292 | 435 | 727 | 726 | 728 | 5 | 77 | 0.22 | 44 | 19 | 37 | 29 | 98 | 106 | 102 | 16% | 88 | 1% | 22% | | | | 4.29 | -6.9 | 14 | 47 | $14 |

## Hechavarria,Adeiny

| Age: 30 | Bats: R | Pos: SS | Health | C | LIMA Plan | D+ |
|---|---|---|---|---|---|---|
| Ht: 6' 0" | Wt: 195 | | PT/Exp | C | Rand Var | 0 |
| | | | Consist | B | MM | 1423 |

As a GB hitter with plus speed, once offered BA value even with restrained running game. But now launch angle project has taken wing, with poor early results. Optimistic xPX offset by PX, hr/f that hint he lacks the juice. BA/xBA look stagnant; hamstring woes hit Spd. Age, AB trend, multiple home addresses add to gloomy outlook.

| Yr Tm | AB | R | HR | RBI | SB | BA | xBA | OBP | SLG | OPS | vL | vR | bb% | ct% | Eye | G | L | F | h% | HctX | PX | xPX | hr/f | Spd | SBO | SB% | #Wk | DOM | DIS | RC/G | RAR | BPV | BPX | R$ |
|---|---|---|---|---|---|---|---|---|---|---|---|---|---|---|---|---|---|---|---|---|---|---|---|---|---|---|---|---|---|---|---|---|---|---|
| 14 MIA | 536 | 53 | 1 | 34 | 7 | 276 | 262 | 308 | 356 | 664 | 742 | 645 | 5 | 84 | 0.30 | 54 | 22 | 24 | 33 | 100 | 55 | 73 | 1% | 173 | 8% | 58% | 25 | 40% | 44% | 3.80 | 9.6 | 43 | 116 | $11 |
| 15 MIA | 470 | 54 | 5 | 48 | 7 | 281 | 253 | 315 | 374 | 689 | 912 | 637 | 5 | 83 | 0.29 | 51 | 20 | 29 | 33 | 92 | 58 | 83 | 5% | 136 | 7% | 78% | 22 | 27% | 32% | 4.19 | -2.8 | 32 | 86 | $13 |
| 16 MIA | 508 | 52 | 3 | 38 | 1 | 236 | 254 | 283 | 311 | 594 | 570 | 600 | 6 | 86 | 0.45 | 48 | 22 | 30 | 27 | 112 | 43 | 86 | 2% | 138 | 1% | 100% | 27 | 30% | 26% | 2.95 | -20.6 | 32 | 91 | $1 |
| 17 2 TM | 330 | 37 | 8 | 30 | 4 | 261 | 259 | 289 | 406 | 695 | 747 | 678 | 4 | 80 | 0.19 | 49 | 20 | 32 | 31 | 116 | 79 | 74 | 10% | 141 | 7% | 80% | 19 | 32% | 47% | 4.05 | -5.5 | 34 | 103 | $6 |
| 18 3 TM | 296 | 34 | 6 | 31 | 2 | 247 | 241 | 279 | 345 | 624 | 755 | 573 | 5 | 80 | 0.28 | 38 | 25 | 37 | 29 | 106 | 59 | 112 | 7% | 99 | 3% | 100% | 24 | 21% | 46% | 3.36 | -6.4 | 11 | 37 | $4 |
| 1st Half | 162 | 18 | 3 | 18 | 0 | 259 | 245 | 287 | 340 | 627 | 803 | 544 | 5 | 83 | 0.30 | 41 | 25 | 34 | 30 | 115 | 45 | 117 | 6% | 98 | 0% | 0% | 11 | 18% | 27% | 3.44 | -2.5 | 10 | 33 | $4 |
| 2nd Half | 134 | 16 | 3 | 13 | 2 | 231 | 235 | 269 | 351 | 620 | 673 | 604 | 6 | 77 | 0.26 | 34 | 25 | 42 | 28 | 94 | 78 | 107 | 7% | 103 | 7% | 100% | 13 | 23% | 62% | 3.27 | -2.8 | 14 | 47 | $4 |
| 19 Proj | 332 | 37 | 6 | 31 | 3 | 250 | 245 | 285 | 357 | 642 | 724 | 615 | 5 | 81 | 0.28 | 43 | 23 | 34 | 29 | 107 | 63 | 95 | 6% | 126 | 4% | 86% | | | | 3.52 | -4.4 | 13 | 42 | $7 |

## Hedges,Austin

| Age: 26 | Bats: R | Pos: CA | Health | B | LIMA Plan | C |
|---|---|---|---|---|---|---|
| Ht: 6' 1" | Wt: 206 | | PT/Exp | D | Rand Var | -3 |
| | | | Consist | B | MM | 4213 |

14-37-.231 in 303 AB at SD. Miserable April ended with long DL stint (elbow tendinitis). But a different hitter returned in late June. Legit power continued ascent, this time joined by ct% and HctX. Superior glove bolsters outlook. Health, 2nd-half skills need confirmation. With that... UP: 25 HR, .250 BA.

| Yr Tm | AB | R | HR | RBI | SB | BA | xBA | OBP | SLG | OPS | vL | vR | bb% | ct% | Eye | G | L | F | h% | HctX | PX | xPX | hr/f | Spd | SBO | SB% | #Wk | DOM | DIS | RC/G | RAR | BPV | BPX | R$ |
|---|---|---|---|---|---|---|---|---|---|---|---|---|---|---|---|---|---|---|---|---|---|---|---|---|---|---|---|---|---|---|---|---|---|---|
| 14 aa | 427 | 26 | 5 | 36 | 1 | 196 | | 231 | 276 | 507 | | | 4 | 77 | 0.19 | | | | 25 | | 63 | | | 91 | 5% | 20% | | | | 1.95 | | -4 | -11 | -$4 |
| 15 SD * | 208 | 21 | 4 | 21 | 1 | 202 | 226 | 250 | 308 | 558 | 420 | 483 | 6 | 77 | 0.28 | 45 | 19 | 36 | 24 | 67 | 74 | 55 | 8% | 76 | 2% | 100% | 23 | 17% | 74% | 2.47 | -8.7 | 4 | 11 | -$2 |
| 16 SD * | 337 | 39 | 13 | 56 | 1 | 256 | 219 | 275 | 433 | 708 | 1000 | 148 | 2 | 80 | 0.13 | 44 | 6 | 50 | 28 | 109 | 104 | 59 | 0% | 77 | 5% | 24% | 3 | 33% | 67% | 3.96 | -4.3 | 35 | 100 | $7 |
| 17 SD | 387 | 36 | 18 | 55 | 4 | 214 | 223 | 262 | 398 | 660 | 600 | 684 | 6 | 68 | 0.19 | 37 | 18 | 46 | 26 | 92 | 116 | 114 | 15% | 69 | 7% | 80% | 24 | 38% | 54% | 3.34 | -8.5 | 0 | 0 | $3 |
| 18 SD * | 330 | 34 | 16 | 44 | 3 | 239 | 235 | 288 | 445 | 734 | 675 | 726 | 6 | 69 | 0.23 | 38 | 18 | 44 | 30 | 94 | 133 | 116 | 15% | 93 | 4% | 100% | 21 | 38% | 43% | 4.35 | 8.2 | 26 | 87 | $7 |
| 1st Half | 118 | 11 | 4 | 18 | 0 | 209 | 193 | 266 | 364 | 630 | 563 | 502 | 7 | 60 | 0.19 | 36 | 18 | 45 | 31 | 64 | 124 | 82 | 8% | 91 | 0% | 0% | 8 | 13% | 63% | 3.12 | -1.2 | -18 | -60 | -$3 |
| 2nd Half | 212 | 23 | 12 | 26 | 3 | 255 | 256 | 303 | 491 | 793 | 726 | 820 | 6 | 75 | 0.26 | 38 | 18 | 43 | 29 | 109 | 137 | 128 | 18% | 100 | 7% | 100% | 13 | 54% | 31% | 5.13 | 10.4 | 52 | 173 | $13 |
| 19 Proj | 397 | 40 | 19 | 54 | 4 | 243 | 235 | 286 | 439 | 725 | 677 | 746 | 5 | 71 | 0.20 | 38 | 18 | 43 | 30 | 88 | 124 | 103 | 15% | 85 | 6% | 84% | | | | 4.23 | 9.2 | 16 | 53 | $11 |

## Heredia,Guillermo

| Age: 28 | Bats: R | Pos: CF LF | Health | A | LIMA Plan | D |
|---|---|---|---|---|---|---|
| Ht: 5' 10" | Wt: 180 | | PT/Exp | D | Rand Var | +1 |
| | | | Consist | A | MM | 1121 |

5-19-.236 in 292 AB at SEA. Career .223 hitter vR with anemic pop teased improvement out of the gate, earning an early AB uptick. But .418 OPS in June cemented part-timer role for the remainder. Defense, plate skills, speed and career .272 BA vL can earn an MLB paycheck, but not a fantasy roster spot.

| Yr Tm | AB | R | HR | RBI | SB | BA | xBA | OBP | SLG | OPS | vL | vR | bb% | ct% | Eye | G | L | F | h% | HctX | PX | xPX | hr/f | Spd | SBO | SB% | #Wk | DOM | DIS | RC/G | RAR | BPV | BPX | R$ |
|---|---|---|---|---|---|---|---|---|---|---|---|---|---|---|---|---|---|---|---|---|---|---|---|---|---|---|---|---|---|---|---|---|---|---|
| 14 | | | | | | | | | | | | | | | | | | | | | | | | | | | | | | | | | | |
| 15 | | | | | | | | | | | | | | | | | | | | | | | | | | | | | | | | | | |
| 16 SEA * | 435 | 66 | 4 | 50 | 5 | 254 | 241 | 332 | 325 | 657 | 658 | 669 | 10 | 83 | 0.70 | 49 | 20 | 31 | 30 | 56 | 43 | 13 | 4% | 131 | 8% | 43% | 10 | 30% | 60% | 3.53 | -10.9 | 30 | 86 | $8 |
| 17 SEA | 386 | 43 | 6 | 24 | 1 | 249 | 233 | 315 | 337 | 652 | 794 | 582 | 6 | 83 | 0.42 | 47 | 18 | 35 | 28 | 69 | 52 | 38 | 6% | 113 | 6% | 17% | 26 | 27% | 35% | 3.22 | -17.6 | 24 | 73 | $3 |
| 18 SEA * | 321 | 32 | 5 | 20 | 3 | 235 | 250 | 310 | 334 | 643 | 671 | 652 | 9 | 83 | 0.63 | 43 | 23 | 33 | 27 | 82 | 61 | 64 | 6% | 104 | 10% | 40% | 27 | 33% | 37% | 3.27 | -7.5 | 31 | 103 | $2 |
| 1st Half | 184 | 17 | 2 | 9 | 1 | 239 | 231 | 334 | 325 | 659 | 553 | 720 | 12 | 80 | 0.70 | 41 | 22 | 37 | 29 | 73 | 55 | 66 | 4% | 127 | 9% | 19% | 14 | 36% | 36% | 3.35 | -4.5 | 27 | 90 | $0 |
| 2nd Half | 137 | 14 | 3 | 11 | 2 | 229 | 277 | 275 | 346 | 620 | 795 | 515 | 6 | 87 | 0.48 | 46 | 25 | 29 | 24 | 94 | 68 | 61 | 10% | 80 | 11% | 71% | 13 | 31% | 38% | 3.12 | -4.3 | 39 | 130 | $4 |
| 19 Proj | 225 | 25 | 4 | 16 | 2 | 241 | 248 | 313 | 341 | 654 | 715 | 601 | 8 | 84 | 0.53 | 46 | 21 | 33 | 27 | 75 | 60 | 47 | 6% | 106 | 8% | 38% | | | | 3.30 | -5.7 | 16 | 53 | $4 |

JOCK THOMPSON

## Hernandez,Cesar

Age: 29 Bats: B Pos: 2B | Ht: 5' 10" Wt: 160
Health B | PT/Exp A | Consist B
LIMA Plan B | Rand Var -1 | MM 1525

Proof there's no such thing as a free launch (angle). Padded his power stats with extra fly balls, but swing change included costly whiffs that resulted in a BA/xBA nosedive. R$ remained stable due to uptick in AB and SB, but BPV, RAR and RC/G all prefer the 2017 version. Lacking HctX or xPX support, you should, too.

| Yr | Tm | AB | R | HR | RBI | SB | BA | xBA | OBP | SLG | OPS | vL | vR | bb% | ct% | Eye | G | L | F | h% | HctX | PX | xPX | hr/f | Spd | SBO | SB% | #Wk | DOM | DIS | RC/G | RAR | BPV | BPX | R$ |
|---|---|---|---|---|---|---|---|---|---|---|---|---|---|---|---|---|---|---|---|---|---|---|---|---|---|---|---|---|---|---|---|---|---|---|---|
| 14 | PHI * | 373 | 40 | 4 | 22 | 7 | 242 | 246 | 299 | 314 | 613 | 626 | 551 | 7 | 76 | 0.34 | 53 | 26 | 21 | 31 | 63 | 54 | 50 | 6% | 135 | 15% | 44% | 16 | 19% | 56% | 2.92 | -5.3 | 5 | 14 | $5 |
| 15 | PHI | 405 | 57 | 1 | 35 | 19 | 272 | 257 | 339 | 348 | 687 | 769 | 653 | 9 | 79 | 0.47 | 54 | 24 | 22 | 34 | 80 | 58 | 67 | 2% | 149 | 19% | 79% | 24 | 38% | 42% | 4.19 | 0.3 | 26 | 70 | $14 |
| 16 | PHI | 547 | 67 | 6 | 39 | 17 | 294 | 262 | 371 | 393 | 764 | 789 | 756 | 11 | 79 | 0.57 | 55 | 24 | 21 | 36 | 83 | 55 | 59 | 7% | 186 | 15% | 57% | 27 | 26% | 33% | 5.01 | 2.1 | 38 | 109 | $20 |
| 17 | PHI | 511 | 85 | 9 | 34 | 15 | 294 | 273 | 373 | 421 | 793 | 810 | 786 | 11 | 80 | 0.59 | 53 | 23 | 25 | 35 | 71 | 74 | 61 | 9% | 185 | 12% | 75% | 22 | 41% | 18% | 5.60 | 8.3 | 56 | 170 | $19 |
| 18 | PHI | 605 | 91 | 15 | 60 | 19 | 253 | 225 | 356 | 362 | 718 | 700 | 725 | 13 | 74 | 0.61 | 46 | 21 | 34 | 32 | 66 | 65 | 63 | 10% | 145 | 12% | 76% | 28 | 29% | 36% | 4.42 | 2.6 | 22 | 73 | $20 |
| 1st Half | | 310 | 57 | 8 | 27 | 12 | 271 | 234 | 378 | 394 | 772 | 748 | 780 | 15 | 75 | 0.68 | 45 | 22 | 34 | 34 | 78 | 77 | 83 | 11% | 139 | 12% | 86% | 15 | 27% | 33% | 5.37 | 10.7 | 33 | 110 | $25 |
| 2nd Half | | 295 | 34 | 7 | 33 | 7 | 234 | 214 | 333 | 329 | 662 | 642 | 669 | 12 | 74 | 0.54 | 47 | 20 | 33 | 29 | 53 | 52 | 43 | 10% | 154 | 11% | 64% | 13 | 31% | 38% | 3.53 | -5.8 | 11 | 37 | $15 |
| **19** | **Proj** | **526** | **76** | **10** | **45** | **16** | **268** | **242** | **355** | **375** | **731** | **740** | **727** | **12** | **77** | **0.56** | **50** | **22** | **28** | **33** | **69** | **64** | **59** | **9%** | **163** | **13%** | **70%** | | | | **4.57** | **6.1** | **15** | **51** | **$17** |

## Hernandez,Enrique

Age: 27 Bats: R Pos: CF 2B SS | Ht: 5' 11" Wt: 200
Health B | PT/Exp D | Consist C
LIMA Plan B+ | Rand Var 0 | MM 3335

Increased MLB plate appearances each year, and signs of growth are emerging. Year-long success against RHP closed the platoon gap; significantly more 2nd half contact, HctX drove overall skills bump; fly balls are on the rise. Real-life versatility may cap current AB level, but with opportunity ... UP: 25 HR, .285 BA

| Yr | Tm | AB | R | HR | RBI | SB | BA | xBA | OBP | SLG | OPS | vL | vR | bb% | ct% | Eye | G | L | F | h% | HctX | PX | xPX | hr/f | Spd | SBO | SB% | #Wk | DOM | DIS | RC/G | RAR | BPV | BPX | R$ |
|---|---|---|---|---|---|---|---|---|---|---|---|---|---|---|---|---|---|---|---|---|---|---|---|---|---|---|---|---|---|---|---|---|---|---|---|
| 14 | 2 TM * | 497 | 55 | 10 | 45 | 4 | 266 | 264 | 313 | 401 | 714 | 581 | 796 | 6 | 87 | 0.52 | 38 | 21 | 41 | 29 | 94 | 92 | 115 | 7% | 113 | 9% | 39% | 9 | 56% | 22% | 4.16 | 5.4 | 69 | 186 | $12 |
| 15 | LA * | 261 | 28 | 8 | 29 | 1 | 269 | 261 | 306 | 427 | 733 | 1215 | 592 | 5 | 76 | 0.22 | 46 | 23 | 30 | 33 | 110 | 106 | 98 | 15% | 118 | 5% | 27% | 20 | 45% | 40% | 4.42 | -2.2 | 37 | 100 | $5 |
| 16 | LA | 216 | 25 | 7 | 18 | 2 | 190 | 211 | 283 | 324 | 607 | 668 | 524 | 11 | 70 | 0.44 | 41 | 17 | 42 | 23 | 79 | 89 | 91 | 11% | 87 | 4% | 100% | 23 | 26% | 48% | 2.93 | -11.6 | 4 | 11 | -$2 |
| 17 | LA | 297 | 46 | 11 | 37 | 3 | 215 | 259 | 308 | 421 | 729 | 946 | 499 | 12 | 73 | 0.51 | 42 | 19 | 40 | 26 | 116 | 132 | 122 | 13% | 93 | 4% | 100% | 27 | 48% | 37% | 4.31 | -8.6 | 52 | 158 | $3 |
| 18 | LA | 402 | 67 | 21 | 52 | 3 | 256 | 260 | 336 | 470 | 806 | 780 | 833 | 11 | 81 | 0.64 | 38 | 19 | 44 | 27 | 105 | 115 | 105 | 15% | 105 | 3% | 100% | 28 | 61% | 14% | 5.50 | 10.5 | 70 | 233 | $13 |
| 1st Half | | 202 | 33 | 14 | 30 | 1 | 238 | 246 | 316 | 485 | 801 | 821 | 780 | 11 | 75 | 0.48 | 32 | 17 | 51 | 25 | 84 | 136 | 112 | 18% | 93 | 2% | 100% | 15 | 53% | 20% | 5.20 | 3.6 | 61 | 203 | $13 |
| 2nd Half | | 200 | 34 | 7 | 22 | 2 | 275 | 276 | 357 | 455 | 812 | 737 | 882 | 12 | 86 | 0.93 | 42 | 20 | 38 | 29 | 126 | 97 | 98 | 11% | 115 | 3% | 100% | 13 | 69% | 8% | 5.81 | 6.9 | 81 | 270 | $13 |
| **19** | **Proj** | **405** | **61** | **18** | **47** | **3** | **256** | **259** | **337** | **457** | **794** | **853** | **737** | **11** | **79** | **0.60** | **40** | **19** | **41** | **28** | **106** | **115** | **107** | **14%** | **103** | **3%** | **89%** | | | | **5.34** | **14.2** | **58** | **193** | **$13** |

## Hernandez,Gorkys

Age: 31 Bats: R Pos: CF LF | Ht: 6' 1" Wt: 196
Health A | PT/Exp C | Consist A
LIMA Plan D+ | Rand Var -1 | MM 1313

Talk about false expectations: 1st half h% and hr/f combo papered over mushrooming swing-and-miss issues. The correction hit HARD come July, and he limped to the finish (.469 OPS in Aug/Sep). League-average HctX/xPX is noteworthy, but void of more loft and/or contact, he still is destined to disappoint.

| Yr | Tm | AB | R | HR | RBI | SB | BA | xBA | OBP | SLG | OPS | vL | vR | bb% | ct% | Eye | G | L | F | h% | HctX | PX | xPX | hr/f | Spd | SBO | SB% | #Wk | DOM | DIS | RC/G | RAR | BPV | BPX | R$ |
|---|---|---|---|---|---|---|---|---|---|---|---|---|---|---|---|---|---|---|---|---|---|---|---|---|---|---|---|---|---|---|---|---|---|---|---|
| 14 | aaa | 189 | 12 | 0 | 6 | 5 | 174 | | 212 | 213 | 426 | | | 5 | 69 | 0.16 | | | | 25 | | 45 | | | 93 | 18% | 80% | | | | 1.44 | | -46 | -124 | -$4 |
| 15 | PIT * | 345 | 40 | 4 | 33 | 14 | 232 | 253 | 297 | 320 | 618 | 0 | 0 | 8 | 73 | 0.34 | 100 | 0 | 0 | 31 | 0 | 65 | -16 | 0% | 104 | 20% | 80% | 3 | 0% | 0% | 3.23 | -11.2 | -4 | -11 | $7 |
| 16 | SF * | 491 | 59 | 7 | 40 | 14 | 238 | 221 | 297 | 336 | 633 | 788 | 714 | 8 | 78 | 0.37 | 39 | 20 | 41 | 29 | 125 | 64 | 152 | 12% | 130 | 25% | 45% | 6 | 67% | 33% | 2.97 | -25.8 | 18 | 51 | $9 |
| 17 | SF | 310 | 40 | 0 | 22 | 12 | 255 | 237 | 327 | 326 | 652 | 610 | 684 | 9 | 76 | 0.42 | 47 | 22 | 31 | 33 | 78 | 56 | 66 | 0% | 108 | 18% | 75% | 27 | 19% | 44% | 3.63 | -13.1 | 3 | 9 | $6 |
| 18 | SF | 414 | 52 | 15 | 40 | 8 | 234 | 232 | 285 | 391 | 676 | 673 | 678 | 6 | 73 | 0.24 | 48 | 16 | 36 | 29 | 104 | 97 | 103 | 14% | 115 | 14% | 62% | 28 | 32% | 57% | 3.56 | -8.5 | 17 | 57 | $9 |
| 1st Half | | 209 | 28 | 10 | 24 | 4 | 287 | 242 | 341 | 474 | 814 | 729 | 869 | 7 | 69 | 0.25 | 46 | 21 | 33 | 37 | 101 | 116 | 99 | 22% | 128 | 9% | 80% | 15 | 33% | 53% | 5.73 | 9.4 | 25 | 83 | $15 |
| 2nd Half | | 205 | 24 | 5 | 16 | 4 | 180 | 221 | 227 | 307 | 535 | 605 | 500 | 5 | 76 | 0.22 | 51 | 11 | 38 | 21 | 106 | 79 | 106 | 8% | 100 | 24% | 50% | 13 | 31% | 62% | 1.97 | -14.6 | 10 | 33 | $3 |
| **19** | **Proj** | **326** | **39** | **7** | **27** | **8** | **231** | **229** | **288** | **354** | **642** | **642** | **643** | **7** | **75** | **0.29** | **47** | **18** | **35** | **29** | **98** | **80** | **98** | **9%** | **113** | **17%** | **59%** | | | | **3.21** | **-9.3** | **7** | **22** | **$7** |

## Hernandez,Teoscar

Age: 26 Bats: R Pos: LF RF | Ht: 6' 2" Wt: 180
Health A | PT/Exp C | Consist B
LIMA Plan B | Rand Var 0 | MM 4315

Skilled but flawed for sure. The power's real, given the heavy fly ball lean and year-long xPX, hr/f. Raw speed is too, but chances dried up due to poor execution. Contact issues are the darkest shadow, especially when viewed as 1st half/2nd half splits. Speculation worthy—but with strong bust potential.

| Yr | Tm | AB | R | HR | RBI | SB | BA | xBA | OBP | SLG | OPS | vL | vR | bb% | ct% | Eye | G | L | F | h% | HctX | PX | xPX | hr/f | Spd | SBO | SB% | #Wk | DOM | DIS | RC/G | RAR | BPV | BPX | R$ |
|---|---|---|---|---|---|---|---|---|---|---|---|---|---|---|---|---|---|---|---|---|---|---|---|---|---|---|---|---|---|---|---|---|---|---|---|
| 14 | aa | 95 | 9 | 3 | 8 | 2 | 252 | | 264 | 409 | 673 | | | 2 | 57 | 0.04 | | | | 41 | | 146 | | | 109 | 27% | 32% | | | | 3.12 | | -16 | -43 | $1 |
| 15 | aa | 470 | 70 | 14 | 36 | 25 | 191 | | 231 | 310 | 541 | | | 5 | 69 | 0.17 | | | | 24 | | 81 | | | 124 | 37% | 76% | | | | 2.26 | | -7 | -19 | $9 |
| 16 | HOU * | 523 | 75 | 12 | 54 | 28 | 262 | 234 | 323 | 404 | 727 | 881 | 632 | 8 | 76 | 0.38 | 48 | 12 | 40 | 32 | 102 | 94 | 75 | 14% | 134 | 34% | 59% | 9 | 56% | 22% | 4.12 | -2.4 | 39 | 111 | $21 |
| 17 | 2 AL * | 488 | 79 | 25 | 81 | 15 | 252 | 246 | 321 | 488 | 809 | 647 | 1014 | 9 | 69 | 0.33 | 28 | 23 | 49 | 31 | 80 | 149 | 139 | 31% | 124 | 22% | 60% | 7 | 57% | 43% | 5.06 | -5.6 | 55 | 167 | $19 |
| 18 | TOR | 476 | 67 | 22 | 57 | 5 | 239 | 238 | 302 | 468 | 771 | 744 | 783 | 8 | 66 | 0.25 | 36 | 20 | 44 | 32 | 90 | 157 | 149 | 16% | 158 | 10% | 50% | 26 | 65% | 27% | 4.55 | -0.4 | 54 | 180 | $12 |
| 1st Half | | 261 | 37 | 13 | 33 | 3 | 257 | 266 | 309 | 513 | 822 | 839 | 813 | 6 | 72 | 0.23 | 38 | 21 | 41 | 31 | 100 | 161 | 140 | 17% | 151 | 15% | 43% | 13 | 77% | 8% | 5.03 | 3.3 | 75 | 250 | $16 |
| 2nd Half | | 215 | 30 | 9 | 24 | 2 | 219 | 204 | 295 | 414 | 709 | 613 | 749 | 10 | 59 | 0.27 | 34 | 19 | 48 | 32 | 79 | 150 | 162 | 15% | 155 | 6% | 67% | 13 | 54% | 46% | 3.98 | -4.1 | 23 | 77 | $8 |
| **19** | **Proj** | **450** | **66** | **22** | **55** | **7** | **238** | **234** | **300** | **460** | **760** | **677** | **797** | **8** | **67** | **0.27** | **35** | **20** | **46** | **31** | **87** | **148** | **137** | **16%** | **151** | **14%** | **51%** | | | | **4.42** | **-2.4** | **37** | **124** | **$14** |

## Herrera,Odubel

Age: 27 Bats: L Pos: CF | Ht: 5' 11" Wt: 205
Health A | PT/Exp A | Consist B
LIMA Plan B+ | Rand Var +1 | MM 2325

Appeared to be racing to stardom by June 1 (.862 OPS), but fell way off the pace afterwards (.655), dashing hopes of a hr/f uptick. We should have known, as his quality of contact (and the resulting power) has never been an asset, and both plate and speed skills are devoid of growth. BPV confirms he's stuck in neutral.

| Yr | Tm | AB | R | HR | RBI | SB | BA | xBA | OBP | SLG | OPS | vL | vR | bb% | ct% | Eye | G | L | F | h% | HctX | PX | xPX | hr/f | Spd | SBO | SB% | #Wk | DOM | DIS | RC/G | RAR | BPV | BPX | R$ |
|---|---|---|---|---|---|---|---|---|---|---|---|---|---|---|---|---|---|---|---|---|---|---|---|---|---|---|---|---|---|---|---|---|---|---|---|
| 14 | aa | 368 | 37 | 2 | 37 | 10 | 289 | | 331 | 359 | 690 | | | 6 | 79 | 0.30 | | | | 36 | | 55 | | | 110 | 16% | 55% | | | | 4.04 | | 7 | 19 | $12 |
| 15 | PHI | 495 | 64 | 8 | 41 | 16 | 297 | 248 | 344 | 418 | 762 | 720 | 776 | 5 | 74 | 0.22 | 47 | 23 | 29 | 39 | 85 | 93 | 83 | 8% | 129 | 18% | 67% | 27 | 44% | 30% | 4.94 | 8.7 | 21 | 57 | $20 |
| 16 | PHI | 583 | 87 | 15 | 49 | 25 | 286 | 249 | 361 | 420 | 781 | 599 | 841 | 10 | 77 | 0.47 | 46 | 22 | 32 | 35 | 85 | 79 | 88 | 11% | 150 | 17% | 78% | 27 | 26% | 26% | 5.38 | 12.2 | 37 | 106 | $26 |
| 17 | PHI | 526 | 67 | 14 | 56 | 8 | 281 | 265 | 325 | 452 | 778 | 794 | 771 | 6 | 76 | 0.25 | 44 | 21 | 35 | 35 | 90 | 110 | 79 | 10% | 95 | 11% | 62% | 25 | 40% | 36% | 5.04 | -0.2 | 34 | 103 | $16 |
| 18 | PHI | 550 | 64 | 22 | 71 | 5 | 255 | 245 | 310 | 420 | 730 | 740 | 727 | 6 | 78 | 0.31 | 45 | 18 | 37 | 29 | 71 | 93 | 64 | 14% | 110 | 5% | 71% | 28 | 25% | 46% | 4.33 | 1.5 | 33 | 110 | $15 |
| 1st Half | | 308 | 42 | 14 | 46 | 4 | 286 | 265 | 340 | 481 | 821 | 846 | 811 | 7 | 78 | 0.32 | 44 | 21 | 35 | 33 | 77 | 111 | 66 | 17% | 109 | 8% | 67% | 15 | 27% | 33% | 5.65 | 13.1 | 49 | 163 | $25 |
| 2nd Half | | 242 | 22 | 8 | 25 | 1 | 215 | 215 | 272 | 343 | 615 | 547 | 631 | 6 | 78 | 0.30 | 45 | 15 | 40 | 24 | 64 | 70 | 62 | 11% | 109 | 2% | 100% | 13 | 23% | 62% | 2.96 | -8.8 | 14 | 47 | $3 |
| **19** | **Proj** | **523** | **63** | **16** | **57** | **9** | **264** | **246** | **319** | **416** | **735** | **710** | **743** | **7** | **77** | **0.31** | **45** | **20** | **35** | **31** | **78** | **91** | **73** | **11%** | **112** | **10%** | **70%** | | | | **4.46** | **5.0** | **24** | **80** | **$17** |

## Herrera,Rosell

Age: 26 Bats: B Pos: RF | Ht: 6' 3" Wt: 195
Health A | PT/Exp C | Consist B
LIMA Plan D | Rand Var +4 | MM 1331

1-20-.234 in 278 AB at CIN/KC. The hard contact skills and line-drive stroke would seem to be worth something. But with so many batted balls on the ground, and with the brakes (rightfully) applied to his SB chances, this isn't going to be an easy path to MLB—let alone fantasy—relevance. At 26, window is closing fast.

| Yr | Tm | AB | R | HR | RBI | SB | BA | xBA | OBP | SLG | OPS | vL | vR | bb% | ct% | Eye | G | L | F | h% | HctX | PX | xPX | hr/f | Spd | SBO | SB% | #Wk | DOM | DIS | RC/G | RAR | BPV | BPX | R$ |
|---|---|---|---|---|---|---|---|---|---|---|---|---|---|---|---|---|---|---|---|---|---|---|---|---|---|---|---|---|---|---|---|---|---|---|---|
| 14 | | | | | | | | | | | | | | | | | | | | | | | | | | | | | | | | | | | |
| 15 | | | | | | | | | | | | | | | | | | | | | | | | | | | | | | | | | | | |
| 16 | aa | 425 | 50 | 5 | 54 | 30 | 283 | | 353 | 368 | 721 | | | 10 | 81 | 0.58 | | | | 34 | | 52 | | | 104 | 27% | 77% | | | | 4.70 | | 20 | 57 | $21 |
| 17 | aaa | 320 | 41 | 2 | 19 | 14 | 247 | | 300 | 348 | 648 | | | 7 | 77 | 0.33 | | | | 32 | | 66 | | | 129 | 26% | 67% | | | | 3.43 | | 15 | 45 | $7 |
| 18 | 2 TM * | 404 | 39 | 4 | 32 | 7 | 235 | 270 | 283 | 355 | 637 | 506 | 649 | 6 | 80 | 0.33 | 57 | 22 | 22 | 29 | 109 | 76 | 77 | 2% | 115 | 17% | 51% | 20 | 25% | 40% | 3.15 | -16.8 | 29 | 97 | $4 |
| 1st Half | | 185 | 15 | 3 | 18 | 5 | 236 | 274 | 272 | 412 | 685 | 737 | 539 | 5 | 79 | 0.24 | 48 | 22 | 30 | 29 | 124 | 106 | 130 | 0% | 117 | 31% | 56% | 7 | 14% | 57% | 3.47 | -5.6 | 47 | 157 | $4 |
| 2nd Half | | 219 | 24 | 1 | 14 | 2 | 233 | 255 | 296 | 306 | 602 | 447 | 678 | 8 | 80 | 0.42 | 59 | 21 | 20 | 29 | 105 | 51 | 63 | 3% | 107 | 9% | 40% | 13 | 31% | 31% | 2.83 | -10.9 | 12 | 40 | $4 |
| **19** | **Proj** | **227** | **25** | **1** | **18** | **6** | **246** | **255** | **303** | **337** | **640** | **596** | **660** | **7** | **79** | **0.38** | **54** | **22** | **24** | **31** | **113** | **61** | **90** | **2%** | **116** | **17%** | **57%** | | | | **3.28** | **-8.1** | **15** | **50** | **$5** |

## Heyward,Jason

Age: 29 Bats: L Pos: RF CF | Ht: 6' 5" Wt: 240
Health B | PT/Exp B | Consist B
LIMA Plan B | Rand Var 0 | MM 1235

Think positive: What would a late-career surge look like? 1) FB% inches towards 40%; 2) HctX and xPX both improve to hover around league average; 3) Contact rate nears elite level. That'd be good, right? Well, take 2018's first half, double the results and you have ... not much. Reality stinks sometimes.

| Yr | Tm | AB | R | HR | RBI | SB | BA | xBA | OBP | SLG | OPS | vL | vR | bb% | ct% | Eye | G | L | F | h% | HctX | PX | xPX | hr/f | Spd | SBO | SB% | #Wk | DOM | DIS | RC/G | RAR | BPV | BPX | R$ |
|---|---|---|---|---|---|---|---|---|---|---|---|---|---|---|---|---|---|---|---|---|---|---|---|---|---|---|---|---|---|---|---|---|---|---|---|
| 14 | ATL | 573 | 74 | 11 | 58 | 20 | 271 | 251 | 351 | 384 | 735 | 477 | 820 | 10 | 83 | 0.68 | 45 | 19 | 36 | 31 | 95 | 80 | 80 | 6% | 116 | 13% | 83% | 26 | 50% | 12% | 4.75 | 10.8 | 53 | 143 | $21 |
| 15 | STL | 547 | 79 | 13 | 60 | 23 | 293 | 288 | 359 | 439 | 797 | 709 | 835 | 9 | 84 | 0.62 | 57 | 19 | 23 | 33 | 105 | 94 | 73 | 12% | 112 | 16% | 88% | 27 | 48% | 19% | 5.84 | 14.9 | 63 | 170 | $27 |
| 16 | CHC | 530 | 61 | 7 | 49 | 11 | 230 | 249 | 306 | 325 | 631 | 586 | 647 | 9 | 82 | 0.58 | 46 | 21 | 33 | 27 | 88 | 62 | 72 | 5% | 89 | 11% | 73% | 27 | 26% | 37% | 3.25 | -23.1 | 26 | 74 | $6 |
| 17 | CHC | 432 | 59 | 11 | 59 | 4 | 259 | 262 | 326 | 389 | 715 | 662 | 734 | 9 | 84 | 0.61 | 47 | 20 | 33 | 29 | 87 | 66 | 70 | 9% | 113 | 7% | 50% | 24 | 33% | 17% | 4.22 | -12.2 | 44 | 133 | $10 |
| 18 | CHC | 440 | 67 | 8 | 57 | 1 | 270 | 260 | 335 | 395 | 731 | 716 | 735 | 9 | 86 | 0.70 | 48 | 18 | 34 | 30 | 94 | 71 | 69 | 6% | 106 | 2% | 50% | 26 | 54% | 8% | 4.59 | 2.4 | 53 | 177 | $11 |
| 1st Half | | 234 | 38 | 5 | 37 | 0 | 291 | 268 | 349 | 440 | 789 | 637 | 831 | 8 | 88 | 0.72 | 43 | 19 | 38 | 32 | 110 | 83 | 97 | 6% | 102 | 1% | 0% | 15 | 67% | 7% | 5.43 | 6.4 | 66 | 220 | $15 |
| 2nd Half | | 206 | 29 | 3 | 20 | 1 | 248 | 250 | 320 | 345 | 665 | 815 | 628 | 9 | 85 | 0.68 | 54 | 17 | 29 | 28 | 77 | 57 | 36 | 6% | 107 | 2% | 100% | 11 | 36% | 9% | 3.73 | -4.4 | 38 | 127 | $7 |
| **19** | **Proj** | **447** | **62** | **9** | **53** | **5** | **260** | **257** | **327** | **379** | **706** | **676** | **716** | **9** | **85** | **0.63** | **49** | **19** | **33** | **29** | **90** | **68** | **66** | **7%** | **105** | **6%** | **69%** | | | | **4.22** | **-3.1** | **40** | **134** | **$13** |

BRENT HERSHEY

## Hicks,Aaron

Age: 29 Bats: B Pos: CF | Ht: 6' 1" Wt: 202
Health: D | PT/Exp: C | Consist: D
LIMA Plan: B+ | Rand Var: 0 | MM: 4345

Power surge fully supported by rising xPX, as he built upon 2017's gains. Aside from two weeks lost in April to strained intercostal, health returned, and Spd, too. Hit rate vL dragged down BA, but rising Eye, HctX say BA rebound is likely. Repeat of 2018 is probable; could exceed with increased playing time.

| Yr | Tm | AB | R | HR | RBI | SB | BA | xBA | OBP | SLG | OPS | vL | vR | bb% | ct% | Eye | G | L | F | h% | HctX | PX | xPX | hr/f | Spd | SBO | SB% | #Wk | DOM | DIS | RC/G | RAR | BPV | BPX | R$ |
|---|---|---|---|---|---|---|---|---|---|---|---|---|---|---|---|---|---|---|---|---|---|---|---|---|---|---|---|---|---|---|---|---|---|---|---|
| 14 | MIN * | 406 | 52 | 5 | 41 | 6 | 235 | 241 | 340 | 330 | 670 | 792 | 512 | 14 | 75 | 0.64 | 54 | 20 | 26 | 30 | 78 | 81 | 45 | 3% | 103 | 11% | 45% | 16 | 25% | 56% | 3.57 | -4.0 | 26 | 70 | $6 |
| 15 | MIN * | 501 | 69 | 13 | 49 | 15 | 268 | 259 | 331 | 418 | 750 | 870 | 661 | 9 | 80 | 0.48 | 42 | 23 | 35 | 31 | 90 | 94 | 93 | 11% | 125 | 13% | 78% | 18 | 39% | 22% | 4.84 | 4.8 | 52 | 141 | $17 |
| 16 | NYY | 327 | 32 | 8 | 31 | 3 | 217 | 232 | 281 | 336 | 617 | 484 | 691 | 8 | 79 | 0.44 | 46 | 17 | 37 | 25 | 93 | 72 | 104 | 8% | 92 | 9% | 43% | 25 | 28% | 36% | 2.98 | -14.1 | 21 | 60 | $1 |
| 17 | NYY * | 325 | 60 | 16 | 54 | 11 | 267 | 266 | 370 | 481 | 852 | 903 | 816 | 14 | 78 | 0.76 | 44 | 16 | 40 | 30 | 98 | 122 | 119 | 16% | 92 | 15% | 68% | 19 | 47% | 26% | 6.08 | 12.7 | 68 | 206 | $14 |
| 18 | NYY | 480 | 90 | 27 | 79 | 11 | 248 | 264 | 366 | 467 | 833 | 801 | 845 | 15 | 77 | 0.81 | 40 | 22 | 38 | 27 | 112 | 122 | 131 | 19% | 111 | 8% | 85% | 27 | 41% | 30% | 5.87 | 26.1 | 71 | 237 | $21 |
| 1st Half | | 225 | 36 | 11 | 34 | 6 | 249 | 257 | 337 | 458 | 795 | 825 | 781 | 12 | 77 | 0.59 | 40 | 19 | 41 | 28 | 121 | 118 | 142 | 15% | 108 | 11% | 86% | 14 | 43% | 29% | 5.32 | 7.8 | 62 | 207 | $16 |
| 2nd Half | | 255 | 54 | 16 | 45 | 5 | 247 | 270 | 390 | 475 | 864 | 778 | 897 | 19 | 76 | 1.00 | 40 | 24 | 36 | 26 | 104 | 125 | 121 | 23% | 111 | 6% | 83% | 13 | 38% | 31% | 6.33 | 16.6 | 79 | 263 | $25 |
| **19** | **Proj** | **512** | **87** | **29** | **76** | **12** | **256** | **266** | **359** | **480** | **840** | **829** | **844** | **14** | **78** | **0.72** | **42** | **20** | **39** | **28** | **102** | **126** | **117** | **19%** | **104** | **10%** | **72%** | | | | **5.88** | **26.4** | **69** | **230** | **$21** |

## Hicks,John

Age: 29 Bats: R Pos: 1B CA | Ht: 6' 2" Wt: 230
Health: B | PT/Exp: D | Consist: A
LIMA Plan: D | Rand Var: -5 | MM: 2111

Backup catcher fell into some AB at first base when Miguel Cabrera went down, then season ended due to an August groin injury. xPX, HctX confirm league average power, but poor skills vR (0.19 Eye, 84 PX) cap BA and limit usefulness to deep leagues only. Probably most valuable as short-side of a platoon.

| Yr | Tm | AB | R | HR | RBI | SB | BA | xBA | OBP | SLG | OPS | vL | vR | bb% | ct% | Eye | G | L | F | h% | HctX | PX | xPX | hr/f | Spd | SBO | SB% | #Wk | DOM | DIS | RC/G | RAR | BPV | BPX | R$ |
|---|---|---|---|---|---|---|---|---|---|---|---|---|---|---|---|---|---|---|---|---|---|---|---|---|---|---|---|---|---|---|---|---|---|---|---|
| 14 | a/a | 290 | 29 | 3 | 33 | 5 | 232 | | 278 | 313 | 590 | | | 6 | 72 | 0.23 | | | | 31 | | 65 | | | 100 | 12% | 58% | | | | 2.80 | | -15 | -41 | $3 |
| 15 | SEA * | 330 | 26 | 4 | 24 | 7 | 174 | 197 | 202 | 249 | 451 | 200 | 178 | 3 | 67 | 0.11 | 14 | 36 | 50 | 24 | 117 | 63 | 198 | 0% | 78 | 20% | 67% | 6 | 17% | 67% | 1.52 | -36.9 | -46 | -124 | -$4 |
| 16 | DET * | 325 | 36 | 8 | 36 | 3 | 255 | 330 | 292 | 392 | 684 | 0 | 3000 | 5 | 74 | 0.20 | 50 | 50 | 0 | 33 | 0 | 95 | -24 | 0% | 82 | 6% | 72% | 1 | 100% | 0% | 3.91 | -9.0 | 7 | 20 | $5 |
| 17 | DET * | 381 | 42 | 12 | 51 | 6 | 246 | 243 | 277 | 399 | 676 | 731 | 784 | 4 | 70 | 0.14 | 51 | 20 | 30 | 32 | 99 | 100 | 86 | 17% | 66 | 14% | 57% | 19 | 32% | 37% | 3.60 | -20.3 | -9 | -27 | $7 |
| 18 | DET | 288 | 35 | 9 | 32 | 0 | 260 | 221 | 312 | 403 | 715 | 822 | 672 | 7 | 71 | 0.26 | 43 | 19 | 38 | 34 | 96 | 93 | 98 | 12% | 107 | 1% | 0% | 19 | 32% | 47% | 4.28 | -1.1 | 6 | 20 | $5 |
| 1st Half | | 204 | 27 | 7 | 26 | 0 | 284 | 226 | 329 | 446 | 775 | 948 | 721 | 6 | 70 | 0.23 | 42 | 19 | 39 | 38 | 103 | 107 | 129 | 13% | 111 | 0% | 0% | 14 | 36% | 43% | 5.25 | 2.8 | 14 | 47 | $9 |
| 2nd Half | | 84 | 8 | 2 | 6 | 0 | 202 | 208 | 272 | 298 | 569 | 641 | 523 | 9 | 73 | 0.35 | 46 | 20 | 34 | 25 | 79 | 59 | 26 | 10% | 90 | 5% | 0% | 5 | 20% | 60% | 2.45 | -6.2 | -16 | -53 | -$5 |
| **19** | **Proj** | **230** | **25** | **7** | **24** | **2** | **238** | **229** | **288** | **381** | **669** | **695** | **655** | **6** | **71** | **0.23** | **47** | **20** | **34** | **30** | **93** | **93** | **76** | **13%** | **89** | **7%** | **46%** | | | | **3.52** | **-8.7** | **-9** | **-31** | **$5** |

## Hiura,Keston

Age: 22 Bats: R Pos: 2B | Ht: 5' 11" Wt: 190
Health: A | PT/Exp: F | Consist: F
LIMA Plan: D+ | Rand Var: 0 | MM: 3433

#9 overall pick in 2017 continued mashing his way through the Brewers system, reaching Double-A after ~400 PA. Scouts love his hit tool, but issues recognizing breaking pitches may slow initial contribution in majors. Long-term, he has batting title potential with a smattering of power and speed, too.

| Yr | Tm | AB | R | HR | RBI | SB | BA | xBA | OBP | SLG | OPS | vL | vR | bb% | ct% | Eye | G | L | F | h% | HctX | PX | xPX | hr/f | Spd | SBO | SB% | #Wk | DOM | DIS | RC/G | RAR | BPV | BPX | R$ |
|---|---|---|---|---|---|---|---|---|---|---|---|---|---|---|---|---|---|---|---|---|---|---|---|---|---|---|---|---|---|---|---|---|---|---|---|
| 14 | | | | | | | | | | | | | | | | | | | | | | | | | | | | | | | | | | | |
| 15 | | | | | | | | | | | | | | | | | | | | | | | | | | | | | | | | | | | |
| 16 | | | | | | | | | | | | | | | | | | | | | | | | | | | | | | | | | | | |
| 17 | | | | | | | | | | | | | | | | | | | | | | | | | | | | | | | | | | | |
| 18 | aa | 279 | 34 | 6 | 19 | 10 | 264 | | 315 | 408 | 723 | | | 7 | 78 | 0.34 | | | | 32 | | 92 | | | 112 | 23% | 66% | | | | 4.30 | | 36 | 120 | $8 |
| 1st Half | | 92 | 15 | 2 | 4 | 6 | 317 | | 350 | 504 | 854 | | | 5 | 79 | 0.24 | | | | 39 | | 133 | | | 108 | 27% | 100% | | | | 7.02 | | 65 | 217 | $5 |
| 2nd Half | | 187 | 19 | 4 | 15 | 5 | 239 | | 298 | 362 | 660 | | | 8 | 78 | 0.38 | | | | 29 | | 72 | | | 128 | 21% | 47% | | | | 3.29 | | 26 | 87 | $9 |
| **19** | **Proj** | **261** | **33** | **7** | **17** | **9** | **263** | **255** | **313** | **426** | **739** | **739** | **739** | **7** | **76** | **0.31** | **45** | **20** | **35** | **32** | | **106** | | **10%** | **118** | **22%** | **68%** | | | | **4.49** | **2.4** | **38** | **125** | **$9** |

## Holt,Brock

Age: 31 Bats: L Pos: 2B SS | Ht: 5' 10" Wt: 180
Health: D | PT/Exp: D | Consist: F
LIMA Plan: D | Rand Var: -3 | MM: 1231

After vertigo-plauged 2017, part-timer bounced back to previous levels as health, HctX, PX returned. Above average BA is his only asset, supported by xBA. Spd is average but declining SB% points to an end to running game. Some will ignore, but he can accumulate sneaky value if he falls into playing time.

| Yr | Tm | AB | R | HR | RBI | SB | BA | xBA | OBP | SLG | OPS | vL | vR | bb% | ct% | Eye | G | L | F | h% | HctX | PX | xPX | hr/f | Spd | SBO | SB% | #Wk | DOM | DIS | RC/G | RAR | BPV | BPX | R$ |
|---|---|---|---|---|---|---|---|---|---|---|---|---|---|---|---|---|---|---|---|---|---|---|---|---|---|---|---|---|---|---|---|---|---|---|---|
| 14 | BOS * | 557 | 84 | 5 | 34 | 17 | 280 | 272 | 327 | 384 | 711 | 763 | 682 | 6 | 80 | 0.35 | 50 | 26 | 23 | 34 | 97 | 80 | 66 | 5% | 144 | 13% | 84% | 19 | 42% | 26% | 4.53 | 18.1 | 42 | 114 | $19 |
| 15 | BOS | 454 | 56 | 2 | 45 | 8 | 280 | 263 | 349 | 379 | 727 | 807 | 701 | 9 | 79 | 0.47 | 53 | 24 | 24 | 35 | 88 | 74 | 62 | 2% | 128 | 7% | 89% | 26 | 31% | 35% | 4.72 | 5.6 | 32 | 86 | $12 |
| 16 | BOS * | 315 | 47 | 7 | 36 | 4 | 258 | 276 | 325 | 382 | 707 | 342 | 762 | 9 | 80 | 0.49 | 54 | 24 | 22 | 30 | 75 | 81 | 50 | 14% | 99 | 8% | 57% | 22 | 41% | 32% | 4.17 | -5.1 | 33 | 94 | $7 |
| 17 | BOS * | 222 | 28 | 2 | 14 | 2 | 193 | 226 | 274 | 253 | 527 | 680 | 518 | 10 | 77 | 0.48 | 60 | 17 | 23 | 24 | 66 | 40 | 18 | 0% | 104 | 5% | 67% | 15 | 33% | 53% | 2.19 | -17.1 | -8 | -24 | -$3 |
| 18 | BOS | 321 | 41 | 7 | 46 | 7 | 277 | 266 | 362 | 411 | 774 | 718 | 788 | 10 | 77 | 0.51 | 51 | 24 | 25 | 34 | 83 | 86 | 56 | 11% | 102 | 14% | 50% | 27 | 41% | 37% | 4.82 | 6.9 | 31 | 103 | $10 |
| 1st Half | | 141 | 17 | 1 | 19 | 3 | 298 | 287 | 377 | 418 | 795 | 1092 | 745 | 11 | 80 | 0.61 | 54 | 26 | 19 | 37 | 77 | 86 | 32 | 5% | 95 | 11% | 60% | 14 | 36% | 29% | 5.52 | 5.3 | 41 | 137 | $6 |
| 2nd Half | | 180 | 24 | 6 | 27 | 4 | 261 | 248 | 351 | 406 | 757 | 549 | 826 | 10 | 75 | 0.44 | 49 | 22 | 29 | 32 | 88 | 85 | 77 | 15% | 112 | 17% | 44% | 13 | 46% | 46% | 4.31 | 0.7 | 24 | 80 | $14 |
| **19** | **Proj** | **221** | **29** | **4** | **25** | **4** | **262** | **261** | **342** | **379** | **721** | **682** | **731** | **10** | **79** | **0.51** | **52** | **23** | **25** | **31** | **79** | **73** | **48** | **10%** | **105** | **11%** | **55%** | | | | **4.23** | **0.4** | **18** | **61** | **$7** |

## Hoskins,Rhys

Age: 26 Bats: R Pos: LF | Ht: 6' 4" Wt: 225
Health: A | PT/Exp: A | Consist: D
LIMA Plan: B+ | Rand Var: 0 | MM: 5145

Sophomore couldn't match 2017's outlandish HR pace, but still produced nice follow-up to 2017. Solid Eye boosts OBP, avoids BA drain of many sluggers. Poor Spd, SBO mean SB could vanish. PX, xPX are elite and support strong hr/f—combined with terrific fly ball rate, homers will be plentiful. UP: 45 MLB HR

| Yr | Tm | AB | R | HR | RBI | SB | BA | xBA | OBP | SLG | OPS | vL | vR | bb% | ct% | Eye | G | L | F | h% | HctX | PX | xPX | hr/f | Spd | SBO | SB% | #Wk | DOM | DIS | RC/G | RAR | BPV | BPX | R$ |
|---|---|---|---|---|---|---|---|---|---|---|---|---|---|---|---|---|---|---|---|---|---|---|---|---|---|---|---|---|---|---|---|---|---|---|---|
| 14 | | | | | | | | | | | | | | | | | | | | | | | | | | | | | | | | | | | |
| 15 | | | | | | | | | | | | | | | | | | | | | | | | | | | | | | | | | | | |
| 16 | aa | 498 | 71 | 31 | 87 | 6 | 240 | | 313 | 470 | 783 | | | 10 | 71 | 0.36 | | | | 28 | | 144 | | | 82 | 8% | 64% | | | | 4.87 | | 43 | 123 | $15 |
| 17 | PHI * | 571 | 104 | 45 | 126 | 5 | 258 | 288 | 361 | 557 | 918 | 1006 | 1016 | 14 | 76 | 0.69 | 31 | 24 | 45 | 26 | 143 | 160 | 178 | 32% | 85 | 5% | 71% | 9 | 56% | 33% | 6.88 | 27.1 | 89 | 270 | $24 |
| 18 | PHI | 558 | 89 | 34 | 96 | 5 | 246 | 256 | 354 | 496 | 850 | 665 | 902 | 13 | 73 | 0.58 | 29 | 19 | 52 | 28 | 93 | 157 | 145 | 16% | 73 | 5% | 63% | 28 | 54% | 32% | 5.76 | 19.2 | 68 | 227 | $21 |
| 1st Half | | 253 | 45 | 14 | 50 | 4 | 257 | 251 | 374 | 498 | 872 | 846 | 880 | 15 | 70 | 0.58 | 26 | 23 | 51 | 31 | 87 | 163 | 151 | 15% | 90 | 9% | 57% | 15 | 53% | 33% | 6.15 | 11.6 | 68 | 227 | $22 |
| 2nd Half | | 305 | 44 | 20 | 46 | 1 | 236 | 259 | 336 | 495 | 831 | 511 | 921 | 12 | 76 | 0.58 | 32 | 16 | 52 | 25 | 97 | 153 | 141 | 17% | 67 | 1% | 100% | 13 | 54% | 31% | 5.45 | 7.8 | 73 | 243 | $20 |
| **19** | **Proj** | **549** | **90** | **38** | **103** | **4** | **254** | **266** | **356** | **525** | **881** | **766** | **915** | **13** | **74** | **0.57** | **31** | **20** | **49** | **27** | **108** | **161** | **158** | **19%** | **79** | **4%** | **62%** | | | | **6.21** | **26.1** | **71** | **237** | **$24** |

## Hosmer,Eric

Age: 29 Bats: L Pos: 1B | Ht: 6' 4" Wt: 225
Health: A | PT/Exp: A | Consist: F
LIMA Plan: B | Rand Var: +2 | MM: 2245

Lost value across the board, as plate skills oscillated back to 2016 levels. With FB% dropping to alarming level, historically great hr/f may not deliver 20 HR, even with all that PT. Would have expected some decline with move to SD, but he held his own at home, instead, cratering on road (.223/.287/.348). If bidding passes $20, drop.

| Yr | Tm | AB | R | HR | RBI | SB | BA | xBA | OBP | SLG | OPS | vL | vR | bb% | ct% | Eye | G | L | F | h% | HctX | PX | xPX | hr/f | Spd | SBO | SB% | #Wk | DOM | DIS | RC/G | RAR | BPV | BPX | R$ |
|---|---|---|---|---|---|---|---|---|---|---|---|---|---|---|---|---|---|---|---|---|---|---|---|---|---|---|---|---|---|---|---|---|---|---|---|
| 14 | KC | 503 | 54 | 9 | 58 | 4 | 270 | 259 | 318 | 398 | 716 | 676 | 732 | 6 | 82 | 0.38 | 51 | 17 | 32 | 32 | 117 | 99 | 100 | 7% | 82 | 5% | 67% | 23 | 35% | 26% | 4.39 | 2.9 | 45 | 122 | $13 |
| 15 | KC | 599 | 98 | 18 | 93 | 7 | 297 | 290 | 363 | 459 | 822 | 730 | 885 | 9 | 82 | 0.56 | 52 | 24 | 24 | 34 | 116 | 102 | 94 | 15% | 107 | 5% | 70% | 27 | 48% | 19% | 6.00 | 10.4 | 62 | 168 | $27 |
| 16 | KC | 605 | 80 | 25 | 104 | 5 | 266 | 263 | 328 | 433 | 761 | 656 | 813 | 9 | 78 | 0.43 | 59 | 16 | 25 | 30 | 109 | 97 | 89 | 21% | 77 | 5% | 63% | 26 | 46% | 27% | 4.91 | -7.5 | 33 | 94 | $19 |
| 17 | KC | 603 | 98 | 25 | 94 | 6 | 318 | 298 | 385 | 498 | 882 | 760 | 938 | 10 | 83 | 0.63 | 56 | 22 | 22 | 35 | 99 | 96 | 65 | 23% | 91 | 3% | 86% | 27 | 70% | 7% | 7.21 | 21.0 | 57 | 173 | $30 |
| 18 | SD | 613 | 72 | 18 | 69 | 7 | 253 | 266 | 322 | 398 | 720 | 527 | 829 | 9 | 77 | 0.44 | 60 | 20 | 20 | 30 | 98 | 90 | 68 | 19% | 86 | 7% | 64% | 28 | 43% | 43% | 4.32 | -14.2 | 25 | 83 | $15 |
| 1st Half | | 311 | 37 | 9 | 36 | 3 | 273 | 277 | 347 | 434 | 781 | 654 | 841 | 10 | 76 | 0.47 | 60 | 22 | 18 | 33 | 108 | 105 | 68 | 21% | 79 | 7% | 50% | 15 | 47% | 33% | 5.15 | 3.4 | 35 | 117 | $17 |
| 2nd Half | | 302 | 35 | 9 | 33 | 4 | 232 | 253 | 296 | 361 | 657 | 423 | 816 | 8 | 77 | 0.40 | 61 | 17 | 22 | 27 | 87 | 75 | 68 | 18% | 97 | 6% | 80% | 13 | 38% | 54% | 3.55 | -11.1 | 17 | 57 | $13 |
| **19** | **Proj** | **606** | **80** | **20** | **81** | **6** | **264** | **270** | **329** | **415** | **745** | **588** | **829** | **9** | **79** | **0.47** | **58** | **20** | **22** | **31** | **100** | **90** | **73** | **19%** | **88** | **5%** | **70%** | | | | **4.72** | **-0.9** | **29** | **98** | **$20** |

## Hundley,Nick

Age: 35 Bats: R Pos: CA | Ht: 6' 0" Wt: 203
Health: B | PT/Exp: D | Consist: B
LIMA Plan: D | Rand Var: 0 | MM: 3123

Never anyone's first choice at CA, yet returns positive value each year. Low ct% seems the new normal, so don't expect BA rebound. HctX and xPX are average or better, but vR, contact and power have decreased for three straight years to unsightly levels (68% ct%, 86 PX). Playing time could decrease even further.

| Yr | Tm | AB | R | HR | RBI | SB | BA | xBA | OBP | SLG | OPS | vL | vR | bb% | ct% | Eye | G | L | F | h% | HctX | PX | xPX | hr/f | Spd | SBO | SB% | #Wk | DOM | DIS | RC/G | RAR | BPV | BPX | R$ |
|---|---|---|---|---|---|---|---|---|---|---|---|---|---|---|---|---|---|---|---|---|---|---|---|---|---|---|---|---|---|---|---|---|---|---|---|
| 14 | 2 TM | 218 | 18 | 6 | 22 | 1 | 243 | 219 | 273 | 358 | 631 | 570 | 641 | 4 | 71 | 0.16 | 37 | 23 | 40 | 32 | 98 | 89 | 109 | 10% | 76 | 2% | 100% | 27 | 22% | 52% | 3.35 | -0.6 | -10 | -27 | $2 |
| 15 | COL | 366 | 45 | 10 | 43 | 5 | 301 | 267 | 339 | 467 | 807 | 727 | 832 | 5 | 79 | 0.28 | 43 | 23 | 34 | 36 | 97 | 108 | 107 | 10% | 126 | 12% | 45% | 23 | 57% | 26% | 5.46 | 16.9 | 54 | 146 | $14 |
| 16 | COL | 289 | 30 | 10 | 48 | 0 | 260 | 256 | 320 | 439 | 759 | 923 | 674 | 8 | 78 | 0.38 | 46 | 18 | 36 | 30 | 118 | 115 | 109 | 12% | 84 | 0% | 0% | 22 | 50% | 32% | 4.82 | 3.4 | 45 | 129 | $6 |
| 17 | SF | 287 | 27 | 9 | 35 | 0 | 244 | 242 | 272 | 418 | 691 | 904 | 584 | 4 | 72 | 0.15 | 42 | 19 | 38 | 31 | 98 | 119 | 101 | 11% | 75 | 0% | 0% | 27 | 41% | 37% | 3.87 | -1.5 | 15 | 45 | $2 |
| 18 | SF | 282 | 34 | 10 | 31 | 2 | 241 | 240 | 298 | 408 | 706 | 828 | 619 | 7 | 70 | 0.26 | 36 | 27 | 37 | 31 | 111 | 109 | 103 | 14% | 92 | 5% | 67% | 28 | 25% | 46% | 4.03 | 4.3 | 11 | 37 | $4 |
| 1st Half | | 127 | 18 | 8 | 23 | 0 | 252 | 263 | 291 | 504 | 795 | 950 | 661 | 5 | 72 | 0.19 | 31 | 25 | 44 | 29 | 107 | 152 | 124 | 20% | 85 | 0% | 0% | 15 | 40% | 40% | 5.00 | 5.8 | 46 | 153 | $7 |
| 2nd Half | | 155 | 16 | 2 | 8 | 2 | 232 | 224 | 304 | 329 | 633 | 707 | 588 | 9 | 68 | 0.31 | 41 | 28 | 31 | 33 | 114 | 71 | 86 | 6% | 105 | 7% | 67% | 13 | 8% | 54% | 3.26 | -0.9 | -19 | -63 | $3 |
| **19** | **Proj** | **262** | **28** | **8** | **31** | **1** | **247** | **241** | **296** | **406** | **702** | **835** | **627** | **6** | **72** | **0.24** | **40** | **23** | **37** | **31** | **108** | **106** | **103** | **11%** | **89** | **3%** | **63%** | | | | **4.03** | **4.5** | **6** | **20** | **$6** |

ARIK FLORIMONTE

## Iannetta,Chris

Age: 36 Bats: R Pos: CA | Ht: 6' 0" Wt: 230
Health A | PT/Exp D | Consist F | LIMA Plan D | Rand Var 0 | MM 3113

COL homecoming not enough to keep 2017's HR surge afloat, as hr/f fell back to career levels while playing time dwindled down the stretch. Plate skills actually took a step forward, and 2nd half BA shouldn't have been this low. Not likely to incite a bidding war on draft day, but there are worse CA options.

| Yr | Tm | AB | R | HR | RBI | SB | BA | xBA | OBP | SLG | OPS | vL | vR | bb% | ct% | Eye | G | L | F | h% | HctX | PX | xPX | hr/f | Spd | SBO | SB% | #Wk | DOM | DIS | RC/G | RAR | BPV | BPX | R$ |
|---|---|---|---|---|---|---|---|---|---|---|---|---|---|---|---|---|---|---|---|---|---|---|---|---|---|---|---|---|---|---|---|---|---|---|---|
| 14 | LAA | 306 | 41 | 7 | 43 | 3 | 252 | 233 | 373 | 392 | 765 | 880 | 697 | 14 | 70 | 0.59 | 38 | 20 | 41 | 34 | 93 | 125 | 100 | 8% | 74 | 3% | 100% | 26 | 46% | 35% | 4.93 | 13.2 | 34 | 92 | $7 |
| 15 | LAA | 272 | 28 | 10 | 34 | 0 | 188 | 196 | 293 | 335 | 628 | 764 | 575 | 13 | 69 | 0.49 | 39 | 13 | 48 | 23 | 80 | 105 | 105 | 11% | 73 | 1% | 0% | 26 | 31% | 54% | 3.04 | -6.7 | 12 | 32 | -$2 |
| 16 | SEA | 295 | 23 | 7 | 24 | 0 | 210 | 224 | 303 | 329 | 631 | 740 | 557 | 11 | 72 | 0.46 | 41 | 22 | 36 | 27 | 102 | 83 | 94 | 9% | 68 | 0% | 0% | 26 | 27% | 58% | 3.19 | -11.1 | 0 | 0 | -$2 |
| 17 | ARI | 272 | 38 | 17 | 43 | 0 | 254 | 259 | 354 | 511 | 865 | 967 | 823 | 12 | 68 | 0.43 | 37 | 20 | 42 | 31 | 98 | 166 | 131 | 22% | 65 | 0% | 0% | 26 | 54% | 35% | 5.99 | 15.4 | 50 | 152 | $6 |
| 18 | COL | 299 | 36 | 11 | 36 | 0 | 224 | 232 | 345 | 385 | 730 | 700 | 748 | 14 | 71 | 0.57 | 38 | 23 | 39 | 28 | 102 | 103 | 133 | 13% | 74 | 0% | 0% | 28 | 39% | 46% | 4.24 | 6.5 | 18 | 60 | $3 |
| 1st Half | | 165 | 20 | 6 | 20 | 0 | 242 | 242 | 354 | 406 | 760 | 589 | 874 | 13 | 70 | 0.50 | 41 | 25 | 34 | 31 | 103 | 112 | 136 | 15% | 63 | 0% | 0% | 15 | 47% | 33% | 4.68 | 6.0 | 16 | 53 | $4 |
| 2nd Half | | 134 | 16 | 5 | 16 | 0 | 201 | 221 | 335 | 358 | 694 | 856 | 608 | 16 | 72 | 0.68 | 35 | 20 | 44 | 24 | 100 | 93 | 129 | 11% | 91 | 0% | 0% | 13 | 31% | 62% | 3.74 | 1.2 | 25 | 83 | $2 |
| 19 | Proj | **273** | **32** | **11** | **34** | **0** | **233** | **233** | **344** | **409** | **753** | **810** | **722** | **13** | **70** | **0.52** | **38** | **21** | **41** | **29** | **99** | **115** | **123** | **14%** | **74** | **0%** | **73%** | | | | **4.56** | **9.2** | **12** | **40** | **$3** |

## Iglesias,Jose

Age: 29 Bats: R Pos: SS | Ht: 5' 11" Wt: 194
Health C | PT/Exp B | Consist A | LIMA Plan B+ | Rand Var +1 | MM 1355

Season-ending abdominal strain in August didn't stop him from tying career-high R$, thanks mostly to brighter green light from new manager. Top-shelf ct% ensures decent BA floor, while xBA hints that he can do better. 1st half SBO/SB% may be difficult to repeat, but a viable late draft option nonetheless.

| Yr | Tm | AB | R | HR | RBI | SB | BA | xBA | OBP | SLG | OPS | vL | vR | bb% | ct% | Eye | G | L | F | h% | HctX | PX | xPX | hr/f | Spd | SBO | SB% | #Wk | DOM | DIS | RC/G | RAR | BPV | BPX | R$ |
|---|---|---|---|---|---|---|---|---|---|---|---|---|---|---|---|---|---|---|---|---|---|---|---|---|---|---|---|---|---|---|---|---|---|---|---|
| 14 | | | | | | | | | | | | | | | | | | | | | | | | | | | | | | | | | | | |
| 15 | DET | 416 | 44 | 2 | 23 | 11 | 300 | 273 | 347 | 370 | 717 | 889 | 663 | 6 | 89 | 0.57 | 56 | 21 | 23 | 33 | 65 | 46 | 30 | 2% | 135 | 15% | 58% | 22 | 36% | 18% | 4.40 | 0.0 | 48 | 130 | $13 |
| 16 | DET | 467 | 57 | 4 | 32 | 7 | 255 | 271 | 306 | 336 | 643 | 704 | 618 | 5 | 89 | 0.56 | 51 | 21 | 28 | 28 | 65 | 53 | 28 | 3% | 109 | 9% | 64% | 26 | 46% | 27% | 3.37 | -12.9 | 45 | 129 | $7 |
| 17 | DET | 463 | 56 | 6 | 54 | 7 | 255 | 287 | 288 | 369 | 657 | 651 | 659 | 4 | 86 | 0.32 | 50 | 23 | 26 | 29 | 99 | 71 | 46 | 6% | 77 | 11% | 64% | 26 | 46% | 27% | 3.56 | -14.5 | 34 | 103 | $9 |
| 18 | DET | 432 | 43 | 5 | 48 | 15 | 269 | 279 | 310 | 389 | 699 | 865 | 656 | 4 | 89 | 0.40 | 44 | 23 | 34 | 29 | 88 | 73 | 45 | 4% | 105 | 22% | 71% | 23 | 57% | 22% | 3.99 | -1.3 | 57 | 190 | $13 |
| 1st Half | | 278 | 27 | 2 | 28 | 12 | 270 | 274 | 311 | 381 | 692 | 879 | 653 | 4 | 88 | 0.38 | 43 | 23 | 33 | 30 | 80 | 68 | 43 | 2% | 113 | 25% | 75% | 15 | 47% | 27% | 3.97 | 0.1 | 53 | 177 | $16 |
| 2nd Half | | 154 | 16 | 3 | 20 | 3 | 266 | 287 | 309 | 403 | 712 | 847 | 664 | 4 | 90 | 0.47 | 44 | 22 | 34 | 28 | 104 | 82 | 48 | 6% | 91 | 15% | 60% | 8 | 75% | 13% | 4.03 | 0.3 | 65 | 217 | $7 |
| 19 | Proj | **502** | **55** | **6** | **52** | **12** | **266** | **280** | **306** | **376** | **683** | **784** | **652** | **4** | **89** | **0.41** | **48** | **22** | **30** | **29** | **88** | **68** | **42** | **5%** | **99** | **15%** | **66%** | | | | **3.81** | **-2.2** | **47** | **157** | **$15** |

## Inciarte,Ender

Age: 28 Bats: L Pos: CF | Ht: 5' 11" Wt: 190
Health A | PT/Exp A | Consist B | LIMA Plan B+ | Rand Var +1 | MM 1445

Blazing April (13 SB, 47% SBO) carried season's final SB total, while slowly slipping Spd makes a 2019 repeat unlikely. However, with swing change leading the way for 2nd half HctX/xPX improvements, plus rising FB% trend, a new career-high in HR wouldn't be surprising. A well-rounded fantasy asset.

| Yr | Tm | AB | R | HR | RBI | SB | BA | xBA | OBP | SLG | OPS | vL | vR | bb% | ct% | Eye | G | L | F | h% | HctX | PX | xPX | hr/f | Spd | SBO | SB% | #Wk | DOM | DIS | RC/G | RAR | BPV | BPX | R$ |
|---|---|---|---|---|---|---|---|---|---|---|---|---|---|---|---|---|---|---|---|---|---|---|---|---|---|---|---|---|---|---|---|---|---|---|---|
| 14 | ARI * | 527 | 68 | 5 | 35 | 23 | 273 | 271 | 314 | 358 | 671 | 646 | 691 | 6 | 85 | 0.40 | 52 | 24 | 25 | 31 | 87 | 60 | 51 | 5% | 125 | 20% | 81% | 23 | 43% | 22% | 4.02 | 2.9 | 40 | 108 | $19 |
| 15 | ARI | 524 | 73 | 6 | 45 | 21 | 303 | 284 | 338 | 408 | 747 | 530 | 826 | 5 | 89 | 0.45 | 52 | 22 | 26 | 33 | 102 | 66 | 72 | 5% | 129 | 21% | 68% | 23 | 43% | 13% | 4.88 | 8.4 | 59 | 159 | $24 |
| 16 | ATL | 522 | 85 | 3 | 29 | 16 | 291 | 275 | 351 | 381 | 732 | 749 | 726 | 8 | 87 | 0.66 | 49 | 24 | 27 | 33 | 80 | 53 | 50 | 2% | 157 | 14% | 70% | 24 | 46% | 33% | 4.71 | 0.9 | 55 | 157 | $18 |
| 17 | ATL | 662 | 93 | 11 | 57 | 22 | 304 | 274 | 350 | 409 | 759 | 712 | 773 | 7 | 86 | 0.52 | 47 | 24 | 29 | 34 | 77 | 57 | 54 | 7% | 135 | 15% | 71% | 27 | 41% | 30% | 5.21 | 2.7 | 45 | 136 | $29 |
| 18 | ATL | 597 | 83 | 10 | 61 | 28 | 265 | 269 | 325 | 380 | 705 | 665 | 719 | 7 | 86 | 0.57 | 45 | 24 | 31 | 30 | 100 | 65 | 68 | 6% | 121 | 26% | 67% | 28 | 43% | 29% | 4.08 | -2.8 | 47 | 157 | $24 |
| 1st Half | | 323 | 47 | 5 | 31 | 21 | 251 | 255 | 314 | 347 | 660 | 541 | 706 | 8 | 86 | 0.59 | 49 | 20 | 32 | 28 | 80 | 54 | 54 | 6% | 119 | 31% | 75% | 15 | 33% | 33% | 3.65 | -4.8 | 39 | 130 | $27 |
| 2nd Half | | 274 | 36 | 5 | 30 | 7 | 281 | 285 | 338 | 420 | 757 | 833 | 733 | 7 | 85 | 0.55 | 41 | 29 | 30 | 31 | 122 | 78 | 85 | 7% | 117 | 19% | 50% | 13 | 54% | 23% | 4.62 | 3.8 | 56 | 187 | $20 |
| 19 | Proj | **553** | **78** | **12** | **49** | **20** | **283** | **274** | **336** | **412** | **748** | **710** | **761** | **7** | **86** | **0.54** | **44** | **24** | **31** | **31** | **96** | **71** | **63** | **8%** | **130** | **19%** | **66%** | | | | **4.73** | **9.5** | **52** | **172** | **$24** |

## Jackson,Austin

Age: 32 Bats: R Pos: CF | Ht: 6' 1" Wt: 198
Health F | PT/Exp D | Consist F | LIMA Plan F | Rand Var -5 | MM 1301

Got off to slow start with SF (.195 xBA, 58 xPX) before eventually catching on with NYM. Contact ability fell off the table, and only lofty h% kept BA from complete despair. With generally fading skill set, quest for AB looks all the more daunting. Such is life on the fringes of MLB (and fantasy) relevance.

| Yr | Tm | AB | R | HR | RBI | SB | BA | xBA | OBP | SLG | OPS | vL | vR | bb% | ct% | Eye | G | L | F | h% | HctX | PX | xPX | hr/f | Spd | SBO | SB% | #Wk | DOM | DIS | RC/G | RAR | BPV | BPX | R$ |
|---|---|---|---|---|---|---|---|---|---|---|---|---|---|---|---|---|---|---|---|---|---|---|---|---|---|---|---|---|---|---|---|---|---|---|---|
| 14 | 2 AL | 597 | 71 | 4 | 47 | 20 | 256 | 238 | 308 | 347 | 655 | 735 | 622 | 7 | 76 | 0.33 | 42 | 26 | 33 | 33 | 86 | 75 | 87 | 3% | 137 | 16% | 77% | 27 | 30% | 44% | 3.72 | -1.8 | 21 | 57 | $16 |
| 15 | 2 TM * | 529 | 58 | 9 | 49 | 18 | 261 | 248 | 303 | 372 | 675 | 770 | 657 | 6 | 73 | 0.22 | 51 | 24 | 25 | 34 | 95 | 83 | 76 | 10% | 105 | 21% | 64% | 25 | 32% | 60% | 3.75 | -8.7 | 4 | 11 | $16 |
| 16 | CHW | 181 | 24 | 0 | 18 | 2 | 254 | 256 | 318 | 343 | 661 | 411 | 741 | 8 | 78 | 0.44 | 37 | 30 | 32 | 32 | 109 | 66 | 97 | 0% | 129 | 6% | 67% | 10 | 40% | 40% | 3.70 | -4.9 | 24 | 69 | $1 |
| 17 | CLE * | 307 | 47 | 8 | 38 | 4 | 314 | 267 | 383 | 480 | 863 | 1013 | 756 | 10 | 77 | 0.48 | 48 | 21 | 31 | 39 | 99 | 102 | 88 | 10% | 126 | 6% | 82% | 22 | 55% | 41% | 6.86 | 14.9 | 48 | 145 | $12 |
| 18 | 2 NL | 347 | 29 | 3 | 32 | 3 | 245 | 194 | 299 | 326 | 624 | 580 | 653 | 7 | 62 | 0.20 | 46 | 23 | 31 | 39 | 70 | 71 | 71 | 5% | 121 | 7% | 50% | 26 | 12% | 81% | 3.19 | -10.8 | -43 | -143 | $3 |
| 1st Half | | 144 | 10 | 0 | 13 | 2 | 236 | 188 | 306 | 285 | 591 | 664 | 504 | 9 | 60 | 0.24 | 46 | 26 | 28 | 40 | 71 | 54 | 62 | 0% | 100 | 7% | 67% | 15 | 13% | 80% | 2.88 | -5.5 | -68 | -227 | -$2 |
| 2nd Half | | 203 | 19 | 3 | 19 | 1 | 251 | 200 | 293 | 355 | 648 | 461 | 721 | 6 | 63 | 0.16 | 46 | 20 | 33 | 38 | 69 | 84 | 77 | 7% | 129 | 6% | 33% | 11 | 9% | 82% | 3.41 | -4.4 | -29 | -97 | $6 |
| 19 | Proj | **161** | **18** | **2** | **16** | **2** | **234** | **225** | **295** | **338** | **633** | **640** | **629** | **8** | **69** | **0.28** | **45** | **24** | **31** | **33** | **85** | **80** | **80** | **5%** | **121** | **8%** | **63%** | | | | **3.27** | **-4.2** | **-17** | **-55** | **$3** |

## Jankowski,Travis

Age: 28 Bats: L Pos: RF CF LF | Ht: 6' 2" Wt: 185
Health C | PT/Exp D | Consist D | LIMA Plan D+ | Rand Var -2 | MM 0513

4-17-.259 with 24 SB in 347 AB at SD. Put 2017 foot injury behind him en route to career-best season. The problem: steady AB continue to elude him as struggles vL (career .174 BA, 65% ct%) persist. More valuable in daily formats; but regardless, elite Spd worth flyer in this SB-starved environment.

| Yr | Tm | AB | R | HR | RBI | SB | BA | xBA | OBP | SLG | OPS | vL | vR | bb% | ct% | Eye | G | L | F | h% | HctX | PX | xPX | hr/f | Spd | SBO | SB% | #Wk | DOM | DIS | RC/G | RAR | BPV | BPX | R$ |
|---|---|---|---|---|---|---|---|---|---|---|---|---|---|---|---|---|---|---|---|---|---|---|---|---|---|---|---|---|---|---|---|---|---|---|---|
| 14 | aa | 100 | 11 | 0 | 8 | 8 | 207 | | 256 | 257 | 513 | | | 6 | 84 | 0.41 | | | | 25 | | 39 | | | 111 | 45% | 78% | | | | 2.22 | | 15 | 41 | $1 |
| 15 | SD * | 469 | 59 | 3 | 30 | 25 | 268 | 236 | 325 | 349 | 674 | 650 | 572 | 8 | 82 | 0.47 | 63 | 10 | 27 | 32 | 47 | 52 | 12 | 12% | 175 | 28% | 65% | 8 | 38% | 50% | 3.78 | -13.1 | 39 | 105 | $17 |
| 16 | SD | 335 | 53 | 2 | 12 | 30 | 245 | 244 | 332 | 313 | 646 | 398 | 727 | 11 | 70 | 0.42 | 58 | 26 | 16 | 34 | 68 | 53 | 28 | 6% | 152 | 39% | 71% | 27 | 15% | 74% | 3.47 | -11.9 | -6 | -17 | $13 |
| 17 | SD * | 214 | 23 | 0 | 8 | 9 | 198 | 202 | 268 | 231 | 499 | 347 | 536 | 9 | 71 | 0.33 | 62 | 14 | 24 | 28 | 105 | 27 | 45 | 0% | 138 | 18% | 88% | 6 | 17% | 83% | 2.11 | -21.2 | -34 | -103 | -$1 |
| 18 | SD * | 427 | 56 | 5 | 24 | 27 | 263 | 250 | 332 | 345 | 677 | 512 | 716 | 9 | 77 | 0.44 | 58 | 22 | 20 | 33 | 73 | 53 | 36 | 8% | 148 | 28% | 71% | 22 | 27% | 36% | 3.93 | -8.6 | 14 | 47 | $16 |
| 1st Half | | 251 | 33 | 2 | 14 | 15 | 280 | 248 | 351 | 352 | 703 | 605 | 741 | 10 | 75 | 0.44 | 63 | 21 | 16 | 37 | 61 | 49 | 25 | 5% | 146 | 25% | 68% | 10 | 20% | 30% | 4.28 | -2.3 | 6 | 20 | $18 |
| 2nd Half | | 176 | 23 | 3 | 10 | 12 | 239 | 254 | 306 | 335 | 641 | 425 | 691 | 9 | 78 | 0.45 | 54 | 23 | 23 | 29 | 85 | 58 | 47 | 10% | 134 | 33% | 75% | 12 | 33% | 42% | 3.45 | -6.2 | 20 | 67 | $13 |
| 19 | Proj | **286** | **37** | **3** | **14** | **18** | **244** | **238** | **317** | **319** | **636** | **472** | **679** | **9** | **75** | **0.41** | **59** | **19** | **21** | **32** | **79** | **50** | **36** | **6%** | **145** | **29%** | **75%** | | | | **3.42** | **-9.1** | **-3** | **-9** | **$10** |

## Jansen,Danny

Age: 24 Bats: R Pos: CA | Ht: 6' 2" Wt: 225
Health A | PT/Exp F | Consist B | LIMA Plan C | Rand Var 0 | MM 3433

3-8-.247 in 81 AB at TOR. Larger-framed backstop, known mostly for hit tool and on-base ability, held his own during first taste of majors. PX/xPX (118/69) gap in brief MLB sample warns against projecting plus power, and Sept struggles (.178 BA) suggest road ahead could be bumpy. Be wary, is all.

| Yr | Tm | AB | R | HR | RBI | SB | BA | xBA | OBP | SLG | OPS | vL | vR | bb% | ct% | Eye | G | L | F | h% | HctX | PX | xPX | hr/f | Spd | SBO | SB% | #Wk | DOM | DIS | RC/G | RAR | BPV | BPX | R$ |
|---|---|---|---|---|---|---|---|---|---|---|---|---|---|---|---|---|---|---|---|---|---|---|---|---|---|---|---|---|---|---|---|---|---|---|---|
| 14 | | | | | | | | | | | | | | | | | | | | | | | | | | | | | | | | | | | |
| 15 | | | | | | | | | | | | | | | | | | | | | | | | | | | | | | | | | | | |
| 16 | | | | | | | | | | | | | | | | | | | | | | | | | | | | | | | | | | | |
| 17 | a/a | 246 | 29 | 5 | 28 | 1 | 294 | | 372 | 447 | 819 | | | 11 | 89 | 1.11 | | | | 32 | | 86 | | | 98 | 1% | 100% | | | | 6.04 | | 78 | 236 | $6 |
| 18 | TOR * | 379 | 52 | 14 | 59 | 4 | 257 | 256 | 340 | 441 | 781 | 707 | 801 | 11 | 82 | 0.68 | 32 | 20 | 48 | 28 | 60 | 111 | 69 | 10% | 102 | 4% | 100% | 7 | 43% | 43% | 5.22 | 20.4 | 70 | 233 | $11 |
| 1st Half | | 194 | 26 | 4 | 34 | 4 | 283 | 275 | 367 | 450 | 817 | | | 12 | 83 | 0.79 | | | | 32 | | 105 | | | 86 | 6% | 100% | | | | 6.00 | | 68 | 227 | $13 |
| 2nd Half | | 185 | 25 | 9 | 25 | 1 | 229 | 255 | 312 | 432 | 744 | 707 | 801 | 11 | 80 | 0.59 | 32 | 20 | 48 | 24 | 59 | 116 | 69 | 10% | 104 | 2% | 100% | 7 | 43% | 43% | 4.49 | 5.8 | 66 | 220 | $9 |
| 19 | Proj | **311** | **40** | **8** | **42** | **3** | **255** | **255** | **360** | **415** | **775** | **749** | **782** | **11** | **81** | **0.65** | **38** | **20** | **42** | **29** | **71** | **101** | **62** | **8%** | **114** | **3%** | **100%** | | | | **4.86** | **12.8** | **50** | **167** | **$9** |

## Jay,Jon

Age: 34 Bats: L Pos: RF LF CF | Ht: 5' 11" Wt: 195
Health C | PT/Exp C | Consist B | LIMA Plan D | Rand Var 0 | MM 1341

Traded from KC to ARI when BA was .307; the Royals must've looked at his xBA history and sold high. Surprising career high in HctX was wasted on career-low FB%, and despite solid Spd, the dream of more than a handful of SB died long ago. Aspire for something less mediocre. You deserve it.

| Yr | Tm | AB | R | HR | RBI | SB | BA | xBA | OBP | SLG | OPS | vL | vR | bb% | ct% | Eye | G | L | F | h% | HctX | PX | xPX | hr/f | Spd | SBO | SB% | #Wk | DOM | DIS | RC/G | RAR | BPV | BPX | R$ |
|---|---|---|---|---|---|---|---|---|---|---|---|---|---|---|---|---|---|---|---|---|---|---|---|---|---|---|---|---|---|---|---|---|---|---|---|
| 14 | STL | 413 | 52 | 3 | 46 | 6 | 303 | 269 | 372 | 378 | 750 | 859 | 721 | 6 | 81 | 0.36 | 52 | 28 | 20 | 37 | 94 | 57 | 63 | 4% | 116 | 7% | 67% | 26 | 19% | 50% | 4.75 | 10.9 | 19 | 51 | $15 |
| 15 | STL | 210 | 25 | 1 | 10 | 0 | 210 | 248 | 306 | 257 | 563 | 414 | 596 | 8 | 83 | 0.53 | 60 | 22 | 18 | 25 | 84 | 32 | 46 | 3% | 111 | 4% | 0% | 18 | 17% | 56% | 2.18 | -16.6 | 8 | 22 | -$3 |
| 16 | SD | 347 | 49 | 2 | 26 | 2 | 291 | 267 | 339 | 389 | 728 | 752 | 713 | 5 | 78 | 0.24 | 55 | 24 | 21 | 37 | 93 | 76 | 65 | 4% | 106 | 2% | 100% | 16 | 25% | 44% | 4.63 | 0.0 | 15 | 43 | $8 |
| 17 | CHC | 379 | 65 | 2 | 34 | 6 | 296 | 266 | 374 | 375 | 749 | 751 | 748 | 9 | 79 | 0.46 | 47 | 29 | 24 | 37 | 81 | 52 | 54 | 3% | 121 | 6% | 75% | 27 | 26% | 44% | 4.87 | -4.0 | 13 | 39 | $12 |
| 18 | 2 TM | 527 | 74 | 3 | 40 | 4 | 268 | 273 | 330 | 347 | 678 | 604 | 705 | 6 | 82 | 0.35 | 59 | 24 | 17 | 32 | 107 | 48 | 52 | 4% | 130 | 5% | 57% | 28 | 25% | 43% | 3.71 | -13.6 | 18 | 60 | $10 |
| 1st Half | | 324 | 45 | 2 | 27 | 3 | 287 | 264 | 355 | 364 | 719 | 616 | 756 | 7 | 81 | 0.43 | 61 | 22 | 17 | 35 | 103 | 49 | 63 | 5% | 121 | 6% | 50% | 15 | 20% | 40% | 4.32 | -2.5 | 17 | 57 | $15 |
| 2nd Half | | 203 | 29 | 1 | 13 | 1 | 236 | 283 | 291 | 320 | 611 | 587 | 619 | 3 | 83 | 0.21 | 56 | 28 | 16 | 28 | 113 | 46 | 35 | 4% | 128 | 2% | 100% | 13 | 31% | 46% | 2.82 | -10.8 | 17 | 57 | $2 |
| 19 | Proj | **165** | **24** | **1** | **13** | **1** | **271** | **269** | **334** | **353** | **687** | **659** | **697** | **6** | **81** | **0.33** | **55** | **26** | **19** | **33** | **98** | **52** | **52** | **4%** | **114** | **5%** | **69%** | | | | **3.87** | **-2.8** | **9** | **29** | **$4** |

BRIAN SLACK

## Jimenez,Eloy

**Age:** 22 **Bats:** R **Pos:** DH | **Ht:** 6' 4" **Wt:** 205
**Health** A | **PT/Exp** F | **Consist** B
**LIMA Plan** B | **Rand Var** 0 | **MM** 3053

More service time shenanigans will likely keep top prospect in minors 'til at least mid-April; once he arrives, BA, PX history offer reason to believe he'll be worth the wait. Contact rate got even better upon promotion to AAA, and power held firm. Rookies are never a sure thing, but this one looks like he's ready.

| Yr | Tm | AB | R | HR | RBI | SB | BA | xBA | OBP | SLG | OPS | vL | vR | bb% | ct% | Eye | G | L | F | h% | HctX | PX | xPX | hr/f | Spd | SBO | SB% | #Wk | DOM | DIS | RC/G | RAR | BPV | BPX | R$ |
|---|---|---|---|---|---|---|---|---|---|---|---|---|---|---|---|---|---|---|---|---|---|---|---|---|---|---|---|---|---|---|---|---|---|---|---|
| 14 | | | | | | | | | | | | | | | | | | | | | | | | | | | | | | | | | | | |
| 15 | | | | | | | | | | | | | | | | | | | | | | | | | | | | | | | | | | | |
| 16 | | | | | | | | | | | | | | | | | | | | | | | | | | | | | | | | | | | |
| 17 | aa | 68 | 11 | 3 | 7 | 1 | 342 | | 388 | 553 | 942 | | | 7 | 74 | 0.29 | | | | 43 | | 130 | | | 99 | 10% | 48% | | | | 7.95 | | 47 | 142 | $2 |
| 18 | a/a | 416 | 58 | 21 | 68 | 0 | 315 | | 361 | 544 | 905 | | | 7 | 81 | 0.39 | | | | 35 | | 128 | | | 95 | 1% | 0% | | | | 7.23 | | 72 | 240 | $19 |
| 1st Half | | 246 | 36 | 12 | 41 | 0 | 292 | | 349 | 508 | 857 | | | 8 | 80 | 0.44 | | | | 33 | | 123 | | | 113 | 2% | 0% | | | | 6.28 | | 71 | 237 | $21 |
| 2nd Half | | 170 | 22 | 10 | 26 | 0 | 348 | | 379 | 596 | 974 | | | 5 | 83 | 0.30 | | | | 37 | | 135 | | | 107 | 0% | 0% | | | | 8.82 | | 86 | 287 | $17 |
| 19 | Proj | 328 | 45 | 14 | 52 | 0 | 295 | 278 | 339 | 503 | 841 | 841 | 841 | 6 | 82 | 0.37 | 41 | 21 | 38 | 32 | | 117 | | 14% | 111 | 1% | 0% | | | | 6.11 | 14.6 | 53 | 178 | $12 |

## Jones,Adam

**Age:** 33 **Bats:** R **Pos:** CF RF | **Ht:** 6' 2" **Wt:** 215
**Health** A | **PT/Exp** A | **Consist** B
**LIMA Plan** B+ | **Rand Var** -1 | **MM** 2235

While previous PX declines were about being passed up by rising league average, big drop in hr/f suggests this latest one's more of a red flag. Still managed to post career-best ct%, and salvaged 2nd half by tapping into long-dormant baserunning savvy, so he's not done yet. But 20+ HR might be.

| Yr | Tm | AB | R | HR | RBI | SB | BA | xBA | OBP | SLG | OPS | vL | vR | bb% | ct% | Eye | G | L | F | h% | HctX | PX | xPX | hr/f | Spd | SBO | SB% | #Wk | DOM | DIS | RC/G | RAR | BPV | BPX | R$ |
|---|---|---|---|---|---|---|---|---|---|---|---|---|---|---|---|---|---|---|---|---|---|---|---|---|---|---|---|---|---|---|---|---|---|---|---|
| 14 | BAL | 644 | 88 | 29 | 96 | 7 | 281 | 270 | 311 | 469 | 780 | 1003 | 709 | 3 | 79 | 0.14 | 47 | 17 | 36 | 32 | 113 | 127 | 119 | 16% | 104 | 6% | 88% | 27 | 52% | 30% | 5.05 | 20.9 | 58 | 157 | $29 |
| 15 | BAL | 546 | 74 | 27 | 82 | 3 | 269 | 274 | 308 | 474 | 782 | 754 | 792 | 4 | 81 | 0.24 | 46 | 18 | 36 | 29 | 109 | 122 | 120 | 17% | 97 | 3% | 75% | 25 | 44% | 36% | 4.96 | 2.9 | 62 | 168 | $20 |
| 16 | BAL | 619 | 86 | 29 | 83 | 2 | 265 | 248 | 310 | 436 | 746 | 580 | 798 | 6 | 81 | 0.34 | 43 | 17 | 41 | 28 | 108 | 92 | 110 | 14% | 85 | 1% | 100% | 27 | 44% | 26% | 4.69 | -0.3 | 39 | 111 | $18 |
| 17 | BAL | 597 | 82 | 26 | 73 | 2 | 285 | 271 | 322 | 466 | 787 | 739 | 803 | 4 | 81 | 0.24 | 45 | 21 | 34 | 31 | 102 | 97 | 84 | 16% | 101 | 2% | 67% | 26 | 38% | 15% | 5.22 | 4.9 | 43 | 130 | $19 |
| 18 | BAL | 580 | 54 | 15 | 63 | 7 | 281 | 260 | 313 | 419 | 732 | 714 | 739 | 4 | 84 | 0.26 | 43 | 21 | 37 | 31 | 97 | 83 | 81 | 8% | 73 | 6% | 88% | 28 | 43% | 21% | 4.64 | 2.0 | 34 | 113 | $17 |
| 1st Half | | 324 | 34 | 10 | 32 | 0 | 287 | 260 | 311 | 438 | 749 | 691 | 774 | 3 | 83 | 0.16 | 40 | 22 | 38 | 32 | 97 | 89 | 84 | 10% | 74 | 0% | 0% | 15 | 47% | 20% | 4.80 | 3.1 | 33 | 110 | $18 |
| 2nd Half | | 256 | 20 | 5 | 31 | 7 | 273 | 257 | 316 | 395 | 711 | 747 | 698 | 6 | 85 | 0.39 | 47 | 19 | 35 | 31 | 97 | 75 | 76 | 7% | 76 | 13% | 88% | 13 | 38% | 23% | 4.43 | -0.2 | 37 | 123 | $16 |
| 19 | Proj | 534 | 60 | 19 | 65 | 6 | 278 | 260 | 316 | 435 | 751 | 723 | 761 | 5 | 83 | 0.28 | 44 | 19 | 36 | 31 | 101 | 90 | 89 | 12% | 86 | 5% | 85% | | | | 4.81 | 10.3 | 34 | 113 | $19 |

## Jones,JaCoby

**Age:** 27 **Bats:** R **Pos:** CF LF | **Ht:** 6' 2" **Wt:** 201
**Health** A | **PT/Exp** C | **Consist** A
**LIMA Plan** D+ | **Rand Var** +3 | **MM** 3503

It's never a good sign when a .230 xBA represents a step forward in your career path. Defense earned him a long look, but contact issues that have plagued him everywhere make his job security as shaky as his BA history. So don't put too much faith in another round of double-digit HR and SB. DN: JaCoby who?

| Yr | Tm | AB | R | HR | RBI | SB | BA | xBA | OBP | SLG | OPS | vL | vR | bb% | ct% | Eye | G | L | F | h% | HctX | PX | xPX | hr/f | Spd | SBO | SB% | #Wk | DOM | DIS | RC/G | RAR | BPV | BPX | R$ |
|---|---|---|---|---|---|---|---|---|---|---|---|---|---|---|---|---|---|---|---|---|---|---|---|---|---|---|---|---|---|---|---|---|---|---|---|
| 14 | | | | | | | | | | | | | | | | | | | | | | | | | | | | | | | | | | | |
| 15 | aa | 146 | 22 | 5 | 18 | 9 | 241 | | 311 | 408 | 719 | | | 9 | 63 | 0.27 | | | | 35 | | 130 | | | 120 | 33% | 73% | | | | 4.18 | | 11 | 30 | $5 |
| 16 | DET * | 397 | 38 | 6 | 37 | 10 | 228 | 221 | 279 | 358 | 637 | 294 | 909 | 7 | 64 | 0.20 | 44 | 25 | 31 | 34 | 97 | 98 | 147 | 0% | 146 | 19% | 65% | 5 | 20% | 40% | 3.21 | -14.0 | -5 | -14 | $4 |
| 17 | DET * | 492 | 64 | 11 | 52 | 17 | 208 | 213 | 264 | 330 | 594 | 562 | 491 | 7 | 64 | 0.21 | 51 | 19 | 31 | 30 | 78 | 86 | 90 | 13% | 117 | 22% | 72% | 14 | 14% | 79% | 2.78 | -30.5 | -24 | -73 | $6 |
| 18 | DET | 429 | 54 | 11 | 34 | 13 | 207 | 230 | 266 | 364 | 630 | 618 | 634 | 5 | 67 | 0.17 | 43 | 24 | 33 | 28 | 89 | 108 | 88 | 12% | 153 | 24% | 72% | 27 | 22% | 41% | 2.87 | -15.6 | 12 | 40 | $7 |
| 1st Half | | 253 | 30 | 5 | 19 | 7 | 217 | 233 | 267 | 364 | 631 | 578 | 649 | 4 | 70 | 0.14 | 43 | 23 | 34 | 29 | 89 | 99 | 79 | 8% | 161 | 26% | 64% | 15 | 27% | 33% | 2.84 | -10.3 | 18 | 60 | $7 |
| 2nd Half | | 176 | 24 | 6 | 15 | 6 | 193 | 227 | 264 | 364 | 628 | 672 | 612 | 7 | 63 | 0.20 | 43 | 26 | 31 | 27 | 90 | 123 | 104 | 18% | 127 | 23% | 86% | 12 | 17% | 50% | 2.92 | -6.8 | 2 | 7 | $6 |
| 19 | Proj | 360 | 46 | 9 | 34 | 12 | 211 | 222 | 280 | 359 | 640 | 666 | 631 | 7 | 65 | 0.20 | 46 | 22 | 32 | 30 | 85 | 106 | 92 | 13% | 139 | 24% | 73% | | | | 3.03 | -12.6 | 1 | 2 | $8 |

## Jones,Ryder

**Age:** 25 **Bats:** L **Pos:** 1B | **Ht:** 6' 2" **Wt:** 221
**Health** A | **PT/Exp** C | **Consist** C
**LIMA Plan** D | **Rand Var** +4 | **MM** 1201

2-3-.375 in 8 AB at SF. Before you look at 2018 HctX, xPX, and hr/f and decide to blow your entire budget on "the next Babe Ruth", be aware that's MLB-only data. Eight at-bats. Reality is, he's got some pop, but injuries and increased Ks as he's moved up the ladder keep getting in the way. Needs more development time.

| Yr | Tm | AB | R | HR | RBI | SB | BA | xBA | OBP | SLG | OPS | vL | vR | bb% | ct% | Eye | G | L | F | h% | HctX | PX | xPX | hr/f | Spd | SBO | SB% | #Wk | DOM | DIS | RC/G | RAR | BPV | BPX | R$ |
|---|---|---|---|---|---|---|---|---|---|---|---|---|---|---|---|---|---|---|---|---|---|---|---|---|---|---|---|---|---|---|---|---|---|---|---|
| 14 | | | | | | | | | | | | | | | | | | | | | | | | | | | | | | | | | | | |
| 15 | | | | | | | | | | | | | | | | | | | | | | | | | | | | | | | | | | | |
| 16 | aa | 474 | 45 | 11 | 61 | 1 | 229 | | 266 | 353 | 619 | | | 5 | 82 | 0.28 | | | | 26 | | 77 | | | 77 | 3% | 30% | | | | 3.05 | | 24 | 69 | $3 |
| 17 | SF * | 387 | 49 | 11 | 42 | 7 | 236 | 218 | 298 | 399 | 696 | 397 | 549 | 8 | 71 | 0.31 | 38 | 14 | 47 | 30 | 82 | 104 | 90 | 4% | 107 | 8% | 100% | 12 | 8% | 67% | 4.06 | -21.4 | 18 | 55 | $6 |
| 18 | SF * | 449 | 43 | 8 | 45 | 1 | 229 | 293 | 265 | 342 | 607 | 0 | 1714 | 5 | 72 | 0.17 | 0 | 67 | 33 | 30 | 176 | 75 | 306 | 200% | 102 | 4% | 38% | 3 | 67% | 33% | 2.94 | -29.6 | -11 | -37 | $3 |
| 1st Half | | 263 | 24 | 4 | 27 | 1 | 246 | 215 | 279 | 345 | 624 | | | 4 | 73 | 0.17 | | | | 32 | | 65 | | | 101 | 4% | 55% | | | | 3.21 | | -15 | -50 | $6 |
| 2nd Half | | 186 | 18 | 4 | 19 | 0 | 206 | 288 | 244 | 340 | 584 | 0 | 1714 | 5 | 70 | 0.16 | 0 | 67 | 33 | 27 | 171 | 90 | 306 | 200% | 105 | 3% | 0% | 3 | 67% | 33% | 2.58 | -12.8 | -7 | -23 | $0 |
| 19 | Proj | 165 | 17 | 2 | 18 | 1 | 227 | 195 | 288 | 333 | 621 | 487 | 656 | 6 | 73 | 0.23 | 38 | 14 | 47 | 30 | 74 | 73 | 81 | 4% | 101 | 5% | 71% | | | | 2.98 | -8.9 | -13 | -42 | $2 |

## Joseph,Caleb

**Age:** 33 **Bats:** R **Pos:** CA | **Ht:** 6' 3" **Wt:** 180
**Health** A | **PT/Exp** F | **Consist** F
**LIMA Plan** D | **Rand Var** 0 | **MM** 1303

3-17-.219 with 2 SB in 280 AB at BAL. Used to have power skills worth owning, but those numbers have faded with age. Now he's just another interchangeable backup CA. Seriously, if we switched his stats out with Roberto Perez's, would anyone know the difference? Including the players themselves? Or perhaps their parents? I doubt it.

| Yr | Tm | AB | R | HR | RBI | SB | BA | xBA | OBP | SLG | OPS | vL | vR | bb% | ct% | Eye | G | L | F | h% | HctX | PX | xPX | hr/f | Spd | SBO | SB% | #Wk | DOM | DIS | RC/G | RAR | BPV | BPX | R$ |
|---|---|---|---|---|---|---|---|---|---|---|---|---|---|---|---|---|---|---|---|---|---|---|---|---|---|---|---|---|---|---|---|---|---|---|---|
| 14 | BAL * | 338 | 27 | 10 | 35 | 0 | 205 | 224 | 247 | 340 | 588 | 643 | 603 | 5 | 72 | 0.20 | 33 | 22 | 46 | 25 | 93 | 106 | 138 | 11% | 86 | 2% | 0% | 21 | 24% | 57% | 2.66 | -6.9 | 9 | 24 | $0 |
| 15 | BAL | 320 | 38 | 11 | 49 | 0 | 234 | 249 | 299 | 394 | 693 | 712 | 683 | 8 | 78 | 0.38 | 33 | 23 | 43 | 27 | 104 | 105 | 121 | 10% | 99 | 0% | 0% | 26 | 42% | 42% | 3.85 | 1.1 | 41 | 111 | $4 |
| 16 | BAL * | 193 | 10 | 1 | 4 | 0 | 184 | 189 | 222 | 213 | 435 | 191 | 494 | 5 | 77 | 0.21 | 41 | 19 | 39 | 23 | 68 | 22 | 88 | 0% | 120 | 3% | 0% | 20 | 15% | 55% | 1.42 | -15.1 | -25 | -71 | -$6 |
| 17 | BAL | 254 | 31 | 8 | 28 | 0 | 256 | 253 | 287 | 413 | 700 | 787 | 672 | 4 | 72 | 0.14 | 46 | 24 | 30 | 33 | 82 | 101 | 74 | 15% | 114 | 0% | 0% | 26 | 42% | 46% | 4.02 | -0.8 | 11 | 33 | $3 |
| 18 | BAL * | 353 | 35 | 5 | 27 | 2 | 218 | 216 | 252 | 313 | 565 | 540 | 591 | 4 | 74 | 0.17 | 41 | 21 | 39 | 28 | 66 | 64 | 73 | 4% | 121 | 4% | 67% | 24 | 25% | 54% | 2.56 | -8.7 | -5 | -17 | $1 |
| 1st Half | | 196 | 14 | 3 | 14 | 0 | 194 | 218 | 226 | 298 | 524 | 480 | 522 | 4 | 73 | 0.15 | 37 | 23 | 40 | 25 | 64 | 70 | 75 | 3% | 118 | 3% | 0% | 11 | 45% | 45% | 2.07 | -8.6 | -8 | -27 | -$3 |
| 2nd Half | | 157 | 21 | 2 | 13 | 2 | 248 | 215 | 292 | 331 | 623 | 614 | 625 | 5 | 76 | 0.21 | 43 | 19 | 38 | 32 | 67 | 58 | 71 | 4% | 113 | 5% | 100% | 13 | 8% | 62% | 3.27 | -0.8 | -5 | -17 | $6 |
| 19 | Proj | 301 | 31 | 6 | 21 | 1 | 226 | 223 | 266 | 332 | 598 | 567 | 611 | 5 | 74 | 0.19 | 41 | 22 | 37 | 29 | 73 | 70 | 81 | 7% | 121 | 3% | 66% | | | | 2.85 | -5.4 | -17 | -56 | $3 |

## Judge,Aaron

**Age:** 27 **Bats:** R **Pos:** RF | **Ht:** 6' 7" **Wt:** 282
**Health** C | **PT/Exp** B | **Consist** F
**LIMA Plan** B+ | **Rand Var** -4 | **MM** 5235

Late July wrist fracture cost him nearly eight weeks of production, and 41 AB after return diluted 2nd half data. That said, 1st half skills still had notable drops in FB%, xPX that put lower ceiling on HR upside and revive BA risk we've seen in past. Don't let that "52" anchor your expectations. Right now, it looks like more of an outlier.

| Yr | Tm | AB | R | HR | RBI | SB | BA | xBA | OBP | SLG | OPS | vL | vR | bb% | ct% | Eye | G | L | F | h% | HctX | PX | xPX | hr/f | Spd | SBO | SB% | #Wk | DOM | DIS | RC/G | RAR | BPV | BPX | R$ |
|---|---|---|---|---|---|---|---|---|---|---|---|---|---|---|---|---|---|---|---|---|---|---|---|---|---|---|---|---|---|---|---|---|---|---|---|
| 14 | | | | | | | | | | | | | | | | | | | | | | | | | | | | | | | | | | | |
| 15 | a/a | 478 | 55 | 20 | 63 | 6 | 238 | | 306 | 422 | 728 | | | 9 | 66 | 0.29 | | | | 31 | | 138 | | | 91 | 7% | 74% | | | | 4.31 | | 23 | 62 | $11 |
| 16 | NYY * | 436 | 65 | 24 | 68 | 4 | 237 | 215 | 317 | 446 | 763 | 289 | 679 | 10 | 65 | 0.33 | 35 | 14 | 51 | 31 | 129 | 142 | 196 | 18% | 74 | 5% | 82% | 6 | 33% | 50% | 4.74 | 0.3 | 18 | 51 | $11 |
| 17 | NYY | 542 | 128 | 52 | 114 | 9 | 284 | 267 | 422 | 627 | 1049 | 934 | 1079 | 19 | 62 | 0.61 | 35 | 22 | 43 | 36 | 113 | 223 | 175 | 36% | 94 | 6% | 69% | 26 | 58% | 23% | 9.29 | 67.0 | 93 | 282 | $33 |
| 18 | NYY | 413 | 77 | 27 | 67 | 6 | 278 | 251 | 392 | 528 | 919 | 967 | 901 | 15 | 63 | 0.50 | 42 | 23 | 35 | 38 | 112 | 175 | 126 | 29% | 76 | 6% | 67% | 22 | 45% | 36% | 7.21 | 31.8 | 48 | 160 | $20 |
| 1st Half | | 290 | 54 | 21 | 54 | 4 | 272 | 258 | 390 | 552 | 942 | 799 | 998 | 16 | 62 | 0.51 | 44 | 21 | 35 | 36 | 111 | 199 | 126 | 32% | 68 | 6% | 67% | 15 | 60% | 20% | 7.46 | 25.1 | 64 | 213 | $28 |
| 2nd Half | | 123 | 23 | 6 | 13 | 2 | 293 | 236 | 395 | 472 | 866 | 1435 | 683 | 14 | 65 | 0.47 | 37 | 29 | 34 | 41 | 114 | 119 | 125 | 21% | 99 | 7% | 67% | 7 | 14% | 71% | 6.59 | 7.3 | 15 | 50 | $3 |
| 19 | Proj | 508 | 95 | 38 | 92 | 7 | 273 | 254 | 381 | 548 | 928 | 1003 | 905 | 15 | 64 | 0.47 | 39 | 23 | 38 | 35 | 115 | 184 | 153 | 31% | 85 | 6% | 69% | | | | 7.20 | 40.1 | 55 | 185 | $28 |

## Kelly,Carson

**Age:** 24 **Bats:** R **Pos:** CA | **Ht:** 6'2" **Wt:** 220
**Health** A | **PT/Exp** D | **Consist** A
**LIMA Plan** D | **Rand Var** -1 | **MM** 1011

0-3-.114 in 35 AB at STL. Third straight year where his cup of coffee turned bitter, and he now has career .187 xBA in 117 MLB AB. But big picture shows growth in plate discipline that should eventually start paying off for highly-touted prospect. Catchers often develop more slowly; put him on your 2021 watchlist.

| Yr | Tm | AB | R | HR | RBI | SB | BA | xBA | OBP | SLG | OPS | vL | vR | bb% | ct% | Eye | G | L | F | h% | HctX | PX | xPX | hr/f | Spd | SBO | SB% | #Wk | DOM | DIS | RC/G | RAR | BPV | BPX | R$ |
|---|---|---|---|---|---|---|---|---|---|---|---|---|---|---|---|---|---|---|---|---|---|---|---|---|---|---|---|---|---|---|---|---|---|---|---|
| 14 | | | | | | | | | | | | | | | | | | | | | | | | | | | | | | | | | | | |
| 15 | | | | | | | | | | | | | | | | | | | | | | | | | | | | | | | | | | | |
| 16 | STL * | 342 | 36 | 5 | 27 | 0 | 259 | 210 | 300 | 349 | 649 | 1667 | 91 | 6 | 80 | 0.30 | 64 | 9 | 27 | 31 | 59 | 61 | -2 | 0% | 93 | 1% | 0% | 5 | 20% | 40% | 3.55 | -8.5 | 10 | 29 | $3 |
| 17 | STL * | 313 | 35 | 8 | 40 | 0 | 235 | 242 | 305 | 356 | 661 | 282 | 487 | 9 | 83 | 0.58 | 56 | 16 | 28 | 26 | 109 | 69 | 123 | 0% | 68 | 3% | 0% | 12 | 42% | 33% | 3.51 | -5.1 | 26 | 79 | $2 |
| 18 | STL * | 329 | 30 | 5 | 34 | 0 | 217 | 186 | 300 | 304 | 604 | 182 | 375 | 10 | 82 | 0.64 | 54 | 7 | 39 | 25 | 87 | 53 | 98 | 0% | 82 | 0% | 0% | 5 | 0% | 80% | 2.97 | -5.5 | 16 | 53 | $0 |
| 1st Half | | 167 | 13 | 4 | 22 | 0 | 211 | 206 | 280 | 336 | 616 | 200 | 243 | 9 | 84 | 0.59 | 58 | 5 | 37 | 23 | 117 | 74 | 144 | 0% | 81 | 0% | 0% | 3 | 0% | 100% | 3.04 | -2.1 | 38 | 127 | $0 |
| 2nd Half | | 162 | 17 | 1 | 12 | 0 | 223 | 166 | 319 | 271 | 591 | 0 | 586 | 12 | 79 | 0.69 | 44 | 11 | 44 | 27 | 29 | 30 | 1 | 0% | 99 | 0% | 0% | 2 | 0% | 50% | 2.84 | -3.0 | -2 | -7 | $0 |
| 19 | Proj | 158 | 16 | 3 | 17 | 0 | 229 | 227 | 320 | 321 | 641 | 505 | 694 | 9 | 82 | 0.56 | 50 | 17 | 33 | 27 | 98 | 57 | 136 | 6% | 91 | 1% | 0% | | | | 3.16 | -1.4 | 3 | 9 | $2 |

BRANDON KRUSE

## Kemp,Anthony

**Age:** 27 **Bats:** L **Pos:** LF CF
**Ht:** 5' 6" **Wt:** 165

| Health | A | LIMA Plan | D+ |
|---|---|---|---|
| PT/Exp | C | Rand Var | 0 |
| Consist | B | MM | 1333 |

6-30-.263 with 9 SB in 255 AB at HOU. His best MLB performance yet, but... 1) Strong ct%, LD% slid to league average in 2nd half, his largest AB sample in majors; 2) Mediocre SB% history raises questions about SB stability; 3) "Improvement" vL was really just a 35% hit rate. Deep league value could be short-lived.

| Yr | Tm | AB | R | HR | RBI | SB | BA | xBA | OBP | SLG | OPS | vL | vR | bb% | ct% | Eye | G | L | F | h% | HctX | PX | xPX | hr/f | Spd | SBO | SB% | #Wk | DOM | DIS | RC/G | RAR | BPV | BPX | R$ |
|---|---|---|---|---|---|---|---|---|---|---|---|---|---|---|---|---|---|---|---|---|---|---|---|---|---|---|---|---|---|---|---|---|---|---|---|
| 14 | aa | 233 | 32 | 3 | 16 | 10 | 253 | | 316 | 364 | 680 | | | 8 | 84 | 0.58 | | | | 29 | | 74 | | | 131 | 26% | 59% | | | | 3.69 | | 54 | 146 | $6 |
| 15 | a/a | 464 | 56 | 2 | 35 | 25 | 259 | | 319 | 324 | 642 | | | 8 | 83 | 0.52 | | | | 31 | | 44 | | | 118 | 30% | 61% | | | | 3.33 | | 22 | 59 | $15 |
| 16 | HOU * | 375 | 43 | 3 | 26 | 10 | 247 | 250 | 319 | 334 | 653 | 440 | 660 | 10 | 82 | 0.58 | 45 | 24 | 31 | 30 | 108 | 50 | 77 | 4% | 133 | 18% | 49% | 15 | 40% | 47% | 3.35 | -10.6 | 28 | 80 | $6 |
| 17 | HOU * | 541 | 66 | 7 | 43 | 16 | 247 | 215 | 277 | 335 | 613 | 522 | 491 | 4 | 89 | 0.39 | 44 | 9 | 47 | 27 | 90 | 45 | 75 | 0% | 143 | 20% | 65% | 7 | 14% | 43% | 3.06 | -39.0 | 45 | 136 | $11 |
| 18 | HOU * | 416 | 59 | 6 | 43 | 18 | 259 | 261 | 331 | 363 | 694 | 671 | 770 | 9 | 85 | 0.70 | 45 | 23 | 32 | 29 | 95 | 61 | 80 | 9% | 107 | 19% | 76% | 21 | 48% | 29% | 4.16 | -5.1 | 41 | 137 | $14 |
| 1st Half | | 255 | 34 | 1 | 25 | 12 | 274 | 276 | 335 | 349 | 684 | 908 | 753 | 8 | 89 | 0.80 | 47 | 27 | 27 | 31 | 96 | 44 | 51 | 5% | 123 | 19% | 77% | 8 | 50% | 13% | 4.15 | -3.3 | 45 | 150 | $17 |
| 2nd Half | | 161 | 25 | 5 | 18 | 6 | 236 | 254 | 332 | 385 | 717 | 572 | 781 | 12 | 79 | 0.62 | 43 | 21 | 36 | 27 | 89 | 92 | 99 | 11% | 91 | 18% | 75% | 13 | 46% | 38% | 4.17 | -2.1 | 42 | 140 | $10 |
| **19** | **Proj** | **288** | **39** | **5** | **26** | **11** | **250** | **255** | **317** | **360** | **677** | **593** | **702** | **8** | **82** | **0.50** | **45** | **24** | **31** | **29** | **98** | **65** | **78** | **7%** | **111** | **20%** | **67%** | | | | **3.75** | **-7.3** | **31** | **104** | **$7** |

## Kemp,Matt

**Age:** 34 **Bats:** R **Pos:** LF RF
**Ht:** 6' 4" **Wt:** 210

| Health | B | LIMA Plan | B |
|---|---|---|---|
| PT/Exp | B | Rand Var | -3 |
| Consist | B | MM | 3135 |

Restored FB% and revived power, at least for a while: .340 BA/.957 OPS on June 16; hit .247/.698 after. Then again, in 2017: .352 BA/1.001 OPS on June 2; .225/.634 after. Could be an age/stamina issue, could be a coincidence. Could be that you'll think about selling high if he gets off to another hot start.

| Yr | Tm | AB | R | HR | RBI | SB | BA | xBA | OBP | SLG | OPS | vL | vR | bb% | ct% | Eye | G | L | F | h% | HctX | PX | xPX | hr/f | Spd | SBO | SB% | #Wk | DOM | DIS | RC/G | RAR | BPV | BPX | R$ |
|---|---|---|---|---|---|---|---|---|---|---|---|---|---|---|---|---|---|---|---|---|---|---|---|---|---|---|---|---|---|---|---|---|---|---|---|
| 14 | LA | 541 | 77 | 25 | 89 | 8 | 287 | 287 | 346 | 506 | 852 | 781 | 879 | 9 | 73 | 0.36 | 43 | 26 | 31 | 35 | 128 | 168 | 139 | 20% | 91 | 9% | 62% | 27 | 67% | 15% | 6.18 | 36.7 | 74 | 200 | $27 |
| 15 | SD | 596 | 80 | 23 | 100 | 12 | 265 | 258 | 312 | 443 | 755 | 824 | 736 | 6 | 75 | 0.27 | 44 | 21 | 35 | 32 | 135 | 119 | 149 | 14% | 94 | 10% | 86% | 26 | 38% | 35% | 4.82 | 1.7 | 39 | 105 | $23 |
| 16 | 2 NL | 623 | 89 | 35 | 108 | 1 | 268 | 270 | 304 | 499 | 803 | 954 | 761 | 5 | 75 | 0.23 | 40 | 20 | 40 | 31 | 109 | 143 | 136 | 18% | 70 | 1% | 100% | 27 | 37% | 15% | 5.37 | 13.2 | 48 | 137 | $21 |
| 17 | ATL | 438 | 47 | 19 | 64 | 0 | 276 | 273 | 318 | 463 | 781 | 684 | 808 | 6 | 77 | 0.27 | 49 | 23 | 28 | 32 | 109 | 107 | 104 | 20% | 81 | 2% | 0% | 23 | 35% | 30% | 5.10 | -2.0 | 33 | 100 | $11 |
| 18 | LA | 462 | 62 | 21 | 85 | 0 | 290 | 265 | 338 | 481 | 818 | 828 | 812 | 7 | 75 | 0.31 | 35 | 27 | 38 | 35 | 120 | 117 | 143 | 16% | 66 | 0% | 0% | 28 | 43% | 29% | 5.89 | 16.5 | 30 | 100 | $18 |
| 1st Half | | 251 | 34 | 13 | 47 | 0 | 303 | 268 | 342 | 522 | 864 | 962 | 811 | 6 | 75 | 0.25 | 36 | 24 | 40 | 36 | 119 | 136 | 155 | 17% | 77 | 0% | 0% | 15 | 47% | 20% | 6.58 | 13.6 | 45 | 150 | $22 |
| 2nd Half | | 211 | 28 | 8 | 38 | 0 | 275 | 263 | 333 | 431 | 765 | 704 | 811 | 9 | 75 | 0.38 | 34 | 30 | 36 | 33 | 122 | 95 | 128 | 14% | 64 | 0% | 0% | 13 | 38% | 38% | 5.12 | 3.1 | 16 | 53 | $14 |
| **19** | **Proj** | **456** | **59** | **20** | **78** | **1** | **280** | **264** | **327** | **467** | **794** | **785** | **798** | **7** | **76** | **0.30** | **40** | **25** | **35** | **33** | **117** | **115** | **130** | **16%** | **75** | **1%** | **53%** | | | | **5.42** | **10.7** | **22** | **74** | **$18** |

## Kendrick,Howie

**Age:** 35 **Bats:** R **Pos:** 2B
**Ht:** 5' 11" **Wt:** 220

| Health | F | LIMA Plan | C+ |
|---|---|---|---|
| PT/Exp | D | Rand Var | -1 |
| Consist | C | MM | 2253 |

Ruptured Achilles ended season in mid-May and led to his greatest fantasy contribution for 2018: creating an opening for Juan Soto. Prior to that, was up to his old tricks, riding consistent ct% and flurry of LD to top-notch BA. But you have to wonder what impact injury will have on already-shaky SB skills.

| Yr | Tm | AB | R | HR | RBI | SB | BA | xBA | OBP | SLG | OPS | vL | vR | bb% | ct% | Eye | G | L | F | h% | HctX | PX | xPX | hr/f | Spd | SBO | SB% | #Wk | DOM | DIS | RC/G | RAR | BPV | BPX | R$ |
|---|---|---|---|---|---|---|---|---|---|---|---|---|---|---|---|---|---|---|---|---|---|---|---|---|---|---|---|---|---|---|---|---|---|---|---|
| 14 | LAA | 617 | 85 | 7 | 75 | 14 | 293 | 272 | 347 | 397 | 744 | 834 | 714 | 7 | 82 | 0.44 | 60 | 19 | 21 | 35 | 133 | 78 | 88 | 7% | 102 | 10% | 74% | 27 | 26% | 22% | 4.92 | 26.4 | 38 | 103 | $25 |
| 15 | LA | 464 | 64 | 9 | 54 | 6 | 295 | 286 | 336 | 409 | 746 | 721 | 753 | 5 | 82 | 0.33 | 59 | 24 | 17 | 34 | 108 | 75 | 71 | 14% | 93 | 6% | 75% | 22 | 27% | 36% | 4.94 | 10.0 | 30 | 81 | $17 |
| 16 | LA | 487 | 65 | 8 | 40 | 10 | 255 | 272 | 326 | 366 | 691 | 626 | 722 | 9 | 80 | 0.52 | 61 | 19 | 20 | 30 | 110 | 72 | 63 | 10% | 95 | 9% | 83% | 26 | 31% | 38% | 4.11 | -10.8 | 28 | 80 | $10 |
| 17 | 2 NL | 305 | 40 | 9 | 41 | 12 | 315 | 285 | 368 | 475 | 844 | 901 | 819 | 7 | 78 | 0.32 | 58 | 22 | 20 | 38 | 99 | 93 | 84 | 19% | 110 | 19% | 71% | 19 | 37% | 32% | 6.24 | 10.3 | 33 | 100 | $16 |
| 18 | WAS | 152 | 17 | 4 | 12 | 1 | 303 | 287 | 331 | 474 | 805 | 669 | 860 | 3 | 81 | 0.17 | 48 | 24 | 28 | 35 | 118 | 112 | 82 | 11% | 73 | 6% | 50% | 8 | 50% | 25% | 5.51 | 5.2 | 43 | 143 | $3 |
| 1st Half | | 152 | 17 | 4 | 12 | 1 | 303 | 287 | 331 | 474 | 805 | 669 | 860 | 3 | 81 | 0.17 | 48 | 24 | 28 | 35 | 118 | 112 | 82 | 11% | 73 | 6% | 50% | 8 | 50% | 25% | 5.51 | 5.6 | 43 | 143 | $3 |
| 2nd Half | | | | | | | | | | | | | | | | | | | | | | | | | | | | | | | | | | | |
| **19** | **Proj** | **329** | **42** | **7** | **33** | **5** | **291** | **278** | **338** | **431** | **769** | **726** | **786** | **6** | **80** | **0.33** | **56** | **22** | **22** | **34** | **112** | **88** | **77** | **13%** | **91** | **9%** | **68%** | | | | **5.11** | **8.6** | **30** | **100** | **$13** |

## Kepler,Max

**Age:** 26 **Bats:** L **Pos:** RF CF
**Ht:** 6' 4" **Wt:** 205

| Health | A | LIMA Plan | A |
|---|---|---|---|
| PT/Exp | B | Rand Var | +4 |
| Consist | A | MM | 3235 |

Three good developments in a disappointing season: 1) career-best Eye; 2) continued FB% growth; 3) 76% contact and 119 PX vL. Efforts were also hurt by unlucky h%, though xBA shows promise of 2015 MLE is still out of reach. If you can live with middling BA, he's at the right age for step up in power... UP: 30 HR

| Yr | Tm | AB | R | HR | RBI | SB | BA | xBA | OBP | SLG | OPS | vL | vR | bb% | ct% | Eye | G | L | F | h% | HctX | PX | xPX | hr/f | Spd | SBO | SB% | #Wk | DOM | DIS | RC/G | RAR | BPV | BPX | R$ |
|---|---|---|---|---|---|---|---|---|---|---|---|---|---|---|---|---|---|---|---|---|---|---|---|---|---|---|---|---|---|---|---|---|---|---|---|
| 14 | | | | | | | | | | | | | | | | | | | | | | | | | | | | | | | | | | | |
| 15 | MIN * | 414 | 58 | 7 | 54 | 14 | 288 | 280 | 365 | 457 | 822 | 0 | 333 | 11 | 83 | 0.72 | 75 | 0 | 25 | 33 | 90 | 107 | -16 | 0% | 129 | 15% | 76% | 2 | 0% | 100% | 5.96 | 14.0 | 81 | 219 | $17 |
| 16 | MIN * | 506 | 66 | 18 | 80 | 7 | 243 | 259 | 319 | 426 | 744 | 595 | 792 | 10 | 79 | 0.52 | 47 | 16 | 36 | 28 | 106 | 105 | 103 | 15% | 112 | 8% | 69% | 22 | 55% | 36% | 4.54 | -2.5 | 54 | 154 | $12 |
| 17 | MIN | 511 | 67 | 19 | 69 | 6 | 243 | 256 | 312 | 425 | 737 | 453 | 828 | 8 | 78 | 0.41 | 43 | 18 | 40 | 28 | 104 | 107 | 93 | 12% | 93 | 6% | 86% | 26 | 46% | 35% | 4.41 | -7.8 | 43 | 130 | $10 |
| 18 | MIN | 532 | 80 | 20 | 58 | 4 | 224 | 249 | 319 | 408 | 727 | 745 | 720 | 12 | 82 | 0.74 | 38 | 16 | 46 | 24 | 112 | 104 | 120 | 10% | 105 | 7% | 44% | 28 | 68% | 14% | 4.10 | -6.6 | 68 | 227 | $10 |
| 1st Half | | 271 | 32 | 8 | 29 | 3 | 221 | 245 | 307 | 391 | 698 | 941 | 602 | 11 | 83 | 0.72 | 37 | 16 | 48 | 24 | 115 | 100 | 123 | 7% | 98 | 8% | 60% | 15 | 73% | 13% | 3.89 | -4.8 | 64 | 213 | $7 |
| 2nd Half | | 261 | 48 | 12 | 29 | 1 | 226 | 253 | 331 | 425 | 756 | 530 | 839 | 12 | 81 | 0.76 | 39 | 16 | 45 | 24 | 109 | 109 | 117 | 13% | 117 | 6% | 25% | 13 | 62% | 15% | 4.33 | -1.0 | 74 | 247 | $13 |
| **19** | **Proj** | **564** | **82** | **24** | **71** | **7** | **247** | **256** | **330** | **448** | **778** | **637** | **830** | **10** | **80** | **0.59** | **39** | **17** | **44** | **27** | **108** | **114** | **108** | **12%** | **107** | **7%** | **62%** | | | | **4.86** | **6.8** | **64** | **212** | **$18** |

## Kieboom,Spencer

**Age:** 28 **Bats:** R **Pos:** CA
**Ht:** 6' 0" **Wt:** 210

| Health | A | LIMA Plan | D |
|---|---|---|---|
| PT/Exp | F | Rand Var | 0 |
| Consist | A | MM | 1011 |

2-13-.232 in 143 AB at WAS. Solid on defense, but skills suggest that hearing his last name announced over PA system is the closest he'll get to any kind of explosion at the plate. And he'll soon likely be overshadowed by more talented younger brother Carter. No one aspires to be the next Wilton Guerrero.

| Yr | Tm | AB | R | HR | RBI | SB | BA | xBA | OBP | SLG | OPS | vL | vR | bb% | ct% | Eye | G | L | F | h% | HctX | PX | xPX | hr/f | Spd | SBO | SB% | #Wk | DOM | DIS | RC/G | RAR | BPV | BPX | R$ |
|---|---|---|---|---|---|---|---|---|---|---|---|---|---|---|---|---|---|---|---|---|---|---|---|---|---|---|---|---|---|---|---|---|---|---|---|
| 14 | | | | | | | | | | | | | | | | | | | | | | | | | | | | | | | | | | | |
| 15 | | | | | | | | | | | | | | | | | | | | | | | | | | | | | | | | | | | |
| 16 | WAS * | 309 | 24 | 4 | 26 | 0 | 202 | 211 | 288 | 273 | 561 | 0 | 1000 | 11 | 78 | 0.55 | 44 | 20 | 36 | 25 | 0 | 47 | -24 | 0% | 80 | 0% | 0% | 1 | 0% | 100% | 2.51 | -18.3 | -2 | -6 | -$4 |
| 17 | a/a | 220 | 18 | 4 | 19 | 0 | 211 | | 275 | 319 | 594 | | | 8 | 77 | 0.38 | | | | 26 | | 70 | | | 84 | 0% | 0% | | | | 2.83 | | 8 | 24 | -$2 |
| 18 | WAS * | 209 | 22 | 3 | 21 | 0 | 224 | 234 | 303 | 304 | 607 | 745 | 603 | 10 | 81 | 0.60 | 41 | 23 | 36 | 26 | 67 | 52 | 81 | 6% | 87 | 0% | 0% | 20 | 25% | 40% | 3.03 | -3.0 | 14 | 47 | $0 |
| 1st Half | | 126 | 8 | 1 | 11 | 0 | 212 | 256 | 285 | 274 | 559 | 222 | 645 | 9 | 83 | 0.59 | 39 | 29 | 32 | 25 | 57 | 43 | 86 | 0% | 75 | 0% | 0% | 8 | 13% | 38% | 2.53 | -3.6 | 8 | 27 | -$3 |
| 2nd Half | | 83 | 14 | 2 | 10 | 0 | 241 | 228 | 333 | 349 | 683 | 927 | 580 | 12 | 78 | 0.61 | 42 | 20 | 38 | 29 | 70 | 66 | 78 | 8% | 105 | 0% | 0% | 12 | 33% | 42% | 3.87 | 1.0 | 23 | 77 | $3 |
| **19** | **Proj** | **221** | **23** | **3** | **21** | **0** | **218** | **233** | **298** | **303** | **601** | **671** | **576** | **10** | **79** | **0.51** | **41** | **24** | **35** | **26** | **65** | **56** | **81** | **5%** | **91** | **0%** | **0%** | | | | **2.92** | **-3.6** | **-11** | **-35** | **$1** |

## Kiermaier,Kevin

**Age:** 29 **Bats:** L **Pos:** CF
**Ht:** 6' 1" **Wt:** 215

| Health | F | LIMA Plan | C+ |
|---|---|---|---|
| PT/Exp | C | Rand Var | +3 |
| Consist | C | MM | 2523 |

You can see toll that injuries are taking on him—just look at the trend lines for xBA, ct%, HctX, and BPV/BPX. With enough AB, still has a potentially valuable power/speed combo, but try saying "I really think Kiermaier will stay healthy this year" at your draft or auction. Your league mates could use a good laugh.

| Yr | Tm | AB | R | HR | RBI | SB | BA | xBA | OBP | SLG | OPS | vL | vR | bb% | ct% | Eye | G | L | F | h% | HctX | PX | xPX | hr/f | Spd | SBO | SB% | #Wk | DOM | DIS | RC/G | RAR | BPV | BPX | R$ |
|---|---|---|---|---|---|---|---|---|---|---|---|---|---|---|---|---|---|---|---|---|---|---|---|---|---|---|---|---|---|---|---|---|---|---|---|
| 14 | TAM * | 459 | 58 | 12 | 46 | 14 | 264 | 270 | 314 | 436 | 750 | 507 | 837 | 7 | 79 | 0.34 | 53 | 17 | 31 | 31 | 92 | 116 | 82 | 13% | 139 | 18% | 73% | 22 | 45% | 32% | 4.69 | 10.7 | 65 | 176 | $16 |
| 15 | TAM | 505 | 62 | 10 | 40 | 18 | 263 | 275 | 298 | 420 | 718 | 625 | 754 | 4 | 81 | 0.25 | 48 | 23 | 29 | 31 | 88 | 96 | 58 | 8% | 148 | 21% | 78% | 26 | 46% | 31% | 4.31 | -2.8 | 57 | 154 | $16 |
| 16 | TAM | 366 | 55 | 12 | 37 | 21 | 246 | 260 | 331 | 410 | 741 | 816 | 718 | 10 | 80 | 0.54 | 42 | 21 | 38 | 28 | 102 | 98 | 77 | 11% | 96 | 25% | 88% | 19 | 42% | 26% | 4.62 | 2.7 | 48 | 137 | $14 |
| 17 | TAM | 380 | 56 | 15 | 39 | 16 | 276 | 252 | 338 | 450 | 788 | 682 | 851 | 7 | 74 | 0.31 | 50 | 18 | 32 | 34 | 95 | 99 | 70 | 17% | 132 | 22% | 70% | 17 | 18% | 29% | 5.10 | 3.9 | 31 | 94 | $16 |
| 18 | TAM | 332 | 44 | 7 | 29 | 10 | 217 | 240 | 282 | 370 | 653 | 548 | 694 | 7 | 73 | 0.27 | 50 | 19 | 31 | 28 | 84 | 91 | 70 | 10% | 149 | 22% | 67% | 19 | 16% | 47% | 3.19 | -8.7 | 23 | 77 | $5 |
| 1st Half | | 81 | 12 | 1 | 5 | 4 | 160 | 177 | 269 | 259 | 528 | 486 | 544 | 11 | 62 | 0.32 | 55 | 10 | 35 | 24 | 64 | 62 | 54 | 6% | 142 | 21% | 100% | 7 | 0% | 57% | 2.20 | -5.2 | -37 | -123 | -$8 |
| 2nd Half | | 251 | 32 | 6 | 24 | 6 | 235 | 260 | 287 | 406 | 693 | 571 | 739 | 6 | 76 | 0.25 | 48 | 22 | 30 | 29 | 91 | 98 | 74 | 11% | 139 | 22% | 55% | 12 | 25% | 42% | 3.54 | -4.7 | 38 | 127 | $9 |
| **19** | **Proj** | **387** | **54** | **10** | **35** | **15** | **235** | **241** | **304** | **391** | **696** | **617** | **729** | **8** | **74** | **0.32** | **49** | **18** | **33** | **29** | **88** | **93** | **69** | **11%** | **140** | **22%** | **75%** | | | | **3.83** | **-3.6** | **31** | **103** | **$12** |

## Kiner-Falefa,Isiah

**Age:** 24 **Bats:** R **Pos:** 3B CA 2B
**Ht:** 5'10" **Wt:** 176

| Health | A | LIMA Plan | D+ |
|---|---|---|---|
| PT/Exp | B | Rand Var | 0 |
| Consist | C | MM | 1253 |

CA eligibility is a game-changer, as BA, SB potential put him above most other #2 options, at least in deep leagues. 2nd half ct%, LD% gains are encouraging, especially after league had a good look at him, and vL success seems legit (90% ct, 1.25 Eye). Won't make or break your season, but he's nice depth.

| Yr | Tm | AB | R | HR | RBI | SB | BA | xBA | OBP | SLG | OPS | vL | vR | bb% | ct% | Eye | G | L | F | h% | HctX | PX | xPX | hr/f | Spd | SBO | SB% | #Wk | DOM | DIS | RC/G | RAR | BPV | BPX | R$ |
|---|---|---|---|---|---|---|---|---|---|---|---|---|---|---|---|---|---|---|---|---|---|---|---|---|---|---|---|---|---|---|---|---|---|---|---|
| 14 | | | | | | | | | | | | | | | | | | | | | | | | | | | | | | | | | | | |
| 15 | | | | | | | | | | | | | | | | | | | | | | | | | | | | | | | | | | | |
| 16 | aa | 402 | 48 | 0 | 24 | 5 | 245 | | 308 | 274 | 583 | | | 8 | 87 | 0.70 | | | | 28 | | 18 | | | 125 | 9% | 45% | | | | 2.74 | | 19 | 54 | $3 |
| 17 | aa | 513 | 51 | 5 | 42 | 15 | 280 | | 329 | 377 | 707 | | | 7 | 85 | 0.51 | | | | 32 | | 60 | | | 100 | 15% | 70% | | | | 4.35 | | 36 | 109 | $14 |
| 18 | TEX | 356 | 43 | 4 | 34 | 7 | 261 | 271 | 325 | 357 | 682 | 801 | 622 | 7 | 83 | 0.45 | 51 | 25 | 24 | 31 | 89 | 60 | 34 | 6% | 117 | 12% | 58% | 25 | 32% | 44% | 3.76 | 4.1 | 30 | 100 | $8 |
| 1st Half | | 211 | 30 | 2 | 22 | 5 | 251 | 257 | 326 | 355 | 682 | 697 | 675 | 9 | 81 | 0.50 | 46 | 24 | 30 | 30 | 98 | 67 | 51 | 4% | 125 | 16% | 56% | 13 | 31% | 38% | 3.66 | 1.3 | 35 | 117 | $9 |
| 2nd Half | | 145 | 13 | 2 | 12 | 2 | 276 | 287 | 323 | 359 | 681 | 925 | 535 | 5 | 85 | 0.36 | 58 | 28 | 15 | 31 | 76 | 51 | 12 | 11% | 103 | 8% | 67% | 12 | 33% | 50% | 3.92 | 2.0 | 23 | 77 | $5 |
| **19** | **Proj** | **293** | **32** | **4** | **24** | **6** | **267** | **281** | **328** | **363** | **690** | **858** | **601** | **7** | **85** | **0.49** | **53** | **26** | **21** | **31** | **85** | **58** | **28** | **7%** | **103** | **12%** | **63%** | | | | **3.94** | **-4.9** | **25** | **82** | **$8** |

BRANDON KRUSE

## Kingery,Scott

| | | | |
|---|---|---|---|
| Age: 25 Bats: R Pos: SS | Health A | LIMA Plan B | |
| Ht: 5' 10" Wt: 180 | PT/Exp C | Rand Var 0 | |
| | Consist F | MM 2515 | |

Hyped prospect fell far short of expecations. Alleged stock in trade—making consistent, hard contact—failed to materialize amid move from 2B to SS. Corrections start with improving plate discipline that was among worst in MLB. On the plus side, he has wheels and a full year of experience. It may take him a while.

| Yr Tm | AB | R | HR | RBI | SB | BA | xBA | OBP | SLG | OPS | vL | vR | bb% | ct% | Eye | G | L | F | h% | HctX | PX | xPX | hr/f | Spd | SBO | SB% | #Wk | DOM | DIS | RC/G | RAR | BPV | BPX | R$ |
|---|---|---|---|---|---|---|---|---|---|---|---|---|---|---|---|---|---|---|---|---|---|---|---|---|---|---|---|---|---|---|---|---|---|---|
| 14 | | | | | | | | | | | | | | | | | | | | | | | | | | | | | | | | | | |
| 15 | | | | | | | | | | | | | | | | | | | | | | | | | | | | | | | | | | |
| 16 aa | 156 | 12 | 2 | 14 | 3 | 213 | | 232 | 282 | 514 | | | 2 | 73 | 0.09 | | | | 28 | | 51 | | | 88 | 18% | 58% | | | | 2.03 | | -31 | -89 | -$1 |
| 17 a/a | 543 | 88 | 25 | 56 | 25 | 277 | | 322 | 485 | 807 | | | 6 | 77 | 0.28 | | | | 32 | | 114 | | | 133 | 23% | 82% | | | | 5.55 | | 52 | 158 | $26 |
| 18 PHI | 452 | 55 | 8 | 35 | 10 | 226 | 220 | 267 | 338 | 605 | 587 | 612 | 5 | 72 | 0.19 | 35 | 24 | 41 | 30 | 71 | 79 | 101 | 6% | 122 | 14% | 77% | 28 | 18% | 57% | 2.96 | -18.1 | 0 | 0 | $7 |
| 1st Half | 260 | 30 | 4 | 24 | 7 | 231 | 231 | 280 | 342 | 622 | 525 | 660 | 6 | 74 | 0.25 | 38 | 25 | 38 | 30 | 73 | 79 | 103 | 6% | 112 | 16% | 78% | 15 | 13% | 47% | 3.17 | -7.9 | 6 | 20 | $9 |
| 2nd Half | 192 | 25 | 4 | 11 | 3 | 219 | 204 | 248 | 333 | 581 | 676 | 547 | 4 | 70 | 0.12 | 31 | 23 | 46 | 29 | 68 | 79 | 100 | 7% | 133 | 11% | 75% | 13 | 23% | 69% | 2.67 | -8.9 | -9 | -30 | $4 |
| **19 Proj** | **433** | **56** | **13** | **37** | **13** | **241** | **234** | **279** | **387** | **667** | **698** | **655** | **5** | **75** | **0.21** | **34** | **24** | **42** | **29** | **70** | **91** | **101** | **9%** | **130** | **18%** | **77%** | | | | **3.61** | **-4.6** | **22** | **72** | **$10** |

## Kinsler,Ian

| | | | |
|---|---|---|---|
| Age: 37 Bats: R Pos: 2B | Health B | LIMA Plan B+ | |
| Ht: 6' 0" Wt: 200 | PT/Exp A | Rand Var +3 | |
| | Consist C | MM 2335 | |

This is a model of aging gracefully and subtly. While no longer outperforming xBA, his Eye and bat-on-ball skills remain fine, and with hard hits less frequent, he retains basepath acumen and capitalizes on SBO. In 13 seasons, he's reached double-digit HR/SB in twelve of them. Next year, he'll make it a baker's dozen.

| Yr Tm | AB | R | HR | RBI | SB | BA | xBA | OBP | SLG | OPS | vL | vR | bb% | ct% | Eye | G | L | F | h% | HctX | PX | xPX | hr/f | Spd | SBO | SB% | #Wk | DOM | DIS | RC/G | RAR | BPV | BPX | R$ |
|---|---|---|---|---|---|---|---|---|---|---|---|---|---|---|---|---|---|---|---|---|---|---|---|---|---|---|---|---|---|---|---|---|---|---|
| 14 DET | 684 | 100 | 17 | 92 | 15 | 275 | 267 | 307 | 420 | 727 | 740 | 722 | 4 | 88 | 0.37 | 38 | 20 | 43 | 29 | 92 | 96 | 84 | 7% | 118 | 12% | 79% | 27 | 59% | 4% | 4.50 | 21.7 | 76 | 205 | $28 |
| 15 DET | 624 | 94 | 11 | 73 | 10 | 296 | 265 | 342 | 428 | 770 | 798 | 763 | 6 | 87 | 0.54 | 34 | 25 | 41 | 33 | 102 | 81 | 94 | 5% | 129 | 9% | 63% | 26 | 42% | 15% | 5.20 | 16.0 | 67 | 181 | $25 |
| 16 DET | 618 | 117 | 28 | 83 | 14 | 288 | 264 | 348 | 484 | 831 | 893 | 809 | 7 | 81 | 0.39 | 32 | 24 | 45 | 32 | 112 | 109 | 122 | 13% | 123 | 12% | 70% | 27 | 56% | 15% | 5.74 | 17.7 | 65 | 186 | $29 |
| 17 DET | 551 | 90 | 22 | 52 | 14 | 236 | 257 | 313 | 412 | 725 | 896 | 680 | 9 | 84 | 0.64 | 33 | 21 | 46 | 24 | 126 | 90 | 119 | 10% | 109 | 14% | 74% | 25 | 48% | 16% | 4.17 | -7.5 | 62 | 188 | $13 |
| 18 2 AL | 487 | 66 | 14 | 48 | 16 | 240 | 259 | 301 | 380 | 681 | 486 | 756 | 7 | 87 | 0.63 | 37 | 21 | 42 | 25 | 94 | 79 | 81 | 8% | 84 | 20% | 70% | 26 | 46% | 27% | 3.73 | -5.0 | 53 | 177 | $14 |
| 1st Half | 280 | 34 | 11 | 22 | 7 | 218 | 263 | 280 | 389 | 669 | 534 | 712 | 8 | 89 | 0.77 | 38 | 17 | 45 | 21 | 103 | 90 | 97 | 10% | 89 | 17% | 70% | 14 | 57% | 0% | 3.47 | -6.2 | 73 | 243 | $12 |
| 2nd Half | 207 | 32 | 3 | 26 | 9 | 271 | 254 | 330 | 367 | 698 | 439 | 823 | 8 | 84 | 0.50 | 34 | 28 | 38 | 31 | 81 | 62 | 58 | 5% | 82 | 22% | 69% | 12 | 33% | 58% | 4.10 | -0.4 | 26 | 87 | $17 |
| **19 Proj** | **452** | **70** | **14** | **50** | **13** | **255** | **256** | **319** | **403** | **722** | **645** | **750** | **8** | **85** | **0.56** | **35** | **23** | **43** | **27** | **103** | **83** | **94** | **8%** | **100** | **16%** | **70%** | | | | **4.27** | **1.2** | **54** | **180** | **$17** |

## Kipnis,Jason

| | | | |
|---|---|---|---|
| Age: 32 Bats: L Pos: 2B | Health C | LIMA Plan B+ | |
| Ht: 5' 11" Wt: 195 | PT/Exp B | Rand Var +2 | |
| | Consist C | MM 3235 | |

Yearly stat outcomes have been all over the place, challenging fanalytics. But 2018 was driven by four-year GB/FB reversal that boosted HR while dampening BA. Repressed Spd/SBO likely a carryover from 2017 hamstring woes, so as confidently as possible, we say that 2019 will look like 2nd half of 2018. Or not.

| Yr Tm | AB | R | HR | RBI | SB | BA | xBA | OBP | SLG | OPS | vL | vR | bb% | ct% | Eye | G | L | F | h% | HctX | PX | xPX | hr/f | Spd | SBO | SB% | #Wk | DOM | DIS | RC/G | RAR | BPV | BPX | R$ |
|---|---|---|---|---|---|---|---|---|---|---|---|---|---|---|---|---|---|---|---|---|---|---|---|---|---|---|---|---|---|---|---|---|---|---|
| 14 CLE | 500 | 61 | 6 | 41 | 22 | 240 | 249 | 310 | 330 | 640 | 500 | 710 | 9 | 80 | 0.50 | 46 | 23 | 31 | 29 | 92 | 72 | 84 | 5% | 94 | 18% | 88% | 23 | 30% | 30% | 3.58 | 2.8 | 26 | 70 | $13 |
| 15 CLE | 565 | 86 | 9 | 52 | 12 | 303 | 284 | 372 | 451 | 823 | 679 | 908 | 9 | 81 | 0.53 | 45 | 27 | 28 | 36 | 109 | 103 | 97 | 7% | 118 | 12% | 60% | 24 | 50% | 21% | 5.87 | 25.1 | 62 | 168 | $23 |
| 16 CLE | 610 | 91 | 23 | 82 | 15 | 275 | 267 | 343 | 469 | 811 | 790 | 822 | 9 | 76 | 0.41 | 39 | 24 | 37 | 33 | 110 | 123 | 122 | 13% | 91 | 11% | 83% | 27 | 52% | 26% | 5.66 | 16.3 | 49 | 140 | $24 |
| 17 CLE * | 372 | 44 | 13 | 37 | 6 | 223 | 253 | 278 | 400 | 679 | 632 | 744 | 7 | 78 | 0.34 | 36 | 20 | 44 | 25 | 95 | 109 | 122 | 10% | 93 | 11% | 75% | 18 | 44% | 28% | 3.64 | -11.2 | 41 | 124 | $4 |
| 18 CLE | 530 | 65 | 18 | 75 | 7 | 230 | 243 | 315 | 389 | 704 | 646 | 725 | 10 | 79 | 0.54 | 34 | 22 | 45 | 26 | 101 | 95 | 120 | 10% | 69 | 6% | 88% | 28 | 43% | 32% | 4.01 | -0.9 | 34 | 113 | $12 |
| 1st Half | 290 | 33 | 7 | 33 | 2 | 217 | 228 | 296 | 341 | 638 | 715 | 611 | 10 | 78 | 0.48 | 35 | 21 | 44 | 26 | 105 | 80 | 132 | 7% | 69 | 4% | 67% | 15 | 33% | 40% | 3.24 | -8.3 | 16 | 53 | $7 |
| 2nd Half | 240 | 32 | 11 | 42 | 5 | 246 | 261 | 337 | 446 | 783 | 570 | 866 | 11 | 80 | 0.62 | 32 | 23 | 45 | 26 | 97 | 113 | 106 | 13% | 78 | 8% | 100% | 13 | 54% | 23% | 5.06 | 6.3 | 59 | 197 | $18 |
| **19 Proj** | **508** | **65** | **17** | **66** | **8** | **241** | **252** | **316** | **411** | **728** | **644** | **765** | **9** | **78** | **0.47** | **36** | **22** | **42** | **28** | **100** | **104** | **116** | **10%** | **84** | **8%** | **81%** | | | | **4.34** | **2.5** | **44** | **147** | **$15** |

## Knapp,Andrew

| | | | |
|---|---|---|---|
| Age: 27 Bats: B Pos: CA | Health A | LIMA Plan D | |
| Ht: 6' 1" Wt: 195 | PT/Exp D | Rand Var +1 | |
| | Consist D | MM 2401 | |

Several years ago I drafted Knapp because we attended the same college and he hit .360 in AA during the 2nd half of 2015. That allegiance ended in 2018 as his xBA over two seasons straddled the Mendoza Line. I'm probably just fickle; he'll likely turn out to be a servicable second CA... which is to say, not all that good.

| Yr Tm | AB | R | HR | RBI | SB | BA | xBA | OBP | SLG | OPS | vL | vR | bb% | ct% | Eye | G | L | F | h% | HctX | PX | xPX | hr/f | Spd | SBO | SB% | #Wk | DOM | DIS | RC/G | RAR | BPV | BPX | R$ |
|---|---|---|---|---|---|---|---|---|---|---|---|---|---|---|---|---|---|---|---|---|---|---|---|---|---|---|---|---|---|---|---|---|---|---|
| 14 | | | | | | | | | | | | | | | | | | | | | | | | | | | | | | | | | | |
| 15 aa | 214 | 30 | 9 | 43 | 1 | 311 | | 361 | 540 | 901 | | | 7 | 76 | 0.33 | | | | 37 | | 160 | | | 86 | 1% | 100% | | | | 7.24 | | 74 | 200 | $9 |
| 16 aaa | 403 | 49 | 8 | 41 | 2 | 235 | | 293 | 349 | 642 | | | 8 | 68 | 0.26 | | | | 32 | | 85 | | | 90 | 4% | 44% | | | | 3.35 | | -13 | -37 | $4 |
| 17 PHI | 171 | 26 | 3 | 13 | 1 | 257 | 222 | 368 | 368 | 736 | 623 | 767 | 15 | 67 | 0.55 | 59 | 17 | 24 | 37 | 105 | 78 | 102 | 11% | 124 | 2% | 100% | 22 | 23% | 50% | 4.74 | 3.4 | 1 | 3 | $1 |
| 18 PHI | 187 | 19 | 4 | 15 | 1 | 198 | 196 | 294 | 316 | 610 | 642 | 601 | 11 | 60 | 0.32 | 38 | 26 | 36 | 31 | 72 | 88 | 113 | 10% | 131 | 2% | 100% | 26 | 23% | 69% | 2.93 | -3.4 | -25 | -83 | -$2 |
| 1st Half | 103 | 11 | 2 | 9 | 1 | 214 | 191 | 299 | 320 | 620 | 431 | 662 | 11 | 60 | 0.32 | 41 | 24 | 35 | 33 | 70 | 80 | 108 | 9% | 126 | 3% | 100% | 14 | 21% | 71% | 3.19 | -0.8 | -33 | -110 | -$2 |
| 2nd Half | 84 | 8 | 2 | 6 | 0 | 179 | 203 | 289 | 310 | 598 | 955 | 528 | 12 | 60 | 0.32 | 35 | 29 | 37 | 27 | 73 | 99 | 121 | 11% | 124 | 0% | 0% | 12 | 25% | 67% | 2.63 | -2.2 | -20 | -67 | -$2 |
| **19 Proj** | **217** | **26** | **5** | **20** | **1** | **227** | **214** | **319** | **350** | **668** | **677** | **665** | **11** | **65** | **0.37** | **46** | **23** | **31** | **33** | **85** | **91** | **110** | **10%** | **119** | **2%** | **86%** | | | | **3.66** | **1.4** | **-22** | **-74** | **$3** |

## Lagares,Juan

| | | | |
|---|---|---|---|
| Age: 30 Bats: R Pos: CF | Health F | LIMA Plan D | |
| Ht: 6' 1" Wt: 215 | PT/Exp F | Rand Var -5 | |
| | Consist C | MM 1521 | |

Missing 273 days to injury over the past three years virtually presses the reset button here. In seasons prior, he displayed passable small-ball skills, striking the ball on the ground and ulitizing his speed. But it was more his defense that earned him PT, and glovework isn't a fantasy category. Nor are DL days.

| Yr Tm | AB | R | HR | RBI | SB | BA | xBA | OBP | SLG | OPS | vL | vR | bb% | ct% | Eye | G | L | F | h% | HctX | PX | xPX | hr/f | Spd | SBO | SB% | #Wk | DOM | DIS | RC/G | RAR | BPV | BPX | R$ |
|---|---|---|---|---|---|---|---|---|---|---|---|---|---|---|---|---|---|---|---|---|---|---|---|---|---|---|---|---|---|---|---|---|---|---|
| 14 NYM | 416 | 46 | 4 | 47 | 13 | 281 | 249 | 321 | 382 | 703 | 875 | 658 | 4 | 79 | 0.23 | 46 | 22 | 32 | 35 | 93 | 81 | 89 | 4% | 112 | 16% | 76% | 22 | 41% | 36% | 4.27 | 5.2 | 26 | 70 | $14 |
| 15 NYM | 441 | 47 | 6 | 41 | 7 | 259 | 236 | 289 | 358 | 647 | 771 | 599 | 3 | 80 | 0.18 | 55 | 14 | 31 | 31 | 107 | 64 | 72 | 6% | 127 | 10% | 70% | 27 | 26% | 41% | 3.48 | -10.7 | 19 | 51 | $9 |
| 16 NYM | 142 | 15 | 3 | 9 | 4 | 239 | 259 | 301 | 380 | 682 | 650 | 715 | 7 | 81 | 0.41 | 42 | 22 | 35 | 28 | 71 | 83 | 68 | 7% | 124 | 18% | 67% | 19 | 32% | 42% | 3.66 | -4.2 | 43 | 123 | $1 |
| 17 NYM * | 281 | 40 | 3 | 15 | 7 | 245 | 250 | 281 | 348 | 629 | 604 | 687 | 5 | 77 | 0.22 | 51 | 20 | 29 | 31 | 93 | 67 | 77 | 5% | 137 | 16% | 70% | 18 | 28% | 56% | 3.26 | -15.1 | 16 | 48 | $4 |
| 18 NYM | 59 | 9 | 0 | 6 | 3 | 339 | 255 | 375 | 390 | 765 | 664 | 870 | 5 | 85 | 0.33 | 56 | 22 | 22 | 40 | 73 | 26 | -7 | 0% | 141 | 19% | 75% | 8 | 13% | 63% | 5.58 | 2.1 | 13 | 43 | $1 |
| 1st Half | 59 | 9 | 0 | 6 | 3 | 339 | 255 | 375 | 390 | 765 | 664 | 870 | 5 | 85 | 0.33 | 56 | 22 | 22 | 40 | 73 | 26 | -7 | 0% | 141 | 19% | 75% | 8 | 13% | 63% | 5.58 | 2.3 | 14 | 47 | $1 |
| 2nd Half | | | | | | | | | | | | | | | | | | | | | | | | | | | | | | | | | | |
| **19 Proj** | **200** | **26** | **2** | **16** | **7** | **268** | **248** | **308** | **362** | **669** | **642** | **688** | **5** | **81** | **0.26** | **50** | **21** | **29** | **32** | **84** | **56** | **50** | **4%** | **142** | **18%** | **72%** | | | | **3.76** | **-2.2** | **17** | **57** | **$7** |

## Lamb,Jake

| | | | |
|---|---|---|---|
| Age: 28 Bats: L Pos: 3B | Health F | LIMA Plan B | |
| Ht: 6' 3" Wt: 215 | PT/Exp B | Rand Var 0 | |
| | Consist C | MM 4215 | |

Attempted to play through bum shoulder that cost him four months and required surgery. And even when in the lineup, PX, hr/f were sapped, though HctX and xPX both held up. This makes the prospect of a rebound sound reasonable, but if impotence vL continues, that comeback might be staged in significantly fewer AB.

| Yr Tm | AB | R | HR | RBI | SB | BA | xBA | OBP | SLG | OPS | vL | vR | bb% | ct% | Eye | G | L | F | h% | HctX | PX | xPX | hr/f | Spd | SBO | SB% | #Wk | DOM | DIS | RC/G | RAR | BPV | BPX | R$ |
|---|---|---|---|---|---|---|---|---|---|---|---|---|---|---|---|---|---|---|---|---|---|---|---|---|---|---|---|---|---|---|---|---|---|---|
| 14 ARI * | 518 | 59 | 15 | 70 | 2 | 268 | 258 | 323 | 451 | 774 | 364 | 692 | 8 | 70 | 0.27 | 52 | 17 | 31 | 36 | 98 | 153 | 105 | 14% | 101 | 3% | 71% | 9 | 33% | 56% | 5.07 | 20.2 | 50 | 135 | $15 |
| 15 ARI | 350 | 38 | 6 | 34 | 3 | 263 | 234 | 331 | 386 | 716 | 541 | 743 | 9 | 72 | 0.37 | 45 | 23 | 32 | 35 | 115 | 87 | 114 | 7% | 124 | 5% | 60% | 21 | 29% | 57% | 4.37 | -3.0 | 16 | 43 | $6 |
| 16 ARI | 523 | 81 | 29 | 91 | 6 | 249 | 271 | 332 | 509 | 840 | 625 | 898 | 11 | 71 | 0.42 | 46 | 17 | 37 | 30 | 113 | 164 | 149 | 21% | 112 | 6% | 86% | 27 | 67% | 22% | 5.73 | 11.6 | 70 | 200 | $17 |
| 17 ARI | 536 | 89 | 30 | 105 | 6 | 248 | 264 | 357 | 487 | 844 | 557 | 938 | 14 | 72 | 0.57 | 41 | 21 | 38 | 29 | 104 | 142 | 125 | 20% | 96 | 6% | 60% | 27 | 48% | 26% | 5.74 | 6.9 | 58 | 176 | $17 |
| 18 ARI | 207 | 34 | 6 | 31 | 1 | 222 | 216 | 307 | 348 | 655 | 493 | 702 | 11 | 69 | 0.40 | 51 | 18 | 31 | 29 | 107 | 86 | 127 | 13% | 109 | 5% | 33% | 13 | 31% | 38% | 3.41 | -8.0 | 0 | 0 | $2 |
| 1st Half | 143 | 22 | 6 | 25 | 1 | 238 | 233 | 333 | 399 | 732 | 513 | 779 | 13 | 71 | 0.51 | 49 | 19 | 32 | 29 | 115 | 100 | 151 | 18% | 103 | 7% | 33% | 10 | 40% | 30% | 4.27 | -1.0 | 24 | 80 | $5 |
| 2nd Half | 64 | 12 | 0 | 6 | 0 | 188 | 180 | 243 | 234 | 477 | 455 | 485 | 7 | 63 | 0.21 | 59 | 15 | 27 | 30 | 90 | 49 | 64 | 0% | 116 | 0% | 0% | 3 | 0% | 67% | 1.81 | -5.5 | -59 | -197 | -$4 |
| **19 Proj** | **407** | **68** | **18** | **69** | **3** | **247** | **239** | **326** | **443** | **769** | **558** | **837** | **11** | **69** | **0.38** | **45** | **19** | **35** | **31** | **104** | **128** | **114** | **19%** | **111** | **4%** | **55%** | | | | **4.83** | **3.9** | **26** | **85** | **$14** |

## Laureano,Ramon

| | | | |
|---|---|---|---|
| Age: 24 Bats: R Pos: CF | Health A | LIMA Plan C+ | |
| Ht: 5'11" Wt: 185 | PT/Exp D | Rand Var -3 | |
| | Consist F | MM 2515 | |

5-19-.288 with 7 SB in 156 AB at OAK. Fine debut warrants a long look heading into 2019, but small MLB sample size poses questions about BA (40% h%, .251 xBA), power (137 PX vs. 86 xPX), and contact. On the other hand, legit speed should play immediately. Pay for steals, hedge your bets on the rest.

| Yr Tm | AB | R | HR | RBI | SB | BA | xBA | OBP | SLG | OPS | vL | vR | bb% | ct% | Eye | G | L | F | h% | HctX | PX | xPX | hr/f | Spd | SBO | SB% | #Wk | DOM | DIS | RC/G | RAR | BPV | BPX | R$ |
|---|---|---|---|---|---|---|---|---|---|---|---|---|---|---|---|---|---|---|---|---|---|---|---|---|---|---|---|---|---|---|---|---|---|---|
| 14 | | | | | | | | | | | | | | | | | | | | | | | | | | | | | | | | | | |
| 15 | | | | | | | | | | | | | | | | | | | | | | | | | | | | | | | | | | |
| 16 aa | 124 | 17 | 4 | 11 | 9 | 300 | | 385 | 508 | 893 | | | 12 | 70 | 0.45 | | | | 40 | | 141 | | | 116 | 30% | 73% | | | | 6.95 | | 52 | 149 | $6 |
| 17 aa | 463 | 56 | 10 | 47 | 21 | 201 | | 255 | 323 | 578 | | | 7 | 74 | 0.27 | | | | 25 | | 74 | | | 119 | 28% | 79% | | | | 2.67 | | 5 | 15 | $6 |
| 18 OAK * | 402 | 62 | 15 | 47 | 16 | 269 | 247 | 335 | 449 | 784 | 789 | 849 | 9 | 68 | 0.31 | 44 | 25 | 31 | 36 | 100 | 124 | 86 | 15% | 120 | 18% | 83% | 10 | 30% | 50% | 5.32 | 14.9 | 27 | 90 | $17 |
| 1st Half | 138 | 15 | 4 | 13 | 4 | 204 | 216 | 277 | 316 | 593 | | | 9 | 72 | 0.36 | | | | 26 | | 72 | | | 102 | 18% | 64% | | | | 2.73 | | -4 | -13 | -$5 |
| 2nd Half | 264 | 47 | 12 | 33 | 12 | 303 | 255 | 366 | 520 | 886 | 789 | 849 | 9 | 66 | 0.29 | 44 | 25 | 31 | 42 | 97 | 154 | 86 | 15% | 125 | 17% | 92% | 10 | 30% | 50% | 7.18 | 22.1 | 45 | 150 | $29 |
| **19 Proj** | **415** | **57** | **12** | **44** | **15** | **247** | **233** | **316** | **396** | **711** | **663** | **730** | **9** | **70** | **0.32** | **42** | **23** | **35** | **32** | **87** | **100** | **77** | **11%** | **124** | **18%** | **79%** | | | | **4.21** | **0.9** | **17** | **55** | **$15** |

ROB CARROLL

## LeMahieu,DJ

| | | | |
|---|---|---|---|
| Age: 30 Bats: R Pos: 2B | Health B | LIMA Plan B+ | |
| Ht: 6' 4" Wt: 215 | PT/Exp A | Rand Var +2 | |
| | Consist D | MM 1255 | |

Sing-song stream of consistent production can lead to inattention, so maybe you don't notice the declining Spd or slipping Eye. Or that power comes and goes. But what you should heed are his career splits at Coors (.330/.387/.448) and away (.264/.311/.364) in light of his free agency. That'll put you back in the moment.

| Yr | Tm | AB | R | HR | RBI | SB | BA | xBA | OBP | SLG | OPS | vL | vR | bb% | ct% | Eye | G | L | F | h% | HctX | PX | xPX | hr/f | Spd | SBO | SB% | #Wk | DOM | DIS | RC/G | RAR | BPV | BPX | R$ |
|---|---|---|---|---|---|---|---|---|---|---|---|---|---|---|---|---|---|---|---|---|---|---|---|---|---|---|---|---|---|---|---|---|---|---|---|
| 14 | COL | 494 | 59 | 5 | 42 | 10 | 267 | 250 | 315 | 348 | 663 | 669 | 660 | 6 | 80 | 0.34 | 56 | 21 | 23 | 32 | 98 | 57 | 84 | 5% | 143 | 14% | 50% | 26 | 27% | 46% | 3.58 | 2.7 | 24 | 65 | $13 |
| 15 | COL | 564 | 85 | 6 | 61 | 23 | 301 | 271 | 358 | 388 | 746 | 757 | 743 | 8 | 81 | 0.47 | 54 | 26 | 19 | 36 | 95 | 58 | 75 | 7% | 135 | 14% | 88% | 26 | 38% | 35% | 5.26 | 16.9 | 29 | 78 | $27 |
| 16 | COL | 552 | 104 | 11 | 66 | 11 | 348 | 303 | 416 | 495 | 911 | 931 | 903 | 10 | 86 | 0.83 | 51 | 27 | 23 | 39 | 122 | 84 | 95 | 10% | 149 | 9% | 61% | 26 | 62% | 19% | 7.87 | 43.2 | 77 | 220 | $32 |
| 17 | COL | 609 | 95 | 8 | 64 | 6 | 310 | 289 | 374 | 409 | 783 | 961 | 724 | 9 | 85 | 0.66 | 56 | 25 | 20 | 35 | 105 | 56 | 60 | 8% | 112 | 5% | 55% | 27 | 37% | 30% | 5.51 | 8.1 | 39 | 118 | $23 |
| 18 | COL | 533 | 90 | 15 | 62 | 6 | 276 | 280 | 321 | 428 | 749 | 900 | 675 | 6 | 85 | 0.45 | 50 | 21 | 29 | 30 | 109 | 88 | 97 | 11% | 103 | 8% | 55% | 25 | 56% | 24% | 4.74 | 7.1 | 55 | 183 | $18 |
| 1st Half | | 247 | 42 | 8 | 30 | 4 | 275 | 282 | 326 | 437 | 763 | 906 | 698 | 7 | 84 | 0.50 | 48 | 22 | 30 | 30 | 117 | 95 | 125 | 13% | 87 | 11% | 57% | 13 | 62% | 23% | 4.92 | 5.3 | 54 | 180 | $17 |
| 2nd Half | | 286 | 48 | 7 | 32 | 2 | 276 | 277 | 317 | 420 | 737 | 893 | 654 | 6 | 85 | 0.40 | 51 | 20 | 29 | 30 | 102 | 82 | 74 | 10% | 117 | 6% | 50% | 12 | 50% | 25% | 4.58 | 3.4 | 55 | 183 | $19 |
| 19 | Proj | 517 | 79 | 11 | 55 | 7 | 286 | 281 | 341 | 414 | 755 | 877 | 705 | 8 | 85 | 0.54 | 52 | 23 | 25 | 32 | 108 | 75 | 84 | 10% | 118 | 8% | 59% | | | | 4.94 | 11.2 | 43 | 145 | $17 |

## Leon,Sandy

| | | | |
|---|---|---|---|
| Age: 30 Bats: B Pos: CA | Health A | LIMA Plan D | |
| Ht: 5' 10" Wt: 225 | PT/Exp D | Rand Var +5 | |
| | Consist D | MM 1103 | |

In 2016, he hit 7-35-.310 in 252 AB at age 27. In 745 other career AB, he's hit 13 HR with .197 BA, so 2018 wasn't a fluke. Yes, this is an exercise in validating performance and assessing skills, so we'll dutifully point out that he had one error in 814 chances behind the plate. Bummer for him our game isn't real baseball.

| Yr | Tm | AB | R | HR | RBI | SB | BA | xBA | OBP | SLG | OPS | vL | vR | bb% | ct% | Eye | G | L | F | h% | HctX | PX | xPX | hr/f | Spd | SBO | SB% | #Wk | DOM | DIS | RC/G | RAR | BPV | BPX | R$ |
|---|---|---|---|---|---|---|---|---|---|---|---|---|---|---|---|---|---|---|---|---|---|---|---|---|---|---|---|---|---|---|---|---|---|---|---|
| 14 | WAS * | 234 | 26 | 4 | 21 | 1 | 182 | 225 | 254 | 275 | 528 | 511 | 413 | 9 | 74 | 0.37 | 53 | 19 | 28 | 23 | 67 | 74 | 38 | 8% | 62 | 1% | 100% | 10 | 20% | 70% | 2.18 | -9.5 | -5 | -14 | -$3 |
| 15 | BOS * | 213 | 15 | 1 | 14 | 0 | 209 | 188 | 262 | 248 | 510 | 118 | 569 | 7 | 74 | 0.28 | 45 | 19 | 36 | 28 | 45 | 34 | 28 | 0% | 69 | 4% | 0% | 19 | 16% | 63% | 1.99 | -11.6 | -38 | -103 | -$4 |
| 16 | BOS * | 367 | 46 | 9 | 46 | 0 | 283 | 253 | 341 | 424 | 765 | 1062 | 764 | 8 | 75 | 0.35 | 45 | 24 | 31 | 36 | 95 | 93 | 80 | 12% | 116 | 0% | 0% | 18 | 39% | 39% | 5.15 | 13.2 | 26 | 74 | $9 |
| 17 | BOS | 271 | 32 | 7 | 39 | 0 | 225 | 239 | 290 | 354 | 644 | 732 | 612 | 8 | 73 | 0.34 | 37 | 25 | 38 | 28 | 88 | 84 | 65 | 9% | 51 | 0% | 0% | 26 | 19% | 62% | 3.39 | -6.1 | -7 | -21 | $1 |
| 18 | BOS | 265 | 30 | 5 | 22 | 1 | 177 | 203 | 232 | 279 | 511 | 466 | 527 | 5 | 72 | 0.20 | 41 | 17 | 41 | 23 | 70 | 72 | 74 | 6% | 63 | 2% | 100% | 28 | 14% | 57% | 1.93 | -12.2 | -23 | -77 | -$3 |
| 1st Half | | 110 | 15 | 4 | 16 | 1 | 255 | 224 | 297 | 409 | 706 | 626 | 734 | 4 | 72 | 0.16 | 38 | 19 | 42 | 32 | 94 | 100 | 117 | 12% | 74 | 4% | 100% | 15 | 20% | 60% | 4.06 | 2.0 | 0 | 0 | $3 |
| 2nd Half | | 155 | 15 | 1 | 6 | 0 | 123 | 187 | 186 | 187 | 373 | 360 | 376 | 6 | 72 | 0.23 | 44 | 15 | 41 | 16 | 53 | 52 | 43 | 2% | 66 | 0% | 0% | 13 | 8% | 54% | 0.96 | -13.3 | -38 | -127 | -$7 |
| 19 | Proj | 261 | 30 | 6 | 27 | 1 | 206 | 219 | 264 | 319 | 583 | 599 | 577 | 7 | 73 | 0.26 | 42 | 20 | 38 | 26 | 77 | 77 | 68 | 8% | 67 | 1% | 81% | | | | 2.65 | -6.5 | -17 | -55 | $2 |

## Lindor,Francisco

| | | | |
|---|---|---|---|
| Age: 25 Bats: B Pos: SS | Health A | LIMA Plan C | |
| Ht: 5' 11" Wt: 190 | PT/Exp A | Rand Var +1 | |
| | Consist A | MM 4355 | |

Had a shot at going 30-30-.300 until he hit a bit of turbulence toward the end. But that's a weak sideswipe for major talent who's continued to pump up the power without selling out xBA. Only 25(!) with solid plate skills a constant (see Eye), even a slight pullback won't interrupt the insane run of BPX. Pony up.

| Yr | Tm | AB | R | HR | RBI | SB | BA | xBA | OBP | SLG | OPS | vL | vR | bb% | ct% | Eye | G | L | F | h% | HctX | PX | xPX | hr/f | Spd | SBO | SB% | #Wk | DOM | DIS | RC/G | RAR | BPV | BPX | R$ |
|---|---|---|---|---|---|---|---|---|---|---|---|---|---|---|---|---|---|---|---|---|---|---|---|---|---|---|---|---|---|---|---|---|---|---|---|
| 14 | a/a | 507 | 61 | 9 | 51 | 23 | 248 | | 301 | 342 | 643 | | | 7 | 79 | 0.36 | | | | 30 | | 67 | | | 104 | 29% | 57% | | | | 3.20 | | 16 | 43 | $16 |
| 15 | CLE * | 619 | 73 | 14 | 71 | 20 | 298 | 274 | 349 | 443 | 793 | 890 | 804 | 7 | 82 | 0.45 | 51 | 21 | 29 | 34 | 92 | 92 | 75 | 13% | 136 | 17% | 68% | 17 | 71% | 18% | 5.49 | 19.1 | 61 | 165 | $28 |
| 16 | CLE | 604 | 99 | 15 | 78 | 19 | 301 | 282 | 358 | 435 | 794 | 748 | 816 | 8 | 85 | 0.65 | 49 | 22 | 28 | 33 | 95 | 77 | 74 | 10% | 117 | 13% | 79% | 27 | 44% | 19% | 5.78 | 24.6 | 57 | 163 | $29 |
| 17 | CLE | 651 | 99 | 33 | 89 | 15 | 273 | 289 | 337 | 505 | 842 | 891 | 817 | 8 | 86 | 0.65 | 39 | 18 | 42 | 28 | 122 | 120 | 122 | 14% | 100 | 11% | 83% | 27 | 74% | 7% | 5.97 | 25.0 | 87 | 264 | $26 |
| 18 | CLE | 661 | 129 | 38 | 92 | 25 | 277 | 292 | 352 | 519 | 871 | 1006 | 821 | 9 | 84 | 0.65 | 39 | 22 | 40 | 28 | 129 | 131 | 135 | 17% | 92 | 20% | 71% | 28 | 68% | 25% | 6.20 | 40.1 | 88 | 293 | $38 |
| 1st Half | | 331 | 66 | 20 | 46 | 10 | 290 | 291 | 365 | 547 | 911 | 1055 | 853 | 10 | 80 | 0.52 | 38 | 22 | 40 | 31 | 122 | 149 | 132 | 19% | 90 | 15% | 77% | 15 | 67% | 33% | 6.99 | 28.2 | 86 | 287 | $38 |
| 2nd Half | | 330 | 63 | 18 | 46 | 15 | 264 | 294 | 339 | 491 | 830 | 948 | 791 | 10 | 88 | 0.88 | 39 | 21 | 40 | 25 | 135 | 115 | 138 | 16% | 99 | 26% | 68% | 13 | 69% | 15% | 5.47 | 14.8 | 94 | 313 | $38 |
| 19 | Proj | 605 | 104 | 33 | 81 | 21 | 286 | 287 | 353 | 517 | 870 | 938 | 841 | 9 | 85 | 0.65 | 39 | 21 | 40 | 29 | 119 | 123 | 117 | 16% | 104 | 18% | 72% | | | | 6.37 | 41.6 | 90 | 300 | $34 |

## Longoria,Evan

| | | | |
|---|---|---|---|
| Age: 33 Bats: R Pos: 3B | Health B | LIMA Plan B+ | |
| Ht: 6' 1" Wt: 215 | PT/Exp A | Rand Var +1 | |
| | Consist B | MM 3235 | |

Excluding 2016's HR total, this box is the realm he now inhabits. In 2018, uncooperative home venue was predictable drag on sock, and he was further undone by hand fracture that tanked 2nd half HctX and PX. Assuming lame 2nd half vL was a fluke and age-related issues are minimal, tack on a similar line for 2019.

| Yr | Tm | AB | R | HR | RBI | SB | BA | xBA | OBP | SLG | OPS | vL | vR | bb% | ct% | Eye | G | L | F | h% | HctX | PX | xPX | hr/f | Spd | SBO | SB% | #Wk | DOM | DIS | RC/G | RAR | BPV | BPX | R$ |
|---|---|---|---|---|---|---|---|---|---|---|---|---|---|---|---|---|---|---|---|---|---|---|---|---|---|---|---|---|---|---|---|---|---|---|---|
| 14 | TAM | 624 | 83 | 22 | 91 | 5 | 253 | 249 | 320 | 404 | 724 | 824 | 691 | 8 | 79 | 0.43 | 39 | 20 | 41 | 29 | 109 | 105 | 118 | 11% | 90 | 3% | 100% | 27 | 44% | 19% | 4.40 | 12.5 | 44 | 119 | $19 |
| 15 | TAM | 604 | 74 | 21 | 73 | 3 | 270 | 253 | 328 | 435 | 764 | 960 | 695 | 8 | 78 | 0.39 | 39 | 21 | 40 | 31 | 105 | 111 | 121 | 11% | 87 | 3% | 75% | 27 | 44% | 33% | 4.97 | 4.9 | 45 | 122 | $18 |
| 16 | TAM | 633 | 81 | 36 | 98 | 0 | 273 | 276 | 318 | 521 | 840 | 753 | 864 | 6 | 77 | 0.29 | 32 | 21 | 47 | 30 | 113 | 148 | 146 | 16% | 96 | 2% | 0% | 27 | 59% | 26% | 5.71 | 13.2 | 70 | 200 | $21 |
| 17 | TAM | 613 | 71 | 20 | 86 | 6 | 261 | 266 | 313 | 424 | 737 | 678 | 760 | 7 | 82 | 0.42 | 43 | 20 | 37 | 29 | 114 | 91 | 91 | 11% | 83 | 5% | 86% | 27 | 37% | 22% | 4.60 | -12.5 | 42 | 127 | $15 |
| 18 | SF | 480 | 51 | 16 | 54 | 3 | 244 | 250 | 281 | 413 | 694 | 744 | 669 | 4 | 79 | 0.22 | 42 | 18 | 39 | 28 | 120 | 99 | 114 | 11% | 102 | 4% | 75% | 23 | 43% | 39% | 3.84 | -11.7 | 36 | 120 | $9 |
| 1st Half | | 256 | 28 | 10 | 34 | 1 | 246 | 253 | 278 | 434 | 711 | 882 | 623 | 4 | 78 | 0.18 | 43 | 17 | 40 | 28 | 133 | 114 | 132 | 13% | 74 | 2% | 100% | 12 | 50% | 33% | 4.04 | -3.5 | 34 | 113 | $11 |
| 2nd Half | | 224 | 23 | 6 | 20 | 2 | 241 | 246 | 285 | 388 | 674 | 579 | 720 | 5 | 80 | 0.27 | 42 | 20 | 38 | 28 | 105 | 82 | 94 | 9% | 132 | 6% | 67% | 11 | 36% | 45% | 3.62 | -5.9 | 39 | 130 | $7 |
| 19 | Proj | 528 | 60 | 19 | 66 | 3 | 254 | 254 | 299 | 427 | 726 | 716 | 730 | 6 | 80 | 0.30 | 41 | 20 | 40 | 29 | 114 | 101 | 111 | 11% | 101 | 4% | 72% | | | | 4.31 | -3.0 | 36 | 120 | $14 |

## Lowe,Brandon

| | | | |
|---|---|---|---|
| Age: 24 Bats: L Pos: 2B | Health A | LIMA Plan C+ | |
| Ht: 6' 0" Wt: 185 | PT/Exp F | Rand Var 0 | |
| | Consist F | MM 4323 | |

6-25-.233 with 2 SB in 129 AB at TAM. College product boosted bb% amid burgeoning power during ascent through minors. Those skills held up in first exposure to big league pitching (11% bb%, 136 PX), and he had but one error while playing both IF and OF. Needs to make better contact, but pop is worthy of another look.

| Yr | Tm | AB | R | HR | RBI | SB | BA | xBA | OBP | SLG | OPS | vL | vR | bb% | ct% | Eye | G | L | F | h% | HctX | PX | xPX | hr/f | Spd | SBO | SB% | #Wk | DOM | DIS | RC/G | RAR | BPV | BPX | R$ |
|---|---|---|---|---|---|---|---|---|---|---|---|---|---|---|---|---|---|---|---|---|---|---|---|---|---|---|---|---|---|---|---|---|---|---|---|
| 14 | | | | | | | | | | | | | | | | | | | | | | | | | | | | | | | | | | | |
| 15 | | | | | | | | | | | | | | | | | | | | | | | | | | | | | | | | | | | |
| 16 | | | | | | | | | | | | | | | | | | | | | | | | | | | | | | | | | | | |
| 17 | aa | 95 | 7 | 2 | 10 | 1 | 224 | | 238 | 340 | 578 | | | 2 | 68 | 0.06 | | | | 31 | | 79 | | | 107 | 12% | 44% | | | | 2.53 | | -25 | -76 | -$1 |
| 18 | TAM * | 509 | 78 | 24 | 89 | 9 | 251 | 254 | 335 | 467 | 802 | 704 | 794 | 11 | 69 | 0.40 | 43 | 22 | 35 | 32 | 88 | 146 | 100 | 19% | 100 | 10% | 66% | 9 | 33% | 33% | 5.25 | 17.8 | 45 | 150 | $19 |
| 1st Half | | 287 | 47 | 13 | 54 | 7 | 266 | 252 | 357 | 486 | 842 | | | 12 | 67 | 0.43 | | | | 35 | | 157 | | | 96 | 13% | 66% | | | | 5.90 | | 49 | 163 | $26 |
| 2nd Half | | 222 | 30 | 11 | 35 | 2 | 232 | 253 | 306 | 444 | 750 | 704 | 794 | 10 | 71 | 0.36 | 43 | 22 | 35 | 28 | 90 | 131 | 100 | 19% | 114 | 6% | 67% | 9 | 33% | 33% | 4.47 | 2.0 | 42 | 140 | $11 |
| 19 | Proj | 343 | 50 | 14 | 58 | 5 | 246 | 247 | 334 | 440 | 774 | 689 | 799 | 11 | 69 | 0.39 | 43 | 22 | 35 | 32 | 81 | 129 | 90 | 17% | 105 | 8% | 69% | | | | 4.83 | 6.7 | 31 | 102 | $12 |

## Lowrie,Jed

| | | | |
|---|---|---|---|
| Age: 35 Bats: B Pos: 2B | Health D | LIMA Plan B | |
| Ht: 6' 0" Wt: 180 | PT/Exp A | Rand Var -2 | |
| | Consist C | MM 2035 | |

Did his 2017 breakout one better, the payoff for all of those abbreviated seasons and near-misses. HctX and PX/xPX conspired with perennial plate and LD skills to drive middle-of-order value. Still iffy health grade and encroaching age do toss some cold water onto this feel-good story. Sure beats the prequels, though.

| Yr | Tm | AB | R | HR | RBI | SB | BA | xBA | OBP | SLG | OPS | vL | vR | bb% | ct% | Eye | G | L | F | h% | HctX | PX | xPX | hr/f | Spd | SBO | SB% | #Wk | DOM | DIS | RC/G | RAR | BPV | BPX | R$ |
|---|---|---|---|---|---|---|---|---|---|---|---|---|---|---|---|---|---|---|---|---|---|---|---|---|---|---|---|---|---|---|---|---|---|---|---|
| 14 | OAK | 502 | 59 | 6 | 50 | 0 | 249 | 250 | 321 | 355 | 676 | 598 | 707 | 9 | 84 | 0.65 | 31 | 24 | 44 | 29 | 107 | 79 | 112 | 3% | 109 | 0% | 0% | 25 | 40% | 16% | 3.83 | 6.5 | 53 | 143 | $7 |
| 15 | HOU | 230 | 35 | 9 | 30 | 1 | 222 | 263 | 312 | 400 | 712 | 908 | 641 | 11 | 81 | 0.65 | 35 | 21 | 44 | 24 | 128 | 115 | 153 | 11% | 88 | 2% | 100% | 15 | 60% | 27% | 4.04 | -1.6 | 67 | 181 | $2 |
| 16 | OAK | 338 | 30 | 2 | 27 | 0 | 263 | 239 | 314 | 322 | 637 | 667 | 627 | 7 | 81 | 0.40 | 43 | 25 | 32 | 32 | 92 | 40 | 82 | 2% | 111 | 0% | 0% | 17 | 24% | 53% | 3.53 | -11.7 | 5 | 14 | $3 |
| 17 | OAK | 567 | 86 | 14 | 69 | 0 | 277 | 280 | 360 | 448 | 808 | 750 | 825 | 11 | 82 | 0.73 | 29 | 27 | 43 | 32 | 115 | 103 | 115 | 7% | 100 | 1% | 0% | 27 | 63% | 15% | 5.64 | 16.3 | 67 | 203 | $14 |
| 18 | OAK | 596 | 78 | 23 | 99 | 0 | 267 | 260 | 353 | 448 | 801 | 713 | 841 | 11 | 79 | 0.61 | 33 | 23 | 43 | 31 | 116 | 110 | 125 | 11% | 96 | 0% | 0% | 28 | 46% | 29% | 5.48 | 24.0 | 56 | 187 | $19 |
| 1st Half | | 326 | 36 | 14 | 56 | 0 | 291 | 266 | 351 | 500 | 851 | 749 | 902 | 8 | 78 | 0.42 | 35 | 21 | 43 | 34 | 113 | 128 | 127 | 13% | 100 | 0% | 0% | 15 | 60% | 20% | 6.32 | 19.4 | 64 | 213 | $24 |
| 2nd Half | | 270 | 42 | 9 | 43 | 0 | 237 | 252 | 355 | 385 | 740 | 662 | 773 | 15 | 79 | 0.84 | 31 | 26 | 43 | 27 | 120 | 89 | 122 | 10% | 89 | 0% | 0% | 13 | 31% | 38% | 4.53 | 2.9 | 46 | 153 | $13 |
| 19 | Proj | 499 | 67 | 14 | 68 | 0 | 262 | 258 | 344 | 411 | 755 | 708 | 774 | 11 | 80 | 0.63 | 33 | 25 | 42 | 30 | 113 | 92 | 116 | 8% | 99 | 0% | 33% | | | | 4.86 | 9.9 | 31 | 104 | $14 |

## Lucroy,Jonathan

| | | | |
|---|---|---|---|
| Age: 33 Bats: R Pos: CA | Health A | LIMA Plan C | |
| Ht: 6'0" Wt: 200 | PT/Exp B | Rand Var +3 | |
| | Consist D | MM 1335 | |

Veteran is fading into #2 CA territory with two boring years. Plate skills aren't far off premier marks, but where did the power go? What's with the LD%-BA disconnect? Could it be he's just not as good anymore? Answering questions with more questions is uncool, but they're just about all we've got at the moment.

| Yr | Tm | AB | R | HR | RBI | SB | BA | xBA | OBP | SLG | OPS | vL | vR | bb% | ct% | Eye | G | L | F | h% | HctX | PX | xPX | hr/f | Spd | SBO | SB% | #Wk | DOM | DIS | RC/G | RAR | BPV | BPX | R$ |
|---|---|---|---|---|---|---|---|---|---|---|---|---|---|---|---|---|---|---|---|---|---|---|---|---|---|---|---|---|---|---|---|---|---|---|---|
| 14 | MIL | 585 | 73 | 13 | 69 | 4 | 301 | 298 | 373 | 465 | 837 | 838 | 837 | 10 | 88 | 0.93 | 42 | 22 | 36 | 33 | 132 | 119 | 128 | 7% | 96 | 5% | 50% | 27 | 78% | 4% | 6.19 | 46.4 | 98 | 265 | $23 |
| 15 | MIL | 371 | 51 | 7 | 43 | 1 | 264 | 275 | 326 | 391 | 717 | 639 | 743 | 9 | 83 | 0.56 | 44 | 26 | 29 | 30 | 124 | 83 | 104 | 8% | 95 | 1% | 100% | 21 | 38% | 29% | 4.48 | 7.9 | 45 | 122 | $8 |
| 16 | 2 TM | 490 | 67 | 24 | 81 | 5 | 292 | 276 | 355 | 500 | 855 | 796 | 874 | 9 | 80 | 0.47 | 37 | 24 | 39 | 33 | 114 | 118 | 131 | 16% | 105 | 4% | 100% | 27 | 48% | 22% | 6.44 | 35.0 | 63 | 180 | $21 |
| 17 | 2 TM | 423 | 45 | 6 | 40 | 1 | 265 | 270 | 345 | 371 | 716 | 644 | 741 | 10 | 88 | 0.90 | 53 | 19 | 28 | 29 | 80 | 59 | 46 | 6% | 102 | 1% | 100% | 27 | 48% | 26% | 4.35 | 2.6 | 51 | 155 | $6 |
| 18 | OAK | 415 | 41 | 4 | 51 | 0 | 241 | 254 | 291 | 325 | 617 | 660 | 598 | 6 | 84 | 0.45 | 42 | 25 | 33 | 28 | 108 | 55 | 78 | 3% | 82 | 0% | 0% | 28 | 32% | 46% | 3.18 | -2.4 | 21 | 70 | $4 |
| 1st Half | | 221 | 22 | 1 | 23 | 0 | 258 | 255 | 315 | 339 | 655 | 552 | 699 | 7 | 84 | 0.47 | 45 | 24 | 31 | 30 | 122 | 56 | 87 | 2% | 85 | 0% | 0% | 15 | 27% | 47% | 3.63 | 1.2 | 21 | 70 | $4 |
| 2nd Half | | 194 | 19 | 3 | 28 | 0 | 222 | 253 | 264 | 309 | 573 | 789 | 486 | 6 | 85 | 0.41 | 38 | 25 | 36 | 25 | 92 | 53 | 68 | 5% | 80 | 0% | 0% | 13 | 38% | 46% | 2.71 | -4.4 | 20 | 67 | $4 |
| 19 | Proj | 419 | 46 | 7 | 52 | 1 | 256 | 261 | 317 | 369 | 686 | 694 | 683 | 8 | 85 | 0.56 | 44 | 23 | 33 | 29 | 102 | 67 | 81 | 6% | 92 | 1% | 88% | | | | 3.99 | 6.6 | 27 | 89 | $9 |

ROB CARROLL

## Lugo,Dawel

Age: 24 Bats: R Pos: 2B | Ht: 6' 0" Wt: 190
Health A | PT/Exp C | Consist C
LIMA Plan D+ | Rand Var +3 | MM 1351

1-8-.213 in 94 AB at DET. Want to buy a Dawel? Only 9 BB in 523 PA in first Triple-A tour, so he doesn't like to lose a turn at bat. Makes good contact, so skill set not bankrupt, but has yet to solve puzzle of turning decent Spd into SB. Only 24, so fortune may turn; that's when to take a spin. For now, move on to next contestant.

| Yr | Tm | AB | R | HR | RBI | SB | BA | xBA | OBP | SLG | OPS | vL | vR | bb% | ct% | Eye | G | L | F | h% | HctX | PX | xPX | hr/f | Spd | SBO | SB% | #Wk | DOM | DIS | RC/G | RAR | BPV | BPX | R$ |
|---|---|---|---|---|---|---|---|---|---|---|---|---|---|---|---|---|---|---|---|---|---|---|---|---|---|---|---|---|---|---|---|---|---|---|---|
| 14 | | | | | | | | | | | | | | | | | | | | | | | | | | | | | | | | | | | |
| 15 | | | | | | | | | | | | | | | | | | | | | | | | | | | | | | | | | | | |
| 16 | aa | 173 | 22 | 4 | 18 | 1 | 302 | | 316 | 449 | 765 | | | 2 | 91 | 0.22 | | | | 32 | | 77 | | | 115 | 5% | 46% | | | | 5.08 | | 65 | 186 | $4 |
| 17 | aa | 516 | 50 | 11 | 56 | 3 | 259 | | 297 | 394 | 691 | | | 5 | 86 | 0.38 | | | | 28 | | 72 | | | 111 | 3% | 70% | | | | 4.01 | | 45 | 136 | $8 |
| 18 | DET * | 603 | 60 | 4 | 60 | 11 | 245 | 280 | 263 | 325 | 588 | 806 | 526 | 2 | 85 | 0.17 | 66 | 19 | 15 | 28 | 93 | 50 | 24 | 9% | 120 | 12% | 71% | 6 | 33% | 17% | 2.87 | -21.7 | 24 | 80 | $11 |
| 1st Half | | 311 | 35 | 2 | 27 | 4 | 259 | 249 | 269 | 352 | 621 | | | 1 | 86 | 0.10 | | | | 30 | | 57 | | | 129 | 11% | 67% | | | | 3.22 | | 34 | 113 | $11 |
| 2nd Half | | 292 | 25 | 2 | 33 | 6 | 230 | 267 | 257 | 296 | 553 | 806 | 526 | 3 | 84 | 0.23 | 66 | 19 | 15 | 27 | 92 | 42 | 24 | 9% | 107 | 13% | 74% | 6 | 33% | 17% | 2.52 | -14.7 | 11 | 37 | $10 |
| 19 | Proj | 237 | 24 | 2 | 25 | 3 | 257 | 285 | 281 | 354 | 635 | 842 | 592 | 3 | 86 | 0.24 | 66 | 19 | 15 | 29 | 83 | 58 | 22 | 8% | 123 | 7% | 70% | | | | 3.39 | -5.4 | 26 | 86 | $3 |

## Luplow,Jordan

Age: 25 Bats: R Pos: LF | Ht: 6' 1" Wt: 195
Health A | PT/Exp F | Consist C
LIMA Plan D+ | Rand Var 0 | MM 2213

3-7-.185 with 2 SB in 92 AB at PIT. 2017 power outburst set expectations he couldn't live up to in first full season at Triple-A. And while he's flashed some pop in two brief MLB stints, the rest has been lousy: .644 OPS, .225 xBA in 170 AB. Emerging Spd is something to keep an eye on, but for now, he looks overmatched.

| Yr | Tm | AB | R | HR | RBI | SB | BA | xBA | OBP | SLG | OPS | vL | vR | bb% | ct% | Eye | G | L | F | h% | HctX | PX | xPX | hr/f | Spd | SBO | SB% | #Wk | DOM | DIS | RC/G | RAR | BPV | BPX | R$ |
|---|---|---|---|---|---|---|---|---|---|---|---|---|---|---|---|---|---|---|---|---|---|---|---|---|---|---|---|---|---|---|---|---|---|---|---|
| 14 | | | | | | | | | | | | | | | | | | | | | | | | | | | | | | | | | | | |
| 15 | | | | | | | | | | | | | | | | | | | | | | | | | | | | | | | | | | | |
| 16 | | | | | | | | | | | | | | | | | | | | | | | | | | | | | | | | | | | |
| 17 | PIT * | 492 | 71 | 22 | 60 | 4 | 263 | 243 | 326 | 455 | 781 | 664 | 658 | 8 | 78 | 0.41 | 38 | 16 | 46 | 30 | 88 | 107 | 103 | 12% | 98 | 8% | 44% | 8 | 38% | 38% | 4.95 | -3.4 | 44 | 133 | $13 |
| 18 | PIT * | 406 | 48 | 9 | 45 | 7 | 231 | 232 | 300 | 379 | 679 | 707 | 577 | 9 | 78 | 0.44 | 42 | 15 | 42 | 28 | 66 | 91 | 75 | 10% | 121 | 12% | 63% | 12 | 33% | 33% | 3.70 | -8.6 | 40 | 133 | $7 |
| 1st Half | | 264 | 27 | 6 | 35 | 5 | 249 | 253 | 321 | 406 | 727 | | | 10 | 77 | 0.46 | | | | 30 | | 103 | | | 109 | 10% | 82% | 1 | 0% | 0% | 4.46 | | 44 | 147 | $11 |
| 2nd Half | | 142 | 21 | 3 | 10 | 2 | 198 | 221 | 262 | 328 | 590 | 707 | 577 | 8 | 79 | 0.42 | 42 | 15 | 42 | 23 | 67 | 69 | 75 | 10% | 165 | 17% | 39% | 11 | 36% | 36% | 2.51 | -9.0 | 40 | 133 | -$1 |
| 19 | Proj | 320 | 43 | 10 | 34 | 4 | 237 | 238 | 312 | 398 | 711 | 756 | 683 | 9 | 78 | 0.43 | 40 | 17 | 42 | 27 | 75 | 94 | 86 | 9% | 121 | 10% | 51% | | | | 3.90 | -6.8 | 36 | 120 | $8 |

## Machado,Manny

Age: 26 Bats: R Pos: SS | Ht: 6' 3" Wt: 185
Health A | PT/Exp A | Consist D
LIMA Plan D+ | Rand Var -2 | MM 4345

To-do list for entering free agency: Boost walk, contact rates? Check. Maintain power skills, fly ball tilt? Check. Improve SB success rate? Check. Reach 690 PA for fifth time? Check. Don't have a 27th birthday? Check. Unless cashing in makes him fat and happy, little to worry about here.

| Yr | Tm | AB | R | HR | RBI | SB | BA | xBA | OBP | SLG | OPS | vL | vR | bb% | ct% | Eye | G | L | F | h% | HctX | PX | xPX | hr/f | Spd | SBO | SB% | #Wk | DOM | DIS | RC/G | RAR | BPV | BPX | R$ |
|---|---|---|---|---|---|---|---|---|---|---|---|---|---|---|---|---|---|---|---|---|---|---|---|---|---|---|---|---|---|---|---|---|---|---|---|
| 14 | BAL | 327 | 38 | 12 | 32 | 2 | 278 | 262 | 324 | 431 | 755 | 642 | 802 | 6 | 79 | 0.29 | 49 | 20 | 31 | 32 | 100 | 106 | 101 | 15% | 112 | 2% | 100% | 16 | 56% | 25% | 4.91 | 14.9 | 49 | 132 | $10 |
| 15 | BAL | 633 | 102 | 35 | 86 | 20 | 286 | 279 | 359 | 502 | 861 | 763 | 894 | 10 | 82 | 0.63 | 44 | 18 | 38 | 30 | 119 | 127 | 122 | 18% | 113 | 15% | 71% | 27 | 63% | 4% | 6.30 | 45.7 | 87 | 235 | $35 |
| 16 | BAL | 640 | 105 | 37 | 96 | 0 | 294 | 283 | 343 | 533 | 876 | 919 | 862 | 7 | 81 | 0.40 | 37 | 20 | 43 | 31 | 117 | 136 | 118 | 17% | 111 | 2% | 0% | 27 | 63% | 4% | 6.47 | 33.0 | 83 | 237 | $27 |
| 17 | BAL | 630 | 81 | 33 | 95 | 9 | 259 | 266 | 310 | 471 | 782 | 826 | 767 | 7 | 82 | 0.43 | 42 | 16 | 42 | 27 | 131 | 112 | 131 | 15% | 108 | 9% | 69% | 27 | 59% | 22% | 5.02 | 9.3 | 66 | 200 | $20 |
| 18 | 2 TM | 632 | 84 | 37 | 107 | 14 | 297 | 281 | 367 | 538 | 905 | 921 | 897 | 10 | 84 | 0.67 | 40 | 18 | 42 | 31 | 119 | 128 | 115 | 16% | 109 | 9% | 88% | 28 | 64% | 14% | 7.25 | 60.0 | 91 | 303 | $34 |
| 1st Half | | 315 | 40 | 20 | 57 | 5 | 308 | 278 | 376 | 556 | 931 | 821 | 976 | 10 | 85 | 0.75 | 36 | 18 | 47 | 31 | 115 | 128 | 120 | 16% | 112 | 6% | 83% | 15 | 67% | 13% | 7.78 | 32.8 | 98 | 327 | $35 |
| 2nd Half | | 317 | 44 | 17 | 50 | 9 | 287 | 285 | 358 | 521 | 878 | 1013 | 817 | 10 | 82 | 0.61 | 44 | 18 | 38 | 30 | 123 | 128 | 110 | 17% | 109 | 11% | 90% | 13 | 62% | 15% | 6.74 | 24.8 | 86 | 287 | $34 |
| 19 | Proj | 614 | 85 | 34 | 98 | 11 | 285 | 275 | 346 | 511 | 856 | 887 | 844 | 9 | 82 | 0.53 | 41 | 18 | 41 | 30 | 121 | 123 | 119 | 16% | 111 | 8% | 79% | | | | 6.30 | 40.6 | 72 | 240 | $30 |

## Mahtook,Mikie

Age: 29 Bats: R Pos: LF | Ht: 6' 1" Wt: 216
Health A | PT/Exp D | Consist F
LIMA Plan D | Rand Var +2 | MM 3411

9-29-.202 with 4 SB in 223 AB at DET. Looked like late bloomer in 2017, but struggled in spring (9-for-56), earned quick April demotion, then did little in AAA to force way back. Last year's ct% now looks like fluke, Eye has never been strong, and hr/f raises doubts about 9 HR in Aug/Sept. At 29, window to regular PT may be shut.

| Yr | Tm | AB | R | HR | RBI | SB | BA | xBA | OBP | SLG | OPS | vL | vR | bb% | ct% | Eye | G | L | F | h% | HctX | PX | xPX | hr/f | Spd | SBO | SB% | #Wk | DOM | DIS | RC/G | RAR | BPV | BPX | R$ |
|---|---|---|---|---|---|---|---|---|---|---|---|---|---|---|---|---|---|---|---|---|---|---|---|---|---|---|---|---|---|---|---|---|---|---|---|
| 14 | aaa | 489 | 46 | 9 | 56 | 15 | 251 | | 305 | 386 | 691 | | | 7 | 67 | 0.24 | | | | 36 | | 119 | | | 101 | 17% | 72% | | | | 3.96 | | 9 | 24 | $13 |
| 15 | TAM * | 490 | 50 | 12 | 54 | 12 | 225 | 221 | 260 | 367 | 627 | 1030 | 856 | 5 | 69 | 0.15 | 33 | 23 | 44 | 30 | 120 | 109 | 192 | 28% | 113 | 18% | 74% | 12 | 58% | 17% | 3.12 | -19.2 | 9 | 24 | $8 |
| 16 | TAM * | 290 | 30 | 4 | 17 | 4 | 218 | 183 | 262 | 318 | 580 | 678 | 438 | 6 | 66 | 0.18 | 38 | 14 | 47 | 31 | 86 | 77 | 94 | 5% | 122 | 10% | 66% | 13 | 15% | 85% | 2.68 | -14.3 | -23 | -66 | $0 |
| 17 | DET | 348 | 50 | 12 | 38 | 6 | 276 | 264 | 330 | 457 | 787 | 793 | 783 | 6 | 77 | 0.29 | 46 | 20 | 33 | 33 | 119 | 99 | 112 | 13% | 151 | 7% | 100% | 25 | 40% | 36% | 5.27 | -1.7 | 48 | 145 | $10 |
| 18 | DET * | 506 | 55 | 18 | 56 | 9 | 206 | 218 | 264 | 368 | 632 | 507 | 683 | 7 | 68 | 0.25 | 44 | 18 | 38 | 27 | 65 | 101 | 67 | 15% | 151 | 14% | 59% | 16 | 38% | 50% | 3.02 | -24.9 | 14 | 47 | $7 |
| 1st Half | | 280 | 30 | 6 | 23 | 6 | 209 | 212 | 259 | 345 | 604 | 368 | 530 | 6 | 68 | 0.21 | 40 | 21 | 38 | 29 | 62 | 88 | 40 | 0% | 142 | 17% | 61% | 7 | 29% | 57% | 2.79 | -16.0 | -2 | -7 | $6 |
| 2nd Half | | 226 | 25 | 11 | 33 | 3 | 201 | 226 | 271 | 396 | 667 | 562 | 751 | 9 | 68 | 0.30 | 46 | 17 | 37 | 24 | 67 | 116 | 80 | 23% | 144 | 10% | 55% | 9 | 44% | 44% | 3.32 | -9.1 | 26 | 87 | $9 |
| 19 | Proj | 228 | 26 | 8 | 25 | 4 | 227 | 228 | 287 | 402 | 689 | 705 | 680 | 7 | 70 | 0.24 | 42 | 19 | 39 | 29 | 87 | 107 | 93 | 14% | 137 | 12% | 70% | | | | 3.67 | -6.5 | 14 | 48 | $5 |

## Maldonado,Martin

Age: 32 Bats: R Pos: CA | Ht: 6' 0" Wt: 230
Health A | PT/Exp C | Consist A
LIMA Plan D | Rand Var 0 | MM 1003

HOU picked him up for defense, and he delivered, thwarting 5 of 8 SB attempts. But glove/arm keeping him on field is a double-edge sword for fantasy owners: is occasional HR worth BA pinned in mid-.220s? (Before you say "no," check out rest of catcher pool.) Nonetheless, there's no upside to be mined here.

| Yr | Tm | AB | R | HR | RBI | SB | BA | xBA | OBP | SLG | OPS | vL | vR | bb% | ct% | Eye | G | L | F | h% | HctX | PX | xPX | hr/f | Spd | SBO | SB% | #Wk | DOM | DIS | RC/G | RAR | BPV | BPX | R$ |
|---|---|---|---|---|---|---|---|---|---|---|---|---|---|---|---|---|---|---|---|---|---|---|---|---|---|---|---|---|---|---|---|---|---|---|---|
| 14 | MIL | 111 | 14 | 4 | 16 | 0 | 234 | 223 | 320 | 387 | 707 | 721 | 693 | 9 | 71 | 0.34 | 36 | 18 | 46 | 29 | 86 | 119 | 107 | 12% | 84 | 0% | 0% | 26 | 31% | 54% | 3.91 | 2.0 | 24 | 65 | $1 |
| 15 | MIL | 229 | 19 | 4 | 22 | 0 | 210 | 205 | 282 | 293 | 575 | 810 | 503 | 9 | 72 | 0.35 | 47 | 20 | 33 | 28 | 91 | 62 | 99 | 8% | 53 | 2% | 0% | 25 | 12% | 68% | 2.61 | -8.0 | -27 | -73 | -$2 |
| 16 | MIL | 208 | 21 | 8 | 21 | 1 | 202 | 225 | 332 | 351 | 683 | 677 | 685 | 14 | 73 | 0.63 | 44 | 18 | 38 | 24 | 84 | 92 | 90 | 14% | 51 | 2% | 100% | 25 | 44% | 40% | 3.58 | -1.8 | 11 | 31 | -$1 |
| 17 | LAA | 429 | 43 | 14 | 38 | 0 | 221 | 221 | 276 | 368 | 645 | 632 | 649 | 3 | 72 | 0.13 | 49 | 15 | 37 | 27 | 78 | 91 | 78 | 13% | 72 | 3% | 0% | 26 | 19% | 50% | 2.92 | -16.0 | -7 | -21 | $1 |
| 18 | 2 AL | 373 | 39 | 9 | 44 | 0 | 225 | 227 | 276 | 351 | 627 | 648 | 618 | 4 | 74 | 0.16 | 41 | 21 | 38 | 28 | 86 | 83 | 86 | 9% | 67 | 1% | 0% | 27 | 15% | 63% | 2.93 | -4.9 | -8 | -27 | $3 |
| 1st Half | | 218 | 22 | 5 | 32 | 0 | 243 | 229 | 303 | 367 | 669 | 594 | 693 | 5 | 73 | 0.19 | 37 | 23 | 40 | 31 | 85 | 86 | 92 | 8% | 64 | 2% | 0% | 15 | 13% | 60% | 3.38 | -0.4 | -9 | -30 | $6 |
| 2nd Half | | 155 | 17 | 4 | 12 | 0 | 200 | 227 | 238 | 329 | 567 | 690 | 474 | 3 | 75 | 0.13 | 46 | 18 | 36 | 24 | 86 | 79 | 77 | 10% | 82 | 0% | 0% | 12 | 17% | 67% | 2.36 | -5.3 | -5 | -17 | -$1 |
| 19 | Proj | 330 | 34 | 8 | 34 | 0 | 223 | 218 | 285 | 342 | 627 | 668 | 608 | 6 | 73 | 0.22 | 44 | 18 | 37 | 28 | 84 | 78 | 85 | 9% | 67 | 1% | 24% | | | | 2.96 | -4.9 | -18 | -59 | $3 |

## Mancini,Trey

Age: 27 Bats: R Pos: LF 1B | Ht: 6'4" Wt: 215
Health A | PT/Exp A | Consist D
LIMA Plan B | Rand Var +5 | MM 3135

Once again defied heavy ground ball tilt to match 2017 HR total; chances of that continuing seem remote (but we said that last year). Hit rate luck DID run out; 2018's BA is closer to who he is. After power dipped in 2H of 2017, skills remained nothing special in 2018. That means if hr/f finally falls... DN: 15 HR, still

| Yr | Tm | AB | R | HR | RBI | SB | BA | xBA | OBP | SLG | OPS | vL | vR | bb% | ct% | Eye | G | L | F | h% | HctX | PX | xPX | hr/f | Spd | SBO | SB% | #Wk | DOM | DIS | RC/G | RAR | BPV | BPX | R$ |
|---|---|---|---|---|---|---|---|---|---|---|---|---|---|---|---|---|---|---|---|---|---|---|---|---|---|---|---|---|---|---|---|---|---|---|---|
| 14 | | | | | | | | | | | | | | | | | | | | | | | | | | | | | | | | | | | |
| 15 | aa | 326 | 52 | 12 | 49 | 2 | 332 | | 368 | 540 | 908 | | | 5 | 81 | 0.30 | | | | 38 | | 137 | | | 94 | 3% | 61% | | | | 7.52 | | 73 | 197 | $17 |
| 16 | BAL * | 560 | 69 | 20 | 63 | 2 | 243 | 220 | 309 | 392 | 701 | 1800 | 650 | 9 | 70 | 0.31 | 40 | 20 | 40 | 31 | 169 | 94 | 250 | 75% | 124 | 3% | 43% | 2 | 50% | 50% | 4.03 | -4.1 | 10 | 29 | $9 |
| 17 | BAL | 543 | 65 | 24 | 78 | 1 | 293 | 263 | 338 | 488 | 826 | 742 | 860 | 6 | 74 | 0.24 | 51 | 19 | 30 | 36 | 103 | 112 | 113 | 20% | 127 | 1% | 100% | 27 | 37% | 37% | 5.88 | 6.4 | 39 | 118 | $19 |
| 18 | BAL | 582 | 69 | 24 | 58 | 0 | 242 | 249 | 299 | 416 | 715 | 651 | 741 | 7 | 74 | 0.29 | 55 | 19 | 26 | 29 | 91 | 104 | 95 | 21% | 108 | 1% | 0% | 28 | 25% | 39% | 4.10 | -8.3 | 26 | 87 | $11 |
| 1st Half | | 293 | 36 | 10 | 23 | 0 | 232 | 233 | 304 | 375 | 679 | 647 | 696 | 9 | 73 | 0.36 | 56 | 19 | 26 | 29 | 85 | 91 | 82 | 18% | 98 | 1% | 0% | 15 | 27% | 47% | 3.70 | -7.9 | 13 | 43 | $7 |
| 2nd Half | | 289 | 33 | 14 | 35 | 0 | 253 | 263 | 294 | 457 | 750 | 657 | 781 | 5 | 75 | 0.21 | 53 | 19 | 27 | 29 | 98 | 117 | 108 | 23% | 116 | 0% | 0% | 13 | 23% | 31% | 4.51 | -0.7 | 39 | 130 | $15 |
| 19 | Proj | 556 | 68 | 21 | 67 | 1 | 265 | 252 | 317 | 437 | 754 | 683 | 783 | 7 | 74 | 0.27 | 53 | 19 | 28 | 32 | 97 | 104 | 104 | 19% | 105 | 1% | 51% | | | | 4.73 | -0.6 | 13 | 44 | $16 |

## Margot,Manuel

Age: 24 Bats: R Pos: CF | Ht: 5'11" Wt: 180
Health B | PT/Exp B | Consist B
LIMA Plan B | Rand Var 0 | MM 2535

After strong finish to 2017, first two months of 2018 were buzzkill. Still, foundation is forming, as seen in gains in ct% and HctX, while xPX hints at latent power. SB% alarming, but Spd is strong enough to keep getting him chances. Steady growth is likeliest scenario; however, if skills coalesce more quickly, he's got HR/SB upside.

| Yr | Tm | AB | R | HR | RBI | SB | BA | xBA | OBP | SLG | OPS | vL | vR | bb% | ct% | Eye | G | L | F | h% | HctX | PX | xPX | hr/f | Spd | SBO | SB% | #Wk | DOM | DIS | RC/G | RAR | BPV | BPX | R$ |
|---|---|---|---|---|---|---|---|---|---|---|---|---|---|---|---|---|---|---|---|---|---|---|---|---|---|---|---|---|---|---|---|---|---|---|---|
| 14 | | | | | | | | | | | | | | | | | | | | | | | | | | | | | | | | | | | |
| 15 | aa | 258 | 31 | 2 | 27 | 16 | 263 | | 309 | 403 | 712 | | | 6 | 85 | 0.45 | | | | 30 | | 98 | | | 104 | 42% | 65% | | | | 4.02 | | 65 | 176 | $9 |
| 16 | SD * | 554 | 72 | 4 | 41 | 23 | 258 | 301 | 289 | 350 | 639 | 769 | 583 | 4 | 86 | 0.32 | 63 | 23 | 13 | 29 | 140 | 53 | 51 | 0% | 173 | 27% | 65% | 3 | 33% | 67% | 3.33 | -21.8 | 49 | 140 | $16 |
| 17 | SD | 487 | 53 | 13 | 39 | 17 | 263 | 251 | 313 | 409 | 721 | 833 | 683 | 7 | 78 | 0.33 | 41 | 23 | 36 | 31 | 80 | 79 | 75 | 9% | 167 | 19% | 71% | 22 | 27% | 32% | 4.34 | -10.3 | 41 | 124 | $14 |
| 18 | SD | 477 | 50 | 8 | 51 | 11 | 245 | 251 | 292 | 384 | 675 | 656 | 685 | 6 | 82 | 0.36 | 43 | 20 | 37 | 29 | 118 | 81 | 106 | 6% | 148 | 20% | 52% | 28 | 36% | 25% | 3.56 | -9.8 | 50 | 167 | $10 |
| 1st Half | | 233 | 23 | 3 | 24 | 6 | 240 | 249 | 302 | 373 | 675 | 639 | 687 | 8 | 81 | 0.43 | 47 | 16 | 36 | 28 | 113 | 84 | 96 | 4% | 130 | 23% | 50% | 15 | 27% | 33% | 3.45 | -5.0 | 48 | 160 | $8 |
| 2nd Half | | 244 | 27 | 5 | 27 | 5 | 250 | 252 | 281 | 393 | 675 | 666 | 681 | 5 | 82 | 0.30 | 39 | 23 | 38 | 29 | 123 | 78 | 114 | 6% | 162 | 17% | 56% | 13 | 46% | 15% | 3.67 | -3.4 | 51 | 170 | $13 |
| 19 | Proj | 493 | 55 | 11 | 47 | 16 | 254 | 255 | 298 | 400 | 697 | 720 | 687 | 6 | 82 | 0.35 | 42 | 22 | 37 | 29 | 103 | 83 | 94 | 7% | 146 | 23% | 62% | | | | 3.89 | -3.7 | 45 | 149 | $16 |

KRISTOPHER OLSON

## Marisnick,Jake

| Age: 28 | Bats: R | Pos: CF | Health | B | LIMA Plan | D |
|---|---|---|---|---|---|---|
| Ht: 6' 4" | Wt: 220 | | PT/Exp | F | Rand Var | -1 |
| | | | Consist | D | MM | 4511 |

10-28-.211 with 6 SB in 213 AB at HOU. Reclaimed some lost line drives, but quest to gain relevancy through trajectory still ill-fated. Don't let 2nd half "surge" fool you: h% elevated, xPX not sold on power. Given that lousy plate skills show no signs of life, fate as fifth OF, frequent AAA flyer are all but sealed.

| Yr | Tm | AB | R | HR | RBI | SB | BA | xBA | OBP | SLG | OPS | vL | vR | bb% | ct% | Eye | G | L | F | h% | HctX | PX | xPX | hr/f | Spd | SBO | SB% | #Wk | DOM | DIS | RC/G | RAR | BPV | BPX | R$ |
|---|---|---|---|---|---|---|---|---|---|---|---|---|---|---|---|---|---|---|---|---|---|---|---|---|---|---|---|---|---|---|---|---|---|---|---|
| 14 | 2 TM * | 564 | 55 | 9 | 46 | 27 | 237 | 223 | 263 | 334 | 597 | 738 | 568 | 3 | 75 | 0.14 | 39 | 22 | 39 | 30 | 74 | 75 | 73 | 5% | 129 | 31% | 74% | 12 | 25% | 67% | 2.90 | -16.0 | 9 | 24 | $15 |
| 15 | HOU | 339 | 46 | 9 | 36 | 24 | 236 | 223 | 281 | 383 | 665 | 669 | 662 | 5 | 69 | 0.17 | 42 | 20 | 38 | 32 | 72 | 107 | 93 | 10% | 136 | 47% | 73% | 25 | 32% | 48% | 3.40 | -11.6 | 14 | 38 | $13 |
| 16 | HOU * | 314 | 42 | 5 | 22 | 11 | 204 | 224 | 245 | 321 | 566 | 701 | 519 | 5 | 70 | 0.18 | 45 | 19 | 36 | 28 | 74 | 90 | 68 | 7% | 114 | 31% | 64% | 26 | 19% | 50% | 2.40 | -19.7 | -2 | -6 | $2 |
| 17 | HOU | 230 | 50 | 16 | 35 | 9 | 243 | 227 | 319 | 496 | 815 | 817 | 813 | 8 | 61 | 0.22 | 37 | 15 | 48 | 32 | 71 | 171 | 119 | 25% | 107 | 26% | 69% | 24 | 50% | 42% | 4.91 | 1.1 | 30 | 91 | $9 |
| 18 | HOU * | 292 | 48 | 13 | 38 | 9 | 225 | 219 | 273 | 423 | 697 | 693 | 655 | 6 | 64 | 0.18 | 32 | 23 | 45 | 31 | 68 | 140 | 123 | 18% | 135 | 22% | 73% | 24 | 33% | 63% | 3.75 | -2.5 | 21 | 70 | $8 |
| 1st Half | | 167 | 26 | 8 | 22 | 2 | 195 | 200 | 233 | 382 | 615 | 602 | 615 | 5 | 56 | 0.12 | 28 | 26 | 46 | 27 | 64 | 136 | 130 | 19% | 121 | 11% | 67% | 15 | 33% | 60% | 2.78 | -7.2 | -11 | -37 | $6 |
| 2nd Half | | 125 | 21 | 5 | 16 | 7 | 263 | 243 | 322 | 473 | 795 | 884 | 737 | 8 | 71 | 0.30 | 38 | 19 | 44 | 34 | 71 | 141 | 113 | 14% | 131 | 32% | 76% | 9 | 33% | 67% | 5.19 | 3.9 | 52 | 173 | $12 |
| 19 | Proj | 196 | 33 | 9 | 24 | 8 | 224 | 227 | 286 | 429 | 715 | 759 | 681 | 6 | 66 | 0.20 | 37 | 20 | 44 | 29 | 70 | 141 | 108 | 16% | 128 | 30% | 72% | | | | 3.77 | -2.2 | 32 | 107 | $5 |

## Markakis,Nick

| Age: 35 | Bats: L | Pos: RF | Health | A | LIMA Plan | B+ |
|---|---|---|---|---|---|---|
| Ht: 6' 1" | Wt: 210 | | PT/Exp | A | Rand Var | 0 |
| | | | Consist | B | MM | 1045 |

Rare success vL, spike in hit rate, hr/f in 1st half fueled first All-Star nod, but Fountain of Youth ran dry. Boring-but-effective self returned in 2nd half. Plate skills still robust, LD% boost interesting, but at 35, best to expect 2nd half times two (unless Daniel Poncedeleon becomes a teammate, we suppose).

| Yr | Tm | AB | R | HR | RBI | SB | BA | xBA | OBP | SLG | OPS | vL | vR | bb% | ct% | Eye | G | L | F | h% | HctX | PX | xPX | hr/f | Spd | SBO | SB% | #Wk | DOM | DIS | RC/G | RAR | BPV | BPX | R$ |
|---|---|---|---|---|---|---|---|---|---|---|---|---|---|---|---|---|---|---|---|---|---|---|---|---|---|---|---|---|---|---|---|---|---|---|---|
| 14 | BAL | 642 | 81 | 14 | 50 | 4 | 276 | 258 | 342 | 386 | 729 | 673 | 751 | 9 | 87 | 0.74 | 46 | 20 | 34 | 30 | 103 | 74 | 85 | 7% | 103 | 3% | 67% | 27 | 41% | 11% | 4.60 | 9.1 | 57 | 154 | $18 |
| 15 | ATL | 612 | 73 | 3 | 53 | 2 | 296 | 261 | 370 | 376 | 746 | 635 | 795 | 10 | 86 | 0.84 | 52 | 21 | 27 | 34 | 97 | 60 | 55 | 2% | 95 | 1% | 67% | 27 | 44% | 19% | 5.00 | 2.4 | 45 | 122 | $16 |
| 16 | ATL | 599 | 67 | 13 | 89 | 0 | 269 | 259 | 346 | 397 | 744 | 613 | 800 | 10 | 83 | 0.70 | 43 | 22 | 35 | 31 | 111 | 82 | 105 | 7% | 62 | 1% | 0% | 27 | 44% | 19% | 4.73 | 0.9 | 40 | 114 | $13 |
| 17 | ATL | 593 | 76 | 8 | 76 | 0 | 275 | 260 | 354 | 384 | 738 | 722 | 743 | 10 | 81 | 0.62 | 49 | 22 | 29 | 33 | 109 | 71 | 71 | 6% | 77 | 1% | 0% | 27 | 33% | 26% | 4.66 | -8.8 | 28 | 85 | $13 |
| 18 | ATL | 623 | 78 | 14 | 93 | 1 | 297 | 293 | 366 | 440 | 806 | 765 | 828 | 10 | 87 | 0.90 | 43 | 27 | 30 | 32 | 130 | 84 | 89 | 8% | 86 | 1% | 50% | 28 | 50% | 14% | 5.87 | 25.4 | 64 | 213 | $22 |
| 1st Half | | 319 | 49 | 9 | 56 | 1 | 326 | 307 | 391 | 492 | 883 | 923 | 860 | 10 | 88 | 1.00 | 43 | 27 | 30 | 35 | 133 | 97 | 96 | 10% | 85 | 2% | 50% | 15 | 67% | 0% | 7.31 | 24.2 | 80 | 267 | $31 |
| 2nd Half | | 304 | 29 | 5 | 37 | 0 | 266 | 278 | 340 | 385 | 725 | 602 | 794 | 10 | 86 | 0.81 | 43 | 26 | 30 | 30 | 128 | 70 | 81 | 6% | 89 | 0% | 0% | 13 | 31% | 31% | 4.58 | 1.1 | 49 | 163 | $12 |
| 19 | Proj | 535 | 64 | 10 | 72 | 1 | 277 | 275 | 349 | 401 | 751 | 692 | 777 | 10 | 85 | 0.77 | 45 | 24 | 31 | 31 | 119 | 76 | 84 | 7% | 82 | 1% | 33% | | | | 4.91 | 6.9 | 37 | 123 | $16 |

## Marte,Jefry

| Age: 28 | Bats: R | Pos: 1B | Health | B | LIMA Plan | D |
|---|---|---|---|---|---|---|
| Ht: 6' 1" | Wt: 220 | | PT/Exp | D | Rand Var | +3 |
| | | | Consist | B | MM | 2121 |

All signs point to regular MLB role just not happening for him, even as weak-side platoon player. Hard to survive as corner IF/OF by sustaining below-average power and adding ground balls each season. Versatility may keep him employed, but he's unlikely to offer much fantasy help.

| Yr | Tm | AB | R | HR | RBI | SB | BA | xBA | OBP | SLG | OPS | vL | vR | bb% | ct% | Eye | G | L | F | h% | HctX | PX | xPX | hr/f | Spd | SBO | SB% | #Wk | DOM | DIS | RC/G | RAR | BPV | BPX | R$ |
|---|---|---|---|---|---|---|---|---|---|---|---|---|---|---|---|---|---|---|---|---|---|---|---|---|---|---|---|---|---|---|---|---|---|---|---|
| 14 | aa | 405 | 39 | 7 | 41 | 7 | 222 | | 285 | 313 | 598 | | | 8 | 81 | 0.48 | | | | 26 | | 67 | | | 82 | 10% | 68% | | | | 2.90 | | 22 | 59 | $4 |
| 15 | DET * | 437 | 46 | 15 | 60 | 6 | 233 | 266 | 285 | 409 | 694 | 920 | 506 | 7 | 79 | 0.35 | 46 | 19 | 35 | 26 | 114 | 115 | 102 | 20% | 82 | 13% | 52% | 11 | 45% | 45% | 3.72 | -16.2 | 49 | 132 | $8 |
| 16 | LAA * | 420 | 54 | 17 | 61 | 4 | 237 | 246 | 293 | 418 | 712 | 783 | 793 | 7 | 76 | 0.33 | 46 | 15 | 39 | 27 | 113 | 114 | 109 | 19% | 74 | 11% | 43% | 21 | 48% | 29% | 3.91 | -12.0 | 33 | 94 | $8 |
| 17 | LAA * | 312 | 27 | 10 | 40 | 5 | 191 | 241 | 248 | 326 | 574 | 634 | 515 | 7 | 76 | 0.33 | 47 | 19 | 34 | 22 | 86 | 79 | 83 | 13% | 63 | 10% | 80% | 13 | 38% | 54% | 2.57 | -27.8 | 4 | 12 | $0 |
| 18 | LAA | 194 | 28 | 7 | 22 | 1 | 216 | 250 | 273 | 371 | 644 | 649 | 635 | 6 | 79 | 0.32 | 55 | 15 | 30 | 24 | 87 | 87 | 45 | 15% | 90 | 5% | 50% | 26 | 42% | 46% | 3.15 | -7.5 | 26 | 87 | $1 |
| 1st Half | | 84 | 11 | 3 | 10 | 0 | 262 | 267 | 311 | 440 | 752 | 917 | 570 | 7 | 80 | 0.35 | 40 | 24 | 36 | 30 | 83 | 101 | 59 | 13% | 106 | 0% | 0% | 13 | 54% | 38% | 4.73 | -0.1 | 47 | 157 | $0 |
| 2nd Half | | 110 | 17 | 4 | 12 | 1 | 182 | 238 | 244 | 318 | 562 | 495 | 711 | 6 | 78 | 0.29 | 66 | 8 | 26 | 20 | 90 | 76 | 34 | 18% | 75 | 10% | 50% | 13 | 31% | 54% | 2.21 | -9.1 | 10 | 33 | $2 |
| 19 | Proj | 163 | 20 | 7 | 20 | 2 | 213 | 250 | 277 | 382 | 659 | 682 | 633 | 7 | 78 | 0.33 | 51 | 16 | 33 | 23 | 93 | 97 | 69 | 16% | 80 | 8% | 59% | | | | 3.25 | -7.7 | 27 | 89 | $3 |

## Marte,Ketel

| Age: 25 | Bats: B | Pos: 2B SS | Health | A | LIMA Plan | A |
|---|---|---|---|---|---|---|
| Ht: 6' 1" | Wt: 165 | | PT/Exp | B | Rand Var | +2 |
| | | | Consist | B | MM | 2555 |

To-do list on the way to fantasy impact: better AB vR, manager's nod to unleash robust speed skills. Otherwise, encouraging signs abound: rising HctX, PX/xPX, and walk rate, especially in 2nd half. Perhaps a few too many ground balls to threaten 20/20 just yet, but this is a growth stock worth buying.

| Yr | Tm | AB | R | HR | RBI | SB | BA | xBA | OBP | SLG | OPS | vL | vR | bb% | ct% | Eye | G | L | F | h% | HctX | PX | xPX | hr/f | Spd | SBO | SB% | #Wk | DOM | DIS | RC/G | RAR | BPV | BPX | R$ |
|---|---|---|---|---|---|---|---|---|---|---|---|---|---|---|---|---|---|---|---|---|---|---|---|---|---|---|---|---|---|---|---|---|---|---|---|
| 14 | a/a | 523 | 59 | 3 | 41 | 22 | 263 | | 289 | 347 | 636 | | | 4 | 83 | 0.22 | | | | 31 | | 67 | | | 104 | 27% | 66% | | | | 3.34 | | 26 | 70 | $16 |
| 15 | SEA * | 487 | 58 | 4 | 39 | 24 | 279 | 266 | 333 | 375 | 708 | 720 | 780 | 7 | 84 | 0.50 | 52 | 22 | 26 | 33 | 82 | 66 | 45 | 4% | 150 | 23% | 71% | 11 | 55% | 18% | 4.35 | 2.6 | 49 | 132 | $19 |
| 16 | SEA * | 465 | 59 | 1 | 35 | 13 | 254 | 253 | 284 | 318 | 602 | 525 | 651 | 4 | 82 | 0.23 | 52 | 22 | 26 | 31 | 71 | 47 | 41 | 1% | 126 | 16% | 72% | 22 | 14% | 41% | 3.07 | -24.7 | 12 | 34 | $9 |
| 17 | ARI * | 534 | 70 | 9 | 45 | 8 | 277 | 273 | 333 | 417 | 750 | 721 | 748 | 8 | 86 | 0.59 | 45 | 21 | 34 | 31 | 98 | 76 | 77 | 8% | 155 | 7% | 69% | 15 | 53% | 7% | 4.86 | -2.3 | 68 | 206 | $14 |
| 18 | ARI | 520 | 68 | 14 | 59 | 6 | 260 | 285 | 332 | 437 | 768 | 971 | 651 | 9 | 85 | 0.68 | 51 | 20 | 29 | 28 | 113 | 93 | 84 | 11% | 149 | 5% | 86% | 28 | 61% | 7% | 4.98 | 10.8 | 79 | 263 | $14 |
| 1st Half | | 286 | 38 | 6 | 31 | 2 | 245 | 285 | 298 | 413 | 710 | 867 | 621 | 7 | 86 | 0.54 | 56 | 17 | 28 | 27 | 112 | 87 | 81 | 9% | 153 | 3% | 100% | 15 | 53% | 7% | 4.17 | -0.1 | 77 | 257 | $11 |
| 2nd Half | | 234 | 30 | 8 | 28 | 4 | 278 | 285 | 370 | 466 | 836 | 1093 | 687 | 12 | 83 | 0.83 | 45 | 24 | 31 | 31 | 114 | 102 | 89 | 13% | 138 | 7% | 80% | 13 | 69% | 8% | 6.06 | 12.6 | 81 | 270 | $17 |
| 19 | Proj | 515 | 66 | 15 | 50 | 10 | 276 | 282 | 336 | 446 | 782 | 897 | 720 | 8 | 84 | 0.56 | 49 | 21 | 30 | 30 | 100 | 92 | 73 | 11% | 145 | 9% | 75% | | | | 5.25 | 15.9 | 64 | 212 | $19 |

## Marte,Starling

| Age: 30 | Bats: R | Pos: CF | Health | A | LIMA Plan | D+ |
|---|---|---|---|---|---|---|
| Ht: 6' 1" | Wt: 190 | | PT/Exp | B | Rand Var | 0 |
| | | | Consist | B | MM | 2545 |

Had 20-HR, 50-SB upside attached to him in last two Forecasters. He half-delivered in 2018; as power skills of 2015 have returned, and he could do it again despite ground ball tilt. Low walk rate doesn't help chances to ascend SB peak and now on wrong side of 30, but Spd remains robust, so never say never.

| Yr | Tm | AB | R | HR | RBI | SB | BA | xBA | OBP | SLG | OPS | vL | vR | bb% | ct% | Eye | G | L | F | h% | HctX | PX | xPX | hr/f | Spd | SBO | SB% | #Wk | DOM | DIS | RC/G | RAR | BPV | BPX | R$ |
|---|---|---|---|---|---|---|---|---|---|---|---|---|---|---|---|---|---|---|---|---|---|---|---|---|---|---|---|---|---|---|---|---|---|---|---|
| 14 | PIT | 495 | 73 | 13 | 56 | 30 | 291 | 264 | 356 | 453 | 808 | 781 | 814 | 6 | 74 | 0.25 | 47 | 23 | 29 | 37 | 105 | 125 | 113 | 13% | 165 | 32% | 73% | 26 | 50% | 35% | 5.33 | 21.2 | 58 | 157 | $28 |
| 15 | PIT | 579 | 84 | 19 | 81 | 30 | 287 | 283 | 337 | 444 | 780 | 717 | 798 | 4 | 79 | 0.22 | 54 | 24 | 23 | 34 | 101 | 103 | 94 | 19% | 117 | 28% | 75% | 27 | 48% | 22% | 4.98 | 11.1 | 43 | 116 | $32 |
| 16 | PIT | 489 | 71 | 9 | 46 | 47 | 311 | 274 | 362 | 456 | 818 | 730 | 837 | 4 | 79 | 0.22 | 48 | 23 | 28 | 38 | 111 | 95 | 98 | 8% | 147 | 46% | 80% | 25 | 36% | 40% | 5.79 | 15.6 | 46 | 131 | $35 |
| 17 | PIT * | 345 | 51 | 8 | 33 | 23 | 275 | 245 | 317 | 376 | 694 | 404 | 808 | 6 | 79 | 0.30 | 49 | 21 | 30 | 33 | 84 | 54 | 77 | 10% | 141 | 28% | 85% | 15 | 20% | 40% | 4.39 | -6.6 | 15 | 45 | $16 |
| 18 | PIT | 559 | 81 | 20 | 72 | 33 | 277 | 272 | 327 | 460 | 787 | 725 | 808 | 6 | 81 | 0.32 | 51 | 17 | 32 | 31 | 99 | 105 | 106 | 14% | 138 | 35% | 70% | 28 | 57% | 18% | 4.97 | 12.0 | 61 | 203 | $31 |
| 1st Half | | 273 | 43 | 9 | 34 | 18 | 267 | 257 | 319 | 443 | 762 | 630 | 803 | 7 | 77 | 0.33 | 48 | 18 | 33 | 32 | 84 | 103 | 97 | 13% | 161 | 32% | 82% | 15 | 53% | 27% | 5.01 | 7.0 | 55 | 183 | $29 |
| 2nd Half | | 286 | 38 | 11 | 38 | 15 | 287 | 285 | 336 | 476 | 811 | 807 | 812 | 5 | 84 | 0.30 | 53 | 16 | 31 | 31 | 114 | 108 | 114 | 15% | 111 | 38% | 60% | 13 | 62% | 8% | 4.93 | 6.6 | 67 | 223 | $33 |
| 19 | Proj | 562 | 81 | 17 | 65 | 37 | 284 | 265 | 336 | 440 | 777 | 654 | 814 | 6 | 80 | 0.29 | 50 | 20 | 30 | 33 | 99 | 92 | 98 | 12% | 140 | 35% | 75% | | | | 4.98 | 13.7 | 45 | 150 | $34 |

## Martin,Leonys

| Age: 31 | Bats: L | Pos: CF | Health | D | LIMA Plan | C+ |
|---|---|---|---|---|---|---|
| Ht: 6' 2" | Wt: 200 | | PT/Exp | C | Rand Var | -2 |
| | | | Consist | C | MM | 2513 |

Life-threatening bacterial infection ended his season in August. Prior to illness, was on pace for career-high HR total due to FB% increase, which didn't come at expense of contact rate. SB dip mainly a function of SBO; Spd still strong. Stars would have to align (health, role), but... UP: 20 HR, 25 SB

| Yr | Tm | AB | R | HR | RBI | SB | BA | xBA | OBP | SLG | OPS | vL | vR | bb% | ct% | Eye | G | L | F | h% | HctX | PX | xPX | hr/f | Spd | SBO | SB% | #Wk | DOM | DIS | RC/G | RAR | BPV | BPX | R$ |
|---|---|---|---|---|---|---|---|---|---|---|---|---|---|---|---|---|---|---|---|---|---|---|---|---|---|---|---|---|---|---|---|---|---|---|---|
| 14 | TEX | 533 | 68 | 7 | 40 | 31 | 274 | 242 | 325 | 364 | 689 | 581 | 725 | 7 | 79 | 0.34 | 50 | 22 | 28 | 34 | 88 | 60 | 68 | 6% | 155 | 27% | 72% | 27 | 26% | 44% | 4.08 | 2.9 | 24 | 65 | $23 |
| 15 | TEX * | 325 | 31 | 6 | 28 | 15 | 221 | 230 | 266 | 325 | 591 | 566 | 582 | 6 | 77 | 0.27 | 52 | 15 | 33 | 27 | 79 | 74 | 62 | 7% | 88 | 31% | 71% | 19 | 21% | 63% | 2.78 | -17.5 | 8 | 22 | $6 |
| 16 | SEA | 518 | 72 | 15 | 47 | 24 | 247 | 224 | 306 | 378 | 684 | 684 | 684 | 8 | 71 | 0.30 | 43 | 20 | 37 | 32 | 85 | 84 | 79 | 11% | 130 | 22% | 80% | 25 | 36% | 56% | 3.98 | -6.0 | 8 | 23 | $17 |
| 17 | 2 TM * | 488 | 60 | 11 | 37 | 25 | 219 | 212 | 255 | 348 | 603 | 857 | 444 | 5 | 69 | 0.15 | 46 | 15 | 39 | 30 | 70 | 85 | 100 | 9% | 120 | 39% | 68% | 11 | 27% | 45% | 2.77 | -30.4 | -9 | -27 | $10 |
| 18 | 2 AL | 318 | 48 | 11 | 33 | 7 | 255 | 231 | 323 | 425 | 747 | 575 | 799 | 8 | 76 | 0.39 | 36 | 18 | 46 | 30 | 106 | 102 | 120 | 10% | 130 | 13% | 64% | 19 | 42% | 53% | 4.52 | 4.5 | 43 | 143 | $9 |
| 1st Half | | 273 | 44 | 9 | 28 | 7 | 256 | 233 | 327 | 432 | 759 | 589 | 808 | 9 | 75 | 0.40 | 35 | 18 | 47 | 31 | 110 | 108 | 126 | 10% | 129 | 14% | 70% | 15 | 47% | 47% | 4.73 | 4.8 | 47 | 157 | $12 |
| 2nd Half | | 45 | 4 | 2 | 5 | 0 | 244 | 205 | 300 | 378 | 678 | 490 | 738 | 6 | 78 | 0.30 | 42 | 15 | 42 | 27 | 80 | 66 | 86 | 14% | 110 | 8% | 0% | 4 | 25% | 75% | 3.35 | -1.1 | 11 | 37 | -$10 |
| 19 | Proj | 325 | 44 | 10 | 29 | 14 | 243 | 227 | 302 | 397 | 699 | 677 | 706 | 7 | 74 | 0.29 | 43 | 17 | 40 | 30 | 85 | 95 | 94 | 11% | 128 | 25% | 72% | | | | 3.90 | -2.3 | 23 | 77 | $12 |

## Martin,Russell

| Age: 36 | Bats: R | Pos: CA 3B | Health | B | LIMA Plan | D |
|---|---|---|---|---|---|---|
| Ht: 5'10" | Wt: 205 | | PT/Exp | C | Rand Var | +3 |
| | | | Consist | B | MM | 2011 |

Many take up new hobbies as retirement nears; he tried his hand at shortstop. Has a year left on contract, but with HctX, PX in decline and ability to work walks now his most potent "weapon," there's little incentive to ask him to earn his keep. If spending $1 on second CA, look for one with less wear on tires.

| Yr | Tm | AB | R | HR | RBI | SB | BA | xBA | OBP | SLG | OPS | vL | vR | bb% | ct% | Eye | G | L | F | h% | HctX | PX | xPX | hr/f | Spd | SBO | SB% | #Wk | DOM | DIS | RC/G | RAR | BPV | BPX | R$ |
|---|---|---|---|---|---|---|---|---|---|---|---|---|---|---|---|---|---|---|---|---|---|---|---|---|---|---|---|---|---|---|---|---|---|---|---|
| 14 | PIT | 379 | 45 | 11 | 67 | 4 | 290 | 255 | 402 | 430 | 832 | 693 | 865 | 13 | 79 | 0.76 | 49 | 19 | 32 | 34 | 109 | 102 | 91 | 11% | 81 | 6% | 50% | 23 | 39% | 39% | 5.81 | 26.6 | 51 | 138 | $16 |
| 15 | TOR | 441 | 76 | 23 | 77 | 4 | 240 | 272 | 329 | 458 | 787 | 937 | 747 | 10 | 76 | 0.50 | 51 | 16 | 33 | 27 | 97 | 140 | 113 | 21% | 89 | 8% | 44% | 27 | 48% | 26% | 4.77 | 13.8 | 65 | 176 | $14 |
| 16 | TOR | 455 | 62 | 20 | 74 | 2 | 231 | 223 | 335 | 398 | 733 | 700 | 743 | 12 | 67 | 0.43 | 46 | 18 | 36 | 30 | 92 | 111 | 128 | 18% | 65 | 2% | 67% | 27 | 37% | 44% | 4.28 | 5.7 | 4 | 11 | $8 |
| 17 | TOR | 307 | 49 | 13 | 35 | 1 | 221 | 256 | 343 | 388 | 731 | 581 | 772 | 14 | 73 | 0.60 | 48 | 24 | 28 | 26 | 89 | 98 | 84 | 21% | 69 | 3% | 33% | 22 | 36% | 50% | 4.11 | -0.2 | 20 | 61 | $3 |
| 18 | TOR | 289 | 37 | 10 | 25 | 0 | 194 | 201 | 338 | 325 | 663 | 683 | 657 | 16 | 72 | 0.68 | 51 | 14 | 35 | 23 | 79 | 81 | 83 | 14% | 87 | 3% | 0% | 24 | 38% | 46% | 3.21 | -1.4 | 11 | 37 | $0 |
| 1st Half | | 175 | 20 | 6 | 16 | 0 | 171 | 193 | 329 | 297 | 626 | 585 | 638 | 17 | 70 | 0.71 | 49 | 14 | 37 | 21 | 84 | 78 | 91 | 13% | 72 | 4% | 0% | 15 | 40% | 47% | 2.77 | -3.9 | 2 | 7 | -$2 |
| 2nd Half | | 114 | 17 | 4 | 9 | 0 | 228 | 220 | 353 | 368 | 721 | 820 | 686 | 14 | 74 | 0.63 | 55 | 14 | 31 | 28 | 71 | 86 | 71 | 15% | 103 | 3% | 0% | 9 | 33% | 44% | 3.98 | 1.9 | 25 | 83 | $2 |
| 19 | Proj | 211 | 30 | 8 | 24 | 1 | 219 | 227 | 341 | 372 | 714 | 698 | 718 | 14 | 72 | 0.59 | 50 | 17 | 32 | 26 | 84 | 95 | 90 | 17% | 86 | 3% | 24% | | | | 3.88 | 2.8 | 6 | 20 | $4 |

KRISTOPHER OLSON

## Martinez,J.D.

| Age: 31 | Bats: R | Pos: DH LF RF | Health | C | LIMA Plan | C |
|---|---|---|---|---|---|---|
| Ht: 6' 3" | Wt: 220 | | PT/Exp | B | Rand Var | -4 |
| | | | Consist | C | MM | 5355 |

Sometimes there's a man—well, he's the man for his time and place. Nearly took home Triple Crown by pairing elite power with improved ct%, chipping in a handful of SB for good measure. xBA and lofty h% suggest betting against a full BA repeat, though really, betting against this dude seems like a bad idea. Hear that, Ron?

| Yr | Tm | AB | R | HR | RBI | SB | BA | xBA | OBP | SLG | OPS | vL | vR | bb% | ct% | Eye | G | L | F | h% | HctX | PX | xPX | hr/f | Spd | SBO | SB% | #Wk | DOM | DIS | RC/G | RAR | BPV | BPX | R$ |
|---|---|---|---|---|---|---|---|---|---|---|---|---|---|---|---|---|---|---|---|---|---|---|---|---|---|---|---|---|---|---|---|---|---|---|---|
| 14 | DET * | 506 | 69 | 30 | 92 | 7 | 308 | 287 | 349 | 568 | 917 | 1003 | 880 | 6 | 71 | 0.22 | 40 | 23 | 37 | 38 | 133 | 196 | 159 | 19% | 111 | 9% | 71% | 24 | 54% | 33% | 7.23 | 44.1 | 89 | 241 | $31 |
| 15 | DET | 596 | 93 | 38 | 102 | 3 | 282 | 265 | 344 | 535 | 879 | 915 | 870 | 8 | 70 | 0.30 | 34 | 22 | 43 | 34 | 131 | 175 | 182 | 21% | 96 | 3% | 60% | 27 | 56% | 30% | 6.42 | 16.3 | 68 | 184 | $28 |
| 16 | DET * | 496 | 71 | 22 | 72 | 2 | 300 | 265 | 364 | 517 | 881 | 861 | 925 | 9 | 71 | 0.35 | 42 | 21 | 36 | 38 | 119 | 147 | 144 | 18% | 92 | 3% | 47% | 21 | 48% | 14% | 6.78 | 17.5 | 51 | 146 | $20 |
| 17 | 2 TM | 432 | 85 | 45 | 104 | 4 | 303 | 305 | 376 | 690 | 1066 | 1356 | 985 | 11 | 70 | 0.41 | 38 | 19 | 43 | 33 | 140 | 224 | 190 | 34% | 98 | 4% | 100% | 22 | 73% | 9% | 9.65 | 56.4 | 114 | 345 | $27 |
| 18 | BOS | 569 | 111 | 43 | 130 | 6 | 330 | 298 | 402 | 629 | 1031 | 966 | 1051 | 11 | 74 | 0.47 | 43 | 23 | 34 | 38 | 123 | 178 | 148 | 29% | 109 | 4% | 86% | 28 | 71% | 7% | 9.68 | 77.4 | 96 | 320 | $41 |
| 1st Half | | 306 | 58 | 25 | 67 | 2 | 327 | 303 | 392 | 641 | 1033 | 881 | 1081 | 10 | 74 | 0.42 | 46 | 23 | 32 | 37 | 135 | 185 | 166 | 34% | 109 | 3% | 67% | 15 | 73% | 7% | 9.45 | 40.1 | 99 | 330 | $43 |
| 2nd Half | | 263 | 53 | 18 | 63 | 4 | 335 | 289 | 413 | 616 | 1029 | 1076 | 1016 | 12 | 75 | 0.54 | 41 | 23 | 37 | 39 | 108 | 169 | 128 | 25% | 105 | 5% | 100% | 13 | 69% | 8% | 9.92 | 37.2 | 91 | 303 | $38 |
| 19 | Proj | **561** | **103** | **42** | **121** | **5** | **302** | **288** | **378** | **601** | **978** | **1022** | **965** | **11** | **73** | **0.45** | **41** | **21** | **38** | **35** | **125** | **182** | **158** | **27%** | **105** | **4%** | **85%** | | | | **8.32** | **58.7** | **85** | **284** | **$33** |

## Martinez,Jose

| Age: 30 | Bats: R | Pos: 1B RF | Health | A | LIMA Plan | B |
|---|---|---|---|---|---|---|
| Ht: 6' 6" | Wt: 215 | | PT/Exp | C | Rand Var | -3 |
| | | | Consist | F | MM | 2045 |

Late bloomer had a nice follow-up to 2017 breakout. Low FB% leaves HR output subject to even tiny fluctuations—see how xPX moves in sync with changes in fly ball rate. Despite xBA slippage, could approach .300 mark, but woeful defense really serves as biggest threat to playing time. Upside, yes, but not without risk.

| Yr | Tm | AB | R | HR | RBI | SB | BA | xBA | OBP | SLG | OPS | vL | vR | bb% | ct% | Eye | G | L | F | h% | HctX | PX | xPX | hr/f | Spd | SBO | SB% | #Wk | DOM | DIS | RC/G | RAR | BPV | BPX | R$ |
|---|---|---|---|---|---|---|---|---|---|---|---|---|---|---|---|---|---|---|---|---|---|---|---|---|---|---|---|---|---|---|---|---|---|---|---|
| 14 | | | | | | | | | | | | | | | | | | | | | | | | | | | | | | | | | | | |
| 15 | aaa | 341 | 43 | 7 | 45 | 6 | 324 | | 388 | 467 | 854 | | | 9 | 81 | 0.55 | | | | 38 | | 97 | | | 95 | 7% | 71% | | | | 6.78 | | 51 | 138 | $16 |
| 16 | STL * | 458 | 40 | 7 | 42 | 8 | 226 | 266 | 271 | 328 | 599 | 1083 | 750 | 6 | 80 | 0.32 | 60 | 20 | 20 | 27 | 152 | 67 | 9 | 0% | 87 | 9% | 86% | 5 | 20% | 0% | 2.97 | -23.1 | 15 | 43 | $3 |
| 17 | STL | 272 | 47 | 14 | 46 | 4 | 309 | 286 | 379 | 518 | 897 | 1340 | 773 | 10 | 78 | 0.53 | 42 | 27 | 31 | 35 | 117 | 115 | 123 | 21% | 112 | 5% | 100% | 24 | 42% | 33% | 7.41 | 15.9 | 60 | 182 | $13 |
| 18 | STL | 534 | 64 | 17 | 83 | 0 | 305 | 273 | 364 | 457 | 821 | 776 | 834 | 8 | 81 | 0.47 | 46 | 26 | 28 | 35 | 120 | 91 | 101 | 14% | 84 | 2% | 0% | 28 | 46% | 29% | 5.96 | 19.9 | 39 | 130 | $20 |
| 1st Half | | 280 | 35 | 13 | 52 | 0 | 300 | 295 | 368 | 500 | 868 | 711 | 901 | 10 | 84 | 0.65 | 46 | 25 | 29 | 32 | 127 | 112 | 113 | 19% | 79 | 4% | 0% | 15 | 60% | 27% | 6.42 | 14.3 | 69 | 230 | $25 |
| 2nd Half | | 254 | 29 | 4 | 31 | 0 | 311 | 252 | 359 | 409 | 768 | 817 | 748 | 7 | 77 | 0.33 | 46 | 27 | 27 | 39 | 112 | 67 | 88 | 8% | 96 | 0% | 0% | 13 | 31% | 31% | 5.44 | 5.8 | 7 | 23 | $16 |
| 19 | Proj | **416** | **53** | **15** | **60** | **0** | **297** | **277** | **356** | **464** | **819** | **964** | **775** | **9** | **79** | **0.46** | **45** | **26** | **29** | **34** | **118** | **99** | **108** | **16%** | **101** | **1%** | **22%** | | | | **5.93** | **13.4** | **27** | **91** | **$17** |

## Martinez,Victor

| Age: 40 | Bats: B | Pos: DH | Health | C | LIMA Plan | F |
|---|---|---|---|---|---|---|
| Ht: 6' 2" | Wt: 235 | | PT/Exp | B | Rand Var | +2 |
| | | | Consist | C | MM | 0000 |

The switch-hitting Venezuelan calls it quits after an illustrious 16-year career. A 5-time All-Star and 2-time Silver Slugger, he ends with 295 HR and a career .295/.360/.455 line. His power fell off these past couple seasons, but his elite contact ability never wavered. Truly a pleasure watching him hit.

| Yr | Tm | AB | R | HR | RBI | SB | BA | xBA | OBP | SLG | OPS | vL | vR | bb% | ct% | Eye | G | L | F | h% | HctX | PX | xPX | hr/f | Spd | SBO | SB% | #Wk | DOM | DIS | RC/G | RAR | BPV | BPX | R$ |
|---|---|---|---|---|---|---|---|---|---|---|---|---|---|---|---|---|---|---|---|---|---|---|---|---|---|---|---|---|---|---|---|---|---|---|---|
| 14 | DET | 561 | 87 | 32 | 103 | 3 | 335 | 320 | 409 | 565 | 974 | 1123 | 923 | 11 | 93 | 1.67 | 41 | 21 | 38 | 32 | 158 | 135 | 147 | 16% | 76 | 3% | 60% | 26 | 88% | 4% | 8.79 | 69.7 | 125 | 338 | $38 |
| 15 | DET | 440 | 39 | 11 | 64 | 0 | 245 | 256 | 301 | 366 | 667 | 870 | 616 | 6 | 88 | 0.60 | 40 | 21 | 39 | 26 | 116 | 73 | 110 | 7% | 51 | 0% | 0% | 23 | 43% | 26% | 3.65 | -23.3 | 41 | 111 | $6 |
| 16 | DET | 553 | 65 | 27 | 86 | 0 | 289 | 276 | 351 | 476 | 826 | 812 | 832 | 8 | 84 | 0.56 | 37 | 24 | 39 | 31 | 132 | 100 | 132 | 15% | 53 | 0% | 0% | 27 | 48% | 30% | 5.94 | 6.8 | 49 | 140 | $20 |
| 17 | DET | 392 | 38 | 10 | 47 | 0 | 255 | 259 | 324 | 372 | 697 | 626 | 719 | 8 | 84 | 0.57 | 42 | 24 | 34 | 28 | 135 | 64 | 117 | 9% | 65 | 0% | 0% | 20 | 35% | 40% | 4.05 | -9.3 | 25 | 76 | $5 |
| 18 | DET | 467 | 32 | 9 | 54 | 0 | 251 | 266 | 297 | 353 | 651 | 686 | 638 | 6 | 90 | 0.65 | 39 | 25 | 36 | 26 | 122 | 58 | 91 | 6% | 54 | 0% | 0% | 26 | 38% | 15% | 3.59 | -12.5 | 35 | 117 | $6 |
| 1st Half | | 261 | 15 | 4 | 26 | 0 | 241 | 246 | 297 | 326 | 623 | 644 | 616 | 7 | 89 | 0.72 | 41 | 23 | 36 | 26 | 125 | 48 | 84 | 5% | 49 | 0% | 0% | 15 | 27% | 13% | 3.26 | -9.7 | 26 | 87 | $3 |
| 2nd Half | | 206 | 17 | 5 | 28 | 0 | 262 | 288 | 297 | 388 | 686 | 731 | 667 | 5 | 90 | 0.55 | 37 | 27 | 36 | 27 | 117 | 70 | 100 | 7% | 69 | 0% | 0% | 11 | 55% | 18% | 4.02 | -2.9 | 50 | 167 | $9 |
| 19 | Proj | | | | | | | | | | | | | | | | | | | | | | | | | | | | | | | | | | |

## Martini,Nick

| Age: 29 | Bats: L | Pos: LF | Health | A | LIMA Plan | D |
|---|---|---|---|---|---|---|
| Ht: 5' 11" | Wt: 205 | | PT/Exp | C | Rand Var | -4 |
| | | | Consist | B | MM | 1221 |

1-19-.296 in 152 AB at OAK. Career minor leaguer forced way onto roster with 65-game AAA on-base streak. Penchant for BB landed him atop lineup vR, but lack of carrying tool casts doubt on playing time and fantasy impact. Unless he shakes things up, don't let your emotions get... (yep, we're doing this) ...stirred.

| Yr | Tm | AB | R | HR | RBI | SB | BA | xBA | OBP | SLG | OPS | vL | vR | bb% | ct% | Eye | G | L | F | h% | HctX | PX | xPX | hr/f | Spd | SBO | SB% | #Wk | DOM | DIS | RC/G | RAR | BPV | BPX | R$ |
|---|---|---|---|---|---|---|---|---|---|---|---|---|---|---|---|---|---|---|---|---|---|---|---|---|---|---|---|---|---|---|---|---|---|---|---|
| 14 | | | | | | | | | | | | | | | | | | | | | | | | | | | | | | | | | | | |
| 15 | a/a | 369 | 37 | 4 | 33 | 6 | 231 | | 313 | 321 | 635 | | | 11 | 81 | 0.61 | | | | 28 | | 61 | | | 105 | 14% | 44% | | | | 3.13 | | 26 | 70 | $3 |
| 16 | a/a | 401 | 44 | 4 | 29 | 8 | 217 | | 289 | 291 | 580 | | | 9 | 81 | 0.55 | | | | 26 | | 47 | | | 108 | 8% | 86% | | | | 2.80 | | 16 | 46 | $2 |
| 17 | a/a | 459 | 57 | 6 | 54 | 5 | 245 | | 319 | 344 | 663 | | | 10 | 76 | 0.46 | | | | 31 | | 63 | | | 107 | 4% | 79% | | | | 3.73 | | 8 | 24 | $6 |
| 18 | OAK * | 428 | 58 | 5 | 48 | 4 | 258 | 242 | 345 | 359 | 705 | 489 | 829 | 12 | 72 | 0.48 | 49 | 26 | 25 | 35 | 100 | 69 | 90 | 3% | 104 | 4% | 75% | 15 | 33% | 33% | 4.27 | -3.8 | 1 | 3 | $9 |
| 1st Half | | 259 | 30 | 3 | 29 | 4 | 245 | 191 | 330 | 335 | 665 | 0 | 222 | 11 | 72 | 0.46 | 50 | 10 | 40 | 33 | 160 | 62 | 73 | 0% | 98 | 6% | 75% | 3 | 0% | 33% | 3.74 | -6.6 | -8 | -27 | $9 |
| 2nd Half | | 169 | 28 | 2 | 19 | 0 | 278 | 252 | 370 | 397 | 767 | 543 | 867 | 13 | 72 | 0.52 | 49 | 28 | 23 | 38 | 95 | 80 | 92 | 4% | 112 | 0% | 0% | 12 | 42% | 33% | 5.19 | 2.8 | 14 | 47 | $8 |
| 19 | Proj | **187** | **24** | **1** | **20** | **2** | **249** | **250** | **348** | **333** | **681** | **472** | **692** | **11** | **75** | **0.50** | **49** | **28** | **23** | **32** | **86** | **58** | **83** | **4%** | **101** | **5%** | **73%** | | | | **3.76** | **-4.7** | **-1** | **-2** | **$4** |

## Mauer,Joe

| Age: 36 | Bats: L | Pos: 1B DH | Health | B | LIMA Plan | B |
|---|---|---|---|---|---|---|
| Ht: 6' 5" | Wt: 225 | | PT/Exp | A | Rand Var | 0 |
| | | | Consist | C | MM | 1145 |

Looks like end could be near for this 6-time All-Star. Won three batting titles and owns one of the best ever fantasy seasons from CA position (.365 BA, 28 HR, 94 R, 96 RBI in 2009), maintaining top-shelf plate skills throughout. If he does decide to stick around, LD%/HctX suggest there's still some life left in his bat.

| Yr | Tm | AB | R | HR | RBI | SB | BA | xBA | OBP | SLG | OPS | vL | vR | bb% | ct% | Eye | G | L | F | h% | HctX | PX | xPX | hr/f | Spd | SBO | SB% | #Wk | DOM | DIS | RC/G | RAR | BPV | BPX | R$ |
|---|---|---|---|---|---|---|---|---|---|---|---|---|---|---|---|---|---|---|---|---|---|---|---|---|---|---|---|---|---|---|---|---|---|---|---|
| 14 | MIN | 455 | 60 | 4 | 55 | 3 | 277 | 269 | 361 | 371 | 732 | 654 | 776 | 12 | 79 | 0.63 | 51 | 27 | 22 | 34 | 96 | 79 | 70 | 5% | 90 | 2% | 100% | 22 | 45% | 32% | 4.78 | 8.2 | 31 | 84 | $12 |
| 15 | MIN | 592 | 69 | 10 | 66 | 2 | 265 | 275 | 338 | 380 | 718 | 720 | 718 | 10 | 81 | 0.60 | 56 | 24 | 20 | 31 | 108 | 80 | 80 | 10% | 85 | 2% | 67% | 26 | 38% | 27% | 4.47 | -7.9 | 36 | 97 | $12 |
| 16 | MIN | 494 | 68 | 11 | 49 | 2 | 261 | 283 | 363 | 389 | 752 | 610 | 793 | 14 | 81 | 0.85 | 52 | 27 | 21 | 30 | 103 | 75 | 76 | 13% | 104 | 1% | 100% | 26 | 38% | 35% | 4.90 | 0.5 | 45 | 129 | $9 |
| 17 | MIN | 525 | 69 | 7 | 71 | 2 | 305 | 285 | 384 | 417 | 801 | 754 | 816 | 11 | 84 | 0.80 | 51 | 25 | 24 | 35 | 124 | 70 | 70 | 7% | 89 | 2% | 67% | 27 | 44% | 22% | 5.84 | 6.6 | 44 | 133 | $17 |
| 18 | MIN | 486 | 64 | 6 | 48 | 0 | 282 | 273 | 351 | 379 | 729 | 744 | 724 | 9 | 82 | 0.59 | 51 | 27 | 22 | 33 | 136 | 63 | 113 | 7% | 80 | 1% | 0% | 25 | 44% | 32% | 4.67 | 3.4 | 24 | 80 | $11 |
| 1st Half | | 187 | 24 | 2 | 21 | 0 | 267 | 273 | 370 | 358 | 728 | 871 | 685 | 13 | 85 | 1.04 | 51 | 26 | 23 | 31 | 125 | 60 | 102 | 5% | 67 | 0% | 0% | 12 | 58% | 25% | 4.56 | -1.1 | 37 | 123 | $4 |
| 2nd Half | | 299 | 40 | 4 | 27 | 0 | 291 | 273 | 337 | 391 | 729 | 675 | 750 | 7 | 81 | 0.38 | 51 | 28 | 21 | 35 | 143 | 66 | 119 | 8% | 93 | 1% | 0% | 13 | 31% | 38% | 4.71 | -0.4 | 19 | 63 | $16 |
| 19 | Proj | | | | | | | | | | | | | | | | | | | | | | | | | | | | | | | | | | |

## Maybin,Cameron

| Age: 32 | Bats: R | Pos: LF CF RF | Health | C | LIMA Plan | D |
|---|---|---|---|---|---|---|
| Ht: 6' 3" | Wt: 215 | | PT/Exp | C | Rand Var | 0 |
| | | | Consist | B | MM | 1423 |

Part-time starter with MIA before deadline trade to SEA, where he soon fell into reserve role. LD stroke returned and HctX enjoyed a nice boost, but 2017's SBO now a clear outlier. Yearly BPV and AB trends say struggle for fantasy relevance will only get tougher. Roster only in a pinch.

| Yr | Tm | AB | R | HR | RBI | SB | BA | xBA | OBP | SLG | OPS | vL | vR | bb% | ct% | Eye | G | L | F | h% | HctX | PX | xPX | hr/f | Spd | SBO | SB% | #Wk | DOM | DIS | RC/G | RAR | BPV | BPX | R$ |
|---|---|---|---|---|---|---|---|---|---|---|---|---|---|---|---|---|---|---|---|---|---|---|---|---|---|---|---|---|---|---|---|---|---|---|---|
| 14 | SD * | 304 | 28 | 2 | 18 | 5 | 226 | 242 | 280 | 319 | 599 | 575 | 646 | 7 | 77 | 0.33 | 57 | 17 | 26 | 29 | 97 | 72 | 60 | 2% | 139 | 11% | 60% | 20 | 15% | 55% | 2.88 | -8.8 | 24 | 65 | $1 |
| 15 | ATL | 505 | 65 | 10 | 59 | 23 | 267 | 266 | 327 | 370 | 697 | 711 | 692 | 8 | 80 | 0.44 | 58 | 22 | 20 | 32 | 75 | 67 | 46 | 12% | 100 | 19% | 79% | 26 | 31% | 38% | 4.28 | -3.2 | 21 | 57 | $20 |
| 16 | DET * | 434 | 76 | 6 | 51 | 18 | 282 | 269 | 352 | 392 | 744 | 802 | 801 | 10 | 79 | 0.52 | 57 | 22 | 22 | 35 | 80 | 69 | 48 | 7% | 142 | 18% | 71% | 19 | 21% | 26% | 4.86 | 6.1 | 37 | 106 | $18 |
| 17 | 2 AL | 395 | 63 | 10 | 35 | 33 | 228 | 254 | 318 | 365 | 683 | 640 | 701 | 11 | 76 | 0.54 | 58 | 14 | 28 | 27 | 84 | 83 | 65 | 12% | 117 | 38% | 80% | 24 | 29% | 54% | 3.94 | -9.8 | 31 | 94 | $16 |
| 18 | 2 TM | 342 | 32 | 4 | 28 | 10 | 249 | 244 | 326 | 336 | 662 | 638 | 681 | 10 | 78 | 0.51 | 49 | 24 | 28 | 31 | 96 | 57 | 62 | 5% | 110 | 15% | 67% | 28 | 25% | 43% | 3.64 | -4.0 | 13 | 43 | $6 |
| 1st Half | | 183 | 13 | 0 | 15 | 3 | 230 | 247 | 302 | 301 | 603 | 692 | 534 | 9 | 78 | 0.48 | 47 | 26 | 27 | 29 | 99 | 55 | 58 | 0% | 89 | 14% | 43% | 15 | 20% | 47% | 2.81 | -7.5 | 4 | 13 | $1 |
| 2nd Half | | 159 | 19 | 4 | 13 | 7 | 270 | 241 | 352 | 377 | 729 | 578 | 854 | 11 | 78 | 0.54 | 51 | 21 | 28 | 33 | 93 | 58 | 65 | 11% | 133 | 15% | 88% | 13 | 31% | 38% | 4.77 | 2.9 | 22 | 73 | $13 |
| 19 | Proj | **252** | **32** | **4** | **23** | **9** | **243** | **248** | **322** | **349** | **671** | **623** | **699** | **10** | **78** | **0.51** | **53** | **20** | **26** | **30** | **89** | **66** | **60** | **8%** | **120** | **17%** | **70%** | | | | **3.72** | **-6.6** | **18** | **58** | **$7** |

## Mazara,Nomar

| Age: 24 | Bats: L | Pos: RF | Health | A | LIMA Plan | B+ |
|---|---|---|---|---|---|---|
| Ht: 6'4" | Wt: 215 | | PT/Exp | A | Rand Var | 0 |
| | | | Consist | A | MM | 3135 |

On one hand, tempting to focus on gains vL while chalking up brutal 2nd half to lingering thumb injury. On the other, GB/FB trending in wrong direction, plate skills stagnant, and final line bailed out by obscene May (10 HR, 59% hr/f). Loads of MLB experience for his age, but growth is proceeding at a glacial pace.

| Yr | Tm | AB | R | HR | RBI | SB | BA | xBA | OBP | SLG | OPS | vL | vR | bb% | ct% | Eye | G | L | F | h% | HctX | PX | xPX | hr/f | Spd | SBO | SB% | #Wk | DOM | DIS | RC/G | RAR | BPV | BPX | R$ |
|---|---|---|---|---|---|---|---|---|---|---|---|---|---|---|---|---|---|---|---|---|---|---|---|---|---|---|---|---|---|---|---|---|---|---|---|
| 14 | aa | 85 | 9 | 3 | 14 | 0 | 293 | | 352 | 484 | 837 | | | 8 | 73 | 0.34 | | | | 37 | | 152 | | | 96 | 0% | 0% | | | | 6.16 | | 63 | 170 | $2 |
| 15 | a/a | 490 | 56 | 11 | 57 | 2 | 272 | | 333 | 398 | 731 | | | 8 | 78 | 0.42 | | | | 33 | | 85 | | | 91 | 1% | 100% | | | | 4.67 | | 27 | 73 | $12 |
| 16 | TEX | 516 | 59 | 20 | 64 | 0 | 266 | 254 | 320 | 419 | 739 | 548 | 791 | 7 | 78 | 0.35 | 49 | 21 | 30 | 30 | 91 | 84 | 77 | 16% | 119 | 1% | 0% | 26 | 38% | 35% | 4.53 | -2.6 | 32 | 91 | $12 |
| 17 | TEX | 554 | 64 | 20 | 101 | 2 | 253 | 256 | 323 | 422 | 745 | 603 | 786 | 9 | 77 | 0.43 | 47 | 19 | 34 | 29 | 102 | 99 | 87 | 14% | 83 | 3% | 50% | 27 | 33% | 19% | 4.57 | -5.8 | 32 | 97 | $13 |
| 18 | TEX | 489 | 61 | 20 | 77 | 1 | 258 | 260 | 317 | 436 | 753 | 697 | 783 | 7 | 76 | 0.34 | 55 | 18 | 27 | 30 | 105 | 108 | 80 | 20% | 91 | 1% | 100% | 23 | 48% | 39% | 4.71 | 2.8 | 36 | 120 | $14 |
| 1st Half | | 308 | 45 | 15 | 55 | 1 | 282 | 279 | 342 | 484 | 826 | 787 | 845 | 8 | 77 | 0.36 | 53 | 22 | 24 | 33 | 109 | 118 | 78 | 26% | 101 | 1% | 100% | 15 | 53% | 33% | 5.84 | 12.0 | 49 | 163 | $24 |
| 2nd Half | | 181 | 16 | 5 | 22 | 0 | 215 | 212 | 274 | 354 | 628 | 563 | 668 | 7 | 76 | 0.32 | 58 | 12 | 30 | 26 | 99 | 90 | 85 | 12% | 85 | 0% | 0% | 8 | 38% | 50% | 3.12 | -7.4 | 17 | 57 | -$3 |
| 19 | Proj | **549** | **65** | **23** | **84** | **1** | **264** | **255** | **324** | **444** | **769** | **659** | **814** | **8** | **77** | **0.37** | **52** | **18** | **30** | **31** | **101** | **107** | **83** | **18%** | **96** | **1%** | **57%** | | | | **4.93** | **7.5** | **24** | **78** | **$18** |

BRIAN SLACK

## McCann,Brian

| Age: 35 Bats: L Pos: CA | Health | D | LIMA Plan | D+ |
|---|---|---|---|---|
| Ht: 6' 3" Wt: 225 | PT/Exp | D | Rand Var | +3 |
| | Consist | B | MM | 2013 |

Lingering 2017 knee issues finally resulted in June surgery, costing him two months. On the field, combining FB% uptick with diminished underlying power proved to be an unappetizing recipe. Age, health, and BA drain now impossible to ignore, but still a potential late-round power source if knee repair enables power recovery.

| Yr | Tm | AB | R | HR | RBI | SB | BA | xBA | OBP | SLG | OPS | vL | vR | bb% | ct% | Eye | G | L | F | h% | HctX | PX | xPX | hr/f | Spd | SBO | SB% | #Wk | DOM | DIS | RC/G | RAR | BPV | BPX | R$ |
|---|---|---|---|---|---|---|---|---|---|---|---|---|---|---|---|---|---|---|---|---|---|---|---|---|---|---|---|---|---|---|---|---|---|---|---|
| 14 | NYY | 495 | 57 | 23 | 75 | 0 | 232 | 266 | 286 | 406 | 692 | 850 | 633 | 6 | 84 | 0.42 | 33 | 22 | 45 | 23 | 113 | 106 | 127 | 12% | 66 | 0% | 0% | 26 | 58% | 23% | 3.76 | 6.5 | 56 | 151 | $11 |
| 15 | NYY | 465 | 68 | 26 | 94 | 0 | 232 | 248 | 320 | 437 | 756 | 753 | 757 | 10 | 79 | 0.54 | 36 | 17 | 47 | 24 | 110 | 120 | 131 | 15% | 64 | 0% | 0% | 27 | 48% | 30% | 4.49 | 10.5 | 53 | 143 | $12 |
| 16 | NYY | 429 | 56 | 20 | 58 | 1 | 242 | 242 | 335 | 413 | 748 | 662 | 770 | 11 | 77 | 0.55 | 34 | 21 | 44 | 27 | 111 | 97 | 120 | 14% | 70 | 1% | 100% | 27 | 44% | 41% | 4.56 | 8.8 | 30 | 86 | $8 |
| 17 | HOU | 349 | 47 | 18 | 62 | 1 | 241 | 261 | 323 | 436 | 759 | 737 | 767 | 10 | 83 | 0.66 | 41 | 17 | 41 | 24 | 99 | 97 | 98 | 15% | 76 | 1% | 100% | 26 | 50% | 12% | 4.63 | 5.1 | 55 | 167 | $7 |
| 18 | HOU * | 211 | 23 | 8 | 25 | 0 | 204 | 218 | 276 | 327 | 603 | 600 | 651 | 9 | 78 | 0.45 | 28 | 22 | 50 | 22 | 74 | 66 | 74 | 9% | 77 | 2% | 0% | 19 | 32% | 47% | 2.83 | -3.5 | 7 | 23 | $0 |
| 1st Half | | 155 | 17 | 5 | 17 | 0 | 206 | 218 | 283 | 323 | 606 | 612 | 602 | 8 | 78 | 0.38 | 28 | 22 | 50 | 23 | 80 | 64 | 72 | 8% | 86 | 0% | 0% | 14 | 36% | 50% | 2.78 | -3.2 | 7 | 23 | $0 |
| 2nd Half | | 56 | 6 | 3 | 8 | 0 | 196 | 216 | 296 | 341 | 637 | 400 | 820 | 12 | 78 | 0.64 | 28 | 21 | 52 | 20 | 49 | 72 | 85 | 13% | 74 | 6% | 0% | 5 | 20% | 40% | 2.97 | -0.9 | 18 | 60 | -$1 |
| **19** | **Proj** | **315** | **38** | **15** | **46** | **0** | **220** | **235** | **314** | **386** | **699** | **631** | **717** | **10** | **80** | **0.55** | **33** | **20** | **47** | **23** | **83** | **87** | **95** | **13%** | **69** | **2%** | **17%** | | | | **3.68** | **2.2** | **20** | **67** | **$4** |

## McCann,James

| Age: 29 Bats: R Pos: CA | Health | A | LIMA Plan | D |
|---|---|---|---|---|
| Ht: 6' 3" Wt: 225 | PT/Exp | C | Rand Var | +1 |
| | Consist | D | MM | 2013 |

Bulked up in offseason ready to take production to new level, only to post worst season yet—despite career-high 112 starts behind the dish. Plate skills and xPX drop-offs weren't as steep, and lowly 22% h% vL should recover, putting modest rebound very much in play. Just, y'know, don't get too excited.

| Yr | Tm | AB | R | HR | RBI | SB | BA | xBA | OBP | SLG | OPS | vL | vR | bb% | ct% | Eye | G | L | F | h% | HctX | PX | xPX | hr/f | Spd | SBO | SB% | #Wk | DOM | DIS | RC/G | RAR | BPV | BPX | R$ |
|---|---|---|---|---|---|---|---|---|---|---|---|---|---|---|---|---|---|---|---|---|---|---|---|---|---|---|---|---|---|---|---|---|---|---|---|
| 14 | DET * | 429 | 40 | 6 | 42 | 8 | 256 | 323 | 289 | 366 | 655 | 333 | 833 | 4 | 77 | 0.20 | 20 | 60 | 20 | 32 | 33 | 95 | 10 | 0% | 74 | 11% | 78% | 3 | 33% | 33% | 3.64 | 4.0 | 16 | 43 | $9 |
| 15 | DET | 401 | 32 | 7 | 41 | 0 | 264 | 254 | 297 | 387 | 683 | 916 | 609 | 4 | 78 | 0.18 | 50 | 23 | 27 | 33 | 90 | 82 | 63 | 8% | 103 | 1% | 0% | 27 | 30% | 48% | 3.87 | 1.6 | 16 | 43 | $6 |
| 16 | DET * | 366 | 33 | 12 | 50 | 0 | 212 | 204 | 267 | 341 | 607 | 848 | 511 | 7 | 68 | 0.23 | 41 | 18 | 41 | 28 | 94 | 83 | 112 | 13% | 94 | 1% | 0% | 25 | 20% | 56% | 2.90 | -10.9 | -15 | -43 | $1 |
| 17 | DET | 352 | 39 | 13 | 49 | 1 | 253 | 260 | 318 | 415 | 733 | 928 | 650 | 7 | 75 | 0.29 | 38 | 28 | 34 | 30 | 116 | 93 | 101 | 14% | 99 | 1% | 100% | 25 | 24% | 28% | 4.32 | 1.9 | 18 | 55 | $6 |
| 18 | DET | 427 | 31 | 8 | 39 | 0 | 220 | 211 | 267 | 314 | 581 | 514 | 602 | 6 | 73 | 0.22 | 38 | 22 | 39 | 28 | 98 | 63 | 90 | 7% | 66 | 3% | 0% | 28 | 11% | 54% | 2.63 | -9.8 | -24 | -80 | $1 |
| 1st Half | | 222 | 17 | 4 | 22 | 0 | 230 | 222 | 279 | 324 | 603 | 792 | 547 | 6 | 77 | 0.30 | 39 | 22 | 39 | 28 | 107 | 61 | 83 | 6% | 69 | 4% | 0% | 15 | 13% | 47% | 2.87 | -3.9 | -6 | -20 | $1 |
| 2nd Half | | 205 | 14 | 4 | 17 | 0 | 210 | 200 | 253 | 302 | 556 | 230 | 663 | 5 | 68 | 0.17 | 38 | 23 | 40 | 29 | 88 | 66 | 99 | 7% | 77 | 2% | 0% | 13 | 8% | 62% | 2.38 | -6.8 | -41 | -137 | $0 |
| **19** | **Proj** | **363** | **31** | **10** | **40** | **1** | **230** | **228** | **280** | **359** | **639** | **712** | **612** | **6** | **72** | **0.22** | **40** | **23** | **37** | **29** | **100** | **82** | **95** | **11%** | **83** | **3%** | **29%** | | | | **3.21** | **-2.6** | **-20** | **-67** | **$5** |

## McCutchen,Andrew

| Age: 32 Bats: R Pos: RF | Health | A | LIMA Plan | B |
|---|---|---|---|---|
| Ht: 5' 11" Wt: 195 | PT/Exp | A | Rand Var | 0 |
| | Consist | C | MM | 3235 |

Career-worst BA, alarming SB%, and lowest HR/RBI totals since 2011. Not exactly Hype Machine material. But wait: HctX/xPX still well above league-average, growing patience, and Sept in NYY (5 HR, 123 PX) shows upside in hitters' park. Still a valuable profile, even if different than in years past.

| Yr | Tm | AB | R | HR | RBI | SB | BA | xBA | OBP | SLG | OPS | vL | vR | bb% | ct% | Eye | G | L | F | h% | HctX | PX | xPX | hr/f | Spd | SBO | SB% | #Wk | DOM | DIS | RC/G | RAR | BPV | BPX | R$ |
|---|---|---|---|---|---|---|---|---|---|---|---|---|---|---|---|---|---|---|---|---|---|---|---|---|---|---|---|---|---|---|---|---|---|---|---|
| 14 | PIT | 548 | 89 | 25 | 83 | 18 | 314 | 284 | 410 | 542 | 952 | 912 | 962 | 13 | 79 | 0.73 | 40 | 19 | 41 | 36 | 139 | 159 | 155 | 14% | 128 | 11% | 86% | 26 | 62% | 12% | 8.27 | 64.9 | 110 | 297 | $36 |
| 15 | PIT | 566 | 91 | 23 | 96 | 11 | 292 | 268 | 401 | 488 | 889 | 918 | 881 | 14 | 77 | 0.74 | 38 | 24 | 38 | 35 | 131 | 132 | 158 | 14% | 107 | 8% | 69% | 27 | 59% | 30% | 6.88 | 33.6 | 74 | 200 | $28 |
| 16 | PIT | 598 | 81 | 24 | 79 | 6 | 256 | 249 | 336 | 430 | 766 | 741 | 772 | 10 | 76 | 0.48 | 36 | 22 | 42 | 30 | 111 | 104 | 134 | 13% | 107 | 8% | 46% | 27 | 37% | 30% | 4.73 | 0.4 | 42 | 120 | $16 |
| 17 | PIT | 570 | 94 | 28 | 88 | 11 | 279 | 276 | 363 | 486 | 849 | 1131 | 769 | 11 | 80 | 0.63 | 41 | 22 | 37 | 31 | 114 | 113 | 109 | 16% | 92 | 9% | 69% | 27 | 56% | 15% | 6.13 | 19.5 | 61 | 185 | $24 |
| 18 | 2 TM | 569 | 83 | 20 | 65 | 14 | 255 | 250 | 368 | 424 | 792 | 819 | 777 | 14 | 75 | 0.66 | 41 | 23 | 36 | 31 | 119 | 105 | 125 | 13% | 101 | 12% | 61% | 27 | 44% | 19% | 5.10 | 9.9 | 42 | 140 | $19 |
| 1st Half | | 304 | 47 | 9 | 37 | 6 | 266 | 255 | 351 | 441 | 792 | 818 | 777 | 11 | 74 | 0.48 | 35 | 27 | 39 | 33 | 130 | 117 | 148 | 10% | 120 | 10% | 67% | 15 | 47% | 33% | 5.25 | 7.1 | 49 | 163 | $21 |
| 2nd Half | | 265 | 36 | 11 | 28 | 8 | 242 | 244 | 386 | 404 | 789 | 819 | 776 | 18 | 75 | 0.88 | 49 | 19 | 33 | 28 | 107 | 93 | 98 | 17% | 86 | 14% | 57% | 12 | 42% | 0% | 4.90 | 3.6 | 40 | 133 | $18 |
| **19** | **Proj** | **516** | **77** | **23** | **67** | **8** | **264** | **259** | **368** | **455** | **822** | **891** | **797** | **13** | **76** | **0.65** | **41** | **22** | **37** | **31** | **117** | **113** | **122** | **15%** | **99** | **9%** | **55%** | | | | **5.53** | **16.2** | **48** | **159** | **$20** |

## McKinney,Billy

| Age: 24 Bats: L Pos: LF | Health | B | LIMA Plan | D+ |
|---|---|---|---|---|
| Ht: 6' 1" Wt: 205 | PT/Exp | C | Rand Var | +5 |
| | Consist | C | MM | 4133 |

6-13-.252 in 119 AB at NYY/TOR. Unsung prospect landed in TOR via trade, arriving with a bang (3 HR, 38 AB) in August before cooling down the stretch. MiLB power uptick aided by swing change, but small-sample PX/xPX (136/79) gap in MLB warns of caution. A dart throw, preferably with BA cushion.

| Yr | Tm | AB | R | HR | RBI | SB | BA | xBA | OBP | SLG | OPS | vL | vR | bb% | ct% | Eye | G | L | F | h% | HctX | PX | xPX | hr/f | Spd | SBO | SB% | #Wk | DOM | DIS | RC/G | RAR | BPV | BPX | R$ |
|---|---|---|---|---|---|---|---|---|---|---|---|---|---|---|---|---|---|---|---|---|---|---|---|---|---|---|---|---|---|---|---|---|---|---|---|
| 14 | | | | | | | | | | | | | | | | | | | | | | | | | | | | | | | | | | | |
| 15 | aa | 274 | 23 | 3 | 32 | 0 | 260 | | 315 | 381 | 696 | | | 8 | 81 | 0.43 | | | | 31 | | 95 | | | 82 | 0% | 0% | | | | 4.14 | | 42 | 114 | $3 |
| 16 | aa | 426 | 49 | 4 | 41 | 4 | 235 | | 323 | 321 | 643 | | | 12 | 75 | 0.52 | | | | 30 | | 59 | | | 105 | 8% | 37% | | | | 3.29 | | 5 | 14 | $3 |
| 17 | a/a | 441 | 61 | 17 | 59 | 2 | 259 | | 315 | 457 | 772 | | | 8 | 76 | 0.35 | | | | 30 | | 115 | | | 113 | 3% | 63% | | | | 4.93 | | 48 | 145 | $10 |
| 18 | 2 AL * | 413 | 47 | 19 | 47 | 2 | 217 | 253 | 283 | 433 | 716 | 551 | 829 | 8 | 72 | 0.33 | 37 | 24 | 39 | 25 | 88 | 130 | 79 | 18% | 114 | 4% | 62% | 9 | 33% | 44% | 3.97 | -6.9 | 44 | 147 | $6 |
| 1st Half | | 164 | 19 | 9 | 21 | 1 | 207 | 252 | 268 | 450 | 717 | 0 | 500 | 8 | 74 | 0.31 | 67 | 0 | 33 | 22 | 0 | 139 | -27 | 0% | 126 | 7% | 43% | 1 | 0% | 100% | 3.77 | -3.5 | 62 | 207 | $3 |
| 2nd Half | | 249 | 28 | 10 | 26 | 1 | 224 | 245 | 293 | 422 | 715 | 551 | 843 | 9 | 70 | 0.33 | 36 | 25 | 39 | 28 | 90 | 124 | 83 | 18% | 109 | 2% | 100% | 8 | 38% | 38% | 4.08 | -2.8 | 33 | 110 | $8 |
| **19** | **Proj** | **320** | **37** | **14** | **37** | **2** | **235** | **260** | **304** | **445** | **749** | **568** | **789** | **9** | **74** | **0.37** | **36** | **25** | **39** | **27** | **104** | **126** | **75** | **15%** | **100** | **4%** | **56%** | | | | **4.41** | **-1.8** | **42** | **139** | **$7** |

## McMahon,Ryan

| Age: 24 Bats: L Pos: 1B | Health | A | LIMA Plan | C+ |
|---|---|---|---|---|
| Ht: 6' 2" Wt: 185 | PT/Exp | C | Rand Var | +1 |
| | Consist | F | MM | 3233 |

5-19-.232 in 181 AB at COL. Failed to earn steady AB despite cracking Opening Day roster, riding shuttle to/from AAA while working at 2B/3B to improve versatility. Power recovered in 2nd half, and still owns 2017's MiLB breakout skills, with ct% rebound now the missing ingredient. Could emerge quickly.

| Yr | Tm | AB | R | HR | RBI | SB | BA | xBA | OBP | SLG | OPS | vL | vR | bb% | ct% | Eye | G | L | F | h% | HctX | PX | xPX | hr/f | Spd | SBO | SB% | #Wk | DOM | DIS | RC/G | RAR | BPV | BPX | R$ |
|---|---|---|---|---|---|---|---|---|---|---|---|---|---|---|---|---|---|---|---|---|---|---|---|---|---|---|---|---|---|---|---|---|---|---|---|
| 14 | | | | | | | | | | | | | | | | | | | | | | | | | | | | | | | | | | | |
| 15 | | | | | | | | | | | | | | | | | | | | | | | | | | | | | | | | | | | |
| 16 | aa | 466 | 42 | 11 | 64 | 9 | 247 | | 316 | 403 | 719 | | | 9 | 67 | 0.30 | | | | 35 | | 114 | | | 99 | 13% | 60% | | | | 4.18 | | 8 | 23 | $9 |
| 17 | COL * | 489 | 59 | 17 | 69 | 9 | 331 | 290 | 379 | 532 | 911 | 200 | 635 | 7 | 80 | 0.38 | 86 | 0 | 14 | 39 | 69 | 118 | 81 | 0% | 102 | 8% | 72% | 7 | 14% | 71% | 7.62 | 22.2 | 60 | 182 | $25 |
| 18 | COL * | 405 | 42 | 13 | 49 | 3 | 243 | 242 | 292 | 410 | 701 | 967 | 618 | 6 | 68 | 0.21 | 46 | 24 | 30 | 33 | 85 | 114 | 99 | 14% | 98 | 6% | 56% | 21 | 29% | 67% | 3.96 | -13.8 | 8 | 27 | $8 |
| 1st Half | | 221 | 20 | 5 | 24 | 0 | 220 | 233 | 278 | 369 | 647 | 851 | 553 | 7 | 64 | 0.22 | 52 | 25 | 23 | 32 | 62 | 109 | 67 | 14% | 113 | 2% | 0% | 11 | 27% | 73% | 3.28 | -10.1 | -6 | -20 | $3 |
| 2nd Half | | 184 | 22 | 7 | 26 | 3 | 271 | 253 | 308 | 459 | 767 | 1170 | 683 | 5 | 73 | 0.20 | 39 | 23 | 38 | 34 | 113 | 121 | 133 | 14% | 94 | 10% | 72% | 10 | 30% | 60% | 4.90 | 0.7 | 30 | 100 | $13 |
| **19** | **Proj** | **359** | **39** | **12** | **48** | **5** | **273** | **259** | **330** | **455** | **784** | **730** | **796** | **7** | **73** | **0.27** | **45** | **24** | **32** | **35** | **93** | **119** | **107** | **14%** | **95** | **9%** | **68%** | | | | **5.09** | **3.3** | **29** | **96** | **$13** |

## McNeil,Jeff

| Age: 27 Bats: L Pos: 2B | Health | A | LIMA Plan | B+ |
|---|---|---|---|---|
| Ht: 6' 1" Wt: 195 | PT/Exp | F | Rand Var | -1 |
| | Consist | F | MM | 1535 |

3-19-.329 with 7 SB in 225 AB at NYM. Burst onto scene after tearing up AA/AAA. Near-elite contact skills and underlying power, with makings of a sneaky speed source. Injury history, MLB BA/xBA (.329/.263) gap, and limited MiLB track record urge prudence though. Enjoy, just don't extrapolate.

| Yr | Tm | AB | R | HR | RBI | SB | BA | xBA | OBP | SLG | OPS | vL | vR | bb% | ct% | Eye | G | L | F | h% | HctX | PX | xPX | hr/f | Spd | SBO | SB% | #Wk | DOM | DIS | RC/G | RAR | BPV | BPX | R$ |
|---|---|---|---|---|---|---|---|---|---|---|---|---|---|---|---|---|---|---|---|---|---|---|---|---|---|---|---|---|---|---|---|---|---|---|---|
| 14 | | | | | | | | | | | | | | | | | | | | | | | | | | | | | | | | | | | |
| 15 | | | | | | | | | | | | | | | | | | | | | | | | | | | | | | | | | | | |
| 16 | | | | | | | | | | | | | | | | | | | | | | | | | | | | | | | | | | | |
| 17 | aaa | 71 | 8 | 1 | 4 | 1 | 197 | | 221 | 281 | 502 | | | 3 | 83 | 0.17 | | | | 23 | | 55 | | | 101 | 12% | 100% | | | | 2.04 | | 13 | 39 | -$2 |
| 18 | NYM * | 564 | 85 | 16 | 68 | 11 | 292 | 270 | 339 | 464 | 803 | 812 | 866 | 7 | 86 | 0.52 | 39 | 22 | 40 | 32 | 96 | 92 | 103 | 4% | 141 | 8% | 92% | 11 | 73% | 9% | 5.76 | 23.4 | 76 | 253 | $23 |
| 1st Half | | 274 | 41 | 11 | 39 | 3 | 268 | 279 | 320 | 464 | 784 | | | 7 | 83 | 0.46 | | | | 29 | | 110 | | | 105 | 5% | 100% | | | | 5.26 | | 69 | 230 | $20 |
| 2nd Half | | 290 | 44 | 5 | 29 | 8 | 315 | 268 | 357 | 465 | 822 | 812 | 866 | 6 | 89 | 0.60 | 39 | 22 | 40 | 34 | 99 | 77 | 103 | 4% | 160 | 10% | 88% | 11 | 73% | 9% | 6.27 | 16.4 | 80 | 267 | $26 |
| **19** | **Proj** | **491** | **69** | **9** | **51** | **10** | **276** | **263** | **335** | **422** | **757** | **735** | **764** | **6** | **87** | **0.51** | **39** | **22** | **40** | **30** | **89** | **80** | **93** | **5%** | **146** | **9%** | **91%** | | | | **4.88** | **9.8** | **66** | **219** | **$18** |

## Meadows,Austin

| Age: 24 Bats: L Pos: RF | Health | A | LIMA Plan | B |
|---|---|---|---|---|
| Ht: 6'3" Wt: 210 | PT/Exp | D | Rand Var | 0 |
| | Consist | F | MM | 3543 |

6-17-.287 with 5 SB in 178 AB with PIT/TAM. After two injury-plagued seasons, touted prospect debuted with electric May (4 HR, 3 SB) before PT squeeze and eventual trade. BA contribution hardly assured, but speed and strong xPX make for nice power/speed threat. With AB, potential for... UP: 20 HR, 15 SB

| Yr | Tm | AB | R | HR | RBI | SB | BA | xBA | OBP | SLG | OPS | vL | vR | bb% | ct% | Eye | G | L | F | h% | HctX | PX | xPX | hr/f | Spd | SBO | SB% | #Wk | DOM | DIS | RC/G | RAR | BPV | BPX | R$ |
|---|---|---|---|---|---|---|---|---|---|---|---|---|---|---|---|---|---|---|---|---|---|---|---|---|---|---|---|---|---|---|---|---|---|---|---|
| 14 | | | | | | | | | | | | | | | | | | | | | | | | | | | | | | | | | | | |
| 15 | aa | 25 | 4 | 0 | 1 | 1 | 340 | | 381 | 597 | 979 | | | 6 | 79 | 0.33 | | | | 43 | | 151 | | | 145 | 14% | 100% | | | | 9.08 | | 97 | 262 | -$1 |
| 16 | a/a | 293 | 44 | 10 | 43 | 15 | 261 | | 326 | 514 | 840 | | | 9 | 77 | 0.42 | | | | 31 | | 150 | | | 130 | 33% | 74% | | | | 5.66 | | 87 | 249 | $12 |
| 17 | aaa | 284 | 44 | 3 | 33 | 10 | 236 | | 290 | 337 | 627 | | | 7 | 82 | 0.42 | | | | 28 | | 66 | | | 89 | 20% | 76% | | | | 3.27 | | 22 | 67 | $6 |
| 18 | 2 TM * | 439 | 59 | 16 | 54 | 15 | 276 | 272 | 314 | 463 | 777 | 921 | 707 | 5 | 81 | 0.30 | 41 | 21 | 37 | 31 | 111 | 111 | 139 | 12% | 122 | 19% | 83% | 13 | 31% | 38% | 5.17 | 8.2 | 62 | 207 | $18 |
| 1st Half | | 247 | 31 | 6 | 26 | 11 | 287 | 254 | 322 | 437 | 760 | 1224 | 713 | 5 | 80 | 0.26 | 42 | 20 | 38 | 34 | 123 | 93 | 151 | 14% | 119 | 22% | 84% | 8 | 25% | 38% | 5.13 | 4.7 | 42 | 140 | $20 |
| 2nd Half | | 192 | 28 | 10 | 28 | 4 | 261 | 298 | 304 | 496 | 800 | 454 | 688 | 6 | 82 | 0.35 | 40 | 24 | 36 | 27 | 79 | 134 | 110 | 7% | 117 | 15% | 80% | 5 | 40% | 40% | 5.20 | 4.2 | 85 | 283 | $16 |
| **19** | **Proj** | **327** | **48** | **11** | **42** | **11** | **260** | **272** | **309** | **444** | **753** | **770** | **742** | **7** | **81** | **0.37** | **41** | **22** | **37** | **29** | **97** | **109** | **126** | **11%** | **134** | **20%** | **79%** | | | | **4.73** | **2.7** | **62** | **206** | **$14** |

BRIAN SLACK

## Mejia,Francisco

| | | | |
|---|---|---|---|
| Age: 23 Bats: B Pos: CA | Health A | LIMA Plan D+ | |
| Ht: 5' 10" Wt: 180 | PT/Exp F | Rand Var 0 | |
| | Consist D | MM 4243 | |

3-9-.174 in 54 AB at CLE/SD. Premier prospect changed hands at mid-season and spent most of the year in Triple-A (.293/.338/.471). Has had contact issues in brief MLB turns, but projects as pure hitter. Arm shines but receiving skills lag; has also taken cameo roles at 3B/OF. Good luck getting him this cheap.

| Yr | Tm | AB | R | HR | RBI | SB | BA | xBA | OBP | SLG | OPS | vL | vR | bb% | ct% | Eye | G | L | F | h% | HctX | PX | xPX | hr/f | Spd | SBO | SB% | #Wk | DOM | DIS | RC/G | RAR | BPV | BPX | R$ |
|---|---|---|---|---|---|---|---|---|---|---|---|---|---|---|---|---|---|---|---|---|---|---|---|---|---|---|---|---|---|---|---|---|---|---|---|
| 14 | | | | | | | | | | | | | | | | | | | | | | | | | | | | | | | | | | | |
| 15 | | | | | | | | | | | | | | | | | | | | | | | | | | | | | | | | | | | |
| 16 | | | | | | | | | | | | | | | | | | | | | | | | | | | | | | | | | | | |
| 17 | CLE * | 360 | 44 | 12 | 44 | 6 | 278 | 314 | 318 | 445 | 763 | 333 | 393 | 6 | 83 | 0.36 | 50 | 30 | 20 | 31 | 135 | 92 | 49 | 0% | 92 | 9% | 73% | 4 | 0% | 50% | 4.97 | 1.0 | 48 | 145 | $11 |
| 18 | 2 TM * | 483 | 44 | 12 | 56 | 0 | 234 | 234 | 269 | 373 | 642 | 510 | 757 | 4 | 76 | 0.19 | 54 | 16 | 30 | 28 | 98 | 90 | 74 | 27% | 87 | 0% | 0% | 6 | 33% | 50% | 3.34 | -16.9 | 13 | 43 | $5 |
| 1st Half | | 265 | 20 | 5 | 28 | 0 | 240 | 232 | 273 | 361 | 634 | | | 4 | 76 | 0.19 | | | | 30 | | 83 | | | 93 | 0% | 0% | | | | 3.30 | | 10 | 33 | $4 |
| 2nd Half | | 218 | 24 | 8 | 28 | 0 | 228 | 242 | 264 | 387 | 651 | 510 | 757 | 5 | 76 | 0.20 | 54 | 16 | 30 | 27 | 98 | 98 | 74 | 27% | 94 | 0% | 0% | 6 | 33% | 50% | 3.37 | -7.5 | 21 | 70 | $7 |
| **19** | **Proj** | **366** | **39** | **18** | **44** | **2** | **252** | **272** | **300** | **460** | **760** | **656** | **868** | **5** | **79** | **0.25** | **54** | **16** | **30** | **27** | **88** | **121** | **67** | **21%** | **90** | **5%** | **75%** | | | | **4.52** | **11.6** | **42** | **139** | **$8** |

## Mercer,Jordy

| | | | |
|---|---|---|---|
| Age: 32 Bats: R Pos: SS | Health B | LIMA Plan C | |
| Ht: 6' 3" Wt: 210 | PT/Exp B | Rand Var 0 | |
| | Consist A | MM 2235 | |

Range of predictable outcomes is quite small and kind of drab. Plate skills are decent and he pops one occasionally, but usually fills box scores with 1-for-4s. Ended up losing 2nd half PT, which had negligible impact on value. Don't expect him to break out of his torpor with anything special.

| Yr | Tm | AB | R | HR | RBI | SB | BA | xBA | OBP | SLG | OPS | vL | vR | bb% | ct% | Eye | G | L | F | h% | HctX | PX | xPX | hr/f | Spd | SBO | SB% | #Wk | DOM | DIS | RC/G | RAR | BPV | BPX | R$ |
|---|---|---|---|---|---|---|---|---|---|---|---|---|---|---|---|---|---|---|---|---|---|---|---|---|---|---|---|---|---|---|---|---|---|---|---|
| 14 | PIT | 506 | 56 | 12 | 55 | 4 | 255 | 264 | 305 | 387 | 693 | 803 | 658 | 6 | 82 | 0.39 | 48 | 20 | 32 | 29 | 90 | 94 | 89 | 9% | 106 | 4% | 80% | 27 | 37% | 33% | 4.03 | 10.9 | 51 | 138 | $11 |
| 15 | PIT * | 419 | 36 | 4 | 36 | 3 | 240 | 238 | 288 | 317 | 605 | 738 | 580 | 6 | 81 | 0.35 | 49 | 21 | 31 | 29 | 89 | 58 | 87 | 3% | 86 | 5% | 60% | 23 | 26% | 52% | 3.03 | -9.2 | 11 | 30 | $3 |
| 16 | PIT | 519 | 66 | 11 | 59 | 1 | 256 | 257 | 328 | 374 | 701 | 829 | 669 | 9 | 84 | 0.61 | 49 | 20 | 32 | 29 | 86 | 68 | 60 | 8% | 116 | 1% | 50% | 26 | 31% | 15% | 4.12 | -7.6 | 45 | 129 | $9 |
| 17 | PIT | 502 | 52 | 14 | 58 | 0 | 255 | 268 | 326 | 406 | 733 | 723 | 735 | 9 | 82 | 0.58 | 48 | 21 | 31 | 28 | 104 | 82 | 87 | 11% | 114 | 3% | 0% | 25 | 48% | 20% | 4.36 | -2.3 | 50 | 152 | $7 |
| 18 | PIT | 394 | 43 | 6 | 39 | 2 | 251 | 260 | 315 | 381 | 696 | 754 | 674 | 7 | 78 | 0.37 | 38 | 27 | 34 | 31 | 86 | 89 | 78 | 6% | 98 | 2% | 100% | 26 | 23% | 38% | 4.02 | 2.3 | 29 | 97 | $6 |
| 1st Half | | 254 | 28 | 5 | 26 | 0 | 252 | 251 | 313 | 394 | 707 | 748 | 694 | 7 | 78 | 0.36 | 40 | 23 | 37 | 31 | 83 | 92 | 85 | 7% | 111 | 0% | 0% | 15 | 27% | 53% | 4.11 | 1.1 | 35 | 117 | $7 |
| 2nd Half | | 140 | 15 | 1 | 13 | 2 | 250 | 279 | 318 | 357 | 675 | 763 | 635 | 8 | 78 | 0.39 | 35 | 36 | 29 | 31 | 91 | 83 | 67 | 3% | 78 | 6% | 100% | 11 | 18% | 18% | 3.84 | -0.5 | 19 | 63 | $2 |
| **19** | **Proj** | **451** | **49** | **8** | **47** | **2** | **252** | **263** | **318** | **377** | **695** | **757** | **674** | **8** | **80** | **0.44** | **43** | **25** | **32** | **30** | **92** | **80** | **77** | **7%** | **99** | **3%** | **67%** | | | | **4.01** | **0.6** | **24** | **80** | **$9** |

## Merrifield,Whit

| | | | |
|---|---|---|---|
| Age: 30 Bats: R Pos: 2B CF | Health A | LIMA Plan D+ | |
| Ht: 6' 0" Wt: 195 | PT/Exp B | Rand Var -5 | |
| | Consist C | MM 2545 | |

Value has soared along with SB totals, but there's more. Good ct%, HctX should keep BA floor high even with regression of absurd LD%; bb% increase puts more O in SBO. PX/xPX shows room for a little more power, though his is mostly of inside-the-park variety. Enjoy him for what he is; run with it.

| Yr | Tm | AB | R | HR | RBI | SB | BA | xBA | OBP | SLG | OPS | vL | vR | bb% | ct% | Eye | G | L | F | h% | HctX | PX | xPX | hr/f | Spd | SBO | SB% | #Wk | DOM | DIS | RC/G | RAR | BPV | BPX | R$ |
|---|---|---|---|---|---|---|---|---|---|---|---|---|---|---|---|---|---|---|---|---|---|---|---|---|---|---|---|---|---|---|---|---|---|---|---|
| 14 | a/a | 483 | 57 | 6 | 36 | 12 | 269 | | 309 | 391 | 700 | | | 5 | 82 | 0.31 | | | | 32 | | 96 | | | 103 | 22% | 47% | | | | 3.86 | | 47 | 127 | $13 |
| 15 | aaa | 544 | 63 | 4 | 29 | 24 | 226 | | 266 | 310 | 576 | | | 5 | 86 | 0.39 | | | | 26 | | 57 | | | 122 | 30% | 70% | | | | 2.67 | | 39 | 105 | $9 |
| 16 | KC * | 585 | 76 | 7 | 49 | 22 | 252 | 257 | 293 | 364 | 657 | 891 | 657 | 5 | 77 | 0.25 | 45 | 26 | 30 | 32 | 111 | 81 | 87 | 3% | 123 | 21% | 80% | 17 | 24% | 47% | 3.68 | -18.1 | 21 | 60 | $15 |
| 17 | KC * | 621 | 84 | 21 | 85 | 35 | 291 | 274 | 323 | 469 | 792 | 800 | 780 | 4 | 85 | 0.32 | 38 | 22 | 40 | 31 | 105 | 94 | 111 | 9% | 130 | 30% | 79% | 25 | 44% | 12% | 5.43 | 14.1 | 65 | 197 | $34 |
| 18 | KC | 632 | 88 | 12 | 60 | 45 | 304 | 269 | 367 | 438 | 806 | 945 | 750 | 9 | 82 | 0.54 | 35 | 30 | 35 | 36 | 111 | 85 | 100 | 7% | 107 | 28% | 82% | 28 | 43% | 21% | 6.00 | 33.9 | 47 | 157 | $38 |
| 1st Half | | 304 | 32 | 4 | 24 | 16 | 289 | 260 | 362 | 405 | 766 | 1039 | 629 | 9 | 81 | 0.53 | 35 | 28 | 37 | 35 | 119 | 80 | 110 | 4% | 82 | 22% | 80% | 15 | 40% | 13% | 5.21 | 9.0 | 34 | 113 | $23 |
| 2nd Half | | 328 | 56 | 8 | 36 | 29 | 317 | 278 | 373 | 470 | 842 | 822 | 849 | 9 | 83 | 0.54 | 35 | 32 | 33 | 37 | 104 | 90 | 90 | 9% | 127 | 34% | 83% | 13 | 46% | 31% | 6.77 | 23.4 | 60 | 200 | $52 |
| **19** | **Proj** | **619** | **85** | **13** | **63** | **37** | **293** | **265** | **344** | **434** | **778** | **872** | **747** | **7** | **82** | **0.42** | **37** | **27** | **36** | **34** | **108** | **87** | **101** | **7%** | **122** | **27%** | **80%** | | | | **5.41** | **21.6** | **52** | **174** | **$35** |

## Mesoraco,Devin

| | | | |
|---|---|---|---|
| Age: 31 Bats: R Pos: CA | Health F | LIMA Plan D | |
| Ht: 6' 1" Wt: 229 | PT/Exp F | Rand Var -1 | |
| | Consist C | MM 2111 | |

First things first: zero DL days in 2018. But stripped of that reference point, what do we have? Takes a walk, makes decent contact with average power, and with such a steady dose of FB, some have to clear the fence. Still a huge health risk, so best case for free agent is as short-term solution or #2 CA.

| Yr | Tm | AB | R | HR | RBI | SB | BA | xBA | OBP | SLG | OPS | vL | vR | bb% | ct% | Eye | G | L | F | h% | HctX | PX | xPX | hr/f | Spd | SBO | SB% | #Wk | DOM | DIS | RC/G | RAR | BPV | BPX | R$ |
|---|---|---|---|---|---|---|---|---|---|---|---|---|---|---|---|---|---|---|---|---|---|---|---|---|---|---|---|---|---|---|---|---|---|---|---|
| 14 | CIN | 384 | 54 | 25 | 80 | 1 | 273 | 287 | 359 | 534 | 893 | 925 | 883 | 9 | 73 | 0.40 | 34 | 23 | 43 | 31 | 123 | 192 | 165 | 20% | 59 | 4% | 25% | 24 | 54% | 25% | 6.25 | 30.9 | 85 | 230 | $18 |
| 15 | CIN | 45 | 2 | 0 | 2 | 1 | 178 | 192 | 275 | 244 | 519 | 481 | 536 | 10 | 80 | 0.56 | 42 | 14 | 44 | 22 | 67 | 40 | 67 | 0% | 103 | 9% | 100% | 7 | 43% | 43% | 2.07 | -2.4 | 4 | 11 | -$3 |
| 16 | CIN | 50 | 2 | 0 | 1 | 0 | 140 | 214 | 218 | 160 | 378 | 507 | 320 | 9 | 80 | 0.50 | 48 | 23 | 30 | 18 | 49 | 17 | 7 | 0% | 97 | 9% | 0% | 4 | 25% | 50% | 0.93 | -5.9 | -16 | -46 | -$4 |
| 17 | CIN * | 195 | 21 | 8 | 20 | 1 | 192 | 228 | 285 | 352 | 637 | 645 | 748 | 11 | 71 | 0.45 | 41 | 19 | 39 | 23 | 83 | 93 | 84 | 15% | 88 | 2% | 100% | 16 | 31% | 50% | 3.19 | -5.3 | 11 | 33 | -$2 |
| 18 | 2 NL | 244 | 24 | 11 | 33 | 0 | 221 | 233 | 303 | 398 | 700 | 708 | 697 | 9 | 79 | 0.48 | 36 | 18 | 47 | 24 | 93 | 100 | 98 | 12% | 80 | 0% | 0% | 26 | 38% | 27% | 3.82 | 2.3 | 39 | 130 | $2 |
| 1st Half | | 148 | 17 | 7 | 19 | 0 | 223 | 245 | 311 | 405 | 717 | 738 | 706 | 9 | 80 | 0.50 | 39 | 19 | 42 | 23 | 100 | 102 | 93 | 14% | 83 | 0% | 0% | 15 | 33% | 27% | 3.92 | 2.1 | 46 | 153 | $3 |
| 2nd Half | | 96 | 7 | 4 | 14 | 0 | 219 | 214 | 290 | 385 | 675 | 642 | 684 | 9 | 77 | 0.45 | 31 | 16 | 53 | 24 | 83 | 98 | 106 | 10% | 80 | 0% | 0% | 11 | 45% | 27% | 3.68 | 0.7 | 32 | 107 | $1 |
| **19** | **Proj** | **221** | **23** | **8** | **30** | **0** | **231** | **228** | **316** | **388** | **704** | **699** | **704** | **10** | **75** | **0.44** | **38** | **19** | **43** | **27** | **85** | **95** | **89** | **12%** | **84** | **1%** | **65%** | | | | **3.94** | **3.3** | **9** | **30** | **$4** |

## Miller,Bradley

| | | | |
|---|---|---|---|
| Age: 29 Bats: L Pos: 1B 2B | Health B | LIMA Plan D | |
| Ht: 6' 2" Wt: 215 | PT/Exp C | Rand Var -4 | |
| | Consist B | MM 3301 | |

7-29-.248 in 230 AB at TAM/MIL. Sure, extrapolating output into full season produces decent MI line. But severe contact issues are derailing opportunities to do so, dragging down xBA and reducing xPX to a tease. In 2018, BPV was under zero in two of every three weeks. In 2019, playing time will follow suit.

| Yr | Tm | AB | R | HR | RBI | SB | BA | xBA | OBP | SLG | OPS | vL | vR | bb% | ct% | Eye | G | L | F | h% | HctX | PX | xPX | hr/f | Spd | SBO | SB% | #Wk | DOM | DIS | RC/G | RAR | BPV | BPX | R$ |
|---|---|---|---|---|---|---|---|---|---|---|---|---|---|---|---|---|---|---|---|---|---|---|---|---|---|---|---|---|---|---|---|---|---|---|---|
| 14 | SEA | 367 | 47 | 10 | 36 | 4 | 221 | 236 | 288 | 365 | 653 | 542 | 692 | 8 | 74 | 0.36 | 42 | 19 | 39 | 27 | 98 | 105 | 105 | 10% | 117 | 7% | 67% | 27 | 37% | 52% | 3.40 | 0.0 | 34 | 92 | $4 |
| 15 | SEA | 438 | 44 | 11 | 46 | 13 | 258 | 254 | 329 | 402 | 730 | 513 | 803 | 9 | 77 | 0.47 | 48 | 20 | 31 | 31 | 106 | 97 | 97 | 10% | 108 | 14% | 76% | 27 | 22% | 41% | 4.57 | 5.1 | 39 | 105 | $12 |
| 16 | TAM | 548 | 73 | 30 | 81 | 6 | 243 | 268 | 304 | 482 | 786 | 682 | 812 | 8 | 73 | 0.32 | 45 | 19 | 37 | 28 | 104 | 147 | 116 | 20% | 99 | 9% | 60% | 26 | 62% | 19% | 4.81 | -0.9 | 56 | 160 | $15 |
| 17 | TAM | 338 | 43 | 9 | 40 | 5 | 201 | 214 | 327 | 337 | 664 | 679 | 659 | 15 | 67 | 0.57 | 47 | 17 | 36 | 27 | 105 | 88 | 94 | 11% | 120 | 8% | 63% | 22 | 32% | 45% | 3.48 | -16.4 | 9 | 27 | $1 |
| 18 | 2 TM * | 257 | 23 | 8 | 30 | 1 | 236 | 210 | 300 | 391 | 691 | 653 | 736 | 8 | 64 | 0.25 | 40 | 20 | 40 | 34 | 98 | 114 | 150 | 12% | 106 | 1% | 100% | 17 | 18% | 65% | 3.93 | -2.5 | -3 | -10 | $2 |
| 1st Half | | 204 | 20 | 7 | 26 | 1 | 243 | 218 | 313 | 409 | 722 | 685 | 786 | 9 | 64 | 0.29 | 37 | 21 | 42 | 34 | 98 | 123 | 154 | 12% | 102 | 1% | 100% | 14 | 21% | 57% | 4.33 | 0.9 | 7 | 23 | $5 |
| 2nd Half | | 53 | 3 | 1 | 4 | 0 | 208 | 179 | 250 | 321 | 571 | 400 | 588 | 5 | 60 | 0.14 | 50 | 16 | 34 | 32 | 97 | 77 | 137 | 9% | 117 | 0% | 0% | 3 | 0% | 100% | 2.58 | -2.6 | -49 | -163 | -$6 |
| **19** | **Proj** | **191** | **19** | **6** | **21** | **2** | **222** | **214** | **294** | **372** | **665** | **609** | **678** | **9** | **66** | **0.30** | **45** | **18** | **37** | **30** | **101** | **101** | **123** | **12%** | **113** | **5%** | **67%** | | | | **3.56** | **-7.1** | **-8** | **-28** | **$3** |

## Molina,Yadier

| | | | |
|---|---|---|---|
| Age: 36 Bats: R Pos: CA | Health B | LIMA Plan B | |
| Ht: 5' 11" Wt: 205 | PT/Exp B | Rand Var +1 | |
| | Consist B | MM 2145 | |

Late-career surge continues, highlighted by three-year PX/xPX hike that may have produced career-high HR had he not missed a month (groin). Skills remain vintage across the board despite age and rigors of the position. The end is out there somewhere, but it's not within view quite yet, so ride the wave.

| Yr | Tm | AB | R | HR | RBI | SB | BA | xBA | OBP | SLG | OPS | vL | vR | bb% | ct% | Eye | G | L | F | h% | HctX | PX | xPX | hr/f | Spd | SBO | SB% | #Wk | DOM | DIS | RC/G | RAR | BPV | BPX | R$ |
|---|---|---|---|---|---|---|---|---|---|---|---|---|---|---|---|---|---|---|---|---|---|---|---|---|---|---|---|---|---|---|---|---|---|---|---|
| 14 | STL | 404 | 40 | 7 | 38 | 1 | 282 | 271 | 333 | 386 | 719 | 795 | 695 | 6 | 86 | 0.51 | 51 | 23 | 27 | 31 | 115 | 75 | 95 | 7% | 73 | 2% | 50% | 20 | 45% | 25% | 4.48 | 11.6 | 42 | 114 | $10 |
| 15 | STL | 488 | 34 | 4 | 61 | 3 | 270 | 253 | 310 | 350 | 660 | 577 | 689 | 6 | 88 | 0.54 | 48 | 20 | 32 | 30 | 99 | 54 | 79 | 3% | 77 | 3% | 75% | 25 | 36% | 28% | 3.87 | 0.6 | 32 | 86 | $9 |
| 16 | STL | 534 | 56 | 8 | 58 | 3 | 307 | 282 | 360 | 427 | 787 | 776 | 790 | 7 | 88 | 0.62 | 48 | 22 | 30 | 34 | 111 | 75 | 88 | 6% | 77 | 3% | 60% | 27 | 48% | 26% | 5.52 | 16.2 | 51 | 146 | $17 |
| 17 | STL | 501 | 60 | 18 | 82 | 9 | 273 | 274 | 312 | 439 | 751 | 850 | 724 | 5 | 85 | 0.38 | 42 | 20 | 37 | 29 | 126 | 88 | 118 | 11% | 75 | 11% | 69% | 26 | 42% | 23% | 4.74 | 9.9 | 46 | 139 | $17 |
| 18 | STL | 459 | 55 | 20 | 74 | 4 | 261 | 279 | 314 | 436 | 750 | 801 | 733 | 6 | 86 | 0.44 | 39 | 24 | 37 | 27 | 140 | 92 | 130 | 14% | 63 | 6% | 57% | 23 | 57% | 26% | 4.51 | 13.3 | 49 | 163 | $15 |
| 1st Half | | 190 | 20 | 11 | 32 | 2 | 268 | 292 | 313 | 479 | 791 | 574 | 843 | 5 | 85 | 0.38 | 40 | 25 | 35 | 27 | 142 | 107 | 132 | 19% | 69 | 7% | 67% | 11 | 55% | 27% | 5.09 | 9.0 | 58 | 193 | $12 |
| 2nd Half | | 269 | 35 | 9 | 42 | 2 | 257 | 269 | 315 | 405 | 720 | 911 | 646 | 6 | 86 | 0.49 | 38 | 23 | 39 | 27 | 139 | 82 | 129 | 10% | 65 | 6% | 50% | 12 | 58% | 25% | 4.12 | 5.3 | 45 | 150 | $17 |
| **19** | **Proj** | **462** | **53** | **15** | **69** | **5** | **273** | **274** | **319** | **426** | **745** | **793** | **730** | **6** | **86** | **0.44** | **42** | **23** | **35** | **29** | **129** | **84** | **117** | **11%** | **71** | **7%** | **62%** | | | | **4.63** | **15.7** | **43** | **142** | **$16** |

## Moncada,Yoan

| | | | |
|---|---|---|---|
| Age: 24 Bats: B Pos: 2B | Health A | LIMA Plan B | |
| Ht: 6'2" Wt: 205 | PT/Exp C | Rand Var -1 | |
| | Consist A | MM 4405 | |

Season of estimation for precocious talent, whose K total led MLB and caused severe BA/xBA turbulence. PX/xPX suggest he maxed out on power, while strong bb% helped keep SB opportunities from crashing. 20/20 seasons loom... as well as the possibility of BA hijacking a career about to take flight.

| Yr | Tm | AB | R | HR | RBI | SB | BA | xBA | OBP | SLG | OPS | vL | vR | bb% | ct% | Eye | G | L | F | h% | HctX | PX | xPX | hr/f | Spd | SBO | SB% | #Wk | DOM | DIS | RC/G | RAR | BPV | BPX | R$ |
|---|---|---|---|---|---|---|---|---|---|---|---|---|---|---|---|---|---|---|---|---|---|---|---|---|---|---|---|---|---|---|---|---|---|---|---|
| 14 | | | | | | | | | | | | | | | | | | | | | | | | | | | | | | | | | | | |
| 15 | | | | | | | | | | | | | | | | | | | | | | | | | | | | | | | | | | | |
| 16 | BOS * | 196 | 33 | 9 | 24 | 7 | 259 | 273 | 339 | 457 | 796 | 500 | 517 | 11 | 60 | 0.30 | 71 | 29 | 0 | 39 | 70 | 144 | 11 | 0% | 129 | 21% | 64% | 3 | 0% | 67% | 5.11 | 2.2 | 18 | 51 | $7 |
| 17 | CHW * | 508 | 78 | 19 | 52 | 17 | 244 | 214 | 337 | 403 | 740 | 641 | 804 | 12 | 63 | 0.38 | 46 | 19 | 35 | 35 | 91 | 105 | 112 | 18% | 142 | 18% | 61% | 11 | 36% | 36% | 4.40 | -3.4 | 4 | 12 | $15 |
| 18 | CHW | 578 | 73 | 17 | 61 | 12 | 235 | 213 | 315 | 400 | 714 | 585 | 759 | 10 | 62 | 0.31 | 37 | 23 | 40 | 35 | 85 | 123 | 113 | 12% | 128 | 12% | 67% | 27 | 26% | 44% | 4.13 | 0.9 | 9 | 30 | $14 |
| 1st Half | | 295 | 36 | 10 | 34 | 8 | 224 | 213 | 292 | 400 | 692 | 440 | 766 | 9 | 61 | 0.24 | 39 | 22 | 39 | 33 | 94 | 134 | 142 | 14% | 126 | 15% | 80% | 14 | 29% | 50% | 3.85 | -2.9 | 7 | 23 | $13 |
| 2nd Half | | 283 | 37 | 7 | 27 | 4 | 247 | 215 | 337 | 399 | 737 | 702 | 751 | 12 | 64 | 0.39 | 36 | 24 | 41 | 36 | 75 | 113 | 84 | 9% | 125 | 10% | 50% | 13 | 23% | 38% | 4.41 | 2.0 | 11 | 37 | $14 |
| **19** | **Proj** | **559** | **80** | **19** | **59** | **15** | **243** | **213** | **332** | **410** | **742** | **635** | **786** | **11** | **62** | **0.34** | **40** | **21** | **38** | **36** | **86** | **120** | **110** | **14%** | **136** | **15%** | **62%** | | | | **4.40** | **3.9** | **5** | **16** | **$18** |

ROB CARROLL

## Mondesi,Adalberto

| | | | | | |
|---|---|---|---|---|---|
| Age: 23 | Bats: B | Pos: SS | PT/Exp D | Rand Var -2 | |
| Ht: 6' 1" | Wt: 190 | | Consist B | MM 3515 | |
| Health B | LIMA Plan B | | | | |

14-37-.276 with 32 SB in 275 AB at KC. 2nd half (esp. 8 HR/14 SB Sept.) has hype train chugging; but track hasn't been fully laid down yet. Plate skills perilously bad. Obscene SBO with sub-.300 OBP came on a team with nothing to lose—it won't happen again. xPX supportive of pop, but that's based on <500 career MLB ABs. CAUTION.

| Yr | Tm | AB | R | HR | RBI | SB | BA | xBA | OBP | SLG | OPS | vL | vR | bb% | ct% | Eye | G | L | F | h% | HctX | PX | xPX | hr/f | Spd | SBO | SB% | #Wk | DOM | DIS | RC/G | RAR | BPV | BPX | R$ |
|---|---|---|---|---|---|---|---|---|---|---|---|---|---|---|---|---|---|---|---|---|---|---|---|---|---|---|---|---|---|---|---|---|---|---|---|
| 14 | | | | | | | | | | | | | | | | | | | | | | | | | | | | | | | | | | | |
| 15 | aa | 304 | 30 | 5 | 27 | 16 | 230 | | 264 | 344 | 608 | | | 4 | 71 | 0.15 | | | | 31 | | 80 | | | 128 | 35% | 71% | | | | 2.94 | | -4 | -11 | $7 |
| 16 | KC * | 307 | 41 | 7 | 35 | 28 | 232 | 208 | 275 | 375 | 651 | 434 | 546 | 6 | 68 | 0.19 | 49 | 12 | 39 | 32 | 86 | 89 | 137 | 7% | 168 | 45% | 93% | 10 | 20% | 80% | 3.76 | -5.0 | 6 | 17 | $13 |
| 17 | KC * | 374 | 47 | 11 | 46 | 22 | 270 | 260 | 302 | 454 | 756 | 462 | 459 | 4 | 70 | 0.16 | 34 | 34 | 31 | 36 | 73 | 115 | 120 | 11% | 142 | 35% | 81% | 10 | 10% | 70% | 4.82 | 2.0 | 26 | 79 | $17 |
| 18 | KC * | 395 | 62 | 18 | 54 | 40 | 262 | 254 | 293 | 479 | 772 | 834 | 789 | 4 | 72 | 0.16 | 41 | 21 | 38 | 32 | 115 | 132 | 130 | 20% | 133 | 61% | 85% | 16 | 44% | 31% | 4.99 | 10.3 | 46 | 153 | $27 |
| 1st Half | | 155 | 22 | 5 | 21 | 11 | 223 | 249 | 258 | 420 | 678 | 833 | 469 | 5 | 74 | 0.18 | 44 | 16 | 40 | 27 | 115 | 126 | 153 | 10% | 128 | 51% | 92% | 3 | 33% | 67% | 3.77 | -0.9 | 45 | 150 | $7 |
| 2nd Half | | 240 | 40 | 13 | 33 | 29 | 288 | 256 | 317 | 517 | 834 | 834 | 834 | 4 | 72 | 0.15 | 41 | 22 | 37 | 35 | 114 | 137 | 127 | 21% | 133 | 66% | 83% | 13 | 46% | 23% | 5.89 | 13.4 | 46 | 153 | $41 |
| 19 | Proj | **571** | **77** | **16** | **64** | **38** | **257** | **236** | **289** | **427** | **716** | **788** | **686** | **4** | **70** | **0.14** | **44** | **20** | **36** | **34** | **99** | **109** | **131** | **11%** | **144** | **39%** | **83%** | | | | **4.29** | **5.5** | **30** | **99** | **$27** |

## Morales,Kendrys

| | | | | | |
|---|---|---|---|---|---|
| Age: 36 | Bats: B | Pos: DH | PT/Exp A | Rand Var 0 | |
| Ht: 6' 1" | Wt: 225 | | Consist A | MM 3025 | |
| Health A | LIMA Plan B | | | | |

April hamstring injury may have led to slow start, but he was back to old self by May. 2nd half highlighted by HR in 7 straight games, better luck vR, and improved walk rate, and xPX says don't write him off just yet. Sure, with age comes some risk, but stats of overlooked, unsexy veterans still count.

| Yr | Tm | AB | R | HR | RBI | SB | BA | xBA | OBP | SLG | OPS | vL | vR | bb% | ct% | Eye | G | L | F | h% | HctX | PX | xPX | hr/f | Spd | SBO | SB% | #Wk | DOM | DIS | RC/G | RAR | BPV | BPX | R$ |
|---|---|---|---|---|---|---|---|---|---|---|---|---|---|---|---|---|---|---|---|---|---|---|---|---|---|---|---|---|---|---|---|---|---|---|---|
| 14 | 2 AL | 367 | 28 | 8 | 42 | 0 | 218 | 238 | 274 | 338 | 612 | 661 | 584 | 7 | 81 | 0.40 | 49 | 18 | 33 | 25 | 106 | 89 | 102 | 8% | 64 | 0% | 0% | 17 | 41% | 41% | 2.99 | -11.8 | 32 | 86 | $1 |
| 15 | KC | 569 | 81 | 22 | 106 | 0 | 290 | 282 | 362 | 485 | 847 | 771 | 901 | 9 | 82 | 0.56 | 45 | 20 | 35 | 32 | 126 | 126 | 134 | 13% | 67 | 0% | 0% | 27 | 63% | 11% | 6.20 | 11.8 | 69 | 186 | $23 |
| 16 | KC | 558 | 65 | 30 | 93 | 0 | 263 | 262 | 327 | 468 | 795 | 930 | 730 | 8 | 78 | 0.40 | 44 | 20 | 36 | 29 | 131 | 117 | 140 | 19% | 42 | 0% | 0% | 27 | 37% | 26% | 5.21 | -4.6 | 38 | 109 | $16 |
| 17 | TOR | 557 | 67 | 28 | 85 | 0 | 250 | 253 | 308 | 445 | 753 | 1000 | 680 | 7 | 76 | 0.33 | 48 | 18 | 33 | 28 | 117 | 110 | 117 | 20% | 57 | 0% | 0% | 26 | 42% | 35% | 4.59 | -4.5 | 27 | 82 | $12 |
| 18 | TOR | 413 | 47 | 21 | 57 | 2 | 249 | 246 | 331 | 438 | 769 | 582 | 860 | 11 | 77 | 0.53 | 46 | 18 | 36 | 28 | 115 | 107 | 135 | 18% | 59 | 4% | 40% | 27 | 30% | 41% | 4.81 | 3.6 | 34 | 113 | $11 |
| 1st Half | | 206 | 18 | 8 | 26 | 2 | 233 | 236 | 297 | 398 | 695 | 639 | 724 | 9 | 75 | 0.38 | 46 | 17 | 36 | 27 | 119 | 103 | 129 | 14% | 65 | 6% | 67% | 15 | 33% | 33% | 3.95 | -3.5 | 21 | 70 | $6 |
| 2nd Half | | 207 | 29 | 13 | 31 | 0 | 266 | 255 | 364 | 478 | 842 | 517 | 985 | 13 | 79 | 0.70 | 45 | 19 | 36 | 28 | 111 | 111 | 141 | 22% | 62 | 3% | 0% | 12 | 25% | 50% | 5.74 | 7.4 | 52 | 173 | $15 |
| 19 | Proj | **444** | **52** | **22** | **66** | **1** | **251** | **251** | **325** | **442** | **767** | **719** | **787** | **9** | **78** | **0.47** | **46** | **19** | **35** | **28** | **118** | **108** | **130** | **18%** | **57** | **2%** | **33%** | | | | **4.78** | **3.5** | **26** | **88** | **$13** |

## Moran,Colin

| | | | | | |
|---|---|---|---|---|---|
| Age: 26 | Bats: L | Pos: 3B | PT/Exp C | Rand Var 0 | |
| Ht: 6' 4" | Wt: 205 | | Consist C | MM 1035 | |
| Health B | LIMA Plan B | | | | |

Didn't ace first MLB test but earned passing grade, thanks to solid plate skills. But power is underwhelming for corner INF; 2nd half FB% suggests that's not changing soon. Shielding from LHP (62 AB) may continue, given results. He's got time, but unless skills pop to greater degree, hold on PT may be tenuous.

| Yr | Tm | AB | R | HR | RBI | SB | BA | xBA | OBP | SLG | OPS | vL | vR | bb% | ct% | Eye | G | L | F | h% | HctX | PX | xPX | hr/f | Spd | SBO | SB% | #Wk | DOM | DIS | RC/G | RAR | BPV | BPX | R$ |
|---|---|---|---|---|---|---|---|---|---|---|---|---|---|---|---|---|---|---|---|---|---|---|---|---|---|---|---|---|---|---|---|---|---|---|---|
| 14 | aa | 112 | 9 | 2 | 17 | 0 | 267 | | 311 | 358 | 669 | | | 6 | 77 | 0.27 | | | | 34 | | 75 | | | 84 | 4% | 0% | | | | 3.71 | | 5 | 14 | $1 |
| 15 | aa | 366 | 36 | 8 | 52 | 1 | 268 | | 328 | 399 | 728 | | | 8 | 75 | 0.36 | | | | 34 | | 97 | | | 88 | 1% | 100% | | | | 4.58 | | 23 | 62 | $8 |
| 16 | HOU * | 482 | 41 | 8 | 57 | 2 | 218 | 263 | 275 | 306 | 581 | 0 | 374 | 7 | 68 | 0.24 | 47 | 40 | 13 | 31 | 73 | 65 | 76 | 0% | 91 | 4% | 51% | 4 | 25% | 75% | 2.71 | -33.7 | -33 | -94 | $1 |
| 17 | HOU * | 313 | 37 | 13 | 44 | 0 | 243 | 262 | 289 | 415 | 704 | 1400 | 1095 | 6 | 78 | 0.30 | 50 | 20 | 30 | 27 | 95 | 93 | 74 | 33% | 111 | 5% | 0% | 3 | 67% | 33% | 3.83 | -13.9 | 35 | 106 | $4 |
| 18 | PIT | 415 | 49 | 11 | 58 | 0 | 277 | 265 | 340 | 407 | 747 | 503 | 790 | 8 | 80 | 0.48 | 45 | 26 | 29 | 32 | 97 | 78 | 91 | 11% | 103 | 2% | 0% | 28 | 43% | 25% | 4.78 | 1.3 | 33 | 110 | $11 |
| 1st Half | | 221 | 27 | 7 | 29 | 0 | 267 | 261 | 346 | 416 | 763 | 623 | 782 | 11 | 81 | 0.60 | 42 | 24 | 35 | 30 | 96 | 90 | 99 | 11% | 94 | 3% | 0% | 15 | 47% | 13% | 4.81 | 1.9 | 45 | 150 | $11 |
| 2nd Half | | 194 | 22 | 4 | 29 | 0 | 289 | 271 | 332 | 397 | 729 | 395 | 800 | 6 | 80 | 0.33 | 48 | 29 | 23 | 34 | 97 | 64 | 81 | 11% | 118 | 0% | 0% | 13 | 38% | 38% | 4.74 | 1.3 | 21 | 70 | $11 |
| 19 | Proj | **519** | **57** | **12** | **72** | **0** | **268** | **257** | **322** | **388** | **710** | **460** | **756** | **7** | **77** | **0.35** | **45** | **27** | **28** | **33** | **97** | **73** | **88** | **11%** | **108** | **2%** | **11%** | | | | **4.23** | **-4.1** | **-3** | **-11** | **$14** |

## Moreland,Mitch

| | | | | | |
|---|---|---|---|---|---|
| Age: 33 | Bats: L | Pos: 1B | PT/Exp B | Rand Var +1 | |
| Ht: 6' 2" | Wt: 230 | | Consist A | MM 4135 | |
| Health B | LIMA Plan B | | | | |

In 1st half, seemed that off-season arthroscopic knee surgery had done the trick (with slight h% assist), but knee started barking in July, HctX tanked, stats followed suit. If he enters 2019 healthy, another season like 2016-2017 should be in reach, as plate and power skills appear intact. Give him another shot.

| Yr | Tm | AB | R | HR | RBI | SB | BA | xBA | OBP | SLG | OPS | vL | vR | bb% | ct% | Eye | G | L | F | h% | HctX | PX | xPX | hr/f | Spd | SBO | SB% | #Wk | DOM | DIS | RC/G | RAR | BPV | BPX | R$ |
|---|---|---|---|---|---|---|---|---|---|---|---|---|---|---|---|---|---|---|---|---|---|---|---|---|---|---|---|---|---|---|---|---|---|---|---|
| 14 | TEX | 167 | 18 | 2 | 23 | 0 | 246 | 235 | 297 | 347 | 644 | 374 | 692 | 7 | 74 | 0.28 | 45 | 22 | 33 | 32 | 136 | 86 | 143 | 5% | 74 | 0% | 0% | 10 | 30% | 60% | 3.48 | -3.2 | 3 | 8 | $1 |
| 15 | TEX | 471 | 51 | 23 | 85 | 1 | 278 | 265 | 330 | 482 | 812 | 681 | 876 | 6 | 76 | 0.29 | 46 | 20 | 35 | 32 | 120 | 135 | 131 | 18% | 61 | 1% | 100% | 26 | 38% | 38% | 5.53 | 7.9 | 46 | 124 | $17 |
| 16 | TEX | 460 | 49 | 22 | 60 | 1 | 233 | 252 | 298 | 422 | 720 | 799 | 700 | 7 | 74 | 0.30 | 42 | 21 | 37 | 27 | 110 | 116 | 111 | 17% | 61 | 1% | 100% | 26 | 38% | 31% | 4.03 | -11.4 | 24 | 69 | $7 |
| 17 | BOS | 508 | 73 | 22 | 79 | 0 | 246 | 264 | 326 | 443 | 769 | 684 | 784 | 10 | 76 | 0.48 | 43 | 20 | 36 | 28 | 120 | 118 | 119 | 15% | 59 | 1% | 0% | 26 | 35% | 42% | 4.79 | -8.8 | 39 | 118 | $10 |
| 18 | BOS | 404 | 57 | 15 | 68 | 2 | 245 | 252 | 325 | 433 | 758 | 684 | 780 | 11 | 75 | 0.49 | 43 | 20 | 37 | 29 | 96 | 116 | 121 | 13% | 70 | 2% | 100% | 28 | 39% | 25% | 4.83 | 4.9 | 37 | 123 | $11 |
| 1st Half | | 221 | 36 | 11 | 40 | 1 | 285 | 279 | 354 | 538 | 892 | 825 | 916 | 10 | 76 | 0.44 | 40 | 21 | 38 | 33 | 111 | 151 | 147 | 17% | 81 | 2% | 100% | 15 | 60% | 20% | 6.85 | 12.9 | 69 | 230 | $18 |
| 2nd Half | | 183 | 21 | 4 | 28 | 1 | 197 | 215 | 291 | 306 | 597 | 456 | 632 | 12 | 74 | 0.54 | 46 | 17 | 36 | 24 | 78 | 73 | 90 | 8% | 56 | 2% | 100% | 13 | 15% | 31% | 2.91 | -10.7 | -3 | -10 | $2 |
| 19 | Proj | **474** | **65** | **21** | **74** | **1** | **245** | **257** | **319** | **444** | **763** | **683** | **784** | **10** | **75** | **0.43** | **44** | **20** | **37** | **28** | **105** | **122** | **117** | **16%** | **64** | **1%** | **86%** | | | | **4.78** | **0.2** | **37** | **123** | **$14** |

## Morrison,Logan

| | | | | | |
|---|---|---|---|---|---|
| Age: 31 | Bats: L | Pos: 1B DH | PT/Exp C | Rand Var +5 | |
| Ht: 6' 3" | Wt: 245 | | Consist F | MM 3113 | |
| Health D | LIMA Plan D+ | | | | |

August hip surgery ended disappointing encore to 2017 breakout, recovery time (4-8 months) puts Opening Day availability in doubt. As bad as 2018 was, hit rate did him no favors, and there were glimmers of 2017 power in short 2nd half. Tons of risk, but if healing goes well, may be worth a late flyer.

| Yr | Tm | AB | R | HR | RBI | SB | BA | xBA | OBP | SLG | OPS | vL | vR | bb% | ct% | Eye | G | L | F | h% | HctX | PX | xPX | hr/f | Spd | SBO | SB% | #Wk | DOM | DIS | RC/G | RAR | BPV | BPX | R$ |
|---|---|---|---|---|---|---|---|---|---|---|---|---|---|---|---|---|---|---|---|---|---|---|---|---|---|---|---|---|---|---|---|---|---|---|---|
| 14 | SEA * | 401 | 49 | 13 | 43 | 6 | 257 | 272 | 310 | 407 | 717 | 846 | 695 | 7 | 83 | 0.44 | 40 | 24 | 36 | 28 | 113 | 104 | 92 | 11% | 61 | 8% | 76% | 20 | 35% | 20% | 4.33 | 3.3 | 49 | 132 | $11 |
| 15 | SEA | 457 | 47 | 17 | 54 | 8 | 225 | 250 | 302 | 383 | 685 | 500 | 767 | 9 | 82 | 0.58 | 45 | 16 | 39 | 24 | 110 | 92 | 120 | 12% | 85 | 10% | 67% | 27 | 48% | 37% | 3.70 | -24.4 | 49 | 132 | $8 |
| 16 | TAM | 353 | 45 | 14 | 43 | 4 | 238 | 256 | 319 | 414 | 733 | 739 | 731 | 9 | 75 | 0.42 | 44 | 21 | 35 | 28 | 104 | 110 | 100 | 15% | 63 | 7% | 67% | 22 | 41% | 50% | 4.26 | -13.1 | 27 | 77 | $6 |
| 17 | TAM | 512 | 75 | 38 | 85 | 2 | 246 | 261 | 353 | 516 | 868 | 761 | 905 | 13 | 71 | 0.54 | 33 | 20 | 46 | 27 | 107 | 156 | 144 | 22% | 58 | 1% | 100% | 27 | 56% | 26% | 6.11 | 18.8 | 55 | 167 | $15 |
| 18 | MIN | 318 | 41 | 15 | 39 | 1 | 186 | 233 | 276 | 368 | 644 | 624 | 650 | 9 | 75 | 0.43 | 33 | 19 | 47 | 20 | 104 | 108 | 125 | 13% | 45 | 2% | 100% | 19 | 42% | 37% | 3.06 | -14.6 | 20 | 67 | $2 |
| 1st Half | | 237 | 29 | 9 | 28 | 1 | 190 | 236 | 290 | 354 | 645 | 637 | 648 | 11 | 76 | 0.54 | 33 | 20 | 46 | 21 | 104 | 101 | 115 | 11% | 49 | 2% | 100% | 15 | 33% | 40% | 3.15 | -10.2 | 26 | 87 | $3 |
| 2nd Half | | 81 | 12 | 6 | 11 | 0 | 173 | 225 | 230 | 407 | 637 | 563 | 655 | 5 | 70 | 0.17 | 35 | 15 | 51 | 16 | 105 | 133 | 159 | 21% | 68 | 0% | 0% | 4 | 75% | 25% | 2.66 | -4.9 | 20 | 67 | -$2 |
| 19 | Proj | **254** | **35** | **13** | **34** | **1** | **235** | **236** | **315** | **429** | **744** | **706** | **755** | **9** | **74** | **0.39** | **36** | **19** | **45** | **27** | **106** | **115** | **132** | **16%** | **57** | **3%** | **77%** | | | | **4.37** | **-3.0** | **22** | **73** | **$7** |

## Moustakas,Mike

| | | | | | |
|---|---|---|---|---|---|
| Age: 30 | Bats: L | Pos: 3B | PT/Exp C | Rand Var +1 | |
| Ht: 6' 0" | Wt: 225 | | Consist B | MM 3045 | |
| Health C | LIMA Plan B+ | | | | |

Aside from dip in hr/f, 2018 looked a lot like 2017 breakout. OK, maybe 2nd half slippage in ct%, xPX bears watching, especially as he hits wrong side of 30, but rebound of HctX good to see. Probably not going flirt with 40 HR again, but given that additional flyballs have stuck around, 30 is a pretty safe bet.

| Yr | Tm | AB | R | HR | RBI | SB | BA | xBA | OBP | SLG | OPS | vL | vR | bb% | ct% | Eye | G | L | F | h% | HctX | PX | xPX | hr/f | Spd | SBO | SB% | #Wk | DOM | DIS | RC/G | RAR | BPV | BPX | R$ |
|---|---|---|---|---|---|---|---|---|---|---|---|---|---|---|---|---|---|---|---|---|---|---|---|---|---|---|---|---|---|---|---|---|---|---|---|
| 14 | KC * | 488 | 47 | 16 | 57 | 1 | 217 | 258 | 272 | 365 | 638 | 554 | 653 | 7 | 83 | 0.46 | 39 | 20 | 41 | 23 | 114 | 100 | 120 | 9% | 55 | 1% | 100% | 26 | 50% | 31% | 3.25 | -6.9 | 46 | 124 | $5 |
| 15 | KC | 549 | 73 | 22 | 82 | 1 | 284 | 274 | 348 | 470 | 817 | 823 | 814 | 7 | 86 | 0.57 | 40 | 19 | 41 | 30 | 117 | 112 | 114 | 11% | 64 | 2% | 33% | 27 | 63% | 19% | 5.55 | 13.5 | 70 | 189 | $20 |
| 16 | KC | 104 | 12 | 7 | 13 | 0 | 240 | 301 | 301 | 500 | 801 | 842 | 791 | 8 | 88 | 0.69 | 42 | 19 | 40 | 21 | 133 | 134 | 135 | 19% | 71 | 5% | 0% | 7 | 71% | 29% | 4.84 | -0.3 | 96 | 274 | $1 |
| 17 | KC | 555 | 75 | 38 | 85 | 0 | 272 | 279 | 314 | 521 | 835 | 763 | 862 | 6 | 83 | 0.36 | 35 | 20 | 46 | 27 | 107 | 124 | 120 | 18% | 67 | 0% | 0% | 27 | 59% | 15% | 5.73 | 6.6 | 65 | 197 | $18 |
| 18 | 2 TM | 573 | 66 | 28 | 95 | 4 | 251 | 264 | 315 | 459 | 774 | 721 | 798 | 8 | 82 | 0.48 | 34 | 20 | 46 | 26 | 124 | 116 | 130 | 13% | 70 | 4% | 80% | 28 | 54% | 14% | 4.85 | 3.1 | 59 | 197 | $18 |
| 1st Half | | 310 | 37 | 16 | 53 | 3 | 261 | 278 | 317 | 477 | 794 | 686 | 848 | 7 | 84 | 0.51 | 33 | 23 | 44 | 27 | 137 | 116 | 140 | 14% | 85 | 4% | 100% | 15 | 67% | 13% | 5.27 | 6.9 | 72 | 240 | $23 |
| 2nd Half | | 263 | 29 | 12 | 42 | 1 | 240 | 244 | 313 | 437 | 750 | 768 | 743 | 8 | 79 | 0.44 | 36 | 16 | 49 | 26 | 110 | 116 | 118 | 12% | 57 | 3% | 50% | 13 | 38% | 15% | 4.39 | -0.9 | 47 | 157 | $13 |
| 19 | Proj | **585** | **70** | **32** | **90** | **2** | **264** | **269** | **320** | **484** | **803** | **771** | **816** | **7** | **83** | **0.45** | **36** | **19** | **45** | **27** | **119** | **120** | **125** | **15%** | **64** | **3%** | **54%** | | | | **5.25** | **12.6** | **56** | **186** | **$21** |

## Mullins II,Cedric

| | | | | | |
|---|---|---|---|---|---|
| Age: 24 | Bats: B | Pos: CF | PT/Exp D | Rand Var 0 | |
| Ht: 5'8" | Wt: 175 | | Consist A | MM 1335 | |
| Health A | LIMA Plan B+ | | | | |

4-11-.235 with 2 SB in 170 AB at BAL. Desperate for ray of hope, BAL promoted him in Aug, despite .771 OPS in AAA; he started hot, then closed on 2-for-36 skid. Speed is his best asset, but power is less certain, given groundball rate. Growing pains? Sure. But contact skills should minimize complete crash potential.

| Yr | Tm | AB | R | HR | RBI | SB | BA | xBA | OBP | SLG | OPS | vL | vR | bb% | ct% | Eye | G | L | F | h% | HctX | PX | xPX | hr/f | Spd | SBO | SB% | #Wk | DOM | DIS | RC/G | RAR | BPV | BPX | R$ |
|---|---|---|---|---|---|---|---|---|---|---|---|---|---|---|---|---|---|---|---|---|---|---|---|---|---|---|---|---|---|---|---|---|---|---|---|
| 14 | | | | | | | | | | | | | | | | | | | | | | | | | | | | | | | | | | | |
| 15 | | | | | | | | | | | | | | | | | | | | | | | | | | | | | | | | | | | |
| 16 | | | | | | | | | | | | | | | | | | | | | | | | | | | | | | | | | | | |
| 17 | aa | 309 | 43 | 11 | 30 | 7 | 238 | | 288 | 407 | 696 | | | 7 | 80 | 0.35 | | | | 26 | | 95 | | | 100 | 23% | 49% | | | | 3.61 | | 41 | 124 | $6 |
| 18 | BAL * | 613 | 83 | 14 | 48 | 18 | 247 | 246 | 300 | 389 | 689 | 452 | 751 | 7 | 82 | 0.41 | 51 | 12 | 37 | 28 | 81 | 84 | 65 | 9% | 134 | 16% | 82% | 9 | 44% | 44% | 4.00 | -0.6 | 51 | 170 | $17 |
| 1st Half | | 313 | 45 | 8 | 32 | 10 | 256 | 267 | 302 | 415 | 717 | | | 6 | 84 | 0.40 | | | | 28 | | 90 | | | 121 | 16% | 90% | | | | 4.41 | | 58 | 193 | $20 |
| 2nd Half | | 300 | 39 | 7 | 16 | 8 | 238 | 232 | 298 | 362 | 660 | 452 | 751 | 8 | 80 | 0.43 | 51 | 12 | 37 | 28 | 79 | 76 | 65 | 9% | 135 | 15% | 73% | 9 | 44% | 44% | 3.60 | -4.9 | 39 | 130 | $13 |
| 19 | Proj | **554** | **76** | **9** | **46** | **16** | **243** | **252** | **302** | **356** | **658** | **453** | **733** | **7** | **81** | **0.39** | **52** | **18** | **30** | **29** | **71** | **71** | **59** | **7%** | **112** | **18%** | **66%** | | | | **3.46** | **-11.4** | **29** | **97** | **$15** |

KRISTOPHER OLSON

## Muncy,Max

| Muncy,Max | | | Health | A | LIMA Plan | B |
|---|---|---|---|---|---|---|
| Age: 28 | Bats: L | Pos: 1B 3B | PT/Exp | D | Rand Var | -3 |
| Ht: 6' 0" | Wt: 210 | | Consist | F | MM | 4125 |

35-79-.263 in 395 AB at LA. Support of xBA, HctX, and xPX says this was not a fluke. A surprise, yes, though perhaps also a reminder that for hitters, bb% is a skill that can lead to bigger things. Still, 2nd half exposed possible issues vL (57% ct, 0.23 Eye), and hr/f will be tough to repeat. Expect some pullback.

| Yr | Tm | AB | R | HR | RBI | SB | BA | xBA | OBP | SLG | OPS | vL | vR | bb% | ct% | Eye | G | L | F | h% | HctX | PX | xPX | hr/f | Spd | SBO | SB% | #Wk | DOM | DIS | RC/G | RAR | BPV | BPX | R$ |
|---|---|---|---|---|---|---|---|---|---|---|---|---|---|---|---|---|---|---|---|---|---|---|---|---|---|---|---|---|---|---|---|---|---|---|---|
| 14 | aa | 435 | 45 | 5 | 48 | 5 | 225 | | 331 | 318 | 648 | | | 14 | 76 | 0.66 | | | | 28 | | 74 | | | 96 | 5% | 70% | | | | 3.46 | | 23 | 62 | $4 |
| 15 | OAK * | 314 | 33 | 6 | 37 | 0 | 226 | 196 | 293 | 361 | 654 | 500 | 660 | 9 | 69 | 0.31 | 32 | 13 | 55 | 31 | 108 | 109 | 209 | 8% | 78 | 2% | 0% | 17 | 29% | 47% | 3.43 | -18.5 | 8 | 22 | $1 |
| 16 | OAK * | 336 | 39 | 8 | 28 | 4 | 202 | 227 | 299 | 304 | 603 | 400 | 572 | 12 | 75 | 0.55 | 51 | 19 | 30 | 25 | 89 | 61 | 74 | 8% | 109 | 4% | 100% | 15 | 13% | 53% | 2.96 | -24.9 | 7 | 20 | $0 |
| 17 | aaa | 320 | 46 | 9 | 33 | 2 | 250 | | 330 | 391 | 721 | | | 11 | 67 | 0.36 | | | | 34 | | 97 | | | 95 | 10% | 23% | | | | 4.04 | | -1 | -3 | $5 |
| 18 | LA * | 427 | 80 | 36 | 82 | 3 | 262 | 267 | 382 | 571 | 953 | 891 | 1001 | 16 | 68 | 0.60 | 34 | 21 | 45 | 30 | 118 | 192 | 176 | 29% | 80 | 2% | 100% | 25 | 60% | 12% | 7.59 | 30.6 | 83 | 277 | $21 |
| 1st Half | | 206 | 35 | 18 | 38 | 2 | 261 | 274 | 394 | 576 | 970 | 1078 | 987 | 18 | 72 | 0.77 | 35 | 18 | 47 | 27 | 124 | 187 | 192 | 30% | 71 | 3% | 100% | 12 | 75% | 8% | 7.91 | 18.8 | 95 | 317 | $19 |
| 2nd Half | | 221 | 45 | 18 | 44 | 1 | 262 | 258 | 379 | 566 | 944 | 757 | 1013 | 15 | 64 | 0.48 | 34 | 23 | 43 | 32 | 113 | 197 | 163 | 29% | 97 | 1% | 100% | 13 | 46% | 15% | 7.28 | 16.1 | 75 | 250 | $23 |
| 19 | Proj | **453** | **75** | **26** | **70** | **3** | **249** | **243** | **354** | **478** | **832** | **881** | **824** | **14** | **69** | **0.51** | **37** | **20** | **43** | **30** | **106** | **145** | **145** | **20%** | **88** | **4%** | **55%** | | | | **5.63** | **11.6** | **43** | **144** | **$14** |

## Munoz,Yairo

| Munoz,Yairo | | | Health | A | LIMA Plan | D+ |
|---|---|---|---|---|---|---|
| Age: 24 | Bats: R | Pos: SS 2B 3B | PT/Exp | C | Rand Var | -2 |
| Ht: 6' 1" | Wt: 201 | | Consist | B | MM | 2241 |

8-42-.276 with 5 SB in 293 AB at STL. Utility INF/OF turned opportunity into showcase for sneaky power and speed. HR might have more of a future than SB—as SB% shows, he's a lousy basestealer. 2nd half growth in bb%, HctX, xPX are all great to see. Roll the dice, hope more opportunity comes his way.

| Yr | Tm | AB | R | HR | RBI | SB | BA | xBA | OBP | SLG | OPS | vL | vR | bb% | ct% | Eye | G | L | F | h% | HctX | PX | xPX | hr/f | Spd | SBO | SB% | #Wk | DOM | DIS | RC/G | RAR | BPV | BPX | R$ |
|---|---|---|---|---|---|---|---|---|---|---|---|---|---|---|---|---|---|---|---|---|---|---|---|---|---|---|---|---|---|---|---|---|---|---|---|
| 14 | | | | | | | | | | | | | | | | | | | | | | | | | | | | | | | | | | | |
| 15 | | | | | | | | | | | | | | | | | | | | | | | | | | | | | | | | | | | |
| 16 | aa | 387 | 38 | 7 | 34 | 5 | 222 | | 259 | 330 | 590 | | | 5 | 80 | 0.25 | | | | 26 | | 66 | | | 106 | 16% | 41% | | | | 2.60 | | 15 | 43 | $2 |
| 17 | a/a | 446 | 53 | 10 | 56 | 18 | 272 | | 298 | 410 | 709 | | | 4 | 80 | 0.19 | | | | 32 | | 80 | | | 106 | 24% | 77% | | | | 4.27 | | 27 | 82 | $16 |
| 18 | STL * | 392 | 48 | 10 | 52 | 6 | 269 | 260 | 327 | 400 | 727 | 838 | 731 | 8 | 77 | 0.37 | 54 | 22 | 23 | 33 | 105 | 83 | 85 | 15% | 90 | 11% | 49% | 24 | 21% | 42% | 4.36 | 6.1 | 19 | 63 | $11 |
| 1st Half | | 220 | 19 | 5 | 26 | 4 | 266 | 242 | 307 | 374 | 681 | 708 | 705 | 6 | 75 | 0.23 | 55 | 22 | 23 | 33 | 96 | 66 | 62 | 14% | 121 | 13% | 49% | 12 | 8% | 42% | 3.77 | -1.2 | 3 | 10 | $10 |
| 2nd Half | | 172 | 30 | 5 | 26 | 2 | 272 | 281 | 352 | 434 | 786 | 912 | 752 | 11 | 79 | 0.58 | 53 | 23 | 24 | 32 | 113 | 105 | 101 | 16% | 75 | 8% | 50% | 12 | 33% | 42% | 5.19 | 6.1 | 46 | 153 | $13 |
| 19 | Proj | **225** | **28** | **6** | **28** | **5** | **264** | **274** | **331** | **413** | **743** | **824** | **709** | **8** | **79** | **0.42** | **54** | **22** | **23** | **31** | **106** | **90** | **85** | **15%** | **98** | **14%** | **63%** | | | | **4.50** | **3.6** | **32** | **107** | **$8** |

## Murphy,Daniel

| Murphy,Daniel | | | Health | D | LIMA Plan | B |
|---|---|---|---|---|---|---|
| Age: 34 | Bats: L | Pos: 2B | PT/Exp | B | Rand Var | 0 |
| Ht: 6' 1" | Wt: 221 | | Consist | D | MM | 3255 |

12-42-.299 in 328 AB at WAS/CHC. Knee surgery that kept him out of action til mid-May likely left him rusty upon return to majors (60 HctX, 46 xPX in June/July). May have also been root cause of decline vL, where PX plunged to 28. Modest rebound is a reasonable expectation; rebound to 2016-17 levels is not.

| Yr | Tm | AB | R | HR | RBI | SB | BA | xBA | OBP | SLG | OPS | vL | vR | bb% | ct% | Eye | G | L | F | h% | HctX | PX | xPX | hr/f | Spd | SBO | SB% | #Wk | DOM | DIS | RC/G | RAR | BPV | BPX | R$ |
|---|---|---|---|---|---|---|---|---|---|---|---|---|---|---|---|---|---|---|---|---|---|---|---|---|---|---|---|---|---|---|---|---|---|---|---|
| 14 | NYM | 596 | 79 | 9 | 57 | 13 | 289 | 285 | 332 | 403 | 734 | 695 | 747 | 6 | 86 | 0.45 | 42 | 28 | 29 | 33 | 106 | 84 | 89 | 6% | 93 | 11% | 72% | 26 | 50% | 23% | 4.77 | 23.1 | 51 | 138 | $22 |
| 15 | NYM | 499 | 56 | 14 | 73 | 2 | 281 | 299 | 322 | 449 | 770 | 633 | 817 | 6 | 92 | 0.82 | 43 | 21 | 36 | 28 | 124 | 101 | 108 | 8% | 62 | 3% | 50% | 24 | 63% | 4% | 5.07 | 12.7 | 82 | 222 | $15 |
| 16 | WAS | 531 | 88 | 25 | 104 | 5 | 347 | 314 | 390 | 595 | 985 | 924 | 1010 | 6 | 89 | 0.61 | 36 | 22 | 42 | 35 | 138 | 135 | 138 | 12% | 105 | 6% | 63% | 26 | 77% | 0% | 8.86 | 54.8 | 111 | 317 | $34 |
| 17 | WAS | 534 | 94 | 23 | 93 | 2 | 322 | 307 | 384 | 543 | 928 | 823 | 960 | 9 | 86 | 0.68 | 33 | 28 | 39 | 34 | 123 | 119 | 120 | 13% | 86 | 1% | 100% | 27 | 63% | 19% | 7.84 | 40.0 | 83 | 252 | $27 |
| 18 | 2 NL * | 365 | 46 | 13 | 47 | 3 | 288 | 278 | 332 | 444 | 776 | 563 | 864 | 6 | 88 | 0.54 | 35 | 26 | 39 | 30 | 84 | 82 | 82 | 11% | 78 | 3% | 100% | 17 | 53% | 18% | 5.33 | 10.8 | 54 | 180 | $12 |
| 1st Half | | 87 | 7 | 1 | 11 | 0 | 196 | 262 | 250 | 287 | 536 | 778 | 404 | 7 | 87 | 0.57 | 32 | 27 | 41 | 21 | 51 | 53 | 1 | 0% | 84 | 0% | 0% | 4 | 50% | 25% | 2.27 | -5.2 | 32 | 107 | -$13 |
| 2nd Half | | 278 | 39 | 12 | 36 | 3 | 317 | 285 | 355 | 493 | 847 | 537 | 955 | 6 | 88 | 0.53 | 36 | 26 | 39 | 33 | 90 | 92 | 96 | 13% | 79 | 4% | 100% | 13 | 54% | 15% | 6.66 | 18.6 | 62 | 207 | $20 |
| 19 | Proj | **489** | **68** | **19** | **73** | **3** | **295** | **291** | **344** | **483** | **827** | **742** | **854** | **7** | **87** | **0.59** | **35** | **26** | **39** | **31** | **100** | **102** | **90** | **12%** | **86** | **3%** | **82%** | | | | **6.02** | **25.0** | **67** | **224** | **$22** |

## Murphy,John

| Murphy,John | | | Health | A | LIMA Plan | D |
|---|---|---|---|---|---|---|
| Age: 28 | Bats: R | Pos: CA | PT/Exp | F | Rand Var | 0 |
| Ht: 5' 11" | Wt: 205 | | Consist | B | MM | 2003 |

Made changes in approach to join launch angle revolution, and it worked... for two months. .457 OPS after June 1, and 2nd half ct% shows pitchers found holes in his plan pretty quickly. So we're left with as hearty a test of "Once you display a skill, you own it" as you'll find in this book. Worth a fingers-crossed flyer.

| Yr | Tm | AB | R | HR | RBI | SB | BA | xBA | OBP | SLG | OPS | vL | vR | bb% | ct% | Eye | G | L | F | h% | HctX | PX | xPX | hr/f | Spd | SBO | SB% | #Wk | DOM | DIS | RC/G | RAR | BPV | BPX | R$ |
|---|---|---|---|---|---|---|---|---|---|---|---|---|---|---|---|---|---|---|---|---|---|---|---|---|---|---|---|---|---|---|---|---|---|---|---|
| 14 | NYY * | 260 | 20 | 6 | 30 | 0 | 234 | 240 | 273 | 348 | 622 | 686 | 690 | 5 | 73 | 0.20 | 36 | 27 | 37 | 30 | 54 | 91 | 53 | 5% | 77 | 0% | 0% | 15 | 40% | 53% | 3.17 | -2.2 | 1 | 3 | $2 |
| 15 | NYY | 155 | 21 | 3 | 14 | 0 | 277 | 244 | 327 | 406 | 734 | 770 | 696 | 7 | 72 | 0.28 | 47 | 23 | 30 | 37 | 102 | 98 | 95 | 9% | 109 | 0% | 0% | 26 | 35% | 54% | 4.72 | 4.0 | 16 | 43 | $2 |
| 16 | MIN * | 345 | 25 | 4 | 37 | 0 | 198 | 198 | 247 | 275 | 522 | 481 | 381 | 6 | 79 | 0.31 | 38 | 16 | 46 | 24 | 82 | 55 | 63 | 3% | 69 | 0% | 0% | 10 | 10% | 60% | 2.16 | -24.3 | -6 | -17 | -$4 |
| 17 | ARI * | 268 | 16 | 4 | 22 | 0 | 186 | 208 | 237 | 261 | 499 | 0 | 429 | 6 | 80 | 0.34 | 50 | 17 | 33 | 22 | 163 | 45 | 140 | 0% | 82 | 0% | 0% | 3 | 33% | 67% | 1.94 | -18.0 | -2 | -6 | -$5 |
| 18 | ARI | 208 | 19 | 9 | 24 | 0 | 202 | 209 | 244 | 375 | 619 | 688 | 561 | 5 | 66 | 0.15 | 31 | 19 | 50 | 26 | 99 | 119 | 150 | 13% | 77 | 0% | 0% | 28 | 25% | 68% | 2.90 | -3.9 | -5 | -17 | $0 |
| 1st Half | | 132 | 18 | 9 | 22 | 0 | 250 | 248 | 296 | 500 | 796 | 911 | 711 | 6 | 70 | 0.21 | 24 | 21 | 54 | 29 | 120 | 154 | 198 | 18% | 82 | 0% | 0% | 15 | 40% | 47% | 4.98 | 5.9 | 43 | 143 | $5 |
| 2nd Half | | 76 | 1 | 0 | 2 | 0 | 118 | 111 | 152 | 158 | 310 | 370 | 243 | 4 | 58 | 0.09 | 47 | 14 | 40 | 20 | 62 | 45 | 43 | 0% | 86 | 0% | 0% | 13 | 8% | 92% | 0.69 | -7.2 | -97 | -323 | -$10 |
| 19 | Proj | **265** | **18** | **7** | **25** | **0** | **210** | **204** | **253** | **329** | **582** | **652** | **528** | **5** | **71** | **0.20** | **36** | **20** | **44** | **27** | **95** | **81** | **88** | **8%** | **77** | **0%** | **0%** | | | | **2.69** | **-6.2** | **-36** | **-121** | **$1** |

## Murphy,Tom

| Murphy,Tom | | | Health | B | LIMA Plan | D+ |
|---|---|---|---|---|---|---|
| Age: 28 | Bats: R | Pos: CA | PT/Exp | F | Rand Var | +4 |
| Ht: 6' 1" | Wt: 220 | | Consist | F | MM | 4203 |

2-11-.226 in 93 AB at COL. If you can't manage more than a .204 xBA, 73 HctX, and 85 xPX with half your games at Coors in a peak age season, maybe hitting's not your thing. Poor ct%, Eye second that notion. Minor league history of plus power means we can't give up on him, but he's an end-gamer now.

| Yr | Tm | AB | R | HR | RBI | SB | BA | xBA | OBP | SLG | OPS | vL | vR | bb% | ct% | Eye | G | L | F | h% | HctX | PX | xPX | hr/f | Spd | SBO | SB% | #Wk | DOM | DIS | RC/G | RAR | BPV | BPX | R$ |
|---|---|---|---|---|---|---|---|---|---|---|---|---|---|---|---|---|---|---|---|---|---|---|---|---|---|---|---|---|---|---|---|---|---|---|---|
| 14 | aa | 94 | 12 | 4 | 11 | 0 | 199 | | 280 | 378 | 658 | | | 10 | 70 | 0.38 | | | | 23 | | 136 | | | 93 | 0% | 0% | | | | 3.37 | | 39 | 105 | -$1 |
| 15 | COL * | 429 | 44 | 19 | 54 | 4 | 232 | 228 | 273 | 433 | 705 | 417 | 1362 | 5 | 68 | 0.18 | 33 | 17 | 50 | 29 | 142 | 146 | 213 | 25% | 95 | 9% | 51% | 4 | 50% | 25% | 3.81 | 0.0 | 31 | 84 | $8 |
| 16 | COL * | 347 | 46 | 20 | 56 | 2 | 297 | 274 | 327 | 584 | 911 | 651 | 1157 | 4 | 71 | 0.16 | 28 | 24 | 48 | 37 | 139 | 184 | 225 | 42% | 122 | 4% | 60% | 6 | 83% | 17% | 6.85 | 23.5 | 79 | 226 | $14 |
| 17 | COL * | 165 | 16 | 3 | 14 | 0 | 195 | 190 | 232 | 318 | 551 | 276 | 0 | 5 | 57 | 0.12 | 40 | 20 | 40 | 32 | 46 | 106 | 40 | 0% | 86 | 0% | 0% | 6 | 0% | 83% | 2.34 | -8.8 | -48 | -145 | -$3 |
| 18 | COL * | 329 | 29 | 13 | 40 | 2 | 214 | 234 | 252 | 415 | 667 | 637 | 637 | 5 | 60 | 0.13 | 31 | 33 | 37 | 31 | 73 | 154 | 85 | 11% | 101 | 12% | 41% | 13 | 15% | 62% | 3.25 | -2.7 | 6 | 20 | $3 |
| 1st Half | | 231 | 22 | 10 | 33 | 1 | 246 | 266 | 282 | 467 | 749 | 667 | 802 | 5 | 64 | 0.14 | 36 | 36 | 28 | 34 | 113 | 162 | 123 | 0% | 97 | 7% | 21% | 4 | 0% | 75% | 4.27 | 5.7 | 26 | 87 | $8 |
| 2nd Half | | 98 | 6 | 3 | 7 | 2 | 140 | 178 | 182 | 295 | 477 | 610 | 510 | 5 | 52 | 0.11 | 25 | 29 | 46 | 23 | 32 | 130 | 46 | 18% | 121 | 27% | 60% | 9 | 22% | 56% | 1.52 | -6.5 | -40 | -133 | -$7 |
| 19 | Proj | **332** | **31** | **9** | **36** | **3** | **237** | **206** | **276** | **403** | **679** | **677** | **680** | **5** | **60** | **0.14** | **38** | **20** | **42** | **36** | **71** | **130** | **77** | **11%** | **100** | **7%** | **60%** | | | | **3.66** | **2.2** | **-14** | **-48** | **$6** |

## Myers,Wil

| Myers,Wil | | | Health | F | LIMA Plan | B |
|---|---|---|---|---|---|---|
| Age: 28 | Bats: R | Pos: 3B LF | PT/Exp | B | Rand Var | 0 |
| Ht: 6' 3" | Wt: 205 | | Consist | A | MM | 4435 |

Back stiffness, nerve irritation in right arm, and oblique strain sabotaged first half, and served as reminder that health is always a risk with him. Shifts in LD/FB caused slide in HR, but history of each gives reason to think he'll revert to more typical levels. Speed drives his value now, and maybe... UP: 30 SB

| Yr | Tm | AB | R | HR | RBI | SB | BA | xBA | OBP | SLG | OPS | vL | vR | bb% | ct% | Eye | G | L | F | h% | HctX | PX | xPX | hr/f | Spd | SBO | SB% | #Wk | DOM | DIS | RC/G | RAR | BPV | BPX | R$ |
|---|---|---|---|---|---|---|---|---|---|---|---|---|---|---|---|---|---|---|---|---|---|---|---|---|---|---|---|---|---|---|---|---|---|---|---|
| 14 | TAM * | 349 | 40 | 8 | 40 | 9 | 221 | 216 | 301 | 329 | 630 | 532 | 649 | 10 | 72 | 0.41 | 48 | 16 | 36 | 29 | 98 | 88 | 96 | 7% | 106 | 10% | 89% | 16 | 25% | 50% | 3.33 | -4.0 | 12 | 32 | $6 |
| 15 | SD | 225 | 40 | 8 | 29 | 5 | 253 | 254 | 336 | 427 | 763 | 793 | 751 | 11 | 76 | 0.49 | 48 | 17 | 36 | 30 | 115 | 119 | 107 | 14% | 112 | 11% | 71% | 12 | 50% | 33% | 4.82 | 0.9 | 54 | 146 | $7 |
| 16 | SD | 599 | 99 | 28 | 94 | 28 | 259 | 263 | 336 | 461 | 797 | 814 | 791 | 10 | 73 | 0.43 | 44 | 22 | 34 | 31 | 100 | 125 | 111 | 19% | 121 | 21% | 82% | 27 | 52% | 33% | 5.37 | 6.9 | 52 | 149 | $28 |
| 17 | SD | 567 | 80 | 30 | 74 | 20 | 243 | 242 | 328 | 464 | 792 | 790 | 792 | 11 | 68 | 0.39 | 38 | 20 | 43 | 30 | 114 | 138 | 144 | 18% | 126 | 18% | 77% | 26 | 46% | 31% | 5.09 | -3.6 | 45 | 136 | $19 |
| 18 | SD | 312 | 39 | 11 | 39 | 13 | 253 | 266 | 318 | 446 | 763 | 805 | 735 | 9 | 70 | 0.32 | 44 | 28 | 29 | 33 | 120 | 137 | 121 | 17% | 95 | 19% | 93% | 19 | 42% | 42% | 5.03 | 3.3 | 37 | 123 | $11 |
| 1st Half | | 72 | 9 | 2 | 7 | 2 | 278 | 262 | 307 | 431 | 737 | 489 | 889 | 4 | 74 | 0.16 | 42 | 28 | 30 | 35 | 123 | 105 | 109 | 13% | 97 | 13% | 100% | 7 | 43% | 43% | 4.83 | 0.7 | 18 | 60 | -$6 |
| 2nd Half | | 240 | 30 | 9 | 32 | 11 | 246 | 268 | 321 | 450 | 771 | 892 | 687 | 10 | 69 | 0.36 | 44 | 27 | 28 | 32 | 119 | 147 | 124 | 19% | 97 | 21% | 92% | 12 | 42% | 42% | 5.09 | 4.2 | 44 | 147 | $16 |
| 19 | Proj | **509** | **70** | **20** | **65** | **19** | **253** | **254** | **321** | **444** | **764** | **749** | **771** | **9** | **71** | **0.34** | **42** | **24** | **34** | **32** | **114** | **128** | **122** | **17%** | **107** | **18%** | **86%** | | | | **4.95** | **6.7** | **38** | **126** | **$21** |

## Naquin,Tyler

| Naquin,Tyler | | | Health | D | LIMA Plan | D |
|---|---|---|---|---|---|---|
| Age: 28 | Bats: L | Pos: RF | PT/Exp | D | Rand Var | 0 |
| Ht: 6'2" | Wt: 195 | | Consist | C | MM | 2231 |

August hip surgery cost him final two months of season; skills say we didn't miss much. Still chasing the promise of that 2016 power, though changes in GB/FB distribution have made that an uphill climb. Only 52 (10%) of his career AB have come vL—that limits upside to deep league speculative material.

| Yr | Tm | AB | R | HR | RBI | SB | BA | xBA | OBP | SLG | OPS | vL | vR | bb% | ct% | Eye | G | L | F | h% | HctX | PX | xPX | hr/f | Spd | SBO | SB% | #Wk | DOM | DIS | RC/G | RAR | BPV | BPX | R$ |
|---|---|---|---|---|---|---|---|---|---|---|---|---|---|---|---|---|---|---|---|---|---|---|---|---|---|---|---|---|---|---|---|---|---|---|---|
| 14 | aa | 304 | 43 | 3 | 24 | 11 | 274 | | 324 | 361 | 685 | | | 7 | 73 | 0.28 | | | | 36 | | 69 | | | 123 | 16% | 77% | | | | 4.14 | | 1 | 3 | $10 |
| 15 | a/a | 327 | 44 | 6 | 24 | 11 | 279 | | 347 | 416 | 764 | | | 9 | 76 | 0.44 | | | | 35 | | 106 | | | 99 | 16% | 77% | | | | 5.13 | | 39 | 105 | $11 |
| 16 | CLE * | 391 | 57 | 15 | 50 | 7 | 289 | 253 | 359 | 486 | 845 | 775 | 898 | 10 | 67 | 0.34 | 46 | 23 | 30 | 40 | 105 | 133 | 127 | 22% | 132 | 11% | 56% | 26 | 50% | 46% | 6.06 | 15.0 | 37 | 106 | $15 |
| 17 | CLE * | 332 | 37 | 8 | 41 | 4 | 257 | 254 | 311 | 391 | 702 | 500 | 523 | 7 | 72 | 0.28 | 59 | 21 | 21 | 33 | 91 | 84 | 69 | 0% | 113 | 10% | 46% | 9 | 22% | 56% | 3.99 | -9.1 | 7 | 21 | $6 |
| 18 | CLE | 174 | 22 | 3 | 23 | 1 | 264 | 242 | 295 | 356 | 651 | 563 | 660 | 3 | 76 | 0.14 | 54 | 23 | 23 | 33 | 107 | 61 | 63 | 10% | 90 | 5% | 50% | 14 | 29% | 50% | 3.50 | -5.0 | -11 | -37 | $2 |
| 1st Half | | 112 | 11 | 2 | 15 | 0 | 277 | 231 | 305 | 375 | 680 | 538 | 698 | 3 | 72 | 0.13 | 52 | 23 | 24 | 37 | 104 | 69 | 55 | 10% | 103 | 4% | 0% | 11 | 27% | 55% | 3.83 | -2.0 | -16 | -53 | $2 |
| 2nd Half | | 62 | 11 | 1 | 8 | 1 | 242 | 260 | 277 | 323 | 600 | 667 | 596 | 3 | 82 | 0.18 | 57 | 22 | 22 | 28 | 113 | 48 | 76 | 9% | 90 | 7% | 100% | 3 | 33% | 33% | 2.96 | -2.8 | 3 | 10 | $2 |
| 19 | Proj | **231** | **32** | **6** | **28** | **3** | **263** | **254** | **311** | **401** | **712** | **649** | **718** | **6** | **75** | **0.23** | **52** | **23** | **26** | **33** | **108** | **86** | **91** | **15%** | **100** | **9%** | **65%** | | | | **4.15** | **-2.1** | **7** | **25** | **$8** |

BRANDON KRUSE

## Narvaez,Omar

| Age: 27 | Bats: B | Pos: CA | Health | A | LIMA Plan | D |
|---|---|---|---|---|---|---|
| Ht: 5' 11" | Wt: 220 | | PT/Exp | D | Rand Var | -3 |
| | | | Consist | C | MM | 1033 |

Sneaky HR source down the stretch, but plenty of reasons to be skeptical: mediocre HctX, xPX not enough to support lofty hr/f; entered 2nd half with 11 HR in more than 2,000 career AB. LD% stroke, xBA history suggest he can be a #2 catcher who won't hurt your BA, and OBP helps too, but don't buy into this power surge.

| Yr | Tm | AB | R | HR | RBI | SB | BA | xBA | OBP | SLG | OPS | vL | vR | bb% | ct% | Eye | G | L | F | h% | HctX | PX | xPX | hr/f | Spd | SBO | SB% | #Wk | DOM | DIS | RC/G | RAR | BPV | BPX | R$ |
|---|---|---|---|---|---|---|---|---|---|---|---|---|---|---|---|---|---|---|---|---|---|---|---|---|---|---|---|---|---|---|---|---|---|---|---|
| 14 | | | | | | | | | | | | | | | | | | | | | | | | | | | | | | | | | | | |
| 15 | | | | | | | | | | | | | | | | | | | | | | | | | | | | | | | | | | | |
| 16 | CHW * | 289 | 27 | 3 | 23 | 0 | 227 | 263 | 289 | 293 | 582 | 947 | 617 | 8 | 85 | 0.58 | 40 | 28 | 31 | 26 | 50 | 43 | 40 | 4% | 80 | 0% | 0% | 11 | 36% | 27% | 2.80 | -9.3 | 16 | 46 | -$1 |
| 17 | CHW | 253 | 23 | 2 | 14 | 0 | 277 | 257 | 373 | 340 | 713 | 668 | 723 | 13 | 82 | 0.84 | 44 | 28 | 29 | 33 | 65 | 41 | 27 | 3% | 76 | 0% | 0% | 26 | 23% | 38% | 4.45 | 2.2 | 12 | 36 | $2 |
| 18 | CHW | 280 | 30 | 9 | 30 | 0 | 275 | 270 | 366 | 429 | 794 | 567 | 837 | 12 | 77 | 0.58 | 42 | 29 | 29 | 33 | 81 | 94 | 84 | 15% | 77 | 2% | 0% | 26 | 38% | 35% | 5.30 | 15.5 | 31 | 103 | $6 |
| 1st Half | | 123 | 8 | 1 | 10 | 0 | 252 | 248 | 333 | 341 | 675 | 403 | 719 | 11 | 78 | 0.56 | 42 | 26 | 32 | 32 | 70 | 67 | 65 | 3% | 82 | 5% | 0% | 14 | 29% | 36% | 3.63 | 0.7 | 14 | 47 | -$2 |
| 2nd Half | | 157 | 22 | 8 | 20 | 0 | 293 | 286 | 390 | 497 | 887 | 668 | 933 | 13 | 76 | 0.61 | 42 | 31 | 27 | 34 | 89 | 116 | 99 | 25% | 79 | 0% | 0% | 12 | 50% | 33% | 6.87 | 14.9 | 47 | 157 | $12 |
| **19** | **Proj** | **247** | **25** | **5** | **21** | **0** | **269** | **258** | **358** | **381** | **739** | **661** | **755** | **12** | **80** | **0.67** | **43** | **26** | **30** | **32** | **71** | **69** | **58** | **9%** | **76** | **1%** | **0%** | | | | **4.67** | **8.7** | **9** | **30** | **$3** |

## Newman,Kevin

| Age: 25 | Bats: R | Pos: SS | Health | A | LIMA Plan | D+ |
|---|---|---|---|---|---|---|
| Ht: 6' 1" | Wt: 180 | | PT/Exp | C | Rand Var | 0 |
| | | | Consist | A | MM | 1441 |

0-6-.209 in 91 AB at PIT. Increased aggressiveness led to SB spike, but a lot of work to do elsewhere: Struggled vR in both AAA and majors; SB% and bb% way too low for a speedster; power is non-existent. Combo of wheels and solid ct% may provide eventual path to roto value, but not yet. Check back in a year.

| Yr | Tm | AB | R | HR | RBI | SB | BA | xBA | OBP | SLG | OPS | vL | vR | bb% | ct% | Eye | G | L | F | h% | HctX | PX | xPX | hr/f | Spd | SBO | SB% | #Wk | DOM | DIS | RC/G | RAR | BPV | BPX | R$ |
|---|---|---|---|---|---|---|---|---|---|---|---|---|---|---|---|---|---|---|---|---|---|---|---|---|---|---|---|---|---|---|---|---|---|---|---|
| 14 | | | | | | | | | | | | | | | | | | | | | | | | | | | | | | | | | | | |
| 15 | | | | | | | | | | | | | | | | | | | | | | | | | | | | | | | | | | | |
| 16 | aa | 233 | 34 | 2 | 23 | 5 | 261 | | 324 | 340 | 664 | | | 9 | 89 | 0.86 | | | | 29 | | 47 | | | 110 | 12% | 60% | | | | 3.70 | | 46 | 131 | $5 |
| 17 | a/a | 509 | 57 | 3 | 36 | 10 | 244 | | 280 | 330 | 610 | | | 5 | 87 | 0.38 | | | | 28 | | 52 | | | 112 | 11% | 74% | | | | 3.11 | | 34 | 103 | $6 |
| 18 | PIT * | 528 | 64 | 3 | 33 | 22 | 250 | 263 | 288 | 326 | 613 | 866 | 405 | 5 | 85 | 0.35 | 55 | 20 | 25 | 29 | 59 | 51 | 45 | 0% | 114 | 28% | 61% | 8 | 13% | 88% | 3.01 | -13.0 | 27 | 90 | $14 |
| 1st Half | | 289 | 37 | 1 | 16 | 15 | 263 | 242 | 301 | 328 | 629 | | | 5 | 86 | 0.39 | | | | 30 | | 47 | | | 115 | 32% | 61% | | | | 3.19 | | 29 | 97 | $17 |
| 2nd Half | | 239 | 27 | 2 | 17 | 7 | 233 | 261 | 271 | 322 | 594 | 866 | 405 | 5 | 83 | 0.31 | 55 | 20 | 25 | 27 | 58 | 56 | 45 | 0% | 122 | 22% | 61% | 8 | 13% | 88% | 2.79 | -8.6 | 27 | 90 | $10 |
| **19** | **Proj** | **232** | **28** | **1** | **17** | **7** | **247** | **268** | **292** | **330** | **622** | **1070** | **537** | **5** | **86** | **0.41** | **55** | **20** | **25** | **28** | **52** | **53** | **41** | **3%** | **119** | **18%** | **66%** | | | | **3.15** | **-5.7** | **30** | **100** | **$6** |

## Nido,Tomas

| Age: 25 | Bats: R | Pos: CA | Health | A | LIMA Plan | D |
|---|---|---|---|---|---|---|
| Ht: 6' 0" | Wt: 210 | | PT/Exp | F | Rand Var | +3 |
| | | | Consist | B | MM | 1021 |

1-9-.167 in 84 AB at NYM. Posted solid .320/.357/.459 line at Single-A in 2016, but bat has stalled as he's moved up the ranks. Power has been slow to develop, and plate approach just took a turn for the worse. Still worth keeping an eye on, but for now, he's likely to be a BA/OBP drag with very little pop.

| Yr | Tm | AB | R | HR | RBI | SB | BA | xBA | OBP | SLG | OPS | vL | vR | bb% | ct% | Eye | G | L | F | h% | HctX | PX | xPX | hr/f | Spd | SBO | SB% | #Wk | DOM | DIS | RC/G | RAR | BPV | BPX | R$ |
|---|---|---|---|---|---|---|---|---|---|---|---|---|---|---|---|---|---|---|---|---|---|---|---|---|---|---|---|---|---|---|---|---|---|---|---|
| 14 | | | | | | | | | | | | | | | | | | | | | | | | | | | | | | | | | | | |
| 15 | | | | | | | | | | | | | | | | | | | | | | | | | | | | | | | | | | | |
| 16 | | | | | | | | | | | | | | | | | | | | | | | | | | | | | | | | | | | |
| 17 | NYM * | 377 | 40 | 8 | 62 | 0 | 218 | 287 | 276 | 333 | 609 | 0 | 778 | 7 | 81 | 0.42 | 25 | 38 | 38 | 25 | 82 | 69 | 161 | 0% | 76 | 0% | 0% | 4 | 25% | 25% | 3.00 | -12.2 | 18 | 55 | $1 |
| 18 | NYM * | 316 | 28 | 4 | 31 | 0 | 204 | 252 | 230 | 312 | 542 | 627 | 395 | 3 | 77 | 0.15 | 51 | 24 | 25 | 25 | 91 | 75 | 74 | 7% | 91 | 0% | 0% | 13 | 8% | 62% | 2.30 | -11.9 | 4 | 13 | -$1 |
| 1st Half | | 153 | 12 | 1 | 12 | 0 | 186 | 233 | 220 | 265 | 486 | 697 | 305 | 4 | 72 | 0.15 | 55 | 24 | 21 | 26 | 100 | 67 | 128 | 0% | 85 | 0% | 0% | 7 | 0% | 71% | 1.83 | -7.9 | -24 | -80 | -$6 |
| 2nd Half | | 163 | 17 | 4 | 19 | 0 | 221 | 268 | 240 | 356 | 596 | 500 | 489 | 2 | 82 | 0.14 | 47 | 23 | 30 | 25 | 81 | 82 | 23 | 11% | 101 | 0% | 0% | 6 | 17% | 50% | 2.79 | -3.3 | 31 | 103 | $3 |
| **19** | **Proj** | **167** | **16** | **3** | **21** | **0** | **230** | **249** | **260** | **347** | **607** | **834** | **559** | **5** | **79** | **0.23** | **48** | **22** | **30** | **27** | **89** | **76** | **65** | **8%** | **94** | **0%** | **0%** | | | | **3.05** | **-2.0** | **1** | **5** | **$2** |

## Nimmo,Brandon

| Age: 26 | Bats: L | Pos: RF CF LF | Health | C | LIMA Plan | B |
|---|---|---|---|---|---|---|
| Ht: 6' 3" | Wt: 207 | | PT/Exp | C | Rand Var | -3 |
| | | | Consist | C | MM | 4225 |

Quickly forced way into starting role with big 1st half before pair of finger injuries slowed him down. Sure, early power might be a little over his head, and ct%, particularly vL (62%), is a concern. But bb%, Spd make him ideal fit at top of the order, and if pre-injury 1st half line really was a breakout... UP: 25 HR, 15 SB

| Yr | Tm | AB | R | HR | RBI | SB | BA | xBA | OBP | SLG | OPS | vL | vR | bb% | ct% | Eye | G | L | F | h% | HctX | PX | xPX | hr/f | Spd | SBO | SB% | #Wk | DOM | DIS | RC/G | RAR | BPV | BPX | R$ |
|---|---|---|---|---|---|---|---|---|---|---|---|---|---|---|---|---|---|---|---|---|---|---|---|---|---|---|---|---|---|---|---|---|---|---|---|
| 14 | aa | 240 | 28 | 5 | 19 | 4 | 200 | | 280 | 320 | 600 | | | 10 | 75 | 0.43 | | | | 25 | | 91 | | | 116 | 8% | 77% | | | | 2.87 | | 28 | 76 | $0 |
| 15 | a/a | 360 | 35 | 4 | 19 | 4 | 237 | | 304 | 324 | 628 | | | 9 | 76 | 0.41 | | | | 30 | | 61 | | | 122 | 11% | 37% | | | | 3.09 | | 11 | 30 | $2 |
| 16 | NYM * | 465 | 61 | 9 | 47 | 5 | 279 | 261 | 337 | 398 | 735 | 661 | 667 | 8 | 76 | 0.36 | 42 | 30 | 28 | 35 | 87 | 76 | 79 | 7% | 123 | 10% | 33% | 10 | 20% | 50% | 4.42 | -3.0 | 19 | 54 | $12 |
| 17 | NYM * | 340 | 42 | 7 | 33 | 2 | 221 | 226 | 333 | 353 | 686 | 530 | 878 | 14 | 65 | 0.48 | 43 | 24 | 33 | 32 | 92 | 98 | 106 | 13% | 101 | 2% | 100% | 13 | 31% | 69% | 3.89 | -12.1 | 0 | 0 | $1 |
| 18 | NYM | 433 | 77 | 17 | 47 | 9 | 263 | 254 | 404 | 483 | 886 | 742 | 946 | 15 | 68 | 0.57 | 45 | 22 | 33 | 35 | 93 | 148 | 114 | 18% | 145 | 11% | 60% | 26 | 46% | 35% | 6.15 | 24.4 | 64 | 213 | $16 |
| 1st Half | | 211 | 40 | 12 | 25 | 7 | 270 | 249 | 389 | 540 | 929 | 766 | 1008 | 12 | 66 | 0.41 | 39 | 19 | 42 | 35 | 103 | 169 | 159 | 21% | 174 | 15% | 78% | 15 | 47% | 33% | 6.74 | 15.9 | 79 | 263 | $20 |
| 2nd Half | | 222 | 37 | 5 | 22 | 2 | 257 | 259 | 417 | 428 | 845 | 713 | 891 | 19 | 69 | 0.74 | 50 | 24 | 25 | 35 | 83 | 128 | 74 | 13% | 113 | 7% | 33% | 11 | 45% | 36% | 5.52 | 9.2 | 51 | 170 | $12 |
| **19** | **Proj** | **483** | **72** | **18** | **58** | **7** | **260** | **252** | **377** | **457** | **834** | **665** | **887** | **14** | **69** | **0.52** | **44** | **23** | **33** | **34** | **95** | **131** | **103** | **16%** | **122** | **8%** | **55%** | | | | **5.55** | **15.6** | **40** | **132** | **$17** |

## Nunez,Eduardo

| Age: 32 | Bats: R | Pos: 2B 3B | Health | B | LIMA Plan | B |
|---|---|---|---|---|---|---|
| Ht: 6' 0" | Wt: 195 | | PT/Exp | B | Rand Var | +1 |
| | | | Consist | C | MM | 1443 |

Off-season knee surgery didn't do the trick, as it supposedly bothered him for most of year. SBO completely dried up, but after awful 1st half, ct%, HctX, and even Spd were about as strong as ever. Obviously carries some risk, but if knee is back to 100 percent, discounted price could yield pretty nice profit.

| Yr | Tm | AB | R | HR | RBI | SB | BA | xBA | OBP | SLG | OPS | vL | vR | bb% | ct% | Eye | G | L | F | h% | HctX | PX | xPX | hr/f | Spd | SBO | SB% | #Wk | DOM | DIS | RC/G | RAR | BPV | BPX | R$ |
|---|---|---|---|---|---|---|---|---|---|---|---|---|---|---|---|---|---|---|---|---|---|---|---|---|---|---|---|---|---|---|---|---|---|---|---|
| 14 | MIN * | 253 | 32 | 5 | 28 | 10 | 251 | 265 | 274 | 377 | 651 | 586 | 716 | 3 | 83 | 0.19 | 56 | 16 | 27 | 29 | 80 | 78 | 42 | 9% | 148 | 25% | 78% | 20 | 40% | 40% | 3.52 | 1.0 | 47 | 127 | $7 |
| 15 | MIN | 188 | 23 | 4 | 20 | 8 | 282 | 284 | 327 | 431 | 758 | 649 | 809 | 6 | 85 | 0.41 | 57 | 16 | 27 | 32 | 93 | 100 | 68 | 10% | 101 | 26% | 67% | 24 | 50% | 25% | 4.78 | 2.7 | 62 | 168 | $7 |
| 16 | 2 TM | 553 | 73 | 16 | 67 | 40 | 288 | 264 | 325 | 432 | 758 | 750 | 760 | 5 | 84 | 0.33 | 50 | 17 | 34 | 32 | 95 | 80 | 85 | 10% | 142 | 35% | 80% | 26 | 50% | 31% | 5.04 | 4.9 | 55 | 157 | $32 |
| 17 | 2 TM | 467 | 60 | 12 | 58 | 24 | 313 | 292 | 341 | 460 | 801 | 751 | 821 | 4 | 88 | 0.33 | 53 | 17 | 29 | 33 | 96 | 83 | 67 | 10% | 101 | 26% | 77% | 22 | 50% | 14% | 5.74 | 14.3 | 60 | 182 | $26 |
| 18 | BOS | 480 | 56 | 10 | 44 | 7 | 265 | 262 | 289 | 388 | 677 | 641 | 691 | 3 | 86 | 0.23 | 49 | 19 | 32 | 29 | 86 | 70 | 47 | 7% | 122 | 8% | 78% | 28 | 43% | 14% | 3.88 | -2.7 | 44 | 147 | $12 |
| 1st Half | | 268 | 31 | 5 | 19 | 4 | 250 | 244 | 283 | 354 | 637 | 526 | 681 | 4 | 81 | 0.22 | 50 | 19 | 32 | 29 | 79 | 66 | 40 | 7% | 104 | 10% | 67% | 15 | 33% | 20% | 3.33 | -6.8 | 19 | 63 | $10 |
| 2nd Half | | 212 | 25 | 5 | 25 | 3 | 283 | 281 | 298 | 429 | 727 | 797 | 703 | 2 | 91 | 0.26 | 48 | 19 | 33 | 29 | 95 | 74 | 55 | 8% | 135 | 6% | 100% | 13 | 54% | 8% | 4.66 | 2.9 | 70 | 233 | $14 |
| **19** | **Proj** | **405** | **50** | **10** | **44** | **10** | **280** | **271** | **307** | **418** | **725** | **694** | **737** | **3** | **87** | **0.27** | **51** | **18** | **31** | **30** | **91** | **77** | **60** | **9%** | **122** | **15%** | **72%** | | | | **4.47** | **3.5** | **47** | **158** | **$16** |

## Nunez,Renato

| Age: 25 | Bats: R | Pos: 3B | Health | A | LIMA Plan | D+ |
|---|---|---|---|---|---|---|
| Ht: 6' 1" | Wt: 220 | | PT/Exp | C | Rand Var | -4 |
| | | | Consist | B | MM | 2305 |

8-22-.258 in 236 AB at TEX/BAL. Return of ct% appeared to sap his power for most of season, but finished strong (.313 BA, 5 HR in Sept). He'll need to combine 2017 power with 2018 ct% in order to make an impact. Given inconsistencies in both and supbar BPV history, odds are against for 2019. But has some time.

| Yr | Tm | AB | R | HR | RBI | SB | BA | xBA | OBP | SLG | OPS | vL | vR | bb% | ct% | Eye | G | L | F | h% | HctX | PX | xPX | hr/f | Spd | SBO | SB% | #Wk | DOM | DIS | RC/G | RAR | BPV | BPX | R$ |
|---|---|---|---|---|---|---|---|---|---|---|---|---|---|---|---|---|---|---|---|---|---|---|---|---|---|---|---|---|---|---|---|---|---|---|---|
| 14 | | | | | | | | | | | | | | | | | | | | | | | | | | | | | | | | | | | |
| 15 | aa | 381 | 47 | 13 | 46 | 1 | 243 | | 283 | 398 | 681 | | | 5 | 82 | 0.30 | | | | 27 | | 100 | | | 82 | 1% | 100% | | | | 3.80 | | 43 | 116 | $7 |
| 16 | OAK * | 520 | 51 | 18 | 63 | 2 | 203 | 271 | 240 | 347 | 587 | 333 | 0 | 5 | 76 | 0.20 | 75 | 17 | 8 | 23 | 26 | 87 | -3 | 0% | 86 | 2% | 100% | 3 | 0% | 100% | 2.68 | -34.4 | 9 | 26 | $1 |
| 17 | OAK * | 488 | 60 | 25 | 65 | 2 | 216 | 279 | 273 | 426 | 699 | 636 | 650 | 7 | 67 | 0.23 | 29 | 43 | 29 | 27 | 77 | 135 | 116 | 50% | 93 | 3% | 59% | 4 | 0% | 75% | 3.76 | -16.4 | 20 | 61 | $5 |
| 18 | 2 AL * | 465 | 51 | 13 | 46 | 1 | 262 | 220 | 321 | 403 | 723 | 670 | 778 | 8 | 74 | 0.33 | 39 | 17 | 43 | 33 | 74 | 94 | 78 | 11% | 108 | 1% | 100% | 16 | 38% | 19% | 4.47 | 1.8 | 20 | 67 | $9 |
| 1st Half | | 218 | 21 | 3 | 18 | 1 | 245 | 173 | 305 | 342 | 647 | 639 | 411 | 8 | 72 | 0.31 | 40 | 8 | 52 | 33 | 74 | 71 | 73 | 8% | 108 | 1% | 100% | 4 | 25% | 25% | 3.55 | -6.2 | -5 | -17 | $3 |
| 2nd Half | | 247 | 30 | 10 | 28 | 0 | 278 | 239 | 334 | 455 | 790 | 679 | 829 | 8 | 75 | 0.34 | 39 | 19 | 42 | 33 | 75 | 112 | 79 | 11% | 100 | 0% | 0% | 12 | 42% | 17% | 5.38 | 6.1 | 39 | 130 | $15 |
| **19** | **Proj** | **423** | **48** | **13** | **48** | **1** | **241** | **220** | **304** | **393** | **697** | **676** | **710** | **7** | **73** | **0.28** | **40** | **16** | **44** | **30** | **75** | **99** | **77** | **10%** | **109** | **1%** | **84%** | | | | **3.90** | **-7.6** | **3** | **11** | **$9** |

## O Hearn,Ryan

| Age: 25 | Bats: L | Pos: 1B | Health | A | LIMA Plan | D+ |
|---|---|---|---|---|---|---|
| Ht: 6'3" | Wt: 200 | | PT/Exp | B | Rand Var | +2 |
| | | | Consist | A | MM | 4113 |

12-30-.262 in 149 AB at KC. Surprising power source over final two months, but a couple red flags here: MLB BA doesn't jibe with minors history and ct% baseline; 2nd half power well above previous levels, aided by sky-high hr/f. The 2,000+ AB minor league track record suggests he's unlikely to pick up where he left off.

| Yr | Tm | AB | R | HR | RBI | SB | BA | xBA | OBP | SLG | OPS | vL | vR | bb% | ct% | Eye | G | L | F | h% | HctX | PX | xPX | hr/f | Spd | SBO | SB% | #Wk | DOM | DIS | RC/G | RAR | BPV | BPX | R$ |
|---|---|---|---|---|---|---|---|---|---|---|---|---|---|---|---|---|---|---|---|---|---|---|---|---|---|---|---|---|---|---|---|---|---|---|---|
| 14 | | | | | | | | | | | | | | | | | | | | | | | | | | | | | | | | | | | |
| 15 | | | | | | | | | | | | | | | | | | | | | | | | | | | | | | | | | | | |
| 16 | aa | 414 | 45 | 12 | 55 | 3 | 247 | | 318 | 410 | 728 | | | 9 | 67 | 0.31 | | | | 34 | | 121 | | | 89 | 8% | 34% | | | | 4.21 | | 11 | 31 | $7 |
| 17 | a/a | 479 | 45 | 16 | 53 | 1 | 227 | | 293 | 393 | 686 | | | 9 | 68 | 0.30 | | | | 30 | | 110 | | | 91 | 1% | 100% | | | | 3.80 | | 8 | 24 | $3 |
| 18 | KC * | 502 | 59 | 20 | 70 | 2 | 219 | 230 | 295 | 408 | 703 | 465 | 1108 | 10 | 70 | 0.36 | 35 | 19 | 46 | 27 | 108 | 127 | 160 | 25% | 86 | 1% | 100% | 10 | 70% | 10% | 3.95 | -7.2 | 27 | 90 | $8 |
| 1st Half | | 264 | 28 | 7 | 33 | 1 | 216 | 229 | 286 | 357 | 643 | | | 9 | 72 | 0.35 | | | | 27 | | 95 | | | 100 | 1% | 100% | | | | 3.34 | | 13 | 43 | $5 |
| 2nd Half | | 238 | 31 | 13 | 37 | 1 | 222 | 245 | 305 | 465 | 770 | 465 | 1108 | 11 | 67 | 0.36 | 35 | 19 | 46 | 27 | 105 | 164 | 160 | 25% | 91 | 2% | 100% | 10 | 70% | 10% | 4.67 | -0.7 | 51 | 170 | $12 |
| **19** | **Proj** | **380** | **42** | **13** | **50** | **1** | **219** | **227** | **297** | **396** | **693** | **323** | **814** | **10** | **67** | **0.32** | **38** | **20** | **42** | **29** | **95** | **124** | **144** | **13%** | **83** | **3%** | **68%** | | | | **3.78** | **-11.5** | **10** | **33** | **$6** |

BRIAN RUDD

## O Neill,Tyler

Age: 24 Bats: R Pos: RF
Ht: 5' 11" Wt: 210

Health A | LIMA Plan C+
PT/Exp B | Rand Var -2
Consist D | MM 4505

9-23-.254 in 130 AB at STL. Explosive MLB debut just another point along a straight power-growth line. Already packed near-elite punch at 23, but sub-60% MLB ct% introduces risk to both BA and HR totals (see Sano, M). Non-sluggerish speed adds to intrigue and upside, but establishing bat-to-ball is Job One.

| Yr | Tm | AB | R | HR | RBI | SB | BA | xBA | OBP | SLG | OPS | vL | vR | bb% | ct% | Eye | G | L | F | h% | HctX | PX | xPX | hr/f | Spd | SBO | SB% | #Wk | DOM | DIS | RC/G | RAR | BPV | BPX | R$ |
|---|---|---|---|---|---|---|---|---|---|---|---|---|---|---|---|---|---|---|---|---|---|---|---|---|---|---|---|---|---|---|---|---|---|---|---|
| 14 | | | | | | | | | | | | | | | | | | | | | | | | | | | | | | | | | | | |
| 15 | | | | | | | | | | | | | | | | | | | | | | | | | | | | | | | | | | | |
| 16 | aa | 492 | 61 | 22 | 92 | 11 | 272 | | 345 | 468 | 813 | | | 10 | 66 | 0.33 | | | | 37 | | 135 | | | 90 | 9% | 83% | | | | 5.70 | | 21 | 60 | $20 |
| 17 | aaa | 495 | 65 | 25 | 80 | 12 | 222 | | 286 | 429 | 715 | | | 8 | 68 | 0.28 | | | | 28 | | 131 | | | 94 | 13% | 84% | | | | 4.06 | | 21 | 64 | $11 |
| 18 | STL * | 368 | 77 | 28 | 73 | 4 | 265 | 240 | 319 | 539 | 858 | 800 | 804 | 7 | 64 | 0.22 | 29 | 23 | 48 | 33 | 107 | 179 | 169 | 25% | 117 | 7% | 79% | 15 | 33% | 53% | 5.96 | 16.6 | 51 | 170 | $18 |
| 1st Half | | 222 | 42 | 17 | 45 | 2 | 260 | 271 | 306 | 531 | 837 | 0 | 881 | 6 | 67 | 0.20 | 29 | 38 | 33 | 31 | 93 | 169 | 139 | 43% | 90 | 7% | 68% | 6 | 33% | 67% | 5.53 | 7.0 | 43 | 143 | $21 |
| 2nd Half | | 146 | 35 | 11 | 28 | 2 | 272 | 227 | 338 | 553 | 890 | 953 | 765 | 9 | 60 | 0.25 | 30 | 17 | 54 | 37 | 107 | 195 | 181 | 21% | 131 | 5% | 100% | 9 | 33% | 44% | 6.63 | 9.0 | 57 | 190 | $14 |
| 19 | Proj | **417** | **73** | **22** | **76** | **7** | **239** | **215** | **312** | **452** | **764** | **730** | **773** | **8** | **60** | **0.23** | **32** | **22** | **45** | **34** | **101** | **155** | **164** | **20%** | **129** | **9%** | **86%** | | | | **4.61** | **1.9** | **18** | **60** | **$14** |

## Odor,Rougned

Age: 25 Bats: L Pos: 2B
Ht: 5' 11" Wt: 195

Health B | LIMA Plan B+
PT/Exp A | Rand Var -2
Consist D | MM 3225

Did he start to re-figure some things out? Better patience, hard-contact surge are hopeful signs, and was arguably his team's best hitter over the summer before Sept fade. Some real risk that the SB total could dry up, as success rate stooped to a new low. But still only 25, and his stock is rising again.

| Yr | Tm | AB | R | HR | RBI | SB | BA | xBA | OBP | SLG | OPS | vL | vR | bb% | ct% | Eye | G | L | F | h% | HctX | PX | xPX | hr/f | Spd | SBO | SB% | #Wk | DOM | DIS | RC/G | RAR | BPV | BPX | R$ |
|---|---|---|---|---|---|---|---|---|---|---|---|---|---|---|---|---|---|---|---|---|---|---|---|---|---|---|---|---|---|---|---|---|---|---|---|
| 14 | TEX * | 515 | 57 | 14 | 62 | 9 | 260 | 249 | 292 | 404 | 695 | 626 | 727 | 4 | 82 | 0.24 | 49 | 15 | 36 | 29 | 90 | 90 | 68 | 8% | 133 | 16% | 47% | 22 | 41% | 23% | 3.78 | 6.0 | 49 | 132 | $15 |
| 15 | TEX * | 534 | 76 | 20 | 77 | 9 | 273 | 277 | 316 | 486 | 802 | 781 | 781 | 6 | 83 | 0.37 | 46 | 15 | 40 | 30 | 106 | 126 | 102 | 12% | 132 | 14% | 51% | 22 | 55% | 18% | 5.14 | 13.3 | 86 | 232 | $21 |
| 16 | TEX | 605 | 89 | 33 | 88 | 14 | 271 | 269 | 296 | 502 | 798 | 763 | 811 | 3 | 78 | 0.14 | 40 | 18 | 42 | 30 | 112 | 135 | 131 | 17% | 89 | 19% | 67% | 26 | 54% | 19% | 5.00 | 4.8 | 53 | 151 | $25 |
| 17 | TEX | 607 | 79 | 30 | 75 | 15 | 204 | 239 | 252 | 397 | 649 | 452 | 719 | 5 | 73 | 0.20 | 42 | 16 | 42 | 23 | 109 | 109 | 116 | 16% | 92 | 21% | 71% | 27 | 30% | 41% | 3.05 | -30.2 | 20 | 61 | $9 |
| 18 | TEX | 474 | 76 | 18 | 63 | 12 | 253 | 238 | 326 | 424 | 751 | 711 | 773 | 8 | 73 | 0.34 | 41 | 20 | 39 | 31 | 122 | 107 | 121 | 14% | 101 | 20% | 50% | 25 | 24% | 40% | 4.22 | 2.1 | 27 | 90 | $17 |
| 1st Half | | 188 | 26 | 4 | 19 | 3 | 229 | 204 | 300 | 351 | 651 | 766 | 600 | 7 | 71 | 0.28 | 40 | 15 | 45 | 30 | 110 | 83 | 113 | 7% | 116 | 18% | 38% | 12 | 17% | 33% | 3.00 | -6.9 | 3 | 10 | $1 |
| 2nd Half | | 286 | 50 | 14 | 44 | 9 | 269 | 259 | 344 | 472 | 816 | 683 | 902 | 9 | 74 | 0.38 | 42 | 22 | 36 | 32 | 130 | 122 | 125 | 18% | 91 | 21% | 56% | 13 | 31% | 46% | 5.16 | 8.3 | 43 | 143 | $28 |
| 19 | Proj | **590** | **87** | **26** | **78** | **10** | **245** | **244** | **302** | **435** | **736** | **668** | **768** | **6** | **75** | **0.27** | **42** | **18** | **40** | **29** | **115** | **113** | **117** | **15%** | **100** | **16%** | **50%** | | | | **4.06** | **-2.1** | **34** | **113** | **$20** |

## Ohtani,Shohei

Age: 24 Bats: L Pos: DH
Ht: 6' 4" Wt: 200

Health A | LIMA Plan B
PT/Exp D | Rand Var 0
Consist A | MM 5345

Elbow woes aside, "second coming of Babe Ruth" lived up to the hype, and then some. Now, following Tommy John surgery, he's expected to DH full time in 2019. Booming power more than offsets shaky ct%. Showed a marked platoon split, so more AB vL could hurt rate stats. Still, this is a skill set to own—pitching or not.

| Yr | Tm | AB | R | HR | RBI | SB | BA | xBA | OBP | SLG | OPS | vL | vR | bb% | ct% | Eye | G | L | F | h% | HctX | PX | xPX | hr/f | Spd | SBO | SB% | #Wk | DOM | DIS | RC/G | RAR | BPV | BPX | R$ |
|---|---|---|---|---|---|---|---|---|---|---|---|---|---|---|---|---|---|---|---|---|---|---|---|---|---|---|---|---|---|---|---|---|---|---|---|
| 14 | for | 212 | 31 | 6 | 30 | 1 | 255 | | 310 | 434 | 744 | | | 7 | 79 | 0.37 | | | | 30 | | 136 | | | 95 | 2% | 100% | | | | 4.63 | 3.6 | 68 | 184 | $5 |
| 15 | for | 109 | 15 | 3 | 17 | 1 | 188 | | 233 | 307 | 541 | | | 6 | 63 | 0.16 | | | | 27 | | 97 | | | 90 | 4% | 100% | | | | 2.29 | -10.9 | -30 | -81 | -$1 |
| 16 | for | 323 | 63 | 13 | 65 | 6 | 300 | | 383 | 488 | 871 | | | 12 | 71 | 0.47 | | | | 39 | | 123 | | | 93 | 8% | 74% | | | | 6.78 | 11.5 | 37 | 106 | $16 |
| 17 | for | 191 | 22 | 5 | 30 | 0 | 312 | | 371 | 482 | 852 | | | 8 | 70 | 0.31 | | | | 42 | | 116 | | | 96 | 2% | 0% | | | | 6.47 | 8.3 | 22 | 67 | $6 |
| 18 | LAA | 326 | 59 | 22 | 61 | 10 | 285 | 279 | 361 | 564 | 925 | 654 | 1043 | 10 | 69 | 0.36 | 44 | 24 | 33 | 35 | 109 | 181 | 129 | 30% | 117 | 16% | 71% | 25 | 60% | 28% | 7.08 | 23.9 | 77 | 257 | $19 |
| 1st Half | | 114 | 17 | 6 | 20 | 1 | 289 | 280 | 372 | 535 | 907 | 451 | 1057 | 12 | 71 | 0.45 | 51 | 22 | 27 | 36 | 110 | 158 | 108 | 27% | 116 | 3% | 100% | 12 | 50% | 33% | 7.21 | 8.6 | 71 | 237 | $3 |
| 2nd Half | | 212 | 42 | 16 | 41 | 9 | 283 | 276 | 354 | 580 | 935 | 734 | 1035 | 9 | 67 | 0.32 | 40 | 24 | 36 | 35 | 109 | 193 | 141 | 31% | 118 | 25% | 69% | 13 | 69% | 23% | 6.97 | 15.1 | 80 | 267 | $27 |
| 19 | Proj | **443** | **72** | **26** | **79** | **6** | **282** | **276** | **354** | **542** | **896** | **629** | **1010** | **10** | **70** | **0.35** | **44** | **23** | **33** | **35** | **109** | **168** | **128** | **26%** | **117** | **8%** | **63%** | | | | **6.64** | **26.9** | **62** | **208** | **$23** |

## Olson,Matt

Age: 25 Bats: L Pos: 1B
Ht: 6' 5" Wt: 230

Health A | LIMA Plan B+
PT/Exp B | Rand Var 0
Consist B | MM 4225

Power regressed a bit—as expected. Overall, though, a solid first full MLB season. Plate skills growth was encouraging, and finished especially well after mid-season struggles. Two-year xPX totals and fly-ball lean point to more power upside. A consistent 30-HR threat with a BA that doesn't offend (these days).

| Yr | Tm | AB | R | HR | RBI | SB | BA | xBA | OBP | SLG | OPS | vL | vR | bb% | ct% | Eye | G | L | F | h% | HctX | PX | xPX | hr/f | Spd | SBO | SB% | #Wk | DOM | DIS | RC/G | RAR | BPV | BPX | R$ |
|---|---|---|---|---|---|---|---|---|---|---|---|---|---|---|---|---|---|---|---|---|---|---|---|---|---|---|---|---|---|---|---|---|---|---|---|
| 14 | | | | | | | | | | | | | | | | | | | | | | | | | | | | | | | | | | | |
| 15 | aa | 466 | 62 | 12 | 57 | 4 | 217 | | 331 | 366 | 697 | | | 15 | 68 | 0.54 | | | | 29 | | 123 | | | 81 | 4% | 78% | | | | 3.96 | | 28 | 76 | $5 |
| 16 | OAK * | 485 | 61 | 13 | 51 | 1 | 207 | 203 | 302 | 359 | 661 | 0 | 527 | 12 | 71 | 0.46 | 47 | 6 | 47 | 26 | 51 | 110 | -10 | 0% | 88 | 1% | 100% | 4 | 50% | 25% | 3.49 | -20.6 | 24 | 69 | $0 |
| 17 | OAK * | 483 | 78 | 41 | 93 | 2 | 246 | 257 | 326 | 539 | 865 | 758 | 1081 | 11 | 69 | 0.38 | 38 | 16 | 46 | 27 | 112 | 170 | 178 | 41% | 80 | 2% | 100% | 16 | 44% | 44% | 5.97 | 8.4 | 58 | 176 | $16 |
| 18 | OAK | 580 | 85 | 29 | 84 | 2 | 247 | 247 | 335 | 453 | 788 | 701 | 830 | 11 | 72 | 0.43 | 36 | 21 | 43 | 29 | 125 | 132 | 140 | 16% | 81 | 2% | 67% | 28 | 46% | 25% | 5.01 | 10.1 | 41 | 137 | $17 |
| 1st Half | | 305 | 45 | 18 | 43 | 2 | 239 | 242 | 321 | 459 | 780 | 709 | 813 | 9 | 71 | 0.34 | 35 | 20 | 45 | 28 | 137 | 136 | 171 | 19% | 79 | 4% | 67% | 15 | 47% | 13% | 4.70 | -0.6 | 36 | 120 | $19 |
| 2nd Half | | 275 | 40 | 11 | 41 | 0 | 255 | 252 | 350 | 447 | 797 | 691 | 848 | 13 | 73 | 0.54 | 36 | 22 | 41 | 31 | 112 | 128 | 107 | 13% | 89 | 0% | 0% | 13 | 46% | 38% | 5.34 | 4.6 | 49 | 163 | $15 |
| 19 | Proj | **557** | **81** | **33** | **83** | **2** | **253** | **250** | **349** | **487** | **835** | **708** | **887** | **12** | **71** | **0.44** | **37** | **19** | **44** | **30** | **118** | **149** | **151** | **19%** | **81** | **2%** | **80%** | | | | **5.64** | **14.2** | **41** | **137** | **$20** |

## Osuna,Jose

Age: 26 Bats: R Pos: 1B
Ht: 6' 3" Wt: 240

Health A | LIMA Plan D+
PT/Exp D | Rand Var 0
Consist A | MM 3151

3-11-.226 in 106 AB at PIT. "Makes consistent contact" is both a truism and the best compliment one can make for this skill set. If you squint hard enough, you can find 1) 2nd-half spurts in HctX, xPX, FB%; 2) established double-digit hr/f; 3) solid xBA history. But the whole package is decidedly uninspiring. And my eyes hurt.

| Yr | Tm | AB | R | HR | RBI | SB | BA | xBA | OBP | SLG | OPS | vL | vR | bb% | ct% | Eye | G | L | F | h% | HctX | PX | xPX | hr/f | Spd | SBO | SB% | #Wk | DOM | DIS | RC/G | RAR | BPV | BPX | R$ |
|---|---|---|---|---|---|---|---|---|---|---|---|---|---|---|---|---|---|---|---|---|---|---|---|---|---|---|---|---|---|---|---|---|---|---|---|
| 14 | | | | | | | | | | | | | | | | | | | | | | | | | | | | | | | | | | | |
| 15 | aa | 323 | 37 | 6 | 42 | 5 | 253 | | 283 | 371 | 654 | | | 4 | 80 | 0.21 | | | | 30 | | 83 | | | 91 | 12% | 59% | | | | 3.48 | | 23 | 62 | $7 |
| 16 | a/a | 473 | 53 | 11 | 60 | 3 | 254 | | 300 | 408 | 709 | | | 6 | 82 | 0.37 | | | | 29 | | 97 | | | 93 | 7% | 37% | | | | 4.04 | | 47 | 134 | $8 |
| 17 | PIT * | 251 | 36 | 7 | 31 | 1 | 231 | 283 | 270 | 416 | 686 | 740 | 660 | 5 | 80 | 0.27 | 53 | 18 | 29 | 26 | 96 | 106 | 65 | 14% | 97 | 5% | 43% | 25 | 56% | 36% | 3.66 | -11.6 | 46 | 139 | $2 |
| 18 | PIT * | 408 | 48 | 10 | 56 | 4 | 258 | 272 | 303 | 404 | 707 | 834 | 447 | 6 | 80 | 0.33 | 47 | 24 | 29 | 30 | 94 | 96 | 79 | 12% | 69 | 8% | 51% | 15 | 40% | 40% | 4.10 | -3.5 | 32 | 107 | $10 |
| 1st Half | | 192 | 21 | 5 | 31 | 1 | 265 | 276 | 307 | 437 | 745 | 671 | 471 | 6 | 80 | 0.31 | 53 | 19 | 28 | 31 | 82 | 115 | 63 | 20% | 69 | 8% | 24% | 7 | 43% | 29% | 4.43 | -0.1 | 47 | 157 | $8 |
| 2nd Half | | 216 | 28 | 5 | 25 | 3 | 251 | 266 | 299 | 375 | 675 | 996 | 435 | 6 | 80 | 0.35 | 43 | 27 | 31 | 29 | 102 | 80 | 90 | 7% | 76 | 8% | 72% | 8 | 38% | 50% | 3.81 | -4.1 | 22 | 73 | $11 |
| 19 | Proj | **231** | **29** | **7** | **30** | **2** | **249** | **278** | **295** | **422** | **717** | **859** | **576** | **6** | **80** | **0.30** | **49** | **21** | **29** | **28** | **95** | **106** | **73** | **13%** | **80** | **8%** | **57%** | | | | **4.09** | **-4.6** | **43** | **142** | **$6** |

## Owings,Christopher

Age: 27 Bats: R Pos: RF
Ht: 5'10" Wt: 185

Health C | LIMA Plan C+
PT/Exp C | Rand Var +3
Consist C | MM 2323

4-22-.206 with 11 SB in 281 AB at ARI. What went wrong? Two theories: 1) Just an epic run of bad luck, as HctX / xPX / Eye all reached new peaks, but were buried by h% and hr/f. 2) Nick Ahmed tricked him into some sort of "Freaky Friday" body swap. We're not totally ruling out #2, but Rand Var says there's nice profit in #1.

| Yr | Tm | AB | R | HR | RBI | SB | BA | xBA | OBP | SLG | OPS | vL | vR | bb% | ct% | Eye | G | L | F | h% | HctX | PX | xPX | hr/f | Spd | SBO | SB% | #Wk | DOM | DIS | RC/G | RAR | BPV | BPX | R$ |
|---|---|---|---|---|---|---|---|---|---|---|---|---|---|---|---|---|---|---|---|---|---|---|---|---|---|---|---|---|---|---|---|---|---|---|---|
| 14 | ARI * | 350 | 38 | 6 | 27 | 10 | 255 | 257 | 287 | 386 | 673 | 829 | 672 | 4 | 78 | 0.21 | 45 | 24 | 31 | 31 | 90 | 93 | 77 | 8% | 163 | 14% | 91% | 18 | 33% | 50% | 3.89 | -2.0 | 46 | 124 | $8 |
| 15 | ARI | 515 | 59 | 4 | 43 | 16 | 227 | 227 | 264 | 322 | 587 | 495 | 614 | 5 | 72 | 0.18 | 39 | 26 | 34 | 31 | 94 | 76 | 93 | 3% | 117 | 19% | 80% | 27 | 30% | 63% | 2.85 | -31.6 | -4 | -11 | $7 |
| 16 | ARI | 437 | 52 | 5 | 49 | 21 | 277 | 273 | 315 | 416 | 731 | 826 | 700 | 4 | 80 | 0.23 | 50 | 23 | 27 | 34 | 97 | 84 | 75 | 5% | 159 | 23% | 91% | 22 | 36% | 27% | 4.72 | 0.5 | 46 | 131 | $17 |
| 17 | ARI | 362 | 41 | 12 | 51 | 12 | 268 | 262 | 299 | 442 | 741 | 685 | 759 | 4 | 76 | 0.20 | 43 | 22 | 36 | 32 | 97 | 108 | 109 | 12% | 99 | 18% | 86% | 18 | 28% | 28% | 4.70 | -5.0 | 31 | 94 | $12 |
| 18 | ARI * | 372 | 43 | 5 | 28 | 12 | 207 | 219 | 257 | 299 | 556 | 702 | 465 | 6 | 74 | 0.26 | 39 | 22 | 38 | 27 | 106 | 65 | 123 | 5% | 108 | 23% | 64% | 25 | 24% | 64% | 2.39 | -23.7 | -4 | -13 | $4 |
| 1st Half | | 205 | 25 | 3 | 17 | 6 | 195 | 210 | 265 | 293 | 558 | 631 | 509 | 8 | 71 | 0.31 | 43 | 19 | 39 | 26 | 91 | 73 | 100 | 5% | 106 | 20% | 67% | 15 | 20% | 73% | 2.37 | -13.8 | -7 | -23 | $3 |
| 2nd Half | | 167 | 18 | 2 | 11 | 6 | 222 | 236 | 252 | 307 | 559 | 828 | 285 | 4 | 78 | 0.18 | 31 | 31 | 38 | 28 | 141 | 56 | 177 | 4% | 105 | 27% | 61% | 10 | 30% | 50% | 2.41 | -10.7 | -3 | -10 | $5 |
| 19 | Proj | **333** | **38** | **8** | **32** | **12** | **256** | **247** | **294** | **396** | **690** | **794** | **625** | **5** | **76** | **0.22** | **40** | **25** | **35** | **32** | **109** | **89** | **120** | **9%** | **88** | **21%** | **73%** | | | | **3.94** | **-8.2** | **20** | **68** | **$11** |

## Ozuna,Marcell

Age: 28 Bats: R Pos: LF
Ht: 6'1" Wt: 225

Health A | LIMA Plan B
PT/Exp A | Rand Var -1
Consist F | MM 3235

Played through a year-long cranky shoulder. He says it didn't affect his bat; skills back that: tough to bump ct% / HctX / xPX with a bad wing. In fact, despite R$, the story here is stability: 2014/16/18 set baseline, 2015/17 are just cases where hr/f got wonky in either direction. Fade the shoulder narrative, pay for a repeat only.

| Yr | Tm | AB | R | HR | RBI | SB | BA | xBA | OBP | SLG | OPS | vL | vR | bb% | ct% | Eye | G | L | F | h% | HctX | PX | xPX | hr/f | Spd | SBO | SB% | #Wk | DOM | DIS | RC/G | RAR | BPV | BPX | R$ |
|---|---|---|---|---|---|---|---|---|---|---|---|---|---|---|---|---|---|---|---|---|---|---|---|---|---|---|---|---|---|---|---|---|---|---|---|
| 14 | MIA | 565 | 72 | 23 | 85 | 3 | 269 | 252 | 317 | 455 | 772 | 728 | 783 | 7 | 71 | 0.25 | 49 | 18 | 34 | 34 | 117 | 140 | 133 | 17% | 126 | 3% | 75% | 26 | 42% | 38% | 5.05 | 20.4 | 49 | 132 | $20 |
| 15 | MIA * | 579 | 64 | 14 | 53 | 3 | 263 | 255 | 310 | 402 | 712 | 888 | 646 | 6 | 77 | 0.29 | 48 | 21 | 31 | 32 | 115 | 102 | 106 | 9% | 79 | 4% | 48% | 23 | 30% | 43% | 4.24 | -8.1 | 26 | 70 | $12 |
| 16 | MIA | 557 | 75 | 23 | 76 | 0 | 266 | 262 | 321 | 452 | 773 | 923 | 732 | 7 | 79 | 0.37 | 44 | 20 | 37 | 30 | 120 | 105 | 121 | 14% | 134 | 2% | 0% | 26 | 38% | 31% | 4.89 | 4.2 | 58 | 166 | $14 |
| 17 | MIA | 613 | 93 | 37 | 124 | 1 | 312 | 275 | 376 | 548 | 924 | 804 | 955 | 9 | 77 | 0.44 | 47 | 19 | 34 | 36 | 121 | 130 | 106 | 23% | 90 | 2% | 25% | 27 | 52% | 22% | 7.52 | 37.6 | 58 | 176 | $31 |
| 18 | STL | 582 | 69 | 23 | 88 | 3 | 280 | 248 | 325 | 433 | 758 | 895 | 716 | 6 | 81 | 0.35 | 47 | 18 | 35 | 31 | 135 | 81 | 112 | 14% | 95 | 2% | 100% | 26 | 38% | 38% | 5.00 | 6.5 | 32 | 107 | $21 |
| 1st Half | | 298 | 32 | 10 | 44 | 2 | 285 | 240 | 330 | 419 | 750 | 856 | 722 | 6 | 80 | 0.33 | 48 | 18 | 33 | 33 | 135 | 74 | 103 | 13% | 102 | 2% | 100% | 15 | 27% | 60% | 4.98 | 3.2 | 22 | 73 | $20 |
| 2nd Half | | 284 | 37 | 13 | 44 | 1 | 275 | 256 | 320 | 447 | 767 | 925 | 709 | 6 | 83 | 0.37 | 46 | 18 | 36 | 29 | 135 | 89 | 120 | 15% | 88 | 1% | 100% | 11 | 55% | 9% | 5.02 | 3.4 | 43 | 143 | $21 |
| 19 | Proj | **557** | **70** | **26** | **86** | **2** | **282** | **257** | **329** | **467** | **796** | **871** | **774** | **6** | **79** | **0.33** | **46** | **19** | **36** | **32** | **127** | **102** | **113** | **16%** | **113** | **2%** | **58%** | | | | **5.41** | **12.8** | **31** | **103** | **$22** |

ROD TRUESDELL

## Palka,Daniel

| Age: 27 | Bats: L | Pos: DH RF LF | Health | A | LIMA Plan | D+ |
|---|---|---|---|---|---|---|
| Ht: 6' 2" | Wt: 220 | | PT/Exp | C | Rand Var | 0 |
| | | | Consist | A | MM | 4113 |

27-67-.240 in 417 AB at CHW. Surprise power source after being claimed on waivers before 2018. Tons of punch, but poor plate approach seals BA fate, HctX and high GB% both point to possible HR downside (see xPX), 250-pt OPS platoon split won't gain him many AB vL. This pony's trick is a risky one. DN: 15 HR

| Yr | Tm | AB | R | HR | RBI | SB | BA | xBA | OBP | SLG | OPS | vL | vR | bb% | ct% | Eye | G | L | F | h% | HctX | PX | xPX | hr/f | Spd | SBO | SB% | #Wk | DOM | DIS | RC/G | RAR | BPV | BPX | R$ |
|---|---|---|---|---|---|---|---|---|---|---|---|---|---|---|---|---|---|---|---|---|---|---|---|---|---|---|---|---|---|---|---|---|---|---|---|
| 14 | | | | | | | | | | | | | | | | | | | | | | | | | | | | | | | | | | | |
| 15 | | | | | | | | | | | | | | | | | | | | | | | | | | | | | | | | | | | |
| 16 | a/a | 503 | 61 | 28 | 76 | 8 | 227 | | 292 | 453 | 745 | | | 8 | 60 | 0.23 | | | | 31 | | 166 | | | 96 | 12% | 57% | | | | 4.22 | | 20 | 57 | $11 |
| 17 | aaa | 332 | 42 | 10 | 38 | 1 | 251 | | 301 | 395 | 696 | | | 7 | 73 | 0.27 | | | | 31 | | 84 | | | 116 | 4% | 28% | | | | 3.94 | | 10 | 30 | $5 |
| 18 | CHW * | 480 | 64 | 29 | 72 | 3 | 239 | 230 | 295 | 472 | 767 | 570 | 824 | 7 | 63 | 0.21 | 46 | 16 | 38 | 31 | 84 | 157 | 115 | 27% | 103 | 6% | 45% | 24 | 50% | 33% | 4.55 | 0.5 | 24 | 80 | $14 |
| 1st Half | | 236 | 28 | 9 | 29 | 3 | 236 | 225 | 296 | 426 | 722 | 836 | 704 | 8 | 65 | 0.24 | 45 | 18 | 37 | 32 | 88 | 129 | 104 | 16% | 112 | 12% | 45% | 11 | 55% | 27% | 4.01 | -3.2 | 13 | 43 | $9 |
| 2nd Half | | 244 | 36 | 20 | 43 | 0 | 242 | 230 | 299 | 516 | 816 | 418 | 913 | 7 | 61 | 0.19 | 47 | 15 | 39 | 30 | 80 | 187 | 123 | 35% | 88 | 0% | 0% | 13 | 46% | 38% | 5.10 | 4.7 | 34 | 113 | $19 |
| 19 | Proj | 389 | 51 | 20 | 55 | 2 | 239 | 227 | 298 | 442 | 740 | 552 | 781 | 7 | 66 | 0.23 | 46 | 16 | 38 | 31 | 83 | 133 | 115 | 21% | 105 | 6% | 48% | | | | 4.27 | -2.8 | 9 | 30 | $9 |

## Panik,Joe

| Age: 28 | Bats: L | Pos: 2B | Health | D | LIMA Plan | B |
|---|---|---|---|---|---|---|
| Ht: 6' 1" | Wt: 200 | | PT/Exp | B | Rand Var | +2 |
| | | | Consist | C | MM | 1345 |

Weird: When reaching a 90+ percent contact rate, somehow he hits worse! Now, before you go crossing out the Forecaster Encyclopedia's entry on ct%/BA correlation, note that xBA and H% show ill fortune has played a part. And in 2018, thumb and groin sprains surely contributed as well. With health, should be good for a BA rebound.

| Yr | Tm | AB | R | HR | RBI | SB | BA | xBA | OBP | SLG | OPS | vL | vR | bb% | ct% | Eye | G | L | F | h% | HctX | PX | xPX | hr/f | Spd | SBO | SB% | #Wk | DOM | DIS | RC/G | RAR | BPV | BPX | R$ |
|---|---|---|---|---|---|---|---|---|---|---|---|---|---|---|---|---|---|---|---|---|---|---|---|---|---|---|---|---|---|---|---|---|---|---|---|
| 14 | SF * | 562 | 64 | 4 | 48 | 2 | 281 | 263 | 323 | 358 | 680 | 839 | 655 | 6 | 87 | 0.48 | 50 | 23 | 27 | 32 | 90 | 53 | 51 | 2% | 136 | 3% | 46% | 17 | 24% | 24% | 4.04 | 10.3 | 45 | 122 | $13 |
| 15 | SF | 382 | 59 | 8 | 37 | 3 | 312 | 288 | 378 | 455 | 833 | 769 | 852 | 9 | 89 | 0.90 | 43 | 23 | 34 | 33 | 115 | 91 | 89 | 7% | 106 | 4% | 60% | 18 | 72% | 11% | 6.24 | 21.5 | 80 | 216 | $15 |
| 16 | SF | 464 | 67 | 10 | 62 | 5 | 239 | 270 | 315 | 379 | 695 | 595 | 734 | 10 | 90 | 1.06 | 45 | 18 | 37 | 25 | 94 | 73 | 87 | 6% | 122 | 4% | 100% | 24 | 67% | 13% | 4.04 | -11.3 | 75 | 214 | $8 |
| 17 | SF | 511 | 60 | 10 | 53 | 4 | 288 | 282 | 347 | 421 | 768 | 697 | 799 | 8 | 89 | 0.85 | 44 | 22 | 34 | 31 | 94 | 70 | 78 | 6% | 116 | 3% | 80% | 27 | 59% | 15% | 5.23 | 3.0 | 67 | 203 | $14 |
| 18 | SF | 358 | 38 | 4 | 24 | 4 | 254 | 271 | 307 | 332 | 639 | 489 | 706 | 7 | 92 | 0.87 | 48 | 23 | 30 | 27 | 105 | 44 | 56 | 4% | 97 | 6% | 67% | 21 | 43% | 10% | 3.44 | -8.7 | 46 | 153 | $5 |
| 1st Half | | 180 | 24 | 4 | 12 | 1 | 250 | 278 | 325 | 367 | 692 | 521 | 797 | 9 | 93 | 1.38 | 47 | 21 | 32 | 25 | 101 | 59 | 64 | 7% | 117 | 6% | 33% | 11 | 55% | 0% | 3.82 | -1.9 | 74 | 247 | $4 |
| 2nd Half | | 178 | 14 | 0 | 12 | 3 | 258 | 264 | 287 | 298 | 585 | 433 | 630 | 4 | 90 | 0.47 | 48 | 25 | 27 | 29 | 110 | 29 | 48 | 0% | 79 | 6% | 100% | 10 | 30% | 20% | 3.07 | -5.7 | 19 | 63 | $5 |
| 19 | Proj | 455 | 52 | 6 | 40 | 5 | 276 | 270 | 329 | 373 | 702 | 597 | 744 | 7 | 90 | 0.80 | 46 | 22 | 32 | 30 | 101 | 54 | 67 | 4% | 105 | 5% | 77% | | | | 4.31 | 1.8 | 45 | 149 | $12 |

## Parra,Gerardo

| Age: 32 | Bats: L | Pos: LF | Health | C | LIMA Plan | D |
|---|---|---|---|---|---|---|
| Ht: 5' 11" | Wt: 210 | | PT/Exp | C | Rand Var | -2 |
| | | | Consist | D | MM | 1233 |

Just look at that second-half power "output." That's despite a solid Eye and other mostly unchanged peripherals; the 3% hr/f hints at a hidden injury. Line-drive stroke and solid HctX sets good BA floor: now owns a career .683 road (mostly non-Coors/Chase) OPS. So consider home park wisely before drafting.

| Yr | Tm | AB | R | HR | RBI | SB | BA | xBA | OBP | SLG | OPS | vL | vR | bb% | ct% | Eye | G | L | F | h% | HctX | PX | xPX | hr/f | Spd | SBO | SB% | #Wk | DOM | DIS | RC/G | RAR | BPV | BPX | R$ |
|---|---|---|---|---|---|---|---|---|---|---|---|---|---|---|---|---|---|---|---|---|---|---|---|---|---|---|---|---|---|---|---|---|---|---|---|
| 14 | 2 NL | 529 | 64 | 9 | 40 | 9 | 261 | 266 | 308 | 369 | 677 | 554 | 704 | 6 | 81 | 0.32 | 54 | 22 | 24 | 31 | 96 | 76 | 85 | 9% | 103 | 12% | 56% | 28 | 25% | 43% | 3.72 | -0.9 | 29 | 78 | $13 |
| 15 | 2 TM | 547 | 83 | 14 | 51 | 14 | 291 | 287 | 328 | 452 | 780 | 658 | 809 | 5 | 83 | 0.30 | 47 | 24 | 29 | 33 | 109 | 104 | 97 | 11% | 113 | 14% | 78% | 27 | 44% | 22% | 5.27 | 8.5 | 61 | 165 | $23 |
| 16 | COL * | 394 | 47 | 7 | 41 | 6 | 247 | 271 | 265 | 384 | 649 | 634 | 684 | 2 | 79 | 0.12 | 55 | 19 | 26 | 29 | 103 | 90 | 100 | 9% | 91 | 14% | 60% | 19 | 53% | 37% | 3.34 | -15.1 | 24 | 69 | $6 |
| 17 | COL | 392 | 56 | 10 | 71 | 2 | 309 | 277 | 341 | 452 | 793 | 806 | 788 | 5 | 83 | 0.30 | 47 | 23 | 30 | 35 | 117 | 83 | 113 | 10% | 75 | 7% | 29% | 24 | 42% | 29% | 5.43 | 1.9 | 32 | 97 | $16 |
| 18 | COL | 401 | 52 | 6 | 53 | 11 | 284 | 254 | 342 | 372 | 714 | 510 | 776 | 7 | 81 | 0.43 | 47 | 25 | 28 | 34 | 102 | 55 | 96 | 7% | 68 | 12% | 73% | 28 | 25% | 50% | 4.46 | -1.6 | 6 | 20 | $14 |
| 1st Half | | 239 | 32 | 5 | 37 | 6 | 301 | 264 | 340 | 418 | 758 | 459 | 866 | 5 | 82 | 0.30 | 47 | 24 | 29 | 35 | 109 | 73 | 102 | 9% | 73 | 13% | 67% | 15 | 47% | 40% | 5.04 | 3.0 | 19 | 63 | $19 |
| 2nd Half | | 162 | 20 | 1 | 16 | 5 | 259 | 241 | 346 | 302 | 648 | 610 | 657 | 10 | 81 | 0.61 | 46 | 27 | 27 | 32 | 92 | 29 | 86 | 3% | 71 | 11% | 83% | 13 | 0% | 62% | 3.62 | -4.7 | -9 | -30 | $7 |
| 19 | Proj | 263 | 34 | 5 | 34 | 5 | 280 | 260 | 327 | 386 | 713 | 629 | 738 | 6 | 81 | 0.35 | 48 | 24 | 28 | 33 | 104 | 66 | 99 | 8% | 78 | 11% | 66% | | | | 4.35 | -1.9 | 17 | 57 | $10 |

## Pearce,Steve

| Age: 36 | Bats: R | Pos: 1B DH | Health | F | LIMA Plan | D+ |
|---|---|---|---|---|---|---|
| Ht: 5' 11" | Wt: 200 | | PT/Exp | D | Rand Var | -2 |
| | | | Consist | F | MM | 4043 |

Return to lefty-killing ways carved out terrific per-AB value. Of course, in a short-side platoon, those at-bats were relatively few. Couple that with his propensity for injury, and can't even bet on 2018's AB total going forward. Worth a late-round pick in sim leagues, or spot him in DFS games vLHP.

| Yr | Tm | AB | R | HR | RBI | SB | BA | xBA | OBP | SLG | OPS | vL | vR | bb% | ct% | Eye | G | L | F | h% | HctX | PX | xPX | hr/f | Spd | SBO | SB% | #Wk | DOM | DIS | RC/G | RAR | BPV | BPX | R$ |
|---|---|---|---|---|---|---|---|---|---|---|---|---|---|---|---|---|---|---|---|---|---|---|---|---|---|---|---|---|---|---|---|---|---|---|---|
| 14 | BAL | 338 | 51 | 21 | 49 | 5 | 293 | 294 | 373 | 556 | 930 | 1109 | 856 | 10 | 78 | 0.53 | 35 | 19 | 46 | 32 | 116 | 188 | 130 | 18% | 77 | 5% | 100% | 26 | 62% | 35% | 7.48 | 35.5 | 107 | 289 | $18 |
| 15 | BAL | 294 | 42 | 15 | 40 | 1 | 218 | 252 | 289 | 422 | 711 | 623 | 765 | 7 | 77 | 0.33 | 34 | 20 | 46 | 23 | 101 | 129 | 132 | 14% | 84 | 3% | 50% | 22 | 50% | 36% | 3.73 | -6.0 | 51 | 138 | $4 |
| 16 | 2 AL | 264 | 35 | 13 | 35 | 0 | 288 | 266 | 374 | 492 | 867 | 1022 | 798 | 11 | 80 | 0.63 | 43 | 19 | 38 | 32 | 112 | 117 | 118 | 16% | 114 | 4% | 0% | 21 | 48% | 38% | 6.23 | 14.6 | 71 | 203 | $8 |
| 17 | TOR * | 335 | 40 | 13 | 38 | 0 | 241 | 257 | 299 | 414 | 713 | 730 | 767 | 7 | 78 | 0.37 | 41 | 21 | 38 | 27 | 109 | 99 | 99 | 14% | 80 | 0% | 0% | 20 | 45% | 35% | 4.15 | -12.8 | 32 | 97 | $4 |
| 18 | 2 AL | 215 | 35 | 11 | 42 | 0 | 284 | 283 | 378 | 512 | 890 | 959 | 828 | 12 | 81 | 0.71 | 44 | 20 | 36 | 31 | 110 | 129 | 122 | 17% | 94 | 0% | 0% | 21 | 48% | 29% | 6.72 | 12.9 | 80 | 267 | $8 |
| 1st Half | | 83 | 16 | 4 | 16 | 0 | 301 | 311 | 356 | 530 | 886 | 933 | 807 | 8 | 82 | 0.47 | 38 | 29 | 32 | 33 | 129 | 135 | 164 | 18% | 93 | 0% | 0% | 9 | 44% | 22% | 6.88 | 5.2 | 81 | 270 | $4 |
| 2nd Half | | 132 | 19 | 7 | 26 | 0 | 273 | 266 | 391 | 500 | 891 | 982 | 835 | 14 | 80 | 0.85 | 47 | 15 | 38 | 29 | 99 | 126 | 95 | 17% | 95 | 0% | 0% | 12 | 50% | 33% | 6.60 | 7.6 | 81 | 270 | $10 |
| 19 | Proj | 251 | 37 | 12 | 40 | 0 | 271 | 272 | 354 | 484 | 838 | 905 | 795 | 10 | 80 | 0.56 | 42 | 20 | 38 | 30 | 110 | 122 | 117 | 16% | 94 | 1% | 33% | | | | 5.81 | 7.6 | 53 | 177 | $10 |

## Pederson,Joc

| Age: 27 | Bats: L | Pos: LF CF | Health | B | LIMA Plan | B+ |
|---|---|---|---|---|---|---|
| Ht: 6' 1" | Wt: 220 | | PT/Exp | C | Rand Var | +2 |
| | | | Consist | F | MM | 4135 |

The evolution continues. Slipped a bit in Sept, but overall, 2018 continued his steady upward trend in making contact—and hard contact at that. Surging xBA gives hope for a respectable BA in his future, too. No, he still can't hit lefties, and he's not turning into Ichiro Jr. or anything. But there's sneaky value here.

| Yr | Tm | AB | R | HR | RBI | SB | BA | xBA | OBP | SLG | OPS | vL | vR | bb% | ct% | Eye | G | L | F | h% | HctX | PX | xPX | hr/f | Spd | SBO | SB% | #Wk | DOM | DIS | RC/G | RAR | BPV | BPX | R$ |
|---|---|---|---|---|---|---|---|---|---|---|---|---|---|---|---|---|---|---|---|---|---|---|---|---|---|---|---|---|---|---|---|---|---|---|---|
| 14 | LA * | 473 | 68 | 22 | 49 | 19 | 239 | 217 | 335 | 416 | 751 | 167 | 561 | 13 | 61 | 0.37 | 35 | 24 | 41 | 34 | 73 | 148 | 103 | 0% | 96 | 23% | 56% | 5 | 20% | 80% | 4.34 | 7.5 | 18 | 49 | $18 |
| 15 | LA | 480 | 67 | 26 | 54 | 4 | 210 | 224 | 346 | 417 | 763 | 691 | 784 | 16 | 65 | 0.54 | 42 | 16 | 42 | 26 | 104 | 152 | 147 | 20% | 84 | 7% | 36% | 27 | 41% | 37% | 4.34 | 0.5 | 39 | 105 | $7 |
| 16 | LA | 406 | 64 | 25 | 68 | 6 | 246 | 261 | 352 | 495 | 847 | 469 | 918 | 13 | 68 | 0.48 | 40 | 21 | 40 | 30 | 107 | 169 | 134 | 23% | 77 | 7% | 75% | 25 | 56% | 36% | 5.81 | 14.0 | 59 | 169 | $13 |
| 17 | LA * | 338 | 50 | 13 | 42 | 5 | 199 | 258 | 288 | 378 | 667 | 597 | 768 | 11 | 75 | 0.51 | 47 | 19 | 34 | 22 | 100 | 110 | 101 | 15% | 72 | 10% | 61% | 23 | 43% | 35% | 3.41 | -17.6 | 33 | 100 | $2 |
| 18 | LA | 395 | 65 | 25 | 56 | 1 | 248 | 281 | 321 | 522 | 843 | 503 | 893 | 9 | 78 | 0.47 | 39 | 17 | 44 | 26 | 122 | 156 | 134 | 18% | 89 | 7% | 17% | 28 | 68% | 14% | 5.33 | 12.9 | 85 | 283 | $13 |
| 1st Half | | 190 | 32 | 11 | 32 | 1 | 258 | 288 | 341 | 537 | 878 | 276 | 979 | 11 | 83 | 0.75 | 36 | 17 | 48 | 26 | 132 | 151 | 162 | 14% | 96 | 7% | 33% | 15 | 73% | 0% | 6.07 | 10.8 | 107 | 357 | $13 |
| 2nd Half | | 205 | 33 | 14 | 24 | 0 | 239 | 272 | 302 | 507 | 810 | 747 | 814 | 7 | 74 | 0.30 | 43 | 17 | 39 | 25 | 112 | 162 | 104 | 23% | 85 | 8% | 0% | 13 | 62% | 31% | 4.68 | 3.4 | 68 | 227 | $12 |
| 19 | Proj | 439 | 69 | 25 | 60 | 4 | 255 | 264 | 342 | 496 | 838 | 593 | 884 | 10 | 74 | 0.45 | 42 | 18 | 40 | 29 | 111 | 147 | 124 | 19% | 82 | 9% | 44% | | | | 5.44 | 11.0 | 57 | 191 | $17 |

## Pedroia,Dustin

| Age: 35 | Bats: R | Pos: 2B | Health | F | LIMA Plan | C |
|---|---|---|---|---|---|---|
| Ht: 5'9" | Wt: 175 | | PT/Exp | C | Rand Var | +5 |
| | | | Consist | F | MM | 1143 |

Return from left knee surgery obviously didn't go as hoped, and he needed another cleanup procedure in July. He and the club hope he'll be ready to go by spring. But consider that he's only managed one full season in the last four. Still has the skills to contribute if he can get on the field, but that's a massive "if."

| Yr | Tm | AB | R | HR | RBI | SB | BA | xBA | OBP | SLG | OPS | vL | vR | bb% | ct% | Eye | G | L | F | h% | HctX | PX | xPX | hr/f | Spd | SBO | SB% | #Wk | DOM | DIS | RC/G | RAR | BPV | BPX | R$ |
|---|---|---|---|---|---|---|---|---|---|---|---|---|---|---|---|---|---|---|---|---|---|---|---|---|---|---|---|---|---|---|---|---|---|---|---|
| 14 | BOS | 551 | 72 | 7 | 53 | 6 | 278 | 276 | 337 | 376 | 712 | 727 | 707 | 8 | 86 | 0.68 | 48 | 24 | 28 | 31 | 112 | 75 | 88 | 5% | 95 | 7% | 50% | 24 | 50% | 13% | 4.37 | 15.4 | 53 | 143 | $16 |
| 15 | BOS | 381 | 46 | 12 | 42 | 2 | 291 | 270 | 356 | 441 | 797 | 834 | 785 | 9 | 87 | 0.75 | 50 | 18 | 32 | 31 | 96 | 90 | 92 | 11% | 118 | 3% | 50% | 19 | 58% | 16% | 5.56 | 13.7 | 74 | 200 | $12 |
| 16 | BOS | 633 | 105 | 15 | 74 | 7 | 318 | 294 | 376 | 449 | 825 | 812 | 827 | 9 | 88 | 0.84 | 49 | 24 | 27 | 34 | 115 | 75 | 82 | 10% | 106 | 5% | 64% | 27 | 52% | 4% | 6.26 | 26.1 | 65 | 186 | $28 |
| 17 | BOS | 406 | 46 | 7 | 62 | 4 | 293 | 273 | 369 | 392 | 760 | 929 | 729 | 11 | 88 | 1.02 | 49 | 22 | 29 | 32 | 92 | 55 | 58 | 7% | 86 | 5% | 57% | 23 | 52% | 26% | 5.14 | 5.8 | 46 | 139 | $13 |
| 18 | BOS | 11 | 1 | 0 | 0 | 0 | 91 | 257 | 231 | 91 | 322 | 250 | 347 | 15 | 91 | 2.00 | 40 | 30 | 30 | 10 | 67 | 0 | -2 | 0% | 96 | 0% | 0% | 2 | 50% | 50% | 0.59 | -1.3 | 25 | 83 | -$3 |
| 1st Half | | 11 | 1 | 0 | 0 | 0 | 91 | 257 | 231 | 91 | 322 | 250 | 347 | 15 | 91 | 2.00 | 40 | 30 | 30 | 10 | 67 | 0 | -2 | 0% | 96 | 0% | 0% | 2 | 50% | 50% | 0.59 | -1.4 | 25 | 83 | -$3 |
| 2nd Half | | | | | | | | | | | | | | | | | | | | | | | | | | | | | | | | | | | |
| 19 | Proj | 286 | 37 | 6 | 35 | 2 | 295 | 272 | 360 | 417 | 777 | 828 | 763 | 9 | 87 | 0.82 | 49 | 21 | 29 | 32 | 101 | 69 | 79 | 9% | 68 | 5% | 55% | | | | 5.35 | 4.7 | 41 | 138 | $11 |

## Pence,Hunter

| Age: 36 | Bats: R | Pos: LF | Health | F | LIMA Plan | D |
|---|---|---|---|---|---|---|
| Ht: 6'4" | Wt: 230 | | PT/Exp | C | Rand Var | +2 |
| | | | Consist | D | MM | 1321 |

4-24-.226 with 5 SB in 235 AB at SF. Missed time with a sprained right thumb. But that injury is less the cause and more the latest data point in a series of maladies that has led to this decline. Even second-half "rebound" shows there's little left in the tank. A sentimental favorite, but sentiment doesn't win your league. DN: Retires.

| Yr | Tm | AB | R | HR | RBI | SB | BA | xBA | OBP | SLG | OPS | vL | vR | bb% | ct% | Eye | G | L | F | h% | HctX | PX | xPX | hr/f | Spd | SBO | SB% | #Wk | DOM | DIS | RC/G | RAR | BPV | BPX | R$ |
|---|---|---|---|---|---|---|---|---|---|---|---|---|---|---|---|---|---|---|---|---|---|---|---|---|---|---|---|---|---|---|---|---|---|---|---|
| 14 | SF | 650 | 106 | 20 | 74 | 13 | 277 | 264 | 332 | 445 | 777 | 770 | 779 | 7 | 80 | 0.40 | 52 | 14 | 34 | 32 | 97 | 112 | 88 | 11% | 160 | 11% | 68% | 27 | 59% | 26% | 5.11 | 24.6 | 74 | 200 | $27 |
| 15 | SF | 207 | 30 | 9 | 40 | 4 | 275 | 279 | 327 | 478 | 806 | 570 | 861 | 7 | 77 | 0.33 | 54 | 17 | 29 | 32 | 119 | 135 | 117 | 20% | 85 | 10% | 80% | 11 | 73% | 9% | 5.52 | 4.7 | 57 | 154 | $8 |
| 16 | SF * | 419 | 62 | 15 | 62 | 1 | 290 | 258 | 356 | 460 | 816 | 821 | 802 | 9 | 76 | 0.43 | 55 | 17 | 28 | 35 | 93 | 108 | 79 | 15% | 100 | 2% | 50% | 20 | 40% | 35% | 5.84 | 14.2 | 42 | 120 | $15 |
| 17 | SF | 493 | 55 | 13 | 67 | 2 | 260 | 239 | 315 | 385 | 701 | 776 | 670 | 7 | 79 | 0.39 | 57 | 13 | 29 | 30 | 94 | 66 | 76 | 11% | 143 | 4% | 40% | 24 | 33% | 42% | 4.10 | -16.7 | 30 | 91 | $9 |
| 18 | SF * | 338 | 26 | 5 | 32 | 5 | 224 | 225 | 257 | 312 | 568 | 566 | 609 | 4 | 73 | 0.16 | 50 | 21 | 29 | 29 | 82 | 61 | 64 | 8% | 106 | 8% | 83% | 22 | 27% | 55% | 2.66 | -20.0 | -15 | -50 | $2 |
| 1st Half | | 201 | 12 | 1 | 17 | 2 | 213 | 185 | 253 | 250 | 504 | 447 | 520 | 5 | 68 | 0.17 | 50 | 20 | 30 | 31 | 61 | 33 | 45 | 0% | 94 | 4% | 100% | 9 | 11% | 56% | 2.10 | -15.5 | -62 | -207 | -$1 |
| 2nd Half | | 137 | 14 | 4 | 15 | 3 | 241 | 275 | 261 | 401 | 662 | 643 | 678 | 3 | 81 | 0.15 | 50 | 21 | 29 | 27 | 101 | 95 | 75 | 13% | 109 | 17% | 75% | 13 | 38% | 54% | 3.51 | -4.5 | 41 | 137 | $7 |
| 19 | Proj | 165 | 18 | 4 | 20 | 2 | 251 | 243 | 294 | 378 | 672 | 649 | 685 | 6 | 77 | 0.27 | 53 | 18 | 29 | 30 | 91 | 78 | 73 | 10% | 125 | 7% | 71% | | | | 3.78 | -4.0 | 8 | 28 | $4 |

ROD TRUESDELL

## Peralta,David

Age: 31 | Bats: L | Pos: LF
Ht: 6' 1" | Wt: 210

| Health | C | LIMA Plan | A |
|---|---|---|---|
| PT/Exp | C | Rand Var | -2 |
| Consist | C | MM | 3355 |

What humidor? (.988 home OPS.) Third among MLB qualifiers in hard-contact percentage, and that spike surged right through season's end. Sure, groundball tilt means this was probably his HR peak. But xBA confirms solid BA floor; even factoring in some power regression, a $20 bid looks safe here.

| Yr Tm | AB | R | HR | RBI | SB | BA | xBA | OBP | SLG | OPS | vL | vR | bb% | ct% | Eye | G | L | F | h% | HctX | PX | xPX | hr/f | Spd | SBO | SB% | #Wk | DOM | DIS | RC/G | RAR | BPV | BPX | R$ |
|---|---|---|---|---|---|---|---|---|---|---|---|---|---|---|---|---|---|---|---|---|---|---|---|---|---|---|---|---|---|---|---|---|---|---|
| 14 ARI * | 531 | 64 | 13 | 69 | 7 | 271 | 282 | 309 | 430 | 739 | 510 | 848 | 5 | 84 | 0.34 | 48 | 21 | 31 | 30 | 110 | 104 | 90 | 10% | 110 | 8% | 71% | 17 | 59% | 18% | 4.61 | 12.6 | 64 | 173 | $17 |
| 15 ARI | 462 | 61 | 17 | 78 | 9 | 312 | 286 | 371 | 522 | 893 | 686 | 936 | 9 | 77 | 0.41 | 52 | 21 | 27 | 38 | 118 | 133 | 115 | 18% | 123 | 10% | 69% | 26 | 46% | 15% | 7.08 | 29.8 | 70 | 189 | $24 |
| 16 ARI * | 206 | 28 | 4 | 17 | 2 | 244 | 269 | 281 | 414 | 696 | 717 | 731 | 5 | 76 | 0.22 | 51 | 21 | 28 | 30 | 107 | 107 | 99 | 11% | 116 | 8% | 62% | 10 | 30% | 30% | 3.87 | -4.6 | 36 | 103 | $2 |
| 17 ARI | 525 | 82 | 14 | 57 | 8 | 293 | 278 | 352 | 444 | 796 | 711 | 825 | 7 | 82 | 0.46 | 55 | 18 | 26 | 34 | 106 | 86 | 80 | 12% | 115 | 8% | 67% | 26 | 46% | 23% | 5.49 | 3.3 | 49 | 148 | $19 |
| 18 ARI | 560 | 75 | 30 | 87 | 4 | 293 | 280 | 352 | 516 | 868 | 693 | 946 | 8 | 78 | 0.39 | 51 | 20 | 29 | 33 | 139 | 124 | 120 | 23% | 107 | 3% | 100% | 27 | 52% | 22% | 6.54 | 30.0 | 60 | 200 | $25 |
| 1st Half | 295 | 37 | 15 | 44 | 2 | 281 | 276 | 349 | 508 | 857 | 670 | 935 | 9 | 76 | 0.40 | 51 | 19 | 30 | 32 | 131 | 132 | 120 | 22% | 112 | 3% | 100% | 15 | 53% | 27% | 6.25 | 13.7 | 64 | 213 | $23 |
| 2nd Half | 265 | 38 | 15 | 43 | 2 | 306 | 284 | 355 | 525 | 880 | 716 | 958 | 7 | 80 | 0.37 | 50 | 22 | 28 | 34 | 149 | 116 | 120 | 25% | 99 | 3% | 100% | 12 | 50% | 17% | 6.88 | 16.5 | 57 | 190 | $26 |
| **19 Proj** | **520** | **73** | **22** | **69** | **5** | **287** | **280** | **342** | **487** | **829** | **697** | **879** | **7** | **79** | **0.37** | **52** | **20** | **28** | **33** | **125** | **113** | **105** | **19%** | **112** | **5%** | **76%** | | | | **5.88** | **18.7** | **52** | **175** | **$20** |

## Peraza,Jose

Age: 25 | Bats: R | Pos: SS
Ht: 6' 0" | Wt: 196

| Health | A | LIMA Plan | B |
|---|---|---|---|
| PT/Exp | B | Rand Var | -2 |
| Consist | C | MM | 1545 |

Fine growth season for a SS who makes terrific contact with a line-drive swing that's getting more oomph as he matures. SB totals would benefit from a few more walks, but that's less likely than a return to past SBO. If HctX growth, FB trends continue, and that light gets a little greener... UP: 20 HR, 35 SB

| Yr Tm | AB | R | HR | RBI | SB | BA | xBA | OBP | SLG | OPS | vL | vR | bb% | ct% | Eye | G | L | F | h% | HctX | PX | xPX | hr/f | Spd | SBO | SB% | #Wk | DOM | DIS | RC/G | RAR | BPV | BPX | R$ |
|---|---|---|---|---|---|---|---|---|---|---|---|---|---|---|---|---|---|---|---|---|---|---|---|---|---|---|---|---|---|---|---|---|---|---|
| 14 aa | 185 | 30 | 1 | 14 | 21 | 315 | | 336 | 391 | 727 | | | 3 | 91 | 0.35 | | | | 34 | | 49 | | | 130 | 55% | 71% | | | | 4.61 | | 50 | 135 | $13 |
| 15 LA * | 503 | 54 | 3 | 35 | 30 | 255 | 231 | 276 | 324 | 599 | 779 | 125 | 3 | 90 | 0.28 | 37 | 21 | 42 | 28 | 37 | 40 | 37 | 0% | 132 | 31% | 79% | 5 | 40% | 20% | 3.11 | -9.7 | 38 | 103 | $16 |
| 16 CIN * | 529 | 61 | 5 | 44 | 30 | 292 | 268 | 325 | 378 | 703 | 793 | 754 | 5 | 85 | 0.33 | 43 | 28 | 29 | 34 | 73 | 52 | 55 | 5% | 144 | 32% | 63% | 18 | 28% | 39% | 4.14 | -7.4 | 35 | 100 | $24 |
| 17 CIN | 487 | 50 | 5 | 37 | 23 | 259 | 248 | 297 | 324 | 622 | 655 | 609 | 4 | 86 | 0.29 | 47 | 22 | 31 | 29 | 74 | 33 | 43 | 4% | 150 | 24% | 74% | 26 | 23% | 38% | 3.21 | -18.9 | 24 | 73 | $14 |
| 18 CIN | 632 | 85 | 14 | 58 | 23 | 288 | 269 | 326 | 416 | 742 | 774 | 728 | 4 | 88 | 0.39 | 37 | 26 | 38 | 31 | 96 | 70 | 57 | 7% | 114 | 18% | 79% | 28 | 46% | 18% | 4.78 | 17.2 | 53 | 177 | $27 |
| 1st Half | 316 | 45 | 4 | 23 | 14 | 272 | 262 | 316 | 364 | 680 | 626 | 702 | 5 | 89 | 0.47 | 39 | 26 | 35 | 30 | 97 | 52 | 56 | 4% | 115 | 19% | 88% | 15 | 40% | 13% | 4.09 | 1.2 | 43 | 143 | $23 |
| 2nd Half | 316 | 40 | 10 | 35 | 9 | 304 | 277 | 336 | 468 | 805 | 917 | 755 | 4 | 88 | 0.31 | 34 | 25 | 41 | 32 | 94 | 89 | 59 | 9% | 114 | 17% | 69% | 13 | 54% | 23% | 5.52 | 13.7 | 65 | 217 | $31 |
| **19 Proj** | **604** | **74** | **15** | **52** | **28** | **279** | **265** | **317** | **406** | **723** | **765** | **707** | **4** | **87** | **0.34** | **39** | **24** | **37** | **30** | **90** | **67** | **52** | **8%** | **131** | **25%** | **73%** | | | | **4.36** | **6.9** | **49** | **162** | **$28** |

## Perez,Hernan

Age: 28 | Bats: R | Pos: 2B RF 3B
Ht: 6' 1" | Wt: 215

| Health | A | LIMA Plan | C |
|---|---|---|---|
| PT/Exp | C | Rand Var | -1 |
| Consist | A | MM | 2523 |

Consistent, yes—but for a 28-year-old? Let's call it "stagnant." That's what these skills are at what should be his peak, and troubles vR continue to mount. It leaves us with a mediocre bat whose one potential plus skill, speed, is shunted by a combination of poor OBP and life in a short-side platoon. Meh.

| Yr Tm | AB | R | HR | RBI | SB | BA | xBA | OBP | SLG | OPS | vL | vR | bb% | ct% | Eye | G | L | F | h% | HctX | PX | xPX | hr/f | Spd | SBO | SB% | #Wk | DOM | DIS | RC/G | RAR | BPV | BPX | R$ |
|---|---|---|---|---|---|---|---|---|---|---|---|---|---|---|---|---|---|---|---|---|---|---|---|---|---|---|---|---|---|---|---|---|---|---|
| 14 DET * | 552 | 56 | 5 | 42 | 17 | 258 | 207 | 297 | 363 | 659 | 0 | 833 | 5 | 87 | 0.43 | 50 | 0 | 50 | 29 | 189 | 72 | -15 | 0% | 130 | 18% | 72% | 4 | 25% | 75% | 3.66 | 4.3 | 59 | 159 | $14 |
| 15 2 TM | 263 | 14 | 1 | 21 | 5 | 243 | 233 | 257 | 327 | 584 | 635 | 552 | 2 | 78 | 0.08 | 43 | 22 | 34 | 31 | 102 | 66 | 98 | 1% | 91 | 12% | 83% | 26 | 23% | 58% | 2.87 | -10.1 | -3 | -8 | $1 |
| 16 MIL * | 466 | 57 | 14 | 64 | 35 | 273 | 249 | 303 | 424 | 727 | 787 | 699 | 4 | 77 | 0.19 | 43 | 20 | 36 | 33 | 100 | 91 | 97 | 12% | 118 | 39% | 83% | 24 | 33% | 29% | 4.62 | -3.3 | 27 | 77 | $25 |
| 17 MIL | 432 | 47 | 14 | 51 | 13 | 259 | 263 | 289 | 414 | 704 | 789 | 673 | 4 | 82 | 0.25 | 48 | 18 | 34 | 29 | 100 | 83 | 81 | 12% | 99 | 18% | 76% | 27 | 37% | 37% | 4.15 | -11.0 | 34 | 103 | $12 |
| 18 MIL | 316 | 36 | 9 | 29 | 11 | 253 | 237 | 290 | 386 | 676 | 783 | 612 | 5 | 78 | 0.24 | 42 | 21 | 37 | 30 | 99 | 77 | 104 | 10% | 137 | 19% | 79% | 28 | 29% | 46% | 3.86 | -3.8 | 25 | 83 | $9 |
| 1st Half | 165 | 15 | 4 | 16 | 6 | 248 | 239 | 273 | 370 | 643 | 516 | 697 | 4 | 79 | 0.17 | 43 | 20 | 37 | 29 | 95 | 76 | 93 | 8% | 111 | 20% | 86% | 15 | 33% | 40% | 3.53 | -3.2 | 18 | 60 | $7 |
| 2nd Half | 151 | 21 | 5 | 13 | 5 | 258 | 236 | 309 | 404 | 713 | 972 | 495 | 7 | 76 | 0.31 | 41 | 22 | 37 | 31 | 102 | 79 | 117 | 12% | 155 | 18% | 71% | 13 | 23% | 54% | 4.23 | 0.2 | 30 | 100 | $11 |
| **19 Proj** | **266** | **30** | **8** | **27** | **10** | **258** | **246** | **293** | **398** | **692** | **804** | **630** | **5** | **79** | **0.25** | **44** | **20** | **36** | **30** | **100** | **81** | **98** | **10%** | **124** | **21%** | **78%** | | | | **4.05** | **-1.0** | **26** | **88** | **$10** |

## Perez,Michael

Age: 26 | Bats: L | Pos: CA
Ht: 5' 11" | Wt: 180

| Health | B | LIMA Plan | D |
|---|---|---|---|
| PT/Exp | F | Rand Var | -1 |
| Consist | C | MM | 1003 |

1-11-.284 in 74 AB at TAM. Strained hammy ended journeyman's debut before it really got rolling. But then, to paraphrase the great Bob Uecker, that just means it'll take longer for them to figure out he's not that good. Those 2017 skills are the BEST of his career. Still young as catchers go, but safe to ignore for now.

| Yr Tm | AB | R | HR | RBI | SB | BA | xBA | OBP | SLG | OPS | vL | vR | bb% | ct% | Eye | G | L | F | h% | HctX | PX | xPX | hr/f | Spd | SBO | SB% | #Wk | DOM | DIS | RC/G | RAR | BPV | BPX | R$ |
|---|---|---|---|---|---|---|---|---|---|---|---|---|---|---|---|---|---|---|---|---|---|---|---|---|---|---|---|---|---|---|---|---|---|---|
| 14 | | | | | | | | | | | | | | | | | | | | | | | | | | | | | | | | | | |
| 15 | | | | | | | | | | | | | | | | | | | | | | | | | | | | | | | | | | |
| 16 aa | 122 | 6 | 3 | 9 | 0 | 194 | | 231 | 312 | 543 | | | 5 | 74 | 0.19 | | | | 24 | | 73 | | | 108 | 5% | 0% | | | | 2.17 | | -2 | -6 | -$3 |
| 17 a/a | 271 | 22 | 4 | 32 | 0 | 245 | | 310 | 381 | 692 | | | 9 | 74 | 0.36 | | | | 32 | | 96 | | | 84 | 4% | 0% | | | | 3.85 | | 17 | 52 | $1 |
| 18 TAM * | 292 | 27 | 4 | 28 | 0 | 230 | 215 | 267 | 319 | 586 | 890 | 654 | 5 | 77 | 0.22 | 37 | 21 | 42 | 29 | 112 | 59 | 126 | 4% | 128 | 2% | 0% | 6 | 33% | 50% | 2.76 | -6.6 | 4 | 13 | $0 |
| 1st Half | 175 | 17 | 3 | 15 | 0 | 217 | 229 | 263 | 311 | 574 | | | 6 | 80 | 0.31 | | | | 26 | | 58 | | | 109 | 0% | 0% | | | | 2.66 | | 14 | 47 | $0 |
| 2nd Half | 117 | 10 | 2 | 13 | 0 | 249 | 201 | 275 | 331 | 605 | 890 | 654 | 3 | 71 | 0.12 | 37 | 21 | 42 | 34 | 104 | 61 | 126 | 4% | 125 | 5% | 0% | 6 | 33% | 50% | 2.93 | -1.8 | -20 | -67 | $2 |
| **19 Proj** | **264** | **21** | **3** | **27** | **0** | **233** | **215** | **271** | **329** | **600** | **785** | **560** | **6** | **74** | **0.24** | **37** | **21** | **42** | **30** | **94** | **69** | **113** | **4%** | **139** | **3%** | **0%** | | | | **2.94** | **-4.0** | **-22** | **-74** | **$2** |

## Perez,Roberto

Age: 30 | Bats: R | Pos: CA
Ht: 5' 11" | Wt: 220

| Health | B | LIMA Plan | F |
|---|---|---|---|
| PT/Exp | F | Rand Var | +3 |
| Consist | C | MM | 2101 |

Continues to get 200+ PA a season. Should we look at that as an indictment on catching talent in baseball? Perhaps. But instead, let's focus on a positive: He's got enough... something (moxie? incriminating photos?) to continue to pull in a big-league salary despite making Mario Mendoza look like a guy who hit for average.

| Yr Tm | AB | R | HR | RBI | SB | BA | xBA | OBP | SLG | OPS | vL | vR | bb% | ct% | Eye | G | L | F | h% | HctX | PX | xPX | hr/f | Spd | SBO | SB% | #Wk | DOM | DIS | RC/G | RAR | BPV | BPX | R$ |
|---|---|---|---|---|---|---|---|---|---|---|---|---|---|---|---|---|---|---|---|---|---|---|---|---|---|---|---|---|---|---|---|---|---|---|
| 14 CLE * | 259 | 31 | 7 | 36 | 1 | 257 | 217 | 324 | 397 | 721 | 397 | 786 | 9 | 66 | 0.29 | 45 | 17 | 38 | 36 | 85 | 125 | 123 | 5% | 79 | 1% | 100% | 13 | 31% | 62% | 4.42 | 8.3 | 7 | 19 | $5 |
| 15 CLE | 184 | 30 | 7 | 21 | 0 | 228 | 237 | 348 | 402 | 751 | 841 | 715 | 15 | 65 | 0.52 | 53 | 20 | 27 | 31 | 89 | 134 | 121 | 21% | 92 | 0% | 0% | 26 | 38% | 50% | 4.59 | 4.7 | 27 | 73 | $1 |
| 16 CLE | 153 | 14 | 3 | 17 | 0 | 183 | 213 | 285 | 294 | 579 | 683 | 528 | 13 | 71 | 0.52 | 54 | 15 | 31 | 24 | 72 | 75 | 94 | 9% | 82 | 0% | 0% | 15 | 33% | 53% | 2.66 | -5.8 | -2 | -6 | -$3 |
| 17 CLE | 217 | 22 | 8 | 38 | 0 | 207 | 222 | 291 | 373 | 664 | 807 | 596 | 10 | 67 | 0.37 | 50 | 17 | 32 | 27 | 87 | 112 | 94 | 17% | 50 | 2% | 0% | 26 | 23% | 54% | 3.44 | -4.7 | -2 | -6 | $0 |
| 18 CLE | 179 | 16 | 2 | 19 | 1 | 168 | 182 | 256 | 263 | 519 | 650 | 489 | 10 | 61 | 0.30 | 50 | 15 | 36 | 26 | 91 | 81 | 106 | 5% | 69 | 3% | 100% | 26 | 23% | 73% | 2.08 | -7.5 | -48 | -160 | -$3 |
| 1st Half | 92 | 8 | 1 | 6 | 0 | 141 | 169 | 231 | 228 | 459 | 708 | 417 | 10 | 58 | 0.26 | 55 | 13 | 32 | 23 | 93 | 71 | 67 | 6% | 95 | 0% | 0% | 14 | 21% | 79% | 1.53 | -5.9 | -63 | -210 | -$7 |
| 2nd Half | 87 | 8 | 1 | 13 | 1 | 195 | 194 | 283 | 299 | 582 | 611 | 572 | 11 | 64 | 0.35 | 44 | 17 | 39 | 29 | 90 | 91 | 144 | 5% | 58 | 5% | 100% | 12 | 25% | 67% | 2.76 | -1.9 | -28 | -93 | $0 |
| **19 Proj** | **156** | **15** | **3** | **20** | **1** | **190** | **202** | **278** | **312** | **591** | **701** | **553** | **11** | **65** | **0.35** | **50** | **16** | **34** | **27** | **87** | **94** | **106** | **9%** | **68** | **2%** | **76%** | | | | **2.75** | **-3.5** | **-26** | **-87** | **$0** |

## Perez,Salvador

Age: 29 | Bats: R | Pos: CA DH
Ht: 6' 4" | Wt: 240

| Health | B | LIMA Plan | B+ |
|---|---|---|---|
| PT/Exp | B | Rand Var | +2 |
| Consist | C | MM | 3035 |

27-80-.235 in 510 AB at KC. The only real difference between 2018 and recent past seasons was that aberrant first-half hit rate. In fact, he took his power game up another notch. That FB lean also means he's not going to ever hit much better than .260. But there's still some HR/RBI upside to mine. UP: 2nd half times 2

| Yr Tm | AB | R | HR | RBI | SB | BA | xBA | OBP | SLG | OPS | vL | vR | bb% | ct% | Eye | G | L | F | h% | HctX | PX | xPX | hr/f | Spd | SBO | SB% | #Wk | DOM | DIS | RC/G | RAR | BPV | BPX | R$ |
|---|---|---|---|---|---|---|---|---|---|---|---|---|---|---|---|---|---|---|---|---|---|---|---|---|---|---|---|---|---|---|---|---|---|---|
| 14 KC | 578 | 57 | 17 | 70 | 1 | 260 | 265 | 289 | 403 | 692 | 632 | 710 | 4 | 85 | 0.26 | 39 | 21 | 40 | 28 | 115 | 95 | 106 | 9% | 74 | 1% | 100% | 27 | 52% | 15% | 3.99 | 11.1 | 49 | 132 | $14 |
| 15 KC | 531 | 52 | 21 | 70 | 1 | 260 | 268 | 280 | 426 | 706 | 560 | 775 | 2 | 85 | 0.16 | 42 | 21 | 37 | 27 | 88 | 99 | 87 | 12% | 66 | 1% | 100% | 27 | 48% | 22% | 4.08 | 5.2 | 44 | 119 | $13 |
| 16 KC | 514 | 57 | 22 | 64 | 0 | 247 | 246 | 288 | 438 | 725 | 763 | 710 | 4 | 77 | 0.18 | 35 | 18 | 47 | 28 | 105 | 116 | 107 | 12% | 68 | 0% | 0% | 27 | 44% | 26% | 4.12 | 3.8 | 31 | 89 | $9 |
| 17 KC | 471 | 57 | 27 | 80 | 1 | 268 | 266 | 297 | 495 | 792 | 788 | 794 | 3 | 80 | 0.18 | 33 | 20 | 47 | 28 | 123 | 121 | 142 | 15% | 56 | 1% | 100% | 24 | 63% | 29% | 5.06 | 12.4 | 42 | 127 | $14 |
| 18 KC * | 534 | 55 | 28 | 84 | 1 | 238 | 258 | 262 | 444 | 706 | 702 | 717 | 3 | 79 | 0.15 | 35 | 20 | 45 | 25 | 134 | 116 | 149 | 15% | 50 | 2% | 50% | 24 | 54% | 25% | 3.87 | 7.9 | 33 | 110 | $13 |
| 1st Half | 265 | 28 | 12 | 36 | 1 | 220 | 247 | 246 | 401 | 647 | 611 | 649 | 3 | 80 | 0.17 | 36 | 19 | 45 | 23 | 130 | 100 | 137 | 13% | 65 | 5% | 50% | 11 | 36% | 36% | 3.18 | -2.2 | 29 | 97 | $9 |
| 2nd Half | 269 | 27 | 16 | 48 | 0 | 257 | 267 | 293 | 487 | 780 | 776 | 780 | 3 | 78 | 0.14 | 33 | 21 | 45 | 27 | 138 | 131 | 159 | 16% | 49 | 0% | 0% | 13 | 69% | 15% | 4.64 | 9.4 | 41 | 137 | $18 |
| **19 Proj** | **508** | **55** | **26** | **78** | **1** | **251** | **257** | **285** | **455** | **740** | **729** | **744** | **3** | **80** | **0.16** | **35** | **20** | **45** | **27** | **124** | **115** | **136** | **14%** | **56** | **1%** | **66%** | | | | **4.25** | **12.0** | **30** | **101** | **$15** |

## Pham,Thomas

Age: 31 | Bats: R | Pos: CF LF
Ht: 6' 1" | Wt: 210

| Health | C | LIMA Plan | C+ |
|---|---|---|---|
| PT/Exp | C | Rand Var | -1 |
| Consist | F | MM | 4535 |

We expected some regression from 2017 breakout, but this was another solid year. Probably still out over his hit-rate skis a bit, but gains in hard contact should help offset that. Got his running shoes back on with 5 SB in Sept, too. Should again contribute across the board, with some sneaky value upside in one spot... UP: 30 SB

| Yr Tm | AB | R | HR | RBI | SB | BA | xBA | OBP | SLG | OPS | vL | vR | bb% | ct% | Eye | G | L | F | h% | HctX | PX | xPX | hr/f | Spd | SBO | SB% | #Wk | DOM | DIS | RC/G | RAR | BPV | BPX | R$ |
|---|---|---|---|---|---|---|---|---|---|---|---|---|---|---|---|---|---|---|---|---|---|---|---|---|---|---|---|---|---|---|---|---|---|---|
| 14 STL * | 348 | 43 | 7 | 30 | 14 | 259 | 225 | 309 | 376 | 685 | 0 | 0 | 7 | 72 | 0.26 | 44 | 20 | 36 | 34 | 0 | 91 | -15 | 0% | 133 | 18% | 85% | 4 | 0% | 100% | 4.10 | 3.1 | 15 | 41 | $11 |
| 15 STL * | 324 | 48 | 9 | 45 | 8 | 262 | 258 | 334 | 427 | 761 | 783 | 833 | 10 | 73 | 0.40 | 51 | 21 | 27 | 33 | 120 | 111 | 119 | 16% | 113 | 9% | 100% | 12 | 42% | 33% | 5.09 | 3.5 | 35 | 95 | $11 |
| 16 STL * | 283 | 39 | 12 | 31 | 8 | 214 | 228 | 301 | 383 | 684 | 734 | 784 | 11 | 62 | 0.32 | 45 | 25 | 30 | 30 | 107 | 124 | 126 | 35% | 102 | 19% | 58% | 18 | 33% | 56% | 3.56 | -9.4 | 0 | 0 | $5 |
| 17 STL * | 536 | 107 | 26 | 87 | 29 | 292 | 277 | 384 | 496 | 880 | 964 | 922 | 13 | 73 | 0.56 | 52 | 22 | 26 | 36 | 105 | 121 | 104 | 27% | 107 | 22% | 73% | 22 | 55% | 23% | 6.74 | 22.7 | 49 | 148 | $33 |
| 18 2 TM | 494 | 102 | 21 | 63 | 15 | 275 | 258 | 367 | 464 | 830 | 877 | 815 | 12 | 72 | 0.48 | 48 | 24 | 28 | 35 | 128 | 113 | 123 | 21% | 150 | 14% | 68% | 27 | 41% | 37% | 5.79 | 17.2 | 47 | 157 | $24 |
| 1st Half | 271 | 54 | 12 | 26 | 9 | 244 | 247 | 327 | 406 | 733 | 767 | 724 | 11 | 72 | 0.43 | 52 | 21 | 27 | 30 | 120 | 98 | 104 | 23% | 107 | 19% | 60% | 15 | 33% | 40% | 4.25 | -2.9 | 21 | 70 | $21 |
| 2nd Half | 223 | 48 | 9 | 37 | 6 | 314 | 268 | 413 | 534 | 947 | 967 | 938 | 13 | 72 | 0.54 | 43 | 27 | 30 | 40 | 137 | 131 | 145 | 19% | 164 | 9% | 86% | 12 | 50% | 33% | 8.12 | 21.3 | 69 | 230 | $27 |
| **19 Proj** | **494** | **93** | **23** | **68** | **19** | **274** | **262** | **366** | **479** | **845** | **856** | **841** | **12** | **71** | **0.45** | **48** | **24** | **28** | **34** | **119** | **126** | **121** | **24%** | **137** | **17%** | **72%** | | | | **5.97** | **26.2** | **49** | **163** | **$27** |

ROD TRUESDELL

## Phillips,Brett

| | | | | | |
|---|---|---|---|---|---|
| Age: 25 | Bats: L | Pos: CF | Health | A | LIMA Plan D+ |
| Ht: 6' 0" | Wt: 185 | | PT/Exp | C | Rand Var +1 |
| | | | Consist | D | MM 3503 |

2-11-.187 in 134 AB at KC and MIL. Those historical power and speed skills sure look tasty... until you see the burgeoning holes in his swing. We can't expect improvement there given multi-year ct% erosion. Still owns multi-category tools, but any HR/SB will be paired with a BA in the low .200s. A dart throw.

| Yr | Tm | AB | R | HR | RBI | SB | BA | xBA | OBP | SLG | OPS | vL | vR | bb% | ct% | Eye | G | L | F | h% | HctX | PX | xPX | hr/f | Spd | SBO | SB% | #Wk | DOM | DIS | RC/G | RAR | BPV | BPX | R$ |
|---|---|---|---|---|---|---|---|---|---|---|---|---|---|---|---|---|---|---|---|---|---|---|---|---|---|---|---|---|---|---|---|---|---|---|---|
| 14 | | | | | | | | | | | | | | | | | | | | | | | | | | | | | | | | | | | |
| 15 | aa | 214 | 33 | 1 | 22 | 8 | 285 | | 347 | 421 | 768 | | | 9 | 72 | 0.34 | | | | 39 | | 103 | | | 133 | 19% | 72% | | | | 5.15 | | 31 | 84 | $7 |
| 16 | aa | 441 | 59 | 18 | 61 | 12 | 230 | | 330 | 410 | 740 | | | 13 | 63 | 0.40 | | | | 32 | | 124 | | | 122 | 15% | 62% | | | | 4.35 | | 14 | 40 | $11 |
| 17 | MIL * | 470 | 65 | 19 | 67 | 11 | 266 | 226 | 324 | 464 | 789 | 311 | 855 | 8 | 61 | 0.22 | 38 | 25 | 38 | 40 | 73 | 139 | 101 | 20% | 147 | 11% | 91% | 11 | 18% | 64% | 5.32 | 3.6 | 18 | 55 | $16 |
| 18 | 2 TM * | 392 | 42 | 6 | 27 | 8 | 192 | 190 | 257 | 314 | 572 | 382 | 625 | 8 | 56 | 0.20 | 49 | 21 | 31 | 32 | 76 | 97 | 87 | 9% | 153 | 11% | 89% | 15 | 13% | 80% | 2.61 | -20.2 | -32 | -107 | $1 |
| 1st Half | | 232 | 22 | 3 | 13 | 6 | 198 | 172 | 262 | 306 | 568 | 0 | 364 | 8 | 56 | 0.20 | 40 | 20 | 40 | 34 | 83 | 86 | 123 | 0% | 150 | 13% | 100% | 3 | 0% | 100% | 2.68 | -10.7 | -44 | -147 | $1 |
| 2nd Half | | 160 | 20 | 3 | 14 | 2 | 184 | 199 | 251 | 326 | 577 | 413 | 657 | 8 | 57 | 0.20 | 49 | 21 | 30 | 30 | 76 | 112 | 85 | 10% | 141 | 9% | 62% | 12 | 17% | 75% | 2.52 | -8.3 | -23 | -77 | $0 |
| 19 | Proj | **383** | **48** | **11** | **40** | **9** | **223** | **211** | **297** | **383** | **680** | **396** | **756** | **9** | **60** | **0.24** | **45** | **22** | **33** | **34** | **75** | **117** | **91** | **14%** | **146** | **12%** | **78%** | | | | **3.69** | **-5.3** | **-7** | **-23** | **$6** |

## Pillar,Kevin

| | | | | | |
|---|---|---|---|---|---|
| Age: 30 | Bats: R | Pos: CF | Health | A | LIMA Plan B+ |
| Ht: 6' 0" | Wt: 205 | | PT/Exp | A | Rand Var +1 |
| | | | Consist | A | MM 2345 |

Modest multi-category guys like this are easy to overlook. In fact, he went undrafted in many leagues last year (336 ADP). History cements 15 HR / 15 SB in profile thanks to acumen on basepaths, concurrent power growth, health history. And xBA trend puts BA boost in cards too. UP: .280-20-20

| Yr | Tm | AB | R | HR | RBI | SB | BA | xBA | OBP | SLG | OPS | vL | vR | bb% | ct% | Eye | G | L | F | h% | HctX | PX | xPX | hr/f | Spd | SBO | SB% | #Wk | DOM | DIS | RC/G | RAR | BPV | BPX | R$ |
|---|---|---|---|---|---|---|---|---|---|---|---|---|---|---|---|---|---|---|---|---|---|---|---|---|---|---|---|---|---|---|---|---|---|---|---|
| 14 | TOR * | 521 | 64 | 11 | 54 | 22 | 285 | 285 | 312 | 445 | 757 | 783 | 631 | 4 | 84 | 0.24 | 51 | 16 | 33 | 32 | 98 | 122 | 82 | 7% | 101 | 29% | 72% | 12 | 17% | 50% | 4.82 | 13.9 | 72 | 195 | $23 |
| 15 | TOR | 586 | 76 | 12 | 56 | 25 | 278 | 261 | 314 | 399 | 713 | 684 | 723 | 4 | 85 | 0.33 | 41 | 22 | 37 | 31 | 92 | 78 | 72 | 7% | 108 | 20% | 86% | 27 | 33% | 22% | 4.51 | 0.0 | 48 | 130 | $24 |
| 16 | TOR | 548 | 59 | 7 | 53 | 14 | 266 | 259 | 303 | 376 | 679 | 709 | 668 | 4 | 84 | 0.27 | 46 | 20 | 34 | 31 | 92 | 72 | 73 | 5% | 100 | 16% | 70% | 25 | 32% | 28% | 3.83 | -8.5 | 32 | 91 | $14 |
| 17 | TOR | 587 | 72 | 16 | 42 | 15 | 256 | 269 | 300 | 404 | 704 | 940 | 628 | 5 | 84 | 0.35 | 43 | 20 | 36 | 28 | 93 | 85 | 69 | 9% | 104 | 16% | 71% | 26 | 38% | 12% | 4.03 | -12.4 | 47 | 142 | $14 |
| 18 | TOR | 512 | 65 | 15 | 59 | 14 | 252 | 273 | 282 | 426 | 708 | 686 | 717 | 3 | 81 | 0.18 | 36 | 27 | 38 | 29 | 101 | 108 | 90 | 9% | 95 | 19% | 82% | 26 | 50% | 23% | 4.05 | 0.2 | 47 | 157 | $16 |
| 1st Half | | 307 | 38 | 7 | 29 | 10 | 251 | 275 | 284 | 414 | 698 | 618 | 735 | 4 | 80 | 0.23 | 39 | 27 | 34 | 29 | 103 | 105 | 78 | 8% | 102 | 19% | 91% | 15 | 47% | 33% | 4.10 | -0.3 | 46 | 153 | $17 |
| 2nd Half | | 205 | 27 | 8 | 30 | 4 | 254 | 274 | 279 | 444 | 723 | 811 | 692 | 2 | 82 | 0.11 | 31 | 26 | 43 | 28 | 99 | 114 | 108 | 11% | 86 | 18% | 67% | 11 | 55% | 9% | 3.96 | -1.1 | 51 | 170 | $14 |
| 19 | Proj | **573** | **71** | **15** | **60** | **15** | **258** | **268** | **292** | **413** | **705** | **774** | **679** | **4** | **83** | **0.22** | **39** | **23** | **37** | **29** | **97** | **95** | **84** | **9%** | **98** | **18%** | **75%** | | | | **4.03** | **-1.8** | **46** | **153** | **$19** |

## Pina,Manny

| | | | | | |
|---|---|---|---|---|---|
| Age: 32 | Bats: R | Pos: CA | Health | A | LIMA Plan D+ |
| Ht: 6' 0" | Wt: 215 | | PT/Exp | D | Rand Var 0 |
| | | | Consist | B | MM 2223 |

Reliable backup backstop ready for an everyday gig? PRO: Late OPS vR surge, good xPX in two prior seasons, keeps hitting more liners. CON: Two-year drop in FB% lowers HR ceiling, more futile than not vL, marginal plate discipline. Given age, best to fall on side of pessimism and view this as best-case forecast.

| Yr | Tm | AB | R | HR | RBI | SB | BA | xBA | OBP | SLG | OPS | vL | vR | bb% | ct% | Eye | G | L | F | h% | HctX | PX | xPX | hr/f | Spd | SBO | SB% | #Wk | DOM | DIS | RC/G | RAR | BPV | BPX | R$ |
|---|---|---|---|---|---|---|---|---|---|---|---|---|---|---|---|---|---|---|---|---|---|---|---|---|---|---|---|---|---|---|---|---|---|---|---|
| 14 | a/a | 213 | 21 | 4 | 20 | 1 | 213 | | 260 | 296 | 556 | | | 6 | 84 | 0.40 | | | | 24 | | 58 | | | 85 | 3% | 100% | | | | 2.52 | | 23 | 62 | -$1 |
| 15 | aaa | 256 | 20 | 5 | 27 | 1 | 241 | | 289 | 356 | 645 | | | 6 | 84 | 0.43 | | | | 27 | | 79 | | | 76 | 2% | 100% | | | | 3.48 | | 38 | 103 | $1 |
| 16 | MIL * | 308 | 26 | 6 | 39 | 1 | 250 | 224 | 297 | 381 | 678 | 555 | 840 | 6 | 78 | 0.31 | 36 | 16 | 48 | 30 | 97 | 88 | 118 | 7% | 80 | 4% | 22% | 10 | 30% | 30% | 3.73 | -6.1 | 23 | 66 | $3 |
| 17 | MIL | 330 | 45 | 9 | 43 | 2 | 279 | 245 | 327 | 424 | 751 | 706 | 769 | 6 | 76 | 0.25 | 35 | 23 | 42 | 34 | 105 | 92 | 131 | 8% | 88 | 2% | 100% | 25 | 32% | 36% | 4.84 | 7.3 | 17 | 52 | $8 |
| 18 | MIL | 306 | 39 | 9 | 28 | 2 | 252 | 260 | 307 | 395 | 702 | 577 | 739 | 6 | 80 | 0.34 | 40 | 26 | 34 | 29 | 99 | 83 | 103 | 11% | 87 | 3% | 100% | 26 | 31% | 38% | 4.07 | 5.0 | 26 | 87 | $5 |
| 1st Half | | 181 | 23 | 5 | 15 | 0 | 227 | 260 | 295 | 370 | 665 | 606 | 677 | 7 | 80 | 0.38 | 43 | 24 | 33 | 26 | 105 | 86 | 107 | 10% | 81 | 0% | 0% | 14 | 29% | 36% | 3.44 | 0.0 | 28 | 93 | $3 |
| 2nd Half | | 125 | 16 | 4 | 13 | 2 | 288 | 260 | 324 | 432 | 756 | 552 | 846 | 5 | 80 | 0.28 | 37 | 28 | 35 | 33 | 91 | 79 | 96 | 11% | 97 | 6% | 100% | 12 | 33% | 42% | 5.14 | 5.9 | 25 | 83 | $8 |
| 19 | Proj | **329** | **39** | **10** | **36** | **2** | **262** | **251** | **309** | **408** | **717** | **596** | **764** | **6** | **79** | **0.30** | **37** | **24** | **39** | **31** | **100** | **88** | **114** | **9%** | **87** | **3%** | **88%** | | | | **4.32** | **8.3** | **23** | **76** | **$9** |

## Pinder,Chad

| | | | | | |
|---|---|---|---|---|---|
| Age: 27 | Bats: R | Pos: LF 2B | Health | B | LIMA Plan D+ |
| Ht: 6' 2" | Wt: 195 | | PT/Exp | D | Rand Var -2 |
| | | | Consist | B | MM 3213 |

Even in current HR-happy age, sneaky pop from keystone can help you move the needle. Fine xPX in two of three prior seasons puts 20 HR in sight, even if steadily subpar ct% caps ceiling. Concurrent upticks in bb%, Spd worth watching if green light ever materializes. Not for risk-averse, but... UP: 20 HR, 10 SB

| Yr | Tm | AB | R | HR | RBI | SB | BA | xBA | OBP | SLG | OPS | vL | vR | bb% | ct% | Eye | G | L | F | h% | HctX | PX | xPX | hr/f | Spd | SBO | SB% | #Wk | DOM | DIS | RC/G | RAR | BPV | BPX | R$ |
|---|---|---|---|---|---|---|---|---|---|---|---|---|---|---|---|---|---|---|---|---|---|---|---|---|---|---|---|---|---|---|---|---|---|---|---|
| 14 | | | | | | | | | | | | | | | | | | | | | | | | | | | | | | | | | | | |
| 15 | aa | 477 | 53 | 10 | 64 | 5 | 272 | | 302 | 403 | 706 | | | 4 | 76 | 0.18 | | | | 34 | | 96 | | | 85 | 10% | 48% | | | | 4.10 | | 18 | 49 | $13 |
| 16 | OAK * | 477 | 62 | 11 | 45 | 4 | 226 | 224 | 262 | 360 | 622 | 810 | 448 | 5 | 72 | 0.17 | 50 | 13 | 37 | 29 | 132 | 91 | 173 | 7% | 114 | 6% | 78% | 8 | 38% | 38% | 3.11 | -23.1 | 8 | 23 | $4 |
| 17 | OAK * | 346 | 38 | 16 | 44 | 4 | 235 | 231 | 282 | 431 | 713 | 738 | 753 | 6 | 66 | 0.19 | 41 | 19 | 40 | 31 | 88 | 128 | 119 | 19% | 112 | 8% | 62% | 18 | 50% | 39% | 3.99 | -9.7 | 13 | 39 | $5 |
| 18 | OAK | 298 | 43 | 13 | 27 | 0 | 258 | 233 | 332 | 436 | 769 | 835 | 713 | 8 | 70 | 0.31 | 44 | 19 | 37 | 32 | 120 | 112 | 136 | 17% | 122 | 3% | 0% | 26 | 38% | 38% | 4.67 | 1.3 | 26 | 87 | $6 |
| 1st Half | | 170 | 24 | 7 | 17 | 0 | 247 | 231 | 312 | 429 | 741 | 847 | 646 | 7 | 69 | 0.25 | 48 | 17 | 36 | 32 | 130 | 119 | 142 | 17% | 128 | 3% | 0% | 14 | 43% | 29% | 4.26 | -1.0 | 25 | 83 | $6 |
| 2nd Half | | 128 | 19 | 6 | 10 | 0 | 273 | 238 | 359 | 445 | 804 | 817 | 794 | 10 | 73 | 0.40 | 39 | 23 | 39 | 33 | 107 | 103 | 128 | 17% | 107 | 3% | 0% | 12 | 33% | 50% | 5.23 | 2.8 | 27 | 90 | $6 |
| 19 | Proj | **326** | **43** | **14** | **33** | **3** | **251** | **236** | **312** | **436** | **748** | **798** | **713** | **7** | **71** | **0.26** | **43** | **19** | **38** | **31** | **109** | **117** | **134** | **16%** | **116** | **6%** | **56%** | | | | **4.43** | **-1.6** | **14** | **47** | **$9** |

## Pirela,Jose

| | | | | | |
|---|---|---|---|---|---|
| Age: 29 | Bats: R | Pos: 2B LF | Health | A | LIMA Plan D |
| Ht: 6' 0" | Wt: 220 | | PT/Exp | D | Rand Var 0 |
| | | | Consist | F | MM 1231 |

Predictably couldn't follow-up '17 mini-breakout, as hr/f receded to its prior comfort zone. In fact, only seven bats had a *lower* FB distance in '18, which cements fact that prior power ain't coming back. Stagnant plate skills zap hope for steals too. As he nears 30, his window of opportunity is closing quickly.

| Yr | Tm | AB | R | HR | RBI | SB | BA | xBA | OBP | SLG | OPS | vL | vR | bb% | ct% | Eye | G | L | F | h% | HctX | PX | xPX | hr/f | Spd | SBO | SB% | #Wk | DOM | DIS | RC/G | RAR | BPV | BPX | R$ |
|---|---|---|---|---|---|---|---|---|---|---|---|---|---|---|---|---|---|---|---|---|---|---|---|---|---|---|---|---|---|---|---|---|---|---|---|
| 14 | NYY * | 559 | 69 | 8 | 46 | 11 | 256 | 247 | 292 | 362 | 654 | 2167 | 488 | 5 | 83 | 0.31 | 53 | 16 | 32 | 30 | 108 | 68 | 51 | 0% | 153 | 14% | 57% | 2 | 100% | 0% | 3.48 | 1.5 | 45 | 122 | $13 |
| 15 | NYY * | 315 | 41 | 4 | 24 | 5 | 264 | 263 | 314 | 355 | 669 | 752 | 286 | 7 | 85 | 0.50 | 56 | 19 | 25 | 30 | 105 | 62 | 56 | 7% | 94 | 9% | 69% | 14 | 7% | 50% | 3.83 | -3.0 | 35 | 95 | $6 |
| 16 | SD * | 176 | 14 | 1 | 10 | 1 | 185 | 201 | 214 | 266 | 480 | 556 | 328 | 4 | 80 | 0.19 | 53 | 7 | 40 | 22 | 95 | 53 | 84 | 0% | 114 | 10% | 22% | 4 | 25% | 50% | 1.66 | -18.2 | 8 | 23 | -$4 |
| 17 | SD * | 493 | 66 | 18 | 66 | 9 | 273 | 281 | 323 | 470 | 793 | 928 | 805 | 7 | 79 | 0.35 | 47 | 21 | 32 | 32 | 108 | 113 | 97 | 13% | 121 | 14% | 57% | 16 | 50% | 31% | 5.12 | 1.5 | 57 | 173 | $16 |
| 18 | SD | 438 | 54 | 5 | 32 | 6 | 249 | 253 | 300 | 345 | 645 | 724 | 605 | 6 | 80 | 0.34 | 53 | 21 | 26 | 30 | 101 | 64 | 61 | 6% | 87 | 8% | 67% | 28 | 25% | 46% | 3.44 | -10.7 | 11 | 37 | $7 |
| 1st Half | | 312 | 43 | 2 | 25 | 4 | 263 | 249 | 310 | 353 | 662 | 743 | 630 | 6 | 79 | 0.31 | 55 | 19 | 26 | 33 | 108 | 62 | 62 | 3% | 91 | 9% | 57% | 15 | 20% | 47% | 3.66 | -4.7 | 9 | 30 | $11 |
| 2nd Half | | 126 | 11 | 3 | 7 | 2 | 214 | 262 | 277 | 325 | 603 | 698 | 519 | 7 | 80 | 0.40 | 50 | 25 | 25 | 24 | 85 | 67 | 60 | 12% | 74 | 7% | 100% | 13 | 31% | 46% | 2.95 | -4.8 | 13 | 43 | -$3 |
| 19 | Proj | **164** | **18** | **4** | **14** | **2** | **239** | **262** | **288** | **369** | **657** | **734** | **610** | **6** | **80** | **0.33** | **51** | **22** | **28** | **28** | **101** | **78** | **73** | **10%** | **98** | **10%** | **64%** | | | | **3.47** | **-3.5** | **23** | **77** | **$3** |

## Piscotty,Stephen

| | | | | | |
|---|---|---|---|---|---|
| Age: 28 | Bats: R | Pos: RF | Health | A | LIMA Plan B+ |
| Ht: 6' 3" | Wt: 210 | | PT/Exp | B | Rand Var +1 |
| | | | Consist | C | MM 4145 |

Fine rebound season. Huge second half will cause near-300 2017 ADP to rise sharply. But will he follow up? Spikes in Hctx, xPX and dip in Ks all vote yes. But driving force was that hr/f, and below-average FB distance says don't bank on that over long haul. That's reason to cap your bidding at $20.

| Yr | Tm | AB | R | HR | RBI | SB | BA | xBA | OBP | SLG | OPS | vL | vR | bb% | ct% | Eye | G | L | F | h% | HctX | PX | xPX | hr/f | Spd | SBO | SB% | #Wk | DOM | DIS | RC/G | RAR | BPV | BPX | R$ |
|---|---|---|---|---|---|---|---|---|---|---|---|---|---|---|---|---|---|---|---|---|---|---|---|---|---|---|---|---|---|---|---|---|---|---|---|
| 14 | aaa | 500 | 50 | 6 | 50 | 8 | 244 | | 288 | 339 | 626 | | | 6 | 86 | 0.45 | | | | 27 | | 71 | | | 81 | 12% | 58% | | | | 3.20 | | 40 | 108 | $8 |
| 15 | STL * | 553 | 69 | 15 | 69 | 6 | 259 | 264 | 326 | 428 | 753 | 887 | 841 | 9 | 76 | 0.42 | 45 | 21 | 34 | 31 | 127 | 119 | 136 | 12% | 136 | 10% | 42% | 12 | 50% | 33% | 4.57 | -4.7 | 61 | 165 | $14 |
| 16 | STL | 582 | 86 | 22 | 85 | 7 | 273 | 264 | 343 | 457 | 800 | 952 | 748 | 8 | 77 | 0.38 | 44 | 20 | 36 | 32 | 100 | 114 | 105 | 13% | 116 | 8% | 58% | 27 | 48% | 19% | 5.21 | 8.3 | 52 | 149 | $20 |
| 17 | STL * | 380 | 46 | 12 | 45 | 3 | 235 | 239 | 335 | 384 | 719 | 723 | 704 | 13 | 75 | 0.60 | 49 | 18 | 33 | 28 | 99 | 90 | 112 | 11% | 84 | 8% | 33% | 22 | 27% | 45% | 4.07 | -12.9 | 24 | 73 | $4 |
| 18 | OAK | 546 | 78 | 27 | 88 | 2 | 267 | 287 | 331 | 491 | 821 | 776 | 841 | 7 | 79 | 0.37 | 45 | 22 | 33 | 29 | 124 | 134 | 113 | 19% | 72 | 2% | 100% | 28 | 64% | 18% | 5.48 | 15.2 | 61 | 203 | $20 |
| 1st Half | | 261 | 35 | 7 | 33 | 0 | 253 | 259 | 320 | 406 | 726 | 568 | 797 | 8 | 78 | 0.39 | 47 | 21 | 32 | 30 | 118 | 101 | 90 | 11% | 81 | 0% | 0% | 15 | 53% | 27% | 4.31 | -1.1 | 35 | 117 | $10 |
| 2nd Half | | 285 | 43 | 20 | 55 | 2 | 281 | 310 | 341 | 568 | 909 | 974 | 881 | 7 | 80 | 0.35 | 43 | 23 | 34 | 29 | 129 | 164 | 133 | 26% | 73 | 3% | 100% | 13 | 77% | 8% | 6.65 | 17.6 | 88 | 293 | $29 |
| 19 | Proj | **542** | **74** | **24** | **82** | **4** | **265** | **272** | **339** | **465** | **804** | **826** | **796** | **9** | **78** | **0.44** | **46** | **21** | **34** | **30** | **115** | **121** | **115** | **17%** | **85** | **5%** | **52%** | | | | **5.23** | **12.2** | **46** | **155** | **$20** |

## Plawecki,Kevin

| | | | | | |
|---|---|---|---|---|---|
| Age: 28 | Bats: R | Pos: CA | Health | B | LIMA Plan D |
| Ht: 6'2" | Wt: 210 | | PT/Exp | D | Rand Var +1 |
| | | | Consist | C | MM 2011 |

Managed to stay in majors all season for first time in career, which reminded us why he was a fringe major-leaguer to begin with. GB stroke, marginal HctX trump PX/xPX growth for time being. And .220-ish xBA in three of last four seasons reveals his batting average downside. A marginal speculation at best.

| Yr | Tm | AB | R | HR | RBI | SB | BA | xBA | OBP | SLG | OPS | vL | vR | bb% | ct% | Eye | G | L | F | h% | HctX | PX | xPX | hr/f | Spd | SBO | SB% | #Wk | DOM | DIS | RC/G | RAR | BPV | BPX | R$ |
|---|---|---|---|---|---|---|---|---|---|---|---|---|---|---|---|---|---|---|---|---|---|---|---|---|---|---|---|---|---|---|---|---|---|---|---|
| 14 | a/a | 376 | 38 | 8 | 42 | 0 | 246 | | 283 | 357 | 641 | | | 5 | 85 | 0.34 | | | | 27 | | 80 | | | 80 | 0% | 0% | | | | 3.42 | | 39 | 105 | $5 |
| 15 | NYM * | 318 | 23 | 4 | 27 | 0 | 208 | 218 | 252 | 288 | 540 | 411 | 609 | 6 | 77 | 0.26 | 46 | 20 | 34 | 26 | 97 | 60 | 88 | 5% | 105 | 0% | 0% | 22 | 27% | 55% | 2.34 | -14.6 | 0 | 0 | -$3 |
| 16 | NYM * | 322 | 23 | 6 | 36 | 0 | 215 | 232 | 274 | 319 | 592 | 651 | 530 | 7 | 82 | 0.45 | 56 | 17 | 27 | 24 | 64 | 64 | 44 | 4% | 83 | 2% | 0% | 15 | 13% | 67% | 2.78 | -16.1 | 22 | 63 | -$1 |
| 17 | NYM * | 347 | 36 | 9 | 44 | 1 | 256 | 272 | 306 | 390 | 697 | 643 | 805 | 7 | 81 | 0.39 | 49 | 24 | 27 | 29 | 98 | 78 | 78 | 13% | 79 | 1% | 100% | 14 | 29% | 36% | 4.11 | 0.5 | 26 | 79 | $5 |
| 18 | NYM | 238 | 33 | 7 | 30 | 0 | 210 | 229 | 315 | 370 | 685 | 700 | 681 | 10 | 73 | 0.43 | 48 | 14 | 38 | 26 | 95 | 104 | 95 | 11% | 110 | 2% | 0% | 21 | 48% | 43% | 3.44 | -0.5 | 29 | 97 | $1 |
| 1st Half | | 79 | 11 | 1 | 8 | 0 | 228 | 240 | 358 | 380 | 738 | 871 | 702 | 14 | 71 | 0.57 | 61 | 11 | 29 | 31 | 112 | 115 | 89 | 6% | 118 | 5% | 0% | 9 | 67% | 33% | 4.02 | 1.4 | 41 | 137 | -$5 |
| 2nd Half | | 159 | 22 | 6 | 22 | 0 | 201 | 224 | 293 | 365 | 658 | 613 | 670 | 9 | 74 | 0.36 | 42 | 16 | 42 | 23 | 87 | 98 | 98 | 12% | 104 | 0% | 0% | 12 | 33% | 50% | 3.15 | -1.5 | 23 | 77 | $4 |
| 19 | Proj | **223** | **26** | **5** | **27** | **0** | **225** | **239** | **311** | **358** | **669** | **661** | **671** | **9** | **77** | **0.42** | **50** | **18** | **33** | **27** | **92** | **84** | **82** | **9%** | **107** | **2%** | **19%** | | | | **3.41** | **-0.2** | **12** | **39** | **$3** |

STEPHEN NICKRAND

## Polanco,Gregory

| | | | | | |
|---|---|---|---|---|---|
| Age: 27 | Bats: L | Pos: RF | Health B | LIMA Plan B | |
| Ht: 6' 5" | Wt: 235 | | PT/Exp B | Rand Var 0 | |
| | | | Consist C | MM 3333 | |

Perennial failed breakout target actually showed best skills of career... and if you view 2017 as anomaly, a shiny BPV trend emerges. Bumps in FB%, bb%, and second-half Spd remind us again of what could be. Torn labrum may sideline him to begin season, but if you want to roll the dice again... UP: 30 HR, 20 SB

| Yr Tm | AB | R | HR | RBI | SB | BA | xBA | OBP | SLG | OPS | vL | vR | bb% | ct% | Eye | G | L | F | h% | HctX | PX | xPX | hr/f | Spd | SBO | SB% | #Wk | DOM | DIS | RC/G | RAR | BPV | BPX | R$ |
|---|---|---|---|---|---|---|---|---|---|---|---|---|---|---|---|---|---|---|---|---|---|---|---|---|---|---|---|---|---|---|---|---|---|---|
| 14 PIT * | 551 | 89 | 12 | 72 | 26 | 258 | 252 | 320 | 377 | 697 | 466 | 727 | 8 | 80 | 0.45 | 50 | 19 | 31 | 31 | 84 | 85 | 86 | 10% | 101 | 25% | 69% | 17 | 35% | 47% | 4.05 | -0.7 | 35 | 95 | $24 |
| 15 PIT | 593 | 83 | 9 | 52 | 27 | 256 | 250 | 320 | 381 | 701 | 528 | 747 | 8 | 80 | 0.45 | 45 | 20 | 35 | 31 | 103 | 87 | 95 | 6% | 116 | 24% | 73% | 27 | 41% | 22% | 4.14 | -12.6 | 42 | 114 | $20 |
| 16 PIT | 527 | 79 | 22 | 86 | 17 | 258 | 274 | 323 | 463 | 786 | 781 | 786 | 9 | 77 | 0.45 | 39 | 24 | 37 | 30 | 112 | 125 | 110 | 14% | 84 | 18% | 74% | 26 | 58% | 23% | 5.13 | 7.1 | 55 | 157 | $21 |
| 17 PIT | 379 | 39 | 11 | 35 | 8 | 251 | 262 | 305 | 391 | 695 | 586 | 730 | 7 | 84 | 0.45 | 42 | 20 | 38 | 27 | 88 | 78 | 77 | 9% | 80 | 10% | 89% | 23 | 39% | 30% | 4.06 | -12.5 | 38 | 115 | $7 |
| 18 PIT | 461 | 75 | 23 | 81 | 12 | 254 | 257 | 340 | 499 | 839 | 771 | 864 | 11 | 75 | 0.52 | 33 | 19 | 48 | 29 | 93 | 150 | 123 | 14% | 106 | 12% | 86% | 24 | 67% | 21% | 5.88 | 20.1 | 75 | 250 | $20 |
| 1st Half | 245 | 40 | 11 | 41 | 3 | 237 | 253 | 346 | 469 | 815 | 906 | 791 | 14 | 72 | 0.59 | 33 | 19 | 48 | 28 | 96 | 153 | 112 | 13% | 92 | 8% | 60% | 15 | 60% | 20% | 5.30 | 6.3 | 69 | 230 | $16 |
| 2nd Half | 216 | 35 | 12 | 40 | 9 | 273 | 263 | 333 | 532 | 866 | 671 | 965 | 9 | 77 | 0.43 | 33 | 18 | 48 | 30 | 91 | 146 | 135 | 15% | 121 | 17% | 100% | 9 | 78% | 22% | 6.58 | 13.0 | 82 | 273 | $24 |
| 19 Proj | **381** | **55** | **15** | **56** | **11** | **256** | **258** | **326** | **457** | **783** | **686** | **816** | **9** | **78** | **0.47** | **38** | **20** | **42** | **29** | **95** | **119** | **108** | **12%** | **99** | **14%** | **83%** | | | | **5.16** | **7.9** | **63** | **211** | **$14** |

## Polanco,Jorge

| | | | | | |
|---|---|---|---|---|---|
| Age: 25 | Bats: B | Pos: SS | Health A | LIMA Plan B+ | |
| Ht: 5' 11" | Wt: 200 | | PT/Exp C | Rand Var -5 | |
| | | | Consist A | MM 2235 | |

Just when we thought he was ready to break out, drug suspension dashed those hopes. PRO: Gains vR give reason to speculate again. CON: Steady losses vL put full-time role in doubt; poor SB% keeps SB upside at bay; BA driven by a hit rate that won't repeat. Still owns that upside, may still be a year away.

| Yr Tm | AB | R | HR | RBI | SB | BA | xBA | OBP | SLG | OPS | vL | vR | bb% | ct% | Eye | G | L | F | h% | HctX | PX | xPX | hr/f | Spd | SBO | SB% | #Wk | DOM | DIS | RC/G | RAR | BPV | BPX | R$ |
|---|---|---|---|---|---|---|---|---|---|---|---|---|---|---|---|---|---|---|---|---|---|---|---|---|---|---|---|---|---|---|---|---|---|---|
| 14 MIN * | 152 | 13 | 1 | 16 | 6 | 262 | 252 | 304 | 335 | 639 | 1000 | 1262 | 6 | 79 | 0.30 | 50 | 25 | 25 | 33 | 86 | 59 | 172 | 0% | 103 | 22% | 64% | 3 | 67% | 33% | 3.40 | 1.0 | 9 | 24 | $3 |
| 15 MIN * | 492 | 52 | 5 | 45 | 17 | 266 | 268 | 313 | 350 | 662 | 1333 | 476 | 6 | 84 | 0.43 | 56 | 22 | 22 | 31 | 41 | 56 | -16 | 0% | 101 | 20% | 60% | 2 | 50% | 50% | 3.63 | -11.1 | 27 | 73 | $14 |
| 16 MIN * | 538 | 53 | 12 | 62 | 9 | 272 | 274 | 323 | 428 | 751 | 857 | 718 | 7 | 82 | 0.41 | 33 | 30 | 37 | 31 | 80 | 90 | 65 | 5% | 101 | 12% | 54% | 16 | 50% | 25% | 4.66 | 5.4 | 45 | 129 | $14 |
| 17 MIN | 488 | 60 | 13 | 74 | 13 | 256 | 258 | 313 | 410 | 723 | 669 | 749 | 8 | 84 | 0.53 | 38 | 19 | 43 | 28 | 94 | 86 | 89 | 7% | 96 | 15% | 72% | 26 | 54% | 23% | 4.37 | -3.7 | 51 | 155 | $14 |
| 18 MIN | 302 | 38 | 6 | 42 | 7 | 288 | 255 | 345 | 427 | 773 | 628 | 845 | 8 | 79 | 0.40 | 36 | 26 | 38 | 35 | 94 | 86 | 76 | 7% | 109 | 16% | 50% | 14 | 21% | 21% | 4.90 | 6.9 | 36 | 120 | $10 |
| 1st Half | | | | | | | | | | | | | | | | | | | | | | | | | | | 1 | 0% | 0% | | | | | |
| 2nd Half | 302 | 38 | 6 | 42 | 7 | 288 | 255 | 345 | 427 | 773 | 628 | 845 | 8 | 79 | 0.40 | 36 | 26 | 38 | 35 | 94 | 86 | 76 | 7% | 109 | 16% | 50% | 13 | 23% | 23% | 4.90 | 8.2 | 37 | 123 | $10 |
| 19 Proj | **520** | **52** | **10** | **53** | **10** | **272** | **257** | **326** | **408** | **734** | **702** | **748** | **7** | **82** | **0.42** | **35** | **26** | **39** | **32** | **88** | **81** | **75** | **6%** | **107** | **13%** | **56%** | | | | **4.44** | **7.2** | **35** | **117** | **$16** |

## Pollock,A.J.

| | | | | | |
|---|---|---|---|---|---|
| Age: 31 | Bats: R | Pos: CF | Health F | LIMA Plan B+ | |
| Ht: 6' 1" | Wt: 195 | | PT/Exp D | Rand Var 0 | |
| | | | Consist A | MM 4555 | |

Thumb injury cost him seven weeks this go-round. Flunking health is reason to stop once bidding hits $20, as 2015 breakout was fueled by AB total he hasn't come close to duplicating. If health ever aligns, climbing xPX is where to speculate. Just don't do so without crossing fingers and toes. UP: 30 HR

| Yr Tm | AB | R | HR | RBI | SB | BA | xBA | OBP | SLG | OPS | vL | vR | bb% | ct% | Eye | G | L | F | h% | HctX | PX | xPX | hr/f | Spd | SBO | SB% | #Wk | DOM | DIS | RC/G | RAR | BPV | BPX | R$ |
|---|---|---|---|---|---|---|---|---|---|---|---|---|---|---|---|---|---|---|---|---|---|---|---|---|---|---|---|---|---|---|---|---|---|---|
| 14 ARI * | 314 | 43 | 7 | 29 | 14 | 274 | 281 | 318 | 447 | 764 | 953 | 828 | 6 | 84 | 0.40 | 52 | 14 | 34 | 31 | 109 | 116 | 97 | 9% | 175 | 23% | 82% | 15 | 67% | 13% | 5.04 | 11.0 | 94 | 254 | $13 |
| 15 ARI | 609 | 111 | 20 | 76 | 39 | 315 | 299 | 367 | 498 | 865 | 881 | 860 | 8 | 85 | 0.60 | 50 | 21 | 29 | 34 | 128 | 111 | 99 | 13% | 128 | 26% | 85% | 27 | 70% | 15% | 7.02 | 45.0 | 87 | 235 | $44 |
| 16 ARI | 41 | 9 | 2 | 4 | 4 | 244 | 209 | 326 | 390 | 716 | 425 | 788 | 11 | 80 | 0.63 | 42 | 9 | 48 | 26 | 89 | 71 | 119 | 13% | 122 | 31% | 100% | 3 | 33% | 33% | 4.88 | 0.3 | 39 | 111 | $1 |
| 17 ARI | 425 | 73 | 14 | 49 | 20 | 266 | 299 | 330 | 471 | 801 | 854 | 775 | 8 | 83 | 0.49 | 45 | 23 | 32 | 29 | 118 | 113 | 111 | 12% | 124 | 27% | 77% | 21 | 52% | 19% | 5.22 | 2.0 | 78 | 236 | $18 |
| 18 ARI | 413 | 61 | 21 | 65 | 13 | 257 | 265 | 316 | 484 | 800 | 742 | 830 | 7 | 76 | 0.31 | 42 | 19 | 38 | 29 | 124 | 132 | 146 | 17% | 124 | 17% | 87% | 22 | 59% | 18% | 5.20 | 11.6 | 61 | 203 | $18 |
| 1st Half | 150 | 23 | 11 | 33 | 9 | 293 | 299 | 349 | 620 | 969 | 1060 | 930 | 7 | 75 | 0.32 | 40 | 21 | 39 | 33 | 125 | 189 | 161 | 25% | 121 | 34% | 82% | 9 | 89% | 11% | 7.71 | 15.1 | 103 | 343 | $20 |
| 2nd Half | 263 | 38 | 10 | 32 | 4 | 236 | 244 | 297 | 407 | 704 | 592 | 767 | 7 | 76 | 0.31 | 43 | 18 | 38 | 27 | 124 | 100 | 138 | 13% | 120 | 7% | 100% | 13 | 38% | 23% | 3.98 | -1.3 | 37 | 123 | $17 |
| 19 Proj | **487** | **77** | **22** | **72** | **14** | **271** | **281** | **328** | **491** | **820** | **813** | **823** | **7** | **80** | **0.38** | **45** | **20** | **35** | **30** | **122** | **125** | **126** | **16%** | **131** | **15%** | **80%** | | | | **5.55** | **19.9** | **76** | **253** | **$23** |

## Posey,Buster

| | | | | | |
|---|---|---|---|---|---|
| Age: 32 | Bats: R | Pos: CA | Health B | LIMA Plan C+ | |
| Ht: 6' 1" | Wt: 210 | | PT/Exp B | Rand Var 0 | |
| | | | Consist D | MM 1143 | |

Catchers with this kind of mileage on their bodies generally don't age well. August hip surgery puts start of 2019 in doubt, but with this AB trend, durability was in question anyway. The healthy version's skills are as rock-solid as they come among backstops, but given injury, this might be his last CA-eligible season.

| Yr Tm | AB | R | HR | RBI | SB | BA | xBA | OBP | SLG | OPS | vL | vR | bb% | ct% | Eye | G | L | F | h% | HctX | PX | xPX | hr/f | Spd | SBO | SB% | #Wk | DOM | DIS | RC/G | RAR | BPV | BPX | R$ |
|---|---|---|---|---|---|---|---|---|---|---|---|---|---|---|---|---|---|---|---|---|---|---|---|---|---|---|---|---|---|---|---|---|---|---|
| 14 SF | 547 | 72 | 22 | 89 | 0 | 311 | 298 | 364 | 490 | 854 | 875 | 844 | 8 | 87 | 0.68 | 42 | 24 | 34 | 32 | 131 | 113 | 121 | 13% | 84 | 1% | 0% | 27 | 70% | 19% | 6.57 | 46.2 | 83 | 224 | $27 |
| 15 SF | 557 | 74 | 19 | 95 | 2 | 318 | 287 | 379 | 470 | 849 | 854 | 847 | 9 | 91 | 1.08 | 44 | 22 | 34 | 33 | 137 | 87 | 113 | 11% | 61 | 1% | 100% | 27 | 67% | 11% | 6.71 | 43.1 | 70 | 189 | $27 |
| 16 SF | 539 | 82 | 14 | 80 | 6 | 288 | 289 | 362 | 434 | 796 | 899 | 752 | 10 | 87 | 0.94 | 49 | 22 | 30 | 31 | 128 | 84 | 111 | 10% | 93 | 4% | 86% | 27 | 59% | 11% | 5.68 | 19.2 | 68 | 194 | $19 |
| 17 SF | 494 | 62 | 12 | 67 | 6 | 320 | 285 | 400 | 462 | 861 | 1019 | 799 | 11 | 87 | 0.92 | 44 | 23 | 33 | 35 | 116 | 81 | 113 | 8% | 81 | 4% | 86% | 27 | 52% | 11% | 6.87 | 37.2 | 59 | 179 | $21 |
| 18 SF | 398 | 47 | 5 | 41 | 3 | 284 | 264 | 359 | 382 | 741 | 829 | 698 | 10 | 87 | 0.85 | 47 | 22 | 31 | 32 | 116 | 61 | 93 | 5% | 79 | 4% | 60% | 22 | 50% | 23% | 4.81 | 14.5 | 41 | 137 | $10 |
| 1st Half | 255 | 36 | 5 | 26 | 3 | 290 | 274 | 367 | 420 | 786 | 886 | 734 | 10 | 87 | 0.88 | 47 | 21 | 32 | 32 | 127 | 76 | 114 | 7% | 86 | 5% | 75% | 15 | 67% | 7% | 5.47 | 14.4 | 57 | 190 | $15 |
| 2nd Half | 143 | 11 | 0 | 15 | 0 | 273 | 244 | 346 | 315 | 661 | 713 | 637 | 10 | 86 | 0.80 | 46 | 24 | 29 | 32 | 95 | 32 | 54 | 0% | 74 | 2% | 0% | 7 | 14% | 57% | 3.71 | 1.1 | 14 | 47 | $1 |
| 19 Proj | **378** | **45** | **6** | **47** | **3** | **281** | **269** | **356** | **391** | **747** | **834** | **709** | **10** | **87** | **0.86** | **46** | **23** | **31** | **31** | **116** | **66** | **96** | **6%** | **80** | **3%** | **66%** | | | | **4.88** | **15.4** | **38** | **127** | **$12** |

## Profar,Jurickson

| | | | | | |
|---|---|---|---|---|---|
| Age: 26 | Bats: B | Pos: SS 3B 1B | Health D | LIMA Plan A | |
| Ht: 6' 0" | Wt: 190 | | PT/Exp C | Rand Var +1 | |
| | | | Consist B | MM 3455 | |

Former #1 prospect once again looked the part. As strength in shoulder returned, so did power that he once seemed to own so easily. Fact that it got better as season went along bodes well for more growth there, and if he gets the green light more often, multi-category upside would bloom. UP: 25+ HR, 15+ SB

| Yr Tm | AB | R | HR | RBI | SB | BA | xBA | OBP | SLG | OPS | vL | vR | bb% | ct% | Eye | G | L | F | h% | HctX | PX | xPX | hr/f | Spd | SBO | SB% | #Wk | DOM | DIS | RC/G | RAR | BPV | BPX | R$ |
|---|---|---|---|---|---|---|---|---|---|---|---|---|---|---|---|---|---|---|---|---|---|---|---|---|---|---|---|---|---|---|---|---|---|---|
| 14 | | | | | | | | | | | | | | | | | | | | | | | | | | | | | | | | | | |
| 15 | | | | | | | | | | | | | | | | | | | | | | | | | | | | | | | | | | |
| 16 TEX * | 441 | 57 | 9 | 40 | 5 | 244 | 247 | 311 | 350 | 661 | 461 | 728 | 9 | 80 | 0.48 | 53 | 19 | 28 | 29 | 78 | 62 | 47 | 8% | 121 | 8% | 54% | 20 | 25% | 65% | 3.59 | -15.9 | 25 | 71 | $7 |
| 17 TEX * | 385 | 45 | 5 | 39 | 5 | 241 | 275 | 317 | 347 | 663 | 733 | 479 | 10 | 87 | 0.85 | 41 | 25 | 34 | 27 | 92 | 64 | 82 | 0% | 91 | 5% | 83% | 7 | 43% | 57% | 3.72 | -13.0 | 48 | 145 | $4 |
| 18 TEX | 524 | 82 | 20 | 77 | 10 | 254 | 288 | 335 | 458 | 793 | 795 | 792 | 9 | 83 | 0.61 | 44 | 22 | 34 | 27 | 114 | 115 | 98 | 13% | 110 | 8% | 100% | 28 | 61% | 11% | 5.18 | 12.9 | 78 | 260 | $19 |
| 1st Half | 274 | 42 | 8 | 44 | 6 | 241 | 291 | 325 | 438 | 763 | 875 | 720 | 9 | 84 | 0.60 | 42 | 24 | 35 | 26 | 100 | 114 | 85 | 10% | 92 | 10% | 100% | 15 | 53% | 13% | 4.64 | 1.1 | 75 | 250 | $18 |
| 2nd Half | 250 | 40 | 12 | 33 | 4 | 268 | 283 | 346 | 480 | 826 | 728 | 883 | 10 | 82 | 0.62 | 46 | 20 | 34 | 28 | 130 | 116 | 112 | 17% | 132 | 6% | 100% | 13 | 69% | 8% | 5.82 | 9.4 | 83 | 277 | $20 |
| 19 Proj | **506** | **74** | **19** | **66** | **9** | **266** | **283** | **345** | **450** | **795** | **844** | **780** | **10** | **84** | **0.66** | **44** | **22** | **33** | **28** | **103** | **103** | **86** | **13%** | **108** | **7%** | **88%** | | | | **5.31** | **19.7** | **68** | **228** | **$19** |

## Puig,Yasiel

| | | | | | |
|---|---|---|---|---|---|
| Age: 28 | Bats: R | Pos: RF | Health C | LIMA Plan B | |
| Ht: 6' 2" | Wt: 240 | | PT/Exp C | Rand Var 0 | |
| | | | Consist B | MM 4345 | |

Foot, oblique issues reminded us why his $30 tools always seem to come with a $10 penalty. Still, growing xPX, huge second half prove his upside remains, and soaring OPS vR points to more growth. If health finally cooperates, there's still a $30 season here. UP: 30 HR, 20 SB

| Yr Tm | AB | R | HR | RBI | SB | BA | xBA | OBP | SLG | OPS | vL | vR | bb% | ct% | Eye | G | L | F | h% | HctX | PX | xPX | hr/f | Spd | SBO | SB% | #Wk | DOM | DIS | RC/G | RAR | BPV | BPX | R$ |
|---|---|---|---|---|---|---|---|---|---|---|---|---|---|---|---|---|---|---|---|---|---|---|---|---|---|---|---|---|---|---|---|---|---|---|
| 14 LA | 558 | 92 | 16 | 69 | 11 | 296 | 272 | 382 | 480 | 863 | 736 | 901 | 10 | 78 | 0.54 | 52 | 15 | 33 | 36 | 116 | 134 | 110 | 11% | 139 | 11% | 61% | 28 | 54% | 36% | 6.29 | 34.3 | 83 | 224 | $26 |
| 15 LA | 282 | 30 | 11 | 38 | 3 | 255 | 249 | 322 | 436 | 758 | 924 | 704 | 8 | 77 | 0.39 | 44 | 17 | 39 | 30 | 107 | 114 | 89 | 13% | 104 | 8% | 50% | 18 | 39% | 22% | 4.60 | -2.0 | 48 | 130 | $7 |
| 16 LA * | 403 | 54 | 14 | 54 | 5 | 268 | 252 | 316 | 428 | 743 | 784 | 715 | 6 | 79 | 0.34 | 48 | 16 | 35 | 31 | 100 | 92 | 90 | 12% | 101 | 8% | 61% | 22 | 27% | 32% | 4.62 | -0.6 | 35 | 100 | $12 |
| 17 LA | 499 | 72 | 28 | 74 | 15 | 263 | 277 | 346 | 487 | 833 | 592 | 909 | 11 | 80 | 0.64 | 48 | 16 | 36 | 28 | 107 | 119 | 95 | 19% | 94 | 15% | 71% | 27 | 56% | 22% | 5.75 | 8.2 | 68 | 206 | $20 |
| 18 LA | 405 | 60 | 23 | 63 | 15 | 267 | 278 | 327 | 494 | 820 | 636 | 921 | 8 | 79 | 0.41 | 43 | 21 | 36 | 29 | 111 | 129 | 107 | 20% | 83 | 20% | 75% | 26 | 58% | 31% | 5.54 | 13.5 | 60 | 200 | $20 |
| 1st Half | 230 | 34 | 9 | 27 | 7 | 257 | 256 | 323 | 435 | 758 | 593 | 845 | 9 | 79 | 0.47 | 43 | 18 | 39 | 29 | 100 | 108 | 102 | 13% | 81 | 17% | 70% | 14 | 57% | 36% | 4.75 | 2.0 | 46 | 153 | $17 |
| 2nd Half | 175 | 26 | 14 | 36 | 8 | 280 | 303 | 332 | 571 | 903 | 694 | 1021 | 7 | 78 | 0.34 | 42 | 25 | 33 | 28 | 125 | 156 | 114 | 31% | 92 | 25% | 80% | 12 | 58% | 25% | 6.64 | 10.9 | 81 | 270 | $24 |
| 19 Proj | **448** | **64** | **25** | **70** | **14** | **269** | **275** | **334** | **492** | **826** | **679** | **891** | **9** | **79** | **0.44** | **45** | **19** | **35** | **29** | **110** | **125** | **102** | **20%** | **96** | **16%** | **73%** | | | | **5.61** | **15.1** | **64** | **212** | **$23** |

## Pujols,Albert

| | | | | | |
|---|---|---|---|---|---|
| Age: 39 | Bats: R | Pos: 1B DH | Health B | LIMA Plan C+ | |
| Ht: 6' 3" | Wt: 240 | | PT/Exp A | Rand Var +2 | |
| | | | Consist B | MM 2143 | |

Active leader in career Roto dollars at $553, and 4th overall since 1980. But two years of below replacement-level value confirms the writing is on the wall. As FB rate continues to dip, expect another cut in HR. Nagging knee, elbow ailments as he nears 40 puts everyday ability in jeopardy. DN: 300 AB, 10 HR, 50 RBI

| Yr Tm | AB | R | HR | RBI | SB | BA | xBA | OBP | SLG | OPS | vL | vR | bb% | ct% | Eye | G | L | F | h% | HctX | PX | xPX | hr/f | Spd | SBO | SB% | #Wk | DOM | DIS | RC/G | RAR | BPV | BPX | R$ |
|---|---|---|---|---|---|---|---|---|---|---|---|---|---|---|---|---|---|---|---|---|---|---|---|---|---|---|---|---|---|---|---|---|---|---|
| 14 LAA | 633 | 89 | 28 | 105 | 5 | 272 | 299 | 324 | 466 | 790 | 737 | 807 | 7 | 89 | 0.68 | 46 | 19 | 35 | 27 | 139 | 122 | 110 | 14% | 59 | 4% | 83% | 27 | 70% | 0% | 5.29 | 20.7 | 86 | 232 | $26 |
| 15 LAA | 602 | 85 | 40 | 95 | 5 | 244 | 286 | 307 | 480 | 787 | 753 | 799 | 8 | 88 | 0.69 | 42 | 16 | 42 | 22 | 127 | 125 | 130 | 18% | 57 | 6% | 63% | 27 | 70% | 11% | 4.83 | -1.8 | 86 | 232 | $21 |
| 16 LAA | 593 | 71 | 31 | 119 | 4 | 268 | 269 | 323 | 457 | 780 | 811 | 770 | 8 | 87 | 0.65 | 44 | 17 | 40 | 26 | 129 | 95 | 132 | 15% | 57 | 3% | 100% | 26 | 50% | 23% | 5.20 | 5.8 | 60 | 171 | $21 |
| 17 LAA | 593 | 53 | 23 | 101 | 3 | 241 | 251 | 286 | 386 | 672 | 608 | 692 | 6 | 84 | 0.40 | 43 | 18 | 38 | 25 | 120 | 72 | 105 | 12% | 49 | 2% | 100% | 27 | 30% | 22% | 3.73 | -28.9 | 23 | 70 | $10 |
| 18 LAA | 465 | 50 | 19 | 64 | 1 | 245 | 272 | 289 | 411 | 700 | 674 | 708 | 6 | 86 | 0.43 | 40 | 22 | 37 | 25 | 134 | 88 | 122 | 13% | 54 | 1% | 100% | 22 | 41% | 14% | 4.01 | -5.6 | 44 | 147 | $10 |
| 1st Half | 310 | 31 | 12 | 44 | 0 | 245 | 268 | 281 | 403 | 685 | 462 | 739 | 5 | 85 | 0.32 | 39 | 23 | 38 | 25 | 130 | 85 | 119 | 12% | 59 | 0% | 0% | 15 | 33% | 20% | 3.81 | -8.7 | 36 | 120 | $13 |
| 2nd Half | 155 | 19 | 7 | 20 | 1 | 245 | 278 | 304 | 426 | 730 | 927 | 635 | 8 | 88 | 0.72 | 43 | 20 | 37 | 24 | 143 | 92 | 126 | 14% | 58 | 3% | 100% | 7 | 57% | 0% | 4.40 | -1.7 | 62 | 207 | $4 |
| 19 Proj | **392** | **44** | **17** | **61** | **2** | **249** | **266** | **300** | **419** | **719** | **748** | **709** | **7** | **87** | **0.53** | **43** | **20** | **38** | **25** | **132** | **88** | **120** | **13%** | **55** | **2%** | **94%** | | | | **4.28** | **-5.6** | **45** | **149** | **$11** |

STEPHEN NICKRAND

## Quinn,Roman

Age: 26 Bats: B Pos: CF | Ht: 5' 10" Wt: 170
Health A | PT/Exp F | Consist B
LIMA Plan D+ | Rand Var -2 | MM 1513

2-12-.267 with 10 SB in 131 AB at PHI. Long history of ailments in minors made this his first extended MLB look. What we saw is what we should expect: elite wheels, so-so BA, very little pop, big L/R splits. Still, with another year of growth vR... UP: 40 SB

| Yr | Tm | AB | R | HR | RBI | SB | BA | xBA | OBP | SLG | OPS | vL | vR | bb% | ct% | Eye | G | L | F | h% | HctX | PX | xPX | hr/f | Spd | SBO | SB% | #Wk | DOM | DIS | RC/G | RAR | BPV | BPX | R$ |
|---|---|---|---|---|---|---|---|---|---|---|---|---|---|---|---|---|---|---|---|---|---|---|---|---|---|---|---|---|---|---|---|---|---|---|---|
| 14 | | | | | | | | | | | | | | | | | | | | | | | | | | | | | | | | | | | |
| 15 | aa | 232 | 35 | 4 | 12 | 23 | 272 | | 314 | 378 | 692 | | | 6 | 79 | 0.30 | | | | 33 | | 62 | | | 165 | 53% | 67% | | | | 3.82 | | 29 | 78 | $12 |
| 16 | PHI * | 343 | 53 | 5 | 25 | 28 | 246 | 247 | 307 | 357 | 664 | 911 | 633 | 8 | 71 | 0.31 | 57 | 22 | 22 | 33 | 51 | 77 | 50 | 0% | 170 | 42% | 74% | 3 | 33% | 33% | 3.67 | -10.2 | 15 | 43 | $14 |
| 17 | aaa | 175 | 21 | 2 | 11 | 9 | 245 | | 306 | 345 | 651 | | | 8 | 67 | 0.27 | | | | 36 | | 69 | | | 133 | 28% | 66% | | | | 3.43 | | -18 | -55 | $3 |
| 18 | PHI * | 232 | 25 | 4 | 21 | 20 | 256 | 236 | 307 | 394 | 702 | 884 | 653 | 7 | 74 | 0.29 | 49 | 18 | 33 | 33 | 59 | 81 | 79 | 7% | 183 | 43% | 80% | 11 | 45% | 27% | 4.22 | -0.1 | 33 | 110 | $10 |
| 1st Half | | 90 | 11 | 2 | 9 | 10 | 250 | 223 | 295 | 378 | 673 | | | 6 | 74 | 0.25 | | | | 32 | | 69 | | | 153 | 48% | 89% | | | | 4.13 | | 13 | 43 | $6 |
| 2nd Half | | 142 | 15 | 2 | 12 | 11 | 263 | 241 | 319 | 410 | 729 | 884 | 653 | 8 | 74 | 0.32 | 49 | 18 | 33 | 34 | 59 | 89 | 79 | 7% | 173 | 41% | 73% | 11 | 45% | 27% | 4.41 | 1.2 | 38 | 127 | $13 |
| **19** | **Proj** | **292** | **36** | **2** | **23** | **23** | **255** | **230** | **322** | **356** | **678** | **840** | **608** | **7** | **73** | **0.29** | **52** | **20** | **28** | **34** | **56** | **65** | **67** | **4%** | **183** | **40%** | **75%** | | | | **3.77** | **-3.3** | **7** | **22** | **$12** |

## Ramirez,Jose

Age: 26 Bats: B Pos: 3B | Ht: 5' 9" Wt: 165
Health A | PT/Exp A | Consist C
LIMA Plan C | Rand Var +3 | MM 4455

Emergence as top-5 bat backed by surging skills across the board, including *doubling* of walk rate. Heck, he would've posted a .300 BA too if not for a fluky hit rate. Soaring FB%, elite plate discipline, acumen on basepaths all cement him as a multi-category stud for years to come. Peak age, too. UP: MVP

| Yr | Tm | AB | R | HR | RBI | SB | BA | xBA | OBP | SLG | OPS | vL | vR | bb% | ct% | Eye | G | L | F | h% | HctX | PX | xPX | hr/f | Spd | SBO | SB% | #Wk | DOM | DIS | RC/G | RAR | BPV | BPX | R$ |
|---|---|---|---|---|---|---|---|---|---|---|---|---|---|---|---|---|---|---|---|---|---|---|---|---|---|---|---|---|---|---|---|---|---|---|---|
| 14 | CLE * | 482 | 57 | 6 | 40 | 25 | 265 | 274 | 312 | 366 | 677 | 676 | 632 | 6 | 86 | 0.47 | 47 | 24 | 28 | 30 | 85 | 72 | 71 | 4% | 120 | 30% | 66% | 15 | 47% | 27% | 3.77 | 1.5 | 51 | 138 | $18 |
| 15 | CLE * | 489 | 76 | 7 | 38 | 23 | 240 | 264 | 306 | 355 | 661 | 574 | 655 | 9 | 90 | 0.96 | 48 | 16 | 36 | 25 | 94 | 71 | 69 | 6% | 135 | 25% | 74% | 20 | 35% | 20% | 3.63 | -13.9 | 77 | 208 | $14 |
| 16 | CLE | 565 | 84 | 11 | 76 | 22 | 312 | 290 | 363 | 462 | 825 | 841 | 818 | 7 | 89 | 0.71 | 41 | 23 | 36 | 34 | 97 | 91 | 77 | 6% | 110 | 18% | 76% | 27 | 81% | 7% | 6.15 | 21.0 | 78 | 223 | $30 |
| 17 | CLE | 585 | 107 | 29 | 83 | 17 | 318 | 320 | 374 | 583 | 957 | 953 | 958 | 8 | 88 | 0.75 | 39 | 21 | 40 | 32 | 121 | 138 | 102 | 14% | 117 | 15% | 77% | 27 | 85% | 4% | 8.09 | 51.2 | 116 | 352 | $35 |
| 18 | CLE | 578 | 110 | 39 | 105 | 34 | 270 | 299 | 387 | 552 | 939 | 809 | 991 | 15 | 86 | 1.33 | 33 | 21 | 46 | 25 | 115 | 146 | 119 | 17% | 101 | 22% | 85% | 28 | 79% | 4% | 7.53 | 53.6 | 124 | 413 | $40 |
| 1st Half | | 302 | 56 | 24 | 53 | 14 | 291 | 313 | 398 | 603 | 1000 | 840 | 1063 | 14 | 86 | 1.19 | 33 | 22 | 44 | 27 | 120 | 160 | 136 | 21% | 97 | 17% | 88% | 15 | 93% | 0% | 8.69 | 35.5 | 131 | 437 | $42 |
| 2nd Half | | 276 | 54 | 15 | 52 | 20 | 246 | 283 | 375 | 496 | 872 | 777 | 912 | 17 | 87 | 1.49 | 34 | 19 | 48 | 24 | 109 | 130 | 102 | 13% | 110 | 28% | 83% | 13 | 62% | 8% | 6.40 | 15.8 | 119 | 397 | $37 |
| **19** | **Proj** | **587** | **104** | **34** | **99** | **29** | **287** | **305** | **373** | **552** | **925** | **862** | **953** | **12** | **87** | **1.05** | **37** | **21** | **42** | **28** | **110** | **139** | **102** | **16%** | **108** | **22%** | **81%** | | | | **7.34** | **47.2** | **122** | **408** | **$39** |

## Ramos,Wilson

Age: 31 Bats: R Pos: CA | Ht: 6' 1" Wt: 245
Health D | PT/Exp C | Consist F
LIMA Plan B | Rand Var -5 | MM 2035

Groundball-hitting backstop continues to rely on friendly hr/f as path to value. But with FB distance in bottom quartile, low FB rate, and pessimistic xPX, 10 HR is more likely than 20. And we can't bet on that hit rate repeating again, so BA also at risk. Combined with "D" health, he'll likely be overvalued.

| Yr | Tm | AB | R | HR | RBI | SB | BA | xBA | OBP | SLG | OPS | vL | vR | bb% | ct% | Eye | G | L | F | h% | HctX | PX | xPX | hr/f | Spd | SBO | SB% | #Wk | DOM | DIS | RC/G | RAR | BPV | BPX | R$ |
|---|---|---|---|---|---|---|---|---|---|---|---|---|---|---|---|---|---|---|---|---|---|---|---|---|---|---|---|---|---|---|---|---|---|---|---|
| 14 | WAS | 341 | 32 | 11 | 47 | 0 | 267 | 263 | 299 | 399 | 698 | 820 | 661 | 5 | 83 | 0.30 | 55 | 22 | 23 | 29 | 99 | 86 | 88 | 17% | 47 | 0% | 0% | 22 | 32% | 50% | 4.18 | 7.1 | 28 | 76 | $9 |
| 15 | WAS | 475 | 41 | 15 | 68 | 0 | 229 | 240 | 258 | 358 | 616 | 620 | 615 | 4 | 79 | 0.21 | 55 | 20 | 25 | 26 | 93 | 81 | 84 | 16% | 54 | 0% | 0% | 26 | 27% | 42% | 3.10 | -10.2 | 6 | 16 | $5 |
| 16 | WAS | 482 | 58 | 22 | 80 | 0 | 307 | 280 | 354 | 496 | 850 | 1008 | 806 | 7 | 84 | 0.44 | 54 | 20 | 25 | 33 | 120 | 105 | 97 | 21% | 54 | 0% | 0% | 26 | 62% | 23% | 6.46 | 26.8 | 50 | 143 | $20 |
| 17 | TAM * | 236 | 22 | 13 | 39 | 0 | 252 | 258 | 287 | 444 | 731 | 809 | 708 | 5 | 84 | 0.31 | 52 | 18 | 30 | 25 | 113 | 94 | 106 | 21% | 49 | 0% | 0% | 15 | 40% | 47% | 4.34 | 1.9 | 38 | 115 | $4 |
| 18 | 2 TM | 382 | 39 | 15 | 70 | 0 | 306 | 266 | 358 | 487 | 845 | 916 | 818 | 8 | 79 | 0.40 | 55 | 20 | 25 | 36 | 114 | 107 | 90 | 20% | 63 | 0% | 0% | 24 | 25% | 38% | 6.44 | 30.4 | 38 | 127 | $15 |
| 1st Half | | 254 | 24 | 11 | 43 | 0 | 291 | 259 | 338 | 461 | 799 | 888 | 762 | 7 | 79 | 0.34 | 51 | 23 | 26 | 33 | 116 | 96 | 97 | 21% | 57 | 0% | 0% | 15 | 20% | 47% | 5.61 | 15.2 | 26 | 87 | $17 |
| 2nd Half | | 128 | 15 | 4 | 27 | 0 | 336 | 281 | 396 | 539 | 935 | 984 | 919 | 10 | 79 | 0.52 | 62 | 16 | 22 | 40 | 110 | 130 | 77 | 17% | 74 | 0% | 0% | 9 | 33% | 22% | 8.31 | 16.2 | 63 | 210 | $10 |
| **19** | **Proj** | **423** | **44** | **13** | **57** | **0** | **269** | **260** | **317** | **420** | **737** | **798** | **715** | **7** | **81** | **0.40** | **56** | **19** | **26** | **31** | **112** | **90** | **92** | **14%** | **64** | **0%** | **0%** | | | | **4.68** | **15.0** | **22** | **72** | **$12** |

## Realmuto,Jacob

Age: 28 Bats: R Pos: CA | Ht: 6' 1" Wt: 210
Health A | PT/Exp B | Consist A
LIMA Plan B | Rand Var -1 | MM 3345

In short, best skills of career. Simultaneous increases in HR, xPX give him a firm 15-HR floor now. Legs still slick enough for return to double-digit bags too, if red light would even flicker green. Combined with excellent durability and consistency, he's a premium get at a hitting-starved position.

| Yr | Tm | AB | R | HR | RBI | SB | BA | xBA | OBP | SLG | OPS | vL | vR | bb% | ct% | Eye | G | L | F | h% | HctX | PX | xPX | hr/f | Spd | SBO | SB% | #Wk | DOM | DIS | RC/G | RAR | BPV | BPX | R$ |
|---|---|---|---|---|---|---|---|---|---|---|---|---|---|---|---|---|---|---|---|---|---|---|---|---|---|---|---|---|---|---|---|---|---|---|---|
| 14 | MIA * | 404 | 54 | 5 | 56 | 14 | 258 | 291 | 313 | 386 | 699 | 2000 | 563 | 7 | 82 | 0.44 | 43 | 33 | 24 | 30 | 101 | 91 | 57 | 0% | 126 | 19% | 71% | 6 | 17% | 67% | 4.10 | 7.7 | 55 | 149 | $13 |
| 15 | MIA | 441 | 49 | 10 | 47 | 8 | 259 | 269 | 290 | 406 | 696 | 791 | 671 | 4 | 84 | 0.27 | 45 | 21 | 34 | 29 | 106 | 88 | 105 | 8% | 125 | 13% | 67% | 25 | 44% | 16% | 3.96 | 1.8 | 55 | 149 | $11 |
| 16 | MIA | 509 | 60 | 11 | 48 | 12 | 303 | 261 | 343 | 428 | 771 | 617 | 806 | 5 | 80 | 0.28 | 49 | 20 | 30 | 36 | 97 | 82 | 86 | 9% | 103 | 11% | 75% | 26 | 27% | 35% | 5.29 | 12.4 | 30 | 86 | $20 |
| 17 | MIA | 532 | 68 | 17 | 65 | 8 | 278 | 267 | 332 | 451 | 783 | 837 | 768 | 6 | 80 | 0.34 | 48 | 18 | 34 | 32 | 108 | 97 | 98 | 12% | 126 | 8% | 80% | 27 | 37% | 37% | 5.17 | 16.9 | 50 | 152 | $17 |
| 18 | MIA | 477 | 74 | 21 | 74 | 3 | 277 | 272 | 340 | 484 | 825 | 651 | 875 | 7 | 78 | 0.37 | 40 | 23 | 37 | 32 | 111 | 123 | 110 | 15% | 108 | 4% | 60% | 24 | 63% | 13% | 5.58 | 28.0 | 60 | 200 | $18 |
| 1st Half | | 232 | 39 | 10 | 35 | 1 | 306 | 294 | 364 | 543 | 907 | 589 | 1007 | 6 | 79 | 0.33 | 42 | 24 | 34 | 35 | 129 | 141 | 114 | 16% | 122 | 4% | 50% | 12 | 83% | 0% | 6.91 | 22.0 | 82 | 273 | $20 |
| 2nd Half | | 245 | 35 | 11 | 39 | 2 | 249 | 250 | 319 | 429 | 747 | 716 | 756 | 8 | 77 | 0.39 | 37 | 22 | 41 | 28 | 94 | 105 | 106 | 14% | 86 | 5% | 67% | 12 | 42% | 25% | 4.49 | 7.6 | 37 | 123 | $17 |
| **19** | **Proj** | **524** | **72** | **20** | **71** | **7** | **273** | **267** | **328** | **458** | **786** | **712** | **806** | **6** | **79** | **0.34** | **43** | **21** | **36** | **31** | **106** | **109** | **103** | **13%** | **115** | **8%** | **71%** | | | | **5.10** | **24.9** | **48** | **160** | **$20** |

## Reddick,Josh

Age: 32 Bats: L Pos: RF LF | Ht: 6' 2" Wt: 195
Health C | PT/Exp C | Consist F
LIMA Plan B+ | Rand Var +1 | MM 2335

As that LD% returned closer to prior norm, hit rate fell with it, which took down BA. History suggests the hit rate will improve, but xBA confirms he won't add much value. And four straight seasons of subpar underlying power from a player with mediocre health is not a recipe for another $20 season.

| Yr | Tm | AB | R | HR | RBI | SB | BA | xBA | OBP | SLG | OPS | vL | vR | bb% | ct% | Eye | G | L | F | h% | HctX | PX | xPX | hr/f | Spd | SBO | SB% | #Wk | DOM | DIS | RC/G | RAR | BPV | BPX | R$ |
|---|---|---|---|---|---|---|---|---|---|---|---|---|---|---|---|---|---|---|---|---|---|---|---|---|---|---|---|---|---|---|---|---|---|---|---|
| 14 | OAK | 363 | 53 | 12 | 54 | 1 | 264 | 250 | 316 | 446 | 763 | 533 | 849 | 7 | 83 | 0.44 | 33 | 18 | 50 | 29 | 103 | 115 | 118 | 8% | 139 | 2% | 50% | 21 | 62% | 14% | 4.87 | 10.2 | 80 | 216 | $11 |
| 15 | OAK | 526 | 67 | 20 | 77 | 10 | 272 | 276 | 333 | 449 | 781 | 654 | 826 | 8 | 88 | 0.75 | 38 | 21 | 41 | 28 | 99 | 100 | 93 | 11% | 113 | 8% | 83% | 26 | 58% | 12% | 5.29 | 7.8 | 83 | 224 | $20 |
| 16 | 2 TM * | 423 | 54 | 11 | 38 | 8 | 270 | 259 | 333 | 392 | 725 | 366 | 871 | 9 | 85 | 0.63 | 41 | 22 | 37 | 30 | 105 | 70 | 90 | 8% | 120 | 9% | 73% | 22 | 50% | 27% | 4.55 | -1.9 | 52 | 149 | $11 |
| 17 | HOU | 477 | 77 | 13 | 82 | 7 | 314 | 275 | 363 | 484 | 847 | 762 | 867 | 8 | 85 | 0.60 | 34 | 24 | 42 | 35 | 107 | 95 | 97 | 7% | 117 | 7% | 70% | 26 | 58% | 12% | 6.63 | 22.0 | 69 | 209 | $23 |
| 18 | HOU | 433 | 63 | 17 | 47 | 7 | 242 | 241 | 318 | 400 | 718 | 827 | 669 | 10 | 82 | 0.64 | 37 | 19 | 44 | 26 | 91 | 83 | 91 | 11% | 107 | 7% | 78% | 27 | 52% | 22% | 4.31 | -2.5 | 50 | 167 | $11 |
| 1st Half | | 198 | 34 | 6 | 21 | 3 | 263 | 239 | 339 | 394 | 733 | 797 | 708 | 11 | 82 | 0.67 | 35 | 21 | 44 | 29 | 93 | 75 | 95 | 8% | 114 | 6% | 75% | 14 | 50% | 21% | 4.67 | 1.2 | 45 | 150 | $10 |
| 2nd Half | | 235 | 29 | 11 | 26 | 4 | 226 | 242 | 300 | 404 | 704 | 847 | 631 | 10 | 83 | 0.61 | 39 | 16 | 45 | 23 | 89 | 89 | 88 | 13% | 104 | 8% | 80% | 13 | 54% | 23% | 4.01 | -3.2 | 54 | 180 | $12 |
| **19** | **Proj** | **445** | **64** | **15** | **56** | **7** | **266** | **252** | **331** | **424** | **756** | **727** | **766** | **9** | **84** | **0.63** | **37** | **20** | **43** | **29** | **98** | **86** | **94** | **10%** | **112** | **7%** | **75%** | | | | **4.92** | **6.0** | **51** | **170** | **$16** |

## Reed,A.J.

Age: 26 Bats: L Pos: 1B | Ht: 6' 4" Wt: 275
Health A | PT/Exp C | Consist A
LIMA Plan D | Rand Var +1 | MM 4001

0-0-.000 in 3 AB at HOU. Former top-15 prospect still waiting for extended look in bigs. Impressive power and patience over two stints at Triple-A remind us of ceiling. Chronically spotty contact, struggles vL confirm he still has work to do. Even with warts, a $1 post-hype speculation worth taking... UP: 30 HR

| Yr | Tm | AB | R | HR | RBI | SB | BA | xBA | OBP | SLG | OPS | vL | vR | bb% | ct% | Eye | G | L | F | h% | HctX | PX | xPX | hr/f | Spd | SBO | SB% | #Wk | DOM | DIS | RC/G | RAR | BPV | BPX | R$ |
|---|---|---|---|---|---|---|---|---|---|---|---|---|---|---|---|---|---|---|---|---|---|---|---|---|---|---|---|---|---|---|---|---|---|---|---|
| 14 | | | | | | | | | | | | | | | | | | | | | | | | | | | | | | | | | | | |
| 15 | aa | 205 | 30 | 9 | 36 | 0 | 298 | | 364 | 506 | 871 | | | 9 | 73 | 0.38 | | | | 37 | | 144 | | | 90 | 0% | 0% | | | | 6.71 | | 54 | 146 | $8 |
| 16 | HOU * | 383 | 45 | 15 | 49 | 0 | 227 | 220 | 306 | 411 | 718 | 243 | 572 | 10 | 67 | 0.34 | 49 | 12 | 39 | 30 | 87 | 131 | 119 | 10% | 67 | 0% | 0% | 15 | 13% | 73% | 4.16 | -8.1 | 15 | 43 | $4 |
| 17 | HOU * | 482 | 58 | 23 | 67 | 0 | 202 | 177 | 271 | 384 | 654 | 0 | 0 | 9 | 64 | 0.26 | 60 | 0 | 40 | 26 | 0 | 120 | -26 | 0% | 52 | 0% | 0% | 1 | 0% | 100% | 3.32 | -31.0 | -12 | -36 | $2 |
| 18 | HOU * | 465 | 49 | 20 | 73 | 0 | 199 | 179 | 266 | 376 | 642 | 0 | 0 | 8 | 67 | 0.27 | 50 | 0 | 50 | 25 | 0 | 117 | -27 | 0% | 68 | 0% | 0% | 1 | 0% | 100% | 3.19 | -17.9 | 0 | 0 | $5 |
| 1st Half | | 269 | 31 | 13 | 45 | 0 | 205 | 185 | 289 | 391 | 680 | 0 | 0 | 11 | 69 | 0.38 | 50 | 0 | 50 | 25 | 0 | 115 | -27 | 0% | 77 | 0% | 0% | 1 | 0% | 100% | 3.63 | -9.5 | 14 | 47 | $9 |
| 2nd Half | | 196 | 17 | 7 | 28 | 0 | 191 | 217 | 233 | 356 | 589 | | | 5 | 64 | 0.15 | | | | 26 | | 120 | | | 66 | 0% | 0% | | | | 2.61 | | -16 | -53 | $0 |
| **19** | **Proj** | **193** | **25** | **10** | **34** | **0** | **232** | **226** | **294** | **443** | **737** | **289** | **800** | **8** | **66** | **0.27** | **36** | **18** | **46** | **29** | **78** | **140** | **107** | **17%** | **72** | **0%** | **0%** | | | | **4.36** | **-2.3** | **10** | **34** | **$5** |

## Rendon,Anthony

Age: 29 Bats: R Pos: 3B | Ht: 6' 1" Wt: 200
Health B | PT/Exp A | Consist C
LIMA Plan A | Rand Var -2 | MM 4255

Prior injury-prone label firmly is in the rear view now. 3 reasons he hasn't reached his ceiling yet... 1) Barrel rate soared from middle-of-pack to top 40; 2) GB% steadily declining; 3) Keeps showing more thump against righties. A $25 bid could net $10 of profit. UP: 30 HR

| Yr | Tm | AB | R | HR | RBI | SB | BA | xBA | OBP | SLG | OPS | vL | vR | bb% | ct% | Eye | G | L | F | h% | HctX | PX | xPX | hr/f | Spd | SBO | SB% | #Wk | DOM | DIS | RC/G | RAR | BPV | BPX | R$ |
|---|---|---|---|---|---|---|---|---|---|---|---|---|---|---|---|---|---|---|---|---|---|---|---|---|---|---|---|---|---|---|---|---|---|---|---|
| 14 | WAS | 613 | 111 | 21 | 83 | 17 | 287 | 279 | 351 | 473 | 824 | 825 | 824 | 8 | 83 | 0.56 | 40 | 20 | 40 | 32 | 136 | 126 | 146 | 10% | 122 | 12% | 85% | 27 | 67% | 11% | 5.97 | 38.9 | 88 | 238 | $32 |
| 15 | WAS * | 335 | 44 | 5 | 25 | 1 | 261 | 238 | 337 | 361 | 698 | 750 | 697 | 10 | 78 | 0.52 | 45 | 21 | 33 | 32 | 111 | 76 | 104 | 6% | 106 | 3% | 33% | 16 | 19% | 44% | 4.11 | -5.5 | 26 | 70 | $5 |
| 16 | WAS | 567 | 91 | 20 | 85 | 12 | 270 | 258 | 348 | 450 | 797 | 817 | 792 | 10 | 79 | 0.56 | 36 | 21 | 44 | 31 | 118 | 111 | 116 | 10% | 107 | 11% | 67% | 26 | 58% | 12% | 5.33 | 5.7 | 61 | 174 | $21 |
| 17 | WAS | 508 | 81 | 25 | 100 | 7 | 301 | 282 | 403 | 533 | 937 | 1131 | 887 | 14 | 84 | 1.02 | 34 | 19 | 47 | 32 | 116 | 127 | 112 | 12% | 91 | 5% | 78% | 27 | 67% | 15% | 7.79 | 34.8 | 94 | 285 | $25 |
| 18 | WAS | 529 | 88 | 24 | 92 | 2 | 308 | 291 | 374 | 535 | 909 | 931 | 901 | 9 | 84 | 0.67 | 33 | 24 | 44 | 33 | 118 | 129 | 122 | 12% | 94 | 2% | 67% | 26 | 73% | 19% | 7.33 | 38.3 | 90 | 300 | $26 |
| 1st Half | | 236 | 34 | 11 | 35 | 0 | 292 | 296 | 356 | 530 | 886 | 991 | 846 | 10 | 81 | 0.57 | 29 | 25 | 45 | 32 | 121 | 145 | 126 | 13% | 78 | 2% | 0% | 13 | 77% | 15% | 6.76 | 14.9 | 86 | 287 | $16 |
| 2nd Half | | 293 | 54 | 13 | 57 | 2 | 321 | 291 | 387 | 539 | 927 | 872 | 943 | 9 | 87 | 0.79 | 35 | 23 | 42 | 33 | 115 | 118 | 119 | 12% | 109 | 2% | 100% | 13 | 69% | 23% | 7.83 | 25.9 | 96 | 320 | $34 |
| **19** | **Proj** | **594** | **97** | **25** | **101** | **6** | **298** | **278** | **374** | **507** | **881** | **941** | **864** | **11** | **83** | **0.71** | **34** | **22** | **44** | **32** | **118** | **121** | **119** | **11%** | **99** | **5%** | **72%** | | | | **6.83** | **38.3** | **77** | **257** | **$30** |

STEPHEN NICKRAND

## Renfroe,Hunter

| | | | |
|---|---|---|---|
| Age: 27 | Bats: R | Pos: LF RF | Health B / LIMA Plan B |
| Ht: 6' 1" | Wt: 220 | | PT/Exp C / Rand Var +3 |
| | | | Consist B / MM 4235 |

26-68-.248 in 403 AB at SD. The light finally turned on in 2nd half for this former top prospect; witness steady climb of HctX and xPX. He's no longer just a lefty-masher either, as shown by elite PX vR. With another year of Eye growth, there's something big lurking here...finally. UP: .270-40-100

| Yr | Tm | AB | R | HR | RBI | SB | BA | xBA | OBP | SLG | OPS | vL | vR | bb% | ct% | Eye | G | L | F | h% | HctX | PX | xPX | hr/f | Spd | SBO | SB% | #Wk | DOM | DIS | RC/G | RAR | BPV | BPX | R$ |
|---|---|---|---|---|---|---|---|---|---|---|---|---|---|---|---|---|---|---|---|---|---|---|---|---|---|---|---|---|---|---|---|---|---|---|---|
| 14 | aa | 224 | 14 | 4 | 19 | 2 | 202 | | 271 | 301 | 572 | | | 9 | 73 | 0.35 | | | | 26 | | 83 | | | 82 | 5% | 60% | | | | 2.58 | | 4 | 11 | -$2 |
| 15 | a/a | 511 | 48 | 15 | 57 | 4 | 231 | | 271 | 380 | 651 | | | 5 | 70 | 0.18 | | | | 30 | | 108 | | | 97 | 5% | 77% | | | | 3.41 | | 6 | 16 | $6 |
| 16 | SD * | 568 | 72 | 23 | 84 | 3 | 255 | 242 | 275 | 443 | 718 | 1178 | 1192 | 3 | 76 | 0.11 | 43 | 13 | 43 | 30 | 82 | 116 | 125 | 31% | 90 | 6% | 59% | 3 | 100% | 0% | 4.12 | -8.4 | 31 | 89 | $14 |
| 17 | SD * | 500 | 63 | 29 | 70 | 4 | 252 | 251 | 296 | 493 | 789 | 1077 | 636 | 6 | 70 | 0.21 | 38 | 17 | 45 | 30 | 98 | 149 | 131 | 19% | 87 | 4% | 100% | 22 | 41% | 36% | 5.02 | -3.4 | 40 | 121 | $13 |
| 18 | SD * | 444 | 57 | 27 | 71 | 2 | 241 | 259 | 291 | 483 | 773 | 809 | 803 | 6 | 73 | 0.26 | 37 | 20 | 43 | 27 | 126 | 148 | 136 | 20% | 82 | 3% | 67% | 23 | 52% | 26% | 4.69 | 1.1 | 49 | 163 | $13 |
| 1st Half | | 180 | 25 | 5 | 23 | 1 | 233 | 250 | 293 | 408 | 700 | 919 | 689 | 8 | 71 | 0.29 | 40 | 24 | 36 | 30 | 128 | 123 | 113 | 11% | 105 | 3% | 100% | 10 | 50% | 30% | 3.99 | -3.3 | 32 | 107 | $2 |
| 2nd Half | | 264 | 32 | 22 | 48 | 1 | 246 | 265 | 288 | 534 | 822 | 754 | 866 | 6 | 74 | 0.23 | 36 | 18 | 46 | 25 | 126 | 164 | 148 | 24% | 67 | 4% | 50% | 13 | 54% | 23% | 5.16 | 4.4 | 60 | 200 | $21 |
| 19 | Proj | **494** | **70** | **30** | **90** | **3** | **252** | **258** | **300** | **498** | **799** | **919** | **738** | **6** | **72** | **0.23** | **38** | **19** | **43** | **29** | **115** | **151** | **132** | **20%** | **86** | **4%** | **75%** | | | | **5.01** | **6.0** | **46** | **154** | **$17** |

## Reyes,Franmil

| | | | |
|---|---|---|---|
| Age: 23 | Bats: R | Pos: RF | Health A / LIMA Plan C+ |
| Ht: 6' 5" | Wt: 275 | | PT/Exp D / Rand Var -2 |
| | | | Consist D / MM 4025 |

16-31-.280 in 261 AB at SD. A young bat whose ability to barrel the ball generates power in bursts. Still, flyball distance didn't even crack MLB top 250, so that 30% hr/f is headed south, which will bring homers down with it. And large frame gives swing large holes to close. A high-upside work-in-progress.

| Yr | Tm | AB | R | HR | RBI | SB | BA | xBA | OBP | SLG | OPS | vL | vR | bb% | ct% | Eye | G | L | F | h% | HctX | PX | xPX | hr/f | Spd | SBO | SB% | #Wk | DOM | DIS | RC/G | RAR | BPV | BPX | R$ |
|---|---|---|---|---|---|---|---|---|---|---|---|---|---|---|---|---|---|---|---|---|---|---|---|---|---|---|---|---|---|---|---|---|---|---|---|
| 14 | | | | | | | | | | | | | | | | | | | | | | | | | | | | | | | | | | | |
| 15 | | | | | | | | | | | | | | | | | | | | | | | | | | | | | | | | | | | |
| 16 | | | | | | | | | | | | | | | | | | | | | | | | | | | | | | | | | | | |
| 17 | aa | 507 | 74 | 22 | 95 | 4 | 243 | | 305 | 430 | 735 | | | 8 | 71 | 0.31 | | | | 30 | | 116 | | | 83 | 7% | 47% | | | | 4.29 | | 20 | 61 | $12 |
| 18 | SD * | 471 | 71 | 27 | 68 | 0 | 275 | 246 | 345 | 487 | 832 | 1028 | 748 | 10 | 68 | 0.34 | 49 | 21 | 30 | 35 | 111 | 135 | 115 | 30% | 75 | 0% | 0% | 18 | 33% | 44% | 5.91 | 20.1 | 25 | 83 | $17 |
| 1st Half | | 260 | 42 | 16 | 38 | 0 | 260 | 241 | 324 | 485 | 808 | 808 | 684 | 9 | 66 | 0.28 | 47 | 19 | 34 | 33 | 101 | 147 | 138 | 33% | 82 | 0% | 0% | 6 | 17% | 50% | 5.41 | 7.2 | 25 | 83 | $19 |
| 2nd Half | | 211 | 29 | 11 | 29 | 0 | 293 | 248 | 370 | 491 | 861 | 1115 | 785 | 11 | 71 | 0.42 | 50 | 22 | 28 | 36 | 119 | 121 | 105 | 28% | 72 | 0% | 0% | 12 | 42% | 42% | 6.55 | 12.2 | 27 | 90 | $15 |
| 19 | Proj | **412** | **57** | **21** | **61** | **1** | **258** | **249** | **327** | **459** | **786** | **962** | **704** | **9** | **70** | **0.34** | **49** | **21** | **30** | **32** | **112** | **128** | **118** | **24%** | **73** | **2%** | **50%** | | | | **5.12** | **7.9** | **17** | **55** | **$14** |

## Reyes,Jose

| | | | |
|---|---|---|---|
| Age: 36 | Bats: B | Pos: 3B SS | Health A / LIMA Plan D |
| Ht: 6' 0" | Wt: 195 | | PT/Exp C / Rand Var +5 |
| | | | Consist B / MM 2431 |

Just when we thought he found fountain of youth, already eroding hit rate totally bottomed out. In fact, only 28 batters had a lower exit velocity, so we can't assume full regression is in order. That leaves power and legs. xPX gives little hope for former, and age makes latter unlikely. UP: 2016 DN: Retirement

| Yr | Tm | AB | R | HR | RBI | SB | BA | xBA | OBP | SLG | OPS | vL | vR | bb% | ct% | Eye | G | L | F | h% | HctX | PX | xPX | hr/f | Spd | SBO | SB% | #Wk | DOM | DIS | RC/G | RAR | BPV | BPX | R$ |
|---|---|---|---|---|---|---|---|---|---|---|---|---|---|---|---|---|---|---|---|---|---|---|---|---|---|---|---|---|---|---|---|---|---|---|---|
| 14 | TOR | 610 | 94 | 9 | 51 | 30 | 287 | 268 | 328 | 398 | 726 | 709 | 732 | 6 | 88 | 0.52 | 42 | 23 | 36 | 31 | 89 | 77 | 66 | 5% | 132 | 19% | 94% | 26 | 42% | 8% | 4.93 | 26.3 | 67 | 181 | $29 |
| 15 | 2 TM | 481 | 57 | 7 | 53 | 24 | 274 | 258 | 310 | 378 | 688 | 700 | 683 | 5 | 87 | 0.42 | 44 | 20 | 36 | 30 | 73 | 68 | 58 | 5% | 104 | 24% | 80% | 24 | 38% | 25% | 4.20 | 0.5 | 46 | 124 | $20 |
| 16 | NYM * | 317 | 53 | 9 | 27 | 12 | 251 | 248 | 315 | 408 | 723 | 1196 | 664 | 9 | 81 | 0.51 | 35 | 22 | 43 | 28 | 96 | 88 | 100 | 9% | 132 | 18% | 78% | 12 | 67% | 25% | 4.39 | -4.4 | 55 | 157 | $9 |
| 17 | NYM | 501 | 75 | 15 | 58 | 24 | 246 | 258 | 315 | 413 | 728 | 843 | 692 | 9 | 84 | 0.63 | 37 | 20 | 43 | 27 | 91 | 87 | 88 | 8% | 137 | 24% | 80% | 26 | 54% | 19% | 4.43 | -8.8 | 67 | 203 | $17 |
| 18 | NYM | 228 | 30 | 4 | 16 | 5 | 189 | 251 | 260 | 320 | 580 | 635 | 560 | 9 | 83 | 0.56 | 44 | 19 | 37 | 21 | 80 | 77 | 71 | 6% | 105 | 15% | 71% | 27 | 37% | 37% | 2.60 | -12.1 | 44 | 147 | $0 |
| 1st Half | | 104 | 13 | 1 | 4 | 4 | 183 | 248 | 261 | 250 | 511 | 523 | 506 | 10 | 88 | 0.85 | 47 | 20 | 33 | 20 | 74 | 42 | 46 | 3% | 81 | 20% | 80% | 14 | 29% | 50% | 2.11 | -7.0 | 29 | 97 | -$3 |
| 2nd Half | | 124 | 17 | 3 | 12 | 1 | 194 | 254 | 259 | 379 | 638 | 750 | 603 | 8 | 79 | 0.42 | 41 | 18 | 41 | 22 | 85 | 109 | 94 | 8% | 115 | 10% | 50% | 13 | 46% | 23% | 3.02 | -4.6 | 56 | 187 | $2 |
| 19 | Proj | **96** | **14** | **2** | **8** | **3** | **221** | **252** | **287** | **367** | **654** | **758** | **620** | **8** | **83** | **0.55** | **41** | **20** | **40** | **25** | **86** | **82** | **81** | **7%** | **109** | **19%** | **77%** | | | | **3.47** | **-3.1** | **56** | **185** | **$2** |

## Reyes,Victor

| | | | |
|---|---|---|---|
| Age: 24 | Bats: B | Pos: LF DH CF | Health A / LIMA Plan D |
| Ht: 6' 5" | Wt: 194 | | PT/Exp F / Rand Var +2 |
| | | | Consist D / MM 0533 |

One-trick pony showed off those speed skills in debut. Problem is, when you neither draw walks nor make contact, opportunity to put wheels to use will remain limited. And even a bad team won't give him another 200 AB if he can't hit ball out of the infield. Only worthy of a SB dart-throw in very deep 5x5 leagues.

| Yr | Tm | AB | R | HR | RBI | SB | BA | xBA | OBP | SLG | OPS | vL | vR | bb% | ct% | Eye | G | L | F | h% | HctX | PX | xPX | hr/f | Spd | SBO | SB% | #Wk | DOM | DIS | RC/G | RAR | BPV | BPX | R$ |
|---|---|---|---|---|---|---|---|---|---|---|---|---|---|---|---|---|---|---|---|---|---|---|---|---|---|---|---|---|---|---|---|---|---|---|---|
| 14 | | | | | | | | | | | | | | | | | | | | | | | | | | | | | | | | | | | |
| 15 | | | | | | | | | | | | | | | | | | | | | | | | | | | | | | | | | | | |
| 16 | | | | | | | | | | | | | | | | | | | | | | | | | | | | | | | | | | | |
| 17 | aa | 479 | 49 | 3 | 42 | 15 | 278 | | 311 | 384 | 695 | | | 5 | 82 | 0.26 | | | | 33 | | 65 | | | 114 | 21% | 61% | | | | 4.01 | | 25 | 76 | $13 |
| 18 | DET | 212 | 35 | 1 | 12 | 9 | 222 | 246 | 239 | 288 | 526 | 486 | 535 | 2 | 78 | 0.11 | 50 | 26 | 24 | 28 | 100 | 39 | 63 | 3% | 154 | 23% | 90% | 26 | 12% | 62% | 2.38 | -10.7 | -2 | -7 | $3 |
| 1st Half | | 68 | 15 | 0 | 6 | 5 | 206 | 263 | 206 | 279 | 485 | 909 | 404 | 0 | 78 | 0.00 | 57 | 27 | 16 | 26 | 103 | 37 | 46 | 0% | 161 | 45% | 100% | 14 | 14% | 43% | 2.11 | -4.3 | -8 | -27 | $0 |
| 2nd Half | | 144 | 20 | 1 | 6 | 4 | 229 | 239 | 253 | 292 | 545 | 308 | 596 | 3 | 78 | 0.16 | 47 | 25 | 27 | 29 | 98 | 39 | 70 | 3% | 131 | 16% | 80% | 12 | 8% | 83% | 2.50 | -7.2 | -7 | -23 | $4 |
| 19 | Proj | **272** | **39** | **1** | **20** | **11** | **243** | **259** | **263** | **321** | **584** | **576** | **586** | **3** | **80** | **0.15** | **51** | **26** | **23** | **30** | **100** | **48** | **60** | **2%** | **138** | **24%** | **79%** | | | | **2.89** | **-14.0** | **12** | **40** | **$8** |

## Reynolds,Mark

| | | | |
|---|---|---|---|
| Age: 35 | Bats: R | Pos: 1B | Health A / LIMA Plan D |
| Ht: 6' 2" | Wt: 220 | | PT/Exp C / Rand Var 0 |
| | | | Consist B / MM 4111 |

13-40-.248 in 206 AB at WAS. Not often that a 30-HR season will net you a pinch-hitting role, but that's what happened. Yo-yo h% confirms BA projection is an educated guess, especially given chronic contact struggles. Buy him for power—just use 10-15 HR as baseline.

| Yr | Tm | AB | R | HR | RBI | SB | BA | xBA | OBP | SLG | OPS | vL | vR | bb% | ct% | Eye | G | L | F | h% | HctX | PX | xPX | hr/f | Spd | SBO | SB% | #Wk | DOM | DIS | RC/G | RAR | BPV | BPX | R$ |
|---|---|---|---|---|---|---|---|---|---|---|---|---|---|---|---|---|---|---|---|---|---|---|---|---|---|---|---|---|---|---|---|---|---|---|---|
| 14 | MIL | 378 | 47 | 22 | 45 | 5 | 196 | 223 | 287 | 394 | 681 | 573 | 719 | 11 | 68 | 0.39 | 38 | 14 | 48 | 22 | 94 | 146 | 155 | 18% | 89 | 7% | 83% | 26 | 46% | 42% | 3.58 | -7.2 | 38 | 103 | $6 |
| 15 | STL | 382 | 35 | 13 | 48 | 2 | 230 | 229 | 315 | 398 | 713 | 753 | 697 | 10 | 68 | 0.36 | 41 | 19 | 40 | 30 | 92 | 126 | 117 | 13% | 88 | 5% | 40% | 27 | 48% | 41% | 3.98 | -16.1 | 23 | 62 | $4 |
| 16 | COL | 393 | 61 | 14 | 53 | 1 | 282 | 256 | 356 | 450 | 806 | 673 | 865 | 10 | 72 | 0.38 | 42 | 26 | 33 | 36 | 84 | 115 | 99 | 15% | 93 | 3% | 33% | 23 | 48% | 48% | 5.53 | 2.2 | 27 | 77 | $12 |
| 17 | COL | 520 | 82 | 30 | 97 | 2 | 267 | 245 | 352 | 487 | 839 | 760 | 869 | 12 | 66 | 0.39 | 42 | 22 | 36 | 35 | 93 | 138 | 133 | 24% | 81 | 2% | 67% | 26 | 38% | 46% | 5.96 | 0.8 | 25 | 76 | $18 |
| 18 | WAS * | 245 | 28 | 14 | 43 | 0 | 237 | 222 | 311 | 442 | 753 | 858 | 773 | 9 | 67 | 0.33 | 41 | 18 | 41 | 29 | 89 | 131 | 121 | 22% | 65 | 0% | 0% | 21 | 38% | 43% | 4.60 | -3.6 | 14 | 47 | $5 |
| 1st Half | | 129 | 13 | 8 | 15 | 0 | 218 | 198 | 281 | 413 | 694 | 763 | 783 | 8 | 66 | 0.26 | 45 | 14 | 42 | 26 | 94 | 118 | 165 | 26% | 78 | 0% | 0% | 8 | 50% | 38% | 3.78 | -3.9 | 2 | 7 | $2 |
| 2nd Half | | 116 | 15 | 6 | 28 | 0 | 259 | 243 | 351 | 474 | 825 | 966 | 767 | 11 | 68 | 0.41 | 38 | 21 | 41 | 33 | 85 | 146 | 85 | 18% | 70 | 0% | 0% | 13 | 31% | 46% | 5.60 | 2.8 | 35 | 117 | $8 |
| 19 | Proj | **220** | **29** | **12** | **38** | **0** | **251** | **237** | **330** | **460** | **790** | **784** | **792** | **10** | **68** | **0.36** | **41** | **20** | **39** | **32** | **89** | **136** | **120** | **20%** | **77** | **2%** | **56%** | | | | **5.12** | **2.3** | **14** | **47** | **$8** |

## Rickard,Joey

| | | | |
|---|---|---|---|
| Age: 28 | Bats: R | Pos: RF LF | Health B / LIMA Plan D+ |
| Ht: 6' 1" | Wt: 185 | | PT/Exp D / Rand Var 0 |
| | | | Consist C / MM 2423 |

8-23-.244 in 213 AB at BAL. When looking for a 4th or 5th OF, target one with a high ceiling or intriguing underlying or power/speed skills. If you're looking here, it's time to move along. He can only hit lefties, and he doesn't do that particularly well either. What, you're still here? Move along!

| Yr | Tm | AB | R | HR | RBI | SB | BA | xBA | OBP | SLG | OPS | vL | vR | bb% | ct% | Eye | G | L | F | h% | HctX | PX | xPX | hr/f | Spd | SBO | SB% | #Wk | DOM | DIS | RC/G | RAR | BPV | BPX | R$ |
|---|---|---|---|---|---|---|---|---|---|---|---|---|---|---|---|---|---|---|---|---|---|---|---|---|---|---|---|---|---|---|---|---|---|---|---|
| 14 | aa | 206 | 26 | 1 | 13 | 7 | 208 | | 286 | 252 | 538 | | | 10 | 78 | 0.51 | | | | 26 | | 39 | | | 99 | 20% | 62% | | | | 2.27 | | -3 | -8 | $1 |
| 15 | a/a | 325 | 43 | 2 | 35 | 16 | 287 | | 365 | 406 | 770 | | | 11 | 77 | 0.54 | | | | 37 | | 87 | | | 120 | 20% | 78% | | | | 5.35 | | 39 | 105 | $13 |
| 16 | BAL | 257 | 32 | 5 | 19 | 4 | 268 | 240 | 319 | 377 | 696 | 861 | 618 | 6 | 79 | 0.33 | 42 | 21 | 37 | 32 | 83 | 72 | 83 | 7% | 129 | 7% | 80% | 16 | 25% | 25% | 4.19 | -3.8 | 27 | 77 | $5 |
| 17 | BAL * | 308 | 35 | 5 | 22 | 8 | 230 | 238 | 272 | 329 | 601 | 687 | 563 | 5 | 76 | 0.24 | 35 | 27 | 38 | 29 | 77 | 65 | 64 | 5% | 108 | 13% | 89% | 24 | 21% | 58% | 3.04 | -17.5 | 2 | 6 | $3 |
| 18 | BAL * | 366 | 47 | 10 | 44 | 6 | 238 | 235 | 305 | 383 | 687 | 789 | 668 | 9 | 76 | 0.40 | 35 | 22 | 43 | 29 | 82 | 93 | 101 | 12% | 105 | 9% | 76% | 22 | 32% | 50% | 3.91 | -6.6 | 30 | 100 | $8 |
| 1st Half | | 196 | 26 | 7 | 29 | 2 | 227 | 217 | 304 | 375 | 679 | 708 | 628 | 10 | 76 | 0.46 | 34 | 17 | 49 | 27 | 76 | 88 | 87 | 17% | 103 | 5% | 100% | 9 | 44% | 44% | 3.83 | -3.8 | 28 | 93 | $8 |
| 2nd Half | | 170 | 20 | 3 | 15 | 4 | 250 | 248 | 306 | 391 | 697 | 887 | 682 | 7 | 76 | 0.34 | 36 | 25 | 39 | 31 | 85 | 98 | 109 | 8% | 112 | 15% | 67% | 13 | 23% | 54% | 3.99 | -2.4 | 33 | 110 | $7 |
| 19 | Proj | **259** | **32** | **7** | **24** | **6** | **242** | **242** | **305** | **386** | **691** | **766** | **640** | **7** | **77** | **0.34** | **36** | **23** | **40** | **29** | **80** | **92** | **85** | **9%** | **118** | **12%** | **77%** | | | | **3.87** | **-4.5** | **24** | **79** | **$7** |

## Riddle,J.T.

| | | | |
|---|---|---|---|
| Age: 27 | Bats: L | Pos: SS | Health D / LIMA Plan D |
| Ht: 6' 1" | Wt: 180 | | PT/Exp D / Rand Var +1 |
| | | | Consist A / MM 2133 |

9-36-.232 in 311 AB at MIA. Just when we thought there was nothing to see here, he rides 1st half hr/f all the way to... 6 HR. Predictably it didn't stick, and there crashed his value, along with the title hopes of his two owners. Has there ever been a more uninspiring end to a Forecaster page? Riddle me that!

| Yr | Tm | AB | R | HR | RBI | SB | BA | xBA | OBP | SLG | OPS | vL | vR | bb% | ct% | Eye | G | L | F | h% | HctX | PX | xPX | hr/f | Spd | SBO | SB% | #Wk | DOM | DIS | RC/G | RAR | BPV | BPX | R$ |
|---|---|---|---|---|---|---|---|---|---|---|---|---|---|---|---|---|---|---|---|---|---|---|---|---|---|---|---|---|---|---|---|---|---|---|---|
| 14 | | | | | | | | | | | | | | | | | | | | | | | | | | | | | | | | | | | |
| 15 | a/a | 176 | 23 | 4 | 16 | 0 | 260 | | 294 | 363 | 657 | | | 5 | 85 | 0.31 | | | | 29 | | 61 | | | 109 | 0% | 0% | | | | 3.68 | | 32 | 86 | $2 |
| 16 | a/a | 445 | 45 | 3 | 45 | 5 | 239 | | 286 | 314 | 599 | | | 6 | 78 | 0.30 | | | | 30 | | 51 | | | 101 | 6% | 81% | | | | 3.02 | | -1 | -3 | $4 |
| 17 | MIA * | 291 | 27 | 4 | 36 | 1 | 247 | 251 | 279 | 362 | 640 | 581 | 657 | 4 | 79 | 0.21 | 53 | 18 | 28 | 30 | 106 | 71 | 97 | 6% | 115 | 5% | 29% | 13 | 23% | 46% | 3.32 | -10.3 | 19 | 58 | $2 |
| 18 | MIA * | 396 | 41 | 11 | 51 | 2 | 241 | 255 | 288 | 383 | 671 | 466 | 707 | 6 | 78 | 0.30 | 48 | 23 | 29 | 28 | 92 | 80 | 87 | 13% | 115 | 5% | 34% | 20 | 35% | 55% | 3.60 | -2.6 | 25 | 83 | $6 |
| 1st Half | | 192 | 23 | 6 | 30 | 2 | 267 | 267 | 305 | 419 | 724 | 478 | 787 | 5 | 74 | 0.21 | 55 | 25 | 20 | 33 | 95 | 91 | 89 | 27% | 114 | 6% | 61% | 7 | 43% | 43% | 4.39 | 2.4 | 17 | 57 | $10 |
| 2nd Half | | 204 | 18 | 5 | 21 | 0 | 216 | 251 | 271 | 348 | 620 | 460 | 666 | 7 | 81 | 0.42 | 44 | 22 | 34 | 24 | 92 | 70 | 86 | 9% | 121 | 4% | 0% | 13 | 31% | 62% | 2.95 | -6.5 | 34 | 113 | $3 |
| 19 | Proj | **298** | **30** | **8** | **35** | **1** | **242** | **258** | **281** | **382** | **662** | **525** | **705** | **6** | **79** | **0.28** | **51** | **21** | **28** | **28** | **98** | **80** | **91** | **12%** | **116** | **5%** | **43%** | | | | **3.56** | **-3.6** | **16** | **52** | **$6** |

STEPHEN NICKRAND

## Riley,Austin

Age: 22 Bats: R Pos: 3B
Ht: 6' 3" Wt: 220

| Health | A | LIMA Plan | D |
|---|---|---|---|
| PT/Exp | F | Rand Var | 0 |
| Consist | D | MM | 4413 |

Impressive .282/.346/.464 slash line in 291 Triple-A AB, though knee sprain in June cost him a month. Elevated h% hid some underlying contact issues, but the power is legit and PX says it could translate immediately. Not far from making it to Atlanta, but long swing hints at BA risk and rocky short-term transition.

| Yr | Tm | AB | R | HR | RBI | SB | BA | xBA | OBP | SLG | OPS | vL | vR | bb% | ct% | Eye | G | L | F | h% | HctX | PX | xPX | hr/f | Spd | SBO | SB% | #Wk | DOM | DIS | RC/G | RAR | BPV | BPX | R$ |
|---|---|---|---|---|---|---|---|---|---|---|---|---|---|---|---|---|---|---|---|---|---|---|---|---|---|---|---|---|---|---|---|---|---|---|---|
| 14 | | | | | | | | | | | | | | | | | | | | | | | | | | | | | | | | | | | |
| 15 | | | | | | | | | | | | | | | | | | | | | | | | | | | | | | | | | | | |
| 16 | | | | | | | | | | | | | | | | | | | | | | | | | | | | | | | | | | | |
| 17 | aa | 178 | 28 | 8 | 27 | 2 | 318 | | 384 | 517 | 901 | | | 10 | 71 | 0.37 | | | | 41 | | 121 | | | 100 | 3% | 100% | | | | 7.51 | | 34 | 103 | $8 |
| 18 | a/a | 390 | 51 | 16 | 59 | 1 | 280 | | 329 | 484 | 813 | | | 7 | 67 | 0.22 | | | | 38 | | 144 | | | 94 | 1% | 100% | | | | 5.66 | | 26 | 87 | $13 |
| 1st Half | | 201 | 24 | 9 | 34 | 1 | 294 | | 343 | 513 | 856 | | | 7 | 65 | 0.22 | | | | 41 | | 154 | | | 110 | 2% | 100% | | | | 6.38 | | 33 | 110 | $15 |
| 2nd Half | | 189 | 27 | 7 | 26 | 0 | 266 | | 315 | 452 | 767 | | | 7 | 68 | 0.22 | | | | 36 | | 134 | | | 88 | 0% | 0% | | | | 4.95 | | 22 | 73 | $11 |
| **19** | **Proj** | **257** | **37** | **10** | **39** | **1** | **263** | **238** | **322** | **450** | **773** | **773** | **773** | **8** | **69** | **0.28** | **38** | **22** | **40** | **35** | | **129** | | **14%** | **99** | **2%** | **100%** | | | | **5.06** | **4.1** | **18** | **60** | **$6** |

## Rivera,T.J.

Age: 30 Bats: R Pos: 2B 3B
Ht: 6' 1" Wt: 203

| Health | F | LIMA Plan | D |
|---|---|---|---|
| PT/Exp | F | Rand Var | 0 |
| Consist | B | MM | 1241 |

Never recovered from Sept 2017 Tommy John surgery, as July setback ended season after just 22 PA in Single-A/AAA. Pre-injury contact skills, LD% swing keep him relevant, but there's little power to speak of. Best case is an empty BA at multiple positions, but even that's a stretch given 20-month layoff. Not worth waiting for.

| Yr | Tm | AB | R | HR | RBI | SB | BA | xBA | OBP | SLG | OPS | vL | vR | bb% | ct% | Eye | G | L | F | h% | HctX | PX | xPX | hr/f | Spd | SBO | SB% | #Wk | DOM | DIS | RC/G | RAR | BPV | BPX | R$ |
|---|---|---|---|---|---|---|---|---|---|---|---|---|---|---|---|---|---|---|---|---|---|---|---|---|---|---|---|---|---|---|---|---|---|---|---|
| 14 | aa | 201 | 19 | 1 | 19 | 1 | 281 | | 307 | 343 | 650 | | | 4 | 83 | 0.22 | | | | 34 | | 54 | | | 85 | 1% | 100% | | | | 3.76 | | 9 | 24 | $3 |
| 15 | a/a | 403 | 45 | 5 | 34 | 1 | 254 | | 279 | 349 | 628 | | | 3 | 85 | 0.23 | | | | 29 | | 66 | | | 89 | 2% | 36% | | | | 3.29 | | 29 | 78 | $5 |
| 16 | NYM * | 510 | 51 | 10 | 67 | 2 | 270 | 259 | 295 | 386 | 680 | 457 | 997 | 3 | 82 | 0.20 | 42 | 24 | 34 | 31 | 90 | 72 | 92 | 10% | 104 | 5% | 31% | 8 | 25% | 25% | 3.85 | -16.6 | 25 | 71 | $11 |
| 17 | NYM * | 235 | 29 | 6 | 30 | 1 | 282 | 270 | 310 | 421 | 731 | 696 | 780 | 4 | 85 | 0.27 | 35 | 25 | 40 | 31 | 102 | 78 | 101 | 7% | 99 | 2% | 100% | 17 | 41% | 47% | 4.67 | -4.2 | 41 | 124 | $5 |
| 18 | | | | | | | | | | | | | | | | | | | | | | | | | | | | | | | | | | | |
| 1st Half | | | | | | | | | | | | | | | | | | | | | | | | | | | | | | | | | | | |
| 2nd Half | | | | | | | | | | | | | | | | | | | | | | | | | | | | | | | | | | | |
| **19** | **Proj** | **135** | **15** | **3** | **15** | **0** | **270** | **265** | **302** | **405** | **707** | **523** | **775** | **4** | **84** | **0.23** | **38** | **25** | **37** | **30** | **97** | **79** | **97** | **8%** | **101** | **3%** | **60%** | | | | **4.16** | **0.0** | **24** | **80** | **$4** |

## Rizzo,Anthony

Age: 29 Bats: L Pos: 1B
Ht: 6' 3" Wt: 240

| Health | A | LIMA Plan | B+ |
|---|---|---|---|
| PT/Exp | A | Rand Var | 0 |
| Consist | B | MM | 3155 |

Brutal start (.149 BA, 1 HR through April) driven mostly by fluky h%; finished with another strong R$ anyway. Ironclad plate skills, LD% stroke cement strong BA, but FB% and xPX trends ding once-stable power profile. BPX history is elite, so bid on repeat, just know it might not come with another 30 HR.

| Yr | Tm | AB | R | HR | RBI | SB | BA | xBA | OBP | SLG | OPS | vL | vR | bb% | ct% | Eye | G | L | F | h% | HctX | PX | xPX | hr/f | Spd | SBO | SB% | #Wk | DOM | DIS | RC/G | RAR | BPV | BPX | R$ |
|---|---|---|---|---|---|---|---|---|---|---|---|---|---|---|---|---|---|---|---|---|---|---|---|---|---|---|---|---|---|---|---|---|---|---|---|
| 14 | CHC | 524 | 89 | 32 | 78 | 5 | 286 | 286 | 386 | 527 | 913 | 928 | 907 | 12 | 78 | 0.63 | 36 | 22 | 42 | 31 | 106 | 164 | 135 | 19% | 74 | 6% | 56% | 25 | 72% | 4% | 6.90 | 40.2 | 91 | 246 | $28 |
| 15 | CHC | 586 | 94 | 31 | 101 | 17 | 278 | 285 | 387 | 512 | 899 | 881 | 905 | 11 | 82 | 0.74 | 35 | 22 | 44 | 29 | 121 | 143 | 131 | 15% | 76 | 14% | 74% | 27 | 70% | 15% | 6.51 | 19.1 | 90 | 243 | $31 |
| 16 | CHC | 583 | 94 | 32 | 109 | 3 | 292 | 294 | 385 | 544 | 928 | 832 | 970 | 11 | 81 | 0.69 | 38 | 21 | 41 | 31 | 114 | 145 | 120 | 16% | 72 | 5% | 38% | 27 | 74% | 7% | 7.07 | 28.4 | 88 | 251 | $26 |
| 17 | CHC | 572 | 99 | 32 | 109 | 10 | 273 | 291 | 392 | 507 | 899 | 881 | 906 | 13 | 84 | 1.01 | 41 | 20 | 39 | 28 | 117 | 119 | 107 | 17% | 69 | 8% | 71% | 27 | 70% | 7% | 6.58 | 11.0 | 81 | 245 | $25 |
| 18 | CHC | 566 | 74 | 25 | 101 | 6 | 283 | 286 | 376 | 470 | 846 | 684 | 902 | 11 | 86 | 0.88 | 38 | 25 | 37 | 29 | 108 | 100 | 93 | 14% | 76 | 6% | 60% | 27 | 59% | 22% | 5.95 | 13.6 | 69 | 230 | $24 |
| 1st Half | | 273 | 35 | 12 | 55 | 3 | 249 | 278 | 346 | 421 | 767 | 629 | 810 | 10 | 85 | 0.80 | 37 | 25 | 38 | 25 | 104 | 90 | 90 | 13% | 60 | 6% | 60% | 14 | 57% | 29% | 4.62 | -1.2 | 54 | 180 | $20 |
| 2nd Half | | 293 | 39 | 13 | 46 | 3 | 314 | 293 | 404 | 515 | 919 | 728 | 992 | 11 | 86 | 0.95 | 39 | 24 | 37 | 33 | 111 | 109 | 96 | 14% | 94 | 5% | 60% | 13 | 62% | 15% | 7.42 | 21.1 | 86 | 287 | $28 |
| **19** | **Proj** | **589** | **88** | **29** | **106** | **7** | **284** | **286** | **381** | **494** | **876** | **777** | **912** | **11** | **84** | **0.82** | **39** | **23** | **38** | **30** | **112** | **114** | **105** | **15%** | **75** | **7%** | **62%** | | | | **6.34** | **26.3** | **74** | **247** | **$28** |

## Robertson,Daniel

Age: 25 Bats: R Pos: 2B SS
Ht: 5' 11" Wt: 200

| Health | D | LIMA Plan | D |
|---|---|---|---|
| PT/Exp | D | Rand Var | -2 |
| Consist | B | MM | 2113 |

Modest step forward in utility role, then August thumb sprain shelved him for season. Several reasons for caution here... Power outlook muted by subpar xPX, lack of FBs. xBA still subpar despite ct% gains. Ineffective on basepaths. Patience is his best skill, but you shouldn't exercise much of it with him.

| Yr | Tm | AB | R | HR | RBI | SB | BA | xBA | OBP | SLG | OPS | vL | vR | bb% | ct% | Eye | G | L | F | h% | HctX | PX | xPX | hr/f | Spd | SBO | SB% | #Wk | DOM | DIS | RC/G | RAR | BPV | BPX | R$ |
|---|---|---|---|---|---|---|---|---|---|---|---|---|---|---|---|---|---|---|---|---|---|---|---|---|---|---|---|---|---|---|---|---|---|---|---|
| 14 | | | | | | | | | | | | | | | | | | | | | | | | | | | | | | | | | | | |
| 15 | aa | 299 | 40 | 3 | 33 | 2 | 244 | | 306 | 361 | 667 | | | 8 | 78 | 0.41 | | | | 30 | | 83 | | | 113 | 7% | 33% | | | | 3.59 | | 32 | 86 | $3 |
| 16 | aaa | 436 | 47 | 5 | 40 | 2 | 242 | | 327 | 329 | 656 | | | 11 | 74 | 0.49 | | | | 32 | | 61 | | | 101 | 2% | 63% | | | | 3.61 | | 1 | 3 | $3 |
| 17 | TAM * | 261 | 28 | 6 | 20 | 1 | 229 | 209 | 313 | 346 | 658 | 646 | 629 | 11 | 69 | 0.39 | 46 | 18 | 36 | 31 | 94 | 74 | 100 | 9% | 116 | 4% | 32% | 20 | 15% | 70% | 3.48 | -9.1 | -6 | -18 | $0 |
| 18 | TAM | 282 | 46 | 9 | 34 | 2 | 262 | 241 | 382 | 415 | 797 | 834 | 783 | 13 | 73 | 0.56 | 51 | 19 | 30 | 33 | 93 | 102 | 77 | 14% | 94 | 4% | 50% | 19 | 37% | 47% | 5.07 | 8.2 | 28 | 93 | $7 |
| 1st Half | | 197 | 32 | 7 | 20 | 1 | 264 | 235 | 384 | 421 | 805 | 887 | 769 | 15 | 73 | 0.65 | 47 | 19 | 34 | 33 | 91 | 102 | 80 | 14% | 105 | 1% | 100% | 15 | 33% | 53% | 5.51 | 7.6 | 36 | 120 | $9 |
| 2nd Half | | 85 | 14 | 2 | 14 | 1 | 259 | 254 | 379 | 400 | 779 | 644 | 812 | 9 | 73 | 0.35 | 59 | 19 | 22 | 33 | 98 | 101 | 68 | 14% | 84 | 14% | 33% | 4 | 50% | 25% | 4.08 | -0.2 | 17 | 57 | $2 |
| **19** | **Proj** | **250** | **35** | **7** | **28** | **2** | **248** | **237** | **356** | **391** | **747** | **733** | **752** | **11** | **73** | **0.45** | **51** | **18** | **31** | **32** | **95** | **95** | **84** | **12%** | **99** | **6%** | **40%** | | | | **4.24** | **0.5** | **9** | **29** | **$6** |

## Robles,Victor

Age: 22 Bats: R Pos: CF
Ht: 6' 0" Wt: 190

| Health | A | LIMA Plan | B |
|---|---|---|---|
| PT/Exp | F | Rand Var | -2 |
| Consist | C | MM | 3535 |

3-10-.288 with 3 SB in 59 AB at WAS. April elbow injury cost him three months which squashed odds of making MLB impact. Big impact is inevitable, though, as he pairs blinding speed with decent contact and just enough power to produce across the board. Should graduate as a top-five prospect in 2019.

| Yr | Tm | AB | R | HR | RBI | SB | BA | xBA | OBP | SLG | OPS | vL | vR | bb% | ct% | Eye | G | L | F | h% | HctX | PX | xPX | hr/f | Spd | SBO | SB% | #Wk | DOM | DIS | RC/G | RAR | BPV | BPX | R$ |
|---|---|---|---|---|---|---|---|---|---|---|---|---|---|---|---|---|---|---|---|---|---|---|---|---|---|---|---|---|---|---|---|---|---|---|---|
| 14 | | | | | | | | | | | | | | | | | | | | | | | | | | | | | | | | | | | |
| 15 | | | | | | | | | | | | | | | | | | | | | | | | | | | | | | | | | | | |
| 16 | | | | | | | | | | | | | | | | | | | | | | | | | | | | | | | | | | | |
| 17 | WAS * | 163 | 23 | 3 | 16 | 10 | 300 | 266 | 342 | 459 | 801 | 0 | 833 | 6 | 82 | 0.36 | 53 | 12 | 35 | 35 | 105 | 94 | 135 | 0% | 131 | 33% | 70% | 5 | 40% | 40% | 5.49 | 2.0 | 57 | 173 | $7 |
| 18 | WAS * | 217 | 30 | 5 | 19 | 16 | 271 | 237 | 332 | 411 | 743 | 970 | 804 | 8 | 82 | 0.51 | 27 | 24 | 49 | 31 | 107 | 84 | 106 | 14% | 130 | 40% | 65% | 5 | 20% | 20% | 4.44 | 1.3 | 52 | 173 | $9 |
| 1st Half | | 13 | 3 | 0 | 1 | 2 | 369 | 219 | 445 | 369 | 814 | | | 12 | 92 | 1.68 | | | | 40 | | 0 | | | 117 | 44% | 63% | | | | 5.92 | | 29 | 97 | -$15 |
| 2nd Half | | 204 | 28 | 5 | 18 | 14 | 265 | 239 | 325 | 414 | 739 | 970 | 804 | 8 | 81 | 0.47 | 27 | 24 | 49 | 31 | 106 | 90 | 106 | 14% | 129 | 40% | 65% | 5 | 20% | 20% | 4.35 | 1.3 | 54 | 180 | $11 |
| **19** | **Proj** | **455** | **63** | **13** | **42** | **24** | **279** | **263** | **344** | **461** | **805** | **933** | **712** | **7** | **82** | **0.42** | **37** | **21** | **42** | **32** | **95** | **107** | **95** | **8%** | **144** | **32%** | **67%** | | | | **5.12** | **13.1** | **69** | **230** | **$23** |

## Rodgers,Brendan

Age: 22 Bats: R Pos: SS
Ht: 6' 0" Wt: 180

| Health | A | LIMA Plan | D |
|---|---|---|---|
| PT/Exp | F | Rand Var | 0 |
| Consist | A | MM | 2221 |

Talented prospect made it to Triple-A, where he struggled in limited late sample (.232 BA, 0 HR in 69 AB). Power is the main draw, which we saw with early PX, and makes enough contact to drive a decent BA. 2nd half BPV, low bb% suggest he needs more seasoning, so don't bet on more than a late-season Colorado cameo.

| Yr | Tm | AB | R | HR | RBI | SB | BA | xBA | OBP | SLG | OPS | vL | vR | bb% | ct% | Eye | G | L | F | h% | HctX | PX | xPX | hr/f | Spd | SBO | SB% | #Wk | DOM | DIS | RC/G | RAR | BPV | BPX | R$ |
|---|---|---|---|---|---|---|---|---|---|---|---|---|---|---|---|---|---|---|---|---|---|---|---|---|---|---|---|---|---|---|---|---|---|---|---|
| 14 | | | | | | | | | | | | | | | | | | | | | | | | | | | | | | | | | | | |
| 15 | | | | | | | | | | | | | | | | | | | | | | | | | | | | | | | | | | | |
| 16 | | | | | | | | | | | | | | | | | | | | | | | | | | | | | | | | | | | |
| 17 | aa | 150 | 17 | 6 | 15 | 0 | 261 | | 294 | 408 | 702 | | | 4 | 76 | 0.20 | | | | 31 | | 83 | | | 96 | 6% | 0% | | | | 3.88 | | 12 | 36 | $1 |
| 18 | a/a | 426 | 39 | 14 | 49 | 9 | 250 | | 289 | 416 | 705 | | | 5 | 78 | 0.25 | | | | 29 | | 102 | | | 92 | 14% | 73% | | | | 4.05 | | 34 | 113 | $11 |
| 1st Half | | 290 | 33 | 13 | 44 | 7 | 275 | | 314 | 501 | 815 | | | 5 | 78 | 0.26 | | | | 31 | | 136 | | | 111 | 16% | 78% | | | | 5.50 | | 67 | 223 | $19 |
| 2nd Half | | 136 | 9 | 2 | 9 | 2 | 225 | | 269 | 303 | 572 | | | 6 | 79 | 0.29 | | | | 27 | | 52 | | | 104 | 10% | 67% | | | | 2.66 | | 3 | 10 | -$6 |
| **19** | **Proj** | **133** | **13** | **5** | **13** | **1** | **253** | **246** | **291** | **410** | **701** | **701** | **701** | **5** | **78** | **0.25** | **42** | **20** | **38** | **29** | | **94** | | **12%** | **108** | **9%** | **54%** | | | | **3.95** | **0.0** | **15** | **50** | **$3** |

## Rodriguez,Ronny

Age: 27 Bats: R Pos: SS
Ht: 6'0" Wt: 170

| Health | A | LIMA Plan | D |
|---|---|---|---|
| PT/Exp | C | Rand Var | -1 |
| Consist | A | MM | 2213 |

5-20-.225 with 2 SB in 191 AB at DET. Hit for the cycle and got The Call on same day, but highlights end there. The bat-to-ball skills exist, but they're muted by hollow contact and lack of patience. SB% should snip that green light, and without a .300+ OBP on this page, can't bank on regular playing time.

| Yr | Tm | AB | R | HR | RBI | SB | BA | xBA | OBP | SLG | OPS | vL | vR | bb% | ct% | Eye | G | L | F | h% | HctX | PX | xPX | hr/f | Spd | SBO | SB% | #Wk | DOM | DIS | RC/G | RAR | BPV | BPX | R$ |
|---|---|---|---|---|---|---|---|---|---|---|---|---|---|---|---|---|---|---|---|---|---|---|---|---|---|---|---|---|---|---|---|---|---|---|---|
| 14 | aa | 413 | 42 | 4 | 27 | 3 | 202 | | 238 | 287 | 526 | | | 5 | 75 | 0.19 | | | | 26 | | 76 | | | 90 | 11% | 37% | | | | 2.07 | | 0 | 0 | -$2 |
| 15 | aa | 269 | 31 | 10 | 26 | 4 | 272 | | 295 | 460 | 756 | | | 3 | 76 | 0.14 | | | | 32 | | 123 | | | 111 | 17% | 40% | | | | 4.40 | | 46 | 124 | $7 |
| 16 | aaa | 450 | 48 | 9 | 49 | 3 | 240 | | 270 | 366 | 637 | | | 4 | 80 | 0.22 | | | | 28 | | 79 | | | 98 | 9% | 43% | | | | 3.20 | | 25 | 71 | $5 |
| 17 | aaa | 447 | 48 | 14 | 51 | 12 | 261 | | 291 | 399 | 690 | | | 4 | 77 | 0.18 | | | | 31 | | 80 | | | 93 | 17% | 68% | | | | 3.91 | | 8 | 24 | $12 |
| 18 | DET * | 451 | 52 | 13 | 53 | 10 | 266 | 251 | 295 | 428 | 722 | 730 | 537 | 4 | 79 | 0.19 | 45 | 18 | 37 | 31 | 102 | 96 | 82 | 9% | 135 | 20% | 53% | 17 | 35% | 65% | 4.09 | -0.1 | 43 | 143 | $14 |
| 1st Half | | 281 | 37 | 8 | 34 | 8 | 279 | 275 | 298 | 456 | 754 | 571 | 53 | 3 | 79 | 0.13 | 47 | 24 | 29 | 33 | 85 | 104 | 134 | 0% | 146 | 31% | 47% | 5 | 0% | 100% | 4.24 | 2.3 | 50 | 167 | $20 |
| 2nd Half | | 170 | 15 | 5 | 19 | 2 | 246 | 233 | 291 | 381 | 671 | 754 | 607 | 6 | 79 | 0.30 | 45 | 17 | 38 | 28 | 105 | 81 | 75 | 10% | 102 | 5% | 100% | 12 | 50% | 50% | 3.80 | -0.8 | 27 | 90 | $4 |
| **19** | **Proj** | **268** | **29** | **7** | **30** | **3** | **255** | **238** | **286** | **397** | **683** | **807** | **635** | **4** | **78** | **0.21** | **45** | **17** | **38** | **30** | **95** | **86** | **68** | **9%** | **106** | **9%** | **54%** | | | | **3.80** | **-1.3** | **15** | **52** | **$7** |

RYAN BLOOMFIELD

## Rojas,Miguel

| | | | | | |
|---|---|---|---|---|---|
| Age: 30 | Bats: R | Pos: SS 1B 3B | Health | B | LIMA Plan D+ |
| Ht: 5' 11" | Wt: 195 | | PT/Exp | D | Rand Var +1 |
| | | | Consist | D | MM 1243 |

Burst out of the gate with 7 HR in first 163 AB, but power quickly dried up. Offers respectable BA floor thanks to solid ct% and line drive stroke, but PX/xPX history says early power was a fluke. Multi-position eligibility likely his best asset, which is all you need to know about mixed league viability.

| Yr | Tm | AB | R | HR | RBI | SB | BA | xBA | OBP | SLG | OPS | vL | vR | bb% | ct% | Eye | G | L | F | h% | HctX | PX | xPX | hr/f | Spd | SBO | SB% | #Wk | DOM | DIS | RC/G | RAR | BPV | BPX | R$ |
|---|---|---|---|---|---|---|---|---|---|---|---|---|---|---|---|---|---|---|---|---|---|---|---|---|---|---|---|---|---|---|---|---|---|---|---|
| 14 | LA * | 308 | 32 | 4 | 17 | 4 | 205 | 221 | 243 | 271 | 515 | 283 | 516 | 5 | 82 | 0.29 | 68 | 8 | 24 | 24 | 50 | 50 | 34 | 4% | 96 | 12% | 53% | 18 | 6% | 61% | 2.05 | -16.2 | 10 | 27 | -$1 |
| 15 | MIA * | 391 | 39 | 3 | 35 | 2 | 268 | 289 | 307 | 369 | 676 | 327 | 768 | 5 | 88 | 0.47 | 55 | 24 | 21 | 30 | 88 | 64 | 42 | 4% | 110 | 9% | 19% | 16 | 38% | 31% | 3.67 | -11.6 | 50 | 135 | $6 |
| 16 | MIA | 194 | 27 | 1 | 14 | 2 | 247 | 266 | 288 | 325 | 613 | 697 | 579 | 5 | 86 | 0.41 | 54 | 20 | 26 | 28 | 70 | 55 | 37 | 2% | 97 | 7% | 67% | 27 | 37% | 44% | 3.15 | -10.5 | 30 | 86 | $1 |
| 17 | MIA | 272 | 37 | 1 | 26 | 2 | 290 | 285 | 361 | 375 | 736 | 712 | 745 | 9 | 88 | 0.84 | 48 | 25 | 27 | 33 | 72 | 52 | 32 | 2% | 115 | 3% | 67% | 18 | 22% | 28% | 4.76 | -4.1 | 49 | 148 | $6 |
| 18 | MIA | 488 | 44 | 11 | 53 | 6 | 252 | 260 | 297 | 346 | 643 | 629 | 648 | 5 | 86 | 0.35 | 47 | 24 | 29 | 27 | 85 | 51 | 45 | 9% | 71 | 7% | 67% | 27 | 33% | 44% | 3.36 | -18.8 | 17 | 57 | $10 |
| 1st Half | | 273 | 23 | 7 | 30 | 3 | 245 | 256 | 303 | 348 | 651 | 582 | 677 | 6 | 85 | 0.41 | 48 | 23 | 29 | 27 | 92 | 55 | 51 | 10% | 77 | 6% | 75% | 15 | 33% | 40% | 3.41 | -8.9 | 21 | 70 | $10 |
| 2nd Half | | 215 | 21 | 4 | 23 | 3 | 260 | 264 | 289 | 344 | 633 | 703 | 613 | 3 | 87 | 0.25 | 46 | 25 | 29 | 28 | 75 | 46 | 37 | 7% | 75 | 9% | 60% | 12 | 33% | 50% | 3.29 | -7.7 | 16 | 53 | $9 |
| **19** | **Proj** | **330** | **37** | **5** | **32** | **4** | **261** | **267** | **308** | **352** | **661** | **654** | **663** | **6** | **87** | **0.44** | **50** | **23** | **27** | **29** | **76** | **54** | **39** | **6%** | **95** | **7%** | **61%** | | | | **3.62** | **-3.3** | **23** | **75** | **$5** |

## Romine,Austin

| | | | | | |
|---|---|---|---|---|---|
| Age: 30 | Bats: R | Pos: CA | Health | A | LIMA Plan D |
| Ht: 6' 1" | Wt: 220 | | PT/Exp | F | Rand Var -3 |
| | | | Consist | C | MM 2221 |

Skills were surprisingly solid during small-sample 1st half, but ct% abandoned him and was back to sub-.600 OPS over final two months. That hr/f sure looks like an outlier, so can't expect the power to repeat, and he's proven to be both a BA and OBP drag. This is not the second catcher you are looking for.

| Yr | Tm | AB | R | HR | RBI | SB | BA | xBA | OBP | SLG | OPS | vL | vR | bb% | ct% | Eye | G | L | F | h% | HctX | PX | xPX | hr/f | Spd | SBO | SB% | #Wk | DOM | DIS | RC/G | RAR | BPV | BPX | R$ |
|---|---|---|---|---|---|---|---|---|---|---|---|---|---|---|---|---|---|---|---|---|---|---|---|---|---|---|---|---|---|---|---|---|---|---|---|
| 14 | NYY * | 298 | 25 | 5 | 24 | 1 | 196 | 247 | 240 | 292 | 532 | 3000 | 333 | 5 | 77 | 0.25 | 56 | 22 | 22 | 24 | 184 | 78 | 152 | 0% | 73 | 1% | 100% | 5 | 20% | 60% | 2.24 | -10.1 | 4 | 11 | -$2 |
| 15 | NYY * | 340 | 30 | 6 | 39 | 0 | 219 | 355 | 258 | 321 | 579 | 0 | 0 | 5 | 81 | 0.28 | 50 | 50 | 0 | 25 | 0 | 70 | -16 | 0% | 68 | 2% | 0% | 1 | 0% | 0% | 2.66 | -11.2 | 12 | 32 | $0 |
| 16 | NYY | 165 | 17 | 4 | 26 | 1 | 242 | 260 | 269 | 382 | 650 | 725 | 551 | 4 | 81 | 0.23 | 47 | 19 | 33 | 28 | 88 | 90 | 100 | 9% | 78 | 3% | 100% | 26 | 38% | 42% | 3.54 | -1.5 | 30 | 86 | $1 |
| 17 | NYY | 229 | 19 | 2 | 21 | 0 | 218 | 235 | 272 | 293 | 565 | 499 | 586 | 6 | 75 | 0.28 | 45 | 25 | 30 | 28 | 84 | 50 | 66 | 4% | 82 | 0% | 0% | 27 | 11% | 56% | 2.57 | -10.9 | -19 | -58 | -$2 |
| 18 | NYY | 242 | 30 | 10 | 42 | 1 | 244 | 243 | 295 | 417 | 713 | 714 | 712 | 6 | 72 | 0.25 | 49 | 19 | 32 | 30 | 95 | 111 | 89 | 18% | 63 | 2% | 100% | 25 | 28% | 48% | 4.15 | 5.6 | 12 | 40 | $5 |
| 1st Half | | 95 | 13 | 4 | 20 | 0 | 274 | 270 | 340 | 474 | 813 | 733 | 849 | 10 | 80 | 0.53 | 42 | 21 | 38 | 31 | 111 | 121 | 90 | 14% | 58 | 0% | 0% | 13 | 38% | 54% | 5.70 | 6.1 | 55 | 183 | $3 |
| 2nd Half | | 147 | 17 | 6 | 22 | 1 | 224 | 225 | 266 | 381 | 647 | 697 | 632 | 5 | 67 | 0.15 | 54 | 18 | 28 | 29 | 85 | 103 | 88 | 21% | 78 | 3% | 100% | 12 | 17% | 42% | 3.29 | -0.7 | -14 | -47 | $6 |
| **19** | **Proj** | **230** | **25** | **6** | **33** | **1** | **234** | **242** | **283** | **369** | **652** | **654** | **650** | **6** | **75** | **0.26** | **47** | **21** | **31** | **28** | **90** | **87** | **83** | **12%** | **72** | **1%** | **95%** | | | | **3.47** | **0.2** | **-2** | **-7** | **$4** |

## Rondon,Jose

| | | | | | |
|---|---|---|---|---|---|
| Age: 25 | Bats: R | Pos: DH | Health | A | LIMA Plan D |
| Ht: 6' 1" | Wt: 195 | | PT/Exp | D | Rand Var 0 |
| | | | Consist | A | MM 3221 |

6-14-.230 with 2 SB in 100 AB at CHW. With change in teams came new approach, as he traded contact for power. Added pop may not be enough, as OBP still abysmal, hr/f is sure to regress, and low efficiency limits SB potential. Needs skills consolidation for shot at regular PT in middle infield, which seems unlikely.

| Yr | Tm | AB | R | HR | RBI | SB | BA | xBA | OBP | SLG | OPS | vL | vR | bb% | ct% | Eye | G | L | F | h% | HctX | PX | xPX | hr/f | Spd | SBO | SB% | #Wk | DOM | DIS | RC/G | RAR | BPV | BPX | R$ |
|---|---|---|---|---|---|---|---|---|---|---|---|---|---|---|---|---|---|---|---|---|---|---|---|---|---|---|---|---|---|---|---|---|---|---|---|
| 14 | | | | | | | | | | | | | | | | | | | | | | | | | | | | | | | | | | | |
| 15 | aa | 100 | 5 | 0 | 7 | 1 | 171 | | 198 | 204 | 402 | | | 3 | 83 | 0.20 | | | | 21 | | 22 | | | 111 | 23% | 21% | | | | 1.03 | | -6 | -16 | -$4 |
| 16 | SD * | 481 | 43 | 4 | 43 | 10 | 247 | 231 | 267 | 328 | 595 | 0 | 310 | 3 | 82 | 0.15 | 62 | 10 | 29 | 29 | 32 | 55 | 11 | 0% | 98 | 15% | 65% | 3 | 33% | 67% | 2.90 | -24.7 | 8 | 23 | $7 |
| 17 | a/a | 300 | 31 | 4 | 33 | 2 | 252 | | 293 | 363 | 655 | | | 5 | 77 | 0.26 | | | | 31 | | 72 | | | 101 | 5% | 68% | | | | 3.60 | | 11 | 33 | $3 |
| 18 | CHW * | 413 | 48 | 22 | 45 | 6 | 221 | 252 | 258 | 440 | 699 | 636 | 847 | 5 | 70 | 0.16 | 41 | 23 | 36 | 26 | 95 | 137 | 128 | 24% | 127 | 20% | 44% | 14 | 43% | 29% | 3.45 | -8.4 | 38 | 127 | $9 |
| 1st Half | | 203 | 26 | 10 | 20 | 4 | 232 | 247 | 270 | 452 | 722 | 527 | 954 | 5 | 68 | 0.16 | 41 | 22 | 38 | 29 | 99 | 142 | 137 | 25% | 144 | 22% | 57% | 8 | 25% | 25% | 3.84 | -0.8 | 41 | 137 | $9 |
| 2nd Half | | 210 | 22 | 12 | 25 | 2 | 211 | 258 | 247 | 429 | 676 | 721 | 726 | 5 | 71 | 0.16 | 41 | 24 | 35 | 24 | 92 | 133 | 121 | 23% | 104 | 18% | 27% | 6 | 67% | 33% | 3.09 | -5.8 | 33 | 110 | $8 |
| **19** | **Proj** | **167** | **13** | **6** | **14** | **2** | **233** | **242** | **268** | **409** | **676** | **601** | **743** | **5** | **73** | **0.17** | **44** | **20** | **36** | **28** | **95** | **110** | **127** | **15%** | **115** | **14%** | **47%** | | | | **3.45** | **-5.4** | **9** | **28** | **$3** |

## Rosario,Amed

| | | | | | |
|---|---|---|---|---|---|
| Age: 23 | Bats: R | Pos: SS | Health | A | LIMA Plan B |
| Ht: 6' 2" | Wt: 189 | | PT/Exp | C | Rand Var +2 |
| | | | Consist | B | MM 2535 |

Took a long time to get going, but final 209 PA yielded .303 BA with 5 HR, 13 SB. Elite speed on full display in 2nd half, and 8-for-9 SB in Sept bodes well for continued green light. Importantly, made strides in ct% and LD% after the break also. If in-season SB% gains hold ... UP: 40 SB

| Yr | Tm | AB | R | HR | RBI | SB | BA | xBA | OBP | SLG | OPS | vL | vR | bb% | ct% | Eye | G | L | F | h% | HctX | PX | xPX | hr/f | Spd | SBO | SB% | #Wk | DOM | DIS | RC/G | RAR | BPV | BPX | R$ |
|---|---|---|---|---|---|---|---|---|---|---|---|---|---|---|---|---|---|---|---|---|---|---|---|---|---|---|---|---|---|---|---|---|---|---|---|
| 14 | | | | | | | | | | | | | | | | | | | | | | | | | | | | | | | | | | | |
| 15 | | | | | | | | | | | | | | | | | | | | | | | | | | | | | | | | | | | |
| 16 | aa | 214 | 33 | 2 | 27 | 5 | 307 | | 362 | 422 | 783 | | | 8 | 72 | 0.31 | | | | 42 | | 83 | | | 114 | 11% | 71% | | | | 5.55 | | 7 | 20 | $8 |
| 17 | NYM * | 558 | 65 | 9 | 53 | 21 | 268 | 247 | 294 | 383 | 678 | 829 | 617 | 4 | 77 | 0.16 | 51 | 20 | 29 | 33 | 75 | 65 | 73 | 12% | 171 | 23% | 68% | 10 | 20% | 50% | 3.82 | -11.5 | 21 | 64 | $18 |
| 18 | NYM | 554 | 76 | 9 | 51 | 24 | 256 | 253 | 295 | 381 | 676 | 743 | 654 | 5 | 79 | 0.24 | 50 | 21 | 30 | 31 | 80 | 75 | 71 | 7% | 162 | 27% | 69% | 28 | 25% | 43% | 3.71 | -1.8 | 34 | 113 | $19 |
| 1st Half | | 248 | 29 | 4 | 21 | 4 | 246 | 235 | 285 | 363 | 648 | 621 | 658 | 5 | 77 | 0.21 | 48 | 18 | 34 | 31 | 78 | 76 | 68 | 6% | 143 | 15% | 50% | 15 | 20% | 53% | 3.27 | -5.2 | 21 | 70 | $6 |
| 2nd Half | | 306 | 47 | 5 | 30 | 20 | 265 | 267 | 304 | 395 | 699 | 860 | 650 | 5 | 80 | 0.28 | 51 | 23 | 26 | 32 | 82 | 75 | 73 | 8% | 169 | 36% | 74% | 13 | 31% | 31% | 4.09 | 1.1 | 44 | 147 | $30 |
| **19** | **Proj** | **599** | **80** | **12** | **59** | **28** | **269** | **254** | **309** | **405** | **714** | **800** | **687** | **5** | **78** | **0.23** | **50** | **21** | **29** | **33** | **78** | **81** | **72** | **9%** | **164** | **27%** | **70%** | | | | **4.19** | **3.9** | **30** | **101** | **$26** |

## Rosario,Eddie

| | | | | | |
|---|---|---|---|---|---|
| Age: 27 | Bats: L | Pos: LF | Health | A | LIMA Plan B+ |
| Ht: 6' 1" | Wt: 180 | | PT/Exp | B | Rand Var -2 |
| | | | Consist | B | MM 3335 |

Built on 2017 finish with even better 1st half, as LD%/FB% surged. But then: HctX plunged, GBs returned, and he stopped running. Sore shoulder in late June cost him just one game, but may help explain collapse, and quad injury ended season early. Should bounce back with health, and could be the year for... UP: 30 HR.

| Yr | Tm | AB | R | HR | RBI | SB | BA | xBA | OBP | SLG | OPS | vL | vR | bb% | ct% | Eye | G | L | F | h% | HctX | PX | xPX | hr/f | Spd | SBO | SB% | #Wk | DOM | DIS | RC/G | RAR | BPV | BPX | R$ |
|---|---|---|---|---|---|---|---|---|---|---|---|---|---|---|---|---|---|---|---|---|---|---|---|---|---|---|---|---|---|---|---|---|---|---|---|
| 14 | aa | 316 | 32 | 6 | 28 | 6 | 213 | | 245 | 347 | 592 | | | 4 | 77 | 0.18 | | | | 26 | | 103 | | | 103 | 20% | 59% | | | | 2.64 | | 31 | 84 | $2 |
| 15 | MIN * | 548 | 69 | 15 | 60 | 12 | 259 | 242 | 284 | 438 | 722 | 811 | 727 | 3 | 75 | 0.14 | 39 | 20 | 41 | 32 | 96 | 110 | 110 | 10% | 173 | 17% | 62% | 22 | 41% | 27% | 4.13 | -4.3 | 49 | 132 | $16 |
| 16 | MIN * | 495 | 75 | 16 | 54 | 9 | 275 | 257 | 301 | 441 | 742 | 594 | 752 | 3 | 76 | 0.15 | 46 | 19 | 34 | 33 | 93 | 106 | 102 | 12% | 128 | 14% | 63% | 18 | 28% | 50% | 4.54 | 3.8 | 37 | 106 | $16 |
| 17 | MIN | 542 | 79 | 27 | 78 | 9 | 290 | 281 | 328 | 507 | 836 | 682 | 906 | 6 | 80 | 0.33 | 42 | 20 | 37 | 32 | 103 | 119 | 121 | 16% | 107 | 13% | 53% | 27 | 52% | 22% | 5.79 | 5.3 | 63 | 191 | $23 |
| 18 | MIN | 559 | 87 | 24 | 77 | 8 | 288 | 259 | 323 | 479 | 803 | 726 | 838 | 5 | 81 | 0.29 | 36 | 20 | 44 | 32 | 109 | 108 | 126 | 12% | 105 | 7% | 80% | 26 | 62% | 27% | 5.57 | 15.5 | 56 | 187 | $24 |
| 1st Half | | 311 | 56 | 18 | 52 | 6 | 315 | 289 | 355 | 576 | 930 | 779 | 1000 | 6 | 82 | 0.35 | 31 | 23 | 45 | 34 | 118 | 145 | 136 | 16% | 106 | 11% | 75% | 15 | 73% | 27% | 7.53 | 24.8 | 91 | 303 | $37 |
| 2nd Half | | 248 | 31 | 6 | 25 | 2 | 254 | 217 | 284 | 359 | 642 | 659 | 635 | 4 | 80 | 0.22 | 41 | 17 | 42 | 30 | 99 | 61 | 113 | 7% | 105 | 3% | 100% | 11 | 45% | 27% | 3.55 | -7.6 | 12 | 40 | $9 |
| **19** | **Proj** | **562** | **81** | **26** | **71** | **9** | **284** | **262** | **322** | **486** | **807** | **719** | **845** | **6** | **80** | **0.29** | **39** | **20** | **41** | **32** | **103** | **115** | **118** | **14%** | **114** | **10%** | **66%** | | | | **5.50** | **14.5** | **51** | **169** | **$25** |

## Russell,Addison

| | | | | | |
|---|---|---|---|---|---|
| Age: 25 | Bats: R | Pos: SS | Health | B | LIMA Plan D+ |
| Ht: 6' 0" | Wt: 200 | | PT/Exp | B | Rand Var 0 |
| | | | Consist | A | MM 2323 |

High h% kept him afloat early on, but xBA, PX, and hr/f were down from the start. Shoulder, finger woes likely played role in 2nd half power outage, but off-field issues complicate matters, and will cost him first month of 2019. Age, pedigree say we can't give up yet, but not as much upside as we once thought.

| Yr | Tm | AB | R | HR | RBI | SB | BA | xBA | OBP | SLG | OPS | vL | vR | bb% | ct% | Eye | G | L | F | h% | HctX | PX | xPX | hr/f | Spd | SBO | SB% | #Wk | DOM | DIS | RC/G | RAR | BPV | BPX | R$ |
|---|---|---|---|---|---|---|---|---|---|---|---|---|---|---|---|---|---|---|---|---|---|---|---|---|---|---|---|---|---|---|---|---|---|---|---|
| 14 | aa | 241 | 31 | 10 | 35 | 4 | 277 | | 316 | 466 | 782 | | | 5 | 80 | 0.29 | | | | 31 | | 130 | | | 89 | 15% | 48% | | | | 4.90 | | 64 | 173 | $9 |
| 15 | CHC * | 519 | 66 | 14 | 61 | 5 | 246 | 226 | 303 | 393 | 696 | 527 | 746 | 8 | 70 | 0.27 | 41 | 18 | 41 | 33 | 83 | 115 | 105 | 10% | 96 | 6% | 61% | 25 | 36% | 40% | 3.98 | 3.2 | 17 | 46 | $11 |
| 16 | CHC | 525 | 67 | 21 | 95 | 5 | 238 | 252 | 321 | 417 | 738 | 801 | 715 | 9 | 74 | 0.41 | 41 | 21 | 37 | 28 | 88 | 111 | 94 | 14% | 110 | 5% | 83% | 27 | 44% | 33% | 4.35 | -4.1 | 39 | 111 | $12 |
| 17 | CHC | 352 | 52 | 12 | 43 | 2 | 239 | 256 | 304 | 418 | 722 | 821 | 687 | 8 | 74 | 0.32 | 40 | 23 | 37 | 29 | 97 | 109 | 83 | 13% | 111 | 4% | 67% | 22 | 32% | 45% | 4.13 | -4.0 | 34 | 103 | $5 |
| 18 | CHC | 420 | 52 | 5 | 38 | 4 | 250 | 236 | 317 | 340 | 657 | 744 | 626 | 9 | 76 | 0.40 | 42 | 25 | 33 | 32 | 82 | 63 | 79 | 5% | 115 | 3% | 100% | 26 | 31% | 46% | 3.71 | -1.3 | 10 | 33 | $7 |
| 1st Half | | 246 | 38 | 5 | 26 | 3 | 285 | 244 | 355 | 407 | 762 | 839 | 735 | 10 | 76 | 0.45 | 36 | 27 | 37 | 36 | 88 | 80 | 107 | 7% | 136 | 4% | 100% | 15 | 47% | 33% | 5.20 | 8.5 | 32 | 107 | $14 |
| 2nd Half | | 174 | 14 | 0 | 12 | 1 | 201 | 220 | 261 | 247 | 508 | 619 | 465 | 7 | 76 | 0.34 | 52 | 21 | 27 | 26 | 72 | 40 | 39 | 0% | 90 | 2% | 100% | 11 | 9% | 64% | 2.08 | -10.2 | -19 | -63 | -$4 |
| **19** | **Proj** | **322** | **40** | **10** | **36** | **3** | **239** | **247** | **304** | **396** | **700** | **772** | **674** | **8** | **75** | **0.35** | **41** | **23** | **36** | **29** | **85** | **98** | **78** | **12%** | **109** | **4%** | **80%** | | | | **3.98** | **0.2** | **20** | **66** | **$7** |

## Saladino,Tyler

| | | | | | |
|---|---|---|---|---|---|
| Age: 29 | Bats: R | Pos: SS | Health | C | LIMA Plan D |
| Ht: 6'0" | Wt: 200 | | PT/Exp | D | Rand Var -2 |
| | | | Consist | F | MM 2411 |

5-16-.246 with 2 SB in 126 AB at CHW/MIL. May ankle injury halted hot start, but track record says good times weren't going to last long anyway. Speed remains intact, but ct% slide has crippled OBP, and small sample 1st half power metrics are clear outliers. Two straight years of underwater BPVs = stay away.

| Yr | Tm | AB | R | HR | RBI | SB | BA | xBA | OBP | SLG | OPS | vL | vR | bb% | ct% | Eye | G | L | F | h% | HctX | PX | xPX | hr/f | Spd | SBO | SB% | #Wk | DOM | DIS | RC/G | RAR | BPV | BPX | R$ |
|---|---|---|---|---|---|---|---|---|---|---|---|---|---|---|---|---|---|---|---|---|---|---|---|---|---|---|---|---|---|---|---|---|---|---|---|
| 14 | aaa | 294 | 27 | 6 | 28 | 5 | 248 | | 293 | 373 | 666 | | | 6 | 79 | 0.31 | | | | 29 | | 89 | | | 103 | 8% | 79% | | | | 3.72 | | 33 | 89 | $5 |
| 15 | CHW * | 432 | 55 | 7 | 43 | 28 | 219 | 257 | 270 | 322 | 592 | 650 | 585 | 7 | 79 | 0.33 | 54 | 23 | 23 | 26 | 61 | 63 | 32 | 9% | 129 | 32% | 86% | 14 | 43% | 50% | 3.00 | -10.2 | 19 | 51 | $12 |
| 16 | CHW | 298 | 33 | 8 | 38 | 11 | 282 | 257 | 315 | 409 | 725 | 799 | 698 | 4 | 79 | 0.21 | 51 | 20 | 29 | 33 | 83 | 79 | 58 | 12% | 90 | 21% | 69% | 25 | 20% | 36% | 4.41 | -1.7 | 17 | 49 | $11 |
| 17 | CHW | 253 | 23 | 0 | 10 | 5 | 178 | 198 | 254 | 229 | 484 | 567 | 441 | 8 | 74 | 0.34 | 46 | 17 | 37 | 24 | 66 | 37 | 38 | 0% | 137 | 16% | 56% | 21 | 5% | 62% | 1.69 | -23.4 | -16 | -48 | -$5 |
| 18 | 2 TM * | 256 | 26 | 7 | 27 | 8 | 218 | 209 | 278 | 340 | 618 | 498 | 800 | 8 | 70 | 0.27 | 33 | 25 | 42 | 29 | 105 | 77 | 120 | 14% | 124 | 16% | 80% | 19 | 21% | 63% | 3.11 | -5.5 | -5 | -17 | $4 |
| 1st Half | | 89 | 13 | 4 | 12 | 3 | 264 | 249 | 311 | 442 | 754 | 643 | 1041 | 9 | 69 | 0.22 | 31 | 34 | 34 | 34 | 139 | 115 | 145 | 27% | 109 | 14% | 100% | 9 | 33% | 56% | 4.97 | 2.6 | 16 | 53 | $4 |
| 2nd Half | | 167 | 13 | 3 | 15 | 5 | 193 | 184 | 260 | 285 | 545 | 430 | 656 | 8 | 70 | 0.30 | 34 | 19 | 47 | 26 | 84 | 57 | 105 | 8% | 128 | 17% | 71% | 10 | 10% | 70% | 2.34 | -8.7 | -18 | -60 | $4 |
| **19** | **Proj** | **228** | **23** | **6** | **21** | **6** | **222** | **228** | **280** | **355** | **634** | **555** | **671** | **7** | **73** | **0.27** | **41** | **22** | **37** | **28** | **88** | **82** | **82** | **11%** | **122** | **16%** | **71%** | | | | **3.16** | **-5.6** | **1** | **4** | **$5** |

BRIAN RUDD

## Sanchez,Gary

| Age: 26 | Bats: R | Pos: CA | Health | C | LIMA Plan | B |
|---|---|---|---|---|---|---|
| Ht: 6' 2" | Wt: 230 | | PT/Exp | C | Rand Var | +5 |
| | | | Consist | C | MM | 4135 |

18-53-.186 in 323 AB at NYY. Groin strains started in late June and likely slowed production; brutal h% didn't oblige either. Jump in whiffs, FBs say we might not see full BA rebound, but the power is real, as pre-injury xPX supports a run at 30 HR. Health permitting, his track record says to buy low.

| Yr | Tm | AB | R | HR | RBI | SB | BA | xBA | OBP | SLG | OPS | vL | vR | bb% | ct% | Eye | G | L | F | h% | HctX | PX | xPX | hr/f | Spd | SBO | SB% | #Wk | DOM | DIS | RC/G | RAR | BPV | BPX | R$ |
|---|---|---|---|---|---|---|---|---|---|---|---|---|---|---|---|---|---|---|---|---|---|---|---|---|---|---|---|---|---|---|---|---|---|---|---|
| 14 | aa | 429 | 39 | 12 | 53 | 1 | 245 | | 303 | 367 | 669 | | | 8 | 76 | 0.35 | | | | 29 | | 90 | | | 78 | 2% | 43% | | | | 3.72 | | 18 | 49 | $7 |
| 15 | NYY * | 367 | 44 | 18 | 55 | 6 | 255 | 164 | 304 | 459 | 763 | 0 | 0 | 7 | 76 | 0.29 | 0 | 0 | 100 | 29 | 0 | 135 | -16 | 0% | 69 | 10% | 74% | 2 | 0% | 50% | 4.74 | 10.8 | 48 | 130 | $12 |
| 16 | NYY * | 485 | 69 | 31 | 87 | 7 | 275 | 288 | 334 | 530 | 864 | 868 | 1093 | 8 | 78 | 0.40 | 49 | 16 | 34 | 30 | 132 | 150 | 159 | 40% | 72 | 7% | 87% | 11 | 45% | 36% | 6.27 | 33.2 | 70 | 200 | $21 |
| 17 | NYY | 471 | 79 | 33 | 90 | 2 | 278 | 275 | 345 | 531 | 876 | 882 | 874 | 8 | 75 | 0.33 | 42 | 21 | 37 | 31 | 111 | 140 | 114 | 25% | 83 | 3% | 67% | 23 | 39% | 22% | 6.25 | 28.2 | 52 | 158 | $20 |
| 18 | NYY * | 351 | 54 | 22 | 56 | 1 | 184 | 241 | 279 | 417 | 695 | 872 | 636 | 11 | 70 | 0.44 | 43 | 14 | 43 | 19 | 91 | 147 | 115 | 18% | 49 | 1% | 100% | 22 | 36% | 32% | 3.64 | 3.0 | 37 | 123 | $5 |
| 1st Half | | 231 | 36 | 14 | 41 | 0 | 190 | 248 | 291 | 433 | 723 | 936 | 653 | 12 | 73 | 0.49 | 41 | 14 | 45 | 19 | 97 | 151 | 128 | 18% | 48 | 0% | 0% | 14 | 43% | 29% | 3.90 | 3.3 | 52 | 173 | $8 |
| 2nd Half | | 120 | 18 | 8 | 15 | 1 | 172 | 223 | 264 | 386 | 650 | 735 | 587 | 11 | 64 | 0.35 | 48 | 15 | 37 | 19 | 80 | 138 | 82 | 17% | 80 | 4% | 100% | 8 | 25% | 38% | 3.17 | -1.1 | 16 | 53 | -$1 |
| 19 | Proj | **475** | **71** | **31** | **77** | **3** | **237** | **255** | **316** | **477** | **793** | **836** | **777** | **10** | **72** | **0.37** | **45** | **17** | **38** | **26** | **102** | **145** | **114** | **24%** | **68** | **3%** | **84%** | | | | **4.95** | **21.3** | **41** | **137** | **$14** |

## Sanchez,Yolmer

| Age: 27 | Bats: B | Pos: 3B | Health | A | LIMA Plan | C+ |
|---|---|---|---|---|---|---|
| Ht: 5' 11" | Wt: 185 | | PT/Exp | B | Rand Var | +1 |
| | | | Consist | B | MM | 1325 |

Found success on the basepaths, but BA/HR dips kept R$ stuck in neutral. Several reasons for caution: previous SB%, inability to get on base questions SB repeat; weaker contact, GB% cap his HR ceiling; weak skills vL (69% ct%, 36 PX) put another 600 AB in question. Best left for deep leagues.

| Yr | Tm | AB | R | HR | RBI | SB | BA | xBA | OBP | SLG | OPS | vL | vR | bb% | ct% | Eye | G | L | F | h% | HctX | PX | xPX | hr/f | Spd | SBO | SB% | #Wk | DOM | DIS | RC/G | RAR | BPV | BPX | R$ |
|---|---|---|---|---|---|---|---|---|---|---|---|---|---|---|---|---|---|---|---|---|---|---|---|---|---|---|---|---|---|---|---|---|---|---|---|
| 14 | CHW * | 537 | 48 | 5 | 45 | 12 | 248 | 240 | 288 | 331 | 619 | 867 | 423 | 5 | 77 | 0.25 | 42 | 26 | 32 | 31 | 84 | 64 | 87 | 0% | 123 | 13% | 69% | 8 | 25% | 75% | 3.20 | -3.1 | 11 | 30 | $9 |
| 15 | CHW * | 520 | 54 | 7 | 45 | 6 | 244 | 261 | 276 | 349 | 624 | 606 | 591 | 4 | 78 | 0.20 | 54 | 23 | 23 | 30 | 76 | 79 | 48 | 7% | 89 | 10% | 59% | 23 | 22% | 61% | 3.18 | -17.0 | 12 | 32 | $7 |
| 16 | CHW * | 389 | 40 | 11 | 44 | 8 | 217 | 232 | 255 | 362 | 617 | 405 | 662 | 5 | 73 | 0.18 | 39 | 21 | 40 | 27 | 67 | 95 | 75 | 9% | 102 | 19% | 59% | 17 | 35% | 53% | 2.88 | -22.3 | 8 | 23 | $4 |
| 17 | CHW | 484 | 63 | 12 | 59 | 8 | 267 | 251 | 319 | 413 | 732 | 660 | 755 | 7 | 77 | 0.32 | 45 | 22 | 34 | 32 | 75 | 81 | 72 | 9% | 160 | 14% | 47% | 27 | 33% | 33% | 4.28 | -4.9 | 36 | 109 | $13 |
| 18 | CHW | 600 | 62 | 8 | 55 | 14 | 242 | 254 | 306 | 372 | 678 | 517 | 724 | 7 | 77 | 0.36 | 49 | 22 | 29 | 30 | 80 | 83 | 67 | 6% | 114 | 14% | 70% | 28 | 29% | 39% | 3.70 | -6.8 | 25 | 83 | $12 |
| 1st Half | | 300 | 31 | 5 | 36 | 8 | 260 | 265 | 306 | 410 | 716 | 563 | 758 | 5 | 80 | 0.27 | 51 | 21 | 29 | 31 | 80 | 84 | 63 | 7% | 126 | 15% | 80% | 15 | 33% | 27% | 4.22 | 0.4 | 37 | 123 | $16 |
| 2nd Half | | 300 | 31 | 3 | 19 | 6 | 223 | 243 | 307 | 333 | 640 | 474 | 690 | 10 | 74 | 0.42 | 47 | 24 | 30 | 29 | 80 | 81 | 72 | 5% | 105 | 13% | 60% | 13 | 23% | 54% | 3.20 | -9.0 | 14 | 47 | $8 |
| 19 | Proj | **457** | **50** | **6** | **45** | **9** | **243** | **245** | **300** | **363** | **662** | **561** | **695** | **7** | **76** | **0.31** | **47** | **22** | **31** | **31** | **77** | **77** | **70** | **6%** | **120** | **14%** | **61%** | | | | **3.50** | **-13.9** | **15** | **49** | **$10** |

## Sano,Miguel

| Age: 26 | Bats: R | Pos: 3B | Health | C | LIMA Plan | B |
|---|---|---|---|---|---|---|
| Ht: 6' 4" | Wt: 260 | | PT/Exp | C | Rand Var | +3 |
| | | | Consist | D | MM | 4205 |

13-41-.199 in 266 AB at MIN. Early hamstring strain, demotion to Single-A, September leg injury all led to disastrous season. That ct% can dampen your whole roster's BA. But 2nd half hr/f snapped right back and xPX baseline supports HR recovery. Off-field issues further cloud outlook, so be ready to embrace some risk.

| Yr | Tm | AB | R | HR | RBI | SB | BA | xBA | OBP | SLG | OPS | vL | vR | bb% | ct% | Eye | G | L | F | h% | HctX | PX | xPX | hr/f | Spd | SBO | SB% | #Wk | DOM | DIS | RC/G | RAR | BPV | BPX | R$ |
|---|---|---|---|---|---|---|---|---|---|---|---|---|---|---|---|---|---|---|---|---|---|---|---|---|---|---|---|---|---|---|---|---|---|---|---|
| 14 | | | | | | | | | | | | | | | | | | | | | | | | | | | | | | | | | | | |
| 15 | MIN * | 520 | 88 | 29 | 89 | 5 | 257 | 249 | 357 | 496 | 853 | 881 | 929 | 13 | 63 | 0.43 | 33 | 25 | 42 | 35 | 122 | 188 | 175 | 26% | 90 | 5% | 70% | 15 | 53% | 20% | 6.04 | 22.4 | 60 | 162 | $20 |
| 16 | MIN * | 462 | 60 | 27 | 68 | 1 | 231 | 224 | 317 | 459 | 776 | 818 | 771 | 11 | 59 | 0.31 | 34 | 20 | 46 | 32 | 96 | 173 | 157 | 21% | 81 | 1% | 100% | 24 | 38% | 42% | 4.84 | 0.6 | 24 | 69 | $9 |
| 17 | MIN | 424 | 75 | 28 | 77 | 0 | 264 | 229 | 352 | 507 | 859 | 992 | 817 | 11 | 59 | 0.31 | 39 | 21 | 40 | 38 | 107 | 166 | 148 | 27% | 104 | 0% | 0% | 22 | 36% | 41% | 6.10 | 15.2 | 25 | 76 | $14 |
| 18 | MIN * | 296 | 34 | 15 | 45 | 0 | 204 | 201 | 290 | 404 | 695 | 643 | 693 | 11 | 58 | 0.29 | 44 | 15 | 41 | 29 | 91 | 156 | 121 | 21% | 75 | 0% | 0% | 17 | 24% | 65% | 3.76 | -5.2 | 4 | 13 | $3 |
| 1st Half | | 164 | 19 | 9 | 30 | 0 | 217 | 201 | 289 | 432 | 721 | 476 | 743 | 9 | 58 | 0.24 | 40 | 13 | 47 | 31 | 85 | 170 | 135 | 18% | 76 | 0% | 0% | 9 | 22% | 67% | 4.06 | -2.2 | 10 | 33 | $5 |
| 2nd Half | | 132 | 15 | 6 | 16 | 0 | 188 | 201 | 293 | 369 | 662 | 831 | 627 | 13 | 59 | 0.36 | 49 | 17 | 34 | 26 | 99 | 139 | 105 | 25% | 80 | 0% | 0% | 8 | 25% | 63% | 3.39 | -4.7 | -2 | -7 | $0 |
| 19 | Proj | **527** | **73** | **28** | **83** | **1** | **227** | **215** | **316** | **436** | **752** | **789** | **740** | **12** | **59** | **0.32** | **41** | **18** | **41** | **32** | **100** | **157** | **137** | **22%** | **86** | **1%** | **77%** | | | | **4.55** | **0.7** | **1** | **4** | **$13** |

## Santana,Carlos

| Age: 33 | Bats: B | Pos: 1B | Health | A | LIMA Plan | A |
|---|---|---|---|---|---|---|
| Ht: 5' 11" | Wt: 210 | | PT/Exp | A | Rand Var | +3 |
| | | | Consist | B | MM | 3235 |

Elite Eye continues to cement strong OBP foundation, even when h% took a dive. His xBA points to some BA recovery despite slipping hard contact. While 2nd half xPX sunk, he still has enough muscle for 20 HR. Steady R$, BPV concur he's a high-floor/low-ceiling pick, and he should find a few more hits.

| Yr | Tm | AB | R | HR | RBI | SB | BA | xBA | OBP | SLG | OPS | vL | vR | bb% | ct% | Eye | G | L | F | h% | HctX | PX | xPX | hr/f | Spd | SBO | SB% | #Wk | DOM | DIS | RC/G | RAR | BPV | BPX | R$ |
|---|---|---|---|---|---|---|---|---|---|---|---|---|---|---|---|---|---|---|---|---|---|---|---|---|---|---|---|---|---|---|---|---|---|---|---|
| 14 | CLE | 541 | 68 | 27 | 85 | 5 | 231 | 262 | 365 | 427 | 792 | 864 | 757 | 17 | 77 | 0.91 | 40 | 19 | 40 | 25 | 117 | 136 | 125 | 16% | 67 | 4% | 71% | 27 | 56% | 22% | 5.15 | 15.7 | 73 | 197 | $15 |
| 15 | CLE | 550 | 72 | 19 | 85 | 11 | 231 | 252 | 357 | 395 | 752 | 755 | 750 | 16 | 78 | 0.89 | 45 | 18 | 37 | 26 | 101 | 108 | 95 | 12% | 73 | 8% | 79% | 27 | 56% | 22% | 4.71 | -11.0 | 54 | 146 | $14 |
| 16 | CLE | 582 | 89 | 34 | 87 | 5 | 259 | 281 | 366 | 498 | 865 | 742 | 915 | 14 | 83 | 1.00 | 43 | 16 | 41 | 26 | 122 | 129 | 122 | 17% | 79 | 4% | 71% | 27 | 74% | 7% | 6.28 | 15.9 | 90 | 257 | $20 |
| 17 | CLE | 571 | 90 | 23 | 79 | 5 | 259 | 278 | 363 | 455 | 818 | 777 | 844 | 13 | 84 | 0.94 | 41 | 20 | 39 | 28 | 112 | 106 | 102 | 12% | 86 | 3% | 83% | 27 | 63% | 11% | 5.64 | -4.5 | 73 | 221 | $16 |
| 18 | PHI | 560 | 82 | 24 | 86 | 2 | 229 | 253 | 352 | 414 | 766 | 816 | 747 | 16 | 83 | 1.18 | 40 | 16 | 44 | 23 | 101 | 101 | 112 | 12% | 81 | 2% | 67% | 28 | 64% | 14% | 4.86 | -4.2 | 73 | 243 | $13 |
| 1st Half | | 279 | 47 | 14 | 48 | 1 | 222 | 254 | 360 | 434 | 794 | 758 | 807 | 18 | 84 | 1.35 | 39 | 13 | 48 | 22 | 116 | 114 | 156 | 12% | 91 | 1% | 100% | 15 | 73% | 7% | 5.19 | 3.6 | 91 | 303 | $16 |
| 2nd Half | | 281 | 35 | 10 | 38 | 1 | 235 | 254 | 343 | 395 | 738 | 888 | 691 | 15 | 83 | 1.02 | 41 | 19 | 40 | 25 | 85 | 89 | 69 | 11% | 72 | 2% | 50% | 13 | 54% | 23% | 4.52 | -2.1 | 57 | 190 | $11 |
| 19 | Proj | **504** | **74** | **22** | **74** | **3** | **242** | **262** | **357** | **434** | **790** | **797** | **787** | **15** | **83** | **1.04** | **41** | **18** | **41** | **25** | **106** | **106** | **107** | **13%** | **80** | **3%** | **73%** | | | | **5.21** | **6.6** | **68** | **226** | **$15** |

## Santana,Domingo

| Age: 26 | Bats: R | Pos: RF | Health | B | LIMA Plan | C |
|---|---|---|---|---|---|---|
| Ht: 6' 5" | Wt: 220 | | PT/Exp | C | Rand Var | -1 |
| | | | Consist | D | MM | 4313 |

5-20-.265 in 211 AB at MIL. Followed up 2017's breakout with a clunker that included May demotion. Power plummeted (2nd half xPX skewed by 22-AB sample); ditto for contact, xBA, and green light. All those GBs put pressure on hr/f, and a lot of his value hinges on holding sky-high h%, so aim between 2017-18.

| Yr | Tm | AB | R | HR | RBI | SB | BA | xBA | OBP | SLG | OPS | vL | vR | bb% | ct% | Eye | G | L | F | h% | HctX | PX | xPX | hr/f | Spd | SBO | SB% | #Wk | DOM | DIS | RC/G | RAR | BPV | BPX | R$ |
|---|---|---|---|---|---|---|---|---|---|---|---|---|---|---|---|---|---|---|---|---|---|---|---|---|---|---|---|---|---|---|---|---|---|---|---|
| 14 | HOU * | 460 | 47 | 12 | 60 | 4 | 245 | 224 | 317 | 384 | 701 | 100 | 0 | 10 | 60 | 0.26 | 33 | 33 | 33 | 38 | 86 | 133 | 235 | 0% | 94 | 7% | 50% | 3 | 0% | 100% | 4.00 | -1.2 | -4 | -11 | $10 |
| 15 | 2 TM * | 514 | 74 | 21 | 81 | 5 | 271 | 237 | 347 | 457 | 803 | 950 | 681 | 10 | 64 | 0.32 | 52 | 19 | 29 | 39 | 92 | 146 | 135 | 28% | 114 | 8% | 45% | 11 | 55% | 36% | 5.33 | 7.0 | 29 | 78 | $19 |
| 16 | MIL | 246 | 34 | 11 | 32 | 2 | 256 | 252 | 345 | 447 | 792 | 937 | 726 | 11 | 63 | 0.35 | 44 | 30 | 26 | 36 | 98 | 143 | 107 | 28% | 86 | 7% | 40% | 17 | 29% | 47% | 5.04 | 2.6 | 17 | 49 | $6 |
| 17 | MIL | 525 | 88 | 30 | 85 | 15 | 278 | 266 | 371 | 505 | 875 | 892 | 870 | 12 | 66 | 0.41 | 45 | 27 | 28 | 37 | 106 | 148 | 120 | 31% | 96 | 12% | 79% | 26 | 46% | 35% | 6.54 | 20.3 | 38 | 115 | $25 |
| 18 | MIL * | 398 | 40 | 11 | 42 | 2 | 245 | 209 | 318 | 391 | 709 | 539 | 816 | 10 | 57 | 0.25 | 49 | 23 | 28 | 40 | 85 | 123 | 95 | 13% | 117 | 3% | 69% | 18 | 28% | 50% | 4.19 | -2.4 | -15 | -50 | $6 |
| 1st Half | | 212 | 17 | 3 | 19 | 1 | 244 | 210 | 312 | 348 | 660 | 352 | 767 | 9 | 63 | 0.27 | 51 | 23 | 26 | 37 | 94 | 87 | 89 | 9% | 108 | 3% | 50% | 13 | 15% | 54% | 3.62 | -5.3 | -27 | -90 | $3 |
| 2nd Half | | 186 | 22 | 8 | 22 | 1 | 246 | 198 | 324 | 440 | 765 | 1198 | 1611 | 10 | 51 | 0.24 | 29 | 29 | 43 | 44 | 67 | 173 | 151 | 33% | 120 | 3% | 100% | 5 | 60% | 40% | 4.87 | 2.3 | 2 | 7 | $10 |
| 19 | Proj | **376** | **48** | **14** | **48** | **6** | **257** | **229** | **339** | **431** | **770** | **791** | **762** | **11** | **60** | **0.29** | **48** | **26** | **27** | **39** | **98** | **135** | **108** | **23%** | **110** | **9%** | **67%** | | | | **4.89** | **4.8** | **-3** | **-10** | **$13** |

## Schebler,Scott

| Age: 28 | Bats: L | Pos: RF | Health | C | LIMA Plan | B+ |
|---|---|---|---|---|---|---|
| Ht: 6' 0" | Wt: 228 | | PT/Exp | C | Rand Var | 0 |
| | | | Consist | A | MM | 4135 |

17-49-.255 in 380 AB at CIN. Right shoulder sprain in July likely slowed 2nd half power skills. Pre-injury profile was worth buying, as 1st half xBA mirrored 2016-17 and HctX says there was plenty of thump despite fewer FBs. If shoulder heals, he's an off-season launch-angle lesson away from returning to 30 HR.

| Yr | Tm | AB | R | HR | RBI | SB | BA | xBA | OBP | SLG | OPS | vL | vR | bb% | ct% | Eye | G | L | F | h% | HctX | PX | xPX | hr/f | Spd | SBO | SB% | #Wk | DOM | DIS | RC/G | RAR | BPV | BPX | R$ |
|---|---|---|---|---|---|---|---|---|---|---|---|---|---|---|---|---|---|---|---|---|---|---|---|---|---|---|---|---|---|---|---|---|---|---|---|
| 14 | aa | 489 | 57 | 21 | 51 | 7 | 229 | | 273 | 425 | 698 | | | 6 | 73 | 0.23 | | | | 27 | | 137 | | | 124 | 12% | 60% | | | | 3.73 | | 54 | 146 | $11 |
| 15 | LA * | 468 | 48 | 13 | 41 | 13 | 201 | 215 | 249 | 335 | 584 | 200 | 905 | 6 | 74 | 0.25 | 52 | 9 | 39 | 24 | 125 | 87 | 136 | 33% | 113 | 18% | 80% | 7 | 43% | 43% | 2.68 | -30.1 | 13 | 35 | $4 |
| 16 | CIN * | 546 | 69 | 21 | 76 | 4 | 269 | 270 | 313 | 462 | 775 | 608 | 791 | 6 | 76 | 0.27 | 53 | 18 | 29 | 32 | 103 | 116 | 78 | 16% | 102 | 6% | 48% | 15 | 47% | 27% | 4.92 | 4.7 | 42 | 120 | $16 |
| 17 | CIN | 473 | 63 | 30 | 67 | 5 | 233 | 268 | 307 | 484 | 791 | 782 | 794 | 7 | 74 | 0.31 | 46 | 16 | 38 | 25 | 117 | 144 | 132 | 22% | 76 | 9% | 63% | 26 | 50% | 27% | 4.60 | -9.3 | 49 | 148 | $10 |
| 18 | CIN * | 432 | 59 | 18 | 51 | 4 | 243 | 255 | 314 | 415 | 728 | 789 | 770 | 9 | 74 | 0.40 | 49 | 22 | 30 | 29 | 104 | 106 | 94 | 20% | 74 | 5% | 67% | 22 | 36% | 32% | 4.35 | -3.2 | 24 | 80 | $11 |
| 1st Half | | 241 | 39 | 10 | 32 | 2 | 268 | 273 | 326 | 454 | 780 | 917 | 790 | 8 | 77 | 0.37 | 49 | 22 | 28 | 31 | 117 | 115 | 103 | 20% | 73 | 3% | 100% | 14 | 50% | 21% | 5.21 | 4.2 | 38 | 127 | $16 |
| 2nd Half | | 191 | 19 | 8 | 20 | 2 | 212 | 229 | 299 | 365 | 664 | 640 | 735 | 11 | 71 | 0.43 | 48 | 20 | 32 | 26 | 85 | 95 | 78 | 21% | 82 | 8% | 50% | 8 | 13% | 50% | 3.43 | -7.0 | 9 | 30 | $4 |
| 19 | Proj | **514** | **64** | **26** | **64** | **5** | **247** | **258** | **322** | **451** | **773** | **748** | **782** | **8** | **74** | **0.34** | **48** | **19** | **33** | **29** | **105** | **123** | **102** | **20%** | **83** | **7%** | **62%** | | | | **4.64** | **2.7** | **34** | **114** | **$16** |

## Schoop,Jonathan

| Age: 27 | Bats: R | Pos: 2B | Health | B | LIMA Plan | B+ |
|---|---|---|---|---|---|---|
| Ht: 6' 1" | Wt: 225 | | PT/Exp | A | Rand Var | +3 |
| | | | Consist | D | MM | 3135 |

Right oblique strain in April probably drove 1st half power outage, and ugly h% didn't help. Power skills, xBA returned to normal in 2nd half, and while HR total should bounce back, struggles vL likely prevent a full BA recovery. 2017 sure looks like peak, but 2nd half pace seems like a reasonable expectation.

| Yr | Tm | AB | R | HR | RBI | SB | BA | xBA | OBP | SLG | OPS | vL | vR | bb% | ct% | Eye | G | L | F | h% | HctX | PX | xPX | hr/f | Spd | SBO | SB% | #Wk | DOM | DIS | RC/G | RAR | BPV | BPX | R$ |
|---|---|---|---|---|---|---|---|---|---|---|---|---|---|---|---|---|---|---|---|---|---|---|---|---|---|---|---|---|---|---|---|---|---|---|---|
| 14 | BAL | 455 | 48 | 16 | 45 | 2 | 209 | 228 | 244 | 354 | 598 | 529 | 625 | 3 | 73 | 0.11 | 49 | 14 | 37 | 25 | 82 | 109 | 95 | 13% | 75 | 3% | 100% | 27 | 33% | 44% | 2.65 | -10.4 | 10 | 27 | $4 |
| 15 | BAL * | 330 | 36 | 18 | 44 | 2 | 274 | 264 | 295 | 493 | 788 | 573 | 892 | 3 | 74 | 0.11 | 43 | 19 | 38 | 32 | 115 | 147 | 123 | 17% | 65 | 3% | 100% | 15 | 47% | 27% | 5.14 | 9.2 | 41 | 111 | $11 |
| 16 | BAL | 615 | 82 | 25 | 82 | 1 | 267 | 266 | 298 | 454 | 752 | 688 | 772 | 3 | 78 | 0.15 | 45 | 20 | 35 | 31 | 84 | 116 | 74 | 15% | 81 | 2% | 33% | 27 | 41% | 26% | 4.53 | -6.0 | 36 | 103 | $17 |
| 17 | BAL | 622 | 92 | 32 | 105 | 1 | 293 | 270 | 338 | 503 | 841 | 955 | 805 | 5 | 77 | 0.25 | 42 | 21 | 37 | 33 | 113 | 120 | 113 | 18% | 66 | 1% | 100% | 27 | 41% | 19% | 6.00 | 16.9 | 37 | 112 | $25 |
| 18 | 2 TM | 473 | 61 | 21 | 61 | 1 | 233 | 249 | 266 | 416 | 682 | 646 | 698 | 4 | 76 | 0.17 | 45 | 18 | 37 | 26 | 78 | 110 | 79 | 16% | 72 | 2% | 50% | 25 | 36% | 32% | 3.60 | -9.5 | 22 | 73 | $10 |
| 1st Half | | 249 | 31 | 8 | 21 | 0 | 197 | 232 | 242 | 345 | 587 | 600 | 580 | 5 | 78 | 0.22 | 48 | 14 | 38 | 22 | 70 | 88 | 59 | 11% | 89 | 2% | 0% | 12 | 42% | 25% | 2.51 | -13.1 | 20 | 67 | $2 |
| 2nd Half | | 224 | 30 | 13 | 40 | 1 | 272 | 266 | 294 | 496 | 789 | 695 | 833 | 3 | 73 | 0.12 | 42 | 23 | 35 | 32 | 86 | 135 | 103 | 22% | 65 | 2% | 100% | 13 | 31% | 38% | 5.14 | 6.2 | 28 | 93 | $18 |
| 19 | Proj | **571** | **76** | **27** | **82** | **1** | **258** | **256** | **293** | **453** | **747** | **714** | **759** | **4** | **76** | **0.17** | **44** | **20** | **36** | **30** | **91** | **117** | **93** | **17%** | **70** | **2%** | **66%** | | | | **4.47** | **5.0** | **23** | **77** | **$19** |

BRANT CHESSER

## Schwarber,Kyle

**Age:** 26 **Bats:** L **Pos:** LF | **Ht:** 6' 0" **Wt:** 235

| Health | D | LIMA Plan | B |
|---|---|---|---|
| PT/Exp | D | Rand Var | -4 |
| Consist | F | MM | 4115 |

Improved plate discipline and h% correction got BA up to passable level, but GB spike took a toll on power production and PT fell off down the stretch. More than 1,000 AB sample says elite hr/f likely here to stay. Unfortunately, so is ineptitude vL, which caps upside—especially if FB% doesn't return.

| Yr Tm | AB | R | HR | RBI | SB | BA | xBA | OBP | SLG | OPS | vL | vR | bb% | ct% | Eye | G | L | F | h% | HctX | PX | xPX | hr/f | Spd | SBO | SB% | #Wk | DOM | DIS | RC/G | RAR | BPV | BPX | R$ |
|---|---|---|---|---|---|---|---|---|---|---|---|---|---|---|---|---|---|---|---|---|---|---|---|---|---|---|---|---|---|---|---|---|---|---|
| 14 | | | | | | | | | | | | | | | | | | | | | | | | | | | | | | | | | | |
| 15 CHC * | 489 | 88 | 29 | 82 | 4 | 271 | 247 | 368 | 505 | 873 | 481 | 953 | 13 | 68 | 0.48 | 40 | 17 | 42 | 34 | 116 | 164 | 157 | 24% | 94 | 4% | 56% | 14 | 57% | 21% | 6.41 | 23.8 | 59 | 159 | $21 |
| 16 CHC | 4 | 0 | 0 | 0 | 0 | 0 | 0 | 200 | 0 | 200 | 0 | 200 | 20 | 50 | 0.50 | 100 | 0 | 0 | 0 | 203 | 0 | -24 | 0% | 88 | 0% | 0% | 1 | 0% | 100% | 0.00 | -0.6 | -131 | -374 | -$2 |
| 17 CHC * | 457 | 74 | 33 | 66 | 1 | 217 | 234 | 315 | 476 | 791 | 648 | 814 | 12 | 64 | 0.40 | 38 | 15 | 46 | 25 | 94 | 163 | 125 | 24% | 71 | 2% | 50% | 26 | 42% | 23% | 4.86 | -5.6 | 35 | 106 | $8 |
| 18 CHC | 428 | 64 | 26 | 61 | 4 | 238 | 243 | 356 | 467 | 823 | 654 | 859 | 15 | 67 | 0.56 | 44 | 19 | 37 | 29 | 100 | 143 | 119 | 25% | 94 | 5% | 57% | 28 | 43% | 36% | 5.48 | 11.3 | 44 | 147 | $13 |
| 1st Half | 234 | 37 | 16 | 37 | 3 | 239 | 250 | 372 | 487 | 859 | 682 | 901 | 17 | 68 | 0.66 | 46 | 18 | 36 | 28 | 103 | 152 | 117 | 28% | 89 | 6% | 60% | 15 | 47% | 33% | 5.96 | 9.6 | 58 | 193 | $17 |
| 2nd Half | 194 | 27 | 10 | 24 | 1 | 237 | 232 | 335 | 443 | 778 | 608 | 810 | 13 | 66 | 0.44 | 41 | 21 | 38 | 31 | 96 | 131 | 122 | 21% | 97 | 4% | 50% | 13 | 38% | 38% | 4.92 | 1.9 | 26 | 87 | $9 |
| **19 Proj** | **423** | **66** | **27** | **61** | **3** | **235** | **239** | **343** | **477** | **820** | **627** | **865** | **14** | **66** | **0.46** | **41** | **18** | **41** | **29** | **100** | **154** | **127** | **24%** | **86** | **4%** | **55%** | | | | **5.33** | **9.4** | **38** | **126** | **$11** |

## Seager,Corey

**Age:** 25 **Bats:** L **Pos:** SS | **Ht:** 6' 4" **Wt:** 220

| Health | F | LIMA Plan | B+ |
|---|---|---|---|
| PT/Exp | B | Rand Var | +4 |
| Consist | C | MM | 3255 |

Passed on elbow surgery after 2017 season; lingering soreness led to April Tommy John surgery. Also underwent hip procedure, but appears on track for spring. Deserves pass for power plunge, and h% dip kept BA down, but multitude of recent ailments say we can't pencil him in for full return to form.

| Yr Tm | AB | R | HR | RBI | SB | BA | xBA | OBP | SLG | OPS | vL | vR | bb% | ct% | Eye | G | L | F | h% | HctX | PX | xPX | hr/f | Spd | SBO | SB% | #Wk | DOM | DIS | RC/G | RAR | BPV | BPX | R$ |
|---|---|---|---|---|---|---|---|---|---|---|---|---|---|---|---|---|---|---|---|---|---|---|---|---|---|---|---|---|---|---|---|---|---|---|
| 14 aa | 148 | 21 | 2 | 21 | 1 | 304 | | 337 | 457 | 793 | | | 5 | 70 | 0.17 | | | | 42 | | 142 | | | 97 | 5% | 41% | | | | 5.49 | | 36 | 97 | $4 |
| 15 LA * | 599 | 86 | 20 | 82 | 5 | 280 | 296 | 328 | 462 | 790 | 926 | 1028 | 7 | 83 | 0.42 | 53 | 20 | 27 | 31 | 168 | 118 | 139 | 19% | 91 | 5% | 83% | 6 | 83% | 17% | 5.39 | 27.4 | 69 | 186 | $22 |
| 16 LA | 627 | 105 | 26 | 72 | 3 | 308 | 290 | 365 | 512 | 877 | 722 | 948 | 8 | 79 | 0.41 | 46 | 24 | 29 | 36 | 127 | 122 | 130 | 18% | 112 | 3% | 50% | 27 | 59% | 19% | 6.75 | 36.4 | 64 | 183 | $27 |
| 17 LA | 539 | 85 | 22 | 77 | 4 | 295 | 271 | 375 | 479 | 854 | 916 | 826 | 11 | 76 | 0.51 | 42 | 25 | 33 | 35 | 135 | 111 | 136 | 16% | 77 | 4% | 67% | 27 | 52% | 33% | 6.42 | 28.5 | 39 | 118 | $21 |
| 18 LA | 101 | 13 | 2 | 13 | 0 | 267 | 281 | 348 | 396 | 744 | 660 | 787 | 10 | 83 | 0.65 | 45 | 28 | 27 | 30 | 108 | 74 | 79 | 9% | 106 | 0% | 0% | 6 | 33% | 17% | 4.68 | 2.5 | 45 | 150 | $0 |
| 1st Half | 101 | 13 | 2 | 13 | 0 | 267 | 281 | 348 | 396 | 744 | 660 | 787 | 10 | 83 | 0.65 | 45 | 28 | 27 | 30 | 108 | 74 | 79 | 9% | 106 | 0% | 0% | 6 | 33% | 17% | 4.68 | 2.1 | 45 | 150 | $0 |
| 2nd Half | | | | | | | | | | | | | | | | | | | | | | | | | | | | | | | | | | |
| **19 Proj** | **480** | **71** | **19** | **63** | **3** | **289** | **285** | **355** | **487** | **842** | **770** | **880** | **9** | **79** | **0.45** | **45** | **25** | **30** | **33** | **129** | **117** | **117** | **17%** | **100** | **4%** | **70%** | | | | **6.09** | **28.5** | **54** | **179** | **$20** |

## Seager,Kyle

**Age:** 31 **Bats:** L **Pos:** 3B | **Ht:** 6' 0" **Wt:** 210

| Health | A | LIMA Plan | B+ |
|---|---|---|---|
| PT/Exp | A | Rand Var | +3 |
| Consist | C | MM | 3135 |

Declining h% levels were a factor in recent BA fades, but eroding Eye and HctX say it wasn't all bad luck. Broken toe in late June may help explain 2nd half hr/f, PX dips, so while power should rebound some, high FB% could prevent BA from returning to previous levels. This skill set isn't hard to find in today's game.

| Yr Tm | AB | R | HR | RBI | SB | BA | xBA | OBP | SLG | OPS | vL | vR | bb% | ct% | Eye | G | L | F | h% | HctX | PX | xPX | hr/f | Spd | SBO | SB% | #Wk | DOM | DIS | RC/G | RAR | BPV | BPX | R$ |
|---|---|---|---|---|---|---|---|---|---|---|---|---|---|---|---|---|---|---|---|---|---|---|---|---|---|---|---|---|---|---|---|---|---|---|
| 14 SEA | 590 | 71 | 25 | 96 | 7 | 268 | 268 | 334 | 454 | 788 | 661 | 862 | 8 | 80 | 0.44 | 37 | 22 | 41 | 30 | 131 | 124 | 141 | 13% | 85 | 8% | 58% | 27 | 56% | 26% | 5.07 | 23.9 | 63 | 170 | $23 |
| 15 SEA | 623 | 85 | 26 | 74 | 6 | 266 | 280 | 328 | 451 | 779 | 835 | 747 | 8 | 84 | 0.55 | 35 | 24 | 41 | 28 | 122 | 113 | 112 | 12% | 81 | 8% | 50% | 27 | 70% | 15% | 4.95 | 6.9 | 69 | 186 | $20 |
| 16 SEA | 597 | 89 | 30 | 99 | 3 | 278 | 281 | 359 | 499 | 859 | 728 | 932 | 10 | 82 | 0.64 | 36 | 22 | 42 | 30 | 129 | 125 | 135 | 15% | 72 | 2% | 75% | 27 | 67% | 11% | 6.21 | 24.0 | 72 | 206 | $22 |
| 17 SEA | 578 | 72 | 27 | 88 | 2 | 249 | 251 | 323 | 450 | 773 | 766 | 776 | 9 | 81 | 0.53 | 31 | 17 | 52 | 27 | 117 | 110 | 142 | 11% | 78 | 2% | 67% | 27 | 48% | 7% | 4.84 | -0.3 | 55 | 167 | $13 |
| 18 SEA | 583 | 62 | 22 | 78 | 2 | 221 | 248 | 273 | 400 | 673 | 702 | 658 | 6 | 76 | 0.28 | 34 | 21 | 45 | 25 | 104 | 112 | 127 | 11% | 64 | 4% | 50% | 28 | 36% | 32% | 3.48 | -15.3 | 28 | 93 | $9 |
| 1st Half | 324 | 38 | 15 | 49 | 1 | 228 | 250 | 281 | 429 | 710 | 783 | 672 | 6 | 77 | 0.26 | 36 | 19 | 46 | 25 | 105 | 123 | 133 | 13% | 72 | 3% | 50% | 15 | 53% | 27% | 3.83 | -6.6 | 40 | 133 | $15 |
| 2nd Half | 259 | 24 | 7 | 29 | 1 | 212 | 245 | 263 | 363 | 626 | 597 | 640 | 6 | 76 | 0.29 | 32 | 25 | 44 | 25 | 102 | 98 | 120 | 8% | 63 | 4% | 50% | 13 | 15% | 38% | 3.06 | -11.6 | 17 | 57 | $2 |
| **19 Proj** | **582** | **68** | **26** | **82** | **3** | **240** | **257** | **302** | **437** | **739** | **718** | **749** | **8** | **79** | **0.39** | **33** | **21** | **45** | **26** | **113** | **116** | **131** | **12%** | **70** | **4%** | **57%** | | | | **4.32** | **-3.1** | **41** | **138** | **$15** |

## Segura,Jean

**Age:** 29 **Bats:** R **Pos:** SS | **Ht:** 5' 10" **Wt:** 205

| Health | B | LIMA Plan | B |
|---|---|---|---|
| PT/Exp | A | Rand Var | -2 |
| Consist | B | MM | 1445 |

Huge h% swing played key role in 1st/2nd half splits, but wasn't the whole problem: 2nd half ct% jump came with big dip in HctX; SB% limited contributions on basepaths. Minor bumps and bruises (hand, ribs, shin) may have played role in late struggles, but track record confirms he's worthy of early investment.

| Yr Tm | AB | R | HR | RBI | SB | BA | xBA | OBP | SLG | OPS | vL | vR | bb% | ct% | Eye | G | L | F | h% | HctX | PX | xPX | hr/f | Spd | SBO | SB% | #Wk | DOM | DIS | RC/G | RAR | BPV | BPX | R$ |
|---|---|---|---|---|---|---|---|---|---|---|---|---|---|---|---|---|---|---|---|---|---|---|---|---|---|---|---|---|---|---|---|---|---|---|
| 14 MIL | 513 | 61 | 5 | 31 | 20 | 246 | 265 | 289 | 326 | 614 | 511 | 643 | 5 | 86 | 0.40 | 59 | 18 | 23 | 28 | 79 | 51 | 51 | 5% | 160 | 22% | 69% | 27 | 33% | 41% | 3.07 | -1.6 | 46 | 124 | $12 |
| 15 MIL | 560 | 57 | 6 | 50 | 25 | 257 | 252 | 281 | 336 | 616 | 679 | 594 | 2 | 83 | 0.14 | 59 | 17 | 24 | 30 | 71 | 49 | 48 | 5% | 128 | 24% | 81% | 26 | 19% | 38% | 3.21 | -19.5 | 18 | 49 | $17 |
| 16 ARI | 637 | 102 | 20 | 64 | 33 | 319 | 296 | 368 | 499 | 867 | 763 | 900 | 6 | 84 | 0.39 | 53 | 19 | 28 | 35 | 101 | 103 | 93 | 14% | 143 | 25% | 77% | 27 | 41% | 15% | 6.63 | 40.3 | 75 | 214 | $39 |
| 17 SEA | 524 | 80 | 11 | 45 | 22 | 300 | 279 | 349 | 427 | 776 | 819 | 762 | 6 | 84 | 0.41 | 54 | 19 | 26 | 34 | 96 | 73 | 66 | 9% | 120 | 20% | 73% | 23 | 35% | 22% | 5.27 | 9.3 | 45 | 136 | $24 |
| 18 SEA | 586 | 91 | 10 | 63 | 20 | 304 | 272 | 341 | 415 | 755 | 803 | 737 | 5 | 88 | 0.46 | 51 | 19 | 29 | 33 | 84 | 63 | 59 | 7% | 123 | 18% | 65% | 27 | 52% | 22% | 4.98 | 14.4 | 52 | 173 | $27 |
| 1st Half | 321 | 59 | 6 | 45 | 14 | 336 | 290 | 364 | 477 | 841 | 885 | 824 | 5 | 85 | 0.34 | 53 | 22 | 26 | 38 | 91 | 85 | 63 | 8% | 119 | 22% | 70% | 15 | 53% | 27% | 6.55 | 22.2 | 57 | 190 | $39 |
| 2nd Half | 265 | 32 | 4 | 18 | 6 | 264 | 247 | 312 | 340 | 652 | 707 | 630 | 6 | 92 | 0.73 | 50 | 17 | 33 | 28 | 74 | 38 | 54 | 5% | 126 | 15% | 55% | 12 | 50% | 17% | 3.43 | -4.2 | 49 | 163 | $13 |
| **19 Proj** | **562** | **82** | **11** | **52** | **21** | **294** | **272** | **338** | **414** | **752** | **772** | **745** | **6** | **87** | **0.44** | **53** | **19** | **28** | **32** | **87** | **67** | **64** | **8%** | **129** | **20%** | **69%** | | | | **4.87** | **14.4** | **47** | **158** | **$27** |

## Semien,Marcus

**Age:** 28 **Bats:** R **Pos:** SS | **Ht:** 6' 0" **Wt:** 195

| Health | C | LIMA Plan | B+ |
|---|---|---|---|
| PT/Exp | A | Rand Var | 0 |
| Consist | A | MM | 2325 |

Career year in terms of R$ thanks in large part to high AB total padding the counting stats. Power was down most of year, but returned to peak levels over final two months, while ct%, LD% were up all season. May not get back to 20+ HR, but stable skills make him good bet to repeat, minus a few runs and RBI.

| Yr Tm | AB | R | HR | RBI | SB | BA | xBA | OBP | SLG | OPS | vL | vR | bb% | ct% | Eye | G | L | F | h% | HctX | PX | xPX | hr/f | Spd | SBO | SB% | #Wk | DOM | DIS | RC/G | RAR | BPV | BPX | R$ |
|---|---|---|---|---|---|---|---|---|---|---|---|---|---|---|---|---|---|---|---|---|---|---|---|---|---|---|---|---|---|---|---|---|---|---|
| 14 CHW * | 534 | 68 | 17 | 62 | 8 | 224 | 245 | 301 | 383 | 684 | 735 | 637 | 10 | 74 | 0.42 | 40 | 21 | 39 | 27 | 78 | 119 | 75 | 10% | 136 | 8% | 77% | 15 | 33% | 53% | 3.79 | 10.0 | 53 | 143 | $10 |
| 15 OAK | 556 | 65 | 15 | 45 | 11 | 257 | 242 | 310 | 405 | 715 | 879 | 653 | 7 | 76 | 0.32 | 38 | 23 | 39 | 31 | 98 | 96 | 119 | 9% | 138 | 11% | 69% | 27 | 37% | 30% | 4.24 | -2.5 | 39 | 105 | $14 |
| 16 OAK | 568 | 72 | 27 | 75 | 10 | 238 | 249 | 300 | 435 | 735 | 813 | 707 | 8 | 76 | 0.37 | 39 | 17 | 43 | 27 | 88 | 119 | 115 | 15% | 110 | 9% | 83% | 27 | 41% | 22% | 4.40 | 1.5 | 49 | 140 | $14 |
| 17 OAK | 342 | 53 | 10 | 40 | 12 | 249 | 237 | 325 | 398 | 722 | 670 | 743 | 10 | 75 | 0.45 | 37 | 20 | 42 | 30 | 92 | 92 | 110 | 9% | 108 | 14% | 92% | 16 | 38% | 38% | 4.52 | -1.0 | 28 | 85 | $10 |
| 18 OAK | 632 | 89 | 15 | 70 | 14 | 255 | 248 | 318 | 388 | 706 | 758 | 682 | 9 | 79 | 0.47 | 39 | 23 | 38 | 30 | 95 | 83 | 90 | 8% | 107 | 12% | 70% | 28 | 36% | 25% | 4.21 | 2.0 | 35 | 117 | $19 |
| 1st Half | 338 | 46 | 7 | 31 | 7 | 249 | 240 | 302 | 364 | 666 | 692 | 654 | 8 | 79 | 0.39 | 41 | 22 | 37 | 30 | 83 | 72 | 85 | 7% | 113 | 13% | 64% | 15 | 20% | 33% | 3.70 | -2.7 | 23 | 77 | $17 |
| 2nd Half | 294 | 43 | 8 | 39 | 7 | 262 | 256 | 336 | 415 | 751 | 833 | 714 | 10 | 80 | 0.56 | 37 | 24 | 40 | 30 | 108 | 95 | 95 | 9% | 101 | 11% | 78% | 13 | 54% | 15% | 4.84 | 7.5 | 48 | 160 | $22 |
| **19 Proj** | **572** | **81** | **16** | **67** | **12** | **250** | **244** | **318** | **397** | **716** | **754** | **699** | **9** | **77** | **0.44** | **39** | **21** | **39** | **30** | **94** | **92** | **100** | **9%** | **111** | **10%** | **77%** | | | | **4.32** | **6.0** | **32** | **106** | **$18** |

## Senzel,Nick

**Age:** 24 **Bats:** R **Pos:** 2B | **Ht:** 6' 1" **Wt:** 205

| Health | C | LIMA Plan | C+ |
|---|---|---|---|
| PT/Exp | F | Rand Var | 0 |
| Consist | F | MM | 3333 |

Top prospect can't catch a break. Second bout of vertigo sidelined him in May, and a few weeks after return, torn finger tendon ended his season. Also had elbow surgery in October, but expected to be 100% by spring. Power/speed combo with decent ct% hints at immediate impact, but beware the health risk.

| Yr Tm | AB | R | HR | RBI | SB | BA | xBA | OBP | SLG | OPS | vL | vR | bb% | ct% | Eye | G | L | F | h% | HctX | PX | xPX | hr/f | Spd | SBO | SB% | #Wk | DOM | DIS | RC/G | RAR | BPV | BPX | R$ |
|---|---|---|---|---|---|---|---|---|---|---|---|---|---|---|---|---|---|---|---|---|---|---|---|---|---|---|---|---|---|---|---|---|---|---|
| 14 | | | | | | | | | | | | | | | | | | | | | | | | | | | | | | | | | | |
| 15 | | | | | | | | | | | | | | | | | | | | | | | | | | | | | | | | | | |
| 16 | | | | | | | | | | | | | | | | | | | | | | | | | | | | | | | | | | |
| 17 aa | 209 | 42 | 12 | 36 | 5 | 345 | | 422 | 588 | 1010 | | | 12 | 78 | 0.61 | | | | 40 | | 138 | | | 98 | 13% | 56% | | | | 9.19 | | 77 | 233 | $13 |
| 18 aaa | 171 | 19 | 5 | 21 | 7 | 280 | | 342 | 457 | 799 | | | 9 | 74 | 0.36 | | | | 35 | | 114 | | | 102 | 19% | 75% | | | | 5.50 | | 37 | 123 | $5 |
| 1st Half | 171 | 19 | 5 | 21 | 7 | 280 | | 342 | 457 | 799 | | | 9 | 74 | 0.36 | | | | 35 | | 114 | | | 109 | 19% | 75% | | | | 5.50 | | 39 | 130 | $5 |
| 2nd Half | | | | | | | | | | | | | | | | | | | | | | | | | | | | | | | | | | |
| **19 Proj** | **377** | **52** | **14** | **50** | **13** | **280** | **261** | **353** | **470** | **823** | **823** | **823** | **10** | **75** | **0.46** | **42** | **22** | **36** | **34** | | **120** | | **14%** | **101** | **17%** | **70%** | | | | **5.76** | **17.2** | **48** | **161** | **$18** |

## Severino,Pedro

**Age:** 25 **Bats:** R **Pos:** CA | **Ht:** 6' 1" **Wt:** 219

| Health | A | LIMA Plan | D |
|---|---|---|---|
| PT/Exp | F | Rand Var | +5 |
| Consist | B | MM | 1101 |

2-15-.168 in 190 AB at WAS. Was given semi-regular AB in 1st half, but fell flat on his face. Power was non-existent, and low h% took BA from bad to worse. PX, ct% were better in 2nd half (mostly at AAA), but he's only hanging around for his defense. Even if he lucks into more PT, not worth your time.

| Yr Tm | AB | R | HR | RBI | SB | BA | xBA | OBP | SLG | OPS | vL | vR | bb% | ct% | Eye | G | L | F | h% | HctX | PX | xPX | hr/f | Spd | SBO | SB% | #Wk | DOM | DIS | RC/G | RAR | BPV | BPX | R$ |
|---|---|---|---|---|---|---|---|---|---|---|---|---|---|---|---|---|---|---|---|---|---|---|---|---|---|---|---|---|---|---|---|---|---|---|
| 14 | | | | | | | | | | | | | | | | | | | | | | | | | | | | | | | | | | |
| 15 WAS * | 333 | 29 | 4 | 29 | 1 | 229 | 271 | 265 | 305 | 570 | 0 | 750 | 5 | 84 | 0.30 | 33 | 33 | 33 | 26 | 120 | 53 | 233 | 0% | 76 | 4% | 28% | 2 | 50% | 50% | 2.61 | -12.2 | 11 | 30 | $0 |
| 16 WAS * | 319 | 30 | 4 | 24 | 3 | 263 | 212 | 313 | 345 | 658 | 1229 | 1010 | 7 | 84 | 0.45 | 60 | 8 | 32 | 30 | 82 | 53 | 76 | 25% | 99 | 8% | 39% | 9 | 56% | 33% | 3.57 | -7.8 | 24 | 69 | $4 |
| 17 WAS * | 240 | 14 | 4 | 26 | 1 | 208 | 193 | 252 | 279 | 531 | 571 | 390 | 6 | 76 | 0.24 | 47 | 16 | 37 | 26 | 65 | 41 | 66 | 0% | 80 | 3% | 42% | 8 | 13% | 75% | 2.22 | -13.7 | -26 | -79 | -$2 |
| 18 WAS * | 320 | 26 | 7 | 26 | 1 | 197 | 230 | 248 | 309 | 557 | 560 | 478 | 6 | 77 | 0.30 | 40 | 21 | 38 | 23 | 63 | 71 | 49 | 4% | 74 | 2% | 100% | 18 | 17% | 61% | 2.45 | -10.7 | 2 | 7 | -$2 |
| 1st Half | 160 | 11 | 0 | 11 | 1 | 175 | 213 | 265 | 231 | 496 | 563 | 469 | 9 | 74 | 0.39 | 41 | 23 | 36 | 24 | 62 | 50 | 32 | 0% | 73 | 3% | 100% | 14 | 21% | 57% | 1.81 | -8.5 | -20 | -67 | -$7 |
| 2nd Half | 160 | 15 | 7 | 15 | 0 | 218 | 220 | 247 | 387 | 634 | 533 | 514 | 4 | 80 | 0.19 | 39 | 13 | 48 | 23 | 61 | 90 | 136 | 18% | 91 | 0% | 0% | 4 | 0% | 75% | 3.11 | -1.6 | 28 | 93 | $3 |
| **19 Proj** | **165** | **13** | **3** | **15** | **1** | **221** | **211** | **273** | **320** | **593** | **737** | **551** | **6** | **79** | **0.29** | **40** | **17** | **43** | **26** | **61** | **60** | **94** | **6%** | **79** | **3%** | **53%** | | | | **2.77** | **-3.4** | **-10** | **-33** | **$1** |

BRIAN RUDD

## Shaw,Chris

| | | | | | |
|---|---|---|---|---|---|
| Age: 25 | Bats: L | Pos: LF | Health: A | LIMA Plan: D+ | |
| Ht: 6' 3" | Wt: 226 | | PT/Exp: C | Rand Var: -1 | |
| | | | Consist: C | MM: 4303 | |

1-7-.185 in 54 AB at SF. Missed three weeks with groin strain; finished top 10 in Pacific Coast League with 24 HR anyway. PX confirms the power should translate well to majors, but mounting Ks and downard batting Eye are major hurdles to short-term impact. Check back if the whiffs die down.

| Yr | Tm | | AB | R | HR | RBI | SB | BA | xBA | OBP | SLG | OPS | vL | vR | bb% | ct% | Eye | G | L | F | h% | HctX | PX | xPX | hr/f | Spd | SBO | SB% | #Wk | DOM | DIS | RC/G | RAR | BPV | BPX | R$ |
|---|---|---|---|---|---|---|---|---|---|---|---|---|---|---|---|---|---|---|---|---|---|---|---|---|---|---|---|---|---|---|---|---|---|---|---|---|
| 14 | | | | | | | | | | | | | | | | | | | | | | | | | | | | | | | | | | | | |
| 15 | | | | | | | | | | | | | | | | | | | | | | | | | | | | | | | | | | | | |
| 16 | aa | | 232 | 23 | 4 | 27 | 0 | 230 | | 286 | 382 | 667 | | | 7 | 74 | 0.30 | | | | 30 | | 101 | | | 114 | 0% | 0% | | | | 3.61 | | 27 | 77 | $0 |
| 17 | a/a | | 469 | 50 | 17 | 68 | 0 | 256 | | 304 | 436 | 740 | | | 6 | 68 | 0.22 | | | | 34 | | 124 | | | 81 | 0% | 0% | | | | 4.54 | | 10 | 30 | $9 |
| 18 | SF | * | 448 | 40 | 15 | 53 | 1 | 202 | 187 | 239 | 352 | 592 | 619 | 541 | 5 | 57 | 0.11 | 38 | 19 | 44 | 32 | 72 | 121 | 121 | 7% | 81 | 1% | 100% | 5 | 0% | 80% | 2.70 | -26.6 | -39 | -130 | $2 |
| 1st Half | | | 233 | 24 | 9 | 30 | 0 | 199 | 196 | 223 | 371 | 594 | | | 3 | 53 | 0.06 | | | | 33 | | 150 | | | 88 | 0% | 0% | | | | 2.63 | | -32 | -107 | $3 |
| 2nd Half | | | 215 | 16 | 6 | 23 | 1 | 205 | 184 | 256 | 332 | 589 | 619 | 541 | 6 | 61 | 0.17 | 38 | 19 | 44 | 31 | 77 | 94 | 121 | 7% | 86 | 2% | 100% | 5 | 0% | 80% | 2.75 | -12.3 | -41 | -137 | $2 |
| **19** | **Proj** | | **363** | **35** | **15** | **46** | **1** | **225** | **214** | **265** | **411** | **676** | **700** | **673** | **6** | **61** | **0.16** | **40** | **20** | **40** | **32** | **69** | **139** | **109** | **16%** | **82** | **1%** | **100%** | | | | **3.65** | **-10.5** | **-12** | **-39** | **$3** |

## Shaw,Travis

| | | | | | |
|---|---|---|---|---|---|
| Age: 29 | Bats: L | Pos: 3B 2B | Health: A | LIMA Plan: B+ | |
| Ht: 6' 4" | Wt: 230 | | PT/Exp: A | Rand Var: +3 | |
| | | | Consist: C | MM: 4235 | |

Almost a full repeat of 2017 breakout; too bad h% plunge had to get in the way. More FBs say the BA drop wasn't all bad luck, but he cut down on the whiffs and PX/xPX baseline says he'll flirt with 30 HR again. Issues vL might ding PT and 2017's SB isn't coming back, but this is a level he can sustain—now with 2B eligibility.

| Yr | Tm | | AB | R | HR | RBI | SB | BA | xBA | OBP | SLG | OPS | vL | vR | bb% | ct% | Eye | G | L | F | h% | HctX | PX | xPX | hr/f | Spd | SBO | SB% | #Wk | DOM | DIS | RC/G | RAR | BPV | BPX | R$ |
|---|---|---|---|---|---|---|---|---|---|---|---|---|---|---|---|---|---|---|---|---|---|---|---|---|---|---|---|---|---|---|---|---|---|---|---|---|
| 14 | a/a | | 490 | 61 | 16 | 61 | 6 | 252 | | 315 | 415 | 730 | | | 8 | 78 | 0.41 | | | | 30 | | 122 | | | 87 | 7% | 62% | | | | 4.39 | | 53 | 143 | $14 |
| 15 | BOS | * | 515 | 56 | 17 | 61 | 0 | 248 | 237 | 302 | 397 | 699 | 975 | 723 | 7 | 77 | 0.34 | 37 | 20 | 43 | 29 | 98 | 98 | 128 | 18% | 87 | 2% | 0% | 16 | 31% | 31% | 3.99 | -2.7 | 29 | 78 | $9 |
| 16 | BOS | | 480 | 63 | 16 | 71 | 5 | 242 | 240 | 306 | 421 | 726 | 599 | 762 | 8 | 72 | 0.32 | 36 | 19 | 45 | 30 | 98 | 123 | 122 | 10% | 80 | 6% | 83% | 26 | 35% | 38% | 4.32 | -7.8 | 30 | 86 | $10 |
| 17 | MIL | | 538 | 84 | 31 | 101 | 10 | 273 | 274 | 349 | 513 | 862 | 776 | 892 | 10 | 74 | 0.43 | 43 | 20 | 38 | 31 | 112 | 141 | 128 | 21% | 76 | 7% | 100% | 26 | 69% | 19% | 6.35 | 20.5 | 55 | 167 | $23 |
| 18 | MIL | | 498 | 73 | 32 | 86 | 5 | 241 | 263 | 345 | 480 | 825 | 599 | 894 | 13 | 78 | 0.72 | 37 | 18 | 45 | 25 | 115 | 133 | 132 | 18% | 60 | 5% | 71% | 28 | 71% | 4% | 5.52 | 18.6 | 66 | 220 | $18 |
| 1st Half | | | 264 | 40 | 14 | 47 | 0 | 239 | 267 | 344 | 470 | 814 | 537 | 901 | 14 | 79 | 0.75 | 39 | 18 | 43 | 25 | 105 | 138 | 113 | 16% | 63 | 3% | 0% | 15 | 67% | 7% | 5.24 | 8.5 | 74 | 247 | $16 |
| 2nd Half | | | 234 | 33 | 18 | 39 | 5 | 244 | 257 | 345 | 491 | 837 | 668 | 886 | 13 | 78 | 0.69 | 36 | 18 | 46 | 24 | 126 | 128 | 154 | 21% | 73 | 7% | 100% | 13 | 77% | 0% | 5.84 | 11.6 | 64 | 213 | $20 |
| **19** | **Proj** | | **529** | **76** | **31** | **88** | **7** | **258** | **260** | **342** | **487** | **830** | **717** | **867** | **11** | **76** | **0.53** | **38** | **19** | **43** | **28** | **111** | **134** | **132** | **18%** | **71** | **6%** | **85%** | | | | **5.74** | **19.0** | **57** | **189** | **$22** |

## Sierra,Magneuris

| | | | | | |
|---|---|---|---|---|---|
| Age: 23 | Bats: L | Pos: CF | Health: A | LIMA Plan: D | |
| Ht: 5' 11" | Wt: 160 | | PT/Exp: F | Rand Var: +1 | |
| | | | Consist: C | MM: 0521 | |

0-7-.187 with 3 SB in 150 AB at MIA. There's bad; then there's -37 BPV in the majors bad. Sure, the speed looks great, but 2nd half SB% says it didn't translate to bags. Tack on an awful batting Eye with zero hard contact and that OBP baseline, and there's little hope for 2019 fantasy relevance.

| Yr | Tm | | AB | R | HR | RBI | SB | BA | xBA | OBP | SLG | OPS | vL | vR | bb% | ct% | Eye | G | L | F | h% | HctX | PX | xPX | hr/f | Spd | SBO | SB% | #Wk | DOM | DIS | RC/G | RAR | BPV | BPX | R$ |
|---|---|---|---|---|---|---|---|---|---|---|---|---|---|---|---|---|---|---|---|---|---|---|---|---|---|---|---|---|---|---|---|---|---|---|---|---|
| 14 | | | | | | | | | | | | | | | | | | | | | | | | | | | | | | | | | | | | |
| 15 | | | | | | | | | | | | | | | | | | | | | | | | | | | | | | | | | | | | |
| 16 | | | | | | | | | | | | | | | | | | | | | | | | | | | | | | | | | | | | |
| 17 | STL | * | 386 | 39 | 1 | 36 | 17 | 264 | 273 | 303 | 327 | 631 | 923 | 610 | 5 | 80 | 0.28 | 53 | 28 | 19 | 33 | 21 | 43 | -3 | 0% | 159 | 24% | 70% | 8 | 0% | 88% | 3.39 | -19.0 | 16 | 48 | $11 |
| 18 | MIA | * | 493 | 51 | 2 | 21 | 15 | 219 | 240 | 245 | 272 | 517 | 745 | 381 | 3 | 76 | 0.14 | 57 | 23 | 19 | 29 | 55 | 36 | 18 | 0% | 176 | 21% | 67% | 11 | 9% | 73% | 2.13 | -32.4 | -6 | -20 | $5 |
| 1st Half | | | 293 | 36 | 2 | 13 | 12 | 227 | 206 | 255 | 289 | 544 | | | 4 | 74 | 0.15 | | | | 30 | | 42 | | | 154 | 25% | 73% | | | | 2.43 | | -13 | -43 | $9 |
| 2nd Half | | | 200 | 15 | 0 | 9 | 3 | 207 | 236 | 230 | 247 | 478 | 745 | 381 | 3 | 77 | 0.13 | 57 | 23 | 19 | 27 | 56 | 27 | 18 | 0% | 163 | 15% | 49% | 11 | 9% | 73% | 1.74 | -15.2 | -13 | -43 | -$2 |
| **19** | **Proj** | | **235** | **23** | **1** | **15** | **8** | **234** | **251** | **266** | **291** | **557** | **918** | **482** | **4** | **78** | **0.19** | **56** | **25** | **19** | **30** | **42** | **39** | **10** | **2%** | **158** | **21%** | **68%** | | | | **2.53** | **-11.6** | **-15** | **-51** | **$4** |

## Simmons,Andrelton

| | | | | | |
|---|---|---|---|---|---|
| Age: 29 | Bats: R | Pos: SS | Health: B | LIMA Plan: B+ | |
| Ht: 6' 2" | Wt: 200 | | PT/Exp: A | Rand Var: -1 | |
| | | | Consist: A | MM: 1455 | |

Led majors with dazzling ct%; career-high HctX says its quality improved as well. GB% stroke caps any hope for HR gains, which xPX confirms, but xBA foundation is about as consistent as it gets. Spd/SB% upticks hint at some untapped value with his legs, so he could pair that BA with... UP: 25 SB.

| Yr | Tm | | AB | R | HR | RBI | SB | BA | xBA | OBP | SLG | OPS | vL | vR | bb% | ct% | Eye | G | L | F | h% | HctX | PX | xPX | hr/f | Spd | SBO | SB% | #Wk | DOM | DIS | RC/G | RAR | BPV | BPX | R$ |
|---|---|---|---|---|---|---|---|---|---|---|---|---|---|---|---|---|---|---|---|---|---|---|---|---|---|---|---|---|---|---|---|---|---|---|---|---|
| 14 | ATL | | 540 | 44 | 7 | 46 | 4 | 244 | 250 | 286 | 331 | 617 | 679 | 603 | 6 | 89 | 0.53 | 52 | 16 | 31 | 26 | 102 | 56 | 87 | 5% | 128 | 7% | 44% | 26 | 54% | 23% | 3.11 | -1.1 | 52 | 141 | $6 |
| 15 | ATL | | 535 | 60 | 4 | 44 | 5 | 265 | 279 | 321 | 338 | 660 | 565 | 683 | 7 | 91 | 0.81 | 56 | 22 | 22 | 29 | 92 | 47 | 61 | 4% | 105 | 5% | 63% | 27 | 56% | 22% | 3.67 | -11.2 | 49 | 132 | $10 |
| 16 | LAA | | 448 | 48 | 4 | 44 | 10 | 281 | 282 | 324 | 366 | 690 | 752 | 671 | 6 | 92 | 0.74 | 55 | 20 | 26 | 30 | 87 | 51 | 54 | 4% | 107 | 9% | 91% | 23 | 48% | 9% | 4.30 | 0.0 | 53 | 151 | $12 |
| 17 | LAA | | 589 | 77 | 14 | 69 | 19 | 278 | 286 | 331 | 421 | 752 | 690 | 770 | 7 | 89 | 0.70 | 50 | 19 | 31 | 30 | 105 | 78 | 82 | 8% | 102 | 16% | 76% | 27 | 56% | 15% | 4.93 | 5.0 | 64 | 194 | $22 |
| 18 | LAA | | 554 | 68 | 11 | 75 | 10 | 292 | 281 | 337 | 417 | 754 | 751 | 756 | 6 | 92 | 0.80 | 50 | 19 | 31 | 30 | 122 | 65 | 82 | 7% | 136 | 8% | 83% | 27 | 56% | 7% | 5.07 | 14.9 | 75 | 250 | $21 |
| 1st Half | | | 270 | 41 | 5 | 38 | 5 | 322 | 288 | 383 | 444 | 828 | 867 | 812 | 9 | 95 | 1.86 | 50 | 19 | 31 | 33 | 128 | 64 | 68 | 6% | 135 | 8% | 71% | 15 | 73% | 0% | 6.34 | 17.3 | 91 | 303 | $25 |
| 2nd Half | | | 284 | 27 | 6 | 37 | 5 | 264 | 273 | 291 | 391 | 682 | 650 | 697 | 3 | 89 | 0.30 | 50 | 19 | 31 | 28 | 117 | 66 | 97 | 8% | 132 | 8% | 100% | 12 | 33% | 17% | 3.98 | 0.1 | 58 | 193 | $17 |
| **19** | **Proj** | | **592** | **69** | **11** | **71** | **13** | **281** | **278** | **326** | **399** | **724** | **715** | **728** | **6** | **91** | **0.68** | **51** | **19** | **30** | **30** | **110** | **64** | **79** | **7%** | **121** | **10%** | **81%** | | | | **4.61** | **11.0** | **57** | **191** | **$22** |

## Sisco,Chance

| | | | | | |
|---|---|---|---|---|---|
| Age: 24 | Bats: L | Pos: CA | Health: A | LIMA Plan: D | |
| Ht: 6' 2" | Wt: 195 | | PT/Exp: D | Rand Var: 0 | |
| | | | Consist: C | MM: 2103 | |

2-16-.181 in 160 AB at BAL. Top CA prospect made Opening Day roster, then took several rides on AAA shuttle. Steady erosion of contact skills is worrisome, particularly without the PX to make for up for it. Catchers tend to develop late, so be patient, but BPV trend says odds of 2019 impact are slim to none.

| Yr | Tm | | AB | R | HR | RBI | SB | BA | xBA | OBP | SLG | OPS | vL | vR | bb% | ct% | Eye | G | L | F | h% | HctX | PX | xPX | hr/f | Spd | SBO | SB% | #Wk | DOM | DIS | RC/G | RAR | BPV | BPX | R$ |
|---|---|---|---|---|---|---|---|---|---|---|---|---|---|---|---|---|---|---|---|---|---|---|---|---|---|---|---|---|---|---|---|---|---|---|---|---|
| 14 | | | | | | | | | | | | | | | | | | | | | | | | | | | | | | | | | | | | |
| 15 | aa | | 74 | 8 | 2 | 7 | 0 | 248 | | 321 | 379 | 700 | | | 10 | 81 | 0.56 | | | | 28 | | 87 | | | 94 | 5% | 0% | | | | 3.89 | | 42 | 114 | -$1 |
| 16 | a/a | | 426 | 52 | 5 | 46 | 2 | 282 | | 370 | 363 | 733 | | | 12 | 76 | 0.59 | | | | 36 | | 55 | | | 91 | 3% | 45% | | | | 4.71 | | 3 | 9 | $10 |
| 17 | BAL | * | 362 | 45 | 9 | 46 | 2 | 255 | 224 | 314 | 390 | 704 | 167 | 1639 | 8 | 69 | 0.28 | 45 | 18 | 36 | 34 | 179 | 96 | 223 | 50% | 86 | 4% | 45% | 5 | 20% | 40% | 4.11 | -0.2 | -1 | -3 | $6 |
| 18 | BAL | * | 288 | 32 | 5 | 26 | 1 | 199 | 176 | 267 | 292 | 558 | 651 | 548 | 8 | 64 | 0.25 | 47 | 13 | 40 | 29 | 78 | 74 | 126 | 5% | 88 | 1% | 100% | 18 | 17% | 72% | 2.49 | -7.9 | -40 | -133 | -$1 |
| 1st Half | | | 144 | 14 | 3 | 18 | 1 | 226 | 180 | 297 | 342 | 639 | 812 | 628 | 9 | 59 | 0.25 | 49 | 14 | 37 | 36 | 71 | 100 | 113 | 7% | 89 | 3% | 100% | 14 | 21% | 71% | 3.38 | -0.3 | -35 | -117 | $1 |
| 2nd Half | | | 144 | 18 | 2 | 8 | 0 | 172 | 156 | 236 | 242 | 478 | 0 | 225 | 8 | 68 | 0.26 | 40 | 10 | 50 | 24 | 88 | 52 | 172 | 0% | 102 | 0% | 0% | 4 | 0% | 75% | 1.76 | -7.9 | -38 | -127 | -$3 |
| **19** | **Proj** | | **255** | **30** | **6** | **26** | **1** | **229** | **188** | **328** | **351** | **678** | **798** | **666** | **9** | **68** | **0.30** | **44** | **11** | **45** | **31** | **81** | **87** | **148** | **8%** | **87** | **3%** | **60%** | | | | **3.43** | **-0.2** | **-24** | **-81** | **$4** |

## Slater,Austin

| | | | | | |
|---|---|---|---|---|---|
| Age: 26 | Bats: R | Pos: LF 1B | Health: B | LIMA Plan: C | |
| Ht: 6' 2" | Wt: 197 | | PT/Exp: D | Rand Var: -1 | |
| | | | Consist: A | MM: 1313 | |

1-23-.251 with 7 SB in 199 AB at SF. Got an extended look from July onward, but failed to impress. GB% stroke, PX baseline squash his power ceiling, while 2nd half ct% and xBA—all against MLB pitching—went in the tank. Given SB% history, can't trust speed gains yet either, so he's safe to avoid.

| Yr | Tm | | AB | R | HR | RBI | SB | BA | xBA | OBP | SLG | OPS | vL | vR | bb% | ct% | Eye | G | L | F | h% | HctX | PX | xPX | hr/f | Spd | SBO | SB% | #Wk | DOM | DIS | RC/G | RAR | BPV | BPX | R$ |
|---|---|---|---|---|---|---|---|---|---|---|---|---|---|---|---|---|---|---|---|---|---|---|---|---|---|---|---|---|---|---|---|---|---|---|---|---|
| 14 | | | | | | | | | | | | | | | | | | | | | | | | | | | | | | | | | | | | |
| 15 | aa | | 199 | 20 | 0 | 12 | 1 | 279 | | 324 | 344 | 668 | | | 6 | 73 | 0.25 | | | | 38 | | 58 | | | 106 | 4% | 46% | | | | 3.87 | | -14 | -38 | $2 |
| 16 | a/a | | 390 | 47 | 12 | 56 | 7 | 265 | | 347 | 413 | 759 | | | 11 | 74 | 0.48 | | | | 33 | | 95 | | | 87 | 12% | 46% | | | | 4.68 | | 21 | 60 | $11 |
| 17 | SF | * | 301 | 37 | 6 | 38 | 3 | 276 | 236 | 321 | 390 | 712 | 813 | 709 | 6 | 75 | 0.27 | 61 | 14 | 25 | 35 | 73 | 71 | 48 | 14% | 121 | 8% | 48% | 9 | 22% | 56% | 4.27 | -8.5 | 8 | 24 | $7 |
| 18 | SF | * | 394 | 43 | 4 | 45 | 13 | 263 | 251 | 323 | 371 | 694 | 657 | 629 | 8 | 70 | 0.30 | 63 | 21 | 16 | 37 | 97 | 83 | 31 | 5% | 107 | 14% | 84% | 17 | 12% | 76% | 4.23 | -4.2 | -1 | -3 | $11 |
| 1st Half | | | 214 | 25 | 3 | 25 | 8 | 284 | 312 | 344 | 441 | 785 | 1159 | 863 | 8 | 75 | 0.37 | 79 | 21 | 0 | 37 | 99 | 116 | 27 | 0% | 124 | 18% | 76% | 6 | 33% | 67% | 5.38 | 4.8 | 49 | 163 | $14 |
| 2nd Half | | | 180 | 18 | 1 | 20 | 5 | 239 | 204 | 312 | 289 | 600 | 605 | 598 | 8 | 65 | 0.24 | 61 | 21 | 18 | 36 | 90 | 38 | 31 | 5% | 111 | 10% | 100% | 11 | 0% | 82% | 3.03 | -8.4 | -59 | -197 | $7 |
| **19** | **Proj** | | **387** | **43** | **7** | **45** | **8** | **265** | **231** | **335** | **378** | **713** | **727** | **705** | **8** | **72** | **0.30** | **51** | **20** | **29** | **35** | **83** | **79** | **38** | **8%** | **106** | **11%** | **71%** | | | | **4.20** | **-4.5** | **-6** | **-21** | **$12** |

## Smith,Dominic

| | | | | | |
|---|---|---|---|---|---|
| Age: 24 | Bats: L | Pos: 1B | Health: A | LIMA Plan: D | |
| Ht: 6'0" | Wt: 239 | | PT/Exp: B | Rand Var: +3 | |
| | | | Consist: C | MM: 4221 | |

5-11-.224 in 143 AB at NYM. Shuttled between Vegas and Queens with call-ups in four separate months. A step back along the way: Fewest HR since 2015; spiraling bb%/ct% magnifies BA/OBP risk. Career 133 PX in majors offers hope for power rebound, but regular PT seems unlikely unless plate skills improve.

| Yr | Tm | | AB | R | HR | RBI | SB | BA | xBA | OBP | SLG | OPS | vL | vR | bb% | ct% | Eye | G | L | F | h% | HctX | PX | xPX | hr/f | Spd | SBO | SB% | #Wk | DOM | DIS | RC/G | RAR | BPV | BPX | R$ |
|---|---|---|---|---|---|---|---|---|---|---|---|---|---|---|---|---|---|---|---|---|---|---|---|---|---|---|---|---|---|---|---|---|---|---|---|---|
| 14 | | | | | | | | | | | | | | | | | | | | | | | | | | | | | | | | | | | | |
| 15 | | | | | | | | | | | | | | | | | | | | | | | | | | | | | | | | | | | | |
| 16 | aa | | 484 | 56 | 13 | 79 | 2 | 272 | | 337 | 410 | 748 | | | 9 | 82 | 0.56 | | | | 31 | | 83 | | | 82 | 2% | 61% | | | | 4.83 | | 40 | 114 | $13 |
| 17 | NYM | * | 624 | 74 | 21 | 82 | 1 | 257 | 243 | 306 | 416 | 722 | 437 | 708 | 7 | 76 | 0.29 | 50 | 16 | 34 | 31 | 114 | 97 | 112 | 23% | 50 | 1% | 40% | 9 | 33% | 44% | 4.34 | -28.5 | 11 | 33 | $12 |
| 18 | NYM | * | 480 | 48 | 9 | 38 | 2 | 208 | 228 | 251 | 328 | 579 | 583 | 688 | 5 | 71 | 0.20 | 34 | 26 | 40 | 27 | 80 | 86 | 105 | 13% | 72 | 2% | 100% | 14 | 43% | 50% | 2.67 | -36.2 | -10 | -33 | $1 |
| 1st Half | | | 264 | 29 | 2 | 17 | 0 | 207 | 246 | 263 | 304 | 567 | 833 | 615 | 7 | 72 | 0.27 | 46 | 29 | 25 | 28 | 142 | 74 | 151 | 14% | 76 | 0% | 0% | 6 | 33% | 50% | 2.57 | -18.0 | -14 | -47 | -$2 |
| 2nd Half | | | 216 | 20 | 7 | 21 | 2 | 210 | 227 | 236 | 357 | 593 | 382 | 718 | 3 | 71 | 0.11 | 29 | 25 | 46 | 27 | 54 | 101 | 87 | 13% | 70 | 6% | 100% | 8 | 50% | 50% | 2.76 | -13.4 | -7 | -23 | $4 |
| **19** | **Proj** | | **165** | **18** | **7** | **19** | **1** | **235** | **250** | **287** | **427** | **714** | **578** | **739** | **6** | **71** | **0.22** | **42** | **22** | **36** | **29** | **100** | **124** | **113** | **17%** | **89** | **2%** | **82%** | | | | **3.99** | **-3.8** | **14** | **45** | **$3** |

RYAN BLOOMFIELD

## Smith,Kevan

Age: 31 Bats: R Pos: CA
Ht: 6' 4" Wt: 230

Health B | LIMA Plan D
PT/Exp F | Rand Var -2
Consist C | MM 1221

3-21-.292 in 171 AB at CHW. Called up in June after a pair of ankle injuries; provided nice little BA boost in semi-regular role. While contact trend is encouraging, xPX/GB% combo points toward more infield groundouts than hits, which xBA confirms. Best case: a "can't hurt you" end-gamer in two-CA leagues.

| Yr | Tm | AB | R | HR | RBI | SB | BA | xBA | OBP | SLG | OPS | vL | vR | bb% | ct% | Eye | G | L | F | h% | HctX | PX | xPX | hr/f | Spd | SBO | SB% | #Wk | DOM | DIS | RC/G | RAR | BPV | BPX | R$ |
|---|---|---|---|---|---|---|---|---|---|---|---|---|---|---|---|---|---|---|---|---|---|---|---|---|---|---|---|---|---|---|---|---|---|---|---|
| 14 | aa | 389 | 31 | 8 | 34 | 1 | 235 | | 297 | 347 | 643 | | | 8 | 79 | 0.41 | | | | 28 | | 83 | | | 94 | 2% | 37% | | | | 3.39 | | 27 | 73 | $3 |
| 15 | aaa | 319 | 32 | 5 | 28 | 0 | 211 | | 266 | 298 | 565 | | | 7 | 74 | 0.29 | | | | 27 | | 62 | | | 100 | 2% | 0% | | | | 2.52 | | -8 | -22 | -$2 |
| 16 | CHW * | 199 | 15 | 6 | 18 | 0 | 170 | 199 | 220 | 300 | 520 | 200 | 333 | 6 | 74 | 0.24 | 60 | 10 | 30 | 20 | 180 | 82 | 150 | 0% | 84 | 0% | 0% | 5 | 0% | 80% | 2.03 | -11.8 | 0 | 0 | -$4 |
| 17 | CHW * | 329 | 30 | 4 | 41 | 0 | 284 | 254 | 312 | 386 | 698 | 615 | 751 | 4 | 82 | 0.23 | 57 | 19 | 23 | 33 | 75 | 67 | 43 | 7% | 69 | 0% | 0% | 23 | 26% | 39% | 4.29 | 1.4 | 13 | 39 | $6 |
| 18 | CHW * | 283 | 30 | 6 | 33 | 1 | 258 | 251 | 298 | 355 | 653 | 1106 | 578 | 5 | 85 | 0.38 | 63 | 16 | 21 | 28 | 75 | 54 | 52 | 9% | 84 | 1% | 100% | 17 | 41% | 29% | 3.66 | 2.4 | 22 | 73 | $4 |
| 1st Half | | 170 | 16 | 3 | 17 | 1 | 254 | 241 | 283 | 338 | 622 | 1154 | 630 | 4 | 83 | 0.24 | 56 | 19 | 25 | 29 | 58 | 49 | 45 | 0% | 101 | 2% | 100% | 5 | 20% | 40% | 3.31 | -0.7 | 9 | 30 | $4 |
| 2nd Half | | 113 | 14 | 3 | 16 | 0 | 265 | 257 | 339 | 381 | 719 | 1092 | 548 | 7 | 89 | 0.75 | 67 | 15 | 19 | 28 | 87 | 60 | 56 | 16% | 79 | 0% | 0% | 12 | 50% | 25% | 4.22 | 2.5 | 46 | 153 | $5 |
| **19** | **Proj** | **198** | **20** | **3** | **23** | **0** | **249** | **243** | **302** | **338** | **640** | **778** | **574** | **6** | **83** | **0.33** | **60** | **18** | **22** | **29** | **75** | **56** | **48** | **8%** | **80** | **1%** | **82%** | | | | **3.33** | **-0.7** | **-2** | **-7** | **$1** |

## Smith,Mallex

Age: 26 Bats: L Pos: CF RF LF
Ht: 5' 10" Wt: 180

Health C | LIMA Plan D+
PT/Exp C | Rand Var -2
Consist C | MM 1535

Delivered on the SB he was drafted for; BA gains were icing on the cake. A 45% h% vL won't hold, so not likely to sniff .300 again, but plate skill surge—especially in 2nd half—suggests the pullback will be light. Now with the goods to hold full-time gig, elite Spd and green light make him a SB game-changer.

| Yr | Tm | AB | R | HR | RBI | SB | BA | xBA | OBP | SLG | OPS | vL | vR | bb% | ct% | Eye | G | L | F | h% | HctX | PX | xPX | hr/f | Spd | SBO | SB% | #Wk | DOM | DIS | RC/G | RAR | BPV | BPX | R$ |
|---|---|---|---|---|---|---|---|---|---|---|---|---|---|---|---|---|---|---|---|---|---|---|---|---|---|---|---|---|---|---|---|---|---|---|---|
| 14 | | | | | | | | | | | | | | | | | | | | | | | | | | | | | | | | | | | |
| 15 | a/a | 484 | 75 | 2 | 31 | 51 | 283 | | 346 | 353 | 699 | | | 9 | 80 | 0.48 | | | | 35 | | 47 | | | 148 | 41% | 78% | | | | 4.49 | | 21 | 57 | $30 |
| 16 | ATL * | 220 | 37 | 3 | 26 | 20 | 258 | 253 | 331 | 388 | 719 | 299 | 819 | 10 | 74 | 0.42 | 61 | 16 | 23 | 34 | 58 | 79 | 59 | 11% | 149 | 45% | 68% | 15 | 27% | 40% | 4.18 | -3.3 | 25 | 71 | $11 |
| 17 | TAM * | 442 | 56 | 5 | 21 | 35 | 256 | 238 | 315 | 353 | 668 | 603 | 699 | 8 | 74 | 0.33 | 50 | 22 | 28 | 34 | 64 | 57 | 29 | 4% | 188 | 39% | 71% | 19 | 21% | 47% | 3.72 | -16.1 | 16 | 48 | $18 |
| 18 | TAM | 480 | 65 | 2 | 40 | 40 | 296 | 265 | 367 | 406 | 773 | 817 | 761 | 9 | 80 | 0.48 | 50 | 25 | 25 | 37 | 79 | 70 | 57 | 2% | 157 | 35% | 77% | 27 | 41% | 37% | 5.31 | 10.9 | 41 | 137 | $27 |
| 1st Half | | 241 | 24 | 0 | 16 | 15 | 266 | 245 | 331 | 349 | 679 | 633 | 690 | 8 | 77 | 0.38 | 50 | 24 | 26 | 35 | 72 | 57 | 58 | 0% | 143 | 32% | 68% | 15 | 27% | 47% | 3.81 | -4.7 | 14 | 47 | $15 |
| 2nd Half | | 239 | 41 | 2 | 24 | 25 | 326 | 285 | 402 | 464 | 867 | 969 | 836 | 10 | 82 | 0.62 | 50 | 26 | 25 | 39 | 87 | 82 | 56 | 4% | 158 | 37% | 83% | 12 | 58% | 25% | 7.16 | 17.6 | 64 | 213 | $39 |
| **19** | **Proj** | **542** | **78** | **5** | **43** | **48** | **282** | **255** | **351** | **394** | **745** | **679** | **761** | **9** | **78** | **0.44** | **51** | **23** | **26** | **36** | **72** | **68** | **47** | **4%** | **164** | **38%** | **75%** | | | | **4.82** | **10.9** | **33** | **111** | **$33** |

## Smoak,Justin

Age: 32 Bats: B Pos: 1B
Ht: 6' 4" Wt: 220

Health A | LIMA Plan B+
PT/Exp B | Rand Var 0
Consist D | MM 4025

Not a complete collapse, but never came close to repeat of previous year's breakout. The whiffs returned, which drove down xBA, and 2017 looks like the clear outlier with string of subpar ct% on this page. Power remains legit and he has plenty of loft, so while another 30 HR is in reach, he's likely to keep dragging BA.

| Yr | Tm | AB | R | HR | RBI | SB | BA | xBA | OBP | SLG | OPS | vL | vR | bb% | ct% | Eye | G | L | F | h% | HctX | PX | xPX | hr/f | Spd | SBO | SB% | #Wk | DOM | DIS | RC/G | RAR | BPV | BPX | R$ |
|---|---|---|---|---|---|---|---|---|---|---|---|---|---|---|---|---|---|---|---|---|---|---|---|---|---|---|---|---|---|---|---|---|---|---|---|
| 14 | SEA * | 453 | 46 | 11 | 55 | 0 | 224 | 223 | 292 | 349 | 641 | 618 | 611 | 9 | 73 | 0.37 | 42 | 18 | 39 | 28 | 116 | 101 | 145 | 10% | 65 | 3% | 0% | 18 | 33% | 44% | 3.23 | -12.6 | 14 | 38 | $4 |
| 15 | TOR | 296 | 44 | 18 | 59 | 0 | 226 | 274 | 299 | 470 | 768 | 839 | 757 | 9 | 71 | 0.34 | 43 | 24 | 34 | 26 | 112 | 166 | 141 | 25% | 72 | 0% | 0% | 27 | 52% | 33% | 4.57 | -3.2 | 58 | 157 | $7 |
| 16 | TOR | 299 | 33 | 14 | 34 | 1 | 217 | 223 | 314 | 391 | 705 | 621 | 738 | 12 | 63 | 0.36 | 30 | 27 | 42 | 29 | 99 | 123 | 144 | 18% | 80 | 1% | 100% | 26 | 27% | 58% | 3.97 | -8.1 | -1 | -3 | $2 |
| 17 | TOR | 560 | 85 | 38 | 90 | 0 | 270 | 277 | 355 | 529 | 883 | 977 | 856 | 11 | 77 | 0.57 | 34 | 21 | 44 | 29 | 123 | 141 | 158 | 20% | 68 | 1% | 0% | 27 | 56% | 19% | 6.49 | 17.8 | 67 | 203 | $19 |
| 18 | TOR | 505 | 67 | 25 | 77 | 0 | 242 | 239 | 350 | 457 | 808 | 688 | 867 | 14 | 69 | 0.53 | 39 | 18 | 43 | 30 | 86 | 147 | 140 | 17% | 69 | 1% | 0% | 27 | 44% | 30% | 5.32 | 13.5 | 45 | 150 | $13 |
| 1st Half | | 260 | 36 | 11 | 40 | 0 | 235 | 229 | 359 | 438 | 797 | 799 | 796 | 16 | 69 | 0.61 | 39 | 15 | 46 | 30 | 84 | 143 | 141 | 13% | 74 | 1% | 0% | 15 | 53% | 27% | 5.13 | 2.8 | 47 | 157 | $12 |
| 2nd Half | | 245 | 31 | 14 | 37 | 0 | 249 | 249 | 341 | 478 | 818 | 538 | 935 | 12 | 69 | 0.45 | 40 | 21 | 39 | 30 | 89 | 150 | 140 | 21% | 72 | 0% | 0% | 12 | 33% | 33% | 5.52 | 5.4 | 44 | 147 | $14 |
| **19** | **Proj** | **522** | **69** | **28** | **78** | **0** | **244** | **247** | **339** | **464** | **802** | **717** | **837** | **12** | **70** | **0.47** | **37** | **21** | **42** | **29** | **101** | **141** | **146** | **18%** | **70** | **1%** | **23%** | | | | **5.24** | **7.4** | **28** | **95** | **$15** |

## Solarte,Yangervis

Age: 31 Bats: B Pos: 3B 2B
Ht: 5' 11" Wt: 205

Health C | LIMA Plan B
PT/Exp B | Rand Var +4
Consist C | MM 2035

On his way to last year's "UP: 25 HR" until August oblique injury cost him a month and likely played role in 2nd half power collapse. Hit rate didn't help either, as it cratered BA, but rock-solid ct% stayed intact. Traded back fly balls for line drives, so not much room for power growth, but still a prime rebound candidate.

| Yr | Tm | AB | R | HR | RBI | SB | BA | xBA | OBP | SLG | OPS | vL | vR | bb% | ct% | Eye | G | L | F | h% | HctX | PX | xPX | hr/f | Spd | SBO | SB% | #Wk | DOM | DIS | RC/G | RAR | BPV | BPX | R$ |
|---|---|---|---|---|---|---|---|---|---|---|---|---|---|---|---|---|---|---|---|---|---|---|---|---|---|---|---|---|---|---|---|---|---|---|---|
| 14 | 2 TM | 469 | 56 | 10 | 48 | 0 | 260 | 254 | 336 | 369 | 705 | 760 | 673 | 10 | 88 | 0.91 | 45 | 19 | 35 | 28 | 99 | 72 | 71 | 7% | 81 | 1% | 0% | 26 | 42% | 12% | 4.23 | 7.5 | 54 | 146 | $10 |
| 15 | SD | 526 | 63 | 14 | 63 | 1 | 270 | 280 | 320 | 428 | 748 | 667 | 771 | 6 | 89 | 0.61 | 44 | 19 | 37 | 28 | 118 | 94 | 96 | 8% | 90 | 1% | 100% | 27 | 59% | 15% | 4.71 | 2.1 | 73 | 197 | $13 |
| 16 | SD | 405 | 55 | 15 | 71 | 1 | 286 | 282 | 341 | 467 | 808 | 772 | 819 | 7 | 84 | 0.48 | 41 | 22 | 37 | 31 | 112 | 104 | 91 | 12% | 66 | 2% | 50% | 22 | 45% | 18% | 5.56 | 8.6 | 56 | 160 | $14 |
| 17 | SD | 466 | 49 | 18 | 64 | 3 | 255 | 257 | 314 | 416 | 731 | 564 | 794 | 7 | 87 | 0.61 | 42 | 16 | 42 | 26 | 109 | 82 | 98 | 10% | 71 | 3% | 100% | 22 | 50% | 14% | 4.46 | -5.4 | 51 | 155 | $10 |
| 18 | TOR | 468 | 50 | 17 | 54 | 1 | 226 | 260 | 277 | 378 | 655 | 692 | 638 | 6 | 85 | 0.43 | 43 | 21 | 37 | 23 | 88 | 83 | 70 | 12% | 66 | 4% | 25% | 23 | 39% | 39% | 3.33 | -14.3 | 39 | 130 | $6 |
| 1st Half | | 313 | 40 | 15 | 45 | 1 | 256 | 281 | 313 | 454 | 767 | 783 | 757 | 7 | 85 | 0.52 | 40 | 22 | 38 | 26 | 96 | 107 | 90 | 15% | 64 | 3% | 50% | 15 | 53% | 20% | 4.78 | 2.5 | 60 | 200 | $16 |
| 2nd Half | | 155 | 10 | 2 | 9 | 0 | 168 | 216 | 202 | 226 | 428 | 457 | 420 | 4 | 85 | 0.25 | 48 | 17 | 34 | 19 | 73 | 33 | 30 | 4% | 83 | 7% | 0% | 8 | 13% | 75% | 1.27 | -16.6 | -1 | -3 | -$12 |
| **19** | **Proj** | **460** | **48** | **19** | **54** | **1** | **250** | **263** | **300** | **417** | **717** | **684** | **731** | **6** | **86** | **0.46** | **42** | **20** | **38** | **26** | **96** | **89** | **74** | **12%** | **71** | **3%** | **35%** | | | | **4.13** | **-5.1** | **38** | **126** | **$11** |

## Soler,Jorge

Age: 27 Bats: R Pos: RF
Ht: 6' 4" Wt: 230

Health F | LIMA Plan C+
PT/Exp D | Rand Var -3
Consist C | MM 4215

Scorching start (.324 BA, 5 HR in first 108 AB), then broken toe ended season in June. Can't glean much from limited sample, but PX/xPX gains were encouraging, and a bit more contact drove xBA to respectable level. Still carries some (post) post-hype profit potential, so he's worth a late dart throw.

| Yr | Tm | AB | R | HR | RBI | SB | BA | xBA | OBP | SLG | OPS | vL | vR | bb% | ct% | Eye | G | L | F | h% | HctX | PX | xPX | hr/f | Spd | SBO | SB% | #Wk | DOM | DIS | RC/G | RAR | BPV | BPX | R$ |
|---|---|---|---|---|---|---|---|---|---|---|---|---|---|---|---|---|---|---|---|---|---|---|---|---|---|---|---|---|---|---|---|---|---|---|---|
| 14 | CHC * | 264 | 38 | 16 | 59 | 1 | 296 | 312 | 365 | 594 | 960 | 701 | 964 | 10 | 73 | 0.41 | 52 | 12 | 36 | 35 | 128 | 230 | 131 | 21% | 91 | 3% | 47% | 6 | 67% | 33% | 7.76 | 27.2 | 127 | 343 | $14 |
| 15 | CHC | 366 | 39 | 10 | 47 | 3 | 262 | 236 | 324 | 399 | 723 | 730 | 720 | 8 | 67 | 0.26 | 42 | 28 | 30 | 37 | 110 | 107 | 123 | 14% | 97 | 4% | 75% | 20 | 30% | 50% | 4.43 | -10.7 | 0 | 0 | $8 |
| 16 | CHC * | 264 | 40 | 12 | 33 | 0 | 224 | 215 | 325 | 394 | 719 | 812 | 749 | 13 | 68 | 0.47 | 40 | 17 | 43 | 28 | 86 | 112 | 91 | 17% | 84 | 0% | 0% | 19 | 47% | 37% | 4.20 | -10.3 | 15 | 43 | $3 |
| 17 | KC * | 370 | 45 | 19 | 52 | 1 | 205 | 217 | 300 | 395 | 695 | 577 | 459 | 12 | 65 | 0.39 | 38 | 18 | 44 | 25 | 82 | 122 | 88 | 7% | 63 | 1% | 100% | 13 | 0% | 69% | 3.81 | -12.2 | 4 | 12 | $2 |
| 18 | KC | 223 | 27 | 9 | 28 | 3 | 265 | 251 | 354 | 466 | 820 | 1064 | 742 | 11 | 69 | 0.41 | 47 | 19 | 34 | 34 | 109 | 144 | 110 | 17% | 93 | 7% | 75% | 12 | 42% | 42% | 5.59 | 7.0 | 43 | 143 | $5 |
| 1st Half | | 223 | 27 | 9 | 28 | 3 | 265 | 251 | 354 | 466 | 820 | 1064 | 742 | 11 | 69 | 0.41 | 47 | 19 | 34 | 34 | 109 | 144 | 110 | 17% | 93 | 7% | 75% | 12 | 42% | 42% | 5.59 | 7.0 | 44 | 147 | $5 |
| 2nd Half | | | | | | | | | | | | | | | | | | | | | | | | | | | | | | | | | | | |
| **19** | **Proj** | **405** | **52** | **16** | **56** | **3** | **245** | **231** | **333** | **421** | **754** | **814** | **730** | **11** | **68** | **0.39** | **43** | **19** | **38** | **32** | **100** | **122** | **105** | **15%** | **88** | **3%** | **74%** | | | | **4.67** | **2.6** | **10** | **35** | **$11** |

## Soto,Juan

Age: 20 Bats: L Pos: LF
Ht: 6' 1" Wt: 185

Health A | LIMA Plan B+
PT/Exp F | Rand Var -1
Consist F | MM 4345

22-70-.292 in 414 AB at WAS. Meteoric rise from Single-A to majors took just six weeks, and he didn't flinch all year. Sure, we can point to GB% stroke, and xPX questions a similar HR pace for 2019. We can also point to advanced plate patience, strong xBA, and elite BPX. As a TEENAGER. Kid will be here for a while.

| Yr | Tm | AB | R | HR | RBI | SB | BA | xBA | OBP | SLG | OPS | vL | vR | bb% | ct% | Eye | G | L | F | h% | HctX | PX | xPX | hr/f | Spd | SBO | SB% | #Wk | DOM | DIS | RC/G | RAR | BPV | BPX | R$ |
|---|---|---|---|---|---|---|---|---|---|---|---|---|---|---|---|---|---|---|---|---|---|---|---|---|---|---|---|---|---|---|---|---|---|---|---|
| 14 | | | | | | | | | | | | | | | | | | | | | | | | | | | | | | | | | | | |
| 15 | | | | | | | | | | | | | | | | | | | | | | | | | | | | | | | | | | | |
| 16 | | | | | | | | | | | | | | | | | | | | | | | | | | | | | | | | | | | |
| 17 | | | | | | | | | | | | | | | | | | | | | | | | | | | | | | | | | | | |
| 18 | WAS * | 445 | 80 | 24 | 79 | 6 | 293 | 277 | 404 | 519 | 922 | 846 | 949 | 16 | 76 | 0.78 | 54 | 17 | 29 | 34 | 98 | 135 | 105 | 25% | 109 | 5% | 75% | 21 | 71% | 19% | 7.54 | 36.4 | 78 | 260 | $23 |
| 1st Half | | 151 | 28 | 10 | 30 | 2 | 321 | 291 | 423 | 588 | 1011 | 1202 | 961 | 15 | 77 | 0.75 | 46 | 21 | 34 | 37 | 110 | 159 | 119 | 26% | 109 | 3% | 100% | 8 | 88% | 0% | 9.45 | 19.5 | 98 | 327 | $14 |
| 2nd Half | | 294 | 52 | 14 | 49 | 4 | 279 | 269 | 394 | 483 | 877 | 673 | 945 | 16 | 76 | 0.79 | 57 | 16 | 27 | 33 | 92 | 122 | 98 | 24% | 113 | 6% | 67% | 13 | 62% | 31% | 6.68 | 17.5 | 69 | 230 | $28 |
| **19** | **Proj** | **532** | **96** | **25** | **95** | **7** | **290** | **272** | **400** | **496** | **897** | **858** | **910** | **16** | **76** | **0.78** | **52** | **18** | **30** | **34** | **99** | **126** | **106** | **21%** | **109** | **5%** | **77%** | | | | **7.14** | **37.8** | **61** | **205** | **$28** |

## Souza,Steven

Age: 30 Bats: R Pos: RF
Ht: 6' 4" Wt: 225

Health F | LIMA Plan B
PT/Exp C | Rand Var +3
Consist D | MM 4415

The injury bug bit back, as a pair of pectoral strains cost him 11 weeks. Power outage just a small-sample blip—HctX/xPX were strong as ever—while efficient SB% should keep the wheels churning. Can't bank on ct% trend to continue, but even a leveling-off should help HR/SB flourish... if he can stay on the field.

| Yr | Tm | AB | R | HR | RBI | SB | BA | xBA | OBP | SLG | OPS | vL | vR | bb% | ct% | Eye | G | L | F | h% | HctX | PX | xPX | hr/f | Spd | SBO | SB% | #Wk | DOM | DIS | RC/G | RAR | BPV | BPX | R$ |
|---|---|---|---|---|---|---|---|---|---|---|---|---|---|---|---|---|---|---|---|---|---|---|---|---|---|---|---|---|---|---|---|---|---|---|---|
| 14 | WAS * | 369 | 48 | 14 | 57 | 19 | 284 | 254 | 356 | 465 | 820 | 2071 | 105 | 10 | 75 | 0.44 | 50 | 13 | 38 | 35 | 122 | 136 | 141 | 33% | 79 | 25% | 70% | 9 | 22% | 78% | 5.72 | 17.3 | 54 | 146 | $21 |
| 15 | TAM | 373 | 59 | 16 | 40 | 12 | 225 | 220 | 318 | 399 | 717 | 730 | 712 | 11 | 61 | 0.32 | 45 | 20 | 35 | 32 | 92 | 138 | 100 | 21% | 104 | 18% | 67% | 21 | 24% | 48% | 3.98 | -10.1 | 11 | 30 | $10 |
| 16 | TAM | 430 | 58 | 17 | 49 | 7 | 247 | 224 | 303 | 409 | 713 | 664 | 731 | 7 | 63 | 0.19 | 41 | 25 | 35 | 35 | 83 | 118 | 112 | 18% | 119 | 13% | 54% | 24 | 25% | 58% | 3.95 | -9.4 | -2 | -6 | $10 |
| 17 | TAM | 523 | 78 | 30 | 78 | 16 | 239 | 246 | 351 | 459 | 810 | 785 | 819 | 14 | 66 | 0.47 | 45 | 21 | 34 | 30 | 91 | 139 | 100 | 26% | 96 | 13% | 80% | 27 | 48% | 26% | 5.33 | 2.2 | 32 | 97 | $17 |
| 18 | ARI | 241 | 21 | 5 | 29 | 6 | 220 | 229 | 309 | 369 | 678 | 776 | 624 | 10 | 69 | 0.37 | 37 | 24 | 39 | 30 | 112 | 106 | 122 | 8% | 106 | 12% | 86% | 18 | 33% | 56% | 3.70 | -5.1 | 15 | 50 | $2 |
| 1st Half | | 43 | 1 | 0 | 1 | 1 | 163 | 143 | 234 | 186 | 420 | 1196 | 265 | 9 | 70 | 0.31 | 47 | 10 | 43 | 23 | 103 | 22 | 81 | 0% | 100 | 20% | 50% | 5 | 0% | 80% | 1.25 | -4.6 | -54 | -180 | -$13 |
| 2nd Half | | 198 | 20 | 5 | 28 | 5 | 232 | 242 | 324 | 409 | 734 | 738 | 730 | 11 | 69 | 0.39 | 35 | 27 | 38 | 31 | 114 | 125 | 131 | 10% | 104 | 10% | 100% | 13 | 46% | 46% | 4.43 | -0.2 | 30 | 100 | $6 |
| **19** | **Proj** | **408** | **53** | **17** | **54** | **11** | **241** | **233** | **326** | **432** | **758** | **871** | **712** | **10** | **66** | **0.34** | **42** | **21** | **37** | **32** | **99** | **131** | **107** | **17%** | **110** | **14%** | **80%** | | | | **4.66** | **2.5** | **24** | **81** | **$14** |

RYAN BLOOMFIELD

## Span,Denard

Age: 35 Bats: L Pos: LF
Ht: 6' 0" Wt: 210

| Health | C | LIMA Plan | B+ |
|---|---|---|---|
| PT/Exp | A | Rand Var | 0 |
| Consist | A | MM | 2345 |

Skills and R$ have been stable the past few seasons, but starting to show small signs of decline: lowest ct% of career; pedestrian SB% eating into green light. Small-sample vL gains likely just a blip, so don't be surprised if AB total continues trending downard, and he falls short of double digit HR and SB.

| Yr Tm | AB | R | HR | RBI | SB | BA | xBA | OBP | SLG | OPS | vL | vR | bb% | ct% | Eye | G | L | F | h% | HctX | PX | xPX | hr/f | Spd | SBO | SB% | #Wk | DOM | DIS | RC/G | RAR | BPV | BPX | R$ |
|---|---|---|---|---|---|---|---|---|---|---|---|---|---|---|---|---|---|---|---|---|---|---|---|---|---|---|---|---|---|---|---|---|---|---|
| 14 WAS | 610 | 94 | 5 | 37 | 31 | 302 | 288 | 355 | 416 | 771 | 694 | 802 | 7 | 89 | 0.77 | 46 | 24 | 30 | 33 | 98 | 80 | 52 | 3% | 134 | 21% | 82% | 27 | 56% | 7% | 5.49 | 30.5 | 78 | 211 | $30 |
| 15 WAS | 246 | 38 | 5 | 22 | 11 | 301 | 301 | 365 | 431 | 796 | 542 | 880 | 9 | 89 | 0.96 | 50 | 24 | 26 | 32 | 95 | 84 | 72 | 9% | 102 | 14% | 100% | 13 | 54% | 23% | 6.07 | 11.3 | 76 | 205 | $11 |
| 16 SF | 572 | 70 | 11 | 53 | 12 | 266 | 282 | 331 | 381 | 712 | 566 | 781 | 8 | 86 | 0.67 | 52 | 23 | 25 | 29 | 87 | 64 | 51 | 9% | 96 | 11% | 63% | 27 | 52% | 30% | 4.25 | -0.4 | 43 | 123 | $15 |
| 17 SF | 497 | 73 | 12 | 43 | 12 | 272 | 283 | 329 | 427 | 756 | 576 | 804 | 7 | 86 | 0.58 | 45 | 21 | 34 | 30 | 88 | 84 | 74 | 8% | 116 | 15% | 63% | 25 | 52% | 20% | 4.73 | -10.4 | 63 | 191 | $15 |
| 18 2 AL | 437 | 63 | 11 | 58 | 9 | 261 | 272 | 341 | 419 | 760 | 830 | 742 | 10 | 82 | 0.65 | 40 | 26 | 33 | 30 | 93 | 89 | 61 | 9% | 103 | 10% | 69% | 28 | 43% | 21% | 4.84 | 3.2 | 52 | 173 | $14 |
| 1st Half | 232 | 40 | 7 | 39 | 6 | 259 | 271 | 352 | 409 | 761 | 730 | 771 | 13 | 81 | 0.77 | 40 | 27 | 33 | 29 | 102 | 88 | 74 | 11% | 84 | 12% | 67% | 15 | 53% | 20% | 4.90 | 2.1 | 47 | 157 | $18 |
| 2nd Half | 205 | 23 | 4 | 19 | 3 | 263 | 274 | 329 | 429 | 758 | 998 | 712 | 8 | 83 | 0.49 | 41 | 26 | 34 | 30 | 84 | 89 | 45 | 7% | 115 | 8% | 75% | 13 | 31% | 23% | 4.74 | 0.9 | 55 | 183 | $9 |
| 19 Proj | **414** | **57** | **9** | **43** | **9** | **269** | **277** | **337** | **418** | **755** | **684** | **775** | **9** | **84** | **0.63** | **44** | **24** | **32** | **30** | **90** | **83** | **61** | **8%** | **108** | **10%** | **74%** | | | | **4.84** | **3.0** | **59** | **197** | **$12** |

## Spangenberg,Cory

Age: 28 Bats: L Pos: 2B 3B
Ht: 6' 0" Wt: 195

| Health | D | LIMA Plan | D |
|---|---|---|---|
| PT/Exp | D | Rand Var | -3 |
| Consist | B | MM | 2513 |

7-25-.235 with 6 SB in 298 AB at SD. PX/SB% gains led to some early value, but all the whiffs were too much to overcome. Still hard to buy into hr/f given modest power, and doesn't hit many FB anyway. Needs ct% rebound to put wheels to use. Odds are, he'll do more shuffling between Triple-A and majors.

| Yr Tm | AB | R | HR | RBI | SB | BA | xBA | OBP | SLG | OPS | vL | vR | bb% | ct% | Eye | G | L | F | h% | HctX | PX | xPX | hr/f | Spd | SBO | SB% | #Wk | DOM | DIS | RC/G | RAR | BPV | BPX | R$ |
|---|---|---|---|---|---|---|---|---|---|---|---|---|---|---|---|---|---|---|---|---|---|---|---|---|---|---|---|---|---|---|---|---|---|---|
| 14 SD * | 343 | 38 | 4 | 27 | 15 | 291 | 250 | 320 | 415 | 735 | 667 | 795 | 4 | 75 | 0.17 | 45 | 26 | 30 | 38 | 86 | 93 | 113 | 14% | 135 | 32% | 56% | 5 | 20% | 40% | 4.30 | 5.9 | 23 | 62 | $14 |
| 15 SD * | 341 | 42 | 5 | 24 | 12 | 260 | 262 | 321 | 385 | 706 | 703 | 738 | 8 | 76 | 0.38 | 50 | 25 | 25 | 33 | 84 | 86 | 74 | 8% | 143 | 17% | 75% | 20 | 40% | 45% | 4.25 | -4.2 | 35 | 95 | $9 |
| 16 SD | 48 | 6 | 1 | 8 | 1 | 229 | 251 | 302 | 354 | 656 | 1074 | 448 | 8 | 73 | 0.31 | 69 | 16 | 16 | 29 | 51 | 72 | 15 | 20% | 119 | 8% | 100% | 3 | 0% | 67% | 3.49 | -2.1 | 2 | 6 | -$1 |
| 17 SD * | 510 | 62 | 14 | 51 | 13 | 265 | 247 | 314 | 395 | 709 | 487 | 811 | 7 | 73 | 0.27 | 49 | 23 | 28 | 34 | 86 | 79 | 76 | 15% | 119 | 14% | 70% | 24 | 17% | 58% | 4.25 | -15.7 | 6 | 18 | $14 |
| 18 SD * | 386 | 44 | 9 | 35 | 8 | 241 | 224 | 294 | 381 | 675 | 417 | 725 | 7 | 62 | 0.20 | 48 | 27 | 25 | 36 | 81 | 102 | 93 | 15% | 142 | 10% | 89% | 26 | 15% | 62% | 3.83 | -9.6 | -11 | -37 | $7 |
| 1st Half | 223 | 27 | 7 | 25 | 6 | 229 | 232 | 252 | 386 | 638 | 464 | 686 | 3 | 64 | 0.09 | 43 | 30 | 27 | 32 | 84 | 105 | 102 | 20% | 124 | 16% | 85% | 14 | 21% | 57% | 3.25 | -8.5 | -14 | -47 | $10 |
| 2nd Half | 163 | 17 | 2 | 11 | 2 | 259 | 212 | 347 | 375 | 722 | 379 | 773 | 12 | 59 | 0.33 | 56 | 23 | 21 | 42 | 77 | 97 | 79 | 6% | 150 | 5% | 100% | 12 | 8% | 67% | 4.57 | 0.3 | -15 | -50 | $4 |
| 19 Proj | **292** | **34** | **6** | **25** | **7** | **244** | **236** | **304** | **376** | **680** | **476** | **741** | **7** | **68** | **0.25** | **50** | **25** | **25** | **34** | **83** | **90** | **86** | **12%** | **139** | **14%** | **74%** | | | | **3.80** | **-3.3** | **-4** | **-14** | **$7** |

## Springer,George

Age: 29 Bats: R Pos: CF RF
Ht: 6' 3" Wt: 215

| Health | C | LIMA Plan | B |
|---|---|---|---|
| PT/Exp | A | Rand Var | 0 |
| Consist | C | MM | 3235 |

While thumb, quad injuries surely played role in 2nd half power dip, wasn't quite himself in 1st half, either. PX, HctX a notch below usual levels; low LD% held down h% and BA. Power should return, but low SB% says SB likely won't. His floor is rock solid, but ceiling seems to be lowering with each passing year.

| Yr Tm | AB | R | HR | RBI | SB | BA | xBA | OBP | SLG | OPS | vL | vR | bb% | ct% | Eye | G | L | F | h% | HctX | PX | xPX | hr/f | Spd | SBO | SB% | #Wk | DOM | DIS | RC/G | RAR | BPV | BPX | R$ |
|---|---|---|---|---|---|---|---|---|---|---|---|---|---|---|---|---|---|---|---|---|---|---|---|---|---|---|---|---|---|---|---|---|---|---|
| 14 HOU * | 346 | 57 | 22 | 57 | 8 | 239 | 241 | 328 | 475 | 802 | 774 | 811 | 11 | 62 | 0.34 | 45 | 15 | 39 | 32 | 105 | 191 | 161 | 28% | 129 | 11% | 80% | 14 | 50% | 36% | 5.23 | 13.9 | 63 | 170 | $14 |
| 15 HOU | 388 | 59 | 16 | 41 | 16 | 276 | 261 | 367 | 459 | 826 | 936 | 767 | 11 | 72 | 0.46 | 45 | 24 | 30 | 35 | 106 | 127 | 112 | 19% | 120 | 17% | 80% | 19 | 58% | 32% | 5.84 | 14.8 | 49 | 132 | $18 |
| 16 HOU | 644 | 116 | 29 | 82 | 9 | 261 | 259 | 359 | 457 | 815 | 945 | 769 | 12 | 72 | 0.49 | 48 | 20 | 31 | 32 | 99 | 122 | 111 | 20% | 125 | 10% | 47% | 27 | 41% | 26% | 5.27 | 17.2 | 50 | 143 | $22 |
| 17 HOU | 548 | 112 | 34 | 85 | 5 | 283 | 285 | 367 | 522 | 889 | 972 | 860 | 10 | 80 | 0.58 | 48 | 18 | 34 | 30 | 119 | 128 | 112 | 23% | 99 | 8% | 42% | 25 | 64% | 8% | 6.38 | 25.5 | 73 | 221 | $24 |
| 18 HOU | 544 | 102 | 22 | 71 | 6 | 265 | 249 | 346 | 434 | 780 | 834 | 757 | 10 | 78 | 0.52 | 49 | 16 | 35 | 31 | 95 | 101 | 100 | 15% | 111 | 6% | 60% | 28 | 46% | 25% | 5.07 | 16.3 | 47 | 157 | $20 |
| 1st Half | 328 | 60 | 15 | 42 | 5 | 253 | 259 | 332 | 442 | 775 | 907 | 715 | 10 | 79 | 0.52 | 49 | 15 | 35 | 28 | 100 | 110 | 114 | 16% | 105 | 9% | 63% | 15 | 47% | 20% | 4.84 | 6.8 | 57 | 190 | $24 |
| 2nd Half | 216 | 42 | 7 | 29 | 1 | 282 | 234 | 366 | 421 | 787 | 705 | 817 | 11 | 75 | 0.53 | 49 | 17 | 34 | 35 | 88 | 86 | 78 | 13% | 119 | 3% | 50% | 13 | 46% | 31% | 5.40 | 7.7 | 31 | 103 | $14 |
| 19 Proj | **562** | **106** | **26** | **77** | **7** | **271** | **256** | **356** | **460** | **816** | **863** | **798** | **11** | **76** | **0.50** | **49** | **18** | **34** | **32** | **102** | **112** | **105** | **18%** | **115** | **7%** | **56%** | | | | **5.49** | **22.1** | **41** | **137** | **$24** |

## Stanton,Giancarlo

Age: 29 Bats: R Pos: DH RF LF
Ht: 6' 6" Wt: 245

| Health | B | LIMA Plan | B+ |
|---|---|---|---|
| PT/Exp | A | Rand Var | -2 |
| Consist | F | MM | 5235 |

Looks like power took a step back, but 50-HR seasons are outliers and the extent of this drop-off is historically typical. Previous year's uptick in hr/f, ct% proved unsustainable, and downward xPX trend could be concerning. Still, we know immense power is lurking. Best news: took another step toward shedding injury-prone tag.

| Yr Tm | AB | R | HR | RBI | SB | BA | xBA | OBP | SLG | OPS | vL | vR | bb% | ct% | Eye | G | L | F | h% | HctX | PX | xPX | hr/f | Spd | SBO | SB% | #Wk | DOM | DIS | RC/G | RAR | BPV | BPX | R$ |
|---|---|---|---|---|---|---|---|---|---|---|---|---|---|---|---|---|---|---|---|---|---|---|---|---|---|---|---|---|---|---|---|---|---|---|
| 14 MIA | 539 | 89 | 37 | 105 | 13 | 288 | 278 | 395 | 555 | 950 | 1075 | 920 | 15 | 68 | 0.55 | 41 | 20 | 39 | 36 | 120 | 206 | 145 | 26% | 81 | 8% | 93% | 24 | 75% | 13% | 7.94 | 58.8 | 94 | 254 | $35 |
| 15 MIA | 279 | 47 | 27 | 67 | 4 | 265 | 282 | 346 | 606 | 952 | 1172 | 893 | 11 | 66 | 0.36 | 35 | 20 | 45 | 30 | 142 | 236 | 209 | 32% | 90 | 9% | 67% | 12 | 75% | 25% | 7.14 | 13.7 | 103 | 278 | $16 |
| 16 MIA | 413 | 56 | 27 | 74 | 0 | 240 | 243 | 326 | 489 | 815 | 947 | 779 | 11 | 66 | 0.36 | 40 | 17 | 43 | 29 | 115 | 167 | 156 | 23% | 85 | 0% | 0% | 24 | 46% | 46% | 5.28 | -2.6 | 47 | 134 | $10 |
| 17 MIA | 597 | 123 | 59 | 132 | 2 | 281 | 296 | 376 | 631 | 1007 | 1213 | 950 | 12 | 73 | 0.52 | 45 | 16 | 39 | 29 | 114 | 197 | 131 | 34% | 59 | 2% | 50% | 27 | 74% | 15% | 8.23 | 56.8 | 93 | 282 | $32 |
| 18 NYY | 617 | 102 | 38 | 100 | 5 | 266 | 250 | 343 | 509 | 852 | 1036 | 792 | 10 | 66 | 0.33 | 45 | 19 | 37 | 34 | 103 | 164 | 113 | 25% | 105 | 3% | 100% | 27 | 52% | 37% | 6.07 | 27.8 | 48 | 160 | $26 |
| 1st Half | 308 | 47 | 19 | 46 | 2 | 263 | 245 | 338 | 503 | 841 | 1199 | 713 | 9 | 65 | 0.29 | 49 | 17 | 34 | 34 | 104 | 162 | 125 | 27% | 116 | 3% | 100% | 15 | 53% | 33% | 5.79 | 11.4 | 44 | 147 | $24 |
| 2nd Half | 309 | 55 | 19 | 54 | 3 | 269 | 253 | 348 | 515 | 863 | 849 | 867 | 11 | 67 | 0.38 | 41 | 20 | 39 | 34 | 101 | 167 | 102 | 23% | 91 | 4% | 100% | 12 | 50% | 42% | 6.35 | 16.4 | 52 | 173 | $29 |
| 19 Proj | **592** | **102** | **43** | **110** | **4** | **267** | **261** | **351** | **540** | **890** | **1047** | **844** | **11** | **68** | **0.39** | **43** | **18** | **39** | **32** | **110** | **176** | **129** | **27%** | **87** | **3%** | **84%** | | | | **6.55** | **34.7** | **55** | **185** | **$29** |

## Stassi,Max

Age: 28 Bats: R Pos: CA
Ht: 5' 10" Wt: 200

| Health | B | LIMA Plan | D |
|---|---|---|---|
| PT/Exp | F | Rand Var | -2 |
| Consist | B | MM | 2101 |

Teased with early power in first extended MLB opportunity, especially vL. But then he crashed. GB tilt became more extreme, while hr/f plummeted; ct% woes persisted; went 5-for-60 vL in last four months. Power potential remains in question, but can confirm he'll be a BA drag—if he even gets another shot.

| Yr Tm | AB | R | HR | RBI | SB | BA | xBA | OBP | SLG | OPS | vL | vR | bb% | ct% | Eye | G | L | F | h% | HctX | PX | xPX | hr/f | Spd | SBO | SB% | #Wk | DOM | DIS | RC/G | RAR | BPV | BPX | R$ |
|---|---|---|---|---|---|---|---|---|---|---|---|---|---|---|---|---|---|---|---|---|---|---|---|---|---|---|---|---|---|---|---|---|---|---|
| 14 HOU * | 412 | 37 | 7 | 36 | 1 | 214 | 231 | 243 | 316 | 559 | 1000 | 765 | 4 | 70 | 0.13 | 21 | 36 | 43 | 29 | 86 | 88 | 128 | 0% | 88 | 1% | 100% | 4 | 50% | 50% | 2.50 | -10.4 | -14 | -38 | $0 |
| 15 HOU * | 309 | 29 | 11 | 31 | 1 | 184 | 234 | 230 | 318 | 548 | 667 | 1278 | 6 | 63 | 0.16 | 30 | 40 | 30 | 25 | 74 | 98 | 59 | 33% | 100 | 3% | 37% | 5 | 20% | 80% | 2.25 | -14.7 | -25 | -68 | -$2 |
| 16 HOU * | 256 | 17 | 5 | 25 | 1 | 187 | 218 | 233 | 298 | 531 | 0 | 200 | 6 | 67 | 0.18 | 75 | 13 | 13 | 26 | 34 | 80 | -24 | 0% | 90 | 2% | 100% | 6 | 0% | 67% | 2.19 | -13.6 | -26 | -74 | -$4 |
| 17 HOU * | 274 | 47 | 12 | 30 | 1 | 211 | 201 | 299 | 392 | 691 | 731 | 806 | 11 | 67 | 0.38 | 38 | 10 | 52 | 26 | 91 | 117 | 105 | 18% | 80 | 3% | 37% | 6 | 33% | 50% | 3.73 | -3.4 | 12 | 36 | $2 |
| 18 HOU | 221 | 28 | 8 | 27 | 0 | 226 | 224 | 316 | 394 | 710 | 681 | 729 | 9 | 67 | 0.31 | 52 | 18 | 31 | 30 | 88 | 121 | 112 | 18% | 82 | 0% | 0% | 28 | 29% | 57% | 3.88 | 3.4 | 8 | 27 | $2 |
| 1st Half | 138 | 21 | 7 | 22 | 0 | 254 | 243 | 335 | 486 | 821 | 936 | 734 | 9 | 66 | 0.30 | 48 | 15 | 36 | 33 | 93 | 168 | 132 | 21% | 87 | 0% | 0% | 15 | 47% | 40% | 5.35 | 7.7 | 45 | 150 | $6 |
| 2nd Half | 83 | 7 | 1 | 5 | 0 | 181 | 197 | 284 | 241 | 525 | 205 | 720 | 10 | 67 | 0.33 | 57 | 21 | 21 | 25 | 80 | 44 | 80 | 8% | 90 | 0% | 0% | 13 | 8% | 77% | 1.96 | -4.0 | -46 | -153 | -$5 |
| 19 Proj | **223** | **26** | **6** | **23** | **0** | **215** | **219** | **304** | **347** | **650** | **525** | **733** | **9** | **67** | **0.30** | **54** | **19** | **27** | **29** | **85** | **93** | **101** | **15%** | **86** | **1%** | **62%** | | | | **3.20** | **-1.7** | **-24** | **-81** | **$2** |

## Stewart,Christin

Age: 25 Bats: L Pos: LF
Ht: 6' 0" Wt: 205

| Health | A | LIMA Plan | D+ |
|---|---|---|---|
| PT/Exp | C | Rand Var | -1 |
| Consist | B | MM | 3003 |

2-10-.267 in 60 AB at DET. Hit 13 HR through May at Triple-A, but couldn't sustain power all year. Eye gains encouraging and held strong after September call-up, though still has work to do in order to boost BA. Should be ready for spring after October abdominal surgery, but at least a year away from making major impact.

| Yr Tm | AB | R | HR | RBI | SB | BA | xBA | OBP | SLG | OPS | vL | vR | bb% | ct% | Eye | G | L | F | h% | HctX | PX | xPX | hr/f | Spd | SBO | SB% | #Wk | DOM | DIS | RC/G | RAR | BPV | BPX | R$ |
|---|---|---|---|---|---|---|---|---|---|---|---|---|---|---|---|---|---|---|---|---|---|---|---|---|---|---|---|---|---|---|---|---|---|---|
| 14 | | | | | | | | | | | | | | | | | | | | | | | | | | | | | | | | | | |
| 15 | | | | | | | | | | | | | | | | | | | | | | | | | | | | | | | | | | |
| 16 aa | 87 | 13 | 5 | 15 | 0 | 188 | | 267 | 368 | 635 | | | 10 | 68 | 0.34 | | | | 22 | | 111 | | | 96 | 0% | 0% | | | | 3.09 | | 10 | 29 | -$1 |
| 17 aa | 485 | 55 | 23 | 71 | 2 | 228 | | 294 | 438 | 733 | | | 9 | 69 | 0.31 | | | | 28 | | 131 | | | 95 | 2% | 100% | | | | 4.29 | | 30 | 91 | $7 |
| 18 DET * | 504 | 66 | 22 | 75 | 0 | 240 | 235 | 328 | 425 | 753 | 629 | 822 | 12 | 74 | 0.51 | 38 | 19 | 44 | 28 | 97 | 110 | 108 | 10% | 104 | 0% | 0% | 3 | 67% | 33% | 4.68 | 1.4 | 40 | 133 | $12 |
| 1st Half | 268 | 33 | 13 | 38 | 0 | 241 | 258 | 314 | 448 | 762 | | | 10 | 75 | 0.43 | | | | 27 | | 122 | | | 101 | 0% | 0% | | | | 4.73 | | 50 | 167 | $13 |
| 2nd Half | 236 | 32 | 9 | 37 | 0 | 238 | 221 | 343 | 399 | 743 | 629 | 822 | 14 | 73 | 0.59 | 38 | 19 | 44 | 29 | 95 | 95 | 108 | 10% | 109 | 0% | 0% | 3 | 67% | 33% | 4.59 | 0.0 | 29 | 97 | $11 |
| 19 Proj | **375** | **46** | **14** | **56** | **1** | **235** | **226** | **323** | **403** | **726** | **547** | **760** | **11** | **72** | **0.43** | **38** | **19** | **44** | **29** | **86** | **105** | **97** | **12%** | **98** | **2%** | **38%** | | | | **4.24** | **-4.0** | **15** | **49** | **$8** |

## Story,Trevor

Age: 26 Bats: R Pos: SS
Ht: 6' 1" Wt: 210

| Health | B | LIMA Plan | D+ |
|---|---|---|---|
| PT/Exp | B | Rand Var | -2 |
| Consist | F | MM | 5435 |

Power/speed combo has always been outstanding, but huge leaps in ct%, SBO took game to another level, especially in 2nd half. Track record says we can't expect full BA/SB repeat, but SB% supports green light, and the landing should be softer this time around. Assuming elbow is ok, looks like an upper tier option.

| Yr Tm | AB | R | HR | RBI | SB | BA | xBA | OBP | SLG | OPS | vL | vR | bb% | ct% | Eye | G | L | F | h% | HctX | PX | xPX | hr/f | Spd | SBO | SB% | #Wk | DOM | DIS | RC/G | RAR | BPV | BPX | R$ |
|---|---|---|---|---|---|---|---|---|---|---|---|---|---|---|---|---|---|---|---|---|---|---|---|---|---|---|---|---|---|---|---|---|---|---|
| 14 aa | 205 | 23 | 8 | 16 | 2 | 192 | | 269 | 356 | 625 | | | 10 | 59 | 0.26 | | | | 28 | | 147 | | | 108 | 8% | 69% | | | | 3.00 | | 8 | 22 | $0 |
| 15 a/a | 512 | 60 | 16 | 58 | 16 | 259 | | 309 | 463 | 771 | | | 7 | 73 | 0.26 | | | | 33 | | 144 | | | 117 | 18% | 83% | | | | 4.96 | | 56 | 151 | $17 |
| 16 COL | 372 | 67 | 27 | 72 | 8 | 272 | 259 | 341 | 567 | 909 | 975 | 883 | 8 | 65 | 0.27 | 29 | 24 | 47 | 34 | 119 | 200 | 191 | 24% | 111 | 15% | 62% | 17 | 53% | 12% | 6.41 | 19.3 | 72 | 206 | $18 |
| 17 COL | 503 | 68 | 24 | 82 | 7 | 239 | 224 | 308 | 457 | 765 | 1034 | 668 | 9 | 62 | 0.26 | 34 | 18 | 48 | 33 | 101 | 156 | 166 | 16% | 116 | 8% | 78% | 26 | 38% | 38% | 4.69 | 2.5 | 27 | 82 | $12 |
| 18 COL | 598 | 88 | 37 | 108 | 27 | 291 | 271 | 348 | 567 | 914 | 1069 | 852 | 7 | 72 | 0.28 | 34 | 23 | 43 | 35 | 118 | 172 | 155 | 20% | 117 | 24% | 82% | 28 | 57% | 25% | 6.99 | 53.5 | 77 | 257 | $38 |
| 1st Half | 318 | 44 | 16 | 58 | 10 | 274 | 256 | 339 | 519 | 858 | 967 | 806 | 8 | 71 | 0.32 | 32 | 22 | 46 | 34 | 122 | 156 | 160 | 15% | 128 | 19% | 71% | 15 | 60% | 27% | 5.97 | 18.5 | 67 | 223 | $33 |
| 2nd Half | 280 | 44 | 21 | 50 | 17 | 311 | 289 | 358 | 621 | 979 | 1216 | 899 | 6 | 73 | 0.23 | 37 | 23 | 40 | 36 | 113 | 190 | 150 | 26% | 102 | 31% | 89% | 13 | 54% | 23% | 8.29 | 33.1 | 87 | 290 | $45 |
| 19 Proj | **582** | **86** | **35** | **100** | **19** | **271** | **255** | **331** | **537** | **868** | **1047** | **801** | **8** | **68** | **0.26** | **34** | **21** | **45** | **34** | **112** | **175** | **164** | **20%** | **119** | **19%** | **80%** | | | | **6.13** | **36.5** | **66** | **220** | **$32** |

BRIAN RUDD

## Suarez,Eugenio

| | | | | | |
|---|---|---|---|---|---|
| Age: 27 | Bats: R | Pos: 3B | Health A | LIMA Plan B | |
| Ht: 5' 11" | Wt: 213 | | PT/Exp A | Rand Var -3 | |
| | | | Consist C | MM 4135 | |

Big step forward that came with plenty of skill support. HR spike driven by PX/xPX gains that held all year; HctX confirms he mashed; no longer a liability vR. Line drive stroke sets a decent BA floor, so we're not too worried about 2nd half ct% dip. Breakouts rarely get repeated, but he should come close.

| Yr Tm | AB | R | HR | RBI | SB | BA | xBA | OBP | SLG | OPS | vL | vR | bb% | ct% | Eye | G | L | F | h% | HctX | PX | xPX | hr/f | Spd | SBO | SB% | #Wk | DOM | DIS | RC/G | RAR | BPV | BPX | R$ |
|---|---|---|---|---|---|---|---|---|---|---|---|---|---|---|---|---|---|---|---|---|---|---|---|---|---|---|---|---|---|---|---|---|---|---|
| 14 DET * | 442 | 57 | 10 | 50 | 10 | 246 | 231 | 306 | 379 | 685 | 656 | 650 | 8 | 74 | 0.33 | 35 | 22 | 43 | 31 | 87 | 107 | 109 | 5% | 97 | 13% | 70% | 17 | 29% | 59% | 3.88 | 2.2 | 26 | 70 | $11 |
| 15 CIN * | 575 | 67 | 21 | 69 | 7 | 263 | 248 | 310 | 429 | 739 | 819 | 744 | 6 | 75 | 0.28 | 41 | 21 | 38 | 32 | 95 | 111 | 105 | 12% | 107 | 9% | 54% | 18 | 39% | 39% | 4.47 | -3.4 | 37 | 100 | $17 |
| 16 CIN | 565 | 78 | 21 | 70 | 11 | 248 | 241 | 317 | 411 | 728 | 882 | 683 | 8 | 73 | 0.33 | 41 | 22 | 38 | 31 | 103 | 104 | 105 | 13% | 93 | 11% | 69% | 27 | 30% | 37% | 4.26 | -12.0 | 20 | 57 | $15 |
| 17 CIN | 534 | 87 | 26 | 82 | 4 | 260 | 258 | 367 | 461 | 828 | 896 | 806 | 13 | 72 | 0.57 | 39 | 24 | 37 | 31 | 99 | 118 | 116 | 18% | 82 | 5% | 44% | 27 | 37% | 37% | 5.58 | 4.3 | 37 | 112 | $16 |
| 18 CIN | 527 | 79 | 34 | 104 | 1 | 283 | 269 | 366 | 526 | 892 | 1020 | 840 | 11 | 73 | 0.45 | 38 | 25 | 37 | 33 | 131 | 143 | 150 | 23% | 93 | 1% | 50% | 27 | 56% | 26% | 6.70 | 30.1 | 58 | 193 | $25 |
| 1st Half | 248 | 38 | 16 | 60 | 1 | 306 | 289 | 391 | 569 | 960 | 1079 | 911 | 12 | 79 | 0.62 | 37 | 25 | 39 | 34 | 144 | 145 | 147 | 21% | 107 | 1% | 100% | 14 | 71% | 14% | 8.14 | 24.5 | 88 | 293 | $28 |
| 2nd Half | 279 | 41 | 18 | 44 | 0 | 262 | 250 | 344 | 487 | 831 | 967 | 775 | 10 | 68 | 0.35 | 40 | 24 | 35 | 32 | 119 | 140 | 152 | 26% | 78 | 1% | 0% | 13 | 38% | 38% | 5.57 | 8.6 | 30 | 100 | $21 |
| 19 Proj | 563 | 84 | 30 | 93 | 4 | 267 | 256 | 352 | 477 | 829 | 939 | 789 | 11 | 73 | 0.44 | 39 | 24 | 37 | 32 | 114 | 127 | 130 | 19% | 90 | 5% | 57% | | | | 5.65 | 18.7 | 34 | 114 | $21 |

## Suzuki,Ichiro

| | | | | | |
|---|---|---|---|---|---|
| Age: 45 | Bats: L | Pos: LF | Health A | LIMA Plan F | |
| Ht: 5' 11" | Wt: 175 | | PT/Exp F | Rand Var +1 | |
| | | | Consist B | MM 0000 | |

Might get an early-season swan song, but this seems like the end. If so, let's tip our cap: $407 in career earnings, including a $32 average from 2004-10; 600+ AB every season from 2001-12; some mind-blowing career BA/SB skills in majors: 89% ct%, .311 BA, 179 Spd. Destination: Cooperstown.

| Yr Tm | AB | R | HR | RBI | SB | BA | xBA | OBP | SLG | OPS | vL | vR | bb% | ct% | Eye | G | L | F | h% | HctX | PX | xPX | hr/f | Spd | SBO | SB% | #Wk | DOM | DIS | RC/G | RAR | BPV | BPX | R$ |
|---|---|---|---|---|---|---|---|---|---|---|---|---|---|---|---|---|---|---|---|---|---|---|---|---|---|---|---|---|---|---|---|---|---|---|
| 14 NYY | 359 | 42 | 1 | 22 | 15 | 284 | 255 | 324 | 340 | 664 | 807 | 632 | 5 | 81 | 0.31 | 58 | 22 | 20 | 35 | 67 | 45 | 22 | 2% | 135 | 17% | 83% | 27 | 22% | 48% | 4.03 | 3.5 | 14 | 38 | $12 |
| 15 MIA | 398 | 45 | 1 | 21 | 11 | 229 | 250 | 282 | 279 | 561 | 723 | 514 | 7 | 87 | 0.61 | 58 | 18 | 23 | 26 | 52 | 26 | 28 | 1% | 178 | 15% | 69% | 27 | 22% | 44% | 2.61 | -21.8 | 39 | 105 | $3 |
| 16 MIA | 327 | 48 | 1 | 22 | 10 | 291 | 286 | 354 | 376 | 730 | 859 | 700 | 8 | 87 | 0.71 | 48 | 28 | 24 | 33 | 77 | 51 | 50 | 1% | 138 | 12% | 83% | 27 | 44% | 22% | 4.82 | 5.0 | 49 | 140 | $10 |
| 17 MIA | 196 | 19 | 3 | 20 | 1 | 255 | 240 | 318 | 332 | 649 | 796 | 603 | 8 | 82 | 0.49 | 57 | 19 | 24 | 30 | 62 | 44 | 25 | 8% | 90 | 3% | 50% | 27 | 33% | 41% | 3.52 | -11.0 | 8 | 24 | $1 |
| 18 SEA | 44 | 5 | 0 | 0 | 0 | 205 | 187 | 255 | 205 | 460 | 1136 | 278 | 6 | 84 | 0.43 | 56 | 14 | 31 | 24 | 42 | 0 | 42 | 0% | 120 | 0% | 0% | 6 | 0% | 83% | 1.67 | -3.9 | -12 | -40 | -$3 |
| 1st Half | 44 | 5 | 0 | 0 | 0 | 205 | 187 | 255 | 205 | 460 | 1136 | 278 | 6 | 84 | 0.43 | 56 | 14 | 31 | 24 | 42 | 0 | 42 | 0% | 120 | 0% | 0% | 6 | 0% | 83% | 1.67 | -4.0 | -13 | -43 | -$3 |
| 2nd Half | | | | | | | | | | | | | | | | | | | | | | | | | | | | | | | | | | |
| 19 Proj | | | | | | | | | | | | | | | | | | | | | | | | | | | | | | | | | | |

## Suzuki,Kurt

| | | | | | |
|---|---|---|---|---|---|
| Age: 35 | Bats: R | Pos: CA | Health A | LIMA Plan D+ | |
| Ht: 5' 11" | Wt: 210 | | PT/Exp D | Rand Var 0 | |
| | | | Consist D | MM 2043 | |

Couldn't repeat 2017 HR spike, but kept late-career surge going with worthy encore. Traded fly balls for line drives, which cut into power despite another HctX uptick. Bat-to-ball skills build the foundation for another strong BA, and should approach double-digit HR. You could do far worse as your second catcher.

| Yr Tm | AB | R | HR | RBI | SB | BA | xBA | OBP | SLG | OPS | vL | vR | bb% | ct% | Eye | G | L | F | h% | HctX | PX | xPX | hr/f | Spd | SBO | SB% | #Wk | DOM | DIS | RC/G | RAR | BPV | BPX | R$ |
|---|---|---|---|---|---|---|---|---|---|---|---|---|---|---|---|---|---|---|---|---|---|---|---|---|---|---|---|---|---|---|---|---|---|---|
| 14 MIN | 452 | 37 | 3 | 61 | 0 | 288 | 268 | 345 | 383 | 727 | 810 | 695 | 7 | 90 | 0.74 | 44 | 22 | 34 | 32 | 100 | 76 | 82 | 2% | 69 | 1% | 0% | 27 | 56% | 15% | 4.58 | 14.2 | 56 | 151 | $11 |
| 15 MIN | 433 | 36 | 5 | 50 | 0 | 240 | 229 | 296 | 314 | 610 | 658 | 587 | 6 | 86 | 0.49 | 43 | 19 | 38 | 27 | 100 | 50 | 84 | 4% | 75 | 0% | 0% | 26 | 38% | 35% | 3.03 | -10.0 | 22 | 59 | $3 |
| 16 MIN | 345 | 34 | 8 | 49 | 0 | 258 | 270 | 301 | 403 | 704 | 745 | 685 | 5 | 86 | 0.38 | 40 | 21 | 39 | 28 | 103 | 88 | 79 | 7% | 57 | 0% | 0% | 26 | 54% | 27% | 4.08 | -3.2 | 44 | 126 | $5 |
| 17 ATL | 276 | 38 | 19 | 50 | 0 | 283 | 284 | 351 | 536 | 887 | 1191 | 806 | 6 | 86 | 0.44 | 35 | 18 | 47 | 27 | 116 | 123 | 124 | 17% | 61 | 0% | 0% | 27 | 56% | 33% | 6.18 | 16.5 | 73 | 221 | $10 |
| 18 ATL | 347 | 45 | 12 | 50 | 0 | 271 | 281 | 332 | 444 | 776 | 822 | 761 | 6 | 88 | 0.51 | 35 | 23 | 41 | 28 | 125 | 97 | 105 | 9% | 49 | 0% | 0% | 27 | 56% | 19% | 4.88 | 13.5 | 56 | 187 | $9 |
| 1st Half | 188 | 28 | 8 | 28 | 0 | 287 | 293 | 352 | 484 | 836 | 923 | 805 | 7 | 89 | 0.67 | 34 | 24 | 42 | 29 | 122 | 106 | 94 | 11% | 58 | 0% | 0% | 15 | 67% | 13% | 5.83 | 12.5 | 73 | 243 | $12 |
| 2nd Half | 159 | 17 | 4 | 22 | 0 | 252 | 267 | 309 | 396 | 705 | 694 | 708 | 5 | 86 | 0.36 | 37 | 22 | 40 | 27 | 128 | 86 | 118 | 7% | 54 | 0% | 0% | 12 | 42% | 25% | 3.88 | 2.0 | 41 | 137 | $5 |
| 19 Proj | 297 | 35 | 11 | 45 | 0 | 269 | 272 | 328 | 440 | 768 | 850 | 740 | 6 | 87 | 0.45 | 37 | 21 | 42 | 28 | 117 | 95 | 105 | 10% | 57 | 0% | 0% | | | | 4.75 | 11.1 | 45 | 150 | $9 |

## Swanson,Dansby

| | | | | | |
|---|---|---|---|---|---|
| Age: 25 | Bats: R | Pos: SS | Health A | LIMA Plan B | |
| Ht: 6' 1" | Wt: 190 | | PT/Exp C | Rand Var 0 | |
| | | | Consist B | MM 1315 | |

Wrist injury slowed hot start (.289 BA through April), and while this was a step forward, it's hard to see further gains. Stagnant xBA offers zero BA upside, power skills question attempt to add loft and shaky SB% caps SB ceiling. Still has time, but another year removed from prospect hype with few signs he'll deliver.

| Yr Tm | AB | R | HR | RBI | SB | BA | xBA | OBP | SLG | OPS | vL | vR | bb% | ct% | Eye | G | L | F | h% | HctX | PX | xPX | hr/f | Spd | SBO | SB% | #Wk | DOM | DIS | RC/G | RAR | BPV | BPX | R$ |
|---|---|---|---|---|---|---|---|---|---|---|---|---|---|---|---|---|---|---|---|---|---|---|---|---|---|---|---|---|---|---|---|---|---|---|
| 14 | | | | | | | | | | | | | | | | | | | | | | | | | | | | | | | | | | |
| 15 | | | | | | | | | | | | | | | | | | | | | | | | | | | | | | | | | | |
| 16 ATL * | 462 | 74 | 10 | 62 | 10 | 258 | 243 | 331 | 382 | 713 | 1015 | 771 | 10 | 75 | 0.44 | 46 | 23 | 31 | 32 | 106 | 75 | 97 | 10% | 162 | 9% | 82% | 8 | 25% | 63% | 4.39 | -3.0 | 31 | 89 | $13 |
| 17 ATL * | 526 | 63 | 7 | 55 | 4 | 230 | 239 | 314 | 323 | 636 | 741 | 610 | 11 | 75 | 0.49 | 47 | 23 | 29 | 29 | 89 | 60 | 73 | 6% | 107 | 4% | 56% | 26 | 19% | 42% | 3.32 | -19.2 | 5 | 15 | $4 |
| 18 ATL | 478 | 51 | 14 | 59 | 10 | 238 | 240 | 304 | 395 | 699 | 662 | 709 | 8 | 74 | 0.36 | 42 | 20 | 38 | 29 | 98 | 99 | 89 | 10% | 121 | 12% | 71% | 26 | 31% | 23% | 3.98 | 2.2 | 32 | 107 | $11 |
| 1st Half | 258 | 29 | 7 | 31 | 3 | 252 | 247 | 301 | 422 | 723 | 683 | 735 | 6 | 72 | 0.24 | 42 | 22 | 36 | 32 | 92 | 113 | 106 | 10% | 128 | 7% | 75% | 14 | 29% | 29% | 4.28 | 2.4 | 33 | 110 | $11 |
| 2nd Half | 220 | 22 | 7 | 28 | 7 | 223 | 231 | 307 | 364 | 670 | 634 | 680 | 11 | 77 | 0.53 | 43 | 18 | 39 | 26 | 105 | 83 | 70 | 10% | 110 | 17% | 70% | 12 | 33% | 17% | 3.63 | -2.3 | 30 | 100 | $11 |
| 19 Proj | 506 | 60 | 11 | 60 | 9 | 236 | 236 | 309 | 361 | 670 | 702 | 662 | 10 | 75 | 0.43 | 45 | 21 | 34 | 29 | 97 | 79 | 82 | 9% | 120 | 9% | 70% | | | | 3.72 | -3.7 | 13 | 44 | $12 |

## Swihart,Blake

| | | | | | |
|---|---|---|---|---|---|
| Age: 27 | Bats: B | Pos: CA | Health D | LIMA Plan D | |
| Ht: 6' 1" | Wt: 200 | | PT/Exp F | Rand Var -2 | |
| | | | Consist D | MM 1301 | |

Played every position except SS and CF, but couldn't find regular AB. For a change, that wasn't because of injury. Given years of low AB totals, it's no surprise that plate approach remains subpar; and most recent sighting of plus power is about to scroll out of this box. He remains qualified at C, so at least the bar for rosterability is low.

| Yr Tm | AB | R | HR | RBI | SB | BA | xBA | OBP | SLG | OPS | vL | vR | bb% | ct% | Eye | G | L | F | h% | HctX | PX | xPX | hr/f | Spd | SBO | SB% | #Wk | DOM | DIS | RC/G | RAR | BPV | BPX | R$ |
|---|---|---|---|---|---|---|---|---|---|---|---|---|---|---|---|---|---|---|---|---|---|---|---|---|---|---|---|---|---|---|---|---|---|---|
| 14 a/a | 416 | 44 | 10 | 53 | 7 | 279 | | 321 | 433 | 754 | | | 6 | 80 | 0.30 | | | | 33 | | 116 | | | 92 | 8% | 86% | | | | 4.95 | | 52 | 141 | $14 |
| 15 BOS * | 369 | 54 | 5 | 40 | 5 | 281 | 249 | 323 | 384 | 708 | 603 | 754 | 6 | 74 | 0.24 | 46 | 27 | 28 | 37 | 91 | 81 | 71 | 9% | 106 | 8% | 61% | 22 | 23% | 41% | 4.33 | 6.2 | 8 | 22 | $11 |
| 16 BOS * | 165 | 21 | 1 | 12 | 2 | 246 | 231 | 352 | 326 | 677 | 1657 | 629 | 14 | 79 | 0.77 | 46 | 22 | 33 | 31 | 83 | 46 | 95 | 0% | 144 | 7% | 47% | 5 | 20% | 20% | 3.76 | -0.4 | 25 | 71 | $1 |
| 17 BOS * | 200 | 20 | 3 | 20 | 1 | 179 | 86 | 229 | 269 | 497 | 0 | 629 | 6 | 69 | 0.21 | 0 | 0 | 100 | 24 | 0 | 59 | -26 | 0% | 109 | 2% | 100% | 5 | 0% | 100% | 1.93 | -14.2 | -28 | -85 | -$4 |
| 18 BOS | 192 | 28 | 3 | 18 | 6 | 229 | 212 | 285 | 328 | 613 | 319 | 748 | 7 | 70 | 0.26 | 41 | 21 | 38 | 31 | 77 | 74 | 89 | 6% | 99 | 15% | 86% | 26 | 19% | 65% | 3.18 | -1.0 | -12 | -40 | $2 |
| 1st Half | 77 | 6 | 0 | 3 | 2 | 156 | 176 | 217 | 182 | 399 | 419 | 388 | 7 | 69 | 0.25 | 36 | 23 | 42 | 23 | 86 | 25 | 109 | 0% | 92 | 19% | 67% | 14 | 14% | 79% | 1.19 | -5.8 | -61 | -203 | -$8 |
| 2nd Half | 115 | 22 | 3 | 15 | 4 | 278 | 237 | 331 | 426 | 757 | 235 | 967 | 7 | 71 | 0.27 | 45 | 20 | 35 | 37 | 70 | 106 | 76 | 10% | 108 | 13% | 100% | 12 | 25% | 50% | 5.20 | 5.7 | 19 | 63 | $9 |
| 19 Proj | 194 | 25 | 4 | 18 | 4 | 225 | 223 | 283 | 333 | 617 | 515 | 647 | 8 | 72 | 0.30 | 44 | 22 | 34 | 29 | 81 | 74 | 89 | 7% | 108 | 10% | 80% | | | | 3.15 | -1.7 | -6 | -21 | $4 |

## Tapia,Raimel

| | | | | | |
|---|---|---|---|---|---|
| Age: 25 | Bats: L | Pos: CF | Health A | LIMA Plan C+ | |
| Ht: 6' 2" | Wt: 180 | | PT/Exp C | Rand Var -1 | |
| | | | Consist C | MM 3543 | |

1-6-.200 in 25 AB at COL. Impressive AAA campaign (.302 BA, 21-for-24 on bases) netted just a quick cup of coffee. Elite Spd is the draw, while contact and GB% stroke (49% in Triple-A) let it flourish. Growing PX says he's got some pop too, so while we'd like to see more patience, he can make an early impact.

| Yr Tm | AB | R | HR | RBI | SB | BA | xBA | OBP | SLG | OPS | vL | vR | bb% | ct% | Eye | G | L | F | h% | HctX | PX | xPX | hr/f | Spd | SBO | SB% | #Wk | DOM | DIS | RC/G | RAR | BPV | BPX | R$ |
|---|---|---|---|---|---|---|---|---|---|---|---|---|---|---|---|---|---|---|---|---|---|---|---|---|---|---|---|---|---|---|---|---|---|---|
| 14 | | | | | | | | | | | | | | | | | | | | | | | | | | | | | | | | | | |
| 15 | | | | | | | | | | | | | | | | | | | | | | | | | | | | | | | | | | |
| 16 COL * | 566 | 79 | 7 | 42 | 22 | 322 | 292 | 349 | 441 | 791 | 500 | 570 | 4 | 88 | 0.34 | 37 | 33 | 30 | 36 | 76 | 65 | 59 | 0% | 166 | 24% | 55% | 6 | 0% | 67% | 5.30 | 10.6 | 62 | 177 | $28 |
| 17 COL * | 423 | 59 | 4 | 38 | 14 | 324 | 283 | 351 | 469 | 820 | 640 | 798 | 4 | 81 | 0.22 | 42 | 28 | 29 | 39 | 71 | 86 | 69 | 6% | 155 | 16% | 76% | 19 | 42% | 42% | 6.19 | 10.5 | 50 | 152 | $20 |
| 18 COL * | 459 | 57 | 9 | 45 | 13 | 261 | 229 | 296 | 424 | 719 | 393 | 874 | 5 | 79 | 0.23 | 24 | 24 | 53 | 32 | 64 | 100 | 120 | 11% | 131 | 18% | 80% | 9 | 44% | 44% | 4.34 | -3.6 | 45 | 150 | $13 |
| 1st Half | 316 | 39 | 7 | 30 | 11 | 269 | 264 | 302 | 444 | 746 | | | 5 | 79 | 0.23 | | | | 32 | | 106 | | | 137 | 19% | 91% | 1 | 100% | 0% | 4.81 | | 54 | 180 | $19 |
| 2nd Half | 143 | 18 | 2 | 15 | 2 | 242 | 219 | 282 | 380 | 661 | 393 | 874 | 5 | 77 | 0.24 | 24 | 24 | 53 | 30 | 63 | 88 | 120 | 11% | 128 | 14% | 46% | 8 | 38% | 50% | 3.40 | -5.2 | 30 | 100 | $1 |
| 19 Proj | 267 | 35 | 7 | 25 | 10 | 289 | 271 | 324 | 470 | 794 | 537 | 893 | 4 | 81 | 0.24 | 46 | 20 | 34 | 34 | 66 | 106 | 100 | 9% | 139 | 20% | 80% | | | | 5.41 | 9.6 | 60 | 199 | $12 |

## Tatis Jr.,Fernando

| | | | | | |
|---|---|---|---|---|---|
| Age: 20 | Bats: R | Pos: SS | Health A | LIMA Plan D | |
| Ht: 6' 3" | Wt: 185 | | PT/Exp F | Rand Var 0 | |
| | | | Consist D | MM 4421 | |

Surgery on broken thumb ended season in July; likely to be a full go by spring. Excellent power stroke comes with SB prowess, making his keeper star as bright as any. Struck out 109 times in Double-A though, so expect some short-term bumps in the road. Candidate for a 2nd half call to SD, but might not deliver right away.

| Yr Tm | AB | R | HR | RBI | SB | BA | xBA | OBP | SLG | OPS | vL | vR | bb% | ct% | Eye | G | L | F | h% | HctX | PX | xPX | hr/f | Spd | SBO | SB% | #Wk | DOM | DIS | RC/G | RAR | BPV | BPX | R$ |
|---|---|---|---|---|---|---|---|---|---|---|---|---|---|---|---|---|---|---|---|---|---|---|---|---|---|---|---|---|---|---|---|---|---|---|
| 14 | | | | | | | | | | | | | | | | | | | | | | | | | | | | | | | | | | |
| 15 | | | | | | | | | | | | | | | | | | | | | | | | | | | | | | | | | | |
| 16 | | | | | | | | | | | | | | | | | | | | | | | | | | | | | | | | | | |
| 17 aa | 55 | 6 | 1 | 6 | 3 | 264 | | 291 | 337 | 628 | | | 4 | 69 | 0.12 | | | | 37 | | 46 | | | 104 | 21% | 100% | | | | 3.70 | | -45 | -136 | $0 |
| 18 aa | 353 | 70 | 14 | 39 | 14 | 274 | | 331 | 472 | 803 | | | 8 | 67 | 0.26 | | | | 37 | | 136 | | | 122 | 22% | 74% | | | | 5.40 | | 32 | 107 | $17 |
| 1st Half | 309 | 63 | 12 | 33 | 12 | 273 | | 335 | 475 | 811 | | | 9 | 67 | 0.28 | | | | 37 | | 140 | | | 135 | 20% | 74% | | | | 5.52 | | 39 | 130 | $20 |
| 2nd Half | 44 | 6 | 2 | 6 | 3 | 283 | | 298 | 446 | 743 | | | 2 | 71 | 0.07 | | | | 36 | | 105 | | | 101 | 39% | 72% | | | | 4.53 | | 5 | 17 | -$11 |
| 19 Proj | 161 | 30 | 6 | 15 | 5 | 245 | 246 | 306 | 428 | 734 | 734 | 734 | 8 | 70 | 0.29 | 40 | 25 | 35 | 31 | | 121 | | 15% | 127 | 17% | 71% | | | | 4.35 | 1.9 | 34 | 114 | $6 |

RYAN BLOOMFIELD

## Taylor,Chris

Age: 28 Bats: R Pos: SS CF LF
Ht: 6' 1" Wt: 195

Health A | LIMA Plan B
PT/Exp C | Rand Var -3
Consist C | MM 4425

Something happened in July. Whether it was the remnants of a June hamstring injury or the role change upon Manny Machado's arrival, his contact rate plummeted, bottoming out at 59% during an August in which he hit .185. Sept recovery salvaged season but Ks remain a new problem. His 2nd half xBA raises a red flag.

| Yr Tm | AB | R | HR | RBI | SB | BA | xBA | OBP | SLG | OPS | vL | vR | bb% | ct% | Eye | G | L | F | h% | HctX | PX | xPX | hr/f | Spd | SBO | SB% | #Wk | DOM | DIS | RC/G | RAR | BPV | BPX | R$ |
|---|---|---|---|---|---|---|---|---|---|---|---|---|---|---|---|---|---|---|---|---|---|---|---|---|---|---|---|---|---|---|---|---|---|---|
| 14 SEA * | 438 | 59 | 3 | 34 | 15 | 271 | 219 | 324 | 371 | 695 | 699 | 687 | 7 | 71 | 0.26 | 41 | 21 | 38 | 38 | 52 | 91 | 62 | 0% | 155 | 20% | 62% | 11 | 18% | 55% | 4.04 | 8.3 | 18 | 49 | $14 |
| 15 SEA * | 437 | 47 | 3 | 22 | 14 | 221 | 210 | 285 | 302 | 586 | 635 | 358 | 8 | 75 | 0.36 | 32 | 24 | 44 | 29 | 126 | 60 | 161 | 0% | 133 | 23% | 54% | 10 | 10% | 70% | 2.63 | -21.2 | 8 | 22 | $4 |
| 16 2 TM * | 365 | 45 | 3 | 35 | 13 | 258 | 243 | 312 | 380 | 693 | 644 | 606 | 7 | 74 | 0.30 | 44 | 22 | 33 | 34 | 79 | 87 | 98 | 7% | 133 | 21% | 69% | 12 | 17% | 50% | 3.99 | -9.4 | 22 | 63 | $9 |
| 17 LA * | 557 | 91 | 22 | 76 | 18 | 280 | 263 | 343 | 483 | 826 | 837 | 855 | 9 | 73 | 0.36 | 42 | 23 | 36 | 35 | 96 | 123 | 103 | 16% | 143 | 17% | 73% | 25 | 40% | 24% | 5.80 | 12.5 | 54 | 164 | $25 |
| 18 LA | 536 | 85 | 17 | 63 | 9 | 254 | 238 | 331 | 444 | 775 | 754 | 786 | 9 | 67 | 0.31 | 34 | 28 | 39 | 35 | 94 | 134 | 117 | 12% | 153 | 11% | 60% | 28 | 46% | 32% | 4.78 | 8.0 | 40 | 133 | $16 |
| 1st Half | 292 | 47 | 9 | 30 | 3 | 250 | 249 | 332 | 452 | 784 | 827 | 765 | 10 | 71 | 0.36 | 34 | 26 | 40 | 32 | 89 | 129 | 116 | 11% | 166 | 11% | 38% | 15 | 60% | 27% | 4.66 | 4.3 | 58 | 193 | $15 |
| 2nd Half | 244 | 38 | 8 | 33 | 6 | 258 | 227 | 330 | 434 | 764 | 685 | 815 | 9 | 62 | 0.26 | 34 | 29 | 38 | 38 | 101 | 139 | 119 | 14% | 124 | 11% | 86% | 13 | 31% | 38% | 4.91 | 5.3 | 16 | 53 | $18 |
| **19 Proj** | **479** | **72** | **14** | **56** | **8** | **250** | **242** | **321** | **426** | **747** | **725** | **758** | **9** | **70** | **0.31** | **37** | **25** | **37** | **33** | **93** | **121** | **111** | **11%** | **147** | **10%** | **66%** | | | | **4.51** | **7.9** | **29** | **96** | **$12** |

## Taylor,Michael

Age: 28 Bats: R Pos: CF
Ht: 6' 4" Wt: 212

Health A | LIMA Plan D
PT/Exp D | Rand Var +1
Consist D | MM 3503

2017's favorable hr/f went 'poof' but he managed to hold together some value by running wild for half a season before losing his job altogether. Best assets are wheels and efficiency on basepaths, and newfound GB% tilt is a step in the right direction. But awful batting eye ensures those bags will come at a cost.

| Yr Tm | AB | R | HR | RBI | SB | BA | xBA | OBP | SLG | OPS | vL | vR | bb% | ct% | Eye | G | L | F | h% | HctX | PX | xPX | hr/f | Spd | SBO | SB% | #Wk | DOM | DIS | RC/G | RAR | BPV | BPX | R$ |
|---|---|---|---|---|---|---|---|---|---|---|---|---|---|---|---|---|---|---|---|---|---|---|---|---|---|---|---|---|---|---|---|---|---|---|
| 14 WAS * | 467 | 65 | 17 | 52 | 27 | 258 | 240 | 323 | 417 | 739 | 1095 | 553 | 9 | 63 | 0.25 | 55 | 23 | 23 | 38 | 49 | 139 | 65 | 20% | 115 | 31% | 69% | 6 | 17% | 50% | 4.45 | 8.7 | 16 | 43 | $22 |
| 15 WAS * | 498 | 52 | 15 | 66 | 18 | 235 | 219 | 290 | 364 | 654 | 667 | 633 | 7 | 66 | 0.23 | 46 | 22 | 32 | 33 | 90 | 96 | 115 | 15% | 111 | 18% | 81% | 26 | 19% | 54% | 3.58 | -11.0 | -9 | -24 | $14 |
| 16 WAS * | 338 | 43 | 8 | 24 | 20 | 215 | 228 | 269 | 335 | 604 | 755 | 596 | 7 | 66 | 0.22 | 44 | 27 | 30 | 30 | 85 | 90 | 81 | 17% | 109 | 33% | 83% | 22 | 18% | 64% | 3.04 | -16.9 | -14 | -40 | $8 |
| 17 WAS * | 425 | 57 | 20 | 56 | 19 | 262 | 243 | 311 | 474 | 785 | 849 | 794 | 7 | 66 | 0.21 | 43 | 20 | 37 | 35 | 90 | 141 | 109 | 20% | 131 | 28% | 73% | 21 | 38% | 43% | 4.99 | -0.8 | 30 | 91 | $17 |
| 18 WAS | 353 | 46 | 6 | 28 | 24 | 227 | 227 | 287 | 357 | 644 | 616 | 659 | 8 | 67 | 0.25 | 51 | 18 | 31 | 32 | 80 | 99 | 83 | 9% | 127 | 38% | 80% | 28 | 21% | 61% | 3.43 | -8.7 | 3 | 10 | $11 |
| 1st Half | 254 | 32 | 5 | 24 | 23 | 240 | 241 | 301 | 386 | 687 | 671 | 693 | 8 | 69 | 0.28 | 52 | 20 | 29 | 33 | 85 | 109 | 90 | 10% | 126 | 47% | 85% | 15 | 27% | 53% | 4.10 | -0.3 | 17 | 57 | $18 |
| 2nd Half | 99 | 14 | 1 | 4 | 1 | 192 | 187 | 252 | 283 | 535 | 517 | 549 | 7 | 64 | 0.19 | 49 | 15 | 36 | 29 | 67 | 70 | 63 | 5% | 120 | 15% | 33% | 13 | 15% | 69% | 2.01 | -6.8 | -38 | -127 | -$7 |
| **19 Proj** | **292** | **39** | **8** | **25** | **13** | **235** | **222** | **292** | **382** | **674** | **666** | **678** | **7** | **66** | **0.22** | **47** | **20** | **33** | **33** | **81** | **107** | **88** | **12%** | **123** | **28%** | **73%** | | | | **3.64** | **-4.4** | **2** | **8** | **$10** |

## Tellez,Rowdy

Age: 24 Bats: L Pos: 1B
Ht: 6' 4" Wt: 220

Health A | LIMA Plan D
PT/Exp B | Rand Var 0
Consist F | MM 4241

4-14-.314 in 70 AB at TOR. Has a slugger's build, but power laid dormant for 1.5 years in Triple-A. Finally sparked in 2nd half, and carried over to Sept callup. That cameo was likely enough to earn him more opportunities, but beware getting sucked in by MLB debut. Make him show it again before buying.

| Yr Tm | AB | R | HR | RBI | SB | BA | xBA | OBP | SLG | OPS | vL | vR | bb% | ct% | Eye | G | L | F | h% | HctX | PX | xPX | hr/f | Spd | SBO | SB% | #Wk | DOM | DIS | RC/G | RAR | BPV | BPX | R$ |
|---|---|---|---|---|---|---|---|---|---|---|---|---|---|---|---|---|---|---|---|---|---|---|---|---|---|---|---|---|---|---|---|---|---|---|
| 14 | | | | | | | | | | | | | | | | | | | | | | | | | | | | | | | | | | |
| 15 | | | | | | | | | | | | | | | | | | | | | | | | | | | | | | | | | | |
| 16 aa | 438 | 61 | 21 | 70 | 3 | 285 | | 364 | 504 | 868 | | | 11 | 77 | 0.55 | | | | 33 | | 134 | | | 87 | 5% | 52% | | | | 6.41 | | 67 | 191 | $16 |
| 17 aaa | 445 | 44 | 6 | 55 | 6 | 223 | | 296 | 337 | 633 | | | 9 | 78 | 0.47 | | | | 27 | | 77 | | | 83 | 6% | 85% | | | | 3.31 | | 19 | 58 | $3 |
| 18 TOR * | 463 | 48 | 15 | 58 | 6 | 263 | 268 | 318 | 431 | 748 | 324 | 1200 | 7 | 78 | 0.37 | 38 | 26 | 36 | 31 | 115 | 106 | 138 | 22% | 84 | 9% | 59% | 5 | 40% | 60% | 4.62 | 2.7 | 40 | 133 | $13 |
| 1st Half | 242 | 22 | 5 | 25 | 4 | 233 | 248 | 304 | 362 | 666 | | | 9 | 80 | 0.52 | | | | 27 | | 83 | | | 87 | 11% | 52% | | | | 3.53 | | 35 | 117 | $7 |
| 2nd Half | 221 | 26 | 10 | 33 | 3 | 295 | 277 | 333 | 506 | 839 | 324 | 1200 | 5 | 76 | 0.24 | 38 | 26 | 36 | 35 | 112 | 133 | 138 | 22% | 86 | 7% | 71% | 5 | 40% | 60% | 6.05 | 7.9 | 48 | 160 | $19 |
| **19 Proj** | **193** | **21** | **9** | **26** | **3** | **256** | **270** | **314** | **461** | **774** | **405** | **926** | **8** | **78** | **0.41** | **40** | **22** | **38** | **29** | **101** | **125** | **124** | **15%** | **90** | **8%** | **70%** | | | | **4.97** | **1.2** | **45** | **151** | **$6** |

## Thames,Eric

Age: 32 Bats: L Pos: RF 1B
Ht: 6' 0" Wt: 210

Health C | LIMA Plan B
PT/Exp C | Rand Var +3
Consist C | MM 5323

Left thumb injury (torn UCL) shelved him for two months in 1st half. Returned to a logjam which resulted in far less PT. Elite power profile is intact, as are the problematic ct% and xBA. Platoon role can minimize the downside, and position versatility helps him find AB. Put him on the (very long) list of cheap power sources.

| Yr Tm | AB | R | HR | RBI | SB | BA | xBA | OBP | SLG | OPS | vL | vR | bb% | ct% | Eye | G | L | F | h% | HctX | PX | xPX | hr/f | Spd | SBO | SB% | #Wk | DOM | DIS | RC/G | RAR | BPV | BPX | R$ |
|---|---|---|---|---|---|---|---|---|---|---|---|---|---|---|---|---|---|---|---|---|---|---|---|---|---|---|---|---|---|---|---|---|---|---|
| 14 for | 443 | 93 | 22 | 118 | 10 | 320 | | 385 | 580 | 965 | | | 10 | 79 | 0.50 | | | | 36 | | 175 | | | 113 | 10% | 82% | | | | 8.38 | 55.2 | 110 | 297 | $34 |
| 15 for | 472 | 127 | 28 | 137 | 36 | 355 | | 452 | 656 | 1108 | | | 15 | 82 | 0.96 | | | | 39 | | 184 | | | 104 | 26% | 80% | | | | 11.70 | 87.6 | 137 | 370 | $54 |
| 16 for | 436 | 115 | 24 | 118 | 12 | 299 | | 383 | 555 | 938 | | | 12 | 78 | 0.61 | | | | 34 | | 151 | | | 101 | 12% | 72% | | | | 7.65 | 38.8 | 88 | 251 | $30 |
| 17 MIL | 469 | 83 | 31 | 63 | 4 | 247 | 256 | 359 | 518 | 877 | 664 | 936 | 14 | 65 | 0.46 | 38 | 20 | 41 | 31 | 110 | 174 | 162 | 25% | 98 | 5% | 67% | 27 | 48% | 44% | 6.12 | 12.0 | 59 | 179 | $14 |
| 18 MIL | 247 | 41 | 16 | 37 | 7 | 219 | 228 | 306 | 478 | 783 | 612 | 804 | 10 | 61 | 0.30 | 33 | 20 | 47 | 28 | 103 | 180 | 186 | 23% | 108 | 13% | 100% | 21 | 48% | 38% | 4.84 | 1.8 | 42 | 140 | $8 |
| 1st Half | 119 | 19 | 11 | 24 | 5 | 235 | 259 | 331 | 563 | 894 | 953 | 885 | 11 | 68 | 0.39 | 32 | 16 | 52 | 24 | 118 | 197 | 201 | 26% | 88 | 19% | 100% | 9 | 67% | 11% | 6.27 | 6.0 | 81 | 270 | $11 |
| 2nd Half | 128 | 22 | 5 | 13 | 2 | 203 | 201 | 282 | 398 | 680 | 167 | 731 | 10 | 54 | 0.24 | 35 | 25 | 41 | 33 | 89 | 160 | 168 | 18% | 122 | 7% | 100% | 12 | 33% | 58% | 3.67 | -3.7 | 2 | 7 | $4 |
| **19 Proj** | **377** | **72** | **22** | **65** | **7** | **248** | **244** | **342** | **503** | **844** | **644** | **879** | **12** | **66** | **0.38** | **36** | **21** | **44** | **32** | **105** | **168** | **174** | **21%** | **102** | **9%** | **84%** | | | | **5.76** | **14.6** | **62** | **208** | **$17** |

## Tilson,Charlie

Age: 26 Bats: L Pos: LF
Ht: 6' 0" Wt: 185

Health F | LIMA Plan D
PT/Exp F | Rand Var 0
Consist C | MM 0511

0-11-.264 in 106 AB at CHW. Missed 2017 season due to foot and ankle fractures. Speed and ability to make contact were his top skills pre-injury. Even if we give a mulligan and project recovery as he gains distance from those injuries, the ceiling here is just some dirt-cheap SB in deeper leagues.

| Yr Tm | AB | R | HR | RBI | SB | BA | xBA | OBP | SLG | OPS | vL | vR | bb% | ct% | Eye | G | L | F | h% | HctX | PX | xPX | hr/f | Spd | SBO | SB% | #Wk | DOM | DIS | RC/G | RAR | BPV | BPX | R$ |
|---|---|---|---|---|---|---|---|---|---|---|---|---|---|---|---|---|---|---|---|---|---|---|---|---|---|---|---|---|---|---|---|---|---|---|
| 14 aa | 139 | 15 | 2 | 13 | 2 | 211 | | 237 | 282 | 519 | | | 3 | 79 | 0.16 | | | | 26 | | 51 | | | 107 | 17% | 33% | | | | 1.94 | | -4 | -11 | -$1 |
| 15 aa | 539 | 63 | 3 | 24 | 34 | 250 | | 296 | 320 | 616 | | | 6 | 84 | 0.41 | | | | 29 | | 45 | | | 147 | 39% | 61% | | | | 2.96 | | 31 | 84 | $17 |
| 16 CHW * | 353 | 40 | 3 | 25 | 11 | 244 | 294 | 294 | 342 | 635 | 0 | 1000 | 6 | 84 | 0.44 | 100 | 0 | 0 | 28 | 171 | 56 | -24 | 0% | 138 | 17% | 77% | 1 | 0% | 0% | 3.40 | -13.1 | 38 | 109 | $6 |
| 17 | | | | | | | | | | | | | | | | | | | | | | | | | | | | | | | | | | |
| 18 CHW * | 376 | 28 | 0 | 31 | 11 | 219 | 225 | 264 | 253 | 517 | 347 | 672 | 6 | 78 | 0.28 | 65 | 16 | 19 | 28 | 42 | 27 | 11 | 0% | 113 | 17% | 66% | 8 | 0% | 75% | 2.16 | -22.0 | -19 | -63 | $2 |
| 1st Half | 254 | 16 | 0 | 15 | 8 | 232 | 240 | 276 | 270 | 545 | 369 | 707 | 6 | 81 | 0.31 | 64 | 18 | 17 | 29 | 41 | 27 | 6 | 0% | 121 | 19% | 66% | 7 | 0% | 71% | 2.43 | -13.4 | -6 | -20 | $4 |
| 2nd Half | 122 | 12 | 0 | 16 | 2 | 192 | 153 | 240 | 218 | 458 | 0 | 452 | 6 | 72 | 0.22 | 67 | 0 | 33 | 27 | 53 | 25 | 56 | 0% | 99 | 13% | 67% | 1 | 0% | 100% | 1.64 | -9.8 | -49 | -163 | $0 |
| **19 Proj** | **132** | **13** | **1** | **11** | **6** | **238** | **231** | **286** | **300** | **586** | **356** | **631** | **6** | **79** | **0.30** | **55** | **18** | **23** | **29** | **37** | **40** | **5** | **3%** | **126** | **24%** | **74%** | | | | **2.84** | **-7.1** | **-5** | **-17** | **$4** |

## Torres,Gleyber

Age: 22 Bats: R Pos: 2B SS
Ht: 6'1" Wt: 200

Health A | LIMA Plan B
PT/Exp F | Rand Var -2
Consist A | MM 4225

24-77-.271 in 431 AB at NYY. Strong rookie season lived up to the top-prospect clippings. What looks like a 2nd-half fade is more like a Sept crash (.233 BA, 56 xPX); certainly not the first rookie to hit The Wall near season's end. We will still need to see what he looks like when/if he adjusts. But there's this... UP: 30 HR/15 SB, .275 BA.

| Yr Tm | AB | R | HR | RBI | SB | BA | xBA | OBP | SLG | OPS | vL | vR | bb% | ct% | Eye | G | L | F | h% | HctX | PX | xPX | hr/f | Spd | SBO | SB% | #Wk | DOM | DIS | RC/G | RAR | BPV | BPX | R$ |
|---|---|---|---|---|---|---|---|---|---|---|---|---|---|---|---|---|---|---|---|---|---|---|---|---|---|---|---|---|---|---|---|---|---|---|
| 14 | | | | | | | | | | | | | | | | | | | | | | | | | | | | | | | | | | |
| 15 | | | | | | | | | | | | | | | | | | | | | | | | | | | | | | | | | | |
| 16 | | | | | | | | | | | | | | | | | | | | | | | | | | | | | | | | | | |
| 17 a/a | 201 | 29 | 8 | 32 | 7 | 278 | | 371 | 473 | 844 | | | 13 | 75 | 0.60 | | | | 34 | | 117 | | | 101 | 21% | 51% | | | | 5.70 | | 52 | 158 | $8 |
| 18 NYY * | 480 | 59 | 25 | 87 | 7 | 276 | 247 | 340 | 479 | 819 | 912 | 785 | 9 | 72 | 0.35 | 33 | 25 | 43 | 33 | 102 | 122 | 115 | 18% | 105 | 7% | 69% | 22 | 32% | 14% | 5.68 | 22.0 | 37 | 123 | $21 |
| 1st Half | 257 | 32 | 15 | 49 | 3 | 294 | 262 | 344 | 528 | 872 | 989 | 842 | 7 | 73 | 0.28 | 31 | 26 | 43 | 35 | 109 | 139 | 137 | 22% | 107 | 7% | 58% | 11 | 45% | 9% | 6.42 | 16.1 | 52 | 173 | $25 |
| 2nd Half | 223 | 27 | 10 | 38 | 4 | 256 | 229 | 337 | 422 | 759 | 832 | 734 | 11 | 71 | 0.42 | 35 | 23 | 43 | 32 | 96 | 101 | 95 | 14% | 100 | 7% | 80% | 11 | 18% | 18% | 4.88 | 4.6 | 20 | 67 | $16 |
| **19 Proj** | **531** | **70** | **25** | **91** | **10** | **269** | **246** | **350** | **468** | **819** | **908** | **785** | **11** | **72** | **0.44** | **35** | **23** | **42** | **33** | **101** | **123** | **112** | **15%** | **93** | **11%** | **62%** | | | | **5.55** | **12.1** | **36** | **122** | **$23** |

## Travis,Devon

Age: 28 Bats: R Pos: 2B
Ht: 5'9" Wt: 190

Health F | LIMA Plan D+
PT/Exp D | Rand Var +5
Consist C | MM 2243

11-44-.232 in 357 AB at TOR. PRO: appeared in 103 games, after missing 270 games from 2015-17. CON: "Chronically injured players don't suddenly get healthy" is one of our truisms for a reason; formerly-interesting power and speed didn't survive intact. 2nd half flickers of life in his bat keep us interested... barely.

| Yr Tm | AB | R | HR | RBI | SB | BA | xBA | OBP | SLG | OPS | vL | vR | bb% | ct% | Eye | G | L | F | h% | HctX | PX | xPX | hr/f | Spd | SBO | SB% | #Wk | DOM | DIS | RC/G | RAR | BPV | BPX | R$ |
|---|---|---|---|---|---|---|---|---|---|---|---|---|---|---|---|---|---|---|---|---|---|---|---|---|---|---|---|---|---|---|---|---|---|---|
| 14 aa | 396 | 49 | 7 | 37 | 11 | 259 | | 306 | 391 | 697 | | | 6 | 84 | 0.42 | | | | 29 | | 86 | | | 129 | 17% | 68% | | | | 4.02 | | 58 | 157 | $11 |
| 15 TOR * | 260 | 42 | 8 | 36 | 4 | 282 | 277 | 340 | 447 | 787 | 974 | 812 | 8 | 79 | 0.42 | 50 | 22 | 28 | 33 | 95 | 116 | 109 | 16% | 89 | 7% | 79% | 12 | 58% | 8% | 5.41 | 8.4 | 52 | 141 | $9 |
| 16 TOR * | 432 | 56 | 11 | 53 | 4 | 298 | 261 | 329 | 448 | 777 | 617 | 838 | 4 | 79 | 0.22 | 46 | 19 | 34 | 35 | 94 | 98 | 81 | 10% | 109 | 5% | 80% | 20 | 25% | 25% | 5.36 | 7.5 | 39 | 111 | $15 |
| 17 TOR | 185 | 22 | 5 | 24 | 4 | 259 | 284 | 291 | 438 | 729 | 1013 | 670 | 4 | 79 | 0.18 | 37 | 26 | 36 | 30 | 104 | 115 | 131 | 9% | 75 | 19% | 67% | 10 | 40% | 40% | 4.21 | -2.2 | 41 | 124 | $4 |
| 18 TOR * | 419 | 48 | 12 | 47 | 4 | 225 | 264 | 256 | 359 | 615 | 742 | 623 | 4 | 83 | 0.24 | 50 | 21 | 29 | 25 | 93 | 73 | 79 | 13% | 112 | 7% | 66% | 23 | 39% | 30% | 2.99 | -13.8 | 33 | 110 | $6 |
| 1st Half | 221 | 24 | 6 | 20 | 2 | 209 | 261 | 238 | 332 | 571 | 706 | 610 | 4 | 81 | 0.20 | 58 | 19 | 23 | 23 | 76 | 67 | 57 | 17% | 125 | 7% | 64% | 12 | 42% | 42% | 2.52 | -11.4 | 24 | 80 | $3 |
| 2nd Half | 198 | 24 | 6 | 27 | 2 | 242 | 270 | 282 | 389 | 671 | 772 | 634 | 4 | 85 | 0.30 | 44 | 23 | 33 | 26 | 106 | 80 | 96 | 11% | 97 | 7% | 67% | 11 | 36% | 18% | 3.57 | -3.6 | 43 | 143 | $9 |
| **19 Proj** | **335** | **41** | **10** | **41** | **5** | **254** | **273** | **292** | **416** | **708** | **795** | **680** | **4** | **82** | **0.24** | **46** | **22** | **32** | **28** | **97** | **96** | **96** | **12%** | **92** | **10%** | **68%** | | | | **4.02** | **-1.5** | **40** | **133** | **$10** |

GREG PYRON

## Trout,Mike

| Age: 27 | Bats: R | Pos: CF | Health | B | LIMA Plan | C |
|---|---|---|---|---|---|---|
| Ht: 6' 2" | Wt: 235 | | PT/Exp | A | Rand Var | -2 |
| | | | Consist | B | MM | 5545 |

Logged another near-$40 season despite missing most of August with right wrist inflammation. This is a phenomenal collection of skills, as evidenced by BPX column (393!). If 2nd half loft somehow sticks, could unlock another power level, but at BA's expense (see xBA). Either way, still best in the game and at peak.

| Yr | Tm | AB | R | HR | RBI | SB | BA | xBA | OBP | SLG | OPS | vL | vR | bb% | ct% | Eye | G | L | F | h% | HctX | PX | xPX | hr/f | Spd | SBO | SB% | #Wk | DOM | DIS | RC/G | RAR | BPV | BPX | R$ |
|---|---|---|---|---|---|---|---|---|---|---|---|---|---|---|---|---|---|---|---|---|---|---|---|---|---|---|---|---|---|---|---|---|---|---|---|
| 14 | LAA | 602 | 115 | 36 | 111 | 16 | 287 | 272 | 377 | 561 | 939 | 910 | 948 | 12 | 69 | 0.45 | 34 | 19 | 47 | 36 | 115 | 209 | 151 | 18% | 145 | 10% | 89% | 27 | 67% | 11% | 7.61 | 62.8 | 114 | 308 | $38 |
| 15 | LAA | 575 | 104 | 41 | 90 | 11 | 299 | 289 | 402 | 590 | 991 | 1032 | 978 | 13 | 73 | 0.58 | 37 | 24 | 38 | 35 | 129 | 190 | 152 | 25% | 121 | 10% | 61% | 27 | 70% | 7% | 8.27 | 60.4 | 107 | 289 | $35 |
| 16 | LAA | 549 | 123 | 29 | 100 | 30 | 315 | 276 | 441 | 550 | 991 | 971 | 996 | 17 | 75 | 0.85 | 41 | 22 | 37 | 38 | 127 | 142 | 142 | 19% | 118 | 17% | 81% | 27 | 63% | 19% | 8.99 | 69.4 | 85 | 243 | $42 |
| 17 | LAA | 402 | 92 | 33 | 72 | 22 | 306 | 296 | 442 | 629 | 1071 | 907 | 1113 | 19 | 78 | 1.04 | 37 | 18 | 45 | 32 | 120 | 173 | 133 | 23% | 116 | 17% | 85% | 22 | 73% | 9% | 10.26 | 61.1 | 123 | 373 | $31 |
| 18 | LAA | 471 | 101 | 39 | 79 | 24 | 312 | 281 | 460 | 628 | 1088 | 992 | 1118 | 20 | 74 | 0.98 | 31 | 23 | 45 | 35 | 121 | 182 | 156 | 25% | 119 | 13% | 92% | 26 | 69% | 15% | 10.89 | 87.6 | 118 | 393 | $38 |
| 1st Half | | 290 | 66 | 24 | 49 | 13 | 317 | 295 | 461 | 641 | 1102 | 1184 | 1082 | 20 | 75 | 1.03 | 33 | 25 | 41 | 35 | 123 | 184 | 152 | 26% | 119 | 11% | 93% | 15 | 73% | 13% | 11.22 | 55.3 | 126 | 420 | $45 |
| 2nd Half | | 181 | 35 | 15 | 30 | 11 | 304 | 262 | 458 | 608 | 1065 | 784 | 1186 | 21 | 71 | 0.92 | 28 | 20 | 52 | 35 | 116 | 180 | 161 | 22% | 110 | 15% | 92% | 11 | 64% | 18% | 10.38 | 31.1 | 106 | 353 | $26 |
| 19 | Proj | **500** | **107** | **38** | **86** | **26** | **308** | **277** | **443** | **605** | **1049** | **920** | **1090** | **19** | **74** | **0.89** | **34** | **21** | **45** | **35** | **121** | **173** | **148** | **23%** | **122** | **15%** | **87%** | | | | **9.96** | **80.0** | **111** | **370** | **$38** |

## Trumbo,Mark

| Age: 33 | Bats: R | Pos: DH | Health | D | LIMA Plan | C+ |
|---|---|---|---|---|---|---|
| Ht: 6' 4" | Wt: 225 | | PT/Exp | B | Rand Var | -1 |
| | | | Consist | C | MM | 3215 |

17-44-.261 in 330 AB at BAL. Missed April with a quad strain; underwent season-ending right knee surgery in late-August (expected ready for start of 2019). While the 2014-16 power was useful, we've since seen almost 1000 AB of "meh" power, and he isn't helpful without that now-missing elite pop.

| Yr | Tm | AB | R | HR | RBI | SB | BA | xBA | OBP | SLG | OPS | vL | vR | bb% | ct% | Eye | G | L | F | h% | HctX | PX | xPX | hr/f | Spd | SBO | SB% | #Wk | DOM | DIS | RC/G | RAR | BPV | BPX | R$ |
|---|---|---|---|---|---|---|---|---|---|---|---|---|---|---|---|---|---|---|---|---|---|---|---|---|---|---|---|---|---|---|---|---|---|---|---|
| 14 | ARI | 328 | 37 | 14 | 61 | 2 | 235 | 241 | 293 | 415 | 707 | 796 | 679 | 8 | 73 | 0.31 | 45 | 15 | 40 | 28 | 111 | 133 | 135 | 14% | 89 | 7% | 40% | 18 | 39% | 44% | 3.94 | -1.0 | 42 | 114 | $8 |
| 15 | 2 TM | 508 | 62 | 22 | 64 | 0 | 262 | 244 | 310 | 449 | 759 | 856 | 709 | 7 | 74 | 0.27 | 42 | 18 | 40 | 31 | 107 | 124 | 122 | 14% | 118 | 0% | 0% | 27 | 52% | 30% | 4.82 | -9.2 | 46 | 124 | $13 |
| 16 | BAL | 613 | 94 | 47 | 108 | 2 | 256 | 268 | 316 | 533 | 850 | 608 | 932 | 8 | 72 | 0.30 | 40 | 17 | 43 | 28 | 115 | 166 | 147 | 25% | 84 | 2% | 100% | 27 | 52% | 30% | 5.75 | 4.4 | 64 | 183 | $22 |
| 17 | BAL | 559 | 79 | 23 | 65 | 1 | 234 | 228 | 289 | 397 | 686 | 763 | 658 | 7 | 73 | 0.28 | 43 | 16 | 41 | 28 | 90 | 96 | 87 | 14% | 86 | 1% | 100% | 26 | 19% | 50% | 3.82 | -17.6 | 12 | 36 | $8 |
| 18 | BAL * | 354 | 42 | 17 | 46 | 0 | 254 | 247 | 304 | 434 | 737 | 782 | 758 | 7 | 74 | 0.27 | 42 | 23 | 35 | 30 | 109 | 107 | 111 | 20% | 80 | 0% | 0% | 17 | 41% | 47% | 4.50 | 0.0 | 19 | 63 | $8 |
| 1st Half | | 204 | 22 | 8 | 25 | 0 | 244 | 254 | 294 | 414 | 708 | 637 | 814 | 7 | 74 | 0.27 | 41 | 25 | 35 | 29 | 113 | 108 | 110 | 17% | 67 | 0% | 0% | 10 | 50% | 40% | 4.11 | -2.4 | 17 | 57 | $7 |
| 2nd Half | | 150 | 20 | 9 | 21 | 0 | 267 | 239 | 313 | 460 | 773 | 1025 | 699 | 7 | 73 | 0.28 | 45 | 21 | 35 | 31 | 104 | 106 | 113 | 23% | 100 | 0% | 0% | 7 | 29% | 57% | 5.07 | 2.4 | 24 | 80 | $10 |
| 19 | Proj | **423** | **56** | **20** | **58** | **1** | **246** | **238** | **301** | **425** | **726** | **753** | **716** | **7** | **73** | **0.29** | **43** | **19** | **38** | **29** | **104** | **107** | **113** | **17%** | **89** | **1%** | **73%** | | | | **4.31** | **-2.5** | **8** | **26** | **$12** |

## Tucker,Kyle

| Age: 22 | Bats: L | Pos: LF | Health | A | LIMA Plan | C+ |
|---|---|---|---|---|---|---|
| Ht: 6' 4" | Wt: 190 | | PT/Exp | F | Rand Var | 0 |
| | | | Consist | A | MM | 2323 |

0-4-.141 in 64 AB at HOU. Though MLB cup of coffee didn't go well, former first-round pick's future is bright. Hefty GB% in tiny MLB sample wasn't present in minors, so expect more power as he fills out physically. Near-term growing pains likely, but there is eventual 25 HR/15 SB potential here.

| Yr | Tm | AB | R | HR | RBI | SB | BA | xBA | OBP | SLG | OPS | vL | vR | bb% | ct% | Eye | G | L | F | h% | HctX | PX | xPX | hr/f | Spd | SBO | SB% | #Wk | DOM | DIS | RC/G | RAR | BPV | BPX | R$ |
|---|---|---|---|---|---|---|---|---|---|---|---|---|---|---|---|---|---|---|---|---|---|---|---|---|---|---|---|---|---|---|---|---|---|---|---|
| 14 | | | | | | | | | | | | | | | | | | | | | | | | | | | | | | | | | | | |
| 15 | | | | | | | | | | | | | | | | | | | | | | | | | | | | | | | | | | | |
| 16 | | | | | | | | | | | | | | | | | | | | | | | | | | | | | | | | | | | |
| 17 | aa | 287 | 35 | 15 | 43 | 7 | 249 | | 297 | 480 | 777 | | | 6 | 76 | 0.29 | | | | 28 | | 135 | | | 86 | 21% | 63% | | | | 4.65 | | 54 | 164 | $8 |
| 18 | HOU * | 471 | 73 | 19 | 73 | 16 | 264 | 256 | 323 | 447 | 770 | 988 | 309 | 8 | 77 | 0.38 | 49 | 16 | 35 | 31 | 95 | 109 | 76 | 0% | 113 | 18% | 74% | 9 | 33% | 33% | 4.96 | 5.2 | 47 | 157 | $21 |
| 1st Half | | 311 | 45 | 10 | 46 | 10 | 262 | 251 | 317 | 427 | 744 | | | 7 | 75 | 0.33 | | | | 32 | | 107 | | | 105 | 18% | 75% | 1 | 0% | 100% | 4.66 | | 35 | 117 | $25 |
| 2nd Half | | 160 | 29 | 9 | 27 | 5 | 270 | 269 | 335 | 488 | 823 | 988 | 309 | 9 | 80 | 0.49 | 49 | 16 | 35 | 29 | 99 | 112 | 76 | 0% | 140 | 18% | 72% | 8 | 38% | 25% | 5.61 | 4.7 | 73 | 243 | $14 |
| 19 | Proj | **324** | **48** | **10** | **51** | **9** | **258** | **249** | **331** | **416** | **747** | **1837** | **500** | **7** | **78** | **0.36** | **37** | **24** | **39** | **31** | **89** | **96** | **68** | **10%** | **113** | **17%** | **70%** | | | | **4.41** | **-1.8** | **37** | **124** | **$13** |

## Tulowitzki,Troy

| Age: 34 | Bats: R | Pos: DH | Health | F | LIMA Plan | D+ |
|---|---|---|---|---|---|---|
| Ht: 6' 3" | Wt: 205 | | PT/Exp | D | Rand Var | 0 |
| | | | Consist | C | MM | 2133 |

Recovered from right ankle compression fracture and ligament tear suffered in July 2017, but April surgery to remove bone spurs in both feet cost him the entire 2018 season. When last seen in action, steep declines in xPX, LD and xBA plagued his performance. Rust won't likely help those issues. A gamble for someone else.

| Yr | Tm | AB | R | HR | RBI | SB | BA | xBA | OBP | SLG | OPS | vL | vR | bb% | ct% | Eye | G | L | F | h% | HctX | PX | xPX | hr/f | Spd | SBO | SB% | #Wk | DOM | DIS | RC/G | RAR | BPV | BPX | R$ |
|---|---|---|---|---|---|---|---|---|---|---|---|---|---|---|---|---|---|---|---|---|---|---|---|---|---|---|---|---|---|---|---|---|---|---|---|
| 14 | COL | 315 | 71 | 21 | 52 | 1 | 340 | 310 | 432 | 603 | 1035 | 1348 | 930 | 13 | 82 | 0.88 | 38 | 23 | 39 | 36 | 150 | 170 | 163 | 21% | 105 | 2% | 50% | 16 | 75% | 13% | 9.94 | 55.4 | 124 | 335 | $23 |
| 15 | 2 TM | 486 | 77 | 17 | 70 | 1 | 280 | 254 | 337 | 440 | 777 | 940 | 735 | 7 | 77 | 0.33 | 41 | 22 | 37 | 34 | 126 | 110 | 126 | 12% | 88 | 1% | 100% | 25 | 44% | 36% | 5.19 | 10.9 | 37 | 100 | $17 |
| 16 | TOR | 492 | 54 | 24 | 79 | 1 | 254 | 256 | 318 | 443 | 761 | 767 | 759 | 8 | 79 | 0.43 | 41 | 19 | 40 | 28 | 109 | 108 | 113 | 15% | 77 | 1% | 100% | 25 | 52% | 24% | 4.77 | 6.6 | 45 | 129 | $12 |
| 17 | TOR | 241 | 16 | 7 | 26 | 0 | 249 | 220 | 300 | 378 | 678 | 479 | 750 | 7 | 83 | 0.43 | 52 | 14 | 33 | 27 | 102 | 70 | 68 | 10% | 74 | 2% | 0% | 13 | 46% | 15% | 3.76 | -6.1 | 27 | 82 | $1 |
| 18 | | | | | | | | | | | | | | | | | | | | | | | | | | | | | | | | | | | |
| 1st Half | | | | | | | | | | | | | | | | | | | | | | | | | | | | | | | | | | | |
| 2nd Half | | | | | | | | | | | | | | | | | | | | | | | | | | | | | | | | | | | |
| 19 | Proj | **258** | **34** | **10** | **36** | **0** | **255** | **254** | **319** | **424** | **743** | **776** | **733** | **8** | **80** | **0.44** | **44** | **19** | **37** | **28** | **105** | **98** | **112** | **14%** | **88** | **1%** | **48%** | | | | **4.55** | **0.3** | **28** | **92** | **$7** |

## Turner,Justin

| Age: 34 | Bats: R | Pos: 3B | Health | D | LIMA Plan | B+ |
|---|---|---|---|---|---|---|
| Ht: 5' 11" | Wt: 205 | | PT/Exp | B | Rand Var | -2 |
| | | | Consist | C | MM | 4255 |

Another injury-marred year. Didn't make 2018 debut until May 15 (broken left wrist on spring HBP), then hampered by groin strain in July. Despite sluggish start, again displayed terrific plate control; wide PX/xPX gap hints at a few more HR. Stellar 2nd half, but putting together two halves like that in a year is getting less likely.

| Yr | Tm | AB | R | HR | RBI | SB | BA | xBA | OBP | SLG | OPS | vL | vR | bb% | ct% | Eye | G | L | F | h% | HctX | PX | xPX | hr/f | Spd | SBO | SB% | #Wk | DOM | DIS | RC/G | RAR | BPV | BPX | R$ |
|---|---|---|---|---|---|---|---|---|---|---|---|---|---|---|---|---|---|---|---|---|---|---|---|---|---|---|---|---|---|---|---|---|---|---|---|
| 14 | LA | 288 | 46 | 7 | 43 | 6 | 340 | 283 | 404 | 493 | 897 | 911 | 890 | 9 | 80 | 0.48 | 49 | 23 | 28 | 41 | 115 | 117 | 105 | 11% | 98 | 7% | 86% | 26 | 46% | 31% | 7.67 | 29.6 | 62 | 168 | $17 |
| 15 | LA | 385 | 55 | 16 | 60 | 5 | 294 | 291 | 370 | 491 | 861 | 751 | 904 | 8 | 82 | 0.51 | 36 | 28 | 36 | 33 | 113 | 126 | 117 | 14% | 74 | 7% | 71% | 25 | 40% | 28% | 6.23 | 16.7 | 68 | 184 | $17 |
| 16 | LA | 556 | 79 | 27 | 90 | 4 | 275 | 283 | 339 | 493 | 832 | 640 | 919 | 8 | 81 | 0.45 | 36 | 24 | 40 | 30 | 123 | 125 | 123 | 15% | 91 | 4% | 80% | 27 | 56% | 26% | 5.77 | 12.6 | 68 | 194 | $20 |
| 17 | LA | 457 | 72 | 21 | 71 | 7 | 322 | 282 | 415 | 530 | 945 | 1181 | 837 | 11 | 88 | 1.05 | 31 | 21 | 48 | 33 | 138 | 108 | 154 | 11% | 68 | 5% | 88% | 25 | 64% | 12% | 8.01 | 32.9 | 82 | 248 | $24 |
| 18 | LA | 365 | 62 | 14 | 52 | 2 | 312 | 290 | 406 | 518 | 924 | 1028 | 872 | 11 | 85 | 0.87 | 29 | 26 | 44 | 34 | 141 | 119 | 154 | 10% | 77 | 3% | 67% | 21 | 62% | 14% | 7.47 | 27.7 | 83 | 277 | $16 |
| 1st Half | | 126 | 16 | 5 | 15 | 1 | 262 | 251 | 356 | 429 | 785 | 975 | 700 | 11 | 90 | 1.23 | 33 | 17 | 50 | 26 | 122 | 86 | 130 | 9% | 85 | 3% | 100% | 8 | 50% | 13% | 5.16 | 2.4 | 78 | 260 | $0 |
| 2nd Half | | 239 | 46 | 9 | 37 | 1 | 339 | 307 | 432 | 565 | 997 | 1048 | 970 | 11 | 83 | 0.76 | 27 | 32 | 41 | 38 | 152 | 139 | 167 | 11% | 70 | 3% | 50% | 13 | 69% | 15% | 8.94 | 27.6 | 89 | 297 | $24 |
| 19 | Proj | **440** | **70** | **21** | **65** | **4** | **307** | **291** | **392** | **533** | **925** | **1010** | **885** | **10** | **85** | **0.75** | **32** | **24** | **44** | **32** | **134** | **126** | **144** | **13%** | **81** | **4%** | **79%** | | | | **7.42** | **35.0** | **83** | **277** | **$23** |

## Turner,Trea

| Age: 26 | Bats: R | Pos: SS | Health | B | LIMA Plan | D+ |
|---|---|---|---|---|---|---|
| Ht: 6'2" | Wt: 185 | | PT/Exp | A | Rand Var | 0 |
| | | | Consist | B | MM | 2535 |

Just missed $40 season despite huge AB total. Elite Spd/SB% is the engine here, even as SBO% settles to a mere mortal level. Low LD%/xBA say he isn't a .300 BA threat, while xPX/GB% cap HR, but those are accessories here. Only two players have more SB from 2017-18; neither notched double-digit HR.

| Yr | Tm | AB | R | HR | RBI | SB | BA | xBA | OBP | SLG | OPS | vL | vR | bb% | ct% | Eye | G | L | F | h% | HctX | PX | xPX | hr/f | Spd | SBO | SB% | #Wk | DOM | DIS | RC/G | RAR | BPV | BPX | R$ |
|---|---|---|---|---|---|---|---|---|---|---|---|---|---|---|---|---|---|---|---|---|---|---|---|---|---|---|---|---|---|---|---|---|---|---|---|
| 14 | | | | | | | | | | | | | | | | | | | | | | | | | | | | | | | | | | | |
| 15 | WAS * | 494 | 64 | 7 | 48 | 27 | 295 | 248 | 345 | 405 | 750 | 819 | 570 | 7 | 77 | 0.33 | 50 | 21 | 29 | 37 | 36 | 79 | 11 | 13% | 121 | 24% | 76% | 8 | 13% | 50% | 5.06 | 18.1 | 22 | 59 | $25 |
| 16 | WAS * | 638 | 111 | 18 | 71 | 57 | 313 | 276 | 362 | 498 | 860 | 751 | 985 | 7 | 78 | 0.36 | 43 | 25 | 32 | 38 | 111 | 109 | 122 | 17% | 203 | 36% | 87% | 14 | 64% | 21% | 6.98 | 41.3 | 78 | 223 | $49 |
| 17 | WAS | 412 | 75 | 11 | 45 | 46 | 284 | 268 | 338 | 451 | 789 | 630 | 836 | 7 | 81 | 0.38 | 52 | 15 | 34 | 33 | 87 | 94 | 85 | 10% | 183 | 51% | 85% | 18 | 61% | 28% | 5.59 | 12.7 | 68 | 206 | $30 |
| 18 | WAS | 664 | 103 | 19 | 73 | 43 | 271 | 253 | 344 | 416 | 760 | 796 | 748 | 9 | 80 | 0.52 | 49 | 18 | 33 | 31 | 93 | 82 | 79 | 11% | 158 | 26% | 83% | 28 | 50% | 18% | 5.07 | 24.2 | 54 | 180 | $36 |
| 1st Half | | 322 | 47 | 9 | 29 | 22 | 270 | 249 | 354 | 410 | 764 | 708 | 784 | 11 | 79 | 0.57 | 51 | 16 | 33 | 32 | 101 | 82 | 78 | 11% | 142 | 25% | 88% | 15 | 60% | 20% | 5.26 | 12.1 | 47 | 157 | $31 |
| 2nd Half | | 342 | 56 | 10 | 44 | 21 | 272 | 257 | 334 | 421 | 755 | 885 | 713 | 8 | 81 | 0.47 | 47 | 19 | 34 | 31 | 86 | 82 | 80 | 11% | 166 | 28% | 78% | 13 | 38% | 15% | 4.89 | 9.3 | 59 | 197 | $40 |
| 19 | Proj | **579** | **94** | **18** | **64** | **46** | **275** | **261** | **337** | **438** | **775** | **722** | **792** | **8** | **80** | **0.43** | **49** | **18** | **33** | **32** | **93** | **94** | **88** | **11%** | **150** | **35%** | **83%** | | | | **5.28** | **8.7** | **60** | **200** | **$37** |

## Upton,Justin

| Age: 31 | Bats: R | Pos: LF | Health | A | LIMA Plan | B |
|---|---|---|---|---|---|---|
| Ht: 6'2" | Wt: 205 | | PT/Exp | A | Rand Var | -2 |
| | | | Consist | D | MM | 4225 |

A year ago we wrote "keep .260 BA, 30 HR as your baseline", and he nailed it. Lacerated left index finger and concussion suffered in late-Aug/early Sept likely influenced brutal final month (.197 BA; 58% ct%). At his age, it's unlikely the 2nd half Spd holds, but he's still capable of sprinkling in the SB. Same baseline applies.

| Yr | Tm | AB | R | HR | RBI | SB | BA | xBA | OBP | SLG | OPS | vL | vR | bb% | ct% | Eye | G | L | F | h% | HctX | PX | xPX | hr/f | Spd | SBO | SB% | #Wk | DOM | DIS | RC/G | RAR | BPV | BPX | R$ |
|---|---|---|---|---|---|---|---|---|---|---|---|---|---|---|---|---|---|---|---|---|---|---|---|---|---|---|---|---|---|---|---|---|---|---|---|
| 14 | ATL | 566 | 77 | 29 | 102 | 8 | 270 | 262 | 342 | 491 | 833 | 981 | 794 | 9 | 70 | 0.35 | 40 | 20 | 40 | 34 | 115 | 173 | 159 | 18% | 95 | 8% | 67% | 26 | 62% | 19% | 5.77 | 33.9 | 67 | 181 | $26 |
| 15 | SD | 542 | 85 | 26 | 81 | 19 | 251 | 240 | 336 | 454 | 790 | 558 | 848 | 11 | 71 | 0.43 | 39 | 17 | 44 | 31 | 108 | 140 | 131 | 15% | 127 | 16% | 79% | 26 | 50% | 38% | 5.19 | 12.7 | 57 | 154 | $23 |
| 16 | DET | 570 | 81 | 31 | 87 | 9 | 246 | 242 | 310 | 465 | 775 | 754 | 783 | 8 | 69 | 0.28 | 39 | 18 | 43 | 30 | 106 | 144 | 127 | 18% | 97 | 10% | 69% | 27 | 44% | 48% | 4.76 | 8.1 | 37 | 106 | $17 |
| 17 | 2 AL | 557 | 100 | 35 | 109 | 14 | 273 | 263 | 361 | 540 | 901 | 1155 | 828 | 12 | 68 | 0.41 | 37 | 20 | 44 | 34 | 112 | 176 | 151 | 21% | 75 | 13% | 74% | 27 | 52% | 26% | 6.72 | 20.5 | 59 | 179 | $27 |
| 18 | LAA | 533 | 80 | 30 | 85 | 8 | 257 | 239 | 344 | 463 | 808 | 593 | 875 | 10 | 67 | 0.36 | 42 | 22 | 36 | 33 | 108 | 132 | 137 | 23% | 103 | 7% | 80% | 26 | 31% | 42% | 5.37 | 12.2 | 27 | 90 | $21 |
| 1st Half | | 302 | 47 | 17 | 44 | 4 | 255 | 237 | 345 | 457 | 802 | 656 | 835 | 12 | 68 | 0.41 | 43 | 20 | 37 | 32 | 118 | 128 | 152 | 22% | 84 | 4% | 100% | 15 | 27% | 40% | 5.44 | 7.4 | 24 | 80 | $23 |
| 2nd Half | | 231 | 33 | 13 | 41 | 4 | 260 | 241 | 344 | 472 | 815 | 541 | 935 | 9 | 66 | 0.30 | 42 | 24 | 35 | 34 | 95 | 137 | 116 | 25% | 126 | 10% | 67% | 11 | 36% | 45% | 5.27 | 4.6 | 32 | 107 | $18 |
| 19 | Proj | **566** | **88** | **31** | **95** | **7** | **260** | **242** | **342** | **477** | **819** | **745** | **843** | **10** | **68** | **0.35** | **40** | **21** | **39** | **33** | **107** | **143** | **137** | **20%** | **103** | **7%** | **64%** | | | | **5.45** | **14.1** | **29** | **96** | **$24** |

GREG PYRON

## Urias,Luis

| | | | | | |
|---|---|---|---|---|---|
| Age: 22 | Bats: R | Pos: 2B | Health A | LIMA Plan C | |
| Ht: 5' 9" | Wt: 185 | | PT/Exp D | Rand Var 0 | |
| | | | Consist B | MM 1335 | |

2-5-.208 in 48 AB at SD. Walked more than he struck out prior to 2018, but ct% fell in first real exposure to Triple-A. Despite power gains, heavy GB tilt (also present in minors) will provide a hard ceiling on further gains there. Owns decent Spd, but not seen on the bases yet. Lots more work to be done here, but he's got time.

| Yr | Tm | AB | R | HR | RBI | SB | BA | xBA | OBP | SLG | OPS | vL | vR | bb% | ct% | Eye | G | L | F | h% | HctX | PX | xPX | hr/f | Spd | SBO | SB% | #Wk | DOM | DIS | RC/G | RAR | BPV | BPX | R$ |
|---|---|---|---|---|---|---|---|---|---|---|---|---|---|---|---|---|---|---|---|---|---|---|---|---|---|---|---|---|---|---|---|---|---|---|---|
| 14 | | | | | | | | | | | | | | | | | | | | | | | | | | | | | | | | | | | |
| 15 | | | | | | | | | | | | | | | | | | | | | | | | | | | | | | | | | | | |
| 16 | | | | | | | | | | | | | | | | | | | | | | | | | | | | | | | | | | | |
| 17 | aa | 442 | 74 | 3 | 37 | 7 | 290 | | 381 | 369 | 750 | | | 13 | 84 | 0.95 | | | | 34 | | 48 | | | 126 | 7% | 56% | | | | 4.94 | | 41 | 124 | $13 |
| 18 | SD * | 498 | 65 | 8 | 37 | 2 | 248 | 243 | 318 | 366 | 685 | 1231 | 400 | 9 | 73 | 0.38 | 63 | 16 | 21 | 33 | 83 | 81 | 78 | 25% | 119 | 3% | 69% | 3 | 67% | 33% | 3.95 | -4.6 | 14 | 47 | $7 |
| 1st Half | | 288 | 34 | 4 | 22 | 1 | 233 | 218 | 313 | 333 | 646 | | | 10 | 73 | 0.43 | | | | 31 | | 70 | | | 112 | 2% | 39% | | | | 3.43 | | 5 | 17 | $6 |
| 2nd Half | | 210 | 31 | 3 | 16 | 2 | 270 | 257 | 326 | 413 | 739 | 1231 | 400 | 8 | 74 | 0.32 | 63 | 16 | 21 | 35 | 83 | 96 | 78 | 25% | 129 | 3% | 100% | 3 | 67% | 33% | 4.75 | 3.4 | 27 | 90 | $10 |
| 19 | Proj | **407** | **60** | **8** | **32** | **4** | **269** | **255** | **351** | **395** | **746** | **1521** | **474** | **10** | **78** | **0.52** | **50** | **22** | **28** | **33** | **75** | **79** | **70** | **9%** | **119** | **5%** | **66%** | | | | **4.73** | **6.6** | **25** | **83** | **$9** |

## Utley,Chase

| | | | | | |
|---|---|---|---|---|---|
| Age: 40 | Bats: L | Pos: 2B | Health C | LIMA Plan F | |
| Ht: 6' 1" | Wt: 195 | | PT/Exp C | Rand Var +3 | |
| | | | Consist C | MM 0000 | |

Retiring after a 16-year run, he notched five straight seasons (2005-2009) with an OPS better than .900 and at least $25 in roto value. Serious knee issues got in the way thereafter, but he hangs 'em up with a career .275/.358/.465 slash line. Helped to usher in the era of the patience-and-power middle infielders.

| Yr | Tm | AB | R | HR | RBI | SB | BA | xBA | OBP | SLG | OPS | vL | vR | bb% | ct% | Eye | G | L | F | h% | HctX | PX | xPX | hr/f | Spd | SBO | SB% | #Wk | DOM | DIS | RC/G | RAR | BPV | BPX | R$ |
|---|---|---|---|---|---|---|---|---|---|---|---|---|---|---|---|---|---|---|---|---|---|---|---|---|---|---|---|---|---|---|---|---|---|---|---|
| 14 | PHI | 589 | 74 | 11 | 78 | 10 | 270 | 276 | 339 | 407 | 746 | 682 | 775 | 8 | 86 | 0.62 | 39 | 25 | 36 | 30 | 113 | 96 | 106 | 6% | 105 | 7% | 91% | 27 | 67% | 22% | 4.77 | 23.3 | 69 | 186 | $19 |
| 15 | 2 NL | 373 | 37 | 8 | 39 | 4 | 212 | 257 | 286 | 343 | 629 | 557 | 655 | 8 | 83 | 0.50 | 44 | 20 | 36 | 24 | 112 | 86 | 106 | 7% | 91 | 5% | 100% | 22 | 45% | 45% | 3.10 | -12.3 | 45 | 122 | $1 |
| 16 | LA | 512 | 79 | 14 | 52 | 2 | 252 | 255 | 319 | 396 | 716 | 470 | 768 | 7 | 78 | 0.35 | 44 | 22 | 34 | 30 | 119 | 90 | 101 | 11% | 101 | 3% | 50% | 27 | 30% | 30% | 4.09 | -11.7 | 29 | 83 | $10 |
| 17 | LA | 309 | 43 | 8 | 34 | 6 | 236 | 264 | 324 | 405 | 728 | 661 | 734 | 9 | 82 | 0.56 | 43 | 19 | 38 | 27 | 120 | 95 | 134 | 8% | 113 | 10% | 86% | 27 | 52% | 26% | 4.21 | -7.4 | 56 | 170 | $5 |
| 18 | LA | 164 | 18 | 1 | 14 | 3 | 213 | 241 | 305 | 305 | 610 | 450 | 625 | 9 | 79 | 0.50 | 41 | 24 | 35 | 26 | 100 | 65 | 80 | 2% | 90 | 10% | 75% | 23 | 35% | 43% | 2.85 | -7.1 | 16 | 53 | -$1 |
| 1st Half | | 120 | 13 | 1 | 14 | 2 | 225 | 251 | 304 | 325 | 629 | 523 | 637 | 10 | 80 | 0.54 | 39 | 27 | 34 | 27 | 94 | 67 | 64 | 3% | 92 | 6% | 100% | 13 | 23% | 46% | 3.31 | -3.2 | 23 | 77 | $0 |
| 2nd Half | | 44 | 5 | 0 | 0 | 1 | 182 | 211 | 308 | 250 | 558 | 333 | 589 | 8 | 77 | 0.40 | 47 | 15 | 38 | 24 | 117 | 58 | 127 | 0% | 93 | 22% | 50% | 10 | 50% | 40% | 1.82 | -3.4 | 2 | 7 | -$3 |
| 19 | Proj | | | | | | | | | | | | | | | | | | | | | | | | | | | | | | | | | | |

## Vazquez,Christian

| | | | | | |
|---|---|---|---|---|---|
| Age: 28 | Bats: R | Pos: CA | Health F | LIMA Plan D+ | |
| Ht: 5' 9" | Wt: 195 | | PT/Exp D | Rand Var +5 | |
| | | | Consist D | MM 0223 | |

Right pinkie fracture shelved him for most of 2nd half. Seemed to try to hop on the launch angle bandwagon, drastically increasing FB, but BA/xBA/h% all crashed. Bat-on-ball remains a foundational skill, but continues to stand alone: HctX and xPX impugn the quality of that contact. Will rebound some, but don't expect 2017.

| Yr | Tm | AB | R | HR | RBI | SB | BA | xBA | OBP | SLG | OPS | vL | vR | bb% | ct% | Eye | G | L | F | h% | HctX | PX | xPX | hr/f | Spd | SBO | SB% | #Wk | DOM | DIS | RC/G | RAR | BPV | BPX | R$ |
|---|---|---|---|---|---|---|---|---|---|---|---|---|---|---|---|---|---|---|---|---|---|---|---|---|---|---|---|---|---|---|---|---|---|---|---|
| 14 | BOS * | 419 | 42 | 3 | 36 | 0 | 249 | 230 | 308 | 335 | 643 | 539 | 638 | 8 | 78 | 0.39 | 57 | 17 | 26 | 31 | 82 | 77 | 58 | 3% | 78 | 1% | 0% | 12 | 33% | 42% | 3.46 | 1.7 | 16 | 43 | $4 |
| 15 | | | | | | | | | | | | | | | | | | | | | | | | | | | | | | | | | | | |
| 16 | BOS * | 324 | 38 | 3 | 26 | 2 | 240 | 271 | 291 | 329 | 620 | 804 | 527 | 7 | 77 | 0.32 | 60 | 25 | 15 | 30 | 88 | 65 | 53 | 5% | 91 | 2% | 100% | 16 | 13% | 56% | 3.25 | -5.9 | 4 | 11 | $2 |
| 17 | BOS | 324 | 43 | 5 | 32 | 7 | 290 | 268 | 330 | 404 | 735 | 748 | 732 | 5 | 80 | 0.27 | 47 | 25 | 28 | 35 | 86 | 70 | 58 | 7% | 91 | 10% | 78% | 27 | 41% | 44% | 4.74 | 5.4 | 16 | 48 | $10 |
| 18 | BOS | 251 | 24 | 3 | 16 | 4 | 207 | 237 | 257 | 283 | 540 | 603 | 518 | 5 | 84 | 0.32 | 42 | 21 | 36 | 24 | 85 | 48 | 51 | 4% | 79 | 10% | 80% | 20 | 20% | 50% | 2.26 | -8.6 | 9 | 30 | -$1 |
| 1st Half | | 195 | 18 | 3 | 12 | 1 | 221 | 240 | 259 | 313 | 571 | 662 | 539 | 3 | 85 | 0.23 | 43 | 20 | 37 | 25 | 83 | 57 | 50 | 5% | 80 | 5% | 50% | 15 | 27% | 40% | 2.49 | -5.8 | 17 | 57 | $0 |
| 2nd Half | | 56 | 6 | 0 | 4 | 3 | 161 | 220 | 254 | 179 | 433 | 371 | 448 | 10 | 80 | 0.55 | 40 | 27 | 33 | 20 | 92 | 15 | 56 | 0% | 94 | 21% | 100% | 5 | 0% | 80% | 1.53 | -3.5 | -17 | -57 | -$2 |
| 19 | Proj | **360** | **40** | **3** | **28** | **5** | **234** | **245** | **292** | **308** | **600** | **612** | **596** | **7** | **81** | **0.36** | **47** | **24** | **29** | **28** | **87** | **50** | **55** | **4%** | **85** | **7%** | **84%** | | | | **2.96** | **-5.3** | **2** | **8** | **$5** |

## Verdugo,Alex

| | | | | | |
|---|---|---|---|---|---|
| Age: 23 | Bats: L | Pos: RF | Health A | LIMA Plan C+ | |
| Ht: 6' 0" | Wt: 205 | | PT/Exp C | Rand Var -2 | |
| | | | Consist B | MM 1233 | |

1-4-.260 in 77 AB at LA. Good strike zone judgment and ability to make contact should result in a BA asset. Scouts say dearth of HR is due to spraying the ball to all fields as opposed to shortage of power and believe he could eventually hit 20+ HR. He also owns enough speed to contribute around 10 SB. A keeper league gem.

| Yr | Tm | AB | R | HR | RBI | SB | BA | xBA | OBP | SLG | OPS | vL | vR | bb% | ct% | Eye | G | L | F | h% | HctX | PX | xPX | hr/f | Spd | SBO | SB% | #Wk | DOM | DIS | RC/G | RAR | BPV | BPX | R$ |
|---|---|---|---|---|---|---|---|---|---|---|---|---|---|---|---|---|---|---|---|---|---|---|---|---|---|---|---|---|---|---|---|---|---|---|---|
| 14 | | | | | | | | | | | | | | | | | | | | | | | | | | | | | | | | | | | |
| 15 | | | | | | | | | | | | | | | | | | | | | | | | | | | | | | | | | | | |
| 16 | aa | 477 | 51 | 12 | 56 | 2 | 256 | | 308 | 381 | 688 | | | 7 | 85 | 0.50 | | | | 28 | | 73 | | | 84 | 7% | 22% | | | | 3.81 | | 39 | 111 | $8 |
| 17 | LA * | 456 | 57 | 6 | 53 | 8 | 279 | 327 | 342 | 386 | 728 | 400 | 583 | 9 | 87 | 0.73 | 58 | 32 | 11 | 31 | 74 | 61 | 40 | 50% | 92 | 9% | 64% | 6 | 17% | 33% | 4.60 | -5.9 | 43 | 130 | $12 |
| 18 | LA * | 420 | 47 | 9 | 40 | 6 | 287 | 265 | 341 | 409 | 750 | 556 | 748 | 7 | 84 | 0.52 | 62 | 16 | 22 | 32 | 121 | 73 | 68 | 7% | 96 | 7% | 74% | 10 | 30% | 40% | 4.98 | 8.7 | 41 | 137 | $12 |
| 1st Half | | 248 | 26 | 5 | 25 | 3 | 295 | 287 | 334 | 427 | 760 | 615 | 729 | 5 | 84 | 0.37 | 68 | 18 | 14 | 33 | 96 | 83 | 26 | 0% | 87 | 5% | 100% | 3 | 67% | 33% | 5.24 | 7.6 | 43 | 143 | $14 |
| 2nd Half | | 172 | 20 | 4 | 14 | 3 | 276 | 240 | 350 | 383 | 734 | 400 | 758 | 10 | 84 | 0.73 | 57 | 14 | 29 | 31 | 142 | 60 | 101 | 10% | 108 | 9% | 59% | 7 | 14% | 43% | 4.61 | 2.4 | 40 | 133 | $9 |
| 19 | Proj | **322** | **37** | **9** | **33** | **5** | **277** | **264** | **335** | **417** | **753** | **556** | **806** | **8** | **85** | **0.60** | **48** | **19** | **33** | **30** | **124** | **80** | **71** | **10%** | **105** | **8%** | **63%** | | | | **4.85** | **3.6** | **42** | **140** | **$11** |

## Villanueva,Christian

| | | | | | |
|---|---|---|---|---|---|
| Age: 28 | Bats: R | Pos: 3B | Health F | LIMA Plan D | |
| Ht: 5' 11" | Wt: 210 | | PT/Exp F | Rand Var 0 | |
| | | | Consist B | MM 3123 | |

Belted 15 HR through 170 AB, but that new level of performance proved unsustainable, as he hit just 5 HR over his next 185 AB. Extended playing time exposed flaws and pitchers adjusted. Fourteen of his 20 HR came vL; was totally inept vR. Low ct%/high FB% and xBA history add to the gloom. Just a short-side platoon option.

| Yr | Tm | AB | R | HR | RBI | SB | BA | xBA | OBP | SLG | OPS | vL | vR | bb% | ct% | Eye | G | L | F | h% | HctX | PX | xPX | hr/f | Spd | SBO | SB% | #Wk | DOM | DIS | RC/G | RAR | BPV | BPX | R$ |
|---|---|---|---|---|---|---|---|---|---|---|---|---|---|---|---|---|---|---|---|---|---|---|---|---|---|---|---|---|---|---|---|---|---|---|---|
| 14 | a/a | 457 | 39 | 7 | 43 | 1 | 199 | | 249 | 322 | 572 | | | 6 | 74 | 0.25 | | | | 25 | | 110 | | | 79 | 5% | 40% | | | | 2.51 | | 21 | 57 | -$2 |
| 15 | a/a | 479 | 46 | 16 | 72 | 2 | 221 | | 267 | 369 | 636 | | | 6 | 79 | 0.30 | | | | 25 | | 93 | | | 84 | 5% | 31% | | | | 3.13 | | 31 | 84 | $5 |
| 16 | | | | | | | | | | | | | | | | | | | | | | | | | | | | | | | | | | | |
| 17 | SD * | 430 | 50 | 16 | 63 | 3 | 237 | 238 | 283 | 410 | 693 | 1231 | 1000 | 6 | 74 | 0.24 | 50 | 14 | 36 | 28 | 95 | 105 | 167 | 50% | 105 | 6% | 51% | 2 | 100% | 0% | 3.80 | -19.4 | 24 | 73 | $7 |
| 18 | SD | 351 | 42 | 20 | 46 | 3 | 236 | 237 | 299 | 450 | 750 | 1118 | 574 | 6 | 70 | 0.22 | 32 | 21 | 47 | 28 | 84 | 133 | 108 | 17% | 68 | 4% | 100% | 22 | 45% | 50% | 4.31 | -3.7 | 22 | 73 | $9 |
| 1st Half | | 229 | 30 | 16 | 39 | 1 | 231 | 240 | 295 | 485 | 780 | 1143 | 609 | 7 | 69 | 0.23 | 31 | 17 | 52 | 26 | 86 | 158 | 125 | 20% | 70 | 2% | 100% | 15 | 47% | 47% | 4.55 | 0.3 | 39 | 130 | $13 |
| 2nd Half | | 122 | 12 | 4 | 7 | 2 | 246 | 238 | 308 | 385 | 694 | 1069 | 507 | 5 | 73 | 0.21 | 34 | 27 | 39 | 31 | 79 | 89 | 77 | 11% | 84 | 7% | 100% | 7 | 43% | 57% | 3.82 | -2.5 | 1 | 3 | $0 |
| 19 | Proj | **296** | **32** | **13** | **36** | **2** | **232** | **242** | **296** | **416** | **712** | **1063** | **542** | **6** | **73** | **0.24** | **33** | **23** | **44** | **27** | **82** | **114** | **96** | **14%** | **71** | **5%** | **77%** | | | | **3.84** | **-6.0** | **15** | **49** | **$7** |

## Villar,Jonathan

| | | | | | |
|---|---|---|---|---|---|
| Age: 28 | Bats: B | Pos: 2B | Health B | LIMA Plan C+ | |
| Ht: 6'1" | Wt: 215 | | PT/Exp B | Rand Var -2 | |
| | | | Consist D | MM 2415 | |

Thrived after deadline deal to BAL (8 HR/21 SB in 209 AB). Though shaky ct% limits BA capability, blend of plus Spd, SBO and SB% helps him maximize opportunities. Doesn't hit many flyballs, but makes them count (lifetime 17% hr/f). He's still young, and 2nd half looks a fair amount like 2016, so... UP: return to 60 SB.

| Yr | Tm | AB | R | HR | RBI | SB | BA | xBA | OBP | SLG | OPS | vL | vR | bb% | ct% | Eye | G | L | F | h% | HctX | PX | xPX | hr/f | Spd | SBO | SB% | #Wk | DOM | DIS | RC/G | RAR | BPV | BPX | R$ |
|---|---|---|---|---|---|---|---|---|---|---|---|---|---|---|---|---|---|---|---|---|---|---|---|---|---|---|---|---|---|---|---|---|---|---|---|
| 14 | HOU * | 453 | 55 | 9 | 46 | 34 | 213 | 218 | 279 | 325 | 604 | 644 | 608 | 8 | 67 | 0.27 | 51 | 19 | 30 | 30 | 84 | 92 | 108 | 13% | 100 | 41% | 76% | 19 | 21% | 47% | 2.96 | -6.1 | -10 | -27 | $14 |
| 15 | HOU * | 396 | 58 | 6 | 33 | 31 | 242 | 239 | 293 | 356 | 649 | 761 | 742 | 7 | 70 | 0.24 | 57 | 20 | 23 | 33 | 75 | 85 | 44 | 10% | 139 | 45% | 71% | 15 | 33% | 40% | 3.41 | -10.6 | 5 | 14 | $16 |
| 16 | MIL | 589 | 92 | 19 | 63 | 62 | 285 | 264 | 369 | 457 | 826 | 930 | 786 | 12 | 70 | 0.45 | 56 | 20 | 24 | 36 | 101 | 120 | 103 | 19% | 110 | 43% | 78% | 27 | 44% | 48% | 6.04 | 22.5 | 36 | 103 | $43 |
| 17 | MIL | 403 | 49 | 11 | 40 | 23 | 241 | 240 | 293 | 372 | 665 | 607 | 689 | 7 | 67 | 0.23 | 57 | 21 | 22 | 33 | 90 | 89 | 83 | 19% | 105 | 32% | 74% | 25 | 20% | 64% | 3.63 | -12.2 | -12 | -36 | $13 |
| 18 | 2 TM | 466 | 54 | 14 | 46 | 35 | 260 | 235 | 325 | 384 | 709 | 728 | 702 | 8 | 70 | 0.30 | 56 | 20 | 24 | 34 | 80 | 79 | 71 | 18% | 111 | 30% | 88% | 26 | 23% | 50% | 4.47 | 5.4 | -3 | -10 | $23 |
| 1st Half | | 229 | 19 | 6 | 22 | 11 | 258 | 241 | 302 | 380 | 682 | 886 | 633 | 6 | 68 | 0.19 | 63 | 21 | 16 | 35 | 80 | 82 | 57 | 25% | 106 | 22% | 85% | 15 | 20% | 60% | 4.03 | -1.0 | -17 | -57 | $13 |
| 2nd Half | | 237 | 35 | 8 | 24 | 24 | 262 | 227 | 346 | 388 | 734 | 632 | 777 | 10 | 73 | 0.42 | 49 | 18 | 32 | 33 | 80 | 76 | 84 | 15% | 113 | 36% | 89% | 11 | 27% | 36% | 4.91 | 5.1 | 8 | 27 | $32 |
| 19 | Proj | **545** | **70** | **16** | **54** | **42** | **256** | **239** | **321** | **390** | **711** | **711** | **711** | **8** | **70** | **0.30** | **56** | **20** | **25** | **34** | **86** | **89** | **80** | **17%** | **97** | **35%** | **81%** | | | | **4.37** | **-6.4** | **5** | **16** | **$29** |

## Vogelbach,Daniel

| | | | | | |
|---|---|---|---|---|---|
| Age: 26 | Bats: L | Pos: 1B | Health A | LIMA Plan D+ | |
| Ht: 6'0" | Wt: 250 | | PT/Exp C | Rand Var 0 | |
| | | | Consist B | MM 4023 | |

4-13-.207 in 87 AB at SEA. Power/patience profile is well established, but despite a .290 BA in 342 games at AAA, he hasn't yet put it together in MLB. Issues defensively and vL are impediments to an everyday role. However, if opportunity arises, he profiles as a cheap power source. Number 37,156 on that list.

| Yr | Tm | AB | R | HR | RBI | SB | BA | xBA | OBP | SLG | OPS | vL | vR | bb% | ct% | Eye | G | L | F | h% | HctX | PX | xPX | hr/f | Spd | SBO | SB% | #Wk | DOM | DIS | RC/G | RAR | BPV | BPX | R$ |
|---|---|---|---|---|---|---|---|---|---|---|---|---|---|---|---|---|---|---|---|---|---|---|---|---|---|---|---|---|---|---|---|---|---|---|---|
| 14 | | | | | | | | | | | | | | | | | | | | | | | | | | | | | | | | | | | |
| 15 | aa | 254 | 32 | 6 | 31 | 1 | 241 | | 356 | 371 | 727 | | | 15 | 73 | 0.66 | | | | 31 | | 98 | | | 91 | 2% | 41% | | | | 4.39 | | 29 | 78 | $3 |
| 16 | SEA * | 471 | 63 | 19 | 77 | 0 | 246 | 255 | 353 | 417 | 771 | 0 | 258 | 14 | 73 | 0.62 | 67 | 17 | 17 | 30 | 0 | 108 | -24 | 0% | 56 | 0% | 0% | 4 | 0% | 75% | 4.99 | 1.8 | 26 | 74 | $10 |
| 17 | SEA * | 487 | 51 | 14 | 69 | 2 | 242 | 272 | 330 | 371 | 701 | 500 | 546 | 12 | 73 | 0.49 | 32 | 37 | 32 | 30 | 141 | 81 | 145 | 0% | 55 | 2% | 67% | 7 | 29% | 71% | 4.11 | -18.4 | 0 | 0 | $7 |
| 18 | SEA * | 384 | 49 | 19 | 58 | 0 | 229 | 246 | 349 | 416 | 764 | 274 | 815 | 15 | 74 | 0.71 | 44 | 21 | 34 | 26 | 143 | 112 | 161 | 19% | 57 | 1% | 0% | 13 | 23% | 38% | 4.73 | 3.6 | 35 | 117 | $8 |
| 1st Half | | 229 | 32 | 12 | 29 | 0 | 216 | 251 | 351 | 413 | 764 | 302 | 839 | 17 | 72 | 0.74 | 48 | 23 | 30 | 25 | 132 | 122 | 129 | 17% | 64 | 0% | 0% | 7 | 29% | 57% | 4.71 | -0.4 | 40 | 133 | $8 |
| 2nd Half | | 155 | 17 | 7 | 29 | 0 | 248 | 234 | 345 | 420 | 765 | 0 | 758 | 13 | 77 | 0.65 | 38 | 19 | 43 | 28 | 162 | 97 | 222 | 22% | 62 | 2% | 0% | 6 | 17% | 17% | 4.76 | 0.0 | 32 | 107 | $7 |
| 19 | Proj | **241** | **29** | **13** | **37** | **0** | **242** | **252** | **354** | **453** | **807** | **346** | **896** | **14** | **74** | **0.62** | **42** | **20** | **38** | **27** | **150** | **125** | **185** | **20%** | **85** | **1%** | **33%** | | | | **5.24** | **3.4** | **33** | **111** | **$7** |

GREG PYRON

## Vogt,Stephen

**Age:** 34 **Bats:** L **Pos:** DH | **Ht:** 6' 0" **Wt:** 225

**Health** F | **PT/Exp** D | **Consist** A | **LIMA Plan** D | **Rand Var** 0 | **MM** 2021

Spring shoulder injury ulimately required mid-May surgery to repair damage to his shoulder capsule, rotator cuff and labrum. Hopes to be ready by spring 2019, but this was his second major shoulder surgery, so there is some worry that it could be career-ending. Rerun of 2017 may be the best-case scenario.

| Yr | Tm | AB | R | HR | RBI | SB | BA | xBA | OBP | SLG | OPS | vL | vR | bb% | ct% | Eye | G | L | F | h% | HctX | PX | xPX | hr/f | Spd | SBO | SB% | #Wk | DOM | DIS | RC/G | RAR | BPV | BPX | R$ |
|---|---|---|---|---|---|---|---|---|---|---|---|---|---|---|---|---|---|---|---|---|---|---|---|---|---|---|---|---|---|---|---|---|---|---|---|
| 14 | OAK * | 357 | 37 | 11 | 46 | 2 | 275 | 254 | 315 | 428 | 744 | 647 | 770 | 6 | 86 | 0.42 | 33 | 20 | 47 | 30 | 123 | 97 | 144 | 8% | 100 | 2% | 100% | 17 | 53% | 35% | 4.78 | 13.4 | 65 | 176 | $11 |
| 15 | OAK | 445 | 58 | 18 | 71 | 0 | 261 | 258 | 341 | 443 | 783 | 631 | 832 | 11 | 78 | 0.58 | 38 | 22 | 40 | 30 | 96 | 115 | 110 | 13% | 86 | 2% | 0% | 25 | 48% | 32% | 5.15 | 17.3 | 55 | 149 | $12 |
| 16 | OAK | 490 | 54 | 14 | 56 | 0 | 251 | 260 | 305 | 406 | 711 | 549 | 748 | 7 | 83 | 0.42 | 30 | 23 | 46 | 28 | 90 | 93 | 106 | 7% | 69 | 0% | 0% | 27 | 52% | 26% | 4.16 | -3.5 | 42 | 120 | $7 |
| 17 | 2 TM | 279 | 25 | 12 | 40 | 0 | 233 | 255 | 285 | 423 | 708 | 509 | 732 | 7 | 80 | 0.38 | 38 | 19 | 44 | 25 | 106 | 105 | 122 | 12% | 83 | 2% | 0% | 23 | 57% | 26% | 3.97 | -0.7 | 44 | 133 | $2 |
| 18 | | | | | | | | | | | | | | | | | | | | | | | | | | | | | | | | | | | |
| 1st Half | | | | | | | | | | | | | | | | | | | | | | | | | | | | | | | | | | | |
| 2nd Half | | | | | | | | | | | | | | | | | | | | | | | | | | | | | | | | | | | |
| 19 | Proj | **193** | **21** | **7** | **27** | **0** | **242** | **248** | **303** | **407** | **709** | **573** | **739** | **8** | **80** | **0.43** | **36** | **21** | **44** | **27** | **102** | **96** | **118** | **10%** | **83** | **1%** | **24%** | | | | **4.11** | **-2.3** | **29** | **97** | **$2** |

## Voit,Luke

**Age:** 28 **Bats:** R **Pos:** 1B | **Ht:** 6' 3" **Wt:** 225

**Health** A | **PT/Exp** C | **Consist** B | **LIMA Plan** B | **Rand Var** 0 | **MM** 4045

15-36-.322 in 143 AB at STL/NYY. Unheralded prospect was blocked in STL, but July trade to NYY opened door. Erased GB% tilt to better tap into raw power, though hr/f can't stay THAT high. He also makes enough contact to support a respectable BA. Plenty to like here, just be careful not to extrapolate production and overpay.

| Yr | Tm | AB | R | HR | RBI | SB | BA | xBA | OBP | SLG | OPS | vL | vR | bb% | ct% | Eye | G | L | F | h% | HctX | PX | xPX | hr/f | Spd | SBO | SB% | #Wk | DOM | DIS | RC/G | RAR | BPV | BPX | R$ |
|---|---|---|---|---|---|---|---|---|---|---|---|---|---|---|---|---|---|---|---|---|---|---|---|---|---|---|---|---|---|---|---|---|---|---|---|
| 14 | | | | | | | | | | | | | | | | | | | | | | | | | | | | | | | | | | | |
| 15 | | | | | | | | | | | | | | | | | | | | | | | | | | | | | | | | | | | |
| 16 | aa | 482 | 57 | 15 | 60 | 1 | 259 | | 318 | 404 | 722 | | | 8 | 81 | 0.45 | | | | 29 | | 82 | | | 105 | 2% | 26% | | | | 4.34 | | 39 | 111 | $10 |
| 17 | STL * | 383 | 45 | 14 | 57 | 1 | 266 | 260 | 318 | 451 | 769 | 797 | 713 | 7 | 76 | 0.31 | 48 | 18 | 34 | 32 | 126 | 115 | 142 | 14% | 73 | 2% | 39% | 14 | 36% | 50% | 4.92 | -10.8 | 33 | 100 | $9 |
| 18 | 2 TM * | 412 | 60 | 25 | 68 | 0 | 276 | 274 | 347 | 512 | 859 | 1169 | 1015 | 10 | 73 | 0.40 | 35 | 28 | 37 | 32 | 126 | 141 | 158 | 41% | 112 | 1% | 0% | 14 | 50% | 29% | 6.19 | 20.7 | 59 | 197 | $16 |
| 1st Half | | 180 | 19 | 6 | 22 | 0 | 228 | 218 | 295 | 381 | 676 | 1000 | 333 | 9 | 73 | 0.36 | 43 | 14 | 43 | 28 | 116 | 100 | 116 | 33% | 99 | 3% | 0% | 4 | 25% | 50% | 3.60 | -6.4 | 22 | 73 | $1 |
| 2nd Half | | 232 | 41 | 20 | 46 | 0 | 313 | 294 | 387 | 614 | 1000 | 1195 | 1046 | 11 | 73 | 0.44 | 34 | 29 | 37 | 36 | 127 | 174 | 161 | 41% | 110 | 0% | 0% | 10 | 60% | 20% | 8.82 | 25.3 | 86 | 287 | $28 |
| 19 | Proj | **415** | **55** | **22** | **64** | **1** | **262** | **268** | **336** | **486** | **823** | **891** | **792** | **9** | **74** | **0.36** | **41** | **24** | **35** | **31** | **127** | **137** | **153** | **20%** | **105** | **2%** | **32%** | | | | **5.45** | **8.2** | **38** | **128** | **$15** |

## Votto,Joey

**Age:** 35 **Bats:** L **Pos:** 1B | **Ht:** 6' 2" **Wt:** 220

**Health** B | **PT/Exp** A | **Consist** F | **LIMA Plan** B+ | **Rand Var** +1 | **MM** 3255

Posted his lowest BA and HR tally in a season of at least 300 AB, but skills say he deserved better. Good ct% and career best LD% say he's still a .300 hitter. Stable xPX paired with career-low hr/f suggests positive regression ahead, but don't count on a return to 30 HR. If price drops too far, don't hesitate to pounce.

| Yr | Tm | AB | R | HR | RBI | SB | BA | xBA | OBP | SLG | OPS | vL | vR | bb% | ct% | Eye | G | L | F | h% | HctX | PX | xPX | hr/f | Spd | SBO | SB% | #Wk | DOM | DIS | RC/G | RAR | BPV | BPX | R$ |
|---|---|---|---|---|---|---|---|---|---|---|---|---|---|---|---|---|---|---|---|---|---|---|---|---|---|---|---|---|---|---|---|---|---|---|---|
| 14 | CIN | 220 | 32 | 6 | 23 | 1 | 255 | 276 | 390 | 409 | 799 | 969 | 736 | 17 | 78 | 0.96 | 41 | 27 | 33 | 30 | 109 | 122 | 146 | 11% | 66 | 2% | 50% | 11 | 64% | 18% | 5.35 | 7.5 | 65 | 176 | $4 |
| 15 | CIN | 545 | 95 | 29 | 80 | 11 | 314 | 285 | 459 | 541 | 1000 | 1009 | 997 | 21 | 75 | 1.06 | 42 | 25 | 33 | 37 | 126 | 151 | 150 | 22% | 81 | 6% | 79% | 27 | 59% | 22% | 9.20 | 56.7 | 89 | 241 | $33 |
| 16 | CIN | 556 | 101 | 29 | 97 | 8 | 326 | 298 | 434 | 550 | 985 | 861 | 1033 | 16 | 78 | 0.90 | 43 | 27 | 30 | 37 | 123 | 133 | 134 | 22% | 84 | 4% | 89% | 27 | 52% | 22% | 9.13 | 55.9 | 79 | 226 | $33 |
| 17 | CIN | 559 | 106 | 36 | 100 | 5 | 320 | 309 | 454 | 578 | 1032 | 988 | 1048 | 19 | 85 | 1.61 | 39 | 23 | 38 | 33 | 125 | 130 | 141 | 20% | 84 | 2% | 83% | 27 | 81% | 11% | 9.82 | 58.4 | 110 | 333 | $32 |
| 18 | CIN | 503 | 67 | 12 | 67 | 2 | 284 | 276 | 417 | 419 | 837 | 758 | 880 | 17 | 80 | 1.07 | 38 | 31 | 31 | 34 | 121 | 83 | 129 | 10% | 80 | 1% | 100% | 27 | 44% | 26% | 6.17 | 15.0 | 47 | 157 | $16 |
| 1st Half | | 290 | 43 | 8 | 42 | 1 | 297 | 292 | 429 | 448 | 877 | 731 | 951 | 18 | 82 | 1.21 | 37 | 33 | 30 | 34 | 125 | 88 | 117 | 11% | 82 | 1% | 100% | 15 | 53% | 20% | 6.89 | 17.0 | 61 | 203 | $21 |
| 2nd Half | | 213 | 24 | 4 | 25 | 1 | 268 | 255 | 402 | 380 | 782 | 790 | 775 | 17 | 77 | 0.92 | 39 | 28 | 33 | 33 | 114 | 76 | 146 | 7% | 80 | 1% | 100% | 12 | 33% | 33% | 5.27 | 3.1 | 30 | 100 | $8 |
| 19 | Proj | **552** | **91** | **25** | **85** | **3** | **301** | **288** | **423** | **502** | **925** | **868** | **953** | **17** | **80** | **1.03** | **39** | **28** | **33** | **34** | **121** | **116** | **137** | **17%** | **82** | **2%** | **83%** | | | | **7.69** | **44.4** | **67** | **223** | **$27** |

## Walker,Neil

**Age:** 33 **Bats:** B **Pos:** 1B 2B 3B | **Ht:** 6' 3" **Wt:** 210

**Health** C | **PT/Exp** C | **Consist** C | **LIMA Plan** D+ | **Rand Var** +3 | **MM** 2123

Move to NYY excited fantasy thrift shoppers, but floundered in 1st half and finished with his first sub-.250 BA. Though he struck out more, plus bb% and PX/xPX gap points to some HR upside. Deepening issues vL may force platoon, but track record and swiss-army eligibility keep him worthy of deep-league speculation.

| Yr | Tm | AB | R | HR | RBI | SB | BA | xBA | OBP | SLG | OPS | vL | vR | bb% | ct% | Eye | G | L | F | h% | HctX | PX | xPX | hr/f | Spd | SBO | SB% | #Wk | DOM | DIS | RC/G | RAR | BPV | BPX | R$ |
|---|---|---|---|---|---|---|---|---|---|---|---|---|---|---|---|---|---|---|---|---|---|---|---|---|---|---|---|---|---|---|---|---|---|---|---|
| 14 | PIT | 512 | 74 | 23 | 76 | 2 | 271 | 283 | 342 | 467 | 809 | 727 | 831 | 8 | 83 | 0.51 | 38 | 23 | 39 | 29 | 102 | 127 | 105 | 14% | 81 | 3% | 50% | 26 | 65% | 12% | 5.33 | 28.6 | 75 | 203 | $20 |
| 15 | PIT | 543 | 69 | 16 | 71 | 4 | 269 | 261 | 328 | 427 | 756 | 575 | 793 | 7 | 80 | 0.40 | 42 | 21 | 37 | 31 | 112 | 105 | 113 | 10% | 96 | 4% | 80% | 27 | 44% | 22% | 4.83 | 8.6 | 48 | 130 | $16 |
| 16 | NYM | 412 | 57 | 23 | 55 | 3 | 282 | 255 | 347 | 476 | 823 | 1001 | 766 | 9 | 80 | 0.50 | 35 | 21 | 43 | 30 | 116 | 102 | 136 | 16% | 100 | 3% | 75% | 21 | 52% | 24% | 5.87 | 13.3 | 50 | 143 | $15 |
| 17 | 2 NL | 385 | 59 | 14 | 49 | 0 | 265 | 260 | 362 | 439 | 801 | 610 | 854 | 12 | 80 | 0.71 | 36 | 22 | 42 | 30 | 106 | 97 | 114 | 11% | 95 | 2% | 0% | 21 | 71% | 24% | 5.33 | 7.8 | 53 | 161 | $9 |
| 18 | NYY | 347 | 48 | 11 | 46 | 0 | 219 | 235 | 309 | 354 | 664 | 477 | 713 | 11 | 75 | 0.48 | 37 | 24 | 39 | 26 | 105 | 82 | 124 | 11% | 84 | 0% | 0% | 28 | 32% | 57% | 3.51 | -5.9 | 14 | 47 | $4 |
| 1st Half | | 162 | 22 | 2 | 14 | 0 | 185 | 201 | 261 | 259 | 520 | 348 | 564 | 9 | 75 | 0.39 | 41 | 18 | 40 | 24 | 97 | 52 | 111 | 4% | 100 | 0% | 0% | 15 | 20% | 80% | 2.10 | -10.8 | -10 | -33 | -$4 |
| 2nd Half | | 185 | 26 | 9 | 32 | 0 | 249 | 264 | 349 | 438 | 786 | 580 | 842 | 12 | 75 | 0.57 | 34 | 29 | 37 | 28 | 111 | 108 | 135 | 17% | 75 | 0% | 0% | 13 | 46% | 31% | 5.07 | 4.9 | 36 | 120 | $11 |
| 19 | Proj | **344** | **49** | **13** | **46** | **1** | **247** | **248** | **332** | **409** | **741** | **621** | **774** | **11** | **78** | **0.53** | **37** | **23** | **40** | **28** | **107** | **93** | **123** | **12%** | **88** | **1%** | **46%** | | | | **4.50** | **-2.7** | **24** | **81** | **$9** |

## Ward,Taylor

**Age:** 25 **Bats:** R **Pos:** 3B | **Ht:** 6' 1" **Wt:** 200

**Health** A | **PT/Exp** F | **Consist** A | **LIMA Plan** D | **Rand Var** -3 | **MM** 2211

6-15-.178 in 135 AB at LAA. Shift from catcher to third base and reported swing adjustments jump-started his bat. Traded ct% for increased power as he pulled the ball more than ever. Suddenly active on basepaths after registering 0 SB in 2016-17. Trouble vR wasn't present in minors. More work to do, but we're intrigued.

| Yr | Tm | AB | R | HR | RBI | SB | BA | xBA | OBP | SLG | OPS | vL | vR | bb% | ct% | Eye | G | L | F | h% | HctX | PX | xPX | hr/f | Spd | SBO | SB% | #Wk | DOM | DIS | RC/G | RAR | BPV | BPX | R$ |
|---|---|---|---|---|---|---|---|---|---|---|---|---|---|---|---|---|---|---|---|---|---|---|---|---|---|---|---|---|---|---|---|---|---|---|---|
| 14 | | | | | | | | | | | | | | | | | | | | | | | | | | | | | | | | | | | |
| 15 | | | | | | | | | | | | | | | | | | | | | | | | | | | | | | | | | | | |
| 16 | | | | | | | | | | | | | | | | | | | | | | | | | | | | | | | | | | | |
| 17 | aa | 119 | 13 | 3 | 18 | 0 | 261 | | 367 | 353 | 720 | | | 14 | 84 | 1.03 | | | | 29 | | 47 | | | 93 | 0% | 0% | | | | 4.47 | | 31 | 94 | $1 |
| 18 | LAA * | 510 | 62 | 16 | 58 | 15 | 255 | 213 | 326 | 396 | 722 | 758 | 489 | 10 | 69 | 0.34 | 35 | 21 | 44 | 34 | 76 | 97 | 99 | 15% | 79 | 13% | 80% | 8 | 38% | 63% | 4.47 | 1.9 | -2 | -7 | $17 |
| 1st Half | | 244 | 30 | 8 | 28 | 11 | 268 | 228 | 342 | 414 | 756 | | | 10 | 70 | 0.38 | | | | 35 | | 98 | | | 92 | 16% | 90% | | | | 5.12 | | 10 | 33 | $19 |
| 2nd Half | | 266 | 33 | 8 | 30 | 4 | 243 | 208 | 312 | 380 | 691 | 758 | 489 | 9 | 67 | 0.30 | 35 | 21 | 44 | 33 | 74 | 97 | 99 | 15% | 83 | 9% | 63% | 8 | 38% | 63% | 3.92 | -4.7 | -10 | -33 | $15 |
| 19 | Proj | **217** | **24** | **8** | **26** | **4** | **238** | **231** | **336** | **392** | **729** | **943** | **622** | **11** | **75** | **0.51** | **35** | **21** | **44** | **28** | **67** | **93** | **89** | **12%** | **82** | **7%** | **82%** | | | | **4.30** | **-1.4** | **14** | **45** | **$6** |

## Wendle,Joe

**Age:** 29 **Bats:** L **Pos:** 2B 3B | **Ht:** 6' 1" **Wt:** 190

**Health** A | **PT/Exp** B | **Consist** C | **LIMA Plan** B | **Rand Var** -3 | **MM** 2445

Late-bloomer enjoyed best season of his pro career, thanks to a 2nd half surge that was fueled by substantial ct% and LD% gains. Subpar xPX says he may not reach double-digit HR, but Spd/SBO/SB% backs continued SB contributions. Multi-position eligibility adds to value, and if 2nd half gains stick ... UP: 12 HR/20 SB.

| Yr | Tm | AB | R | HR | RBI | SB | BA | xBA | OBP | SLG | OPS | vL | vR | bb% | ct% | Eye | G | L | F | h% | HctX | PX | xPX | hr/f | Spd | SBO | SB% | #Wk | DOM | DIS | RC/G | RAR | BPV | BPX | R$ |
|---|---|---|---|---|---|---|---|---|---|---|---|---|---|---|---|---|---|---|---|---|---|---|---|---|---|---|---|---|---|---|---|---|---|---|---|
| 14 | aa | 336 | 36 | 6 | 39 | 3 | 216 | | 259 | 342 | 601 | | | 6 | 81 | 0.30 | | | | 25 | | 92 | | | 100 | 8% | 58% | | | | 2.82 | | 39 | 105 | $2 |
| 15 | aaa | 577 | 64 | 7 | 45 | 10 | 252 | | 274 | 380 | 654 | | | 3 | 78 | 0.14 | | | | 31 | | 93 | | | 112 | 11% | 81% | | | | 3.56 | | 27 | 73 | $10 |
| 16 | OAK * | 587 | 74 | 9 | 58 | 13 | 240 | 256 | 272 | 361 | 633 | 745 | 572 | 4 | 76 | 0.18 | 54 | 21 | 25 | 30 | 94 | 78 | 65 | 5% | 144 | 14% | 73% | 6 | 0% | 50% | 3.28 | -25.6 | 19 | 54 | $10 |
| 17 | OAK * | 491 | 52 | 6 | 45 | 10 | 235 | 257 | 257 | 354 | 611 | 0 | 973 | 3 | 80 | 0.15 | 50 | 20 | 30 | 28 | 129 | 70 | 124 | 33% | 126 | 16% | 66% | 4 | 50% | 25% | 2.97 | -24.7 | 20 | 61 | $6 |
| 18 | TAM | 487 | 62 | 7 | 61 | 16 | 300 | 261 | 354 | 435 | 789 | 809 | 784 | 7 | 80 | 0.39 | 46 | 22 | 32 | 36 | 109 | 86 | 76 | 5% | 105 | 15% | 80% | 28 | 36% | 29% | 5.57 | 20.3 | 37 | 123 | $21 |
| 1st Half | | 227 | 22 | 2 | 21 | 6 | 260 | 219 | 302 | 344 | 646 | 636 | 648 | 5 | 73 | 0.20 | 52 | 19 | 29 | 35 | 95 | 53 | 59 | 4% | 129 | 14% | 75% | 15 | 13% | 53% | 3.52 | -4.4 | -14 | -47 | $8 |
| 2nd Half | | 260 | 40 | 5 | 40 | 10 | 335 | 297 | 397 | 515 | 912 | 897 | 916 | 9 | 87 | 0.71 | 41 | 24 | 34 | 37 | 122 | 110 | 90 | 6% | 93 | 15% | 83% | 13 | 62% | 0% | 7.85 | 25.2 | 81 | 270 | $32 |
| 19 | Proj | **490** | **65** | **8** | **60** | **13** | **270** | **268** | **319** | **408** | **727** | **800** | **711** | **7** | **83** | **0.41** | **45** | **22** | **32** | **31** | **104** | **82** | **72** | **6%** | **114** | **14%** | **76%** | | | | **4.53** | **5.1** | **49** | **163** | **$18** |

## White,Tyler

**Age:** 28 **Bats:** R **Pos:** 1B DH | **Ht:** 5' 11" **Wt:** 225

**Health** A | **PT/Exp** C | **Consist** B | **LIMA Plan** D+ | **Rand Var** -1 | **MM** 3023

12-42-.276 in 210 AB at HOU. Bided time at AAA awaiting an opening at the MLB level and made the most of it when it arrived. Improved plate skills are a plus, but roughly average HctX and xPX (92 and 111, respectively) in 520 lifetime MLB AB calls into question his upside. Take a wait-and-see approach outside of deep leagues.

| Yr | Tm | AB | R | HR | RBI | SB | BA | xBA | OBP | SLG | OPS | vL | vR | bb% | ct% | Eye | G | L | F | h% | HctX | PX | xPX | hr/f | Spd | SBO | SB% | #Wk | DOM | DIS | RC/G | RAR | BPV | BPX | R$ |
|---|---|---|---|---|---|---|---|---|---|---|---|---|---|---|---|---|---|---|---|---|---|---|---|---|---|---|---|---|---|---|---|---|---|---|---|
| 14 | | | | | | | | | | | | | | | | | | | | | | | | | | | | | | | | | | | |
| 15 | a/a | 403 | 50 | 11 | 70 | 1 | 268 | | 363 | 404 | 766 | | | 13 | 78 | 0.67 | | | | 32 | | 93 | | | 81 | 1% | 37% | | | | 5.06 | | 38 | 103 | $11 |
| 16 | HOU * | 423 | 45 | 18 | 50 | 2 | 210 | 245 | 270 | 387 | 657 | 798 | 591 | 8 | 76 | 0.34 | 43 | 18 | 39 | 23 | 96 | 107 | 104 | 11% | 75 | 3% | 60% | 21 | 33% | 38% | 3.35 | -28.2 | 29 | 83 | $2 |
| 17 | HOU * | 497 | 59 | 19 | 65 | 4 | 229 | 219 | 276 | 391 | 667 | 1333 | 780 | 6 | 71 | 0.22 | 26 | 22 | 52 | 28 | 125 | 100 | 185 | 13% | 77 | 9% | 47% | 8 | 38% | 50% | 3.45 | -21.5 | 1 | 3 | $7 |
| 18 | HOU * | 465 | 62 | 21 | 76 | 1 | 261 | 256 | 337 | 466 | 803 | 1010 | 837 | 10 | 79 | 0.53 | 39 | 19 | 43 | 29 | 95 | 118 | 101 | 17% | 88 | 2% | 22% | 15 | 53% | 33% | 5.32 | 11.0 | 57 | 190 | $14 |
| 1st Half | | 245 | 31 | 9 | 29 | 1 | 251 | 256 | 332 | 410 | 742 | 775 | 730 | 11 | 79 | 0.59 | 55 | 18 | 27 | 28 | 106 | 95 | -4 | 0% | 86 | 3% | 33% | 4 | 25% | 75% | 4.55 | 0.3 | 42 | 140 | $10 |
| 2nd Half | | 220 | 31 | 13 | 47 | 0 | 272 | 272 | 342 | 529 | 871 | 1047 | 841 | 10 | 78 | 0.47 | 38 | 19 | 44 | 30 | 93 | 145 | 108 | 18% | 96 | 2% | 0% | 11 | 64% | 18% | 6.22 | 10.8 | 77 | 257 | $19 |
| 19 | Proj | **254** | **32** | **11** | **40** | **1** | **255** | **248** | **327** | **449** | **776** | **938** | **717** | **9** | **76** | **0.42** | **39** | **19** | **42** | **29** | **102** | **115** | **126** | **14%** | **83** | **4%** | **42%** | | | | **4.88** | **0.9** | **34** | **112** | **$8** |

GREG PYRON

## Wieters,Matt

Age: 33 Bats: B Pos: CA
Ht: 6' 5" Wt: 235
Health: F | PT/Exp: C | Consist: B
LIMA Plan: D+ | Rand Var: +1 | MM: 2023

Oblique injury delayed start of his season, hamstring surgery cost him two months in the middle. When in the lineup, there are signs here of the classic mid-30s catcher power spike: xPX endorses his new launch angle, and bb% growth dates back to 2nd half of 2017. With health... UP: 20 HR.

| Yr | Tm | AB | R | HR | RBI | SB | BA | xBA | OBP | SLG | OPS | vL | vR | bb% | ct% | Eye | G | L | F | h% | HctX | PX | xPX | hr/f | Spd | SBO | SB% | #Wk | DOM | DIS | RC/G | RAR | BPV | BPX | R$ |
|---|---|---|---|---|---|---|---|---|---|---|---|---|---|---|---|---|---|---|---|---|---|---|---|---|---|---|---|---|---|---|---|---|---|---|---|
| 14 | BAL | 104 | 13 | 5 | 18 | 0 | 308 | 293 | 339 | 500 | 839 | 799 | 849 | 5 | 82 | 0.32 | 28 | 30 | 43 | 34 | 138 | 127 | 160 | 14% | 81 | 4% | 0% | 6 | 67% | 33% | 6.11 | 7.6 | 66 | 178 | $4 |
| 15 | BAL | 258 | 24 | 8 | 25 | 0 | 267 | 255 | 319 | 422 | 742 | 728 | 746 | 7 | 74 | 0.31 | 43 | 25 | 32 | 33 | 101 | 109 | 113 | 13% | 77 | 0% | 0% | 19 | 53% | 37% | 4.74 | 6.8 | 23 | 62 | $4 |
| 16 | BAL | 423 | 48 | 17 | 66 | 1 | 243 | 261 | 302 | 409 | 711 | 645 | 733 | 7 | 80 | 0.38 | 36 | 24 | 40 | 27 | 106 | 94 | 113 | 13% | 82 | 1% | 100% | 27 | 41% | 44% | 4.10 | -3.7 | 35 | 100 | $8 |
| 17 | WAS | 422 | 43 | 10 | 52 | 1 | 225 | 239 | 288 | 344 | 632 | 687 | 619 | 8 | 78 | 0.40 | 42 | 21 | 36 | 27 | 86 | 72 | 100 | 8% | 66 | 1% | 100% | 27 | 30% | 41% | 3.28 | -9.9 | 7 | 21 | $2 |
| 18 | WAS | 235 | 24 | 8 | 30 | 0 | 238 | 234 | 330 | 374 | 704 | 705 | 703 | 11 | 81 | 0.67 | 34 | 21 | 45 | 26 | 102 | 76 | 137 | 9% | 82 | 1% | 0% | 18 | 39% | 22% | 4.00 | 3.4 | 33 | 110 | $2 |
| 1st Half | | 65 | 6 | 3 | 7 | 0 | 231 | 239 | 342 | 385 | 727 | 725 | 727 | 13 | 82 | 0.83 | 36 | 21 | 43 | 24 | 68 | 78 | 100 | 13% | 86 | 5% | 0% | 6 | 33% | 0% | 4.00 | 1.1 | 43 | 143 | -$5 |
| 2nd Half | | 170 | 18 | 5 | 23 | 0 | 241 | 233 | 325 | 371 | 695 | 693 | 695 | 11 | 81 | 0.61 | 33 | 21 | 46 | 27 | 115 | 76 | 151 | 8% | 86 | 0% | 0% | 12 | 42% | 33% | 4.00 | 2.8 | 32 | 107 | $5 |
| **19** | **Proj** | **316** | **33** | **11** | **41** | **0** | **240** | **242** | **316** | **381** | **697** | **699** | **696** | **10** | **80** | **0.52** | **37** | **22** | **41** | **27** | **97** | **81** | **121** | **10%** | **77** | **2%** | **21%** | | | | **3.95** | **4.7** | **12** | **39** | **$4** |

## Williams,Mason

Age: 27 Bats: L Pos: RF
Ht: 6' 1" Wt: 195
Health: D | PT/Exp: D | Consist: B
LIMA Plan: D | Rand Var: 0 | MM: 1221

2-6-.293 in 123 AB at CIN. Bull Durham prospect has interesting wheels, but ct%/PX combo shows there's nothing going on with his bat. Hard contact spike is an isolated blip in an otherwise pedestrian skill set and is probably a small sample anomaly. Could stick as a backup OF, but more likely he'll just keep making the AAA rounds.

| Yr | Tm | AB | R | HR | RBI | SB | BA | xBA | OBP | SLG | OPS | vL | vR | bb% | ct% | Eye | G | L | F | h% | HctX | PX | xPX | hr/f | Spd | SBO | SB% | #Wk | DOM | DIS | RC/G | RAR | BPV | BPX | R$ |
|---|---|---|---|---|---|---|---|---|---|---|---|---|---|---|---|---|---|---|---|---|---|---|---|---|---|---|---|---|---|---|---|---|---|---|---|
| 14 | aa | 507 | 53 | 4 | 32 | 17 | 195 | | 251 | 262 | 513 | | | 7 | 85 | 0.49 | | | | 22 | | 47 | | | 112 | 22% | 65% | | | | 2.04 | | 27 | 73 | $2 |
| 15 | NYY * | 222 | 26 | 1 | 22 | 11 | 288 | 283 | 359 | 377 | 736 | 0 | 933 | 10 | 87 | 0.84 | 53 | 24 | 24 | 33 | 63 | 67 | 57 | 25% | 93 | 27% | 59% | 2 | 100% | 0% | 4.52 | -2.1 | 50 | 135 | $8 |
| 16 | NYY * | 152 | 21 | 0 | 22 | 1 | 269 | 308 | 294 | 330 | 624 | 625 | 666 | 3 | 76 | 0.15 | 33 | 53 | 13 | 35 | 96 | 50 | 59 | 0% | 104 | 5% | 43% | 4 | 0% | 100% | 3.30 | -6.0 | -15 | -43 | $2 |
| 17 | NYY * | 415 | 40 | 2 | 26 | 18 | 227 | 196 | 271 | 271 | 542 | 400 | 606 | 6 | 81 | 0.31 | 57 | 7 | 36 | 28 | 70 | 26 | 45 | 0% | 141 | 22% | 75% | 3 | 0% | 67% | 2.46 | -34.9 | 0 | 0 | $5 |
| 18 | CIN * | 441 | 49 | 7 | 29 | 5 | 248 | 254 | 295 | 358 | 653 | 513 | 769 | 6 | 77 | 0.29 | 48 | 25 | 26 | 31 | 131 | 69 | 77 | 8% | 119 | 15% | 29% | 11 | 36% | 55% | 3.23 | -15.7 | 15 | 50 | $6 |
| 1st Half | | 243 | 29 | 5 | 19 | 3 | 228 | 236 | 272 | 349 | 620 | | | 6 | 78 | 0.27 | | | | 27 | | 76 | | | 114 | 17% | 33% | | | | 2.83 | | 18 | 60 | $6 |
| 2nd Half | | 198 | 21 | 2 | 10 | 2 | 273 | 249 | 324 | 369 | 693 | 513 | 769 | 7 | 77 | 0.33 | 48 | 25 | 26 | 35 | 130 | 61 | 77 | 8% | 127 | 13% | 24% | 11 | 36% | 55% | 3.76 | -4.1 | 12 | 40 | $6 |
| **19** | **Proj** | **164** | **18** | **2** | **13** | **4** | **248** | **249** | **294** | **346** | **640** | **455** | **674** | **6** | **77** | **0.28** | **48** | **25** | **26** | **31** | **107** | **62** | **69** | **7%** | **111** | **17%** | **50%** | | | | **3.24** | **-6.1** | **-2** | **-6** | **$4** |

## Williams,Nick

Age: 25 Bats: L Pos: RF
Ht: 6' 3" Wt: 195
Health: A | PT/Exp: B | Consist: B
LIMA Plan: C+ | Rand Var: 0 | MM: 3235

Made some adjustments, with mixed results. PRO: Concurrent GB% reduction, bb% and ct% growth are steps toward unlocking power. CON: More contact didn't mean more quality contact (see HctX), xPX also unmoved. Red light on bases understandable given long-shaky SB%. Back to the drawing board.

| Yr | Tm | AB | R | HR | RBI | SB | BA | xBA | OBP | SLG | OPS | vL | vR | bb% | ct% | Eye | G | L | F | h% | HctX | PX | xPX | hr/f | Spd | SBO | SB% | #Wk | DOM | DIS | RC/G | RAR | BPV | BPX | R$ |
|---|---|---|---|---|---|---|---|---|---|---|---|---|---|---|---|---|---|---|---|---|---|---|---|---|---|---|---|---|---|---|---|---|---|---|---|
| 14 | aa | 62 | 3 | 0 | 3 | 1 | 208 | | 229 | 266 | 494 | | | 3 | 64 | 0.07 | | | | 32 | | 53 | | | 115 | 16% | 43% | | | | 1.82 | | -58 | -157 | -$2 |
| 15 | aa | 475 | 61 | 15 | 43 | 10 | 270 | | 310 | 432 | 742 | | | 6 | 77 | 0.25 | | | | 32 | | 106 | | | 114 | 17% | 54% | | | | 4.42 | | 38 | 103 | $15 |
| 16 | aaa | 497 | 73 | 13 | 60 | 6 | 239 | | 265 | 398 | 663 | | | 3 | 69 | 0.11 | | | | 32 | | 113 | | | 106 | 11% | 56% | | | | 3.43 | | 7 | 20 | $9 |
| 17 | PHI * | 595 | 82 | 26 | 93 | 5 | 271 | 251 | 310 | 469 | 779 | 738 | 838 | 5 | 66 | 0.17 | 50 | 23 | 27 | 37 | 90 | 128 | 87 | 20% | 131 | 9% | 45% | 15 | 27% | 53% | 4.90 | -6.2 | 18 | 55 | $19 |
| 18 | PHI | 407 | 53 | 17 | 50 | 3 | 256 | 248 | 324 | 425 | 749 | 625 | 780 | 7 | 73 | 0.29 | 44 | 24 | 32 | 31 | 81 | 99 | 87 | 18% | 114 | 5% | 60% | 28 | 29% | 50% | 4.46 | -1.7 | 21 | 70 | $11 |
| 1st Half | | 190 | 21 | 9 | 26 | 2 | 232 | 254 | 305 | 421 | 726 | 637 | 750 | 7 | 71 | 0.27 | 48 | 23 | 29 | 28 | 76 | 116 | 71 | 23% | 90 | 7% | 67% | 15 | 40% | 40% | 3.98 | -3.6 | 21 | 70 | $7 |
| 2nd Half | | 217 | 32 | 8 | 24 | 1 | 276 | 243 | 340 | 429 | 769 | 612 | 806 | 7 | 74 | 0.30 | 40 | 26 | 34 | 34 | 85 | 86 | 101 | 15% | 139 | 3% | 50% | 13 | 15% | 62% | 4.90 | 1.9 | 24 | 80 | $14 |
| **19** | **Proj** | **428** | **58** | **18** | **54** | **4** | **260** | **252** | **315** | **444** | **760** | **658** | **790** | **6** | **71** | **0.22** | **46** | **24** | **30** | **33** | **85** | **114** | **88** | **20%** | **119** | **8%** | **54%** | | | | **4.53** | **0.9** | **17** | **56** | **$14** |

## Williamson,Mac

Age: 28 Bats: R Pos: LF
Ht: 6' 4" Wt: 237
Health: C | PT/Exp: D | Consist: B
LIMA Plan: D | Rand Var: +3 | MM: 3223

4-11-.213 in 94 AB at SF. Called up in late April after a much-ballyhooed swing adjustment. Hit 3 HR in 5 games, then missed a month with concussion. Managed just 1 HR in 75 AB upon return, got sent back down; eventually shut down after concussion symptoms returned. Worth checking in on him come spring.

| Yr | Tm | AB | R | HR | RBI | SB | BA | xBA | OBP | SLG | OPS | vL | vR | bb% | ct% | Eye | G | L | F | h% | HctX | PX | xPX | hr/f | Spd | SBO | SB% | #Wk | DOM | DIS | RC/G | RAR | BPV | BPX | R$ |
|---|---|---|---|---|---|---|---|---|---|---|---|---|---|---|---|---|---|---|---|---|---|---|---|---|---|---|---|---|---|---|---|---|---|---|---|
| 14 | | | | | | | | | | | | | | | | | | | | | | | | | | | | | | | | | | | |
| 15 | SF * | 480 | 63 | 9 | 60 | 3 | 231 | 246 | 293 | 350 | 643 | 321 | 690 | 8 | 72 | 0.31 | 52 | 24 | 24 | 31 | 124 | 89 | 74 | 0% | 92 | 4% | 73% | 3 | 0% | 67% | 3.40 | -19.0 | 3 | 8 | $6 |
| 16 | SF * | 320 | 41 | 13 | 47 | 2 | 220 | 238 | 271 | 387 | 658 | 722 | 731 | 6 | 69 | 0.23 | 56 | 17 | 27 | 28 | 106 | 113 | 76 | 29% | 71 | 6% | 41% | 18 | 28% | 39% | 3.34 | -12.6 | 3 | 9 | $3 |
| 17 | SF * | 419 | 49 | 12 | 44 | 4 | 202 | 211 | 245 | 332 | 577 | 882 | 621 | 5 | 65 | 0.16 | 60 | 12 | 28 | 28 | 86 | 93 | 73 | 25% | 90 | 8% | 65% | 9 | 22% | 67% | 2.57 | -35.4 | -24 | -73 | $0 |
| 18 | SF * | 276 | 34 | 11 | 40 | 2 | 204 | 233 | 273 | 364 | 636 | 839 | 609 | 9 | 70 | 0.32 | 55 | 16 | 28 | 25 | 73 | 101 | 96 | 21% | 82 | 4% | 62% | 7 | 43% | 43% | 3.15 | -12.5 | 5 | 17 | $3 |
| 1st Half | | 169 | 29 | 10 | 29 | 1 | 238 | 253 | 318 | 459 | 777 | 839 | 609 | 10 | 69 | 0.37 | 55 | 16 | 28 | 29 | 72 | 140 | 96 | 21% | 90 | 5% | 50% | 7 | 43% | 43% | 4.80 | 1.0 | 37 | 123 | $8 |
| 2nd Half | | 107 | 6 | 2 | 12 | 1 | 152 | 195 | 200 | 218 | 418 | | | 6 | 72 | 0.22 | | | | 19 | | 43 | | | 85 | 3% | 100% | | | | 1.33 | | -38 | -127 | -$6 |
| **19** | **Proj** | **293** | **33** | **14** | **38** | **2** | **223** | **244** | **281** | **408** | **689** | **772** | **633** | **7** | **69** | **0.24** | **52** | **20** | **28** | **27** | **89** | **117** | **82** | **25%** | **81** | **5%** | **69%** | | | | **3.68** | **-8.2** | **4** | **13** | **$6** |

## Winker,Jesse

Age: 25 Bats: L Pos: RF LF
Ht: 6' 3" Wt: 215
Health: C | PT/Exp: C | Consist: B
LIMA Plan: B | Rand Var: -3 | MM: 3055

Torn labrum in shoulder ended his season in July, just as he was starting to translate his elite plate discipline into power. Full-season growth in HctX, FB%, xPX show the progress, but the monthly trends were even more exciting. Hit .362/.465/.554 over 130 AB in June+July. Injury may delay breakout, but it's coming.

| Yr | Tm | AB | R | HR | RBI | SB | BA | xBA | OBP | SLG | OPS | vL | vR | bb% | ct% | Eye | G | L | F | h% | HctX | PX | xPX | hr/f | Spd | SBO | SB% | #Wk | DOM | DIS | RC/G | RAR | BPV | BPX | R$ |
|---|---|---|---|---|---|---|---|---|---|---|---|---|---|---|---|---|---|---|---|---|---|---|---|---|---|---|---|---|---|---|---|---|---|---|---|
| 14 | aa | 77 | 12 | 2 | 6 | 0 | 186 | | 288 | 316 | 604 | | | 13 | 68 | 0.45 | | | | 25 | | 116 | | | 99 | 0% | 0% | | | | 2.85 | | 21 | 57 | -$2 |
| 15 | aa | 443 | 60 | 13 | 48 | 7 | 264 | | 359 | 407 | 766 | | | 13 | 78 | 0.69 | | | | 31 | | 96 | | | 95 | 8% | 62% | | | | 4.98 | | 47 | 127 | $13 |
| 16 | aaa | 380 | 35 | 3 | 40 | 0 | 280 | | 369 | 357 | 726 | | | 12 | 82 | 0.80 | | | | 33 | | 55 | | | 80 | 0% | 0% | | | | 4.67 | | 24 | 69 | $6 |
| 17 | CIN * | 420 | 48 | 9 | 49 | 3 | 283 | 248 | 355 | 410 | 765 | 354 | 1042 | 10 | 81 | 0.60 | 53 | 16 | 31 | 33 | 118 | 78 | 100 | 23% | 80 | 6% | 32% | 13 | 54% | 15% | 4.96 | -2.7 | 34 | 103 | $11 |
| 18 | CIN | 281 | 38 | 7 | 43 | 0 | 299 | 265 | 405 | 431 | 836 | 690 | 874 | 15 | 84 | 1.07 | 42 | 24 | 34 | 34 | 135 | 79 | 107 | 9% | 67 | 0% | 0% | 18 | 56% | 22% | 6.31 | 14.8 | 49 | 163 | $9 |
| 1st Half | | 229 | 27 | 6 | 32 | 0 | 266 | 251 | 381 | 389 | 770 | 705 | 788 | 15 | 83 | 1.03 | 42 | 23 | 35 | 30 | 127 | 71 | 101 | 9% | 71 | 0% | 0% | 15 | 60% | 27% | 5.10 | 4.3 | 41 | 137 | $10 |
| 2nd Half | | 52 | 11 | 1 | 11 | 0 | 442 | 322 | 517 | 615 | 1132 | 571 | 1214 | 13 | 88 | 1.33 | 43 | 28 | 28 | 49 | 170 | 111 | 130 | 8% | 85 | 0% | 0% | 3 | 33% | 0% | 14.54 | 11.5 | 97 | 323 | $3 |
| **19** | **Proj** | **490** | **70** | **18** | **72** | **1** | **296** | **283** | **386** | **481** | **866** | **473** | **953** | **13** | **84** | **0.87** | **47** | **22** | **31** | **32** | **126** | **108** | **111** | **14%** | **68** | **2%** | **23%** | | | | **6.61** | **29.2** | **56** | **187** | **$21** |

## Wisdom,Patrick

Age: 27 Bats: R Pos: 3B
Ht: 6' 2" Wt: 220
Health: A | PT/Exp: C | Consist: B
LIMA Plan: D | Rand Var: -4 | MM: 4201

4-10-.260 in 50 AB at STL. Former first-rounder finally found the power stroke in 2017... but don't get too excited: 26-year-olds better hit for power in their second time around the PCL. Contact rate dips suggest he's selling out to generate that power, and there just isn't enough of it. Pass.

| Yr | Tm | AB | R | HR | RBI | SB | BA | xBA | OBP | SLG | OPS | vL | vR | bb% | ct% | Eye | G | L | F | h% | HctX | PX | xPX | hr/f | Spd | SBO | SB% | #Wk | DOM | DIS | RC/G | RAR | BPV | BPX | R$ |
|---|---|---|---|---|---|---|---|---|---|---|---|---|---|---|---|---|---|---|---|---|---|---|---|---|---|---|---|---|---|---|---|---|---|---|---|
| 14 | aa | 452 | 38 | 10 | 41 | 4 | 187 | | 237 | 307 | 544 | | | 6 | 64 | 0.18 | | | | 26 | | 104 | | | 102 | 6% | 78% | | | | 2.28 | | -14 | -38 | -$2 |
| 15 | aa | 414 | 37 | 10 | 44 | 8 | 193 | | 241 | 316 | 557 | | | 6 | 69 | 0.20 | | | | 26 | | 91 | | | 99 | 15% | 70% | | | | 2.38 | | -7 | -19 | $0 |
| 16 | aaa | 262 | 21 | 4 | 22 | 4 | 194 | | 248 | 304 | 552 | | | 7 | 69 | 0.23 | | | | 27 | | 88 | | | 87 | 10% | 76% | | | | 2.39 | | -11 | -31 | -$2 |
| 17 | aaa | 456 | 52 | 23 | 69 | 2 | 201 | | 249 | 400 | 648 | | | 6 | 62 | 0.17 | | | | 26 | | 137 | | | 82 | 5% | 39% | | | | 3.10 | | -2 | -6 | $3 |
| 18 | STL * | 421 | 58 | 14 | 54 | 10 | 234 | 217 | 295 | 387 | 682 | 810 | 930 | 8 | 64 | 0.24 | 35 | 26 | 39 | 33 | 106 | 113 | 134 | 33% | 93 | 13% | 74% | 8 | 50% | 50% | 3.79 | -11.2 | -8 | -27 | $11 |
| 1st Half | | 271 | 37 | 8 | 35 | 6 | 239 | 215 | 300 | 386 | 685 | | | 8 | 64 | 0.24 | | | | 34 | | 109 | | | 93 | 12% | 84% | | | | 3.93 | | -11 | -37 | $14 |
| 2nd Half | | 150 | 21 | 6 | 19 | 3 | 225 | 218 | 286 | 389 | 676 | 810 | 930 | 8 | 63 | 0.23 | 35 | 26 | 39 | 31 | 104 | 120 | 134 | 33% | 94 | 17% | 61% | 8 | 50% | 50% | 3.54 | -4.5 | -7 | -23 | $5 |
| **19** | **Proj** | **130** | **15** | **5** | **16** | **2** | **215** | **221** | **294** | **394** | **688** | **631** | **728** | **7** | **64** | **0.21** | **37** | **22** | **41** | **29** | **94** | **128** | **121** | **16%** | **97** | **11%** | **69%** | | | | **3.42** | **-4.4** | **-2** | **-6** | **$3** |

## Wolters,Tony

Age: 27 Bats: L Pos: CA
Ht: 5'10" Wt: 200
Health: A | PT/Exp: F | Consist: C
LIMA Plan: D | Rand Var: +5 | MM: 1321

Sure, small sample size caveats apply, but that 7-pt ct% bump has to be a good thing, right? Slide your eye over to HctX. Didn't move at all, which means that additional contact was bad contact, which in turn means that 19% hit rate isn't quite as unlucky as it looks. Mine for your 2nd catcher elsewhere.

| Yr | Tm | AB | R | HR | RBI | SB | BA | xBA | OBP | SLG | OPS | vL | vR | bb% | ct% | Eye | G | L | F | h% | HctX | PX | xPX | hr/f | Spd | SBO | SB% | #Wk | DOM | DIS | RC/G | RAR | BPV | BPX | R$ |
|---|---|---|---|---|---|---|---|---|---|---|---|---|---|---|---|---|---|---|---|---|---|---|---|---|---|---|---|---|---|---|---|---|---|---|---|
| 14 | aa | 341 | 29 | 1 | 28 | 2 | 221 | | 279 | 276 | 556 | | | 7 | 76 | 0.33 | | | | 29 | | 50 | | | 95 | 5% | 53% | | | | 2.49 | | -10 | -27 | -$1 |
| 15 | aa | 239 | 21 | 2 | 15 | 3 | 198 | | 256 | 263 | 518 | | | 7 | 72 | 0.28 | | | | 27 | | 49 | | | 111 | 9% | 55% | | | | 2.09 | | -21 | -57 | -$3 |
| 16 | COL | 205 | 27 | 3 | 30 | 4 | 259 | 258 | 327 | 395 | 723 | 579 | 757 | 9 | 74 | 0.40 | 48 | 23 | 29 | 34 | 64 | 98 | 72 | 7% | 102 | 9% | 80% | 25 | 36% | 44% | 4.48 | 0.4 | 26 | 74 | $4 |
| 17 | COL * | 283 | 34 | 1 | 22 | 0 | 239 | 236 | 323 | 312 | 635 | 496 | 661 | 11 | 75 | 0.49 | 55 | 22 | 24 | 31 | 64 | 51 | 42 | 0% | 97 | 2% | 0% | 24 | 21% | 54% | 3.27 | -6.6 | -6 | -18 | $0 |
| 18 | COL | 182 | 19 | 3 | 27 | 2 | 170 | 246 | 292 | 286 | 577 | 603 | 571 | 12 | 82 | 0.79 | 57 | 15 | 28 | 19 | 64 | 58 | 38 | 7% | 119 | 4% | 100% | 28 | 39% | 29% | 2.46 | -6.2 | 36 | 120 | -$2 |
| 1st Half | | 103 | 9 | 2 | 11 | 2 | 146 | 204 | 264 | 214 | 478 | 485 | 476 | 11 | 80 | 0.62 | 57 | 12 | 30 | 16 | 60 | 36 | 28 | 8% | 87 | 8% | 100% | 15 | 20% | 47% | 1.62 | -6.3 | -2 | -7 | -$4 |
| 2nd Half | | 79 | 10 | 1 | 16 | 0 | 203 | 285 | 326 | 380 | 706 | 722 | 701 | 14 | 85 | 1.08 | 57 | 19 | 24 | 23 | 69 | 86 | 51 | 6% | 121 | 0% | 0% | 13 | 62% | 8% | 3.83 | 0.9 | 75 | 250 | $1 |
| **19** | **Proj** | **186** | **21** | **2** | **24** | **1** | **220** | **250** | **317** | **336** | **654** | **594** | **670** | **11** | **79** | **0.59** | **55** | **19** | **26** | **27** | **65** | **67** | **46** | **7%** | **108** | **4%** | **71%** | | | | **3.38** | **-0.4** | **23** | **76** | **$2** |

RAY MURPHY

## Wong,Kolten

**Age:** 28 **Bats:** L **Pos:** 2B
**Ht:** 5' 9" **Wt:** 185

| Health | B | LIMA Plan | C+ |
|---|---|---|---|
| PT/Exp | C | Rand Var | +1 |
| Consist | C | MM | 1343 |

We've long touted his latent SB potential, but once again injuries (hamstring, knee) and an inability to reach first base kept that skill under wraps. Speed is a skill of the young; he's creeping toward age 30. We may see more periodic flashes, like 2nd half, where health and h% align. But that is now the extent of his upside.

| Yr | Tm | AB | R | HR | RBI | SB | BA | xBA | OBP | SLG | OPS | vL | vR | bb% | ct% | Eye | G | L | F | h% | HctX | PX | xPX | hr/f | Spd | SBO | SB% | #Wk | DOM | DIS | RC/G | RAR | BPV | BPX | R$ |
|---|---|---|---|---|---|---|---|---|---|---|---|---|---|---|---|---|---|---|---|---|---|---|---|---|---|---|---|---|---|---|---|---|---|---|---|
| 14 | STL * | 477 | 63 | 14 | 51 | 24 | 257 | 262 | 294 | 395 | 689 | 790 | 656 | 5 | 83 | 0.30 | 47 | 19 | 34 | 28 | 93 | 90 | 82 | 11% | 106 | 25% | 86% | 23 | 48% | 30% | 4.10 | 9.9 | 47 | 127 | $20 |
| 15 | STL | 557 | 71 | 11 | 61 | 15 | 262 | 262 | 321 | 386 | 707 | 552 | 772 | 6 | 83 | 0.38 | 45 | 22 | 33 | 30 | 98 | 80 | 86 | 7% | 106 | 17% | 65% | 27 | 30% | 26% | 3.99 | -2.9 | 41 | 111 | $17 |
| 16 | STL * | 341 | 46 | 8 | 31 | 8 | 249 | 253 | 323 | 384 | 707 | 653 | 689 | 9 | 83 | 0.63 | 46 | 20 | 34 | 28 | 87 | 67 | 79 | 6% | 155 | 8% | 100% | 26 | 35% | 38% | 4.35 | -5.1 | 52 | 149 | $7 |
| 17 | STL | 354 | 55 | 4 | 42 | 8 | 285 | 270 | 376 | 412 | 788 | 703 | 810 | 10 | 83 | 0.68 | 48 | 20 | 32 | 33 | 95 | 79 | 72 | 4% | 112 | 9% | 80% | 22 | 55% | 18% | 5.33 | 3.1 | 51 | 155 | $11 |
| 18 | STL | 353 | 41 | 9 | 38 | 6 | 249 | 263 | 332 | 388 | 720 | 614 | 752 | 8 | 83 | 0.52 | 49 | 20 | 31 | 28 | 86 | 80 | 59 | 10% | 96 | 12% | 55% | 25 | 44% | 36% | 3.93 | -3.5 | 42 | 140 | $7 |
| 1st Half | | 190 | 20 | 6 | 16 | 1 | 189 | 228 | 292 | 321 | 613 | 392 | 664 | 8 | 79 | 0.40 | 55 | 12 | 33 | 21 | 74 | 72 | 46 | 13% | 106 | 10% | 25% | 15 | 40% | 47% | 2.38 | -11.1 | 23 | 77 | $1 |
| 2nd Half | | 163 | 21 | 3 | 22 | 5 | 319 | 301 | 379 | 466 | 845 | 784 | 870 | 8 | 88 | 0.75 | 43 | 28 | 29 | 35 | 100 | 89 | 72 | 8% | 93 | 14% | 71% | 10 | 50% | 20% | 6.49 | 10.3 | 69 | 230 | $15 |
| 19 | Proj | **385** | **51** | **8** | **43** | **9** | **268** | **266** | **346** | **403** | **749** | **673** | **771** | **8** | **84** | **0.56** | **47** | **21** | **32** | **30** | **91** | **79** | **69** | **8%** | **107** | **12%** | **71%** | | | | **4.60** | **4.8** | **48** | **159** | **$11** |

## Wright,David

**Age:** 36 **Bats:** R **Pos:** 3B
**Ht:** 6' 0" **Wt:** 205

| Health | F | LIMA Plan | F |
|---|---|---|---|
| PT/Exp | F | Rand Var | +5 |
| Consist | F | MM | 0000 |

He made it back to say one last goodbye during the season's final weekend, long after the career's worth of good times had scrolled out of this box. And there were some very good times: 2007's 34-107-.325 ($37) was the headliner, but he was a consistent $25+ player from 2005-12. Best wishes for a healthy retirement, David!

| Yr | Tm | AB | R | HR | RBI | SB | BA | xBA | OBP | SLG | OPS | vL | vR | bb% | ct% | Eye | G | L | F | h% | HctX | PX | xPX | hr/f | Spd | SBO | SB% | #Wk | DOM | DIS | RC/G | RAR | BPV | BPX | R$ |
|---|---|---|---|---|---|---|---|---|---|---|---|---|---|---|---|---|---|---|---|---|---|---|---|---|---|---|---|---|---|---|---|---|---|---|---|
| 14 | NYM | 535 | 54 | 8 | 63 | 8 | 269 | 245 | 324 | 374 | 698 | 921 | 634 | 7 | 79 | 0.37 | 40 | 23 | 37 | 33 | 116 | 84 | 113 | 5% | 83 | 9% | 62% | 24 | 38% | 46% | 4.13 | 6.4 | 24 | 65 | $15 |
| 15 | NYM | 152 | 24 | 5 | 17 | 2 | 289 | 247 | 379 | 434 | 814 | 1023 | 746 | 13 | 76 | 0.61 | 37 | 24 | 39 | 35 | 120 | 98 | 132 | 11% | 87 | 6% | 67% | 9 | 22% | 44% | 5.86 | 5.1 | 37 | 100 | $4 |
| 16 | NYM | 137 | 18 | 7 | 14 | 3 | 226 | 228 | 350 | 438 | 788 | 714 | 814 | 16 | 60 | 0.47 | 23 | 28 | 49 | 32 | 116 | 165 | 228 | 18% | 79 | 12% | 60% | 8 | 38% | 50% | 4.91 | -0.2 | 29 | 83 | $2 |
| 17 | | | | | | | | | | | | | | | | | | | | | | | | | | | | | | | | | | | |
| 18 | NYM | 2 | 0 | 0 | 0 | 0 | 0 | 0 | 333 | 0 | 333 | 0 | 333 | 33 | 100 | 0.00 | 50 | 0 | 50 | 0 | 0 | 0 | -27 | 0% | 88 | 0% | 0% | 1 | 100% | 0% | 0.00 | -0.3 | 95 | 317 | -$3 |
| 1st Half | | | | | | | | | | | | | | | | | | | | | | | | | | | | | | | | | | | |
| 2nd Half | | 2 | 0 | 0 | 0 | 0 | 0 | 0 | 333 | 0 | 333 | 0 | 333 | 33 | 100 | 0.00 | 50 | 0 | 50 | 0 | 0 | 0 | -27 | 0% | 88 | 0% | 0% | 1 | 100% | 0% | 0.00 | -0.4 | 95 | 317 | -$3 |
| 19 | Proj | | | | | | | | | | | | | | | | | | | | | | | | | | | | | | | | | | |

## Yelich,Christian

**Age:** 27 **Bats:** L **Pos:** LF RF CF
**Ht:** 6' 3" **Wt:** 195

| Health | A | LIMA Plan | D+ |
|---|---|---|---|
| PT/Exp | A | Rand Var | -4 |
| Consist | D | MM | 4455 |

Missed two weeks in April (oblique); clearly it hampered him all summer... or not. Park factors in MIA-to-MIL move were strongly in his favor, but don't support this hr/f silliness. By month: 18%-22%-33%-50%-44%-43%. xBA, Spd+SB%, HctX confirm a five-category contributor. Just don't pay for another 30 HR with 25% FB.

| Yr | Tm | AB | R | HR | RBI | SB | BA | xBA | OBP | SLG | OPS | vL | vR | bb% | ct% | Eye | G | L | F | h% | HctX | PX | xPX | hr/f | Spd | SBO | SB% | #Wk | DOM | DIS | RC/G | RAR | BPV | BPX | R$ |
|---|---|---|---|---|---|---|---|---|---|---|---|---|---|---|---|---|---|---|---|---|---|---|---|---|---|---|---|---|---|---|---|---|---|---|---|
| 14 | MIA | 582 | 94 | 9 | 54 | 21 | 284 | 271 | 362 | 402 | 764 | 819 | 747 | 11 | 76 | 0.51 | 61 | 21 | 18 | 36 | 113 | 91 | 97 | 12% | 137 | 15% | 75% | 25 | 44% | 16% | 5.16 | 17.7 | 43 | 116 | $25 |
| 15 | MIA | 476 | 63 | 7 | 44 | 16 | 300 | 282 | 366 | 416 | 782 | 703 | 812 | 9 | 79 | 0.47 | 62 | 23 | 15 | 37 | 114 | 85 | 82 | 13% | 121 | 14% | 76% | 25 | 48% | 32% | 5.52 | 8.7 | 39 | 105 | $20 |
| 16 | MIA | 578 | 78 | 21 | 98 | 9 | 298 | 289 | 376 | 483 | 859 | 716 | 908 | 11 | 76 | 0.52 | 57 | 23 | 20 | 36 | 117 | 118 | 97 | 24% | 93 | 7% | 69% | 27 | 52% | 22% | 6.52 | 29.6 | 51 | 146 | $25 |
| 17 | MIA | 602 | 100 | 18 | 81 | 16 | 282 | 272 | 369 | 439 | 807 | 722 | 837 | 12 | 77 | 0.58 | 55 | 19 | 25 | 34 | 110 | 94 | 77 | 15% | 109 | 9% | 89% | 27 | 48% | 30% | 5.83 | 10.9 | 42 | 127 | $25 |
| 18 | MIL | 574 | 118 | 36 | 110 | 22 | 326 | 310 | 402 | 598 | 1000 | 983 | 1007 | 10 | 76 | 0.50 | 52 | 25 | 24 | 37 | 134 | 156 | 128 | 35% | 134 | 15% | 85% | 27 | 56% | 22% | 9.05 | 71.3 | 94 | 313 | $44 |
| 1st Half | | 263 | 52 | 11 | 34 | 10 | 289 | 273 | 364 | 471 | 835 | 729 | 874 | 10 | 75 | 0.43 | 52 | 24 | 24 | 35 | 123 | 108 | 120 | 23% | 133 | 14% | 91% | 14 | 43% | 21% | 6.26 | 13.3 | 46 | 153 | $26 |
| 2nd Half | | 311 | 66 | 25 | 76 | 12 | 357 | 341 | 435 | 704 | 1139 | 1158 | 1130 | 11 | 78 | 0.57 | 52 | 25 | 23 | 39 | 143 | 194 | 135 | 45% | 134 | 15% | 80% | 13 | 69% | 23% | 11.90 | 59.3 | 132 | 440 | $59 |
| 19 | Proj | **593** | **107** | **27** | **100** | **21** | **306** | **291** | **385** | **519** | **903** | **866** | **918** | **11** | **77** | **0.52** | **51** | **24** | **25** | **36** | **124** | **127** | **107** | **24%** | **121** | **13%** | **84%** | | | | **7.34** | **44.8** | **70** | **232** | **$38** |

## Zimmer,Bradley

**Age:** 26 **Bats:** L **Pos:** CF
**Ht:** 6' 5" **Wt:** 220

| Health | A | LIMA Plan | D |
|---|---|---|---|
| PT/Exp | D | Rand Var | -1 |
| Consist | C | MM | 2403 |

2-9-.226 with 4 SB in 106 AB at CLE. Labrum surgery ended his season in July, and likely impacts his first half of 2019. Prior to injury, flimsy sample size confirmed what we already knew: speed is calling card skill; power also intrigues. But both are only theoretical assets until he figures out consistent contact. Check back in a year.

| Yr | Tm | AB | R | HR | RBI | SB | BA | xBA | OBP | SLG | OPS | vL | vR | bb% | ct% | Eye | G | L | F | h% | HctX | PX | xPX | hr/f | Spd | SBO | SB% | #Wk | DOM | DIS | RC/G | RAR | BPV | BPX | R$ |
|---|---|---|---|---|---|---|---|---|---|---|---|---|---|---|---|---|---|---|---|---|---|---|---|---|---|---|---|---|---|---|---|---|---|---|---|
| 14 | | | | | | | | | | | | | | | | | | | | | | | | | | | | | | | | | | | |
| 15 | aa | 187 | 22 | 6 | 22 | 11 | 208 | | 270 | 354 | 624 | | | 8 | 70 | 0.28 | | | | 27 | | 108 | | | 95 | 33% | 83% | | | | 3.18 | | 11 | 30 | $4 |
| 16 | a/a | 468 | 62 | 13 | 51 | 31 | 230 | | 324 | 382 | 706 | | | 12 | 63 | 0.38 | | | | 33 | | 115 | | | 105 | 36% | 67% | | | | 3.91 | | 4 | 11 | $17 |
| 17 | CLE * | 425 | 58 | 12 | 50 | 25 | 248 | 234 | 309 | 409 | 718 | 624 | 714 | 8 | 65 | 0.25 | 48 | 20 | 32 | 35 | 88 | 114 | 83 | 13% | 121 | 29% | 85% | 18 | 17% | 61% | 4.42 | -4.0 | 6 | 18 | $16 |
| 18 | CLE * | 136 | 16 | 3 | 10 | 6 | 208 | 195 | 259 | 306 | 565 | 770 | 548 | 6 | 58 | 0.16 | 48 | 24 | 28 | 33 | 94 | 82 | 123 | 13% | 102 | 24% | 86% | 9 | 11% | 78% | 2.66 | -5.8 | -55 | -183 | $0 |
| 1st Half | | 136 | 16 | 3 | 10 | 6 | 208 | 195 | 259 | 306 | 565 | 770 | 548 | 6 | 58 | 0.16 | 48 | 24 | 28 | 33 | 93 | 82 | 123 | 13% | 103 | 24% | 86% | 9 | 11% | 78% | 2.66 | -6.3 | -56 | -187 | $0 |
| 2nd Half | | | | | | | | | | | | | | | | | | | | | | | | | | | | | | | | | | | |
| 19 | Proj | **255** | **32** | **6** | **26** | **15** | **231** | **218** | **305** | **361** | **666** | **736** | **640** | **9** | **63** | **0.26** | **48** | **23** | **29** | **34** | **91** | **100** | **107** | **13%** | **110** | **30%** | **76%** | | | | **3.60** | **-4.2** | **-12** | **-38** | **$9** |

## Zimmerman,Ryan

**Age:** 34 **Bats:** R **Pos:** 1B
**Ht:** 6' 3" **Wt:** 215

| Health | F | LIMA Plan | C+ |
|---|---|---|---|
| PT/Exp | C | Rand Var | +1 |
| Consist | F | MM | 4043 |

2017 was an anomaly, let us count the ways: 1) stayed healthy enough for 500+ AB, 2) hr/f was nearly double the rest of the numbers in that column; 3) lofty hit% fed BA spike. He'll be lucky to see any one of those three numbers again, let alone all three at the same time. Don't pay for more than a 2018 repeat.

| Yr | Tm | AB | R | HR | RBI | SB | BA | xBA | OBP | SLG | OPS | vL | vR | bb% | ct% | Eye | G | L | F | h% | HctX | PX | xPX | hr/f | Spd | SBO | SB% | #Wk | DOM | DIS | RC/G | RAR | BPV | BPX | R$ |
|---|---|---|---|---|---|---|---|---|---|---|---|---|---|---|---|---|---|---|---|---|---|---|---|---|---|---|---|---|---|---|---|---|---|---|---|
| 14 | WAS | 214 | 26 | 5 | 38 | 0 | 280 | 284 | 342 | 449 | 790 | 779 | 794 | 9 | 83 | 0.59 | 44 | 21 | 35 | 32 | 121 | 128 | 115 | 8% | 81 | 0% | 0% | 13 | 69% | 15% | 5.52 | 8.1 | 78 | 211 | $6 |
| 15 | WAS | 346 | 43 | 16 | 73 | 1 | 249 | 275 | 308 | 465 | 773 | 1058 | 672 | 8 | 77 | 0.42 | 48 | 17 | 35 | 28 | 124 | 146 | 141 | 16% | 77 | 1% | 100% | 17 | 47% | 35% | 4.97 | -3.9 | 67 | 181 | $10 |
| 16 | WAS | 427 | 60 | 15 | 46 | 4 | 218 | 243 | 272 | 370 | 642 | 683 | 632 | 6 | 76 | 0.28 | 49 | 17 | 35 | 25 | 106 | 94 | 99 | 13% | 91 | 6% | 80% | 24 | 46% | 46% | 3.24 | -27.5 | 20 | 57 | $4 |
| 17 | WAS | 524 | 90 | 36 | 108 | 1 | 303 | 289 | 358 | 573 | 930 | 1038 | 895 | 8 | 76 | 0.35 | 46 | 20 | 34 | 34 | 124 | 152 | 138 | 26% | 87 | 1% | 100% | 27 | 59% | 30% | 7.50 | 22.8 | 69 | 209 | $26 |
| 18 | WAS | 288 | 33 | 13 | 51 | 1 | 264 | 282 | 337 | 486 | 824 | 1143 | 718 | 9 | 81 | 0.55 | 49 | 17 | 34 | 29 | 118 | 129 | 128 | 16% | 94 | 3% | 50% | 18 | 61% | 22% | 5.56 | 3.7 | 76 | 253 | $8 |
| 1st Half | | 115 | 11 | 5 | 16 | 0 | 217 | 262 | 280 | 409 | 689 | 945 | 563 | 7 | 79 | 0.38 | 44 | 22 | 34 | 23 | 122 | 99 | 124 | 16% | 138 | 0% | 0% | 7 | 43% | 43% | 3.65 | -3.9 | 54 | 180 | -$2 |
| 2nd Half | | 173 | 22 | 8 | 35 | 1 | 295 | 289 | 374 | 538 | 911 | 1360 | 802 | 11 | 82 | 0.68 | 52 | 15 | 33 | 32 | 116 | 148 | 131 | 17% | 74 | 4% | 50% | 11 | 73% | 9% | 7.10 | 11.2 | 93 | 310 | $15 |
| 19 | Proj | **308** | **41** | **13** | **54** | **0** | **260** | **269** | **325** | **464** | **789** | **996** | **723** | **8** | **79** | **0.43** | **48** | **18** | **34** | **29** | **118** | **122** | **126** | **16%** | **92** | **1%** | **20%** | | | | **5.12** | **3.2** | **46** | **152** | **$10** |

## Zobrist,Ben

**Age:** 38 **Bats:** B **Pos:** 2B RF LF
**Ht:** 6' 3" **Wt:** 210

| Health | B | LIMA Plan | B |
|---|---|---|---|
| PT/Exp | B | Rand Var | -4 |
| Consist | F | MM | 1145 |

Turned back the clock to his prime years, on the strength of a career-best h% at age 38. Sure, there were a few more line drives mixed in there, and HctX ticked up a few points. But xBA shows that the BA is largely a fluke, and there aren't any plus skills left. An empty .270 BA isn't worth much, even with position flexibility.

| Yr | Tm | AB | R | HR | RBI | SB | BA | xBA | OBP | SLG | OPS | vL | vR | bb% | ct% | Eye | G | L | F | h% | HctX | PX | xPX | hr/f | Spd | SBO | SB% | #Wk | DOM | DIS | RC/G | RAR | BPV | BPX | R$ |
|---|---|---|---|---|---|---|---|---|---|---|---|---|---|---|---|---|---|---|---|---|---|---|---|---|---|---|---|---|---|---|---|---|---|---|---|
| 14 | TAM | 570 | 83 | 10 | 52 | 10 | 272 | 267 | 354 | 395 | 749 | 873 | 703 | 11 | 85 | 0.89 | 49 | 18 | 33 | 30 | 103 | 88 | 89 | 6% | 112 | 8% | 67% | 25 | 60% | 16% | 4.88 | 12.9 | 70 | 189 | $18 |
| 15 | 2 AL | 467 | 76 | 13 | 56 | 3 | 276 | 293 | 359 | 450 | 809 | 926 | 753 | 12 | 88 | 1.11 | 49 | 19 | 32 | 29 | 107 | 108 | 85 | 10% | 105 | 5% | 43% | 23 | 61% | 9% | 5.58 | 9.6 | 95 | 257 | $15 |
| 16 | CHC | 523 | 94 | 18 | 76 | 6 | 272 | 288 | 386 | 446 | 831 | 856 | 823 | 15 | 84 | 1.17 | 48 | 22 | 30 | 29 | 111 | 99 | 94 | 13% | 99 | 5% | 60% | 27 | 52% | 19% | 5.92 | 18.7 | 79 | 226 | $18 |
| 17 | CHC | 435 | 58 | 12 | 50 | 2 | 232 | 257 | 318 | 375 | 693 | 553 | 737 | 11 | 84 | 0.76 | 51 | 16 | 33 | 25 | 109 | 76 | 84 | 10% | 108 | 3% | 50% | 26 | 54% | 27% | 3.90 | -16.9 | 52 | 158 | $4 |
| 18 | CHC | 455 | 67 | 9 | 58 | 3 | 305 | 277 | 378 | 440 | 817 | 787 | 828 | 11 | 87 | 0.92 | 48 | 22 | 30 | 34 | 114 | 78 | 95 | 7% | 111 | 5% | 43% | 27 | 52% | 15% | 5.99 | 19.9 | 66 | 220 | $17 |
| 1st Half | | 212 | 38 | 6 | 32 | 1 | 297 | 274 | 394 | 439 | 832 | 662 | 891 | 14 | 85 | 1.06 | 44 | 24 | 32 | 33 | 117 | 79 | 111 | 10% | 102 | 4% | 33% | 14 | 50% | 14% | 6.10 | 9.7 | 63 | 210 | $17 |
| 2nd Half | | 243 | 29 | 3 | 26 | 2 | 313 | 280 | 363 | 440 | 803 | 893 | 770 | 8 | 88 | 0.75 | 52 | 19 | 29 | 34 | 111 | 77 | 82 | 5% | 114 | 5% | 50% | 13 | 54% | 15% | 5.87 | 9.4 | 68 | 227 | $17 |
| 19 | Proj | **465** | **69** | **8** | **57** | **3** | **273** | **267** | **354** | **399** | **754** | **745** | **757** | **11** | **86** | **0.90** | **49** | **20** | **31** | **30** | **111** | **75** | **91** | **7%** | **108** | **5%** | **50%** | | | | **4.89** | **9.6** | **49** | **163** | **$15** |

## Zunino,Mike

**Age:** 28 **Bats:** R **Pos:** CA
**Ht:** 6'2" **Wt:** 220

| Health | B | LIMA Plan | D+ |
|---|---|---|---|
| PT/Exp | C | Rand Var | +1 |
| Consist | D | MM | 5003 |

Hit the DL twice (oblique, ankle). As 2016 reminds us, there's an Eye threshold where the power is useful enough to carry the BA at a weak position. Or as 2017 shows, a favorable h% can paper over the ct% problems. 2018 is what happens when you lose the Eye and the h%. In 2019, the BA risk outweighs the power payoff.

| Yr | Tm | AB | R | HR | RBI | SB | BA | xBA | OBP | SLG | OPS | vL | vR | bb% | ct% | Eye | G | L | F | h% | HctX | PX | xPX | hr/f | Spd | SBO | SB% | #Wk | DOM | DIS | RC/G | RAR | BPV | BPX | R$ |
|---|---|---|---|---|---|---|---|---|---|---|---|---|---|---|---|---|---|---|---|---|---|---|---|---|---|---|---|---|---|---|---|---|---|---|---|
| 14 | SEA | 438 | 51 | 22 | 60 | 0 | 199 | 226 | 254 | 404 | 658 | 722 | 632 | 4 | 64 | 0.11 | 34 | 17 | 49 | 25 | 86 | 170 | 143 | 16% | 90 | 5% | 0% | 27 | 30% | 37% | 2.83 | -6.8 | 28 | 76 | $5 |
| 15 | SEA * | 391 | 33 | 13 | 33 | 0 | 183 | 186 | 224 | 315 | 539 | 522 | 534 | 5 | 64 | 0.15 | 33 | 17 | 50 | 25 | 81 | 102 | 121 | 10% | 79 | 1% | 0% | 21 | 14% | 62% | 2.17 | -19.6 | -27 | -73 | -$4 |
| 16 | SEA * | 444 | 53 | 26 | 76 | 0 | 228 | 227 | 304 | 446 | 749 | 835 | 769 | 10 | 66 | 0.32 | 29 | 18 | 53 | 28 | 95 | 146 | 155 | 23% | 90 | 1% | 0% | 14 | 36% | 43% | 4.42 | 7.4 | 31 | 89 | $8 |
| 17 | SEA * | 428 | 57 | 29 | 73 | 1 | 250 | 245 | 317 | 515 | 832 | 883 | 827 | 9 | 61 | 0.25 | 32 | 22 | 46 | 34 | 96 | 186 | 141 | 24% | 82 | 1% | 100% | 24 | 50% | 50% | 5.56 | 17.9 | 38 | 115 | $11 |
| 18 | SEA | 373 | 37 | 20 | 44 | 0 | 201 | 212 | 259 | 410 | 669 | 575 | 714 | 6 | 60 | 0.16 | 37 | 19 | 44 | 27 | 87 | 156 | 131 | 20% | 74 | 0% | 0% | 22 | 32% | 45% | 3.26 | -1.2 | 0 | 0 | $3 |
| 1st Half | | 194 | 20 | 12 | 29 | 0 | 191 | 201 | 251 | 412 | 664 | 577 | 698 | 5 | 57 | 0.12 | 35 | 16 | 49 | 26 | 85 | 167 | 153 | 22% | 78 | 0% | 0% | 12 | 25% | 58% | 2.99 | -2.8 | -4 | -13 | $4 |
| 2nd Half | | 179 | 17 | 8 | 15 | 0 | 212 | 225 | 268 | 408 | 676 | 572 | 734 | 7 | 63 | 0.21 | 39 | 21 | 39 | 29 | 90 | 146 | 111 | 18% | 84 | 0% | 0% | 10 | 40% | 30% | 3.56 | 0.6 | 11 | 37 | $2 |
| 19 | Proj | **390** | **43** | **23** | **52** | **0** | **223** | **225** | **290** | **450** | **740** | **691** | **759** | **7** | **62** | **0.20** | **35** | **20** | **46** | **29** | **91** | **164** | **136** | **21%** | **88** | **1%** | **42%** | | | | **4.09** | **7.7** | **2** | **7** | **$8** |

RAY MURPHY

The preceding section provided player boxes and analysis for 441 batters. As we know, far more than 441 batters will play in the major leagues in 2019. Many of those additional hitters are covered in the minor league section, but that still leaves a gap: established major leaguers who don't play enough, or well enough, to merit a player box.

This section looks to fill that gap. Here, you will find "The Next Tier" of batters who are mostly past their growth years, but who are likely to see some playing time in 2019. We are including their 2017-18 statline here for reference for you to do your own analysis. This way, if Craig Gentry stumbles into some playing time in June, a quick check would show that his Spd skills were an asset even in 2018. Or if you're dredging through the catcher pool in May and Chris Herrmann has come upon some MLB playing time, this is a good reminder that he could be able to provide some short-term pop behind the plate.

| Batter | Yr | B | Age | Pos | AB | R | HR | RBI | SB | BA | xBA | OPS | VL | VR | bb% | ct% | Eye | GLF | HctX | PX | xPX | SPD | SBO | SB% | BPV |
|---|---|---|---|---|---|---|---|---|---|---|---|---|---|---|---|---|---|---|---|---|---|---|---|---|---|
| Adduci, James | 17* | L | 32 | 39 | 298 | 40 | 4 | 32 | 9 | 238 | 221 | 657 | 664 | 728 | 8 | 67 | 0.26 | 53/16/31 | 136 | 86 | 92 | 106 | 19 | 65 | -12 |
| | 18* | L | 33 | | 448 | 49 | 8 | 55 | 7 | 257 | 236 | 677 | 200 | 736 | 5 | 74 | 0.19 | 49/18/33 | 89 | 87 | 60 | 100 | 8 | 85 | 6 |
| Almonte, Abraham | 17* | B | 28 | 897 | 249 | 34 | 5 | 18 | 4 | 229 | 259 | 681 | 561 | 723 | 11 | 75 | 0.51 | 51/22/27 | 88 | 84 | 84 | 117 | 10 | 66 | 27 |
| | 18 | B | 29 | | 134 | 15 | 3 | 9 | 2 | 179 | 203 | 544 | 353 | 625 | 10 | 73 | 0.42 | 51/14/35 | 102 | 55 | 82 | 112 | 12 | 50 | -7 |
| Blanco, Gregor | 17 | L | 33 | 789 | 224 | 43 | 3 | 13 | 15 | 246 | 230 | 694 | 525 | 752 | 12 | 74 | 0.53 | 43/22/35 | 84 | 70 | 90 | 155 | 23 | 94 | 23 |
| | 18* | L | 34 | | 359 | 32 | 4 | 20 | 7 | 200 | 221 | 547 | 499 | 594 | 7 | 69 | 0.24 | 42/27/30 | 75 | 63 | 45 | 112 | 14 | 69 | -22 |
| Butera, Drew | 17 | R | 33 | 2 | 163 | 18 | 3 | 14 | 0 | 227 | 215 | 603 | 596 | 606 | 7 | 75 | 0.29 | 30/25/45 | 86 | 53 | 90 | 105 | 0 | 0 | -10 |
| | 18 | R | 34 | | 163 | 13 | 3 | 21 | 0 | 190 | 213 | 564 | 649 | 521 | 8 | 76 | 0.38 | 35/19/46 | 82 | 76 | 84 | 82 | 0 | 0 | 8 |
| Cuthbert, Cheslor | 17* | R | 24 | 53 | 202 | 18 | 5 | 25 | 0 | 232 | 240 | 644 | 606 | 591 | 7 | 75 | 0.28 | 42/23/35 | 86 | 80 | 102 | 91 | 0 | 0 | 5 |
| | 18 | R | 25 | | 103 | 11 | 3 | 7 | 0 | 194 | 194 | 583 | 710 | 507 | 9 | 78 | 0.48 | 48/11/41 | 88 | 60 | 41 | 82 | 4 | 0 | 4 |
| Flaherty, Ryan | 17* | L | 30 | 5 | 76 | 18 | 2 | 8 | 0 | 261 | 237 | 721 | 347 | 590 | 13 | 82 | 0.81 | 54/14/32 | 47 | 61 | 27 | 95 | 0 | 0 | 32 |
| | 18* | L | 31 | | 191 | 19 | 2 | 16 | 4 | 216 | 230 | 569 | 481 | 601 | 9 | 73 | 0.36 | 61/21/18 | 61 | 49 | 34 | 75 | 12 | 67 | -27 |
| Freese, David | 17 | R | 34 | 53 | 426 | 44 | 10 | 52 | 0 | 263 | 225 | 739 | 839 | 704 | 12 | 73 | 0.50 | 57/20/23 | 94 | 68 | 80 | 86 | 1 | 0 | -3 |
| | 18 | R | 35 | | 280 | 38 | 11 | 51 | 0 | 296 | 259 | 830 | 876 | 786 | 8 | 74 | 0.33 | 52/22/26 | 99 | 105 | 104 | 117 | 0 | 0 | 34 |
| Garcia, Greg | 17 | L | 27 | 546 | 241 | 27 | 2 | 20 | 2 | 253 | 253 | 697 | 342 | 758 | 13 | 73 | 0.58 | 48/30/22 | 50 | 52 | 41 | 120 | 4 | 67 | 0 |
| | 18 | L | 28 | | 181 | 15 | 3 | 15 | 3 | 221 | 232 | 613 | 617 | 611 | 10 | 80 | 0.54 | 46/22/32 | 82 | 51 | 68 | 100 | 8 | 75 | 10 |
| Gentry, Craig | 17* | R | 33 | 978 | 249 | 29 | 3 | 23 | 10 | 220 | 234 | 586 | 786 | 626 | 7 | 73 | 0.28 | 51/22/27 | 87 | 59 | 78 | 137 | 29 | 55 | -4 |
| | 18 | R | 34 | | 156 | 13 | 1 | 11 | 12 | 269 | 249 | 668 | 677 | 658 | 7 | 80 | 0.35 | 49/25/26 | 75 | 46 | 55 | 143 | 33 | 80 | 15 |
| Goins, Ryan | 17 | L | 29 | 64 | 418 | 37 | 9 | 62 | 3 | 237 | 229 | 643 | 607 | 650 | 7 | 77 | 0.32 | 50/15/35 | 86 | 74 | 70 | 95 | 5 | 60 | 11 |
| | 18* | L | 30 | | 242 | 24 | 2 | 12 | 3 | 196 | 226 | 515 | 450 | 589 | 5 | 70 | 0.19 | 45/27/29 | 71 | 63 | 63 | 102 | 9 | 69 | -24 |
| Guyer, Brandon | 17 | R | 31 | 97 | 165 | 23 | 2 | 20 | 2 | 236 | 229 | 654 | 691 | 577 | 8 | 74 | 0.35 | 39/25/36 | 67 | 60 | 59 | 116 | 5 | 100 | -3 |
| | 18 | R | 32 | | 238 | 31 | 8 | 28 | 1 | 181 | 236 | 566 | 804 | 513 | 6 | 76 | 0.28 | 40/20/41 | 105 | 93 | 102 | 73 | 5 | 50 | 15 |
| Headley, Chase | 17 | B | 33 | 53 | 512 | 77 | 12 | 61 | 9 | 273 | 252 | 758 | 704 | 779 | 10 | 74 | 0.45 | 43/25/32 | 90 | 86 | 78 | 104 | 7 | 82 | 19 |
| | 18 | B | 34 | | 52 | 2 | 0 | 4 | 0 | 115 | 159 | 368 | 220 | 415 | 10 | 62 | 0.30 | 50/22/28 | 85 | 21 | 51 | 79 | 0 | 0 | -90 |
| Herrmann, Chris | 17 | L | 29 | 27 | 226 | 35 | 10 | 27 | 5 | 181 | 227 | 619 | 503 | 645 | 11 | 70 | 0.43 | 44/18/38 | 98 | 97 | 126 | 93 | 9 | 100 | 12 |
| | 18* | L | 30 | | 212 | 24 | 6 | 23 | 0 | 208 | 195 | 669 | 839 | 726 | 14 | 62 | 0.43 | 34/23/43 | 95 | 98 | 128 | 104 | 0 | 0 | -12 |
| Holaday, Bryan | 17* | R | 29 | 2 | 338 | 26 | 10 | 42 | 0 | 222 | 241 | 623 | 400 | 583 | 5 | 80 | 0.26 | 46/18/36 | 47 | 83 | 10 | 63 | 6 | 0 | 19 |
| | 18 | R | 30 | | 151 | 7 | 1 | 16 | 0 | 205 | 219 | 519 | 418 | 558 | 4 | 81 | 0.34 | 39/23/38 | 64 | 36 | 45 | 80 | 0 | 0 | -9 |
| Holliday, Matt | 17 | R | 37 | 07 | 373 | 50 | 19 | 64 | 1 | 231 | 234 | 748 | 843 | 719 | 11 | 69 | 0.40 | 48/15/38 | 89 | 125 | 97 | 69 | 1 | 100 | 22 |
| | 18* | R | 38 | | 105 | 10 | 4 | 11 | 0 | 274 | 246 | 811 | 856 | 836 | 14 | 72 | 0.59 | 40/26/34 | 122 | 103 | 123 | 70 | 0 | 0 | 23 |
| Joyce, Matt | 17 | L | 32 | 97 | 469 | 78 | 25 | 68 | 4 | 243 | 268 | 808 | 537 | 855 | 12 | 76 | 0.58 | 38/19/43 | 93 | 136 | 127 | 69 | 4 | 80 | 59 |
| | 18* | L | 33 | | 239 | 37 | 7 | 17 | 0 | 209 | 242 | 659 | 673 | 675 | 13 | 75 | 0.63 | 35/26/39 | 99 | 87 | 134 | 75 | 3 | 0 | 21 |
| Kratz, Erik | 17* | R | 37 | 2 | 284 | 27 | 10 | 29 | 4 | 225 | 190 | 667 | 2000 | 3000 | 8 | 72 | 0.29 | 50/0/50 | 145 | 100 | 348 | 79 | 8 | 74 | 8 |
| | 18* | R | 38 | | 255 | 25 | 9 | 27 | 1 | 232 | 235 | 636 | 611 | 644 | 4 | 79 | 0.21 | 44/19/38 | 135 | 78 | 139 | 67 | 2 | 100 | 9 |
| La Stella, Tommy | 17* | L | 28 | 54 | 235 | 28 | 6 | 26 | 0 | 232 | 250 | 657 | 1000 | 845 | 10 | 81 | 0.60 | 43/23/34 | 105 | 65 | 95 | 78 | 2 | 0 | 21 |
| | 18 | L | 29 | | 169 | 23 | 1 | 19 | 0 | 266 | 258 | 672 | 384 | 707 | 9 | 84 | 0.63 | 53/24/23 | 96 | 45 | 56 | 86 | 2 | 0 | 18 |
| LaMarre, Ryan | 17* | R | 28 | 87 | 177 | 12 | 0 | 13 | 6 | 185 | 151 | 466 | 0 | 250 | 7 | 58 | 0.17 | 75/0/25 | 59 | 30 | -26 | 140 | 34 | 45 | -86 |
| | 18* | R | 29 | | 258 | 24 | 2 | 23 | 4 | 253 | 219 | 651 | 815 | 625 | 6 | 65 | 0.18 | 47/26/27 | 85 | 83 | 70 | 107 | 10 | 68 | -28 |
| Machado, Dixon | 17 | R | 25 | 46 | 166 | 17 | 1 | 11 | 1 | 259 | 238 | 621 | 437 | 695 | 6 | 81 | 0.31 | 57/19/24 | 95 | 37 | 48 | 132 | 2 | 100 | 5 |
| | 18 | R | 26 | | 361 | 36 | 2 | 28 | 4 | 201 | 240 | 531 | 706 | 514 | 7 | 80 | 0.40 | 43/25/32 | 94 | 49 | 72 | 99 | 9 | 57 | 5 |
| Maile, Luke | 17 | R | 26 | 2 | 184 | 15 | 2 | 8 | 1 | 148 | 178 | 384 | 476 | 375 | 3 | 74 | 0.14 | 51/9/40 | 65 | 40 | 74 | 93 | 4 | 100 | -36 |
| | 18 | R | 27 | | 202 | 22 | 3 | 27 | 2 | 248 | 216 | 700 | 820 | 656 | 11 | 67 | 0.37 | 46/20/34 | 84 | 94 | 100 | 123 | 3 | 100 | 3 |
| Mathis, Jeff | 17 | R | 34 | 2 | 186 | 13 | 2 | 11 | 1 | 215 | 217 | 600 | 677 | 573 | 7 | 67 | 0.23 | 42/23/35 | 84 | 78 | 94 | 105 | 3 | 100 | -21 |
| | 18 | R | 35 | | 195 | 15 | 1 | 20 | 0 | 200 | 195 | 544 | 615 | 504 | 9 | 66 | 0.30 | 37/24/39 | 98 | 60 | 126 | 82 | 0 | 0 | -42 |
| Orlando, Paulo | 17* | R | 31 | 98 | 243 | 22 | 3 | 22 | 2 | 229 | 229 | 586 | 646 | 501 | 5 | 75 | 0.20 | 43/22/35 | 110 | 64 | 97 | 74 | 12 | 41 | -14 |
| | 18* | R | 32 | | 379 | 38 | 8 | 34 | 1 | 201 | 235 | 548 | 432 | 366 | 4 | 74 | 0.15 | 49/20/31 | 68 | 76 | 34 | 112 | 2 | 100 | 2 |

# THE NEXT TIER (*=includes MLEs)                                           Batters

| Batter | Yr | B | Age | Pos | AB | R | HR | RBI | SB | BA | xBA | OPS | VL | VR | bb% | ct% | Eye | GLF | HctX | PX | xPX | SPD | SBO | SB% | BPV |
|--------|----|---|-----|-----|----|----|----|-----|----|----|-----|-----|----|----|-----|-----|-----|-----|------|----|-----|-----|-----|-----|-----|
| Ortega, Rafael | 17* | L | 26 | 97 | 419 | 45 | 4 | 34 | 17 | 246 | 257 | 647 | 0 | 0 | 7 | 85 | 0.49 | 44/20/36 | 0 | 62 | -26 | 113 | 25 | 66 | 40 |
| | 18* | L | 27 | | 413 | 49 | 1 | 28 | 14 | 225 | 245 | 602 | 708 | 526 | 10 | 85 | 0.72 | 46/22/32 | 88 | 40 | 37 | 177 | 15 | 81 | 47 |
| Peterson, Jace | 17* | L | 27 | 5749 | 314 | 31 | 4 | 37 | 8 | 216 | 223 | 624 | 529 | 644 | 13 | 75 | 0.58 | 58/12/30 | 89 | 60 | 80 | 98 | 9 | 86 | 4 |
| | 18 | L | 28 | | 210 | 21 | 3 | 28 | 13 | 200 | 232 | 634 | 391 | 681 | 13 | 72 | 0.53 | 48/19/34 | 74 | 88 | 65 | 79 | 29 | 81 | 11 |
| Phegley, Joshua | 17* | R | 29 | 2 | 178 | 15 | 4 | 13 | 0 | 208 | 235 | 591 | 600 | 582 | 5 | 82 | 0.32 | 35/17/48 | 96 | 82 | 91 | 50 | 3 | 0 | 21 |
| | 18* | R | 30 | | 212 | 21 | 4 | 27 | 0 | 192 | 208 | 576 | 504 | 645 | 7 | 69 | 0.25 | 44/15/41 | 64 | 95 | 87 | 103 | 0 | 0 | 0 |
| Prado, Martin | 17 | R | 33 | 5 | 140 | 13 | 2 | 12 | 0 | 250 | 256 | 636 | 658 | 630 | 4 | 84 | 0.27 | 49/20/31 | 66 | 67 | 58 | 72 | 0 | 0 | 22 |
| | 18 | R | 34 | | 197 | 16 | 1 | 18 | 1 | 244 | 247 | 592 | 523 | 608 | 5 | 82 | 0.31 | 47/25/28 | 92 | 44 | 58 | 83 | 4 | 50 | 2 |
| Ramirez, Hanley | 17 | R | 33 | 3 | 496 | 58 | 23 | 62 | 1 | 242 | 257 | 750 | 679 | 769 | 9 | 77 | 0.44 | 42/21/37 | 109 | 107 | 109 | 54 | 3 | 25 | 29 |
| | 18 | R | 34 | | 177 | 25 | 6 | 29 | 4 | 254 | 243 | 708 | 854 | 664 | 7 | 80 | 0.40 | 51/15/34 | 92 | 81 | 68 | 90 | 11 | 80 | 29 |
| Rivera, Rene | 17 | R | 33 | 2 | 218 | 23 | 10 | 35 | 0 | 252 | 239 | 736 | 753 | 730 | 6 | 68 | 0.20 | 36/25/39 | 99 | 113 | 139 | 55 | 2 | 0 | -7 |
| | 18 | R | 34 | | 86 | 8 | 4 | 11 | 0 | 233 | 223 | 693 | 523 | 800 | 4 | 59 | 0.11 | 28/28/44 | 94 | 142 | 138 | 65 | 0 | 0 | -18 |
| Robinson, Drew | 17* | L | 25 | 85 | 372 | 46 | 14 | 42 | 5 | 230 | 238 | 735 | 956 | 713 | 11 | 66 | 0.37 | 46/18/35 | 87 | 127 | 120 | 109 | 13 | 44 | 24 |
| | 18* | L | 26 | | 328 | 51 | 11 | 32 | 6 | 231 | 205 | 721 | 922 | 526 | 10 | 52 | 0.24 | 40/30/30 | 73 | 158 | 98 | 116 | 18 | 44 | -9 |
| Rodriguez, Sean | 17* | R | 32 | 4o6 | 162 | 20 | 5 | 10 | 1 | 146 | 177 | 494 | 774 | 431 | 11 | 56 | 0.28 | 39/22/39 | 81 | 80 | 132 | 85 | 3 | 100 | -61 |
| | 18* | R | 33 | | 186 | 24 | 6 | 24 | 2 | 171 | 186 | 586 | 790 | 506 | 12 | 61 | 0.35 | 33/19/48 | 60 | 103 | 105 | 110 | 7 | 57 | -13 |
| Romine, Andrew | 17 | L | 31 | 48536 | 318 | 45 | 4 | 25 | 6 | 233 | 264 | 625 | 674 | 613 | 6 | 79 | 0.33 | 47/26/27 | 94 | 65 | 76 | 101 | 14 | 60 | 13 |
| | 18 | L | 32 | | 119 | 15 | 0 | 2 | 1 | 210 | 180 | 504 | 465 | 524 | 5 | 67 | 0.18 | 42/23/35 | 35 | 25 | 8 | 132 | 3 | 100 | -58 |
| Rua, Ryan | 17* | R | 27 | 73 | 306 | 36 | 9 | 32 | 4 | 218 | 220 | 622 | 695 | 567 | 6 | 62 | 0.18 | 43/27/30 | 93 | 96 | 74 | 97 | 9 | 67 | -30 |
| | 18* | R | 28 | | 219 | 26 | 8 | 25 | 6 | 194 | 209 | 587 | 722 | 450 | 5 | 63 | 0.13 | 43/20/38 | 83 | 111 | 79 | 106 | 19 | 85 | -16 |
| Sandoval, Pablo | 17* | B | 30 | 53 | 365 | 35 | 10 | 37 | 0 | 204 | 226 | 576 | 391 | 704 | 6 | 79 | 0.29 | 47/16/36 | 104 | 70 | 87 | 33 | 1 | 0 | -4 |
| | 18 | B | 31 | | 230 | 22 | 9 | 40 | 0 | 248 | 255 | 727 | 440 | 816 | 8 | 77 | 0.37 | 50/20/30 | 116 | 99 | 94 | 45 | 0 | 0 | 19 |
| Sogard, Eric | 17* | L | 31 | 46 | 340 | 56 | 5 | 28 | 6 | 266 | 279 | 745 | 745 | 771 | 14 | 84 | 1.02 | 39/29/33 | 90 | 68 | 62 | 94 | 8 | 67 | 49 |
| | 18* | L | 32 | | 186 | 13 | 0 | 8 | 3 | 146 | 214 | 398 | 500 | 392 | 9 | 76 | 0.40 | 36/27/36 | 96 | 28 | 101 | 75 | 11 | 70 | -30 |
| Sucre, Jesus | 17 | R | 29 | 2 | 176 | 20 | 7 | 29 | 2 | 256 | 254 | 699 | 734 | 689 | 4 | 80 | 0.20 | 39/22/39 | 110 | 82 | 105 | 63 | 5 | 100 | 14 |
| | 18 | R | 30 | | 182 | 9 | 1 | 17 | 1 | 209 | 220 | 500 | 443 | 528 | 5 | 84 | 0.31 | 45/21/35 | 99 | 29 | 57 | 77 | 2 | 100 | -5 |
| Thompson, Trayce | 17* | R | 26 | 9 | 388 | 39 | 8 | 27 | 2 | 166 | 205 | 497 | 339 | 634 | 6 | 65 | 0.18 | 46/19/35 | 112 | 76 | 147 | 136 | 13 | 28 | -23 |
| | 18* | R | 27 | | 288 | 32 | 6 | 20 | 5 | 147 | 169 | 456 | 426 | 340 | 6 | 58 | 0.16 | 38/15/47 | 48 | 93 | 68 | 87 | 18 | 71 | -52 |
| Tomlinson, Kelby | 17* | R | 27 | 456 | 302 | 45 | 1 | 17 | 16 | 252 | 250 | 631 | 695 | 614 | 10 | 80 | 0.54 | 50/25/24 | 63 | 33 | 26 | 161 | 20 | 82 | 16 |
| | 18* | R | 28 | | 321 | 19 | 0 | 17 | 5 | 221 | 219 | 520 | 523 | 536 | 6 | 72 | 0.23 | 60/23/16 | 62 | 22 | 14 | 138 | 14 | 40 | -39 |
| Tucker, Preston | 17* | L | 26 | 7 | 492 | 51 | 15 | 58 | 1 | 183 | 231 | 561 | 0 | 0 | 7 | 74 | 0.30 | 44/20/36 | 0 | 77 | -26 | 112 | 5 | 25 | 8 |
| | 18* | L | 27 | | 235 | 24 | 6 | 32 | 0 | 220 | 249 | 627 | 380 | 741 | 6 | 78 | 0.28 | 45/21/34 | 111 | 91 | 76 | 70 | 0 | 0 | 19 |
| Valaika, Pat | 17* | R | 24 | 643 | 227 | 32 | 14 | 48 | 0 | 254 | 247 | 786 | 927 | 729 | 4 | 71 | 0.15 | 33/17/50 | 99 | 147 | 145 | 81 | 0 | 0 | 38 |
| | 18* | R | 25 | | 261 | 16 | 7 | 17 | 1 | 167 | 220 | 497 | 539 | 365 | 5 | 76 | 0.21 | 39/20/41 | 53 | 73 | 56 | 100 | 4 | 34 | 3 |
| Valbuena, Luis | 17 | L | 31 | 53 | 347 | 42 | 22 | 65 | 0 | 199 | 230 | 727 | 423 | 765 | 12 | 69 | 0.45 | 38/14/47 | 101 | 140 | 144 | 40 | 3 | 0 | 28 |
| | 18 | L | 32 | | 266 | 23 | 9 | 33 | 3 | 199 | 193 | 588 | 661 | 576 | 7 | 62 | 0.19 | 36/20/44 | 86 | 98 | 95 | 69 | 6 | 100 | -35 |
| Valencia, Danny | 17 | R | 32 | 3590 | 450 | 54 | 15 | 66 | 2 | 256 | 247 | 725 | 804 | 693 | 8 | 73 | 0.33 | 48/21/31 | 88 | 93 | 79 | 118 | 3 | 50 | 20 |
| | 18 | R | 33 | | 255 | 28 | 9 | 28 | 1 | 263 | 254 | 723 | 873 | 610 | 8 | 79 | 0.42 | 44/23/32 | 96 | 81 | 99 | 100 | 3 | 50 | 29 |
| Wilson, Bobby | 17* | R | 34 | 2 | 243 | 24 | 8 | 31 | 0 | 184 | 221 | 554 | 0 | 0 | 6 | 70 | 0.23 | 44/20/36 | 0 | 85 | -26 | 75 | 0 | 0 | -12 |
| | 18* | R | 35 | | 175 | 14 | 2 | 18 | 0 | 161 | 187 | 469 | 469 | 540 | 7 | 70 | 0.27 | 47/15/38 | 71 | 66 | 65 | 49 | 0 | 0 | -35 |
| Young, Chris | 17 | R | 33 | 7098 | 243 | 30 | 7 | 25 | 3 | 235 | 234 | 709 | 590 | 793 | 11 | 77 | 0.55 | 35/19/46 | 93 | 88 | 89 | 101 | 8 | 60 | 34 |
| | 18 | R | 34 | 0 | 113 | 17 | 6 | 13 | 2 | 168 | 207 | 615 | 680 | 568 | 9 | 67 | 0.30 | 29/19/52 | 67 | 117 | 90 | 123 | 10 | 100 | 19 |

The following section contains player boxes for every pitcher who had significant playing time in 2018 and/or is expected to get fantasy roster-worthy innings in 2019. You will find some prospects here, specifically the most impactful names who we project to play in 2019. For more complete prospect coverage, see our Prospects section.

## Snapshot Section

**The top band of each player box contains the following information:**

**Age** as of Opening Day 2019.

**Throws** right (R) or left (L).

**Role:** Starters (SP) are those projected to face 20+ batters per game; the rest are relievers (RP).

**Ht/Wt:** Each batter's height and weight.

**Type** evaluates the extent to which a pitcher allows the ball to be put into play and his ground ball or fly ball tendency. CON (contact) represents pitchers who allow the ball to be put into play a great deal. PWR (power) represents those with high strikeout and/or walk totals who keep the ball out of play. GB are those who have a ground ball rate more than 50%; xGB are those who have a GB rate more than 55%. FB are those who have a fly ball rate more than 40%; xFB are those who have a FB rate more than 45%.

**Reliability Grades** analyze each pitcher's forecast risk, on an A-F scale. High grades go to those who have accumulated few disabled list days (Health), have a history of substantial and regular major league playing time (PT/Exp) and have displayed consistent performance over the past three years, using xERA (Consist).

**LIMA Plan Grade** evaluates how well that pitcher would be a good fit for a team using the LIMA Plan draft strategy. Best grades go to pitchers who have excellent base skills and had a 2018 dollar value less than $20. Lowest grades will go to poor skills and values more than $20.

**Random Variance Score (Rand Var)** measures the impact random variance had on the pitcher's 2018 stats and the probability that his 2019 performance will exceed or fall short of 2018. The variables tracked are those prone to regression—H%, S%, hr/f and xERA to ERA variance. Players are rated on a scale of –5 to +5 with positive scores indicating rebounds and negative scores indicating corrections. Note that this score is computer-generated and the projections will override it on occasion.

**Mayberry Method (MM)** acknowledges the imprecision of the forecasting process by projecting player performance in broad strokes. The four digits of MM each represent a fantasy-relevant skill—ERA, strikeout rate, saves potential and playing time (IP)—and are all on a scale of 0 to 5.

**Commentaries** for each pitcher provide a brief analysis of his skills and the potential impact on performance in 2019. MLB statistics are listed first for those who played only a portion of 2018 at the major league level. Note that these commentaries generally look at performance related issues only. Role and playing time expectations may impact these analyses, so you will have to adjust accordingly. Upside (UP) and downside (DN) statistical potential appears for some players; these are less grounded in hard data and more speculative of skills potential.

## Player Stat Section

The past five years' statistics represent the total accumulated in the majors as well as in Triple-A, Double-A ball and various foreign leagues during each year. All non-major league stats have been converted to a major league equivalent (MLE) performance level. Minor league levels below Double-A are not included.

Nearly all baseball publications separate a player's statistical experiences in the major leagues from the minor leagues and outside leagues. While this may be appropriate for official record-keeping purposes, it is not an easy-to-analyze snapshot of a player's complete performance for a given year.

Bill James has proven that minor league statistics (converted to MLEs), at Double-A level or above, provide as accurate a record of a player's performance as major league statistics. Other researchers have also devised conversion factors for foreign leagues. Since these are adequate barometers, we include them in the pool of historical data for each year.

**Team designations:** An asterisk (*) appearing with a team name means that Triple-A and/or Double-A numbers are included in that year's stat line. Any stints of less than 10 IP are not included (to screen out most rehab appearances). A designation of "a/a" means the stats were accumulated at both AA and AAA levels that year. "for" represents a foreign or independent league. The designation "2TM" appears whenever a player was on more than one major league team, crossing leagues, in a season. "2AL" and "2NL" represent more than one team in the same league. Players who were cut during the season and finished 2018 as a free agent are designated as FAA (Free agent, AL) and FAN (Free agent, NL).

**Stats:** Descriptions of all the categories appear in the Encyclopedia.

- The leading decimal point has been suppressed on some categories to conserve space.
- Data for platoons (vL, vR), balls-in-play (G/L/F) and consistency (Wk#, DOM, DIS) and velocity (Vel) are for major league performance only.
- Formulas that use BIP data, like xERA and BPV, are used for years in which G/L/F data is available. Where feasible, older versions of these formulas are used otherwise.

Earned run average is presented alongside skills-based xERA. WHIP appears next, followed by opponents' overall OPS (oOPS). OPS splits vs. left-handed and right-handed batters appear to the right of oOPS. Batters faced per game (BF/G) provide a quick view of a pitcher's role—starters will generally have levels over 20.

Basic pitching skills are measured with Control, or walk rate (Ctl), Dominance, or strikeout rate (Dom), and Command, or strikeout-to-walk rate (Cmd). First-pitch strike rate (FpK) and Swinging strike rate (SwK) are also presented with these basic skills. Our research shows that FpK serves as a useful tool for validating Ctl, and SwK serves as a similar check on Dom. Vel is the pitcher's average fastball velocity.

Once the ball leaves the bat, it will either be a (G)round ball, (L)ine drive or (F)ly ball.

Random variance indicators include hit rate (H%)—often referred to as batting average on balls-in-play (BABIP)—which tends to regress to 30%. Normal strand rates (S%) fall within the tolerances of 65% to 80%. The ratio of home runs to fly balls (hr/f) is another sanity check; levels far from the league average of 14% are prone to regression.

In looking at consistency for starting pitchers, we track games started (GS), average pitch counts (APC) for all outings (for starters and relievers), the percentage of DOMinating starts (PQS 4 or 5) and DISaster starts (PQS 0 or 1). The larger the variance between DOM and DIS, the greater the consistency.

For relievers, we look at their saves success rate (Sv%) and Leverage Index (LI). A Doug Dennis study showed little correlation between saves success and future opportunity. However, you can increase your odds by prospecting for pitchers who have *both* a high saves percentage (80% or better) *and* high skills. Relievers with LI levels over 1.0 are being used more often by managers to win ballgames.

The final section includes several overall performance measures: runs above replacement (RAR), Base performance value (BPV), Base performance index (BPX, which is BPV indexed to each year's league average) and the Rotisserie value (R$).

## 2019 Projections

Forecasts are computed from a player's trends over the past five years. Adjustments were made for leading indicators and variances between skill and statistical output. After reviewing the leading indicators, you might opt to make further adjustments.

Although each year's numbers include all playing time at the Double-A level or above, the 2019 forecast only represents potential playing time at the major league level, and again is highly preliminary.

Note that the projected Rotisserie values in this book will not necessarily align with each player's historical actuals. Since we currently have no idea who is going to close games for the Angels, or whether Brent Honeywell is going to break camp with the Rays, it is impossible to create a finite pool of playing time, something which is required for valuation. So the projections are roughly based on a 12-team AL/NL league, and include an inflated number of innings, league-wide. This serves to flatten the spread of values and depress individual player dollar projections. In truth, a $25 player in this book might actually be worth $21, or $28. This level of precision is irrelevant in a process that is driven by market forces anyway. So, don't obsess over it.

Be aware of other sources that publish perfectly calibrated Rotisserie values over the winter. They are likely making arbitrary decisions as to where free agents are going to sign and who is going to land jobs in the spring. We do not make those leaps of faith here.

Bottom line… It is far too early to be making definitive projections for 2019, especially on playing time. Focus on the skill levels and trends, then consult BaseballHQ.com for playing time revisions as players change teams and roles become more defined. A free projections update will be available online in March.

## Do-it-yourself analysis

Here are some data points you can look at in doing your own player analysis:

- Variance between vLH and vRH opposition OPS
- Variance in 2018 hr/f rate from 14%
- Variance in 2018 hit rate (H%) from 30%
- Variance in 2018 strand rate (S%) to tolerances (65% - 80%)
- Variance between ERA and xERA each year
- Growth or decline in Base Performance Value (BPV)
- Spikes in innings pitched
- Trends in average pitch counts (APC)
- Trends in DOM/DIS splits
- Trends in saves success rate (Sv%)
- Variance between Dom changes and corresponding SwK levels
- Variance between Ctl changes and corresponding FpK levels
- Improvement or decline in velocity

## Alcantara,Sandy

| Alcantara,Sandy | | | | Health | C | LIMA Plan | D+ |
|---|---|---|---|---|---|---|---|
| Age: 23 | Th: R | Role | SP | PT/Exp | D | Rand Var | 0 |
| Ht: 6' 4" | Wt: 170 | Type | Pwr GB | Consist | C | MM | 0101 |

2-3, 3.44 ERA in 34 IP at MIA. Nice on the surface, but had 5.00 xERA and more BB than K in half his starts. Despite ideal frame and easy heat, has yet to find path to strikeouts, and may eventually move to pen. More MiLB time could breed confidence in secondary offerings, so keep an eye on his progress.

| Yr Tm | W | Sv | IP | K | ERA | xERA | WHIP | oOPS | vL | vR | BF/G | Ctl | Dom | Cmd | FpK | SwK | Vel | G | L | F | H% | S% | hr/f | GS | APC | DOM% | DIS% | Sv% | LI | RAR | BPV | BPX | R$ |
|---|---|---|---|---|---|---|---|---|---|---|---|---|---|---|---|---|---|---|---|---|---|---|---|---|---|---|---|---|---|---|---|---|---|
| 14 | | | | | | | | | | | | | | | | | | | | | | | | | | | | | | | | | |
| 15 | | | | | | | | | | | | | | | | | | | | | | | | | | | | | | | | | |
| 16 | | | | | | | | | | | | | | | | | | | | | | | | | | | | | | | | | |
| 17 STL * | 7 | 0 | 134 | 100 | 5.20 | 5.23 | 1.58 | 869 | 817 | 933 | 17.8 | 4.0 | 6.7 | 1.7 | 56% | 17% | 98.3 | 26 | 43 | 30 | 33% | 69% | 29% | 0 | 19 | | | 0 | 0.08 | -13.9 | 41 | 50 | -$7 |
| 18 MIA * | 8 | 0 | 151 | 106 | 4.13 | 3.93 | 1.36 | 706 | 627 | 798 | 25.3 | 3.6 | 6.3 | 1.7 | 61% | 11% | 95.5 | 48 | 16 | 36 | 29% | 70% | 9% | 6 | 95 | 33% | 33% | | | 0.4 | 57 | 65 | $1 |
| 1st Half | 6 | 0 | 90 | 57 | 4.05 | 3.82 | 1.38 | 694 | 111 | 1208 | 25.2 | 3.9 | 5.7 | 1.5 | 41% | 6% | 94.0 | 43 | 14 | 43 | 29% | 71% | 0% | 1 | 98 | 0% | 0% | | | 1.2 | 53 | 61 | $2 |
| 2nd Half | 2 | 0 | 61 | 49 | 4.25 | 4.09 | 1.32 | 708 | 699 | 715 | 25.3 | 3.2 | 7.2 | 2.2 | 64% | 12% | 95.8 | 49 | 16 | 35 | 30% | 70% | 12% | 5 | 94 | 40% | 40% | | | -0.8 | 64 | 73 | -$1 |
| **19 Proj** | **5** | **0** | **123** | **91** | **4.57** | **4.57** | **1.44** | **754** | **738** | **773** | **21.6** | **3.7** | **6.6** | **1.8** | **64%** | **12%** | **95.8** | **49** | **16** | **35** | **31%** | **70%** | **9%** | **24** | | | | | | **-6.3** | **46** | **53** | **-$4** |

## Alexander,Scott

| Alexander,Scott | | | | Health | B | LIMA Plan | B+ |
|---|---|---|---|---|---|---|---|
| Age: 29 | Th: L | Role | RP | PT/Exp | D | Rand Var | +4 |
| Ht: 6' 2" | Wt: 190 | Type | Pwr xGB | Consist | C | MM | 4210 |

As with many RP, he's more valuable in real baseball than in our game. Provides few counting stats and you only take notice when something goes awry, usually when facing RHB. Other than extreme GB tilt, skills are very average. A placeholder who's invariably nudged aside by someone better.

| Yr Tm | W | Sv | IP | K | ERA | xERA | WHIP | oOPS | vL | vR | BF/G | Ctl | Dom | Cmd | FpK | SwK | Vel | G | L | F | H% | S% | hr/f | GS | APC | DOM% | DIS% | Sv% | LI | RAR | BPV | BPX | R$ |
|---|---|---|---|---|---|---|---|---|---|---|---|---|---|---|---|---|---|---|---|---|---|---|---|---|---|---|---|---|---|---|---|---|---|
| 14 a/a | 2 | 3 | 68 | 38 | 5.33 | 4.88 | 1.50 | | | | 6.4 | 3.5 | 5.1 | 1.5 | | | | | | | 31% | 65% | | | | | | | | -13.3 | 31 | 36 | -$7 |
| 15 KC * | 2 | 14 | 69 | 42 | 3.49 | 3.48 | 1.24 | 598 | 762 | 533 | 6.3 | 2.7 | 5.4 | 2.0 | 48% | 8% | 92.8 | 78 | 17 | 6 | 28% | 74% | 0% | 0 | 22 | | | 78 | 0.03 | 4.1 | 57 | 68 | $5 |
| 16 KC * | 2 | 1 | 49 | 34 | 3.64 | 5.35 | 1.66 | 790 | 761 | 814 | 5.6 | 3.2 | 6.3 | 1.9 | 63% | 13% | 90.7 | 68 | 8 | 23 | 37% | 79% | 7% | 0 | 19 | | | 25 | 0.52 | 3.3 | 53 | 63 | -$4 |
| 17 KC | 5 | 4 | 69 | 59 | 2.48 | 3.13 | 1.30 | 647 | 681 | 633 | 4.9 | 3.7 | 7.7 | 2.1 | 61% | 14% | 93.2 | 74 | 15 | 11 | 30% | 82% | 14% | 0 | 18 | | | 67 | 1.38 | 16.0 | 92 | 110 | $6 |
| 18 LA | 2 | 3 | 66 | 56 | 3.68 | 3.09 | 1.27 | 667 | 460 | 812 | 3.7 | 3.7 | 7.6 | 2.1 | 63% | 12% | 93.3 | 71 | 18 | 12 | 29% | 71% | 19% | 1 | 13 | 0% | 100% | 50 | 1.09 | 3.8 | 87 | 100 | $0 |
| 1st Half | 1 | 0 | 36 | 27 | 4.04 | 3.42 | 1.40 | 691 | 547 | 793 | 4.2 | 4.3 | 6.8 | 1.6 | 57% | 11% | 92.9 | 73 | 17 | 11 | 30% | 71% | 18% | 1 | 15 | 0% | 100% | 0 | 0.92 | 0.5 | 58 | 66 | -$4 |
| 2nd Half | 1 | 3 | 30 | 29 | 3.26 | 2.73 | 1.12 | 637 | 348 | 835 | 3.2 | 3.0 | 8.6 | 2.9 | 69% | 13% | 93.9 | 68 | 19 | 13 | 28% | 72% | 20% | 0 | 12 | | | 50 | 1.25 | 3.3 | 121 | 139 | $6 |
| **19 Proj** | **2** | **2** | **65** | **55** | **3.40** | **3.16** | **1.36** | **703** | **550** | **789** | **4.3** | **3.7** | **7.6** | **2.0** | **63%** | **13%** | **93.3** | **72** | **17** | **11** | **31%** | **76%** | **18%** | **0** | | | | | | **6.1** | **86** | **98** | **$0** |

## Allard,Kolby

| Allard,Kolby | | | | Health | A | LIMA Plan | C |
|---|---|---|---|---|---|---|---|
| Age: 21 | Th: L | Role | SP | PT/Exp | D | Rand Var | +2 |
| Ht: 6' 1" | Wt: 190 | Type | | Consist | A | MM | 1000 |

1-1, 12.38 ERA in 8 IP at ATL. Strong 2.73 ERA, 1.21 WHIP in full season at Triple-A, and made MLB debut at age 20. Concern over Dom fade during ascent through minors is partly allayed by plus-plus curveball and poise. Consensus is that in time, he'll be fine. It's just not his time quite yet.

| Yr Tm | W | Sv | IP | K | ERA | xERA | WHIP | oOPS | vL | vR | BF/G | Ctl | Dom | Cmd | FpK | SwK | Vel | G | L | F | H% | S% | hr/f | GS | APC | DOM% | DIS% | Sv% | LI | RAR | BPV | BPX | R$ |
|---|---|---|---|---|---|---|---|---|---|---|---|---|---|---|---|---|---|---|---|---|---|---|---|---|---|---|---|---|---|---|---|---|---|
| 14 | | | | | | | | | | | | | | | | | | | | | | | | | | | | | | | | | |
| 15 | | | | | | | | | | | | | | | | | | | | | | | | | | | | | | | | | |
| 16 | | | | | | | | | | | | | | | | | | | | | | | | | | | | | | | | | |
| 17 aa | 8 | 0 | 150 | 114 | 4.34 | 4.76 | 1.46 | | | | 23.8 | 2.7 | 6.8 | 2.5 | | | | | | | 34% | 72% | | | | | | | | 0.4 | 66 | 79 | $0 |
| 18 ATL * | 7 | 0 | 121 | 80 | 3.77 | 4.39 | 1.39 | 1253 | 1482 | 1133 | 23.2 | 2.6 | 5.9 | 2.2 | 62% | 4% | 89.4 | 32 | 29 | 39 | 32% | 74% | 20% | 1 | 54 | 0% | 100% | 0 | 0.56 | 5.7 | 61 | 70 | $0 |
| 1st Half | 5 | 0 | 92 | 61 | 3.43 | 3.74 | 1.28 | | | | 25.1 | 2.5 | 6.0 | 2.4 | | | | | | | 30% | 74% | 0% | 0 | | | | | | 8.2 | 69 | 80 | $4 |
| 2nd Half | 2 | 0 | 29 | 19 | 4.85 | 6.42 | 1.75 | 1253 | 1482 | 1133 | 19.0 | 3.0 | 5.7 | 1.9 | 62% | 4% | 89.4 | 32 | 29 | 39 | 38% | 74% | 20% | 1 | 54 | 0% | 100% | 0 | 0.56 | -2.5 | 35 | 41 | -$13 |
| **19 Proj** | **3** | **0** | **51** | **35** | **4.32** | **4.42** | **1.48** | | | | **21.8** | **2.4** | **6.3** | **2.6** | **61%** | **10%** | | **44** | **20** | **36** | **34%** | **72%** | **7%** | **10** | | | | | | **-1.0** | **69** | **79** | **-$4** |

## Allen,Cody

| Allen,Cody | | | | Health | A | LIMA Plan | B+ |
|---|---|---|---|---|---|---|---|
| Age: 30 | Th: R | Role | RP | PT/Exp | B | Rand Var | +1 |
| Ht: 6' 1" | Wt: 210 | Type | Pwr xFB | Consist | B | MM | 3520 |

No skill was spared from erosion in 2018. HR damage was fait accompli amid flyball trend and command issues, ulitimately reducing him to co-closer—bad timing for an impending free agent. If rising xERA doesn't do an about-face, and upheaval vL isn't a one-off, then... DN: pricey setup.

| Yr Tm | W | Sv | IP | K | ERA | xERA | WHIP | oOPS | vL | vR | BF/G | Ctl | Dom | Cmd | FpK | SwK | Vel | G | L | F | H% | S% | hr/f | GS | APC | DOM% | DIS% | Sv% | LI | RAR | BPV | BPX | R$ |
|---|---|---|---|---|---|---|---|---|---|---|---|---|---|---|---|---|---|---|---|---|---|---|---|---|---|---|---|---|---|---|---|---|---|
| 14 CLE | 6 | 24 | 70 | 91 | 2.07 | 3.08 | 1.06 | 601 | 451 | 757 | 3.7 | 3.4 | 11.8 | 3.5 | 63% | 14% | 95.3 | 36 | 15 | 48 | 28% | 87% | 9% | 0 | 15 | | | 86 | 1.43 | 14.4 | 135 | 161 | $18 |
| 15 CLE | 2 | 34 | 69 | 99 | 2.99 | 3.01 | 1.17 | 596 | 512 | 676 | 4.1 | 3.2 | 12.9 | 4.0 | 60% | 14% | 94.9 | 33 | 26 | 41 | 36% | 73% | 3% | 0 | 16 | | | 89 | 1.23 | 8.3 | 155 | 184 | $18 |
| 16 CLE | 3 | 32 | 68 | 87 | 2.51 | 3.09 | 1.00 | 584 | 677 | 501 | 3.9 | 3.6 | 11.5 | 3.2 | 55% | 14% | 94.2 | 46 | 18 | 36 | 24% | 82% | 15% | 0 | 17 | | | 91 | 1.25 | 14.0 | 135 | 160 | $21 |
| 17 CLE | 3 | 30 | 67 | 92 | 2.94 | 3.59 | 1.16 | 649 | 545 | 727 | 4.1 | 2.8 | 12.3 | 4.4 | 59% | 15% | 94.3 | 34 | 20 | 46 | 33% | 81% | 12% | 0 | 17 | | | 88 | 1.26 | 11.8 | 158 | 189 | $18 |
| 18 CLE | 4 | 27 | 67 | 80 | 4.70 | 4.43 | 1.36 | 740 | 800 | 685 | 4.1 | 4.4 | 10.7 | 2.4 | 53% | 13% | 93.5 | 30 | 19 | 51 | 30% | 70% | 13% | 0 | 17 | | | 84 | 1.36 | -4.6 | 82 | 94 | $9 |
| 1st Half | 2 | 16 | 32 | 39 | 3.62 | 3.89 | 1.05 | 630 | 869 | 433 | 3.9 | 3.3 | 10.9 | 3.3 | 52% | 14% | 93.6 | 33 | 14 | 53 | 25% | 72% | 13% | 0 | 16 | | | 94 | 1.39 | 2.1 | 116 | 133 | $15 |
| 2nd Half | 2 | 11 | 35 | 41 | 5.71 | 4.96 | 1.64 | 833 | 747 | 917 | 4.4 | 5.5 | 10.6 | 2.0 | 55% | 13% | 93.4 | 28 | 23 | 49 | 35% | 69% | 13% | 0 | 18 | | | 73 | 1.34 | -6.7 | 50 | 58 | $3 |
| **19 Proj** | **3** | **22** | **65** | **83** | **3.80** | **3.58** | **1.25** | **690** | **685** | **694** | **4.0** | **3.9** | **11.4** | **2.9** | **56%** | **14%** | **94.0** | **34** | **20** | **47** | **31%** | **75%** | **13%** | **0** | | | | | | **5.8** | **112** | **129** | **$11** |

## Alvarado,Jose

| Alvarado,Jose | | | | Health | A | LIMA Plan | B+ |
|---|---|---|---|---|---|---|---|
| Age: 24 | Th: L | Role | RP | PT/Exp | D | Rand Var | -3 |
| Ht: 6' 2" | Wt: 245 | Type | Pwr GB | Consist | B | MM | 5520 |

Fine follow-up to strong rookie season. Might have been even better with more 0-1 counts, but that's picking a nit when you allow only one HR in 64 IP. High-octane, wood-averse, ground ball profile points to more 9th innings ahead. Shedding a few BB could make him elite. Grab him if you still can. UP: 35 Sv

| Yr Tm | W | Sv | IP | K | ERA | xERA | WHIP | oOPS | vL | vR | BF/G | Ctl | Dom | Cmd | FpK | SwK | Vel | G | L | F | H% | S% | hr/f | GS | APC | DOM% | DIS% | Sv% | LI | RAR | BPV | BPX | R$ |
|---|---|---|---|---|---|---|---|---|---|---|---|---|---|---|---|---|---|---|---|---|---|---|---|---|---|---|---|---|---|---|---|---|---|
| 14 | | | | | | | | | | | | | | | | | | | | | | | | | | | | | | | | | |
| 15 | | | | | | | | | | | | | | | | | | | | | | | | | | | | | | | | | |
| 16 | | | | | | | | | | | | | | | | | | | | | | | | | | | | | | | | | |
| 17 TAM * | 2 | 1 | 59 | 65 | 3.90 | 2.38 | 1.16 | 570 | 736 | 449 | 3.9 | 4.1 | 9.9 | 2.4 | 65% | 11% | 98.2 | 54 | 16 | 30 | 27% | 66% | 4% | 0 | 13 | | | 33 | 1.15 | 3.3 | 110 | 133 | $2 |
| 18 TAM | 1 | 8 | 64 | 80 | 2.39 | 3.13 | 1.11 | 525 | 582 | 495 | 3.8 | 4.1 | 11.3 | 2.8 | 55% | 13% | 97.4 | 55 | 17 | 28 | 29% | 77% | 2% | 0 | 15 | | | 67 | 1.48 | 13.9 | 125 | 144 | $8 |
| 1st Half | 0 | 2 | 34 | 38 | 2.88 | 3.69 | 1.28 | 577 | 643 | 536 | 4.1 | 4.7 | 10.0 | 2.1 | 54% | 11% | 97.6 | 58 | 13 | 30 | 30% | 77% | 4% | 0 | 16 | | | 50 | 1.58 | 5.4 | 88 | 101 | $2 |
| 2nd Half | 1 | 6 | 30 | 42 | 1.82 | 2.54 | 0.91 | 461 | 485 | 451 | 3.4 | 3.3 | 12.7 | 3.8 | 56% | 16% | 97.1 | 51 | 24 | 25 | 28% | 78% | 0% | 0 | 14 | | | 75 | 1.37 | 8.5 | 168 | 193 | $13 |
| **19 Proj** | **5** | **20** | **65** | **79** | **2.94** | **2.93** | **1.10** | **539** | **620** | **499** | **3.7** | **4.0** | **10.9** | **2.7** | **55%** | **14%** | **97.3** | **54** | **19** | **27** | **28%** | **72%** | **4%** | **0** | | | | | | **11.9** | **120** | **138** | **$14** |

## Alvarez,Jose

| Alvarez,Jose | | | | Health | A | LIMA Plan | B |
|---|---|---|---|---|---|---|---|
| Age: 30 | Th: L | Role | RP | PT/Exp | D | Rand Var | -3 |
| Ht: 5' 11" | Wt: 180 | Type | Pwr | Consist | A | MM | 2210 |

Runs hot and cold, but final numbers are usually palatable. He manages to outperform xERA with just enough agility to ensure continued usage. 2018's trick was holding batters to .323 Slg, but can't count on tiny hr/f every year. Unremarkable, but health, consistency make him decent filler. Like, say, hummus?

| Yr Tm | W | Sv | IP | K | ERA | xERA | WHIP | oOPS | vL | vR | BF/G | Ctl | Dom | Cmd | FpK | SwK | Vel | G | L | F | H% | S% | hr/f | GS | APC | DOM% | DIS% | Sv% | LI | RAR | BPV | BPX | R$ |
|---|---|---|---|---|---|---|---|---|---|---|---|---|---|---|---|---|---|---|---|---|---|---|---|---|---|---|---|---|---|---|---|---|---|
| 14 LAA * | 0 | 0 | 31 | 15 | 5.64 | 5.65 | 1.53 | 667 | 0 | 2000 | 17.0 | 3.5 | 4.3 | 1.2 | 67% | 20% | 89.0 | 50 | 0 | 50 | 29% | 67% | 0% | 0 | 5 | | | 0 | 1.79 | -7.3 | 0 | 0 | -$7 |
| 15 LAA | 4 | 0 | 67 | 59 | 3.49 | 3.74 | 1.21 | 642 | 575 | 690 | 4.4 | 3.1 | 7.9 | 2.6 | 69% | 11% | 90.9 | 51 | 19 | 30 | 29% | 72% | 9% | 0 | 16 | | | 0 | 0.89 | 3.9 | 88 | 105 | $2 |
| 16 LAA | 1 | 0 | 57 | 51 | 3.45 | 4.25 | 1.50 | 745 | 671 | 811 | 4.0 | 2.4 | 8.0 | 3.4 | 64% | 10% | 90.6 | 44 | 24 | 32 | 38% | 78% | 7% | 0 | 15 | | | 0 | 0.94 | 5.2 | 103 | 122 | -$2 |
| 17 LAA | 0 | 1 | 49 | 45 | 3.88 | 4.18 | 1.27 | 733 | 715 | 749 | 3.2 | 2.2 | 8.3 | 3.8 | 60% | 11% | 91.1 | 39 | 24 | 37 | 32% | 75% | 13% | 0 | 12 | | | 33 | 1.02 | 2.8 | 107 | 128 | -$2 |
| 18 LAA | 6 | 1 | 63 | 59 | 2.71 | 3.97 | 1.16 | 613 | 604 | 624 | 3.4 | 3.1 | 8.4 | 2.7 | 62% | 11% | 91.6 | 45 | 20 | 35 | 29% | 77% | 5% | 0 | 13 | | | 25 | 1.24 | 11.2 | 90 | 103 | $5 |
| 1st Half | 3 | 0 | 37 | 36 | 2.95 | 3.92 | 1.15 | 630 | 648 | 606 | 3.6 | 2.7 | 8.8 | 3.3 | 61% | 11% | 91.8 | 43 | 18 | 38 | 30% | 75% | 5% | 0 | 14 | | | 0 | 1.13 | 5.4 | 108 | 124 | $5 |
| 2nd Half | 3 | 1 | 26 | 23 | 2.39 | 4.05 | 1.18 | 588 | 546 | 654 | 3.2 | 3.8 | 7.9 | 2.1 | 63% | 11% | 91.3 | 47 | 24 | 29 | 27% | 80% | 5% | 0 | 12 | | | 100 | 1.38 | 5.7 | 65 | 75 | $6 |
| **19 Proj** | **2** | **1** | **65** | **58** | **3.53** | **3.80** | **1.26** | **676** | **643** | **713** | **3.5** | **2.9** | **8.0** | **2.8** | **63%** | **11%** | **91.2** | **44** | **22** | **33** | **31%** | **74%** | **9%** | **0** | | | | | | **2.5** | **88** | **101** | **$1** |

## Anderson,Brett

| Anderson,Brett | | | | Health | F | LIMA Plan | C |
|---|---|---|---|---|---|---|---|
| Age: 31 | Th: L | Role | SP | PT/Exp | D | Rand Var | +2 |
| Ht: 6' 3" | Wt: 230 | Type | Con xGB | Consist | B | MM | 2000 |

4-5, 4.48 ERA in 80 IP at OAK. Wow, he's still around? How many days injured? Only 68? Certainly better than the 243 days lost in 2016-17. Coulda pitched worse, right? Never been much of a strikeout guy, was he? He's what, 40 now? Really, only 31? Next year he puts it all together, whaddaya think? No? C'mon, how come?

| Yr Tm | W | Sv | IP | K | ERA | xERA | WHIP | oOPS | vL | vR | BF/G | Ctl | Dom | Cmd | FpK | SwK | Vel | G | L | F | H% | S% | hr/f | GS | APC | DOM% | DIS% | Sv% | LI | RAR | BPV | BPX | R$ |
|---|---|---|---|---|---|---|---|---|---|---|---|---|---|---|---|---|---|---|---|---|---|---|---|---|---|---|---|---|---|---|---|---|---|
| 14 COL | 1 | 0 | 43 | 29 | 2.91 | 3.55 | 1.32 | 688 | 724 | 675 | 22.5 | 2.7 | 6.0 | 2.2 | 62% | 9% | 89.8 | 61 | 17 | 22 | 32% | 77% | 3% | 8 | 83 | 25% | 25% | | | 4.5 | 75 | 89 | -$1 |
| 15 LA | 10 | 0 | 180 | 116 | 3.69 | 3.53 | 1.33 | 726 | 698 | 737 | 24.2 | 2.3 | 5.8 | 2.5 | 58% | 8% | 90.7 | 66 | 15 | 19 | 31% | 75% | 17% | 31 | 88 | 13% | 39% | | | 6.0 | 86 | 103 | $5 |
| 16 LA | 1 | 0 | 11 | 5 | 11.91 | 6.13 | 2.56 | 1208 | 1267 | 1178 | 15.5 | 3.2 | 4.0 | 1.3 | 67% | 6% | 91.3 | 50 | 29 | 21 | 44% | 56% | 36% | 3 | 52 | 0% | 100% | 0 | 0.71 | -10.8 | 14 | 16 | -$9 |
| 17 2 TM * | 7 | 0 | 92 | 51 | 6.10 | 5.98 | 1.74 | 872 | 1078 | 830 | 20.1 | 3.4 | 5.0 | 1.5 | 57% | 9% | 90.5 | 49 | 29 | 22 | 36% | 64% | 12% | 13 | 69 | 0% | 46% | | | -19.8 | 28 | 33 | -$12 |
| 18 OAK * | 6 | 0 | 113 | 73 | 4.25 | 4.51 | 1.34 | 770 | 725 | 782 | 19.6 | 1.6 | 5.8 | 3.7 | 58% | 8% | 90.3 | 56 | 20 | 25 | 33% | 69% | 15% | 17 | 71 | 12% | 47% | | | -1.3 | 85 | 98 | -$1 |
| 1st Half | 1 | 0 | 44 | 30 | 4.92 | 5.87 | 1.66 | 1022 | 803 | 1097 | 19.5 | 2.2 | 6.3 | 2.9 | 51% | 8% | 91.1 | 55 | 21 | 24 | 39% | 70% | 21% | 4 | 63 | 0% | 75% | | | -4.1 | 68 | 78 | -$16 |
| 2nd Half | 5 | 0 | 72 | 43 | 3.70 | 3.46 | 1.10 | 702 | 696 | 703 | 20.2 | 1.2 | 5.3 | 4.6 | 60% | 8% | 90.2 | 56 | 19 | 25 | 28% | 69% | 13% | 13 | 73 | 15% | 38% | | | 4.0 | 106 | 122 | $9 |
| **19 Proj** | **4** | **0** | **65** | **40** | **4.49** | **3.96** | **1.43** | **772** | **771** | **772** | **20.7** | **2.2** | **5.6** | **2.5** | **57%** | **8%** | **90.5** | **56** | **21** | **23** | **33%** | **69%** | **11%** | **13** | | | | | | **0.9** | **74** | **85** | **-$4** |

ROB CARROLL

## Anderson,Chase

| | | | | | | | | | |
|---|---|---|---|---|---|---|---|---|---|
| Age: 31 | Th: R | Role | SP | Health | D | LIMA Plan | B |
| Ht: 6' 1" | Wt: 200 | Type | Pwr FB | PT/Exp | A | Rand Var | -1 |
| | | | | Consist | B | MM | 1203 |

Had longball-induced nightmares while most of 2017's gains ebbed away. May not be able to dispel that HR specter in light of rising FB rate and return of middling Dom and SwK. He generally outpitches xERA, but no single skill stands out. Dream of 2017, but you'll wake up to more of 2018.

| Yr Tm | W | Sv | IP | K | ERA | xERA | WHIP | oOPS | vL | vR | BF/G | Ctl | Dom | Cmd | FpK | SwK | Vel | G | L | F | H% | S% | hr/f | GS | APC | DOM% | DIS% | Sv% | LI | RAR | BPV | BPX | R$ |
|---|---|---|---|---|---|---|---|---|---|---|---|---|---|---|---|---|---|---|---|---|---|---|---|---|---|---|---|---|---|---|---|---|---|
| 14 ARI * | 13 | 0 | 153 | 135 | 3.23 | 3.79 | 1.25 | 779 | 714 | 831 | 23.1 | 2.7 | 7.9 | 2.9 | 63% | 10% | 91.0 | 40 | 24 | 36 | 30% | 78% | 14% | 21 | 90 | 10% | 33% | | | 9.7 | 82 | 98 | $9 |
| 15 ARI | 6 | 0 | 153 | 111 | 4.30 | 4.16 | 1.30 | 754 | 746 | 761 | 23.7 | 2.4 | 6.5 | 2.8 | 62% | 8% | 91.5 | 42 | 24 | 34 | 30% | 69% | 11% | 27 | 91 | 11% | 26% | | | -6.4 | 74 | 88 | $0 |
| 16 MIL | 9 | 0 | 152 | 120 | 4.39 | 4.78 | 1.37 | 819 | 664 | 935 | 20.9 | 3.1 | 7.1 | 2.3 | 58% | 9% | 91.1 | 36 | 23 | 41 | 29% | 74% | 15% | 30 | 85 | 13% | 47% | 0 | 0.78 | -3.8 | 57 | 68 | $1 |
| 17 MIL | 12 | 0 | 141 | 133 | 2.74 | 4.15 | 1.09 | 647 | 607 | 679 | 22.8 | 2.6 | 8.5 | 3.2 | 61% | 11% | 93.1 | 39 | 18 | 43 | 27% | 79% | 9% | 25 | 90 | 36% | 20% | | | 28.2 | 99 | 119 | $20 |
| 18 MIL | 9 | 0 | 158 | 128 | 3.93 | 4.63 | 1.19 | 731 | 677 | 785 | 21.5 | 3.2 | 7.3 | 2.2 | 63% | 10% | 92.4 | 34 | 21 | 44 | 24% | 75% | 15% | 30 | 87 | 10% | 40% | | | 4.3 | 56 | 64 | $8 |
| 1st Half | 6 | 0 | 88 | 68 | 4.18 | 4.67 | 1.13 | 699 | 637 | 765 | 22.3 | 3.6 | 6.9 | 1.9 | 62% | 9% | 92.4 | 36 | 20 | 44 | 21% | 71% | 16% | 16 | 89 | 13% | 38% | | | -0.3 | 42 | 49 | $10 |
| 2nd Half | 3 | 0 | 70 | 60 | 3.62 | 4.57 | 1.26 | 769 | 729 | 807 | 20.6 | 2.8 | 7.8 | 2.7 | 64% | 10% | 92.3 | 33 | 22 | 45 | 28% | 80% | 14% | 14 | 84 | 7% | 43% | | | 4.6 | 74 | 85 | $6 |
| **19 Proj** | **10** | **0** | **152** | **129** | **3.88** | **4.15** | **1.21** | **735** | **674** | **789** | **21.3** | **2.9** | **7.6** | **2.6** | **62%** | **10%** | **92.3** | **36** | **21** | **43** | **27%** | **75%** | **14%** | **29** | | | | | | **5.1** | **72** | **83** | **$9** |

## Anderson,Justin

| | | | | | | | | | |
|---|---|---|---|---|---|---|---|---|---|
| Age: 26 | Th: R | Role | RP | Health | A | LIMA Plan | D+ |
| Ht: 6' 3" | Wt: 220 | Type | Pwr GB | PT/Exp | D | Rand Var | 0 |
| | | | | Consist | F | MM | 1310 |

Older rookie came out of nowhere to walk a boatload of batters. He struck out a bunch, too, but the final tally was a lot of sloppy outings. He did keep the ball on the ground and his wildness could be intimidating, but these guys are a dime a dozen. He may vanish as unobtrusively as he arrived.

| Yr Tm | W | Sv | IP | K | ERA | xERA | WHIP | oOPS | vL | vR | BF/G | Ctl | Dom | Cmd | FpK | SwK | Vel | G | L | F | H% | S% | hr/f | GS | APC | DOM% | DIS% | Sv% | LI | RAR | BPV | BPX | R$ |
|---|---|---|---|---|---|---|---|---|---|---|---|---|---|---|---|---|---|---|---|---|---|---|---|---|---|---|---|---|---|---|---|---|---|
| 14 | | | | | | | | | | | | | | | | | | | | | | | | | | | | | | | | | |
| 15 | | | | | | | | | | | | | | | | | | | | | | | | | | | | | | | | | |
| 16 | | | | | | | | | | | | | | | | | | | | | | | | | | | | | | | | | |
| 17 aa | 3 | 1 | 59 | 30 | 7.27 | 6.25 | 1.76 | | | | 6.4 | 4.9 | 4.6 | 0.9 | | | | | | | 32% | 59% | | | | | | | | -21.1 | 0 | 0 | -$12 |
| 18 LAA | 3 | 4 | 55 | 67 | 4.07 | 4.03 | 1.48 | 634 | 665 | 612 | 4.2 | 6.5 | 10.9 | 1.7 | 52% | 14% | 97.3 | 51 | 19 | 30 | 30% | 72% | 8% | 0 | 18 | | | 67 | 1.06 | 0.6 | 49 | 57 | -$1 |
| 1st Half | 2 | 3 | 29 | 37 | 3.68 | 4.21 | 1.60 | 714 | 782 | 665 | 4.6 | 6.1 | 11.4 | 1.9 | 52% | 15% | 97.7 | 42 | 23 | 35 | 34% | 80% | 12% | 0 | 20 | | | 75 | 1.00 | 1.7 | 59 | 68 | -$2 |
| 2nd Half | 1 | 1 | 26 | 30 | 4.50 | 3.79 | 1.35 | 535 | 519 | 545 | 3.9 | 6.9 | 10.4 | 1.5 | 51% | 13% | 96.9 | 61 | 14 | 25 | 26% | 63% | 0% | 0 | 17 | | | 50 | 1.12 | -1.1 | 39 | 45 | -$1 |
| **19 Proj** | **3** | **5** | **58** | **61** | **4.29** | **4.16** | **1.55** | **744** | **748** | **740** | **4.8** | **5.9** | **9.4** | **1.6** | **52%** | **14%** | **97.2** | **54** | **17** | **29** | **31%** | **74%** | **14%** | **0** | | | | | | **-1.0** | **41** | **47** | **-$2** |

## Anderson,Tyler

| | | | | | | | | | |
|---|---|---|---|---|---|---|---|---|---|
| Age: 29 | Th: L | Role | SP | Health | D | LIMA Plan | B+ |
| Ht: 6' 4" | Wt: 210 | Type | Pwr | PT/Exp | B | Rand Var | +2 |
| | | | | Consist | A | MM | 2203 |

Quietly effective in 2018. PRO: Unfazed by home venue (career 3.73 ERA at Coors) or batters' handedness; strong FpK suggests bb% should rebound. CON: FB/GB trends aren't reassuring; average Dom/SwK caps upside; health remains an issue. VERDICT: Of the Pitching Andersons, this is the one you want.

| Yr Tm | W | Sv | IP | K | ERA | xERA | WHIP | oOPS | vL | vR | BF/G | Ctl | Dom | Cmd | FpK | SwK | Vel | G | L | F | H% | S% | hr/f | GS | APC | DOM% | DIS% | Sv% | LI | RAR | BPV | BPX | R$ |
|---|---|---|---|---|---|---|---|---|---|---|---|---|---|---|---|---|---|---|---|---|---|---|---|---|---|---|---|---|---|---|---|---|---|
| 14 aa | 7 | 0 | 118 | 83 | 2.94 | 3.64 | 1.38 | | | | 21.6 | 3.4 | 6.3 | 1.8 | | | | | | | 31% | 78% | | | | | | | | 11.7 | 68 | 81 | $3 |
| 15 | | | | | | | | | | | | | | | | | | | | | | | | | | | | | | | | | |
| 16 COL * | 7 | 0 | 141 | 116 | 3.48 | 4.08 | 1.32 | 742 | 607 | 783 | 24.4 | 2.4 | 7.4 | 3.1 | 64% | 11% | 90.9 | 51 | 20 | 29 | 32% | 76% | 12% | 19 | 94 | 16% | 11% | | | 12.3 | 84 | 100 | $6 |
| 17 COL | 6 | 0 | 86 | 81 | 4.81 | 4.07 | 1.33 | 820 | 740 | 848 | 21.3 | 2.7 | 8.5 | 3.1 | 65% | 12% | 92.0 | 44 | 23 | 33 | 31% | 69% | 20% | 15 | 83 | 13% | 33% | 0 | 0.78 | -4.8 | 101 | 121 | $0 |
| 18 COL | 7 | 0 | 176 | 164 | 4.55 | 4.30 | 1.27 | 756 | 827 | 737 | 23.0 | 3.0 | 8.4 | 2.8 | 65% | 12% | 91.8 | 37 | 24 | 39 | 29% | 70% | 15% | 32 | 89 | 25% | 34% | | | -8.7 | 84 | 97 | $2 |
| 1st Half | 5 | 0 | 94 | 85 | 4.23 | 4.37 | 1.28 | 757 | 998 | 697 | 23.1 | 3.0 | 8.2 | 2.7 | 62% | 13% | 91.7 | 36 | 24 | 40 | 29% | 72% | 14% | 17 | 90 | 24% | 35% | | | -0.9 | 80 | 92 | $4 |
| 2nd Half | 2 | 0 | 82 | 79 | 4.92 | 4.21 | 1.26 | 755 | 660 | 784 | 23.0 | 3.1 | 8.6 | 2.8 | 68% | 12% | 92.0 | 38 | 24 | 38 | 28% | 66% | 17% | 15 | 88 | 27% | 33% | | | -7.8 | 89 | 102 | $0 |
| **19 Proj** | **8** | **0** | **174** | **165** | **3.93** | **3.77** | **1.28** | **754** | **719** | **765** | **23.6** | **2.9** | **8.5** | **2.9** | **65%** | **12%** | **91.8** | **41** | **23** | **36** | **30%** | **75%** | **15%** | **30** | | | | | | **4.7** | **95** | **109** | **$8** |

## Andriese,Matt

| | | | | | | | | | |
|---|---|---|---|---|---|---|---|---|---|
| Age: 29 | Th: R | Role | RP | Health | D | LIMA Plan | C+ |
| Ht: 6' 2" | Wt: 225 | Type | Pwr | PT/Exp | C | Rand Var | +5 |
| | | | | Consist | A | MM | 2301 |

Transitioned to RP role, first as part of TAM's "opener" experiment, then as more traditional RP for ARI in Aug/Sept. Skills mostly benefitted from the move (see full-season SwK, xERA, BPV); he became essentially a two-pitch guy (FB/CH). Gopheritis was his undoing, especially w/ARI. But bullpen seems to suit him.

| Yr Tm | W | Sv | IP | K | ERA | xERA | WHIP | oOPS | vL | vR | BF/G | Ctl | Dom | Cmd | FpK | SwK | Vel | G | L | F | H% | S% | hr/f | GS | APC | DOM% | DIS% | Sv% | LI | RAR | BPV | BPX | R$ |
|---|---|---|---|---|---|---|---|---|---|---|---|---|---|---|---|---|---|---|---|---|---|---|---|---|---|---|---|---|---|---|---|---|---|
| 14 aaa | 11 | 0 | 162 | 107 | 4.83 | 4.94 | 1.46 | | | | 24.8 | 2.9 | 5.9 | 2.1 | | | | | | | 32% | 69% | | | | | | | | -21.8 | 44 | 53 | -$7 |
| 15 TAM * | 6 | 2 | 131 | 105 | 3.59 | 4.31 | 1.36 | 728 | 785 | 677 | 14.4 | 2.0 | 7.3 | 3.7 | 59% | 9% | 91.3 | 48 | 17 | 35 | 35% | 75% | 11% | 8 | 44 | 13% | 50% | 100 | 0.77 | 6.0 | 97 | 115 | $3 |
| 16 TAM * | 9 | 1 | 162 | 145 | 4.49 | 4.24 | 1.27 | 720 | 706 | 732 | 19.0 | 1.8 | 8.0 | 4.3 | 66% | 11% | 91.8 | 43 | 19 | 38 | 33% | 67% | 11% | 19 | 68 | 11% | 26% | 100 | 0.81 | -6.1 | 107 | 127 | $4 |
| 17 TAM | 5 | 1 | 86 | 76 | 4.50 | 4.44 | 1.37 | 795 | 617 | 931 | 20.8 | 2.9 | 8.0 | 2.7 | 61% | 11% | 92.1 | 45 | 20 | 35 | 31% | 74% | 17% | 17 | 80 | 12% | 41% | 100 | 0.73 | -1.5 | 87 | 105 | $0 |
| 18 2 TM | 3 | 0 | 79 | 78 | 5.26 | 3.84 | 1.39 | 819 | 726 | 891 | 8.3 | 2.9 | 8.9 | 3.1 | 58% | 13% | 92.2 | 49 | 20 | 31 | 32% | 67% | 21% | 5 | 33 | 0% | 60% | 0 | 0.86 | -10.8 | 110 | 127 | -$6 |
| 1st Half | 1 | 0 | 47 | 43 | 4.02 | 3.64 | 1.17 | 701 | 512 | 820 | 9.3 | 2.1 | 8.2 | 3.9 | 57% | 12% | 92.2 | 51 | 18 | 31 | 30% | 68% | 12% | 3 | 37 | 0% | 67% | 0 | 1.11 | 0.7 | 120 | 138 | -$2 |
| 2nd Half | 2 | 0 | 32 | 35 | 7.11 | 4.14 | 1.71 | 983 | 953 | 1012 | 7.3 | 4.0 | 9.9 | 2.5 | 58% | 14% | 92.2 | 45 | 24 | 31 | 36% | 66% | 34% | 2 | 28 | 0% | 50% | 0 | 0.60 | -11.5 | 95 | 109 | -$11 |
| **19 Proj** | **5** | **0** | **87** | **85** | **4.12** | **3.67** | **1.35** | **763** | **699** | **816** | **10.8** | **2.9** | **8.8** | **3.1** | **60%** | **12%** | **92.0** | **46** | **20** | **33** | **32%** | **75%** | **16%** | **3** | | | | | | **5.0** | **105** | **121** | **$0** |

## Arano,Victor

| | | | | | | | | | |
|---|---|---|---|---|---|---|---|---|---|
| Age: 24 | Th: R | Role | RP | Health | B | LIMA Plan | B+ |
| Ht: 6' 2" | Wt: 200 | Type | Pwr FB | PT/Exp | D | Rand Var | -4 |
| | | | | Consist | D | MM | 2310 |

Wowed 'em in Philly and it's easy to see why. But absurd SwK and sturdy Cmd were mostly at the expense of RHB, and xERA confirms that he was clearly sputtering by season's end. There are more Ks in the forecast, but until he proves that he can get lefties out consistently, his role will be limited.

| Yr Tm | W | Sv | IP | K | ERA | xERA | WHIP | oOPS | vL | vR | BF/G | Ctl | Dom | Cmd | FpK | SwK | Vel | G | L | F | H% | S% | hr/f | GS | APC | DOM% | DIS% | Sv% | LI | RAR | BPV | BPX | R$ |
|---|---|---|---|---|---|---|---|---|---|---|---|---|---|---|---|---|---|---|---|---|---|---|---|---|---|---|---|---|---|---|---|---|---|
| 14 | | | | | | | | | | | | | | | | | | | | | | | | | | | | | | | | | |
| 15 | | | | | | | | | | | | | | | | | | | | | | | | | | | | | | | | | |
| 16 aa | 1 | 1 | 17 | 22 | 2.22 | 2.28 | 0.91 | | | | 5.7 | 2.0 | 11.8 | 5.9 | | | | | | | 27% | 84% | | | | | | | | 4.1 | 178 | 212 | $0 |
| 17 PHI * | 2 | 9 | 49 | 47 | 4.35 | 4.74 | 1.33 | 475 | 861 | 339 | 4.9 | 2.8 | 8.7 | 3.1 | 55% | 20% | 93.4 | 44 | 20 | 36 | 31% | 73% | 0% | 0 | 17 | | | 82 | 0.76 | 0.1 | 73 | 87 | $2 |
| 18 PHI | 1 | 3 | 59 | 60 | 2.73 | 4.01 | 1.20 | 673 | 829 | 567 | 4.1 | 2.6 | 9.1 | 3.5 | 60% | 16% | 93.7 | 39 | 20 | 41 | 31% | 82% | 9% | 0 | 16 | | | 60 | 0.96 | 10.4 | 111 | 128 | $3 |
| 1st Half | 1 | 0 | 28 | 30 | 2.57 | 3.62 | 1.07 | 564 | 643 | 500 | 4.5 | 2.3 | 9.6 | 4.3 | 62% | 16% | 93.3 | 38 | 26 | 36 | 31% | 76% | 4% | 0 | 16 | | | 0 | 0.63 | 5.5 | 129 | 148 | $2 |
| 2nd Half | 0 | 3 | 31 | 30 | 2.87 | 4.37 | 1.31 | 773 | 1033 | 620 | 3.8 | 2.9 | 8.6 | 3.0 | 57% | 16% | 94.0 | 39 | 15 | 46 | 31% | 86% | 12% | 0 | 16 | | | 60 | 1.21 | 4.9 | 95 | 109 | $3 |
| **19 Proj** | **2** | **2** | **65** | **64** | **3.40** | **3.81** | **1.26** | **733** | **911** | **613** | **4.3** | **2.7** | **8.9** | **3.3** | **59%** | **16%** | **93.7** | **39** | **19** | **42** | **31%** | **79%** | **12%** | **0** | | | | | | **2.7** | **104** | **120** | **$2** |

## Archer,Chris

| | | | | | | | | | |
|---|---|---|---|---|---|---|---|---|---|
| Age: 30 | Th: R | Role | SP | Health | C | LIMA Plan | A |
| Ht: 6' 2" | Wt: 195 | Type | Pwr | PT/Exp | A | Rand Var | +4 |
| | | | | Consist | A | MM | 4405 |

Narrative of underperformance, letdowns reached its nadir. Missed a month with abdominal strain, but injury and league change didn't dampen 2nd half skills. They're right in line with 2016-17, and the annual Ks are a given. Yes, you've been burned thrice, but he's still too young to write off.

| Yr Tm | W | Sv | IP | K | ERA | xERA | WHIP | oOPS | vL | vR | BF/G | Ctl | Dom | Cmd | FpK | SwK | Vel | G | L | F | H% | S% | hr/f | GS | APC | DOM% | DIS% | Sv% | LI | RAR | BPV | BPX | R$ |
|---|---|---|---|---|---|---|---|---|---|---|---|---|---|---|---|---|---|---|---|---|---|---|---|---|---|---|---|---|---|---|---|---|---|
| 14 TAM | 10 | 0 | 195 | 173 | 3.33 | 3.68 | 1.28 | 650 | 624 | 685 | 25.7 | 3.3 | 8.0 | 2.4 | 57% | 10% | 94.6 | 47 | 22 | 31 | 31% | 75% | 7% | 32 | 99 | 31% | 19% | | | 9.9 | 79 | 94 | $9 |
| 15 TAM | 12 | 0 | 212 | 252 | 3.23 | 3.12 | 1.14 | 613 | 604 | 622 | 25.5 | 2.8 | 10.7 | 3.8 | 64% | 13% | 95.2 | 46 | 20 | 34 | 31% | 74% | 10% | 34 | 101 | 44% | 15% | | | 19.2 | 141 | 168 | $22 |
| 16 TAM | 9 | 0 | 201 | 233 | 4.02 | 3.52 | 1.24 | 703 | 698 | 708 | 25.8 | 3.0 | 10.4 | 3.5 | 58% | 13% | 94.3 | 48 | 18 | 35 | 31% | 73% | 16% | 33 | 103 | 36% | 27% | | | 4.1 | 133 | 158 | $12 |
| 17 TAM | 10 | 0 | 201 | 249 | 4.07 | 3.54 | 1.26 | 710 | 760 | 666 | 25.1 | 2.7 | 11.1 | 4.2 | 62% | 14% | 95.5 | 42 | 22 | 36 | 34% | 72% | 14% | 34 | 100 | 35% | 12% | | | 7.0 | 148 | 178 | $14 |
| 18 2 TM | 6 | 0 | 148 | 162 | 4.31 | 3.72 | 1.38 | 767 | 809 | 734 | 23.6 | 3.0 | 9.8 | 3.3 | 62% | 13% | 94.7 | 45 | 23 | 32 | 35% | 72% | 14% | 27 | 93 | 26% | 33% | | | -2.9 | 120 | 138 | $0 |
| 1st Half | 3 | 0 | 76 | 76 | 4.24 | 3.90 | 1.34 | 746 | 839 | 674 | 24.7 | 3.1 | 9.0 | 2.9 | 58% | 13% | 94.6 | 44 | 23 | 33 | 32% | 71% | 13% | 13 | 95 | 31% | 31% | | | -0.9 | 100 | 115 | -$1 |
| 2nd Half | 3 | 0 | 72 | 86 | 4.38 | 3.52 | 1.42 | 787 | 777 | 795 | 22.6 | 2.9 | 10.8 | 3.7 | 66% | 14% | 94.9 | 46 | 23 | 31 | 37% | 73% | 16% | 14 | 91 | 21% | 36% | | | -2.0 | 139 | 160 | $1 |
| **19 Proj** | **8** | **0** | **189** | **216** | **3.87** | **3.24** | **1.23** | **693** | **715** | **675** | **23.1** | **2.9** | **10.3** | **3.5** | **62%** | **13%** | **94.9** | **45** | **22** | **33** | **32%** | **73%** | **15%** | **33** | | | | | | **24.3** | **130** | **149** | **$12** |

## Arrieta,Jake

| | | | | | | | | | |
|---|---|---|---|---|---|---|---|---|---|
| Age: 33 | Th: R | Role | SP | Health | A | LIMA Plan | B |
| Ht: 6' 4" | Wt: 225 | Type | Pwr | PT/Exp | A | Rand Var | +1 |
| | | | | Consist | A | MM | 2205 |

If only Reliability Grades were the end-all, be-all ... but they're not. Unsavory trends in xERA, Dom, Cmd, SwK are difficult to ignore, and ERA has finally regressed to skill level. Still, he recovered some in 2nd half, so with reasonable workload and no age-related surprises, could reclaim some lost value.

| Yr Tm | W | Sv | IP | K | ERA | xERA | WHIP | oOPS | vL | vR | BF/G | Ctl | Dom | Cmd | FpK | SwK | Vel | G | L | F | H% | S% | hr/f | GS | APC | DOM% | DIS% | Sv% | LI | RAR | BPV | BPX | R$ |
|---|---|---|---|---|---|---|---|---|---|---|---|---|---|---|---|---|---|---|---|---|---|---|---|---|---|---|---|---|---|---|---|---|---|
| 14 CHC | 10 | 0 | 157 | 167 | 2.53 | 2.79 | 0.99 | 535 | 553 | 520 | 24.6 | 2.4 | 9.6 | 4.1 | 59% | 11% | 93.5 | 49 | 22 | 28 | 28% | 74% | 8% | 25 | 97 | 60% | 12% | | | 23.4 | 136 | 162 | $20 |
| 15 CHC | 22 | 0 | 229 | 236 | 1.77 | 2.62 | 0.86 | 507 | 449 | 557 | 26.4 | 1.9 | 9.3 | 4.9 | 60% | 11% | 94.6 | 56 | 21 | 23 | 25% | 81% | 8% | 33 | 104 | 67% | 3% | | | 62.0 | 150 | 179 | $51 |
| 16 CHC | 18 | 0 | 197 | 190 | 3.10 | 3.57 | 1.08 | 583 | 612 | 557 | 25.6 | 3.5 | 8.7 | 2.5 | 59% | 11% | 93.7 | 53 | 20 | 28 | 25% | 74% | 11% | 31 | 101 | 42% | 19% | | | 26.5 | 93 | 111 | $26 |
| 17 CHC | 14 | 0 | 168 | 163 | 3.53 | 4.04 | 1.22 | 716 | 843 | 610 | 23.6 | 2.9 | 8.7 | 3.0 | 58% | 9% | 92.1 | 45 | 21 | 34 | 29% | 76% | 14% | 30 | 91 | 20% | 27% | | | 17.2 | 100 | 121 | $16 |
| 18 PHI | 10 | 0 | 173 | 138 | 3.96 | 4.03 | 1.29 | 724 | 812 | 656 | 23.4 | 3.0 | 7.2 | 2.4 | 62% | 8% | 93.0 | 52 | 20 | 29 | 29% | 73% | 14% | 31 | 89 | 23% | 39% | | | 4.0 | 79 | 91 | $6 |
| 1st Half | 5 | 0 | 84 | 59 | 3.54 | 4.16 | 1.27 | 704 | 735 | 681 | 23.5 | 2.9 | 6.3 | 2.2 | 61% | 8% | 93.0 | 55 | 17 | 28 | 29% | 76% | 13% | 15 | 89 | 27% | 40% | | | 6.4 | 69 | 79 | $6 |
| 2nd Half | 5 | 0 | 89 | 79 | 4.36 | 3.92 | 1.30 | 744 | 877 | 632 | 23.3 | 3.0 | 8.0 | 2.6 | 63% | 9% | 93.1 | 48 | 22 | 29 | 30% | 70% | 16% | 16 | 90 | 19% | 38% | | | -2.3 | 88 | 102 | $6 |
| **19 Proj** | **13** | **0** | **181** | **158** | **3.73** | **3.73** | **1.24** | **697** | **781** | **630** | **24.2** | **3.1** | **7.8** | **2.6** | **60%** | **9%** | **93.0** | **48** | **21** | **31** | **29%** | **73%** | **13%** | **30** | | | | | | **8.2** | **84** | **97** | **$13** |

ROB CARROLL

## Baez,Pedro

| | | | | | |
|---|---|---|---|---|---|
| Age: 31 | Th: R | Role RP | Health D | LIMA Plan B+ | |
| Ht: 6' 0" | Wt: 230 | Type Pwr FB | PT/Exp C | Rand Var -3 | |
| | | | Consist C | MM 2300 | |

Recaptured some lost Dom and tightened strike zone a bit, but LI and holds drop (23 in 2017, 7 in 2018) affect a sense of unease. Maybe it's the rising FB%, the something's-gotta-give ERA/xERA chasm, or his fluctuating Cmd and FpK. Swing-and-miss sometimes saves the day, but he's just tough to get behind.

| Yr Tm | W | Sv | IP | K | ERA | xERA | WHIP | oOPS | vL | vR | BF/G | Ctl | Dom | Cmd | FpK | SwK | Vel | G | L | F | H% | S% | hr/f | GS | APC | DOM% | DIS% | Sv% | LI | RAR | BPV | BPX | R$ |
|---|---|---|---|---|---|---|---|---|---|---|---|---|---|---|---|---|---|---|---|---|---|---|---|---|---|---|---|---|---|---|---|---|---|
| 14 LA * | 2 | 12 | 66 | 49 | 3.28 | 3.40 | 1.16 | 537 | 578 | 501 | 4.4 | 2.2 | 6.7 | 3.0 | 61% | 10% | 95.3 | 37 | 15 | 49 | 28% | 75% | 9% | 0 | 18 | | | 100 | 0.46 | 3.7 | 81 | 97 | $6 |
| 15 LA | 4 | 0 | 51 | 60 | 3.35 | 3.27 | 1.14 | 693 | 735 | 678 | 4.0 | 1.9 | 10.6 | 5.5 | 66% | 16% | 97.1 | 38 | 19 | 44 | 34% | 72% | 7% | 0 | 16 | | | 0 | 1.20 | 3.8 | 154 | 184 | $2 |
| 16 LA | 3 | 0 | 74 | 83 | 3.04 | 3.42 | 1.00 | 615 | 553 | 649 | 4.0 | 2.7 | 10.1 | 3.8 | 63% | 15% | 96.7 | 43 | 20 | 38 | 25% | 78% | 16% | 0 | 16 | | | 0 | 1.02 | 10.5 | 130 | 155 | $7 |
| 17 LA | 3 | 0 | 64 | 64 | 2.95 | 4.85 | 1.33 | 728 | 678 | 763 | 4.2 | 4.1 | 9.0 | 2.2 | 58% | 16% | 97.0 | 35 | 22 | 43 | 29% | 84% | 11% | 0 | 18 | | | 0 | 1.00 | 11.1 | 65 | 78 | $2 |
| 18 LA | 4 | 0 | 56 | 62 | 2.88 | 4.17 | 1.22 | 652 | 608 | 672 | 4.3 | 3.7 | 9.9 | 2.7 | 62% | 16% | 96.0 | 35 | 22 | 44 | 30% | 78% | 6% | 0 | 18 | | | 0 | 0.78 | 8.9 | 92 | 106 | $2 |
| 1st Half | 3 | 0 | 31 | 36 | 3.23 | 4.38 | 1.50 | 745 | 768 | 729 | 4.6 | 4.7 | 10.6 | 2.3 | 57% | 14% | 95.6 | 35 | 24 | 41 | 36% | 80% | 6% | 0 | 19 | | | 0 | 0.80 | 3.5 | 76 | 88 | $0 |
| 2nd Half | 1 | 0 | 26 | 26 | 2.45 | 3.92 | 0.90 | 531 | 327 | 607 | 4.0 | 2.5 | 9.1 | 3.7 | 69% | 18% | 96.6 | 34 | 19 | 46 | 23% | 76% | 6% | 0 | 16 | | | 0 | 0.76 | 5.4 | 110 | 127 | $6 |
| 19 Proj | 3 | 0 | 58 | 61 | 3.37 | 3.82 | 1.25 | 700 | 640 | 731 | 4.1 | 3.3 | 9.5 | 2.9 | 62% | 16% | 96.5 | 36 | 21 | 43 | 31% | 76% | 9% | 0 | | | | | | 5.6 | 95 | 110 | $1 |

## Bailey,Homer

| | | | | | |
|---|---|---|---|---|---|
| Age: 33 | Th: R | Role SP | Health F | LIMA Plan D+ | |
| Ht: 6' 4" | Wt: 223 | Type | PT/Exp D | Rand Var +4 | |
| | | | Consist F | MM 1101 | |

1-14, 6.09 ERA in 106 IP at CIN. Caps off to the Reds, who for the past four seasons have abided 429 DL days for 231 IP. Many of those innings have been unwatchable, and it's nearly impossible to know what he is now other than extremely hittable. Moving forward, it's foolish to expect anything but.

| Yr Tm | W | Sv | IP | K | ERA | xERA | WHIP | oOPS | vL | vR | BF/G | Ctl | Dom | Cmd | FpK | SwK | Vel | G | L | F | H% | S% | hr/f | GS | APC | DOM% | DIS% | Sv% | LI | RAR | BPV | BPX | R$ |
|---|---|---|---|---|---|---|---|---|---|---|---|---|---|---|---|---|---|---|---|---|---|---|---|---|---|---|---|---|---|---|---|---|---|
| 14 CIN | 9 | 0 | 146 | 124 | 3.71 | 3.46 | 1.23 | 703 | 750 | 666 | 26.3 | 2.8 | 7.7 | 2.8 | 62% | 11% | 94.2 | 51 | 21 | 29 | 29% | 73% | 13% | 23 | 99 | 35% | 26% | | | 0.6 | 92 | 109 | $5 |
| 15 CIN | 0 | 0 | 11 | 3 | 5.56 | 5.64 | 1.76 | 1009 | 1424 | 707 | 25.5 | 3.2 | 2.4 | 0.8 | 63% | 7% | 91.1 | 52 | 17 | 31 | 31% | 76% | 23% | 2 | 86 | 0% | 100% | | | -2.2 | -13 | -15 | -$6 |
| 16 CIN * | 3 | 0 | 51 | 44 | 7.51 | 9.32 | 2.13 | 816 | 968 | 706 | 18.0 | 3.7 | 7.7 | 2.1 | 54% | 10% | 92.7 | 45 | 30 | 25 | 43% | 69% | 11% | 6 | 76 | 17% | 33% | | | -20.9 | -1 | -1 | -$15 |
| 17 CIN | 6 | 0 | 91 | 67 | 6.43 | 5.11 | 1.69 | 875 | 817 | 931 | 23.3 | 4.2 | 6.6 | 1.6 | 61% | 10% | 93.5 | 45 | 27 | 28 | 35% | 62% | 13% | 18 | 88 | 6% | 61% | | | -23.2 | 30 | 36 | -$12 |
| 18 CIN * | 3 | 0 | 146 | 96 | 6.24 | 6.82 | 1.66 | 901 | 949 | 858 | 24.2 | 2.8 | 5.9 | 2.1 | 62% | 9% | 93.1 | 43 | 24 | 33 | 35% | 66% | 19% | 20 | 89 | 15% | 65% | | | -37.5 | 17 | 20 | -$22 |
| 1st Half | 1 | 0 | 78 | 43 | 7.81 | 7.88 | 1.76 | 933 | 923 | 943 | 23.8 | 3.0 | 4.9 | 1.6 | 60% | 8% | 92.9 | 41 | 22 | 37 | 34% | 60% | 18% | 12 | 86 | 8% | 75% | | | -35.2 | -21 | -24 | -$37 |
| 2nd Half | 2 | 0 | 68 | 54 | 4.43 | 5.60 | 1.55 | 857 | 990 | 751 | 24.6 | 2.5 | 7.1 | 2.9 | 66% | 12% | 93.4 | 45 | 28 | 27 | 36% | 74% | 20% | 8 | 94 | 25% | 50% | | | -2.3 | 64 | 74 | -$6 |
| 19 Proj | 3 | 0 | 73 | 54 | 5.88 | 4.52 | 1.68 | 907 | 932 | 885 | 22.7 | 3.2 | 6.7 | 2.1 | 62% | 10% | 93.4 | 45 | 25 | 30 | 36% | 68% | 17% | 14 | | | | | | -15.5 | 57 | 65 | -$11 |

## Barnes,Jacob

| | | | | | |
|---|---|---|---|---|---|
| Age: 29 | Th: R | Role RP | Health B | LIMA Plan C | |
| Ht: 6' 2" | Wt: 220 | Type Pwr GB | PT/Exp D | Rand Var -1 | |
| | | | Consist B | MM 2310 | |

A season of regression. Dom and GB mastery faded just enough to to generate significant xERA slippage. FpK/Ctl problems keep him on a tightrope, Cmd now showing serious loss of footing. If 2nd half is extension of a trend, the act is going to be over quickly. There are so many others guys with the same act. Next!

| Yr Tm | W | Sv | IP | K | ERA | xERA | WHIP | oOPS | vL | vR | BF/G | Ctl | Dom | Cmd | FpK | SwK | Vel | G | L | F | H% | S% | hr/f | GS | APC | DOM% | DIS% | Sv% | LI | RAR | BPV | BPX | R$ |
|---|---|---|---|---|---|---|---|---|---|---|---|---|---|---|---|---|---|---|---|---|---|---|---|---|---|---|---|---|---|---|---|---|---|
| 14 aa | 2 | 0 | 106 | 63 | 5.25 | 4.56 | 1.43 | | | | 19.5 | 3.5 | 5.4 | 1.6 | | | | | | | 30% | 64% | | | | | | | | -19.6 | 35 | 42 | -$9 |
| 15 aa | 4 | 0 | 75 | 68 | 4.85 | 5.20 | 1.73 | | | | 8.7 | 4.1 | 8.2 | 2.0 | | | | | | | 39% | 70% | | | | | | | | -8.2 | 74 | 88 | -$8 |
| 16 MIL * | 2 | 2 | 52 | 48 | 2.09 | 2.62 | 1.11 | 612 | 820 | 437 | 4.3 | 2.4 | 8.3 | 3.5 | 62% | 16% | 94.6 | 49 | 21 | 31 | 30% | 83% | 5% | 0 | 15 | | | 67 | 0.55 | 13.4 | 120 | 142 | $5 |
| 17 MIL | 3 | 2 | 72 | 80 | 4.00 | 3.63 | 1.25 | 664 | 686 | 645 | 4.2 | 4.1 | 10.0 | 2.4 | 60% | 16% | 96.7 | 53 | 20 | 27 | 28% | 71% | 16% | 0 | 17 | | | 29 | 1.10 | 3.2 | 100 | 120 | $2 |
| 18 MIL | 0 | 2 | 49 | 47 | 3.33 | 4.23 | 1.52 | 723 | 761 | 689 | 4.4 | 4.3 | 8.7 | 2.0 | 58% | 14% | 95.2 | 50 | 22 | 28 | 34% | 80% | 10% | 0 | 17 | | | 50 | 0.68 | 4.9 | 70 | 80 | -$3 |
| 1st Half | 0 | 2 | 32 | 32 | 2.53 | 3.95 | 1.41 | 665 | 719 | 612 | 4.6 | 3.9 | 9.0 | 2.3 | 57% | 16% | 95.2 | 51 | 22 | 27 | 33% | 84% | 8% | 0 | 18 | | | 50 | 0.79 | 6.4 | 84 | 97 | -$1 |
| 2nd Half | 0 | 0 | 17 | 15 | 4.86 | 4.80 | 1.74 | 828 | 851 | 811 | 4.1 | 4.9 | 8.1 | 1.7 | 59% | 11% | 95.1 | 49 | 23 | 28 | 36% | 74% | 13% | 0 | 16 | | | 0 | 0.51 | -1.5 | 42 | 48 | -$7 |
| 19 Proj | 3 | 1 | 58 | 56 | 3.78 | 3.82 | 1.44 | 718 | 751 | 690 | 4.5 | 4.0 | 8.7 | 2.2 | 59% | 14% | 95.8 | 51 | 21 | 28 | 33% | 76% | 11% | 0 | | | | | | 2.6 | 76 | 88 | -$1 |

## Barnes,Matt

| | | | | | |
|---|---|---|---|---|---|
| Age: 29 | Th: R | Role RP | Health A | LIMA Plan A | |
| Ht: 6' 4" | Wt: 210 | Type Pwr | PT/Exp C | Rand Var +3 | |
| | | | Consist B | MM 5510 | |

Not only did he strike out three every two innings, he nearly reduced opposing bats to props. Steady Dom rise, shrinking oOPS foretold this skills breakout; SwK, GB% ushered it in, though H% kept it hidden behind ERA. Has still found no cure for wildness and may be too late for him to find it, but if he does... UP: 30 Sv

| Yr Tm | W | Sv | IP | K | ERA | xERA | WHIP | oOPS | vL | vR | BF/G | Ctl | Dom | Cmd | FpK | SwK | Vel | G | L | F | H% | S% | hr/f | GS | APC | DOM% | DIS% | Sv% | LI | RAR | BPV | BPX | R$ |
|---|---|---|---|---|---|---|---|---|---|---|---|---|---|---|---|---|---|---|---|---|---|---|---|---|---|---|---|---|---|---|---|---|---|
| 14 BOS * | 8 | 0 | 137 | 93 | 4.98 | 4.57 | 1.50 | 861 | 1000 | 762 | 21.1 | 3.3 | 6.1 | 1.8 | 67% | 13% | 93.9 | 31 | 21 | 48 | 33% | 66% | 7% | 0 | 31 | | | 0 | 0.27 | -21.0 | 54 | 64 | -$9 |
| 15 BOS * | 4 | 0 | 81 | 72 | 5.68 | 6.34 | 1.77 | 887 | 800 | 959 | 7.6 | 4.5 | 8.1 | 1.8 | 58% | 10% | 94.8 | 39 | 22 | 40 | 37% | 71% | 16% | 2 | 25 | 0% | 100% | 0 | 0.88 | -17.1 | 37 | 44 | -$12 |
| 16 BOS | 4 | 1 | 67 | 71 | 4.05 | 4.01 | 1.40 | 711 | 741 | 693 | 4.6 | 4.2 | 9.6 | 2.3 | 58% | 11% | 96.8 | 46 | 21 | 33 | 32% | 72% | 10% | 0 | 19 | | | 50 | 1.08 | 1.1 | 84 | 99 | $0 |
| 17 BOS | 7 | 1 | 70 | 83 | 3.88 | 3.38 | 1.22 | 655 | 792 | 577 | 4.1 | 3.6 | 10.7 | 3.0 | 57% | 13% | 95.2 | 49 | 23 | 28 | 31% | 71% | 14% | 0 | 17 | | | 33 | 0.95 | 4.1 | 122 | 147 | $5 |
| 18 BOS | 6 | 0 | 62 | 96 | 3.65 | 2.88 | 1.26 | 624 | 643 | 610 | 4.3 | 4.5 | 14.0 | 3.1 | 56% | 15% | 96.6 | 53 | 14 | 33 | 35% | 73% | 11% | 0 | 18 | | | 0 | 1.08 | 3.8 | 161 | 185 | $3 |
| 1st Half | 2 | 0 | 35 | 48 | 2.60 | 2.84 | 1.07 | 505 | 754 | 371 | 4.2 | 4.7 | 12.5 | 2.7 | 58% | 12% | 96.2 | 56 | 19 | 25 | 27% | 75% | 6% | 0 | 17 | | | 0 | 1.22 | 6.6 | 132 | 152 | $5 |
| 2nd Half | 4 | 0 | 27 | 48 | 5.00 | 2.94 | 1.52 | 758 | 543 | 925 | 4.4 | 4.3 | 16.0 | 3.7 | 54% | 18% | 97.2 | 49 | 8 | 43 | 46% | 70% | 15% | 0 | 18 | | | 0 | 0.92 | -2.8 | 198 | 228 | $1 |
| 19 Proj | 6 | 5 | 65 | 91 | 3.58 | 2.95 | 1.24 | 624 | 627 | 622 | 4.3 | 4.3 | 12.5 | 2.9 | 56% | 14% | 96.2 | 49 | 17 | 34 | 32% | 74% | 14% | 0 | | | | | | 13.4 | 137 | 157 | $6 |

## Barraclough,Kyle

| | | | | | |
|---|---|---|---|---|---|
| Age: 29 | Th: R | Role RP | Health C | LIMA Plan B | |
| Ht: 6' 3" | Wt: 225 | Type Pwr | PT/Exp C | Rand Var 0 | |
| | | | Consist B | MM 1411 | |

Virtually every skill is minimally in two-year decline, despite May-June when opposing batters went 3-for-82. Deposed as closer with back, shoulder woes partially to blame, but annual walk rate is indefensible—and unacceptable with HR barrage. Now scraping by on early reputation and incredibly cool name.

| Yr Tm | W | Sv | IP | K | ERA | xERA | WHIP | oOPS | vL | vR | BF/G | Ctl | Dom | Cmd | FpK | SwK | Vel | G | L | F | H% | S% | hr/f | GS | APC | DOM% | DIS% | Sv% | LI | RAR | BPV | BPX | R$ |
|---|---|---|---|---|---|---|---|---|---|---|---|---|---|---|---|---|---|---|---|---|---|---|---|---|---|---|---|---|---|---|---|---|---|
| 14 | | | | | | | | | | | | | | | | | | | | | | | | | | | | | | | | | |
| 15 MIA * | 4 | 10 | 53 | 59 | 3.12 | 2.74 | 1.44 | 563 | 656 | 497 | 4.3 | 6.9 | 10.1 | 1.5 | 48% | 15% | 95.6 | 32 | 26 | 42 | 28% | 77% | 5% | 0 | 19 | | | 83 | 1.15 | 5.5 | 102 | 122 | $4 |
| 16 MIA | 6 | 0 | 73 | 113 | 2.85 | 2.84 | 1.22 | 538 | 584 | 492 | 4.1 | 5.4 | 14.0 | 2.6 | 57% | 14% | 95.6 | 52 | 21 | 27 | 32% | 75% | 3% | 0 | 18 | | | 0 | 1.21 | 12.0 | 135 | 160 | $7 |
| 17 MIA | 6 | 1 | 66 | 76 | 3.00 | 4.23 | 1.38 | 638 | 581 | 702 | 4.3 | 5.2 | 10.4 | 2.0 | 56% | 12% | 94.8 | 43 | 23 | 34 | 30% | 80% | 9% | 0 | 18 | | | 20 | 0.95 | 11.1 | 68 | 81 | $4 |
| 18 MIA | 1 | 10 | 56 | 60 | 4.20 | 4.35 | 1.33 | 675 | 607 | 737 | 4.0 | 5.5 | 9.7 | 1.8 | 50% | 11% | 93.6 | 45 | 20 | 34 | 25% | 73% | 16% | 0 | 17 | | | 59 | 0.99 | -0.4 | 49 | 57 | $1 |
| 1st Half | 0 | 8 | 36 | 39 | 0.99 | 3.49 | 0.74 | 374 | 454 | 300 | 3.7 | 4.2 | 9.7 | 2.3 | 57% | 13% | 93.5 | 47 | 17 | 36 | 11% | 92% | 7% | 0 | 16 | | | 80 | 0.88 | 14.2 | 86 | 98 | $12 |
| 2nd Half | 1 | 2 | 19 | 21 | 10.24 | 6.15 | 2.43 | 1076 | 809 | 1326 | 4.5 | 7.9 | 9.8 | 1.2 | 42% | 9% | 93.7 | 43 | 25 | 32 | 42% | 61% | 29% | 0 | 18 | | | 29 | 1.17 | -14.5 | -17 | -19 | -$19 |
| 19 Proj | 4 | 5 | 73 | 82 | 4.38 | 4.07 | 1.51 | 722 | 627 | 815 | 4.0 | 5.6 | 10.2 | 1.8 | 51% | 12% | 94.3 | 45 | 22 | 33 | 31% | 74% | 15% | 0 | | | | | | 0.8 | 54 | 63 | -$1 |

## Barria,Jaime

| | | | | | |
|---|---|---|---|---|---|
| Age: 22 | Th: R | Role SP | Health A | LIMA Plan B+ | |
| Ht: 6' 1" | Wt: 210 | Type FB | PT/Exp D | Rand Var -1 | |
| | | | Consist A | MM 1103 | |

10-9. 3.41 ERA in 129 IP at LAA. No skill is exceptional, but results more arresting given age and prior experience (20 starts above Single-A). Not shown here is grit; in high leverage situations, oOPS was .285. He'll need more of that if 2nd-half xERA and Cmd bleed into 2019. Literally learning on the job, so be patient.

| Yr Tm | W | Sv | IP | K | ERA | xERA | WHIP | oOPS | vL | vR | BF/G | Ctl | Dom | Cmd | FpK | SwK | Vel | G | L | F | H% | S% | hr/f | GS | APC | DOM% | DIS% | Sv% | LI | RAR | BPV | BPX | R$ |
|---|---|---|---|---|---|---|---|---|---|---|---|---|---|---|---|---|---|---|---|---|---|---|---|---|---|---|---|---|---|---|---|---|---|
| 14 | | | | | | | | | | | | | | | | | | | | | | | | | | | | | | | | | |
| 15 | | | | | | | | | | | | | | | | | | | | | | | | | | | | | | | | | |
| 16 | | | | | | | | | | | | | | | | | | | | | | | | | | | | | | | | | |
| 17 a/a | 3 | 0 | 76 | 53 | 3.42 | 4.04 | 1.26 | | | | 20.8 | 2.0 | 6.3 | 3.2 | | | | | | | 31% | 76% | | | | | | | | 8.9 | 78 | 93 | $2 |
| 18 LAA * | 10 | 0 | 147 | 115 | 3.37 | 4.02 | 1.27 | 719 | 614 | 824 | 19.5 | 3.1 | 7.0 | 2.2 | 55% | 11% | 91.2 | 37 | 20 | 43 | 28% | 78% | 10% | 26 | 84 | 15% | 42% | | | 14.2 | 61 | 70 | $9 |
| 1st Half | 5 | 0 | 74 | 63 | 3.32 | 4.26 | 1.23 | 734 | 608 | 863 | 18.6 | 2.5 | 7.7 | 3.1 | 56% | 12% | 91.6 | 39 | 20 | 42 | 29% | 80% | 15% | 11 | 86 | 27% | 45% | | | 7.5 | 73 | 84 | $9 |
| 2nd Half | 5 | 0 | 74 | 52 | 3.42 | 5.16 | 1.32 | 707 | 618 | 795 | 20.5 | 3.8 | 6.4 | 1.7 | 54% | 10% | 90.9 | 36 | 20 | 45 | 27% | 77% | 7% | 15 | 82 | 7% | 40% | | | 6.6 | 26 | 30 | $8 |
| 19 Proj | 9 | 0 | 160 | 126 | 3.95 | 4.42 | 1.33 | 762 | 654 | 871 | 20.3 | 2.9 | 7.1 | 2.4 | 55% | 11% | 91.2 | 37 | 20 | 43 | 30% | 74% | 10% | 33 | | | | | | -4.2 | 64 | 74 | $5 |

## Bauer,Trevor

| | | | | | |
|---|---|---|---|---|---|
| Age: 28 | Th: R | Role SP | Health C | LIMA Plan C | |
| Ht: 6' 1" | Wt: 190 | Type Pwr | PT/Exp A | Rand Var -4 | |
| | | | Consist A | MM 4405 | |

Flirtations with greatness turned into full-blown affair that even a fractured fibula couldn't restrain. Check out those skills, but more pertinent: Can he do it again? Yearly trends in xERA/Ctl/Cmd are very convincing and unaffected by splits. He can give some back and still be an ace, but if the band plays on... UP: Cy Young

| Yr Tm | W | Sv | IP | K | ERA | xERA | WHIP | oOPS | vL | vR | BF/G | Ctl | Dom | Cmd | FpK | SwK | Vel | G | L | F | H% | S% | hr/f | GS | APC | DOM% | DIS% | Sv% | LI | RAR | BPV | BPX | R$ |
|---|---|---|---|---|---|---|---|---|---|---|---|---|---|---|---|---|---|---|---|---|---|---|---|---|---|---|---|---|---|---|---|---|---|
| 14 CLE * | 9 | 0 | 199 | 181 | 3.77 | 3.97 | 1.33 | 737 | 729 | 744 | 25.0 | 3.3 | 8.2 | 2.5 | 56% | 9% | 94.0 | 35 | 23 | 41 | 31% | 74% | 9% | 26 | 100 | 31% | 38% | | | -0.7 | 77 | 91 | $4 |
| 15 CLE | 11 | 0 | 176 | 170 | 4.55 | 4.21 | 1.31 | 713 | 705 | 721 | 24.0 | 4.0 | 8.7 | 2.2 | 59% | 10% | 92.8 | 39 | 20 | 41 | 28% | 68% | 12% | 30 | 93 | 40% | 27% | 0 | 0.76 | -12.8 | 64 | 77 | $2 |
| 16 CLE | 12 | 0 | 190 | 168 | 4.26 | 4.09 | 1.31 | 712 | 690 | 732 | 23.2 | 3.3 | 8.0 | 2.4 | 60% | 9% | 93.2 | 49 | 20 | 31 | 30% | 69% | 12% | 28 | 88 | 25% | 39% | 0 | 0.74 | -1.7 | 81 | 96 | $7 |
| 17 CLE | 17 | 0 | 176 | 196 | 4.19 | 3.72 | 1.37 | 774 | 839 | 717 | 23.4 | 3.1 | 10.0 | 3.3 | 57% | 9% | 94.0 | 46 | 22 | 32 | 34% | 74% | 16% | 31 | 98 | 19% | 23% | 0 | 0.77 | 3.8 | 121 | 146 | $11 |
| 18 CLE | 12 | 1 | 175 | 221 | 2.21 | 3.16 | 1.09 | 582 | 570 | 595 | 25.6 | 2.9 | 11.3 | 3.9 | 64% | 14% | 94.5 | 45 | 21 | 34 | 31% | 81% | 6% | 27 | 102 | 59% | 11% | 100 | 0.80 | 42.0 | 148 | 171 | $28 |
| 1st Half | 7 | 0 | 114 | 148 | 2.45 | 3.08 | 1.09 | 591 | 564 | 614 | 27.5 | 2.9 | 11.7 | 4.1 | 64% | 14% | 94.5 | 46 | 20 | 34 | 32% | 78% | 5% | 17 | 109 | 65% | 6% | | | 23.8 | 158 | 181 | $34 |
| 2nd Half | 5 | 1 | 62 | 73 | 1.75 | 3.33 | 1.09 | 566 | 579 | 548 | 22.6 | 3.1 | 10.7 | 3.5 | 63% | 14% | 94.6 | 42 | 24 | 34 | 29% | 87% | 8% | 10 | 90 | 50% | 20% | 100 | 0.83 | 18.2 | 129 | 148 | $18 |
| 19 Proj | 15 | 0 | 203 | 230 | 3.12 | 3.25 | 1.20 | 660 | 666 | 654 | 23.2 | 3.0 | 10.2 | 3.4 | 62% | 12% | 94.1 | 44 | 22 | 34 | 32% | 77% | 11% | 35 | | | | | | 25.5 | 126 | 144 | $23 |

ROB CARROLL

## Bedrosian,Cam

| | | | | | | |
|---|---|---|---|---|---|---|
| Age: 27 | Th: R | Role RP | Health | D | LIMA Plan | C |
| Ht: 6' 0" | Wt: 230 | Type Pwr | PT/Exp | D | Rand Var | 0 |
| | | | Consist | B | MM | 2300 |

xERA, BPV, and Cmd trends all show a pitcher moving further away from saves consideration at age when skills should be peaking. And Dom/SwK drop, ongoing loss of velocity only further the concern. FpK indicates Ctl should improve, but even so, most likely outcome is season of slightly above average relief.

| Yr Tm | W | Sv | IP | K | ERA | xERA | WHIP | oOPS | vL | vR | BF/G | Ctl | Dom | Cmd | FpK | SwK | Vel | G | L | F | H% | S% | hr/f | GS | APC | DOM% | DIS% | Sv% | LI | RAR | BPV | BPX | R$ |
|---|---|---|---|---|---|---|---|---|---|---|---|---|---|---|---|---|---|---|---|---|---|---|---|---|---|---|---|---|---|---|---|---|---|
| 14 LAA * | 2 | 17 | 59 | 78 | 3.66 | 2.05 | 1.10 | 801 | 1055 | 531 | 4.2 | 4.0 | 11.9 | 3.0 | 61% | 11% | 94.5 | 41 | 21 | 38 | 29% | 66% | 9% | 0 | 24 | | | 81 | 0.67 | 0.6 | 139 | 166 | $8 |
| 15 LAA * | 2 | 3 | 69 | 70 | 3.99 | 4.18 | 1.52 | 833 | 1047 | 719 | 5.2 | 4.1 | 9.1 | 2.2 | 55% | 7% | 94.4 | 43 | 23 | 34 | 36% | 73% | 9% | 0 | 19 | | | 60 | 0.73 | -0.3 | 90 | 107 | -$3 |
| 16 LAA | 2 | 1 | 40 | 51 | 1.12 | 2.94 | 1.09 | 532 | 583 | 485 | 3.6 | 3.1 | 11.4 | 3.6 | 62% | 11% | 95.3 | 49 | 21 | 29 | 32% | 91% | 4% | 0 | 15 | | | 50 | 0.78 | 15.3 | 147 | 175 | $5 |
| 17 LAA | 6 | 6 | 45 | 53 | 4.43 | 3.95 | 1.30 | 705 | 778 | 639 | 4.0 | 3.4 | 10.7 | 3.1 | 61% | 13% | 93.9 | 43 | 17 | 40 | 33% | 68% | 10% | 0 | 16 | | | 55 | 1.12 | -0.4 | 121 | 145 | $3 |
| 18 LAA | 5 | 1 | 64 | 57 | 3.80 | 4.18 | 1.39 | 738 | 749 | 731 | 3.8 | 3.7 | 8.0 | 2.2 | 65% | 9% | 93.1 | 47 | 21 | 32 | 31% | 76% | 12% | 0 | 15 | | | 13 | 0.96 | 2.8 | 71 | 81 | -$1 |
| 1st Half | 3 | 1 | 37 | 31 | 3.38 | 4.36 | 1.42 | 755 | 688 | 798 | 4.0 | 3.9 | 7.5 | 1.9 | 68% | 9% | 93.7 | 49 | 20 | 31 | 30% | 81% | 15% | 0 | 15 | | | 20 | 0.89 | 3.6 | 57 | 66 | $0 |
| 2nd Half | 2 | 0 | 27 | 26 | 4.39 | 3.93 | 1.35 | 714 | 840 | 637 | 3.6 | 3.4 | 8.8 | 2.6 | 61% | 8% | 92.4 | 44 | 22 | 33 | 33% | 68% | 8% | 0 | 14 | | | 0 | 1.06 | -0.8 | 89 | 103 | -$1 |
| **19 Proj** | **5** | **0** | **58** | **59** | **3.65** | **3.66** | **1.29** | **682** | **744** | **638** | **3.8** | **3.4** | **9.1** | **2.7** | **62%** | **10%** | **93.7** | **46** | **20** | **34** | **32%** | **73%** | **9%** | **0** | | | | | | **3.6** | **96** | **111** | **$1** |

## Beeks,Jalen

| | | | | | | |
|---|---|---|---|---|---|---|
| Age: 25 | Th: L | Role SP | Health | A | LIMA Plan | C |
| Ht: 5' 11" | Wt: 195 | Type Pwr xGB | PT/Exp | D | Rand Var | 0 |
| | | | Consist | B | MM | 2201 |

5-1, 5.51 ERA in 51 IP at BOS/TAM. Intriguing rookie struggled in MLB debut, but rising Dom, Cmd plus healthy GB% make him an arm worth watching long-term. In short-term, however, FpK and SwK are at odds, suggesting Ctl may undermine Ks a little longer. Give him another year to develop.

| Yr Tm | W | Sv | IP | K | ERA | xERA | WHIP | oOPS | vL | vR | BF/G | Ctl | Dom | Cmd | FpK | SwK | Vel | G | L | F | H% | S% | hr/f | GS | APC | DOM% | DIS% | Sv% | LI | RAR | BPV | BPX | R$ |
|---|---|---|---|---|---|---|---|---|---|---|---|---|---|---|---|---|---|---|---|---|---|---|---|---|---|---|---|---|---|---|---|---|---|
| 14 | | | | | | | | | | | | | | | | | | | | | | | | | | | | | | | | | |
| 15 | | | | | | | | | | | | | | | | | | | | | | | | | | | | | | | | | |
| 16 aa | 5 | 0 | 65 | 46 | 6.09 | 6.03 | 1.77 | | | | 23.1 | 4.1 | 6.3 | 1.6 | | | | | | | 36% | 66% | | | | | | | | -15.3 | 34 | 40 | -$10 |
| 17 a/a | 11 | 0 | 145 | 125 | 4.65 | 4.60 | 1.46 | | | | 23.9 | 3.7 | 7.7 | 2.1 | | | | | | | 32% | 70% | | | | | | | | -5.2 | 62 | 74 | $1 |
| 18 2AL * | 10 | 0 | 139 | 134 | 4.73 | 4.75 | 1.41 | 794 | 586 | 857 | 19.6 | 3.4 | 8.7 | 2.6 | 54% | 12% | 91.8 | 47 | 21 | 32 | 33% | 69% | 13% | 1 | 63 | 0% | 100% | 0 | 0.88 | -9.9 | 71 | 81 | -$2 |
| 1st Half | 5 | 0 | 82 | 84 | 4.76 | 4.82 | 1.41 | 1244 | 4500 | 871 | 23.1 | 3.1 | 9.2 | 3.0 | 50% | 7% | 92.0 | 20 | 33 | 47 | 34% | 69% | 14% | 1 | 88 | 0% | 100% | | | -6.1 | 80 | 92 | -$3 |
| 2nd Half | 5 | 0 | 57 | 50 | 4.68 | 4.65 | 1.41 | 745 | 411 | 855 | 16.0 | 3.7 | 7.9 | 2.1 | 55% | 13% | 91.8 | 50 | 20 | 30 | 31% | 70% | 12% | 0 | 61 | | | 0 | 0.89 | -3.7 | 59 | 68 | $0 |
| **19 Proj** | **7** | **0** | **87** | **81** | **4.45** | **3.91** | **1.41** | **721** | **387** | **831** | **20.3** | **3.6** | **8.4** | **2.3** | **55%** | **13%** | **91.8** | **50** | **20** | **30** | **32%** | **72%** | **14%** | **18** | | | | | | **-3.2** | **82** | **94** | **-$1** |

## Berrios,Jose

| | | | | | | |
|---|---|---|---|---|---|---|
| Age: 25 | Th: R | Role SP | Health | A | LIMA Plan | C |
| Ht: 6' 0" | Wt: 185 | Type Pwr | PT/Exp | B | Rand Var | +1 |
| | | | Consist | B | MM | 2305 |

At MLB-only level, this was a solid step forward over 2017's 4.29 xERA, 2.9 Cmd, and 92 BPV. Walks got away from him down the stretch (4.7 Ctl in Aug/Sept), but FpK shows there isn't much to worry about; perhaps it was fatigue from first full season in bigs. With that under his belt... UP: 16 Wins, 3.25 ERA

| Yr Tm | W | Sv | IP | K | ERA | xERA | WHIP | oOPS | vL | vR | BF/G | Ctl | Dom | Cmd | FpK | SwK | Vel | G | L | F | H% | S% | hr/f | GS | APC | DOM% | DIS% | Sv% | LI | RAR | BPV | BPX | R$ |
|---|---|---|---|---|---|---|---|---|---|---|---|---|---|---|---|---|---|---|---|---|---|---|---|---|---|---|---|---|---|---|---|---|---|
| 14 a/a | 3 | 0 | 44 | 27 | 5.36 | 3.71 | 1.35 | | | | 20.2 | 3.0 | 5.5 | 1.9 | | | | | | | 31% | 58% | | | | | | | | -8.7 | 61 | 73 | -$4 |
| 15 a/a | 14 | 0 | 166 | 147 | 3.41 | 3.11 | 1.14 | | | | 24.4 | 2.0 | 7.9 | 4.0 | | | | | | | 30% | 72% | | | | | | | | 11.4 | 118 | 140 | $15 |
| 16 MIN * | 13 | 0 | 170 | 152 | 5.05 | 4.36 | 1.40 | 932 | 837 | 1034 | 23.1 | 3.8 | 8.0 | 2.1 | 55% | 9% | 93.3 | 38 | 22 | 40 | 30% | 66% | 16% | 14 | 82 | 7% | 50% | | | -18.0 | 61 | 72 | -$1 |
| 17 MIN * | 17 | 0 | 185 | 171 | 3.43 | 3.29 | 1.18 | 693 | 783 | 616 | 23.2 | 2.8 | 8.3 | 3.0 | 59% | 10% | 93.5 | 39 | 21 | 40 | 29% | 74% | 9% | 25 | 92 | 32% | 32% | 0 | 0.78 | 21.3 | 95 | 114 | $21 |
| 18 MIN | 12 | 0 | 192 | 202 | 3.84 | 3.79 | 1.14 | 665 | 681 | 649 | 24.9 | 2.9 | 9.5 | 3.3 | 64% | 12% | 93.2 | 42 | 20 | 38 | 28% | 71% | 13% | 32 | 96 | 38% | 25% | | | 7.4 | 113 | 130 | $16 |
| 1st Half | 8 | 0 | 107 | 111 | 3.52 | 3.55 | 1.00 | 629 | 618 | 640 | 25.2 | 2.0 | 9.3 | 4.6 | 66% | 12% | 93.2 | 40 | 21 | 39 | 26% | 70% | 13% | 17 | 94 | 41% | 24% | | | 8.3 | 131 | 151 | $25 |
| 2nd Half | 4 | 0 | 85 | 91 | 4.24 | 4.10 | 1.33 | 710 | 756 | 660 | 24.5 | 3.9 | 9.6 | 2.5 | 63% | 11% | 93.2 | 43 | 19 | 38 | 30% | 72% | 13% | 15 | 98 | 33% | 27% | | | -0.9 | 89 | 102 | $4 |
| **19 Proj** | **13** | **0** | **189** | **187** | **3.74** | **3.69** | **1.19** | **677** | **701** | **654** | **23.1** | **2.9** | **9.0** | **3.0** | **63%** | **12%** | **93.3** | **40** | **21** | **39** | **29%** | **72%** | **11%** | **33** | | | | | | **9.4** | **100** | **115** | **$15** |

## Betances,Dellin

| | | | | | | |
|---|---|---|---|---|---|---|
| Age: 31 | Th: R | Role RP | Health | A | LIMA Plan | A |
| Ht: 6' 8" | Wt: 265 | Type Pwr | PT/Exp | C | Rand Var | +4 |
| | | | Consist | C | MM | 5520 |

2018 rankings, among pitchers with at least 50 IP: xERA, 2nd; Dom, 3rd; BPV, 3rd. And if he's finally mastered Ctl, as career-best 2nd half FpK seems to indicate, that's simply unfair. Seems only thing left he can't control is whether he gets save opps, and those could come at any time. Be ready.

| Yr Tm | W | Sv | IP | K | ERA | xERA | WHIP | oOPS | vL | vR | BF/G | Ctl | Dom | Cmd | FpK | SwK | Vel | G | L | F | H% | S% | hr/f | GS | APC | DOM% | DIS% | Sv% | LI | RAR | BPV | BPX | R$ |
|---|---|---|---|---|---|---|---|---|---|---|---|---|---|---|---|---|---|---|---|---|---|---|---|---|---|---|---|---|---|---|---|---|---|
| 14 NYY | 5 | 1 | 90 | 135 | 1.40 | 2.03 | 0.78 | 442 | 405 | 482 | 4.9 | 2.4 | 13.5 | 5.6 | 66% | 13% | 96.6 | 47 | 20 | 33 | 26% | 85% | 7% | 0 | 20 | | | 20 | 1.19 | 26.0 | 203 | 242 | $18 |
| 15 NYY | 6 | 9 | 84 | 131 | 1.50 | 2.43 | 1.01 | 510 | 454 | 558 | 4.5 | 4.3 | 14.0 | 3.3 | 59% | 15% | 97.0 | 48 | 21 | 32 | 27% | 90% | 12% | 0 | 19 | | | 69 | 1.42 | 25.5 | 163 | 194 | $19 |
| 16 NYY | 3 | 12 | 73 | 126 | 3.08 | 2.09 | 1.12 | 577 | 634 | 532 | 4.1 | 3.5 | 15.5 | 4.5 | 61% | 16% | 97.7 | 54 | 19 | 27 | 38% | 74% | 13% | 0 | 17 | | | 71 | 1.19 | 10.0 | 218 | 260 | $12 |
| 17 NYY | 3 | 10 | 60 | 100 | 2.87 | 3.19 | 1.22 | 538 | 441 | 623 | 4.0 | 6.6 | 15.1 | 2.3 | 52% | 13% | 98.5 | 49 | 13 | 38 | 28% | 77% | 8% | 0 | 17 | | | 77 | 1.09 | 11.0 | 119 | 143 | $9 |
| 18 NYY | 4 | 4 | 67 | 115 | 2.70 | 2.18 | 1.05 | 578 | 613 | 553 | 4.1 | 3.5 | 15.5 | 4.4 | 61% | 15% | 97.8 | 44 | 28 | 28 | 34% | 79% | 21% | 0 | 17 | | | 57 | 1.09 | 11.9 | 207 | 238 | $9 |
| 1st Half | 1 | 0 | 35 | 62 | 2.83 | 2.11 | 1.03 | 542 | 572 | 522 | 4.2 | 4.1 | 15.9 | 3.9 | 51% | 15% | 97.9 | 48 | 23 | 28 | 30% | 78% | 24% | 0 | 18 | | | 0 | 0.95 | 5.7 | 202 | 232 | $6 |
| 2nd Half | 3 | 4 | 32 | 53 | 2.56 | 2.24 | 1.07 | 617 | 651 | 589 | 4.0 | 2.8 | 15.1 | 5.3 | 71% | 16% | 97.7 | 40 | 33 | 27 | 37% | 81% | 18% | 0 | 16 | | | 57 | 1.22 | 6.2 | 212 | 244 | $13 |
| **19 Proj** | **4** | **11** | **65** | **110** | **2.66** | **2.23** | **1.09** | **564** | **557** | **570** | **3.9** | **4.2** | **15.2** | **3.6** | **62%** | **15%** | **97.8** | **47** | **23** | **31** | **33%** | **79%** | **15%** | **0** | | | | | | **26.2** | **185** | **212** | **$12** |

## Bettis,Chad

| | | | | | | |
|---|---|---|---|---|---|---|
| Age: 30 | Th: R | Role RP | Health | F | LIMA Plan | D+ |
| Ht: 6' 1" | Wt: 200 | Type | PT/Exp | B | Rand Var | +2 |
| | | | Consist | C | MM | 0000 |

Even at his peak, simply didn't have the tools to deliver more than modest deep league value, and he's lost a little on his fastball since then. 2nd half move to pen only made things worse, and career 1.8 Cmd in away games says problem ain't just Coors. A 20th century skill set in a 21st century game.

| Yr Tm | W | Sv | IP | K | ERA | xERA | WHIP | oOPS | vL | vR | BF/G | Ctl | Dom | Cmd | FpK | SwK | Vel | G | L | F | H% | S% | hr/f | GS | APC | DOM% | DIS% | Sv% | LI | RAR | BPV | BPX | R$ |
|---|---|---|---|---|---|---|---|---|---|---|---|---|---|---|---|---|---|---|---|---|---|---|---|---|---|---|---|---|---|---|---|---|---|
| 14 COL * | 3 | 3 | 80 | 56 | 5.37 | 4.87 | 1.58 | 1020 | 901 | 1138 | 8.6 | 3.5 | 6.3 | 1.8 | 50% | 6% | 93.2 | 46 | 24 | 30 | 35% | 65% | 14% | 0 | 24 | | | 60 | 0.70 | -16.1 | 53 | 64 | -$8 |
| 15 COL * | 11 | 0 | 157 | 125 | 4.29 | 4.79 | 1.46 | 771 | 737 | 806 | 24.1 | 3.2 | 7.1 | 2.3 | 58% | 10% | 92.0 | 49 | 22 | 28 | 33% | 73% | 11% | 20 | 94 | 20% | 40% | | | -6.4 | 58 | 69 | -$2 |
| 16 COL | 14 | 0 | 186 | 138 | 4.79 | 4.26 | 1.41 | 775 | 694 | 854 | 25.4 | 2.9 | 6.7 | 2.3 | 63% | 9% | 91.7 | 51 | 22 | 27 | 32% | 68% | 14% | 32 | 95 | 19% | 44% | | | -13.8 | 72 | 86 | $0 |
| 17 COL * | 2 | 0 | 70 | 42 | 5.56 | 5.90 | 1.52 | 828 | 797 | 856 | 20.2 | 2.5 | 5.4 | 2.1 | 60% | 10% | 90.2 | 48 | 19 | 33 | 32% | 67% | 16% | 9 | 82 | 11% | 44% | | | -10.3 | 23 | 27 | -$8 |
| 18 COL | 5 | 0 | 120 | 80 | 5.01 | 4.73 | 1.40 | 791 | 726 | 839 | 19.2 | 3.5 | 6.0 | 1.7 | 61% | 9% | 90.5 | 49 | 19 | 32 | 28% | 67% | 15% | 20 | 71 | 5% | 40% | 0 | 0.75 | -12.8 | 40 | 46 | -$6 |
| 1st Half | 5 | 0 | 92 | 67 | 5.07 | 4.53 | 1.40 | 797 | 718 | 862 | 24.7 | 3.5 | 6.5 | 1.9 | 64% | 9% | 90.5 | 49 | 20 | 30 | 29% | 68% | 17% | 16 | 94 | 6% | 38% | | | -10.5 | 50 | 57 | -$6 |
| 2nd Half | 0 | 0 | 28 | 13 | 4.82 | 5.45 | 1.39 | 773 | 757 | 779 | 11.2 | 3.5 | 4.2 | 1.2 | 54% | 7% | 90.5 | 49 | 16 | 35 | 27% | 67% | 9% | 4 | 39 | 0% | 50% | 0 | 0.66 | -2.3 | 7 | 8 | -$9 |
| **19 Proj** | **2** | **0** | **58** | **36** | **5.05** | **4.53** | **1.44** | **815** | **770** | **850** | **16.0** | **3.2** | **5.6** | **1.8** | **59%** | **9%** | **90.8** | **49** | **19** | **32** | **30%** | **68%** | **13%** | **9** | | | | | | **-1.7** | **42** | **49** | **-$6** |

## Biagini,Joe

| | | | | | | |
|---|---|---|---|---|---|---|
| Age: 29 | Th: R | Role RP | Health | A | LIMA Plan | C |
| Ht: 6' 5" | Wt: 240 | Type GB | PT/Exp | D | Rand Var | +5 |
| | | | Consist | C | MM | 1100 |

4-7, 6.00 ERA in 72 IP at TOR. Inability to repeat 2016 skills has kept him shuttling between majors and minors, and cost him a rotation spot. Move back to bullpen didn't revive Dom/SwK, even with an increase in velocity. High GB% helps limit the damage, but that's not exactly a selling point, is it?

| Yr Tm | W | Sv | IP | K | ERA | xERA | WHIP | oOPS | vL | vR | BF/G | Ctl | Dom | Cmd | FpK | SwK | Vel | G | L | F | H% | S% | hr/f | GS | APC | DOM% | DIS% | Sv% | LI | RAR | BPV | BPX | R$ |
|---|---|---|---|---|---|---|---|---|---|---|---|---|---|---|---|---|---|---|---|---|---|---|---|---|---|---|---|---|---|---|---|---|---|
| 14 | | | | | | | | | | | | | | | | | | | | | | | | | | | | | | | | | |
| 15 aa | 10 | 0 | 130 | 70 | 3.35 | 3.89 | 1.38 | | | | 23.8 | 2.6 | 4.8 | 1.8 | | | | | | | 31% | 75% | | | | | | | | 9.8 | 55 | 66 | $4 |
| 16 TOR | 4 | 1 | 68 | 62 | 3.06 | 3.72 | 1.30 | 678 | 725 | 644 | 4.9 | 2.5 | 8.2 | 3.3 | 69% | 12% | 94.3 | 52 | 21 | 26 | 34% | 76% | 6% | 0 | 19 | | | 33 | 0.91 | 9.4 | 110 | 131 | $3 |
| 17 TOR * | 4 | 1 | 137 | 108 | 5.30 | 4.62 | 1.40 | 752 | 788 | 724 | 12.1 | 3.2 | 7.1 | 2.2 | 64% | 9% | 93.8 | 56 | 18 | 27 | 31% | 64% | 15% | 18 | 44 | 17% | 39% | 33 | 1.22 | -15.9 | 54 | 65 | -$5 |
| 18 TOR * | 4 | 0 | 95 | 63 | 6.08 | 6.22 | 1.63 | 913 | 960 | 873 | 7.8 | 3.2 | 5.9 | 1.9 | 65% | 9% | 94.3 | 48 | 20 | 32 | 34% | 65% | 18% | 4 | 25 | 0% | 100% | 0 | 0.69 | -22.6 | 24 | 28 | -$14 |
| 1st Half | 0 | 0 | 59 | 37 | 6.43 | 6.43 | 1.71 | 949 | 984 | 912 | 11.7 | 3.3 | 5.6 | 1.7 | 64% | 9% | 93.3 | 50 | 21 | 29 | 35% | 63% | 19% | 4 | 35 | 0% | 100% | 0 | 0.85 | -16.6 | 22 | 25 | -$21 |
| 2nd Half | 4 | 0 | 36 | 26 | 5.50 | 4.65 | 1.50 | 873 | 926 | 837 | 5.0 | 3.0 | 6.5 | 2.2 | 67% | 9% | 95.2 | 46 | 19 | 36 | 32% | 68% | 18% | 0 | 18 | | | 0 | 0.59 | -6.0 | 60 | 68 | -$3 |
| **19 Proj** | **3** | **0** | **58** | **42** | **4.74** | **4.13** | **1.40** | **759** | **804** | **725** | **7.4** | **3.0** | **6.6** | **2.2** | **66%** | **9%** | **94.2** | **51** | **19** | **30** | **31%** | **69%** | **14%** | **0** | | | | | | **0.1** | **67** | **77** | **-$4** |

## Bieber,Shane

| | | | | | | |
|---|---|---|---|---|---|---|
| Age: 24 | Th: R | Role SP | Health | A | LIMA Plan | B |
| Ht: 6' 3" | Wt: 195 | Type | PT/Exp | D | Rand Var | 0 |
| | | | Consist | A | MM | 3203 |

11-5, 4.55 ERA in 115 IP at CLE. From Low-A ball at start of 2017 to majors in a little over a year thanks to pinpoint Ctl. 36% hit rate undermined his debut, so his 3.53 MLB xERA may slip under the radar. Still some Dom uncertainty, but otherwise this is a skilled young SP looking at a potential breakout year.

| Yr Tm | W | Sv | IP | K | ERA | xERA | WHIP | oOPS | vL | vR | BF/G | Ctl | Dom | Cmd | FpK | SwK | Vel | G | L | F | H% | S% | hr/f | GS | APC | DOM% | DIS% | Sv% | LI | RAR | BPV | BPX | R$ |
|---|---|---|---|---|---|---|---|---|---|---|---|---|---|---|---|---|---|---|---|---|---|---|---|---|---|---|---|---|---|---|---|---|---|
| 14 | | | | | | | | | | | | | | | | | | | | | | | | | | | | | | | | | |
| 15 | | | | | | | | | | | | | | | | | | | | | | | | | | | | | | | | | |
| 16 | | | | | | | | | | | | | | | | | | | | | | | | | | | | | | | | | |
| 17 aa | 2 | 0 | 54 | 42 | 2.99 | 4.11 | 1.31 | | | | 24.9 | 0.9 | 7.0 | 8.0 | | | | | | | 36% | 77% | | | | | | | | 9.2 | 194 | 233 | $0 |
| 18 CLE * | 17 | 0 | 196 | 183 | 3.45 | 3.64 | 1.16 | 787 | 909 | 655 | 23.6 | 1.4 | 8.4 | 6.0 | 66% | 12% | 93.1 | 47 | 22 | 31 | 33% | 73% | 12% | 19 | 90 | 42% | 21% | 0 | 0.79 | 16.9 | 154 | 178 | $19 |
| 1st Half | 9 | 0 | 103 | 88 | 1.80 | 2.69 | 1.00 | 743 | 937 | 500 | 24.5 | 0.9 | 7.7 | 8.4 | 59% | 13% | 92.6 | 51 | 19 | 30 | 30% | 86% | 10% | 4 | 93 | 25% | 0% | | | 29.8 | 212 | 243 | $36 |
| 2nd Half | 8 | 0 | 93 | 95 | 5.27 | 4.68 | 1.35 | 799 | 900 | 693 | 22.9 | 1.9 | 9.2 | 4.7 | 68% | 12% | 93.2 | 45 | 23 | 32 | 36% | 62% | 13% | 15 | 90 | 47% | 27% | 0 | 0.80 | -12.9 | 121 | 139 | $4 |
| **19 Proj** | **11** | **0** | **160** | **143** | **3.43** | **3.38** | **1.17** | **694** | **821** | **552** | **23.6** | **1.4** | **8.1** | **5.8** | **65%** | **12%** | **93.0** | **45** | **22** | **33** | **33%** | **73%** | **9%** | **27** | | | | | | **13.7** | **131** | **150** | **$14** |

BRANDON KRUSE

## Blach,Ty

| Age: 28 | Th: L | Role RP | Health | A | LIMA Plan | D+ |
|---|---|---|---|---|---|---|
| Ht: 6' 1" | Wt: 213 | Type Con GB | PT/Exp | B | Rand Var | 0 |
| | | | Consist | C | MM | 1001 |

Another run of mediocre skills and forgettable stats got him demoted to bullpen, where Dom rose, but stagnant SwK, Vel, make it look like small sample fluke. If he can't cut it in pen, next step is off the roster. When BPV, RAR keep saying you're replaceable, eventually teams will find someone to replace you.

| Yr Tm | W | Sv | IP | K | ERA | xERA | WHIP | oOPS | vL | vR | BF/G | Ctl | Dom | Cmd | FpK | SwK | Vel | G | L | F | H% | S% | hr/f | GS | APC | DOM% | DIS% | Sv% | LI | RAR | BPV | BPX | R$ |
|---|---|---|---|---|---|---|---|---|---|---|---|---|---|---|---|---|---|---|---|---|---|---|---|---|---|---|---|---|---|---|---|---|---|
| 14 aa | 8 | 0 | 141 | 76 | 3.53 | 4.20 | 1.41 | | | | 23.9 | 2.5 | 4.9 | 1.9 | | | | | | | 32% | 75% | | | | | | | | 3.7 | 54 | 65 | $0 |
| 15 aaa | 11 | 0 | 165 | 77 | 4.82 | 4.94 | 1.46 | | | | 26.2 | 1.7 | 4.2 | 2.5 | | | | | | | 34% | 67% | | | | | | | | -17.5 | 49 | 58 | -$7 |
| 16 SF * | 15 | 0 | 180 | 101 | 3.89 | 3.56 | 1.28 | 445 | 374 | 495 | 24.5 | 2.3 | 5.0 | 2.2 | 65% | 6% | 91.1 | 58 | 9 | 33 | 30% | 69% | 7% | 2 | 60 | 50% | 50% | 0 | 0.40 | 6.7 | 65 | 77 | $9 |
| 17 SF | 8 | 0 | 164 | 73 | 4.78 | 5.16 | 1.36 | 766 | 592 | 831 | 20.4 | 2.4 | 4.0 | 1.7 | 62% | 7% | 90.1 | 47 | 21 | 32 | 29% | 66% | 10% | 24 | 74 | 8% | 38% | 0 | 0.72 | -8.6 | 33 | 40 | -$1 |
| 18 SF | 6 | 0 | 119 | 75 | 4.25 | 4.38 | 1.47 | 746 | 723 | 757 | 10.9 | 3.1 | 5.7 | 1.8 | 62% | 7% | 90.0 | 54 | 23 | 23 | 32% | 71% | 9% | 13 | 40 | 0% | 62% | 0 | 0.89 | -1.4 | 50 | 58 | -$4 |
| 1st Half | 5 | 0 | 82 | 43 | 4.06 | 4.55 | 1.46 | 736 | 697 | 756 | 15.3 | 3.0 | 4.7 | 1.6 | 63% | 7% | 89.8 | 55 | 23 | 22 | 32% | 72% | 8% | 12 | 55 | 0% | 58% | 0 | 0.99 | 0.9 | 38 | 44 | -$3 |
| 2nd Half | 1 | 0 | 37 | 32 | 4.66 | 4.03 | 1.47 | 770 | 790 | 761 | 6.6 | 3.4 | 7.9 | 2.3 | 61% | 7% | 90.4 | 51 | 24 | 25 | 34% | 69% | 11% | 1 | 26 | 0% | 100% | 0 | 0.80 | -2.3 | 78 | 89 | -$6 |
| **19 Proj** | **4** | **0** | **87** | **53** | **4.41** | **4.29** | **1.41** | **750** | **685** | **778** | **12.2** | **2.8** | **5.5** | **2.0** | **62%** | **7%** | **90.1** | **50** | **23** | **27** | **32%** | **69%** | **9%** | **7** | | | | | | **-2.8** | **53** | **61** | **-$3** |

## Black,Ray

| Age: 29 | Th: R | Role RP | Health | F | LIMA Plan | A |
|---|---|---|---|---|---|---|
| Ht: 6' 5" | Wt: 225 | Type Pwr xFB | PT/Exp | F | Rand Var | +5 |
| | | | Consist | C | MM | 4500 |

2-2, 6.17 ERA in 23 IP at SF. Electric stuff—including fastball that touches triple digits—undermined by injury history that nearly caused him to quit the game. 48% strand rate ruined MLB debut, where xERA was 3.32, though FpK, FB% show there's still reason for caution. Closer upside, DL downside.

| Yr Tm | W | Sv | IP | K | ERA | xERA | WHIP | oOPS | vL | vR | BF/G | Ctl | Dom | Cmd | FpK | SwK | Vel | G | L | F | H% | S% | hr/f | GS | APC | DOM% | DIS% | Sv% | LI | RAR | BPV | BPX | R$ |
|---|---|---|---|---|---|---|---|---|---|---|---|---|---|---|---|---|---|---|---|---|---|---|---|---|---|---|---|---|---|---|---|---|---|
| 14 | | | | | | | | | | | | | | | | | | | | | | | | | | | | | | | | | |
| 15 | | | | | | | | | | | | | | | | | | | | | | | | | | | | | | | | | |
| 16 aa | 1 | 6 | 31 | 43 | 6.71 | 3.88 | 1.85 | | | | 4.2 | 10.4 | 12.2 | 1.2 | | | | | | | 31% | 61% | | | | | | | | -9.7 | 105 | 124 | -$5 |
| 17 | | | | | | | | | | | | | | | | | | | | | | | | | | | | | | | | | |
| 18 SF * | 5 | 5 | 61 | 83 | 4.22 | 2.41 | 1.05 | 728 | 998 | 623 | 3.8 | 3.4 | 12.4 | 3.6 | 52% | 16% | 97.9 | 39 | 12 | 49 | 28% | 61% | 17% | 0 | 16 | | | 71 | 0.87 | -0.5 | 141 | 162 | $5 |
| 1st Half | 1 | 5 | 31 | 40 | 2.86 | 1.39 | 0.90 | | | | 3.9 | 3.1 | 11.6 | 3.7 | | | | | | | 24% | 69% | 0% | 0 | | | | | | 5.0 | 154 | 177 | $8 |
| 2nd Half | 4 | 0 | 29 | 43 | 5.67 | 3.49 | 1.20 | 728 | 998 | 623 | 3.7 | 3.7 | 13.2 | 3.5 | 52% | 16% | 97.9 | 39 | 12 | 49 | 32% | 54% | 17% | 0 | 16 | | | 0 | 0.87 | -5.5 | 127 | 146 | $3 |
| **19 Proj** | **3** | **0** | **44** | **60** | **3.64** | **3.30** | **1.13** | **600** | **804** | **520** | **3.7** | **3.9** | **12.4** | **3.2** | **52%** | **16%** | **97.9** | **39** | **12** | **49** | **29%** | **70%** | **9%** | **0** | | | | | | **2.7** | **134** | **154** | **$1** |

## Borucki,Ryan

| Age: 25 | Th: L | Role SP | Health | A | LIMA Plan | B+ |
|---|---|---|---|---|---|---|
| Ht: 6' 4" | Wt: 175 | Type GB | PT/Exp | D | Rand Var | 0 |
| | | | Consist | C | MM | 1003 |

4-6, 3.87 ERA in 97 IP at TOR. Gets by on mix of ground balls and good Ctl, though the latter took a step back in 2018 as he faced higher-level competition. Platoon splits don't reflect disparity in Cmd (4.0 vL, 1.7 vR), and low hr/f hid a lot of damage; 4.68 xERA in majors means he'll likely be overvalued.

| Yr Tm | W | Sv | IP | K | ERA | xERA | WHIP | oOPS | vL | vR | BF/G | Ctl | Dom | Cmd | FpK | SwK | Vel | G | L | F | H% | S% | hr/f | GS | APC | DOM% | DIS% | Sv% | LI | RAR | BPV | BPX | R$ |
|---|---|---|---|---|---|---|---|---|---|---|---|---|---|---|---|---|---|---|---|---|---|---|---|---|---|---|---|---|---|---|---|---|---|
| 14 | | | | | | | | | | | | | | | | | | | | | | | | | | | | | | | | | |
| 15 | | | | | | | | | | | | | | | | | | | | | | | | | | | | | | | | | |
| 16 | | | | | | | | | | | | | | | | | | | | | | | | | | | | | | | | | |
| 17 a/a | 2 | 0 | 52 | 40 | 2.37 | 2.56 | 1.06 | | | | 25.4 | 1.7 | 6.9 | 4.1 | | | | | | | 29% | 79% | | | | | | | | 12.8 | 123 | 148 | $3 |
| 18 TOR * | 10 | 0 | 175 | 115 | 4.12 | 4.02 | 1.35 | 705 | 639 | 728 | 24.3 | 3.3 | 5.9 | 1.8 | 53% | 8% | 91.5 | 47 | 19 | 34 | 30% | 70% | 7% | 17 | 93 | 24% | 41% | | | 0.6 | 54 | 63 | $2 |
| 1st Half | 6 | 0 | 83 | 51 | 4.34 | 4.25 | 1.41 | 805 | 833 | 793 | 25.1 | 3.7 | 5.5 | 1.5 | 44% | 6% | 92.0 | 35 | 25 | 40 | 29% | 70% | 0% | 1 | 95 | 0% | 100% | | | -2.0 | 43 | 49 | -$2 |
| 2nd Half | 4 | 0 | 92 | 64 | 3.93 | 4.54 | 1.30 | 698 | 627 | 723 | 24.3 | 2.8 | 6.3 | 2.2 | 54% | 8% | 91.5 | 48 | 19 | 33 | 30% | 71% | 7% | 16 | 93 | 25% | 38% | | | 2.5 | 62 | 71 | $6 |
| **19 Proj** | **7** | **0** | **145** | **102** | **4.17** | **4.18** | **1.27** | **668** | **605** | **691** | **24.9** | **2.6** | **6.3** | **2.4** | **54%** | **8%** | **91.5** | **48** | **19** | **33** | **29%** | **70%** | **10%** | **24** | | | | | | **-0.3** | **69** | **80** | **$3** |

## Boxberger,Brad

| Age: 31 | Th: R | Role RP | Health | F | LIMA Plan | C+ |
|---|---|---|---|---|---|---|
| Ht: 6' 2" | Wt: 205 | Type Pwr FB | PT/Exp | C | Rand Var | +3 |
| | | | Consist | C | MM | 3520 |

Skill inconsistency—particularly Ctl—remains an issue, and big reason why he can't seem to hold down closer role. Even staying healthy for first time since 2015 couldn't prevent swing in value from 1st half to 2nd. When he's on, he's good, but that happens far too rarely for any kind of sizable investment.

| Yr Tm | W | Sv | IP | K | ERA | xERA | WHIP | oOPS | vL | vR | BF/G | Ctl | Dom | Cmd | FpK | SwK | Vel | G | L | F | H% | S% | hr/f | GS | APC | DOM% | DIS% | Sv% | LI | RAR | BPV | BPX | R$ |
|---|---|---|---|---|---|---|---|---|---|---|---|---|---|---|---|---|---|---|---|---|---|---|---|---|---|---|---|---|---|---|---|---|---|
| 14 TAM | 5 | 2 | 65 | 104 | 2.37 | 2.08 | 0.84 | 538 | 402 | 659 | 3.9 | 2.8 | 14.5 | 5.2 | 67% | 15% | 93.1 | 41 | 17 | 42 | 24% | 82% | 19% | 0 | 17 | | | 40 | 1.23 | 11.0 | 204 | 243 | $11 |
| 15 TAM | 4 | 41 | 63 | 74 | 3.71 | 3.98 | 1.37 | 703 | 657 | 759 | 3.9 | 4.6 | 10.6 | 2.3 | 56% | 13% | 92.7 | 36 | 21 | 43 | 30% | 78% | 13% | 0 | 17 | | | 87 | 1.58 | 1.9 | 81 | 96 | $17 |
| 16 TAM | 4 | 0 | 24 | 22 | 4.81 | 5.57 | 1.73 | 728 | 750 | 711 | 4.2 | 7.0 | 8.1 | 1.2 | 58% | 10% | 92.0 | 48 | 15 | 37 | 30% | 74% | 12% | 0 | 17 | | | 0 | 1.15 | -1.9 | -17 | -21 | -$4 |
| 17 TAM | 4 | 0 | 29 | 40 | 3.38 | 3.39 | 1.16 | 665 | 584 | 753 | 4.0 | 3.4 | 12.3 | 3.6 | 59% | 13% | 92.3 | 42 | 16 | 42 | 31% | 77% | 14% | 0 | 17 | | | 0 | 1.14 | 3.6 | 150 | 180 | $0 |
| 18 ARI | 3 | 32 | 53 | 71 | 4.39 | 3.89 | 1.43 | 732 | 844 | 655 | 3.9 | 5.4 | 12.0 | 2.2 | 61% | 11% | 91.4 | 46 | 16 | 38 | 31% | 75% | 18% | 0 | 16 | | | 80 | 1.31 | -1.6 | 94 | 108 | $10 |
| 1st Half | 1 | 19 | 29 | 39 | 3.68 | 3.54 | 1.33 | 736 | 851 | 655 | 4.0 | 4.6 | 12.0 | 2.6 | 61% | 10% | 90.8 | 51 | 11 | 37 | 29% | 82% | 23% | 0 | 16 | | | 83 | 1.27 | 1.7 | 121 | 138 | $13 |
| 2nd Half | 2 | 13 | 24 | 32 | 5.25 | 4.35 | 1.54 | 728 | 836 | 654 | 3.9 | 6.4 | 12.0 | 1.9 | 60% | 13% | 92.0 | 40 | 21 | 40 | 32% | 68% | 13% | 0 | 16 | | | 76 | 1.35 | -3.3 | 62 | 71 | $7 |
| **19 Proj** | **4** | **14** | **58** | **76** | **3.97** | **3.53** | **1.33** | **695** | **704** | **687** | **3.8** | **4.9** | **11.9** | **2.4** | **60%** | **12%** | **92.2** | **41** | **18** | **41** | **30%** | **75%** | **16%** | **0** | | | | | | **5.9** | **102** | **117** | **$6** |

## Boyd,Matt

| Age: 28 | Th: L | Role SP | Health | A | LIMA Plan | B |
|---|---|---|---|---|---|---|
| Ht: 6' 3" | Wt: 234 | Type Pwr xFB | PT/Exp | B | Rand Var | 0 |
| | | | Consist | B | MM | 1205 |

Threw slider, his best strikeout pitch, three times as often, leading to career-high Dom, Cmd, and even greater heights in 2nd half. But gains were offset by sky-high FB%, and FpK wasn't at level that would support elite 2nd half Ctl. Still, seeds are here for sub-4 ERA, and he's at right age to make it happen.

| Yr Tm | W | Sv | IP | K | ERA | xERA | WHIP | oOPS | vL | vR | BF/G | Ctl | Dom | Cmd | FpK | SwK | Vel | G | L | F | H% | S% | hr/f | GS | APC | DOM% | DIS% | Sv% | LI | RAR | BPV | BPX | R$ |
|---|---|---|---|---|---|---|---|---|---|---|---|---|---|---|---|---|---|---|---|---|---|---|---|---|---|---|---|---|---|---|---|---|---|
| 14 aa | 1 | 0 | 43 | 39 | 8.72 | 7.05 | 1.82 | | | | 19.8 | 2.8 | 8.2 | 2.9 | | | | | | | 42% | 51% | | | | | | | | -26.2 | 56 | 67 | -$13 |
| 15 2AL * | 10 | 0 | 172 | 128 | 3.84 | 3.77 | 1.17 | 979 | 1134 | 913 | 21.5 | 2.5 | 6.7 | 2.6 | 59% | 9% | 91.1 | 32 | 16 | 52 | 26% | 73% | 18% | 12 | 77 | 0% | 50% | 0 | 0.74 | 2.6 | 63 | 74 | $9 |
| 16 DET * | 8 | 0 | 161 | 127 | 3.95 | 4.39 | 1.31 | 765 | 598 | 800 | 21.5 | 2.7 | 7.1 | 2.6 | 63% | 10% | 91.2 | 38 | 17 | 45 | 30% | 75% | 13% | 18 | 84 | 22% | 44% | 0 | 0.87 | 4.8 | 60 | 72 | $5 |
| 17 DET * | 9 | 0 | 186 | 150 | 5.00 | 5.06 | 1.46 | 826 | 712 | 847 | 23.4 | 3.3 | 7.3 | 2.2 | 59% | 10% | 92.0 | 38 | 22 | 40 | 32% | 69% | 11% | 25 | 91 | 12% | 48% | 0 | 0.74 | -14.7 | 49 | 59 | -$3 |
| 18 DET | 9 | 0 | 170 | 159 | 4.39 | 4.55 | 1.16 | 704 | 654 | 718 | 22.9 | 2.7 | 8.4 | 3.1 | 58% | 11% | 90.4 | 29 | 21 | 50 | 27% | 67% | 11% | 31 | 92 | 16% | 26% | | | -4.9 | 85 | 98 | $8 |
| 1st Half | 4 | 0 | 88 | 76 | 4.18 | 4.78 | 1.21 | 667 | 624 | 679 | 23.1 | 3.6 | 7.7 | 2.2 | 56% | 10% | 89.3 | 30 | 24 | 46 | 27% | 67% | 8% | 16 | 92 | 6% | 19% | | | -0.3 | 51 | 59 | $5 |
| 2nd Half | 5 | 0 | 82 | 83 | 4.61 | 4.33 | 1.10 | 741 | 685 | 757 | 22.7 | 1.8 | 9.1 | 5.2 | 61% | 11% | 91.4 | 27 | 18 | 54 | 27% | 67% | 14% | 15 | 92 | 27% | 33% | | | -4.6 | 122 | 140 | $10 |
| **19 Proj** | **10** | **0** | **189** | **168** | **4.30** | **4.24** | **1.28** | **747** | **706** | **757** | **24.8** | **2.7** | **8.0** | **2.9** | **60%** | **10%** | **91.1** | **33** | **20** | **47** | **30%** | **71%** | **11%** | **27** | | | | | | **-1.9** | **81** | **93** | **$6** |

## Brach,Brad

| Age: 33 | Th: R | Role RP | Health | A | LIMA Plan | B+ |
|---|---|---|---|---|---|---|
| Ht: 6' 6" | Wt: 215 | Type Pwr | PT/Exp | C | Rand Var | 0 |
| | | | Consist | B | MM | 2310 |

Unfortunately for him, save opps came after season with his most closer-worthy skills; xERA, Cmd, and BPV all say he's been fading fast. Meanwhile, an improbable run of fortunate S%, hr/f rates has been making him look better than he is. As he hits mid-30s, wouldn't take much for this to all fall apart.

| Yr Tm | W | Sv | IP | K | ERA | xERA | WHIP | oOPS | vL | vR | BF/G | Ctl | Dom | Cmd | FpK | SwK | Vel | G | L | F | H% | S% | hr/f | GS | APC | DOM% | DIS% | Sv% | LI | RAR | BPV | BPX | R$ |
|---|---|---|---|---|---|---|---|---|---|---|---|---|---|---|---|---|---|---|---|---|---|---|---|---|---|---|---|---|---|---|---|---|---|
| 14 BAL * | 10 | 1 | 86 | 86 | 3.47 | 3.63 | 1.30 | 640 | 776 | 543 | 5.6 | 3.3 | 9.1 | 2.7 | 58% | 13% | 93.4 | 36 | 19 | 45 | 32% | 75% | 8% | 0 | 23 | | | 50 | 0.82 | 2.9 | 95 | 113 | $4 |
| 15 BAL | 5 | 1 | 79 | 89 | 2.72 | 3.61 | 1.20 | 627 | 534 | 729 | 5.2 | 4.3 | 10.1 | 2.3 | 58% | 14% | 94.0 | 45 | 19 | 36 | 27% | 81% | 10% | 0 | 21 | | | 50 | 0.99 | 12.1 | 88 | 105 | $7 |
| 16 BAL | 10 | 2 | 79 | 92 | 2.05 | 3.38 | 1.04 | 578 | 784 | 399 | 4.4 | 2.8 | 10.5 | 3.7 | 60% | 15% | 94.5 | 41 | 21 | 38 | 28% | 85% | 10% | 0 | 18 | | | 29 | 1.05 | 20.8 | 131 | 155 | $14 |
| 17 BAL | 4 | 18 | 68 | 70 | 3.18 | 4.05 | 1.13 | 620 | 559 | 675 | 4.1 | 3.4 | 9.3 | 2.7 | 58% | 13% | 95.0 | 42 | 19 | 39 | 27% | 76% | 10% | 0 | 18 | | | 75 | 1.06 | 9.9 | 94 | 113 | $13 |
| 18 2TM | 2 | 12 | 63 | 60 | 3.59 | 4.51 | 1.60 | 754 | 838 | 692 | 4.2 | 4.0 | 8.6 | 2.1 | 57% | 13% | 93.9 | 46 | 24 | 30 | 36% | 79% | 8% | 0 | 17 | | | 75 | 1.08 | 4.3 | 71 | 81 | $1 |
| 1st Half | 0 | 10 | 32 | 33 | 3.62 | 4.74 | 1.67 | 751 | 834 | 693 | 4.4 | 4.7 | 9.2 | 1.9 | 56% | 15% | 93.2 | 42 | 25 | 33 | 38% | 79% | 6% | 0 | 17 | | | 83 | 1.06 | 2.1 | 58 | 66 | $0 |
| 2nd Half | 2 | 2 | 30 | 27 | 3.56 | 4.26 | 1.52 | 757 | 841 | 689 | 3.9 | 3.3 | 8.0 | 2.5 | 59% | 11% | 94.6 | 50 | 22 | 28 | 35% | 79% | 11% | 0 | 17 | | | 50 | 1.10 | 2.2 | 84 | 97 | $1 |
| **19 Proj** | **4** | **2** | **58** | **59** | **3.67** | **3.79** | **1.35** | **704** | **753** | **664** | **4.1** | **3.6** | **9.1** | **2.5** | **58%** | **13%** | **94.3** | **44** | **21** | **34** | **32%** | **76%** | **11%** | **0** | | | | | | **2.6** | **89** | **102** | **$1** |

## Bracho,Silvino

| Age: 26 | Th: R | Role RP | Health | A | LIMA Plan | B+ |
|---|---|---|---|---|---|---|
| Ht: 5' 10" | Wt: 190 | Type Pwr xFB | PT/Exp | D | Rand Var | +1 |
| | | | Consist | B | MM | 2310 |

2-0, 3.19 ERA in 31 IP at ARI. Dom, SwK rates show he can miss bats at major league level, and while Ctl hasn't been consistent, it's been enough to make him viable. Extreme FB% has been holding him back, though trend suggests he's working on it. Note the 1st half; that could be his best-case scenario.

| Yr Tm | W | Sv | IP | K | ERA | xERA | WHIP | oOPS | vL | vR | BF/G | Ctl | Dom | Cmd | FpK | SwK | Vel | G | L | F | H% | S% | hr/f | GS | APC | DOM% | DIS% | Sv% | LI | RAR | BPV | BPX | R$ |
|---|---|---|---|---|---|---|---|---|---|---|---|---|---|---|---|---|---|---|---|---|---|---|---|---|---|---|---|---|---|---|---|---|---|
| 14 | | | | | | | | | | | | | | | | | | | | | | | | | | | | | | | | | |
| 15 ARI * | 2 | 17 | 57 | 67 | 2.15 | 3.04 | 1.10 | 680 | 988 | 486 | 4.5 | 2.1 | 10.6 | 5.0 | 52% | 16% | 92.9 | 18 | 25 | 57 | 32% | 86% | 13% | 0 | 17 | | | 89 | 0.55 | 12.8 | 151 | 180 | $12 |
| 16 ARI * | 0 | 15 | 58 | 53 | 6.35 | 5.50 | 1.51 | 951 | 920 | 970 | 4.1 | 2.8 | 8.1 | 2.9 | 62% | 11% | 92.7 | 29 | 21 | 51 | 35% | 59% | 16% | 0 | 18 | | | 88 | 0.57 | -15.5 | 63 | 75 | -$3 |
| 17 ARI * | 3 | 8 | 56 | 64 | 4.87 | 4.48 | 1.24 | 725 | 572 | 822 | 4.2 | 3.8 | 10.3 | 2.7 | 56% | 13% | 93.6 | 44 | 9 | 47 | 26% | 70% | 19% | 0 | 17 | | | 80 | 0.44 | -3.5 | 65 | 77 | $2 |
| 18 ARI * | 4 | 8 | 66 | 75 | 3.68 | 3.71 | 1.29 | 670 | 714 | 638 | 4.7 | 2.6 | 10.3 | 3.9 | 60% | 16% | 93.3 | 35 | 22 | 43 | 36% | 72% | 6% | 0 | 16 | | | 62 | 0.99 | 3.8 | 128 | 147 | $4 |
| 1st Half | 3 | 5 | 36 | 44 | 3.34 | 1.95 | 1.02 | 416 | 563 | 301 | 5.1 | 2.4 | 11.1 | 4.6 | 66% | 19% | 93.1 | 45 | 14 | 41 | 32% | 65% | 0% | 0 | 18 | | | 83 | 1.02 | 3.6 | 170 | 196 | $8 |
| 2nd Half | 1 | 3 | 33 | 31 | 3.79 | 5.17 | 1.49 | 819 | 814 | 819 | 4.5 | 2.7 | 8.5 | 3.2 | 56% | 14% | 93.4 | 31 | 25 | 44 | 37% | 78% | 8% | 0 | 15 | | | 43 | 0.98 | 1.4 | 83 | 96 | -$1 |
| **19 Proj** | **2** | **4** | **58** | **62** | **3.88** | **3.87** | **1.25** | **667** | **646** | **678** | **4.4** | **2.9** | **9.6** | **3.3** | **56%** | **14%** | **93.4** | **31** | **25** | **44** | **31%** | **73%** | **10%** | **0** | | | | | | **2.1** | **104** | **119** | **$1** |

BRANDON KRUSE

## Bradford,Chase

Age: 29 | Th: R | Role: RP | Health: A | LIMA Plan: C
Ht: 6' 1" | Wt: 229 | Type: GB | PT/Exp: D | Rand Var: 0 | Consist: B | MM: 1000

Fewer first pitch and swinging strikes, more FB, and his ERA gets BETTER? Nope, no one's gonna buy that. The 1st half tandem of 25% hit rate and 86% strand rate provided a faux foundation from which his lack of dominance chipped away at his surface stats the rest of the year. His xERA column is all you need to see.

| Yr Tm | W | Sv | IP | K | ERA | xERA | WHIP | oOPS | vL | vR | BF/G | Ctl | Dom | Cmd | FpK | SwK | Vel | G | L | F | H% | S% | hr/f | GS | APC | DOM% | DIS% | Sv% | LI | RAR | BPV | BPX | R$ |
|---|---|---|---|---|---|---|---|---|---|---|---|---|---|---|---|---|---|---|---|---|---|---|---|---|---|---|---|---|---|---|---|---|---|
| 14 a/a | 4 | 16 | 73 | 55 | 2.75 | 3.99 | 1.26 | | | | 5.2 | 1.1 | 6.8 | 6.1 | | | | | | | 34% | 80% | | | | | | | | 8.9 | 148 | 176 | $9 |
| 15 aaa | 5 | 7 | 64 | 37 | 4.14 | 5.71 | 1.68 | | | | 5.4 | 1.9 | 5.3 | 2.8 | | | | | | | 39% | 75% | | | | | | | | -1.4 | 64 | 77 | -$3 |
| 16 aaa | 5 | 5 | 66 | 44 | 5.05 | 5.77 | 1.64 | | | | 5.2 | 1.9 | 6.1 | 3.2 | | | | | | | 39% | 69% | | | | | | | | -6.9 | 71 | 85 | -$4 |
| 17 NYM * | 3 | 11 | 69 | 49 | 4.09 | 4.99 | 1.51 | 657 | 715 | 596 | 4.9 | 2.6 | 6.3 | 2.4 | 65% | 13% | 90.6 | 56 | 15 | 29 | 35% | 74% | 10% | 0 | 18 | | | 73 | 0.63 | 2.3 | 60 | 72 | $2 |
| 18 SEA | 5 | 0 | 54 | 38 | 3.69 | 4.54 | 1.29 | 758 | 750 | 762 | 5.0 | 2.3 | 6.4 | 2.7 | 62% | 11% | 90.8 | 47 | 17 | 36 | 29% | 78% | 14% | 0 | 19 | | | 0 | 0.61 | 3.0 | 76 | 88 | $0 |
| 1st Half | 5 | 0 | 32 | 26 | 2.81 | 3.96 | 1.06 | 701 | 701 | 701 | 4.6 | 2.0 | 7.3 | 3.7 | 60% | 13% | 91.0 | 46 | 16 | 38 | 25% | 86% | 17% | 0 | 18 | | | 0 | 0.74 | 5.3 | 103 | 118 | $5 |
| 2nd Half | 0 | 0 | 22 | 12 | 4.98 | 5.47 | 1.62 | 831 | 833 | 829 | 5.7 | 2.9 | 5.0 | 1.7 | 64% | 8% | 90.5 | 47 | 19 | 35 | 34% | 72% | 11% | 0 | 20 | | | 0 | 0.42 | -2.2 | 36 | 42 | -$8 |
| 19 Proj | **3** | **0** | **51** | **34** | **4.20** | **4.29** | **1.47** | **803** | **817** | **795** | **5.0** | **2.4** | **6.1** | **2.6** | **64%** | **11%** | **90.7** | **50** | **16** | **33** | **34%** | **74%** | **11%** | **0** | | | | | | **-0.3** | **74** | **85** | **-$4** |

## Bradley,Archie

Age: 26 | Th: R | Role: RP | Health: C | LIMA Plan: A
Ht: 6' 4" | Wt: 225 | Type: Pwr | PT/Exp: C | Rand Var: +1 | Consist: B | MM: 4320

Had to reduce curveball usage because it cracks nail on his right forefinger, and half-season shifts in SwK probably reflect him adjusting to new pitch mix. 2nd half Cmd growth was offset by FB% increase, though all of it was buried under ERA inflated by bad luck, including 43% hit rate vR. Still looks like a closer-in-waiting.

| Yr Tm | W | Sv | IP | K | ERA | xERA | WHIP | oOPS | vL | vR | BF/G | Ctl | Dom | Cmd | FpK | SwK | Vel | G | L | F | H% | S% | hr/f | GS | APC | DOM% | DIS% | Sv% | LI | RAR | BPV | BPX | R$ |
|---|---|---|---|---|---|---|---|---|---|---|---|---|---|---|---|---|---|---|---|---|---|---|---|---|---|---|---|---|---|---|---|---|---|
| 14 a/a | 3 | 0 | 79 | 60 | 4.76 | 3.83 | 1.53 | | | | 20.2 | 5.0 | 6.8 | 1.3 | | | | | | | 31% | 66% | | | | | | | | -9.9 | 66 | 78 | -$6 |
| 15 ARI * | 3 | 0 | 57 | 40 | 4.70 | 4.90 | 1.57 | 768 | 587 | 985 | 20.8 | 4.2 | 6.3 | 1.5 | 55% | 6% | 92.2 | 58 | 14 | 28 | 32% | 71% | 10% | 8 | 81 | 0% | 63% | | | -5.2 | 41 | 49 | -$6 |
| 16 ARI * | 13 | 0 | 182 | 182 | 4.42 | 4.29 | 1.47 | 802 | 936 | 666 | 23.7 | 4.2 | 9.0 | 2.1 | 57% | 9% | 92.4 | 45 | 25 | 30 | 34% | 71% | 13% | 26 | 99 | 15% | 38% | | | -5.2 | 78 | 92 | $1 |
| 17 ARI | 3 | 1 | 73 | 79 | 1.73 | 3.31 | 1.04 | 567 | 579 | 556 | 4.6 | 2.6 | 9.7 | 3.8 | 59% | 11% | 96.4 | 48 | 23 | 29 | 29% | 86% | 7% | 0 | 18 | | | 14 | 1.29 | 23.7 | 131 | 158 | $10 |
| 18 ARI | 4 | 3 | 72 | 75 | 3.64 | 3.51 | 1.14 | 672 | 490 | 795 | 3.9 | 2.5 | 9.4 | 3.8 | 68% | 9% | 95.6 | 49 | 17 | 33 | 29% | 73% | 14% | 0 | 16 | | | 27 | 1.37 | 4.5 | 129 | 148 | $4 |
| 1st Half | 2 | 3 | 39 | 35 | 2.08 | 3.45 | 0.95 | 556 | 432 | 631 | 3.8 | 2.5 | 8.1 | 3.2 | 69% | 8% | 95.6 | 54 | 16 | 30 | 23% | 85% | 13% | 0 | 16 | | | 60 | 1.22 | 10.0 | 109 | 125 | $10 |
| 2nd Half | 2 | 0 | 33 | 40 | 5.51 | 3.57 | 1.38 | 793 | 544 | 977 | 4.0 | 2.5 | 11.0 | 4.4 | 66% | 11% | 95.7 | 43 | 20 | 37 | 37% | 63% | 15% | 0 | 17 | | | 0 | 1.54 | -5.5 | 153 | 176 | -$3 |
| 19 Proj | **3** | **23** | **58** | **60** | **3.33** | **3.29** | **1.20** | **677** | **591** | **747** | **5.0** | **2.7** | **9.4** | **3.5** | **64%** | **9%** | **95.0** | **48** | **20** | **32** | **31%** | **76%** | **12%** | **0** | | | | | | **5.9** | **123** | **141** | **$11** |

## Brasier,Ryan

Age: 31 | Th: R | Role: RP | Health: C | LIMA Plan: B+
Ht: 6' 0" | Wt: 225 | Type: FB | PT/Exp: D | Rand Var: -4 | Consist: D | MM: 2100

2-0, 1.60 ERA in 34 IP at BOS. What a story: MLB debut in 2013, misses 2014 after TJ surgery, restarts in minors, plays in Japan, then posts best skills of career in half-season w/BOS at age 30. It'd seem fluky if not for elite FpK, SwK, which hint that he could do even better. There may be something worth tracking here.

| Yr Tm | W | Sv | IP | K | ERA | xERA | WHIP | oOPS | vL | vR | BF/G | Ctl | Dom | Cmd | FpK | SwK | Vel | G | L | F | H% | S% | hr/f | GS | APC | DOM% | DIS% | Sv% | LI | RAR | BPV | BPX | R$ |
|---|---|---|---|---|---|---|---|---|---|---|---|---|---|---|---|---|---|---|---|---|---|---|---|---|---|---|---|---|---|---|---|---|---|
| 14 | | | | | | | | | | | | | | | | | | | | | | | | | | | | | | | | | |
| 15 | | | | | | | | | | | | | | | | | | | | | | | | | | | | | | | | | |
| 16 aaa | 5 | 1 | 61 | 50 | 4.85 | 4.57 | 1.43 | | | | 5.6 | 3.2 | 7.4 | 2.3 | | | | | | | 33% | 68% | | | | | | | | -4.9 | 63 | 75 | -$2 |
| 17 for | 2 | 1 | 30 | 18 | 3.73 | 5.39 | 1.48 | | | | 5.0 | 3.0 | 5.4 | 1.8 | | | | | | | 31% | 81% | | | | | | | | 2.3 | 23 | 28 | -$3 |
| 18 BOS * | 4 | 13 | 75 | 57 | 1.92 | 2.42 | 1.04 | 482 | 647 | 313 | 4.2 | 2.0 | 6.9 | 3.4 | 70% | 16% | 96.9 | 40 | 20 | 40 | 27% | 83% | 6% | 0 | 14 | | | 81 | 1.13 | 20.6 | 111 | 128 | $14 |
| 1st Half | 2 | 11 | 38 | 27 | 2.34 | 3.76 | 1.32 | | | | 5.1 | 2.3 | 6.4 | 2.7 | | | | | | | 33% | 83% | 0% | 0 | | | | | | 8.5 | 86 | 99 | $12 |
| 2nd Half | 2 | 2 | 37 | 30 | 1.47 | 1.02 | 0.75 | 482 | 647 | 313 | 3.5 | 1.7 | 7.5 | 4.3 | 70% | 16% | 96.9 | 40 | 20 | 40 | 20% | 84% | 6% | 0 | 14 | | | 50 | 1.13 | 12.1 | 143 | 165 | $16 |
| 19 Proj | **4** | **0** | **58** | **46** | **3.22** | **4.00** | **1.13** | **684** | **901** | **462** | **4.5** | **2.0** | **7.1** | **3.5** | **70%** | **16%** | **96.9** | **40** | **20** | **40** | **27%** | **77%** | **10%** | **0** | | | | | | **6.7** | **91** | **105** | **$2** |

## Brault,Steven

Age: 27 | Th: L | Role: RP | Health: A | LIMA Plan: D+
Ht: 6' 0" | Wt: 200 | Type: Pwr | PT/Exp: C | Rand Var: 0 | Consist: D | MM: 0100

Whatever edge his deceptive delivery and arm slot gives him is being negated by inability to master the strike zone (career 5.0 Ctl, 1.5 Cmd in MLB). And history of struggles vR will likely keep him relegated to pen. "Lefty specialist with control issues, subpar strikeout rate" is not the résumé you want in this reliever job market.

| Yr Tm | W | Sv | IP | K | ERA | xERA | WHIP | oOPS | vL | vR | BF/G | Ctl | Dom | Cmd | FpK | SwK | Vel | G | L | F | H% | S% | hr/f | GS | APC | DOM% | DIS% | Sv% | LI | RAR | BPV | BPX | R$ |
|---|---|---|---|---|---|---|---|---|---|---|---|---|---|---|---|---|---|---|---|---|---|---|---|---|---|---|---|---|---|---|---|---|---|
| 14 | | | | | | | | | | | | | | | | | | | | | | | | | | | | | | | | | |
| 15 aa | 9 | 0 | 90 | 65 | 2.32 | 2.46 | 1.11 | | | | 23.6 | 1.8 | 6.5 | 3.5 | | | | | | | 30% | 78% | | | | | | | | 18.3 | 117 | 139 | $11 |
| 16 PIT * | 2 | 0 | 105 | 93 | 5.42 | 5.93 | 1.78 | 893 | 828 | 902 | 20.0 | 4.9 | 8.0 | 1.7 | 48% | 10% | 91.0 | 45 | 26 | 29 | 37% | 71% | 15% | 7 | 83 | 0% | 71% | 0 | 0.71 | -15.9 | 45 | 53 | -$13 |
| 17 PIT * | 11 | 1 | 155 | 109 | 3.11 | 3.63 | 1.35 | 790 | 657 | 832 | 20.2 | 3.6 | 6.3 | 1.7 | 52% | 8% | 91.9 | 42 | 20 | 38 | 30% | 78% | 7% | 4 | 58 | 25% | 50% | 100 | 0.49 | 23.8 | 64 | 76 | $11 |
| 18 PIT | 6 | 0 | 92 | 82 | 4.61 | 4.86 | 1.54 | 749 | 640 | 799 | 9.2 | 5.6 | 8.1 | 1.4 | 57% | 11% | 92.5 | 48 | 19 | 33 | 30% | 72% | 12% | 5 | 37 | 0% | 60% | 0 | 0.83 | -5.3 | 20 | 23 | -$5 |
| 1st Half | 5 | 0 | 57 | 51 | 4.42 | 4.66 | 1.37 | 678 | 523 | 742 | 10.7 | 5.4 | 8.1 | 1.5 | 57% | 11% | 92.3 | 49 | 15 | 36 | 26% | 68% | 9% | 5 | 42 | 0% | 60% | 0 | 0.91 | -1.9 | 27 | 31 | -$2 |
| 2nd Half | 1 | 0 | 35 | 31 | 4.93 | 5.19 | 1.82 | 851 | 781 | 889 | 7.6 | 6.0 | 8.0 | 1.3 | 56% | 10% | 92.8 | 46 | 26 | 28 | 34% | 76% | 17% | 0 | 31 | | | 0 | 0.76 | -3.3 | 8 | 9 | -$11 |
| 19 Proj | **2** | **0** | **44** | **36** | **4.19** | **4.61** | **1.53** | **739** | **644** | **774** | **11.6** | **4.7** | **7.5** | **1.6** | **54%** | **10%** | **92.1** | **45** | **22** | **33** | **32%** | **74%** | **9%** | **3** | | | | | | **-2.0** | **31** | **36** | **-$4** |

## Brebbia,John

Age: 29 | Th: R | Role: RP | Health: A | LIMA Plan: C+
Ht: 6' 1" | Wt: 185 | Type: Pwr xFB | PT/Exp: D | Rand Var: 0 | Consist: F | MM: 2300

3-3, 3.20 ERA in 51 IP at STL. Unheralded relief arm made nice follow-up to impressive debut. 2nd half slips in Ctl, FpK likely caused by forearm tightness that sent him to DL in August; posted 2.5 Ctl, 70% FpK in September return. Extreme fly ball rate might be the last obstacle between him and higher-leverage work.

| Yr Tm | W | Sv | IP | K | ERA | xERA | WHIP | oOPS | vL | vR | BF/G | Ctl | Dom | Cmd | FpK | SwK | Vel | G | L | F | H% | S% | hr/f | GS | APC | DOM% | DIS% | Sv% | LI | RAR | BPV | BPX | R$ |
|---|---|---|---|---|---|---|---|---|---|---|---|---|---|---|---|---|---|---|---|---|---|---|---|---|---|---|---|---|---|---|---|---|---|
| 14 | | | | | | | | | | | | | | | | | | | | | | | | | | | | | | | | | |
| 15 | | | | | | | | | | | | | | | | | | | | | | | | | | | | | | | | | |
| 16 a/a | 5 | 2 | 68 | 52 | 6.31 | 6.72 | 1.76 | | | | 7.2 | 2.6 | 6.9 | 2.6 | | | | | | | 39% | 65% | | | | | | | | -17.8 | 43 | 51 | -$10 |
| 17 STL * | 1 | 3 | 78 | 73 | 2.34 | 2.55 | 0.93 | 640 | 737 | 575 | 4.5 | 1.9 | 8.4 | 4.5 | 71% | 13% | 94.2 | 25 | 19 | 56 | 24% | 84% | 10% | 0 | 16 | | | 75 | 0.68 | 19.5 | 123 | 148 | $11 |
| 18 STL * | 5 | 4 | 66 | 78 | 3.63 | 3.99 | 1.26 | 647 | 785 | 525 | 4.8 | 2.8 | 10.6 | 3.9 | 70% | 13% | 94.6 | 33 | 20 | 48 | 34% | 75% | 8% | 0 | 19 | | | 100 | 0.48 | 4.2 | 116 | 133 | $3 |
| 1st Half | 1 | 4 | 38 | 42 | 3.78 | 3.94 | 1.22 | 625 | 635 | 613 | 5.5 | 1.9 | 9.9 | 5.2 | 75% | 13% | 94.2 | 30 | 20 | 49 | 34% | 72% | 5% | 0 | 20 | | | 100 | 0.44 | 1.7 | 141 | 162 | $2 |
| 2nd Half | 4 | 0 | 28 | 36 | 3.43 | 4.06 | 1.30 | 679 | 1100 | 432 | 4.1 | 3.9 | 11.6 | 3.0 | 63% | 13% | 95.2 | 37 | 18 | 45 | 32% | 80% | 14% | 0 | 17 | | | 0 | 0.52 | 2.5 | 101 | 116 | $5 |
| 19 Proj | **2** | **0** | **36** | **38** | **3.58** | **3.88** | **1.22** | **723** | **898** | **594** | **4.8** | **2.6** | **9.4** | **3.7** | **69%** | **13%** | **94.5** | **30** | **19** | **51** | **31%** | **75%** | **10%** | **0** | | | | | | **1.3** | **109** | **125** | **-$1** |

## Brice,Austin

Age: 27 | Th: R | Role: RP | Health: D | LIMA Plan: C
Ht: 6' 4" | Wt: 235 | Type: Pwr GB | PT/Exp: D | Rand Var: +5 | Consist: B | MM: 2100

2-3, 5.79 ERA in 37 IP at CIN. Results aren't going to improve unless he generates fewer walks or more strikeouts, and FpK, SwK don't offer much hope for either outcome. That leaves him stuck in a rut, albeit one that comes with a six-figure salary and the chance to play in the majors. That's a pretty nice rut.

| Yr Tm | W | Sv | IP | K | ERA | xERA | WHIP | oOPS | vL | vR | BF/G | Ctl | Dom | Cmd | FpK | SwK | Vel | G | L | F | H% | S% | hr/f | GS | APC | DOM% | DIS% | Sv% | LI | RAR | BPV | BPX | R$ |
|---|---|---|---|---|---|---|---|---|---|---|---|---|---|---|---|---|---|---|---|---|---|---|---|---|---|---|---|---|---|---|---|---|---|
| 14 | | | | | | | | | | | | | | | | | | | | | | | | | | | | | | | | | |
| 15 aa | 6 | 0 | 125 | 105 | 5.67 | 4.73 | 1.61 | | | | 22.2 | 5.1 | 7.6 | 1.5 | | | | | | | 33% | 64% | | | | | | | | -26.4 | 55 | 66 | -$13 |
| 16 MIA * | 4 | 4 | 116 | 90 | 3.82 | 3.27 | 1.22 | 598 | 620 | 566 | 10.0 | 2.8 | 7.0 | 2.5 | 56% | 13% | 94.1 | 53 | 16 | 32 | 29% | 69% | 17% | 0 | 14 | | | 100 | 0.47 | 5.3 | 81 | 96 | $6 |
| 17 CIN * | 2 | 1 | 57 | 46 | 4.95 | 4.76 | 1.46 | 756 | 718 | 780 | 6.1 | 2.9 | 7.3 | 2.5 | 63% | 11% | 93.8 | 51 | 17 | 32 | 34% | 67% | 19% | 0 | 23 | | | 50 | 0.56 | -4.2 | 65 | 78 | -$4 |
| 18 CIN * | 5 | 1 | 61 | 52 | 4.69 | 4.95 | 1.34 | 876 | 1049 | 762 | 5.1 | 3.1 | 7.6 | 2.5 | 52% | 10% | 94.0 | 51 | 19 | 30 | 29% | 71% | 26% | 0 | 18 | | | 100 | 0.65 | -4.1 | 49 | 56 | -$2 |
| 1st Half | 1 | 0 | 32 | 29 | 6.03 | 6.05 | 1.54 | 892 | 1193 | 703 | 5.0 | 4.0 | 8.2 | 2.1 | 52% | 10% | 93.9 | 51 | 20 | 29 | 31% | 66% | 24% | 0 | 19 | | | 0 | 0.66 | -7.5 | 30 | 34 | -$10 |
| 2nd Half | 4 | 1 | 29 | 22 | 3.20 | 3.72 | 1.12 | 820 | 607 | 985 | 5.2 | 2.0 | 6.9 | 3.4 | 53% | 8% | 94.4 | 52 | 15 | 33 | 27% | 79% | 33% | 0 | 17 | | | 100 | 0.62 | 3.4 | 80 | 92 | $8 |
| 19 Proj | **2** | **0** | **29** | **23** | **4.51** | **4.02** | **1.38** | **749** | **878** | **669** | **6.4** | **3.3** | **7.3** | **2.2** | **56%** | **11%** | **93.9** | **51** | **19** | **30** | **31%** | **70%** | **14%** | **0** | | | | | | **0.4** | **70** | **80** | **-$4** |

## Britton,Zach

Age: 31 | Th: L | Role: RP | Health: F | LIMA Plan: A
Ht: 6' 3" | Wt: 195 | Type: Pwr xGB | PT/Exp: B | Rand Var: +2 | Consist: B | MM: 5220

Recovery from torn Achilles kept him out until mid-June, and neither skills nor velocity ever came all the way back. Thankfully, elite GB% has kept performance from falling off a cliff these last two seasons. Free agency and health questions create too many unknowns. Any 2019 bid on him has to be considered speculative.

| Yr Tm | W | Sv | IP | K | ERA | xERA | WHIP | oOPS | vL | vR | BF/G | Ctl | Dom | Cmd | FpK | SwK | Vel | G | L | F | H% | S% | hr/f | GS | APC | DOM% | DIS% | Sv% | LI | RAR | BPV | BPX | R$ |
|---|---|---|---|---|---|---|---|---|---|---|---|---|---|---|---|---|---|---|---|---|---|---|---|---|---|---|---|---|---|---|---|---|---|
| 14 BAL | 3 | 37 | 76 | 62 | 1.65 | 2.44 | 0.90 | 500 | 386 | 559 | 4.0 | 2.7 | 7.3 | 2.7 | 55% | 13% | 95.1 | 75 | 13 | 12 | 22% | 85% | 17% | 0 | 15 | | | 90 | 1.41 | 19.7 | 111 | 133 | $24 |
| 15 BAL | 4 | 36 | 66 | 79 | 1.92 | 1.75 | 0.99 | 547 | 325 | 636 | 4.0 | 1.9 | 10.8 | 5.6 | 64% | 17% | 95.9 | 79 | 11 | 9 | 31% | 82% | 20% | 0 | 14 | | | 90 | 1.17 | 16.5 | 200 | 238 | $23 |
| 16 BAL | 2 | 47 | 67 | 74 | 0.54 | 1.95 | 0.84 | 430 | 495 | 410 | 3.7 | 2.4 | 9.9 | 4.1 | 56% | 18% | 96.3 | 80 | 11 | 9 | 24% | 95% | 7% | 0 | 15 | | | 100 | 1.31 | 30.2 | 172 | 204 | $32 |
| 17 BAL | 2 | 15 | 37 | 29 | 2.89 | 3.56 | 1.53 | 690 | 717 | 680 | 4.2 | 4.3 | 7.0 | 1.6 | 56% | 12% | 96.1 | 73 | 19 | 8 | 33% | 80% | 11% | 0 | 15 | | | 88 | 1.05 | 6.7 | 60 | 72 | $4 |
| 18 2 AL | 2 | 7 | 41 | 34 | 3.10 | 3.31 | 1.23 | 609 | 689 | 573 | 4.1 | 4.6 | 7.5 | 1.6 | 50% | 13% | 94.9 | 73 | 16 | 11 | 24% | 77% | 25% | 0 | 16 | | | 70 | 0.86 | 5.3 | 61 | 70 | $2 |
| 1st Half | 0 | 1 | 9 | 7 | 6.23 | 4.95 | 1.73 | 844 | 1016 | 703 | 4.3 | 7.3 | 7.3 | 1.0 | 49% | 11% | 93.8 | 54 | 29 | 17 | 29% | 64% | 25% | 0 | 16 | | | 50 | 0.55 | -2.2 | -33 | -38 | -$14 |
| 2nd Half | 2 | 6 | 32 | 27 | 2.25 | 2.90 | 1.09 | 541 | 536 | 543 | 4.1 | 3.9 | 7.6 | 1.9 | 50% | 13% | 95.2 | 78 | 13 | 9 | 23% | 82% | 25% | 0 | 16 | | | 75 | 0.94 | 7.5 | 87 | 99 | $6 |
| 19 Proj | **3** | **15** | **58** | **55** | **2.62** | **2.51** | **1.13** | **571** | **537** | **583** | **4.0** | **3.2** | **8.5** | **2.7** | **55%** | **15%** | **95.8** | **77** | **13** | **9** | **28%** | **77%** | **16%** | **0** | | | | | | **11.1** | **122** | **140** | **$10** |

BRANDON KRUSE

## Buchholz,Clay

| Age: 34 | Th: R | Role SP | Health | F | LIMA Plan | B+ |
|---|---|---|---|---|---|---|
| Ht: 6' 3" | Wt: 190 | Type | PT/Exp | C | Rand Var | -5 |
| | | | Consist | F | MM | 1101 |

7-2, 2.01 ERA in 98 IP at ARI. Who is this, and what did he do with Clay? Cmd spike came out of the blue, but did have support from FpK. September elbow strain brought good times to abrupt end—guess it really WAS Clay. Less velocity, another year older... just how often do you think lightning finds bottle?

| Yr Tm | W | Sv | IP | K | ERA | xERA | WHIP | oOPS | vL | vR | BF/G | Ctl | Dom | Cmd | FpK | SwK | Vel | G | L | F | H% | S% | hr/f | GS | APC | DOM% | DIS% | Sv% | LI | RAR | BPV | BPX | R$ |
|---|---|---|---|---|---|---|---|---|---|---|---|---|---|---|---|---|---|---|---|---|---|---|---|---|---|---|---|---|---|---|---|---|---|
| 14 BOS | 8 | 0 | 170 | 132 | 5.34 | 3.99 | 1.39 | 751 | 793 | 696 | 26.3 | 2.9 | 7.0 | 2.4 | 60% | 9% | 91.6 | 47 | 19 | 34 | 32% | 62% | 9% | 28 | 98 | 29% | 32% | | | -33.5 | 74 | 88 | -$9 |
| 15 BOS | 7 | 0 | 113 | 107 | 3.26 | 3.36 | 1.21 | 664 | 610 | 725 | 26.1 | 1.8 | 8.5 | 4.7 | 65% | 11% | 92.0 | 48 | 21 | 31 | 34% | 73% | 6% | 18 | 95 | 50% | 17% | | | 9.9 | 130 | 154 | $7 |
| 16 BOS | 8 | 0 | 139 | 93 | 4.78 | 5.13 | 1.33 | 742 | 788 | 695 | 15.9 | 3.6 | 6.0 | 1.7 | 62% | 10% | 92.1 | 41 | 16 | 43 | 27% | 68% | 11% | 21 | 60 | 14% | 48% | 0 | 0.72 | -10.1 | 31 | 37 | -$1 |
| 17 PHI | 0 | 0 | 7 | 5 | 12.27 | 7.39 | 2.59 | 1161 | 1195 | 1122 | 20.0 | 3.7 | 6.1 | 1.7 | 71% | 7% | 90.6 | 28 | 25 | 47 | 49% | 50% | 7% | 2 | 72 | 0% | 100% | | | -7.2 | 17 | 20 | -$8 |
| 18 ARI * | 8 | 0 | 128 | 95 | 2.30 | 3.01 | 1.11 | 620 | 552 | 686 | 23.9 | 2.5 | 6.7 | 2.7 | 68% | 10% | 90.2 | 43 | 21 | 37 | 27% | 83% | 9% | 16 | 89 | 31% | 19% | | | 29.2 | 83 | 96 | $15 |
| 1st Half | 3 | 0 | 68 | 45 | 2.86 | 3.08 | 1.13 | 623 | 512 | 738 | 22.4 | 2.6 | 6.0 | 2.3 | 67% | 10% | 90.4 | 41 | 19 | 41 | 26% | 78% | 9% | 7 | 80 | 29% | 29% | | | 10.8 | 69 | 79 | $11 |
| 2nd Half | 5 | 0 | 60 | 50 | 1.66 | 3.90 | 1.09 | 619 | 579 | 655 | 26.7 | 2.3 | 7.5 | 3.3 | 68% | 10% | 90.0 | 44 | 22 | 34 | 28% | 90% | 9% | 9 | 86 | 33% | 11% | | | 18.3 | 96 | 111 | $20 |
| **19 Proj** | **5** | **0** | **87** | **67** | **3.82** | **4.11** | **1.26** | **727** | **701** | **753** | **21.8** | **2.7** | **6.9** | **2.6** | **65%** | **10%** | **91.1** | **43** | **19** | **37** | **29%** | **73%** | **11%** | **16** | | | | | | **3.6** | **74** | **86** | **$2** |

## Buehler,Walker

| Age: 24 | Th: R | Role SP | Health | C | LIMA Plan | C |
|---|---|---|---|---|---|---|
| Ht: 6' 2" | Wt: 175 | Type Pwr | PT/Exp | D | Rand Var | -2 |
| | | | Consist | B | MM | 4403 |

But for rib injury that cost him a few weeks, first full MLB season could have hardly gone better. Ground ball tilt, equal platoon splits, and worst news for hitters may be 2nd half SwK/Dom bump. Too much H%, S% luck in 2nd half to say "that, times two"; but no reason he couldn't do... UP: 15 Wins, 220 K.

| Yr Tm | W | Sv | IP | K | ERA | xERA | WHIP | oOPS | vL | vR | BF/G | Ctl | Dom | Cmd | FpK | SwK | Vel | G | L | F | H% | S% | hr/f | GS | APC | DOM% | DIS% | Sv% | LI | RAR | BPV | BPX | R$ |
|---|---|---|---|---|---|---|---|---|---|---|---|---|---|---|---|---|---|---|---|---|---|---|---|---|---|---|---|---|---|---|---|---|---|
| 14 | | | | | | | | | | | | | | | | | | | | | | | | | | | | | | | | | |
| 15 | | | | | | | | | | | | | | | | | | | | | | | | | | | | | | | | | |
| 16 | | | | | | | | | | | | | | | | | | | | | | | | | | | | | | | | | |
| 17 LA * | 4 | 1 | 82 | 97 | 4.83 | 3.95 | 1.35 | 932 | 503 | 1270 | 11.0 | 3.6 | 10.6 | 3.0 | 59% | 10% | 98.1 | 67 | 17 | 17 | 34% | 65% | 50% | 0 | 24 | | | 100 | 0.33 | -4.8 | 103 | 124 | $0 |
| 18 LA | 8 | 0 | 137 | 151 | 2.62 | 3.14 | 0.96 | 556 | 569 | 544 | 22.5 | 2.4 | 9.9 | 4.1 | 63% | 12% | 96.2 | 50 | 18 | 32 | 26% | 77% | 11% | 23 | 91 | 39% | 9% | 0 | 0.79 | 25.9 | 141 | 162 | $21 |
| 1st Half | 4 | 0 | 52 | 54 | 3.44 | 3.19 | 1.05 | 590 | 638 | 549 | 21.1 | 2.1 | 9.3 | 4.5 | 64% | 10% | 95.9 | 54 | 18 | 29 | 30% | 67% | 7% | 9 | 84 | 33% | 11% | 0 | 0.80 | 4.6 | 143 | 164 | $6 |
| 2nd Half | 4 | 0 | 85 | 97 | 2.12 | 3.12 | 0.91 | 535 | 527 | 542 | 23.6 | 2.6 | 10.3 | 3.9 | 63% | 13% | 96.4 | 48 | 19 | 34 | 23% | 84% | 13% | 14 | 95 | 43% | 7% | | | 21.3 | 139 | 160 | $29 |
| **19 Proj** | **12** | **0** | **174** | **197** | **3.13** | **3.04** | **1.12** | **631** | **647** | **616** | **20.3** | **2.9** | **10.2** | **3.6** | **63%** | **12%** | **96.2** | **50** | **18** | **32** | **29%** | **75%** | **12%** | **28** | | | | | | **22.0** | **134** | **154** | **$21** |

## Bumgarner,Madison

| Age: 29 | Th: L | Role SP | Health | F | LIMA Plan | B |
|---|---|---|---|---|---|---|
| Ht: 6' 4" | Wt: 242 | Type Pwr | PT/Exp | A | Rand Var | -2 |
| | | | Consist | A | MM | 2203 |

Hand injury delayed debut until June, but then all was well, right? Not quite. Years of xERA decline paints grim picture, as does sudden drop in Cmd, SwK. ERA doesn't reflect that, which means market won't price it in; and yet, age, freak nature of injuries may aid rebound, so you don't get stuck with a lemon.

| Yr Tm | W | Sv | IP | K | ERA | xERA | WHIP | oOPS | vL | vR | BF/G | Ctl | Dom | Cmd | FpK | SwK | Vel | G | L | F | H% | S% | hr/f | GS | APC | DOM% | DIS% | Sv% | LI | RAR | BPV | BPX | R$ |
|---|---|---|---|---|---|---|---|---|---|---|---|---|---|---|---|---|---|---|---|---|---|---|---|---|---|---|---|---|---|---|---|---|---|
| 14 SF | 18 | 0 | 217 | 219 | 2.98 | 3.08 | 1.09 | 653 | 539 | 684 | 26.5 | 1.8 | 9.1 | 5.1 | 66% | 12% | 92.1 | 44 | 20 | 36 | 31% | 76% | 10% | 33 | 102 | 48% | 15% | | | 20.4 | 137 | 163 | $23 |
| 15 SF | 18 | 0 | 218 | 234 | 2.93 | 3.10 | 1.01 | 612 | 539 | 627 | 27.2 | 1.6 | 9.6 | 6.0 | 64% | 13% | 92.1 | 42 | 23 | 36 | 30% | 75% | 10% | 32 | 104 | 59% | 6% | | | 27.9 | 150 | 179 | $32 |
| 16 SF | 15 | 0 | 227 | 251 | 2.74 | 3.54 | 1.03 | 619 | 513 | 645 | 26.8 | 2.1 | 10.0 | 4.6 | 65% | 12% | 90.9 | 40 | 19 | 41 | 28% | 79% | 11% | 34 | 105 | 56% | 9% | | | 40.5 | 140 | 166 | $34 |
| 17 SF | 4 | 0 | 111 | 101 | 3.32 | 4.05 | 1.09 | 704 | 530 | 740 | 26.5 | 1.6 | 8.2 | 5.1 | 67% | 11% | 91.0 | 41 | 18 | 41 | 28% | 77% | 13% | 17 | 98 | 53% | 12% | | | 14.2 | 123 | 147 | $10 |
| 18 SF | 6 | 0 | 130 | 109 | 3.26 | 4.35 | 1.24 | 694 | 635 | 707 | 26.2 | 3.0 | 7.6 | 2.5 | 64% | 9% | 90.9 | 43 | 22 | 35 | 29% | 78% | 10% | 21 | 98 | 29% | 14% | | | 14.2 | 77 | 88 | $7 |
| 1st Half | 1 | 0 | 32 | 25 | 2.51 | 4.26 | 1.02 | 631 | 408 | 679 | 26.0 | 2.5 | 7.0 | 2.8 | 60% | 8% | 90.6 | 45 | 17 | 38 | 24% | 80% | 8% | 5 | 97 | 40% | 40% | | | 6.6 | 80 | 92 | -$3 |
| 2nd Half | 5 | 0 | 97 | 84 | 3.51 | 4.37 | 1.32 | 713 | 705 | 715 | 26.3 | 3.1 | 7.8 | 2.5 | 65% | 10% | 91.0 | 42 | 24 | 34 | 30% | 77% | 11% | 16 | 98 | 25% | 6% | | | 7.6 | 75 | 86 | $10 |
| **19 Proj** | **11** | **0** | **174** | **159** | **3.61** | **3.75** | **1.20** | **714** | **588** | **742** | **25.8** | **2.5** | **8.2** | **3.2** | **64%** | **10%** | **91.0** | **42** | **20** | **38** | **29%** | **75%** | **13%** | **27** | | | | | | **11.6** | **99** | **114** | **$14** |

## Bummer,Aaron

| Age: 25 | Th: L | Role RP | Health | A | LIMA Plan | C |
|---|---|---|---|---|---|---|
| Ht: 6' 3" | Wt: 200 | Type Pwr xGB | PT/Exp | F | Rand Var | +1 |
| | | | Consist | A | MM | 3200 |

0-1, 4.26 ERA in 32 IP at CHW. What's that? You posted far stronger skills in 2nd MLB tour, but due to 42% H%, no one noticed? Unfortunate, dude. Big step forward was with Ctl; FpK casts doubt, though combo of GB%, Dom is mildly intriguing. May never close, but don't rule out future LIMA-worthiness.

| Yr Tm | W | Sv | IP | K | ERA | xERA | WHIP | oOPS | vL | vR | BF/G | Ctl | Dom | Cmd | FpK | SwK | Vel | G | L | F | H% | S% | hr/f | GS | APC | DOM% | DIS% | Sv% | LI | RAR | BPV | BPX | R$ |
|---|---|---|---|---|---|---|---|---|---|---|---|---|---|---|---|---|---|---|---|---|---|---|---|---|---|---|---|---|---|---|---|---|---|
| 14 | | | | | | | | | | | | | | | | | | | | | | | | | | | | | | | | | |
| 15 | | | | | | | | | | | | | | | | | | | | | | | | | | | | | | | | | |
| 16 | | | | | | | | | | | | | | | | | | | | | | | | | | | | | | | | | |
| 17 CHW * | 2 | 3 | 60 | 50 | 4.00 | 4.21 | 1.46 | 692 | 618 | 778 | 5.1 | 5.1 | 7.5 | 1.5 | 51% | 11% | 93.2 | 54 | 14 | 32 | 29% | 75% | 22% | 0 | 12 | | | 75 | 1.55 | 2.7 | 54 | 64 | -$2 |
| 18 CHW * | 2 | 0 | 64 | 60 | 3.72 | 4.16 | 1.48 | 730 | 600 | 816 | 4.0 | 3.1 | 8.5 | 2.7 | 53% | 11% | 93.1 | 61 | 22 | 16 | 37% | 73% | 6% | 0 | 16 | | | 0 | 0.92 | 3.4 | 101 | 117 | -$3 |
| 1st Half | 1 | 0 | 32 | 33 | 4.17 | 4.90 | 1.68 | 743 | 790 | 710 | 3.9 | 3.6 | 9.3 | 2.6 | 52% | 11% | 92.8 | 60 | 25 | 14 | 42% | 72% | 0% | 0 | 15 | | | 0 | 0.99 | -0.1 | 103 | 119 | -$7 |
| 2nd Half | 1 | 0 | 32 | 27 | 3.29 | 3.43 | 1.29 | 709 | 255 | 991 | 4.2 | 2.6 | 7.6 | 2.9 | 57% | 10% | 93.8 | 63 | 17 | 20 | 33% | 74% | 14% | 0 | 21 | | | 0 | 0.75 | 3.4 | 101 | 116 | $2 |
| **19 Proj** | **1** | **0** | **44** | **41** | **3.86** | **3.53** | **1.29** | **546** | **603** | **507** | **4.3** | **3.4** | **8.4** | **2.4** | **52%** | **11%** | **92.8** | **53** | **24** | **23** | **30%** | **71%** | **11%** | **0** | | | | | | **3.1** | **90** | **103** | **-$2** |

## Bundy,Dylan

| Age: 26 | Th: R | Role SP | Health | B | LIMA Plan | C |
|---|---|---|---|---|---|---|
| Ht: 6' 1" | Wt: 200 | Type Pwr xFB | PT/Exp | A | Rand Var | +4 |
| | | | Consist | A | MM | 2303 |

"Reward" for best skills in MLB career? Horrid luck with 2nd half H%, S%, hr/f ballooned his ERA. Velocity trend needs to be watched, but otherwise, Dom, Cmd, and BPX all headed in right direction. You should be able to get him cheap, providing ample profit in the event of... UP: 15 Wins, 3.75 ERA, 200+ K

| Yr Tm | W | Sv | IP | K | ERA | xERA | WHIP | oOPS | vL | vR | BF/G | Ctl | Dom | Cmd | FpK | SwK | Vel | G | L | F | H% | S% | hr/f | GS | APC | DOM% | DIS% | Sv% | LI | RAR | BPV | BPX | R$ |
|---|---|---|---|---|---|---|---|---|---|---|---|---|---|---|---|---|---|---|---|---|---|---|---|---|---|---|---|---|---|---|---|---|---|
| 14 | | | | | | | | | | | | | | | | | | | | | | | | | | | | | | | | | |
| 15 aa | 0 | 0 | 22 | 21 | 4.91 | 3.74 | 1.39 | | | | 11.6 | 2.1 | 8.5 | 4.0 | | | | | | | 38% | 61% | | | | | | | | -2.6 | 131 | 156 | -$5 |
| 16 BAL | 10 | 0 | 110 | 104 | 4.02 | 4.55 | 1.38 | 766 | 756 | 776 | 13.2 | 3.4 | 8.5 | 2.5 | 61% | 11% | 93.8 | 36 | 22 | 42 | 31% | 77% | 13% | 14 | 54 | 14% | 43% | 0 | 0.82 | 2.3 | 75 | 89 | $3 |
| 17 BAL | 13 | 0 | 170 | 152 | 4.24 | 4.62 | 1.20 | 721 | 773 | 674 | 24.9 | 2.7 | 8.1 | 3.0 | 60% | 12% | 92.2 | 33 | 20 | 47 | 28% | 69% | 11% | 28 | 101 | 25% | 29% | | | 2.4 | 83 | 100 | $12 |
| 18 BAL | 8 | 0 | 172 | 184 | 5.45 | 4.37 | 1.41 | 855 | 938 | 770 | 24.2 | 2.8 | 9.6 | 3.4 | 62% | 13% | 91.6 | 34 | 20 | 46 | 33% | 69% | 18% | 31 | 92 | 35% | 32% | | | -27.6 | 109 | 126 | -$7 |
| 1st Half | 6 | 0 | 96 | 108 | 3.75 | 3.98 | 1.21 | 739 | 849 | 633 | 25.0 | 2.7 | 10.1 | 3.7 | 64% | 14% | 91.6 | 35 | 18 | 46 | 30% | 78% | 15% | 16 | 94 | 56% | 19% | | | 4.7 | 122 | 140 | $8 |
| 2nd Half | 2 | 0 | 76 | 76 | 7.61 | 4.87 | 1.67 | 987 | 1035 | 936 | 23.3 | 3.0 | 9.0 | 3.0 | 60% | 12% | 91.6 | 33 | 22 | 46 | 36% | 60% | 21% | 15 | 90 | 13% | 47% | | | -32.3 | 93 | 107 | -$28 |
| **19 Proj** | **11** | **0** | **174** | **176** | **3.98** | **3.99** | **1.33** | **793** | **847** | **738** | **20.8** | **2.8** | **9.1** | **3.3** | **61%** | **12%** | **92.2** | **34** | **20** | **46** | **31%** | **78%** | **15%** | **35** | | | | | | **3.4** | **100** | **115** | **$7** |

## Burnes,Corbin

| Age: 24 | Th: R | Role RP | Health | A | LIMA Plan | B |
|---|---|---|---|---|---|---|
| Ht: 6' 3" | Wt: 205 | Type Pwr GB | PT/Exp | D | Rand Var | +1 |
| | | | Consist | B | MM | 2201 |

7-0, 2.61 ERA in 38 IP at MIL. Shone as win vulture in back end of MIL bullpen in MLB debut, though expected to revert to SP in 2019. Sometimes, role changes can be rocky, but GB% should limit blowup potential, and SwK hints at more strikeouts on horizon. You may want to get in on ground floor.

| Yr Tm | W | Sv | IP | K | ERA | xERA | WHIP | oOPS | vL | vR | BF/G | Ctl | Dom | Cmd | FpK | SwK | Vel | G | L | F | H% | S% | hr/f | GS | APC | DOM% | DIS% | Sv% | LI | RAR | BPV | BPX | R$ |
|---|---|---|---|---|---|---|---|---|---|---|---|---|---|---|---|---|---|---|---|---|---|---|---|---|---|---|---|---|---|---|---|---|---|
| 14 | | | | | | | | | | | | | | | | | | | | | | | | | | | | | | | | | |
| 15 | | | | | | | | | | | | | | | | | | | | | | | | | | | | | | | | | |
| 16 | | | | | | | | | | | | | | | | | | | | | | | | | | | | | | | | | |
| 17 aa | 3 | 0 | 86 | 73 | 3.28 | 3.40 | 1.28 | | | | 21.9 | 2.4 | 7.6 | 3.2 | | | | | | | 33% | 74% | | | | | | | | 11.4 | 105 | 126 | $3 |
| 18 MIL * | 10 | 1 | 118 | 103 | 4.33 | 3.99 | 1.32 | 595 | 512 | 638 | 10.0 | 3.0 | 7.9 | 2.6 | 57% | 16% | 95.3 | 49 | 21 | 30 | 31% | 68% | 13% | 0 | 19 | | | 33 | 0.96 | -2.6 | 80 | 92 | $2 |
| 1st Half | 3 | 0 | 77 | 67 | 5.34 | 4.84 | 1.50 | | | | 19.6 | 3.4 | 7.8 | 2.3 | | | | | | | 35% | 64% | 0% | 0 | | | | | | -11.4 | 68 | 78 | -$6 |
| 2nd Half | 7 | 1 | 41 | 37 | 2.41 | 2.40 | 0.98 | 595 | 512 | 638 | 4.9 | 2.4 | 8.1 | 3.3 | 57% | 16% | 95.3 | 49 | 21 | 30 | 24% | 81% | 13% | 0 | 19 | | | 50 | 0.96 | 8.8 | 107 | 123 | $19 |
| **19 Proj** | **8** | **0** | **102** | **89** | **3.49** | **3.68** | **1.23** | **629** | **546** | **672** | **10.0** | **2.7** | **7.9** | **3.0** | **57%** | **16%** | **95.3** | **49** | **21** | **30** | **31%** | **73%** | **7%** | **0** | | | | | | **5.1** | **97** | **111** | **$7** |

## Butler,Eddie

| Age: 28 | Th: R | Role RP | Health | F | LIMA Plan | D |
|---|---|---|---|---|---|---|
| Ht: 6' 2" | Wt: 180 | Type Con | PT/Exp | D | Rand Var | +4 |
| | | | Consist | D | MM | 0000 |

Held MIA to 1 ER in 7 IP as RP on 3/30, but things devolved rapidly. Lost three months to groin injury; upon return, resumed role as worst guy in your FA pool, and even without Coors, attained "vintage" oOPS in 2nd half. If you want to stop reading to grab a bat, we'd understand. Really, go for it. We'll wait.

| Yr Tm | W | Sv | IP | K | ERA | xERA | WHIP | oOPS | vL | vR | BF/G | Ctl | Dom | Cmd | FpK | SwK | Vel | G | L | F | H% | S% | hr/f | GS | APC | DOM% | DIS% | Sv% | LI | RAR | BPV | BPX | R$ |
|---|---|---|---|---|---|---|---|---|---|---|---|---|---|---|---|---|---|---|---|---|---|---|---|---|---|---|---|---|---|---|---|---|---|
| 14 COL * | 7 | 0 | 129 | 57 | 5.08 | 5.24 | 1.52 | 973 | 1310 | 760 | 25.5 | 3.0 | 4.0 | 1.3 | 49% | 5% | 93.1 | 52 | 25 | 23 | 31% | 68% | 13% | 3 | 86 | 0% | 100% | | | -21.4 | 16 | 19 | -$11 |
| 15 COL * | 5 | 0 | 143 | 72 | 6.21 | 6.32 | 1.77 | 952 | 1073 | 831 | 24.3 | 4.3 | 4.5 | 1.1 | 57% | 7% | 93.4 | 50 | 22 | 28 | 33% | 66% | 17% | 16 | 85 | 0% | 69% | | | -39.5 | 3 | 4 | -$24 |
| 16 COL * | 10 | 0 | 153 | 73 | 6.76 | 6.49 | 1.68 | 944 | 894 | 977 | 21.5 | 3.0 | 4.3 | 1.5 | 58% | 8% | 92.9 | 46 | 25 | 30 | 34% | 62% | 20% | 9 | 63 | 11% | 67% | 0 | 0.78 | -48.6 | 0 | 0 | -$21 |
| 17 CHC * | 6 | 0 | 100 | 54 | 3.34 | 4.27 | 1.49 | 715 | 665 | 748 | 20.6 | 3.7 | 4.8 | 1.3 | 60% | 7% | 93.4 | 44 | 22 | 33 | 31% | 78% | 7% | 11 | 71 | 0% | 64% | 0 | 0.65 | 12.6 | 43 | 51 | $1 |
| 18 2 TM | 2 | 2 | 50 | 29 | 5.62 | 5.17 | 1.57 | 852 | 783 | 892 | 7.6 | 3.4 | 5.3 | 1.5 | 64% | 7% | 93.6 | 52 | 18 | 30 | 30% | 70% | 21% | 0 | 28 | | | 100 | 0.92 | -9.0 | 32 | 36 | -$8 |
| 1st Half | 0 | 0 | 15 | 10 | 4.30 | 3.85 | 1.16 | 564 | 429 | 639 | 10.2 | 3.1 | 6.1 | 2.0 | 70% | 10% | 92.6 | 67 | 11 | 22 | 26% | 63% | 10% | 0 | 36 | | | 0 | 1.44 | -0.3 | 72 | 83 | -$7 |
| 2nd Half | 2 | 2 | 35 | 19 | 6.17 | 5.71 | 1.74 | 962 | 918 | 986 | 7.0 | 3.6 | 4.9 | 1.4 | 62% | 6% | 93.9 | 47 | 21 | 33 | 32% | 73% | 23% | 0 | 26 | | | 100 | 0.80 | -8.7 | 15 | 18 | -$8 |
| **19 Proj** | **3** | **0** | **58** | **30** | **5.18** | **5.14** | **1.66** | **893** | **873** | **905** | **13.0** | **3.5** | **4.6** | **1.3** | **60%** | **7%** | **93.4** | **46** | **23** | **31** | **32%** | **73%** | **15%** | **6** | | | | | | **-3.6** | **13** | **15** | **-$8** |

KRISTOPHER OLSON

## Buttrey,Ty

| | | | | | | |
|---|---|---|---|---|---|---|
| | | | Health | A | LIMA Plan | B+ |
| Age: 26 | Th: R | Role: RP | PT/Exp | D | Rand Var | -3 |
| Ht: 6' 6" | Wt: 230 | Type: Pwr xGB | Consist | C | MM | 3320 |

0-1, 3.31 ERA with 4 Sv in 16 IP at LAA. Did LAA pilfer future closer candidate in Kinsler deal? Maybe. Needs to refine slider to pair with fastball, but he already gets grounders, misses bats. Ctl took step forward, too, though FpK casts doubt on whether that'll stick. Still, he's one to watch.

| Yr | Tm | W | Sv | IP | K | ERA | xERA | WHIP | oOPS | vL | vR | BF/G | Ctl | Dom | Cmd | FpK | SwK | Vel | G | L | F | H% | S% | hr/f | GS | APC | DOM% | DIS% | Sv% | LI | RAR | BPV | BPX | R$ |
|---|---|---|---|---|---|---|---|---|---|---|---|---|---|---|---|---|---|---|---|---|---|---|---|---|---|---|---|---|---|---|---|---|---|---|
| 14 | | | | | | | | | | | | | | | | | | | | | | | | | | | | | | | | | | |
| 15 | | | | | | | | | | | | | | | | | | | | | | | | | | | | | | | | | | |
| 16 | aa | 1 | 0 | 79 | 43 | 5.78 | 5.75 | 1.83 | | | | 11.1 | 5.5 | 4.9 | 0.9 | | | | | | | 33% | 68% | | | | | | | | -15.5 | 19 | 23 | -$14 |
| 17 | a/a | 2 | 4 | 64 | 60 | 6.79 | 5.23 | 1.74 | | | | 7.3 | 5.0 | 8.4 | 1.7 | | | | | | | 37% | 59% | | | | | | | | -19.1 | 66 | 79 | -$10 |
| 18 | LAA * | 1 | 5 | 64 | 79 | 2.41 | 2.75 | 1.13 | 591 | 797 | 404 | 4.9 | 2.5 | 11.0 | 4.3 | 59% | 14% | 96.0 | 57 | 23 | 20 | 33% | 80% | 0% | 0 | 19 | | | 50 | 1.41 | 13.8 | 151 | 174 | $6 |
| 1st Half | | 1 | 0 | 36 | 46 | 1.88 | 3.09 | 1.13 | | | | 5.5 | 2.6 | 11.6 | 4.4 | | | | | | | 33% | 89% | 0% | 0 | | | | | | 10.1 | 145 | 167 | $7 |
| 2nd Half | | 0 | 5 | 28 | 32 | 3.10 | 2.32 | 1.13 | 591 | 797 | 404 | 4.3 | 2.4 | 10.3 | 4.2 | 59% | 14% | 96.0 | 57 | 23 | 20 | 34% | 70% | 0% | 0 | 19 | | | 63 | 1.41 | 3.7 | 159 | 183 | $6 |
| 19 | Proj | **1** | **11** | **58** | **58** | **3.51** | **3.50** | **1.31** | **610** | **806** | **431** | **5.9** | **3.9** | **9.1** | **2.3** | **59%** | **14%** | **96.0** | **54** | **22** | **24** | **31%** | **75%** | **12%** | **0** | | | | | | **4.6** | **90** | **104** | **$4** |

## Cahill,Trevor

| | | | | | | |
|---|---|---|---|---|---|---|
| | | | Health | F | LIMA Plan | B+ |
| Age: 31 | Th: R | Role: RP | PT/Exp | D | Rand Var | +1 |
| Ht: 6' 4" | Wt: 240 | Type: Pwr GB | Consist | B | MM | 2201 |

7-4, 3.76 ERA in 110 IP at OAK. Let's check 2018's injury roll call: elbow, Achilles, back. Again posted tantalizing skills in 1st half, but FpK hinted Ctl was due for crash, and crash it did. GB% minimizes blowup potential, but Cmd shows lack of upside, and he's only useful during windows of health. Good luck finding them.

| Yr | Tm | W | Sv | IP | K | ERA | xERA | WHIP | oOPS | vL | vR | BF/G | Ctl | Dom | Cmd | FpK | SwK | Vel | G | L | F | H% | S% | hr/f | GS | APC | DOM% | DIS% | Sv% | LI | RAR | BPV | BPX | R$ |
|---|---|---|---|---|---|---|---|---|---|---|---|---|---|---|---|---|---|---|---|---|---|---|---|---|---|---|---|---|---|---|---|---|---|---|
| 14 | ARI * | 5 | 1 | 139 | 126 | 5.21 | 4.77 | 1.58 | 791 | 929 | 657 | 16.1 | 4.8 | 8.2 | 1.7 | 57% | 11% | 90.0 | 48 | 24 | 27 | 33% | 67% | 10% | 17 | 60 | 18% | 35% | 50 | 0.67 | -25.2 | 60 | 72 | -$11 |
| 15 | 2 NL * | 2 | 0 | 80 | 55 | 5.72 | 4.86 | 1.55 | 725 | 684 | 751 | 9.4 | 3.9 | 6.2 | 1.6 | 59% | 10% | 91.5 | 63 | 19 | 18 | 32% | 63% | 17% | 3 | 26 | 0% | 100% | 0 | 0.63 | -17.3 | 44 | 52 | -$11 |
| 16 | CHC * | 4 | 0 | 85 | 85 | 3.35 | 4.38 | 1.49 | 621 | 660 | 594 | 6.6 | 5.1 | 9.0 | 1.8 | 54% | 12% | 92.0 | 57 | 22 | 22 | 31% | 82% | 18% | 1 | 23 | 0% | 0% | 0 | 0.70 | 8.8 | 65 | 77 | $1 |
| 17 | 2 TM | 4 | 0 | 84 | 87 | 4.93 | 4.22 | 1.62 | 850 | 767 | 915 | 18.1 | 4.8 | 9.3 | 1.9 | 60% | 12% | 90.9 | 56 | 18 | 26 | 33% | 75% | 25% | 14 | 73 | 21% | 29% | 0 | 0.66 | -5.9 | 72 | 86 | -$6 |
| 18 | OAK * | 7 | 0 | 125 | 112 | 3.69 | 2.88 | 1.19 | 653 | 675 | 633 | 20.9 | 3.6 | 8.1 | 2.2 | 57% | 12% | 91.8 | 53 | 19 | 27 | 27% | 69% | 10% | 20 | 85 | 25% | 20% | 0 | 0.77 | 7.0 | 89 | 103 | $7 |
| 1st Half | | 1 | 0 | 60 | 54 | 3.07 | 2.23 | 1.02 | 621 | 554 | 668 | 23.0 | 2.8 | 8.1 | 2.9 | 57% | 13% | 91.3 | 60 | 18 | 22 | 25% | 71% | 15% | 8 | 94 | 38% | 13% | | | 8.0 | 106 | 122 | $8 |
| 2nd Half | | 6 | 0 | 65 | 58 | 4.27 | 3.49 | 1.35 | 675 | 746 | 595 | 19.4 | 4.3 | 8.0 | 1.9 | 57% | 11% | 92.2 | 49 | 20 | 31 | 30% | 68% | 8% | 12 | 80 | 17% | 25% | 0 | 0.77 | -1.0 | 78 | 90 | $6 |
| 19 | Proj | **6** | **0** | **116** | **108** | **4.17** | **3.78** | **1.39** | **724** | **728** | **721** | **14.3** | **4.2** | **8.4** | **2.0** | **58%** | **12%** | **91.5** | **55** | **20** | **26** | **30%** | **72%** | **15%** | **15** | | | | | | **-0.2** | **69** | **80** | **$0** |

## Carrasco,Carlos

| | | | | | | |
|---|---|---|---|---|---|---|
| | | | Health | D | LIMA Plan | C+ |
| Age: 32 | Th: R | Role: SP | PT/Exp | A | Rand Var | +1 |
| Ht: 6' 3" | Wt: 212 | Type: Pwr | Consist | A | MM | 5405 |

June recurrence of elbow woes precluded second 200-IP season, but once he shook those, skills took off. In fact, no pitcher's BPV was higher in August. Other than health grade, little not to like here, with strong skills validated by sub-indicators across the board. If he can just keep elbow from barking... UP: Cy Young Award

| Yr | Tm | W | Sv | IP | K | ERA | xERA | WHIP | oOPS | vL | vR | BF/G | Ctl | Dom | Cmd | FpK | SwK | Vel | G | L | F | H% | S% | hr/f | GS | APC | DOM% | DIS% | Sv% | LI | RAR | BPV | BPX | R$ |
|---|---|---|---|---|---|---|---|---|---|---|---|---|---|---|---|---|---|---|---|---|---|---|---|---|---|---|---|---|---|---|---|---|---|---|
| 14 | CLE | 8 | 1 | 134 | 140 | 2.55 | 2.73 | 0.99 | 543 | 516 | 566 | 13.2 | 1.9 | 9.4 | 4.8 | 63% | 14% | 95.3 | 53 | 20 | 28 | 29% | 75% | 7% | 14 | 49 | 43% | 0% | 100 | 0.63 | 19.6 | 148 | 176 | $17 |
| 15 | CLE | 14 | 0 | 184 | 216 | 3.63 | 2.75 | 1.07 | 646 | 639 | 651 | 24.3 | 2.1 | 10.6 | 5.0 | 67% | 14% | 94.5 | 51 | 19 | 30 | 31% | 69% | 13% | 30 | 93 | 57% | 20% | | | 7.6 | 163 | 194 | $19 |
| 16 | CLE | 11 | 0 | 146 | 150 | 3.32 | 3.42 | 1.15 | 711 | 739 | 688 | 24.0 | 2.1 | 9.2 | 4.4 | 62% | 13% | 93.8 | 49 | 20 | 31 | 30% | 78% | 16% | 25 | 90 | 32% | 20% | | | 15.7 | 137 | 162 | $15 |
| 17 | CLE | 18 | 0 | 200 | 226 | 3.29 | 3.26 | 1.10 | 674 | 727 | 629 | 24.9 | 2.1 | 10.2 | 4.9 | 63% | 14% | 94.3 | 45 | 22 | 33 | 31% | 74% | 12% | 32 | 96 | 50% | 13% | | | 26.5 | 150 | 180 | $28 |
| 18 | CLE | 17 | 0 | 192 | 231 | 3.38 | 3.07 | 1.13 | 669 | 703 | 634 | 24.5 | 2.0 | 10.8 | 5.4 | 65% | 16% | 93.5 | 47 | 21 | 32 | 33% | 74% | 13% | 30 | 93 | 47% | 17% | 0 | 0.80 | 18.4 | 165 | 191 | $23 |
| 1st Half | | 8 | 0 | 91 | 96 | 4.24 | 3.59 | 1.17 | 689 | 697 | 682 | 25.0 | 2.2 | 9.5 | 4.4 | 66% | 14% | 93.3 | 42 | 22 | 36 | 31% | 67% | 12% | 15 | 94 | 40% | 33% | | | -1.0 | 132 | 152 | $11 |
| 2nd Half | | 9 | 0 | 101 | 135 | 2.59 | 2.62 | 1.08 | 651 | 707 | 579 | 24.1 | 1.9 | 12.1 | 6.4 | 64% | 18% | 93.7 | 51 | 20 | 28 | 34% | 81% | 14% | 15 | 92 | 53% | 0% | 0 | 0.84 | 19.3 | 196 | 225 | $34 |
| 19 | Proj | **16** | **0** | **189** | **219** | **3.25** | **2.86** | **1.11** | **668** | **702** | **635** | **22.8** | **2.0** | **10.4** | **5.1** | **64%** | **15%** | **93.9** | **48** | **21** | **31** | **32%** | **75%** | **14%** | **32** | | | | | | **20.9** | **159** | **182** | **$24** |

## Cashner,Andrew

| | | | | | | |
|---|---|---|---|---|---|---|
| | | | Health | D | LIMA Plan | D+ |
| Age: 32 | Th: R | Role: SP | PT/Exp | A | Rand Var | +1 |
| Ht: 6' 6" | Wt: 235 | Type: | Consist | A | MM | 0003 |

"Heed BPX trend," we warned last year. Alas, BAL didn't, and endured realignment of ERA and xERA. Hit DL twice in 1st half (back, neck), knee injury ended season in Sept. Even if health improves, scary signs abound: flagging velocity, subpar Cmd for three years running, no looming recovery seen in FpK, SwK. Heed all of it.

| Yr | Tm | W | Sv | IP | K | ERA | xERA | WHIP | oOPS | vL | vR | BF/G | Ctl | Dom | Cmd | FpK | SwK | Vel | G | L | F | H% | S% | hr/f | GS | APC | DOM% | DIS% | Sv% | LI | RAR | BPV | BPX | R$ |
|---|---|---|---|---|---|---|---|---|---|---|---|---|---|---|---|---|---|---|---|---|---|---|---|---|---|---|---|---|---|---|---|---|---|---|
| 14 | SD | 5 | 0 | 123 | 93 | 2.55 | 3.60 | 1.13 | 623 | 675 | 573 | 26.6 | 2.1 | 6.8 | 3.2 | 63% | 8% | 94.3 | 48 | 20 | 31 | 29% | 79% | 6% | 19 | 95 | 32% | 26% | | | 18.1 | 91 | 108 | $10 |
| 15 | SD | 6 | 0 | 185 | 165 | 4.34 | 3.95 | 1.44 | 772 | 896 | 669 | 25.9 | 3.2 | 8.0 | 2.5 | 62% | 9% | 94.8 | 47 | 23 | 30 | 34% | 72% | 12% | 31 | 100 | 23% | 26% | | | -8.6 | 83 | 99 | -$4 |
| 16 | 2 NL | 5 | 0 | 132 | 112 | 5.25 | 4.62 | 1.53 | 849 | 903 | 794 | 21.0 | 4.1 | 7.6 | 1.9 | 55% | 8% | 93.5 | 46 | 20 | 33 | 32% | 68% | 15% | 27 | 85 | 11% | 37% | 0 | 1.05 | -17.3 | 51 | 61 | -$8 |
| 17 | TEX | 11 | 0 | 167 | 86 | 3.40 | 5.18 | 1.32 | 692 | 701 | 683 | 25.1 | 3.5 | 4.6 | 1.3 | 58% | 6% | 93.4 | 49 | 19 | 32 | 27% | 77% | 9% | 28 | 94 | 7% | 43% | | | 19.7 | 17 | 21 | $10 |
| 18 | BAL | 4 | 0 | 153 | 99 | 5.29 | 5.36 | 1.58 | 856 | 852 | 860 | 24.3 | 3.8 | 5.8 | 1.5 | 56% | 7% | 92.4 | 40 | 23 | 36 | 31% | 70% | 14% | 28 | 95 | 7% | 57% | | | -21.6 | 20 | 23 | -$15 |
| 1st Half | | 2 | 0 | 88 | 71 | 4.48 | 4.97 | 1.57 | 855 | 826 | 881 | 24.4 | 4.1 | 7.2 | 1.8 | 56% | 8% | 92.8 | 41 | 23 | 36 | 32% | 76% | 14% | 16 | 97 | 6% | 56% | | | -3.6 | 39 | 45 | -$13 |
| 2nd Half | | 2 | 0 | 65 | 28 | 6.40 | 5.90 | 1.59 | 858 | 883 | 827 | 24.2 | 3.5 | 3.9 | 1.1 | 55% | 7% | 91.8 | 40 | 24 | 36 | 30% | 62% | 13% | 12 | 91 | 8% | 58% | | | -18.0 | -6 | -7 | -$20 |
| 19 | Proj | **6** | **0** | **145** | **91** | **5.05** | **4.80** | **1.48** | **800** | **826** | **775** | **23.7** | **3.6** | **5.7** | **1.6** | **57%** | **7%** | **92.9** | **44** | **22** | **34** | **30%** | **68%** | **12%** | **26** | | | | | | **-7.3** | **27** | **31** | **-$8** |

## Castillo,Diego

| | | | | | | |
|---|---|---|---|---|---|---|
| | | | Health | A | LIMA Plan | A |
| Age: 25 | Th: R | Role: RP | PT/Exp | F | Rand Var | 0 |
| Ht: 6' 3" | Wt: 240 | Type: Pwr FB | Consist | C | MM | 4410 |

4-2, 3.18 ERA in 57 IP at TAM. Young fireballer closed MLB debut with flourish: 22/2 K/BB, 99.4 mph fastball in September. Ctl defied shaky FpK, which is a concern. So is his role, at least for fantasy, as TAM has used him more in 1st than 9th. But buy skills (and electric arms), not roles. If "opener" gets opening... UP: 25 Sv

| Yr | Tm | W | Sv | IP | K | ERA | xERA | WHIP | oOPS | vL | vR | BF/G | Ctl | Dom | Cmd | FpK | SwK | Vel | G | L | F | H% | S% | hr/f | GS | APC | DOM% | DIS% | Sv% | LI | RAR | BPV | BPX | R$ |
|---|---|---|---|---|---|---|---|---|---|---|---|---|---|---|---|---|---|---|---|---|---|---|---|---|---|---|---|---|---|---|---|---|---|---|
| 14 | | | | | | | | | | | | | | | | | | | | | | | | | | | | | | | | | | |
| 15 | | | | | | | | | | | | | | | | | | | | | | | | | | | | | | | | | | |
| 16 | | | | | | | | | | | | | | | | | | | | | | | | | | | | | | | | | | |
| 17 | a/a | 4 | 15 | 72 | 80 | 3.52 | 3.25 | 1.25 | | | | 5.7 | 2.6 | 10.0 | 3.9 | | | | | | | 35% | 71% | | | | | | | | 7.4 | 133 | 160 | $10 |
| 18 | TAM * | 4 | 4 | 84 | 93 | 2.55 | 1.99 | 0.94 | 554 | 516 | 581 | 5.1 | 2.7 | 10.0 | 3.7 | 48% | 14% | 97.7 | 45 | 18 | 37 | 25% | 77% | 12% | 11 | 21 | 0% | 36% | 57 | 1.20 | 16.5 | 132 | 152 | $12 |
| 1st Half | | 1 | 4 | 41 | 43 | 1.47 | 1.52 | 0.89 | 482 | 390 | 542 | 5.3 | 2.4 | 9.3 | 3.8 | 52% | 14% | 96.6 | 49 | 17 | 34 | 24% | 87% | 8% | 0 | 22 | | | 80 | 1.16 | 13.7 | 141 | 162 | $15 |
| 2nd Half | | 3 | 0 | 42 | 50 | 3.61 | 3.32 | 0.99 | 578 | 554 | 594 | 5.1 | 3.0 | 10.6 | 3.6 | 47% | 14% | 98.2 | 44 | 19 | 37 | 25% | 68% | 13% | 11 | 20 | 0% | 36% | 0 | 1.21 | 2.8 | 133 | 153 | $10 |
| 19 | Proj | **3** | **5** | **58** | **65** | **3.36** | **3.30** | **1.11** | **586** | **538** | **621** | **5.4** | **2.7** | **10.1** | **3.7** | **50%** | **14%** | **98.2** | **44** | **19** | **37** | **29%** | **73%** | **10%** | **0** | | | | | | **6.8** | **131** | **150** | **$5** |

## Castillo,Jose

| | | | | | | |
|---|---|---|---|---|---|---|
| | | | Health | B | LIMA Plan | A |
| Age: 23 | Th: L | Role: RP | PT/Exp | F | Rand Var | 0 |
| Ht: 6' 5" | Wt: 246 | Type: Pwr FB | Consist | F | MM | 5510 |

3-3, 3.29 ERA in 38 IP at SD. In rock solid debut, brought improved Cmd up to MLB, and FpK and SwK say it was totally legit. Was deadly vL, but may have turned corner vR in 2nd half, too. Fly ball tilt, handedness may militate against use in 9th, but if he got a shot, skills say he could get the job done... UP: 20 Sv

| Yr | Tm | W | Sv | IP | K | ERA | xERA | WHIP | oOPS | vL | vR | BF/G | Ctl | Dom | Cmd | FpK | SwK | Vel | G | L | F | H% | S% | hr/f | GS | APC | DOM% | DIS% | Sv% | LI | RAR | BPV | BPX | R$ |
|---|---|---|---|---|---|---|---|---|---|---|---|---|---|---|---|---|---|---|---|---|---|---|---|---|---|---|---|---|---|---|---|---|---|---|
| 14 | | | | | | | | | | | | | | | | | | | | | | | | | | | | | | | | | | |
| 15 | | | | | | | | | | | | | | | | | | | | | | | | | | | | | | | | | | |
| 16 | | | | | | | | | | | | | | | | | | | | | | | | | | | | | | | | | | |
| 17 | | | | | | | | | | | | | | | | | | | | | | | | | | | | | | | | | | |
| 18 | SD * | 6 | 8 | 65 | 86 | 2.79 | 2.00 | 1.00 | 520 | 353 | 603 | 4.2 | 2.9 | 11.9 | 4.0 | 70% | 15% | 94.8 | 38 | 20 | 43 | 29% | 73% | 9% | 0 | 17 | | | 80 | 1.11 | 11.0 | 156 | 180 | $11 |
| 1st Half | | 4 | 8 | 35 | 46 | 2.39 | 2.17 | 1.04 | 528 | 243 | 715 | 4.5 | 2.9 | 11.7 | 4.0 | 79% | 19% | 94.8 | 26 | 26 | 48 | 30% | 79% | 9% | 0 | 15 | | | 89 | 0.83 | 7.6 | 155 | 178 | $15 |
| 2nd Half | | 2 | 0 | 30 | 41 | 3.26 | 1.81 | 0.96 | 517 | 409 | 565 | 4.0 | 2.9 | 12.0 | 4.1 | 66% | 14% | 94.8 | 42 | 17 | 41 | 28% | 67% | 8% | 0 | 18 | | | 0 | 1.24 | 3.3 | 158 | 182 | $7 |
| 19 | Proj | **6** | **5** | **65** | **87** | **3.16** | **2.89** | **1.00** | **492** | **400** | **533** | **4.2** | **2.9** | **12.0** | **4.1** | **66%** | **14%** | **94.8** | **42** | **17** | **41** | **29%** | **69%** | **6%** | **0** | | | | | | **13.5** | **158** | **182** | **$9** |

## Castillo,Luis

| | | | | | | |
|---|---|---|---|---|---|---|
| | | | Health | A | LIMA Plan | B+ |
| Age: 26 | Th: R | Role: SP | PT/Exp | C | Rand Var | +3 |
| Ht: 6' 2" | Wt: 190 | Type: Pwr GB | Consist | A | MM | 3303 |

Strong finish to rookie 2017 season spawned off-the-charts expectations, making 1st half a profound disappointment. But velocity was up in 2nd half, as was FpK, which reined in Ctl; main thing missing was 2017's ground ball rate. MLB Dom was down, but SwK suggests that may be temporary. Let the hype build anew.

| Yr | Tm | W | Sv | IP | K | ERA | xERA | WHIP | oOPS | vL | vR | BF/G | Ctl | Dom | Cmd | FpK | SwK | Vel | G | L | F | H% | S% | hr/f | GS | APC | DOM% | DIS% | Sv% | LI | RAR | BPV | BPX | R$ |
|---|---|---|---|---|---|---|---|---|---|---|---|---|---|---|---|---|---|---|---|---|---|---|---|---|---|---|---|---|---|---|---|---|---|---|
| 14 | | | | | | | | | | | | | | | | | | | | | | | | | | | | | | | | | | |
| 15 | | | | | | | | | | | | | | | | | | | | | | | | | | | | | | | | | | |
| 16 | | | | | | | | | | | | | | | | | | | | | | | | | | | | | | | | | | |
| 17 | CIN * | 7 | 0 | 170 | 166 | 3.72 | 3.72 | 1.22 | 638 | 630 | 646 | 23.6 | 2.6 | 8.8 | 3.4 | 57% | 13% | 97.5 | 59 | 12 | 29 | 31% | 73% | 17% | 15 | 99 | 40% | 20% | | | 13.3 | 99 | 119 | $12 |
| 18 | CIN | 10 | 0 | 170 | 165 | 4.30 | 3.77 | 1.22 | 732 | 882 | 587 | 22.8 | 2.6 | 8.8 | 3.4 | 61% | 14% | 95.8 | 46 | 22 | 32 | 29% | 70% | 18% | 31 | 90 | 26% | 32% | | | -3.1 | 111 | 128 | $7 |
| 1st Half | | 5 | 0 | 88 | 85 | 5.85 | 4.20 | 1.41 | 807 | 891 | 727 | 22.5 | 3.4 | 8.7 | 2.6 | 58% | 14% | 95.3 | 45 | 21 | 34 | 31% | 63% | 20% | 17 | 91 | 6% | 35% | | | -18.4 | 89 | 102 | -$8 |
| 2nd Half | | 5 | 0 | 82 | 80 | 2.63 | 3.32 | 1.01 | 645 | 871 | 428 | 23.3 | 1.8 | 8.8 | 5.0 | 65% | 14% | 96.4 | 47 | 23 | 30 | 27% | 81% | 15% | 14 | 89 | 50% | 29% | | | 15.3 | 136 | 156 | $23 |
| 19 | Proj | **11** | **0** | **174** | **170** | **3.66** | **3.34** | **1.21** | **732** | **837** | **634** | **22.8** | **2.5** | **8.8** | **3.5** | **60%** | **14%** | **96.6** | **51** | **18** | **31** | **30%** | **75%** | **16%** | **31** | | | | | | **17.0** | **120** | **138** | **$13** |

KRISTOPHER OLSON

## Castro,Miguel

| Age: 24 | Th: R | Role RP | Health B | LIMA Plan D |
|---|---|---|---|---|
| Ht: 6' 7" | Wt: 205 | Type Pwr | PT/Exp D | Rand Var -3 |
| | | | Consist F | MM 0001 |

Given "success" as multi-inning reliever (hey, first digit of ERA is under 4!), may earn another shot at starting. Don't be fooled. Sure, velocity is decent, but he has no idea where it's going, and doesn't miss bats. Effective enough vR and in inducing GBs to be OK middle man, maybe, but he's a long way from relevant.

| Yr Tm | W | Sv | IP | K | ERA | xERA | WHIP | oOPS | vL | vR | BF/G | Ctl | Dom | Cmd | FpK | SwK | Vel | G | L | F | H% | S% | hr/f | GS | APC | DOM% | DIS% | Sv% | LI | RAR | BPV | BPX | R$ |
|---|---|---|---|---|---|---|---|---|---|---|---|---|---|---|---|---|---|---|---|---|---|---|---|---|---|---|---|---|---|---|---|---|---|
| 14 | | | | | | | | | | | | | | | | | | | | | | | | | | | | | | | | | |
| 15 2 TM * | 3 | 4 | 51 | 43 | 4.57 | 5.75 | 1.67 | 937 | 920 | 952 | 5.4 | 5.0 | 7.5 | 1.5 | 58% | 11% | 96.4 | 33 | 24 | 43 | 32% | 77% | 17% | 0 | 16 | | | 36 | 1.04 | -3.9 | 30 | 35 | -$5 |
| 16 COL * | 2 | 0 | 30 | 24 | 10.27 | 8.39 | 1.84 | 880 | 1111 | 772 | 4.0 | 3.7 | 7.1 | 1.9 | 42% | 10% | 96.1 | 54 | 19 | 27 | 35% | 46% | 23% | 0 | 13 | | | 0 | 1.27 | -22.7 | -17 | -21 | -$12 |
| 17 BAL * | 6 | 0 | 91 | 47 | 4.06 | 3.59 | 1.26 | 682 | 848 | 573 | 8.2 | 3.4 | 4.7 | 1.4 | 58% | 10% | 95.6 | 49 | 17 | 34 | 25% | 70% | 12% | 1 | 26 | 0% | 100% | 0 | 0.90 | 3.3 | 37 | 44 | $2 |
| 18 BAL | 2 | 0 | 86 | 57 | 3.96 | 5.25 | 1.45 | 714 | 777 | 669 | 6.0 | 5.2 | 5.9 | 1.1 | 58% | 10% | 95.5 | 49 | 19 | 32 | 26% | 75% | 11% | 1 | 23 | 0% | 100% | 0 | 0.99 | 2.0 | -7 | -8 | -$4 |
| 1st Half | 2 | 0 | 49 | 32 | 2.96 | 5.27 | 1.40 | 633 | 697 | 592 | 6.4 | 5.2 | 5.9 | 1.1 | 60% | 11% | 95.5 | 48 | 19 | 33 | 27% | 79% | 4% | 0 | 25 | | | 0 | 1.03 | 7.2 | -8 | -9 | -$1 |
| 2nd Half | 0 | 0 | 38 | 25 | 5.26 | 5.21 | 1.51 | 818 | 868 | 779 | 5.5 | 5.3 | 6.0 | 1.1 | 55% | 9% | 95.5 | 51 | 18 | 31 | 26% | 70% | 19% | 1 | 22 | 0% | 100% | 0 | 0.95 | -5.1 | -6 | -6 | -$9 |
| **19 Proj** | **4** | **0** | **87** | **58** | **4.79** | **4.82** | **1.49** | **812** | **930** | **730** | **5.7** | **4.5** | **6.0** | **1.3** | **58%** | **10%** | **95.6** | **49** | **18** | **33** | **28%** | **72%** | **15%** | **0** | | | | | | **-6.8** | **14** | **16** | **-$6** |

## Chacin,Jhoulys

| Age: 31 | Th: R | Role SP | Health C | LIMA Plan C |
|---|---|---|---|---|
| Ht: 6' 3" | Wt: 215 | Type Pwr | PT/Exp A | Rand Var -2 |
| | | | Consist A | MM 1105 |

Anatomy of prime auction nominee: Recent history of outpacing xERA, partly via H% luck? Check. Higher profile from playoff run? Check. Healthy win total? Check. Velocity dip, FB% rise haven't caught up to him, thanks to hr/f? Check. If you budget to 4.30 xERAs, he'll end up on someone else's roster. And that's fine.

| Yr Tm | W | Sv | IP | K | ERA | xERA | WHIP | oOPS | vL | vR | BF/G | Ctl | Dom | Cmd | FpK | SwK | Vel | G | L | F | H% | S% | hr/f | GS | APC | DOM% | DIS% | Sv% | LI | RAR | BPV | BPX | R$ |
|---|---|---|---|---|---|---|---|---|---|---|---|---|---|---|---|---|---|---|---|---|---|---|---|---|---|---|---|---|---|---|---|---|---|
| 14 COL | 1 | 0 | 63 | 42 | 5.40 | 4.56 | 1.44 | 790 | 751 | 821 | 24.7 | 4.0 | 6.0 | 1.5 | 63% | 9% | 88.0 | 33 | 22 | 35 | 29% | 64% | 12% | 11 | 93 | 9% | 73% | | | -13.0 | 21 | 25 | -$7 |
| 15 ARI * | 9 | 0 | 155 | 89 | 3.39 | 3.82 | 1.35 | 729 | 982 | 497 | 25.9 | 3.1 | 5.2 | 1.7 | 55% | 10% | 88.6 | 47 | 19 | 33 | 30% | 76% | 15% | 4 | 85 | 50% | 50% | 0 | 0.84 | 11.0 | 51 | 61 | $4 |
| 16 2 TM | 6 | 0 | 144 | 119 | 4.81 | 4.31 | 1.44 | 745 | 762 | 728 | 18.6 | 3.4 | 7.4 | 2.2 | 61% | 8% | 90.8 | 48 | 23 | 29 | 33% | 68% | 11% | 22 | 70 | 18% | 59% | 0 | 0.68 | -11.1 | 67 | 80 | -$4 |
| 17 SD | 13 | 0 | 180 | 153 | 3.89 | 4.35 | 1.27 | 693 | 789 | 602 | 23.9 | 3.6 | 7.6 | 2.1 | 59% | 8% | 91.4 | 49 | 19 | 32 | 28% | 72% | 11% | 32 | 92 | 22% | 28% | | | 10.4 | 67 | 81 | $12 |
| 18 MIL | 15 | 0 | 193 | 156 | 3.50 | 4.34 | 1.16 | 655 | 781 | 528 | 22.7 | 3.3 | 7.3 | 2.2 | 58% | 9% | 90.1 | 42 | 22 | 36 | 26% | 72% | 9% | 35 | 86 | 23% | 34% | | | 15.4 | 62 | 71 | $17 |
| 1st Half | 6 | 0 | 97 | 76 | 3.71 | 4.78 | 1.34 | 692 | 771 | 607 | 23.0 | 4.0 | 7.1 | 1.8 | 60% | 9% | 89.8 | 40 | 23 | 37 | 29% | 73% | 7% | 18 | 84 | 17% | 33% | | | 5.2 | 38 | 43 | $7 |
| 2nd Half | 9 | 0 | 96 | 80 | 3.29 | 3.91 | 0.98 | 616 | 790 | 448 | 22.5 | 2.6 | 7.5 | 2.9 | 56% | 9% | 90.4 | 44 | 21 | 35 | 22% | 71% | 12% | 17 | 88 | 29% | 35% | | | 10.1 | 87 | 99 | $28 |
| **19 Proj** | **12** | **0** | **189** | **152** | **4.05** | **4.08** | **1.27** | **718** | **811** | **628** | **21.9** | **3.4** | **7.2** | **2.2** | **59%** | **9%** | **90.4** | **45** | **21** | **34** | **28%** | **71%** | **12%** | **35** | | | | | | **2.2** | **63** | **72** | **$9** |

## Chafin,Andrew

| Age: 29 | Th: L | Role RP | Health C | LIMA Plan C |
|---|---|---|---|---|
| Ht: 6' 2" | Wt: 225 | Type Pwr GB | PT/Exp D | Rand Var -3 |
| | | | Consist B | MM 3310 |

As LI shows, he's been trusted in late innings, finding success with comforting combo of SwK-backed Dom, GB bent. Main wart is Ctl, which FpK validates is a legit issue. Don't buy newfound success vR—it was H%-fueled mirage. You can't count on him for saves, but don't be shocked if a few fall his way, either.

| Yr Tm | W | Sv | IP | K | ERA | xERA | WHIP | oOPS | vL | vR | BF/G | Ctl | Dom | Cmd | FpK | SwK | Vel | G | L | F | H% | S% | hr/f | GS | APC | DOM% | DIS% | Sv% | LI | RAR | BPV | BPX | R$ |
|---|---|---|---|---|---|---|---|---|---|---|---|---|---|---|---|---|---|---|---|---|---|---|---|---|---|---|---|---|---|---|---|---|---|
| 14 ARI * | 9 | 0 | 162 | 105 | 4.50 | 5.21 | 1.58 | 685 | 641 | 701 | 24.5 | 3.5 | 5.8 | 1.6 | 58% | 7% | 90.7 | 54 | 18 | 28 | 33% | 73% | 0% | 3 | 86 | 0% | 0% | | | -15.1 | 38 | 45 | -$10 |
| 15 ARI | 5 | 2 | 75 | 58 | 2.76 | 3.70 | 1.15 | 587 | 524 | 631 | 4.6 | 3.6 | 7.0 | 1.9 | 54% | 9% | 92.5 | 58 | 19 | 23 | 26% | 76% | 6% | 0 | 18 | | | 100 | 1.29 | 11.1 | 64 | 76 | $6 |
| 16 ARI | 0 | 0 | 23 | 28 | 6.75 | 3.35 | 1.46 | 703 | 569 | 824 | 3.1 | 4.4 | 11.1 | 2.5 | 60% | 15% | 92.8 | 51 | 24 | 25 | 37% | 50% | 7% | 0 | 11 | | | 0 | 0.94 | -7.2 | 111 | 132 | -$6 |
| 17 ARI | 1 | 0 | 51 | 61 | 3.51 | 3.26 | 1.34 | 699 | 565 | 792 | 3.1 | 3.7 | 10.7 | 2.9 | 52% | 12% | 93.7 | 56 | 21 | 22 | 34% | 77% | 17% | 0 | 12 | | | 0 | 1.02 | 5.4 | 127 | 153 | -$1 |
| 18 ARI | 1 | 0 | 49 | 53 | 3.10 | 3.71 | 1.34 | 621 | 664 | 575 | 2.7 | 4.6 | 9.7 | 2.1 | 57% | 15% | 93.5 | 50 | 26 | 24 | 32% | 74% | 0% | 0 | 11 | | | 0 | 1.20 | 6.4 | 79 | 91 | -$1 |
| 1st Half | 1 | 0 | 29 | 32 | 1.84 | 3.82 | 1.16 | 559 | 545 | 572 | 3.1 | 4.3 | 9.8 | 2.3 | 56% | 14% | 93.4 | 45 | 22 | 33 | 28% | 82% | 0% | 0 | 13 | | | 0 | 1.09 | 8.4 | 84 | 96 | $2 |
| 2nd Half | 0 | 0 | 20 | 21 | 4.95 | 3.55 | 1.60 | 706 | 804 | 580 | 2.4 | 5.0 | 9.5 | 1.9 | 60% | 15% | 93.7 | 57 | 30 | 13 | 37% | 66% | 0% | 0 | 10 | | | 0 | 1.32 | -2.0 | 72 | 82 | -$6 |
| **19 Proj** | **1** | **2** | **51** | **51** | **3.59** | **3.48** | **1.38** | **671** | **657** | **683** | **3.2** | **4.2** | **9.1** | **2.2** | **55%** | **13%** | **93.5** | **55** | **24** | **22** | **33%** | **73%** | **7%** | **0** | | | | | | **3.5** | **84** | **97** | **-$1** |

## Chapman,Aroldis

| Age: 31 | Th: L | Role RP | Health D | LIMA Plan B |
|---|---|---|---|---|
| Ht: 6' 4" | Wt: 212 | Type Pwr | PT/Exp B | Rand Var -1 |
| | | | Consist B | MM 5530 |

Fought knee tendinitis for months before hitting DL in Aug, which may explain walk rate spike, slight dip in velocity. When healthy, was same old guy, racking up Ks, converting saves, though bad H%, hr/f luck hurt 2nd half results. But wear and tear are piling up, adding uncertainty. Risk-reward may be near tipping point.

| Yr Tm | W | Sv | IP | K | ERA | xERA | WHIP | oOPS | vL | vR | BF/G | Ctl | Dom | Cmd | FpK | SwK | Vel | G | L | F | H% | S% | hr/f | GS | APC | DOM% | DIS% | Sv% | LI | RAR | BPV | BPX | R$ |
|---|---|---|---|---|---|---|---|---|---|---|---|---|---|---|---|---|---|---|---|---|---|---|---|---|---|---|---|---|---|---|---|---|---|
| 14 CIN | 0 | 36 | 54 | 106 | 2.00 | 1.52 | 0.83 | 406 | 372 | 415 | 3.7 | 4.0 | 17.7 | 4.4 | 58% | 21% | 100.3 | 43 | 22 | 35 | 30% | 75% | 4% | 0 | 17 | | | 95 | 1.44 | 11.6 | 231 | 275 | $21 |
| 15 CIN | 4 | 33 | 66 | 116 | 1.63 | 2.55 | 1.15 | 527 | 451 | 554 | 4.3 | 4.5 | 15.7 | 3.5 | 56% | 20% | 99.5 | 37 | 22 | 41 | 36% | 88% | 6% | 0 | 18 | | | 92 | 1.24 | 19.1 | 177 | 211 | $23 |
| 16 2 TM | 4 | 36 | 58 | 90 | 1.55 | 2.25 | 0.86 | 452 | 462 | 448 | 3.8 | 2.8 | 14.0 | 5.0 | 57% | 19% | 100.4 | 46 | 25 | 29 | 29% | 83% | 6% | 0 | 17 | | | 92 | 1.39 | 18.9 | 200 | 238 | $25 |
| 17 NYY | 4 | 22 | 50 | 69 | 3.22 | 3.17 | 1.13 | 584 | 577 | 588 | 4.0 | 3.6 | 12.3 | 3.5 | 62% | 14% | 100.1 | 49 | 16 | 35 | 32% | 72% | 7% | 0 | 17 | | | 85 | 1.14 | 7.1 | 153 | 183 | $13 |
| 18 NYY | 3 | 32 | 51 | 93 | 2.45 | 2.48 | 1.05 | 493 | 468 | 501 | 3.9 | 5.3 | 16.3 | 3.1 | 58% | 16% | 98.9 | 44 | 19 | 37 | 30% | 77% | 6% | 0 | 17 | | | 94 | 1.10 | 10.7 | 173 | 200 | $19 |
| 1st Half | 3 | 23 | 35 | 60 | 1.29 | 2.27 | 0.86 | 455 | 618 | 414 | 3.9 | 3.9 | 15.4 | 4.0 | 60% | 18% | 99.1 | 45 | 17 | 38 | 27% | 86% | 5% | 0 | 17 | | | 96 | 1.22 | 12.4 | 196 | 226 | $29 |
| 2nd Half | 0 | 9 | 16 | 33 | 4.96 | 2.98 | 1.47 | 562 | 334 | 711 | 3.8 | 8.3 | 18.2 | 2.2 | 55% | 12% | 98.6 | 42 | 23 | 35 | 38% | 65% | 11% | 0 | 17 | | | 90 | 0.90 | -1.6 | 124 | 143 | $0 |
| **19 Proj** | **3** | **29** | **58** | **99** | **2.81** | **2.38** | **1.07** | **498** | **430** | **525** | **3.6** | **5.0** | **15.4** | **3.1** | **58%** | **16%** | **99.5** | **45** | **20** | **35** | **30%** | **74%** | **8%** | **0** | | | | | | **21.7** | **165** | **190** | **$18** |

## Chatwood,Tyler

| Age: 29 | Th: R | Role RP | Health D | LIMA Plan D |
|---|---|---|---|---|
| Ht: 6' 0" | Wt: 185 | Type Pwr xGB | PT/Exp B | Rand Var 0 |
| | | | Consist B | MM 0101 |

He just needs to get out of thin air... or not. Left what little Ctl he had in Rockies; mountains of trouble ensued. Lost starting role, LHB clubbed him, dealt with hip injury... but hey, he became a dad, so season wasn't a total loss. (What's that? You're wondering if he's already taught his son to walk? That's just mean.)

| Yr Tm | W | Sv | IP | K | ERA | xERA | WHIP | oOPS | vL | vR | BF/G | Ctl | Dom | Cmd | FpK | SwK | Vel | G | L | F | H% | S% | hr/f | GS | APC | DOM% | DIS% | Sv% | LI | RAR | BPV | BPX | R$ |
|---|---|---|---|---|---|---|---|---|---|---|---|---|---|---|---|---|---|---|---|---|---|---|---|---|---|---|---|---|---|---|---|---|---|
| 14 COL | 1 | 0 | 24 | 20 | 4.50 | 3.56 | 1.21 | 711 | 472 | 1015 | 25.3 | 3.0 | 7.5 | 2.5 | 50% | 10% | 92.6 | 46 | 29 | 26 | 26% | 68% | 22% | 4 | 89 | 25% | 50% | | | -2.2 | 78 | 93 | -$3 |
| 15 | | | | | | | | | | | | | | | | | | | | | | | | | | | | | | | | | |
| 16 COL | 12 | 0 | 158 | 117 | 3.87 | 4.24 | 1.37 | 723 | 751 | 693 | 24.8 | 4.0 | 6.7 | 1.7 | 54% | 8% | 92.2 | 57 | 17 | 26 | 29% | 74% | 12% | 27 | 94 | 22% | 37% | | | 6.2 | 47 | 56 | $5 |
| 17 COL | 8 | 1 | 148 | 120 | 4.69 | 4.27 | 1.44 | 788 | 837 | 736 | 19.1 | 4.7 | 7.3 | 1.6 | 53% | 10% | 94.7 | 58 | 20 | 22 | 28% | 70% | 22% | 25 | 75 | 16% | 52% | 100 | 0.72 | -6.1 | 41 | 49 | -$1 |
| 18 CHC | 4 | 0 | 104 | 85 | 5.30 | 5.81 | 1.80 | 774 | 923 | 578 | 20.3 | 8.2 | 7.4 | 0.9 | 50% | 8% | 93.1 | 54 | 18 | 28 | 29% | 71% | 11% | 20 | 81 | 0% | 45% | 0 | 0.63 | -14.7 | -58 | -67 | -$14 |
| 1st Half | 3 | 0 | 73 | 70 | 4.54 | 5.32 | 1.75 | 738 | 872 | 559 | 22.7 | 8.1 | 8.6 | 1.1 | 52% | 9% | 93.0 | 54 | 18 | 28 | 29% | 74% | 9% | 15 | 93 | 0% | 27% | | | -3.5 | -32 | -36 | -$13 |
| 2nd Half | 1 | 0 | 30 | 15 | 7.12 | 7.06 | 1.95 | 860 | 1045 | 620 | 16.2 | 8.6 | 4.5 | 0.5 | 46% | 7% | 93.3 | 54 | 19 | 28 | 27% | 64% | 15% | 5 | 61 | 0% | 100% | 0 | 0.44 | -11.1 | -121 | -139 | -$18 |
| **19 Proj** | **4** | **0** | **87** | **69** | **5.27** | **4.90** | **1.64** | **792** | **898** | **667** | **19.1** | **6.4** | **7.1** | **1.1** | **51%** | **9%** | **93.5** | **56** | **19** | **25** | **29%** | **69%** | **15%** | **18** | | | | | | **-6.3** | **-12** | **-13** | **-$9** |

## Chavez,Jesse

| Age: 35 | Th: R | Role RP | Health B | LIMA Plan B |
|---|---|---|---|---|
| Ht: 6' 2" | Wt: 175 | Type Pwr | PT/Exp B | Rand Var -3 |
| | | | Consist B | MM 3200 |

If new RP posted these skills at 24, we'd salivate about role change. At 34, it's more like, "Congrats on your continued employment." Getting ahead of hitters keyed career-best Ctl, Cmd; rest of package stable. Even handled handful of save opps, and may again have value in spurts, as team faces emergency, breaks glass.

| Yr Tm | W | Sv | IP | K | ERA | xERA | WHIP | oOPS | vL | vR | BF/G | Ctl | Dom | Cmd | FpK | SwK | Vel | G | L | F | H% | S% | hr/f | GS | APC | DOM% | DIS% | Sv% | LI | RAR | BPV | BPX | R$ |
|---|---|---|---|---|---|---|---|---|---|---|---|---|---|---|---|---|---|---|---|---|---|---|---|---|---|---|---|---|---|---|---|---|---|
| 14 OAK | 8 | 0 | 146 | 136 | 3.45 | 3.72 | 1.31 | 692 | 663 | 729 | 19.4 | 3.0 | 8.4 | 2.8 | 63% | 9% | 91.3 | 42 | 23 | 35 | 31% | 78% | 11% | 21 | 75 | 29% | 24% | 0 | 0.66 | 5.2 | 89 | 106 | $5 |
| 15 OAK | 7 | 1 | 157 | 136 | 4.18 | 4.04 | 1.35 | 730 | 825 | 616 | 22.4 | 2.8 | 7.8 | 2.8 | 61% | 9% | 91.2 | 43 | 23 | 34 | 32% | 72% | 11% | 26 | 86 | 23% | 38% | 100 | 0.74 | -4.3 | 87 | 104 | $1 |
| 16 2 TM | 2 | 0 | 67 | 63 | 4.43 | 4.10 | 1.33 | 779 | 836 | 740 | 4.5 | 2.4 | 8.5 | 3.5 | 64% | 10% | 93.2 | 43 | 18 | 39 | 32% | 73% | 15% | 0 | 18 | | | 0 | 0.90 | -2.0 | 108 | 128 | -$2 |
| 17 LAA | 7 | 0 | 138 | 119 | 5.35 | 4.52 | 1.40 | 826 | 779 | 867 | 15.4 | 2.9 | 7.8 | 2.6 | 62% | 8% | 92.0 | 41 | 22 | 37 | 31% | 67% | 18% | 21 | 61 | 10% | 43% | 0 | 0.74 | -16.8 | 79 | 95 | -$3 |
| 18 2 TM | 5 | 5 | 95 | 92 | 2.55 | 3.54 | 1.06 | 645 | 651 | 642 | 6.1 | 1.6 | 8.7 | 5.4 | 64% | 11% | 93.0 | 44 | 20 | 36 | 29% | 84% | 14% | 0 | 24 | | | 83 | 0.83 | 18.8 | 135 | 155 | $12 |
| 1st Half | 3 | 1 | 52 | 47 | 3.31 | 3.88 | 1.16 | 721 | 795 | 682 | 8.5 | 1.7 | 8.2 | 4.7 | 61% | 12% | 92.8 | 45 | 19 | 37 | 29% | 80% | 16% | 0 | 32 | | | 100 | 0.55 | 5.4 | 123 | 141 | $8 |
| 2nd Half | 2 | 4 | 44 | 45 | 1.65 | 3.13 | 0.94 | 548 | 458 | 591 | 4.5 | 1.4 | 9.3 | 6.4 | 68% | 10% | 93.2 | 44 | 22 | 34 | 28% | 89% | 11% | 0 | 18 | | | 80 | 1.02 | 13.5 | 150 | 172 | $17 |
| **19 Proj** | **5** | **0** | **58** | **54** | **3.54** | **3.56** | **1.20** | **707** | **712** | **704** | **6.9** | **2.2** | **8.4** | **3.9** | **64%** | **10%** | **92.7** | **43** | **21** | **36** | **30%** | **77%** | **15%** | **4** | | | | | | **3.9** | **114** | **131** | **$2** |

## Chen,Wei-Yin

| Age: 33 | Th: L | Role RP | Health F | LIMA Plan C |
|---|---|---|---|---|
| Ht: 6' 0" | Wt: 200 | Type FB | PT/Exp C | Rand Var 0 |
| | | | Consist A | MM 1103 |

After late start due to lingering issues with partially torn UCL, early performance was rough, especially vR. With some h% help, results improved in 2nd half as Ctl returned, but Dom gain is hard to buy, given SwK. If elbow holds up (a big "if," perhaps), he can be marginally useful. Faint praise, indeed.

| Yr Tm | W | Sv | IP | K | ERA | xERA | WHIP | oOPS | vL | vR | BF/G | Ctl | Dom | Cmd | FpK | SwK | Vel | G | L | F | H% | S% | hr/f | GS | APC | DOM% | DIS% | Sv% | LI | RAR | BPV | BPX | R$ |
|---|---|---|---|---|---|---|---|---|---|---|---|---|---|---|---|---|---|---|---|---|---|---|---|---|---|---|---|---|---|---|---|---|---|
| 14 BAL | 16 | 0 | 186 | 136 | 3.54 | 3.86 | 1.23 | 727 | 670 | 746 | 24.9 | 1.7 | 6.6 | 3.9 | 61% | 8% | 91.8 | 41 | 22 | 38 | 30% | 76% | 10% | 31 | 96 | 23% | 29% | | | 4.6 | 92 | 109 | $10 |
| 15 BAL | 11 | 0 | 191 | 153 | 3.34 | 4.01 | 1.22 | 758 | 576 | 815 | 25.5 | 1.9 | 7.2 | 3.7 | 68% | 9% | 91.4 | 40 | 20 | 39 | 30% | 79% | 12% | 31 | 97 | 26% | 19% | | | 14.7 | 95 | 114 | $13 |
| 16 MIA | 5 | 0 | 123 | 100 | 4.96 | 4.27 | 1.28 | 789 | 778 | 791 | 23.6 | 1.8 | 7.3 | 4.2 | 64% | 10% | 90.7 | 40 | 21 | 38 | 31% | 66% | 15% | 22 | 87 | 27% | 27% | | | -11.8 | 102 | 121 | -$1 |
| 17 MIA | 2 | 0 | 33 | 25 | 3.82 | 4.60 | 1.03 | 612 | 523 | 646 | 14.7 | 2.5 | 6.8 | 2.8 | 63% | 10% | 90.9 | 37 | 19 | 44 | 24% | 65% | 7% | 5 | 55 | 0% | 40% | 0 | 0.52 | 2.2 | 71 | 86 | -$1 |
| 18 MIA | 6 | 0 | 133 | 111 | 4.79 | 4.81 | 1.34 | 749 | 558 | 797 | 22.0 | 3.2 | 7.5 | 2.4 | 63% | 9% | 91.1 | 37 | 20 | 43 | 30% | 67% | 11% | 26 | 86 | 27% | 46% | | | -10.6 | 64 | 74 | -$3 |
| 1st Half | 2 | 0 | 56 | 41 | 6.14 | 5.65 | 1.62 | 872 | 608 | 941 | 21.2 | 4.0 | 6.6 | 1.6 | 63% | 9% | 90.7 | 35 | 20 | 45 | 32% | 65% | 12% | 12 | 80 | 25% | 58% | | | -13.7 | 23 | 27 | -$21 |
| 2nd Half | 4 | 0 | 78 | 70 | 3.82 | 4.24 | 1.13 | 653 | 515 | 686 | 22.7 | 2.5 | 8.1 | 3.2 | 63% | 9% | 91.5 | 38 | 19 | 42 | 28% | 70% | 10% | 14 | 91 | 29% | 36% | | | 3.1 | 94 | 108 | $8 |
| **19 Proj** | **7** | **0** | **145** | **117** | **4.42** | **4.18** | **1.24** | **720** | **580** | **758** | **19.4** | **2.6** | **7.2** | **2.8** | **63%** | **9%** | **91.1** | **38** | **20** | **42** | **29%** | **68%** | **11%** | **29** | | | | | | **-0.4** | **75** | **87** | **$4** |

KRISTOPHER OLSON

## Chirinos,Yonny

| | | | | | |
|---|---|---|---|---|---|
| Age: 25 | Th: R | Role: SP | Health: C | LIMA Plan: B | |
| Ht: 6' 2" | Wt: 235 | Type: | PT/Exp: D | Rand Var: 0 | |
| | | | Consist: C | MM: 2103 | |

5-5, 3.51 ERA in 90 IP at TAM. Rays' 2017 MiLB Pitcher of the Year flashed stellar control in MLB debut, and SwK points to room for more K. Hard contact a mild concern, as he owned 11th-worst rate (out of 173) among pitchers with 80+ IP. If usage questions keep price low, potential profit here.

| Yr | Tm | W | Sv | IP | K | ERA | xERA | WHIP | oOPS | vL | vR | BF/G | Ctl | Dom | Cmd | FpK | SwK | Vel | G | L | F | H% | S% | hr/f | GS | APC | DOM% | DIS% | Sv% | LI | RAR | BPV | BPX | R$ |
|---|---|---|---|---|---|---|---|---|---|---|---|---|---|---|---|---|---|---|---|---|---|---|---|---|---|---|---|---|---|---|---|---|---|---|
| 14 | | | | | | | | | | | | | | | | | | | | | | | | | | | | | | | | | | |
| 15 | | | | | | | | | | | | | | | | | | | | | | | | | | | | | | | | | | |
| 16 | aa | 5 | 0 | 67 | 38 | 5.39 | 4.96 | 1.47 | | | | 20.4 | 1.7 | 5.1 | 3.1 | | | | | | | 35% | 63% | | | | | | | | -9.8 | 66 | 78 | -$5 |
| 17 | a/a | 13 | 0 | 168 | 123 | 3.54 | 3.60 | 1.15 | | | | 24.8 | 1.5 | 6.6 | 4.5 | | | | | | | 30% | 72% | | | | | | | | 16.9 | 109 | 130 | $16 |
| 18 | TAM * | 5 | 0 | 122 | 101 | 4.29 | 4.36 | 1.30 | 687 | 679 | 694 | 19.3 | 2.4 | 7.5 | 3.1 | 64% | 11% | 93.7 | 44 | 24 | 32 | 32% | 70% | 8% | 7 | 73 | 29% | 43% | 0 | 0.90 | -2.1 | 79 | 91 | $0 |
| 1st Half | | 0 | 0 | 47 | 37 | 5.80 | 5.59 | 1.48 | 708 | 677 | 746 | 18.3 | 2.7 | 7.1 | 2.6 | 68% | 10% | 93.2 | 42 | 25 | 34 | 33% | 64% | 8% | 5 | 68 | 20% | 40% | 0 | 1.02 | -9.5 | 48 | 56 | -$17 |
| 2nd Half | | 5 | 0 | 75 | 65 | 3.34 | 3.60 | 1.19 | 678 | 680 | 677 | 20.0 | 2.2 | 7.8 | 3.6 | 62% | 12% | 93.8 | 45 | 24 | 32 | 30% | 75% | 9% | 2 | 75 | 50% | 50% | 0 | 0.84 | 7.5 | 100 | 115 | $11 |
| **19** | **Proj** | **8** | **0** | **131** | **105** | **3.72** | **3.76** | **1.24** | **753** | **748** | **758** | **20.9** | **2.0** | **7.2** | **3.6** | **65%** | **11%** | **93.6** | **43** | **24** | **32** | **31%** | **74%** | **12%** | **25** | | | | | | **6.9** | **98** | **112** | **$6** |

## Cimber,Adam

| | | | | | |
|---|---|---|---|---|---|
| Age: 28 | Th: R | Role: RP | Health: A | LIMA Plan: B+ | |
| Ht: 6' 4" | Wt: 180 | Type: Con xGB | PT/Exp: D | Rand Var: 0 | |
| | | | Consist: B | MM: 3001 | |

Rookie enjoyed fine start (9.5 Dom, 5.1 Cmd) with SD before fading (3.2 Dom, 1.0 Cmd) after July trade to CLE. MiLB profile supports above-average control and GB tilt, though lowly velocity and 2nd half SwK warn strikeouts will be hard to come by. Despite acceptable surface stats, a marginal fantasy commodity.

| Yr | Tm | W | Sv | IP | K | ERA | xERA | WHIP | oOPS | vL | vR | BF/G | Ctl | Dom | Cmd | FpK | SwK | Vel | G | L | F | H% | S% | hr/f | GS | APC | DOM% | DIS% | Sv% | LI | RAR | BPV | BPX | R$ |
|---|---|---|---|---|---|---|---|---|---|---|---|---|---|---|---|---|---|---|---|---|---|---|---|---|---|---|---|---|---|---|---|---|---|---|
| 14 | | | | | | | | | | | | | | | | | | | | | | | | | | | | | | | | | | |
| 15 | a/a | 4 | 1 | 59 | 39 | 3.31 | 4.54 | 1.41 | | | | 5.4 | 2.3 | 5.9 | 2.6 | | | | | | | 33% | 79% | | | | | | | | 4.7 | 64 | 76 | -$1 |
| 16 | a/a | 3 | 3 | 57 | 24 | 4.62 | 4.57 | 1.44 | | | | 5.3 | 2.4 | 3.8 | 1.6 | | | | | | | 31% | 68% | | | | | | | | -3.1 | 32 | 38 | -$3 |
| 17 | a/a | 5 | 5 | 81 | 52 | 3.49 | 3.60 | 1.07 | | | | 6.4 | 1.2 | 5.7 | 4.9 | | | | | | | 27% | 74% | | | | | | | | 8.6 | 104 | 125 | $8 |
| 18 | 2 TM | 3 | 0 | 68 | 58 | 3.42 | 3.39 | 1.24 | 743 | 1062 | 610 | 4.1 | 2.2 | 7.6 | 3.4 | 64% | 10% | 86.5 | 57 | 21 | 21 | 32% | 74% | 12% | 0 | 14 | | | 0 | 0.88 | 6.1 | 112 | 129 | $1 |
| 1st Half | | 3 | 0 | 40 | 45 | 3.38 | 2.86 | 1.13 | 665 | 1016 | 464 | 4.8 | 1.6 | 10.1 | 6.4 | 68% | 13% | 86.3 | 47 | 28 | 25 | 35% | 68% | 4% | 0 | 17 | | | 0 | 0.80 | 3.8 | 165 | 189 | $4 |
| 2nd Half | | 0 | 0 | 28 | 13 | 3.49 | 4.25 | 1.41 | 847 | 1169 | 766 | 3.4 | 3.2 | 4.1 | 1.3 | 59% | 7% | 86.8 | 68 | 14 | 18 | 28% | 81% | 24% | 0 | 11 | | | 0 | 0.94 | 2.3 | 35 | 40 | -$4 |
| **19** | **Proj** | **3** | **0** | **73** | **47** | **3.61** | **3.60** | **1.27** | **786** | **1094** | **677** | **4.5** | **2.2** | **5.9** | **2.7** | **62%** | **9%** | **86.6** | **60** | **20** | **21** | **30%** | **75%** | **16%** | **0** | | | | | | **4.9** | **85** | **98** | **$0** |

## Cingrani,Tony

| | | | | | |
|---|---|---|---|---|---|
| Age: 29 | Th: L | Role: RP | Health: F | LIMA Plan: C+ | |
| Ht: 6' 4" | Wt: 214 | Type: Pwr | PT/Exp: D | Rand Var: +5 | |
| | | | Consist: C | MM: 4500 | |

Another year, another ERA over 4.00. But wait: brutal S% paired with unsightly H% to do much of the damage, while two years of improving Cmd paint brighter picture. FpK doesn't support this level of Ctl, and continued shoulder issues hard to overlook. Still, with health, could post career-best season.

| Yr | Tm | W | Sv | IP | K | ERA | xERA | WHIP | oOPS | vL | vR | BF/G | Ctl | Dom | Cmd | FpK | SwK | Vel | G | L | F | H% | S% | hr/f | GS | APC | DOM% | DIS% | Sv% | LI | RAR | BPV | BPX | R$ |
|---|---|---|---|---|---|---|---|---|---|---|---|---|---|---|---|---|---|---|---|---|---|---|---|---|---|---|---|---|---|---|---|---|---|---|
| 14 | CIN | 2 | 0 | 63 | 61 | 4.55 | 4.51 | 1.53 | 811 | 613 | 862 | 21.5 | 5.0 | 8.7 | 1.7 | 54% | 9% | 91.3 | 35 | 22 | 44 | 30% | 76% | 15% | 11 | 86 | 9% | 64% | 0 | 0.85 | -6.3 | 35 | 41 | -$5 |
| 15 | CIN * | 0 | 0 | 58 | 66 | 4.33 | 4.67 | 1.62 | 811 | 915 | 751 | 5.9 | 5.8 | 10.2 | 1.8 | 50% | 12% | 91.8 | 38 | 27 | 35 | 34% | 75% | 10% | 1 | 19 | 0% | 100% | 0 | 1.24 | -2.6 | 75 | 89 | -$7 |
| 16 | CIN | 2 | 17 | 63 | 49 | 4.14 | 5.07 | 1.44 | 719 | 674 | 743 | 4.2 | 5.3 | 7.0 | 1.3 | 55% | 9% | 94.2 | 47 | 16 | 38 | 28% | 72% | 7% | 0 | 17 | | | 74 | 1.16 | 0.4 | 8 | 10 | $4 |
| 17 | 2 NL | 0 | 0 | 43 | 52 | 4.22 | 3.64 | 1.22 | 791 | 838 | 750 | 3.7 | 2.5 | 11.0 | 4.3 | 62% | 14% | 94.4 | 41 | 16 | 43 | 31% | 76% | 21% | 0 | 15 | | | 0 | 0.67 | 0.7 | 148 | 178 | -$2 |
| 18 | LA | 1 | 0 | 23 | 36 | 4.76 | 2.47 | 1.10 | 644 | 749 | 564 | 3.2 | 2.4 | 14.3 | 6.0 | 53% | 14% | 93.5 | 50 | 13 | 38 | 38% | 57% | 11% | 0 | 14 | | | 0 | 1.12 | -1.7 | 221 | 254 | -$3 |
| 1st Half | | 1 | 0 | 22 | 36 | 4.84 | 2.41 | 1.03 | 612 | 753 | 506 | 3.3 | 2.4 | 14.5 | 6.0 | 53% | 14% | 93.6 | 51 | 9 | 40 | 36% | 52% | 11% | 0 | 14 | | | 0 | 1.19 | -1.9 | 225 | 258 | -$3 |
| 2nd Half | | 0 | 0 | 0 | 0 | 0.00 | 0.00 | 6.00 | 1417 | 500 | 2000 | 2.0 | 0.0 | 0.0 | 0.0 | 50% | 12% | 92.7 | 33 | 67 | 0 | 68% | 100% | 0% | 0 | 9 | | | 0 | 0.01 | 0.2 | 11 | 13 | -$7 |
| **19** | **Proj** | **1** | **0** | **44** | **55** | **3.61** | **3.24** | **1.22** | **698** | **747** | **668** | **4.1** | **3.5** | **11.3** | **3.2** | **55%** | **12%** | **93.4** | **44** | **16** | **40** | **31%** | **75%** | **14%** | **0** | | | | | | **2.9** | **131** | **151** | **-$1** |

## Cishek,Steve

| | | | | | |
|---|---|---|---|---|---|
| Age: 33 | Th: R | Role: RP | Health: B | LIMA Plan: B+ | |
| Ht: 6' 6" | Wt: 215 | Type: Pwr | PT/Exp: C | Rand Var: -5 | |
| | | | Consist: A | MM: 4310 | |

Side-arming veteran landed some save opps, but never fully seized role though he has both the chops and experience. Ctl survived despite shaky FpK, and while ERA/xERA gap suggests regression, that BPV line is aging well. Boring and cheap to roster, likely with modest ROI in the end. The Baltic Avenue of MLB relievers.

| Yr | Tm | W | Sv | IP | K | ERA | xERA | WHIP | oOPS | vL | vR | BF/G | Ctl | Dom | Cmd | FpK | SwK | Vel | G | L | F | H% | S% | hr/f | GS | APC | DOM% | DIS% | Sv% | LI | RAR | BPV | BPX | R$ |
|---|---|---|---|---|---|---|---|---|---|---|---|---|---|---|---|---|---|---|---|---|---|---|---|---|---|---|---|---|---|---|---|---|---|---|
| 14 | MIA | 4 | 39 | 65 | 84 | 3.17 | 2.84 | 1.21 | 643 | 586 | 713 | 4.1 | 2.9 | 11.6 | 4.0 | 67% | 10% | 91.7 | 43 | 26 | 31 | 35% | 74% | 6% | 0 | 17 | | | 91 | 1.61 | 4.6 | 151 | 180 | $18 |
| 15 | 2 NL | 2 | 4 | 55 | 48 | 3.58 | 4.42 | 1.48 | 720 | 754 | 696 | 4.1 | 4.4 | 7.8 | 1.8 | 64% | 10% | 90.8 | 46 | 22 | 32 | 32% | 77% | 8% | 0 | 16 | | | 44 | 0.91 | 2.6 | 46 | 55 | -$1 |
| 16 | SEA | 4 | 25 | 64 | 76 | 2.81 | 3.39 | 1.02 | 600 | 728 | 498 | 4.2 | 3.0 | 10.7 | 3.6 | 61% | 12% | 91.4 | 44 | 17 | 39 | 26% | 79% | 13% | 0 | 17 | | | 78 | 1.52 | 10.9 | 135 | 160 | $17 |
| 17 | 2 AL | 3 | 1 | 45 | 41 | 2.01 | 3.38 | 0.90 | 491 | 663 | 413 | 3.6 | 2.8 | 8.3 | 2.9 | 64% | 11% | 90.3 | 56 | 18 | 26 | 21% | 81% | 10% | 0 | 15 | | | 25 | 1.16 | 12.9 | 107 | 128 | $6 |
| 18 | CHC | 4 | 4 | 70 | 78 | 2.18 | 3.51 | 1.04 | 593 | 724 | 528 | 3.6 | 3.6 | 10.0 | 2.8 | 55% | 12% | 90.3 | 47 | 18 | 35 | 25% | 82% | 8% | 0 | 14 | | | 57 | 1.46 | 17.1 | 108 | 124 | $10 |
| 1st Half | | 2 | 2 | 36 | 40 | 1.75 | 3.36 | 1.06 | 563 | 732 | 480 | 3.8 | 4.3 | 10.0 | 2.4 | 55% | 11% | 90.5 | 55 | 17 | 29 | 25% | 84% | 4% | 0 | 16 | | | 50 | 1.36 | 10.7 | 98 | 113 | $10 |
| 2nd Half | | 2 | 2 | 34 | 38 | 2.62 | 3.64 | 1.02 | 624 | 713 | 578 | 3.4 | 2.9 | 10.0 | 3.5 | 54% | 13% | 90.1 | 40 | 19 | 41 | 25% | 81% | 11% | 0 | 13 | | | 67 | 1.55 | 6.5 | 119 | 137 | $10 |
| **19** | **Proj** | **4** | **2** | **65** | **70** | **2.40** | **3.21** | **1.03** | **582** | **702** | **515** | **3.5** | **3.2** | **9.6** | **3.0** | **59%** | **11%** | **90.6** | **48** | **18** | **34** | **25%** | **80%** | **10%** | **0** | | | | | | **8.1** | **112** | **129** | **$8** |

## Claudio,Alexander

| | | | | | |
|---|---|---|---|---|---|
| Age: 27 | Th: L | Role: RP | Health: F | LIMA Plan: C | |
| Ht: 6' 3" | Wt: 180 | Type: Con xGB | PT/Exp: C | Rand Var: +3 | |
| | | | Consist: B | MM: 3010 | |

Passed over for 9th inning and then fell flat out of the gate (8.44 April ERA). GB/Ctl combo creates nice floor, and modest H% regression should put sub-4.00 ERA back in play. 86-mph-throwing lefty hardly screams "closer material" though, and no Ks/no saves makes for a questionable path to value.

| Yr | Tm | W | Sv | IP | K | ERA | xERA | WHIP | oOPS | vL | vR | BF/G | Ctl | Dom | Cmd | FpK | SwK | Vel | G | L | F | H% | S% | hr/f | GS | APC | DOM% | DIS% | Sv% | LI | RAR | BPV | BPX | R$ |
|---|---|---|---|---|---|---|---|---|---|---|---|---|---|---|---|---|---|---|---|---|---|---|---|---|---|---|---|---|---|---|---|---|---|---|
| 14 | TEX * | 2 | 0 | 55 | 38 | 2.63 | 2.82 | 1.13 | 693 | 465 | 855 | 8.7 | 1.3 | 6.2 | 4.8 | 46% | 12% | 84.3 | 58 | 25 | 17 | 31% | 75% | 0% | 0 | 14 | | | 0 | 0.41 | 7.5 | 137 | 163 | $2 |
| 15 | TEX * | 4 | 0 | 56 | 42 | 3.38 | 4.48 | 1.35 | 762 | 716 | 813 | 4.9 | 2.2 | 6.8 | 3.1 | 65% | 11% | 84.1 | 51 | 16 | 33 | 33% | 79% | 27% | 0 | 14 | | | 0 | 1.16 | 4.0 | 75 | 89 | -$1 |
| 16 | TEX * | 4 | 1 | 68 | 40 | 2.28 | 2.78 | 1.14 | 662 | 449 | 752 | 6.0 | 1.9 | 5.4 | 2.8 | 65% | 11% | 85.5 | 63 | 17 | 20 | 29% | 80% | 6% | 0 | 20 | | | 100 | 0.72 | 16.0 | 89 | 106 | $6 |
| 17 | TEX | 4 | 11 | 83 | 56 | 2.50 | 3.23 | 1.04 | 591 | 368 | 694 | 4.6 | 1.6 | 6.1 | 3.7 | 63% | 10% | 86.7 | 67 | 17 | 17 | 27% | 78% | 12% | 1 | 16 | 0% | 100% | 73 | 1.18 | 18.9 | 111 | 133 | $13 |
| 18 | TEX | 4 | 1 | 68 | 41 | 4.48 | 3.80 | 1.52 | 827 | 602 | 933 | 4.5 | 1.7 | 5.4 | 3.2 | 63% | 12% | 86.0 | 61 | 23 | 16 | 36% | 70% | 11% | 1 | 16 | 0% | 100% | 33 | 1.14 | -2.8 | 90 | 104 | -$5 |
| 1st Half | | 4 | 1 | 35 | 17 | 4.93 | 3.99 | 1.59 | 838 | 538 | 998 | 4.6 | 1.0 | 4.4 | 4.3 | 64% | 10% | 86.1 | 61 | 23 | 16 | 38% | 67% | 5% | 0 | 15 | | | 33 | 1.31 | -3.3 | 90 | 104 | -$7 |
| 2nd Half | | 0 | 0 | 34 | 24 | 4.01 | 3.61 | 1.46 | 815 | 684 | 869 | 4.5 | 2.4 | 6.4 | 2.7 | 61% | 13% | 85.9 | 61 | 23 | 16 | 34% | 74% | 18% | 1 | 17 | 0% | 100% | 0 | 0.97 | 0.6 | 90 | 103 | -$4 |
| **19** | **Proj** | **3** | **2** | **65** | **42** | **3.87** | **3.50** | **1.35** | **745** | **526** | **844** | **4.9** | **1.8** | **5.8** | **3.2** | **63%** | **11%** | **86.2** | **61** | **22** | **17** | **33%** | **71%** | **10%** | **0** | | | | | | **3.4** | **95** | **109** | **-$1** |

## Clevinger,Michael

| | | | | | |
|---|---|---|---|---|---|
| Age: 28 | Th: R | Role: SP | Health: A | LIMA Plan: D+ | |
| Ht: 6' 4" | Wt: 210 | Type: Pwr | PT/Exp: B | Rand Var: -1 | |
| | | | Consist: B | MM: 2305 | |

Rode improved curve/slider to new heights, first 200-K season. Repeatable? Big Ctl improvement backed by impressive FpK, and Velocity/SwK suggest K will keep flowing. Struggles vL (12 HR, .479 SLG) resurfaced in 2nd half; if he solves those, watch out. Borderline ace sans the name-brand price tag.

| Yr | Tm | W | Sv | IP | K | ERA | xERA | WHIP | oOPS | vL | vR | BF/G | Ctl | Dom | Cmd | FpK | SwK | Vel | G | L | F | H% | S% | hr/f | GS | APC | DOM% | DIS% | Sv% | LI | RAR | BPV | BPX | R$ |
|---|---|---|---|---|---|---|---|---|---|---|---|---|---|---|---|---|---|---|---|---|---|---|---|---|---|---|---|---|---|---|---|---|---|---|
| 14 | | | | | | | | | | | | | | | | | | | | | | | | | | | | | | | | | | |
| 15 | aa | 9 | 0 | 158 | 114 | 3.95 | 3.82 | 1.31 | | | | 24.2 | 2.5 | 6.5 | 2.6 | | | | | | | 32% | 70% | | | | | | | | 0.3 | 76 | 91 | $3 |
| 16 | CLE * | 14 | 0 | 146 | 119 | 4.73 | 4.91 | 1.53 | 768 | 505 | 976 | 18.7 | 4.3 | 7.4 | 1.7 | 61% | 10% | 93.4 | 38 | 22 | 40 | 31% | 72% | 13% | 10 | 57 | 0% | 60% | 0 | 0.84 | -9.8 | 45 | 54 | -$2 |
| 17 | CLE * | 15 | 0 | 156 | 167 | 3.27 | 3.63 | 1.32 | 667 | 819 | 570 | 19.0 | 4.4 | 9.6 | 2.2 | 63% | 13% | 92.5 | 39 | 24 | 36 | 29% | 79% | 12% | 21 | 78 | 33% | 24% | 0 | 0.71 | 20.8 | 83 | 100 | $15 |
| 18 | CLE | 13 | 0 | 200 | 207 | 3.02 | 3.85 | 1.16 | 655 | 726 | 586 | 25.3 | 3.0 | 9.3 | 3.1 | 64% | 12% | 93.6 | 40 | 20 | 39 | 29% | 78% | 10% | 32 | 102 | 31% | 13% | | | 28.0 | 104 | 120 | $22 |
| 1st Half | | 6 | 0 | 104 | 94 | 3.03 | 3.98 | 1.18 | 649 | 638 | 657 | 26.2 | 2.9 | 8.1 | 2.8 | 67% | 11% | 93.1 | 45 | 19 | 37 | 29% | 76% | 7% | 16 | 104 | 38% | 19% | | | 14.4 | 90 | 103 | $19 |
| 2nd Half | | 7 | 0 | 96 | 113 | 3.00 | 3.70 | 1.13 | 662 | 803 | 494 | 24.4 | 3.1 | 10.6 | 3.4 | 60% | 13% | 94.2 | 36 | 22 | 42 | 28% | 81% | 14% | 16 | 100 | 25% | 6% | | | 13.6 | 121 | 139 | $25 |
| **19** | **Proj** | **15** | **0** | **189** | **192** | **3.43** | **3.75** | **1.22** | **685** | **737** | **641** | **24.3** | **3.3** | **9.2** | **2.7** | **63%** | **12%** | **93.3** | **39** | **22** | **39** | **29%** | **76%** | **11%** | **31** | | | | | | **9.4** | **92** | **105** | **$17** |

## Clippard,Tyler

| | | | | | |
|---|---|---|---|---|---|
| Age: 34 | Th: R | Role: RP | Health: A | LIMA Plan: B+ | |
| Ht: 6' 3" | Wt: 200 | Type: Pwr xFB | PT/Exp: C | Rand Var: 0 | |
| | | | Consist: A | MM: 2510 | |

Fell briefly into closer's gig, blowing 6 of 13 chances before returning to setup role. Ctl moved back to palatable levels, and career-high FpK says it could stick. Extreme FB% with mediocre hr/f keep xERA over 4.00 though, limiting chances at closing games again. Unappealing fantasy option at this point.

| Yr | Tm | W | Sv | IP | K | ERA | xERA | WHIP | oOPS | vL | vR | BF/G | Ctl | Dom | Cmd | FpK | SwK | Vel | G | L | F | H% | S% | hr/f | GS | APC | DOM% | DIS% | Sv% | LI | RAR | BPV | BPX | R$ |
|---|---|---|---|---|---|---|---|---|---|---|---|---|---|---|---|---|---|---|---|---|---|---|---|---|---|---|---|---|---|---|---|---|---|---|
| 14 | WAS | 7 | 1 | 70 | 82 | 2.18 | 3.26 | 1.00 | 541 | 642 | 423 | 3.7 | 2.9 | 10.5 | 3.6 | 63% | 15% | 91.8 | 37 | 14 | 49 | 27% | 82% | 6% | 0 | 15 | | | 14 | 1.34 | 13.6 | 124 | 148 | $10 |
| 15 | 2 TM | 5 | 19 | 71 | 64 | 2.92 | 4.96 | 1.13 | 599 | 468 | 745 | 4.4 | 3.9 | 8.1 | 2.1 | 56% | 12% | 91.5 | 21 | 18 | 61 | 23% | 79% | 7% | 0 | 18 | | | 76 | 1.25 | 9.2 | 39 | 46 | $13 |
| 16 | 2 TM | 4 | 3 | 63 | 72 | 3.57 | 4.22 | 1.27 | 716 | 753 | 679 | 3.8 | 3.7 | 10.3 | 2.8 | 57% | 13% | 91.1 | 31 | 19 | 50 | 29% | 79% | 13% | 0 | 15 | | | 50 | 1.05 | 4.8 | 94 | 112 | $3 |
| 17 | 3 AL | 2 | 5 | 60 | 72 | 4.77 | 4.66 | 1.29 | 711 | 677 | 735 | 3.9 | 4.6 | 10.7 | 2.3 | 59% | 14% | 91.1 | 32 | 17 | 51 | 27% | 68% | 13% | 0 | 17 | | | 45 | 1.11 | -3.1 | 78 | 94 | $1 |
| 18 | TOR | 4 | 7 | 69 | 85 | 3.67 | 4.25 | 1.17 | 719 | 597 | 824 | 3.9 | 3.0 | 11.1 | 3.7 | 65% | 15% | 90.9 | 19 | 20 | 60 | 29% | 78% | 13% | 1 | 16 | 0% | 100% | 54 | 1.02 | 4.1 | 116 | 134 | $6 |
| 1st Half | | 4 | 5 | 39 | 46 | 3.20 | 4.52 | 1.14 | 692 | 584 | 788 | 3.9 | 3.7 | 10.5 | 2.9 | 65% | 15% | 91.0 | 20 | 17 | 64 | 25% | 82% | 11% | 0 | 16 | | | 56 | 1.13 | 4.6 | 88 | 102 | $10 |
| 2nd Half | | 0 | 2 | 29 | 39 | 4.30 | 3.91 | 1.19 | 755 | 613 | 866 | 3.9 | 2.1 | 12.0 | 5.6 | 65% | 16% | 90.9 | 18 | 25 | 57 | 33% | 72% | 14% | 1 | 16 | 0% | 100% | 50 | 0.88 | -0.5 | 154 | 177 | $1 |
| **19** | **Proj** | **4** | **3** | **65** | **79** | **3.91** | **3.82** | **1.21** | **708** | **638** | **767** | **3.7** | **3.4** | **10.9** | **3.2** | **62%** | **15%** | **91.1** | **25** | **19** | **55** | **29%** | **75%** | **13%** | **0** | | | | | | **3.2** | **106** | **122** | **$3** |

BRIAN SLACK

## Cobb,Alex

| Cobb,Alex | | | | Health | F | LIMA Plan | C |
|---|---|---|---|---|---|---|---|
| Age: 31 | Th: R | Role | SP | PT/Exp | B | Rand Var | +2 |
| Ht: 6' 3" | Wt: 205 | Type | | Consist | F | MM | 1003 |

2017 xERA foretold of ERA downturn, while underlying skills stayed stagnant, putting 2013-14 peak further into rear view. Post-All-Star break return of once-nasty splitter offers glimmer of hope, but tidy 2nd half ERA mostly the product of S%/H% good fortune. Unless Dom/SwK recovers, probably best to watch from afar.

| Yr Tm | W | Sv | IP | K | ERA | xERA | WHIP | oOPS | vL | vR | BF/G | Ctl | Dom | Cmd | FpK | SwK | Vel | G | L | F | H% | S% | hr/f | GS | APC | DOM% | DIS% | Sv% | LI | RAR | BPV | BPX | R$ |
|---|---|---|---|---|---|---|---|---|---|---|---|---|---|---|---|---|---|---|---|---|---|---|---|---|---|---|---|---|---|---|---|---|---|
| 14 TAM | 10 | 0 | 166 | 149 | 2.87 | 3.16 | 1.14 | 619 | 590 | 646 | 25.2 | 2.5 | 8.1 | 3.2 | 59% | 11% | 91.7 | 56 | 16 | 27 | 29% | 76% | 9% | 27 | 97 | 44% | 22% | | | 17.9 | 110 | 132 | $14 |
| 15 | | | | | | | | | | | | | | | | | | | | | | | | | | | | | | | | | |
| 16 TAM * | 1 | 0 | 37 | 24 | 9.18 | 9.27 | 2.12 | 968 | 1206 | 737 | 20.3 | 3.2 | 5.8 | 1.8 | 65% | 8% | 90.4 | 53 | 19 | 29 | 41% | 59% | 22% | 5 | 77 | 20% | 60% | | | -22.8 | -15 | -18 | -$15 |
| 17 TAM | 12 | 0 | 179 | 128 | 3.66 | 4.27 | 1.22 | 709 | 678 | 731 | 25.6 | 2.2 | 6.4 | 2.9 | 59% | 7% | 91.7 | 48 | 22 | 30 | 29% | 74% | 13% | 29 | 98 | 38% | 17% | | | 15.4 | 82 | 98 | $14 |
| 18 BAL | 5 | 0 | 152 | 102 | 4.90 | 4.57 | 1.41 | 814 | 771 | 857 | 23.6 | 2.5 | 6.0 | 2.4 | 60% | 8% | 92.0 | 50 | 19 | 31 | 31% | 69% | 15% | 28 | 87 | 21% | 36% | | | -14.2 | 68 | 78 | -$7 |
| 1st Half | 2 | 0 | 75 | 50 | 6.75 | 4.83 | 1.67 | 937 | 971 | 908 | 24.5 | 2.5 | 6.0 | 2.4 | 60% | 7% | 92.0 | 51 | 18 | 31 | 36% | 62% | 17% | 14 | 89 | 21% | 43% | | | -23.9 | 69 | 79 | -$25 |
| 2nd Half | 3 | 0 | 78 | 52 | 3.13 | 4.31 | 1.16 | 681 | 591 | 789 | 22.7 | 2.5 | 6.0 | 2.4 | 61% | 8% | 92.0 | 48 | 20 | 32 | 26% | 79% | 13% | 14 | 85 | 21% | 29% | | | 9.8 | 66 | 75 | $11 |
| **19 Proj** | **8** | **0** | **174** | **122** | **4.46** | **4.15** | **1.42** | **817** | **771** | **859** | **22.9** | **2.6** | **6.3** | **2.5** | **60%** | **8%** | **91.8** | **50** | **20** | **30** | **32%** | **73%** | **15%** | **32** | | | | | | **-6.7** | **72** | **83** | **-$2** |

## Cole,Gerrit

| Cole,Gerrit | | | | Health | D | LIMA Plan | D+ |
|---|---|---|---|---|---|---|---|
| Age: 28 | Th: R | Role | SP | PT/Exp | A | Rand Var | 0 |
| Ht: 6' 4" | Wt: 225 | Type | Pwr FB | Consist | B | MM | 4505 |

Former #1 pick re-established himself among elite SP as SwK/Dom soared, FpK stayed pretty, and 200 IP threshold met for 3rd time in four years. Dropped sinkers for more four-seam fastballs upon move to HOU, so GB/FB trade-off now likely part of the package. A prime foundational piece to anchor your staff.

| Yr Tm | W | Sv | IP | K | ERA | xERA | WHIP | oOPS | vL | vR | BF/G | Ctl | Dom | Cmd | FpK | SwK | Vel | G | L | F | H% | S% | hr/f | GS | APC | DOM% | DIS% | Sv% | LI | RAR | BPV | BPX | R$ |
|---|---|---|---|---|---|---|---|---|---|---|---|---|---|---|---|---|---|---|---|---|---|---|---|---|---|---|---|---|---|---|---|---|---|
| 14 PIT * | 14 | 0 | 160 | 151 | 3.44 | 3.33 | 1.21 | 693 | 729 | 659 | 24.9 | 2.5 | 8.5 | 3.4 | 62% | 10% | 95.5 | 49 | 19 | 32 | 31% | 73% | 9% | 22 | 100 | 45% | 14% | | | 6.0 | 107 | 128 | $10 |
| 15 PIT | 19 | 0 | 208 | 202 | 2.60 | 3.16 | 1.09 | 623 | 597 | 648 | 26.0 | 1.9 | 8.7 | 4.6 | 62% | 11% | 95.6 | 48 | 22 | 30 | 31% | 77% | 7% | 32 | 101 | 59% | 13% | | | 35.0 | 132 | 157 | $30 |
| 16 PIT | 7 | 0 | 116 | 98 | 3.88 | 4.15 | 1.44 | 754 | 870 | 652 | 24.1 | 2.8 | 7.6 | 2.7 | 60% | 9% | 95.2 | 46 | 25 | 29 | 35% | 73% | 7% | 21 | 92 | 24% | 29% | | | 4.4 | 85 | 102 | $1 |
| 17 PIT | 12 | 0 | 203 | 196 | 4.26 | 3.92 | 1.25 | 739 | 794 | 689 | 25.7 | 2.4 | 8.7 | 3.6 | 63% | 10% | 96.0 | 46 | 21 | 34 | 31% | 71% | 16% | 33 | 100 | 24% | 18% | | | 2.6 | 115 | 138 | $12 |
| 18 HOU | 15 | 0 | 200 | 276 | 2.88 | 3.13 | 1.03 | 600 | 519 | 676 | 25.0 | 2.9 | 12.4 | 4.3 | 63% | 15% | 96.6 | 36 | 21 | 43 | 30% | 76% | 10% | 32 | 102 | 50% | 0% | | | 31.5 | 160 | 184 | $31 |
| 1st Half | 9 | 0 | 112 | 151 | 2.50 | 3.08 | 0.92 | 561 | 566 | 557 | 25.4 | 2.9 | 12.2 | 4.2 | 64% | 14% | 96.3 | 35 | 20 | 44 | 25% | 80% | 13% | 17 | 104 | 59% | 0% | | | 22.7 | 154 | 177 | $41 |
| 2nd Half | 6 | 0 | 89 | 125 | 3.35 | 3.19 | 1.17 | 646 | 463 | 811 | 24.5 | 2.8 | 12.7 | 4.5 | 63% | 16% | 96.8 | 37 | 22 | 41 | 36% | 72% | 7% | 15 | 100 | 40% | 0% | | | 8.8 | 166 | 191 | $19 |
| **19 Proj** | **16** | **0** | **203** | **242** | **3.23** | **3.22** | **1.14** | **652** | **632** | **672** | **24.0** | **2.7** | **10.7** | **4.0** | **63%** | **13%** | **96.1** | **38** | **22** | **40** | **31%** | **75%** | **10%** | **33** | | | | | | **23.1** | **137** | **157** | **$25** |

## Colome,Alexander

| Colome,Alexander | | | | Health | B | LIMA Plan | B |
|---|---|---|---|---|---|---|---|
| Age: 30 | Th: R | Role | RP | PT/Exp | A | Rand Var | 0 |
| Ht: 6' 1" | Wt: 220 | Type | Pwr | Consist | C | MM | 4310 |

Began season 11-for-13 in Sv chances for TAM, only to be shipped to SEA, where setup role awaited. Cutter reliance (55% usage, 23% SwK) fell back closer to breakout 2016 levels (48%, 25%, respectively), and SwK/FpK growth means return to 4.0 Cmd can't be ruled out. A capable closer, if opportunity arises.

| Yr Tm | W | Sv | IP | K | ERA | xERA | WHIP | oOPS | vL | vR | BF/G | Ctl | Dom | Cmd | FpK | SwK | Vel | G | L | F | H% | S% | hr/f | GS | APC | DOM% | DIS% | Sv% | LI | RAR | BPV | BPX | R$ |
|---|---|---|---|---|---|---|---|---|---|---|---|---|---|---|---|---|---|---|---|---|---|---|---|---|---|---|---|---|---|---|---|---|---|
| 14 TAM * | 9 | 0 | 110 | 73 | 4.36 | 4.12 | 1.49 | 590 | 566 | 612 | 23.6 | 3.5 | 6.0 | 1.7 | 67% | 9% | 94.2 | 38 | 22 | 41 | 33% | 69% | 3% | 3 | 77 | 67% | 0% | 0 | 0.68 | -8.4 | 64 | 76 | -$4 |
| 15 TAM | 8 | 0 | 110 | 88 | 3.94 | 4.06 | 1.30 | 698 | 736 | 658 | 10.6 | 2.5 | 7.2 | 2.8 | 62% | 11% | 94.1 | 40 | 25 | 35 | 32% | 71% | 8% | 13 | 40 | 8% | 38% | 0 | 1.06 | 0.3 | 79 | 94 | $2 |
| 16 TAM | 2 | 37 | 57 | 71 | 1.91 | 2.86 | 1.02 | 572 | 479 | 638 | 4.0 | 2.4 | 11.3 | 4.7 | 63% | 16% | 94.7 | 47 | 23 | 30 | 29% | 88% | 15% | 0 | 15 | | | 93 | 1.23 | 16.0 | 164 | 194 | $22 |
| 17 TAM | 2 | 47 | 67 | 58 | 3.24 | 4.25 | 1.20 | 636 | 677 | 596 | 4.3 | 3.1 | 7.8 | 2.5 | 60% | 12% | 95.1 | 49 | 18 | 34 | 29% | 74% | 6% | 0 | 15 | | | 89 | 1.41 | 9.2 | 84 | 101 | $23 |
| 18 2AL | 7 | 12 | 68 | 72 | 3.04 | 3.49 | 1.18 | 645 | 488 | 761 | 4.0 | 2.8 | 9.5 | 3.4 | 63% | 14% | 95.1 | 46 | 24 | 30 | 30% | 78% | 13% | 0 | 16 | | | 71 | 1.37 | 9.3 | 120 | 139 | $10 |
| 1st Half | 2 | 12 | 34 | 33 | 4.72 | 3.85 | 1.37 | 735 | 541 | 885 | 4.1 | 2.9 | 8.7 | 3.0 | 64% | 13% | 95.1 | 47 | 27 | 25 | 33% | 67% | 15% | 0 | 16 | | | 75 | 1.39 | -2.4 | 103 | 118 | $5 |
| 2nd Half | 5 | 0 | 34 | 39 | 1.34 | 3.15 | 0.98 | 539 | 424 | 621 | 3.9 | 2.7 | 10.4 | 3.9 | 62% | 15% | 95.2 | 45 | 20 | 35 | 26% | 93% | 11% | 0 | 15 | | | 0 | 1.36 | 11.7 | 138 | 159 | $15 |
| **19 Proj** | **5** | **4** | **65** | **68** | **2.99** | **3.25** | **1.15** | **637** | **570** | **693** | **4.3** | **2.7** | **9.4** | **3.5** | **62%** | **14%** | **95.0** | **46** | **22** | **32** | **30%** | **78%** | **12%** | **0** | | | | | | **9.3** | **122** | **140** | **$7** |

## Colon,Bartolo

| Colon,Bartolo | | | | Health | D | LIMA Plan | D+ |
|---|---|---|---|---|---|---|---|
| Age: 46 | Th: R | Role | SP | PT/Exp | A | Rand Var | +5 |
| Ht: 5' 11" | Wt: 285 | Type | Con | Consist | B | MM | 0001 |

21-year veteran got off to a solid start (3.55 ERA, 5.7 Cmd in April/May), only to post second consecutive season of negative R$ while finishing out year in bullpen. Despite an expressed desire to keep playing, this may be the end of the road; even if not, you'd be best served to steer clear.

| Yr Tm | W | Sv | IP | K | ERA | xERA | WHIP | oOPS | vL | vR | BF/G | Ctl | Dom | Cmd | FpK | SwK | Vel | G | L | F | H% | S% | hr/f | GS | APC | DOM% | DIS% | Sv% | LI | RAR | BPV | BPX | R$ |
|---|---|---|---|---|---|---|---|---|---|---|---|---|---|---|---|---|---|---|---|---|---|---|---|---|---|---|---|---|---|---|---|---|---|
| 14 NYM | 15 | 0 | 202 | 151 | 4.09 | 3.82 | 1.23 | 716 | 681 | 755 | 27.3 | 1.3 | 6.7 | 5.0 | 66% | 6% | 88.7 | 39 | 22 | 39 | 32% | 69% | 9% | 31 | 97 | 52% | 39% | | | -8.8 | 102 | 121 | $6 |
| 15 NYM | 14 | 0 | 195 | 136 | 4.16 | 4.05 | 1.24 | 741 | 735 | 748 | 24.7 | 1.1 | 6.3 | 5.7 | 66% | 7% | 88.3 | 42 | 21 | 37 | 32% | 70% | 11% | 31 | 82 | 29% | 35% | 0 | 0.76 | -4.8 | 103 | 123 | $7 |
| 16 NYM | 15 | 0 | 192 | 128 | 3.43 | 4.28 | 1.21 | 729 | 795 | 664 | 23.3 | 1.5 | 6.0 | 4.0 | 63% | 6% | 87.9 | 43 | 23 | 34 | 30% | 76% | 11% | 33 | 84 | 24% | 30% | 0 | 0.78 | 18.0 | 89 | 105 | $15 |
| 17 2TM | 7 | 0 | 143 | 89 | 6.48 | 5.40 | 1.59 | 909 | 910 | 908 | 23.1 | 2.2 | 5.6 | 2.5 | 65% | 6% | 87.8 | 42 | 19 | 39 | 34% | 62% | 14% | 28 | 82 | 11% | 61% | | | -37.5 | 61 | 74 | -$15 |
| 18 TEX | 7 | 0 | 146 | 81 | 5.78 | 4.84 | 1.35 | 866 | 774 | 942 | 22.4 | 1.5 | 5.0 | 3.2 | 64% | 6% | 87.4 | 42 | 23 | 35 | 30% | 62% | 18% | 24 | 80 | 13% | 67% | 0 | 0.68 | -29.4 | 68 | 78 | -$9 |
| 1st Half | 5 | 0 | 93 | 56 | 4.76 | 4.49 | 1.22 | 803 | 782 | 819 | 22.8 | 1.5 | 5.4 | 3.7 | 64% | 6% | 87.5 | 44 | 22 | 34 | 28% | 69% | 19% | 15 | 82 | 20% | 60% | 0 | 0.70 | -7.0 | 81 | 92 | -$4 |
| 2nd Half | 2 | 0 | 54 | 25 | 7.55 | 5.44 | 1.57 | 967 | 763 | 1156 | 21.9 | 1.7 | 4.2 | 2.5 | 63% | 5% | 87.3 | 39 | 24 | 37 | 33% | 54% | 16% | 9 | 76 | 0% | 78% | 0 | 0.65 | -22.5 | 47 | 54 | -$23 |
| **19 Proj** | **5** | **0** | **94** | **50** | **5.95** | **4.73** | **1.47** | **894** | **831** | **953** | **29.1** | **2.0** | **4.8** | **2.4** | **63%** | **5%** | **87.7** | **42** | **22** | **36** | **31%** | **64%** | **16%** | **14** | | | | | | **-3.6** | **53** | **61** | **-$9** |

## Conley,Adam

| Conley,Adam | | | | Health | B | LIMA Plan | B+ |
|---|---|---|---|---|---|---|---|
| Age: 29 | Th: L | Role | RP | PT/Exp | C | Rand Var | +2 |
| Ht: 6' 3" | Wt: 200 | Type | Pwr | Consist | C | MM | 2211 |

3-4, 4.09 ERA with 3 Sv in 51 IP at MIA. Failed SP looked much improved after transition to bullpen, with noticeable boost in velocity/SwK, plus MLB Dom was 8.9. Snagged a few Sv, and while nothing points to impending stint as closer, could emerge as a weapon—just more likely in real-life than fantasy.

| Yr Tm | W | Sv | IP | K | ERA | xERA | WHIP | oOPS | vL | vR | BF/G | Ctl | Dom | Cmd | FpK | SwK | Vel | G | L | F | H% | S% | hr/f | GS | APC | DOM% | DIS% | Sv% | LI | RAR | BPV | BPX | R$ |
|---|---|---|---|---|---|---|---|---|---|---|---|---|---|---|---|---|---|---|---|---|---|---|---|---|---|---|---|---|---|---|---|---|---|
| 14 aaa | 3 | 0 | 60 | 39 | 6.12 | 4.57 | 1.57 | | | | 21.9 | 3.7 | 5.9 | 1.6 | | | | | | | 34% | 58% | | | | | | | | -17.6 | 55 | 65 | -$9 |
| 15 MIA * | 13 | 0 | 174 | 123 | 3.51 | 3.72 | 1.35 | 723 | 767 | 714 | 21.3 | 3.3 | 6.4 | 1.9 | 58% | 11% | 91.3 | 41 | 19 | 41 | 30% | 75% | 9% | 11 | 73 | 18% | 36% | 0 | 0.72 | 9.6 | 65 | 77 | $7 |
| 16 MIA | 8 | 0 | 133 | 124 | 3.85 | 4.68 | 1.40 | 738 | 759 | 731 | 23.4 | 4.2 | 8.4 | 2.0 | 64% | 10% | 91.0 | 38 | 21 | 41 | 31% | 75% | 8% | 25 | 91 | 24% | 32% | | | 5.6 | 54 | 64 | $3 |
| 17 MIA * | 11 | 0 | 165 | 105 | 6.46 | 5.91 | 1.63 | 852 | 822 | 861 | 21.6 | 3.8 | 5.7 | 1.5 | 58% | 10% | 89.5 | 40 | 19 | 42 | 32% | 62% | 14% | 20 | 78 | 15% | 55% | 0 | 0.83 | -42.8 | 17 | 21 | -$16 |
| 18 MIA * | 5 | 3 | 91 | 69 | 5.15 | 4.59 | 1.39 | 642 | 584 | 687 | 6.4 | 3.3 | 6.9 | 2.1 | 62% | 15% | 95.3 | 44 | 20 | 36 | 30% | 65% | 11% | 0 | 15 | | | 60 | 1.26 | -11.2 | 53 | 61 | -$4 |
| 1st Half | 4 | 0 | 57 | 37 | 5.00 | 5.37 | 1.49 | 537 | 490 | 579 | 9.9 | 3.1 | 5.9 | 1.9 | 65% | 15% | 94.8 | 50 | 21 | 29 | 32% | 69% | 17% | 0 | 15 | | | 0 | 0.83 | -6.0 | 33 | 38 | -$7 |
| 2nd Half | 1 | 3 | 33 | 32 | 5.40 | 4.22 | 1.23 | 692 | 633 | 736 | 3.9 | 3.8 | 8.6 | 2.3 | 61% | 15% | 95.5 | 42 | 19 | 39 | 28% | 55% | 9% | 0 | 15 | | | 60 | 1.47 | -5.1 | 73 | 84 | -$1 |
| **19 Proj** | **4** | **7** | **73** | **66** | **4.30** | **3.96** | **1.27** | **739** | **675** | **771** | **8.1** | **3.2** | **8.2** | **2.6** | **61%** | **13%** | **92.8** | **42** | **20** | **38** | **29%** | **69%** | **12%** | **0** | | | | | | **1.5** | **81** | **93** | **$3** |

## Corbin,Patrick

| Corbin,Patrick | | | | Health | D | LIMA Plan | C |
|---|---|---|---|---|---|---|---|
| Age: 29 | Th: L | Role | SP | PT/Exp | A | Rand Var | 0 |
| Ht: 6' 3" | Wt: 210 | Type | Pwr | Consist | B | MM | 5405 |

Topped 2017's strong 2nd half with ace-level season, as filthy slider (30% SwK) and new curveball (13% SwK) yielded huge SwK bump, while May velocity concerns never really affected bottom line. Lack of venue splits—.603 home OPS vs. .611 away—encouraging too. Even with slight pullback, an attractive asset.

| Yr Tm | W | Sv | IP | K | ERA | xERA | WHIP | oOPS | vL | vR | BF/G | Ctl | Dom | Cmd | FpK | SwK | Vel | G | L | F | H% | S% | hr/f | GS | APC | DOM% | DIS% | Sv% | LI | RAR | BPV | BPX | R$ |
|---|---|---|---|---|---|---|---|---|---|---|---|---|---|---|---|---|---|---|---|---|---|---|---|---|---|---|---|---|---|---|---|---|---|
| 14 | | | | | | | | | | | | | | | | | | | | | | | | | | | | | | | | | |
| 15 ARI * | 7 | 0 | 101 | 87 | 3.63 | 4.07 | 1.28 | 743 | 574 | 788 | 21.9 | 2.0 | 7.7 | 3.9 | 61% | 11% | 92.4 | 47 | 23 | 30 | 33% | 74% | 12% | 16 | 78 | 25% | 19% | | | 4.2 | 100 | 119 | $3 |
| 16 ARI | 5 | 1 | 156 | 131 | 5.15 | 4.34 | 1.56 | 825 | 743 | 851 | 19.5 | 3.8 | 7.6 | 2.0 | 57% | 10% | 91.7 | 54 | 19 | 27 | 33% | 70% | 18% | 24 | 71 | 21% | 42% | 100 | 0.89 | -18.4 | 65 | 78 | -$9 |
| 17 ARI | 14 | 0 | 190 | 178 | 4.03 | 4.06 | 1.42 | 792 | 651 | 830 | 25.0 | 2.9 | 8.4 | 2.9 | 62% | 11% | 92.4 | 50 | 20 | 30 | 34% | 76% | 15% | 32 | 93 | 31% | 28% | 0 | 0.76 | 7.6 | 102 | 122 | $8 |
| 18 ARI | 11 | 0 | 200 | 246 | 3.15 | 2.81 | 1.05 | 607 | 692 | 583 | 24.2 | 2.2 | 11.1 | 5.1 | 64% | 16% | 90.8 | 48 | 24 | 27 | 32% | 72% | 11% | 33 | 95 | 39% | 0% | | | 24.7 | 167 | 192 | $25 |
| 1st Half | 6 | 0 | 106 | 134 | 3.14 | 2.84 | 0.99 | 586 | 767 | 538 | 24.6 | 2.4 | 11.4 | 4.8 | 63% | 15% | 90.5 | 46 | 25 | 30 | 29% | 72% | 15% | 17 | 96 | 41% | 0% | | | 13.2 | 164 | 189 | $29 |
| 2nd Half | 5 | 0 | 94 | 112 | 3.16 | 2.79 | 1.12 | 629 | 617 | 632 | 23.8 | 1.9 | 10.7 | 5.6 | 65% | 17% | 91.1 | 51 | 24 | 24 | 35% | 71% | 7% | 16 | 94 | 38% | 0% | | | 11.5 | 171 | 196 | $21 |
| **19 Proj** | **13** | **0** | **189** | **209** | **3.53** | **2.96** | **1.17** | **674** | **640** | **684** | **22.2** | **2.4** | **10.0** | **4.3** | **62%** | **14%** | **91.5** | **50** | **22** | **28** | **32%** | **73%** | **14%** | **34** | | | | | | **30.8** | **144** | **166** | **$18** |

## Covey,Dylan

| Covey,Dylan | | | | Health | D | LIMA Plan | D+ |
|---|---|---|---|---|---|---|---|
| Age: 27 | Th: R | Role | SP | PT/Exp | D | Rand Var | +1 |
| Ht: 6' 2" | Wt: 195 | Type | GB | Consist | C | MM | 0001 |

5-14, 5.18 ERA in 122 IP at CHW. Some early success with velocity uptick and increased sinker usage, then moved to/from bullpen as numbers tanked. Career MLB stats: 5-21, 6.10 ERA, 1.55 WHIP in roughly full season's IP. But really, alarming DIS% says it all. Stack against him in DFS.

| Yr Tm | W | Sv | IP | K | ERA | xERA | WHIP | oOPS | vL | vR | BF/G | Ctl | Dom | Cmd | FpK | SwK | Vel | G | L | F | H% | S% | hr/f | GS | APC | DOM% | DIS% | Sv% | LI | RAR | BPV | BPX | R$ |
|---|---|---|---|---|---|---|---|---|---|---|---|---|---|---|---|---|---|---|---|---|---|---|---|---|---|---|---|---|---|---|---|---|---|
| 14 | | | | | | | | | | | | | | | | | | | | | | | | | | | | | | | | | |
| 15 | | | | | | | | | | | | | | | | | | | | | | | | | | | | | | | | | |
| 16 aa | 2 | 0 | 29 | 20 | 2.33 | 3.76 | 1.46 | | | | 20.9 | 5.4 | 6.2 | 1.2 | | | | | | | 27% | 86% | | | | | | | | 6.7 | 51 | 60 | -$2 |
| 17 CHW | 0 | 0 | 70 | 41 | 7.71 | 5.62 | 1.67 | 979 | 894 | 1055 | 17.2 | 4.4 | 5.3 | 1.2 | 56% | 7% | 92.6 | 48 | 16 | 35 | 29% | 59% | 25% | 12 | 64 | 0% | 58% | 0 | 0.66 | -29.0 | 3 | 3 | -$16 |
| 18 CHW * | 8 | 0 | 162 | 119 | 4.63 | 4.68 | 1.47 | 733 | 790 | 669 | 20.4 | 3.8 | 6.6 | 1.7 | 60% | 7% | 94.1 | 55 | 20 | 25 | 31% | 70% | 13% | 21 | 76 | 24% | 52% | 0 | 0.79 | -9.5 | 49 | 56 | -$5 |
| 1st Half | 6 | 0 | 87 | 64 | 3.96 | 4.88 | 1.51 | 756 | 848 | 633 | 23.5 | 4.2 | 6.6 | 1.6 | 60% | 8% | 93.9 | 58 | 15 | 27 | 31% | 77% | 15% | 9 | 87 | 33% | 56% | | | 2.0 | 43 | 50 | -$2 |
| 2nd Half | 2 | 0 | 75 | 55 | 5.40 | 4.37 | 1.43 | 719 | 748 | 689 | 18.4 | 3.5 | 6.6 | 1.9 | 60% | 7% | 94.3 | 53 | 23 | 24 | 31% | 62% | 12% | 12 | 70 | 17% | 50% | 0 | 0.78 | -11.6 | 56 | 65 | -$9 |
| **19 Proj** | **3** | **0** | **102** | **69** | **4.98** | **4.59** | **1.54** | **808** | **806** | **810** | **27.5** | **4.0** | **6.1** | **1.5** | **58%** | **7%** | **93.5** | **53** | **18** | **29** | **31%** | **71%** | **17%** | **11** | | | | | | **-3.7** | **32** | **37** | **-$8** |

BRIAN SLACK

## Crick,Kyle

| | | | | | |
|---|---|---|---|---|---|
| Age: 26 | Th: R | Role RP | Health | A | LIMA Plan B |
| Ht: 6' 4" | Wt: 220 | Type Pwr | PT/Exp | D | Rand Var -4 |
| | | | Consist | D | MM 1300 |

Prospect of some note with SF enjoyed productive PIT debut, working into higher-leverage situations as season wore on. Ctl issues part of MiLB profile, and while those might appear somewhat cured, take a peek at that unsightly FpK. Even with strikeout ability, hard to view him as closer-in-waiting at this point.

| Yr Tm | W | Sv | IP | K | ERA | xERA | WHIP | oOPS | vL | vR | BF/G | Ctl | Dom | Cmd | FpK | SwK | Vel | G | L | F | H% | S% | hr/f | GS | APC | DOM% | DIS% | Sv% | LI | RAR | BPV | BPX | R$ |
|---|---|---|---|---|---|---|---|---|---|---|---|---|---|---|---|---|---|---|---|---|---|---|---|---|---|---|---|---|---|---|---|---|---|
| 14 aa | 6 | 0 | 90 | 97 | 4.10 | 4.19 | 1.59 | | | | 17.3 | 5.9 | 9.6 | 1.6 | | | | | | | 33% | 74% | | | | | | | | -4.0 | 80 | 96 | -$4 |
| 15 aa | 3 | 0 | 63 | 63 | 4.37 | 4.96 | 2.03 | | | | 8.5 | 10.2 | 9.0 | 0.9 | | | | | | | 32% | 77% | | | | | | | | -3.2 | 70 | 84 | -$10 |
| 16 aa | 4 | 0 | 109 | 72 | 6.63 | 5.84 | 1.89 | | | | 22.3 | 6.0 | 5.9 | 1.0 | | | | | | | 35% | 64% | | | | | | | | -32.8 | 31 | 37 | -$20 |
| 17 SF * | 1 | 6 | 62 | 60 | 3.20 | 3.04 | 1.31 | 596 | 524 | 648 | 4.7 | 4.4 | 8.7 | 2.0 | 56% | 12% | 95.5 | 38 | 16 | 46 | 29% | 76% | 5% | 0 | 20 | | | 55 | 0.56 | 8.8 | 91 | 109 | $3 |
| 18 PIT | 3 | 2 | 60 | 65 | 2.39 | 3.80 | 1.13 | 569 | 673 | 475 | 4.0 | 3.4 | 9.7 | 2.8 | 52% | 12% | 95.9 | 40 | 25 | 35 | 29% | 80% | 5% | 0 | 16 | | | 67 | 0.92 | 13.1 | 100 | 115 | $5 |
| 1st Half | 0 | 1 | 29 | 30 | 2.51 | 4.43 | 1.29 | 580 | 664 | 515 | 4.0 | 4.4 | 9.4 | 2.1 | 53% | 11% | 95.7 | 39 | 23 | 38 | 30% | 81% | 3% | 0 | 16 | | | 100 | 0.82 | 5.8 | 68 | 78 | $0 |
| 2nd Half | 3 | 1 | 32 | 35 | 2.27 | 3.26 | 0.98 | 558 | 680 | 429 | 3.9 | 2.6 | 9.9 | 3.9 | 51% | 13% | 96.1 | 41 | 28 | 32 | 27% | 79% | 8% | 0 | 16 | | | 50 | 1.02 | 7.3 | 128 | 148 | $11 |
| 19 Proj | 2 | 0 | 44 | 45 | 3.82 | 4.13 | 1.39 | 717 | 772 | 670 | 5.1 | 4.4 | 9.3 | 2.1 | 53% | 12% | 95.8 | 39 | 22 | 39 | 31% | 75% | 10% | 0 | | | | | | 1.8 | 64 | 74 | -$2 |

## Cueto,Johnny

| | | | | | |
|---|---|---|---|---|---|
| Age: 33 | Th: R | Role SP | Health | F | LIMA Plan B+ |
| Ht: 5' 11" | Wt: 229 | Type | PT/Exp | A | Rand Var -2 |
| | | | Consist | B | MM 2100 |

Frustrating season in four acts: 1) Sub-1.00 ERA through 5 starts, 2) Two-month DL stint with elbow strain, 3) Over-6.00 ERA in 4 July starts, 4) Season-ending Tommy John surgery in August. Still owns fine skills when healthy, but with return date uncertain, too many question marks to invest in re-draft leagues.

| Yr Tm | W | Sv | IP | K | ERA | xERA | WHIP | oOPS | vL | vR | BF/G | Ctl | Dom | Cmd | FpK | SwK | Vel | G | L | F | H% | S% | hr/f | GS | APC | DOM% | DIS% | Sv% | LI | RAR | BPV | BPX | R$ |
|---|---|---|---|---|---|---|---|---|---|---|---|---|---|---|---|---|---|---|---|---|---|---|---|---|---|---|---|---|---|---|---|---|---|
| 14 CIN | 20 | 0 | 244 | 242 | 2.25 | 3.07 | 0.96 | 574 | 561 | 585 | 28.3 | 2.4 | 8.9 | 3.7 | 63% | 10% | 93.1 | 46 | 19 | 35 | 25% | 82% | 10% | 34 | 108 | 56% | 6% | | | 44.7 | 120 | 143 | $38 |
| 15 2 TM | 11 | 0 | 212 | 176 | 3.44 | 3.76 | 1.13 | 675 | 598 | 743 | 27.1 | 2.0 | 7.5 | 3.8 | 63% | 10% | 92.5 | 43 | 22 | 36 | 29% | 73% | 9% | 32 | 102 | 34% | 28% | | | 13.7 | 103 | 122 | $17 |
| 16 SF | 18 | 0 | 220 | 198 | 2.79 | 3.42 | 1.09 | 633 | 670 | 601 | 27.5 | 1.8 | 8.1 | 4.4 | 68% | 10% | 91.5 | 50 | 21 | 29 | 30% | 76% | 8% | 32 | 103 | 53% | 16% | | | 38.0 | 124 | 148 | $30 |
| 17 SF | 8 | 0 | 147 | 136 | 4.52 | 4.53 | 1.45 | 814 | 833 | 793 | 25.9 | 3.2 | 8.3 | 2.6 | 64% | 11% | 91.3 | 39 | 25 | 36 | 33% | 73% | 14% | 25 | 101 | 20% | 40% | | | -2.9 | 79 | 95 | $0 |
| 18 SF | 3 | 0 | 53 | 38 | 3.23 | 4.21 | 1.11 | 702 | 701 | 703 | 23.8 | 2.2 | 6.5 | 2.9 | 63% | 10% | 89.4 | 44 | 19 | 37 | 25% | 78% | 14% | 9 | 88 | 33% | 56% | | | 6.0 | 79 | 90 | $1 |
| 1st Half | 3 | 0 | 32 | 26 | 0.84 | 3.45 | 0.69 | 421 | 394 | 451 | 23.4 | 1.7 | 7.3 | 4.3 | 63% | 11% | 90.2 | 45 | 18 | 38 | 19% | 90% | 3% | 5 | 95 | 60% | 40% | | | 13.1 | 109 | 125 | $10 |
| 2nd Half | 0 | 0 | 21 | 12 | 6.86 | 5.45 | 1.76 | 1050 | 1240 | 921 | 24.3 | 3.0 | 5.1 | 1.7 | 63% | 8% | 88.4 | 42 | 22 | 36 | 33% | 70% | 26% | 4 | 79 | 0% | 75% | | | -7.0 | 31 | 36 | -$12 |
| 19 Proj | 1 | 0 | 29 | 23 | 4.06 | 4.03 | 1.30 | 777 | 805 | 751 | 24.6 | 2.5 | 7.1 | 2.8 | 64% | 10% | 90.4 | 43 | 21 | 35 | 30% | 75% | 15% | 5 | | | | | | 0.3 | 81 | 93 | -$3 |

## Darvish,Yu

| | | | | | |
|---|---|---|---|---|---|
| Age: 32 | Th: R | Role SP | Health | F | LIMA Plan C+ |
| Ht: 6' 5" | Wt: 220 | Type Pwr | PT/Exp | C | Rand Var +3 |
| | | | Consist | A | MM 3503 |

Shelved in May with arm injury, then relatively minor elbow surgery in Aug; expecting full health by spring training. Velocity remained, BPX/Cmd history keeps ceiling intact, and should come cheap(er). Then again, F Health grade mostly arm-related, and what if 2017 Ctl loss is real? A WIDE range of possible outcomes.

| Yr Tm | W | Sv | IP | K | ERA | xERA | WHIP | oOPS | vL | vR | BF/G | Ctl | Dom | Cmd | FpK | SwK | Vel | G | L | F | H% | S% | hr/f | GS | APC | DOM% | DIS% | Sv% | LI | RAR | BPV | BPX | R$ |
|---|---|---|---|---|---|---|---|---|---|---|---|---|---|---|---|---|---|---|---|---|---|---|---|---|---|---|---|---|---|---|---|---|---|
| 14 TEX | 10 | 0 | 144 | 182 | 3.06 | 3.18 | 1.26 | 679 | 721 | 605 | 27.5 | 3.1 | 11.3 | 3.7 | 62% | 11% | 92.4 | 36 | 23 | 41 | 35% | 79% | 9% | 22 | 105 | 50% | 9% | | | 12.2 | 136 | 162 | $10 |
| 15 | | | | | | | | | | | | | | | | | | | | | | | | | | | | | | | | | |
| 16 TEX * | 8 | 0 | 127 | 154 | 3.42 | 3.21 | 1.16 | 636 | 607 | 662 | 21.1 | 3.1 | 10.9 | 3.6 | 58% | 13% | 93.3 | 40 | 20 | 40 | 30% | 75% | 12% | 17 | 93 | 47% | 12% | | | 12.0 | 119 | 141 | $12 |
| 17 2 TM | 10 | 0 | 187 | 209 | 3.86 | 3.70 | 1.16 | 689 | 778 | 600 | 24.7 | 2.8 | 10.1 | 3.6 | 59% | 13% | 94.2 | 41 | 22 | 37 | 29% | 72% | 15% | 31 | 99 | 35% | 26% | | | 11.5 | 125 | 150 | $17 |
| 18 CHC | 1 | 0 | 40 | 49 | 4.95 | 4.15 | 1.43 | 766 | 842 | 692 | 22.5 | 4.7 | 11.0 | 2.3 | 55% | 11% | 93.9 | 38 | 23 | 40 | 31% | 70% | 18% | 8 | 93 | 13% | 50% | | | -3.9 | 87 | 100 | -$5 |
| 1st Half | 1 | 0 | 40 | 49 | 4.95 | 4.15 | 1.43 | 766 | 842 | 692 | 22.5 | 4.7 | 11.0 | 2.3 | 55% | 11% | 93.9 | 38 | 23 | 40 | 31% | 70% | 18% | 8 | 93 | 13% | 50% | | | -3.9 | 86 | 99 | -$5 |
| 2nd Half | | | | | | | | | | | | | | | | | | | | | | | | | | | | | | | | | |
| 19 Proj | 7 | 0 | 145 | 175 | 3.90 | 3.44 | 1.25 | 696 | 735 | 656 | 22.4 | 3.5 | 10.8 | 3.1 | 58% | 12% | 93.5 | 39 | 22 | 39 | 31% | 73% | 14% | 26 | | | | | | 4.4 | 118 | 135 | $8 |

## Davies,Zachary

| | | | | | |
|---|---|---|---|---|---|
| Age: 26 | Th: R | Role SP | Health | F | LIMA Plan B+ |
| Ht: 6' 0" | Wt: 155 | Type | PT/Exp | B | Rand Var +4 |
| | | | Consist | A | MM 1103 |

2-7, 4.77 ERA in 66 IP at MIL. Wins-driven R$ from 2017 took nosedive as shoulder/back issues plagued him much of the year. Enjoyed nice September, but history of single-digit SwK, underwhelming velocity caps K upside. S% should recover, and decent Ctl/GB combo keep him halfway relevant, though only in deep leagues.

| Yr Tm | W | Sv | IP | K | ERA | xERA | WHIP | oOPS | vL | vR | BF/G | Ctl | Dom | Cmd | FpK | SwK | Vel | G | L | F | H% | S% | hr/f | GS | APC | DOM% | DIS% | Sv% | LI | RAR | BPV | BPX | R$ |
|---|---|---|---|---|---|---|---|---|---|---|---|---|---|---|---|---|---|---|---|---|---|---|---|---|---|---|---|---|---|---|---|---|---|
| 14 aa | 10 | 0 | 110 | 94 | 3.70 | 3.98 | 1.32 | | | | 21.7 | 2.5 | 7.7 | 3.1 | | | | | | | 33% | 73% | | | | | | | | 0.6 | 90 | 107 | $3 |
| 15 MIL * | 9 | 0 | 162 | 112 | 3.53 | 3.71 | 1.36 | 614 | 434 | 740 | 22.6 | 3.2 | 6.2 | 1.9 | 60% | 11% | 88.8 | 58 | 21 | 21 | 31% | 74% | 10% | 6 | 90 | 33% | 50% | | | 8.7 | 67 | 80 | $4 |
| 16 MIL | 11 | 0 | 163 | 135 | 3.97 | 3.99 | 1.25 | 728 | 768 | 691 | 24.4 | 2.1 | 7.4 | 3.6 | 62% | 9% | 89.3 | 45 | 22 | 33 | 31% | 72% | 12% | 28 | 92 | 25% | 29% | | | 4.5 | 100 | 119 | $8 |
| 17 MIL | 17 | 0 | 191 | 124 | 3.90 | 4.48 | 1.35 | 755 | 787 | 724 | 24.8 | 2.6 | 5.8 | 2.3 | 57% | 8% | 89.7 | 50 | 23 | 27 | 31% | 74% | 12% | 33 | 94 | 12% | 48% | | | 10.7 | 63 | 76 | $10 |
| 18 MIL * | 3 | 0 | 94 | 70 | 5.35 | 4.46 | 1.43 | 768 | 782 | 753 | 20.0 | 3.6 | 6.7 | 1.9 | 58% | 9% | 89.9 | 48 | 22 | 30 | 31% | 63% | 13% | 13 | 86 | 8% | 38% | | | -13.9 | 54 | 62 | -$8 |
| 1st Half | 2 | 0 | 49 | 36 | 4.97 | 4.94 | 1.44 | 843 | 857 | 830 | 20.9 | 3.5 | 6.6 | 1.9 | 53% | 9% | 89.5 | 48 | 21 | 31 | 30% | 68% | 17% | 8 | 92 | 0% | 50% | | | -5.0 | 42 | 48 | -$9 |
| 2nd Half | 1 | 0 | 45 | 34 | 5.68 | 3.86 | 1.40 | 618 | 662 | 568 | 19.0 | 3.7 | 6.7 | 1.8 | 69% | 9% | 90.5 | 47 | 25 | 28 | 31% | 57% | 5% | 5 | 77 | 20% | 20% | | | -8.5 | 68 | 79 | -$7 |
| 19 Proj | 9 | 0 | 160 | 118 | 4.32 | 4.11 | 1.38 | 754 | 769 | 740 | 21.5 | 3.1 | 6.6 | 2.1 | 61% | 9% | 89.8 | 49 | 23 | 28 | 31% | 71% | 12% | 31 | | | | | | 0.7 | 63 | 72 | $1 |

## Davis,Wade

| | | | | | |
|---|---|---|---|---|---|
| Age: 33 | Th: R | Role RP | Health | C | LIMA Plan C+ |
| Ht: 6' 5" | Wt: 225 | Type Pwr | PT/Exp | B | Rand Var +1 |
| | | | Consist | A | MM 3530 |

NL Saves leader held role despite midseason rough patch and S% misfortune; claimed to have spotted mechanical flaw in early Aug. Don't let 2nd half Ctl fool you though, as FpK reached ulcer-inducing levels. Velocity fade continues and H% won't always be around to help. Leash should be long, just note the risk.

| Yr Tm | W | Sv | IP | K | ERA | xERA | WHIP | oOPS | vL | vR | BF/G | Ctl | Dom | Cmd | FpK | SwK | Vel | G | L | F | H% | S% | hr/f | GS | APC | DOM% | DIS% | Sv% | LI | RAR | BPV | BPX | R$ |
|---|---|---|---|---|---|---|---|---|---|---|---|---|---|---|---|---|---|---|---|---|---|---|---|---|---|---|---|---|---|---|---|---|---|
| 14 KC | 9 | 3 | 72 | 109 | 1.00 | 2.08 | 0.85 | 408 | 513 | 298 | 3.9 | 2.9 | 13.6 | 4.7 | 61% | 15% | 95.7 | 48 | 22 | 30 | 29% | 87% | 0% | 0 | 17 | | | 50 | 1.23 | 24.3 | 194 | 231 | $17 |
| 15 KC | 8 | 17 | 67 | 78 | 0.94 | 3.04 | 0.79 | 451 | 453 | 449 | 3.6 | 2.7 | 10.4 | 3.9 | 61% | 12% | 95.9 | 38 | 21 | 41 | 21% | 92% | 5% | 0 | 15 | | | 94 | 1.22 | 25.1 | 131 | 157 | $23 |
| 16 KC | 2 | 27 | 43 | 47 | 1.87 | 3.47 | 1.13 | 537 | 489 | 586 | 3.9 | 3.3 | 9.8 | 2.9 | 53% | 13% | 94.9 | 49 | 18 | 33 | 30% | 82% | 0% | 0 | 16 | | | 90 | 1.00 | 12.4 | 113 | 134 | $14 |
| 17 CHC | 4 | 32 | 59 | 79 | 2.30 | 3.50 | 1.14 | 600 | 493 | 690 | 4.1 | 4.3 | 12.1 | 2.8 | 59% | 15% | 94.3 | 40 | 21 | 38 | 28% | 85% | 12% | 0 | 18 | | | 97 | 1.15 | 14.9 | 120 | 144 | $20 |
| 18 COL | 3 | 43 | 65 | 78 | 4.13 | 3.54 | 1.06 | 615 | 485 | 739 | 3.8 | 3.6 | 10.7 | 3.0 | 49% | 12% | 93.8 | 42 | 18 | 40 | 25% | 64% | 13% | 0 | 16 | | | 88 | 1.21 | 0.1 | 117 | 134 | $20 |
| 1st Half | 0 | 23 | 33 | 36 | 4.41 | 4.13 | 1.22 | 659 | 428 | 888 | 3.9 | 5.0 | 9.9 | 2.0 | 48% | 11% | 93.8 | 44 | 15 | 41 | 24% | 67% | 13% | 0 | 16 | | | 85 | 1.26 | -1.0 | 66 | 76 | $15 |
| 2nd Half | 3 | 20 | 33 | 42 | 3.86 | 3.02 | 0.89 | 569 | 540 | 594 | 3.7 | 2.2 | 11.6 | 5.3 | 51% | 14% | 93.8 | 39 | 21 | 39 | 25% | 60% | 13% | 0 | 16 | | | 91 | 1.15 | 1.2 | 166 | 191 | $24 |
| 19 Proj | 4 | 36 | 58 | 70 | 3.46 | 3.33 | 1.15 | 620 | 531 | 704 | 3.8 | 3.8 | 10.8 | 2.8 | 54% | 12% | 94.3 | 42 | 20 | 38 | 28% | 72% | 10% | 0 | | | | | | 7.1 | 112 | 129 | $18 |

## De Los Santos,Enyel

| | | | | | |
|---|---|---|---|---|---|
| Age: 23 | Th: R | Role SP | Health | A | LIMA Plan D+ |
| Ht: 6' 3" | Wt: 170 | Type | PT/Exp | D | Rand Var 0 |
| | | | Consist | A | MM 1100 |

1-0, 4.74 ERA in 19 IP at PHI. Made pair of spot starts before moving to pen in August/September. Impressive year at Triple-A, while scouting reports suggest serviceable back-of-rotation arm, with good control and underwhelming stuff. Interesting keeper speculation, but likely limited fantasy production for 2019.

| Yr Tm | W | Sv | IP | K | ERA | xERA | WHIP | oOPS | vL | vR | BF/G | Ctl | Dom | Cmd | FpK | SwK | Vel | G | L | F | H% | S% | hr/f | GS | APC | DOM% | DIS% | Sv% | LI | RAR | BPV | BPX | R$ |
|---|---|---|---|---|---|---|---|---|---|---|---|---|---|---|---|---|---|---|---|---|---|---|---|---|---|---|---|---|---|---|---|---|---|
| 14 | | | | | | | | | | | | | | | | | | | | | | | | | | | | | | | | | |
| 15 | | | | | | | | | | | | | | | | | | | | | | | | | | | | | | | | | |
| 16 | | | | | | | | | | | | | | | | | | | | | | | | | | | | | | | | | |
| 17 aa | 10 | 0 | 150 | 122 | 4.90 | 4.14 | 1.36 | | | | 24.1 | 3.0 | 7.3 | 2.4 | | | | | | | 32% | 64% | | | | | | | | -10.0 | 72 | 87 | $1 |
| 18 PHI * | 11 | 0 | 147 | 113 | 3.40 | 4.08 | 1.31 | 836 | 513 | 1121 | 21.0 | 3.2 | 6.9 | 2.2 | 59% | 11% | 94.7 | 47 | 25 | 27 | 29% | 78% | 13% | 2 | 48 | 50% | 50% | 0 | 0.31 | 13.6 | 60 | 69 | $8 |
| 1st Half | 8 | 0 | 90 | 76 | 2.22 | 3.74 | 1.22 | | | | 24.3 | 3.1 | 7.5 | 2.4 | | | | | | | 28% | 89% | 0% | 0 | | | | | | 21.5 | 71 | 81 | $17 |
| 2nd Half | 3 | 0 | 57 | 37 | 5.27 | 4.63 | 1.44 | 836 | 513 | 1121 | 17.4 | 3.4 | 5.9 | 1.7 | 59% | 11% | 94.7 | 47 | 25 | 27 | 31% | 64% | 13% | 2 | 48 | 50% | 50% | 0 | 0.31 | -7.9 | 45 | 51 | -$11 |
| 19 Proj | 3 | 0 | 44 | 33 | 4.54 | 4.32 | 1.35 | 801 | 463 | 1100 | 21.2 | 3.1 | 6.9 | 2.2 | 59% | 11% | 94.7 | 44 | 23 | 34 | 29% | 71% | 13% | 9 | | | | | | -0.7 | 61 | 70 | -$3 |

## deGrom,Jacob

| | | | | | |
|---|---|---|---|---|---|
| Age: 31 | Th: R | Role SP | Health | B | LIMA Plan D+ |
| Ht: 6' 4" | Wt: 180 | Type Pwr | PT/Exp | A | Rand Var -5 |
| | | | Consist | A | MM 5405 |

Wildly talented pitcher posts ridiculous R$ despite lack of run support? Improves underlying skills in pretty much every way? Um, yes please. Had S% and hr/f working in his favor so expect at least a little bit of pullback. But make no mistake: now with back-to-back 200 IP seasons, this profile is as good as they come.

| Yr Tm | W | Sv | IP | K | ERA | xERA | WHIP | oOPS | vL | vR | BF/G | Ctl | Dom | Cmd | FpK | SwK | Vel | G | L | F | H% | S% | hr/f | GS | APC | DOM% | DIS% | Sv% | LI | RAR | BPV | BPX | R$ |
|---|---|---|---|---|---|---|---|---|---|---|---|---|---|---|---|---|---|---|---|---|---|---|---|---|---|---|---|---|---|---|---|---|---|
| 14 NYM * | 13 | 0 | 179 | 168 | 2.59 | 2.83 | 1.16 | 613 | 639 | 594 | 24.5 | 2.6 | 8.4 | 3.2 | 63% | 12% | 93.5 | 45 | 23 | 31 | 30% | 79% | 6% | 22 | 102 | 50% | 18% | | | 25.4 | 113 | 135 | $18 |
| 15 NYM | 14 | 0 | 191 | 205 | 2.54 | 3.04 | 0.98 | 574 | 663 | 475 | 25.0 | 1.8 | 9.7 | 5.4 | 68% | 13% | 95.0 | 44 | 21 | 35 | 29% | 78% | 9% | 30 | 99 | 63% | 13% | | | 33.4 | 148 | 176 | $30 |
| 16 NYM | 7 | 0 | 148 | 143 | 3.04 | 3.57 | 1.20 | 685 | 624 | 749 | 25.2 | 2.2 | 8.7 | 4.0 | 64% | 11% | 93.4 | 46 | 23 | 32 | 32% | 79% | 12% | 24 | 98 | 38% | 13% | | | 21.0 | 121 | 144 | $13 |
| 17 NYM | 15 | 0 | 201 | 239 | 3.53 | 3.40 | 1.19 | 682 | 693 | 671 | 26.7 | 2.6 | 10.7 | 4.1 | 64% | 14% | 95.2 | 45 | 21 | 34 | 32% | 76% | 16% | 31 | 102 | 48% | 23% | | | 20.5 | 144 | 173 | $22 |
| 18 NYM | 10 | 0 | 217 | 269 | 1.70 | 2.75 | 0.91 | 521 | 579 | 460 | 26.1 | 1.9 | 11.2 | 5.8 | 66% | 16% | 96.0 | 46 | 22 | 32 | 29% | 84% | 6% | 32 | 100 | 75% | 0% | | | 65.6 | 173 | 200 | $44 |
| 1st Half | 5 | 0 | 107 | 134 | 1.84 | 2.81 | 1.02 | 559 | 651 | 465 | 25.1 | 2.3 | 11.2 | 4.8 | 65% | 16% | 95.4 | 47 | 25 | 28 | 31% | 84% | 8% | 17 | 95 | 65% | 0% | | | 30.5 | 164 | 188 | $40 |
| 2nd Half | 5 | 0 | 110 | 135 | 1.56 | 2.70 | 0.81 | 482 | 508 | 455 | 27.3 | 1.5 | 11.1 | 7.5 | 68% | 16% | 96.6 | 46 | 19 | 35 | 28% | 82% | 5% | 15 | 106 | 87% | 0% | | | 35.0 | 183 | 211 | $49 |
| 19 Proj | 14 | 0 | 196 | 227 | 2.66 | 2.85 | 1.03 | 592 | 616 | 569 | 25.4 | 2.1 | 10.5 | 4.9 | 65% | 14% | 95.3 | 46 | 22 | 33 | 30% | 77% | 10% | 30 | | | | | | 36.6 | 155 | 178 | $31 |

BRIAN SLACK

## DeSclafani,Anthony

| | | | |
|---|---|---|---|
| Age: 29 Th: R Role SP | Health F | LIMA Plan B+ | |
| Ht: 6' 1" Wt: 195 Type | PT/Exp D | Rand Var +2 | |
| | Consist B | MM 2203 | |

7-8, 4.93 ERA in 115 IP at CIN. Missed 320 games in last three years to injuries, so his 21 starts in 2018 were a feat. More impressive was BPV that increased each month, with 2nd half Dom and Cmd levels heretofore unseen. HR vL are an issue and health concerns will persist, but he's put himself back on the map.

| Yr | Tm | W | Sv | IP | K | ERA | xERA | WHIP | oOPS | vL | vR | BF/G | Ctl | Dom | Cmd | FpK | SwK | Vel | G | L | F | H% | S% | hr/f | GS | APC | DOM% | DIS% | Sv% | LI | RAR | BPV | BPX | R$ |
|---|---|---|---|---|---|---|---|---|---|---|---|---|---|---|---|---|---|---|---|---|---|---|---|---|---|---|---|---|---|---|---|---|---|---|
| 14 | MIA * | 8 | 0 | 135 | 104 | 4.63 | 3.86 | 1.31 | 801 | 893 | 710 | 16.9 | 2.3 | 6.9 | 3.0 | 66% | 9% | 92.5 | 36 | 24 | 40 | 32% | 64% | 9% | 5 | 42 | 20% | 60% | 0 | 0.40 | -14.8 | 87 | 103 | -$2 |
| 15 | CIN | 9 | 0 | 185 | 151 | 4.05 | 4.04 | 1.35 | 742 | 783 | 697 | 25.3 | 2.7 | 7.4 | 2.7 | 63% | 10% | 92.5 | 45 | 21 | 34 | 32% | 72% | 9% | 31 | 94 | 29% | 23% | | | -1.9 | 83 | 99 | $2 |
| 16 | CIN * | 9 | 0 | 140 | 118 | 3.93 | 4.43 | 1.23 | 723 | 837 | 585 | 23.7 | 2.0 | 7.6 | 3.8 | 58% | 10% | 92.9 | 42 | 23 | 35 | 30% | 75% | 13% | 20 | 98 | 25% | 30% | | | 4.6 | 80 | 95 | $7 |
| 17 | | | | | | | | | | | | | | | | | | | | | | | | | | | | | | | | | | |
| 18 | CIN * | 7 | 0 | 135 | 125 | 5.15 | 5.42 | 1.32 | 792 | 917 | 676 | 22.4 | 2.2 | 8.3 | 3.7 | 63% | 10% | 93.6 | 41 | 22 | 36 | 31% | 69% | 20% | 21 | 85 | 14% | 24% | | | -16.6 | 66 | 76 | -$3 |
| 1st Half | | 3 | 0 | 48 | 41 | 5.26 | 5.99 | 1.36 | 773 | 729 | 813 | 22.5 | 2.3 | 7.7 | 3.3 | 63% | 9% | 93.2 | 39 | 21 | 40 | 30% | 71% | 18% | 5 | 88 | 20% | 0% | | | -6.6 | 41 | 47 | -$10 |
| 2nd Half | | 4 | 0 | 87 | 84 | 5.09 | 3.87 | 1.29 | 798 | 978 | 633 | 22.9 | 2.2 | 8.7 | 4.0 | 63% | 11% | 93.7 | 42 | 23 | 35 | 31% | 67% | 20% | 16 | 84 | 13% | 31% | | | -10.0 | 118 | 136 | $1 |
| 19 | Proj | 10 | 0 | 174 | 151 | 4.46 | 3.86 | 1.30 | 790 | 883 | 696 | 22.3 | 2.3 | 7.8 | 3.4 | 62% | 10% | 93.1 | 41 | 22 | 36 | 31% | 72% | 17% | 32 | | | | | | -6.7 | 99 | 114 | $4 |

## Devenski,Chris

| | | | |
|---|---|---|---|
| Age: 28 Th: R Role RP | Health B | LIMA Plan C+ | |
| Ht: 6' 3" Wt: 210 Type Pwr FB | PT/Exp C | Rand Var +2 | |
| | Consist A | MM 4400 | |

Was stepping up to a new level until two July outings (8 ER, retired 0) and hamstring injury befouled the rest of his season. Until then, Cmd and Dom were on point and FpK was surging, again reducing baserunners to an endangered species. If fully healthy, expect more of what you saw in 2016-2017, with a bullet.

| Yr | Tm | W | Sv | IP | K | ERA | xERA | WHIP | oOPS | vL | vR | BF/G | Ctl | Dom | Cmd | FpK | SwK | Vel | G | L | F | H% | S% | hr/f | GS | APC | DOM% | DIS% | Sv% | LI | RAR | BPV | BPX | R$ |
|---|---|---|---|---|---|---|---|---|---|---|---|---|---|---|---|---|---|---|---|---|---|---|---|---|---|---|---|---|---|---|---|---|---|---|
| 14 | aa | 5 | 0 | 41 | 32 | 4.50 | 4.56 | 1.34 | | | | 17.2 | 3.9 | 6.9 | 1.7 | | | | | | | 26% | 73% | | | | | | | | -3.9 | 34 | 41 | -$2 |
| 15 | aa | 7 | 2 | 120 | 87 | 3.54 | 4.76 | 1.42 | | | | 21.1 | 2.5 | 6.5 | 2.6 | | | | | | | 33% | 79% | | | | | | | | 6.2 | 60 | 71 | $2 |
| 16 | HOU | 4 | 1 | 108 | 104 | 2.16 | 3.54 | 0.91 | 551 | 639 | 465 | 8.5 | 1.7 | 8.6 | 5.2 | 64% | 14% | 92.4 | 33 | 26 | 41 | 27% | 77% | 4% | 5 | 33 | 40% | 40% | 100 | 0.91 | 27.1 | 122 | 145 | $17 |
| 17 | HOU | 8 | 4 | 81 | 100 | 2.68 | 3.45 | 0.94 | 588 | 414 | 762 | 5.1 | 2.9 | 11.2 | 3.8 | 65% | 17% | 94.1 | 40 | 15 | 45 | 23% | 80% | 14% | 0 | 20 | | | 40 | 1.51 | 16.7 | 141 | 169 | $15 |
| 18 | HOU | 2 | 2 | 47 | 51 | 4.18 | 3.94 | 1.16 | 719 | 712 | 726 | 3.9 | 2.5 | 9.7 | 3.9 | 61% | 15% | 94.2 | 34 | 20 | 46 | 29% | 72% | 16% | 1 | 16 | 0% | 100% | 40 | 1.35 | -0.2 | 120 | 138 | $0 |
| 1st Half | | 2 | 2 | 34 | 40 | 1.34 | 2.92 | 0.83 | 518 | 502 | 538 | 3.7 | 1.9 | 10.7 | 5.7 | 65% | 16% | 94.4 | 41 | 19 | 40 | 26% | 88% | 7% | 0 | 15 | | | 67 | 1.62 | 11.7 | 161 | 185 | $7 |
| 2nd Half | | 0 | 0 | 14 | 11 | 11.20 | 6.66 | 1.98 | 1083 | 1153 | 1009 | 4.4 | 4.0 | 7.2 | 1.8 | 54% | 14% | 93.9 | 24 | 22 | 55 | 34% | 50% | 25% | 1 | 18 | 0% | 100% | 0 | 0.76 | -11.9 | 25 | 29 | -$18 |
| 19 | Proj | 4 | 0 | 65 | 70 | 3.02 | 3.22 | 1.00 | 620 | 604 | 637 | 6.1 | 2.2 | 9.7 | 4.4 | 65% | 15% | 93.5 | 39 | 21 | 40 | 28% | 73% | 9% | 0 | | | | | | 9.1 | 132 | 152 | $6 |

## Diaz,Edwin

| | | | |
|---|---|---|---|
| Age: 25 Th: R Role RP | Health A | LIMA Plan C | |
| Ht: 6' 3" Wt: 165 Type Pwr | PT/Exp B | Rand Var -1 | |
| | Consist C | MM 5530 | |

Cy Young-caliber season will be hard to repeat. Then again, the sheer insanity of his 2nd half numbers makes you giggle and ask, why not? Nobody is immune from regression, though in his case, only potential overuse or injury seem viable as immediate threats. You may have to overpay in 2019, but these skills are elite.

| Yr | Tm | W | Sv | IP | K | ERA | xERA | WHIP | oOPS | vL | vR | BF/G | Ctl | Dom | Cmd | FpK | SwK | Vel | G | L | F | H% | S% | hr/f | GS | APC | DOM% | DIS% | Sv% | LI | RAR | BPV | BPX | R$ |
|---|---|---|---|---|---|---|---|---|---|---|---|---|---|---|---|---|---|---|---|---|---|---|---|---|---|---|---|---|---|---|---|---|---|---|
| 14 | | | | | | | | | | | | | | | | | | | | | | | | | | | | | | | | | | |
| 15 | aa | 5 | 0 | 104 | 93 | 4.88 | 3.76 | 1.36 | | | | 21.8 | 2.9 | 8.1 | 2.8 | | | | | | | 34% | 62% | | | | | | | | -11.8 | 96 | 114 | -$4 |
| 16 | SEA * | 3 | 19 | 92 | 137 | 2.73 | 3.03 | 1.12 | 627 | 604 | 643 | 5.6 | 2.1 | 13.3 | 6.2 | 58% | 19% | 97.3 | 47 | 23 | 31 | 37% | 79% | 15% | 0 | 17 | | | 86 | 1.34 | 16.7 | 194 | 230 | $18 |
| 17 | SEA | 4 | 34 | 66 | 89 | 3.27 | 3.83 | 1.15 | 619 | 655 | 590 | 4.2 | 4.4 | 12.1 | 2.8 | 56% | 17% | 97.3 | 39 | 15 | 46 | 26% | 79% | 14% | 0 | 17 | | | 87 | 1.64 | 8.8 | 118 | 141 | $20 |
| 18 | SEA | 0 | 57 | 73 | 124 | 1.96 | 2.01 | 0.79 | 470 | 444 | 488 | 3.8 | 2.1 | 15.2 | 7.3 | 67% | 20% | 97.3 | 44 | 20 | 35 | 30% | 79% | 11% | 0 | 16 | | | 93 | 1.40 | 19.8 | 240 | 276 | $36 |
| 1st Half | | 0 | 31 | 43 | 68 | 2.51 | 2.22 | 0.88 | 488 | 454 | 512 | 3.9 | 2.7 | 14.2 | 5.2 | 65% | 19% | 97.4 | 46 | 22 | 32 | 30% | 72% | 8% | 0 | 17 | | | 91 | 1.46 | 8.7 | 206 | 237 | $37 |
| 2nd Half | | 0 | 26 | 30 | 56 | 1.19 | 1.75 | 0.66 | 443 | 428 | 453 | 3.8 | 1.2 | 16.6 | 14.0 | 71% | 21% | 97.1 | 42 | 17 | 40 | 31% | 94% | 14% | 0 | 15 | | | 96 | 1.30 | 11.1 | 287 | 330 | $33 |
| 19 | Proj | 2 | 41 | 65 | 99 | 2.58 | 2.38 | 0.97 | 550 | 546 | 553 | 4.3 | 2.6 | 13.7 | 5.2 | 62% | 19% | 97.3 | 43 | 18 | 39 | 31% | 78% | 12% | 0 | | | | | | 12.7 | 196 | 226 | $24 |

## Diekman,Jake

| | | | |
|---|---|---|---|
| Age: 32 Th: L Role RP | Health C | LIMA Plan C | |
| Ht: 6' 4" Wt: 200 Type Pwr | PT/Exp D | Rand Var +2 | |
| | Consist B | MM 3500 | |

LOOGY suddenly couldn't live up to his handle in 2018, and by season's end his S% luck had run out. Disregarding injury-riddled 2017, xERA has advanced as strikeouts have become less of a weapon against phalanx of walks. On-again, off-again GB% adds to unreliability. Dicey end-of-draft option.

| Yr | Tm | W | Sv | IP | K | ERA | xERA | WHIP | oOPS | vL | vR | BF/G | Ctl | Dom | Cmd | FpK | SwK | Vel | G | L | F | H% | S% | hr/f | GS | APC | DOM% | DIS% | Sv% | LI | RAR | BPV | BPX | R$ |
|---|---|---|---|---|---|---|---|---|---|---|---|---|---|---|---|---|---|---|---|---|---|---|---|---|---|---|---|---|---|---|---|---|---|---|
| 14 | PHI | 5 | 0 | 71 | 100 | 3.80 | 2.99 | 1.42 | 692 | 577 | 748 | 4.3 | 4.4 | 12.7 | 2.9 | 55% | 14% | 96.9 | 43 | 26 | 30 | 38% | 73% | 8% | 0 | 18 | | | 0 | 1.14 | -0.5 | 129 | 154 | $0 |
| 15 | 2 TM | 2 | 0 | 58 | 69 | 4.01 | 3.54 | 1.44 | 689 | 729 | 660 | 3.9 | 4.8 | 10.6 | 2.2 | 59% | 12% | 96.5 | 56 | 15 | 28 | 33% | 73% | 11% | 0 | 16 | | | 0 | 0.86 | -0.4 | 96 | 115 | -$3 |
| 16 | TEX | 4 | 4 | 53 | 59 | 3.40 | 3.73 | 1.17 | 594 | 625 | 578 | 3.3 | 4.4 | 10.0 | 2.3 | 53% | 11% | 95.1 | 48 | 20 | 32 | 26% | 72% | 9% | 0 | 14 | | | 80 | 1.08 | 5.2 | 87 | 104 | $4 |
| 17 | TEX | 0 | 1 | 11 | 13 | 2.53 | 4.36 | 1.31 | 523 | 466 | 560 | 4.1 | 8.4 | 11.0 | 1.3 | 53% | 12% | 94.7 | 59 | 14 | 27 | 15% | 85% | 17% | 0 | 17 | | | 100 | 1.10 | 2.4 | 7 | 8 | -$3 |
| 18 | 2 TM | 1 | 2 | 53 | 66 | 4.73 | 3.94 | 1.50 | 717 | 882 | 624 | 3.4 | 5.2 | 11.1 | 2.1 | 56% | 12% | 95.0 | 48 | 20 | 32 | 35% | 68% | 9% | 0 | 14 | | | 67 | 1.07 | -3.8 | 85 | 98 | -$5 |
| 1st Half | | 1 | 2 | 28 | 35 | 3.81 | 4.16 | 1.55 | 691 | 930 | 571 | 3.7 | 5.7 | 11.1 | 1.9 | 54% | 11% | 94.5 | 47 | 21 | 32 | 35% | 76% | 8% | 0 | 16 | | | 67 | 1.06 | 1.2 | 70 | 81 | -$4 |
| 2nd Half | | 0 | 0 | 25 | 31 | 5.76 | 3.70 | 1.44 | 745 | 831 | 689 | 3.2 | 4.7 | 11.2 | 2.4 | 57% | 12% | 95.5 | 49 | 19 | 32 | 35% | 59% | 10% | 0 | 13 | | | 0 | 1.08 | -5.0 | 102 | 117 | -$6 |
| 19 | Proj | 2 | 0 | 44 | 53 | 4.32 | 3.51 | 1.39 | 684 | 764 | 639 | 3.3 | 4.8 | 10.9 | 2.3 | 56% | 12% | 95.5 | 49 | 20 | 31 | 33% | 69% | 10% | 0 | | | | | | 4.2 | 94 | 108 | -$3 |

## Dominguez,Seranthony

| | | | |
|---|---|---|---|
| Age: 24 Th: R Role RP | Health A | LIMA Plan B | |
| Ht: 6' 1" Wt: 185 Type Pwr xGB | PT/Exp F | Rand Var 0 | |
| | Consist F | MM 5520 | |

2-5, 2.95 ERA with 16 Sv in 58 IP at PHI. Called up in May, converted SP racked up holds (14) and saves even as sheen dulled in 2nd half. While Dom and GB% are right out of the closer catalog, Ctl and Cmd may be on back-order for retooling. Will need time for components to coalesce, but you want these skills.

| Yr | Tm | W | Sv | IP | K | ERA | xERA | WHIP | oOPS | vL | vR | BF/G | Ctl | Dom | Cmd | FpK | SwK | Vel | G | L | F | H% | S% | hr/f | GS | APC | DOM% | DIS% | Sv% | LI | RAR | BPV | BPX | R$ |
|---|---|---|---|---|---|---|---|---|---|---|---|---|---|---|---|---|---|---|---|---|---|---|---|---|---|---|---|---|---|---|---|---|---|---|
| 14 | | | | | | | | | | | | | | | | | | | | | | | | | | | | | | | | | | |
| 15 | | | | | | | | | | | | | | | | | | | | | | | | | | | | | | | | | | |
| 16 | | | | | | | | | | | | | | | | | | | | | | | | | | | | | | | | | | |
| 17 | | | | | | | | | | | | | | | | | | | | | | | | | | | | | | | | | | |
| 18 | PHI * | 4 | 16 | 76 | 92 | 2.67 | 1.24 | 0.87 | 501 | 630 | 374 | 4.4 | 3.0 | 10.9 | 3.7 | 62% | 16% | 98.1 | 56 | 15 | 29 | 23% | 70% | 11% | 0 | 18 | | | 76 | 1.48 | 13.9 | 151 | 174 | $17 |
| 1st Half | | 3 | 7 | 46 | 54 | 1.90 | 0.36 | 0.67 | 411 | 496 | 327 | 4.7 | 1.4 | 10.7 | 7.7 | 63% | 18% | 98.1 | 51 | 20 | 29 | 23% | 71% | 6% | 0 | 18 | | | 78 | 1.61 | 12.7 | 244 | 280 | $23 |
| 2nd Half | | 1 | 9 | 31 | 38 | 3.82 | 3.43 | 1.17 | 574 | 738 | 410 | 4.3 | 5.3 | 11.2 | 2.1 | 62% | 14% | 98.0 | 60 | 11 | 29 | 24% | 70% | 14% | 0 | 17 | | | 75 | 1.37 | 1.3 | 96 | 110 | $8 |
| 19 | Proj | 3 | 18 | 65 | 79 | 3.08 | 2.76 | 0.97 | 507 | 638 | 376 | 4.3 | 3.7 | 11.0 | 2.9 | 62% | 16% | 98.0 | 56 | 15 | 29 | 23% | 69% | 11% | 0 | | | | | | 13.6 | 131 | 150 | $13 |

## Doolittle,Sean

| | | | |
|---|---|---|---|
| Age: 32 Th: L Role RP | Health F | LIMA Plan B | |
| Ht: 6' 2" Wt: 204 Type Pwr xFB | PT/Exp C | Rand Var -5 | |
| | Consist B | MM 5530 | |

Long duration of yearly DL stints (60 days in 2018) make other annual productions—stellar Ctl, Dom, and Cmd—all the more impresssive. Tack on FpK, SwK, BPV and microscopic oOBP (.200 in 2017-2018), and you have by all standards a top-tier closer. If only those injuries would stop crashing the party.

| Yr | Tm | W | Sv | IP | K | ERA | xERA | WHIP | oOPS | vL | vR | BF/G | Ctl | Dom | Cmd | FpK | SwK | Vel | G | L | F | H% | S% | hr/f | GS | APC | DOM% | DIS% | Sv% | LI | RAR | BPV | BPX | R$ |
|---|---|---|---|---|---|---|---|---|---|---|---|---|---|---|---|---|---|---|---|---|---|---|---|---|---|---|---|---|---|---|---|---|---|---|
| 14 | OAK | 2 | 22 | 63 | 89 | 2.73 | 2.61 | 0.73 | 459 | 276 | 550 | 3.9 | 1.1 | 12.8 | 11.1 | 72% | 17% | 94.0 | 23 | 18 | 59 | 27% | 66% | 6% | 0 | 15 | | | 85 | 1.29 | 7.8 | 200 | 238 | $17 |
| 15 | OAK | 1 | 4 | 14 | 15 | 3.95 | 3.99 | 1.24 | 651 | 1065 | 531 | 4.8 | 3.3 | 9.9 | 3.0 | 65% | 10% | 92.4 | 32 | 19 | 49 | 32% | 69% | 6% | 0 | 21 | | | 80 | 0.75 | 0.0 | 99 | 118 | -$2 |
| 16 | OAK | 2 | 4 | 39 | 45 | 3.23 | 3.77 | 1.05 | 705 | 584 | 798 | 3.5 | 1.8 | 10.4 | 5.6 | 70% | 16% | 94.8 | 29 | 16 | 55 | 29% | 77% | 12% | 0 | 14 | | | 67 | 1.18 | 4.6 | 144 | 171 | $3 |
| 17 | 2 TM | 2 | 24 | 51 | 62 | 2.81 | 3.53 | 0.86 | 517 | 371 | 559 | 3.7 | 1.8 | 10.9 | 6.2 | 71% | 16% | 94.7 | 31 | 19 | 50 | 26% | 72% | 8% | 0 | 15 | | | 92 | 1.26 | 9.8 | 157 | 189 | $16 |
| 18 | WAS | 3 | 25 | 45 | 60 | 1.60 | 2.73 | 0.60 | 391 | 205 | 436 | 3.8 | 1.2 | 12.0 | 10.0 | 70% | 18% | 93.9 | 32 | 19 | 48 | 21% | 79% | 7% | 0 | 14 | | | 96 | 1.40 | 14.2 | 194 | 223 | $19 |
| 1st Half | | 2 | 21 | 34 | 44 | 1.60 | 2.90 | 0.53 | 393 | 115 | 463 | 3.8 | 0.8 | 11.8 | 14.7 | 73% | 19% | 94.2 | 24 | 20 | 56 | 19% | 80% | 8% | 0 | 14 | | | 95 | 1.35 | 10.6 | 192 | 221 | $26 |
| 2nd Half | | 1 | 4 | 11 | 16 | 1.59 | 2.09 | 0.79 | 384 | 476 | 358 | 3.9 | 2.4 | 12.7 | 5.3 | 63% | 15% | 92.9 | 59 | 18 | 23 | 27% | 78% | 0% | 0 | 14 | | | 100 | 1.54 | 3.6 | 201 | 231 | $0 |
| 19 | Proj | 3 | 25 | 58 | 73 | 2.58 | 2.94 | 0.81 | 540 | 416 | 597 | 3.5 | 1.4 | 11.3 | 8.0 | 71% | 17% | 94.5 | 27 | 18 | 55 | 26% | 75% | 9% | 0 | | | | | | 10.8 | 170 | 195 | $18 |

## Drake,Oliver

| | | | |
|---|---|---|---|
| Age: 32 Th: R Role RP | Health A | LIMA Plan C | |
| Ht: 6' 4" Wt: 215 Type Pwr | PT/Exp D | Rand Var +5 | |
| | Consist A | MM 3400 | |

Poor guy is still waiting for all his forwarded mail to find him. Alternately courted for K potential and GB% only to be dispatched for Ctl and Cmd, in 2018 was the literal embodiment of "pedestrian." Last of five stops was his best showing, so maybe for first part of 2019, he won't feel like a chameleon on plaid.

| Yr | Tm | W | Sv | IP | K | ERA | xERA | WHIP | oOPS | vL | vR | BF/G | Ctl | Dom | Cmd | FpK | SwK | Vel | G | L | F | H% | S% | hr/f | GS | APC | DOM% | DIS% | Sv% | LI | RAR | BPV | BPX | R$ |
|---|---|---|---|---|---|---|---|---|---|---|---|---|---|---|---|---|---|---|---|---|---|---|---|---|---|---|---|---|---|---|---|---|---|---|
| 14 | aa | 2 | 31 | 53 | 55 | 3.80 | 3.34 | 1.30 | | | | 4.3 | 3.1 | 9.3 | 3.0 | | | | | | | 34% | 70% | | | | | | | | -0.4 | 111 | 132 | $11 |
| 15 | BAL * | 1 | 23 | 60 | 66 | 1.78 | 3.03 | 1.31 | 708 | 609 | 774 | 4.5 | 4.4 | 10.0 | 2.3 | 56% | 14% | 90.6 | 48 | 15 | 37 | 31% | 88% | 6% | 0 | 23 | | | 100 | 0.48 | 16.0 | 105 | 125 | $12 |
| 16 | BAL * | 2 | 10 | 74 | 82 | 4.30 | 4.73 | 1.54 | 595 | 598 | 589 | 5.3 | 4.9 | 9.9 | 2.0 | 62% | 15% | 90.3 | 49 | 14 | 37 | 33% | 75% | 13% | 0 | 21 | | | 77 | 0.72 | -1.0 | 71 | 84 | $1 |
| 17 | 2 TM | 3 | 1 | 56 | 62 | 4.66 | 3.95 | 1.57 | 808 | 693 | 1030 | 3.9 | 4.0 | 10.0 | 2.5 | 63% | 12% | 91.9 | 49 | 25 | 26 | 37% | 72% | 14% | 0 | 16 | | | 25 | 0.75 | -2.1 | 98 | 118 | -$4 |
| 18 | 5 TM | 1 | 0 | 48 | 51 | 5.29 | 3.78 | 1.45 | 758 | 861 | 671 | 4.8 | 3.2 | 9.6 | 3.0 | 59% | 13% | 92.5 | 45 | 26 | 29 | 37% | 63% | 10% | 0 | 19 | | | 0 | 0.41 | -6.7 | 110 | 126 | -$6 |
| 1st Half | | 1 | 0 | 20 | 23 | 8.24 | 4.35 | 1.98 | 945 | 1017 | 888 | 5.1 | 4.6 | 10.5 | 2.3 | 57% | 13% | 92.6 | 39 | 33 | 28 | 45% | 57% | 12% | 0 | 19 | | | 0 | 0.49 | -9.9 | 83 | 96 | -$15 |
| 2nd Half | | 0 | 0 | 28 | 28 | 3.21 | 3.38 | 1.07 | 605 | 741 | 485 | 4.5 | 2.3 | 9.0 | 4.0 | 60% | 14% | 92.4 | 49 | 21 | 29 | 29% | 71% | 9% | 0 | 18 | | | 0 | 0.34 | 3.2 | 129 | 148 | $1 |
| 19 | Proj | 1 | 0 | 44 | 47 | 4.69 | 3.59 | 1.47 | 758 | 757 | 759 | 4.5 | 3.7 | 9.8 | 2.6 | 61% | 13% | 92.3 | 47 | 26 | 28 | 36% | 69% | 12% | 0 | | | | | | 3.3 | 100 | 115 | -$5 |

ROB CARROLL

## Duffy,Danny

| | | | | | | |
|---|---|---|---|---|---|---|
| Age: 30 | Th: L | Role SP | Health | D | LIMA Plan | C |
| Ht: 6' 3" | Wt: 205 | Type Pwr FB | PT/Exp | A | Rand Var | 0 |
| | | | Consist | B | MM | 1203 |

Shoulder problems likely played a role in Ctl, FpK, SwK slides, but what we said in last year's book still applies: "There's just one sub-4.00 xERA and 160+ IP season in this box." Also hasn't been able to tame RHB, who have hit 92% of his career HR allowed. He's gone from budding ace to late-round flyer.

| Yr Tm | W | Sv | IP | K | ERA | xERA | WHIP | oOPS | vL | vR | BF/G | Ctl | Dom | Cmd | FpK | SwK | Vel | G | L | F | H% | S% | hr/f | GS | APC | DOM% | DIS% | Sv% | LI | RAR | BPV | BPX | R$ |
|---|---|---|---|---|---|---|---|---|---|---|---|---|---|---|---|---|---|---|---|---|---|---|---|---|---|---|---|---|---|---|---|---|---|
| 14 KC | 9 | 0 | 149 | 113 | 2.53 | 4.24 | 1.11 | 605 | 386 | 670 | 19.5 | 3.2 | 6.8 | 2.1 | 59% | 8% | 93.2 | 36 | 18 | 46 | 25% | 81% | 6% | 25 | 78 | 32% | 24% | 0 | 0.87 | 22.3 | 50 | 60 | $14 |
| 15 KC | 7 | 1 | 137 | 102 | 4.08 | 4.56 | 1.39 | 746 | 593 | 785 | 19.6 | 3.5 | 6.7 | 1.9 | 57% | 9% | 93.8 | 39 | 25 | 36 | 30% | 73% | 10% | 24 | 79 | 8% | 29% | 100 | 0.75 | -2.0 | 44 | 52 | $0 |
| 16 KC | 12 | 0 | 180 | 188 | 3.51 | 3.79 | 1.14 | 710 | 449 | 760 | 17.4 | 2.1 | 9.4 | 4.5 | 62% | 13% | 94.8 | 36 | 21 | 43 | 30% | 76% | 13% | 26 | 64 | 38% | 15% | 0 | 0.72 | 15.1 | 127 | 151 | $17 |
| 17 KC | 9 | 0 | 146 | 130 | 3.81 | 4.38 | 1.26 | 709 | 451 | 766 | 25.4 | 2.5 | 8.0 | 3.2 | 65% | 12% | 92.8 | 39 | 20 | 41 | 32% | 71% | 8% | 24 | 95 | 38% | 25% | | | 9.8 | 93 | 111 | $9 |
| 18 KC | 8 | 0 | 155 | 141 | 4.88 | 5.01 | 1.49 | 767 | 661 | 790 | 24.7 | 4.1 | 8.2 | 2.0 | 58% | 10% | 93.1 | 35 | 22 | 43 | 32% | 71% | 11% | 28 | 99 | 11% | 39% | | | -13.9 | 51 | 58 | -$6 |
| 1st Half | 4 | 0 | 95 | 83 | 4.94 | 5.31 | 1.49 | 803 | 610 | 839 | 24.6 | 4.4 | 7.9 | 1.8 | 59% | 10% | 93.2 | 32 | 21 | 47 | 30% | 72% | 13% | 17 | 100 | 12% | 47% | | | -9.3 | 34 | 39 | -$8 |
| 2nd Half | 4 | 0 | 60 | 58 | 4.77 | 4.55 | 1.49 | 713 | 720 | 711 | 24.8 | 3.6 | 8.7 | 2.4 | 56% | 9% | 93.1 | 41 | 23 | 36 | 35% | 68% | 7% | 11 | 99 | 9% | 27% | | | -4.6 | 78 | 90 | -$3 |
| **19 Proj** | **9** | **0** | **160** | **146** | **4.23** | **4.16** | **1.36** | **726** | **578** | **761** | **22.2** | **3.2** | **8.3** | **2.6** | **60%** | **11%** | **93.3** | **38** | **21** | **41** | **32%** | **72%** | **10%** | **30** | | | | | | **-1.6** | **77** | **89** | **$3** |

## Dyson,Sam

| | | | | | | |
|---|---|---|---|---|---|---|
| Age: 31 | Th: R | Role RP | Health | A | LIMA Plan | B |
| Ht: 6' 1" | Wt: 212 | Type xGB | PT/Exp | B | Rand Var | -2 |
| | | | Consist | D | MM | 3110 |

Blamed 2017 on losing feel for sinker, which he was able to restore in SF. And while he's posted four sub-3 ERAs in five years, only one was supported by xERA, and skills say he hasn't been closer-worthy since 2015. Of course, that was 55 saves ago, and LI suggests he'll get more chances; just know he's good, not great.

| Yr Tm | W | Sv | IP | K | ERA | xERA | WHIP | oOPS | vL | vR | BF/G | Ctl | Dom | Cmd | FpK | SwK | Vel | G | L | F | H% | S% | hr/f | GS | APC | DOM% | DIS% | Sv% | LI | RAR | BPV | BPX | R$ |
|---|---|---|---|---|---|---|---|---|---|---|---|---|---|---|---|---|---|---|---|---|---|---|---|---|---|---|---|---|---|---|---|---|---|
| 14 MIA * | 5 | 1 | 67 | 49 | 2.33 | 3.20 | 1.33 | 653 | 781 | 553 | 6.3 | 3.3 | 6.5 | 2.0 | 60% | 11% | 95.6 | 63 | 19 | 18 | 31% | 81% | 4% | 0 | 22 | | | 33 | 0.68 | 11.7 | 80 | 96 | $3 |
| 15 2 TM | 5 | 2 | 75 | 71 | 2.63 | 2.74 | 1.14 | 603 | 557 | 633 | 4.1 | 2.5 | 8.5 | 3.4 | 60% | 13% | 95.8 | 69 | 17 | 14 | 30% | 78% | 13% | 0 | 15 | | | 50 | 1.02 | 12.4 | 132 | 157 | $7 |
| 16 TEX | 3 | 38 | 70 | 55 | 2.43 | 3.29 | 1.22 | 658 | 740 | 593 | 3.9 | 2.9 | 7.0 | 2.4 | 61% | 9% | 95.3 | 65 | 19 | 16 | 29% | 83% | 16% | 0 | 14 | | | 88 | 1.32 | 15.3 | 90 | 107 | $20 |
| 17 2 TM | 4 | 14 | 55 | 34 | 6.09 | 5.13 | 1.77 | 860 | 924 | 811 | 4.7 | 4.9 | 5.6 | 1.1 | 53% | 8% | 95.1 | 63 | 17 | 20 | 33% | 67% | 21% | 0 | 17 | | | 67 | 1.32 | -11.7 | 8 | 10 | -$3 |
| 18 SF | 4 | 3 | 70 | 56 | 2.69 | 3.34 | 1.08 | 652 | 735 | 607 | 3.7 | 2.6 | 7.2 | 2.8 | 61% | 12% | 93.6 | 61 | 15 | 24 | 26% | 77% | 11% | 0 | 13 | | | 38 | 1.08 | 12.7 | 99 | 114 | $7 |
| 1st Half | 2 | 3 | 38 | 30 | 3.35 | 3.47 | 1.14 | 729 | 748 | 717 | 3.7 | 2.6 | 7.2 | 2.7 | 64% | 10% | 93.2 | 62 | 14 | 24 | 27% | 74% | 15% | 0 | 14 | | | 43 | 1.00 | 3.7 | 98 | 112 | $5 |
| 2nd Half | 2 | 0 | 33 | 26 | 1.93 | 3.19 | 1.01 | 557 | 713 | 483 | 3.6 | 2.5 | 7.2 | 2.9 | 58% | 14% | 94.0 | 61 | 17 | 23 | 26% | 81% | 5% | 0 | 13 | | | 0 | 1.17 | 9.0 | 101 | 116 | $9 |
| **19 Proj** | **4** | **5** | **58** | **47** | **3.07** | **3.33** | **1.23** | **675** | **753** | **626** | **4.0** | **2.8** | **7.3** | **2.6** | **60%** | **11%** | **94.5** | **63** | **17** | **21** | **30%** | **76%** | **11%** | **0** | | | | | | **7.7** | **96** | **111** | **$4** |

## Edwards,Carl

| | | | | | | |
|---|---|---|---|---|---|---|
| Age: 27 | Th: R | Role RP | Health | C | LIMA Plan | B+ |
| Ht: 6' 3" | Wt: 170 | Type Pwr | PT/Exp | D | Rand Var | -5 |
| | | | Consist | C | MM | 3500 |

Shoulder inflammation caused him to miss all of June and likely explains 2nd half skill collapse. 1st half was promising, though given his Ctl history, adding more fly balls is like storing gasoline next to a malfunctioning electrical outlet: one day it's all gonna blow. This has been a message from the Fire & Pitcher Safety Council.

| Yr Tm | W | Sv | IP | K | ERA | xERA | WHIP | oOPS | vL | vR | BF/G | Ctl | Dom | Cmd | FpK | SwK | Vel | G | L | F | H% | S% | hr/f | GS | APC | DOM% | DIS% | Sv% | LI | RAR | BPV | BPX | R$ |
|---|---|---|---|---|---|---|---|---|---|---|---|---|---|---|---|---|---|---|---|---|---|---|---|---|---|---|---|---|---|---|---|---|---|
| 14 aa | 1 | 0 | 48 | 40 | 2.72 | 2.04 | 1.13 | | | | 19.0 | 3.9 | 7.4 | 1.9 | | | | | | | 25% | 75% | | | | | | | | 6.0 | 94 | 112 | $1 |
| 15 CHC * | 5 | 6 | 60 | 67 | 3.30 | 2.02 | 1.30 | 566 | 929 | 350 | 6.0 | 6.8 | 10.1 | 1.5 | 63% | 10% | 93.5 | 58 | 25 | 17 | 24% | 73% | 0% | 0 | 14 | | | 67 | 0.19 | 4.9 | 109 | 130 | $4 |
| 16 CHC * | 1 | 3 | 61 | 81 | 4.15 | 1.97 | 1.07 | 456 | 425 | 475 | 4.0 | 4.6 | 11.9 | 2.6 | 56% | 18% | 95.2 | 50 | 21 | 29 | 24% | 61% | 19% | 0 | 17 | | | 75 | 0.95 | 0.3 | 126 | 149 | $3 |
| 17 CHC | 5 | 0 | 66 | 94 | 2.98 | 3.20 | 1.01 | 506 | 437 | 574 | 3.6 | 5.2 | 12.8 | 2.5 | 57% | 15% | 95.2 | 44 | 19 | 36 | 20% | 74% | 13% | 0 | 15 | | | 0 | 1.13 | 11.2 | 112 | 135 | $8 |
| 18 CHC | 3 | 0 | 52 | 67 | 2.60 | 4.25 | 1.31 | 583 | 652 | 534 | 3.8 | 5.5 | 11.6 | 2.1 | 60% | 15% | 94.5 | 29 | 27 | 44 | 30% | 80% | 4% | 0 | 16 | | | 0 | 1.21 | 10.0 | 66 | 76 | $2 |
| 1st Half | 2 | 0 | 25 | 40 | 2.88 | 3.31 | 1.20 | 598 | 641 | 569 | 4.2 | 4.3 | 14.4 | 3.3 | 61% | 18% | 94.6 | 30 | 23 | 47 | 34% | 79% | 8% | 0 | 18 | | | 0 | 0.97 | 3.9 | 151 | 173 | $2 |
| 2nd Half | 1 | 0 | 27 | 27 | 2.33 | 5.28 | 1.41 | 567 | 658 | 496 | 3.5 | 6.7 | 9.0 | 1.4 | 60% | 13% | 94.4 | 28 | 31 | 41 | 27% | 82% | 0% | 0 | 15 | | | 0 | 1.40 | 6.1 | -12 | -14 | $2 |
| **19 Proj** | **3** | **0** | **58** | **74** | **3.10** | **3.54** | **1.19** | **578** | **588** | **571** | **3.9** | **5.1** | **11.4** | **2.3** | **59%** | **15%** | **94.8** | **37** | **24** | **39** | **27%** | **76%** | **8%** | **0** | | | | | | **7.5** | **85** | **97** | **$3** |

## Eflin,Zach

| | | | | | | |
|---|---|---|---|---|---|---|
| Age: 25 | Th: R | Role SP | Health | D | LIMA Plan | B |
| Ht: 6' 6" | Wt: 215 | Type Pwr | PT/Exp | D | Rand Var | 0 |
| | | | Consist | F | MM | 2203 |

11-8, 4.36 ERA in 128 IP at PHI. Increased fastball velocity, added movement on slider were keys to unlocking higher Dom, then July blister problems, 2nd half hr/f shifts knocked him off track. 1st half was so good, PHI reportedly declined to trade him for Manny Machado. That speaks to his upside; for now, he's a sleeper.

| Yr Tm | W | Sv | IP | K | ERA | xERA | WHIP | oOPS | vL | vR | BF/G | Ctl | Dom | Cmd | FpK | SwK | Vel | G | L | F | H% | S% | hr/f | GS | APC | DOM% | DIS% | Sv% | LI | RAR | BPV | BPX | R$ |
|---|---|---|---|---|---|---|---|---|---|---|---|---|---|---|---|---|---|---|---|---|---|---|---|---|---|---|---|---|---|---|---|---|---|
| 14 | | | | | | | | | | | | | | | | | | | | | | | | | | | | | | | | | |
| 15 aa | 8 | 0 | 132 | 62 | 4.09 | 4.31 | 1.29 | | | | 23.5 | 1.5 | 4.2 | 2.8 | | | | | | | 30% | 70% | | | | | | | | -2.0 | 54 | 64 | $1 |
| 16 PHI * | 8 | 0 | 132 | 80 | 4.67 | 3.62 | 1.17 | 828 | 939 | 723 | 23.9 | 2.0 | 5.5 | 2.8 | 62% | 6% | 92.3 | 36 | 24 | 40 | 28% | 62% | 13% | 11 | 90 | 18% | 64% | | | -7.9 | 66 | 79 | $3 |
| 17 PHI * | 2 | 0 | 108 | 69 | 6.06 | 6.01 | 1.53 | 896 | 926 | 856 | 24.6 | 2.3 | 5.7 | 2.5 | 64% | 7% | 92.7 | 44 | 18 | 38 | 33% | 64% | 19% | 11 | 93 | 0% | 36% | | | -22.6 | 29 | 35 | -$11 |
| 18 PHI * | 13 | 0 | 148 | 136 | 4.46 | 4.29 | 1.32 | 746 | 842 | 667 | 21.9 | 2.6 | 8.3 | 3.2 | 65% | 11% | 94.3 | 41 | 21 | 38 | 33% | 68% | 11% | 24 | 85 | 29% | 29% | | | -5.6 | 89 | 103 | $4 |
| 1st Half | 8 | 0 | 77 | 70 | 3.56 | 3.30 | 1.21 | 649 | 752 | 568 | 22.1 | 2.3 | 8.2 | 3.6 | 64% | 11% | 94.3 | 36 | 24 | 40 | 32% | 70% | 6% | 10 | 90 | 40% | 0% | | | 5.6 | 116 | 133 | $11 |
| 2nd Half | 5 | 0 | 71 | 66 | 5.43 | 4.37 | 1.44 | 818 | 907 | 742 | 22.5 | 2.9 | 8.3 | 2.9 | 65% | 11% | 94.4 | 45 | 18 | 37 | 33% | 66% | 15% | 14 | 81 | 21% | 50% | | | -11.2 | 94 | 109 | -$4 |
| **19 Proj** | **11** | **0** | **167** | **147** | **3.99** | **3.88** | **1.27** | **743** | **810** | **675** | **22.5** | **2.3** | **7.9** | **3.4** | **64%** | **11%** | **93.4** | **42** | **20** | **39** | **31%** | **73%** | **12%** | **30** | | | | | | **4.9** | **98** | **113** | **$8** |

## Eickhoff,Jerad

| | | | | | | |
|---|---|---|---|---|---|---|
| Age: 28 | Th: R | Role SP | Health | F | LIMA Plan | C |
| Ht: 6' 4" | Wt: 245 | Type Pwr | PT/Exp | B | Rand Var | 0 |
| | | | Consist | B | MM | 1201 |

0-1, 6.75 ERA in 5 IP at PHI. Spring training lat strain cost him nearly a whole season, and after injury-plagued 2017, leaves us with muddied skills data (including 2018 FpK, SwK that should be ignored). Going back to 2016, Ctl was likely a bit flukish, so mid-4s ERA seems about his speed. But first he needs to stay healthy.

| Yr Tm | W | Sv | IP | K | ERA | xERA | WHIP | oOPS | vL | vR | BF/G | Ctl | Dom | Cmd | FpK | SwK | Vel | G | L | F | H% | S% | hr/f | GS | APC | DOM% | DIS% | Sv% | LI | RAR | BPV | BPX | R$ |
|---|---|---|---|---|---|---|---|---|---|---|---|---|---|---|---|---|---|---|---|---|---|---|---|---|---|---|---|---|---|---|---|---|---|
| 14 aa | 10 | 0 | 154 | 118 | 5.11 | 4.30 | 1.34 | | | | 23.8 | 3.2 | 6.9 | 2.2 | | | | | | | 30% | 64% | | | | | | | | -26.1 | 55 | 66 | -$5 |
| 15 PHI * | 15 | 0 | 184 | 155 | 4.14 | 4.08 | 1.27 | 621 | 830 | 458 | 24.3 | 2.6 | 7.6 | 2.9 | 65% | 11% | 91.0 | 38 | 22 | 40 | 30% | 71% | 9% | 8 | 92 | 50% | 13% | | | -4.1 | 75 | 89 | $7 |
| 16 PHI | 11 | 0 | 197 | 167 | 3.65 | 4.11 | 1.16 | 740 | 822 | 645 | 24.6 | 1.9 | 7.6 | 4.0 | 61% | 10% | 91.0 | 40 | 20 | 39 | 29% | 75% | 13% | 33 | 92 | 24% | 24% | | | 13.2 | 103 | 123 | $15 |
| 17 PHI | 4 | 0 | 128 | 118 | 4.71 | 4.96 | 1.52 | 794 | 900 | 670 | 24.0 | 3.7 | 8.3 | 2.2 | 57% | 9% | 90.4 | 38 | 22 | 40 | 34% | 72% | 10% | 24 | 89 | 17% | 38% | | | -5.6 | 65 | 78 | -$4 |
| 18 PHI * | 0 | 0 | 30 | 21 | 4.00 | 5.86 | 1.62 | 1038 | 1235 | 667 | 16.5 | 3.1 | 6.5 | 2.1 | 81% | 19% | 91.3 | 20 | 40 | 40 | 35% | 78% | 17% | 1 | 33 | 0% | 0% | 0 | 0.28 | 0.5 | 43 | 49 | -$6 |
| 1st Half | 0 | 0 | 7 | 2 | 4.98 | 8.13 | 1.92 | | | | 16.9 | 2.8 | 3.0 | 1.1 | | | | | | | 36% | 79% | 0% | 0 | | | | | | -0.7 | -27 | -31 | -$12 |
| 2nd Half | 0 | 0 | 23 | 19 | 3.69 | 5.14 | 1.52 | 1039 | 1235 | 667 | 16.3 | 3.1 | 7.6 | 2.4 | 81% | 19% | 91.3 | 20 | 40 | 40 | 35% | 78% | 17% | 1 | 33 | 0% | 0% | 0 | 0.28 | 1.3 | 65 | 74 | -$5 |
| **19 Proj** | **3** | **0** | **87** | **74** | **4.07** | **4.22** | **1.37** | **775** | **926** | **624** | **20.8** | **2.9** | **7.7** | **2.6** | **61%** | **10%** | **90.8** | **38** | **22** | **40** | **32%** | **74%** | **10%** | **18** | | | | | | **-0.7** | **76** | **87** | **-$1** |

## Eovaldi,Nathan

| | | | | | | |
|---|---|---|---|---|---|---|
| Age: 29 | Th: R | Role SP | Health | F | LIMA Plan | B+ |
| Ht: 6' 2" | Wt: 225 | Type | PT/Exp | C | Rand Var | 0 |
| | | | Consist | B | MM | 3203 |

Seems fair to say that return from Tommy John surgery went well, with career-best skills across the board. Would also seem fair to expect a little Ctl regression, which might push ERA just over 4.00. And if we were to remind you that Health grade tempers expectations as much as skill resurgence raises them? Fair enough.

| Yr Tm | W | Sv | IP | K | ERA | xERA | WHIP | oOPS | vL | vR | BF/G | Ctl | Dom | Cmd | FpK | SwK | Vel | G | L | F | H% | S% | hr/f | GS | APC | DOM% | DIS% | Sv% | LI | RAR | BPV | BPX | R$ |
|---|---|---|---|---|---|---|---|---|---|---|---|---|---|---|---|---|---|---|---|---|---|---|---|---|---|---|---|---|---|---|---|---|---|
| 14 MIA | 6 | 0 | 200 | 142 | 4.37 | 3.90 | 1.33 | 732 | 768 | 688 | 25.9 | 1.9 | 6.4 | 3.3 | 63% | 9% | 95.7 | 45 | 22 | 33 | 33% | 67% | 7% | 33 | 97 | 33% | 30% | | | -15.5 | 86 | 102 | -$3 |
| 15 NYY | 14 | 0 | 154 | 121 | 4.20 | 3.98 | 1.45 | 716 | 781 | 656 | 24.9 | 2.9 | 7.1 | 2.5 | 60% | 9% | 96.7 | 52 | 22 | 26 | 34% | 71% | 8% | 27 | 98 | 19% | 30% | | | -4.5 | 80 | 95 | $1 |
| 16 NYY | 9 | 0 | 125 | 97 | 4.76 | 4.26 | 1.31 | 778 | 871 | 705 | 21.9 | 2.9 | 7.0 | 2.4 | 65% | 10% | 97.1 | 50 | 18 | 32 | 28% | 69% | 19% | 21 | 86 | 19% | 38% | 0 | 0.70 | -8.8 | 76 | 90 | $1 |
| 17 | | | | | | | | | | | | | | | | | | | | | | | | | | | | | | | | | |
| 18 2 AL | 6 | 0 | 111 | 101 | 3.81 | 3.75 | 1.13 | 685 | 737 | 633 | 20.7 | 1.6 | 8.2 | 5.1 | 64% | 11% | 97.2 | 46 | 19 | 35 | 30% | 70% | 12% | 21 | 82 | 24% | 19% | 0 | 0.75 | 4.6 | 128 | 147 | $6 |
| 1st Half | 2 | 0 | 35 | 30 | 4.08 | 3.61 | 0.82 | 649 | 671 | 631 | 22.3 | 1.3 | 7.6 | 6.0 | 66% | 10% | 97.0 | 47 | 12 | 40 | 19% | 62% | 21% | 6 | 93 | 17% | 0% | | | 0.3 | 129 | 148 | $0 |
| 2nd Half | 4 | 0 | 76 | 71 | 3.69 | 3.81 | 1.27 | 700 | 761 | 634 | 20.1 | 1.8 | 8.4 | 4.7 | 62% | 12% | 97.3 | 45 | 22 | 33 | 35% | 72% | 8% | 15 | 78 | 27% | 27% | 0 | 0.75 | 4.3 | 127 | 146 | $9 |
| **19 Proj** | **10** | **0** | **160** | **136** | **3.95** | **3.63** | **1.22** | **716** | **775** | **661** | **21.5** | **2.1** | **7.7** | **3.6** | **63%** | **10%** | **97.0** | **48** | **19** | **33** | **30%** | **72%** | **14%** | **30** | | | | | | **8.7** | **106** | **122** | **$9** |

## Erlin,Robert

| | | | | | | |
|---|---|---|---|---|---|---|
| Age: 28 | Th: L | Role RP | Health | F | LIMA Plan | A |
| Ht: 6' 0" | Wt: 190 | Type | PT/Exp | D | Rand Var | +2 |
| | | | Consist | A | MM | 2101 |

Came back from Tommy John surgery to turn in by far the best performance of his career, but low S% made it look pretty run-of-the-mill. Made major strides vR, including 6.7 Dom, 8.1 Cmd, that could bode well for chances of full-time return to starting. Just beware if he ever leaves SD—career road ERA is 6.21.

| Yr Tm | W | Sv | IP | K | ERA | xERA | WHIP | oOPS | vL | vR | BF/G | Ctl | Dom | Cmd | FpK | SwK | Vel | G | L | F | H% | S% | hr/f | GS | APC | DOM% | DIS% | Sv% | LI | RAR | BPV | BPX | R$ |
|---|---|---|---|---|---|---|---|---|---|---|---|---|---|---|---|---|---|---|---|---|---|---|---|---|---|---|---|---|---|---|---|---|---|
| 14 SD * | 4 | 0 | 82 | 61 | 5.28 | 5.32 | 1.53 | 787 | 755 | 799 | 19.9 | 2.2 | 6.7 | 3.0 | 65% | 9% | 89.7 | 41 | 27 | 32 | 36% | 66% | 10% | 11 | 77 | 18% | 45% | 0 | 0.70 | -15.7 | 68 | 81 | -$8 |
| 15 SD * | 8 | 0 | 142 | 99 | 5.41 | 5.53 | 1.50 | 663 | 1000 | 592 | 22.8 | 2.3 | 6.2 | 2.7 | 65% | 9% | 90.1 | 47 | 25 | 27 | 34% | 67% | 7% | 3 | 73 | 33% | 33% | | | -25.5 | 47 | 56 | -$11 |
| 16 SD | 1 | 0 | 16 | 13 | 4.02 | 3.50 | 0.96 | 750 | 426 | 882 | 19.3 | 1.7 | 7.5 | 4.3 | 57% | 10% | 88.0 | 43 | 24 | 33 | 22% | 67% | 21% | 2 | 68 | 50% | 50% | 0 | 0.74 | 0.3 | 109 | 129 | -$2 |
| 17 | | | | | | | | | | | | | | | | | | | | | | | | | | | | | | | | | |
| 18 SD | 4 | 0 | 109 | 88 | 4.21 | 3.63 | 1.14 | 695 | 713 | 688 | 11.3 | 1.0 | 7.3 | 7.3 | 64% | 10% | 90.3 | 47 | 23 | 30 | 31% | 65% | 12% | 12 | 41 | 0% | 50% | 0 | 0.67 | -0.8 | 129 | 149 | $3 |
| 1st Half | 1 | 0 | 48 | 40 | 4.15 | 3.41 | 1.07 | 705 | 903 | 615 | 8.5 | 0.9 | 7.6 | 8.0 | 65% | 10% | 89.8 | 48 | 22 | 30 | 30% | 64% | 15% | 2 | 31 | 0% | 100% | 0 | 0.55 | 0.0 | 137 | 157 | $0 |
| 2nd Half | 3 | 0 | 61 | 48 | 4.26 | 3.80 | 1.19 | 688 | 553 | 738 | 14.8 | 1.0 | 7.0 | 6.9 | 63% | 9% | 90.7 | 46 | 24 | 31 | 32% | 66% | 10% | 10 | 54 | 0% | 40% | 0 | 0.82 | -0.8 | 123 | 141 | $5 |
| **19 Proj** | **5** | **0** | **102** | **79** | **4.09** | **3.71** | **1.24** | **737** | **728** | **740** | **14.8** | **1.7** | **7.0** | **4.2** | **64%** | **10%** | **90.1** | **45** | **23** | **32** | **31%** | **70%** | **13%** | **13** | | | | | | **4.3** | **104** | **120** | **$2** |

BRANDON KRUSE

### Estrada,Marco

| | | | | | | | |
|---|---|---|---|---|---|---|---|
| Age: 35 | Th: R | Role | SP | Health | C | LIMA Plan | D+ |
| Ht: 6' 0" | Wt: 180 | Type | Pwr xFB | PT/Exp | A | Rand Var | 0 |
| | | | | Consist | B | MM | 0103 |

Season bookended by back woes; results suggest pain may never have left him. Also went on DL with hip injury, thus might need to demonstrate health to extend career. In SwK, there's faint glimmer of hope that Dom could rebound, but when extreme flyballers start to get hit hard, end is near... if not already here.

| Yr | Tm | W | Sv | IP | K | ERA | xERA | WHIP | oOPS | vL | vR | BF/G | Ctl | Dom | Cmd | FpK | SwK | Vel | G | L | F | H% | S% | hr/f | GS | APC | DOM% | DIS% | Sv% | LI | RAR | BPV | BPX | R$ |
|---|---|---|---|---|---|---|---|---|---|---|---|---|---|---|---|---|---|---|---|---|---|---|---|---|---|---|---|---|---|---|---|---|---|---|
| 14 | MIL | 7 | 0 | 151 | 127 | 4.36 | 4.15 | 1.20 | 752 | 719 | 781 | 16.0 | 2.6 | 7.6 | 2.9 | 61% | 11% | 89.0 | 33 | 18 | 50 | 27% | 71% | 13% | 18 | 65 | 11% | 50% | 0 | 0.63 | -11.5 | 77 | 91 | $2 |
| 15 | TOR | 13 | 0 | 181 | 131 | 3.13 | 4.61 | 1.04 | 633 | 638 | 626 | 21.3 | 2.7 | 6.5 | 2.4 | 57% | 10% | 89.3 | 32 | 16 | 52 | 22% | 76% | 9% | 28 | 86 | 21% | 29% | 0 | 0.76 | 18.5 | 53 | 64 | $20 |
| 16 | TOR | 9 | 0 | 176 | 165 | 3.48 | 4.52 | 1.12 | 639 | 602 | 680 | 24.9 | 3.3 | 8.4 | 2.5 | 59% | 11% | 88.1 | 33 | 18 | 48 | 25% | 74% | 10% | 29 | 98 | 34% | 17% | | | 15.5 | 73 | 87 | $16 |
| 17 | TOR | 10 | 0 | 186 | 176 | 4.98 | 5.09 | 1.38 | 785 | 686 | 864 | 24.4 | 3.4 | 8.5 | 2.5 | 59% | 11% | 89.9 | 30 | 19 | 50 | 31% | 68% | 11% | 33 | 98 | 21% | 30% | | | -14.4 | 69 | 82 | $1 |
| 18 | TOR | 7 | 0 | 144 | 103 | 5.64 | 5.76 | 1.43 | 852 | 759 | 922 | 22.4 | 3.1 | 6.5 | 2.1 | 63% | 11% | 88.6 | 24 | 20 | 56 | 29% | 65% | 11% | 28 | 89 | 4% | 43% | | | -26.4 | 34 | 39 | -$10 |
| 1st Half | | 4 | 0 | 89 | 69 | 4.53 | 5.19 | 1.30 | 798 | 731 | 848 | 23.4 | 2.4 | 7.0 | 2.9 | 65% | 11% | 89.0 | 26 | 20 | 54 | 30% | 70% | 9% | 16 | 96 | 6% | 31% | | | -4.2 | 64 | 73 | -$3 |
| 2nd Half | | 3 | 0 | 54 | 34 | 7.45 | 6.77 | 1.64 | 937 | 804 | 1034 | 21.1 | 4.3 | 5.6 | 1.3 | 61% | 11% | 87.9 | 21 | 21 | 58 | 29% | 59% | 14% | 12 | 81 | 0% | 58% | | | -22.1 | -16 | -18 | -$20 |
| **19** | **Proj** | **8** | **0** | **145** | **116** | **4.97** | **4.91** | **1.40** | **816** | **722** | **893** | **21.8** | **3.4** | **7.2** | **2.1** | **61%** | **11%** | **88.8** | **27** | **20** | **53** | **29%** | **70%** | **12%** | **28** | | | | | | **-14.7** | **43** | **49** | **-$3** |

### Familia,Jeurys

| | | | | | | | |
|---|---|---|---|---|---|---|---|
| Age: 29 | Th: R | Role | RP | Health | F | LIMA Plan | B |
| Ht: 6' 3" | Wt: 240 | Type | Pwr GB | PT/Exp | B | Rand Var | -2 |
| | | | | Consist | B | MM | 4420 |

Further he's gotten from 2017 blood clot in shoulder, more he's looked like his old self, though heavy ground ball tilt still somewhat AWOL. Still, 2nd half SwK is a positive sign, as is rebound in FpK. As a free agent, he's likely to find a suitor to give him ball in ninth, and if health holds, he should be able to earn his keep.

| Yr | Tm | W | Sv | IP | K | ERA | xERA | WHIP | oOPS | vL | vR | BF/G | Ctl | Dom | Cmd | FpK | SwK | Vel | G | L | F | H% | S% | hr/f | GS | APC | DOM% | DIS% | Sv% | LI | RAR | BPV | BPX | R$ |
|---|---|---|---|---|---|---|---|---|---|---|---|---|---|---|---|---|---|---|---|---|---|---|---|---|---|---|---|---|---|---|---|---|---|---|
| 14 | NYM | 2 | 5 | 77 | 73 | 2.21 | 3.36 | 1.18 | 587 | 821 | 377 | 4.2 | 3.7 | 8.5 | 2.3 | 53% | 13% | 96.4 | 57 | 15 | 28 | 28% | 82% | 5% | 0 | 16 | | | 50 | 1.18 | 14.6 | 87 | 104 | $7 |
| 15 | NYM | 2 | 43 | 78 | 86 | 1.85 | 2.62 | 1.00 | 569 | 616 | 531 | 4.1 | 2.2 | 9.9 | 4.5 | 61% | 16% | 97.1 | 58 | 20 | 22 | 28% | 86% | 14% | 0 | 15 | | | 90 | 1.29 | 20.4 | 155 | 185 | $27 |
| 16 | NYM | 3 | 51 | 78 | 84 | 2.55 | 3.02 | 1.21 | 574 | 629 | 526 | 4.1 | 3.6 | 9.7 | 2.7 | 57% | 15% | 96.2 | 63 | 18 | 19 | 31% | 77% | 3% | 0 | 16 | | | 91 | 1.22 | 15.7 | 119 | 142 | $27 |
| 17 | NYM | 2 | 6 | 25 | 25 | 4.38 | 4.05 | 1.46 | 636 | 760 | 542 | 4.3 | 5.5 | 9.1 | 1.7 | 44% | 10% | 95.9 | 60 | 21 | 19 | 31% | 69% | 8% | 0 | 16 | | | 86 | 1.08 | -0.1 | 54 | 65 | -$1 |
| 18 | 2 TM | 8 | 18 | 72 | 83 | 3.13 | 3.58 | 1.22 | 601 | 722 | 495 | 4.3 | 3.5 | 10.4 | 3.0 | 55% | 15% | 96.2 | 46 | 21 | 33 | 32% | 74% | 5% | 0 | 17 | | | 75 | 1.28 | 9.1 | 116 | 134 | $13 |
| 1st Half | | 3 | 14 | 34 | 37 | 3.48 | 3.75 | 1.43 | 689 | 896 | 513 | 4.5 | 3.5 | 9.9 | 2.8 | 48% | 12% | 95.7 | 52 | 17 | 32 | 37% | 74% | 3% | 0 | 18 | | | 78 | 1.51 | 2.8 | 114 | 131 | $10 |
| 2nd Half | | 5 | 4 | 38 | 46 | 2.82 | 3.44 | 1.04 | 516 | 561 | 477 | 4.2 | 3.5 | 10.8 | 3.1 | 61% | 17% | 96.6 | 41 | 25 | 34 | 27% | 74% | 6% | 0 | 17 | | | 67 | 1.07 | 6.3 | 118 | 136 | $16 |
| **19** | **Proj** | **5** | **23** | **65** | **72** | **3.09** | **3.09** | **1.17** | **607** | **713** | **515** | **4.1** | **3.4** | **10.0** | **3.0** | **56%** | **15%** | **96.4** | **53** | **20** | **27** | **30%** | **75%** | **10%** | **0** | | | | | | **8.5** | **120** | **138** | **$14** |

### Faria,Jake

| | | | | | | | |
|---|---|---|---|---|---|---|---|
| Age: 25 | Th: R | Role | RP | Health | F | LIMA Plan | B+ |
| Ht: 6' 4" | Wt: 235 | Type | Pwr FB | PT/Exp | D | Rand Var | +2 |
| | | | | Consist | B | MM | 1201 |

4-4, 5.40 ERA in 65 IP at TAM. May oblique injury tore two-plus months out of encore to promising MLB debut, and he never got on track. History of strikeout ability should lessen concern about Dom drop, bump in FpK fosters hope of better Ctl ahead. He's got work to do, but there's time to resume his progression.

| Yr | Tm | W | Sv | IP | K | ERA | xERA | WHIP | oOPS | vL | vR | BF/G | Ctl | Dom | Cmd | FpK | SwK | Vel | G | L | F | H% | S% | hr/f | GS | APC | DOM% | DIS% | Sv% | LI | RAR | BPV | BPX | R$ |
|---|---|---|---|---|---|---|---|---|---|---|---|---|---|---|---|---|---|---|---|---|---|---|---|---|---|---|---|---|---|---|---|---|---|---|
| 14 | | | | | | | | | | | | | | | | | | | | | | | | | | | | | | | | | | |
| 15 | aa | 7 | 0 | 75 | 85 | 2.80 | 2.58 | 1.14 | | | | 22.9 | 3.4 | 10.2 | 3.0 | | | | | | | 29% | 77% | | | | | | | | 10.8 | 118 | 141 | $7 |
| 16 | a/a | 5 | 0 | 151 | 138 | 5.07 | 3.56 | 1.34 | | | | 23.2 | 4.3 | 8.2 | 1.9 | | | | | | | 29% | 62% | | | | | | | | -16.3 | 74 | 88 | -$3 |
| 17 | TAM * | 11 | 0 | 145 | 157 | 3.71 | 3.70 | 1.24 | 677 | 559 | 729 | 21.8 | 3.4 | 9.7 | 2.9 | 54% | 13% | 91.8 | 38 | 22 | 40 | 30% | 75% | 12% | 14 | 90 | 36% | 29% | 0 | 0.76 | 11.6 | 91 | 109 | $12 |
| 18 | TAM * | 6 | 0 | 95 | 74 | 5.51 | 4.76 | 1.44 | 776 | 813 | 743 | 16.9 | 4.4 | 7.0 | 1.6 | 57% | 9% | 91.5 | 34 | 23 | 43 | 28% | 64% | 11% | 12 | 66 | 17% | 50% | 0 | 0.67 | -15.9 | 38 | 44 | -$7 |
| 1st Half | | 3 | 0 | 48 | 37 | 5.48 | 5.22 | 1.32 | 748 | 726 | 757 | 20.3 | 4.2 | 7.0 | 1.7 | 55% | 9% | 91.4 | 32 | 23 | 45 | 26% | 61% | 11% | 10 | 81 | 20% | 40% | | | -7.8 | 24 | 27 | -$7 |
| 2nd Half | | 3 | 0 | 47 | 37 | 5.54 | 5.39 | 1.56 | 847 | 1060 | 709 | 14.8 | 4.7 | 7.0 | 1.5 | 63% | 7% | 91.9 | 41 | 22 | 37 | 30% | 68% | 10% | 2 | 44 | 0% | 100% | 0 | 0.49 | -8.1 | 31 | 35 | -$7 |
| **19** | **Proj** | **8** | **0** | **116** | **109** | **4.32** | **4.22** | **1.34** | **741** | **775** | **717** | **18.8** | **3.9** | **8.5** | **2.2** | **58%** | **10%** | **91.7** | **38** | **22** | **40** | **29%** | **71%** | **12%** | **23** | | | | | | **-2.4** | **62** | **71** | **$2** |

### Farmer,Buck

| | | | | | | | |
|---|---|---|---|---|---|---|---|
| Age: 28 | Th: R | Role | RP | Health | A | LIMA Plan | D+ |
| Ht: 6' 4" | Wt: 232 | Type | Pwr FB | PT/Exp | C | Rand Var | -2 |
| | | | | Consist | B | MM | 0100 |

We know a thing or two because we've seen a thing or two. Move to pen spiking velocity but torpedoing Ctl? Seen it, covered it. Worm turn in 2nd half that is fool's gold, fueled by H%, hr/f? Seen it, covered it. Hopes for MLB career slamming up against limits of talent? Seen it, covered it. Bum ba-dum bum bum bum BUM.

| Yr | Tm | W | Sv | IP | K | ERA | xERA | WHIP | oOPS | vL | vR | BF/G | Ctl | Dom | Cmd | FpK | SwK | Vel | G | L | F | H% | S% | hr/f | GS | APC | DOM% | DIS% | Sv% | LI | RAR | BPV | BPX | R$ |
|---|---|---|---|---|---|---|---|---|---|---|---|---|---|---|---|---|---|---|---|---|---|---|---|---|---|---|---|---|---|---|---|---|---|---|
| 14 | DET * | 2 | 0 | 29 | 21 | 8.12 | 6.03 | 1.70 | 1054 | 1189 | 880 | 16.2 | 4.1 | 6.7 | 1.6 | 70% | 11% | 93.1 | 33 | 15 | 52 | 35% | 51% | 14% | 2 | 49 | 0% | 100% | 0 | 0.42 | -15.5 | 30 | 35 | -$8 |
| 15 | DET * | 7 | 0 | 127 | 84 | 5.70 | 5.29 | 1.53 | 986 | 1067 | 920 | 18.4 | 3.0 | 5.9 | 2.0 | 60% | 8% | 92.5 | 45 | 15 | 40 | 33% | 64% | 18% | 5 | 50 | 0% | 80% | 0 | 0.58 | -27.2 | 38 | 45 | -$12 |
| 16 | DET * | 5 | 0 | 129 | 100 | 5.11 | 5.57 | 1.60 | 771 | 903 | 604 | 16.8 | 3.5 | 7.0 | 2.0 | 60% | 11% | 92.9 | 52 | 11 | 37 | 34% | 71% | 13% | 1 | 36 | 0% | 100% | 0 | 0.28 | -14.7 | 42 | 49 | -$9 |
| 17 | DET * | 11 | 0 | 172 | 136 | 6.20 | 6.12 | 1.68 | 843 | 875 | 803 | 24.1 | 2.9 | 7.1 | 2.4 | 64% | 11% | 91.7 | 32 | 21 | 47 | 38% | 64% | 13% | 11 | 82 | 18% | 64% | | | -38.9 | 50 | 60 | -$16 |
| 18 | DET | 3 | 0 | 69 | 57 | 4.15 | 5.29 | 1.56 | 754 | 612 | 864 | 4.7 | 5.3 | 7.4 | 1.4 | 65% | 11% | 94.5 | 40 | 23 | 37 | 31% | 75% | 8% | 1 | 19 | 0% | 0% | 0 | 0.73 | 0.0 | 7 | 9 | -$5 |
| 1st Half | | 3 | 0 | 38 | 39 | 4.74 | 4.86 | 1.68 | 847 | 686 | 964 | 4.4 | 5.4 | 9.2 | 1.7 | 60% | 12% | 94.5 | 41 | 22 | 37 | 35% | 75% | 13% | 0 | 18 | | | 0 | 0.87 | -2.8 | 38 | 44 | -$6 |
| 2nd Half | | 0 | 0 | 31 | 18 | 3.45 | 5.81 | 1.40 | 636 | 524 | 729 | 5.0 | 5.2 | 5.2 | 1.0 | 71% | 10% | 94.4 | 39 | 23 | 37 | 26% | 74% | 3% | 1 | 20 | 0% | 0% | 0 | 0.54 | 2.7 | -29 | -33 | -$2 |
| **19** | **Proj** | **2** | **0** | **51** | **38** | **5.03** | **4.99** | **1.57** | **793** | **759** | **823** | **7.7** | **4.2** | **6.8** | **1.6** | **64%** | **11%** | **93.2** | **38** | **21** | **41** | **33%** | **69%** | **8%** | **0** | | | | | | **-4.0** | **25** | **29** | **-$6** |

### Fedde,Erick

| | | | | | | | |
|---|---|---|---|---|---|---|---|
| Age: 26 | Th: R | Role | SP | Health | D | LIMA Plan | C |
| Ht: 6' 4" | Wt: 195 | Type | Pwr GB | PT/Exp | D | Rand Var | +5 |
| | | | | Consist | B | MM | 2101 |

2-4, 5.54 ERA in 50 IP at WAS. Missed two months with stiff shoulder, so former first-rounder's MLB resume still thin. We know he can induce GBs; step one for better results: positive turn of hr/f. For next trick, needs to improve Ctl (no sign yet in FpK), miss more bats (no sign yet in SwK). Too soon to write him off.

| Yr | Tm | W | Sv | IP | K | ERA | xERA | WHIP | oOPS | vL | vR | BF/G | Ctl | Dom | Cmd | FpK | SwK | Vel | G | L | F | H% | S% | hr/f | GS | APC | DOM% | DIS% | Sv% | LI | RAR | BPV | BPX | R$ |
|---|---|---|---|---|---|---|---|---|---|---|---|---|---|---|---|---|---|---|---|---|---|---|---|---|---|---|---|---|---|---|---|---|---|---|
| 14 | | | | | | | | | | | | | | | | | | | | | | | | | | | | | | | | | | |
| 15 | | | | | | | | | | | | | | | | | | | | | | | | | | | | | | | | | | |
| 16 | aa | 2 | 0 | 29 | 24 | 5.30 | 5.47 | 1.72 | | | | 26.7 | 3.3 | 7.3 | 2.2 | | | | | | | 40% | 67% | | | | | | | | -4.0 | 69 | 83 | -$6 |
| 17 | WAS * | 4 | 0 | 106 | 80 | 5.34 | 5.02 | 1.46 | 1106 | 836 | 1445 | 14.1 | 2.7 | 6.8 | 2.5 | 71% | 6% | 92.9 | 62 | 17 | 21 | 33% | 65% | 50% | 3 | 99 | 0% | 100% | | | -12.8 | 57 | 68 | -$6 |
| 18 | WAS * | 5 | 0 | 122 | 105 | 5.58 | 5.61 | 1.63 | 846 | 878 | 820 | 21.8 | 3.2 | 7.8 | 2.4 | 55% | 9% | 93.7 | 53 | 22 | 24 | 38% | 66% | 22% | 11 | 86 | 9% | 64% | | | -21.6 | 65 | 75 | -$13 |
| 1st Half | | 4 | 0 | 85 | 68 | 6.20 | 6.32 | 1.72 | 936 | 862 | 1008 | 24.2 | 2.7 | 7.2 | 2.7 | 56% | 9% | 94.4 | 52 | 25 | 23 | 39% | 64% | 25% | 5 | 98 | 0% | 80% | | | -21.6 | 60 | 69 | -$20 |
| 2nd Half | | 1 | 0 | 40 | 37 | 4.16 | 3.78 | 1.37 | 737 | 900 | 629 | 18.4 | 4.2 | 8.5 | 2.0 | 52% | 9% | 93.0 | 55 | 18 | 27 | 31% | 70% | 19% | 6 | 76 | 17% | 50% | | | -0.1 | 80 | 92 | -$1 |
| **19** | **Proj** | **4** | **0** | **102** | **84** | **4.52** | **4.00** | **1.56** | **864** | **938** | **805** | **23.2** | **3.4** | **7.5** | **2.2** | **54%** | **9%** | **93.6** | **54** | **21** | **25** | **35%** | **74%** | **16%** | **15** | | | | | | **1.6** | **73** | **84** | **-$6** |

### Feliz,Michael

| | | | | | | | |
|---|---|---|---|---|---|---|---|
| Age: 26 | Th: R | Role | RP | Health | C | LIMA Plan | C |
| Ht: 6' 4" | Wt: 230 | Type | Pwr FB | PT/Exp | D | Rand Var | +5 |
| | | | | Consist | B | MM | 2400 |

Plan had been for him to fill key setup role—skills in 2016-2017 suggested he was ready—but velocity receded, took Dom with it. Shoulder issue that led to June DL stint may have been a factor. H%/S% luck has been lousy for two years running, and FpK says Ctl not a lost cause. Still owns 2016 skills, so keep a tab on him.

| Yr | Tm | W | Sv | IP | K | ERA | xERA | WHIP | oOPS | vL | vR | BF/G | Ctl | Dom | Cmd | FpK | SwK | Vel | G | L | F | H% | S% | hr/f | GS | APC | DOM% | DIS% | Sv% | LI | RAR | BPV | BPX | R$ |
|---|---|---|---|---|---|---|---|---|---|---|---|---|---|---|---|---|---|---|---|---|---|---|---|---|---|---|---|---|---|---|---|---|---|---|
| 14 | | | | | | | | | | | | | | | | | | | | | | | | | | | | | | | | | | |
| 15 | HOU * | 6 | 1 | 87 | 69 | 2.91 | 2.50 | 1.03 | 884 | 868 | 898 | 16.7 | 2.4 | 7.2 | 3.0 | 66% | 13% | 93.5 | 38 | 31 | 31 | 25% | 75% | 25% | 0 | 35 | | | 100 | 0.05 | 11.2 | 95 | 114 | $9 |
| 16 | HOU | 8 | 0 | 65 | 95 | 4.43 | 2.98 | 1.18 | 659 | 705 | 619 | 5.7 | 3.0 | 13.2 | 4.3 | 51% | 14% | 94.9 | 42 | 21 | 37 | 34% | 67% | 18% | 0 | 24 | | | 0 | 0.99 | -1.9 | 175 | 207 | $4 |
| 17 | HOU | 4 | 0 | 48 | 70 | 5.63 | 3.95 | 1.56 | 854 | 879 | 839 | 4.7 | 4.1 | 13.1 | 3.2 | 63% | 15% | 96.2 | 31 | 27 | 42 | 41% | 67% | 15% | 0 | 20 | | | 0 | 0.67 | -7.5 | 134 | 161 | -$4 |
| 18 | PIT | 1 | 0 | 48 | 55 | 5.66 | 4.44 | 1.51 | 776 | 730 | 815 | 4.6 | 4.3 | 10.4 | 2.4 | 61% | 10% | 94.7 | 32 | 29 | 39 | 35% | 64% | 11% | 0 | 20 | | | 0 | 0.76 | -8.9 | 80 | 92 | -$7 |
| 1st Half | | 0 | 0 | 33 | 39 | 5.51 | 4.20 | 1.47 | 793 | 772 | 810 | 4.4 | 4.4 | 10.7 | 2.4 | 60% | 10% | 94.9 | 31 | 32 | 38 | 34% | 65% | 15% | 0 | 19 | | | 0 | 0.82 | -5.5 | 83 | 95 | -$8 |
| 2nd Half | | 1 | 0 | 15 | 16 | 6.00 | 4.97 | 1.60 | 743 | 640 | 823 | 5.2 | 4.2 | 9.6 | 2.3 | 63% | 11% | 94.5 | 35 | 23 | 42 | 38% | 61% | 5% | 0 | 22 | | | 0 | 0.62 | -3.4 | 73 | 84 | -$5 |
| **19** | **Proj** | **3** | **0** | **44** | **51** | **4.02** | **3.82** | **1.35** | **697** | **673** | **715** | **4.9** | **4.3** | **10.6** | **2.5** | **61%** | **13%** | **95.2** | **34** | **26** | **40** | **31%** | **74%** | **12%** | **0** | | | | | | **2.1** | **87** | **100** | **-$2** |

### Ferguson,Caleb

| | | | | | | | |
|---|---|---|---|---|---|---|---|
| Age: 22 | Th: L | Role | RP | Health | A | LIMA Plan | B+ |
| Ht: 6' 3" | Wt: 215 | Type | Pwr | PT/Exp | F | Rand Var | 0 |
| | | | | Consist | F | MM | 4401 |

7-2, 3.49 ERA with 2 Sv in 49 IP at LA. 21-year-old rocketed through minors, got three June starts, then pitched out of pen into playoffs. Skills show plenty of promise, with velocity creeping up in 2nd half and Cmd spiking, while hr/f inflated MLB ERA. Deployment remains to be seen, but should help in almost any role.

| Yr | Tm | W | Sv | IP | K | ERA | xERA | WHIP | oOPS | vL | vR | BF/G | Ctl | Dom | Cmd | FpK | SwK | Vel | G | L | F | H% | S% | hr/f | GS | APC | DOM% | DIS% | Sv% | LI | RAR | BPV | BPX | R$ |
|---|---|---|---|---|---|---|---|---|---|---|---|---|---|---|---|---|---|---|---|---|---|---|---|---|---|---|---|---|---|---|---|---|---|---|
| 14 | | | | | | | | | | | | | | | | | | | | | | | | | | | | | | | | | | |
| 15 | | | | | | | | | | | | | | | | | | | | | | | | | | | | | | | | | | |
| 16 | | | | | | | | | | | | | | | | | | | | | | | | | | | | | | | | | | |
| 17 | | | | | | | | | | | | | | | | | | | | | | | | | | | | | | | | | | |
| 18 | LA * | 10 | 2 | 96 | 105 | 2.57 | 3.26 | 1.14 | 688 | 733 | 661 | 9.7 | 2.5 | 9.8 | 3.9 | 62% | 12% | 93.9 | 45 | 25 | 30 | 30% | 82% | 21% | 3 | 29 | 0% | 67% | 67 | 0.79 | 18.7 | 121 | 139 | $13 |
| 1st Half | | 4 | 0 | 64 | 67 | 2.60 | 2.97 | 1.19 | 694 | 1111 | 512 | 17.0 | 3.1 | 9.4 | 3.0 | 62% | 13% | 92.9 | 46 | 27 | 27 | 31% | 80% | 18% | 3 | 61 | 0% | 67% | 0 | 0.69 | 12.1 | 113 | 129 | $13 |
| 2nd Half | | 6 | 2 | 32 | 38 | 2.51 | 2.98 | 1.05 | 683 | 580 | 755 | 5.4 | 1.4 | 10.6 | 7.6 | 62% | 11% | 94.4 | 45 | 24 | 32 | 30% | 89% | 22% | 0 | 22 | | | 67 | 0.81 | 6.6 | 176 | 202 | $13 |
| **19** | **Proj** | **6** | **0** | **73** | **82** | **3.14** | **3.10** | **1.13** | **669** | **736** | **630** | **7.3** | **2.3** | **10.1** | **4.4** | **62%** | **12%** | **93.8** | **42** | **24** | **34** | **30%** | **79%** | **16%** | **5** | | | | | | **10.5** | **140** | **161** | **$6** |

KRISTOPHER OLSON

## Fiers,Mike

| | | | |
|---|---|---|---|
| Age: 34 Th: R Role SP | Health B | LIMA Plan C+ | |
| Ht: 6' 2" Wt: 202 Type | PT/Exp A | Rand Var -1 | |
| | Consist A | MM 2203 | |

Every once in a while, a player posts a rebound season fully supported by underlying skills, with no luck whatsoever. This is not one of those cases. 2nd half FpK is eye-popping, but fortunate S%/H% deserve plenty of credit for ERA/R$ goodness. xERA/BPX history says this is the same guy, which sounds about right.

| Yr Tm | W | Sv | IP | K | ERA | xERA | WHIP | oOPS | vL | vR | BF/G | Ctl | Dom | Cmd | FpK | SwK | Vel | G | L | F | H% | S% | hr/f | GS | APC | DOM% | DIS% | Sv% | LI | RAR | BPV | BPX | R$ |
|---|---|---|---|---|---|---|---|---|---|---|---|---|---|---|---|---|---|---|---|---|---|---|---|---|---|---|---|---|---|---|---|---|---|
| 14 MIL * | 14 | 0 | 174 | 174 | 2.90 | 3.07 | 1.08 | 531 | 517 | 542 | 21.9 | 1.9 | 9.0 | 4.7 | 58% | 10% | 89.6 | 33 | 20 | 47 | 29% | 78% | 8% | 10 | 80 | 60% | 0% | 0 | 0.74 | 18.0 | 131 | 156 | $19 |
| 15 2 TM | 7 | 0 | 180 | 180 | 3.69 | 4.00 | 1.25 | 713 | 664 | 756 | 24.5 | 3.2 | 9.0 | 2.8 | 60% | 10% | 89.4 | 38 | 20 | 42 | 30% | 75% | 11% | 30 | 98 | 20% | 20% | 0 | 0.78 | 6.0 | 91 | 109 | $8 |
| 16 HOU | 11 | 0 | 169 | 134 | 4.48 | 4.24 | 1.36 | 801 | 749 | 843 | 23.4 | 2.2 | 7.2 | 3.2 | 63% | 9% | 89.6 | 42 | 26 | 32 | 32% | 71% | 15% | 30 | 89 | 30% | 40% | 0 | 0.76 | -6.1 | 88 | 105 | $2 |
| 17 HOU | 8 | 0 | 153 | 146 | 5.22 | 4.48 | 1.43 | 827 | 809 | 844 | 23.1 | 3.6 | 8.6 | 2.4 | 60% | 10% | 89.7 | 43 | 20 | 37 | 30% | 70% | 20% | 28 | 91 | 18% | 36% | 0 | 0.75 | -16.4 | 77 | 92 | -$3 |
| 18 2 AL | 12 | 0 | 172 | 139 | 3.56 | 4.41 | 1.18 | 746 | 707 | 787 | 23.0 | 1.9 | 7.3 | 3.8 | 66% | 9% | 89.4 | 39 | 17 | 43 | 28% | 79% | 14% | 30 | 87 | 20% | 40% | 0 | 0.76 | 12.6 | 96 | 110 | $13 |
| 1st Half | 5 | 0 | 85 | 63 | 4.04 | 4.80 | 1.29 | 793 | 789 | 797 | 24.2 | 2.0 | 6.7 | 3.3 | 63% | 9% | 88.5 | 38 | 17 | 45 | 30% | 76% | 13% | 15 | 90 | 20% | 47% | | | 1.2 | 82 | 94 | $4 |
| 2nd Half | 7 | 0 | 87 | 76 | 3.09 | 4.04 | 1.08 | 699 | 630 | 776 | 21.9 | 1.9 | 7.8 | 4.2 | 69% | 9% | 90.3 | 41 | 17 | 42 | 26% | 82% | 15% | 15 | 83 | 20% | 33% | 0 | 0.76 | 11.4 | 110 | 126 | $22 |
| **19 Proj** | **10** | **0** | **167** | **142** | **4.04** | **4.01** | **1.26** | **766** | **728** | **804** | **22.3** | **2.5** | **7.6** | **3.0** | **64%** | **9%** | **89.6** | **41** | **20** | **40** | **29%** | **75%** | **15%** | **30** | | | | | | **2.2** | **88** | **101** | **$7** |

## Fillmyer,Heath

| | | | |
|---|---|---|---|
| Age: 25 Th: R Role SP | Health A | LIMA Plan D+ | |
| Ht: 6' 1" Wt: 195 Type | PT/Exp D | Rand Var +2 | |
| | Consist C | MM 0001 | |

4-2, 4.26 ERA in 82 IP at KC. Bumpy MLB debut for converted SS, whose pinpoint Ctl from 2016 in Double-A slipped farther into rear view. Unless that returns, expect turbulence given his lack of dominant stuff. A faint hope? Went +7 IP in 4 of 5 September starts, 107 BPV. Don't bet the rent on that tiny data parse.

| Yr Tm | W | Sv | IP | K | ERA | xERA | WHIP | oOPS | vL | vR | BF/G | Ctl | Dom | Cmd | FpK | SwK | Vel | G | L | F | H% | S% | hr/f | GS | APC | DOM% | DIS% | Sv% | LI | RAR | BPV | BPX | R$ |
|---|---|---|---|---|---|---|---|---|---|---|---|---|---|---|---|---|---|---|---|---|---|---|---|---|---|---|---|---|---|---|---|---|---|
| 14 | | | | | | | | | | | | | | | | | | | | | | | | | | | | | | | | | |
| 15 | | | | | | | | | | | | | | | | | | | | | | | | | | | | | | | | | |
| 16 aa | 2 | 0 | 39 | 24 | 3.02 | 2.98 | 1.10 | | | | 19.1 | 1.8 | 5.5 | 3.1 | | | | | | | 27% | 75% | | | | | | | | 5.6 | 85 | 100 | $1 |
| 17 aa | 11 | 0 | 150 | 95 | 4.09 | 5.33 | 1.53 | | | | 22.5 | 3.0 | 5.7 | 1.9 | | | | | | | 33% | 77% | | | | | | | | 5.0 | 36 | 44 | $0 |
| 18 KC * | 8 | 0 | 150 | 95 | 5.56 | 5.30 | 1.57 | 721 | 648 | 808 | 22.0 | 3.6 | 5.7 | 1.6 | 59% | 9% | 92.5 | 46 | 22 | 31 | 33% | 65% | 14% | 13 | 78 | 23% | 46% | 0 | 0.72 | -26.2 | 34 | 39 | -$14 |
| 1st Half | 4 | 0 | 74 | 41 | 6.79 | 6.20 | 1.78 | 642 | 393 | 767 | 22.7 | 3.7 | 5.0 | 1.3 | 35% | 8% | 92.1 | 50 | 17 | 33 | 36% | 60% | 17% | 0 | 42 | | | 0 | 0.17 | -24.2 | 25 | 28 | -$28 |
| 2nd Half | 4 | 0 | 76 | 54 | 4.36 | 4.59 | 1.36 | 727 | 659 | 812 | 21.4 | 3.5 | 6.4 | 1.8 | 61% | 9% | 92.6 | 46 | 23 | 31 | 28% | 71% | 14% | 13 | 83 | 23% | 46% | 0 | 0.79 | -2.0 | 43 | 50 | $0 |
| **19 Proj** | **7** | **0** | **116** | **74** | **4.55** | **4.76** | **1.47** | **714** | **651** | **793** | **21.6** | **3.1** | **5.7** | **1.8** | **61%** | **9%** | **92.6** | **44** | **21** | **35** | **32%** | **71%** | **9%** | **23** | | | | | | **-5.7** | **41** | **47** | **-$4** |

## Fister,Doug

| | | | |
|---|---|---|---|
| Age: 35 Th: R Role SP | Health F | LIMA Plan D+ | |
| Ht: 6' 8" Wt: 210 Type | PT/Exp C | Rand Var +2 | |
| | Consist B | MM 1001 | |

Couldn't replicate 2017's K spike (8.3 Dom at MLB), falling back to career levels as SwK hit new low. The bigger issue was health, as hip/knee injuries wrecked his season. That leaves us with an aging soft-tosser whose Ctl/GB combo may keep him MLB viable, but hardly useful for even deep-league fantasy rosters.

| Yr Tm | W | Sv | IP | K | ERA | xERA | WHIP | oOPS | vL | vR | BF/G | Ctl | Dom | Cmd | FpK | SwK | Vel | G | L | F | H% | S% | hr/f | GS | APC | DOM% | DIS% | Sv% | LI | RAR | BPV | BPX | R$ |
|---|---|---|---|---|---|---|---|---|---|---|---|---|---|---|---|---|---|---|---|---|---|---|---|---|---|---|---|---|---|---|---|---|---|
| 14 WAS | 16 | 0 | 164 | 98 | 2.41 | 3.75 | 1.08 | 654 | 690 | 618 | 26.5 | 1.3 | 5.4 | 4.1 | 65% | 6% | 87.9 | 49 | 17 | 34 | 27% | 84% | 10% | 25 | 99 | 36% | 36% | | | 26.8 | 88 | 105 | $19 |
| 15 WAS | 5 | 1 | 103 | 63 | 4.19 | 4.49 | 1.40 | 796 | 738 | 860 | 18.0 | 2.1 | 5.5 | 2.6 | 62% | 6% | 86.2 | 45 | 21 | 34 | 32% | 74% | 12% | 15 | 66 | 20% | 47% | 100 | 0.86 | -3.0 | 65 | 78 | -$3 |
| 16 HOU | 12 | 0 | 180 | 115 | 4.64 | 4.88 | 1.43 | 788 | 946 | 606 | 24.3 | 3.1 | 5.7 | 1.9 | 60% | 6% | 87.0 | 45 | 20 | 34 | 30% | 70% | 12% | 32 | 94 | 22% | 47% | | | -10.1 | 43 | 51 | -$1 |
| 17 BOS * | 6 | 0 | 106 | 90 | 4.83 | 4.12 | 1.41 | 726 | 862 | 589 | 21.3 | 3.7 | 7.7 | 2.1 | 60% | 8% | 89.8 | 51 | 21 | 29 | 32% | 66% | 12% | 15 | 85 | 33% | 33% | 0 | 1.06 | -6.2 | 70 | 84 | -$2 |
| 18 TEX | 1 | 0 | 66 | 40 | 4.50 | 4.51 | 1.39 | 795 | 736 | 844 | 24.1 | 2.6 | 5.5 | 2.1 | 59% | 5% | 88.4 | 50 | 23 | 26 | 30% | 73% | 19% | 12 | 93 | 8% | 42% | | | -2.8 | 56 | 65 | -$5 |
| 1st Half | 1 | 0 | 66 | 40 | 4.50 | 4.51 | 1.39 | 795 | 736 | 844 | 24.1 | 2.6 | 5.5 | 2.1 | 59% | 5% | 88.4 | 50 | 23 | 26 | 30% | 73% | 19% | 12 | 93 | 8% | 42% | | | -2.8 | 57 | 65 | -$5 |
| 2nd Half | | | | | | | | | | | | | | | | | | | | | | | | | | | | | | | | | |
| **19 Proj** | **5** | **0** | **102** | **67** | **4.61** | **4.33** | **1.38** | **769** | **816** | **723** | **22.1** | **2.8** | **6.0** | **2.1** | **60%** | **6%** | **87.9** | **47** | **21** | **32** | **30%** | **70%** | **13%** | **19** | | | | | | **-5.8** | **56** | **65** | **-$3** |

## Flaherty,Jack

| | | | |
|---|---|---|---|
| Age: 23 Th: R Role SP | Health A | LIMA Plan C+ | |
| Ht: 6' 4" Wt: 205 Type Pwr | PT/Exp D | Rand Var 0 | |
| | Consist B | MM 3405 | |

8-9, 3.34 ERA in 151 IP at STL. Budding prospect rode GIF-worthy slider to lights-out year, with elite K ability fully supported by SwK. Control issues from 2017 debut (4.2 Ctl in MLB) improved, but still present—and shaky FpK says he's not out of the woods just yet. Despite upside, hype might outweigh profit in 2019.

| Yr Tm | W | Sv | IP | K | ERA | xERA | WHIP | oOPS | vL | vR | BF/G | Ctl | Dom | Cmd | FpK | SwK | Vel | G | L | F | H% | S% | hr/f | GS | APC | DOM% | DIS% | Sv% | LI | RAR | BPV | BPX | R$ |
|---|---|---|---|---|---|---|---|---|---|---|---|---|---|---|---|---|---|---|---|---|---|---|---|---|---|---|---|---|---|---|---|---|---|
| 14 | | | | | | | | | | | | | | | | | | | | | | | | | | | | | | | | | |
| 15 | | | | | | | | | | | | | | | | | | | | | | | | | | | | | | | | | |
| 16 | | | | | | | | | | | | | | | | | | | | | | | | | | | | | | | | | |
| 17 STL * | 14 | 0 | 170 | 144 | 3.05 | 3.48 | 1.19 | 843 | 1096 | 588 | 22.0 | 2.3 | 7.6 | 3.3 | 63% | 14% | 93.2 | 48 | 22 | 30 | 30% | 78% | 21% | 5 | 60 | 0% | 80% | 0 | 0.65 | 27.4 | 94 | 113 | $19 |
| 18 STL * | 12 | 0 | 184 | 216 | 3.17 | 2.83 | 1.07 | 635 | 610 | 660 | 21.7 | 3.2 | 10.6 | 3.3 | 57% | 14% | 92.7 | 42 | 21 | 37 | 27% | 76% | 15% | 28 | 92 | 21% | 18% | | | 22.3 | 115 | 132 | $23 |
| 1st Half | 7 | 0 | 95 | 107 | 2.73 | 2.78 | 1.02 | 645 | 650 | 640 | 22.8 | 2.3 | 10.1 | 4.3 | 55% | 13% | 92.3 | 44 | 19 | 36 | 28% | 79% | 16% | 11 | 96 | 27% | 27% | | | 16.6 | 134 | 154 | $27 |
| 2nd Half | 5 | 0 | 89 | 109 | 3.63 | 3.55 | 1.13 | 628 | 580 | 674 | 21.4 | 4.1 | 11.0 | 2.7 | 59% | 15% | 92.9 | 40 | 22 | 37 | 26% | 72% | 14% | 17 | 90 | 18% | 12% | | | 5.8 | 105 | 120 | $18 |
| **19 Proj** | **13** | **0** | **181** | **205** | **3.53** | **3.39** | **1.18** | **677** | **650** | **703** | **22.0** | **3.3** | **10.2** | **3.1** | **57%** | **14%** | **92.7** | **42** | **21** | **37** | **29%** | **74%** | **13%** | **33** | | | | | | **19.3** | **115** | **132** | **$17** |

## Floro,Dylan

| | | | |
|---|---|---|---|
| Age: 28 Th: R Role RP | Health A | LIMA Plan B | |
| Ht: 6' 2" Wt: 205 Type GB | PT/Exp D | Rand Var -5 | |
| | Consist D | MM 2100 | |

Midseason acquisition rose up pecking order after July trade, posting 2.69 ERA, 10.1 Dom in 28 IP at LA. Got support from healthy 2nd half SwK boost while maintaining GB%, and struggles vL were exaggerated by 38% H%. Fortunate S%, indeed, but sneaky upside if he can rediscover impressive Ctl he flashed at MiLB level.

| Yr Tm | W | Sv | IP | K | ERA | xERA | WHIP | oOPS | vL | vR | BF/G | Ctl | Dom | Cmd | FpK | SwK | Vel | G | L | F | H% | S% | hr/f | GS | APC | DOM% | DIS% | Sv% | LI | RAR | BPV | BPX | R$ |
|---|---|---|---|---|---|---|---|---|---|---|---|---|---|---|---|---|---|---|---|---|---|---|---|---|---|---|---|---|---|---|---|---|---|
| 14 aa | 11 | 0 | 179 | 95 | 4.04 | 4.66 | 1.47 | | | | 27.4 | 1.2 | 4.8 | 3.9 | | | | | | | 36% | 71% | | | | | | | | -6.5 | 96 | 114 | -$4 |
| 15 aaa | 9 | 0 | 133 | 68 | 6.38 | 5.89 | 1.62 | | | | 23.6 | 1.5 | 4.6 | 3.1 | | | | | | | 37% | 59% | | | | | | | | -39.6 | 55 | 66 | -$18 |
| 16 TAM * | 1 | 7 | 65 | 47 | 4.12 | 6.03 | 1.64 | 813 | 777 | 836 | 6.6 | 2.1 | 6.5 | 3.1 | 67% | 9% | 92.5 | 55 | 21 | 25 | 38% | 78% | 0% | 0 | 21 | | | 78 | 0.77 | 0.6 | 61 | 72 | -$3 |
| 17 CHC * | 3 | 2 | 70 | 36 | 5.36 | 6.82 | 1.66 | 971 | 1021 | 955 | 8.7 | 1.7 | 4.7 | 2.8 | 58% | 9% | 91.3 | 50 | 19 | 31 | 36% | 72% | 18% | 0 | 44 | | | 67 | 0.15 | -8.6 | 25 | 30 | -$7 |
| 18 2 NL | 6 | 0 | 64 | 58 | 2.25 | 3.79 | 1.25 | 634 | 757 | 561 | 5.0 | 3.2 | 8.2 | 2.5 | 61% | 12% | 93.3 | 55 | 18 | 26 | 31% | 83% | 6% | 0 | 18 | | | 0 | 1.06 | 15.0 | 92 | 106 | $5 |
| 1st Half | 2 | 0 | 34 | 25 | 2.91 | 4.32 | 1.41 | 735 | 878 | 627 | 6.5 | 2.9 | 6.6 | 2.3 | 64% | 9% | 92.8 | 56 | 16 | 28 | 33% | 80% | 6% | 0 | 23 | | | 0 | 0.78 | 5.2 | 75 | 86 | -$2 |
| 2nd Half | 4 | 0 | 30 | 33 | 1.50 | 3.23 | 1.07 | 509 | 543 | 493 | 3.9 | 3.6 | 9.9 | 2.8 | 57% | 15% | 93.9 | 53 | 22 | 25 | 27% | 87% | 6% | 0 | 15 | | | 0 | 1.27 | 9.8 | 112 | 129 | $10 |
| **19 Proj** | **4** | **0** | **58** | **44** | **3.50** | **3.70** | **1.31** | **724** | **846** | **656** | **6.0** | **2.5** | **6.9** | **2.7** | **60%** | **12%** | **93.4** | **55** | **20** | **26** | **31%** | **75%** | **11%** | **0** | | | | | | **2.5** | **89** | **102** | **$0** |

## Flynn,Brian

| | | | |
|---|---|---|---|
| Age: 29 Th: L Role RP | Health F | LIMA Plan D+ | |
| Ht: 6' 7" Wt: 255 Type GB | PT/Exp D | Rand Var -1 | |
| | Consist F | MM 0001 | |

Imposing lefty missed much of 2017 after... [double-checks notes]... falling through barn roof. Passed over for saves chances midway through 2018, and hard to see him knocking on door anytime soon. Nice GB%, but SwK/Dom uninspiring and FpK says Ctl actually could have been worse. Avoid until further notice.

| Yr Tm | W | Sv | IP | K | ERA | xERA | WHIP | oOPS | vL | vR | BF/G | Ctl | Dom | Cmd | FpK | SwK | Vel | G | L | F | H% | S% | hr/f | GS | APC | DOM% | DIS% | Sv% | LI | RAR | BPV | BPX | R$ |
|---|---|---|---|---|---|---|---|---|---|---|---|---|---|---|---|---|---|---|---|---|---|---|---|---|---|---|---|---|---|---|---|---|---|
| 14 MIA * | 8 | 0 | 147 | 91 | 4.37 | 5.48 | 1.66 | 929 | 667 | 987 | 24.3 | 3.1 | 5.6 | 1.8 | 60% | 4% | 90.4 | 50 | 27 | 23 | 36% | 74% | 0% | 1 | 70 | 0% | 100% | 0 | 0.61 | -11.5 | 44 | 52 | -$10 |
| 15 | | | | | | | | | | | | | | | | | | | | | | | | | | | | | | | | | |
| 16 KC * | 3 | 0 | 79 | 66 | 2.97 | 3.18 | 1.27 | 598 | 585 | 605 | 7.2 | 4.0 | 7.5 | 1.8 | 55% | 11% | 92.6 | 55 | 18 | 27 | 27% | 79% | 13% | 1 | 23 | 0% | 100% | 0 | 0.87 | 11.9 | 73 | 87 | $4 |
| 17 KC * | 5 | 0 | 52 | 38 | 7.05 | 8.46 | 1.95 | 1250 | 1200 | 1333 | 10.9 | 2.3 | 6.5 | 2.9 | 75% | 0% | 92.6 | 38 | 25 | 38 | 42% | 67% | 0% | 0 | 29 | | | 0 | 0.46 | -17.4 | 22 | 27 | -$12 |
| 18 KC | 3 | 1 | 76 | 47 | 4.04 | 5.07 | 1.61 | 790 | 776 | 796 | 7.0 | 4.2 | 5.6 | 1.3 | 48% | 9% | 91.8 | 50 | 21 | 29 | 33% | 75% | 7% | 0 | 26 | | | 50 | 0.63 | 1.0 | 16 | 19 | -$6 |
| 1st Half | 0 | 1 | 35 | 20 | 4.15 | 5.45 | 1.73 | 844 | 905 | 821 | 7.2 | 4.4 | 5.2 | 1.2 | 48% | 9% | 92.0 | 45 | 25 | 30 | 35% | 76% | 6% | 0 | 27 | | | 50 | 0.59 | 0.0 | -3 | -3 | -$12 |
| 2nd Half | 3 | 0 | 41 | 27 | 3.95 | 4.75 | 1.51 | 743 | 683 | 771 | 6.8 | 4.0 | 5.9 | 1.5 | 49% | 9% | 91.7 | 54 | 18 | 28 | 32% | 75% | 8% | 0 | 25 | | | 0 | 0.67 | 1.0 | 32 | 37 | -$2 |
| **19 Proj** | **4** | **0** | **73** | **49** | **4.66** | **4.73** | **1.70** | **886** | **860** | **898** | **8.5** | **4.0** | **6.1** | **1.5** | **51%** | **10%** | **92.1** | **52** | **20** | **28** | **35%** | **74%** | **11%** | **0** | | | | | | **-3.5** | **32** | **37** | **-$7** |

## Foltynewicz,Mike

| | | | |
|---|---|---|---|
| Age: 27 Th: R Role SP | Health C | LIMA Plan D+ | |
| Ht: 6' 4" Wt: 200 Type Pwr | PT/Exp B | Rand Var -3 | |
| | Consist B | MM 2305 | |

Best season yet for post-hype SP, using more effective slider (27% usage, 19% SwK) en route to 200-K season. SwK doesn't support quite that much Dom, and modest H%/S% pullback likely coming. Still, premium velocity paired with improving Cmd/GB paint an optimistic picture. A fine addition—just don't go overboard.

| Yr Tm | W | Sv | IP | K | ERA | xERA | WHIP | oOPS | vL | vR | BF/G | Ctl | Dom | Cmd | FpK | SwK | Vel | G | L | F | H% | S% | hr/f | GS | APC | DOM% | DIS% | Sv% | LI | RAR | BPV | BPX | R$ |
|---|---|---|---|---|---|---|---|---|---|---|---|---|---|---|---|---|---|---|---|---|---|---|---|---|---|---|---|---|---|---|---|---|---|
| 14 HOU * | 7 | 0 | 121 | 103 | 5.36 | 4.77 | 1.53 | 864 | 1062 | 659 | 14.3 | 4.2 | 7.6 | 1.8 | 52% | 10% | 96.7 | 29 | 21 | 51 | 33% | 66% | 9% | 0 | 20 | | | 0 | 0.38 | -24.2 | 55 | 66 | -$9 |
| 15 ATL * | 5 | 0 | 143 | 132 | 5.26 | 5.96 | 1.62 | 896 | 950 | 843 | 22.7 | 3.6 | 8.3 | 2.3 | 63% | 10% | 95.0 | 33 | 23 | 44 | 36% | 72% | 14% | 15 | 82 | 13% | 40% | 0 | 0.99 | -22.9 | 46 | 55 | -$13 |
| 16 ATL * | 10 | 0 | 150 | 132 | 3.93 | 3.89 | 1.28 | 761 | 775 | 750 | 22.8 | 3.0 | 7.9 | 2.6 | 63% | 10% | 95.2 | 41 | 21 | 37 | 30% | 73% | 13% | 22 | 96 | 23% | 32% | | | 4.8 | 75 | 89 | $7 |
| 17 ATL | 10 | 0 | 154 | 143 | 4.79 | 4.68 | 1.48 | 795 | 879 | 716 | 23.9 | 3.4 | 8.4 | 2.4 | 62% | 10% | 95.3 | 39 | 24 | 36 | 34% | 70% | 12% | 28 | 96 | 18% | 36% | 0 | 0.76 | -8.2 | 74 | 89 | -$1 |
| 18 ATL | 13 | 0 | 183 | 202 | 2.85 | 3.70 | 1.08 | 600 | 618 | 580 | 24.0 | 3.3 | 9.9 | 3.0 | 62% | 11% | 96.4 | 43 | 19 | 38 | 26% | 77% | 10% | 31 | 98 | 39% | 23% | | | 29.3 | 110 | 126 | $25 |
| 1st Half | 5 | 0 | 84 | 98 | 2.14 | 3.60 | 1.13 | 593 | 651 | 530 | 23.0 | 4.0 | 10.5 | 2.6 | 63% | 10% | 96.5 | 44 | 21 | 34 | 27% | 84% | 8% | 15 | 98 | 27% | 27% | | | 20.8 | 104 | 120 | $23 |
| 2nd Half | 8 | 0 | 99 | 104 | 3.45 | 3.79 | 1.04 | 605 | 589 | 621 | 24.9 | 2.8 | 9.5 | 3.4 | 60% | 11% | 96.4 | 42 | 16 | 41 | 26% | 71% | 10% | 16 | 98 | 50% | 19% | | | 8.5 | 114 | 131 | $27 |
| **19 Proj** | **12** | **0** | **181** | **186** | **3.49** | **3.69** | **1.22** | **675** | **708** | **644** | **22.1** | **3.3** | **9.3** | **2.8** | **62%** | **10%** | **95.8** | **41** | **21** | **38** | **29%** | **75%** | **11%** | **33** | | | | | | **10.5** | **96** | **111** | **$15** |

BRIAN SLACK

## Font,Wilmer

| Font,Wilmer | | Health | F | LIMA Plan | C |
|---|---|---|---|---|---|
| Age: 29 | Th: R Role RP | PT/Exp | D | Rand Var | +5 |
| Ht: 6' 4" | Wt: 265 Type Pwr xFB | Consist | B | MM | 1101 |

Finally stuck in majors, but it wasn't pretty. Doesn't miss enough bats for a bullpen arm and only 22 pitchers gave up a higher exit velocity. Combined with wobbly control foundation and injury history, there's still no reason for optimism. His window of opportunity is closing quickly.

| Yr Tm | W | Sv | IP | K | ERA | xERA | WHIP | oOPS | vL | vR | BF/G | Ctl | Dom | Cmd | FpK | SwK | Vel | G | L | F | H% | S% | hr/f | GS | APC | DOM% | DIS% | Sv% | LI | RAR | BPV | BPX | R$ |
|---|---|---|---|---|---|---|---|---|---|---|---|---|---|---|---|---|---|---|---|---|---|---|---|---|---|---|---|---|---|---|---|---|---|
| 14 aa | 2 | 3 | 31 | 25 | 4.36 | 4.22 | 1.53 | | | | 4.7 | 5.2 | 7.4 | 1.4 | | | | | | | 31% | 72% | | | | | | | | -2.4 | 58 | 70 | -$3 |
| 15 | | | | | | | | | | | | | | | | | | | | | | | | | | | | | | | | | |
| 16 a/a | 4 | 0 | 66 | 44 | 5.38 | 5.40 | 1.42 | | | | 23.3 | 1.9 | 6.0 | 3.2 | | | | | | | 33% | 66% | | | | | | | | -9.7 | 53 | 63 | -$5 |
| 17 LA * | 10 | 0 | 138 | 144 | 4.55 | 4.24 | 1.34 | 1389 | 946 | 1662 | 20.5 | 2.6 | 9.4 | 3.7 | 59% | 11% | 93.8 | 27 | 27 | 47 | 35% | 68% | 29% | 0 | 30 | | | 0 | 0.33 | -3.3 | 106 | 127 | $4 |
| 18 3 TM | 2 | 0 | 44 | 36 | 5.93 | 4.88 | 1.41 | 842 | 835 | 847 | 10.1 | 3.3 | 7.4 | 2.3 | 57% | 10% | 94.4 | 43 | 14 | 42 | 28% | 66% | 20% | 5 | 44 | 20% | 0% | 0 | 0.54 | -9.7 | 65 | 75 | -$7 |
| 1st Half | 2 | 0 | 44 | 36 | 5.93 | 4.88 | 1.41 | 842 | 835 | 847 | 10.1 | 3.3 | 7.4 | 2.3 | 57% | 10% | 94.4 | 43 | 14 | 42 | 28% | 66% | 20% | 5 | 44 | 20% | 0% | 0 | 0.54 | -9.7 | 65 | 75 | -$7 |
| 2nd Half | | | | | | | | | | | | | | | | | | | | | | | | | | | | | | | | | |
| 19 Proj | 4 | 0 | 73 | 59 | 5.21 | 4.50 | 1.42 | 719 | 701 | 731 | 11.3 | 2.9 | 7.3 | 2.5 | 57% | 10% | 94.4 | 43 | 14 | 42 | 31% | 67% | 12% | 4 | | | | | | -9.4 | 73 | 84 | -$5 |

## Freeland,Kyle

| Freeland,Kyle | | Health | A | LIMA Plan | D |
|---|---|---|---|---|---|
| Age: 26 | Th: L Role SP | PT/Exp | B | Rand Var | -3 |
| Ht: 6' 3" | Wt: 170 Type | Consist | B | MM | 1103 |

One of 2018's top SP profit centers (ADP 491), he even posted a 2.40 ERA at Coors Field. Three reasons he'll be overvalued: 1) FpK gains offset by high ball%; 2) that strand rate won't stick; 3) improving BPV still below average and unsupportive of such a low ERA. xERA tells the true tale. That's the prudent baseline.

| Yr Tm | W | Sv | IP | K | ERA | xERA | WHIP | oOPS | vL | vR | BF/G | Ctl | Dom | Cmd | FpK | SwK | Vel | G | L | F | H% | S% | hr/f | GS | APC | DOM% | DIS% | Sv% | LI | RAR | BPV | BPX | R$ |
|---|---|---|---|---|---|---|---|---|---|---|---|---|---|---|---|---|---|---|---|---|---|---|---|---|---|---|---|---|---|---|---|---|---|
| 14 | | | | | | | | | | | | | | | | | | | | | | | | | | | | | | | | | |
| 15 | | | | | | | | | | | | | | | | | | | | | | | | | | | | | | | | | |
| 16 a/a | 11 | 0 | 162 | 84 | 5.76 | 5.94 | 1.60 | | | | 27.6 | 2.7 | 4.7 | 1.7 | | | | | | | 33% | 66% | | | | | | | | -31.4 | 16 | 19 | -$14 |
| 17 COL | 11 | 0 | 156 | 107 | 4.10 | 4.72 | 1.49 | 792 | 755 | 803 | 20.8 | 3.6 | 6.2 | 1.7 | 55% | 8% | 92.0 | 54 | 19 | 28 | 31% | 75% | 13% | 28 | 78 | 14% | 68% | 0 | 0.69 | 5.0 | 45 | 54 | $2 |
| 18 COL | 17 | 0 | 202 | 173 | 2.85 | 4.19 | 1.25 | 666 | 519 | 704 | 25.6 | 3.1 | 7.7 | 2.5 | 62% | 10% | 91.6 | 46 | 19 | 35 | 29% | 80% | 8% | 33 | 98 | 33% | 21% | | | 32.5 | 78 | 90 | $21 |
| 1st Half | 7 | 0 | 98 | 81 | 3.29 | 4.09 | 1.22 | 685 | 640 | 700 | 25.3 | 2.9 | 7.4 | 2.5 | 60% | 9% | 91.2 | 49 | 17 | 33 | 28% | 77% | 12% | 16 | 98 | 38% | 25% | | | 10.4 | 82 | 94 | $15 |
| 2nd Half | 10 | 0 | 104 | 92 | 2.42 | 4.29 | 1.27 | 648 | 335 | 707 | 25.9 | 3.3 | 8.0 | 2.4 | 64% | 10% | 92.0 | 43 | 21 | 36 | 30% | 83% | 6% | 17 | 99 | 29% | 18% | | | 22.2 | 76 | 87 | $27 |
| 19 Proj | 14 | 0 | 174 | 130 | 3.84 | 4.21 | 1.39 | 746 | 636 | 776 | 23.4 | 3.3 | 6.7 | 2.1 | 60% | 10% | 91.8 | 49 | 19 | 32 | 31% | 75% | 10% | 31 | | | | | | 6.6 | 60 | 69 | $6 |

## Fried,Max

| Fried,Max | | Health | C | LIMA Plan | B+ |
|---|---|---|---|---|---|
| Age: 25 | Th: L Role SP | PT/Exp | D | Rand Var | +5 |
| Ht: 6' 4" | Wt: 190 Type Pwr | Consist | C | MM | 2303 |

1-4, 2.94 ERA in 34 IP at ATL. Former top prospect finally showing signs of tapping into that upside. Soaring FpK and SwK put further Cmd growth on table, which will keep BPV trending up. And GB tilt gives him some cushion with command. With another year of growth vR... UP: 3.60 ERA, 180 Ks

| Yr Tm | W | Sv | IP | K | ERA | xERA | WHIP | oOPS | vL | vR | BF/G | Ctl | Dom | Cmd | FpK | SwK | Vel | G | L | F | H% | S% | hr/f | GS | APC | DOM% | DIS% | Sv% | LI | RAR | BPV | BPX | R$ |
|---|---|---|---|---|---|---|---|---|---|---|---|---|---|---|---|---|---|---|---|---|---|---|---|---|---|---|---|---|---|---|---|---|---|
| 14 | | | | | | | | | | | | | | | | | | | | | | | | | | | | | | | | | |
| 15 | | | | | | | | | | | | | | | | | | | | | | | | | | | | | | | | | |
| 16 | | | | | | | | | | | | | | | | | | | | | | | | | | | | | | | | | |
| 17 ATL * | 3 | 0 | 119 | 98 | 6.63 | 5.37 | 1.65 | 818 | 684 | 875 | 17.7 | 4.4 | 7.5 | 1.7 | 49% | 9% | 92.4 | 65 | 18 | 17 | 35% | 59% | 21% | 4 | 47 | 0% | 75% | 0 | 0.38 | -33.2 | 48 | 58 | -$15 |
| 18 ATL * | 4 | 0 | 113 | 115 | 4.40 | 4.12 | 1.46 | 688 | 836 | 633 | 16.7 | 4.3 | 9.2 | 2.1 | 57% | 14% | 93.0 | 51 | 28 | 20 | 34% | 70% | 20% | 5 | 41 | 20% | 20% | 0 | 0.64 | -3.4 | 85 | 98 | -$4 |
| 1st Half | 3 | 0 | 75 | 71 | 4.34 | 4.28 | 1.45 | 710 | 844 | 640 | 20.0 | 3.9 | 8.5 | 2.2 | 56% | 14% | 92.4 | 54 | 22 | 24 | 34% | 70% | 33% | 2 | 46 | 50% | 0% | 0 | 0.83 | -1.8 | 80 | 91 | -$4 |
| 2nd Half | 1 | 0 | 40 | 45 | 4.25 | 3.43 | 1.38 | 662 | 800 | 626 | 13.0 | 4.9 | 10.0 | 2.0 | 59% | 15% | 93.8 | 49 | 35 | 16 | 31% | 69% | 0% | 3 | 37 | 0% | 33% | 0 | 0.50 | -0.5 | 96 | 110 | -$4 |
| 19 Proj | 8 | 0 | 131 | 131 | 4.10 | 3.66 | 1.35 | 703 | 846 | 655 | 21.1 | 4.4 | 9.0 | 2.0 | 58% | 14% | 93.2 | 48 | 30 | 22 | 31% | 70% | 10% | 32 | | | | | | 0.8 | 69 | 80 | $3 |

## Fry,Jace

| Fry,Jace | | Health | A | LIMA Plan | A |
|---|---|---|---|---|---|
| Age: 25 | Th: L Role RP | PT/Exp | D | Rand Var | +4 |
| Ht: 6' 1" | Wt: 190 Type Pwr | Consist | D | MM | 3520 |

Earned late-inning trust (see 2nd-half LI), and it was no fluke. Surge in Ks came with support of SwK. Post-July FpK lays foundation for further Ctl reduction. And 3.0 Cmd vR cements closer upside, even as a lefty. Ignore 2nd-half ERA, as it was product of fluky H% and S%. UP: 40 saves

| Yr Tm | W | Sv | IP | K | ERA | xERA | WHIP | oOPS | vL | vR | BF/G | Ctl | Dom | Cmd | FpK | SwK | Vel | G | L | F | H% | S% | hr/f | GS | APC | DOM% | DIS% | Sv% | LI | RAR | BPV | BPX | R$ |
|---|---|---|---|---|---|---|---|---|---|---|---|---|---|---|---|---|---|---|---|---|---|---|---|---|---|---|---|---|---|---|---|---|---|
| 14 | | | | | | | | | | | | | | | | | | | | | | | | | | | | | | | | | |
| 15 | | | | | | | | | | | | | | | | | | | | | | | | | | | | | | | | | |
| 16 | | | | | | | | | | | | | | | | | | | | | | | | | | | | | | | | | |
| 17 CHW * | 2 | 3 | 52 | 47 | 4.86 | 4.92 | 1.74 | 1085 | 932 | 1196 | 5.4 | 5.7 | 8.2 | 1.4 | 61% | 12% | 93.6 | 43 | 32 | 25 | 36% | 71% | 14% | 0 | 12 | | | 75 | 0.36 | -3.2 | 66 | 79 | -$6 |
| 18 CHW | 2 | 4 | 51 | 70 | 4.38 | 3.12 | 1.11 | 567 | 408 | 690 | 3.6 | 3.5 | 12.3 | 3.5 | 61% | 15% | 92.9 | 45 | 21 | 34 | 31% | 60% | 10% | 1 | 15 | 0% | 100% | 80 | 1.49 | -1.5 | 149 | 172 | $1 |
| 1st Half | 0 | 1 | 25 | 32 | 1.82 | 3.33 | 0.89 | 434 | 241 | 622 | 3.9 | 3.6 | 11.7 | 3.2 | 57% | 15% | 92.4 | 41 | 19 | 41 | 23% | 81% | 5% | 0 | 16 | | | 100 | 1.19 | 7.1 | 130 | 150 | $3 |
| 2nd Half | 2 | 3 | 27 | 38 | 6.75 | 2.92 | 1.31 | 678 | 586 | 736 | 3.4 | 3.4 | 12.8 | 3.8 | 65% | 15% | 93.4 | 49 | 23 | 28 | 37% | 47% | 17% | 1 | 15 | 0% | 100% | 75 | 1.70 | -8.6 | 167 | 192 | -$1 |
| 19 Proj | 2 | 20 | 58 | 69 | 3.52 | 3.33 | 1.24 | 620 | 465 | 736 | 3.9 | 3.9 | 10.7 | 2.7 | 62% | 15% | 93.0 | 46 | 21 | 33 | 31% | 73% | 10% | 0 | | | | | | 7.0 | 110 | 127 | $9 |

## Fulmer,Michael

| Fulmer,Michael | | Health | D | LIMA Plan | C |
|---|---|---|---|---|---|
| Age: 26 | Th: R Role SP | PT/Exp | B | Rand Var | +2 |
| Ht: 6' 3" | Wt: 246 Type | Consist | A | MM | 2103 |

Former budding rotation anchor's struggles to stay healthy derailing a once-promising future. Even when upright, eroding Cmd has driven inflating ERA. While solid command sub-indicators give hope, ugly xERA, BPV trends confirm we can't bet on a rebound. DOM/DIS% underscores risk. DN: 5.00 ERA

| Yr Tm | W | Sv | IP | K | ERA | xERA | WHIP | oOPS | vL | vR | BF/G | Ctl | Dom | Cmd | FpK | SwK | Vel | G | L | F | H% | S% | hr/f | GS | APC | DOM% | DIS% | Sv% | LI | RAR | BPV | BPX | R$ |
|---|---|---|---|---|---|---|---|---|---|---|---|---|---|---|---|---|---|---|---|---|---|---|---|---|---|---|---|---|---|---|---|---|---|
| 14 | | | | | | | | | | | | | | | | | | | | | | | | | | | | | | | | | |
| 15 aa | 10 | 0 | 118 | 95 | 2.53 | 3.32 | 1.22 | | | | 22.6 | 2.3 | 7.3 | 3.1 | | | | | | | 31% | 81% | | | | | | | | 20.8 | 96 | 115 | $11 |
| 16 DET * | 12 | 0 | 174 | 148 | 3.26 | 3.40 | 1.16 | 652 | 621 | 684 | 23.9 | 2.4 | 7.7 | 3.1 | 61% | 11% | 94.8 | 49 | 19 | 32 | 28% | 76% | 11% | 26 | 95 | 35% | 31% | | | 20.0 | 89 | 105 | $17 |
| 17 DET | 10 | 0 | 165 | 114 | 3.83 | 4.19 | 1.15 | 644 | 677 | 616 | 27.0 | 2.2 | 6.2 | 2.9 | 61% | 10% | 95.8 | 49 | 22 | 29 | 28% | 68% | 9% | 25 | 99 | 36% | 32% | | | 10.8 | 80 | 96 | $12 |
| 18 DET | 3 | 0 | 132 | 110 | 4.69 | 4.29 | 1.31 | 758 | 794 | 715 | 23.3 | 3.1 | 7.5 | 2.4 | 63% | 11% | 95.8 | 44 | 22 | 34 | 29% | 68% | 15% | 24 | 90 | 25% | 33% | | | -8.9 | 72 | 83 | -$3 |
| 1st Half | 3 | 0 | 94 | 80 | 4.20 | 4.03 | 1.25 | 711 | 716 | 704 | 24.5 | 2.9 | 7.6 | 2.7 | 61% | 11% | 95.8 | 46 | 22 | 32 | 29% | 69% | 13% | 16 | 95 | 31% | 31% | | | -0.6 | 84 | 97 | $1 |
| 2nd Half | 0 | 0 | 38 | 30 | 5.92 | 4.95 | 1.47 | 871 | 993 | 739 | 20.8 | 3.8 | 7.1 | 1.9 | 65% | 12% | 95.9 | 39 | 23 | 38 | 29% | 65% | 18% | 8 | 79 | 13% | 38% | | | -8.3 | 43 | 49 | -$14 |
| 19 Proj | 6 | 0 | 160 | 126 | 4.31 | 3.99 | 1.28 | 734 | 783 | 684 | 23.0 | 2.9 | 7.1 | 2.5 | 63% | 11% | 95.7 | 46 | 22 | 33 | 29% | 70% | 13% | 28 | | | | | | 2.6 | 74 | 85 | $3 |

## Gallardo,Yovani

| Gallardo,Yovani | | Health | C | LIMA Plan | D |
|---|---|---|---|---|---|
| Age: 33 | Th: R Role SP | PT/Exp | B | Rand Var | +3 |
| Ht: 6' 2" | Wt: 205 Type | Consist | A | MM | 0001 |

Talk about wearing out your welcome. There's a reason he's been on five clubs in five seasons: He hasn't been good for years. Three straight seasons of negative value, blowups in more than half his starts, some of worst skills of any SP in game all are reasons to stay far, far away.

| Yr Tm | W | Sv | IP | K | ERA | xERA | WHIP | oOPS | vL | vR | BF/G | Ctl | Dom | Cmd | FpK | SwK | Vel | G | L | F | H% | S% | hr/f | GS | APC | DOM% | DIS% | Sv% | LI | RAR | BPV | BPX | R$ |
|---|---|---|---|---|---|---|---|---|---|---|---|---|---|---|---|---|---|---|---|---|---|---|---|---|---|---|---|---|---|---|---|---|---|
| 14 MIL | 8 | 0 | 192 | 146 | 3.51 | 3.72 | 1.29 | 698 | 637 | 742 | 25.5 | 2.5 | 6.8 | 2.7 | 57% | 7% | 91.4 | 51 | 20 | 29 | 31% | 76% | 12% | 32 | 101 | 28% | 28% | | | 5.5 | 84 | 100 | $5 |
| 15 TEX | 13 | 0 | 184 | 121 | 3.42 | 4.46 | 1.42 | 729 | 765 | 694 | 24.0 | 3.3 | 5.9 | 1.8 | 59% | 7% | 90.4 | 49 | 22 | 29 | 31% | 78% | 9% | 33 | 98 | 6% | 42% | | | 12.4 | 44 | 52 | $5 |
| 16 BAL | 6 | 0 | 118 | 85 | 5.42 | 5.33 | 1.58 | 813 | 808 | 815 | 22.9 | 4.7 | 6.5 | 1.4 | 54% | 7% | 89.5 | 43 | 20 | 37 | 31% | 68% | 12% | 23 | 92 | 9% | 52% | | | -17.8 | 12 | 14 | -$9 |
| 17 SEA | 5 | 1 | 131 | 94 | 5.72 | 5.31 | 1.52 | 820 | 787 | 852 | 20.6 | 4.1 | 6.5 | 1.6 | 58% | 9% | 92.2 | 44 | 19 | 37 | 29% | 66% | 16% | 22 | 82 | 9% | 59% | 100 | 0.73 | -21.9 | 27 | 32 | -$9 |
| 18 2 TM * | 10 | 0 | 146 | 86 | 5.99 | 5.50 | 1.63 | 866 | 777 | 948 | 20.9 | 4.0 | 5.3 | 1.3 | 63% | 6% | 91.6 | 44 | 23 | 33 | 33% | 63% | 14% | 18 | 79 | 6% | 61% | 0 | 0.68 | -33.0 | 28 | 32 | -$16 |
| 1st Half | 4 | 0 | 71 | 44 | 6.30 | 5.47 | 1.64 | 884 | 837 | 928 | 19.9 | 3.4 | 5.6 | 1.6 | 69% | 7% | 91.6 | 37 | 27 | 36 | 35% | 60% | 17% | 3 | 60 | 33% | 67% | 0 | 0.50 | -18.9 | 41 | 47 | -$22 |
| 2nd Half | 6 | 0 | 74 | 42 | 5.69 | 5.47 | 1.61 | 861 | 759 | 954 | 21.9 | 4.5 | 5.1 | 1.1 | 61% | 6% | 91.5 | 46 | 22 | 32 | 30% | 66% | 13% | 15 | 87 | 0% | 60% | | | -14.1 | -6 | -7 | -$11 |
| 19 Proj | 6 | 0 | 102 | 66 | 5.56 | 4.96 | 1.56 | 817 | 766 | 862 | 21.3 | 4.0 | 5.9 | 1.4 | 60% | 7% | 91.4 | 44 | 22 | 34 | 31% | 66% | 12% | 21 | | | | | | -6.6 | 18 | 21 | -$9 |

## Gant,John

| Gant,John | | Health | D | LIMA Plan | D+ |
|---|---|---|---|---|---|
| Age: 26 | Th: R Role SP | PT/Exp | D | Rand Var | -2 |
| Ht: 6' 3" | Wt: 200 Type Pwr | Consist | B | MM | 1101 |

7-6, 3.47 ERA in 114 IP at STL. PRO: FpK, SwK give hope for better Cmd; xERA says he can keep ERA under 4.00. CON: ERA fueled by H%/S%; has never posted rotation-worthy skills; low ceiling visible in DOM/DIS%. Shiny MLB stats will make him a target, but best viewed as an end-rotation speculation.

| Yr Tm | W | Sv | IP | K | ERA | xERA | WHIP | oOPS | vL | vR | BF/G | Ctl | Dom | Cmd | FpK | SwK | Vel | G | L | F | H% | S% | hr/f | GS | APC | DOM% | DIS% | Sv% | LI | RAR | BPV | BPX | R$ |
|---|---|---|---|---|---|---|---|---|---|---|---|---|---|---|---|---|---|---|---|---|---|---|---|---|---|---|---|---|---|---|---|---|---|
| 14 | | | | | | | | | | | | | | | | | | | | | | | | | | | | | | | | | |
| 15 aa | 8 | 0 | 100 | 76 | 4.28 | 4.28 | 1.53 | | | | 24.2 | 3.8 | 6.9 | 1.8 | | | | | | | 34% | 71% | | | | | | | | -3.9 | 69 | 82 | -$4 |
| 16 ATL * | 4 | 0 | 106 | 99 | 5.17 | 5.30 | 1.60 | 831 | 765 | 909 | 14.6 | 3.9 | 8.4 | 2.2 | 60% | 10% | 91.8 | 42 | 24 | 34 | 36% | 69% | 14% | 7 | 47 | 14% | 29% | 0 | 0.46 | -12.8 | 60 | 72 | -$8 |
| 17 STL * | 6 | 0 | 121 | 90 | 4.68 | 5.24 | 1.50 | 884 | 987 | 808 | 20.9 | 2.6 | 6.7 | 2.5 | 61% | 10% | 93.0 | 54 | 13 | 33 | 34% | 71% | 22% | 2 | 41 | 0% | 100% | 0 | 0.38 | -4.9 | 56 | 67 | -$4 |
| 18 STL * | 12 | 0 | 163 | 128 | 3.01 | 3.70 | 1.33 | 646 | 662 | 629 | 19.9 | 4.0 | 7.1 | 1.7 | 61% | 12% | 93.3 | 45 | 21 | 34 | 28% | 80% | 8% | 19 | 72 | 16% | 26% | 0 | 0.79 | 22.9 | 63 | 73 | $11 |
| 1st Half | 7 | 0 | 83 | 65 | 2.57 | 3.62 | 1.29 | 547 | 565 | 518 | 20.0 | 3.3 | 7.0 | 2.1 | 64% | 12% | 93.1 | 51 | 15 | 34 | 30% | 83% | 3% | 4 | 62 | 25% | 0% | 0 | 0.85 | 16.1 | 73 | 84 | $14 |
| 2nd Half | 5 | 0 | 80 | 63 | 3.47 | 4.93 | 1.37 | 687 | 714 | 663 | 20.2 | 4.8 | 7.1 | 1.5 | 60% | 12% | 93.4 | 43 | 23 | 34 | 27% | 77% | 10% | 15 | 77 | 13% | 33% | 0 | 0.76 | 6.7 | 18 | 20 | $8 |
| 19 Proj | 5 | 0 | 87 | 69 | 3.95 | 4.37 | 1.44 | 763 | 740 | 790 | 20.4 | 3.7 | 7.2 | 1.9 | 61% | 11% | 92.7 | 45 | 22 | 34 | 31% | 74% | 9% | 18 | | | | | | -1.9 | 51 | 59 | -$1 |

STEPHEN NICKRAND

## Garcia,Jaime

| | | | | | | |
|---|---|---|---|---|---|---|
| Age: 32 | Th: L | Role RP | PT/Exp | B | Rand Var | +3 |
| Ht: 6' 2" | Wt: 215 | Type Pwr GB | Consist | B | MM | 1201 |
| | | | Health | D | LIMA Plan | D+ |

It's hard to give up on pitchers who used to provide value. But now's the time to cut the cord here. Cmd, BPV, xERA trends all are stacked against him. Chronic shoulder woes add even further risk into the mix. There's a reason he has been on five MLB teams in two seasons: He's just not good anymore.

| Yr Tm | W | Sv | IP | K | ERA | xERA | WHIP | oOPS | vL | vR | BF/G | Ctl | Dom | Cmd | FpK | SwK | Vel | G | L | F | H% | S% | hr/f | GS | APC | DOM% | DIS% | Sv% | LI | RAR | BPV | BPX | R$ |
|---|---|---|---|---|---|---|---|---|---|---|---|---|---|---|---|---|---|---|---|---|---|---|---|---|---|---|---|---|---|---|---|---|---|
| 14 STL | 3 | 0 | 44 | 39 | 4.12 | 2.89 | 1.05 | 696 | 881 | 631 | 25.3 | 1.4 | 8.0 | 5.6 | 60% | 13% | 90.6 | 55 | 20 | 25 | 28% | 65% | 19% | 7 | 90 | 43% | 14% | | | -2.1 | 139 | 165 | $0 |
| 15 STL | 10 | 0 | 130 | 97 | 2.43 | 3.25 | 1.05 | 574 | 630 | 557 | 25.5 | 2.1 | 6.7 | 3.2 | 59% | 9% | 90.2 | 61 | 16 | 22 | 27% | 78% | 7% | 20 | 93 | 50% | 10% | | | 24.5 | 104 | 124 | $17 |
| 16 STL | 10 | 0 | 172 | 150 | 4.67 | 3.78 | 1.37 | 779 | 702 | 798 | 23.2 | 3.0 | 7.9 | 2.6 | 60% | 10% | 90.5 | 57 | 18 | 25 | 31% | 70% | 20% | 30 | 81 | 17% | 40% | 0 | 0.74 | -10.1 | 96 | 114 | $1 |
| 17 3 TM | 5 | 0 | 157 | 129 | 4.41 | 4.28 | 1.41 | 759 | 683 | 781 | 24.9 | 3.7 | 7.4 | 2.0 | 56% | 11% | 90.7 | 55 | 19 | 27 | 31% | 71% | 14% | 27 | 90 | 22% | 44% | | | -1.1 | 67 | 81 | $0 |
| 18 2 TM | 3 | 0 | 82 | 73 | 5.82 | 5.05 | 1.54 | 811 | 613 | 887 | 11.2 | 4.8 | 8.0 | 1.7 | 54% | 9% | 89.3 | 43 | 18 | 39 | 30% | 65% | 14% | 14 | 42 | 7% | 50% | 0 | 0.89 | -16.9 | 35 | 40 | -$10 |
| 1st Half | 2 | 0 | 61 | 56 | 6.16 | 5.03 | 1.61 | 877 | 782 | 907 | 21.6 | 4.5 | 8.2 | 1.8 | 54% | 9% | 89.2 | 42 | 19 | 39 | 32% | 66% | 16% | 13 | 82 | 8% | 46% | | | -15.2 | 45 | 52 | -$13 |
| 2nd Half | 1 | 0 | 21 | 17 | 4.79 | 5.11 | 1.31 | 594 | 281 | 803 | 4.4 | 5.7 | 7.4 | 1.3 | 57% | 10% | 89.6 | 46 | 14 | 39 | 24% | 62% | 5% | 1 | 16 | 0% | 100% | 0 | 0.98 | -1.6 | 5 | 6 | -$2 |
| **19 Proj** | **4** | **0** | **87** | **74** | **5.11** | **4.21** | **1.41** | **745** | **556** | **818** | **10.1** | **4.1** | **7.6** | **1.8** | **57%** | **10%** | **90.0** | **50** | **17** | **32** | **30%** | **65%** | **12%** | **0** | | | | | | **-10.3** | **54** | **62** | **-$5** |

## Garcia,Luis

| | | | | | | |
|---|---|---|---|---|---|---|
| Age: 32 | Th: R | Role RP | PT/Exp | D | Rand Var | +5 |
| Ht: 6' 3" | Wt: 230 | Type Pwr GB | Consist | B | MM | 4300 |
| | | | Health | D | LIMA Plan | C+ |

The pullback we thought would happen, but for the wrong reasons. Behind grisly surface stats were best skills of career. Steady gains in FpK say improved control can stick, and now missing bats at an elite clip. Ugly hit and strand rates won't repeat. A $1 speculative stash in very deep leagues.

| Yr Tm | W | Sv | IP | K | ERA | xERA | WHIP | oOPS | vL | vR | BF/G | Ctl | Dom | Cmd | FpK | SwK | Vel | G | L | F | H% | S% | hr/f | GS | APC | DOM% | DIS% | Sv% | LI | RAR | BPV | BPX | R$ |
|---|---|---|---|---|---|---|---|---|---|---|---|---|---|---|---|---|---|---|---|---|---|---|---|---|---|---|---|---|---|---|---|---|---|
| 14 PHI * | 3 | 22 | 61 | 54 | 2.39 | 3.51 | 1.43 | 815 | 628 | 1042 | 5.0 | 4.5 | 8.0 | 1.8 | 49% | 12% | 95.0 | 70 | 12 | 19 | 32% | 83% | 25% | 0 | 22 | | | 88 | 0.42 | 10.1 | 82 | 98 | $9 |
| 15 PHI | 4 | 2 | 67 | 63 | 3.51 | 3.80 | 1.64 | 748 | 878 | 660 | 4.2 | 5.0 | 8.5 | 1.7 | 52% | 12% | 95.5 | 63 | 22 | 15 | 35% | 79% | 13% | 0 | 16 | | | 50 | 1.03 | 3.7 | 59 | 71 | -$3 |
| 16 PHI * | 7 | 13 | 70 | 55 | 4.01 | 4.79 | 1.59 | 895 | 1009 | 751 | 4.8 | 4.8 | 7.1 | 1.5 | 55% | 12% | 96.5 | 55 | 15 | 30 | 32% | 77% | 13% | 0 | 17 | | | 81 | 0.90 | 1.5 | 48 | 57 | $3 |
| 17 PHI | 2 | 2 | 71 | 60 | 2.65 | 3.94 | 1.22 | 593 | 729 | 472 | 4.5 | 3.3 | 7.6 | 2.3 | 58% | 13% | 97.2 | 56 | 18 | 26 | 29% | 79% | 6% | 0 | 15 | | | 29 | 0.85 | 15.0 | 82 | 98 | $5 |
| 18 PHI | 3 | 1 | 46 | 51 | 6.07 | 3.65 | 1.46 | 773 | 768 | 777 | 3.5 | 3.5 | 10.0 | 2.8 | 62% | 15% | 97.2 | 48 | 24 | 27 | 36% | 57% | 11% | 0 | 13 | | | 25 | 1.29 | -10.9 | 111 | 127 | -$6 |
| 1st Half | 2 | 1 | 25 | 23 | 4.74 | 3.45 | 1.09 | 634 | 483 | 737 | 3.2 | 2.2 | 8.4 | 3.8 | 62% | 15% | 97.0 | 49 | 22 | 28 | 29% | 56% | 11% | 0 | 12 | | | 33 | 1.55 | -1.8 | 119 | 137 | -$3 |
| 2nd Half | 1 | 0 | 21 | 28 | 7.59 | 3.86 | 1.88 | 919 | 1058 | 821 | 3.7 | 5.1 | 11.8 | 2.3 | 61% | 15% | 97.5 | 48 | 26 | 26 | 45% | 58% | 13% | 0 | 14 | | | 0 | 0.99 | -9.1 | 101 | 117 | -$10 |
| **19 Proj** | **3** | **0** | **58** | **62** | **3.85** | **3.29** | **1.30** | **669** | **737** | **618** | **3.7** | **3.7** | **9.6** | **2.6** | **59%** | **14%** | **97.0** | **53** | **22** | **25** | **32%** | **71%** | **11%** | **0** | | | | | | **2.2** | **106** | **122** | **$0** |

## Garrett,Amir

| | | | | | | |
|---|---|---|---|---|---|---|
| Age: 27 | Th: L | Role RP | PT/Exp | D | Rand Var | +1 |
| Ht: 6' 5" | Wt: 228 | Type Pwr FB | Consist | F | MM | 1300 |
| | | | Health | B | LIMA Plan | C |

Once-promising prospect firmly at a crossroads now. Transition to bullpen role looked good at first, not so much after return from Achilles and foot issues. Consistently bad FpK will keep preventing him from finding plate. Without control, he won't stick in any role. A true wild card.

| Yr Tm | W | Sv | IP | K | ERA | xERA | WHIP | oOPS | vL | vR | BF/G | Ctl | Dom | Cmd | FpK | SwK | Vel | G | L | F | H% | S% | hr/f | GS | APC | DOM% | DIS% | Sv% | LI | RAR | BPV | BPX | R$ |
|---|---|---|---|---|---|---|---|---|---|---|---|---|---|---|---|---|---|---|---|---|---|---|---|---|---|---|---|---|---|---|---|---|---|
| 14 | | | | | | | | | | | | | | | | | | | | | | | | | | | | | | | | | |
| 15 | | | | | | | | | | | | | | | | | | | | | | | | | | | | | | | | | |
| 16 a/a | 7 | 0 | 145 | 114 | 3.60 | 3.30 | 1.33 | | | | 24.0 | 4.2 | 7.1 | 1.7 | | | | | | | 28% | 73% | | | | | | | | 10.4 | 70 | 84 | $6 |
| 17 CIN * | 5 | 0 | 138 | 114 | 7.46 | 6.80 | 1.72 | 937 | 954 | 933 | 20.9 | 4.3 | 7.4 | 1.7 | 56% | 9% | 91.7 | 43 | 18 | 38 | 33% | 60% | 28% | 14 | 77 | 14% | 50% | 0 | 0.77 | -52.9 | 12 | 14 | -$22 |
| 18 CIN | 1 | 0 | 63 | 71 | 4.29 | 3.83 | 1.29 | 734 | 726 | 740 | 4.0 | 3.6 | 10.1 | 2.8 | 53% | 14% | 95.1 | 38 | 25 | 37 | 31% | 70% | 13% | 0 | 15 | | | 0 | 0.97 | -1.1 | 102 | 118 | -$2 |
| 1st Half | 0 | 0 | 42 | 49 | 2.76 | 3.13 | 1.02 | 623 | 793 | 470 | 4.3 | 2.8 | 10.4 | 3.8 | 54% | 14% | 94.9 | 43 | 23 | 35 | 26% | 79% | 15% | 0 | 17 | | | 0 | 0.99 | 7.2 | 134 | 154 | $2 |
| 2nd Half | 1 | 0 | 21 | 22 | 7.40 | 5.34 | 1.84 | 919 | 603 | 1158 | 3.6 | 5.2 | 9.6 | 1.8 | 51% | 14% | 95.3 | 30 | 28 | 42 | 39% | 60% | 11% | 0 | 13 | | | 0 | 0.94 | -8.3 | 39 | 45 | -$12 |
| **19 Proj** | **2** | **0** | **65** | **62** | **4.69** | **4.31** | **1.43** | **788** | **677** | **848** | **6.2** | **4.0** | **8.6** | **2.2** | **54%** | **12%** | **93.8** | **37** | **23** | **40** | **31%** | **71%** | **14%** | **0** | | | | | | **-4.4** | **62** | **72** | **-$4** |

## Gausman,Kevin

| | | | | | | |
|---|---|---|---|---|---|---|
| Age: 28 | Th: R | Role SP | PT/Exp | A | Rand Var | 0 |
| Ht: 6' 3" | Wt: 190 | Type Pwr | Consist | A | MM | 2205 |
| | | | Health | C | LIMA Plan | B |

Perennial failed breakout target got fresh start after trade, and results followed. Can they stick? PRO: 3.0+ Cmd in 3 of 4 seasons; prior hr/f struggles improved after deal. CON: One good BPV in 5 years; DOM/DIS% tilted towards disaster. UP: $5 bid nets a $15 profit. DN: $5 bid nets a $5 loss.

| Yr Tm | W | Sv | IP | K | ERA | xERA | WHIP | oOPS | vL | vR | BF/G | Ctl | Dom | Cmd | FpK | SwK | Vel | G | L | F | H% | S% | hr/f | GS | APC | DOM% | DIS% | Sv% | LI | RAR | BPV | BPX | R$ |
|---|---|---|---|---|---|---|---|---|---|---|---|---|---|---|---|---|---|---|---|---|---|---|---|---|---|---|---|---|---|---|---|---|---|
| 14 BAL * | 8 | 0 | 157 | 125 | 3.60 | 3.92 | 1.35 | 685 | 700 | 662 | 21.1 | 3.2 | 7.2 | 2.2 | 57% | 9% | 94.8 | 41 | 23 | 35 | 31% | 75% | 6% | 20 | 98 | 35% | 25% | | | 2.8 | 71 | 85 | $2 |
| 15 BAL * | 4 | 0 | 130 | 118 | 4.28 | 4.42 | 1.25 | 739 | 643 | 843 | 18.2 | 2.5 | 8.2 | 3.3 | 55% | 12% | 95.3 | 44 | 17 | 38 | 30% | 72% | 13% | 17 | 75 | 35% | 24% | 0 | 0.72 | -5.2 | 74 | 88 | $0 |
| 16 BAL | 9 | 0 | 180 | 174 | 3.61 | 3.86 | 1.28 | 742 | 659 | 812 | 25.2 | 2.4 | 8.7 | 3.7 | 57% | 11% | 94.7 | 44 | 21 | 35 | 32% | 78% | 15% | 30 | 104 | 30% | 20% | | | 12.9 | 115 | 137 | $11 |
| 17 BAL | 11 | 0 | 187 | 179 | 4.68 | 4.44 | 1.49 | 808 | 807 | 808 | 24.0 | 3.4 | 8.6 | 2.5 | 60% | 11% | 95.0 | 43 | 22 | 35 | 34% | 73% | 15% | 34 | 99 | 29% | 35% | | | -7.3 | 84 | 101 | $0 |
| 18 2 TM | 10 | 0 | 184 | 148 | 3.92 | 4.21 | 1.30 | 753 | 717 | 786 | 25.0 | 2.5 | 7.3 | 3.0 | 57% | 12% | 93.6 | 46 | 21 | 33 | 31% | 75% | 14% | 31 | 97 | 26% | 42% | | | 5.2 | 88 | 102 | $6 |
| 1st Half | 3 | 0 | 94 | 88 | 4.20 | 3.91 | 1.37 | 802 | 723 | 861 | 25.4 | 2.4 | 8.4 | 3.5 | 55% | 12% | 93.5 | 47 | 21 | 32 | 33% | 75% | 18% | 16 | 100 | 25% | 38% | | | -0.6 | 112 | 129 | $1 |
| 2nd Half | 7 | 0 | 89 | 60 | 3.63 | 4.53 | 1.23 | 700 | 711 | 687 | 24.7 | 2.5 | 6.0 | 2.4 | 60% | 11% | 93.8 | 45 | 20 | 35 | 28% | 74% | 10% | 15 | 94 | 27% | 47% | | | 5.8 | 63 | 73 | $14 |
| **19 Proj** | **10** | **0** | **181** | **156** | **4.03** | **3.94** | **1.34** | **758** | **726** | **787** | **23.6** | **2.7** | **7.7** | **2.8** | **58%** | **11%** | **94.3** | **44** | **21** | **35** | **31%** | **74%** | **14%** | **32** | | | | | | **4.1** | **88** | **101** | **$6** |

## Gaviglio,Sam

| | | | | | | |
|---|---|---|---|---|---|---|
| Age: 29 | Th: R | Role SP | PT/Exp | D | Rand Var | +1 |
| Ht: 6' 2" | Wt: 195 | Type | Consist | A | MM | 1101 |
| | | | Health | A | LIMA Plan | C |

3-10, 5.31 ERA in 124 IP at TOR. If you're pressed for time when looking for arms, scan the BPV column. If you don't see any triple-digits, then look at xERA. If you see nothing under 4.00, look for signs of a double-digit SwK as last beacon of hope. Still nothing? Move on.

| Yr Tm | W | Sv | IP | K | ERA | xERA | WHIP | oOPS | vL | vR | BF/G | Ctl | Dom | Cmd | FpK | SwK | Vel | G | L | F | H% | S% | hr/f | GS | APC | DOM% | DIS% | Sv% | LI | RAR | BPV | BPX | R$ |
|---|---|---|---|---|---|---|---|---|---|---|---|---|---|---|---|---|---|---|---|---|---|---|---|---|---|---|---|---|---|---|---|---|---|
| 14 aa | 5 | 0 | 137 | 102 | 4.93 | 5.12 | 1.60 | | | | 24.2 | 3.0 | 6.7 | 2.3 | | | | | | | 37% | 68% | | | | | | | | -20.0 | 65 | 78 | -$12 |
| 15 aaa | 8 | 0 | 102 | 67 | 4.82 | 4.47 | 1.35 | | | | 20.2 | 2.8 | 5.9 | 2.1 | | | | | | | 30% | 67% | | | | | | | | -10.8 | 45 | 54 | -$3 |
| 16 a/a | 8 | 0 | 165 | 102 | 4.99 | 4.80 | 1.43 | | | | 25.0 | 2.1 | 5.5 | 2.7 | | | | | | | 33% | 66% | | | | | | | | -16.2 | 58 | 69 | -$5 |
| 17 2 AL * | 7 | 0 | 146 | 96 | 4.64 | 4.99 | 1.39 | 849 | 838 | 859 | 21.3 | 2.4 | 5.9 | 2.4 | 61% | 8% | 88.6 | 49 | 18 | 32 | 31% | 71% | 21% | 13 | 73 | 0% | 54% | 0 | 0.64 | -5.0 | 44 | 53 | -$1 |
| 18 TOR * | 3 | 0 | 153 | 127 | 4.83 | 5.19 | 1.38 | 804 | 801 | 808 | 20.7 | 2.5 | 7.5 | 3.0 | 64% | 9% | 88.0 | 49 | 19 | 32 | 32% | 70% | 17% | 24 | 79 | 8% | 54% | 0 | 0.81 | -12.8 | 59 | 68 | -$6 |
| 1st Half | 2 | 0 | 77 | 67 | 3.51 | 4.19 | 1.17 | 712 | 666 | 747 | 20.4 | 2.2 | 7.8 | 3.6 | 70% | 10% | 88.5 | 49 | 16 | 35 | 28% | 78% | 17% | 8 | 75 | 0% | 25% | 0 | 0.88 | 6.1 | 80 | 92 | $4 |
| 2nd Half | 1 | 0 | 76 | 60 | 6.16 | 4.57 | 1.59 | 857 | 869 | 846 | 21.8 | 2.8 | 7.1 | 2.5 | 61% | 8% | 87.6 | 49 | 21 | 30 | 35% | 64% | 17% | 16 | 81 | 13% | 69% | | | -18.8 | 78 | 90 | -$18 |
| **19 Proj** | **4** | **0** | **116** | **86** | **4.78** | **4.12** | **1.42** | **811** | **804** | **817** | **21.6** | **2.5** | **6.6** | **2.7** | **63%** | **8%** | **88.2** | **49** | **19** | **32** | **32%** | **70%** | **14%** | **23** | | | | | | **0.3** | **79** | **91** | **-$5** |

## German,Domingo

| | | | | | | |
|---|---|---|---|---|---|---|
| Age: 26 | Th: R | Role SP | PT/Exp | D | Rand Var | +5 |
| Ht: 6' 2" | Wt: 175 | Type Pwr FB | Consist | B | MM | 2401 |
| | | | Health | B | LIMA Plan | C |

Demoted due to ugly ERA, then sidelined with elbow pain. Before arm issue, skills supported a sub-4 ERA. In fact, glossy 1st-half Cmd came with full support, including top-tier SwK. History of good Cmd in minors gives foundation for more growth. A premium buy-low target. UP: 3.50 ERA, 200 Ks

| Yr Tm | W | Sv | IP | K | ERA | xERA | WHIP | oOPS | vL | vR | BF/G | Ctl | Dom | Cmd | FpK | SwK | Vel | G | L | F | H% | S% | hr/f | GS | APC | DOM% | DIS% | Sv% | LI | RAR | BPV | BPX | R$ |
|---|---|---|---|---|---|---|---|---|---|---|---|---|---|---|---|---|---|---|---|---|---|---|---|---|---|---|---|---|---|---|---|---|---|
| 14 | | | | | | | | | | | | | | | | | | | | | | | | | | | | | | | | | |
| 15 | | | | | | | | | | | | | | | | | | | | | | | | | | | | | | | | | |
| 16 | | | | | | | | | | | | | | | | | | | | | | | | | | | | | | | | | |
| 17 NYY * | 8 | 0 | 124 | 117 | 4.12 | 4.57 | 1.42 | 661 | 622 | 696 | 19.4 | 3.3 | 8.5 | 2.5 | 61% | 11% | 96.4 | 55 | 21 | 24 | 33% | 74% | 13% | 0 | 36 | | | 0 | 0.35 | 3.6 | 72 | 87 | $3 |
| 18 NYY | 2 | 0 | 86 | 102 | 5.57 | 3.98 | 1.33 | 774 | 834 | 717 | 17.9 | 3.5 | 10.7 | 3.1 | 62% | 15% | 94.7 | 37 | 22 | 40 | 32% | 62% | 16% | 14 | 70 | 14% | 36% | 0 | 0.68 | -15.0 | 114 | 132 | -$6 |
| 1st Half | 2 | 0 | 64 | 75 | 5.32 | 3.67 | 1.21 | 735 | 684 | 779 | 18.2 | 2.9 | 10.5 | 3.6 | 63% | 16% | 94.9 | 39 | 24 | 37 | 30% | 60% | 17% | 9 | 71 | 22% | 33% | 0 | 0.67 | -9.3 | 127 | 146 | -$4 |
| 2nd Half | 0 | 0 | 21 | 27 | 6.33 | 4.94 | 1.69 | 880 | 1182 | 515 | 17.0 | 5.1 | 11.4 | 2.3 | 59% | 13% | 94.3 | 32 | 18 | 50 | 38% | 66% | 13% | 5 | 68 | 0% | 40% | 0 | 0.71 | -5.7 | 79 | 90 | -$11 |
| **19 Proj** | **6** | **0** | **102** | **113** | **4.14** | **3.86** | **1.32** | **751** | **922** | **568** | **21.3** | **3.5** | **10.0** | **2.9** | **60%** | **14%** | **94.5** | **35** | **20** | **45** | **31%** | **74%** | **13%** | **17** | | | | | | **4.1** | **99** | **114** | **$2** |

## Gibson,Kyle

| | | | | | | |
|---|---|---|---|---|---|---|
| Age: 31 | Th: R | Role SP | PT/Exp | B | Rand Var | +1 |
| Ht: 6' 6" | Wt: 215 | Type Pwr GB | Consist | C | MM | 2103 |
| | | | Health | C | LIMA Plan | B |

Tightened slider gave him putaway pitch he was missing. Combined with uptick in FB velocity, it was a recipe for a mini-breakout. Missing piece to sub-3.50 ERA is improved control. With chronically subpar FpK, hope for that is slim. xERA confirms it: use 4.00 ERA as your baseline.

| Yr Tm | W | Sv | IP | K | ERA | xERA | WHIP | oOPS | vL | vR | BF/G | Ctl | Dom | Cmd | FpK | SwK | Vel | G | L | F | H% | S% | hr/f | GS | APC | DOM% | DIS% | Sv% | LI | RAR | BPV | BPX | R$ |
|---|---|---|---|---|---|---|---|---|---|---|---|---|---|---|---|---|---|---|---|---|---|---|---|---|---|---|---|---|---|---|---|---|---|
| 14 MIN | 13 | 0 | 179 | 107 | 4.47 | 4.01 | 1.31 | 679 | 705 | 650 | 24.4 | 2.9 | 5.4 | 1.9 | 57% | 9% | 91.3 | 54 | 19 | 27 | 29% | 65% | 8% | 31 | 90 | 19% | 35% | | | -16.0 | 51 | 61 | -$1 |
| 15 MIN | 11 | 0 | 195 | 145 | 3.84 | 3.94 | 1.29 | 698 | 702 | 693 | 25.7 | 3.0 | 6.7 | 2.2 | 61% | 10% | 91.8 | 53 | 20 | 27 | 29% | 72% | 11% | 32 | 101 | 31% | 31% | | | 3.0 | 71 | 84 | $7 |
| 16 MIN | 6 | 0 | 147 | 104 | 5.07 | 4.65 | 1.56 | 820 | 886 | 760 | 26.1 | 3.4 | 6.4 | 1.9 | 59% | 10% | 91.0 | 49 | 23 | 29 | 33% | 70% | 14% | 25 | 99 | 16% | 56% | | | -16.0 | 51 | 60 | -$9 |
| 17 MIN * | 13 | 0 | 175 | 137 | 4.93 | 5.35 | 1.53 | 826 | 832 | 821 | 23.8 | 3.4 | 7.1 | 2.1 | 59% | 10% | 92.0 | 51 | 23 | 26 | 33% | 71% | 18% | 29 | 90 | 17% | 45% | | | -12.3 | 43 | 52 | -$3 |
| 18 MIN | 10 | 0 | 197 | 179 | 3.62 | 3.95 | 1.30 | 701 | 733 | 670 | 25.8 | 3.6 | 8.2 | 2.3 | 58% | 12% | 93.0 | 50 | 22 | 28 | 29% | 76% | 15% | 32 | 101 | 22% | 28% | | | 13.0 | 78 | 90 | $10 |
| 1st Half | 2 | 0 | 96 | 93 | 3.48 | 3.90 | 1.24 | 660 | 648 | 670 | 25.0 | 3.8 | 8.7 | 2.3 | 58% | 11% | 92.8 | 48 | 22 | 30 | 28% | 75% | 13% | 16 | 98 | 25% | 25% | | | 7.9 | 82 | 94 | $7 |
| 2nd Half | 8 | 0 | 101 | 86 | 3.74 | 4.00 | 1.36 | 738 | 801 | 669 | 26.6 | 3.5 | 7.7 | 2.2 | 57% | 12% | 93.3 | 52 | 22 | 26 | 30% | 77% | 17% | 16 | 104 | 19% | 31% | | | 5.1 | 74 | 85 | $12 |
| **19 Proj** | **10** | **0** | **174** | **142** | **3.97** | **3.97** | **1.40** | **752** | **783** | **721** | **25.0** | **3.4** | **7.4** | **2.1** | **58%** | **11%** | **92.3** | **50** | **22** | **27** | **31%** | **75%** | **15%** | **29** | | | | | | **3.1** | **68** | **78** | **$4** |

STEPHEN NICKRAND

## Giles,Ken

| Age: 28 | Th: R | Role: RP | Health: A | LIMA Plan: A |
|---|---|---|---|---|
| Ht: 6' 2" | Wt: 205 | Type: Pwr | PT/Exp: B | Rand Var: +5 |
| | | | Consist: A | MM: 5530 |

Three reasons not to be put off by second 4+ ERA in 3 years: 1) Base skills still showing no wear; 2) Zero blown saves; 3) FpK surged to elite levels late. History of yo-yo hit rate gives him more volatility than top-tier stoppers, but that's the only issue here. With full-time save opps, finally... UP: 40 Sv

| Yr Tm | W | Sv | IP | K | ERA | xERA | WHIP | oOPS | vL | vR | BF/G | Ctl | Dom | Cmd | FpK | SwK | Vel | G | L | F | H% | S% | hr/f | GS | APC | DOM% | DIS% | Sv% | LI | RAR | BPV | BPX | R$ |
|---|---|---|---|---|---|---|---|---|---|---|---|---|---|---|---|---|---|---|---|---|---|---|---|---|---|---|---|---|---|---|---|---|---|
| 14 PHI * | 5 | 13 | 74 | 97 | 1.56 | 1.22 | 0.94 | 450 | 436 | 461 | 4.1 | 2.9 | 11.7 | 4.0 | 63% | 16% | 97.2 | 44 | 15 | 41 | 28% | 83% | 3% | 0 | 16 | | | 93 | 1.15 | 20.0 | 170 | 203 | $17 |
| 15 PHI | 6 | 15 | 70 | 87 | 1.80 | 3.24 | 1.20 | 569 | 574 | 565 | 4.3 | 3.2 | 11.2 | 3.5 | 60% | 15% | 96.5 | 45 | 22 | 33 | 34% | 85% | 3% | 0 | 17 | | | 75 | 1.15 | 18.7 | 138 | 164 | $14 |
| 16 HOU | 2 | 15 | 66 | 102 | 4.11 | 3.00 | 1.29 | 709 | 590 | 823 | 4.1 | 3.4 | 14.0 | 4.1 | 64% | 20% | 97.2 | 40 | 25 | 36 | 38% | 71% | 15% | 0 | 16 | | | 75 | 1.25 | 0.6 | 177 | 210 | $7 |
| 17 HOU | 1 | 34 | 63 | 83 | 2.30 | 3.14 | 1.04 | 566 | 583 | 551 | 3.9 | 3.0 | 11.9 | 4.0 | 62% | 17% | 98.1 | 44 | 18 | 38 | 30% | 80% | 7% | 0 | 15 | | | 89 | 1.11 | 15.9 | 155 | 186 | $21 |
| 18 2 AL | 0 | 26 | 50 | 53 | 4.65 | 3.54 | 1.21 | 722 | 654 | 788 | 3.9 | 1.3 | 9.5 | 7.6 | 66% | 16% | 97.3 | 44 | 20 | 36 | 35% | 64% | 11% | 0 | 14 | | | 100 | 0.99 | -3.1 | 159 | 183 | $7 |
| 1st Half | 0 | 11 | 29 | 28 | 4.08 | 3.65 | 1.22 | 691 | 674 | 703 | 3.8 | 0.9 | 8.8 | 9.3 | 61% | 16% | 97.5 | 40 | 24 | 36 | 37% | 65% | 3% | 0 | 14 | | | 100 | 0.75 | 0.2 | 151 | 174 | $6 |
| 2nd Half | 0 | 15 | 22 | 25 | 5.40 | 3.37 | 1.20 | 765 | 633 | 925 | 3.9 | 1.7 | 10.4 | 6.3 | 73% | 16% | 97.1 | 50 | 15 | 35 | 32% | 62% | 23% | 0 | 14 | | | 100 | 1.29 | -3.3 | 170 | 195 | $9 |
| 19 Proj | 1 | 32 | 58 | 72 | 3.49 | 2.91 | 1.11 | 647 | 592 | 699 | 3.7 | 2.3 | 11.1 | 4.9 | 65% | 17% | 97.4 | 44 | 19 | 36 | 32% | 73% | 13% | 0 | | | | | | 4.8 | 161 | 185 | $15 |

## Giolito,Lucas

| Age: 24 | Th: R | Role: SP | Health: A | LIMA Plan: D+ |
|---|---|---|---|---|
| Ht: 6' 6" | Wt: 245 | Type: Pwr | PT/Exp: C | Rand Var: +5 |
| | | | Consist: A | MM: 0103 |

Sabotaged staffs in first half when it all fell apart. As FB velo returned late, so did flashes of prior top-prospect upside (129 BPV in Aug). But fell apart again in Sept, and overall skill foundation keeps getting more cracks each year. Age still is on his side; just don't roster him without a bench.

| Yr Tm | W | Sv | IP | K | ERA | xERA | WHIP | oOPS | vL | vR | BF/G | Ctl | Dom | Cmd | FpK | SwK | Vel | G | L | F | H% | S% | hr/f | GS | APC | DOM% | DIS% | Sv% | LI | RAR | BPV | BPX | R$ |
|---|---|---|---|---|---|---|---|---|---|---|---|---|---|---|---|---|---|---|---|---|---|---|---|---|---|---|---|---|---|---|---|---|---|
| 14 | | | | | | | | | | | | | | | | | | | | | | | | | | | | | | | | | |
| 15 aa | 4 | 0 | 47 | 38 | 4.63 | 4.44 | 1.52 | | | | 25.7 | 3.3 | 7.3 | 2.2 | | | | | | | 36% | 68% | | | | | | | | -3.9 | 76 | 90 | -$4 |
| 16 WAS * | 6 | 0 | 130 | 108 | 4.31 | 4.93 | 1.57 | 988 | 881 | 1112 | 21.1 | 4.1 | 7.5 | 1.8 | 55% | 6% | 93.4 | 41 | 27 | 32 | 34% | 74% | 29% | 4 | 66 | 0% | 75% | 0 | 0.68 | -1.9 | 55 | 65 | -$4 |
| 17 CHW * | 9 | 0 | 174 | 151 | 4.49 | 4.63 | 1.39 | 645 | 638 | 650 | 23.6 | 3.8 | 7.8 | 2.1 | 62% | 11% | 92.1 | 45 | 20 | 35 | 29% | 72% | 18% | 7 | 101 | 29% | 14% | | | -2.8 | 51 | 62 | $3 |
| 18 CHW | 10 | 0 | 173 | 125 | 6.13 | 5.29 | 1.48 | 794 | 832 | 754 | 24.2 | 4.7 | 6.5 | 1.4 | 55% | 9% | 92.4 | 44 | 18 | 37 | 28% | 60% | 13% | 32 | 94 | 16% | 41% | | | -42.3 | 13 | 15 | -$14 |
| 1st Half | 5 | 0 | 85 | 51 | 6.59 | 6.20 | 1.58 | 821 | 919 | 713 | 24.2 | 5.4 | 5.4 | 1.0 | 54% | 8% | 91.8 | 39 | 18 | 44 | 27% | 60% | 11% | 16 | 92 | 6% | 44% | | | -25.5 | -32 | -37 | -$24 |
| 2nd Half | 5 | 0 | 89 | 74 | 5.68 | 4.46 | 1.38 | 768 | 745 | 792 | 24.3 | 4.0 | 7.5 | 1.9 | 57% | 9% | 93.0 | 50 | 19 | 31 | 28% | 61% | 17% | 16 | 96 | 25% | 38% | | | -16.8 | 56 | 65 | -$5 |
| 19 Proj | 10 | 0 | 174 | 138 | 4.73 | 4.55 | 1.47 | 801 | 825 | 777 | 23.2 | 4.2 | 7.1 | 1.7 | 58% | 9% | 92.4 | 45 | 19 | 36 | 30% | 71% | 13% | 32 | | | | | | -12.5 | 40 | 45 | -$3 |

## Givens,Mychal

| Age: 29 | Th: R | Role: RP | Health: A | LIMA Plan: A |
|---|---|---|---|---|
| Ht: 6' 0" | Wt: 210 | Type: Pwr | PT/Exp: C | Rand Var: -1 |
| | | | Consist: A | MM: 3421 |

Will be viewed as a sneaky Sv source given late cameo in that role. Problem is, that second half hit rate hid some warts. Rip off the bandage, and you're left with a 4.00-ERA bullpen arm whose xERA keeps getting worse. Chronically subpar FpK won't allow late control to stick. A risky bet to stick as stopper.

| Yr Tm | W | Sv | IP | K | ERA | xERA | WHIP | oOPS | vL | vR | BF/G | Ctl | Dom | Cmd | FpK | SwK | Vel | G | L | F | H% | S% | hr/f | GS | APC | DOM% | DIS% | Sv% | LI | RAR | BPV | BPX | R$ |
|---|---|---|---|---|---|---|---|---|---|---|---|---|---|---|---|---|---|---|---|---|---|---|---|---|---|---|---|---|---|---|---|---|---|
| 14 aa | 0 | 0 | 25 | 23 | 4.53 | 3.92 | 1.77 | | | | 6.5 | 8.2 | 8.2 | 1.0 | | | | | | | 31% | 72% | | | | | | | | -2.5 | 78 | 93 | -$6 |
| 15 BAL * | 6 | 15 | 87 | 101 | 2.19 | 2.07 | 1.05 | 538 | 555 | 527 | 5.9 | 2.4 | 10.4 | 4.3 | 63% | 13% | 94.3 | 39 | 30 | 31 | 31% | 79% | 5% | 0 | 21 | | | 88 | 0.79 | 19.0 | 157 | 187 | $18 |
| 16 BAL | 8 | 0 | 75 | 96 | 3.13 | 3.65 | 1.27 | 664 | 1025 | 504 | 4.7 | 4.3 | 11.6 | 2.7 | 59% | 15% | 94.3 | 35 | 25 | 39 | 32% | 78% | 9% | 0 | 20 | | | 0 | 1.10 | 9.7 | 104 | 124 | $6 |
| 17 BAL | 8 | 0 | 79 | 88 | 2.75 | 3.66 | 1.04 | 617 | 619 | 615 | 4.6 | 2.9 | 10.1 | 3.5 | 57% | 13% | 95.6 | 43 | 17 | 40 | 26% | 81% | 13% | 0 | 19 | | | 0 | 1.13 | 15.6 | 125 | 150 | $11 |
| 18 BAL | 0 | 9 | 77 | 79 | 3.99 | 4.08 | 1.19 | 622 | 689 | 581 | 4.6 | 3.5 | 9.3 | 2.6 | 56% | 12% | 95.1 | 36 | 24 | 39 | 29% | 66% | 5% | 0 | 18 | | | 69 | 1.34 | 1.5 | 86 | 99 | $3 |
| 1st Half | 0 | 1 | 43 | 50 | 4.81 | 4.34 | 1.51 | 724 | 874 | 626 | 5.2 | 4.8 | 10.5 | 2.2 | 54% | 12% | 95.1 | 37 | 24 | 39 | 37% | 66% | 2% | 0 | 21 | | | 33 | 1.52 | -3.5 | 73 | 84 | -$5 |
| 2nd Half | 0 | 8 | 34 | 29 | 2.94 | 3.74 | 0.77 | 473 | 401 | 512 | 3.9 | 1.9 | 7.8 | 4.1 | 58% | 13% | 95.2 | 36 | 24 | 40 | 20% | 65% | 9% | 0 | 15 | | | 80 | 1.13 | 5.0 | 103 | 119 | $14 |
| 19 Proj | 4 | 15 | 73 | 78 | 3.59 | 3.53 | 1.16 | 665 | 730 | 628 | 4.6 | 3.1 | 9.7 | 3.1 | 58% | 13% | 95.1 | 38 | 23 | 39 | 29% | 72% | 11% | 0 | | | | | | 5.0 | 106 | 122 | $9 |

## Glasnow,Tyler

| Age: 25 | Th: R | Role: SP | Health: B | LIMA Plan: B+ |
|---|---|---|---|---|
| Ht: 6' 8" | Wt: 220 | Type: Pwr | PT/Exp: C | Rand Var: +4 |
| | | | Consist: C | MM: 3403 |

Finally signs of life from this former frontline prospect. Strong 3.4 Cmd as starter confirms it wasn't the product of shorter stints. GB tilt, rising FB velocity, and high rate of getting strike one in 2nd half all position him for more growth—if he can build on 2nd-half FpK surge. UP: 3.00 ERA, 200 Ks

| Yr Tm | W | Sv | IP | K | ERA | xERA | WHIP | oOPS | vL | vR | BF/G | Ctl | Dom | Cmd | FpK | SwK | Vel | G | L | F | H% | S% | hr/f | GS | APC | DOM% | DIS% | Sv% | LI | RAR | BPV | BPX | R$ |
|---|---|---|---|---|---|---|---|---|---|---|---|---|---|---|---|---|---|---|---|---|---|---|---|---|---|---|---|---|---|---|---|---|---|
| 14 | | | | | | | | | | | | | | | | | | | | | | | | | | | | | | | | | |
| 15 a/a | 7 | 0 | 104 | 108 | 2.78 | 2.52 | 1.19 | | | | 20.8 | 3.4 | 9.3 | 2.7 | | | | | | | 30% | 76% | | | | | | | | 15.2 | 116 | 138 | $9 |
| 16 PIT * | 8 | 0 | 140 | 141 | 2.82 | 3.03 | 1.36 | 774 | 810 | 744 | 20.2 | 5.5 | 9.1 | 1.7 | 61% | 12% | 93.5 | 48 | 21 | 32 | 28% | 80% | 10% | 4 | 63 | 0% | 50% | 0 | 0.55 | 23.6 | 87 | 104 | $10 |
| 17 PIT * | 11 | 0 | 155 | 169 | 4.62 | 4.57 | 1.48 | 997 | 1047 | 943 | 22.2 | 4.5 | 9.8 | 2.2 | 56% | 8% | 94.6 | 43 | 21 | 36 | 33% | 71% | 18% | 13 | 81 | 8% | 54% | 0 | 0.81 | -5.1 | 73 | 87 | $2 |
| 18 2 TM | 2 | 0 | 112 | 136 | 4.27 | 3.44 | 1.27 | 688 | 681 | 694 | 10.4 | 4.3 | 11.0 | 2.6 | 58% | 12% | 96.6 | 50 | 20 | 30 | 29% | 70% | 18% | 11 | 41 | 27% | 9% | 0 | 0.56 | -1.7 | 110 | 127 | $1 |
| 1st Half | 1 | 0 | 45 | 56 | 4.40 | 3.35 | 1.31 | 670 | 758 | 597 | 7.3 | 4.6 | 11.2 | 2.4 | 51% | 12% | 96.4 | 55 | 17 | 28 | 30% | 69% | 17% | 0 | 29 | | | 0 | 0.48 | -1.4 | 110 | 127 | -$4 |
| 2nd Half | 1 | 0 | 67 | 80 | 4.19 | 3.49 | 1.25 | 700 | 638 | 776 | 14.6 | 4.1 | 10.8 | 2.7 | 63% | 12% | 96.7 | 46 | 22 | 32 | 28% | 71% | 19% | 11 | 58 | 27% | 9% | 0 | 0.67 | -0.3 | 109 | 126 | $4 |
| 19 Proj | 8 | 0 | 145 | 165 | 3.75 | 3.59 | 1.33 | 686 | 708 | 663 | 32.6 | 4.4 | 10.2 | 2.3 | 57% | 11% | 95.8 | 47 | 20 | 32 | 30% | 75% | 14% | 23 | | | | | | 11.5 | 90 | 103 | $7 |

## Glover,Koda

| Age: 26 | Th: R | Role: RP | Health: F | LIMA Plan: D+ |
|---|---|---|---|---|
| Ht: 6' 5" | Wt: 215 | Type: Pwr FB | PT/Exp: D | Rand Var: -5 |
| | | | Consist: C | MM: 0110 |

Chronic shoulder balkiness has limited him to 100 IP.. over the last three seasons combined. The healthy version has shown command expected from late-inning arm. But lack of put-away stuff, recent FpK futility put that into question too. Shoulder injuries usually just don't go away either. Pass.

| Yr Tm | W | Sv | IP | K | ERA | xERA | WHIP | oOPS | vL | vR | BF/G | Ctl | Dom | Cmd | FpK | SwK | Vel | G | L | F | H% | S% | hr/f | GS | APC | DOM% | DIS% | Sv% | LI | RAR | BPV | BPX | R$ |
|---|---|---|---|---|---|---|---|---|---|---|---|---|---|---|---|---|---|---|---|---|---|---|---|---|---|---|---|---|---|---|---|---|---|
| 14 | | | | | | | | | | | | | | | | | | | | | | | | | | | | | | | | | |
| 15 | | | | | | | | | | | | | | | | | | | | | | | | | | | | | | | | | |
| 16 WAS * | 5 | 6 | 66 | 59 | 4.14 | 3.35 | 1.17 | 664 | 635 | 687 | 5.1 | 2.4 | 8.1 | 3.3 | 66% | 11% | 96.6 | 42 | 17 | 41 | 29% | 66% | 13% | 0 | 16 | | | 75 | 0.86 | 0.4 | 97 | 116 | $4 |
| 17 WAS | 0 | 8 | 19 | 17 | 5.12 | 4.04 | 1.24 | 647 | 709 | 595 | 3.5 | 1.9 | 7.9 | 4.3 | 56% | 11% | 96.5 | 44 | 22 | 34 | 34% | 57% | 5% | 0 | 14 | | | 80 | 1.58 | -1.8 | 114 | 137 | -$1 |
| 18 WAS | 1 | 1 | 16 | 9 | 3.31 | 6.03 | 1.41 | 607 | 392 | 726 | 3.4 | 5.5 | 5.0 | 0.9 | 46% | 10% | 95.5 | 37 | 25 | 37 | 24% | 77% | 5% | 0 | 13 | | | 100 | 1.10 | 1.7 | -45 | -51 | -$4 |
| 1st Half | | | | | | | | | | | | | | | | | | | | | | | | | | | | | | | | | |
| 2nd Half | 1 | 1 | 16 | 9 | 3.31 | 6.03 | 1.41 | 607 | 392 | 726 | 3.4 | 5.5 | 5.0 | 0.9 | 46% | 10% | 95.5 | 37 | 25 | 37 | 24% | 77% | 5% | 0 | 13 | | | 100 | 1.10 | 1.7 | -44 | -51 | -$4 |
| 19 Proj | 4 | 2 | 58 | 43 | 3.93 | 4.61 | 1.29 | 607 | 326 | 761 | 3.8 | 3.7 | 6.7 | 1.8 | 46% | 10% | 95.5 | 40 | 21 | 39 | 27% | 73% | 9% | 0 | | | | | | -2.4 | 39 | 45 | $0 |

## Godley,Zachary

| Age: 29 | Th: R | Role: SP | Health: A | LIMA Plan: C |
|---|---|---|---|---|
| Ht: 6' 3" | Wt: 240 | Type: Pwr GB | PT/Exp: B | Rand Var: +3 |
| | | | Consist: F | MM: 2303 |

After looking like budding anchor in 2017, he lost two mph on fastball and prior wildness returned. xERA tells us he wasn't as bad as he showed, so there's hope for a rebound. But there's nothing here to suggest it will be to 2017 levels. To err on the safe side, use 2017 + 2018 and divide by two.

| Yr Tm | W | Sv | IP | K | ERA | xERA | WHIP | oOPS | vL | vR | BF/G | Ctl | Dom | Cmd | FpK | SwK | Vel | G | L | F | H% | S% | hr/f | GS | APC | DOM% | DIS% | Sv% | LI | RAR | BPV | BPX | R$ |
|---|---|---|---|---|---|---|---|---|---|---|---|---|---|---|---|---|---|---|---|---|---|---|---|---|---|---|---|---|---|---|---|---|---|
| 14 | | | | | | | | | | | | | | | | | | | | | | | | | | | | | | | | | |
| 15 ARI * | 7 | 0 | 61 | 44 | 4.10 | 3.90 | 1.36 | 688 | 528 | 809 | 15.9 | 4.1 | 6.5 | 1.6 | 58% | 12% | 91.4 | 46 | 22 | 32 | 27% | 72% | 13% | 6 | 64 | 50% | 33% | 0 | 0.74 | -1.0 | 50 | 59 | -$1 |
| 16 ARI * | 9 | 0 | 157 | 115 | 5.64 | 5.63 | 1.58 | 844 | 891 | 804 | 16.4 | 3.1 | 6.6 | 2.1 | 55% | 12% | 90.8 | 54 | 18 | 28 | 34% | 66% | 19% | 9 | 43 | 0% | 56% | 0 | 0.85 | -28.0 | 41 | 48 | -$12 |
| 17 ARI * | 10 | 0 | 183 | 188 | 3.30 | 2.80 | 1.15 | 657 | 648 | 664 | 23.4 | 3.5 | 9.2 | 2.7 | 61% | 14% | 91.9 | 55 | 19 | 26 | 28% | 73% | 15% | 25 | 94 | 40% | 8% | 0 | 0.77 | 24.0 | 101 | 122 | $20 |
| 18 ARI | 15 | 0 | 178 | 185 | 4.74 | 3.97 | 1.45 | 733 | 732 | 735 | 24.0 | 4.1 | 9.3 | 2.3 | 60% | 12% | 89.9 | 49 | 23 | 28 | 34% | 68% | 11% | 32 | 91 | 28% | 25% | 0 | 0.81 | -13.1 | 85 | 97 | $0 |
| 1st Half | 9 | 0 | 88 | 87 | 4.58 | 4.19 | 1.52 | 776 | 787 | 764 | 24.7 | 4.6 | 8.9 | 1.9 | 58% | 11% | 90.0 | 52 | 20 | 28 | 32% | 73% | 17% | 16 | 98 | 19% | 38% | | | -4.7 | 66 | 76 | -$3 |
| 2nd Half | 6 | 0 | 90 | 98 | 4.90 | 3.75 | 1.38 | 692 | 678 | 705 | 23.3 | 3.6 | 9.8 | 2.7 | 62% | 13% | 89.8 | 45 | 26 | 28 | 35% | 63% | 6% | 16 | 85 | 38% | 13% | 0 | 0.85 | -8.3 | 102 | 118 | $2 |
| 19 Proj | 13 | 0 | 174 | 168 | 4.05 | 3.69 | 1.35 | 712 | 703 | 719 | 23.3 | 3.7 | 8.7 | 2.3 | 59% | 13% | 90.7 | 50 | 21 | 28 | 31% | 71% | 12% | 31 | | | | | | 9.5 | 84 | 96 | $7 |

## Gohara,Luiz

| Age: 22 | Th: L | Role: RP | Health: D | LIMA Plan: C |
|---|---|---|---|---|
| Ht: 6' 3" | Wt: 265 | Type: Pwr xFB | PT/Exp: D | Rand Var: +4 |
| | | | Consist: C | MM: 0200 |

0-1, 5.95 ERA in 20 IP at ATL. Green southpaw got more seasoning in the minors before shoulder issue ended year in August. Those 2017 skills started to reappear late, so if healthy, he'll be worthy of speculation again. As a flyball pitcher with "D" health, he's not for the risk-averse though.

| Yr Tm | W | Sv | IP | K | ERA | xERA | WHIP | oOPS | vL | vR | BF/G | Ctl | Dom | Cmd | FpK | SwK | Vel | G | L | F | H% | S% | hr/f | GS | APC | DOM% | DIS% | Sv% | LI | RAR | BPV | BPX | R$ |
|---|---|---|---|---|---|---|---|---|---|---|---|---|---|---|---|---|---|---|---|---|---|---|---|---|---|---|---|---|---|---|---|---|---|
| 14 | | | | | | | | | | | | | | | | | | | | | | | | | | | | | | | | | |
| 15 | | | | | | | | | | | | | | | | | | | | | | | | | | | | | | | | | |
| 16 | | | | | | | | | | | | | | | | | | | | | | | | | | | | | | | | | |
| 17 ATL * | 5 | 0 | 117 | 124 | 4.04 | 3.97 | 1.37 | 800 | 348 | 892 | 20.3 | 3.2 | 9.6 | 3.0 | 62% | 14% | 96.3 | 35 | 21 | 44 | 35% | 71% | 6% | 5 | 86 | 20% | 20% | | | 4.5 | 102 | 122 | $3 |
| 18 ATL * | 3 | 1 | 80 | 68 | 5.81 | 4.97 | 1.37 | 727 | 807 | 698 | 15.2 | 2.9 | 7.7 | 2.7 | 61% | 13% | 94.1 | 25 | 18 | 56 | 31% | 60% | 10% | 1 | 34 | 0% | 0% | 100 | 0.51 | -16.4 | 59 | 67 | -$7 |
| 1st Half | 1 | 1 | 44 | 37 | 6.81 | 6.24 | 1.63 | 796 | 951 | 739 | 13.9 | 4.2 | 7.6 | 1.8 | 62% | 12% | 94.2 | 21 | 21 | 57 | 33% | 61% | 7% | 1 | 35 | 0% | 0% | 100 | 0.62 | -14.4 | 25 | 29 | -$15 |
| 2nd Half | 2 | 0 | 36 | 32 | 4.60 | 3.43 | 1.06 | 385 | 0 | 500 | 17.5 | 1.2 | 7.9 | 6.5 | 54% | 15% | 93.7 | 50 | 0 | 50 | 29% | 59% | 25% | 0 | 30 | | | 0 | 0.12 | -2.0 | 157 | 180 | $3 |
| 19 Proj | 2 | 0 | 51 | 48 | 4.87 | 4.64 | 1.32 | 727 | 897 | 664 | 17.3 | 2.8 | 8.5 | 3.1 | 62% | 12% | 94.2 | 21 | 21 | 57 | 32% | 65% | 7% | 9 | | | | | | -2.9 | 78 | 89 | -$3 |

STEPHEN NICKRAND

## Gomber,Austin

| | | | | | |
|---|---|---|---|---|---|
| Age: 25 | Th: L | Role RP | Health A | LIMA Plan B+ | |
| Ht: 6' 5" | Wt: 230 | Type Pwr | PT/Exp D | Rand Var 0 | |
| | | | Consist C | MM 1201 | |

6-2, 4.44 ERA in 75 IP at STL. Injuries opened rotation door. He didn't implode in MLB debut, and that LIMA grade does give him hint of hidden value. But under closer exam, he's a pitcher that is more bad than good (see DOM/DIS%), and marginal FpK points to more control woes. A low-upside dart throw.

| Yr Tm | W | Sv | IP | K | ERA | xERA | WHIP | oOPS | vL | vR | BF/G | Ctl | Dom | Cmd | FpK | SwK | Vel | G | L | F | H% | S% | hr/f | GS | APC | DOM% | DIS% | Sv% | LI | RAR | BPV | BPX | R$ |
|---|---|---|---|---|---|---|---|---|---|---|---|---|---|---|---|---|---|---|---|---|---|---|---|---|---|---|---|---|---|---|---|---|---|
| 14 | | | | | | | | | | | | | | | | | | | | | | | | | | | | | | | | | |
| 15 | | | | | | | | | | | | | | | | | | | | | | | | | | | | | | | | | |
| 16 aa | 1 | 0 | 19 | 12 | 1.74 | 1.81 | 1.14 | | | | 19.1 | 4.2 | 5.7 | 1.3 | | | | | | | 23% | 83% | | | | | | | | 5.8 | 79 | 94 | -$1 |
| 17 aa | 10 | 0 | 143 | 114 | 4.24 | 4.25 | 1.34 | | | | 22.9 | 3.3 | 7.2 | 2.2 | | | | | | | 29% | 72% | | | | | | | | 2.0 | 57 | 69 | $5 |
| 18 STL * | 13 | 0 | 144 | 127 | 4.18 | 4.73 | 1.44 | 786 | 744 | 804 | 15.0 | 3.2 | 8.0 | 2.5 | 58% | 10% | 92.5 | 38 | 27 | 35 | 33% | 73% | 9% | 11 | 42 | 18% | 27% | 0 | 0.95 | -0.5 | 69 | 80 | $2 |
| 1st Half | 4 | 0 | 69 | 60 | 4.10 | 4.66 | 1.41 | 693 | 1055 | 322 | 12.6 | 3.1 | 7.9 | 2.5 | 54% | 12% | 93.6 | 26 | 43 | 31 | 33% | 74% | 9% | 0 | 15 | | | 0 | 1.17 | 0.4 | 69 | 80 | -$3 |
| 2nd Half | 9 | 0 | 75 | 67 | 4.25 | 4.79 | 1.46 | 803 | 635 | 864 | 18.0 | 3.3 | 8.0 | 2.4 | 59% | 9% | 92.2 | 40 | 24 | 35 | 34% | 73% | 9% | 11 | 68 | 18% | 27% | 0 | 0.74 | -0.9 | 69 | 80 | $6 |
| 19 Proj | 9 | 0 | 102 | 86 | 4.21 | 4.28 | 1.40 | 697 | 533 | 757 | 17.6 | 3.3 | 7.6 | 2.3 | 59% | 9% | 92.2 | 40 | 24 | 35 | 32% | 73% | 10% | 18 | | | | | | -0.7 | 68 | 78 | $1 |

## Gonsalves,Stephen

| | | | | | |
|---|---|---|---|---|---|
| Age: 24 | Th: L | Role SP | Health A | LIMA Plan B | |
| Ht: 6' 5" | Wt: 213 | Type Pwr | PT/Exp D | Rand Var -1 | |
| | | | Consist D | MM 1101 | |

2-2, 6.57 ERA in 25 IP at MIN. As a youngster who relies more on deception than stuff, his margin for error is razor thin. That fact is apparent in his mediocre SwK and FpK combo. And his low rate of first-pitch strikes is no fluke, as he has struggled to find plate in minors. Spend your buck elsewhere.

| Yr Tm | W | Sv | IP | K | ERA | xERA | WHIP | oOPS | vL | vR | BF/G | Ctl | Dom | Cmd | FpK | SwK | Vel | G | L | F | H% | S% | hr/f | GS | APC | DOM% | DIS% | Sv% | LI | RAR | BPV | BPX | R$ |
|---|---|---|---|---|---|---|---|---|---|---|---|---|---|---|---|---|---|---|---|---|---|---|---|---|---|---|---|---|---|---|---|---|---|
| 14 | | | | | | | | | | | | | | | | | | | | | | | | | | | | | | | | | |
| 15 | | | | | | | | | | | | | | | | | | | | | | | | | | | | | | | | | |
| 16 aa | 8 | 0 | 74 | 73 | 2.34 | 2.06 | 1.18 | | | | 22.9 | 4.5 | 8.8 | 2.0 | | | | | | | 27% | 79% | | | | | | | | 17.0 | 106 | 126 | $9 |
| 17 a/a | 9 | 0 | 110 | 97 | 4.80 | 4.75 | 1.39 | | | | 23.2 | 2.8 | 7.9 | 2.9 | | | | | | | 33% | 68% | | | | | | | | -6.0 | 70 | 84 | $0 |
| 18 MIN * | 14 | 0 | 147 | 113 | 4.16 | 3.81 | 1.44 | 822 | 1017 | 773 | 20.9 | 5.6 | 6.9 | 1.2 | 52% | 6% | 89.8 | 37 | 34 | 29 | 27% | 72% | 8% | 4 | 73 | 0% | 100% | 0 | 0.80 | -0.2 | 55 | 63 | $2 |
| 1st Half | 8 | 0 | 74 | 64 | 4.74 | 4.12 | 1.48 | | | | 21.3 | 6.1 | 7.7 | 1.3 | | | | | | | 26% | 70% | 0% | 0 | | | | | | -5.4 | 52 | 59 | -$2 |
| 2nd Half | 6 | 0 | 73 | 49 | 3.57 | 3.49 | 1.41 | 822 | 1017 | 773 | 20.5 | 4.9 | 6.1 | 1.2 | 52% | 6% | 89.8 | 37 | 34 | 29 | 28% | 74% | 8% | 4 | 73 | 0% | 100% | 0 | 0.80 | 5.2 | 58 | 67 | $6 |
| 19 Proj | 8 | 0 | 87 | 72 | 4.26 | 4.42 | 1.38 | 611 | 797 | 564 | 21.9 | 4.4 | 7.5 | 1.7 | 52% | 6% | 89.8 | 37 | 34 | 29 | 29% | 70% | 9% | 17 | | | | | | -1.2 | 32 | 37 | $0 |

## Gonzales,Marco

| | | | | | |
|---|---|---|---|---|---|
| Age: 27 | Th: L | Role SP | Health B | LIMA Plan B | |
| Ht: 6' 1" | Wt: 195 | Type | PT/Exp C | Rand Var 0 | |
| | | | Consist B | MM 2103 | |

Another year of control improvement netted him best skills of career. Can they stick? Big jump in FpK supports Ctl-fueled command surge. Keeps getting better against righties too, which supports continued BPV growth. Even with a modest ceiling, there's some upside profit here. UP: 3.50 ERA

| Yr Tm | W | Sv | IP | K | ERA | xERA | WHIP | oOPS | vL | vR | BF/G | Ctl | Dom | Cmd | FpK | SwK | Vel | G | L | F | H% | S% | hr/f | GS | APC | DOM% | DIS% | Sv% | LI | RAR | BPV | BPX | R$ |
|---|---|---|---|---|---|---|---|---|---|---|---|---|---|---|---|---|---|---|---|---|---|---|---|---|---|---|---|---|---|---|---|---|---|
| 14 STL * | 11 | 0 | 119 | 103 | 3.36 | 3.78 | 1.27 | 737 | 397 | 827 | 19.5 | 2.9 | 7.8 | 2.7 | 61% | 10% | 89.6 | 36 | 23 | 41 | 30% | 77% | 10% | 5 | 62 | 0% | 40% | 0 | 1.07 | 5.6 | 80 | 95 | $6 |
| 15 STL * | 1 | 0 | 79 | 52 | 5.67 | 6.53 | 1.75 | 1286 | 500 | 1286 | 21.1 | 2.8 | 5.9 | 2.1 | 75% | 3% | 89.4 | 36 | 36 | 29 | 38% | 69% | 25% | 1 | 66 | 0% | 100% | | | -16.5 | 32 | 38 | -$14 |
| 16 | | | | | | | | | | | | | | | | | | | | | | | | | | | | | | | | | |
| 17 2 TM * | 9 | 0 | 120 | 88 | 4.57 | 4.65 | 1.38 | 924 | 835 | 954 | 21.1 | 2.5 | 6.6 | 2.6 | 60% | 10% | 91.5 | 45 | 23 | 32 | 32% | 69% | 18% | 8 | 64 | 0% | 75% | 0 | 0.59 | -3.1 | 60 | 72 | $1 |
| 18 SEA | 13 | 0 | 167 | 145 | 4.00 | 3.71 | 1.22 | 720 | 692 | 726 | 23.7 | 1.7 | 7.8 | 4.5 | 66% | 10% | 90.1 | 45 | 25 | 30 | 32% | 70% | 11% | 29 | 88 | 28% | 14% | | | 3.2 | 117 | 135 | $9 |
| 1st Half | 8 | 0 | 100 | 87 | 3.77 | 3.58 | 1.23 | 725 | 689 | 732 | 24.1 | 1.8 | 7.8 | 4.4 | 68% | 10% | 90.4 | 46 | 26 | 27 | 32% | 72% | 12% | 17 | 93 | 24% | 12% | | | 4.7 | 116 | 133 | $13 |
| 2nd Half | 5 | 0 | 66 | 58 | 4.34 | 3.90 | 1.22 | 713 | 697 | 717 | 23.0 | 1.6 | 7.9 | 4.8 | 64% | 10% | 89.6 | 43 | 23 | 34 | 32% | 66% | 10% | 12 | 82 | 33% | 17% | | | -1.6 | 119 | 137 | $4 |
| 19 Proj | 10 | 0 | 160 | 128 | 3.94 | 3.88 | 1.31 | 728 | 647 | 750 | 21.6 | 2.2 | 7.2 | 3.3 | 63% | 10% | 90.4 | 43 | 24 | 33 | 32% | 73% | 12% | 31 | | | | | | 4.2 | 93 | 107 | $6 |

## Gonzalez,Gio

| | | | | | |
|---|---|---|---|---|---|
| Age: 33 | Th: L | Role SP | Health A | LIMA Plan D+ | |
| Ht: 6' 0" | Wt: 203 | Type Pwr | PT/Exp A | Rand Var 0 | |
| | | | Consist A | MM 1203 | |

Exhibit A for why you shouldn't pay for past results when warning signs abound. That nifty ERA in 2017 was proven to be phony as hit rate normalized. Waning ability to get strike one tells us the decline isn't over, especially as he struggles to reach 90 mph. Heed the xERA trend. DN: 5.00 ERA

| Yr Tm | W | Sv | IP | K | ERA | xERA | WHIP | oOPS | vL | vR | BF/G | Ctl | Dom | Cmd | FpK | SwK | Vel | G | L | F | H% | S% | hr/f | GS | APC | DOM% | DIS% | Sv% | LI | RAR | BPV | BPX | R$ |
|---|---|---|---|---|---|---|---|---|---|---|---|---|---|---|---|---|---|---|---|---|---|---|---|---|---|---|---|---|---|---|---|---|---|
| 14 WAS | 10 | 0 | 159 | 162 | 3.57 | 3.41 | 1.20 | 647 | 628 | 653 | 24.2 | 3.2 | 9.2 | 2.9 | 58% | 11% | 92.0 | 45 | 19 | 37 | 30% | 71% | 7% | 27 | 97 | 41% | 26% | | | 3.3 | 103 | 122 | $9 |
| 15 WAS | 11 | 0 | 176 | 169 | 3.79 | 3.66 | 1.42 | 711 | 641 | 732 | 24.5 | 3.5 | 8.7 | 2.4 | 60% | 10% | 92.0 | 54 | 20 | 27 | 35% | 73% | 6% | 31 | 95 | 23% | 29% | | | 3.7 | 92 | 110 | $4 |
| 16 WAS | 11 | 0 | 177 | 171 | 4.57 | 3.85 | 1.34 | 730 | 633 | 756 | 23.9 | 3.0 | 8.7 | 2.9 | 57% | 10% | 90.8 | 48 | 23 | 30 | 33% | 68% | 13% | 32 | 97 | 28% | 31% | | | -8.3 | 101 | 120 | $3 |
| 17 WAS | 15 | 0 | 201 | 188 | 2.96 | 4.15 | 1.18 | 642 | 507 | 681 | 25.8 | 3.5 | 8.4 | 2.4 | 55% | 9% | 89.9 | 46 | 19 | 35 | 27% | 79% | 11% | 32 | 105 | 38% | 16% | | | 34.8 | 80 | 96 | $25 |
| 18 2 NL | 10 | 0 | 171 | 148 | 4.21 | 4.57 | 1.44 | 734 | 597 | 766 | 23.3 | 4.2 | 7.8 | 1.9 | 54% | 10% | 89.8 | 45 | 23 | 32 | 31% | 73% | 10% | 32 | 94 | 13% | 38% | | | -1.3 | 50 | 57 | $0 |
| 1st Half | 6 | 0 | 86 | 82 | 3.68 | 4.22 | 1.42 | 732 | 576 | 769 | 23.3 | 4.1 | 8.6 | 2.1 | 54% | 10% | 89.3 | 50 | 19 | 31 | 32% | 77% | 12% | 16 | 96 | 19% | 38% | | | 5.0 | 72 | 83 | $3 |
| 2nd Half | 4 | 0 | 85 | 66 | 4.75 | 4.92 | 1.46 | 736 | 618 | 763 | 23.3 | 4.3 | 7.0 | 1.6 | 53% | 10% | 90.3 | 41 | 26 | 34 | 30% | 68% | 9% | 16 | 92 | 6% | 38% | | | -6.3 | 27 | 31 | -$4 |
| 19 Proj | 10 | 0 | 160 | 142 | 4.40 | 4.17 | 1.40 | 745 | 611 | 779 | 23.7 | 4.0 | 8.0 | 2.0 | 55% | 10% | 90.2 | 45 | 22 | 34 | 30% | 71% | 13% | 28 | | | | | | -0.3 | 60 | 69 | $1 |

## Goody,Nicholas

| | | | | | |
|---|---|---|---|---|---|
| Age: 27 | Th: R | Role RP | Health F | LIMA Plan C | |
| Ht: 5' 11" | Wt: 195 | Type Pwr xFB | PT/Exp D | Rand Var +5 | |
| | | | Consist C | MM 1400 | |

Elbow injury, eventually leading to surgery, makes last year's 12 IP a non-element in his data sample. Ability to miss bats is cemented in his profile. The roadblock is his inconsistent control. Improving velocity and SwK show he's throwing harder but eroding FpK questions improvement in command. FB rate is flammable.

| Yr Tm | W | Sv | IP | K | ERA | xERA | WHIP | oOPS | vL | vR | BF/G | Ctl | Dom | Cmd | FpK | SwK | Vel | G | L | F | H% | S% | hr/f | GS | APC | DOM% | DIS% | Sv% | LI | RAR | BPV | BPX | R$ |
|---|---|---|---|---|---|---|---|---|---|---|---|---|---|---|---|---|---|---|---|---|---|---|---|---|---|---|---|---|---|---|---|---|---|
| 14 aa | 0 | 0 | 16 | 16 | 7.95 | 8.08 | 2.06 | | | | 5.2 | 5.7 | 9.2 | 1.6 | | | | | | | 40% | 64% | | | | | | | | -8.3 | 16 | 19 | -$7 |
| 15 NYY * | 2 | 8 | 68 | 74 | 2.39 | 2.98 | 1.26 | 794 | 833 | 729 | 5.5 | 3.4 | 9.8 | 2.8 | 69% | 11% | 90.9 | 47 | 21 | 32 | 32% | 82% | 0% | 0 | 17 | | | 73 | 0.66 | 13.2 | 115 | 137 | $7 |
| 16 NYY * | 0 | 5 | 52 | 63 | 3.82 | 4.55 | 1.18 | 878 | 1097 | 758 | 4.7 | 2.8 | 10.8 | 3.8 | 59% | 15% | 90.9 | 23 | 21 | 56 | 28% | 81% | 16% | 0 | 20 | | | 100 | 0.45 | 2.4 | 85 | 101 | $2 |
| 17 CLE | 1 | 0 | 55 | 72 | 2.80 | 3.67 | 1.08 | 632 | 590 | 651 | 3.9 | 3.3 | 11.9 | 3.6 | 58% | 17% | 91.7 | 28 | 23 | 48 | 28% | 81% | 12% | 0 | 16 | | | 0 | 0.55 | 10.5 | 130 | 157 | $4 |
| 18 CLE | 0 | 0 | 12 | 12 | 6.94 | 5.58 | 1.71 | 1016 | 826 | 1122 | 4.8 | 3.9 | 9.3 | 2.4 | 55% | 14% | 91.3 | 28 | 21 | 51 | 34% | 69% | 20% | 0 | 17 | | | 0 | 1.57 | -4.0 | 68 | 79 | -$7 |
| 1st Half | 0 | 0 | 12 | 12 | 6.94 | 5.58 | 1.71 | 1016 | 826 | 1122 | 4.8 | 3.9 | 9.3 | 2.4 | 55% | 14% | 91.3 | 28 | 21 | 51 | 34% | 69% | 20% | 0 | 17 | | | 0 | 1.57 | -4.0 | 69 | 79 | -$7 |
| 2nd Half | | | | | | | | | | | | | | | | | | | | | | | | | | | | | | | | | |
| 19 Proj | 1 | 0 | 44 | 49 | 4.12 | 4.11 | 1.33 | 723 | 685 | 740 | 4.8 | 3.6 | 10.2 | 2.8 | 58% | 17% | 91.7 | 28 | 23 | 48 | 31% | 75% | 12% | 0 | | | | | | 0.3 | 91 | 105 | -$3 |

## Grace,Matt

| | | | | | |
|---|---|---|---|---|---|
| Age: 30 | Th: L | Role RP | Health D | LIMA Plan B+ | |
| Ht: 6' 4" | Wt: 215 | Type GB | PT/Exp D | Rand Var -2 | |
| | | | Consist B | MM 2000 | |

Posted first roster-worthy skills of career just before he turned 30. But his club still didn't trust him in key spots (see mediocre LI), and neither should you. Even with FpK-supported solid control now, he hasn't generated any whiffs in years, so command should continue to be on a yo-yo. Pass.

| Yr Tm | W | Sv | IP | K | ERA | xERA | WHIP | oOPS | vL | vR | BF/G | Ctl | Dom | Cmd | FpK | SwK | Vel | G | L | F | H% | S% | hr/f | GS | APC | DOM% | DIS% | Sv% | LI | RAR | BPV | BPX | R$ |
|---|---|---|---|---|---|---|---|---|---|---|---|---|---|---|---|---|---|---|---|---|---|---|---|---|---|---|---|---|---|---|---|---|---|
| 14 a/a | 5 | 3 | 77 | 48 | 1.36 | 2.82 | 1.23 | | | | 6.2 | 2.8 | 5.6 | 2.0 | | | | | | | 29% | 89% | | | | | | | | 22.6 | 77 | 92 | $8 |
| 15 WAS * | 2 | 1 | 66 | 38 | 3.63 | 4.85 | 1.66 | 855 | 649 | 1071 | 4.6 | 3.7 | 5.2 | 1.4 | 52% | 6% | 91.1 | 59 | 23 | 18 | 35% | 76% | 0% | 0 | 12 | | | 17 | 1.35 | 2.7 | 49 | 59 | -$5 |
| 16 WAS * | 1 | 1 | 50 | 28 | 4.31 | 5.89 | 1.75 | 200 | 333 | 0 | 5.7 | 2.0 | 5.1 | 2.5 | 40% | 18% | 89.1 | 67 | 0 | 33 | 40% | 74% | 0% | 0 | 8 | | | 50 | 0.52 | -0.8 | 61 | 72 | -$6 |
| 17 WAS * | 2 | 2 | 70 | 46 | 4.56 | 4.67 | 1.51 | 702 | 550 | 817 | 5.7 | 3.5 | 6.0 | 1.7 | 61% | 8% | 91.0 | 61 | 18 | 20 | 33% | 70% | 9% | 1 | 19 | 0% | 0% | 100 | 0.60 | -1.7 | 48 | 58 | -$4 |
| 18 WAS | 1 | 0 | 60 | 48 | 2.87 | 3.92 | 1.14 | 638 | 620 | 650 | 4.4 | 2.0 | 7.2 | 3.7 | 65% | 8% | 91.2 | 48 | 20 | 31 | 29% | 78% | 9% | 0 | 15 | | | 0 | 0.70 | 9.5 | 103 | 119 | $2 |
| 1st Half | 0 | 0 | 24 | 20 | 3.38 | 3.79 | 1.00 | 648 | 619 | 662 | 4.7 | 1.5 | 7.5 | 5.0 | 67% | 8% | 90.9 | 47 | 13 | 40 | 26% | 71% | 11% | 0 | 17 | | | 0 | 0.54 | 2.3 | 120 | 137 | -$2 |
| 2nd Half | 1 | 0 | 36 | 28 | 2.52 | 4.01 | 1.23 | 632 | 620 | 642 | 4.3 | 2.3 | 7.1 | 3.1 | 63% | 9% | 91.3 | 49 | 25 | 26 | 31% | 81% | 7% | 0 | 14 | | | 0 | 0.80 | 7.2 | 93 | 107 | $4 |
| 19 Proj | 1 | 0 | 51 | 36 | 3.81 | 3.99 | 1.35 | 722 | 654 | 769 | 4.9 | 2.5 | 6.4 | 2.6 | 63% | 8% | 91.1 | 51 | 19 | 29 | 32% | 72% | 7% | 0 | | | | | | 0.7 | 78 | 89 | -$3 |

## Gray,Jonathan

| | | | | | |
|---|---|---|---|---|---|
| Age: 27 | Th: R | Role SP | Health D | LIMA Plan C+ | |
| Ht: 6' 4" | Wt: 235 | Type Pwr | PT/Exp A | Rand Var +5 | |
| | | | Consist A | MM 3305 | |

One of game's most underperforming pitchers might be completely avoided after this debacle. Three reasons you shouldn't: 1) Both SwK and FpK have never been better; 2) 100+ BPV in 5 of 6 months; 3) GB lean, high hr/f mean HR totals should drop. A wildcard who still carries... UP: 3.00 ERA

| Yr Tm | W | Sv | IP | K | ERA | xERA | WHIP | oOPS | vL | vR | BF/G | Ctl | Dom | Cmd | FpK | SwK | Vel | G | L | F | H% | S% | hr/f | GS | APC | DOM% | DIS% | Sv% | LI | RAR | BPV | BPX | R$ |
|---|---|---|---|---|---|---|---|---|---|---|---|---|---|---|---|---|---|---|---|---|---|---|---|---|---|---|---|---|---|---|---|---|---|
| 14 aa | 10 | 0 | 124 | 92 | 5.58 | 4.70 | 1.44 | | | | 22.1 | 3.2 | 6.6 | 2.1 | | | | | | | 32% | 62% | | | | | | | | -28.2 | 51 | 60 | -$8 |
| 15 COL * | 6 | 0 | 155 | 123 | 5.35 | 5.68 | 1.67 | 856 | 755 | 949 | 23.2 | 3.2 | 7.1 | 2.2 | 58% | 10% | 94.4 | 42 | 25 | 33 | 37% | 68% | 10% | 9 | 76 | 22% | 33% | | | -26.5 | 55 | 65 | -$16 |
| 16 COL | 10 | 0 | 168 | 185 | 4.61 | 3.59 | 1.26 | 703 | 694 | 712 | 24.6 | 3.2 | 9.9 | 3.1 | 62% | 12% | 95.1 | 44 | 24 | 32 | 32% | 65% | 13% | 29 | 96 | 41% | 34% | | | -8.7 | 115 | 137 | $6 |
| 17 COL | 10 | 0 | 110 | 112 | 3.67 | 3.62 | 1.30 | 716 | 695 | 744 | 23.1 | 2.4 | 9.1 | 3.7 | 61% | 9% | 96.0 | 49 | 23 | 29 | 34% | 74% | 11% | 20 | 92 | 35% | 20% | | | 9.4 | 125 | 151 | $8 |
| 18 COL | 12 | 0 | 172 | 183 | 5.12 | 3.64 | 1.35 | 773 | 831 | 717 | 24.0 | 2.7 | 9.6 | 3.5 | 63% | 13% | 94.8 | 47 | 22 | 30 | 34% | 65% | 18% | 31 | 90 | 29% | 29% | | | -20.6 | 124 | 142 | -$1 |
| 1st Half | 7 | 0 | 92 | 119 | 5.77 | 3.28 | 1.49 | 795 | 833 | 752 | 24.2 | 2.8 | 11.6 | 4.1 | 63% | 14% | 95.1 | 46 | 26 | 28 | 41% | 62% | 15% | 17 | 93 | 24% | 18% | | | -18.4 | 157 | 180 | -$6 |
| 2nd Half | 5 | 0 | 80 | 64 | 4.37 | 4.05 | 1.18 | 746 | 828 | 677 | 23.6 | 2.6 | 7.2 | 2.8 | 63% | 12% | 94.3 | 49 | 18 | 33 | 26% | 71% | 21% | 14 | 88 | 36% | 43% | | | -2.2 | 87 | 100 | $8 |
| 19 Proj | 13 | 0 | 189 | 189 | 4.05 | 3.46 | 1.29 | 738 | 749 | 726 | 25.1 | 2.8 | 9.0 | 3.3 | 62% | 12% | 95.0 | 47 | 22 | 31 | 32% | 73% | 15% | 31 | | | | | | 16.1 | 113 | 130 | $10 |

STEPHEN NICKRAND

## Gray,Sonny

Age: 29 | Th: R | Role: RP | Ht: 5' 10" | Wt: 190 | Type: Pwr GB
Health: D | PT/Exp: B | Consist: A | LIMA Plan: C | Rand Var: +3 | MM: 2203

Just when we thought he figured it out *again*, Yankee Stadium happened. Near-7.00 ERA there was result of HRs and ugly 1.3 Cmd. On road, he was great (3.17 ERA, 3.5 Cmd). Overall xERA in recent seasons says we need to use 4.00 mark as new baseline. But if he finds a new club, there's profit here.

| Yr | Tm | W | Sv | IP | K | ERA | xERA | WHIP | oOPS | vL | vR | BF/G | Ctl | Dom | Cmd | FpK | SwK | Vel | G | L | F | H% | S% | hr/f | GS | APC | DOM% | DIS% | Sv% | LI | RAR | BPV | BPX | R$ |
|---|---|---|---|---|---|---|---|---|---|---|---|---|---|---|---|---|---|---|---|---|---|---|---|---|---|---|---|---|---|---|---|---|---|---|
| 14 | OAK | 14 | 0 | 219 | 183 | 3.08 | 3.36 | 1.19 | 627 | 639 | 614 | 27.2 | 3.0 | 7.5 | 2.5 | 58% | 9% | 93.0 | 56 | 18 | 26 | 28% | 76% | 9% | 33 | 100 | 36% | 21% | | | 17.8 | 87 | 104 | $16 |
| 15 | OAK | 14 | 0 | 208 | 169 | 2.73 | 3.62 | 1.08 | 590 | 579 | 601 | 26.8 | 2.6 | 7.3 | 2.9 | 59% | 10% | 92.9 | 53 | 17 | 31 | 26% | 78% | 9% | 31 | 99 | 42% | 23% | | | 31.7 | 94 | 112 | $26 |
| 16 | OAK | 5 | 0 | 117 | 94 | 5.69 | 4.25 | 1.50 | 818 | 757 | 880 | 23.5 | 3.2 | 7.2 | 2.2 | 61% | 8% | 92.7 | 54 | 19 | 27 | 33% | 64% | 17% | 22 | 89 | 9% | 45% | | | -21.7 | 75 | 89 | -$9 |
| 17 | 2 AL | 10 | 0 | 162 | 153 | 3.55 | 3.82 | 1.21 | 668 | 645 | 687 | 25.1 | 3.2 | 8.5 | 2.7 | 62% | 12% | 93.0 | 53 | 20 | 28 | 28% | 75% | 15% | 27 | 99 | 37% | 30% | | | 16.2 | 98 | 118 | $14 |
| 18 | NYY | 11 | 0 | 130 | 123 | 4.90 | 4.14 | 1.50 | 768 | 725 | 808 | 19.4 | 3.9 | 8.5 | 2.2 | 57% | 10% | 93.3 | 50 | 23 | 27 | 34% | 69% | 13% | 23 | 75 | 22% | 43% | 0 | 0.72 | -12.1 | 75 | 86 | -$4 |
| 1st Half | | 5 | 0 | 83 | 73 | 5.44 | 4.42 | 1.51 | 786 | 730 | 836 | 23.1 | 3.9 | 7.9 | 2.0 | 57% | 10% | 93.2 | 48 | 23 | 30 | 33% | 65% | 13% | 16 | 88 | 19% | 44% | | | -13.2 | 63 | 72 | -$9 |
| 2nd Half | | 6 | 0 | 48 | 50 | 3.97 | 3.66 | 1.47 | 738 | 716 | 758 | 15.1 | 4.0 | 9.4 | 2.4 | 58% | 11% | 93.3 | 54 | 24 | 22 | 35% | 74% | 13% | 7 | 60 | 29% | 43% | 0 | 0.67 | 1.1 | 95 | 109 | $4 |
| 19 | Proj | **11** | **0** | **145** | **135** | **4.06** | **3.68** | **1.38** | **731** | **698** | **761** | **19.9** | **3.5** | **8.4** | **2.4** | **59%** | **11%** | **93.1** | **53** | **21** | **26** | **32%** | **73%** | **14%** | **30** | | | | | | **1.6** | **86** | **99** | **$4** |

## Green,Chad

Age: 28 | Th: R | Role: RP | Ht: 6' 3" | Wt: 210 | Type: Pwr FB
Health: B | PT/Exp: D | Consist: C | LIMA Plan: B | Rand Var: -3 | MM: 3411

Emergence as elite middleman validated. Sure, strand rate regression will push ERA north a bit, and FB tilt is risky fit in HR-friendly park. But elite skills, strike-one ability, and plenty of whiffs all suggest he can take on a higher profile role if opportunity aligns. UP: Finds save opps DN: LIMA stash

| Yr | Tm | W | Sv | IP | K | ERA | xERA | WHIP | oOPS | vL | vR | BF/G | Ctl | Dom | Cmd | FpK | SwK | Vel | G | L | F | H% | S% | hr/f | GS | APC | DOM% | DIS% | Sv% | LI | RAR | BPV | BPX | R$ |
|---|---|---|---|---|---|---|---|---|---|---|---|---|---|---|---|---|---|---|---|---|---|---|---|---|---|---|---|---|---|---|---|---|---|---|
| 14 | | | | | | | | | | | | | | | | | | | | | | | | | | | | | | | | | | |
| 15 | aa | 5 | 0 | 149 | 108 | 4.84 | 5.48 | 1.65 | | | | 24.6 | 2.8 | 6.5 | 2.4 | | | | | | | 38% | 70% | | | | | | | | -16.2 | 61 | 73 | -$13 |
| 16 | NYY * | 9 | 1 | 140 | 135 | 3.01 | 3.88 | 1.25 | 852 | 1014 | 704 | 20.4 | 2.5 | 8.6 | 3.5 | 60% | 13% | 94.3 | 41 | 21 | 38 | 31% | 81% | 25% | 8 | 70 | 25% | 38% | 100 | 0.68 | 20.4 | 97 | 115 | $12 |
| 17 | NYY * | 7 | 0 | 96 | 130 | 3.24 | 2.51 | 1.10 | 454 | 411 | 476 | 8.3 | 2.8 | 12.2 | 4.4 | 66% | 16% | 95.8 | 26 | 27 | 47 | 33% | 71% | 7% | 1 | 29 | 0% | 0% | 0 | 0.95 | 13.2 | 160 | 193 | $11 |
| 18 | NYY | 8 | 0 | 76 | 94 | 2.50 | 3.36 | 1.04 | 641 | 645 | 637 | 4.7 | 1.8 | 11.2 | 6.3 | 69% | 14% | 96.2 | 31 | 23 | 46 | 32% | 83% | 10% | 0 | 20 | | | 0 | 1.12 | 15.4 | 162 | 187 | $10 |
| 1st Half | | 4 | 0 | 38 | 52 | 2.11 | 3.12 | 1.02 | 622 | 725 | 532 | 4.8 | 1.9 | 12.2 | 6.5 | 68% | 15% | 96.1 | 29 | 25 | 46 | 32% | 86% | 10% | 0 | 20 | | | 0 | 1.28 | 9.6 | 176 | 202 | $11 |
| 2nd Half | | 4 | 0 | 37 | 42 | 2.89 | 3.62 | 1.07 | 661 | 573 | 752 | 4.7 | 1.7 | 10.1 | 6.0 | 70% | 12% | 96.2 | 33 | 21 | 45 | 31% | 80% | 11% | 0 | 20 | | | 0 | 0.97 | 5.8 | 148 | 170 | $10 |
| 19 | Proj | **6** | **2** | **73** | **84** | **3.03** | **3.38** | **1.15** | **681** | **702** | **665** | **6.8** | **2.2** | **10.5** | **4.7** | **67%** | **14%** | **95.8** | **31** | **24** | **45** | **33%** | **78%** | **9%** | **0** | | | | | | **10.1** | **138** | **158** | **$7** |

## Greene,Shane

Age: 30 | Th: R | Role: RP | Ht: 6' 4" | Wt: 197 | Type: Pwr
Health: C | PT/Exp: C | Consist: A | LIMA Plan: B | Rand Var: +4 | MM: 2320

Looked closer-worthy early before it came crashing down late. That's what happens when you don't have a real strikeout pitch. With FB rate climbing just as he misses ever-fewer bats, margin for error only gets slimmer. And history suggests that FpK spike won't stick. A poor bet to stay a stopper.

| Yr | Tm | W | Sv | IP | K | ERA | xERA | WHIP | oOPS | vL | vR | BF/G | Ctl | Dom | Cmd | FpK | SwK | Vel | G | L | F | H% | S% | hr/f | GS | APC | DOM% | DIS% | Sv% | LI | RAR | BPV | BPX | R$ |
|---|---|---|---|---|---|---|---|---|---|---|---|---|---|---|---|---|---|---|---|---|---|---|---|---|---|---|---|---|---|---|---|---|---|---|
| 14 | NYY * | 10 | 0 | 145 | 127 | 4.53 | 5.05 | 1.59 | 715 | 765 | 661 | 21.3 | 3.5 | 7.9 | 2.3 | 59% | 11% | 93.1 | 50 | 22 | 28 | 37% | 72% | 13% | 14 | 90 | 36% | 36% | 0 | 0.70 | -14.1 | 69 | 82 | -$7 |
| 15 | DET * | 5 | 0 | 119 | 66 | 6.29 | 5.60 | 1.58 | 897 | 1017 | 757 | 20.9 | 3.0 | 5.0 | 1.7 | 62% | 7% | 91.7 | 44 | 23 | 33 | 33% | 61% | 14% | 16 | 74 | 25% | 56% | 0 | 0.70 | -34.1 | 24 | 28 | -$17 |
| 16 | DET | 5 | 2 | 60 | 59 | 5.82 | 3.87 | 1.33 | 680 | 788 | 586 | 5.1 | 3.3 | 8.8 | 2.7 | 58% | 13% | 94.0 | 48 | 20 | 32 | 33% | 53% | 6% | 3 | 20 | 0% | 33% | 67 | 1.26 | -12.1 | 96 | 114 | -$3 |
| 17 | DET | 4 | 9 | 68 | 73 | 2.66 | 4.04 | 1.24 | 631 | 758 | 542 | 4.0 | 4.5 | 9.7 | 2.1 | 59% | 10% | 95.0 | 47 | 18 | 35 | 27% | 82% | 10% | 0 | 15 | | | 69 | 1.18 | 14.2 | 78 | 93 | $9 |
| 18 | DET | 4 | 32 | 63 | 65 | 5.12 | 4.16 | 1.37 | 787 | 745 | 834 | 4.2 | 2.7 | 9.2 | 3.4 | 66% | 9% | 94.3 | 41 | 21 | 39 | 33% | 68% | 16% | 0 | 16 | | | 84 | 1.21 | -7.5 | 112 | 129 | $9 |
| 1st Half | | 2 | 19 | 37 | 42 | 4.14 | 3.88 | 1.27 | 731 | 782 | 652 | 4.2 | 2.7 | 10.2 | 3.8 | 66% | 10% | 94.7 | 43 | 16 | 42 | 32% | 75% | 16% | 0 | 16 | | | 86 | 1.36 | 0.1 | 132 | 152 | $13 |
| 2nd Half | | 2 | 13 | 26 | 23 | 6.49 | 4.58 | 1.52 | 864 | 679 | 1013 | 4.3 | 2.7 | 7.9 | 2.9 | 67% | 8% | 93.9 | 38 | 27 | 35 | 35% | 60% | 17% | 0 | 16 | | | 81 | 1.00 | -7.6 | 84 | 97 | $3 |
| 19 | Proj | **4** | **12** | **65** | **64** | **4.30** | **3.80** | **1.32** | **723** | **735** | **712** | **4.4** | **3.3** | **8.8** | **2.7** | **63%** | **10%** | **94.2** | **44** | **21** | **35** | **31%** | **71%** | **14%** | **0** | | | | | | **-1.2** | **91** | **105** | **$4** |

## Greinke,Zack

Age: 35 | Th: R | Role: SP | Ht: 6' 2" | Wt: 200 | Type: Pwr
Health: C | PT/Exp: A | Consist: A | LIMA Plan: C | Rand Var: 0 | MM: 4305

Even as he keeps losing zip on his fastball, he finds new ways to keep hitters off balance. Credit increased use of curveball and refined slider. Elite rate of first-pitch Ks in 2 of 3 years means his plus command and high-level skills should stay a while. An ace that should continue to come at SP2 prices.

| Yr | Tm | W | Sv | IP | K | ERA | xERA | WHIP | oOPS | vL | vR | BF/G | Ctl | Dom | Cmd | FpK | SwK | Vel | G | L | F | H% | S% | hr/f | GS | APC | DOM% | DIS% | Sv% | LI | RAR | BPV | BPX | R$ |
|---|---|---|---|---|---|---|---|---|---|---|---|---|---|---|---|---|---|---|---|---|---|---|---|---|---|---|---|---|---|---|---|---|---|---|
| 14 | LA | 17 | 0 | 202 | 207 | 2.71 | 2.93 | 1.15 | 660 | 627 | 689 | 25.7 | 1.9 | 9.2 | 4.8 | 63% | 12% | 91.9 | 49 | 23 | 29 | 32% | 80% | 12% | 32 | 100 | 41% | 13% | | | 25.6 | 141 | 168 | $21 |
| 15 | LA | 19 | 0 | 223 | 200 | 1.66 | 3.14 | 0.84 | 507 | 535 | 482 | 26.3 | 1.6 | 8.1 | 5.0 | 64% | 13% | 91.8 | 48 | 19 | 33 | 24% | 84% | 7% | 32 | 101 | 56% | 3% | | | 63.3 | 128 | 152 | $49 |
| 16 | ARI | 13 | 0 | 159 | 134 | 4.37 | 4.12 | 1.27 | 750 | 745 | 756 | 25.7 | 2.3 | 7.6 | 3.3 | 68% | 11% | 91.3 | 46 | 20 | 35 | 31% | 70% | 14% | 26 | 96 | 31% | 35% | | | -3.5 | 98 | 116 | $6 |
| 17 | ARI | 17 | 0 | 202 | 215 | 3.20 | 3.44 | 1.07 | 659 | 657 | 662 | 25.0 | 2.0 | 9.6 | 4.8 | 62% | 13% | 91.0 | 47 | 18 | 35 | 29% | 76% | 13% | 32 | 99 | 50% | 22% | | | 28.8 | 143 | 172 | $29 |
| 18 | ARI | 15 | 0 | 208 | 199 | 3.21 | 3.53 | 1.08 | 665 | 641 | 685 | 25.4 | 1.9 | 8.6 | 4.6 | 67% | 11% | 89.6 | 45 | 23 | 32 | 28% | 77% | 13% | 33 | 97 | 45% | 15% | | | 24.2 | 128 | 147 | $25 |
| 1st Half | | 8 | 0 | 103 | 108 | 3.41 | 3.53 | 1.11 | 702 | 693 | 708 | 24.8 | 1.7 | 9.4 | 5.7 | 67% | 12% | 89.3 | 42 | 22 | 37 | 30% | 77% | 15% | 17 | 96 | 41% | 18% | | | 9.4 | 145 | 166 | $23 |
| 2nd Half | | 7 | 0 | 105 | 91 | 3.01 | 3.52 | 1.05 | 628 | 597 | 658 | 26.1 | 2.1 | 7.8 | 3.8 | 67% | 11% | 90.0 | 48 | 24 | 27 | 27% | 77% | 15% | 16 | 99 | 50% | 13% | | | 14.7 | 112 | 128 | $27 |
| 19 | Proj | **16** | **0** | **203** | **195** | **3.26** | **3.26** | **1.10** | **666** | **654** | **677** | **24.8** | **2.0** | **8.6** | **4.4** | **65%** | **12%** | **90.5** | **46** | **21** | **33** | **29%** | **76%** | **14%** | **32** | | | | | | **21.3** | **126** | **145** | **$25** |

## Gsellman,Robert

Age: 25 | Th: R | Role: RP | Ht: 6' 4" | Wt: 205 | Type:
Health: C | PT/Exp: C | Consist: D | LIMA Plan: B | Rand Var: 0 | MM: 1121

Former SP worked entire season out of bullpen. Those late saves will draw bidders in, but velocity uptick didn't result in stopper-worthy SwK. Without strikeouts, he's left as a GB pitcher with marginal control. Not exactly the recipe for a budding closer. Let others speculate on his save chances.

| Yr | Tm | W | Sv | IP | K | ERA | xERA | WHIP | oOPS | vL | vR | BF/G | Ctl | Dom | Cmd | FpK | SwK | Vel | G | L | F | H% | S% | hr/f | GS | APC | DOM% | DIS% | Sv% | LI | RAR | BPV | BPX | R$ |
|---|---|---|---|---|---|---|---|---|---|---|---|---|---|---|---|---|---|---|---|---|---|---|---|---|---|---|---|---|---|---|---|---|---|---|
| 14 | | | | | | | | | | | | | | | | | | | | | | | | | | | | | | | | | | |
| 15 | aa | 7 | 0 | 92 | 43 | 4.01 | 3.82 | 1.35 | | | | 24.0 | 2.5 | 4.2 | 1.7 | | | | | | | 30% | 69% | | | | | | | | -0.5 | 48 | 58 | -$1 |
| 16 | NYM * | 8 | 0 | 160 | 121 | 3.75 | 3.85 | 1.33 | 639 | 589 | 682 | 23.6 | 2.7 | 6.8 | 2.6 | 61% | 10% | 93.7 | 54 | 23 | 23 | 32% | 72% | 4% | 7 | 89 | 29% | 14% | 0 | 1.01 | 8.7 | 77 | 91 | $6 |
| 17 | NYM * | 9 | 0 | 138 | 92 | 5.19 | 5.51 | 1.57 | 807 | 813 | 803 | 20.2 | 3.3 | 6.0 | 1.8 | 64% | 8% | 92.7 | 49 | 22 | 29 | 33% | 69% | 14% | 22 | 82 | 14% | 45% | 0 | 0.78 | -14.2 | 34 | 41 | -$7 |
| 18 | NYM | 6 | 13 | 80 | 70 | 4.28 | 4.15 | 1.30 | 700 | 717 | 687 | 5.1 | 3.2 | 7.9 | 2.5 | 60% | 10% | 94.1 | 49 | 19 | 32 | 30% | 69% | 11% | 0 | 19 | | | 68 | 1.14 | -1.2 | 84 | 96 | $5 |
| 1st Half | | 5 | 3 | 48 | 47 | 4.28 | 3.96 | 1.32 | 686 | 693 | 682 | 5.6 | 3.7 | 8.8 | 2.4 | 61% | 12% | 93.6 | 51 | 19 | 30 | 30% | 69% | 12% | 0 | 21 | | | 43 | 1.21 | -0.8 | 86 | 99 | $5 |
| 2nd Half | | 1 | 10 | 32 | 23 | 4.26 | 4.42 | 1.26 | 720 | 747 | 694 | 4.4 | 2.3 | 6.5 | 2.9 | 59% | 8% | 94.7 | 47 | 19 | 34 | 30% | 68% | 9% | 0 | 17 | | | 83 | 1.07 | -0.4 | 81 | 93 | $6 |
| 19 | Proj | **4** | **14** | **73** | **54** | **4.40** | **4.08** | **1.37** | **738** | **741** | **736** | **7.7** | **2.9** | **6.7** | **2.3** | **62%** | **9%** | **93.6** | **50** | **20** | **30** | **31%** | **69%** | **10%** | **0** | | | | | | **0.5** | **69** | **80** | **$4** |

## Guerra,Junior

Age: 34 | Th: R | Role: RP | Ht: 6' 0" | Wt: 205 | Type: Pwr
Health: D | PT/Exp: C | Consist: D | LIMA Plan: D+ | Rand Var: 0 | MM: 1201

That shiny ERA from 2016 is becoming a distant memory. Inconsistent FpK cements wildness into his profile. And as results are 3x more likely to result in disaster than dominance, his risk is building. Now in his mid-30s, it's hard to expect a rebound. A fifth or six starter in deep leagues...at best.

| Yr | Tm | W | Sv | IP | K | ERA | xERA | WHIP | oOPS | vL | vR | BF/G | Ctl | Dom | Cmd | FpK | SwK | Vel | G | L | F | H% | S% | hr/f | GS | APC | DOM% | DIS% | Sv% | LI | RAR | BPV | BPX | R$ |
|---|---|---|---|---|---|---|---|---|---|---|---|---|---|---|---|---|---|---|---|---|---|---|---|---|---|---|---|---|---|---|---|---|---|---|
| 14 | | | | | | | | | | | | | | | | | | | | | | | | | | | | | | | | | | |
| 15 | CHW * | 4 | 7 | 87 | 83 | 4.63 | 4.59 | 1.49 | 1033 | 1000 | 1044 | 11.1 | 4.4 | 8.6 | 1.9 | 63% | 11% | 94.1 | 57 | 21 | 21 | 32% | 71% | 33% | 0 | 22 | | | 88 | 0.22 | -7.2 | 62 | 74 | -$2 |
| 16 | MIL * | 9 | 0 | 148 | 119 | 3.20 | 2.88 | 1.16 | 633 | 618 | 645 | 23.6 | 3.3 | 7.2 | 2.2 | 58% | 11% | 93.1 | 45 | 19 | 36 | 26% | 75% | 8% | 20 | 93 | 30% | 20% | | | 18.1 | 77 | 92 | $13 |
| 17 | MIL * | 3 | 0 | 105 | 85 | 4.54 | 5.55 | 1.58 | 817 | 812 | 820 | 16.6 | 5.2 | 7.3 | 1.4 | 54% | 11% | 91.9 | 34 | 23 | 44 | 29% | 78% | 21% | 14 | 59 | 0% | 57% | 0 | 0.58 | -2.3 | 22 | 26 | -$5 |
| 18 | MIL | 6 | 0 | 141 | 136 | 4.09 | 4.30 | 1.40 | 767 | 800 | 733 | 19.7 | 3.5 | 8.7 | 2.5 | 63% | 11% | 93.3 | 43 | 20 | 37 | 32% | 75% | 13% | 26 | 74 | 12% | 35% | 0 | 0.78 | 1.1 | 82 | 95 | $0 |
| 1st Half | | 4 | 0 | 83 | 80 | 3.05 | 4.22 | 1.20 | 677 | 692 | 660 | 22.9 | 3.4 | 8.7 | 2.6 | 63% | 10% | 93.1 | 39 | 19 | 41 | 27% | 80% | 11% | 15 | 90 | 13% | 7% | | | 11.2 | 83 | 95 | $10 |
| 2nd Half | | 2 | 0 | 58 | 56 | 5.55 | 4.40 | 1.70 | 883 | 945 | 820 | 16.7 | 3.7 | 8.6 | 2.3 | 64% | 12% | 93.5 | 48 | 21 | 31 | 38% | 70% | 16% | 11 | 60 | 9% | 73% | 0 | 0.80 | -10.1 | 81 | 93 | -$14 |
| 19 | Proj | **4** | **0** | **102** | **91** | **4.35** | **4.40** | **1.47** | **786** | **806** | **768** | **17.2** | **4.0** | **8.1** | **2.0** | **59%** | **11%** | **92.8** | **41** | **21** | **38** | **31%** | **74%** | **13%** | **18** | | | | | | **-2.8** | **55** | **64** | **-$3** |

## Guerrero,Tayron

Age: 28 | Th: R | Role: RP | Ht: 6' 8" | Wt: 210 | Type: Pwr
Health: B | PT/Exp: D | Consist: F | LIMA Plan: D+ | Rand Var: +5 | MM: 0210

Flame-thrower still can't find home plate, and even when he curbed walks late in season, tiny FpK shows it was a mirage. Marginal rate of whiffs for a bullpen arm puts double-digit Dom at risk, too. Even with regression from fluky hit rate, there are too many warts here to do anything except watch from afar.

| Yr | Tm | W | Sv | IP | K | ERA | xERA | WHIP | oOPS | vL | vR | BF/G | Ctl | Dom | Cmd | FpK | SwK | Vel | G | L | F | H% | S% | hr/f | GS | APC | DOM% | DIS% | Sv% | LI | RAR | BPV | BPX | R$ |
|---|---|---|---|---|---|---|---|---|---|---|---|---|---|---|---|---|---|---|---|---|---|---|---|---|---|---|---|---|---|---|---|---|---|---|
| 14 | | | | | | | | | | | | | | | | | | | | | | | | | | | | | | | | | | |
| 15 | a/a | 1 | 14 | 56 | 53 | 3.25 | 3.11 | 1.34 | | | | 4.8 | 4.8 | 8.5 | 1.8 | | | | | | | 28% | 76% | | | | | | | | 4.9 | 84 | 100 | $5 |
| 16 | SD * | 1 | 4 | 52 | 43 | 5.44 | 4.53 | 1.53 | 944 | 1000 | 833 | 5.0 | 4.2 | 7.4 | 1.7 | 56% | 0% | 95.2 | 50 | 0 | 50 | 33% | 64% | 0% | 0 | 22 | | | 80 | 0.13 | -8.0 | 60 | 71 | -$5 |
| 17 | a/a | 3 | 0 | 31 | 27 | 6.13 | 6.44 | 1.96 | | | | 5.0 | 8.3 | 7.7 | 0.9 | | | | | | | 30% | 72% | | | | | | | | -6.9 | 18 | 22 | -$8 |
| 18 | MIA | 1 | 0 | 58 | 68 | 5.43 | 4.15 | 1.62 | 797 | 961 | 668 | 4.5 | 4.7 | 10.6 | 2.3 | 52% | 11% | 98.8 | 45 | 23 | 32 | 37% | 69% | 15% | 0 | 19 | | | 0 | 0.67 | -9.2 | 87 | 100 | -$9 |
| 1st Half | | 1 | 0 | 38 | 52 | 4.50 | 3.49 | 1.55 | 742 | 874 | 640 | 4.4 | 5.2 | 12.3 | 2.4 | 53% | 13% | 98.4 | 49 | 25 | 26 | 38% | 71% | 12% | 0 | 18 | | | 0 | 0.62 | -1.6 | 108 | 124 | -$7 |
| 2nd Half | | 0 | 0 | 20 | 16 | 7.20 | 5.41 | 1.75 | 891 | 1114 | 716 | 4.5 | 3.6 | 7.2 | 2.0 | 49% | 8% | 99.5 | 39 | 21 | 40 | 35% | 63% | 18% | 0 | 20 | | | 0 | 0.76 | -7.5 | 49 | 56 | -$12 |
| 19 | Proj | **2** | **5** | **58** | **55** | **4.92** | **4.61** | **1.61** | **749** | **922** | **613** | **4.5** | **5.3** | **8.5** | **1.6** | **51%** | **10%** | **99.0** | **43** | **23** | **34** | **32%** | **73%** | **16%** | **0** | | | | | | **-3.1** | **31** | **36** | **-$5** |

STEPHEN NICKRAND

## Hader,Josh

| Age: 25 | Th: L | Role: RP | Health | A | LIMA Plan | C |
|---|---|---|---|---|---|---|
| Ht: 6' 3" | Wt: 185 | Type: Pwr xFB | PT/Exp | C | Rand Var | -1 |
| | | | Consist | C | MM | 4521 |

Swiss Army knife posted top-5 skills in majors that were backed by tons of whiffs, so top-tier K rate is here to stay. And 2nd-half surge in first-pitch strikes gives hope for even better control. Even as that hit rate moves north, xERA confirms he's firmly elite. With more 9th-inning opps... UP: 40 saves

| Yr Tm | W | Sv | IP | K | ERA | xERA | WHIP | oOPS | vL | vR | BF/G | Ctl | Dom | Cmd | FpK | SwK | Vel | G | L | F | H% | S% | hr/f | GS | APC | DOM% | DIS% | Sv% | LI | RAR | BPV | BPX | R$ |
|---|---|---|---|---|---|---|---|---|---|---|---|---|---|---|---|---|---|---|---|---|---|---|---|---|---|---|---|---|---|---|---|---|---|
| 14 aa | 1 | 0 | 20 | 22 | 6.74 | 4.30 | 1.60 | | | | 17.7 | 6.7 | 9.9 | 1.5 | | | | | | | 30% | 57% | | | | | | | | -7.4 | 71 | 85 | -$5 |
| 15 aa | 4 | 1 | 104 | 104 | 4.07 | 4.06 | 1.36 | | | | 18.1 | 3.2 | 9.0 | 2.8 | | | | | | | 33% | 72% | | | | | | | | -1.4 | 89 | 106 | $0 |
| 16 a/a | 3 | 0 | 126 | 142 | 4.01 | 3.52 | 1.36 | | | | 21.1 | 3.9 | 10.1 | 2.6 | | | | | | | 34% | 70% | | | | | | | | 2.7 | 104 | 124 | $2 |
| 17 MIL * | 5 | 0 | 100 | 112 | 3.96 | 4.12 | 1.30 | 554 | 454 | 608 | 8.7 | 4.6 | 10.1 | 2.2 | 59% | 18% | 94.3 | 34 | 14 | 51 | 26% | 77% | 9% | 0 | 22 | | | 0 | 1.14 | 4.9 | 67 | 81 | $4 |
| 18 MIL | 6 | 12 | 81 | 143 | 2.43 | 2.37 | 0.81 | 484 | 355 | 548 | 5.6 | 3.3 | 15.8 | 4.8 | 60% | 20% | 94.5 | 29 | 23 | 48 | 24% | 77% | 15% | 0 | 24 | | | 71 | 1.31 | 17.2 | 202 | 233 | $21 |
| 1st Half | 2 | 7 | 42 | 81 | 1.30 | 2.06 | 0.77 | 380 | 266 | 433 | 5.5 | 3.7 | 17.5 | 4.8 | 56% | 22% | 94.1 | 24 | 24 | 52 | 26% | 87% | 7% | 0 | 24 | | | 78 | 1.40 | 14.7 | 218 | 250 | $24 |
| 2nd Half | 4 | 5 | 40 | 62 | 3.63 | 2.71 | 0.86 | 588 | 437 | 664 | 5.7 | 2.9 | 14.1 | 4.8 | 65% | 17% | 95.0 | 32 | 22 | 46 | 22% | 67% | 21% | 0 | 24 | | | 63 | 1.21 | 2.5 | 184 | 211 | $17 |
| 19 Proj | 5 | 18 | 87 | 122 | 2.93 | 3.10 | 1.07 | 655 | 496 | 737 | 7.6 | 3.5 | 12.7 | 3.6 | 60% | 19% | 94.5 | 31 | 19 | 49 | 28% | 79% | 12% | 0 | | | | | | 13.1 | 143 | 165 | $17 |

## Hamels,Cole

| Age: 35 | Th: L | Role: SP | Health | D | LIMA Plan | B |
|---|---|---|---|---|---|---|
| Ht: 6' 4" | Wt: 205 | Type: Pwr | PT/Exp | A | Rand Var | +2 |
| | | | Consist | B | MM | 2205 |

Just when we thought eroding ERA and skills signaled end was near, refined cutter and change-up reversed SwK slide. Remove 2017 and you've got a consistent arm who is wily enough to find new tricks. Be aware of age and health, but should be good for at least another year at this level.

| Yr Tm | W | Sv | IP | K | ERA | xERA | WHIP | oOPS | vL | vR | BF/G | Ctl | Dom | Cmd | FpK | SwK | Vel | G | L | F | H% | S% | hr/f | GS | APC | DOM% | DIS% | Sv% | LI | RAR | BPV | BPX | R$ |
|---|---|---|---|---|---|---|---|---|---|---|---|---|---|---|---|---|---|---|---|---|---|---|---|---|---|---|---|---|---|---|---|---|---|
| 14 PHI | 9 | 0 | 205 | 198 | 2.46 | 3.20 | 1.15 | 641 | 636 | 641 | 27.6 | 2.6 | 8.7 | 3.4 | 61% | 13% | 92.3 | 46 | 22 | 31 | 30% | 81% | 8% | 30 | 105 | 57% | 10% | | | 32.3 | 111 | 132 | $20 |
| 15 2 TM | 13 | 0 | 212 | 215 | 3.65 | 3.39 | 1.19 | 669 | 646 | 675 | 27.5 | 2.6 | 9.1 | 3.5 | 61% | 14% | 92.6 | 48 | 21 | 31 | 30% | 72% | 12% | 32 | 104 | 44% | 19% | | | 8.3 | 119 | 142 | $16 |
| 16 TEX | 15 | 0 | 201 | 200 | 3.32 | 3.81 | 1.31 | 699 | 605 | 722 | 26.5 | 3.5 | 9.0 | 2.6 | 57% | 13% | 92.6 | 50 | 20 | 31 | 31% | 79% | 14% | 32 | 102 | 34% | 25% | | | 21.5 | 96 | 114 | $16 |
| 17 TEX | 11 | 0 | 148 | 105 | 4.20 | 4.59 | 1.20 | 693 | 483 | 749 | 25.6 | 3.2 | 6.4 | 2.0 | 56% | 10% | 92.0 | 48 | 19 | 34 | 26% | 68% | 12% | 24 | 96 | 25% | 33% | | | 3.0 | 54 | 65 | $9 |
| 18 2 TM | 9 | 0 | 191 | 188 | 3.78 | 3.79 | 1.26 | 746 | 666 | 763 | 25.2 | 3.1 | 8.9 | 2.9 | 60% | 12% | 92.1 | 45 | 23 | 32 | 30% | 76% | 17% | 32 | 96 | 28% | 19% | | | 8.8 | 100 | 115 | $10 |
| 1st Half | 4 | 0 | 97 | 97 | 3.61 | 4.01 | 1.27 | 769 | 770 | 769 | 26.0 | 3.4 | 9.0 | 2.6 | 60% | 12% | 91.2 | 43 | 22 | 35 | 27% | 82% | 21% | 16 | 99 | 19% | 13% | | | 6.5 | 90 | 104 | $9 |
| 2nd Half | 5 | 0 | 93 | 91 | 3.95 | 3.55 | 1.25 | 722 | 572 | 757 | 24.4 | 2.7 | 8.8 | 3.3 | 59% | 13% | 92.8 | 47 | 25 | 28 | 32% | 70% | 13% | 16 | 92 | 38% | 25% | | | 2.3 | 110 | 126 | $10 |
| 19 Proj | 11 | 0 | 189 | 173 | 3.76 | 3.68 | 1.24 | 714 | 594 | 743 | 24.8 | 3.1 | 8.3 | 2.7 | 59% | 12% | 92.2 | 47 | 22 | 32 | 29% | 74% | 14% | 31 | | | | | | 9.1 | 90 | 104 | $12 |

## Hammel,Jason

| Age: 36 | Th: R | Role: RP | Health | A | LIMA Plan | C |
|---|---|---|---|---|---|---|
| Ht: 6' 6" | Wt: 225 | Type: | PT/Exp | A | Rand Var | +4 |
| | | | Consist | B | MM | 0101 |

It'd be easy to blame worst hit rate since rookie season for this disaster. But that mark was fueled by high rate of exit velocity and barrels, so we can't assume full regression. Escalating xERA before this debacle made return to sub-4.00 ERA days a very poor bet anyway. No longer worthy of your attention.

| Yr Tm | W | Sv | IP | K | ERA | xERA | WHIP | oOPS | vL | vR | BF/G | Ctl | Dom | Cmd | FpK | SwK | Vel | G | L | F | H% | S% | hr/f | GS | APC | DOM% | DIS% | Sv% | LI | RAR | BPV | BPX | R$ |
|---|---|---|---|---|---|---|---|---|---|---|---|---|---|---|---|---|---|---|---|---|---|---|---|---|---|---|---|---|---|---|---|---|---|
| 14 2 TM | 10 | 0 | 176 | 158 | 3.47 | 3.53 | 1.12 | 680 | 691 | 670 | 23.8 | 2.2 | 8.1 | 3.6 | 57% | 10% | 92.3 | 40 | 22 | 38 | 28% | 74% | 12% | 29 | 93 | 48% | 21% | 0 | 0.75 | 5.9 | 103 | 122 | $12 |
| 15 CHC | 10 | 0 | 171 | 172 | 3.74 | 3.57 | 1.16 | 714 | 696 | 728 | 22.9 | 2.1 | 9.1 | 4.3 | 61% | 11% | 92.3 | 38 | 25 | 37 | 30% | 73% | 13% | 31 | 89 | 32% | 23% | | | 4.6 | 122 | 146 | $12 |
| 16 CHC | 15 | 0 | 167 | 144 | 3.83 | 4.22 | 1.21 | 729 | 797 | 679 | 23.1 | 2.9 | 7.8 | 2.7 | 60% | 11% | 92.1 | 42 | 20 | 38 | 27% | 74% | 14% | 30 | 87 | 33% | 30% | | | 7.3 | 83 | 98 | $13 |
| 17 KC | 8 | 0 | 180 | 145 | 5.29 | 4.97 | 1.43 | 773 | 775 | 771 | 25.1 | 2.4 | 7.2 | 3.0 | 62% | 10% | 92.1 | 38 | 21 | 41 | 33% | 65% | 11% | 32 | 95 | 13% | 28% | | | -20.7 | 82 | 98 | -$4 |
| 18 KC | 4 | 0 | 127 | 92 | 6.02 | 5.24 | 1.63 | 867 | 732 | 985 | 14.9 | 2.8 | 6.5 | 2.4 | 66% | 10% | 91.8 | 37 | 23 | 40 | 36% | 65% | 10% | 18 | 53 | 22% | 56% | 0 | 0.93 | -29.3 | 58 | 66 | -$17 |
| 1st Half | 2 | 0 | 100 | 66 | 5.56 | 5.29 | 1.54 | 816 | 741 | 879 | 26.7 | 2.7 | 5.9 | 2.2 | 66% | 9% | 91.4 | 38 | 23 | 39 | 34% | 65% | 8% | 17 | 95 | 24% | 53% | | | -17.5 | 50 | 57 | -$18 |
| 2nd Half | 2 | 0 | 27 | 26 | 7.76 | 5.04 | 1.95 | 1045 | 706 | 1390 | 5.9 | 3.0 | 8.8 | 2.9 | 67% | 12% | 93.3 | 34 | 26 | 40 | 42% | 64% | 19% | 1 | 21 | 0% | 100% | 0 | 1.06 | -11.9 | 88 | 101 | -$14 |
| 19 Proj | 5 | 0 | 87 | 70 | 5.70 | 4.56 | 1.57 | 860 | 745 | 967 | 11.8 | 2.9 | 7.2 | 2.5 | 64% | 11% | 92.3 | 37 | 23 | 40 | 35% | 67% | 13% | 6 | | | | | | -16.6 | 67 | 77 | -$9 |

## Hand,Brad

| Age: 29 | Th: L | Role: RP | Health | A | LIMA Plan | C+ |
|---|---|---|---|---|---|---|
| Ht: 6' 3" | Wt: 228 | Type: Pwr | PT/Exp | B | Rand Var | 0 |
| | | | Consist | A | MM | 5530 |

Late-season trade dried up save opps a bit, but under the hood, this remains a premium reliever. Ability to miss bats at a high clip provides foundation for more of same. Average FpK and Ctl may cap further growth; that, along with nouveau bullpen use are only reasons for hesitation. Still... UP: 50 saves

| Yr Tm | W | Sv | IP | K | ERA | xERA | WHIP | oOPS | vL | vR | BF/G | Ctl | Dom | Cmd | FpK | SwK | Vel | G | L | F | H% | S% | hr/f | GS | APC | DOM% | DIS% | Sv% | LI | RAR | BPV | BPX | R$ |
|---|---|---|---|---|---|---|---|---|---|---|---|---|---|---|---|---|---|---|---|---|---|---|---|---|---|---|---|---|---|---|---|---|---|
| 14 MIA * | 5 | 1 | 133 | 85 | 4.21 | 4.00 | 1.34 | 732 | 594 | 789 | 15.4 | 3.2 | 5.7 | 1.8 | 59% | 7% | 92.4 | 50 | 18 | 32 | 29% | 70% | 9% | 16 | 56 | 13% | 31% | 100 | 0.58 | -7.6 | 50 | 60 | -$2 |
| 15 MIA | 4 | 0 | 93 | 67 | 5.30 | 4.39 | 1.49 | 784 | 512 | 887 | 10.7 | 3.1 | 6.5 | 2.1 | 52% | 9% | 92.1 | 46 | 23 | 30 | 33% | 65% | 10% | 12 | 41 | 8% | 50% | 0 | 0.60 | -15.4 | 57 | 68 | -$8 |
| 16 SD | 4 | 1 | 89 | 111 | 2.92 | 3.36 | 1.11 | 589 | 421 | 689 | 4.4 | 3.6 | 11.2 | 3.1 | 59% | 13% | 92.8 | 47 | 17 | 36 | 28% | 77% | 10% | 0 | 18 | | | 14 | 1.30 | 14.0 | 128 | 153 | $9 |
| 17 SD | 3 | 21 | 79 | 104 | 2.16 | 2.81 | 0.93 | 580 | 590 | 577 | 4.3 | 2.3 | 11.8 | 5.2 | 58% | 14% | 93.5 | 46 | 20 | 34 | 27% | 85% | 15% | 0 | 17 | | | 81 | 1.35 | 21.6 | 175 | 210 | $21 |
| 18 2 TM | 2 | 32 | 72 | 106 | 2.75 | 2.83 | 1.11 | 656 | 537 | 729 | 4.4 | 3.5 | 13.3 | 3.8 | 59% | 14% | 93.6 | 45 | 21 | 34 | 31% | 81% | 15% | 0 | 18 | | | 82 | 1.36 | 12.4 | 167 | 192 | $19 |
| 1st Half | 1 | 23 | 40 | 58 | 3.12 | 2.78 | 1.09 | 672 | 489 | 760 | 4.4 | 3.3 | 12.9 | 3.9 | 58% | 14% | 93.7 | 47 | 21 | 31 | 30% | 77% | 18% | 0 | 18 | | | 85 | 1.52 | 5.1 | 168 | 193 | $24 |
| 2nd Half | 1 | 9 | 32 | 48 | 2.27 | 2.90 | 1.14 | 637 | 580 | 679 | 4.3 | 3.7 | 13.6 | 3.7 | 60% | 14% | 93.6 | 42 | 20 | 38 | 33% | 85% | 12% | 0 | 17 | | | 75 | 1.17 | 7.3 | 166 | 191 | $13 |
| 19 Proj | 2 | 35 | 65 | 86 | 2.76 | 2.83 | 1.10 | 635 | 538 | 689 | 4.5 | 3.2 | 11.9 | 3.7 | 58% | 13% | 93.3 | 46 | 20 | 35 | 30% | 80% | 13% | 0 | | | | | | 14.1 | 152 | 174 | $20 |

## Happ,J.A.

| Age: 36 | Th: L | Role: SP | Health | D | LIMA Plan | C+ |
|---|---|---|---|---|---|---|
| Ht: 6' 5" | Wt: 205 | Type: Pwr | PT/Exp | A | Rand Var | 0 |
| | | | Consist | A | MM | 2303 |

It's not often that you see surging skills from a SP in his mid-30s, but that's what we have here. Replaced sliders with sinkers that stymied batters. There are no signs that he won't continue near-3.0 Cmd baseline, which makes him one of the more unheralded middle-rotation arms in the game.

| Yr Tm | W | Sv | IP | K | ERA | xERA | WHIP | oOPS | vL | vR | BF/G | Ctl | Dom | Cmd | FpK | SwK | Vel | G | L | F | H% | S% | hr/f | GS | APC | DOM% | DIS% | Sv% | LI | RAR | BPV | BPX | R$ |
|---|---|---|---|---|---|---|---|---|---|---|---|---|---|---|---|---|---|---|---|---|---|---|---|---|---|---|---|---|---|---|---|---|---|
| 14 TOR | 11 | 0 | 158 | 133 | 4.22 | 4.03 | 1.34 | 770 | 874 | 743 | 22.4 | 2.9 | 7.6 | 2.6 | 62% | 8% | 92.7 | 41 | 20 | 40 | 31% | 72% | 12% | 26 | 90 | 23% | 31% | 0 | 0.82 | -9.2 | 77 | 92 | $1 |
| 15 2 TM | 11 | 0 | 172 | 151 | 3.61 | 3.83 | 1.27 | 698 | 680 | 705 | 22.4 | 2.4 | 7.9 | 3.4 | 60% | 9% | 91.9 | 42 | 24 | 34 | 32% | 74% | 9% | 31 | 89 | 23% | 26% | 0 | 0.78 | 7.5 | 99 | 117 | $9 |
| 16 TOR | 20 | 0 | 195 | 163 | 3.18 | 4.14 | 1.17 | 665 | 651 | 669 | 24.9 | 2.8 | 7.5 | 2.7 | 60% | 10% | 91.6 | 42 | 22 | 36 | 27% | 77% | 11% | 32 | 95 | 31% | 25% | | | 24.2 | 81 | 96 | $22 |
| 17 TOR | 10 | 0 | 145 | 142 | 3.53 | 4.13 | 1.31 | 700 | 553 | 735 | 25.0 | 2.8 | 8.8 | 3.1 | 62% | 10% | 91.8 | 47 | 19 | 34 | 32% | 77% | 12% | 25 | 99 | 24% | 28% | | | 14.9 | 106 | 128 | $10 |
| 18 2 AL | 17 | 0 | 178 | 193 | 3.65 | 3.81 | 1.13 | 677 | 487 | 722 | 23.6 | 2.6 | 9.8 | 3.8 | 61% | 11% | 92.0 | 40 | 17 | 42 | 29% | 74% | 13% | 31 | 98 | 26% | 23% | | | 11.0 | 124 | 143 | $19 |
| 1st Half | 10 | 0 | 97 | 106 | 3.62 | 3.58 | 1.06 | 627 | 423 | 677 | 24.6 | 2.5 | 9.8 | 3.9 | 59% | 11% | 91.7 | 45 | 15 | 40 | 27% | 71% | 13% | 16 | 100 | 38% | 19% | | | 6.4 | 133 | 153 | $23 |
| 2nd Half | 7 | 0 | 81 | 87 | 3.68 | 4.08 | 1.21 | 735 | 562 | 775 | 22.7 | 2.7 | 9.7 | 3.6 | 63% | 11% | 92.3 | 34 | 20 | 46 | 30% | 77% | 14% | 15 | 96 | 13% | 27% | | | 4.7 | 114 | 131 | $14 |
| 19 Proj | 13 | 0 | 174 | 172 | 3.68 | 3.67 | 1.21 | 695 | 571 | 725 | 23.0 | 2.7 | 8.9 | 3.3 | 61% | 10% | 91.9 | 41 | 19 | 39 | 30% | 75% | 13% | 30 | | | | | | 10.3 | 106 | 122 | $14 |

## Hardy,Blaine

| Age: 32 | Th: L | Role: RP | Health | C | LIMA Plan | B+ |
|---|---|---|---|---|---|---|
| Ht: 6' 2" | Wt: 218 | Type: FB | PT/Exp | D | Rand Var | 0 |
| | | | Consist | F | MM | 1103 |

4-5, 3.56 ERA in 86 IP at DET. Shiny stats in transition to full-time SP, but will they stick? PRO: BPV trend reached new heights late; strong FpK in 3 of 4 years supports Ctl. CON: Thin margin for error as lefty soft-tosser; poor 6.3 K/9 as SP; "F" Consistency reflected in yo-yo xERA. End-rotation fodder.

| Yr Tm | W | Sv | IP | K | ERA | xERA | WHIP | oOPS | vL | vR | BF/G | Ctl | Dom | Cmd | FpK | SwK | Vel | G | L | F | H% | S% | hr/f | GS | APC | DOM% | DIS% | Sv% | LI | RAR | BPV | BPX | R$ |
|---|---|---|---|---|---|---|---|---|---|---|---|---|---|---|---|---|---|---|---|---|---|---|---|---|---|---|---|---|---|---|---|---|---|
| 14 DET * | 5 | 0 | 86 | 70 | 3.11 | 3.26 | 1.31 | 611 | 553 | 657 | 6.1 | 3.6 | 7.3 | 2.0 | 54% | 8% | 89.1 | 52 | 19 | 28 | 30% | 76% | 3% | 0 | 17 | | | 0 | 1.04 | 6.7 | 82 | 97 | $2 |
| 15 DET | 5 | 0 | 61 | 55 | 3.08 | 4.21 | 1.35 | 704 | 631 | 770 | 3.8 | 3.2 | 8.1 | 2.5 | 68% | 11% | 88.3 | 39 | 24 | 37 | 33% | 77% | 3% | 0 | 14 | | | 0 | 1.08 | 6.7 | 75 | 89 | $1 |
| 16 DET * | 2 | 1 | 57 | 34 | 2.99 | 3.23 | 1.23 | 707 | 643 | 743 | 4.4 | 2.8 | 5.3 | 1.9 | 64% | 9% | 88.4 | 48 | 18 | 34 | 28% | 77% | 7% | 0 | 21 | | | 100 | 0.57 | 8.5 | 61 | 73 | $1 |
| 17 DET * | 8 | 3 | 74 | 60 | 5.48 | 5.29 | 1.51 | 925 | 843 | 970 | 4.6 | 2.3 | 7.3 | 3.1 | 57% | 10% | 89.9 | 33 | 23 | 44 | 36% | 65% | 14% | 0 | 17 | | | 100 | 0.68 | -10.2 | 71 | 86 | -$2 |
| 18 DET * | 7 | 1 | 113 | 90 | 3.08 | 3.12 | 1.11 | 698 | 682 | 703 | 11.4 | 2.1 | 7.2 | 3.3 | 67% | 9% | 87.9 | 42 | 16 | 42 | 28% | 75% | 9% | 13 | 46 | 23% | 46% | 100 | 0.92 | 14.9 | 97 | 112 | $10 |
| 1st Half | 6 | 0 | 73 | 55 | 2.74 | 3.02 | 1.11 | 744 | 592 | 800 | 14.3 | 2.2 | 6.8 | 3.1 | 67% | 9% | 87.6 | 40 | 17 | 42 | 27% | 78% | 10% | 8 | 57 | 25% | 50% | 0 | 1.09 | 12.7 | 92 | 105 | $15 |
| 2nd Half | 1 | 1 | 40 | 35 | 3.70 | 3.31 | 1.12 | 639 | 816 | 584 | 8.4 | 2.0 | 7.8 | 3.9 | 67% | 10% | 88.3 | 44 | 15 | 41 | 29% | 70% | 9% | 5 | 37 | 20% | 40% | 100 | 0.79 | 2.2 | 108 | 124 | $2 |
| 19 Proj | 9 | 0 | 145 | 114 | 4.00 | 4.20 | 1.31 | 737 | 712 | 750 | 6.3 | 2.6 | 7.1 | 2.8 | 63% | 10% | 88.6 | 41 | 19 | 40 | 31% | 73% | 10% | 0 | | | | | | -0.7 | 77 | 88 | $5 |

## Harris,Will

| Age: 34 | Th: R | Role: RP | Health | C | LIMA Plan | A |
|---|---|---|---|---|---|---|
| Ht: 6' 4" | Wt: 250 | Type: Pwr GB | PT/Exp | C | Rand Var | 0 |
| | | | Consist | A | MM | 5400 |

One of four arms in the majors who can claim a 150+ BPV in three straight seasons (Chapman, Giles, Scherzer). With heavy dose of groundballs and whiffs, this LIMA gem has the goods to continue this run. But balky shoulder likely will keep curbing durability, so keep using 60 IP as baseline.

| Yr Tm | W | Sv | IP | K | ERA | xERA | WHIP | oOPS | vL | vR | BF/G | Ctl | Dom | Cmd | FpK | SwK | Vel | G | L | F | H% | S% | hr/f | GS | APC | DOM% | DIS% | Sv% | LI | RAR | BPV | BPX | R$ |
|---|---|---|---|---|---|---|---|---|---|---|---|---|---|---|---|---|---|---|---|---|---|---|---|---|---|---|---|---|---|---|---|---|---|
| 14 ARI * | 3 | 1 | 75 | 67 | 2.37 | 3.58 | 1.30 | 740 | 721 | 757 | 4.3 | 3.6 | 8.1 | 2.3 | 55% | 11% | 91.7 | 35 | 25 | 40 | 30% | 85% | 10% | 0 | 17 | | | 33 | 0.76 | 12.6 | 80 | 95 | $3 |
| 15 HOU | 5 | 2 | 71 | 68 | 1.90 | 3.25 | 0.90 | 525 | 455 | 586 | 4.1 | 2.8 | 8.6 | 3.1 | 60% | 9% | 91.8 | 51 | 20 | 30 | 20% | 88% | 15% | 0 | 17 | | | 33 | 1.28 | 18.0 | 109 | 130 | $12 |
| 16 HOU | 1 | 12 | 64 | 69 | 2.25 | 2.89 | 1.05 | 560 | 513 | 603 | 3.9 | 2.1 | 9.7 | 4.6 | 64% | 14% | 92.4 | 58 | 17 | 25 | 31% | 80% | 7% | 0 | 16 | | | 80 | 1.17 | 15.3 | 154 | 183 | $11 |
| 17 HOU | 3 | 2 | 45 | 52 | 2.98 | 3.10 | 0.97 | 613 | 606 | 619 | 3.8 | 1.4 | 10.3 | 7.4 | 60% | 14% | | 48 | 16 | 35 | 28% | 78% | 17% | 0 | 15 | | | 50 | 1.33 | 7.7 | 174 | 209 | $4 |
| 18 HOU | 5 | 0 | 57 | 64 | 3.49 | 2.95 | 1.09 | 591 | 672 | 506 | 3.8 | 2.2 | 10.2 | 4.6 | 60% | 14% | 92.3 | 50 | 27 | 24 | 32% | 68% | 9% | 0 | 15 | | | 0 | 0.77 | 4.6 | 151 | 174 | $3 |
| 1st Half | 3 | 0 | 30 | 37 | 4.15 | 2.70 | 1.22 | 677 | 793 | 516 | 3.5 | 2.1 | 11.0 | 5.3 | 64% | 15% | | 51 | 27 | 22 | 36% | 68% | 18% | 0 | 14 | | | 0 | 0.85 | 0.0 | 171 | 196 | $1 |
| 2nd Half | 2 | 0 | 26 | 27 | 2.73 | 3.23 | 0.95 | 487 | 472 | 496 | 4.1 | 2.4 | 9.2 | 3.9 | 56% | 13% | 92.3 | 48 | 26 | 26 | 28% | 68% | 0% | 0 | 15 | | | 0 | 0.67 | 4.6 | 127 | 146 | $6 |
| 19 Proj | 4 | 0 | 58 | 63 | 3.10 | 2.82 | 1.04 | 581 | 599 | 564 | 3.7 | 2.1 | 9.8 | 4.6 | 60% | 13% | 50.7 | 50 | 22 | 28 | 30% | 72% | 11% | 0 | | | | | | 10.4 | 148 | 170 | $4 |

STEPHEN NICKRAND

| Harvey,Matt | | | | Health | F | LIMA Plan | C |
|---|---|---|---|---|---|---|---|
| Age: 30 | Th: R | Role | SP | PT/Exp | B | Rand Var | +2 |
| Ht: 6' 4" | Wt: 215 | Type | Pwr | Consist | C | MM | 2203 |

Looked rejuvenated post-trade, which will draw bidders in again. Hope for 2015 redux? PRO: Elite late Cmd backed by FpK, SwK, velocity upticks; 3.0+ Cmd vL/R (1st time since 2015). CON: DOM/DIS% questions upside; bottom quartile exit velocity and barrel rates; "F" health. A total wildcard.

| Yr Tm | W | Sv | IP | K | ERA | xERA | WHIP | oOPS | vL | vR | BF/G | Ctl | Dom | Cmd | FpK | SwK | Vel | G | L | F | H% | S% | hr/f | GS | APC | DOM% | DIS% | Sv% | LI | RAR | BPV | BPX | R$ |
|---|---|---|---|---|---|---|---|---|---|---|---|---|---|---|---|---|---|---|---|---|---|---|---|---|---|---|---|---|---|---|---|---|---|
| 14 | | | | | | | | | | | | | | | | | | | | | | | | | | | | | | | | | |
| 15 NYM | 13 | 0 | 189 | 188 | 2.71 | 3.25 | 1.02 | 609 | 676 | 544 | 26.0 | 1.8 | 8.9 | 5.1 | 68% | 12% | 95.9 | 46 | 18 | 36 | 29% | 78% | 10% | 29 | 96 | 55% | 14% | | | 29.2 | 137 | 164 | $26 |
| 16 NYM | 4 | 0 | 93 | 76 | 4.86 | 4.36 | 1.47 | 797 | 864 | 724 | 23.6 | 2.4 | 7.4 | 3.0 | 66% | 11% | 94.5 | 41 | 25 | 34 | 36% | 67% | 8% | 17 | 89 | 18% | 41% | | | -7.6 | 86 | 103 | -$5 |
| 17 NYM | 5 | 0 | 93 | 67 | 6.70 | 5.53 | 1.69 | 890 | 1025 | 774 | 22.7 | 4.6 | 6.5 | 1.4 | 58% | 8% | 93.8 | 43 | 23 | 34 | 31% | 65% | 21% | 18 | 89 | 0% | 61% | 0 | 0.79 | -26.8 | 15 | 18 | -$13 |
| 18 2 NL | 7 | 0 | 155 | 131 | 4.94 | 4.28 | 1.30 | 783 | 803 | 762 | 20.7 | 2.1 | 7.6 | 3.5 | 63% | 10% | 94.0 | 42 | 20 | 38 | 31% | 67% | 15% | 28 | 79 | 25% | 25% | 0 | 0.74 | -15.0 | 99 | 114 | -$2 |
| 1st Half | 3 | 0 | 75 | 54 | 5.28 | 4.59 | 1.32 | 795 | 873 | 719 | 18.9 | 2.5 | 6.5 | 2.6 | 61% | 8% | 93.6 | 41 | 23 | 36 | 29% | 64% | 15% | 13 | 74 | 15% | 23% | 0 | 0.69 | -10.5 | 68 | 78 | -$8 |
| 2nd Half | 4 | 0 | 80 | 77 | 4.61 | 4.01 | 1.29 | 772 | 744 | 805 | 22.7 | 1.8 | 8.7 | 4.8 | 65% | 11% | 94.5 | 43 | 17 | 39 | 33% | 70% | 15% | 15 | 85 | 33% | 27% | | | -4.6 | 129 | 148 | $4 |
| **19 Proj** | **8** | **0** | **160** | **139** | **4.10** | **3.88** | **1.31** | **762** | **814** | **709** | **21.1** | **2.5** | **7.9** | **3.1** | **63%** | **10%** | **94.3** | **43** | **21** | **36** | **31%** | **75%** | **15%** | **31** | | | | | | **1.0** | **95** | **109** | **$5** |

| Heaney,Andrew | | | | Health | F | LIMA Plan | B+ |
|---|---|---|---|---|---|---|---|
| Age: 28 | Th: L | Role | SP | PT/Exp | C | Rand Var | +2 |
| Ht: 6' 2" | Wt: 185 | Type | Pwr | Consist | F | MM | 2203 |

Finally flashed upside after years of various arm issues. If you can stomach flunking health grade, there's something good here. Top-tier Cmd came with good sub-support, first full-season 3.0+ Cmd vR. Skills surged even more in second half. If healthy again... UP: 3.50 ERA, 200 Ks

| Yr Tm | W | Sv | IP | K | ERA | xERA | WHIP | oOPS | vL | vR | BF/G | Ctl | Dom | Cmd | FpK | SwK | Vel | G | L | F | H% | S% | hr/f | GS | APC | DOM% | DIS% | Sv% | LI | RAR | BPV | BPX | R$ |
|---|---|---|---|---|---|---|---|---|---|---|---|---|---|---|---|---|---|---|---|---|---|---|---|---|---|---|---|---|---|---|---|---|---|
| 14 MIA * | 9 | 0 | 167 | 139 | 3.89 | 3.59 | 1.22 | 847 | 611 | 944 | 21.7 | 2.2 | 7.5 | 3.4 | 60% | 10% | 90.4 | 45 | 19 | 35 | 31% | 70% | 18% | 5 | 68 | 0% | 60% | 0 | 0.66 | -3.1 | 95 | 113 | $5 |
| 15 LAA * | 12 | 0 | 184 | 141 | 3.94 | 3.92 | 1.35 | 679 | 568 | 723 | 24.0 | 2.5 | 6.9 | 2.8 | 62% | 9% | 91.4 | 38 | 22 | 40 | 33% | 71% | 7% | 18 | 91 | 22% | 28% | | | 0.5 | 84 | 100 | $4 |
| 16 LAA | 0 | 0 | 6 | 7 | 6.00 | 3.21 | 1.17 | 840 | 833 | 842 | 25.0 | 0.0 | 10.5 | 0.0 | 60% | 14% | 90.8 | 44 | 17 | 39 | 34% | 60% | 29% | 1 | 87 | 0% | 0% | | | -1.3 | 211 | 251 | -$4 |
| 17 LAA * | 2 | 0 | 39 | 38 | 5.38 | 7.13 | 1.50 | 1108 | 780 | 1184 | 21.1 | 2.9 | 8.8 | 3.0 | 61% | 14% | 91.9 | 30 | 22 | 48 | 31% | 79% | 40% | 5 | 83 | 0% | 60% | | | -4.9 | 16 | 20 | -$5 |
| 18 LAA | 9 | 0 | 180 | 180 | 4.15 | 3.75 | 1.20 | 719 | 542 | 769 | 25.0 | 2.3 | 9.0 | 4.0 | 65% | 12% | 92.0 | 41 | 24 | 35 | 31% | 70% | 15% | 30 | 92 | 37% | 13% | | | 0.0 | 120 | 138 | $9 |
| 1st Half | 4 | 0 | 82 | 76 | 3.95 | 4.06 | 1.21 | 717 | 492 | 772 | 24.4 | 2.6 | 8.3 | 3.2 | 66% | 11% | 91.8 | 40 | 22 | 38 | 29% | 72% | 13% | 14 | 90 | 29% | 14% | | | 2.0 | 97 | 112 | $5 |
| 2nd Half | 5 | 0 | 98 | 104 | 4.32 | 3.50 | 1.19 | 721 | 576 | 767 | 25.5 | 1.9 | 9.6 | 5.0 | 65% | 13% | 92.1 | 42 | 25 | 33 | 32% | 69% | 18% | 16 | 93 | 44% | 13% | | | -2.0 | 140 | 161 | $12 |
| **19 Proj** | **9** | **0** | **174** | **164** | **3.88** | **3.71** | **1.26** | **756** | **585** | **812** | **22.8** | **2.3** | **8.5** | **3.6** | **64%** | **11%** | **91.7** | **40** | **23** | **37** | **31%** | **75%** | **15%** | **31** | | | | | | **5.9** | **107** | **123** | **$9** |

| Hellickson,Jeremy | | | | Health | D | LIMA Plan | B |
|---|---|---|---|---|---|---|---|
| Age: 32 | Th: R | Role | SP | PT/Exp | A | Rand Var | -1 |
| Ht: 6' 1" | Wt: 190 | Type | | Consist | C | MM | 1003 |

Hamstring, wrist issues kept him on the shelf more often than not. While it's tempting to bid on 2016, it ain't coming back. As velocity dips below 90 mph, he's at the mercy of his defense even if that higher FpK sticks. Keep the past in the rear view and value him for what he is: a 4.00-ERA innings-eater.

| Yr Tm | W | Sv | IP | K | ERA | xERA | WHIP | oOPS | vL | vR | BF/G | Ctl | Dom | Cmd | FpK | SwK | Vel | G | L | F | H% | S% | hr/f | GS | APC | DOM% | DIS% | Sv% | LI | RAR | BPV | BPX | R$ |
|---|---|---|---|---|---|---|---|---|---|---|---|---|---|---|---|---|---|---|---|---|---|---|---|---|---|---|---|---|---|---|---|---|---|
| 14 TAM * | 2 | 0 | 88 | 75 | 5.36 | 6.12 | 1.71 | 759 | 585 | 966 | 21.1 | 2.7 | 7.7 | 2.8 | 63% | 10% | 90.2 | 36 | 23 | 41 | 40% | 69% | 10% | 13 | 91 | 8% | 46% | | | -17.6 | 67 | 79 | -$12 |
| 15 ARI | 9 | 0 | 146 | 121 | 4.62 | 4.22 | 1.33 | 781 | 790 | 774 | 23.6 | 2.7 | 7.5 | 2.8 | 63% | 11% | 90.1 | 42 | 21 | 36 | 31% | 69% | 13% | 27 | 92 | 11% | 37% | | | -11.9 | 83 | 98 | -$1 |
| 16 PHI | 12 | 0 | 189 | 154 | 3.71 | 4.03 | 1.15 | 709 | 751 | 672 | 24.1 | 2.1 | 7.3 | 3.4 | 61% | 11% | 90.1 | 41 | 25 | 34 | 28% | 72% | 13% | 32 | 91 | 34% | 31% | | | 11.1 | 93 | 111 | $15 |
| 17 2 TM | 8 | 0 | 164 | 96 | 5.43 | 5.40 | 1.26 | 808 | 819 | 800 | 23.2 | 2.6 | 5.3 | 2.0 | 59% | 9% | 90.2 | 35 | 21 | 44 | 25% | 63% | 15% | 30 | 87 | 10% | 50% | | | -21.7 | 38 | 46 | -$2 |
| 18 WAS | 5 | 0 | 91 | 65 | 3.45 | 4.04 | 1.07 | 677 | 643 | 717 | 19.5 | 2.0 | 6.4 | 3.3 | 66% | 9% | 89.7 | 46 | 21 | 33 | 26% | 72% | 12% | 19 | 73 | 16% | 32% | | | 7.9 | 86 | 99 | $6 |
| 1st Half | 2 | 0 | 48 | 38 | 2.63 | 3.59 | 1.02 | 678 | 742 | 579 | 18.7 | 1.5 | 7.1 | 4.8 | 67% | 9% | 89.4 | 44 | 26 | 30 | 27% | 80% | 12% | 10 | 71 | 20% | 30% | | | 9.0 | 110 | 126 | $8 |
| 2nd Half | 3 | 0 | 43 | 27 | 4.36 | 4.56 | 1.13 | 676 | 506 | 825 | 20.3 | 2.5 | 5.6 | 2.3 | 66% | 8% | 89.9 | 48 | 16 | 36 | 25% | 65% | 13% | 9 | 75 | 11% | 33% | | | -1.1 | 59 | 68 | $3 |
| **19 Proj** | **8** | **0** | **145** | **101** | **4.25** | **4.11** | **1.18** | **731** | **693** | **768** | **20.5** | **2.3** | **6.3** | **2.8** | **63%** | **9%** | **89.9** | **42** | **21** | **37** | **27%** | **69%** | **13%** | **28** | | | | | | **-1.8** | **71** | **82** | **$6** |

| Hembree,Heath | | | | Health | A | LIMA Plan | C+ |
|---|---|---|---|---|---|---|---|
| Age: 30 | Th: R | Role | RP | PT/Exp | D | Rand Var | +2 |
| Ht: 6' 4" | Wt: 210 | Type | Pwr FB | Consist | A | MM | 2400 |

Most will continue to ignore him, especially given climbing ERA and lack of save opps. That said, potent SwK, soaring FpK in second half support return to 2017 Cmd. OPS vR inflated by 22% hr/f, and improving xERA hints at return to sub-4 ERA. A viable $1 staff-filler in deep leagues.

| Yr Tm | W | Sv | IP | K | ERA | xERA | WHIP | oOPS | vL | vR | BF/G | Ctl | Dom | Cmd | FpK | SwK | Vel | G | L | F | H% | S% | hr/f | GS | APC | DOM% | DIS% | Sv% | LI | RAR | BPV | BPX | R$ |
|---|---|---|---|---|---|---|---|---|---|---|---|---|---|---|---|---|---|---|---|---|---|---|---|---|---|---|---|---|---|---|---|---|---|
| 14 BOS * | 1 | 20 | 56 | 50 | 4.80 | 5.40 | 1.62 | 846 | 962 | 799 | 4.6 | 3.9 | 8.1 | 2.0 | 75% | 10% | 91.9 | 28 | 22 | 50 | 36% | 72% | 6% | 0 | 29 | | | 83 | 0.81 | -7.3 | 56 | 66 | $1 |
| 15 BOS * | 2 | 8 | 57 | 40 | 3.47 | 4.06 | 1.33 | 795 | 862 | 741 | 4.6 | 3.3 | 6.4 | 2.0 | 63% | 9% | 94.3 | 27 | 25 | 48 | 29% | 77% | 13% | 0 | 18 | | | 73 | 0.45 | 3.5 | 54 | 64 | $2 |
| 16 BOS | 4 | 0 | 51 | 47 | 2.65 | 4.57 | 1.33 | 695 | 890 | 591 | 5.9 | 3.0 | 8.3 | 2.8 | 59% | 10% | 93.9 | 36 | 24 | 40 | 32% | 85% | 10% | 0 | 23 | | | 0 | 0.93 | 9.7 | 82 | 98 | $2 |
| 17 BOS | 2 | 0 | 62 | 70 | 3.63 | 4.11 | 1.45 | 803 | 803 | 803 | 4.4 | 2.6 | 10.2 | 3.9 | 61% | 15% | 95.4 | 39 | 21 | 41 | 37% | 81% | 14% | 0 | 18 | | | 0 | 1.18 | 5.6 | 129 | 155 | -$1 |
| 18 BOS | 4 | 0 | 60 | 76 | 4.20 | 3.90 | 1.33 | 734 | 551 | 847 | 3.9 | 4.1 | 11.4 | 2.8 | 62% | 15% | 94.5 | 39 | 19 | 41 | 32% | 74% | 16% | 0 | 16 | | | 0 | 1.15 | -0.4 | 113 | 130 | -$1 |
| 1st Half | 3 | 0 | 35 | 44 | 3.60 | 3.71 | 1.23 | 671 | 598 | 707 | 4.2 | 4.1 | 11.3 | 2.8 | 57% | 15% | 94.6 | 43 | 17 | 40 | 30% | 74% | 12% | 0 | 18 | | | 0 | 0.82 | 2.4 | 114 | 130 | $1 |
| 2nd Half | 1 | 0 | 25 | 32 | 5.04 | 4.16 | 1.48 | 816 | 506 | 1063 | 3.5 | 4.0 | 11.5 | 2.9 | 67% | 14% | 94.5 | 35 | 22 | 43 | 34% | 74% | 20% | 0 | 15 | | | 0 | 1.51 | -2.7 | 113 | 130 | -$4 |
| **19 Proj** | **3** | **0** | **58** | **66** | **3.95** | **3.67** | **1.30** | **710** | **614** | **760** | **4.0** | **3.5** | **10.2** | **2.9** | **62%** | **14%** | **94.7** | **38** | **21** | **41** | **31%** | **76%** | **15%** | **0** | | | | | | **3.9** | **106** | **122** | **$0** |

| Hendricks,Kyle | | | | Health | C | LIMA Plan | C+ |
|---|---|---|---|---|---|---|---|
| Age: 29 | Th: R | Role | SP | PT/Exp | A | Rand Var | 0 |
| Ht: 6' 3" | Wt: 190 | Type | | Consist | A | MM | 3105 |

Continues to stave off critics who think an implosion is coming due to mid-80s velocity. Change-up remains his bread-and-butter and is showing no signs of losing its deception. Pinpoint control legitimized by FpK, so it's here to stay too. xERA confirms downside isn't steep. A low-risk #2 SP.

| Yr Tm | W | Sv | IP | K | ERA | xERA | WHIP | oOPS | vL | vR | BF/G | Ctl | Dom | Cmd | FpK | SwK | Vel | G | L | F | H% | S% | hr/f | GS | APC | DOM% | DIS% | Sv% | LI | RAR | BPV | BPX | R$ |
|---|---|---|---|---|---|---|---|---|---|---|---|---|---|---|---|---|---|---|---|---|---|---|---|---|---|---|---|---|---|---|---|---|---|
| 14 CHC * | 17 | 0 | 183 | 127 | 3.45 | 3.42 | 1.23 | 610 | 584 | 633 | 24.7 | 1.9 | 6.3 | 3.3 | 64% | 8% | 87.9 | 48 | 19 | 33 | 31% | 72% | 5% | 13 | 89 | 31% | 23% | | | 6.5 | 94 | 112 | $11 |
| 15 CHC | 8 | 0 | 180 | 167 | 3.95 | 3.28 | 1.16 | 677 | 797 | 580 | 23.1 | 2.2 | 8.4 | 3.9 | 63% | 9% | 88.3 | 51 | 22 | 27 | 30% | 68% | 13% | 32 | 87 | 31% | 22% | | | 0.3 | 121 | 144 | $9 |
| 16 CHC | 16 | 0 | 190 | 170 | 2.13 | 3.48 | 0.98 | 581 | 616 | 555 | 24.0 | 2.1 | 8.1 | 3.9 | 68% | 10% | 87.8 | 48 | 20 | 31 | 26% | 82% | 9% | 30 | 93 | 33% | 7% | 0 | 0.76 | 48.2 | 115 | 136 | $34 |
| 17 CHC | 7 | 0 | 140 | 123 | 3.03 | 3.83 | 1.19 | 670 | 706 | 639 | 23.8 | 2.6 | 7.9 | 3.1 | 63% | 9% | 85.8 | 50 | 21 | 29 | 29% | 80% | 15% | 24 | 95 | 21% | 17% | | | 22.9 | 101 | 121 | $13 |
| 18 CHC | 14 | 0 | 199 | 161 | 3.44 | 3.85 | 1.15 | 685 | 664 | 703 | 24.6 | 2.0 | 7.3 | 3.7 | 65% | 10% | 86.9 | 47 | 21 | 32 | 29% | 74% | 12% | 33 | 92 | 24% | 30% | | | 17.5 | 102 | 118 | $18 |
| 1st Half | 5 | 0 | 92 | 70 | 4.21 | 4.25 | 1.23 | 735 | 749 | 724 | 23.9 | 2.8 | 6.8 | 2.4 | 64% | 9% | 86.8 | 47 | 21 | 32 | 26% | 72% | 18% | 16 | 88 | 19% | 38% | | | -0.6 | 72 | 82 | $3 |
| 2nd Half | 9 | 0 | 107 | 91 | 2.78 | 3.52 | 1.07 | 642 | 600 | 683 | 25.2 | 1.3 | 7.7 | 6.1 | 66% | 10% | 87.0 | 47 | 22 | 31 | 31% | 75% | 6% | 17 | 96 | 29% | 24% | | | 18.1 | 129 | 148 | $30 |
| **19 Proj** | **13** | **0** | **189** | **159** | **3.26** | **3.49** | **1.13** | **662** | **669** | **657** | **23.7** | **2.1** | **7.6** | **3.6** | **65%** | **9%** | **86.9** | **48** | **21** | **31** | **29%** | **75%** | **11%** | **31** | | | | | | **13.0** | **106** | **122** | **$20** |

| Hernandez,David | | | | Health | F | LIMA Plan | B+ |
|---|---|---|---|---|---|---|---|
| Age: 34 | Th: R | Role | RP | PT/Exp | C | Rand Var | -5 |
| Ht: 6' 3" | Wt: 245 | Type | Pwr FB | Consist | A | MM | 3310 |

Best season since 2012 as he continues to try to shed injury-prone past. Three reasons he could be worthy of more than just a LIMA stash: 1) Peppered strike zone early in counts, especially in second half; 2) near-elite skills in high-leverage duty late; 3) dominant against both LH/RHers. UP: 25 saves

| Yr Tm | W | Sv | IP | K | ERA | xERA | WHIP | oOPS | vL | vR | BF/G | Ctl | Dom | Cmd | FpK | SwK | Vel | G | L | F | H% | S% | hr/f | GS | APC | DOM% | DIS% | Sv% | LI | RAR | BPV | BPX | R$ |
|---|---|---|---|---|---|---|---|---|---|---|---|---|---|---|---|---|---|---|---|---|---|---|---|---|---|---|---|---|---|---|---|---|---|
| 14 | | | | | | | | | | | | | | | | | | | | | | | | | | | | | | | | | |
| 15 ARI | 1 | 0 | 34 | 33 | 4.28 | 3.94 | 1.31 | 778 | 739 | 803 | 3.6 | 2.9 | 8.8 | 3.0 | 55% | 11% | 94.3 | 39 | 19 | 41 | 30% | 74% | 15% | 0 | 15 | | | 0 | 0.86 | -1.3 | 96 | 115 | -$3 |
| 16 PHI | 3 | 1 | 73 | 80 | 3.84 | 4.26 | 1.50 | 785 | 852 | 730 | 4.6 | 4.0 | 9.9 | 2.5 | 58% | 12% | 94.0 | 37 | 25 | 38 | 35% | 80% | 14% | 0 | 18 | | | 33 | 0.85 | 3.1 | 86 | 103 | -$1 |
| 17 2 TM | 3 | 2 | 55 | 52 | 3.11 | 3.72 | 1.04 | 611 | 618 | 605 | 3.3 | 1.5 | 8.5 | 5.8 | 59% | 13% | 93.7 | 43 | 17 | 40 | 30% | 72% | 7% | 0 | 12 | | | 50 | 0.89 | 8.5 | 134 | 161 | $5 |
| 18 CIN | 5 | 0 | 64 | 65 | 2.53 | 3.89 | 0.98 | 635 | 676 | 600 | 4.5 | 2.4 | 9.1 | 3.8 | 65% | 12% | 93.0 | 33 | 21 | 46 | 26% | 79% | 8% | 0 | 17 | | | 0 | 1.20 | 12.8 | 111 | 128 | $7 |
| 1st Half | 3 | 0 | 29 | 31 | 1.57 | 3.98 | 1.01 | 532 | 709 | 368 | 5.0 | 3.8 | 9.7 | 2.6 | 59% | 10% | 92.8 | 30 | 29 | 41 | 25% | 83% | 0% | 0 | 20 | | | 0 | 0.94 | 9.1 | 81 | 94 | $7 |
| 2nd Half | 2 | 0 | 35 | 34 | 3.31 | 3.83 | 0.96 | 717 | 645 | 776 | 4.1 | 1.3 | 8.7 | 6.8 | 70% | 14% | 93.3 | 35 | 15 | 50 | 26% | 75% | 13% | 0 | 15 | | | 0 | 1.37 | 3.7 | 135 | 155 | $7 |
| **19 Proj** | **4** | **5** | **65** | **66** | **3.09** | **3.60** | **1.11** | **673** | **696** | **654** | **3.9** | **2.4** | **9.0** | **3.8** | **62%** | **12%** | **93.5** | **37** | **20** | **43** | **29%** | **77%** | **10%** | **0** | | | | | | **4.5** | **113** | **130** | **$7** |

| Hernandez,Elieser | | | | Health | D | LIMA Plan | D |
|---|---|---|---|---|---|---|---|
| Age: 24 | Th: R | Role | RP | PT/Exp | D | Rand Var | 0 |
| Ht: 6' 0" | Wt: 210 | Type | xFB | Consist | F | MM | 0000 |

Rule-5 pick showed why he can't stick on a 40-man roster. There's no reason to expect anything better either, as skills were among worst in majors. Flyball pitchers that don't miss many bats and can't get the ball over the plate simply don't belong anywhere near any roster, especially yours.

| Yr Tm | W | Sv | IP | K | ERA | xERA | WHIP | oOPS | vL | vR | BF/G | Ctl | Dom | Cmd | FpK | SwK | Vel | G | L | F | H% | S% | hr/f | GS | APC | DOM% | DIS% | Sv% | LI | RAR | BPV | BPX | R$ |
|---|---|---|---|---|---|---|---|---|---|---|---|---|---|---|---|---|---|---|---|---|---|---|---|---|---|---|---|---|---|---|---|---|---|
| 14 | | | | | | | | | | | | | | | | | | | | | | | | | | | | | | | | | |
| 15 | | | | | | | | | | | | | | | | | | | | | | | | | | | | | | | | | |
| 16 | | | | | | | | | | | | | | | | | | | | | | | | | | | | | | | | | |
| 17 | | | | | | | | | | | | | | | | | | | | | | | | | | | | | | | | | |
| 18 MIA | 2 | 0 | 66 | 45 | 5.21 | 5.69 | 1.45 | 809 | 884 | 731 | 8.9 | 3.7 | 6.2 | 1.7 | 56% | 9% | 90.7 | 28 | 21 | 51 | 29% | 68% | 10% | 6 | 35 | 0% | 67% | 0 | 0.69 | -8.6 | 17 | 20 | -$7 |
| 1st Half | 0 | 0 | 36 | 22 | 5.05 | 5.85 | 1.54 | 862 | 981 | 712 | 13.0 | 3.5 | 5.6 | 1.6 | 54% | 9% | 90.3 | 27 | 22 | 50 | 31% | 70% | 9% | 5 | 52 | 0% | 60% | 0 | 0.60 | -3.9 | 10 | 11 | -$11 |
| 2nd Half | 2 | 0 | 30 | 23 | 5.40 | 5.51 | 1.33 | 745 | 736 | 750 | 6.4 | 3.9 | 6.9 | 1.8 | 59% | 9% | 91.1 | 29 | 19 | 53 | 25% | 65% | 13% | 1 | 25 | 0% | 100% | 0 | 0.75 | -4.6 | 25 | 29 | -$3 |
| **19 Proj** | **2** | **0** | **58** | **41** | **5.26** | **5.20** | **1.42** | **792** | **848** | **737** | **7.9** | **3.8** | **6.4** | **1.7** | **57%** | **9%** | **90.8** | **28** | **20** | **52** | **28%** | **67%** | **11%** | **0** | | | | | | **-5.3** | **19** | **22** | **-$6** |

STEPHEN NICKRAND

## Hernandez,Felix

| Age: 33 | Th: R | Role: SP | Health | F | LIMA Plan | C |
|---|---|---|---|---|---|---|
| Ht: 6' 3" | Wt: 225 | Type: Pwr | PT/Exp | B | Rand Var | +5 |
| | | | Consist | A | MM | 1103 |

The slide continues. Sure, aberrant strand rate didn't help, but career lows in velocity, SwK, and Dom. You can refute it, but 1,150 IP by age 24 had a role in this premature downfall. FB velocity has been in steady, nearly consistent decline since his debut (95.8mph in 2005). We warned you this was coming back in #BF13.

| Yr | Tm | W | Sv | IP | K | ERA | xERA | WHIP | oOPS | vL | vR | BF/G | Ctl | Dom | Cmd | FpK | SwK | Vel | G | L | F | H% | S% | hr/f | GS | APC | DOM% | DIS% | Sv% | LI | RAR | BPV | BPX | R$ |
|---|---|---|---|---|---|---|---|---|---|---|---|---|---|---|---|---|---|---|---|---|---|---|---|---|---|---|---|---|---|---|---|---|---|---|
| 14 | SEA | 15 | 0 | 236 | 248 | 2.14 | 2.54 | 0.92 | 546 | 519 | 584 | 26.8 | 1.8 | 9.5 | 5.4 | 65% | 13% | 92.4 | 56 | 18 | 26 | 27% | 80% | 10% | 34 | 101 | 65% | 9% | | | 46.7 | 157 | 187 | $38 |
| 15 | SEA | 18 | 0 | 202 | 191 | 3.53 | 3.25 | 1.18 | 682 | 699 | 665 | 26.6 | 2.6 | 8.5 | 3.3 | 63% | 11% | 91.8 | 56 | 17 | 27 | 29% | 74% | 15% | 31 | 98 | 61% | 16% | | | 10.8 | 118 | 140 | $18 |
| 16 | SEA | 11 | 0 | 153 | 122 | 3.82 | 4.30 | 1.32 | 718 | 739 | 702 | 26.2 | 3.8 | 7.2 | 1.9 | 59% | 10% | 90.5 | 50 | 21 | 29 | 28% | 75% | 15% | 25 | 98 | 16% | 40% | | | 7.1 | 54 | 64 | $7 |
| 17 | SEA | 6 | 0 | 87 | 78 | 4.36 | 4.00 | 1.29 | 791 | 854 | 743 | 23.0 | 2.7 | 8.1 | 3.0 | 61% | 10% | 90.5 | 47 | 23 | 30 | 29% | 74% | 22% | 16 | 86 | 13% | 31% | | | 0.0 | 98 | 118 | $2 |
| 18 | SEA | 8 | 0 | 156 | 125 | 5.55 | 4.55 | 1.40 | 798 | 835 | 771 | 23.6 | 3.4 | 7.2 | 2.1 | 63% | 8% | 89.3 | 47 | 19 | 34 | 30% | 64% | 17% | 28 | 88 | 11% | 50% | 0 | 0.81 | -26.9 | 63 | 73 | -$8 |
| 1st Half | | 8 | 0 | 100 | 85 | 5.11 | 4.32 | 1.36 | 764 | 786 | 747 | 24.4 | 3.2 | 7.6 | 2.4 | 62% | 9% | 89.2 | 46 | 22 | 33 | 30% | 65% | 14% | 18 | 91 | 11% | 39% | | | -11.9 | 74 | 85 | -$3 |
| 2nd Half | | 0 | 0 | 55 | 40 | 6.34 | 4.98 | 1.48 | 859 | 924 | 812 | 22.4 | 3.7 | 6.5 | 1.7 | 64% | 7% | 89.6 | 49 | 15 | 36 | 28% | 62% | 20% | 10 | 84 | 10% | 70% | 0 | 0.81 | -15.0 | 43 | 49 | -$17 |
| **19** | **Proj** | **7** | **0** | **145** | **118** | **4.75** | **4.18** | **1.39** | **798** | **835** | **770** | **23.3** | **3.4** | **7.4** | **2.2** | **62%** | **9%** | **90.1** | **46** | **20** | **34** | **30%** | **71%** | **17%** | **26** | | | | | | **-10.7** | **65** | **75** | **-$2** |

## Herrera,Kelvin

| Age: 29 | Th: R | Role: RP | Health | D | LIMA Plan | B+ |
|---|---|---|---|---|---|---|
| Ht: 5' 10" | Wt: 200 | Type: Pwr | PT/Exp | B | Rand Var | -5 |
| | | | Consist | B | MM | 3210 |

Two-run gap between ERA and xERA shows this wasn't the rebound it appears. Hot start obscured gradual fade before Sept foot surgery. Still throwing hard, but FB% spike and Dom dip concerning. So were second-half shoulder woes, his 2nd straight year with arm issues. DN: 4.50 ERA, more DL time

| Yr | Tm | W | Sv | IP | K | ERA | xERA | WHIP | oOPS | vL | vR | BF/G | Ctl | Dom | Cmd | FpK | SwK | Vel | G | L | F | H% | S% | hr/f | GS | APC | DOM% | DIS% | Sv% | LI | RAR | BPV | BPX | R$ |
|---|---|---|---|---|---|---|---|---|---|---|---|---|---|---|---|---|---|---|---|---|---|---|---|---|---|---|---|---|---|---|---|---|---|---|
| 14 | KC | 4 | 0 | 70 | 59 | 1.41 | 3.43 | 1.14 | 561 | 617 | 508 | 4.1 | 3.3 | 7.6 | 2.3 | 55% | 13% | 98.1 | 49 | 27 | 24 | 28% | 86% | 0% | 0 | 16 | | | 0 | 1.14 | 20.1 | 73 | 87 | $7 |
| 15 | KC | 4 | 0 | 70 | 64 | 2.71 | 3.79 | 1.12 | 578 | 470 | 677 | 4.0 | 3.4 | 8.3 | 2.5 | 61% | 14% | 98.1 | 45 | 23 | 33 | 26% | 78% | 8% | 0 | 15 | | | 0 | 1.17 | 10.7 | 81 | 97 | $5 |
| 16 | KC | 2 | 12 | 72 | 86 | 2.75 | 2.90 | 0.96 | 590 | 557 | 625 | 3.9 | 1.5 | 10.8 | 7.2 | 65% | 16% | 97.1 | 44 | 23 | 33 | 30% | 75% | 10% | 0 | 15 | | | 80 | 1.22 | 12.8 | 175 | 208 | $13 |
| 17 | KC | 3 | 26 | 59 | 56 | 4.25 | 4.31 | 1.35 | 784 | 840 | 720 | 4.0 | 3.0 | 8.5 | 2.8 | 60% | 12% | 97.5 | 48 | 18 | 34 | 31% | 73% | 15% | 0 | 16 | | | 84 | 1.09 | 0.8 | 97 | 116 | $10 |
| 18 | 2 TM | 2 | 17 | 44 | 38 | 2.44 | 4.34 | 1.20 | 689 | 684 | 692 | 3.8 | 2.0 | 7.7 | 3.8 | 67% | 13% | 96.5 | 36 | 21 | 43 | 30% | 87% | 11% | 0 | 15 | | | 89 | 1.11 | 9.4 | 98 | 113 | $8 |
| 1st Half | | 2 | 14 | 31 | 26 | 1.47 | 3.70 | 0.85 | 519 | 502 | 530 | 3.6 | 1.2 | 7.6 | 6.5 | 67% | 14% | 96.4 | 39 | 19 | 42 | 24% | 91% | 9% | 0 | 14 | | | 88 | 1.19 | 10.1 | 123 | 141 | $15 |
| 2nd Half | | 0 | 3 | 14 | 12 | 4.61 | 5.83 | 1.98 | 986 | 931 | 1041 | 4.3 | 4.0 | 7.9 | 2.0 | 68% | 11% | 96.8 | 29 | 25 | 46 | 40% | 83% | 14% | 0 | 16 | | | 100 | 0.96 | -0.8 | 43 | 49 | -$8 |
| **19** | **Proj** | **3** | **9** | **58** | **52** | **3.61** | **3.56** | **1.15** | **676** | **670** | **680** | **3.8** | **2.2** | **8.1** | **3.7** | **63%** | **14%** | **97.2** | **44** | **21** | **35** | **29%** | **72%** | **11%** | **0** | | | | | | **3.9** | **108** | **124** | **$5** |

## Hess,David

| Age: 25 | Th: R | Role: SP | Health | A | LIMA Plan | D+ |
|---|---|---|---|---|---|---|
| Ht: 6' 2" | Wt: 180 | Type: xFB | PT/Exp | D | Rand Var | 0 |
| | | | Consist | C | MM | 0001 |

3-10, 4.88 ERA in 103 IP at BAL. Tends to leaves his fringy stuff up in the zone. That often results in a barrage of hard-hit flyballs, many of which leave the yard. Without a swing-and-miss pitch (see SwK), he's a blow-up ready to happen (see DOM%) with little upside (see DIS%). Avoid him, see?

| Yr | Tm | W | Sv | IP | K | ERA | xERA | WHIP | oOPS | vL | vR | BF/G | Ctl | Dom | Cmd | FpK | SwK | Vel | G | L | F | H% | S% | hr/f | GS | APC | DOM% | DIS% | Sv% | LI | RAR | BPV | BPX | R$ |
|---|---|---|---|---|---|---|---|---|---|---|---|---|---|---|---|---|---|---|---|---|---|---|---|---|---|---|---|---|---|---|---|---|---|---|
| 14 | | | | | | | | | | | | | | | | | | | | | | | | | | | | | | | | | | |
| 15 | | | | | | | | | | | | | | | | | | | | | | | | | | | | | | | | | | |
| 16 | aa | 5 | 0 | 127 | 75 | 6.49 | 7.03 | 1.80 | | | | 23.5 | 3.0 | 5.3 | 1.8 | | | | | | | 37% | 66% | | | | | | | | -36.1 | 11 | 13 | -$21 |
| 17 | aa | 11 | 0 | 154 | 99 | 4.89 | 4.72 | 1.42 | | | | 24.2 | 3.2 | 5.8 | 1.8 | | | | | | | 30% | 68% | | | | | | | | -10.2 | 37 | 45 | -$1 |
| 18 | BAL * | 6 | 0 | 151 | 109 | 4.66 | 5.03 | 1.40 | 821 | 831 | 811 | 21.2 | 3.5 | 6.5 | 1.9 | 61% | 9% | 91.9 | 35 | 19 | 47 | 29% | 72% | 14% | 19 | 83 | 5% | 58% | 0 | 0.74 | -9.4 | 34 | 39 | -$5 |
| 1st Half | | 4 | 0 | 78 | 49 | 4.67 | 4.90 | 1.41 | 860 | 855 | 866 | 22.1 | 3.7 | 5.6 | 1.5 | 65% | 9% | 92.1 | 35 | 18 | 47 | 28% | 71% | 13% | 9 | 87 | 0% | 89% | | | -5.0 | 24 | 28 | -$6 |
| 2nd Half | | 2 | 0 | 72 | 60 | 4.64 | 5.18 | 1.40 | 787 | 812 | 761 | 20.3 | 3.2 | 7.4 | 2.3 | 58% | 9% | 91.8 | 34 | 20 | 46 | 30% | 73% | 15% | 10 | 81 | 10% | 30% | 0 | 0.69 | -4.4 | 45 | 51 | -$3 |
| **19** | **Proj** | **5** | **0** | **102** | **70** | **4.93** | **5.02** | **1.47** | **820** | **814** | **826** | **22.4** | **3.3** | **6.2** | **1.9** | **61%** | **9%** | **91.9** | **34** | **19** | **46** | **31%** | **70%** | **10%** | **19** | | | | | | **-9.7** | **35** | **40** | **-$6** |

## Hicks,Jordan

| Age: 22 | Th: R | Role: RP | Health | A | LIMA Plan | B |
|---|---|---|---|---|---|---|
| Ht: 6' 2" | Wt: 185 | Type: Pwr xGB | PT/Exp | D | Rand Var | -1 |
| | | | Consist | F | MM | 2211 |

PRO: Power two-seamer averages over 100 mph (!) AND gets tons of GB; dominates RHB; durable so far. CON: Doesn't miss as many bats as you'd expect; that plus poor Ctl equates to just so-so overall skills. Still some kinks to work out, but any 22-year-old who throws this hard is worth watching.

| Yr | Tm | W | Sv | IP | K | ERA | xERA | WHIP | oOPS | vL | vR | BF/G | Ctl | Dom | Cmd | FpK | SwK | Vel | G | L | F | H% | S% | hr/f | GS | APC | DOM% | DIS% | Sv% | LI | RAR | BPV | BPX | R$ |
|---|---|---|---|---|---|---|---|---|---|---|---|---|---|---|---|---|---|---|---|---|---|---|---|---|---|---|---|---|---|---|---|---|---|---|
| 14 | | | | | | | | | | | | | | | | | | | | | | | | | | | | | | | | | | |
| 15 | | | | | | | | | | | | | | | | | | | | | | | | | | | | | | | | | | |
| 16 | | | | | | | | | | | | | | | | | | | | | | | | | | | | | | | | | | |
| 17 | | | | | | | | | | | | | | | | | | | | | | | | | | | | | | | | | | |
| 18 | STL | 3 | 6 | 78 | 70 | 3.59 | 3.95 | 1.34 | 587 | 715 | 457 | 4.6 | 5.2 | 8.1 | 1.6 | 59% | 10% | 100.5 | 61 | 21 | 19 | 28% | 72% | 5% | 0 | 17 | | | 46 | 1.25 | 5.3 | 44 | 51 | $2 |
| 1st Half | | 3 | 1 | 41 | 34 | 2.66 | 4.07 | 1.16 | 525 | 668 | 382 | 4.5 | 5.1 | 7.5 | 1.5 | 61% | 11% | 99.9 | 59 | 18 | 23 | 22% | 76% | 4% | 0 | 16 | | | 25 | 1.25 | 7.5 | 35 | 40 | $6 |
| 2nd Half | | 0 | 5 | 37 | 36 | 4.62 | 3.81 | 1.54 | 650 | 759 | 532 | 4.8 | 5.4 | 8.8 | 1.6 | 56% | 9% | 101.1 | 63 | 23 | 14 | 33% | 68% | 7% | 0 | 19 | | | 56 | 1.25 | -2.2 | 54 | 62 | -$1 |
| **19** | **Proj** | **2** | **9** | **73** | **67** | **3.84** | **3.74** | **1.39** | **603** | **726** | **476** | **4.5** | **5.2** | **8.3** | **1.6** | **58%** | **10%** | **100.6** | **61** | **21** | **18** | **29%** | **71%** | **5%** | **0** | | | | | | **3.3** | **46** | **53** | **$2** |

## Hildenberger,Trevor

| Age: 28 | Th: R | Role: RP | Health | A | LIMA Plan | C |
|---|---|---|---|---|---|---|
| Ht: 6' 2" | Wt: 211 | Type: Pwr | PT/Exp | D | Rand Var | +5 |
| | | | Consist | C | MM | 2220 |

PRO: Skills similar to 2017 debut, and even missed a few more bats; unlucky second half drove most of ERA spike. CON: Missed his spots more, as shown by FpK dip and Ctl, hr/f spike, notable drop in GB rate. Still owns fine 2016-17 control; that with projected near-9.0 Dom could give... UP: 3.25 ERA, 25 saves

| Yr | Tm | W | Sv | IP | K | ERA | xERA | WHIP | oOPS | vL | vR | BF/G | Ctl | Dom | Cmd | FpK | SwK | Vel | G | L | F | H% | S% | hr/f | GS | APC | DOM% | DIS% | Sv% | LI | RAR | BPV | BPX | R$ |
|---|---|---|---|---|---|---|---|---|---|---|---|---|---|---|---|---|---|---|---|---|---|---|---|---|---|---|---|---|---|---|---|---|---|---|
| 14 | | | | | | | | | | | | | | | | | | | | | | | | | | | | | | | | | | |
| 15 | | | | | | | | | | | | | | | | | | | | | | | | | | | | | | | | | | |
| 16 | aa | 2 | 16 | 39 | 34 | 0.98 | 1.73 | 0.86 | | | | 4.5 | 1.5 | 7.9 | 5.2 | | | | | | | 25% | 95% | | | | | | | | 15.3 | 155 | 184 | $12 |
| 17 | MIN * | 5 | 7 | 73 | 70 | 3.28 | 3.77 | 1.26 | 664 | 637 | 680 | 5.1 | 1.9 | 8.7 | 4.5 | 65% | 12% | 88.8 | 59 | 18 | 24 | 34% | 76% | 15% | 0 | 17 | | | 70 | 1.06 | 9.6 | 127 | 153 | $7 |
| 18 | MIN | 4 | 7 | 73 | 70 | 5.42 | 3.99 | 1.38 | 803 | 810 | 799 | 4.4 | 3.2 | 8.6 | 2.7 | 57% | 13% | 89.6 | 46 | 25 | 28 | 32% | 64% | 19% | 0 | 16 | | | 64 | 1.03 | -11.5 | 93 | 107 | -$3 |
| 1st Half | | 1 | 0 | 40 | 33 | 3.18 | 3.92 | 1.11 | 695 | 617 | 738 | 4.4 | 2.7 | 7.5 | 2.8 | 59% | 14% | 89.7 | 49 | 22 | 30 | 26% | 77% | 15% | 0 | 16 | | | 0 | 0.99 | 4.8 | 88 | 101 | $1 |
| 2nd Half | | 3 | 7 | 33 | 37 | 8.10 | 4.07 | 1.71 | 917 | 982 | 870 | 4.3 | 3.8 | 10.0 | 2.6 | 56% | 13% | 89.6 | 44 | 29 | 27 | 39% | 54% | 25% | 0 | 16 | | | 64 | 1.07 | -16.2 | 99 | 114 | -$6 |
| **19** | **Proj** | **4** | **12** | **58** | **55** | **3.75** | **3.65** | **1.34** | **765** | **772** | **760** | **4.6** | **2.9** | **8.6** | **2.9** | **60%** | **13%** | **89.3** | **47** | **23** | **30** | **32%** | **76%** | **15%** | **0** | | | | | | **3.4** | **100** | **115** | **$5** |

## Hill,Rich

| Age: 39 | Th: L | Role: RP | Health | F | LIMA Plan | B |
|---|---|---|---|---|---|---|
| Ht: 6' 5" | Wt: 220 | Type: Pwr FB | PT/Exp | B | Rand Var | +1 |
| | | | Consist | A | MM | 3403 |

Got past first-half blister problems to post terrific, 10-win second half. Remarkably consistent in this late-career renaissance—including annual DL trips. So don't even speculate on that second half times two. Instead, set bid based on last three years' skills AND IP totals... and cross your fingers for more.

| Yr | Tm | W | Sv | IP | K | ERA | xERA | WHIP | oOPS | vL | vR | BF/G | Ctl | Dom | Cmd | FpK | SwK | Vel | G | L | F | H% | S% | hr/f | GS | APC | DOM% | DIS% | Sv% | LI | RAR | BPV | BPX | R$ |
|---|---|---|---|---|---|---|---|---|---|---|---|---|---|---|---|---|---|---|---|---|---|---|---|---|---|---|---|---|---|---|---|---|---|---|
| 14 | 2 AL * | 3 | 2 | 48 | 50 | 3.69 | 3.51 | 1.51 | 801 | 679 | 1125 | 4.6 | 4.9 | 9.3 | 1.9 | 41% | 14% | 90.3 | 38 | 31 | 31 | 35% | 73% | 0% | 0 | 7 | | | 67 | 1.07 | 0.3 | 100 | 119 | -$2 |
| 15 | BOS * | 7 | 0 | 83 | 81 | 3.53 | 3.57 | 1.36 | 410 | 358 | 423 | 10.2 | 4.6 | 8.8 | 1.9 | 61% | 12% | 90.2 | 48 | 16 | 35 | 29% | 76% | 9% | 4 | 109 | 50% | 0% | | | 4.4 | 77 | 92 | $2 |
| 16 | 2 TM | 12 | 0 | 110 | 129 | 2.12 | 3.21 | 1.00 | 530 | 522 | 532 | 22.0 | 2.7 | 10.5 | 3.9 | 60% | 11% | 90.2 | 45 | 19 | 36 | 29% | 79% | 4% | 20 | 91 | 40% | 10% | | | 28.2 | 140 | 166 | $20 |
| 17 | LA | 12 | 0 | 136 | 166 | 3.32 | 3.72 | 1.09 | 639 | 845 | 583 | 22.1 | 3.3 | 11.0 | 3.4 | 62% | 12% | 89.0 | 37 | 17 | 46 | 27% | 75% | 13% | 25 | 89 | 28% | 24% | | | 17.4 | 125 | 151 | $18 |
| 18 | LA | 11 | 0 | 133 | 150 | 3.66 | 3.66 | 1.12 | 689 | 694 | 686 | 21.9 | 2.8 | 10.2 | 3.7 | 65% | 11% | 89.3 | 39 | 21 | 40 | 28% | 74% | 15% | 24 | 84 | 29% | 17% | 0 | 0.81 | 8.0 | 125 | 144 | $12 |
| 1st Half | | 1 | 0 | 42 | 46 | 4.68 | 4.29 | 1.42 | 834 | 611 | 902 | 21.0 | 3.4 | 9.8 | 2.9 | 62% | 9% | 89.0 | 35 | 22 | 43 | 32% | 75% | 18% | 9 | 80 | 22% | 44% | | | -2.8 | 97 | 112 | -$15 |
| 2nd Half | | 10 | 0 | 90 | 104 | 3.19 | 3.37 | 0.99 | 614 | 726 | 574 | 22.4 | 2.5 | 10.4 | 4.2 | 67% | 12% | 89.4 | 41 | 20 | 39 | 26% | 73% | 13% | 15 | 86 | 33% | 0% | 0 | 0.82 | 10.7 | 138 | 159 | $25 |
| **19** | **Proj** | **11** | **0** | **131** | **149** | **3.75** | **3.42** | **1.14** | **662** | **718** | **644** | **16.8** | **3.1** | **10.3** | **3.3** | **63%** | **11%** | **89.3** | **39** | **19** | **42** | **29%** | **71%** | **12%** | **21** | | | | | | **13.4** | **118** | **136** | **$12** |

## Hill,Tim

| Age: 29 | Th: L | Role: RP | Health | A | LIMA Plan | C |
|---|---|---|---|---|---|---|
| Ht: 6' 2" | Wt: 200 | Type: Pwr xGB | PT/Exp | D | Rand Var | +4 |
| | | | Consist | C | MM | 4210 |

Jump to majors went well, as he flashed steady skills despite ERA volatility. Really took to LOOGY role with aplomb (46 IP in 70 games), holding lefty hitters to paltry .230/.288/.284 slash. But as .774 OPS vR shows, didn't fare as well against starboard-siders. That doesn't bode well for saves upside.

| Yr | Tm | W | Sv | IP | K | ERA | xERA | WHIP | oOPS | vL | vR | BF/G | Ctl | Dom | Cmd | FpK | SwK | Vel | G | L | F | H% | S% | hr/f | GS | APC | DOM% | DIS% | Sv% | LI | RAR | BPV | BPX | R$ |
|---|---|---|---|---|---|---|---|---|---|---|---|---|---|---|---|---|---|---|---|---|---|---|---|---|---|---|---|---|---|---|---|---|---|---|
| 14 | | | | | | | | | | | | | | | | | | | | | | | | | | | | | | | | | | |
| 15 | | | | | | | | | | | | | | | | | | | | | | | | | | | | | | | | | | |
| 16 | aa | 2 | 1 | 45 | 37 | 4.67 | 6.12 | 1.68 | | | | 6.5 | 4.0 | 7.5 | 1.9 | | | | | | | 35% | 77% | | | | | | | | -2.7 | 32 | 38 | -$5 |
| 17 | aa | 1 | 4 | 69 | 57 | 6.17 | 5.90 | 1.78 | | | | 8.8 | 2.9 | 7.4 | 2.6 | | | | | | | 42% | 63% | | | | | | | | -15.4 | 75 | 91 | -$10 |
| 18 | KC | 1 | 2 | 46 | 42 | 4.53 | 3.38 | 1.31 | 691 | 571 | 774 | 2.8 | 2.8 | 8.3 | 3.0 | 66% | 9% | 91.0 | 62 | 19 | 19 | 33% | 66% | 15% | 0 | 11 | | | 50 | 1.16 | -2.2 | 114 | 132 | -$3 |
| 1st Half | | 1 | 1 | 24 | 24 | 5.70 | 3.51 | 1.44 | 748 | 669 | 791 | 3.1 | 3.4 | 9.1 | 2.7 | 72% | 10% | 91.4 | 60 | 18 | 22 | 35% | 59% | 13% | 0 | 12 | | | 50 | 1.00 | -4.5 | 110 | 127 | -$6 |
| 2nd Half | | 0 | 1 | 22 | 18 | 3.27 | 3.24 | 1.18 | 627 | 492 | 748 | 2.6 | 2.0 | 7.4 | 3.6 | 59% | 7% | 90.5 | 63 | 21 | 16 | 30% | 75% | 18% | 0 | 10 | | | 50 | 1.32 | 2.4 | 119 | 136 | $1 |
| **19** | **Proj** | **1** | **2** | **58** | **50** | **3.57** | **3.27** | **1.31** | **673** | **552** | **763** | **3.9** | **2.9** | **7.8** | **2.7** | **64%** | **9%** | **90.9** | **62** | **19** | **19** | **32%** | **74%** | **15%** | **0** | | | | | | **5.4** | **101** | **116** | **-$1** |

ROD TRUESDELL

## Hirano,Yoshihisa

| | | | | | | | | | |
|---|---|---|---|---|---|---|---|---|---|
| Age: | 35 | Th: | R | Role | RP | Health | A | LIMA Plan | B |
| Ht: | 6' 1" | Wt: | 185 | Type | Pwr | PT/Exp | B | Rand Var | -5 |
| | | | | | | Consist | C | MM | 3210 |

Skills about as expected in 34-year-old's "rookie" season, if not a bit better. But they weren't THAT good. A silly first-half strand rate artificially suppressed ERA; expect a spike to xERA levels. Keeps ball on the ground, but Cmd is only middling. And certainly don't expect many saves.

| Yr | Tm | W | Sv | IP | K | ERA | xERA | WHIP | oOPS | vL | vR | BF/G | Ctl | Dom | Cmd | FpK | SwK | Vel | G | L | F | H% | S% | hr/f | GS | APC | DOM% | DIS% | Sv% | LI | RAR | BPV | BPX | R$ |
|---|---|---|---|---|---|---|---|---|---|---|---|---|---|---|---|---|---|---|---|---|---|---|---|---|---|---|---|---|---|---|---|---|---|---|
| 14 | for | 1 | 40 | 60 | 66 | 4.26 | 4.02 | 1.19 | | | | 3.9 | 2.4 | 9.9 | 4.1 | | | | | | | 31% | 70% | | | | | | | | -3.9 | 107 | 127 | $14 |
| 15 | for | 13 | 0 | 145 | 102 | 2.39 | 2.54 | 0.99 | | | | 26.3 | 1.8 | 6.3 | 3.6 | | | | | | | 25% | 81% | | | | | | | | 28.1 | 99 | 118 | $22 |
| 16 | for | 4 | 0 | 92 | 80 | 3.05 | 4.57 | 1.29 | | | | 26.9 | 2.8 | 7.8 | 2.8 | | | | | | | 29% | 86% | | | | | | | | 12.9 | 60 | 71 | $4 |
| 17 | for | 14 | 0 | 188 | 177 | 2.79 | 3.09 | 1.08 | | | | 27.1 | 1.4 | 8.5 | 6.2 | | | | | | | 31% | 77% | | | | | | | | 36.3 | 163 | 196 | $27 |
| 18 | ARI | 4 | 3 | 66 | 59 | 2.44 | 3.81 | 1.09 | 615 | 603 | 624 | 3.5 | 3.1 | 8.0 | 2.6 | 61% | 13% | 91.4 | 50 | 16 | 34 | 25% | 82% | 10% | 0 | 15 | | | 43 | 1.44 | 14.0 | 88 | 101 | $7 |
| 1st Half | | 2 | 0 | 37 | 34 | 1.23 | 3.41 | 0.95 | 521 | 568 | 489 | 3.5 | 3.2 | 8.3 | 2.6 | 55% | 13% | 91.6 | 52 | 18 | 30 | 22% | 91% | 7% | 0 | 15 | | | 0 | 1.25 | 13.2 | 94 | 108 | $10 |
| 2nd Half | | 2 | 3 | 30 | 25 | 3.94 | 4.30 | 1.25 | 720 | 645 | 766 | 3.5 | 3.0 | 7.6 | 2.5 | 67% | 13% | 91.2 | 48 | 14 | 38 | 28% | 73% | 12% | 0 | 14 | | | 50 | 1.65 | 0.8 | 81 | 93 | $3 |
| 19 | Proj | 4 | 4 | 58 | 52 | 3.54 | 3.59 | 1.17 | 700 | 664 | 724 | 5.8 | 2.5 | 8.0 | 3.2 | 62% | 13% | 91.4 | 50 | 15 | 35 | 29% | 74% | 12% | 0 | | | | | | 4.4 | 104 | 120 | $3 |

## Holder,Jonathan

| | | | | | | | | | |
|---|---|---|---|---|---|---|---|---|---|
| Age: | 26 | Th: | R | Role | RP | Health | A | LIMA Plan | B+ |
| Ht: | 6' 2" | Wt: | 235 | Type | Pwr xFB | PT/Exp | D | Rand Var | -3 |
| | | | | | | Consist | D | MM | 1310 |

Extreme flyballer's lucky first-half hit rate, plus a rather fortunate hr/f (especially given his home park), helped hold down the ERA early. When H% regressed—not to mention a nasty Cmd dip—we saw what happened. FpK shows the Cmd should be okay, but if that hr/f normalizes... DN: 4.50 ERA

| Yr | Tm | W | Sv | IP | K | ERA | xERA | WHIP | oOPS | vL | vR | BF/G | Ctl | Dom | Cmd | FpK | SwK | Vel | G | L | F | H% | S% | hr/f | GS | APC | DOM% | DIS% | Sv% | LI | RAR | BPV | BPX | R$ |
|---|---|---|---|---|---|---|---|---|---|---|---|---|---|---|---|---|---|---|---|---|---|---|---|---|---|---|---|---|---|---|---|---|---|---|
| 14 | | | | | | | | | | | | | | | | | | | | | | | | | | | | | | | | | | |
| 15 | | | | | | | | | | | | | | | | | | | | | | | | | | | | | | | | | | |
| 16 | NYY * | 5 | 16 | 70 | 86 | 2.80 | 1.92 | 0.88 | 753 | 411 | 851 | 5.4 | 1.5 | 11.1 | 7.4 | 64% | 11% | 93.0 | 33 | 7 | 59 | 29% | 71% | 6% | 0 | 18 | | | 94 | 0.88 | 12.0 | 216 | 257 | $16 |
| 17 | NYY * | 1 | 1 | 55 | 58 | 3.45 | 4.91 | 1.46 | 770 | 967 | 709 | 4.8 | 2.7 | 9.4 | 3.4 | 67% | 13% | 92.7 | 42 | 18 | 40 | 37% | 80% | 11% | 0 | 18 | | | 25 | 0.71 | 6.2 | 94 | 112 | -$1 |
| 18 | NYY | 1 | 0 | 66 | 60 | 3.14 | 4.60 | 1.09 | 589 | 568 | 608 | 4.5 | 2.6 | 8.2 | 3.2 | 64% | 11% | 92.7 | 29 | 20 | 51 | 28% | 72% | 4% | 1 | 17 | 0% | 0% | 0 | 0.90 | 8.3 | 84 | 97 | $2 |
| 1st Half | | 1 | 0 | 31 | 30 | 2.01 | 3.80 | 0.73 | 462 | 382 | 524 | 4.4 | 1.1 | 8.6 | 7.5 | 64% | 13% | 92.7 | 33 | 16 | 51 | 24% | 73% | 2% | 0 | 17 | | | 0 | 0.86 | 8.3 | 135 | 155 | $8 |
| 2nd Half | | 0 | 0 | 35 | 30 | 4.15 | 5.39 | 1.41 | 690 | 696 | 685 | 4.6 | 3.9 | 7.8 | 2.0 | 64% | 10% | 92.7 | 26 | 24 | 50 | 31% | 72% | 6% | 1 | 17 | 0% | 0% | 0 | 0.93 | 0.0 | 39 | 45 | -$2 |
| 19 | Proj | 2 | 2 | 65 | 62 | 3.82 | 4.04 | 1.25 | 710 | 728 | 699 | 4.7 | 2.9 | 8.6 | 3.0 | 65% | 12% | 92.7 | 34 | 20 | 46 | 30% | 74% | 11% | 0 | | | | | | 2.6 | 90 | 103 | $1 |

## Holland,Derek

| | | | | | | | | | |
|---|---|---|---|---|---|---|---|---|---|
| Age: | 32 | Th: | L | Role | SP | Health | F | LIMA Plan | B |
| Ht: | 6' 2" | Wt: | 213 | Type | Pwr | PT/Exp | B | Rand Var | 0 |
| | | | | | | Consist | C | MM | 1203 |

Surprising bounce-back season. Dominated lefties as in salad days, and righties didn't kill him, either. In fact, you don't have to squint hard for this to look a lot like pre-2014, pre-knee-injury skills—including best K rate of career. A regression seems most likely, but with health, he could repeat this.

| Yr | Tm | W | Sv | IP | K | ERA | xERA | WHIP | oOPS | vL | vR | BF/G | Ctl | Dom | Cmd | FpK | SwK | Vel | G | L | F | H% | S% | hr/f | GS | APC | DOM% | DIS% | Sv% | LI | RAR | BPV | BPX | R$ |
|---|---|---|---|---|---|---|---|---|---|---|---|---|---|---|---|---|---|---|---|---|---|---|---|---|---|---|---|---|---|---|---|---|---|---|
| 14 | TEX * | 4 | 0 | 57 | 45 | 2.90 | 4.38 | 1.37 | 601 | 618 | 596 | 20.0 | 2.5 | 7.1 | 2.8 | 66% | 10% | 92.3 | 41 | 17 | 41 | 33% | 82% | 0% | 5 | 95 | 80% | 0% | 0 | 0.66 | 5.9 | 74 | 89 | $1 |
| 15 | TEX | 4 | 0 | 59 | 41 | 4.91 | 4.25 | 1.30 | 828 | 740 | 848 | 24.5 | 2.6 | 6.3 | 2.4 | 63% | 7% | 92.9 | 42 | 23 | 35 | 28% | 68% | 17% | 10 | 91 | 20% | 50% | | | -6.9 | 63 | 75 | -$3 |
| 16 | TEX | 7 | 0 | 107 | 67 | 4.95 | 5.17 | 1.41 | 770 | 578 | 812 | 21.0 | 2.9 | 5.6 | 1.9 | 62% | 8% | 91.7 | 38 | 22 | 40 | 30% | 68% | 11% | 20 | 83 | 15% | 50% | 0 | 0.74 | -10.0 | 38 | 45 | -$3 |
| 17 | CHW | 7 | 0 | 135 | 104 | 6.20 | 5.84 | 1.71 | 918 | 719 | 974 | 21.6 | 5.0 | 6.9 | 1.4 | 63% | 7% | 91.1 | 38 | 22 | 40 | 31% | 69% | 18% | 26 | 85 | 15% | 54% | 0 | 0.69 | -30.7 | 6 | 7 | -$15 |
| 18 | SF | 7 | 0 | 171 | 169 | 3.57 | 4.17 | 1.29 | 718 | 440 | 798 | 20.2 | 3.5 | 8.9 | 2.5 | 63% | 11% | 91.6 | 40 | 24 | 36 | 30% | 76% | 11% | 30 | 81 | 27% | 23% | 0 | 0.71 | 12.2 | 83 | 95 | $8 |
| 1st Half | | 5 | 0 | 85 | 79 | 4.24 | 4.47 | 1.31 | 759 | 386 | 853 | 22.4 | 3.5 | 8.4 | 2.4 | 60% | 10% | 91.4 | 38 | 21 | 42 | 29% | 72% | 12% | 16 | 91 | 25% | 31% | | | -0.9 | 72 | 83 | $4 |
| 2nd Half | | 2 | 0 | 86 | 90 | 2.92 | 3.87 | 1.27 | 678 | 483 | 740 | 18.5 | 3.5 | 9.4 | 2.6 | 65% | 11% | 91.7 | 42 | 28 | 30 | 31% | 80% | 10% | 14 | 73 | 29% | 14% | 0 | 0.68 | 13.1 | 93 | 107 | $12 |
| 19 | Proj | 8 | 0 | 174 | 154 | 3.99 | 4.22 | 1.38 | 771 | 554 | 831 | 22.7 | 3.6 | 8.0 | 2.2 | 63% | 9% | 91.6 | 39 | 23 | 37 | 30% | 76% | 13% | 30 | | | | | | 3.5 | 64 | 73 | $4 |

## Holland,Greg

| | | | | | | | | | |
|---|---|---|---|---|---|---|---|---|---|
| Age: | 33 | Th: | R | Role | RP | Health | C | LIMA Plan | C |
| Ht: | 5' 10" | Wt: | 205 | Type | Pwr | PT/Exp | C | Rand Var | -2 |
| | | | | | | Consist | C | MM | 2410 |

Roller-coaster year for late-spring signing by STL. Miserable out of the gate, got hurt, blew up again, got cut. Then WAS picked him up, and he put up a sub-1.00 ERA down the stretch. But FpK shows even that was a tightrope every time out. Hot streaks aside, hasn't been consistently good since 2014.

| Yr | Tm | W | Sv | IP | K | ERA | xERA | WHIP | oOPS | vL | vR | BF/G | Ctl | Dom | Cmd | FpK | SwK | Vel | G | L | F | H% | S% | hr/f | GS | APC | DOM% | DIS% | Sv% | LI | RAR | BPV | BPX | R$ |
|---|---|---|---|---|---|---|---|---|---|---|---|---|---|---|---|---|---|---|---|---|---|---|---|---|---|---|---|---|---|---|---|---|---|---|
| 14 | KC | 1 | 46 | 62 | 90 | 1.44 | 2.29 | 0.91 | 472 | 494 | 444 | 3.7 | 2.9 | 13.0 | 4.5 | 57% | 15% | 95.8 | 48 | 17 | 35 | 28% | 87% | 7% | 0 | 15 | | | 96 | 1.21 | 17.7 | 182 | 217 | $26 |
| 15 | KC | 3 | 32 | 45 | 49 | 3.83 | 3.88 | 1.46 | 692 | 777 | 615 | 4.0 | 5.2 | 9.9 | 1.9 | 63% | 15% | 93.6 | 49 | 22 | 29 | 32% | 73% | 6% | 0 | 15 | | | 86 | 1.23 | 0.7 | 63 | 75 | $11 |
| 16 | | | | | | | | | | | | | | | | | | | | | | | | | | | | | | | | | | |
| 17 | COL | 3 | 41 | 57 | 70 | 3.61 | 3.94 | 1.15 | 623 | 533 | 721 | 3.9 | 4.1 | 11.0 | 2.7 | 61% | 16% | 93.5 | 42 | 13 | 45 | 26% | 73% | 11% | 0 | 14 | | | 91 | 1.33 | 5.3 | 108 | 129 | $20 |
| 18 | 2 NL | 2 | 3 | 46 | 47 | 4.66 | 5.06 | 1.62 | 697 | 656 | 728 | 3.8 | 6.2 | 9.1 | 1.5 | 50% | 14% | 93.0 | 40 | 25 | 35 | 33% | 70% | 4% | 0 | 15 | | | 50 | 0.84 | -2.9 | 15 | 17 | -$5 |
| 1st Half | | 0 | 0 | 18 | 17 | 7.00 | 6.27 | 2.06 | 851 | 618 | 1083 | 4.0 | 7.5 | 8.5 | 1.1 | 58% | 12% | 93.0 | 36 | 29 | 34 | 38% | 64% | 5% | 0 | 15 | | | 0 | 0.77 | -6.3 | -35 | -41 | -$17 |
| 2nd Half | | 2 | 3 | 28 | 30 | 3.18 | 4.35 | 1.34 | 584 | 689 | 507 | 3.7 | 5.4 | 9.5 | 1.8 | 43% | 15% | 93.0 | 43 | 22 | 35 | 29% | 76% | 4% | 0 | 14 | | | 75 | 0.90 | 3.4 | 47 | 54 | $2 |
| 19 | Proj | 2 | 2 | 51 | 57 | 3.97 | 4.02 | 1.41 | 660 | 625 | 692 | 3.7 | 5.2 | 10.1 | 1.9 | 55% | 15% | 93.5 | 43 | 21 | 36 | 31% | 72% | 7% | 0 | | | | | | 0.9 | 61 | 71 | -$1 |

## Honeywell,Brent

| | | | | | | | | | |
|---|---|---|---|---|---|---|---|---|---|
| Age: | 24 | Th: | R | Role | SP | Health | F | LIMA Plan | A |
| Ht: | 6' 2" | Wt: | 180 | Type | Pwr | PT/Exp | F | Rand Var | 0 |
| | | | | | | Consist | C | MM | 3301 |

Top prospect underwent Tommy John surgery in February. Before his injury, he was boasting among the best skills in the high minors. Certainly, he'll need some low-pressure time on the farm to prove he's healthy. Don't count on much in 2019, but definitely hang onto him in keeper leagues.

| Yr | Tm | W | Sv | IP | K | ERA | xERA | WHIP | oOPS | vL | vR | BF/G | Ctl | Dom | Cmd | FpK | SwK | Vel | G | L | F | H% | S% | hr/f | GS | APC | DOM% | DIS% | Sv% | LI | RAR | BPV | BPX | R$ |
|---|---|---|---|---|---|---|---|---|---|---|---|---|---|---|---|---|---|---|---|---|---|---|---|---|---|---|---|---|---|---|---|---|---|---|
| 14 | | | | | | | | | | | | | | | | | | | | | | | | | | | | | | | | | | |
| 15 | | | | | | | | | | | | | | | | | | | | | | | | | | | | | | | | | | |
| 16 | aa | 3 | 0 | 59 | 48 | 2.67 | 3.33 | 1.20 | | | | 23.8 | 2.1 | 7.3 | 3.4 | | | | | | | 31% | 80% | | | | | | | | 11.1 | 101 | 120 | $3 |
| 17 | a/a | 13 | 0 | 137 | 156 | 4.35 | 4.53 | 1.40 | | | | 22.2 | 2.3 | 10.3 | 4.4 | | | | | | | 38% | 70% | | | | | | | | 0.1 | 125 | 150 | $6 |
| 18 | | | | | | | | | | | | | | | | | | | | | | | | | | | | | | | | | | |
| 1st Half | | | | | | | | | | | | | | | | | | | | | | | | | | | | | | | | | | |
| 2nd Half | | | | | | | | | | | | | | | | | | | | | | | | | | | | | | | | | | |
| 19 | Proj | 7 | 0 | 87 | 85 | 3.70 | 3.55 | 1.25 | | | | 27.7 | 2.5 | 8.8 | 3.5 | 61% | 10% | | 45 | 20 | 35 | 32% | 73% | 11% | 13 | | | | | | 6.2 | 114 | 131 | $4 |

## Hudson,Dakota

| | | | | | | | | | |
|---|---|---|---|---|---|---|---|---|---|
| Age: | 24 | Th: | R | Role | RP | Health | A | LIMA Plan | D+ |
| Ht: | 6' 5" | Wt: | 215 | Type | xGB | PT/Exp | D | Rand Var | -4 |
| | | | | | | Consist | B | MM | 1001 |

4-1, 2.63 ERA in 27 IP at STL. Sparkling ERA in majors not supported by skills. Power sinker/curve combo gets plenty of GB, but poor 1.1 Cmd in MLB shows he still needs work. Owns an intriguing profile, but until he can command the plate, best leave him to develop on someone else's roster.

| Yr | Tm | W | Sv | IP | K | ERA | xERA | WHIP | oOPS | vL | vR | BF/G | Ctl | Dom | Cmd | FpK | SwK | Vel | G | L | F | H% | S% | hr/f | GS | APC | DOM% | DIS% | Sv% | LI | RAR | BPV | BPX | R$ |
|---|---|---|---|---|---|---|---|---|---|---|---|---|---|---|---|---|---|---|---|---|---|---|---|---|---|---|---|---|---|---|---|---|---|---|
| 14 | | | | | | | | | | | | | | | | | | | | | | | | | | | | | | | | | | |
| 15 | | | | | | | | | | | | | | | | | | | | | | | | | | | | | | | | | | |
| 16 | | | | | | | | | | | | | | | | | | | | | | | | | | | | | | | | | | |
| 17 | a/a | 10 | 0 | 153 | 80 | 3.63 | 4.18 | 1.43 | | | | 25.9 | 2.9 | 4.7 | 1.6 | | | | | | | 32% | 74% | | | | | | | | 13.6 | 48 | 58 | $4 |
| 18 | STL * | 17 | 0 | 141 | 90 | 2.75 | 3.45 | 1.38 | 559 | 759 | 406 | 13.1 | 3.5 | 5.7 | 1.6 | 59% | 10% | 96.0 | 61 | 20 | 19 | 31% | 78% | 0% | 0 | 17 | | | 0 | 1.35 | 24.3 | 70 | 81 | $12 |
| 1st Half | | 11 | 0 | 95 | 58 | 2.34 | 3.69 | 1.40 | | | | 26.7 | 3.1 | 5.5 | 1.8 | | | | | | | 32% | 82% | 0% | 0 | | | | | | 21.2 | 68 | 78 | $17 |
| 2nd Half | | 6 | 0 | 45 | 32 | 3.59 | 2.94 | 1.34 | 559 | 759 | 406 | 6.3 | 4.3 | 6.3 | 1.5 | 59% | 10% | 96.0 | 61 | 20 | 19 | 29% | 70% | 0% | 0 | 17 | | | 0 | 1.35 | 3.1 | 77 | 88 | $3 |
| 19 | Proj | 4 | 0 | 73 | 44 | 3.92 | 4.09 | 1.39 | 640 | 878 | 465 | 12.5 | 3.4 | 5.5 | 1.6 | 59% | 10% | 96.0 | 61 | 20 | 19 | 31% | 70% | 3% | 6 | | | | | | 0.4 | 45 | 51 | -$2 |

## Hughes,Jared

| | | | | | | | | | |
|---|---|---|---|---|---|---|---|---|---|
| Age: | 33 | Th: | R | Role | RP | Health | B | LIMA Plan | C+ |
| Ht: | 6' 7" | Wt: | 240 | Type | xGB | PT/Exp | C | Rand Var | -5 |
| | | | | | | Consist | B | MM | 3010 |

PRO: Posted best skills of career, as taking a tad off to throw more strikes worked wonders. CON: Unless pact with a malevolent supreme being truly is involved, the ERA/xERA gap will close—someday. Despite skills gains, the sub-2.00 ERA and handful of saves means he'll probably still be overvalued.

| Yr | Tm | W | Sv | IP | K | ERA | xERA | WHIP | oOPS | vL | vR | BF/G | Ctl | Dom | Cmd | FpK | SwK | Vel | G | L | F | H% | S% | hr/f | GS | APC | DOM% | DIS% | Sv% | LI | RAR | BPV | BPX | R$ |
|---|---|---|---|---|---|---|---|---|---|---|---|---|---|---|---|---|---|---|---|---|---|---|---|---|---|---|---|---|---|---|---|---|---|---|
| 14 | PIT | 7 | 0 | 64 | 36 | 1.96 | 3.34 | 1.09 | 609 | 592 | 622 | 4.1 | 2.7 | 5.0 | 1.9 | 60% | 11% | 92.4 | 65 | 19 | 17 | 24% | 85% | 13% | 0 | 14 | | | 0 | 1.09 | 14.1 | 62 | 74 | $7 |
| 15 | PIT | 3 | 0 | 67 | 36 | 2.28 | 3.86 | 1.33 | 720 | 684 | 741 | 3.7 | 2.6 | 4.8 | 1.9 | 61% | 10% | 93.1 | 64 | 18 | 19 | 30% | 84% | 8% | 0 | 13 | | | 0 | 1.14 | 13.9 | 60 | 72 | $2 |
| 16 | PIT | 1 | 1 | 59 | 34 | 3.03 | 4.54 | 1.42 | 794 | 849 | 751 | 3.8 | 3.3 | 5.2 | 1.5 | 60% | 10% | 93.0 | 58 | 16 | 26 | 30% | 82% | 12% | 0 | 14 | | | 33 | 0.72 | 8.5 | 39 | 46 | -$1 |
| 17 | MIL | 5 | 1 | 60 | 48 | 3.02 | 3.63 | 1.22 | 723 | 912 | 628 | 3.6 | 3.6 | 7.2 | 2.0 | 57% | 12% | 93.5 | 62 | 19 | 19 | 27% | 77% | 13% | 0 | 14 | | | 25 | 0.92 | 9.9 | 73 | 87 | $4 |
| 18 | CIN | 4 | 7 | 79 | 59 | 1.94 | 3.13 | 1.02 | 566 | 561 | 569 | 4.1 | 2.6 | 6.8 | 2.6 | 66% | 12% | 91.8 | 65 | 17 | 18 | 25% | 83% | 11% | 0 | 16 | | | 64 | 1.30 | 21.4 | 93 | 108 | $12 |
| 1st Half | | 2 | 5 | 43 | 30 | 1.27 | 3.23 | 1.03 | 549 | 471 | 605 | 4.6 | 2.3 | 6.3 | 2.7 | 64% | 13% | 92.1 | 65 | 16 | 19 | 26% | 88% | 5% | 0 | 17 | | | 83 | 1.34 | 15.2 | 94 | 108 | $15 |
| 2nd Half | | 2 | 2 | 36 | 29 | 2.75 | 3.02 | 1.00 | 587 | 686 | 529 | 3.7 | 3.0 | 7.3 | 2.4 | 69% | 12% | 91.5 | 66 | 18 | 16 | 22% | 76% | 20% | 0 | 14 | | | 40 | 1.27 | 6.2 | 93 | 107 | $10 |
| 19 | Proj | 4 | 5 | 65 | 47 | 3.46 | 3.51 | 1.24 | 705 | 766 | 667 | 4.0 | 3.0 | 6.5 | 2.2 | 63% | 12% | 92.4 | 63 | 17 | 19 | 28% | 73% | 12% | 0 | | | | | | 3.7 | 77 | 88 | $3 |

ROD TRUESDELL

## Hunter,Tommy

Age: 32 | Th: R | Role: RP | Ht: 6' 3" | Wt: 250 | Type:
Health: D | PT/Exp: D | Consist: B
LIMA Plan: A | Rand Var: 0 | MM: 3110

It figures with relievers: Best two skills months (an abbreviated April, full June) were his worst ERA months. So let's cut past the noise. Dom drop didn't correspond with meaningful SwK or FB Vel drops; at the same time, 2017's K/9 looks like the outlier. Another year similar to 2018 seems likely.

| Yr Tm | W | Sv | IP | K | ERA | xERA | WHIP | oOPS | vL | vR | BF/G | Ctl | Dom | Cmd | FpK | SwK | Vel | G | L | F | H% | S% | hr/f | GS | APC | DOM% | DIS% | Sv% | LI | RAR | BPV | BPX | R$ |
|---|---|---|---|---|---|---|---|---|---|---|---|---|---|---|---|---|---|---|---|---|---|---|---|---|---|---|---|---|---|---|---|---|---|
| 14 BAL | 3 | 11 | 61 | 45 | 2.97 | 3.27 | 1.10 | 643 | 639 | 647 | 4.0 | 1.8 | 6.7 | 3.8 | 65% | 8% | 96.1 | 51 | 24 | 25 | 29% | 75% | 9% | 0 | 14 | | | 65 | 1.16 | 5.8 | 101 | 120 | $7 |
| 15 2 TM | 4 | 1 | 60 | 47 | 4.18 | 3.93 | 1.24 | 711 | 754 | 674 | 4.3 | 2.1 | 7.0 | 3.4 | 66% | 11% | 96.2 | 45 | 21 | 35 | 30% | 69% | 11% | 0 | 15 | | | 50 | 0.82 | -1.6 | 93 | 111 | -$1 |
| 16 2 AL * | 4 | 1 | 49 | 30 | 3.67 | 4.23 | 1.34 | 678 | 715 | 656 | 4.3 | 1.9 | 5.4 | 2.8 | 65% | 10% | 94.5 | 50 | 25 | 26 | 32% | 74% | 4% | 0 | 15 | | | 33 | 0.77 | 3.1 | 67 | 80 | $0 |
| 17 TAM | 3 | 1 | 59 | 64 | 2.61 | 3.33 | 0.97 | 588 | 501 | 649 | 3.7 | 2.1 | 9.8 | 4.6 | 65% | 12% | 96.3 | 44 | 21 | 35 | 27% | 78% | 12% | 0 | 14 | | | 100 | 1.21 | 12.7 | 141 | 169 | $7 |
| 18 PHI | 5 | 4 | 64 | 51 | 3.80 | 3.98 | 1.25 | 745 | 739 | 749 | 4.2 | 2.1 | 7.2 | 3.4 | 64% | 11% | 95.9 | 52 | 17 | 31 | 31% | 72% | 10% | 0 | 15 | | | 67 | 1.28 | 2.8 | 102 | 118 | $2 |
| 1st Half | 2 | 1 | 25 | 25 | 5.04 | 3.32 | 1.48 | 807 | 681 | 936 | 3.9 | 1.4 | 9.0 | 6.3 | 57% | 11% | 95.7 | 52 | 27 | 21 | 41% | 66% | 12% | 0 | 14 | | | 50 | 1.18 | -2.7 | 154 | 176 | -$7 |
| 2nd Half | 3 | 3 | 39 | 26 | 3.00 | 4.41 | 1.10 | 699 | 785 | 615 | 4.4 | 2.5 | 6.0 | 2.4 | 69% | 11% | 96.0 | 52 | 10 | 38 | 25% | 77% | 9% | 0 | 15 | | | 75 | 1.36 | 5.5 | 69 | 79 | $8 |
| 19 Proj | 5 | 9 | 65 | 55 | 3.47 | 3.55 | 1.19 | 704 | 691 | 715 | 4.0 | 2.1 | 7.6 | 3.6 | 65% | 11% | 95.8 | 49 | 20 | 31 | 30% | 73% | 10% | 0 | | | | | | 5.5 | 107 | 123 | $6 |

## Iglesias,Raisel

Age: 29 | Th: R | Role: RP | Ht: 6' 2" | Wt: 188 | Type: Pwr
Health: D | PT/Exp: B | Consist: A
LIMA Plan: C+ | Rand Var: -5 | MM: 4431

Skills about as consistent as you'll see, which SHOULD make him easy to forecast. But that never seems to be the case for relievers, even when peripherals are steady. This one's outpitched his skills for three years running, so ERA appears (over)due for a bit of a jump. But that shouldn't affect save totals, which is why you buy him.

| Yr Tm | W | Sv | IP | K | ERA | xERA | WHIP | oOPS | vL | vR | BF/G | Ctl | Dom | Cmd | FpK | SwK | Vel | G | L | F | H% | S% | hr/f | GS | APC | DOM% | DIS% | Sv% | LI | RAR | BPV | BPX | R$ |
|---|---|---|---|---|---|---|---|---|---|---|---|---|---|---|---|---|---|---|---|---|---|---|---|---|---|---|---|---|---|---|---|---|---|
| 14 | | | | | | | | | | | | | | | | | | | | | | | | | | | | | | | | | |
| 15 CIN * | 4 | 0 | 124 | 122 | 4.26 | 3.75 | 1.21 | 682 | 753 | 618 | 20.9 | 2.7 | 8.8 | 3.3 | 62% | 13% | 91.7 | 47 | 21 | 32 | 30% | 68% | 14% | 16 | 87 | 38% | 25% | 0 | 0.72 | -4.6 | 93 | 110 | $2 |
| 16 CIN | 3 | 6 | 78 | 83 | 2.53 | 3.80 | 1.14 | 623 | 777 | 483 | 8.8 | 3.0 | 9.5 | 3.2 | 54% | 12% | 93.0 | 41 | 21 | 38 | 29% | 82% | 9% | 5 | 34 | 20% | 20% | 75 | 1.01 | 16.1 | 110 | 131 | $9 |
| 17 CIN | 3 | 28 | 76 | 92 | 2.49 | 3.38 | 1.11 | 576 | 709 | 452 | 4.9 | 3.2 | 10.9 | 3.4 | 65% | 15% | 96.4 | 42 | 25 | 32 | 30% | 80% | 8% | 0 | 20 | | | 93 | 0.99 | 17.5 | 130 | 156 | $20 |
| 18 CIN | 2 | 30 | 72 | 80 | 2.38 | 3.59 | 1.07 | 644 | 663 | 625 | 4.4 | 3.1 | 10.0 | 3.2 | 59% | 16% | 95.2 | 38 | 26 | 35 | 25% | 89% | 19% | 0 | 17 | | | 88 | 1.02 | 15.8 | 112 | 129 | $19 |
| 1st Half | 1 | 15 | 35 | 38 | 2.08 | 3.55 | 1.04 | 597 | 797 | 396 | 4.3 | 3.1 | 9.9 | 3.2 | 59% | 15% | 95.1 | 38 | 26 | 36 | 25% | 88% | 13% | 0 | 17 | | | 88 | 0.93 | 8.9 | 109 | 125 | $19 |
| 2nd Half | 1 | 15 | 37 | 42 | 2.65 | 3.63 | 1.10 | 686 | 543 | 830 | 4.6 | 3.1 | 10.1 | 3.2 | 60% | 16% | 95.3 | 39 | 27 | 34 | 24% | 91% | 24% | 0 | 18 | | | 88 | 1.10 | 6.9 | 115 | 132 | $19 |
| 19 Proj | 2 | 29 | 73 | 81 | 2.64 | 3.27 | 1.10 | 636 | 695 | 580 | 5.2 | 3.1 | 10.0 | 3.3 | 60% | 15% | 94.8 | 41 | 25 | 35 | 27% | 83% | 15% | 0 | | | | | | 13.5 | 116 | 134 | $18 |

## Jackson,Edwin

Age: 35 | Th: R | Role: RP | Ht: 6' 2" | Wt: 215 | Type: Pwr
Health: C | PT/Exp: C | Consist: B
LIMA Plan: D+ | Rand Var: 0 | MM: 0001

6-3, 3.33 ERA in 92 IP with OAK. Savior for the A's down the stretch after languishing in WAS farm system. But that doesn't mean he's found a fountain of youth. His 4.85 xERA in the majors was right in line with recent seasons, and there's nothing new in these skills. It'll get him a new contract, though.

| Yr Tm | W | Sv | IP | K | ERA | xERA | WHIP | oOPS | vL | vR | BF/G | Ctl | Dom | Cmd | FpK | SwK | Vel | G | L | F | H% | S% | hr/f | GS | APC | DOM% | DIS% | Sv% | LI | RAR | BPV | BPX | R$ |
|---|---|---|---|---|---|---|---|---|---|---|---|---|---|---|---|---|---|---|---|---|---|---|---|---|---|---|---|---|---|---|---|---|---|
| 14 CHC | 6 | 0 | 141 | 123 | 6.33 | 4.32 | 1.64 | 869 | 930 | 816 | 22.6 | 4.0 | 7.9 | 2.0 | 55% | 11% | 92.7 | 39 | 26 | 35 | 35% | 62% | 12% | 27 | 89 | 11% | 56% | 0 | 0.77 | -45.0 | 50 | 59 | -$19 |
| 15 2 NL | 4 | 1 | 56 | 40 | 3.07 | 4.41 | 1.17 | 622 | 565 | 657 | 4.9 | 3.4 | 6.5 | 1.9 | 54% | 11% | 93.9 | 41 | 22 | 37 | 25% | 75% | 7% | 0 | 19 | | | 50 | 0.77 | 6.1 | 44 | 52 | $2 |
| 16 2 NL | 5 | 0 | 84 | 61 | 5.89 | 5.34 | 1.58 | 857 | 786 | 914 | 17.8 | 4.4 | 6.5 | 1.5 | 53% | 10% | 91.9 | 40 | 21 | 39 | 31% | 66% | 14% | 13 | 67 | 15% | 54% | 0 | 0.78 | -17.6 | 17 | 20 | -$9 |
| 17 2 TM * | 7 | 2 | 117 | 88 | 4.27 | 5.44 | 1.52 | 891 | 792 | 983 | 15.3 | 4.0 | 6.8 | 1.7 | 55% | 10% | 93.5 | 37 | 16 | 47 | 30% | 78% | 18% | 13 | 81 | 15% | 46% | 67 | 0.70 | 1.2 | 27 | 32 | -$1 |
| 18 OAK * | 10 | 0 | 164 | 113 | 3.94 | 4.26 | 1.39 | 687 | 703 | 669 | 23.0 | 3.9 | 6.2 | 1.6 | 54% | 9% | 93.2 | 36 | 24 | 40 | 29% | 74% | 11% | 17 | 87 | 24% | 24% | | | 4.2 | 46 | 53 | $2 |
| 1st Half | 5 | 0 | 85 | 58 | 4.34 | 4.60 | 1.47 | 533 | 538 | 526 | 24.2 | 3.6 | 6.2 | 1.7 | 49% | 11% | 93.1 | 22 | 25 | 53 | 31% | 72% | 12% | 2 | 83 | 50% | 0% | | | -1.9 | 49 | 56 | -$4 |
| 2nd Half | 5 | 0 | 79 | 55 | 3.52 | 5.10 | 1.31 | 709 | 728 | 687 | 22.3 | 4.2 | 6.2 | 1.5 | 55% | 9% | 93.2 | 38 | 24 | 38 | 25% | 78% | 11% | 15 | 88 | 20% | 27% | | | 6.2 | 15 | 18 | $8 |
| 19 Proj | 5 | 0 | 87 | 63 | 4.34 | 4.84 | 1.45 | 779 | 752 | 801 | 16.9 | 4.0 | 6.5 | 1.6 | 55% | 10% | 93.0 | 39 | 22 | 39 | 29% | 74% | 11% | 15 | | | | | | -2.0 | 26 | 29 | -$3 |

## Jansen,Kenley

Age: 31 | Th: R | Role: RP | Ht: 6' 5" | Wt: 275 | Type: Pwr xFB
Health: C | PT/Exp: A | Consist: B
LIMA Plan: C+ | Rand Var: -2 | MM: 5530

Slight Cmd wobble, losing some strikes and a touch off his heater. It didn't hurt in saves dept, but it's worth watching for signs of mortality. Irregular heartbeat resurfaced at altitude in COL, and he skipped a series there late, but seemed fine otherwise—and hey, maybe he'll get to avoid Coors forever!

| Yr Tm | W | Sv | IP | K | ERA | xERA | WHIP | oOPS | vL | vR | BF/G | Ctl | Dom | Cmd | FpK | SwK | Vel | G | L | F | H% | S% | hr/f | GS | APC | DOM% | DIS% | Sv% | LI | RAR | BPV | BPX | R$ |
|---|---|---|---|---|---|---|---|---|---|---|---|---|---|---|---|---|---|---|---|---|---|---|---|---|---|---|---|---|---|---|---|---|---|
| 14 LA | 2 | 44 | 65 | 101 | 2.76 | 2.43 | 1.13 | 610 | 710 | 521 | 3.9 | 2.6 | 13.9 | 5.3 | 67% | 17% | 93.7 | 35 | 28 | 37 | 38% | 78% | 9% | 0 | 16 | | | 90 | 1.27 | 7.9 | 193 | 230 | $21 |
| 15 LA | 2 | 36 | 52 | 80 | 2.41 | 2.46 | 0.78 | 513 | 566 | 459 | 3.7 | 1.4 | 13.8 | 10.0 | 70% | 18% | 92.5 | 35 | 11 | 54 | 29% | 77% | 10% | 0 | 15 | | | 95 | 1.22 | 10.0 | 223 | 266 | $22 |
| 16 LA | 3 | 47 | 69 | 104 | 1.83 | 2.60 | 0.67 | 446 | 542 | 352 | 3.5 | 1.4 | 13.6 | 9.5 | 68% | 18% | 93.6 | 30 | 15 | 55 | 26% | 76% | 6% | 0 | 14 | | | 89 | 1.21 | 19.9 | 214 | 255 | $33 |
| 17 LA | 5 | 41 | 68 | 109 | 1.32 | 2.26 | 0.75 | 476 | 640 | 315 | 4.0 | 0.9 | 14.4 | 15.6 | 73% | 19% | 93.3 | 38 | 21 | 41 | 32% | 89% | 9% | 0 | 16 | | | 98 | 1.30 | 25.6 | 250 | 300 | $34 |
| 18 LA | 1 | 38 | 72 | 82 | 3.01 | 3.62 | 0.99 | 635 | 569 | 693 | 4.2 | 2.1 | 10.3 | 4.8 | 65% | 14% | 92.3 | 35 | 21 | 44 | 25% | 81% | 16% | 0 | 17 | | | 90 | 1.15 | 10.0 | 141 | 162 | $21 |
| 1st Half | 0 | 21 | 38 | 37 | 2.37 | 3.85 | 0.92 | 519 | 563 | 475 | 4.2 | 2.1 | 8.8 | 4.1 | 65% | 13% | 92.3 | 38 | 22 | 40 | 24% | 81% | 10% | 0 | 17 | | | 91 | 1.10 | 8.4 | 116 | 134 | $24 |
| 2nd Half | 1 | 17 | 34 | 45 | 3.74 | 3.39 | 1.07 | 766 | 576 | 905 | 4.2 | 2.1 | 12.0 | 5.6 | 66% | 15% | 92.4 | 32 | 20 | 49 | 28% | 81% | 23% | 0 | 16 | | | 89 | 1.21 | 1.7 | 168 | 194 | $18 |
| 19 Proj | 2 | 36 | 65 | 90 | 2.73 | 2.66 | 0.93 | 604 | 617 | 591 | 3.8 | 1.7 | 12.4 | 7.2 | 68% | 16% | 92.8 | 35 | 20 | 46 | 30% | 79% | 14% | 0 | | | | | | 16.5 | 189 | 218 | $22 |

## Jeffress,Jeremy

Age: 31 | Th: R | Role: RP | Ht: 6' 0" | Wt: 205 | Type: Pwr xGB
Health: B | PT/Exp: B | Consist: C
LIMA Plan: D+ | Rand Var: -5 | MM: 4320

Playoff hiccups aside, career rebirth continued back where it began in MIL. No, he won't post a sub-1.50 ERA again. But xERA, Dom spikes show this was legit, thanks to heavy use of whiff-inducing curve. Still, FpK points out a Ctl-spike risk. He'll probably be fine... but consistency isn't his strong suit.

| Yr Tm | W | Sv | IP | K | ERA | xERA | WHIP | oOPS | vL | vR | BF/G | Ctl | Dom | Cmd | FpK | SwK | Vel | G | L | F | H% | S% | hr/f | GS | APC | DOM% | DIS% | Sv% | LI | RAR | BPV | BPX | R$ |
|---|---|---|---|---|---|---|---|---|---|---|---|---|---|---|---|---|---|---|---|---|---|---|---|---|---|---|---|---|---|---|---|---|---|
| 14 2 TM * | 5 | 5 | 74 | 65 | 2.33 | 3.68 | 1.44 | 709 | 967 | 509 | 5.1 | 3.7 | 7.9 | 2.1 | 60% | 7% | 96.4 | 59 | 26 | 16 | 34% | 83% | 7% | 0 | 16 | | | 63 | 0.85 | 12.9 | 90 | 107 | $4 |
| 15 MIL | 5 | 0 | 68 | 67 | 2.65 | 3.08 | 1.26 | 666 | 752 | 617 | 4.0 | 2.9 | 8.9 | 3.0 | 56% | 12% | 95.4 | 58 | 24 | 18 | 32% | 81% | 15% | 0 | 15 | | | 0 | 1.15 | 11.0 | 117 | 139 | $4 |
| 16 2 TM | 3 | 27 | 58 | 42 | 2.33 | 3.54 | 1.26 | 656 | 906 | 475 | 4.1 | 2.8 | 6.5 | 2.3 | 61% | 10% | 95.1 | 60 | 24 | 16 | 30% | 82% | 7% | 0 | 15 | | | 96 | 1.08 | 13.3 | 80 | 95 | $14 |
| 17 2 TM | 5 | 0 | 65 | 51 | 4.68 | 4.64 | 1.64 | 830 | 871 | 810 | 4.8 | 4.7 | 7.0 | 1.5 | 53% | 10% | 94.5 | 59 | 17 | 24 | 32% | 75% | 21% | 1 | 19 | 0% | 100% | 0 | 0.85 | -2.6 | 37 | 44 | -$5 |
| 18 MIL | 8 | 15 | 77 | 89 | 1.29 | 2.85 | 0.99 | 530 | 469 | 568 | 4.1 | 3.2 | 10.4 | 3.3 | 50% | 14% | 95.3 | 56 | 20 | 24 | 26% | 92% | 12% | 0 | 17 | | | 75 | 1.52 | 27.0 | 136 | 157 | $21 |
| 1st Half | 5 | 3 | 40 | 43 | 1.12 | 2.84 | 0.82 | 486 | 368 | 551 | 3.8 | 2.7 | 9.6 | 3.6 | 49% | 13% | 94.7 | 54 | 21 | 24 | 20% | 93% | 13% | 0 | 15 | | | 50 | 1.74 | 15.1 | 133 | 152 | $21 |
| 2nd Half | 3 | 12 | 36 | 46 | 1.49 | 2.84 | 1.18 | 574 | 556 | 586 | 4.5 | 3.7 | 11.4 | 3.1 | 51% | 15% | 96.0 | 59 | 18 | 23 | 32% | 90% | 10% | 0 | 18 | | | 86 | 1.25 | 11.9 | 141 | 162 | $21 |
| 19 Proj | 5 | 18 | 58 | 57 | 3.06 | 3.24 | 1.25 | 649 | 683 | 628 | 4.3 | 3.6 | 8.9 | 2.5 | 53% | 12% | 95.2 | 58 | 20 | 22 | 30% | 78% | 14% | 0 | | | | | | 6.4 | 100 | 115 | $10 |

## Jimenez,Joe

Age: 24 | Th: R | Role: RP | Ht: 6' 3" | Wt: 272 | Type: Pwr FB
Health: A | PT/Exp: D | Consist: F
LIMA Plan: A | Rand Var: 0 | MM: 2410

PRO: Hard thrower misses plenty of bats; dominated RH hitters; finished strong (8 IP, 13 K, 1 BB in Sept).
CON: Control deserted him in Jul/Aug (6.1/7.3 Ctl) just as he got shot to close; FB tilt means HR ball always a risk. Future still bright, but the late-summer issues likely nix big saves chances for now.

| Yr Tm | W | Sv | IP | K | ERA | xERA | WHIP | oOPS | vL | vR | BF/G | Ctl | Dom | Cmd | FpK | SwK | Vel | G | L | F | H% | S% | hr/f | GS | APC | DOM% | DIS% | Sv% | LI | RAR | BPV | BPX | R$ |
|---|---|---|---|---|---|---|---|---|---|---|---|---|---|---|---|---|---|---|---|---|---|---|---|---|---|---|---|---|---|---|---|---|---|
| 14 | | | | | | | | | | | | | | | | | | | | | | | | | | | | | | | | | |
| 15 | | | | | | | | | | | | | | | | | | | | | | | | | | | | | | | | | |
| 16 a/a | 3 | 20 | 36 | 42 | 2.63 | 1.57 | 0.98 | | | | 3.6 | 3.0 | 10.5 | 3.6 | | | | | | | 27% | 72% | | | | | | | | 7.0 | 147 | 175 | $11 |
| 17 DET * | 1 | 4 | 44 | 47 | 6.46 | 5.85 | 1.73 | 999 | 635 | 1234 | 4.0 | 4.5 | 9.6 | 2.2 | 62% | 13% | 95.3 | 34 | 23 | 43 | 39% | 63% | 13% | 0 | 17 | | | 67 | 0.55 | -11.4 | 64 | 77 | -$7 |
| 18 DET | 5 | 3 | 63 | 78 | 4.31 | 3.83 | 1.20 | 645 | 703 | 595 | 4.1 | 3.2 | 11.2 | 3.5 | 53% | 14% | 95.6 | 36 | 19 | 45 | 33% | 64% | 7% | 0 | 17 | | | 43 | 1.08 | -1.2 | 130 | 150 | $2 |
| 1st Half | 3 | 2 | 39 | 44 | 2.77 | 3.82 | 1.08 | 611 | 615 | 608 | 3.9 | 2.1 | 10.2 | 4.9 | 55% | 14% | 95.5 | 35 | 19 | 46 | 32% | 75% | 4% | 0 | 16 | | | 50 | 1.22 | 6.6 | 140 | 160 | $7 |
| 2nd Half | 2 | 1 | 24 | 34 | 6.85 | 3.85 | 1.39 | 697 | 810 | 567 | 4.0 | 4.9 | 12.9 | 2.6 | 50% | 14% | 95.6 | 37 | 19 | 44 | 34% | 50% | 12% | 0 | 18 | | | 33 | 0.86 | -7.9 | 114 | 131 | -$4 |
| 19 Proj | 4 | 7 | 65 | 77 | 3.93 | 3.70 | 1.28 | 672 | 750 | 598 | 3.7 | 3.6 | 10.6 | 2.9 | 52% | 14% | 95.6 | 36 | 19 | 45 | 32% | 71% | 8% | 0 | | | | | | 4.2 | 106 | 122 | $4 |

## Johnson,Brian

Age: 28 | Th: L | Role: RP | Ht: 6' 4" | Wt: 235 | Type: Pwr FB
Health: B | PT/Exp: D | Consist: C
LIMA Plan: D+ | Rand Var: 0 | MM: 0101

Soft-tossing swingman ate some much-needed innings for BOS. But that's about all he's good for: FB lean, low SwK rate, and so-so FpK make him a blowup risk every time out. Showed better skills as a reliever, and could one day convert into a useful LOOGY. But that's not valuable to you, either. Pass.

| Yr Tm | W | Sv | IP | K | ERA | xERA | WHIP | oOPS | vL | vR | BF/G | Ctl | Dom | Cmd | FpK | SwK | Vel | G | L | F | H% | S% | hr/f | GS | APC | DOM% | DIS% | Sv% | LI | RAR | BPV | BPX | R$ |
|---|---|---|---|---|---|---|---|---|---|---|---|---|---|---|---|---|---|---|---|---|---|---|---|---|---|---|---|---|---|---|---|---|---|
| 14 aa | 10 | 0 | 118 | 81 | 2.26 | 2.51 | 1.08 | | | | 23.0 | 2.6 | 6.2 | 2.4 | | | | | | | 26% | 81% | | | | | | | | 21.5 | 83 | 99 | $13 |
| 15 BOS * | 9 | 0 | 100 | 76 | 3.91 | 3.92 | 1.39 | 583 | 0 | 662 | 22.2 | 3.6 | 6.8 | 1.9 | 47% | 7% | 87.5 | 33 | 42 | 25 | 31% | 73% | 0% | 1 | 87 | 0% | 0% | | | 0.7 | 64 | 76 | $1 |
| 16 aaa | 5 | 0 | 77 | 42 | 6.87 | 7.09 | 1.93 | | | | 24.4 | 5.2 | 4.9 | 0.9 | | | | | | | 34% | 66% | | | | | | | | -25.5 | -7 | -8 | -$16 |
| 17 BOS * | 5 | 0 | 117 | 74 | 4.85 | 5.95 | 1.60 | 817 | 308 | 882 | 23.6 | 3.2 | 5.7 | 1.8 | 62% | 8% | 87.3 | 36 | 18 | 46 | 33% | 74% | 12% | 5 | 90 | 20% | 80% | | | -7.1 | 21 | 26 | -$7 |
| 18 BOS | 4 | 0 | 99 | 87 | 4.17 | 4.86 | 1.43 | 773 | 665 | 810 | 11.4 | 3.4 | 7.9 | 2.3 | 59% | 9% | 88.5 | 37 | 20 | 43 | 31% | 76% | 12% | 13 | 45 | 8% | 54% | 0 | 0.70 | -0.2 | 64 | 74 | -$3 |
| 1st Half | 1 | 0 | 40 | 35 | 4.28 | 4.36 | 1.40 | 748 | 600 | 802 | 7.5 | 2.5 | 7.9 | 3.2 | 62% | 8% | 88.5 | 41 | 22 | 37 | 34% | 73% | 11% | 2 | 29 | 0% | 100% | 0 | 0.58 | -0.6 | 94 | 108 | -$7 |
| 2nd Half | 3 | 0 | 59 | 52 | 4.10 | 5.22 | 1.45 | 789 | 712 | 814 | 17.5 | 4.1 | 7.9 | 1.9 | 57% | 9% | 88.6 | 35 | 18 | 47 | 29% | 79% | 13% | 11 | 69 | 9% | 45% | 0 | 0.88 | 0.4 | 44 | 51 | $0 |
| 19 Proj | 5 | 0 | 102 | 79 | 4.55 | 4.67 | 1.46 | 784 | 674 | 821 | 15.0 | 3.3 | 7.0 | 2.1 | 59% | 9% | 88.5 | 37 | 20 | 43 | 31% | 73% | 11% | 15 | | | | | | -5.1 | 51 | 59 | -$4 |

ROD TRUESDELL

## Jones,Nate

| Jones,Nate | | | | Health | F | LIMA Plan | C |
|---|---|---|---|---|---|---|---|
| Age: 33 | Th: R | Role | RP | PT/Exp | D | Rand Var | -4 |
| Ht: 6' 5" | Wt: 220 | Type | Pwr | Consist | B | MM | 3410 |

Struggled with control early after return from ulnar nerve surgery, then missed three more months with a pronator muscle strain. Terrific when right, but how seldom that's been—just one full season in the last five. Still owns double-digit saves upside, but health makes him a late-round dart throw.

| Yr Tm | W | Sv | IP | K | ERA | xERA | WHIP | oOPS | vL | vR | BF/G | Ctl | Dom | Cmd | FpK | SwK | Vel | G | L | F | H% | S% | hr/f | GS | APC | DOM% | DIS% | Sv% | LI | RAR | BPV | BPX | R$ |
|---|---|---|---|---|---|---|---|---|---|---|---|---|---|---|---|---|---|---|---|---|---|---|---|---|---|---|---|---|---|---|---|---|---|
| 14 CHW | 0 | 0 | 0 | 0 | 0.00 | 0.00 | 0.00 | | 3000 | 2000 | 2.5 | 0.0 | 0.0 | 0.0 | | | 95.8 | | | | 0% | 20% | 0% | 0 | 15 | | | 0 | 1.50 | 0.0 | -22 | -26 | -$5 |
| 15 CHW | 2 | 0 | 19 | 27 | 3.32 | 2.51 | 0.95 | 695 | 567 | 770 | 3.8 | 2.8 | 12.8 | 4.5 | 59% | 16% | 97.6 | 46 | 14 | 41 | 21% | 85% | 33% | 0 | 15 | | | 0 | 1.17 | 1.5 | 177 | 211 | -$1 |
| 16 CHW | 5 | 3 | 71 | 80 | 2.29 | 3.00 | 0.89 | 552 | 667 | 477 | 3.9 | 1.9 | 10.2 | 5.3 | 64% | 15% | 96.8 | 46 | 21 | 33 | 26% | 80% | 12% | 0 | 14 | | | 25 | 1.53 | 16.5 | 156 | 185 | $12 |
| 17 CHW | 1 | 0 | 12 | 15 | 2.31 | 3.25 | 1.29 | 675 | 514 | 881 | 4.5 | 4.6 | 11.6 | 2.5 | 59% | 12% | 97.2 | 54 | 19 | 27 | 31% | 86% | 14% | 0 | 18 | | | 0 | 1.12 | 2.9 | 115 | 138 | -$3 |
| 18 CHW | 2 | 5 | 30 | 32 | 3.00 | 4.59 | 1.43 | 723 | 806 | 657 | 4.2 | 4.5 | 9.6 | 2.1 | 58% | 14% | 97.2 | 40 | 21 | 40 | 31% | 85% | 12% | 0 | 16 | | | 63 | 1.06 | 4.3 | 69 | 80 | $0 |
| 1st Half | 2 | 4 | 25 | 27 | 2.55 | 4.62 | 1.38 | 677 | 798 | 589 | 4.1 | 5.1 | 9.9 | 1.9 | 54% | 15% | 97.2 | 39 | 21 | 40 | 29% | 87% | 11% | 0 | 16 | | | 57 | 1.22 | 4.9 | 56 | 65 | $1 |
| 2nd Half | 0 | 1 | 5 | 5 | 5.06 | 4.50 | 1.69 | 902 | 833 | 968 | 4.2 | 1.7 | 8.4 | 5.0 | 72% | 12% | 97.3 | 42 | 21 | 37 | 41% | 75% | 14% | 0 | 13 | | | 100 | 0.33 | -0.6 | 126 | 145 | -$7 |
| **19 Proj** | **3** | **2** | **44** | **48** | **3.07** | **3.55** | **1.18** | **631** | **750** | **548** | **3.8** | **3.8** | **10.0** | **2.6** | **58%** | **15%** | **97.0** | **42** | **21** | **37** | **27%** | **79%** | **12%** | **0** | | | | | | **5.8** | **96** | **110** | **$2** |

## Junis,Jakob

| Junis,Jakob | | | | Health | A | LIMA Plan | A |
|---|---|---|---|---|---|---|---|
| Age: 26 | Th: R | Role | SP | PT/Exp | C | Rand Var | +2 |
| Ht: 6' 2" | Wt: 225 | Type | | Consist | B | MM | 2203 |

PRO: Growing Cmd, GB rates; durability; again finished fast (135 BPV over Aug/Sept). CON: Fastball is hittable; Cmd dip vL (2.8 vL, 5.2 vR) lead to a modest split. Solid, but needs a second pitch to go with superb slider. Two-seamer has shown promise in past; if that can develop... UP: 3.50 ERA

| Yr Tm | W | Sv | IP | K | ERA | xERA | WHIP | oOPS | vL | vR | BF/G | Ctl | Dom | Cmd | FpK | SwK | Vel | G | L | F | H% | S% | hr/f | GS | APC | DOM% | DIS% | Sv% | LI | RAR | BPV | BPX | R$ |
|---|---|---|---|---|---|---|---|---|---|---|---|---|---|---|---|---|---|---|---|---|---|---|---|---|---|---|---|---|---|---|---|---|---|
| 14 | | | | | | | | | | | | | | | | | | | | | | | | | | | | | | | | | |
| 15 | | | | | | | | | | | | | | | | | | | | | | | | | | | | | | | | | |
| 16 a/a | 10 | 0 | 149 | 115 | 5.37 | 5.22 | 1.46 | | | | 23.6 | 2.2 | 6.9 | 3.2 | | | | | | | 35% | 65% | | | | | | | | -21.7 | 68 | 81 | -$6 |
| 17 KC * | 12 | 0 | 169 | 148 | 4.06 | 4.21 | 1.27 | 762 | 783 | 740 | 21.7 | 2.2 | 7.9 | 3.6 | 62% | 9% | 91.2 | 40 | 20 | 40 | 32% | 72% | 12% | 16 | 76 | 19% | 31% | 0 | 0.88 | 6.2 | 91 | 109 | $10 |
| 18 KC | 9 | 0 | 177 | 164 | 4.37 | 4.06 | 1.27 | 773 | 786 | 760 | 25.3 | 2.2 | 8.3 | 3.8 | 63% | 10% | 91.1 | 42 | 21 | 37 | 31% | 72% | 16% | 30 | 95 | 23% | 30% | | | -4.9 | 111 | 128 | $4 |
| 1st Half | 5 | 0 | 96 | 90 | 4.67 | 4.39 | 1.27 | 783 | 761 | 800 | 25.8 | 2.5 | 8.4 | 3.3 | 63% | 10% | 91.0 | 39 | 17 | 44 | 29% | 72% | 17% | 16 | 95 | 19% | 31% | | | -6.2 | 100 | 115 | $2 |
| 2nd Half | 4 | 0 | 81 | 74 | 4.02 | 3.67 | 1.28 | 762 | 810 | 699 | 24.6 | 1.8 | 8.3 | 4.6 | 63% | 10% | 91.1 | 46 | 25 | 29 | 33% | 72% | 14% | 14 | 94 | 29% | 29% | | | 1.3 | 124 | 143 | $6 |
| **19 Proj** | **10** | **0** | **174** | **154** | **4.20** | **3.82** | **1.30** | **770** | **794** | **745** | **23.1** | **2.1** | **8.0** | **3.7** | **62%** | **10%** | **91.1** | **42** | **21** | **37** | **32%** | **72%** | **13%** | **31** | | | | | | **-1.1** | **105** | **121** | **$6** |

## Karns,Nathan

| Karns,Nathan | | | | Health | F | LIMA Plan | B+ |
|---|---|---|---|---|---|---|---|
| Age: 31 | Th: R | Role | SP | PT/Exp | D | Rand Var | 0 |
| Ht: 6' 3" | Wt: 225 | Type | Pwr | Consist | B | MM | 2301 |

Thoracic outlet surgery ended 2017 early, then after a strong spring, missed entire 2018 season with elbow inflammation. Skills were ramping up before his injuries, and was a sleeper late-round target entering last year. If finally healthy, throw another dollar his way... UP: 3.50 ERA

| Yr Tm | W | Sv | IP | K | ERA | xERA | WHIP | oOPS | vL | vR | BF/G | Ctl | Dom | Cmd | FpK | SwK | Vel | G | L | F | H% | S% | hr/f | GS | APC | DOM% | DIS% | Sv% | LI | RAR | BPV | BPX | R$ |
|---|---|---|---|---|---|---|---|---|---|---|---|---|---|---|---|---|---|---|---|---|---|---|---|---|---|---|---|---|---|---|---|---|---|
| 14 TAM * | 10 | 0 | 157 | 134 | 6.62 | 5.65 | 1.65 | 661 | 384 | 859 | 24.3 | 4.2 | 7.7 | 1.8 | 49% | 10% | 93.2 | 43 | 13 | 43 | 35% | 60% | 23% | 2 | 103 | 50% | 50% | | | -55.9 | 44 | 53 | -$21 |
| 15 TAM | 7 | 0 | 147 | 145 | 3.67 | 3.89 | 1.28 | 699 | 690 | 708 | 23.0 | 3.4 | 8.9 | 2.6 | 58% | 10% | 91.6 | 42 | 22 | 37 | 30% | 76% | 13% | 26 | 90 | 15% | 27% | 0 | 0.80 | 5.2 | 87 | 104 | $6 |
| 16 SEA | 6 | 1 | 94 | 101 | 5.15 | 4.31 | 1.48 | 760 | 628 | 875 | 19.0 | 4.3 | 9.6 | 2.2 | 57% | 11% | 93.0 | 40 | 23 | 37 | 34% | 67% | 11% | 15 | 76 | 40% | 27% | 100 | 0.62 | -11.2 | 76 | 90 | -$4 |
| 17 KC | 2 | 0 | 45 | 51 | 4.17 | 3.62 | 1.19 | 743 | 804 | 698 | 20.9 | 2.6 | 10.1 | 3.9 | 58% | 13% | 92.9 | 50 | 12 | 38 | 29% | 73% | 20% | 8 | 83 | 25% | 38% | 0 | 0.72 | 1.1 | 141 | 169 | -$1 |
| 18 | | | | | | | | | | | | | | | | | | | | | | | | | | | | | | | | | |
| 1st Half | | | | | | | | | | | | | | | | | | | | | | | | | | | | | | | | | |
| 2nd Half | | | | | | | | | | | | | | | | | | | | | | | | | | | | | | | | | |
| **19 Proj** | **5** | **0** | **102** | **104** | **4.12** | **3.80** | **1.35** | **749** | **728** | **766** | **21.0** | **3.5** | **9.2** | **2.7** | **58%** | **11%** | **92.4** | **44** | **19** | **37** | **31%** | **74%** | **14%** | **20** | | | | | | **0.4** | **95** | **109** | **$1** |

## Kela,Keone

| Kela,Keone | | | | Health | D | LIMA Plan | B |
|---|---|---|---|---|---|---|---|
| Age: 26 | Th: R | Role | RP | PT/Exp | C | Rand Var | 0 |
| Ht: 6' 1" | Wt: 215 | Type | Pwr FB | Consist | A | MM | 4510 |

Electric arm limited by shaky control, plus occasional bouts with gopheritis and injury. As FpK trend shows, control issues aren't likely to go away anytime soon. Did manage to avoid the DL in 2018, though. Still owns 20-save upside, and when healthy, a reliable source of Ksss—appropriately enough.

| Yr Tm | W | Sv | IP | K | ERA | xERA | WHIP | oOPS | vL | vR | BF/G | Ctl | Dom | Cmd | FpK | SwK | Vel | G | L | F | H% | S% | hr/f | GS | APC | DOM% | DIS% | Sv% | LI | RAR | BPV | BPX | R$ |
|---|---|---|---|---|---|---|---|---|---|---|---|---|---|---|---|---|---|---|---|---|---|---|---|---|---|---|---|---|---|---|---|---|---|
| 14 aa | 2 | 5 | 39 | 47 | 2.22 | 2.45 | 1.34 | | | | 4.5 | 6.3 | 11.1 | 1.8 | | | | | | | 28% | 83% | | | | | | | | 7.3 | 114 | 135 | $2 |
| 15 TEX | 7 | 1 | 60 | 68 | 2.39 | 3.01 | 1.16 | 615 | 739 | 527 | 3.6 | 2.7 | 10.1 | 3.8 | 58% | 14% | 95.6 | 51 | 21 | 29 | 32% | 82% | 9% | 0 | 15 | | | 25 | 1.21 | 11.7 | 139 | 166 | $7 |
| 16 TEX | 5 | 0 | 34 | 45 | 6.09 | 3.56 | 1.38 | 779 | 577 | 872 | 4.3 | 4.5 | 11.9 | 2.6 | 55% | 12% | 95.7 | 44 | 22 | 34 | 32% | 59% | 21% | 0 | 18 | | | 0 | 0.84 | -8.0 | 115 | 137 | -$3 |
| 17 TEX | 4 | 2 | 39 | 51 | 2.79 | 3.86 | 0.91 | 479 | 644 | 370 | 3.9 | 4.0 | 11.9 | 3.0 | 57% | 11% | 96.5 | 30 | 12 | 57 | 19% | 74% | 9% | 0 | 16 | | | 67 | 0.90 | 7.5 | 115 | 138 | $5 |
| 18 2 TM | 3 | 24 | 52 | 66 | 3.29 | 3.48 | 1.10 | 605 | 780 | 474 | 3.9 | 3.3 | 11.4 | 3.5 | 52% | 13% | 96.8 | 37 | 23 | 40 | 28% | 73% | 10% | 0 | 16 | | | 92 | 1.09 | 5.5 | 132 | 152 | $12 |
| 1st Half | 3 | 20 | 29 | 36 | 3.41 | 3.67 | 1.10 | 597 | 916 | 373 | 3.8 | 3.4 | 11.2 | 3.3 | 50% | 12% | 96.8 | 37 | 19 | 44 | 29% | 70% | 6% | 0 | 16 | | | 100 | 1.07 | 2.6 | 124 | 143 | $19 |
| 2nd Half | 0 | 4 | 23 | 30 | 3.13 | 3.24 | 1.09 | 615 | 623 | 600 | 4.1 | 3.1 | 11.7 | 3.8 | 54% | 14% | 96.8 | 38 | 29 | 34 | 29% | 77% | 16% | 0 | 16 | | | 67 | 1.12 | 2.9 | 142 | 163 | $4 |
| **19 Proj** | **4** | **7** | **58** | **75** | **3.47** | **3.21** | **1.11** | **601** | **690** | **540** | **3.8** | **3.7** | **11.6** | **3.1** | **54%** | **13%** | **96.4** | **38** | **21** | **41** | **27%** | **72%** | **12%** | **0** | | | | | | **8.6** | **123** | **142** | **$7** |

## Keller,Brad

| Keller,Brad | | | | Health | A | LIMA Plan | C+ |
|---|---|---|---|---|---|---|---|
| Age: 23 | Th: R | Role | RP | PT/Exp | D | Rand Var | -3 |
| Ht: 6' 5" | Wt: 230 | Type | xGB | Consist | C | MM | 1003 |

Strong GB lean keeps the ball in the yard, but the rest of these skills shout "mediocre" at best. Low SwK means lots of balls in play, and only threw 41% of his pitches in the zone, so Ctl may spike as well. Lefties hit him hard, too. Other owners will see that ERA and pounce. Let them.

| Yr Tm | W | Sv | IP | K | ERA | xERA | WHIP | oOPS | vL | vR | BF/G | Ctl | Dom | Cmd | FpK | SwK | Vel | G | L | F | H% | S% | hr/f | GS | APC | DOM% | DIS% | Sv% | LI | RAR | BPV | BPX | R$ |
|---|---|---|---|---|---|---|---|---|---|---|---|---|---|---|---|---|---|---|---|---|---|---|---|---|---|---|---|---|---|---|---|---|---|
| 14 | | | | | | | | | | | | | | | | | | | | | | | | | | | | | | | | | |
| 15 | | | | | | | | | | | | | | | | | | | | | | | | | | | | | | | | | |
| 16 | | | | | | | | | | | | | | | | | | | | | | | | | | | | | | | | | |
| 17 aa | 10 | 0 | 131 | 96 | 6.27 | 5.72 | 1.77 | | | | 23.1 | 4.2 | 6.6 | 1.6 | | | | | | | 37% | 63% | | | | | | | | -30.8 | 46 | 55 | -$15 |
| 18 KC | 9 | 0 | 140 | 96 | 3.08 | 4.24 | 1.30 | 653 | 730 | 587 | 14.2 | 3.2 | 6.2 | 1.9 | 59% | 9% | 93.9 | 54 | 19 | 27 | 30% | 77% | 6% | 20 | 54 | 30% | 25% | 0 | 0.97 | 18.6 | 56 | 65 | $8 |
| 1st Half | 2 | 0 | 48 | 30 | 2.25 | 4.06 | 1.23 | 592 | 489 | 640 | 7.5 | 3.4 | 5.6 | 1.7 | 56% | 9% | 94.6 | 61 | 17 | 22 | 28% | 81% | 3% | 5 | 29 | 20% | 20% | 0 | 1.09 | 11.2 | 49 | 56 | $1 |
| 2nd Half | 7 | 0 | 92 | 66 | 3.51 | 4.34 | 1.34 | 683 | 805 | 549 | 25.9 | 3.1 | 6.4 | 2.1 | 60% | 9% | 93.6 | 51 | 20 | 29 | 31% | 75% | 7% | 15 | 99 | 33% | 27% | | | 7.3 | 61 | 70 | $11 |
| **19 Proj** | **10** | **0** | **145** | **102** | **4.24** | **4.27** | **1.49** | **735** | **808** | **675** | **15.8** | **3.6** | **6.3** | **1.7** | **59%** | **9%** | **94.0** | **55** | **19** | **26** | **33%** | **71%** | **7%** | **23** | | | | | | **-1.5** | **49** | **56** | **-$1** |

## Keller,Mitch

| Keller,Mitch | | | | Health | A | LIMA Plan | B+ |
|---|---|---|---|---|---|---|---|
| Age: 23 | Th: R | Role | SP | PT/Exp | F | Rand Var | 0 |
| Ht: 6' 3" | Wt: 195 | Type | Pwr | Consist | C | MM | 2200 |

Top prospect hasn't dominated during his steady ascent through the minors. But he projects for more, and solid command and groundball tilt are strong assets. Some 2018 struggles at Triple-A highlight need for more seasoning, but should be ready to contribute in PIT soon, and owns #2 SP upside.

| Yr Tm | W | Sv | IP | K | ERA | xERA | WHIP | oOPS | vL | vR | BF/G | Ctl | Dom | Cmd | FpK | SwK | Vel | G | L | F | H% | S% | hr/f | GS | APC | DOM% | DIS% | Sv% | LI | RAR | BPV | BPX | R$ |
|---|---|---|---|---|---|---|---|---|---|---|---|---|---|---|---|---|---|---|---|---|---|---|---|---|---|---|---|---|---|---|---|---|---|
| 14 | | | | | | | | | | | | | | | | | | | | | | | | | | | | | | | | | |
| 15 | | | | | | | | | | | | | | | | | | | | | | | | | | | | | | | | | |
| 16 | | | | | | | | | | | | | | | | | | | | | | | | | | | | | | | | | |
| 17 aa | 2 | 0 | 35 | 38 | 4.01 | 2.91 | 1.17 | | | | 23.1 | 2.9 | 9.9 | 3.4 | | | | | | | 31% | 66% | | | | | | | | 1.5 | 121 | 146 | -$1 |
| 18 a/a | 12 | 0 | 139 | 111 | 4.10 | 4.02 | 1.38 | | | | 24.3 | 3.4 | 7.2 | 2.1 | | | | | | | 31% | 71% | | | | | | | | 0.8 | 70 | 81 | $3 |
| 1st Half | 9 | 0 | 90 | 66 | 3.98 | 3.76 | 1.29 | | | | 24.7 | 3.3 | 6.6 | 2.0 | | | | | | | 29% | 71% | | | | | | | | 1.8 | 62 | 71 | $7 |
| 2nd Half | 3 | 0 | 51 | 45 | 4.13 | 4.16 | 1.46 | | | | 24.4 | 3.5 | 7.9 | 2.3 | | | | | | | 35% | 71% | | | | | | | | 0.1 | 85 | 97 | -$3 |
| **19 Proj** | **4** | **0** | **58** | **54** | **4.28** | **3.88** | **1.30** | | | | **23.9** | **3.2** | **8.4** | **2.6** | **61%** | **10%** | | **44** | **20** | **36** | **30%** | **69%** | **11%** | **10** | | | | | | **1.8** | **86** | **98** | **-$1** |

## Kelley,Shawn

| Kelley,Shawn | | | | Health | F | LIMA Plan | A |
|---|---|---|---|---|---|---|---|
| Age: 35 | Th: R | Role | RP | PT/Exp | D | Rand Var | -4 |
| Ht: 6' 2" | Wt: 237 | Type | Pwr xFB | Consist | F | MM | 2300 |

DFA'd in WAS due to outburst during mop-up duty—not to mention some ill-timed HR. Those went away in OAK and, overall, skills rebounded. But not to peak, and lucky H% held down ERA. DL time getting routine, too. LIMA option when healthy, but watch Dom: more HR will fly if this is its new level.

| Yr Tm | W | Sv | IP | K | ERA | xERA | WHIP | oOPS | vL | vR | BF/G | Ctl | Dom | Cmd | FpK | SwK | Vel | G | L | F | H% | S% | hr/f | GS | APC | DOM% | DIS% | Sv% | LI | RAR | BPV | BPX | R$ |
|---|---|---|---|---|---|---|---|---|---|---|---|---|---|---|---|---|---|---|---|---|---|---|---|---|---|---|---|---|---|---|---|---|---|
| 14 NYY | 3 | 4 | 52 | 67 | 4.53 | 3.30 | 1.26 | 663 | 612 | 709 | 3.7 | 3.5 | 11.7 | 3.4 | 61% | 15% | 92.2 | 34 | 23 | 44 | 34% | 65% | 9% | 0 | 15 | | | 57 | 1.33 | -5.0 | 128 | 152 | $0 |
| 15 SD | 2 | 0 | 51 | 63 | 2.45 | 3.04 | 1.09 | 596 | 667 | 536 | 3.9 | 2.6 | 11.0 | 4.2 | 72% | 15% | 91.9 | 43 | 19 | 38 | 31% | 81% | 9% | 0 | 15 | | | 0 | 0.88 | 9.5 | 149 | 177 | $3 |
| 16 WAS | 3 | 7 | 58 | 80 | 2.64 | 3.05 | 0.90 | 635 | 792 | 539 | 3.3 | 1.7 | 12.4 | 7.3 | 66% | 16% | 92.4 | 36 | 14 | 50 | 28% | 81% | 14% | 0 | 14 | | | 78 | 1.23 | 11.1 | 191 | 227 | $10 |
| 17 WAS | 3 | 4 | 26 | 25 | 7.27 | 5.92 | 1.54 | 963 | 780 | 1098 | 3.7 | 3.8 | 8.7 | 2.3 | 72% | 14% | 91.8 | 26 | 14 | 60 | 26% | 68% | 24% | 0 | 16 | | | 67 | 0.90 | -9.3 | 57 | 68 | -$4 |
| 18 2 TM | 2 | 0 | 49 | 50 | 2.94 | 4.02 | 0.90 | 618 | 635 | 605 | 3.5 | 2.0 | 9.2 | 4.5 | 57% | 12% | 91.2 | 30 | 16 | 54 | 23% | 76% | 10% | 0 | 14 | | | 0 | 0.85 | 7.3 | 119 | 137 | $3 |
| 1st Half | 0 | 0 | 19 | 21 | 3.72 | 4.47 | 1.03 | 784 | 653 | 823 | 3.4 | 2.3 | 9.8 | 4.2 | 58% | 12% | 91.8 | 27 | 10 | 63 | 23% | 80% | 15% | 0 | 13 | | | 0 | 1.00 | 1.0 | 118 | 136 | -$4 |
| 2nd Half | 2 | 0 | 30 | 29 | 2.43 | 3.72 | 0.81 | 502 | 629 | 412 | 3.6 | 1.8 | 8.8 | 4.8 | 55% | 12% | 90.7 | 32 | 20 | 47 | 23% | 73% | 6% | 0 | 14 | | | 0 | 0.74 | 6.3 | 120 | 137 | $9 |
| **19 Proj** | **2** | **0** | **51** | **51** | **3.49** | **3.74** | **1.08** | **674** | **735** | **635** | **3.5** | **2.5** | **9.1** | **3.6** | **62%** | **12%** | **91.7** | **34** | **17** | **49** | **27%** | **73%** | **10%** | **0** | | | | | | **2.6** | **107** | **123** | **$1** |

ROD TRUESDELL

## Kelly,Joe

| | | | | | | |
|---|---|---|---|---|---|---|
| Age: 31 | Th: R | Role: RP | Health | D | LIMA Plan | C |
| Ht: 6' 1" | Wt: 190 | Type: Pwr | PT/Exp | D | Rand Var | 0 |
| | | | Consist | A | MM | 2310 |

Early H% tried to keep him on path to 2017 repeat; poor skills eventually won out. All those free passes heighten ratio risk, FpK dip hints they aren't going away, and high-end velocity hasn't generated enough Ks to make up for it. Can't count on saves with that BPV string.

| Yr | Tm | W | Sv | IP | K | ERA | xERA | WHIP | oOPS | vL | vR | BF/G | Ctl | Dom | Cmd | FpK | SwK | Vel | G | L | F | H% | S% | hr/f | GS | APC | DOM% | DIS% | Sv% | LI | RAR | BPV | BPX | R$ |
|---|---|---|---|---|---|---|---|---|---|---|---|---|---|---|---|---|---|---|---|---|---|---|---|---|---|---|---|---|---|---|---|---|---|---|
| 14 | 2 TM | 6 | 0 | 96 | 66 | 4.20 | 4.00 | 1.35 | 693 | 689 | 695 | 24.4 | 3.9 | 6.2 | 1.6 | 57% | 7% | 94.7 | 55 | 21 | 24 | 28% | 70% | 11% | 17 | 93 | 18% | 35% | | | -5.5 | 38 | 45 | -$2 |
| 15 | BOS * | 11 | 0 | 153 | 124 | 4.76 | 4.53 | 1.44 | 768 | 702 | 836 | 22.5 | 3.3 | 7.3 | 2.2 | 62% | 8% | 95.4 | 46 | 25 | 29 | 32% | 68% | 12% | 25 | 95 | 8% | 40% | | | -15.2 | 61 | 73 | -$3 |
| 16 | BOS * | 5 | 2 | 75 | 82 | 4.02 | 4.92 | 1.58 | 828 | 899 | 791 | 8.9 | 3.8 | 9.8 | 2.6 | 52% | 11% | 96.3 | 47 | 28 | 25 | 38% | 76% | 18% | 6 | 37 | 17% | 67% | 67 | 1.11 | 1.5 | 87 | 103 | -$1 |
| 17 | BOS | 4 | 0 | 58 | 52 | 2.79 | 4.07 | 1.19 | 573 | 671 | 509 | 4.4 | 4.2 | 8.1 | 1.9 | 64% | 11% | 99.0 | 51 | 23 | 26 | 26% | 77% | 7% | 0 | 19 | | | 0 | 1.09 | 11.2 | 61 | 73 | $4 |
| 18 | BOS | 4 | 2 | 66 | 68 | 4.39 | 3.96 | 1.36 | 662 | 610 | 703 | 3.9 | 4.4 | 9.3 | 2.1 | 58% | 11% | 98.1 | 47 | 25 | 28 | 31% | 67% | 8% | 0 | 16 | | | 29 | 1.05 | -1.9 | 74 | 86 | -$1 |
| 1st Half | | 3 | 2 | 35 | 34 | 3.38 | 3.86 | 1.10 | 560 | 303 | 750 | 3.9 | 4.2 | 8.8 | 2.1 | 58% | 10% | 97.9 | 46 | 24 | 30 | 24% | 69% | 7% | 0 | 16 | | | 50 | 1.31 | 3.3 | 71 | 81 | $4 |
| 2nd Half | | 1 | 0 | 31 | 34 | 5.52 | 4.07 | 1.65 | 763 | 880 | 650 | 3.9 | 4.6 | 9.9 | 2.1 | 57% | 12% | 98.3 | 48 | 27 | 26 | 38% | 65% | 9% | 0 | 16 | | | 0 | 0.80 | -5.2 | 78 | 90 | -$7 |
| 19 | Proj | **4** | **1** | **58** | **57** | **4.09** | **3.77** | **1.39** | **683** | **705** | **667** | **4.7** | **4.2** | **8.9** | **2.1** | **58%** | **11%** | **97.8** | **48** | **25** | **27** | **32%** | **71%** | **9%** | **0** | | | | | | **0.4** | **73** | **84** | **-$1** |

## Kennedy,Ian

| | | | | | | |
|---|---|---|---|---|---|---|
| Age: 34 | Th: R | Role: SP | Health | F | LIMA Plan | C |
| Ht: 6' 0" | Wt: 205 | Type: Pwr FB | PT/Exp | A | Rand Var | 0 |
| | | | Consist | A | MM | 1203 |

Strained oblique in July cost him two months, and strong finish (2.88 Sept ERA) was propped up by 6% hr/f. Holding FpK bump is his best shot at league-average ratios, as FB% elevates HR risk, SwK continued its steady decline. A best-case innings eater, but IP trend suggests even that's a reach.

| Yr | Tm | W | Sv | IP | K | ERA | xERA | WHIP | oOPS | vL | vR | BF/G | Ctl | Dom | Cmd | FpK | SwK | Vel | G | L | F | H% | S% | hr/f | GS | APC | DOM% | DIS% | Sv% | LI | RAR | BPV | BPX | R$ |
|---|---|---|---|---|---|---|---|---|---|---|---|---|---|---|---|---|---|---|---|---|---|---|---|---|---|---|---|---|---|---|---|---|---|---|
| 14 | SD | 13 | 0 | 201 | 207 | 3.63 | 3.56 | 1.29 | 698 | 689 | 706 | 25.6 | 3.1 | 9.3 | 3.0 | 64% | 11% | 91.8 | 40 | 23 | 38 | 32% | 73% | 8% | 33 | 103 | 33% | 15% | | | 2.8 | 100 | 119 | $9 |
| 15 | SD | 9 | 0 | 168 | 174 | 4.28 | 3.74 | 1.30 | 815 | 842 | 788 | 23.8 | 2.8 | 9.3 | 3.3 | 61% | 11% | 91.3 | 38 | 23 | 39 | 31% | 74% | 17% | 30 | 97 | 13% | 27% | | | -6.5 | 108 | 129 | $4 |
| 16 | KC | 11 | 0 | 196 | 184 | 3.68 | 4.47 | 1.22 | 722 | 709 | 735 | 24.8 | 3.0 | 8.5 | 2.8 | 62% | 10% | 92.2 | 33 | 20 | 47 | 28% | 77% | 13% | 33 | 102 | 30% | 27% | | | 12.3 | 81 | 97 | $14 |
| 17 | KC | 5 | 0 | 154 | 131 | 5.38 | 5.10 | 1.32 | 804 | 818 | 791 | 21.8 | 3.6 | 7.7 | 2.1 | 58% | 10% | 91.9 | 36 | 16 | 48 | 26% | 66% | 16% | 30 | 88 | 13% | 57% | | | -19.3 | 56 | 67 | -$3 |
| 18 | KC | 3 | 0 | 120 | 105 | 4.66 | 4.82 | 1.38 | 779 | 750 | 806 | 23.5 | 3.0 | 7.9 | 2.6 | 63% | 9% | 91.9 | 30 | 26 | 44 | 31% | 71% | 13% | 22 | 94 | 14% | 45% | | | -7.6 | 69 | 79 | -$4 |
| 1st Half | | 1 | 0 | 92 | 84 | 5.11 | 4.84 | 1.42 | 807 | 796 | 815 | 23.6 | 3.2 | 8.2 | 2.5 | 62% | 9% | 92.0 | 30 | 26 | 44 | 31% | 69% | 14% | 17 | 95 | 18% | 41% | | | -10.8 | 69 | 79 | -$6 |
| 2nd Half | | 2 | 0 | 28 | 21 | 3.21 | 4.76 | 1.25 | 687 | 639 | 761 | 23.2 | 2.3 | 6.8 | 3.0 | 65% | 9% | 91.4 | 31 | 26 | 43 | 30% | 78% | 8% | 5 | 91 | 0% | 60% | | | 3.2 | 69 | 80 | $1 |
| 19 | Proj | **7** | **0** | **145** | **125** | **4.59** | **4.32** | **1.32** | **768** | **744** | **794** | **22.8** | **3.0** | **7.8** | **2.6** | **62%** | **9%** | **91.8** | **33** | **22** | **45** | **30%** | **71%** | **13%** | **26** | | | | | | **-7.8** | **71** | **82** | **$0** |

## Kershaw,Clayton

| | | | | | | |
|---|---|---|---|---|---|---|
| Age: 31 | Th: L | Role: SP | Health | F | LIMA Plan | C+ |
| Ht: 6' 4" | Wt: 228 | Type: Pwr | PT/Exp | A | Rand Var | -1 |
| | | | Consist | A | MM | 5403 |

Missed time with biceps/back injuries in May/June, but flashed vintage value in the 2nd half. Elite FpK backs pinpoint control, but his velocity waned, and fewer whiffs have cut into once-pristine DOM%. This is still an ace-level profile, but BPV trend, recent IP volume say he's ceded top SP status.

| Yr | Tm | W | Sv | IP | K | ERA | xERA | WHIP | oOPS | vL | vR | BF/G | Ctl | Dom | Cmd | FpK | SwK | Vel | G | L | F | H% | S% | hr/f | GS | APC | DOM% | DIS% | Sv% | LI | RAR | BPV | BPX | R$ |
|---|---|---|---|---|---|---|---|---|---|---|---|---|---|---|---|---|---|---|---|---|---|---|---|---|---|---|---|---|---|---|---|---|---|---|
| 14 | LA | 21 | 0 | 198 | 239 | 1.77 | 2.27 | 0.86 | 521 | 477 | 531 | 27.7 | 1.4 | 10.8 | 7.7 | 69% | 15% | 93.0 | 52 | 19 | 29 | 29% | 81% | 7% | 27 | 101 | 81% | 4% | | | 48.2 | 187 | 223 | $40 |
| 15 | LA | 16 | 0 | 233 | 301 | 2.13 | 2.31 | 0.88 | 521 | 554 | 511 | 27.0 | 1.6 | 11.6 | 7.2 | 68% | 16% | 93.6 | 50 | 22 | 28 | 29% | 79% | 10% | 33 | 103 | 76% | 3% | | | 52.6 | 194 | 231 | $47 |
| 16 | LA | 12 | 0 | 149 | 172 | 1.69 | 2.46 | 0.72 | 472 | 309 | 529 | 25.9 | 0.7 | 10.4 | 15.6 | 70% | 16% | 93.1 | 49 | 20 | 30 | 26% | 80% | 8% | 21 | 98 | 76% | 5% | | | 45.9 | 196 | 233 | $35 |
| 17 | LA | 18 | 0 | 175 | 202 | 2.31 | 3.02 | 0.95 | 604 | 734 | 570 | 25.1 | 1.5 | 10.4 | 6.7 | 69% | 15% | 92.7 | 48 | 19 | 33 | 28% | 85% | 16% | 27 | 93 | 56% | 7% | | | 44.1 | 171 | 206 | $36 |
| 18 | LA | 9 | 0 | 161 | 155 | 2.73 | 3.36 | 1.04 | 630 | 679 | 615 | 25.0 | 1.6 | 8.6 | 5.3 | 70% | 12% | 90.9 | 48 | 23 | 30 | 29% | 79% | 13% | 26 | 91 | 35% | 8% | | | 28.2 | 138 | 159 | $21 |
| 1st Half | | 1 | 0 | 57 | 63 | 2.84 | 3.19 | 1.14 | 671 | 878 | 608 | 23.2 | 1.9 | 9.9 | 5.3 | 69% | 12% | 90.9 | 45 | 25 | 29 | 32% | 81% | 16% | 10 | 86 | 40% | 10% | | | 9.2 | 151 | 174 | $3 |
| 2nd Half | | 8 | 0 | 104 | 92 | 2.67 | 3.45 | 0.99 | 606 | 558 | 619 | 26.1 | 1.5 | 7.9 | 5.4 | 71% | 11% | 90.8 | 49 | 21 | 30 | 27% | 77% | 11% | 16 | 94 | 31% | 6% | | | 19.0 | 130 | 150 | $31 |
| 19 | Proj | **13** | **0** | **174** | **187** | **2.66** | **2.78** | **0.99** | **607** | **640** | **598** | **24.6** | **1.5** | **9.7** | **6.6** | **70%** | **13%** | **91.9** | **48** | **21** | **30** | **29%** | **78%** | **13%** | **27** | | | | | | **32.1** | **161** | **185** | **$28** |

## Keuchel,Dallas

| | | | | | | |
|---|---|---|---|---|---|---|
| Age: 31 | Th: L | Role: SP | Health | D | LIMA Plan | B |
| Ht: 6' 3" | Wt: 205 | Type: xGB | PT/Exp | A | Rand Var | 0 |
| | | | Consist | B | MM | 3105 |

Returned to 200 IP, which is most of the good news. Gave back ERA gains despite help from 2nd half hr/f. GB% profile pairs well with Ctl foundation to bolster ratio floor, though SwK drop questions much Dom recovery. While those sub-3.00 ERAs in the past provide hope, his skills support something more likely in the mid-3s.

| Yr | Tm | W | Sv | IP | K | ERA | xERA | WHIP | oOPS | vL | vR | BF/G | Ctl | Dom | Cmd | FpK | SwK | Vel | G | L | F | H% | S% | hr/f | GS | APC | DOM% | DIS% | Sv% | LI | RAR | BPV | BPX | R$ |
|---|---|---|---|---|---|---|---|---|---|---|---|---|---|---|---|---|---|---|---|---|---|---|---|---|---|---|---|---|---|---|---|---|---|---|
| 14 | HOU | 12 | 0 | 200 | 146 | 2.93 | 3.07 | 1.18 | 655 | 595 | 674 | 27.9 | 2.2 | 6.6 | 3.0 | 65% | 9% | 89.7 | 64 | 17 | 19 | 30% | 76% | 10% | 29 | 104 | 41% | 17% | | | 20.1 | 102 | 121 | $15 |
| 15 | HOU | 20 | 0 | 232 | 216 | 2.48 | 2.80 | 1.02 | 575 | 461 | 606 | 27.6 | 2.0 | 8.4 | 4.2 | 61% | 11% | 89.6 | 62 | 19 | 20 | 28% | 79% | 14% | 33 | 106 | 42% | 6% | | | 42.3 | 137 | 164 | $37 |
| 16 | HOU | 9 | 0 | 168 | 144 | 4.55 | 3.61 | 1.29 | 736 | 603 | 772 | 27.0 | 2.6 | 7.7 | 3.0 | 63% | 10% | 88.6 | 57 | 19 | 24 | 31% | 67% | 16% | 26 | 103 | 35% | 19% | | | -7.5 | 104 | 124 | $3 |
| 17 | HOU | 14 | 0 | 146 | 125 | 2.90 | 3.23 | 1.12 | 619 | 435 | 666 | 25.4 | 2.9 | 7.7 | 2.7 | 60% | 11% | 88.7 | 67 | 15 | 18 | 26% | 78% | 21% | 23 | 95 | 30% | 22% | | | 26.1 | 106 | 127 | $19 |
| 18 | HOU | 12 | 0 | 205 | 153 | 3.74 | 4.02 | 1.31 | 704 | 707 | 703 | 25.7 | 2.6 | 6.7 | 2.6 | 60% | 9% | 89.3 | 54 | 22 | 24 | 31% | 73% | 11% | 34 | 97 | 21% | 29% | | | 10.4 | 84 | 97 | $8 |
| 1st Half | | 4 | 0 | 102 | 80 | 4.22 | 3.94 | 1.34 | 730 | 791 | 713 | 26.1 | 2.5 | 7.0 | 2.9 | 61% | 9% | 89.0 | 54 | 22 | 23 | 32% | 71% | 15% | 17 | 101 | 18% | 24% | | | -0.9 | 92 | 106 | $1 |
| 2nd Half | | 8 | 0 | 102 | 73 | 3.25 | 4.09 | 1.29 | 677 | 583 | 694 | 25.4 | 2.6 | 6.4 | 2.4 | 59% | 8% | 89.6 | 53 | 22 | 25 | 31% | 75% | 7% | 17 | 94 | 24% | 35% | | | 11.3 | 75 | 87 | $17 |
| 19 | Proj | **13** | **0** | **189** | **156** | **3.50** | **3.44** | **1.24** | **677** | **593** | **698** | **25.3** | **2.6** | **7.5** | **2.9** | **61%** | **10%** | **89.1** | **55** | **21** | **23** | **30%** | **74%** | **13%** | **30** | | | | | | **13.6** | **97** | **112** | **$14** |

## Kikuchi,Yusei

| | | | | | | |
|---|---|---|---|---|---|---|
| Age: 28 | Th: L | Role: SP | Health | A | LIMA Plan | C+ |
| Ht: 6' 0" | Wt: 192 | Type: Pwr | PT/Exp | A | Rand Var | -1 |
| | | | Consist | C | MM | 2203 |

Left shoulder stiffness led to early DL trip, stalled repeat of 2017 breakout. Still posted a 2.48 ERA over his last two seasons in Japan's NPB league with more Ks than innings pitched (stats below are MLEs). Early-career control issues add risk, but if health holds, fastball/slider combo could result in decent stateside transition.

| Yr | Tm | W | Sv | IP | K | ERA | xERA | WHIP | oOPS | vL | vR | BF/G | Ctl | Dom | Cmd | FpK | SwK | Vel | G | L | F | H% | S% | hr/f | GS | APC | DOM% | DIS% | Sv% | LI | RAR | BPV | BPX | R$ |
|---|---|---|---|---|---|---|---|---|---|---|---|---|---|---|---|---|---|---|---|---|---|---|---|---|---|---|---|---|---|---|---|---|---|---|
| 14 | for | 5 | 0 | 140 | 105 | 4.40 | 5.14 | 1.71 | | | | 27.5 | 6.2 | 6.8 | 1.1 | | | | | | | 31% | 76% | | | | | | | | -11.4 | 37 | 44 | -$12 |
| 15 | for | 9 | 0 | 133 | 116 | 3.53 | 3.46 | 1.30 | | | | 23.8 | 4.6 | 7.8 | 1.7 | | | | | | | 26% | 76% | | | | | | | | 7.1 | 64 | 76 | $6 |
| 16 | for | 12 | 0 | 143 | 120 | 3.20 | 3.86 | 1.46 | | | | 27.8 | 5.2 | 7.6 | 1.4 | | | | | | | 29% | 80% | | | | | | | | 17.4 | 62 | 73 | $7 |
| 17 | for | 16 | 0 | 188 | 206 | 2.44 | 2.78 | 1.02 | | | | 27.7 | 2.9 | 9.9 | 3.4 | | | | | | | 24% | 85% | | | | | | | | 44.4 | 108 | 129 | $33 |
| 18 | for | 14 | 0 | 164 | 145 | 3.82 | 3.70 | 1.15 | | | | 28.3 | 3.1 | 8.0 | 2.6 | | | | | | | 25% | 73% | | | | | | | | 6.6 | 69 | 79 | $13 |
| 1st Half | | | | | | | | | | | | | | | | | | | | | | | | | | | | | | | | | | |
| 2nd Half | | | | | | | | | | | | | | | | | | | | | | | | | | | | | | | | | | |
| 19 | Proj | **9** | **0** | **145** | **137** | **3.76** | **3.93** | **1.28** | | | | **23.9** | **3.7** | **8.5** | **2.3** | **61%** | **10%** | | **44** | **20** | **36** | **28%** | **74%** | **12%** | **25** | | | | | | **3.7** | **74** | **85** | **$8** |

## Kimbrel,Craig

| | | | | | | |
|---|---|---|---|---|---|---|
| Age: 31 | Th: R | Role: RP | Health | B | LIMA Plan | C+ |
| Ht: 6' 0" | Wt: 210 | Type: Pwr xFB | PT/Exp | A | Rand Var | -3 |
| | | | Consist | C | MM | 5530 |

Saves total, H% covered for R$, but he's missing the zone enough to now question elite status. There's enough swing-and-miss to offset the Ctl loss, as electric Dom offers stability, but all those FBs keep HR risk hanging around. BPV shows he's still an effective closer, even if 2nd half ratios become the norm.

| Yr | Tm | W | Sv | IP | K | ERA | xERA | WHIP | oOPS | vL | vR | BF/G | Ctl | Dom | Cmd | FpK | SwK | Vel | G | L | F | H% | S% | hr/f | GS | APC | DOM% | DIS% | Sv% | LI | RAR | BPV | BPX | R$ |
|---|---|---|---|---|---|---|---|---|---|---|---|---|---|---|---|---|---|---|---|---|---|---|---|---|---|---|---|---|---|---|---|---|---|---|
| 14 | ATL | 0 | 47 | 62 | 95 | 1.61 | 2.36 | 0.91 | 430 | 425 | 436 | 3.9 | 3.8 | 13.9 | 3.7 | 58% | 17% | 97.1 | 41 | 23 | 35 | 26% | 83% | 5% | 0 | 17 | | | 92 | 1.44 | 16.2 | 166 | 198 | $26 |
| 15 | SD | 4 | 39 | 59 | 87 | 2.58 | 2.61 | 1.04 | 569 | 629 | 508 | 3.9 | 3.3 | 13.2 | 4.0 | 61% | 16% | 97.3 | 46 | 20 | 34 | 30% | 80% | 14% | 0 | 17 | | | 91 | 1.49 | 10.1 | 171 | 204 | $22 |
| 16 | BOS | 2 | 31 | 53 | 83 | 3.23 | 3.36 | 1.09 | 539 | 514 | 559 | 3.9 | 5.1 | 14.1 | 2.8 | 68% | 15% | 97.3 | 29 | 23 | 48 | 27% | 72% | 8% | 0 | 16 | | | 94 | 1.50 | 6.3 | 123 | 146 | $16 |
| 17 | BOS | 5 | 35 | 69 | 126 | 1.43 | 1.90 | 0.68 | 444 | 572 | 335 | 3.8 | 1.8 | 16.4 | 9.0 | 63% | 20% | 98.3 | 37 | 19 | 44 | 28% | 88% | 13% | 0 | 17 | | | 90 | 1.34 | 24.9 | 262 | 314 | $32 |
| 18 | BOS | 5 | 42 | 62 | 96 | 2.74 | 3.16 | 0.99 | 565 | 631 | 508 | 3.9 | 4.5 | 13.9 | 3.1 | 56% | 18% | 97.1 | 28 | 25 | 47 | 23% | 78% | 13% | 0 | 18 | | | 89 | 1.39 | 10.8 | 135 | 155 | $25 |
| 1st Half | | 1 | 24 | 33 | 49 | 2.16 | 2.99 | 0.87 | 566 | 701 | 460 | 3.7 | 3.5 | 13.2 | 3.8 | 58% | 19% | 96.7 | 33 | 20 | 47 | 20% | 88% | 17% | 0 | 17 | | | 92 | 1.59 | 8.2 | 154 | 177 | $28 |
| 2nd Half | | 4 | 18 | 29 | 47 | 3.41 | 3.37 | 1.14 | 562 | 552 | 566 | 4.1 | 5.6 | 14.6 | 2.6 | 54% | 16% | 97.6 | 23 | 30 | 47 | 27% | 71% | 8% | 0 | 19 | | | 86 | 1.17 | 2.6 | 112 | 129 | $22 |
| 19 | Proj | **4** | **38** | **58** | **94** | **3.13** | **2.60** | **1.00** | **554** | **608** | **505** | **3.8** | **4.0** | **14.6** | **3.7** | **60%** | **18%** | **97.5** | **31** | **24** | **45** | **28%** | **72%** | **11%** | **0** | | | | | | **18.0** | **165** | **190** | **$22** |

## Kingham,Nick

| | | | | | | |
|---|---|---|---|---|---|---|
| Age: 27 | Th: R | Role: SP | Health | A | LIMA Plan | D+ |
| Ht: 6' 5" | Wt: 225 | Type: | PT/Exp | D | Rand Var | +2 |
| | | | Consist | A | MM | 0000 |

5-7, 5.21 ERA in 76 IP at PIT. Improved slider boosted 1st half skills, but lost feel for the zone, while HR bug contributed to ugly 2nd half. Has work to do vL (1.6 Cmd), while his below-average Dom further reduces margin for error. BPV, xERA baseline confirm he's not yet mixed-league relevant.

| Yr | Tm | W | Sv | IP | K | ERA | xERA | WHIP | oOPS | vL | vR | BF/G | Ctl | Dom | Cmd | FpK | SwK | Vel | G | L | F | H% | S% | hr/f | GS | APC | DOM% | DIS% | Sv% | LI | RAR | BPV | BPX | R$ |
|---|---|---|---|---|---|---|---|---|---|---|---|---|---|---|---|---|---|---|---|---|---|---|---|---|---|---|---|---|---|---|---|---|---|---|
| 14 | a/a | 6 | 0 | 159 | 97 | 3.40 | 3.17 | 1.23 | | | | 24.7 | 2.6 | 5.5 | 2.1 | | | | | | | 29% | 72% | | | | | | | | 6.6 | 70 | 84 | $5 |
| 15 | aaa | 1 | 0 | 31 | 25 | 5.61 | 5.43 | 1.54 | | | | 22.8 | 2.1 | 7.3 | 3.5 | | | | | | | 38% | 64% | | | | | | | | -6.4 | 81 | 97 | -$7 |
| 16 | | | | | | | | | | | | | | | | | | | | | | | | | | | | | | | | | | |
| 17 | aaa | 9 | 0 | 113 | 72 | 5.77 | 5.64 | 1.63 | | | | 25.2 | 2.6 | 5.7 | 2.2 | | | | | | | 37% | 64% | | | | | | | | -19.8 | 48 | 57 | -$9 |
| 18 | PIT * | 9 | 0 | 144 | 116 | 5.11 | 5.20 | 1.41 | 837 | 959 | 722 | 19.7 | 2.8 | 7.2 | 2.6 | 61% | 11% | 92.2 | 38 | 22 | 40 | 32% | 68% | 19% | 15 | 72 | 27% | 40% | 0 | 0.68 | -17.1 | 52 | 60 | -$5 |
| 1st Half | | 6 | 0 | 90 | 76 | 3.57 | 2.99 | 1.12 | 623 | 706 | 545 | 22.3 | 2.2 | 7.6 | 3.4 | 67% | 13% | 92.3 | 36 | 20 | 44 | 29% | 69% | 9% | 6 | 92 | 50% | 17% | | | 6.5 | 106 | 122 | $7 |
| 2nd Half | | 3 | 0 | 54 | 39 | 7.71 | 8.92 | 1.90 | 1002 | 1152 | 859 | 16.9 | 3.7 | 6.6 | 1.8 | 56% | 10% | 92.1 | 40 | 23 | 37 | 36% | 66% | 27% | 9 | 63 | 11% | 56% | 0 | 0.62 | -23.6 | -25 | -29 | -$29 |
| 19 | Proj | **3** | **0** | **58** | **42** | **5.68** | **4.68** | **1.55** | **861** | **981** | **747** | **21.0** | **2.7** | **6.5** | **2.4** | **60%** | **11%** | **92.2** | **38** | **22** | **40** | **34%** | **66%** | **11%** | **12** | | | | | | **-2.7** | **60** | **69** | **-$7** |

BRANT CHESSER

## Kintzler,Brandon

| | | | | | | |
|---|---|---|---|---|---|---|
| Age: 34 | Th: R | Role: RP | Health | D | LIMA Plan | C |
| Ht: 6' 0" | Wt: 194 | Type: GB | PT/Exp | C | Rand Var | 0 |
| | | | Consist | A | MM | 2000 |

Forearm injury led to DL trip in June, as saves vanished and sent R$ into free fall. SwK says he isn't fooling anybody, which makes him dependent upon GBs, Ctl for success, and even those are trending in the wrong direction. While FpK hints at fewer walks, xERA baseline keeps him far from the ninth.

| Yr Tm | W | Sv | IP | K | ERA | xERA | WHIP | oOPS | vL | vR | BF/G | Ctl | Dom | Cmd | FpK | SwK | Vel | G | L | F | H% | S% | hr/f | GS | APC | DOM% | DIS% | Sv% | LI | RAR | BPV | BPX | R$ |
|---|---|---|---|---|---|---|---|---|---|---|---|---|---|---|---|---|---|---|---|---|---|---|---|---|---|---|---|---|---|---|---|---|---|
| 14 MIL | 3 | 0 | 58 | 31 | 3.24 | 3.87 | 1.34 | 781 | 648 | 859 | 3.7 | 2.5 | 4.8 | 1.9 | 60% | 7% | 92.1 | 57 | 18 | 25 | 29% | 81% | 17% | 0 | 14 | | | 0 | 1.04 | 3.6 | 54 | 65 | -$1 |
| 15 MIL * | 1 | 0 | 26 | 17 | 6.46 | 6.58 | 1.94 | 1021 | 1017 | 1000 | 5.4 | 3.3 | 6.0 | 1.8 | 56% | 9% | 90.8 | 63 | 29 | 8 | 42% | 64% | 50% | 0 | 21 | | | 0 | 0.59 | -8.0 | 47 | 56 | -$9 |
| 16 MIN * | 4 | 17 | 70 | 43 | 3.73 | 4.21 | 1.33 | 705 | 673 | 730 | 4.5 | 1.5 | 5.5 | 3.7 | 65% | 7% | 92.7 | 62 | 18 | 20 | 33% | 73% | 14% | 0 | 15 | | | 81 | 1.01 | 4.0 | 87 | 104 | $7 |
| 17 2 TM | 4 | 29 | 71 | 39 | 3.03 | 4.25 | 1.15 | 638 | 535 | 734 | 4.0 | 2.0 | 4.9 | 2.4 | 62% | 6% | 93.4 | 55 | 19 | 27 | 27% | 75% | 8% | 0 | 15 | | | 83 | 1.17 | 11.7 | 67 | 81 | $17 |
| 18 2 NL | 3 | 2 | 61 | 43 | 4.60 | 4.46 | 1.47 | 787 | 862 | 739 | 3.8 | 3.3 | 6.4 | 2.0 | 62% | 7% | 92.6 | 50 | 22 | 28 | 33% | 69% | 9% | 0 | 14 | | | 40 | 1.05 | -3.4 | 55 | 63 | -$4 |
| 1st Half | 1 | 2 | 29 | 21 | 4.30 | 4.45 | 1.43 | 767 | 872 | 682 | 3.9 | 3.7 | 6.4 | 1.8 | 60% | 6% | 92.4 | 45 | 27 | 27 | 32% | 68% | 4% | 0 | 15 | | | 50 | 1.19 | -0.5 | 40 | 46 | -$5 |
| 2nd Half | 2 | 0 | 31 | 22 | 4.88 | 4.47 | 1.50 | 804 | 849 | 779 | 3.6 | 2.9 | 6.3 | 2.2 | 64% | 9% | 92.8 | 53 | 18 | 29 | 33% | 70% | 13% | 0 | 14 | | | 0 | 0.94 | -2.8 | 68 | 78 | -$4 |
| 19 Proj | 3 | 0 | 58 | 39 | 3.97 | 3.99 | 1.36 | 757 | 738 | 770 | 3.9 | 2.6 | 6.0 | 2.3 | 63% | 7% | 92.8 | 54 | 20 | 26 | 31% | 73% | 12% | 0 | | | | | | 1.3 | 71 | 81 | -$2 |

## Kittredge,Andrew

| | | | | | | |
|---|---|---|---|---|---|---|
| Age: 29 | Th: R | Role: RP | Health | A | LIMA Plan | C |
| Ht: 6' 1" | Wt: 200 | Type: Pwr | PT/Exp | D | Rand Var | +5 |
| | | | Consist | F | MM | 2200 |

3-2, 7.75 ERA in 38 IP at TAM. Rode the Triple-A shuttle early and ran into hr/f, H% buzzsaw; though xERA says he would have struggled anyway. Late jump in whiffs suggests league-average Dom can stick, and GBs point to serviceable ERA if luck factors correct. Even so, he's just an -only league dart throw.

| Yr Tm | W | Sv | IP | K | ERA | xERA | WHIP | oOPS | vL | vR | BF/G | Ctl | Dom | Cmd | FpK | SwK | Vel | G | L | F | H% | S% | hr/f | GS | APC | DOM% | DIS% | Sv% | LI | RAR | BPV | BPX | R$ |
|---|---|---|---|---|---|---|---|---|---|---|---|---|---|---|---|---|---|---|---|---|---|---|---|---|---|---|---|---|---|---|---|---|---|
| 14 | | | | | | | | | | | | | | | | | | | | | | | | | | | | | | | | | |
| 15 a/a | 2 | 0 | 75 | 51 | 4.46 | 4.34 | 1.45 | | | | 8.9 | 3.2 | 6.1 | 1.9 | | | | | | | 32% | 69% | | | | | | | | -4.6 | 56 | 66 | -$5 |
| 16 a/a | 3 | 7 | 72 | 69 | 4.38 | 5.17 | 1.56 | | | | 8.5 | 2.5 | 8.7 | 3.5 | | | | | | | 39% | 72% | | | | | | | | -1.7 | 96 | 114 | -$1 |
| 17 TAM * | 6 | 2 | 84 | 78 | 2.02 | 3.15 | 1.21 | 665 | 733 | 627 | 6.0 | 2.6 | 8.4 | 3.2 | 65% | 13% | 94.5 | 47 | 19 | 35 | 31% | 85% | 13% | 0 | 16 | | | 50 | 0.61 | 24.1 | 108 | 130 | $10 |
| 18 TAM * | 9 | 2 | 84 | 76 | 5.57 | 5.88 | 1.63 | 956 | 741 | 1074 | 7.0 | 3.3 | 8.1 | 2.5 | 59% | 10% | 93.1 | 50 | 24 | 25 | 37% | 67% | 21% | 3 | 19 | 0% | 100% | 67 | 0.77 | -14.7 | 60 | 69 | -$7 |
| 1st Half | 3 | 2 | 46 | 38 | 5.96 | 5.72 | 1.68 | 983 | 557 | 1183 | 7.9 | 3.6 | 7.5 | 2.1 | 60% | 7% | 93.5 | 54 | 22 | 24 | 37% | 64% | 20% | 3 | 24 | 0% | 100% | 100 | 0.90 | -10.2 | 57 | 65 | -$13 |
| 2nd Half | 6 | 0 | 41 | 38 | 4.81 | 5.57 | 1.49 | 934 | 869 | 974 | 6.3 | 2.7 | 8.4 | 3.1 | 58% | 13% | 92.6 | 47 | 26 | 26 | 35% | 72% | 22% | 0 | 17 | | | 0 | 0.67 | -3.3 | 69 | 79 | $0 |
| 19 Proj | 5 | 0 | 58 | 52 | 4.24 | 3.79 | 1.34 | 697 | 578 | 762 | 6.8 | 3.0 | 8.0 | 2.7 | 58% | 11% | 93.0 | 47 | 23 | 30 | 32% | 70% | 11% | 0 | | | | | | -0.7 | 88 | 101 | -$1 |

## Kluber,Corey

| | | | | | | |
|---|---|---|---|---|---|---|
| Age: 33 | Th: R | Role: SP | Health | C | LIMA Plan | D+ |
| Ht: 6' 4" | Wt: 215 | Type: Pwr | PT/Exp | A | Rand Var | 0 |
| | | | Consist | B | MM | 5405 |

200-IP streak continued, even with a right knee injury in July. Dom regression was the only dent in otherwise sturdy armor, though 2nd half SwK rebound eases concerns, and plenty of early strikes back pinpoint Ctl. Consistently elite BPV baseline points to yet another $30 season.

| Yr Tm | W | Sv | IP | K | ERA | xERA | WHIP | oOPS | vL | vR | BF/G | Ctl | Dom | Cmd | FpK | SwK | Vel | G | L | F | H% | S% | hr/f | GS | APC | DOM% | DIS% | Sv% | LI | RAR | BPV | BPX | R$ |
|---|---|---|---|---|---|---|---|---|---|---|---|---|---|---|---|---|---|---|---|---|---|---|---|---|---|---|---|---|---|---|---|---|---|
| 14 CLE | 18 | 0 | 236 | 269 | 2.44 | 2.74 | 1.09 | 624 | 687 | 553 | 28.0 | 1.9 | 10.3 | 5.3 | 64% | 12% | 93.2 | 48 | 21 | 31 | 33% | 80% | 7% | 34 | 103 | 62% | 12% | | | 37.7 | 158 | 189 | $30 |
| 15 CLE | 9 | 0 | 222 | 245 | 3.49 | 3.07 | 1.05 | 650 | 740 | 549 | 27.7 | 1.8 | 9.9 | 5.4 | 63% | 13% | 92.8 | 42 | 22 | 36 | 30% | 70% | 11% | 32 | 102 | 47% | 13% | | | 13.0 | 150 | 178 | $22 |
| 16 CLE | 18 | 0 | 215 | 227 | 3.14 | 3.48 | 1.06 | 631 | 648 | 615 | 26.9 | 2.4 | 9.5 | 4.0 | 62% | 13% | 92.5 | 44 | 19 | 36 | 28% | 74% | 11% | 32 | 100 | 59% | 16% | | | 27.8 | 129 | 153 | $29 |
| 17 CLE | 18 | 0 | 204 | 265 | 2.25 | 2.70 | 0.87 | 556 | 575 | 539 | 26.8 | 1.6 | 11.7 | 7.4 | 64% | 16% | 92.6 | 45 | 22 | 33 | 28% | 81% | 13% | 29 | 102 | 66% | 14% | | | 52.9 | 191 | 229 | $45 |
| 18 CLE | 20 | 0 | 215 | 222 | 2.89 | 3.22 | 0.99 | 624 | 677 | 575 | 25.5 | 1.4 | 9.3 | 6.5 | 63% | 12% | 92.0 | 44 | 22 | 33 | 29% | 77% | 13% | 33 | 96 | 58% | 9% | | | 33.5 | 151 | 174 | $35 |
| 1st Half | 11 | 0 | 113 | 115 | 2.54 | 2.98 | 0.86 | 575 | 579 | 572 | 25.2 | 1.0 | 9.1 | 8.8 | 63% | 11% | 92.1 | 48 | 21 | 31 | 25% | 80% | 17% | 17 | 96 | 71% | 6% | | | 22.5 | 162 | 186 | $44 |
| 2nd Half | 9 | 0 | 102 | 107 | 3.28 | 3.50 | 1.14 | 676 | 771 | 578 | 25.9 | 1.9 | 9.5 | 5.1 | 64% | 14% | 91.9 | 41 | 24 | 35 | 32% | 74% | 9% | 16 | 97 | 44% | 13% | | | 11.0 | 139 | 160 | $25 |
| 19 Proj | 18 | 0 | 218 | 239 | 2.99 | 2.90 | 1.00 | 616 | 665 | 570 | 25.5 | 1.7 | 9.9 | 5.8 | 63% | 14% | 92.3 | 44 | 22 | 34 | 29% | 74% | 12% | 33 | | | | | | 31.2 | 154 | 177 | $34 |

## Knebel,Corey

| | | | | | | |
|---|---|---|---|---|---|---|
| Age: 27 | Th: R | Role: RP | Health | D | LIMA Plan | B+ |
| Ht: 6' 4" | Wt: 220 | Type: Pwr | PT/Exp | B | Rand Var | +5 |
| | | | Consist | B | MM | 5520 |

Rocky follow-up featured hamstring strain in April and Triple-A demotion in August. But don't worry, this was driven by fluky hr/f. Closer-worthy skills are there with plenty of swings and misses, especially if GB% bump holds. Control is still a hurdle, but xERA, BPV say he can hold down a late-inning role.

| Yr Tm | W | Sv | IP | K | ERA | xERA | WHIP | oOPS | vL | vR | BF/G | Ctl | Dom | Cmd | FpK | SwK | Vel | G | L | F | H% | S% | hr/f | GS | APC | DOM% | DIS% | Sv% | LI | RAR | BPV | BPX | R$ |
|---|---|---|---|---|---|---|---|---|---|---|---|---|---|---|---|---|---|---|---|---|---|---|---|---|---|---|---|---|---|---|---|---|---|
| 14 DET * | 5 | 3 | 54 | 64 | 3.06 | 2.28 | 1.13 | 776 | 733 | 826 | 5.1 | 4.1 | 10.6 | 2.6 | 59% | 9% | 94.3 | 48 | 16 | 36 | 27% | 74% | 0% | 0 | 21 | | | 50 | 0.37 | 4.6 | 119 | 142 | $4 |
| 15 MIL * | 1 | 6 | 66 | 76 | 3.67 | 3.92 | 1.27 | 744 | 764 | 728 | 4.2 | 3.3 | 10.4 | 3.2 | 58% | 10% | 94.9 | 49 | 20 | 31 | 32% | 76% | 20% | 0 | 17 | | | 75 | 0.49 | 2.3 | 99 | 118 | $2 |
| 16 MIL | 1 | 2 | 33 | 38 | 4.68 | 4.14 | 1.47 | 708 | 510 | 909 | 4.1 | 4.4 | 10.5 | 2.4 | 61% | 8% | 95.2 | 42 | 21 | 37 | 35% | 69% | 9% | 0 | 17 | | | 50 | 1.00 | -2.0 | 89 | 106 | -$3 |
| 17 MIL | 1 | 39 | 76 | 126 | 1.78 | 3.03 | 1.16 | 568 | 510 | 629 | 4.1 | 4.7 | 14.9 | 3.2 | 51% | 15% | 97.4 | 38 | 17 | 45 | 32% | 89% | 10% | 0 | 18 | | | 87 | 1.49 | 24.2 | 157 | 188 | $27 |
| 18 MIL | 4 | 16 | 55 | 88 | 3.58 | 2.44 | 1.08 | 659 | 613 | 710 | 3.9 | 3.6 | 14.3 | 4.0 | 56% | 14% | 96.9 | 48 | 21 | 31 | 31% | 72% | 21% | 0 | 17 | | | 84 | 1.21 | 3.9 | 187 | 215 | $10 |
| 1st Half | 1 | 8 | 19 | 29 | 3.38 | 2.52 | 1.02 | 630 | 683 | 550 | 3.7 | 4.3 | 14.0 | 3.2 | 57% | 13% | 96.6 | 49 | 23 | 29 | 20% | 80% | 40% | 0 | 16 | | | 80 | 1.32 | 1.8 | 161 | 185 | $4 |
| 2nd Half | 3 | 8 | 37 | 59 | 3.68 | 2.41 | 1.12 | 674 | 571 | 772 | 4.0 | 3.2 | 14.5 | 4.5 | 56% | 14% | 97.1 | 47 | 20 | 32 | 36% | 68% | 13% | 0 | 18 | | | 89 | 1.16 | 2.1 | 200 | 230 | $13 |
| 19 Proj | 3 | 11 | 58 | 87 | 3.11 | 2.73 | 1.15 | 615 | 555 | 678 | 3.9 | 4.2 | 13.5 | 3.2 | 56% | 13% | 96.6 | 45 | 20 | 35 | 31% | 76% | 13% | 0 | | | | | | 15.3 | 152 | 175 | $8 |

## Koch,Matt

| | | | | | | |
|---|---|---|---|---|---|---|
| Age: 28 | Th: R | Role: RP | Health | A | LIMA Plan | D+ |
| Ht: 6' 3" | Wt: 215 | Type: Con | PT/Exp | D | Rand Var | +2 |
| | | | Consist | F | MM | 0000 |

5-5, 4.15 ERA in 87 IP at ARI. Severe 1st/2nd half ERA swing, but three reasons to trust the latter: 1) In age of strikeouts, inability to miss bats sets him back, 2) three straight 5.00+ xERAs, 3) flunking DOM%/DIS% say he's only hurting your roster. String of negative R$ confirms: stay away.

| Yr Tm | W | Sv | IP | K | ERA | xERA | WHIP | oOPS | vL | vR | BF/G | Ctl | Dom | Cmd | FpK | SwK | Vel | G | L | F | H% | S% | hr/f | GS | APC | DOM% | DIS% | Sv% | LI | RAR | BPV | BPX | R$ |
|---|---|---|---|---|---|---|---|---|---|---|---|---|---|---|---|---|---|---|---|---|---|---|---|---|---|---|---|---|---|---|---|---|---|
| 14 | | | | | | | | | | | | | | | | | | | | | | | | | | | | | | | | | |
| 15 aa | 5 | 0 | 96 | 50 | 4.30 | 4.80 | 1.47 | | | | 11.4 | 1.9 | 4.7 | 2.4 | | | | | | | 34% | 71% | | | | | | | | -4.0 | 55 | 65 | -$5 |
| 16 ARI * | 7 | 1 | 139 | 69 | 5.11 | 5.51 | 1.53 | 463 | 349 | 544 | 21.7 | 1.6 | 4.4 | 2.8 | 67% | 9% | 92.0 | 41 | 16 | 43 | 35% | 67% | 5% | 2 | 33 | 0% | 0% | 100 | 1.17 | -15.9 | 48 | 57 | -$8 |
| 17 ARI * | 2 | 0 | 45 | 19 | 10.09 | 9.76 | 2.17 | | 3000 | 2000 | 20.4 | 3.3 | 3.9 | 1.2 | | | 91.6 | | | | 39% | 55% | 0% | 0 | 9 | | | 0 | 0.02 | -31.8 | -46 | -55 | -$19 |
| 18 ARI * | 7 | 0 | 142 | 74 | 4.79 | 5.48 | 1.37 | 816 | 688 | 922 | 19.8 | 2.1 | 4.7 | 2.2 | 61% | 7% | 91.3 | 44 | 22 | 33 | 29% | 71% | 20% | 14 | 68 | 7% | 64% | 0 | 0.63 | -11.2 | 18 | 21 | -$5 |
| 1st Half | 5 | 0 | 91 | 44 | 3.96 | 4.74 | 1.21 | 808 | 655 | 942 | 22.8 | 2.0 | 4.4 | 2.2 | 60% | 7% | 91.3 | 42 | 23 | 36 | 25% | 76% | 19% | 12 | 84 | 8% | 58% | 0 | 0.75 | 2.1 | 21 | 24 | $3 |
| 2nd Half | 2 | 0 | 51 | 29 | 6.26 | 6.80 | 1.65 | 853 | 863 | 845 | 16.3 | 2.4 | 5.2 | 2.1 | 63% | 10% | 91.9 | 58 | 21 | 21 | 35% | 65% | 30% | 2 | 35 | 0% | 100% | 0 | 0.37 | -13.3 | 15 | 17 | -$16 |
| 19 Proj | 2 | 0 | 44 | 22 | 5.15 | 4.86 | 1.57 | 855 | 786 | 905 | 17.8 | 2.4 | 4.5 | 1.9 | 62% | 8% | 91.6 | 46 | 22 | 33 | 33% | 70% | 12% | 8 | | | | | | -1.9 | 41 | 47 | -$7 |

## Lauer,Eric

| | | | | | | |
|---|---|---|---|---|---|---|
| Age: 24 | Th: L | Role: SP | Health | C | LIMA Plan | B+ |
| Ht: 6' 3" | Wt: 205 | Type: Pwr | PT/Exp | D | Rand Var | 0 |
| | | | Consist | A | MM | 1103 |

6-7, 4.34 ERA in 112 IP at SD. Left forearm strain took up most of August before excellent post-injury finish (3 ER in last 25.1 IP). Seeds of deep-league value exist, as SwK/FpK spikes supported 2nd-half ratios. Lack of GBs in minors, xERA hint at some short-term bumps, but he's worth a late flyer.

| Yr Tm | W | Sv | IP | K | ERA | xERA | WHIP | oOPS | vL | vR | BF/G | Ctl | Dom | Cmd | FpK | SwK | Vel | G | L | F | H% | S% | hr/f | GS | APC | DOM% | DIS% | Sv% | LI | RAR | BPV | BPX | R$ |
|---|---|---|---|---|---|---|---|---|---|---|---|---|---|---|---|---|---|---|---|---|---|---|---|---|---|---|---|---|---|---|---|---|---|
| 14 | | | | | | | | | | | | | | | | | | | | | | | | | | | | | | | | | |
| 15 | | | | | | | | | | | | | | | | | | | | | | | | | | | | | | | | | |
| 16 | | | | | | | | | | | | | | | | | | | | | | | | | | | | | | | | | |
| 17 aa | 4 | 0 | 55 | 42 | 5.09 | 4.85 | 1.44 | | | | 23.4 | 2.9 | 6.9 | 2.4 | | | | | | | 33% | 66% | | | | | | | | -5.0 | 57 | 68 | -$4 |
| 18 SD * | 8 | 0 | 134 | 119 | 4.01 | 4.73 | 1.45 | 800 | 844 | 787 | 21.2 | 3.6 | 8.0 | 2.2 | 59% | 9% | 91.2 | 38 | 28 | 35 | 32% | 75% | 13% | 23 | 88 | 13% | 43% | | | 2.2 | 63 | 73 | $0 |
| 1st Half | 5 | 0 | 80 | 70 | 4.59 | 5.53 | 1.57 | 883 | 774 | 910 | 22.0 | 3.6 | 7.9 | 2.2 | 57% | 8% | 90.7 | 36 | 29 | 36 | 35% | 74% | 14% | 13 | 88 | 8% | 54% | | | -4.4 | 53 | 61 | -$5 |
| 2nd Half | 3 | 0 | 54 | 49 | 3.16 | 3.55 | 1.27 | 689 | 921 | 612 | 20.1 | 3.6 | 8.1 | 2.2 | 62% | 10% | 91.9 | 41 | 25 | 34 | 29% | 78% | 11% | 10 | 88 | 20% | 30% | | | 6.6 | 78 | 90 | $6 |
| 19 Proj | 8 | 0 | 145 | 122 | 4.04 | 4.25 | 1.41 | 751 | 846 | 722 | 25.4 | 3.4 | 7.6 | 2.3 | 60% | 9% | 91.4 | 39 | 27 | 35 | 32% | 75% | 12% | 24 | | | | | | -1.6 | 62 | 71 | $2 |

## Leake,Mike

| | | | | | | |
|---|---|---|---|---|---|---|
| Age: 31 | Th: R | Role: SP | Health | B | LIMA Plan | B+ |
| Ht: 5' 10" | Wt: 170 | Type: Con GB | PT/Exp | A | Rand Var | +1 |
| | | | Consist | A | MM | 2005 |

Different year, same old story. Inducing GBs and limiting walks have only taken him so far, as SwK caps his Dom and R$. Without a bunch of Ks, this profile points to league-average ratios that are, admittedly, serviceable in deep leagues. Reliability grades, IP totals say there's plenty more mediocrity to come.

| Yr Tm | W | Sv | IP | K | ERA | xERA | WHIP | oOPS | vL | vR | BF/G | Ctl | Dom | Cmd | FpK | SwK | Vel | G | L | F | H% | S% | hr/f | GS | APC | DOM% | DIS% | Sv% | LI | RAR | BPV | BPX | R$ |
|---|---|---|---|---|---|---|---|---|---|---|---|---|---|---|---|---|---|---|---|---|---|---|---|---|---|---|---|---|---|---|---|---|---|
| 14 CIN | 11 | 0 | 214 | 164 | 3.70 | 3.45 | 1.25 | 730 | 801 | 674 | 27.3 | 2.1 | 6.9 | 3.3 | 60% | 8% | 90.7 | 53 | 20 | 26 | 31% | 73% | 13% | 33 | 97 | 30% | 27% | | | 1.2 | 98 | 117 | $7 |
| 15 2 NL | 11 | 0 | 192 | 119 | 3.70 | 3.95 | 1.16 | 686 | 727 | 635 | 25.9 | 2.3 | 5.6 | 2.4 | 61% | 7% | 90.9 | 52 | 22 | 27 | 26% | 72% | 14% | 30 | 92 | 27% | 33% | | | 6.1 | 68 | 81 | $11 |
| 16 STL | 9 | 0 | 177 | 125 | 4.69 | 3.89 | 1.32 | 756 | 761 | 752 | 25.2 | 1.5 | 6.4 | 4.2 | 62% | 7% | 90.6 | 54 | 21 | 25 | 33% | 66% | 14% | 30 | 89 | 23% | 33% | | | -10.8 | 105 | 125 | $1 |
| 17 2 TM | 10 | 0 | 186 | 130 | 3.92 | 3.98 | 1.28 | 742 | 785 | 700 | 25.2 | 1.8 | 6.3 | 3.5 | 63% | 9% | 90.1 | 54 | 22 | 25 | 31% | 72% | 14% | 31 | 90 | 29% | 26% | | | 10.1 | 97 | 116 | $9 |
| 18 SEA | 10 | 0 | 186 | 119 | 4.36 | 4.25 | 1.30 | 762 | 735 | 786 | 25.3 | 1.6 | 5.8 | 3.5 | 65% | 8% | 88.7 | 49 | 22 | 29 | 31% | 69% | 13% | 31 | 90 | 23% | 35% | | | -4.9 | 86 | 99 | $2 |
| 1st Half | 8 | 0 | 108 | 66 | 4.01 | 4.31 | 1.21 | 735 | 697 | 772 | 26.0 | 2.0 | 5.5 | 2.8 | 65% | 8% | 89.0 | 49 | 21 | 30 | 28% | 71% | 14% | 17 | 94 | 29% | 35% | | | 1.8 | 72 | 83 | $10 |
| 2nd Half | 2 | 0 | 78 | 53 | 4.85 | 4.18 | 1.42 | 798 | 794 | 800 | 24.4 | 1.2 | 6.1 | 5.3 | 65% | 7% | 88.3 | 49 | 23 | 28 | 36% | 67% | 10% | 14 | 85 | 14% | 36% | | | -6.7 | 105 | 121 | -$7 |
| 19 Proj | 9 | 0 | 189 | 128 | 4.12 | 3.79 | 1.31 | 757 | 763 | 752 | 25.4 | 1.6 | 6.1 | 3.7 | 64% | 8% | 89.5 | 51 | 22 | 27 | 32% | 71% | 13% | 31 | | | | | | 5.7 | 94 | 108 | $5 |

BRANT CHESSER

## LeBlanc,Wade

| | | | |
|---|---|---|---|
| Age: 34 Th: L Role SP | Health B | LIMA Plan B | |
| Ht: 6' 3" Wt: 205 Type | PT/Exp C | Rand Var 0 | |
| | Consist B | MM 1101 | |

Moved back to starting role in May on way to career-high IP; more than he'd thrown in past four years combined. Still doing a nice job of limiting BB, but fly balls returned, and velocity was lowest among all SP. Walking very fine line with these skills, and odds are stacked against repeating workload or ERA.

| Yr Tm | W | Sv | IP | K | ERA | xERA | WHIP | oOPS | vL | vR | BF/G | Ctl | Dom | Cmd | FpK | SwK | Vel | G | L | F | H% | S% | hr/f | GS | APC | DOM% | DIS% | Sv% | LI | RAR | BPV | BPX | R$ |
|---|---|---|---|---|---|---|---|---|---|---|---|---|---|---|---|---|---|---|---|---|---|---|---|---|---|---|---|---|---|---|---|---|---|
| 14 2 AL * | 11 | 0 | 158 | 110 | 4.14 | 4.52 | 1.45 | 625 | 627 | 623 | 20.4 | 2.6 | 6.3 | 2.4 | 59% | 9% | 87.8 | 40 | 24 | 36 | 34% | 72% | 6% | 3 | 41 | 0% | 33% | 0 | 0.53 | -7.7 | 67 | 80 | -$3 |
| 15 | | | | | | | | | | | | | | | | | | | | | | | | | | | | | | | | | |
| 16 2 TM * | 11 | 2 | 152 | 114 | 3.25 | 5.07 | 1.45 | 776 | 680 | 801 | 19.6 | 2.2 | 6.8 | 3.0 | 63% | 10% | 86.9 | 34 | 21 | 45 | 34% | 82% | 17% | 8 | 50 | 0% | 38% | 100 | 0.62 | 17.6 | 66 | 78 | $7 |
| 17 PIT | 5 | 1 | 68 | 54 | 4.50 | 4.19 | 1.19 | 717 | 833 | 658 | 5.7 | 2.3 | 7.1 | 3.2 | 60% | 10% | 87.3 | 46 | 23 | 31 | 28% | 66% | 15% | 0 | 21 | | | 33 | 0.71 | -1.2 | 92 | 110 | $1 |
| 18 SEA | 9 | 0 | 162 | 130 | 3.72 | 4.45 | 1.18 | 712 | 698 | 717 | 20.7 | 2.2 | 7.2 | 3.3 | 63% | 10% | 86.3 | 37 | 20 | 43 | 28% | 74% | 12% | 27 | 77 | 11% | 30% | 0 | 0.69 | 8.5 | 85 | 98 | $10 |
| 1st Half | 3 | 0 | 72 | 56 | 3.38 | 4.46 | 1.21 | 701 | 761 | 681 | 18.6 | 1.9 | 7.0 | 3.7 | 68% | 9% | 86.4 | 36 | 23 | 41 | 30% | 77% | 10% | 11 | 68 | 9% | 36% | 0 | 0.62 | 6.9 | 89 | 102 | $5 |
| 2nd Half | 6 | 0 | 90 | 74 | 4.00 | 4.45 | 1.16 | 721 | 650 | 747 | 22.8 | 2.5 | 7.4 | 3.0 | 59% | 10% | 86.2 | 37 | 18 | 44 | 26% | 72% | 13% | 16 | 85 | 13% | 25% | | | 1.7 | 81 | 93 | $14 |
| **19 Proj** | **7** | **0** | **116** | **91** | **4.06** | **4.08** | **1.25** | **752** | **781** | **741** | **20.6** | **2.3** | **7.0** | **3.1** | **62%** | **10%** | **86.7** | **40** | **21** | **39** | **29%** | **73%** | **13%** | **15** | | | | | | **1.4** | **83** | **95** | **$4** |

## Leclerc,Jose

| | | | |
|---|---|---|---|
| Age: 25 Th: R Role RP | Health B | LIMA Plan B | |
| Ht: 6' 0" Wt: 190 Type Pwr xFB | PT/Exp D | Rand Var -5 | |
| | Consist D | MM 3530 | |

More trouble finding plate in 1st half, but then... FpK/Ctl took dramatic turns; SwK/Dom became elite; 12 for 12 in Sv opps in final two months. A little luck also helped, and short track record as closer, Ctl history, FB tilt say he's far from a sure thing. But that will all keep price tag in check, too... you'd hope. UP: 40 Sv.

| Yr Tm | W | Sv | IP | K | ERA | xERA | WHIP | oOPS | vL | vR | BF/G | Ctl | Dom | Cmd | FpK | SwK | Vel | G | L | F | H% | S% | hr/f | GS | APC | DOM% | DIS% | Sv% | LI | RAR | BPV | BPX | R$ |
|---|---|---|---|---|---|---|---|---|---|---|---|---|---|---|---|---|---|---|---|---|---|---|---|---|---|---|---|---|---|---|---|---|---|
| 14 | | | | | | | | | | | | | | | | | | | | | | | | | | | | | | | | | |
| 15 aa | 6 | 0 | 103 | 83 | 6.59 | 5.07 | 1.76 | | | | 18.2 | 6.4 | 7.2 | 1.1 | | | | | | | 32% | 61% | | | | | | | | -33.4 | 46 | 55 | -$18 |
| 16 TEX * | 2 | 2 | 81 | 79 | 3.50 | 3.07 | 1.39 | 710 | 1068 | 507 | 6.7 | 5.9 | 8.8 | 1.5 | 58% | 12% | 94.3 | 29 | 26 | 45 | 27% | 75% | 0% | 0 | 22 | | | 29 | 0.26 | 6.9 | 82 | 97 | $1 |
| 17 TEX | 2 | 2 | 46 | 60 | 3.94 | 4.94 | 1.38 | 585 | 688 | 513 | 4.3 | 7.9 | 11.8 | 1.5 | 55% | 16% | 95.8 | 40 | 10 | 50 | 22% | 73% | 8% | 0 | 18 | | | 67 | 0.90 | 2.3 | 18 | 22 | -$1 |
| 18 TEX | 2 | 12 | 58 | 85 | 1.56 | 3.04 | 0.85 | 431 | 448 | 421 | 3.8 | 3.9 | 13.3 | 3.4 | 57% | 18% | 95.3 | 32 | 21 | 47 | 23% | 81% | 2% | 0 | 16 | | | 75 | 1.30 | 18.4 | 143 | 165 | $14 |
| 1st Half | 2 | 0 | 30 | 41 | 2.43 | 3.65 | 1.04 | 470 | 559 | 426 | 3.9 | 5.2 | 12.4 | 2.4 | 52% | 16% | 94.6 | 32 | 21 | 47 | 25% | 74% | 0% | 0 | 16 | | | 0 | 1.42 | 6.3 | 94 | 108 | $7 |
| 2nd Half | 0 | 12 | 28 | 44 | 0.64 | 2.46 | 0.64 | 388 | 354 | 412 | 3.7 | 2.6 | 14.1 | 5.5 | 63% | 20% | 96.1 | 33 | 20 | 47 | 20% | 94% | 4% | 0 | 16 | | | 92 | 1.16 | 12.1 | 196 | 225 | $22 |
| **19 Proj** | **3** | **30** | **65** | **87** | **2.84** | **3.43** | **1.13** | **622** | **681** | **584** | **4.5** | **4.5** | **12.0** | **2.7** | **57%** | **17%** | **95.6** | **35** | **17** | **48** | **27%** | **79%** | **9%** | **0** | | | | | | **10.6** | **108** | **124** | **$18** |

## Leone,Dominic

| | | | |
|---|---|---|---|
| Age: 27 Th: R Role RP | Health F | LIMA Plan C | |
| Ht: 5' 11" Wt: 210 Type Pwr | PT/Exp D | Rand Var +3 | |
| | Consist C | MM 2300 | |

Nerve damage in biceps wiped out majority of his season. Swing and miss stuff from 2017 held firm, but FpK took another dip. Can probably chalk up sky-high LD% and H% to small sample, but given xERA history, he's probably a long way from saves. Should be safe to watch from a distance.

| Yr Tm | W | Sv | IP | K | ERA | xERA | WHIP | oOPS | vL | vR | BF/G | Ctl | Dom | Cmd | FpK | SwK | Vel | G | L | F | H% | S% | hr/f | GS | APC | DOM% | DIS% | Sv% | LI | RAR | BPV | BPX | R$ |
|---|---|---|---|---|---|---|---|---|---|---|---|---|---|---|---|---|---|---|---|---|---|---|---|---|---|---|---|---|---|---|---|---|---|
| 14 SEA | 8 | 0 | 66 | 70 | 2.17 | 2.98 | 1.16 | 624 | 800 | 511 | 4.8 | 3.4 | 9.5 | 2.8 | 56% | 14% | 94.6 | 55 | 21 | 25 | 29% | 84% | 10% | 0 | 19 | | | 0 | 0.98 | 12.8 | 112 | 134 | $7 |
| 15 2 TM * | 2 | 1 | 52 | 39 | 6.33 | 4.56 | 1.55 | 884 | 668 | 1083 | 5.7 | 4.4 | 6.7 | 1.5 | 62% | 10% | 93.3 | 45 | 22 | 33 | 32% | 58% | 11% | 0 | 22 | | | 25 | 1.26 | -15.2 | 52 | 61 | -$9 |
| 16 ARI * | 5 | 1 | 62 | 52 | 5.02 | 5.90 | 1.57 | 1095 | 1170 | 1044 | 4.7 | 3.4 | 7.6 | 2.3 | 61% | 12% | 93.1 | 47 | 17 | 36 | 34% | 73% | 21% | 0 | 19 | | | 33 | 0.49 | -6.4 | 38 | 45 | -$4 |
| 17 TOR | 3 | 1 | 70 | 81 | 2.56 | 3.69 | 1.05 | 625 | 627 | 624 | 4.3 | 2.9 | 10.4 | 3.5 | 57% | 15% | 94.4 | 40 | 18 | 42 | 28% | 79% | 8% | 0 | 17 | | | 20 | 1.12 | 15.6 | 125 | 150 | $8 |
| 18 STL | 1 | 0 | 24 | 26 | 4.50 | 4.20 | 1.46 | 727 | 831 | 623 | 3.7 | 3.0 | 9.8 | 3.3 | 54% | 15% | 93.8 | 30 | 34 | 37 | 37% | 72% | 12% | 0 | 13 | | | 0 | 0.93 | -1.0 | 103 | 118 | -$5 |
| 1st Half | 1 | 0 | 13 | 15 | 4.15 | 3.85 | 1.38 | 817 | 930 | 702 | 3.7 | 2.1 | 10.4 | 5.0 | 53% | 16% | 94.0 | 24 | 35 | 41 | 36% | 80% | 20% | 0 | 12 | | | 0 | 1.28 | 0.0 | 133 | 153 | -$5 |
| 2nd Half | 0 | 0 | 11 | 11 | 4.91 | 4.66 | 1.55 | 629 | 718 | 541 | 3.6 | 4.1 | 9.0 | 2.2 | 55% | 15% | 93.6 | 35 | 32 | 32 | 37% | 65% | 0% | 0 | 14 | | | 0 | 0.52 | -1.0 | 65 | 74 | -$4 |
| **19 Proj** | **3** | **0** | **51** | **51** | **4.00** | **3.68** | **1.31** | **751** | **852** | **696** | **4.8** | **3.3** | **9.1** | **2.8** | **57%** | **14%** | **94.5** | **46** | **19** | **35** | **32%** | **72%** | **10%** | **0** | | | | | | **1.0** | **100** | **114** | **-$1** |

## Lester,Jon

| | | | |
|---|---|---|---|
| Age: 35 Th: L Role SP | Health B | LIMA Plan C+ | |
| Ht: 6' 4" Wt: 240 Type Pwr | PT/Exp A | Rand Var -2 | |
| | Consist B | MM 2205 | |

A bounce back year on the surface, but in reality, a continuation of his decline. Struggled to generate both GB and swinging strikes, while career-long dominance vL came to screeching halt. 11 straight years of 30+ starts is impressive, but comes with far fewer IP and Ks these days. DN: 2nd half x2.

| Yr Tm | W | Sv | IP | K | ERA | xERA | WHIP | oOPS | vL | vR | BF/G | Ctl | Dom | Cmd | FpK | SwK | Vel | G | L | F | H% | S% | hr/f | GS | APC | DOM% | DIS% | Sv% | LI | RAR | BPV | BPX | R$ |
|---|---|---|---|---|---|---|---|---|---|---|---|---|---|---|---|---|---|---|---|---|---|---|---|---|---|---|---|---|---|---|---|---|---|
| 14 2 AL | 16 | 0 | 220 | 220 | 2.46 | 3.19 | 1.10 | 635 | 697 | 617 | 27.7 | 2.0 | 9.0 | 4.6 | 61% | 10% | 91.8 | 42 | 21 | 37 | 31% | 81% | 7% | 32 | 109 | 59% | 9% | | | 34.8 | 129 | 154 | $26 |
| 15 CHC | 11 | 0 | 205 | 207 | 3.34 | 3.13 | 1.12 | 661 | 658 | 662 | 25.9 | 2.1 | 9.1 | 4.4 | 61% | 11% | 92.0 | 49 | 22 | 29 | 31% | 72% | 10% | 32 | 100 | 44% | 16% | | | 15.8 | 135 | 161 | $19 |
| 16 CHC | 19 | 0 | 203 | 197 | 2.44 | 3.43 | 1.02 | 602 | 540 | 620 | 24.9 | 2.3 | 8.7 | 3.8 | 63% | 11% | 92.1 | 47 | 20 | 33 | 26% | 82% | 12% | 32 | 99 | 50% | 16% | | | 43.7 | 120 | 143 | $34 |
| 17 CHC | 13 | 0 | 181 | 180 | 4.33 | 3.95 | 1.32 | 750 | 554 | 808 | 23.8 | 3.0 | 9.0 | 3.0 | 58% | 11% | 91.1 | 46 | 21 | 32 | 32% | 71% | 16% | 32 | 98 | 25% | 34% | | | 0.5 | 105 | 126 | $9 |
| 18 CHC | 18 | 0 | 182 | 149 | 3.32 | 4.47 | 1.31 | 733 | 878 | 696 | 23.8 | 3.2 | 7.4 | 2.3 | 57% | 9% | 91.0 | 38 | 26 | 36 | 29% | 80% | 12% | 32 | 98 | 22% | 31% | | | 18.6 | 63 | 73 | $14 |
| 1st Half | 10 | 0 | 95 | 74 | 2.18 | 4.36 | 1.08 | 627 | 688 | 610 | 23.9 | 3.0 | 7.0 | 2.3 | 59% | 9% | 90.9 | 39 | 23 | 38 | 24% | 86% | 10% | 16 | 97 | 31% | 19% | | | 23.1 | 61 | 70 | $28 |
| 2nd Half | 8 | 0 | 87 | 75 | 4.57 | 4.57 | 1.56 | 841 | 1096 | 779 | 23.7 | 3.3 | 7.8 | 2.3 | 55% | 8% | 91.1 | 37 | 29 | 34 | 34% | 75% | 15% | 16 | 98 | 13% | 44% | | | -4.5 | 65 | 75 | $1 |
| **19 Proj** | **14** | **0** | **189** | **167** | **3.78** | **3.95** | **1.31** | **728** | **746** | **723** | **26.4** | **3.1** | **8.0** | **2.5** | **58%** | **10%** | **91.3** | **42** | **24** | **34** | **30%** | **75%** | **13%** | **29** | | | | | | **4.1** | **78** | **90** | **$11** |

## Liriano,Francisco

| | | | |
|---|---|---|---|
| Age: 35 Th: L Role SP | Health D | LIMA Plan D+ | |
| Ht: 6' 3" Wt: 218 Type Pwr | PT/Exp B | Rand Var +1 | |
| | Consist B | MM 1201 | |

Hit rate helped keep head above water in 1st half, but poor skills caught up with him. Cmd continued downward spiral, and mediocre SwK, deteriorating FpK say any rebound would be minor. A future LOOGY perhaps? Nah, 20% H% was driving factor in small sample success vL. The end is near.

| Yr Tm | W | Sv | IP | K | ERA | xERA | WHIP | oOPS | vL | vR | BF/G | Ctl | Dom | Cmd | FpK | SwK | Vel | G | L | F | H% | S% | hr/f | GS | APC | DOM% | DIS% | Sv% | LI | RAR | BPV | BPX | R$ |
|---|---|---|---|---|---|---|---|---|---|---|---|---|---|---|---|---|---|---|---|---|---|---|---|---|---|---|---|---|---|---|---|---|---|
| 14 PIT | 7 | 0 | 162 | 175 | 3.38 | 3.33 | 1.30 | 644 | 735 | 622 | 23.8 | 4.5 | 9.7 | 2.2 | 56% | 14% | 92.6 | 54 | 19 | 27 | 29% | 76% | 12% | 29 | 94 | 28% | 28% | | | 7.2 | 85 | 102 | $6 |
| 15 PIT | 12 | 0 | 187 | 205 | 3.38 | 3.21 | 1.21 | 631 | 592 | 641 | 24.9 | 3.4 | 9.9 | 2.9 | 57% | 15% | 92.5 | 51 | 22 | 26 | 30% | 74% | 12% | 31 | 96 | 45% | 13% | | | 13.5 | 116 | 138 | $15 |
| 16 2 TM | 8 | 0 | 163 | 168 | 4.69 | 4.17 | 1.48 | 773 | 739 | 783 | 23.6 | 4.7 | 9.3 | 2.0 | 56% | 12% | 92.8 | 52 | 18 | 30 | 31% | 73% | 19% | 29 | 90 | 24% | 45% | 0 | 0.74 | -10.1 | 70 | 83 | -$2 |
| 17 2 AL | 6 | 0 | 97 | 85 | 5.66 | 5.11 | 1.63 | 824 | 655 | 878 | 11.6 | 4.9 | 7.9 | 1.6 | 54% | 10% | 92.9 | 45 | 20 | 35 | 33% | 66% | 11% | 18 | 46 | 17% | 50% | 0 | 0.86 | -15.6 | 32 | 39 | -$8 |
| 18 DET | 5 | 0 | 134 | 110 | 4.58 | 4.72 | 1.50 | 771 | 516 | 824 | 21.7 | 4.9 | 7.4 | 1.5 | 53% | 10% | 92.0 | 48 | 22 | 30 | 29% | 73% | 16% | 26 | 84 | 12% | 54% | 0 | 0.79 | -7.1 | 27 | 31 | -$6 |
| 1st Half | 3 | 0 | 68 | 52 | 3.99 | 4.81 | 1.30 | 698 | 444 | 765 | 23.2 | 4.8 | 6.9 | 1.4 | 56% | 10% | 91.9 | 45 | 18 | 37 | 24% | 73% | 13% | 12 | 90 | 17% | 58% | | | 1.3 | 18 | 21 | $0 |
| 2nd Half | 2 | 0 | 66 | 58 | 5.18 | 4.63 | 1.70 | 838 | 616 | 873 | 20.5 | 5.0 | 7.9 | 1.6 | 51% | 10% | 92.2 | 51 | 25 | 24 | 34% | 73% | 21% | 14 | 79 | 7% | 50% | 0 | 0.80 | -8.4 | 36 | 41 | -$11 |
| **19 Proj** | **5** | **0** | **102** | **88** | **4.81** | **4.40** | **1.52** | **780** | **620** | **819** | **20.9** | **4.8** | **7.8** | **1.6** | **54%** | **11%** | **92.4** | **49** | **21** | **30** | **31%** | **71%** | **15%** | **19** | | | | | | **-2.7** | **38** | **44** | **-$6** |

## Loaisiga,Jonathan

| | | | |
|---|---|---|---|
| Age: 24 Th: R Role SP | Health A | LIMA Plan A | |
| Ht: 5' 11" Wt: 165 Type Pwr | PT/Exp F | Rand Var +5 | |
| | Consist F | MM 3401 | |

2-0, 5.11 ERA in 25 IP at NYY. Flashed electric stuff in four starts after June promotion, then hit DL with bum shoulder. Ratios were ugly, but high Dom was fully supported by SwK, and GB% adds to intrigue. Can't expect hefty workload, but he's a low cost, upside target to round out your future rotation.

| Yr Tm | W | Sv | IP | K | ERA | xERA | WHIP | oOPS | vL | vR | BF/G | Ctl | Dom | Cmd | FpK | SwK | Vel | G | L | F | H% | S% | hr/f | GS | APC | DOM% | DIS% | Sv% | LI | RAR | BPV | BPX | R$ |
|---|---|---|---|---|---|---|---|---|---|---|---|---|---|---|---|---|---|---|---|---|---|---|---|---|---|---|---|---|---|---|---|---|---|
| 14 | | | | | | | | | | | | | | | | | | | | | | | | | | | | | | | | | |
| 15 | | | | | | | | | | | | | | | | | | | | | | | | | | | | | | | | | |
| 16 | | | | | | | | | | | | | | | | | | | | | | | | | | | | | | | | | |
| 17 | | | | | | | | | | | | | | | | | | | | | | | | | | | | | | | | | |
| 18 NYY * | 5 | 0 | 60 | 67 | 5.18 | 5.96 | 1.51 | 789 | 792 | 787 | 14.4 | 2.8 | 10.1 | 3.6 | 63% | 14% | 96.0 | 49 | 27 | 24 | 37% | 71% | 20% | 4 | 55 | 25% | 50% | 0 | 0.44 | -7.6 | 79 | 91 | -$5 |
| 1st Half | 5 | 0 | 39 | 45 | 4.46 | 5.19 | 1.43 | 540 | 492 | 575 | 18.4 | 2.6 | 10.4 | 4.0 | 67% | 14% | 95.9 | 58 | 29 | 13 | 37% | 73% | 0% | 3 | 87 | 33% | 33% | | | -1.5 | 104 | 119 | -$2 |
| 2nd Half | 0 | 0 | 21 | 22 | 6.53 | 7.40 | 1.66 | 1052 | 1048 | 1056 | 10.3 | 3.2 | 9.4 | 3.0 | 59% | 13% | 96.1 | 41 | 25 | 34 | 37% | 68% | 27% | 1 | 40 | 0% | 100% | 0 | 0.29 | -6.1 | 35 | 40 | -$11 |
| **19 Proj** | **5** | **0** | **73** | **80** | **3.79** | **3.44** | **1.24** | | | | **21.7** | **3.1** | **9.9** | **3.2** | **62%** | **13%** | | **42** | **23** | **35** | **31%** | **74%** | **15%** | **14** | | | | | | **7.0** | **114** | **132** | **$2** |

## Lopez,Jorge

| | | | |
|---|---|---|---|
| Age: 26 Th: R Role RP | Health A | LIMA Plan D+ | |
| Ht: 6' 3" Wt: 195 Type Pwr | PT/Exp D | Rand Var +2 | |
| | Consist C | MM 0101 | |

2-5, 5.03 ERA in 54 IP at MIL/KC. Back and forth between SP and RP past couple years, but hasn't performed well in either role. Improved Ctl after July trade, but FpK went in wrong direction, as did SwK and FB%. Recent ERA/xERA history says no reason he should be on your radar for 2019.

| Yr Tm | W | Sv | IP | K | ERA | xERA | WHIP | oOPS | vL | vR | BF/G | Ctl | Dom | Cmd | FpK | SwK | Vel | G | L | F | H% | S% | hr/f | GS | APC | DOM% | DIS% | Sv% | LI | RAR | BPV | BPX | R$ |
|---|---|---|---|---|---|---|---|---|---|---|---|---|---|---|---|---|---|---|---|---|---|---|---|---|---|---|---|---|---|---|---|---|---|
| 14 | | | | | | | | | | | | | | | | | | | | | | | | | | | | | | | | | |
| 15 MIL * | 13 | 0 | 153 | 128 | 3.22 | 3.56 | 1.32 | 860 | 971 | 793 | 24.4 | 3.6 | 7.5 | 2.1 | 57% | 10% | 93.6 | 57 | 23 | 20 | 30% | 77% | 0% | 2 | 94 | 0% | 50% | | | 14.0 | 75 | 90 | $10 |
| 16 a/a | 3 | 0 | 125 | 98 | 7.20 | 7.26 | 1.96 | | | | 23.8 | 5.3 | 7.0 | 1.3 | | | | | | | 37% | 65% | | | | | | | | -46.3 | 12 | 14 | -$27 |
| 17 MIL * | 8 | 7 | 106 | 89 | 6.73 | 5.41 | 1.63 | 1056 | 1100 | 1000 | 11.8 | 3.9 | 7.6 | 2.0 | 60% | 6% | 94.8 | 44 | 33 | 22 | 36% | 58% | 0% | 0 | 35 | | | 78 | 0.04 | -31.0 | 53 | 64 | -$9 |
| 18 2 TM * | 6 | 5 | 93 | 65 | 5.64 | 5.21 | 1.51 | 763 | 728 | 814 | 9.4 | 3.3 | 6.3 | 1.9 | 61% | 9% | 93.7 | 45 | 23 | 32 | 33% | 64% | 11% | 7 | 52 | 29% | 71% | 71 | 0.57 | -17.0 | 43 | 49 | -$7 |
| 1st Half | 3 | 5 | 38 | 28 | 4.58 | 4.13 | 1.48 | 812 | 702 | 937 | 6.0 | 4.4 | 6.6 | 1.5 | 67% | 11% | 94.1 | 53 | 22 | 25 | 31% | 68% | 11% | 0 | 33 | | | 71 | 0.21 | -2.0 | 60 | 69 | -$3 |
| 2nd Half | 3 | 0 | 55 | 37 | 6.36 | 5.95 | 1.53 | 747 | 730 | 772 | 15.0 | 2.5 | 6.0 | 2.5 | 59% | 8% | 93.5 | 43 | 23 | 34 | 34% | 60% | 11% | 7 | 66 | 29% | 71% | 0 | 0.82 | -15.1 | 36 | 41 | -$10 |
| **19 Proj** | **5** | **0** | **73** | **55** | **5.28** | **4.64** | **1.53** | **722** | **701** | **751** | **11.7** | **3.7** | **6.9** | **1.9** | **59%** | **8%** | **93.5** | **43** | **23** | **34** | **33%** | **67%** | **10%** | **5** | | | | | | **-3.4** | **45** | **52** | **-$6** |

BRIAN RUDD

### Lopez,Pablo

| | | | | | | |
|---|---|---|---|---|---|---|
| Age: 23 | Th: R | Role: SP | Health | C | LIMA Plan | B+ |
| Ht: 6' 3" | Wt: 200 | Type: GB | PT/Exp | F | Rand Var | 0 |
| | | | Consist | F | MM | 2101 |

2-4, 4.14 ERA in 59 IP at MIA. Made rapid ascension from Double-A to majors, where he held his own until August shoulder strain ended season. Minor league track record says there isn't much K upside, but GB lean and 1.5 career Ctl set a firm foundation. A good place to speculate in your end game.

| Yr Tm | W | Sv | IP | K | ERA | xERA | WHIP | oOPS | vL | vR | BF/G | Ctl | Dom | Cmd | FpK | SwK | Vel | G | L | F | H% | S% | hr/f | GS | APC | DOM% | DIS% | Sv% | LI | RAR | BPV | BPX | R$ |
|---|---|---|---|---|---|---|---|---|---|---|---|---|---|---|---|---|---|---|---|---|---|---|---|---|---|---|---|---|---|---|---|---|---|
| 14 | | | | | | | | | | | | | | | | | | | | | | | | | | | | | | | | | |
| 15 | | | | | | | | | | | | | | | | | | | | | | | | | | | | | | | | | |
| 16 | | | | | | | | | | | | | | | | | | | | | | | | | | | | | | | | | |
| 17 | | | | | | | | | | | | | | | | | | | | | | | | | | | | | | | | | |
| 18 MIA * | 4 | 0 | 124 | 104 | 2.77 | 3.24 | 1.10 | 745 | 679 | 809 | 22.1 | 2.2 | 7.6 | 3.5 | 62% | 11% | 92.4 | 50 | 21 | 29 | 27% | 80% | 16% | 10 | 95 | 10% | 40% | | | 21.1 | 97 | 112 | $11 |
| 1st Half | 3 | 0 | 71 | 63 | 1.67 | 2.70 | 0.97 | 857 | 200 | 1352 | 20.8 | 1.6 | 8.0 | 4.9 | 68% | 7% | 92.4 | 56 | 17 | 28 | 26% | 91% | 40% | 1 | 97 | 0% | 0% | | | 21.9 | 133 | 153 | $21 |
| 2nd Half | 1 | 0 | 53 | 41 | 4.27 | 4.11 | 1.27 | 732 | 725 | 738 | 24.7 | 2.9 | 7.0 | 2.4 | 62% | 12% | 92.4 | 49 | 22 | 29 | 29% | 69% | 13% | 9 | 95 | 11% | 44% | | | -0.8 | 75 | 86 | -$2 |
| **19 Proj** | **5** | **0** | **102** | **81** | **3.93** | **3.80** | **1.21** | **673** | **664** | **681** | **23.0** | **2.4** | **7.2** | **3.0** | **62%** | **10%** | **92.4** | **48** | **22** | **31** | **29%** | **71%** | **12%** | **18** | | | | | | **2.8** | **90** | **104** | **$3** |

### Lopez,Reynaldo

| | | | | | | |
|---|---|---|---|---|---|---|
| Age: 25 | Th: R | Role: SP | Health | A | LIMA Plan | C+ |
| Ht: 6' 1" | Wt: 200 | Type: Pwr xFB | PT/Exp | B | Rand Var | -2 |
| | | | Consist | A | MM | 1203 |

Some good fortune was about all he had going for him in 1st half, but eventually showed some positive signs, leading to 1.13 ERA, 9.2 Dom in final six starts. Pedigree offers hope he can put it all together, but high FB%, spotty Ctl, and sub-2.0 Cmd vL say there will be more bumps in the road.

| Yr Tm | W | Sv | IP | K | ERA | xERA | WHIP | oOPS | vL | vR | BF/G | Ctl | Dom | Cmd | FpK | SwK | Vel | G | L | F | H% | S% | hr/f | GS | APC | DOM% | DIS% | Sv% | LI | RAR | BPV | BPX | R$ |
|---|---|---|---|---|---|---|---|---|---|---|---|---|---|---|---|---|---|---|---|---|---|---|---|---|---|---|---|---|---|---|---|---|---|
| 14 | | | | | | | | | | | | | | | | | | | | | | | | | | | | | | | | | |
| 15 | | | | | | | | | | | | | | | | | | | | | | | | | | | | | | | | | |
| 16 WAS * | 10 | 0 | 153 | 151 | 4.51 | 4.46 | 1.40 | 772 | 666 | 885 | 21.6 | 3.5 | 8.9 | 2.5 | 56% | 10% | 95.8 | 41 | 23 | 35 | 33% | 71% | 9% | 6 | 73 | 17% | 50% | 0 | 0.62 | -6.1 | 74 | 88 | $1 |
| 17 CHW * | 9 | 0 | 169 | 144 | 4.51 | 4.45 | 1.35 | 741 | 808 | 676 | 23.5 | 3.4 | 7.7 | 2.2 | 61% | 9% | 94.5 | 30 | 22 | 48 | 29% | 71% | 9% | 8 | 96 | 0% | 50% | | | -3.3 | 56 | 68 | $3 |
| 18 CHW | 7 | 0 | 189 | 151 | 3.91 | 5.05 | 1.27 | 713 | 703 | 724 | 25.0 | 3.6 | 7.2 | 2.0 | 60% | 10% | 95.5 | 33 | 20 | 47 | 27% | 73% | 9% | 32 | 96 | 31% | 28% | | | 5.5 | 44 | 51 | $6 |
| 1st Half | 3 | 0 | 94 | 67 | 3.73 | 5.37 | 1.28 | 711 | 745 | 671 | 24.9 | 3.7 | 6.4 | 1.7 | 63% | 10% | 95.4 | 34 | 17 | 49 | 26% | 74% | 8% | 16 | 94 | 25% | 31% | | | 4.8 | 26 | 30 | $4 |
| 2nd Half | 4 | 0 | 95 | 84 | 4.09 | 4.74 | 1.27 | 714 | 656 | 768 | 25.1 | 3.4 | 8.0 | 2.3 | 57% | 10% | 95.7 | 32 | 23 | 45 | 28% | 73% | 11% | 16 | 99 | 38% | 25% | | | 0.7 | 62 | 71 | $8 |
| **19 Proj** | **8** | **0** | **174** | **149** | **4.24** | **4.47** | **1.32** | **726** | **726** | **725** | **23.5** | **3.5** | **7.7** | **2.2** | **59%** | **10%** | **95.2** | **33** | **21** | **45** | **29%** | **72%** | **10%** | **31** | | | | | | **-1.9** | **55** | **63** | **$4** |

### Lorenzen,Michael

| | | | | | | |
|---|---|---|---|---|---|---|
| Age: 27 | Th: R | Role: RP | Health | F | LIMA Plan | B |
| Ht: 6' 3" | Wt: 217 | Type: Pwr GB | PT/Exp | C | Rand Var | -3 |
| | | | Consist | B | MM | 2101 |

Shoulder strain kept him out until late May; skills never got on track despite solid ERA. With lower velocity, SwK dropped on all of his pitches, while GB% became less extreme. Even took a step back vR, as Dom fell. September trial as SP puts future role up in the air, but either way, value will be minimal.

| Yr Tm | W | Sv | IP | K | ERA | xERA | WHIP | oOPS | vL | vR | BF/G | Ctl | Dom | Cmd | FpK | SwK | Vel | G | L | F | H% | S% | hr/f | GS | APC | DOM% | DIS% | Sv% | LI | RAR | BPV | BPX | R$ |
|---|---|---|---|---|---|---|---|---|---|---|---|---|---|---|---|---|---|---|---|---|---|---|---|---|---|---|---|---|---|---|---|---|---|
| 14 aa | 4 | 0 | 121 | 76 | 3.50 | 4.16 | 1.38 | | | | 21.1 | 3.2 | 5.7 | 1.8 | | | | | | | 30% | 77% | | | | | | | | 3.6 | 48 | 58 | -$1 |
| 15 CIN * | 8 | 0 | 156 | 100 | 4.59 | 5.12 | 1.52 | 882 | 1007 | 784 | 20.5 | 3.8 | 5.8 | 1.5 | 57% | 9% | 94.0 | 41 | 28 | 31 | 31% | 73% | 16% | 21 | 74 | 0% | 57% | 0 | 0.69 | -12.1 | 28 | 33 | -$8 |
| 16 CIN | 2 | 0 | 50 | 48 | 2.88 | 2.80 | 1.08 | 630 | 548 | 708 | 5.8 | 2.3 | 8.6 | 3.7 | 63% | 10% | 96.2 | 63 | 21 | 16 | 28% | 78% | 23% | 0 | 22 | | | 0 | 0.84 | 8.1 | 133 | 158 | $3 |
| 17 CIN | 8 | 2 | 83 | 80 | 4.45 | 3.91 | 1.35 | 695 | 770 | 635 | 5.2 | 3.7 | 8.7 | 2.4 | 52% | 11% | 96.4 | 55 | 20 | 25 | 31% | 69% | 15% | 0 | 20 | | | 29 | 1.00 | -0.9 | 90 | 108 | $2 |
| 18 CIN | 4 | 1 | 81 | 54 | 3.11 | 4.50 | 1.38 | 707 | 801 | 638 | 7.6 | 3.8 | 6.0 | 1.6 | 59% | 7% | 95.1 | 50 | 25 | 25 | 29% | 79% | 10% | 3 | 29 | 0% | 33% | 50 | 0.84 | 10.4 | 34 | 39 | $1 |
| 1st Half | 1 | 1 | 23 | 12 | 1.93 | 4.67 | 1.20 | 617 | 727 | 525 | 6.3 | 3.9 | 4.6 | 1.2 | 54% | 6% | 95.3 | 50 | 26 | 24 | 25% | 82% | 0% | 0 | 24 | | | 50 | 0.96 | 6.4 | 7 | 8 | -$2 |
| 2nd Half | 3 | 0 | 58 | 42 | 3.59 | 4.43 | 1.46 | 740 | 831 | 676 | 8.3 | 3.7 | 6.6 | 1.8 | 60% | 8% | 95.1 | 50 | 24 | 25 | 31% | 78% | 13% | 3 | 31 | 0% | 33% | 0 | 0.77 | 4.0 | 45 | 52 | $2 |
| **19 Proj** | **4** | **0** | **73** | **56** | **3.78** | **3.96** | **1.36** | **716** | **779** | **665** | **6.7** | **3.5** | **6.9** | **2.0** | **57%** | **9%** | **95.5** | **52** | **23** | **24** | **30%** | **74%** | **12%** | **0** | | | | | | **3.3** | **60** | **69** | **$0** |

### Lucchesi,Joey

| | | | | | | |
|---|---|---|---|---|---|---|
| Age: 26 | Th: L | Role: SP | Health | C | LIMA Plan | A |
| Ht: 6' 5" | Wt: 204 | Type: Pwr | PT/Exp | D | Rand Var | +4 |
| | | | Consist | A | MM | 3303 |

Solid debut could have been even better if not for a punishing hr/f. Hip strain cost him a month, but surprising swing and miss stuff improved in 2nd half, including 28% SwK on change-up in last seven GS. Lack of third pitch prevents us from going all in, but most signs point to strong encore with plenty of Ks.

| Yr Tm | W | Sv | IP | K | ERA | xERA | WHIP | oOPS | vL | vR | BF/G | Ctl | Dom | Cmd | FpK | SwK | Vel | G | L | F | H% | S% | hr/f | GS | APC | DOM% | DIS% | Sv% | LI | RAR | BPV | BPX | R$ |
|---|---|---|---|---|---|---|---|---|---|---|---|---|---|---|---|---|---|---|---|---|---|---|---|---|---|---|---|---|---|---|---|---|---|
| 14 | | | | | | | | | | | | | | | | | | | | | | | | | | | | | | | | | |
| 15 | | | | | | | | | | | | | | | | | | | | | | | | | | | | | | | | | |
| 16 | | | | | | | | | | | | | | | | | | | | | | | | | | | | | | | | | |
| 17 aa | 5 | 1 | 60 | 45 | 2.42 | 3.18 | 1.19 | | | | 24.2 | 2.3 | 6.7 | 3.0 | | | | | | | 30% | 81% | | | | | | | | 14.4 | 92 | 110 | $5 |
| 18 SD | 8 | 0 | 130 | 145 | 4.08 | 3.57 | 1.29 | 766 | 630 | 800 | 21.1 | 3.0 | 10.0 | 3.4 | 59% | 11% | 90.4 | 45 | 23 | 33 | 32% | 75% | 20% | 26 | 83 | 15% | 31% | | | 1.0 | 123 | 142 | $4 |
| 1st Half | 4 | 0 | 58 | 60 | 3.26 | 3.71 | 1.22 | 711 | 565 | 751 | 19.8 | 3.6 | 9.3 | 2.6 | 57% | 10% | 90.1 | 47 | 21 | 32 | 27% | 82% | 21% | 12 | 80 | 8% | 42% | | | 6.4 | 97 | 111 | $6 |
| 2nd Half | 4 | 0 | 72 | 85 | 4.75 | 3.46 | 1.35 | 808 | 686 | 836 | 22.1 | 2.5 | 10.6 | 4.3 | 60% | 12% | 90.7 | 43 | 24 | 33 | 35% | 70% | 20% | 14 | 86 | 21% | 21% | | | -5.3 | 144 | 166 | $3 |
| **19 Proj** | **10** | **0** | **152** | **153** | **3.73** | **3.48** | **1.25** | **724** | **616** | **751** | **21.9** | **2.7** | **9.0** | **3.4** | **59%** | **11%** | **90.4** | **44** | **23** | **33** | **31%** | **75%** | **15%** | **28** | | | | | | **12.6** | **113** | **130** | **$9** |

### Lugo,Seth

| | | | | | | |
|---|---|---|---|---|---|---|
| Age: 29 | Th: R | Role: RP | Health | D | LIMA Plan | B |
| Ht: 6' 4" | Wt: 225 | Type: Pwr | PT/Exp | C | Rand Var | -2 |
| | | | Consist | B | MM | 3211 |

Was used as multi-inning RP for most of season, and thrived. Increased velocity, curveball usage fueled Dom spike, and he racked up the occasional save as added bonus. Though xERA isn't fully buying in yet, stellar final two months (27/3 K/BB in 25.2 IP) suggests more save opps may be on the horizon.

| Yr Tm | W | Sv | IP | K | ERA | xERA | WHIP | oOPS | vL | vR | BF/G | Ctl | Dom | Cmd | FpK | SwK | Vel | G | L | F | H% | S% | hr/f | GS | APC | DOM% | DIS% | Sv% | LI | RAR | BPV | BPX | R$ |
|---|---|---|---|---|---|---|---|---|---|---|---|---|---|---|---|---|---|---|---|---|---|---|---|---|---|---|---|---|---|---|---|---|---|
| 14 | | | | | | | | | | | | | | | | | | | | | | | | | | | | | | | | | |
| 15 a/a | 8 | 0 | 136 | 103 | 4.27 | 4.41 | 1.39 | | | | 23.9 | 2.3 | 6.8 | 2.9 | | | | | | | 34% | 70% | | | | | | | | -5.3 | 77 | 92 | -$1 |
| 16 NYM * | 8 | 0 | 137 | 96 | 4.80 | 5.14 | 1.50 | 666 | 672 | 661 | 15.6 | 2.8 | 6.3 | 2.3 | 64% | 10% | 92.1 | 43 | 19 | 38 | 33% | 70% | 10% | 8 | 57 | 13% | 38% | 0 | 0.65 | -10.3 | 48 | 57 | -$5 |
| 17 NYM | 7 | 0 | 101 | 85 | 4.71 | 4.37 | 1.37 | 770 | 772 | 768 | 22.9 | 2.2 | 7.5 | 3.4 | 59% | 9% | 91.1 | 42 | 24 | 34 | 33% | 68% | 12% | 18 | 86 | 17% | 33% | 0 | 0.79 | -4.4 | 96 | 115 | $0 |
| 18 NYM | 3 | 3 | 101 | 103 | 2.66 | 3.54 | 1.08 | 595 | 552 | 633 | 7.6 | 2.5 | 9.1 | 3.7 | 64% | 11% | 93.9 | 46 | 20 | 33 | 28% | 79% | 10% | 5 | 30 | 20% | 40% | 75 | 0.93 | 18.6 | 122 | 140 | $11 |
| 1st Half | 2 | 0 | 59 | 63 | 2.91 | 3.45 | 1.09 | 622 | 550 | 680 | 9.3 | 2.3 | 9.7 | 4.2 | 66% | 11% | 93.5 | 46 | 20 | 34 | 29% | 79% | 13% | 5 | 36 | 20% | 40% | 0 | 0.86 | 8.9 | 136 | 156 | $11 |
| 2nd Half | 1 | 3 | 43 | 40 | 2.32 | 3.66 | 1.05 | 555 | 555 | 557 | 6.0 | 2.7 | 8.4 | 3.1 | 61% | 10% | 94.4 | 47 | 20 | 32 | 27% | 79% | 5% | 0 | 24 | | | 100 | 1.01 | 9.6 | 103 | 119 | $11 |
| **19 Proj** | **4** | **8** | **87** | **81** | **3.29** | **3.49** | **1.16** | **661** | **651** | **670** | **10.2** | **2.3** | **8.4** | **3.7** | **62%** | **10%** | **92.7** | **45** | **21** | **34** | **30%** | **75%** | **10%** | **0** | | | | | | **6.6** | **112** | **129** | **$9** |

### Luzardo,Jesus

| | | | | | | |
|---|---|---|---|---|---|---|
| Age: 21 | Th: L | Role: SP | Health | A | LIMA Plan | B+ |
| Ht: 6' 1" | Wt: 205 | Type: Pwr | PT/Exp | F | Rand Var | 0 |
| | | | Consist | F | MM | 2203 |

Two years removed from Tommy John surgery, OAK's cautious approach prevented September call-up. Stock soared during dominant season—most of which was spent as youngest pitcher in Double-A—that included 51 IP, 3 ER mid-year stretch. Workload will surely be monitored, but he looks ready to make an impact.

| Yr Tm | W | Sv | IP | K | ERA | xERA | WHIP | oOPS | vL | vR | BF/G | Ctl | Dom | Cmd | FpK | SwK | Vel | G | L | F | H% | S% | hr/f | GS | APC | DOM% | DIS% | Sv% | LI | RAR | BPV | BPX | R$ |
|---|---|---|---|---|---|---|---|---|---|---|---|---|---|---|---|---|---|---|---|---|---|---|---|---|---|---|---|---|---|---|---|---|---|
| 14 | | | | | | | | | | | | | | | | | | | | | | | | | | | | | | | | | |
| 15 | | | | | | | | | | | | | | | | | | | | | | | | | | | | | | | | | |
| 16 | | | | | | | | | | | | | | | | | | | | | | | | | | | | | | | | | |
| 17 | | | | | | | | | | | | | | | | | | | | | | | | | | | | | | | | | |
| 18 a/a | 8 | 0 | 96 | 89 | 3.47 | 3.34 | 1.19 | | | | 19.3 | 2.2 | 8.3 | 3.8 | | | | | | | 32% | 72% | | | | | | | | 8.1 | 116 | 133 | $6 |
| 1st Half | 4 | 0 | 54 | 51 | 3.32 | 3.11 | 1.14 | | | | 19.5 | 2.2 | 8.5 | 3.9 | | | | | | | 31% | 72% | | | | | | | | 5.6 | 121 | 139 | $7 |
| 2nd Half | 4 | 0 | 42 | 38 | 3.61 | 3.58 | 1.24 | | | | 18.9 | 2.2 | 8.1 | 3.6 | | | | | | | 32% | 71% | | | | | | | | 2.8 | 110 | 126 | $5 |
| **19 Proj** | **8** | **0** | **131** | **117** | **4.07** | **3.66** | **1.30** | | | | **23.0** | **2.4** | **8.1** | **3.4** | **63%** | **10%** | | **46** | **22** | **32** | **33%** | **70%** | **9%** | **17** | | | | | | **7.1** | **106** | **121** | **$4** |

### Lyles,Jordan

| | | | | | | |
|---|---|---|---|---|---|---|
| Age: 28 | Th: R | Role: RP | Health | F | LIMA Plan | C |
| Ht: 6' 4" | Wt: 230 | Type: Pwr | PT/Exp | D | Rand Var | 0 |
| | | | Consist | C | MM | 2200 |

FpK was up all year, and after returning from mid-year forearm issue, throwing more curves helped drive SwK surge. However, can't buy into success vL, which was aided by 22% H%; and late-season run was a tiny sample. There's some hope if he stays in the 'pen, but be ready to jump ship quickly.

| Yr Tm | W | Sv | IP | K | ERA | xERA | WHIP | oOPS | vL | vR | BF/G | Ctl | Dom | Cmd | FpK | SwK | Vel | G | L | F | H% | S% | hr/f | GS | APC | DOM% | DIS% | Sv% | LI | RAR | BPV | BPX | R$ |
|---|---|---|---|---|---|---|---|---|---|---|---|---|---|---|---|---|---|---|---|---|---|---|---|---|---|---|---|---|---|---|---|---|---|
| 14 COL | 7 | 0 | 127 | 90 | 4.33 | 3.90 | 1.37 | 750 | 844 | 654 | 24.8 | 3.3 | 6.4 | 2.0 | 57% | 8% | 91.3 | 52 | 23 | 26 | 30% | 70% | 12% | 22 | 95 | 5% | 32% | | | -9.3 | 57 | 68 | -$2 |
| 15 COL | 2 | 0 | 49 | 30 | 5.14 | 4.45 | 1.49 | 751 | 797 | 697 | 21.2 | 3.5 | 5.5 | 1.6 | 58% | 8% | 92.1 | 50 | 26 | 25 | 32% | 63% | 5% | 10 | 77 | 0% | 30% | | | -7.1 | 33 | 39 | -$6 |
| 16 COL * | 8 | 1 | 103 | 53 | 6.80 | 6.56 | 1.87 | 790 | 902 | 713 | 10.1 | 4.2 | 4.6 | 1.1 | 60% | 7% | 92.9 | 51 | 24 | 25 | 36% | 63% | 8% | 5 | 24 | 20% | 80% | 25 | 0.98 | -33.3 | 10 | 11 | -$18 |
| 17 2 NL * | 2 | 0 | 90 | 71 | 7.06 | 6.48 | 1.65 | 948 | 1030 | 879 | 9.3 | 3.0 | 7.1 | 2.4 | 55% | 10% | 93.8 | 49 | 19 | 32 | 36% | 59% | 21% | 5 | 33 | 0% | 40% | 0 | 0.44 | -29.9 | 33 | 40 | -$15 |
| 18 2 NL | 3 | 0 | 88 | 84 | 4.11 | 4.07 | 1.27 | 718 | 568 | 837 | 10.6 | 2.9 | 8.6 | 3.0 | 67% | 11% | 93.6 | 46 | 17 | 37 | 30% | 72% | 13% | 8 | 40 | 38% | 50% | 0 | 0.65 | 0.5 | 102 | 117 | $0 |
| 1st Half | 2 | 0 | 67 | 56 | 4.46 | 4.25 | 1.28 | 746 | 569 | 896 | 13.4 | 2.4 | 7.6 | 3.1 | 68% | 9% | 93.3 | 47 | 16 | 37 | 29% | 71% | 16% | 8 | 49 | 38% | 50% | 0 | 0.51 | -2.5 | 95 | 109 | $0 |
| 2nd Half | 1 | 0 | 21 | 28 | 3.00 | 3.50 | 1.24 | 621 | 556 | 661 | 6.4 | 4.3 | 12.0 | 2.8 | 66% | 15% | 94.5 | 41 | 22 | 37 | 34% | 73% | 0% | 0 | 24 | | | 0 | 0.86 | 3.0 | 119 | 137 | $0 |
| **19 Proj** | **2** | **0** | **58** | **53** | **4.42** | **3.83** | **1.36** | **746** | **748** | **745** | **8.9** | **3.0** | **8.2** | **2.7** | **62%** | **11%** | **93.6** | **47** | **21** | **33** | **32%** | **69%** | **11%** | **0** | | | | | | **2.1** | **90** | **103** | **-$3** |

BRIAN RUDD

## Lynn,Lance

| | | | | | | |
|---|---|---|---|---|---|---|
| Age: 32 | Th: R | Role SP | Health | F | LIMA Plan | C |
| Ht: 6' 5" | Wt: 280 | Type Pwr | PT/Exp | B | Rand Var | +3 |
| | | | Consist | B | MM | 2203 |

Second season after Tommy John a big step back from first. Luck factors (H%/S%) certainly hurt, but walks did plenty of damage too, and FpK plunge questions 2nd half Ctl "gains." It's not all bad news—he set career highs in GB% and SwK—so while xERA says to expect a rebound, don't bet on a return to 2017's line.

| Yr Tm | W | Sv | IP | K | ERA | xERA | WHIP | oOPS | vL | vR | BF/G | Ctl | Dom | Cmd | FpK | SwK | Vel | G | L | F | H% | S% | hr/f | GS | APC | DOM% | DIS% | Sv% | LI | RAR | BPV | BPX | R$ |
|---|---|---|---|---|---|---|---|---|---|---|---|---|---|---|---|---|---|---|---|---|---|---|---|---|---|---|---|---|---|---|---|---|---|
| 14 STL | 15 | 0 | 204 | 181 | 2.74 | 3.81 | 1.26 | 662 | 697 | 635 | 26.2 | 3.2 | 8.0 | 2.5 | 60% | 9% | 92.4 | 44 | 20 | 36 | 30% | 80% | 6% | 33 | 105 | 30% | 18% | | | 25.2 | 80 | 95 | $16 |
| 15 STL | 12 | 0 | 175 | 167 | 3.03 | 3.95 | 1.37 | 708 | 809 | 623 | 24.2 | 3.5 | 8.6 | 2.5 | 56% | 9% | 91.7 | 44 | 22 | 34 | 33% | 80% | 8% | 31 | 98 | 32% | 29% | | | 20.2 | 82 | 98 | $11 |
| 16 | | | | | | | | | | | | | | | | | | | | | | | | | | | | | | | | | |
| 17 STL | 11 | 0 | 186 | 153 | 3.43 | 4.59 | 1.23 | 707 | 818 | 601 | 23.5 | 3.8 | 7.4 | 2.0 | 55% | 9% | 91.8 | 44 | 20 | 36 | 25% | 78% | 14% | 33 | 95 | 15% | 42% | | | 21.3 | 53 | 64 | $16 |
| 18 2 AL | 10 | 0 | 157 | 161 | 4.77 | 4.08 | 1.53 | 744 | 841 | 670 | 22.6 | 4.4 | 9.2 | 2.1 | 54% | 11% | 93.2 | 50 | 23 | 27 | 35% | 69% | 11% | 29 | 95 | 17% | 34% | 0 | 0.79 | -11.9 | 77 | 88 | -$5 |
| 1st Half | 5 | 0 | 79 | 81 | 4.81 | 4.26 | 1.61 | 767 | 844 | 715 | 23.7 | 5.4 | 9.3 | 1.7 | 57% | 11% | 92.9 | 52 | 22 | 25 | 34% | 71% | 12% | 15 | 98 | 20% | 27% | | | -6.4 | 52 | 60 | -$10 |
| 2nd Half | 5 | 0 | 78 | 80 | 4.73 | 3.92 | 1.44 | 721 | 839 | 620 | 21.5 | 3.3 | 9.2 | 2.8 | 51% | 10% | 93.5 | 47 | 24 | 29 | 35% | 68% | 10% | 14 | 92 | 14% | 43% | 0 | 0.79 | -5.6 | 101 | 116 | $0 |
| **19 Proj** | **10** | **0** | **160** | **152** | **3.97** | **3.90** | **1.37** | **710** | **806** | **630** | **22.5** | **3.9** | **8.6** | **2.2** | **55%** | **10%** | **92.6** | **47** | **22** | **31** | **31%** | **73%** | **11%** | **30** | | | | | | **3.6** | **74** | **85** | **$5** |

## Maeda,Kenta

| | | | | | | |
|---|---|---|---|---|---|---|
| Age: 31 | Th: R | Role RP | Health | C | LIMA Plan | B+ |
| Ht: 6' 1" | Wt: 175 | Type Pwr | PT/Exp | A | Rand Var | +2 |
| | | | Consist | A | MM | 3403 |

Demoted to bullpen by season's end (again), but skills were better than ever: Dom boost got full backing from now-elite SwK; Ctl snapped back to normal down the stretch; BPV surged in 2nd half despite ERA spike. LD%/h% combo unlikely to wreak havoc again, so if he sticks in rotation... UP: 3.25 ERA, 200 K.

| Yr Tm | W | Sv | IP | K | ERA | xERA | WHIP | oOPS | vL | vR | BF/G | Ctl | Dom | Cmd | FpK | SwK | Vel | G | L | F | H% | S% | hr/f | GS | APC | DOM% | DIS% | Sv% | LI | RAR | BPV | BPX | R$ |
|---|---|---|---|---|---|---|---|---|---|---|---|---|---|---|---|---|---|---|---|---|---|---|---|---|---|---|---|---|---|---|---|---|---|
| 14 | | | | | | | | | | | | | | | | | | | | | | | | | | | | | | | | | |
| 15 for | 15 | 0 | 176 | 170 | 4.32 | 4.37 | 1.27 | | | | 24.8 | 3.2 | 8.7 | 2.7 | | | | | | | 28% | 73% | | | | | | | | -7.7 | 65 | 77 | $7 |
| 16 LA | 16 | 0 | 176 | 179 | 3.48 | 3.65 | 1.14 | 649 | 730 | 580 | 22.4 | 2.6 | 9.2 | 3.6 | 61% | 12% | 90.0 | 44 | 20 | 36 | 29% | 73% | 12% | 32 | 92 | 25% | 19% | | | 15.3 | 118 | 140 | $19 |
| 17 LA | 13 | 1 | 134 | 140 | 4.22 | 3.94 | 1.15 | 714 | 781 | 647 | 19.2 | 2.3 | 9.4 | 4.1 | 64% | 13% | 91.5 | 38 | 22 | 40 | 29% | 69% | 15% | 25 | 75 | 24% | 36% | 100 | 0.73 | 2.3 | 123 | 148 | $12 |
| 18 LA | 8 | 2 | 125 | 153 | 3.81 | 3.52 | 1.26 | 706 | 820 | 608 | 13.6 | 3.1 | 11.0 | 3.6 | 63% | 15% | 91.9 | 40 | 24 | 35 | 34% | 72% | 11% | 20 | 53 | 35% | 45% | 100 | 1.04 | 5.3 | 132 | 152 | $7 |
| 1st Half | 5 | 0 | 75 | 89 | 3.36 | 3.70 | 1.28 | 686 | 767 | 603 | 21.3 | 3.5 | 10.7 | 3.1 | 65% | 14% | 91.7 | 38 | 27 | 35 | 33% | 76% | 9% | 14 | 81 | 29% | 43% | 0 | 0.79 | 7.3 | 114 | 131 | $10 |
| 2nd Half | 3 | 2 | 50 | 64 | 4.47 | 3.26 | 1.23 | 736 | 919 | 614 | 8.9 | 2.5 | 11.4 | 4.6 | 61% | 16% | 92.1 | 43 | 21 | 36 | 34% | 67% | 15% | 6 | 35 | 50% | 50% | 100 | 1.20 | -2.0 | 160 | 184 | $4 |
| **19 Proj** | **12** | **1** | **152** | **172** | **3.72** | **3.34** | **1.21** | **699** | **799** | **613** | **14.4** | **2.7** | **10.2** | **3.7** | **63%** | **14%** | **91.5** | **41** | **22** | **37** | **32%** | **73%** | **13%** | **19** | | | | | | **8.0** | **128** | **147** | **$13** |

## Magill,Matthew

| | | | | | | |
|---|---|---|---|---|---|---|
| Age: 29 | Th: R | Role RP | Health | A | LIMA Plan | D+ |
| Ht: 6' 3" | Wt: 210 | Type Pwr FB | PT/Exp | D | Rand Var | -1 |
| | | | Consist | C | MM | 0200 |

Called up from Triple-A in April and stuck in bullpen all year. Early success was fueled by Ctl gains, but FpK says they were a mirage, as he couldn't hit water from a boat in 2nd half. FB% tilt further elevates risk, so while the swing-and-miss is nice, xERA baseline says there's not enough here to bank on higher-leverage role.

| Yr Tm | W | Sv | IP | K | ERA | xERA | WHIP | oOPS | vL | vR | BF/G | Ctl | Dom | Cmd | FpK | SwK | Vel | G | L | F | H% | S% | hr/f | GS | APC | DOM% | DIS% | Sv% | LI | RAR | BPV | BPX | R$ |
|---|---|---|---|---|---|---|---|---|---|---|---|---|---|---|---|---|---|---|---|---|---|---|---|---|---|---|---|---|---|---|---|---|---|
| 14 aaa | 7 | 0 | 85 | 58 | 4.45 | 4.16 | 1.51 | | | | 10.2 | 5.2 | 6.2 | 1.2 | | | | | | | 29% | 71% | | | | | | | | -7.4 | 46 | 55 | -$4 |
| 15 | | | | | | | | | | | | | | | | | | | | | | | | | | | | | | | | | |
| 16 CIN * | 4 | 1 | 56 | 49 | 7.22 | 7.26 | 2.00 | 1098 | 1067 | 1067 | 6.3 | 6.0 | 7.8 | 1.3 | 60% | 7% | 92.8 | 23 | 23 | 54 | 37% | 66% | 14% | 0 | 16 | | | 33 | 0.26 | -21.1 | 16 | 19 | -$13 |
| 17 aaa | 6 | 0 | 96 | 57 | 4.18 | 5.84 | 1.68 | | | | 22.6 | 3.8 | 5.3 | 1.4 | | | | | | | 34% | 78% | | | | | | | | 2.1 | 21 | 25 | -$5 |
| 18 MIN | 3 | 0 | 57 | 56 | 3.81 | 4.65 | 1.43 | 809 | 830 | 791 | 6.2 | 3.7 | 8.9 | 2.4 | 53% | 12% | 94.7 | 35 | 22 | 43 | 31% | 81% | 15% | 0 | 25 | | | 0 | 0.87 | 2.4 | 74 | 86 | -$2 |
| 1st Half | 2 | 0 | 30 | 29 | 3.00 | 3.80 | 0.97 | 698 | 697 | 697 | 7.1 | 1.2 | 8.7 | 7.3 | 55% | 11% | 94.5 | 39 | 14 | 47 | 25% | 83% | 15% | 0 | 27 | | | 0 | 0.65 | 4.3 | 141 | 162 | $2 |
| 2nd Half | 1 | 0 | 27 | 27 | 4.73 | 5.76 | 1.95 | 917 | 973 | 874 | 5.6 | 6.4 | 9.1 | 1.4 | 51% | 12% | 94.9 | 31 | 29 | 40 | 37% | 81% | 15% | 0 | 24 | | | 0 | 1.03 | -1.9 | 0 | 0 | -$8 |
| **19 Proj** | **3** | **0** | **58** | **52** | **4.58** | **4.91** | **1.65** | **851** | **881** | **825** | **7.7** | **4.6** | **8.1** | **1.8** | **52%** | **12%** | **94.7** | **34** | **23** | **43** | **34%** | **77%** | **12%** | **0** | | | | | | **-3.0** | **34** | **40** | **-$6** |

## Mahle,Tyler

| | | | | | | |
|---|---|---|---|---|---|---|
| Age: 24 | Th: R | Role SP | Health | A | LIMA Plan | D+ |
| Ht: 6' 3" | Wt: 210 | Type Pwr | PT/Exp | D | Rand Var | +1 |
| | | | Consist | F | MM | 1103 |

7-9, 4.98 ERA in 112 IP at CIN. Wheels fell off after 1st half, as August demotion preceded tender shoulder that ended season in September. Brutal hr/f didn't help, but neither does xERA that hints at more bumps ahead. Decent FpK/SwK keeps him relevant, but without a plus skill on this page, it's tough to expect much growth.

| Yr Tm | W | Sv | IP | K | ERA | xERA | WHIP | oOPS | vL | vR | BF/G | Ctl | Dom | Cmd | FpK | SwK | Vel | G | L | F | H% | S% | hr/f | GS | APC | DOM% | DIS% | Sv% | LI | RAR | BPV | BPX | R$ |
|---|---|---|---|---|---|---|---|---|---|---|---|---|---|---|---|---|---|---|---|---|---|---|---|---|---|---|---|---|---|---|---|---|---|
| 14 | | | | | | | | | | | | | | | | | | | | | | | | | | | | | | | | | |
| 15 | | | | | | | | | | | | | | | | | | | | | | | | | | | | | | | | | |
| 16 aa | 6 | 0 | 71 | 58 | 6.70 | 6.90 | 1.65 | | | | 22.8 | 2.8 | 7.4 | 2.6 | | | | | | | 36% | 64% | | | | | | | | -22.0 | 26 | 31 | -$10 |
| 17 CIN * | 11 | 0 | 164 | 134 | 2.90 | 3.43 | 1.22 | 684 | 893 | 598 | 23.7 | 2.4 | 7.4 | 3.0 | 61% | 7% | 92.9 | 52 | 15 | 33 | 30% | 79% | 0% | 4 | 92 | 0% | 25% | | | 29.5 | 91 | 110 | $17 |
| 18 CIN * | 9 | 0 | 143 | 127 | 4.62 | 5.53 | 1.51 | 848 | 990 | 703 | 22.1 | 4.1 | 8.0 | 2.0 | 62% | 10% | 92.4 | 39 | 25 | 36 | 31% | 75% | 18% | 23 | 90 | 9% | 39% | | | -8.3 | 38 | 44 | -$5 |
| 1st Half | 6 | 0 | 92 | 93 | 3.83 | 4.26 | 1.42 | 792 | 973 | 616 | 23.3 | 3.8 | 9.1 | 2.4 | 61% | 11% | 92.6 | 39 | 25 | 36 | 31% | 80% | 18% | 17 | 95 | 12% | 24% | | | 3.6 | 78 | 89 | $0 |
| 2nd Half | 3 | 0 | 52 | 34 | 6.03 | 6.52 | 1.67 | 1052 | 1047 | 1053 | 21.1 | 4.5 | 5.9 | 1.3 | 68% | 7% | 92.0 | 39 | 25 | 36 | 31% | 69% | 21% | 6 | 77 | 0% | 83% | | | -11.9 | 2 | 2 | -$18 |
| **19 Proj** | **11** | **0** | **160** | **129** | **4.50** | **4.41** | **1.46** | **732** | **779** | **679** | **22.5** | **3.4** | **7.3** | **2.1** | **62%** | **9%** | **92.2** | **41** | **23** | **36** | **31%** | **74%** | **14%** | **30** | | | | | | **-4.1** | **58** | **66** | **-$1** |

## Manaea,Sean

| | | | | | | |
|---|---|---|---|---|---|---|
| Age: 27 | Th: L | Role SP | Health | D | LIMA Plan | C+ |
| Ht: 6' 5" | Wt: 245 | Type | PT/Exp | B | Rand Var | -1 |
| | | | Consist | A | MM | 2100 |

Rollercoaster year started with no-hitter, 1.00 April ERA; ended with shoulder surgery that puts 2019 return in question. In between, he was stingy with the free pass, but strikeouts waned as velocity/SwK eroded, while xERA remained unimpressed. Not enough volume for redraft impact, so check back in #BF20.

| Yr Tm | W | Sv | IP | K | ERA | xERA | WHIP | oOPS | vL | vR | BF/G | Ctl | Dom | Cmd | FpK | SwK | Vel | G | L | F | H% | S% | hr/f | GS | APC | DOM% | DIS% | Sv% | LI | RAR | BPV | BPX | R$ |
|---|---|---|---|---|---|---|---|---|---|---|---|---|---|---|---|---|---|---|---|---|---|---|---|---|---|---|---|---|---|---|---|---|---|
| 14 | | | | | | | | | | | | | | | | | | | | | | | | | | | | | | | | | |
| 15 aa | 6 | 0 | 50 | 51 | 2.49 | 3.59 | 1.33 | | | | 22.9 | 3.6 | 9.2 | 2.6 | | | | | | | 32% | 84% | | | | | | | | 9.0 | 95 | 114 | $3 |
| 16 OAK * | 9 | 0 | 163 | 141 | 3.63 | 3.78 | 1.20 | 713 | 526 | 754 | 23.3 | 2.3 | 7.8 | 3.4 | 65% | 12% | 92.3 | 44 | 21 | 35 | 29% | 74% | 14% | 24 | 87 | 33% | 29% | 0 | 0.78 | 11.2 | 89 | 105 | $11 |
| 17 OAK | 12 | 0 | 159 | 140 | 4.37 | 4.49 | 1.40 | 763 | 593 | 809 | 23.9 | 3.1 | 7.9 | 2.5 | 60% | 12% | 91.6 | 44 | 21 | 35 | 33% | 71% | 11% | 29 | 93 | 17% | 38% | | | -0.2 | 81 | 97 | $4 |
| 18 OAK | 12 | 0 | 161 | 108 | 3.59 | 4.24 | 1.08 | 663 | 627 | 673 | 24.2 | 1.8 | 6.0 | 3.4 | 64% | 10% | 90.5 | 44 | 21 | 35 | 26% | 72% | 12% | 27 | 88 | 26% | 41% | | | 11.2 | 82 | 95 | $14 |
| 1st Half | 8 | 0 | 107 | 77 | 3.38 | 4.08 | 0.97 | 625 | 598 | 631 | 25.3 | 1.7 | 6.5 | 3.9 | 60% | 10% | 90.6 | 43 | 22 | 35 | 23% | 72% | 13% | 17 | 92 | 35% | 41% | | | 10.2 | 92 | 106 | $22 |
| 2nd Half | 4 | 0 | 54 | 31 | 4.00 | 4.59 | 1.30 | 738 | 683 | 752 | 22.4 | 2.0 | 5.2 | 2.6 | 72% | 10% | 90.2 | 46 | 20 | 34 | 30% | 72% | 10% | 10 | 81 | 10% | 40% | | | 1.0 | 63 | 72 | -$3 |
| **19 Proj** | **1** | **0** | **15** | **11** | **3.77** | **3.97** | **1.24** | **713** | **606** | **741** | **23.0** | **2.4** | **6.9** | **2.9** | **64%** | **11%** | **91.1** | **44** | **21** | **35** | **30%** | **73%** | **11%** | **3** | | | | | | **0.2** | **82** | **94** | **-$4** |

## Marquez,German

| | | | | | | |
|---|---|---|---|---|---|---|
| Age: 24 | Th: R | Role SP | Health | A | LIMA Plan | C+ |
| Ht: 6' 1" | Wt: 185 | Type Pwr | PT/Exp | A | Rand Var | +2 |
| | | | Consist | B | MM | 3305 |

Looked like another Coors casualty before stunning 2nd half. The late surge came with full support: leaned on revamped slider to drive SwK, Dom gains; induced more GBs; pounded the zone en route to elite Ctl. Next step: sustaining it, but xERA/BPV combos at this age are hard to find, no matter where he calls home.

| Yr Tm | W | Sv | IP | K | ERA | xERA | WHIP | oOPS | vL | vR | BF/G | Ctl | Dom | Cmd | FpK | SwK | Vel | G | L | F | H% | S% | hr/f | GS | APC | DOM% | DIS% | Sv% | LI | RAR | BPV | BPX | R$ |
|---|---|---|---|---|---|---|---|---|---|---|---|---|---|---|---|---|---|---|---|---|---|---|---|---|---|---|---|---|---|---|---|---|---|
| 14 | | | | | | | | | | | | | | | | | | | | | | | | | | | | | | | | | |
| 15 | | | | | | | | | | | | | | | | | | | | | | | | | | | | | | | | | |
| 16 COL * | 12 | 0 | 187 | 139 | 4.58 | 4.88 | 1.43 | 932 | 933 | 931 | 24.9 | 2.3 | 6.7 | 2.9 | 63% | 10% | 93.3 | 55 | 30 | 15 | 34% | 70% | 18% | 3 | 59 | 0% | 33% | 0 | 0.51 | -9.1 | 65 | 77 | $0 |
| 17 COL | 11 | 0 | 162 | 147 | 4.39 | 4.23 | 1.38 | 806 | 757 | 853 | 24.2 | 2.7 | 8.2 | 3.0 | 60% | 10% | 95.0 | 45 | 22 | 33 | 32% | 73% | 15% | 29 | 92 | 10% | 34% | | | -0.6 | 97 | 116 | $5 |
| 18 COL | 14 | 0 | 196 | 230 | 3.77 | 3.22 | 1.20 | 698 | 796 | 591 | 24.8 | 2.6 | 10.6 | 4.0 | 65% | 13% | 95.2 | 47 | 23 | 30 | 32% | 73% | 16% | 33 | 95 | 36% | 18% | | | 9.3 | 144 | 166 | $16 |
| 1st Half | 6 | 0 | 91 | 93 | 5.14 | 4.18 | 1.44 | 796 | 828 | 757 | 23.8 | 3.5 | 9.2 | 2.7 | 60% | 10% | 95.1 | 43 | 22 | 34 | 33% | 68% | 16% | 17 | 91 | 18% | 35% | | | -11.1 | 93 | 107 | -$9 |
| 2nd Half | 8 | 0 | 105 | 137 | 2.57 | 2.45 | 1.00 | 605 | 763 | 450 | 25.8 | 1.9 | 11.7 | 6.2 | 69% | 16% | 95.3 | 52 | 23 | 25 | 32% | 78% | 15% | 16 | 98 | 56% | 0% | | | 20.4 | 190 | 219 | $33 |
| **19 Proj** | **13** | **0** | **189** | **193** | **3.64** | **3.31** | **1.25** | **725** | **768** | **679** | **23.7** | **2.5** | **9.2** | **3.7** | **63%** | **12%** | **95.1** | **47** | **23** | **31** | **32%** | **75%** | **14%** | **32** | | | | | | **20.0** | **125** | **143** | **$14** |

## Martin,Christopher

| | | | | | | |
|---|---|---|---|---|---|---|
| Age: 33 | Th: R | Role RP | Health | D | LIMA Plan | C+ |
| Ht: 6' 8" | Wt: 215 | Type | PT/Exp | D | Rand Var | +4 |
| | | | Consist | C | MM | 3200 |

Successful two-year stint in Japan (1.12 ERA in 88.1 NPB innings) was met with... pain. Forearm, hamstring, and groin injuries sent him to the DL three times, while H%/S% combo inflated ERA. FpK says those control gains have legs, but doesn't miss enough bats to be relevant, especially given health woes at this age.

| Yr Tm | W | Sv | IP | K | ERA | xERA | WHIP | oOPS | vL | vR | BF/G | Ctl | Dom | Cmd | FpK | SwK | Vel | G | L | F | H% | S% | hr/f | GS | APC | DOM% | DIS% | Sv% | LI | RAR | BPV | BPX | R$ |
|---|---|---|---|---|---|---|---|---|---|---|---|---|---|---|---|---|---|---|---|---|---|---|---|---|---|---|---|---|---|---|---|---|---|
| 14 COL * | 1 | 5 | 42 | 40 | 6.08 | 6.69 | 1.82 | 915 | 866 | 943 | 4.8 | 2.9 | 8.6 | 2.9 | 71% | 9% | 94.3 | 61 | 20 | 20 | 43% | 67% | 20% | 0 | 16 | | | 83 | 0.61 | -12.2 | 69 | 82 | -$7 |
| 15 NYY * | 0 | 3 | 49 | 37 | 5.16 | 5.47 | 1.67 | 777 | 581 | 872 | 5.0 | 3.3 | 6.8 | 2.0 | 65% | 6% | 94.2 | 53 | 27 | 20 | 37% | 69% | 13% | 0 | 16 | | | 75 | 0.62 | -7.3 | 56 | 66 | -$8 |
| 16 for | 2 | 0 | 51 | 54 | 1.54 | 0.86 | 0.70 | | | | 3.4 | 1.5 | 9.6 | 6.2 | | | | | | | 21% | 83% | | | | | | | | 16.5 | 194 | 231 | $8 |
| 17 for | 0 | 0 | 38 | 32 | 1.48 | 1.51 | 0.80 | | | | 3.4 | 1.8 | 7.7 | 4.3 | | | | | | | 21% | 89% | | | | | | | | 13.4 | 133 | 160 | $4 |
| 18 TEX | 1 | 0 | 42 | 37 | 4.54 | 3.77 | 1.22 | 722 | 788 | 689 | 3.8 | 1.1 | 8.0 | 7.4 | 66% | 10% | 95.2 | 40 | 27 | 32 | 34% | 65% | 12% | 0 | 15 | | | 0 | 0.90 | -2.0 | 133 | 153 | -$3 |
| 1st Half | 1 | 0 | 24 | 21 | 4.13 | 3.62 | 1.21 | 689 | 700 | 683 | 3.7 | 1.1 | 7.9 | 7.0 | 61% | 10% | 94.8 | 42 | 27 | 30 | 34% | 67% | 9% | 0 | 14 | | | 0 | 1.02 | 0.1 | 132 | 151 | -$3 |
| 2nd Half | 0 | 0 | 18 | 16 | 5.09 | 3.99 | 1.25 | 765 | 871 | 698 | 4.1 | 1.0 | 8.2 | 8.0 | 71% | 10% | 95.7 | 38 | 28 | 34 | 33% | 63% | 15% | 0 | 17 | | | 0 | 0.73 | -2.1 | 135 | 155 | -$4 |
| **19 Proj** | **1** | **0** | **58** | **52** | **3.67** | **3.45** | **1.16** | **661** | **755** | **610** | **3.8** | **1.7** | **8.1** | **4.9** | **67%** | **10%** | **95.3** | **40** | **28** | **33** | **31%** | **71%** | **11%** | **0** | | | | | | **4.5** | **119** | **137** | **$0** |

RYAN BLOOMFIELD

| Martinez,Carlos | | | | Health | D | LIMA Plan | B |
|---|---|---|---|---|---|---|---|
| Age: 27 | Th: R | Role | RP | PT/Exp | A | Rand Var | -3 |
| Ht: 6' 0" | Wt: 190 | Type | Pwr GB | Consist | A | MM | 3303 |

Hot start (1.62 ERA in 8 GS) gave way to trio of DL stints (lat, oblique, shoulder), then ended season as closer. Bailed out by hr/f, but 1st half wildness, GB% erosion, and velocity dip hint this could've been much worse. Ctl history says he should recover and whiffs held firm, but can no longer pencil in 2016-17 volume.

| Yr Tm | W | Sv | IP | K | ERA | xERA | WHIP | oOPS | vL | vR | BF/G | Ctl | Dom | Cmd | FpK | SwK | Vel | G | L | F | H% | S% | hr/f | GS | APC | DOM% | DIS% | Sv% | LI | RAR | BPV | BPX | R$ |
|---|---|---|---|---|---|---|---|---|---|---|---|---|---|---|---|---|---|---|---|---|---|---|---|---|---|---|---|---|---|---|---|---|---|
| 14 STL | 2 | 1 | 89 | 84 | 4.03 | 3.54 | 1.41 | 713 | 849 | 609 | 6.8 | 3.6 | 8.5 | 2.3 | 58% | 14% | 96.7 | 51 | 22 | 27 | 34% | 70% | 6% | 7 | 24 | 14% | 14% | 17 | 1.34 | -3.2 | 83 | 99 | -$3 |
| 15 STL | 14 | 0 | 180 | 184 | 3.01 | 3.28 | 1.29 | 687 | 756 | 623 | 24.4 | 3.2 | 9.2 | 2.9 | 63% | 11% | 95.3 | 54 | 20 | 25 | 32% | 78% | 11% | 29 | 92 | 41% | 21% | 0 | 0.82 | 21.2 | 113 | 134 | $15 |
| 16 STL | 16 | 0 | 195 | 174 | 3.04 | 3.64 | 1.22 | 643 | 730 | 540 | 26.1 | 3.2 | 8.0 | 2.5 | 62% | 10% | 95.6 | 56 | 18 | 26 | 29% | 77% | 11% | 31 | 98 | 32% | 23% | | | 27.7 | 91 | 108 | $20 |
| 17 STL | 12 | 0 | 205 | 217 | 3.64 | 3.63 | 1.22 | 694 | 783 | 608 | 26.8 | 3.1 | 9.5 | 3.1 | 59% | 11% | 95.6 | 51 | 19 | 30 | 30% | 75% | 16% | 32 | 98 | 41% | 19% | | | 18.1 | 116 | 140 | $18 |
| 18 STL | 8 | 5 | 119 | 117 | 3.11 | 4.22 | 1.35 | 647 | 685 | 596 | 15.8 | 4.6 | 8.9 | 2.0 | 60% | 11% | 93.6 | 49 | 19 | 32 | 30% | 77% | 5% | 18 | 60 | 33% | 28% | 100 | 0.97 | 15.2 | 64 | 74 | $9 |
| 1st Half | 4 | 0 | 73 | 73 | 3.22 | 4.44 | 1.43 | 659 | 624 | 710 | 25.1 | 5.3 | 9.0 | 1.7 | 59% | 11% | 93.5 | 49 | 18 | 33 | 31% | 77% | 5% | 13 | 95 | 23% | 23% | | | 8.3 | 46 | 52 | $6 |
| 2nd Half | 4 | 5 | 46 | 44 | 2.93 | 3.89 | 1.22 | 626 | 793 | 442 | 9.8 | 3.3 | 8.6 | 2.6 | 63% | 13% | 93.7 | 50 | 20 | 30 | 30% | 76% | 5% | 5 | 37 | 60% | 40% | 100 | 1.09 | 6.9 | 93 | 107 | $12 |
| **19 Proj** | **11** | **0** | **160** | **157** | **3.53** | **3.53** | **1.24** | **670** | **756** | **575** | **15.1** | **3.4** | **8.9** | **2.6** | **61%** | **11%** | **94.7** | **50** | **19** | **31** | **30%** | **74%** | **11%** | **22** | | | | | | **12.3** | **96** | **111** | **$12** |

| Maton,Phil | | | | Health | C | LIMA Plan | C+ |
|---|---|---|---|---|---|---|---|
| Age: 26 | Th: R | Role | RP | PT/Exp | D | Rand Var | +1 |
| Ht: 6' 3" | Wt: 220 | Type | Pwr | Consist | A | MM | 3410 |

Missed over a month with May lat strain; ERA tanked upon return. Not all is lost: swing-and-miss stuff held strong, so Ks should come; 2.0 career Ctl in minors, above-average FpK suggest BBs were just a blip. No need to speculate early, but with Triple-A closer experience, early success could net higher-leverage role.

| Yr Tm | W | Sv | IP | K | ERA | xERA | WHIP | oOPS | vL | vR | BF/G | Ctl | Dom | Cmd | FpK | SwK | Vel | G | L | F | H% | S% | hr/f | GS | APC | DOM% | DIS% | Sv% | LI | RAR | BPV | BPX | R$ |
|---|---|---|---|---|---|---|---|---|---|---|---|---|---|---|---|---|---|---|---|---|---|---|---|---|---|---|---|---|---|---|---|---|---|
| 14 | | | | | | | | | | | | | | | | | | | | | | | | | | | | | | | | | |
| 15 | | | | | | | | | | | | | | | | | | | | | | | | | | | | | | | | | |
| 16 | | | | | | | | | | | | | | | | | | | | | | | | | | | | | | | | | |
| 17 SD * | 4 | 14 | 68 | 72 | 3.66 | 4.15 | 1.25 | 778 | 912 | 679 | 4.0 | 2.8 | 9.5 | 3.4 | 61% | 14% | 93.0 | 45 | 22 | 32 | 31% | 77% | 26% | 0 | 16 | | | 100 | 0.99 | 5.9 | 91 | 109 | $8 |
| 18 SD | 0 | 0 | 47 | 55 | 4.37 | 4.42 | 1.54 | 757 | 725 | 783 | 4.8 | 4.4 | 10.5 | 2.4 | 63% | 15% | 91.1 | 36 | 23 | 41 | 37% | 71% | 6% | 0 | 19 | | | 0 | 0.85 | -1.3 | 84 | 97 | -$6 |
| 1st Half | 0 | 0 | 18 | 18 | 1.53 | 4.56 | 1.58 | 728 | 764 | 700 | 4.8 | 4.1 | 9.2 | 2.3 | 64% | 15% | 90.8 | 40 | 25 | 36 | 39% | 89% | 0% | 0 | 20 | | | 0 | 1.03 | 5.7 | 73 | 83 | -$5 |
| 2nd Half | 0 | 0 | 30 | 37 | 6.07 | 4.34 | 1.52 | 775 | 705 | 840 | 4.7 | 4.6 | 11.2 | 2.5 | 62% | 15% | 91.3 | 33 | 22 | 45 | 37% | 60% | 9% | 0 | 18 | | | 0 | 0.75 | -7.0 | 91 | 104 | -$6 |
| **19 Proj** | **1** | **2** | **58** | **65** | **3.67** | **3.47** | **1.22** | **673** | **700** | **651** | **4.1** | **3.1** | **10.0** | **3.2** | **62%** | **14%** | **91.8** | **40** | **23** | **38** | **31%** | **74%** | **12%** | **0** | | | | | | **3.4** | **114** | **131** | **$1** |

| Matz,Steven | | | | Health | F | LIMA Plan | B+ |
|---|---|---|---|---|---|---|---|
| Age: 28 | Th: L | Role | SP | PT/Exp | B | Rand Var | +2 |
| Ht: 6' 2" | Wt: 200 | Type | Pwr | Consist | C | MM | 2303 |

Just one DL stint this time (Aug forearm), a minor miracle given recent arm issues. Skills-wise, a mixed bag: SwK uptick drove Dom gains down the stretch, but FpK trend doesn't bode well for Ctl recovery, and gave up more FBs in 2nd half. ERA/xERA were in lockstep, so a repeat seems likely along with a few more wins.

| Yr Tm | W | Sv | IP | K | ERA | xERA | WHIP | oOPS | vL | vR | BF/G | Ctl | Dom | Cmd | FpK | SwK | Vel | G | L | F | H% | S% | hr/f | GS | APC | DOM% | DIS% | Sv% | LI | RAR | BPV | BPX | R$ |
|---|---|---|---|---|---|---|---|---|---|---|---|---|---|---|---|---|---|---|---|---|---|---|---|---|---|---|---|---|---|---|---|---|---|
| 14 aa | 6 | 0 | 71 | 60 | 2.25 | 2.97 | 1.15 | | | | 23.6 | 1.6 | 7.6 | 4.7 | | | | | | | 32% | 81% | | | | | | | | 13.1 | 137 | 164 | $6 |
| 15 NYM * | 12 | 0 | 137 | 122 | 2.13 | 2.75 | 1.12 | 650 | 650 | 644 | 23.5 | 2.7 | 8.0 | 2.9 | 62% | 9% | 94.3 | 46 | 21 | 34 | 28% | 84% | 12% | 6 | 96 | 17% | 17% | | | 31.1 | 100 | 119 | $19 |
| 16 NYM | 9 | 0 | 132 | 129 | 3.40 | 3.38 | 1.21 | 689 | 698 | 686 | 24.9 | 2.1 | 8.8 | 4.2 | 65% | 10% | 93.6 | 51 | 21 | 28 | 32% | 75% | 14% | 22 | 98 | 36% | 23% | | | 12.9 | 130 | 154 | $10 |
| 17 NYM | 2 | 0 | 67 | 48 | 6.08 | 4.73 | 1.53 | 860 | 763 | 887 | 22.9 | 2.6 | 6.5 | 2.5 | 59% | 7% | 93.1 | 47 | 22 | 31 | 34% | 63% | 17% | 13 | 90 | 8% | 38% | | | -14.1 | 72 | 87 | -$8 |
| 18 NYM | 5 | 0 | 154 | 152 | 3.97 | 3.98 | 1.25 | 730 | 675 | 743 | 21.8 | 3.4 | 8.9 | 2.6 | 56% | 10% | 93.4 | 49 | 15 | 36 | 28% | 74% | 17% | 30 | 90 | 30% | 27% | | | 3.3 | 95 | 110 | $5 |
| 1st Half | 3 | 0 | 78 | 70 | 3.69 | 3.97 | 1.24 | 741 | 626 | 774 | 21.8 | 3.5 | 8.1 | 2.3 | 57% | 8% | 93.1 | 53 | 15 | 33 | 26% | 77% | 19% | 15 | 89 | 27% | 27% | | | 4.4 | 83 | 95 | $5 |
| 2nd Half | 2 | 0 | 76 | 82 | 4.26 | 3.99 | 1.25 | 720 | 741 | 716 | 21.8 | 3.3 | 9.7 | 2.9 | 56% | 11% | 93.7 | 45 | 16 | 39 | 29% | 71% | 15% | 15 | 90 | 33% | 27% | | | -1.1 | 108 | 124 | $5 |
| **19 Proj** | **7** | **0** | **160** | **154** | **3.87** | **3.64** | **1.29** | **714** | **691** | **720** | **21.9** | **3.0** | **8.7** | **2.9** | **59%** | **10%** | **93.5** | **48** | **18** | **34** | **31%** | **74%** | **13%** | **30** | | | | | | **5.5** | **102** | **117** | **$6** |

| Maurer,Brandon | | | | Health | B | LIMA Plan | D+ |
|---|---|---|---|---|---|---|---|
| Age: 28 | Th: R | Role | RP | PT/Exp | C | Rand Var | +5 |
| Ht: 6' 5" | Wt: 225 | Type | Pwr | Consist | D | MM | 1200 |

1 save, 7.76 ERA in 31 IP at KC. Former closer was sent to Triple-A after just five outings. Resurfaced in June, but control went M.I.A. and SwK/Dom continued their steady descents. Sure, we could note brutal H%/S% and hr/f, but xERA says it didn't really matter. Even if skills rebound, save chances are likely long gone.

| Yr Tm | W | Sv | IP | K | ERA | xERA | WHIP | oOPS | vL | vR | BF/G | Ctl | Dom | Cmd | FpK | SwK | Vel | G | L | F | H% | S% | hr/f | GS | APC | DOM% | DIS% | Sv% | LI | RAR | BPV | BPX | R$ |
|---|---|---|---|---|---|---|---|---|---|---|---|---|---|---|---|---|---|---|---|---|---|---|---|---|---|---|---|---|---|---|---|---|---|
| 14 SEA * | 2 | 3 | 89 | 75 | 4.23 | 4.06 | 1.34 | 705 | 631 | 759 | 7.4 | 2.6 | 7.6 | 2.9 | 63% | 10% | 94.4 | 39 | 18 | 43 | 33% | 69% | 6% | 7 | 30 | 0% | 43% | 75 | 0.72 | -5.4 | 84 | 100 | -$2 |
| 15 SD | 7 | 0 | 51 | 39 | 3.00 | 3.83 | 1.06 | 568 | 427 | 711 | 3.9 | 2.6 | 6.9 | 2.6 | 61% | 13% | 95.1 | 48 | 22 | 30 | 26% | 73% | 7% | 0 | 15 | | | 0 | 1.15 | 6.1 | 78 | 93 | $4 |
| 16 SD | 0 | 13 | 70 | 72 | 4.52 | 4.22 | 1.26 | 686 | 648 | 722 | 4.2 | 3.0 | 9.3 | 3.1 | 60% | 12% | 95.3 | 38 | 20 | 42 | 32% | 65% | 8% | 0 | 17 | | | 68 | 1.02 | -2.9 | 103 | 123 | $3 |
| 17 2 TM | 3 | 22 | 59 | 59 | 6.52 | 4.47 | 1.55 | 838 | 757 | 902 | 3.9 | 2.9 | 8.9 | 3.1 | 67% | 11% | 96.6 | 39 | 26 | 35 | 38% | 58% | 12% | 0 | 15 | | | 85 | 1.06 | -15.8 | 100 | 120 | $2 |
| 18 KC * | 1 | 6 | 54 | 49 | 7.65 | 7.31 | 2.05 | 1012 | 1085 | 930 | 4.7 | 6.6 | 8.2 | 1.2 | 59% | 10% | 96.0 | 43 | 19 | 38 | 38% | 63% | 18% | 0 | 18 | | | 43 | 0.94 | -23.4 | 26 | 30 | -$15 |
| 1st Half | 1 | 5 | 31 | 25 | 8.38 | 7.58 | 2.05 | 1265 | 1217 | 1290 | 5.3 | 6.2 | 7.3 | 1.2 | 64% | 12% | 95.2 | 41 | 14 | 45 | 37% | 59% | 31% | 0 | 18 | | | 50 | 0.90 | -16.3 | 14 | 16 | -$19 |
| 2nd Half | 0 | 1 | 23 | 24 | 6.65 | 5.74 | 2.04 | 919 | 1057 | 712 | 4.3 | 7.0 | 9.4 | 1.3 | 57% | 10% | 96.4 | 44 | 21 | 36 | 39% | 68% | 12% | 0 | 18 | | | 25 | 0.96 | -7.1 | 1 | 1 | -$12 |
| **19 Proj** | **2** | **0** | **58** | **55** | **5.09** | **4.53** | **1.59** | **804** | **821** | **787** | **4.2** | **4.8** | **8.6** | **1.8** | **61%** | **11%** | **95.8** | **41** | **22** | **37** | **33%** | **71%** | **13%** | **0** | | | | | | **-2.6** | **45** | **51** | **-$7** |

| May,Trevor | | | | Health | F | LIMA Plan | A |
|---|---|---|---|---|---|---|---|
| Age: 29 | Th: R | Role | RP | PT/Exp | D | Rand Var | +4 |
| Ht: 6' 5" | Wt: 240 | Type | Pwr | Consist | C | MM | 3510 |

3 Sv, 3.20 ERA in 25 IP at MIN. Shook off early rust in return from Tommy John surgery with great finish. SwK picked up where it left off after 2016 switch to 'pen, which backs 2nd half Dom surge, while 1.8 Ctl in majors helped him snag closer gig by Sept. Still in small-sample mode, but if late gains hold... UP: 25 Sv.

| Yr Tm | W | Sv | IP | K | ERA | xERA | WHIP | oOPS | vL | vR | BF/G | Ctl | Dom | Cmd | FpK | SwK | Vel | G | L | F | H% | S% | hr/f | GS | APC | DOM% | DIS% | Sv% | LI | RAR | BPV | BPX | R$ |
|---|---|---|---|---|---|---|---|---|---|---|---|---|---|---|---|---|---|---|---|---|---|---|---|---|---|---|---|---|---|---|---|---|---|
| 14 MIN * | 11 | 0 | 144 | 118 | 5.06 | 4.42 | 1.49 | 900 | 892 | 907 | 22.2 | 4.0 | 7.4 | 1.9 | 62% | 10% | 91.9 | 36 | 23 | 41 | 33% | 66% | 12% | 9 | 84 | 0% | 44% | 0 | 0.70 | -23.4 | 62 | 74 | -$7 |
| 15 MIN | 8 | 0 | 115 | 110 | 4.00 | 3.86 | 1.33 | 752 | 759 | 743 | 10.3 | 2.0 | 8.6 | 4.2 | 63% | 11% | 92.9 | 39 | 21 | 40 | 35% | 72% | 8% | 16 | 39 | 25% | 31% | 0 | 0.87 | -0.6 | 117 | 140 | $2 |
| 16 MIN | 2 | 0 | 43 | 60 | 5.27 | 3.64 | 1.31 | 757 | 547 | 872 | 4.3 | 3.6 | 12.7 | 3.5 | 62% | 14% | 93.9 | 31 | 26 | 43 | 35% | 63% | 15% | 0 | 19 | | | 0 | 1.18 | -5.7 | 140 | 166 | -$3 |
| 17 | | | | | | | | | | | | | | | | | | | | | | | | | | | | | | | | | |
| 18 MIN * | 4 | 5 | 52 | 54 | 4.92 | 5.09 | 1.53 | 646 | 616 | 670 | 6.2 | 4.2 | 9.3 | 2.2 | 58% | 16% | 94.1 | 41 | 22 | 37 | 34% | 70% | 18% | 1 | 19 | 0% | 100% | 100 | 1.05 | -4.9 | 66 | 76 | -$3 |
| 1st Half | 0 | 2 | 19 | 12 | 9.17 | 8.58 | 2.32 | | | | 14.1 | 7.5 | 5.4 | 0.7 | | | | | | | 37% | 60% | 0% | 0 | | | | | | -11.9 | -9 | -11 | -$29 |
| 2nd Half | 4 | 3 | 35 | 42 | 2.29 | 2.68 | 1.00 | 646 | 616 | 670 | 4.5 | 2.2 | 10.8 | 4.9 | 58% | 16% | 94.1 | 41 | 22 | 37 | 28% | 84% | 18% | 1 | 19 | 0% | 100% | 100 | 1.05 | 8.2 | 150 | 172 | $4 |
| **19 Proj** | **4** | **8** | **58** | **71** | **3.74** | **3.34** | **1.23** | **677** | **649** | **701** | **6.1** | **3.3** | **11.1** | **3.3** | **61%** | **13%** | **93.3** | **38** | **23** | **40** | **31%** | **74%** | **13%** | **0** | | | | | | **7.1** | **125** | **144** | **$5** |

| Mayers,Mike | | | | Health | B | LIMA Plan | C |
|---|---|---|---|---|---|---|---|
| Age: 27 | Th: R | Role | RP | PT/Exp | D | Rand Var | +3 |
| Ht: 6' 3" | Wt: 200 | Type | Pwr | Consist | C | MM | 1200 |

Transition to full-time relief role started out well, but luck can giveth (S%, hr/f in 1st half) and luck can taketh away (everything in 2nd half). Picked up a few ticks on his fastball, which led to now passable Dom, and while Ctl is fine, xERA baseline confirms there's not much here worth targeting.

| Yr Tm | W | Sv | IP | K | ERA | xERA | WHIP | oOPS | vL | vR | BF/G | Ctl | Dom | Cmd | FpK | SwK | Vel | G | L | F | H% | S% | hr/f | GS | APC | DOM% | DIS% | Sv% | LI | RAR | BPV | BPX | R$ |
|---|---|---|---|---|---|---|---|---|---|---|---|---|---|---|---|---|---|---|---|---|---|---|---|---|---|---|---|---|---|---|---|---|---|
| 14 a/a | 6 | 0 | 81 | 46 | 3.33 | 4.53 | 1.48 | | | | 25.0 | 2.5 | 5.1 | 2.1 | | | | | | | 34% | 77% | | | | | | | | 4.1 | 57 | 68 | -$1 |
| 15 aa | 1 | 0 | 47 | 31 | 7.17 | 6.21 | 1.70 | | | | 21.1 | 4.0 | 6.0 | 1.5 | | | | | | | 34% | 59% | | | | | | | | -18.5 | 17 | 21 | -$12 |
| 16 STL * | 10 | 0 | 149 | 101 | 4.74 | 5.04 | 1.52 | 1438 | 1248 | 1600 | 22.4 | 3.2 | 6.1 | 1.9 | 77% | 8% | 93.1 | 48 | 28 | 24 | 33% | 70% | 43% | 1 | 30 | 0% | 100% | 0 | 0.43 | -10.1 | 45 | 53 | -$5 |
| 17 STL * | 5 | 0 | 114 | 79 | 4.41 | 5.93 | 1.63 | 1427 | 1762 | 1056 | 15.0 | 2.9 | 6.2 | 2.1 | 64% | 9% | 94.2 | 28 | 22 | 50 | 36% | 76% | 22% | 0 | 34 | | | 0 | 0.12 | -0.7 | 38 | 45 | -$6 |
| 18 STL | 2 | 1 | 52 | 49 | 4.70 | 4.17 | 1.43 | 822 | 721 | 907 | 4.5 | 2.6 | 8.5 | 3.3 | 63% | 11% | 96.1 | 42 | 23 | 35 | 35% | 70% | 13% | 0 | 18 | | | 100 | 0.61 | -3.5 | 103 | 119 | -$4 |
| 1st Half | 2 | 1 | 26 | 25 | 2.81 | 4.04 | 1.13 | 695 | 572 | 818 | 4.8 | 2.1 | 8.8 | 4.2 | 65% | 10% | 95.7 | 39 | 19 | 42 | 30% | 81% | 10% | 0 | 20 | | | 100 | 0.63 | 4.3 | 118 | 136 | $1 |
| 2nd Half | 0 | 0 | 26 | 24 | 6.58 | 4.31 | 1.73 | 937 | 885 | 975 | 4.3 | 3.1 | 8.3 | 2.7 | 61% | 11% | 96.4 | 45 | 26 | 29 | 39% | 63% | 17% | 0 | 17 | | | 0 | 0.60 | -7.8 | 89 | 102 | -$10 |
| **19 Proj** | **2** | **0** | **58** | **50** | **4.56** | **4.11** | **1.47** | **823** | **732** | **897** | **7.0** | **2.9** | **7.7** | **2.7** | **63%** | **11%** | **96.1** | **43** | **23** | **34** | **34%** | **72%** | **12%** | **0** | | | | | | **0.3** | **82** | **95** | **-$4** |

| McAllister,Zach | | | | Health | B | LIMA Plan | C |
|---|---|---|---|---|---|---|---|
| Age: 31 | Th: R | Role | RP | PT/Exp | D | Rand Var | +5 |
| Ht: 6' 6" | Wt: 240 | Type | Pwr | Consist | A | MM | 2300 |

ERA nearly tripled and was DFA'd twice in Aug... safe to say he's had better years. On the plus side, he kept limiting the free pass with plenty of FpK support, while H%/S% threw surface stats out of whack. But steady Dom decline, three straight 4.00+ xERAs say there's little fantasy relevance, even if he gets another shot.

| Yr Tm | W | Sv | IP | K | ERA | xERA | WHIP | oOPS | vL | vR | BF/G | Ctl | Dom | Cmd | FpK | SwK | Vel | G | L | F | H% | S% | hr/f | GS | APC | DOM% | DIS% | Sv% | LI | RAR | BPV | BPX | R$ |
|---|---|---|---|---|---|---|---|---|---|---|---|---|---|---|---|---|---|---|---|---|---|---|---|---|---|---|---|---|---|---|---|---|---|
| 14 CLE * | 11 | 0 | 155 | 121 | 4.04 | 3.95 | 1.34 | 750 | 789 | 715 | 19.5 | 2.5 | 7.0 | 2.9 | 62% | 8% | 92.9 | 42 | 21 | 37 | 33% | 70% | 7% | 15 | 66 | 13% | 47% | 0 | 0.91 | -5.6 | 84 | 100 | $2 |
| 15 CLE | 4 | 1 | 69 | 84 | 3.00 | 3.37 | 1.35 | 702 | 632 | 764 | 4.9 | 3.0 | 11.0 | 3.7 | 57% | 11% | 95.3 | 43 | 21 | 36 | 36% | 81% | 10% | 1 | 20 | 0% | 0% | 50 | 0.87 | 8.2 | 137 | 163 | $2 |
| 16 CLE | 3 | 0 | 52 | 54 | 3.44 | 4.63 | 1.45 | 742 | 692 | 788 | 4.4 | 4.0 | 9.3 | 2.3 | 60% | 10% | 94.2 | 36 | 22 | 43 | 33% | 80% | 9% | 2 | 18 | 0% | 50% | 0 | 0.96 | 4.8 | 74 | 88 | -$1 |
| 17 CLE | 2 | 0 | 62 | 66 | 2.61 | 4.02 | 1.19 | 670 | 843 | 535 | 5.0 | 3.0 | 9.6 | 3.1 | 64% | 10% | 95.3 | 36 | 21 | 43 | 29% | 85% | 12% | 0 | 20 | | | 0 | 0.51 | 13.3 | 104 | 125 | $4 |
| 18 2 AL | 1 | 0 | 45 | 39 | 6.20 | 4.38 | 1.49 | 880 | 993 | 793 | 4.5 | 2.0 | 7.8 | 3.9 | 67% | 10% | 95.2 | 41 | 22 | 38 | 36% | 61% | 15% | 0 | 18 | | | 0 | 0.74 | -11.4 | 105 | 121 | -$8 |
| 1st Half | 0 | 0 | 32 | 28 | 5.85 | 4.23 | 1.36 | 899 | 969 | 845 | 4.3 | 1.9 | 7.8 | 4.0 | 64% | 11% | 95.1 | 41 | 20 | 38 | 32% | 62% | 18% | 0 | 17 | | | 0 | 0.82 | -6.8 | 107 | 123 | -$9 |
| 2nd Half | 1 | 0 | 13 | 11 | 7.11 | 4.76 | 1.82 | 836 | 1045 | 677 | 5.0 | 2.1 | 7.8 | 3.7 | 75% | 10% | 95.6 | 40 | 24 | 36 | 43% | 59% | 6% | 0 | 19 | | | 0 | 0.53 | -4.6 | 101 | 116 | -$7 |
| **19 Proj** | **2** | **0** | **51** | **50** | **3.99** | **3.88** | **1.35** | **766** | **796** | **742** | **4.8** | **2.9** | **8.9** | **3.1** | **62%** | **10%** | **94.7** | **39** | **21** | **40** | **33%** | **75%** | **12%** | **0** | | | | | | **1.7** | **100** | **115** | **-$2** |

RYAN BLOOMFIELD

## McCarthy,Kevin

| | | | | | |
|---|---|---|---|---|---|
| Age: 27 | Th: R | Role RP | Health | A | LIMA Plan B+ |
| Ht: 6' 3" | Wt: 215 | Type Con xGB | PT/Exp | D | Rand Var +2 |
| | | | Consist | B | MM 2000 |

More sinkers led to big jump in already strong GB%, and even started missing some bats in 2nd half. But unappealing Dom history, declining velocity, and ineptitude vL (1.3 career Cmd) suggest this was about as good as it's gonna get. He's just a run-of-the-mill middle reliever with no real path to R$.

| Yr | Tm | W | Sv | IP | K | ERA | xERA | WHIP | oOPS | vL | vR | BF/G | Ctl | Dom | Cmd | FpK | SwK | Vel | G | L | F | H% | S% | hr/f | GS | APC | DOM% | DIS% | Sv% | LI | RAR | BPV | BPX | R$ |
|---|---|---|---|---|---|---|---|---|---|---|---|---|---|---|---|---|---|---|---|---|---|---|---|---|---|---|---|---|---|---|---|---|---|---|
| 14 | | | | | | | | | | | | | | | | | | | | | | | | | | | | | | | | | | |
| 15 | aa | 1 | 0 | 17 | 7 | 6.89 | 7.12 | 2.05 | | | | 7.7 | 4.1 | 3.8 | 0.9 | | | | | | | 39% | 65% | | | | | | | | -6.3 | 10 | 11 | -$8 |
| 16 | KC * | 6 | 16 | 76 | 54 | 4.15 | 4.35 | 1.40 | 857 | 1040 | 663 | 5.7 | 3.6 | 6.4 | 1.8 | 59% | 5% | 93.7 | 54 | 25 | 21 | 30% | 73% | 17% | 0 | 17 | | | 70 | 1.04 | 0.4 | 48 | 57 | $6 |
| 17 | KC * | 2 | 2 | 77 | 40 | 3.51 | 4.72 | 1.44 | 704 | 840 | 618 | 5.7 | 2.6 | 4.7 | 1.8 | 63% | 9% | 93.0 | 54 | 19 | 27 | 32% | 78% | 10% | 0 | 22 | | | 100 | 0.30 | 8.0 | 38 | 46 | -$1 |
| 18 | KC | 5 | 0 | 72 | 46 | 3.25 | 3.57 | 1.25 | 703 | 817 | 636 | 4.5 | 2.5 | 5.8 | 2.3 | 62% | 10% | 91.7 | 64 | 19 | 16 | 29% | 77% | 19% | 0 | 16 | | | 0 | 1.23 | 8.0 | 78 | 90 | $2 |
| 1st Half | | 4 | 0 | 35 | 21 | 3.31 | 3.66 | 1.13 | 590 | 825 | 476 | 4.5 | 3.1 | 5.3 | 1.8 | 60% | 9% | 92.2 | 63 | 22 | 14 | 25% | 71% | 13% | 0 | 16 | | | 0 | 1.36 | 3.7 | 55 | 63 | $3 |
| 2nd Half | | 1 | 0 | 37 | 25 | 3.19 | 3.48 | 1.36 | 804 | 811 | 800 | 4.5 | 2.0 | 6.1 | 3.1 | 63% | 12% | 91.3 | 65 | 17 | 18 | 32% | 82% | 24% | 0 | 15 | | | 0 | 1.12 | 4.3 | 100 | 115 | $1 |
| **19** | **Proj** | **3** | **0** | **65** | **40** | **3.74** | **3.87** | **1.35** | **726** | **843** | **653** | **5.0** | **2.6** | **5.5** | **2.1** | **62%** | **10%** | **92.2** | **60** | **19** | **21** | **30%** | **75%** | **15%** | **0** | | | | | | **3.3** | **66** | **76** | **-$1** |

## McCullers,Lance

| | | | | | |
|---|---|---|---|---|---|
| Age: 25 | Th: R | Role RP | Health | F | LIMA Plan B+ |
| Ht: 6' 1" | Wt: 205 | Type Pwr GB | PT/Exp | B | Rand Var +2 |
| | | | Consist | A | MM 4500 |

BPV, xERA history plus typical combo of high GB% and Dom show we can count on the skills. First half was what we've been waiting for—no missed starts. But then injury struck again—this time the elbow. Tommy John surgery in November means we won't likely see him again until 2020.

| Yr | Tm | W | Sv | IP | K | ERA | xERA | WHIP | oOPS | vL | vR | BF/G | Ctl | Dom | Cmd | FpK | SwK | Vel | G | L | F | H% | S% | hr/f | GS | APC | DOM% | DIS% | Sv% | LI | RAR | BPV | BPX | R$ |
|---|---|---|---|---|---|---|---|---|---|---|---|---|---|---|---|---|---|---|---|---|---|---|---|---|---|---|---|---|---|---|---|---|---|---|
| 14 | | | | | | | | | | | | | | | | | | | | | | | | | | | | | | | | | | |
| 15 | HOU * | 9 | 1 | 158 | 172 | 2.70 | 2.69 | 1.14 | 659 | 590 | 729 | 21.5 | 3.2 | 9.8 | 3.0 | 57% | 10% | 94.5 | 46 | 22 | 32 | 29% | 79% | 9% | 22 | 96 | 36% | 18% | | | 24.6 | 115 | 137 | $18 |
| 16 | HOU | 6 | 0 | 81 | 106 | 3.22 | 3.18 | 1.54 | 736 | 751 | 722 | 25.1 | 5.0 | 11.8 | 2.4 | 57% | 13% | 93.8 | 57 | 22 | 21 | 38% | 80% | 12% | 14 | 96 | 21% | 14% | | | 9.7 | 112 | 133 | $2 |
| 17 | HOU | 7 | 0 | 119 | 132 | 4.25 | 3.09 | 1.30 | 696 | 605 | 764 | 23.3 | 3.0 | 10.0 | 3.3 | 55% | 12% | 94.2 | 61 | 19 | 20 | 34% | 67% | 13% | 22 | 92 | 32% | 18% | | | 1.6 | 137 | 165 | $5 |
| 18 | HOU | 10 | 0 | 128 | 142 | 3.86 | 3.28 | 1.17 | 653 | 571 | 731 | 21.1 | 3.5 | 10.0 | 2.8 | 60% | 14% | 94.3 | 55 | 18 | 27 | 29% | 69% | 13% | 22 | 84 | 36% | 27% | 0 | 0.91 | 4.6 | 118 | 135 | $9 |
| 1st Half | | 9 | 0 | 101 | 106 | 3.55 | 3.35 | 1.15 | 651 | 566 | 738 | 24.2 | 3.4 | 9.4 | 2.8 | 59% | 13% | 94.2 | 55 | 18 | 27 | 28% | 72% | 14% | 17 | 98 | 41% | 24% | | | 7.5 | 111 | 128 | $15 |
| 2nd Half | | 1 | 0 | 27 | 36 | 5.00 | 3.03 | 1.22 | 663 | 595 | 708 | 14.4 | 4.0 | 12.0 | 3.0 | 61% | 16% | 94.6 | 54 | 17 | 29 | 32% | 58% | 11% | 5 | 56 | 20% | 40% | 0 | 1.18 | -2.8 | 140 | 161 | -$11 |
| **19** | **Proj** | **1** | **0** | **15** | **17** | **4.02** | **3.04** | **1.27** | **676** | **613** | **728** | **19.2** | **3.7** | **10.7** | **2.9** | **58%** | **14%** | **94.3** | **54** | **20** | **26** | **32%** | **69%** | **12%** | **3** | | | | | | **0.2** | **125** | **144** | **-$4** |

## McGee,Jake

| | | | | | |
|---|---|---|---|---|---|
| Age: 32 | Th: L | Role RP | Health | D | LIMA Plan C |
| Ht: 6' 3" | Wt: 230 | Type Pwr | PT/Exp | C | Rand Var +5 |
| | | | Consist | B | MM 1200 |

Skills drop-off wasn't quite as severe as surface stats would suggest, as trifecta of bad luck, particularly in 2nd half, caused ERA to skyrocket. Even so, pre-2016 Cmd and BPV look like a distant memory. Can pretty much forget about consistent save opps, and even helpful ratios look increasingly less likely.

| Yr | Tm | W | Sv | IP | K | ERA | xERA | WHIP | oOPS | vL | vR | BF/G | Ctl | Dom | Cmd | FpK | SwK | Vel | G | L | F | H% | S% | hr/f | GS | APC | DOM% | DIS% | Sv% | LI | RAR | BPV | BPX | R$ |
|---|---|---|---|---|---|---|---|---|---|---|---|---|---|---|---|---|---|---|---|---|---|---|---|---|---|---|---|---|---|---|---|---|---|---|
| 14 | TAM | 5 | 19 | 71 | 90 | 1.89 | 2.68 | 0.90 | 486 | 572 | 452 | 3.8 | 2.0 | 11.4 | 5.6 | 65% | 14% | 96.3 | 38 | 19 | 43 | 29% | 79% | 3% | 0 | 16 | | | 83 | 1.38 | 16.3 | 166 | 198 | $18 |
| 15 | TAM | 1 | 6 | 37 | 48 | 2.41 | 2.95 | 0.94 | 544 | 607 | 513 | 3.8 | 1.9 | 11.6 | 6.0 | 62% | 13% | 94.5 | 39 | 16 | 46 | 30% | 78% | 7% | 0 | 16 | | | 60 | 1.30 | 7.1 | 173 | 206 | $5 |
| 16 | COL | 2 | 15 | 46 | 38 | 4.73 | 4.78 | 1.58 | 887 | 821 | 922 | 3.6 | 3.2 | 7.5 | 2.4 | 66% | 9% | 93.1 | 40 | 22 | 38 | 34% | 76% | 16% | 0 | 15 | | | 79 | 0.78 | -3.0 | 68 | 80 | $1 |
| 17 | COL | 0 | 3 | 57 | 58 | 3.61 | 3.91 | 1.10 | 624 | 690 | 585 | 3.7 | 2.5 | 9.1 | 3.6 | 62% | 10% | 94.9 | 41 | 19 | 41 | 29% | 68% | 6% | 0 | 15 | | | 50 | 1.09 | 5.3 | 115 | 138 | $2 |
| 18 | COL | 2 | 1 | 51 | 47 | 6.49 | 4.51 | 1.46 | 883 | 942 | 847 | 3.7 | 2.8 | 8.2 | 2.9 | 62% | 11% | 93.8 | 40 | 21 | 39 | 33% | 58% | 16% | 0 | 14 | | | 33 | 0.80 | -14.8 | 91 | 104 | -$8 |
| 1st Half | | 1 | 1 | 30 | 27 | 5.70 | 4.49 | 1.43 | 846 | 1012 | 748 | 3.9 | 2.1 | 8.1 | 3.9 | 64% | 10% | 93.4 | 38 | 22 | 40 | 35% | 63% | 13% | 0 | 15 | | | 50 | 0.95 | -5.7 | 105 | 121 | -$8 |
| 2nd Half | | 1 | 0 | 21 | 20 | 7.59 | 4.54 | 1.50 | 938 | 838 | 994 | 3.4 | 3.8 | 8.4 | 2.2 | 60% | 11% | 94.2 | 43 | 19 | 38 | 31% | 52% | 21% | 0 | 14 | | | 0 | 0.62 | -9.1 | 70 | 81 | -$8 |
| **19** | **Proj** | **2** | **0** | **51** | **46** | **4.71** | **4.09** | **1.36** | **800** | **822** | **787** | **3.6** | **3.0** | **8.2** | **2.7** | **63%** | **11%** | **94.2** | **40** | **20** | **40** | **31%** | **69%** | **13%** | **0** | | | | | | **-3.5** | **84** | **96** | **-$4** |

## McHugh,Collin

| | | | | | |
|---|---|---|---|---|---|
| Age: 32 | Th: R | Role RP | Health | F | LIMA Plan B |
| Ht: 6' 2" | Wt: 190 | Type Pwr FB | PT/Exp | C | Rand Var -5 |
| | | | Consist | B | MM 4501 |

Shift to 'pen worked out well. Elite in 1st half, as velocity bump helped Dom reach new heights, GB% returned, and luck was on his side. Was good, not great, in 2nd half, as Ctl and FB% went in wrong direction, and S% returned to usual level. Should be a strong LIMA option in 2019, but use 2nd half as your baseline.

| Yr | Tm | W | Sv | IP | K | ERA | xERA | WHIP | oOPS | vL | vR | BF/G | Ctl | Dom | Cmd | FpK | SwK | Vel | G | L | F | H% | S% | hr/f | GS | APC | DOM% | DIS% | Sv% | LI | RAR | BPV | BPX | R$ |
|---|---|---|---|---|---|---|---|---|---|---|---|---|---|---|---|---|---|---|---|---|---|---|---|---|---|---|---|---|---|---|---|---|---|---|
| 14 | HOU * | 11 | 0 | 174 | 167 | 2.91 | 2.49 | 1.05 | 588 | 609 | 556 | 22.4 | 2.4 | 8.7 | 3.5 | 58% | 11% | 91.6 | 42 | 24 | 34 | 27% | 74% | 9% | 25 | 99 | 40% | 12% | | | 17.8 | 118 | 141 | $18 |
| 15 | HOU | 19 | 0 | 204 | 171 | 3.89 | 3.90 | 1.28 | 705 | 648 | 755 | 26.8 | 2.3 | 7.6 | 3.2 | 62% | 11% | 90.4 | 45 | 20 | 35 | 32% | 71% | 9% | 32 | 101 | 41% | 25% | | | 1.8 | 96 | 114 | $12 |
| 16 | HOU | 13 | 0 | 185 | 177 | 4.34 | 4.18 | 1.41 | 790 | 804 | 777 | 24.1 | 2.6 | 8.6 | 3.3 | 67% | 11% | 90.2 | 41 | 21 | 38 | 34% | 73% | 12% | 33 | 96 | 27% | 27% | | | -3.4 | 103 | 123 | $4 |
| 17 | HOU * | 5 | 0 | 79 | 71 | 4.05 | 4.59 | 1.42 | 747 | 809 | 694 | 19.8 | 2.9 | 8.0 | 2.8 | 63% | 13% | 90.2 | 33 | 22 | 45 | 34% | 74% | 9% | 12 | 90 | 25% | 33% | | | 3.0 | 78 | 94 | $0 |
| 18 | HOU | 6 | 0 | 72 | 94 | 1.99 | 3.18 | 0.91 | 542 | 695 | 416 | 4.9 | 2.6 | 11.7 | 4.5 | 62% | 14% | 92.1 | 35 | 22 | 44 | 26% | 83% | 8% | 0 | 21 | | | 0 | 0.87 | 19.3 | 153 | 176 | $12 |
| 1st Half | | 3 | 0 | 37 | 51 | 0.97 | 2.62 | 0.81 | 474 | 608 | 341 | 5.4 | 2.2 | 12.4 | 5.7 | 64% | 13% | 92.0 | 42 | 21 | 37 | 26% | 93% | 7% | 0 | 24 | | | 0 | 0.48 | 14.5 | 184 | 212 | $15 |
| 2nd Half | | 3 | 0 | 35 | 43 | 3.06 | 3.78 | 1.02 | 611 | 805 | 480 | 4.4 | 3.1 | 11.0 | 3.6 | 59% | 14% | 92.2 | 27 | 23 | 50 | 26% | 75% | 10% | 0 | 18 | | | 0 | 1.19 | 4.8 | 120 | 138 | $9 |
| **19** | **Proj** | **5** | **0** | **73** | **88** | **3.00** | **3.25** | **1.14** | **677** | **770** | **597** | **7.8** | **2.6** | **10.9** | **4.2** | **62%** | **13%** | **91.2** | **35** | **22** | **43** | **31%** | **78%** | **11%** | **0** | | | | | | **9.7** | **140** | **161** | **$6** |

## Mejia,Adalberto

| | | | | | |
|---|---|---|---|---|---|
| Age: 26 | Th: L | Role RP | Health | D | LIMA Plan D+ |
| Ht: 6' 3" | Wt: 195 | Type FB | PT/Exp | D | Rand Var -1 |
| | | | Consist | B | MM 0000 |

2-0, 2.01 ERA in 22 IP at MIN. Missed a month in 1st half with blister, then elbow injury ended season in August. More mediocrity when on the mound, as seen in low GB%, shaky Cmd, and subpar SwK. Without a plus skill anywhere on the page, there are better places to speculate when rounding out your rotation.

| Yr | Tm | W | Sv | IP | K | ERA | xERA | WHIP | oOPS | vL | vR | BF/G | Ctl | Dom | Cmd | FpK | SwK | Vel | G | L | F | H% | S% | hr/f | GS | APC | DOM% | DIS% | Sv% | LI | RAR | BPV | BPX | R$ |
|---|---|---|---|---|---|---|---|---|---|---|---|---|---|---|---|---|---|---|---|---|---|---|---|---|---|---|---|---|---|---|---|---|---|---|
| 14 | aa | 7 | 0 | 108 | 72 | 5.00 | 4.58 | 1.46 | | | | 21.0 | 2.5 | 6.0 | 2.4 | | | | | | | 34% | 65% | | | | | | | | -16.8 | 65 | 77 | -$7 |
| 15 | aa | 5 | 0 | 51 | 33 | 3.20 | 2.99 | 1.25 | | | | 17.4 | 3.3 | 5.9 | 1.8 | | | | | | | 28% | 74% | | | | | | | | 4.8 | 69 | 82 | $1 |
| 16 | MIN * | 9 | 0 | 134 | 101 | 4.16 | 4.48 | 1.35 | 1098 | 2500 | 808 | 24.4 | 2.2 | 6.8 | 3.1 | 62% | 5% | 90.3 | 33 | 25 | 42 | 33% | 72% | 0% | 0 | 42 | | | 0 | 0.05 | 0.5 | 75 | 90 | $2 |
| 17 | MIN * | 5 | 0 | 127 | 103 | 4.47 | 5.08 | 1.54 | 822 | 812 | 824 | 20.5 | 3.6 | 7.3 | 2.0 | 57% | 11% | 92.5 | 39 | 23 | 38 | 34% | 73% | 11% | 21 | 83 | 5% | 38% | | | -1.7 | 53 | 64 | -$4 |
| 18 | MIN * | 7 | 0 | 86 | 62 | 4.10 | 4.04 | 1.39 | 561 | 328 | 624 | 18.2 | 3.3 | 6.4 | 2.0 | 54% | 9% | 92.4 | 34 | 27 | 39 | 32% | 70% | 4% | 4 | 71 | 0% | 50% | 0 | 0.66 | 0.6 | 65 | 75 | -$1 |
| 1st Half | | 4 | 0 | 54 | 40 | 4.39 | 4.55 | 1.51 | 874 | 800 | 900 | 19.5 | 3.5 | 6.7 | 1.9 | 50% | 9% | 92.6 | 33 | 40 | 27 | 34% | 70% | 0% | 1 | 79 | 0% | 100% | | | -1.6 | 65 | 74 | -$3 |
| 2nd Half | | 3 | 0 | 32 | 21 | 3.60 | 3.20 | 1.19 | 483 | 143 | 562 | 16.2 | 2.9 | 6.0 | 2.0 | 56% | 9% | 92.3 | 35 | 23 | 42 | 27% | 71% | 5% | 3 | 70 | 0% | 33% | 0 | 0.64 | 2.2 | 67 | 77 | $4 |
| **19** | **Proj** | **4** | **0** | **58** | **42** | **4.26** | **4.59** | **1.38** | **778** | **514** | **838** | **19.1** | **3.1** | **6.5** | **2.1** | **56%** | **10%** | **92.4** | **37** | **23** | **41** | **30%** | **73%** | **10%** | **12** | | | | | | **-2.3** | **49** | **57** | **-$2** |

## Melancon,Mark

| | | | | | |
|---|---|---|---|---|---|
| Age: 34 | Th: R | Role RP | Health | F | LIMA Plan C |
| Ht: 6' 2" | Wt: 215 | Type GB | PT/Exp | C | Rand Var -1 |
| | | | Consist | B | MM 3110 |

Sore elbow sidelined him through May, and never got back to looking like himself. Usual keys to success no longer a sure thing, as pinpoint Ctl evaded him, and GB% continued steady decline. Track record, contract could help vault him back into the saves mix, but BPV drop, Health Grade, and age all say to bet against it.

| Yr | Tm | W | Sv | IP | K | ERA | xERA | WHIP | oOPS | vL | vR | BF/G | Ctl | Dom | Cmd | FpK | SwK | Vel | G | L | F | H% | S% | hr/f | GS | APC | DOM% | DIS% | Sv% | LI | RAR | BPV | BPX | R$ |
|---|---|---|---|---|---|---|---|---|---|---|---|---|---|---|---|---|---|---|---|---|---|---|---|---|---|---|---|---|---|---|---|---|---|---|
| 14 | PIT | 3 | 33 | 71 | 71 | 1.90 | 2.50 | 0.87 | 473 | 415 | 524 | 3.8 | 1.4 | 9.0 | 6.5 | 69% | 14% | 92.8 | 57 | 20 | 23 | 27% | 78% | 5% | 0 | 14 | | | 89 | 1.37 | 16.1 | 159 | 190 | $22 |
| 15 | PIT | 3 | 51 | 77 | 62 | 2.23 | 3.00 | 0.93 | 541 | 380 | 673 | 3.8 | 1.6 | 7.3 | 4.4 | 62% | 12% | 91.5 | 58 | 20 | 23 | 26% | 78% | 8% | 0 | 14 | | | 96 | 1.35 | 16.4 | 123 | 146 | $30 |
| 16 | 2 NL | 2 | 47 | 71 | 65 | 1.64 | 2.99 | 0.90 | 511 | 560 | 471 | 3.6 | 1.5 | 8.2 | 5.4 | 66% | 11% | 91.8 | 54 | 21 | 25 | 26% | 84% | 6% | 0 | 14 | | | 92 | 1.04 | 22.4 | 139 | 165 | $29 |
| 17 | SF | 1 | 11 | 30 | 29 | 4.50 | 3.59 | 1.43 | 794 | 715 | 883 | 4.1 | 1.8 | 8.7 | 4.8 | 56% | 10% | 92.2 | 53 | 22 | 26 | 38% | 70% | 13% | 0 | 16 | | | 69 | 1.12 | -0.5 | 139 | 167 | $1 |
| 18 | SF | 1 | 3 | 39 | 31 | 3.23 | 4.17 | 1.59 | 771 | 770 | 771 | 4.2 | 3.2 | 7.2 | 2.2 | 57% | 10% | 91.5 | 52 | 26 | 22 | 37% | 80% | 7% | 0 | 16 | | | 43 | 1.24 | 4.4 | 72 | 82 | -$3 |
| 1st Half | | 0 | 1 | 10 | 8 | 2.61 | 4.22 | 1.26 | 633 | 500 | 692 | 3.9 | 2.6 | 7.0 | 2.7 | 49% | 11% | 90.8 | 48 | 16 | 35 | 32% | 77% | 0% | 0 | 14 | | | 33 | 0.99 | 2.0 | 81 | 93 | -$6 |
| 2nd Half | | 1 | 2 | 29 | 23 | 3.45 | 4.16 | 1.71 | 816 | 843 | 800 | 4.4 | 3.5 | 7.2 | 2.1 | 60% | 10% | 91.8 | 53 | 29 | 18 | 38% | 81% | 12% | 0 | 17 | | | 50 | 1.33 | 2.5 | 68 | 78 | -$2 |
| **19** | **Proj** | **1** | **9** | **44** | **36** | **3.70** | **3.53** | **1.27** | **675** | **642** | **701** | **3.9** | **2.4** | **7.5** | **3.2** | **62%** | **10%** | **91.9** | **50** | **24** | **25** | **32%** | **71%** | **8%** | **0** | | | | | | **2.8** | **100** | **115** | **$2** |

## Mendez,Yohander

| | | | | | |
|---|---|---|---|---|---|
| Age: 24 | Th: L | Role SP | Health | A | LIMA Plan D+ |
| Ht: 6' 5" | Wt: 200 | Type xFB | PT/Exp | D | Rand Var 0 |
| | | | Consist | F | MM 0001 |

2-2, 5.53 ERA in 28 IP at TEX. Development hit another snag, as Cmd deserted him early on, and FB tilt led to major HR problems (2.4 hr/9 in minors). At least took a step in right direction in 2nd half, but ugly xERA, FpK shows plenty of work left to do. Don't write him off yet, but he's a long shot to contribute in 2019.

| Yr | Tm | W | Sv | IP | K | ERA | xERA | WHIP | oOPS | vL | vR | BF/G | Ctl | Dom | Cmd | FpK | SwK | Vel | G | L | F | H% | S% | hr/f | GS | APC | DOM% | DIS% | Sv% | LI | RAR | BPV | BPX | R$ |
|---|---|---|---|---|---|---|---|---|---|---|---|---|---|---|---|---|---|---|---|---|---|---|---|---|---|---|---|---|---|---|---|---|---|---|
| 14 | | | | | | | | | | | | | | | | | | | | | | | | | | | | | | | | | | |
| 15 | | | | | | | | | | | | | | | | | | | | | | | | | | | | | | | | | | |
| 16 | TEX * | 8 | 0 | 81 | 58 | 3.18 | 2.54 | 1.20 | 878 | 1300 | 664 | 17.1 | 3.7 | 6.4 | 1.7 | 41% | 11% | 91.4 | 33 | 20 | 47 | 27% | 72% | 0% | 0 | 37 | | | 0 | 0.29 | 10.1 | 78 | 93 | $6 |
| 17 | TEX * | 7 | 0 | 150 | 111 | 5.30 | 5.25 | 1.37 | 869 | 528 | 1040 | 20.3 | 3.1 | 6.7 | 2.1 | 52% | 9% | 92.5 | 34 | 20 | 46 | 28% | 68% | 16% | 0 | 27 | | | 0 | 0.75 | -17.4 | 27 | 32 | -$3 |
| 18 | TEX * | 3 | 0 | 120 | 85 | 6.25 | 6.57 | 1.64 | 789 | 916 | 755 | 20.5 | 3.9 | 6.4 | 1.6 | 42% | 9% | 91.8 | 38 | 17 | 45 | 32% | 67% | 10% | 5 | 62 | 0% | 80% | 0 | 0.60 | -31.0 | 8 | 9 | -$18 |
| 1st Half | | 0 | 0 | 56 | 34 | 6.94 | 7.65 | 1.85 | 1108 | 900 | 1181 | 21.7 | 4.3 | 5.5 | 1.3 | 33% | 4% | 91.9 | 33 | 33 | 33 | 34% | 67% | 17% | 1 | 43 | 0% | 100% | 0 | 0.41 | -19.2 | -12 | -14 | -$31 |
| 2nd Half | | 3 | 0 | 64 | 51 | 5.48 | 5.48 | 1.42 | 721 | 921 | 671 | 19.4 | 3.5 | 7.2 | 2.1 | 44% | 11% | 91.7 | 39 | 13 | 49 | 29% | 67% | 9% | 4 | 68 | 0% | 75% | 0 | 0.66 | -10.5 | 30 | 34 | -$9 |
| **19** | **Proj** | **3** | **0** | **73** | **53** | **5.36** | **5.10** | **1.46** | **801** | **997** | **753** | **21.1** | **3.6** | **6.5** | **1.8** | **44%** | **11%** | **91.7** | **39** | **13** | **49** | **29%** | **68%** | **11%** | **10** | | | | | | **-6.2** | **38** | **44** | **-$6** |

BRIAN RUDD

## Mengden,Daniel

| | | | | | | |
|---|---|---|---|---|---|---|
| Mengden,Daniel | | | Health | D | LIMA Plan | B |
| Age: 26 | Th: R | Role: SP | PT/Exp | D | Rand Var | 0 |
| Ht: 6' 2" | Wt: 190 | Type: FB | Consist | B | MM | 1003 |

7-6, 4.05 ERA in 116 IP at OAK. Mid-season rough patch (foot sprain, demotion) was book-ended by H%-fueled success. Inconsistency will continue to be part of the package given FB lean and mediocre, downward trending Dom. Solid Ctl could make him serviceable back-end SP, but one completely devoid of upside.

| Yr Tm | W | Sv | IP | K | ERA | xERA | WHIP | oOPS | vL | vR | BF/G | Ctl | Dom | Cmd | FpK | SwK | Vel | G | L | F | H% | S% | hr/f | GS | APC | DOM% | DIS% | Sv% | LI | RAR | BPV | BPX | R$ |
|---|---|---|---|---|---|---|---|---|---|---|---|---|---|---|---|---|---|---|---|---|---|---|---|---|---|---|---|---|---|---|---|---|---|
| 14 | | | | | | | | | | | | | | | | | | | | | | | | | | | | | | | | | |
| 15 | | | | | | | | | | | | | | | | | | | | | | | | | | | | | | | | | |
| 16 OAK * | 12 | 0 | 170 | 148 | 3.77 | 3.66 | 1.32 | 819 | 824 | 815 | 22.7 | 3.3 | 7.8 | 2.4 | 61% | 10% | 92.1 | 40 | 24 | 36 | 31% | 72% | 11% | 14 | 94 | 21% | 36% | | | 8.9 | 81 | 97 | $9 |
| 17 OAK * | 5 | 0 | 84 | 62 | 4.02 | 4.18 | 1.30 | 650 | 734 | 560 | 21.6 | 2.9 | 6.6 | 2.3 | 58% | 9% | 92.1 | 39 | 19 | 42 | 29% | 73% | 11% | 7 | 93 | 29% | 57% | | | 3.5 | 56 | 67 | $1 |
| 18 OAK * | 11 | 0 | 162 | 99 | 3.91 | 3.62 | 1.13 | 699 | 638 | 748 | 20.6 | 1.8 | 5.5 | 3.0 | 62% | 8% | 92.2 | 40 | 22 | 38 | 27% | 69% | 13% | 17 | 81 | 24% | 35% | 0 | 0.74 | 4.7 | 68 | 78 | $10 |
| 1st Half | 6 | 0 | 91 | 55 | 4.47 | 4.71 | 1.17 | 731 | 645 | 802 | 23.7 | 1.9 | 5.5 | 2.9 | 64% | 8% | 92.1 | 40 | 23 | 37 | 26% | 67% | 14% | 16 | 87 | 25% | 38% | | | -3.5 | 65 | 75 | $7 |
| 2nd Half | 5 | 0 | 71 | 44 | 3.21 | 2.89 | 1.07 | 573 | 612 | 544 | 18.5 | 1.8 | 5.6 | 3.1 | 53% | 9% | 92.6 | 39 | 14 | 46 | 27% | 72% | 9% | 1 | 63 | 0% | 0% | 0 | 0.64 | 8.3 | 87 | 100 | $15 |
| **19 Proj** | **10** | **0** | **152** | **106** | **4.07** | **4.30** | **1.21** | **698** | **727** | **673** | **27.5** | **2.4** | **6.3** | **2.6** | **58%** | **9%** | **92.3** | **39** | **19** | **41** | **28%** | **69%** | **9%** | **22** | | | | | | **1.6** | **65** | **75** | **$7** |

## Middleton,Keynan

| | | | | | | |
|---|---|---|---|---|---|---|
| Middleton,Keynan | | | Health | F | LIMA Plan | C |
| Age: 25 | Th: R | Role: RP | PT/Exp | D | Rand Var | -5 |
| Ht: 6' 2" | Wt: 215 | Type: Pwr FB | Consist | B | MM | 1310 |

With six saves in April, it appeared he may run with closer gig. But then elbow soreness popped up, and by the end of May he'd gone under the knife for Tommy John surgery. Swing-and-miss stuff from 2017 makes him worth tracking, but even with expected late-season return, he's unlikely to be a factor in 2019.

| Yr Tm | W | Sv | IP | K | ERA | xERA | WHIP | oOPS | vL | vR | BF/G | Ctl | Dom | Cmd | FpK | SwK | Vel | G | L | F | H% | S% | hr/f | GS | APC | DOM% | DIS% | Sv% | LI | RAR | BPV | BPX | R$ |
|---|---|---|---|---|---|---|---|---|---|---|---|---|---|---|---|---|---|---|---|---|---|---|---|---|---|---|---|---|---|---|---|---|---|
| 14 | | | | | | | | | | | | | | | | | | | | | | | | | | | | | | | | | |
| 15 | | | | | | | | | | | | | | | | | | | | | | | | | | | | | | | | | |
| 16 a/a | 0 | 8 | 30 | 28 | 3.59 | 3.39 | 1.23 | | | | 5.7 | 2.4 | 8.5 | 3.6 | | | | | | | 32% | 72% | | | | | | | | 2.2 | 112 | 133 | $1 |
| 17 LAA | 6 | 3 | 58 | 63 | 3.86 | 4.14 | 1.34 | 791 | 733 | 834 | 3.8 | 2.8 | 9.7 | 3.5 | 57% | 17% | 96.8 | 38 | 21 | 41 | 33% | 79% | 16% | 0 | 15 | | | 60 | 0.96 | 3.6 | 116 | 139 | $3 |
| 18 LAA | 0 | 6 | 18 | 16 | 2.04 | 4.57 | 1.30 | 688 | 749 | 612 | 4.4 | 4.6 | 8.2 | 1.8 | 61% | 11% | 96.1 | 33 | 24 | 42 | 28% | 86% | 5% | 0 | 19 | | | 86 | 1.53 | 4.6 | 34 | 39 | -$1 |
| 1st Half | 0 | 6 | 18 | 16 | 2.04 | 4.57 | 1.30 | 688 | 749 | 612 | 4.4 | 4.6 | 8.2 | 1.8 | 61% | 11% | 96.1 | 33 | 24 | 42 | 28% | 86% | 5% | 0 | 19 | | | 86 | 1.53 | 4.6 | 34 | 39 | -$1 |
| 2nd Half | | | | | | | | | | | | | | | | | | | | | | | | | | | | | | | | | |
| **19 Proj** | **1** | **2** | **15** | **14** | **3.39** | **4.16** | **1.32** | **733** | **743** | **722** | **4.2** | **3.9** | **8.8** | **2.3** | **59%** | **13%** | **96.4** | **35** | **23** | **42** | **30%** | **78%** | **10%** | **0** | | | | | | **1.4** | **67** | **77** | **-$3** |

## Mikolas,Miles

| | | | | | | |
|---|---|---|---|---|---|---|
| Mikolas,Miles | | | Health | A | LIMA Plan | C |
| Age: 30 | Th: R | Role: SP | PT/Exp | A | Rand Var | -1 |
| Ht: 6' 5" | Wt: 220 | Type: | Consist | C | MM | 3105 |

Armed with vast pitch mix (four over 20% usage), return to majors was a resounding success. Combined impeccable Ctl with GB tilt, while 2nd half SwK bump and numbers in Japan hint at more Dom potential. Likely hr/f correction could send ERA up just a bit, but all signs point to a strong follow-up.

| Yr Tm | W | Sv | IP | K | ERA | xERA | WHIP | oOPS | vL | vR | BF/G | Ctl | Dom | Cmd | FpK | SwK | Vel | G | L | F | H% | S% | hr/f | GS | APC | DOM% | DIS% | Sv% | LI | RAR | BPV | BPX | R$ |
|---|---|---|---|---|---|---|---|---|---|---|---|---|---|---|---|---|---|---|---|---|---|---|---|---|---|---|---|---|---|---|---|---|---|
| 14 TEX * | 7 | 2 | 102 | 68 | 5.17 | 4.95 | 1.42 | 769 | 732 | 815 | 16.6 | 1.9 | 6.0 | 3.2 | 62% | 8% | 92.7 | 40 | 23 | 37 | 34% | 65% | 11% | 10 | 93 | 20% | 40% | | | -18.0 | 69 | 82 | -$6 |
| 15 for | 13 | 0 | 145 | 102 | 2.39 | 2.54 | 0.99 | | | | 26.3 | 1.8 | 6.3 | 3.6 | | | | | | | 25% | 81% | | | | | | | | 28.1 | 99 | 118 | $22 |
| 16 for | 4 | 0 | 92 | 80 | 3.05 | 4.57 | 1.29 | | | | 26.9 | 2.8 | 7.8 | 2.8 | | | | | | | 29% | 86% | | | | | | | | 12.9 | 60 | 71 | $4 |
| 17 for | 14 | 0 | 188 | 177 | 2.79 | 3.09 | 1.08 | | | | 27.1 | 1.4 | 8.5 | 6.2 | | | | | | | 31% | 77% | | | | | | | | 36.3 | 163 | 196 | $27 |
| 18 STL | 18 | 0 | 201 | 146 | 2.83 | 3.71 | 1.07 | 628 | 722 | 504 | 25.3 | 1.3 | 6.5 | 5.0 | 71% | 10% | 93.9 | 49 | 22 | 28 | 29% | 76% | 9% | 32 | 94 | 38% | 22% | | | 32.8 | 110 | 126 | $27 |
| 1st Half | 8 | 0 | 103 | 72 | 2.61 | 3.62 | 0.99 | 590 | 717 | 439 | 25.7 | 1.1 | 6.3 | 5.5 | 72% | 9% | 94.1 | 52 | 22 | 27 | 27% | 77% | 9% | 16 | 94 | 44% | 19% | | | 19.6 | 112 | 129 | $29 |
| 2nd Half | 10 | 0 | 97 | 74 | 3.05 | 3.81 | 1.16 | 667 | 727 | 581 | 24.8 | 1.5 | 6.8 | 4.6 | 69% | 11% | 93.8 | 47 | 23 | 30 | 31% | 76% | 9% | 16 | 94 | 31% | 25% | | | 13.2 | 108 | 124 | $25 |
| **19 Proj** | **15** | **0** | **189** | **151** | **3.26** | **3.53** | **1.12** | **651** | **685** | **608** | **24.8** | **1.6** | **7.2** | **4.4** | **67%** | **10%** | **93.4** | **45** | **22** | **32** | **29%** | **75%** | **11%** | **30** | | | | | | **20.8** | **109** | **126** | **$21** |

## Miley,Wade

| | | | | | | |
|---|---|---|---|---|---|---|
| Miley,Wade | | | Health | F | LIMA Plan | B+ |
| Age: 32 | Th: L | Role: SP | PT/Exp | B | Rand Var | -2 |
| Ht: 6' 0" | Wt: 220 | Type: | Consist | B | MM | 2103 |

5-2, 2.57 ERA in 81 IP at MIL. Groin, oblique injuries limited him early on, but returned with shocking 2nd half. New cutter-heavy approach gave him weapon vR, and should help prevent total crash. But FpK didn't support Ctl rebound, and he got a lot of help from hr/f. Bottom line: bet the over on 4.00 ERA.

| Yr Tm | W | Sv | IP | K | ERA | xERA | WHIP | oOPS | vL | vR | BF/G | Ctl | Dom | Cmd | FpK | SwK | Vel | G | L | F | H% | S% | hr/f | GS | APC | DOM% | DIS% | Sv% | LI | RAR | BPV | BPX | R$ |
|---|---|---|---|---|---|---|---|---|---|---|---|---|---|---|---|---|---|---|---|---|---|---|---|---|---|---|---|---|---|---|---|---|---|
| 14 ARI | 8 | 0 | 201 | 183 | 4.34 | 3.59 | 1.40 | 746 | 727 | 752 | 26.2 | 3.4 | 8.2 | 2.4 | 63% | 10% | 91.2 | 51 | 21 | 28 | 32% | 71% | 14% | 33 | 97 | 24% | 24% | | | -14.8 | 86 | 102 | -$3 |
| 15 BOS | 11 | 0 | 194 | 147 | 4.46 | 4.16 | 1.37 | 740 | 674 | 760 | 26.0 | 3.0 | 6.8 | 2.3 | 61% | 9% | 90.8 | 49 | 21 | 30 | 32% | 68% | 9% | 32 | 100 | 34% | 28% | | | -11.9 | 70 | 83 | -$1 |
| 16 2AL | 9 | 0 | 166 | 137 | 5.37 | 4.12 | 1.42 | 808 | 671 | 842 | 23.7 | 2.7 | 7.4 | 2.8 | 60% | 9% | 90.3 | 47 | 23 | 30 | 33% | 65% | 16% | 30 | 91 | 13% | 37% | | | -24.1 | 87 | 103 | -$6 |
| 17 BAL | 8 | 0 | 157 | 142 | 5.61 | 4.90 | 1.73 | 841 | 663 | 875 | 22.8 | 5.3 | 8.1 | 1.5 | 54% | 8% | 91.0 | 50 | 23 | 27 | 34% | 70% | 19% | 32 | 95 | 16% | 63% | | | -24.2 | 31 | 37 | -$13 |
| 18 MIL * | 6 | 0 | 107 | 71 | 3.33 | 4.02 | 1.33 | 636 | 605 | 645 | 19.3 | 2.7 | 6.0 | 2.2 | 58% | 9% | 90.8 | 53 | 24 | 24 | 31% | 76% | 5% | 16 | 81 | 19% | 44% | | | 10.8 | 64 | 73 | $3 |
| 1st Half | 2 | 0 | 23 | 19 | 6.76 | 8.32 | 1.93 | 557 | 286 | 633 | 15.8 | 3.0 | 7.3 | 2.4 | 54% | 7% | 91.0 | 47 | 26 | 26 | 41% | 69% | 0% | 2 | 58 | 0% | 50% | | | -7.5 | 20 | 23 | -$22 |
| 2nd Half | 4 | 0 | 83 | 52 | 2.37 | 2.81 | 1.16 | 643 | 630 | 646 | 20.8 | 2.6 | 5.6 | 2.1 | 58% | 10% | 90.8 | 53 | 23 | 23 | 28% | 80% | 6% | 14 | 84 | 21% | 43% | | | 18.3 | 77 | 88 | $12 |
| **19 Proj** | **7** | **0** | **131** | **97** | **4.20** | **4.03** | **1.36** | **743** | **653** | **767** | **21.2** | **3.0** | **6.7** | **2.3** | **59%** | **9%** | **90.8** | **49** | **22** | **28** | **31%** | **71%** | **13%** | **26** | | | | | | **1.5** | **68** | **78** | **$1** |

## Miller,Andrew

| | | | | | | |
|---|---|---|---|---|---|---|
| Miller,Andrew | | | Health | F | LIMA Plan | B |
| Age: 34 | Th: L | Role: RP | PT/Exp | C | Rand Var | +3 |
| Ht: 6' 7" | Wt: 205 | Type: Pwr | Consist | B | MM | 5510 |

An injury-riddled season, as he spent time on DL with hamstring, knee, and shoulder issues. Inflated H% deserves some of the blame, and 2nd half FpK/Ctl rebound a promising sign, so this looks like a good chance to buy low. Just don't count on full recovery, because at this age, injuries are unlikely to completely go away.

| Yr Tm | W | Sv | IP | K | ERA | xERA | WHIP | oOPS | vL | vR | BF/G | Ctl | Dom | Cmd | FpK | SwK | Vel | G | L | F | H% | S% | hr/f | GS | APC | DOM% | DIS% | Sv% | LI | RAR | BPV | BPX | R$ |
|---|---|---|---|---|---|---|---|---|---|---|---|---|---|---|---|---|---|---|---|---|---|---|---|---|---|---|---|---|---|---|---|---|---|
| 14 2AL | 5 | 1 | 62 | 103 | 2.02 | 1.80 | 0.80 | 456 | 467 | 446 | 3.3 | 2.5 | 14.9 | 6.1 | 59% | 15% | 93.9 | 47 | 22 | 31 | 29% | 77% | 9% | 0 | 14 | | | 50 | 1.54 | 13.2 | 226 | 270 | $11 |
| 15 NYY | 3 | 36 | 62 | 100 | 2.04 | 2.14 | 0.86 | 475 | 602 | 444 | 4.1 | 2.9 | 14.6 | 5.0 | 66% | 18% | 94.3 | 48 | 18 | 33 | 27% | 81% | 13% | 0 | 16 | | | 95 | 1.22 | 14.6 | 210 | 250 | $24 |
| 16 2AL | 10 | 12 | 74 | 123 | 1.45 | 1.67 | 0.69 | 487 | 523 | 474 | 3.9 | 1.1 | 14.9 | 13.7 | 62% | 17% | 94.5 | 54 | 17 | 29 | 28% | 91% | 20% | 0 | 16 | | | 86 | 1.23 | 25.1 | 271 | 322 | $25 |
| 17 CLE | 4 | 2 | 63 | 95 | 1.44 | 2.61 | 0.83 | 440 | 481 | 424 | 4.3 | 3.0 | 13.6 | 4.5 | 63% | 17% | 94.0 | 40 | 24 | 36 | 26% | 86% | 7% | 0 | 17 | | | 50 | 1.29 | 22.6 | 181 | 218 | $13 |
| 18 CLE | 2 | 2 | 34 | 45 | 4.24 | 3.45 | 1.38 | 729 | 556 | 813 | 4.2 | 4.2 | 11.9 | 2.8 | 65% | 14% | 93.1 | 48 | 21 | 31 | 35% | 70% | 11% | 0 | 16 | | | 40 | 1.27 | -0.4 | 126 | 145 | -$2 |
| 1st Half | 1 | 1 | 14 | 23 | 4.40 | 3.31 | 1.60 | 823 | 722 | 862 | 3.9 | 6.3 | 14.4 | 2.3 | 61% | 14% | 93.0 | 50 | 17 | 33 | 41% | 73% | 10% | 0 | 15 | | | 25 | 1.60 | -0.4 | 118 | 136 | -$5 |
| 2nd Half | 1 | 1 | 20 | 22 | 4.12 | 3.55 | 1.22 | 661 | 465 | 773 | 4.4 | 2.7 | 10.1 | 3.7 | 67% | 14% | 93.1 | 46 | 23 | 30 | 32% | 68% | 12% | 0 | 17 | | | 100 | 1.00 | 0.1 | 132 | 151 | $0 |
| **19 Proj** | **4** | **8** | **58** | **85** | **3.02** | **2.40** | **1.00** | **548** | **506** | **566** | **4.3** | **3.2** | **13.1** | **4.2** | **64%** | **16%** | **93.9** | **47** | **21** | **32** | **29%** | **73%** | **13%** | **0** | | | | | | **18.3** | **177** | **203** | **$10** |

## Miller,Justin

| | | | | | | |
|---|---|---|---|---|---|---|
| Miller,Justin | | | Health | A | LIMA Plan | B+ |
| Age: 32 | Th: R | Role: RP | PT/Exp | D | Rand Var | -2 |
| Ht: 6' 3" | Wt: 215 | Type: Pwr xFB | Consist | F | MM | 1210 |

7-1, 3.61 ERA in 51 IP at WAS. Fast start at Triple-A led to recall, and success carried over initially thanks to elite SwK and some good fortune. But couldn't hold the whiffs in 2nd half, while xFB lean led to HR issues. A nice arm with K potential, but 4.00 MLB xERA says don't expect ratios to repeat; or wins, for that matter.

| Yr Tm | W | Sv | IP | K | ERA | xERA | WHIP | oOPS | vL | vR | BF/G | Ctl | Dom | Cmd | FpK | SwK | Vel | G | L | F | H% | S% | hr/f | GS | APC | DOM% | DIS% | Sv% | LI | RAR | BPV | BPX | R$ |
|---|---|---|---|---|---|---|---|---|---|---|---|---|---|---|---|---|---|---|---|---|---|---|---|---|---|---|---|---|---|---|---|---|---|
| 14 DET * | 3 | 5 | 57 | 34 | 3.01 | 3.28 | 1.19 | 829 | 708 | 900 | 5.0 | 2.5 | 5.3 | 2.2 | 55% | 5% | 91.8 | 38 | 18 | 44 | 27% | 77% | 10% | 0 | 24 | | | 83 | 0.25 | 5.2 | 62 | 74 | $3 |
| 15 COL * | 4 | 8 | 71 | 68 | 3.37 | 2.77 | 1.15 | 553 | 542 | 558 | 4.4 | 3.1 | 8.5 | 2.7 | 62% | 13% | 94.2 | 38 | 24 | 39 | 28% | 72% | 6% | 0 | 16 | | | 73 | 0.89 | 5.2 | 101 | 120 | $6 |
| 16 COL | 1 | 0 | 43 | 45 | 5.70 | 4.57 | 1.64 | 885 | 1125 | 740 | 4.9 | 4.2 | 9.5 | 2.3 | 60% | 11% | 93.1 | 35 | 27 | 38 | 37% | 67% | 13% | 0 | 19 | | | 0 | 0.50 | -7.9 | 70 | 83 | -$7 |
| 17 aaa | 5 | 9 | 46 | 28 | 6.22 | 5.74 | 1.48 | | | | 5.2 | 1.6 | 5.4 | 3.4 | | | | | | | 34% | 60% | | | | | | | | -10.6 | 54 | 65 | -$2 |
| 18 WAS * | 9 | 3 | 68 | 77 | 2.80 | 2.77 | 0.99 | 705 | 823 | 631 | 4.3 | 2.7 | 10.2 | 3.7 | 60% | 13% | 94.0 | 34 | 13 | 54 | 24% | 81% | 14% | 0 | 17 | | | 75 | 0.99 | 11.3 | 116 | 133 | $11 |
| 1st Half | 7 | 1 | 36 | 49 | 1.49 | 0.96 | 0.74 | 577 | 776 | 467 | 5.4 | 2.4 | 12.1 | 5.1 | 60% | 17% | 93.5 | 28 | 12 | 60 | 21% | 87% | 12% | 0 | 22 | | | 100 | 1.24 | 11.9 | 183 | 210 | $17 |
| 2nd Half | 2 | 2 | 31 | 28 | 4.31 | 4.82 | 1.28 | 783 | 847 | 738 | 3.7 | 3.2 | 8.0 | 2.5 | 60% | 11% | 94.3 | 36 | 13 | 51 | 27% | 76% | 15% | 0 | 15 | | | 67 | 0.89 | -0.6 | 74 | 85 | $0 |
| **19 Proj** | **5** | **2** | **58** | **54** | **4.33** | **4.11** | **1.26** | **790** | **952** | **694** | **4.5** | **2.8** | **8.3** | **3.0** | **60%** | **12%** | **93.7** | **34** | **19** | **46** | **29%** | **73%** | **14%** | **0** | | | | | | **0.3** | **88** | **101** | **$1** |

## Miller,Shelby

| | | | | | | |
|---|---|---|---|---|---|---|
| Miller,Shelby | | | Health | F | LIMA Plan | C |
| Age: 28 | Th: R | Role: SP | PT/Exp | D | Rand Var | +5 |
| Ht: 6' 3" | Wt: 225 | Type: Pwr | Consist | B | MM | 1201 |

Return from Tommy John surgery didn't quite go as planned, as he made just four starts with awful results before suffering setback with elbow. Maintaining Dom and velocity is encouraging, and token Sept relief outing bodes well for starting healthy in 2019. But he's a very high-risk dart throw at this point.

| Yr Tm | W | Sv | IP | K | ERA | xERA | WHIP | oOPS | vL | vR | BF/G | Ctl | Dom | Cmd | FpK | SwK | Vel | G | L | F | H% | S% | hr/f | GS | APC | DOM% | DIS% | Sv% | LI | RAR | BPV | BPX | R$ |
|---|---|---|---|---|---|---|---|---|---|---|---|---|---|---|---|---|---|---|---|---|---|---|---|---|---|---|---|---|---|---|---|---|---|
| 14 STL | 10 | 0 | 183 | 127 | 3.74 | 4.44 | 1.27 | 697 | 707 | 690 | 23.9 | 3.6 | 6.2 | 1.7 | 60% | 7% | 93.5 | 40 | 19 | 41 | 26% | 74% | 10% | 31 | 89 | 23% | 42% | 0 | 0.75 | 0.1 | 33 | 40 | $5 |
| 15 ATL | 6 | 0 | 205 | 171 | 3.02 | 4.02 | 1.25 | 663 | 732 | 594 | 26.1 | 3.2 | 7.5 | 2.3 | 61% | 10% | 94.0 | 48 | 18 | 34 | 29% | 77% | 6% | 33 | 98 | 30% | 24% | | | 23.7 | 75 | 89 | $13 |
| 16 ARI * | 8 | 0 | 152 | 114 | 5.69 | 5.68 | 1.62 | 867 | 943 | 767 | 24.0 | 3.1 | 6.7 | 2.2 | 59% | 8% | 93.0 | 42 | 23 | 35 | 36% | 66% | 12% | 20 | 87 | 5% | 50% | | | -28.2 | 46 | 54 | -$13 |
| 17 ARI | 2 | 0 | 22 | 20 | 4.09 | 5.05 | 1.45 | 668 | 840 | 421 | 24.8 | 4.9 | 8.2 | 1.7 | 55% | 10% | 94.9 | 44 | 21 | 35 | 31% | 71% | 4% | 4 | 97 | 25% | 25% | | | 0.7 | 37 | 44 | -$4 |
| 18 ARI | 0 | 0 | 16 | 19 | 10.69 | 4.37 | 2.00 | 1048 | 819 | 1286 | 15.8 | 4.5 | 10.7 | 2.4 | 48% | 9% | 94.5 | 49 | 20 | 31 | 42% | 48% | 31% | 4 | 66 | 0% | 50% | 0 | 0.93 | -12.9 | 98 | 113 | -$11 |
| 1st Half | 0 | 0 | 9 | 11 | 11.42 | 3.90 | 2.08 | 1034 | 897 | 1167 | 22.0 | 3.1 | 11.4 | 3.7 | 55% | 8% | 94.5 | 48 | 24 | 28 | 47% | 47% | 38% | 2 | 91 | 0% | 50% | | | -7.8 | 148 | 170 | -$13 |
| 2nd Half | 0 | 0 | 7 | 8 | 9.82 | 4.99 | 1.91 | 1067 | 725 | 1467 | 11.7 | 6.1 | 9.8 | 1.6 | 40% | 10% | 94.5 | 50 | 14 | 36 | 36% | 50% | 25% | 2 | 49 | 0% | 50% | 0 | 0.99 | -5.1 | 39 | 45 | -$7 |
| **19 Proj** | **5** | **0** | **102** | **86** | **4.25** | **4.31** | **1.42** | **752** | **810** | **691** | **22.3** | **3.6** | **7.6** | **2.1** | **60%** | **8%** | **93.5** | **43** | **20** | **37** | **32%** | **72%** | **10%** | **16** | | | | | | **-1.7** | **61** | **70** | **-$2** |

BRIAN RUDD

## Minaya,Juan

| | | | | | | | |
|---|---|---|---|---|---|---|---|
| Age: 28 | Th: R | Role | RP | Health | B | LIMA Plan | C |
| Ht: 6' 4" | Wt: 210 | Type | Pwr | PT/Exp | D | Rand Var | -1 |
| | | | | Consist | A | MM | 1310 |

2-2, 3.28 ERA in 47 IP at CHW. After some early Triple-A shuttling, he thrived during 2nd half in the majors. Dom spike came with support from SwK, but xERA questions the whole thing since late S%, hr/f won't always be on his side. FpK says the control issues will linger, so not enough here to warrant saves speculation.

| Yr | Tm | W | Sv | IP | K | ERA | xERA | WHIP | oOPS | vL | vR | BF/G | Ctl | Dom | Cmd | FpK | SwK | Vel | G | L | F | H% | S% | hr/f | GS | APC | DOM% | DIS% | Sv% | LI | RAR | BPV | BPX | R$ |
|---|---|---|---|---|---|---|---|---|---|---|---|---|---|---|---|---|---|---|---|---|---|---|---|---|---|---|---|---|---|---|---|---|---|---|
| 14 | | | | | | | | | | | | | | | | | | | | | | | | | | | | | | | | | | |
| 15 | a/a | 1 | 1 | 55 | 49 | 3.13 | 3.72 | 1.40 | | | | 6.6 | 3.4 | 8.1 | 2.4 | | | | | | | 34% | 77% | | | | | | | | 5.6 | 90 | 107 | -$1 |
| 16 | CHW * | 6 | 1 | 62 | 45 | 4.58 | 4.50 | 1.55 | 712 | 660 | 764 | 6.1 | 4.0 | 6.5 | 1.6 | 55% | 10% | 94.2 | 24 | 24 | 53 | 33% | 70% | 0% | 0 | 16 | | | 20 | 0.43 | -3.0 | 56 | 66 | -$3 |
| 17 | CHW * | 4 | 9 | 63 | 63 | 3.71 | 4.03 | 1.35 | 765 | 767 | 764 | 4.9 | 3.7 | 9.0 | 2.5 | 55% | 12% | 94.2 | 35 | 22 | 43 | 31% | 76% | 15% | 0 | 20 | | | 90 | 1.09 | 5.0 | 81 | 97 | $4 |
| 18 | CHW * | 3 | 3 | 71 | 79 | 4.06 | 4.17 | 1.42 | 673 | 634 | 697 | 4.2 | 4.9 | 10.1 | 2.1 | 57% | 12% | 95.0 | 41 | 21 | 38 | 31% | 74% | 7% | 0 | 18 | | | 43 | 1.11 | 0.8 | 79 | 91 | -$1 |
| 1st Half | | 1 | 2 | 39 | 43 | 5.00 | 4.46 | 1.46 | 609 | 421 | 758 | 5.0 | 5.1 | 9.8 | 1.9 | 55% | 11% | 95.2 | 56 | 13 | 31 | 30% | 68% | 0% | 0 | 23 | | | 67 | 0.41 | -4.1 | 70 | 80 | -$5 |
| 2nd Half | | 2 | 1 | 31 | 36 | 2.87 | 4.25 | 1.37 | 707 | 779 | 668 | 3.6 | 4.6 | 10.3 | 2.3 | 59% | 12% | 94.9 | 33 | 25 | 42 | 31% | 83% | 9% | 0 | 15 | | | 25 | 1.40 | 4.9 | 73 | 84 | $4 |
| 19 | Proj | **3** | **3** | **58** | **59** | **4.12** | **4.17** | **1.41** | **761** | **737** | **776** | **4.7** | **4.3** | **9.1** | **2.1** | **56%** | **12%** | **94.7** | **40** | **21** | **39** | **31%** | **75%** | **12%** | **0** | | | | | | **0.3** | **66** | **76** | **-$1** |

## Minor,Mike

| | | | | | | | |
|---|---|---|---|---|---|---|---|
| Age: 31 | Th: L | Role | SP | Health | F | LIMA Plan | C+ |
| Ht: 6' 4" | Wt: 210 | Type | Pwr FB | PT/Exp | C | Rand Var | 0 |
| | | | | Consist | F | MM | 1203 |

Handled workload spike in transition back to rotation, but otherwise took a step back: lost a tick on the fastball and threw fewer sliders, which sunk Dom from 2017's peak; pinpoint Ctl is on shaky ground given FpK collapse; flyball tilt became more extreme. A back-end innings eater without much room for growth.

| Yr | Tm | W | Sv | IP | K | ERA | xERA | WHIP | oOPS | vL | vR | BF/G | Ctl | Dom | Cmd | FpK | SwK | Vel | G | L | F | H% | S% | hr/f | GS | APC | DOM% | DIS% | Sv% | LI | RAR | BPV | BPX | R$ |
|---|---|---|---|---|---|---|---|---|---|---|---|---|---|---|---|---|---|---|---|---|---|---|---|---|---|---|---|---|---|---|---|---|---|---|
| 14 | ATL * | 8 | 0 | 163 | 132 | 5.00 | 5.34 | 1.45 | 798 | 887 | 774 | 23.9 | 2.6 | 7.3 | 2.8 | 61% | 8% | 90.3 | 41 | 23 | 36 | 33% | 70% | 13% | 25 | 97 | 24% | 28% | | | -25.3 | 54 | 64 | -$8 |
| 15 | | | | | | | | | | | | | | | | | | | | | | | | | | | | | | | | | | |
| 16 | a/a | 0 | 0 | 42 | 32 | 8.51 | 7.67 | 1.96 | | | | 20.2 | 5.5 | 6.9 | 1.3 | | | | | | | 35% | 59% | | | | | | | | -22.5 | -4 | -5 | -$14 |
| 17 | KC | 6 | 6 | 78 | 88 | 2.55 | 3.58 | 1.02 | 585 | 423 | 664 | 4.7 | 2.5 | 10.2 | 4.0 | 65% | 13% | 94.4 | 42 | 16 | 41 | 28% | 77% | 6% | 0 | 18 | | | 67 | 1.20 | 17.3 | 135 | 162 | $13 |
| 18 | TEX | 12 | 0 | 157 | 132 | 4.18 | 4.39 | 1.12 | 733 | 799 | 717 | 22.9 | 2.2 | 7.6 | 3.5 | 58% | 10% | 92.8 | 34 | 21 | 45 | 27% | 68% | 12% | 28 | 91 | 14% | 43% | | | -0.7 | 89 | 103 | $10 |
| 1st Half | | 6 | 0 | 85 | 70 | 4.64 | 4.42 | 1.17 | 767 | 691 | 783 | 23.5 | 2.0 | 7.4 | 3.7 | 59% | 10% | 92.3 | 36 | 20 | 44 | 29% | 64% | 11% | 15 | 94 | 13% | 40% | | | -5.2 | 92 | 106 | $6 |
| 2nd Half | | 6 | 0 | 72 | 62 | 3.64 | 4.35 | 1.06 | 691 | 919 | 634 | 22.1 | 2.4 | 7.8 | 3.3 | 56% | 10% | 93.3 | 33 | 22 | 46 | 24% | 75% | 14% | 13 | 88 | 15% | 46% | | | 4.5 | 87 | 99 | $16 |
| 19 | Proj | **10** | **0** | **160** | **136** | **4.21** | **4.16** | **1.26** | **763** | **724** | **776** | **20.9** | **2.8** | **7.7** | **2.7** | **61%** | **11%** | **93.1** | **38** | **20** | **42** | **29%** | **72%** | **12%** | **28** | | | | | | **-1.1** | **77** | **89** | **$6** |

## Minter,A.J.

| | | | | | | | |
|---|---|---|---|---|---|---|---|
| Age: 25 | Th: L | Role | RP | Health | A | LIMA Plan | B+ |
| Ht: 6' 0" | Wt: 215 | Type | Pwr | PT/Exp | D | Rand Var | 0 |
| | | | | Consist | B | MM | 3420 |

Strong full-season debut; even began to get some saves in July. Minuscule hr/f certainly helped and xERA doesn't fully buy in, but knockout slider (21% SwK) and premium velocity led to plenty of whiffs. Even cut down on walks in 2nd half, though FpK says that's likely a blip. Still, tools are here to hold down the ninth.

| Yr | Tm | W | Sv | IP | K | ERA | xERA | WHIP | oOPS | vL | vR | BF/G | Ctl | Dom | Cmd | FpK | SwK | Vel | G | L | F | H% | S% | hr/f | GS | APC | DOM% | DIS% | Sv% | LI | RAR | BPV | BPX | R$ |
|---|---|---|---|---|---|---|---|---|---|---|---|---|---|---|---|---|---|---|---|---|---|---|---|---|---|---|---|---|---|---|---|---|---|---|
| 14 | | | | | | | | | | | | | | | | | | | | | | | | | | | | | | | | | | |
| 15 | | | | | | | | | | | | | | | | | | | | | | | | | | | | | | | | | | |
| 16 | aa | 1 | 0 | 19 | 28 | 3.53 | 2.62 | 1.26 | | | | 4.2 | 3.4 | 13.3 | 3.9 | | | | | | | 40% | 69% | | | | | | | | 1.5 | 170 | 202 | -$2 |
| 17 | ATL * | 1 | 0 | 33 | 42 | 4.30 | 3.91 | 1.42 | 595 | 418 | 696 | 3.9 | 3.9 | 11.5 | 3.0 | 63% | 19% | 95.9 | 38 | 22 | 41 | 37% | 70% | 8% | 0 | 16 | | | 0 | 0.87 | 0.2 | 116 | 139 | -$3 |
| 18 | ATL | 4 | 15 | 61 | 69 | 3.23 | 3.78 | 1.29 | 642 | 529 | 700 | 4.0 | 3.2 | 10.1 | 3.1 | 58% | 15% | 96.6 | 37 | 28 | 35 | 34% | 75% | 5% | 0 | 16 | | | 88 | 1.08 | 7.0 | 110 | 127 | $8 |
| 1st Half | | 3 | 2 | 34 | 36 | 2.91 | 3.92 | 1.29 | 636 | 510 | 706 | 3.8 | 3.7 | 9.5 | 2.6 | 59% | 16% | 96.5 | 36 | 30 | 34 | 33% | 77% | 3% | 0 | 15 | | | 100 | 1.11 | 5.2 | 85 | 98 | $5 |
| 2nd Half | | 1 | 13 | 27 | 33 | 3.62 | 3.62 | 1.28 | 648 | 554 | 692 | 4.3 | 2.6 | 10.9 | 4.1 | 58% | 14% | 96.7 | 39 | 25 | 36 | 36% | 73% | 7% | 0 | 17 | | | 87 | 1.05 | 1.8 | 142 | 163 | $11 |
| 19 | Proj | **3** | **20** | **65** | **76** | **3.59** | **3.39** | **1.18** | **618** | **475** | **690** | **3.8** | **3.4** | **10.4** | **3.1** | **58%** | **15%** | **96.6** | **40** | **22** | **38** | **30%** | **73%** | **11%** | **0** | | | | | | **4.5** | **115** | **132** | **$10** |

## Mitchell,Bryan

| | | | | | | | |
|---|---|---|---|---|---|---|---|
| Age: 28 | Th: R | Role | SP | Health | F | LIMA Plan | D+ |
| Ht: 6' 3" | Wt: 210 | Type | GB | PT/Exp | D | Rand Var | +1 |
| | | | | Consist | B | MM | 0001 |

June elbow injury knocked him out for two months, but with more walks than strikeouts, did anyone really miss him? 2nd half ERA was a small-sample mirage built on lucky H%/S%, and while the GBs are nice, he was the only MLB pitcher with that bad of a FpK/SwK combo all season (min. 70 IP). Move along...

| Yr | Tm | W | Sv | IP | K | ERA | xERA | WHIP | oOPS | vL | vR | BF/G | Ctl | Dom | Cmd | FpK | SwK | Vel | G | L | F | H% | S% | hr/f | GS | APC | DOM% | DIS% | Sv% | LI | RAR | BPV | BPX | R$ |
|---|---|---|---|---|---|---|---|---|---|---|---|---|---|---|---|---|---|---|---|---|---|---|---|---|---|---|---|---|---|---|---|---|---|---|
| 14 | NYY * | 6 | 0 | 114 | 88 | 4.73 | 5.21 | 1.58 | 751 | 1013 | 554 | 19.3 | 3.8 | 7.0 | 1.8 | 59% | 10% | 94.0 | 55 | 26 | 19 | 34% | 72% | 0% | 1 | 52 | 0% | 100% | 0 | 0.30 | -13.9 | 47 | 56 | -$8 |
| 15 | NYY * | 5 | 1 | 105 | 81 | 4.83 | 4.64 | 1.63 | 817 | 757 | 861 | 13.3 | 4.8 | 6.9 | 1.4 | 57% | 9% | 96.1 | 50 | 28 | 22 | 34% | 69% | 19% | 2 | 30 | 0% | 100% | 100 | 0.57 | -11.2 | 57 | 68 | -$9 |
| 16 | NYY * | 1 | 0 | 41 | 28 | 3.59 | 4.41 | 1.52 | 741 | 750 | 735 | 19.6 | 3.9 | 6.1 | 1.6 | 53% | 7% | 94.8 | 48 | 19 | 33 | 32% | 77% | 4% | 5 | 78 | 0% | 60% | | | 3.0 | 52 | 62 | -$3 |
| 17 | NYY * | 4 | 1 | 96 | 70 | 5.10 | 4.66 | 1.53 | 783 | 792 | 779 | 12.3 | 2.6 | 6.6 | 2.5 | 58% | 7% | 96.0 | 54 | 25 | 20 | 36% | 64% | 8% | 1 | 27 | 0% | 100% | 100 | 0.27 | -8.8 | 76 | 92 | -$6 |
| 18 | SD | 2 | 0 | 73 | 38 | 5.42 | 5.85 | 1.75 | 868 | 825 | 903 | 21.1 | 5.3 | 4.7 | 0.9 | 53% | 6% | 94.1 | 48 | 25 | 28 | 30% | 72% | 17% | 11 | 77 | 9% | 64% | 0 | 0.57 | -11.5 | -33 | -38 | -$13 |
| 1st Half | | 0 | 0 | 48 | 23 | 7.08 | 6.65 | 2.03 | 957 | 826 | 1059 | 19.8 | 6.5 | 4.3 | 0.7 | 51% | 6% | 94.1 | 47 | 26 | 27 | 32% | 67% | 20% | 7 | 72 | 0% | 71% | 0 | 0.50 | -17.4 | -74 | -85 | -$24 |
| 2nd Half | | 2 | 0 | 25 | 15 | 2.19 | 4.46 | 1.22 | 670 | 820 | 521 | 25.0 | 2.9 | 5.5 | 1.9 | 57% | 8% | 94.3 | 49 | 21 | 30 | 26% | 89% | 13% | 4 | 91 | 25% | 50% | | | 6.0 | 47 | 54 | $5 |
| 19 | Proj | **3** | **0** | **73** | **46** | **4.74** | **4.61** | **1.55** | **774** | **797** | **758** | **21.2** | **4.0** | **5.8** | **1.4** | **56%** | **7%** | **94.9** | **51** | **24** | **25** | **31%** | **72%** | **14%** | **15** | | | | | | **-2.7** | **25** | **28** | **-$6** |

## Montas,Frankie

| | | | | | | | |
|---|---|---|---|---|---|---|---|
| Age: 26 | Th: R | Role | SP | Health | D | LIMA Plan | D+ |
| Ht: 6' 2" | Wt: 255 | Type | Pwr | PT/Exp | D | Rand Var | 0 |
| | | | | Consist | D | MM | 1101 |

5-4, 3.88 ERA in 65 IP at OAK. Fortunate hr/f kept MLB ERA afloat, as he moved to SP role and bounced between Triple-A and majors all season. Last year, we said SwK kept a glimmer of hope, but velocity dip and less effective slider say that's starting to dim. Lefties still mash him, BPV confirms: speculate elsewhere.

| Yr | Tm | W | Sv | IP | K | ERA | xERA | WHIP | oOPS | vL | vR | BF/G | Ctl | Dom | Cmd | FpK | SwK | Vel | G | L | F | H% | S% | hr/f | GS | APC | DOM% | DIS% | Sv% | LI | RAR | BPV | BPX | R$ |
|---|---|---|---|---|---|---|---|---|---|---|---|---|---|---|---|---|---|---|---|---|---|---|---|---|---|---|---|---|---|---|---|---|---|---|
| 14 | | | | | | | | | | | | | | | | | | | | | | | | | | | | | | | | | | |
| 15 | CHW * | 5 | 0 | 127 | 117 | 3.85 | 3.47 | 1.41 | 699 | 921 | 560 | 17.9 | 4.3 | 8.3 | 1.9 | 53% | 13% | 96.7 | 38 | 16 | 46 | 32% | 71% | 6% | 2 | 41 | 0% | 50% | 0 | 0.31 | 1.8 | 86 | 102 | $0 |
| 16 | a/a | 0 | 0 | 16 | 19 | 2.59 | 3.23 | 1.15 | | | | 9.1 | 1.5 | 10.7 | 7.0 | | | | | | | 36% | 80% | | | | | | | | 3.2 | 196 | 233 | -$2 |
| 17 | OAK * | 1 | 0 | 61 | 66 | 6.62 | 5.95 | 1.55 | 974 | 1267 | 751 | 8.4 | 4.0 | 9.7 | 2.5 | 63% | 12% | 97.7 | 35 | 24 | 41 | 34% | 61% | 26% | 0 | 27 | | | 0 | 0.43 | -17.1 | 47 | 56 | -$9 |
| 18 | OAK * | 9 | 0 | 138 | 92 | 4.77 | 4.76 | 1.47 | 796 | 885 | 707 | 21.2 | 3.1 | 6.0 | 1.9 | 59% | 9% | 95.8 | 44 | 25 | 31 | 32% | 68% | 7% | 11 | 77 | 27% | 36% | 0 | 0.64 | -10.5 | 50 | 58 | -$5 |
| 1st Half | | 5 | 0 | 78 | 48 | 4.57 | 4.93 | 1.49 | 757 | 738 | 773 | 22.3 | 3.0 | 5.6 | 1.8 | 56% | 8% | 95.4 | 46 | 27 | 28 | 33% | 70% | 6% | 6 | 92 | 50% | 33% | | | -4.0 | 44 | 51 | -$6 |
| 2nd Half | | 4 | 0 | 61 | 43 | 5.02 | 4.53 | 1.44 | 846 | 1071 | 618 | 19.8 | 3.2 | 6.4 | 2.0 | 62% | 11% | 96.3 | 41 | 23 | 37 | 32% | 65% | 9% | 5 | 64 | 0% | 40% | 0 | 0.54 | -6.5 | 58 | 67 | -$4 |
| 19 | Proj | **4** | **0** | **94** | **77** | **4.54** | **4.41** | **1.45** | **783** | **947** | **637** | **20.9** | **3.6** | **7.4** | **2.1** | **61%** | **11%** | **96.6** | **40** | **24** | **36** | **31%** | **72%** | **13%** | **13** | | | | | | **-2.5** | **54** | **62** | **-$4** |

## Montgomery,Jordan

| | | | | | | | |
|---|---|---|---|---|---|---|---|
| Age: 26 | Th: L | Role | SP | Health | F | LIMA Plan | C |
| Ht: 6' 6" | Wt: 225 | Type | Pwr | PT/Exp | C | Rand Var | -1 |
| | | | | Consist | A | MM | 1200 |

Velocity drop and loss of control were red flags through six starts, then bam: Tommy John surgery in June. Pre-injury whiff rate was intriguing despite middling FpK/Ctl and FB% tilt, but xERA ultimately pinned him with mid-rotation upside, at best. A long shot to return any 2019 value, even if he makes late-season cameo.

| Yr | Tm | W | Sv | IP | K | ERA | xERA | WHIP | oOPS | vL | vR | BF/G | Ctl | Dom | Cmd | FpK | SwK | Vel | G | L | F | H% | S% | hr/f | GS | APC | DOM% | DIS% | Sv% | LI | RAR | BPV | BPX | R$ |
|---|---|---|---|---|---|---|---|---|---|---|---|---|---|---|---|---|---|---|---|---|---|---|---|---|---|---|---|---|---|---|---|---|---|---|
| 14 | | | | | | | | | | | | | | | | | | | | | | | | | | | | | | | | | | |
| 15 | | | | | | | | | | | | | | | | | | | | | | | | | | | | | | | | | | |
| 16 | a/a | 14 | 0 | 139 | 113 | 3.02 | 4.24 | 1.46 | | | | 23.9 | 3.2 | 7.3 | 2.3 | | | | | | | 34% | 80% | | | | | | | | 20.2 | 76 | 90 | $8 |
| 17 | NYY | 9 | 0 | 155 | 144 | 3.88 | 4.46 | 1.23 | 684 | 662 | 687 | 22.4 | 3.0 | 8.3 | 2.8 | 60% | 12% | 92.0 | 41 | 18 | 42 | 29% | 73% | 11% | 29 | 87 | 17% | 28% | | | 9.1 | 89 | 107 | $10 |
| 18 | NYY | 2 | 0 | 27 | 23 | 3.62 | 4.67 | 1.35 | 675 | 0 | 750 | 19.3 | 4.0 | 7.6 | 1.9 | 60% | 10% | 90.3 | 46 | 16 | 38 | 29% | 76% | 10% | 6 | 76 | 0% | 17% | | | 1.8 | 54 | 62 | -$3 |
| 1st Half | | 2 | 0 | 27 | 23 | 3.62 | 4.67 | 1.35 | 675 | 0 | 750 | 19.3 | 4.0 | 7.6 | 1.9 | 60% | 10% | 90.3 | 46 | 16 | 38 | 29% | 76% | 10% | 6 | 76 | 0% | 17% | | | 1.8 | 53 | 61 | -$3 |
| 2nd Half | | | | | | | | | | | | | | | | | | | | | | | | | | | | | | | | | | |
| 19 | Proj | **5** | **0** | **58** | **49** | **4.23** | **4.26** | **1.37** | **736** | **358** | **788** | **21.4** | **3.4** | **7.7** | **2.2** | **60%** | **11%** | **90.9** | **44** | **17** | **40** | **30%** | **74%** | **13%** | **11** | | | | | | **-0.7** | **67** | **77** | **-$1** |

## Montgomery,Mike

| | | | | | | | |
|---|---|---|---|---|---|---|---|
| Age: 30 | Th: L | Role | RP | Health | A | LIMA Plan | C |
| Ht: 6' 5" | Wt: 215 | Type | GB | PT/Exp | B | Rand Var | 0 |
| | | | | Consist | A | MM | 2101 |

Couldn't repeat 2016-17 success as he transitioned to full-time SP in May. Hit rate correction finally shrunk ERA/xERA gap, and while SwK hints at slight Dom uptick, it's unlikely to move the needle. Low FB%, good control should keep ratios in check, but inability to go deep (0 starts over 6 IP) caps Wins, R$ ceiling.

| Yr | Tm | W | Sv | IP | K | ERA | xERA | WHIP | oOPS | vL | vR | BF/G | Ctl | Dom | Cmd | FpK | SwK | Vel | G | L | F | H% | S% | hr/f | GS | APC | DOM% | DIS% | Sv% | LI | RAR | BPV | BPX | R$ |
|---|---|---|---|---|---|---|---|---|---|---|---|---|---|---|---|---|---|---|---|---|---|---|---|---|---|---|---|---|---|---|---|---|---|---|
| 14 | aaa | 10 | 0 | 126 | 81 | 5.49 | 4.72 | 1.53 | | | | 21.9 | 3.7 | 5.8 | 1.6 | | | | | | | 33% | 63% | | | | | | | | -27.2 | 45 | 54 | -$10 |
| 15 | SEA * | 8 | 0 | 155 | 112 | 4.33 | 3.95 | 1.34 | 754 | 841 | 725 | 24.0 | 3.1 | 6.5 | 2.1 | 63% | 9% | 90.9 | 51 | 20 | 29 | 30% | 69% | 13% | 16 | 91 | 19% | 50% | | | -7.1 | 62 | 73 | -$1 |
| 16 | 2 TM | 4 | 0 | 100 | 92 | 2.52 | 3.33 | 1.17 | 652 | 570 | 691 | 8.4 | 3.4 | 8.3 | 2.4 | 56% | 12% | 93.6 | 58 | 23 | 19 | 27% | 82% | 16% | 7 | 31 | 0% | 14% | 0 | 0.75 | 20.6 | 93 | 110 | $9 |
| 17 | CHC | 7 | 3 | 131 | 100 | 3.38 | 4.12 | 1.21 | 632 | 631 | 632 | 12.3 | 3.8 | 6.9 | 1.8 | 60% | 9% | 92.2 | 58 | 17 | 25 | 26% | 74% | 11% | 14 | 47 | 7% | 29% | 100 | 0.93 | 15.8 | 58 | 69 | $11 |
| 18 | CHC | 5 | 0 | 124 | 86 | 3.99 | 4.29 | 1.37 | 724 | 676 | 743 | 14.1 | 2.8 | 6.2 | 2.2 | 61% | 10% | 91.5 | 52 | 22 | 27 | 31% | 72% | 10% | 19 | 51 | 5% | 42% | 0 | 0.69 | 2.4 | 66 | 76 | -$1 |
| 1st Half | | 3 | 0 | 66 | 45 | 3.55 | 4.21 | 1.21 | 643 | 719 | 606 | 11.0 | 3.0 | 6.1 | 2.0 | 64% | 10% | 91.9 | 56 | 15 | 28 | 27% | 73% | 11% | 7 | 41 | 14% | 29% | 0 | 0.66 | 4.9 | 64 | 73 | $4 |
| 2nd Half | | 2 | 0 | 58 | 41 | 4.50 | 4.37 | 1.55 | 810 | 606 | 866 | 19.9 | 2.6 | 6.4 | 2.4 | 58% | 9% | 91.2 | 47 | 28 | 25 | 36% | 71% | 8% | 12 | 72 | 0% | 50% | 0 | 0.73 | -2.5 | 68 | 78 | -$6 |
| 19 | Proj | **5** | **0** | **102** | **76** | **3.77** | **3.91** | **1.33** | **705** | **655** | **724** | **13.0** | **3.2** | **6.7** | **2.1** | **60%** | **10%** | **91.9** | **54** | **21** | **25** | **30%** | **73%** | **10%** | **10** | | | | | | **2.3** | **66** | **76** | **$1** |

RYAN BLOOMFIELD

## Moore,Matt

| | | | | | | | |
|---|---|---|---|---|---|---|---|
| Age: 30 | Th: L | Role RP | | Health | D | LIMA Plan | D+ |
| Ht: 6' 3" | Wt: 210 | Type Pwr FB | | PT/Exp | A | Rand Var | +5 |
| | | | | Consist | A | MM | 0201 |

Right knee injury in May cut into IP, while bad fortune added to terrible line before he was banished to 'pen in June. Even with more first-pitch strikes, Cmd remained on life support, and xERA history says to expect more inflated ratios. Lofty prospect status now a distant memory; he'll be lucky to grab a rotation spot.

| Yr Tm | W | Sv | IP | K | ERA | xERA | WHIP | oOPS | vL | vR | BF/G | Ctl | Dom | Cmd | FpK | SwK | Vel | G | L | F | H% | S% | hr/f | GS | APC | DOM% | DIS% | Sv% | LI | RAR | BPV | BPX | R$ |
|---|---|---|---|---|---|---|---|---|---|---|---|---|---|---|---|---|---|---|---|---|---|---|---|---|---|---|---|---|---|---|---|---|---|
| 14 TAM | 0 | 0 | 10 | 6 | 2.70 | 4.75 | 1.50 | 777 | 1010 | 703 | 22.0 | 4.5 | 5.4 | 1.2 | 44% | 7% | 91.5 | 45 | 27 | 27 | 29% | 86% | 11% | 2 | 92 | 0% | 50% | | | 1.3 | -1 | -2 | -$3 |
| 15 TAM * | 5 | 0 | 103 | 93 | 5.12 | 5.22 | 1.48 | 839 | 785 | 866 | 23.4 | 3.1 | 8.1 | 2.6 | 60% | 10% | 92.0 | 39 | 22 | 39 | 34% | 69% | 11% | 12 | 88 | 17% | 67% | | | -14.7 | 59 | 71 | -$7 |
| 16 2 TM | 13 | 0 | 198 | 178 | 4.08 | 4.51 | 1.29 | 694 | 654 | 706 | 25.4 | 3.3 | 8.1 | 2.5 | 62% | 11% | 92.8 | 38 | 20 | 42 | 29% | 72% | 10% | 33 | 100 | 36% | 33% | | | 2.6 | 73 | 87 | $9 |
| 17 SF | 6 | 0 | 174 | 148 | 5.52 | 5.19 | 1.53 | 835 | 1047 | 767 | 24.7 | 3.5 | 7.6 | 2.2 | 61% | 9% | 92.0 | 38 | 20 | 42 | 33% | 67% | 12% | 31 | 90 | 16% | 42% | 0 | 0.75 | -25.1 | 60 | 72 | -$9 |
| 18 TEX | 3 | 0 | 102 | 86 | 6.79 | 5.18 | 1.66 | 911 | 868 | 920 | 12.1 | 3.6 | 7.6 | 2.1 | 65% | 10% | 92.4 | 38 | 21 | 41 | 35% | 61% | 14% | 12 | 46 | 8% | 67% | 0 | 0.68 | -33.3 | 55 | 63 | -$18 |
| 1st Half | 1 | 0 | 62 | 48 | 7.51 | 5.80 | 1.93 | 953 | 977 | 948 | 19.2 | 3.9 | 6.9 | 1.8 | 65% | 10% | 92.0 | 38 | 21 | 41 | 40% | 61% | 10% | 12 | 72 | 8% | 67% | 0 | 0.65 | -25.8 | 35 | 40 | -$29 |
| 2nd Half | 2 | 0 | 40 | 38 | 5.67 | 4.24 | 1.24 | 831 | 685 | 867 | 7.1 | 3.2 | 8.6 | 2.7 | 63% | 11% | 92.9 | 38 | 21 | 41 | 25% | 62% | 22% | 0 | 28 | | | 0 | 0.70 | -7.4 | 85 | 98 | -$1 |
| **19 Proj** | **4** | **0** | **94** | **81** | **5.71** | **4.54** | **1.50** | **842** | **850** | **840** | **13.7** | **3.6** | **7.7** | **2.1** | **63%** | **10%** | **92.4** | **38** | **21** | **41** | **32%** | **65%** | **14%** | **11** | | | | | | **-18.1** | **58** | **66** | **-$9** |

## Moronta,Reyes

| | | | | | | | |
|---|---|---|---|---|---|---|---|
| Age: 26 | Th: R | Role RP | | Health | A | LIMA Plan | B |
| Ht: 5' 11" | Wt: 241 | Type Pwr FB | | PT/Exp | D | Rand Var | -5 |
| | | | | Consist | A | MM | 2500 |

Skills didn't support results, as H%, hr/f drove a major wedge between ERA and xERA. Lack of FpK suggests the Ctl struggles should continue, though his elite velocity and easy swing-and-miss will bring plenty more strikeouts. The Ks can keep value afloat, but wildness excludes him from closer conversation.

| Yr Tm | W | Sv | IP | K | ERA | xERA | WHIP | oOPS | vL | vR | BF/G | Ctl | Dom | Cmd | FpK | SwK | Vel | G | L | F | H% | S% | hr/f | GS | APC | DOM% | DIS% | Sv% | LI | RAR | BPV | BPX | R$ |
|---|---|---|---|---|---|---|---|---|---|---|---|---|---|---|---|---|---|---|---|---|---|---|---|---|---|---|---|---|---|---|---|---|---|
| 14 | | | | | | | | | | | | | | | | | | | | | | | | | | | | | | | | | |
| 15 | | | | | | | | | | | | | | | | | | | | | | | | | | | | | | | | | |
| 16 | | | | | | | | | | | | | | | | | | | | | | | | | | | | | | | | | |
| 17 SF * | 3 | 5 | 42 | 47 | 3.69 | 4.07 | 1.51 | 656 | 476 | 721 | 4.6 | 5.1 | 10.1 | 2.0 | 62% | 15% | 95.7 | 47 | 20 | 33 | 34% | 76% | 20% | 0 | 16 | | | 50 | 0.26 | 3.4 | 88 | 106 | $0 |
| 18 SF | 5 | 1 | 65 | 79 | 2.49 | 3.89 | 1.09 | 507 | 608 | 445 | 3.8 | 5.1 | 10.9 | 2.1 | 56% | 14% | 96.8 | 42 | 16 | 42 | 22% | 79% | 7% | 0 | 16 | | | 17 | 1.34 | 13.3 | 79 | 90 | $7 |
| 1st Half | 4 | 1 | 37 | 42 | 1.96 | 3.89 | 1.04 | 452 | 426 | 467 | 3.8 | 4.7 | 10.3 | 2.2 | 55% | 14% | 96.7 | 42 | 16 | 41 | 23% | 81% | 3% | 0 | 16 | | | 50 | 1.07 | 9.9 | 80 | 92 | $11 |
| 2nd Half | 1 | 0 | 28 | 37 | 3.18 | 3.89 | 1.16 | 579 | 849 | 417 | 3.7 | 5.7 | 11.8 | 2.1 | 56% | 14% | 97.1 | 42 | 15 | 43 | 22% | 77% | 12% | 0 | 16 | | | 0 | 1.67 | 3.4 | 77 | 88 | $3 |
| **19 Proj** | **4** | **0** | **58** | **69** | **3.69** | **3.96** | **1.37** | **701** | **926** | **563** | **4.1** | **5.2** | **10.8** | **2.1** | **56%** | **14%** | **96.9** | **42** | **16** | **42** | **30%** | **76%** | **10%** | **0** | | | | | | **3.3** | **72** | **83** | **$0** |

## Morrow,Brandon

| | | | | | | | |
|---|---|---|---|---|---|---|---|
| Age: 34 | Th: R | Role RP | | Health | F | LIMA Plan | B |
| Ht: 6' 3" | Wt: 205 | Type Pwr | | PT/Exp | D | Rand Var | -5 |
| | | | | Consist | F | MM | 3320 |

Right biceps inflammation ended season in mid-July after S%, saves boosted early R$. Throwing consistent strike one supports useful Ctl, and even with dip in SwK, he can keep the Ks coming. A swing in fortune should push ERA closer to xERA, however, and injuries are likely to stand in the way of consistent saves.

| Yr Tm | W | Sv | IP | K | ERA | xERA | WHIP | oOPS | vL | vR | BF/G | Ctl | Dom | Cmd | FpK | SwK | Vel | G | L | F | H% | S% | hr/f | GS | APC | DOM% | DIS% | Sv% | LI | RAR | BPV | BPX | R$ |
|---|---|---|---|---|---|---|---|---|---|---|---|---|---|---|---|---|---|---|---|---|---|---|---|---|---|---|---|---|---|---|---|---|---|
| 14 TOR | 1 | 0 | 33 | 30 | 5.67 | 4.15 | 1.65 | 832 | 948 | 708 | 11.4 | 4.9 | 8.1 | 1.7 | 52% | 9% | 94.0 | 51 | 19 | 30 | 35% | 64% | 7% | 6 | 48 | 0% | 33% | 0 | 0.68 | -7.9 | 44 | 52 | -$6 |
| 15 SD | 2 | 0 | 33 | 23 | 2.73 | 3.65 | 1.09 | 681 | 613 | 761 | 25.2 | 1.9 | 6.3 | 3.3 | 53% | 11% | 93.4 | 47 | 21 | 32 | 27% | 79% | 10% | 5 | 97 | 20% | 20% | | | 5.0 | 86 | 103 | $0 |
| 16 SD * | 2 | 2 | 47 | 26 | 6.63 | 8.26 | 2.06 | 769 | 966 | 660 | 7.2 | 3.3 | 4.9 | 1.5 | 53% | 10% | 94.2 | 44 | 26 | 30 | 40% | 70% | 13% | 0 | 13 | | | 50 | 0.69 | -14.3 | -3 | -3 | -$12 |
| 17 LA * | 6 | 8 | 64 | 66 | 4.36 | 3.67 | 1.22 | 454 | 308 | 532 | 4.0 | 2.0 | 9.4 | 4.6 | 69% | 17% | 97.7 | 45 | 24 | 31 | 34% | 65% | 0% | 0 | 14 | | | 73 | 0.85 | 0.0 | 131 | 158 | $5 |
| 18 CHC | 0 | 22 | 31 | 31 | 1.47 | 3.20 | 1.08 | 555 | 432 | 667 | 3.5 | 2.6 | 9.1 | 3.4 | 66% | 13% | 97.5 | 52 | 23 | 25 | 28% | 90% | 10% | 0 | 14 | | | 92 | 1.28 | 10.1 | 122 | 141 | $9 |
| 1st Half | 0 | 17 | 23 | 25 | 1.54 | 3.18 | 1.16 | 560 | 481 | 629 | 3.4 | 3.5 | 9.6 | 2.8 | 64% | 13% | 97.5 | 53 | 25 | 22 | 29% | 88% | 8% | 0 | 14 | | | 94 | 1.23 | 7.5 | 110 | 127 | $12 |
| 2nd Half | 0 | 5 | 7 | 6 | 1.23 | 3.24 | 0.82 | 536 | 286 | 786 | 4.0 | 0.0 | 7.4 | 0.0 | 71% | 15% | 97.6 | 50 | 18 | 32 | 25% | 100% | 14% | 0 | 15 | | | 83 | 1.46 | 2.6 | 161 | 184 | $0 |
| **19 Proj** | **2** | **25** | **51** | **50** | **3.27** | **3.43** | **1.23** | **688** | **658** | **714** | **5.1** | **3.0** | **8.8** | **2.9** | **60%** | **12%** | **95.6** | **49** | **23** | **28** | **30%** | **76%** | **12%** | **0** | | | | | | **5.5** | **104** | **120** | **$11** |

## Morton,Charlie

| | | | | | | | |
|---|---|---|---|---|---|---|---|
| Age: 35 | Th: R | Role SP | | Health | F | LIMA Plan | C |
| Ht: 6' 5" | Wt: 235 | Type Pwr GB | | PT/Exp | B | Rand Var | 0 |
| | | | | Consist | A | MM | 4403 |

Eclipsed 200 Ks for the first time despite shoulder discomfort in August. GB% waned again, but it still pairs well with increased velocity and SwK, while passable control bolsters the ratio floor. Can't bank on a repeat, but assuming shoulder checks out, skills are here for a line that echoes 2017 success.

| Yr Tm | W | Sv | IP | K | ERA | xERA | WHIP | oOPS | vL | vR | BF/G | Ctl | Dom | Cmd | FpK | SwK | Vel | G | L | F | H% | S% | hr/f | GS | APC | DOM% | DIS% | Sv% | LI | RAR | BPV | BPX | R$ |
|---|---|---|---|---|---|---|---|---|---|---|---|---|---|---|---|---|---|---|---|---|---|---|---|---|---|---|---|---|---|---|---|---|---|
| 14 PIT | 6 | 0 | 157 | 126 | 3.72 | 3.45 | 1.27 | 682 | 664 | 698 | 25.6 | 3.3 | 7.2 | 2.2 | 61% | 8% | 91.1 | 56 | 21 | 23 | 30% | 71% | 9% | 26 | 96 | 31% | 19% | | | 0.4 | 76 | 90 | -$3 |
| 15 PIT * | 11 | 0 | 149 | 112 | 4.41 | 4.16 | 1.37 | 769 | 894 | 633 | 24.1 | 2.9 | 6.7 | 2.3 | 62% | 8% | 92.0 | 57 | 21 | 21 | 32% | 69% | 15% | 23 | 87 | 22% | 26% | | | -8.3 | 66 | 79 | $0 |
| 16 PHI | 1 | 0 | 17 | 19 | 4.15 | 3.01 | 1.33 | 651 | 743 | 559 | 17.8 | 4.2 | 9.9 | 2.4 | 62% | 13% | 94.3 | 63 | 21 | 16 | 32% | 68% | 14% | 4 | 69 | 50% | 25% | | | 0.1 | 106 | 126 | -$3 |
| 17 HOU | 14 | 0 | 147 | 163 | 3.62 | 3.44 | 1.19 | 692 | 561 | 805 | 24.7 | 3.1 | 10.0 | 3.3 | 61% | 11% | 95.0 | 52 | 19 | 29 | 31% | 72% | 13% | 25 | 95 | 40% | 16% | | | 13.3 | 127 | 153 | $15 |
| 18 HOU | 15 | 0 | 167 | 201 | 3.13 | 3.26 | 1.16 | 659 | 695 | 629 | 23.2 | 3.4 | 10.8 | 3.1 | 61% | 12% | 95.7 | 47 | 22 | 30 | 29% | 77% | 15% | 30 | 90 | 27% | 17% | | | 21.1 | 127 | 146 | $20 |
| 1st Half | 10 | 0 | 96 | 122 | 2.54 | 3.00 | 1.11 | 626 | 620 | 632 | 24.6 | 3.7 | 11.5 | 3.1 | 62% | 13% | 96.0 | 51 | 21 | 28 | 27% | 83% | 18% | 16 | 95 | 38% | 13% | | | 19.0 | 137 | 157 | $29 |
| 2nd Half | 5 | 0 | 71 | 79 | 3.91 | 3.60 | 1.23 | 703 | 814 | 626 | 21.5 | 3.2 | 10.0 | 3.2 | 60% | 10% | 95.3 | 43 | 24 | 33 | 31% | 70% | 11% | 14 | 84 | 14% | 21% | | | 2.1 | 115 | 132 | $7 |
| **19 Proj** | **13** | **0** | **160** | **174** | **3.62** | **3.21** | **1.22** | **691** | **707** | **678** | **22.8** | **3.2** | **9.8** | **3.1** | **61%** | **11%** | **94.4** | **50** | **21** | **28** | **31%** | **73%** | **13%** | **28** | | | | | | **20.1** | **118** | **136** | **$14** |

## Musgrove,Joe

| | | | | | | | |
|---|---|---|---|---|---|---|---|
| Age: 26 | Th: R | Role SP | | Health | D | LIMA Plan | B+ |
| Ht: 6' 5" | Wt: 260 | Type | | PT/Exp | C | Rand Var | +1 |
| | | | | Consist | A | MM | 3203 |

6-9, 4.06 ERA in 115 IP at PIT. Right shoulder injury kept him out until late May, and he was somewhat effective until pelvis/abdomen injury in September. Skills point to something more: 1) SwK hints at room for Dom growth; 2) FpK, pinpoint Ctl provide ratio support; 3) with health, 2nd half BPV hints at... UP: 3.50 ERA.

| Yr Tm | W | Sv | IP | K | ERA | xERA | WHIP | oOPS | vL | vR | BF/G | Ctl | Dom | Cmd | FpK | SwK | Vel | G | L | F | H% | S% | hr/f | GS | APC | DOM% | DIS% | Sv% | LI | RAR | BPV | BPX | R$ |
|---|---|---|---|---|---|---|---|---|---|---|---|---|---|---|---|---|---|---|---|---|---|---|---|---|---|---|---|---|---|---|---|---|---|
| 14 | | | | | | | | | | | | | | | | | | | | | | | | | | | | | | | | | |
| 15 aa | 4 | 1 | 45 | 29 | 2.49 | 3.47 | 1.00 | | | | 21.5 | 1.2 | 5.8 | 4.9 | | | | | | | 24% | 88% | | | | | | | | 8.2 | 99 | 118 | $4 |
| 16 HOU * | 11 | 0 | 147 | 131 | 3.63 | 4.01 | 1.20 | 758 | 822 | 710 | 21.9 | 1.6 | 8.0 | 5.0 | 62% | 10% | 91.7 | 43 | 21 | 36 | 32% | 74% | 14% | 10 | 89 | 30% | 30% | 0 | 0.78 | 10.1 | 120 | 143 | $11 |
| 17 HOU | 7 | 2 | 109 | 98 | 4.77 | 4.10 | 1.33 | 798 | 763 | 829 | 12.2 | 2.3 | 8.1 | 3.5 | 64% | 12% | 92.9 | 45 | 21 | 34 | 32% | 69% | 16% | 15 | 46 | 13% | 53% | 50 | 0.89 | -5.6 | 106 | 127 | $2 |
| 18 PIT * | 7 | 0 | 132 | 112 | 4.17 | 3.61 | 1.16 | 687 | 777 | 613 | 23.8 | 1.7 | 7.6 | 4.4 | 68% | 12% | 93.0 | 46 | 20 | 34 | 31% | 66% | 10% | 19 | 86 | 26% | 11% | | | -0.3 | 116 | 133 | $5 |
| 1st Half | 4 | 0 | 57 | 48 | 4.13 | 3.94 | 1.29 | 733 | 837 | 655 | 23.2 | 2.1 | 7.6 | 3.6 | 63% | 11% | 93.2 | 46 | 19 | 35 | 33% | 68% | 7% | 7 | 81 | 29% | 14% | | | 0.2 | 102 | 118 | $0 |
| 2nd Half | 3 | 0 | 75 | 64 | 4.20 | 3.35 | 1.07 | 662 | 746 | 587 | 25.8 | 1.4 | 7.7 | 5.3 | 72% | 13% | 92.9 | 46 | 21 | 33 | 29% | 63% | 12% | 12 | 88 | 25% | 8% | | | -0.5 | 123 | 141 | $9 |
| **19 Proj** | **9** | **0** | **145** | **123** | **4.06** | **3.60** | **1.19** | **721** | **763** | **688** | **20.6** | **1.8** | **7.6** | **4.3** | **66%** | **12%** | **92.8** | **45** | **21** | **34** | **30%** | **70%** | **13%** | **25** | | | | | | **8.3** | **112** | **129** | **$8** |

## Neris,Hector

| | | | | | | | |
|---|---|---|---|---|---|---|---|
| Age: 30 | Th: R | Role RP | | Health | A | LIMA Plan | B+ |
| Ht: 6' 2" | Wt: 215 | Type Pwr FB | | PT/Exp | C | Rand Var | +5 |
| | | | | Consist | B | MM | 4520 |

11 Sv, 5.10 ERA in 48 IP at PHI. Mowed down batters with ease, but FB profile, hr/f led to disastrous 1st half and demotion. He flashed closer-worthy skills upon return with elite swing-and-miss stuff, which xERA confirms. Not as good or bad as either half, but recent string of BPX says he's good enough to close again.

| Yr Tm | W | Sv | IP | K | ERA | xERA | WHIP | oOPS | vL | vR | BF/G | Ctl | Dom | Cmd | FpK | SwK | Vel | G | L | F | H% | S% | hr/f | GS | APC | DOM% | DIS% | Sv% | LI | RAR | BPV | BPX | R$ |
|---|---|---|---|---|---|---|---|---|---|---|---|---|---|---|---|---|---|---|---|---|---|---|---|---|---|---|---|---|---|---|---|---|---|
| 14 PHI * | 7 | 2 | 78 | 60 | 4.16 | 3.92 | 1.30 | 0 | 0 | 0 | 6.6 | 3.4 | 6.9 | 2.0 | 100% | 22% | 93.0 | 50 | 0 | 50 | 28% | 71% | 0% | 0 | 9 | | | 40 | 1.97 | -4.0 | 57 | 68 | $1 |
| 15 PHI * | 3 | 1 | 78 | 70 | 4.21 | 5.00 | 1.56 | 772 | 770 | 772 | 5.8 | 4.2 | 8.1 | 1.9 | 52% | 14% | 93.2 | 39 | 15 | 46 | 34% | 76% | 15% | 0 | 21 | | | 33 | 0.69 | -2.4 | 56 | 67 | -$5 |
| 16 PHI | 4 | 2 | 80 | 102 | 2.58 | 3.23 | 1.11 | 620 | 632 | 607 | 4.2 | 3.4 | 11.4 | 3.4 | 52% | 16% | 94.1 | 42 | 25 | 34 | 29% | 83% | 14% | 0 | 17 | | | 33 | 1.11 | 16.0 | 135 | 160 | $9 |
| 17 PHI | 4 | 26 | 75 | 86 | 3.01 | 4.13 | 1.26 | 689 | 716 | 660 | 4.3 | 3.1 | 10.4 | 3.3 | 59% | 17% | 94.7 | 33 | 23 | 44 | 32% | 81% | 10% | 0 | 17 | | | 90 | 1.10 | 12.4 | 113 | 136 | $16 |
| 18 PHI * | 3 | 12 | 68 | 100 | 4.14 | 3.90 | 1.21 | 803 | 896 | 713 | 3.8 | 3.2 | 13.3 | 4.1 | 59% | 20% | 94.6 | 31 | 24 | 45 | 34% | 72% | 23% | 0 | 15 | | | 75 | 0.81 | 0.1 | 131 | 151 | $6 |
| 1st Half | 1 | 10 | 32 | 43 | 6.47 | 6.85 | 1.47 | 981 | 1005 | 955 | 3.9 | 3.4 | 12.0 | 3.5 | 57% | 19% | 94.1 | 29 | 24 | 46 | 33% | 67% | 31% | 0 | 15 | | | 77 | 0.86 | -9.2 | 52 | 59 | -$3 |
| 2nd Half | 2 | 2 | 36 | 58 | 2.06 | 1.28 | 0.97 | 466 | 655 | 306 | 3.7 | 3.0 | 14.4 | 4.8 | 64% | 22% | 95.3 | 34 | 24 | 41 | 34% | 77% | 0% | 0 | 14 | | | 67 | 0.74 | 9.3 | 205 | 236 | $13 |
| **19 Proj** | **3** | **12** | **58** | **76** | **3.45** | **3.23** | **1.21** | **680** | **752** | **611** | **4.1** | **3.2** | **11.8** | **3.6** | **58%** | **18%** | **94.5** | **35** | **23** | **42** | **32%** | **76%** | **13%** | **0** | | | | | | **8.7** | **138** | **159** | **$7** |

## Neshek,Pat

| | | | | | | | |
|---|---|---|---|---|---|---|---|
| Age: 38 | Th: R | Role RP | | Health | F | LIMA Plan | A |
| Ht: 6' 3" | Wt: 220 | Type xFB | | PT/Exp | D | Rand Var | -5 |
| | | | | Consist | C | MM | 2210 |

Shoulder, forearm injuries cost him 1st half before he added a handful of saves. In a small sample, he still threw consistent FpK, but less effective slider led to Dom/BPV drop. He still misses enough bats for Ks to rebound and elite control should keep ratios in check, so even with FB risk, he's a decent LIMA play.

| Yr Tm | W | Sv | IP | K | ERA | xERA | WHIP | oOPS | vL | vR | BF/G | Ctl | Dom | Cmd | FpK | SwK | Vel | G | L | F | H% | S% | hr/f | GS | APC | DOM% | DIS% | Sv% | LI | RAR | BPV | BPX | R$ |
|---|---|---|---|---|---|---|---|---|---|---|---|---|---|---|---|---|---|---|---|---|---|---|---|---|---|---|---|---|---|---|---|---|---|
| 14 STL | 7 | 6 | 67 | 68 | 1.87 | 3.21 | 0.79 | 480 | 541 | 442 | 3.6 | 1.2 | 9.1 | 7.6 | 67% | 13% | 90.3 | 35 | 11 | 54 | 25% | 80% | 4% | 0 | 14 | | | 60 | 1.38 | 15.5 | 144 | 172 | $14 |
| 15 HOU | 3 | 1 | 55 | 51 | 3.62 | 3.87 | 1.12 | 709 | 768 | 673 | 3.4 | 2.0 | 8.4 | 4.3 | 69% | 11% | 90.0 | 32 | 22 | 46 | 28% | 74% | 11% | 0 | 13 | | | 25 | 1.32 | 2.3 | 108 | 128 | $2 |
| 16 HOU | 2 | 0 | 47 | 43 | 3.06 | 4.07 | 0.94 | 606 | 967 | 463 | 3.1 | 2.1 | 8.2 | 3.9 | 71% | 11% | 89.2 | 33 | 21 | 46 | 23% | 74% | 10% | 0 | 12 | | | 0 | 1.20 | 6.5 | 102 | 122 | $3 |
| 17 2 NL | 5 | 1 | 62 | 69 | 1.59 | 3.35 | 0.87 | 536 | 614 | 486 | 3.3 | 0.9 | 10.0 | 11.5 | 71% | 14% | 90.3 | 36 | 18 | 46 | 30% | 84% | 4% | 0 | 13 | | | 20 | 1.11 | 21.3 | 170 | 204 | $12 |
| 18 PHI | 3 | 5 | 24 | 15 | 2.59 | 5.00 | 1.15 | 663 | 900 | 551 | 3.4 | 1.8 | 5.5 | 3.0 | 73% | 11% | 89.1 | 38 | 16 | 46 | 28% | 81% | 6% | 0 | 12 | | | 83 | 1.24 | 4.7 | 66 | 76 | $1 |
| 1st Half | | | | | | | | | | | | | | | | | | | | | | | | | | | | | | | | | |
| 2nd Half | 3 | 5 | 24 | 15 | 2.59 | 5.00 | 1.15 | 663 | 900 | 551 | 3.4 | 1.8 | 5.5 | 3.0 | 73% | 11% | 89.1 | 38 | 16 | 46 | 28% | 81% | 6% | 0 | 12 | | | 83 | 1.24 | 4.7 | 66 | 76 | $1 |
| **19 Proj** | **5** | **5** | **65** | **57** | **3.00** | **3.79** | **1.08** | **691** | **889** | **590** | **3.2** | **1.7** | **7.9** | **4.7** | **71%** | **12%** | **89.6** | **35** | **18** | **47** | **28%** | **79%** | **11%** | **0** | | | | | | **2.5** | **110** | **127** | **$7** |

BRANT CHESSER

## Newcomb,Sean

| | | | | | | | |
|---|---|---|---|---|---|---|---|
| Age: | 26 | Th: | L | Role | SP | Health | A |
| Ht: | 6' 5" | Wt: | 255 | Type | Pwr | PT/Exp | C |
| | | | | | | Consist | A |

LIMA Plan C+ · Rand Var 0 · MM 1303

Early success crumbled when walks piled up, GB% dropped, and good fortune ran dry in 2nd half. With meager FpK, expect his poor control to continue, even though SwK supports Dom repeat. Shaky Cmd history, xERA baseline hint we'll see something closer to the 2nd-half version than the 1st.

| Yr | Tm | W | Sv | IP | K | ERA | xERA | WHIP | oOPS | vL | vR | BF/G | Ctl | Dom | Cmd | FpK | SwK | Vel | G | L | F | H% | S% | hr/f | GS | APC | DOM% | DIS% | Sv% | LI | RAR | BPV | BPX | R$ |
|---|---|---|---|---|---|---|---|---|---|---|---|---|---|---|---|---|---|---|---|---|---|---|---|---|---|---|---|---|---|---|---|---|---|---|
| 14 | | | | | | | | | | | | | | | | | | | | | | | | | | | | | | | | | | |
| 15 | aa | 2 | 0 | 36 | 35 | 3.40 | 2.98 | 1.37 | | | | 21.6 | 6.0 | 8.7 | 1.4 | | | | | | | 26% | 76% | | | | | | | | 2.5 | 82 | 97 | -$2 |
| 16 | aa | 8 | 0 | 140 | 135 | 5.64 | 4.25 | 1.62 | | | | 23.0 | 5.3 | 8.7 | 1.6 | | | | | | | 35% | 63% | | | | | | | | -25.1 | 79 | 93 | -$10 |
| 17 | ATL * | 7 | 0 | 158 | 169 | 4.13 | 4.40 | 1.55 | 780 | 753 | 790 | 23.0 | 5.1 | 9.6 | 1.9 | 59% | 12% | 93.7 | 44 | 23 | 33 | 34% | 74% | 11% | 19 | 96 | 11% | 26% | | | 4.4 | 78 | 93 | $0 |
| 18 | ATL | 12 | 0 | 164 | 160 | 3.90 | 4.38 | 1.33 | 679 | 712 | 670 | 22.5 | 4.4 | 8.8 | 2.0 | 54% | 11% | 93.0 | 43 | 21 | 36 | 28% | 74% | 11% | 30 | 94 | 17% | 27% | 0 | 0.77 | 5.1 | 59 | 68 | $7 |
| 1st Half | | 8 | 0 | 93 | 90 | 2.71 | 3.99 | 1.18 | 615 | 800 | 576 | 23.6 | 3.9 | 8.7 | 2.3 | 56% | 11% | 92.8 | 47 | 19 | 34 | 27% | 80% | 8% | 16 | 98 | 19% | 19% | | | 16.5 | 77 | 89 | $19 |
| 2nd Half | | 4 | 0 | 71 | 70 | 5.45 | 4.90 | 1.52 | 756 | 642 | 797 | 21.2 | 5.2 | 8.9 | 1.7 | 51% | 10% | 93.3 | 39 | 23 | 38 | 30% | 67% | 14% | 14 | 90 | 14% | 36% | 0 | 0.74 | -11.4 | 37 | 42 | -$8 |
| **19** | **Proj** | **10** | **0** | **174** | **174** | **4.30** | **4.28** | **1.46** | **712** | **699** | **717** | **24.2** | **5.0** | **9.0** | **1.8** | **55%** | **11%** | **93.3** | **43** | **22** | **35** | **31%** | **72%** | **10%** | **31** | | | | | | **-3.2** | **47** | **54** | **$1** |

## Nicasio,Juan

| | | | | | | | |
|---|---|---|---|---|---|---|---|
| Age: | 32 | Th: | R | Role | RP | Health | D |
| Ht: | 6' 4" | Wt: | 252 | Type | Pwr | PT/Exp | C |
| | | | | | | Consist | A |

LIMA Plan C+ · Rand Var +5 · MM 3410

Bone chips in knee shelved him in June, eventually ended ugly season in August. With H%/S% correction, ratios should approach league average, while SwK says the Ks will keep coming. Luck won't fix everything, as GB% dip and likely Ctl regression prevent a big step forward, which leaves him stuck in middle relief.

| Yr | Tm | W | Sv | IP | K | ERA | xERA | WHIP | oOPS | vL | vR | BF/G | Ctl | Dom | Cmd | FpK | SwK | Vel | G | L | F | H% | S% | hr/f | GS | APC | DOM% | DIS% | Sv% | LI | RAR | BPV | BPX | R$ |
|---|---|---|---|---|---|---|---|---|---|---|---|---|---|---|---|---|---|---|---|---|---|---|---|---|---|---|---|---|---|---|---|---|---|---|
| 14 | COL * | 9 | 1 | 129 | 89 | 5.50 | 6.06 | 1.59 | 860 | 900 | 827 | 13.3 | 3.3 | 6.2 | 1.9 | 59% | 8% | 92.7 | 46 | 20 | 34 | 33% | 70% | 18% | 14 | 49 | 7% | 50% | 100 | 0.76 | -28.0 | 21 | 25 | -$12 |
| 15 | LA | 1 | 1 | 58 | 65 | 3.86 | 4.04 | 1.56 | 742 | 969 | 634 | 4.9 | 4.9 | 10.0 | 2.0 | 62% | 12% | 95.1 | 43 | 25 | 32 | 37% | 73% | 2% | 1 | 20 | 0% | 100% | 33 | 1.05 | 0.8 | 68 | 81 | -$4 |
| 16 | PIT | 10 | 0 | 118 | 138 | 4.50 | 3.71 | 1.37 | 774 | 934 | 638 | 9.9 | 3.4 | 10.5 | 3.1 | 63% | 11% | 93.6 | 44 | 22 | 35 | 34% | 70% | 14% | 12 | 42 | 25% | 50% | 0 | 0.89 | -4.5 | 119 | 141 | $3 |
| 17 | 3 NL | 5 | 6 | 72 | 72 | 2.61 | 3.64 | 1.08 | 610 | 544 | 664 | 3.8 | 2.5 | 9.0 | 3.6 | 67% | 12% | 95.4 | 46 | 22 | 33 | 29% | 78% | 8% | 0 | 16 | | | 60 | 1.18 | 15.6 | 118 | 142 | $10 |
| 18 | SEA | 1 | 1 | 42 | 53 | 6.00 | 3.52 | 1.38 | 828 | 752 | 881 | 4.0 | 1.1 | 11.4 | 10.6 | 63% | 12% | 93.8 | 36 | 21 | 43 | 42% | 58% | 12% | 0 | 17 | | | 14 | 1.33 | -9.6 | 190 | 218 | -$6 |
| 1st Half | | 1 | 1 | 33 | 41 | 6.00 | 3.50 | 1.30 | 789 | 668 | 880 | 4.0 | 0.8 | 11.2 | 13.7 | 59% | 13% | 93.6 | 34 | 21 | 45 | 41% | 54% | 10% | 0 | 17 | | | 20 | 1.44 | -7.5 | 191 | 220 | -$6 |
| 2nd Half | | 0 | 0 | 9 | 12 | 6.00 | 3.58 | 1.67 | 962 | 1098 | 885 | 3.8 | 2.0 | 12.0 | 6.0 | 76% | 9% | 94.4 | 43 | 21 | 36 | 45% | 69% | 20% | 0 | 15 | | | 0 | 1.00 | -2.1 | 183 | 210 | -$6 |
| **19** | **Proj** | **3** | **1** | **65** | **72** | **3.47** | **3.40** | **1.24** | **714** | **736** | **698** | **5.0** | **2.7** | **9.9** | **3.7** | **62%** | **11%** | **94.1** | **41** | **22** | **37** | **32%** | **76%** | **12%** | **0** | | | | | | **5.5** | **125** | **144** | **$3** |

## Nix,Jacob

| | | | | | | | |
|---|---|---|---|---|---|---|---|
| Age: | 23 | Th: | R | Role | SP | Health | A |
| Ht: | 6' 4" | Wt: | 220 | Type | Con FB | PT/Exp | F |
| | | | | | | Consist | C |

LIMA Plan D+ · Rand Var +1 · MM 0003

2-5, 7.02 ERA in 42 IP at SD. Groin injury delayed start of season until late May, and 56% S% didn't help MLB results. He's not fooling hitters, as minuscule SwK won't lead to many strikeouts, and FpK doesn't jibe with elite Ctl. Too early to give up, but 2nd-half xERA, BPV suggest 2019 owners should exercise patience.

| Yr | Tm | W | Sv | IP | K | ERA | xERA | WHIP | oOPS | vL | vR | BF/G | Ctl | Dom | Cmd | FpK | SwK | Vel | G | L | F | H% | S% | hr/f | GS | APC | DOM% | DIS% | Sv% | LI | RAR | BPV | BPX | R$ |
|---|---|---|---|---|---|---|---|---|---|---|---|---|---|---|---|---|---|---|---|---|---|---|---|---|---|---|---|---|---|---|---|---|---|---|
| 14 | | | | | | | | | | | | | | | | | | | | | | | | | | | | | | | | | | |
| 15 | | | | | | | | | | | | | | | | | | | | | | | | | | | | | | | | | | |
| 16 | | | | | | | | | | | | | | | | | | | | | | | | | | | | | | | | | | |
| 17 | aa | 1 | 0 | 28 | 20 | 7.10 | 5.07 | 1.69 | | | | 20.8 | 3.0 | 6.4 | 2.1 | | | | | | | 39% | 53% | | | | | | | | -9.3 | 73 | 88 | -$8 |
| 18 | SD * | 5 | 0 | 103 | 60 | 4.00 | 3.69 | 1.17 | 907 | 978 | 807 | 21.6 | 1.9 | 5.2 | 2.8 | 58% | 7% | 93.0 | 40 | 21 | 39 | 28% | 68% | 14% | 9 | 73 | 0% | 67% | | | 1.8 | 66 | 76 | $2 |
| 1st Half | | 1 | 0 | 29 | 18 | 1.46 | 0.82 | 0.75 | | | | 20.8 | 1.8 | 5.4 | 3.0 | | | | | | | 19% | 82% | 0% | 0 | | | | | | 9.7 | 108 | 124 | $6 |
| 2nd Half | | 4 | 0 | 73 | 42 | 5.08 | 4.92 | 1.36 | 907 | 978 | 807 | 21.9 | 1.9 | 5.2 | 2.7 | 58% | 7% | 93.0 | 40 | 21 | 39 | 31% | 65% | 14% | 9 | 73 | 0% | 67% | | | -8.4 | 48 | 55 | $1 |
| **19** | **Proj** | **6** | **0** | **131** | **77** | **4.67** | **4.84** | **1.39** | **768** | **826** | **685** | **23.0** | **2.6** | **5.3** | **2.0** | **58%** | **7%** | **93.0** | **40** | **21** | **39** | **29%** | **71%** | **12%** | **24** | | | | | | **-8.3** | **43** | **49** | **-$3** |

## Nola,Aaron

| | | | | | | | |
|---|---|---|---|---|---|---|---|
| Age: | 26 | Th: | R | Role | SP | Health | B |
| Ht: | 6' 2" | Wt: | 195 | Type | Pwr GB | PT/Exp | A |
| | | | | | | Consist | A |

LIMA Plan D+ · Rand Var -3 · MM 4305

A true breakout season, as he added tons of whiffs and plenty of volume to already-stable Ctl/GB% profile. As he joins the ace conversation, use xERA as a guide since good fortune helped his cause. He won't fall far—FpK/SwK combo backs elite Cmd and recent BPVs say he's a rotation anchor—just bid between 2017-18.

| Yr | Tm | W | Sv | IP | K | ERA | xERA | WHIP | oOPS | vL | vR | BF/G | Ctl | Dom | Cmd | FpK | SwK | Vel | G | L | F | H% | S% | hr/f | GS | APC | DOM% | DIS% | Sv% | LI | RAR | BPV | BPX | R$ |
|---|---|---|---|---|---|---|---|---|---|---|---|---|---|---|---|---|---|---|---|---|---|---|---|---|---|---|---|---|---|---|---|---|---|---|
| 14 | aa | 2 | 0 | 24 | 14 | 2.86 | 5.09 | 1.32 | | | | 19.9 | 1.8 | 5.1 | 2.8 | | | | | | | 29% | 88% | | | | | | | | 2.6 | 38 | 46 | -$2 |
| 15 | PHI * | 16 | 0 | 187 | 151 | 3.10 | 3.58 | 1.17 | 703 | 834 | 618 | 24.1 | 1.8 | 7.2 | 4.1 | 64% | 9% | 90.5 | 48 | 20 | 32 | 30% | 77% | 15% | 13 | 86 | 31% | 23% | | | 19.9 | 105 | 126 | $19 |
| 16 | PHI | 6 | 0 | 111 | 121 | 4.78 | 3.22 | 1.31 | 712 | 703 | 720 | 24.2 | 2.4 | 9.8 | 4.2 | 61% | 10% | 90.1 | 55 | 20 | 25 | 36% | 64% | 13% | 20 | 90 | 35% | 15% | | | -8.1 | 146 | 174 | $0 |
| 17 | PHI | 12 | 0 | 168 | 184 | 3.54 | 3.50 | 1.21 | 679 | 741 | 624 | 25.7 | 2.6 | 9.9 | 3.8 | 64% | 11% | 92.0 | 50 | 19 | 31 | 32% | 74% | 13% | 27 | 99 | 44% | 15% | | | 17.0 | 135 | 162 | $16 |
| 18 | PHI | 17 | 0 | 212 | 224 | 2.37 | 3.17 | 0.97 | 570 | 559 | 582 | 25.2 | 2.5 | 9.5 | 3.9 | 69% | 13% | 92.4 | 51 | 19 | 30 | 26% | 79% | 11% | 33 | 97 | 52% | 15% | | | 46.5 | 134 | 154 | $38 |
| 1st Half | | 10 | 0 | 109 | 107 | 2.48 | 3.31 | 1.01 | 560 | 560 | 558 | 25.0 | 2.6 | 8.8 | 3.5 | 68% | 12% | 92.2 | 51 | 19 | 30 | 27% | 77% | 7% | 17 | 98 | 47% | 18% | | | 22.5 | 119 | 137 | $37 |
| 2nd Half | | 7 | 0 | 103 | 117 | 2.26 | 3.02 | 0.94 | 581 | 556 | 605 | 25.4 | 2.4 | 10.2 | 4.3 | 71% | 14% | 92.7 | 50 | 19 | 31 | 25% | 83% | 14% | 16 | 97 | 56% | 13% | | | 24.0 | 148 | 170 | $39 |
| **19** | **Proj** | **16** | **0** | **189** | **199** | **3.08** | **3.05** | **1.10** | **633** | **648** | **619** | **24.3** | **2.4** | **9.5** | **3.9** | **66%** | **12%** | **91.8** | **51** | **19** | **30** | **29%** | **75%** | **12%** | **30** | | | | | | **27.0** | **135** | **155** | **$25** |

## Norris,Bud

| | | | | | | | |
|---|---|---|---|---|---|---|---|
| Age: | 34 | Th: | R | Role | RP | Health | D |
| Ht: | 6' 0" | Wt: | 215 | Type | Pwr | PT/Exp | B |
| | | | | | | Consist | A |

LIMA Plan C+ · Rand Var +1 · MM 2310

Stellar 1st half featured elite SwK and uncharacteristic Ctl, but skills crashed and he lost the closer role in September. Subpar FpK, xERA say the ratio risks persist, though his newfound cutter backs 2017-18 SwK bump. We can count on the strikeouts, but more ninth-inning looks? Not so much.

| Yr | Tm | W | Sv | IP | K | ERA | xERA | WHIP | oOPS | vL | vR | BF/G | Ctl | Dom | Cmd | FpK | SwK | Vel | G | L | F | H% | S% | hr/f | GS | APC | DOM% | DIS% | Sv% | LI | RAR | BPV | BPX | R$ |
|---|---|---|---|---|---|---|---|---|---|---|---|---|---|---|---|---|---|---|---|---|---|---|---|---|---|---|---|---|---|---|---|---|---|---|
| 14 | BAL | 15 | 0 | 165 | 139 | 3.65 | 3.77 | 1.22 | 710 | 753 | 659 | 24.5 | 2.8 | 7.6 | 2.7 | 60% | 8% | 93.4 | 42 | 21 | 37 | 28% | 74% | 11% | 28 | 98 | 29% | 25% | | | 1.9 | 80 | 95 | $9 |
| 15 | 2 TM | 3 | 0 | 83 | 71 | 6.72 | 4.42 | 1.58 | 895 | 899 | 890 | 9.9 | 3.4 | 7.7 | 2.3 | 58% | 10% | 93.8 | 43 | 23 | 34 | 34% | 59% | 17% | 11 | 39 | 9% | 64% | 0 | 0.82 | -28.3 | 69 | 82 | -$14 |
| 16 | 2 NL | 6 | 0 | 113 | 102 | 5.10 | 4.32 | 1.46 | 763 | 915 | 646 | 14.1 | 3.9 | 8.1 | 2.1 | 62% | 10% | 93.5 | 48 | 22 | 31 | 32% | 67% | 14% | 19 | 57 | 26% | 37% | 0 | 0.75 | -12.7 | 67 | 79 | -$4 |
| 17 | LAA | 2 | 19 | 62 | 74 | 4.21 | 3.72 | 1.34 | 693 | 540 | 798 | 4.5 | 3.9 | 10.7 | 2.7 | 53% | 13% | 94.1 | 45 | 25 | 31 | 32% | 72% | 16% | 3 | 18 | 0% | 0% | 83 | 1.14 | 1.1 | 111 | 133 | $7 |
| 18 | STL | 3 | 28 | 58 | 67 | 3.59 | 3.58 | 1.25 | 694 | 559 | 847 | 3.8 | 3.3 | 10.5 | 3.2 | 58% | 13% | 94.6 | 43 | 23 | 34 | 31% | 77% | 16% | 0 | 15 | | | 85 | 1.27 | 4.0 | 121 | 139 | $12 |
| 1st Half | | 3 | 15 | 35 | 45 | 3.12 | 2.72 | 0.98 | 613 | 477 | 776 | 3.9 | 1.3 | 11.7 | 9.0 | 63% | 16% | 94.6 | 39 | 27 | 34 | 32% | 73% | 14% | 0 | 16 | | | 88 | 1.42 | 4.4 | 192 | 221 | $17 |
| 2nd Half | | 0 | 13 | 23 | 22 | 4.30 | 5.17 | 1.65 | 800 | 673 | 935 | 3.8 | 6.3 | 8.6 | 1.4 | 53% | 8% | 94.5 | 47 | 18 | 35 | 30% | 79% | 17% | 0 | 15 | | | 81 | 1.08 | -0.4 | 11 | 13 | $2 |
| **19** | **Proj** | **2** | **5** | **58** | **62** | **3.78** | **3.76** | **1.39** | **721** | **648** | **789** | **4.7** | **4.0** | **9.6** | **2.4** | **57%** | **11%** | **94.2** | **45** | **22** | **33** | **32%** | **76%** | **14%** | **0** | | | | | | **3.0** | **87** | **100** | **$0** |

## Norris,Daniel

| | | | | | | | |
|---|---|---|---|---|---|---|---|
| Age: | 26 | Th: | L | Role | SP | Health | F |
| Ht: | 6' 2" | Wt: | 185 | Type | Pwr FB | PT/Exp | C |
| | | | | | | Consist | B |

LIMA Plan C · Rand Var +5 · MM 1303

Lost most of season with groin surgery in May, so take small-sample BPV growth with a grain of salt. Velocity drop adds some concern, especially when combined with GB% loss and poor control. DIS%-heavy baseline says he'll do more harm than good, so let someone else take the plunge.

| Yr | Tm | W | Sv | IP | K | ERA | xERA | WHIP | oOPS | vL | vR | BF/G | Ctl | Dom | Cmd | FpK | SwK | Vel | G | L | F | H% | S% | hr/f | GS | APC | DOM% | DIS% | Sv% | LI | RAR | BPV | BPX | R$ |
|---|---|---|---|---|---|---|---|---|---|---|---|---|---|---|---|---|---|---|---|---|---|---|---|---|---|---|---|---|---|---|---|---|---|---|
| 14 | TOR * | 6 | 0 | 65 | 83 | 4.98 | 4.14 | 1.35 | 667 | 594 | 719 | 15.0 | 4.1 | 11.5 | 2.8 | 43% | 7% | 91.2 | 35 | 20 | 45 | 32% | 66% | 11% | 1 | 28 | 0% | 0% | 0 | 0.85 | -10.0 | 95 | 113 | -$2 |
| 15 | 2 AL * | 6 | 0 | 151 | 114 | 5.03 | 4.96 | 1.55 | 732 | 880 | 680 | 22.7 | 3.7 | 6.8 | 1.8 | 53% | 9% | 91.9 | 39 | 17 | 43 | 33% | 68% | 11% | 13 | 80 | 15% | 46% | | | -19.9 | 49 | 58 | -$11 |
| 16 | DET * | 10 | 0 | 149 | 140 | 4.50 | 4.81 | 1.51 | 762 | 648 | 800 | 22.3 | 3.2 | 8.4 | 2.6 | 64% | 11% | 93.1 | 38 | 23 | 39 | 36% | 71% | 12% | 13 | 85 | 23% | 31% | 0 | 0.72 | -5.7 | 76 | 91 | -$1 |
| 17 | DET | 5 | 0 | 102 | 86 | 5.31 | 5.19 | 1.61 | 840 | 928 | 813 | 20.9 | 3.9 | 7.6 | 2.0 | 55% | 9% | 93.2 | 39 | 22 | 39 | 35% | 68% | 10% | 18 | 83 | 6% | 44% | 0 | 0.65 | -12.0 | 49 | 59 | -$8 |
| 18 | DET | 0 | 0 | 44 | 51 | 5.68 | 4.40 | 1.47 | 791 | 872 | 768 | 18.2 | 3.9 | 10.4 | 2.7 | 58% | 11% | 90.2 | 30 | 29 | 41 | 34% | 65% | 15% | 8 | 74 | 0% | 25% | 0 | 0.72 | -8.4 | 90 | 104 | -$7 |
| 1st Half | | 0 | 0 | 15 | 18 | 5.87 | 4.68 | 1.63 | 801 | 713 | 843 | 14.6 | 5.3 | 10.6 | 2.0 | 60% | 12% | 89.0 | 41 | 20 | 39 | 34% | 68% | 18% | 2 | 56 | 0% | 50% | 0 | 0.60 | -3.3 | 66 | 76 | -$11 |
| 2nd Half | | 0 | 0 | 29 | 33 | 5.59 | 4.25 | 1.38 | 786 | 1061 | 733 | 21.2 | 3.1 | 10.2 | 3.3 | 57% | 10% | 90.7 | 24 | 33 | 43 | 34% | 63% | 14% | 6 | 89 | 0% | 17% | | | -5.1 | 103 | 118 | -$5 |
| **19** | **Proj** | **8** | **0** | **131** | **126** | **4.80** | **4.23** | **1.42** | **761** | **804** | **748** | **24.6** | **3.7** | **8.7** | **2.4** | **58%** | **10%** | **91.5** | **35** | **25** | **40** | **32%** | **70%** | **13%** | **23** | | | | | | **-1.3** | **70** | **80** | **-$2** |

## Nova,Ivan

| | | | | | | | |
|---|---|---|---|---|---|---|---|
| Age: | 32 | Th: | R | Role | SP | Health | D |
| Ht: | 6' 5" | Wt: | 250 | Type | Con | PT/Exp | A |
| | | | | | | Consist | A |

LIMA Plan B+ · Rand Var +1 · MM 2005

Missed some time with strained ligament in right index finger in May; ratio results remained eerily consistent. Without many strikeouts, he's entirely dependent upon Ctl, as once-heavy GB% tilt has slipped and struggles vL cap his usefulness. 2016-18 ERA makes for a simple, yet not all that exciting, projection.

| Yr | Tm | W | Sv | IP | K | ERA | xERA | WHIP | oOPS | vL | vR | BF/G | Ctl | Dom | Cmd | FpK | SwK | Vel | G | L | F | H% | S% | hr/f | GS | APC | DOM% | DIS% | Sv% | LI | RAR | BPV | BPX | R$ |
|---|---|---|---|---|---|---|---|---|---|---|---|---|---|---|---|---|---|---|---|---|---|---|---|---|---|---|---|---|---|---|---|---|---|---|
| 14 | NYY | 2 | 0 | 21 | 12 | 8.27 | 4.53 | 1.84 | 1033 | 764 | 1444 | 24.0 | 2.6 | 5.2 | 2.0 | 64% | 5% | 91.9 | 49 | 20 | 31 | 36% | 59% | 26% | 4 | 82 | 0% | 75% | | | -11.6 | 51 | 60 | -$7 |
| 15 | NYY | 6 | 0 | 94 | 63 | 5.07 | 4.50 | 1.40 | 793 | 899 | 682 | 24.3 | 3.2 | 6.0 | 1.9 | 55% | 8% | 93.0 | 49 | 19 | 32 | 30% | 66% | 13% | 17 | 90 | 18% | 53% | | | -12.9 | 50 | 60 | -$5 |
| 16 | 2 TM | 12 | 1 | 162 | 127 | 4.17 | 3.73 | 1.25 | 778 | 857 | 716 | 21.4 | 1.6 | 7.1 | 4.5 | 62% | 10% | 92.6 | 54 | 19 | 28 | 32% | 71% | 16% | 26 | 72 | 31% | 42% | 100 | 0.74 | 0.5 | 117 | 139 | $8 |
| 17 | PIT | 11 | 0 | 187 | 131 | 4.14 | 4.29 | 1.28 | 781 | 858 | 713 | 25.3 | 1.7 | 6.3 | 3.6 | 64% | 9% | 92.8 | 46 | 23 | 31 | 31% | 73% | 16% | 31 | 86 | 19% | 29% | | | 5.1 | 91 | 109 | $9 |
| 18 | PIT | 9 | 0 | 161 | 114 | 4.19 | 4.38 | 1.28 | 769 | 835 | 707 | 23.6 | 2.0 | 6.4 | 3.3 | 57% | 9% | 92.9 | 46 | 20 | 34 | 30% | 73% | 15% | 29 | 87 | 17% | 41% | | | -0.8 | 86 | 99 | $3 |
| 1st Half | | 4 | 0 | 87 | 68 | 4.02 | 4.06 | 1.20 | 737 | 764 | 711 | 24.5 | 1.5 | 7.0 | 4.5 | 57% | 10% | 93.0 | 47 | 19 | 34 | 30% | 71% | 13% | 15 | 91 | 27% | 47% | | | 1.4 | 110 | 126 | $5 |
| 2nd Half | | 5 | 0 | 74 | 46 | 4.40 | 4.77 | 1.37 | 805 | 926 | 704 | 22.5 | 2.4 | 5.6 | 2.3 | 58% | 9% | 92.7 | 43 | 23 | 34 | 29% | 75% | 17% | 14 | 83 | 7% | 36% | | | -2.3 | 57 | 65 | $1 |
| **19** | **Proj** | **10** | **0** | **189** | **132** | **4.29** | **3.99** | **1.30** | **780** | **862** | **707** | **22.8** | **2.0** | **6.3** | **3.1** | **60%** | **9%** | **92.8** | **47** | **21** | **32** | **30%** | **72%** | **15%** | **34** | | | | | | **2.6** | **84** | **97** | **$4** |

BRANT CHESSER

## Oberg,Scott

| Age: 29 | Th: R | Role RP | Health C | LIMA Plan A |
|---|---|---|---|---|
| Ht: 6' 2" | Wt: 205 | Type Pwr xGB | PT/Exp D | Rand Var 0 |
| | | | Consist C | MM 4200 |

8-1, 2.45 ERA in 59 IP at COL. Demoted after 5 ER outing on 4/23, returned in late May, then went three months (minus short DL stint) before giving up 5 more. Always had GB tilt, but 2nd half brought leap in Dom, Cmd, with SwK/FpK backing. Not an old dog, so if new tricks stick, might even get save or two.

| Yr Tm | W | Sv | IP | K | ERA | xERA | WHIP | oOPS | vL | vR | BF/G | Ctl | Dom | Cmd | FpK | SwK | Vel | G | L | F | H% | S% | hr/f | GS | APC | DOM% | DIS% | Sv% | LI | RAR | BPV | BPX | R$ |
|---|---|---|---|---|---|---|---|---|---|---|---|---|---|---|---|---|---|---|---|---|---|---|---|---|---|---|---|---|---|---|---|---|---|
| 14 aa | 0 | 15 | 27 | 17 | 3.84 | 3.62 | 1.27 | | | | 4.1 | 2.2 | 5.5 | 2.5 | | | | | | | 31% | 70% | | | | | | | | -0.3 | 72 | 86 | $3 |
| 15 COL | 3 | 1 | 58 | 44 | 5.09 | 4.51 | 1.53 | 839 | 781 | 872 | 4.0 | 4.8 | 6.8 | 1.4 | 55% | 9% | 95.0 | 54 | 18 | 28 | 28% | 71% | 21% | 0 | 16 | | | 33 | 1.00 | -8.1 | 25 | 30 | -$6 |
| 16 COL * | 2 | 10 | 56 | 46 | 4.35 | 3.30 | 1.27 | 713 | 993 | 549 | 4.5 | 3.8 | 7.5 | 2.0 | 55% | 10% | 94.5 | 56 | 11 | 33 | 28% | 66% | 11% | 0 | 18 | | | 83 | 0.63 | -1.1 | 73 | 87 | $2 |
| 17 COL | 0 | 0 | 58 | 55 | 4.94 | 4.08 | 1.61 | 800 | 816 | 790 | 4.0 | 3.7 | 8.5 | 2.3 | 69% | 13% | 96.3 | 57 | 19 | 24 | 38% | 69% | 9% | 0 | 15 | | | 0 | 0.90 | -4.2 | 88 | 105 | -$7 |
| 18 COL * | 9 | 3 | 75 | 67 | 2.38 | 2.63 | 1.03 | 571 | 633 | 524 | 4.2 | 1.7 | 8.1 | 4.7 | 68% | 14% | 95.3 | 56 | 25 | 19 | 28% | 80% | 13% | 0 | 16 | | | 38 | 1.28 | 16.3 | 138 | 158 | $12 |
| 1st Half | 2 | 3 | 35 | 23 | 3.03 | 3.17 | 1.22 | 591 | 804 | 449 | 4.7 | 2.4 | 5.9 | 2.5 | 63% | 13% | 94.8 | 52 | 30 | 18 | 30% | 75% | 0% | 0 | 20 | | | 50 | 1.33 | 4.9 | 82 | 95 | $3 |
| 2nd Half | 7 | 0 | 40 | 44 | 1.82 | 2.27 | 0.86 | 558 | 548 | 566 | 3.7 | 1.1 | 10.0 | 8.8 | 72% | 14% | 95.6 | 59 | 21 | 20 | 27% | 87% | 21% | 0 | 15 | | | 0 | 1.26 | 11.4 | 186 | 214 | $20 |
| **19 Proj** | **3** | **0** | **44** | **39** | **3.14** | **3.26** | **1.20** | **661** | **687** | **642** | **4.0** | **2.8** | **8.1** | **2.9** | **66%** | **12%** | **95.6** | **56** | **22** | **22** | **30%** | **76%** | **13%** | **0** | | | | | | **5.4** | **104** | **120** | **$1** |

## Odorizzi,Jake

| Age: 29 | Th: R | Role SP | Health C | LIMA Plan B+ |
|---|---|---|---|---|
| Ht: 6' 2" | Wt: 190 | Type Pwr xFB | PT/Exp A | Rand Var 0 |
| | | | Consist A | MM 1203 |

New team, same old Ctl woes. Not only that, but fly ball rate stayed on upswing; only hr/f saved him from worse fate. Has always gotten swings and misses, but one of these years, luck—in 2018, it was S%—is going to run out, closing ERA/xERA gap. Whatever buzz there once was has fizzled. Bid accordingly.

| Yr Tm | W | Sv | IP | K | ERA | xERA | WHIP | oOPS | vL | vR | BF/G | Ctl | Dom | Cmd | FpK | SwK | Vel | G | L | F | H% | S% | hr/f | GS | APC | DOM% | DIS% | Sv% | LI | RAR | BPV | BPX | R$ |
|---|---|---|---|---|---|---|---|---|---|---|---|---|---|---|---|---|---|---|---|---|---|---|---|---|---|---|---|---|---|---|---|---|---|
| 14 TAM | 11 | 0 | 168 | 174 | 4.13 | 3.96 | 1.28 | 692 | 663 | 726 | 23.2 | 3.2 | 9.3 | 2.9 | 61% | 10% | 90.3 | 30 | 21 | 49 | 31% | 71% | 9% | 31 | 98 | 35% | 32% | | | -8.0 | 90 | 108 | $4 |
| 15 TAM | 9 | 0 | 169 | 150 | 3.35 | 3.99 | 1.15 | 680 | 630 | 745 | 25.0 | 2.4 | 8.0 | 3.3 | 60% | 11% | 91.3 | 37 | 22 | 41 | 29% | 75% | 9% | 28 | 98 | 25% | 11% | | | 12.8 | 92 | 110 | $13 |
| 16 TAM | 10 | 0 | 188 | 166 | 3.69 | 4.39 | 1.19 | 715 | 578 | 814 | 23.4 | 2.6 | 8.0 | 3.1 | 58% | 10% | 91.6 | 37 | 19 | 44 | 28% | 75% | 12% | 33 | 100 | 21% | 42% | | | 11.5 | 88 | 105 | $13 |
| 17 TAM | 10 | 0 | 143 | 127 | 4.14 | 5.06 | 1.24 | 736 | 686 | 773 | 21.6 | 3.8 | 8.0 | 2.1 | 54% | 12% | 91.6 | 31 | 22 | 47 | 24% | 76% | 16% | 28 | 94 | 11% | 50% | | | 3.8 | 49 | 59 | $8 |
| 18 MIN | 7 | 0 | 164 | 162 | 4.49 | 4.82 | 1.34 | 743 | 764 | 726 | 22.2 | 3.8 | 8.9 | 2.3 | 57% | 11% | 91.1 | 28 | 23 | 49 | 30% | 69% | 9% | 32 | 96 | 28% | 31% | | | -6.9 | 62 | 72 | $0 |
| 1st Half | 3 | 0 | 86 | 88 | 4.62 | 4.84 | 1.44 | 811 | 847 | 782 | 22.1 | 4.1 | 9.2 | 2.3 | 57% | 12% | 91.0 | 27 | 24 | 49 | 31% | 72% | 12% | 17 | 96 | 12% | 35% | | | -5.0 | 61 | 70 | -$4 |
| 2nd Half | 4 | 0 | 79 | 74 | 4.35 | 4.79 | 1.25 | 668 | 676 | 662 | 22.4 | 3.5 | 8.5 | 2.4 | 57% | 10% | 91.2 | 30 | 22 | 48 | 29% | 65% | 6% | 15 | 96 | 47% | 27% | | | -1.9 | 65 | 74 | $5 |
| **19 Proj** | **9** | **0** | **174** | **163** | **4.61** | **4.38** | **1.32** | **752** | **723** | **776** | **21.9** | **3.7** | **8.4** | **2.3** | **57%** | **11%** | **91.3** | **31** | **22** | **47** | **29%** | **69%** | **12%** | **33** | | | | | | **-9.8** | **62** | **71** | **$3** |

## Oh,Seung-Hwan

| Age: 36 | Th: R | Role RP | Health A | LIMA Plan B+ |
|---|---|---|---|---|
| Ht: 5' 10" | Wt: 205 | Type Pwr xFB | PT/Exp B | Rand Var -3 |
| | | | Consist D | MM 3400 |

Shook off rough pre-season (contract, visa issues) to have bounce-back year, especially with Dom, though 2nd half H% luck helped, too. Toyed with return to Korea; if he stays stateside, he'll likely remain "Semifinal Boss," due to issues with LHB, FB bent, diminishing velocity. Still, there's some useful IP to be had here.

| Yr Tm | W | Sv | IP | K | ERA | xERA | WHIP | oOPS | vL | vR | BF/G | Ctl | Dom | Cmd | FpK | SwK | Vel | G | L | F | H% | S% | hr/f | GS | APC | DOM% | DIS% | Sv% | LI | RAR | BPV | BPX | R$ |
|---|---|---|---|---|---|---|---|---|---|---|---|---|---|---|---|---|---|---|---|---|---|---|---|---|---|---|---|---|---|---|---|---|---|
| 14 for | 2 | 39 | 67 | 77 | 2.18 | 2.22 | 0.90 | | | | 3.9 | 2.2 | 10.4 | 4.8 | | | | | | | 24% | 85% | | | | | | | | 12.9 | 146 | 174 | $23 |
| 15 for | 2 | 41 | 69 | 63 | 3.39 | 4.23 | 1.28 | | | | 4.5 | 2.6 | 8.1 | 3.2 | | | | | | | 31% | 79% | | | | | | | | 4.9 | 79 | 94 | $17 |
| 16 STL | 6 | 19 | 80 | 103 | 1.92 | 3.02 | 0.92 | 510 | 455 | 555 | 4.1 | 2.0 | 11.6 | 5.7 | 67% | 18% | 92.8 | 40 | 19 | 41 | 29% | 82% | 7% | 0 | 17 | | | 83 | 1.30 | 22.3 | 173 | 205 | $22 |
| 17 STL | 1 | 20 | 59 | 54 | 4.10 | 5.04 | 1.40 | 794 | 1006 | 642 | 4.3 | 2.3 | 8.2 | 3.6 | 63% | 14% | 92.9 | 29 | 22 | 49 | 34% | 77% | 11% | 0 | 17 | | | 83 | 1.35 | 1.9 | 93 | 112 | $6 |
| 18 2 TM | 6 | 3 | 68 | 79 | 2.63 | 3.77 | 1.01 | 620 | 915 | 459 | 3.8 | 2.2 | 10.4 | 4.6 | 65% | 15% | 91.6 | 30 | 20 | 50 | 28% | 80% | 9% | 0 | 16 | | | 33 | 1.06 | 12.8 | 135 | 155 | $9 |
| 1st Half | 4 | 2 | 38 | 46 | 3.05 | 3.88 | 1.12 | 653 | 915 | 527 | 4.1 | 2.3 | 10.8 | 4.6 | 64% | 15% | 91.5 | 31 | 19 | 51 | 31% | 79% | 10% | 0 | 17 | | | 40 | 0.98 | 5.2 | 140 | 160 | $9 |
| 2nd Half | 2 | 1 | 30 | 33 | 2.10 | 3.63 | 0.87 | 573 | 911 | 351 | 3.4 | 2.1 | 9.9 | 4.7 | 65% | 16% | 91.8 | 29 | 21 | 50 | 24% | 83% | 8% | 0 | 14 | | | 25 | 1.16 | 7.6 | 129 | 148 | $10 |
| **19 Proj** | **3** | **0** | **58** | **63** | **3.45** | **3.56** | **1.12** | **662** | **872** | **524** | **3.8** | **2.2** | **9.9** | **4.5** | **64%** | **15%** | **92.3** | **31** | **21** | **48** | **30%** | **74%** | **10%** | **0** | | | | | | **5.0** | **127** | **145** | **$3** |

## Olson,Tyler

| Age: 29 | Th: L | Role RP | Health C | LIMA Plan C |
|---|---|---|---|---|
| Ht: 6' 3" | Wt: 195 | Type Pwr FB | PT/Exp D | Rand Var +5 |
| | | | Consist F | MM 2300 |

In and around trips to Triple-A and DL, posted strong skills as lefty specialist cloaked by conspiracy among H%, S%, hr/f. Hit rate of 41% vR says he shouldn't be THAT ineffective against righties, but 2.1 Cmd vR suggests role expansion not likely, either. Good for ERA/WHIP maintenance, maybe, but little more.

| Yr Tm | W | Sv | IP | K | ERA | xERA | WHIP | oOPS | vL | vR | BF/G | Ctl | Dom | Cmd | FpK | SwK | Vel | G | L | F | H% | S% | hr/f | GS | APC | DOM% | DIS% | Sv% | LI | RAR | BPV | BPX | R$ |
|---|---|---|---|---|---|---|---|---|---|---|---|---|---|---|---|---|---|---|---|---|---|---|---|---|---|---|---|---|---|---|---|---|---|
| 14 aa | 10 | 0 | 125 | 84 | 3.94 | 4.13 | 1.33 | | | | 23.7 | 1.7 | 6.0 | 3.5 | | | | | | | 33% | 70% | | | | | | | | -3.1 | 89 | 106 | $1 |
| 15 SEA * | 4 | 1 | 68 | 52 | 4.51 | 5.45 | 1.60 | 1056 | 1058 | 1055 | 8.3 | 3.4 | 6.9 | 2.0 | 68% | 7% | 88.6 | 44 | 21 | 35 | 35% | 74% | 13% | 0 | 20 | | | 33 | 1.28 | -4.6 | 47 | 56 | -$6 |
| 16 NYY * | 2 | 0 | 47 | 23 | 7.61 | 7.57 | 2.04 | 885 | 143 | 1917 | 8.8 | 4.1 | 4.4 | 1.1 | 46% | 13% | 87.9 | 27 | 18 | 55 | 39% | 62% | 0% | 0 | 47 | | | 0 | 0.67 | -19.8 | 0 | -1 | -$14 |
| 17 CLE * | 3 | 3 | 62 | 59 | 3.25 | 3.63 | 1.17 | 481 | 460 | 504 | 3.9 | 3.2 | 8.6 | 2.7 | 64% | 10% | 89.1 | 53 | 22 | 25 | 26% | 80% | 0% | 0 | 10 | | | 100 | 1.05 | 8.5 | 76 | 92 | $4 |
| 18 CLE | 2 | 0 | 27 | 40 | 4.94 | 3.23 | 1.39 | 756 | 595 | 926 | 2.7 | 4.0 | 13.2 | 3.3 | 63% | 15% | 88.6 | 43 | 22 | 35 | 37% | 68% | 17% | 0 | 11 | | | 0 | 1.04 | -2.7 | 151 | 174 | -$4 |
| 1st Half | 1 | 0 | 17 | 23 | 7.27 | 3.90 | 1.62 | 862 | 653 | 1083 | 2.8 | 4.2 | 11.9 | 2.9 | 65% | 12% | 88.6 | 43 | 19 | 38 | 40% | 56% | 17% | 0 | 11 | | | 0 | 1.00 | -6.7 | 123 | 142 | -$9 |
| 2nd Half | 1 | 0 | 10 | 17 | 0.90 | 2.16 | 1.00 | 542 | 478 | 610 | 2.6 | 3.6 | 15.3 | 4.3 | 59% | 21% | 88.7 | 44 | 28 | 28 | 31% | 100% | 20% | 0 | 10 | | | 0 | 1.11 | 4.0 | 201 | 230 | $2 |
| **19 Proj** | **2** | **0** | **44** | **46** | **3.74** | **3.91** | **1.37** | **687** | **522** | **863** | **4.5** | **3.6** | **9.5** | **2.7** | **65%** | **12%** | **88.6** | **43** | **19** | **38** | **32%** | **78%** | **12%** | **0** | | | | | | **1.4** | **95** | **109** | **-$2** |

## Osuna,Roberto

| Age: 24 | Th: R | Role RP | Health A | LIMA Plan B+ |
|---|---|---|---|---|
| Ht: 6' 2" | Wt: 215 | Type Pwr | PT/Exp B | Rand Var -3 |
| | | | Consist B | MM 5430 |

Skills mostly held up, even with lengthy suspension, trade. Yes, Dom was down, but SwK urges not to worry too much about that, and while give back of GB gains is a concern, he's still a far cry from past fly ball issues. Should be solid bet to keep saves rolling in, this time over a full season.

| Yr Tm | W | Sv | IP | K | ERA | xERA | WHIP | oOPS | vL | vR | BF/G | Ctl | Dom | Cmd | FpK | SwK | Vel | G | L | F | H% | S% | hr/f | GS | APC | DOM% | DIS% | Sv% | LI | RAR | BPV | BPX | R$ |
|---|---|---|---|---|---|---|---|---|---|---|---|---|---|---|---|---|---|---|---|---|---|---|---|---|---|---|---|---|---|---|---|---|---|
| 14 | | | | | | | | | | | | | | | | | | | | | | | | | | | | | | | | | |
| 15 TOR | 1 | 20 | 70 | 75 | 2.58 | 3.41 | 0.92 | 591 | 638 | 537 | 4.0 | 2.1 | 9.7 | 4.7 | 63% | 15% | 95.6 | 34 | 20 | 46 | 25% | 77% | 9% | 0 | 16 | | | 87 | 1.36 | 11.8 | 131 | 156 | $15 |
| 16 TOR | 4 | 36 | 74 | 82 | 2.68 | 3.54 | 0.93 | 603 | 729 | 480 | 4.0 | 1.7 | 10.0 | 5.9 | 70% | 16% | 95.8 | 33 | 20 | 47 | 27% | 78% | 10% | 0 | 16 | | | 86 | 1.39 | 13.8 | 145 | 172 | $24 |
| 17 TOR | 3 | 39 | 64 | 83 | 3.38 | 2.70 | 0.86 | 507 | 505 | 509 | 3.8 | 1.3 | 11.7 | 9.2 | 64% | 17% | 94.6 | 48 | 18 | 34 | 31% | 60% | 6% | 0 | 15 | | | 80 | 1.36 | 7.8 | 202 | 242 | $24 |
| 18 2 AL | 2 | 21 | 38 | 32 | 2.37 | 3.53 | 0.97 | 578 | 699 | 441 | 3.9 | 0.9 | 7.6 | 8.0 | 75% | 15% | 95.2 | 41 | 25 | 34 | 30% | 75% | 3% | 0 | 14 | | | 95 | 1.10 | 8.4 | 130 | 149 | $10 |
| 1st Half | 0 | 9 | 15 | 13 | 2.93 | 3.43 | 1.11 | 618 | 612 | 628 | 4.2 | 0.6 | 7.6 | 13.0 | 78% | 12% | 95.2 | 39 | 33 | 28 | 35% | 71% | 0% | 0 | 15 | | | 90 | 1.06 | 2.3 | 139 | 159 | $3 |
| 2nd Half | 2 | 12 | 23 | 19 | 1.99 | 3.60 | 0.88 | 549 | 776 | 328 | 3.8 | 1.2 | 7.5 | 6.3 | 74% | 17% | 95.2 | 43 | 19 | 38 | 26% | 79% | 4% | 0 | 13 | | | 100 | 1.12 | 6.1 | 124 | 143 | $15 |
| **19 Proj** | **3** | **32** | **58** | **65** | **2.69** | **2.87** | **0.95** | **569** | **657** | **479** | **3.8** | **1.4** | **10.1** | **7.2** | **70%** | **16%** | **95.2** | **41** | **22** | **37** | **30%** | **73%** | **6%** | **0** | | | | | | **10.3** | **163** | **187** | **$19** |

## Otero,Dan

| Age: 34 | Th: R | Role RP | Health A | LIMA Plan C+ |
|---|---|---|---|---|
| Ht: 6' 3" | Wt: 205 | Type Con xGB | PT/Exp C | Rand Var +5 |
| | | | Consist A | MM 4000 |

Knows how to find the strike zone; perhaps too well. His hr/f last two years suggests a Home Run Derby contestant should ask him to come along. That, along with H%, S%, is what tanked his results. Strong skills, GB lean should make him harmless back-of-roster warm body anew, but that's about it.

| Yr Tm | W | Sv | IP | K | ERA | xERA | WHIP | oOPS | vL | vR | BF/G | Ctl | Dom | Cmd | FpK | SwK | Vel | G | L | F | H% | S% | hr/f | GS | APC | DOM% | DIS% | Sv% | LI | RAR | BPV | BPX | R$ |
|---|---|---|---|---|---|---|---|---|---|---|---|---|---|---|---|---|---|---|---|---|---|---|---|---|---|---|---|---|---|---|---|---|---|
| 14 OAK | 8 | 1 | 87 | 45 | 2.28 | 3.50 | 1.10 | 607 | 698 | 539 | 4.8 | 1.6 | 4.7 | 3.0 | 69% | 7% | 90.2 | 56 | 24 | 20 | 28% | 80% | 7% | 0 | 17 | | | 25 | 1.26 | 15.6 | 76 | 91 | $9 |
| 15 OAK * | 4 | 0 | 74 | 42 | 5.25 | 5.08 | 1.42 | 886 | 884 | 887 | 5.6 | 1.3 | 5.0 | 3.9 | 73% | 7% | 89.7 | 49 | 23 | 28 | 34% | 64% | 15% | 0 | 18 | | | 0 | 0.77 | -11.8 | 75 | 89 | -$7 |
| 16 CLE | 5 | 1 | 71 | 57 | 1.53 | 2.90 | 0.91 | 526 | 522 | 529 | 4.3 | 1.3 | 7.3 | 5.7 | 67% | 8% | 90.3 | 62 | 18 | 20 | 27% | 84% | 5% | 0 | 16 | | | 50 | 0.79 | 23.2 | 136 | 162 | $12 |
| 17 CLE | 3 | 0 | 60 | 38 | 2.85 | 3.29 | 1.20 | 693 | 872 | 581 | 4.7 | 1.4 | 5.7 | 4.2 | 68% | 8% | 90.0 | 64 | 24 | 12 | 30% | 80% | 26% | 0 | 16 | | | 0 | 0.54 | 11.2 | 108 | 130 | $2 |
| 18 CLE | 2 | 1 | 59 | 43 | 5.22 | 3.35 | 1.26 | 826 | 993 | 721 | 4.0 | 0.8 | 6.6 | 8.6 | 66% | 9% | 90.0 | 59 | 22 | 19 | 32% | 65% | 32% | 0 | 15 | | | 33 | 0.84 | -7.7 | 135 | 155 | -$4 |
| 1st Half | 1 | 0 | 30 | 21 | 6.07 | 3.47 | 1.08 | 787 | 1091 | 634 | 4.1 | 0.9 | 6.4 | 7.0 | 69% | 7% | 90.0 | 60 | 17 | 22 | 26% | 48% | 32% | 0 | 16 | | | 0 | 1.06 | -7.0 | 128 | 147 | -$6 |
| 2nd Half | 1 | 1 | 29 | 22 | 4.34 | 3.22 | 1.45 | 866 | 918 | 825 | 4.0 | 0.6 | 6.8 | 11.0 | 63% | 11% | 90.0 | 57 | 27 | 16 | 37% | 76% | 31% | 0 | 15 | | | 50 | 0.63 | -0.7 | 141 | 162 | -$2 |
| **19 Proj** | **3** | **0** | **58** | **41** | **3.37** | **3.15** | **1.21** | **746** | **857** | **671** | **4.2** | **1.0** | **6.3** | **6.1** | **67%** | **8%** | **90.1** | **60** | **23** | **18** | **31%** | **78%** | **24%** | **0** | | | | | | **5.1** | **123** | **142** | **$1** |

## Ottavino,Adam

| Age: 33 | Th: R | Role RP | Health F | LIMA Plan B |
|---|---|---|---|---|
| Ht: 6' 5" | Wt: 220 | Type Pwr | PT/Exp C | Rand Var -3 |
| | | | Consist F | MM 4510 |

Before oblique felled him, skills were off the charts. Wasn't quite the same upon return, as GB gains evaporated, Ctl concerns deepened. Free agent could thrive away from COL, though injury concerns will be ever-present. If you throw out lost 2017, skills say he could even close—but first, needs to stay on the field.

| Yr Tm | W | Sv | IP | K | ERA | xERA | WHIP | oOPS | vL | vR | BF/G | Ctl | Dom | Cmd | FpK | SwK | Vel | G | L | F | H% | S% | hr/f | GS | APC | DOM% | DIS% | Sv% | LI | RAR | BPV | BPX | R$ |
|---|---|---|---|---|---|---|---|---|---|---|---|---|---|---|---|---|---|---|---|---|---|---|---|---|---|---|---|---|---|---|---|---|---|
| 14 COL | 1 | 1 | 65 | 70 | 3.60 | 3.09 | 1.28 | 735 | 943 | 645 | 3.6 | 2.2 | 9.7 | 4.4 | 61% | 12% | 94.3 | 47 | 19 | 34 | 35% | 74% | 10% | 0 | 14 | | | 17 | 1.31 | 1.1 | 140 | 166 | $0 |
| 15 COL | 1 | 3 | 10 | 13 | 0.00 | 1.89 | 0.48 | 265 | 321 | 217 | 3.5 | 1.7 | 11.3 | 6.5 | 51% | 13% | 95.7 | 63 | 5 | 32 | 16% | 100% | 0% | 0 | 14 | | | 100 | 1.05 | 5.0 | 198 | 236 | $1 |
| 16 COL | 1 | 7 | 27 | 35 | 2.67 | 2.29 | 0.93 | 528 | 780 | 350 | 3.1 | 2.3 | 11.7 | 5.0 | 52% | 11% | 93.8 | 62 | 17 | 21 | 27% | 77% | 23% | 0 | 13 | | | 58 | 1.28 | 5.1 | 187 | 222 | $4 |
| 17 COL | 2 | 0 | 53 | 63 | 5.06 | 5.00 | 1.63 | 786 | 898 | 727 | 3.9 | 6.6 | 10.6 | 1.6 | 47% | 10% | 94.4 | 37 | 22 | 41 | 31% | 72% | 14% | 0 | 17 | | | 0 | 0.89 | -4.6 | 29 | 34 | -$6 |
| 18 COL | 6 | 6 | 78 | 112 | 2.43 | 2.95 | 0.99 | 509 | 560 | 467 | 4.1 | 4.2 | 13.0 | 3.1 | 60% | 13% | 93.9 | 43 | 19 | 38 | 25% | 78% | 9% | 0 | 17 | | | 55 | 1.21 | 16.4 | 142 | 163 | $14 |
| 1st Half | 4 | 2 | 38 | 59 | 1.42 | 2.15 | 0.82 | 406 | 463 | 362 | 4.0 | 3.8 | 14.0 | 3.7 | 63% | 13% | 94.0 | 56 | 14 | 30 | 23% | 83% | 5% | 0 | 17 | | | 50 | 1.20 | 12.8 | 183 | 210 | $18 |
| 2nd Half | 2 | 4 | 40 | 53 | 3.40 | 3.73 | 1.16 | 597 | 642 | 559 | 4.2 | 4.5 | 12.0 | 2.7 | 58% | 12% | 93.8 | 34 | 22 | 44 | 27% | 74% | 10% | 0 | 17 | | | 57 | 1.22 | 3.7 | 106 | 122 | $10 |
| **19 Proj** | **3** | **2** | **51** | **67** | **3.09** | **3.16** | **1.19** | **642** | **714** | **598** | **3.7** | **4.0** | **11.9** | **2.9** | **59%** | **12%** | **94.1** | **42** | **20** | **38** | **30%** | **78%** | **12%** | **0** | | | | | | **8.3** | **126** | **145** | **$3** |

KRISTOPHER OLSON

### Pagan,Emilio

| | | | | | | | |
|---|---|---|---|---|---|---|---|
| Age: 28 | Th: R | Role | RP | Health | A | LIMA Plan | C |
| | | | | PT/Exp | D | Rand Var | 0 |
| Ht: 6' 3" | Wt: 210 | Type | Pwr xFB | Consist | D | MM | 1300 |

FB/SL combo garners plenty of swings and misses, which kept his Cmd in good shape despite an uptick in free passes. However, extreme FB% isn't likely to work in launch angle era (1.9 hr/9 in 2018) and his struggles vL have deepened. Until he fixes those issues, fantasy relevance figures to elude him.

| Yr | Tm | W | Sv | IP | K | ERA | xERA | WHIP | oOPS | vL | vR | BF/G | Ctl | Dom | Cmd | FpK | SwK | Vel | G | L | F | H% | S% | hr/f | GS | APC | DOM% | DIS% | Sv% | LI | RAR | BPV | BPX | R$ |
|---|---|---|---|---|---|---|---|---|---|---|---|---|---|---|---|---|---|---|---|---|---|---|---|---|---|---|---|---|---|---|---|---|---|---|
| 14 | | | | | | | | | | | | | | | | | | | | | | | | | | | | | | | | | | |
| 15 | | | | | | | | | | | | | | | | | | | | | | | | | | | | | | | | | | |
| 16 | a/a | 5 | 10 | 65 | 71 | 3.05 | 3.78 | 1.32 | | | | 6.6 | 4.1 | 9.8 | 2.4 | | | | | | | 30% | 82% | | | | | | | | 9.1 | 84 | 100 | $7 |
| 17 | SEA * | 4 | 5 | 82 | 86 | 3.20 | 2.30 | 0.96 | 610 | 825 | 502 | 5.4 | 1.8 | 9.4 | 5.2 | 63% | 14% | 93.6 | 22 | 21 | 57 | 27% | 69% | 9% | 0 | 21 | | | 83 | 1.09 | 11.7 | 156 | 187 | $11 |
| 18 | OAK | 3 | 0 | 62 | 63 | 4.35 | 4.63 | 1.19 | 767 | 1031 | 628 | 4.8 | 2.8 | 9.1 | 3.3 | 57% | 15% | 93.8 | 27 | 18 | 55 | 27% | 72% | 14% | 0 | 19 | | | 0 | 0.56 | -1.6 | 95 | 110 | -$1 |
| 1st Half | | 1 | 0 | 35 | 35 | 2.86 | 4.62 | 1.21 | 750 | 1078 | 591 | 5.3 | 3.1 | 9.1 | 2.9 | 58% | 15% | 93.6 | 31 | 17 | 52 | 28% | 86% | 12% | 0 | 21 | | | 0 | 0.56 | 5.5 | 88 | 101 | $1 |
| 2nd Half | | 2 | 0 | 27 | 28 | 6.26 | 4.65 | 1.17 | 787 | 977 | 677 | 4.3 | 2.3 | 9.2 | 4.0 | 56% | 14% | 94.1 | 22 | 19 | 58 | 27% | 52% | 16% | 0 | 17 | | | 0 | 0.57 | -7.1 | 104 | 119 | -$2 |
| 19 | Proj | 3 | 0 | 51 | 53 | 4.37 | 4.11 | 1.25 | 768 | 1018 | 637 | 5.1 | 2.6 | 9.4 | 3.6 | 59% | 14% | 93.8 | 24 | 19 | 56 | 30% | 71% | 12% | 0 | | | | | | -1.4 | 101 | 116 | -$1 |

### Pannone,Thomas

| | | | | | | | |
|---|---|---|---|---|---|---|---|
| Age: 25 | Th: L | Role | SP | Health | A | LIMA Plan | C |
| | | | | PT/Exp | D | Rand Var | 0 |
| Ht: 6' 0" | Wt: 195 | Type | xFB | Consist | C | MM | 0101 |

4-1, 4.19 ERA in 43 IP at TOR. Lacks a plus offering, but demonstrated the ability in minors to locate each of his three pitches and keep batters off balance by adding/subtracting velocity. Given his repertoire and FB tilt, HR figure to be an ongoing problem. Low ceiling, high blowup potential.

| Yr | Tm | W | Sv | IP | K | ERA | xERA | WHIP | oOPS | vL | vR | BF/G | Ctl | Dom | Cmd | FpK | SwK | Vel | G | L | F | H% | S% | hr/f | GS | APC | DOM% | DIS% | Sv% | LI | RAR | BPV | BPX | R$ |
|---|---|---|---|---|---|---|---|---|---|---|---|---|---|---|---|---|---|---|---|---|---|---|---|---|---|---|---|---|---|---|---|---|---|---|
| 14 | | | | | | | | | | | | | | | | | | | | | | | | | | | | | | | | | | |
| 15 | | | | | | | | | | | | | | | | | | | | | | | | | | | | | | | | | | |
| 16 | | | | | | | | | | | | | | | | | | | | | | | | | | | | | | | | | | |
| 17 | aa | 7 | 0 | 117 | 92 | 3.78 | 4.21 | 1.26 | | | | 23.9 | 2.3 | 7.1 | 3.0 | | | | | | | 30% | 75% | | | | | | | | 8.4 | 71 | 85 | $6 |
| 18 | TOR * | 4 | 0 | 90 | 72 | 5.04 | 5.33 | 1.38 | 719 | 795 | 689 | 19.0 | 2.8 | 7.2 | 2.6 | 56% | 10% | 88.1 | 35 | 15 | 50 | 30% | 69% | 10% | 6 | 58 | 17% | 33% | 0 | 0.52 | -9.9 | 43 | 50 | -$5 |
| 1st Half | | 0 | 0 | 4 | 4 | 2.92 | 5.80 | 1.78 | | | | 18.4 | 2.4 | 9.2 | 3.9 | | | | | | | 46% | 82% | 0% | 0 | | | | | | 0.6 | 122 | 140 | -$16 |
| 2nd Half | | 4 | 0 | 86 | 68 | 5.14 | 5.31 | 1.36 | 719 | 795 | 689 | 19.0 | 2.8 | 7.1 | 2.5 | 56% | 10% | 88.1 | 35 | 15 | 50 | 29% | 69% | 10% | 6 | 58 | 17% | 33% | 0 | 0.52 | -10.5 | 40 | 46 | -$5 |
| 19 | Proj | 5 | 0 | 87 | 69 | 4.78 | 4.68 | 1.32 | 745 | 837 | 709 | 20.7 | 2.6 | 7.1 | 2.7 | 56% | 10% | 88.1 | 35 | 15 | 50 | 30% | 69% | 11% | 17 | | | | | | -6.8 | 70 | 80 | -$2 |

### Parker,Blake

| | | | | | | | |
|---|---|---|---|---|---|---|---|
| Age: 34 | Th: R | Role | RP | Health | A | LIMA Plan | B+ |
| | | | | PT/Exp | C | Rand Var | -2 |
| Ht: 6' 3" | Wt: 225 | Type | Pwr FB | Consist | B | MM | 3310 |

Follow-up to career year was a rocky ride, as he bounced in and out of the closer job. GB lean of 2016-17 vanished; with added flyballs came HR issues and a jump in xERA. 2nd half drop in SwK/Dom/Velo heightens the concern. May vie for late-inning role, but outside of 2017 hasn't shown skills to hold it.

| Yr | Tm | W | Sv | IP | K | ERA | xERA | WHIP | oOPS | vL | vR | BF/G | Ctl | Dom | Cmd | FpK | SwK | Vel | G | L | F | H% | S% | hr/f | GS | APC | DOM% | DIS% | Sv% | LI | RAR | BPV | BPX | R$ |
|---|---|---|---|---|---|---|---|---|---|---|---|---|---|---|---|---|---|---|---|---|---|---|---|---|---|---|---|---|---|---|---|---|---|---|
| 14 | CHC * | 1 | 25 | 57 | 63 | 3.33 | 4.41 | 1.38 | 784 | 559 | 939 | 4.5 | 3.0 | 10.1 | 3.4 | 56% | 12% | 90.5 | 32 | 22 | 46 | 36% | 80% | 10% | 0 | 20 | | | 93 | 0.50 | 2.8 | 101 | 120 | $8 |
| 15 | | | | | | | | | | | | | | | | | | | | | | | | | | | | | | | | | | |
| 16 | 2 AL * | 2 | 20 | 57 | 58 | 3.89 | 3.31 | 1.21 | 707 | 701 | 712 | 4.2 | 3.4 | 9.1 | 2.7 | 60% | 11% | 92.2 | 48 | 13 | 38 | 29% | 70% | 5% | 0 | 20 | | | 91 | 1.26 | 2.1 | 93 | 110 | $8 |
| 17 | LAA | 3 | 8 | 67 | 86 | 2.54 | 2.81 | 0.83 | 527 | 483 | 568 | 3.6 | 2.1 | 11.5 | 5.4 | 60% | 14% | 93.5 | 47 | 18 | 35 | 24% | 76% | 13% | 0 | 15 | | | 73 | 1.20 | 15.1 | 174 | 209 | $13 |
| 18 | LAA | 2 | 14 | 66 | 70 | 3.26 | 4.04 | 1.24 | 751 | 779 | 725 | 4.1 | 2.6 | 9.5 | 3.7 | 60% | 11% | 92.2 | 34 | 23 | 43 | 30% | 83% | 15% | 0 | 17 | | | 82 | 0.84 | 7.3 | 113 | 131 | $7 |
| 1st Half | | 1 | 9 | 40 | 47 | 3.12 | 3.80 | 1.17 | 702 | 805 | 612 | 4.2 | 2.9 | 10.5 | 3.6 | 59% | 13% | 92.6 | 30 | 25 | 45 | 30% | 80% | 13% | 0 | 17 | | | 82 | 0.97 | 5.1 | 119 | 137 | $10 |
| 2nd Half | | 1 | 5 | 26 | 23 | 3.46 | 4.43 | 1.35 | 819 | 743 | 886 | 4.1 | 2.1 | 8.0 | 3.8 | 61% | 9% | 91.5 | 38 | 21 | 41 | 31% | 86% | 18% | 0 | 18 | | | 83 | 0.66 | 2.2 | 103 | 118 | $3 |
| 19 | Proj | 2 | 9 | 65 | 70 | 3.91 | 3.62 | 1.26 | 745 | 725 | 763 | 4.0 | 2.7 | 9.6 | 3.6 | 60% | 12% | 92.6 | 38 | 22 | 41 | 32% | 74% | 14% | 0 | | | | | | 1.9 | 116 | 133 | $4 |

### Paulino,David

| | | | | | | | |
|---|---|---|---|---|---|---|---|
| Age: 25 | Th: R | Role | RP | Health | C | LIMA Plan | A |
| | | | | PT/Exp | D | Rand Var | +1 |
| Ht: 6' 7" | Wt: 222 | Type | Pwr | Consist | B | MM | 2301 |

1-0, 1.35 ERA in 7 IP at TOR. How a prospect's pedigree goes sideways: 80-game PED suspension (July 2017), surgery to remove bone spurs in his elbow (Sept 2017), multiple DL stints for shoulder issues (2018). Four plus pitches preserve the upside but needs to stay on the mound to reach it.

| Yr | Tm | W | Sv | IP | K | ERA | xERA | WHIP | oOPS | vL | vR | BF/G | Ctl | Dom | Cmd | FpK | SwK | Vel | G | L | F | H% | S% | hr/f | GS | APC | DOM% | DIS% | Sv% | LI | RAR | BPV | BPX | R$ |
|---|---|---|---|---|---|---|---|---|---|---|---|---|---|---|---|---|---|---|---|---|---|---|---|---|---|---|---|---|---|---|---|---|---|---|
| 14 | | | | | | | | | | | | | | | | | | | | | | | | | | | | | | | | | | |
| 15 | | | | | | | | | | | | | | | | | | | | | | | | | | | | | | | | | | |
| 16 | HOU * | 5 | 1 | 85 | 85 | 2.76 | 2.81 | 1.13 | 665 | 770 | 393 | 16.8 | 2.0 | 9.0 | 4.4 | 59% | 6% | 92.1 | 43 | 13 | 43 | 32% | 76% | 0% | 1 | 42 | 0% | 100% | 100 | 0.36 | 15.0 | 140 | 167 | $8 |
| 17 | HOU | 2 | 0 | 29 | 34 | 6.52 | 4.30 | 1.48 | 914 | 843 | 984 | 21.3 | 2.2 | 10.6 | 4.9 | 59% | 11% | 92.6 | 30 | 19 | 51 | 37% | 63% | 19% | 6 | 88 | 0% | 33% | | | -7.7 | 139 | 167 | -$6 |
| 18 | TOR * | 1 | 0 | 25 | 25 | 4.30 | 4.01 | 1.19 | 686 | 626 | 728 | 9.0 | 2.4 | 9.2 | 3.9 | 61% | 9% | 93.1 | 50 | 10 | 40 | 30% | 69% | 13% | 0 | 18 | | | 0 | 0.15 | -0.4 | 101 | 116 | -$4 |
| 1st Half | | 0 | 0 | 18 | 19 | 5.39 | 4.03 | 1.18 | | | | 18.0 | 2.3 | 9.6 | 4.3 | | | | | | | 31% | 57% | 0% | 0 | | | | | | -2.8 | 111 | 127 | -$5 |
| 2nd Half | | 1 | 0 | 7 | 6 | 1.35 | 4.22 | 1.20 | 686 | 626 | 728 | 4.0 | 2.7 | 8.1 | 3.0 | 61% | 9% | 93.1 | 50 | 10 | 40 | 28% | 100% | 13% | 0 | 18 | | | 0 | 0.15 | 2.3 | 101 | 116 | $1 |
| 19 | Proj | 3 | 0 | 116 | 114 | 4.01 | 3.64 | 1.22 | | | | 17.8 | 2.6 | 8.8 | 3.4 | 61% | 10% | | 42 | 20 | 38 | 31% | 70% | 11% | 20 | | | | | | 7.2 | 108 | 125 | $3 |

### Paxton,James

| | | | | | | | |
|---|---|---|---|---|---|---|---|
| Age: 30 | Th: L | Role | SP | Health | F | LIMA Plan | C+ |
| | | | | PT/Exp | B | Rand Var | +2 |
| Ht: 6' 4" | Wt: 235 | Type | Pwr | Consist | A | MM | 4403 |

Another year marred by multiple DL stints (back stiffness, left forearm contusion); at least the injuries were minor this time. Again showcased ace-like skills when on the mound, spiking Cmd as driver of career-best BPV and xERA. Pay for another brilliant 150 IP, no more.

| Yr | Tm | W | Sv | IP | K | ERA | xERA | WHIP | oOPS | vL | vR | BF/G | Ctl | Dom | Cmd | FpK | SwK | Vel | G | L | F | H% | S% | hr/f | GS | APC | DOM% | DIS% | Sv% | LI | RAR | BPV | BPX | R$ |
|---|---|---|---|---|---|---|---|---|---|---|---|---|---|---|---|---|---|---|---|---|---|---|---|---|---|---|---|---|---|---|---|---|---|---|
| 14 | SEA | 6 | 0 | 74 | 59 | 3.04 | 3.50 | 1.20 | 612 | 527 | 629 | 23.3 | 3.5 | 7.2 | 2.0 | 54% | 8% | 94.8 | 55 | 23 | 23 | 28% | 74% | 6% | 13 | 91 | 23% | 8% | | | 6.4 | 67 | 80 | $4 |
| 15 | SEA | 3 | 0 | 67 | 56 | 3.90 | 4.47 | 1.43 | 704 | 1054 | 606 | 22.8 | 3.9 | 7.5 | 1.9 | 53% | 7% | 94.2 | 48 | 17 | 34 | 31% | 76% | 11% | 13 | 85 | 15% | 38% | | | 0.5 | 56 | 67 | -$3 |
| 16 | SEA * | 10 | 0 | 172 | 159 | 4.06 | 4.19 | 1.33 | 717 | 733 | 714 | 23.0 | 2.1 | 8.3 | 4.0 | 62% | 12% | 96.8 | 48 | 22 | 30 | 35% | 71% | 8% | 20 | 98 | 30% | 15% | | | 2.7 | 107 | 127 | $6 |
| 17 | SEA | 12 | 0 | 136 | 156 | 2.98 | 3.38 | 1.10 | 602 | 463 | 630 | 23.0 | 2.4 | 10.3 | 4.2 | 65% | 13% | 95.4 | 45 | 22 | 33 | 31% | 74% | 8% | 24 | 95 | 54% | 21% | | | 23.2 | 143 | 171 | $19 |
| 18 | SEA | 11 | 0 | 160 | 208 | 3.76 | 3.22 | 1.10 | 662 | 874 | 617 | 23.0 | 2.4 | 11.7 | 5.0 | 66% | 15% | 95.4 | 40 | 19 | 41 | 31% | 71% | 14% | 28 | 93 | 32% | 18% | | | 7.7 | 165 | 189 | $16 |
| 1st Half | | 7 | 0 | 104 | 134 | 3.65 | 3.30 | 1.11 | 654 | 943 | 585 | 24.6 | 2.6 | 11.6 | 4.5 | 64% | 14% | 95.5 | 38 | 21 | 41 | 31% | 72% | 13% | 17 | 100 | 41% | 18% | | | 6.4 | 155 | 178 | $21 |
| 2nd Half | | 4 | 0 | 57 | 74 | 3.97 | 3.08 | 1.08 | 675 | 690 | 673 | 20.5 | 1.9 | 11.8 | 6.2 | 71% | 17% | 95.2 | 43 | 15 | 42 | 31% | 71% | 18% | 11 | 81 | 18% | 18% | | | 1.3 | 181 | 208 | $7 |
| 19 | Proj | 13 | 0 | 152 | 176 | 3.44 | 3.09 | 1.13 | 645 | 702 | 633 | 21.9 | 2.4 | 10.4 | 4.4 | 65% | 14% | 95.5 | 44 | 20 | 36 | 31% | 73% | 12% | 28 | | | | | | 23.0 | 145 | 167 | $17 |

### Pazos,James

| | | | | | | | |
|---|---|---|---|---|---|---|---|
| Age: 28 | Th: L | Role | RP | Health | A | LIMA Plan | B+ |
| | | | | PT/Exp | D | Rand Var | -3 |
| Ht: 6' 2" | Wt: 235 | Type | Pwr | Consist | B | MM | 2300 |

Found an answer vR and appeared on his way to a breakout with a strong 1st half BPX. While there was no report of injury, the sudden steep declines in FpK/SwK and velocity that befell him in 2nd half are worrisome and cloud his 2019 outlook. If healthy, could again notch Holds, but this is a pedestrian skill set.

| Yr | Tm | W | Sv | IP | K | ERA | xERA | WHIP | oOPS | vL | vR | BF/G | Ctl | Dom | Cmd | FpK | SwK | Vel | G | L | F | H% | S% | hr/f | GS | APC | DOM% | DIS% | Sv% | LI | RAR | BPV | BPX | R$ |
|---|---|---|---|---|---|---|---|---|---|---|---|---|---|---|---|---|---|---|---|---|---|---|---|---|---|---|---|---|---|---|---|---|---|---|
| 14 | aa | 0 | 6 | 42 | 36 | 1.77 | 2.26 | 1.22 | | | | 6.1 | 4.1 | 7.8 | 1.9 | | | | | | | 28% | 84% | | | | | | | | 10.2 | 99 | 117 | $3 |
| 15 | NYY * | 3 | 3 | 48 | 44 | 1.55 | 2.67 | 1.23 | 476 | 606 | 250 | 5.1 | 3.7 | 8.4 | 2.3 | 43% | 6% | 93.8 | 43 | 14 | 43 | 29% | 88% | 0% | 0 | 8 | | | 75 | 0.44 | 14.2 | 100 | 119 | $5 |
| 16 | NYY * | 3 | 1 | 31 | 37 | 4.84 | 5.25 | 1.75 | 1408 | 1250 | 1569 | 4.7 | 6.6 | 10.8 | 1.7 | 53% | 12% | 95.4 | 46 | 23 | 31 | 36% | 74% | 50% | 0 | 8 | | | 50 | 0.46 | -2.5 | 70 | 84 | -$4 |
| 17 | SEA | 4 | 0 | 54 | 65 | 3.86 | 3.61 | 1.40 | 723 | 561 | 821 | 4.1 | 4.0 | 10.9 | 2.7 | 63% | 13% | 95.5 | 51 | 22 | 27 | 34% | 76% | 18% | 0 | 16 | | | 0 | 1.11 | 3.3 | 117 | 140 | $0 |
| 18 | SEA | 4 | 0 | 50 | 45 | 2.88 | 3.97 | 1.24 | 686 | 800 | 609 | 3.5 | 2.7 | 8.1 | 3.0 | 56% | 10% | 93.7 | 45 | 21 | 34 | 31% | 79% | 8% | 0 | 13 | | | 0 | 1.05 | 7.8 | 96 | 110 | $1 |
| 1st Half | | 2 | 0 | 29 | 27 | 1.84 | 3.27 | 0.99 | 618 | 625 | 613 | 3.4 | 1.2 | 8.3 | 6.8 | 61% | 11% | 94.5 | 41 | 28 | 31 | 30% | 82% | 4% | 0 | 13 | | | 0 | 1.14 | 8.4 | 135 | 155 | $4 |
| 2nd Half | | 2 | 0 | 21 | 18 | 4.35 | 5.02 | 1.60 | 773 | 1023 | 604 | 3.7 | 4.8 | 7.8 | 1.6 | 49% | 8% | 92.7 | 50 | 13 | 38 | 32% | 77% | 13% | 0 | 14 | | | 0 | 0.93 | -0.5 | 40 | 46 | -$3 |
| 19 | Proj | 4 | 0 | 51 | 52 | 3.68 | 3.64 | 1.35 | 704 | 736 | 683 | 3.8 | 3.5 | 9.2 | 2.6 | 58% | 11% | 94.3 | 48 | 20 | 32 | 32% | 75% | 12% | 0 | | | | | | 3.3 | 96 | 111 | $0 |

### Peacock,Brad

| | | | | | | | |
|---|---|---|---|---|---|---|---|
| Age: 31 | Th: R | Role | RP | Health | D | LIMA Plan | A |
| | | | | PT/Exp | C | Rand Var | +4 |
| Ht: 6' 1" | Wt: 210 | Type | Pwr FB | Consist | C | MM | 4511 |

Missed about two weeks in Sept with Hand, Foot and Mouth disease. Move to full-time bullpen role suited him well as skills reached elite status. Surface stats tanked in 2nd half (thank you, 41% hit rate, 22% hr/f), but BPX and xERA remained in fine shape. Should continue to supply lots of strikeouts and ERA/WHIP help.

| Yr | Tm | W | Sv | IP | K | ERA | xERA | WHIP | oOPS | vL | vR | BF/G | Ctl | Dom | Cmd | FpK | SwK | Vel | G | L | F | H% | S% | hr/f | GS | APC | DOM% | DIS% | Sv% | LI | RAR | BPV | BPX | R$ |
|---|---|---|---|---|---|---|---|---|---|---|---|---|---|---|---|---|---|---|---|---|---|---|---|---|---|---|---|---|---|---|---|---|---|---|
| 14 | HOU | 4 | 0 | 132 | 119 | 4.72 | 4.59 | 1.56 | 801 | 793 | 811 | 21.0 | 4.8 | 8.1 | 1.7 | 57% | 9% | 92.1 | 37 | 21 | 42 | 31% | 74% | 12% | 24 | 85 | 13% | 46% | 0 | 0.81 | -15.8 | 32 | 38 | -$9 |
| 15 | HOU | 0 | 0 | 5 | 3 | 5.40 | 5.05 | 1.40 | 808 | 1167 | 422 | 22.0 | 3.6 | 5.4 | 1.5 | 68% | 6% | 89.9 | 31 | 31 | 38 | 31% | 57% | 0% | 1 | 85 | 0% | 100% | | | -0.9 | 9 | 11 | -$5 |
| 16 | HOU * | 5 | 0 | 149 | 123 | 5.13 | 5.27 | 1.55 | 700 | 718 | 686 | 20.3 | 3.5 | 7.4 | 2.2 | 58% | 9% | 91.8 | 41 | 9 | 49 | 34% | 69% | 14% | 5 | 49 | 20% | 60% | 0 | 0.40 | -17.3 | 52 | 62 | -$9 |
| 17 | HOU | 13 | 0 | 132 | 161 | 3.00 | 3.72 | 1.19 | 615 | 759 | 501 | 16.1 | 3.9 | 11.0 | 2.8 | 63% | 12% | 92.1 | 44 | 19 | 38 | 30% | 77% | 8% | 21 | 66 | 24% | 14% | 0 | 0.68 | 22.1 | 115 | 138 | $17 |
| 18 | HOU | 3 | 3 | 65 | 96 | 3.46 | 3.04 | 1.17 | 722 | 953 | 587 | 4.5 | 2.8 | 13.3 | 4.8 | 63% | 14% | 92.7 | 38 | 22 | 40 | 34% | 78% | 18% | 1 | 19 | 0% | 100% | 50 | 0.88 | 5.5 | 180 | 208 | $4 |
| 1st Half | | 1 | 1 | 35 | 50 | 2.06 | 2.91 | 0.89 | 567 | 801 | 383 | 4.2 | 2.1 | 12.9 | 6.3 | 64% | 14% | 93.2 | 37 | 20 | 43 | 27% | 88% | 15% | 0 | 18 | | | 33 | 1.13 | 9.0 | 191 | 219 | $8 |
| 2nd Half | | 2 | 2 | 30 | 46 | 5.10 | 3.18 | 1.50 | 891 | 1204 | 763 | 4.7 | 3.6 | 13.8 | 3.8 | 61% | 13% | 92.3 | 38 | 25 | 37 | 41% | 72% | 22% | 1 | 20 | 0% | 100% | 67 | 0.59 | -3.5 | 168 | 192 | -$1 |
| 19 | Proj | 4 | 2 | 73 | 97 | 3.44 | 3.10 | 1.19 | 673 | 799 | 586 | 6.8 | 3.3 | 12.0 | 3.6 | 62% | 13% | 92.4 | 40 | 20 | 41 | 32% | 75% | 12% | 0 | | | | | | 12.5 | 144 | 165 | $5 |

GREG PYRON

### Pena,Felix

| Age: 29 | Th: R | Role: RP | Health | A | LIMA Plan | B+ |
|---|---|---|---|---|---|---|
| Ht: 6' 2" | Wt: 185 | Type: Pwr FB | PT/Exp | D | Rand Var | +1 |
| | | | Consist | F | MM | 2201 |

3-5, 4.18 ERA in 93 IP at LAA. RP turned SP, flashed promise. Heavily reduced four-seam FB usage, opting for new sinker 50% of the time and a highly effective slider (20% SwK), which resulted in still-solid Dom and a sharp reduction in FB%. There's sleeper potential here, especially in deep leagues.

| Yr Tm | W | Sv | IP | K | ERA | xERA | WHIP | oOPS | vL | vR | BF/G | Ctl | Dom | Cmd | FpK | SwK | Vel | G | L | F | H% | S% | hr/f | GS | APC | DOM% | DIS% | Sv% | LI | RAR | BPV | BPX | R$ |
|---|---|---|---|---|---|---|---|---|---|---|---|---|---|---|---|---|---|---|---|---|---|---|---|---|---|---|---|---|---|---|---|---|---|
| 14 aa | 2 | 0 | 28 | 22 | 8.53 | 6.72 | 1.85 | | | | 21.6 | 5.6 | 7.2 | 1.3 | | | | | | | 34% | 54% | | | | | | | | -16.3 | 14 | 16 | -$9 |
| 15 aa | 7 | 0 | 130 | 116 | 4.58 | 4.18 | 1.41 | | | | 22.0 | 3.6 | 8.0 | 2.2 | | | | | | | 32% | 68% | | | | | | | | -9.9 | 73 | 87 | -$3 |
| 16 CHC * | 3 | 4 | 72 | 79 | 3.87 | 2.82 | 1.17 | 479 | 286 | 511 | 6.1 | 3.3 | 9.8 | 2.9 | 60% | 17% | 93.5 | 39 | 17 | 44 | 30% | 67% | 13% | 0 | 12 | | | 80 | 1.00 | 2.9 | 112 | 133 | $4 |
| 17 CHC * | 3 | 6 | 73 | 73 | 6.08 | 6.13 | 1.63 | 866 | 796 | 922 | 6.7 | 4.1 | 8.9 | 2.2 | 49% | 12% | 94.3 | 35 | 14 | 51 | 35% | 67% | 16% | 0 | 24 | | | 50 | 0.34 | -15.6 | 41 | 49 | -$6 |
| 18 LAA * | 4 | 0 | 127 | 114 | 3.98 | 3.96 | 1.29 | 699 | 780 | 618 | 18.0 | 3.1 | 8.1 | 2.7 | 62% | 11% | 92.4 | 43 | 24 | 33 | 30% | 72% | 13% | 17 | 74 | 18% | 12% | 0 | 0.71 | 2.7 | 80 | 92 | $2 |
| 1st Half | 2 | 0 | 51 | 48 | 3.53 | 4.47 | 1.43 | 796 | 955 | 686 | 14.5 | 3.5 | 8.5 | 2.4 | 65% | 14% | 92.9 | 50 | 18 | 32 | 34% | 78% | 19% | 3 | 56 | 33% | 0% | 0 | 0.53 | 3.9 | 77 | 89 | -$3 |
| 2nd Half | 2 | 0 | 76 | 66 | 4.28 | 4.09 | 1.19 | 675 | 747 | 598 | 22.4 | 2.7 | 7.9 | 2.9 | 61% | 10% | 92.3 | 41 | 25 | 34 | 28% | 67% | 12% | 14 | 81 | 14% | 14% | | | -1.2 | 86 | 99 | $5 |
| **19 Proj** | **4** | **0** | **102** | **97** | **3.94** | **3.89** | **1.28** | **710** | **740** | **682** | **16.4** | **3.0** | **8.6** | **2.9** | **60%** | **12%** | **93.2** | **41** | **19** | **40** | **30%** | **74%** | **12%** | **16** | | | | | | **2.7** | **93** | **107** | **$2** |

### Peralta,Freddy

| Age: 23 | Th: R | Role: RP | Health | A | LIMA Plan | B+ |
|---|---|---|---|---|---|---|
| Ht: 5' 11" | Wt: 175 | Type: Pwr xFB | PT/Exp | D | Rand Var | +1 |
| | | | Consist | A | MM | 1503 |

6-4, 4.25 ERA in 78 IP at MIL. Racked up lots of strikeouts, despite no real dynamite offering. Deceptive delivery helped four-seam FB (77% usage!) play up, but batters seemed to begin to adjust in 2nd half. Poor Ctl, extreme FB% and issues vL add to risk. Jury is still out, both on long-term role and ceiling.

| Yr Tm | W | Sv | IP | K | ERA | xERA | WHIP | oOPS | vL | vR | BF/G | Ctl | Dom | Cmd | FpK | SwK | Vel | G | L | F | H% | S% | hr/f | GS | APC | DOM% | DIS% | Sv% | LI | RAR | BPV | BPX | R$ |
|---|---|---|---|---|---|---|---|---|---|---|---|---|---|---|---|---|---|---|---|---|---|---|---|---|---|---|---|---|---|---|---|---|---|
| 14 | | | | | | | | | | | | | | | | | | | | | | | | | | | | | | | | | |
| 15 | | | | | | | | | | | | | | | | | | | | | | | | | | | | | | | | | |
| 16 | | | | | | | | | | | | | | | | | | | | | | | | | | | | | | | | | |
| 17 aa | 2 | 1 | 64 | 81 | 3.42 | 2.84 | 1.30 | | | | 20.2 | 4.9 | 11.4 | 2.3 | | | | | | | 31% | 73% | | | | | | | | 7.3 | 118 | 141 | $2 |
| 18 MIL * | 12 | 0 | 139 | 173 | 3.72 | 2.61 | 1.18 | 622 | 864 | 396 | 19.2 | 4.2 | 11.2 | 2.6 | 58% | 12% | 90.8 | 31 | 18 | 52 | 29% | 69% | 9% | 14 | 86 | 29% | 14% | 0 | 0.75 | 7.5 | 120 | 138 | $12 |
| 1st Half | 9 | 0 | 82 | 109 | 2.38 | 1.77 | 1.06 | 351 | 499 | 167 | 19.8 | 3.7 | 12.0 | 3.3 | 56% | 15% | 91.3 | 33 | 18 | 49 | 30% | 77% | 5% | 4 | 95 | 75% | 0% | | | 17.8 | 152 | 174 | $25 |
| 2nd Half | 3 | 0 | 58 | 64 | 5.61 | 3.81 | 1.35 | 721 | 1027 | 465 | 18.5 | 5.0 | 9.9 | 2.0 | 59% | 10% | 90.6 | 30 | 17 | 53 | 28% | 59% | 10% | 10 | 83 | 10% | 20% | 0 | 0.72 | -10.4 | 80 | 91 | -$6 |
| **19 Proj** | **7** | **0** | **145** | **173** | **4.30** | **4.04** | **1.30** | **723** | **1004** | **450** | **19.7** | **4.6** | **10.8** | **2.3** | **58%** | **12%** | **90.8** | **31** | **18** | **51** | **29%** | **70%** | **10%** | **29** | | | | | | **-2.7** | **78** | **89** | **$5** |

### Peralta,Wily

| Age: 30 | Th: R | Role: RP | Health | D | LIMA Plan | D+ |
|---|---|---|---|---|---|---|
| Ht: 6' 1" | Wt: 255 | Type: Pwr | PT/Exp | D | Rand Var | +1 |
| | | | Consist | A | MM | 0210 |

14 Sv, 3.67 ERA in 34 IP at KC. Starter-turned-reliever began season in the minors, but was anointed to MLB closer gig in late June. Don't be fooled by the pristine Sv%. These horrid skills (Ctl, BPX, xERA) don't belong anywhere near that role. Stay far away, especially if he benefits from March proclamations.

| Yr Tm | W | Sv | IP | K | ERA | xERA | WHIP | oOPS | vL | vR | BF/G | Ctl | Dom | Cmd | FpK | SwK | Vel | G | L | F | H% | S% | hr/f | GS | APC | DOM% | DIS% | Sv% | LI | RAR | BPV | BPX | R$ |
|---|---|---|---|---|---|---|---|---|---|---|---|---|---|---|---|---|---|---|---|---|---|---|---|---|---|---|---|---|---|---|---|---|---|
| 14 MIL | 17 | 0 | 199 | 154 | 3.53 | 3.62 | 1.30 | 714 | 820 | 606 | 26.2 | 2.8 | 7.0 | 2.5 | 58% | 9% | 95.8 | 54 | 19 | 28 | 30% | 77% | 14% | 32 | 100 | 28% | 31% | | | 5.1 | 83 | 99 | $9 |
| 15 MIL | 5 | 0 | 109 | 60 | 4.72 | 4.67 | 1.54 | 844 | 889 | 796 | 23.9 | 3.1 | 5.0 | 1.6 | 57% | 7% | 94.3 | 52 | 20 | 28 | 32% | 72% | 13% | 20 | 88 | 10% | 55% | | | -10.2 | 37 | 44 | -$8 |
| 16 MIL * | 8 | 0 | 169 | 124 | 5.47 | 5.98 | 1.64 | 855 | 880 | 832 | 22.8 | 3.2 | 6.6 | 2.0 | 56% | 9% | 94.8 | 50 | 23 | 27 | 35% | 69% | 17% | 23 | 93 | 13% | 57% | | | -26.6 | 35 | 42 | -$14 |
| 17 MIL * | 6 | 1 | 73 | 60 | 7.01 | 6.09 | 1.79 | 947 | 1030 | 874 | 10.6 | 5.2 | 7.3 | 1.4 | 64% | 9% | 96.0 | 45 | 22 | 34 | 35% | 61% | 16% | 8 | 59 | 25% | 50% | 50 | 0.74 | -23.9 | 32 | 38 | -$12 |
| 18 KC * | 1 | 15 | 69 | 63 | 4.91 | 5.59 | 1.77 | 737 | 687 | 791 | 5.8 | 6.1 | 8.2 | 1.3 | 62% | 10% | 96.2 | 46 | 19 | 35 | 34% | 74% | 13% | 0 | 16 | | | 100 | 0.82 | -6.5 | 47 | 55 | -$5 |
| 1st Half | 0 | 3 | 40 | 34 | 5.63 | 6.49 | 1.99 | 538 | 429 | 558 | 8.3 | 6.4 | 7.7 | 1.2 | 75% | 12% | 96.7 | 44 | 11 | 44 | 38% | 72% | 0% | 0 | 17 | | | 100 | 1.37 | -7.2 | 41 | 47 | -$14 |
| 2nd Half | 1 | 12 | 30 | 29 | 3.94 | 4.64 | 1.48 | 767 | 702 | 850 | 4.0 | 5.8 | 8.8 | 1.5 | 60% | 10% | 96.1 | 46 | 20 | 34 | 28% | 78% | 15% | 0 | 16 | | | 100 | 0.73 | 0.8 | 27 | 31 | $8 |
| **19 Proj** | **3** | **10** | **58** | **49** | **4.84** | **4.71** | **1.68** | **848** | **863** | **833** | **7.6** | **5.1** | **7.6** | **1.5** | **59%** | **9%** | **95.5** | **48** | **21** | **31** | **33%** | **73%** | **13%** | **0** | | | | | | **-4.9** | **26** | **30** | **-$3** |

### Perez,Martin

| Age: 28 | Th: L | Role: SP | Health | F | LIMA Plan | D+ |
|---|---|---|---|---|---|---|
| Ht: 6' 0" | Wt: 200 | Type: GB | PT/Exp | A | Rand Var | +5 |
| | | | Consist | A | MM | 0001 |

Missed most of 1st half due to complications following off-season surgery on non-throwing elbow. The on-field results continued to go in the wrong direction. He hasn't produced positive R$ since 2013. Pitiful BPX and rising xERA trend say that he should be handled only with a hazmat suit.

| Yr Tm | W | Sv | IP | K | ERA | xERA | WHIP | oOPS | vL | vR | BF/G | Ctl | Dom | Cmd | FpK | SwK | Vel | G | L | F | H% | S% | hr/f | GS | APC | DOM% | DIS% | Sv% | LI | RAR | BPV | BPX | R$ |
|---|---|---|---|---|---|---|---|---|---|---|---|---|---|---|---|---|---|---|---|---|---|---|---|---|---|---|---|---|---|---|---|---|---|
| 14 TEX | 4 | 0 | 51 | 35 | 4.38 | 3.73 | 1.34 | 743 | 707 | 753 | 25.9 | 3.3 | 6.1 | 1.8 | 60% | 8% | 90.3 | 53 | 23 | 25 | 30% | 67% | 8% | 8 | 97 | 13% | 38% | | | -4.1 | 52 | 61 | -$2 |
| 15 TEX * | 3 | 0 | 104 | 68 | 4.73 | 4.69 | 1.49 | 729 | 537 | 777 | 22.5 | 2.3 | 5.9 | 2.5 | 65% | 8% | 91.8 | 60 | 18 | 22 | 35% | 67% | 5% | 14 | 87 | 21% | 50% | | | -9.9 | 66 | 79 | -$8 |
| 16 TEX | 10 | 0 | 199 | 103 | 4.39 | 4.84 | 1.41 | 741 | 537 | 786 | 25.9 | 3.4 | 4.7 | 1.4 | 64% | 8% | 92.7 | 53 | 20 | 26 | 29% | 70% | 10% | 33 | 93 | 12% | 48% | | | -5.0 | 22 | 26 | -$1 |
| 17 TEX | 13 | 0 | 185 | 115 | 4.82 | 4.89 | 1.54 | 812 | 666 | 849 | 25.3 | 3.1 | 5.6 | 1.8 | 59% | 7% | 93.1 | 47 | 25 | 28 | 33% | 71% | 13% | 32 | 97 | 9% | 66% | | | -10.5 | 43 | 52 | -$4 |
| 18 TEX | 2 | 0 | 85 | 52 | 6.22 | 5.25 | 1.78 | 916 | 746 | 966 | 18.0 | 3.8 | 5.5 | 1.4 | 59% | 7% | 92.7 | 51 | 20 | 29 | 35% | 68% | 18% | 15 | 64 | 0% | 73% | 0 | 0.83 | -21.8 | 25 | 29 | -$17 |
| 1st Half | 2 | 0 | 22 | 13 | 9.67 | 6.57 | 2.37 | 1132 | 830 | 1213 | 23.8 | 4.8 | 5.2 | 1.1 | 55% | 5% | 91.8 | 48 | 18 | 34 | 40% | 63% | 23% | 5 | 83 | 0% | 80% | | | -15.2 | -10 | -11 | -$26 |
| 2nd Half | 0 | 0 | 63 | 39 | 5.00 | 4.79 | 1.57 | 825 | 714 | 858 | 16.4 | 3.4 | 5.6 | 1.6 | 61% | 8% | 93.1 | 52 | 21 | 27 | 32% | 71% | 16% | 10 | 58 | 0% | 70% | 0 | 0.86 | -6.6 | 38 | 43 | -$14 |
| **19 Proj** | **6** | **0** | **116** | **70** | **5.13** | **4.74** | **1.61** | **837** | **673** | **881** | **21.0** | **3.6** | **5.4** | **1.5** | **60%** | **7%** | **92.6** | **51** | **21** | **28** | **33%** | **71%** | **15%** | **25** | | | | | | **-5.1** | **30** | **35** | **-$10** |

### Perez,Oliver

| Age: 37 | Th: L | Role: RP | Health | A | LIMA Plan | A |
|---|---|---|---|---|---|---|
| Ht: 6' 3" | Wt: 225 | Type: Pwr | PT/Exp | D | Rand Var | -5 |
| | | | Consist | B | MM | 5500 |

Signed with CLE on June 2 and enjoyed terrific season, including career-best ERA/xERA/BPX. Pounded strike zone while paring down pitch mix to essentially four-seam FB and nasty slider (20% SwK). Expect some obvious pullback (37 year-olds don't repeat sub-1.50 ERAs), but he figures to remain effective a little longer.

| Yr Tm | W | Sv | IP | K | ERA | xERA | WHIP | oOPS | vL | vR | BF/G | Ctl | Dom | Cmd | FpK | SwK | Vel | G | L | F | H% | S% | hr/f | GS | APC | DOM% | DIS% | Sv% | LI | RAR | BPV | BPX | R$ |
|---|---|---|---|---|---|---|---|---|---|---|---|---|---|---|---|---|---|---|---|---|---|---|---|---|---|---|---|---|---|---|---|---|---|
| 14 ARI | 3 | 0 | 59 | 76 | 2.91 | 3.03 | 1.26 | 679 | 780 | 602 | 3.8 | 3.7 | 11.7 | 3.2 | 62% | 13% | 91.3 | 44 | 22 | 34 | 33% | 80% | 10% | 0 | 15 | | | 0 | 1.09 | 6.0 | 132 | 158 | $2 |
| 15 2 TM | 2 | 0 | 41 | 51 | 4.17 | 3.61 | 1.32 | 681 | 517 | 881 | 2.6 | 3.3 | 11.2 | 3.4 | 66% | 13% | 91.9 | 36 | 24 | 40 | 35% | 70% | 9% | 0 | 10 | | | 0 | 1.11 | -1.1 | 127 | 151 | -$2 |
| 16 WAS | 2 | 0 | 40 | 46 | 4.95 | 4.19 | 1.45 | 751 | 720 | 790 | 2.8 | 4.5 | 10.4 | 2.3 | 54% | 10% | 91.7 | 39 | 23 | 38 | 34% | 67% | 10% | 0 | 11 | | | 0 | 1.03 | -3.8 | 82 | 97 | -$4 |
| 17 WAS | 0 | 1 | 33 | 39 | 4.64 | 4.26 | 1.33 | 772 | 665 | 888 | 2.9 | 3.3 | 10.6 | 3.3 | 64% | 11% | 93.0 | 33 | 18 | 49 | 34% | 68% | 9% | 0 | 12 | | | 100 | 1.06 | -1.1 | 114 | 137 | -$3 |
| 18 CLE | 1 | 0 | 32 | 43 | 1.39 | 2.57 | 0.74 | 417 | 490 | 322 | 2.4 | 1.9 | 12.0 | 6.1 | 64% | 16% | 91.7 | 41 | 24 | 35 | 25% | 83% | 4% | 0 | 9 | | | 0 | 0.93 | 11.0 | 182 | 209 | $4 |
| 1st Half | 0 | 0 | 10 | 11 | 0.90 | 3.05 | 0.60 | 314 | 368 | 243 | 2.8 | 1.8 | 9.9 | 5.5 | 58% | 14% | 91.6 | 39 | 22 | 39 | 19% | 83% | 0% | 0 | 9 | | | 0 | 0.78 | 4.0 | 147 | 169 | -$3 |
| 2nd Half | 1 | 0 | 22 | 32 | 1.61 | 2.36 | 0.81 | 462 | 541 | 358 | 2.3 | 2.0 | 12.9 | 6.4 | 67% | 17% | 91.8 | 42 | 24 | 33 | 28% | 82% | 7% | 0 | 9 | | | 0 | 0.99 | 7.0 | 198 | 227 | $6 |
| **19 Proj** | **2** | **0** | **44** | **55** | **3.36** | **2.97** | **1.08** | **623** | **600** | **650** | **2.5** | **2.6** | **11.4** | **4.4** | **62%** | **13%** | **92.0** | **39** | **22** | **39** | **31%** | **71%** | **9%** | **0** | | | | | | **8.1** | **152** | **174** | **$1** |

### Petit,Yusmeiro

| Age: 34 | Th: R | Role: RP | Health | A | LIMA Plan | B+ |
|---|---|---|---|---|---|---|
| Ht: 6' 1" | Wt: 255 | Type: xFB | PT/Exp | C | Rand Var | -3 |
| | | | Consist | B | MM | 2201 |

Another year of quality middle relief work despite some skills erosion. Vastly upgraded cutter was the driving force behind 2017 SwK/Dom growth, but it didn't draw nearly as many whiffs in 2018 (2017: 16% SwK; 2018: 6% SwK). Heed warning signs of wide xERA/ERA gap from 2017-18.

| Yr Tm | W | Sv | IP | K | ERA | xERA | WHIP | oOPS | vL | vR | BF/G | Ctl | Dom | Cmd | FpK | SwK | Vel | G | L | F | H% | S% | hr/f | GS | APC | DOM% | DIS% | Sv% | LI | RAR | BPV | BPX | R$ |
|---|---|---|---|---|---|---|---|---|---|---|---|---|---|---|---|---|---|---|---|---|---|---|---|---|---|---|---|---|---|---|---|---|---|
| 14 SF | 5 | 0 | 117 | 133 | 3.69 | 3.03 | 1.02 | 635 | 777 | 510 | 11.8 | 1.7 | 10.2 | 6.0 | 69% | 13% | 88.9 | 36 | 21 | 43 | 30% | 66% | 9% | 12 | 43 | 17% | 17% | 0 | 0.52 | 0.7 | 152 | 182 | $8 |
| 15 SF | 1 | 1 | 76 | 59 | 3.67 | 4.34 | 1.18 | 743 | 828 | 680 | 7.5 | 1.8 | 7.0 | 3.9 | 62% | 10% | 88.5 | 33 | 21 | 46 | 29% | 75% | 10% | 1 | 27 | 0% | 100% | 100 | 0.84 | 2.7 | 89 | 106 | $1 |
| 16 WAS | 3 | 1 | 62 | 49 | 4.50 | 4.56 | 1.32 | 793 | 925 | 698 | 7.4 | 2.2 | 7.1 | 3.3 | 65% | 9% | 88.6 | 42 | 17 | 41 | 30% | 73% | 15% | 1 | 27 | 0% | 0% | 50 | 0.82 | -2.4 | 89 | 106 | -$2 |
| 17 LAA | 5 | 4 | 91 | 101 | 2.76 | 3.74 | 0.95 | 571 | 645 | 514 | 5.9 | 1.8 | 10.0 | 5.6 | 64% | 11% | 89.6 | 33 | 18 | 49 | 28% | 76% | 8% | 1 | 22 | 100% | 0% | 80 | 0.92 | 18.0 | 142 | 171 | $14 |
| 18 OAK | 7 | 0 | 93 | 76 | 3.00 | 4.22 | 1.01 | 649 | 611 | 679 | 5.0 | 1.7 | 7.4 | 4.2 | 65% | 9% | 89.3 | 36 | 20 | 44 | 25% | 78% | 11% | 0 | 18 | | | 0 | 1.06 | 13.2 | 99 | 114 | $10 |
| 1st Half | 2 | 0 | 47 | 31 | 3.66 | 4.47 | 1.16 | 686 | 615 | 738 | 5.0 | 1.5 | 6.0 | 3.9 | 63% | 10% | 88.9 | 41 | 20 | 39 | 28% | 73% | 11% | 0 | 17 | | | 0 | 1.26 | 2.8 | 85 | 97 | $0 |
| 2nd Half | 5 | 0 | 46 | 45 | 2.33 | 3.98 | 0.86 | 608 | 607 | 608 | 4.9 | 1.9 | 8.7 | 4.5 | 67% | 9% | 89.6 | 30 | 20 | 50 | 21% | 85% | 11% | 0 | 19 | | | 0 | 0.84 | 10.4 | 113 | 129 | $17 |
| **19 Proj** | **5** | **0** | **80** | **73** | **3.50** | **3.76** | **1.11** | **692** | **724** | **667** | **5.7** | **1.8** | **8.2** | **4.5** | **65%** | **10%** | **89.2** | **35** | **19** | **46** | **29%** | **74%** | **11%** | **0** | | | | | | **3.5** | **112** | **128** | **$5** |

### Petricka,Jacob

| Age: 31 | Th: R | Role: RP | Health | F | LIMA Plan | C |
|---|---|---|---|---|---|---|
| Ht: 6' 5" | Wt: 220 | Type: Pwr xGB | PT/Exp | D | Rand Var | -1 |
| | | | Consist | C | MM | 3210 |

3-1, 4.53 ERA in 46 IP at TOR. Injuries, most recently Oct 2017 nerve transposition surgery, have limited him recently. Small signs of life in 2nd half: Increased usage of revamped slider and velocity uptick yielded SwK gains and 100+ BPV in Aug/Sept. Still work to do vL, but there's a glimmer of hope overall.

| Yr Tm | W | Sv | IP | K | ERA | xERA | WHIP | oOPS | vL | vR | BF/G | Ctl | Dom | Cmd | FpK | SwK | Vel | G | L | F | H% | S% | hr/f | GS | APC | DOM% | DIS% | Sv% | LI | RAR | BPV | BPX | R$ |
|---|---|---|---|---|---|---|---|---|---|---|---|---|---|---|---|---|---|---|---|---|---|---|---|---|---|---|---|---|---|---|---|---|---|
| 14 CHW | 1 | 14 | 73 | 55 | 2.96 | 3.57 | 1.37 | 671 | 830 | 549 | 4.6 | 4.1 | 6.8 | 1.7 | 61% | 8% | 94.2 | 63 | 17 | 19 | 30% | 78% | 7% | 0 | 18 | | | 78 | 1.52 | 7.0 | 53 | 63 | $5 |
| 15 CHW | 4 | 2 | 52 | 33 | 3.63 | 3.77 | 1.42 | 716 | 851 | 666 | 3.5 | 3.1 | 5.7 | 1.8 | 65% | 9% | 94.1 | 65 | 18 | 17 | 32% | 74% | 7% | 0 | 13 | | | 67 | 1.16 | 2.1 | 62 | 73 | -$5 |
| 16 CHW | 0 | 0 | 8 | 7 | 4.50 | 5.54 | 2.00 | 854 | 650 | 886 | 4.3 | 9.0 | 7.9 | 0.9 | 54% | 8% | 94.2 | 70 | 9 | 22 | 31% | 80% | 20% | 0 | 17 | | | 0 | 1.04 | -0.3 | -53 | -63 | -$5 |
| 17 CHW | 1 | 0 | 26 | 26 | 7.01 | 4.10 | 1.75 | 947 | 928 | 959 | 4.5 | 2.1 | 9.1 | 4.3 | 62% | 7% | 94.2 | 47 | 26 | 27 | 42% | 64% | 25% | 0 | 18 | | | 0 | 0.94 | -8.4 | 132 | 159 | -$8 |
| 18 TOR * | 3 | 2 | 69 | 51 | 3.42 | 5.61 | 1.59 | 897 | 902 | 895 | 5.3 | 2.9 | 6.7 | 2.3 | 57% | 11% | 94.9 | 51 | 24 | 25 | 36% | 82% | 17% | 0 | 19 | | | 100 | 0.96 | 6.2 | 53 | 61 | -$3 |
| 1st Half | 0 | 2 | 28 | 15 | 2.56 | 6.59 | 1.76 | 1003 | 1067 | 967 | 5.9 | 2.2 | 4.9 | 2.2 | 51% | 8% | 93.2 | 57 | 24 | 19 | 39% | 88% | 14% | 0 | 20 | | | 100 | 0.47 | 5.5 | 39 | 44 | -$8 |
| 2nd Half | 3 | 0 | 40 | 36 | 4.02 | 4.92 | 1.46 | 867 | 861 | 871 | 4.9 | 3.4 | 8.0 | 2.3 | 59% | 12% | 95.4 | 49 | 24 | 27 | 33% | 76% | 17% | 0 | 19 | | | 0 | 1.10 | 0.7 | 63 | 72 | -$1 |
| **19 Proj** | **3** | **1** | **58** | **50** | **3.58** | **3.57** | **1.44** | **781** | **872** | **722** | **4.4** | **3.1** | **7.8** | **2.5** | **61%** | **10%** | **94.6** | **59** | **20** | **22** | **34%** | **76%** | **11%** | **0** | | | | | | **3.6** | **92** | **105** | **-$1** |

GREG PYRON

## Pineda,Michael

| Age: 30 | Th: R | Role SP | Health | F | LIMA Plan | A |
|---|---|---|---|---|---|---|
| Ht: 6' 7" | Wt: 260 | Type Pwr | PT/Exp | C | Rand Var | 0 |
| | | | Consist | A | MM | 3301 |

Recovering from July 2017 Tommy John surgery, made four minor league appearances before needing surgery to repair a torn meniscus in right knee. Even when last in action, he displayed his typically strong skills, but a sky-high hr/f wreaked havoc on ERA. Prior skills are certainly worth a look if he answers spring bell in MIN.

| Yr Tm | W | Sv | IP | K | ERA | xERA | WHIP | oOPS | vL | vR | BF/G | Ctl | Dom | Cmd | FpK | SwK | Vel | G | L | F | H% | S% | hr/f | GS | APC | DOM% | DIS% | Sv% | LI | RAR | BPV | BPX | R$ |
|---|---|---|---|---|---|---|---|---|---|---|---|---|---|---|---|---|---|---|---|---|---|---|---|---|---|---|---|---|---|---|---|---|---|
| 14 NYY | 5 | 0 | 76 | 59 | 1.89 | 3.39 | 0.83 | 526 | 533 | 518 | 22.3 | 0.8 | 7.0 | 8.4 | 67% | 12% | 92.5 | 39 | 19 | 42 | 25% | 81% | 5% | 13 | 88 | 38% | 23% | | | 17.5 | 120 | 143 | $11 |
| 15 NYY | 12 | 0 | 161 | 156 | 4.37 | 3.21 | 1.23 | 752 | 741 | 762 | 24.7 | 1.2 | 8.7 | 7.4 | 64% | 12% | 92.8 | 48 | 22 | 30 | 34% | 68% | 15% | 27 | 94 | 30% | 37% | | | -8.1 | 152 | 180 | $6 |
| 16 NYY | 6 | 0 | 176 | 207 | 4.82 | 3.47 | 1.35 | 784 | 801 | 770 | 23.6 | 2.7 | 10.6 | 3.9 | 67% | 15% | 94.1 | 46 | 22 | 33 | 35% | 68% | 17% | 32 | 94 | 9% | 25% | | | -13.6 | 142 | 168 | $1 |
| 17 NYY | 8 | 0 | 96 | 92 | 4.39 | 3.77 | 1.29 | 769 | 760 | 777 | 24.1 | 2.0 | 8.6 | 4.4 | 65% | 13% | 93.9 | 51 | 19 | 31 | 32% | 74% | 22% | 17 | 91 | 35% | 29% | | | -0.4 | 131 | 157 | $3 |
| 18 | | | | | | | | | | | | | | | | | | | | | | | | | | | | | | | | | |
| 1st Half | | | | | | | | | | | | | | | | | | | | | | | | | | | | | | | | | |
| 2nd Half | | | | | | | | | | | | | | | | | | | | | | | | | | | | | | | | | |
| 19 Proj | 7 | 0 | 102 | 99 | 4.00 | 3.53 | 1.28 | 744 | 739 | 748 | 23.6 | 2.3 | 8.8 | 3.8 | 65% | 13% | 93.3 | 45 | 20 | 34 | 32% | 74% | 15% | 18 | | | | | | 1.8 | 120 | 138 | $3 |

## Pivetta,Nick

| Age: 26 | Th: R | Role SP | Health | A | LIMA Plan | A |
|---|---|---|---|---|---|---|
| Ht: 6' 5" | Wt: 220 | Type Pwr | PT/Exp | C | Rand Var | +5 |
| | | | Consist | C | MM | 3303 |

Bloated ERA hid significant growth (see xERA/BPX). Heightened focus on getting ahead in the count and pounding the zone led to better Ctl and hints at possible further gains. New spike grip turned curve into top offering, boosting SwK. RandVar says he deserved a better fate. Skills are here for... UP: 15 wins, 3.40 ERA.

| Yr Tm | W | Sv | IP | K | ERA | xERA | WHIP | oOPS | vL | vR | BF/G | Ctl | Dom | Cmd | FpK | SwK | Vel | G | L | F | H% | S% | hr/f | GS | APC | DOM% | DIS% | Sv% | LI | RAR | BPV | BPX | R$ |
|---|---|---|---|---|---|---|---|---|---|---|---|---|---|---|---|---|---|---|---|---|---|---|---|---|---|---|---|---|---|---|---|---|---|
| 14 | | | | | | | | | | | | | | | | | | | | | | | | | | | | | | | | | |
| 15 aa | 2 | 0 | 43 | 28 | 8.13 | 7.25 | 1.92 | | | | 20.5 | 5.6 | 5.8 | 1.0 | | | | | | | 33% | 60% | | | | | | | | -22.3 | -9 | -10 | -$14 |
| 16 a/a | 12 | 0 | 149 | 121 | 3.90 | 3.94 | 1.33 | | | | 22.9 | 3.1 | 7.4 | 2.4 | | | | | | | 31% | 73% | | | | | | | | 5.4 | 72 | 85 | $7 |
| 17 PHI * | 13 | 0 | 165 | 172 | 5.22 | 4.91 | 1.42 | 846 | 701 | 983 | 22.5 | 3.2 | 9.4 | 2.9 | 59% | 9% | 94.4 | 44 | 20 | 36 | 34% | 67% | 18% | 26 | 94 | 12% | 31% | | | -17.5 | 75 | 90 | $1 |
| 18 PHI | 7 | 0 | 164 | 188 | 4.77 | 3.53 | 1.30 | 743 | 786 | 709 | 21.0 | 2.8 | 10.3 | 3.7 | 63% | 13% | 94.8 | 47 | 19 | 35 | 34% | 67% | 16% | 32 | 86 | 31% | 38% | 0 | 0.80 | -12.6 | 135 | 156 | $1 |
| 1st Half | 4 | 0 | 86 | 103 | 4.71 | 3.56 | 1.31 | 751 | 847 | 671 | 21.6 | 2.7 | 10.8 | 4.0 | 64% | 13% | 94.7 | 43 | 19 | 38 | 35% | 68% | 15% | 17 | 88 | 47% | 41% | | | -5.9 | 141 | 163 | $0 |
| 2nd Half | 3 | 0 | 78 | 85 | 4.85 | 3.49 | 1.29 | 733 | 712 | 749 | 20.4 | 2.9 | 9.8 | 3.4 | 62% | 12% | 95.0 | 51 | 18 | 31 | 33% | 66% | 17% | 15 | 84 | 13% | 33% | 0 | 0.84 | -6.7 | 127 | 146 | $1 |
| 19 Proj | 10 | 0 | 167 | 177 | 3.80 | 3.50 | 1.28 | 718 | 680 | 749 | 20.7 | 3.0 | 9.6 | 3.2 | 61% | 11% | 94.7 | 46 | 19 | 35 | 32% | 75% | 14% | 33 | | | | | | 7.2 | 114 | 131 | $9 |

## Plutko,Adam

| Age: 27 | Th: R | Role SP | Health | A | LIMA Plan | D+ |
|---|---|---|---|---|---|---|
| Ht: 6' 3" | Wt: 200 | Type xFB | PT/Exp | D | Rand Var | 0 |
| | | | Consist | F | MM | 0001 |

4-5, 5.28 ERA in 77 IP at CLE. First extended MLB look didn't go well, and his skill set doesn't figure to be successful in today's launch angle climate. The extreme flyball pitcher was touched up for a whopping 2.5 hr/9 while sporting a subpar Dom/SwK and struggling mightily vL. Unlikely to have fantasy relevance.

| Yr Tm | W | Sv | IP | K | ERA | xERA | WHIP | oOPS | vL | vR | BF/G | Ctl | Dom | Cmd | FpK | SwK | Vel | G | L | F | H% | S% | hr/f | GS | APC | DOM% | DIS% | Sv% | LI | RAR | BPV | BPX | R$ |
|---|---|---|---|---|---|---|---|---|---|---|---|---|---|---|---|---|---|---|---|---|---|---|---|---|---|---|---|---|---|---|---|---|---|
| 14 | | | | | | | | | | | | | | | | | | | | | | | | | | | | | | | | | |
| 15 aa | 9 | 0 | 116 | 72 | 4.05 | 3.97 | 1.25 | | | | 24.9 | 1.9 | 5.6 | 2.9 | | | | | | | 30% | 70% | | | | | | | | -1.2 | 68 | 81 | $3 |
| 16 CLE * | 9 | 0 | 165 | 98 | 5.30 | 5.13 | 1.52 | 951 | 333 | 1300 | 23.9 | 3.0 | 5.3 | 1.8 | 44% | 4% | 90.9 | 23 | 15 | 62 | 33% | 66% | 13% | 0 | 40 | | | 0 | 0.10 | -22.7 | 35 | 42 | -$9 |
| 17 aaa | 7 | 0 | 136 | 82 | 8.43 | 7.93 | 1.91 | | | | 26.7 | 4.1 | 5.4 | 1.3 | | | | | | | 36% | 58% | | | | | | | | -68.2 | -16 | -19 | -$31 |
| 18 CLE * | 11 | 1 | 163 | 123 | 3.71 | 3.75 | 1.11 | 869 | 1049 | 706 | 20.6 | 2.3 | 6.8 | 3.0 | 61% | 9% | 91.1 | 27 | 16 | 57 | 25% | 74% | 15% | 12 | 75 | 17% | 42% | 100 | 0.55 | 8.8 | 66 | 76 | $13 |
| 1st Half | 9 | 0 | 96 | 62 | 3.35 | 3.04 | 0.98 | 833 | 979 | 693 | 22.7 | 1.9 | 5.9 | 3.0 | 59% | 9% | 91.2 | 28 | 16 | 56 | 22% | 73% | 14% | 6 | 79 | 17% | 33% | 0 | 0.67 | 9.4 | 71 | 82 | $22 |
| 2nd Half | 2 | 1 | 67 | 61 | 4.22 | 4.75 | 1.28 | 900 | 1110 | 715 | 18.4 | 2.8 | 8.1 | 2.9 | 64% | 9% | 91.0 | 26 | 16 | 58 | 29% | 75% | 17% | 6 | 72 | 17% | 50% | 100 | 0.47 | -0.6 | 60 | 69 | $2 |
| 19 Proj | 4 | 0 | 73 | 51 | 5.01 | 5.16 | 1.41 | 849 | 1028 | 687 | 22.5 | 2.9 | 6.3 | 2.2 | 62% | 9% | 91.0 | 27 | 16 | 57 | 30% | 71% | 11% | 14 | | | | | | -7.7 | 41 | 47 | -$5 |

## Pomeranz,Drew

| Age: 30 | Th: L | Role RP | Health | F | LIMA Plan | D+ |
|---|---|---|---|---|---|---|
| Ht: 6' 6" | Wt: 240 | Type Pwr | PT/Exp | B | Rand Var | 0 |
| | | | Consist | C | MM | 0201 |

2-6, 6.20 ERA in 74 IP at BOS. Began 2018 on DL (forearm flexor strain), missed another seven weeks near mid-season due to biceps tendinitis, and was demoted to bullpen in early August. Skills have been in rapid decline since 2nd half 2017. Velocity drop is also a concern. Make him show something before you invest.

| Yr Tm | W | Sv | IP | K | ERA | xERA | WHIP | oOPS | vL | vR | BF/G | Ctl | Dom | Cmd | FpK | SwK | Vel | G | L | F | H% | S% | hr/f | GS | APC | DOM% | DIS% | Sv% | LI | RAR | BPV | BPX | R$ |
|---|---|---|---|---|---|---|---|---|---|---|---|---|---|---|---|---|---|---|---|---|---|---|---|---|---|---|---|---|---|---|---|---|---|
| 14 OAK * | 8 | 0 | 115 | 106 | 2.90 | 3.48 | 1.24 | 586 | 664 | 563 | 16.7 | 3.3 | 8.3 | 2.5 | 52% | 9% | 91.1 | 46 | 18 | 36 | 29% | 81% | 10% | 10 | 57 | 50% | 20% | 0 | 0.75 | 12.0 | 82 | 97 | $7 |
| 15 OAK | 5 | 3 | 86 | 82 | 3.66 | 3.84 | 1.19 | 651 | 438 | 749 | 6.7 | 3.2 | 8.6 | 2.6 | 58% | 12% | 91.5 | 43 | 21 | 36 | 28% | 71% | 9% | 9 | 27 | 22% | 33% | 50 | 1.27 | 3.2 | 88 | 105 | $5 |
| 16 2 TM | 11 | 0 | 171 | 186 | 3.32 | 3.73 | 1.18 | 658 | 643 | 663 | 22.7 | 3.4 | 9.8 | 2.9 | 56% | 12% | 90.3 | 46 | 17 | 37 | 28% | 77% | 14% | 30 | 92 | 30% | 27% | 0 | 0.83 | 18.3 | 108 | 128 | $16 |
| 17 BOS | 17 | 0 | 174 | 174 | 3.32 | 4.22 | 1.35 | 711 | 778 | 692 | 23.1 | 3.6 | 9.0 | 2.5 | 60% | 10% | 91.3 | 43 | 22 | 35 | 32% | 79% | 11% | 32 | 96 | 19% | 22% | | | 22.3 | 87 | 104 | $16 |
| 18 BOS * | 3 | 0 | 101 | 77 | 6.35 | 6.70 | 1.76 | 894 | 705 | 947 | 14.5 | 5.6 | 6.9 | 1.2 | 53% | 7% | 89.2 | 37 | 24 | 39 | 31% | 69% | 13% | 11 | 56 | 0% | 64% | 0 | 0.63 | -27.5 | 4 | 5 | -$18 |
| 1st Half | 2 | 0 | 48 | 40 | 6.37 | 6.66 | 1.81 | 936 | 844 | 956 | 22.3 | 5.9 | 7.4 | 1.2 | 55% | 8% | 88.8 | 38 | 20 | 42 | 32% | 68% | 15% | 8 | 91 | 0% | 63% | | | -13.2 | 13 | 15 | -$20 |
| 2nd Half | 1 | 0 | 53 | 38 | 6.33 | 6.74 | 1.71 | 850 | 604 | 935 | 10.9 | 5.3 | 6.4 | 1.2 | 52% | 7% | 89.7 | 36 | 28 | 36 | 29% | 69% | 12% | 3 | 40 | 0% | 67% | 0 | 0.56 | -14.3 | -4 | -5 | -$16 |
| 19 Proj | 6 | 0 | 116 | 103 | 4.42 | 4.55 | 1.51 | 813 | 688 | 851 | 15.4 | 4.5 | 8.0 | 1.8 | 55% | 9% | 90.2 | 41 | 22 | 37 | 30% | 76% | 16% | 18 | | | | | | -5.1 | 41 | 47 | -$3 |

## Poncedeleon,Daniel

| Age: 27 | Th: R | Role SP | Health | A | LIMA Plan | D+ |
|---|---|---|---|---|---|---|
| Ht: 6' 4" | Wt: 185 | Type Pwr FB | PT/Exp | D | Rand Var | -3 |
| | | | Consist | A | MM | 0100 |

0-2, 2.73 ERA in 33 IP at STL. Great to see him back on the mound after 2017 season was cut short by line drive to the head. PRO: Growing Dom trend; improved change-up has helped immensely vL, MiLB history of keeping ball in yard. CON: Inconsistent mechanics have led to poor Ctl. There are better gambles out there.

| Yr Tm | W | Sv | IP | K | ERA | xERA | WHIP | oOPS | vL | vR | BF/G | Ctl | Dom | Cmd | FpK | SwK | Vel | G | L | F | H% | S% | hr/f | GS | APC | DOM% | DIS% | Sv% | LI | RAR | BPV | BPX | R$ |
|---|---|---|---|---|---|---|---|---|---|---|---|---|---|---|---|---|---|---|---|---|---|---|---|---|---|---|---|---|---|---|---|---|---|
| 14 | | | | | | | | | | | | | | | | | | | | | | | | | | | | | | | | | |
| 15 | | | | | | | | | | | | | | | | | | | | | | | | | | | | | | | | | |
| 16 aa | 9 | 0 | 151 | 97 | 4.47 | 4.01 | 1.40 | | | | 23.6 | 3.5 | 5.8 | 1.7 | | | | | | | 30% | 68% | | | | | | | | -5.1 | 52 | 62 | -$1 |
| 17 aaa | 2 | 0 | 29 | 20 | 2.66 | 3.19 | 1.27 | | | | 19.8 | 4.1 | 6.2 | 1.5 | | | | | | | 26% | 81% | | | | | | | | 6.1 | 59 | 71 | -$1 |
| 18 STL * | 9 | 1 | 130 | 117 | 2.64 | 3.04 | 1.29 | 596 | 457 | 728 | 17.8 | 4.4 | 8.1 | 1.8 | 56% | 13% | 93.4 | 34 | 24 | 41 | 28% | 80% | 6% | 4 | 53 | 0% | 0% | 100 | 0.78 | 24.2 | 85 | 98 | $11 |
| 1st Half | 7 | 0 | 77 | 71 | 3.02 | 4.11 | 1.52 | | | | 20.9 | 5.1 | 8.3 | 1.6 | | | | | | | 32% | 81% | 0% | 0 | | | | | | 10.7 | 74 | 85 | $9 |
| 2nd Half | 2 | 1 | 53 | 46 | 2.09 | 1.49 | 0.96 | 596 | 457 | 728 | 14.3 | 3.4 | 7.8 | 2.3 | 56% | 13% | 93.4 | 34 | 24 | 41 | 22% | 79% | 6% | 4 | 53 | 0% | 0% | 100 | 0.78 | 13.5 | 105 | 121 | $16 |
| 19 Proj | 3 | 0 | 65 | 52 | 3.81 | 4.67 | 1.35 | 706 | 548 | 856 | 22.5 | 3.8 | 7.1 | 1.9 | 56% | 13% | 93.4 | 36 | 23 | 40 | 28% | 76% | 10% | 12 | | | | | | -3.3 | 39 | 45 | -$1 |

## Porcello,Rick

| Age: 30 | Th: R | Role SP | Health | A | LIMA Plan | B |
|---|---|---|---|---|---|---|
| Ht: 6' 5" | Wt: 205 | Type Pwr | PT/Exp | A | Rand Var | +2 |
| | | | Consist | B | MM | 2205 |

Rebounded from rough 2017, as xERA fell in line with past performance. Changes in pitch mix (13% fewer four-seam FB in 1st half; 10% reduction in sinkers in 2nd half) drove GB% fluctuations. Dom spike wasn't supported by SwK, so expect pullback there. Discount 2017 and use consistent xERA history as your guide.

| Yr Tm | W | Sv | IP | K | ERA | xERA | WHIP | oOPS | vL | vR | BF/G | Ctl | Dom | Cmd | FpK | SwK | Vel | G | L | F | H% | S% | hr/f | GS | APC | DOM% | DIS% | Sv% | LI | RAR | BPV | BPX | R$ |
|---|---|---|---|---|---|---|---|---|---|---|---|---|---|---|---|---|---|---|---|---|---|---|---|---|---|---|---|---|---|---|---|---|---|
| 14 DET | 15 | 0 | 205 | 129 | 3.43 | 3.74 | 1.23 | 712 | 732 | 686 | 26.3 | 1.8 | 5.7 | 3.1 | 64% | 8% | 90.4 | 49 | 22 | 29 | 30% | 74% | 9% | 31 | 95 | 32% | 32% | 0 | 0.83 | 7.9 | 80 | 96 | $10 |
| 15 BOS | 9 | 0 | 172 | 149 | 4.92 | 3.77 | 1.36 | 787 | 815 | 751 | 26.3 | 2.0 | 7.8 | 3.9 | 60% | 9% | 91.0 | 46 | 22 | 33 | 34% | 67% | 14% | 28 | 98 | 43% | 32% | | | -20.3 | 111 | 132 | -$4 |
| 16 BOS | 22 | 0 | 223 | 189 | 3.15 | 3.77 | 1.01 | 635 | 600 | 672 | 27.0 | 1.3 | 7.6 | 5.9 | 64% | 9% | 90.2 | 43 | 19 | 38 | 28% | 73% | 9% | 33 | 103 | 55% | 9% | | | 28.6 | 123 | 147 | $32 |
| 17 BOS | 11 | 0 | 203 | 181 | 4.65 | 4.54 | 1.40 | 826 | 856 | 798 | 26.8 | 2.1 | 8.0 | 3.8 | 67% | 10% | 91.1 | 39 | 21 | 40 | 34% | 73% | 15% | 33 | 103 | 30% | 24% | | | -7.3 | 104 | 125 | $3 |
| 18 BOS | 17 | 0 | 191 | 190 | 4.28 | 3.79 | 1.18 | 698 | 727 | 672 | 24.5 | 2.3 | 8.9 | 4.0 | 67% | 9% | 90.4 | 44 | 20 | 36 | 30% | 68% | 14% | 33 | 94 | 27% | 24% | | | -3.1 | 122 | 140 | $13 |
| 1st Half | 9 | 0 | 105 | 99 | 3.60 | 3.76 | 1.13 | 654 | 702 | 618 | 26.0 | 2.1 | 8.5 | 4.1 | 67% | 9% | 90.4 | 46 | 19 | 34 | 30% | 71% | 10% | 17 | 99 | 29% | 18% | | | 7.1 | 122 | 140 | $19 |
| 2nd Half | 8 | 0 | 86 | 91 | 5.11 | 3.82 | 1.23 | 751 | 751 | 751 | 22.9 | 2.5 | 9.5 | 3.8 | 66% | 9% | 90.4 | 41 | 21 | 37 | 30% | 64% | 19% | 16 | 88 | 25% | 31% | | | -10.2 | 122 | 141 | $7 |
| 19 Proj | 15 | 0 | 189 | 172 | 3.97 | 3.68 | 1.24 | 736 | 751 | 722 | 24.3 | 2.2 | 8.2 | 3.8 | 66% | 9% | 90.6 | 43 | 21 | 37 | 31% | 73% | 14% | 31 | | | | | | 10.0 | 110 | 126 | $13 |

## Pressly,Ryan

| Age: 30 | Th: R | Role RP | Health | C | LIMA Plan | B+ |
|---|---|---|---|---|---|---|
| Ht: 6' 3" | Wt: 210 | Type Pwr GB | PT/Exp | C | Rand Var | 0 |
| | | | Consist | B | MM | 5411 |

Built upon 2017 skills gains to produce a breakout season. Slider was key, as it became a dominant offering (32% SwK%, 69% GB%) and its usage rose from 18% to 27%, leading to Dom/SwK spike. Tremendous 2nd half fueled by fewer four-seam FB, more CB and improved FpK/Ctl. If given the chance... UP: 40 Sv

| Yr Tm | W | Sv | IP | K | ERA | xERA | WHIP | oOPS | vL | vR | BF/G | Ctl | Dom | Cmd | FpK | SwK | Vel | G | L | F | H% | S% | hr/f | GS | APC | DOM% | DIS% | Sv% | LI | RAR | BPV | BPX | R$ |
|---|---|---|---|---|---|---|---|---|---|---|---|---|---|---|---|---|---|---|---|---|---|---|---|---|---|---|---|---|---|---|---|---|---|
| 14 MIN * | 3 | 6 | 89 | 63 | 3.65 | 4.26 | 1.47 | 779 | 887 | 715 | 6.3 | 3.1 | 6.3 | 2.0 | 59% | 9% | 93.3 | 47 | 27 | 26 | 34% | 75% | 12% | 0 | 15 | | | 75 | 0.81 | 1.0 | 66 | 79 | -$1 |
| 15 MIN | 3 | 0 | 28 | 22 | 2.93 | 4.39 | 1.41 | 645 | 678 | 626 | 4.4 | 3.9 | 7.2 | 1.8 | 59% | 9% | 94.2 | 47 | 20 | 33 | 33% | 77% | 0% | 0 | 16 | | | 0 | 0.93 | 3.5 | 48 | 58 | -$2 |
| 16 MIN | 6 | 1 | 75 | 67 | 3.70 | 4.38 | 1.35 | 725 | 659 | 767 | 4.6 | 2.7 | 8.0 | 2.9 | 57% | 12% | 95.1 | 39 | 24 | 36 | 33% | 76% | 10% | 0 | 17 | | | 17 | 1.19 | 4.5 | 87 | 103 | $2 |
| 17 MIN | 2 | 0 | 61 | 61 | 4.70 | 3.71 | 1.16 | 697 | 816 | 618 | 4.4 | 2.8 | 9.0 | 3.2 | 58% | 13% | 95.8 | 51 | 17 | 33 | 27% | 64% | 19% | 0 | 16 | | | 0 | 0.94 | -2.6 | 115 | 138 | -$1 |
| 18 2 AL | 2 | 2 | 71 | 101 | 2.54 | 2.71 | 1.11 | 604 | 516 | 657 | 3.8 | 2.8 | 12.8 | 4.6 | 61% | 18% | 95.8 | 52 | 17 | 32 | 34% | 81% | 12% | 0 | 14 | | | 25 | 1.16 | 14.1 | 185 | 213 | $7 |
| 1st Half | 1 | 0 | 38 | 55 | 4.06 | 3.16 | 1.43 | 744 | 679 | 775 | 4.0 | 3.8 | 13.1 | 3.4 | 59% | 18% | 95.8 | 46 | 22 | 32 | 39% | 76% | 17% | 0 | 16 | | | 0 | 1.07 | 0.4 | 158 | 181 | -$1 |
| 2nd Half | 1 | 2 | 33 | 46 | 0.81 | 2.22 | 0.75 | 426 | 346 | 482 | 3.5 | 1.6 | 12.4 | 7.7 | 63% | 18% | 96.0 | 58 | 11 | 31 | 27% | 92% | 5% | 0 | 13 | | | 50 | 1.25 | 13.7 | 216 | 248 | $16 |
| 19 Proj | 3 | 5 | 73 | 84 | 3.03 | 2.98 | 1.12 | 626 | 616 | 632 | 4.0 | 2.7 | 10.4 | 3.9 | 59% | 15% | 95.7 | 50 | 17 | 32 | 31% | 77% | 12% | 0 | | | | | | 12.2 | 144 | 165 | $7 |

GREG PYRON

## Price,David

| Price,David | | Health | F | LIMA Plan | C+ |
|---|---|---|---|---|---|
| Age: 33 | Th: L Role SP | PT/Exp | A | Rand Var | 0 |
| Ht: 6' 5" | Wt: 215 Type Pwr | Consist | A | MM | 3303 |

Managed to avoid DL following injury-plagued 2017. Sputtered out of the gate, but really hit his stride in June (120 BPV) and boasted vintage skills in the 2nd half. While the drop in velocity is notable, he has had success in the past at similar levels. 2015 ERA isn't coming back, but this performance is very repeatable.

| Yr Tm | W | Sv | IP | K | ERA | xERA | WHIP | oOPS | vL | vR | BF/G | Ctl | Dom | Cmd | FpK | SwK | Vel | G | L | F | H% | S% | hr/f | GS | APC | DOM% | DIS% | Sv% | LI | RAR | BPV | BPX | R$ |
|---|---|---|---|---|---|---|---|---|---|---|---|---|---|---|---|---|---|---|---|---|---|---|---|---|---|---|---|---|---|---|---|---|---|
| 14 2 AL | 15 | 0 | 248 | 271 | 3.26 | 3.00 | 1.08 | 647 | 657 | 644 | 29.7 | 1.4 | 9.8 | 7.1 | 70% | 11% | 93.2 | 41 | 21 | 38 | 32% | 73% | 10% | 34 | 110 | 59% | 3% | | | 14.7 | 159 | 189 | $23 |
| 15 2 AL | 18 | 0 | 220 | 225 | 2.45 | 3.36 | 1.08 | 621 | 658 | 609 | 27.8 | 1.9 | 9.2 | 4.8 | 67% | 12% | 94.2 | 40 | 23 | 36 | 30% | 80% | 8% | 32 | 106 | 63% | 9% | | | 41.1 | 132 | 157 | $33 |
| 16 BOS | 17 | 0 | 230 | 228 | 3.99 | 3.63 | 1.20 | 721 | 749 | 712 | 27.2 | 2.0 | 8.9 | 4.6 | 65% | 12% | 92.9 | 44 | 22 | 34 | 32% | 71% | 14% | 35 | 103 | 40% | 23% | | | 5.6 | 130 | 154 | $17 |
| 17 BOS | 6 | 0 | 75 | 76 | 3.38 | 4.17 | 1.19 | 652 | 494 | 697 | 19.8 | 2.9 | 9.2 | 3.2 | 67% | 13% | 94.3 | 40 | 22 | 39 | 30% | 75% | 10% | 11 | 78 | 27% | 36% | 0 | 0.85 | 9.1 | 105 | 126 | $5 |
| 18 BOS | 16 | 0 | 176 | 177 | 3.58 | 3.86 | 1.14 | 691 | 672 | 695 | 24.1 | 2.6 | 9.1 | 3.5 | 62% | 10% | 92.7 | 40 | 21 | 39 | 28% | 74% | 13% | 30 | 91 | 43% | 27% | | | 12.4 | 112 | 129 | $18 |
| 1st Half | 9 | 0 | 93 | 89 | 3.66 | 4.19 | 1.21 | 685 | 678 | 686 | 23.9 | 3.2 | 8.6 | 2.7 | 61% | 9% | 92.7 | 40 | 18 | 41 | 29% | 73% | 9% | 16 | 89 | 31% | 25% | | | 5.6 | 87 | 100 | $16 |
| 2nd Half | 7 | 0 | 83 | 88 | 3.48 | 3.51 | 1.06 | 699 | 665 | 705 | 24.3 | 1.9 | 9.6 | 5.2 | 64% | 11% | 92.8 | 40 | 23 | 37 | 28% | 77% | 18% | 14 | 93 | 57% | 29% | | | 6.8 | 140 | 161 | $20 |
| **19 Proj** | **14** | **0** | **174** | **177** | **3.51** | **3.45** | **1.15** | **681** | **634** | **693** | **22.6** | **2.4** | **9.2** | **3.9** | **65%** | **11%** | **93.2** | **41** | **22** | **38** | **29%** | **75%** | **13%** | **31** | | | | | | **13.8** | **120** | **137** | **$18** |

## Pruitt,Austin

| Pruitt,Austin | | Health | A | LIMA Plan | C+ |
|---|---|---|---|---|---|
| Age: 29 | Th: R Role RP | PT/Exp | D | Rand Var | +2 |
| Ht: 5' 10" | Wt: 180 Type | Consist | C | MM | 2101 |

2-3, 4.65 ERA in 70 IP at TAM. Though the surface stats are rather bland, there are some fairly encouraging signs beneath. GB% lean, history of good Ctl provide a foundation, while SwK suggests average Dom upside. If he could land a starting rotation gig, there's potential deep league value here.

| Yr Tm | W | Sv | IP | K | ERA | xERA | WHIP | oOPS | vL | vR | BF/G | Ctl | Dom | Cmd | FpK | SwK | Vel | G | L | F | H% | S% | hr/f | GS | APC | DOM% | DIS% | Sv% | LI | RAR | BPV | BPX | R$ |
|---|---|---|---|---|---|---|---|---|---|---|---|---|---|---|---|---|---|---|---|---|---|---|---|---|---|---|---|---|---|---|---|---|---|
| 14 | | | | | | | | | | | | | | | | | | | | | | | | | | | | | | | | | |
| 15 aa | 10 | 0 | 160 | 100 | 3.76 | 4.16 | 1.44 | | | | 26.2 | 2.2 | 5.6 | 2.5 | | | | | | | 35% | 72% | | | | | | | | 4.1 | 77 | 91 | $0 |
| 16 aaa | 8 | 0 | 163 | 120 | 5.47 | 6.04 | 1.54 | | | | 25.3 | 1.8 | 6.7 | 3.8 | | | | | | | 36% | 68% | | | | | | | | -25.6 | 65 | 78 | -$11 |
| 17 TAM * | 7 | 2 | 108 | 92 | 4.96 | 4.89 | 1.39 | 827 | 704 | 925 | 11.6 | 2.0 | 7.7 | 3.8 | 66% | 10% | 91.6 | 48 | 21 | 32 | 35% | 67% | 13% | 8 | 44 | 25% | 13% | 67 | 0.61 | -7.9 | 88 | 106 | $0 |
| 18 TAM * | 5 | 5 | 111 | 80 | 4.40 | 3.51 | 1.18 | 712 | 691 | 723 | 12.0 | 2.0 | 6.5 | 3.3 | 63% | 10% | 91.9 | 48 | 18 | 33 | 29% | 63% | 9% | 0 | 45 | | | 83 | 0.53 | -3.4 | 90 | 104 | $4 |
| 1st Half | 3 | 1 | 62 | 41 | 4.70 | 3.88 | 1.22 | 677 | 761 | 630 | 12.5 | 1.8 | 5.9 | 3.3 | 61% | 9% | 91.9 | 50 | 15 | 35 | 30% | 62% | 10% | 0 | 48 | | | 50 | 0.48 | -4.2 | 81 | 93 | $1 |
| 2nd Half | 2 | 4 | 49 | 40 | 4.01 | 3.04 | 1.13 | 821 | 451 | 997 | 11.4 | 2.2 | 7.3 | 3.3 | 71% | 11% | 91.9 | 44 | 28 | 28 | 29% | 65% | 6% | 0 | 36 | | | 100 | 0.64 | 0.8 | 101 | 117 | $7 |
| **19 Proj** | **4** | **0** | **73** | **60** | **4.20** | **3.69** | **1.30** | **713** | **576** | **797** | **13.7** | **2.0** | **7.5** | **3.7** | **66%** | **10%** | **91.8** | **47** | **22** | **31** | **33%** | **69%** | **10%** | **8** | | | | | | **-0.5** | **106** | **122** | **-$1** |

## Quintana,Jose

| Quintana,Jose | | Health | A | LIMA Plan | B |
|---|---|---|---|---|---|
| Age: 30 | Th: L Role SP | PT/Exp | A | Rand Var | +1 |
| Ht: 6' 1" | Wt: 220 Type Pwr | Consist | A | MM | 2205 |

1st half struggles largely due to wildness, especially vR (12% BB%, 1.7 Cmd). However, with a renewed focus on throwing strikes and a tweak to pitch mix, he looked more like himself in Aug-Sept (3.65 ERA, 2.2 Ctl in 67 IP). DIS% trend is unnerving, but there's still enough left here to sneak back under 4.00 ERA.

| Yr Tm | W | Sv | IP | K | ERA | xERA | WHIP | oOPS | vL | vR | BF/G | Ctl | Dom | Cmd | FpK | SwK | Vel | G | L | F | H% | S% | hr/f | GS | APC | DOM% | DIS% | Sv% | LI | RAR | BPV | BPX | R$ |
|---|---|---|---|---|---|---|---|---|---|---|---|---|---|---|---|---|---|---|---|---|---|---|---|---|---|---|---|---|---|---|---|---|---|
| 14 CHW | 9 | 0 | 200 | 178 | 3.32 | 3.51 | 1.24 | 662 | 686 | 653 | 25.9 | 2.3 | 8.0 | 3.4 | 66% | 9% | 91.6 | 45 | 22 | 33 | 33% | 73% | 5% | 32 | 105 | 25% | 19% | | | 10.3 | 104 | 124 | $9 |
| 15 CHW | 9 | 0 | 206 | 177 | 3.36 | 3.60 | 1.27 | 722 | 663 | 740 | 26.9 | 1.9 | 7.7 | 4.0 | 69% | 9% | 91.6 | 47 | 23 | 30 | 33% | 75% | 9% | 32 | 105 | 38% | 16% | | | 15.4 | 112 | 134 | $11 |
| 16 CHW | 13 | 0 | 208 | 181 | 3.20 | 4.02 | 1.16 | 687 | 650 | 698 | 26.2 | 2.2 | 7.8 | 3.6 | 65% | 8% | 92.1 | 40 | 21 | 39 | 30% | 76% | 10% | 32 | 103 | 47% | 19% | | | 25.3 | 101 | 119 | $21 |
| 17 2 TM | 11 | 0 | 189 | 207 | 4.15 | 3.72 | 1.22 | 701 | 584 | 732 | 24.7 | 2.9 | 9.9 | 3.4 | 67% | 9% | 92.1 | 45 | 21 | 34 | 31% | 69% | 13% | 32 | 99 | 31% | 22% | | | 4.8 | 122 | 147 | $13 |
| 18 CHC | 13 | 0 | 174 | 158 | 4.03 | 4.27 | 1.32 | 737 | 696 | 748 | 23.1 | 3.5 | 8.2 | 2.3 | 65% | 8% | 91.6 | 43 | 22 | 34 | 29% | 74% | 15% | 32 | 91 | 28% | 34% | | | 2.7 | 73 | 84 | $7 |
| 1st Half | 6 | 0 | 86 | 80 | 4.31 | 4.44 | 1.41 | 754 | 670 | 781 | 23.3 | 4.2 | 8.4 | 2.0 | 65% | 8% | 91.4 | 44 | 22 | 33 | 30% | 73% | 15% | 16 | 92 | 31% | 44% | | | -1.7 | 60 | 69 | $0 |
| 2nd Half | 7 | 0 | 89 | 78 | 3.76 | 4.10 | 1.23 | 719 | 727 | 717 | 22.9 | 2.8 | 7.9 | 2.8 | 65% | 8% | 91.7 | 42 | 22 | 35 | 28% | 75% | 15% | 16 | 90 | 25% | 25% | | | 4.3 | 86 | 99 | $13 |
| **19 Proj** | **12** | **0** | **189** | **173** | **3.89** | **3.79** | **1.26** | **714** | **663** | **729** | **23.6** | **3.0** | **8.2** | **2.8** | **66%** | **8%** | **91.8** | **43** | **22** | **35** | **30%** | **73%** | **13%** | **33** | | | | | | **6.1** | **90** | **103** | **$11** |

## Ramirez,Erasmo

| Ramirez,Erasmo | | Health | F | LIMA Plan | C |
|---|---|---|---|---|---|
| Age: 29 | Th: R Role RP | PT/Exp | C | Rand Var | +4 |
| Ht: 5' 10" | Wt: 215 Type | Consist | A | MM | 1101 |

2-4, 6.50 ERA in 46 IP at SEA. Missed most of 2018 with a teres major muscle strain (shoulder); explains the reduced velocity. Even when healthy in 2017, these were run-of-the-mill skills plagued by extreme difficulty vL and a touch of gopheritis. With these skills, "a touch" of gopheritis is more than enough. Avoid.

| Yr Tm | W | Sv | IP | K | ERA | xERA | WHIP | oOPS | vL | vR | BF/G | Ctl | Dom | Cmd | FpK | SwK | Vel | G | L | F | H% | S% | hr/f | GS | APC | DOM% | DIS% | Sv% | LI | RAR | BPV | BPX | R$ |
|---|---|---|---|---|---|---|---|---|---|---|---|---|---|---|---|---|---|---|---|---|---|---|---|---|---|---|---|---|---|---|---|---|---|
| 14 SEA * | 7 | 0 | 162 | 117 | 4.34 | 4.66 | 1.38 | 815 | 790 | 848 | 21.2 | 2.5 | 6.5 | 2.6 | 61% | 11% | 91.1 | 38 | 19 | 43 | 32% | 72% | 13% | 14 | 76 | 14% | 50% | 0 | 0.63 | -12.0 | 59 | 70 | -$4 |
| 15 TAM | 11 | 0 | 163 | 126 | 3.75 | 3.76 | 1.13 | 655 | 567 | 753 | 19.6 | 2.2 | 6.9 | 3.2 | 65% | 11% | 90.9 | 48 | 21 | 32 | 28% | 69% | 10% | 27 | 71 | 19% | 33% | 0 | 0.70 | 4.3 | 91 | 109 | $11 |
| 16 TAM | 7 | 2 | 91 | 63 | 3.77 | 4.25 | 1.28 | 766 | 905 | 685 | 5.9 | 2.6 | 6.3 | 2.4 | 63% | 9% | 91.3 | 53 | 15 | 32 | 28% | 76% | 16% | 1 | 21 | 0% | 0% | 33 | 1.43 | 4.7 | 74 | 88 | $4 |
| 17 2 AL | 5 | 1 | 131 | 109 | 4.39 | 4.29 | 1.17 | 733 | 829 | 670 | 14.6 | 2.1 | 7.5 | 3.5 | 62% | 11% | 91.6 | 43 | 19 | 38 | 28% | 68% | 15% | 19 | 54 | 11% | 26% | 50 | 1.00 | -0.4 | 98 | 118 | $6 |
| 18 SEA * | 2 | 0 | 70 | 51 | 5.23 | 5.23 | 1.28 | 916 | 965 | 871 | 17.9 | 2.0 | 6.6 | 3.4 | 67% | 9% | 89.9 | 40 | 21 | 40 | 29% | 66% | 23% | 10 | 75 | 0% | 50% | | | -9.3 | 52 | 60 | -$5 |
| 1st Half | 0 | 0 | 21 | 12 | 5.81 | 6.54 | 1.18 | 1332 | 1436 | 1103 | 20.9 | 0.9 | 5.0 | 5.5 | 64% | 7% | 89.3 | 38 | 16 | 46 | 23% | 68% | 41% | 2 | 75 | 0% | 50% | | | -4.3 | 41 | 47 | -$11 |
| 2nd Half | 2 | 0 | 49 | 40 | 4.97 | 4.65 | 1.33 | 793 | 735 | 834 | 16.9 | 2.4 | 7.3 | 3.0 | 68% | 9% | 90.0 | 40 | 22 | 38 | 31% | 65% | 16% | 8 | 75 | 0% | 50% | | | -5.0 | 69 | 79 | -$3 |
| **19 Proj** | **4** | **0** | **109** | **86** | **4.51** | **4.05** | **1.30** | **807** | **812** | **803** | **13.4** | **2.2** | **7.1** | **3.2** | **64%** | **10%** | **90.9** | **42** | **20** | **38** | **30%** | **72%** | **17%** | **11** | | | | | | **1.0** | **88** | **102** | **-$1** |

## Ramirez,Neil

| Ramirez,Neil | | Health | D | LIMA Plan | C+ |
|---|---|---|---|---|---|
| Age: 30 | Th: R Role RP | PT/Exp | D | Rand Var | +1 |
| Ht: 6' 4" | Wt: 215 Type Pwr xFB | Consist | A | MM | 2500 |

0-3, 4.54 ERA in 42 IP at CLE. August back spasms may have influenced horrid Sept (6.5 Ctl, 5.35 xERA, 37 BPV). Overall, saw velocity uptick, replaced curve with more sliders (21% SwK) and enhanced effort to pound zone sparked Ctl gains. HRs are an issue, but if career-best velocity/Ctl sticks, he could be a Holds asset.

| Yr Tm | W | Sv | IP | K | ERA | xERA | WHIP | oOPS | vL | vR | BF/G | Ctl | Dom | Cmd | FpK | SwK | Vel | G | L | F | H% | S% | hr/f | GS | APC | DOM% | DIS% | Sv% | LI | RAR | BPV | BPX | R$ |
|---|---|---|---|---|---|---|---|---|---|---|---|---|---|---|---|---|---|---|---|---|---|---|---|---|---|---|---|---|---|---|---|---|---|
| 14 CHC | 3 | 3 | 44 | 53 | 1.44 | 3.44 | 1.05 | 550 | 591 | 522 | 3.5 | 3.5 | 10.9 | 3.1 | 58% | 14% | 94.3 | 26 | 24 | 50 | 28% | 89% | 4% | 0 | 15 | | | 60 | 0.97 | 12.4 | 106 | 126 | $6 |
| 15 CHC | 1 | 0 | 14 | 15 | 3.21 | 4.11 | 1.29 | 673 | 577 | 737 | 3.2 | 3.9 | 9.6 | 2.5 | 52% | 12% | 93.0 | 38 | 18 | 44 | 31% | 76% | 6% | 0 | 13 | | | 0 | 0.39 | 1.3 | 85 | 102 | -$3 |
| 16 3 TM * | 0 | 0 | 44 | 44 | 5.45 | 5.50 | 1.52 | 967 | 1192 | 766 | 5.7 | 5.3 | 8.9 | 1.7 | 64% | 11% | 92.0 | 27 | 14 | 59 | 27% | 72% | 21% | 0 | 26 | | | 0 | 0.61 | -6.9 | 29 | 34 | -$6 |
| 17 2 NL | 0 | 0 | 31 | 44 | 7.18 | 5.05 | 1.79 | 826 | 655 | 944 | 5.3 | 6.0 | 12.6 | 2.1 | 60% | 13% | 93.1 | 31 | 20 | 49 | 40% | 62% | 14% | 0 | 22 | | | 0 | 0.56 | -10.9 | 74 | 88 | -$9 |
| 18 CLE * | 2 | 3 | 63 | 76 | 4.51 | 4.92 | 1.29 | 774 | 831 | 741 | 4.2 | 3.3 | 10.8 | 3.3 | 61% | 16% | 95.3 | 35 | 19 | 47 | 30% | 74% | 18% | 0 | 16 | | | 60 | 1.06 | -2.8 | 77 | 89 | -$1 |
| 1st Half | 2 | 3 | 35 | 39 | 2.88 | 3.24 | 1.05 | 590 | 476 | 631 | 4.4 | 1.9 | 10.0 | 5.1 | 61% | 18% | 95.6 | 31 | 22 | 47 | 29% | 80% | 10% | 0 | 13 | | | 100 | 0.78 | 5.5 | 141 | 162 | $6 |
| 2nd Half | 0 | 0 | 28 | 36 | 6.51 | 6.96 | 1.57 | 885 | 988 | 818 | 3.9 | 5.0 | 11.9 | 2.4 | 60% | 15% | 95.2 | 37 | 16 | 47 | 31% | 70% | 24% | 0 | 18 | | | 0 | 1.24 | -8.0 | 28 | 32 | -$9 |
| **19 Proj** | **3** | **0** | **58** | **72** | **3.88** | **3.85** | **1.39** | **776** | **732** | **802** | **4.3** | **3.9** | **11.1** | **2.8** | **60%** | **14%** | **94.4** | **32** | **20** | **48** | **33%** | **80%** | **16%** | **0** | | | | | | **2.6** | **105** | **120** | **-$1** |

## Ramirez,Noe

| Ramirez,Noe | | Health | A | LIMA Plan | B+ |
|---|---|---|---|---|---|
| Age: 29 | Th: R Role RP | PT/Exp | D | Rand Var | +4 |
| Ht: 6' 3" | Wt: 195 Type Pwr | Consist | C | MM | 2301 |

Lacks velocity, but deceptive delivery has helped keep batters off balance. Of his sinker/slider/change-up mix, the change-up has been by far his most effective offering (21% SwK/59% GB%) and the only one garnering a double-digit SwK. 2017 and 2nd half 2018 FpK hints at possible Ctl downside. Filler.

| Yr Tm | W | Sv | IP | K | ERA | xERA | WHIP | oOPS | vL | vR | BF/G | Ctl | Dom | Cmd | FpK | SwK | Vel | G | L | F | H% | S% | hr/f | GS | APC | DOM% | DIS% | Sv% | LI | RAR | BPV | BPX | R$ |
|---|---|---|---|---|---|---|---|---|---|---|---|---|---|---|---|---|---|---|---|---|---|---|---|---|---|---|---|---|---|---|---|---|---|
| 14 aa | 2 | 18 | 67 | 45 | 2.82 | 3.14 | 1.28 | | | | 6.6 | 2.3 | 6.0 | 2.6 | | | | | | | 32% | 76% | | | | | | | | 7.7 | 92 | 110 | $8 |
| 15 BOS * | 4 | 3 | 56 | 43 | 3.63 | 4.36 | 1.52 | 803 | 533 | 867 | 5.1 | 4.5 | 7.0 | 1.5 | 65% | 12% | 89.8 | 41 | 18 | 41 | 32% | 77% | 19% | 0 | 15 | | | 75 | 1.02 | 2.3 | 56 | 66 | -$1 |
| 16 BOS * | 2 | 7 | 57 | 56 | 3.88 | 5.97 | 1.66 | 1059 | 862 | 1109 | 5.8 | 3.5 | 8.8 | 2.5 | 61% | 12% | 89.7 | 36 | 22 | 42 | 38% | 81% | 27% | 0 | 16 | | | 88 | 0.59 | 2.1 | 59 | 70 | -$1 |
| 17 2 AL * | 3 | 5 | 66 | 61 | 3.39 | 3.47 | 1.17 | 520 | 1178 | 351 | 5.4 | 3.1 | 8.4 | 2.7 | 53% | 15% | 89.8 | 47 | 17 | 37 | 27% | 77% | 18% | 0 | 18 | | | 83 | 0.90 | 7.9 | 80 | 96 | $5 |
| 18 LAA | 7 | 1 | 83 | 95 | 4.54 | 3.73 | 1.26 | 752 | 787 | 729 | 5.1 | 3.2 | 10.3 | 3.2 | 56% | 12% | 90.1 | 43 | 19 | 38 | 30% | 70% | 18% | 1 | 20 | 0% | 100% | 25 | 0.72 | -4.0 | 118 | 136 | $1 |
| 1st Half | 3 | 0 | 47 | 59 | 4.37 | 3.64 | 1.27 | 743 | 750 | 739 | 5.2 | 3.4 | 11.2 | 3.3 | 57% | 12% | 90.1 | 42 | 18 | 40 | 32% | 70% | 15% | 0 | 20 | | | 0 | 0.90 | -1.3 | 130 | 149 | $1 |
| 2nd Half | 4 | 1 | 36 | 36 | 4.75 | 3.85 | 1.25 | 764 | 825 | 714 | 5.0 | 3.0 | 9.0 | 3.0 | 53% | 11% | 90.0 | 45 | 20 | 35 | 28% | 70% | 23% | 1 | 20 | 0% | 100% | 50 | 0.49 | -2.7 | 104 | 119 | $3 |
| **19 Proj** | **5** | **0** | **73** | **73** | **4.04** | **3.77** | **1.31** | **749** | **794** | **718** | **5.2** | **3.2** | **9.0** | **2.8** | **55%** | **11%** | **90.1** | **44** | **19** | **37** | **31%** | **75%** | **15%** | **0** | | | | | | **3.4** | **97** | **111** | **$1** |

## Ramirez,Yefry

| Ramirez,Yefry | | Health | A | LIMA Plan | D+ |
|---|---|---|---|---|---|
| Age: 25 | Th: R Role RP | PT/Exp | D | Rand Var | +3 |
| Ht: 6' 2" | Wt: 215 Type Pwr xFB | Consist | A | MM | 0201 |

1-8, 5.92 ERA in 65 IP at BAL. Originally an infielder, he transitioned to pitching in 2012 and has been used predominantly as a starter since 2013. FpK and SwK suggest potential Ctl and Dom upside. However, FB% makes him susceptible to HR problems and vL looks dangerous. Take a wait-and-see approach for now.

| Yr Tm | W | Sv | IP | K | ERA | xERA | WHIP | oOPS | vL | vR | BF/G | Ctl | Dom | Cmd | FpK | SwK | Vel | G | L | F | H% | S% | hr/f | GS | APC | DOM% | DIS% | Sv% | LI | RAR | BPV | BPX | R$ |
|---|---|---|---|---|---|---|---|---|---|---|---|---|---|---|---|---|---|---|---|---|---|---|---|---|---|---|---|---|---|---|---|---|---|
| 14 | | | | | | | | | | | | | | | | | | | | | | | | | | | | | | | | | |
| 15 | | | | | | | | | | | | | | | | | | | | | | | | | | | | | | | | | |
| 16 | | | | | | | | | | | | | | | | | | | | | | | | | | | | | | | | | |
| 17 aa | 15 | 0 | 124 | 94 | 4.42 | 4.76 | 1.42 | | | | 22.0 | 3.7 | 6.8 | 1.8 | | | | | | | 29% | 73% | | | | | | | | -0.9 | 41 | 49 | $4 |
| 18 BAL * | 4 | 0 | 137 | 119 | 5.60 | 5.01 | 1.47 | 802 | 926 | 694 | 19.0 | 3.9 | 7.8 | 2.0 | 61% | 11% | 92.6 | 34 | 21 | 45 | 31% | 64% | 13% | 12 | 72 | 8% | 50% | 0 | 0.73 | -24.6 | 49 | 57 | -$11 |
| 1st Half | 3 | 0 | 81 | 66 | 5.03 | 4.59 | 1.36 | 581 | 494 | 652 | 21.3 | 2.9 | 7.3 | 2.5 | 59% | 11% | 91.9 | 46 | 17 | 38 | 31% | 65% | 11% | 1 | 75 | 0% | 0% | 0 | 1.46 | -8.8 | 63 | 72 | -$7 |
| 2nd Half | 1 | 0 | 56 | 53 | 6.43 | 5.50 | 1.63 | 835 | 993 | 700 | 17.1 | 5.5 | 8.5 | 1.6 | 61% | 11% | 92.7 | 32 | 21 | 46 | 31% | 63% | 13% | 11 | 72 | 9% | 55% | 0 | 0.63 | -15.7 | 16 | 18 | -$16 |
| **19 Proj** | **7** | **0** | **116** | **103** | **4.72** | **4.66** | **1.40** | **726** | **859** | **618** | **19.2** | **3.6** | **8.0** | **2.2** | **61%** | **11%** | **92.7** | **32** | **21** | **46** | **30%** | **71%** | **12%** | **23** | | | | | | **-6.4** | **56** | **64** | **-$2** |

GREG PYRON

## Ramos,A.J.

| Age: 32 | Th: R | Role RP | Health | F | LIMA Plan | D |
|---|---|---|---|---|---|---|
| Ht: 5' 10" | Wt: 200 | Type Pwr FB | PT/Exp | B | Rand Var | +4 |
| | | | Consist | B | MM | 0410 |

Sept 2017 struggles—sagging Dom/Vel, soaring walks/FB%/ERA, biceps tendinitis—foreshadowed 2018. Strained shoulder DL'd him in May. Season-ending surgery in June left him with a mid-2019 return shot at best. SwK, saves history keep him in the book. Health, chronic Ctl woes keep him off our spring radars.

| Yr Tm | W | Sv | IP | K | ERA | xERA | WHIP | oOPS | vL | vR | BF/G | Ctl | Dom | Cmd | FpK | SwK | Vel | G | L | F | H% | S% | hr/f | GS | APC | DOM% | DIS% | Sv% | LI | RAR | BPV | BPX | R$ |
|---|---|---|---|---|---|---|---|---|---|---|---|---|---|---|---|---|---|---|---|---|---|---|---|---|---|---|---|---|---|---|---|---|---|
| 14 MIA | 7 | 0 | 64 | 73 | 2.11 | 3.89 | 1.23 | 543 | 522 | 555 | 4.0 | 6.0 | 10.3 | 1.7 | 57% | 14% | 91.3 | 42 | 19 | 39 | 25% | 82% | 2% | 0 | 16 | | | 0 | 1.36 | 12.9 | 42 | 49 | $6 |
| 15 MIA | 2 | 32 | 70 | 87 | 2.30 | 3.10 | 1.01 | 562 | 602 | 529 | 3.9 | 3.3 | 11.1 | 3.3 | 59% | 17% | 92.6 | 43 | 16 | 40 | 26% | 82% | 9% | 0 | 15 | | | 84 | 1.27 | 14.4 | 132 | 157 | $21 |
| 16 MIA | 1 | 40 | 64 | 73 | 2.81 | 4.23 | 1.36 | 600 | 578 | 627 | 4.1 | 4.9 | 10.3 | 2.1 | 60% | 12% | 91.9 | 36 | 26 | 38 | 32% | 78% | 2% | 0 | 17 | | | 93 | 1.15 | 10.9 | 66 | 78 | $18 |
| 17 2 NL | 2 | 27 | 59 | 72 | 3.99 | 4.32 | 1.41 | 694 | 656 | 738 | 4.2 | 5.2 | 11.0 | 2.1 | 52% | 12% | 92.3 | 40 | 20 | 39 | 31% | 75% | 12% | 0 | 18 | | | 90 | 1.07 | 2.7 | 76 | 91 | $10 |
| 18 NYM | 2 | 0 | 20 | 22 | 6.41 | 5.50 | 1.63 | 766 | 917 | 660 | 3.1 | 6.9 | 10.1 | 1.5 | 52% | 11% | 91.4 | 27 | 20 | 53 | 29% | 62% | 12% | 0 | 13 | | | 0 | 1.20 | -5.5 | 1 | 1 | -$6 |
| 1st Half | 2 | 0 | 20 | 22 | 6.41 | 5.50 | 1.63 | 766 | 917 | 660 | 3.1 | 6.9 | 10.1 | 1.5 | 52% | 11% | 91.4 | 27 | 20 | 53 | 29% | 62% | 12% | 0 | 13 | | | 0 | 1.20 | -5.5 | 0 | 0 | -$6 |
| 2nd Half | | | | | | | | | | | | | | | | | | | | | | | | | | | | | | | | | |
| **19 Proj** | **2** | **2** | **29** | **32** | **4.60** | **4.66** | **1.49** | **676** | **702** | **652** | **3.7** | **6.4** | **9.9** | **1.6** | **56%** | **13%** | **91.9** | **36** | **21** | **43** | **29%** | **70%** | **8%** | **0** | | | | | | **-1.6** | **20** | **23** | **-$3** |

## Ramos,Edubray

| Age: 26 | Th: R | Role RP | Health | C | LIMA Plan | B+ |
|---|---|---|---|---|---|---|
| Ht: 6' 0" | Wt: 160 | Type Pwr | PT/Exp | D | Rand Var | -5 |
| | | | Consist | B | MM | 2300 |

Big 1st-half S%, HR avoidance were unsustainable—particularly given season-long FB% spike. Wasn't as fortunate in 2nd half, as injuries (shoulder, knee, finger) took a toll and Swk/Dom plunged. ERA volatility hasn't been just a season-to-season thing. Inconsistency might be his most predictable skill.

| Yr Tm | W | Sv | IP | K | ERA | xERA | WHIP | oOPS | vL | vR | BF/G | Ctl | Dom | Cmd | FpK | SwK | Vel | G | L | F | H% | S% | hr/f | GS | APC | DOM% | DIS% | Sv% | LI | RAR | BPV | BPX | R$ |
|---|---|---|---|---|---|---|---|---|---|---|---|---|---|---|---|---|---|---|---|---|---|---|---|---|---|---|---|---|---|---|---|---|---|
| 14 | | | | | | | | | | | | | | | | | | | | | | | | | | | | | | | | | |
| 15 aa | 1 | 0 | 20 | 16 | 4.04 | 3.25 | 1.42 | | | | 4.8 | 4.4 | 7.0 | 1.6 | | | | | | | 31% | 68% | | | | | | | | -0.2 | 81 | 96 | -$4 |
| 16 PHI * | 3 | 10 | 79 | 75 | 2.64 | 2.52 | 1.01 | 687 | 794 | 572 | 4.4 | 1.7 | 8.6 | 5.0 | 59% | 11% | 95.2 | 37 | 25 | 38 | 28% | 77% | 12% | 0 | 15 | | | 71 | 1.09 | 15.0 | 145 | 173 | $12 |
| 17 PHI | 2 | 0 | 58 | 75 | 4.21 | 3.99 | 1.47 | 699 | 856 | 580 | 4.3 | 4.4 | 11.7 | 2.7 | 61% | 12% | 94.4 | 37 | 27 | 36 | 38% | 72% | 7% | 0 | 17 | | | 0 | 0.93 | 1.0 | 108 | 129 | -$2 |
| 18 PHI | 3 | 1 | 43 | 42 | 2.32 | 4.30 | 1.15 | 599 | 597 | 600 | 3.3 | 3.2 | 8.9 | 2.8 | 58% | 11% | 93.3 | 33 | 20 | 46 | 28% | 84% | 8% | 0 | 14 | | | 50 | 1.00 | 9.6 | 85 | 98 | $2 |
| 1st Half | 2 | 1 | 29 | 32 | 1.24 | 3.94 | 1.14 | 594 | 623 | 579 | 3.5 | 3.4 | 9.9 | 2.9 | 59% | 12% | 93.5 | 31 | 24 | 45 | 29% | 94% | 6% | 0 | 15 | | | 50 | 1.12 | 10.4 | 96 | 110 | $5 |
| 2nd Half | 1 | 0 | 14 | 10 | 4.61 | 5.10 | 1.17 | 608 | 529 | 641 | 3.1 | 2.6 | 6.6 | 2.5 | 57% | 9% | 92.9 | 37 | 14 | 49 | 26% | 64% | 10% | 0 | 12 | | | 0 | 0.80 | -0.8 | 63 | 72 | -$4 |
| **19 Proj** | **2** | **0** | **44** | **45** | **3.78** | **3.82** | **1.26** | **697** | **822** | **598** | **4.1** | **3.2** | **9.2** | **2.9** | **59%** | **11%** | **94.4** | **35** | **25** | **40** | **31%** | **74%** | **11%** | **0** | | | | | | **2.0** | **93** | **107** | **-$1** |

## Ray,Robbie

| Age: 27 | Th: L | Role SP | Health | D | LIMA Plan | A |
|---|---|---|---|---|---|---|
| Ht: 6' 2" | Wt: 195 | Type Pwr | PT/Exp | A | Rand Var | +2 |
| | | | Consist | A | MM | 3503 |

Combination of shaky control, hint of H%/S% regression was a red flag. Ctl began, ended badly. Oblique strain that cost him 8 weeks was a crusher. Finished Aug/Sept with 58 IP, 37 walks, sub-3 ERA, positive H%/S% reversal. SwK/Dom is a big enabler, but too much must align for another 2017.

| Yr Tm | W | Sv | IP | K | ERA | xERA | WHIP | oOPS | vL | vR | BF/G | Ctl | Dom | Cmd | FpK | SwK | Vel | G | L | F | H% | S% | hr/f | GS | APC | DOM% | DIS% | Sv% | LI | RAR | BPV | BPX | R$ |
|---|---|---|---|---|---|---|---|---|---|---|---|---|---|---|---|---|---|---|---|---|---|---|---|---|---|---|---|---|---|---|---|---|---|
| 14 DET * | 8 | 0 | 129 | 79 | 5.85 | 5.78 | 1.73 | 993 | 889 | 1038 | 20.2 | 4.0 | 5.5 | 1.4 | 54% | 6% | 91.3 | 35 | 24 | 41 | 35% | 66% | 12% | 6 | 61 | 17% | 50% | 0 | 0.65 | -33.5 | 30 | 36 | -$17 |
| 15 ARI * | 7 | 0 | 169 | 166 | 3.55 | 3.86 | 1.42 | 731 | 723 | 733 | 22.5 | 3.9 | 8.8 | 2.3 | 61% | 9% | 93.3 | 44 | 22 | 35 | 34% | 75% | 7% | 23 | 98 | 22% | 26% | | | 8.6 | 88 | 104 | $3 |
| 16 ARI | 8 | 0 | 174 | 218 | 4.90 | 3.62 | 1.47 | 770 | 684 | 797 | 24.3 | 3.7 | 11.3 | 3.1 | 56% | 12% | 94.1 | 46 | 22 | 33 | 37% | 69% | 15% | 32 | 99 | 22% | 19% | | | -15.4 | 128 | 152 | -$2 |
| 17 ARI | 15 | 0 | 162 | 218 | 2.89 | 3.49 | 1.15 | 646 | 622 | 651 | 23.8 | 3.9 | 12.1 | 3.1 | 60% | 15% | 94.3 | 40 | 19 | 40 | 28% | 82% | 16% | 28 | 97 | 43% | 25% | | | 29.4 | 130 | 156 | $24 |
| 18 ARI | 6 | 0 | 124 | 165 | 3.93 | 3.75 | 1.35 | 706 | 455 | 780 | 21.9 | 5.1 | 12.0 | 2.4 | 59% | 13% | 93.7 | 39 | 22 | 39 | 30% | 76% | 17% | 24 | 95 | 17% | 25% | | | 3.4 | 96 | 110 | $3 |
| 1st Half | 3 | 0 | 34 | 51 | 4.01 | 3.57 | 1.37 | 695 | 723 | 688 | 20.7 | 5.1 | 13.6 | 2.7 | 62% | 14% | 93.0 | 35 | 21 | 44 | 33% | 76% | 16% | 7 | 85 | 14% | 29% | | | 0.6 | 121 | 139 | -$6 |
| 2nd Half | 3 | 0 | 90 | 114 | 3.90 | 3.82 | 1.34 | 711 | 364 | 817 | 22.4 | 5.1 | 11.4 | 2.2 | 57% | 13% | 93.9 | 41 | 23 | 36 | 29% | 77% | 18% | 17 | 100 | 18% | 24% | | | 2.8 | 86 | 99 | $7 |
| **19 Proj** | **11** | **0** | **174** | **224** | **3.90** | **3.49** | **1.34** | **714** | **593** | **749** | **25.9** | **4.5** | **11.6** | **2.6** | **59%** | **13%** | **93.8** | **40** | **21** | **38** | **32%** | **76%** | **15%** | **28** | | | | | | **5.4** | **106** | **122** | **$10** |

## Reed,Addison

| Age: 30 | Th: R | Role RP | Health | B | LIMA Plan | C+ |
|---|---|---|---|---|---|---|
| Ht: 6' 4" | Wt: 230 | Type FB | PT/Exp | C | Rand Var | 0 |
| | | | Consist | B | MM | 2211 |

Early SwK decline, FB%/xERA spikes warned something was off. Eventually regained G/L/F footing, but HR barrage and Dom plunge began in June, never relented. Triceps woes shelved him for 3 weeks in July. Velocity ticked downward along with Aug/Sept usage. Reliability has taken a hit; health is a red flag.

| Yr Tm | W | Sv | IP | K | ERA | xERA | WHIP | oOPS | vL | vR | BF/G | Ctl | Dom | Cmd | FpK | SwK | Vel | G | L | F | H% | S% | hr/f | GS | APC | DOM% | DIS% | Sv% | LI | RAR | BPV | BPX | R$ |
|---|---|---|---|---|---|---|---|---|---|---|---|---|---|---|---|---|---|---|---|---|---|---|---|---|---|---|---|---|---|---|---|---|---|
| 14 ARI | 1 | 32 | 59 | 69 | 4.25 | 3.51 | 1.21 | 740 | 610 | 863 | 4.1 | 2.3 | 10.5 | 4.6 | 66% | 14% | 92.4 | 29 | 23 | 48 | 32% | 72% | 14% | 0 | 16 | | | 84 | 1.25 | -3.7 | 134 | 160 | $11 |
| 15 2 NL | 3 | 4 | 56 | 51 | 3.38 | 4.15 | 1.38 | 714 | 699 | 726 | 4.4 | 3.1 | 8.2 | 2.7 | 57% | 9% | 92.6 | 43 | 18 | 39 | 34% | 76% | 5% | 0 | 17 | | | 50 | 1.18 | 4.1 | 86 | 103 | $1 |
| 16 NYM | 4 | 1 | 78 | 91 | 1.97 | 3.13 | 0.94 | 536 | 532 | 538 | 3.8 | 1.5 | 10.5 | 7.0 | 70% | 12% | 92.4 | 39 | 23 | 38 | 30% | 81% | 5% | 0 | 15 | | | 20 | 1.23 | 21.3 | 166 | 197 | $12 |
| 17 2 TM | 2 | 19 | 76 | 76 | 2.84 | 3.88 | 1.05 | 656 | 662 | 651 | 4.0 | 1.8 | 9.0 | 5.1 | 67% | 14% | 92.3 | 41 | 18 | 41 | 28% | 81% | 13% | 0 | 15 | | | 90 | 1.30 | 14.2 | 133 | 160 | $15 |
| 18 MIN | 1 | 0 | 56 | 44 | 4.50 | 4.98 | 1.43 | 855 | 976 | 772 | 4.4 | 2.4 | 7.1 | 2.9 | 63% | 11% | 90.9 | 32 | 21 | 47 | 32% | 75% | 13% | 0 | 16 | | | 0 | 1.02 | -2.4 | 72 | 83 | -$5 |
| 1st Half | 1 | 0 | 38 | 33 | 4.26 | 4.91 | 1.42 | 817 | 1043 | 687 | 4.4 | 3.1 | 7.8 | 2.5 | 66% | 11% | 91.2 | 28 | 21 | 51 | 32% | 75% | 11% | 0 | 17 | | | 0 | 1.31 | -0.5 | 64 | 73 | -$5 |
| 2nd Half | 0 | 0 | 18 | 11 | 5.00 | 5.14 | 1.44 | 922 | 874 | 967 | 4.4 | 1.0 | 5.5 | 5.5 | 58% | 10% | 90.0 | 37 | 21 | 42 | 32% | 76% | 18% | 0 | 16 | | | 0 | 0.42 | -1.9 | 87 | 100 | -$6 |
| **19 Proj** | **2** | **5** | **73** | **64** | **3.74** | **3.91** | **1.25** | **765** | **783** | **750** | **4.1** | **1.9** | **8.0** | **4.3** | **64%** | **12%** | **91.4** | **37** | **20** | **43** | **31%** | **77%** | **13%** | **0** | | | | | | **1.9** | **108** | **124** | **$2** |

## Reed,Cody

| Age: 26 | Th: L | Role RP | Health | A | LIMA Plan | C |
|---|---|---|---|---|---|---|
| Ht: 6' 5" | Wt: 230 | Type Pwr xGB | PT/Exp | D | Rand Var | +3 |
| | | | Consist | A | MM | 2201 |

1-3, 3.98 ERA in 43 IP at CIN. Once-top prospect dialed back some velocity, reversed hellacious 2017 Ctl problems. Owns elite GB%, plus SwK; flashed skills in back-to-back Sept starts (11 IP, no runs, 16/2 K/BB). Chronic HR woes, elevated H%, consistency still impede the next step up. Watch from a distance.

| Yr Tm | W | Sv | IP | K | ERA | xERA | WHIP | oOPS | vL | vR | BF/G | Ctl | Dom | Cmd | FpK | SwK | Vel | G | L | F | H% | S% | hr/f | GS | APC | DOM% | DIS% | Sv% | LI | RAR | BPV | BPX | R$ |
|---|---|---|---|---|---|---|---|---|---|---|---|---|---|---|---|---|---|---|---|---|---|---|---|---|---|---|---|---|---|---|---|---|---|
| 14 | | | | | | | | | | | | | | | | | | | | | | | | | | | | | | | | | |
| 15 aa | 8 | 0 | 78 | 72 | 3.32 | 3.53 | 1.29 | | | | 24.8 | 2.9 | 8.3 | 2.9 | | | | | | | 32% | 75% | | | | | | | | 6.2 | 96 | 115 | $4 |
| 16 CIN * | 6 | 0 | 121 | 100 | 5.42 | 6.02 | 1.61 | 968 | 782 | 1022 | 23.2 | 3.1 | 7.5 | 2.4 | 59% | 10% | 92.8 | 52 | 21 | 27 | 36% | 70% | 28% | 10 | 88 | 10% | 40% | | | -18.3 | 44 | 52 | -$10 |
| 17 CIN * | 5 | 1 | 124 | 104 | 4.66 | 5.48 | 1.79 | 780 | 551 | 873 | 17.3 | 6.1 | 7.6 | 1.2 | 38% | 14% | 94.3 | 60 | 14 | 26 | 34% | 75% | 27% | 1 | 28 | 0% | 100% | 100 | 0.47 | -4.6 | 44 | 52 | -$9 |
| 18 CIN * | 5 | 0 | 150 | 130 | 4.74 | 5.53 | 1.51 | 729 | 560 | 774 | 18.6 | 2.9 | 7.8 | 2.7 | 58% | 11% | 92.4 | 61 | 16 | 23 | 35% | 72% | 17% | 7 | 42 | 29% | 57% | 0 | 0.81 | -11.0 | 59 | 68 | -$8 |
| 1st Half | 2 | 0 | 74 | 59 | 5.93 | 7.06 | 1.73 | 832 | 0 | 1153 | 21.0 | 3.3 | 7.2 | 2.2 | 61% | 12% | 92.8 | 33 | 20 | 47 | 36% | 70% | 29% | 1 | 25 | 0% | 100% | 0 | 0.40 | -16.3 | 23 | 27 | -$23 |
| 2nd Half | 3 | 0 | 76 | 71 | 3.59 | 4.05 | 1.31 | 713 | 667 | 725 | 16.6 | 2.6 | 8.4 | 3.3 | 58% | 11% | 92.4 | 65 | 15 | 20 | 33% | 75% | 14% | 6 | 48 | 33% | 50% | 0 | 0.93 | 5.3 | 96 | 111 | $5 |
| **19 Proj** | **5** | **0** | **116** | **100** | **4.57** | **3.80** | **1.56** | **785** | **694** | **809** | **19.1** | **3.7** | **7.8** | **2.1** | **58%** | **11%** | **92.6** | **60** | **18** | **23** | **34%** | **73%** | **18%** | **24** | | | | | | **4.3** | **77** | **89** | **-$5** |

## Reid-Foley,Sean

| Age: 23 | Th: R | Role SP | Health | A | LIMA Plan | D+ |
|---|---|---|---|---|---|---|
| Ht: 6' 3" | Wt: 220 | Type Pwr FB | PT/Exp | D | Rand Var | +3 |
| | | | Consist | F | MM | 1201 |

2-4, 5.13 ERA in 33 IP at TOR. Conquered Double-A (2.03 ERA, 44 IP) in second effort; proceeded to Triple-A, MLB debut from there. Dom/SwK say stuff stepped forward, but throwing strikes remains an effort. Secondaries need consistency, G/L/F needs taming. More minor league IP likely; bullpen role is an option.

| Yr Tm | W | Sv | IP | K | ERA | xERA | WHIP | oOPS | vL | vR | BF/G | Ctl | Dom | Cmd | FpK | SwK | Vel | G | L | F | H% | S% | hr/f | GS | APC | DOM% | DIS% | Sv% | LI | RAR | BPV | BPX | R$ |
|---|---|---|---|---|---|---|---|---|---|---|---|---|---|---|---|---|---|---|---|---|---|---|---|---|---|---|---|---|---|---|---|---|---|
| 14 | | | | | | | | | | | | | | | | | | | | | | | | | | | | | | | | | |
| 15 | | | | | | | | | | | | | | | | | | | | | | | | | | | | | | | | | |
| 16 | | | | | | | | | | | | | | | | | | | | | | | | | | | | | | | | | |
| 17 aa | 10 | 0 | 133 | 104 | 6.36 | 6.48 | 1.69 | | | | 22.1 | 3.7 | 7.1 | 1.9 | | | | | | | 35% | 66% | | | | | | | | -32.7 | 24 | 29 | -$13 |
| 18 TOR * | 14 | 0 | 165 | 168 | 4.38 | 4.03 | 1.38 | 794 | 749 | 846 | 22.3 | 4.0 | 9.2 | 2.3 | 57% | 12% | 93.8 | 37 | 26 | 37 | 32% | 70% | 19% | 7 | 91 | 29% | 43% | | | -4.8 | 83 | 95 | $4 |
| 1st Half | 9 | 0 | 88 | 85 | 3.85 | 3.54 | 1.31 | | | | 22.8 | 3.6 | 8.6 | 2.4 | | | | | | | 31% | 71% | 0% | 0 | | | | | | 3.3 | 90 | 103 | $9 |
| 2nd Half | 5 | 0 | 76 | 83 | 5.00 | 4.60 | 1.47 | 794 | 749 | 846 | 21.8 | 4.5 | 9.8 | 2.2 | 57% | 12% | 93.8 | 37 | 26 | 37 | 33% | 68% | 19% | 7 | 91 | 29% | 43% | | | -8.0 | 75 | 86 | -$1 |
| **19 Proj** | **6** | **0** | **73** | **68** | **5.25** | **4.45** | **1.51** | **740** | **684** | **803** | **22.2** | **4.0** | **8.4** | **2.1** | **57%** | **12%** | **93.8** | **37** | **26** | **37** | **33%** | **68%** | **11%** | **14** | | | | | | **-2.5** | **60** | **69** | **-$5** |

## Reyes,Alex

| Age: 24 | Th: R | Role SP | Health | F | LIMA Plan | B+ |
|---|---|---|---|---|---|---|
| Ht: 6' 3" | Wt: 175 | Type Pwr xFB | PT/Exp | F | Rand Var | -5 |
| | | | Consist | F | MM | 2401 |

0-0, 0.00 ERA in 4 IP at STL. Followed up 2017 Tommy John surgery hiatus with season-ending lat surgery after just one MLB start. Pre-injury, both Dom, Ctl say elite stuff remains intact. But even if healthy, IP limit, short-term role questions cap his 2019 upside. Triple-F reliability is scary; needs to log some MLB innings.

| Yr Tm | W | Sv | IP | K | ERA | xERA | WHIP | oOPS | vL | vR | BF/G | Ctl | Dom | Cmd | FpK | SwK | Vel | G | L | F | H% | S% | hr/f | GS | APC | DOM% | DIS% | Sv% | LI | RAR | BPV | BPX | R$ |
|---|---|---|---|---|---|---|---|---|---|---|---|---|---|---|---|---|---|---|---|---|---|---|---|---|---|---|---|---|---|---|---|---|---|
| 14 | | | | | | | | | | | | | | | | | | | | | | | | | | | | | | | | | |
| 15 aa | 3 | 0 | 35 | 48 | 3.24 | 1.87 | 1.13 | | | | 17.1 | 4.4 | 12.4 | 2.8 | | | | | | | 30% | 70% | | | | | | | | 3.1 | 144 | 172 | $1 |
| 16 STL * | 6 | 1 | 111 | 129 | 3.84 | 3.57 | 1.39 | 578 | 672 | 509 | 18.0 | 4.3 | 10.4 | 2.4 | 56% | 12% | 96.5 | 43 | 15 | 41 | 34% | 72% | 2% | 5 | 66 | 20% | 0% | 100 | 0.95 | 4.8 | 103 | 123 | $4 |
| 17 | | | | | | | | | | | | | | | | | | | | | | | | | | | | | | | | | |
| 18 STL * | 2 | 0 | 20 | 23 | 0.00 | 0.00 | 0.55 | 650 | 629 | 661 | 22.7 | 2.6 | 10.3 | 4.0 | 53% | 4% | 94.8 | 40 | 20 | 40 | 13% | 100% | 0% | 1 | 73 | 0% | 0% | | | 10.4 | 183 | 211 | $3 |
| 1st Half | 2 | 0 | 20 | 23 | 0.00 | 0.00 | 0.55 | 650 | 629 | 661 | 22.7 | 2.6 | 10.3 | 4.0 | 53% | 4% | 94.8 | 40 | 20 | 40 | 13% | 100% | 0% | 1 | 73 | 0% | 0% | | | 10.4 | 183 | 211 | $3 |
| 2nd Half | | | | | | | | | | | | | | | | | | | | | | | | | | | | | | | | | |
| **19 Proj** | **8** | **0** | **102** | **116** | **3.79** | **3.71** | **1.26** | **677** | **686** | **672** | **23.6** | **3.8** | **10.3** | **2.7** | **56%** | **12%** | **96.5** | **43** | **15** | **41** | **29%** | **75%** | **13%** | **18** | | | | | | **6.3** | **105** | **120** | **$6** |

JOCK THOMPSON

## Richard,Clayton

| Age: 35 | Th: L | Role: RP | Health | D | LIMA Plan | D+ |
|---|---|---|---|---|---|---|
| Ht: 6' 5" | Wt: 240 | Type: xGB | PT/Exp | A | Rand Var | +5 |
| | | | Consist | A | MM | 1003 |

Reportedly pitched through pain in both knees for most of the season; shut it down in late August and underwent two surgeries to clean up various issues. Flashed tolerable skills in 1st half, but crashed hard afterwards. Expected ready for spring, but he isn't viable as anything more than a periodic matchup play.

| Yr Tm | W | Sv | IP | K | ERA | xERA | WHIP | oOPS | vL | vR | BF/G | Ctl | Dom | Cmd | FpK | SwK | Vel | G | L | F | H% | S% | hr/f | GS | APC | DOM% | DIS% | Sv% | LI | RAR | BPV | BPX | R$ |
|---|---|---|---|---|---|---|---|---|---|---|---|---|---|---|---|---|---|---|---|---|---|---|---|---|---|---|---|---|---|---|---|---|---|
| 14 a/a | 1 | 0 | 21 | 6 | 7.45 | 9.82 | 2.27 | | | | 27.1 | 2.3 | 2.5 | 1.1 | | | | | | | 42% | 69% | | | | | | | | -9.8 | -37 | -44 | -$9 |
| 15 CHC * | 9 | 0 | 105 | 44 | 2.99 | 4.13 | 1.34 | 714 | 534 | 820 | 13.3 | 1.9 | 3.7 | 2.0 | 61% | 7% | 91.0 | 59 | 26 | 15 | 31% | 79% | 14% | 3 | 27 | 0% | 33% | 0 | 0.90 | 12.7 | 45 | 53 | $4 |
| 16 2 NL | 3 | 1 | 68 | 41 | 3.33 | 4.46 | 1.66 | 761 | 654 | 799 | 8.5 | 4.1 | 5.5 | 1.3 | 63% | 9% | 90.8 | 65 | 17 | 18 | 34% | 81% | 10% | 9 | 30 | 11% | 33% | 100 | 0.64 | 7.2 | 30 | 35 | -$3 |
| 17 SD | 8 | 0 | 197 | 151 | 4.79 | 3.90 | 1.52 | 842 | 676 | 899 | 26.8 | 2.7 | 6.9 | 2.6 | 62% | 9% | 90.7 | 59 | 21 | 20 | 35% | 71% | 19% | 32 | 95 | 25% | 38% | | | -10.5 | 88 | 106 | -$4 |
| 18 SD | 7 | 0 | 159 | 108 | 5.33 | 4.18 | 1.38 | 770 | 663 | 799 | 25.3 | 3.4 | 6.1 | 1.8 | 61% | 9% | 90.1 | 57 | 22 | 22 | 29% | 63% | 18% | 27 | 88 | 22% | 48% | | | -23.1 | 53 | 61 | -$8 |
| 1st Half | 7 | 0 | 107 | 84 | 4.29 | 3.68 | 1.23 | 708 | 648 | 727 | 26.4 | 2.8 | 7.1 | 2.5 | 61% | 10% | 90.1 | 58 | 21 | 22 | 29% | 66% | 14% | 17 | 94 | 35% | 29% | | | -1.8 | 88 | 101 | $3 |
| 2nd Half | 0 | 0 | 52 | 24 | 7.49 | 5.31 | 1.68 | 895 | 706 | 932 | 23.3 | 4.7 | 4.2 | 0.9 | 63% | 6% | 90.0 | 55 | 23 | 22 | 30% | 56% | 24% | 10 | 78 | 0% | 80% | | | -21.3 | -19 | -21 | -$29 |
| **19 Proj** | **6** | **0** | **160** | **107** | **4.54** | **4.09** | **1.46** | **792** | **638** | **840** | **17.7** | **3.2** | **6.0** | **1.9** | **62%** | **8%** | **90.4** | **56** | **22** | **22** | **31%** | **71%** | **16%** | **30** | | | | | | **-7.6** | **55** | **64** | **-$4** |

## Richards,Garrett

| Age: 31 | Th: R | Role: SP | Health | F | LIMA Plan | B+ |
|---|---|---|---|---|---|---|
| Ht: 6' 3" | Wt: 210 | Type: Pwr GB | PT/Exp | D | Rand Var | +2 |
| | | | Consist | A | MM | 3300 |

Spent a month on DL with a hamstring strain, but then his time-bomb UCL (diagnosed May 2016) finally gave out, triggering Tommy John surgery in July. Expected to miss most of 2019. When healthy, he induces lots of GB and racks up plenty of strikeouts, but the IP column highlights the rarity of such occasions.

| Yr Tm | W | Sv | IP | K | ERA | xERA | WHIP | oOPS | vL | vR | BF/G | Ctl | Dom | Cmd | FpK | SwK | Vel | G | L | F | H% | S% | hr/f | GS | APC | DOM% | DIS% | Sv% | LI | RAR | BPV | BPX | R$ |
|---|---|---|---|---|---|---|---|---|---|---|---|---|---|---|---|---|---|---|---|---|---|---|---|---|---|---|---|---|---|---|---|---|---|
| 14 LAA | 13 | 0 | 169 | 164 | 2.61 | 3.08 | 1.04 | 529 | 519 | 542 | 26.1 | 2.7 | 8.8 | 3.2 | 55% | 11% | 96.3 | 51 | 21 | 28 | 28% | 74% | 4% | 26 | 101 | 58% | 8% | | | 23.4 | 113 | 135 | $21 |
| 15 LAA | 15 | 0 | 207 | 176 | 3.65 | 3.75 | 1.24 | 664 | 628 | 707 | 27.0 | 3.3 | 7.6 | 2.3 | 60% | 12% | 95.5 | 55 | 17 | 28 | 28% | 73% | 12% | 32 | 102 | 34% | 31% | | | 8.1 | 81 | 97 | $13 |
| 16 LAA | 1 | 0 | 35 | 34 | 2.34 | 3.99 | 1.33 | 683 | 483 | 858 | 24.7 | 3.9 | 8.8 | 2.3 | 57% | 11% | 95.6 | 46 | 25 | 29 | 31% | 84% | 7% | 6 | 103 | 33% | 0% | | | 7.9 | 78 | 92 | $0 |
| 17 LAA | 0 | 0 | 28 | 27 | 2.28 | 3.34 | 0.90 | 494 | 517 | 470 | 18.0 | 2.3 | 8.8 | 3.9 | 61% | 13% | 95.8 | 54 | 17 | 29 | 25% | 75% | 5% | 6 | 71 | 17% | 17% | | | 7.1 | 129 | 154 | $0 |
| 18 LAA | 5 | 0 | 76 | 87 | 3.66 | 3.68 | 1.28 | 686 | 652 | 724 | 20.3 | 4.0 | 10.3 | 2.6 | 55% | 12% | 95.9 | 49 | 19 | 31 | 29% | 77% | 17% | 16 | 82 | 13% | 44% | | | 4.7 | 103 | 119 | $2 |
| 1st Half | 4 | 0 | 68 | 78 | 3.42 | 3.72 | 1.29 | 666 | 647 | 688 | 20.8 | 4.2 | 10.3 | 2.4 | 55% | 12% | 95.9 | 50 | 19 | 31 | 30% | 78% | 14% | 14 | 85 | 14% | 43% | | | 6.1 | 99 | 114 | $3 |
| 2nd Half | 1 | 0 | 8 | 9 | 5.63 | 3.39 | 1.25 | 857 | 692 | 980 | 16.5 | 2.3 | 10.1 | 4.5 | 50% | 9% | 95.4 | 43 | 24 | 33 | 27% | 71% | 43% | 2 | 61 | 0% | 50% | | | -1.5 | 142 | 164 | -$10 |
| **19 Proj** | **1** | **0** | **15** | **14** | **3.78** | **3.54** | **1.24** | **649** | **591** | **713** | **23.4** | **3.6** | **8.8** | **2.4** | **57%** | **12%** | **95.8** | **51** | **20** | **29** | **29%** | **71%** | **11%** | **3** | | | | | | **0.7** | **91** | **104** | **-$4** |

## Richards,Trevor

| Age: 26 | Th: R | Role: SP | Health | A | LIMA Plan | B+ |
|---|---|---|---|---|---|---|
| Ht: 6' 2" | Wt: 190 | Type: Pwr | PT/Exp | D | Rand Var | 0 |
| | | | Consist | A | MM | 2203 |

4-10, 4.52 ERA in 131 IP at MIA. Signed out of indy ball in 2016. Spent most of 2018 in MLB, despite having not pitched above Double-A previously. 2nd half Dom surged as he threw plus change-up more (26% SwK, 38% usage), but it's his only pitch with >7% SwK. Lack of velocity curbs further optimism for this average skill set.

| Yr Tm | W | Sv | IP | K | ERA | xERA | WHIP | oOPS | vL | vR | BF/G | Ctl | Dom | Cmd | FpK | SwK | Vel | G | L | F | H% | S% | hr/f | GS | APC | DOM% | DIS% | Sv% | LI | RAR | BPV | BPX | R$ |
|---|---|---|---|---|---|---|---|---|---|---|---|---|---|---|---|---|---|---|---|---|---|---|---|---|---|---|---|---|---|---|---|---|---|
| 14 | | | | | | | | | | | | | | | | | | | | | | | | | | | | | | | | | |
| 15 | | | | | | | | | | | | | | | | | | | | | | | | | | | | | | | | | |
| 16 | | | | | | | | | | | | | | | | | | | | | | | | | | | | | | | | | |
| 17 aa | 5 | 0 | 75 | 65 | 3.94 | 4.10 | 1.37 | | | | 22.5 | 2.4 | 7.8 | 3.3 | | | | | | | 35% | 71% | | | | | | | | 3.9 | 97 | 117 | $1 |
| 18 MIA * | 7 | 0 | 166 | 161 | 3.92 | 3.99 | 1.29 | 754 | 668 | 829 | 22.1 | 3.1 | 8.7 | 2.8 | 62% | 11% | 90.8 | 36 | 25 | 39 | 31% | 73% | 11% | 25 | 89 | 32% | 32% | | | 4.6 | 84 | 97 | $5 |
| 1st Half | 5 | 0 | 88 | 74 | 3.84 | 3.78 | 1.26 | 769 | 613 | 905 | 22.5 | 2.7 | 7.5 | 2.8 | 58% | 9% | 91.1 | 40 | 23 | 37 | 31% | 71% | 8% | 10 | 87 | 20% | 50% | | | 3.4 | 84 | 96 | $6 |
| 2nd Half | 2 | 0 | 78 | 87 | 4.02 | 4.17 | 1.33 | 745 | 702 | 782 | 22.5 | 3.7 | 10.0 | 2.7 | 64% | 12% | 90.6 | 33 | 27 | 40 | 31% | 74% | 13% | 15 | 91 | 40% | 20% | | | 1.2 | 92 | 105 | $4 |
| **19 Proj** | **6** | **0** | **131** | **123** | **4.09** | **4.02** | **1.36** | **775** | **680** | **858** | **22.4** | **3.0** | **8.5** | **2.9** | **61%** | **11%** | **90.8** | **36** | **25** | **39** | **33%** | **73%** | **11%** | **24** | | | | | | **0.9** | **86** | **99** | **$2** |

## Roark,Tanner

| Age: 32 | Th: R | Role: SP | Health | A | LIMA Plan | B+ |
|---|---|---|---|---|---|---|
| Ht: 6' 2" | Wt: 229 | Type: | PT/Exp | A | Rand Var | 0 |
| | | | Consist | A | MM | 2105 |

PRO: Curbed free passes; improved Cmd vL (2.7). CON: 2nd half 2017 Dom/SwK growth (9.2 Dom, 11% SwK) vanished as quickly as it appeared; lost GB lean; alarming DIS% trend. Ordinary skill set leaves him open to H%, hr/f swings. Those swung in his favor in 2014, 2016, but tough to bet on them again.

| Yr Tm | W | Sv | IP | K | ERA | xERA | WHIP | oOPS | vL | vR | BF/G | Ctl | Dom | Cmd | FpK | SwK | Vel | G | L | F | H% | S% | hr/f | GS | APC | DOM% | DIS% | Sv% | LI | RAR | BPV | BPX | R$ |
|---|---|---|---|---|---|---|---|---|---|---|---|---|---|---|---|---|---|---|---|---|---|---|---|---|---|---|---|---|---|---|---|---|---|
| 14 WAS | 15 | 0 | 199 | 138 | 2.85 | 3.80 | 1.09 | 632 | 672 | 591 | 25.7 | 1.8 | 6.3 | 3.5 | 65% | 9% | 91.1 | 41 | 21 | 38 | 28% | 77% | 7% | 31 | 97 | 29% | 26% | | | 21.7 | 84 | 100 | $19 |
| 15 WAS | 4 | 1 | 111 | 70 | 4.38 | 4.17 | 1.31 | 784 | 866 | 709 | 11.7 | 2.1 | 5.7 | 2.7 | 60% | 8% | 92.8 | 48 | 22 | 31 | 30% | 71% | 15% | 12 | 45 | 17% | 50% | 50 | 0.90 | -5.7 | 71 | 85 | -$2 |
| 16 WAS | 16 | 0 | 210 | 172 | 2.83 | 3.97 | 1.17 | 634 | 617 | 648 | 25.1 | 3.1 | 7.4 | 2.4 | 58% | 9% | 92.1 | 49 | 20 | 31 | 27% | 79% | 9% | 33 | 99 | 36% | 18% | 0 | 0.81 | 35.3 | 75 | 89 | $24 |
| 17 WAS | 13 | 0 | 181 | 166 | 4.67 | 4.19 | 1.33 | 729 | 836 | 618 | 24.3 | 3.2 | 8.2 | 2.6 | 59% | 10% | 92.2 | 48 | 20 | 32 | 31% | 68% | 14% | 30 | 101 | 23% | 30% | 0 | 0.76 | -6.9 | 89 | 106 | $6 |
| 18 WAS | 9 | 0 | 180 | 146 | 4.34 | 4.37 | 1.28 | 741 | 767 | 716 | 24.5 | 2.5 | 7.3 | 2.9 | 60% | 9% | 91.5 | 41 | 22 | 38 | 30% | 70% | 12% | 30 | 95 | 30% | 40% | 0 | 0.83 | -4.3 | 83 | 95 | $3 |
| 1st Half | 3 | 0 | 99 | 84 | 4.10 | 4.35 | 1.27 | 733 | 782 | 678 | 24.5 | 3.3 | 7.7 | 2.3 | 60% | 9% | 91.0 | 42 | 21 | 36 | 28% | 71% | 13% | 16 | 98 | 38% | 38% | 0 | 0.88 | 0.6 | 70 | 80 | $3 |
| 2nd Half | 6 | 0 | 82 | 62 | 4.63 | 4.40 | 1.30 | 749 | 746 | 751 | 24.6 | 1.5 | 6.8 | 4.4 | 61% | 8% | 92.0 | 39 | 22 | 39 | 32% | 67% | 11% | 14 | 92 | 21% | 43% | | | -4.8 | 98 | 113 | $4 |
| **19 Proj** | **11** | **0** | **181** | **148** | **4.26** | **3.94** | **1.27** | **720** | **762** | **681** | **24.2** | **2.6** | **7.3** | **2.9** | **60%** | **9%** | **91.9** | **44** | **21** | **35** | **30%** | **69%** | **12%** | **31** | | | | | | **3.8** | **85** | **97** | **$7** |

## Robertson,David

| Age: 34 | Th: R | Role: RP | Health | A | LIMA Plan | B |
|---|---|---|---|---|---|---|
| Ht: 5' 11" | Wt: 195 | Type: Pwr | PT/Exp | B | Rand Var | 0 |
| | | | Consist | B | MM | 5520 |

As expected, regression grabbed hold of 2017 ERA and shook it, but there is still useful fantasy production here. Elite Dom, average Ctl and ability to dominate both vR and vL comprise a collection of still-closer-worthy skills. Watch where he lands in free agency. With opportunity, UP: 30 saves

| Yr Tm | W | Sv | IP | K | ERA | xERA | WHIP | oOPS | vL | vR | BF/G | Ctl | Dom | Cmd | FpK | SwK | Vel | G | L | F | H% | S% | hr/f | GS | APC | DOM% | DIS% | Sv% | LI | RAR | BPV | BPX | R$ |
|---|---|---|---|---|---|---|---|---|---|---|---|---|---|---|---|---|---|---|---|---|---|---|---|---|---|---|---|---|---|---|---|---|---|
| 14 NYY | 4 | 39 | 64 | 96 | 3.08 | 2.38 | 1.06 | 588 | 437 | 765 | 4.1 | 3.2 | 13.4 | 4.2 | 61% | 13% | 91.8 | 44 | 23 | 33 | 31% | 75% | 16% | 0 | 17 | | | 89 | 1.67 | 5.3 | 177 | 211 | $20 |
| 15 CHW | 6 | 34 | 63 | 86 | 3.41 | 2.60 | 0.93 | 573 | 462 | 651 | 4.2 | 1.8 | 12.2 | 6.6 | 68% | 14% | 92.2 | 36 | 30 | 34 | 30% | 67% | 14% | 0 | 16 | | | 83 | 1.35 | 4.3 | 184 | 219 | $21 |
| 16 CHW | 5 | 37 | 62 | 75 | 3.47 | 3.95 | 1.36 | 684 | 610 | 756 | 4.3 | 4.6 | 10.8 | 2.3 | 61% | 13% | 91.8 | 45 | 14 | 40 | 32% | 77% | 10% | 0 | 17 | | | 84 | 1.44 | 5.6 | 93 | 111 | $17 |
| 17 2 AL | 9 | 14 | 68 | 98 | 1.84 | 2.74 | 0.85 | 488 | 441 | 527 | 4.3 | 3.0 | 12.9 | 4.3 | 59% | 17% | 91.6 | 47 | 16 | 37 | 23% | 85% | 12% | 0 | 17 | | | 88 | 1.19 | 21.2 | 176 | 211 | $21 |
| 18 NYY | 8 | 5 | 70 | 91 | 3.23 | 3.22 | 1.03 | 595 | 618 | 574 | 4.1 | 3.4 | 11.8 | 3.5 | 56% | 14% | 92.3 | 45 | 17 | 37 | 27% | 72% | 12% | 0 | 17 | | | 56 | 1.20 | 7.9 | 144 | 166 | $10 |
| 1st Half | 5 | 1 | 36 | 44 | 3.47 | 3.41 | 1.07 | 593 | 565 | 612 | 4.1 | 3.2 | 10.9 | 3.4 | 58% | 14% | 92.1 | 44 | 20 | 36 | 29% | 68% | 6% | 0 | 17 | | | 20 | 1.26 | 3.1 | 131 | 151 | $8 |
| 2nd Half | 3 | 4 | 33 | 47 | 2.97 | 3.03 | 0.99 | 598 | 663 | 520 | 4.1 | 3.5 | 12.7 | 3.6 | 54% | 14% | 92.5 | 47 | 14 | 39 | 24% | 79% | 18% | 0 | 17 | | | 100 | 1.13 | 4.9 | 159 | 183 | $12 |
| **19 Proj** | **7** | **16** | **65** | **88** | **2.89** | **2.81** | **1.03** | **582** | **566** | **597** | **4.0** | **3.4** | **12.1** | **3.6** | **58%** | **15%** | **92.1** | **46** | **17** | **37** | **27%** | **76%** | **13%** | **0** | | | | | | **14.6** | **150** | **172** | **$15** |

## Robles,Hansel

| Age: 28 | Th: R | Role: RP | Health | B | LIMA Plan | C |
|---|---|---|---|---|---|---|
| Ht: 5' 11" | Wt: 185 | Type: Pwr FB | PT/Exp | D | Rand Var | -1 |
| | | | Consist | B | MM | 1310 |

Claimed by LAA off waivers from NYM in late-June. Change of coast seemed to help, as FpK and velocity spiked in 2nd half. Returned from brief August DL stint (shoulder impingement) using change-up more (9% vs. 3% earlier in 2018) during impressive Sept (1.74 ERA, 3.5 Ctl, 10.5 Dom). An intriguing late-inning speculation.

| Yr Tm | W | Sv | IP | K | ERA | xERA | WHIP | oOPS | vL | vR | BF/G | Ctl | Dom | Cmd | FpK | SwK | Vel | G | L | F | H% | S% | hr/f | GS | APC | DOM% | DIS% | Sv% | LI | RAR | BPV | BPX | R$ |
|---|---|---|---|---|---|---|---|---|---|---|---|---|---|---|---|---|---|---|---|---|---|---|---|---|---|---|---|---|---|---|---|---|---|
| 14 aa | 7 | 0 | 111 | 91 | 4.36 | 4.18 | 1.39 | | | | 15.5 | 3.3 | 7.4 | 2.3 | | | | | | | 32% | 70% | | | | | | | | -8.4 | 69 | 83 | -$3 |
| 15 NYM | 4 | 0 | 54 | 61 | 3.67 | 3.64 | 1.02 | 655 | 560 | 717 | 3.8 | 3.0 | 10.2 | 3.4 | 60% | 13% | 95.7 | 33 | 18 | 49 | 24% | 70% | 12% | 0 | 16 | | | 0 | 1.02 | 2.0 | 113 | 135 | $3 |
| 16 NYM | 6 | 1 | 78 | 85 | 3.48 | 4.33 | 1.35 | 703 | 586 | 784 | 4.9 | 4.2 | 9.8 | 2.4 | 59% | 12% | 95.2 | 30 | 29 | 41 | 32% | 77% | 8% | 0 | 20 | | | 33 | 1.07 | 6.8 | 73 | 86 | $3 |
| 17 NYM * | 7 | 4 | 80 | 78 | 5.30 | 5.15 | 1.51 | 750 | 712 | 771 | 5.4 | 4.9 | 8.7 | 1.8 | 54% | 9% | 94.9 | 34 | 22 | 44 | 30% | 70% | 15% | 0 | 21 | | | 50 | 1.11 | -9.2 | 44 | 53 | -$2 |
| 18 2 TM | 2 | 2 | 56 | 59 | 3.70 | 4.41 | 1.39 | 771 | 865 | 704 | 4.6 | 4.0 | 9.5 | 2.4 | 57% | 11% | 96.0 | 35 | 24 | 41 | 31% | 80% | 14% | 0 | 18 | | | 67 | 0.99 | 3.1 | 75 | 87 | -$1 |
| 1st Half | 2 | 0 | 23 | 26 | 5.01 | 4.50 | 1.54 | 970 | 1217 | 790 | 5.2 | 4.2 | 10.0 | 2.4 | 53% | 11% | 95.0 | 33 | 22 | 44 | 30% | 82% | 29% | 0 | 20 | | | 0 | 0.86 | -2.5 | 77 | 89 | -$7 |
| 2nd Half | 0 | 2 | 33 | 33 | 2.76 | 4.34 | 1.29 | 626 | 608 | 639 | 4.2 | 3.9 | 9.1 | 2.4 | 60% | 11% | 96.6 | 36 | 26 | 39 | 31% | 78% | 3% | 0 | 17 | | | 67 | 1.06 | 5.6 | 73 | 84 | $3 |
| **19 Proj** | **3** | **2** | **58** | **60** | **3.77** | **4.07** | **1.34** | **762** | **769** | **758** | **4.8** | **3.7** | **9.3** | **2.5** | **57%** | **11%** | **95.6** | **34** | **24** | **43** | **30%** | **78%** | **13%** | **0** | | | | | | **0.6** | **79** | **91** | **$0** |

## Rodney,Fernando

| Age: 42 | Th: R | Role: RP | Health | B | LIMA Plan | B |
|---|---|---|---|---|---|---|
| Ht: 5' 11" | Wt: 230 | Type: Pwr | PT/Exp | B | Rand Var | 0 |
| | | | Consist | A | MM | 2420 |

Boasted best Ctl since 2012 in 1st half, then lost the zone again. Threw top pitch, a change-up, less in 2018 (23% SwK, 29% usage) and upped sinker usage (51%), resulting in SwK/Dom dip. GB% decay is scary; 2nd half Ctl plus LD% are giant warning light to get off this train. Only S% kept it from being a lot worse.

| Yr Tm | W | Sv | IP | K | ERA | xERA | WHIP | oOPS | vL | vR | BF/G | Ctl | Dom | Cmd | FpK | SwK | Vel | G | L | F | H% | S% | hr/f | GS | APC | DOM% | DIS% | Sv% | LI | RAR | BPV | BPX | R$ |
|---|---|---|---|---|---|---|---|---|---|---|---|---|---|---|---|---|---|---|---|---|---|---|---|---|---|---|---|---|---|---|---|---|---|
| 14 SEA | 1 | 48 | 66 | 76 | 2.85 | 3.19 | 1.34 | 646 | 726 | 530 | 4.1 | 3.8 | 10.3 | 2.7 | 60% | 11% | 94.9 | 49 | 24 | 27 | 34% | 79% | 6% | 0 | 16 | | | 94 | 1.36 | 7.3 | 110 | 131 | $19 |
| 15 2 TM | 7 | 16 | 63 | 58 | 4.74 | 4.05 | 1.40 | 776 | 845 | 721 | 4.1 | 4.2 | 8.3 | 2.0 | 59% | 10% | 94.7 | 51 | 18 | 31 | 30% | 70% | 16% | 0 | 16 | | | 70 | 1.22 | -6.0 | 66 | 79 | $4 |
| 16 2 NL | 2 | 25 | 65 | 74 | 3.44 | 3.58 | 1.39 | 668 | 726 | 611 | 4.2 | 5.1 | 10.2 | 2.0 | 57% | 13% | 94.4 | 55 | 22 | 23 | 31% | 77% | 14% | 0 | 17 | | | 89 | 1.13 | 6.0 | 79 | 94 | $10 |
| 17 ARI | 5 | 39 | 55 | 65 | 4.23 | 3.61 | 1.19 | 582 | 662 | 497 | 3.8 | 4.2 | 10.6 | 2.5 | 59% | 13% | 94.6 | 52 | 16 | 32 | 29% | 63% | 7% | 0 | 16 | | | 87 | 1.28 | 0.9 | 106 | 127 | $19 |
| 18 2 AL | 4 | 25 | 64 | 70 | 3.36 | 4.14 | 1.46 | 703 | 572 | 827 | 4.2 | 4.5 | 9.8 | 2.2 | 57% | 11% | 94.2 | 44 | 24 | 32 | 33% | 80% | 12% | 0 | 17 | | | 78 | 1.21 | 6.3 | 77 | 89 | $10 |
| 1st Half | 2 | 17 | 27 | 31 | 2.96 | 3.81 | 1.21 | 603 | 356 | 782 | 4.0 | 3.6 | 10.2 | 2.8 | 57% | 13% | 94.2 | 44 | 18 | 38 | 29% | 80% | 11% | 0 | 17 | | | 81 | 1.28 | 4.0 | 108 | 125 | $15 |
| 2nd Half | 2 | 8 | 37 | 39 | 3.65 | 4.40 | 1.65 | 774 | 692 | 866 | 4.3 | 5.1 | 9.5 | 1.9 | 57% | 11% | 94.1 | 44 | 28 | 28 | 36% | 81% | 13% | 0 | 18 | | | 73 | 1.15 | 2.3 | 55 | 64 | $6 |
| **19 Proj** | **3** | **15** | **51** | **54** | **4.17** | **3.78** | **1.44** | **717** | **683** | **751** | **4.0** | **4.5** | **9.6** | **2.2** | **58%** | **12%** | **94.4** | **49** | **21** | **30** | **32%** | **73%** | **13%** | **0** | | | | | | **2.5** | **79** | **91** | **$4** |

GREG PYRON

## Rodon,Carlos

| Age: 26 | Th: L | Role: SP | Health | F | LIMA Plan | B+ |
|---|---|---|---|---|---|---|
| Ht: 6' 3" | Wt: 235 | Type: Pwr | PT/Exp | B | Rand Var | -3 |
| | | | Consist | B | MM | 1203 |

Recovery from off-season shoulder surgery (bursitis) cost him first two months. After shaking off the rust, he had a really nice 6-start run in July/August, but then unraveled again down the stretch. Ctl is the key: When he has it for stretches like those 6 starts, he's an asset. But FpK shows little sign of him finding a compass.

| Yr Tm | W | Sv | IP | K | ERA | xERA | WHIP | oOPS | vL | vR | BF/G | Ctl | Dom | Cmd | FpK | SwK | Vel | G | L | F | H% | S% | hr/f | GS | APC | DOM% | DIS% | Sv% | LI | RAR | BPV | BPX | R$ |
|---|---|---|---|---|---|---|---|---|---|---|---|---|---|---|---|---|---|---|---|---|---|---|---|---|---|---|---|---|---|---|---|---|---|
| 14 | | | | | | | | | | | | | | | | | | | | | | | | | | | | | | | | | |
| 15 CHW | 9 | 0 | 139 | 139 | 3.75 | 4.00 | 1.44 | 725 | 524 | 799 | 23.3 | 4.6 | 9.0 | 2.0 | 53% | 11% | 93.4 | 47 | 23 | 30 | 32% | 75% | 10% | 23 | 94 | 26% | 26% | 0 | 0.87 | 3.7 | 63 | 75 | $2 |
| 16 CHW | 9 | 0 | 165 | 168 | 4.04 | 3.97 | 1.39 | 763 | 609 | 799 | 25.5 | 2.9 | 9.2 | 3.1 | 54% | 11% | 93.4 | 44 | 21 | 35 | 34% | 75% | 14% | 28 | 100 | 18% | 25% | | | 3.1 | 107 | 128 | $4 |
| 17 CHW | 2 | 0 | 69 | 76 | 4.15 | 4.06 | 1.37 | 770 | 746 | 777 | 24.8 | 4.0 | 9.9 | 2.5 | 56% | 11% | 93.1 | 44 | 22 | 34 | 30% | 76% | 19% | 12 | 98 | 33% | 25% | | | 1.7 | 91 | 109 | -$1 |
| 18 CHW | 6 | 0 | 121 | 90 | 4.18 | 5.00 | 1.26 | 698 | 860 | 654 | 25.6 | 4.1 | 6.7 | 1.6 | 58% | 9% | 93.0 | 41 | 16 | 43 | 25% | 70% | 10% | 20 | 98 | 30% | 30% | | | -0.4 | 29 | 33 | $2 |
| 1st Half | 1 | 0 | 30 | 22 | 4.55 | 5.20 | 1.18 | 712 | 764 | 694 | 25.4 | 2.7 | 6.7 | 2.4 | 61% | 9% | 93.4 | 35 | 12 | 53 | 24% | 69% | 12% | 5 | 97 | 20% | 40% | | | -1.5 | 60 | 69 | -$10 |
| 2nd Half | 5 | 0 | 91 | 68 | 4.05 | 4.94 | 1.29 | 693 | 898 | 640 | 25.6 | 4.5 | 6.7 | 1.5 | 56% | 9% | 92.9 | 44 | 17 | 39 | 25% | 70% | 9% | 15 | 99 | 33% | 27% | | | 1.1 | 20 | 23 | $6 |
| **19 Proj** | **7** | **0** | **160** | **143** | **4.15** | **4.18** | **1.32** | **730** | **746** | **725** | **24.3** | **3.8** | **8.1** | **2.1** | **57%** | **10%** | **93.2** | **43** | **18** | **39** | **28%** | **73%** | **13%** | **27** | | | | | | **0.1** | **63** | **73** | **$4** |

## Rodriguez,Dereck

| Age: 27 | Th: R | Role: SP | Health | A | LIMA Plan | B |
|---|---|---|---|---|---|---|
| Ht: 6' 1" | Wt: 215 | Type: | PT/Exp | D | Rand Var | -2 |
| | | | Consist | F | MM | 1003 |

6-4, 2.81 ERA in 118 IP at SF. Out-of-nowhere breakout in terms of prospect pedigree and prior MLEs. Skills also skeptical: FpK questions Ctl; H% and hr/f papered over 2nd half skills collapse. That 2nd half was all MLB work; those skills (plus full-year MLB-only xERA of 4.43) represent reality here. Expect significant pullback.

| Yr Tm | W | Sv | IP | K | ERA | xERA | WHIP | oOPS | vL | vR | BF/G | Ctl | Dom | Cmd | FpK | SwK | Vel | G | L | F | H% | S% | hr/f | GS | APC | DOM% | DIS% | Sv% | LI | RAR | BPV | BPX | R$ |
|---|---|---|---|---|---|---|---|---|---|---|---|---|---|---|---|---|---|---|---|---|---|---|---|---|---|---|---|---|---|---|---|---|---|
| 14 | | | | | | | | | | | | | | | | | | | | | | | | | | | | | | | | | |
| 15 | | | | | | | | | | | | | | | | | | | | | | | | | | | | | | | | | |
| 16 | | | | | | | | | | | | | | | | | | | | | | | | | | | | | | | | | |
| 17 aa | 5 | 0 | 75 | 49 | 5.86 | 6.29 | 1.68 | | | | 22.6 | 3.6 | 5.8 | 1.6 | | | | | | | 34% | 68% | | | | | | | | -14.0 | 17 | 20 | -$9 |
| 18 SF * | 10 | 0 | 169 | 131 | 3.06 | 3.53 | 1.18 | 667 | 706 | 632 | 22.6 | 2.5 | 7.0 | 2.8 | 57% | 9% | 91.4 | 39 | 23 | 37 | 28% | 78% | 7% | 19 | 89 | 32% | 21% | 0 | 0.81 | 22.9 | 79 | 90 | $15 |
| 1st Half | 7 | 0 | 88 | 75 | 3.42 | 4.59 | 1.30 | 739 | 770 | 711 | 22.7 | 2.0 | 7.7 | 3.8 | 59% | 11% | 92.2 | 41 | 26 | 34 | 32% | 79% | 8% | 6 | 88 | 33% | 17% | 0 | 0.72 | 7.9 | 89 | 102 | $12 |
| 2nd Half | 3 | 0 | 81 | 56 | 2.66 | 4.58 | 1.05 | 630 | 672 | 592 | 23.2 | 3.0 | 6.2 | 2.1 | 57% | 9% | 91.0 | 39 | 22 | 39 | 23% | 77% | 7% | 13 | 89 | 31% | 23% | 0 | 0.85 | 15.0 | 48 | 55 | $18 |
| **19 Proj** | **9** | **0** | **160** | **114** | **4.31** | **4.46** | **1.37** | **808** | **844** | **776** | **22.6** | **3.0** | **6.4** | **2.1** | **58%** | **10%** | **91.5** | **40** | **23** | **37** | **30%** | **71%** | **11%** | **30** | | | | | | **-3.1** | **53** | **60** | **$2** |

## Rodriguez,Eduardo

| Age: 26 | Th: L | Role: SP | Health | F | LIMA Plan | B |
|---|---|---|---|---|---|---|
| Ht: 6' 2" | Wt: 220 | Type: Pwr FB | PT/Exp | B | Rand Var | 0 |
| | | | Consist | A | MM | 2303 |

Some promising concurrent trends here: stable Ctl and rising Dom pushing Cmd into the good zone, all while continuing to make progress vR. Chronic leg issues (knee problem in spring, ankle in 2nd half) likely will continue to cap his innings, but paying for a repeat will leave you with some room for potential profit.

| Yr Tm | W | Sv | IP | K | ERA | xERA | WHIP | oOPS | vL | vR | BF/G | Ctl | Dom | Cmd | FpK | SwK | Vel | G | L | F | H% | S% | hr/f | GS | APC | DOM% | DIS% | Sv% | LI | RAR | BPV | BPX | R$ |
|---|---|---|---|---|---|---|---|---|---|---|---|---|---|---|---|---|---|---|---|---|---|---|---|---|---|---|---|---|---|---|---|---|---|
| 14 aa | 6 | 0 | 120 | 93 | 4.42 | 4.35 | 1.46 | | | | 23.3 | 2.8 | 7.0 | 2.5 | | | | | | | 35% | 69% | | | | | | | | -10.0 | 77 | 92 | -$5 |
| 15 BOS * | 14 | 0 | 170 | 136 | 3.92 | 3.95 | 1.30 | 701 | 820 | 662 | 24.1 | 2.4 | 7.2 | 3.1 | 57% | 9% | 94.0 | 43 | 24 | 33 | 32% | 71% | 10% | 21 | 96 | 33% | 33% | | | 0.9 | 84 | 100 | $7 |
| 16 BOS * | 3 | 0 | 145 | 120 | 4.75 | 4.51 | 1.31 | 726 | 711 | 730 | 22.2 | 3.0 | 7.4 | 2.5 | 59% | 11% | 93.5 | 31 | 23 | 46 | 29% | 69% | 11% | 20 | 93 | 30% | 35% | | | -10.0 | 55 | 65 | -$2 |
| 17 BOS | 6 | 0 | 137 | 150 | 4.19 | 4.26 | 1.28 | 736 | 808 | 718 | 23.3 | 3.3 | 9.8 | 3.0 | 61% | 12% | 93.3 | 35 | 22 | 43 | 31% | 71% | 12% | 24 | 98 | 17% | 21% | 0 | 0.77 | 2.8 | 101 | 122 | $6 |
| 18 BOS | 13 | 0 | 130 | 146 | 3.82 | 3.97 | 1.26 | 681 | 691 | 679 | 20.5 | 3.1 | 10.1 | 3.2 | 61% | 11% | 93.3 | 39 | 20 | 41 | 32% | 74% | 11% | 23 | 86 | 30% | 26% | 0 | 0.81 | 5.3 | 115 | 132 | $9 |
| 1st Half | 9 | 0 | 88 | 94 | 4.11 | 4.09 | 1.30 | 708 | 760 | 696 | 23.7 | 2.9 | 9.7 | 3.4 | 61% | 12% | 93.2 | 40 | 19 | 41 | 33% | 73% | 12% | 16 | 101 | 19% | 25% | | | 0.5 | 114 | 131 | $10 |
| 2nd Half | 4 | 0 | 42 | 52 | 3.21 | 3.74 | 1.19 | 621 | 534 | 640 | 15.8 | 3.6 | 11.1 | 3.1 | 63% | 11% | 93.6 | 36 | 22 | 42 | 30% | 76% | 9% | 7 | 64 | 57% | 29% | 0 | 0.84 | 4.8 | 116 | 133 | $6 |
| **19 Proj** | **12** | **0** | **145** | **154** | **3.71** | **3.77** | **1.27** | **698** | **718** | **694** | **22.9** | **3.2** | **9.6** | **3.0** | **61%** | **11%** | **93.4** | **36** | **22** | **42** | **31%** | **75%** | **11%** | **26** | | | | | | **7.9** | **100** | **115** | **$10** |

## Rodriguez,Jefry

| Age: 25 | Th: R | Role: SP | Health | A | LIMA Plan | D |
|---|---|---|---|---|---|---|
| Ht: 6' 6" | Wt: 232 | Type: Pwr FB | PT/Exp | D | Rand Var | +1 |
| | | | Consist | F | MM | 0101 |

3-3, 5.71 ERA in 52 IP at WAS. Big guy with big arm and potentially plus stuff who has struggled to find that elusive last piece of the puzzle, Cmd. Not much sign of that clicking right now, but there's enough here to make it worth checking back periodically. In particular, sit up and pay attention if he shifts to pen role.

| Yr Tm | W | Sv | IP | K | ERA | xERA | WHIP | oOPS | vL | vR | BF/G | Ctl | Dom | Cmd | FpK | SwK | Vel | G | L | F | H% | S% | hr/f | GS | APC | DOM% | DIS% | Sv% | LI | RAR | BPV | BPX | R$ |
|---|---|---|---|---|---|---|---|---|---|---|---|---|---|---|---|---|---|---|---|---|---|---|---|---|---|---|---|---|---|---|---|---|---|
| 14 | | | | | | | | | | | | | | | | | | | | | | | | | | | | | | | | | |
| 15 | | | | | | | | | | | | | | | | | | | | | | | | | | | | | | | | | |
| 16 | | | | | | | | | | | | | | | | | | | | | | | | | | | | | | | | | |
| 17 | | | | | | | | | | | | | | | | | | | | | | | | | | | | | | | | | |
| 18 WAS * | 10 | 0 | 154 | 121 | 4.86 | 4.53 | 1.51 | 784 | 899 | 680 | 20.2 | 4.8 | 7.1 | 1.5 | 49% | 9% | 95.4 | 42 | 17 | 41 | 30% | 69% | 13% | 8 | 65 | 0% | 50% | 0 | 0.77 | -13.4 | 50 | 57 | -$6 |
| 1st Half | 5 | 0 | 87 | 71 | 4.78 | 4.72 | 1.49 | 887 | 973 | 817 | 22.0 | 4.4 | 7.4 | 1.7 | 61% | 11% | 95.4 | 37 | 16 | 47 | 31% | 70% | 17% | 2 | 85 | 0% | 50% | 0 | 0.93 | -6.7 | 51 | 58 | -$7 |
| 2nd Half | 5 | 0 | 68 | 50 | 4.96 | 4.29 | 1.54 | 746 | 873 | 626 | 18.4 | 5.4 | 6.6 | 1.2 | 45% | 8% | 95.4 | 44 | 17 | 39 | 29% | 67% | 12% | 6 | 60 | 0% | 50% | 0 | 0.73 | -6.7 | 50 | 58 | -$5 |
| **19 Proj** | **6** | **0** | **94** | **73** | **4.87** | **5.05** | **1.52** | **715** | **830** | **607** | **21.8** | **5.0** | **6.9** | **1.4** | **45%** | **8%** | **95.4** | **44** | **17** | **39** | **30%** | **68%** | **7%** | **16** | | | | | | **-8.1** | **12** | **13** | **-$5** |

## Rodriguez,Richard

| Age: 29 | Th: R | Role: RP | Health | A | LIMA Plan | B+ |
|---|---|---|---|---|---|---|
| Ht: 6' 4" | Wt: 205 | Type: Pwr xFB | PT/Exp | D | Rand Var | -3 |
| | | | Consist | C | MM | 3411 |

Older rookie blossomed without a pitch mix change, just changed orgs and better harnessed his existing offerings. First two months were other-worldly, briefly slowed by shoulder injury in June, then was a mere mortal rest of the way. Yet another helpful bullpen piece, with some saves potential if you really squint.

| Yr Tm | W | Sv | IP | K | ERA | xERA | WHIP | oOPS | vL | vR | BF/G | Ctl | Dom | Cmd | FpK | SwK | Vel | G | L | F | H% | S% | hr/f | GS | APC | DOM% | DIS% | Sv% | LI | RAR | BPV | BPX | R$ |
|---|---|---|---|---|---|---|---|---|---|---|---|---|---|---|---|---|---|---|---|---|---|---|---|---|---|---|---|---|---|---|---|---|---|
| 14 a/a | 2 | 0 | 49 | 44 | 3.68 | 3.04 | 1.07 | | | | 7.1 | 1.5 | 8.0 | 5.5 | | | | | | | 30% | 67% | | | | | | | | 0.4 | 146 | 174 | $0 |
| 15 a/a | 7 | 0 | 84 | 59 | 3.68 | 4.16 | 1.27 | | | | 7.4 | 2.7 | 6.3 | 2.4 | | | | | | | 28% | 76% | | | | | | | | 2.9 | 53 | 63 | $2 |
| 16 aaa | 6 | 2 | 82 | 67 | 3.83 | 4.35 | 1.45 | | | | 7.3 | 3.5 | 7.4 | 2.1 | | | | | | | 33% | 75% | | | | | | | | 3.6 | 66 | 79 | $1 |
| 17 BAL * | 4 | 10 | 76 | 63 | 4.34 | 5.08 | 1.44 | 1516 | 222 | 1986 | 6.9 | 2.8 | 7.5 | 2.7 | 48% | 7% | 93.8 | 46 | 13 | 42 | 33% | 74% | 40% | 0 | 24 | | | 83 | 0.27 | 0.2 | 59 | 70 | $2 |
| 18 PIT | 4 | 0 | 69 | 88 | 2.47 | 3.38 | 1.07 | 596 | 439 | 730 | 4.4 | 2.5 | 11.4 | 4.6 | 70% | 14% | 92.9 | 38 | 15 | 48 | 32% | 80% | 7% | 0 | 18 | | | 0 | 0.81 | 14.4 | 155 | 178 | $7 |
| 1st Half | 1 | 0 | 31 | 42 | 2.03 | 3.10 | 0.97 | 615 | 468 | 727 | 4.7 | 0.9 | 12.2 | 14.0 | 74% | 15% | 92.9 | 34 | 12 | 53 | 35% | 85% | 8% | 0 | 19 | | | 0 | 0.51 | 8.1 | 208 | 239 | $5 |
| 2nd Half | 3 | 0 | 38 | 46 | 2.82 | 3.64 | 1.15 | 578 | 417 | 729 | 4.3 | 3.8 | 10.8 | 2.9 | 66% | 14% | 92.9 | 40 | 17 | 43 | 30% | 76% | 5% | 0 | 17 | | | 0 | 1.03 | 6.3 | 111 | 128 | $9 |
| **19 Proj** | **4** | **2** | **73** | **80** | **3.29** | **3.59** | **1.18** | **686** | **490** | **855** | **5.3** | **2.7** | **10.0** | **3.7** | **70%** | **14%** | **92.9** | **38** | **15** | **47** | **31%** | **77%** | **10%** | **0** | | | | | | **5.5** | **122** | **140** | **$5** |

## Roe,Chaz

| Age: 32 | Th: R | Role: RP | Health | F | LIMA Plan | A |
|---|---|---|---|---|---|---|
| Ht: 6' 5" | Wt: 190 | Type: Pwr | PT/Exp | D | Rand Var | 0 |
| | | | Consist | C | MM | 3310 |

Finally turned previously-established skills into an MLB role that stuck, eventually thriving in setup work (31 Holds). 2nd half profile showed some wobble, but that's a small sample due to an August knee injury. Even before that injury, these aren't blow-you-away skills for today's game, but they can still be helpful.

| Yr Tm | W | Sv | IP | K | ERA | xERA | WHIP | oOPS | vL | vR | BF/G | Ctl | Dom | Cmd | FpK | SwK | Vel | G | L | F | H% | S% | hr/f | GS | APC | DOM% | DIS% | Sv% | LI | RAR | BPV | BPX | R$ |
|---|---|---|---|---|---|---|---|---|---|---|---|---|---|---|---|---|---|---|---|---|---|---|---|---|---|---|---|---|---|---|---|---|---|
| 14 NYY * | 3 | 14 | 66 | 58 | 4.22 | 3.76 | 1.35 | 1239 | 1500 | 1111 | 5.5 | 3.3 | 7.9 | 2.4 | 62% | 15% | 91.5 | 17 | 17 | 67 | 32% | 69% | 0% | 0 | 15 | | | 78 | 0.10 | -3.9 | 82 | 98 | $3 |
| 15 BAL * | 8 | 2 | 67 | 54 | 4.06 | 4.09 | 1.45 | 798 | 912 | 716 | 5.3 | 3.8 | 7.2 | 1.9 | 61% | 10% | 92.7 | 52 | 20 | 28 | 33% | 72% | 12% | 0 | 20 | | | 40 | 0.98 | -0.8 | 69 | 82 | $0 |
| 16 2 TM * | 3 | 4 | 67 | 71 | 3.79 | 3.30 | 1.31 | 672 | 971 | 410 | 4.4 | 3.7 | 9.5 | 2.6 | 69% | 13% | 92.6 | 58 | 8 | 34 | 33% | 71% | 8% | 0 | 16 | | | 80 | 1.01 | 3.3 | 104 | 123 | $2 |
| 17 2 TM * | 0 | 4 | 33 | 41 | 5.01 | 4.45 | 1.48 | 585 | 741 | 494 | 4.7 | 3.4 | 11.2 | 3.3 | 61% | 14% | 92.8 | 56 | 20 | 24 | 40% | 66% | 17% | 0 | 14 | | | 67 | 0.69 | -2.6 | 116 | 140 | -$3 |
| 18 TAM | 1 | 1 | 50 | 53 | 3.58 | 3.36 | 1.01 | 629 | 804 | 572 | 3.3 | 2.9 | 9.5 | 3.3 | 57% | 11% | 92.4 | 48 | 19 | 33 | 25% | 69% | 15% | 0 | 13 | | | 50 | 1.39 | 3.6 | 119 | 137 | $1 |
| 1st Half | 1 | 1 | 33 | 37 | 2.73 | 3.09 | 0.97 | 583 | 675 | 559 | 3.3 | 2.7 | 10.1 | 3.7 | 61% | 13% | 92.6 | 50 | 17 | 33 | 25% | 76% | 12% | 0 | 13 | | | 100 | 1.39 | 5.8 | 136 | 156 | $4 |
| 2nd Half | 0 | 0 | 17 | 16 | 5.19 | 3.88 | 1.10 | 712 | 958 | 600 | 3.4 | 3.1 | 8.3 | 2.7 | 50% | 9% | 91.9 | 43 | 24 | 33 | 23% | 56% | 20% | 0 | 13 | | | 0 | 1.40 | -2.2 | 87 | 100 | -$5 |
| **19 Proj** | **1** | **5** | **58** | **61** | **3.70** | **3.37** | **1.23** | **707** | **883** | **621** | **3.8** | **3.2** | **9.5** | **3.0** | **57%** | **10%** | **92.4** | **49** | **20** | **31** | **30%** | **72%** | **12%** | **0** | | | | | | **5.9** | **111** | **127** | **$2** |

## Rogers,Taylor

| Age: 28 | Th: L | Role: RP | Health | A | LIMA Plan | B+ |
|---|---|---|---|---|---|---|
| Ht: 6' 3" | Wt: 170 | Type: Pwr | PT/Exp | D | Rand Var | -1 |
| | | | Consist | B | MM | 4321 |

Unlocked a new skill level when he introduced a slider to his arsenal in May. Besides spiking his Dom and SwK, it also gave him the weapon vs. RH batters that he was lacking (see 2H vR). Newfound Dom, GB tilt, answers vs. both sides of the plate, improved FpK... this is now a premium closer-in-waiting. UP: 35 saves.

| Yr Tm | W | Sv | IP | K | ERA | xERA | WHIP | oOPS | vL | vR | BF/G | Ctl | Dom | Cmd | FpK | SwK | Vel | G | L | F | H% | S% | hr/f | GS | APC | DOM% | DIS% | Sv% | LI | RAR | BPV | BPX | R$ |
|---|---|---|---|---|---|---|---|---|---|---|---|---|---|---|---|---|---|---|---|---|---|---|---|---|---|---|---|---|---|---|---|---|---|
| 14 aa | 11 | 0 | 145 | 91 | 4.09 | 4.45 | 1.48 | | | | 26.0 | 2.4 | 5.6 | 2.4 | | | | | | | 35% | 71% | | | | | | | | -6.3 | 71 | 84 | -$3 |
| 15 aaa | 11 | 0 | 174 | 98 | 5.56 | 5.58 | 1.65 | | | | 27.8 | 2.4 | 5.1 | 2.1 | | | | | | | 37% | 65% | | | | | | | | -34.3 | 46 | 55 | -$18 |
| 16 MIN * | 3 | 0 | 79 | 75 | 4.61 | 4.97 | 1.48 | 719 | 547 | 811 | 5.3 | 2.6 | 8.5 | 3.3 | 56% | 8% | 92.6 | 51 | 20 | 28 | 37% | 71% | 14% | 0 | 18 | | | 0 | 0.84 | -4.1 | 88 | 104 | -$4 |
| 17 MIN | 7 | 0 | 56 | 49 | 3.07 | 4.27 | 1.31 | 693 | 560 | 766 | 3.4 | 3.4 | 7.9 | 2.3 | 58% | 9% | 93.2 | 45 | 24 | 31 | 30% | 81% | 12% | 0 | 13 | | | 0 | 1.23 | 8.8 | 74 | 89 | $3 |
| 18 MIN | 1 | 2 | 68 | 75 | 2.63 | 2.98 | 0.95 | 553 | 428 | 643 | 3.3 | 2.1 | 9.9 | 4.7 | 64% | 12% | 93.4 | 45 | 26 | 30 | 28% | 73% | 6% | 0 | 14 | | | 50 | 1.04 | 12.8 | 144 | 166 | $7 |
| 1st Half | 1 | 0 | 32 | 33 | 4.22 | 3.19 | 1.28 | 711 | 548 | 824 | 3.8 | 1.7 | 9.3 | 5.5 | 65% | 10% | 93.1 | 45 | 28 | 26 | 37% | 67% | 9% | 0 | 15 | | | 0 | 0.93 | -0.3 | 145 | 167 | -$3 |
| 2nd Half | 0 | 2 | 36 | 42 | 1.24 | 2.80 | 0.66 | 390 | 311 | 449 | 3.4 | 2.5 | 10.4 | 4.2 | 64% | 13% | 93.9 | 43 | 22 | 34 | 18% | 83% | 4% | 0 | 13 | | | 100 | 1.14 | 13.0 | 142 | 163 | $15 |
| **19 Proj** | **4** | **16** | **73** | **77** | **3.17** | **3.17** | **1.15** | **643** | **498** | **734** | **4.1** | **2.4** | **9.5** | **3.9** | **63%** | **12%** | **93.3** | **46** | **24** | **30** | **31%** | **74%** | **8%** | **0** | | | | | | **9.3** | **129** | **148** | **$11** |

RAY MURPHY

## Romano,Sal

| Age: | 25 | Th: | R | Role | SP | Health | A | LIMA Plan | D+ |
|---|---|---|---|---|---|---|---|---|---|
| Ht: | 6' 5" | Wt: | 270 | Type | | PT/Exp | C | Rand Var | +2 |
| | | | | | | Consist | A | MM | 1103 |

Nudged his Cmd to the 2.0 level. A decade ago, that might have made him interesting. Today, it's not even the minimum standard. Velocity is enough to keep him employed, but subpar FpK/SwK are enough to keep him off fantasy rosters. If that doesn't get the point across, go look at DOM%/DIS%. Then find a palette cleanser.

| Yr Tm | W | Sv | IP | K | ERA | xERA | WHIP | oOPS | vL | vR | BF/G | Ctl | Dom | Cmd | FpK | SwK | Vel | G | L | F | H% | S% | hr/f | GS | APC | DOM% | DIS% | Sv% | LI | RAR | BPV | BPX | R$ |
|---|---|---|---|---|---|---|---|---|---|---|---|---|---|---|---|---|---|---|---|---|---|---|---|---|---|---|---|---|---|---|---|---|---|
| 14 | | | | | | | | | | | | | | | | | | | | | | | | | | | | | | | | | |
| 15 aa | 0 | 0 | 23 | 8 | 13.77 | 9.68 | 2.32 | | | | 16.9 | 4.9 | 3.2 | 0.7 | | | | | | | 39% | 38% | | | | | | | | -27.8 | -49 | -59 | -$17 |
| 16 aa | 6 | 0 | 156 | 127 | 5.01 | 5.09 | 1.51 | | | | 25.0 | 2.2 | 7.3 | 3.3 | | | | | | | 37% | 67% | | | | | | | | -15.9 | 82 | 97 | -$7 |
| 17 CIN * | 6 | 0 | 136 | 100 | 4.46 | 4.56 | 1.51 | 799 | 793 | 805 | 22.7 | 3.6 | 6.6 | 1.8 | 55% | 9% | 95.3 | 50 | 20 | 30 | 33% | 71% | 12% | 16 | 94 | 6% | 31% | | | -1.6 | 56 | 68 | -$3 |
| 18 CIN | 8 | 0 | 146 | 105 | 5.31 | 4.81 | 1.43 | 784 | 900 | 681 | 16.5 | 3.3 | 6.5 | 2.0 | 58% | 8% | 94.2 | 45 | 21 | 33 | 30% | 66% | 15% | 25 | 62 | 8% | 56% | 0 | 0.81 | -20.9 | 51 | 59 | -$8 |
| 1st Half | 4 | 0 | 90 | 67 | 5.30 | 4.84 | 1.49 | 808 | 869 | 752 | 23.5 | 3.8 | 6.7 | 1.8 | 59% | 8% | 94.2 | 45 | 23 | 31 | 30% | 68% | 16% | 17 | 89 | 12% | 65% | | | -12.8 | 41 | 47 | -$11 |
| 2nd Half | 4 | 0 | 56 | 38 | 5.34 | 4.77 | 1.33 | 746 | 952 | 572 | 11.1 | 2.4 | 6.1 | 2.5 | 57% | 9% | 94.2 | 46 | 18 | 36 | 30% | 62% | 12% | 8 | 40 | 0% | 38% | 0 | 0.84 | -8.1 | 69 | 79 | -$3 |
| 19 Proj | 7 | 0 | 131 | 96 | 4.96 | 4.52 | 1.50 | 797 | 882 | 722 | 20.5 | 3.6 | 6.6 | 1.8 | 57% | 9% | 94.6 | 46 | 20 | 33 | 32% | 69% | 11% | 26 | | | | | | -13.0 | 47 | 54 | -$6 |

## Romero,Fernando

| Age: | 24 | Th: | R | Role | SP | Health | A | LIMA Plan | D+ |
|---|---|---|---|---|---|---|---|---|---|
| Ht: | 6' 0" | Wt: | 215 | Type | | PT/Exp | D | Rand Var | +1 |
| | | | | | | Consist | A | MM | 0003 |

3-3, 4.69 ERA in 52 IP at MIN. Rookie made a quick splash after callup, allowing total of 6 ER across first 5 MLB starts. But that was way out over his skis. Velocity is there already, and SwK says Dom should eventually follow. But Ctl and FpK say "not yet." A worthy dynasty stash, if you can overlook the near-term peril.

| Yr Tm | W | Sv | IP | K | ERA | xERA | WHIP | oOPS | vL | vR | BF/G | Ctl | Dom | Cmd | FpK | SwK | Vel | G | L | F | H% | S% | hr/f | GS | APC | DOM% | DIS% | Sv% | LI | RAR | BPV | BPX | R$ |
|---|---|---|---|---|---|---|---|---|---|---|---|---|---|---|---|---|---|---|---|---|---|---|---|---|---|---|---|---|---|---|---|---|---|
| 14 | | | | | | | | | | | | | | | | | | | | | | | | | | | | | | | | | |
| 15 | | | | | | | | | | | | | | | | | | | | | | | | | | | | | | | | | |
| 16 | | | | | | | | | | | | | | | | | | | | | | | | | | | | | | | | | |
| 17 aa | 11 | 0 | 125 | 99 | 5.03 | 4.98 | 1.63 | | | | 23.2 | 3.5 | 7.1 | 2.0 | | | | | | | 37% | 67% | | | | | | | | -10.4 | 68 | 81 | -$5 |
| 18 MIN * | 8 | 0 | 148 | 100 | 4.97 | 4.89 | 1.51 | 770 | 812 | 734 | 23.7 | 3.3 | 6.1 | 1.9 | 55% | 11% | 95.4 | 46 | 23 | 31 | 33% | 67% | 11% | 11 | 87 | 18% | 55% | | | -14.9 | 50 | 57 | -$8 |
| 1st Half | 4 | 0 | 78 | 61 | 4.05 | 4.38 | 1.43 | 747 | 812 | 696 | 22.2 | 3.7 | 7.0 | 1.9 | 55% | 11% | 95.4 | 45 | 22 | 33 | 31% | 73% | 12% | 10 | 88 | 20% | 50% | | | 1.0 | 58 | 67 | -$3 |
| 2nd Half | 4 | 0 | 70 | 40 | 6.01 | 5.46 | 1.60 | 978 | 818 | 1129 | 25.6 | 2.8 | 5.1 | 1.8 | 52% | 9% | 95.4 | 55 | 30 | 15 | 35% | 61% | 0% | 1 | 78 | 0% | 100% | | | -15.9 | 40 | 46 | -$14 |
| 19 Proj | 8 | 0 | 145 | 103 | 4.61 | 4.58 | 1.48 | 763 | 832 | 709 | 23.2 | 3.3 | 6.4 | 1.9 | 55% | 11% | 95.4 | 45 | 22 | 33 | 32% | 72% | 11% | 27 | | | | | | -8.2 | 50 | 57 | -$4 |

## Romo,Sergio

| Age: | 36 | Th: | R | Role | RP | Health | D | LIMA Plan | B+ |
|---|---|---|---|---|---|---|---|---|---|
| Ht: | 5' 11" | Wt: | 185 | Type | Pwr FB | PT/Exp | C | Rand Var | +1 |
| | | | | | | Consist | A | MM | 3420 |

Turned back the clock with jack-of-all-trades workload: opener, closer, middleman. Late-career shift to more slider/change-up combo and less fastball has plugged holes vL, and mitigates velocity loss. Ctl/Dom/Cmd are in fine shape, and say he can continue to handle the 9th if asked. Just plan for periodic interruptions from hr/f.

| Yr Tm | W | Sv | IP | K | ERA | xERA | WHIP | oOPS | vL | vR | BF/G | Ctl | Dom | Cmd | FpK | SwK | Vel | G | L | F | H% | S% | hr/f | GS | APC | DOM% | DIS% | Sv% | LI | RAR | BPV | BPX | R$ |
|---|---|---|---|---|---|---|---|---|---|---|---|---|---|---|---|---|---|---|---|---|---|---|---|---|---|---|---|---|---|---|---|---|---|
| 14 SF | 6 | 23 | 58 | 59 | 3.72 | 3.27 | 0.95 | 622 | 777 | 528 | 3.6 | 1.9 | 9.2 | 4.9 | 69% | 15% | 88.0 | 37 | 18 | 45 | 25% | 67% | 13% | 0 | 14 | | | 82 | 1.26 | 0.1 | 130 | 154 | $13 |
| 15 SF | 0 | 2 | 57 | 71 | 2.98 | 2.70 | 1.06 | 622 | 929 | 467 | 3.3 | 1.6 | 11.1 | 7.1 | 70% | 17% | 87.5 | 45 | 23 | 32 | 35% | 72% | 7% | 0 | 13 | | | 50 | 1.26 | 6.9 | 181 | 216 | $3 |
| 16 SF | 1 | 4 | 31 | 33 | 2.64 | 3.58 | 1.08 | 709 | 790 | 674 | 2.9 | 2.1 | 9.7 | 4.7 | 65% | 15% | 85.8 | 38 | 14 | 47 | 28% | 86% | 14% | 0 | 12 | | | 100 | 1.27 | 5.9 | 135 | 160 | $2 |
| 17 2 TM | 3 | 0 | 56 | 59 | 3.56 | 4.04 | 1.10 | 661 | 733 | 633 | 4.1 | 3.1 | 9.5 | 3.1 | 59% | 15% | 86.1 | 37 | 20 | 43 | 25% | 75% | 15% | 0 | 17 | | | 0 | 0.88 | 5.5 | 104 | 125 | $3 |
| 18 TAM | 3 | 25 | 67 | 75 | 4.14 | 3.96 | 1.26 | 718 | 713 | 720 | 3.9 | 2.7 | 10.0 | 3.8 | 63% | 14% | 86.3 | 36 | 20 | 44 | 32% | 73% | 14% | 5 | 15 | 0% | 40% | 76 | 1.29 | 0.1 | 122 | 141 | $10 |
| 1st Half | 1 | 7 | 34 | 38 | 4.46 | 3.93 | 1.31 | 699 | 701 | 695 | 3.9 | 3.4 | 10.0 | 2.9 | 61% | 12% | 85.9 | 42 | 20 | 38 | 32% | 68% | 11% | 5 | 16 | 0% | 40% | 64 | 1.33 | -1.3 | 107 | 123 | $3 |
| 2nd Half | 2 | 18 | 33 | 37 | 3.82 | 3.99 | 1.21 | 737 | 720 | 748 | 3.9 | 1.9 | 10.1 | 5.3 | 65% | 16% | 86.8 | 31 | 19 | 51 | 32% | 79% | 15% | 0 | 15 | | | 82 | 1.25 | 1.4 | 139 | 160 | $17 |
| 19 Proj | 3 | 18 | 65 | 72 | 3.93 | 3.52 | 1.16 | 696 | 743 | 672 | 3.6 | 2.5 | 9.9 | 3.9 | 63% | 15% | 86.4 | 37 | 19 | 44 | 30% | 73% | 14% | 0 | | | | | | 1.8 | 125 | 144 | $9 |

## Rondon,Hector

| Age: | 31 | Th: | R | Role | RP | Health | B | LIMA Plan | B+ |
|---|---|---|---|---|---|---|---|---|---|
| Ht: | 6' 3" | Wt: | 230 | Type | Pwr | PT/Exp | C | Rand Var | 0 |
| | | | | | | Consist | A | MM | 3410 |

Seems like good news: Changed teams, pulled ERA back under 4, even worked his way into the saves picture. Skills-wise, all that really changed was getting hr/f back into single digits. It's a nice skill set, but BPX column is instructive here: the bar is being raised, and he's not keeping up. There are lots of others like him.

| Yr Tm | W | Sv | IP | K | ERA | xERA | WHIP | oOPS | vL | vR | BF/G | Ctl | Dom | Cmd | FpK | SwK | Vel | G | L | F | H% | S% | hr/f | GS | APC | DOM% | DIS% | Sv% | LI | RAR | BPV | BPX | R$ |
|---|---|---|---|---|---|---|---|---|---|---|---|---|---|---|---|---|---|---|---|---|---|---|---|---|---|---|---|---|---|---|---|---|---|
| 14 CHC | 4 | 29 | 63 | 63 | 2.42 | 2.99 | 1.06 | 526 | 616 | 454 | 4.0 | 2.1 | 9.0 | 4.2 | 65% | 12% | 95.7 | 49 | 23 | 28 | 30% | 77% | 4% | 0 | 16 | | | 88 | 1.16 | 10.4 | 131 | 156 | $17 |
| 15 CHC | 6 | 30 | 70 | 69 | 1.67 | 3.04 | 1.00 | 568 | 640 | 503 | 3.9 | 1.9 | 8.9 | 4.6 | 63% | 11% | 96.4 | 52 | 20 | 27 | 28% | 86% | 8% | 0 | 15 | | | 88 | 1.51 | 19.8 | 138 | 164 | $23 |
| 16 CHC | 2 | 18 | 51 | 58 | 3.53 | 2.99 | 0.98 | 641 | 743 | 569 | 3.7 | 1.4 | 10.2 | 7.3 | 72% | 11% | 96.0 | 46 | 20 | 34 | 28% | 71% | 18% | 0 | 15 | | | 78 | 1.09 | 4.2 | 170 | 202 | $10 |
| 17 CHC | 4 | 0 | 57 | 69 | 4.24 | 3.48 | 1.22 | 724 | 810 | 677 | 3.9 | 3.1 | 10.8 | 3.5 | 64% | 12% | 96.4 | 48 | 17 | 35 | 30% | 72% | 20% | 0 | 16 | | | 0 | 0.72 | 0.8 | 136 | 164 | $1 |
| 18 HOU | 2 | 15 | 59 | 67 | 3.20 | 3.61 | 1.32 | 695 | 711 | 680 | 4.0 | 3.1 | 10.2 | 3.4 | 61% | 14% | 97.2 | 46 | 22 | 33 | 35% | 77% | 8% | 0 | 16 | | | 68 | 1.19 | 6.9 | 126 | 145 | $6 |
| 1st Half | 1 | 5 | 30 | 38 | 1.50 | 3.10 | 1.17 | 614 | 509 | 714 | 3.7 | 2.7 | 11.4 | 4.2 | 63% | 15% | 97.0 | 45 | 23 | 32 | 35% | 88% | 4% | 0 | 15 | | | 71 | 0.89 | 9.8 | 155 | 178 | $8 |
| 2nd Half | 1 | 10 | 29 | 29 | 4.97 | 4.17 | 1.48 | 772 | 908 | 647 | 4.3 | 3.4 | 9.0 | 2.6 | 59% | 13% | 97.4 | 47 | 20 | 33 | 35% | 68% | 10% | 0 | 17 | | | 67 | 1.53 | -2.9 | 94 | 108 | $3 |
| 19 Proj | 3 | 9 | 58 | 65 | 3.58 | 3.31 | 1.27 | 694 | 758 | 644 | 3.9 | 3.1 | 10.1 | 3.3 | 63% | 13% | 96.7 | 47 | 20 | 33 | 33% | 75% | 13% | 0 | | | | | | 6.8 | 124 | 142 | $4 |

## Rosario,Randy

| Age: | 25 | Th: | L | Role | RP | Health | A | LIMA Plan | D+ |
|---|---|---|---|---|---|---|---|---|---|
| Ht: | 6' 1" | Wt: | 200 | Type | GB | PT/Exp | F | Rand Var | -3 |
| | | | | | | Consist | F | MM | 1000 |

4-0, 3.66 ERA in 47 IP at CHC. Called up early in year to serve as lefty specialist, he danced around trouble for a while (14 BB/14 K in MLB over first half) but eventually got exposed. Skills actually showed improvement in 2nd half, and he's left-handed, so he's got about 13,787 more chances to prove himself.

| Yr Tm | W | Sv | IP | K | ERA | xERA | WHIP | oOPS | vL | vR | BF/G | Ctl | Dom | Cmd | FpK | SwK | Vel | G | L | F | H% | S% | hr/f | GS | APC | DOM% | DIS% | Sv% | LI | RAR | BPV | BPX | R$ |
|---|---|---|---|---|---|---|---|---|---|---|---|---|---|---|---|---|---|---|---|---|---|---|---|---|---|---|---|---|---|---|---|---|---|
| 14 | | | | | | | | | | | | | | | | | | | | | | | | | | | | | | | | | |
| 15 | | | | | | | | | | | | | | | | | | | | | | | | | | | | | | | | | |
| 16 | | | | | | | | | | | | | | | | | | | | | | | | | | | | | | | | | |
| 17 MIN * | 1 | 1 | 60 | 39 | 6.80 | 5.97 | 1.73 | 1390 | 650 | 1700 | 8.0 | 3.7 | 5.9 | 1.6 | 40% | 5% | 93.5 | 67 | 8 | 25 | 36% | 60% | 33% | 0 | 32 | | | 33 | 0.26 | -18.0 | 31 | 37 | -$12 |
| 18 CHC * | 4 | 1 | 71 | 42 | 2.70 | 3.50 | 1.27 | 721 | 597 | 801 | 4.9 | 3.6 | 5.4 | 1.5 | 59% | 10% | 93.3 | 52 | 23 | 25 | 26% | 82% | 14% | 0 | 17 | | | 50 | 1.07 | 12.7 | 49 | 56 | $3 |
| 1st Half | 3 | 0 | 40 | 22 | 1.15 | 2.07 | 1.06 | 633 | 725 | 561 | 5.4 | 3.6 | 4.9 | 1.3 | 54% | 10% | 93.5 | 45 | 28 | 27 | 21% | 92% | 13% | 0 | 18 | | | 0 | 1.43 | 14.8 | 62 | 71 | $10 |
| 2nd Half | 1 | 1 | 31 | 21 | 4.72 | 5.37 | 1.54 | 781 | 493 | 941 | 4.5 | 3.5 | 6.0 | 1.7 | 61% | 9% | 93.2 | 57 | 19 | 24 | 32% | 72% | 14% | 0 | 16 | | | 100 | 0.84 | -2.1 | 34 | 39 | -$4 |
| 19 Proj | 2 | 0 | 58 | 37 | 4.63 | 4.44 | 1.49 | 739 | 587 | 836 | 5.7 | 3.6 | 5.7 | 1.6 | 59% | 10% | 93.3 | 52 | 22 | 25 | 31% | 70% | 12% | 0 | | | | | | -1.3 | 35 | 41 | -$5 |

## Ross,Joe

| Age: | 26 | Th: | R | Role | SP | Health | F | LIMA Plan | B |
|---|---|---|---|---|---|---|---|---|---|
| Ht: | 6' 4" | Wt: | 220 | Type | | PT/Exp | D | Rand Var | +2 |
| | | | | | | Consist | D | MM | 2103 |

0-2, 5.06 ERA in 16 IP at WAS. Recovery from July 2017 Tommy John surgery cost him the season, save a three-start September cameo. The skills he flashed then are irrelevant, but the velocity is encouraging. He'll come to spring training healthy, looking to recapture the 2015-16 skills that previously had our attention.

| Yr Tm | W | Sv | IP | K | ERA | xERA | WHIP | oOPS | vL | vR | BF/G | Ctl | Dom | Cmd | FpK | SwK | Vel | G | L | F | H% | S% | hr/f | GS | APC | DOM% | DIS% | Sv% | LI | RAR | BPV | BPX | R$ |
|---|---|---|---|---|---|---|---|---|---|---|---|---|---|---|---|---|---|---|---|---|---|---|---|---|---|---|---|---|---|---|---|---|---|
| 14 aa | 2 | 0 | 20 | 17 | 3.89 | 4.51 | 1.28 | | | | 20.5 | 0.4 | 7.7 | 17.8 | | | | | | | 37% | 72% | | | | | | | | -0.4 | 388 | 462 | -$2 |
| 15 WAS * | 10 | 0 | 153 | 127 | 3.45 | 3.09 | 1.15 | 628 | 809 | 461 | 20.2 | 2.4 | 7.5 | 3.1 | 59% | 12% | 93.4 | 50 | 16 | 34 | 29% | 72% | 10% | 13 | 72 | 38% | 15% | 0 | 0.71 | 9.6 | 96 | 115 | $11 |
| 16 WAS | 7 | 0 | 105 | 93 | 3.43 | 3.95 | 1.30 | 713 | 824 | 611 | 23.5 | 2.5 | 8.0 | 3.2 | 56% | 11% | 92.7 | 43 | 27 | 30 | 33% | 76% | 10% | 19 | 90 | 26% | 32% | | | 9.9 | 97 | 116 | $5 |
| 17 WAS * | 7 | 0 | 101 | 86 | 5.32 | 6.05 | 1.54 | 867 | 923 | 806 | 24.5 | 2.5 | 7.6 | 3.0 | 64% | 10% | 91.4 | 38 | 25 | 38 | 35% | 70% | 19% | 13 | 93 | 31% | 46% | | | -12.1 | 51 | 62 | -$5 |
| 18 WAS * | 2 | 0 | 34 | 15 | 4.80 | 4.53 | 1.31 | 870 | 736 | 1023 | 23.6 | 2.2 | 4.0 | 1.8 | 62% | 9% | 93.1 | 36 | 22 | 42 | 29% | 66% | 13% | 3 | 83 | 0% | 33% | | | -2.7 | 29 | 33 | -$5 |
| 1st Half | | | | | | | | | | | | | | | | | | | | | | | | | | | | | | | | | |
| 2nd Half | 2 | 0 | 34 | 15 | 4.80 | 4.53 | 1.31 | 871 | 736 | 1023 | 23.6 | 2.2 | 4.0 | 1.8 | 62% | 9% | 93.1 | 36 | 22 | 42 | 29% | 66% | 13% | 3 | 83 | 0% | 33% | | | -2.7 | 29 | 33 | -$5 |
| 19 Proj | 9 | 0 | 145 | 122 | 3.84 | 3.95 | 1.29 | 755 | 790 | 717 | 22.7 | 2.5 | 7.6 | 3.0 | 60% | 11% | 92.7 | 41 | 23 | 36 | 31% | 74% | 12% | 26 | | | | | | 3.1 | 88 | 101 | $6 |

## Ross,Tyson

| Age: | 32 | Th: | R | Role | SP | Health | F | LIMA Plan | B |
|---|---|---|---|---|---|---|---|---|---|
| Ht: | 6' 6" | Wt: | 245 | Type | Pwr GB | PT/Exp | C | Rand Var | +1 |
| | | | | | | Consist | F | MM | 1100 |

Stayed off the DL for the entire year. Yay? Being healthy is not the same as being effective, and skills couldn't handle the workload. BPV by month: 113-94-47-(-30)-(-18). That got him released in August and turned him into a reliever in STL, which stopped the carnage. Tough to envision more than flashes of value here.

| Yr Tm | W | Sv | IP | K | ERA | xERA | WHIP | oOPS | vL | vR | BF/G | Ctl | Dom | Cmd | FpK | SwK | Vel | G | L | F | H% | S% | hr/f | GS | APC | DOM% | DIS% | Sv% | LI | RAR | BPV | BPX | R$ |
|---|---|---|---|---|---|---|---|---|---|---|---|---|---|---|---|---|---|---|---|---|---|---|---|---|---|---|---|---|---|---|---|---|---|
| 14 SD | 13 | 0 | 196 | 195 | 2.81 | 3.02 | 1.21 | 634 | 635 | 632 | 26.2 | 3.3 | 9.0 | 2.7 | 58% | 13% | 93.2 | 57 | 21 | 22 | 30% | 79% | 11% | 31 | 101 | 48% | 23% | | | 22.6 | 107 | 127 | $16 |
| 15 SD | 10 | 0 | 196 | 212 | 3.26 | 3.07 | 1.31 | 652 | 721 | 584 | 24.9 | 3.9 | 9.7 | 2.5 | 58% | 13% | 92.8 | 62 | 19 | 20 | 32% | 75% | 9% | 33 | 98 | 33% | 18% | | | 17.0 | 111 | 132 | $12 |
| 16 SD | 0 | 0 | 5 | 5 | 11.81 | 3.59 | 1.88 | 986 | 1033 | 873 | 27.0 | 1.7 | 8.4 | 5.0 | 70% | 15% | 92.5 | 47 | 37 | 16 | 47% | 30% | 0% | 1 | 94 | 0% | 0% | | | -5.0 | 131 | 156 | -$6 |
| 17 TEX * | 6 | 0 | 79 | 51 | 8.06 | 6.78 | 1.97 | 856 | 759 | 952 | 21.1 | 6.4 | 5.8 | 0.9 | 46% | 7% | 91.6 | 47 | 19 | 35 | 34% | 59% | 13% | 10 | 81 | 0% | 60% | 0 | 0.65 | -36.2 | 8 | 10 | -$19 |
| 18 2 NL | 8 | 0 | 150 | 122 | 4.15 | 4.26 | 1.30 | 712 | 848 | 565 | 20.5 | 3.7 | 7.3 | 2.0 | 57% | 9% | 91.1 | 46 | 26 | 28 | 28% | 71% | 14% | 23 | 81 | 22% | 30% | 0 | 0.99 | 0.0 | 55 | 64 | $3 |
| 1st Half | 5 | 0 | 95 | 90 | 3.32 | 3.88 | 1.19 | 665 | 814 | 514 | 24.8 | 3.3 | 8.5 | 2.6 | 57% | 10% | 90.9 | 43 | 27 | 30 | 28% | 76% | 13% | 16 | 99 | 25% | 13% | | | 9.8 | 85 | 98 | $9 |
| 2nd Half | 3 | 0 | 55 | 32 | 5.60 | 5.00 | 1.48 | 794 | 900 | 660 | 15.9 | 4.4 | 5.3 | 1.2 | 57% | 7% | 91.5 | 50 | 26 | 24 | 28% | 64% | 16% | 7 | 61 | 14% | 71% | 0 | 1.24 | -9.8 | 3 | 3 | -$14 |
| 19 Proj | 3 | 0 | 44 | 34 | 4.51 | 4.38 | 1.49 | 769 | 819 | 716 | 20.2 | 4.5 | 7.1 | 1.6 | 54% | 9% | 91.8 | 50 | 23 | 27 | 30% | 72% | 13% | 9 | | | | | | -1.0 | 35 | 40 | -$4 |

RAY MURPHY

## Ryu,Hyun-Jin

| | | | | | |
|---|---|---|---|---|---|
| Age: 32 | Th: L | Role SP | Health | F | LIMA Plan B |
| Ht: 6' 3" | Wt: 250 | Type Pwr | PT/Exp | C | Rand Var -5 |
| | | | Consist | C | MM 4301 |

Missed three months with a groin injury. On either side of that absence, he had short bursts of brilliance. Unfortunately, short bursts are all you can count on here: 105 more DL days brings his five-year total to 524. If you bet on "more innings than DL days," you would have lost 3 times in 5 years. Bid accordingly.

| Yr Tm | W | Sv | IP | K | ERA | xERA | WHIP | oOPS | vL | vR | BF/G | Ctl | Dom | Cmd | FpK | SwK | Vel | G | L | F | H% | S% | hr/f | GS | APC | DOM% | DIS% | Sv% | LI | RAR | BPV | BPX | R$ |
|---|---|---|---|---|---|---|---|---|---|---|---|---|---|---|---|---|---|---|---|---|---|---|---|---|---|---|---|---|---|---|---|---|---|
| 14 LA | 14 | 0 | 152 | 139 | 3.38 | 3.23 | 1.19 | 658 | 665 | 656 | 24.3 | 1.7 | 8.2 | 4.8 | 62% | 9% | 90.9 | 47 | 22 | 30 | 33% | 72% | 6% | 26 | 94 | 42% | 27% | | | 6.9 | 127 | 151 | $11 |
| 15 | | | | | | | | | | | | | | | | | | | | | | | | | | | | | | | | | |
| 16 LA | 0 | 0 | 5 | 4 | 11.57 | 5.52 | 2.14 | 1144 | 800 | 1238 | 24.0 | 3.9 | 7.7 | 2.0 | 54% | 11% | 89.8 | 41 | 24 | 35 | 43% | 44% | 17% | 1 | 89 | 0% | 100% | | | -4.2 | 54 | 64 | -$6 |
| 17 LA | 5 | 1 | 127 | 116 | 3.77 | 4.23 | 1.37 | 792 | 962 | 730 | 21.6 | 3.2 | 8.2 | 2.6 | 60% | 11% | 90.3 | 45 | 23 | 32 | 31% | 79% | 19% | 24 | 85 | 13% | 33% | 100 | 0.76 | 9.3 | 85 | 102 | $4 |
| 18 LA | 7 | 0 | 82 | 89 | 1.97 | 3.23 | 1.01 | 622 | 720 | 591 | 21.6 | 1.6 | 9.7 | 5.9 | 58% | 12% | 90.2 | 46 | 19 | 35 | 29% | 88% | 12% | 15 | 83 | 40% | 20% | | | 22.2 | 155 | 178 | $13 |
| 1st Half | 3 | 0 | 30 | 36 | 2.12 | 2.86 | 0.88 | 543 | 534 | 541 | 19.2 | 3.0 | 10.9 | 3.6 | 56% | 11% | 90.2 | 57 | 12 | 31 | 21% | 83% | 14% | 6 | 78 | 33% | 17% | | | 7.4 | 149 | 172 | $6 |
| 2nd Half | 4 | 0 | 53 | 53 | 1.88 | 3.41 | 1.08 | 663 | 807 | 619 | 23.2 | 0.9 | 9.1 | 10.6 | 60% | 13% | 90.3 | 41 | 22 | 37 | 33% | 90% | 11% | 9 | 86 | 44% | 22% | | | 14.7 | 159 | 183 | $16 |
| **19 Proj** | **7** | **0** | **102** | **102** | **3.34** | **3.25** | **1.14** | **683** | **798** | **646** | **21.2** | **2.1** | **9.0** | **4.4** | **60%** | **11%** | **90.3** | **47** | **20** | **33** | **30%** | **75%** | **14%** | **19** | | | | | | **10.1** | **131** | **151** | **$9** |

## Sabathia,CC

| | | | | | |
|---|---|---|---|---|---|
| Age: 38 | Th: L | Role SP | Health | F | LIMA Plan B |
| Ht: 6' 6" | Wt: 300 | Type Pwr | PT/Exp | A | Rand Var 0 |
| | | | Consist | A | MM 2203 |

For half a season, took this whole "guile-fueled late-career resurgence" thing to another level. But then the strand rate gods finally caught up with him. xERA has actually been locked into a narrow range for four years now. Seems like he can keep pitching to that level for a while longer, should he choose to do so.

| Yr Tm | W | Sv | IP | K | ERA | xERA | WHIP | oOPS | vL | vR | BF/G | Ctl | Dom | Cmd | FpK | SwK | Vel | G | L | F | H% | S% | hr/f | GS | APC | DOM% | DIS% | Sv% | LI | RAR | BPV | BPX | R$ |
|---|---|---|---|---|---|---|---|---|---|---|---|---|---|---|---|---|---|---|---|---|---|---|---|---|---|---|---|---|---|---|---|---|---|
| 14 NYY | 3 | 0 | 46 | 48 | 5.28 | 3.29 | 1.48 | 875 | 570 | 921 | 26.1 | 2.0 | 9.4 | 4.8 | 70% | 11% | 88.8 | 48 | 22 | 30 | 37% | 71% | 23% | 8 | 100 | 13% | 25% | | | -8.7 | 142 | 169 | -$5 |
| 15 NYY | 6 | 0 | 167 | 137 | 4.73 | 4.08 | 1.42 | 797 | 516 | 864 | 25.0 | 2.7 | 7.4 | 2.7 | 62% | 9% | 90.1 | 46 | 22 | 32 | 32% | 71% | 17% | 29 | 93 | 17% | 41% | | | -15.9 | 84 | 100 | -$6 |
| 16 NYY | 9 | 0 | 180 | 152 | 3.91 | 4.21 | 1.32 | 713 | 662 | 725 | 25.6 | 3.3 | 7.6 | 2.3 | 61% | 10% | 90.0 | 50 | 17 | 33 | 30% | 74% | 13% | 30 | 97 | 23% | 33% | | | 6.3 | 77 | 92 | $7 |
| 17 NYY | 14 | 0 | 149 | 120 | 3.69 | 4.15 | 1.27 | 715 | 683 | 722 | 23.1 | 3.0 | 7.3 | 2.4 | 61% | 9% | 90.9 | 50 | 22 | 28 | 28% | 76% | 17% | 27 | 87 | 22% | 37% | | | 12.2 | 77 | 93 | $12 |
| 18 NYY | 9 | 0 | 153 | 140 | 3.65 | 4.24 | 1.31 | 715 | 629 | 732 | 22.9 | 3.0 | 8.2 | 2.7 | 61% | 11% | 90.3 | 44 | 20 | 35 | 31% | 76% | 12% | 29 | 86 | 31% | 31% | | | 9.5 | 89 | 103 | $6 |
| 1st Half | 5 | 0 | 83 | 66 | 3.02 | 4.37 | 1.24 | 701 | 677 | 706 | 23.7 | 2.3 | 7.1 | 3.1 | 61% | 11% | 90.2 | 43 | 21 | 37 | 30% | 81% | 10% | 15 | 89 | 33% | 27% | | | 11.6 | 88 | 101 | $11 |
| 2nd Half | 4 | 0 | 70 | 74 | 4.39 | 4.07 | 1.41 | 733 | 552 | 762 | 22.1 | 3.9 | 9.6 | 2.5 | 60% | 12% | 90.5 | 46 | 20 | 34 | 33% | 72% | 14% | 14 | 84 | 29% | 36% | | | -2.1 | 92 | 106 | $2 |
| **19 Proj** | **9** | **0** | **145** | **127** | **4.03** | **3.95** | **1.34** | **732** | **635** | **752** | **22.6** | **3.2** | **7.9** | **2.5** | **61%** | **11%** | **90.3** | **46** | **20** | **33** | **30%** | **74%** | **14%** | **27** | | | | | | **2.2** | **80** | **91** | **$4** |

## Salazar,Danny

| | | | | | |
|---|---|---|---|---|---|
| Age: 29 | Th: R | Role SP | Health | F | LIMA Plan A |
| Ht: 6' 0" | Wt: 195 | Type Pwr | PT/Exp | C | Rand Var 0 |
| | | | Consist | A | MM 3501 |

Fought a shoulder injury right from spring training, eventually having surgery on it in July. He's a unicorn until further notice, but the skills history makes us want to believe in fantastical creatures. If there's good news in the spring, he's instantly worth a speculative bid.

| Yr Tm | W | Sv | IP | K | ERA | xERA | WHIP | oOPS | vL | vR | BF/G | Ctl | Dom | Cmd | FpK | SwK | Vel | G | L | F | H% | S% | hr/f | GS | APC | DOM% | DIS% | Sv% | LI | RAR | BPV | BPX | R$ |
|---|---|---|---|---|---|---|---|---|---|---|---|---|---|---|---|---|---|---|---|---|---|---|---|---|---|---|---|---|---|---|---|---|---|
| 14 CLE * | 10 | 0 | 171 | 184 | 4.25 | 4.63 | 1.43 | 751 | 696 | 786 | 23.4 | 3.3 | 9.7 | 3.0 | 59% | 12% | 94.6 | 34 | 23 | 42 | 35% | 73% | 10% | 20 | 93 | 30% | 25% | | | -10.7 | 89 | 106 | -$2 |
| 15 CLE | 14 | 0 | 185 | 195 | 3.45 | 3.44 | 1.13 | 673 | 724 | 628 | 25.2 | 2.6 | 9.5 | 3.7 | 59% | 12% | 94.8 | 44 | 19 | 37 | 29% | 74% | 12% | 30 | 102 | 33% | 17% | | | 11.6 | 123 | 147 | $18 |
| 16 CLE | 11 | 0 | 137 | 161 | 3.87 | 3.75 | 1.34 | 697 | 628 | 755 | 23.4 | 4.1 | 10.6 | 2.6 | 54% | 12% | 94.7 | 48 | 17 | 35 | 32% | 74% | 13% | 25 | 96 | 36% | 28% | | | 5.5 | 104 | 124 | $8 |
| 17 CLE | 5 | 0 | 103 | 145 | 4.28 | 3.40 | 1.34 | 721 | 780 | 671 | 19.1 | 3.8 | 12.7 | 3.3 | 60% | 17% | 95.1 | 39 | 25 | 36 | 35% | 72% | 16% | 19 | 79 | 26% | 16% | 0 | 0.67 | 1.0 | 141 | 170 | $3 |
| 18 | | | | | | | | | | | | | | | | | | | | | | | | | | | | | | | | | |
| 1st Half | | | | | | | | | | | | | | | | | | | | | | | | | | | | | | | | | |
| 2nd Half | | | | | | | | | | | | | | | | | | | | | | | | | | | | | | | | | |
| **19 Proj** | **6** | **0** | **87** | **103** | **3.70** | **3.40** | **1.28** | **706** | **720** | **695** | **21.9** | **3.4** | **10.7** | **3.2** | **58%** | **13%** | **94.8** | **42** | **21** | **37** | **32%** | **75%** | **13%** | **16** | | | | | | **4.8** | **121** | **139** | **$4** |

## Sale,Chris

| | | | | | |
|---|---|---|---|---|---|
| Age: 30 | Th: L | Role SP | Health | D | LIMA Plan C |
| Ht: 6' 6" | Wt: 180 | Type Pwr | PT/Exp | A | Rand Var -1 |
| | | | Consist | B | MM 5505 |

A couple of bouts of shoulder inflammation ate up his second half, but there are no visible ailments in these skills. Boston was already trying to manage his workload even before the shoulder got cranky, which means the most difficult number in the projection is the IP value. On a per-IP basis, he's platinum.

| Yr Tm | W | Sv | IP | K | ERA | xERA | WHIP | oOPS | vL | vR | BF/G | Ctl | Dom | Cmd | FpK | SwK | Vel | G | L | F | H% | S% | hr/f | GS | APC | DOM% | DIS% | Sv% | LI | RAR | BPV | BPX | R$ |
|---|---|---|---|---|---|---|---|---|---|---|---|---|---|---|---|---|---|---|---|---|---|---|---|---|---|---|---|---|---|---|---|---|---|
| 14 CHW | 12 | 0 | 174 | 208 | 2.17 | 2.81 | 0.97 | 567 | 393 | 608 | 26.3 | 2.0 | 10.8 | 5.3 | 67% | 14% | 93.8 | 41 | 18 | 41 | 29% | 81% | 8% | 26 | 106 | 58% | 4% | | | 33.7 | 158 | 188 | $27 |
| 15 CHW | 13 | 0 | 209 | 274 | 3.41 | 2.74 | 1.09 | 649 | 610 | 657 | 27.5 | 1.8 | 11.8 | 6.5 | 67% | 15% | 94.5 | 43 | 22 | 35 | 34% | 73% | 13% | 31 | 107 | 65% | 10% | | | 14.3 | 185 | 220 | $23 |
| 16 CHW | 17 | 0 | 227 | 233 | 3.34 | 3.47 | 1.04 | 651 | 585 | 663 | 28.3 | 1.8 | 9.3 | 5.2 | 62% | 12% | 92.8 | 41 | 21 | 38 | 29% | 73% | 12% | 32 | 107 | 66% | 13% | | | 23.9 | 137 | 163 | $29 |
| 17 BOS | 17 | 0 | 214 | 308 | 2.90 | 2.86 | 0.97 | 603 | 531 | 617 | 26.6 | 1.8 | 12.9 | 7.2 | 67% | 15% | 94.4 | 39 | 20 | 41 | 32% | 76% | 12% | 32 | 107 | 69% | 3% | | | 38.6 | 201 | 241 | $40 |
| 18 BOS | 12 | 0 | 158 | 237 | 2.11 | 2.40 | 0.86 | 532 | 424 | 555 | 22.9 | 1.9 | 13.5 | 7.0 | 67% | 16% | 94.7 | 44 | 20 | 36 | 30% | 79% | 9% | 27 | 94 | 63% | 11% | | | 39.8 | 213 | 245 | $34 |
| 1st Half | 8 | 0 | 116 | 164 | 2.41 | 2.64 | 0.89 | 545 | 464 | 560 | 25.2 | 2.3 | 12.7 | 5.7 | 68% | 16% | 94.4 | 45 | 18 | 37 | 28% | 77% | 11% | 18 | 101 | 61% | 11% | | | 25.0 | 191 | 219 | $43 |
| 2nd Half | 4 | 0 | 42 | 73 | 1.29 | 1.80 | 0.79 | 496 | 338 | 538 | 18.1 | 1.1 | 15.6 | 14.6 | 66% | 17% | 95.5 | 43 | 24 | 33 | 37% | 84% | 4% | 9 | 79 | 67% | 11% | | | 14.8 | 274 | 314 | $14 |
| **19 Proj** | **15** | **0** | **189** | **266** | **2.37** | **2.40** | **0.94** | **572** | **456** | **596** | **22.3** | **1.9** | **12.7** | **6.8** | **66%** | **15%** | **94.4** | **42** | **21** | **37** | **31%** | **79%** | **10%** | **32** | | | | | | **57.3** | **198** | **227** | **$37** |

## Samardzija,Jeff

| | | | | | |
|---|---|---|---|---|---|
| Age: 34 | Th: R | Role SP | Health | F | LIMA Plan B |
| Ht: 6' 5" | Wt: 240 | Type | PT/Exp | A | Rand Var +2 |
| | | | Consist | B | MM 1103 |

1-5, 6.25 ERA in 45 IP at SF. Strained pectoral delayed start of his season, then shoulder problems ended it early. Skills certainly look like he was hampered all year, though surgery reportedly not required. This projection gives him a mulligan on 2018. Just check on him in spring before extending the same courtesy.

| Yr Tm | W | Sv | IP | K | ERA | xERA | WHIP | oOPS | vL | vR | BF/G | Ctl | Dom | Cmd | FpK | SwK | Vel | G | L | F | H% | S% | hr/f | GS | APC | DOM% | DIS% | Sv% | LI | RAR | BPV | BPX | R$ |
|---|---|---|---|---|---|---|---|---|---|---|---|---|---|---|---|---|---|---|---|---|---|---|---|---|---|---|---|---|---|---|---|---|---|
| 14 2 TM | 7 | 0 | 220 | 202 | 2.99 | 3.05 | 1.07 | 646 | 662 | 631 | 26.6 | 1.8 | 8.3 | 4.7 | 65% | 12% | 94.4 | 50 | 19 | 31 | 29% | 75% | 11% | 33 | 101 | 58% | 9% | | | 20.3 | 129 | 154 | $19 |
| 15 CHW | 11 | 0 | 214 | 163 | 4.96 | 4.25 | 1.29 | 765 | 839 | 689 | 28.4 | 2.1 | 6.9 | 3.3 | 62% | 10% | 94.2 | 39 | 21 | 40 | 31% | 64% | 11% | 32 | 104 | 28% | 28% | | | -26.4 | 85 | 101 | -$2 |
| 16 SF | 12 | 0 | 203 | 167 | 3.81 | 4.01 | 1.20 | 710 | 780 | 639 | 25.9 | 2.4 | 7.4 | 3.1 | 63% | 10% | 94.3 | 46 | 20 | 34 | 29% | 72% | 12% | 32 | 100 | 28% | 34% | | | 9.6 | 93 | 110 | $14 |
| 17 SF | 9 | 0 | 208 | 205 | 4.42 | 3.71 | 1.14 | 734 | 771 | 692 | 26.5 | 1.4 | 8.9 | 6.4 | 65% | 11% | 94.3 | 41 | 22 | 36 | 31% | 65% | 14% | 32 | 102 | 41% | 16% | | | -1.6 | 141 | 170 | $14 |
| 18 SF * | 1 | 0 | 66 | 45 | 6.01 | 5.41 | 1.53 | 789 | 911 | 701 | 19.0 | 4.2 | 6.2 | 1.5 | 55% | 8% | 92.3 | 30 | 24 | 47 | 30% | 63% | 9% | 10 | 81 | 0% | 50% | | | -15.0 | 24 | 28 | -$11 |
| 1st Half | 1 | 0 | 47 | 38 | 6.82 | 5.98 | 1.64 | 813 | 993 | 671 | 18.9 | 4.8 | 7.4 | 1.5 | 58% | 9% | 92.4 | 34 | 21 | 46 | 32% | 61% | 12% | 8 | 84 | 0% | 63% | | | -15.4 | 25 | 29 | -$13 |
| 2nd Half | 0 | 0 | 19 | 7 | 3.58 | 3.66 | 1.20 | 694 | 481 | 802 | 19.1 | 2.5 | 3.3 | 1.3 | 44% | 7% | 91.7 | 16 | 34 | 50 | 25% | 73% | 0% | 2 | 68 | 0% | 0% | | | 1.3 | 26 | 30 | $0 |
| **19 Proj** | **7** | **0** | **160** | **131** | **4.00** | **4.05** | **1.29** | **752** | **840** | **670** | **22.0** | **2.5** | **7.4** | **3.0** | **63%** | **10%** | **93.7** | **41** | **21** | **38** | **31%** | **73%** | **12%** | **30** | | | | | | **1.6** | **86** | **98** | **$5** |

## Sampson,Adrian

| | | | | | |
|---|---|---|---|---|---|
| Age: 27 | Th: R | Role RP | Health | D | LIMA Plan D+ |
| Ht: 6' 2" | Wt: 210 | Type Con xFB | PT/Exp | D | Rand Var +3 |
| | | | Consist | C | MM 0000 |

0-3, 4.30 ERA in 23 IP at TEX. There used to be a place in the game for these good-Ctl, low-Dom types. But that was back when the league-average Dom was in the mid-6s. Now that it's up in the mid-8s, this skill set is just too far below viability... especially without a GB tilt. Yo, Adrian! Work on a strikeout pitch.

| Yr Tm | W | Sv | IP | K | ERA | xERA | WHIP | oOPS | vL | vR | BF/G | Ctl | Dom | Cmd | FpK | SwK | Vel | G | L | F | H% | S% | hr/f | GS | APC | DOM% | DIS% | Sv% | LI | RAR | BPV | BPX | R$ |
|---|---|---|---|---|---|---|---|---|---|---|---|---|---|---|---|---|---|---|---|---|---|---|---|---|---|---|---|---|---|---|---|---|---|
| 14 a/a | 11 | 0 | 167 | 89 | 3.02 | 3.20 | 1.17 | | | | 23.8 | 1.8 | 4.8 | 2.7 | | | | | | | 29% | 75% | | | | | | | | 14.8 | 75 | 90 | $11 |
| 15 aaa | 10 | 0 | 163 | 106 | 4.38 | 4.61 | 1.43 | | | | 24.7 | 1.8 | 5.9 | 3.3 | | | | | | | 35% | 69% | | | | | | | | -8.3 | 82 | 97 | -$3 |
| 16 SEA * | 7 | 0 | 85 | 54 | 4.05 | 4.55 | 1.36 | 1129 | 1500 | 1000 | 25.4 | 1.4 | 5.7 | 4.1 | 48% | 4% | 91.1 | 33 | 39 | 28 | 34% | 72% | 40% | 1 | 85 | 0% | 100% | | | 1.5 | 91 | 108 | $1 |
| 17 | | | | | | | | | | | | | | | | | | | | | | | | | | | | | | | | | |
| 18 TEX * | 8 | 0 | 151 | 79 | 4.89 | 5.85 | 1.52 | 829 | 726 | 974 | 17.3 | 1.9 | 4.7 | 2.5 | 50% | 8% | 91.1 | 36 | 22 | 42 | 34% | 71% | 19% | 4 | 68 | 0% | 50% | 0 | 0.66 | -13.9 | 34 | 39 | -$9 |
| 1st Half | 3 | 0 | 55 | 31 | 7.46 | 7.07 | 1.77 | | | | 12.0 | 2.9 | 5.0 | 1.8 | | | | | | | 36% | 58% | 0% | 0 | | | | | | -22.5 | 11 | 13 | -$29 |
| 2nd Half | 5 | 0 | 96 | 48 | 3.42 | 5.16 | 1.38 | 829 | 726 | 974 | 23.7 | 1.4 | 4.5 | 3.3 | 50% | 8% | 91.1 | 36 | 22 | 42 | 32% | 80% | 19% | 4 | 68 | 0% | 50% | 0 | 0.66 | 8.6 | 57 | 65 | $3 |
| **19 Proj** | **4** | **0** | **58** | **33** | **4.51** | **4.87** | **1.43** | **746** | **657** | **870** | **20.0** | **1.7** | **5.1** | **3.0** | **50%** | **8%** | **91.1** | **36** | **22** | **42** | **33%** | **70%** | **7%** | **12** | | | | | | **-2.9** | **60** | **69** | **-$4** |

## Sanchez,Aaron

| | | | | | |
|---|---|---|---|---|---|
| Age: 27 | Th: R | Role SP | Health | F | LIMA Plan D+ |
| Ht: 6' 4" | Wt: 215 | Type Pwr GB | PT/Exp | B | Rand Var 0 |
| | | | Consist | C | MM 1103 |

Another year, more finger problems. 2017 was ruined by blisters; this year he caught a finger in a suitcase in June and eventually had surgery on it in September. Amid the carnage here, the SwK spike is an eye-catcher. Take that SwK, some Ctl recovery, and five intact digits, and there's still big profit potential here.

| Yr Tm | W | Sv | IP | K | ERA | xERA | WHIP | oOPS | vL | vR | BF/G | Ctl | Dom | Cmd | FpK | SwK | Vel | G | L | F | H% | S% | hr/f | GS | APC | DOM% | DIS% | Sv% | LI | RAR | BPV | BPX | R$ |
|---|---|---|---|---|---|---|---|---|---|---|---|---|---|---|---|---|---|---|---|---|---|---|---|---|---|---|---|---|---|---|---|---|---|
| 14 TOR * | 5 | 3 | 133 | 102 | 3.96 | 3.47 | 1.37 | 367 | 469 | 306 | 12.1 | 4.5 | 6.9 | 1.5 | 53% | 7% | 97.1 | 66 | 15 | 20 | 28% | 71% | 6% | 0 | 19 | | | 100 | 1.17 | -3.6 | 65 | 77 | $0 |
| 15 TOR | 7 | 0 | 92 | 61 | 3.22 | 4.08 | 1.28 | 666 | 878 | 435 | 9.3 | 4.3 | 5.9 | 1.4 | 53% | 7% | 94.9 | 61 | 18 | 22 | 25% | 78% | 16% | 11 | 35 | 0% | 45% | 0 | 1.08 | 8.5 | 30 | 36 | $4 |
| 16 TOR | 15 | 0 | 192 | 161 | 3.00 | 3.72 | 1.17 | 625 | 657 | 592 | 26.3 | 3.0 | 7.5 | 2.6 | 61% | 9% | 94.7 | 54 | 20 | 25 | 28% | 77% | 11% | 30 | 97 | 43% | 17% | | | 28.2 | 88 | 105 | $21 |
| 17 TOR | 1 | 0 | 36 | 24 | 4.25 | 5.60 | 1.72 | 836 | 654 | 955 | 20.9 | 5.0 | 6.0 | 1.2 | 59% | 6% | 94.9 | 48 | 24 | 29 | 32% | 80% | 17% | 8 | 77 | 13% | 75% | | | 0.5 | -1 | -1 | -$6 |
| 18 TOR | 4 | 0 | 105 | 86 | 4.89 | 4.92 | 1.56 | 768 | 876 | 661 | 23.7 | 5.0 | 7.4 | 1.5 | 59% | 10% | 93.7 | 49 | 19 | 32 | 31% | 70% | 11% | 20 | 90 | 10% | 55% | | | -9.5 | 25 | 29 | -$8 |
| 1st Half | 3 | 0 | 80 | 67 | 4.52 | 4.84 | 1.51 | 739 | 873 | 628 | 23.9 | 5.1 | 7.6 | 1.5 | 60% | 10% | 93.8 | 50 | 18 | 32 | 30% | 71% | 11% | 15 | 91 | 7% | 53% | | | -3.6 | 27 | 31 | -$7 |
| 2nd Half | 1 | 0 | 25 | 19 | 6.04 | 5.16 | 1.74 | 858 | 884 | 813 | 23.2 | 4.6 | 6.8 | 1.5 | 54% | 8% | 93.5 | 46 | 23 | 31 | 35% | 66% | 12% | 5 | 87 | 20% | 60% | | | -5.9 | 21 | 24 | -$12 |
| **19 Proj** | **8** | **0** | **131** | **109** | **4.04** | **4.28** | **1.48** | **748** | **771** | **723** | **23.3** | **4.4** | **7.5** | **1.7** | **57%** | **8%** | **94.3** | **50** | **21** | **29** | **31%** | **76%** | **14%** | **24** | | | | | | **-1.8** | **45** | **51** | **$0** |

RAY MURPHY

## Sanchez,Anibal

| | | | | | | | |
|---|---|---|---|---|---|---|---|
| Age: 35 | Th: R | Role RP | | Health F | PT/Exp B | Consist F | |
| Ht: 6' 0" | Wt: 205 | Type Pwr | | LIMA Plan C | Rand Var -3 | MM 2203 | |

What just happened? Chronic hr/f, fading velocity, age and health left him unrosterable. Rearranged broad arsenal to feature cutter, change-up; hiked GB%, enjoyed uncharacteristic H%/S%, health—and the stars aligned. Command, FpK remain attractive, but maintaining this fortunate convergence now? Unlikely.

| Yr Tm | W | Sv | IP | K | ERA | xERA | WHIP | oOPS | vL | vR | BF/G | Ctl | Dom | Cmd | FpK | SwK | Vel | G | L | F | H% | S% | hr/f | GS | APC | DOM% | DIS% | Sv% | LI | RAR | BPV | BPX | R$ |
|---|---|---|---|---|---|---|---|---|---|---|---|---|---|---|---|---|---|---|---|---|---|---|---|---|---|---|---|---|---|---|---|---|---|
| 14 DET | 8 | 0 | 126 | 102 | 3.43 | 3.58 | 1.10 | 597 | 562 | 648 | 23.4 | 2.1 | 7.3 | 3.4 | 60% | 10% | 92.1 | 46 | 19 | 35 | 29% | 67% | 3% | 21 | 95 | 33% | 10% | 0 | 0.75 | 4.9 | 97 | 116 | $8 |
| 15 DET | 10 | 0 | 157 | 138 | 4.99 | 4.11 | 1.28 | 768 | 681 | 866 | 26.4 | 2.8 | 7.9 | 2.8 | 65% | 10% | 91.9 | 40 | 21 | 39 | 29% | 66% | 16% | 25 | 101 | 40% | 24% | | | -19.9 | 85 | 101 | -$1 |
| 16 DET | 7 | 0 | 153 | 135 | 5.87 | 4.63 | 1.46 | 828 | 771 | 888 | 19.1 | 3.1 | 7.9 | 2.5 | 67% | 10% | 91.1 | 40 | 19 | 41 | 32% | 64% | 16% | 26 | 74 | 12% | 38% | 0 | 0.84 | -31.8 | 77 | 91 | -$10 |
| 17 DET * | 3 | 0 | 121 | 118 | 6.56 | 7.08 | 1.64 | 906 | 822 | 989 | 16.9 | 2.6 | 8.8 | 3.3 | 61% | 10% | 90.8 | 36 | 25 | 40 | 37% | 66% | 19% | 17 | 66 | 12% | 35% | 0 | 0.58 | -32.8 | 45 | 54 | -$15 |
| 18 ATL | 7 | 0 | 137 | 135 | 2.83 | 3.77 | 1.08 | 633 | 573 | 686 | 22.1 | 2.8 | 8.9 | 3.2 | 66% | 11% | 90.7 | 45 | 18 | 37 | 27% | 79% | 11% | 24 | 85 | 38% | 29% | 0 | 0.75 | 22.2 | 108 | 125 | $15 |
| 1st Half | 3 | 0 | 47 | 44 | 2.68 | 4.09 | 1.09 | 661 | 724 | 611 | 21.1 | 3.1 | 8.4 | 2.8 | 65% | 10% | 90.4 | 42 | 17 | 41 | 25% | 82% | 12% | 8 | 82 | 38% | 25% | 0 | 0.69 | 8.5 | 89 | 102 | $5 |
| 2nd Half | 4 | 0 | 90 | 91 | 2.91 | 3.60 | 1.08 | 618 | 505 | 730 | 22.7 | 2.6 | 9.1 | 3.5 | 67% | 11% | 90.9 | 47 | 19 | 35 | 28% | 77% | 11% | 16 | 87 | 38% | 31% | | | 13.7 | 119 | 136 | $21 |
| **19 Proj** | **7** | **0** | **145** | **138** | **4.10** | **3.79** | **1.29** | **745** | **686** | **803** | **19.7** | **2.8** | **8.6** | **3.1** | **65%** | **10%** | **90.9** | **43** | **20** | **38** | **31%** | **73%** | **14%** | **29** | | | | | | **0.9** | **100** | **115** | **$4** |

## Santana,Edgar

| | | | | | | | |
|---|---|---|---|---|---|---|---|
| Age: 27 | Th: R | Role RP | | Health A | PT/Exp D | Consist B | |
| Ht: 6' 2" | Wt: 195 | Type | | LIMA Plan B+ | Rand Var 0 | MM 2100 | |

Live-armed rookie came late to both baseball, pitching. Didn't sign professionally until age 22, now with promising results at the highest level. Has yet to fully leverage swing-and-miss slider into whiffs; both repertoire, GB% are works-in-progress. But ahead-of-schedule Ctl buys development time. Watchable.

| Yr Tm | W | Sv | IP | K | ERA | xERA | WHIP | oOPS | vL | vR | BF/G | Ctl | Dom | Cmd | FpK | SwK | Vel | G | L | F | H% | S% | hr/f | GS | APC | DOM% | DIS% | Sv% | LI | RAR | BPV | BPX | R$ |
|---|---|---|---|---|---|---|---|---|---|---|---|---|---|---|---|---|---|---|---|---|---|---|---|---|---|---|---|---|---|---|---|---|---|
| 14 | | | | | | | | | | | | | | | | | | | | | | | | | | | | | | | | | |
| 15 | | | | | | | | | | | | | | | | | | | | | | | | | | | | | | | | | |
| 16 a/a | 2 | 3 | 57 | 40 | 4.74 | 5.00 | 1.51 | | | | 7.3 | 3.0 | 6.2 | 2.1 | | | | | | | 34% | 70% | | | | | | | | -3.9 | 50 | 59 | -$4 |
| 17 PIT * | 1 | 8 | 76 | 62 | 3.81 | 5.32 | 1.59 | 780 | 1164 | 497 | 5.3 | 3.0 | 7.3 | 2.4 | 60% | 14% | 95.1 | 45 | 26 | 30 | 37% | 78% | 14% | 0 | 16 | | | 89 | 0.79 | 5.1 | 64 | 76 | $0 |
| 18 PIT | 3 | 0 | 66 | 54 | 3.26 | 3.90 | 1.10 | 657 | 696 | 619 | 3.9 | 1.6 | 7.3 | 4.5 | 61% | 12% | 94.7 | 46 | 20 | 34 | 29% | 74% | 10% | 0 | 13 | | | 0 | 1.08 | 7.3 | 112 | 129 | $3 |
| 1st Half | 2 | 0 | 34 | 28 | 3.97 | 3.92 | 1.06 | 659 | 768 | 542 | 3.9 | 1.1 | 7.4 | 7.0 | 60% | 13% | 94.6 | 48 | 15 | 37 | 28% | 68% | 13% | 0 | 14 | | | 0 | 1.00 | 0.8 | 130 | 150 | $1 |
| 2nd Half | 1 | 0 | 32 | 26 | 2.51 | 3.89 | 1.14 | 653 | 605 | 698 | 4.0 | 2.2 | 7.2 | 3.3 | 62% | 12% | 94.8 | 44 | 26 | 31 | 29% | 80% | 7% | 0 | 13 | | | 0 | 1.17 | 6.6 | 92 | 105 | $5 |
| **19 Proj** | **2** | **0** | **44** | **35** | **3.58** | **3.95** | **1.34** | **751** | **766** | **737** | **4.6** | **2.4** | **7.2** | **3.0** | **61%** | **12%** | **94.7** | **45** | **21** | **33** | **33%** | **76%** | **9%** | **0** | | | | | | **3.1** | **88** | **102** | **-$2** |

## Santana,Ervin

| | | | | | | | |
|---|---|---|---|---|---|---|---|
| Age: 36 | Th: R | Role SP | | Health F | PT/Exp B | Consist C | |
| Ht: 6' 2" | Wt: 175 | Type FB | | LIMA Plan B | Rand Var +3 | MM 1101 | |

0-1, 8.03 ERA in 25 IP at MIN. Off-season finger surgery shelved workhorse until late July. Ongoing grip issues, velocity plunge fueled 5 disastrous starts before he called it quits. Now hoping off-season plasma rich platelet injections will take. In free-agent limbo, will get opportunity if healthy. March will be an early tell.

| Yr Tm | W | Sv | IP | K | ERA | xERA | WHIP | oOPS | vL | vR | BF/G | Ctl | Dom | Cmd | FpK | SwK | Vel | G | L | F | H% | S% | hr/f | GS | APC | DOM% | DIS% | Sv% | LI | RAR | BPV | BPX | R$ |
|---|---|---|---|---|---|---|---|---|---|---|---|---|---|---|---|---|---|---|---|---|---|---|---|---|---|---|---|---|---|---|---|---|---|
| 14 ATL | 14 | 0 | 196 | 179 | 3.95 | 3.57 | 1.31 | 724 | 763 | 676 | 26.4 | 2.9 | 8.2 | 2.8 | 63% | 12% | 92.3 | 43 | 25 | 33 | 32% | 71% | 9% | 31 | 96 | 32% | 29% | | | -5.0 | 91 | 108 | $5 |
| 15 MIN * | 10 | 0 | 129 | 90 | 3.79 | 4.09 | 1.31 | 729 | 804 | 651 | 26.6 | 2.9 | 6.3 | 2.2 | 61% | 10% | 92.5 | 41 | 22 | 38 | 29% | 74% | 10% | 17 | 99 | 47% | 35% | | | 2.7 | 56 | 67 | $4 |
| 16 MIN | 7 | 0 | 181 | 149 | 3.38 | 4.21 | 1.22 | 682 | 667 | 697 | 24.9 | 2.6 | 7.4 | 2.8 | 59% | 10% | 92.7 | 43 | 22 | 36 | 29% | 76% | 10% | 30 | 98 | 27% | 27% | | | 18.2 | 83 | 99 | $12 |
| 17 MIN | 16 | 0 | 211 | 167 | 3.28 | 4.59 | 1.13 | 678 | 646 | 705 | 26.2 | 2.6 | 7.1 | 2.7 | 64% | 11% | 92.9 | 41 | 16 | 42 | 25% | 78% | 12% | 33 | 98 | 27% | 27% | | | 28.1 | 77 | 92 | $25 |
| 18 MIN * | 0 | 0 | 45 | 27 | 6.85 | 6.69 | 1.37 | 1038 | 885 | 1270 | 20.9 | 2.8 | 5.3 | 1.9 | 68% | 5% | 88.8 | 23 | 17 | 60 | 24% | 60% | 17% | 5 | 86 | 0% | 60% | | | -15.0 | -24 | -27 | -$9 |
| 1st Half | 0 | 0 | 2 | 1 | 12.72 | 17.16 | 2.68 | | | | 11.0 | 0.0 | 3.2 | 0.0 | | | | | | | 45% | 63% | 0% | 0 | | | | | | -2.1 | 0 | 0 | -$12 |
| 2nd Half | 0 | 0 | 43 | 26 | 6.53 | 6.15 | 1.30 | 1038 | 885 | 1270 | 22.1 | 2.9 | 5.4 | 1.9 | 68% | 5% | 88.8 | 23 | 17 | 60 | 22% | 60% | 17% | 5 | 86 | 0% | 60% | | | -12.6 | -17 | -19 | -$9 |
| **19 Proj** | **5** | **0** | **123** | **91** | **4.41** | **4.44** | **1.25** | **762** | **730** | **797** | **24.3** | **2.8** | **6.7** | **2.4** | **63%** | **9%** | **91.5** | **36** | **20** | **44** | **27%** | **71%** | **14%** | **21** | | | | | | **-4.0** | **59** | **68** | **$1** |

## Santiago,Hector

| | | | | | | | |
|---|---|---|---|---|---|---|---|
| Age: 31 | Th: L | Role RP | | Health F | PT/Exp B | Consist B | |
| Ht: 6' 0" | Wt: 215 | Type Pwr xFB | | LIMA Plan D+ | Rand Var 0 | MM 0201 | |

6.12 ERA, 24/23 K/BB over 32 IP as a starter banished him to the pen, where he mopped up, ate innings for one of the AL's worst clubs. Was actually better in relief, as 2nd-half Dom soared, ERA fell; even FpK perked up. But execrable Ctl, big FB% look entrenched; WHIP, xERA history say he's still unrosterable.

| Yr Tm | W | Sv | IP | K | ERA | xERA | WHIP | oOPS | vL | vR | BF/G | Ctl | Dom | Cmd | FpK | SwK | Vel | G | L | F | H% | S% | hr/f | GS | APC | DOM% | DIS% | Sv% | LI | RAR | BPV | BPX | R$ |
|---|---|---|---|---|---|---|---|---|---|---|---|---|---|---|---|---|---|---|---|---|---|---|---|---|---|---|---|---|---|---|---|---|---|
| 14 LAA | 6 | 0 | 127 | 108 | 3.75 | 4.53 | 1.36 | 698 | 606 | 732 | 18.1 | 3.7 | 7.6 | 2.0 | 56% | 8% | 90.9 | 31 | 19 | 50 | 29% | 76% | 8% | 24 | 76 | 8% | 50% | 0 | 0.80 | -0.1 | 45 | 54 | $0 |
| 15 LAA | 9 | 0 | 181 | 162 | 3.59 | 4.74 | 1.26 | 723 | 633 | 752 | 23.5 | 3.5 | 8.1 | 2.3 | 57% | 9% | 90.3 | 30 | 16 | 54 | 27% | 78% | 10% | 32 | 96 | 19% | 31% | 0 | 0.74 | 8.4 | 58 | 69 | $9 |
| 16 2AL | 13 | 0 | 182 | 144 | 4.70 | 5.33 | 1.36 | 774 | 750 | 780 | 23.8 | 3.9 | 7.1 | 1.8 | 55% | 9% | 91.4 | 34 | 16 | 50 | 27% | 71% | 12% | 33 | 96 | 18% | 48% | | | -11.4 | 35 | 41 | $2 |
| 17 MIN * | 5 | 0 | 94 | 69 | 6.54 | 6.14 | 1.64 | 782 | 1521 | 627 | 19.0 | 5.0 | 6.6 | 1.3 | 56% | 8% | 90.7 | 30 | 18 | 51 | 29% | 65% | 13% | 14 | 82 | 14% | 50% | 0 | 0.84 | -25.4 | 5 | 6 | -$12 |
| 18 CHW | 6 | 2 | 102 | 103 | 4.50 | 5.30 | 1.59 | 814 | 831 | 804 | 9.4 | 5.3 | 9.1 | 1.7 | 56% | 9% | 90.8 | 33 | 17 | 50 | 32% | 76% | 11% | 7 | 40 | 0% | 57% | 100 | 0.69 | -4.4 | 32 | 36 | -$5 |
| 1st Half | 2 | 0 | 61 | 48 | 4.70 | 6.08 | 1.63 | 859 | 905 | 838 | 11.1 | 5.4 | 7.0 | 1.3 | 53% | 8% | 90.7 | 34 | 13 | 53 | 29% | 76% | 11% | 7 | 47 | 0% | 57% | 0 | 0.61 | -4.1 | -8 | -9 | -$12 |
| 2nd Half | 4 | 2 | 41 | 55 | 4.20 | 4.20 | 1.52 | 747 | 743 | 747 | 7.6 | 5.1 | 12.2 | 2.4 | 61% | 10% | 90.8 | 32 | 23 | 45 | 36% | 75% | 11% | 0 | 33 | | | 100 | 0.77 | -0.3 | 92 | 105 | $2 |
| **19 Proj** | **5** | **0** | **73** | **69** | **4.90** | **4.89** | **1.53** | **795** | **922** | **752** | **11.9** | **4.8** | **8.6** | **1.8** | **57%** | **9%** | **90.8** | **32** | **18** | **50** | **31%** | **72%** | **12%** | **5** | | | | | | **-6.3** | **34** | **39** | **-$5** |

## Scherzer,Max

| | | | | | | | |
|---|---|---|---|---|---|---|---|
| Age: 34 | Th: R | Role SP | | Health B | PT/Exp A | Consist A | |
| Ht: 6' 3" | Wt: 215 | Type Pwr xFB | | LIMA Plan C | Rand Var -1 | MM 5505 | |

Now just the 6th pitcher ever to record 300 K; also led in MLB IP, second in WHIP. Unsustainable early pace, as 2nd-half S%, Dom downtick and a few more HR combined to make him look less otherworldly. But despite encroaching age and firmly rooted FB%, nothing hints at any drop-off from elite status.

| Yr Tm | W | Sv | IP | K | ERA | xERA | WHIP | oOPS | vL | vR | BF/G | Ctl | Dom | Cmd | FpK | SwK | Vel | G | L | F | H% | S% | hr/f | GS | APC | DOM% | DIS% | Sv% | LI | RAR | BPV | BPX | R$ |
|---|---|---|---|---|---|---|---|---|---|---|---|---|---|---|---|---|---|---|---|---|---|---|---|---|---|---|---|---|---|---|---|---|---|
| 14 DET | 18 | 0 | 220 | 252 | 3.15 | 3.24 | 1.18 | 663 | 685 | 629 | 27.4 | 2.6 | 10.3 | 4.0 | 63% | 12% | 92.8 | 37 | 22 | 42 | 33% | 76% | 8% | 33 | 110 | 39% | 6% | | | 16.2 | 131 | 156 | $20 |
| 15 WAS | 14 | 0 | 229 | 276 | 2.79 | 3.00 | 0.92 | 600 | 657 | 538 | 27.2 | 1.3 | 10.9 | 8.1 | 71% | 16% | 94.2 | 36 | 19 | 45 | 29% | 76% | 11% | 33 | 102 | 58% | 9% | | | 32.9 | 173 | 207 | $37 |
| 16 WAS | 20 | 0 | 228 | 284 | 2.96 | 3.42 | 0.97 | 619 | 757 | 477 | 26.5 | 2.2 | 11.2 | 5.1 | 65% | 16% | 94.3 | 33 | 19 | 48 | 27% | 77% | 12% | 34 | 105 | 65% | 12% | | | 34.7 | 153 | 182 | $38 |
| 17 WAS | 16 | 0 | 201 | 268 | 2.51 | 3.21 | 0.90 | 565 | 690 | 425 | 25.2 | 2.5 | 12.0 | 4.9 | 65% | 16% | 94.1 | 37 | 17 | 47 | 26% | 79% | 11% | 31 | 100 | 65% | 3% | | | 45.7 | 165 | 198 | $41 |
| 18 WAS | 18 | 0 | 221 | 300 | 2.53 | 3.10 | 0.91 | 580 | 609 | 547 | 26.2 | 2.1 | 12.2 | 5.9 | 66% | 17% | 94.4 | 34 | 18 | 48 | 28% | 78% | 10% | 33 | 106 | 67% | 6% | | | 44.1 | 176 | 203 | $44 |
| 1st Half | 10 | 0 | 115 | 165 | 2.04 | 2.88 | 0.85 | 548 | 639 | 447 | 26.2 | 2.1 | 13.0 | 6.1 | 70% | 18% | 94.1 | 36 | 16 | 47 | 28% | 82% | 9% | 17 | 106 | 76% | 6% | | | 29.8 | 190 | 219 | $52 |
| 2nd Half | 8 | 0 | 106 | 135 | 3.06 | 3.35 | 0.97 | 614 | 577 | 652 | 26.3 | 2.0 | 11.5 | 5.6 | 61% | 16% | 94.7 | 32 | 20 | 48 | 29% | 74% | 11% | 16 | 105 | 56% | 6% | | | 14.3 | 161 | 185 | $34 |
| **19 Proj** | **17** | **0** | **203** | **265** | **2.92** | **2.91** | **0.96** | **605** | **669** | **534** | **25.1** | **2.2** | **11.8** | **5.4** | **65%** | **16%** | **94.3** | **35** | **18** | **47** | **29%** | **75%** | **11%** | **31** | | | | | | **40.7** | **166** | **190** | **$35** |

## Scott,Tanner

| | | | | | | | |
|---|---|---|---|---|---|---|---|
| Age: 24 | Th: L | Role RP | | Health A | PT/Exp D | Consist D | |
| Ht: 6' 2" | Wt: 220 | Type Pwr | | LIMA Plan C | Rand Var +5 | MM 3510 | |

Featured fastball/slider combo and some eye-opening peripherals during rocky MLB debut. Ctl is an ongoing project, though 2018 FpK isn't hopeless. Small sample 2nd-half progress vR still leaves plenty of room for improvement. But Dom/SwK and GB% combo point to late-inning upside; xERA has him on our radar.

| Yr Tm | W | Sv | IP | K | ERA | xERA | WHIP | oOPS | vL | vR | BF/G | Ctl | Dom | Cmd | FpK | SwK | Vel | G | L | F | H% | S% | hr/f | GS | APC | DOM% | DIS% | Sv% | LI | RAR | BPV | BPX | R$ |
|---|---|---|---|---|---|---|---|---|---|---|---|---|---|---|---|---|---|---|---|---|---|---|---|---|---|---|---|---|---|---|---|---|---|
| 14 | | | | | | | | | | | | | | | | | | | | | | | | | | | | | | | | | |
| 15 | | | | | | | | | | | | | | | | | | | | | | | | | | | | | | | | | |
| 16 aa | 1 | 0 | 16 | 16 | 6.66 | 6.26 | 2.27 | | | | 5.8 | 9.0 | 9.1 | 1.0 | | | | | | | 41% | 67% | | | | | | | | -4.9 | 69 | 82 | -$7 |
| 17 BAL * | 0 | 0 | 71 | 73 | 2.95 | 3.22 | 1.47 | 873 | 0 | 1171 | 11.7 | 6.3 | 9.4 | 1.5 | 44% | 11% | 98.0 | 20 | 60 | 20 | 29% | 80% | 0% | 0 | 19 | | | 0 | 0.02 | 12.3 | 90 | 108 | $0 |
| 18 BAL | 3 | 0 | 53 | 76 | 5.40 | 3.26 | 1.56 | 777 | 639 | 877 | 4.5 | 4.7 | 12.8 | 2.7 | 56% | 17% | 97.1 | 47 | 27 | 25 | 40% | 66% | 18% | 0 | 18 | | | 0 | 0.87 | -8.2 | 128 | 148 | -$6 |
| 1st Half | 0 | 0 | 21 | 29 | 6.33 | 3.18 | 1.59 | 809 | 529 | 1010 | 4.5 | 4.2 | 12.2 | 2.9 | 56% | 19% | 97.0 | 50 | 26 | 24 | 41% | 59% | 15% | 0 | 18 | | | 0 | 0.99 | -5.7 | 134 | 154 | -$13 |
| 2nd Half | 3 | 0 | 32 | 47 | 4.78 | 3.31 | 1.53 | 756 | 712 | 788 | 4.5 | 5.1 | 13.2 | 2.6 | 57% | 17% | 97.2 | 45 | 29 | 26 | 38% | 71% | 20% | 0 | 18 | | | 0 | 0.78 | -2.5 | 125 | 143 | -$2 |
| **19 Proj** | **2** | **7** | **58** | **73** | **3.96** | **3.47** | **1.35** | **656** | **546** | **735** | **5.6** | **5.0** | **11.4** | **2.3** | **56%** | **17%** | **97.1** | **45** | **23** | **32** | **31%** | **73%** | **13%** | **0** | | | | | | **6.2** | **93** | **107** | **$2** |

## Senzatela,Antonio

| | | | | | | | |
|---|---|---|---|---|---|---|---|
| Age: 24 | Th: R | Role RP | | Health B | PT/Exp C | Consist B | |
| Ht: 6' 1" | Wt: 180 | Type | | LIMA Plan B+ | Rand Var 0 | MM 2101 | |

6-6, 4.38 ERA in 90 IP at COL. Struggled early in April relief (6.23 ERA at COL) before two-month AAA stint; returned to the MLB rotation for good in July. Sept surge (3.25 ERA, 13% SwK over 28 IP) notwithstanding, he's at very best a useful, low-ceiling contributor. Unexciting Cmd keeps our expectations in check.

| Yr Tm | W | Sv | IP | K | ERA | xERA | WHIP | oOPS | vL | vR | BF/G | Ctl | Dom | Cmd | FpK | SwK | Vel | G | L | F | H% | S% | hr/f | GS | APC | DOM% | DIS% | Sv% | LI | RAR | BPV | BPX | R$ |
|---|---|---|---|---|---|---|---|---|---|---|---|---|---|---|---|---|---|---|---|---|---|---|---|---|---|---|---|---|---|---|---|---|---|
| 14 | | | | | | | | | | | | | | | | | | | | | | | | | | | | | | | | | |
| 15 | | | | | | | | | | | | | | | | | | | | | | | | | | | | | | | | | |
| 16 aa | 4 | 0 | 35 | 22 | 2.79 | 3.45 | 1.29 | | | | 20.3 | 2.6 | 5.6 | 2.1 | | | | | | | 30% | 79% | | | | | | | | 6.0 | 70 | 83 | $0 |
| 17 COL | 10 | 0 | 135 | 102 | 4.68 | 4.31 | 1.30 | 756 | 745 | 767 | 15.7 | 3.1 | 6.8 | 2.2 | 62% | 7% | 94.3 | 50 | 22 | 28 | 28% | 67% | 16% | 20 | 62 | 10% | 50% | 0 | 0.64 | -5.3 | 66 | 79 | $3 |
| 18 COL * | 9 | 0 | 130 | 102 | 3.77 | 3.88 | 1.30 | 764 | 696 | 816 | 17.2 | 2.9 | 7.1 | 2.4 | 61% | 9% | 93.7 | 46 | 21 | 33 | 30% | 73% | 11% | 13 | 66 | 15% | 38% | 0 | 0.73 | 6.1 | 74 | 85 | $5 |
| 1st Half | 5 | 0 | 57 | 47 | 3.54 | 3.62 | 1.30 | 838 | 804 | 858 | 12.9 | 2.9 | 7.5 | 2.6 | 63% | 8% | 94.4 | 58 | 12 | 31 | 32% | 73% | 11% | 0 | 34 | | | 0 | 0.67 | 4.2 | 89 | 102 | $3 |
| 2nd Half | 4 | 0 | 73 | 55 | 3.95 | 4.48 | 1.30 | 745 | 671 | 803 | 23.8 | 3.0 | 6.8 | 2.3 | 61% | 9% | 93.4 | 43 | 23 | 33 | 29% | 72% | 11% | 13 | 91 | 15% | 38% | | | 1.8 | 64 | 73 | $6 |
| **19 Proj** | **9** | **0** | **116** | **87** | **4.10** | **4.00** | **1.30** | **722** | **683** | **752** | **17.1** | **2.9** | **6.8** | **2.3** | **62%** | **8%** | **94.0** | **50** | **20** | **31** | **30%** | **71%** | **12%** | **20** | | | | | | **1.6** | **70** | **80** | **$3** |

JOCK THOMPSON

## Severino,Luis

| Severino,Luis | | Health | A | LIMA Plan | C |
|---|---|---|---|---|---|
| Age: 25 | Th: R Role SP | PT/Exp | A | Rand Var | 0 |
| Ht: 6' 2" | Wt: 215 Type Pwr | Consist | B | MM | 4405 |

1st-half Cy Young candidate turned into post-June pumpkin. Ctl, Dom, velocity remained elite all season. But LD% was already surging when 2nd-half H%/S% reversal took over. Nightmarish 7-game stretch (36 IP, 11 HR, 7.50 ERA) preceded tepid Sept rebound. Ace stuff intact; only inconsistency is holding him back.

| Yr Tm | W | Sv | IP | K | ERA | xERA | WHIP | oOPS | vL | vR | BF/G | Ctl | Dom | Cmd | FpK | SwK | Vel | G | L | F | H% | S% | hr/f | GS | APC | DOM% | DIS% | Sv% | LI | RAR | BPV | BPX | R$ |
|---|---|---|---|---|---|---|---|---|---|---|---|---|---|---|---|---|---|---|---|---|---|---|---|---|---|---|---|---|---|---|---|---|---|
| 14 aa | 2 | 0 | 25 | 26 | 2.82 | 2.61 | 1.10 | | | | 16.3 | 2.1 | 9.5 | 4.5 | | | | | | | 32% | 75% | | | | | | | | 2.8 | 148 | 176 | $0 |
| 15 NYY * | 14 | 0 | 162 | 143 | 3.07 | 2.97 | 1.16 | 705 | 705 | 702 | 21.5 | 2.8 | 8.0 | 2.9 | 63% | 10% | 95.4 | 50 | 20 | 30 | 29% | 75% | 17% | 11 | 93 | 9% | 27% | | | 17.7 | 97 | 115 | $17 |
| 16 NYY * | 11 | 0 | 148 | 135 | 5.25 | 4.75 | 1.43 | 812 | 747 | 872 | 18.0 | 2.7 | 8.2 | 3.1 | 59% | 9% | 96.1 | 46 | 24 | 31 | 35% | 64% | 17% | 11 | 58 | 9% | 64% | 0 | 0.70 | -19.4 | 80 | 95 | -$4 |
| 17 NYY | 14 | 0 | 193 | 230 | 2.98 | 3.12 | 1.04 | 603 | 667 | 550 | 25.3 | 2.4 | 10.7 | 4.5 | 65% | 13% | 97.6 | 51 | 19 | 31 | 29% | 76% | 14% | 31 | 99 | 65% | 13% | | | 32.9 | 158 | 189 | $30 |
| 18 NYY | 19 | 0 | 191 | 220 | 3.39 | 3.30 | 1.14 | 666 | 691 | 646 | 24.4 | 2.2 | 10.3 | 4.8 | 69% | 13% | 97.6 | 41 | 26 | 33 | 33% | 74% | 11% | 32 | 99 | 41% | 9% | | | 18.0 | 147 | 169 | $23 |
| 1st Half | 12 | 0 | 112 | 132 | 2.10 | 3.01 | 0.96 | 547 | 537 | 553 | 25.5 | 2.1 | 10.6 | 5.1 | 71% | 13% | 97.8 | 45 | 21 | 34 | 29% | 80% | 7% | 17 | 100 | 59% | 0% | | | 28.3 | 158 | 181 | $41 |
| 2nd Half | 7 | 0 | 80 | 88 | 5.20 | 3.70 | 1.41 | 816 | 839 | 791 | 23.1 | 2.3 | 9.9 | 4.4 | 67% | 12% | 97.5 | 37 | 31 | 32 | 37% | 67% | 17% | 15 | 97 | 20% | 20% | | | -10.3 | 133 | 153 | -$3 |
| **19 Proj** | **16** | **0** | **189** | **205** | **3.44** | **3.13** | **1.15** | **667** | **688** | **647** | **23.3** | **2.4** | **9.8** | **4.1** | **65%** | **12%** | **97.1** | **45** | **24** | **32** | **31%** | **74%** | **13%** | **32** | | | | | | **16.6** | **135** | **155** | **$21** |

## Sheffield,Justus

| Sheffield,Justus | | Health | A | LIMA Plan | D+ |
|---|---|---|---|---|---|
| Age: 23 | Th: L Role SP | PT/Exp | D | Rand Var | +5 |
| Ht: 5' 10" | Wt: 195 Type Pwr | Consist | F | MM | 1101 |

0-0, 10.13 ERA in 3 IP at NYY. Smallish lefty carved up high-minors hitters, posting a 2.48 ERA over 116 IP at AA/AAA before MLB debut. 123/50 K/BB speak to both dominance and work-in-progress control. Inexperience, IP limit cap 2019 upside; could start out in the pen. But he's coming.

| Yr Tm | W | Sv | IP | K | ERA | xERA | WHIP | oOPS | vL | vR | BF/G | Ctl | Dom | Cmd | FpK | SwK | Vel | G | L | F | H% | S% | hr/f | GS | APC | DOM% | DIS% | Sv% | LI | RAR | BPV | BPX | R$ |
|---|---|---|---|---|---|---|---|---|---|---|---|---|---|---|---|---|---|---|---|---|---|---|---|---|---|---|---|---|---|---|---|---|---|
| 14 | | | | | | | | | | | | | | | | | | | | | | | | | | | | | | | | | |
| 15 | | | | | | | | | | | | | | | | | | | | | | | | | | | | | | | | | |
| 16 | | | | | | | | | | | | | | | | | | | | | | | | | | | | | | | | | |
| 17 aa | 7 | 0 | 93 | 73 | 4.52 | 6.53 | 1.63 | | | | 24.4 | 3.5 | 7.0 | 2.0 | | | | | | | 33% | 80% | | | | | | | | -1.9 | 18 | 21 | -$4 |
| 18 NYY * | 7 | 0 | 119 | 108 | 3.33 | 3.25 | 1.31 | 1227 | 700 | 1667 | 17.5 | 4.2 | 8.2 | 2.0 | 36% | 2% | 94.4 | 55 | 18 | 27 | 29% | 75% | 33% | 0 | 19 | | | 0 | 0.14 | 12.0 | 85 | 98 | $6 |
| 1st Half | 2 | 0 | 74 | 72 | 3.26 | 3.04 | 1.27 | | | | 21.7 | 4.2 | 8.8 | 2.1 | | | | | | | 29% | 75% | 0% | 0 | | | | | | 8.2 | 93 | 106 | $6 |
| 2nd Half | 5 | 0 | 47 | 36 | 3.28 | 3.27 | 1.31 | 1227 | 700 | 1667 | 13.8 | 4.0 | 6.9 | 1.7 | 36% | 2% | 94.4 | 55 | 18 | 27 | 28% | 75% | 33% | 0 | 19 | | | 0 | 0.14 | 5.0 | 73 | 84 | $5 |
| **19 Proj** | **5** | **0** | **73** | **60** | **3.78** | **4.38** | **1.42** | | | | **21.5** | **3.8** | **7.4** | **1.9** | **59%** | **9%** | | **44** | **20** | **36** | **31%** | **77%** | **11%** | **14** | | | | | | **3.4** | **52** | **60** | **$0** |

## Shields,James

| Shields,James | | Health | D | LIMA Plan | B |
|---|---|---|---|---|---|
| Age: 37 | Th: R Role SP | PT/Exp | A | Rand Var | -1 |
| Ht: 6' 3" | Wt: 210 Type Pwr FB | Consist | A | MM | 0103 |

Managed to avoid another HR onslaught for an entire half. Return to health aided Ctl rebound and returned him to 200 IP plateau. But more isn't better, fantasy-wise, for an aging past-primer eating innings on an awful team. $16M option with buyout says he's a free agent. Should stay that way in your league.

| Yr Tm | W | Sv | IP | K | ERA | xERA | WHIP | oOPS | vL | vR | BF/G | Ctl | Dom | Cmd | FpK | SwK | Vel | G | L | F | H% | S% | hr/f | GS | APC | DOM% | DIS% | Sv% | LI | RAR | BPV | BPX | R$ |
|---|---|---|---|---|---|---|---|---|---|---|---|---|---|---|---|---|---|---|---|---|---|---|---|---|---|---|---|---|---|---|---|---|---|
| 14 KC | 14 | 0 | 227 | 180 | 3.21 | 3.56 | 1.18 | 702 | 698 | 706 | 27.6 | 1.7 | 7.1 | 4.1 | 63% | 10% | 92.4 | 45 | 21 | 34 | 30% | 76% | 10% | 34 | 107 | 38% | 21% | | | 14.8 | 104 | 124 | $15 |
| 15 SD | 13 | 0 | 202 | 216 | 3.91 | 3.67 | 1.33 | 776 | 890 | 660 | 26.1 | 3.6 | 9.6 | 2.7 | 60% | 13% | 91.0 | 45 | 21 | 34 | 31% | 77% | 18% | 33 | 101 | 30% | 18% | | | 1.2 | 99 | 117 | $8 |
| 16 2 TM | 6 | 0 | 182 | 135 | 5.85 | 5.26 | 1.60 | 891 | 866 | 915 | 24.9 | 4.1 | 6.7 | 1.6 | 54% | 9% | 90.4 | 40 | 21 | 38 | 31% | 69% | 18% | 33 | 95 | 9% | 42% | | | -37.1 | 29 | 34 | -$17 |
| 17 CHW | 5 | 0 | 117 | 103 | 5.23 | 5.18 | 1.44 | 824 | 929 | 724 | 24.6 | 4.1 | 7.9 | 1.9 | 58% | 10% | 90.0 | 38 | 18 | 44 | 28% | 71% | 17% | 21 | 96 | 5% | 33% | | | -12.6 | 49 | 58 | -$4 |
| 18 CHW | 7 | 0 | 205 | 154 | 4.53 | 5.02 | 1.31 | 754 | 686 | 823 | 25.6 | 3.4 | 6.8 | 2.0 | 57% | 11% | 89.4 | 35 | 22 | 43 | 27% | 71% | 13% | 33 | 97 | 27% | 36% | 0 | 0.82 | -9.6 | 42 | 49 | $0 |
| 1st Half | 3 | 0 | 107 | 73 | 4.29 | 5.09 | 1.24 | 675 | 628 | 723 | 25.1 | 3.4 | 6.1 | 1.8 | 57% | 10% | 89.3 | 38 | 20 | 42 | 26% | 68% | 9% | 17 | 96 | 29% | 41% | 0 | 0.85 | -1.8 | 34 | 39 | $1 |
| 2nd Half | 4 | 0 | 98 | 81 | 4.79 | 4.93 | 1.38 | 838 | 747 | 937 | 26.3 | 3.4 | 7.5 | 2.2 | 57% | 12% | 89.5 | 32 | 24 | 45 | 28% | 73% | 17% | 16 | 99 | 25% | 31% | | | -7.7 | 52 | 60 | -$1 |
| **19 Proj** | **5** | **0** | **131** | **106** | **4.84** | **4.55** | **1.39** | **801** | **791** | **811** | **24.7** | **3.6** | **7.3** | **2.0** | **57%** | **11%** | **90.0** | **37** | **21** | **42** | **28%** | **71%** | **15%** | **22** | | | | | | **-11.0** | **49** | **56** | **-$3** |

## Shoemaker,Matthew

| Shoemaker,Matthew | | Health | F | LIMA Plan | C |
|---|---|---|---|---|---|
| Age: 32 | Th: R Role SP | PT/Exp | C | Rand Var | +4 |
| Ht: 6' 2" | Wt: 225 Type Pwr | Consist | B | MM | 2201 |

Another lost season. More forearm discomfort shelved him after March start, eventually leading to more surgery in May. Six Sept starts generated optimistic xERA and Cmd, as FpK, SwK and velocity all emerged intact. A back-of-the-rotation upsider whose miserable health history should inform your bid.

| Yr Tm | W | Sv | IP | K | ERA | xERA | WHIP | oOPS | vL | vR | BF/G | Ctl | Dom | Cmd | FpK | SwK | Vel | G | L | F | H% | S% | hr/f | GS | APC | DOM% | DIS% | Sv% | LI | RAR | BPV | BPX | R$ |
|---|---|---|---|---|---|---|---|---|---|---|---|---|---|---|---|---|---|---|---|---|---|---|---|---|---|---|---|---|---|---|---|---|---|
| 14 LAA * | 17 | 0 | 162 | 144 | 3.47 | 3.54 | 1.17 | 658 | 702 | 610 | 20.2 | 1.8 | 8.0 | 4.5 | 63% | 11% | 90.5 | 41 | 20 | 39 | 31% | 73% | 9% | 20 | 78 | 35% | 20% | 0 | 0.81 | 5.3 | 121 | 144 | $12 |
| 15 LAA | 7 | 0 | 135 | 116 | 4.46 | 4.12 | 1.26 | 758 | 727 | 791 | 22.8 | 2.3 | 7.7 | 3.3 | 60% | 10% | 90.2 | 39 | 18 | 42 | 29% | 71% | 14% | 24 | 84 | 38% | 42% | 0 | 0.76 | -8.2 | 93 | 111 | $1 |
| 16 LAA | 9 | 0 | 160 | 143 | 3.88 | 3.94 | 1.23 | 723 | 705 | 745 | 24.7 | 1.7 | 8.0 | 4.8 | 68% | 13% | 91.5 | 40 | 24 | 36 | 32% | 71% | 10% | 27 | 92 | 26% | 30% | | | 6.1 | 117 | 139 | $9 |
| 17 LAA | 6 | 0 | 78 | 69 | 4.52 | 4.74 | 1.30 | 788 | 791 | 783 | 23.3 | 3.2 | 8.0 | 2.5 | 64% | 12% | 91.5 | 38 | 15 | 47 | 28% | 72% | 15% | 14 | 90 | 21% | 36% | | | -1.5 | 72 | 87 | $1 |
| 18 LAA | 2 | 0 | 31 | 33 | 4.94 | 3.72 | 1.26 | 694 | 608 | 762 | 18.6 | 2.9 | 9.6 | 3.3 | 68% | 13% | 91.3 | 44 | 22 | 34 | 32% | 61% | 10% | 7 | 71 | 0% | 29% | | | -3.0 | 116 | 134 | -$4 |
| 1st Half | 1 | 0 | 6 | 4 | 4.76 | 5.23 | 1.41 | 633 | 231 | 1055 | 24.0 | 6.4 | 6.4 | 1.0 | 71% | 13% | 89.8 | 44 | 31 | 25 | 25% | 63% | 0% | 1 | 90 | 0% | 0% | | | -0.4 | -35 | -41 | -$9 |
| 2nd Half | 1 | 0 | 25 | 29 | 4.97 | 3.46 | 1.22 | 706 | 700 | 709 | 17.7 | 2.1 | 10.3 | 4.8 | 68% | 13% | 91.6 | 43 | 20 | 36 | 34% | 61% | 12% | 6 | 68 | 0% | 33% | | | -2.6 | 149 | 172 | -$3 |
| **19 Proj** | **7** | **0** | **102** | **96** | **4.38** | **3.94** | **1.32** | **747** | **742** | **752** | **26.3** | **2.9** | **8.5** | **2.9** | **66%** | **12%** | **91.2** | **41** | **20** | **40** | **31%** | **71%** | **12%** | **16** | | | | | | **2.5** | **92** | **106** | **$1** |

## Shreve,Chasen

| Shreve,Chasen | | Health | A | LIMA Plan | C |
|---|---|---|---|---|---|
| Age: 28 | Th: L Role RP | PT/Exp | D | Rand Var | 0 |
| Ht: 6' 4" | Wt: 195 Type Pwr FB | Consist | A | MM | 2400 |

Tale of two halves, both overdone. Notably a 2nd half in which he outpitched his xERA by 2+ runs, courtesy of a cartoonish S% and hr/f regression—despite FB% spike and Dom plunge. Elite swing-and-miss is his only consistent skill, though FpK teases at more. For now, chronic Ctl, HR issues, volatility keep him unrosterable.

| Yr Tm | W | Sv | IP | K | ERA | xERA | WHIP | oOPS | vL | vR | BF/G | Ctl | Dom | Cmd | FpK | SwK | Vel | G | L | F | H% | S% | hr/f | GS | APC | DOM% | DIS% | Sv% | LI | RAR | BPV | BPX | R$ |
|---|---|---|---|---|---|---|---|---|---|---|---|---|---|---|---|---|---|---|---|---|---|---|---|---|---|---|---|---|---|---|---|---|---|
| 14 ATL * | 5 | 9 | 76 | 91 | 2.68 | 2.68 | 1.08 | 526 | 652 | 408 | 4.9 | 1.8 | 10.7 | 6.1 | 65% | 12% | 91.5 | 48 | 16 | 35 | 34% | 76% | 0% | 0 | 14 | | | 90 | 0.47 | 10.0 | 185 | 220 | $10 |
| 15 NYY | 6 | 0 | 58 | 64 | 3.09 | 4.13 | 1.41 | 738 | 755 | 727 | 4.3 | 5.1 | 9.9 | 1.9 | 53% | 12% | 91.4 | 46 | 13 | 41 | 28% | 86% | 16% | 0 | 19 | | | 0 | 1.05 | 6.3 | 64 | 77 | $1 |
| 16 NYY * | 2 | 1 | 50 | 49 | 4.24 | 3.42 | 1.11 | 823 | 1058 | 711 | 3.9 | 3.8 | 8.9 | 2.3 | 62% | 14% | 91.6 | 45 | 15 | 40 | 21% | 70% | 22% | 0 | 15 | | | 100 | 0.69 | -0.3 | 66 | 79 | $1 |
| 17 NYY | 4 | 0 | 45 | 58 | 3.77 | 4.36 | 1.32 | 712 | 498 | 829 | 4.5 | 5.0 | 11.5 | 2.3 | 59% | 15% | 92.7 | 37 | 17 | 45 | 28% | 79% | 15% | 0 | 19 | | | 0 | 0.93 | 3.3 | 88 | 106 | $0 |
| 18 2 TM | 3 | 1 | 53 | 62 | 3.93 | 4.35 | 1.52 | 832 | 911 | 780 | 3.9 | 4.6 | 10.6 | 2.3 | 65% | 15% | 92.2 | 40 | 19 | 41 | 33% | 83% | 19% | 0 | 17 | | | 100 | 0.83 | 1.4 | 84 | 97 | -$3 |
| 1st Half | 2 | 0 | 29 | 37 | 4.97 | 4.10 | 1.59 | 852 | 1025 | 759 | 4.4 | 5.0 | 11.5 | 2.3 | 65% | 14% | 92.2 | 46 | 20 | 35 | 34% | 77% | 25% | 0 | 19 | | | 0 | 0.60 | -2.9 | 96 | 111 | -$6 |
| 2nd Half | 1 | 1 | 24 | 25 | 2.66 | 4.63 | 1.44 | 805 | 794 | 815 | 3.4 | 4.2 | 9.5 | 2.3 | 65% | 15% | 92.1 | 32 | 19 | 49 | 31% | 90% | 13% | 0 | 15 | | | 100 | 1.06 | 4.3 | 68 | 78 | $1 |
| **19 Proj** | **3** | **0** | **51** | **59** | **4.00** | **3.91** | **1.37** | **763** | **776** | **756** | **3.9** | **4.4** | **10.4** | **2.4** | **62%** | **14%** | **92.1** | **39** | **18** | **43** | **29%** | **78%** | **17%** | **0** | | | | | | **1.7** | **85** | **98** | **-$1** |

## Sims,Lucas

| Sims,Lucas | | Health | A | LIMA Plan | D+ |
|---|---|---|---|---|---|
| Age: 25 | Th: R Role RP | PT/Exp | D | Rand Var | +1 |
| Ht: 6' 2" | Wt: 230 Type Pwr FB | Consist | A | MM | 1301 |

0-0, 7.47 ERA in 16 IP at ATL/CIN. Dom, SwK returned as velocity ticked up, both in minors and MLB small sample. Posted intriguing 32/5 K/BB over 28 Triple-A IP following the trade. But Ctl has a ton to prove, and FB%, HRs have become a problem. Age gives him time; not exactly a breakthrough profile.

| Yr Tm | W | Sv | IP | K | ERA | xERA | WHIP | oOPS | vL | vR | BF/G | Ctl | Dom | Cmd | FpK | SwK | Vel | G | L | F | H% | S% | hr/f | GS | APC | DOM% | DIS% | Sv% | LI | RAR | BPV | BPX | R$ |
|---|---|---|---|---|---|---|---|---|---|---|---|---|---|---|---|---|---|---|---|---|---|---|---|---|---|---|---|---|---|---|---|---|---|
| 14 | | | | | | | | | | | | | | | | | | | | | | | | | | | | | | | | | |
| 15 aa | 4 | 0 | 48 | 51 | 3.89 | 2.47 | 1.31 | | | | 21.9 | 5.6 | 9.7 | 1.7 | | | | | | | 28% | 68% | | | | | | | | 0.4 | 104 | 124 | -$1 |
| 16 a/a | 7 | 0 | 141 | 144 | 5.88 | 5.27 | 1.74 | | | | 23.0 | 6.5 | 9.2 | 1.4 | | | | | | | 33% | 67% | | | | | | | | -29.5 | 55 | 65 | -$15 |
| 17 ATL * | 10 | 0 | 173 | 155 | 5.01 | 4.82 | 1.35 | 869 | 918 | 827 | 21.2 | 3.0 | 8.0 | 2.7 | 66% | 9% | 91.8 | 38 | 23 | 39 | 30% | 68% | 13% | 10 | 70 | 10% | 60% | 0 | 0.74 | -14.0 | 58 | 69 | $1 |
| 18 2 NL * | 4 | 0 | 118 | 114 | 4.42 | 4.88 | 1.47 | 825 | 817 | 822 | 17.4 | 4.2 | 8.7 | 2.1 | 53% | 12% | 92.5 | 37 | 22 | 41 | 32% | 74% | 16% | 0 | 35 | | | 0 | 0.52 | -3.9 | 60 | 69 | -$4 |
| 1st Half | 4 | 0 | 60 | 50 | 4.07 | 5.34 | 1.71 | 869 | 774 | 962 | 16.9 | 5.6 | 7.6 | 1.4 | 50% | 10% | 92.8 | 42 | 21 | 36 | 33% | 78% | 17% | 0 | 34 | | | 0 | 0.51 | 0.6 | 47 | 54 | -$9 |
| 2nd Half | 0 | 0 | 61 | 64 | 4.59 | 4.13 | 1.18 | 728 | 956 | 607 | 18.6 | 2.7 | 9.5 | 3.6 | 60% | 14% | 91.9 | 23 | 23 | 54 | 28% | 67% | 14% | 0 | 37 | | | 0 | 0.54 | -3.3 | 90 | 103 | -$1 |
| **19 Proj** | **4** | **0** | **87** | **84** | **4.72** | **4.37** | **1.42** | **732** | **790** | **684** | **19.7** | **4.2** | **8.7** | **2.1** | **60%** | **9%** | **91.8** | **38** | **23** | **39** | **31%** | **70%** | **12%** | **18** | | | | | | **-2.2** | **60** | **69** | **-$3** |

## Skaggs,Tyler

| Skaggs,Tyler | | Health | F | LIMA Plan | B+ |
|---|---|---|---|---|---|
| Age: 27 | Th: L Role SP | PT/Exp | C | Rand Var | +2 |
| Ht: 6' 4" | Wt: 200 Type Pwr | Consist | B | MM | 2301 |

Durability-challenged SP made 16 first-half starts flashing broad mid-rotation skills. With S% help, allowed more than 3 earned runs just twice. Strained groin first shelved him in July, then lingered on, torpedoing return efforts. Career-high 125 IP is a positive. With better health... UP: 150 IP, 12 wins, 3.50 ERA.

| Yr Tm | W | Sv | IP | K | ERA | xERA | WHIP | oOPS | vL | vR | BF/G | Ctl | Dom | Cmd | FpK | SwK | Vel | G | L | F | H% | S% | hr/f | GS | APC | DOM% | DIS% | Sv% | LI | RAR | BPV | BPX | R$ |
|---|---|---|---|---|---|---|---|---|---|---|---|---|---|---|---|---|---|---|---|---|---|---|---|---|---|---|---|---|---|---|---|---|---|
| 14 LAA | 5 | 0 | 113 | 86 | 4.30 | 3.59 | 1.21 | 674 | 742 | 655 | 25.8 | 2.4 | 6.8 | 2.9 | 64% | 9% | 92.1 | 50 | 19 | 31 | 30% | 65% | 9% | 18 | 95 | 44% | 22% | | | -7.8 | 87 | 103 | $0 |
| 15 | | | | | | | | | | | | | | | | | | | | | | | | | | | | | | | | | |
| 16 LAA * | 6 | 0 | 82 | 88 | 3.24 | 3.36 | 1.26 | 750 | 804 | 734 | 19.7 | 3.4 | 9.7 | 2.9 | 60% | 9% | 92.8 | 43 | 23 | 34 | 31% | 76% | 10% | 10 | 88 | 30% | 30% | | | 9.6 | 103 | 122 | $5 |
| 17 LAA | 2 | 0 | 85 | 76 | 4.55 | 4.42 | 1.39 | 790 | 734 | 806 | 22.8 | 3.0 | 8.0 | 2.7 | 62% | 8% | 91.9 | 42 | 22 | 37 | 32% | 71% | 14% | 16 | 87 | 25% | 38% | | | -2.0 | 85 | 102 | -$2 |
| 18 LAA | 8 | 0 | 125 | 129 | 4.02 | 3.85 | 1.33 | 736 | 652 | 761 | 22.2 | 2.9 | 9.3 | 3.2 | 63% | 11% | 91.4 | 44 | 21 | 34 | 33% | 73% | 11% | 24 | 90 | 33% | 29% | | | 2.0 | 111 | 128 | $3 |
| 1st Half | 6 | 0 | 92 | 100 | 2.64 | 3.47 | 1.22 | 671 | 485 | 735 | 23.7 | 2.6 | 9.8 | 3.7 | 64% | 12% | 91.6 | 47 | 20 | 33 | 33% | 82% | 10% | 16 | 99 | 38% | 19% | | | 17.1 | 130 | 149 | $11 |
| 2nd Half | 2 | 0 | 33 | 29 | 7.83 | 4.95 | 1.65 | 900 | 1262 | 820 | 19.3 | 3.5 | 7.8 | 2.2 | 60% | 10% | 91.1 | 38 | 24 | 38 | 36% | 53% | 15% | 8 | 73 | 25% | 50% | | | -15.1 | 62 | 70 | -$23 |
| **19 Proj** | **9** | **0** | **123** | **119** | **3.84** | **3.77** | **1.31** | **717** | **758** | **705** | **20.5** | **3.0** | **8.7** | **2.9** | **62%** | **10%** | **91.7** | **43** | **22** | **35** | **32%** | **74%** | **11%** | **25** | | | | | | **5.6** | **96** | **110** | **$6** |

JOCK THOMPSON

## Skoglund,Eric

| | | | |
|---|---|---|---|
| Age: 26 Th: L Role SP | Health F | LIMA Plan D+ | |
| Ht: 6' 7" Wt: 210 Type FB | PT/Exp D | Rand Var +3 | |
| | Consist D | MM 0001 | |

1-6, 5.14 ERA in 70 IP at KC. Horrific start interrupted by UCL strain that shelved him in late May. Plus Ctl fueled marked improvement in September return (1.33 ERA, 0.79 WHIP over 20 IP)—but 15% H%, 93% S% scream regression. Healthy or not, SwK history suggests his MLB rotation days are numbered.

| Yr | Tm | W | Sv | IP | K | ERA | xERA | WHIP | oOPS | vL | vR | BF/G | Ctl | Dom | Cmd | FpK | SwK | Vel | G | L | F | H% | S% | hr/f | GS | APC | DOM% | DIS% | Sv% | LI | RAR | BPV | BPX | R$ |
|---|---|---|---|---|---|---|---|---|---|---|---|---|---|---|---|---|---|---|---|---|---|---|---|---|---|---|---|---|---|---|---|---|---|---|
| 14 | | | | | | | | | | | | | | | | | | | | | | | | | | | | | | | | | | |
| 15 | | | | | | | | | | | | | | | | | | | | | | | | | | | | | | | | | | |
| 16 | aa | 7 | 0 | 156 | 108 | 5.12 | 4.88 | 1.38 | | | | 24.3 | 2.4 | 6.2 | 2.6 | | | | | | | 31% | 66% | | | | | | | | -17.9 | 49 | 59 | -$5 |
| 17 | KC * | 5 | 0 | 122 | 95 | 6.06 | 6.73 | 1.80 | 1027 | 899 | 1043 | 20.9 | 3.4 | 7.0 | 2.0 | 61% | 6% | 91.5 | 36 | 24 | 39 | 38% | 68% | 8% | 5 | 55 | 20% | 80% | 0 | 0.54 | -25.6 | 35 | 42 | -$16 |
| 18 | KC * | 1 | 0 | 88 | 57 | 5.17 | 4.73 | 1.27 | 781 | 815 | 774 | 20.0 | 2.2 | 5.8 | 2.7 | 60% | 8% | 91.3 | 42 | 18 | 40 | 28% | 64% | 14% | 13 | 78 | 15% | 46% | 0 | 0.72 | -11.1 | 46 | 53 | -$6 |
| 1st Half | | 1 | 0 | 50 | 39 | 6.70 | 4.55 | 1.39 | 871 | 1013 | 841 | 24.1 | 2.5 | 7.1 | 2.8 | 61% | 8% | 91.6 | 42 | 20 | 38 | 31% | 54% | 17% | 9 | 88 | 22% | 44% | | | -15.7 | 79 | 90 | -$12 |
| 2nd Half | | 0 | 0 | 38 | 18 | 3.19 | 3.78 | 1.12 | 524 | 237 | 583 | 16.8 | 1.7 | 4.1 | 2.5 | 57% | 5% | 90.7 | 42 | 12 | 46 | 25% | 78% | 7% | 4 | 59 | 0% | 50% | 0 | 0.62 | 4.6 | 45 | 52 | $2 |
| 19 | Proj | 2 | 0 | 73 | 49 | 4.96 | 4.67 | 1.45 | 896 | 741 | 929 | 20.3 | 2.5 | 6.1 | 2.4 | 59% | 7% | 91.0 | 42 | 15 | 42 | 32% | 69% | 11% | 15 | | | | | | -7.3 | 61 | 70 | -$6 |

## Smith,Burch

| | | | |
|---|---|---|---|
| Age: 29 Th: R Role RP | Health D | LIMA Plan C | |
| Ht: 6' 4" Wt: 225 Type Pwr | PT/Exp D | Rand Var +5 | |
| | Consist D | MM 1300 | |

Ex-starter returned as a Rule 5 reliever in his first MLB appearance since 2013. Injury parade led by Tommy John surgery shelved him from 2014 through 2016. Historical Dom still offers hope for a career, as velocity, SwK shake off some rust. A project that still needs work, likely in the minors. Watch from afar.

| Yr | Tm | W | Sv | IP | K | ERA | xERA | WHIP | oOPS | vL | vR | BF/G | Ctl | Dom | Cmd | FpK | SwK | Vel | G | L | F | H% | S% | hr/f | GS | APC | DOM% | DIS% | Sv% | LI | RAR | BPV | BPX | R$ |
|---|---|---|---|---|---|---|---|---|---|---|---|---|---|---|---|---|---|---|---|---|---|---|---|---|---|---|---|---|---|---|---|---|---|---|
| 14 | | | | | | | | | | | | | | | | | | | | | | | | | | | | | | | | | | |
| 15 | | | | | | | | | | | | | | | | | | | | | | | | | | | | | | | | | | |
| 16 | | | | | | | | | | | | | | | | | | | | | | | | | | | | | | | | | | |
| 17 | aaa | 2 | 0 | 16 | 16 | 2.37 | 2.94 | 1.00 | | | | 20.8 | 2.5 | 8.5 | 3.4 | | | | | | | 23% | 87% | | | | | | | | 4.0 | 95 | 113 | -$1 |
| 18 | KC | 1 | 0 | 78 | 77 | 6.92 | 4.89 | 1.67 | 873 | 937 | 816 | 9.4 | 4.6 | 8.9 | 1.9 | 54% | 10% | 93.2 | 40 | 20 | 40 | 34% | 61% | 16% | 6 | 38 | 17% | 67% | 0 | 0.53 | -26.7 | 53 | 61 | -$16 |
| 1st Half | | 0 | 0 | 34 | 36 | 6.03 | 4.96 | 1.66 | 910 | 896 | 917 | 6.7 | 5.5 | 9.4 | 1.7 | 57% | 10% | 93.5 | 39 | 17 | 44 | 32% | 69% | 20% | 0 | 27 | | | 0 | 0.37 | -8.0 | 39 | 44 | -$15 |
| 2nd Half | | 1 | 0 | 44 | 41 | 7.63 | 4.85 | 1.67 | 846 | 956 | 712 | 13.5 | 3.9 | 8.5 | 2.2 | 52% | 11% | 92.9 | 41 | 22 | 37 | 36% | 55% | 13% | 6 | 54 | 17% | 67% | 0 | 0.79 | -18.7 | 65 | 75 | -$16 |
| 19 | Proj | 1 | 0 | 58 | 57 | 5.44 | 4.33 | 1.53 | 823 | 887 | 763 | 9.2 | 4.1 | 8.8 | 2.2 | 54% | 10% | 93.1 | 40 | 20 | 40 | 33% | 69% | 16% | 0 | | | | | | -9.2 | 67 | 77 | -$7 |

## Smith,Caleb

| | | | |
|---|---|---|---|
| Age: 27 Th: L Role SP | Health F | LIMA Plan B+ | |
| Ht: 6' 2" Wt: 205 Type Pwr xFB | PT/Exp D | Rand Var 0 | |
| | Consist B | MM 1301 | |

Unheralded late-bloomer finally turned plus SwK into plus Dom, during MLB rookie season no less. Held his own vR; Cmd, FpK upticks hint at growth potential. Surgery for Grade 3 lat strain ended his season in late June. Scary G/L/F history adds to the list of questions. Health is now first and foremost among these.

| Yr | Tm | W | Sv | IP | K | ERA | xERA | WHIP | oOPS | vL | vR | BF/G | Ctl | Dom | Cmd | FpK | SwK | Vel | G | L | F | H% | S% | hr/f | GS | APC | DOM% | DIS% | Sv% | LI | RAR | BPV | BPX | R$ |
|---|---|---|---|---|---|---|---|---|---|---|---|---|---|---|---|---|---|---|---|---|---|---|---|---|---|---|---|---|---|---|---|---|---|---|
| 14 | | | | | | | | | | | | | | | | | | | | | | | | | | | | | | | | | | |
| 15 | a/a | 10 | 0 | 135 | 81 | 4.75 | 4.91 | 1.59 | | | | 22.9 | 4.1 | 5.4 | 1.3 | | | | | | | 32% | 70% | | | | | | | | -13.2 | 35 | 42 | -$8 |
| 16 | aa | 3 | 3 | 64 | 58 | 5.76 | 5.82 | 1.69 | | | | 10.6 | 3.2 | 8.2 | 2.6 | | | | | | | 39% | 66% | | | | | | | | -12.3 | 67 | 80 | -$7 |
| 17 | NYY * | 9 | 0 | 119 | 101 | 4.28 | 4.66 | 1.41 | 854 | 894 | 833 | 18.0 | 3.5 | 7.6 | 2.2 | 56% | 13% | 94.0 | 28 | 29 | 43 | 31% | 74% | 16% | 2 | 38 | 0% | 100% | 0 | 0.35 | 1.2 | 55 | 66 | $2 |
| 18 | MIA | 5 | 0 | 77 | 88 | 4.19 | 4.36 | 1.24 | 694 | 717 | 684 | 20.4 | 3.8 | 10.2 | 2.7 | 59% | 12% | 92.8 | 28 | 21 | 51 | 29% | 70% | 10% | 16 | 87 | 19% | 25% | | | -0.4 | 87 | 100 | $1 |
| 1st Half | | 5 | 0 | 77 | 88 | 4.19 | 4.36 | 1.24 | 694 | 717 | 684 | 20.4 | 3.8 | 10.2 | 2.7 | 59% | 12% | 92.8 | 28 | 21 | 51 | 29% | 70% | 10% | 16 | 87 | 19% | 25% | | | -0.4 | 87 | 100 | $1 |
| 2nd Half | | | | | | | | | | | | | | | | | | | | | | | | | | | | | | | | | | |
| 19 | Proj | 6 | 0 | 102 | 103 | 4.32 | 4.42 | 1.34 | 717 | 747 | 705 | 20.0 | 3.6 | 9.2 | 2.5 | 59% | 12% | 92.8 | 28 | 21 | 51 | 30% | 73% | 11% | 21 | | | | | | -2.2 | 74 | 85 | $1 |

## Smith,Joe

| | | | |
|---|---|---|---|
| Age: 35 Th: R Role RP | Health D | LIMA Plan A | |
| Ht: 6' 2" Wt: 205 Type Pwr | PT/Exp D | Rand Var 0 | |
| | Consist C | MM 3300 | |

One-time elite GBer now more susceptible to bouts of gopheritis. Mercurial H% took a year-long turn for the better, worked with 2nd-half S%, hr/f correction to fuel in-season turnaround. Ctl still top-shelf if inconsistent; improving SwK cushions GB% fade. Volatility, age make more late inning work less likely.

| Yr | Tm | W | Sv | IP | K | ERA | xERA | WHIP | oOPS | vL | vR | BF/G | Ctl | Dom | Cmd | FpK | SwK | Vel | G | L | F | H% | S% | hr/f | GS | APC | DOM% | DIS% | Sv% | LI | RAR | BPV | BPX | R$ |
|---|---|---|---|---|---|---|---|---|---|---|---|---|---|---|---|---|---|---|---|---|---|---|---|---|---|---|---|---|---|---|---|---|---|---|
| 14 | LAA | 7 | 15 | 75 | 68 | 1.81 | 2.67 | 0.80 | 491 | 584 | 385 | 3.8 | 1.8 | 8.2 | 4.5 | 66% | 8% | 88.7 | 59 | 15 | 26 | 22% | 80% | 8% | 0 | 15 | | | 79 | 1.25 | 17.8 | 136 | 162 | $18 |
| 15 | LAA | 5 | 5 | 65 | 57 | 3.58 | 3.49 | 1.27 | 684 | 786 | 587 | 3.9 | 2.6 | 7.9 | 3.0 | 63% | 8% | 88.3 | 52 | 23 | 25 | 32% | 72% | 9% | 0 | 14 | | | 56 | 1.29 | 3.1 | 101 | 120 | $3 |
| 16 | 2 TM | 2 | 6 | 52 | 40 | 3.46 | 4.00 | 1.25 | 716 | 726 | 708 | 4.0 | 3.1 | 6.9 | 2.2 | 66% | 9% | 88.3 | 50 | 23 | 27 | 27% | 79% | 20% | 0 | 15 | | | 67 | 0.90 | 4.7 | 69 | 81 | $2 |
| 17 | 2 AL | 3 | 1 | 54 | 71 | 3.33 | 2.67 | 1.04 | 601 | 701 | 546 | 3.6 | 1.7 | 11.8 | 7.1 | 67% | 12% | 88.9 | 50 | 21 | 29 | 34% | 69% | 11% | 0 | 14 | | | 50 | 1.22 | 6.8 | 196 | 235 | $4 |
| 18 | HOU | 5 | 0 | 46 | 46 | 3.74 | 3.57 | 1.01 | 645 | 647 | 644 | 3.2 | 2.4 | 9.1 | 3.8 | 63% | 10% | 87.8 | 44 | 18 | 38 | 25% | 69% | 16% | 0 | 12 | | | 0 | 0.93 | 2.3 | 121 | 140 | $2 |
| 1st Half | | 2 | 0 | 20 | 20 | 5.49 | 3.73 | 1.12 | 714 | 812 | 678 | 3.3 | 3.2 | 9.2 | 2.9 | 64% | 12% | 88.1 | 49 | 10 | 41 | 24% | 56% | 20% | 0 | 13 | | | 0 | 0.74 | -3.3 | 105 | 121 | -$5 |
| 2nd Half | | 3 | 0 | 26 | 26 | 2.42 | 3.45 | 0.92 | 593 | 536 | 617 | 3.1 | 1.7 | 9.0 | 5.2 | 63% | 9% | 87.5 | 41 | 23 | 36 | 25% | 81% | 12% | 0 | 12 | | | 0 | 1.07 | 5.5 | 134 | 154 | $7 |
| 19 | Proj | 4 | 0 | 51 | 51 | 3.62 | 3.36 | 1.09 | 645 | 688 | 621 | 3.4 | 2.6 | 9.0 | 3.4 | 65% | 10% | 88.2 | 45 | 20 | 35 | 27% | 71% | 13% | 0 | | | | | | 4.9 | 114 | 131 | $2 |

## Smith,Will

| | | | |
|---|---|---|---|
| Age: 29 Th: L Role RP | Health F | LIMA Plan B | |
| Ht: 6' 5" Wt: 248 Type Pwr | PT/Exp D | Rand Var -1 | |
| | Consist B | MM 5520 | |

Missed 2017 and this past April recovering from Tommy John surgery; parlayed stellar early results into closer role by late June. Velocity returned intact, still misses plenty of bats; previously-shaky Ctl was the surprise. Health, handedness, 2nd-half ERA, closer-go-round point to risk, but job ownership sets price floor.

| Yr | Tm | W | Sv | IP | K | ERA | xERA | WHIP | oOPS | vL | vR | BF/G | Ctl | Dom | Cmd | FpK | SwK | Vel | G | L | F | H% | S% | hr/f | GS | APC | DOM% | DIS% | Sv% | LI | RAR | BPV | BPX | R$ |
|---|---|---|---|---|---|---|---|---|---|---|---|---|---|---|---|---|---|---|---|---|---|---|---|---|---|---|---|---|---|---|---|---|---|---|
| 14 | MIL | 1 | 1 | 66 | 86 | 3.70 | 3.15 | 1.42 | 737 | 516 | 872 | 3.7 | 4.2 | 11.8 | 2.8 | 53% | 13% | 93.0 | 44 | 23 | 33 | 36% | 76% | 11% | 0 | 14 | | | 17 | 1.48 | 0.3 | 119 | 142 | -$1 |
| 15 | MIL | 7 | 0 | 63 | 91 | 2.70 | 2.88 | 1.20 | 649 | 786 | 545 | 3.5 | 3.4 | 12.9 | 3.8 | 60% | 16% | 93.2 | 46 | 15 | 39 | 35% | 80% | 9% | 0 | 14 | | | 0 | 1.15 | 9.9 | 165 | 196 | $6 |
| 16 | 2 NL | 2 | 0 | 40 | 48 | 3.35 | 3.79 | 1.21 | 637 | 627 | 645 | 3.2 | 4.0 | 10.7 | 2.7 | 70% | 12% | 91.9 | 35 | 25 | 40 | 30% | 74% | 8% | 0 | 12 | | | 0 | 1.58 | 4.2 | 97 | 116 | $0 |
| 17 | | | | | | | | | | | | | | | | | | | | | | | | | | | | | | | | | | |
| 18 | SF | 2 | 14 | 53 | 71 | 2.55 | 2.99 | 0.98 | 533 | 440 | 582 | 3.9 | 2.5 | 12.1 | 4.7 | 62% | 15% | 92.7 | 42 | 20 | 38 | 30% | 76% | 7% | 0 | 15 | | | 78 | 1.44 | 10.5 | 168 | 194 | $10 |
| 1st Half | | 0 | 1 | 24 | 33 | 1.13 | 2.79 | 0.71 | 362 | 431 | 294 | 3.5 | 2.6 | 12.4 | 4.7 | 63% | 18% | 92.5 | 40 | 15 | 45 | 22% | 82% | 0% | 0 | 13 | | | 50 | 1.12 | 9.0 | 170 | 196 | $7 |
| 2nd Half | | 2 | 13 | 29 | 38 | 3.72 | 3.16 | 1.21 | 652 | 452 | 724 | 4.2 | 2.5 | 11.8 | 4.8 | 62% | 13% | 92.8 | 42 | 23 | 34 | 35% | 72% | 12% | 0 | 17 | | | 81 | 1.71 | 1.5 | 166 | 190 | $13 |
| 19 | Proj | 3 | 25 | 58 | 76 | 2.95 | 3.00 | 1.13 | 605 | 563 | 632 | 3.5 | 3.2 | 11.8 | 3.7 | 63% | 14% | 92.6 | 41 | 21 | 38 | 32% | 76% | 8% | 0 | | | | | | 10.8 | 145 | 166 | $14 |

## Smyly,Drew

| | | | |
|---|---|---|---|
| Age: 30 Th: L Role SP | Health F | LIMA Plan B+ | |
| Ht: 6' 3" Wt: 190 Type Pwr xFB | PT/Exp D | Rand Var 0 | |
| | Consist F | MM 2301 | |

M.I.A. since March 2016 flexor strain turned into mid-season Tommy John surgery; now expected to be ready for CHC on Opening Day. When healthy, mid-rotation profile with solid Cmd and dominance vL that neutralized xFB lean and unexciting velocity. Now after two years off? This is where March means something.

| Yr | Tm | W | Sv | IP | K | ERA | xERA | WHIP | oOPS | vL | vR | BF/G | Ctl | Dom | Cmd | FpK | SwK | Vel | G | L | F | H% | S% | hr/f | GS | APC | DOM% | DIS% | Sv% | LI | RAR | BPV | BPX | R$ |
|---|---|---|---|---|---|---|---|---|---|---|---|---|---|---|---|---|---|---|---|---|---|---|---|---|---|---|---|---|---|---|---|---|---|---|
| 14 | 2 AL | 9 | 0 | 153 | 133 | 3.24 | 3.79 | 1.16 | 688 | 486 | 763 | 22.1 | 2.5 | 7.8 | 3.2 | 62% | 10% | 89.9 | 37 | 20 | 43 | 28% | 77% | 10% | 25 | 93 | 28% | 32% | 0 | 0.73 | 9.5 | 89 | 106 | $10 |
| 15 | TAM | 5 | 0 | 67 | 77 | 3.11 | 3.53 | 1.17 | 701 | 507 | 751 | 22.9 | 2.7 | 10.4 | 3.9 | 61% | 12% | 90.3 | 37 | 19 | 44 | 30% | 82% | 14% | 12 | 95 | 25% | 33% | | | 7.0 | 129 | 154 | $4 |
| 16 | TAM | 7 | 0 | 175 | 167 | 4.88 | 4.53 | 1.27 | 763 | 724 | 773 | 24.6 | 2.5 | 8.6 | 3.4 | 58% | 11% | 90.2 | 31 | 19 | 49 | 30% | 67% | 13% | 30 | 96 | 27% | 33% | | | -14.9 | 95 | 113 | $2 |
| 17 | | | | | | | | | | | | | | | | | | | | | | | | | | | | | | | | | | |
| 18 | | | | | | | | | | | | | | | | | | | | | | | | | | | | | | | | | | |
| 1st Half | | | | | | | | | | | | | | | | | | | | | | | | | | | | | | | | | | |
| 2nd Half | | | | | | | | | | | | | | | | | | | | | | | | | | | | | | | | | | |
| 19 | Proj | 6 | 0 | 102 | 98 | 3.78 | 3.88 | 1.20 | 718 | 565 | 763 | 22.6 | 2.5 | 8.7 | 3.4 | 60% | 11% | 90.1 | 35 | 20 | 46 | 29% | 75% | 12% | 18 | | | | | | 3.3 | 101 | 116 | $5 |

## Snell,Blake

| | | | |
|---|---|---|---|
| Age: 26 Th: L Role SP | Health A | LIMA Plan D+ | |
| Ht: 6' 4" Wt: 200 Type Pwr | PT/Exp B | Rand Var -5 | |
| | Consist B | MM 4405 | |

Top-shelf stuff finally delivered big upside. 1st half gains only hinted at what was to follow. 63% FpK, 2.5 Ctl over final 62 IP drove 2nd half Cmd. But soaring SwK, Dom, velocity began early and never let up, spiking through Sept. 2nd half GB% helped. Unsustainable momentum, but even a step back leaves him near elite.

| Yr | Tm | W | Sv | IP | K | ERA | xERA | WHIP | oOPS | vL | vR | BF/G | Ctl | Dom | Cmd | FpK | SwK | Vel | G | L | F | H% | S% | hr/f | GS | APC | DOM% | DIS% | Sv% | LI | RAR | BPV | BPX | R$ |
|---|---|---|---|---|---|---|---|---|---|---|---|---|---|---|---|---|---|---|---|---|---|---|---|---|---|---|---|---|---|---|---|---|---|---|
| 14 | | | | | | | | | | | | | | | | | | | | | | | | | | | | | | | | | | |
| 15 | a/a | 12 | 0 | 113 | 119 | 1.97 | 2.49 | 1.12 | | | | 21.2 | 3.3 | 9.4 | 2.8 | | | | | | | 28% | 85% | | | | | | | | 27.8 | 112 | 133 | $18 |
| 16 | TAM * | 9 | 0 | 152 | 176 | 3.77 | 4.57 | 1.61 | 728 | 656 | 747 | 21.7 | 4.9 | 10.4 | 2.1 | 57% | 12% | 93.5 | 37 | 27 | 36 | 38% | 77% | 6% | 19 | 90 | 26% | 37% | | | 7.9 | 90 | 107 | $1 |
| 17 | TAM * | 10 | 0 | 173 | 171 | 3.94 | 4.30 | 1.40 | 707 | 494 | 741 | 23.6 | 3.9 | 8.9 | 2.3 | 54% | 11% | 94.3 | 44 | 18 | 38 | 31% | 75% | 11% | 24 | 95 | 17% | 29% | | | 9.0 | 72 | 87 | $7 |
| 18 | TAM | 21 | 0 | 181 | 221 | 1.89 | 3.17 | 0.97 | 554 | 413 | 588 | 22.6 | 3.2 | 11.0 | 3.5 | 57% | 15% | 95.8 | 45 | 19 | 36 | 25% | 86% | 11% | 31 | 94 | 55% | 19% | | | 50.3 | 135 | 156 | $39 |
| 1st Half | | 10 | 0 | 101 | 113 | 2.31 | 3.68 | 1.04 | 589 | 373 | 653 | 23.6 | 3.6 | 10.0 | 2.8 | 55% | 14% | 95.5 | 41 | 20 | 39 | 24% | 84% | 11% | 17 | 99 | 53% | 24% | | | 23.0 | 104 | 119 | $36 |
| 2nd Half | | 11 | 0 | 79 | 108 | 1.36 | 2.55 | 0.89 | 507 | 492 | 509 | 21.3 | 2.7 | 12.3 | 4.5 | 60% | 17% | 96.4 | 50 | 17 | 33 | 27% | 89% | 9% | 14 | 89 | 57% | 14% | | | 27.3 | 175 | 201 | $43 |
| 19 | Proj | 16 | 0 | 189 | 218 | 3.10 | 3.30 | 1.17 | 646 | 503 | 675 | 22.1 | 3.4 | 10.4 | 3.1 | 58% | 14% | 95.0 | 44 | 20 | 36 | 30% | 77% | 11% | 34 | | | | | | 22.8 | 119 | 136 | $23 |

JOCK THOMPSON

## Soria,Joakim

| | | | | | |
|---|---|---|---|---|---|
| Age: 35 | Th: R | Role: RP | Health | D | LIMA Plan: B+ |
| Ht: 6' 3" | Wt: 200 | Type: Pwr | PT/Exp | C | Rand Var: 0 |
| | | | Consist | B | MM: 3410 |

The rare mid-30s skills bump. Can it stick? PRO: SwK in a straight-line ascent; logged a career-best FpK; xERA consistently in mid-3s. CON: His GB% edge vaporized in an instant; age and health work against him; coming hr/f regression plus new FB lean is a volatile mix. Unlikely to hit double-digit R$ again.

| Yr Tm | W | Sv | IP | K | ERA | xERA | WHIP | oOPS | vL | vR | BF/G | Ctl | Dom | Cmd | FpK | SwK | Vel | G | L | F | H% | S% | hr/f | GS | APC | DOM% | DIS% | Sv% | LI | RAR | BPV | BPX | R$ |
|---|---|---|---|---|---|---|---|---|---|---|---|---|---|---|---|---|---|---|---|---|---|---|---|---|---|---|---|---|---|---|---|---|---|
| 14 2 AL | 2 | 18 | 44 | 48 | 3.25 | 2.93 | 0.99 | 605 | 675 | 503 | 3.8 | 1.2 | 9.7 | 8.0 | 63% | 10% | 90.2 | 43 | 22 | 35 | 32% | 67% | 5% | 0 | 14 | | | 90 | 1.12 | 2.7 | 164 | 195 | $9 |
| 15 2 TM | 3 | 24 | 68 | 64 | 2.53 | 3.54 | 1.09 | 628 | 722 | 536 | 3.8 | 2.5 | 8.5 | 3.4 | 61% | 10% | 92.2 | 42 | 23 | 35 | 27% | 83% | 13% | 0 | 16 | | | 80 | 1.35 | 12.0 | 105 | 125 | $15 |
| 16 KC | 5 | 1 | 67 | 68 | 4.05 | 3.93 | 1.46 | 800 | 669 | 931 | 4.2 | 3.6 | 9.2 | 2.5 | 63% | 12% | 92.7 | 50 | 20 | 30 | 33% | 77% | 18% | 0 | 17 | | | 13 | 1.25 | 1.1 | 95 | 113 | $0 |
| 17 KC | 4 | 1 | 56 | 64 | 3.70 | 3.20 | 1.23 | 592 | 679 | 524 | 3.9 | 3.2 | 10.3 | 3.2 | 58% | 13% | 92.9 | 55 | 22 | 23 | 34% | 68% | 3% | 0 | 17 | | | 13 | 1.14 | 4.6 | 131 | 158 | $2 |
| 18 2 TM | 3 | 16 | 61 | 75 | 3.12 | 3.54 | 1.14 | 619 | 704 | 542 | 3.9 | 2.4 | 11.1 | 4.7 | 66% | 15% | 92.4 | 36 | 23 | 41 | 34% | 74% | 6% | 0 | 16 | | | 76 | 1.13 | 7.7 | 150 | 173 | $10 |
| 1st Half | 0 | 11 | 30 | 33 | 2.70 | 3.74 | 1.10 | 603 | 774 | 430 | 4.1 | 1.8 | 9.9 | 5.5 | 59% | 15% | 92.0 | 38 | 20 | 42 | 33% | 77% | 6% | 0 | 16 | | | 85 | 0.91 | 5.4 | 146 | 167 | $10 |
| 2nd Half | 3 | 5 | 31 | 42 | 3.52 | 3.35 | 1.17 | 634 | 626 | 640 | 3.7 | 2.9 | 12.3 | 4.2 | 74% | 15% | 92.7 | 33 | 26 | 41 | 35% | 71% | 7% | 0 | 15 | | | 63 | 1.33 | 2.4 | 154 | 176 | $10 |
| 19 Proj | **4** | **2** | **58** | **64** | **3.42** | **3.47** | **1.24** | **674** | **720** | **632** | **3.8** | **3.1** | **9.9** | **3.2** | **64%** | **13%** | **92.5** | **41** | **22** | **37** | **32%** | **76%** | **11%** | **0** | | | | | | **5.3** | **114** | **131** | **$3** |

## Soroka,Michael

| | | | | | |
|---|---|---|---|---|---|
| Age: 21 | Th: R | Role: SP | Health | F | LIMA Plan: B+ |
| Ht: 6' 5" | Wt: 225 | Type | PT/Exp | D | Rand Var: 0 |
| | | | Consist | B | MM: 3100 |

2-1, 3.51 ERA in 26 IP at ATL. Performed as advertised in short MLB stint—average Ctl and Dom with a groundball tilt from a workhorse starter's frame. But shoulder inflammation cut his season short and though he avoided surgery, it adds another layer of risk. Youth on his side, but better long-term than 2019 play.

| Yr Tm | W | Sv | IP | K | ERA | xERA | WHIP | oOPS | vL | vR | BF/G | Ctl | Dom | Cmd | FpK | SwK | Vel | G | L | F | H% | S% | hr/f | GS | APC | DOM% | DIS% | Sv% | LI | RAR | BPV | BPX | R$ |
|---|---|---|---|---|---|---|---|---|---|---|---|---|---|---|---|---|---|---|---|---|---|---|---|---|---|---|---|---|---|---|---|---|---|
| 14 | | | | | | | | | | | | | | | | | | | | | | | | | | | | | | | | | |
| 15 | | | | | | | | | | | | | | | | | | | | | | | | | | | | | | | | | |
| 16 | | | | | | | | | | | | | | | | | | | | | | | | | | | | | | | | | |
| 17 aa | 11 | 0 | 154 | 110 | 3.75 | 3.80 | 1.25 | | | | 24.1 | 2.0 | 6.4 | 3.3 | | | | | | | 31% | 71% | | | | | | | | 11.4 | 86 | 104 | $10 |
| 18 ATL * | 4 | 0 | 53 | 48 | 2.91 | 3.15 | 1.23 | 744 | 630 | 857 | 21.3 | 2.1 | 8.2 | 3.8 | 58% | 11% | 92.6 | 44 | 32 | 24 | 34% | 75% | 5% | 5 | 81 | 20% | 40% | | | 8.1 | 127 | 146 | $2 |
| 1st Half | 4 | 0 | 53 | 48 | 2.91 | 3.15 | 1.23 | 744 | 630 | 857 | 21.3 | 2.1 | 8.2 | 3.8 | 58% | 11% | 92.6 | 44 | 32 | 24 | 34% | 75% | 5% | 5 | 81 | 20% | 40% | | | 8.1 | 127 | 145 | $2 |
| 2nd Half | | | | | | | | | | | | | | | | | | | | | | | | | | | | | | | | | |
| 19 Proj | **4** | **0** | **51** | **42** | **3.24** | **3.56** | **1.24** | **615** | **514** | **715** | **22.4** | **2.1** | **7.5** | **3.5** | **58%** | **11%** | **92.6** | **44** | **32** | **24** | **33%** | **74%** | **6%** | **9** | | | | | | **5.7** | **100** | **114** | **$1** |

## Stammen,Craig

| | | | | | |
|---|---|---|---|---|---|
| Age: 35 | Th: R | Role: RP | Health | D | LIMA Plan: B+ |
| Ht: 6' 4" | Wt: 230 | Type: Pwr GB | PT/Exp | D | Rand Var: -1 |
| | | | Consist | D | MM: 4311 |

No indecisiveness here: Rode elite-level FpK, SwK and GB% into high-leverage bullpen role and a top-10 NL finisher in Holds. Arm has been healthy for two seasons, and while overall numbers and hr/f will correct, the floor is higher here than most mid-30s bullpen arms. Can again be a sneaky source of deep-league value.

| Yr Tm | W | Sv | IP | K | ERA | xERA | WHIP | oOPS | vL | vR | BF/G | Ctl | Dom | Cmd | FpK | SwK | Vel | G | L | F | H% | S% | hr/f | GS | APC | DOM% | DIS% | Sv% | LI | RAR | BPV | BPX | R$ |
|---|---|---|---|---|---|---|---|---|---|---|---|---|---|---|---|---|---|---|---|---|---|---|---|---|---|---|---|---|---|---|---|---|---|
| 14 WAS | 4 | 0 | 73 | 56 | 3.84 | 3.49 | 1.27 | 708 | 767 | 660 | 6.2 | 1.7 | 6.9 | 4.0 | 61% | 11% | 91.6 | 48 | 23 | 29 | 33% | 70% | 8% | 0 | 23 | | | 0 | 1.05 | -0.9 | 104 | 124 | $0 |
| 15 WAS | 0 | 0 | 4 | 3 | 0.00 | 5.18 | 1.25 | 525 | 500 | 536 | 3.4 | 6.8 | 6.8 | 1.0 | 71% | 12% | 91.6 | 55 | 9 | 36 | 19% | 100% | 0% | 0 | 13 | | | 0 | 1.63 | 2.0 | -28 | -33 | -$4 |
| 16 a/a | 0 | 0 | 24 | 13 | 5.19 | 6.88 | 1.71 | | | | 5.5 | 2.3 | 4.9 | 2.1 | | | | | | | 36% | 74% | | | | | | | | -3.0 | 11 | 13 | -$6 |
| 17 SD | 2 | 0 | 80 | 74 | 3.14 | 3.90 | 1.20 | 684 | 803 | 592 | 5.5 | 3.1 | 8.3 | 2.6 | 65% | 12% | 91.5 | 52 | 17 | 31 | 27% | 81% | 17% | 0 | 21 | | | 0 | 1.18 | 12.1 | 95 | 114 | $4 |
| 18 SD | 8 | 0 | 79 | 88 | 2.73 | 3.06 | 1.04 | 583 | 657 | 521 | 4.3 | 1.9 | 10.0 | 5.2 | 72% | 14% | 91.7 | 49 | 21 | 30 | 32% | 73% | 5% | 0 | 16 | | | 0 | 1.33 | 13.8 | 155 | 179 | $10 |
| 1st Half | 4 | 0 | 38 | 43 | 2.58 | 3.14 | 1.02 | 555 | 621 | 496 | 4.3 | 1.6 | 10.1 | 6.1 | 67% | 14% | 91.4 | 47 | 20 | 34 | 32% | 74% | 3% | 0 | 17 | | | 0 | 1.37 | 7.4 | 162 | 186 | $9 |
| 2nd Half | 4 | 0 | 41 | 45 | 2.88 | 2.98 | 1.06 | 609 | 690 | 542 | 4.3 | 2.2 | 10.0 | 4.5 | 76% | 14% | 91.9 | 52 | 22 | 26 | 31% | 73% | 7% | 0 | 15 | | | 0 | 1.29 | 6.4 | 149 | 172 | $11 |
| 19 Proj | **5** | **5** | **80** | **79** | **3.05** | **3.18** | **1.13** | **640** | **727** | **570** | **4.8** | **2.4** | **8.9** | **3.8** | **68%** | **13%** | **91.6** | **50** | **20** | **30** | **30%** | **75%** | **10%** | **0** | | | | | | **10.8** | **126** | **145** | **$8** |

## Stanek,Ryne

| | | | | | |
|---|---|---|---|---|---|
| Age: 27 | Th: R | Role: RP | Health | A | LIMA Plan: B+ |
| Ht: 6' 4" | Wt: 215 | Type: Pwr xFB | PT/Exp | D | Rand Var: -3 |
| | | | Consist | A | MM: 1411 |

New World Order: While Ryan Yarborough got the roto-glory (16 W; $9), this one brought the goods. But the skill set is far from perfect: too many fly balls, can't always find the zone, and a sizeable xERA/ERA gap. Velocity and strikeouts are in abundance, but this a more volatile profile than you might think.

| Yr Tm | W | Sv | IP | K | ERA | xERA | WHIP | oOPS | vL | vR | BF/G | Ctl | Dom | Cmd | FpK | SwK | Vel | G | L | F | H% | S% | hr/f | GS | APC | DOM% | DIS% | Sv% | LI | RAR | BPV | BPX | R$ |
|---|---|---|---|---|---|---|---|---|---|---|---|---|---|---|---|---|---|---|---|---|---|---|---|---|---|---|---|---|---|---|---|---|---|
| 14 | | | | | | | | | | | | | | | | | | | | | | | | | | | | | | | | | |
| 15 aa | 4 | 1 | 62 | 35 | 4.75 | 4.45 | 1.47 | | | | 16.5 | 4.5 | 5.1 | 1.1 | | | | | | | 27% | 70% | | | | | | | | -6.0 | 27 | 32 | -$5 |
| 16 a/a | 4 | 3 | 103 | 95 | 5.68 | 4.66 | 1.55 | | | | 13.2 | 4.6 | 8.4 | 1.8 | | | | | | | 33% | 63% | | | | | | | | -18.9 | 62 | 74 | -$8 |
| 17 TAM * | 3 | 8 | 65 | 79 | 2.98 | 3.86 | 1.38 | 985 | 613 | 1269 | 4.7 | 4.2 | 11.0 | 2.6 | 62% | 16% | 98.2 | 35 | 22 | 43 | 34% | 81% | 26% | 0 | 20 | | | 89 | 0.82 | 11.0 | 102 | 123 | $6 |
| 18 TAM | 2 | 0 | 66 | 81 | 2.98 | 3.86 | 1.19 | 618 | 509 | 681 | 4.5 | 3.7 | 11.0 | 3.0 | 58% | 16% | 98.0 | 33 | 15 | 52 | 26% | 78% | 10% | 29 | 18 | 3% | 48% | 0 | 0.89 | 9.5 | 110 | 127 | $4 |
| 1st Half | 1 | 0 | 25 | 30 | 1.78 | 4.07 | 0.95 | 475 | 361 | 527 | 4.7 | 4.6 | 10.7 | 2.3 | 53% | 14% | 98.2 | 35 | 11 | 55 | 18% | 86% | 7% | 9 | 20 | 0% | 33% | 0 | 0.72 | 7.4 | 80 | 92 | $3 |
| 2nd Half | 1 | 0 | 41 | 51 | 3.73 | 3.75 | 1.17 | 702 | 578 | 783 | 4.3 | 3.1 | 11.2 | 3.6 | 61% | 18% | 97.9 | 32 | 17 | 51 | 30% | 74% | 12% | 20 | 18 | 5% | 55% | 0 | 0.98 | 2.1 | 128 | 147 | $5 |
| 19 Proj | **3** | **5** | **73** | **81** | **3.54** | **4.09** | **1.26** | **712** | **588** | **783** | **5.5** | **4.0** | **10.0** | **2.5** | **58%** | **16%** | **98.0** | **33** | **15** | **52** | **28%** | **77%** | **10%** | **0** | | | | | | **0.6** | **82** | **94** | **$4** |

## Steckenrider,Drew

| | | | | | |
|---|---|---|---|---|---|
| Age: 28 | Th: R | Role: RP | Health | A | LIMA Plan: A |
| Ht: 6' 5" | Wt: 215 | Type: Pwr FB | PT/Exp | D | Rand Var: 0 |
| | | | Consist | C | MM: 3521 |

Chic pre-season pick for closer. He gave up nearly a one-quarter of his total earned runs for the year in one mid-May outing and spent rest of season attempting to lower his decimals. Threw more FpK in the 2nd half, which points to some Ctl upside—essential if he wants to compile saves and escape single-digit Rotoland.

| Yr Tm | W | Sv | IP | K | ERA | xERA | WHIP | oOPS | vL | vR | BF/G | Ctl | Dom | Cmd | FpK | SwK | Vel | G | L | F | H% | S% | hr/f | GS | APC | DOM% | DIS% | Sv% | LI | RAR | BPV | BPX | R$ |
|---|---|---|---|---|---|---|---|---|---|---|---|---|---|---|---|---|---|---|---|---|---|---|---|---|---|---|---|---|---|---|---|---|---|
| 14 | | | | | | | | | | | | | | | | | | | | | | | | | | | | | | | | | |
| 15 | | | | | | | | | | | | | | | | | | | | | | | | | | | | | | | | | |
| 16 a/a | 1 | 13 | 42 | 45 | 3.24 | 1.84 | 1.09 | | | | 4.8 | 3.9 | 9.7 | 2.5 | | | | | | | 27% | 69% | | | | | | | | 4.9 | 121 | 144 | $6 |
| 17 MIA * | 1 | 6 | 68 | 90 | 2.18 | 2.96 | 1.15 | 674 | 693 | 661 | 4.3 | 3.5 | 11.9 | 3.4 | 68% | 14% | 95.3 | 42 | 20 | 38 | 30% | 87% | 13% | 0 | 19 | | | 86 | 1.27 | 18.3 | 126 | 151 | $9 |
| 18 MIA | 4 | 5 | 65 | 74 | 3.90 | 4.06 | 1.27 | 664 | 808 | 545 | 3.8 | 3.8 | 10.3 | 2.7 | 61% | 12% | 94.7 | 34 | 24 | 42 | 31% | 72% | 10% | 0 | 16 | | | 50 | 1.09 | 2.0 | 96 | 110 | $2 |
| 1st Half | 3 | 1 | 36 | 42 | 3.28 | 3.72 | 1.15 | 590 | 798 | 438 | 3.7 | 3.8 | 10.6 | 2.8 | 56% | 11% | 94.6 | 33 | 26 | 40 | 29% | 72% | 6% | 0 | 15 | | | 50 | 1.03 | 3.8 | 100 | 115 | $4 |
| 2nd Half | 1 | 4 | 29 | 32 | 4.66 | 4.49 | 1.41 | 746 | 815 | 681 | 4.0 | 3.7 | 9.9 | 2.7 | 66% | 12% | 94.8 | 35 | 21 | 44 | 33% | 72% | 14% | 0 | 18 | | | 50 | 1.16 | -1.8 | 91 | 104 | $0 |
| 19 Proj | **3** | **18** | **73** | **86** | **3.28** | **3.44** | **1.20** | **622** | **705** | **559** | **4.0** | **3.5** | **10.7** | **3.1** | **65%** | **13%** | **95.0** | **37** | **22** | **41** | **30%** | **76%** | **10%** | **0** | | | | | | **7.5** | **115** | **132** | **$11** |

## Stock,Robert

| | | | | | |
|---|---|---|---|---|---|
| Age: 29 | Th: R | Role: RP | Health | A | LIMA Plan: B+ |
| Ht: 6' 1" | Wt: 214 | Type: Pwr GB | PT/Exp | F | Rand Var: -5 |
| | | | Consist | F | MM: 1100 |

1-1 with 2.50 ERA in 40 IP at SD. Former catcher cleaned up mechanics, conditioning after simmering awhile in independent ball. High-90s heat didn't produce the Ks one might expect, but with a dash of FpK and more than a pinch of hr/f fortune, his debut was tasty. Needs better Cmd to fully satisfy, though.

| Yr Tm | W | Sv | IP | K | ERA | xERA | WHIP | oOPS | vL | vR | BF/G | Ctl | Dom | Cmd | FpK | SwK | Vel | G | L | F | H% | S% | hr/f | GS | APC | DOM% | DIS% | Sv% | LI | RAR | BPV | BPX | R$ |
|---|---|---|---|---|---|---|---|---|---|---|---|---|---|---|---|---|---|---|---|---|---|---|---|---|---|---|---|---|---|---|---|---|---|
| 14 | | | | | | | | | | | | | | | | | | | | | | | | | | | | | | | | | |
| 15 | | | | | | | | | | | | | | | | | | | | | | | | | | | | | | | | | |
| 16 | | | | | | | | | | | | | | | | | | | | | | | | | | | | | | | | | |
| 17 aa | 8 | 0 | 45 | 28 | 5.42 | 5.43 | 1.90 | | | | 8.6 | 5.6 | 5.6 | 1.0 | | | | | | | 37% | 68% | | | | | | | | -5.9 | 47 | 57 | -$6 |
| 18 SD * | 2 | 9 | 78 | 70 | 2.26 | 2.88 | 1.19 | 615 | 709 | 531 | 4.9 | 3.3 | 8.1 | 2.5 | 63% | 10% | 97.6 | 50 | 16 | 34 | 29% | 83% | 3% | 0 | 19 | | | 82 | 0.88 | 18.1 | 96 | 110 | $9 |
| 1st Half | 1 | 8 | 36 | 35 | 2.41 | 3.34 | 1.23 | 916 | 1167 | 629 | 4.7 | 3.5 | 8.7 | 2.5 | 62% | 11% | 97.5 | 67 | 17 | 17 | 29% | 84% | 0% | 0 | 19 | | | 89 | 1.12 | 7.7 | 89 | 102 | $9 |
| 2nd Half | 1 | 1 | 42 | 35 | 2.14 | 2.50 | 1.15 | 590 | 668 | 522 | 5.1 | 3.0 | 7.6 | 2.5 | 63% | 10% | 97.6 | 49 | 16 | 35 | 29% | 81% | 3% | 0 | 19 | | | 50 | 0.86 | 10.4 | 102 | 117 | $9 |
| 19 Proj | **6** | **0** | **65** | **54** | **3.52** | **4.19** | **1.37** | **665** | **820** | **529** | **5.9** | **3.3** | **7.5** | **2.2** | **63%** | **10%** | **97.6** | **49** | **16** | **35** | **31%** | **78%** | **11%** | **0** | | | | | | **-0.2** | **72** | **82** | **$1** |

## Strahm,Matt

| | | | | | |
|---|---|---|---|---|---|
| Age: 27 | Th: L | Role: RP | Health | F | LIMA Plan: B+ |
| Ht: 6' 3" | Wt: 185 | Type: Pwr FB | PT/Exp | D | Rand Var: -3 |
| | | | Consist | C | MM: 3401 |

3-4, 2.05 ERA in 61 IP at SD. Started several bullpen games and worked in short stints as he recovered from July 2017 knee surgery, but lots to like: 1) Gets ahead with FpK; 2) solid velocity; K ability from the left side; 3) Skills improved with more work. S%, hr/f should regress, but could have value as starter or reliever.

| Yr Tm | W | Sv | IP | K | ERA | xERA | WHIP | oOPS | vL | vR | BF/G | Ctl | Dom | Cmd | FpK | SwK | Vel | G | L | F | H% | S% | hr/f | GS | APC | DOM% | DIS% | Sv% | LI | RAR | BPV | BPX | R$ |
|---|---|---|---|---|---|---|---|---|---|---|---|---|---|---|---|---|---|---|---|---|---|---|---|---|---|---|---|---|---|---|---|---|---|
| 14 | | | | | | | | | | | | | | | | | | | | | | | | | | | | | | | | | |
| 15 | | | | | | | | | | | | | | | | | | | | | | | | | | | | | | | | | |
| 16 KC * | 5 | 0 | 124 | 114 | 4.49 | 5.24 | 1.48 | 484 | 641 | 411 | 12.4 | 2.7 | 8.3 | 3.1 | 53% | 13% | 93.8 | 47 | 24 | 29 | 35% | 73% | 0% | 0 | 21 | | | 0 | 1.66 | -4.6 | 72 | 86 | -$3 |
| 17 KC | 2 | 0 | 35 | 37 | 5.45 | 4.99 | 1.50 | 779 | 728 | 794 | 6.4 | 5.7 | 9.6 | 1.7 | 59% | 11% | 93.6 | 37 | 19 | 44 | 28% | 67% | 15% | 3 | 27 | 0% | 33% | 0 | 0.81 | -4.7 | 34 | 40 | -$5 |
| 18 SD * | 4 | 0 | 76 | 86 | 2.27 | 2.67 | 1.07 | 564 | 773 | 473 | 6.0 | 3.0 | 10.2 | 3.4 | 66% | 13% | 93.5 | 35 | 21 | 44 | 28% | 84% | 9% | 5 | 24 | 20% | 40% | 0 | 0.91 | 17.8 | 121 | 139 | $9 |
| 1st Half | 3 | 0 | 41 | 42 | 2.70 | 3.09 | 1.20 | 561 | 1036 | 361 | 6.8 | 3.4 | 9.4 | 2.8 | 68% | 13% | 93.4 | 31 | 22 | 46 | 30% | 80% | 6% | 5 | 28 | 20% | 40% | 0 | 0.67 | 7.3 | 103 | 118 | $6 |
| 2nd Half | 1 | 0 | 36 | 44 | 1.77 | 3.21 | 0.93 | 567 | 585 | 558 | 5.4 | 2.5 | 11.1 | 4.4 | 65% | 13% | 93.5 | 38 | 21 | 41 | 25% | 90% | 12% | 0 | 22 | | | 0 | 1.05 | 10.5 | 148 | 169 | $11 |
| 19 Proj | **5** | **0** | **102** | **116** | **3.46** | **3.54** | **1.19** | **694** | **805** | **651** | **14.0** | **3.1** | **10.3** | **3.3** | **63%** | **12%** | **93.5** | **36** | **20** | **44** | **30%** | **76%** | **12%** | **12** | | | | | | **8.8** | **116** | **133** | **$7** |

BRENT HERSHEY

## Straily,Dan

| | | | | | | | | |
|---|---|---|---|---|---|---|---|---|
| Age: 30 | Th: R | Role SP | Health | C | LIMA Plan | B |
| Ht: 6' 2" | Wt: 220 | Type Pwr FB | PT/Exp | A | Rand Var | -1 |
| | | | Consist | A | MM | 1205 |

Forearm, oblique injuries wiped out most of Apr and Sept, so there are questions of health. Sat 5 games for retaliation after sluggers Buster Posey and Gorkys Hernandez took him deep, so questions of stuff, judgment. Cmd, xERA, BPV trends tepid, so questions of skills. Outside of very deep leagues, answer should be obvious.

| Yr Tm | W | Sv | IP | K | ERA | xERA | WHIP | oOPS | vL | vR | BF/G | Ctl | Dom | Cmd | FpK | SwK | Vel | G | L | F | H% | S% | hr/f | GS | APC | DOM% | DIS% | Sv% | LI | RAR | BPV | BPX | R$ |
|---|---|---|---|---|---|---|---|---|---|---|---|---|---|---|---|---|---|---|---|---|---|---|---|---|---|---|---|---|---|---|---|---|---|
| 14 2 TM * | 8 | 0 | 170 | 147 | 5.75 | 5.34 | 1.53 | 832 | 765 | 906 | 21.8 | 3.9 | 7.8 | 2.0 | 47% | 12% | 88.7 | 35 | 16 | 49 | 32% | 65% | 13% | 8 | 63 | 13% | 25% | 0 | 0.60 | -42.2 | 44 | 52 | -$15 |
| 15 HOU * | 10 | 0 | 139 | 113 | 5.31 | 5.66 | 1.57 | 747 | 796 | 681 | 23.5 | 2.1 | 7.3 | 3.4 | 47% | 10% | 89.3 | 42 | 21 | 38 | 38% | 67% | 10% | 3 | 73 | 0% | 67% | 0 | 0.64 | -23.2 | 75 | 89 | -$10 |
| 16 CIN | 14 | 0 | 191 | 162 | 3.76 | 4.77 | 1.19 | 712 | 645 | 763 | 23.3 | 3.4 | 7.6 | 2.2 | 61% | 11% | 89.3 | 32 | 20 | 48 | 25% | 75% | 12% | 31 | 90 | 16% | 16% | 0 | 0.77 | 10.1 | 54 | 65 | $15 |
| 17 MIA | 10 | 0 | 182 | 170 | 4.26 | 4.67 | 1.30 | 783 | 761 | 807 | 23.3 | 3.0 | 8.4 | 2.8 | 62% | 13% | 90.3 | 34 | 20 | 46 | 30% | 73% | 13% | 33 | 93 | 18% | 33% | | | 2.2 | 83 | 100 | $8 |
| 18 MIA | 5 | 0 | 122 | 99 | 4.12 | 4.90 | 1.30 | 754 | 830 | 669 | 22.5 | 3.8 | 7.3 | 1.9 | 60% | 10% | 90.4 | 32 | 26 | 42 | 26% | 74% | 14% | 23 | 93 | 17% | 30% | | | 0.5 | 38 | 44 | $1 |
| 1st Half | 3 | 0 | 52 | 45 | 4.82 | 4.91 | 1.39 | 811 | 854 | 753 | 20.9 | 4.3 | 7.7 | 1.8 | 58% | 11% | 90.5 | 31 | 31 | 38 | 26% | 74% | 21% | 11 | 88 | 18% | 45% | | | -4.3 | 32 | 37 | -$6 |
| 2nd Half | 2 | 0 | 70 | 54 | 3.60 | 4.89 | 1.23 | 710 | 809 | 613 | 24.0 | 3.5 | 6.9 | 2.0 | 61% | 10% | 90.3 | 33 | 21 | 46 | 26% | 74% | 9% | 12 | 97 | 17% | 17% | | | 4.7 | 42 | 48 | $6 |
| 19 Proj | 9 | 0 | 181 | 154 | 4.37 | 4.47 | 1.32 | 783 | 801 | 763 | 22.4 | 3.5 | 7.6 | 2.2 | 59% | 11% | 90.0 | 33 | 22 | 45 | 28% | 73% | 13% | 34 | | | | | | -5.0 | 55 | 63 | $4 |

## Strasburg,Stephen

| | | | | | | |
|---|---|---|---|---|---|---|
| Age: 30 | Th: R | Role SP | Health | F | LIMA Plan | B+ |
| Ht: 6' 5" | Wt: 235 | Type Pwr | PT/Exp | A | Rand Var | +2 |
| | | | Consist | A | MM | 4503 |

There was a time when such a Reliability Grade (tarnished by neck, shoulder in 2018) was a bright red flag. But in today's milieu, is it really? The skills profile is elite and stable; the workload reality is 145 IP and 24 GS (his four-year averages). When he pitches, you know what you're getting. Price it all in.

| Yr Tm | W | Sv | IP | K | ERA | xERA | WHIP | oOPS | vL | vR | BF/G | Ctl | Dom | Cmd | FpK | SwK | Vel | G | L | F | H% | S% | hr/f | GS | APC | DOM% | DIS% | Sv% | LI | RAR | BPV | BPX | R$ |
|---|---|---|---|---|---|---|---|---|---|---|---|---|---|---|---|---|---|---|---|---|---|---|---|---|---|---|---|---|---|---|---|---|---|
| 14 WAS | 14 | 0 | 215 | 242 | 3.14 | 2.78 | 1.12 | 672 | 653 | 687 | 25.5 | 1.8 | 10.1 | 5.6 | 65% | 12% | 94.8 | 46 | 23 | 31 | 32% | 76% | 13% | 34 | 97 | 47% | 9% | | | 16.0 | 158 | 188 | $20 |
| 15 WAS | 11 | 0 | 127 | 155 | 3.46 | 2.94 | 1.11 | 653 | 572 | 737 | 22.7 | 1.8 | 11.0 | 6.0 | 66% | 12% | 95.4 | 42 | 23 | 34 | 33% | 72% | 12% | 23 | 89 | 39% | 22% | | | 7.8 | 168 | 200 | $13 |
| 16 WAS | 15 | 0 | 148 | 183 | 3.60 | 3.34 | 1.10 | 637 | 615 | 658 | 24.9 | 2.7 | 11.2 | 4.2 | 65% | 12% | 94.9 | 40 | 21 | 39 | 31% | 70% | 11% | 24 | 99 | 58% | 13% | | | 10.8 | 146 | 174 | $17 |
| 17 WAS | 15 | 0 | 175 | 204 | 2.52 | 3.27 | 1.02 | 581 | 573 | 589 | 25.0 | 2.4 | 10.5 | 4.3 | 63% | 13% | 95.6 | 47 | 19 | 34 | 29% | 78% | 9% | 28 | 98 | 46% | 11% | | | 39.9 | 148 | 178 | $31 |
| 18 WAS | 10 | 0 | 130 | 156 | 3.74 | 3.34 | 1.20 | 711 | 723 | 697 | 24.7 | 2.6 | 10.8 | 4.1 | 61% | 12% | 94.5 | 44 | 22 | 34 | 32% | 74% | 16% | 22 | 98 | 36% | 5% | | | 6.6 | 145 | 167 | $10 |
| 1st Half | 6 | 0 | 81 | 95 | 3.46 | 3.12 | 1.09 | 680 | 635 | 733 | 25.2 | 2.1 | 10.6 | 5.0 | 62% | 12% | 95.3 | 44 | 24 | 32 | 30% | 75% | 18% | 13 | 98 | 46% | 8% | | | 6.9 | 156 | 179 | $15 |
| 2nd Half | 4 | 0 | 49 | 61 | 4.20 | 3.71 | 1.38 | 757 | 883 | 647 | 24.1 | 3.5 | 11.1 | 3.2 | 59% | 13% | 93.5 | 43 | 19 | 38 | 36% | 73% | 12% | 9 | 99 | 22% | 0% | | | -0.3 | 127 | 146 | $1 |
| 19 Proj | 13 | 0 | 160 | 191 | 3.45 | 3.07 | 1.16 | 672 | 688 | 657 | 23.7 | 2.7 | 10.8 | 4.1 | 62% | 13% | 94.8 | 44 | 21 | 35 | 32% | 74% | 13% | 27 | | | | | | 13.8 | 145 | 166 | $17 |

## Stratton,Chris

| | | | | | | |
|---|---|---|---|---|---|---|
| Age: 28 | Th: R | Role SP | Health | A | LIMA Plan | D+ |
| Ht: 6' 2" | Wt: 211 | Type | PT/Exp | D | Rand Var | 0 |
| | | | Consist | B | MM | 1101 |

10-10, 5.09 ERA in 145 IP at SF. Skills stuck in neutral at an age/experience level where one hopes to see growth. If you squint, there is a 2nd half FpK spike, but below-average whiffs and Cmd, a disturbing LD history and increasing oOPS which quickly negate any optimism. Hard to see him getting another 26 MLB starts.

| Yr Tm | W | Sv | IP | K | ERA | xERA | WHIP | oOPS | vL | vR | BF/G | Ctl | Dom | Cmd | FpK | SwK | Vel | G | L | F | H% | S% | hr/f | GS | APC | DOM% | DIS% | Sv% | LI | RAR | BPV | BPX | R$ |
|---|---|---|---|---|---|---|---|---|---|---|---|---|---|---|---|---|---|---|---|---|---|---|---|---|---|---|---|---|---|---|---|---|---|
| 14 aa | 1 | 0 | 23 | 15 | 3.97 | 6.53 | 1.95 | | | | 21.9 | 4.8 | 5.9 | 1.2 | | | | | | | 38% | 80% | | | | | | | | -0.6 | 29 | 35 | -$5 |
| 15 a/a | 5 | 0 | 148 | 92 | 4.80 | 4.06 | 1.46 | | | | 24.4 | 4.0 | 5.6 | 1.4 | | | | | | | 30% | 66% | | | | | | | | -15.3 | 50 | 59 | -$8 |
| 16 SF * | 13 | 0 | 136 | 89 | 4.63 | 4.35 | 1.48 | 767 | 687 | 850 | 20.8 | 3.1 | 5.9 | 1.9 | 42% | 8% | 91.3 | 41 | 16 | 44 | 33% | 67% | 7% | 0 | 24 | | | 0 | 0.31 | -7.4 | 60 | 71 | -$1 |
| 17 SF * | 8 | 1 | 138 | 106 | 5.28 | 5.60 | 1.64 | 738 | 811 | 670 | 22.0 | 3.4 | 6.9 | 2.1 | 59% | 9% | 91.6 | 43 | 28 | 29 | 36% | 69% | 10% | 10 | 80 | 20% | 30% | 50 | 0.68 | -15.6 | 49 | 59 | -$8 |
| 18 SF * | 13 | 0 | 169 | 130 | 4.85 | 4.90 | 1.45 | 791 | 834 | 740 | 22.5 | 3.3 | 6.9 | 2.1 | 62% | 9% | 91.1 | 43 | 25 | 32 | 32% | 69% | 13% | 26 | 88 | 23% | 38% | 0 | 0.80 | -14.5 | 51 | 58 | -$3 |
| 1st Half | 8 | 0 | 91 | 70 | 4.45 | 4.66 | 1.40 | 763 | 772 | 750 | 22.8 | 3.5 | 6.9 | 2.0 | 58% | 9% | 91.1 | 39 | 27 | 34 | 31% | 69% | 10% | 17 | 91 | 18% | 35% | | | -3.4 | 49 | 56 | $0 |
| 2nd Half | 5 | 0 | 78 | 60 | 5.31 | 5.57 | 1.51 | 838 | 946 | 727 | 22.5 | 3.1 | 7.0 | 2.2 | 68% | 10% | 91.1 | 48 | 23 | 29 | 33% | 68% | 20% | 9 | 83 | 33% | 44% | 0 | 0.83 | -11.2 | 42 | 48 | -$7 |
| 19 Proj | 6 | 0 | 87 | 64 | 4.98 | 4.41 | 1.51 | 805 | 876 | 731 | 22.3 | 3.3 | 6.6 | 2.0 | 62% | 9% | 91.3 | 44 | 26 | 30 | 33% | 68% | 11% | 17 | | | | | | -8.9 | 51 | 59 | -$5 |

## Strickland,Hunter

| | | | | | | |
|---|---|---|---|---|---|---|
| Age: 30 | Th: R | Role RP | Health | D | LIMA Plan | B |
| Ht: 6' 3" | Wt: 225 | Type Pwr | PT/Exp | C | Rand Var | -1 |
| | | | Consist | B | MM | 1210 |

Closers and Frustration in Four Acts: I) Debuts as high-velocity strike-thrower and bat-misser; II) Skills steadily deteriorate, though good fortune extends hope; III) Claims stopper role, saves begin to pile up; IV) Breaks finger in blown save tirade; misses 2 months; club moves on. The heart is a lonely hunter. Sort of.

| Yr Tm | W | Sv | IP | K | ERA | xERA | WHIP | oOPS | vL | vR | BF/G | Ctl | Dom | Cmd | FpK | SwK | Vel | G | L | F | H% | S% | hr/f | GS | APC | DOM% | DIS% | Sv% | LI | RAR | BPV | BPX | R$ |
|---|---|---|---|---|---|---|---|---|---|---|---|---|---|---|---|---|---|---|---|---|---|---|---|---|---|---|---|---|---|---|---|---|---|
| 14 SF * | 2 | 12 | 43 | 48 | 1.98 | 2.10 | 0.90 | 440 | 500 | 400 | 3.4 | 0.9 | 10.0 | 11.2 | 84% | 13% | 98.1 | 56 | 25 | 19 | 30% | 81% | 0% | 0 | 11 | | | 100 | 0.45 | 9.2 | 289 | 345 | $9 |
| 15 SF * | 4 | 5 | 73 | 70 | 2.28 | 1.63 | 0.87 | 543 | 509 | 562 | 3.8 | 1.6 | 8.6 | 5.3 | 65% | 15% | 96.9 | 40 | 20 | 40 | 25% | 76% | 8% | 0 | 13 | | | 71 | 1.28 | 15.1 | 164 | 196 | $12 |
| 16 SF | 3 | 3 | 61 | 57 | 3.10 | 3.70 | 1.13 | 589 | 741 | 515 | 3.5 | 2.8 | 8.4 | 3.0 | 57% | 12% | 96.8 | 47 | 22 | 30 | 29% | 74% | 8% | 0 | 14 | | | 38 | 1.29 | 8.2 | 101 | 120 | $5 |
| 17 SF | 4 | 1 | 61 | 58 | 2.64 | 5.00 | 1.43 | 702 | 876 | 587 | 3.9 | 4.3 | 8.5 | 2.0 | 62% | 11% | 95.7 | 39 | 17 | 44 | 32% | 83% | 5% | 0 | 14 | | | 33 | 1.37 | 13.0 | 55 | 66 | $2 |
| 18 SF | 3 | 14 | 45 | 37 | 3.97 | 5.10 | 1.41 | 758 | 627 | 884 | 4.1 | 4.2 | 7.3 | 1.8 | 56% | 11% | 94.9 | 38 | 22 | 40 | 29% | 75% | 9% | 0 | 16 | | | 78 | 1.07 | 1.0 | 36 | 41 | $3 |
| 1st Half | 3 | 13 | 32 | 29 | 2.84 | 4.48 | 1.23 | 619 | 409 | 831 | 4.0 | 3.7 | 8.2 | 2.2 | 56% | 11% | 95.4 | 40 | 23 | 37 | 28% | 78% | 6% | 0 | 16 | | | 76 | 1.32 | 5.1 | 66 | 76 | $7 |
| 2nd Half | 0 | 1 | 14 | 8 | 6.59 | 6.66 | 1.83 | 1055 | 1126 | 992 | 4.4 | 5.3 | 5.3 | 1.0 | 56% | 12% | 93.8 | 35 | 21 | 44 | 31% | 68% | 14% | 0 | 17 | | | 100 | 0.50 | -4.1 | -34 | -39 | -$13 |
| 19 Proj | 3 | 2 | 44 | 38 | 4.14 | 4.28 | 1.39 | 724 | 722 | 725 | 3.8 | 4.0 | 8.0 | 2.0 | 59% | 12% | 96.2 | 42 | 21 | 37 | 30% | 73% | 10% | 0 | | | | | | -0.6 | 55 | 63 | -$2 |

## Stripling,Ross

| | | | | | | |
|---|---|---|---|---|---|---|
| Age: 29 | Th: R | Role SP | Health | C | LIMA Plan | B |
| Ht: 6' 3" | Wt: 210 | Type Pwr | PT/Exp | C | Rand Var | 0 |
| | | | Consist | A | MM | 4303 |

First-half FAAB darling after moving to rotation in early May, though Ctl/FpK spike and S% were skeptical of his staying power. Things re-set after July 1, but from a full-year perspective, this was still a step up. Danced around toe, back injuries in 2nd half, but throws strikes, gets whiffs and GBs, and has SP/RP versatility.

| Yr Tm | W | Sv | IP | K | ERA | xERA | WHIP | oOPS | vL | vR | BF/G | Ctl | Dom | Cmd | FpK | SwK | Vel | G | L | F | H% | S% | hr/f | GS | APC | DOM% | DIS% | Sv% | LI | RAR | BPV | BPX | R$ |
|---|---|---|---|---|---|---|---|---|---|---|---|---|---|---|---|---|---|---|---|---|---|---|---|---|---|---|---|---|---|---|---|---|---|
| 14 | | | | | | | | | | | | | | | | | | | | | | | | | | | | | | | | | |
| 15 aa | 3 | 0 | 67 | 44 | 5.20 | 4.91 | 1.42 | | | | 22.0 | 2.6 | 5.9 | 2.3 | | | | | | | 32% | 65% | | | | | | | | -10.3 | 45 | 54 | -$6 |
| 16 LA * | 5 | 0 | 117 | 87 | 4.06 | 4.09 | 1.30 | 709 | 656 | 752 | 17.8 | 2.5 | 6.7 | 2.7 | 64% | 8% | 90.5 | 51 | 20 | 29 | 31% | 71% | 11% | 14 | 72 | 14% | 50% | 0 | 0.99 | 1.9 | 71 | 84 | $2 |
| 17 LA | 3 | 2 | 74 | 74 | 3.75 | 3.56 | 1.18 | 691 | 554 | 796 | 6.2 | 2.3 | 9.0 | 3.9 | 65% | 12% | 92.9 | 49 | 22 | 29 | 30% | 73% | 17% | 2 | 24 | 50% | 0% | 40 | 0.86 | 5.5 | 126 | 152 | $4 |
| 18 LA | 8 | 0 | 122 | 136 | 3.02 | 3.27 | 1.19 | 722 | 661 | 785 | 15.2 | 1.6 | 10.0 | 6.2 | 69% | 12% | 91.7 | 45 | 22 | 33 | 34% | 82% | 16% | 21 | 61 | 29% | 19% | 0 | 0.83 | 16.9 | 160 | 184 | $11 |
| 1st Half | 6 | 0 | 77 | 89 | 1.98 | 3.08 | 1.07 | 640 | 640 | 640 | 14.0 | 1.4 | 10.4 | 7.4 | 72% | 12% | 91.8 | 48 | 17 | 35 | 33% | 88% | 11% | 11 | 55 | 55% | 18% | 0 | 0.82 | 20.7 | 175 | 201 | $21 |
| 2nd Half | 2 | 0 | 45 | 47 | 4.84 | 3.61 | 1.39 | 855 | 703 | 977 | 17.6 | 2.0 | 9.5 | 4.7 | 64% | 12% | 91.6 | 41 | 30 | 29 | 35% | 73% | 26% | 10 | 72 | 0% | 20% | 0 | 0.86 | -3.8 | 135 | 155 | -$7 |
| 19 Proj | 7 | 0 | 145 | 149 | 3.42 | 3.23 | 1.24 | 715 | 620 | 795 | 20.5 | 2.1 | 9.2 | 4.4 | 66% | 12% | 91.9 | 47 | 23 | 30 | 33% | 77% | 14% | 24 | | | | | | 16.9 | 135 | 155 | $10 |

## Stroman,Marcus

| | | | | | | |
|---|---|---|---|---|---|---|
| Age: 28 | Th: R | Role SP | Health | F | LIMA Plan | C |
| Ht: 5' 8" | Wt: 180 | Type xGB | PT/Exp | A | Rand Var | +5 |
| | | | Consist | A | MM | 3103 |

Pitched through first 7 starts with shoulder inflammation, then out of action for six weeks in May/Jun. By Aug, blister problems led to another DL stint. Skills remained stable throughout and more sedate xERAs show some bounce-back potential, though little further upside. Hope for health, pray for more Ks—but bid on neither.

| Yr Tm | W | Sv | IP | K | ERA | xERA | WHIP | oOPS | vL | vR | BF/G | Ctl | Dom | Cmd | FpK | SwK | Vel | G | L | F | H% | S% | hr/f | GS | APC | DOM% | DIS% | Sv% | LI | RAR | BPV | BPX | R$ |
|---|---|---|---|---|---|---|---|---|---|---|---|---|---|---|---|---|---|---|---|---|---|---|---|---|---|---|---|---|---|---|---|---|---|
| 14 TOR * | 13 | 1 | 166 | 151 | 3.70 | 3.23 | 1.20 | 633 | 646 | 620 | 20.3 | 2.0 | 8.1 | 4.0 | 58% | 9% | 93.5 | 54 | 18 | 28 | 33% | 69% | 6% | 20 | 80 | 45% | 35% | 100 | 0.84 | 0.8 | 124 | 147 | $9 |
| 15 TOR | 4 | 0 | 27 | 18 | 1.67 | 3.13 | 0.96 | 554 | 514 | 646 | 25.8 | 2.0 | 6.0 | 3.0 | 66% | 8% | 92.0 | 64 | 18 | 18 | 24% | 88% | 14% | 4 | 93 | 75% | 25% | | | 7.6 | 96 | 114 | $2 |
| 16 TOR | 9 | 0 | 204 | 166 | 4.37 | 3.48 | 1.29 | 720 | 741 | 698 | 26.7 | 2.4 | 7.3 | 3.1 | 61% | 10% | 92.4 | 60 | 20 | 20 | 31% | 68% | 17% | 32 | 97 | 34% | 31% | | | -4.5 | 106 | 125 | $5 |
| 17 TOR | 13 | 0 | 201 | 164 | 3.09 | 3.58 | 1.31 | 715 | 650 | 769 | 25.3 | 2.8 | 7.3 | 2.6 | 59% | 10% | 93.3 | 62 | 18 | 20 | 31% | 80% | 18% | 33 | 95 | 39% | 27% | | | 31.5 | 97 | 117 | $17 |
| 18 TOR | 4 | 0 | 102 | 77 | 5.54 | 3.93 | 1.48 | 759 | 746 | 772 | 23.6 | 3.2 | 6.8 | 2.1 | 60% | 9% | 92.4 | 62 | 18 | 20 | 33% | 62% | 14% | 19 | 90 | 16% | 42% | | | -17.6 | 76 | 88 | -$9 |
| 1st Half | 1 | 0 | 49 | 41 | 6.02 | 3.89 | 1.52 | 762 | 824 | 678 | 24.6 | 3.5 | 7.5 | 2.2 | 59% | 10% | 92.3 | 63 | 18 | 20 | 34% | 61% | 19% | 9 | 91 | 11% | 33% | | | -11.4 | 82 | 94 | -$14 |
| 2nd Half | 3 | 0 | 53 | 36 | 5.09 | 3.97 | 1.43 | 756 | 657 | 845 | 22.8 | 2.9 | 6.1 | 2.1 | 62% | 9% | 92.4 | 61 | 18 | 20 | 33% | 63% | 9% | 10 | 89 | 20% | 50% | | | -6.2 | 71 | 82 | -$4 |
| 19 Proj | 8 | 0 | 160 | 125 | 4.47 | 3.60 | 1.39 | 734 | 711 | 756 | 23.7 | 3.0 | 7.1 | 2.4 | 60% | 9% | 92.7 | 61 | 18 | 21 | 32% | 69% | 14% | 28 | | | | | | 8.6 | 86 | 99 | $0 |

## Strop,Pedro

| | | | | | | |
|---|---|---|---|---|---|---|
| Age: 34 | Th: R | Role RP | Health | C | LIMA Plan | B |
| Ht: 6' 1" | Wt: 220 | Type Pwr GB | PT/Exp | C | Rand Var | -5 |
| | | | Consist | B | MM | 4310 |

Finally found his way into save opps in the 2nd half until a hamstring injury cut his season short. PRO: Elite SwK says Dom should rebound; velocity sitting pretty in his mid-30s; still death on RHB. CON: FpK gives little hope for Ctl improvement; FB% and xERA inching northward. Even without saves, good source of RP profit.

| Yr Tm | W | Sv | IP | K | ERA | xERA | WHIP | oOPS | vL | vR | BF/G | Ctl | Dom | Cmd | FpK | SwK | Vel | G | L | F | H% | S% | hr/f | GS | APC | DOM% | DIS% | Sv% | LI | RAR | BPV | BPX | R$ |
|---|---|---|---|---|---|---|---|---|---|---|---|---|---|---|---|---|---|---|---|---|---|---|---|---|---|---|---|---|---|---|---|---|---|
| 14 CHC | 2 | 2 | 61 | 71 | 2.21 | 2.65 | 1.07 | 535 | 621 | 478 | 3.8 | 3.7 | 10.5 | 2.8 | 56% | 16% | 95.0 | 55 | 24 | 21 | 27% | 79% | 7% | 0 | 14 | | | 33 | 1.12 | 11.5 | 122 | 145 | $6 |
| 15 CHC | 2 | 3 | 68 | 81 | 2.91 | 2.98 | 1.00 | 538 | 641 | 475 | 3.6 | 3.8 | 10.7 | 2.8 | 58% | 17% | 95.1 | 51 | 20 | 29 | 23% | 73% | 11% | 0 | 14 | | | 60 | 1.30 | 8.8 | 118 | 141 | $7 |
| 16 CHC | 2 | 0 | 47 | 60 | 2.85 | 2.57 | 0.89 | 517 | 608 | 470 | 3.5 | 2.9 | 11.4 | 4.0 | 53% | 16% | 94.9 | 58 | 16 | 25 | 24% | 71% | 15% | 0 | 14 | | | 0 | 0.98 | 7.8 | 164 | 195 | $4 |
| 17 CHC | 5 | 0 | 60 | 65 | 2.83 | 3.56 | 1.18 | 619 | 498 | 705 | 3.6 | 3.9 | 9.7 | 2.5 | 54% | 16% | 96.1 | 59 | 11 | 30 | 28% | 78% | 9% | 0 | 15 | | | 0 | 1.09 | 11.3 | 107 | 128 | $5 |
| 18 CHC | 6 | 13 | 60 | 57 | 2.26 | 3.78 | 0.99 | 541 | 643 | 473 | 4.0 | 3.2 | 8.6 | 2.7 | 58% | 17% | 95.1 | 46 | 18 | 36 | 23% | 80% | 7% | 0 | 15 | | | 76 | 1.31 | 13.9 | 93 | 107 | $13 |
| 1st Half | 3 | 1 | 34 | 34 | 2.62 | 3.93 | 1.08 | 555 | 775 | 421 | 4.0 | 3.4 | 8.9 | 2.6 | 58% | 17% | 94.6 | 39 | 24 | 37 | 26% | 77% | 6% | 0 | 14 | | | 33 | 1.08 | 6.5 | 86 | 99 | $9 |
| 2nd Half | 3 | 12 | 25 | 23 | 1.78 | 3.56 | 0.87 | 523 | 487 | 551 | 4.0 | 2.8 | 8.2 | 2.9 | 56% | 17% | 95.7 | 55 | 11 | 34 | 20% | 85% | 9% | 0 | 15 | | | 86 | 1.62 | 7.4 | 104 | 119 | $19 |
| 19 Proj | 5 | 9 | 65 | 68 | 3.00 | 3.25 | 1.13 | 632 | 649 | 621 | 3.7 | 3.3 | 9.4 | 2.9 | 56% | 16% | 95.4 | 53 | 15 | 31 | 28% | 76% | 11% | 0 | | | | | | 7.6 | 112 | 128 | $9 |

BRENT HERSHEY

## Suarez,Andrew

| | | | | | |
|---|---|---|---|---|---|
| Age: 26 | Th: L | Role SP | Health A | LIMA Plan C | |
| Ht: 6' 0" | Wt: 187 | Type GB | PT/Exp D | Rand Var +2 | |
| | | | Consist B | MM 1003 | |

7-13, 4.49 in 160 IP at SF. Solid 1st half ERA driven by career-high Dom, which SwK didn't support. 2nd half reversion was no surprise, even though ERA rose mostly due to poor S% and elevated hr/f. Excellent G/F ratio should make him a useful innings-eater, but he hasn't shown skills to suggest more than that.

| Yr Tm | W | Sv | IP | K | ERA | xERA | WHIP | oOPS | vL | vR | BF/G | Ctl | Dom | Cmd | FpK | SwK | Vel | G | L | F | H% | S% | hr/f | GS | APC | DOM% | DIS% | Sv% | LI | RAR | BPV | BPX | R$ |
|---|---|---|---|---|---|---|---|---|---|---|---|---|---|---|---|---|---|---|---|---|---|---|---|---|---|---|---|---|---|---|---|---|---|
| 14 | | | | | | | | | | | | | | | | | | | | | | | | | | | | | | | | | |
| 15 | | | | | | | | | | | | | | | | | | | | | | | | | | | | | | | | | |
| 16 aa | 7 | 0 | 114 | 75 | 5.19 | 5.70 | 1.60 | | | | 26.5 | 2.1 | 5.9 | 2.9 | | | | | | | 37% | 68% | | | | | | | | -14.1 | 60 | 71 | -$8 |
| 17 a/a | 10 | 0 | 156 | 110 | 4.23 | 5.16 | 1.58 | | | | 26.3 | 2.6 | 6.3 | 2.5 | | | | | | | 37% | 73% | | | | | | | | 2.4 | 65 | 78 | -$2 |
| 18 SF * | 9 | 0 | 179 | 143 | 4.14 | 4.16 | 1.27 | 767 | 512 | 853 | 22.8 | 2.6 | 7.2 | 2.8 | 61% | 8% | 92.2 | 51 | 22 | 27 | 30% | 71% | 18% | 29 | 86 | 21% | 41% | | | 0.2 | 70 | 80 | $5 |
| 1st Half | 5 | 0 | 89 | 79 | 3.55 | 3.80 | 1.22 | 755 | 484 | 850 | 22.5 | 2.2 | 7.9 | 3.6 | 61% | 8% | 92.4 | 52 | 21 | 27 | 31% | 74% | 16% | 13 | 85 | 23% | 31% | | | 6.6 | 99 | 114 | $10 |
| 2nd Half | 4 | 0 | 89 | 64 | 4.74 | 4.20 | 1.31 | 777 | 536 | 855 | 23.3 | 3.0 | 6.4 | 2.1 | 62% | 8% | 92.0 | 51 | 22 | 27 | 28% | 68% | 19% | 16 | 87 | 19% | 50% | | | -6.4 | 63 | 73 | $1 |
| 19 Proj | 9 | 0 | 160 | 116 | 4.39 | 4.04 | 1.41 | 789 | 552 | 869 | 24.5 | 2.7 | 6.5 | 2.4 | 61% | 8% | 92.2 | 50 | 22 | 28 | 33% | 71% | 12% | 28 | | | | | | -4.6 | 73 | 84 | $0 |

## Suter,Brent

| | | | | | |
|---|---|---|---|---|---|
| Age: 29 | Th: L | Role RP | Health F | LIMA Plan B+ | |
| Ht: 6' 5" | Wt: 195 | Type | PT/Exp C | Rand Var +2 | |
| | | | Consist A | MM 1000 | |

Soft-tosser underwent Tommy John surgery in July. Prior to injury displayed excellent Ctl, supported by FpK—his only standout skill. Low strikeout rate and plummeting GB% leave little margin for error, reflected in mediocre xERA. Without improvements, ERA and WHIP will remain below average. Check back in 2020.

| Yr Tm | W | Sv | IP | K | ERA | xERA | WHIP | oOPS | vL | vR | BF/G | Ctl | Dom | Cmd | FpK | SwK | Vel | G | L | F | H% | S% | hr/f | GS | APC | DOM% | DIS% | Sv% | LI | RAR | BPV | BPX | R$ |
|---|---|---|---|---|---|---|---|---|---|---|---|---|---|---|---|---|---|---|---|---|---|---|---|---|---|---|---|---|---|---|---|---|---|
| 14 aa | 10 | 0 | 152 | 98 | 4.98 | 5.11 | 1.52 | | | | 23.6 | 3.4 | 5.8 | 1.7 | | | | | | | 32% | 69% | | | | | | | | -23.3 | 34 | 40 | -$9 |
| 15 a/a | 8 | 0 | 118 | 66 | 3.04 | 4.32 | 1.46 | | | | 19.5 | 3.3 | 5.0 | 1.5 | | | | | | | 32% | 80% | | | | | | | | 13.4 | 45 | 53 | $2 |
| 16 MIL * | 8 | 2 | 132 | 74 | 3.94 | 5.07 | 1.49 | 773 | 1051 | 592 | 14.2 | 1.3 | 5.1 | 3.8 | 68% | 9% | 83.8 | 43 | 19 | 37 | 36% | 74% | 12% | 2 | 25 | 0% | 100% | 100 | 0.75 | 4.1 | 83 | 98 | $0 |
| 17 MIL * | 6 | 0 | 118 | 93 | 3.97 | 4.69 | 1.39 | 702 | 541 | 755 | 15.6 | 2.3 | 7.1 | 3.1 | 67% | 9% | 85.8 | 45 | 24 | 31 | 33% | 74% | 10% | 14 | 58 | 21% | 43% | 0 | 0.67 | 5.6 | 73 | 88 | $2 |
| 18 MIL | 8 | 0 | 101 | 84 | 4.44 | 4.22 | 1.19 | 754 | 683 | 775 | 21.2 | 1.7 | 7.5 | 4.4 | 69% | 10% | 86.7 | 33 | 29 | 38 | 29% | 69% | 16% | 18 | 82 | 22% | 22% | 0 | 0.83 | -3.6 | 100 | 115 | $3 |
| 1st Half | 8 | 0 | 88 | 73 | 4.28 | 4.16 | 1.15 | 726 | 722 | 728 | 21.5 | 1.8 | 7.4 | 4.1 | 70% | 10% | 86.7 | 34 | 29 | 37 | 28% | 68% | 14% | 15 | 83 | 27% | 20% | 0 | 0.84 | -1.4 | 96 | 111 | $5 |
| 2nd Half | 0 | 0 | 13 | 11 | 5.54 | 4.61 | 1.46 | 923 | 417 | 1060 | 19.3 | 0.7 | 7.6 | 11.0 | 66% | 11% | 86.6 | 27 | 30 | 43 | 35% | 73% | 21% | 3 | 75 | 0% | 33% | | | -2.2 | 124 | 142 | -$15 |
| 19 Proj | 1 | 0 | 15 | 10 | 4.01 | 4.28 | 1.36 | 773 | 691 | 799 | 17.5 | 2.2 | 6.2 | 2.9 | 69% | 10% | 86.3 | 38 | 27 | 35 | 32% | 73% | 10% | 3 | | | | | | 0.2 | 70 | 81 | -$4 |

## Swarzak,Anthony

| | | | | | |
|---|---|---|---|---|---|
| Age: 33 | Th: R | Role RP | Health F | LIMA Plan C | |
| Ht: 6' 4" | Wt: 215 | Type Pwr | PT/Exp D | Rand Var +5 | |
| | | | Consist D | MM 2210 | |

Missed 14 weeks to two different injuries (oblique, shoulder). In resulting short sample, control slipped but FpK history gives hope for recovery. While he appeared to hold Dom gains, SwK drop suggests 2017's surprise breakout is likely an outlier. Skills and age make him a fairly average bullpen arm.

| Yr Tm | W | Sv | IP | K | ERA | xERA | WHIP | oOPS | vL | vR | BF/G | Ctl | Dom | Cmd | FpK | SwK | Vel | G | L | F | H% | S% | hr/f | GS | APC | DOM% | DIS% | Sv% | LI | RAR | BPV | BPX | R$ |
|---|---|---|---|---|---|---|---|---|---|---|---|---|---|---|---|---|---|---|---|---|---|---|---|---|---|---|---|---|---|---|---|---|---|
| 14 MIN | 3 | 0 | 86 | 47 | 4.60 | 4.74 | 1.49 | 752 | 733 | 768 | 7.6 | 2.9 | 4.9 | 1.7 | 60% | 7% | 92.2 | 45 | 20 | 36 | 33% | 68% | 5% | 4 | 28 | 0% | 75% | 0 | 0.82 | -9.2 | 32 | 39 | -$7 |
| 15 CLE | 0 | 0 | 13 | 13 | 3.38 | 3.85 | 1.65 | 799 | 636 | 886 | 6.1 | 2.7 | 8.8 | 3.3 | 74% | 11% | 92.2 | 43 | 32 | 25 | 41% | 81% | 9% | 0 | 20 | | | 0 | 0.29 | 1.0 | 106 | 126 | -$5 |
| 16 NYY * | 2 | 7 | 78 | 63 | 5.88 | 5.87 | 1.44 | 847 | 858 | 839 | 8.1 | 2.0 | 7.3 | 3.7 | 68% | 10% | 93.4 | 46 | 11 | 43 | 33% | 64% | 28% | 0 | 19 | | | 88 | 0.67 | -16.2 | 58 | 69 | -$5 |
| 17 2 TM | 6 | 2 | 77 | 91 | 2.33 | 3.42 | 1.03 | 595 | 575 | 605 | 4.3 | 2.6 | 10.6 | 4.1 | 65% | 15% | 94.7 | 44 | 16 | 41 | 29% | 81% | 8% | 0 | 18 | | | 40 | 1.37 | 19.4 | 144 | 172 | $12 |
| 18 NYM | 0 | 4 | 26 | 31 | 6.15 | 4.43 | 1.59 | 861 | 1048 | 730 | 4.0 | 4.8 | 10.6 | 2.2 | 68% | 9% | 93.9 | 30 | 28 | 42 | 34% | 67% | 21% | 0 | 17 | | | 80 | 1.05 | -6.5 | 70 | 80 | -$6 |
| 1st Half | 0 | 1 | 14 | 16 | 4.50 | 4.07 | 1.64 | 1032 | 1341 | 802 | 4.6 | 3.2 | 10.3 | 3.2 | 64% | 10% | 93.8 | 34 | 24 | 42 | 36% | 89% | 31% | 0 | 19 | | | 50 | 0.98 | -0.6 | 111 | 127 | -$7 |
| 2nd Half | 0 | 3 | 12 | 15 | 8.03 | 4.89 | 1.54 | 662 | 675 | 650 | 3.5 | 6.6 | 10.9 | 1.7 | 71% | 8% | 94.1 | 26 | 32 | 42 | 31% | 44% | 8% | 0 | 15 | | | 100 | 1.11 | -5.9 | 24 | 27 | -$5 |
| 19 Proj | 3 | 2 | 58 | 54 | 3.82 | 3.82 | 1.27 | 744 | 732 | 752 | 6.0 | 2.6 | 8.4 | 3.3 | 66% | 11% | 93.4 | 41 | 20 | 39 | 31% | 75% | 12% | 0 | | | | | | 2.3 | 101 | 117 | $1 |

## Syndergaard,Noah

| | | | | | |
|---|---|---|---|---|---|
| Age: 26 | Th: R | Role SP | Health F | LIMA Plan C+ | |
| Ht: 6' 6" | Wt: 240 | Type Pwr GB | PT/Exp B | Rand Var 0 | |
| | | | Consist A | MM 5303 | |

Missed 7 weeks with strained finger in 1st half. Delivered very good ERA/WHIP, but Dom and Ctl/FpK were off peak. With his injury history, 2nd half fade in Ctl/Dom should be concerning. However, GB%, SwK, and velocity remained and FpK actually improved. Good health is the only barrier to another ace-level season.

| Yr Tm | W | Sv | IP | K | ERA | xERA | WHIP | oOPS | vL | vR | BF/G | Ctl | Dom | Cmd | FpK | SwK | Vel | G | L | F | H% | S% | hr/f | GS | APC | DOM% | DIS% | Sv% | LI | RAR | BPV | BPX | R$ |
|---|---|---|---|---|---|---|---|---|---|---|---|---|---|---|---|---|---|---|---|---|---|---|---|---|---|---|---|---|---|---|---|---|---|
| 14 aaa | 9 | 0 | 133 | 129 | 3.62 | 3.88 | 1.33 | | | | 21.2 | 2.3 | 8.7 | 3.7 | | | | | | | 35% | 73% | | | | | | | | 2.0 | 114 | 136 | $3 |
| 15 NYM * | 12 | 0 | 180 | 195 | 2.99 | 2.87 | 1.03 | 645 | 691 | 601 | 23.8 | 1.9 | 9.8 | 5.1 | 64% | 13% | 97.1 | 46 | 20 | 34 | 29% | 76% | 14% | 24 | 99 | 42% | 17% | | | 21.5 | 145 | 173 | $23 |
| 16 NYM | 14 | 0 | 184 | 218 | 2.60 | 2.89 | 1.15 | 639 | 713 | 581 | 24.0 | 2.1 | 10.7 | 5.1 | 64% | 15% | 98.0 | 51 | 22 | 27 | 34% | 79% | 9% | 30 | 95 | 50% | 10% | 0 | 0.78 | 36.1 | 164 | 195 | $25 |
| 17 NYM | 1 | 0 | 30 | 34 | 2.97 | 2.75 | 1.05 | 573 | 493 | 656 | 17.7 | 0.9 | 10.1 | 11.3 | 56% | 14% | 98.3 | 58 | 19 | 24 | 36% | 69% | 0% | 7 | 66 | 43% | 29% | | | 5.2 | 194 | 232 | $0 |
| 18 NYM | 13 | 0 | 154 | 155 | 3.03 | 3.40 | 1.21 | 651 | 659 | 641 | 25.8 | 2.3 | 9.0 | 4.0 | 59% | 14% | 97.4 | 49 | 24 | 27 | 33% | 76% | 8% | 25 | 96 | 36% | 16% | | | 21.3 | 128 | 148 | $16 |
| 1st Half | 4 | 0 | 65 | 76 | 3.06 | 3.00 | 1.18 | 663 | 703 | 624 | 24.5 | 1.8 | 10.6 | 5.8 | 55% | 15% | 97.4 | 48 | 25 | 28 | 35% | 76% | 10% | 11 | 95 | 27% | 9% | | | 8.7 | 167 | 192 | $10 |
| 2nd Half | 9 | 0 | 90 | 79 | 3.01 | 3.72 | 1.24 | 642 | 631 | 656 | 26.8 | 2.6 | 7.9 | 3.0 | 62% | 13% | 97.4 | 50 | 24 | 26 | 32% | 76% | 6% | 14 | 98 | 43% | 21% | | | 12.6 | 100 | 115 | $21 |
| 19 Proj | 14 | 0 | 167 | 177 | 2.98 | 2.95 | 1.17 | 652 | 648 | 657 | 22.0 | 2.0 | 9.5 | 4.8 | 60% | 14% | 97.7 | 51 | 22 | 27 | 33% | 76% | 10% | 30 | | | | | | 26.2 | 147 | 169 | $20 |

## Taillon,Jameson

| | | | | | |
|---|---|---|---|---|---|
| Age: 27 | Th: R | Role SP | Health C | LIMA Plan C+ | |
| Ht: 6' 5" | Wt: 230 | Type Pwr | PT/Exp B | Rand Var 0 | |
| | | | Consist B | MM 3205 | |

Finally healthy, delivered a full season of ERA and WHIP goodness. FpK supports excellent Ctl, including in-season bump. Debuted brand new slider mid-season and got more SwK; Dom rise could follow. Elevated 2nd half S% drove ERA/xERA split, but even so the pieces are here to repeat ERA and deliver on UP: 200 K

| Yr Tm | W | Sv | IP | K | ERA | xERA | WHIP | oOPS | vL | vR | BF/G | Ctl | Dom | Cmd | FpK | SwK | Vel | G | L | F | H% | S% | hr/f | GS | APC | DOM% | DIS% | Sv% | LI | RAR | BPV | BPX | R$ |
|---|---|---|---|---|---|---|---|---|---|---|---|---|---|---|---|---|---|---|---|---|---|---|---|---|---|---|---|---|---|---|---|---|---|
| 14 | | | | | | | | | | | | | | | | | | | | | | | | | | | | | | | | | |
| 15 | | | | | | | | | | | | | | | | | | | | | | | | | | | | | | | | | |
| 16 PIT * | 9 | 0 | 166 | 133 | 3.25 | 3.21 | 1.09 | 702 | 731 | 671 | 23.1 | 1.3 | 7.2 | 5.5 | 62% | 9% | 94.3 | 52 | 20 | 27 | 30% | 73% | 15% | 18 | 86 | 11% | 28% | | | 19.3 | 139 | 165 | $16 |
| 17 PIT | 8 | 0 | 134 | 125 | 4.44 | 4.11 | 1.48 | 789 | 833 | 751 | 23.5 | 3.1 | 8.4 | 2.7 | 62% | 9% | 95.3 | 47 | 25 | 28 | 36% | 71% | 10% | 25 | 93 | 16% | 32% | | | -1.4 | 93 | 112 | $0 |
| 18 PIT | 14 | 0 | 191 | 179 | 3.20 | 3.66 | 1.18 | 681 | 737 | 617 | 24.5 | 2.2 | 8.4 | 3.9 | 64% | 11% | 95.2 | 46 | 22 | 31 | 31% | 77% | 12% | 32 | 93 | 25% | 16% | | | 22.3 | 117 | 135 | $19 |
| 1st Half | 5 | 0 | 89 | 83 | 3.96 | 3.77 | 1.22 | 689 | 775 | 609 | 23.2 | 2.5 | 8.4 | 3.3 | 62% | 10% | 95.2 | 50 | 17 | 32 | 30% | 70% | 12% | 16 | 89 | 25% | 19% | | | 2.1 | 112 | 128 | $7 |
| 2nd Half | 9 | 0 | 102 | 96 | 2.55 | 3.56 | 1.14 | 674 | 708 | 627 | 25.9 | 1.8 | 8.4 | 4.6 | 65% | 12% | 95.2 | 43 | 27 | 31 | 31% | 82% | 11% | 16 | 96 | 25% | 13% | | | 20.2 | 123 | 141 | $29 |
| 19 Proj | 13 | 0 | 196 | 182 | 3.60 | 3.47 | 1.27 | 722 | 765 | 678 | 23.5 | 2.3 | 8.4 | 3.6 | 63% | 10% | 95.1 | 47 | 23 | 29 | 32% | 74% | 12% | 34 | | | | | | 15.3 | 113 | 130 | $14 |

## Tanaka,Masahiro

| | | | | | |
|---|---|---|---|---|---|
| Age: 30 | Th: R | Role SP | Health D | LIMA Plan B | |
| Ht: 6' 3" | Wt: 215 | Type Pwr | PT/Exp A | Rand Var +3 | |
| | | | Consist A | MM 4303 | |

A month lost to a hamstring injury ensures yet another D health grade, but he consistently delivers excellent xERA and solid IP. After ugly 1st half S%, hr/f gave way to normalization, ERA sparkled. "Homer prone" label is a red herring; G/F remains excellent. As ever, with health this is a nigh-ace.

| Yr Tm | W | Sv | IP | K | ERA | xERA | WHIP | oOPS | vL | vR | BF/G | Ctl | Dom | Cmd | FpK | SwK | Vel | G | L | F | H% | S% | hr/f | GS | APC | DOM% | DIS% | Sv% | LI | RAR | BPV | BPX | R$ |
|---|---|---|---|---|---|---|---|---|---|---|---|---|---|---|---|---|---|---|---|---|---|---|---|---|---|---|---|---|---|---|---|---|---|
| 14 NYY | 13 | 0 | 136 | 141 | 2.77 | 2.76 | 1.06 | 657 | 632 | 687 | 27.1 | 1.4 | 9.3 | 6.7 | 62% | 14% | 91.2 | 47 | 24 | 29 | 31% | 79% | 14% | 20 | 100 | 50% | 5% | | | 16.3 | 155 | 185 | $16 |
| 15 NYY | 12 | 0 | 154 | 139 | 3.51 | 3.34 | 0.99 | 674 | 697 | 654 | 25.4 | 1.6 | 8.1 | 5.1 | 63% | 12% | 91.8 | 47 | 19 | 34 | 25% | 73% | 17% | 24 | 95 | 50% | 21% | | | 8.6 | 129 | 153 | $17 |
| 16 NYY | 14 | 0 | 200 | 165 | 3.07 | 3.69 | 1.08 | 645 | 655 | 635 | 26.0 | 1.6 | 7.4 | 4.6 | 64% | 11% | 90.6 | 48 | 21 | 31 | 28% | 76% | 12% | 31 | 95 | 35% | 16% | | | 27.7 | 116 | 138 | $24 |
| 17 NYY | 13 | 0 | 178 | 194 | 4.74 | 3.53 | 1.24 | 771 | 746 | 790 | 25.1 | 2.1 | 9.8 | 4.7 | 64% | 15% | 92.2 | 49 | 18 | 33 | 32% | 68% | 21% | 30 | 94 | 30% | 23% | | | -8.5 | 147 | 177 | $9 |
| 18 NYY | 12 | 0 | 156 | 159 | 3.75 | 3.44 | 1.13 | 711 | 653 | 758 | 23.5 | 2.0 | 9.2 | 4.5 | 68% | 14% | 91.7 | 47 | 20 | 33 | 29% | 74% | 18% | 27 | 89 | 37% | 33% | | | 7.7 | 136 | 156 | $14 |
| 1st Half | 7 | 0 | 73 | 73 | 4.58 | 3.68 | 1.09 | 724 | 692 | 745 | 22.6 | 2.4 | 9.0 | 3.8 | 67% | 15% | 91.8 | 45 | 16 | 39 | 25% | 67% | 21% | 13 | 86 | 23% | 38% | | | -3.9 | 122 | 140 | $8 |
| 2nd Half | 5 | 0 | 83 | 86 | 3.02 | 3.23 | 1.16 | 701 | 624 | 771 | 24.4 | 1.7 | 9.3 | 5.4 | 69% | 14% | 91.7 | 49 | 22 | 28 | 33% | 78% | 14% | 14 | 92 | 50% | 29% | | | 11.6 | 148 | 170 | $18 |
| 19 Proj | 13 | 0 | 174 | 175 | 3.58 | 3.21 | 1.15 | 700 | 665 | 730 | 23.8 | 2.0 | 9.0 | 4.5 | 66% | 14% | 91.7 | 48 | 20 | 32 | 30% | 74% | 16% | 29 | | | | | | 20.2 | 134 | 155 | $17 |

## Teheran,Julio

| | | | | | |
|---|---|---|---|---|---|
| Age: 28 | Th: R | Role SP | Health B | LIMA Plan C+ | |
| Ht: 6' 2" | Wt: 205 | Type Pwr FB | PT/Exp A | Rand Var -2 | |
| | | | Consist B | MM 1203 | |

On the surface, a passable year with 2nd half improvements. Underneath, both Cmd vL (1.0) and velocity fell to career worsts. Only tiny H% kept ERA, WHIP usable, which delivered most of his value. BPX shows clearly he's a below-average pitcher with skills heading in the wrong direction.

| Yr Tm | W | Sv | IP | K | ERA | xERA | WHIP | oOPS | vL | vR | BF/G | Ctl | Dom | Cmd | FpK | SwK | Vel | G | L | F | H% | S% | hr/f | GS | APC | DOM% | DIS% | Sv% | LI | RAR | BPV | BPX | R$ |
|---|---|---|---|---|---|---|---|---|---|---|---|---|---|---|---|---|---|---|---|---|---|---|---|---|---|---|---|---|---|---|---|---|---|
| 14 ATL | 14 | 0 | 221 | 186 | 2.89 | 3.73 | 1.08 | 639 | 687 | 587 | 26.8 | 2.1 | 7.6 | 3.6 | 60% | 11% | 90.4 | 35 | 21 | 44 | 28% | 77% | 8% | 33 | 99 | 55% | 21% | | | 23.2 | 93 | 111 | $22 |
| 15 ATL | 11 | 0 | 201 | 171 | 4.04 | 4.15 | 1.31 | 737 | 893 | 583 | 25.5 | 3.3 | 7.7 | 2.3 | 57% | 11% | 91.2 | 40 | 24 | 36 | 29% | 73% | 13% | 33 | 99 | 36% | 27% | | | -1.9 | 68 | 81 | $6 |
| 16 ATL | 7 | 0 | 188 | 167 | 3.21 | 4.01 | 1.05 | 650 | 756 | 564 | 25.3 | 2.0 | 8.0 | 4.1 | 62% | 11% | 90.9 | 39 | 19 | 42 | 27% | 74% | 10% | 30 | 99 | 43% | 23% | | | 22.8 | 108 | 128 | $20 |
| 17 ATL | 11 | 0 | 188 | 151 | 4.49 | 4.94 | 1.37 | 772 | 787 | 753 | 25.4 | 3.4 | 7.2 | 2.1 | 64% | 10% | 91.4 | 40 | 20 | 40 | 29% | 72% | 14% | 32 | 96 | 19% | 34% | | | -3.1 | 55 | 66 | $4 |
| 18 ATL | 9 | 0 | 176 | 162 | 3.94 | 4.52 | 1.17 | 672 | 723 | 620 | 23.4 | 4.3 | 8.3 | 1.9 | 61% | 12% | 89.8 | 38 | 20 | 42 | 22% | 72% | 13% | 31 | 90 | 29% | 35% | | | 4.4 | 49 | 57 | $10 |
| 1st Half | 6 | 0 | 88 | 77 | 4.21 | 4.65 | 1.21 | 722 | 786 | 660 | 22.7 | 4.2 | 7.9 | 1.9 | 63% | 11% | 89.6 | 39 | 19 | 43 | 23% | 71% | 15% | 16 | 89 | 25% | 50% | | | -0.6 | 45 | 52 | $8 |
| 2nd Half | 3 | 0 | 88 | 85 | 3.68 | 4.39 | 1.14 | 622 | 660 | 577 | 24.1 | 4.4 | 8.7 | 2.0 | 59% | 13% | 90.0 | 37 | 22 | 42 | 22% | 72% | 12% | 15 | 92 | 33% | 20% | | | 5.1 | 53 | 61 | $13 |
| 19 Proj | 9 | 0 | 174 | 154 | 4.31 | 4.25 | 1.31 | 750 | 805 | 693 | 24.3 | 3.6 | 8.0 | 2.2 | 61% | 11% | 90.5 | 38 | 20 | 41 | 28% | 71% | 13% | 30 | | | | | | -1.9 | 63 | 72 | $4 |

ARIK FLORIMONTE

## Tepera,Ryan

| Tepera,Ryan | | | | Health | B | LIMA Plan | B+ |
|---|---|---|---|---|---|---|---|
| Age: 31 | Th: R | Role | RP | PT/Exp | C | Rand Var | 0 |
| Ht: 6' 2" | Wt: 195 | Type | Pwr | Consist | A | MM | 2310 |

Built on 2017 success with elite 1st half skills (Dom, Cmd, SwK), but late-June elbow injury hung over rest of season. Mid-season fastball performance slid as velocity dropped and Cmd tanked. Strength vR and emerging K/9 establish foundation. If elbow drove 2nd half dip, then full health still offers LIMA upside.

| Yr | Tm | W | Sv | IP | K | ERA | xERA | WHIP | oOPS | vL | vR | BF/G | Ctl | Dom | Cmd | FpK | SwK | Vel | G | L | F | H% | S% | hr/f | GS | APC | DOM% | DIS% | Sv% | LI | RAR | BPV | BPX | R$ |
|---|---|---|---|---|---|---|---|---|---|---|---|---|---|---|---|---|---|---|---|---|---|---|---|---|---|---|---|---|---|---|---|---|---|---|
| 14 | aaa | 7 | 2 | 64 | 54 | 5.11 | 5.90 | 1.76 | | | | 5.7 | 3.8 | 7.6 | 2.0 | | | | | | | 39% | 71% | | | | | | | | -10.8 | 55 | 66 | -$6 |
| 15 | TOR * | 3 | 4 | 67 | 51 | 2.45 | 2.69 | 1.00 | 670 | 568 | 746 | 4.8 | 2.9 | 6.8 | 2.3 | 64% | 10% | 95.0 | 45 | 16 | 38 | 21% | 85% | 22% | 0 | 15 | | | 80 | 0.50 | 12.5 | 68 | 81 | $8 |
| 16 | TOR * | 1 | 18 | 64 | 54 | 3.92 | 4.32 | 1.46 | 635 | 679 | 598 | 4.8 | 4.0 | 7.6 | 1.9 | 45% | 14% | 95.2 | 58 | 15 | 26 | 32% | 75% | 7% | 0 | 15 | | | 95 | 0.67 | 2.1 | 63 | 75 | $4 |
| 17 | TOR | 7 | 2 | 78 | 81 | 3.59 | 4.05 | 1.13 | 633 | 715 | 581 | 4.4 | 3.6 | 9.4 | 2.6 | 62% | 13% | 95.0 | 42 | 18 | 41 | 27% | 70% | 9% | 0 | 17 | | | 50 | 1.00 | 7.3 | 92 | 110 | $7 |
| 18 | TOR | 5 | 7 | 65 | 68 | 3.62 | 3.81 | 1.22 | 738 | 806 | 691 | 3.9 | 3.3 | 9.5 | 2.8 | 59% | 14% | 94.9 | 44 | 17 | 39 | 29% | 76% | 14% | 0 | 15 | | | 47 | 1.29 | 4.2 | 102 | 118 | $5 |
| 1st Half | | 5 | 6 | 39 | 43 | 2.97 | 3.45 | 1.19 | 730 | 744 | 722 | 4.1 | 2.7 | 9.8 | 3.6 | 61% | 15% | 95.3 | 47 | 15 | 37 | 31% | 81% | 14% | 0 | 17 | | | 55 | 1.24 | 5.7 | 128 | 148 | $10 |
| 2nd Half | | 0 | 1 | 25 | 25 | 4.62 | 4.40 | 1.26 | 749 | 893 | 638 | 3.6 | 4.3 | 8.9 | 2.1 | 56% | 14% | 94.2 | 39 | 19 | 42 | 26% | 68% | 14% | 0 | 13 | | | 25 | 1.36 | -1.5 | 62 | 71 | -$4 |
| 19 | Proj | 4 | 9 | 65 | 67 | 3.85 | 3.82 | 1.26 | 723 | 785 | 679 | 4.1 | 3.7 | 9.3 | 2.5 | 60% | 13% | 94.8 | 43 | 18 | 40 | 29% | 73% | 12% | 0 | | | | | | 2.5 | 88 | 102 | $5 |

## Tomlin,Josh

| Tomlin,Josh | | | | Health | F | LIMA Plan | C |
|---|---|---|---|---|---|---|---|
| Age: 34 | Th: R | Role | RP | PT/Exp | B | Rand Var | +4 |
| Ht: 6' 1" | Wt: 190 | Type | Con FB | Consist | B | MM | 1001 |

Teetering skills finally crashed as poor Dom sunk further and perennial HR issues exploded thanks to flyball surge. Good Ctl can only cover so much when you don't do anything else well. Always a marginal profile and now he's a 34-year old with a near-5.00 ERA since 2016 who doesn't miss bats. Run!

| Yr | Tm | W | Sv | IP | K | ERA | xERA | WHIP | oOPS | vL | vR | BF/G | Ctl | Dom | Cmd | FpK | SwK | Vel | G | L | F | H% | S% | hr/f | GS | APC | DOM% | DIS% | Sv% | LI | RAR | BPV | BPX | R$ |
|---|---|---|---|---|---|---|---|---|---|---|---|---|---|---|---|---|---|---|---|---|---|---|---|---|---|---|---|---|---|---|---|---|---|---|
| 14 | CLE * | 8 | 0 | 144 | 119 | 4.24 | 4.54 | 1.24 | 781 | 718 | 848 | 18.8 | 1.6 | 7.4 | 4.8 | 68% | 10% | 89.0 | 37 | 27 | 36 | 31% | 71% | 15% | 16 | 69 | 13% | 38% | 0 | 0.94 | -8.9 | 100 | 119 | $2 |
| 15 | CLE * | 8 | 0 | 90 | 71 | 3.79 | 4.11 | 1.08 | 642 | 448 | 838 | 23.3 | 1.0 | 7.1 | 6.8 | 66% | 10% | 88.4 | 38 | 16 | 46 | 28% | 74% | 15% | 10 | 95 | 50% | 10% | | | 1.9 | 136 | 162 | $6 |
| 16 | CLE | 13 | 0 | 174 | 118 | 4.40 | 4.25 | 1.19 | 778 | 685 | 845 | 24.2 | 1.0 | 6.1 | 5.9 | 68% | 8% | 87.7 | 44 | 21 | 35 | 29% | 71% | 18% | 29 | 87 | 17% | 28% | 0 | 0.74 | -4.4 | 104 | 123 | $8 |
| 17 | CLE | 10 | 0 | 141 | 109 | 4.98 | 4.23 | 1.28 | 807 | 826 | 794 | 22.5 | 0.9 | 7.0 | 7.8 | 69% | 9% | 87.7 | 40 | 23 | 37 | 33% | 65% | 14% | 26 | 80 | 23% | 31% | | | -10.8 | 119 | 143 | $2 |
| 18 | CLE | 2 | 0 | 70 | 46 | 6.14 | 5.42 | 1.48 | 947 | 1125 | 801 | 10.0 | 1.5 | 5.9 | 3.8 | 63% | 9% | 87.8 | 31 | 24 | 45 | 31% | 71% | 21% | 9 | 37 | 0% | 78% | 0 | 0.55 | -17.3 | 73 | 85 | -$10 |
| 1st Half | | 0 | 0 | 45 | 27 | 6.60 | 5.71 | 1.47 | 986 | 1126 | 883 | 10.8 | 1.8 | 5.4 | 3.0 | 62% | 9% | 87.2 | 30 | 23 | 47 | 28% | 70% | 24% | 6 | 39 | 0% | 83% | 0 | 0.42 | -13.6 | 57 | 65 | -$14 |
| 2nd Half | | 2 | 0 | 25 | 19 | 5.33 | 4.91 | 1.50 | 880 | 1124 | 638 | 8.8 | 1.1 | 6.8 | 6.3 | 64% | 9% | 88.8 | 32 | 26 | 42 | 36% | 72% | 16% | 3 | 33 | 0% | 67% | 0 | 0.74 | -3.7 | 103 | 118 | -$3 |
| 19 | Proj | 5 | 0 | 87 | 61 | 5.23 | 4.39 | 1.38 | 861 | 951 | 786 | 12.7 | 1.4 | 6.3 | 4.5 | 65% | 9% | 88.0 | 34 | 24 | 43 | 32% | 70% | 17% | 11 | | | | | | -11.5 | 87 | 100 | -$5 |

## Toussaint,Touki

| Toussaint,Touki | | | | Health | A | LIMA Plan | B+ |
|---|---|---|---|---|---|---|---|
| Age: 23 | Th: R | Role | SP | PT/Exp | D | Rand Var | 0 |
| Ht: 6' 3" | Wt: 185 | Type | Pwr | Consist | C | MM | 2301 |

2-1, 4.03 ERA in 29 IP at ATL. Top prospect flashed electric stuff with 9.9 Dom and 25% H% in MiLB. But he left his career-best 3.5 Ctl behind upon promotion; issued 21 BB in his MLB sample. Walks will breed volatility, but three useful pitches, a GB lean, and consistent ability to miss bats make him a worthy rookie gamble.

| Yr | Tm | W | Sv | IP | K | ERA | xERA | WHIP | oOPS | vL | vR | BF/G | Ctl | Dom | Cmd | FpK | SwK | Vel | G | L | F | H% | S% | hr/f | GS | APC | DOM% | DIS% | Sv% | LI | RAR | BPV | BPX | R$ |
|---|---|---|---|---|---|---|---|---|---|---|---|---|---|---|---|---|---|---|---|---|---|---|---|---|---|---|---|---|---|---|---|---|---|---|
| 14 | | | | | | | | | | | | | | | | | | | | | | | | | | | | | | | | | | |
| 15 | | | | | | | | | | | | | | | | | | | | | | | | | | | | | | | | | | |
| 16 | | | | | | | | | | | | | | | | | | | | | | | | | | | | | | | | | | |
| 17 | aa | 3 | 0 | 40 | 38 | 4.42 | 4.19 | 1.48 | | | | 24.4 | 5.1 | 8.6 | 1.7 | | | | | | | 31% | 72% | | | | | | | | -0.3 | 67 | 81 | -$3 |
| 18 | ATL * | 11 | 0 | 166 | 171 | 3.14 | 2.99 | 1.25 | 619 | 511 | 699 | 21.8 | 3.9 | 9.3 | 2.4 | 52% | 10% | 93.2 | 48 | 28 | 24 | 30% | 75% | 6% | 5 | 68 | 20% | 0% | 0 | 0.67 | 20.8 | 101 | 117 | $14 |
| 1st Half | | 4 | 0 | 86 | 91 | 3.87 | 3.88 | 1.33 | | | | 22.3 | 3.7 | 9.6 | 2.6 | | | | | | | 32% | 73% | 0% | 0 | | | | | | 3.0 | 91 | 104 | $7 |
| 2nd Half | | 7 | 0 | 80 | 80 | 2.58 | 2.28 | 1.20 | 619 | 511 | 699 | 21.5 | 4.2 | 9.0 | 2.1 | 52% | 10% | 93.2 | 48 | 28 | 24 | 28% | 77% | 6% | 5 | 68 | 20% | 0% | 0 | 0.67 | 15.5 | 109 | 125 | $22 |
| 19 | Proj | 6 | 0 | 87 | 89 | 3.80 | 3.98 | 1.35 | 684 | 521 | 804 | 22.8 | 4.4 | 9.2 | 2.1 | 52% | 10% | 93.2 | 44 | 23 | 33 | 31% | 72% | 7% | 16 | | | | | | 3.7 | 69 | 79 | $2 |

## Treinen,Blake

| Treinen,Blake | | | | Health | A | LIMA Plan | D+ |
|---|---|---|---|---|---|---|---|
| Age: 31 | Th: R | Role | RP | PT/Exp | B | Rand Var | -5 |
| Ht: 6' 5" | Wt: 225 | Type | Pwr xGB | Consist | B | MM | 5431 |

Strong 2nd half from 2017 led into brilliant breakout season as everything came together with career-bests in several categories. His GB dominance returned in 2nd half, too. FpK says be a little careful about Ctl gains, but SwK fully backs Dom and rest of skills scream top-shelf closer even with an ERA pushback.

| Yr | Tm | W | Sv | IP | K | ERA | xERA | WHIP | oOPS | vL | vR | BF/G | Ctl | Dom | Cmd | FpK | SwK | Vel | G | L | F | H% | S% | hr/f | GS | APC | DOM% | DIS% | Sv% | LI | RAR | BPV | BPX | R$ |
|---|---|---|---|---|---|---|---|---|---|---|---|---|---|---|---|---|---|---|---|---|---|---|---|---|---|---|---|---|---|---|---|---|---|---|
| 14 | WAS * | 10 | 0 | 131 | 79 | 3.46 | 4.10 | 1.40 | 678 | 798 | 564 | 17.9 | 2.3 | 5.4 | 2.4 | 57% | 8% | 94.8 | 59 | 22 | 19 | 33% | 75% | 3% | 7 | 49 | 0% | 43% | 0 | 0.56 | 4.5 | 69 | 82 | $1 |
| 15 | WAS | 2 | 0 | 68 | 65 | 3.86 | 3.25 | 1.39 | 692 | 934 | 493 | 4.7 | 4.3 | 8.6 | 2.0 | 59% | 11% | 96.3 | 62 | 23 | 15 | 32% | 72% | 15% | 0 | 17 | | | 0 | 0.93 | 0.9 | 81 | 96 | -$2 |
| 16 | WAS | 4 | 1 | 67 | 63 | 2.28 | 3.24 | 1.22 | 648 | 737 | 600 | 3.6 | 4.2 | 8.5 | 2.0 | 57% | 11% | 95.4 | 66 | 14 | 20 | 27% | 84% | 15% | 0 | 14 | | | 33 | 1.23 | 15.8 | 84 | 100 | $6 |
| 17 | 2 TM | 3 | 16 | 76 | 74 | 3.93 | 3.53 | 1.39 | 736 | 875 | 622 | 4.5 | 3.0 | 8.8 | 3.0 | 59% | 13% | 97.2 | 58 | 19 | 23 | 35% | 73% | 12% | 0 | 17 | | | 76 | 1.30 | 4.0 | 114 | 137 | $7 |
| 18 | OAK | 9 | 38 | 80 | 100 | 0.78 | 2.61 | 0.83 | 417 | 462 | 372 | 4.6 | 2.4 | 11.2 | 4.8 | 55% | 19% | 97.4 | 52 | 24 | 24 | 26% | 92% | 4% | 0 | 17 | | | 88 | 1.60 | 33.4 | 168 | 194 | $36 |
| 1st Half | | 4 | 21 | 41 | 49 | 0.89 | 2.97 | 0.91 | 454 | 534 | 382 | 4.9 | 2.7 | 10.8 | 4.1 | 55% | 19% | 97.2 | 47 | 24 | 29 | 27% | 92% | 4% | 0 | 18 | | | 91 | 1.80 | 16.4 | 149 | 171 | $35 |
| 2nd Half | | 5 | 17 | 40 | 51 | 0.68 | 2.25 | 0.76 | 377 | 392 | 360 | 4.4 | 2.0 | 11.6 | 5.7 | 55% | 18% | 97.7 | 57 | 25 | 18 | 25% | 93% | 6% | 0 | 16 | | | 85 | 1.41 | 17.0 | 188 | 216 | $36 |
| 19 | Proj | 6 | 35 | 73 | 81 | 2.44 | 2.79 | 1.08 | 559 | 633 | 495 | 4.4 | 2.8 | 10.1 | 3.5 | 57% | 15% | 96.9 | 55 | 21 | 24 | 30% | 78% | 8% | 0 | | | | | | 13.6 | 137 | 158 | $23 |

## Trivino,Lou

| Trivino,Lou | | | | Health | A | LIMA Plan | B+ |
|---|---|---|---|---|---|---|---|
| Age: 27 | Th: R | Role | RP | PT/Exp | D | Rand Var | -2 |
| Ht: 6' 5" | Wt: 225 | Type | Pwr | Consist | A | MM | 3410 |

LIMA stud emerged out of nowhere as fantastic cutter spurred a great debut. Couldn't ride snazzy H% and S% all year, but 3 disastrous outings totaling 1 IP with 11 ER did most of the damage. Dom held even as 2nd half regression set in. Ctl is the only concern as velocity, a true out pitch, and Ks establish a base.

| Yr | Tm | W | Sv | IP | K | ERA | xERA | WHIP | oOPS | vL | vR | BF/G | Ctl | Dom | Cmd | FpK | SwK | Vel | G | L | F | H% | S% | hr/f | GS | APC | DOM% | DIS% | Sv% | LI | RAR | BPV | BPX | R$ |
|---|---|---|---|---|---|---|---|---|---|---|---|---|---|---|---|---|---|---|---|---|---|---|---|---|---|---|---|---|---|---|---|---|---|---|
| 14 | | | | | | | | | | | | | | | | | | | | | | | | | | | | | | | | | | |
| 15 | | | | | | | | | | | | | | | | | | | | | | | | | | | | | | | | | | |
| 16 | aa | 1 | 1 | 18 | 10 | 2.98 | 3.18 | 1.26 | | | | 6.2 | 3.4 | 4.8 | 1.4 | | | | | | | 27% | 77% | | | | | | | | 2.7 | 51 | 60 | -$2 |
| 17 | a/a | 8 | 5 | 68 | 53 | 3.61 | 3.57 | 1.39 | | | | 6.0 | 2.7 | 7.0 | 2.5 | | | | | | | 35% | 71% | | | | | | | | 6.3 | 94 | 113 | $4 |
| 18 | OAK | 8 | 4 | 74 | 82 | 2.92 | 3.50 | 1.14 | 603 | 648 | 565 | 4.3 | 3.8 | 10.0 | 2.6 | 55% | 15% | 97.6 | 47 | 23 | 31 | 26% | 79% | 14% | 1 | 16 | 0% | 0% | 44 | 1.18 | 11.2 | 103 | 118 | $9 |
| 1st Half | | 6 | 3 | 35 | 39 | 1.56 | 3.05 | 0.95 | 509 | 554 | 474 | 4.7 | 3.4 | 10.1 | 3.0 | 55% | 16% | 97.4 | 53 | 22 | 25 | 22% | 90% | 14% | 0 | 17 | | | 75 | 1.34 | 11.1 | 122 | 140 | $16 |
| 2nd Half | | 2 | 1 | 39 | 43 | 4.12 | 3.90 | 1.30 | 682 | 720 | 647 | 4.1 | 4.1 | 9.8 | 2.4 | 55% | 14% | 97.7 | 41 | 23 | 35 | 29% | 72% | 14% | 1 | 16 | 0% | 0% | 20 | 1.06 | 0.2 | 85 | 98 | $3 |
| 19 | Proj | 6 | 4 | 65 | 74 | 3.25 | 3.31 | 1.25 | 641 | 700 | 592 | 4.8 | 3.4 | 10.1 | 3.0 | 55% | 15% | 97.6 | 46 | 23 | 31 | 32% | 75% | 8% | 0 | | | | | | 7.6 | 115 | 132 | $6 |

## Tropeano,Nicholas

| Tropeano,Nicholas | | | | Health | F | LIMA Plan | D+ |
|---|---|---|---|---|---|---|---|
| Age: 28 | Th: R | Role | SP | PT/Exp | D | Rand Var | +1 |
| Ht: 6' 4" | Wt: 200 | Type | Pwr FB | Consist | A | MM | 1201 |

Missed 2017 with Tommy John surgery and then 2018 was marred by three shoulder-related DL stints. The SwK is still there offering some hope, but since 2016, Cmd (2.1) and HR/9 (1.9) have been major issues. With six DL stints and just 203 IP as a major leaguer, he's an easy pass on draft day.

| Yr | Tm | W | Sv | IP | K | ERA | xERA | WHIP | oOPS | vL | vR | BF/G | Ctl | Dom | Cmd | FpK | SwK | Vel | G | L | F | H% | S% | hr/f | GS | APC | DOM% | DIS% | Sv% | LI | RAR | BPV | BPX | R$ |
|---|---|---|---|---|---|---|---|---|---|---|---|---|---|---|---|---|---|---|---|---|---|---|---|---|---|---|---|---|---|---|---|---|---|---|
| 14 | HOU * | 10 | 0 | 146 | 115 | 3.46 | 2.72 | 1.09 | 626 | 648 | 576 | 21.2 | 2.5 | 7.1 | 2.8 | 54% | 9% | 90.4 | 40 | 13 | 46 | 26% | 70% | 0% | 4 | 92 | 0% | 25% | | | 5.1 | 91 | 109 | $10 |
| 15 | LAA * | 6 | 0 | 126 | 118 | 4.46 | 4.57 | 1.48 | 700 | 712 | 686 | 22.5 | 3.1 | 8.5 | 2.7 | 64% | 12% | 91.2 | 39 | 21 | 40 | 36% | 70% | 5% | 7 | 81 | 29% | 0% | 0 | 0.68 | -7.7 | 85 | 102 | -$4 |
| 16 | LAA | 3 | 0 | 68 | 68 | 3.56 | 4.81 | 1.48 | 843 | 885 | 798 | 22.8 | 4.1 | 9.0 | 2.2 | 60% | 13% | 90.9 | 33 | 17 | 49 | 31% | 85% | 15% | 13 | 93 | 8% | 31% | | | 5.3 | 62 | 74 | -$1 |
| 17 | | | | | | | | | | | | | | | | | | | | | | | | | | | | | | | | | | |
| 18 | LAA | 5 | 0 | 76 | 64 | 4.74 | 4.66 | 1.30 | 807 | 831 | 782 | 22.6 | 3.7 | 7.6 | 2.1 | 56% | 12% | 90.4 | 37 | 22 | 41 | 26% | 71% | 18% | 14 | 84 | 29% | 29% | | | -5.5 | 52 | 60 | -$2 |
| 1st Half | | 3 | 0 | 54 | 44 | 4.83 | 4.76 | 1.35 | 806 | 830 | 782 | 22.4 | 3.3 | 7.3 | 2.2 | 54% | 12% | 90.3 | 35 | 21 | 43 | 29% | 69% | 13% | 10 | 86 | 30% | 30% | | | -4.6 | 55 | 63 | -$3 |
| 2nd Half | | 2 | 0 | 22 | 20 | 4.50 | 4.40 | 1.18 | 813 | 836 | 783 | 23.0 | 4.5 | 8.2 | 1.8 | 61% | 13% | 90.6 | 42 | 25 | 33 | 16% | 79% | 35% | 4 | 79 | 25% | 25% | | | -0.9 | 45 | 52 | $0 |
| 19 | Proj | 5 | 0 | 73 | 66 | 4.59 | 4.36 | 1.38 | 807 | 840 | 771 | 22.6 | 3.8 | 8.1 | 2.2 | 60% | 12% | 90.7 | 37 | 21 | 42 | 29% | 73% | 15% | 14 | | | | | | -1.7 | 60 | 69 | -$2 |

## Tuivailala,Sam

| Tuivailala,Sam | | | | Health | D | LIMA Plan | C |
|---|---|---|---|---|---|---|---|
| Age: 26 | Th: R | Role | RP | PT/Exp | D | Rand Var | 0 |
| Ht: 6' 3" | Wt: 225 | Type | Pwr | Consist | D | MM | 2300 |

A mediocre Dom is an automatic disqualifier for LIMA consideration in today's game as it puts everything on the ERA/WHIP. There isn't a lot here outside of his strong vR work and GB tilt. Knee and Achilles injuries ate up some time, too. Reliability grades tell the story here so without GB or Dom surge, it's a pass.

| Yr | Tm | W | Sv | IP | K | ERA | xERA | WHIP | oOPS | vL | vR | BF/G | Ctl | Dom | Cmd | FpK | SwK | Vel | G | L | F | H% | S% | hr/f | GS | APC | DOM% | DIS% | Sv% | LI | RAR | BPV | BPX | R$ |
|---|---|---|---|---|---|---|---|---|---|---|---|---|---|---|---|---|---|---|---|---|---|---|---|---|---|---|---|---|---|---|---|---|---|---|
| 14 | STL * | 2 | 2 | 23 | 29 | 3.98 | 4.59 | 1.52 | 2075 | 2333 | 1914 | 4.8 | 3.9 | 11.2 | 2.8 | 60% | 14% | 96.9 | 0 | 29 | 71 | 39% | 75% | 40% | 0 | 21 | | | 50 | 1.06 | -0.7 | 103 | 122 | -$2 |
| 15 | STL * | 3 | 17 | 60 | 58 | 2.08 | 2.92 | 1.30 | 744 | 699 | 775 | 4.3 | 5.1 | 8.8 | 1.7 | 60% | 12% | 96.4 | 49 | 19 | 32 | 27% | 87% | 17% | 0 | 19 | | | 100 | 1.05 | 13.9 | 85 | 101 | $10 |
| 16 | STL * | 3 | 17 | 56 | 64 | 5.96 | 4.91 | 1.67 | 759 | 741 | 774 | 4.6 | 4.5 | 10.4 | 2.3 | 57% | 6% | 95.8 | 44 | 25 | 31 | 40% | 62% | 0% | 0 | 18 | | | 74 | 0.10 | -12.1 | 93 | 111 | -$1 |
| 17 | STL * | 4 | 6 | 64 | 51 | 2.21 | 2.65 | 1.01 | 626 | 693 | 589 | 4.4 | 2.0 | 7.2 | 3.6 | 64% | 10% | 95.4 | 49 | 20 | 32 | 26% | 84% | 10% | 0 | 17 | | | 100 | 0.43 | 16.8 | 104 | 125 | $10 |
| 18 | 2 TM | 4 | 0 | 37 | 30 | 3.41 | 4.25 | 1.43 | 743 | 1050 | 528 | 4.6 | 2.9 | 7.3 | 2.5 | 59% | 10% | 95.2 | 49 | 24 | 27 | 34% | 78% | 9% | 0 | 18 | | | 0 | 0.77 | 3.4 | 80 | 92 | -$2 |
| 1st Half | | 1 | 0 | 24 | 21 | 3.33 | 4.36 | 1.44 | 729 | 1070 | 454 | 4.5 | 3.3 | 7.8 | 2.3 | 60% | 9% | 95.0 | 47 | 23 | 31 | 34% | 79% | 9% | 0 | 17 | | | 0 | 0.79 | 2.5 | 75 | 86 | -$3 |
| 2nd Half | | 3 | 0 | 13 | 9 | 3.55 | 4.04 | 1.42 | 767 | 1006 | 642 | 4.8 | 2.1 | 6.4 | 3.0 | 58% | 12% | 95.6 | 53 | 26 | 21 | 34% | 76% | 11% | 0 | 18 | | | 0 | 0.74 | 0.9 | 89 | 102 | $1 |
| 19 | Proj | 2 | 0 | 44 | 42 | 3.96 | 3.86 | 1.41 | 705 | 960 | 523 | 4.4 | 3.7 | 8.7 | 2.3 | 62% | 10% | 95.1 | 48 | 21 | 31 | 33% | 73% | 8% | 0 | | | | | | 1.5 | 81 | 93 | -$3 |

PAUL SPORER

## Turnbull,Spencer

| | | | | | |
|---|---|---|---|---|---|
| Age: 26 | Th: R | Role SP | Health | A | LIMA Plan C |
| Ht: 6' 3" | Wt: 215 | Type Pwr GB | PT/Exp | F | Rand Var +5 |
| | | | Consist | C | MM 2201 |

0-2, 6.06 ERA in 16 IP at DET. Strong 2.9 Cmd across four minor-league levels actually improved to 3.8 in brief MLB sample, but a 50% S% sunk any chance of success. His useful 4-pitch mix along with a career 8.5 MiLB Dom give him the elements of something to build on. Monitor for progress in deep leagues.

| Yr Tm | W | Sv | IP | K | ERA | xERA | WHIP | oOPS | vL | vR | BF/G | Ctl | Dom | Cmd | FpK | SwK | Vel | G | L | F | H% | S% | hr/f | GS | APC | DOM% | DIS% | Sv% | LI | RAR | BPV | BPX | R$ |
|---|---|---|---|---|---|---|---|---|---|---|---|---|---|---|---|---|---|---|---|---|---|---|---|---|---|---|---|---|---|---|---|---|---|
| 14 | | | | | | | | | | | | | | | | | | | | | | | | | | | | | | | | | |
| 15 | | | | | | | | | | | | | | | | | | | | | | | | | | | | | | | | | |
| 16 | | | | | | | | | | | | | | | | | | | | | | | | | | | | | | | | | |
| 17 aa | 0 | 0 | 20 | 17 | 8.28 | 5.72 | 1.76 | | | | 23.3 | 3.8 | 7.6 | 2.0 | | | | | | | 39% | 49% | | | | | | | | -9.8 | 62 | 74 | -$9 |
| 18 DET * | 5 | 0 | 131 | 110 | 5.76 | 4.43 | 1.50 | 658 | 649 | 670 | 22.6 | 3.6 | 7.5 | 2.1 | 64% | 10% | 94.1 | 46 | 28 | 26 | 35% | 59% | 8% | 3 | 71 | 0% | 33% | 0 | 0.89 | -25.9 | 76 | 87 | -$12 |
| 1st Half | 4 | 0 | 68 | 60 | 5.69 | 4.53 | 1.63 | | | | 23.3 | 4.0 | 8.0 | 2.0 | | | | | | | 38% | 61% | 0% | 0 | | | | | | -12.9 | 85 | 98 | -$15 |
| 2nd Half | 1 | 0 | 63 | 49 | 5.59 | 4.15 | 1.34 | 658 | 649 | 670 | 21.7 | 3.0 | 7.1 | 2.4 | 64% | 10% | 94.1 | 46 | 28 | 26 | 31% | 58% | 8% | 3 | 71 | 0% | 33% | 0 | 0.89 | -11.1 | 69 | 79 | -$9 |
| **19 Proj** | **5** | **0** | **116** | **99** | **4.40** | **4.00** | **1.40** | **626** | **600** | **658** | **22.1** | **3.6** | **7.7** | **2.2** | **64%** | **10%** | **94.1** | **46** | **28** | **26** | **32%** | **69%** | **10%** | **22** | | | | | | **-3.5** | **67** | **77** | **-$2** |

## Urena,Jose

| | | | | | |
|---|---|---|---|---|---|
| Age: 27 | Th: R | Role SP | Health | B | LIMA Plan C+ |
| Ht: 6' 2" | Wt: 200 | Type | PT/Exp | B | Rand Var 0 |
| | | | Consist | B | MM 1003 |

ERA was nearly a carbon copy of 2017, but xERA and BPV say look deeper and we find Cmd, GB, and vR boosts. Gains weren't supported by unmoving FpK and SwK so Cmd immediately fell back in 2nd half. There just isn't a major upside path here so he'll always be at the mercy of H% and S%.

| Yr Tm | W | Sv | IP | K | ERA | xERA | WHIP | oOPS | vL | vR | BF/G | Ctl | Dom | Cmd | FpK | SwK | Vel | G | L | F | H% | S% | hr/f | GS | APC | DOM% | DIS% | Sv% | LI | RAR | BPV | BPX | R$ |
|---|---|---|---|---|---|---|---|---|---|---|---|---|---|---|---|---|---|---|---|---|---|---|---|---|---|---|---|---|---|---|---|---|---|
| 14 aa | 13 | 0 | 162 | 100 | 3.78 | 3.82 | 1.24 | | | | 25.3 | 1.6 | 5.6 | 3.5 | | | | | | | 31% | 71% | | | | | | | | -0.7 | 87 | 104 | $5 |
| 15 MIA * | 7 | 0 | 129 | 61 | 4.32 | 4.75 | 1.52 | 818 | 871 | 777 | 18.1 | 3.2 | 4.3 | 1.4 | 58% | 9% | 93.8 | 48 | 20 | 32 | 32% | 72% | 7% | 9 | 50 | 0% | 56% | 0 | 0.59 | -5.7 | 31 | 37 | -$6 |
| 16 MIA * | 7 | 1 | 132 | 92 | 5.33 | 4.62 | 1.45 | 800 | 864 | 725 | 14.1 | 3.5 | 6.3 | 1.8 | 56% | 9% | 94.9 | 48 | 22 | 30 | 31% | 64% | 13% | 12 | 51 | 8% | 50% | 33 | 0.90 | -18.6 | 45 | 53 | -$6 |
| 17 MIA | 14 | 0 | 170 | 113 | 3.82 | 5.06 | 1.27 | 735 | 752 | 719 | 21.3 | 3.4 | 6.0 | 1.8 | 59% | 9% | 95.5 | 43 | 19 | 38 | 26% | 76% | 13% | 28 | 85 | 7% | 46% | 0 | 0.73 | 11.3 | 37 | 45 | $11 |
| 18 MIA | 9 | 0 | 174 | 130 | 3.98 | 4.10 | 1.18 | 690 | 734 | 635 | 23.0 | 2.6 | 6.7 | 2.5 | 59% | 9% | 95.8 | 50 | 18 | 32 | 27% | 69% | 12% | 31 | 90 | 16% | 26% | | | 3.6 | 78 | 90 | $8 |
| 1st Half | 2 | 0 | 94 | 75 | 4.40 | 3.71 | 1.19 | 702 | 759 | 640 | 24.2 | 2.0 | 7.2 | 3.6 | 59% | 9% | 95.7 | 53 | 18 | 29 | 30% | 64% | 11% | 16 | 94 | 19% | 13% | | | -2.9 | 106 | 122 | $3 |
| 2nd Half | 7 | 0 | 80 | 55 | 3.49 | 4.58 | 1.18 | 675 | 707 | 627 | 21.7 | 3.4 | 6.2 | 1.8 | 59% | 9% | 95.9 | 45 | 18 | 36 | 24% | 75% | 12% | 15 | 85 | 13% | 40% | | | 6.5 | 44 | 50 | $15 |
| **19 Proj** | **11** | **0** | **174** | **120** | **4.08** | **4.24** | **1.26** | **721** | **757** | **680** | **24.8** | **3.0** | **6.2** | **2.1** | **58%** | **9%** | **95.4** | **47** | **19** | **34** | **28%** | **71%** | **11%** | **30** | | | | | | **1.4** | **55** | **64** | **$7** |

## Urias,Julio

| | | | | | |
|---|---|---|---|---|---|
| Age: 22 | Th: L | Role SP | Health | F | LIMA Plan C |
| Ht: 6' 0" | Wt: 215 | Type Pwr | PT/Exp | D | Rand Var +5 |
| | | | Consist | C | MM 2201 |

Major shoulder surgery ate up 2018, but finished as key playoff RP. Velocity returned and Ctl stabilized in Sept/Oct. sample (1 BB in 10 IP) after 19 BB in 12 rehab IP. Back in SP role for 2019, but IP will be tightly managed. While sky-high ceiling is dimmed by health, pedigree keeps him firmly on the radar.

| Yr Tm | W | Sv | IP | K | ERA | xERA | WHIP | oOPS | vL | vR | BF/G | Ctl | Dom | Cmd | FpK | SwK | Vel | G | L | F | H% | S% | hr/f | GS | APC | DOM% | DIS% | Sv% | LI | RAR | BPV | BPX | R$ |
|---|---|---|---|---|---|---|---|---|---|---|---|---|---|---|---|---|---|---|---|---|---|---|---|---|---|---|---|---|---|---|---|---|---|
| 14 | | | | | | | | | | | | | | | | | | | | | | | | | | | | | | | | | |
| 15 a/a | 3 | 0 | 73 | 72 | 4.04 | 3.14 | 1.19 | | | | 19.4 | 2.2 | 9.0 | 4.0 | | | | | | | 33% | 65% | | | | | | | | -0.7 | 128 | 153 | $0 |
| 16 LA * | 10 | 0 | 122 | 128 | 2.69 | 3.24 | 1.24 | 728 | 740 | 725 | 17.1 | 2.8 | 9.5 | 3.4 | 63% | 11% | 92.6 | 44 | 27 | 30 | 33% | 80% | 8% | 15 | 79 | 13% | 33% | 0 | 0.73 | 22.5 | 118 | 140 | $13 |
| 17 LA * | 3 | 0 | 55 | 39 | 3.93 | 3.00 | 1.32 | 768 | 1343 | 570 | 20.6 | 4.5 | 6.5 | 1.4 | 52% | 9% | 93.1 | 40 | 28 | 32 | 27% | 69% | 4% | 5 | 82 | 20% | 40% | | | 2.9 | 69 | 83 | -$1 |
| 18 LA | 0 | 0 | 4 | 7 | 0.00 | 1.23 | 0.25 | 154 | 0 | 200 | 4.3 | 0.0 | 15.8 | 0.0 | 62% | 22% | 93.1 | 50 | 17 | 33 | 19% | 0% | 0% | 0 | 19 | | | 0 | 0.00 | 2.0 | 312 | 359 | -$3 |
| 1st Half | | | | | | | | | | | | | | | | | | | | | | | | | | | | | | | | | |
| 2nd Half | 0 | 0 | 4 | 7 | 0.00 | 1.23 | 0.25 | 154 | 0 | 200 | 4.3 | 0.0 | 15.8 | 0.0 | 62% | 22% | 93.1 | 50 | 17 | 33 | 19% | 0% | 0% | 0 | 19 | | | 0 | 0.00 | 2.0 | 312 | 358 | -$3 |
| **19 Proj** | **5** | **0** | **87** | **79** | **3.70** | **3.80** | **1.26** | **617** | **677** | **601** | **21.2** | **3.2** | **8.2** | **2.5** | **63%** | **11%** | **92.6** | **44** | **27** | **30** | **30%** | **73%** | **10%** | **14** | | | | | | **4.8** | **82** | **95** | **$3** |

## Vargas,Jason

| | | | | | |
|---|---|---|---|---|---|
| Age: 36 | Th: L | Role SP | Health | F | LIMA Plan C |
| Ht: 6' 0" | Wt: 215 | Type Pwr | PT/Exp | C | Rand Var +5 |
| | | | Consist | B | MM 1103 |

Ugly 1st half plagued by a HR issue (2.6 HR/9) and injuries to his hand and calf. Home runs leveled off and Dom jumped, fueling 2nd half rebound. Crafty vet seems to put up a rosterable period or two each year, but timing it right is always the key as ever-present HRs and hit-per-inning career rate can sting quickly.

| Yr Tm | W | Sv | IP | K | ERA | xERA | WHIP | oOPS | vL | vR | BF/G | Ctl | Dom | Cmd | FpK | SwK | Vel | G | L | F | H% | S% | hr/f | GS | APC | DOM% | DIS% | Sv% | LI | RAR | BPV | BPX | R$ |
|---|---|---|---|---|---|---|---|---|---|---|---|---|---|---|---|---|---|---|---|---|---|---|---|---|---|---|---|---|---|---|---|---|---|
| 14 KC | 11 | 0 | 187 | 128 | 3.71 | 4.13 | 1.27 | 713 | 661 | 731 | 26.3 | 2.0 | 6.2 | 3.1 | 63% | 9% | 87.3 | 38 | 23 | 39 | 31% | 74% | 8% | 30 | 100 | 27% | 30% | | | 0.8 | 74 | 88 | $5 |
| 15 KC | 5 | 0 | 43 | 27 | 3.98 | 4.71 | 1.35 | 740 | 809 | 712 | 20.3 | 2.5 | 5.7 | 2.3 | 65% | 8% | 87.7 | 41 | 19 | 40 | 30% | 74% | 9% | 9 | 76 | 0% | 22% | | | -0.1 | 53 | 63 | -$2 |
| 16 KC * | 0 | 0 | 28 | 25 | 5.78 | 6.29 | 1.42 | 552 | 1333 | 430 | 17.0 | 1.3 | 7.9 | 5.9 | 64% | 11% | 86.3 | 36 | 15 | 48 | 34% | 67% | 6% | 3 | 70 | 33% | 0% | | | -5.5 | 94 | 112 | -$6 |
| 17 KC | 18 | 0 | 180 | 134 | 4.16 | 4.88 | 1.33 | 766 | 843 | 747 | 23.6 | 2.9 | 6.7 | 2.3 | 66% | 10% | 85.6 | 40 | 19 | 40 | 29% | 74% | 12% | 32 | 91 | 22% | 41% | | | 4.4 | 60 | 73 | $10 |
| 18 NYM | 7 | 0 | 92 | 84 | 5.77 | 4.46 | 1.41 | 819 | 725 | 847 | 20.2 | 2.9 | 8.2 | 2.8 | 64% | 11% | 86.4 | 39 | 21 | 39 | 32% | 63% | 17% | 20 | 78 | 20% | 55% | | | -18.4 | 86 | 99 | -$6 |
| 1st Half | 2 | 0 | 38 | 32 | 8.60 | 5.24 | 1.83 | 1017 | 1013 | 1018 | 20.0 | 3.3 | 7.6 | 2.3 | 64% | 10% | 87.0 | 36 | 23 | 41 | 37% | 57% | 21% | 9 | 73 | 11% | 67% | | | -20.7 | 62 | 71 | -$27 |
| 2nd Half | 5 | 0 | 54 | 52 | 3.81 | 3.94 | 1.12 | 661 | 415 | 724 | 20.4 | 2.7 | 8.6 | 3.3 | 63% | 12% | 86.0 | 42 | 20 | 38 | 27% | 70% | 13% | 11 | 81 | 27% | 45% | | | 2.3 | 104 | 119 | $6 |
| **19 Proj** | **12** | **0** | **138** | **111** | **4.87** | **4.38** | **1.43** | **806** | **780** | **814** | **21.2** | **3.0** | **7.3** | **2.5** | **64%** | **10%** | **86.5** | **40** | **20** | **40** | **32%** | **70%** | **13%** | **28** | | | | | | **-3.2** | **69** | **79** | **-$1** |

## Vazquez,Felipe

| | | | | | |
|---|---|---|---|---|---|
| Age: 27 | Th: L | Role RP | Health | A | LIMA Plan C+ |
| Ht: 6' 2" | Wt: 210 | Type Pwr | PT/Exp | B | Rand Var -1 |
| | | | Consist | A | MM 5531 |

Massive H% and Ctl trouble yielded bumpy 1st half, but the latter returned in 2nd half and soaring S% offered cover as hits kept falling. Elite Dom and SwK plus post-All Star rebound keep him firmly among the elite closer candidates, especially if FpK boost is real.

| Yr Tm | W | Sv | IP | K | ERA | xERA | WHIP | oOPS | vL | vR | BF/G | Ctl | Dom | Cmd | FpK | SwK | Vel | G | L | F | H% | S% | hr/f | GS | APC | DOM% | DIS% | Sv% | LI | RAR | BPV | BPX | R$ |
|---|---|---|---|---|---|---|---|---|---|---|---|---|---|---|---|---|---|---|---|---|---|---|---|---|---|---|---|---|---|---|---|---|---|
| 14 aa | 2 | 0 | 44 | 31 | 4.34 | 4.60 | 1.49 | | | | 18.8 | 3.5 | 6.4 | 1.9 | | | | | | | 33% | 72% | | | | | | | | -3.2 | 54 | 65 | -$4 |
| 15 WAS | 2 | 2 | 48 | 43 | 2.79 | 3.41 | 0.95 | 544 | 486 | 600 | 3.9 | 2.0 | 8.0 | 3.9 | 62% | 12% | 95.4 | 45 | 21 | 33 | 26% | 70% | 5% | 0 | 16 | | | 67 | 1.10 | 7.0 | 112 | 133 | $4 |
| 16 2 NL | 1 | 1 | 77 | 92 | 4.09 | 3.44 | 1.29 | 671 | 765 | 626 | 4.4 | 3.9 | 10.8 | 2.8 | 57% | 15% | 95.8 | 48 | 22 | 30 | 32% | 70% | 12% | 0 | 17 | | | 25 | 1.04 | 0.9 | 115 | 137 | $0 |
| 17 PIT | 5 | 21 | 75 | 88 | 1.67 | 2.99 | 0.89 | 473 | 255 | 571 | 4.1 | 2.4 | 10.5 | 4.4 | 58% | 16% | 98.5 | 53 | 19 | 28 | 26% | 84% | 8% | 0 | 16 | | | 91 | 1.21 | 25.0 | 156 | 187 | $23 |
| 18 PIT | 4 | 37 | 70 | 89 | 2.70 | 3.32 | 1.24 | 618 | 454 | 666 | 4.2 | 3.1 | 11.4 | 3.7 | 63% | 15% | 98.1 | 43 | 25 | 32 | 35% | 80% | 7% | 0 | 17 | | | 88 | 1.28 | 12.5 | 144 | 165 | $20 |
| 1st Half | 3 | 16 | 33 | 42 | 3.78 | 3.66 | 1.38 | 592 | 385 | 645 | 4.4 | 4.1 | 11.3 | 2.8 | 63% | 15% | 97.2 | 40 | 33 | 27 | 37% | 71% | 4% | 0 | 18 | | | 80 | 1.37 | 1.5 | 112 | 129 | $14 |
| 2nd Half | 1 | 21 | 37 | 47 | 1.72 | 3.02 | 1.12 | 643 | 509 | 688 | 4.1 | 2.2 | 11.5 | 5.2 | 62% | 15% | 98.9 | 46 | 17 | 37 | 34% | 89% | 9% | 0 | 16 | | | 95 | 1.19 | 11.0 | 172 | 198 | $25 |
| **19 Proj** | **4** | **35** | **73** | **86** | **2.91** | **3.01** | **1.15** | **599** | **474** | **649** | **4.2** | **2.9** | **10.7** | **3.7** | **61%** | **15%** | **97.6** | **47** | **22** | **32** | **32%** | **76%** | **8%** | **0** | | | | | | **12.1** | **138** | **159** | **$20** |

## Velasquez,Vincent

| | | | | | |
|---|---|---|---|---|---|
| Age: 27 | Th: R | Role SP | Health | F | LIMA Plan C |
| Ht: 6' 3" | Wt: 205 | Type Pwr | PT/Exp | B | Rand Var +2 |
| | | | Consist | B | MM 2303 |

Another frustrating season as Dom, SwK, BPV were squandered by HR trouble. His perennial injury struck in the 2nd half (forearm) while Ks fell and LD soared, rendering hr/f correction moot. Still young enough to be something, but Ks are only building block. Health keeps price in check, but also limits ceiling.

| Yr Tm | W | Sv | IP | K | ERA | xERA | WHIP | oOPS | vL | vR | BF/G | Ctl | Dom | Cmd | FpK | SwK | Vel | G | L | F | H% | S% | hr/f | GS | APC | DOM% | DIS% | Sv% | LI | RAR | BPV | BPX | R$ |
|---|---|---|---|---|---|---|---|---|---|---|---|---|---|---|---|---|---|---|---|---|---|---|---|---|---|---|---|---|---|---|---|---|---|
| 14 | | | | | | | | | | | | | | | | | | | | | | | | | | | | | | | | | |
| 15 HOU * | 5 | 0 | 89 | 97 | 3.54 | 3.01 | 1.20 | 720 | 644 | 808 | 12.7 | 3.4 | 9.9 | 2.9 | 61% | 11% | 94.6 | 31 | 22 | 47 | 30% | 72% | 7% | 7 | 51 | 14% | 0% | 0 | 0.64 | 4.6 | 108 | 129 | $4 |
| 16 PHI | 8 | 0 | 131 | 152 | 4.12 | 3.85 | 1.33 | 765 | 780 | 750 | 23.0 | 3.1 | 10.4 | 3.4 | 60% | 12% | 93.7 | 35 | 24 | 41 | 33% | 75% | 15% | 24 | 92 | 17% | 13% | | | 1.1 | 117 | 140 | $5 |
| 17 PHI | 2 | 0 | 72 | 68 | 5.13 | 4.63 | 1.50 | 851 | 879 | 824 | 21.0 | 4.3 | 8.5 | 2.0 | 63% | 10% | 93.9 | 43 | 23 | 35 | 30% | 72% | 21% | 15 | 85 | 7% | 40% | | | -6.8 | 59 | 71 | -$5 |
| 18 PHI | 9 | 0 | 147 | 161 | 4.85 | 4.11 | 1.34 | 747 | 890 | 607 | 20.3 | 3.6 | 9.9 | 2.7 | 59% | 12% | 93.8 | 38 | 21 | 41 | 33% | 65% | 10% | 30 | 80 | 27% | 30% | 0 | 0.83 | -12.6 | 96 | 111 | $0 |
| 1st Half | 5 | 0 | 88 | 107 | 4.69 | 3.83 | 1.29 | 738 | 835 | 641 | 22.1 | 3.5 | 10.9 | 3.1 | 57% | 13% | 94.0 | 39 | 19 | 42 | 32% | 67% | 14% | 17 | 88 | 35% | 24% | | | -5.8 | 120 | 138 | $2 |
| 2nd Half | 4 | 0 | 58 | 54 | 5.09 | 4.55 | 1.42 | 760 | 975 | 555 | 18.2 | 3.9 | 8.3 | 2.2 | 61% | 12% | 93.6 | 36 | 25 | 39 | 33% | 63% | 5% | 13 | 69 | 15% | 38% | 0 | 0.88 | -6.8 | 60 | 68 | -$5 |
| **19 Proj** | **8** | **0** | **145** | **151** | **4.35** | **3.95** | **1.35** | **757** | **837** | **678** | **22.3** | **3.7** | **9.4** | **2.5** | **61%** | **11%** | **93.9** | **37** | **23** | **40** | **31%** | **71%** | **12%** | **27** | | | | | | **3.6** | **83** | **96** | **$3** |

## Velazquez,Hector

| | | | | | |
|---|---|---|---|---|---|
| Age: 30 | Th: R | Role RP | Health | A | LIMA Plan B |
| Ht: 6' 0" | Wt: 180 | Type Con GB | PT/Exp | D | Rand Var -3 |
| | | | Consist | A | MM 1001 |

Sinkerballing soft-tosser rode a strong S% and passable Ctl, but xERA tells the real story. Dom/SwK history takes away any hope of late-inning impact potential, so we're left with a swingman/long-reliever who doesn't miss bats. A non-factor everywhere except for 15-team "Guys with Last Names Including a Z" leagues.

| Yr Tm | W | Sv | IP | K | ERA | xERA | WHIP | oOPS | vL | vR | BF/G | Ctl | Dom | Cmd | FpK | SwK | Vel | G | L | F | H% | S% | hr/f | GS | APC | DOM% | DIS% | Sv% | LI | RAR | BPV | BPX | R$ |
|---|---|---|---|---|---|---|---|---|---|---|---|---|---|---|---|---|---|---|---|---|---|---|---|---|---|---|---|---|---|---|---|---|---|
| 14 | | | | | | | | | | | | | | | | | | | | | | | | | | | | | | | | | |
| 15 | | | | | | | | | | | | | | | | | | | | | | | | | | | | | | | | | |
| 16 | | | | | | | | | | | | | | | | | | | | | | | | | | | | | | | | | |
| 17 BOS * | 11 | 0 | 127 | 76 | 3.58 | 4.42 | 1.35 | 707 | 905 | 595 | 19.6 | 2.6 | 5.4 | 2.1 | 60% | 9% | 89.6 | 43 | 23 | 34 | 30% | 77% | 17% | 3 | 48 | 0% | 33% | 0 | 0.98 | 12.1 | 45 | 54 | $6 |
| 18 BOS | 7 | 0 | 85 | 53 | 3.18 | 4.57 | 1.45 | 766 | 806 | 734 | 7.9 | 2.8 | 5.6 | 2.0 | 64% | 8% | 90.7 | 50 | 22 | 28 | 33% | 80% | 9% | 8 | 30 | 0% | 50% | 0 | 0.61 | 10.2 | 55 | 63 | $1 |
| 1st Half | 6 | 0 | 43 | 28 | 2.32 | 4.37 | 1.38 | 735 | 753 | 723 | 8.0 | 1.9 | 5.9 | 3.1 | 68% | 9% | 90.6 | 48 | 21 | 31 | 34% | 86% | 7% | 2 | 29 | 0% | 0% | 0 | 0.64 | 9.6 | 81 | 93 | $5 |
| 2nd Half | 1 | 0 | 42 | 25 | 4.04 | 4.78 | 1.51 | 797 | 846 | 747 | 7.8 | 3.6 | 5.3 | 1.5 | 60% | 8% | 90.9 | 52 | 23 | 26 | 31% | 75% | 11% | 6 | 30 | 0% | 67% | 0 | 0.57 | 0.6 | 28 | 32 | -$4 |
| **19 Proj** | **6** | **0** | **73** | **44** | **3.91** | **4.32** | **1.42** | **775** | **832** | **727** | **10.1** | **2.8** | **5.5** | **2.0** | **63%** | **8%** | **90.8** | **50** | **22** | **28** | **31%** | **75%** | **12%** | **5** | | | | | | **-0.9** | **52** | **60** | **-$1** |

PAUL SPORER

## VerHagen,Drew

| | | | | | |
|---|---|---|---|---|---|
| Age: 28 | Th: R | Role RP | Health | F | LIMA Plan B+ |
| Ht: 6' 6" | Wt: 230 | Type Pwr | PT/Exp | D | Rand Var +1 |
| | | | Consist | F | MM 2201 |

3-3, 4.63 ERA in 56 IP at DET. Dom-challenged SP finally healthy, reborn as a reliever? Flagship sinker produced another solid GB%; SwK, Cmd jumped unexpectedly as once-lagging secondaries stepped up. Improved 2nd-half H%/S% luck fueled huge performance surge. Atypical season needs 2019 confirmation.

| Yr Tm | W | Sv | IP | K | ERA | xERA | WHIP | oOPS | vL | vR | BF/G | Ctl | Dom | Cmd | FpK | SwK | Vel | G | L | F | H% | S% | hr/f | GS | APC | DOM% | DIS% | Sv% | LI | RAR | BPV | BPX | R$ |
|---|---|---|---|---|---|---|---|---|---|---|---|---|---|---|---|---|---|---|---|---|---|---|---|---|---|---|---|---|---|---|---|---|---|
| 14 DET * | 6 | 0 | 115 | 54 | 4.64 | 4.76 | 1.50 | 753 | 822 | 500 | 24.9 | 2.3 | 4.2 | 1.8 | 59% | 10% | 90.6 | 42 | 33 | 25 | 34% | 68% | 0% | 1 | 82 | 0% | 100% | | | -12.8 | 43 | 51 | -$8 |
| 15 DET * | 5 | 3 | 61 | 33 | 3.27 | 3.43 | 1.38 | 559 | 691 | 487 | 6.4 | 4.1 | 4.9 | 1.2 | 58% | 6% | 93.9 | 75 | 16 | 9 | 28% | 76% | 14% | 0 | 20 | | | 60 | 0.99 | 5.2 | 51 | 60 | $1 |
| 16 DET | 1 | 0 | 19 | 10 | 7.11 | 5.12 | 1.84 | 968 | 1111 | 876 | 4.7 | 3.3 | 4.7 | 1.4 | 55% | 6% | 94.4 | 60 | 14 | 26 | 36% | 63% | 16% | 0 | 18 | | | 0 | 0.66 | -6.8 | 34 | 40 | -$7 |
| 17 DET * | 7 | 0 | 132 | 76 | 7.14 | 7.13 | 1.89 | 967 | 1090 | 911 | 14.4 | 4.1 | 5.2 | 1.3 | 57% | 10% | 94.0 | 50 | 15 | 34 | 37% | 63% | 26% | 2 | 22 | 0% | 100% | 0 | 0.92 | -45.2 | 5 | 6 | -$24 |
| 18 DET * | 5 | 0 | 91 | 90 | 3.79 | 2.67 | 1.12 | 645 | 749 | 577 | 7.0 | 3.1 | 9.0 | 2.9 | 58% | 13% | 94.1 | 48 | 11 | 41 | 28% | 66% | 9% | 1 | 22 | 0% | 100% | 0 | 0.78 | 4.0 | 109 | 126 | $5 |
| 1st Half | 2 | 0 | 48 | 49 | 4.72 | 2.82 | 1.18 | 864 | 884 | 848 | 9.1 | 3.5 | 9.2 | 2.6 | 58% | 13% | 94.0 | 48 | 5 | 46 | 29% | 59% | 12% | 1 | 24 | 0% | 100% | 0 | 0.86 | -3.4 | 105 | 120 | $0 |
| 2nd Half | 3 | 0 | 43 | 42 | 2.74 | 2.51 | 1.06 | 527 | 655 | 457 | 5.5 | 2.6 | 8.7 | 3.4 | 58% | 13% | 94.0 | 48 | 15 | 38 | 27% | 76% | 8% | 0 | 21 | | | 0 | 0.74 | 7.4 | 116 | 134 | $10 |
| 19 Proj | 4 | 0 | 73 | 66 | 3.88 | 3.85 | 1.28 | 711 | 799 | 661 | 8.3 | 3.1 | 8.2 | 2.7 | 58% | 12% | 94.1 | 47 | 17 | 36 | 30% | 73% | 11% | 0 | | | | | | 2.5 | 89 | 103 | $1 |

## Verlander,Justin

| | | | | | |
|---|---|---|---|---|---|
| Age: 36 | Th: R | Role SP | Health | C | LIMA Plan D+ |
| Ht: 6' 5" | Wt: 225 | Type Pwr xFB | PT/Exp | A | Rand Var -2 |
| | | | Consist | B | MM 4505 |

New life on a contender. Career-best SwK/Dom, FpK/Ctl never backed off, all continued to soar through the end of the year. Only H%, hr/f over-corrections applied 2nd-half gravity. Age, sliding GB% are likely to stall and turn this unworldly momentum. But even with 2nd half as the benchmark, he's still near-elite at worst.

| Yr Tm | W | Sv | IP | K | ERA | xERA | WHIP | oOPS | vL | vR | BF/G | Ctl | Dom | Cmd | FpK | SwK | Vel | G | L | F | H% | S% | hr/f | GS | APC | DOM% | DIS% | Sv% | LI | RAR | BPV | BPX | R$ |
|---|---|---|---|---|---|---|---|---|---|---|---|---|---|---|---|---|---|---|---|---|---|---|---|---|---|---|---|---|---|---|---|---|---|
| 14 DET | 15 | 0 | 206 | 159 | 4.54 | 4.27 | 1.40 | 756 | 686 | 849 | 27.9 | 2.8 | 6.9 | 2.4 | 62% | 9% | 92.3 | 40 | 20 | 41 | 33% | 68% | 7% | 32 | 107 | 31% | 31% | | | -20.4 | 66 | 79 | -$3 |
| 15 DET | 5 | 0 | 133 | 113 | 3.38 | 4.03 | 1.09 | 634 | 620 | 650 | 26.8 | 2.2 | 7.6 | 3.5 | 64% | 10% | 92.8 | 35 | 20 | 46 | 28% | 72% | 7% | 20 | 108 | 40% | 30% | | | 9.7 | 92 | 110 | $9 |
| 16 DET | 16 | 0 | 228 | 254 | 3.04 | 3.72 | 1.00 | 630 | 603 | 657 | 26.6 | 2.3 | 10.0 | 4.5 | 64% | 13% | 93.5 | 34 | 19 | 48 | 27% | 76% | 11% | 34 | 108 | 62% | 9% | | | 32.2 | 132 | 157 | $33 |
| 17 2AL | 15 | 0 | 206 | 219 | 3.36 | 4.19 | 1.17 | 660 | 712 | 614 | 25.7 | 3.1 | 9.6 | 3.0 | 62% | 11% | 95.2 | 33 | 24 | 43 | 28% | 77% | 11% | 33 | 107 | 55% | 15% | | | 25.3 | 98 | 118 | $24 |
| 18 HOU | 16 | 0 | 214 | 290 | 2.52 | 3.16 | 0.90 | 602 | 583 | 617 | 24.5 | 1.6 | 12.2 | 7.8 | 69% | 15% | 95.1 | 29 | 20 | 51 | 29% | 81% | 11% | 34 | 101 | 62% | 3% | | | 42.9 | 185 | 212 | $42 |
| 1st Half | 9 | 0 | 119 | 144 | 2.12 | 3.54 | 0.86 | 549 | 530 | 563 | 25.6 | 1.8 | 10.9 | 6.0 | 66% | 14% | 94.9 | 29 | 17 | 54 | 26% | 81% | 7% | 18 | 104 | 61% | 0% | | | 29.7 | 155 | 178 | $49 |
| 2nd Half | 7 | 0 | 95 | 146 | 3.02 | 2.72 | 0.95 | 666 | 641 | 688 | 23.3 | 1.2 | 13.8 | 11.2 | 73% | 17% | 95.3 | 29 | 23 | 48 | 33% | 80% | 17% | 16 | 98 | 63% | 6% | | | 13.3 | 222 | 255 | $32 |
| 19 Proj | 15 | 0 | 203 | 247 | 3.02 | 3.17 | 1.03 | 640 | 636 | 644 | 24.3 | 2.1 | 10.9 | 5.2 | 66% | 14% | 94.7 | 32 | 21 | 47 | 29% | 77% | 12% | 32 | | | | | | 28.2 | 150 | 172 | $30 |

## Vincent,Nick

| | | | | | |
|---|---|---|---|---|---|
| Age: 32 | Th: R | Role RP | Health | D | LIMA Plan A |
| Ht: 6' 0" | Wt: 185 | Type Pwr xFB | PT/Exp | C | Rand Var -1 |
| | | | Consist | B | MM 2300 |

Soft-tossing RP offers elite Ctl, plus command. Still sidestepping a HR barrage despite that lofty/risky FB%. Ceiling capped by modestly serviceable Dom, H%/S% swings that can make a difference in half-to-half ERA, WHIP. Age suggests unexciting profile is unlikely to change for the better.

| Yr Tm | W | Sv | IP | K | ERA | xERA | WHIP | oOPS | vL | vR | BF/G | Ctl | Dom | Cmd | FpK | SwK | Vel | G | L | F | H% | S% | hr/f | GS | APC | DOM% | DIS% | Sv% | LI | RAR | BPV | BPX | R$ |
|---|---|---|---|---|---|---|---|---|---|---|---|---|---|---|---|---|---|---|---|---|---|---|---|---|---|---|---|---|---|---|---|---|---|
| 14 SD | 1 | 0 | 55 | 62 | 3.60 | 3.00 | 1.00 | 626 | 825 | 507 | 3.4 | 1.8 | 10.1 | 5.6 | 61% | 12% | 89.8 | 33 | 22 | 45 | 30% | 66% | 8% | 0 | 14 | | | 0 | 1.07 | 1.0 | 145 | 173 | $2 |
| 15 SD * | 5 | 1 | 73 | 75 | 2.98 | 4.31 | 1.45 | 698 | 756 | 649 | 4.7 | 3.1 | 9.1 | 2.9 | 63% | 10% | 89.6 | 32 | 28 | 40 | 36% | 81% | 0% | 0 | 16 | | | 20 | 0.55 | 8.9 | 97 | 115 | $2 |
| 16 SEA | 4 | 3 | 60 | 65 | 3.73 | 3.99 | 1.13 | 700 | 658 | 723 | 4.1 | 2.2 | 9.7 | 4.3 | 69% | 14% | 89.9 | 32 | 20 | 48 | 29% | 75% | 14% | 0 | 16 | | | 33 | 1.26 | 3.4 | 124 | 147 | $4 |
| 17 SEA | 3 | 0 | 65 | 50 | 3.20 | 4.73 | 1.16 | 643 | 672 | 627 | 3.8 | 1.8 | 7.0 | 3.8 | 67% | 11% | 89.9 | 31 | 21 | 48 | 31% | 72% | 3% | 0 | 14 | | | 0 | 1.34 | 9.2 | 85 | 103 | $3 |
| 18 SEA | 4 | 0 | 56 | 56 | 3.99 | 4.45 | 1.15 | 659 | 670 | 653 | 3.9 | 2.4 | 8.9 | 3.7 | 64% | 12% | 89.6 | 30 | 20 | 50 | 29% | 69% | 9% | 1 | 13 | 0% | 0% | 0 | 1.24 | 1.1 | 104 | 120 | $1 |
| 1st Half | 3 | 0 | 25 | 24 | 4.26 | 4.84 | 1.34 | 739 | 731 | 744 | 3.9 | 2.5 | 8.5 | 3.4 | 62% | 13% | 89.7 | 28 | 24 | 49 | 34% | 71% | 8% | 0 | 13 | | | 0 | 1.41 | -0.4 | 92 | 105 | -$3 |
| 2nd Half | 1 | 0 | 31 | 32 | 3.77 | 4.14 | 1.00 | 587 | 596 | 582 | 3.8 | 2.3 | 9.3 | 4.0 | 65% | 12% | 89.5 | 33 | 17 | 51 | 26% | 67% | 10% | 1 | 13 | 0% | 0% | 0 | 1.09 | 1.4 | 115 | 132 | $3 |
| 19 Proj | 3 | 0 | 58 | 56 | 3.83 | 3.88 | 1.15 | 664 | 692 | 649 | 3.7 | 2.2 | 8.7 | 3.9 | 65% | 12% | 89.7 | 31 | 20 | 49 | 30% | 70% | 8% | 0 | | | | | | 2.3 | 105 | 121 | $1 |

## Vizcaino,Arodys

| | | | | | |
|---|---|---|---|---|---|
| Age: 28 | Th: R | Role RP | Health | F | LIMA Plan B |
| Ht: 6' 0" | Wt: 245 | Type Pwr | PT/Exp | C | Rand Var -5 |
| | | | Consist | A | MM 2420 |

Began the season en fuego with more H%/S% help neutralizing funky G/L/F. Balky shoulder knocked him out for 2+ weeks in June, then two more months in the 2nd half. Still brings gas and plus curveball, SwK and passable FpK, but heed xERA warning. Rarely healthy enough to turn it into full-year production.

| Yr Tm | W | Sv | IP | K | ERA | xERA | WHIP | oOPS | vL | vR | BF/G | Ctl | Dom | Cmd | FpK | SwK | Vel | G | L | F | H% | S% | hr/f | GS | APC | DOM% | DIS% | Sv% | LI | RAR | BPV | BPX | R$ |
|---|---|---|---|---|---|---|---|---|---|---|---|---|---|---|---|---|---|---|---|---|---|---|---|---|---|---|---|---|---|---|---|---|---|
| 14 CHC * | 1 | 1 | 37 | 31 | 4.91 | 4.85 | 1.58 | 837 | 200 | 1318 | 4.5 | 4.2 | 7.6 | 1.8 | 59% | 7% | 95.2 | 40 | 20 | 40 | 34% | 69% | 17% | 0 | 19 | | | 50 | 0.02 | -5.3 | 59 | 70 | -$5 |
| 15 ATL | 3 | 9 | 34 | 37 | 1.60 | 3.66 | 1.19 | 615 | 583 | 641 | 3.9 | 3.5 | 9.9 | 2.8 | 58% | 12% | 97.7 | 35 | 28 | 37 | 31% | 87% | 3% | 0 | 15 | | | 90 | 1.12 | 9.8 | 97 | 116 | $6 |
| 16 ATL | 1 | 10 | 39 | 50 | 4.42 | 4.05 | 1.63 | 681 | 607 | 748 | 4.2 | 6.1 | 11.6 | 1.9 | 56% | 14% | 97.4 | 54 | 16 | 30 | 37% | 73% | 10% | 0 | 17 | | | 71 | 1.15 | -1.1 | 78 | 93 | $0 |
| 17 ATL | 5 | 14 | 57 | 64 | 2.83 | 4.08 | 1.10 | 627 | 749 | 527 | 3.8 | 3.3 | 10.0 | 3.0 | 60% | 15% | 97.8 | 39 | 16 | 45 | 26% | 80% | 10% | 0 | 14 | | | 82 | 1.28 | 10.8 | 109 | 131 | $11 |
| 18 ATL | 2 | 16 | 38 | 40 | 2.11 | 4.14 | 1.17 | 652 | 718 | 587 | 4.1 | 3.5 | 9.4 | 2.7 | 60% | 15% | 97.6 | 32 | 27 | 42 | 28% | 88% | 10% | 0 | 16 | | | 89 | 1.06 | 9.6 | 84 | 97 | $8 |
| 1st Half | 2 | 15 | 30 | 33 | 1.82 | 4.02 | 1.15 | 619 | 736 | 509 | 4.1 | 3.6 | 10.0 | 2.8 | 59% | 15% | 97.7 | 29 | 28 | 43 | 26% | 88% | 6% | 0 | 17 | | | 88 | 1.24 | 8.5 | 89 | 103 | $11 |
| 2nd Half | 0 | 1 | 9 | 7 | 3.12 | 4.57 | 1.27 | 760 | 656 | 833 | 4.0 | 3.1 | 7.3 | 2.3 | 64% | 12% | 97.1 | 38 | 23 | 38 | 26% | 89% | 20% | 0 | 15 | | | 100 | 0.46 | 1.1 | 63 | 73 | -$8 |
| 19 Proj | 3 | 20 | 51 | 57 | 3.30 | 3.73 | 1.31 | 649 | 673 | 628 | 3.9 | 4.2 | 10.2 | 2.4 | 58% | 14% | 97.6 | 41 | 22 | 38 | 31% | 76% | 8% | 0 | | | | | | 3.0 | 88 | 101 | $9 |

## Volquez,Edinson

| | | | | | |
|---|---|---|---|---|---|
| Age: 35 | Th: R | Role SP | Health | D | LIMA Plan D+ |
| Ht: 6' 0" | Wt: 220 | Type Pwr | PT/Exp | C | Rand Var 0 |
| | | | Consist | A | MM 1101 |

Missed all of 2018 following 2017 Tommy John surgery. Almost 20 months after, should be ready as of Opening Day. Experience, GB% and inning-eating potential are reasons free agent could get more MLB opportunity—and they aren't enough. Age, health, Cmd history say make him prove something.

| Yr Tm | W | Sv | IP | K | ERA | xERA | WHIP | oOPS | vL | vR | BF/G | Ctl | Dom | Cmd | FpK | SwK | Vel | G | L | F | H% | S% | hr/f | GS | APC | DOM% | DIS% | Sv% | LI | RAR | BPV | BPX | R$ |
|---|---|---|---|---|---|---|---|---|---|---|---|---|---|---|---|---|---|---|---|---|---|---|---|---|---|---|---|---|---|---|---|---|---|
| 14 PIT | 13 | 0 | 193 | 140 | 3.04 | 3.95 | 1.23 | 674 | 728 | 634 | 25.3 | 3.3 | 6.5 | 2.0 | 60% | 9% | 93.2 | 50 | 17 | 33 | 27% | 78% | 9% | 31 | 93 | 29% | 29% | 0 | 0.76 | 16.7 | 56 | 67 | $12 |
| 15 KC | 13 | 0 | 200 | 155 | 3.55 | 4.22 | 1.31 | 692 | 692 | 691 | 25.0 | 3.2 | 7.0 | 2.2 | 58% | 10% | 93.7 | 46 | 21 | 33 | 30% | 74% | 8% | 33 | 97 | 33% | 27% | 0 | 0.77 | 10.2 | 62 | 74 | $10 |
| 16 KC | 10 | 0 | 189 | 139 | 5.37 | 4.68 | 1.55 | 794 | 799 | 788 | 25.1 | 3.6 | 6.6 | 1.8 | 56% | 9% | 93.2 | 51 | 20 | 29 | 33% | 67% | 13% | 34 | 95 | 12% | 41% | | | -27.6 | 50 | 60 | -$11 |
| 17 MIA | 4 | 0 | 92 | 81 | 4.19 | 4.79 | 1.42 | 718 | 810 | 613 | 23.4 | 5.2 | 7.9 | 1.5 | 56% | 9% | 93.1 | 46 | 22 | 33 | 28% | 72% | 10% | 17 | 89 | 18% | 59% | | | 1.9 | 27 | 32 | -$1 |
| 18 | | | | | | | | | | | | | | | | | | | | | | | | | | | | | | | | | |
| 1st Half | | | | | | | | | | | | | | | | | | | | | | | | | | | | | | | | | |
| 2nd Half | | | | | | | | | | | | | | | | | | | | | | | | | | | | | | | | | |
| 19 Proj | 6 | 0 | 102 | 80 | 4.21 | 4.28 | 1.38 | 719 | 756 | 680 | 23.9 | 3.9 | 7.1 | 1.8 | 57% | 9% | 93.3 | 48 | 20 | 32 | 30% | 71% | 10% | 18 | | | | | | -1.3 | 48 | 55 | $0 |

## Wacha,Michael

| | | | | | |
|---|---|---|---|---|---|
| Age: 28 | Th: R | Role SP | Health | F | LIMA Plan B |
| Ht: 6' 6" | Wt: 215 | Type Pwr | PT/Exp | B | Rand Var -2 |
| | | | Consist | A | MM 2203 |

Despite poor Cmd, sagging velocity and problematic G/L/F, H% helped him outpitch xERA early on. HR caught up with him in June, followed by oblique strain that shelved him for 2nd half. Ctl woes look like an aberration historically, but the sum of the metric parts looks mediocre. Durability woes further cap any upside.

| Yr Tm | W | Sv | IP | K | ERA | xERA | WHIP | oOPS | vL | vR | BF/G | Ctl | Dom | Cmd | FpK | SwK | Vel | G | L | F | H% | S% | hr/f | GS | APC | DOM% | DIS% | Sv% | LI | RAR | BPV | BPX | R$ |
|---|---|---|---|---|---|---|---|---|---|---|---|---|---|---|---|---|---|---|---|---|---|---|---|---|---|---|---|---|---|---|---|---|---|
| 14 STL | 5 | 0 | 107 | 94 | 3.20 | 3.70 | 1.20 | 636 | 581 | 687 | 23.5 | 2.8 | 7.9 | 2.8 | 64% | 11% | 93.2 | 42 | 22 | 36 | 30% | 74% | 5% | 19 | 89 | 26% | 21% | | | 7.2 | 87 | 104 | $5 |
| 15 STL | 17 | 0 | 181 | 153 | 3.38 | 3.91 | 1.21 | 672 | 617 | 716 | 25.4 | 2.9 | 7.6 | 2.6 | 63% | 10% | 94.2 | 46 | 22 | 32 | 29% | 76% | 11% | 30 | 98 | 23% | 23% | | | 13.1 | 83 | 99 | $16 |
| 16 STL | 7 | 0 | 138 | 114 | 5.09 | 4.30 | 1.48 | 800 | 733 | 849 | 22.4 | 2.9 | 7.4 | 2.5 | 59% | 9% | 93.2 | 47 | 24 | 30 | 34% | 67% | 12% | 24 | 86 | 25% | 33% | 0 | 0.72 | -15.3 | 80 | 95 | -$6 |
| 17 STL | 12 | 0 | 166 | 158 | 4.13 | 3.99 | 1.36 | 735 | 724 | 745 | 23.4 | 3.0 | 8.6 | 2.9 | 66% | 10% | 95.1 | 48 | 21 | 31 | 33% | 72% | 12% | 30 | 90 | 27% | 30% | | | 4.7 | 100 | 120 | $8 |
| 18 STL | 8 | 0 | 84 | 71 | 3.20 | 4.24 | 1.23 | 646 | 583 | 710 | 23.7 | 3.8 | 7.6 | 2.0 | 53% | 10% | 93.5 | 43 | 29 | 27 | 26% | 78% | 14% | 15 | 95 | 40% | 33% | | | 9.9 | 54 | 62 | $5 |
| 1st Half | 8 | 0 | 84 | 71 | 3.20 | 4.24 | 1.23 | 646 | 583 | 710 | 23.7 | 3.8 | 7.6 | 2.0 | 53% | 10% | 93.5 | 43 | 29 | 27 | 26% | 78% | 14% | 15 | 95 | 40% | 33% | | | 9.9 | 54 | 62 | $5 |
| 2nd Half | | | | | | | | | | | | | | | | | | | | | | | | | | | | | | | | | |
| 19 Proj | 10 | 0 | 131 | 113 | 4.02 | 3.87 | 1.31 | 707 | 652 | 755 | 22.8 | 3.2 | 7.8 | 2.4 | 60% | 10% | 93.8 | 45 | 25 | 30 | 30% | 71% | 11% | 24 | | | | | | 3.8 | 77 | 89 | $5 |

## Wainwright,Adam

| | | | | | |
|---|---|---|---|---|---|
| Age: 37 | Th: R | Role SP | Health | F | LIMA Plan B+ |
| Ht: 6' 7" | Wt: 235 | Type Pwr | PT/Exp | B | Rand Var -1 |
| | | | Consist | B | MM 2201 |

2-4, 4.46 ERA in 40 IP at STL. Elbow issues that ended 2017 campaign never left. First shelved in April, again in May for three months. Small sample September return included velocity uptick, Dom/SwK surge and solid GB% in STL. Age, health are scary, but low-bid profit potential remains. Check back in March.

| Yr Tm | W | Sv | IP | K | ERA | xERA | WHIP | oOPS | vL | vR | BF/G | Ctl | Dom | Cmd | FpK | SwK | Vel | G | L | F | H% | S% | hr/f | GS | APC | DOM% | DIS% | Sv% | LI | RAR | BPV | BPX | R$ |
|---|---|---|---|---|---|---|---|---|---|---|---|---|---|---|---|---|---|---|---|---|---|---|---|---|---|---|---|---|---|---|---|---|---|
| 14 STL | 20 | 0 | 227 | 179 | 2.38 | 3.31 | 1.03 | 580 | 625 | 542 | 28.1 | 2.0 | 7.1 | 3.6 | 61% | 9% | 90.2 | 46 | 24 | 30 | 27% | 78% | 5% | 32 | 102 | 56% | 22% | | | 38.1 | 98 | 117 | $30 |
| 15 STL | 2 | 0 | 28 | 20 | 1.61 | 3.35 | 1.04 | 590 | 661 | 540 | 15.9 | 1.3 | 6.4 | 5.0 | 54% | 8% | 89.6 | 51 | 26 | 23 | 30% | 83% | 0% | 4 | 55 | 25% | 0% | 0 | 0.51 | 8.1 | 110 | 131 | $1 |
| 16 STL | 13 | 0 | 199 | 161 | 4.62 | 4.20 | 1.40 | 785 | 841 | 739 | 25.7 | 2.7 | 7.3 | 2.7 | 61% | 9% | 90.3 | 44 | 25 | 31 | 33% | 69% | 12% | 33 | 97 | 27% | 33% | | | -10.6 | 81 | 96 | $1 |
| 17 STL | 12 | 0 | 123 | 96 | 5.11 | 4.58 | 1.50 | 794 | 821 | 768 | 22.8 | 3.3 | 7.0 | 2.1 | 60% | 8% | 89.7 | 47 | 25 | 28 | 33% | 67% | 13% | 23 | 90 | 27% | 39% | 0 | 0.74 | -11.4 | 62 | 75 | -$2 |
| 18 STL * | 4 | 0 | 59 | 54 | 3.03 | 3.94 | 1.34 | 753 | 747 | 754 | 19.0 | 3.4 | 8.2 | 2.4 | 55% | 9% | 89.3 | 49 | 18 | 33 | 32% | 80% | 13% | 8 | 92 | 25% | 38% | | | 8.2 | 82 | 94 | $1 |
| 1st Half | 2 | 0 | 23 | 16 | 3.13 | 4.41 | 1.54 | 842 | 841 | 831 | 20.1 | 5.5 | 6.4 | 1.2 | 51% | 6% | 88.6 | 55 | 16 | 29 | 29% | 82% | 13% | 4 | 88 | 0% | 50% | | | 2.9 | 45 | 52 | -$6 |
| 2nd Half | 2 | 0 | 36 | 38 | 2.97 | 3.63 | 1.22 | 673 | 662 | 684 | 18.3 | 2.1 | 9.4 | 4.6 | 58% | 12% | 90.0 | 44 | 19 | 37 | 34% | 78% | 13% | 4 | 95 | 50% | 25% | | | 5.3 | 133 | 153 | $4 |
| 19 Proj | 7 | 0 | 87 | 74 | 4.24 | 3.96 | 1.37 | 720 | 736 | 703 | 21.2 | 3.1 | 7.6 | 2.5 | 58% | 9% | 89.7 | 47 | 22 | 32 | 32% | 70% | 10% | 17 | | | | | | 1.8 | 78 | 90 | $0 |

JOCK THOMPSON

## Walker,Taijuan

| | | | | | | | |
|---|---|---|---|---|---|---|---|
| Age: 26 | Th: R | Role SP | | Health | F | LIMA Plan | C |
| Ht: 6' 4" | Wt: 235 | Type Pwr | | PT/Exp | C | Rand Var | -2 |
| | | | | Consist | A | MM | 2201 |

Durability-challenged, once-elite prospect with April Tommy John surgery should be ready sometime after Opening Day. FpK/Ctl have flashed plus skill with volatility; Cmd, GB%, velocity don't look hopeless. Can SwK tick back up again with health? Underachiever has plenty to prove; age keeps him watchable.

| Yr Tm | W | Sv | IP | K | ERA | xERA | WHIP | oOPS | vL | vR | BF/G | Ctl | Dom | Cmd | FpK | SwK | Vel | G | L | F | H% | S% | hr/f | GS | APC | DOM% | DIS% | Sv% | LI | RAR | BPV | BPX | R$ |
|---|---|---|---|---|---|---|---|---|---|---|---|---|---|---|---|---|---|---|---|---|---|---|---|---|---|---|---|---|---|---|---|---|---|
| 14 SEA * | 9 | 0 | 116 | 109 | 3.85 | 3.70 | 1.25 | 642 | 729 | 501 | 20.5 | 3.2 | 8.4 | 2.7 | 61% | 10% | 94.7 | 47 | 27 | 26 | 29% | 73% | 7% | 5 | 78 | 20% | 0% | 0 | 0.57 | -1.5 | 82 | 97 | $4 |
| 15 SEA | 11 | 0 | 170 | 157 | 4.56 | 3.78 | 1.20 | 716 | 714 | 719 | 24.3 | 2.1 | 8.3 | 3.9 | 63% | 11% | 94.3 | 39 | 22 | 39 | 30% | 66% | 13% | 29 | 91 | 34% | 34% | | | -12.6 | 110 | 131 | $5 |
| 16 SEA * | 9 | 0 | 149 | 124 | 4.21 | 4.46 | 1.26 | 767 | 721 | 809 | 21.7 | 2.7 | 7.5 | 2.8 | 64% | 10% | 93.9 | 44 | 18 | 38 | 28% | 74% | 18% | 25 | 92 | 28% | 40% | | | -0.5 | 57 | 67 | $5 |
| 17 ARI | 9 | 0 | 157 | 146 | 3.49 | 4.29 | 1.33 | 732 | 727 | 736 | 24.4 | 3.5 | 8.4 | 2.4 | 59% | 9% | 93.8 | 49 | 18 | 33 | 31% | 77% | 11% | 28 | 98 | 18% | 32% | | | 16.9 | 83 | 100 | $10 |
| 18 ARI | 0 | 0 | 13 | 9 | 3.46 | 4.72 | 1.54 | 749 | 967 | 526 | 18.7 | 3.5 | 6.2 | 1.8 | 68% | 7% | 93.7 | 43 | 28 | 30 | 34% | 79% | 8% | 3 | 75 | 0% | 67% | | | 1.1 | 40 | 46 | -$5 |
| 1st Half | 0 | 0 | 13 | 9 | 3.46 | 4.72 | 1.54 | 749 | 967 | 526 | 18.7 | 3.5 | 6.2 | 1.8 | 68% | 7% | 93.7 | 43 | 28 | 30 | 34% | 79% | 8% | 3 | 75 | 0% | 67% | | | 1.1 | 39 | 45 | -$5 |
| 2nd Half | | | | | | | | | | | | | | | | | | | | | | | | | | | | | | | | | |
| **19 Proj** | **7** | **0** | **102** | **92** | **3.98** | **3.77** | **1.26** | **731** | **732** | **728** | **22.6** | **2.8** | **8.2** | **2.9** | **61%** | **10%** | **94.1** | **44** | **21** | **35** | **30%** | **73%** | **14%** | **18** | | | | | | **2.1** | **94** | **107** | **$4** |

## Warren,Adam

| | | | | | | | |
|---|---|---|---|---|---|---|---|
| Age: 31 | Th: R | Role RP | | Health | F | LIMA Plan | C |
| Ht: 6' 1" | Wt: 224 | Type Pwr | | PT/Exp | D | Rand Var | -3 |
| | | | | Consist | B | MM | 2200 |

More back issues limited him to nine games through June 3; wasn't particularly effective afterward. Ctl always on the edge with shaky FpK; Dom looks capped at "nothing special." Ability to limit H%/S% damage has been a big plus. Return to peak R$ not in the cards without reprise of swing-man role, health.

| Yr Tm | W | Sv | IP | K | ERA | xERA | WHIP | oOPS | vL | vR | BF/G | Ctl | Dom | Cmd | FpK | SwK | Vel | G | L | F | H% | S% | hr/f | GS | APC | DOM% | DIS% | Sv% | LI | RAR | BPV | BPX | R$ |
|---|---|---|---|---|---|---|---|---|---|---|---|---|---|---|---|---|---|---|---|---|---|---|---|---|---|---|---|---|---|---|---|---|---|
| 14 NYY | 3 | 3 | 79 | 76 | 2.97 | 3.31 | 1.11 | 615 | 525 | 690 | 4.7 | 2.7 | 8.7 | 3.2 | 58% | 12% | 94.2 | 45 | 24 | 31 | 29% | 73% | 6% | 0 | 19 | | | 50 | 1.26 | 7.4 | 105 | 126 | $6 |
| 15 NYY | 7 | 1 | 131 | 104 | 3.29 | 3.84 | 1.16 | 648 | 603 | 680 | 12.4 | 2.7 | 7.1 | 2.7 | 60% | 9% | 92.5 | 45 | 23 | 32 | 28% | 73% | 8% | 17 | 50 | 18% | 12% | 100 | 1.01 | 10.9 | 79 | 94 | $9 |
| 16 2 TM | 7 | 0 | 65 | 52 | 4.68 | 4.80 | 1.35 | 742 | 635 | 800 | 4.8 | 4.0 | 7.2 | 1.8 | 60% | 10% | 92.8 | 44 | 17 | 40 | 27% | 70% | 14% | 1 | 20 | 0% | 0% | 0 | 1.05 | -4.0 | 43 | 51 | -$1 |
| 17 NYY | 3 | 1 | 57 | 54 | 2.35 | 3.83 | 0.87 | 491 | 548 | 457 | 4.8 | 2.4 | 8.5 | 3.6 | 52% | 10% | 93.0 | 44 | 17 | 39 | 22% | 76% | 7% | 0 | 20 | | | 25 | 1.11 | 14.2 | 111 | 133 | $8 |
| 18 2 AL | 3 | 0 | 52 | 52 | 3.14 | 4.35 | 1.32 | 694 | 733 | 665 | 4.7 | 3.5 | 9.1 | 2.6 | 56% | 11% | 91.9 | 38 | 23 | 40 | 31% | 81% | 10% | 0 | 21 | | | 0 | 0.67 | 6.5 | 85 | 98 | $0 |
| 1st Half | 0 | 0 | 20 | 24 | 1.35 | 3.62 | 1.20 | 577 | 769 | 409 | 4.9 | 4.1 | 10.8 | 2.7 | 54% | 12% | 91.6 | 44 | 22 | 34 | 30% | 91% | 6% | 0 | 23 | | | 0 | 0.47 | 6.9 | 107 | 123 | -$1 |
| 2nd Half | 3 | 0 | 32 | 28 | 4.26 | 4.81 | 1.39 | 762 | 707 | 798 | 4.7 | 3.1 | 8.0 | 2.5 | 57% | 10% | 92.1 | 34 | 23 | 42 | 31% | 74% | 12% | 0 | 20 | | | 0 | 0.79 | -0.4 | 71 | 82 | $1 |
| **19 Proj** | **4** | **0** | **58** | **55** | **3.46** | **3.81** | **1.19** | **646** | **662** | **636** | **4.7** | **3.2** | **8.5** | **2.7** | **56%** | **11%** | **92.5** | **41** | **20** | **38** | **28%** | **74%** | **10%** | **0** | | | | | | **4.9** | **86** | **99** | **$2** |

## Watson,Tony

| | | | | | | | |
|---|---|---|---|---|---|---|---|
| Age: 34 | Th: L | Role RP | | Health | A | LIMA Plan | B+ |
| Ht: 6' 3" | Wt: 218 | Type Pwr | | PT/Exp | C | Rand Var | -1 |
| | | | | Consist | B | MM | 3310 |

Out of saves consideration, closer-worthy metrics returned. Ctl looked vintage again; Dom rebirth comes with entrenched SwK support. 2nd-half FB% spike left him more hittable; accompanying S% reversal didn't help. But even another year older, LI hints at more late-inning value and another handful of saves.

| Yr Tm | W | Sv | IP | K | ERA | xERA | WHIP | oOPS | vL | vR | BF/G | Ctl | Dom | Cmd | FpK | SwK | Vel | G | L | F | H% | S% | hr/f | GS | APC | DOM% | DIS% | Sv% | LI | RAR | BPV | BPX | R$ |
|---|---|---|---|---|---|---|---|---|---|---|---|---|---|---|---|---|---|---|---|---|---|---|---|---|---|---|---|---|---|---|---|---|---|
| 14 PIT | 10 | 2 | 77 | 81 | 1.63 | 2.76 | 1.02 | 613 | 531 | 646 | 3.9 | 1.7 | 9.4 | 5.4 | 65% | 14% | 94.4 | 48 | 21 | 32 | 30% | 88% | 8% | 0 | 15 | | | 22 | 1.34 | 20.1 | 149 | 177 | $13 |
| 15 PIT | 4 | 1 | 75 | 62 | 1.91 | 3.42 | 0.96 | 525 | 493 | 536 | 3.8 | 2.0 | 7.4 | 3.6 | 66% | 12% | 93.9 | 48 | 21 | 32 | 26% | 81% | 5% | 0 | 14 | | | 33 | 1.38 | 19.1 | 104 | 124 | $10 |
| 16 PIT | 2 | 15 | 68 | 58 | 3.06 | 4.03 | 1.06 | 672 | 577 | 711 | 3.9 | 2.7 | 7.7 | 2.9 | 64% | 13% | 93.2 | 44 | 18 | 38 | 24% | 79% | 14% | 0 | 15 | | | 75 | 1.07 | 9.4 | 89 | 106 | $10 |
| 17 2 NL | 7 | 10 | 67 | 53 | 3.38 | 4.32 | 1.38 | 764 | 691 | 808 | 4.1 | 2.7 | 7.2 | 2.7 | 66% | 13% | 93.6 | 48 | 23 | 30 | 32% | 81% | 15% | 0 | 14 | | | 56 | 1.27 | 8.1 | 82 | 98 | $7 |
| 18 SF | 4 | 0 | 66 | 72 | 2.59 | 3.24 | 1.03 | 599 | 570 | 621 | 3.6 | 1.9 | 9.8 | 5.1 | 69% | 14% | 92.5 | 43 | 23 | 34 | 30% | 77% | 7% | 0 | 13 | | | 0 | 1.50 | 12.7 | 146 | 168 | $6 |
| 1st Half | 2 | 0 | 37 | 40 | 1.69 | 2.91 | 0.94 | 523 | 541 | 508 | 3.9 | 1.7 | 9.6 | 5.7 | 71% | 14% | 92.1 | 47 | 25 | 28 | 29% | 82% | 4% | 0 | 14 | | | 0 | 1.27 | 11.3 | 153 | 175 | $9 |
| 2nd Half | 2 | 0 | 29 | 32 | 3.77 | 3.66 | 1.15 | 691 | 609 | 744 | 3.4 | 2.2 | 10.0 | 4.6 | 66% | 13% | 93.1 | 39 | 21 | 40 | 32% | 70% | 10% | 0 | 12 | | | 0 | 1.75 | 1.4 | 138 | 159 | $3 |
| **19 Proj** | **4** | **2** | **58** | **56** | **2.95** | **3.39** | **1.14** | **664** | **605** | **699** | **3.6** | **2.3** | **8.7** | **3.9** | **67%** | **13%** | **93.1** | **44** | **22** | **34** | **30%** | **78%** | **11%** | **0** | | | | | | **8.6** | **118** | **136** | **$4** |

## Weaver,Luke

| | | | | | | | |
|---|---|---|---|---|---|---|---|
| Age: 25 | Th: R | Role SP | | Health | A | LIMA Plan | C |
| Ht: 6' 2" | Wt: 170 | Type Pwr | | PT/Exp | C | Rand Var | +2 |
| | | | | Consist | B | MM | 2201 |

What a difference a year makes. 1st-half S%, GB% plunge didn't help. But both Ctl and Dom trended poorly throughout, as intermittent bouts of wildness banished him to the pen in late August. Torched by LHB all season; RHB piled on in the 2nd half. SwK/FpK stability, age offer rebound hope, limited upside.

| Yr Tm | W | Sv | IP | K | ERA | xERA | WHIP | oOPS | vL | vR | BF/G | Ctl | Dom | Cmd | FpK | SwK | Vel | G | L | F | H% | S% | hr/f | GS | APC | DOM% | DIS% | Sv% | LI | RAR | BPV | BPX | R$ |
|---|---|---|---|---|---|---|---|---|---|---|---|---|---|---|---|---|---|---|---|---|---|---|---|---|---|---|---|---|---|---|---|---|---|
| 14 | | | | | | | | | | | | | | | | | | | | | | | | | | | | | | | | | |
| 15 | | | | | | | | | | | | | | | | | | | | | | | | | | | | | | | | | |
| 16 STL * | 8 | 0 | 119 | 120 | 2.80 | 3.60 | 1.20 | 870 | 1025 | 761 | 21.8 | 1.8 | 9.0 | 5.0 | 56% | 10% | 91.9 | 31 | 37 | 33 | 33% | 80% | 21% | 8 | 76 | 13% | 38% | 0 | 0.71 | 20.4 | 137 | 163 | $12 |
| 17 STL * | 17 | 0 | 138 | 134 | 3.41 | 3.41 | 1.22 | 699 | 575 | 793 | 19.9 | 2.3 | 8.7 | 3.7 | 59% | 10% | 93.2 | 49 | 24 | 27 | 32% | 73% | 16% | 10 | 80 | 40% | 30% | 0 | 0.64 | 16.1 | 115 | 138 | $16 |
| 18 STL | 7 | 0 | 136 | 121 | 4.95 | 4.63 | 1.50 | 786 | 841 | 724 | 20.3 | 3.6 | 8.0 | 2.2 | 60% | 10% | 93.7 | 42 | 22 | 36 | 33% | 70% | 13% | 25 | 80 | 16% | 40% | 0 | 0.69 | -13.5 | 68 | 78 | -$7 |
| 1st Half | 4 | 0 | 89 | 82 | 5.16 | 4.50 | 1.45 | 766 | 865 | 668 | 23.1 | 3.4 | 8.3 | 2.4 | 62% | 10% | 93.7 | 41 | 23 | 36 | 33% | 67% | 12% | 17 | 92 | 12% | 41% | | | -11.1 | 75 | 87 | -$7 |
| 2nd Half | 3 | 0 | 47 | 39 | 4.56 | 4.89 | 1.58 | 822 | 804 | 845 | 16.6 | 3.8 | 7.4 | 2.0 | 57% | 10% | 93.7 | 45 | 21 | 34 | 34% | 75% | 13% | 8 | 63 | 25% | 38% | 0 | 0.56 | -2.4 | 54 | 62 | -$6 |
| **19 Proj** | **9** | **0** | **116** | **107** | **4.01** | **3.81** | **1.37** | **727** | **729** | **724** | **22.7** | **2.9** | **8.3** | **2.8** | **59%** | **10%** | **93.3** | **44** | **25** | **32** | **33%** | **73%** | **12%** | **21** | | | | | | **4.5** | **92** | **106** | **$3** |

## Wheeler,Zack

| | | | | | | | |
|---|---|---|---|---|---|---|---|
| Age: 29 | Th: R | Role SP | | Health | F | LIMA Plan | C |
| Ht: 6' 4" | Wt: 195 | Type Pwr | | PT/Exp | C | Rand Var | -1 |
| | | | | Consist | B | MM | 3303 |

Why health-ravaged, premium young arms can't be completely counted out. Three years off TJS and ineffective comeback efforts, velocity and Ctl showed life - and then some - beginning in June. 2nd-half H%/S% combo fueled ERA that will regress. Workload is ominous. But now a reasonable risk portfolio pick.

| Yr Tm | W | Sv | IP | K | ERA | xERA | WHIP | oOPS | vL | vR | BF/G | Ctl | Dom | Cmd | FpK | SwK | Vel | G | L | F | H% | S% | hr/f | GS | APC | DOM% | DIS% | Sv% | LI | RAR | BPV | BPX | R$ |
|---|---|---|---|---|---|---|---|---|---|---|---|---|---|---|---|---|---|---|---|---|---|---|---|---|---|---|---|---|---|---|---|---|---|
| 14 NYM | 11 | 0 | 185 | 187 | 3.54 | 3.37 | 1.33 | 678 | 745 | 615 | 24.8 | 3.8 | 9.1 | 2.4 | 54% | 10% | 95.0 | 54 | 19 | 27 | 31% | 75% | 10% | 32 | 103 | 31% | 22% | | | 4.5 | 92 | 109 | $6 |
| 15 | | | | | | | | | | | | | | | | | | | | | | | | | | | | | | | | | |
| 16 | | | | | | | | | | | | | | | | | | | | | | | | | | | | | | | | | |
| 17 NYM | 3 | 0 | 86 | 81 | 5.21 | 4.50 | 1.59 | 828 | 858 | 804 | 22.7 | 4.2 | 8.4 | 2.0 | 61% | 10% | 94.6 | 47 | 23 | 30 | 34% | 71% | 19% | 17 | 92 | 18% | 47% | | | -9.1 | 64 | 77 | -$7 |
| 18 NYM | 12 | 0 | 182 | 179 | 3.31 | 3.74 | 1.12 | 611 | 679 | 549 | 25.7 | 2.7 | 8.8 | 3.3 | 62% | 11% | 95.9 | 44 | 20 | 35 | 29% | 72% | 8% | 29 | 99 | 45% | 28% | | | 19.0 | 108 | 124 | $19 |
| 1st Half | 2 | 0 | 89 | 86 | 4.47 | 4.14 | 1.33 | 683 | 743 | 637 | 25.3 | 3.2 | 8.7 | 2.7 | 63% | 11% | 95.4 | 44 | 19 | 36 | 32% | 68% | 10% | 15 | 97 | 27% | 40% | | | -3.5 | 92 | 106 | -$2 |
| 2nd Half | 10 | 0 | 94 | 93 | 2.21 | 3.37 | 0.93 | 537 | 624 | 439 | 26.0 | 2.2 | 8.9 | 4.0 | 61% | 11% | 96.4 | 44 | 21 | 35 | 26% | 78% | 6% | 14 | 102 | 64% | 14% | | | 22.4 | 123 | 142 | $38 |
| **19 Proj** | **11** | **0** | **160** | **155** | **3.80** | **3.57** | **1.26** | **688** | **738** | **644** | **23.5** | **3.0** | **8.7** | **3.0** | **60%** | **11%** | **95.4** | **47** | **21** | **32** | **31%** | **73%** | **12%** | **28** | | | | | | **11.2** | **102** | **118** | **$10** |

## Whitley,Forrest

| | | | | | | | |
|---|---|---|---|---|---|---|---|
| Age: 21 | Th: R | Role SP | | Health | A | LIMA Plan | C |
| Ht: 6' 7" | Wt: 195 | Type Pwr | | PT/Exp | F | Rand Var | +5 |
| | | | | Consist | F | MM | 2300 |

Lost season began in Feb. with 50-game suspension for recreational drug use. Subsequent oblique, lat strains kept him shelved more often than not. Between DL stints and later in the Arizona Fall League, flashed elite Dom, repertoire with top-of-the-rotation upside. Innings limit and rust likely to cap 2019 value in HOU.

| Yr Tm | W | Sv | IP | K | ERA | xERA | WHIP | oOPS | vL | vR | BF/G | Ctl | Dom | Cmd | FpK | SwK | Vel | G | L | F | H% | S% | hr/f | GS | APC | DOM% | DIS% | Sv% | LI | RAR | BPV | BPX | R$ |
|---|---|---|---|---|---|---|---|---|---|---|---|---|---|---|---|---|---|---|---|---|---|---|---|---|---|---|---|---|---|---|---|---|---|
| 14 | | | | | | | | | | | | | | | | | | | | | | | | | | | | | | | | | |
| 15 | | | | | | | | | | | | | | | | | | | | | | | | | | | | | | | | | |
| 16 | | | | | | | | | | | | | | | | | | | | | | | | | | | | | | | | | |
| 17 | | | | | | | | | | | | | | | | | | | | | | | | | | | | | | | | | |
| 18 aa | 0 | 0 | 27 | 30 | 4.48 | 2.21 | 1.03 | | | | 13.1 | 3.6 | 9.9 | 2.8 | | | | | | | 24% | 56% | | | | | | | | -1.1 | 113 | 130 | -$3 |
| 1st Half | 0 | 0 | 21 | 26 | 5.24 | 2.90 | 1.09 | | | | 16.5 | 2.9 | 10.9 | 3.7 | | | | | | | 29% | 52% | | | | | | | | -2.8 | 126 | 145 | -$4 |
| 2nd Half | 0 | 0 | 6 | 4 | 1.84 | -0.20 | 0.85 | | | | 7.3 | 5.9 | 6.6 | 1.1 | | | | | | | 8% | 76% | | | | | | | | 1.7 | 106 | 121 | -$1 |
| **19 Proj** | **4** | **0** | **58** | **61** | **3.77** | **3.79** | **1.32** | | | | **21.6** | **3.9** | **9.4** | **2.4** | **61%** | **11%** | | **44** | **20** | **36** | **31%** | **74%** | **11%** | **8** | | | | | | **2.7** | **86** | **99** | **$0** |

## Williams,Taylor

| | | | | | | | |
|---|---|---|---|---|---|---|---|
| Age: 27 | Th: R | Role RP | | Health | C | LIMA Plan | D+ |
| Ht: 5' 11" | Wt: 195 | Type Pwr | | PT/Exp | D | Rand Var | +1 |
| | | | | Consist | C | MM | 1300 |

Fast start deteriorated into abysmal finish for converted SP. Lost ability to reach strike three in 2nd half; LD% and H% soared as S% plummeted. Through it all, FpK, SwK and velocity remained stable, and even intriguing. But inexperience, inconsistency and history of poor Ctl, hittability all say he can't be trusted.

| Yr Tm | W | Sv | IP | K | ERA | xERA | WHIP | oOPS | vL | vR | BF/G | Ctl | Dom | Cmd | FpK | SwK | Vel | G | L | F | H% | S% | hr/f | GS | APC | DOM% | DIS% | Sv% | LI | RAR | BPV | BPX | R$ |
|---|---|---|---|---|---|---|---|---|---|---|---|---|---|---|---|---|---|---|---|---|---|---|---|---|---|---|---|---|---|---|---|---|---|
| 14 | | | | | | | | | | | | | | | | | | | | | | | | | | | | | | | | | |
| 15 | | | | | | | | | | | | | | | | | | | | | | | | | | | | | | | | | |
| 16 | | | | | | | | | | | | | | | | | | | | | | | | | | | | | | | | | |
| 17 MIL * | 0 | 0 | 51 | 50 | 4.84 | 5.42 | 1.76 | 633 | 864 | 347 | 8.7 | 4.8 | 8.8 | 1.8 | 70% | 10% | 95.9 | 43 | 43 | 14 | 39% | 72% | 0% | 0 | 16 | | | 0 | 0.09 | -3.0 | 68 | 82 | -$8 |
| 18 MIL | 1 | 0 | 53 | 57 | 4.25 | 4.35 | 1.47 | 747 | 1057 | 567 | 4.2 | 4.2 | 9.7 | 2.3 | 60% | 14% | 95.6 | 36 | 28 | 35 | 34% | 74% | 12% | 0 | 17 | | | 0 | 0.70 | -0.6 | 74 | 85 | -$5 |
| 1st Half | 0 | 0 | 31 | 41 | 2.93 | 3.60 | 1.27 | 616 | 738 | 528 | 4.6 | 5.0 | 12.0 | 2.4 | 58% | 14% | 95.7 | 37 | 31 | 31 | 29% | 81% | 14% | 0 | 19 | | | 0 | 0.44 | 4.6 | 97 | 111 | -$3 |
| 2nd Half | 1 | 0 | 22 | 16 | 6.04 | 5.44 | 1.75 | 906 | 1594 | 605 | 3.9 | 3.2 | 6.4 | 2.0 | 62% | 14% | 95.6 | 36 | 26 | 38 | 37% | 67% | 10% | 0 | 14 | | | 0 | 0.96 | -5.2 | 43 | 49 | -$10 |
| **19 Proj** | **1** | **0** | **44** | **42** | **4.81** | **4.46** | **1.64** | **804** | **1204** | **590** | **5.1** | **4.3** | **8.8** | **2.0** | **60%** | **14%** | **95.6** | **36** | **28** | **36** | **37%** | **71%** | **9%** | **0** | | | | | | **-1.6** | **55** | **63** | **-$7** |

JOCK THOMPSON

## Williams,Trevor

| Age: 27 | Th: R | Role SP | Health A | LIMA Plan D+ |
|---|---|---|---|---|
| Ht: 6' 3" | Wt: 230 | Type | PT/Exp B | Rand Var -3 |
| | | | Consist A | MM 1003 |

Trifecta of luck (H%, S%, hr/f) delivered amazing 2nd half ERA/WHIP, but peripherals scream regression as he doesn't possess a single plus skill. Yielded 20% less hard contact than typical SP but that's unlikely to be repeatable. High xERA, tepid K rates don't indicate a pending breakout.

| Yr Tm | W | Sv | IP | K | ERA | xERA | WHIP | oOPS | vL | vR | BF/G | Ctl | Dom | Cmd | FpK | SwK | Vel | G | L | F | H% | S% | hr/f | GS | APC | DOM% | DIS% | Sv% | LI | RAR | BPV | BPX | R$ |
|---|---|---|---|---|---|---|---|---|---|---|---|---|---|---|---|---|---|---|---|---|---|---|---|---|---|---|---|---|---|---|---|---|---|
| 14 aa | 0 | 0 | 15 | 12 | 6.66 | 6.48 | 1.99 | | | | 24.0 | 3.4 | 7.1 | 2.1 | | | | | | | 44% | 63% | | | | | | | | -5.4 | 68 | 81 | -$6 |
| 15 a/a | 7 | 0 | 131 | 84 | 4.79 | 5.13 | 1.60 | | | | 23.2 | 3.1 | 5.8 | 1.9 | | | | | | | 35% | 70% | | | | | | | | -13.4 | 49 | 59 | -$10 |
| 16 PIT * | 10 | 0 | 123 | 70 | 4.10 | 5.03 | 1.54 | 1054 | 1359 | 885 | 19.9 | 2.8 | 5.1 | 1.8 | 56% | 10% | 92.8 | 45 | 25 | 30 | 34% | 74% | 31% | 1 | 32 | 0% | 100% | 0 | 0.70 | 1.3 | 40 | 48 | -$2 |
| 17 PIT | 7 | 0 | 150 | 117 | 4.07 | 4.43 | 1.31 | 715 | 742 | 688 | 20.7 | 3.1 | 7.0 | 2.3 | 61% | 9% | 92.1 | 48 | 21 | 31 | 30% | 70% | 10% | 25 | 78 | 16% | 24% | 0 | 0.75 | 5.3 | 68 | 82 | $5 |
| 18 PIT | 14 | 0 | 171 | 126 | 3.11 | 4.51 | 1.18 | 659 | 637 | 681 | 22.6 | 2.9 | 6.6 | 2.3 | 61% | 8% | 90.5 | 41 | 22 | 37 | 27% | 76% | 8% | 31 | 88 | 16% | 32% | | | 21.9 | 60 | 69 | $17 |
| 1st Half | 6 | 0 | 92 | 68 | 4.22 | 4.57 | 1.20 | 703 | 711 | 695 | 22.3 | 2.9 | 6.7 | 2.3 | 59% | 9% | 90.5 | 41 | 20 | 39 | 27% | 68% | 11% | 17 | 87 | 12% | 35% | | | -0.8 | 60 | 69 | $9 |
| 2nd Half | 8 | 0 | 79 | 58 | 1.82 | 4.45 | 1.15 | 609 | 563 | 662 | 23.0 | 2.8 | 6.6 | 2.3 | 63% | 8% | 90.4 | 40 | 24 | 36 | 27% | 86% | 5% | 14 | 89 | 21% | 29% | | | 22.7 | 60 | 69 | $26 |
| **19 Proj** | **11** | **0** | **174** | **124** | **4.18** | **4.31** | **1.33** | **766** | **758** | **773** | **21.4** | **3.0** | **6.4** | **2.2** | **61%** | **9%** | **91.1** | **44** | **22** | **35** | **29%** | **72%** | **12%** | **34** | | | | | | **-0.6** | **57** | **66** | **$4** |

## Wilson,Alex

| Age: 32 | Th: R | Role RP | Health D | LIMA Plan B+ |
|---|---|---|---|---|
| Ht: 6' 0" | Wt: 227 | Type | PT/Exp C | Rand Var -1 |
| | | | Consist B | MM 2000 |

Lost a month to 1st half foot injury. 2018 ERA and WHIP were H%-aided, though in-season gains in FpK, SwK backed August-September improvement. Neither platoon split nor 2nd half Cmd is consistent with history, so they could both easily vanish again. He's not much more than bullpen depth.

| Yr Tm | W | Sv | IP | K | ERA | xERA | WHIP | oOPS | vL | vR | BF/G | Ctl | Dom | Cmd | FpK | SwK | Vel | G | L | F | H% | S% | hr/f | GS | APC | DOM% | DIS% | Sv% | LI | RAR | BPV | BPX | R$ |
|---|---|---|---|---|---|---|---|---|---|---|---|---|---|---|---|---|---|---|---|---|---|---|---|---|---|---|---|---|---|---|---|---|---|
| 14 BOS * | 7 | 5 | 70 | 49 | 4.38 | 4.18 | 1.45 | 624 | 787 | 476 | 5.6 | 4.1 | 6.3 | 1.6 | 61% | 8% | 92.5 | 44 | 18 | 38 | 30% | 70% | 10% | 0 | 23 | | | 50 | 0.54 | -5.5 | 52 | 62 | -$1 |
| 15 DET | 3 | 2 | 70 | 38 | 2.19 | 3.98 | 1.03 | 609 | 566 | 645 | 4.6 | 1.4 | 4.9 | 3.5 | 62% | 7% | 92.4 | 50 | 15 | 35 | 26% | 82% | 7% | 1 | 17 | 0% | 0% | 50 | 0.94 | 15.3 | 78 | 93 | $7 |
| 16 DET | 4 | 0 | 73 | 49 | 2.96 | 4.51 | 1.22 | 692 | 728 | 665 | 4.8 | 2.6 | 6.0 | 2.3 | 58% | 9% | 91.9 | 44 | 19 | 37 | 29% | 77% | 6% | 0 | 18 | | | 0 | 1.10 | 11.1 | 61 | 72 | $4 |
| 17 DET | 2 | 2 | 60 | 42 | 4.50 | 4.79 | 1.37 | 764 | 687 | 829 | 3.9 | 2.3 | 6.3 | 2.8 | 55% | 9% | 92.8 | 42 | 23 | 36 | 32% | 69% | 10% | 0 | 14 | | | 29 | 1.00 | -1.0 | 73 | 87 | -$2 |
| 18 DET | 2 | 0 | 62 | 43 | 3.36 | 3.99 | 1.05 | 646 | 829 | 517 | 4.2 | 2.2 | 6.3 | 2.9 | 57% | 9% | 92.1 | 49 | 20 | 31 | 24% | 74% | 14% | 0 | 16 | | | 0 | 1.22 | 6.0 | 81 | 93 | $2 |
| 1st Half | 0 | 0 | 32 | 21 | 3.94 | 4.39 | 1.16 | 702 | 844 | 585 | 4.7 | 2.8 | 5.9 | 2.1 | 52% | 8% | 92.2 | 49 | 18 | 33 | 24% | 72% | 16% | 0 | 18 | | | 0 | 1.45 | 0.8 | 58 | 66 | -$3 |
| 2nd Half | 2 | 0 | 30 | 22 | 2.73 | 3.57 | 0.94 | 584 | 810 | 450 | 3.7 | 1.5 | 6.7 | 4.4 | 63% | 11% | 92.1 | 49 | 23 | 28 | 24% | 76% | 13% | 0 | 14 | | | 0 | 1.01 | 5.2 | 106 | 122 | $7 |
| **19 Proj** | **3** | **0** | **58** | **40** | **3.81** | **3.99** | **1.22** | **735** | **818** | **673** | **4.2** | **2.2** | **6.2** | **2.8** | **58%** | **9%** | **92.3** | **47** | **21** | **33** | **28%** | **74%** | **14%** | **0** | | | | | | **2.4** | **76** | **87** | **$0** |

## Wilson,Justin

| Age: 31 | Th: L | Role RP | Health A | LIMA Plan C |
|---|---|---|---|---|
| Ht: 6' 2" | Wt: 205 | Type Pwr | PT/Exp C | Rand Var -1 |
| | | | Consist A | MM 2500 |

Struggled with Ctl again, and although FpK bounced back to previous levels, it is still below average. High Dom supports elevated S%, as Ks provide margin for error. Combined with his success vR, he's a viable choice in leagues that value setup men, if you can absorb the WHIP.

| Yr Tm | W | Sv | IP | K | ERA | xERA | WHIP | oOPS | vL | vR | BF/G | Ctl | Dom | Cmd | FpK | SwK | Vel | G | L | F | H% | S% | hr/f | GS | APC | DOM% | DIS% | Sv% | LI | RAR | BPV | BPX | R$ |
|---|---|---|---|---|---|---|---|---|---|---|---|---|---|---|---|---|---|---|---|---|---|---|---|---|---|---|---|---|---|---|---|---|---|
| 14 PIT | 3 | 0 | 60 | 61 | 4.20 | 3.68 | 1.32 | 643 | 681 | 622 | 3.7 | 4.5 | 9.2 | 2.0 | 61% | 10% | 95.2 | 51 | 14 | 34 | 29% | 68% | 7% | 0 | 15 | | | 0 | 1.05 | -3.4 | 72 | 86 | -$2 |
| 15 NYY | 5 | 0 | 61 | 66 | 3.10 | 3.17 | 1.13 | 602 | 629 | 588 | 3.3 | 3.0 | 9.7 | 3.3 | 60% | 13% | 95.1 | 44 | 27 | 29 | 30% | 73% | 7% | 0 | 14 | | | 0 | 1.26 | 6.5 | 118 | 140 | $4 |
| 16 DET | 4 | 1 | 59 | 65 | 4.14 | 3.37 | 1.33 | 708 | 772 | 667 | 3.8 | 2.6 | 10.0 | 3.8 | 59% | 13% | 95.1 | 55 | 15 | 30 | 35% | 71% | 12% | 0 | 15 | | | 17 | 1.25 | 0.3 | 142 | 169 | $0 |
| 17 2 TM | 4 | 13 | 58 | 80 | 3.41 | 4.04 | 1.29 | 631 | 701 | 599 | 3.8 | 5.4 | 12.4 | 2.3 | 53% | 13% | 96.0 | 37 | 18 | 44 | 30% | 76% | 9% | 0 | 17 | | | 81 | 1.21 | 6.8 | 92 | 110 | $8 |
| 18 CHC | 4 | 0 | 55 | 69 | 3.46 | 4.19 | 1.43 | 682 | 643 | 707 | 3.3 | 5.4 | 11.4 | 2.1 | 59% | 12% | 94.7 | 35 | 24 | 40 | 32% | 78% | 9% | 0 | 15 | | | 0 | 1.21 | 4.7 | 71 | 81 | -$1 |
| 1st Half | 2 | 0 | 34 | 46 | 3.18 | 4.08 | 1.47 | 684 | 574 | 760 | 4.2 | 6.6 | 12.2 | 1.8 | 59% | 11% | 94.6 | 38 | 26 | 36 | 31% | 81% | 11% | 0 | 18 | | | 0 | 0.91 | 4.1 | 56 | 65 | -$1 |
| 2nd Half | 2 | 0 | 21 | 23 | 3.92 | 4.39 | 1.35 | 677 | 757 | 630 | 2.5 | 3.5 | 10.0 | 2.9 | 59% | 13% | 94.9 | 32 | 23 | 46 | 34% | 73% | 8% | 0 | 11 | | | 0 | 1.50 | 0.6 | 96 | 110 | $0 |
| **19 Proj** | **4** | **0** | **58** | **71** | **3.65** | **3.69** | **1.35** | **668** | **700** | **650** | **3.2** | **4.5** | **11.0** | **2.4** | **58%** | **13%** | **95.2** | **39** | **21** | **40** | **32%** | **75%** | **9%** | **0** | | | | | | **3.6** | **94** | **108** | **$1** |

## Winkler,Daniel

| Age: 29 | Th: R | Role RP | Health F | LIMA Plan A |
|---|---|---|---|---|
| Ht: 6' 3" | Wt: 205 | Type Pwr | PT/Exp D | Rand Var -1 |
| | | | Consist D | MM 3410 |

So much lost time time due to fractured elbow. Had the kind of 1st half that puts you in the closer conversation, backed by excellent Dom and Cmd. Faded big in the 2nd half, which is concerning given injury history and workload. Track record as reliever is brief and volatile, making him a high risk / high reward pick.

| Yr Tm | W | Sv | IP | K | ERA | xERA | WHIP | oOPS | vL | vR | BF/G | Ctl | Dom | Cmd | FpK | SwK | Vel | G | L | F | H% | S% | hr/f | GS | APC | DOM% | DIS% | Sv% | LI | RAR | BPV | BPX | R$ |
|---|---|---|---|---|---|---|---|---|---|---|---|---|---|---|---|---|---|---|---|---|---|---|---|---|---|---|---|---|---|---|---|---|---|
| 14 aa | 5 | 0 | 70 | 57 | 2.06 | 1.89 | 0.87 | | | | 21.5 | 2.4 | 7.3 | 3.0 | | | | | | | 20% | 84% | | | | | | | | 14.5 | 97 | 116 | $9 |
| 15 ATL | 0 | 0 | 2 | 2 | 10.80 | 5.08 | 1.80 | 1518 | 1000 | 2667 | 4.0 | 5.4 | 10.8 | 2.0 | 63% | 12% | 89.4 | 40 | 0 | 60 | 0% | 0% | 67% | 0 | 17 | | | 0 | 0.05 | -1.4 | 67 | 79 | -$5 |
| 16 ATL | 0 | 0 | 2 | 4 | 0.00 | 0.00 | 0.43 | 125 | 0 | 200 | 2.7 | 3.9 | 15.4 | 4.0 | 89% | 21% | 92.0 | 100 | 0 | 0 | 0% | 0% | 0% | 0 | 11 | | | 0 | 1.91 | 1.2 | 252 | 299 | -$3 |
| 17 ATL | 1 | 0 | 14 | 18 | 2.51 | 3.41 | 0.91 | 511 | 311 | 640 | 3.3 | 3.8 | 11.3 | 3.0 | 68% | 12% | 93.6 | 36 | 18 | 46 | 21% | 75% | 8% | 0 | 15 | | | 0 | 1.24 | 3.3 | 116 | 139 | -$2 |
| 18 ATL | 4 | 2 | 60 | 69 | 3.43 | 3.67 | 1.19 | 648 | 898 | 501 | 3.7 | 3.0 | 10.3 | 3.5 | 57% | 13% | 93.3 | 38 | 26 | 36 | 33% | 71% | 5% | 0 | 15 | | | 40 | 1.07 | 5.4 | 121 | 139 | $3 |
| 1st Half | 2 | 1 | 33 | 42 | 2.48 | 2.83 | 0.95 | 513 | 660 | 429 | 3.7 | 2.5 | 11.6 | 4.7 | 60% | 15% | 93.4 | 41 | 30 | 29 | 31% | 71% | 0% | 0 | 16 | | | 33 | 1.10 | 6.7 | 160 | 184 | $6 |
| 2nd Half | 2 | 1 | 28 | 27 | 4.55 | 4.73 | 1.48 | 792 | 1141 | 581 | 3.6 | 3.6 | 8.8 | 2.5 | 54% | 12% | 93.0 | 36 | 21 | 43 | 35% | 71% | 8% | 0 | 14 | | | 50 | 1.03 | -1.4 | 75 | 86 | -$2 |
| **19 Proj** | **5** | **2** | **65** | **75** | **3.73** | **3.38** | **1.15** | **661** | **953** | **488** | **5.2** | **3.3** | **10.3** | **3.1** | **56%** | **13%** | **93.1** | **38** | **25** | **37** | **29%** | **71%** | **12%** | **0** | | | | | | **7.1** | **113** | **129** | **$4** |

## Wisler,Matthew

| Age: 26 | Th: R | Role RP | Health A | LIMA Plan C |
|---|---|---|---|---|
| Ht: 6' 3" | Wt: 210 | Type FB | PT/Exp D | Rand Var +2 |
| | | | Consist B | MM 1101 |

1-1, 4.28 ERA in 40 IP at ATL/CIN. Ctl improved despite decline in FpK and doesn't support gains. 37% hit rate at Triple-A raised ERA, and low Dom inflated xERA. Solid SwK is consistent with much higher Dom, but it has yet to materialize at any level. He still needs several adjustments to make him rosterable.

| Yr Tm | W | Sv | IP | K | ERA | xERA | WHIP | oOPS | vL | vR | BF/G | Ctl | Dom | Cmd | FpK | SwK | Vel | G | L | F | H% | S% | hr/f | GS | APC | DOM% | DIS% | Sv% | LI | RAR | BPV | BPX | R$ |
|---|---|---|---|---|---|---|---|---|---|---|---|---|---|---|---|---|---|---|---|---|---|---|---|---|---|---|---|---|---|---|---|---|---|
| 14 a/a | 10 | 0 | 147 | 121 | 4.06 | 4.32 | 1.32 | | | | 21.7 | 2.3 | 7.4 | 3.2 | | | | | | | 32% | 72% | | | | | | | | -5.7 | 82 | 97 | $2 |
| 15 ATL * | 11 | 0 | 174 | 116 | 5.00 | 4.95 | 1.46 | 819 | 986 | 664 | 23.3 | 2.8 | 6.0 | 2.1 | 59% | 8% | 93.3 | 34 | 23 | 43 | 32% | 68% | 10% | 19 | 89 | 11% | 53% | 0 | 0.74 | -22.2 | 45 | 53 | -$8 |
| 16 ATL * | 9 | 1 | 183 | 134 | 4.97 | 4.69 | 1.34 | 756 | 769 | 741 | 24.6 | 2.7 | 6.6 | 2.5 | 58% | 9% | 92.8 | 40 | 21 | 38 | 30% | 67% | 14% | 26 | 90 | 12% | 35% | 100 | 0.83 | -17.7 | 49 | 58 | -$1 |
| 17 ATL * | 7 | 0 | 126 | 73 | 5.61 | 5.66 | 1.59 | 971 | 1116 | 840 | 14.6 | 2.4 | 5.2 | 2.2 | 58% | 10% | 92.6 | 32 | 19 | 49 | 35% | 65% | 9% | 1 | 28 | 0% | 100% | 0 | 0.25 | -19.4 | 40 | 48 | -$10 |
| 18 2 NL * | 6 | 0 | 131 | 102 | 4.79 | 5.31 | 1.45 | 781 | 780 | 782 | 14.4 | 1.8 | 7.0 | 3.9 | 55% | 11% | 92.3 | 33 | 21 | 47 | 36% | 69% | 14% | 3 | 34 | 33% | 33% | 0 | 0.54 | -10.3 | 86 | 99 | -$6 |
| 1st Half | 3 | 0 | 75 | 58 | 5.31 | 5.30 | 1.36 | 850 | 822 | 879 | 19.5 | 1.7 | 7.0 | 4.1 | 54% | 10% | 92.6 | 29 | 23 | 48 | 33% | 65% | 15% | 3 | 58 | 33% | 33% | 0 | 0.75 | -10.7 | 79 | 91 | -$8 |
| 2nd Half | 3 | 0 | 57 | 45 | 4.09 | 5.32 | 1.56 | 633 | 635 | 632 | 10.8 | 1.9 | 7.1 | 3.7 | 56% | 12% | 91.6 | 40 | 15 | 45 | 39% | 74% | 11% | 0 | 18 | | | 0 | 0.40 | 0.4 | 95 | 109 | -$3 |
| **19 Proj** | **4** | **0** | **73** | **57** | **4.54** | **4.43** | **1.44** | **867** | **915** | **821** | **15.0** | **2.2** | **7.1** | **3.3** | **57%** | **10%** | **92.8** | **34** | **22** | **44** | **33%** | **74%** | **13%** | **10** | | | | | | **-2.0** | **82** | **95** | **-$4** |

## Wood,Alex

| Age: 28 | Th: L | Role SP | Health F | LIMA Plan B+ |
|---|---|---|---|---|
| Ht: 6' 4" | Wt: 215 | Type Pwr | PT/Exp B | Rand Var 0 |
| | | | Consist A | MM 3203 |

10 days on the DL and time in the bullpen led to an identical IP total to 2017. ERA was well supported by SwK, Dom, Ctl, and GB%. Already elite FpK continued upward trend. Should continue to be ERA and WHIP asset if you can afford to fill in for the innings he'll inevitably miss.

| Yr Tm | W | Sv | IP | K | ERA | xERA | WHIP | oOPS | vL | vR | BF/G | Ctl | Dom | Cmd | FpK | SwK | Vel | G | L | F | H% | S% | hr/f | GS | APC | DOM% | DIS% | Sv% | LI | RAR | BPV | BPX | R$ |
|---|---|---|---|---|---|---|---|---|---|---|---|---|---|---|---|---|---|---|---|---|---|---|---|---|---|---|---|---|---|---|---|---|---|
| 14 ATL | 11 | 0 | 172 | 170 | 2.78 | 3.20 | 1.14 | 651 | 667 | 645 | 19.8 | 2.4 | 8.9 | 3.8 | 62% | 10% | 89.8 | 46 | 19 | 35 | 30% | 79% | 10% | 24 | 77 | 42% | 13% | 0 | 0.91 | 20.4 | 121 | 144 | $16 |
| 15 2 NL | 12 | 0 | 190 | 139 | 3.84 | 4.01 | 1.36 | 724 | 517 | 788 | 25.0 | 2.8 | 6.6 | 2.4 | 63% | 8% | 89.1 | 49 | 23 | 28 | 32% | 73% | 9% | 32 | 91 | 28% | 22% | | | 2.8 | 70 | 84 | $5 |
| 16 LA | 1 | 0 | 60 | 66 | 3.73 | 3.30 | 1.26 | 660 | 774 | 620 | 18.2 | 3.0 | 9.8 | 3.3 | 64% | 10% | 90.6 | 53 | 20 | 27 | 33% | 72% | 12% | 10 | 70 | 30% | 20% | 0 | 0.60 | 3.4 | 128 | 152 | $0 |
| 17 LA | 16 | 0 | 152 | 151 | 2.72 | 3.34 | 1.06 | 620 | 607 | 625 | 22.7 | 2.2 | 8.9 | 4.0 | 67% | 12% | 91.8 | 53 | 20 | 27 | 28% | 79% | 14% | 25 | 84 | 44% | 24% | 0 | 0.78 | 30.8 | 131 | 157 | $25 |
| 18 LA | 9 | 0 | 152 | 135 | 3.68 | 3.75 | 1.21 | 664 | 590 | 692 | 19.3 | 2.4 | 8.0 | 3.4 | 69% | 11% | 89.9 | 49 | 22 | 29 | 31% | 72% | 11% | 27 | 74 | 19% | 26% | 0 | 0.81 | 8.8 | 107 | 123 | $9 |
| 1st Half | 4 | 0 | 88 | 81 | 4.00 | 3.67 | 1.16 | 679 | 590 | 707 | 22.8 | 1.6 | 8.3 | 5.1 | 68% | 12% | 90.1 | 46 | 23 | 32 | 31% | 68% | 12% | 16 | 86 | 19% | 19% | | | 1.6 | 129 | 148 | $9 |
| 2nd Half | 5 | 0 | 64 | 54 | 3.23 | 3.88 | 1.27 | 642 | 589 | 666 | 16.1 | 3.4 | 7.6 | 2.3 | 69% | 11% | 89.7 | 53 | 22 | 25 | 30% | 75% | 9% | 11 | 63 | 18% | 36% | 0 | 0.85 | 7.2 | 77 | 89 | $10 |
| **19 Proj** | **11** | **0** | **160** | **149** | **3.57** | **3.37** | **1.17** | **654** | **620** | **667** | **23.9** | **2.4** | **8.4** | **3.5** | **67%** | **11%** | **90.4** | **49** | **21** | **30** | **30%** | **72%** | **11%** | **27** | | | | | | **14.4** | **113** | **130** | **$13** |

## Wood,Hunter

| Age: 25 | Th: R | Role RP | Health A | LIMA Plan B+ |
|---|---|---|---|---|
| Ht: 6' 1" | Wt: 165 | Type Pwr | PT/Exp D | Rand Var 0 |
| | | | Consist D | MM 2311 |

1-1, 3.79 ERA in 41 IP at TAM. Moved to bullpen to begin year, earned July call-up with stellar 13.5 Dom, 6.3 Cmd at Triple-A. Struggled with Ctl in MLB, but excellent SwK backed up Dom in limited sample. Has velocity and pitch mix, but needs to limit walks to reach future as #4 SP or setup man. Worth a late flyer.

| Yr Tm | W | Sv | IP | K | ERA | xERA | WHIP | oOPS | vL | vR | BF/G | Ctl | Dom | Cmd | FpK | SwK | Vel | G | L | F | H% | S% | hr/f | GS | APC | DOM% | DIS% | Sv% | LI | RAR | BPV | BPX | R$ |
|---|---|---|---|---|---|---|---|---|---|---|---|---|---|---|---|---|---|---|---|---|---|---|---|---|---|---|---|---|---|---|---|---|---|
| 14 | | | | | | | | | | | | | | | | | | | | | | | | | | | | | | | | | |
| 15 | | | | | | | | | | | | | | | | | | | | | | | | | | | | | | | | | |
| 16 aa | 6 | 0 | 49 | 43 | 3.97 | 3.48 | 1.26 | | | | 20.1 | 3.8 | 7.9 | 2.1 | | | | | | | 27% | 71% | | | | | | | | 1.3 | 71 | 85 | $1 |
| 17 TAM * | 7 | 0 | 124 | 100 | 5.96 | 5.51 | 1.57 | 0 | 0 | 0 | 17.0 | 3.4 | 7.3 | 2.2 | 0% | 0% | 90.0 | 0 | 0 | 100 | 34% | 63% | 0% | 0 | 5 | | | 0 | 0.11 | -24.4 | 47 | 56 | -$10 |
| 18 TAM * | 3 | 3 | 83 | 96 | 3.79 | 3.56 | 1.23 | 727 | 714 | 734 | 6.3 | 3.1 | 10.4 | 3.3 | 55% | 14% | 94.4 | 44 | 24 | 32 | 32% | 72% | 11% | 8 | 24 | 13% | 75% | 100 | 0.77 | 3.7 | 112 | 129 | $3 |
| 1st Half | 2 | 3 | 44 | 55 | 3.84 | 2.88 | 1.06 | 780 | 762 | 800 | 6.9 | 2.4 | 11.1 | 4.7 | 50% | 5% | 92.3 | 50 | 30 | 20 | 31% | 66% | 0% | 0 | 38 | | | 100 | 0.21 | 1.7 | 149 | 171 | $6 |
| 2nd Half | 1 | 0 | 39 | 41 | 3.72 | 4.05 | 1.42 | 723 | 709 | 731 | 6.0 | 4.0 | 9.5 | 2.4 | 55% | 14% | 94.5 | 44 | 23 | 33 | 33% | 76% | 11% | 8 | 24 | 13% | 75% | 0 | 0.79 | 2.0 | 87 | 100 | -$1 |
| **19 Proj** | **4** | **1** | **73** | **77** | **3.83** | **3.67** | **1.33** | **649** | **630** | **660** | **9.2** | **3.4** | **9.6** | **2.8** | **55%** | **14%** | **94.5** | **44** | **23** | **33** | **32%** | **74%** | **12%** | **0** | | | | | | **4.6** | **101** | **116** | **$1** |

ARIK FLORIMONTE

## Woodruff,Brandon

| | | | | | |
|---|---|---|---|---|---|
| Age: 26 | Th: R | Role RP | Health | C | LIMA Plan B+ |
| Ht: 6' 4" | Wt: 215 | Type Pwr | PT/Exp | D | Rand Var 0 |
| | | | Consist | B | MM 2201 |

3-0, 3.61 in 42 IP at MIL. Shuffled between Triple-A and MLB, where he worked mainly in relief and markedly improved Dom and velocity. Current skills/experience point to success as high-leverage reliever, but he'll need to improve Ctl to make an impact as a starter. There's a bit more time.

| Yr Tm | W | Sv | IP | K | ERA | xERA | WHIP | oOPS | vL | vR | BF/G | Ctl | Dom | Cmd | FpK | SwK | Vel | G | L | F | H% | S% | hr/f | GS | APC | DOM% | DIS% | Sv% | LI | RAR | BPV | BPX | R$ |
|---|---|---|---|---|---|---|---|---|---|---|---|---|---|---|---|---|---|---|---|---|---|---|---|---|---|---|---|---|---|---|---|---|---|
| 14 | | | | | | | | | | | | | | | | | | | | | | | | | | | | | | | | | |
| 15 | | | | | | | | | | | | | | | | | | | | | | | | | | | | | | | | | |
| 16 aa | 10 | 0 | 114 | 107 | 4.52 | 3.53 | 1.29 | | | | 23.4 | 2.7 | 8.5 | 3.2 | | | | | | | 33% | 64% | | | | | | | | -4.6 | 105 | 125 | $3 |
| 17 MIL * | 8 | 0 | 118 | 91 | 4.71 | 4.64 | 1.41 | 719 | 872 | 566 | 20.9 | 2.9 | 6.9 | 2.4 | 62% | 9% | 94.3 | 47 | 19 | 34 | 32% | 69% | 11% | 8 | 90 | 38% | 63% | | | -5.2 | 60 | 72 | -$1 |
| 18 MIL * | 6 | 1 | 114 | 103 | 3.95 | 4.11 | 1.34 | 641 | 622 | 659 | 13.2 | 3.5 | 8.1 | 2.3 | 56% | 11% | 95.3 | 53 | 18 | 29 | 31% | 73% | 12% | 4 | 39 | 0% | 50% | 100 | 0.51 | 2.8 | 73 | 84 | $2 |
| 1st Half | 4 | 0 | 72 | 57 | 3.73 | 3.71 | 1.28 | 685 | 682 | 686 | 16.3 | 3.5 | 7.2 | 2.0 | 55% | 9% | 94.7 | 49 | 19 | 32 | 28% | 73% | 14% | 4 | 51 | 0% | 50% | 0 | 0.56 | 3.7 | 66 | 75 | $3 |
| 2nd Half | 2 | 1 | 45 | 46 | 4.11 | 4.37 | 1.37 | 584 | 536 | 626 | 10.5 | 3.3 | 9.2 | 2.8 | 57% | 14% | 96.4 | 60 | 16 | 24 | 33% | 73% | 9% | 0 | 29 | | | 100 | 0.46 | 0.2 | 86 | 99 | -$1 |
| **19 Proj** | **6** | **0** | **102** | **96** | **3.98** | **3.65** | **1.30** | **708** | **758** | **660** | **15.4** | **3.1** | **8.5** | **2.8** | **57%** | **11%** | **95.1** | **48** | **21** | **31** | **31%** | **72%** | **13%** | **15** | | | | | | **2.1** | **96** | **110** | **$3** |

## Wright,Kyle

| | | | | | |
|---|---|---|---|---|---|
| Age: 23 | Th: R | Role SP | Health | A | LIMA Plan D+ |
| Ht: 6' 4" | Wt: 200 | Type Pwr | PT/Exp | F | Rand Var +5 |
| | | | Consist | F | MM 1100 |

0-0, 4.50 in 6 IP at ATL. 2017's #5 overall pick sprinted through minors (16 IP below Double-A), but without eye-popping numbers. Has utilized four-pitch mix to retire LHB and RHB with equal efficiency. GB tilt (54% in MiLB) should limit HR and speed up ascent, but he's still not likely to contribute much in 2019.

| Yr Tm | W | Sv | IP | K | ERA | xERA | WHIP | oOPS | vL | vR | BF/G | Ctl | Dom | Cmd | FpK | SwK | Vel | G | L | F | H% | S% | hr/f | GS | APC | DOM% | DIS% | Sv% | LI | RAR | BPV | BPX | R$ |
|---|---|---|---|---|---|---|---|---|---|---|---|---|---|---|---|---|---|---|---|---|---|---|---|---|---|---|---|---|---|---|---|---|---|
| 14 | | | | | | | | | | | | | | | | | | | | | | | | | | | | | | | | | |
| 15 | | | | | | | | | | | | | | | | | | | | | | | | | | | | | | | | | |
| 16 | | | | | | | | | | | | | | | | | | | | | | | | | | | | | | | | | |
| 17 | | | | | | | | | | | | | | | | | | | | | | | | | | | | | | | | | |
| 18 ATL * | 8 | 0 | 146 | 116 | 4.33 | 3.98 | 1.37 | 812 | 1306 | 466 | 19.8 | 3.5 | 7.2 | 2.1 | 57% | 10% | 94.0 | 41 | 18 | 41 | 31% | 69% | 29% | 0 | 32 | | | 0 | 0.21 | -3.3 | 69 | 79 | $0 |
| 1st Half | 4 | 0 | 83 | 70 | 5.55 | 5.09 | 1.66 | | | | 23.2 | 3.9 | 7.6 | 1.9 | | | | | | | 37% | 65% | 0% | 0 | | | | | | -14.3 | 69 | 79 | -$12 |
| 2nd Half | 4 | 0 | 63 | 46 | 3.14 | 2.85 | 1.05 | 812 | 1306 | 466 | 16.3 | 3.0 | 6.6 | 2.2 | 57% | 10% | 94.0 | 41 | 18 | 41 | 22% | 76% | 29% | 0 | 32 | | | 0 | 0.21 | 7.9 | 67 | 77 | $15 |
| **19 Proj** | **4** | **0** | **58** | **45** | **4.09** | **4.11** | **1.35** | | | | **22.6** | **3.4** | **7.0** | **2.1** | **60%** | **10%** | | **48** | **22** | **30** | **30%** | **71%** | **10%** | **11** | | | | | | **0.4** | **61** | **70** | **-$1** |

## Wright,Mike

| | | | | | |
|---|---|---|---|---|---|
| Age: 29 | Th: R | Role RP | Health | C | LIMA Plan D+ |
| Ht: 6' 6" | Wt: 215 | Type Pwr | PT/Exp | C | Rand Var +4 |
| | | | Consist | A | MM 0111 |

If you were to look only at ERA or WHIP, you'd say he's a terrible pitcher with no place on your roster. Nothing else here refutes that; he hasn't displayed any skill or trend to speculate on. Though Dom and velocity improved in-season with move to bullpen, SwK stagnated and he was hammered by LHB and RHB alike. Pass.

| Yr Tm | W | Sv | IP | K | ERA | xERA | WHIP | oOPS | vL | vR | BF/G | Ctl | Dom | Cmd | FpK | SwK | Vel | G | L | F | H% | S% | hr/f | GS | APC | DOM% | DIS% | Sv% | LI | RAR | BPV | BPX | R$ |
|---|---|---|---|---|---|---|---|---|---|---|---|---|---|---|---|---|---|---|---|---|---|---|---|---|---|---|---|---|---|---|---|---|---|
| 14 aaa | 5 | 0 | 143 | 85 | 5.17 | 5.08 | 1.54 | | | | 23.9 | 2.6 | 5.3 | 2.1 | | | | | | | 34% | 66% | | | | | | | | -25.1 | 48 | 57 | -$13 |
| 15 BAL * | 12 | 0 | 126 | 76 | 4.44 | 4.62 | 1.43 | 887 | 919 | 855 | 19.8 | 3.4 | 5.5 | 1.6 | 54% | 8% | 93.2 | 38 | 19 | 43 | 29% | 72% | 14% | 9 | 65 | 11% | 78% | 0 | 0.83 | -7.4 | 34 | 40 | -$1 |
| 16 BAL * | 7 | 0 | 151 | 90 | 5.20 | 5.28 | 1.46 | 850 | 990 | 750 | 20.8 | 2.6 | 5.3 | 2.1 | 59% | 7% | 93.1 | 42 | 19 | 39 | 31% | 67% | 13% | 12 | 72 | 8% | 58% | 0 | 0.59 | -18.9 | 30 | 36 | -$7 |
| 17 BAL * | 4 | 0 | 108 | 82 | 5.47 | 5.54 | 1.58 | 830 | 973 | 751 | 16.4 | 3.1 | 6.8 | 2.2 | 65% | 11% | 93.6 | 44 | 23 | 34 | 35% | 67% | 21% | 0 | 32 | | | 0 | 0.36 | -14.9 | 47 | 56 | -$9 |
| 18 BAL | 4 | 0 | 84 | 74 | 5.55 | 4.90 | 1.62 | 837 | 786 | 872 | 8.1 | 3.8 | 7.9 | 2.1 | 58% | 8% | 93.2 | 35 | 29 | 35 | 35% | 68% | 13% | 2 | 33 | 0% | 50% | 0 | 0.62 | -14.6 | 51 | 59 | -$10 |
| 1st Half | 1 | 0 | 44 | 34 | 5.08 | 5.37 | 1.69 | 811 | 760 | 854 | 9.8 | 4.5 | 6.9 | 1.5 | 54% | 8% | 92.1 | 33 | 33 | 34 | 35% | 70% | 8% | 2 | 39 | 0% | 50% | 0 | 0.58 | -5.1 | 14 | 16 | -$14 |
| 2nd Half | 3 | 0 | 40 | 40 | 6.08 | 4.42 | 1.55 | 863 | 820 | 888 | 6.7 | 3.2 | 9.0 | 2.9 | 61% | 9% | 94.3 | 39 | 24 | 37 | 35% | 65% | 17% | 0 | 27 | | | 0 | 0.66 | -9.5 | 94 | 108 | -$7 |
| **19 Proj** | **4** | **2** | **73** | **56** | **5.47** | **4.73** | **1.59** | **879** | **910** | **856** | **10.6** | **3.5** | **7.0** | **2.0** | **58%** | **8%** | **93.3** | **38** | **24** | **38** | **33%** | **69%** | **14%** | **2** | | | | | | **-11.8** | **47** | **54** | **-$7** |

## Wright,Steven

| | | | | | |
|---|---|---|---|---|---|
| Age: 34 | Th: R | Role RP | Health | F | LIMA Plan D+ |
| Ht: 6' 2" | Wt: 215 | Type | PT/Exp | C | Rand Var 0 |
| | | | Consist | C | MM 1001 |

3-1, 2.68 in 54 IP at BOS. Knuckleballer missed 14 weeks over two DL stints related to knee, and another 15 games to suspension. When on the field, struggled with walks but enjoyed good fortune, as MLB H%, S%, hr/f all broke his way. He's well below average in all categories—better to look elsewhere.

| Yr Tm | W | Sv | IP | K | ERA | xERA | WHIP | oOPS | vL | vR | BF/G | Ctl | Dom | Cmd | FpK | SwK | Vel | G | L | F | H% | S% | hr/f | GS | APC | DOM% | DIS% | Sv% | LI | RAR | BPV | BPX | R$ |
|---|---|---|---|---|---|---|---|---|---|---|---|---|---|---|---|---|---|---|---|---|---|---|---|---|---|---|---|---|---|---|---|---|---|
| 14 BOS * | 6 | 0 | 121 | 74 | 4.55 | 5.06 | 1.46 | 632 | 667 | 603 | 23.5 | 2.4 | 5.5 | 2.4 | 56% | 10% | 83.5 | 59 | 21 | 21 | 33% | 71% | 17% | 1 | 58 | 0% | 0% | 0 | 0.26 | -12.1 | 46 | 55 | -$6 |
| 15 BOS * | 7 | 0 | 125 | 83 | 4.95 | 5.17 | 1.54 | 722 | 671 | 770 | 22.6 | 3.3 | 6.0 | 1.8 | 55% | 9% | 83.5 | 43 | 14 | 43 | 33% | 70% | 12% | 9 | 74 | 22% | 56% | 0 | 0.76 | -15.3 | 38 | 46 | -$9 |
| 16 BOS | 13 | 0 | 157 | 127 | 3.33 | 4.42 | 1.24 | 653 | 608 | 686 | 27.3 | 3.3 | 7.3 | 2.2 | 55% | 11% | 83.2 | 44 | 19 | 37 | 29% | 75% | 7% | 24 | 104 | 46% | 25% | | | 16.6 | 65 | 77 | $13 |
| 17 BOS | 1 | 0 | 24 | 13 | 8.25 | 5.60 | 1.88 | 1148 | 1039 | 1210 | 22.8 | 1.9 | 4.9 | 2.6 | 59% | 7% | 83.7 | 41 | 23 | 35 | 36% | 64% | 27% | 5 | 77 | 0% | 60% | | | -11.5 | 56 | 67 | -$10 |
| 18 BOS * | 3 | 1 | 72 | 48 | 3.45 | 4.00 | 1.40 | 643 | 670 | 630 | 12.1 | 3.9 | 6.1 | 1.6 | 60% | 10% | 83.7 | 51 | 16 | 33 | 30% | 76% | 10% | 4 | 41 | 50% | 25% | 100 | 0.75 | 6.2 | 54 | 62 | -$1 |
| 1st Half | 2 | 0 | 56 | 37 | 4.25 | 4.40 | 1.47 | 636 | 637 | 634 | 17.2 | 3.8 | 5.9 | 1.5 | 60% | 10% | 83.3 | 53 | 14 | 33 | 31% | 71% | 11% | 4 | 61 | 50% | 25% | 0 | 0.55 | -0.7 | 49 | 57 | -$3 |
| 2nd Half | 1 | 1 | 16 | 12 | 0.57 | 2.58 | 1.16 | 663 | 754 | 618 | 5.7 | 4.2 | 6.7 | 1.6 | 60% | 9% | 85.8 | 46 | 21 | 33 | 24% | 100% | 8% | 0 | 22 | | | 100 | 0.95 | 6.9 | 72 | 83 | $4 |
| **19 Proj** | **6** | **0** | **102** | **74** | **4.22** | **4.50** | **1.38** | **733** | **707** | **750** | **12.1** | **3.5** | **6.5** | **1.8** | **57%** | **10%** | **83.3** | **47** | **15** | **38** | **29%** | **72%** | **10%** | **13** | | | | | | **-3.2** | **47** | **54** | **-$1** |

## Yarbrough,Ryan

| | | | | | |
|---|---|---|---|---|---|
| Age: 27 | Th: L | Role RP | Health | A | LIMA Plan B |
| Ht: 6' 5" | Wt: 205 | Type Pwr | PT/Exp | C | Rand Var 0 |
| | | | Consist | C | MM 1103 |

Impressive win total drove all of this rookie's value, but don't expect a repeat, with or without unique "bulk RP" deployment. SwK, FpK, Cmd, GB% average or worse, reflected in xERA/BPX. Does this look like the profile of a pitcher who should win 16 games? Or anchor a bullpen? No. No, it does not.

| Yr Tm | W | Sv | IP | K | ERA | xERA | WHIP | oOPS | vL | vR | BF/G | Ctl | Dom | Cmd | FpK | SwK | Vel | G | L | F | H% | S% | hr/f | GS | APC | DOM% | DIS% | Sv% | LI | RAR | BPV | BPX | R$ |
|---|---|---|---|---|---|---|---|---|---|---|---|---|---|---|---|---|---|---|---|---|---|---|---|---|---|---|---|---|---|---|---|---|---|
| 14 | | | | | | | | | | | | | | | | | | | | | | | | | | | | | | | | | |
| 15 | | | | | | | | | | | | | | | | | | | | | | | | | | | | | | | | | |
| 16 aa | 12 | 0 | 128 | 84 | 3.75 | 3.79 | 1.30 | | | | 21.1 | 2.3 | 5.9 | 2.6 | | | | | | | 31% | 71% | | | | | | | | 6.9 | 73 | 86 | $6 |
| 17 aaa | 13 | 0 | 157 | 133 | 4.82 | 5.32 | 1.45 | | | | 25.9 | 2.5 | 7.6 | 3.0 | | | | | | | 34% | 71% | | | | | | | | -9.0 | 63 | 75 | $1 |
| 18 TAM | 16 | 0 | 147 | 128 | 3.91 | 4.41 | 1.29 | 730 | 649 | 757 | 16.5 | 3.1 | 7.8 | 2.6 | 59% | 9% | 89.4 | 38 | 25 | 37 | 30% | 73% | 11% | 6 | 63 | 0% | 50% | 0 | 1.21 | 4.4 | 74 | 86 | $9 |
| 1st Half | 7 | 0 | 79 | 71 | 3.76 | 4.42 | 1.29 | 717 | 686 | 727 | 17.8 | 3.2 | 8.1 | 2.5 | 58% | 9% | 89.4 | 38 | 24 | 37 | 29% | 76% | 13% | 4 | 68 | 0% | 50% | 0 | 1.43 | 3.8 | 76 | 87 | $7 |
| 2nd Half | 9 | 0 | 68 | 57 | 4.08 | 4.40 | 1.29 | 744 | 611 | 794 | 15.3 | 2.9 | 7.5 | 2.6 | 61% | 9% | 89.4 | 38 | 27 | 36 | 30% | 70% | 10% | 2 | 58 | 0% | 50% | 0 | 0.99 | 0.6 | 72 | 83 | $11 |
| **19 Proj** | **10** | **0** | **145** | **121** | **4.10** | **4.16** | **1.35** | **784** | **679** | **820** | **19.1** | **2.7** | **7.5** | **2.8** | **60%** | **9%** | **89.4** | **38** | **24** | **38** | **32%** | **73%** | **11%** | **29** | | | | | | **-0.1** | **78** | **90** | **$4** |

## Yates,Kirby

| | | | | | |
|---|---|---|---|---|---|
| Age: 32 | Th: R | Role RP | Health | C | LIMA Plan B+ |
| Ht: 5' 10" | Wt: 210 | Type Pwr FB | PT/Exp | D | Rand Var -2 |
| | | | Consist | B | MM 5530 |

Superb follow-up to suprising late career breakout, as he improved Ctl and cut FB% while maintaining elite SwK. ERA rose dramatically after taking closer mantle in July, but BPV remained elite. He did benefit from lucky strand rate, but even with regression he's a solid second tier closer.

| Yr Tm | W | Sv | IP | K | ERA | xERA | WHIP | oOPS | vL | vR | BF/G | Ctl | Dom | Cmd | FpK | SwK | Vel | G | L | F | H% | S% | hr/f | GS | APC | DOM% | DIS% | Sv% | LI | RAR | BPV | BPX | R$ |
|---|---|---|---|---|---|---|---|---|---|---|---|---|---|---|---|---|---|---|---|---|---|---|---|---|---|---|---|---|---|---|---|---|---|
| 14 TAM * | 1 | 17 | 61 | 70 | 2.41 | 2.61 | 1.16 | 699 | 844 | 644 | 4.2 | 3.7 | 10.3 | 2.8 | 60% | 9% | 92.4 | 32 | 23 | 45 | 29% | 82% | 9% | 0 | 19 | | | 94 | 0.66 | 10.0 | 115 | 138 | $10 |
| 15 TAM * | 2 | 6 | 46 | 48 | 7.56 | 7.83 | 1.72 | 1004 | 1254 | 840 | 4.8 | 4.0 | 9.4 | 2.3 | 65% | 10% | 92.4 | 25 | 22 | 52 | 34% | 64% | 30% | 0 | 20 | | | 86 | 0.43 | -20.3 | 3 | 4 | -$9 |
| 16 NYY * | 2 | 4 | 58 | 64 | 4.46 | 4.18 | 1.45 | 746 | 584 | 829 | 4.5 | 4.1 | 10.0 | 2.4 | 64% | 12% | 93.2 | 44 | 23 | 34 | 35% | 70% | 14% | 0 | 20 | | | 57 | 0.61 | -1.9 | 91 | 108 | -$1 |
| 17 2 TM | 4 | 1 | 57 | 88 | 3.97 | 3.36 | 1.11 | 698 | 839 | 594 | 3.7 | 3.0 | 14.0 | 4.6 | 63% | 18% | 94.0 | 29 | 15 | 56 | 31% | 75% | 18% | 0 | 16 | | | 25 | 0.85 | 2.7 | 177 | 213 | $4 |
| 18 SD | 5 | 12 | 63 | 90 | 2.14 | 2.72 | 0.92 | 527 | 663 | 412 | 3.8 | 2.4 | 12.9 | 5.3 | 60% | 17% | 94.0 | 43 | 20 | 37 | 29% | 83% | 12% | 0 | 16 | | | 92 | 1.37 | 15.6 | 187 | 215 | $15 |
| 1st Half | 3 | 2 | 34 | 41 | 0.79 | 2.76 | 0.82 | 430 | 725 | 227 | 3.9 | 2.4 | 10.9 | 4.6 | 59% | 14% | 93.6 | 51 | 20 | 29 | 25% | 93% | 4% | 0 | 16 | | | 100 | 1.16 | 14.1 | 160 | 183 | $16 |
| 2nd Half | 2 | 10 | 29 | 49 | 3.72 | 2.68 | 1.03 | 633 | 608 | 659 | 3.8 | 2.5 | 15.2 | 6.1 | 61% | 20% | 94.3 | 32 | 20 | 47 | 34% | 72% | 18% | 0 | 17 | | | 91 | 1.60 | 1.5 | 217 | 249 | $14 |
| **19 Proj** | **4** | **32** | **65** | **92** | **3.02** | **2.84** | **1.05** | **614** | **678** | **568** | **3.8** | **3.0** | **12.7** | **4.3** | **61%** | **16%** | **93.7** | **37** | **20** | **44** | **29%** | **79%** | **16%** | **0** | | | | | | **14.9** | **163** | **188** | **$19** |

## Zimmermann,Jordan

| | | | | | |
|---|---|---|---|---|---|
| Age: 33 | Th: R | Role SP | Health | D | LIMA Plan B+ |
| Ht: 6' 2" | Wt: 225 | Type FB | PT/Exp | B | Rand Var +1 |
| | | | Consist | B | MM 1103 |

Recovered Dom and Ctl to 2015 levels. G/F flipped and those fly balls are more dangerous now. More sliders and fewer fastballs were behind the modest rebound, but given 2nd half Dom fade, we should be skeptical how far he can ride them. He could be good for innings, maybe, but not much else.

| Yr Tm | W | Sv | IP | K | ERA | xERA | WHIP | oOPS | vL | vR | BF/G | Ctl | Dom | Cmd | FpK | SwK | Vel | G | L | F | H% | S% | hr/f | GS | APC | DOM% | DIS% | Sv% | LI | RAR | BPV | BPX | R$ |
|---|---|---|---|---|---|---|---|---|---|---|---|---|---|---|---|---|---|---|---|---|---|---|---|---|---|---|---|---|---|---|---|---|---|
| 14 WAS | 14 | 0 | 200 | 182 | 2.66 | 3.22 | 1.07 | 631 | 655 | 606 | 25.0 | 1.3 | 8.2 | 6.3 | 71% | 11% | 93.8 | 40 | 24 | 36 | 31% | 77% | 6% | 32 | 91 | 50% | 13% | | | 26.6 | 130 | 155 | $22 |
| 15 WAS | 13 | 0 | 202 | 164 | 3.66 | 3.82 | 1.20 | 699 | 776 | 617 | 25.2 | 1.7 | 7.3 | 4.2 | 67% | 9% | 93.0 | 42 | 22 | 36 | 31% | 74% | 11% | 33 | 94 | 27% | 18% | | | 7.5 | 105 | 125 | $13 |
| 16 DET * | 9 | 0 | 126 | 74 | 4.41 | 4.88 | 1.39 | 804 | 738 | 862 | 22.1 | 2.2 | 5.3 | 2.4 | 65% | 8% | 91.8 | 43 | 18 | 39 | 31% | 72% | 10% | 18 | 90 | 17% | 39% | 0 | 0.73 | -3.3 | 43 | 51 | -$1 |
| 17 DET | 8 | 0 | 160 | 103 | 6.08 | 5.50 | 1.55 | 888 | 903 | 872 | 24.6 | 2.5 | 5.8 | 2.3 | 67% | 8% | 92.2 | 33 | 25 | 42 | 33% | 64% | 13% | 29 | 91 | 10% | 48% | | | -33.9 | 48 | 58 | -$13 |
| 18 DET | 7 | 0 | 131 | 111 | 4.52 | 4.48 | 1.26 | 800 | 807 | 793 | 22.2 | 1.8 | 7.6 | 4.3 | 65% | 10% | 91.2 | 35 | 22 | 43 | 30% | 72% | 16% | 25 | 83 | 12% | 28% | | | -6.0 | 102 | 117 | $1 |
| 1st Half | 2 | 0 | 41 | 39 | 4.35 | 4.45 | 1.21 | 699 | 635 | 766 | 19.2 | 2.2 | 8.5 | 3.9 | 66% | 10% | 91.3 | 27 | 27 | 46 | 31% | 67% | 9% | 9 | 73 | 11% | 11% | | | -1.0 | 99 | 114 | -$5 |
| 2nd Half | 5 | 0 | 90 | 72 | 4.60 | 4.49 | 1.29 | 846 | 883 | 806 | 23.9 | 1.6 | 7.2 | 4.5 | 64% | 9% | 91.1 | 38 | 20 | 42 | 30% | 75% | 19% | 16 | 89 | 13% | 38% | | | -5.0 | 103 | 118 | $4 |
| **19 Proj** | **9** | **0** | **160** | **122** | **4.47** | **4.27** | **1.34** | **806** | **805** | **808** | **22.2** | **2.0** | **6.9** | **3.4** | **66%** | **9%** | **91.8** | **36** | **23** | **42** | **31%** | **72%** | **13%** | **30** | | | | | | **-1.8** | **83** | **95** | **$1** |

ARIK FLORIMONTE

## THE NEXT TIER (*=includes MLEs) — Pitchers

The preceding section provided player boxes and analysis for 420 pitchers. As we know, far more than 420 pitchers will play in the major leagues in 2019. Many of those additional pitchers are covered in the minor league section, but that still leaves a gap: established major leaguers who don't play enough, or well enough, to merit a player box.

This section looks to fill that gap. Here, you will find "The Next Tier" of pitchers who are mostly past their growth years, but who are likely to see some playing time in 2019. We are including their 2017-18 statlines here for reference for you to do your own analysis. This way, if Chris Tillman is rumored to be pushing for a rotation spot at some point in 2019, a quick check here would confirm that ... he's still Chris Tillman. Or if Adam Morgan sneaks into a more prominent bullpen role in 2019, this chart shows that he has some scattered elements of high skill in his past that indicate some consolidation would not be unheard of.

| Pitcher | T | Yr | Age | W | Sv | IP | K | ERA | xERA | WHIP | vL | vR | CTL | DOM | CMD | SwK | FpK | G/L/F | H% | S% | BPV |
|---|---|---|---|---|---|---|---|---|---|---|---|---|---|---|---|---|---|---|---|---|---|
| Albers, Matt | R | 17 | 34 | 7 | 2 | 61 | 63 | 1.62 | 3.18 | 0.85 | 583 | 484 | 2.5 | 9.3 | 3.7 | 9 | 62 | 51/19/30 | 21 | 89 | 129 |
| | | 18 | 35 | 3 | 1 | 34 | 32 | 7.34 | 4.35 | 1.66 | 1063 | 893 | 3.1 | 8.4 | 2.7 | 11 | 63 | 46/22/33 | 35 | 62 | 90 |
| Altavilla, Dan | R | 17* | 24 | 3 | 6 | 70 | 83 | 3.45 | 4.34 | 1.41 | 687 | 813 | 4.6 | 10.6 | 2.3 | 14 | 55 | 36/17/47 | 32 | 81 | 80 |
| | | 18 | 25 | 3 | 0 | 21 | 23 | 2.61 | 4.59 | 1.26 | 404 | 778 | 6.5 | 10.0 | 1.5 | 13 | 65 | 39/14/48 | 20 | 83 | 21 |
| Avilan, Luis | L | 17 | 27 | 2 | 0 | 46 | 52 | 2.93 | 3.46 | 1.39 | 571 | 826 | 4.3 | 10.2 | 2.4 | 15 | 54 | 54/25/21 | 34 | 79 | 99 |
| | | 18 | 28 | 2 | 2 | 45 | 51 | 3.77 | 4.11 | 1.37 | 646 | 733 | 3.6 | 10.1 | 2.8 | 11 | 54 | 36/25/39 | 35 | 73 | 100 |
| Axford, John | R | 17 | 34 | 0 | 0 | 21 | 21 | 6.43 | 5.66 | 2.10 | 925 | 860 | 7.3 | 9.0 | 1.2 | 7 | 60 | 50/25/25 | 39 | 71 | -7 |
| | | 18 | 35 | 4 | 0 | 55 | 54 | 5.27 | 3.75 | 1.35 | 560 | 823 | 3.6 | 8.9 | 2.5 | 9 | 60 | 55/17/28 | 31 | 62 | 95 |
| Barnette, Tony | R | 17 | 33 | 2 | 2 | 57 | 57 | 5.49 | 4.45 | 1.50 | 898 | 764 | 3.5 | 8.9 | 2.6 | 13 | 60 | 41/22/36 | 35 | 65 | 87 |
| | | 18 | 34 | 2 | 0 | 26 | 26 | 2.39 | 3.16 | 0.91 | 498 | 631 | 1.7 | 8.9 | 5.2 | 11 | 70 | 51/19/30 | 26 | 77 | 143 |
| Bassitt, Chris | R | 17* | 28 | 4 | 0 | 38 | 23 | 8.03 | 6.22 | 1.83 | - | - | 4.1 | 5.5 | 1.3 | - | - | - | 37 | 54 | 27 |
| | | 18* | 29 | 7 | 0 | 131 | 101 | 4.68 | 4.89 | 1.51 | 575 | 669 | 3.2 | 7.0 | 2.2 | 7 | 59 | 45/22/34 | 34 | 69 | 62 |
| Belisle, Matt | R | 17 | 37 | 2 | 9 | 60 | 54 | 4.03 | 4.36 | 1.16 | 595 | 696 | 3.3 | 8.1 | 2.5 | 11 | 67 | 41/23/38 | 26 | 68 | 75 |
| | | 18 | 38 | 1 | 0 | 34 | 25 | 7.86 | 4.90 | 1.75 | 887 | 987 | 2.9 | 6.6 | 2.3 | 12 | 65 | 46/22/31 | 37 | 56 | 64 |
| Bibens-Dirkx, Austin | R | 17* | 32 | 5 | 0 | 93 | 52 | 4.59 | 5.41 | 1.42 | 782 | 818 | 2.8 | 5.1 | 1.8 | 9 | 61 | 40/21/39 | 29 | 74 | 15 |
| | | 18* | 33 | 5 | 0 | 128 | 89 | 7.38 | 7.55 | 1.80 | 951 | 868 | 3.4 | 6.3 | 1.8 | 10 | 63 | 35/28/38 | 36 | 62 | 6 |
| Biddle, Jesse | L | 17* | 25 | 2 | 2 | 50 | 42 | 4.43 | 5.52 | 1.65 | - | - | 3.2 | 7.6 | 2.3 | - | - | - | 38 | 74 | 64 |
| | | 18 | 26 | 6 | 1 | 64 | 67 | 3.11 | 3.47 | 1.27 | 751 | 586 | 4.4 | 9.5 | 2.2 | 11 | 59 | 56/23/22 | 28 | 79 | 86 |
| Blevins, Jerry | L | 17 | 33 | 6 | 1 | 49 | 69 | 2.94 | 3.66 | 1.37 | 455 | 993 | 4.4 | 12.7 | 2.9 | 13 | 55 | 41/21/38 | 36 | 81 | 128 |
| | | 18 | 34 | 3 | 1 | 43 | 41 | 4.85 | 5.39 | 1.36 | 786 | 682 | 4.6 | 8.6 | 1.9 | 9 | 59 | 22/21/57 | 27 | 67 | 30 |
| Buchter, Ryan | L | 17 | 30 | 4 | 1 | 65 | 65 | 2.89 | 4.68 | 1.07 | 618 | 656 | 3.6 | 9.0 | 2.5 | 11 | 59 | 33/14/54 | 22 | 82 | 75 |
| | | 18 | 31 | 6 | 0 | 39 | 41 | 2.75 | 4.56 | 1.19 | 496 | 842 | 3.4 | 9.4 | 2.7 | 12 | 55 | 25/21/53 | 29 | 81 | 79 |
| Bush, Matt | R | 17 | 31 | 3 | 10 | 52 | 58 | 3.78 | 4.57 | 1.45 | 824 | 699 | 3.3 | 10.0 | 3.1 | 13 | 55 | 37/20/43 | 36 | 78 | 106 |
| | | 18 | 32 | 0 | 0 | 23 | 19 | 4.70 | 5.27 | 1.61 | 671 | 891 | 5.5 | 7.4 | 1.4 | 10 | 54 | 45/23/32 | 30 | 74 | 9 |
| Carle, Shane | R | 17* | 25 | 3 | 1 | 66 | 41 | 7.29 | 7.52 | 1.89 | 818 | 875 | 3.4 | 5.6 | 1.7 | 14 | 84 | 27/20/53 | 38 | 63 | 6 |
| | | 18 | 26 | 4 | 1 | 63 | 43 | 2.86 | 4.44 | 1.22 | 601 | 620 | 3.9 | 6.1 | 1.6 | 13 | 62 | 47/27/26 | 26 | 76 | 31 |
| Casilla, Santiago | R | 17 | 36 | 4 | 16 | 59 | 57 | 4.27 | 4.48 | 1.36 | 803 | 724 | 3.4 | 8.7 | 2.6 | 12 | 55 | 40/22/38 | 31 | 72 | 84 |
| | | 18 | 37 | 0 | 1 | 31 | 22 | 3.16 | 5.32 | 1.21 | 503 | 574 | 5.7 | 6.3 | 1.1 | 9 | 49 | 44/16/40 | 21 | 71 | -19 |
| Cecil, Brett | L | 17 | 30 | 2 | 1 | 67 | 66 | 3.88 | 3.85 | 1.23 | 936 | 561 | 2.1 | 8.8 | 4.1 | 14 | 61 | 43/22/36 | 33 | 71 | 122 |
| | | 18 | 31 | 1 | 0 | 33 | 19 | 6.89 | 6.94 | 1.96 | 862 | 936 | 6.9 | 5.2 | 0.8 | 9 | 58 | 42/20/38 | 32 | 66 | -72 |
| Cole, A.J. | R | 17* | 25 | 7 | 0 | 145 | 108 | 6.24 | 6.62 | 1.86 | 980 | 601 | 4.0 | 6.7 | 1.7 | 10 | 62 | 44/17/39 | 39 | 67 | 33 |
| | | 18 | 26 | 4 | 0 | 48 | 59 | 6.14 | 4.56 | 1.59 | 1174 | 750 | 4.1 | 11.0 | 2.7 | 15 | 60 | 32/20/47 | 34 | 71 | 97 |
| Coulombe, Daniel | L | 17 | 27 | 2 | 0 | 52 | 39 | 3.48 | 4.34 | 1.32 | 596 | 851 | 3.8 | 6.8 | 1.8 | 10 | 52 | 56/17/27 | 28 | 75 | 53 |
| | | 18* | 28 | 3 | 0 | 53 | 46 | 3.87 | 5.67 | 1.53 | 876 | 819 | 3.0 | 7.9 | 2.6 | 13 | 54 | 52/19/29 | 35 | 80 | 55 |
| de la Rosa, Jorge | L | 17 | 36 | 3 | 0 | 51 | 45 | 4.21 | 4.59 | 1.31 | 545 | 821 | 3.7 | 7.9 | 2.1 | 15 | 55 | 45/16/38 | 28 | 72 | 66 |
| | | 18 | 37 | 0 | 1 | 56 | 47 | 3.38 | 4.47 | 1.39 | 686 | 725 | 4.3 | 7.6 | 1.7 | 12 | 59 | 51/19/30 | 29 | 79 | 48 |
| Despaigne, Odrisamer | R | 17* | 30 | 4 | 3 | 128 | 68 | 4.10 | 4.47 | 1.48 | 806 | 546 | 3.7 | 4.7 | 1.3 | 8 | 62 | 38/24/39 | 30 | 73 | 35 |
| | | 18* | 31 | 4 | 2 | 83 | 65 | 6.10 | 6.15 | 1.82 | 871 | 850 | 3.5 | 7.0 | 2.0 | 11 | 62 | 41/32/27 | 40 | 65 | 59 |
| Duensing, Brian | L | 17 | 34 | 1 | 0 | 62 | 61 | 2.74 | 3.81 | 1.22 | 682 | 667 | 2.6 | 8.8 | 3.4 | 11 | 58 | 49/18/34 | 31 | 81 | 115 |
| | | 18 | 35 | 3 | 1 | 38 | 24 | 7.65 | 6.57 | 1.88 | 689 | 1008 | 6.9 | 5.7 | 0.8 | 10 | 56 | 43/23/34 | 30 | 60 | -63 |
| Duke, Zach | L | 17 | 34 | 1 | 0 | 18 | 12 | 3.93 | 4.31 | 1.04 | 661 | 628 | 2.9 | 5.9 | 2.0 | 12 | 64 | 51/19/30 | 20 | 69 | 56 |
| | | 18 | 35 | 5 | 0 | 52 | 51 | 4.15 | 3.67 | 1.50 | 602 | 773 | 3.6 | 8.8 | 2.4 | 11 | 56 | 59/21/20 | 37 | 70 | 98 |
| Dull, Ryan | R | 17 | 27 | 2 | 0 | 42 | 45 | 5.14 | 4.20 | 1.26 | 897 | 639 | 3.4 | 9.6 | 2.8 | 13 | 67 | 39/19/42 | 29 | 63 | 98 |
| | | 18* | 28 | 3 | 1 | 53 | 47 | 4.50 | 4.95 | 1.37 | 587 | 716 | 2.7 | 8.0 | 3.0 | 11 | 65 | 34/24/42 | 32 | 72 | 67 |
| Elias, Roenis | L | 17* | 28 | 1 | 0 | 37 | 20 | 9.97 | 10.17 | 2.06 | 1000 | - | 3.1 | 4.8 | 1.5 | 18 | 50 | - | 37 | 56 | -60 |
| | | 18* | 29 | 6 | 1 | 92 | 65 | 3.73 | 3.58 | 1.35 | 678 | 622 | 3.4 | 6.3 | 1.8 | 10 | 51 | 34/24/42 | 31 | 71 | 71 |
| Fields, Joshua | R | 17 | 31 | 5 | 2 | 57 | 60 | 2.84 | 4.03 | 0.96 | 780 | 530 | 2.4 | 9.5 | 4.0 | 14 | 67 | 30/21/49 | 23 | 82 | 115 |
| | | 18 | 32 | 2 | 2 | 41 | 33 | 2.20 | 4.44 | 0.95 | 501 | 622 | 2.4 | 7.2 | 3.0 | 13 | 57 | 23/26/51 | 23 | 83 | 66 |
| Freeman, Sam | L | 17 | 30 | 2 | 0 | 60 | 59 | 2.55 | 3.80 | 1.25 | 507 | 653 | 4.1 | 8.9 | 2.2 | 12 | 57 | 59/15/26 | 29 | 81 | 87 |
| | | 18 | 31 | 3 | 0 | 50 | 58 | 4.29 | 3.77 | 1.45 | 729 | 624 | 5.7 | 10.4 | 1.8 | 14 | 53 | 52/24/24 | 31 | 70 | 62 |

# THE NEXT TIER (*=includes MLEs)

| Pitcher | T | Yr | Age | W | Sv | IP | K | ERA | xERA | WHIP | vL | vR | CTL | DOM | CMD | SwK | FpK | G/L/F | H% | S% | BPV |
|---|---|---|---|---|---|---|---|---|---|---|---|---|---|---|---|---|---|---|---|---|---|
| Fulmer, Carson | R | 17* | 23 | 10 | 0 | 149 | 101 | 6.43 | 5.88 | 1.68 | 664 | 606 | 4.9 | 6.1 | 1.2 | 9 | 51 | 29/17/55 | 31 | 64 | 15 |
| | | 18* | 24 | 7 | 0 | 102 | 81 | 7.07 | 6.98 | 1.88 | 923 | 947 | 6.1 | 7.2 | 1.2 | 7 | 54 | 32/21/47 | 33 | 65 | 9 |
| Garcia, Jarlin | L | 17 | 24 | 1 | 0 | 53 | 42 | 4.73 | 4.74 | 1.20 | 603 | 783 | 2.9 | 7.1 | 2.5 | 12 | 55 | 39/20/41 | 27 | 62 | 67 |
| | | 18* | 25 | 5 | 0 | 116 | 67 | 5.15 | 5.36 | 1.44 | 799 | 789 | 3.3 | 5.2 | 1.6 | 8 | 51 | 43/20/37 | 29 | 69 | 16 |
| Gearrin, Cory | R | 17 | 31 | 4 | 0 | 68 | 64 | 1.99 | 4.30 | 1.25 | 711 | 607 | 4.6 | 8.5 | 1.8 | 11 | 60 | 48/19/33 | 26 | 86 | 53 |
| | | 18 | 32 | 2 | 1 | 57 | 53 | 3.77 | 4.20 | 1.34 | 747 | 736 | 3.3 | 8.3 | 2.5 | 11 | 59 | 41/24/34 | 31 | 76 | 80 |
| Goeddel, Erik | R | 17* | 28 | 2 | 0 | 59 | 52 | 6.39 | 6.54 | 1.59 | 908 | 844 | 3.7 | 8.0 | 2.2 | 15 | 57 | 43/16/42 | 32 | 66 | 21 |
| | | 18 | 29 | 3 | 0 | 37 | 44 | 2.95 | 3.90 | 1.25 | 501 | 681 | 4.9 | 10.8 | 2.2 | 16 | 58 | 45/17/38 | 27 | 81 | 85 |
| Guerra, Javy | R | 17* | 31 | 3 | 2 | 73 | 45 | 5.38 | 5.41 | 1.58 | 771 | 745 | 3.9 | 5.6 | 1.4 | 6 | 67 | 54/18/28 | 31 | 68 | 24 |
| | | 18* | 32 | 4 | 6 | 54 | 48 | 3.67 | 3.76 | 1.28 | 860 | 812 | 2.6 | 8.0 | 3.1 | 10 | 64 | 45/23/32 | 32 | 72 | 96 |
| Hatcher, Chris | R | 17 | 32 | 1 | 1 | 60 | 63 | 4.22 | 4.56 | 1.32 | 706 | 756 | 3.2 | 9.5 | 3.0 | 13 | 63 | 33/21/46 | 31 | 74 | 97 |
| | | 18 | 33 | 3 | 0 | 36 | 30 | 4.95 | 4.98 | 1.65 | 1091 | 627 | 4.2 | 7.4 | 1.8 | 8 | 58 | 42/26/32 | 33 | 75 | 40 |
| Hudson, Daniel | R | 17 | 30 | 2 | 0 | 62 | 66 | 4.38 | 4.43 | 1.46 | 799 | 727 | 4.8 | 9.6 | 2.0 | 12 | 56 | 43/21/36 | 32 | 72 | 64 |
| | | 18 | 31 | 3 | 0 | 46 | 44 | 4.11 | 4.25 | 1.22 | 524 | 733 | 3.5 | 8.6 | 2.4 | 14 | 65 | 37/27/36 | 27 | 70 | 75 |
| Hughes, Phil | R | 17 | 31 | 4 | 0 | 54 | 38 | 5.87 | 5.60 | 1.58 | 1107 | 766 | 2.2 | 6.4 | 2.9 | 7 | 68 | 30/24/46 | 35 | 68 | 64 |
| | | 18 | 32 | 0 | 0 | 33 | 32 | 6.34 | 5.04 | 1.65 | 967 | 954 | 2.8 | 8.8 | 3.2 | 9 | 61 | 29/24/47 | 35 | 72 | 91 |
| Hutchison, Drew | R | 17* | 26 | 9 | 0 | 159 | 93 | 5.09 | 5.53 | 1.63 | - | - | 3.7 | 5.3 | 1.4 | - | - | - | 33 | 70 | 27 |
| | | 18* | 27 | 6 | 0 | 85 | 62 | 4.70 | 5.41 | 1.60 | 861 | 976 | 4.2 | 6.6 | 1.6 | 9 | 60 | 41/20/39 | 33 | 73 | 38 |
| Jennings, Dan | L | 17 | 30 | 3 | 0 | 63 | 51 | 3.45 | 4.15 | 1.34 | 628 | 701 | 4.5 | 7.3 | 1.6 | 8 | 60 | 60/19/21 | 26 | 79 | 50 |
| | | 18 | 31 | 4 | 1 | 64 | 45 | 3.22 | 4.10 | 1.38 | 570 | 927 | 3.2 | 6.3 | 2.0 | 9 | 58 | 56/21/23 | 31 | 80 | 60 |
| Johnson, Jim | R | 17 | 34 | 6 | 22 | 57 | 61 | 5.56 | 4.19 | 1.48 | 813 | 669 | 4.0 | 9.7 | 2.4 | 10 | 60 | 49/21/31 | 34 | 64 | 94 |
| | | 18 | 35 | 5 | 2 | 63 | 45 | 3.84 | 4.40 | 1.36 | 886 | 632 | 3.1 | 6.4 | 2.0 | 8 | 60 | 49/22/29 | 29 | 77 | 58 |
| Kahnle, Thomas | R | 17 | 27 | 2 | 0 | 63 | 96 | 2.59 | 2.79 | 1.12 | 730 | 525 | 2.4 | 13.8 | 5.6 | 18 | 62 | 41/21/38 | 38 | 79 | 201 |
| | | 18* | 28 | 4 | 2 | 50 | 58 | 6.00 | 5.41 | 1.66 | 660 | 950 | 5.1 | 10.5 | 2.1 | 15 | 57 | 35/24/40 | 37 | 65 | 73 |
| Kuhl, Chad | R | 17 | 24 | 8 | 0 | 157 | 142 | 4.35 | 4.65 | 1.47 | 893 | 698 | 4.1 | 8.1 | 2.0 | 10 | 58 | 42/23/35 | 32 | 72 | 55 |
| | | 18 | 25 | 5 | 0 | 85 | 81 | 4.55 | 4.45 | 1.44 | 866 | 746 | 3.5 | 8.6 | 2.5 | 10 | 56 | 36/26/37 | 32 | 73 | 74 |
| Loup, Aaron | L | 17 | 29 | 2 | 0 | 58 | 64 | 3.75 | 3.98 | 1.53 | 721 | 721 | 4.5 | 10.0 | 2.2 | 10 | 61 | 53/20/26 | 36 | 76 | 89 |
| | | 18 | 30 | 0 | 0 | 40 | 44 | 4.54 | 3.78 | 1.56 | 678 | 935 | 3.2 | 10.0 | 3.1 | 12 | 61 | 49/23/28 | 39 | 72 | 121 |
| Madson, Ryan | R | 17 | 36 | 5 | 2 | 59 | 67 | 1.83 | 2.40 | 0.80 | 506 | 478 | 1.4 | 10.2 | 7.4 | 14 | 59 | 55/24/21 | 27 | 78 | 180 |
| | | 18 | 37 | 2 | 4 | 53 | 54 | 5.47 | 4.00 | 1.41 | 807 | 731 | 2.7 | 9.2 | 3.4 | 14 | 63 | 43/22/35 | 35 | 63 | 113 |
| McFarland, T.J. | L | 17 | 28 | 4 | 0 | 54 | 29 | 5.33 | 4.34 | 1.52 | 548 | 860 | 2.8 | 4.8 | 1.7 | 7 | 53 | 67/15/18 | 33 | 64 | 56 |
| | | 18 | 29 | 2 | 1 | 72 | 42 | 2.00 | 3.71 | 1.19 | 388 | 764 | 2.8 | 5.3 | 1.9 | 8 | 54 | 68/15/17 | 27 | 85 | 66 |
| Milone, Tommy | L | 17* | 30 | 2 | 1 | 68 | 46 | 7.74 | 8.90 | 1.74 | 664 | 1073 | 2.2 | 6.1 | 2.8 | 8 | 66 | 36/24/40 | 34 | 65 | -24 |
| | | 18* | 31 | 8 | 0 | 140 | 107 | 5.90 | 5.78 | 1.49 | 560 | 1026 | 2.0 | 6.9 | 3.5 | 11 | 68 | 28/22/50 | 35 | 62 | 65 |
| Morgan, Adam | L | 17* | 27 | 3 | 0 | 72 | 74 | 4.71 | 4.80 | 1.38 | 597 | 837 | 3.0 | 9.3 | 3.1 | 17 | 62 | 46/20/34 | 33 | 70 | 79 |
| | | 18 | 28 | 0 | 1 | 49 | 50 | 3.83 | 3.90 | 1.44 | 664 | 740 | 4.0 | 9.1 | 2.3 | 12 | 55 | 54/17/29 | 33 | 76 | 88 |
| Moylan, Peter | R | 17 | 38 | 0 | 0 | 59 | 46 | 3.49 | 3.91 | 1.10 | 986 | 479 | 3.8 | 7.0 | 1.8 | 12 | 62 | 61/16/23 | 23 | 69 | 62 |
| | | 18 | 39 | 0 | 0 | 28 | 23 | 4.45 | 4.78 | 1.76 | 812 | 874 | 5.7 | 7.3 | 1.3 | 11 | 55 | 51/27/21 | 33 | 78 | 6 |
| O'Day, Darren | R | 17 | 34 | 2 | 2 | 60 | 76 | 3.43 | 3.31 | 1.08 | 677 | 565 | 3.6 | 11.3 | 3.2 | 11 | 65 | 48/15/38 | 26 | 74 | 133 |
| | | 18 | 35 | 0 | 2 | 20 | 27 | 3.60 | 3.36 | 1.10 | 865 | 637 | 1.8 | 12.2 | 6.8 | 13 | 65 | 25/25/50 | 34 | 74 | 173 |
| Peralta, Wandy | L | 17 | 25 | 3 | 0 | 65 | 57 | 3.76 | 3.93 | 1.19 | 639 | 711 | 3.3 | 7.9 | 2.4 | 16 | 56 | 54/16/30 | 26 | 72 | 85 |
| | | 18* | 26 | 3 | 0 | 60 | 39 | 5.04 | 5.84 | 1.88 | 808 | 763 | 5.8 | 5.8 | 1.0 | 10 | 58 | 48/25/27 | 35 | 72 | 35 |
| Perdomo, Luis | R | 17 | 24 | 8 | 0 | 164 | 118 | 4.67 | 4.22 | 1.51 | 807 | 763 | 3.6 | 6.5 | 1.8 | 9 | 61 | 62/17/21 | 32 | 70 | 60 |
| | | 18* | 25 | 7 | 0 | 120 | 90 | 4.99 | 5.27 | 1.52 | 991 | 782 | 3.1 | 6.7 | 2.1 | 8 | 62 | 43/29/28 | 34 | 69 | 49 |
| Rusin, Chris | L | 17 | 30 | 5 | 2 | 85 | 71 | 2.65 | 3.44 | 1.11 | 703 | 607 | 2.0 | 7.5 | 3.7 | 13 | 59 | 59/17/24 | 28 | 81 | 118 |
| | | 18 | 31 | 2 | 0 | 55 | 47 | 6.09 | 4.24 | 1.50 | 648 | 886 | 4.3 | 7.7 | 1.8 | 10 | 63 | 56/18/26 | 31 | 60 | 58 |
| Salas, Fernando | R | 17 | 32 | 2 | 0 | 59 | 56 | 5.22 | 4.54 | 1.52 | 728 | 817 | 3.4 | 8.6 | 2.5 | 14 | 60 | 47/16/36 | 35 | 67 | 89 |
| | | 18 | 33 | 4 | 0 | 40 | 30 | 4.50 | 4.65 | 1.33 | 1015 | 586 | 2.9 | 6.8 | 2.3 | 10 | 72 | 40/22/38 | 30 | 69 | 61 |
| Sewald, Paul | R | 17 | 27 | 0 | 0 | 65 | 69 | 4.55 | 4.32 | 1.21 | 826 | 627 | 2.9 | 9.5 | 3.3 | 12 | 61 | 32/22/46 | 30 | 65 | 103 |
| | | 18 | 28 | 0 | 2 | 56 | 58 | 6.07 | 4.84 | 1.51 | 861 | 789 | 3.7 | 9.3 | 2.5 | 10 | 61 | 30/23/46 | 35 | 61 | 76 |
| Shaw, Bryan | R | 17 | 29 | 4 | 3 | 77 | 73 | 3.52 | 3.37 | 1.21 | 586 | 693 | 2.6 | 8.6 | 3.3 | 13 | 58 | 56/22/22 | 32 | 72 | 119 |
| | | 18 | 30 | 4 | 0 | 55 | 54 | 5.93 | 4.61 | 1.79 | 773 | 982 | 4.6 | 8.9 | 1.9 | 12 | 56 | 49/21/30 | 38 | 70 | 63 |
| Sipp, Tony | L | 17 | 33 | 0 | 0 | 37 | 39 | 5.79 | 4.34 | 1.39 | 852 | 807 | 3.9 | 9.4 | 2.4 | 13 | 53 | 49/13/38 | 30 | 64 | 92 |
| | | 18 | 34 | 3 | 0 | 39 | 42 | 1.86 | 3.59 | 1.03 | 557 | 608 | 3.0 | 9.8 | 3.2 | 14 | 61 | 41/18/40 | 28 | 82 | 113 |
| Solis, Sammy | L | 17 | 28 | 1 | 1 | 26 | 28 | 5.88 | 4.38 | 1.35 | 640 | 757 | 4.5 | 9.7 | 2.2 | 9 | 56 | 46/15/38 | 28 | 58 | 77 |
| | | 18 | 29 | 1 | 0 | 39 | 44 | 6.41 | 4.02 | 1.55 | 993 | 719 | 4.1 | 10.1 | 2.4 | 13 | 61 | 45/22/33 | 35 | 61 | 93 |
| Tazawa, Junichi | R | 17 | 31 | 3 | 0 | 55 | 38 | 5.69 | 5.32 | 1.39 | 719 | 812 | 3.6 | 6.2 | 1.7 | 9 | 62 | 36/25/40 | 28 | 61 | 29 |
| | | 18 | 32 | 1 | 0 | 28 | 28 | 7.07 | 5.67 | 1.82 | 707 | 1130 | 5.1 | 9.0 | 1.8 | 7 | 59 | 26/27/47 | 35 | 66 | 27 |
| Tillman, Chris | R | 17 | 29 | 1 | 0 | 93 | 63 | 7.84 | 6.15 | 1.89 | 1001 | 962 | 4.9 | 6.1 | 1.2 | 8 | 48 | 40/23/37 | 34 | 63 | -6 |
| | | 18* | 30 | 1 | 0 | 51 | 20 | 10.56 | 10.12 | 2.46 | 1202 | 1017 | 6.1 | 3.6 | 0.6 | 5 | 47 | 42/25/33 | 40 | 57 | -42 |
| Triggs, Andrew | R | 17 | 28 | 5 | 0 | 65 | 50 | 4.27 | 4.48 | 1.33 | 648 | 795 | 2.6 | 6.9 | 2.6 | 10 | 58 | 50/18/33 | 31 | 72 | 81 |
| | | 18 | 29 | 3 | 0 | 41 | 43 | 5.23 | 4.19 | 1.33 | 723 | 739 | 3.9 | 9.4 | 2.4 | 10 | 56 | 47/16/37 | 29 | 65 | 88 |
| Volstad, Chris | R | 17* | 30 | 4 | 1 | 137 | 64 | 7.10 | 7.62 | 1.89 | 882 | 614 | 2.1 | 4.2 | 2.0 | 4 | 66 | 62/12/27 | 39 | 63 | 8 |
| | | 18 | 31 | 1 | 0 | 47 | 29 | 6.27 | 4.56 | 1.63 | 1043 | 850 | 2.3 | 5.5 | 2.4 | 5 | 60 | 55/18/26 | 35 | 65 | 71 |

# MAJOR LEAGUES • INJURIES

## 5-Year Injury Log

The following chart details the disabled list stints for all players during the past five years. Use this as a supplement to our health grades in the player profile boxes as well as the "Risk Management" charts that start on page 260. It's also where to turn when in May you want to check whether, say, Jarrod Dyson's strained right groin should be concerning (answer: Yes, very).

For each injury, the number of days the player missed during the season is listed. A few DL stints are for fewer than 15 days (or fewer than 10 days in 2017 and 2018); these are cases when a player was placed on the DL prior to Opening Day (only in-season time lost is listed).

Abbreviations:
Lt, L = left
Rt, R = right
fx = fractured
R/C = rotator cuff
str = strained
surg = surgery
TJS = Tommy John surgery (ulnar collateral ligament reconstruction)
x 2 = two occurrences of the same injury
x 3 = three occurrences of the same injury

Throughout the spring and all season long, BaseballHQ.com has comprehensive injury coverage.

## FIVE-YEAR INJURY LOG — Hitters

| Batter | Yr | Days | Injury |
|---|---|---|---|
| Abreu, Jose | 14 | 15 | L ankle tendinitis |
| | 18 | 20 | Surg to repair ABD muscle |
| Acuna, Ronald | 18 | 32 | L knee & ACL strain |
| Adams, Matt | 14 | 14 | Tightness in L calf |
| | 15 | 105 | Strained R quad |
| | 16 | 22 | L should inflammation |
| | 18 | 15 | Fractured L index finger |
| Adduci, James | 17 | 54 | Strained R oblique muscle |
| Adrianza, Ehire | 14 | 82 | Strained R hamstring x 2 |
| | 16 | 109 | Fractured L foot |
| | 17 | 48 | R oblique muscle; ab muscle |
| | 18 | 11 | Strained L hamstring |
| Ahmed, Nick | 16 | 72 | R hip impingement |
| | 17 | 95 | Fractured R hand |
| Alberto, Hanser | 17 | 182 | Tightness in R shoulder |
| | 18 | 11 | R hamstring strain |
| Alford, Anthony | 17 | 62 | Fractured L wrist |
| Almonte, Abraham | 17 | 66 | Strained R biceps; L hammy |
| Alonso, Yonder | 14 | 55 | Strained R forearm/R wrist tend |
| | 15 | 46 | Low back strain; bruised R shoulder |
| Altherr, Aaron | 16 | 117 | Repair torn tendon L wrist |
| | 17 | 43 | Strained R hamstring x 2 |
| Altuve, Jose | 18 | 24 | R knee discomfort |
| Amarista, Alexi | 16 | 56 | Strnd R hamstring x 2 |
| Andrus, Elvis | 18 | 67 | Fractured R elbow |
| Aoki, Norichika | 14 | 20 | Strained L groin |
| | 15 | 40 | Concussion; fx fibula |
| Arenado, Nolan | 14 | 40 | Fractured L middle finger |
| Arroyo, Christian | 18 | 30 | Strained L oblique |
| Asche, Cody | 14 | 26 | Strained L hamstring |
| | 16 | 61 | Strained R oblique muscle |
| Austin, Tyler | 17 | 107 | Fx L ankle; strained R ham |
| Avila, Alex | 14 | 5 | Concussion |
| | 15 | 55 | Loose bodies in L knee |
| | 16 | 66 | Strained R hamstring x 2 |
| | 18 | 11 | Strained R hamstring |
| Aybar, Erick | 16 | 15 | Bruised R foot |
| | 17 | 41 | Bruised L foot |
| Baez, Javier | 16 | 12 | Bruised L thumb |
| Bandy, Jett | 17 | 30 | Fractured rib |
| Bautista, Jose | 16 | 53 | Sprnd L knee; L big toe |
| Beckham, Gordon | 14 | 25 | Strained L oblique |
| | 16 | 56 | Strained L hamstring x2 |

## FIVE-YEAR INJURY LOG — Hitters

| Batter | Yr | Days | Injury |
|---|---|---|---|
| Beckham, Tim | 14 | 133 | Rec. from surgery R Knee- torn ACL |
| | 15 | 25 | R hamstring strain |
| | 17 | 10 | Sprained L ankle |
| | 18 | 62 | Strained L groin |
| Bell, Josh | 18 | 12 | Strained L oblique |
| Bellinger, Cody | 17 | 10 | Sprained R ankle |
| Belt, Brandon | 14 | 81 | Concussion x 2/Fx L thumb |
| | 17 | 57 | Concussion |
| | 18 | 35 | Appendectomy; hyperexnd R knee |
| Beltre, Adrian | 14 | 12 | Strained L quadriceps |
| | 15 | 21 | Sprained L thumb |
| | 17 | 68 | Tight R calf; L hammy |
| | 18 | 31 | Strained L hamstring |
| Benintendi, Andrew | 16 | 20 | Sprnd L knee |
| Bethancourt, Christian | 16 | 33 | Strnd L intercostal |
| Betts, Mookie | 15 | 13 | Concussion |
| | 18 | 11 | Pulled abdominal muscle |
| Bird, Gregory | 16 | 183 | Rec fr surg.-torn labrum R should |
| | 17 | 116 | Bruised R ankle |
| | 18 | 59 | R ankle surgery |
| Blackmon, Charlie | 16 | 15 | Turf toe on L foot |
| Blanco, Andres | 16 | 39 | Fractured L index finger |
| Blanco, Gregor | 15 | 9 | Concussion |
| | 16 | 24 | R should impingement |
| Blandino, Alex | 18 | 73 | Torn ACL - R knee |
| Blash, Jabari | 16 | 42 | Sprnd L middle finger |
| Bogaerts, Xander | 14 | 7 | Concussion |
| | 18 | 19 | Stress fracture L ankle |
| Bonifacio, Emilio | 14 | 39 | Strained R ribcage |
| | 15 | 16 | Strained L oblique |
| Bour, Justin | 16 | 62 | Sprnd R ankle |
| | 17 | 55 | BruisedL ankle; strained R oblique |
| | 18 | 11 | Strained L oblique |
| Bourjos, Peter | 16 | 15 | Sprnd R should |
| | 17 | 10 | Elbow injury |
| Bradley, Jackie | 17 | 20 | Sprained R knee; L thumb |
| Brantley, Michael | 16 | 164 | R should fatigue; rec fr R should surg |
| | 17 | 61 | Sprained R ankle x2 |
| | 18 | 9 | Recovery R ankle surgery |
| Brantly, Rob | 15 | 45 | Avulsion fracture, L thumb |
| Braun, Ryan | 14 | 10 | strained R oblique muscle |
| | 17 | 42 | Strained L calf x 2 |
| | 18 | 22 | Mid-back tightness |
| Brinson, Lewis | 18 | 60 | L hip inflammation |

## FIVE-YEAR INJURY LOG — Hitters

| Batter | Yr | Days | Injury |
|---|---|---|---|
| Brito,Socrates | 16 | 42 | Fractured toe R foot |
| | 17 | 74 | Dislocated L ring finger |
| Bruce,Jay | 14 | 16 | Rec from meniscus repair on L knee |
| | 18 | 66 | Sore R hip |
| Bryant,Kris | 18 | 54 | L shoulder inflammation x 2 |
| Buxton,Byron | 15 | 45 | Sprained L thumb |
| | 17 | 17 | Strained L groin |
| | 18 | 57 | Fractured great L toe; migraines |
| Cabrera,Asdrubal | 15 | 16 | Strained R hamstring |
| | 16 | 17 | Strained patella tendon L knee |
| | 17 | 21 | Sprained L thumb x 2 |
| Cabrera,Melky | 14 | 21 | Fractured R pinky finger |
| Cabrera,Miguel | 15 | 41 | L calf strain |
| | 17 | 10 | Strained R groin |
| | 18 | 140 | R ham. strain; Ruptd L biceps tendon |
| Cain,Lorenzo | 14 | 18 | Strained L groin |
| | 16 | 30 | Strained L hamstring |
| | 18 | 13 | L groin strain |
| Calhoun,Kole | 14 | 35 | Sprained R ankle |
| | 18 | 17 | R oblique strain |
| Camargo,Johan | 17 | 27 | Bruised R knee |
| | 18 | 21 | Strained R oblique |
| Candelario,Jeimer | 18 | 12 | L wrist tendinitis |
| Canha,Mark | 16 | 146 | Strained back |
| Cano,Robinson | 17 | 12 | Strained R quadriceps |
| | 18 | 93 | Fractured R hand |
| Carpenter,Matt | 16 | 29 | Strained R oblique muscle |
| Carrera,Ezequiel | 16 | 15 | Strained L Achilles tendon |
| | 17 | 13 | Fractured R foot |
| Casali,Curtis | 14 | 5 | Concussion |
| | 15 | 40 | Strained L hamstring |
| Castellanos,Nick | 16 | 51 | Fractured L hand |
| Castillo,Welington | 14 | 19 | L ribcage inflammation |
| | 17 | 24 | Tendinitis R should; testicular injury |
| | 18 | 11 | R shoulder inflammation |
| Castro,Jason | 15 | 19 | Strained R quad |
| | 17 | 11 | Concussion |
| | 18 | 149 | Torn meniscus - R knee |
| Castro,Starlin | 17 | 52 | Strained R ham x2 |
| Ceciliani,Darrell | 15 | 27 | Strained L hamstring |
| | 17 | 135 | L shoulder subluxation |
| Cervelli,Francisco | 14 | 64 | Hamstring injury |
| | 16 | 38 | Fractured L hand |
| | 17 | 59 | Concussion x2; L wrist inflam; L quad |
| | 18 | 30 | Concussion |
| Cespedes,Yoenis | 16 | 15 | Strained R quadriceps |
| | 17 | 79 | Strained L ham; strained R ham |
| | 18 | 136 | Strained R hip; heel calcifications |
| Chapman,Matt | 17 | 11 | L knee cellulitis |
| | 18 | 18 | R hand soreness |
| Chirinos,Robinson | 15 | 37 | L shoulder strain |
| | 16 | 60 | Fractured R forearm |
| Chisenhall,Lonnie | 16 | 17 | R forearm injury |
| | 17 | 73 | Sprnd R shoulder; concussion; R calf |
| | 18 | 150 | Strained R calf |
| Choo,Shin-Soo | 14 | 35 | Bone spur in L elbow |
| | 16 | 124 | Strnd R calf/L ham/back; FX L 4arm |
| Coghlan,Chris | 16 | 41 | Sore/strained R ribcage |
| | 17 | 57 | Bruised L wrist |
| Colon,Christian | 14 | 12 | fractured R middle finger |
| Conforto,Michael | 17 | 48 | Bruised L hand; Disloc L shoulder |
| | 18 | 8 | Recovery from L shoulder surgery |
| Contreras,Willson | 17 | 32 | Strained R hamstring |

## FIVE-YEAR INJURY LOG — Hitters

| Batter | Yr | Days | Injury |
|---|---|---|---|
| Cooper,Garrett | 17 | 46 | L hamstring tendinitis |
| | 18 | 163 | R wrist contusion |
| Cordero,Franchy | 18 | 140 | L abductor strain; bone spur R elbow |
| Cordoba,Allen | 18 | 95 | Concussion |
| Correa,Carlos | 17 | 47 | Torn ligament in L thumb |
| | 18 | 43 | Lower back soreness |
| Cowart,Kaleb | 18 | 13 | Sprained L ankle |
| Cozart,Zack | 15 | 116 | R knee surgery |
| | 16 | 7 | Sore R knee |
| | 17 | 21 | Strained R quad; L quad |
| | 18 | 109 | Sprained L ankle |
| Cozens,Dylan | 18 | 16 | Strained L quadriceps |
| Crawford,Brandon | 17 | 12 | Strained R groin |
| Crawford,J.P. | 18 | 91 | Strained R elbow |
| Cron,C.J. | 16 | 42 | Fractured L hand |
| | 17 | 15 | Bruised L foot |
| Cruz,Nelson | 18 | 12 | Sprained R ankle |
| Culberson,Charlie | 15 | 67 | Lumbar disc inflammation |
| Cuthbert,Cheslor | 17 | 41 | Sprained L wrist |
| | 18 | 136 | Lower back strain |
| d Arnaud,Travis | 14 | 14 | Concussion |
| | 15 | 88 | Hyperextended L elbow; fx R hand |
| | 16 | 56 | Strained R rotator cuff |
| | 17 | 19 | Bone bruise in R wrist |
| Dahl,David | 17 | 108 | Stress reaction in ribcage |
| | 18 | 123 | Fractured R foot |
| d'Arnaud,Travis | 18 | 174 | TJS |
| Davidson,Matt | 18 | 8 | Back spasms |
| Davidson,Matthew | 16 | 94 | Fractured R foot |
| | 17 | 18 | Bruised R wrist |
| Davis,Chris | 14 | 14 | Strained L oblique |
| | 17 | 29 | Strained R oblique |
| Davis,Khris | 15 | 37 | Torn meniscus, R knee |
| | 18 | 9 | Strained R groin |
| Davis,Rajai | 17 | 10 | Strained L hamstring |
| | 18 | 11 | Medical condition |
| Daza,Yonathan | 18 | 28 | Strained L shoulder |
| Decker,Jaff | 15 | 13 | L calf strain |
| DeJong,Paul | 18 | 50 | Fractured L hand |
| Delmonico,Nicky | 17 | 11 | Sprained R wrist |
| | 18 | 63 | Fractured R hand |
| Descalso,Daniel | 16 | 40 | Fractured L hand |
| DeShields,Delino | 15 | 20 | Strained L hamstring |
| | 18 | 48 | Fx R fing; concussion; Fx L hamate |
| Desmond,Ian | 17 | 72 | Fx L hand; strained R calf x 2 |
| Devers,Rafael | 18 | 40 | L should. inflam; strained L ham. |
| Diaz,Aledmys | 16 | 40 | Fractured R thumb |
| | 18 | 25 | Sprained L ankle |
| Diaz,Elias | 16 | 128 | Disc R elbow, cellulitis L knee |
| Dickerson,Alex | 17 | 182 | Herniated disc |
| | 18 | 187 | TJS |
| Dickerson,Corey | 15 | 98 | Non-displaced rib fx; fasciitis L ft x2 |
| | 18 | 8 | Strained L hamstring |
| Dietrich,Derek | 14 | 53 | Strained R wrist |
| | 16 | 11 | Bruised R knee |
| Donaldson,Josh | 17 | 42 | Strained R calf |
| | 18 | 125 | R shoulder inflam; tight L calf x 2 |
| Dozier,Hunter | 17 | 60 | Strained L oblique |
| Drew,Stephen | 16 | 42 | Vertigo |
| | 17 | 112 | Strained R hamstring |
| Drury,Brandon | 18 | 94 | Severe migraines; fractured L hand |

## FIVE-YEAR INJURY LOG — Hitters

| Batter | Yr | Days | Injury |
|---|---|---|---|
| Duda,Lucas | 15 | 16 | Lower back strain |
| | 16 | 117 | Stress fracture lower back |
| | 17 | 21 | Hyperextended L elbow |
| | 18 | 41 | Plantar fasciitis - R Foot |
| Duffy,Matt | 16 | 78 | Recovering from surg. on L Achilles |
| | 17 | 182 | Recovery surgery L Achilles |
| | 18 | 11 | Strained R hamstring |
| Duggar,Steven | 18 | 34 | Torn labrum - L shoulder |
| Dyson,Jarrod | 16 | 16 | Strained R oblique muscle |
| | 17 | 13 | Strained R groin |
| | 18 | 89 | Strained R groin |
| Eaton,Adam | 14 | 31 | Rt oblique muscle; Rt hamstring |
| | 17 | 155 | Torn ACL in L knee |
| | 18 | 60 | Bone bruise - L ankle |
| Eibner,Brett | 16 | 15 | Sprnd L ankle |
| Ellis,A.J. | 14 | 54 | Sprained R ankle/L knee surgery |
| | 15 | 15 | R knee inflammation |
| Ellsbury,Jacoby | 15 | 49 | R knee sprain |
| | 17 | 33 | Concussion |
| | 18 | 187 | R oblique strain |
| Encarnacion,Edwin | 14 | 39 | Strained R quadriceps |
| | 18 | 11 | L biceps inflammation |
| Escobar,Alcides | 14 | 16 | Sore R shoulder |
| | 15 | 7 | Concussion & L cheek contusion |
| Escobar,Yunel | 16 | 13 | Concussion |
| | 17 | 72 | Strained L ham; R oblique |
| Ethier,Andre | 16 | 160 | Fractured tibia R leg |
| | 17 | 152 | Herniated lumbar disc |
| Evans,Phillip | 18 | 61 | Fractured L tibia |
| Featherston,Taylor | 15 | 16 | Uppen back strain |
| Federowicz,Tim | 15 | 128 | Torn meniscus, R knee |
| Fisher,Derek | 18 | 15 | Gastrointestinal discomfort |
| Flaherty,Ryan | 15 | 30 | Strained R groin x2 |
| | 17 | 88 | Strained R shoulder |
| Flores,Wilmer | 16 | 17 | Strained L hamstring |
| | 17 | 12 | Infection in R knee |
| | 18 | 19 | Lower back soreness |
| Florimon,Pedro | 17 | 26 | Dislocated/sprained R ankle |
| | 18 | 95 | R foot fracture |
| Flowers,Tyler | 16 | 33 | Fractured L hand |
| | 17 | 10 | Bruised L wrist |
| | 18 | 29 | L oblique strain |
| Forsythe,Logan | 16 | 27 | Fractured L scapula |
| | 17 | 34 | Fractured R big toe |
| | 18 | 31 | R shoulder inflammation |
| Fowler,Dexter | 14 | 43 | Strained R intercostal |
| | 16 | 32 | Strained R hamstring |
| | 17 | 25 | Spur R heel; L forearm |
| | 18 | 59 | Strained L foot |
| Fowler,Dustin | 17 | 93 | Ruptured patella tendon in R knee |
| Franco,Maikel | 15 | 48 | Fractured L wrist |
| Franklin,Nick | 15 | 42 | Strained L oblique |
| | 16 | 7 | Concussion |
| | 18 | 146 | Strained R quad |
| Frazier,Adam | 17 | 29 | Strained L ham x 2 |
| Frazier,Clint | 17 | 33 | Strained L oblique |
| | 18 | 113 | Concussion |
| Frazier,Todd | 18 | 54 | Strnd L hammy; strnd L rib cage |
| Freeman,Freddie | 15 | 47 | Strained R oblique; bruised R wrist |
| | 17 | 47 | Fractured L wrist |
| Freese,David | 14 | 17 | Fractured R middle finger |
| | 15 | 40 | Fractured R index finger |
| | 17 | 13 | Strained R hamstring |
| Fuentes,Rey | 17 | 35 | Bruised L thumb |

## FIVE-YEAR INJURY LOG — Hitters

| Batter | Yr | Days | Injury |
|---|---|---|---|
| Gallo,Joey | 17 | 7 | Concussion |
| Galvis,Freddy | 14 | 15 | Staph infection in L knee |
| Garcia,Adonis | 17 | 106 | L Ach tendints; torn ligmt L ring fing |
| Garcia,Avisail | 14 | 128 | Surgery on L shoulder torn labrum |
| | 16 | 14 | Sprnd R knee |
| | 17 | 13 | Sprained R thumb |
| | 18 | 72 | Strained R hamstring x 2 |
| Garcia,Leury | 17 | 70 | Sprained L finger; R thumb |
| | 18 | 75 | Strained L hamstring x 2; spr. L knee |
| Garcia,Willy | 17 | 46 | Concussion |
| Gattis,Evan | 14 | 21 | Bulging thoracic disc in back |
| | 16 | 11 | Rec fr surg. to repair sports hernia |
| | 17 | 30 | Concussion; R wrist |
| Gennett,Scooter | 15 | 14 | L hand laceration |
| | 16 | 14 | Strained R oblique muscle |
| Gentry,Craig | 14 | 39 | Fx R hand; lower back strain |
| | 16 | 90 | Strained R lumbar spine |
| | 17 | 10 | Fractured R finger |
| | 18 | 52 | Fractured L rib |
| Gillaspie,Conor | 14 | 11 | Sore/bruised L hand |
| | 17 | 53 | Back spasms x 2 |
| Gillespie,Cole | 14 | 25 | Strained oblique muscle |
| Gimenez,Chris | 16 | 30 | Infection lower L leg |
| Goins,Ryan | 16 | 30 | Tightness R forearm |
| Goldschmidt,Paul | 14 | 58 | Fractured L hand |
| Gomes,Yan | 14 | 7 | Concussion |
| | 15 | 42 | R knee sprain |
| | 16 | 77 | Separated R should |
| Gomez,Carlos | 15 | 15 | R hamstring strain |
| | 16 | 15 | Bruised L rib cage |
| | 17 | 42 | Strained R ham; cyst R shoulder |
| | 18 | 11 | R groin strain |
| Gomez,Miguel | 17 | 50 | R knee inflammation |
| Gonzalez,Adrian | 17 | 79 | Sore R elbow; hern disk low back |
| Gonzalez,Carlos | 14 | 51 | L knee tendinitis/L finger inflam |
| | 17 | 11 | Strained R shoulder |
| | 18 | 9 | R hamstring strain |
| Goodwin,Brian | 17 | 46 | Strained L groin |
| | 18 | 109 | L wrist contusion; groin strain |
| Gordon,Alex | 15 | 54 | Strained L groin |
| | 16 | 33 | Fractured R wrist |
| | 18 | 15 | L hip labral tear |
| Gordon,Dee | 15 | 11 | Dislocated L thumb |
| | 18 | 10 | Fractured R great toe |
| Gosewisch,Tuffy | 15 | 129 | Torn L ACL |
| Gosselin,Phil | 15 | 105 | Avulsion fracture, L thumb |
| Grandal,Yasmani | 15 | 7 | Concussion |
| | 16 | 9 | Sore R forearm |
| Green,Grant | 14 | 39 | Lumbar strain |
| Gregorius,Didi | 17 | 26 | Strained R shoulder |
| | 18 | 18 | Bruised L heel |
| Grichuk,Randal | 15 | 47 | R elbow strain |
| | 17 | 11 | Strained lower back |
| | 18 | 32 | R knee sprain |
| Grossman,Robbie | 17 | 18 | Fractured L thumb |
| | 18 | 14 | Strained R hamstring |
| Gurriel,Lourdes | 18 | 32 | Concussion; sprained L knee/ankle |
| Gurriel,Yulieski | 18 | 11 | Recov hamate surgery, L hand |
| Gutierrez,Franklin | 17 | 118 | Strained L ham; aRhritis in spine |
| Guyer,Brandon | 14 | 24 | Fractured L thumb |
| | 16 | 23 | Strained L hamstring |
| | 17 | 43 | L wrist injury |
| | 18 | 23 | L cervical strain |
| Guzman,Ronald | 18 | 8 | Concussion |

## FIVE-YEAR INJURY LOG — Hitters

| Batter | Yr | Days | Injury |
|---|---|---|---|
| Gyorko,Jedd | 14 | 52 | Plantar fasciitis in L foot |
| | 17 | 16 | Strained R hamstring |
| | 18 | 29 | Ham strain; R shoulder impinge |
| Hamilton,Billy | 16 | 25 | Strained L oblique; concussion |
| | 17 | 12 | Fractured L thumb |
| Hamilton,Josh | 14 | 55 | Surgery on L thumb torn UCL |
| | 15 | 38 | Jammed & sprianed R Shoulder; |
| | 15 | 89 | L knee infl; L hammy; rec R shld surg |
| | 16 | 142 | Recovering from surg. on L knee |
| Hanigan,Ryan | 14 | 54 | Strained L oblique; Rt hamstring |
| | 15 | 61 | Fractured knuckle, R hand |
| | 16 | 58 | L ankle tendinitis; neck strain |
| | 17 | 16 | Strained L groin |
| Haniger,Mitch | 17 | 66 | Strained R oblique; facial laceration |
| Hanson,Alen | 18 | 20 | L hamstring strain |
| Harper,Bryce | 14 | 64 | Surgery on L thumb |
| | 17 | 44 | Hyperextended L knee |
| Harrison,Josh | 15 | 46 | Torn L thumb ligaments |
| | 16 | 7 | Strained R groin |
| | 17 | 28 | Fractured metacarpal in L hand |
| | 18 | 35 | Fractured metacarpal - L hand |
| Hays,Austin | 18 | 8 | Sprained R ankle |
| Headley,Chase | 14 | 15 | Strained R calf |
| Healy,Ryon | 18 | 18 | Sprained R ankle |
| Hechavarria,Adeiny | 14 | 11 | Strained R triceps |
| | 17 | 59 | Strained IL oblique; L ham |
| | 18 | 30 | Strained R hamstring |
| Hedges,Austin | 17 | 12 | Concussion |
| Heisey,Chris | 17 | 54 | Ruptured R biceps; strained L groin |
| Hernandez,Cesar | 15 | 21 | Dislocated L thumb |
| | 15 | 35 | L hamstring strain |
| | 17 | 36 | Strained L oblique |
| Hernandez,Enrique | 16 | 32 | L ribcage inflammation |
| Hernandez,Gorkys | 15 | 11 | L shoulder discomfort |
| Hernandez,Marco | 17 | 150 | L shoulder subluxation |
| | 18 | 187 | Recovery from L shoulder surgery |
| Hernandez,Teoscar | 17 | 18 | Bruised L knee |
| Herrera,Dilson | 15 | 26 | Fractured R middle finger |
| Herrera,Odubel | 17 | 17 | Strained L hamstring |
| Herrmann,Chris | 16 | 51 | Strained R hamstring; fx L wrist |
| | 18 | 20 | R oblique strain |
| Heyward,Jason | 17 | 24 | Sprained R finger; lacerated R hand |
| | 18 | 28 | Concussion; R hamstring tightness |
| Hicks,Aaron | 14 | 22 | Strained R shoulder;concussion |
| | 15 | 34 | Strained L ham; R forearm |
| | 16 | 15 | Strained R hamstring |
| | 17 | 68 | Strained R oblique; L oblique |
| | 18 | 14 | R intercostal muscle strain |
| Hicks,John | 18 | 55 | Strained R groin |
| Hill,Aaron | 17 | 32 | Strained R forearm |
| Holliday,Matt | 15 | 85 | Strained R quad x 2 |
| | 16 | 52 | Fractured L thumb |
| | 17 | 42 | Viral infection |
| Holt,Brock | 14 | 23 | Concussion |
| | 16 | 42 | Concussion |
| | 17 | 86 | Vertigo |
| | 18 | 12 | Strained L hamstring |
| Hoskins,Rhys | 18 | 10 | Facial injury |
| Hosmer,Eric | 14 | 31 | Stress fracture in R hand |
| Hundley,Nick | 15 | 24 | Cervical strain |
| | 16 | 37 | Strained L oblique; concussion |
| Iannetta,Chris | 17 | 7 | Concussion |

## FIVE-YEAR INJURY LOG — Hitters

| Batter | Yr | Days | Injury |
|---|---|---|---|
| Iglesias,Jose | 14 | 184 | Stress fracture in both shins |
| | 16 | 15 | Strained L hamstring |
| | 17 | 7 | Concussion |
| | 18 | 33 | Lower abdominal strain |
| Inciarte,Ender | 14 | 7 | Concussion |
| | 15 | 31 | Strained R hamstring |
| | 16 | 26 | Strained L hamstring |
| Jackson,Austin | 15 | 22 | Sprained R ankle |
| | 16 | 115 | Torn meniscus L knee |
| | 17 | 52 | Hyperextended L big toe; L quad |
| Jankowski,Travis | 17 | 102 | Bone bruise in R foot |
| Jay,Jon | 15 | 79 | Bone bruise, L wrist + tendon |
| | 16 | 70 | Fractured R forearm |
| Johnson,Micah | 17 | 99 | Fractured L wrist |
| Jones,JaCoby | 17 | 15 | Lacerated lip |
| | 18 | 15 | R hamstring strain |
| Jones,Ryder | 17 | 10 | Bruised R hand/wrist |
| Joseph,Caleb | 16 | 30 | Testicular injury |
| Joyce,Matt | 15 | 35 | Concussion |
| | 18 | 74 | Lumbar strain x 2 |
| Judge,Aaron | 16 | 19 | Strained R oblique |
| | 18 | 50 | Chip fracture, R wrist |
| Kang,Jung-Ho | 15 | 14 | Torn L meniscus, fx L tibia |
| | 16 | 49 | Sore L should; recov L knee surg. |
| Kelly,Carson | 18 | 10 | R hamstring strain |
| Kemp,Matt | 14 | 16 | Recovering from surgery on L ankle |
| | 17 | 31 | Strained R hamstring x 2 |
| Kendrick,Howie | 15 | 56 | Strained L hamstring |
| | 16 | 9 | Strained L calf |
| | 17 | 62 | Strained R Ab; L ham |
| | 18 | 135 | Torn R Achilles |
| Kiermaier,Kevin | 16 | 54 | Fractured L hand |
| | 17 | 70 | Fractured R hip |
| | 18 | 65 | Torn ligament in R rhumb |
| Kim,Hyun-soo | 16 | 15 | Strained R hamstring |
| Kinsler,Ian | 17 | 10 | Strained L hamstring |
| | 18 | 27 | L adductor strain; strained L ham. |
| Kipnis,Jason | 14 | 26 | Strained R oblique |
| | 15 | 15 | R shoulder inflammation |
| | 17 | 72 | R shoulder inflam; R ham x2 |
| Knapp,Andrew | 17 | 37 | Fractured R hand |
| Kratz,Erik | 15 | 36 | Plantar fasciitis, L foot |
| La Stella,Tommy | 15 | 119 | Strained R oblique |
| | 16 | 27 | Strained R hamstring |
| Lagares,Juan | 14 | 39 | Strnd R intercostal/str R hamstring |
| | 16 | 66 | Torn lig L thumb; sprnd L thumb |
| | 17 | 66 | Strained L oblique; L thumb |
| | 18 | 137 | L toe surgery |
| Laird,Gerald | 15 | 130 | Lower back spasms |
| Lamb,Jacob | 15 | 46 | Stress reaction, L foot |
| | 18 | 113 | Sprained L AC joint |
| Lambo,Andrew | 15 | 152 | Plantar fasciitis, L foot |
| | 16 | 91 | Testicular cancer |
| Lavarnway,Ryan | 14 | 76 | Strained L wrist |
| LeMahieu,D.J. | 18 | 40 | Strained R ham; L thumb; L oblique |
| Lind,Adam | 14 | 52 | Fx R foot; lower back tightness |
| Liriano,Rymer | 16 | 183 | Facial bone fractures |
| Lobaton,Jose | 16 | 22 | L elbow tendinitis |
| Longoria,Evan | 18 | 42 | Fractured L hand |
| Lowrie,Jed | 14 | 18 | Fractured R index finger |
| | 15 | 93 | Torn ligament, R thumb |
| | 16 | 74 | Bunion on L foot; bruised R shin |
| Lucroy,Jonathan | 15 | 41 | Broken L toe |
| Machado,Manny | 14 | 79 | Surgery L knee 10/13; R knee surg |

## FIVE-YEAR INJURY LOG — Hitters

| Batter | Yr | Days | Injury |
|---|---|---|---|
| Mahtook,Mikie | 16 | 46 | Fractured L hand |
| Maile,Luke | 17 | 59 | Inflam in R knee |
| Margot,Manuel | 17 | 31 | Strained R calf |
| | 18 | 11 | Bruised ribs |
| Marisnick,Jake | 15 | 16 | Strained L hamstring |
| | 17 | 7 | Concussion |
| | 18 | 22 | L groin discomfort |
| Marrero,Deven | 18 | 39 | Strained L oblique |
| Marte,Jefry | 17 | 23 | Fractured L foot |
| | 18 | 24 | L wrist sprain |
| Marte,Ketel | 16 | 32 | Sprnd L thumb; mono |
| Marte,Starling | 14 | 13 | Concussion |
| | 18 | 9 | Strained R oblique |
| Martin,Leonys | 16 | 14 | Strained L hamstring |
| | 18 | 83 | Strnd L ham x2; bacterial infection |
| Martin,Russell | 14 | 26 | Strained L hamstring |
| | 17 | 45 | Nerve irritation L shoulder; L oblique |
| Martinez,J.D. | 16 | 48 | Fractured R elbow |
| | 17 | 42 | Sprained ligament in R foot |
| Martinez,Jose | 17 | 22 | Strained L groin |
| Martinez,Victor | 15 | 31 | L knee inflammation |
| | 17 | 47 | Irregular heartbeat x2 |
| Mathis,Jeff | 15 | 53 | Fractured R ring finger |
| | 17 | 38 | Fractured R hand |
| Mauer,Joe | 14 | 40 | Strained R oblique muscle |
| | 17 | 10 | strained lower back |
| | 18 | 27 | Concussion |
| Maybin,Cameron | 14 | 29 | Ruptured L biceps tendon |
| | 16 | 60 | Sprnd L thumb; fractured L wrist |
| | 17 | 27 | Strained L oblique; MCL R knee |
| Mazara,Nomar | 18 | 28 | Sprained R thumb |
| McCann,Brian | 14 | 8 | Concussion |
| | 17 | 17 | Concussion; sore R knee |
| | 18 | 72 | Strained R knee |
| McCann,James | 16 | 21 | Sprnd R ankle |
| | 17 | 14 | Laceration on L hand |
| McCutchen,Andrew | 14 | 15 | Fractured L rib |
| McKinney,Billy | 18 | 55 | L AC shoulder sprain |
| Mercer,Jordy | 15 | 34 | Lower leg contusion |
| | 18 | 14 | Strained L calf |
| Mesoraco,Devin | 14 | 20 | strnd L hamstring/strnd L oblique |
| | 15 | 133 | L hip strain |
| | 16 | 154 | Torn labrum L should |
| | 17 | 86 | Rec surg R hip; sprnd L Shld; Fx R foot |
| Middlebrooks,Will | 14 | 94 | Fx Rt index finger; strained Rt calf |
| | 16 | 36 | Strained R lower leg |
| Miller,Brad | 17 | 44 | Strained L ab; L groin |
| | 18 | 12 | Groin strain |
| Molina,Yadier | 14 | 50 | Torn ligament in R thumb |
| | 18 | 31 | Pelvic injury |
| Moncada,Yoan | 17 | 11 | Bone bruise in R shin |
| | 18 | 10 | Tight L hamstring |
| Mondesi,Adalberto | 18 | 33 | R shoulder impingement syndrome |
| Montero,Miguel | 15 | 21 | Sprained L thumb |
| | 17 | 12 | Strained groin |
| Moore,Tyler | 15 | 13 | L ankle sprain |
| Morales,Kendrys | 18 | 11 | Strained R hamstring |
| Moran,Colin | 17 | 56 | Facial fractures |
| Moreland,Mitch | 15 | 14 | L elbow surgery |
| Morrison,Logan | 14 | 56 | Strained R hamstring |
| | 16 | 34 | Strained R forearm,strained L wrist |
| | 18 | 63 | L hip impingement |
| Morse,Michael | 15 | 40 | R ring finger strain |
| | 17 | 124 | Concussion |

## FIVE-YEAR INJURY LOG — Hitters

| Batter | Yr | Days | Injury |
|---|---|---|---|
| Moss,Brandon | 16 | 28 | Sprnd L ankle |
| Motter,Taylor | 18 | 22 | Concussion |
| Moustakas,Mike | 16 | 146 | Torn ACL R knee; fractured L thumb |
| Munoz,Yairo | 18 | 12 | Sprained R wrist |
| Murphy,Daniel | 14 | 11 | Strained R calf |
| | 15 | 25 | Strained L quad |
| | 18 | 76 | Surgery R knee |
| Murphy,Tom | 17 | 74 | Fractured R forearm |
| Myers,Wil | 14 | 80 | Sprained R wrist |
| | 15 | 104 | Bone spurs, L wrist + tend |
| | 18 | 81 | Nerve irrit; bone bruise L Ft; L obliq |
| Napoli,Mike | 14 | 14 | Sprained L ring finger |
| | 17 | 10 | strained lower back |
| Naquin,Tyler | 18 | 101 | R hip strain; strained L ham. |
| Nava,Daniel | 15 | 54 | Strained L thumb |
| | 16 | 51 | Strained L groin; tend. L kneecap |
| | 17 | 57 | Strained L Ham x 2; lower back x 2 |
| Negron,Kristopher | 15 | 21 | Torn labrum Lt shdlr |
| Nicholas,Brett | 17 | 26 | Surg L knee to repair torn meniscus |
| Nieuwenhuis,Kirk | 15 | 30 | Pinched nerve in back |
| Nimmo,Brandon | 17 | 64 | Strained R ham; collapsed lung |
| | 18 | 9 | Bruised L index finger |
| Nunez,Eduardo | 14 | 16 | Strained R hamstring |
| | 15 | 12 | L oblique strain |
| | 17 | 21 | Strained hamstring |
| Nunez,Renato | 18 | 19 | Strained L hamstring |
| O'Neill,Tyler | 18 | 22 | Inflammation in groin area |
| Odor,Rougned | 18 | 32 | Strained L hamstring |
| Ohtani,Shohei | 18 | 26 | Sprained UCL, R elbow |
| Orlando,Paulo | 17 | 82 | Fractured shin |
| Owings,Christopher | 14 | 65 | Strained L shoulder |
| | 16 | 42 | Plantar fasciitis L foot |
| | 17 | 62 | Fractured R middle finger |
| Ozuna,Marcell | 18 | 11 | R shoulder inflammation |
| Pacheco,Jordan | 14 | 33 | R shoulder tendinitis |
| | 16 | 122 | R should tendinitis |
| Panik,Joe | 15 | 54 | Lower back discomfort + inflam |
| | 16 | 29 | Concussion |
| | 17 | 10 | Concussion |
| | 18 | 59 | Sprnd L thumb; L groin strain |
| Parker,Jarrett | 17 | 109 | Fractured R collarbone |
| Parra,Gerardo | 16 | 53 | Sprnd L ankle |
| | 17 | 30 | Strained R quadriceps |
| Pearce,Steven | 15 | 33 | L oblique strain |
| | 16 | 43 | Strnd R ham, strnd flexor R elbow |
| | 17 | 32 | Strained R calf |
| | 18 | 50 | L oblique strain |
| Pederson,Joc | 16 | 18 | Sprnd AC joint R should |
| | 17 | 32 | Strained R groin; concussion |
| Pedroia,Dustin | 14 | 29 | L thumb/wrist surgery |
| | 15 | 67 | R hamstring strain x2 |
| | 17 | 45 | Sprained L wrist; L knee inflam |
| | 18 | 180 | L knee surgery (meniscus) |
| Pena,Brayan | 16 | 147 | L knee inflammation + surg. |
| Pence,Hunter | 15 | 112 | L oblique; Fx L forearm; sore L wrist |
| | 16 | 58 | Strained R hamstring |
| | 17 | 20 | Strained L hamstring |
| | 18 | 44 | Sprained R thumb |
| Pennington,Cliff | 14 | 64 | Sprained ligament in L thumb |
| | 16 | 77 | Strained L hamstring x 2 |
| Peralta,David | 16 | 118 | R wrist inflam; lower back strain |
| Peralta,Jhonny | 16 | 80 | Strained + torn ligament L thumb |
| | 17 | 29 | Upper respiratory ailment |
| Perez,Carlos | 18 | 31 | Sprained R ankle |

## FIVE-YEAR INJURY LOG — Hitters

| Batter | Yr | Days | Injury |
|---|---|---|---|
| Perez,Michael | 18 | 32 | L hamstring strain |
| Perez,Roberto | 16 | 78 | Fractured R thumb |
| Perez,Salvador | 17 | 16 | Strained R intercostal |
| | 18 | 27 | Sprained R MCL |
| Petit,Gregorio | 15 | 37 | R hand contusion |
| Pham,Tommy | 15 | 63 | L quadriceps strain |
| | 16 | 43 | Strained L oblique |
| | 18 | 14 | Fractured R foot |
| Phegley,Josh | 17 | 44 | Concussion; L oblique |
| | 18 | 24 | Fractured R hand |
| Phillips,Brandon | 14 | 38 | Surg torn ligament on L thumb |
| Pillar,Kevin | 16 | 15 | Sprnd L thumb |
| | 18 | 20 | Sprained R shoulder |
| Pina,Manny | 18 | 22 | R calf strain; L biceps strain |
| Pinder,Chad | 17 | 37 | Strained L hamstring |
| | 18 | 20 | Hyperext. L knee; L elbow laceration |
| Pirela,Jose | 15 | 32 | Concussion |
| Piscotty,Stephen | 17 | 32 | Strained R ham; R groin |
| Plawecki,Kevin | 18 | 46 | Hairline fracture - L hand |
| Plouffe,Trevor | 14 | 15 | Strained L oblique |
| | 16 | 73 | Fract L rib; strnd L oblique |
| Polanco,Gregory | 17 | 45 | Strained L ham x 3 |
| | 18 | 14 | Surgery to stabilize L shoulder |
| Pollock,A.J. | 14 | 93 | Fractured R hand |
| | 16 | 146 | Fractured R elbow; strained L groin |
| | 17 | 50 | Strained R groin |
| | 18 | 49 | Fractured L thumb |
| Pompey,Dalton | 17 | 182 | Concussion |
| Posey,Buster | 17 | 7 | Concussion |
| | 18 | 37 | R hip surgery |
| Powell,Boog | 18 | 117 | Sprained R knee |
| Prado,Martin | 14 | 14 | Appendectomy |
| | 15 | 29 | R shoulder sprain |
| | 17 | 136 | Strained R ham x 2; R knee |
| | 18 | 118 | Recovery from R knee surgery |
| Presley,Alex | 14 | 56 | Strained R oblique muscle |
| | 17 | 26 | Concussion; strained R hip |
| Profar,Jurickson | 14 | 183 | Torn muscle in R shoulder |
| | 15 | 183 | Recovery from shoulder surgery |
| Puello,Cesar | 15 | 182 | Stress fracture in lower back |
| Puig,Yasiel | 15 | 79 | Strained R hamstring |
| | 16 | 18 | Strained L hamstring |
| | 18 | 31 | L hip pointer; strained R oblique |
| Pujols,Albert | 18 | 44 | L knee surgery |
| Raburn,Ryan | 14 | 14 | Sore R wrist |
| | 17 | 67 | Strained L trapezius muscle |
| Ramirez,Hanley | 14 | 14 | Strained R oblique |
| | 15 | 30 | R shoulder inflammation |
| Ramos,Wilson | 14 | 50 | Strained R hamstring/Fx L hand |
| | 17 | 85 | Surgery on R knee to repair torn ACL |
| | 18 | 29 | Strained L hamstring |
| Rasmus,Colby | 14 | 33 | Tightness in R hamstring |
| | 16 | 23 | Ear infection |
| | 17 | 51 | Recov surgery on hip; hip tend |
| | 18 | 76 | L hip flexor strain |
| Realmuto,Jacob | 18 | 20 | Lower back bruise |
| Reddick,Josh | 14 | 44 | Strained R knee;hyper Rt knee |
| | 15 | 8 | Strained R oblique |
| | 16 | 39 | Fractured L thumb |
| | 17 | 7 | Concussion |
| | 18 | 15 | Leg infection |
| Reed,Michael | 18 | 30 | Strained lower back |

## FIVE-YEAR INJURY LOG — Hitters

| Batter | Yr | Days | Injury |
|---|---|---|---|
| Rendon,Anthony | 15 | 89 | Strained L quad; Sprain L knee |
| | 18 | 13 | L toe contusion |
| Renfroe,Hunter | 17 | 10 | Strained neck |
| | 18 | 38 | R elbow inflammation |
| Revere,Ben | 16 | 30 | Strained R oblique muscle |
| Reyes,Jose | 14 | 19 | Tightness in L hamstring |
| | 15 | 27 | Cracked L rib |
| | 16 | 14 | Strained L intercostal |
| | 17 | 10 | Strained L oblique |
| Reynolds,Mark | 16 | 19 | Recovering from L wrist surg. |
| Rickard,Joey | 16 | 73 | R thumb ligament injury |
| | 17 | 19 | Sprnd L pinky finger & middle finger |
| Riddle,J.T. | 17 | 68 | L biceps tendinitis |
| | 18 | 36 | Recovery from L shoulder surgery |
| Rivera,Rene | 18 | 88 | R knee inflammation |
| Rivera,T.J. | 17 | 65 | Partially torn UCL in R elbow |
| | 18 | 187 | TJS |
| Rizzo,Anthony | 18 | 9 | Lower back tightness |
| Robertson,Daniel | 17 | 35 | Neck spasms |
| | 18 | 71 | Sprnd L thumb; strnd L hamstring |
| Robinson,Drew | 18 | 16 | Sore L hip |
| Robinson,Shane | 14 | 34 | Surgery on L shoulder |
| | 16 | 48 | Strained R hip flexor; R ankle |
| Rodriguez,Sean | 17 | 106 | Recovery from L shoulder surgery |
| | 18 | 42 | Strained R quad; strained L abdom |
| Rojas,Miguel | 17 | 70 | Fractured R thumb |
| Rosario,Eddie | 16 | 1 | Fractured L thumb |
| Rua,Ryan | 15 | 69 | Sprained R ankle |
| | 18 | 45 | Back spasms |
| Ruggiano,Justin | 14 | 65 | Surgery L ankle/strnd L hamstring |
| | 16 | 53 | L should strain; L hamstring strain |
| Ruiz,Carlos | 14 | 26 | Concussion |
| Russell,Addison | 17 | 44 | Strained R foot |
| | 18 | 11 | Sprained L middle finger |
| Rutledge,Josh | 14 | 11 | Viral infection |
| | 16 | 108 | Patellar tendinitis L knee |
| | 17 | 127 | Strained L ham: concussion |
| Saladino,Tyler | 17 | 48 | Back spasms |
| | 18 | 37 | Sprained L ankle |
| Saltalamacchia,Jarrod | 14 | 17 | Concussion |
| | 15 | 10 | Strained neck |
| Sanchez,Gary | 17 | 27 | Strained R biceps |
| | 18 | 65 | R groin strain |
| Sanchez,Hector | 14 | 37 | Concussion |
| | 15 | 27 | Strained L hamstring |
| | 17 | 57 | Concussion; bruised R foot |
| Sandoval,Pablo | 16 | 173 | Strained L should |
| | 17 | 59 | Sprained R knee; ear infection |
| | 18 | 63 | R hamstring strain |
| Sano,Miguel | 16 | 30 | Strained L hamstring |
| | 17 | 39 | Stress reaction in L shin |
| | 18 | 24 | Strained L hamstring |
| Santana,Carlos | 14 | 10 | Concussion |
| | 14 | 21 | Bone bruise in L knee |
| Santana,Daniel | 16 | 69 | Sprnd AC joint L should; strain ham. |
| | 17 | 54 | Bacterial infection; strained L quad |
| Santana,Domingo | 16 | 85 | Sore R elbow; sore R should |
| Santander,Anthony | 17 | 136 | R elbow inflammation |
| Sardinas,Luis | 18 | 67 | Lower back strain |
| Saunders,Michael | 14 | 74 | Strained Lt oblique; A/C joint inflam |
| | 15 | 168 | L knee inflam; rec L knee surg |
| Schebler,Scott | 17 | 17 | Strained L shoulder |
| | 18 | 51 | R ulnar nerve bruise; sprained R A/C |

## FIVE-YEAR INJURY LOG — Hitters

| Batter | Yr | Days | Injury |
|---|---|---|---|
| Schoop,Jonathan | 15 | 78 | R knee sprain |
|  | 18 | 25 | R oblique strain |
| Schwarber,Kyle | 16 | 178 | Torn ligaments L knee |
| Seager,Corey | 18 | 154 | UCL strain - R elbow |
| Segedin,Robert | 17 | 118 | Strained R big toe |
| Segura,Jean | 15 | 15 | Fractured R pinky finger |
|  | 17 | 33 | Strained R ham; high R ankle sprain |
| Semien,Marcus | 17 | 81 | Bruised R wrist |
| Shuck,J.B. | 15 | 15 | Strained L hamstring |
| Simmons,Andrelton | 16 | 36 | Torn ligament L thumb |
|  | 18 | 11 | Grade 2 R ankle sprain |
| Slater,Austin | 17 | 59 | Strained R groin |
| Smith,Kevan | 16 | 26 | Back injury (sacroiliac joint dysfunct) |
|  | 18 | 24 | Sprained L ankle |
| Smith,Mallex | 16 | 87 | Fractured L thumb |
|  | 17 | 13 | Strained R hamstring |
|  | 18 | 10 | Viral infection |
| Smoak,Justin | 14 | 23 | Strained L quadriceps |
| Smolinski,Jacob | 14 | 53 | Bone bruise in L foot |
|  | 17 | 153 | Recovery surgery R shoulder |
| Smolinski,Jake | 18 | 58 | R arm nerve irritation |
| Sogard,Eric | 16 | 183 | Cervical strain |
|  | 17 | 16 | Strained L ankle |
| Solano,Jhonatan | 18 | 175 | Bone spurs in R elbow |
| Solarte,Yangervis | 16 | 41 | Strained R hamstring |
|  | 17 | 37 | Strained L oblique muscle |
|  | 18 | 29 | Strained R oblique |
| Soler,Jorge | 15 | 56 | L oblique; Sprain L ankle |
|  | 16 | 59 | Strained L hamstring |
|  | 17 | 34 | Strained L oblique |
|  | 18 | 107 | Fractured L toe |
| Soto,Geovany | 14 | 126 | Strained R groin; surg. Rt knee |
|  | 16 | 121 | L knee inf; R knee inf.; torn meniscus |
|  | 17 | 154 | R elbow inflam |
| Souza,Steven | 14 | 22 | Bruised L shoulder |
|  | 15 | 54 | Fractured L hand; cut finger |
|  | 16 | 28 | Brsd/strnd L hip, rec from surg. L hip |
|  | 18 | 81 | Strained R pectoral muscle |
| Span,Denard | 14 | 7 | Concussion |
|  | 15 | 98 | Core muscle surg; back; torn labr. |
|  | 17 | 15 | Sprained R shoulder |
| Spangenberg,Cory | 15 | 45 | L knee contusion |
|  | 16 | 166 | Strained L quadriceps |
| Springer,George | 14 | 68 | L quadriceps injury |
|  | 15 | 70 | Fx R wrist; concussion |
|  | 17 | 12 | L quadriceps injury |
|  | 18 | 12 | Sprained L thumb |
| Stanton,Giancarlo | 15 | 100 | L wrist hamate fracture |
|  | 16 | 23 | Strained L groin |
| Starling,Bubba | 17 | 36 | Strained R oblique |
|  | 18 | 30 | Sprained R UCL |
| Stassi,Max | 16 | 37 | Surg. to repair fractured L wrist |
|  | 17 | 10 | L hand inflammation |
| Stewart,Chris | 14 | 21 | Surgery on R knee |
|  | 15 | 12 | Strained R hamstring |
|  | 16 | 80 | L knee injury |
|  | 17 | 19 | Strained L hamstring |
| Story,Trevor | 16 | 62 | Torn ligament L thumb |
|  | 17 | 12 | Strained L shoulder |
| Stubbs,Drew | 16 | 79 | Sprnd L little toe |
| Suarez,Eugenio | 18 | 18 | Fractured R thumb |
| Sucre,Jesus | 16 | 127 | Fractured fibula leg |
| Susac,Andrew | 15 | 58 | Sprained R wrist |
|  | 17 | 28 | strained trap x 2 |

## FIVE-YEAR INJURY LOG — Hitters

| Batter | Yr | Days | Injury |
|---|---|---|---|
| Swanson,Dansby | 18 | 16 | L wrist inflammation |
| Swihart,Blake | 15 | 17 | Sprained L foot |
|  | 16 | 120 | Sprnd L ankle |
|  | 18 | 12 | Strained R hamstring |
| Szczur,Matthew | 16 | 18 | Strained R hamstring |
| Taylor,Chris | 15 | 14 | Fractured R wrist |
| Taylor,Michael | 17 | 37 | Strained R oblique muscle |
| Tejada,Ruben | 16 | 16 | strnd L quadriceps |
| Thames,Eric | 18 | 58 | Strained R hamstring |
| Thompson,Trayce | 16 | 79 | Lower back injury |
| Tilson,Charlie | 16 | 61 | Torn L hamstring |
|  | 17 | 182 | Stress reaction in R foot |
| Tocci,Carlos | 18 | 41 | Bruised L hip |
| Toles,Andrew | 17 | 144 | Torn ACL in R knee |
| Tomas,Yasmany | 17 | 117 | R groin tendinitis |
| Tomlinson,Kelby | 16 | 31 | Sprnd L thumb |
| Torres,Gleyber | 18 | 22 | Strained R hip |
| Travis,Devon | 15 | 101 | L shoulder strain; inflam |
|  | 16 | 52 | Recovering from surg. on L should |
|  | 17 | 117 | Bone bruise in R knee |
| Trout,Mike | 17 | 46 | Torn ligament in L thumb |
|  | 18 | 15 | R wrist inflammation |
| Trumbo,Mark | 14 | 78 | Stress fracture in L foot |
|  | 17 | 10 | Strained ribcage |
|  | 18 | 77 | Strained R quad muscle |
| Tucker,Preston | 16 | 52 | Strained R should |
| Tulowitzki,Troy | 14 | 69 | Strained L hip flexor |
|  | 16 | 21 | Strained R quadriceps |
|  | 17 | 98 | Strained R ham; sprained R ankle |
|  | 18 | 187 | R heel bone spurs |
| Turner,Justin | 14 | 19 | Strained L hamstring |
|  | 15 | 13 | R thigh skin infection |
|  | 17 | 21 | Strained R hamstring |
|  | 18 | 59 | Recover fr fx L wrist; groin strain |
| Turner,Stuart | 17 | 29 | Strained R hamstring |
| Turner,Trea | 17 | 71 | Strained R ham; fractured R wrist |
| Upton,Justin | 18 | 10 | L index finger laceration |
| Urshela,Giovanny | 18 | 37 | Strained R hamstring |
| Utley,Chase | 15 | 44 | R ankle inflammation |
|  | 18 | 55 | Sprained L thumb; L wrist inflam. |
| Valbuena,Luis | 16 | 66 | Strained R hamstring |
|  | 17 | 31 | Strained R hamstring |
| Valencia,Danny | 14 | 21 | Sprained L hand |
|  | 16 | 14 | Strained L hamstring |
| Van Slyke,Scott | 15 | 15 | L mid-back inflammation |
|  | 16 | 107 | R wrist injury; lower back strain |
| Vazquez,Christian | 15 | 189 | R elbow sprain |
|  | 16 | 12 | Recovering from TJS |
|  | 18 | 56 | R fifth finger fx |
| Villanueva,Christian | 16 | 183 | Fractured fibula R leg |
|  | 18 | 40 | Fractured R middle finger |
| Villar,Jonathan | 17 | 17 | Strained lower back |
|  | 18 | 19 | Sprained R thumb |
| Vogt,Stephen | 17 | 31 | Sprained L knee |
|  | 18 | 187 | R shoulder strain |
| Votto,Joey | 14 | 103 | Strained L quadriceps x 2 |
|  | 18 | 14 | R lower leg contusion |
| Walker,Christian | 18 | 3 | Sinus bone fracture |
| Walker,Neil | 14 | 15 | Appendectomy |
|  | 16 | 27 | Herniated disk lower back |
|  | 17 | 44 | Strained L hamstring |
| Wendle,Joe | 17 | 28 | Strained R shoulder |
| Werth,Jayson | 15 | 78 | Rec. R shldr surg.; L wrist cont. |
|  | 17 | 84 | Bruised L foot |

## FIVE-YEAR INJURY LOG — Hitters

| Batter | Yr | Days | Injury |
|---|---|---|---|
| Wieters,Matt | 14 | 94 | Strained R Elbow; TJS |
| | 15 | 61 | Recovery from R elbow surgery |
| | 18 | 70 | Strained L oblique; strained L ham |
| Wilkerson,Steve | 18 | 50 | L oblique strain |
| Williams,Mason | 15 | 106 | R shoulder inflammation |
| | 16 | 106 | Recovering from surg. on R should |
| Williamson,Mac | 16 | 36 | Strnd L should; strained R quadricep |
| | 17 | 22 | Strained L quadriceps |
| | 18 | 28 | Concussion |
| Wilson,Bobby | 18 | 36 | Sprained R ankle |
| Winker,Jesse | 17 | 19 | Strained L hip flexor |
| | 18 | 68 | R shoulder subluxation |
| Wolters,Tony | 16 | 12 | Concussion |
| | 17 | 13 | Concussion |
| Wong,Kolten | 14 | 15 | Sore L shoulder |
| | 17 | 37 | Strained L elbow; R triceps |
| | 18 | 21 | L knee inflammation |
| Wright,David | 15 | 131 | Strained R hamstring |
| | 16 | 122 | Herniated disc neck |
| | 17 | 182 | Herniated cervical disc |
| | 18 | 181 | Lower back pain |
| Yelich,Christian | 14 | 13 | Strained lower back |
| | 15 | 33 | Rt knee contusion; low back strain |
| | 18 | 10 | Strained R oblique |
| Young Jr.,Eric | 14 | 21 | Strained R hamstring |
| Young,Chris | 14 | 15 | Strained R quadricep |
| | 16 | 76 | Strained R hamstring; R forearm |
| | 18 | 90 | Strained L hamstring |
| Zagunis,Mark | 18 | 28 | R shoulder inflammation |
| Zimmer,Bradley | 18 | 18 | L rib contusion |
| Zimmerman,Ryan | 14 | 110 | Fx R thumb/strained R hamstring |
| | 15 | 47 | Plantar fasciitis, L foot |
| | 16 | 33 | Bruised L wrist; strained L ribcage |
| | 18 | 71 | Strained R oblique |
| Zobrist,Ben | 14 | 15 | Dislocated L thumb |
| | 15 | 30 | Medial meniscus tear, L knee |
| | 17 | 15 | L wrist inflammation |
| | 18 | 8 | Back tightness |
| Zunino,Mike | 18 | 39 | Strained L oblique |

## FIVE-YEAR INJURY LOG — Pitchers

| Pitchers | Yr | Days | Injury |
|---|---|---|---|
| Adleman,Timothy | 16 | 74 | Strnd L oblique |
| Albers,Matt | 14 | 157 | R shoulder tendinitis |
| | 15 | 84 | Broken finger,R hand |
| | 18 | 63 | R shoulder strain |
| Alcantara,Sandy | 18 | 35 | R axillary/armpit infection |
| Alexander,Scott | 17 | 29 | Strained R hamstring |
| Almonte,Miguel | 17 | 40 | R rotator cuff inflam |
| Altavilla,Dan | 18 | 95 | R AC joint inflam; R UCL sprain |
| Alvarez,Dario | 17 | 10 | Strained L elbow |
| Alvarez,Henderson | 14 | 14 | R shoulder inflammation |
| | 15 | 169 | R shoulder inflammation x2 |
| | 16 | 184 | Rec fr surg. on R should |
| Anderson,Brett | 14 | 144 | Strained lower back/fx L finger |
| | 16 | 163 | Rec fr back surg. - bulging disc |
| | 17 | 80 | Strained lower back |
| | 18 | 68 | Strained L shoulder |
| Anderson,Chase | 15 | 19 | R triceps inflammation |
| | 17 | 52 | Strained L oblique muscle |
| | 18 | 9 | Food poisoning |
| Anderson,Cody | 15 | 18 | L oblique strain |
| | 17 | 182 | Surgery on R elbow |
| | 18 | 187 | TJS |
| Anderson,Tyler | 16 | 36 | Strnd R oblique muscle |
| | 17 | 99 | L knee inflammation x2 |
| Andriese,Matt | 17 | 87 | Strained groin; stress reaction R hip |
| Arano,Victor | 18 | 18 | Strained R rotator cuff |
| Araujo,Pedro | 18 | 113 | Sprained UCL - R elbow |
| Archer,Chris | 18 | 35 | L abdominal strain |
| Arrieta,Jake | 14 | 34 | Tightness in R shoulder |
| Atchison,Scott | 15 | 16 | Sprained L ankle |
| Avilan,Luis | 17 | 15 | L triceps soreness |
| Axford,John | 17 | 45 | Strained R shoulder |
| | 18 | 35 | Fractured R fibula |
| Baez,Pedro | 15 | 43 | R pectoral strain |
| | 17 | 12 | Bruised R wrist |
| | 18 | 42 | R biceps tendinitis |
| Bailey,Andrew | 16 | 14 | Strnd L hamstring |
| | 17 | 163 | R shoulder inflam x2 |
| Bailey,Homer | 14 | 16 | Strained flexor tendon in R elbow |
| | 15 | 174 | Torn UCL,R elbow; TJS surgery |
| | 16 | 116 | Rec fr TJS |
| | 17 | 86 | Bone spurs R elbow |
| | 18 | 53 | R knee inflammation |
| Banuelos,Manny | 15 | 35 | L elbow inflammation |
| | 16 | 51 | Rec fr surg. L elbow spur |
| Barbato,Johnny | 18 | 43 | Strained R forearm |
| Barnes,Danny | 17 | 10 | R shoulder impingement |
| | 18 | 41 | L knee tendinitis |
| Barnes,Jacob | 16 | 37 | Sore R elbow |
| Barnes,Matt | 17 | 10 | Strained lower back |
| Barnette,Tony | 17 | 16 | Sprained R ring finger |
| | 18 | 115 | Lower back strain; R shoulder inflam |
| Barraclough,Kyle | 17 | 20 | R shoulder impingement |
| | 18 | 15 | Lower back stiffness |
| Barrett,Aaron | 15 | 86 | R elbow sprain; R biceps |
| | 16 | 183 | Rec fr TJS |
| Barrett,Jake | 17 | 41 | Stiffness in R shoulder |
| Barrios,Yhonathan | 16 | 184 | Strnd R should |
| Bass,Anthony | 14 | 49 | Chest injury/strained R intercostal |
| | 18 | 34 | Viral illness; R mid-thoracic strain |
| Bassitt,Chris | 16 | 157 | Torn ligament R elbow |
| | 17 | 115 | Recovery from TJS |
| Bastardo,Antonio | 17 | 63 | Strained L quadriceps |
| Bauer,Trevor | 18 | 39 | Stress fracture, R fibula |

## FIVE-YEAR INJURY LOG — Pitchers

| Pitchers | Yr | Days | Injury |
|---|---|---|---|
| Baumann,Buddy | 16 | 89 | Strnd lower back |
| | 17 | 112 | Strained L shoulder |
| Beato,Pedro | 17 | 18 | Strained L hamstring |
| Bedrosian,Cam | 16 | 55 | Flexor tendinitis R finger |
| | 17 | 56 | Strained R groin |
| Beeler,Dallas | 15 | 43 | R shoulder inflammation |
| | 16 | 183 | R should inflammation |
| Belisle,Matt | 15 | 74 | R elbow inflammation |
| | 16 | 48 | Strnd R calf |
| | 18 | 26 | R knee chondromalacia |
| Benoit,Joaquin | 16 | 22 | R should inflammation |
| | 17 | 20 | Sprained FT knee; L knee Inflam |
| | 18 | 187 | Strained R forearm |
| Bergman,Christian | 14 | 60 | Fractured L hand/thumb |
| | 15 | 32 | R shoulder fatigue |
| | 16 | 50 | Strnd L oblique |
| Bettis,Chad | 15 | 36 | R elbow inflammation |
| | 17 | 131 | Testicular cancer |
| | 18 | 36 | R middle finger blister |
| Biagini,Joe | 18 | 11 | Strained L oblique |
| Biddle,Jesse | 16 | 183 | Rec fr TJS |
| Black,Ray | 16 | 30 | Bone spur R elbow |
| Blackburn,Clayton | 18 | 187 | TJS |
| Blackburn,Paul | 17 | 37 | Bruised R forearm |
| | 18 | 157 | Strained R forearm |
| Blair,Aaron | 16 | 15 | Strnd L knee |
| Blanton,Joe | 17 | 25 | R shoulder inflammation |
| Blazek,Michael | 15 | 52 | Fractured R hand |
| | 16 | 36 | Strnd R forearm; R elbow imping |
| Bleier,Richard | 18 | 109 | Torn upper lat; L shoulder surgery |
| Blevins,Jerry | 15 | 167 | Fractured L forearm |
| Bolsinger,Michael | 16 | 44 | Strnd L oblique muscle |
| | 17 | 10 | L knee inflammation |
| Bonilla,Lisalverto | 17 | 22 | R elbow inflammation |
| Boshers,Jeffrey | 16 | 22 | L elbow inflammation |
| Bowman,Matthew | 18 | 45 | Blisters pitching hand |
| Boxberger,Brad | 16 | 116 | Strnd L oblique; recov. core surg. |
| | 17 | 89 | Strained R flexor |
| Boyer,Blaine | 15 | 12 | R elbow inflammation |
| | 17 | 26 | Strained R elbow; strained neck |
| | 18 | 75 | R lower back strain |
| Bradley,Archie | 15 | 98 | R shoulder tend; facial bruise |
| Breslow,Craig | 14 | 13 | Strained L shoulder |
| | 17 | 20 | Sore L thoracic rib cage |
| Brewer,Colten | 18 | 37 | Strained L oblique |
| Brice,Austin | 17 | 59 | Ulnar neuritis in R elbow; R lat strain |
| | 18 | 11 | Mid-back strain |
| Britton,Zach | 17 | 76 | Strained L forearm x2 |
| | 18 | 75 | Ruptured R Achilles |
| Brooks,Aaron | 16 | 183 | Bruised hip |
| Buchholz,Clay | 14 | 28 | Hyperextended L knee |
| | 15 | 86 | R flexor strain |
| | 17 | 166 | Torn flexor in R forearm |
| | 18 | 47 | Strained L oblique |
| Buchter,Ryan | 18 | 60 | Strained L shoulder |
| Buehler,Walker | 18 | 32 | R rib microfracture |
| Bumgarner,Madison | 17 | 85 | Bruised ribs, sprained L shoulder |
| | 18 | 69 | Fractured L hand |
| Bundy,Dylan | 15 | 11 | Strained R shoulder |
| | 18 | 11 | L ankle sprain |
| Burdi,Nick | 18 | 157 | TJS |
| Bush,Matt | 17 | 21 | Sprained MCL in R knee |
| | 18 | 109 | Strained R elbow |

## FIVE-YEAR INJURY LOG — Pitchers

| Pitchers | Yr | Days | Injury |
|---|---|---|---|
| Butler,Eddie | 14 | 40 | R rotator cuff inflammation |
| | 18 | 96 | R groin strain |
| Cabrera,Mauricio | 17 | 35 | Strained R elbow |
| Cahill,Trevor | 16 | 32 | Patellar tendinitis R knee |
| | 17 | 85 | Strnd back; R should; R Shld impinge |
| | 18 | 37 | R elbow impingement |
| Caminero,Arquimedes | 16 | 17 | Strnd L quadriceps |
| Campos,Leonel | 17 | 42 | Strained groin |
| Campos,Vicente | 17 | 23 | Recovery surgery ulnar nerve R elbow |
| Capps,Carter | 14 | 97 | Sprained R elbow |
| | 15 | 63 | R elbow strain |
| | 16 | 183 | Rec fr TJS |
| | 17 | 92 | Recovery from TJS; blood clots |
| | 18 | 78 | Recovery from TJS |
| Carle,Shane | 18 | 25 | R shoulder inflammation |
| Carpenter,Ryan | 18 | 56 | Strained R oblique |
| Carrasco,Carlos | 15 | 13 | R shoulder inflammation |
| | 16 | 38 | Strnd L hamstring |
| | 18 | 20 | R elbow contusion |
| Cashner,Andrew | 14 | 82 | Sore R elbow/sore R shoulder |
| | 16 | 37 | Strnd R hamstring; str neck |
| | 17 | 25 | Tendinitis in R biceps; L oblique |
| | 18 | 21 | Lower back strain; strained neck |
| Casilla,Santiago | 14 | 24 | Strained R hamstring |
| | 18 | 14 | R shoulder strain |
| Castillo,Jose | 18 | 22 | R hamstring strain |
| Castro,Miguel | 16 | 26 | R should inflammation |
| Cecil,Brett | 14 | 16 | Strained L groin |
| | 16 | 46 | Strnd L triceps |
| | 18 | 62 | Strained L shoulder; R foot inflam |
| Cedeno,Xavier | 17 | 153 | Tightness in L forearm |
| Cessa,Luis | 17 | 47 | Ribcage injury |
| | 18 | 64 | L oblique strain |
| Chacin,Jhoulys | 14 | 128 | R shoulder inflammation/strain |
| Chafin,Andrew | 16 | 62 | L should tendinitis |
| Chapman,Aroldis | 14 | 41 | Facial fractures,concussion |
| | 17 | 35 | L rotator cuff injury |
| | 18 | 29 | L knee tendinitis |
| Chargois,J.T. | 17 | 26 | R elbow surgery |
| | 18 | 35 | Nerve irritation in neck |
| Chatwood,Tyler | 14 | 168 | Strnd R elbow/strnd L hamstring |
| | 16 | 33 | Tightness upper back x 2 |
| | 17 | 10 | Strained R calf |
| | 18 | 12 | L hip tightness |
| Chavez,Jesse | 15 | 19 | Fractured rib |
| Chen,Wei-Yin | 16 | 57 | Sprnd L elbow |
| | 17 | 122 | L arm fatigue |
| | 18 | 31 | Inflamed L elbow |
| Chirinos,Yonny | 18 | 35 | R forearm strain |
| Cingrani,Tony | 14 | 17 | L shoulder tendinitis |
| | 15 | 37 | Strained L shoulder |
| | 17 | 47 | Strained R oblique |
| | 18 | 114 | Strained rotator cuff L shoulder |
| Cishek,Steve | 16 | 15 | Torn labrum L hip |
| Claudio,Alexander | 16 | 148 | R should stiffness |
| | 18 | 7 | Sprained L ankle |
| Cobb,Alex | 14 | 38 | Strained L oblique muscle |
| | 15 | 183 | R forearm tendinitis; TJS |
| | 16 | 149 | Rec fr TJS |
| | 17 | 15 | Turf toe in R big toe |
| Cole,A.J. | 18 | 13 | L neck strain |
| Cole,Gerrit | 14 | 63 | Tightness R lat/R shoulder fatigue |
| | 16 | 66 | R elbow inflam; R triceps strain |
| Cole,Taylor | 17 | 10 | Fractured R toe |

## FIVE-YEAR INJURY LOG — Pitchers

| Pitchers | Yr | Days | Injury |
|---|---|---|---|
| Coleman,Louis | 14 | 14 | Bone bruised/sprained R mid finger |
| | 16 | 29 | R should fatigue |
| Collins,Tim | 14 | 27 | Strained flexor in L elbow |
| | 15 | 183 | L elbow surgery |
| | 16 | 183 | Rec fr TJS |
| Collmenter,Josh | 16 | 55 | Tightness R should |
| Colome,Alex | 15 | 34 | Pneumonia |
| | 16 | 16 | R biceps tendinitis |
| Colon,Bartolo | 17 | 22 | Strained L oblique |
| | 18 | 9 | Lower back strain |
| Colon,Joseph | 16 | 24 | R should inflammation |
| Conley,Adam | 16 | 43 | L middle finger tendinitis |
| Cook,Ryan | 14 | 39 | Strned R forearm; Rt shoulder inflam |
| | 16 | 183 | Strnd back muscle |
| Corbin,Patrick | 14 | 184 | Recovering from TJS |
| | 15 | 91 | Recovery from L elbow surgery |
| Cosart,Jarred | 15 | 37 | Vertigo |
| | 17 | 142 | Strained R ham; bruised foot |
| Cotham,Caleb | 16 | 125 | R should inflammation |
| Cotton,Jharel | 17 | 24 | Blister on R thumb |
| | 18 | 187 | Recovery from TJS |
| Covey,Dylan | 17 | 80 | Strained L oblique |
| Cravy,Tyler | 15 | 17 | R elbow impingement |
| Crichton,Stefan | 17 | 17 | Strained R shoulder |
| Cruz,Rhiner | 18 | 86 | R groin strain |
| Cueto,Johnny | 17 | 48 | Blisters on R hand |
| | 18 | 133 | Spr R ankle; R elbow inflam x 3; TJS |
| Darvish,Yu | 14 | 61 | Rt elbow inflam; stiff neck |
| | 15 | 183 | R elbow surgery |
| | 16 | 88 | Rec fr TJS; R should strain |
| | 17 | 10 | Lower back tightness |
| | 18 | 138 | Viral infection; R triceps tendinitis |
| Davies,Zach | 18 | 106 | R rotator cuff inflammation |
| Davis,Austin | 18 | 17 | Lower back tightness |
| Davis,Rookie | 17 | 14 | Bruised R forearm |
| | 18 | 152 | Recovery - R hip surgery |
| Davis,Wade | 16 | 48 | Strnd flexor R forearm |
| Dayton,Grant | 17 | 90 | Strained L intercostal; stiff neck x 2 |
| | 18 | 187 | TJS |
| De La Rosa,Jorge | 15 | 15 | Strained L groin |
| | 16 | 27 | Strnd L groin |
| | 18 | 13 | R Achilles bursitis |
| De La Rosa,Rubby | 16 | 105 | R elbow inflammation |
| | 17 | 20 | R shoulder inflammation |
| deGrom,Jacob | 14 | 12 | Tendinitis in R rotator cuff |
| | 18 | 8 | Hyperextended R elbow |
| DeLeon,Jose | 18 | 187 | TJS |
| Delgado,Randall | 15 | 68 | Sprained R ankle |
| | 17 | 77 | R elbow inflammation |
| | 18 | 100 | Strained L oblique |
| DeSclafani,Anthony | 16 | 68 | Strnd oblique muscle |
| | 17 | 182 | Sprained UCL in R elbow |
| | 18 | 69 | L oblique strain |
| Despaigne,Odrisamer | 17 | 10 | Strained L oblique muscle |
| | 18 | 32 | R forearm strain |
| Devenski,Chris | 18 | 27 | L hamstring tightness |
| Diaz,Jairo | 16 | 183 | Rec fr TJS |
| | 17 | 48 | Recovery surgery R elbow |
| Diaz,Jose | 17 | 17 | R arm fatigue |
| Diaz,Miguel | 17 | 67 | Strained R forearm |
| Diekman,Jake | 16 | 16 | Lacerated L index finger |
| | 17 | 156 | Colitis |

## FIVE-YEAR INJURY LOG — Pitchers

| Pitchers | Yr | Days | Injury |
|---|---|---|---|
| Doolittle,Sean | 14 | 36 | Strained R intercostal muscle |
| | 15 | 136 | L shoulder strain; torn rotator cuff |
| | 16 | 64 | Strnd L should |
| | 17 | 38 | Strained L shoulder |
| | 18 | 60 | L toe inflammation |
| Duensing,Brian | 15 | 15 | R intercostal strain |
| | 16 | 75 | Surg. on L elbow |
| | 17 | 12 | Lower back spasms |
| | 18 | 46 | L shoulder fatigue x 2 |
| Duffy,Danny | 15 | 30 | L biceps tendinitis |
| | 17 | 57 | Strained L oblique; L elbow imping |
| | 18 | 11 | L shoulder impingement |
| Duke,Zach | 17 | 114 | Surgery on L elbow |
| Dull,Ryan | 17 | 68 | Strained R knee |
| | 18 | 17 | Strained R shoulder |
| Dunn,Michael | 16 | 58 | Strnd L forearm |
| | 17 | 10 | Back spasms |
| | 18 | 107 | L shoulder surgery; L rhomboid strain |
| Dyson,Sam | 17 | 11 | Bruised R hand |
| Edgin,Josh | 16 | 37 | Rec fr TJS |
| Edwards,Carl | 18 | 38 | R shoulder fatigue |
| Eflin,Zach | 16 | 55 | Patellar tendinopathy both knees |
| | 17 | 50 | Rec surg pat tend both knees; R shldr |
| | 18 | 9 | Blister - R middle finger |
| Eickhoff,Jerad | 17 | 50 | Strnd upper back; nerve irrit R hand |
| | 18 | 159 | R lat strain |
| Elias,Roenis | 14 | 7 | Strained flexor muscle in R elbow |
| | 17 | 138 | R intercostal injury |
| | 18 | 20 | Strained L triceps |
| Enns,Dietrich | 17 | 19 | Strained L shoulder |
| Eovaldi,Nathan | 16 | 52 | R elbow tendon injury |
| | 17 | 183 | Rec. Tommy John surgery |
| | 18 | 63 | Loose bodies R elbow |
| Erlin,Robbie | 14 | 88 | Sore L elbow |
| | 16 | 165 | Strnd L elbow |
| | 17 | 182 | TJS L elbow |
| Escobar,Eduardo | 16 | 16 | Strnd L groin |
| Estevez,Carlos | 18 | 109 | Strained L oblique |
| Estrada,Marco | 16 | 24 | Back strain |
| | 18 | 18 | Strained L glute |
| Familia,Jeurys | 17 | 106 | Blood clot in R shoulder |
| | 18 | 10 | Sore R shoulder |
| Faria,Jacob | 18 | 71 | Strained L oblique |
| | 17 | 26 | Strained L abdominal |
| Farquhar,Danny | 18 | 164 | Brain aneurysm |
| Fedde,Erick | 17 | 27 | Strained flexor in R forearm |
| | 18 | 62 | R shoulder inflammation |
| Feldman,Scott | 14 | 18 | R biceps tendinitis |
| | 15 | 83 | R shoulder sprain; R knee surg |
| | 17 | 69 | R knee inflammation x 2 |
| Feliz,Michael | 17 | 38 | R shoulder injury |
| | 18 | 14 | R shoulder inflammation |
| Feliz,Neftali | 15 | 38 | Axillary abscess on R side |
| | 17 | 13 | Ulnar nerve palsy in R arm |
| Fernandez,Julian | 18 | 187 | TJS |
| Ferrell,Jeff | 16 | 23 | R should impingement |
| Fields,Josh | 14 | 19 | Sore R forearm |
| | 17 | 10 | Strained lower back |
| | 18 | 64 | R shoulder inflammation |
| Fien,Casey | 15 | 29 | R shoulder strain |
| | 16 | 27 | R elbow tendinitis |
| | 17 | 70 | R shoulder impingement |
| Fiers,Michael | 18 | 11 | R lumbar strain |

## FIVE-YEAR INJURY LOG — Pitchers

| Pitchers | Yr | Days | Injury |
|---|---|---|---|
| Finnegan,Brandon | 17 | 168 | Strained L trapezius; torn R labrum |
| | 18 | 17 | Strained L biceps |
| Fister,Doug | 14 | 41 | Strained R lat |
| | 15 | 34 | R forearm tightness |
| | 18 | 130 | Strained R hip; R knee strain |
| Floyd,Gavin | 14 | 143 | Recovery from TJS/fx R elbow |
| | 15 | 149 | R elbow surgery |
| | 16 | 99 | R should injury |
| Flynn,Brian | 17 | 123 | Strained L groin |
| Foltynewicz,Mike | 15 | 13 | Costochondritis |
| | 16 | 26 | Sore R elbow |
| | 18 | 10 | R triceps tightness |
| Font,Wilmer | 18 | 94 | R lat strain |
| Freeland,Kyle | 17 | 10 | Strained L groin |
| Freeman,Sam | 18 | 21 | L shoulder inflammation |
| Frias,Carlos | 15 | 61 | R lower back tightness |
| | 16 | 24 | Strnd R oblique |
| Fried,Max | 18 | 43 | Blister L index finger; L groin strain |
| Friedrich,Christian | 17 | 182 | Strained L lat muscle |
| Fulmer,Michael | 17 | 11 | Ulnar neuritis in R elbow |
| | 18 | 47 | Strndd L oblique; torn meniscs R knee |
| Gadea,Kevin | 17 | 182 | R elbow tendinitis |
| Gallardo,Yovani | 16 | 56 | R biceps tendinitis |
| Gant,John | 16 | 54 | Strnd L oblique |
| | 17 | 47 | Strained R groin |
| Garcia,Jaime | 14 | 69 | L shoulder inflammation x 2 |
| | 15 | 75 | L groin strain; recov L shldr surg |
| | 18 | 32 | L shoulder fatigue |
| Garcia,Jarlin | 17 | 10 | Strained L biceps |
| | 18 | 12 | R ankle contusion |
| Garcia,Luis | 14 | 13 | Strained R forearm |
| | 18 | 36 | Strained R wrist |
| Garcia,Yimi | 16 | 163 | Sore R biceps |
| | 18 | 49 | R forearm inflammation |
| Gardewine,Nick | 18 | 38 | R forearm strain |
| Garrett,Amir | 17 | 10 | R hip inflammation |
| | 18 | 13 | Strained L Achilles |
| Garza,Matt | 14 | 27 | Strained L oblique |
| | 15 | 15 | R shoulder tendinitis |
| | 16 | 70 | Strnd R lat |
| | 17 | 45 | Strained R groin; bruised chest;R leg |
| Gausman,Kevin | 15 | 43 | R shoulder tendinitis |
| | 16 | 22 | R should tendinitis |
| Gearrin,Cory | 14 | 184 | Sprained R elbow |
| | 16 | 43 | Strnd R should |
| Gee,Dillon | 14 | 55 | Tightness in R lat |
| | 15 | 25 | Groin strain |
| Germen,Gonzalez | 14 | 29 | Illness/Flu |
| Gibson,Kyle | 16 | 45 | Sore/strnd R should |
| Glasnow,Tyler | 16 | 35 | Sore R should |
| Glover,Koda | 17 | 128 | L hip imping; lower back strain |
| | 18 | 116 | Tendinitis - R shoulder |
| Goeddel,Erik | 15 | 81 | Strained R elbow |
| | 18 | 57 | R lat inflammation |
| Gohara,Luiz | 18 | 49 | Spr L ankle; L shoulder soreness |
| Gomez,Jeanmar | 17 | 16 | R elbow impingement |
| Gonzales,Marco | 18 | 16 | Cervical neck muscle strain |
| Gonzalez,Chi Chi | 17 | 182 | TJS July 2017 |
| Gonzalez,Gio | 14 | 30 | L shoulder inflammation |
| Gonzalez,Miguel | 14 | 11 | Strained R oblique |
| | 15 | 45 | R shoulder tend; R groin strain |
| | 16 | 25 | Strnd R groin |
| | 17 | 26 | A/C joint inflammation in R shoulder |
| | 18 | 162 | R/C inflammation - R shoulder |

## FIVE-YEAR INJURY LOG — Pitchers

| Pitchers | Yr | Days | Injury |
|---|---|---|---|
| Gonzalez,Rayan | 18 | 187 | TJS |
| Goody,Nick | 18 | 152 | R elbow inflammation |
| Gossett,Daniel | 18 | 119 | TJS |
| Grace,Matt | 18 | 46 | Strained L groin |
| Graveman,Kendall | 15 | 100 | Strained L oblique |
| | 17 | 76 | Strained R shoulder x2 |
| | 18 | 31 | TJS |
| Graves,Brett | 18 | 79 | Strained L oblique |
| Gray,Jonathan | 16 | 20 | Strnd abdominal muscle |
| | 17 | 77 | Stress fracture in L foot |
| Gray,Sonny | 16 | 55 | R forearm; R trap. |
| | 17 | 30 | Strained lat muscle R shoulder |
| Green,Chad | 16 | 26 | Strnd tendon R forearm |
| Greene,Shane | 16 | 37 | Blister on R middle finger |
| | 18 | 12 | R shoulder strain |
| Gregerson,Luke | 16 | 17 | Strnd L oblique |
| | 18 | 142 | R shoulder impinge x 2; torn meniscs |
| Greinke,Zack | 16 | 37 | Strnd L oblique |
| Griffin,A.J. | 14 | 184 | Strained flexor muscle in R elbow |
| | 15 | 172 | R shoulder strain |
| | 16 | 48 | R should stiffness |
| | 17 | 81 | Gout L ankle; L intercostal |
| Grimm,Justin | 15 | 26 | R forearm inflammation |
| | 17 | 14 | Infection in R index finger |
| | 18 | 61 | Back stiffness; R shoulder impinge |
| Grosser,Alec | 16 | 58 | Back strain |
| Gsellman,Robert | 17 | 48 | Strained L hamstring |
| Guerra,Javy | 15 | 16 | R shoulder inflammation |
| Guerra,Junior | 16 | 25 | R elbow inflammation |
| | 17 | 63 | Strained R calf; bruised R shin |
| | 18 | 11 | R forearm tightness |
| Guerrero,Tayron | 18 | 27 | Strained L lumbar spine |
| Guerrieri,Taylor | 17 | 26 | Strained R elbow |
| Gustave,Jandel | 17 | 164 | Tightness in R forearm |
| | 18 | 187 | TJS |
| Hagadone,Nick | 15 | 89 | Lower back strain |
| Hahn,Jesse | 15 | 86 | R forearm strain |
| | 16 | 27 | Strnd R should |
| | 17 | 10 | Strained R triceps |
| | 18 | 187 | Sprained R UCL |
| Hale,David | 15 | 61 | Groin strain |
| Haley,Justin | 17 | 71 | R biceps tendinitis; R shoulder |
| Hamels,Cole | 14 | 27 | L biceps tendinitis |
| | 17 | 54 | Strained R oblique |
| Hancock,Justin | 18 | 98 | R shoulder inflammation |
| Hand,Brad | 14 | 40 | Sprained R ankle |
| Hanhold,Eric | 18 | 7 | Strained L oblique; R shoulder inflam |
| Happ,J.A. | 14 | 18 | Strained back |
| | 17 | 42 | L elbow inflammation |
| | 18 | 8 | Viral infection |
| Hardy,Blaine | 16 | 16 | L should impingement |
| | 18 | 15 | L elbow tendinitis |
| Harrell,Lucas | 16 | 47 | Strnd R groin |
| Harris,Mitch | 15 | 16 | Groin strain |
| | 16 | 183 | Strnd R elbow |
| Harris,Will | 17 | 41 | R shoulder inflam x2 |
| Harrison,Matt | 14 | 55 | Lower back inflam; back surg recov |
| | 15 | 156 | Lower back inflam; back surg |
| | 16 | 183 | Lower back inflammation |
| Harvey,Matt | 14 | 183 | Recovering from TJS |
| | 16 | 90 | Thoracic outlet synd, R should |
| | 17 | 79 | Stress fracture R scapula |

## FIVE-YEAR INJURY LOG — Pitchers

| Pitchers | Yr | Days | Injury |
|---|---|---|---|
| Hatcher,Chris | 15 | 58 | L oblique strain |
| | 16 | 75 | Strnd L oblique |
| | 17 | 51 | R shoulder inflammation |
| Hathaway,Steve | 17 | 182 | Bursitis in L shoulder |
| Heaney,Andrew | 16 | 180 | Strnd L flexor |
| | 17 | 130 | Recovery surgery UCL L elbow |
| | 18 | 16 | L elbow inflammation |
| Heller,Ben | 18 | 183 | Bone spurs - R elbow |
| Hellickson,Jeremy | 14 | 99 | Recovering from surgery on R elbow |
| | 15 | 22 | Strained L hamstring |
| | 18 | 52 | Spr R wrist; strained R hamstring |
| Hembree,Heath | 15 | 37 | R shoulder soreness |
| Hendricks,Kyle | 17 | 46 | R hand tendinitis |
| Hendriks,Liam | 16 | 40 | Strnd R triceps |
| | 18 | 53 | R groin strain |
| Hernandez,David | 14 | 184 | Surgery on R elbow  torn ligament |
| | 15 | 64 | Recovery from R elbow surgery |
| | 18 | 30 | R shoulder inflammation |
| Hernandez,Elieser | 18 | 55 | Finger blister; dental surgery |
| Hernandez,Felix | 16 | 49 | Strnd R calf |
| | 17 | 98 | R shoulder bursitis; R biceps tend |
| | 18 | 12 | Lower back stiffness |
| Herrera,Kelvin | 18 | 50 | Strnd E R/C joint; ligamnt surg L foot |
| Herrera,Ronald | 18 | 187 | R labrum inflammation |
| Heston,Chris | 16 | 96 | Strnd oblique muscle |
| Hill,Rich | 16 | 58 | Blister L finger; L groin |
| | 17 | 39 | Blister L middle finger x 2 |
| | 18 | 52 | Blisters L hand x 2 |
| Hinojosa,Dalier | 16 | 64 | Bruised R hand |
| Hochevar,Luke | 14 | 184 | TJS |
| | 15 | 32 | Recovery from R elbow surgery |
| | 16 | 67 | Thoracic outlet syndrome |
| Holaday,Bryan | 16 | 26 | Bruised L thumb |
| Holland,Derek | 14 | 164 | Recovering from surgery on L knee |
| | 15 | 130 | Subscapular strain in R shoulder |
| | 16 | 62 | L should inflammation |
| Holland,Greg | 15 | 18 | R pectoral strain |
| | 18 | 25 | R hip impingement |
| Hollands,Mario | 14 | 24 | Strained flexor in L elbow |
| | 15 | 183 | Strained flexor tendon,L forearm |
| | 16 | 61 | Rec fr TJS |
| Honeywell,Brent | 18 | 187 | TJS |
| Hoover,J.J. | 17 | 23 | R shoulder inflammation |
| House,T.J. | 15 | 20 | L shoulder inflammation |
| Howell,J.P. | 17 | 72 | Strained L shoulder x2 |
| Hoyt,James | 18 | 10 | Strained L oblique |
| Hudson,Daniel | 14 | 155 | Recovering from TJS |
| | 18 | 49 | R forearm tightness |
| Hughes,Jared | 16 | 27 | Strnd L lat back |
| Hughes,Phil | 15 | 32 | Lower back inflammation |
| | 16 | 115 | L knee injury |
| | 17 | 112 | R biceps tendon inflam; TOS surgery |
| | 18 | 40 | Strained L oblique; R rhomboid strain |
| Hunter,Tommy | 14 | 17 | Strained L groin |
| | 16 | 39 | Back strain; core muscle surg. |
| | 17 | 32 | Strained R calf |
| | 18 | 25 | Strained R hamstring |
| Iglesias,Raisel | 15 | 36 | Strained L oblique |
| | 16 | 51 | R should impingement |
| | 18 | 8 | Strained L biceps |
| Iwakuma,Hisashi | 14 | 35 | Torn tendon in R middle finger |
| | 15 | 73 | R lat strain |
| | 17 | 144 | R shoulder inflam |

## FIVE-YEAR INJURY LOG — Pitchers

| Pitchers | Yr | Days | Injury |
|---|---|---|---|
| Jackson,Edwin | 14 | 29 | Strained R lat |
| | 16 | 31 | Strnd R triceps |
| Jackson,Luke | 16 | 10 | Stress reaction lower back |
| | 17 | 13 | Strained R shoulder |
| Jansen,Kenley | 15 | 40 | L foot surgery |
| | 18 | 11 | Irregular heartbeat |
| Jeffress,Jeremy | 17 | 12 | strained lower back |
| Jennings,Dan | 14 | 24 | Concussion |
| | 15 | 24 | Neck inflammation |
| Jewell,Jake | 18 | 96 | Fractured R fibula |
| Johnson,Brian | 17 | 21 | L shoulder impingement |
| | 18 | 8 | L hip inflammation |
| Johnson,Erik | 16 | 94 | Sprnd R elbow |
| Johnson,Jim | 16 | 24 | Strnd R groin |
| | 18 | 38 | Lumbar strain |
| Jones,Nate | 14 | 184 | Strained L hip;TJS |
| | 15 | 131 | Recovery from R elbow surgery |
| | 17 | 150 | R elbow neuritis |
| | 18 | 90 | Strained pronator muscle - R arm |
| Jones,Zach | 16 | 80 | Sore R should |
| | 18 | 30 | Sore R shoulder |
| Junis,Jake | 18 | 14 | Lower back inflammation |
| Kahnle,Tommy | 14 | 17 | R shoulder inflammation |
| | 18 | 39 | R shoulder tendinitis |
| Karns,Nate | 16 | 65 | Strnd lower back |
| | 17 | 130 | Nerve irritation in R elbow |
| | 18 | 187 | R elbow inflammation |
| Kazmir,Scott | 16 | 31 | Inflammation cervical spine |
| | 17 | 182 | Strained L hip |
| Kela,Keone | 16 | 85 | R elbow impingement |
| | 17 | 60 | Sore R shoulder x2 |
| Kelley,Shawn | 14 | 29 | Strained lumbar spine |
| | 15 | 14 | Strained L calf |
| | 17 | 72 | Str low back;R Trap;bone chips R elb |
| | 18 | 14 | Ulnar nerve irritation, R arm |
| Kelly,Casey | 14 | 184 | Recovering from TJS |
| Kelly,Joe | 14 | 85 | Strained L hamstring |
| | 15 | 8 | R biceps tightness |
| | 16 | 32 | R should impingement |
| | 17 | 21 | Strained L hamstring |
| Kennedy,Ian | 15 | 15 | Strained L hamstring |
| | 17 | 16 | Strained R hamstring |
| | 18 | 68 | Strained L oblique |
| Kershaw,Clayton | 14 | 38 | Back muscle inflam/strnd L shoulder |
| | 16 | 47 | Herniated disc lower back |
| | 17 | 39 | Strained lower back |
| | 18 | 49 | L biceps tendinitis; lower back strain |
| Keuchel,Dallas | 17 | 61 | Pinched nerve in neck; strained neck |
| Kimbrel,Craig | 16 | 23 | Torn meniscus L knee |
| Kintzler,Brandon | 14 | 15 | Strained R rotator cuff |
| | 15 | 75 | L knee tendinitis |
| | 18 | 16 | Flexor muscle strain - R arm |
| Kluber,Corey | 17 | 29 | strained lower back |
| Knebel,Corey | 16 | 67 | Strnd L oblique |
| | 18 | 34 | L hamstring strain |
| Koehler,Tom | 17 | 28 | R shoulder bursitis |
| | 18 | 187 | Strained anterior cuff - R shoulder |
| Kontos,George | 16 | 28 | Strnd flexor R elbow |
| | 17 | 16 | Strained R groin |
| Kopech,Michael | 18 | 24 | TJS |
| Krol,Ian | 14 | 15 | L shoulder inflammation |
| | 17 | 28 | Strained L oblique muscle |
| Kuhl,Chad | 18 | 95 | Strained R forearm |

## FIVE-YEAR INJURY LOG — Pitchers

| Pitchers | Yr | Days | Injury |
|---|---|---|---|
| Lamb,John | 16 | 30 | Rec fr back surg. |
| | 18 | 97 | L elbow surgery |
| Lamet,Dinelson | 18 | 187 | Recovery from TJS |
| Lauer,Eric | 18 | 32 | L forearm strain |
| Law,Derek | 16 | 17 | Strnd R elbow |
| Lazo,Raudel | 16 | 18 | Strnd L should |
| Leake,Mike | 15 | 15 | Strained L hamstring |
| | 16 | 9 | Shingles |
| LeBlanc,Wade | 17 | 14 | Strained L quadriceps |
| Leclerc,Jose | 17 | 25 | Bruised R index finger |
| Lee,Chris | 16 | 18 | Strnd L should |
| Leiter,Mark | 18 | 49 | Strained R forearm |
| Leone,Dominic | 18 | 114 | R upper arm nerve irritation |
| Lester,Jon | 17 | 15 | L shoulder fatigue |
| Lewicki,Artie | 18 | 48 | TJS |
| Lewis,Colby | 16 | 78 | Strnd R lat muscle |
| Liberatore,Adam | 16 | 16 | L elbow inflammation |
| | 17 | 137 | Strained L groin; L forearm tightness |
| Lincecum,Tim | 15 | 95 | R forearm contusion |
| | 18 | 69 | blister pitching hand |
| Lindblom,Josh | 17 | 35 | L side injury |
| Lindgren,Jacob | 15 | 28 | L elbow surgery |
| | 18 | 187 | TJS |
| Liriano,Francisco | 14 | 32 | Strained L oblique |
| | 17 | 22 | L shoulder inflammation |
| | 18 | 25 | Strained R hamstring |
| Lively,Ben | 18 | 14 | Strained lower back |
| Logan,Boone | 14 | 86 | Diverticulitis/L elbow inflam x 3 |
| | 15 | 18 | L elbow inflammation |
| | 16 | 19 | L should inflammation |
| | 17 | 72 | Strained lat muscle |
| | 18 | 43 | Strained L triceps |
| Lopez,Pablo | 18 | 31 | R shoulder strain |
| Lopez,Reynaldo | 17 | 13 | Strained back |
| Lorenzen,Michael | 16 | 80 | Sprnd UCL R elbow |
| | 18 | 56 | R shoulder strain |
| Loup,Aaron | 16 | 55 | Sore L elbow |
| | 18 | 34 | Strained L forearm |
| Lucchesi,Joey | 18 | 37 | R hip strain |
| Luebke,Cory | 14 | 184 | Recovering from TJS |
| | 15 | 183 | Strained L elbow |
| | 16 | 31 | Tightness R hamstring |
| Lugo,Seth | 17 | 82 | Part torn UCL R elb; R shldr imping |
| Lyles,Jordan | 14 | 62 | Fractured L hand |
| | 15 | 126 | Sprained L big toe |
| | 18 | 36 | R elbow inflammation |
| Lynn,Lance | 15 | 13 | Strained R forearm |
| | 16 | 183 | Rec fr TJS |
| Lyons,Tyler | 14 | 36 | Strained L shoulder |
| | 16 | 62 | Stress reaction R knee |
| | 17 | 42 | Rec surg R knee; R intercostal |
| | 18 | 52 | Mid-back strain; sprained L elbow |
| Maddox,Austin | 18 | 187 | R shoulder strain |
| Madson,Ryan | 17 | 15 | Sprained R finger |
| | 18 | 26 | Strnd R pec; lumbar nerve irrit |
| Maeda,Kenta | 17 | 14 | Hamstring tightness |
| | 18 | 15 | R hip strain |
| Manaea,Sean | 16 | 15 | Strnd pronator L forearm |
| | 17 | 15 | Strained L shoulder |
| | 18 | 37 | L shoulder impingement |
| Maness,Seth | 16 | 85 | Strnd R elbow/inflammation |
| Manship,Jeff | 14 | 37 | Strained R quadriceps |
| | 16 | 16 | R wrist tendinitis |
| Marinez,Jhan | 18 | 29 | Strained R hamstring |

## FIVE-YEAR INJURY LOG — Pitchers

| Pitchers | Yr | Days | Injury |
|---|---|---|---|
| Mariot,Michael | 14 | 32 | Strained R hamstring |
| | 16 | 46 | Sprnd R ankle |
| Marshall,Evan | 15 | 27 | Fractured skull |
| | 17 | 88 | Strained R hamstring |
| | 18 | 50 | R elbow inflammation |
| Marshall,Sean | 14 | 127 | Strnd L shoulder/L shoulder inflam |
| Martin,Chris | 15 | 22 | R elbow tendinitis |
| | 18 | 54 | R forearm irrit; str R calf; str L groin |
| Martin,Ethan | 14 | 51 | Strained R shoulder |
| Martinez,Carlos | 15 | 9 | R shoulder strain |
| | 18 | 59 | R lat strain; R oblique strain |
| Maton,Phil | 18 | 40 | R lat strain |
| Matz,Steven | 15 | 53 | Partially torn L lat muscle |
| | 16 | 42 | Tightness L should |
| | 17 | 109 | L elbow inflam; Ulnar nerve irrit |
| | 18 | 14 | L flexor pronator strain |
| Matzek,Tyler | 16 | 46 | Anxiety disorder |
| Maurer,Brandon | 15 | 55 | R shoulder inflammation |
| May,Trevor | 16 | 75 | Strnd lower back x 2 |
| | 17 | 182 | TJS R elbow |
| | 18 | 71 | TJS |
| Mayers,Mike | 18 | 17 | R shoulder inflammation |
| McAllister,Zach | 14 | 27 | Strained lower back |
| | 16 | 22 | R hip injury |
| McCarthy,Brandon | 15 | 161 | Torn UCL,R elbow |
| | 16 | 173 | Rec fr TJS |
| | 17 | 79 | Sore L shldr; R knee tend; blist R hand |
| | 18 | 96 | R knee tendinitis |
| McCullers,Lance | 16 | 103 | Sore R elbow; R should |
| | 17 | 49 | Sore lower back x2 |
| | 18 | 51 | R elbow discomfort |
| McFarland,T.J. | 16 | 57 | L knee inflammation |
| | 17 | 11 | Bruised L ankle |
| | 18 | 12 | L neck strain |
| McGee,Jake | 15 | 86 | Torn L knee menisc rec R elbow surg |
| | 16 | 21 | L knee inflammation |
| | 17 | 10 | Strained mid-back |
| McHugh,Collin | 14 | 15 | R middle finger injury |
| | 17 | 114 | Hypertrophy in R arm |
| McKirahan,Andrew | 16 | 183 | Rec fr TJS |
| Medlen,Kris | 14 | 184 | Recovering from TJS |
| | 15 | 112 | Recovery from R elbow surgery |
| | 16 | 144 | R rotator cuff inflammation |
| Mejia,Adalberto | 17 | 36 | Brachialis strain in L arm |
| | 18 | 53 | Strained L wrist |
| Melancon,Mark | 17 | 56 | R elbow tendinitis x 2 |
| | 18 | 65 | R elbow flexor strain |
| Mella,Keury | 18 | 28 | L oblique strain |
| Mengden,Daniel | 17 | 48 | Fractured R foot |
| | 18 | 18 | L shoulder impingement |
| Merritt,Ryan | 18 | 107 | Sprained L knee x 2 |
| Meyer,Alex | 17 | 77 | Back spasms; R shoulder inflam |
| | 18 | 187 | Recovery from R shoulder surgery |
| Middleton,Keynan | 18 | 151 | R elbow inflammation |
| Miley,Wade | 16 | 12 | Inflammation L should |
| | 17 | 10 | Medical |
| | 18 | 101 | Strained R oblique x 2 |
| Miller,Andrew | 15 | 27 | L flexor forearm muscle strain |
| | 17 | 39 | Patella tendinitis in R knee x2 |
| | 18 | 99 | L shldr; R knee inflam. x 2; str. L ham |
| Miller,Justin | 16 | 59 | Strnd L oblique |
| Miller,Shelby | 16 | 24 | Sprnd R index finger |
| | 17 | 160 | R elbow inflammation |
| | 18 | 169 | Recovery from TJS - R elbow |

# FIVE-YEAR INJURY LOG — Pitchers

| Pitchers | Yr | Days | Injury |
|---|---|---|---|
| Milone,Tommy | 14 | 23 | Neck inflammation |
| | 15 | 13 | Strained L elbow |
| | 16 | 28 | L biceps tendinitis |
| | 17 | 87 | Sprained L knee |
| | 18 | 14 | L shoulder soreness |
| Minaya,Juan | 17 | 24 | Strained R Ab |
| Minor,Mike | 14 | 37 | L shoulder tendinitis |
| | 15 | 185 | L rotator cuff inflammation |
| | 16 | 183 | Rec fr surg. on L should |
| Mitchell,Bryan | 15 | 10 | Concussion,nasal fracture |
| | 16 | 143 | Surg. to repair fractured L big toe |
| | 18 | 74 | R elbow impingement |
| Montas,Frankie | 16 | 113 | Rec fr rib re-section surg. |
| Montero,Rafael | 15 | 158 | R rotator cuff inflammation |
| | 18 | 187 | TJS |
| Montgomery,Jordan | 18 | 151 | TJS |
| Montgomery,Mike | 18 | 14 | L shoulder inflammation |
| Moore,Matt | 14 | 174 | L elbow injury |
| | 15 | 88 | Recovery from L elbow surgery |
| | 18 | 12 | R knee soreness |
| Morales,Franklin | 16 | 103 | L should fatigue |
| Moran,Brian | 14 | 184 | L elbow inflammation |
| Moreno,Diego | 15 | 64 | R elbow inflammation |
| | 17 | 63 | R shoulder bursitis |
| Morgan,Adam | 18 | 11 | Back strain |
| Morin,Michael | 14 | 15 | Lacerated L foot |
| | 15 | 38 | L oblique strain |
| | 17 | 36 | Stiff neck |
| Morris,AJ | 16 | 76 | Strnd R should |
| Morris,Bryan | 15 | 22 | Lower back strain |
| | 16 | 130 | Herniated lumbar disc |
| Morrow,Brandon | 14 | 122 | Torn tendon sheath in R hand |
| | 15 | 153 | R shoulder inflammation |
| | 18 | 83 | R biceps inflam; lower back tightness |
| Morton,Charlie | 14 | 35 | R hip inflammation |
| | 15 | 51 | Hip injury |
| | 16 | 162 | Strnd L hamstring |
| | 17 | 40 | Strained R lat muscle |
| | 18 | 11 | R shoulder discomfort |
| Moscot,Jon | 15 | 111 | L shoulder surgery |
| | 16 | 38 | Strnd R intercostal; L should inflam |
| Motte,Jason | 14 | 77 | Recovery TJS/strained lower back |
| | 15 | 42 | R shoulder strain |
| | 16 | 96 | Strnd R rotator cuff |
| | 17 | 35 | Strained back; R oblique |
| Moylan,Peter | 18 | 76 | Strained R forearm |
| Mujica,Edward | 15 | 28 | Fractured R thumb |
| Mujica,Jose | 18 | 29 | R forearm strain |
| Musgrave,Harrison | 18 | 11 | R hip flexor strain |
| Musgrove,Joe | 17 | 13 | R shoulder injury |
| | 18 | 62 | Strnd R shldr; infected R index finger |
| Nelson,Jimmy | 15 | 13 | Head contusion |
| | 17 | 17 | strained rotator cuff R shoulder |
| | 18 | 187 | Recovery from R rotator cuff surgery |
| Nesbitt,Angel | 16 | 36 | Sprnd R ankle |
| Neshek,Pat | 18 | 94 | R shoulder strain |
| Nicasio,Juan | 15 | 11 | L abdominal strain |
| | 18 | 71 | R knee effusion |
| Nicolino,Justin | 17 | 18 | Bruised L index finger |
| Nola,Aaron | 16 | 61 | Strnd R elbow |
| | 17 | 27 | Strained lower back |
| Nolasco,Ricky | 14 | 38 | Strained R elbow |
| | 15 | 144 | R ankle impinge.; R elbow inflam |

# FIVE-YEAR INJURY LOG — Pitchers

| Pitchers | Yr | Days | Injury |
|---|---|---|---|
| Nolin,Sean | 15 | 41 | Recovery fr. bi-lateral core surgery |
| | 16 | 183 | Strnd L elbow |
| Norris,Bud | 14 | 11 | Strained R groin |
| | 15 | 20 | Bronchitis |
| | 16 | 15 | Strnd mid-back |
| | 17 | 21 | R knee inflam x2 |
| Norris,Daniel | 15 | 27 | R oblique strain |
| | 16 | 52 | Strnd R oblique muscle; lower back |
| | 17 | 57 | Strained L groin |
| | 18 | 125 | L groin strain |
| Nova,Ivan | 14 | 162 | Torn UCL R elbow |
| | 15 | 81 | Recovery from R elbow surgery |
| | 18 | 14 | Sprained R ring finger |
| Nuno,Vidal | 18 | 60 | Strained R hamstring |
| Oberg,Scott | 16 | 42 | Axillary artery thrombosis R arm |
| | 18 | 18 | Back strain |
| O'Day,Darren | 16 | 87 | Strnd R rotator cuff; R hamstring |
| | 17 | 14 | Strained R shoulder |
| | 18 | 129 | Hyperext R elbow; str L hamstring |
| Odorizzi,Jake | 15 | 32 | Strained L oblique |
| | 17 | 30 | Strained L ham; lower back |
| O'Flaherty,Eric | 14 | 95 | Recovering from TJS |
| | 15 | 31 | L shoulder strain |
| | 16 | 78 | L elbow neuritis; strnd R knee |
| | 17 | 53 | Strnd low back; L rotatr cuff tend |
| Ogando,Alexi | 14 | 117 | R elbow inflammation |
| Ogando,Nefi | 16 | 47 | Fractured R rib |
| | 17 | 146 | Strained R hand |
| O'Grady,Chris | 17 | 42 | Strained R oblique |
| | 18 | 166 | Sprained L shoulder |
| Ohtani,Shohei | 18 | 26 | Sprained UCL, R elbow |
| Olmos,Edgar | 15 | 47 | L shoulder impingement |
| Olson,Tyler | 15 | 24 | R knee contusion |
| | 18 | 25 | Strained L lat muscle |
| O'Rourke,Ryan | 17 | 182 | Strained L elbow/forearm |
| Osich,Josh | 16 | 35 | Strnd L forearm |
| | 18 | 14 | Strained R hip |
| O'Sullivan,Sean | 15 | 20 | L knee tendinitis |
| | 16 | 32 | L knee tendinitis |
| Osuna,Roberto | 17 | 10 | Cervical spasms |
| Ottavino,Adam | 15 | 161 | R triceps inflammation |
| | 16 | 138 | Rec fr TJS |
| | 17 | 10 | R shoulder inflammation |
| | 18 | 18 | L oblique strain |
| Outman,Josh | 15 | 120 | L shoulder soreness |
| Palumbo,Joe | 18 | 110 | TJS |
| Parker,Jarrod | 14 | 184 | Recovering from TJS |
| | 15 | 184 | Recovery from R elbow surgery |
| | 16 | 183 | Fractured R elbow |
| Paulino,David | 17 | 44 | R arm inflam; bone spurs R elbow |
| Paxton,James | 14 | 115 | Strained L lat in back |
| | 15 | 107 | Strained tendon in L middle finger |
| | 16 | 16 | Bruised L elbow |
| | 17 | 61 | Strained L forearm; L pec muscle |
| | 18 | 36 | Lower back inflam; L forearm bruise |
| Peacock,Brad | 15 | 184 | L intercostal strain; rec R hip surg |
| Pelfrey,Mike | 14 | 149 | Strained L groin |
| | 16 | 34 | Strnd lower back |
| Peralta,Wily | 15 | 63 | Strained L oblique |
| | 17 | 32 | Strained R calf |
| Perdomo,Luis | 17 | 12 | R shoulder inflammation |
| | 18 | 38 | R shoulder strain |

## FIVE-YEAR INJURY LOG — Pitchers

| Pitchers | Yr | Days | Injury |
|---|---|---|---|
| Perez,Martin | 14 | 141 | L elbow inflammation |
| | 15 | 109 | Recovery from L elbow surgery |
| | 17 | 10 | Fractured R thumb |
| | 18 | 84 | R elbow discomfort |
| Perez,Williams | 15 | 34 | L foot contusion |
| | 16 | 86 | Strnd R rotator cuff |
| Perkins,Glen | 14 | 10 | Strained L Forearm |
| | 16 | 173 | Strnd L should |
| | 17 | 137 | Surgery on L shoulder |
| Petricka,Jacob | 15 | 15 | Strained R forearm |
| | 16 | 151 | R hip impingement |
| | 17 | 115 | Strained R lat; R elbow x2 |
| Phelps,David | 14 | 56 | R elbow inflammation/tendinitis |
| | 15 | 49 | Stress fracture,R forearm |
| | 16 | 33 | Strnd L oblique |
| | 17 | 54 | R elbow imping x2 |
| | 18 | 187 | TJS |
| Pinder,Branden | 16 | 164 | Strnd R elbow |
| Pineda,Michael | 14 | 99 | Strained muscle in R shoulder |
| | 15 | 27 | Strained R forearm |
| | 17 | 79 | Torn UCL in R elbow |
| | 18 | 187 | TJS |
| Pomeranz,Drew | 14 | 26 | Fractured R hand |
| | 15 | 14 | Sprained L AC joint |
| | 17 | 12 | Strained flexor in L forearm |
| | 18 | 73 | L forearm strain; L biceps tendinitis |
| Porcello,Rick | 15 | 24 | Strained R triceps |
| Poyner,Bobby | 18 | 11 | Strained L hamstring |
| Pressly,Ryan | 15 | 91 | R lat strain |
| Price,David | 17 | 106 | Strained L elbow; L elbow inflam |
| Putnam,Zach | 14 | 15 | R shoulder inflammation |
| | 15 | 15 | R groin strain |
| | 16 | 104 | Ulnar neuritis R elbow |
| | 17 | 159 | R elbow inflam |
| Qualls,Chad | 15 | 14 | Pinched nerve |
| | 16 | 27 | Illness |
| | 17 | 32 | R elbow tightness; back spasms |
| Ramirez,Erasmo | 18 | 129 | R shldr/lat strn; R teres major strain |
| Ramirez,J.C. | 17 | 41 | Strained R forearm |
| | 18 | 177 | R elbow surgery |
| Ramirez,Jose | 18 | 167 | R shoulder inflammation |
| Ramirez,Neil | 14 | 12 | Sore R triceps |
| | 15 | 113 | L ab soreness; R shoulder inflam |
| | 18 | 11 | Lower back spasms |
| Ramos,A.J. | 14 | 17 | R shoulder inflammation |
| | 16 | 16 | Fractured R middle finger |
| | 18 | 127 | R shoulder surgery |
| Ramos,Edubray | 18 | 33 | R shldr impinge; R pat tend; fing blist |
| Rasmus,Cory | 15 | 106 | R forearm strain; core muscle surg |
| | 16 | 135 | Strnd R groin; strnd L groin |
| Ravin,Josh | 15 | 34 | L hernia |
| | 16 | 140 | Fractured L forearm; R triceps strain |
| | 17 | 47 | Strained R groin |
| | 18 | 19 | Viral infection |
| Ray,Robbie | 17 | 26 | Concussion |
| | 18 | 59 | Strained R oblique |
| Rea,Colin | 16 | 63 | R elbow injury |
| | 18 | 85 | TJS |
| Reed,Addison | 18 | 20 | R triceps tightness |
| Reed,Cody | 16 | 18 | Back spasms |
| Reyes,Alex | 17 | 182 | Surgery on R elbow |
| | 18 | 187 | Recovery from TJS; back surgery |
| Reynolds,Matt | 14 | 184 | Recovering from TJS |

## FIVE-YEAR INJURY LOG — Pitchers

| Pitchers | Yr | Days | Injury |
|---|---|---|---|
| Richard,Clayton | 16 | 24 | Blister on L middle finger |
| | 18 | 35 | L knee inflammation |
| Richards,Garrett | 14 | 39 | Torn patellar tendon in L knee |
| | 15 | 15 | Recovery from L knee surgery |
| | 16 | 150 | Torn UCL R elbow |
| | 17 | 151 | Strained R biceps |
| | 18 | 103 | Strained L hamstring; TJS |
| Robertson,David | 14 | 14 | Strained L groin |
| Robles,Hansel | 18 | 29 | Sprained R knee |
| Rodgers,Brady | 17 | 29 | TJS |
| | 18 | 107 | TJS |
| Rodon,Carlos | 16 | 22 | Sprnd L wrist |
| | 17 | 95 | Bursitis in L biceps; L shoulder inflam |
| | 18 | 73 | Surgery on L shoulder |
| Rodriguez,Dereck | 18 | 8 | Strained R hamstring |
| Rodriguez,Eduardo | 16 | 59 | Dislocated R kneecap |
| | 17 | 45 | R knee subluxation |
| | 18 | 90 | Recov fr R knee surg.; spr. R ankle |
| Rodriguez,Fernando | 14 | 31 | Recovering from TJS |
| | 16 | 91 | Strnd R should |
| Rodriguez,Paco | 14 | 55 | Strained L shoulder |
| | 15 | 127 | Strained L elbow |
| | 16 | 183 | Rec fr TJS |
| Rodriguez,Ricardo | 18 | 62 | R biceps tendinitis |
| Rodriguez,Richard | 18 | 11 | R shoulder discomfort |
| Rodriguez,Wandy | 14 | 24 | R knee inflammation |
| Roe,Chaz | 15 | 22 | R shoulder injury |
| | 17 | 85 | Strained R lat muscle |
| | 18 | 38 | R groin strain |
| Romero,Enny | 16 | 15 | Strnd back |
| | 17 | 28 | Strained L forearm |
| | 18 | 65 | L shoulder impingement |
| Romo,Sergio | 16 | 81 | Strnd flexor tendon R elbow |
| | 17 | 10 | Sprained L ankle |
| Rondon,Bruce | 14 | 184 | Surgery on R elbow |
| | 15 | 71 | R biceps tendinitis |
| Rondon,Hector | 16 | 18 | Strnd R triceps |
| Rosenthal,Trevor | 16 | 51 | R rotator cuff inflammation |
| | 17 | 56 | Strained R lat; R elbow irritation |
| Ross,Joe | 16 | 77 | R should inflammation |
| | 17 | 79 | TJS |
| | 18 | 160 | TJS |
| Ross,Robbie | 17 | 132 | Flu; L elbow inflam |
| Ross,Tyson | 16 | 178 | R should inflammation |
| | 17 | 94 | Rec surg TOS; blister index finger |
| Rosscup,Zachary | 14 | 31 | Sore L shoulder |
| | 15 | 58 | L shoulder inflammation |
| | 16 | 183 | L should inflammation |
| | 18 | 131 | Blister L middle finger; L calf strain |
| Rucinski,Drew | 18 | 33 | R groin strain |
| Rumbelow,Nick | 16 | 31 | Rec fr TJS |
| Rusin,Chris | 16 | 43 | Strnd L should |
| | 17 | 10 | Strained R oblique muscle |
| | 18 | 27 | R intercostal strain; L plantar fasciitis |
| Ryu,Hyun-Jin | 14 | 35 | Strained R hip/L shoulder inflam |
| | 15 | 183 | L shoulder inflammation |
| | 16 | 171 | L elbow tendinitis; L should surg. |
| | 17 | 30 | Bruised L hip; bruised L foot |
| | 18 | 105 | L groin strain |
| Sabathia,C.C. | 14 | 141 | Fluid in R knee |
| | 15 | 16 | R knee inflammation |
| | 16 | 15 | Strnd L groin |
| | 17 | 29 | Strained L ham; R knee inflam |
| | 18 | 25 | R knee inflammation; R hip strain |

## FIVE-YEAR INJURY LOG — Pitchers

| Pitchers | Yr | Days | Injury |
|---|---|---|---|
| Sadler,Casey | 15 | 34 | R elbow discomfort |
| Salas,Fernando | 14 | 21 | R shoulder inflammation |
| Salazar,Danny | 16 | 15 | R elbow inflammation |
| | 17 | 60 | Sore R shoulder; R elbow inflam |
| | 18 | 187 | R shldr surg, bursa repair and cleanup |
| Sale,Chris | 14 | 30 | Strained flexor muscle in R elbow |
| | 15 | 7 | Fractured R foot |
| | 18 | 38 | Inflamed L shoulder x 2 |
| Samardzija,Jeff | 18 | 141 | Strnd R pec muscle; R shldr tightness |
| Sampson,Adrian | 16 | 101 | Strnd R flexor mass |
| Sanchez,Aaron | 15 | 40 | R lat strain |
| | 17 | 146 | Laceration/blister R middle fing x2 |
| | 18 | 64 | R index finger contusion |
| Sanchez,Anibal | 14 | 66 | Strnd R pectoral muscle;cut Rt fing |
| | 15 | 46 | R rotator cuff inflammation |
| | 17 | 14 | Strained L hamstring |
| | 18 | 42 | R hamstring strain |
| Santana,Dennis | 18 | 116 | Strained R rotator cuff |
| Santana,Ervin | 16 | 16 | Strnd lower back |
| | 18 | 163 | Surgery on R middle finger |
| Santiago,Hector | 17 | 107 | Strained L shoulder |
| Santos,Sergio | 14 | 34 | Strained R elbow/forearm |
| | 15 | 108 | R elbow surgery |
| Saupold,Warwick | 16 | 46 | Strnd R groin |
| Scahill,Rob | 15 | 67 | R forearm tightness |
| Scheppers,Tanner | 14 | 158 | R elbow inflammation x2 |
| | 15 | 29 | L knee inflam; R ankle sprain |
| | 16 | 159 | Torn cartilage L knee |
| | 17 | 13 | Sore L abdominal muscle |
| Scherzer,Max | 17 | 10 | Neck inflammation |
| Schugel,A.J. | 18 | 150 | R shoulder discomfort |
| Schugel,Andrew | 14 | 111 | R hamstring injury |
| | 16 | 10 | R should injury |
| Schultz,Bo | 16 | 48 | Rec fr surg. on L hip |
| | 17 | 182 | Torn UCL in R elbow |
| Scribner,Evan | 16 | 151 | Strnd lat R should |
| | 17 | 129 | Strained R flexor |
| Senzatela,Antonio | 18 | 24 | Finger blister; R shoulder inflam |
| Severino,Luis | 16 | 16 | Strnd R triceps |
| Shackelford,Kevin | 18 | 27 | R forearm strain |
| Shaw,Bryan | 18 | 18 | R calf strain |
| Sherriff,Ryan | 18 | 27 | R big toe fracture |
| Shields,James | 17 | 58 | Strained R lat muscle |
| Shipley,Braden | 18 | 11 | R elbow inflammation |
| Shoemaker,Matt | 14 | 13 | Strained Lt oblique |
| | 16 | 28 | Fractured skull,hematoma |
| | 17 | 106 | Strained R forearm |
| | 18 | 154 | R forearm strain |
| Shreve,Chasen | 16 | 24 | Sprnd AC joint L should |
| Siegrist,Kevin | 14 | 60 | Strained L forearm |
| | 16 | 14 | Mononucleosis |
| | 17 | 43 | Sprnd cervical spine; L forearm tend. |
| Simmons,Shae | 14 | 62 | Strained R shoulder |
| | 16 | 128 | Rec fr TJS |
| | 17 | 154 | Strained flexor in R forearm |
| Sipp,Tony | 17 | 32 | Sore L calf |
| | 18 | 9 | Strained R oblique |
| Skaggs,Tyler | 14 | 81 | Strained L forearm; Rt hammy |
| | 15 | 184 | Recovery from L elbow surgery |
| | 17 | 98 | Strained R oblique muscle |
| | 18 | 55 | L adductor strain |
| Skoglund,Eric | 18 | 102 | Sprained L UCL |
| Slegers,Aaron | 18 | 75 | R shoulder inflammation |

## FIVE-YEAR INJURY LOG — Pitchers

| Pitchers | Yr | Days | Injury |
|---|---|---|---|
| Smith,Caleb | 17 | 15 | Viral infection |
| | 18 | 99 | L lat surgery |
| Smith,Carson | 16 | 167 | Tommy John surg. |
| | 17 | 157 | Recovery from TJS |
| | 18 | 140 | Surgery R should repaired dislocation |
| Smith,Joe | 16 | 39 | Strnd L hamstring |
| | 17 | 33 | R shoulder inflammation |
| | 18 | 24 | R elbow soreness |
| Smith,Will | 16 | 60 | Torn LCL R knee |
| | 17 | 182 | Surgery on L elbow |
| | 18 | 34 | TJS |
| Smoker,Josh | 17 | 36 | Strained L shoulder |
| Smyly,Drew | 15 | 118 | L shoulder soreness x2 |
| | 17 | 182 | Strained flexor in L arm |
| | 18 | 187 | Recovery from L elbow surgery |
| Snell,Blake | 18 | 13 | L shoulder fatigue |
| Solis,Sammy | 15 | 20 | L shoulder inflammation |
| | 16 | 59 | L should inflam; sore R knee |
| | 17 | 73 | L elbow inflammation |
| Soria,Joakim | 14 | 50 | Strained L oblique |
| | 17 | 29 | Strained L oblique |
| | 18 | 15 | R thigh strain |
| Soroka,Michael | 18 | 130 | R shoulder strain |
| Sparkman,Glenn | 17 | 88 | Fractured R thumb |
| Stammen,Craig | 15 | 173 | Torn R flexor tendon |
| Stephens,Jackson | 18 | 37 | Torn lateral meniscus, R knee |
| Stephenson,Robert | 17 | 10 | Bruised R shoulder |
| | 18 | 33 | R shoulder tendinitis |
| Stewart,Brock | 17 | 66 | R shoulder tendinitis |
| | 18 | 30 | R oblique strain |
| Storen,Drew | 16 | 16 | R should inflammation |
| | 17 | 22 | Sprained R elbow |
| Strahm,Matthew | 17 | 92 | Torn patellar tendon in L knee |
| | 18 | 40 | Torn L patellar tendon |
| Straily,Dan | 18 | 33 | R forearm inflammation |
| Strasburg,Stephen | 15 | 58 | L oblique; neck strain |
| | 16 | 33 | Sore R elbow; strnd upper back |
| | 17 | 23 | R elbow nerve impingement |
| | 18 | 71 | R shoulder inflammation |
| Stratton,Chris | 17 | 10 | Dislocated/sprained R ankle |
| Street,Huston | 16 | 94 | R knee inflammation; strnd L oblique |
| | 17 | 170 | Strained R lat; R groin |
| Strickland,Hunter | 18 | 61 | Fractured R hand |
| Stripling,Ross | 18 | 35 | Lower back inflam; R big toe inflam. |
| Stroman,Marcus | 15 | 159 | Torn ACL,L knee |
| | 18 | 60 | R shldr fatigue; fing blisters |
| Strop,Pedro | 14 | 23 | Strained L groin |
| | 16 | 43 | Torn meniscus L knee |
| Stumpf,Daniel | 18 | 34 | L ulnar nerve irritation |
| Surkamp,Eric | 15 | 6 | Strained upper back |
| Suter,Brent | 17 | 19 | strained L rotator cuff |
| | 18 | 80 | Torn UCL - TJS |
| Swarzak,Anthony | 16 | 26 | Strnd R rotator cuff |
| | 18 | 100 | Strained L oblique; R shoulder inflam |
| Syndergaard,Noah | 17 | 145 | Torn R lat muscle |
| | 18 | 57 | Strained R index finger; viral infect |
| Taillon,Jameson | 16 | 15 | R should fatigue |
| | 17 | 37 | Testicular cancer |
| Tanaka,Masahiro | 14 | 74 | R elbow inflammation |
| | 15 | 35 | Strained R forearm |
| | 17 | 10 | R shoulder inflam |
| | 18 | 32 | Strained R and L hamstrings |
| Taylor,Ben | 17 | 35 | Strained L intercostal muscle |

## FIVE-YEAR INJURY LOG — Pitchers

| Pitchers | Yr | Days | Injury |
|---|---|---|---|
| Tazawa,Junichi | 16 | 18 | R should impingement |
| | 17 | 36 | Rib cage inflammation |
| Teheran,Julio | 16 | 17 | Strnd R lat muscle |
| | 18 | 12 | R thumb contusion |
| Tepera,Ryan | 18 | 16 | R elbow inflammation |
| Thatcher,Joe | 14 | 57 | Sprained L ankle |
| Thayer,Dale | 15 | 14 | Strained R shoulder |
| Therrien,Jesen | 17 | 20 | strained R elbow |
| Thornburg,Tyler | 14 | 114 | Sore R elbow |
| | 17 | 182 | R shoulder impingement |
| | 18 | 98 | recovery from R shoulder surgery |
| Thornton,Matt | 16 | 50 | Tendinitis L Achilles |
| Tillman,Chris | 16 | 18 | Bursitis R should |
| | 17 | 35 | Bursitis in R shoulder |
| | 18 | 71 | Lower back strain |
| Tolleson,Shawn | 16 | 41 | Sprnd lower back |
| | 17 | 182 | Strained flexor in R arm |
| Tomlin,Josh | 15 | 117 | R shoulder surgery |
| | 17 | 32 | Strained L hamstring |
| | 18 | 45 | Strained R hamstring |
| Travieso,Nick | 17 | 182 | R shoulder inflammation |
| Triggs,Andrew | 16 | 14 | Bruised L shin |
| | 17 | 113 | Strained L hip |
| | 18 | 137 | Blood clot, L calf |
| Tropeano,Nicholas | 16 | 96 | Torn lig R elbow; strnd R should |
| | 17 | 182 | Surgery on R elbow to repair UCL |
| | 18 | 105 | R shoulder inflammation |
| Tsao,Chin-Hui | 16 | 133 | Strnd R triceps |
| Tuivailala,Sam | 18 | 77 | L knee strain; strained R Achilles |
| Turley,Nik | 18 | 96 | Sprained L elbow |
| Turner,Jacob | 14 | 24 | Strained R shoulder |
| | 15 | 183 | Strained flexor tendon,R elbow |
| Urena,Jose | 15 | 28 | L knee contusion |
| | 18 | 13 | R shoulder impingement |
| Urias,Julio | 18 | 150 | Recovery from L shoulder surgery |
| Valdez,Cesar | 17 | 54 | R shoulder impingement |
| Valdez,Jose | 18 | 133 | R elbow inflammation |
| Vargas,Cesar | 16 | 127 | Sore R elbow |
| Vargas,Jason | 14 | 23 | Appendectomy |
| | 15 | 131 | Torn lig.,L elbow; L flexor strain x2 |
| | 16 | 166 | Rec fr surg. on L elbow |
| | 18 | 65 | Fractured R hand; strained calf |
| Vazquez,Felipe | 15 | 29 | Gastrointestinal bleeding |
| Velasquez,Vincent | 16 | 17 | Strnd R biceps |
| | 17 | 99 | Strnd flexor R elbow; R index fing str |
| | 18 | 11 | Bruised R forearm |
| Velazquez,Hector | 18 | 11 | Lower back strain |
| Venditte,Patrick | 15 | 51 | Strained R shoulder |
| Venters,Jonny | 18 | 31 | Strained R hamstring |
| VerHagen,Drew | 14 | 28 | Stress reaction in spine |
| | 16 | 108 | Thoracic outlet syndrome R should |
| | 18 | 20 | Fractured nose |
| Verlander,Justin | 15 | 66 | Strained R triceps |
| Vincent,Nick | 14 | 34 | R shoulder fatigue |
| | 16 | 39 | Strnd mid-back |
| | 18 | 27 | Strained R groin |
| Vizcaino,Arodys | 16 | 67 | R should inflam; strnd R oblique |
| | 17 | 14 | Strained R index finger |
| | 18 | 73 | R shoulder inflammation |
| Volquez,Edinson | 17 | 96 | Blister R thumb; L knee tendinitis |
| Wacha,Michael | 14 | 74 | Stress reaction in R shoulder |
| | 16 | 36 | R should inflammation |
| | 18 | 103 | L oblique strain |

## FIVE-YEAR INJURY LOG — Pitchers

| Pitchers | Yr | Days | Injury |
|---|---|---|---|
| Wahl,Bobby | 17 | 130 | Strained R shoulder |
| | 18 | 46 | Strained R hamstring |
| Wainwright,Adam | 15 | 162 | Torn L Achilles |
| | 17 | 44 | Tightness mid-back; R elbow imping |
| | 18 | 150 | R elbow inflam x 2; str L hamstring |
| Walker,Taijuan | 14 | 73 | R shoulder impingement |
| | 16 | 31 | R foot tendinitis |
| | 17 | 24 | Blister on R index finger |
| | 18 | 170 | R elbow surgery |
| Wang,Chien-Ming | 16 | 171 | R biceps tendinitis |
| Warren,Adam | 17 | 46 | Strnd trapezius; lower back strain x2 |
| | 18 | 45 | Strained back |
| Webb,Ryan | 16 | 27 | Strnd R pectoral muscle |
| Weber,Ryan | 17 | 122 | Strained R biceps |
| Whalen,Rob | 16 | 40 | R should fatigue |
| | 17 | 27 | Strained calf |
| Wheeler,Zack | 15 | 183 | Torn ligament,R elbow |
| | 16 | 183 | Rec fr TJS |
| | 17 | 83 | R biceps tend; stress reaction R arm |
| Whitley,Chase | 15 | 143 | Sprained R elbow |
| | 16 | 162 | Rec fr TJS |
| | 18 | 20 | R heel infection |
| Wilhelmsen,Tom | 15 | 25 | Hyperextended R elbow |
| | 16 | 15 | Lower back spasms |
| Williams,Taylor | 18 | 11 | R elbow soreness |
| Wilson,Alex | 16 | 14 | Sore R should |
| | 18 | 32 | Strained L plantar fascia |
| Winkler,Daniel | 15 | 158 | Recovery from R elbow surgery |
| | 16 | 175 | Fractured R elbow |
| | 17 | 141 | Recovery surgery fractured R elbow |
| Withrow,Chris | 14 | 127 | TJS |
| | 16 | 24 | R elbow inflammation |
| Wittgren,Nick | 17 | 65 | Strained R elbow |
| | 18 | 21 | Bruised middle finger - R hand |
| Wood,Alex | 16 | 112 | Sore L tricep/elbow; Debride L elbow |
| | 17 | 24 | SC joint inflam L shoulder x 2 |
| | 18 | 11 | L wrist inflammation |
| Wood,Blake | 18 | 162 | TJS |
| Woodruff,Brandon | 17 | 41 | Strained R hamstring |
| Workman,Brandon | 15 | 175 | R elbow soreness |
| | 16 | 183 | Rec fr TJS |
| Wright,Steven | 14 | 70 | Recov surgery sports hernia |
| | 15 | 51 | Concussion |
| | 16 | 15 | Bursitis R should |
| | 17 | 153 | Surgery on L knee |
| | 18 | 68 | Recovery from L knee surgery |
| Yates,Kirby | 15 | 41 | R pectoral strain |
| | 18 | 12 | R ankle tendinitis |
| Ynoa,Gabriel | 17 | 16 | Strained R hamstring |
| | 18 | 187 | Stress reaction R shin |
| Ynoa,Michael | 17 | 12 | Strained flexor in R hip |
| Zastryzny,Rob | 18 | 13 | Back spasms |
| Ziegler,Brad | 17 | 37 | Strained R back |
| Zimmermann,Jordan | 16 | 60 | Strnd R lat; neck |
| | 18 | 40 | R shoulder impingement |
| Zych,Tony | 16 | 112 | R/C tendinitis R should |
| | 17 | 54 | Rec surg R biceps; flexor mass R elb |

## Top 75 Impact Prospects for 2019

*by Rob Gordon and Chris Blessing*

Looking for a rookie infusion in 2019? Here's the place to start. As in past years, in the following pages you'll find skills and narrative profiles of the 75 rookie-eligible prospects most likely to contribute and have an impact in the 2019 season.

We've ranked the Top 40 prospects in terms of projected 2019 rotisserie value from our figures elsewhere in this book. Beyond those 40 players, we provide 35 more, presented in alphabetical order, who could see time in the majors in 2019, but whose raw skill might be less polished or a step below the others in terms of potential 2019 impact. Keep in mind that this list is but one snapshot in time; players develop at different paces and making that one adjustment or catching a playing-time break along the way can make all the difference. (Call this the "Juan Soto Caveat," if you must.) The ranking chart also projects 2019 Mayberry scores to get a quick snapshot of each player.

Below, each of the 75 players is listed in alphabetical order with his own narrative capsule. Consider it a primer on his strengths and weaknesses that attempt to balance raw skill, readiness for the majors and likelihood of 2019 playing time.

For additional information, including profiles of over 1000 minor leaguers, statistics, and our overall HQ100 top prospect list, see our sister publication, the *2019 Minor League Baseball Analyst*—as well as the weekly scouting reports and minor league information on BaseballHQ.com. Happy prospecting!

**Albert Abreu (RHP, NYY)** is a hard thrower, likely to impact fantasy teams as a reliever or spot starter in 2019. He primarily attacks hitters with a high-octane fastball and power curveball, though does flash a change-up. He has struggled with injuries and finding the strike zone, posting a career high 4.0 Ctl in 2018.

**Sandy Alcantara (RHP, MIA)** comes after hitters with a plus 95-99 mph fastball but he also has a hard time finding the strike zone (6.2 Ctl in his MLB debut). The rebuilding Marlins are sure to give Alcantara a spot in their starting rotation next spring, but don't be fooled by his 3.44 ERA in 2018. There is still a lot of work to be done.

**Anthony Alford (OF, TOR)** took a few steps back in development, slashing .240/.312/.344 in 375 Triple-A at-bats. Still a very athletic and toolsy player, he could impact on the base paths, though his contact issues (70% in 2018) will likely prevent a full-time opportunity in 2019.

**Kolby Allard (LHP, ATL)** no longer blows hitters away with a mid-90s fastball; instead he pounds the strike zone and keeps hitters off-balance with a three-pitch mix. Allard got rocked in his MLB debut (12.38 ERA), but had a solid season at Triple-A (2.72 ERA, 2.7 Ctl, 7.1 Dom). The Braves have a lot of young arms, but he represents a value play for owners in deep NL-only formats.

**Logan Allen (LHP, SD)** has emerged as one of the top lefty prospects in the NL after notching a 2.54 ERA, 51 BB/151 K in

148.2 IP. His fastball sits at 91-94 with good late life, and his slider and change-up keep hitters off-balance. The Padres have tons of pitching depth and he profiles as a mid-rotation guy on a team still trying to turn the corner.

**Peter Alonso (1B, NYM)** had a breakout season in 2018, hitting .285 with 31 doubles and 36 HR. Alonso has a solid understanding of the strike zone and posted a .395 OBP, but the Mets chose not call him up last September. He could be on the Ronald Acuna plan for 2019: should see plenty of action and is an early NL ROY candidate.

**Yordan Alvarez (OF, HOU)** is knocking on the door of a full-time MLB opportunity, possibly as soon as mid-season. He hit 20 home runs and slashed .293/.369/.534 between Double-A and Triple-A in 2018. His ability to find barrel should lend itself to immediate contributions in average and, possibly, home runs.

**Ian Anderson (RHP, ATL)** dominated in the High-A Florida State League despite being one of its youngest players and finished the year at Double-A. His best offering is a plus mid-90s fastball that has good late sink and run. The Braves have several arms ahead of Anderson, but he could make an impact in the second half of the season.

**Bo Bichette (SS, TOR)** sports one of the best hit tools in the minor leagues, but posted a career-low .286/.343/.453 slash as a 20-year-old in Double-A. He still cranked out 43 doubles, can handle shortstop defensively, and his bat speed is electric. He won't debut until late 2019 at the earliest, but has the tools to succeed immediately.

**Beau Burrows (RHP, DET)** is a four-pitch pitcher who has struggled adjusting to upper-minors competition. His best pitch is a two-seam FB with arm-side run and drop. He has an idea how to spin the ball, but struggles with secondary pitch effectiveness. Some reliever risk, but could see a 2019 debut.

**Daz Cameron (OF, DET)** is the son of former MLBer Mike Cameron. While his tools aren't as loud as his father's, he's an instinctive player with an incredible work ethic. Instincts play up his hit tool and above-average foot speed. He was 24-for-35 in stolen base attempts in 2018.

**Griffin Canning (RHP, LAA)** was one of the early-2018 breakout pitching performers who cooled off after a promotion to Triple-A. He commands his low-90s fastball down in the zone and mixes in three average-or-better off-speed pitches to keep hitters guessing and off-balance. Polished beyond his years.

**Dylan Cease (RHP, CHW)** was stellar in 10 second-half starts with Double-A Birmingham, with a 13.4 Dom and a .168 OppBA. Hard, mid-90s FB is complemented by a 12-6 power curve, both of which are MLB-ready. Needs his change-up to develop for a SP future, but will bring lots of Ks in any role.

**Michael Chavis (3B, BOS)** lost 80 games in 2018 due to a PED suspension. Upon his return, he continued to club HR, but his ct% was below 70%. He is a power-first bat with 25-30 HR potential and has continued to improve his walk rate. He could struggle breaking into Boston's infield rotation.

**Zack Collins (C, CHW)** is known most for his raw power and OBP skill but his ct% plummeted to a career low 62% in 2018 and he struggled with consistent hard contact. Defensively, he's Gary Sanchez-esque behind the plate—meaning there is real DH risk in his current profile. As a power-first bat, he'll need to make better contact to be an everyday player.

**Yusniel Diaz (OF, BAL)** was the centerpiece of the Manny Machado deal. He is a throwback of sorts: A contact hitter with solid barrel control who lacks the swing trajectory needed to be a big HR hitter. While he has pull tendencies, he keeps defenses honest with ability to hit to the opposite field. He also has an advanced feel for the zone and above-average speed.

**Jon Duplantier (RHP, ARI)** established himself as a top prospect with a dominant campaign in 2017, posting a 1.39 ERA in 136 IP. He proved that was no fluke with a solid 2018, but missed time with a hamstring and biceps injury. He doesn't blow hitters away, relying instead on an impressive four-pitch mix and an advanced understanding of how to pitch.

**Alex Faedo (RHP, DET)** had a successful professional debut split, despite some late-season struggles in Double-A. He has the arsenal to start, but not yet the polish of a third pitch. His borderline plus-plus slider suffered a bit due to substandard fastball command. When he's at his best, he's living in the lower quadrants of the zone.

**Luiz Gohara (LHP, ATL)** is another of the Braves impressive cadre of power arms and has the best velocity in the system. A shoulder injury landed him on the 60-day DL in 2018, but the team used Gohara in relief with mixed results (5.95 ERA). Look for him to reprise that role, but a strong start could land him in the rotation by mid-season.

**Stephen Gonsalves' (LHP, MIN)** stuff was down and he struggled finding the zone during his first taste of big league hitting in 2018. He survives with a below-average fastball due to solid sequencing and his curveball and change-up rate as average or above. Without better fastball command, his stuff will play down at the big league level.

**Nick Gordon (2B/SS, MIN)** busted out early, but struggled mightily against Triple-A pitching late. He's a contact hitter who is at his best working between the gaps with a line drive approach, though struggles to get his bat head out in front of the zone. An above-average runner, he was 20-for-25 in SB attempts.

**Vladimir Guerrero, Jr. (3B, TOR)** was as advertised; he destroyed Eastern (AA) and International (AAA) League pitching with a combined .381/.437/.636 slash line. His hit tool is off the charts, as his ability to barrel a ball is uncanny. He has 30-plus HR ability too, and is a fringe-average runner. There are concerns that he'll have to move off 3B eventually, but he should be the Jays everyday 3B by late April.

**Garrett Hampson (2B, COL)** has an advanced approach at the plate and some of the best speed in the system. Hampson slashed .311/.382/.462 with 36 SB between Double and Triple-A. Hampson will compete with Ryan McMahon and others for the starting 2B role in 2019 and his speed and defense give him the inside edge.

**Monte Harrison (OF, MIA)** is one of the better athletes in the minors with plus speed, a cannon for an arm, and above-average raw power. The only problem is that his overly aggressive approach at the plate results in significant contact issues—he struck out an alarming 215 times in 2018, though he did hit 19 HR and steal 28 bases. Look for him in mid-to-late in 2019.

**Ke'Bryan Hayes (3B, PIT)** has solid all-around skills and an all-fields approach at the plate. He is starting to grow into his power and stroked 31 doubles and a career-high 7 HR at Double-A in 2018. He runs well and is a solid defender at 3B and could see the majors late in 2019.

**Austin Hays (OF, BAL)** regressed from his spectacular 2017 campaign while dealing with shoulder and ankle injuries. A super-aggressive power hitter with solid hand/eye skills and a short, compact swing, he struggles to consistently produce hard contact because of his inability to lay off pitches he cannot handle. There is 30 HR potential in his bat if he can mature.

**Keston Hiura (2B, MIL)** might be the best pure hitter in the minors with a career .313/.374/.502 slash line. He uses a short, compact RH stroke to shoot balls to all fields and should develop at least 15-20 HR power. He isn't a burner on the bases, but gets good reads and uses his speed well. Hiura has plenty of fantasy appeal.

**Brent Honeywell (RHP, TAM)** missed all of 2018 with Tommy John surgery. Known for having the only true screwball in baseball, he has a shot at becoming a top flight starter due to four above-average offerings. His change-up may be his best pitch, with plus deception and fading action. He will likely miss time early in the season due to rehab, but could make his mark by mid-season.

**Dakota Hudson (RHP, STL)** doesn't blow hitters away despite a plus mid-90s heater and a power slider. Instead, he relies on late sink to induce weak contact. His command can come and go (18 BB in 27.1 IP in his MLB debut), but the Cardinals love his competitive approach and he will compete for the 5th spot in their rotation next spring.

**Josh James (RHP, HOU)** broke out big time in 2018, including a stint with the Astros at the end of 2018. He dominates with a mid-to-high 90s fastball and a change-up that positions him nicely for a rotation role. He also features an average slider. Depending on the depth of the Astros rotation, he could either start or relieve in 2019, with a long-term role as a #2-#3 starter.

**Danny Jansen (C, TOR)** provides a shiny new toy for owners in an incredibly depressed catchers market. With solid ct% (84%) and BB% (13%) rates, he took a step forward hitting the ball out of the ballpark. His ability to hit for average will likely lead to widespread ownership coming into the 2019 season.

# Top 75 Impact Prospects for 2019

*Mayberry scores are explained in the Encyclopedia, and here reflect 2019 only, not a player's long-term impact. Batters are dark shaded; pitchers are lighter shaded.*

| RANK/BATTER/POS, TM | POWER | SPEED | BATAVG |
|---|---|---|---|
| RANK/PITCHER/POS, TM | ERA | DOM | SAVES |
| 1 Victor Robles (OF, WAS) | 3 | 4 | 3 |
| 2 Nick Senzel (3B/2B, CIN) | 3 | 1 | 4 |
| 3 Vladimir Guerrero, Jr. (3B, TOR) | 3 | 1 | 5 |
| 4 Garrett Hampson (2B, COL) | 1 | 4 | 3 |
| 5 Kyle Tucker (OF, HOU) | 3 | 2 | 3 |
| 6 Eloy Jimenez (OF, CHW) | 3 | 1 | 3 |
| 7 Brandon Lowe (2B, TAM) | 3 | 2 | 2 |
| 8 Alex Verdugo (OF, LA) | 2 | 1 | 3 |
| 9 Peter Alonso (1B, NYM) | 4 | 1 | 2 |
| 10 Keston Hiura (2B, MIL) | 2 | 2 | 4 |
| 11 Danny Jansen (C, TOR) | 2 | 1 | 3 |
| 12 Luis Urias (2B/SS, SD) | 1 | 1 | 3 |
| 13 Bo Bichette (SS/2B, TOR) | 1 | 2 | 2 |
| 14 Francisco Mejia (C, SD) | 3 | 1 | 3 |
| 15 Christin Stewart (OF, DET) | 3 | 0 | 2 |
| 16 Austin Hays (OF, BAL) | 3 | 1 | 2 |
| 17 Kevin Newman (SS, PIT) | 1 | 3 | 3 |
| 18 Alex Reyes (RHP, STL) | 3 | 5 | 1 |
| 19 Austin Riley (3B, ATL) | 2 | 1 | 2 |
| 20 Fernando Tatis, Jr. (SS, SD) | 4 | 3 | 3 |
| 21 Anthony Alford (OF, TOR) | 1 | 2 | 2 |
| 22 Brent Honeywell (RHP, TAM) | 3 | 3 | 0 |
| 23 Jesus Luzardo (LHP, OAK) | 2 | 3 | 0 |
| 24 Brendan Rodgers (SS, COL) | 3 | 2 | 3 |
| 25 Chris Shaw (OF, SF) | 3 | 1 | 1 |
| 26 Forrest Whitley (RHP, HOU) | 3 | 3 | 0 |
| 27 Touki Toussaint (RHP, ATL) | 2 | 3 | 0 |
| 28 Mike Soroka (RHP, ATL) | 3 | 3 | 0 |
| 29 Jonathan Loaisiga (RHP, NYY) | 2 | 4 | 0 |
| 30 Justus Sheffield (LHP, NYY) | 2 | 3 | 0 |
| 31 Mitch Keller (RHP, PIT) | 3 | 3 | 0 |
| 32 Luiz Gohara (LHP, ATL) | 1 | 3 | 1 |
| 33 Yordan Aivarez (OF, HOU) | 3 | 1 | 3 |
| 34 Sandy Alcantara (RHP, MIA) | 1 | 3 | 0 |
| 35 Kyle Wright (RHP, ATL) | 2 | 2 | 0 |
| 36 Stephen Gonsalves (LHP, MIN) | 1 | 1 | 0 |
| 37 Yusniel Diaz (OF, BAL) | 1 | 2 | 3 |
| 38 Kolby Allard (LHP, ATL) | 3 | 2 | 0 |
| 39 Jon Duplantier (RHP, ARI) | 3 | 2 | 0 |
| 40 Luis Ortiz (RHP, BAL) | 2 | 2 | 0 |

## THE NEXT 35

| BATTER/POS, TM | POWER | SPEED | BATAVG |
|---|---|---|---|
| PITCHER/POS, TM | ERA | DOM | SAVES |
| Albert Abreu (RHP, NYY) | 2 | 3 | 0 |
| Logan Allen (LHP, SD) | 2 | 2 | 0 |
| Ian Anderson (RHP, ATL) | 2 | 2 | 0 |
| Beau Burrows (RHP, DET) | 1 | 2 | 0 |
| Daz Cameron (OF, DET) | 2 | 2 | 1 |
| Griffin Canning (RHP, LAA) | 2 | 3 | 0 |
| Dylan Cease (RHP, CHW) | 2 | 3 | 0 |
| Michael Chavis (3B, BOS) | 2 | 1 | 2 |
| Zack Collins (C, CHW) | 2 | 0 | 1 |
| Alex Faedo (RHP, DET) | 2 | 2 | 0 |
| Nick Gordon (SS/2B, MIN) | 1 | 2 | 2 |
| Monte Harrison (OF, MIA) | 2 | 3 | 1 |
| Ke'Bryan Hayes (3B, PIT) | 1 | 2 | 3 |
| Dakota Hudson (RHP, STL) | 3 | 2 | 2 |
| Josh James (RHP, HOU) | 3 | 3 | 0 |
| Carter Kieboom (SS, WAS) | 1 | 1 | 2 |
| Kevin Kramer (2B, PIT) | 2 | 1 | 2 |
| Peter Lambert (RHP, COL) | 2 | 2 | 0 |
| Shed Long (2B, CIN) | 1 | 2 | 1 |
| Nathaniel Lowe (1B, TAM) | 3 | 0 | 2 |
| Corbin Martin (RHP, HOU) | 2 | 2 | 0 |
| Jorge Mateo (SS/OF, OAK) | 1 | 4 | 1 |
| Triston McKenzie (RHP, CLE) | 3 | 3 | 0 |
| Ryan Mountcastle (3B, BAL) | 2 | 1 | 3 |
| Sean Murphy (C, OAK) | 2 | 1 | 3 |
| Josh Naylor (OF, SD) | 2 | 1 | 1 |
| Cristian Pache (OF, ATL) | 1 | 2 | 2 |
| Chris Paddack (RHP, SD) | 3 | 2 | 0 |
| A.J. Puk (LHP, OAK) | 2 | 4 | 0 |
| Cal Quantrill (RHP, SD) | 2 | 1 | 0 |
| Corey Ray (OF, MIL) | 3 | 3 | 1 |
| Dennis Santana (RHP, LA) | 2 | 3 | 1 |
| Will Smith (C, LA) | 2 | 1 | 1 |
| Dillon Tate (RHP, BAL) | 2 | 2 | 0 |
| Bryse Wilson (RHP, ATL) | 2 | 2 | 1 |

**Eloy Jimenez (OF, CHW)** worked his way up to Triple-A last season, improving his BA, ct% and HR rate. He has big power and an emerging hit tool after making mechanical adjustments early in the season. There is 30-40 plus HR potential here, but he has struggled maintaining health since 2017, with three DL stints.

**Mitch Keller (RHP, PIT)** started 2018 with an impressive stint at Double-A (9-2 with a 2.72 ERA), but found the sledding tough when promoted to Triple-A. He has a plus fastball/curve combination that allows him to dominate against both RHB and LHB, but needs to refine his change-up before he's ready. Look for him to make an impact after the break.

**Carter Kieboom (SS, WAS)** has developed into one of the top SS prospects in the NL. He generates above-average power and in 2018 he hit .280/.357/.444 between High-A and Double-A. He moves well defensively and should be able to stick as short, though the presence of Trea Turner will likely push him over to 2B.

**Kevin Kramer (2B, PIT)** had a breakout season in 2018, hitting .311 with 35 2B, 15 HR, and 13 SB, but scuffled once called to the majors, hitting just .135 in 37 AB. At 25, Kramer isn't an elite prospect, but he does everything well and is a career .293 hitter. Kramer should see plenty of playing time in 2019 and could be a decent end-game play in NL-only formats.

**Peter Lambert (RHP, COL)** has a polished four-pitch mix that is geared more towards inducing weak contact than blowing hitters away. The Rockies have a young and talented starting rotation, so Lambert will open the year back at Triple-A Albuquerque, but an injury could see him in Colorado and he is the Rockies most MLB-ready starting prospect.

**Jonathan Loaisiga (RHP, NYY)** is a three-pitch pitcher who primarily relies on his mid-to-high 90s fastball and mid-80s power curve to rack up swings and misses. However, his change-up continues to get better, and could possibly exceed his curve in effectiveness. Due to limited work in the past, he may be on an innings limit in 2019.

**Shed Long (2B, CIN)** has an aggressive approach at the plate that generates surprising pop from his 5'8" frame, but also results in some swing-and-miss. He knows how to hunt for pitches he can drive, and posted an 11% walk rate while hitting 22 doubles and 12 HR at Double-A. Has the tools to be a 20/20 hitter, especially in Great American Ball Park.

**Brandon Lowe (2B, TAM)** enjoyed a breakout season as his power numbers took a huge jump after some swing path modifications. He also maintained his contact and walk rate despite selling out for more power. With position flexibility, he could maintain a presence in lineups at 2B and in the OF and double-digit SB numbers also possible.

**Nathaniel Lowe (1B, TAM)** has the power and the hit tool to make it as a full-time first baseman. He makes a ton of hard contact and sprays the entire field with line drives. There is some platoon risk against LHPs, but he should hit RHP for power fairly regularly out of the gate.

**Jesus Luzardo (LHP, OAK)** is one of the best pitching prospects in baseball. It's not because his stuff is electric, but he is polished beyond his years. He relies on a late-moving mid-90s two-seam fastball, a repeatable change-up with plus late fade and an above average curve to dominate hitters. An innings cap may cause limitations for his overall value this season.

**Corbin Martin (RHP, HOU)** turned himself into a legit starting pitching prospect in 2018. Each of his four pitches is average or better, led by a fastball that he commands to all corners of the zone. He complements his fastball with two breaking balls, keeping hitters off balance. Might work best in relief early as his change-up continues to evolve.

**Jorge Mateo (SS/OF, OAK)** struggled to get his footing during a full-season Triple-A stint. His hit tool took a step backwards, and he struggled with hard contact rate and a high swing-and-miss rate. Speed is still paramount and carries the profile, but lack of on-base skill and low average may limit opportunities.

**Triston McKenzie (RHP, CLE)** has been on a limited pitch count over the past few seasons as the Indians try to ease his slight frame into a starter's workload. He has three above-average or better pitches, including a low-to-mid 90s 2-seam fastball and a late-fading change-up. His best pitch is a tightly-wound curveball, which misses tons of bats. He could fill multi-inning role in 2019.

**Francisco Mejia (C, SD)** is the top catching prospect in the NL. He slashed .293/.338/.471 with 30 doubles and 14 HR at Triple-A, though he looked overmatched in his MLB debut (.179 in 56 AB). He has a gun for an arm, but is a work in progress behind the plate and should split time with Austin Hedges in 2019.

**Ryan Mountcastle (3B, BAL)** made the conversion from SS to 3B in 2019. After missing a few weeks early due to a broken hand, he didn't miss a beat, as his advanced hit tool drives the profile. However, HR power is beginning to surface in-game. With opportunity, could be up mid-season, maybe sooner.

**Sean Murphy (C, OAK)** had his best year at the plate. An athletic catcher who will stick at the position, he has improved his hard-hit rate while maintaining all-fields hitting approach and on-base skill. Power is still emerging and won't be plentiful early in MLB career.

**Josh Naylor (OF, SD)** has plus raw power from the LH side and is surprisingly discerning at the plate (64 BB/69 K). Naylor came up as a first baseman, and with Eric Hosmer inked to a long-term deal, has transitioned to LF where his bat will have to carry him.

**Kevin Newman (SS, PIT)** has a professional approach at the plate and hit .302 at Triple-A to go along with 28 SB, even though he struggled in his MLB debut. His average bat speed results in below-average power for now, but because of his speed, defense, and versatility, he makes an interesting end-game play in NL-only formats.

**Luis Ortiz (RHP, BAL)** is primarily a three-pitch pitcher, whose best offering is tight slider with swing-and-miss tendencies. He lacks fastball command and it loses velocity from start-to-start; his change-up is playable. He could start the season in the rotation.

**Cristian Pache (OF, ATL)** is a premium athlete with plus speed, but is more of a work-in-progress at the plate. Did hit .279/.307/.410 with a career-high 9 HR in 2018, and had a 32-SB season in 2017. He needs to use his speed more effectively, but his defense is major league ready right now and is his ticket to the show.

**Chris Paddack (RHP, SD)** made a stellar return from Tommy John surgery, going 7-3 with a 2.10 ERA and 8 BB/120 K in 90 IP between High-A and Double-A. He dominates due to his above-average 92-95 mph fastball and plus-plus changeup. His ability to pound the strike zone should land him in the majors by mid-2019.

**A.J. Puk (LHP, OAK)** missed all of 2018 due to Tommy John surgery. When healthy, he's one of the nastiest pitchers in the minors, as his fastball and slider are both plus pitches. However, the lacking sustainability of his change-up and health concerns could put him in a relief role in 2019.

**Cal Quantrill (RHP, SD)** comes after hitters with a plus 92-95 mph fastball and good change-up. He made 28 starts between Double and Triple-A, going 9-6 with a 4.80 ERA. He profiles more as a mid-rotation arm, but Quantrill should get a look at some point in 2019.

**Corey Ray (OF, MIL)** has an enticing blend of speed and power that have him on the verge of his MLB debut. He has an ultra-aggressive approach but also plus power. In 2018 he stroked 32 doubles and 27 HR to go along with 37 SB at Double-A. That blend of speed and power makes him fantasy relevant in all long-term keeper formats, but his career .239 batting average is a significant limitation.

**Alex Reyes (RHP, STL)** has some of the best raw stuff in the minors, but had Tommy John surgery in 2017 and then missed most of 2018 with lat strain. When healthy, his fastball sits in the mid-to-upper 90s with the stuff to be a legit staff ace, though his 2019 role is still to be determined.

**Austin Riley (3B, ATL)** has some of the best raw power in the minors and in 2018 hit .294 with 30 doubles and 19 HR between Double and Triple-A. He's worked hard to make himself an average to above-average defender at 3B where he has a strong arm. A quick start and better plate discipline could force his MLB deubt.

**Victor Robles (OF, WAS)** might be the best pure athlete in the minors with plus-plus speed and outstanding defense, including a rocket arm. His hit tool is above power at present, but the long-term upside is high. He likely will start the year as the club's everyday CF and has tremendous fantasy appeal.

**Brendan Rodgers' (SS, COL)** bat-to-ball skills are excellent and he has the tools to hit for average and power. A shoulder injury in August brought his 2018 season to an early end, but he was productive when healthy (.268/.330/.460 with 17 HR). He has played 2B and 3B in addition to SS and is likely to find an MLB role at some point in 2019.

**Dennis Santana (RHP, LA)** forced his way to the majors in 2018 before being shut down with a strained rotator cuff. He has a plus 93-96 mph fastball and an above-average power slider and owns a career 10.2 Dom. The lack of a consistent change-up and struggles with control could shift him to a relief role, where he could also be successful.

**Nick Senzel (3B/2B, CIN)** was limited to just 44 games and was sidelined with vertigo, a broken finger, and then had elbow surgery in September. When healthy, he is one of the best hitters in the minors and has a career line of .314/.390/.513. He spent the fall in instructional ball learning how to play LF and should be 100% in the spring. Look for a breakout in 2019.

**Chris Shaw (OF, SF)** has plus raw power and blasted his way to the majors, hitting 24 HR in just 394 AB in Triple-A. He is ultra-aggressive at the plate (5% bb%/66% ct%), something that he'll need to tame to get to his power. Shaw should compete for the starting LF job in 2019. Fantasy owners should tread carefully as this is a boom-or-bust profile.

**Justus Sheffield (LHP, NYY)** has a three-pitch mix that proved to be too much for minor league hitters. Both his fastball and slider could be plus offerings with his change-up barely lagging behind. Continued control issues peak up from time to time, and command concerns also exist. The health of Yankees rotation will determine his role.

**Will Smith (C, LA)** is one of the better defensive backstops in the minors and slugged 19 home runs for Double-A Tulsa. He looked overmatched when he moved up to Triple-A, but he is quick and agile behind the plate with a strong, accurate arm. Smith is almost ready and could get a look as the backup to Austin Barnes.

**Mike Soroka (RHP, ATL)** is the Braves top pitching prospect and looked impressive in five big league starts, going 2-1 with a 3.51 ERA. His fastball sits at 92-95 with good sink and run, and his change-up and slider flash as above-average. He was shut down in August with a sore shoulder, but should compete for a rotation spot in the spring and has the stuff and control to make a fantasy impact.

**Christin Stewart (OF, DET)** emerged as the Tigers best position prospect. He has plenty of power, but there are concerns about his hit tool and making enough contact. Playing time is available in Detroit; he could be a solid rookie performer.

**Dillon Tate (RHP, BAL)** throws three pitches, all which have above-average ceilings. Currently, he struggles with inducing swings-and-misses and is at his best keeping the ball in the lower half of the zone to avoid fly balls. Will get a chance to start, though could struggle without a put-away pitch.

**Fernando Tatis, Jr. (SS, SD)** is one of the top-ranked prospects in the NL and has the raw tools to be a future MVP. The 19-year-old should hit for power and average and chip in double-digit steals. Before a thumb injury ended his season early, he was hitting .286/.355/.507 with 22 doubles, 16 HR, and 16 SB at Double-A. He does have some swing-and-miss to his game, but the overall package is elite and if healthy, he should force his way to the majors by mid-2019.

**Touki Toussaint (RHP, ATL)** was dominant in 2018, going 9-6 with a 2.38 ERA while striking out 163 batters in 136.1 IP between Double and Triple-A. The 22-year-old struggles with control at times (21 BB in 29 IP in ATL) but his fastball sits at 92-94 and is backed up by a plus curve and fringe change-up. He will compete for a rotation spot in the spring.

**Kyle Tucker (OF, HOU)** worked his way up through Triple-A to the majors last season, improving his BA, ct% and HR rate. He has big power and an emerging hit tool after making mechanical adjustments early in the season. After being promoted from Double-A, he slashed .355/.399/.597 in 211 Triple-A bats and slugged 22 HRs overall. There is 30-40 plus HR potential. Has struggled maintaining health since 2017, with three DL stints.

**Luis Urias (2B/SS, SD)** struggled in his MLB debut, hitting just .208/.264/.351 in 48 AB. The 21-year-old is a professional hitter and owns a career .306 average, but his lack of power and plus speed limits his fantasy appeal. Urias missed much of the last month with a hamstring injury, but should start the year as the Padres' everyday second baseman.

**Alex Verdugo (OF, LA)** slashed .329/.391/.472 at Triple-A and held his own in limited action with the Dodgers. He is an above-average defender with a plus arm and rarely strikes out (88% ct% rate at Triple-A). If his power develops as it should, he has the potential to hit .290 with 20+ HR.

**Forrest Whitley (RHP, HOU)** missed significant time due to a drug suspension. When on the mound, he flashes four above-average-or better offerings. Both his fastball and slider are plus-plus pitches. He also features a curveball and a change-up. He utilizes his frame well to create some deception to his delivery. Only an innings cap could prevent him from being a starter in Houston.

**Bryse Wilson (RHP, ATL)** uses a bulldog approach on the mound and pounds the zone with an above-average 92-95 mph power sinker. His secondary stuff shows potential, but needs refinement. Given the Braves' starting pitching depth and his aggressive approach, a move to relief seems likely and he could carve out an important role in 2019.

**Kyle Wright (RHP, ATL)** has the best overall stuff of any of the Braves bevy of talented pitching prospects. He can overpower with a plus 95-97 mph fastball and keeps hitters off-balance with two above-average breaking balls and an improving change-up. Wright got into four games with the Braves in 2018 and will battle Mike Soroka, Touki Toussaint, and Sean Newcomb for a spot in the Braves starting rotation. Long-term, he has the highest upside, but his playing time in 2019 could be limited.

## Top International Players for 2019 and Beyond

Since the 2008 edition, the *Baseball Forecaster* has profiled a handful of Japanese prospects who may make the jump to Major League Baseball in the coming years. This provides owners in deep keeper leagues the chance to get the jump on talent before it arrives in the States. For example, that first column in 2008 included names like Koji Uehara (who made his MLB debut in 2009), Norichika Aoki (2012), and even a "hugely talented young pitcher" named Yu Darvish (also 2012).

As more MLB teams now draw regularly from the international player pool, we've expanded our coverage to include both Korean players as well as top Carribean talent—both high-upside teenagers of the past international signing period and Cuban players that could draw the interest of mutliple MLB teams. With each, we list a "possible" MLB ETA—but for most of these, you'll need to be patient.

### Japanese and Korean Players *(by Tom Mulhall)*

Gary Garland, a baseball writer in Japan, wrote an article after Ichiro's first season titled "Note to MLB: There is no 'next Ichiro'". Well, dear *Forecaster* readers, there is no "next Ohtani." He is a once-in-a-generation player. But there are still several players who could help your team if they get a chance.

**Shogo Akiyama (OF, Seibu Lions)** is just the sixth player with a 200-hit season and is the only player to do that since the "deader" ball was introduced in 2011. The durable outfielder has now had three solid five-category years, finishing 2018 at .323 with 24 HR, 82 RBI and 15 SB. He is also an above-average defender. Having just one year left on his contract, it's possible his team will post him. *Possible ETA: 2019*

**Takayuki Kajitani (OF, Yokohama DeNA Baystars)** is similar to Nori Aoki and could provide double-digit SB with a decent BA. The former Central League stolen base champion could be a productive 4th OF in MLB but missed most of 2018 with shoulder surgery. *Possible ETA: 2020*

**Yusei Kikuchi (LHP, Seibu Lions)**, who was posted in early November, won't be the next Ohtani, but could be the closest thing to it. After an elite 2017 season, Kikuchi "slumped" to 14 wins, a 3.08 ERA, 153 strikeouts and just 45 walks in 163.2 IP. His 98 mph fastball is complemented by a highly effective slider that some scouts compare to Clayton Kershaw's. Kikuchi would be the best Japanese pitcher to join MLB this season and is a prime target with the best combination of talent and opportunity. At worst, he should be a solid #3 SP. *Probable ETA: 2019*

**Takayuki Kishi (RHP, Tohoku Rakuten Golden Eagles)** has an unusual overhand delivery and throws a four-seam fastball around 90 mph. He has the typical assortment of complementary pitches, including a change-up, slider and a solid curveball, and could be a decent middle or end-of-the-rotation SP. After a history of injuries, he has now been healthy for two seasons, following up a 2.76 ERA in 2017 with a 2.72 ERA in 2018. He is interested in playing in MLB, so the usual question remains as

to whether his team will let him go. Time is running out for the 34-year-old.
*Possible ETA: 2019*

**Kotaro Kiyomiya (1B/OF, Nippon Ham Fighters)** could be the best power hitter to make the jump to MLB since Hideki Matsui. Kiyomiya holds the Japanese High School Baseball record for most home runs with 111 in three seasons. (You might remember him from the 2012 Little League World Series were he led his team to the championship over Goodlettsville, Tennessee, with an 80 mph fastball.) At 6'1" and 225 pounds, he has the physical strength to become a true power hitter. Just 19 years old, this is a prospect for those with large farm clubs who can protect him for several years.
*Possible ETA: 2022*

**Yoshihiro Maru (OF, Hiroshima Toyo Carp)** comes from a financially strapped team that sometimes posts their players early for financial reasons, as they did with Kenta Maeda. The durable Maru is a superior defender who can handle CF in the majors. He had a power breakout in 2018 with 39 HR and an astonishing .468 OBP. There are a lot of MLB teams with worse 4th outfielders than Maru.
*Possible ETA: 2019*

**Seong-Beom Na (OF, NC Dinos)** is considered the top MLB prospect in Korea. He has good mechanics and raw power, averaging 25 HR and a .300+ BA for the last five years. Na also has a little speed, reaching 23 SB in 2015 but usually swiping around 15. He is eligible to be posted after the 2019 season and wants to try to make the jump to MLB. The question is his defense, which despite his strong arm, may not be MLB caliber. But the muscular and athletic Na could arrive in North America at age 30, his prime power-hitting years.
*Probable ETA: 2020*

**Takahiro Norimoto (RHP, Rakuten Golden Eagles)** was drafted the same year as Ohtani and has pitched in his shadow, even though he won Rookie of the Year. The diminutive pitcher possesses an excellent fastball that sits in the low-to-mid 90s, coupled with a forkball and slider. Despite 186 strikeouts and only 51 walks in 177.1 IP, he had a losing record. That may be good news, as it could lead his team to post him soon. They do have a history of posting their stars early, as they did with Tanaka and Iwakuma.
*Possible ETA: 2019*

**Kodai Senga (RH, SoftBank Hawks)** is a 25-year-old pitcher who has informed his team that he is planning a future move to MLB. Unfortunately, his team has never allowed a player to be posted early, meaning Senga is years away from international free agency. However, there are rumors they may make an exception for him. Senga is major league ready, with a 97 mph fastball and solid forkball and slider. He had 163 strikeouts in 141 IP in 2018.
*Possible ETA: 2020*

**Tomoyuki Sugano (RHP, Yomiuri Giants)** consistently leads the league in ERA, WHIP and strikeouts. He became the first pitcher in 40 years to throw eight shutouts in a season and also lead the league in complete games. Sugano allegedly has command of seven pitches. His best pitches are a slider and curveball, to go

with a fastball in the mid-90s. He signed with the Yomiuri Giants, who were managed by his uncle and are the most popular team in Japan, so the odds of him coming to MLB seem remote. However, he has recently voiced a desire to pitch in North America and the Giants are changing managers. Of all the pitchers in Japan, he could have the biggest impact in the majors if he ever makes the jump.
*Possible ETA: 2020*

**Yoshitomo Tsutsugo (OF, Yokohama DeNA BayStar)** is a multiple All-Star and premier power hitter in Japan who wants to play in the majors. However, defense is something of a challenge so he would be a risky selection for both an MLB team and yours.
*Possible ETA: 2020*

**Tetsuto Yamada (2B/SS, Tokyo Yakult Swallows)** hit for the "Triple 3" (.300 BA, 30+ HR and 30+ SB) in 2015 and 2016 before slumping badly in 2017 due to overwork. He bounced back to his usual elite level in 2018 with yet another Triple 3. Possibly the best all-round offensive player in Japan, Yamada is just 27 years old. His team could post him early as they did Kaz Ishii and Nori Aoki. Yamada is easily capable of going 15/15 and maybe even 20/20, which would make him a top middle infielder.
*Possible ETA: 2020*

**Yuki Yanagita (OF, SoftBank Hawks)** also hit for the legendary "Triple 3" in 2015, but off-season elbow surgery caused issues in 2016. Since then, he has rebounded with two highly successful seasons, including a .352/36/102 season with 21 SB and a .431 OBP in 2018. Along with Yamada, he would have the biggest impact in the MLB as a position player, possibly even as a five category contributor. But he plays for a financially solid team with little incentive to post him early and has two years left on his current contract.
*Possible ETA: 2021.*

Caveat: See the article about Japanese and Korean baseball in the Encyclopedia of Fanalytics regarding style of play and the posting systems.

## Carribean Players *(by Chris Blessing)*

**Victor Victor Mesa (OF, MIA)** headlined this year's July 2nd Caribbean Class, which was considerably weaker than last year's. The 22-year-old Mesa is an athletic OF prospect with bloodlines (Victor Mesa Sr. was a star in Cuba) who was signed in October for $5.25 million. A right-handed hitter, his bat is behind some of the more recent Cuban prospects like Luis Robert. Mesa's hands aren't as loose and quick, which has led to concerns about how he'll fare against premium velocity. His strength is his athletic ability and his plus run tool should help him create havoc on the base paths. Victor Victor Mesa wasn't the only Mesa to sign with the Marlins; 17-year old Victor Mesa Jr. also signed with the club for $1 million.
*Possible ETA: 2021*

**Diego Cartaya (C, LA)** is the top prospect from Venezuela in this class, receiving a $2.5 million signing bonus. The 17-year-old Cartaya is lauded for his high baseball IQ, his defensive ability and his knack for finding barrel at the plate. From an open stance, the right-handed hitter has a short and compact swing, which utilizes the energy created by his lower half. The muscular structure of his legs is beyond his years, indicating strength not normally found in a teenaged prospect. While scouts are conservative with his power projection, Cartaya possesses raw plus power and could become a 20-25 HR bat at projection.

*Possible ETA: 2024*

**Marco Luciano (SS-OF, SF)** is the top Dominican prospect in this class, receiving a $2.6 million signing bonus. While his future position is up for debate, no one can deny the 17-year-old's desire to be the best he can be. The Giants love his makeup. A tireless worker, Luciano's body and ability is beyond his years. At the plate, the right-handed hitter is a line drive machine with big power potential. He has quick wrists and hands and a solid swing path, limiting swing-and-miss issues. A quick-twitch athlete, Luciano is only an average runner. While he possesses solid range at SS, most evaluators think his future is in the OF. The Giants are comfortable trying Luciano at SS until he outgrows the position.

*Possible ETA: 2024*

**Orelvis Martinez (SS, TOR)** has already been comped to Adrian Beltre at the same age. Sure, a Beltre comp is a lofty expectation for a 17-year-old. However, the Blue Jays believe in Martinez, inking him to a $3.5 million signing bonus. As expected, the right-handed hitting Dominican has crazy power potential. From an open stance with a big leg kick, Martinez's swing trajectory is geared for fly-ball contact. He has quick wrists and a short, compact swing, finding barrel more times than not. With a lot of moving parts in his swing and some hitchiness in his load, there are concerns Martinez's hit tool may be below average at maturity. Still, the power plays regardless. Currently a SS, as he adds bulk to his frame, he'll likely move off the position to 3B.

*Possible ETA: 2024*

**Noelvi Marte (SS, SEA)** has the potential to become a big power hitter. While his frame is still a bit wiry, Marte possesses incredible strength, especially in his lower half. Signed for $1.55 million, the 17-year-old Dominican's swing is geared for fly ball

contact. The ball explodes with significant carry off his bat. Marte struggles getting his hands to the hitting zone, causing some swing-and-miss risk. However, with adjustments, there is enough bat speed in the profile to minimize the risk of getting beat in his kitchen. He's presently a below-average runner and could get slower. Defensively, Marte has an outside shot to stick at SS but is likely a 3B long term. With his ability and strength, Marte could be a middle-of-the-order bat at maturity.

*Possible ETA: 2024*

**Gabriel Rodriguez (SS, CLE)** is the best non-catching prospect out of Venezuela this signing period, inking a $2.1 million bonus with the Indians. The 16-year-old right-handed hitter is an impactful player on both sides of the ball. Likely the only profiled SS to stick at the position long-term, Rodriguez has solid instincts and good footwork at short, enabling him to have solid range despite fringe-average speed. At the plate, Rodriguez has an innate ability to find the barrel. He has a good physique to add strength to and could possess above-average power at projection. Overall, he may be the best all-around prospect in the class with no one tool standing out above another.

*Possible ETA: 2024*

**Richard Gallardo (RHP, CHC)** is the best pitching prospect in this year's class. The 17 year-old Venezuelan hurler signed for $1 million in July. Listed at 6'1", evaluators believe he is still growing. Armed with a high-octane fastball that could be plus-plus at maturity, Gallardo has gotten rave reviews for his pitchability and secondary development. His three-pitch mix, including his fastball, an 11-5 curve and a late-fading change-up, dominated hitters during the International Prospect Showcase last February in the Dominican Republic. If he can stay healthy, Gallardo has #1-#2 caliber potential. With advanced command, he could move quicker than most international pitching prospects.

*Possible ETA: 2024*

In his 1985 *Baseball Abstract*, Bill James introduced the concept of major league equivalencies. His assertion was that, with the proper adjustments, a minor leaguer's statistics could be converted to an equivalent major league level performance with a great deal of accuracy.

Because of wide variations in the level of play among different minor leagues, it is difficult to get a true reading on a player's potential. For instance, a .300 batting average achieved in the high-offense Pacific Coast League is not nearly as much of an accomplishment as a similar level in the Eastern League. MLEs normalize these types of variances, for all statistical categories.

The actual MLEs are not projections. They represent how a player's previous performance might look at the major league level. However, the MLE stat line can be used in forecasting future performance in just the same way as a major league stat line would.

The model we use contains a few variations to James' version and updates all of the minor league and ballpark factors. In addition, we designed a module to convert pitching statistics, which is something James did not originally do.

Players are listed if they spent at least part of 2017 or 2018 in Triple-A or Double-A and had at least 100 AB or 30 IP within those two levels (players who split a season at both levels are indicated as a/a). Major league and Single-A (and lower) stats are excluded. Each player is listed in the organization with which they finished the season. Some players over age 30 with major-league experience have been omitted for space.

These charts also provide the unique perspective of looking at two years' worth of data. These are only short-term trends, for sure. But even here we can find small indications of players improving their skills, or struggling, as they rise through more difficult levels of competition. Since players—especially those with any modicum of talent —are promoted rapidly through major league systems, a two-year scan is often all we get to spot any trends. Five-year trends do appear in the *Minor League Baseball Analyst*.

Used correctly, MLEs are excellent indicators of potential. But, just like we cannot take traditional major league statistics at face value, the same goes for MLEs. The underlying measures of base skill—contact rates, pitching command ratios, BPV, etc.—are far more accurate in evaluating future talent than raw home runs, batting averages or ERAs. This chart format focuses more on those underlying gauges.

Here are some things to look for as you scan these charts:

**Target players who...**

- had a full season's worth of playing time in AA and then another full year in AAA
- had consistent playing time from one year to the next
- improved their base skills as they were promoted

**Raise the warning flag for players who...**

- were stuck at the same level both years, or regressed
- displayed marked changes in playing time from one year to the next
- showed large drops in BPIs from one year to the next

| BATTER | yr | b | age | pos | lvl | org | ab | hr | sb | ba | bb% | ct% | px | sx | bpv |
|---|---|---|---|---|---|---|---|---|---|---|---|---|---|---|---|
| Abreu,Osvaldo | 17 | R | 23 | SS | aa | WAS | 431 | 4 | 1 | 220 | 5 | 73 | 49 | 51 | -43 |
| | 18 | R | 24 | SS | aa | WAS | 360 | 6 | 3 | 160 | 7 | 69 | 76 | 74 | -25 |
| Acuna,Ronald | 17 | R | 20 | CF | a/a | ATL | 442 | 16 | 29 | 306 | 8 | 73 | 94 | 113 | 19 |
| | 18 | R | 21 | LF | aaa | ATL | 90 | 1 | 4 | 195 | 9 | 71 | 35 | 73 | -48 |
| Adames,Willy | 17 | R | 22 | SS | aaa | TAM | 506 | 9 | 10 | 258 | 11 | 71 | 84 | 100 | 4 |
| | 18 | R | 23 | SS | aaa | TAM | 245 | 3 | 3 | 256 | 9 | 69 | 70 | 104 | -19 |
| Adams,Lane | 17 | R | 28 | CF | aaa | ATL | 178 | 5 | 12 | 197 | 6 | 55 | 98 | 128 | -47 |
| | 18 | R | 29 | CF | aaa | ATL | 175 | 0 | 8 | 130 | 6 | 51 | 50 | 133 | -100 |
| Adell,Jo | 18 | R | 19 | CF | aa | LAA | 63 | 2 | 2 | 225 | 8 | 63 | 146 | 109 | 20 |
| Aguilera,Eric | 17 | L | 27 | 1B | aa | TEX | 387 | 12 | 1 | 189 | 10 | 64 | 92 | 33 | -37 |
| Ahmed,Mike | 17 | R | 25 | SS | a/a | LA | 137 | 5 | 3 | 229 | 10 | 64 | 94 | 45 | -34 |
| | 18 | R | 26 | 3B | a/a | LA | 234 | 4 | 1 | 199 | 6 | 59 | 83 | 71 | -62 |
| Alberto,Hanser | 17 | R | 25 | SS | a/a | TEX | 20 | 1 | 0 | 306 | 4 | 83 | 86 | 38 | 22 |
| | 18 | R | 26 | SS | aaa | TEX | 361 | 5 | 0 | 280 | 2 | 91 | 52 | 44 | 25 |
| Albies,Ozhaino | 17 | B | 20 | 2B | aaa | ATL | 411 | 8 | 19 | 254 | 6 | 75 | 66 | 157 | 15 |
| Alcantara,Sergio | 18 | B | 22 | SS | aa | DET | 441 | 1 | 7 | 252 | 7 | 78 | 41 | 84 | -14 |
| Alemais,Stephen | 18 | R | 23 | 2B | aa | PIT | 402 | 1 | 13 | 254 | 8 | 82 | 39 | 101 | 8 |
| Alfaro,Jorge | 17 | R | 24 | C | aaa | PHI | 324 | 6 | 1 | 212 | 4 | 59 | 79 | 65 | -70 |
| Alford,Anthony | 17 | R | 23 | CF | a/a | TOR | 257 | 5 | 16 | 297 | 11 | 80 | 73 | 93 | 31 |
| | 18 | R | 24 | CF | aaa | TOR | 375 | 4 | 15 | 222 | 6 | 67 | 79 | 104 | -22 |
| Allday,Forrestt | 17 | L | 26 | RF | a/a | LAA | 302 | 1 | 8 | 244 | 12 | 82 | 24 | 52 | -11 |
| | 18 | L | 27 | RF | a/a | SD | 433 | 3 | 8 | 213 | 8 | 76 | 47 | 95 | -12 |
| Allemand,Blake | 17 | B | 25 | 2B | aa | MIL | 336 | 7 | 2 | 240 | 7 | 78 | 79 | 70 | 13 |
| | 18 | B | 26 | 2B | aa | MIL | 305 | 6 | 2 | 230 | 8 | 76 | 62 | 52 | -13 |
| Allen,Austin | 18 | L | 24 | C | aa | SD | 451 | 17 | 0 | 254 | 6 | 75 | 113 | 20 | 11 |
| Allen,Greg | 17 | B | 24 | CF | aa | CLE | 258 | 2 | 17 | 241 | 7 | 79 | 60 | 117 | 13 |
| | 18 | B | 25 | CF | aaa | CLE | 171 | 2 | 9 | 265 | 8 | 71 | 83 | 90 | -7 |
| Allen,Josh | 18 | R | 27 | 2B | aa | NYM | 153 | 1 | 4 | 195 | 8 | 61 | 85 | 59 | -50 |
| Almanzar,Michael | 17 | R | 27 | 3B | aaa | WAS | 366 | 7 | 0 | 209 | 3 | 70 | 67 | 34 | -49 |
| | 18 | R | 28 | 3B | aaa | WAS | 58 | 0 | 0 | 170 | 3 | 75 | 25 | 16 | -68 |
| Alonso,Peter | 17 | R | 23 | DH | aa | NYM | 45 | 2 | 0 | 290 | 5 | 82 | 138 | 81 | 73 |
| | 18 | R | 24 | 1B | a/a | NYM | 478 | 25 | 0 | 229 | 11 | 68 | 142 | 30 | 17 |
| Altherr,Aaron | 18 | R | 27 | CF | aaa | PHI | 119 | 2 | 3 | 199 | 8 | 61 | 64 | 69 | -67 |
| Alvarez,Eddy | 17 | B | 27 | SS | a/a | CHW | 429 | 3 | 6 | 196 | 12 | 70 | 45 | 72 | -38 |
| | 18 | B | 28 | 2B | aaa | CHW | 308 | 6 | 4 | 201 | 10 | 67 | 107 | 95 | 5 |
| Alvarez,Eliezer | 17 | B | 23 | 2B | aa | STL | 186 | 3 | 7 | 227 | 7 | 68 | 84 | 112 | -10 |
| | 18 | B | 24 | LF | aa | TEX | 408 | 10 | 20 | 205 | 8 | 67 | 90 | 159 | 6 |
| Alvarez,Mandy | 18 | R | 24 | 3B | aa | NYY | 359 | 11 | 2 | 233 | 6 | 85 | 92 | 77 | 49 |
| Alvarez,Yordan | 18 | L | 21 | LF | a/a | HOU | 335 | 17 | 5 | 261 | 9 | 70 | 136 | 66 | 28 |
| Amaral,Beau | 17 | L | 26 | CF | aaa | CIN | 168 | 0 | 2 | 184 | 8 | 71 | 35 | 86 | -45 |
| | 18 | L | 27 | RF | aa | SEA | 384 | 2 | 8 | 200 | 6 | 72 | 45 | 96 | -32 |
| Amburgey,Trey | 18 | R | 24 | LF | aa | NYY | 481 | 16 | 10 | 231 | 4 | 74 | 93 | 101 | 11 |
| Anderson,Brian | 17 | R | 24 | 3B | a/a | MIA | 429 | 18 | 1 | 243 | 9 | 73 | 108 | 64 | 20 |
| Andreoli,John | 17 | R | 27 | CF | aaa | CHC | 430 | 10 | 18 | 194 | 10 | 60 | 103 | 143 | -12 |
| | 18 | R | 28 | RF | aaa | SEA | 327 | 2 | 14 | 222 | 11 | 65 | 64 | 119 | -28 |
| Andujar,Miguel | 17 | R | 22 | 3B | a/a | NYY | 481 | 18 | 5 | 302 | 5 | 84 | 103 | 63 | 49 |
| Aplin,Andrew | 17 | L | 26 | RF | aaa | SEA | 232 | 5 | 4 | 201 | 12 | 72 | 72 | 87 | -3 |
| | 18 | L | 27 | CF | a/a | SEA | 287 | 4 | 1 | 196 | 9 | 75 | 68 | 49 | -10 |
| Aquino,Aristides | 17 | R | 23 | RF | aa | CIN | 459 | 19 | 9 | 215 | 8 | 65 | 125 | 114 | 12 |
| | 18 | R | 24 | RF | aa | CIN | 404 | 18 | 3 | 216 | 7 | 68 | 123 | 55 | 3 |
| Arakawa,Tim | 17 | L | 24 | 2B | a/a | LAA | 240 | 3 | 6 | 208 | 11 | 64 | 39 | 73 | -67 |
| Arcia,Oswaldo | 17 | L | 26 | RF | aaa | ARI | 341 | 16 | 0 | 263 | 8 | 69 | 139 | 76 | 29 |
| Ard,Taylor | 17 | R | 27 | 1B | aa | MIA | 368 | 10 | 3 | 182 | 7 | 62 | 100 | 49 | -42 |
| Arenado,Jonah | 18 | R | 23 | 3B | aa | SF | 340 | 4 | 1 | 179 | 5 | 77 | 62 | 38 | -21 |
| Arozarena,Randy | 17 | R | 22 | LF | aa | STL | 163 | 3 | 7 | 236 | 13 | 78 | 73 | 115 | 34 |
| | 18 | R | 23 | LF | a/a | STL | 358 | 9 | 20 | 237 | 7 | 74 | 83 | 104 | 10 |
| Arraez,Luis | 18 | L | 21 | 2B | aa | MIN | 178 | 2 | 2 | 277 | 6 | 91 | 35 | 55 | 20 |
| Arroyo,Christian | 17 | R | 22 | SS | aaa | SF | 91 | 3 | 2 | 362 | 5 | 85 | 94 | 63 | 48 |
| | 18 | R | 23 | 3B | aaa | TAM | 170 | 2 | 2 | 207 | 4 | 78 | 66 | 62 | -6 |
| Arteaga,Humberto | 17 | R | 23 | SS | aa | KC | 453 | 1 | 4 | 243 | 5 | 85 | 27 | 73 | -6 |
| | 18 | R | 24 | 3B | aaa | KC | 414 | 4 | 2 | 259 | 4 | 81 | 53 | 42 | -13 |
| Asche,Cody | 17 | L | 27 | DH | aaa | CHW | 291 | 11 | 3 | 238 | 12 | 67 | 104 | 57 | -4 |
| | 18 | L | 28 | 3B | aaa | NYM | 328 | 6 | 0 | 153 | 6 | 63 | 81 | 63 | -48 |
| Astudillo,Williams | 17 | R | 26 | C | aaa | ARI | 120 | 3 | 0 | 274 | 2 | 95 | 90 | 44 | 71 |
| | 18 | R | 27 | C | aaa | MIN | 286 | 10 | 6 | 242 | 3 | 94 | 83 | 69 | 72 |
| Asuaje,Carlos | 17 | L | 26 | 2B | aaa | SD | 228 | 2 | 1 | 194 | 10 | 83 | 44 | 85 | 14 |
| | 18 | L | 27 | 2B | aaa | SD | 175 | 1 | 0 | 241 | 6 | 81 | 60 | 91 | 13 |
| Austin,Brett | 17 | B | 25 | C | aa | CHW | 149 | 4 | 0 | 196 | 9 | 61 | 97 | 58 | -39 |
| | 18 | B | 26 | C | aaa | CHW | 34 | 0 | 0 | 193 | 16 | 53 | 59 | 13 | -101 |
| Austin,Tyler | 17 | R | 26 | 1B | a/a | NYY | 185 | 10 | 0 | 254 | 9 | 65 | 169 | 74 | 38 |
| | 18 | R | 27 | 1B | aaa | MIN | 137 | 8 | 0 | 224 | 5 | 65 | 178 | 53 | 30 |
| Avelino,Abiatal | 17 | R | 22 | 2B | a/a | NYY | 291 | 3 | 7 | 245 | 6 | 84 | 55 | 121 | 29 |
| | 18 | R | 23 | SS | a/a | SF | 477 | 10 | 21 | 249 | 5 | 76 | 66 | 139 | 12 |
| Avery,Xavier | 17 | L | 27 | CF | aaa | ATL | 371 | 10 | 17 | 197 | 12 | 45 | 125 | 141 | -54 |
| | 18 | L | 28 | RF | aaa | ATL | 241 | 3 | 7 | 211 | 9 | 53 | 77 | 90 | -79 |
| Aviles Jr.,Luis | 18 | R | 23 | SS | aa | MIL | 207 | 4 | 13 | 238 | 9 | 72 | 91 | 90 | 9 |
| Bader,Harrison | 17 | R | 23 | CF | aaa | STL | 431 | 16 | 12 | 254 | 6 | 71 | 93 | 89 | -2 |
| Baez,Jeffrey | 17 | R | 24 | RF | aa | CHC | 276 | 9 | 6 | 196 | 8 | 76 | 88 | 89 | 18 |
| | 18 | R | 25 | RF | aa | CHC | 256 | 6 | 13 | 228 | 9 | 64 | 96 | 120 | -11 |
| Balaguert ,Yasiel | 17 | R | 24 | 1B | aa | CHC | 477 | 13 | 0 | 231 | 6 | 75 | 84 | 23 | -10 |
| | 18 | R | 25 | 1B | aa | CHC | 449 | 7 | 1 | 198 | 5 | 79 | 62 | 45 | -9 |
| Baldoquin,Roberto | 18 | R | 24 | SS | aa | LAA | 193 | 1 | 3 | 235 | 5 | 72 | 42 | 70 | -43 |
| Bandy,Jett | 17 | R | 27 | C | aaa | MIL | 42 | 2 | 0 | 243 | 7 | 85 | 74 | 40 | 28 |
| | 18 | R | 28 | C | aaa | MIL | 192 | 6 | 2 | 219 | 3 | 78 | 96 | 43 | 11 |
| Barash,Michael | 18 | R | 24 | C | a/a | LAA | 173 | 4 | 1 | 181 | 12 | 70 | 72 | 39 | -25 |
| Barnum,Keon | 17 | L | 24 | 1B | aa | CHW | 333 | 16 | 0 | 196 | 10 | 57 | 138 | 35 | -30 |
| | 18 | L | 25 | 1B | aa | CHW | 272 | 14 | 0 | 182 | 3 | 59 | 135 | 28 | -40 |
| Baron,Steven | 18 | R | 28 | C | aaa | STL | 136 | 0 | 0 | 166 | 4 | 71 | 27 | 25 | -79 |
| Barrera,Luis | 18 | L | 23 | CF | aa | OAK | 131 | 0 | 10 | 295 | 5 | 85 | 65 | 160 | 52 |
| Barreto,Franklin | 17 | R | 21 | SS | aaa | OAK | 469 | 11 | 12 | 264 | 4 | 69 | 86 | 116 | -11 |
| | 18 | R | 22 | 2B | aaa | OAK | 282 | 14 | 4 | 231 | 10 | 60 | 156 | 90 | 13 |
| Barrett,Kyle | 17 | L | 24 | LF | aa | MIA | 126 | 0 | 2 | 209 | 6 | 70 | 40 | 95 | -45 |
| | 18 | L | 25 | LF | aa | MIA | 101 | 0 | 5 | 194 | 7 | 62 | 76 | 144 | -34 |
| Basabe,Luis | 18 | B | 22 | CF | aa | CHW | 231 | 6 | 9 | 239 | 11 | 64 | 98 | 138 | -1 |
| Basto,Nick | 17 | R | 23 | 1B | aa | CHW | 477 | 14 | 0 | 234 | 9 | 69 | 96 | 21 | -24 |
| | 18 | R | 24 | 1B | aa | WAS | 115 | 1 | 0 | 144 | 10 | 59 | 38 | 74 | -91 |
| Batten,Matthew | 18 | R | 23 | 2B | a/a | SD | 187 | 1 | 8 | 219 | 12 | 65 | 46 | 96 | -51 |
| Bauers,Jake | 17 | L | 22 | LF | aaa | TAM | 486 | 12 | 19 | 245 | 13 | 74 | 87 | 102 | 25 |
| | 18 | L | 23 | 1B | aaa | TAM | 197 | 4 | 9 | 247 | 9 | 72 | 91 | 83 | 6 |
| Bautista,Rafael | 17 | R | 24 | CF | aaa | WAS | 176 | 0 | 6 | 220 | 4 | 83 | 37 | 101 | 3 |
| | 18 | R | 25 | CF | a/a | WAS | 109 | 1 | 5 | 266 | 5 | 71 | 41 | 94 | -44 |
| Beaty,Matt | 17 | L | 24 | 1B | aa | LA | 438 | 13 | 2 | 288 | 6 | 86 | 87 | 45 | 39 |
| | 18 | L | 25 | 1B | aaa | LA | 101 | 1 | 0 | 231 | 8 | 80 | 81 | 27 | 10 |
| Beck,Preston | 17 | L | 27 | RF | aaa | TEX | 229 | 1 | 1 | 198 | 7 | 77 | 39 | 72 | -22 |
| | 18 | L | 28 | 1B | aa | TEX | 442 | 10 | 0 | 215 | 6 | 75 | 74 | 45 | -14 |
| Bednar,Brandon | 17 | R | 25 | 3B | aa | SF | 411 | 1 | 2 | 252 | 5 | 82 | 45 | 61 | -4 |
| | 18 | R | 26 | 2B | aa | COL | 272 | 6 | 1 | 253 | 4 | 79 | 80 | 58 | 6 |
| Bemboom,Anthony | 17 | L | 27 | C | aaa | COL | 133 | 3 | 0 | 238 | 11 | 75 | 86 | 59 | 11 |
| | 18 | L | 28 | C | aaa | COL | 211 | 3 | 0 | 181 | 8 | 73 | 58 | 17 | -38 |
| Benedetti,Carmen | 18 | L | 24 | LF | aa | HOU | 271 | 7 | 10 | 246 | 11 | 66 | 109 | 106 | 5 |
| Bernard,Wynton | 17 | R | 27 | CF | aaa | SF | 193 | 1 | 10 | 210 | 5 | 74 | 47 | 141 | -12 |
| | 18 | R | 28 | CF | a/a | CHC | 252 | 2 | 18 | 192 | 5 | 75 | 55 | 141 | -4 |
| Berti,Jon | 17 | R | 27 | 2B | aaa | TOR | 215 | 3 | 20 | 186 | 8 | 71 | 67 | 169 | 5 |
| | 18 | R | 28 | 3B | a/a | TOR | 345 | 6 | 22 | 249 | 8 | 78 | 71 | 151 | 33 |
| Betancourt,Javier | 17 | R | 22 | 2B | aa | MIL | 338 | 7 | 3 | 242 | 6 | 84 | 73 | 84 | 34 |
| Bethancourt,Christian | 18 | R | 27 | C | aaa | MIL | 391 | 14 | 4 | 227 | 3 | 75 | 90 | 55 | -2 |
| Betts,Jordan | 18 | R | 27 | 1B | a/a | BOS | 332 | 8 | 0 | 205 | 5 | 66 | 85 | 20 | -50 |
| Bichette,Bo | 18 | R | 20 | SS | aa | TOR | 539 | 10 | 28 | 281 | 7 | 81 | 104 | 140 | 65 |
| Bichette,Dante | 17 | R | 25 | 3B | aa | NYY | 244 | 4 | 0 | 239 | 12 | 77 | 51 | 32 | -17 |
| Biggio,Cavan | 18 | L | 23 | 2B | aa | TOR | 449 | 22 | 17 | 233 | 16 | 64 | 150 | 114 | 45 |
| Billings,Shane | 18 | R | 24 | LF | aa | STL | 26 | 1 | 0 | 127 | 3 | 79 | 39 | 47 | -32 |
| Biondi,Patrick | 17 | L | 26 | CF | aa | NYM | 264 | 2 | 24 | 204 | 12 | 72 | 24 | 122 | -29 |
| | 18 | L | 27 | CF | a/a | NYM | 217 | 0 | 13 | 164 | 9 | 67 | 21 | 90 | -69 |
| Bird,Gregory | 17 | L | 25 | 1B | aaa | NYY | 47 | 3 | 0 | 269 | 17 | 78 | 150 | 38 | 78 |
| | 18 | L | 26 | 1B | a/a | NYY | 31 | 3 | 0 | 174 | 15 | 66 | 155 | 45 | 34 |
| Birk,Ryne | 17 | L | 23 | 2B | aa | HOU | 126 | 6 | 1 | 221 | 4 | 80 | 78 | 33 | 2 |
| | 18 | L | 24 | 2B | aa | HOU | 412 | 1 | 11 | 190 | 8 | 76 | 34 | 116 | -18 |
| Bishop,Braden | 17 | R | 24 | CF | aa | SEA | 125 | 1 | 5 | 295 | 9 | 86 | 59 | 94 | 39 |
| | 18 | R | 25 | CF | aa | SEA | 345 | 6 | 4 | 238 | 8 | 76 | 70 | 78 | 1 |
| Bladel,Johnny | 18 | R | 27 | LF | aa | BOS | 141 | 0 | 4 | 144 | 10 | 67 | 38 | 86 | -55 |
| Blandino,Alex | 17 | R | 25 | 2B | a/a | CIN | 393 | 12 | 4 | 239 | 13 | 74 | 116 | 53 | 33 |
| Blash,Jabari | 17 | R | 28 | RF | aaa | SD | 235 | 12 | 2 | 211 | 11 | 53 | 168 | 64 | -9 |
| | 18 | R | 29 | RF | aaa | LAA | 287 | 17 | 3 | 221 | 9 | 52 | 194 | 63 | 0 |
| Bohanek,Cody | 18 | R | 23 | 2B | aaa | HOU | 41 | 0 | 1 | 156 | 2 | 53 | 0 | 43 | -170 |
| Bolasky,Devyn | 17 | L | 24 | RF | a/a | NYY | 158 | 1 | 1 | 195 | 6 | 76 | 48 | 99 | -13 |
| | 18 | L | 25 | LF | a/a | NYY | 237 | 0 | 1 | 266 | 6 | 89 | 25 | 64 | 8 |
| Boldt,Ryan | 18 | L | 24 | RF | aa | TAM | 241 | 6 | 10 | 238 | 8 | 71 | 95 | 147 | 23 |
| Bolinger,Royce | 17 | R | 27 | RF | aa | TEX | 325 | 7 | 0 | 199 | 4 | 64 | 88 | 46 | -51 |
| Bolt,Skye | 18 | B | 24 | CF | aa | OAK | 285 | 7 | 8 | 220 | 7 | 71 | 102 | 119 | 15 |
| Bonifacio,Jorge | 17 | R | 24 | RF | aaa | KC | 51 | 2 | 0 | 283 | 8 | 83 | 112 | 59 | 57 |
| | 18 | R | 25 | RF | aaa | KC | 51 | 0 | 0 | 350 | 10 | 74 | 100 | 87 | 22 |
| Booker,Joel | 18 | R | 25 | LF | aa | CHW | 267 | 2 | 11 | 236 | 7 | 66 | 58 | 119 | -37 |
| Borenstein,Zachary | 17 | L | 27 | LF | aaa | ARI | 384 | 15 | 1 | 220 | 7 | 60 | 148 | 98 | 2 |
| | 18 | L | 28 | LF | aaa | NYM | 484 | 14 | 2 | 174 | 9 | 51 | 132 | 58 | -54 |
| Bossart,Austin | 18 | R | 25 | C | aa | PHI | 176 | 6 | 0 | 228 | 4 | 74 | 80 | 26 | -23 |
| Bostick,Christopher | 17 | R | 24 | LF | aaa | PIT | 486 | 6 | 7 | 269 | 8 | 79 | 72 | 80 | 13 |
| | 18 | R | 25 | CF | aaa | MIA | 362 | 3 | 6 | 244 | 6 | 72 | 71 | 79 | -18 |
| Bote,David | 17 | R | 24 | 2B | aa | CHC | 470 | 12 | 4 | 247 | 9 | 75 | 92 | 82 | 20 |
| | 18 | R | 25 | 2B | aaa | CHC | 235 | 9 | 2 | 222 | 8 | 69 | 108 | 72 | 0 |
| Boulware,Garrett | 18 | R | 26 | C | a/a | CIN | 47 | 0 | 0 | 143 | 5 | 51 | 88 | 95 | -83 |
| Bousfield,Auston | 17 | R | 24 | CF | aa | SD | 297 | 3 | 13 | 210 | 8 | 81 | 45 | 96 | 7 |
| | 18 | R | 25 | CF | a/a | SD | 313 | 1 | 5 | 196 | 9 | 73 | 61 | 92 | -13 |
| Boyd,B.J. | 17 | L | 24 | CF | aa | OAK | 533 | 4 | 13 | 283 | 5 | 85 | 52 | 109 | 25 |
| | 18 | L | 25 | LF | aaa | OAK | 391 | 2 | 5 | 231 | 5 | 79 | 42 | 75 | -15 |
| Boyd,Jayce | 17 | R | 27 | LF | aaa | NYM | 246 | 8 | 2 | 223 | 7 | 75 | 94 | 61 | 8 |
| Boykin,Roderick | 18 | R | 23 | LF | aa | SD | 224 | 3 | 7 | 191 | 7 | 47 | 78 | 143 | -91 |
| Bradley,Bobby | 17 | L | 21 | 1B | aa | CLE | 467 | 20 | 3 | 241 | 9 | 75 | 114 | 58 | 29 |
| | 18 | L | 22 | 1B | a/a | CLE | 483 | 23 | 1 | 212 | 9 | 67 | 142 | 60 | 20 |
| Brett,Ryan | 17 | R | 26 | 2B | aaa | TAM | 40 | 0 | 1 | 212 | 0 | 79 | 85 | 54 | 1 |
| | 18 | R | 27 | CF | a/a | CHW | 194 | 3 | 3 | 196 | 3 | 68 | 63 | 111 | -37 |
| Briceno,Jose | 18 | R | 26 | C | aaa | LAA | 112 | 5 | 2 | 204 | 2 | 75 | 94 | 77 | 6 |
| Brigman,Bryson | 18 | R | 23 | 2B | aa | MIA | 42 | 1 | 2 | 273 | 4 | 84 | 59 | 31 | 1 |
| Brinson,Lewis | 17 | R | 23 | CF | aaa | MIL | 299 | 11 | 8 | 284 | 7 | 76 | 112 | 107 | 41 |
| | 18 | R | 24 | CF | a/a | MIA | 50 | 1 | 1 | 153 | 5 | 75 | 51 | 66 | -29 |
| Brito,Socrates | 17 | L | 25 | RF | aaa | ARI | 292 | 3 | 4 | 243 | 4 | 74 | 74 | 110 | 0 |
| | 18 | L | 26 | RF | aaa | ARI | 428 | 9 | 9 | 239 | 6 | 70 | 101 | 107 | 6 |
| Brockmeyer,Cael | 17 | R | 26 | C | a/a | CHC | 204 | 5 | 0 | 159 | 5 | 65 | 76 | 46 | -51 |
| | 18 | R | 27 | C | a/a | LA | 224 | 3 | 2 | 241 | 6 | 64 | 73 | 57 | -57 |
| Brontsema,John | 18 | R | 24 | DH | aa | KC | 109 | 1 | 4 | 206 | 6 | 69 | 73 | 132 | -12 |
| Brosseau,Michael | 18 | R | 24 | 3B | aa | TAM | 370 | 10 | 9 | 226 | 6 | 76 | 96 | 106 | 27 |
| Brown,Cassidy | 18 | R | 24 | C | aa | CIN | 97 | 1 | 0 | 155 | 6 | 55 | 53 | 16 | -119 |
| Brown,Seth | 18 | L | 26 | 1B | aa | OAK | 502 | 10 | 4 | 233 | 6 | 67 | 101 | 84 | -11 |
| Brown,Trevor | 17 | R | 26 | C | aaa | SF | 196 | 1 | 2 | 135 | 3 | 74 | 19 | 46 | -66 |
| | 18 | R | 27 | C | aaa | SF | 128 | 0 | 1 | 187 | 8 | 77 | 21 | 41 | -45 |

| BATTER | yr | b | age | pos | lvl | org | ab | hr | sb | ba | bb% | ct% | px | sx | bpv |
|---|---|---|---|---|---|---|---|---|---|---|---|---|---|---|---|
| Broxton,Keon | 18 | R | 28 | CF | aaa | MIL | 299 | 7 | 16 | 189 | 6 | 49 | 112 | 126 | -64 |
| Brugman,Jaycob | 17 | L | 25 | CF | aaa | OAK | 153 | 1 | 2 | 233 | 9 | 80 | 33 | 69 | -15 |
| | 18 | L | 26 | LF | a/a | BAL | 264 | 7 | 4 | 209 | 7 | 68 | 81 | 106 | -16 |
| Bruno,Stephen | 17 | R | 27 | 3B | aaa | CHC | 219 | 6 | 5 | 209 | 2 | 76 | 73 | 78 | -9 |
| | 18 | R | 28 | 2B | aaa | CHC | 271 | 2 | 3 | 184 | 4 | 79 | 42 | 50 | -25 |
| Bueno,Ronald | 17 | B | 25 | 3B | a/a | CHW | 216 | 6 | 1 | 191 | 10 | 74 | 84 | 57 | 4 |
| Burcham,Scott | 18 | R | 25 | SS | aa | COL | 175 | 2 | 5 | 241 | 7 | 69 | 62 | 61 | -40 |
| Burg,Alex | 18 | R | 31 | 1B | aaa | LA | 47 | 1 | 0 | 175 | 0 | 72 | 68 | 47 | -41 |
| Burks,Charcer | 17 | R | 22 | LF | aa | CHC | 456 | 9 | 15 | 255 | 13 | 74 | 73 | 93 | 11 |
| | 18 | R | 23 | LF | aa | CHC | 437 | 5 | 12 | 207 | 11 | 68 | 60 | 114 | -22 |
| Buxton,Byron | 18 | R | 25 | CF | aaa | MIN | 136 | 4 | 4 | 249 | 5 | 66 | 127 | 111 | 12 |
| Caldwell,Bruce | 17 | L | 26 | 3B | a/a | STL | 339 | 11 | 2 | 205 | 11 | 60 | 94 | 58 | -41 |
| | 18 | L | 27 | 2B | a/a | NYY | 426 | 9 | 1 | 213 | 9 | 65 | 96 | 43 | -29 |
| Calhoun,Willie | 17 | L | 23 | 2B | aaa | TEX | 486 | 24 | 3 | 267 | 6 | 86 | 107 | 81 | 70 |
| | 18 | L | 24 | LF | aaa | TEX | 432 | 7 | 3 | 259 | 5 | 88 | 71 | 61 | 40 |
| Calica,Andrew | 18 | L | 24 | CF | aa | CLE | 421 | 5 | 22 | 257 | 10 | 73 | 66 | 109 | -3 |
| Calixte,Orlando | 17 | R | 25 | SS | aaa | SF | 378 | 9 | 15 | 208 | 4 | 74 | 76 | 139 | 11 |
| | 18 | R | 26 | SS | aaa | SF | 400 | 6 | 10 | 213 | 5 | 71 | 59 | 106 | -24 |
| Call,Alex | 18 | R | 24 | RF | aa | CHW | 236 | 7 | 2 | 219 | 9 | 63 | 123 | 67 | -7 |
| Camargo,Johan | 17 | B | 24 | SS | aaa | ATL | 129 | 3 | 1 | 240 | 5 | 79 | 71 | 69 | 7 |
| | 18 | B | 25 | SS | aaa | ATL | 33 | 2 | 0 | 263 | 6 | 69 | 173 | 25 | 36 |
| Cameron,Daz | 18 | R | 21 | CF | a/a | DET | 257 | 4 | 12 | 259 | 8 | 73 | 103 | 142 | 36 |
| Candelario,Jeimer | 17 | B | 24 | 3B | aaa | DET | 407 | 14 | 1 | 244 | 9 | 72 | 130 | 77 | 38 |
| Canelo,Malquin | 17 | R | 23 | SS | aa | PHI | 389 | 5 | 10 | 199 | 8 | 67 | 73 | 98 | -27 |
| | 18 | R | 24 | SS | aa | PHI | 470 | 8 | 18 | 212 | 6 | 72 | 58 | 123 | -15 |
| Cantwell,Patrick | 17 | R | 27 | C | a/a | TOR | 34 | 0 | 1 | 128 | 0 | 58 | 30 | 55 | -125 |
| | 18 | R | 28 | C | aa | TOR | 127 | 3 | 2 | 229 | 10 | 70 | 77 | 95 | -7 |
| Caratini,Victor | 17 | B | 24 | C | aaa | CHC | 292 | 8 | 1 | 293 | 7 | 81 | 105 | 72 | 44 |
| | 18 | B | 25 | C | aaa | CHC | 115 | 3 | 0 | 260 | 11 | 74 | 85 | 11 | -8 |
| Carbonell,Daniel | 17 | R | 26 | LF | aa | SF | 191 | 3 | 4 | 210 | 5 | 75 | 69 | 97 | -3 |
| Cardona,Jose | 17 | R | 23 | CF | a/a | TEX | 446 | 6 | 13 | 249 | 4 | 88 | 48 | 88 | 26 |
| | 18 | R | 24 | CF | a/a | TEX | 365 | 6 | 10 | 221 | 6 | 80 | 45 | 70 | -8 |
| Carrizales,Omar | 17 | L | 22 | CF | aa | COL | 432 | 5 | 10 | 251 | 9 | 79 | 63 | 93 | 12 |
| | 18 | L | 23 | CF | aa | COL | 279 | 6 | 9 | 221 | 6 | 72 | 93 | 111 | 11 |
| Carter,Jodd | 18 | R | 22 | RF | aa | CLE | 69 | 1 | 0 | 276 | 4 | 81 | 26 | 47 | -30 |
| Casteel,Ryan | 17 | R | 26 | 1B | aa | SEA | 389 | 10 | 1 | 228 | 6 | 73 | 84 | 37 | -14 |
| Castillo,Ali | 17 | R | 28 | 2B | a/a | SF | 345 | 1 | 4 | 221 | 4 | 89 | 31 | 66 | 8 |
| | 18 | R | 29 | 3B | aa | SF | 329 | 1 | 5 | 205 | 5 | 87 | 45 | 93 | 23 |
| Castillo,Erick | 17 | R | 24 | C | aa | CHC | 204 | 1 | 0 | 221 | 8 | 76 | 43 | 19 | -38 |
| | 18 | R | 25 | C | a/a | CHC | 147 | 2 | 0 | 153 | 4 | 83 | 33 | 22 | -25 |
| Castillo,Rusney | 17 | R | 30 | CF | aaa | BOS | 347 | 11 | 11 | 268 | 2 | 82 | 91 | 88 | 36 |
| | 18 | R | 31 | CF | aaa | BOS | 474 | 4 | 9 | 268 | 4 | 80 | 60 | 58 | -5 |
| Castro,Daniel | 17 | R | 25 | SS | aaa | COL | 395 | 2 | 1 | 272 | 4 | 89 | 50 | 33 | 14 |
| | 18 | R | 26 | SS | aaa | COL | 251 | 2 | 1 | 254 | 3 | 89 | 53 | 55 | 24 |
| Castro,Harold | 17 | L | 24 | CF | aa | DET | 414 | 1 | 17 | 258 | 4 | 86 | 35 | 114 | 15 |
| | 18 | L | 25 | 3B | a/a | DET | 351 | 2 | 4 | 232 | 2 | 79 | 34 | 55 | -36 |
| Castro,Willi | 18 | B | 21 | SS | a/a | DET | 497 | 8 | 16 | 250 | 6 | 77 | 80 | 120 | 19 |
| Cave,Jake | 17 | L | 25 | CF | a/a | NYY | 406 | 21 | 2 | 278 | 6 | 67 | 144 | 78 | 21 |
| | 18 | L | 26 | RF | aaa | MIN | 216 | 5 | 3 | 241 | 9 | 71 | 78 | 72 | -10 |
| Cecchini,Garin | 17 | L | 26 | 3B | aaa | KC | 290 | 3 | 2 | 228 | 3 | 77 | 73 | 78 | -3 |
| Cecchini,Gavin | 17 | R | 24 | 2B | aaa | NYM | 453 | 4 | 4 | 211 | 6 | 83 | 51 | 70 | 10 |
| | 18 | R | 25 | 2B | aaa | NYM | 109 | 1 | 1 | 222 | 4 | 83 | 82 | 66 | 27 |
| Cervenka,Martin | 18 | R | 26 | C | aa | BAL | 337 | 11 | 1 | 210 | 6 | 78 | 94 | 30 | 9 |
| Cesar,Randy | 18 | R | 23 | 3B | aa | HOU | 446 | 9 | 3 | 269 | 7 | 72 | 83 | 59 | -13 |
| Chang,Yu-Cheng | 17 | R | 22 | SS | aa | CLE | 439 | 21 | 9 | 210 | 9 | 71 | 131 | 106 | 40 |
| | 18 | R | 23 | SS | aaa | CLE | 457 | 10 | 3 | 236 | 7 | 65 | 105 | 58 | -20 |
| Chapman,Matt | 17 | R | 24 | 3B | aaa | OAK | 175 | 11 | 4 | 218 | 10 | 61 | 161 | 98 | 22 |
| Chavez,Santiago | 18 | R | 23 | C | aa | OAK | 91 | 0 | 0 | 182 | 2 | 80 | 73 | 58 | 2 |
| Chavis,Michael | 17 | R | 22 | 3B | aa | BOS | 248 | 11 | 1 | 239 | 6 | 77 | 128 | 46 | 37 |
| | 18 | R | 23 | 3B | a/a | BOS | 155 | 6 | 2 | 279 | 7 | 68 | 134 | 72 | 16 |
| Chinea,Chris | 18 | R | 24 | 1B | aa | STL | 299 | 10 | 0 | 192 | 4 | 73 | 82 | 31 | -24 |
| Choi,Ji-Man | 17 | L | 26 | 1B | aaa | NYY | 288 | 15 | 3 | 253 | 10 | 65 | 161 | 53 | 25 |
| | 18 | L | 27 | 1B | aaa | TAM | 203 | 5 | 1 | 237 | 14 | 69 | 93 | 29 | -9 |
| Chu,Li-Jen | 18 | R | 24 | C | a/a | CLE | 58 | 2 | 0 | 219 | 4 | 75 | 73 | 12 | -28 |
| Ciuffo,Nick | 17 | L | 22 | C | aa | TAM | 371 | 6 | 2 | 221 | 9 | 71 | 89 | 56 | -7 |
| | 18 | L | 23 | C | aaa | TAM | 221 | 4 | 0 | 232 | 5 | 67 | 75 | 30 | -50 |
| Clement,Ernie | 18 | R | 22 | SS | aa | CLE | 65 | 0 | 1 | 238 | 4 | 89 | 68 | 103 | 49 |
| Coats,Jason | 18 | R | 28 | LF | aaa | TAM | 397 | 11 | 2 | 196 | 4 | 70 | 104 | 89 | -1 |
| Cole,Hunter | 17 | R | 25 | RF | aa | SF | 281 | 5 | 2 | 226 | 9 | 74 | 99 | 90 | 22 |
| | 18 | R | 26 | RF | a/a | TEX | 378 | 12 | 1 | 255 | 8 | 67 | 95 | 50 | -23 |
| Collier,Zach | 17 | L | 27 | CF | a/a | WAS | 205 | 5 | 4 | 221 | 7 | 65 | 101 | 95 | -13 |
| | 18 | L | 28 | RF | aa | WAS | 307 | 4 | 4 | 170 | 9 | 62 | 86 | 97 | -35 |
| Collins,Tyler | 17 | L | 27 | RF | aaa | DET | 260 | 8 | 9 | 249 | 9 | 68 | 98 | 104 | 1 |
| | 18 | L | 28 | RF | aaa | KC | 53 | 0 | 0 | 105 | 9 | 69 | 0 | 34 | -95 |
| Collins,Zack | 17 | L | 22 | C | aa | CHW | 34 | 2 | 0 | 229 | 25 | 64 | 159 | 25 | 44 |
| | 18 | L | 23 | C | aa | CHW | 418 | 15 | 5 | 218 | 19 | 58 | 134 | 69 | -2 |
| Cone,Gene | 18 | L | 24 | CF | aa | NYM | 24 | 0 | 1 | 102 | 3 | 71 | 0 | 61 | -89 |
| Cooper,Garrett | 17 | R | 27 | 1B | a/a | NYY | 306 | 18 | 0 | 314 | 9 | 78 | 148 | 37 | 62 |
| | 18 | R | 28 | 1B | aaa | MIA | 30 | 1 | 0 | 234 | 7 | 79 | 55 | 2 | -24 |
| Coppola,Zachary | 17 | L | 23 | CF | aa | PHI | 325 | 0 | 24 | 222 | 9 | 78 | 21 | 112 | -16 |
| | 18 | L | 24 | CF | aa | PHI | 129 | 0 | 8 | 161 | 13 | 72 | 6 | 83 | -52 |
| Corcino,Edgar | 17 | B | 25 | RF | a/a | MIN | 459 | 5 | 4 | 269 | 7 | 81 | 50 | 63 | 0 |
| | 18 | B | 26 | RF | a/a | MIN | 296 | 6 | 2 | 230 | 6 | 78 | 83 | 91 | 20 |
| Cordell,Ryan | 17 | R | 25 | RF | aaa | MIL | 261 | 8 | 6 | 232 | 6 | 70 | 108 | 116 | 16 |
| | 18 | R | 26 | CF | a/a | CHW | 188 | 4 | 6 | 208 | 5 | 70 | 77 | 98 | -17 |
| Cordero,Franchy | 17 | L | 23 | CF | aaa | SD | 390 | 11 | 10 | 273 | 4 | 66 | 119 | 129 | 7 |
| | 18 | L | 24 | LF | aaa | SD | 26 | 1 | 2 | 217 | 10 | 59 | 84 | 65 | -56 |

| BATTER | yr | b | age | pos | lvl | org | ab | hr | sb | ba | bb% | ct% | px | sx | bpv |
|---|---|---|---|---|---|---|---|---|---|---|---|---|---|---|---|
| Coulter,Clint | 18 | R | 25 | RF | a/a | MIL | 265 | 10 | 1 | 218 | 5 | 64 | 122 | 85 | -9 |
| Cowart,Kaleb | 17 | B | 25 | 3B | aaa | LAA | 367 | 8 | 13 | 245 | 7 | 75 | 78 | 87 | 6 |
| | 18 | B | 26 | SS | aaa | LAA | 258 | 4 | 5 | 210 | 4 | 75 | 76 | 96 | -2 |
| Cozens,Dylan | 17 | L | 23 | RF | aaa | PHI | 476 | 25 | 7 | 192 | 10 | 54 | 141 | 89 | -25 |
| | 18 | L | 24 | RF | aaa | PHI | 297 | 19 | 7 | 218 | 11 | 51 | 215 | 91 | 27 |
| Craig,Will | 18 | R | 24 | 1B | aa | PIT | 480 | 16 | 5 | 219 | 7 | 71 | 110 | 86 | 13 |
| Crawford,J.P. | 17 | L | 22 | SS | aaa | PHI | 474 | 14 | 4 | 224 | 13 | 77 | 83 | 88 | 29 |
| | 18 | L | 23 | SS | aaa | PHI | 58 | 1 | 1 | 231 | 7 | 66 | 71 | 90 | -37 |
| Crawford,Rashad | 17 | L | 24 | CF | aa | NYY | 376 | 5 | 15 | 194 | 6 | 72 | 56 | 143 | -8 |
| | 18 | L | 25 | CF | a/a | NYY | 202 | 2 | 7 | 200 | 7 | 69 | 54 | 93 | -38 |
| Cribbs,Galli | 17 | L | 25 | SS | aa | ARI | 88 | 0 | 2 | 155 | 8 | 51 | 42 | 122 | -106 |
| | 18 | L | 26 | SS | aa | ARI | 308 | 2 | 5 | 178 | 7 | 58 | 69 | 124 | -58 |
| Cron,Kevin | 17 | R | 24 | 1B | aa | ARI | 515 | 21 | 1 | 259 | 8 | 71 | 122 | 35 | 10 |
| | 18 | R | 25 | 3B | aaa | ARI | 392 | 12 | 1 | 235 | 5 | 69 | 108 | 39 | -13 |
| Cronenworth,Jake | 17 | L | 23 | SS | aa | TAM | 158 | 1 | 1 | 255 | 10 | 86 | 31 | 31 | 0 |
| | 18 | L | 24 | SS | a/a | TAM | 443 | 3 | 18 | 219 | 8 | 80 | 49 | 140 | 19 |
| Cronin,Joe | 18 | R | 24 | 2B | aa | MIN | 26 | 0 | 0 | 100 | 10 | 54 | 0 | 42 | -147 |
| Crook,Narciso | 18 | R | 23 | LF | aa | CIN | 161 | 2 | 3 | 261 | 9 | 71 | 54 | 87 | -27 |
| Cruzado,Victor | 17 | B | 25 | CF | aaa | NYM | 301 | 5 | 2 | 204 | 9 | 69 | 59 | 47 | -44 |
| Cuevas,Noel | 17 | R | 26 | RF | aaa | COL | 493 | 11 | 11 | 275 | 3 | 78 | 74 | 124 | 16 |
| | 18 | R | 27 | RF | aaa | COL | 160 | 3 | 2 | 273 | 6 | 84 | 85 | 80 | 40 |
| Culver,Cito | 17 | R | 25 | SS | aaa | NYY | 349 | 12 | 1 | 199 | 7 | 63 | 112 | 62 | -22 |
| | 18 | R | 26 | SS | a/a | MIA | 220 | 3 | 0 | 185 | 8 | 57 | 52 | 47 | -100 |
| Cumberland,Brett | 18 | S | 23 | C | aa | BAL | 60 | 2 | 0 | 145 | 6 | 70 | 66 | 25 | -47 |
| Curcio,Keith | 17 | L | 25 | RF | aa | ATL | 401 | 3 | 9 | 188 | 9 | 80 | 37 | 106 | 2 |
| Curletta,Joey | 18 | R | 24 | 1B | aa | SEA | 465 | 19 | 1 | 242 | 12 | 66 | 113 | 28 | -8 |
| Dahl,David | 17 | L | 23 | LF | aaa | COL | 70 | 2 | 1 | 229 | 3 | 76 | 77 | 118 | 8 |
| | 18 | L | 24 | CF | aaa | COL | 77 | 1 | 1 | 246 | 1 | 74 | 100 | 33 | -12 |
| Dalbec,Bobby | 18 | R | 23 | 3B | aa | BOS | 111 | 4 | 0 | 240 | 4 | 56 | 176 | 56 | -9 |
| Daniel,Andrew | 17 | R | 24 | 2B | aa | ATL | 190 | 2 | 8 | 178 | 11 | 69 | 51 | 105 | -29 |
| Darvill,Wesley | 18 | L | 27 | 3B | a/a | LA | 158 | 1 | 0 | 153 | 5 | 69 | 39 | 54 | -66 |
| Davidson,Austin | 18 | L | 25 | LF | aa | WAS | 267 | 8 | 1 | 247 | 9 | 80 | 95 | 61 | 35 |
| Davis,Dylan | 17 | R | 24 | LF | aa | SF | 327 | 7 | 0 | 194 | 7 | 68 | 81 | 24 | -39 |
| | 18 | R | 25 | LF | a/a | SF | 438 | 8 | 3 | 192 | 5 | 69 | 84 | 73 | -22 |
| Davis,J.D. | 17 | R | 24 | 3B | a/a | HOU | 412 | 19 | 4 | 234 | 7 | 68 | 119 | 46 | -3 |
| | 18 | R | 25 | 3B | aaa | HOU | 333 | 12 | 2 | 273 | 7 | 75 | 112 | 62 | 23 |
| Davis,Jaylin | 18 | R | 24 | RF | aa | MIN | 240 | 5 | 4 | 243 | 6 | 69 | 90 | 83 | -15 |
| Davis,Johnny | 17 | B | 27 | CF | aa | MIL | 505 | 5 | 47 | 236 | 6 | 72 | 44 | 149 | -19 |
| Davis,Jonathan | 17 | R | 25 | CF | aa | TOR | 446 | 9 | 16 | 223 | 11 | 72 | 74 | 108 | 3 |
| | 18 | R | 26 | CF | a/a | TOR | 490 | 8 | 21 | 248 | 7 | 78 | 79 | 141 | 33 |
| Davis,Mason | 18 | B | 25 | SS | aa | MIA | 119 | 0 | 3 | 163 | 5 | 76 | 52 | 145 | 2 |
| Dawson,Ronnie | 18 | L | 23 | CF | aa | HOU | 114 | 6 | 5 | 264 | 4 | 67 | 139 | 120 | 25 |
| Daza,Yonathan | 18 | R | 24 | CF | aa | COL | 219 | 3 | 3 | 289 | 2 | 89 | 86 | 82 | 55 |
| De Goti,Alex | 18 | R | 24 | SS | a/a | HOU | 452 | 10 | 5 | 238 | 5 | 79 | 79 | 68 | 12 |
| De la Calle,Daniel | 18 | R | 26 | DH | aa | TAM | 47 | 2 | 0 | 177 | 0 | 40 | 150 | 56 | -103 |
| De La Guerra,Chad | 17 | L | 25 | SS | aa | BOS | 196 | 3 | 2 | 246 | 8 | 73 | 90 | 57 | 0 |
| | 18 | L | 26 | 2B | a/a | BOS | 389 | 12 | 5 | 212 | 6 | 66 | 94 | 89 | -20 |
| De Leon,Michael | 17 | B | 20 | SS | aa | TEX | 394 | 2 | 3 | 218 | 4 | 88 | 36 | 53 | 6 |
| | 18 | B | 21 | SS | aa | TEX | 503 | 3 | 1 | 248 | 3 | 86 | 40 | 37 | -5 |
| de Oleo,Eduardo | 17 | R | 24 | C | aaa | HOU | 23 | 0 | 0 | 241 | 0 | 73 | 61 | -10 | -60 |
| | 18 | R | 25 | C | a/a | HOU | 137 | 2 | 0 | 210 | 3 | 66 | 60 | 37 | -71 |
| Dean,Austin | 17 | R | 24 | LF | aa | MIA | 234 | 4 | 3 | 257 | 5 | 77 | 80 | 103 | 17 |
| | 18 | R | 25 | LF | a/a | MIA | 397 | 9 | 2 | 292 | 8 | 83 | 73 | 77 | 31 |
| DeCarlo,Joe | 18 | R | 25 | C | aa | SEA | 207 | 6 | 0 | 206 | 8 | 69 | 113 | 47 | -3 |
| Decker,Jaff | 17 | L | 27 | CF | aaa | OAK | 351 | 4 | 11 | 221 | 7 | 69 | 49 | 79 | -44 |
| | 18 | L | 28 | RF | aaa | WAS | 135 | 2 | 2 | 201 | 12 | 56 | 108 | 59 | -44 |
| DeJong,Paul | 17 | R | 24 | SS | aaa | STL | 177 | 10 | 0 | 263 | 4 | 72 | 128 | 31 | 8 |
| Delmonico,Nick | 17 | L | 25 | 3B | aaa | CHW | 378 | 10 | 3 | 222 | 9 | 77 | 76 | 75 | 10 |
| | 18 | L | 26 | LF | a/a | CHW | 35 | 0 | 0 | 266 | 11 | 76 | 84 | 21 | 0 |
| DeLuzio,Ben | 18 | R | 24 | CF | aa | ARI | 263 | 1 | 27 | 229 | 7 | 69 | 58 | 158 | -14 |
| Demeritte,Travis | 17 | R | 23 | 2B | aa | ATL | 458 | 13 | 5 | 203 | 10 | 66 | 86 | 96 | -17 |
| | 18 | R | 24 | LF | aa | ATL | 428 | 15 | 5 | 204 | 10 | 64 | 123 | 108 | 9 |
| DeMuth,Dustin | 17 | L | 26 | 1B | aa | MIL | 377 | 10 | 6 | 224 | 9 | 64 | 96 | 71 | -24 |
| Devers,Rafael | 17 | L | 21 | 3B | a/a | BOS | 322 | 17 | 0 | 307 | 9 | 80 | 134 | 54 | 63 |
| | 18 | L | 22 | 3B | aaa | BOS | 21 | 1 | 0 | 330 | 4 | 71 | 162 | 23 | 29 |
| Dewees,Donnie | 17 | L | 24 | CF | aa | KC | 464 | 7 | 17 | 252 | 8 | 81 | 71 | 124 | 36 |
| | 18 | L | 25 | CF | a/a | KC | 507 | 6 | 12 | 228 | 5 | 80 | 64 | 119 | 18 |
| Diaz,Aledmys | 17 | R | 27 | SS | aaa | STL | 170 | 3 | 2 | 208 | 4 | 80 | 62 | 69 | -1 |
| Diaz,Cesar | 18 | B | 25 | LF | a/a | NYY | 32 | 1 | 2 | 246 | 11 | 74 | 69 | 75 | 0 |
| Diaz,Chris | 17 | R | 27 | SS | aa | MIA | 188 | 0 | 2 | 195 | 9 | 74 | 40 | 76 | -30 |
| | 18 | R | 28 | SS | a/a | MIA | 218 | 0 | 2 | 161 | 11 | 64 | 4 | 42 | -104 |
| Diaz,Edwin | 18 | R | 23 | 3B | aa | OAK | 103 | 1 | 1 | 141 | 6 | 66 | 59 | 33 | -64 |
| Diaz,Elias | 17 | R | 27 | C | aaa | PIT | 218 | 2 | 2 | 227 | 4 | 81 | 40 | 52 | -19 |
| Diaz,Francisco | 17 | B | 27 | C | a/a | NYY | 171 | 0 | 0 | 194 | 5 | 81 | 26 | 32 | -34 |
| | 18 | B | 28 | C | a/a | NYY | 161 | 1 | 0 | 241 | 10 | 72 | 39 | 45 | -46 |
| Diaz,Isan | 18 | L | 22 | 2B | a/a | MIA | 431 | 10 | 12 | 205 | 12 | 64 | 101 | 117 | -2 |
| Diaz,Yandy | 17 | R | 26 | 3B | aaa | CLE | 309 | 4 | 1 | 309 | 14 | 81 | 61 | 42 | 14 |
| | 18 | R | 27 | 3B | aaa | CLE | 348 | 2 | 1 | 249 | 13 | 74 | 66 | 33 | -12 |
| Diaz,Yusniel | 17 | R | 21 | RF | aa | LA | 108 | 3 | 2 | 309 | 7 | 70 | 104 | 49 | -5 |
| | 18 | R | 22 | RF | aa | BAL | 354 | 9 | 9 | 253 | 11 | 80 | 75 | 87 | 30 |
| Dickson,O Koyea | 17 | R | 27 | LF | aaa | LA | 403 | 18 | 3 | 199 | 7 | 70 | 114 | 68 | 9 |
| Didder,Ray-Patrick | 18 | R | 24 | SS | aa | ATL | 131 | 1 | 8 | 253 | 9 | 69 | 64 | 128 | -14 |
| Dini,Nick | 17 | R | 24 | C | aa | KC | 216 | 2 | 7 | 286 | 6 | 87 | 40 | 65 | 14 |
| | 18 | R | 25 | C | a/a | KC | 319 | 8 | 5 | 217 | 3 | 76 | 74 | 81 | -5 |
| Dixon,Brandon | 17 | R | 25 | 3B | aaa | CIN | 440 | 14 | 14 | 228 | 6 | 66 | 116 | 95 | 0 |
| | 18 | R | 26 | 2B | aaa | CIN | 179 | 5 | 7 | 295 | 5 | 63 | 151 | 109 | 18 |
| Dobson,Dillon | 18 | L | 25 | 1B | aa | SF | 180 | 4 | 2 | 145 | 10 | 59 | 83 | 59 | -59 |

| BATTER | yr | b | age | pos | lvl | org | ab | hr | sb | ba | bb% | ct% | px | sx | bpv |
|---|---|---|---|---|---|---|---|---|---|---|---|---|---|---|---|
| Dosch,Drew | 18 | L | 26 | 3B | aaa | BAL | 355 | 6 | 1 | 236 | 7 | 64 | 90 | 46 | -42 |
| Downes,Brandon | 18 | R | 26 | CF | aa | ATL | 168 | 3 | 3 | 167 | 8 | 53 | 82 | 111 | -71 |
| Dozier,Hunter | 17 | R | 26 | 3B | a/a | KC | 100 | 3 | 1 | 200 | 9 | 49 | 160 | 98 | -26 |
| | 18 | R | 27 | 3B | aaa | KC | 118 | 1 | 1 | 212 | 13 | 58 | 73 | 52 | -68 |
| Drake,Blake | 17 | R | 24 | RF | aa | STL | 41 | 2 | 1 | 196 | 9 | 82 | 71 | 43 | 17 |
| | 18 | R | 25 | RF | aa | STL | 289 | 4 | 4 | 193 | 5 | 70 | 74 | 56 | -32 |
| Drury,Brandon | 18 | R | 26 | 3B | a/a | NYY | 218 | 6 | 2 | 246 | 12 | 62 | 102 | 66 | -22 |
| Dubon,Mauricio | 17 | R | 23 | SS | a/a | MIL | 492 | 8 | 31 | 247 | 6 | 83 | 61 | 100 | 23 |
| | 18 | R | 24 | SS | aaa | MIL | 108 | 3 | 4 | 283 | 1 | 79 | 109 | 119 | 43 |
| Duenez,Samir | 17 | L | 21 | 1B | aa | KC | 523 | 14 | 9 | 243 | 6 | 77 | 79 | 86 | 12 |
| | 18 | L | 22 | 1B | aa | KC | 287 | 8 | 4 | 264 | 9 | 75 | 103 | 92 | 31 |
| Dugan,Kelly | 17 | L | 27 | RF | aa | ARI | 313 | 10 | 3 | 221 | 7 | 69 | 111 | 81 | 6 |
| Duggar,Steven | 17 | L | 24 | CF | aaa | SF | 46 | 1 | 2 | 224 | 13 | 70 | 63 | 69 | -22 |
| | 18 | L | 25 | CF | aaa | SF | 316 | 2 | 8 | 222 | 8 | 62 | 100 | 119 | -20 |
| Dunand,Joe | 18 | R | 23 | SS | aa | MIA | 217 | 6 | 0 | 183 | 6 | 63 | 100 | 38 | -43 |
| Dykstra,Luke | 18 | R | 23 | 2B | aa | STL | 151 | 0 | 0 | 193 | 3 | 82 | 23 | 37 | -34 |
| Eaves,Kody | 17 | L | 24 | 3B | a/a | DET | 332 | 11 | 6 | 245 | 8 | 74 | 102 | 103 | 26 |
| | 18 | L | 25 | 3B | a/a | DET | 329 | 3 | 3 | 173 | 9 | 71 | 64 | 86 | -20 |
| Edman,Tommy | 17 | S | 22 | SS | aa | STL | 219 | 2 | 4 | 232 | 6 | 84 | 55 | 84 | 19 |
| | 18 | S | 23 | SS | a/a | STL | 518 | 5 | 23 | 263 | 6 | 81 | 50 | 119 | 15 |
| Elizalde,Sebastian | 17 | L | 26 | RF | aaa | CIN | 506 | 7 | 3 | 234 | 5 | 83 | 43 | 57 | -4 |
| | 18 | L | 27 | RF | aaa | CIN | 71 | 2 | 2 | 209 | 4 | 84 | 87 | 83 | 42 |
| Ely,Andrew | 17 | L | 24 | SS | aa | CHC | 282 | 3 | 1 | 234 | 12 | 76 | 57 | 61 | -5 |
| | 18 | L | 25 | SS | aa | NYM | 179 | 1 | 0 | 131 | 13 | 68 | 36 | 71 | -51 |
| Engel,Adam | 17 | R | 26 | CF | aaa | CHW | 165 | 6 | 3 | 182 | 8 | 62 | 139 | 94 | 7 |
| English,Tanner | 17 | R | 24 | CF | aa | MIN | 62 | 0 | 5 | 121 | 10 | 56 | 50 | 196 | -55 |
| | 18 | R | 25 | CF | aa | MIN | 299 | 3 | 10 | 191 | 5 | 64 | 85 | 144 | -21 |
| Erceg,Lucas | 18 | L | 23 | 3B | aa | MIL | 463 | 13 | 3 | 236 | 7 | 80 | 78 | 58 | 17 |
| Ervin,Phillip | 17 | R | 25 | LF | aaa | CIN | 363 | 6 | 18 | 221 | 8 | 73 | 70 | 103 | -5 |
| | 18 | R | 26 | LF | aaa | CIN | 173 | 4 | 8 | 245 | 8 | 73 | 107 | 120 | 31 |
| Escalera,Alfredo | 17 | R | 22 | LF | aa | KC | 456 | 6 | 13 | 250 | 4 | 74 | 55 | 100 | -20 |
| | 18 | R | 23 | RF | aa | KC | 129 | 3 | 3 | 217 | 6 | 67 | 78 | 87 | -30 |
| Escobar,Elvis | 17 | L | 23 | CF | aa | PIT | 383 | 3 | 4 | 260 | 6 | 81 | 42 | 82 | -4 |
| | 18 | L | 24 | RF | aa | PIT | 106 | 0 | 2 | 135 | 2 | 79 | 19 | 122 | -27 |
| Espinal,Edwin | 17 | R | 23 | 1B | a/a | PIT | 497 | 13 | 1 | 273 | 4 | 85 | 77 | 31 | 21 |
| | 18 | R | 24 | 1B | aaa | DET | 335 | 5 | 0 | 219 | 9 | 79 | 41 | 24 | -23 |
| Espinal,Santiago | 18 | R | 24 | 2B | aa | TOR | 147 | 1 | 2 | 261 | 7 | 83 | 64 | 84 | 27 |
| Esposito,Nathan | 18 | R | 25 | C | aa | KC | 45 | 0 | 1 | 136 | 3 | 63 | 44 | 87 | -77 |
| Estrada,Thairo | 17 | R | 21 | SS | aa | NYY | 495 | 7 | 8 | 294 | 6 | 88 | 48 | 80 | 28 |
| | 18 | R | 22 | SS | aaa | NYY | 33 | 0 | 0 | 135 | 0 | 73 | 23 | 14 | -82 |
| Evans,Phillip | 17 | R | 25 | 3B | aaa | NYM | 466 | 8 | 1 | 217 | 6 | 79 | 62 | 46 | -8 |
| | 18 | R | 26 | 3B | aaa | NYM | 219 | 8 | 2 | 188 | 6 | 76 | 84 | 61 | 2 |
| Ewing,Skyler | 18 | R | 26 | 1B | aa | MIA | 44 | 1 | 0 | 127 | 5 | 46 | 137 | 23 | -88 |
| Farmer,Kyle | 17 | R | 27 | C | a/a | LA | 347 | 8 | 1 | 259 | 6 | 82 | 75 | 40 | 15 |
| | 18 | R | 28 | 3B | aaa | LA | 288 | 5 | 1 | 225 | 4 | 78 | 84 | 50 | 3 |
| Feliz,Anderson | 17 | B | 25 | LF | a/a | PIT | 309 | 4 | 10 | 205 | 9 | 69 | 71 | 106 | -14 |
| | 18 | B | 26 | 3B | a/a | BAL | 438 | 8 | 15 | 231 | 7 | 70 | 67 | 104 | -22 |
| Ferguson,Andrew | 17 | R | 25 | CF | a/a | HOU | 415 | 7 | 13 | 223 | 9 | 71 | 69 | 78 | -19 |
| | 18 | R | 26 | CF | aaa | HOU | 233 | 3 | 4 | 235 | 11 | 68 | 63 | 87 | -28 |
| Fernandez,Jose Migu | 17 | L | 29 | 2B | a/a | LA | 343 | 12 | 0 | 239 | 5 | 87 | 74 | 25 | 26 |
| | 18 | L | 30 | 2B | aaa | LAA | 357 | 10 | 1 | 230 | 5 | 87 | 64 | 45 | 24 |
| Fernandez,Xavier | 18 | R | 23 | C | aa | KC | 119 | 2 | 2 | 304 | 6 | 85 | 91 | 106 | 58 |
| Ficociello,Dominic | 17 | B | 25 | 1B | a/a | DET | 445 | 8 | 10 | 253 | 9 | 70 | 78 | 94 | -8 |
| | 18 | B | 26 | 1B | aa | DET | 366 | 6 | 7 | 227 | 8 | 64 | 72 | 74 | -46 |
| Field,Johnny | 17 | R | 25 | CF | aaa | TAM | 445 | 10 | 11 | 227 | 5 | 74 | 94 | 92 | 10 |
| | 18 | R | 26 | LF | aaa | MIN | 89 | 1 | 2 | 231 | 8 | 77 | 66 | 73 | 2 |
| Fields,Roemon | 17 | L | 27 | CF | a/a | TOR | 406 | 0 | 42 | 248 | 7 | 78 | 35 | 152 | 2 |
| | 18 | L | 28 | CF | aaa | TOR | 328 | 2 | 20 | 200 | 7 | 71 | 41 | 118 | -34 |
| Filia,Eric | 18 | L | 26 | RF | aa | SEA | 296 | 2 | 1 | 224 | 10 | 87 | 38 | 54 | 19 |
| Fisher,Derek | 17 | L | 24 | CF | aaa | HOU | 343 | 14 | 11 | 254 | 6 | 73 | 116 | 78 | 23 |
| | 18 | L | 25 | CF | aaa | HOU | 239 | 7 | 7 | 196 | 10 | 58 | 106 | 101 | -33 |
| Fisher,Jameson | 18 | L | 25 | LF | aa | CHW | 315 | 6 | 3 | 192 | 11 | 58 | 77 | 62 | -63 |
| Fleming,Billy | 17 | R | 25 | 2B | a/a | NYY | 315 | 10 | 4 | 232 | 5 | 85 | 78 | 85 | 40 |
| | 18 | R | 26 | 2B | a/a | NYY | 259 | 6 | 2 | 245 | 6 | 75 | 88 | 56 | 2 |
| Fletcher,David | 17 | R | 23 | 2B | a/a | LAA | 448 | 2 | 16 | 230 | 5 | 86 | 37 | 102 | 14 |
| | 18 | R | 24 | SS | aaa | LAA | 254 | 4 | 4 | 273 | 4 | 90 | 82 | 110 | 67 |
| Flete,Bryant | 18 | L | 25 | 3B | a/a | CHW | 284 | 2 | 3 | 216 | 10 | 68 | 51 | 73 | -45 |
| Flores,Jecksson | 18 | R | 25 | 2B | aa | KC | 459 | 5 | 21 | 278 | 5 | 83 | 72 | 118 | 35 |
| Flores,Ramon | 17 | L | 25 | RF | aaa | LAA | 413 | 7 | 8 | 247 | 10 | 79 | 60 | 91 | 13 |
| | 18 | L | 26 | LF | aaa | BOS | 195 | 2 | 2 | 196 | 9 | 76 | 53 | 52 | -19 |
| Flores,Rudy | 17 | L | 27 | LF | a/a | ARI | 356 | 8 | 1 | 224 | 4 | 64 | 107 | 58 | -32 |
| | 18 | L | 28 | 1B | aa | ARI | 438 | 11 | 1 | 223 | 9 | 65 | 100 | 57 | -24 |
| Fontana,Nolan | 17 | L | 26 | SS | aaa | LAA | 361 | 6 | 9 | 208 | 12 | 66 | 90 | 114 | -4 |
| | 18 | L | 27 | SS | aaa | LAA | 145 | 2 | 2 | 166 | 13 | 67 | 83 | 95 | -10 |
| Ford,Mike | 17 | L | 25 | 1B | a/a | NYY | 429 | 21 | 1 | 246 | 16 | 81 | 105 | 44 | 54 |
| | 18 | L | 26 | 1B | aaa | NYY | 367 | 14 | 1 | 215 | 7 | 77 | 95 | 35 | 12 |
| Fowler,Dustin | 17 | L | 23 | CF | aaa | NYY | 297 | 14 | 12 | 273 | 4 | 76 | 129 | 143 | 62 |
| | 18 | L | 24 | CF | aaa | OAK | 229 | 3 | 10 | 302 | 3 | 80 | 94 | 147 | 47 |
| Fox,Lucius | 18 | B | 21 | SS | aa | TAM | 104 | 1 | 5 | 201 | 6 | 78 | 40 | 123 | -3 |
| France,Ty | 17 | R | 23 | 3B | aa | SD | 363 | 4 | 1 | 259 | 5 | 80 | 60 | 53 | -4 |
| | 18 | R | 24 | 3B | a/a | SD | 509 | 16 | 2 | 223 | 6 | 80 | 88 | 58 | 21 |
| Franco,Carlos | 17 | L | 26 | 1B | a/a | ATL | 461 | 17 | 1 | 204 | 9 | 62 | 87 | 33 | -55 |
| | 18 | L | 27 | 1B | aaa | ATL | 437 | 12 | 1 | 206 | 6 | 58 | 105 | 41 | -56 |
| Franco,J.J. | 18 | R | 26 | 2B | aa | NYM | 50 | 0 | 0 | 94 | 14 | 59 | 36 | 42 | -91 |
| Frazier,Adam | 18 | L | 27 | 2B | aaa | PIT | 121 | 0 | 1 | 182 | 6 | 81 | 38 | 76 | -9 |
| Frazier,Clint | 17 | R | 23 | LF | aaa | NYY | 273 | 13 | 8 | 239 | 11 | 72 | 129 | 100 | 44 |
| | 18 | R | 24 | CF | aaa | NYY | 190 | 10 | 3 | 276 | 9 | 68 | 155 | 107 | 50 |

| BATTER | yr | b | age | pos | lvl | org | ab | hr | sb | ba | bb% | ct% | px | sx | bpv |
|---|---|---|---|---|---|---|---|---|---|---|---|---|---|---|---|
| Freeman,Ronnie | 18 | R | 27 | C | a/a | SF | 232 | 2 | 0 | 204 | 5 | 74 | 37 | 27 | -53 |
| Friedl Jr.,T.J. | 18 | L | 23 | LF | aa | CIN | 261 | 2 | 16 | 251 | 9 | 76 | 49 | 137 | 2 |
| Fuentes,Josh | 17 | R | 24 | 3B | aa | COL | 414 | 13 | 6 | 299 | 4 | 78 | 115 | 97 | 43 |
| | 18 | R | 25 | 3B | aaa | COL | 551 | 10 | 2 | 281 | 2 | 80 | 91 | 88 | 24 |
| Fuentes,Reymond | 17 | L | 26 | CF | aaa | ARI | 175 | 0 | 8 | 278 | 4 | 79 | 54 | 134 | 10 |
| | 18 | L | 27 | CF | aaa | ARI | 302 | 3 | 6 | 193 | 6 | 74 | 50 | 105 | -20 |
| Gaffney,Tyler | 18 | R | 27 | RF | aa | PIT | 124 | 2 | 3 | 159 | 7 | 75 | 51 | 96 | -15 |
| Gallagher,Cameron | 17 | R | 25 | C | aaa | KC | 260 | 4 | 0 | 254 | 5 | 86 | 52 | 21 | 3 |
| | 18 | R | 26 | C | aaa | KC | 268 | 3 | 1 | 224 | 7 | 84 | 49 | 34 | 0 |
| Galloway,Isaac | 17 | R | 28 | CF | a/a | MIA | 117 | 5 | 8 | 264 | 8 | 68 | 108 | 79 | 2 |
| | 18 | R | 29 | RF | aaa | MIA | 324 | 6 | 15 | 199 | 5 | 70 | 83 | 146 | 1 |
| Gamache,Dan | 17 | L | 27 | 1B | aa | WAS | 385 | 4 | 0 | 205 | 7 | 71 | 61 | 42 | -37 |
| | 18 | L | 28 | 2B | aa | WAS | 413 | 4 | 1 | 222 | 9 | 68 | 59 | 32 | -51 |
| Garay,Carlos | 18 | R | 24 | C | a/a | TEX | 218 | 2 | 0 | 270 | 3 | 88 | 47 | 27 | 5 |
| Garcia,Alejandro | 17 | R | 26 | LF | a/a | HOU | 323 | 3 | 4 | 187 | 2 | 83 | 50 | 90 | 3 |
| | 18 | R | 27 | RF | aaa | HOU | 129 | 1 | 0 | 167 | 3 | 88 | 18 | 61 | -6 |
| Garcia,Anthony | 17 | R | 25 | LF | a/a | STL | 386 | 12 | 7 | 246 | 8 | 78 | 85 | 81 | 21 |
| | 18 | R | 26 | DH | aaa | OAK | 480 | 18 | 1 | 209 | 9 | 74 | 108 | 45 | 17 |
| Garcia,Aramis | 17 | R | 24 | C | aa | SF | 78 | 0 | 0 | 257 | 10 | 70 | 128 | 34 | 12 |
| | 18 | R | 25 | C | a/a | SF | 339 | 7 | 0 | 192 | 5 | 70 | 71 | 50 | -37 |
| Garcia,Jose Adolis | 17 | R | 24 | RF | a/a | STL | 445 | 12 | 12 | 258 | 6 | 74 | 103 | 88 | 17 |
| | 18 | R | 25 | RF | aaa | STL | 406 | 16 | 7 | 213 | 2 | 72 | 114 | 110 | 20 |
| Garcia,Rene | 17 | R | 27 | C | a/a | MIL | 166 | 4 | 1 | 281 | 4 | 86 | 57 | 25 | 5 |
| Garlick,Kyle | 17 | R | 25 | LF | aa | LA | 268 | 14 | 1 | 205 | 8 | 66 | 117 | 48 | -11 |
| | 18 | R | 26 | RF | a/a | LA | 402 | 16 | 1 | 209 | 3 | 58 | 133 | 68 | -32 |
| Garver,Mitch | 17 | R | 26 | C | aaa | MIN | 320 | 15 | 2 | 263 | 12 | 71 | 148 | 51 | 44 |
| Gatewood,Jacob | 17 | R | 22 | 3B | aa | MIL | 92 | 5 | 3 | 243 | 8 | 66 | 144 | 106 | 30 |
| | 18 | R | 23 | 1B | aa | MIL | 352 | 19 | 2 | 234 | 7 | 64 | 154 | 60 | 14 |
| George,Jordan | 17 | B | 25 | DH | aa | PIT | 106 | 1 | 1 | 270 | 6 | 88 | 65 | 50 | 32 |
| | 18 | B | 26 | DH | aa | PIT | 342 | 4 | 0 | 223 | 9 | 84 | 39 | 31 | -3 |
| Gerber,Mike | 17 | L | 25 | CF | a/a | DET | 367 | 12 | 8 | 262 | 9 | 72 | 104 | 99 | 21 |
| | 18 | L | 26 | CF | aaa | DET | 287 | 11 | 2 | 186 | 6 | 60 | 127 | 79 | -21 |
| Gettys,Michael | 18 | R | 23 | CF | aa | SD | 430 | 12 | 14 | 204 | 6 | 58 | 114 | 110 | -30 |
| Ghelfi,Mitch | 18 | B | 26 | C | aa | LAA | 131 | 2 | 3 | 210 | 5 | 77 | 59 | 82 | -8 |
| Giambrone,Trent | 18 | R | 25 | 2B | aa | CHC | 398 | 14 | 21 | 218 | 9 | 74 | 97 | 109 | 28 |
| Giardina,Sal | 17 | B | 25 | C | a/a | ATL | 116 | 1 | 1 | 223 | 9 | 67 | 34 | 54 | -68 |
| | 18 | B | 26 | C | a/a | ATL | 128 | 1 | 1 | 202 | 5 | 63 | 41 | 34 | -94 |
| Gibbons,Zach | 17 | R | 24 | LF | aa | LAA | 301 | 3 | 6 | 214 | 7 | 82 | 54 | 68 | 7 |
| | 18 | R | 25 | LF | aa | LAA | 395 | 3 | 5 | 222 | 8 | 82 | 53 | 91 | 17 |
| Gibson,Cam | 18 | L | 24 | LF | aa | DET | 152 | 3 | 5 | 223 | 9 | 70 | 87 | 129 | 7 |
| Gillaspie,Casey | 17 | B | 24 | 1B | aaa | CHW | 458 | 12 | 1 | 192 | 8 | 74 | 76 | 53 | -7 |
| | 18 | B | 25 | 1B | aaa | CHW | 255 | 3 | 0 | 184 | 7 | 58 | 88 | 17 | -78 |
| Gimenez,Andres | 18 | L | 20 | SS | aa | NYM | 137 | 0 | 9 | 250 | 5 | 82 | 52 | 120 | 20 |
| Giron,Ruddy | 18 | R | 21 | SS | aa | SD | 26 | 1 | 0 | 211 | 3 | 62 | 135 | 50 | -20 |
| Gittens,Chris | 18 | R | 24 | 1B | aa | NYY | 183 | 6 | 0 | 176 | 11 | 60 | 103 | 26 | -47 |
| Glenn,Alex | 17 | L | 26 | LF | aa | MIA | 201 | 3 | 2 | 155 | 7 | 59 | 70 | 90 | -64 |
| Godoy,Jose | 18 | L | 24 | C | aa | STL | 31 | 0 | 0 | 190 | 4 | 89 | 20 | 28 | -8 |
| Goeddel,Tyler | 17 | R | 25 | LF | a/a | CIN | 405 | 6 | 14 | 234 | 10 | 75 | 70 | 99 | 11 |
| | 18 | R | 26 | LF | a/a | LA | 237 | 3 | 3 | 175 | 6 | 72 | 51 | 95 | -27 |
| Goetzman,Granden | 17 | R | 25 | LF | a/a | TAM | 159 | 3 | 9 | 229 | 5 | 71 | 83 | 156 | 7 |
| | 18 | R | 26 | RF | aa | STL | 172 | 2 | 2 | 197 | 3 | 74 | 82 | 108 | 0 |
| Goldstein,Jason | 18 | R | 24 | C | a/a | OAK | 55 | 1 | 0 | 138 | 5 | 62 | 58 | 40 | -81 |
| Gomez,Miguel | 17 | B | 25 | 2B | aa | SF | 308 | 6 | 0 | 273 | 3 | 87 | 70 | 60 | 29 |
| | 18 | B | 26 | 2B | a/a | SF | 423 | 4 | 1 | 241 | 2 | 82 | 62 | 61 | 2 |
| Gonzalez,Alfredo | 17 | R | 25 | C | aa | CHW | 216 | 4 | 4 | 189 | 11 | 78 | 50 | 63 | -5 |
| | 18 | R | 26 | C | a/a | CHW | 213 | 2 | 2 | 206 | 7 | 64 | 47 | 47 | -75 |
| Gonzalez,Benji | 17 | B | 27 | SS | aaa | WAS | 291 | 0 | 2 | 195 | 7 | 82 | 25 | 55 | -20 |
| | 18 | B | 28 | SS | aaa | WAS | 312 | 2 | 7 | 198 | 7 | 74 | 49 | 85 | -24 |
| Gonzalez,Erik | 17 | R | 26 | SS | aaa | CLE | 160 | 5 | 4 | 224 | 3 | 65 | 86 | 113 | -27 |
| Gonzalez,Jay | 17 | L | 26 | RF | aa | BAL | 134 | 0 | 10 | 225 | 14 | 69 | 39 | 132 | -22 |
| | 18 | L | 27 | RF | aa | ARI | 181 | 0 | 5 | 235 | 8 | 67 | 41 | 79 | -56 |
| Gonzalez,Luis | 18 | R | 24 | SS | aa | CIN | 391 | 3 | 4 | 216 | 4 | 79 | 43 | 74 | -18 |
| Gonzalez,Miguel | 17 | R | 27 | C | a/a | DET | 164 | 3 | 2 | 184 | 5 | 75 | 38 | 45 | -45 |
| Goodrum,Niko | 17 | B | 25 | RF | aaa | MIN | 461 | 12 | 10 | 246 | 5 | 72 | 92 | 117 | 11 |
| Goodwin,Brian | 17 | L | 27 | RF | aaa | WAS | 90 | 1 | 2 | 210 | 8 | 61 | 68 | 46 | -69 |
| | 18 | L | 28 | LF | a/a | KC | 55 | 2 | 1 | 176 | 8 | 70 | 121 | 69 | 16 |
| Gordon,Nick | 17 | L | 22 | SS | aa | MIN | 519 | 8 | 12 | 262 | 8 | 74 | 83 | 123 | 18 |
| | 18 | L | 23 | SS | a/a | MIN | 544 | 6 | 17 | 230 | 5 | 79 | 58 | 122 | 10 |
| Gore,Jordan | 18 | S | 24 | SS | aa | MIN | 136 | 1 | 1 | 222 | 8 | 77 | 63 | 113 | 9 |
| Gore,Terrance | 17 | R | 26 | LF | a/a | KC | 225 | 1 | 17 | 216 | 6 | 74 | 29 | 161 | -17 |
| | 18 | R | 27 | LF | aaa | CHC | 176 | 0 | 14 | 152 | 7 | 66 | 17 | 163 | -55 |
| Goris,Diego | 17 | R | 27 | SS | aaa | SD | 439 | 7 | 3 | 217 | 4 | 75 | 58 | 55 | -30 |
| | 18 | R | 28 | 3B | aaa | SD | 325 | 4 | 2 | 195 | 3 | 69 | 67 | 64 | -42 |
| Gotta,Cade | 17 | R | 26 | RF | a/a | TAM | 431 | 4 | 33 | 236 | 9 | 77 | 54 | 121 | 6 |
| | 18 | R | 27 | LF | aa | MIA | 142 | 1 | 14 | 205 | 10 | 73 | 63 | 173 | 16 |
| Granite,Zach | 17 | L | 25 | CF | aaa | MIN | 284 | 5 | 14 | 315 | 7 | 87 | 68 | 122 | 56 |
| Granite,Zack | 18 | L | 26 | CF | aaa | MIN | 237 | 0 | 8 | 188 | 7 | 87 | 23 | 85 | 8 |
| Graterol,Juan | 18 | R | 29 | C | aaa | MIN | 206 | 0 | 0 | 252 | 2 | 92 | 32 | 32 | 11 |
| Grayson,Casey | 17 | L | 26 | 1B | aa | STL | 195 | 2 | 0 | 212 | 9 | 64 | 48 | 20 | -80 |
| Green,Zach | 17 | R | 23 | 1B | aa | PHI | 45 | 1 | 0 | 196 | 5 | 49 | 95 | 10 | -113 |
| | 18 | R | 24 | 3B | a/a | PHI | 402 | 18 | 1 | 243 | 7 | 62 | 165 | 64 | 14 |
| Gregor,Conrad | 18 | L | 26 | DH | aa | BOS | 35 | 1 | 0 | 46 | 11 | 62 | 37 | 9 | -98 |
| Greiner,Grayson | 17 | R | 25 | C | a/a | DET | 342 | 12 | 0 | 207 | 9 | 76 | 97 | 28 | 9 |
| | 18 | R | 26 | C | aaa | DET | 158 | 3 | 0 | 233 | 10 | 70 | 83 | 32 | -21 |
| Grisham,Trent | 18 | L | 22 | RF | aa | MIL | 335 | 7 | 10 | 225 | 15 | 72 | 67 | 92 | 0 |
| Grullon,Deivy | 17 | R | 21 | C | aa | PHI | 83 | 4 | 0 | 210 | 5 | 75 | 94 | 24 | -8 |
| | 18 | R | 22 | C | aa | PHI | 326 | 18 | 0 | 244 | 4 | 71 | 127 | 17 | 3 |

| BATTER | yr | b | age | pos | lvl | org | ab | hr | sb | ba | bb% | ct% | px | sx | bpv |
|---|---|---|---|---|---|---|---|---|---|---|---|---|---|---|---|
| Guerra,Javier | 18 | L | 23 | SS | aaa | SD | 430 | 9 | 1 | 182 | 4 | 56 | 98 | 99 | -59 |
| Guerrero Jr.,Vladimir | 18 | R | 19 | 3B | a/a | TOR | 344 | 19 | 3 | 383 | 9 | 89 | 133 | 53 | 98 |
| Guerrero,Emilio | 17 | R | 25 | 1B | aa | TOR | 266 | 3 | 2 | 236 | 5 | 75 | 67 | 72 | -11 |
| Guerrero,Gabriel | 17 | R | 24 | CF | aa | CIN | 501 | 8 | 3 | 265 | 7 | 77 | 66 | 69 | -5 |
| | 18 | R | 25 | RF | a/a | CIN | 502 | 17 | 3 | 256 | 5 | 71 | 100 | 78 | -2 |
| Guillorme,Luis | 17 | L | 23 | 2B | aa | NYM | 481 | 1 | 4 | 262 | 14 | 87 | 31 | 52 | 17 |
| | 18 | L | 24 | SS | aaa | NYM | 247 | 2 | 1 | 236 | 8 | 81 | 54 | 63 | 2 |
| Guillotte,Andrew | 17 | R | 24 | LF | a/a | TOR | 236 | 3 | 7 | 233 | 8 | 75 | 45 | 103 | -13 |
| | 18 | R | 25 | LF | a/a | TOR | 342 | 2 | 8 | 220 | 9 | 76 | 51 | 85 | -8 |
| Gurriel,Lourdes | 17 | R | 24 | 2B | aa | TOR | 170 | 4 | 2 | 220 | 5 | 80 | 74 | 56 | 8 |
| | 18 | R | 25 | SS | a/a | TOR | 206 | 6 | 3 | 270 | 3 | 77 | 90 | 74 | 9 |
| Gushue,Taylor | 18 | B | 25 | C | a/a | WAS | 343 | 8 | 0 | 185 | 8 | 69 | 90 | 43 | -21 |
| Gutierrez,Kelvin | 18 | R | 24 | 3B | aa | KC | 472 | 8 | 16 | 247 | 6 | 75 | 63 | 128 | 3 |
| Guzman,Ronald | 17 | L | 23 | 1B | aaa | TEX | 470 | 9 | 3 | 264 | 7 | 80 | 64 | 76 | 12 |
| Haase,Eric | 17 | R | 25 | C | a/a | CLE | 339 | 22 | 3 | 232 | 10 | 64 | 169 | 90 | 41 |
| | 18 | R | 26 | C | aaa | CLE | 433 | 15 | 2 | 203 | 5 | 61 | 125 | 66 | -22 |
| Hager,Jake | 17 | R | 24 | 2B | aaa | TAM | 271 | 3 | 3 | 205 | 4 | 82 | 47 | 87 | 0 |
| | 18 | R | 25 | SS | a/a | MIL | 335 | 9 | 6 | 241 | 7 | 78 | 100 | 76 | 32 |
| Haggerty,Sam | 18 | B | 24 | 3B | a/a | CLE | 297 | 3 | 21 | 219 | 14 | 69 | 95 | 136 | 22 |
| Hall,Darick | 18 | L | 23 | 1B | aa | PHI | 295 | 13 | 1 | 194 | 5 | 69 | 102 | 54 | -16 |
| Hampson,Garrett | 18 | R | 24 | 2B | a/a | COL | 444 | 8 | 25 | 282 | 8 | 82 | 76 | 139 | 48 |
| Hankins,Todd | 17 | R | 27 | CF | a/a | CLE | 314 | 2 | 13 | 191 | 6 | 68 | 44 | 99 | -50 |
| | 18 | R | 28 | LF | a/a | CLE | 209 | 1 | 11 | 229 | 6 | 65 | 68 | 104 | -40 |
| Hannemann,Jacob | 17 | L | 26 | CF | a/a | CHC | 409 | 5 | 23 | 199 | 7 | 67 | 85 | 127 | -11 |
| | 18 | L | 27 | CF | aaa | CHC | 375 | 4 | 15 | 187 | 5 | 73 | 50 | 114 | -23 |
| Harrison,Monte | 18 | R | 23 | CF | aa | MIA | 521 | 15 | 24 | 209 | 7 | 53 | 109 | 133 | -44 |
| Harrison,Travis | 17 | R | 25 | LF | aa | MIN | 276 | 3 | 3 | 161 | 12 | 62 | 88 | 78 | -33 |
| Haseley,Adam | 18 | L | 22 | CF | aa | PHI | 136 | 5 | 0 | 282 | 9 | 84 | 74 | 32 | 23 |
| Hawkins,Courtney | 17 | R | 24 | LF | aa | CHW | 295 | 10 | 0 | 176 | 7 | 59 | 92 | 51 | -60 |
| | 18 | R | 25 | RF | aa | CIN | 25 | 0 | 0 | 103 | 6 | 53 | 43 | 14 | -134 |
| Hayes,Danny | 17 | L | 27 | 1B | aaa | CHW | 439 | 15 | 0 | 185 | 11 | 59 | 110 | 25 | -43 |
| Hayes,KeBryan | 18 | R | 21 | 3B | aa | PIT | 437 | 6 | 10 | 275 | 10 | 80 | 86 | 110 | 44 |
| Hays,Austin | 17 | R | 22 | CF | aa | BAL | 261 | 14 | 1 | 286 | 4 | 80 | 107 | 57 | 33 |
| | 18 | R | 23 | RF | aa | BAL | 273 | 10 | 4 | 209 | 3 | 77 | 89 | 83 | 11 |
| Heath,Nick | 18 | L | 25 | CF | aa | KC | 105 | 0 | 8 | 230 | 9 | 65 | 55 | 172 | -24 |
| Heathcott,Zachary | 17 | L | 27 | CF | a/a | SF | 416 | 9 | 9 | 222 | 9 | 68 | 85 | 95 | -13 |
| | 18 | L | 28 | 1B | aaa | OAK | 109 | 1 | 3 | 211 | 6 | 59 | 88 | 77 | -57 |
| Heidt,Gunnar | 17 | R | 25 | 3B | aa | TOR | 432 | 11 | 9 | 205 | 8 | 63 | 91 | 84 | -31 |
| | 18 | R | 26 | 1B | a/a | TOR | 347 | 5 | 6 | 210 | 7 | 66 | 86 | 80 | -27 |
| Heim,Jonah | 18 | B | 23 | C | aa | OAK | 137 | 1 | 0 | 157 | 5 | 83 | 28 | 42 | -22 |
| Heineman,Scott | 17 | R | 25 | LF | aa | TEX | 468 | 8 | 10 | 257 | 8 | 71 | 81 | 117 | 4 |
| | 18 | R | 26 | CF | a/a | TEX | 447 | 9 | 13 | 262 | 6 | 75 | 72 | 89 | -1 |
| Heineman,Tyler | 17 | B | 26 | C | aaa | MIL | 199 | 2 | 1 | 222 | 6 | 79 | 72 | 44 | 1 |
| | 18 | B | 27 | C | a/a | MIL | 243 | 3 | 3 | 202 | 10 | 82 | 49 | 49 | 4 |
| Hendrix,Jeff | 17 | L | 24 | CF | aa | NYY | 120 | 0 | 5 | 309 | 9 | 76 | 24 | 81 | -31 |
| | 18 | L | 25 | CF | aa | NYY | 308 | 1 | 7 | 168 | 11 | 57 | 31 | 74 | -101 |
| Hermosillo,Michael | 17 | R | 22 | CF | a/a | LAA | 393 | 7 | 25 | 229 | 9 | 71 | 71 | 117 | -6 |
| | 18 | R | 23 | CF | aaa | LAA | 273 | 8 | 6 | 209 | 6 | 63 | 101 | 102 | -24 |
| Hernandez,Elier | 17 | R | 23 | RF | aa | KC | 62 | 1 | 0 | 319 | 5 | 76 | 74 | 42 | -12 |
| | 18 | R | 24 | RF | a/a | KC | 484 | 2 | 8 | 256 | 4 | 76 | 63 | 74 | -14 |
| Hernandez,Jan | 18 | R | 23 | RF | aa | PHI | 350 | 12 | 5 | 228 | 6 | 60 | 108 | 84 | -35 |
| Hernandez,Oscar | 17 | R | 24 | C | aa | ARI | 233 | 7 | 0 | 180 | 6 | 72 | 83 | 21 | -25 |
| | 18 | R | 25 | C | aaa | BOS | 151 | 1 | 1 | 191 | 7 | 73 | 50 | 48 | -36 |
| Hernandez,Teoscar | 17 | R | 25 | RF | aaa | TOR | 400 | 17 | 15 | 252 | 10 | 71 | 136 | 125 | 53 |
| Herrera,Dilson | 17 | R | 23 | 2B | aaa | CIN | 239 | 6 | 2 | 238 | 5 | 71 | 75 | 60 | -27 |
| | 18 | R | 24 | 2B | aaa | CIN | 185 | 6 | 0 | 263 | 8 | 68 | 103 | 22 | -19 |
| Herrera,Rosell | 17 | B | 25 | LF | aaa | COL | 320 | 2 | 14 | 248 | 7 | 77 | 65 | 126 | 15 |
| | 18 | B | 26 | CF | aaa | KC | 126 | 3 | 4 | 236 | 6 | 80 | 120 | 134 | 71 |
| Herum,Marty | 17 | R | 26 | 3B | aa | ARI | 162 | 2 | 1 | 253 | 3 | 81 | 68 | 66 | 8 |
| | 18 | R | 27 | 3B | aa | ARI | 280 | 3 | 1 | 245 | 5 | 80 | 55 | 45 | -10 |
| Hicks,John | 17 | R | 28 | C | aaa | DET | 208 | 6 | 4 | 227 | 2 | 69 | 85 | 82 | -25 |
| Higashioka,Kyle | 17 | R | 27 | C | aaa | NYY | 53 | 2 | 0 | 226 | 6 | 84 | 94 | 11 | 28 |
| | 18 | R | 28 | C | aaa | NYY | 188 | 4 | 1 | 162 | 6 | 71 | 79 | 56 | -22 |
| Higgins,P.J. | 18 | R | 25 | C | aa | CHC | 145 | 1 | 1 | 204 | 7 | 79 | 38 | 62 | -21 |
| Hill,Logan | 17 | R | 24 | LF | aa | PIT | 79 | 2 | 0 | 254 | 14 | 71 | 84 | 26 | -10 |
| | 18 | R | 25 | LF | aa | PIT | 391 | 13 | 1 | 196 | 8 | 62 | 99 | 49 | -39 |
| Hilliard,Sam | 18 | L | 24 | RF | aa | COL | 435 | 8 | 18 | 247 | 7 | 64 | 89 | 105 | -25 |
| Hinojosa,C.J. | 17 | R | 23 | SS | aa | SF | 373 | 3 | 5 | 247 | 7 | 88 | 39 | 58 | 15 |
| | 18 | R | 24 | SS | aa | SF | 253 | 2 | 4 | 232 | 7 | 88 | 52 | 70 | 30 |
| Hinshaw,Chad | 17 | R | 27 | CF | aaa | MIA | 258 | 3 | 5 | 185 | 7 | 64 | 71 | 84 | -46 |
| Hissey,Ryan | 18 | L | 24 | C | aa | TOR | 110 | 2 | 0 | 155 | 4 | 72 | 48 | 41 | -51 |
| Hiura,Keston | 18 | R | 22 | 2B | aa | MIL | 279 | 6 | 10 | 264 | 7 | 78 | 92 | 105 | 34 |
| Hobson,K.C. | 17 | L | 27 | 1B | aa | SF | 203 | 8 | 1 | 207 | 7 | 67 | 87 | 67 | -26 |
| | 18 | L | 28 | DH | aa | SF | 50 | 2 | 0 | 172 | 10 | 43 | 178 | 38 | -51 |
| Hodges,Jesse | 18 | R | 24 | 3B | aa | CHC | 307 | 3 | 1 | 175 | 6 | 65 | 67 | 48 | -59 |
| Hoenecke,Paul | 17 | L | 27 | C | aa | LA | 173 | 6 | 1 | 180 | 3 | 69 | 101 | 27 | -28 |
| Holder,Kyle | 18 | L | 24 | SS | aa | NYY | 117 | 1 | 0 | 220 | 6 | 85 | 39 | 49 | 0 |
| Hood,Destin | 17 | R | 27 | LF | aaa | MIA | 219 | 10 | 4 | 209 | 10 | 62 | 118 | 79 | -10 |
| | 18 | R | 28 | RF | a/a | TEX | 378 | 11 | 3 | 180 | 5 | 62 | 92 | 73 | -45 |
| Hoskins,Rhys | 17 | R | 24 | 1B | aaa | PHI | 401 | 27 | 3 | 255 | 12 | 78 | 143 | 83 | 78 |
| Houchins,Zach | 17 | R | 25 | 3B | a/a | LAA | 488 | 11 | 5 | 214 | 6 | 79 | 77 | 74 | 14 |
| | 18 | R | 26 | 3B | a/a | LAA | 277 | 10 | 1 | 203 | 4 | 70 | 93 | 55 | -19 |
| Houle,Dustin | 17 | R | 24 | C | aa | MIL | 142 | 1 | 0 | 214 | 10 | 73 | 64 | 23 | -27 |
| | 18 | R | 25 | C | a/a | MIL | 70 | 1 | 1 | 191 | 12 | 71 | 53 | 43 | -33 |
| Howard,Ryan | 18 | R | 24 | SS | aa | SF | 422 | 3 | 8 | 244 | 7 | 85 | 69 | 89 | 40 |
| Hudson,Joe | 17 | R | 26 | C | aa | CIN | 217 | 1 | 0 | 158 | 12 | 73 | 63 | 16 | -29 |
| | 18 | R | 27 | C | a/a | LAA | 167 | 3 | 0 | 225 | 7 | 70 | 73 | 34 | -37 |
| Ibanez,Andy | 18 | R | 25 | 3B | aaa | TEX | 463 | 9 | 1 | 244 | 6 | 82 | 61 | 30 | 0 |
| Ice,Logan | 18 | S | 23 | C | aa | CLE | 48 | 0 | 0 | 235 | 8 | 59 | 103 | 95 | -34 |
| Jackson,Alex | 17 | R | 22 | C | aa | ATL | 110 | 5 | 0 | 232 | 9 | 67 | 90 | 19 | -36 |
| | 18 | R | 23 | C | a/a | ATL | 333 | 7 | 0 | 185 | 7 | 61 | 116 | 66 | -27 |
| Jackson,Bralin | 18 | R | 25 | RF | aa | PIT | 206 | 2 | 4 | 185 | 4 | 66 | 53 | 85 | -58 |
| Jackson,Drew | 17 | R | 24 | 2B | aa | LA | 111 | 1 | 6 | 203 | 7 | 71 | 53 | 137 | -17 |
| | 18 | R | 25 | 2B | aa | LA | 342 | 11 | 16 | 205 | 8 | 68 | 104 | 102 | 3 |
| Jackson,Jhalan | 17 | R | 24 | RF | aa | NYY | 86 | 3 | 1 | 283 | 13 | 64 | 124 | 70 | 6 |
| | 18 | R | 25 | RF | aa | NYY | 346 | 16 | 6 | 182 | 8 | 50 | 163 | 100 | -19 |
| Jagielo,Eric | 17 | L | 25 | 1B | a/a | CIN | 309 | 5 | 0 | 184 | 11 | 68 | 58 | 19 | -49 |
| | 18 | L | 26 | 1B | aa | MIA | 399 | 8 | 1 | 160 | 6 | 58 | 86 | 37 | -72 |
| James,Jared | 17 | L | 23 | LF | aa | ATL | 340 | 5 | 1 | 248 | 9 | 79 | 58 | 81 | 7 |
| James,Mac | 17 | R | 24 | DH | aa | TAM | 154 | 1 | 0 | 209 | 7 | 77 | 30 | 30 | -43 |
| | 18 | R | 25 | C | a/a | TAM | 167 | 0 | 1 | 161 | 10 | 81 | 12 | 40 | -33 |
| Jankowski,Travis | 17 | L | 26 | CF | aaa | SD | 139 | 0 | 5 | 208 | 7 | 76 | 27 | 93 | -29 |
| | 18 | L | 27 | CF | aaa | SD | 80 | 1 | 3 | 280 | 8 | 66 | 52 | 71 | -54 |
| Jansen,Danny | 17 | R | 22 | C | a/a | TOR | 246 | 5 | 1 | 295 | 11 | 89 | 88 | 60 | 67 |
| | 18 | R | 23 | C | aaa | TOR | 298 | 11 | 4 | 260 | 11 | 82 | 109 | 74 | 63 |
| Jebavy,Ronnie | 18 | R | 24 | CF | aa | SF | 238 | 3 | 8 | 148 | 9 | 66 | 51 | 127 | -37 |
| Jhang,Jin-De | 17 | L | 24 | C | aa | PIT | 273 | 2 | 1 | 211 | 5 | 91 | 37 | 66 | 24 |
| | 18 | L | 25 | C | aa | PIT | 122 | 1 | 0 | 279 | 7 | 87 | 52 | 19 | 11 |
| Jimenez,A.J. | 18 | R | 27 | C | aaa | TEX | 196 | 5 | 1 | 197 | 2 | 73 | 70 | 31 | -36 |
| Jimenez,Eloy | 17 | R | 21 | RF | aa | CHW | 68 | 3 | 1 | 346 | 7 | 74 | 131 | 51 | 33 |
| | 18 | R | 22 | LF | a/a | CHW | 416 | 21 | 0 | 315 | 7 | 81 | 128 | 50 | 59 |
| Joe,Connor | 17 | R | 25 | RF | aa | ATL | 294 | 4 | 2 | 187 | 12 | 76 | 50 | 72 | -8 |
| | 18 | R | 26 | 1B | a/a | LA | 364 | 12 | 2 | 243 | 10 | 70 | 116 | 69 | 17 |
| Johnson Jr.,Daniel | 18 | L | 23 | RF | aa | WAS | 356 | 5 | 17 | 240 | 5 | 72 | 79 | 146 | 8 |
| Johnson,Micah | 17 | L | 27 | CF | aaa | ATL | 135 | 1 | 5 | 228 | 10 | 64 | 48 | 119 | -49 |
| | 18 | L | 28 | LF | aaa | TAM | 232 | 4 | 2 | 157 | 5 | 59 | 90 | 103 | -50 |
| Johnson,Sherman | 17 | L | 27 | 1B | a/a | LAA | 395 | 4 | 10 | 205 | 10 | 72 | 55 | 96 | -17 |
| | 18 | L | 28 | 3B | a/a | LAA | 215 | 3 | 2 | 186 | 8 | 62 | 80 | 112 | -37 |
| Jones,Hunter | 17 | R | 26 | CF | aa | CHW | 410 | 7 | 10 | 198 | 8 | 75 | 74 | 102 | 6 |
| | 18 | R | 27 | CF | aa | WAS | 386 | 4 | 10 | 252 | 8 | 77 | 50 | 102 | -4 |
| Jones,JaCoby | 17 | R | 25 | CF | aaa | DET | 351 | 8 | 11 | 220 | 8 | 67 | 88 | 119 | -7 |
| Jones,Jahmai | 18 | R | 21 | 2B | aa | LAA | 184 | 2 | 10 | 223 | 10 | 70 | 77 | 161 | 10 |
| Jones,Matt | 18 | R | 26 | C | aa | ARI | 132 | 2 | 0 | 207 | 7 | 54 | 73 | 29 | -100 |
| Jones,Mylz | 18 | R | 24 | 3B | aa | COL | 404 | 9 | 8 | 236 | 3 | 76 | 78 | 99 | 3 |
| Jones,Ryder | 17 | L | 23 | 3B | aaa | SF | 237 | 9 | 6 | 277 | 9 | 75 | 125 | 115 | 54 |
| | 18 | L | 24 | 3B | aaa | SF | 441 | 6 | 1 | 227 | 5 | 72 | 69 | 71 | -23 |
| Jones,Taylor | 18 | R | 25 | 1B | a/a | HOU | 452 | 14 | 2 | 232 | 9 | 67 | 113 | 54 | -3 |
| Joseph,Tommy | 18 | R | 27 | 1B | a/a | TEX | 345 | 16 | 0 | 237 | 6 | 72 | 124 | 18 | 8 |
| Juengel,Matt | 17 | R | 27 | 1B | aaa | MIA | 200 | 4 | 1 | 202 | 5 | 78 | 76 | 68 | 6 |
| Justus,Connor | 18 | R | 24 | SS | aa | LAA | 247 | 0 | 1 | 146 | 12 | 62 | 35 | 61 | -80 |
| Kaczmarski,Kevin | 17 | L | 26 | RF | aa | NYM | 452 | 5 | 14 | 238 | 12 | 77 | 50 | 99 | 4 |
| | 18 | L | 26 | CF | aaa | NYM | 160 | 0 | 2 | 223 | 6 | 65 | 45 | 76 | -67 |
| Kang,Jung-ho | 18 | R | 31 | 3B | aaa | PIT | 34 | 0 | 0 | 180 | 6 | 82 | 18 | 56 | -28 |
| Katoh,Gosuke | 18 | L | 24 | 1B | aa | NYY | 433 | 5 | 9 | 201 | 11 | 67 | 75 | 83 | -21 |
| Kay,Grant | 17 | R | 24 | 3B | a/a | TAM | 431 | 6 | 12 | 233 | 9 | 75 | 91 | 117 | 27 |
| Keller,Alec | 17 | L | 25 | RF | aa | WAS | 288 | 2 | 5 | 227 | 5 | 76 | 48 | 93 | -18 |
| | 18 | L | 26 | LF | aa | WAS | 223 | 2 | 1 | 287 | 5 | 84 | 53 | 69 | 11 |
| Kelley,Christian | 18 | R | 25 | C | aa | PIT | 311 | 6 | 0 | 203 | 6 | 77 | 65 | 48 | -11 |
| Kelly,Carson | 17 | R | 23 | C | aaa | STL | 244 | 8 | 0 | 254 | 10 | 83 | 81 | 28 | 25 |
| | 18 | R | 24 | C | aaa | STL | 294 | 5 | 0 | 229 | 11 | 82 | 59 | 31 | 7 |
| Kelly,Dalton | 17 | L | 23 | 1B | aa | TAM | 192 | 6 | 5 | 269 | 12 | 65 | 136 | 94 | 23 |
| | 18 | L | 24 | 1B | aa | TAM | 417 | 4 | 18 | 195 | 11 | 71 | 64 | 125 | -3 |
| Kelly,Juan | 18 | B | 24 | 1B | aa | TOR | 290 | 11 | 2 | 199 | 10 | 66 | 115 | 37 | -10 |
| Kemmer,Jon | 17 | L | 27 | LF | aaa | HOU | 304 | 10 | 4 | 224 | 8 | 59 | 114 | 96 | -27 |
| | 18 | L | 28 | DH | aaa | MIN | 410 | 14 | 4 | 209 | 8 | 64 | 124 | 100 | 4 |
| Kemp,Anthony | 17 | L | 26 | 2B | aaa | HOU | 504 | 6 | 15 | 254 | 4 | 89 | 50 | 119 | 42 |
| | 18 | L | 27 | 2B | aaa | HOU | 161 | 0 | 9 | 254 | 7 | 88 | 34 | 144 | 39 |
| Kennedy,A.J. | 17 | R | 23 | C | aa | SD | 101 | 2 | 1 | 64 | 4 | 62 | 40 | 46 | -95 |
| | 18 | R | 24 | C | aaa | SD | 46 | 1 | 0 | 119 | 0 | 52 | 96 | 26 | -104 |
| Kennedy,Garrett | 17 | L | 25 | C | aa | LA | 123 | 3 | 0 | 166 | 8 | 72 | 76 | 39 | -20 |
| | 18 | L | 26 | C | aaa | SEA | 90 | 1 | 0 | 169 | 9 | 60 | 59 | 57 | -76 |
| Kerrigan,Jimmy | 18 | R | 24 | CF | a/a | MIN | 205 | 6 | 0 | 207 | 5 | 64 | 85 | 33 | -57 |
| Kieboom,Carter | 18 | R | 21 | SS | aa | WAS | 248 | 4 | 3 | 247 | 7 | 75 | 83 | 77 | 4 |
| Kieboom,Spencer | 17 | R | 26 | C | a/a | WAS | 220 | 4 | 0 | 210 | 8 | 77 | 69 | 19 | -13 |
| | 18 | R | 27 | C | aaa | WAS | 84 | 1 | 0 | 211 | 9 | 86 | 44 | 19 | 4 |
| Kiner-Falefa,Isiah | 17 | R | 22 | 3B | aa | TEX | 513 | 5 | 15 | 275 | 7 | 85 | 58 | 92 | 31 |
| Kingery,Scott | 17 | R | 23 | 2B | a/a | PHI | 543 | 24 | 25 | 275 | 6 | 77 | 112 | 142 | 54 |
| Knight,Nash | 18 | S | 26 | 3B | aa | TOR | 31 | 1 | 0 | 137 | 5 | 81 | 36 | 30 | -25 |
| Knizner,Andrew | 17 | R | 22 | C | aa | STL | 182 | 3 | 0 | 305 | 6 | 85 | 76 | 35 | 24 |
| | 18 | R | 23 | C | a/a | STL | 335 | 5 | 0 | 273 | 6 | 84 | 58 | 23 | 3 |
| Kohlwey,Taylor | 18 | L | 24 | RF | aa | SD | 204 | 5 | 3 | 232 | 9 | 67 | 88 | 100 | -10 |
| Kramer,Kevin | 17 | L | 24 | 2B | aa | PIT | 202 | 5 | 6 | 273 | 7 | 73 | 116 | 124 | 40 |
| | 18 | L | 25 | 2B | aaa | PIT | 476 | 11 | 10 | 266 | 6 | 70 | 102 | 91 | 2 |
| Kranson,Mitchell | 18 | L | 24 | 3B | aa | MIN | 187 | 2 | 0 | 231 | 10 | 79 | 58 | 29 | -8 |
| Krieger,Tyler | 17 | B | 23 | 2B | aa | CLE | 418 | 5 | 10 | 210 | 8 | 75 | 71 | 89 | 1 |
| | 18 | B | 24 | LF | aa | CLE | 468 | 4 | 16 | 255 | 6 | 79 | 57 | 102 | 7 |
| Kruger,Jack | 18 | R | 24 | C | aa | LAA | 174 | 3 | 2 | 267 | 2 | 79 | 73 | 77 | 4 |
| Kubitza,Kyle | 17 | L | 27 | RF | aaa | ATL | 286 | 4 | 4 | 193 | 10 | 60 | 45 | 107 | -68 |
| La O,Luis | 18 | R | 27 | 2B | aa | TEX | 286 | 2 | 4 | 245 | 4 | 82 | 38 | 71 | -11 |
| Lago,Alay | 18 | R | 27 | 2B | aa | ATL | 295 | 2 | 4 | 213 | 2 | 86 | 41 | 86 | 11 |
| Lara,Luis | 18 | S | 23 | DH | a/a | ARI | 45 | 0 | 0 | 146 | 11 | 63 | 20 | 26 | -100 |
| Laureano,Ramon | 17 | R | 23 | RF | aa | HOU | 463 | 9 | 20 | 206 | 7 | 73 | 78 | 144 | 12 |
| | 18 | R | 24 | RF | aaa | OAK | 246 | 10 | 9 | 256 | 9 | 68 | 117 | 103 | 17 |
| LaValley,Gavin | 17 | R | 23 | 1B | aa | CIN | 247 | 3 | 0 | 248 | 8 | 70 | 80 | 25 | -32 |
| | 18 | R | 24 | 1B | aa | CIN | 393 | 12 | 2 | 187 | 9 | 65 | 87 | 39 | -41 |

| BATTER | yr | b | age | pos | lvl | org | ab | hr | sb | ba | bb% | ct% | px | sx | bpv |
|---|---|---|---|---|---|---|---|---|---|---|---|---|---|---|---|
| Lavarnway,Ryan | 17 | R | 30 | C | aaa | OAK | 264 | 4 | 0 | 180 | 7 | 70 | 47 | 31 | -57 |
| | 18 | R | 31 | C | aaa | PIT | 264 | 6 | 0 | 222 | 7 | 73 | 100 | 25 | -4 |
| Law,Adam | 17 | R | 27 | 2B | aa | SEA | 63 | 0 | 0 | 180 | 1 | 56 | 43 | 47 | -122 |
| | 18 | R | 28 | 2B | a/a | SEA | 383 | 2 | 5 | 196 | 5 | 70 | 57 | 72 | -42 |
| Leblebijian,Jason | 17 | R | 26 | 3B | aaa | TOR | 427 | 10 | 3 | 238 | 7 | 66 | 97 | 87 | -15 |
| | 18 | R | 27 | 3B | aaa | TOR | 282 | 8 | 5 | 189 | 9 | 59 | 88 | 80 | -48 |
| Lee,Braxton | 17 | L | 24 | CF | aa | MIA | 476 | 3 | 19 | 282 | 12 | 75 | 49 | 101 | -6 |
| | 18 | L | 25 | RF | a/a | MIA | 289 | 1 | 6 | 190 | 9 | 77 | 37 | 89 | -15 |
| Lee,Khalil | 18 | L | 20 | CF | aa | KC | 102 | 2 | 2 | 234 | 8 | 72 | 72 | 64 | -16 |
| Leonard,Patrick | 17 | R | 25 | 3B | aaa | TAM | 503 | 10 | 13 | 235 | 7 | 69 | 84 | 99 | -12 |
| | 18 | R | 26 | 3B | aaa | CHW | 430 | 9 | 2 | 200 | 8 | 59 | 108 | 58 | -43 |
| Lester,Josh | 18 | L | 24 | 1B | aa | DET | 464 | 17 | 1 | 229 | 10 | 73 | 103 | 64 | 13 |
| Lewis,Kyle | 18 | R | 23 | CF | aa | SEA | 132 | 3 | 1 | 190 | 10 | 72 | 88 | 49 | -7 |
| Leyba,Domingo | 17 | B | 22 | SS | aa | ARI | 58 | 2 | 0 | 263 | 7 | 89 | 87 | 44 | 54 |
| | 18 | B | 23 | 2B | aa | ARI | 320 | 4 | 4 | 239 | 8 | 84 | 58 | 80 | 25 |
| Lidge,Ryan | 18 | S | 24 | C | aa | NYY | 102 | 1 | 1 | 183 | 13 | 81 | 21 | 34 | -22 |
| Lien,Connor | 17 | R | 23 | CF | aa | ATL | 374 | 9 | 17 | 158 | 6 | 50 | 97 | 135 | -67 |
| | 18 | R | 24 | CF | aa | ATL | 268 | 6 | 7 | 182 | 7 | 54 | 122 | 88 | -44 |
| Lin,Tzu-Wei | 17 | L | 23 | SS | a/a | BOS | 300 | 6 | 8 | 257 | 8 | 81 | 75 | 105 | 33 |
| | 18 | L | 24 | SS | aaa | BOS | 277 | 4 | 3 | 293 | 6 | 75 | 93 | 66 | 11 |
| Lino,Gabriel | 17 | R | 24 | C | a/a | STL | 263 | 4 | 0 | 230 | 7 | 67 | 93 | 32 | -30 |
| Lipka,Matthew | 17 | R | 25 | LF | a/a | TEX | 98 | 0 | 4 | 142 | 2 | 63 | 44 | 180 | -53 |
| | 18 | R | 26 | CF | aa | SF | 304 | 3 | 17 | 207 | 10 | 78 | 55 | 143 | 21 |
| Liriano,Rymer | 17 | R | 26 | RF | aaa | CHW | 449 | 14 | 5 | 213 | 7 | 64 | 86 | 83 | -36 |
| | 18 | R | 27 | LF | aaa | MIL | 352 | 13 | 7 | 193 | 7 | 55 | 114 | 85 | -45 |
| Listi,Austin | 18 | R | 25 | DH | aa | PHI | 217 | 7 | 0 | 234 | 9 | 71 | 87 | 14 | -24 |
| Littlewood,Marcus | 17 | B | 25 | C | aa | SEA | 281 | 8 | 1 | 207 | 4 | 71 | 71 | 40 | -36 |
| | 18 | B | 26 | C | a/a | ARI | 226 | 4 | 1 | 153 | 9 | 68 | 51 | 48 | -53 |
| Locastro,Tim | 17 | R | 25 | CF | a/a | LA | 471 | 8 | 27 | 262 | 4 | 83 | 72 | 135 | 40 |
| | 18 | R | 26 | CF | aaa | LA | 301 | 3 | 13 | 227 | 6 | 79 | 71 | 132 | 26 |
| Lockhart,Daniel | 17 | L | 25 | 2B | aa | ARI | 78 | 1 | 2 | 183 | 10 | 84 | 67 | 90 | 39 |
| | 18 | L | 26 | 3B | aa | ATL | 356 | 5 | 8 | 203 | 9 | 68 | 70 | 116 | -18 |
| Long,Shed | 17 | L | 22 | 2B | aa | CIN | 141 | 4 | 4 | 230 | 13 | 76 | 82 | 97 | 26 |
| | 18 | L | 23 | 2B | aa | CIN | 452 | 11 | 16 | 239 | 10 | 69 | 92 | 119 | 8 |
| Longhi,Nick | 17 | R | 22 | 1B | aa | CIN | 256 | 8 | 0 | 269 | 6 | 81 | 93 | 28 | 21 |
| | 18 | R | 23 | LF | a/a | CIN | 266 | 2 | 1 | 220 | 5 | 72 | 55 | 45 | -42 |
| Loopstok,Sicnarf | 18 | R | 25 | C | aa | CLE | 182 | 7 | 1 | 202 | 14 | 64 | 102 | 67 | -11 |
| Lopes,Christian | 17 | R | 25 | 3B | aaa | TOR | 333 | 6 | 17 | 247 | 11 | 82 | 86 | 113 | 55 |
| | 18 | R | 26 | 2B | aaa | TEX | 429 | 9 | 11 | 220 | 11 | 80 | 69 | 81 | 24 |
| Lopes,Tim | 17 | R | 23 | 2B | aa | TOR | 469 | 6 | 16 | 253 | 8 | 80 | 70 | 92 | 21 |
| | 18 | R | 24 | 2B | aaa | TOR | 354 | 2 | 15 | 256 | 6 | 82 | 56 | 107 | 19 |
| Lopez,Deiner | 17 | B | 23 | SS | aa | BOS | 231 | 2 | 4 | 229 | 5 | 70 | 40 | 100 | -47 |
| | 18 | B | 24 | 2B | a/a | BOS | 183 | 2 | 2 | 214 | 3 | 71 | 99 | 95 | -1 |
| Lopez,Jack | 17 | R | 25 | 2B | a/a | KC | 425 | 4 | 16 | 231 | 4 | 73 | 44 | 98 | -33 |
| | 18 | R | 26 | 2B | aaa | KC | 395 | 5 | 11 | 212 | 3 | 69 | 52 | 112 | -40 |
| Lopez,Nicky | 17 | L | 22 | SS | aa | KC | 232 | 0 | 6 | 248 | 6 | 87 | 23 | 85 | 6 |
| | 18 | L | 23 | SS | a/a | KC | 504 | 7 | 12 | 281 | 9 | 89 | 48 | 104 | 45 |
| Loveless,Derrick | 17 | L | 24 | LF | aa | TOR | 190 | 1 | 2 | 230 | 14 | 67 | 55 | 71 | -34 |
| Lovullo,Nick | 18 | R | 25 | 2B | aa | BOS | 187 | 1 | 1 | 179 | 8 | 77 | 50 | 62 | -16 |
| Lowe,Brandon | 17 | L | 23 | 2B | aa | TAM | 95 | 2 | 1 | 225 | 2 | 68 | 78 | 76 | -35 |
| | 18 | L | 24 | 2B | a/a | TAM | 380 | 18 | 7 | 258 | 11 | 68 | 150 | 80 | 40 |
| Lowe,Nathaniel | 18 | L | 23 | 1B | a/a | TAM | 288 | 14 | 1 | 278 | 11 | 77 | 121 | 56 | 45 |
| Lucena,Isaias | 18 | S | 24 | C | aa | BOS | 20 | 0 | 0 | 223 | 16 | 73 | 0 | -10 | -79 |
| Lugo,Dawel | 17 | R | 22 | 3B | aa | DET | 516 | 11 | 3 | 256 | 5 | 85 | 71 | 79 | 34 |
| | 18 | R | 23 | 2B | aaa | DET | 509 | 3 | 11 | 251 | 2 | 86 | 49 | 101 | 20 |
| Lukes,Nathan | 17 | L | 23 | LF | aa | TAM | 359 | 2 | 5 | 241 | 7 | 77 | 49 | 90 | -9 |
| | 18 | L | 24 | RF | aa | TAM | 435 | 5 | 8 | 240 | 6 | 74 | 72 | 95 | -3 |
| Lund,Brennon | 17 | L | 23 | LF | aa | LAA | 122 | 1 | 1 | 267 | 2 | 69 | 33 | 64 | -71 |
| | 18 | L | 24 | CF | aa | LAA | 401 | 7 | 18 | 230 | 8 | 71 | 77 | 133 | 2 |
| Luplow,Jordan | 17 | R | 24 | LF | a/a | PIT | 414 | 19 | 4 | 274 | 9 | 79 | 106 | 67 | 40 |
| | 18 | R | 25 | LF | aaa | PIT | 314 | 6 | 5 | 245 | 9 | 77 | 93 | 85 | 28 |
| Lusignan,Colby | 18 | L | 26 | 1B | aa | MIA | 30 | 0 | 0 | 162 | 8 | 36 | 99 | 4 | -159 |
| Lux,Gavin | 18 | L | 21 | SS | aa | LA | 105 | 3 | 2 | 287 | 9 | 79 | 79 | 79 | 21 |
| Machado,Dixon | 18 | R | 26 | SS | aaa | DET | 147 | 1 | 3 | 195 | 9 | 79 | 33 | 69 | -18 |
| Machin,Vimael | 18 | L | 25 | 2B | aa | CHC | 250 | 4 | 2 | 190 | 12 | 75 | 59 | 58 | -9 |
| Maddox,Will | 17 | L | 25 | 2B | aa | DET | 64 | 1 | 2 | 257 | 2 | 74 | 30 | 56 | -57 |
| | 18 | L | 26 | 2B | aa | DET | 398 | 3 | 5 | 256 | 4 | 81 | 51 | 96 | 3 |
| Madera,Chris | 18 | R | 26 | CF | aa | BOS | 70 | 0 | 1 | 173 | 2 | 84 | 29 | 124 | 2 |
| Mahtook,Mikie | 18 | R | 29 | CF | aaa | DET | 283 | 9 | 5 | 209 | 6 | 66 | 108 | 115 | -2 |
| Marabell,Connor | 17 | L | 23 | RF | a/a | CLE | 56 | 0 | 0 | 301 | 6 | 81 | 43 | 16 | -25 |
| | 18 | L | 24 | RF | a/a | CLE | 462 | 11 | 4 | 251 | 4 | 82 | 91 | 82 | 37 |
| Marin,Adrian | 17 | R | 23 | 2B | aa | BAL | 433 | 2 | 7 | 223 | 5 | 76 | 34 | 101 | -28 |
| | 18 | R | 24 | SS | a/a | BAL | 340 | 0 | 5 | 193 | 6 | 77 | 25 | 71 | -37 |
| Marincov,Tyler | 17 | R | 26 | RF | aa | OAK | 286 | 6 | 4 | 220 | 7 | 62 | 105 | 83 | -26 |
| | 18 | R | 27 | RF | aa | OAK | 325 | 9 | 8 | 178 | 7 | 59 | 90 | 80 | -51 |
| Maris,Peter | 18 | L | 25 | 3B | aa | TAM | 153 | 5 | 4 | 209 | 10 | 69 | 108 | 95 | 13 |
| Mariscal,Chris | 17 | R | 24 | SS | aa | SEA | 155 | 1 | 0 | 214 | 7 | 77 | 29 | 60 | -34 |
| | 18 | R | 25 | 2B | aa | SEA | 444 | 6 | 4 | 219 | 8 | 64 | 60 | 78 | -54 |
| Marlette,Tyler | 17 | R | 24 | C | aa | SEA | 368 | 10 | 0 | 213 | 7 | 72 | 89 | 48 | -13 |
| | 18 | R | 25 | 1B | aa | ATL | 423 | 10 | 4 | 219 | 9 | 72 | 77 | 70 | -10 |
| Marmolejos,Jose | 17 | L | 24 | LF | aa | WAS | 400 | 11 | 0 | 252 | 8 | 78 | 77 | 59 | 8 |
| | 18 | L | 25 | 1B | aaa | WAS | 493 | 7 | 0 | 235 | 6 | 78 | 60 | 28 | -19 |
| Maron,Camden | 17 | L | 26 | C | aa | MIA | 233 | 4 | 0 | 235 | 12 | 77 | 61 | 32 | -8 |
| Marrero,Deven | 17 | R | 27 | SS | aaa | BOS | 183 | 2 | 1 | 221 | 3 | 68 | 89 | 43 | -37 |
| | 18 | R | 28 | 3B | aaa | ARI | 66 | 1 | 0 | 161 | 6 | 62 | 71 | 71 | -62 |
| Marrero,Emmanuel | 18 | B | 25 | 2B | aa | PHI | 143 | 2 | 2 | 154 | 7 | 60 | 52 | 41 | -89 |
| Mars,Danny | 17 | B | 23 | LF | aa | BOS | 477 | 5 | 10 | 286 | 5 | 79 | 57 | 82 | -2 |
| | 18 | B | 24 | RF | aa | BOS | 411 | 2 | 14 | 231 | 7 | 74 | 57 | 109 | -7 |
| Marte,Ketel | 17 | B | 24 | SS | aaa | ARI | 311 | 4 | 5 | 287 | 5 | 87 | 77 | 118 | 58 |
| Marte,Luis | 17 | R | 24 | 3B | a/a | TEX | 360 | 6 | 7 | 218 | 1 | 83 | 53 | 90 | 6 |
| | 18 | R | 25 | SS | a/a | ATL | 431 | 4 | 8 | 237 | 2 | 79 | 51 | 83 | -13 |
| Martin,Jason | 17 | L | 22 | LF | aa | HOU | 300 | 10 | 6 | 253 | 5 | 69 | 130 | 98 | 21 |
| | 18 | L | 23 | CF | a/a | PIT | 468 | 10 | 10 | 246 | 7 | 74 | 78 | 108 | 8 |
| Martin,Kyle | 17 | L | 25 | 1B | aa | PHI | 436 | 19 | 2 | 164 | 8 | 63 | 106 | 57 | -26 |
| | 18 | L | 26 | 1B | aa | PHI | 143 | 3 | 0 | 156 | 10 | 68 | 96 | 38 | -18 |
| Martin,Richie | 17 | R | 23 | SS | aa | OAK | 286 | 2 | 10 | 198 | 6 | 79 | 46 | 128 | 5 |
| | 18 | R | 24 | SS | aa | OAK | 453 | 4 | 19 | 261 | 7 | 79 | 75 | 131 | 30 |
| Martin,Trey | 17 | R | 25 | CF | aa | CHC | 317 | 4 | 5 | 235 | 3 | 67 | 73 | 79 | -40 |
| | 18 | R | 26 | CF | a/a | CHC | 366 | 5 | 13 | 189 | 9 | 58 | 82 | 106 | -50 |
| Martinez,Alberth | 17 | R | 26 | LF | aa | SD | 395 | 8 | 5 | 212 | 5 | 76 | 78 | 81 | 4 |
| Martinez,Carlos | 18 | R | 23 | C | aa | ATL | 137 | 1 | 0 | 233 | 6 | 87 | 46 | 30 | 9 |
| Martinez,Eddy | 18 | R | 23 | RF | aa | CHC | 411 | 10 | 4 | 198 | 6 | 76 | 84 | 83 | 9 |
| Martinez,Jeremy | 18 | R | 24 | C | a/a | STL | 190 | 4 | 0 | 199 | 7 | 83 | 54 | 23 | -2 |
| Martinez,Jose | 18 | B | 22 | SS | aa | STL | 60 | 0 | 1 | 174 | 8 | 64 | 44 | 38 | -77 |
| Martinez,Valentin | 18 | R | 22 | C | aaa | CIN | 22 | 0 | 0 | 122 | 0 | 70 | 0 | 29 | -110 |
| Martini,Nick | 17 | L | 27 | LF | a/a | STL | 459 | 6 | 5 | 247 | 10 | 77 | 64 | 92 | 7 |
| | 18 | L | 28 | 1B | aaa | OAK | 276 | 4 | 4 | 237 | 12 | 70 | 64 | 82 | -19 |
| Marzilli,Evan | 17 | L | 26 | CF | a/a | ARI | 402 | 5 | 11 | 217 | 10 | 72 | 62 | 121 | -5 |
| | 18 | L | 27 | CF | a/a | ARI | 161 | 1 | 3 | 181 | 9 | 60 | 66 | 106 | -53 |
| Mastrobuoni,Miles | 18 | L | 23 | LF | aa | TAM | 43 | 0 | 1 | 226 | 9 | 81 | 0 | 48 | -42 |
| Mateo,Jorge | 17 | R | 22 | SS | aa | OAK | 257 | 6 | 20 | 272 | 7 | 74 | 108 | 162 | 45 |
| | 18 | R | 23 | SS | aaa | OAK | 470 | 2 | 20 | 209 | 5 | 68 | 70 | 141 | -18 |
| Matheny,Tate | 18 | R | 24 | CF | aa | BOS | 398 | 1 | 9 | 230 | 7 | 66 | 63 | 98 | -41 |
| Mathias,Mark | 17 | R | 23 | 3B | aa | CLE | 104 | 1 | 3 | 196 | 9 | 68 | 64 | 112 | -22 |
| | 18 | R | 24 | 2B | aa | CLE | 397 | 7 | 9 | 215 | 11 | 74 | 87 | 104 | 20 |
| Mathisen,Wyatt | 17 | R | 24 | 3B | aa | PIT | 375 | 4 | 3 | 249 | 9 | 79 | 51 | 62 | -5 |
| | 18 | R | 25 | 1B | a/a | PIT | 268 | 8 | 2 | 224 | 9 | 72 | 95 | 68 | 6 |
| Maxwell III,Bruce | 17 | L | 27 | C | aaa | OAK | 84 | 1 | 0 | 231 | 6 | 81 | 92 | 26 | 18 |
| | 18 | L | 28 | C | aaa | OAK | 178 | 1 | 0 | 172 | 8 | 59 | 49 | 7 | -107 |
| May,Jacob | 17 | B | 25 | CF | aaa | CHW | 415 | 3 | 24 | 210 | 6 | 68 | 41 | 135 | -43 |
| | 18 | B | 26 | CF | aaa | CHW | 314 | 2 | 12 | 210 | 5 | 72 | 57 | 83 | -31 |
| Mayfield,Jack | 17 | R | 27 | 2B | a/a | HOU | 424 | 14 | 7 | 221 | 4 | 74 | 97 | 89 | 9 |
| | 18 | R | 28 | 2B | aaa | HOU | 433 | 11 | 3 | 198 | 5 | 73 | 87 | 58 | -11 |
| Mazeika,Patrick | 17 | L | 24 | DH | aa | NYM | 21 | 0 | 0 | 300 | 9 | 66 | 208 | 33 | 60 |
| | 18 | L | 25 | C | aa | NYM | 295 | 7 | 0 | 188 | 10 | 86 | 57 | 18 | 15 |
| Mazzilli,L.J. | 17 | R | 27 | RF | a/a | NYM | 370 | 4 | 7 | 200 | 10 | 77 | 57 | 74 | -3 |
| | 18 | R | 28 | 2B | aaa | NYY | 236 | 6 | 2 | 197 | 7 | 76 | 84 | 45 | 0 |
| McBroom,Ryan | 17 | R | 25 | 1B | aa | NYY | 486 | 17 | 1 | 226 | 7 | 73 | 90 | 28 | -9 |
| | 18 | R | 26 | 1B | a/a | NYY | 461 | 14 | 1 | 258 | 5 | 65 | 98 | 41 | -35 |
| McCarthy,Joe | 17 | L | 23 | 1B | aa | TAM | 454 | 6 | 17 | 254 | 15 | 76 | 80 | 122 | 37 |
| | 18 | L | 24 | LF | aaa | TAM | 160 | 7 | 3 | 233 | 12 | 68 | 142 | 89 | 37 |
| McCormick,Chas | 18 | R | 23 | RF | aa | HOU | 250 | 2 | 11 | 253 | 8 | 86 | 40 | 95 | 21 |
| McDowell,Max | 18 | R | 24 | C | aa | MIL | 102 | 1 | 3 | 208 | 12 | 80 | 45 | 68 | 2 |
| McElroy Jr.,C.J. | 18 | R | 25 | CF | a/a | CIN | 268 | 3 | 15 | 203 | 4 | 75 | 45 | 124 | -15 |
| McGee,Stephen | 17 | R | 26 | C | aa | SD | 230 | 6 | 0 | 222 | 15 | 66 | 98 | 25 | -17 |
| | 18 | R | 27 | C | aaa | LAA | 87 | 1 | 0 | 128 | 9 | 44 | 88 | 39 | -122 |
| McGuire,Reese | 17 | L | 22 | C | aa | TOR | 115 | 6 | 2 | 266 | 11 | 82 | 105 | 82 | 61 |
| | 18 | L | 23 | C | aaa | TOR | 322 | 6 | 3 | 218 | 8 | 74 | 60 | 61 | -18 |
| McKenna,Ryan | 18 | R | 21 | CF | aa | BAL | 213 | 3 | 3 | 213 | 9 | 72 | 54 | 94 | -18 |
| McKinney,Billy | 17 | L | 23 | RF | a/a | NYY | 441 | 17 | 2 | 260 | 8 | 76 | 115 | 83 | 39 |
| | 18 | L | 24 | RF | a/a | TOR | 294 | 13 | 1 | 203 | 8 | 72 | 129 | 88 | 35 |
| McMahon,Ryan | 17 | L | 23 | 1B | a/a | COL | 470 | 17 | 8 | 340 | 6 | 80 | 120 | 88 | 59 |
| | 18 | L | 24 | 1B | aaa | COL | 224 | 8 | 2 | 252 | 4 | 71 | 121 | 92 | 18 |
| McNeil,Jeff | 17 | L | 25 | 2B | aaa | NYM | 71 | 1 | 1 | 196 | 3 | 82 | 55 | 85 | 7 |
| | 18 | L | 26 | 2B | a/a | NYM | 339 | 13 | 4 | 268 | 7 | 84 | 106 | 103 | 69 |
| McVaney,Jeff | 17 | R | 27 | RF | a/a | DET | 187 | 2 | 2 | 186 | 7 | 77 | 57 | 89 | -6 |
| Meadows,Austin | 17 | L | 22 | CF | aaa | PIT | 284 | 3 | 10 | 236 | 7 | 82 | 66 | 101 | 27 |
| | 18 | L | 23 | CF | aaa | TAM | 261 | 10 | 10 | 268 | 5 | 83 | 117 | 101 | 70 |
| Medrano,Kevin | 17 | L | 27 | 2B | a/a | ARI | 338 | 2 | 1 | 266 | 6 | 81 | 66 | 70 | 11 |
| | 18 | L | 28 | 2B | a/a | ARI | 396 | 2 | 7 | 252 | 5 | 75 | 72 | 104 | 1 |
| Mejia,Alex | 17 | R | 26 | SS | a/a | STL | 433 | 5 | 2 | 249 | 5 | 83 | 66 | 37 | 7 |
| | 18 | R | 27 | 1B | aaa | STL | 322 | 3 | 4 | 220 | 4 | 80 | 22 | 68 | -32 |
| Mejia,Erick | 17 | B | 23 | SS | a/a | LA | 356 | 6 | 21 | 256 | 7 | 75 | 66 | 126 | 7 |
| | 18 | B | 24 | 2B | aa | KC | 540 | 4 | 27 | 238 | 6 | 80 | 60 | 131 | 22 |
| Mejia,Francisco | 17 | B | 22 | C | aa | CLE | 347 | 12 | 6 | 283 | 6 | 85 | 94 | 80 | 53 |
| | 18 | B | 23 | C | aaa | SD | 427 | 9 | 0 | 242 | 4 | 77 | 85 | 38 | -1 |
| Mejias-Brean,Seth | 17 | R | 26 | 3B | a/a | SEA | 422 | 3 | 4 | 222 | 6 | 73 | 41 | 78 | -39 |
| | 18 | R | 27 | 3B | a/a | SEA | 476 | 7 | 4 | 205 | 8 | 74 | 55 | 67 | -21 |
| Mendez,Luis | 17 | B | 24 | 2B | a/a | TEX | 24 | 0 | 2 | 71 | 23 | 69 | 33 | 54 | -35 |
| | 18 | B | 25 | 3B | a/a | TEX | 233 | 4 | 3 | 212 | 7 | 75 | 65 | 72 | -9 |
| Mendick,Danny | 17 | R | 24 | SS | aa | CHW | 147 | 3 | 1 | 182 | 10 | 79 | 54 | 38 | -7 |
| | 18 | R | 25 | SS | aa | CHW | 453 | 13 | 18 | 220 | 10 | 77 | 86 | 79 | 22 |
| Mendoza,Evan | 18 | R | 22 | 3B | aa | STL | 366 | 4 | 1 | 223 | 6 | 77 | 43 | 46 | -29 |
| Mendoza,Yonathan | 17 | B | 23 | 3B | aa | CLE | 51 | 1 | 2 | 182 | 6 | 83 | 52 | 38 | -2 |
| | 18 | B | 24 | SS | aa | SEA | 333 | 0 | 4 | 223 | 10 | 83 | 20 | 77 | -8 |
| Meneses,Heiker | 17 | R | 26 | 2B | a/a | BOS | 307 | 1 | 9 | 251 | 3 | 69 | 49 | 103 | -44 |
| | 18 | R | 27 | 2B | a/a | PHI | 197 | 1 | 1 | 145 | 6 | 69 | 22 | 44 | -80 |
| Meneses,Joey | 17 | R | 25 | 1B | aa | ATL | 360 | 8 | 0 | 253 | 9 | 73 | 51 | 25 | -40 |
| | 18 | R | 26 | 1B | aaa | PHI | 492 | 20 | 0 | 263 | 6 | 72 | 108 | 30 | -2 |
| Mercado,Oscar | 17 | R | 23 | CF | aa | STL | 477 | 11 | 33 | 265 | 5 | 75 | 72 | 127 | 9 |
| | 18 | R | 24 | CF | aaa | CLE | 485 | 6 | 29 | 251 | 7 | 80 | 64 | 112 | 21 |
| Mercedes,Melvin | 17 | B | 25 | 2B | a/a | OAK | 201 | 0 | 4 | 207 | 11 | 80 | 27 | 98 | -5 |
| | 18 | B | 26 | 2B | a/a | OAK | 153 | 0 | 2 | 208 | 9 | 76 | 29 | 107 | -21 |
| Metzler,Ryan | 17 | R | 24 | 3B | aa | COL | 44 | 0 | 1 | 241 | 5 | 66 | 21 | 68 | -88 |
| | 18 | R | 25 | 2B | a/a | COL | 313 | 6 | 10 | 209 | 7 | 68 | 79 | 68 | -28 |

| BATTER | yr | b | age | pos | lvl | org | ab | hr | sb | ba | bb% | ct% | px | sx | bpv |
|---|---|---|---|---|---|---|---|---|---|---|---|---|---|---|---|
| Michael,Levi | 18 | R | 27 | SS | a/a | NYM | 396 | 7 | 9 | 232 | 6 | 69 | 87 | 93 | -13 |
| Michalczewski,Trey | 17 | B | 22 | 3B | aa | CHW | 368 | 9 | 8 | 226 | 10 | 62 | 87 | 93 | -31 |
| | 18 | B | 23 | 2B | aa | CHW | 451 | 6 | 4 | 234 | 5 | 67 | 86 | 92 | -22 |
| Michelena,Arturo | 17 | R | 23 | 3B | aa | HOU | 162 | 1 | 0 | 187 | 5 | 70 | 19 | 36 | -82 |
| | 18 | R | 24 | SS | aa | HOU | 42 | 0 | 0 | 104 | 8 | 79 | 14 | 106 | -25 |
| Mieses,Johan | 17 | R | 22 | CF | aa | LA | 294 | 14 | 0 | 145 | 7 | 57 | 117 | 27 | -55 |
| | 18 | R | 23 | RF | aa | STL | 219 | 6 | 0 | 174 | 4 | 69 | 81 | 47 | -35 |
| Millan,J.C. | 18 | R | 22 | 3B | a/a | MIA | 24 | 0 | 1 | 185 | 10 | 82 | 0 | 83 | -27 |
| Miller,Anderson | 17 | L | 23 | RF | aa | KC | 213 | 2 | 3 | 215 | 4 | 72 | 45 | 51 | -51 |
| | 18 | L | 24 | LF | aa | KC | 432 | 10 | 8 | 228 | 6 | 79 | 81 | 89 | 21 |
| Miller,Brian | 18 | L | 23 | LF | aa | MIA | 262 | 0 | 18 | 235 | 6 | 83 | 26 | 116 | 1 |
| Miller,Ian | 17 | L | 25 | CF | a/a | SEA | 512 | 3 | 35 | 261 | 5 | 76 | 45 | 143 | -6 |
| | 18 | L | 26 | CF | aaa | SEA | 422 | 1 | 24 | 210 | 7 | 74 | 37 | 120 | -24 |
| Miller,Michael | 17 | R | 28 | 2B | aaa | BOS | 280 | 2 | 3 | 231 | 8 | 79 | 46 | 66 | -11 |
| | 18 | R | 29 | SS | aaa | BOS | 320 | 3 | 8 | 241 | 7 | 80 | 42 | 66 | -11 |
| Miller,Sean | 18 | R | 24 | SS | a/a | MIN | 183 | 1 | 1 | 177 | 5 | 74 | 29 | 56 | -52 |
| Milone,Thomas | 18 | L | 23 | CF | aa | TAM | 365 | 3 | 8 | 227 | 5 | 68 | 64 | 124 | -29 |
| Miroglio,Dominic | 18 | R | 23 | C | aa | ARI | 78 | 0 | 0 | 206 | 1 | 83 | 46 | 59 | -9 |
| Molina,Nelson | 18 | L | 23 | 3B | aa | COL | 142 | 2 | 0 | 195 | 3 | 76 | 73 | 49 | -16 |
| Moncada,Yoan | 17 | B | 22 | 2B | aaa | CHW | 309 | 10 | 14 | 255 | 12 | 63 | 95 | 114 | -13 |
| Mondesi,Adalberto | 18 | B | 23 | SS | aaa | KC | 120 | 4 | 8 | 230 | 5 | 73 | 128 | 166 | 58 |
| Mondesi,Raul | 17 | B | 22 | SS | aaa | KC | 321 | 10 | 17 | 286 | 4 | 72 | 122 | 152 | 41 |
| Mondou,Nate | 18 | L | 23 | 3B | aa | OAK | 165 | 0 | 2 | 222 | 8 | 83 | 30 | 41 | -14 |
| Monge,Joseph | 17 | R | 22 | CF | aa | BOS | 193 | 2 | 4 | 229 | 4 | 74 | 64 | 97 | -14 |
| Montgomery,Troy | 17 | L | 23 | CF | aa | LAA | 68 | 0 | 4 | 218 | 12 | 80 | 21 | 113 | -3 |
| | 18 | L | 24 | CF | aa | DET | 209 | 1 | 7 | 222 | 11 | 69 | 49 | 121 | -25 |
| Moon,Logan | 17 | R | 25 | RF | a/a | KC | 373 | 6 | 5 | 238 | 5 | 66 | 85 | 84 | -32 |
| | 18 | R | 26 | LF | aaa | KC | 114 | 0 | 2 | 162 | 4 | 66 | 16 | 59 | -94 |
| Mooney,Peter | 17 | L | 27 | SS | aaa | MIA | 403 | 3 | 2 | 172 | 8 | 81 | 45 | 76 | 0 |
| | 18 | L | 28 | SS | a/a | MIA | 252 | 4 | 2 | 221 | 8 | 82 | 48 | 56 | 0 |
| Moore,Dylan | 17 | R | 25 | SS | aa | ATL | 421 | 6 | 9 | 175 | 9 | 72 | 39 | 70 | -37 |
| | 18 | R | 26 | 3B | a/a | MIL | 408 | 11 | 17 | 250 | 6 | 80 | 106 | 137 | 59 |
| Moore,Logan | 17 | L | 27 | C | aaa | PHI | 210 | 5 | 0 | 193 | 9 | 57 | 81 | 50 | -72 |
| | 18 | L | 28 | C | aaa | PHI | 229 | 2 | 0 | 149 | 9 | 65 | 47 | 21 | -76 |
| Moore,Tyler | 17 | L | 24 | C | aa | NYM | 64 | 0 | 0 | 168 | 13 | 63 | 42 | 38 | -75 |
| | 18 | L | 25 | C | aa | NYM | 51 | 0 | 0 | 94 | 6 | 52 | 41 | 14 | -143 |
| Moorman,Chuck | 18 | R | 24 | C | aa | TEX | 157 | 2 | 0 | 171 | 9 | 58 | 83 | 37 | -70 |
| Mora,Angelo | 17 | B | 24 | 2B | a/a | PHI | 398 | 8 | 4 | 256 | 5 | 77 | 77 | 80 | 4 |
| | 18 | B | 25 | 2B | a/a | LA | 314 | 6 | 4 | 223 | 5 | 76 | 73 | 76 | -4 |
| Mora,John | 17 | L | 24 | CF | aaa | NYM | 30 | 0 | 1 | 126 | 7 | 72 | 83 | 107 | 1 |
| | 18 | L | 25 | CF | aa | NYM | 351 | 4 | 3 | 191 | 8 | 70 | 66 | 89 | -23 |
| Morales,Jonathan | 17 | R | 22 | C | aa | ATL | 130 | 1 | 0 | 151 | 5 | 83 | 23 | 24 | -31 |
| | 18 | R | 23 | C | a/a | ATL | 188 | 1 | 0 | 244 | 5 | 83 | 38 | 40 | -13 |
| Moran,Colin | 17 | L | 25 | 3B | aaa | HOU | 302 | 12 | 0 | 240 | 6 | 77 | 90 | 37 | 5 |
| Moreno,Rando | 17 | B | 25 | SS | aa | SF | 186 | 0 | 3 | 178 | 5 | 85 | 18 | 51 | -19 |
| Morgan,Josh | 18 | R | 23 | C | aa | TEX | 294 | 2 | 1 | 212 | 7 | 82 | 50 | 45 | -1 |
| Morin,Parker | 17 | L | 26 | C | a/a | KC | 128 | 1 | 0 | 147 | 2 | 69 | 35 | 28 | -80 |
| | 18 | L | 27 | C | aaa | KC | 151 | 1 | 1 | 221 | 5 | 74 | 61 | 41 | -32 |
| Moroff,Max | 17 | B | 24 | SS | aaa | PIT | 185 | 11 | 4 | 228 | 16 | 66 | 145 | 56 | 30 |
| | 18 | B | 25 | SS | aaa | PIT | 247 | 6 | 4 | 188 | 12 | 69 | 92 | 94 | 4 |
| Morozowski,Jason | 18 | R | 24 | RF | aa | ARI | 281 | 4 | 3 | 171 | 6 | 66 | 68 | 77 | -44 |
| Motter,Taylor | 17 | R | 28 | SS | aaa | SEA | 100 | 5 | 4 | 279 | 9 | 84 | 110 | 103 | 77 |
| | 18 | R | 29 | 3B | a/a | MIN | 321 | 8 | 5 | 151 | 8 | 73 | 83 | 98 | 5 |
| Mountcastle,Ryan | 17 | R | 20 | 3B | aa | BAL | 153 | 3 | 0 | 181 | 2 | 74 | 68 | 49 | -28 |
| | 18 | R | 21 | 3B | aa | BAL | 394 | 11 | 2 | 267 | 5 | 79 | 81 | 77 | 15 |
| Moya,Steven | 17 | L | 26 | RF | a/a | DET | 375 | 15 | 4 | 185 | 6 | 62 | 106 | 86 | -26 |
| Moyer,Hutton | 17 | B | 24 | SS | aa | LAA | 92 | 0 | 8 | 186 | 7 | 69 | 62 | 140 | -18 |
| | 18 | B | 25 | DH | aa | LAA | 135 | 5 | 6 | 170 | 4 | 55 | 112 | 133 | -40 |
| Mullins II,Cedric | 17 | B | 23 | CF | aa | BAL | 309 | 11 | 7 | 220 | 7 | 78 | 80 | 88 | 18 |
| | 18 | B | 24 | CF | a/a | BAL | 443 | 10 | 16 | 252 | 6 | 83 | 85 | 141 | 58 |
| Muncy,Max | 17 | L | 27 | 3B | aaa | LA | 320 | 9 | 2 | 251 | 10 | 67 | 99 | 55 | -12 |
| | 18 | L | 28 | 1B | aaa | LA | 32 | 1 | 0 | 245 | 11 | 80 | 106 | 33 | 39 |
| Mundell,Brian | 17 | R | 23 | 1B | aa | COL | 172 | 3 | 1 | 297 | 11 | 85 | 73 | 44 | 36 |
| | 18 | R | 24 | 1B | aa | COL | 441 | 6 | 1 | 247 | 9 | 82 | 65 | 33 | 9 |
| Munoz,Yairo | 17 | R | 22 | SS | a/a | OAK | 446 | 10 | 18 | 272 | 4 | 81 | 78 | 118 | 31 |
| | 18 | R | 23 | SS | a/a | STL | 99 | 2 | 1 | 246 | 4 | 80 | 67 | 69 | 4 |
| Murphy,John | 17 | R | 26 | C | aaa | ARI | 261 | 4 | 0 | 186 | 6 | 80 | 42 | 15 | -26 |
| Murphy,Max | 17 | R | 25 | RF | aa | MIN | 206 | 1 | 0 | 231 | 7 | 76 | 65 | 78 | -7 |
| Murphy,Sean | 17 | R | 23 | C | aa | OAK | 191 | 3 | 0 | 183 | 8 | 81 | 47 | 34 | -10 |
| | 18 | R | 24 | C | a/a | OAK | 265 | 6 | 2 | 248 | 7 | 79 | 110 | 101 | 52 |
| Murphy,Tom | 17 | R | 26 | C | aaa | COL | 141 | 3 | 0 | 222 | 4 | 57 | 116 | 63 | -49 |
| | 18 | R | 27 | C | aaa | COL | 236 | 11 | 2 | 210 | 5 | 63 | 153 | 90 | 16 |
| Myers,Connor | 18 | R | 24 | CF | aa | CHC | 129 | 1 | 3 | 200 | 7 | 63 | 34 | 106 | -75 |
| Myers,D Arby | 18 | R | 30 | LF | a/a | BAL | 146 | 0 | 5 | 211 | 4 | 80 | 29 | 100 | -19 |
| Naquin,Tyler | 17 | L | 26 | CF | aaa | CLE | 295 | 8 | 4 | 262 | 8 | 75 | 86 | 80 | 9 |
| Navarreto,Brian | 17 | R | 23 | C | aa | MIN | 102 | 2 | 0 | 195 | 7 | 82 | 38 | 30 | -17 |
| | 18 | R | 24 | C | aa | MIN | 357 | 3 | 0 | 217 | 3 | 83 | 50 | 32 | -12 |
| Nay,Mitch | 18 | R | 25 | 3B | aa | CIN | 221 | 5 | 2 | 230 | 11 | 77 | 71 | 56 | 5 |
| Naylor,Josh | 17 | L | 20 | 1B | aa | SD | 156 | 2 | 2 | 247 | 9 | 77 | 65 | 53 | -6 |
| | 18 | L | 21 | LF | aa | SD | 501 | 14 | 4 | 274 | 10 | 85 | 72 | 48 | 33 |
| Neslony,Tyler | 17 | L | 23 | RF | aa | ATL | 144 | 1 | 0 | 173 | 11 | 78 | 22 | 28 | -36 |
| | 18 | L | 24 | RF | a/a | ATL | 451 | 4 | 8 | 224 | 6 | 74 | 61 | 81 | -18 |
| Neuse,Sheldon | 17 | R | 23 | 3B | aa | OAK | 67 | 0 | 0 | 335 | 7 | 66 | 53 | 24 | -71 |
| | 18 | R | 24 | 3B | aaa | OAK | 499 | 4 | 3 | 228 | 5 | 62 | 69 | 74 | -64 |
| Newman,Kevin | 17 | R | 24 | SS | a/a | PIT | 509 | 3 | 10 | 245 | 5 | 87 | 52 | 105 | 33 |
| | 18 | R | 25 | SS | aaa | PIT | 437 | 3 | 22 | 258 | 5 | 87 | 57 | 114 | 41 |
| Ngoepe,Gift | 17 | R | 27 | SS | aaa | PIT | 264 | 5 | 2 | 188 | 8 | 61 | 99 | 98 | -30 |
| | 18 | R | 28 | SS | aaa | TOR | 131 | 2 | 2 | 141 | 13 | 43 | 74 | 86 | -117 |

| BATTER | yr | b | age | pos | lvl | org | ab | hr | sb | ba | bb% | ct% | px | sx | bpv |
|---|---|---|---|---|---|---|---|---|---|---|---|---|---|---|---|
| Nido,Tomas | 17 | R | 23 | C | aa | NYM | 367 | 8 | 0 | 215 | 8 | 80 | 70 | 39 | 6 |
| | 18 | R | 24 | C | a/a | NYM | 232 | 3 | 0 | 218 | 3 | 80 | 81 | 36 | 5 |
| Nimmo,Brandon | 17 | L | 24 | CF | aaa | NYM | 163 | 2 | 0 | 178 | 13 | 63 | 84 | 38 | -40 |
| Nogowski,John | 17 | R | 24 | 1B | aa | STL | 207 | 2 | 2 | 266 | 10 | 87 | 49 | 55 | 25 |
| | 18 | R | 25 | 1B | aa | STL | 298 | 8 | 0 | 256 | 9 | 92 | 55 | 19 | 37 |
| Noll,Jake | 18 | R | 24 | 3B | aa | WAS | 237 | 2 | 3 | 246 | 5 | 82 | 41 | 81 | -5 |
| Noriega,Gabriel | 17 | R | 27 | 3B | a/a | MIL | 210 | 2 | 0 | 196 | 2 | 72 | 37 | 28 | -68 |
| | 18 | R | 28 | 3B | a/a | MIL | 203 | 2 | 1 | 189 | 4 | 66 | 33 | 34 | -88 |
| Norwood,John | 17 | R | 25 | RF | aa | MIA | 473 | 16 | 4 | 254 | 11 | 67 | 96 | 76 | -11 |
| | 18 | R | 26 | RF | aa | MIA | 396 | 5 | 11 | 199 | 8 | 63 | 66 | 85 | -50 |
| Nottingham,Jacob | 17 | R | 22 | C | aa | MIL | 325 | 10 | 7 | 210 | 10 | 71 | 112 | 93 | 25 |
| | 18 | R | 23 | C | aaa | MIL | 178 | 7 | 1 | 235 | 5 | 62 | 136 | 85 | -7 |
| Numata,Chace | 17 | B | 25 | C | aa | PHI | 305 | 3 | 0 | 210 | 7 | 85 | 51 | 36 | 10 |
| | 18 | B | 26 | C | aa | NYY | 128 | 0 | 1 | 150 | 4 | 77 | 37 | 58 | -35 |
| Nunez,Antonio | 17 | R | 24 | SS | aa | HOU | 363 | 2 | 7 | 196 | 9 | 68 | 29 | 77 | -63 |
| | 18 | R | 25 | SS | aaa | HOU | 217 | 1 | 6 | 144 | 5 | 58 | 44 | 107 | -88 |
| Nunez,Dom | 17 | L | 22 | C | aa | COL | 297 | 10 | 6 | 203 | 13 | 73 | 86 | 75 | 12 |
| | 18 | L | 23 | C | aa | COL | 324 | 8 | 6 | 212 | 10 | 77 | 67 | 47 | -1 |
| Nunez,Jhon | 18 | B | 24 | C | aa | BOS | 232 | 1 | 3 | 218 | 6 | 79 | 42 | 89 | -11 |
| Nunez,Renato | 17 | R | 23 | LF | aaa | OAK | 473 | 23 | 2 | 216 | 7 | 68 | 131 | 61 | 12 |
| | 18 | R | 24 | 3B | aaa | BAL | 229 | 5 | 1 | 266 | 8 | 74 | 81 | 50 | -7 |
| O Brien,Peter | 17 | R | 27 | 1B | a/a | LA | 341 | 12 | 0 | 154 | 7 | 50 | 127 | 40 | -71 |
| | 18 | R | 28 | 1B | a/a | MIA | 356 | 21 | 1 | 166 | 11 | 53 | 163 | 36 | -23 |
| O Conner,Justin | 17 | R | 25 | C | a/a | TAM | 309 | 7 | 3 | 194 | 6 | 64 | 91 | 69 | -37 |
| O Hearn,Ryan | 17 | L | 24 | 1B | a/a | KC | 479 | 16 | 1 | 227 | 8 | 68 | 110 | 49 | -5 |
| | 18 | L | 25 | 1B | aaa | KC | 353 | 8 | 2 | 201 | 9 | 69 | 92 | 58 | -12 |
| O Neill,Tyler | 17 | R | 22 | LF | aaa | STL | 495 | 25 | 12 | 224 | 8 | 68 | 131 | 101 | 27 |
| | 18 | R | 23 | LF | aaa | STL | 238 | 19 | 2 | 270 | 9 | 68 | 175 | 95 | 61 |
| Oberste,Matt | 17 | R | 26 | 1B | aa | NYM | 455 | 5 | 3 | 246 | 10 | 71 | 66 | 71 | -19 |
| | 18 | R | 27 | 3B | a/a | NYM | 218 | 4 | 0 | 135 | 4 | 69 | 42 | 52 | -66 |
| Ochoa,Sebastian | 18 | R | 20 | CF | aaa | SEA | 20 | 0 | 1 | 131 | 0 | 72 | 80 | 215 | 20 |
| Ockimey,Josh | 17 | L | 22 | 1B | aa | BOS | 103 | 2 | 0 | 261 | 12 | 67 | 107 | 14 | -17 |
| | 18 | L | 23 | 1B | aa | BOS | 404 | 16 | 1 | 229 | 12 | 61 | 136 | 46 | -7 |
| Odom,Joseph | 17 | R | 25 | C | a/a | ATL | 64 | 1 | 0 | 221 | 8 | 67 | 45 | 14 | -72 |
| | 18 | R | 26 | C | a/a | SEA | 287 | 4 | 0 | 188 | 6 | 64 | 73 | 21 | -66 |
| O'Grady,Brian | 17 | L | 25 | CF | aa | CIN | 169 | 8 | 7 | 160 | 17 | 60 | 118 | 120 | 5 |
| | 18 | L | 26 | LF | a/a | CIN | 322 | 12 | 7 | 239 | 9 | 70 | 127 | 113 | 35 |
| Ohlman,Mike | 17 | R | 27 | C | aaa | TOR | 282 | 11 | 4 | 196 | 13 | 52 | 150 | 54 | -28 |
| | 18 | R | 28 | C | aaa | BOS | 236 | 8 | 1 | 178 | 10 | 55 | 96 | 34 | -70 |
| Ohtani,Shohei | 17 | L | 23 | OF | for | JPN | 191 | 5 | 0 | 312 | 9 | 70 | 116 | 96 | 22 |
| Okey,Chris | 18 | R | 24 | C | aa | CIN | 263 | 5 | 2 | 176 | 5 | 69 | 72 | 46 | -42 |
| Olloque,Manny | 18 | R | 22 | 3B | aaa | KC | 29 | 0 | 0 | 195 | 3 | 71 | 95 | 38 | -20 |
| Olson,Brian | 18 | R | 25 | C | aa | MIN | 58 | 0 | 0 | 177 | 9 | 64 | 15 | 37 | -102 |
| Olson,Matt | 17 | L | 23 | 1B | aaa | OAK | 294 | 17 | 2 | 236 | 11 | 70 | 138 | 73 | 34 |
| O'Neill,Michael | 17 | R | 25 | LF | aa | TEX | 271 | 7 | 10 | 237 | 8 | 67 | 83 | 122 | -13 |
| | 18 | R | 26 | CF | a/a | TEX | 462 | 9 | 23 | 214 | 7 | 69 | 83 | 113 | -9 |
| Opitz,Shane | 17 | L | 25 | SS | aaa | TOR | 246 | 1 | 6 | 237 | 6 | 83 | 55 | 70 | 12 |
| | 18 | L | 26 | 3B | aaa | MIL | 147 | 1 | 3 | 195 | 8 | 72 | 56 | 105 | -16 |
| Orf,Nate | 17 | R | 27 | 2B | aaa | MIL | 434 | 7 | 5 | 251 | 8 | 78 | 81 | 119 | 30 |
| | 18 | R | 28 | 2B | aaa | MIL | 399 | 4 | 13 | 223 | 7 | 77 | 64 | 104 | 5 |
| Ortega,Angel | 17 | R | 24 | SS | aa | MIL | 471 | 10 | 14 | 238 | 5 | 79 | 56 | 81 | -4 |
| Ortega,Rafael | 17 | L | 26 | CF | aaa | SD | 419 | 4 | 17 | 250 | 6 | 86 | 62 | 113 | 42 |
| | 18 | L | 27 | LF | aaa | MIA | 280 | 1 | 9 | 222 | 11 | 86 | 48 | 144 | 50 |
| Ortiz,Danny | 17 | L | 27 | CF | aaa | PIT | 411 | 12 | 4 | 229 | 4 | 78 | 93 | 65 | 14 |
| | 18 | L | 28 | LF | aaa | PHI | 392 | 12 | 0 | 186 | 4 | 67 | 94 | 27 | -41 |
| Osuna,Jose | 17 | R | 25 | 1B | aaa | PIT | 36 | 0 | 1 | 222 | 11 | 73 | 109 | 78 | 24 |
| | 18 | R | 26 | 3B | aaa | PIT | 302 | 7 | 4 | 269 | 7 | 80 | 91 | 53 | 27 |
| Overstreet,Kyle | 18 | R | 25 | 1B | aa | SD | 470 | 7 | 2 | 233 | 5 | 81 | 57 | 44 | -4 |
| Pabst,Arden | 18 | R | 23 | C | a/a | PIT | 60 | 2 | 0 | 192 | 6 | 71 | 70 | 43 | -30 |
| Pache,Cristian | 18 | R | 20 | CF | aa | ATL | 104 | 1 | 0 | 256 | 4 | 72 | 49 | 66 | -41 |
| Palacios,Jermaine | 18 | R | 22 | SS | aa | TAM | 164 | 1 | 3 | 168 | 5 | 71 | 47 | 84 | -40 |
| Palka,Daniel | 17 | L | 26 | RF | aaa | MIN | 332 | 10 | 1 | 250 | 7 | 74 | 82 | 72 | -3 |
| | 18 | L | 27 | RF | aaa | CHW | 63 | 2 | 1 | 234 | 11 | 58 | 121 | 52 | -29 |
| Panas,Connor | 18 | L | 25 | RF | aa | TOR | 370 | 7 | 3 | 206 | 5 | 74 | 71 | 69 | -13 |
| Pantoja,Alexis | 18 | B | 22 | 3B | aa | CLE | 79 | 0 | 0 | 182 | 3 | 69 | 25 | 41 | -83 |
| Papi,Mike | 17 | L | 25 | RF | a/a | CLE | 415 | 10 | 5 | 231 | 12 | 79 | 67 | 56 | 12 |
| | 18 | L | 26 | RF | aaa | CLE | 243 | 5 | 1 | 214 | 13 | 63 | 111 | 52 | -18 |
| Paredes,Isaac | 18 | R | 19 | 3B | aa | DET | 131 | 3 | 1 | 311 | 11 | 83 | 82 | 42 | 36 |
| Pascual,Oliver | 18 | S | 22 | 2B | aa | NYM | 25 | 0 | 0 | 245 | 0 | 59 | 40 | 7 | -128 |
| Patterson,Jordan | 17 | L | 25 | 1B | aaa | COL | 484 | 20 | 2 | 253 | 5 | 72 | 126 | 80 | 25 |
| | 18 | L | 26 | 1B | aaa | COL | 413 | 17 | 4 | 224 | 6 | 65 | 125 | 75 | -2 |
| Paul,Chris | 18 | R | 26 | 3B | aa | MIN | 338 | 5 | 1 | 215 | 4 | 75 | 72 | 69 | -12 |
| Paulino,Dorssys | 17 | R | 23 | LF | aa | CLE | 315 | 5 | 5 | 239 | 10 | 76 | 59 | 68 | -5 |
| | 18 | R | 24 | RF | a/a | CLE | 144 | 3 | 0 | 176 | 11 | 74 | 70 | 50 | -10 |
| Payton,Mark | 17 | L | 26 | LF | a/a | NYY | 324 | 6 | 3 | 225 | 6 | 75 | 69 | 85 | -2 |
| | 18 | L | 27 | LF | aaa | NYY | 197 | 5 | 2 | 214 | 12 | 69 | 74 | 63 | -18 |
| Paz,Andy | 17 | R | 24 | C | aa | OAK | 179 | 0 | 2 | 217 | 6 | 78 | 16 | 49 | -49 |
| Pena,Roberto | 17 | R | 25 | C | aaa | CHW | 200 | 2 | 0 | 176 | 4 | 83 | 39 | 8 | -25 |
| | 18 | R | 26 | C | aaa | TAM | 43 | 0 | 0 | 233 | 2 | 71 | 18 | 28 | -87 |
| Penalver,Carlos | 17 | R | 23 | SS | aa | CHC | 382 | 3 | 1 | 235 | 4 | 80 | 38 | 81 | -13 |
| | 18 | R | 24 | 2B | aa | CHC | 67 | 1 | 0 | 147 | 7 | 80 | 29 | 94 | -12 |
| Pentecost,Max | 18 | R | 25 | C | aa | TOR | 344 | 8 | 1 | 224 | 3 | 71 | 87 | 62 | -20 |
| Perez,Alex | 17 | L | 25 | 2B | aa | MIN | 125 | 0 | 0 | 248 | 15 | 77 | 30 | 34 | -28 |
| | 18 | L | 26 | 2B | a/a | MIN | 286 | 0 | 2 | 216 | 10 | 74 | 32 | 69 | -35 |
| Perez,Carlos | 17 | R | 27 | C | aaa | LAA | 261 | 3 | 3 | 269 | 7 | 81 | 63 | 69 | 11 |
| | 18 | R | 28 | C | a/a | TEX | 95 | 4 | 0 | 249 | 7 | 79 | 97 | 14 | 11 |
| Perez,Danienger | 18 | R | 22 | 3B | aa | NYY | 27 | 1 | 0 | 210 | 12 | 72 | 61 | 29 | -30 |

| BATTER | yr | b | age | pos | lvl | org | ab | hr | sb | ba | bb% | ct% | px | sx | bpv |
|---|---|---|---|---|---|---|---|---|---|---|---|---|---|---|---|
| Perez,Eury | 18 | R | 28 | RF | aaa | SF | 144 | 1 | 5 | 202 | 3 | 83 | 43 | 129 | 15 |
| Perez,Fernando | 17 | L | 24 | 1B | aa | SD | 212 | 3 | 0 | 195 | 6 | 67 | 57 | 47 | -57 |
| Perez,Juan | 17 | L | 26 | SS | aaa | CIN | 80 | 3 | 5 | 256 | 11 | 72 | 119 | 88 | 35 |
| | 18 | L | 27 | 2B | aaa | CHW | 163 | 3 | 7 | 149 | 5 | 58 | 84 | 142 | -46 |
| Perez,Michael | 17 | L | 25 | C | a/a | ARI | 271 | 4 | 0 | 242 | 9 | 74 | 94 | 33 | 0 |
| | 18 | L | 26 | C | aaa | ARI | 218 | 3 | 0 | 211 | 5 | 77 | 52 | 44 | -23 |
| Perez,Stephen | 17 | B | 27 | 2B | a/a | WAS | 266 | 3 | 7 | 169 | 9 | 65 | 45 | 81 | -60 |
| | 18 | B | 28 | SS | aa | WAS | 103 | 0 | 4 | 172 | 12 | 65 | 8 | 89 | -82 |
| Perez,Yanio | 18 | R | 23 | 3B | aa | TEX | 44 | 0 | 0 | 207 | 12 | 64 | 22 | 44 | -89 |
| Perez,Yefri | 17 | B | 26 | CF | aa | MIA | 248 | 0 | 9 | 147 | 12 | 73 | 35 | 139 | -14 |
| Perio,Noah | 17 | L | 26 | 2B | aa | SD | 430 | 3 | 6 | 249 | 5 | 84 | 39 | 84 | 6 |
| Perkins,Cameron | 17 | R | 27 | CF | aaa | PHI | 257 | 6 | 2 | 239 | 9 | 77 | 83 | 60 | 12 |
| | 18 | R | 28 | 1B | aaa | SEA | 362 | 7 | 6 | 197 | 5 | 75 | 79 | 86 | 2 |
| Peter,Jake | 17 | L | 24 | 2B | a/a | CHW | 463 | 12 | 9 | 250 | 7 | 69 | 80 | 89 | -18 |
| | 18 | L | 25 | 2B | aaa | LA | 329 | 5 | 3 | 200 | 6 | 66 | 61 | 85 | -49 |
| Peters,DJ | 18 | R | 23 | CF | aa | LA | 491 | 22 | 1 | 201 | 6 | 55 | 146 | 62 | -29 |
| Peterson,D.J. | 17 | R | 26 | 3B | aaa | CHW | 468 | 13 | 5 | 209 | 7 | 75 | 72 | 66 | -8 |
| | 18 | R | 26 | 3B | aaa | CIN | 422 | 14 | 2 | 235 | 4 | 66 | 114 | 42 | -20 |
| Peterson,Dustin | 17 | R | 23 | LF | aaa | ATL | 314 | 1 | 1 | 207 | 7 | 71 | 34 | 51 | -59 |
| | 18 | R | 24 | LF | aaa | ATL | 406 | 9 | 2 | 237 | 5 | 74 | 81 | 49 | -14 |
| Peterson,Kort | 18 | L | 24 | RF | aa | KC | 166 | 5 | 5 | 206 | 5 | 60 | 129 | 135 | -3 |
| Phillips,Anthony | 17 | R | 27 | SS | aa | COL | 287 | 3 | 2 | 189 | 5 | 73 | 43 | 29 | -54 |
| | 18 | R | 28 | SS | a/a | COL | 64 | 4 | 1 | 244 | 11 | 75 | 155 | 45 | 60 |
| Phillips,Brett | 17 | L | 23 | RF | aaa | MIL | 383 | 16 | 6 | 263 | 8 | 61 | 144 | 125 | 14 |
| | 18 | L | 24 | RF | aaa | MIL | 258 | 4 | 7 | 195 | 8 | 57 | 98 | 137 | -33 |
| Pinder,Chase | 18 | R | 22 | CF | aa | STL | 30 | 0 | 0 | 235 | 9 | 75 | 0 | 10 | -77 |
| Pineda,Andy | 18 | L | 22 | LF | aa | HOU | 65 | 2 | 3 | 316 | 5 | 73 | 83 | 108 | 3 |
| Pineda,Jeremias | 17 | B | 27 | CF | aa | MIA | 170 | 0 | 8 | 196 | 9 | 60 | 52 | 140 | -57 |
| Pinto,Eduard | 18 | L | 24 | LF | aa | TOR | 124 | 2 | 2 | 195 | 3 | 85 | 36 | 79 | -1 |
| Pintor,Luis | 18 | R | 23 | SS | aa | MIA | 40 | 0 | 0 | 42 | 8 | 61 | 23 | -10 | -121 |
| Pirela,Jose | 17 | R | 28 | 1B | aaa | SD | 181 | 8 | 5 | 249 | 5 | 82 | 97 | 103 | 48 |
| Pizzano,Dario | 17 | L | 26 | LF | a/a | SEA | 412 | 11 | 2 | 226 | 7 | 86 | 64 | 59 | 30 |
| | 18 | L | 27 | DH | aa | SEA | 400 | 8 | 2 | 230 | 8 | 82 | 65 | 51 | 15 |
| Plaia,Colton | 17 | R | 27 | C | aa | NYM | 137 | 1 | 0 | 204 | 12 | 71 | 49 | 34 | -39 |
| | 18 | R | 28 | C | aaa | NYM | 196 | 5 | 0 | 179 | 7 | 58 | 113 | 46 | -47 |
| Plawecki,Kevin | 17 | R | 26 | C | aaa | NYM | 247 | 7 | 0 | 253 | 5 | 80 | 80 | 35 | 5 |
| Polo,Tito | 17 | R | 23 | CF | aa | CHW | 127 | 1 | 13 | 308 | 8 | 80 | 78 | 166 | 48 |
| | 18 | R | 24 | CF | aa | CHW | 163 | 1 | 14 | 223 | 7 | 76 | 51 | 160 | 8 |
| Polonius,John | 18 | R | 27 | 2B | a/a | SF | 100 | 1 | 2 | 174 | 6 | 73 | 53 | 72 | -28 |
| Pompey,Dalton | 18 | B | 26 | RF | a/a | TOR | 160 | 3 | 7 | 219 | 8 | 68 | 80 | 92 | -16 |
| Potts,Hudson | 18 | R | 20 | 3B | aa | SD | 78 | 2 | 1 | 142 | 10 | 55 | 45 | 31 | -112 |
| Powell,Boog | 17 | L | 24 | CF | aaa | OAK | 222 | 4 | 9 | 290 | 9 | 84 | 62 | 108 | 39 |
| | 18 | L | 25 | RF | aaa | OAK | 147 | 0 | 4 | 188 | 11 | 72 | 11 | 61 | -61 |
| Prime,Correlle | 17 | R | 23 | 1B | aa | COL | 272 | 7 | 2 | 269 | 6 | 67 | 76 | 58 | -38 |
| | 18 | R | 24 | 1B | aa | TEX | 144 | 4 | 1 | 230 | 6 | 58 | 120 | 39 | -45 |
| Prince,Joshua | 18 | R | 30 | 1B | a/a | ARI | 305 | 3 | 7 | 205 | 10 | 64 | 65 | 76 | -46 |
| Procyshen,Jordan | 17 | L | 24 | C | aa | BOS | 215 | 3 | 0 | 183 | 9 | 66 | 65 | 31 | -53 |
| Profar,Juremi | 17 | R | 21 | 3B | aa | TEX | 415 | 9 | 1 | 253 | 4 | 86 | 54 | 46 | 10 |
| | 18 | R | 22 | 3B | aa | TEX | 349 | 8 | 1 | 216 | 6 | 86 | 57 | 29 | 12 |
| Profar,Jurickson | 17 | B | 24 | SS | aaa | TEX | 327 | 5 | 4 | 247 | 9 | 89 | 67 | 62 | 48 |
| Puello,Cesar | 17 | R | 26 | RF | aaa | LAA | 346 | 8 | 12 | 253 | 5 | 70 | 95 | 106 | -2 |
| | 18 | R | 27 | LF | aaa | SF | 294 | 3 | 4 | 245 | 8 | 72 | 53 | 84 | -27 |
| Pujols,Jose | 18 | R | 23 | RF | aa | PHI | 89 | 3 | 2 | 235 | 11 | 54 | 106 | 39 | -64 |
| Pullin,Andrew | 17 | L | 24 | LF | a/a | PHI | 504 | 18 | 4 | 238 | 6 | 78 | 114 | 75 | 40 |
| | 18 | L | 25 | LF | aaa | PHI | 117 | 2 | 1 | 145 | 5 | 58 | 85 | 79 | -64 |
| Queliz,Jose | 18 | R | 26 | C | a/a | ARI | 92 | 1 | 0 | 195 | 4 | 50 | 72 | 38 | -119 |
| Querecuto,Juniel | 17 | B | 25 | SS | aaa | SF | 293 | 1 | 5 | 197 | 7 | 75 | 34 | 56 | -41 |
| | 18 | B | 26 | 3B | a/a | ARI | 419 | 1 | 12 | 268 | 5 | 84 | 43 | 96 | 9 |
| Quinn,Roman | 17 | B | 24 | CF | aaa | PHI | 175 | 2 | 9 | 242 | 8 | 67 | 67 | 129 | -21 |
| | 18 | B | 25 | CF | a/a | PHI | 101 | 2 | 10 | 253 | 7 | 76 | 66 | 160 | 19 |
| Quintana,Gabriel | 17 | R | 25 | 1B | aa | DET | 434 | 18 | 1 | 229 | 4 | 68 | 127 | 74 | 5 |
| | 18 | R | 26 | DH | a/a | DET | 152 | 3 | 0 | 151 | 4 | 57 | 69 | 44 | -95 |
| Quiroz,Esteban | 18 | L | 26 | 2B | aa | BOS | 87 | 5 | 1 | 256 | 10 | 75 | 134 | 53 | 44 |
| Rabago,Chris | 18 | R | 25 | C | aa | NYY | 230 | 4 | 7 | 169 | 8 | 69 | 82 | 107 | -10 |
| Rademacher,Bijan | 17 | L | 26 | RF | aaa | CHC | 289 | 5 | 2 | 239 | 9 | 73 | 70 | 61 | -15 |
| | 18 | L | 27 | RF | aaa | CHC | 342 | 1 | 1 | 198 | 7 | 76 | 34 | 26 | -44 |
| Raley,Luke | 18 | L | 24 | 1B | aa | MIN | 484 | 16 | 3 | 244 | 5 | 69 | 101 | 111 | 3 |
| Ramirez,Harold | 17 | R | 23 | RF | aa | TOR | 444 | 5 | 4 | 247 | 6 | 84 | 51 | 63 | 9 |
| | 18 | R | 24 | RF | aa | TOR | 463 | 9 | 13 | 292 | 5 | 79 | 94 | 81 | 26 |
| Ramirez,Tyler | 17 | L | 22 | LF | aa | OAK | 208 | 3 | 2 | 279 | 10 | 73 | 68 | 65 | -12 |
| | 18 | L | 23 | LF | aa | OAK | 512 | 7 | 4 | 253 | 9 | 68 | 91 | 78 | -11 |
| Ramos,Henry | 17 | B | 25 | RF | a/a | LA | 194 | 7 | 2 | 301 | 6 | 83 | 90 | 65 | 36 |
| | 18 | B | 26 | CF | aaa | LA | 357 | 7 | 6 | 242 | 6 | 76 | 82 | 82 | 9 |
| Ramos,Mauricio | 17 | R | 25 | 3B | aa | KC | 356 | 8 | 0 | 231 | 3 | 72 | 63 | 49 | -37 |
| Ramos,Roberto | 18 | L | 24 | 1B | aa | COL | 199 | 13 | 2 | 216 | 9 | 61 | 169 | 31 | 9 |
| Randolph,Cornelius | 18 | L | 21 | LF | aa | PHI | 410 | 4 | 2 | 213 | 9 | 74 | 50 | 45 | -29 |
| Ravelo,Rangel | 17 | R | 25 | 1B | aaa | STL | 306 | 6 | 1 | 272 | 7 | 80 | 87 | 49 | 19 |
| | 18 | R | 26 | 1B | aaa | STL | 347 | 9 | 0 | 253 | 8 | 83 | 75 | 45 | 26 |
| Ray,Corey | 18 | L | 24 | CF | aa | MIL | 532 | 26 | 33 | 227 | 9 | 63 | 164 | 155 | 49 |
| Read,Raudy | 17 | R | 24 | C | aa | WAS | 411 | 13 | 2 | 232 | 5 | 78 | 91 | 43 | 11 |
| | 18 | R | 25 | C | a/a | WAS | 197 | 2 | 0 | 244 | 5 | 78 | 66 | 40 | -12 |
| Reed,A.J. | 17 | L | 24 | 1B | aaa | HOU | 476 | 22 | 0 | 205 | 9 | 62 | 123 | 27 | -24 |
| | 18 | L | 25 | 1B | aaa | HOU | 462 | 20 | 0 | 201 | 8 | 67 | 118 | 42 | -7 |
| Reed,Buddy | 18 | S | 23 | CF | aa | SD | 179 | 1 | 15 | 158 | 5 | 61 | 46 | 130 | -69 |
| Reed,Michael | 17 | R | 25 | LF | aa | MIL | 168 | 8 | 5 | 198 | 16 | 60 | 101 | 58 | -27 |
| | 18 | R | 26 | CF | a/a | ATL | 333 | 9 | 8 | 298 | 13 | 66 | 118 | 73 | 6 |
| Refsnyder,Rob | 17 | R | 26 | 2B | aaa | TOR | 150 | 2 | 2 | 296 | 10 | 75 | 95 | 94 | 27 |
| | 18 | R | 27 | RF | aaa | TAM | 184 | 3 | 0 | 230 | 7 | 68 | 70 | 41 | -43 |
| Reginatto,Leonardo | 17 | R | 27 | 3B | aaa | MIN | 277 | 3 | 0 | 270 | 8 | 79 | 52 | 18 | -18 |
| | 18 | R | 28 | 3B | aaa | MIN | 203 | 2 | 2 | 177 | 5 | 71 | 49 | 78 | -44 |
| Rei,Austin | 18 | R | 25 | C | aa | BOS | 265 | 5 | 1 | 219 | 9 | 70 | 81 | 55 | -19 |
| Reinheimer,Jack | 17 | R | 25 | SS | aaa | ARI | 482 | 3 | 8 | 225 | 6 | 79 | 37 | 82 | -16 |
| | 18 | R | 26 | SS | aaa | NYM | 245 | 3 | 8 | 189 | 6 | 72 | 57 | 105 | -22 |
| Reistetter,Matt | 18 | L | 26 | C | a/a | WAS | 38 | 1 | 0 | 111 | 2 | 61 | 39 | 13 | -116 |
| Reks,Zach | 18 | L | 25 | DH | aa | LA | 260 | 2 | 4 | 236 | 8 | 66 | 62 | 65 | -47 |
| Remillard,Will | 18 | R | 26 | C | a/a | CHC | 79 | 1 | 0 | 166 | 4 | 52 | 73 | 27 | -115 |
| Renda,Tony | 17 | R | 26 | 3B | aaa | ARI | 208 | 1 | 2 | 198 | 4 | 87 | 32 | 56 | 1 |
| | 18 | R | 27 | 2B | a/a | BOS | 267 | 4 | 8 | 277 | 5 | 81 | 76 | 97 | 26 |
| Rengifo,Luis | 18 | S | 21 | SS | a/a | LAA | 341 | 4 | 14 | 246 | 9 | 82 | 68 | 147 | 49 |
| Reyes,Alfredo | 18 | R | 25 | 2B | a/a | PIT | 118 | 1 | 9 | 211 | 7 | 60 | 45 | 110 | -74 |
| Reyes,Franmil | 17 | R | 22 | RF | aa | SD | 507 | 22 | 4 | 246 | 8 | 72 | 114 | 65 | 18 |
| | 18 | R | 23 | RF | aaa | SD | 210 | 11 | 0 | 269 | 11 | 67 | 135 | 48 | 14 |
| Reyes,Pablo | 17 | R | 24 | 2B | aa | PIT | 420 | 8 | 18 | 250 | 10 | 82 | 67 | 103 | 35 |
| | 18 | R | 25 | LF | a/a | PIT | 401 | 6 | 13 | 245 | 6 | 79 | 71 | 103 | 17 |
| Reyes,Victor | 17 | B | 23 | RF | aa | ARI | 479 | 3 | 15 | 276 | 4 | 82 | 65 | 109 | 23 |
| Reynolds,Bryan | 18 | B | 23 | CF | aa | PIT | 331 | 6 | 3 | 275 | 10 | 76 | 76 | 79 | 12 |
| Reynolds,Matt | 17 | R | 27 | LF | aaa | NYM | 128 | 3 | 1 | 242 | 8 | 69 | 84 | 59 | -21 |
| | 18 | R | 28 | SS | aaa | WAS | 309 | 3 | 2 | 219 | 9 | 71 | 101 | 86 | 9 |
| Rice,Ian | 17 | R | 24 | C | aa | CHC | 331 | 15 | 0 | 207 | 14 | 69 | 103 | 31 | -2 |
| | 18 | R | 25 | C | aa | CHC | 272 | 7 | 1 | 216 | 14 | 64 | 99 | 41 | -22 |
| Rickard,Joey | 17 | R | 26 | LF | aaa | BAL | 47 | 1 | 0 | 158 | 17 | 77 | 34 | 34 | -20 |
| | 18 | R | 27 | CF | aaa | BAL | 153 | 2 | 2 | 229 | 12 | 79 | 78 | 84 | 28 |
| Rickles,Nick | 17 | R | 27 | C | a/a | PHI | 128 | 3 | 1 | 211 | 4 | 80 | 81 | 32 | 6 |
| | 18 | R | 28 | C | aaa | PHI | 188 | 6 | 0 | 197 | 3 | 70 | 78 | 6 | -46 |
| Rifaela,Ademar | 18 | L | 24 | LF | aa | BAL | 359 | 6 | 1 | 224 | 6 | 71 | 75 | 47 | -30 |
| Rijo,Wendell | 17 | R | 22 | 2B | aa | MIL | 81 | 0 | 2 | 182 | 8 | 71 | 33 | 118 | -37 |
| | 18 | R | 23 | 2B | aa | NYY | 255 | 4 | 3 | 188 | 10 | 79 | 60 | 64 | 3 |
| Riley,Austin | 17 | R | 20 | 3B | aa | ATL | 178 | 8 | 2 | 296 | 11 | 69 | 103 | 81 | 5 |
| | 18 | R | 21 | 3B | a/a | ATL | 390 | 16 | 1 | 280 | 7 | 67 | 144 | 65 | 17 |
| Riley,John | 18 | R | 24 | 1B | aa | SF | 60 | 1 | 1 | 224 | 9 | 51 | 105 | 105 | -59 |
| Rios,Edwin | 17 | L | 23 | 1B | a/a | LA | 475 | 20 | 1 | 276 | 5 | 73 | 122 | 31 | 13 |
| | 18 | L | 24 | 3B | aaa | LA | 309 | 8 | 0 | 260 | 5 | 58 | 130 | 32 | -41 |
| Ritchie,Jamie | 17 | R | 24 | C | aa | HOU | 242 | 3 | 3 | 226 | 13 | 78 | 42 | 61 | -6 |
| | 18 | R | 25 | C | a/a | HOU | 242 | 2 | 2 | 241 | 9 | 72 | 68 | 58 | -21 |
| Rivas,Webster | 17 | R | 27 | C | aa | SD | 136 | 1 | 0 | 248 | 7 | 70 | 67 | 59 | -33 |
| | 18 | R | 28 | C | aa | SD | 217 | 3 | 1 | 222 | 4 | 73 | 48 | 45 | -47 |
| Rivera,Jeremy | 18 | B | 23 | SS | aa | BOS | 496 | 4 | 9 | 240 | 4 | 82 | 38 | 76 | -10 |
| Rivera,Yadiel | 17 | R | 25 | SS | aaa | MIL | 376 | 4 | 3 | 175 | 5 | 67 | 52 | 78 | -54 |
| Roache,Victor | 17 | R | 26 | LF | aa | LA | 74 | 0 | 2 | 145 | 4 | 58 | 51 | 71 | -96 |
| | 18 | R | 27 | LF | a/a | STL | 433 | 12 | 3 | 171 | 7 | 61 | 77 | 63 | -61 |
| Robbins,Mason | 17 | L | 24 | RF | aa | CHW | 480 | 3 | 4 | 244 | 4 | 88 | 25 | 60 | 1 |
| | 18 | L | 25 | RF | a/a | CHW | 235 | 3 | 3 | 237 | 3 | 75 | 59 | 93 | -18 |
| Robinson,Drew | 17 | L | 25 | 2B | aaa | TEX | 265 | 8 | 5 | 228 | 11 | 69 | 117 | 109 | 24 |
| | 18 | L | 26 | CF | a/a | TEX | 219 | 8 | 4 | 255 | 9 | 54 | 182 | 113 | 14 |
| Robinson,Errol | 17 | R | 23 | SS | aa | LA | 227 | 2 | 9 | 242 | 9 | 75 | 44 | 106 | -13 |
| | 18 | R | 24 | SS | aa | LA | 433 | 7 | 13 | 205 | 6 | 72 | 54 | 77 | -33 |
| Robles,Victor | 17 | R | 20 | CF | aa | WAS | 139 | 3 | 10 | 307 | 7 | 83 | 91 | 118 | 57 |
| | 18 | R | 21 | CF | aaa | WAS | 158 | 2 | 13 | 264 | 9 | 83 | 68 | 115 | 40 |
| Robson,Jake | 18 | L | 24 | CF | a/a | DET | 482 | 9 | 15 | 266 | 10 | 69 | 93 | 107 | 3 |
| Rodgers,Brendan | 17 | R | 21 | SS | aa | COL | 150 | 6 | 0 | 263 | 4 | 77 | 83 | 33 | -5 |
| | 18 | R | 22 | SS | a/a | COL | 426 | 14 | 9 | 250 | 5 | 78 | 102 | 84 | 32 |
| Rodriguez,Aderlin | 17 | R | 26 | 1B | aa | BAL | 484 | 17 | 0 | 221 | 7 | 74 | 78 | 25 | -20 |
| | 18 | R | 27 | 1B | aa | BAL | 483 | 17 | 1 | 229 | 4 | 77 | 83 | 48 | -2 |
| Rodriguez,Alfredo | 18 | R | 24 | SS | aa | CIN | 26 | 0 | 0 | 170 | 6 | 69 | 0 | 59 | -92 |
| Rodriguez,David | 18 | R | 22 | C | aa | TAM | 252 | 3 | 2 | 206 | 7 | 73 | 64 | 56 | -23 |
| Rodriguez,Herlis | 17 | L | 23 | CF | a/a | PHI | 172 | 4 | 3 | 202 | 2 | 71 | 70 | 65 | -35 |
| | 18 | L | 24 | RF | a/a | DET | 94 | 0 | 3 | 173 | 3 | 81 | 48 | 117 | 5 |
| Rodriguez,Luigi | 17 | L | 25 | LF | aa | CLE | 286 | 11 | 6 | 248 | 5 | 66 | 134 | 59 | 2 |
| | 18 | L | 26 | RF | aa | SF | 380 | 9 | 12 | 230 | 8 | 63 | 89 | 119 | -23 |
| Rodriguez,Nellie | 17 | R | 23 | 1B | aaa | CLE | 377 | 15 | 0 | 159 | 11 | 53 | 125 | 13 | -60 |
| | 18 | R | 24 | 1B | a/a | CLE | 346 | 12 | 0 | 208 | 8 | 54 | 139 | 26 | -45 |
| Rodriguez,Ronny | 17 | R | 25 | 2B | aaa | CLE | 447 | 14 | 12 | 261 | 4 | 79 | 78 | 82 | 13 |
| | 18 | R | 26 | 3B | aaa | DET | 260 | 8 | 8 | 300 | 3 | 80 | 114 | 128 | 57 |
| Rogers,Jake | 18 | R | 23 | C | aa | DET | 352 | 14 | 6 | 197 | 9 | 66 | 111 | 95 | 2 |
| Rogers,Wes | 18 | R | 24 | LF | aa | COL | 175 | 2 | 11 | 188 | 6 | 74 | 40 | 114 | -23 |
| Rojas,Jose | 17 | L | 24 | 3B | aa | LAA | 172 | 4 | 0 | 205 | 3 | 76 | 73 | 56 | -11 |
| | 18 | L | 25 | 1B | a/a | LAA | 381 | 12 | 7 | 231 | 6 | 72 | 100 | 92 | 10 |
| Rojas,Josh | 18 | L | 24 | LF | aa | HOU | 390 | 6 | 23 | 222 | 11 | 78 | 75 | 124 | 32 |
| Rollin,Franklin | 18 | R | 23 | LF | a/a | TEX | 101 | 2 | 4 | 234 | 5 | 82 | 81 | 104 | 35 |
| Roman,Mitch | 18 | R | 23 | 2B | aa | CHW | 95 | 0 | 3 | 213 | 3 | 54 | 35 | 89 | -123 |
| Romanski,Jake | 17 | R | 27 | C | a/a | BOS | 176 | 1 | 0 | 219 | 1 | 85 | 23 | 38 | -25 |
| Rondon,Cleuluis | 17 | B | 23 | SS | aa | MIA | 162 | 0 | 1 | 189 | 5 | 70 | 38 | 37 | -66 |
| | 18 | B | 24 | SS | aa | ATL | 75 | 0 | 0 | 110 | 8 | 65 | 36 | 71 | -71 |
| Rondon,Jose | 17 | R | 23 | SS | a/a | SD | 300 | 4 | 2 | 256 | 5 | 78 | 72 | 76 | 7 |
| | 18 | R | 24 | SS | aaa | CHW | 313 | 16 | 4 | 219 | 4 | 70 | 132 | 89 | 21 |
| Rooker,Brent | 18 | R | 24 | 1B | aa | MIN | 503 | 18 | 5 | 224 | 8 | 67 | 121 | 85 | 10 |
| Rosa,Viosergy | 17 | L | 27 | 1B | aa | OAK | 517 | 12 | 0 | 206 | 7 | 69 | 80 | 33 | -33 |
| Rosario,Amed | 17 | R | 22 | SS | aaa | NYM | 393 | 6 | 14 | 274 | 5 | 79 | 59 | 116 | 11 |
| Rose,Matt | 18 | R | 24 | 1B | aa | CHW | 426 | 16 | 0 | 167 | 7 | 61 | 110 | 22 | -46 |
| Rua,Ryan | 17 | R | 27 | LF | aaa | TEX | 177 | 6 | 2 | 216 | 4 | 64 | 97 | 103 | -28 |
| | 18 | R | 28 | LF | a/a | TEX | 80 | 2 | 3 | 194 | 7 | 64 | 111 | 119 | -2 |
| Ruiz,Keibert | 18 | S | 20 | C | aa | LA | 377 | 10 | 0 | 240 | 5 | 90 | 58 | 24 | 27 |
| Ruiz,Rio | 17 | L | 23 | 3B | aaa | ATL | 388 | 13 | 1 | 201 | 9 | 66 | 94 | 54 | -24 |
| | 18 | L | 24 | 3B | aaa | ATL | 498 | 7 | 2 | 238 | 6 | 80 | 63 | 71 | 4 |
| Russell,Michael | 17 | R | 24 | 3B | aa | TAM | 386 | 5 | 17 | 214 | 6 | 74 | 69 | 128 | 4 |
| | 18 | R | 25 | 3B | a/a | TAM | 301 | 2 | 7 | 211 | 5 | 71 | 56 | 114 | -24 |

| BATTER | yr | b | age | pos | lvl | org | ab | hr | sb | ba | bb% | ct% | px | sx | bpv |
|---|---|---|---|---|---|---|---|---|---|---|---|---|---|---|---|
| Ruta,Ben | 18 | L | 24 | LF | aa | NYY | 121 | 0 | 10 | 278 | 7 | 76 | 54 | 120 | 0 |
| Saez,Jorge | 17 | R | 27 | C | aa | NYY | 201 | 9 | 1 | 220 | 12 | 62 | 114 | 42 | -20 |
| | 18 | R | 28 | C | aa | NYY | 152 | 5 | 2 | 195 | 9 | 66 | 73 | 48 | -46 |
| Salazar,Alejandro | 18 | R | 22 | 2B | a/a | ATL | 193 | 0 | 4 | 283 | 4 | 82 | 40 | 85 | -6 |
| Salcedo,Erick | 17 | B | 24 | SS | aa | BAL | 408 | 4 | 2 | 217 | 7 | 85 | 30 | 39 | -7 |
| | 18 | B | 25 | SS | aa | BAL | 432 | 0 | 1 | 184 | 5 | 86 | 32 | 66 | 0 |
| Salter,Blaise | 18 | R | 25 | 1B | aa | DET | 47 | 1 | 0 | 164 | 0 | 65 | 49 | 5 | -97 |
| Salters,Daniel | 18 | L | 25 | C | a/a | CLE | 251 | 4 | 1 | 213 | 5 | 69 | 64 | 28 | -53 |
| Sanchez,Adrian | 17 | R | 27 | SS | a/a | WAS | 274 | 4 | 3 | 201 | 5 | 78 | 58 | 82 | -4 |
| | 18 | R | 28 | SS | aaa | WAS | 269 | 3 | 8 | 193 | 4 | 81 | 58 | 84 | 7 |
| Sanchez,Jesus | 18 | L | 21 | RF | aa | TAM | 98 | 1 | 1 | 191 | 9 | 76 | 76 | 65 | 3 |
| Sandberg,Cord | 17 | L | 22 | LF | aa | PHI | 99 | 4 | 1 | 238 | 3 | 66 | 115 | 44 | -25 |
| | 18 | L | 23 | CF | aa | PHI | 156 | 3 | 2 | 198 | 4 | 74 | 45 | 68 | -38 |
| Sanders,Matt | 18 | R | 22 | SS | aa | SEA | 29 | 0 | 0 | 150 | 3 | 77 | 52 | 51 | -29 |
| Sandoval,Brandon | 18 | R | 23 | RF | aa | LAA | 247 | 2 | 13 | 242 | 8 | 70 | 41 | 89 | -42 |
| Sanger,Brendon | 18 | L | 25 | RF | aa | LAA | 304 | 6 | 3 | 199 | 12 | 72 | 60 | 44 | -25 |
| Santana,Daniel | 18 | B | 28 | CF | aaa | ATL | 322 | 12 | 9 | 214 | 3 | 70 | 118 | 122 | 18 |
| Santana,Domingo | 18 | R | 26 | RF | aaa | MIL | 187 | 6 | 1 | 222 | 11 | 50 | 132 | 74 | -47 |
| Santander,Anthony | 17 | B | 23 | RF | aa | BAL | 50 | 4 | 0 | 320 | 11 | 78 | 168 | 37 | 83 |
| | 18 | B | 24 | RF | a/a | BAL | 253 | 6 | 3 | 213 | 4 | 82 | 71 | 86 | 21 |
| Sardinas,Luis | 17 | B | 24 | 2B | aaa | BAL | 310 | 4 | 5 | 281 | 3 | 85 | 37 | 78 | 2 |
| | 18 | B | 25 | SS | aaa | BAL | 231 | 4 | 2 | 230 | 3 | 80 | 67 | 47 | -3 |
| Sawyer,Wynston | 17 | R | 26 | C | aa | LA | 184 | 3 | 1 | 233 | 5 | 72 | 88 | 45 | -15 |
| | 18 | R | 27 | C | a/a | MIN | 101 | 2 | 0 | 219 | 11 | 76 | 46 | 35 | -25 |
| Scavuzzo,Jacob | 17 | R | 23 | LF | a/a | LA | 278 | 14 | 2 | 210 | 3 | 66 | 119 | 50 | -16 |
| | 18 | R | 24 | LF | a/a | LA | 392 | 20 | 9 | 217 | 5 | 68 | 141 | 88 | 22 |
| Schales,Brian | 18 | R | 22 | 3B | aa | MIA | 422 | 8 | 3 | 230 | 11 | 71 | 87 | 64 | -2 |
| Schrock,Max | 17 | L | 23 | 2B | aa | OAK | 417 | 5 | 3 | 286 | 6 | 89 | 46 | 57 | 25 |
| | 18 | L | 24 | 2B | aaa | STL | 417 | 3 | 8 | 212 | 4 | 90 | 42 | 63 | 24 |
| Schulz,Nick | 17 | R | 26 | CF | a/a | SD | 399 | 12 | 6 | 193 | 8 | 66 | 93 | 67 | -22 |
| | 18 | R | 27 | RF | a/a | SD | 289 | 5 | 3 | 158 | 9 | 57 | 67 | 47 | -84 |
| Schwindel,Frank | 17 | R | 25 | DH | a/a | KC | 529 | 17 | 0 | 291 | 2 | 82 | 103 | 23 | 24 |
| | 18 | R | 26 | DH | aaa | KC | 510 | 16 | 2 | 243 | 5 | 84 | 100 | 40 | 40 |
| Scivicque,Kade | 17 | R | 24 | C | a/a | ATL | 315 | 4 | 0 | 231 | 7 | 76 | 41 | 35 | -39 |
| | 18 | R | 25 | C | a/a | DET | 151 | 2 | 0 | 214 | 5 | 81 | 59 | 6 | -15 |
| Scott,Ryan | 18 | R | 23 | C | aa | SEA | 54 | 0 | 0 | 143 | 11 | 49 | 21 | 48 | -151 |
| Sedio,Chad | 18 | L | 24 | LF | aa | DET | 165 | 2 | 1 | 226 | 6 | 70 | 63 | 74 | -34 |
| Seferina,Darren | 17 | L | 23 | 2B | aa | STL | 173 | 4 | 9 | 255 | 9 | 74 | 67 | 112 | 6 |
| | 18 | L | 24 | 2B | aa | MIL | 96 | 3 | 4 | 136 | 4 | 66 | 73 | 112 | -35 |
| Seitzer,Cameron | 17 | L | 27 | DH | aa | CHW | 227 | 5 | 2 | 191 | 7 | 68 | 83 | 48 | -31 |
| Senzel,Nick | 17 | R | 22 | 3B | aa | CIN | 209 | 12 | 5 | 345 | 12 | 78 | 137 | 86 | 72 |
| | 18 | R | 23 | 2B | aaa | CIN | 171 | 5 | 7 | 280 | 9 | 74 | 114 | 99 | 36 |
| Sergakis,Nick | 18 | R | 25 | 2B | a/a | NYM | 61 | 1 | 0 | 126 | 3 | 61 | 83 | 21 | -75 |
| Sever,Joe | 17 | R | 27 | 3B | a/a | CLE | 442 | 6 | 4 | 243 | 5 | 80 | 54 | 56 | -8 |
| | 18 | R | 28 | 3B | a/a | CLE | 488 | 5 | 7 | 215 | 6 | 78 | 66 | 70 | 0 |
| Severino,Pedro | 17 | R | 24 | C | aaa | WAS | 211 | 4 | 1 | 212 | 6 | 77 | 40 | 27 | -39 |
| | 18 | R | 25 | C | aaa | WAS | 130 | 5 | 0 | 238 | 3 | 80 | 88 | 38 | 10 |
| Seymour,Anfernee | 18 | B | 23 | RF | aa | MIA | 51 | 1 | 3 | 222 | 9 | 80 | 78 | 82 | 27 |
| Shaffer,Richie | 17 | R | 26 | LF | aaa | CLE | 463 | 24 | 3 | 199 | 10 | 58 | 142 | 60 | -15 |
| | 18 | R | 27 | 1B | a/a | MIL | 219 | 8 | 0 | 145 | 6 | 52 | 134 | 38 | -58 |
| Shank,Zach | 17 | R | 26 | RF | aaa | SEA | 368 | 2 | 11 | 174 | 6 | 69 | 51 | 119 | -34 |
| Shaw,Chris | 17 | L | 24 | LF | a/a | SF | 469 | 17 | 0 | 257 | 7 | 68 | 124 | 30 | -6 |
| | 18 | L | 25 | LF | aaa | SF | 394 | 14 | 0 | 204 | 4 | 57 | 127 | 53 | -46 |
| Short,Zack | 18 | R | 23 | SS | aa | CHC | 436 | 15 | 7 | 205 | 14 | 66 | 121 | 83 | 15 |
| Siddall,Brett | 18 | L | 24 | DH | aa | OAK | 253 | 1 | 2 | 176 | 6 | 72 | 47 | 68 | -39 |
| Sierra,Anibal | 18 | R | 24 | SS | aa | HOU | 221 | 2 | 3 | 179 | 5 | 65 | 62 | 90 | -52 |
| Sierra,Magneuris | 17 | L | 21 | RF | aa | STL | 326 | 1 | 15 | 257 | 5 | 82 | 51 | 108 | 11 |
| | 18 | L | 22 | CF | aaa | MIA | 346 | 2 | 12 | 231 | 3 | 76 | 43 | 133 | -12 |
| Silviano,John | 18 | L | 24 | 1B | aa | MIA | 54 | 2 | 0 | 142 | 10 | 49 | 119 | 89 | -60 |
| Simcox,A.J. | 17 | R | 23 | SS | aa | DET | 436 | 7 | 10 | 226 | 5 | 82 | 64 | 117 | 28 |
| | 18 | R | 24 | SS | aa | DET | 166 | 2 | 2 | 182 | 5 | 71 | 47 | 116 | -31 |
| Siri,Jose | 18 | R | 23 | CF | aa | CIN | 253 | 11 | 12 | 211 | 8 | 59 | 147 | 151 | 18 |
| Sisco,Chance | 17 | L | 22 | C | aaa | BAL | 344 | 6 | 2 | 232 | 8 | 67 | 68 | 49 | -44 |
| | 18 | L | 23 | C | aaa | BAL | 128 | 3 | 0 | 221 | 10 | 70 | 68 | 41 | -32 |
| Slater,Austin | 17 | R | 25 | RF | aaa | SF | 184 | 3 | 3 | 274 | 6 | 75 | 74 | 59 | -9 |
| | 18 | R | 26 | RF | aaa | SF | 195 | 3 | 6 | 276 | 7 | 76 | 117 | 103 | 43 |
| Smith,Dominic | 17 | L | 22 | 1B | aaa | NYM | 457 | 13 | 1 | 278 | 7 | 77 | 92 | 47 | 11 |
| | 18 | L | 23 | 1B | aaa | NYM | 337 | 4 | 2 | 202 | 6 | 73 | 64 | 64 | -22 |
| Smith,Dwight | 17 | L | 25 | RF | aaa | TOR | 395 | 8 | 7 | 257 | 10 | 80 | 72 | 69 | 19 |
| | 18 | L | 26 | LF | aaa | TOR | 310 | 5 | 7 | 238 | 10 | 80 | 86 | 75 | 36 |
| Smith,Jordan | 17 | L | 27 | CF | a/a | CLE | 307 | 2 | 6 | 181 | 6 | 74 | 39 | 71 | -37 |
| Smith,Mallex | 17 | L | 24 | CF | aaa | TAM | 186 | 3 | 19 | 237 | 8 | 72 | 66 | 159 | 5 |
| Smith,Tyler | 17 | R | 26 | SS | aaa | TEX | 333 | 4 | 3 | 190 | 8 | 74 | 51 | 41 | -33 |
| | 18 | R | 27 | SS | aaa | ATL | 160 | 3 | 0 | 180 | 7 | 66 | 85 | 36 | -42 |
| Smith,Will | 18 | R | 23 | C | a/a | LA | 352 | 15 | 4 | 200 | 8 | 64 | 126 | 69 | -5 |
| Snyder,Michael | 18 | R | 28 | 1B | aa | ATL | 25 | 0 | 0 | 134 | 8 | 47 | 38 | 95 | -133 |
| Solak,Nick | 17 | R | 22 | 2B | aa | NYY | 119 | 2 | 1 | 275 | 8 | 78 | 89 | 75 | 23 |
| | 18 | R | 23 | 2B | aa | TAM | 478 | 16 | 18 | 250 | 11 | 73 | 85 | 112 | 15 |
| Soler,Jorge | 17 | R | 25 | RF | aaa | KC | 273 | 17 | 1 | 226 | 12 | 66 | 133 | 35 | 8 |
| Sosa,Edmundo | 18 | R | 22 | SS | a/a | STL | 452 | 9 | 5 | 238 | 4 | 78 | 81 | 69 | 5 |
| Sosa,Ruben | 17 | B | 27 | 2B | a/a | KC | 268 | 3 | 13 | 205 | 8 | 73 | 68 | 152 | 11 |
| Soto,Juan | 18 | L | 20 | LF | aa | WAS | 31 | 2 | 1 | 308 | 10 | 76 | 140 | 38 | 51 |
| Sparks,Taylor | 17 | R | 24 | 3B | aa | CIN | 62 | 2 | 0 | 127 | 13 | 62 | 97 | 39 | -36 |
| | 18 | R | 25 | 3B | a/a | CIN | 407 | 12 | 4 | 180 | 7 | 47 | 145 | 110 | -46 |
| Spires,Mitch | 18 | R | 22 | DH | aa | LAA | 61 | 0 | 2 | 223 | 3 | 78 | 12 | 63 | -51 |
| Spitz,Thomas | 18 | R | 26 | LF | aa | STL | 104 | 2 | 1 | 210 | 7 | 57 | 96 | 112 | -44 |
| Sportman,J.P. | 17 | R | 25 | RF | aa | OAK | 513 | 8 | 11 | 234 | 5 | 75 | 69 | 100 | -1 |
| | 18 | R | 26 | 2B | a/a | OAK | 435 | 10 | 14 | 226 | 4 | 75 | 88 | 94 | 10 |

| BATTER | yr | b | age | pos | lvl | org | ab | hr | sb | ba | bb% | ct% | px | sx | bpv |
|---|---|---|---|---|---|---|---|---|---|---|---|---|---|---|---|
| Stallings,Jacob | 17 | R | 28 | C | aaa | PIT | 216 | 3 | 1 | 251 | 6 | 84 | 66 | 50 | 17 |
| | 18 | R | 29 | C | aaa | PIT | 256 | 2 | 1 | 222 | 4 | 75 | 74 | 59 | -11 |
| Stamets,Eric | 17 | R | 26 | SS | a/a | CLE | 374 | 13 | 8 | 229 | 7 | 72 | 112 | 89 | 21 |
| | 18 | R | 27 | 2B | aaa | CLE | 238 | 4 | 4 | 169 | 5 | 69 | 68 | 77 | -36 |
| Stankiewicz,Drew | 17 | L | 24 | 2B | aa | PHI | 149 | 4 | 1 | 264 | 10 | 77 | 67 | 53 | 0 |
| | 18 | L | 25 | 2B | aa | PHI | 156 | 2 | 1 | 162 | 8 | 64 | 72 | 64 | -48 |
| Starling,Bubba | 17 | R | 25 | RF | aaa | KC | 278 | 5 | 4 | 215 | 5 | 74 | 69 | 74 | -15 |
| | 18 | R | 26 | CF | aaa | KC | 35 | 0 | 1 | 219 | 10 | 80 | 43 | 58 | -5 |
| Stassi,Max | 17 | R | 26 | C | a/a | HOU | 250 | 10 | 1 | 216 | 10 | 65 | 115 | 56 | -10 |
| Stevens,River | 17 | L | 25 | 3B | a/a | SD | 161 | 0 | 0 | 193 | 5 | 78 | 38 | 57 | -27 |
| | 18 | L | 26 | 2B | a/a | SD | 162 | 3 | 4 | 208 | 7 | 83 | 34 | 72 | -1 |
| Stevenson,Andrew | 17 | L | 23 | CF | a/a | WAS | 389 | 2 | 9 | 245 | 6 | 74 | 37 | 106 | -28 |
| | 18 | L | 24 | CF | aaa | WAS | 293 | 5 | 10 | 212 | 8 | 72 | 59 | 91 | -21 |
| Stewart,Christin | 17 | L | 24 | LF | aa | DET | 485 | 23 | 2 | 225 | 9 | 69 | 130 | 76 | 22 |
| | 18 | L | 25 | LF | aaa | DET | 444 | 20 | 0 | 236 | 11 | 73 | 114 | 50 | 24 |
| Stewart,D.J. | 17 | L | 24 | LF | aa | BAL | 457 | 17 | 16 | 229 | 11 | 77 | 82 | 101 | 28 |
| | 18 | L | 25 | RF | aaa | BAL | 421 | 11 | 9 | 205 | 9 | 73 | 86 | 87 | 7 |
| Stokes Jr.,Troy | 18 | R | 22 | LF | aa | MIL | 467 | 19 | 18 | 228 | 11 | 66 | 133 | 142 | 38 |
| Straw,Myles | 17 | R | 23 | CF | aa | HOU | 46 | 0 | 2 | 214 | 11 | 77 | 0 | 86 | -40 |
| | 18 | R | 24 | CF | a/a | HOU | 516 | 1 | 55 | 244 | 10 | 77 | 32 | 150 | 0 |
| Strom,Ian | 18 | R | 24 | CF | aa | NYM | 24 | 0 | 0 | 68 | 12 | 67 | 0 | 79 | -84 |
| Stuart,Champ | 17 | R | 25 | CF | aa | NYM | 320 | 5 | 33 | 196 | 11 | 54 | 88 | 144 | -47 |
| | 18 | R | 26 | CF | aa | NYM | 110 | 3 | 8 | 108 | 13 | 49 | 82 | 113 | -78 |
| Stubbs,Garrett | 17 | L | 24 | C | a/a | HOU | 340 | 3 | 8 | 191 | 8 | 79 | 47 | 86 | -1 |
| | 18 | L | 25 | C | aaa | HOU | 297 | 3 | 4 | 244 | 7 | 78 | 66 | 115 | 17 |
| Sturgeon,Cole | 17 | L | 26 | CF | aa | BOS | 406 | 4 | 8 | 233 | 7 | 76 | 65 | 84 | -3 |
| | 18 | L | 27 | RF | a/a | BOS | 364 | 7 | 10 | 230 | 6 | 74 | 64 | 81 | -13 |
| Suchy,Michael | 17 | R | 24 | RF | aa | PIT | 250 | 3 | 2 | 182 | 7 | 59 | 60 | 79 | -75 |
| Suiter,Jerrick | 17 | R | 24 | RF | aa | PIT | 347 | 8 | 6 | 261 | 11 | 74 | 88 | 90 | 18 |
| | 18 | R | 25 | RF | aaa | PIT | 191 | 1 | 5 | 172 | 8 | 58 | 86 | 97 | -52 |
| Sullivan,Brett | 17 | L | 23 | C | aa | TAM | 92 | 0 | 3 | 242 | 3 | 86 | 35 | 90 | 7 |
| | 18 | L | 24 | C | aa | TAM | 421 | 6 | 14 | 230 | 6 | 84 | 54 | 101 | 26 |
| Surum,Ricky | 18 | R | 24 | 2B | a/a | NYY | 40 | 0 | 1 | 196 | 6 | 71 | 35 | 146 | -29 |
| Sweet,Daniel | 18 | B | 24 | CF | a/a | CIN | 96 | 2 | 3 | 138 | 11 | 67 | 67 | 101 | -26 |
| Swihart,Blake | 17 | B | 25 | C | aaa | BOS | 195 | 3 | 1 | 179 | 6 | 70 | 61 | 73 | -36 |
| Tanielu,Nick | 18 | R | 26 | 3B | a/a | HOU | 392 | 7 | 2 | 232 | 5 | 85 | 61 | 56 | 16 |
| Tapia,Raimel | 17 | L | 23 | CF | aaa | COL | 263 | 2 | 9 | 348 | 3 | 84 | 83 | 128 | 49 |
| | 18 | L | 24 | CF | aaa | COL | 434 | 8 | 13 | 264 | 5 | 79 | 97 | 141 | 47 |
| Tarsovich,Jordan | 17 | R | 26 | 3B | aa | OAK | 341 | 2 | 10 | 200 | 9 | 74 | 47 | 108 | -14 |
| Tatis Jr.,Fernando | 17 | R | 18 | SS | aa | SD | 55 | 1 | 3 | 268 | 3 | 71 | 45 | 81 | -48 |
| | 18 | R | 19 | SS | aa | SD | 353 | 14 | 14 | 274 | 8 | 67 | 136 | 145 | 39 |
| Tauchman,Mike | 17 | L | 27 | CF | aaa | COL | 420 | 12 | 11 | 285 | 6 | 81 | 99 | 114 | 51 |
| | 18 | L | 28 | CF | aaa | COL | 403 | 13 | 7 | 259 | 8 | 80 | 101 | 93 | 46 |
| Tavarez,Aneury | 17 | L | 25 | RF | a/a | BOS | 196 | 4 | 7 | 263 | 7 | 80 | 63 | 103 | 20 |
| | 18 | L | 26 | RF | aaa | BOS | 394 | 6 | 7 | 205 | 6 | 71 | 72 | 89 | -20 |
| Taylor,Beau | 17 | L | 27 | C | a/a | OAK | 210 | 3 | 0 | 240 | 9 | 73 | 62 | 52 | -24 |
| | 18 | L | 28 | C | aaa | OAK | 302 | 2 | 1 | 198 | 10 | 64 | 62 | 81 | -46 |
| Taylor,Chuck | 17 | B | 24 | LF | aa | SEA | 471 | 8 | 8 | 239 | 11 | 77 | 65 | 90 | 12 |
| | 18 | B | 25 | LF | aa | SEA | 502 | 2 | 2 | 250 | 9 | 81 | 44 | 55 | -6 |
| Taylor,Kevin | 17 | L | 26 | LF | aa | NYM | 383 | 3 | 2 | 254 | 13 | 83 | 46 | 43 | 8 |
| | 18 | L | 27 | LF | aa | NYM | 437 | 1 | 2 | 207 | 5 | 84 | 34 | 63 | -5 |
| Taylor,Logan | 18 | R | 25 | 3B | a/a | SEA | 230 | 5 | 0 | 228 | 7 | 63 | 80 | 35 | -57 |
| Taylor,Tyrone | 17 | R | 23 | LF | aa | MIL | 85 | 1 | 2 | 241 | 9 | 77 | 85 | 122 | 31 |
| | 18 | R | 24 | CF | aaa | MIL | 446 | 14 | 8 | 228 | 4 | 80 | 92 | 114 | 39 |
| Tebow,Tim | 18 | L | 31 | LF | aa | NYM | 271 | 4 | 1 | 203 | 6 | 49 | 91 | 53 | -101 |
| Telis,Tomas | 17 | B | 26 | C | aaa | MIA | 280 | 4 | 4 | 231 | 5 | 87 | 52 | 90 | 30 |
| | 18 | B | 27 | C | aaa | MIA | 282 | 3 | 2 | 248 | 5 | 87 | 34 | 74 | 9 |
| Tellez,Rowdy | 17 | L | 22 | 1B | aaa | TOR | 445 | 6 | 6 | 223 | 9 | 78 | 78 | 73 | 15 |
| | 18 | L | 23 | 1B | aaa | TOR | 393 | 11 | 6 | 254 | 8 | 80 | 89 | 50 | 23 |
| Tendler,Luke | 17 | L | 26 | DH | aa | TEX | 420 | 11 | 1 | 214 | 8 | 72 | 86 | 52 | -10 |
| | 18 | L | 27 | LF | aa | BOS | 374 | 10 | 1 | 229 | 6 | 71 | 86 | 24 | -27 |
| Thaiss,Matt | 17 | L | 22 | 1B | aa | LAA | 178 | 1 | 4 | 277 | 17 | 69 | 77 | 60 | -11 |
| | 18 | L | 23 | 1B | aa | LAA | 525 | 12 | 6 | 233 | 6 | 77 | 87 | 91 | 19 |
| Thomas,Dillon | 17 | L | 25 | LF | a/a | COL | 273 | 5 | 7 | 207 | 6 | 62 | 85 | 86 | -46 |
| Thomas,Lane | 18 | R | 23 | CF | a/a | STL | 515 | 20 | 13 | 228 | 7 | 71 | 105 | 105 | 17 |
| Thompson,David | 17 | R | 24 | 3B | aa | NYM | 476 | 16 | 8 | 240 | 8 | 77 | 95 | 66 | 23 |
| | 18 | R | 25 | 3B | aaa | NYM | 66 | 1 | 1 | 193 | 4 | 63 | 78 | 78 | -54 |
| Thompson,Trayce | 17 | R | 26 | CF | aaa | LA | 339 | 7 | 2 | 172 | 5 | 67 | 72 | 91 | -35 |
| | 18 | R | 27 | RF | aaa | CHW | 160 | 3 | 2 | 171 | 7 | 56 | 113 | 71 | -49 |
| Tidaback,Sam | 18 | R | 25 | DH | aa | COL | 38 | 0 | 0 | 241 | 6 | 72 | 45 | 42 | -50 |
| Tilson,Charlie | 18 | L | 26 | CF | aaa | CHW | 270 | 0 | 9 | 201 | 5 | 77 | 31 | 83 | -33 |
| Tobias,Josh | 17 | B | 25 | 2B | aa | BOS | 332 | 2 | 3 | 242 | 4 | 76 | 58 | 43 | -26 |
| | 18 | B | 26 | 3B | aa | BOS | 123 | 1 | 1 | 196 | 4 | 71 | 37 | 44 | -65 |
| Tocci,Carlos | 17 | R | 22 | CF | a/a | PHI | 484 | 3 | 4 | 268 | 5 | 82 | 44 | 83 | 0 |
| | 18 | R | 23 | CF | a/a | TEX | 50 | 0 | 2 | 237 | 9 | 79 | 45 | 120 | 7 |
| Toffey,William | 18 | L | 23 | 3B | aa | NYM | 134 | 3 | 2 | 217 | 16 | 69 | 114 | 53 | 17 |
| Toles,Andrew | 18 | L | 26 | LF | aaa | LA | 258 | 5 | 2 | 250 | 3 | 73 | 84 | 73 | -8 |
| Tom,Ka'ai | 18 | L | 24 | CF | aa | CLE | 421 | 10 | 11 | 226 | 8 | 73 | 88 | 94 | 10 |
| Tomas,Yasmany | 18 | R | 28 | LF | aaa | ARI | 355 | 7 | 1 | 186 | 2 | 63 | 91 | 72 | -47 |
| Tomlinson,Kelby | 17 | R | 27 | 2B | aaa | SF | 108 | 0 | 7 | 244 | 9 | 86 | 33 | 90 | 18 |
| | 18 | R | 28 | SS | aaa | SF | 181 | 0 | 5 | 232 | 6 | 69 | 8 | 47 | -88 |
| Tomscha,Damek | 17 | R | 26 | 3B | aa | PHI | 159 | 3 | 1 | 263 | 5 | 86 | 47 | 43 | 7 |
| | 18 | R | 27 | 3B | a/a | PHI | 427 | 14 | 1 | 220 | 5 | 78 | 74 | 40 | -4 |
| Toro-Hernandez,Abra | 18 | S | 22 | 3B | aa | HOU | 178 | 2 | 3 | 211 | 8 | 72 | 96 | 83 | 7 |
| Torres,Gleyber | 17 | R | 21 | SS | a/a | NYY | 201 | 8 | 7 | 280 | 13 | 75 | 117 | 87 | 48 |
| | 18 | R | 22 | 3B | aaa | NYY | 49 | 1 | 1 | 319 | 8 | 77 | 89 | 89 | 25 |
| Torres,Nick | 17 | R | 24 | LF | aa | SD | 437 | 9 | 3 | 255 | 5 | 73 | 64 | 58 | -28 |
| | 18 | R | 25 | 1B | aaa | TEX | 118 | 0 | 1 | 166 | 3 | 65 | 15 | 37 | -109 |

| BATTER | yr | b | age | pos | lvl | org | ab | hr | sb | ba | bb% | ct% | px | sx | bpv |
|---|---|---|---|---|---|---|---|---|---|---|---|---|---|---|---|
| Torres,Ramon | 17 | B | 24 | SS | aaa | KC | 295 | 4 | 13 | 258 | 4 | 88 | 44 | 103 | 28 |
| | 18 | B | 25 | 2B | aaa | KC | 370 | 4 | 5 | 200 | 5 | 82 | 61 | 85 | 15 |
| Toups,Corey | 17 | R | 24 | 2B | a/a | KC | 387 | 6 | 11 | 223 | 8 | 65 | 82 | 123 | -20 |
| | 18 | R | 25 | 3B | a/a | KC | 234 | 4 | 9 | 204 | 9 | 60 | 73 | 105 | -50 |
| Tovar,Wilfredo | 17 | R | 26 | SS | aaa | STL | 360 | 4 | 15 | 213 | 5 | 80 | 53 | 85 | 0 |
| | 18 | R | 27 | SS | aaa | STL | 360 | 3 | 8 | 239 | 4 | 86 | 40 | 66 | 7 |
| Towey,Cal | 17 | L | 27 | 1B | a/a | MIA | 315 | 4 | 2 | 184 | 13 | 57 | 87 | 67 | -55 |
| Trahan,Blake | 17 | R | 24 | SS | aa | CIN | 455 | 2 | 12 | 215 | 11 | 79 | 37 | 76 | -6 |
| | 18 | R | 25 | SS | aaa | CIN | 444 | 2 | 5 | 210 | 8 | 72 | 38 | 63 | -44 |
| Travis,Sam | 17 | R | 24 | 1B | aaa | BOS | 304 | 5 | 5 | 260 | 10 | 80 | 63 | 60 | 10 |
| | 18 | R | 25 | 1B | aaa | BOS | 361 | 6 | 1 | 238 | 6 | 73 | 61 | 27 | -37 |
| Trevino,Jose | 17 | R | 25 | C | aa | TEX | 402 | 6 | 1 | 215 | 4 | 88 | 37 | 33 | 1 |
| | 18 | R | 26 | C | aa | TEX | 184 | 2 | 0 | 201 | 5 | 83 | 47 | 43 | -3 |
| Triunfel,Alberto | 17 | R | 23 | SS | aa | LAA | 301 | 3 | 3 | 225 | 5 | 76 | 45 | 68 | -28 |
| | 18 | R | 24 | SS | aaa | LAA | 117 | 3 | 1 | 210 | 3 | 69 | 81 | 80 | -26 |
| Tromp,Chad | 17 | R | 22 | C | aa | CIN | 113 | 0 | 1 | 205 | 12 | 85 | 26 | 31 | -2 |
| | 18 | R | 23 | C | a/a | CIN | 259 | 2 | 2 | 233 | 8 | 82 | 50 | 51 | 0 |
| Tromp,Jiandido | 17 | R | 24 | RF | a/a | PHI | 465 | 16 | 8 | 250 | 5 | 71 | 112 | 84 | 11 |
| | 18 | R | 25 | RF | a/a | PHI | 304 | 3 | 3 | 187 | 8 | 65 | 62 | 88 | -45 |
| Trosclair,Stefan | 18 | R | 24 | 1B | aa | STL | 101 | 3 | 1 | 225 | 4 | 62 | 78 | 65 | -59 |
| Tucker,Cole | 17 | B | 21 | SS | aa | PIT | 167 | 2 | 10 | 251 | 10 | 81 | 55 | 142 | 34 |
| | 18 | B | 22 | SS | aa | PIT | 517 | 4 | 30 | 240 | 8 | 79 | 53 | 135 | 17 |
| Tucker,Kyle | 17 | L | 20 | CF | aa | HOU | 287 | 15 | 7 | 251 | 6 | 75 | 136 | 83 | 50 |
| | 18 | L | 21 | RF | aaa | HOU | 407 | 19 | 15 | 284 | 8 | 77 | 120 | 109 | 53 |
| Tucker,Preston | 17 | L | 27 | RF | aaa | HOU | 492 | 15 | 1 | 186 | 7 | 73 | 80 | 73 | -5 |
| | 18 | L | 28 | LF | aaa | CIN | 69 | 0 | 0 | 197 | 2 | 87 | 43 | 64 | 8 |
| Twine,Justin | 18 | R | 23 | 2B | aa | MIA | 112 | 3 | 4 | 360 | 2 | 76 | 84 | 98 | 8 |
| Unroe,Riley | 17 | B | 22 | 2B | aa | TAM | 245 | 2 | 5 | 203 | 13 | 68 | 54 | 96 | -27 |
| | 18 | B | 23 | 2B | a/a | LAA | 364 | 3 | 8 | 188 | 9 | 68 | 40 | 75 | -52 |
| Urena,Jhoan | 17 | B | 23 | 1B | aaa | NYM | 44 | 2 | 1 | 185 | 7 | 57 | 113 | 84 | -43 |
| | 18 | B | 24 | RF | aa | NYM | 421 | 11 | 2 | 219 | 7 | 69 | 85 | 45 | -28 |
| Urena,Richard | 17 | B | 21 | SS | aa | TOR | 510 | 5 | 0 | 238 | 5 | 79 | 75 | 42 | 1 |
| | 18 | B | 22 | SS | aaa | TOR | 250 | 4 | 2 | 208 | 4 | 80 | 72 | 91 | 14 |
| Urias,Luis | 17 | R | 20 | SS | aa | SD | 442 | 3 | 7 | 294 | 13 | 85 | 48 | 89 | 32 |
| | 18 | R | 21 | 2B | aaa | SD | 450 | 6 | 1 | 252 | 10 | 73 | 81 | 83 | 1 |
| Urias,Ramon | 18 | R | 24 | 2B | a/a | STL | 311 | 9 | 1 | 254 | 5 | 79 | 108 | 40 | 27 |
| Urshela,Giovanny | 17 | R | 26 | 3B | aaa | CLE | 297 | 5 | 0 | 234 | 5 | 84 | 52 | 34 | 1 |
| | 18 | R | 27 | 3B | aaa | NYY | 224 | 2 | 0 | 234 | 4 | 83 | 55 | 50 | 1 |
| Valentin,Jesmuel | 17 | B | 23 | 2B | aaa | PHI | 96 | 1 | 0 | 205 | 5 | 81 | 35 | 26 | -28 |
| | 18 | B | 24 | 2B | aaa | PHI | 129 | 2 | 2 | 209 | 11 | 75 | 56 | 81 | -6 |
| Valenzuela,Luis | 17 | L | 24 | 2B | a/a | ATL | 266 | 2 | 4 | 230 | 5 | 79 | 50 | 110 | 0 |
| | 18 | L | 25 | SS | aa | ATL | 369 | 2 | 4 | 254 | 3 | 80 | 56 | 82 | -4 |
| Valera,Breyvic | 17 | B | 25 | 2B | aaa | STL | 424 | 6 | 9 | 273 | 7 | 91 | 57 | 92 | 53 |
| | 18 | B | 26 | 2B | aaa | BAL | 341 | 8 | 6 | 224 | 8 | 89 | 61 | 83 | 46 |
| Van Gansen,Peter | 17 | L | 23 | 2B | a/a | SD | 95 | 0 | 2 | 194 | 7 | 71 | 33 | 64 | -52 |
| | 18 | L | 24 | 2B | aa | SD | 336 | 3 | 0 | 221 | 9 | 83 | 48 | 38 | 0 |
| VanMeter,Josh | 17 | L | 22 | 3B | aa | CIN | 475 | 6 | 16 | 257 | 11 | 77 | 70 | 86 | 14 |
| | 18 | L | 23 | 2B | a/a | CIN | 428 | 11 | 8 | 235 | 9 | 76 | 114 | 96 | 43 |
| Vargas,Ildemaro | 17 | B | 26 | 2B | aaa | ARI | 487 | 6 | 5 | 250 | 4 | 90 | 63 | 88 | 46 |
| | 18 | B | 27 | SS | aaa | ARI | 537 | 4 | 6 | 230 | 3 | 89 | 50 | 93 | 33 |
| Vazquez,Jan | 17 | B | 26 | C | a/a | COL | 206 | 6 | 2 | 262 | 8 | 74 | 79 | 71 | -3 |
| | 18 | B | 27 | C | aaa | COL | 148 | 3 | 0 | 184 | 8 | 68 | 68 | 29 | -48 |
| Velazquez,Andrew | 17 | B | 23 | SS | aa | TAM | 374 | 7 | 15 | 209 | 7 | 66 | 80 | 119 | -23 |
| | 18 | B | 24 | SS | a/a | TAM | 458 | 11 | 26 | 222 | 6 | 65 | 90 | 160 | -6 |
| Verdugo,Alex | 17 | L | 21 | CF | aaa | LA | 433 | 5 | 8 | 285 | 8 | 87 | 63 | 87 | 44 |
| | 18 | L | 22 | CF | aaa | LA | 343 | 8 | 6 | 294 | 7 | 85 | 72 | 58 | 30 |
| Vertigan,Brett | 17 | L | 27 | LF | aa | OAK | 249 | 1 | 5 | 233 | 9 | 72 | 63 | 95 | -11 |
| | 18 | L | 28 | LF | a/a | OAK | 364 | 0 | 7 | 198 | 8 | 74 | 44 | 96 | -22 |
| Vielma,Engelb | 17 | B | 23 | SS | a/a | MIN | 415 | 0 | 3 | 220 | 5 | 79 | 35 | 67 | -24 |
| | 18 | B | 24 | SS | aaa | BAL | 38 | 0 | 0 | 162 | 8 | 74 | 57 | 74 | -17 |
| Vigil,Rodrigo | 17 | R | 24 | C | aa | MIA | 85 | 0 | 0 | 279 | 4 | 81 | 27 | 16 | -39 |
| | 18 | R | 25 | C | aa | MIA | 286 | 4 | 1 | 205 | 3 | 85 | 47 | 39 | -4 |
| Villanueva,Christian | 17 | R | 26 | 3B | aaa | SD | 398 | 12 | 3 | 231 | 6 | 75 | 95 | 59 | 9 |
| Villegas,Luis | 17 | R | 25 | C | a/a | KC | 68 | 0 | 0 | 220 | 2 | 74 | 24 | 15 | -74 |
| | 18 | R | 26 | C | a/a | KC | 185 | 3 | 1 | 201 | 6 | 74 | 56 | 58 | -27 |
| Vincej,Zach | 17 | R | 26 | SS | aaa | CIN | 378 | 3 | 3 | 227 | 6 | 84 | 49 | 67 | 9 |
| | 18 | R | 27 | SS | aaa | SEA | 385 | 4 | 5 | 194 | 6 | 79 | 45 | 77 | -12 |
| Vinicio,Jose | 17 | B | 24 | 2B | a/a | CHW | 325 | 4 | 8 | 206 | 3 | 70 | 61 | 110 | -32 |
| | 18 | R | 25 | SS | a/a | ARI | 275 | 2 | 7 | 183 | 3 | 69 | 53 | 122 | -35 |
| Vogelbach,Daniel | 17 | L | 25 | 1B | aaa | SEA | 459 | 14 | 2 | 244 | 11 | 74 | 83 | 40 | 0 |
| | 18 | L | 26 | 1B | aaa | SEA | 297 | 15 | 0 | 235 | 16 | 75 | 116 | 20 | 33 |
| Voit,Luke | 17 | R | 26 | 1B | aaa | STL | 269 | 10 | 1 | 277 | 8 | 78 | 114 | 37 | 30 |
| | 18 | R | 27 | 1B | a/a | NYY | 269 | 10 | 0 | 252 | 9 | 74 | 109 | 43 | 19 |
| Vosler,Jason | 17 | L | 24 | 3B | aa | CHC | 452 | 19 | 1 | 218 | 10 | 70 | 102 | 63 | 1 |
| | 18 | L | 25 | 3B | a/a | CHC | 471 | 18 | 1 | 212 | 8 | 63 | 126 | 53 | -12 |
| Wade,LaMonte | 17 | L | 23 | LF | aa | MIN | 424 | 6 | 8 | 278 | 14 | 83 | 63 | 98 | 40 |
| | 18 | L | 24 | LF | a/a | MIN | 424 | 9 | 8 | 234 | 11 | 81 | 57 | 87 | 20 |
| Wade,Tyler | 17 | L | 23 | SS | aaa | NYY | 339 | 7 | 23 | 287 | 9 | 75 | 88 | 142 | 34 |
| | 18 | L | 24 | SS | aaa | NYY | 364 | 4 | 9 | 223 | 8 | 74 | 60 | 93 | -10 |
| Wagner,Brandon | 18 | L | 23 | 1B | aa | NYY | 130 | 1 | 1 | 236 | 16 | 67 | 66 | 37 | -35 |
| Walding,Mitch | 17 | L | 25 | 3B | aa | PHI | 351 | 22 | 1 | 204 | 9 | 57 | 168 | 71 | 3 |
| | 18 | L | 26 | 3B | aaa | PHI | 388 | 17 | 2 | 224 | 13 | 53 | 150 | 67 | -21 |
| Waldrop,Kyle | 17 | L | 26 | RF | a/a | SEA | 453 | 8 | 3 | 246 | 7 | 74 | 74 | 50 | -15 |
| Walker,Adam | 17 | R | 26 | LF | a/a | CIN | 294 | 14 | 3 | 170 | 5 | 54 | 153 | 76 | -26 |
| | 18 | R | 27 | LF | aa | WAS | 120 | 3 | 1 | 164 | 12 | 50 | 128 | 91 | -45 |
| Walker,Christian | 17 | R | 26 | 1B | aaa | ARI | 514 | 21 | 3 | 250 | 7 | 76 | 117 | 94 | 40 |
| | 18 | R | 27 | 1B | aaa | ARI | 324 | 10 | 1 | 219 | 5 | 66 | 117 | 82 | -5 |

| BATTER | yr | b | age | pos | lvl | org | ab | hr | sb | ba | bb% | ct% | px | sx | bpv |
|---|---|---|---|---|---|---|---|---|---|---|---|---|---|---|---|
| Walker,Ryan | 18 | L | 26 | 2B | aa | MIN | 181 | 3 | 3 | 191 | 8 | 79 | 36 | 52 | -23 |
| Wall,Forrest | 18 | L | 23 | CF | aa | TOR | 299 | 6 | 15 | 217 | 8 | 68 | 83 | 131 | -4 |
| Wallach,Chad | 17 | R | 26 | C | aaa | CIN | 226 | 8 | 1 | 191 | 4 | 67 | 99 | 44 | -30 |
| | 18 | R | 27 | C | aaa | MIA | 147 | 2 | 0 | 177 | 10 | 60 | 68 | 39 | -71 |
| Walsh,Jared | 17 | L | 24 | 1B | aa | LAA | 69 | 3 | 1 | 210 | 4 | 51 | 133 | 50 | -64 |
| | 18 | L | 25 | 1B | a/a | LAA | 327 | 11 | 1 | 221 | 7 | 62 | 131 | 46 | -19 |
| Walton,Donnie | 18 | L | 24 | 2B | aa | SEA | 208 | 1 | 2 | 200 | 8 | 81 | 55 | 71 | 4 |
| Ward,Drew | 17 | L | 23 | 3B | aa | WAS | 413 | 8 | 0 | 210 | 10 | 65 | 75 | 21 | -52 |
| | 18 | L | 24 | 1B | a/a | WAS | 374 | 11 | 1 | 221 | 12 | 66 | 102 | 71 | -8 |
| Ward,Nelson | 17 | L | 25 | 2B | aa | SEA | 264 | 1 | 7 | 226 | 7 | 66 | 44 | 81 | -58 |
| Ward,Taylor | 17 | R | 24 | C | aa | LAA | 119 | 3 | 0 | 260 | 14 | 83 | 47 | 17 | 7 |
| | 18 | R | 25 | 3B | a/a | LAA | 375 | 10 | 13 | 283 | 11 | 69 | 97 | 76 | 1 |
| Washington,David | 17 | L | 27 | 1B | aaa | BAL | 368 | 15 | 6 | 206 | 6 | 53 | 126 | 78 | -51 |
| Wass,Wade | 17 | R | 26 | DH | aa | LAA | 191 | 9 | 8 | 223 | 10 | 56 | 143 | 114 | -6 |
| | 18 | R | 27 | C | a/a | LAA | 72 | 2 | 1 | 124 | 7 | 45 | 115 | 41 | -100 |
| Way,Bo | 17 | L | 26 | CF | a/a | LAA | 364 | 1 | 16 | 205 | 5 | 78 | 25 | 103 | -23 |
| | 18 | L | 27 | CF | a/a | LAA | 234 | 0 | 5 | 239 | 6 | 80 | 36 | 68 | -18 |
| Weeks,Drew | 17 | R | 24 | RF | aa | COL | 471 | 15 | 11 | 236 | 7 | 76 | 90 | 83 | 15 |
| | 18 | R | 25 | LF | a/a | COL | 289 | 8 | 3 | 228 | 6 | 72 | 91 | 98 | 5 |
| Weiss,Erich | 17 | L | 26 | 2B | aaa | PIT | 332 | 5 | 5 | 240 | 9 | 77 | 79 | 102 | 23 |
| | 18 | L | 27 | 1B | aaa | PIT | 219 | 4 | 1 | 190 | 5 | 71 | 76 | 91 | -15 |
| Wendle,Joe | 17 | L | 27 | 2B | aaa | OAK | 478 | 5 | 10 | 232 | 3 | 80 | 66 | 120 | 16 |
| Wernes,Bobby | 18 | R | 24 | 3B | aa | COL | 33 | 0 | 0 | 235 | 2 | 66 | 90 | 86 | -32 |
| Westbrook,Jamie | 17 | R | 22 | LF | aa | ARI | 377 | 7 | 2 | 255 | 3 | 88 | 66 | 67 | 33 |
| | 18 | R | 23 | LF | a/a | ARI | 431 | 12 | 3 | 245 | 4 | 81 | 83 | 84 | 25 |
| White,Eli | 18 | R | 24 | 2B | aa | OAK | 504 | 6 | 14 | 266 | 9 | 74 | 80 | 118 | 15 |
| White,Max | 17 | L | 24 | LF | aa | COL | 371 | 6 | 20 | 236 | 10 | 68 | 92 | 123 | 5 |
| White,Mikey | 18 | R | 25 | 3B | aa | OAK | 225 | 4 | 0 | 180 | 8 | 59 | 62 | 22 | -90 |
| White,T.J. | 17 | R | 25 | 3B | aa | MIN | 366 | 12 | 2 | 251 | 8 | 75 | 112 | 67 | 29 |
| | 18 | R | 26 | 3B | aa | MIN | 134 | 3 | 1 | 156 | 4 | 68 | 63 | 44 | -55 |
| White,Tyler | 17 | R | 27 | 3B | aaa | HOU | 436 | 15 | 4 | 224 | 6 | 69 | 93 | 67 | -14 |
| | 18 | R | 28 | 2B | aaa | HOU | 255 | 9 | 1 | 248 | 10 | 80 | 96 | 40 | 32 |
| Wiel,Zander | 18 | R | 25 | 1B | a/a | MIN | 437 | 8 | 7 | 265 | 7 | 76 | 82 | 80 | 10 |
| Wilkerson,Steve | 17 | B | 25 | 3B | aa | BAL | 245 | 5 | 4 | 239 | 7 | 73 | 54 | 61 | -30 |
| | 18 | B | 26 | 2B | a/a | BAL | 93 | 3 | 0 | 206 | 5 | 74 | 100 | 59 | 7 |
| Wilkins,Andrew | 18 | L | 30 | 1B | a/a | MIN | 210 | 11 | 1 | 160 | 8 | 63 | 123 | 60 | -11 |
| Williams,Jackson | 17 | R | 31 | C | a/a | PIT | 189 | 1 | 0 | 162 | 7 | 72 | 23 | 22 | -72 |
| | 18 | R | 32 | C | a/a | PIT | 86 | 1 | 0 | 170 | 5 | 78 | 39 | 5 | -40 |
| Williams,Justin | 17 | L | 22 | RF | aa | TAM | 366 | 12 | 5 | 274 | 8 | 79 | 93 | 85 | 33 |
| | 18 | L | 23 | RF | aaa | STL | 425 | 8 | 3 | 218 | 5 | 75 | 67 | 45 | -22 |
| Williams,Mason | 17 | L | 26 | CF | aaa | NYY | 399 | 2 | 16 | 228 | 6 | 80 | 27 | 105 | -13 |
| | 18 | L | 27 | CF | aaa | CIN | 318 | 5 | 4 | 231 | 7 | 78 | 71 | 89 | 10 |
| Williams,Nick | 17 | L | 24 | RF | aaa | PHI | 282 | 14 | 4 | 250 | 5 | 63 | 142 | 88 | 2 |
| Williamson,Mac | 17 | R | 27 | RF | aaa | SF | 351 | 9 | 3 | 196 | 5 | 65 | 90 | 70 | -34 |
| | 18 | R | 28 | RF | aaa | SF | 182 | 7 | 1 | 199 | 8 | 69 | 97 | 63 | -9 |
| Wilson,Jacob | 17 | R | 27 | 3B | aa | STL | 431 | 13 | 2 | 209 | 8 | 74 | 80 | 51 | -5 |
| | 18 | R | 28 | 3B | a/a | WAS | 377 | 5 | 1 | 226 | 7 | 75 | 75 | 37 | -10 |
| Wilson,Kenneth | 17 | R | 27 | CF | a/a | OAK | 296 | 2 | 11 | 194 | 6 | 68 | 37 | 107 | -52 |
| | 18 | R | 28 | RF | a/a | DET | 142 | 2 | 8 | 212 | 10 | 61 | 67 | 132 | -39 |
| Wilson,Weston | 18 | R | 24 | 3B | aa | MIL | 46 | 1 | 1 | 221 | 6 | 83 | 46 | 59 | -1 |
| Winker,Jesse | 17 | L | 24 | RF | aaa | CIN | 299 | 2 | 2 | 277 | 10 | 82 | 58 | 29 | 4 |
| Wisdom,Patrick | 17 | R | 26 | 3B | aaa | STL | 456 | 23 | 2 | 203 | 6 | 63 | 137 | 52 | -9 |
| | 18 | R | 27 | 3B | aaa | STL | 371 | 10 | 8 | 231 | 8 | 64 | 105 | 89 | -17 |
| Witte,Jantzen | 17 | R | 27 | 1B | aaa | BOS | 244 | 2 | 2 | 220 | 11 | 76 | 52 | 64 | -12 |
| | 18 | R | 28 | 3B | a/a | BOS | 381 | 9 | 4 | 229 | 7 | 67 | 101 | 82 | -10 |
| Wong,Joey | 17 | L | 29 | SS | a/a | SEA | 426 | 2 | 0 | 185 | 11 | 74 | 26 | 41 | -48 |
| | 18 | L | 30 | SS | a/a | NYM | 102 | 2 | 0 | 137 | 10 | 62 | 70 | 35 | -62 |
| Wong,Kean | 17 | L | 22 | 2B | a/a | TAM | 422 | 4 | 15 | 240 | 7 | 77 | 54 | 77 | -10 |
| | 18 | L | 23 | 2B | aaa | TAM | 451 | 8 | 6 | 250 | 7 | 71 | 73 | 87 | -15 |
| Wood,Eric | 17 | R | 25 | 3B | aaa | PIT | 416 | 13 | 6 | 212 | 9 | 67 | 112 | 111 | 11 |
| | 18 | R | 26 | RF | aaa | PIT | 283 | 8 | 4 | 223 | 5 | 68 | 122 | 91 | 10 |
| Woodrow,Danny | 18 | L | 23 | RF | aa | DET | 342 | 3 | 16 | 285 | 7 | 78 | 48 | 106 | -2 |
| Woodward,Trent | 17 | B | 25 | 3B | a/a | HOU | 157 | 3 | 0 | 207 | 9 | 62 | 75 | 43 | -58 |
| Wren,Kyle | 17 | L | 26 | LF | aaa | MIL | 476 | 4 | 17 | 227 | 7 | 80 | 48 | 130 | 14 |
| | 18 | L | 27 | LF | aaa | BOS | 262 | 2 | 8 | 235 | 8 | 71 | 65 | 91 | -18 |
| Wrenn,Stephen | 18 | R | 24 | RF | aa | HOU | 472 | 8 | 39 | 219 | 7 | 67 | 79 | 153 | -7 |
| Wynns,Austin | 17 | R | 27 | C | aa | BAL | 370 | 8 | 1 | 219 | 10 | 78 | 52 | 48 | -10 |
| | 18 | R | 28 | C | aaa | BAL | 139 | 3 | 0 | 189 | 6 | 68 | 63 | 35 | -55 |
| Yarbrough,Alex | 17 | B | 26 | SS | aa | MIA | 364 | 3 | 4 | 201 | 7 | 65 | 60 | 97 | -44 |
| Yastrzemski,Mike | 17 | L | 27 | RF | a/a | BAL | 354 | 12 | 2 | 213 | 9 | 67 | 92 | 86 | -12 |
| | 18 | L | 28 | LF | a/a | BAL | 428 | 8 | 6 | 198 | 8 | 71 | 85 | 89 | -4 |
| Young,Andy | 18 | R | 24 | 2B | aa | STL | 135 | 6 | 0 | 270 | 4 | 78 | 90 | 44 | 7 |
| Young,Chesny | 17 | R | 25 | 2B | aaa | CHC | 425 | 1 | 5 | 211 | 6 | 80 | 33 | 60 | -21 |
| | 18 | R | 26 | 2B | aaa | CHC | 271 | 0 | 3 | 214 | 4 | 76 | 23 | 71 | -45 |
| Zagunis,Mark | 17 | R | 24 | LF | aaa | CHC | 330 | 10 | 3 | 225 | 14 | 67 | 102 | 57 | -2 |
| | 18 | R | 25 | RF | aaa | CHC | 371 | 5 | 8 | 224 | 13 | 68 | 60 | 75 | -30 |
| Zavala,Seby | 18 | R | 25 | C | a/a | CHW | 380 | 12 | 0 | 224 | 7 | 66 | 104 | 29 | -28 |
| Zehner,Zack | 17 | R | 25 | LF | aa | NYY | 431 | 12 | 7 | 237 | 12 | 67 | 96 | 89 | -5 |
| | 18 | R | 26 | LF | a/a | NYY | 418 | 13 | 2 | 230 | 7 | 64 | 117 | 78 | -12 |
| Zimmer,Bradley | 17 | L | 25 | CF | aaa | CLE | 126 | 4 | 7 | 266 | 8 | 65 | 148 | 129 | 36 |

| PITCHER | yr | t | age | lvl | org | ip | era | whip | bf/g | ctl | dom | cmd | hr/9 | h% | s% | bpv |
|---|---|---|---|---|---|---|---|---|---|---|---|---|---|---|---|---|
| Acevedo,Domingc | 17 | R | 23 | a/a | NYY | 92 | 3.68 | 1.33 | 23.8 | 2.7 | 7.6 | 2.9 | 1.2 | 32 | 77 | 72 |
| | 18 | R | 24 | aa | NYY | 66 | 3.88 | 1.28 | 19.4 | 3.0 | 6.0 | 2.0 | 0.6 | 29 | 70 | 65 |
| Adams,Austin L | 17 | R | 26 | aaa | WAS | 59 | 2.84 | 1.62 | 6.0 | 6.2 | 11.0 | 1.8 | 0.4 | 36 | 83 | 98 |
| | 18 | R | 27 | aaa | WAS | 47 | 4.87 | 1.78 | 5.3 | 4.3 | 11.5 | 2.7 | 0.2 | 45 | 71 | 109 |
| Adams,Chance | 17 | R | 23 | a/a | NYY | 150 | 3.41 | 1.27 | 22.8 | 3.8 | 7.0 | 1.9 | 1.0 | 27 | 77 | 60 |
| | 18 | R | 24 | aaa | NYY | 113 | 6.24 | 1.63 | 18.6 | 4.9 | 7.6 | 1.5 | 1.8 | 31 | 65 | 25 |
| Adams,Spencer | 17 | R | 21 | aa | CHW | 153 | 6.03 | 1.65 | 26.2 | 2.7 | 6.0 | 2.3 | 1.5 | 36 | 66 | 30 |
| | 18 | R | 22 | a/a | CHW | 161 | 4.73 | 1.55 | 25.2 | 3.4 | 4.7 | 1.4 | 1.4 | 31 | 74 | 12 |
| Adcock,Brett | 18 | L | 23 | aa | HOU | 40 | 4.25 | 1.55 | 19.5 | 5.0 | 5.4 | 1.1 | 0.5 | 30 | 72 | 41 |
| Agrazal,Dario | 18 | R | 24 | aa | PIT | 87 | 4.93 | 1.40 | 24.5 | 1.4 | 4.3 | 3.1 | 1.0 | 33 | 66 | 54 |
| Akin,Keegan | 18 | L | 23 | aa | BAL | 139 | 3.68 | 1.32 | 23.1 | 3.7 | 7.5 | 2.1 | 1.2 | 28 | 77 | 59 |
| Alaniz,Ruben | 17 | R | 26 | a/a | DET | 69 | 4.54 | 1.80 | 7.6 | 4.3 | 7.6 | 1.8 | 1.3 | 37 | 78 | 34 |
| | 18 | R | 27 | a/a | TAM | 41 | 4.63 | 1.44 | 6.1 | 3.6 | 8.6 | 2.4 | 0.3 | 35 | 66 | 94 |
| Alcala,Jorge | 18 | R | 23 | aa | MIN | 62 | 5.14 | 1.60 | 19.6 | 4.5 | 7.0 | 1.6 | 0.8 | 33 | 68 | 49 |
| Alcantara,Raul | 17 | R | 25 | aaa | OAK | 34 | 3.20 | 1.46 | 8.0 | 1.9 | 4.6 | 2.4 | 0.0 | 35 | 76 | 72 |
| | 18 | R | 26 | aaa | OAK | 84 | 6.55 | 1.61 | 11.6 | 1.6 | 4.4 | 2.8 | 1.1 | 36 | 59 | 40 |
| Alcantara,Sandy | 17 | R | 22 | aa | STL | 125 | 5.43 | 1.60 | 22.1 | 3.9 | 6.3 | 1.6 | 1.0 | 33 | 67 | 38 |
| | 18 | R | 23 | aaa | MIA | 117 | 4.33 | 1.34 | 25.7 | 2.9 | 5.8 | 2.0 | 0.7 | 30 | 68 | 57 |
| Alcantara,Victor | 17 | R | 24 | a/a | DET | 75 | 4.84 | 1.79 | 8.8 | 6.0 | 7.1 | 1.2 | 0.1 | 35 | 71 | 61 |
| | 18 | R | 25 | aaa | DET | 52 | 3.93 | 1.42 | 7.6 | 1.3 | 6.3 | 4.7 | 0.7 | 36 | 73 | 110 |
| Alexander,Jason | 18 | R | 25 | a/a | LAA | 71 | 4.56 | 1.41 | 20.2 | 2.3 | 4.9 | 2.2 | 0.9 | 32 | 69 | 44 |
| Alexander,Tyler | 17 | L | 23 | aa | DET | 138 | 6.32 | 1.68 | 23.0 | 1.5 | 6.4 | 4.1 | 1.5 | 39 | 64 | 67 |
| | 18 | L | 24 | a/a | DET | 140 | 5.94 | 1.78 | 24.8 | 1.5 | 4.9 | 3.2 | 1.3 | 39 | 68 | 41 |
| Allard,Kolby | 17 | L | 20 | aa | ATL | 150 | 4.34 | 1.49 | 24.0 | 3.0 | 7.2 | 2.4 | 0.8 | 35 | 72 | 68 |
| | 18 | L | 21 | aaa | ATL | 113 | 3.16 | 1.29 | 24.4 | 2.5 | 6.1 | 2.4 | 0.5 | 31 | 76 | 75 |
| Allen,Logan | 18 | L | 21 | a/a | SD | 150 | 2.62 | 1.09 | 23.5 | 2.8 | 8.0 | 2.9 | 0.6 | 27 | 78 | 102 |
| Allie,Stetson | 18 | R | 27 | a/a | LA | 24 | 4.78 | 1.24 | 4.1 | 5.9 | 7.7 | 1.3 | 1.2 | 19 | 64 | 58 |
| Almeida,Adrian | 18 | L | 23 | aa | LAA | 50 | 5.21 | 1.72 | 6.9 | 9.2 | 8.4 | 0.9 | 0.6 | 25 | 69 | 65 |
| Almonte,Miguel | 17 | R | 24 | a/a | KC | 47 | 2.31 | 1.39 | 12.4 | 2.6 | 8.0 | 3.1 | 0.6 | 35 | 86 | 92 |
| | 18 | R | 25 | aaa | LAA | 21 | 9.20 | 2.30 | 4.3 | 5.6 | 7.8 | 1.4 | 1.5 | 44 | 60 | 12 |
| Almonte,Yency | 17 | R | 23 | a/a | COL | 111 | 4.15 | 1.63 | 22.5 | 4.6 | 5.9 | 1.3 | 1.3 | 31 | 78 | 22 |
| | 18 | R | 24 | aaa | COL | 45 | 6.26 | 1.43 | 10.7 | 2.8 | 5.3 | 1.9 | 1.8 | 29 | 60 | 14 |
| Alvarez,Yadier | 17 | R | 21 | aa | LA | 33 | 4.02 | 1.64 | 21.0 | 6.0 | 8.7 | 1.4 | 0.3 | 34 | 74 | 78 |
| | 18 | R | 22 | aa | LA | 49 | 4.73 | 1.56 | 12.7 | 6.9 | 8.4 | 1.2 | 0.3 | 29 | 68 | 76 |
| Alzolay,Adbert | 17 | R | 22 | aa | CHC | 33 | 3.92 | 1.37 | 19.5 | 3.5 | 7.3 | 2.1 | 0.0 | 33 | 68 | 91 |
| | 18 | R | 23 | aaa | CHC | 41 | 5.06 | 1.47 | 22.1 | 2.8 | 5.0 | 1.8 | 0.9 | 32 | 66 | 37 |
| Anderson,Drew | 17 | R | 23 | a/a | PHI | 114 | 4.30 | 1.25 | 21.2 | 3.4 | 6.4 | 1.9 | 1.3 | 26 | 70 | 46 |
| | 18 | R | 24 | aaa | PHI | 106 | 4.80 | 1.32 | 23.1 | 2.6 | 6.2 | 2.4 | 1.5 | 29 | 68 | 44 |
| Anderson,Ian | 18 | R | 20 | aa | ATL | 20 | 2.87 | 1.24 | 20.4 | 3.9 | 9.5 | 2.4 | 0.0 | 31 | 74 | 118 |
| Anderson,Justin | 17 | R | 25 | aa | LAA | 59 | 7.20 | 1.76 | 6.4 | 4.9 | 4.7 | 1.0 | 1.3 | 32 | 60 | 3 |
| Anderson,Shaun | 18 | R | 24 | a/a | SF | 142 | 4.17 | 1.35 | 23.7 | 2.1 | 6.7 | 3.2 | 0.8 | 33 | 70 | 83 |
| Anderson,Tanner | 17 | R | 24 | aa | PIT | 133 | 4.62 | 1.52 | 19.3 | 2.4 | 5.2 | 2.1 | 0.5 | 35 | 69 | 56 |
| | 18 | R | 25 | aaa | PIT | 62 | 3.17 | 1.49 | 6.9 | 2.2 | 5.6 | 2.5 | 0.3 | 35 | 78 | 71 |
| Angulo,Argenis | 18 | R | 24 | aa | CLE | 53 | 7.07 | 2.00 | 5.5 | 5.5 | 9.0 | 1.6 | 0.9 | 41 | 64 | 51 |
| Appel,Mark | 17 | R | 26 | aaa | PHI | 82 | 7.13 | 2.11 | 23.8 | 6.4 | 5.4 | 0.8 | 1.3 | 36 | 67 | 0 |
| Aquino,Jayson | 17 | L | 25 | aaa | BAL | 115 | 5.87 | 1.80 | 25.2 | 3.8 | 5.9 | 1.5 | 1.1 | 37 | 68 | 24 |
| | 18 | L | 26 | a/a | BAL | 59 | 6.51 | 1.79 | 22.7 | 4.3 | 4.7 | 1.1 | 0.2 | 36 | 60 | 37 |
| Arano,Victor | 17 | R | 22 | aa | PHI | 39 | 4.98 | 1.42 | 5.1 | 2.5 | 7.9 | 3.1 | 1.9 | 32 | 72 | 54 |
| Arauz,Harold | 18 | R | 23 | a/a | PHI | 142 | 5.44 | 1.57 | 24.0 | 2.8 | 7.0 | 2.5 | 1.4 | 35 | 68 | 45 |
| Arias,Estarlin | 18 | R | 24 | aa | STL | 34 | 4.91 | 1.75 | 7.4 | 3.8 | 6.7 | 1.8 | 1.2 | 37 | 75 | 30 |
| Armenteros,Roge | 17 | R | 23 | a/a | HOU | 124 | 2.14 | 1.07 | 20.1 | 2.6 | 9.4 | 3.7 | 0.6 | 29 | 83 | 129 |
| | 18 | R | 24 | aaa | HOU | 118 | 3.66 | 1.31 | 22.1 | 3.3 | 8.6 | 2.6 | 1.1 | 31 | 76 | 79 |
| Arredondo,Edgar | 18 | R | 21 | aa | TEX | 45 | 6.11 | 1.53 | 21.8 | 2.1 | 4.6 | 2.1 | 1.0 | 34 | 60 | 35 |
| Ash,Brett | 17 | R | 26 | a/a | SEA | 81 | 9.50 | 2.17 | 19.2 | 3.3 | 4.2 | 1.3 | 1.7 | 41 | 56 | -21 |
| Asher,Alec | 17 | R | 26 | aaa | BAL | 50 | 6.58 | 1.95 | 24.0 | 3.3 | 5.3 | 1.6 | 1.4 | 39 | 68 | 7 |
| | 18 | R | 27 | aaa | MIL | 101 | 6.38 | 1.72 | 20.9 | 3.2 | 3.5 | 1.1 | 1.2 | 34 | 64 | -1 |
| Atkinson,Ryan | 17 | R | 24 | aa | ARI | 36 | 4.49 | 1.61 | 23.0 | 6.4 | 6.8 | 1.1 | 1.0 | 28 | 74 | 40 |
| | 18 | R | 25 | aa | ARI | 109 | 5.96 | 1.64 | 16.8 | 5.1 | 8.2 | 1.6 | 1.2 | 33 | 65 | 48 |
| Aviles,Robbie | 17 | R | 26 | a/a | CLE | 61 | 4.98 | 1.42 | 6.3 | 2.6 | 3.9 | 1.5 | 0.8 | 30 | 65 | 29 |
| Bachar,Lake | 18 | R | 23 | aa | SD | 87 | 6.72 | 1.75 | 19.9 | 4.0 | 5.5 | 1.4 | 1.6 | 34 | 64 | 5 |
| Bacus,Dakota | 17 | R | 26 | aa | WAS | 19 | 3.20 | 1.44 | 7.2 | 2.1 | 6.5 | 3.1 | 1.1 | 34 | 82 | 65 |
| | 18 | R | 27 | a/a | WAS | 37 | 5.23 | 1.62 | 6.3 | 3.5 | 9.0 | 2.6 | 0.3 | 40 | 65 | 93 |
| Baez,Michel | 18 | R | 22 | aa | SD | 19 | 8.33 | 1.92 | 22.6 | 5.6 | 8.7 | 1.6 | 1.9 | 37 | 58 | 19 |
| Baez,Sandy | 18 | R | 25 | aa | DET | 105 | 7.31 | 1.80 | 14.7 | 4.2 | 5.7 | 1.4 | 2.0 | 34 | 62 | -5 |
| Bailey,Brandon | 18 | R | 24 | aa | HOU | 26 | 4.88 | 1.32 | 21.7 | 3.2 | 6.6 | 2.1 | 2.1 | 26 | 72 | 24 |
| Baker,Dylan | 18 | R | 26 | aa | LA | 37 | 6.83 | 1.77 | 5.0 | 3.9 | 4.3 | 1.1 | 1.5 | 33 | 63 | -5 |
| Baldonado,Albert( | 17 | L | 24 | a/a | NYM | 60 | 5.97 | 1.61 | 5.3 | 4.8 | 8.4 | 1.8 | 1.6 | 32 | 66 | 39 |
| | 18 | L | 25 | aaa | CHC | 59 | 5.62 | 1.84 | 7.4 | 5.9 | 8.2 | 1.4 | 0.8 | 37 | 70 | 50 |
| Ball,Matt | 18 | R | 23 | aa | LAA | 20 | 6.76 | 1.63 | 22.5 | 3.1 | 5.0 | 1.6 | 0.0 | 36 | 54 | 56 |
| Ball,Trey | 17 | L | 23 | aa | BOS | 125 | 6.87 | 2.03 | 24.2 | 4.4 | 6.1 | 1.4 | 1.4 | 39 | 68 | 8 |
| | 18 | L | 24 | aa | BOS | 66 | 9.52 | 2.15 | 9.7 | 3.6 | 6.1 | 1.7 | 1.7 | 42 | 56 | 1 |
| Banda,Anthony | 17 | L | 24 | aaa | ARI | 122 | 5.70 | 1.51 | 24.0 | 3.6 | 7.1 | 2.0 | 1.1 | 33 | 63 | 49 |
| | 18 | L | 25 | aaa | TAM | 42 | 4.67 | 1.70 | 23.7 | 4.1 | 9.0 | 2.2 | 0.7 | 39 | 73 | 72 |
| Banks,Tanner | 17 | L | 26 | aa | CHW | 55 | 9.25 | 2.18 | 23 | 3.2 | 5.5 | 1.7 | 1.9 | 42 | 58 | -11 |
| | 18 | L | 27 | aa | CHW | 61 | 3.97 | 1.59 | 26.9 | 2.7 | 5.2 | 1.9 | 1.1 | 34 | 78 | 31 |
| Bannister,Nathan | 17 | R | 24 | aaa | SEA | 23 | 5.10 | 1.38 | 23.8 | 2.0 | 6.2 | 3.1 | 2.2 | 30 | 71 | 34 |
| | 18 | R | 25 | a/a | SEA | 143 | 7.10 | 1.80 | 24.5 | 3.1 | 4.7 | 1.5 | 1.5 | 36 | 62 | 1 |
| Banuelos,Manuel | 17 | L | 26 | aaa | LAA | 95 | 5.11 | 1.73 | 11.1 | 4.4 | 6.7 | 1.5 | 0.3 | 37 | 69 | 55 |
| | 18 | L | 27 | aaa | LA | 110 | 4.38 | 1.56 | 15.6 | 3.4 | 8.2 | 2.4 | 0.9 | 36 | 73 | 69 |
| Barbato,John | 17 | R | 25 | aaa | PIT | 39 | 4.43 | 1.42 | 6.18 | 3.3 | 7.3 | 2.2 | 2.4 | 28 | 81 | 18 |
| | 18 | R | 26 | aaa | DET | 38 | 2.06 | 1.15 | 4.59 | 2.7 | 6.7 | 2.5 | 0.3 | 28 | 83 | 91 |
| Barker,Brandon | 17 | R | 25 | a/a | BAL | 123 | 5.97 | 1.76 | 21.6 | 3.9 | 6.8 | 1.7 | 0.9 | 37 | 66 | 41 |
| Barlow,Scott | 17 | R | 25 | a/a | LA | 140 | 3.92 | 1.22 | 21.7 | 3.6 | 8.5 | 2.3 | 1.1 | 27 | 71 | 78 |
| | 18 | R | 26 | a/a | KC | 51 | 7.46 | 1.83 | 17 | 4.0 | 7.4 | 1.9 | 1.7 | 38 | 61 | 21 |
| Barrett,Jake | 17 | R | 26 | aaa | ARI | 22 | 5.42 | 1.42 | 4.67 | 4.4 | 6.2 | 1.4 | 0.9 | 28 | 62 | 46 |
| | 18 | R | 27 | aaa | ARI | 54 | 2.72 | 1.24 | 5.24 | 4.6 | 8.7 | 1.9 | 0.4 | 27 | 78 | 93 |
| Barria,Jaime | 17 | R | 21 | a/a | LAA | 76 | 3.38 | 1.26 | 20.7 | 2.0 | 6.4 | 3.2 | 0.9 | 31 | 76 | 81 |
| | 18 | R | 22 | aaa | LAA | 18 | 3.09 | 1.31 | 14.9 | 2.1 | 8.4 | 4.0 | 0.8 | 34 | 79 | 110 |

| PITCHER | yr | t | age | lvl | org | ip | era | whip | bf/g | ctl | dom | cmd | hr/9 | h% | s% | bpv |
|---|---|---|---|---|---|---|---|---|---|---|---|---|---|---|---|---|
| Bashlor,Tyler | 18 | R | 25 | aa | NYM | 24 | 3.08 | 1.21 | 4.8 | 4.8 | 9.4 | 2.0 | 0.8 | 25 | 77 | 91 |
| Bassitt,Chris | 17 | R | 28 | aaa | OAK | 38 | 7.95 | 1.82 | 10.3 | 4.1 | 5.4 | 1.3 | 0.8 | 37 | 54 | 27 |
| | 18 | R | 29 | aaa | OAK | 83 | 5.63 | 1.67 | 20.8 | 3.0 | 6.5 | 2.2 | 0.7 | 38 | 66 | 54 |
| Bautista,Gerson | 18 | R | 23 | a/a | NYM | 51 | 4.90 | 1.68 | 6.2 | 3.0 | 10.5 | 3.5 | 0.5 | 44 | 70 | 113 |
| Beasley,Jeremy | 18 | R | 23 | aa | LAA | 45 | 3.03 | 1.15 | 17.9 | 2.8 | 6.4 | 2.3 | 0.7 | 26 | 76 | 74 |
| Beck,Landon | 17 | R | 25 | aa | STL | 41 | 5.04 | 1.70 | 5.0 | 4.0 | 7.6 | 1.9 | 0.8 | 37 | 71 | 55 |
| | 18 | R | 26 | a/a | STL | 65 | 4.62 | 1.51 | 6.6 | 3.2 | 6.1 | 1.9 | 1.0 | 33 | 71 | 45 |
| Beede,Tyler | 17 | R | 24 | aaa | SF | 109 | 5.74 | 1.66 | 25.7 | 3.3 | 5.7 | 1.7 | 1.0 | 35 | 66 | 31 |
| | 18 | R | 25 | aaa | SF | 74 | 7.46 | 1.95 | 10.7 | 6.6 | 7.4 | 1.1 | 1.0 | 36 | 61 | 34 |
| Beeks,Jalen | 17 | L | 24 | a/a | BOS | 145 | 4.69 | 1.48 | 24.0 | 3.8 | 7.7 | 2.0 | 1.0 | 33 | 70 | 60 |
| | 18 | L | 25 | aaa | BOS | 88 | 4.28 | 1.36 | 23.0 | 2.8 | 9.4 | 3.3 | 1.3 | 33 | 73 | 87 |
| Beggs,Dustin | 18 | R | 25 | aa | MIA | 25 | 1.75 | 1.14 | 24.8 | 3.0 | 6.9 | 2.3 | 0.4 | 27 | 86 | 88 |
| Bell,Chadwick | 17 | L | 28 | aaa | DET | 34 | 5.26 | 1.72 | 22.3 | 3.2 | 6.0 | 1.9 | 1.1 | 37 | 71 | 32 |
| | 18 | L | 29 | aaa | ATL | 58 | 7.85 | 1.87 | 8.5 | 3.0 | 6.3 | 2.1 | 1.6 | 39 | 59 | 19 |
| Bellow,Kirby | 18 | L | 27 | a/a | ARI | 48 | 4.11 | 1.51 | 4.4 | 5.5 | 5.1 | 0.9 | 0.3 | 28 | 72 | 46 |
| Beltre,Dario | 18 | R | 26 | aa | LAA | 28 | 6.93 | 1.55 | 5.8 | 5.8 | 8.6 | 1.5 | 0.8 | 30 | 53 | 65 |
| Bencomo,Omar | 17 | R | 28 | a/a | MIA | 93 | 6.91 | 1.78 | 19.4 | 2.7 | 7.0 | 2.6 | 1.7 | 39 | 64 | 31 |
| | 18 | R | 29 | a/a | MIN | 133 | 5.20 | 1.54 | 20.7 | 1.5 | 5.5 | 3.6 | 1.6 | 35 | 71 | 49 |
| Bender,Joel | 18 | L | 27 | aa | CIN | 29 | 2.21 | 1.23 | 6.2 | 2.2 | 6.4 | 3.0 | 0.9 | 30 | 87 | 78 |
| Benjamin,Wes | 18 | L | 25 | aa | TEX | 81 | 4.85 | 1.50 | 23.4 | 2.9 | 6.3 | 2.1 | 1.3 | 33 | 71 | 40 |
| Bergen,Travis | 18 | L | 25 | aa | TOR | 37 | 0.64 | 1.12 | 5.4 | 2.4 | 8.4 | 3.6 | 0.6 | 30 | 99 | 115 |
| Bergjans,Tommy | 17 | R | 25 | a/a | PHI | 56 | 8.58 | 1.79 | 19.8 | 2.9 | 5.9 | 2.0 | 2.9 | 35 | 57 | -22 |
| Bernardino,Brenn | 17 | L | 25 | aa | CIN | 40 | 7.52 | 2.04 | 5.2 | 5.3 | 7.9 | 1.5 | 1.9 | 39 | 66 | 9 |
| | 18 | L | 26 | aa | CIN | 20 | 8.81 | 1.81 | 4.4 | 3.6 | 8.8 | 2.5 | 1.3 | 41 | 50 | 55 |
| Berrios,Jose | 17 | R | 23 | aaa | MIN | 40 | 1.71 | 1.00 | 25.3 | 2.0 | 7.1 | 3.6 | 0.6 | 26 | 87 | 111 |
| Bettencourt,Trevo | 18 | R | 24 | aa | PHI | 17 | 3.66 | 1.47 | 6.6 | 4.8 | 8.3 | 1.7 | 1.2 | 30 | 80 | 54 |
| Biagini,Joe | 17 | R | 27 | aaa | TOR | 17 | 5.10 | 1.48 | 18.6 | 3.8 | 5.7 | 1.5 | 1.6 | 28 | 70 | 18 |
| | 18 | R | 28 | aaa | TOR | 23 | 6.32 | 1.51 | 25.1 | 3.7 | 3.8 | 1.0 | 0.5 | 30 | 56 | 28 |
| Bieber,Shane | 17 | R | 22 | aa | CLE | 54 | 2.99 | 1.31 | 25.0 | 0.9 | 6.3 | 7.2 | 0.4 | 36 | 77 | 171 |
| | 18 | R | 23 | a/a | CLE | 81 | 1.90 | 0.92 | 23.4 | 0.8 | 7.2 | 8.7 | 0.5 | 28 | 83 | 218 |
| Bielak,Brandon | 18 | R | 22 | aa | HOU | 62 | 2.88 | 1.32 | 23.4 | 3.2 | 7.2 | 2.3 | 0.7 | 31 | 80 | 74 |
| Binford,Christian | 17 | R | 25 | a/a | KC | 147 | 8.36 | 1.92 | 25.9 | 3.0 | 5.6 | 1.9 | 1.9 | 38 | 58 | -2 |
| | 18 | R | 26 | aa | DET | 78 | 6.19 | 1.80 | 19.0 | 1.1 | 5.0 | 4.4 | 1.4 | 40 | 68 | 61 |
| Bird,Kyle | 17 | L | 24 | a/a | TAM | 75 | 3.80 | 1.49 | 6.0 | 3.9 | 7.3 | 1.9 | 0.4 | 33 | 74 | 71 |
| | 18 | L | 25 | a/a | TAM | 78 | 2.91 | 1.27 | 7.5 | 4.2 | 8.6 | 2.0 | 0.8 | 28 | 80 | 82 |
| Bivens,Blake | 18 | R | 23 | aa | TAM | 23 | 7.02 | 1.71 | 17.5 | 4.7 | 5.2 | 1.1 | 1.7 | 31 | 61 | 0 |
| Black,Ray | 18 | R | 28 | a/a | SF | 37 | 3.00 | 0.98 | 3.9 | 3.1 | 12.1 | 3.9 | 0.4 | 28 | 69 | 159 |
| Blackburn,Claytor | 17 | R | 24 | aaa | TEX | 96 | 6.09 | 1.57 | 21.1 | 2.6 | 6.0 | 2.3 | 0.5 | 36 | 59 | 61 |
| Blackburn,Paul | 17 | R | 24 | aaa | OAK | 80 | 3.58 | 1.32 | 22.0 | 2.9 | 5.0 | 1.7 | 0.7 | 29 | 74 | 50 |
| Blackham,Matt | 18 | R | 25 | aa | NYM | 27 | 3.90 | 1.43 | 5.2 | 6.0 | 10.0 | 1.7 | 0.7 | 29 | 74 | 86 |
| Blackwood,Nolan | 18 | R | 23 | aa | DET | 61 | 5.21 | 1.61 | 6.0 | 2.9 | 6.6 | 2.3 | 0.9 | 36 | 68 | 54 |
| Blair,Aaron | 17 | R | 25 | aaa | ATL | 127 | 6.58 | 1.80 | 23.5 | 4.5 | 6.3 | 1.4 | 0.8 | 36 | 62 | 36 |
| Blanco,Ronel | 18 | R | 25 | aa | HOU | 21 | 9.00 | 1.89 | 7.6 | 5.0 | 10.5 | 2.1 | 1.6 | 41 | 52 | 50 |
| Blewett,Scott | 18 | R | 22 | aa | KC | 149 | 5.91 | 1.60 | 25.4 | 3.0 | 5.1 | 1.7 | 0.7 | 34 | 62 | 37 |
| Blueberg,Colby | 18 | R | 25 | a/a | SD | 27 | 4.83 | 1.67 | 7.2 | 3.0 | 8.8 | 3.0 | 1.0 | 40 | 73 | 77 |
| Bollinger,Ryan | 18 | L | 27 | a/a | NYY | 113 | 5.42 | 1.51 | 24.5 | 3.0 | 6.1 | 2.0 | 0.8 | 34 | 64 | 50 |
| Bonnell,Bryan | 18 | R | 25 | aa | SEA | 49 | 3.79 | 1.51 | 6.6 | 2.3 | 5.9 | 2.6 | 1.2 | 34 | 79 | 47 |
| Borucki,Ryan | 17 | L | 23 | a/a | TOR | 52 | 2.42 | 1.07 | 25.4 | 1.7 | 7.1 | 4.2 | 0.5 | 29 | 79 | 124 |
| | 18 | L | 24 | aaa | TOR | 77 | 4.45 | 1.39 | 24.9 | 3.5 | 5.6 | 1.6 | 0.9 | 29 | 69 | 43 |
| Bostick,Akeem | 17 | R | 22 | aa | HOU | 80 | 5.54 | 1.62 | 19.8 | 2.2 | 5.9 | 2.7 | 0.9 | 37 | 66 | 55 |
| | 18 | R | 23 | a/a | HOU | 98 | 4.01 | 1.35 | 18.6 | 3.2 | 8.2 | 2.6 | 0.8 | 33 | 72 | 83 |
| Bourque,James | 18 | R | 25 | aa | WAS | 21 | 1.09 | 1.32 | 5.9 | 6.3 | 8.2 | 1.3 | 0.0 | 25 | 91 | 95 |
| Bowman,Matthew | 18 | R | 27 | aaa | STL | 23 | 5.17 | 1.56 | 5.6 | 3.2 | 8.9 | 2.8 | 0.8 | 38 | 67 | 83 |
| Boyd,Matt | 17 | L | 26 | aaa | DET | 51 | 4.17 | 1.20 | 25.6 | 2.7 | 7.2 | 2.7 | 1.7 | 26 | 73 | 57 |
| Bracewell,Ben | 17 | R | 27 | a/a | OAK | 113 | 6.73 | 1.84 | 18.7 | 3.8 | 4.4 | 1.1 | 0.7 | 36 | 62 | 19 |
| | 18 | R | 28 | a/a | OAK | 150 | 4.25 | 1.40 | 25.3 | 1.9 | 5.6 | 3.0 | 0.8 | 33 | 71 | 67 |
| Bracho,Silvino | 17 | R | 25 | aaa | ARI | 35 | 4.41 | 1.25 | 4.4 | 4.2 | 9.9 | 2.4 | 2.1 | 24 | 75 | 58 |
| | 18 | R | 26 | aaa | ARI | 35 | 4.11 | 1.38 | 5.5 | 1.9 | 10.6 | 5.6 | 0.6 | 40 | 70 | 159 |
| Brady,Sean | 18 | L | 24 | a/a | CLE | 148 | 6.05 | 1.68 | 23.8 | 3.7 | 5.0 | 1.4 | 1.4 | 33 | 66 | 11 |
| Bragg,Sam | 17 | R | 24 | aa | OAK | 68 | 3.59 | 1.40 | 6.4 | 2.1 | 5.9 | 2.8 | 0.5 | 34 | 75 | 76 |
| | 18 | R | 25 | a/a | OAK | 75 | 4.62 | 1.66 | 9.9 | 3.1 | 4.6 | 1.5 | 0.6 | 35 | 72 | 31 |
| Brashears,Tyler | 17 | R | 23 | aa | TAM | 37 | 7.26 | 1.94 | 16.0 | 6.1 | 5.1 | 0.8 | 1.6 | 33 | 64 | -6 |
| Brault,Steven | 17 | L | 25 | aaa | PIT | 120 | 2.69 | 1.30 | 23.6 | 3.7 | 6.4 | 1.7 | 0.4 | 28 | 80 | 68 |
| Bray,Tyler | 17 | R | 26 | a/a | STL | 58 | 4.92 | 1.86 | 6.8 | 5.0 | 6.1 | 1.2 | 0.4 | 37 | 72 | 43 |
| Brennan,Brandon | 17 | R | 26 | a/a | CHW | 60 | 6.36 | 1.91 | 6.7 | 5.2 | 6.9 | 1.3 | 0.2 | 39 | 64 | 54 |
| | 18 | R | 27 | a/a | CHW | 76 | 4.48 | 1.34 | 7.2 | 3.3 | 7.5 | 2.2 | 0.7 | 31 | 67 | 76 |
| Breto,Liarvis | 18 | L | 25 | aa | DET | 32 | 4.77 | 1.49 | 15.4 | 1.8 | 6.7 | 3.8 | 0.7 | 37 | 68 | 92 |
| Brice,Austin | 17 | R | 25 | a/a | CIN | 24 | 4.89 | 1.76 | 6.2 | 4.3 | 7.5 | 1.7 | 0.0 | 39 | 69 | 74 |
| | 18 | R | 26 | a/a | CIN | 24 | 2.99 | 1.26 | 5.8 | 2.9 | 7.3 | 2.5 | 1.0 | 29 | 81 | 72 |
| Bridwell,Parker | 17 | R | 26 | a/a | LAA | 40 | 6.21 | 1.58 | 16.1 | 2.3 | 6.8 | 3.0 | 1.7 | 36 | 64 | 45 |
| | 18 | R | 27 | a/a | LAA | 28 | 8.50 | 2.23 | 23.6 | 2.7 | 4.8 | 1.8 | 1.2 | 44 | 61 | 6 |
| Brigham,Jeff | 18 | R | 26 | a/a | MIA | 91 | 3.02 | 1.31 | 23.5 | 2.3 | 7.1 | 3.1 | 0.8 | 32 | 80 | 84 |
| Brooks,Aaron | 17 | R | 27 | aaa | MIL | 146 | 6.93 | 1.74 | 25.5 | 1.8 | 5.2 | 2.9 | 2.1 | 37 | 65 | 12 |
| | 18 | R | 28 | aaa | MIL | 100 | 3.70 | 1.45 | 16.4 | 2.6 | 5.2 | 2.0 | 0.8 | 32 | 76 | 46 |
| Brooks,Craig | 17 | R | 25 | aa | CHC | 40 | 6.14 | 1.75 | 5.58 | 7.3 | 10.7 | 1.5 | 0.3 | 36 | 62 | 92 |
| | 18 | R | 26 | a/a | CHC | 53 | 4.26 | 1.51 | 5.61 | 6.2 | 8.5 | 1.4 | 0.6 | 29 | 72 | 72 |
| Broussard,Joe | 17 | R | 26 | a/a | LA | 63 | 3.98 | 1.38 | 5.54 | 2.7 | 8.4 | 3.1 | 1.1 | 33 | 75 | 81 |
| | 18 | R | 27 | aaa | LA | 67 | 3.68 | 1.43 | 5 | 2.9 | 7.5 | 2.6 | 0.6 | 34 | 75 | 80 |
| Brown,Aaron | 18 | L | 26 | aa | PHI | 24 | 5.86 | 1.80 | 6.16 | 9.1 | 5.3 | 0.6 | 0.5 | 25 | 66 | 42 |
| Brown,Mitch | 17 | R | 23 | aa | CLE | 48 | 8.33 | 1.90 | 6.91 | 7.9 | 5.7 | 0.7 | 0.7 | 30 | 53 | 30 |
| | 18 | R | 24 | aa | CLE | 46 | 2.72 | 1.58 | 5.48 | 7.8 | 8.4 | 1.1 | 0.3 | 26 | 82 | 80 |
| Brown,Zack | 18 | R | 24 | aa | MIL | 127 | 3.52 | 1.27 | 23.7 | 2.9 | 6.9 | 2.4 | 0.8 | 30 | 75 | 72 |
| Broyles,Shane | 17 | R | 26 | a/a | COL | 55 | 2.75 | 1.22 | 4.6 | 3.1 | 9.4 | 3.0 | 1.8 | 28 | 89 | 75 |
| | 18 | R | 27 | aaa | COL | 55 | 6.90 | 1.91 | 6.2 | 4.8 | 7.5 | 1.6 | 1.2 | 38 | 64 | 31 |
| Brubaker,Jonatha | 17 | R | 24 | aa | PIT | 130 | 6.08 | 1.81 | 23.1 | 3.4 | 6.0 | 1.8 | 0.7 | 39 | 66 | 39 |
| | 18 | R | 25 | a/a | PIT | 154 | 3.51 | 1.47 | 23.6 | 2.7 | 6.0 | 2.2 | 0.5 | 34 | 76 | 64 |
| Buchanan,Jake | 17 | R | 28 | aaa | ARI | 106 | 5.21 | 1.57 | 22.1 | 2.5 | 4.6 | 1.8 | 0.7 | 34 | 67 | 36 |
| | 18 | R | 29 | aaa | ARI | 158 | 5.16 | 1.65 | 26.2 | 2.7 | 3.6 | 1.4 | 0.4 | 35 | 67 | 28 |

| PITCHER | yr | t | age | lvl | org | ip | era | whip | bf/g | ctl | dom | cmd | hr/9 | h% | s% | bpv |
|---|---|---|---|---|---|---|---|---|---|---|---|---|---|---|---|---|
| Buckelew,James | 17 | L | 26 | aa | MIA | 33 | 4.69 | 1.14 | 9.34 | 2.5 | 6.2 | 2.5 | 0.7 | 27 | 58 | 78 |
| | 18 | L | 27 | a/a | CHC | 40 | 4.89 | 1.80 | 10.9 | 4.3 | 4.5 | 1.1 | 1.1 | 34 | 75 | 9 |
| Buehler,Walker | 17 | R | 23 | a/a | LA | 72 | 4.41 | 1.24 | 12.8 | 2.9 | 10.5 | 3.6 | 0.8 | 33 | 65 | 121 |
| Bummer,Aaron | 17 | L | 24 | a/a | CHW | 38 | 3.70 | 1.59 | 8.38 | 4.6 | 8.0 | 1.7 | 0.6 | 34 | 77 | 66 |
| | 18 | L | 25 | aaa | CHW | 32 | 3.19 | 1.39 | 4.37 | 3.4 | 7.0 | 2.1 | 0.0 | 33 | 74 | 88 |
| Burdi,Nick | 17 | R | 24 | aa | MIN | 17 | 0.77 | 0.93 | 4.56 | 2.3 | 8.3 | 3.6 | 0.7 | 24 | 99 | 122 |
| Burdi,Zack | 17 | R | 22 | aaa | CHW | 33 | 4.64 | 1.53 | 5 | 4.8 | 12.4 | 2.6 | 0.6 | 39 | 69 | 113 |
| Burke,Brock | 18 | L | 22 | aa | TAM | 56 | 2.28 | 1.03 | 24 | 2.2 | 10.3 | 4.6 | 0.3 | 31 | 78 | 161 |
| Burnes,Corbin | 17 | R | 23 | aa | MIL | 86 | 3.22 | 1.26 | 21.9 | 2.4 | 7.6 | 3.2 | 0.3 | 33 | 74 | 105 |
| | 18 | R | 24 | aaa | MIL | 80 | 5.14 | 1.47 | 18.1 | 3.3 | 7.7 | 2.4 | 0.8 | 34 | 65 | 70 |
| Burr,Ryan | 18 | R | 24 | a/a | CHW | 52 | 3.18 | 1.32 | 5.84 | 4.8 | 7.5 | 1.6 | 0.7 | 27 | 78 | 69 |
| Burrows,Beau | 17 | R | 21 | aa | DET | 76 | 5.70 | 1.61 | 22.5 | 3.9 | 7.5 | 1.9 | 0.6 | 36 | 64 | 62 |
| | 18 | R | 22 | aa | DET | 134 | 5.06 | 1.50 | 22.3 | 3.8 | 7.1 | 1.9 | 0.9 | 33 | 67 | 54 |
| Burrows,Thomas | 18 | L | 24 | aa | ATL | 19 | 1.96 | 0.98 | 4.81 | 2.9 | 10.5 | 3.6 | 0.0 | 28 | 78 | 155 |
| Buttrey,Ty | 17 | R | 24 | a/a | BOS | 64 | 6.85 | 1.77 | 7.31 | 5.2 | 8.4 | 1.6 | 0.5 | 38 | 59 | 64 |
| | 18 | R | 25 | aaa | LAA | 48 | 2.11 | 1.10 | 5.22 | 2.5 | 11.0 | 4.4 | 0.6 | 32 | 84 | 150 |
| Cabrera,Genesis | 17 | L | 21 | aa | TAM | 65 | 4.36 | 1.74 | 24.6 | 3.8 | 6.4 | 1.7 | 0.9 | 37 | 76 | 39 |
| | 18 | L | 22 | a/a | STL | 141 | 4.41 | 1.33 | 21.7 | 4.2 | 8.0 | 1.9 | 0.8 | 29 | 68 | 72 |
| Cabrera,Mauricio | 17 | R | 24 | a/a | ATL | 40 | 9.54 | 2.28 | 5.37 | 11.0 | 6.9 | 0.6 | 0.3 | 33 | 54 | 47 |
| Callahan,Jamie | 17 | R | 23 | a/a | NYM | 52 | 3.58 | 1.43 | 5.39 | 3.3 | 10.2 | 3.1 | 0.8 | 37 | 77 | 103 |
| Camarena,Daniel | 17 | L | 25 | a/a | NYY | 118 | 5.28 | 1.59 | 23.7 | 2.7 | 4.9 | 1.8 | 0.9 | 34 | 68 | 32 |
| | 18 | L | 26 | a/a | SF | 127 | 6.20 | 1.79 | 23.5 | 3.9 | 5.6 | 1.5 | 0.8 | 37 | 65 | 30 |
| Campos,Vicente | 17 | R | 25 | aaa | LAA | 16 | 8.39 | 2.20 | 13.7 | 6.1 | 4.2 | 0.7 | 1.0 | 37 | 61 | -5 |
| | 18 | R | 26 | a/a | LAA | 23 | 7.89 | 2.19 | 9.61 | 4.9 | 6.3 | 1.3 | 1.2 | 42 | 64 | 10 |
| Canning,Griffin | 18 | R | 22 | a/a | LAA | 106 | 4.02 | 1.29 | 19 | 3.1 | 8.4 | 2.7 | 0.6 | 32 | 69 | 93 |
| Caramo,Yender | 17 | R | 26 | aaa | KC | 84 | 6.70 | 1.74 | 15.3 | 1.4 | 2.6 | 1.9 | 1.4 | 36 | 63 | -3 |
| Carle,Shane | 17 | R | 26 | aaa | COL | 62 | 7.51 | 1.93 | 8.17 | 3.6 | 5.3 | 1.5 | 1.6 | 38 | 63 | -1 |
| Carpenter,Ryan | 17 | L | 27 | aaa | COL | 156 | 5.94 | 1.64 | 25.8 | 2.6 | 6.6 | 2.6 | 1.6 | 36 | 67 | 37 |
| | 18 | L | 28 | aaa | DET | 77 | 7.63 | 2.02 | 26.7 | 2.9 | 6.2 | 2.1 | 1.3 | 42 | 63 | 23 |
| Carpenter,Tyler | 17 | R | 25 | aa | LAA | 71 | 6.34 | 1.74 | 23 | 2.9 | 4.3 | 1.5 | 1.0 | 36 | 63 | 16 |
| Carroll,Cody | 17 | R | 25 | aa | NYY | 47 | 3.98 | 1.53 | 7.92 | 4.8 | 9.3 | 1.9 | 1.2 | 33 | 78 | 63 |
| | 18 | R | 26 | aaa | BAL | 47 | 3.74 | 1.37 | 5.33 | 4.7 | 8.5 | 1.8 | 0.0 | 31 | 70 | 98 |
| Carter,Will | 17 | R | 24 | aa | NYY | 47 | 4.77 | 1.76 | 14.3 | 2.8 | 3.7 | 1.3 | 0.9 | 36 | 74 | 10 |
| | 18 | R | 25 | aa | NYY | 31 | 8.01 | 2.16 | 22.2 | 7.4 | 4.8 | 0.6 | 0.4 | 36 | 60 | 20 |
| Case,Andrew | 17 | R | 24 | a/a | TOR | 48 | 3.25 | 1.32 | 5.48 | 2.7 | 4.1 | 1.5 | 0.8 | 28 | 78 | 35 |
| | 18 | R | 25 | a/a | TOR | 49 | 6.73 | 1.84 | 5.7 | 3.0 | 5.2 | 1.7 | 1.8 | 37 | 67 | -2 |
| Cash,Ralston | 17 | R | 26 | aa | SEA | 49 | 6.39 | 1.84 | 6.34 | 3.9 | 9.9 | 2.5 | 0.9 | 43 | 65 | 74 |
| | 18 | R | 27 | a/a | LAA | 68 | 6.65 | 1.77 | 6.66 | 5.2 | 8.1 | 1.5 | 1.4 | 35 | 64 | 35 |
| Casimiro,Ranfi | 17 | R | 25 | aa | PHI | 45 | 4.52 | 1.42 | 9.61 | 2.5 | 5.2 | 2.1 | 1.2 | 31 | 72 | 35 |
| | 18 | R | 26 | a/a | PHI | 88 | 4.48 | 1.61 | 11.9 | 4.4 | 6.3 | 1.4 | 1.3 | 32 | 76 | 27 |
| Castellani,Ryan | 17 | R | 21 | aa | COL | 157 | 7.29 | 1.65 | 26.1 | 3.0 | 6.1 | 2.0 | 1.4 | 35 | 56 | 28 |
| | 18 | R | 22 | aa | COL | 135 | 7.76 | 1.81 | 24.1 | 5.2 | 4.9 | 1.0 | 1.4 | 32 | 57 | 1 |
| Castillo,Cristian | 18 | L | 24 | aa | KC | 23 | 6.50 | 1.22 | 8.52 | 1.6 | 6.9 | 4.2 | 1.2 | 30 | 46 | 94 |
| Castillo,Diego | 17 | R | 23 | a/a | TAM | 72 | 3.55 | 1.26 | 5.73 | 2.7 | 9.9 | 3.7 | 0.4 | 35 | 71 | 129 |
| | 18 | R | 24 | aaa | TAM | 27 | 1.25 | 0.93 | 5.34 | 2.4 | 9.2 | 3.8 | 0.4 | 26 | 89 | 142 |
| Castillo,Jesus | 17 | R | 22 | aa | LAA | 24 | 4.07 | 1.63 | 21.1 | 2.3 | 7.5 | 3.2 | 0.9 | 39 | 77 | 75 |
| | 18 | R | 23 | a/a | LAA | 99 | 6.20 | 1.47 | 20.2 | 2.8 | 4.7 | 1.7 | 0.7 | 32 | 56 | 38 |
| Castillo,Jose | 18 | L | 22 | a/a | SD | 27 | 2.10 | 1.13 | 4.87 | 3.1 | 11.4 | 3.7 | 0.3 | 33 | 82 | 148 |
| Castillo,Luis | 17 | R | 25 | aa | CIN | 80 | 4.34 | 1.38 | 24.1 | 1.8 | 7.7 | 4.2 | 0.9 | 35 | 70 | 102 |
| Caughel,Lindsey | 17 | R | 27 | aa | SEA | 158 | 4.89 | 1.44 | 24.9 | 2.4 | 5.4 | 2.3 | 1.3 | 32 | 69 | 38 |
| | 18 | R | 28 | a/a | SEA | 32 | 8.21 | 1.71 | 10.4 | 3.1 | 5.2 | 1.7 | 1.3 | 35 | 51 | 16 |
| Cavanerio,Jorgan | 18 | R | 24 | aa | MIA | 26 | 5.75 | 1.73 | 9.15 | 2.8 | 7.6 | 2.7 | 1.0 | 40 | 68 | 58 |
| Cease,Dylan | 18 | R | 23 | aa | CHW | 53 | 2.33 | 1.16 | 21.1 | 4.2 | 11.5 | 2.8 | 0.7 | 29 | 83 | 122 |
| Cessa,Luis | 17 | R | 25 | aaa | NYY | 78 | 4.83 | 1.58 | 24.6 | 3.3 | 6.4 | 1.9 | 1.2 | 34 | 72 | 37 |
| | 18 | R | 26 | a/a | NYY | 37 | 3.71 | 1.01 | 17.8 | 1.4 | 7.3 | 5.3 | 0.4 | 29 | 62 | 153 |
| Chacin,Alejandro | 17 | R | 24 | aaa | CIN | 69 | 3.31 | 1.51 | 6.82 | 3.8 | 7.1 | 1.9 | 0.7 | 33 | 79 | 61 |
| | 18 | R | 25 | aa | CIN | 36 | 7.52 | 1.98 | 6.39 | 5.9 | 10.5 | 1.8 | 2.4 | 39 | 67 | 20 |
| Chiang,Shao-Chi | 17 | R | 24 | a/a | CLE | 33 | 8.88 | 1.99 | 26.2 | 3.4 | 4.1 | 1.2 | 1.4 | 38 | 55 | -9 |
| | 18 | R | 25 | a/a | CLE | 138 | 5.27 | 1.41 | 23.4 | 1.7 | 4.9 | 2.8 | 1.1 | 33 | 64 | 51 |
| Chirinos,Yonny | 17 | R | 24 | a/a | TAM | 168 | 3.58 | 1.16 | 24.8 | 1.5 | 6.5 | 4.3 | 0.9 | 30 | 72 | 105 |
| | 18 | R | 25 | aaa | TAM | 32 | 6.44 | 1.55 | 17.6 | 2.1 | 7.4 | 3.6 | 2.2 | 35 | 64 | 44 |
| Chleborad,Tanne | 18 | R | 26 | aa | BAL | 63 | 4.32 | 1.58 | 6.46 | 2.5 | 5.2 | 2.0 | 0.3 | 36 | 71 | 55 |
| Choplick,Adam | 18 | L | 26 | aa | TEX | 37 | 8.50 | 2.26 | 6.48 | 6.3 | 7.9 | 1.3 | 1.0 | 43 | 61 | 29 |
| Church,Andrew | 18 | R | 24 | a/a | NYM | 46 | 6.36 | 1.63 | 22.8 | 1.9 | 6.3 | 3.3 | 1.1 | 38 | 61 | 64 |
| Civale,Aaron | 18 | R | 23 | aa | CLE | 107 | 5.27 | 1.53 | 22.2 | 1.9 | 5.5 | 2.9 | 1.3 | 35 | 68 | 47 |
| Clark,Brian | 17 | L | 24 | aaa | CHW | 49 | 4.79 | 1.67 | 6.15 | 2.6 | 6.9 | 2.7 | 0.8 | 39 | 72 | 62 |
| | 18 | L | 25 | aa | CHW | 63 | 6.74 | 1.65 | 6.88 | 3.5 | 7.8 | 2.2 | 1.0 | 37 | 59 | 56 |
| Clark,Ryan | 18 | R | 25 | a/a | LAA | 61 | 6.26 | 1.61 | 6.19 | 4.3 | 8.0 | 1.9 | 1.3 | 34 | 63 | 45 |
| Clarke,Taylor | 17 | R | 24 | a/a | ARI | 145 | 4.03 | 1.35 | 22.4 | 3.3 | 7.1 | 2.2 | 1.1 | 30 | 73 | 60 |
| | 18 | R | 25 | aaa | ARI | 152 | 3.72 | 1.27 | 23 | 2.4 | 6.0 | 2.5 | 0.5 | 31 | 71 | 75 |
| Clarkin,Ian | 18 | L | 23 | aa | CHW | 70 | 6.69 | 1.79 | 18 | 4.4 | 3.9 | 0.9 | 1.2 | 33 | 63 | -2 |
| Clay,Sam | 18 | L | 25 | aa | MIN | 52 | 7.52 | 1.98 | 7.34 | 6.5 | 8.3 | 1.3 | 0.2 | 39 | 58 | 64 |
| Cleavinger,Garret | 17 | L | 23 | aa | PHI | 54 | 7.28 | 1.82 | 6.59 | 5.4 | 8.7 | 1.6 | 1.0 | 37 | 59 | 50 |
| Clifton,Trevor | 17 | R | 22 | aa | CHC | 100 | 6.73 | 1.80 | 22.1 | 4.3 | 6.8 | 1.6 | 0.8 | 37 | 62 | 40 |
| | 18 | R | 23 | a/a | CHC | 128 | 3.97 | 1.36 | 20.6 | 3.8 | 6.0 | 1.6 | 0.6 | 29 | 71 | 56 |
| Clouse,Corbin | 17 | L | 22 | aa | ATL | 22 | 4.02 | 1.84 | 6.41 | 6.0 | 9.6 | 1.6 | 1.0 | 38 | 80 | 59 |
| | 18 | L | 23 | a/a | ATL | 65 | 2.47 | 1.29 | 5.93 | 3.4 | 9.6 | 2.8 | 0.0 | 34 | 79 | 123 |
| Cochran-Gill,Trey | 18 | R | 26 | aa | OAK | 36 | 6.08 | 1.70 | 7.42 | 3.1 | 4.5 | 1.5 | 0.5 | 36 | 62 | 32 |
| Cole,A.J. | 17 | R | 25 | aaa | WAS | 93 | 7.66 | 2.08 | 25.4 | 3.8 | 6.3 | 1.7 | 0.8 | 43 | 62 | 30 |
| Cole,Taylor | 18 | R | 29 | aaa | LAA | 56 | 5.43 | 1.57 | 7.25 | 4.2 | 7.9 | 1.9 | 0.9 | 34 | 66 | 58 |
| Coley,Austin | 17 | R | 25 | aa | PIT | 144 | 4.20 | 1.51 | 21.5 | 2.2 | 5.6 | 2.6 | 0.7 | 35 | 73 | 58 |
| | 18 | R | 26 | a/a | PIT | 52 | 8.58 | 2.07 | 18.2 | 3.9 | 3.9 | 1.0 | 1.2 | 39 | 58 | -9 |
| Comer,Kevin | 17 | R | 25 | a/a | HOU | 67 | 3.84 | 1.60 | 6.54 | 3.6 | 9.1 | 2.5 | 0.7 | 38 | 77 | 82 |
| | 18 | R | 26 | aaa | DET | 56 | 5.61 | 1.71 | 5.28 | 3.6 | 7.0 | 1.9 | 1.1 | 37 | 68 | 42 |
| Conley,Adam | 17 | L | 27 | aaa | MIA | 62 | 7.00 | 1.81 | 24 | 3.9 | 4.7 | 1.2 | 1.1 | 35 | 61 | 11 |
| | 18 | L | 28 | aaa | MIA | 40 | 6.50 | 1.78 | 23 | 3.5 | 4.4 | 1.2 | 1.4 | 35 | 65 | -2 |
| Conlon,P.J. | 17 | L | 24 | aa | NYM | 136 | 5.09 | 1.59 | 21.4 | 3.2 | 6.3 | 2.0 | 1.3 | 34 | 71 | 33 |
| | 18 | L | 25 | aaa | NYM | 114 | 6.12 | 1.66 | 22.2 | 2.9 | 5.4 | 1.9 | 1.3 | 35 | 65 | 23 |
| Connolly,Michael | 18 | R | 27 | a/a | SF | 100 | 6.85 | 1.77 | 15.9 | 3.6 | 4.8 | 1.3 | 1.1 | 35 | 61 | 15 |
| Coonrod,Sam | 17 | R | 25 | aa | SF | 104 | 6.47 | 1.62 | 19.2 | 4.1 | 6.7 | 1.6 | 0.6 | 35 | 58 | 52 |
| Cooper,Matt | 17 | R | 26 | aa | CHW | 72 | 7.11 | 1.90 | 24.3 | 4.0 | 8.0 | 2.0 | 0.2 | 43 | 59 | 71 |
| Copping,Corey | 17 | R | 23 | aa | LA | 68 | 4.18 | 1.26 | 5.66 | 4.1 | 6.9 | 1.7 | 1.0 | 25 | 69 | 56 |
| | 18 | R | 24 | a/a | TOR | 69 | 3.11 | 1.44 | 6.55 | 4.9 | 8.4 | 1.7 | 0.5 | 31 | 79 | 79 |
| Corcino,Daniel | 17 | R | 27 | aa | LA | 16 | 7.88 | 1.64 | 7.93 | 5.0 | 8.0 | 1.6 | 2.0 | 31 | 54 | 21 |
| | 18 | R | 28 | a/a | LA | 113 | 3.99 | 1.33 | 16.8 | 3.4 | 6.8 | 2.0 | 0.9 | 30 | 72 | 62 |
| Cordero,Jimmy | 17 | R | 26 | aa | WAS | 51 | 9.07 | 2.08 | 6.13 | 7.3 | 5.6 | 0.8 | 1.4 | 33 | 56 | 0 |
| | 18 | R | 27 | aaa | WAS | 46 | 2.77 | 1.76 | 5.14 | 4.9 | 8.0 | 1.6 | 0.0 | 39 | 82 | 77 |
| Cortes,Nestor | 17 | L | 23 | a/a | NYY | 100 | 2.86 | 1.26 | 14.1 | 3.0 | 7.9 | 2.6 | 0.4 | 31 | 77 | 96 |
| | 18 | L | 24 | a/a | NYY | 117 | 4.80 | 1.37 | 20.5 | 3.2 | 6.4 | 2.0 | 1.4 | 29 | 69 | 41 |
| Cosart,Jake | 17 | R | 23 | aa | BOS | 49 | 4.05 | 1.56 | 5.69 | 7.9 | 7.8 | 1.0 | 1.0 | 22 | 77 | 53 |
| | 18 | R | 24 | aa | BOS | 37 | 7.40 | 1.67 | 8.76 | 3.7 | 8.8 | 2.4 | 1.6 | 37 | 57 | 48 |
| Coshow,Cale | 17 | R | 25 | a/a | NYY | 60 | 5.43 | 1.98 | 6.39 | 4.1 | 9.4 | 2.3 | 0.9 | 45 | 73 | 62 |
| | 18 | R | 26 | aaa | NYY | 57 | 6.65 | 1.74 | 6.86 | 4.9 | 8.4 | 1.7 | 2.0 | 34 | 66 | 21 |
| Cotton,Jharel | 17 | R | 25 | aaa | OAK | 21 | 3.54 | 1.01 | 20.4 | 1.7 | 9.2 | 5.4 | 1.2 | 28 | 71 | 142 |
| Coulombe,Daniel | 18 | L | 29 | aaa | OAK | 29 | 3.30 | 1.56 | 5.55 | 2.1 | 6.3 | 3.1 | 1.0 | 36 | 83 | 62 |
| Covey,Dylan | 18 | R | 27 | aaa | CHW | 40 | 2.96 | 1.43 | 24.4 | 3.8 | 6.3 | 1.6 | 0.9 | 30 | 83 | 48 |
| Cozart,Logan | 18 | R | 25 | aa | COL | 70 | 3.29 | 1.28 | 5.33 | 2.4 | 6.1 | 2.5 | 1.2 | 29 | 79 | 57 |
| Crescentini,Marc | 18 | R | 26 | aa | MIA | 26 | 4.71 | 1.85 | 5.3 | 7.1 | 6.7 | 0.9 | 1.8 | 29 | 80 | 6 |
| Crichton,Stefan | 17 | R | 25 | aaa | BAL | 48 | 4.19 | 1.52 | 7.13 | 2.5 | 8.0 | 3.2 | 0.5 | 38 | 72 | 95 |
| | 18 | R | 26 | aaa | ARI | 16 | 9.55 | 1.83 | 5.31 | 5.2 | 7.6 | 1.5 | 1.8 | 35 | 47 | 17 |
| Crick,Kyle | 17 | R | 25 | aaa | SF | 29 | 3.38 | 1.44 | 5.2 | 4.2 | 9.8 | 2.3 | 0.3 | 35 | 76 | 103 |
| Crismatt,Nabil | 18 | R | 24 | a/a | NYM | 146 | 5.01 | 1.51 | 23.5 | 3.4 | 7.4 | 2.2 | 0.9 | 34 | 68 | 61 |
| Crowe,Wil | 18 | R | 24 | aa | WAS | 27 | 7.53 | 1.97 | 26 | 5.5 | 4.1 | 0.7 | 1.5 | 33 | 63 | -16 |
| Crownover,Matthe | 17 | L | 24 | aa | WAS | 84 | 5.72 | 1.71 | 22.4 | 3.8 | 4.0 | 1.0 | 1.3 | 32 | 69 | -1 |
| Cuevas,William | 17 | R | 27 | aaa | MIA | 104 | 6.18 | 1.62 | 19.2 | 4.1 | 5.6 | 1.4 | 1.0 | 32 | 62 | 29 |
| | 18 | R | 28 | aaa | BOS | 136 | 5.39 | 1.57 | 26 | 3.0 | 5.9 | 2.0 | 1.6 | 33 | 69 | 24 |
| Curry,Parker | 18 | R | 25 | aa | LA | 22 | 7.16 | 1.85 | 20.7 | 3.4 | 4.0 | 1.2 | 2.9 | 33 | 69 | -51 |
| Curtis,Zac | 17 | L | 25 | aa | SEA | 51 | 4.42 | 1.39 | 5.28 | 3.5 | 8.9 | 2.6 | 0.6 | 34 | 68 | 91 |
| | 18 | L | 26 | aaa | TEX | 51 | 4.18 | 1.45 | 5.19 | 5.6 | 8.2 | 1.4 | 1.1 | 27 | 74 | 56 |
| Curtiss,John | 17 | R | 24 | a/a | MIN | 49 | 1.91 | 1.10 | 4.95 | 4.4 | 9.8 | 2.2 | 0.0 | 26 | 81 | 125 |
| | 18 | R | 25 | aaa | MIN | 56 | 4.07 | 1.58 | 6.49 | 5.6 | 7.7 | 1.4 | 0.7 | 31 | 75 | 59 |
| Custred,Matt | 18 | R | 25 | a/a | LAA | 56 | 4.56 | 1.52 | 6.42 | 5.8 | 7.6 | 1.3 | 0.3 | 30 | 68 | 71 |
| Cyr,Tyler | 17 | R | 24 | aa | SF | 49 | 2.96 | 1.69 | 4.74 | 4.0 | 8.7 | 2.2 | 0.6 | 39 | 84 | 75 |
| Dahlstrand,Jacob | 17 | R | 25 | aa | BOS | 77 | 9.06 | 2.17 | 13.2 | 5.9 | 3.5 | 0.6 | 1.2 | 36 | 57 | -19 |
| Danish,Tyler | 17 | R | 23 | aaa | CHW | 138 | 6.39 | 1.80 | 24.6 | 3.2 | 4.1 | 1.3 | 1.3 | 35 | 66 | -1 |
| | 18 | R | 24 | aaa | CHW | 73 | 3.66 | 1.43 | 9.42 | 3.7 | 5.6 | 1.5 | 0.9 | 29 | 77 | 40 |
| Darnell,Logan | 17 | L | 28 | aa | TAM | 75 | 5.51 | 1.89 | 29.3 | 2.2 | 5.1 | 2.3 | 1.6 | 39 | 75 | 12 |
| | 18 | L | 29 | a/a | WAS | 123 | 6.85 | 1.86 | 22.2 | 2.5 | 4.6 | 1.9 | 1.5 | 38 | 65 | 7 |
| Davis,Austin | 17 | L | 24 | aa | PHI | 47 | 3.56 | 1.57 | 6.45 | 4.0 | 7.6 | 1.9 | 0.7 | 35 | 79 | 63 |
| | 18 | L | 25 | a/a | PHI | 39 | 3.39 | 1.18 | 5.59 | 2.4 | 9.8 | 4.1 | 0.9 | 32 | 74 | 125 |
| Davis,Rookie | 17 | R | 24 | a/a | CIN | 74 | 6.83 | 1.67 | 23.7 | 2.6 | 6.8 | 2.6 | 2.1 | 36 | 63 | 21 |
| | 18 | R | 25 | aa | CIN | 16 | 7.59 | 1.52 | 11.7 | 1.9 | 5.1 | 2.7 | 2.3 | 32 | 53 | 12 |
| Davis,Tyler | 17 | R | 24 | aa | TEX | 81 | 3.30 | 1.07 | 26.4 | 1.1 | 4.1 | 3.6 | 1.2 | 26 | 75 | 71 |
| | 18 | R | 25 | aa | TEX | 80 | 8.59 | 2.20 | 13 | 3.2 | 4.9 | 1.5 | 1.2 | 43 | 60 | 3 |
| Dawson,Shane | 17 | L | 24 | aa | TOR | 111 | 8.29 | 2.07 | 20.1 | 4.2 | 4.2 | 1.0 | 2.1 | 37 | 53 | -34 |
| De Jong,Chase | 17 | R | 24 | a/a | SEA | 113 | 7.19 | 1.68 | 25.4 | 3.0 | 5.4 | 1.8 | 1.9 | 34 | 60 | 5 |
| | 18 | R | 25 | a/a | MIN | 162 | 4.96 | 1.54 | 25.3 | 2.8 | 5.4 | 2.0 | 1.0 | 34 | 69 | 38 |
| De La Cruz,Oscar | 18 | R | 23 | aa | CHC | 78 | 6.56 | 1.57 | 21.5 | 3.8 | 7.1 | 1.9 | 1.1 | 34 | 58 | 47 |
| De Los Santos,Er | 17 | R | 22 | aa | SD | 150 | 5.16 | 1.39 | 24.3 | 3.0 | 7.0 | 2.4 | 0.8 | 32 | 63 | 67 |
| | 18 | R | 23 | aaa | PHI | 128 | 3.20 | 1.29 | 24 | 3.1 | 6.9 | 2.2 | 1.0 | 29 | 80 | 61 |
| De Los Santos,Sa | 18 | R | 24 | aa | LAA | 34 | 9.23 | 2.36 | 7.05 | 9.5 | 7.2 | 0.8 | 1.6 | 36 | 61 | 3 |
| De Paula,Rafael | 17 | R | 26 | a/a | CIN | 50 | 5.14 | 1.60 | 7.12 | 4.1 | 7.3 | 1.8 | 1.6 | 32 | 72 | 30 |
| | 18 | R | 27 | a/a | CIN | 60 | 4.58 | 1.60 | 6.35 | 5.2 | 8.7 | 1.7 | 1.9 | 31 | 78 | 33 |
| Deetz,Dean | 17 | R | 24 | a/a | HOU | 85 | 4.56 | 1.50 | 14.6 | 5.0 | 8.9 | 1.8 | 0.8 | 32 | 71 | 70 |
| | 18 | R | 25 | a/a | HOU | 39 | 0.78 | 1.15 | 6.49 | 4.0 | 10.5 | 2.6 | 0.2 | 29 | 95 | 126 |
| DeGraaf,Josh | 17 | R | 24 | aa | TOR | 16 | 4.64 | 1.86 | 8.15 | 6.2 | 5.3 | 0.9 | 0.7 | 33 | 76 | 24 |
| | 18 | R | 25 | a/a | TOR | 86 | 5.95 | 1.68 | 19.4 | 2.9 | 6.6 | 2.3 | 1.7 | 36 | 68 | 28 |
| Del Pozo,Miguel | 18 | L | 26 | aa | MIA | 34 | 4.94 | 1.79 | 5.6 | 4.3 | 7.3 | 1.7 | 0.8 | 38 | 73 | 46 |
| DeMasi,Dominic | 18 | R | 25 | a/a | CLE | 88 | 9.26 | 1.87 | 12.5 | 3.0 | 5.1 | 1.7 | 1.6 | 38 | 50 | 5 |
| DeNato,Joey | 17 | L | 25 | a/a | PHI | 51 | 3.43 | 1.74 | 7.05 | 6.0 | 4.9 | 0.8 | 0.7 | 31 | 82 | 26 |
| Derby,Bubba | 17 | R | 23 | a/a | MIL | 113 | 4.03 | 1.35 | 15.8 | 3.0 | 6.5 | 2.2 | 0.8 | 31 | 72 | 62 |
| | 18 | R | 24 | aaa | MIL | 119 | 4.54 | 1.53 | 16.7 | 3.5 | 6.1 | 1.7 | 0.7 | 33 | 71 | 50 |
| Diaz,Carlos | 18 | L | 25 | aa | SF | 41 | 3.94 | 1.54 | 5.6 | 5.4 | 6.4 | 1.2 | 0.2 | 30 | 73 | 62 |
| Diaz,Luis | 17 | R | 25 | a/a | LAA | 111 | 5.46 | 1.66 | 18.5 | 3.8 | 7.4 | 1.9 | 1.1 | 36 | 68 | 46 |
| Diaz,Miguel | 18 | R | 24 | a/a | SD | 79 | 3.62 | 1.40 | 13.9 | 4.8 | 7.8 | 1.6 | 0.7 | 29 | 75 | 69 |
| Dickson,Cody | 17 | L | 25 | a/a | PIT | 72 | 7.26 | 2.15 | 10 | 6.7 | 6.3 | 0.9 | 1.5 | 37 | 68 | 2 |
| Diehl,Phillip | 18 | L | 24 | aa | NYY | 28 | 1.74 | 1.21 | 8.13 | 3.8 | 7.8 | 2.0 | 0.9 | 26 | 92 | 73 |
| Dillon,Justin | 18 | R | 25 | aa | TOR | 74 | 6.58 | 1.53 | 17.9 | 3.2 | 4.0 | 1.3 | 1.2 | 31 | 57 | 11 |
| Diplan,Marcos | 18 | R | 22 | aa | MIL | 57 | 6.43 | 1.91 | 22.5 | 6.1 | 7.9 | 1.3 | 1.3 | 36 | 68 | 29 |
| Diplan,Nattino | 18 | R | 25 | aa | MIL | 15 | 5.30 | 1.54 | 8.29 | 6.1 | 6.4 | 1.0 | 0.9 | 27 | 66 | 42 |
| Dohy,Kyle | 18 | L | 22 | aa | PHI | 24 | 5.76 | 1.46 | 5.76 | 7.9 | 10.1 | 1.3 | 1.2 | 21 | 62 | 71 |
| Dominguez,Seran | 18 | R | 24 | a/a | PHI | 18 | 1.78 | 0.68 | 5.8 | 1.5 | 9.0 | 5.9 | 0.0 | 22 | 71 | 203 |
| Donatella,Justin | 18 | R | 24 | aa | ARI | 130 | 4.22 | 1.38 | 20.2 | 3.4 | 5.9 | 1.8 | 0.6 | 30 | 70 | 56 |
| Dorris,Jacob | 17 | R | 24 | a/a | HOU | 72 | 3.22 | 1.28 | 6.87 | 3.3 | 8.2 | 2.5 | 1.0 | 30 | 79 | 77 |
| | 18 | R | 25 | aaa | HOU | 17 | 7.37 | 1.66 | 6.39 | 4.8 | 5.6 | 1.2 | 1.5 | 30 | 56 | 11 |
| Dowdy,Kyle | 18 | R | 25 | a/a | CLE | 126 | 6.95 | 1.77 | 19.3 | 4.0 | 6.9 | 1.7 | 1.1 | 37 | 61 | 36 |
| Dragmire,Brady | 17 | R | 24 | a/a | WAS | 82 | 5.43 | 1.86 | 10.1 | 4.2 | 3.5 | 0.8 | 1.0 | 35 | 72 | -1 |
| | 18 | R | 25 | a/a | WAS | 151 | 5.97 | 1.59 | 24.7 | 2.2 | 4.7 | 2.1 | 1.2 | 35 | 63 | 29 |
| Duffey,Tyler | 18 | R | 28 | aaa | MIN | 59 | 4.62 | 1.54 | 8.31 | 3.7 | 7.1 | 1.9 | 1.1 | 33 | 73 | 47 |
| Dugger,Robert | 18 | R | 23 | aa | MIA | 110 | 4.39 | 1.36 | 25.6 | 3.0 | 7.6 | 2.5 | 1.0 | 32 | 70 | 69 |
| Dull,Ryan | 18 | R | 29 | aaa | OAK | 28 | 4.72 | 1.57 | 5.34 | 2.9 | 8.4 | 2.9 | 1.8 | 36 | 76 | 52 |
| Duncan,Frank | 17 | R | 25 | a/a | ARI | 152 | 7.73 | 1.88 | 26.4 | 2.9 | 4.6 | 1.6 | 1.4 | 38 | 59 | 4 |
| | 18 | R | 26 | aa | COL | 90 | 7.86 | 1.83 | 18.2 | 3.0 | 2.8 | 0.9 | 1.7 | 34 | 58 | -28 |
| Dunn,Justin | 18 | R | 23 | aa | NYM | 91 | 4.67 | 1.45 | 26 | 3.7 | 9.0 | 2.4 | 0.7 | 35 | 68 | 86 |
| Dunning,Dane | 18 | R | 24 | aa | CHW | 62 | 3.87 | 1.58 | 24.8 | 3.8 | 8.6 | 2.2 | 0.0 | 38 | 73 | 95 |
| Dunshee,Parker | 18 | R | 23 | aa | OAK | 82 | 2.25 | 0.97 | 26 | 1.5 | 7.4 | 5.0 | 0.5 | 27 | 79 | 144 |

| PITCHER | yr | t | age | lvl | org | ip | era | whip | bf/g | ctl | dom | cmd | hr/9 | h% | s% | bpv |
|---|---|---|---|---|---|---|---|---|---|---|---|---|---|---|---|---|
| Duplantier,Jon | 18 | R | 24 | aa | ARI | 67 | 3.27 | 1.34 | 19.9 | 3.9 | 7.6 | 1.9 | 0.5 | 30 | 76 | 76 |
| DuRapau,Montan | 17 | R | 25 | a/a | PIT | 53 | 2.83 | 1.26 | 5.14 | 3.8 | 8.2 | 2.2 | 0.4 | 29 | 78 | 92 |
| | 18 | R | 26 | a/a | PIT | 32 | 6.42 | 1.40 | 7.15 | 3.0 | 8.2 | 2.7 | 1.9 | 31 | 57 | 51 |
| Duval,Max | 18 | R | 27 | aa | MIA | 88 | 9.10 | 1.95 | 17.5 | 3.4 | 6.2 | 1.8 | 2.5 | 38 | 56 | -17 |
| Dykxhoorn,Brock | 17 | R | 23 | aa | HOU | 99 | 5.69 | 1.68 | 17.9 | 3.6 | 6.8 | 1.9 | 0.9 | 36 | 66 | 45 |
| | 18 | R | 24 | a/a | HOU | 129 | 4.34 | 1.23 | 21 | 2.6 | 7.3 | 2.8 | 1.0 | 29 | 67 | 76 |
| Dziedzic,Jonathan | 17 | L | 26 | aaa | KC | 46 | 6.29 | 1.58 | 22.3 | 3.2 | 5.8 | 1.8 | 1.7 | 32 | 64 | 15 |
| | 18 | L | 27 | aaa | KC | 140 | 5.24 | 1.61 | 24.8 | 3.0 | 4.6 | 1.5 | 0.8 | 34 | 67 | 30 |
| Eades,Ryan | 17 | R | 26 | a/a | MIN | 87 | 5.31 | 1.44 | 12.4 | 3.9 | 5.2 | 1.3 | 0.4 | 30 | 61 | 49 |
| | 18 | R | 27 | a/a | MIN | 77 | 5.04 | 1.67 | 9.61 | 2.9 | 7.7 | 2.7 | 0.8 | 39 | 70 | 70 |
| Echemendia,Pedr | 17 | R | 26 | a/a | STL | 75 | 5.42 | 1.64 | 8.58 | 2.3 | 3.8 | 1.6 | 1.3 | 34 | 69 | 8 |
| Eckelman,Matt | 18 | R | 25 | aa | PIT | 26 | 2.21 | 1.44 | 4.86 | 5.5 | 4.6 | 0.8 | 0.4 | 26 | 86 | 43 |
| Ecker,Mark | 17 | R | 22 | aa | DET | 18 | 2.44 | 1.41 | 5.07 | 4.1 | 7.5 | 1.9 | 1.1 | 30 | 88 | 55 |
| | 18 | R | 23 | aa | DET | 59 | 4.62 | 1.41 | 5.68 | 4.8 | 6.3 | 1.3 | 1.2 | 26 | 71 | 36 |
| Effross,Scott | 18 | R | 25 | aa | CHC | 64 | 7.78 | 1.94 | 6.94 | 3.1 | 6.8 | 2.2 | 1.2 | 41 | 60 | 34 |
| Eflin,Zach | 17 | R | 23 | aaa | PHI | 43 | 5.81 | 1.67 | 24.3 | 3.2 | 6.9 | 2.2 | 0.8 | 37 | 65 | 55 |
| | 18 | R | 24 | aaa | PHI | 20 | 5.10 | 1.45 | 21.4 | 2.4 | 5.9 | 2.5 | 0.0 | 35 | 61 | 83 |
| Ege,Cody | 17 | L | 26 | aaa | LAA | 39 | 5.70 | 1.57 | 6.64 | 3.0 | 7.6 | 2.5 | 0.2 | 38 | 61 | 86 |
| Elledge,Seth | 18 | R | 22 | aa | STL | 18 | 4.14 | 1.06 | 5.44 | 2.7 | 8.4 | 3.1 | 1.3 | 24 | 66 | 88 |
| Ellis,Chris | 17 | R | 25 | a/a | STL | 131 | 6.87 | 1.68 | 19.7 | 3.4 | 6.7 | 2.0 | 1.1 | 36 | 59 | 41 |
| | 18 | R | 26 | a/a | STL | 134 | 4.50 | 1.30 | 17.8 | 2.5 | 6.5 | 2.6 | 0.9 | 31 | 66 | 70 |
| Emanuel,Kent | 17 | L | 25 | a/a | HOU | 116 | 6.27 | 1.91 | 22 | 2.8 | 6.0 | 2.2 | 1.1 | 41 | 68 | 32 |
| | 18 | L | 26 | aaa | HOU | 85 | 5.61 | 1.66 | 12.3 | 2.6 | 7.3 | 2.8 | 1.0 | 39 | 67 | 62 |
| Enns,Dietrich | 17 | L | 26 | aaa | MIN | 51 | 3.69 | 1.48 | 21.9 | 2.9 | 6.1 | 2.1 | 0.8 | 33 | 77 | 55 |
| | 18 | L | 27 | a/a | MIN | 131 | 6.51 | 1.73 | 23.9 | 3.3 | 5.5 | 1.7 | 1.1 | 36 | 63 | 24 |
| Eppler,Tyler | 17 | R | 24 | aaa | PIT | 136 | 6.61 | 1.71 | 22.9 | 2.4 | 5.0 | 2.1 | 1.8 | 35 | 64 | 8 |
| | 18 | R | 25 | aaa | PIT | 153 | 4.37 | 1.50 | 23.6 | 2.4 | 5.5 | 2.3 | 0.8 | 34 | 72 | 51 |
| Escobar,Luis | 18 | R | 22 | aa | PIT | 37 | 5.26 | 1.48 | 22.9 | 5.1 | 5.1 | 1.0 | 1.0 | 26 | 66 | 27 |
| Eshelman,Tom | 17 | R | 23 | a/a | PHI | 150 | 2.98 | 1.12 | 25.7 | 1.1 | 5.4 | 4.9 | 1.0 | 28 | 78 | 107 |
| | 18 | R | 24 | aaa | PHI | 141 | 7.31 | 1.93 | 24.8 | 3.0 | 5.8 | 1.9 | 1.7 | 39 | 64 | 7 |
| Esparza,Matt | 17 | R | 23 | aa | CLE | 95 | 6.51 | 1.56 | 24.4 | 3.7 | 5.2 | 1.4 | 1.9 | 29 | 62 | 1 |
| Espinal,Raynel | 17 | R | 26 | aa | NYY | 20 | 0.70 | 0.95 | 8.25 | 4.3 | 10.4 | 2.4 | 0.8 | 19 | 101 | 117 |
| | 18 | R | 27 | aaa | NYY | 67 | 4.30 | 1.50 | 7.07 | 4.0 | 10.1 | 2.5 | 0.8 | 36 | 72 | 91 |
| Espinal,Yoel | 17 | R | 25 | a/a | TAM | 44 | 9.95 | 2.08 | 7.92 | 10.5 | 9.4 | 0.9 | 1.0 | 31 | 49 | 52 |
| | 18 | R | 26 | aa | TAM | 56 | 2.47 | 1.19 | 5.63 | 5.0 | 9.5 | 1.9 | 0.9 | 23 | 84 | 88 |
| Estevez,Carlos | 17 | R | 25 | aaa | COL | 34 | 1.83 | 1.18 | 4.08 | 2.9 | 6.8 | 2.3 | 0.7 | 27 | 89 | 76 |
| | 18 | R | 26 | aaa | COL | 29 | 7.52 | 1.92 | 4.93 | 3.6 | 8.1 | 2.2 | 2.2 | 40 | 65 | 13 |
| Estevez,Wirkin | 17 | R | 25 | aa | WAS | 62 | 4.71 | 1.75 | 25.8 | 4.2 | 4.2 | 1.0 | 0.5 | 34 | 72 | 24 |
| | 18 | R | 26 | aa | WAS | 52 | 5.69 | 1.57 | 20.8 | 3.2 | 5.6 | 1.8 | 1.3 | 33 | 66 | 28 |
| Eubank,Luke | 18 | R | 24 | a/a | CLE | 57 | 4.44 | 1.56 | 5.57 | 4.0 | 7.4 | 1.9 | 0.8 | 34 | 72 | 59 |
| Evans,Jacob | 17 | L | 24 | aa | STL | 18 | 3.34 | 1.85 | 5.89 | 4.3 | 8.5 | 2.0 | 1.2 | 40 | 86 | 47 |
| | 18 | L | 25 | aa | STL | 48 | 5.64 | 1.36 | 6.92 | 2.9 | 5.7 | 1.9 | 0.5 | 31 | 56 | 60 |
| Faedo,Alex | 18 | R | 23 | aa | DET | 60 | 6.24 | 1.43 | 21.3 | 3.4 | 7.2 | 2.1 | 2.6 | 28 | 65 | 10 |
| Faria,Jake | 17 | R | 24 | aaa | TAM | 59 | 4.17 | 1.34 | 22.2 | 3.7 | 11.1 | 3.0 | 1.3 | 33 | 73 | 96 |
| | 18 | R | 25 | aaa | TAM | 30 | 5.74 | 1.46 | 18.4 | 4.1 | 7.1 | 1.7 | 1.7 | 29 | 65 | 31 |
| Farmer,Buck | 17 | R | 26 | aaa | DET | 124 | 5.81 | 1.71 | 26.7 | 2.6 | 6.4 | 2.4 | 0.9 | 38 | 66 | 51 |
| Farrell,Luke | 17 | R | 26 | aaa | CIN | 117 | 6.37 | 1.59 | 23.4 | 4.0 | 7.5 | 1.9 | 1.5 | 33 | 62 | 35 |
| | 18 | R | 27 | aaa | CHC | 55 | 4.32 | 1.43 | 19.5 | 5.0 | 7.7 | 1.5 | 0.7 | 29 | 70 | 65 |
| Farris,James | 17 | R | 25 | a/a | COL | 58 | 5.34 | 1.49 | 5.18 | 3.0 | 8.0 | 2.7 | 2.1 | 32 | 71 | 38 |
| Fasola,John | 18 | R | 27 | aa | TEX | 28 | 5.47 | 1.77 | 6.16 | 4.2 | 6.5 | 1.5 | 0.0 | 38 | 66 | 63 |
| Faulkner,Andrew | 17 | L | 25 | aaa | BAL | 39 | 3.87 | 1.72 | 5.16 | 6.7 | 6.9 | 1.0 | 0.3 | 32 | 76 | 58 |
| | 18 | L | 26 | aaa | BAL | 58 | 6.73 | 1.86 | 5.9 | 5.0 | 6.2 | 1.2 | 1.3 | 35 | 65 | 16 |
| Fedde,Erick | 17 | R | 24 | a/a | WAS | 90 | 4.70 | 1.36 | 13 | 2.4 | 6.5 | 2.7 | 0.8 | 32 | 66 | 72 |
| | 18 | R | 25 | a/a | WAS | 72 | 5.61 | 1.70 | 23.3 | 2.7 | 7.4 | 2.8 | 0.5 | 40 | 65 | 78 |
| Ferguson,Caleb | 18 | L | 22 | a/a | LA | 47 | 1.61 | 1.16 | 18.7 | 2.9 | 8.8 | 3.0 | 0.4 | 30 | 88 | 115 |
| Fernandez,Jose | 17 | L | 24 | a/a | TOR | 46 | 7.32 | 1.98 | 5.43 | 5.4 | 7.8 | 1.4 | 1.0 | 39 | 63 | 36 |
| | 18 | L | 25 | a/a | TOR | 62 | 3.93 | 1.47 | 6.06 | 4.9 | 7.6 | 1.5 | 1.2 | 28 | 78 | 46 |
| Fernandez,Junior | 18 | R | 21 | aa | STL | 21 | 5.33 | 1.64 | 5.85 | 6.2 | 6.2 | 1.0 | 0.4 | 30 | 66 | 52 |
| Fernandez,Pedro | 17 | R | 23 | a/a | KC | 77 | 4.14 | 1.40 | 8.33 | 2.8 | 6.4 | 2.3 | 0.5 | 33 | 70 | 71 |
| | 18 | R | 24 | a/a | KC | 68 | 4.20 | 1.55 | 9.32 | 3.6 | 5.2 | 1.5 | 0.4 | 33 | 72 | 46 |
| Ferrell,Justin | 18 | R | 24 | aa | HOU | 48 | 4.36 | 1.43 | 7.56 | 4.1 | 9.1 | 2.2 | 0.9 | 33 | 71 | 77 |
| Ferrell,Riley | 17 | R | 24 | aa | HOU | 52 | 4.78 | 1.44 | 6.15 | 2.5 | 8.3 | 3.4 | 0.4 | 37 | 65 | 105 |
| | 18 | R | 25 | a/a | HOU | 53 | 5.00 | 1.66 | 5.54 | 5.6 | 9.3 | 1.6 | 0.9 | 34 | 71 | 64 |
| Festa,Matthew | 18 | R | 25 | aa | SEA | 49 | 3.35 | 1.46 | 4.77 | 2.3 | 10.5 | 4.6 | 1.2 | 39 | 82 | 117 |
| Feyereisen,J.P. | 17 | R | 24 | a/a | NYY | 63 | 4.63 | 1.46 | 7.33 | 4.4 | 7.2 | 1.6 | 1.1 | 30 | 71 | 49 |
| | 18 | R | 25 | aaa | NYY | 60 | 4.60 | 1.61 | 7.18 | 4.1 | 7.3 | 1.8 | 1.1 | 34 | 74 | 47 |
| Fierro,Edwin | 17 | R | 24 | a/a | TAM | 89 | 4.76 | 1.53 | 11.8 | 2.5 | 5.8 | 2.3 | 0.6 | 35 | 68 | 60 |
| Fillmyer,Heath | 17 | R | 23 | a/a | OAK | 150 | 4.04 | 1.52 | 22.4 | 3.0 | 5.6 | 1.9 | 1.1 | 33 | 77 | 36 |
| | 18 | R | 24 | aaa | KC | 68 | 7.13 | 1.85 | 24.5 | 3.8 | 5.0 | 1.3 | 0.7 | 37 | 60 | 25 |
| Finnegan,Brandon | 18 | L | 25 | aaa | CIN | 69 | 9.02 | 2.23 | 12.5 | 5.7 | 6.2 | 1.1 | 1.7 | 40 | 60 | -8 |
| Finnegan,Kyle | 17 | R | 26 | a/a | OAK | 60 | 4.77 | 1.64 | 5.85 | 3.8 | 6.5 | 1.7 | 1.2 | 34 | 74 | 33 |
| | 18 | R | 27 | a/a | OAK | 44 | 5.13 | 1.54 | 5.67 | 3.9 | 7.0 | 1.8 | 0.4 | 34 | 65 | 65 |
| Fisk,Conor | 18 | R | 26 | a/a | TOR | 74 | 3.03 | 1.45 | 7.72 | 3.1 | 5.9 | 1.9 | 0.6 | 32 | 81 | 56 |
| Flaa,Jay | 18 | R | 26 | aa | BAL | 65 | 3.35 | 1.09 | 6.2 | 4.0 | 7.1 | 1.8 | 1.2 | 20 | 75 | 63 |
| Flaherty,Jack | 17 | R | 22 | a/a | STL | 149 | 2.66 | 1.16 | 23.7 | 2.1 | 7.4 | 3.5 | 0.8 | 30 | 80 | 116 |
| | 18 | R | 23 | aaa | STL | 33 | 2.39 | 0.93 | 24.9 | 1.8 | 9.2 | 5.1 | 0.5 | 27 | 76 | 162 |
| Flexen,Chris | 17 | R | 23 | aa | NYM | 49 | 2.46 | 0.91 | 25.9 | 1.6 | 8.3 | 5.2 | 1.1 | 25 | 80 | 142 |
| | 18 | R | 24 | aaa | NYM | 92 | 4.03 | 1.51 | 22.1 | 2.8 | 6.5 | 2.3 | 0.9 | 34 | 75 | 57 |
| Flores Jr.,Bernarc | 18 | L | 23 | aa | CHW | 79 | 3.75 | 1.43 | 25.8 | 1.8 | 4.7 | 2.6 | 0.8 | 33 | 75 | 54 |
| Flores,Jose | 17 | R | 28 | a/a | SF | 112 | 4.45 | 1.53 | 15.7 | 3.6 | 6.8 | 1.9 | 0.3 | 35 | 69 | 68 |
| | 18 | R | 29 | a/a | SF | 60 | 8.68 | 2.14 | 15 | 4.8 | 4.9 | 1.0 | 1.0 | 40 | 58 | 4 |
| Floro,Dylan | 17 | R | 27 | aaa | LA | 60 | 5.12 | 1.63 | 8.09 | 1.6 | 4.5 | 2.8 | 1.5 | 36 | 73 | 27 |
| Foley,Jordan | 18 | R | 25 | aa | NYY | 67 | 4.10 | 1.81 | 8.39 | 5.2 | 7.4 | 1.4 | 1.2 | 35 | 81 | 33 |
| Font,Wilmer | 17 | R | 27 | aaa | LA | 134 | 4.17 | 1.28 | 22 | 2.3 | 9.5 | 4.1 | 0.8 | 34 | 69 | 120 |
| Foster,Matt | 18 | R | 23 | aa | CHW | 32 | 5.79 | 1.76 | 6.11 | 4.1 | 7.4 | 1.8 | 1.1 | 37 | 68 | 39 |
| Franco,Daniel | 18 | R | 26 | a/a | ATL | 136 | 5.09 | 1.54 | 20.5 | 3.1 | 6.8 | 2.2 | 1.2 | 34 | 69 | 45 |
| Franco,Mike | 17 | R | 26 | a/a | TAM | 90 | 4.11 | 1.56 | 14.6 | 5.5 | 6.6 | 1.2 | 1.0 | 29 | 76 | 41 |
| | 18 | R | 27 | a/a | TAM | 64 | 4.09 | 1.30 | 6.46 | 3.2 | 7.7 | 2.4 | 1.3 | 29 | 73 | 61 |

| PITCHER | yr | t | age | lvl | org | ip | era | whip | bf/g | ctl | dom | cmd | hr/9 | h% | s% | bpv |
|---|---|---|---|---|---|---|---|---|---|---|---|---|---|---|---|---|
| Frank,Trevor | 18 | R | 27 | a/a | SEA | 42 | 3.98 | 1.21 | 7.38 | 2.5 | 6.8 | 2.7 | 1.5 | 27 | 73 | 59 |
| Frare,Caleb | 17 | L | 24 | aa | NYY | 34 | 6.27 | 1.86 | 6.56 | 10.2 | 9.5 | 0.9 | 0.8 | 26 | 66 | 65 |
| | 18 | L | 25 | a/a | CHW | 60 | 1.00 | 1.07 | 5.47 | 3.7 | 9.6 | 2.6 | 0.2 | 27 | 91 | 123 |
| Frawley,Matt | 18 | R | 23 | aa | NYY | 24 | 6.93 | 1.64 | 7.2 | 4.4 | 5.5 | 1.2 | 2.1 | 29 | 62 | -7 |
| Fried,Max | 17 | L | 23 | a/a | ATL | 93 | 7.42 | 1.71 | 20 | 4.9 | 7.9 | 1.6 | 0.9 | 35 | 55 | 51 |
| | 18 | L | 24 | a/a | ATL | 79 | 5.02 | 1.50 | 22.8 | 3.9 | 8.1 | 2.1 | 0.5 | 34 | 65 | 76 |
| Friedrichs,Kyle | 17 | R | 25 | aa | OAK | 51 | 7.25 | 1.68 | 12.7 | 3.0 | 5.0 | 1.6 | 1.2 | 35 | 57 | 18 |
| | 18 | R | 26 | a/a | OAK | 84 | 6.58 | 1.63 | 23.5 | 2.6 | 5.1 | 1.9 | 1.4 | 34 | 61 | 18 |
| Fry,Paul | 17 | L | 25 | a/a | BAL | 60 | 5.77 | 1.85 | 8.54 | 5.6 | 9.1 | 1.6 | 1.1 | 38 | 70 | 50 |
| | 18 | L | 26 | a/a | BAL | 43 | 4.07 | 1.29 | 6.33 | 3.4 | 9.2 | 2.7 | 1.1 | 31 | 72 | 86 |
| Fulmer,Carson | 17 | R | 24 | aaa | CHW | 126 | 6.90 | 1.77 | 23.1 | 5.0 | 5.9 | 1.2 | 1.5 | 33 | 62 | 11 |
| | 18 | R | 25 | aaa | CHW | 69 | 6.59 | 1.87 | 13 | 5.9 | 6.7 | 1.2 | 1.6 | 33 | 67 | 11 |
| Funkhouser,Kyle | 18 | R | 24 | a/a | DET | 99 | 5.22 | 1.71 | 23.7 | 4.7 | 6.9 | 1.5 | 1.1 | 34 | 71 | 35 |
| Gage,Matt | 17 | L | 24 | a/a | SF | 145 | 5.35 | 1.74 | 25.5 | 2.6 | 4.9 | 1.9 | 0.5 | 38 | 68 | 42 |
| | 18 | L | 25 | a/a | NYM | 103 | 5.37 | 1.78 | 23.7 | 2.3 | 5.8 | 2.6 | 0.6 | 40 | 69 | 57 |
| Gagnon,Drew | 17 | R | 27 | aaa | LAA | 86 | 6.64 | 1.68 | 12.5 | 3.9 | 7.0 | 1.8 | 0.6 | 37 | 58 | 56 |
| | 18 | R | 28 | a/a | NYM | 165 | 4.84 | 1.36 | 24.7 | 2.5 | 7.3 | 2.9 | 1.2 | 32 | 67 | 67 |
| Gallegos,Giovann | 17 | R | 26 | aaa | NYY | 43 | 2.97 | 1.12 | 6.1 | 2.6 | 11.6 | 4.5 | 1.3 | 31 | 81 | 135 |
| | 18 | R | 27 | aaa | STL | 45 | 3.12 | 1.05 | 5.82 | 2.1 | 8.7 | 4.2 | 0.2 | 30 | 69 | 144 |
| Gallen,Zac | 17 | R | 22 | a/a | STL | 92 | 4.54 | 1.44 | 23.1 | 2.4 | 5.3 | 2.2 | 1.0 | 32 | 71 | 42 |
| | 18 | R | 23 | aaa | MIA | 134 | 4.08 | 1.59 | 23.6 | 3.2 | 7.9 | 2.5 | 0.9 | 37 | 76 | 66 |
| Gant,John | 17 | R | 25 | aaa | STL | 103 | 4.83 | 1.52 | 24.9 | 2.3 | 6.7 | 3.0 | 1.0 | 36 | 70 | 67 |
| | 18 | R | 26 | aaa | STL | 49 | 1.94 | 1.41 | 25.9 | 3.0 | 6.0 | 2.0 | 0.9 | 31 | 91 | 50 |
| Garcia,Edgar | 18 | R | 22 | a/a | PHI | 67 | 4.01 | 1.21 | 5.22 | 3.6 | 8.7 | 2.5 | 1.2 | 27 | 71 | 77 |
| Garcia,Elniery | 17 | L | 23 | aa | PHI | 26 | 2.13 | 1.44 | 21.8 | 6.0 | 3.1 | 0.5 | 0.0 | 24 | 84 | 42 |
| | 18 | L | 24 | a/a | STL | 64 | 6.69 | 1.99 | 12.9 | 4.2 | 5.2 | 1.3 | 1.1 | 39 | 67 | 10 |
| Garcia,Jarlin | 18 | L | 25 | aaa | MIA | 50 | 5.48 | 1.61 | 22.2 | 2.6 | 4.9 | 1.9 | 0.9 | 35 | 66 | 34 |
| Garcia,Jason | 17 | R | 25 | aa | BAL | 75 | 6.76 | 1.98 | 9.52 | 5.5 | 7.5 | 1.4 | 0.8 | 39 | 65 | 38 |
| | 18 | R | 26 | aa | COL | 20 | 13.74 | 2.69 | 7.42 | 8.0 | 5.7 | 0.7 | 2.0 | 42 | 47 | -35 |
| Garcia,Onelki | 17 | L | 28 | a/a | KC | 85 | 6.94 | 1.93 | 18.4 | 4.0 | 5.4 | 1.3 | 1.0 | 38 | 64 | 16 |
| Garcia,Rico | 18 | R | 24 | aa | COL | 67 | 3.38 | 1.38 | 25.6 | 3.1 | 6.4 | 2.1 | 1.6 | 29 | 83 | 36 |
| Garcia,Yeudy | 17 | R | 25 | aa | PIT | 72 | 7.34 | 2.05 | 12.1 | 6.4 | 6.5 | 1.0 | 1.2 | 36 | 64 | 15 |
| | 18 | R | 26 | aa | PIT | 54 | 6.77 | 1.86 | 6.84 | 5.8 | 8.7 | 1.5 | 0.6 | 38 | 62 | 62 |
| Garrett,Amir | 17 | L | 25 | aaa | CIN | 68 | 7.46 | 1.82 | 22.4 | 3.5 | 6.8 | 1.9 | 1.2 | 39 | 59 | 33 |
| Garrett,Reed | 17 | R | 24 | aa | TEX | 69 | 7.07 | 1.78 | 7.18 | 4.6 | 7.4 | 1.6 | 1.7 | 35 | 63 | 19 |
| | 18 | R | 25 | a/a | TEX | 63 | 2.64 | 1.41 | 5.25 | 3.2 | 6.8 | 2.1 | 0.5 | 33 | 83 | 70 |
| Garza,Ralph | 17 | R | 23 | a/a | HOU | 27 | 5.53 | 1.62 | 7.58 | 6.1 | 7.3 | 1.2 | 1.3 | 29 | 68 | 36 |
| | 18 | R | 24 | a/a | HOU | 68 | 3.82 | 1.37 | 8.16 | 4.1 | 8.2 | 2.0 | 0.4 | 31 | 71 | 85 |
| Gatto,Joe | 18 | R | 23 | aa | LAA | 78 | 7.13 | 1.74 | 22.3 | 4.2 | 4.9 | 1.2 | 1.1 | 34 | 59 | 14 |
| Gaviglio,Sam | 17 | R | 27 | aaa | SEA | 72 | 4.82 | 1.40 | 23.4 | 1.6 | 5.8 | 3.6 | 0.7 | 34 | 65 | 83 |
| | 18 | R | 28 | aaa | TOR | 29 | 2.76 | 1.14 | 23 | 1.5 | 6.8 | 4.6 | 1.7 | 28 | 87 | 91 |
| Gavin,Grant | 18 | R | 23 | aa | KC | 31 | 4.04 | 1.59 | 6.51 | 5.0 | 7.2 | 1.4 | 1.2 | 31 | 78 | 38 |
| German,Domingo | 17 | R | 25 | a/a | NYY | 109 | 4.17 | 1.40 | 23.1 | 3.0 | 8.1 | 2.7 | 1.1 | 33 | 74 | 71 |
| Gibaut,Ian | 17 | R | 24 | aa | TAM | 53 | 2.82 | 1.27 | 5.02 | 4.7 | 9.3 | 2.0 | 1.1 | 26 | 84 | 76 |
| | 18 | R | 25 | aaa | TAM | 56 | 2.68 | 1.16 | 4.64 | 3.6 | 10.3 | 2.9 | 0.5 | 29 | 78 | 118 |
| Gibson,Daniel | 17 | L | 26 | a/a | ARI | 35 | 4.52 | 1.95 | 6.19 | 5.4 | 5.1 | 0.9 | 0.6 | 36 | 77 | 22 |
| | 18 | L | 27 | a/a | ARI | 30 | 5.62 | 1.63 | 5.16 | 3.3 | 7.2 | 2.2 | 0.6 | 37 | 64 | 65 |
| Gilbert,Tyler | 18 | L | 25 | a/a | PHI | 72 | 3.82 | 1.10 | 5.92 | 2.0 | 7.3 | 3.7 | 1.1 | 28 | 69 | 97 |
| Gillies,Darin | 17 | R | 25 | aa | SEA | 60 | 4.18 | 1.49 | 6.59 | 3.9 | 6.0 | 1.5 | 0.7 | 31 | 73 | 47 |
| | 18 | R | 26 | a/a | SEA | 64 | 6.13 | 1.45 | 6.69 | 3.7 | 8.0 | 2.2 | 1.4 | 31 | 59 | 52 |
| Ginkel,Kevin | 18 | R | 24 | aa | ARI | 44 | 1.98 | 0.90 | 4.84 | 1.9 | 10.1 | 5.3 | 0.6 | 27 | 82 | 170 |
| Giolito,Lucas | 17 | R | 23 | aaa | CHW | 129 | 5.23 | 1.56 | 23.5 | 4.4 | 8.3 | 1.9 | 1.3 | 33 | 69 | 49 |
| Girodo,Chad | 17 | L | 26 | aaa | TOR | 48 | 4.84 | 2.01 | 7.67 | 3.9 | 5.3 | 1.4 | 0.9 | 40 | 77 | 18 |
| | 18 | L | 27 | a/a | LA | 26 | 6.37 | 1.43 | 7.03 | 2.0 | 5.9 | 3.0 | 3.3 | 28 | 68 | -6 |
| Glasnow,Tyler | 17 | R | 24 | aaa | PIT | 93 | 2.61 | 1.13 | 24.6 | 3.4 | 10.7 | 3.2 | 0.7 | 29 | 80 | 124 |
| Gohara,Luiz | 17 | L | 21 | a/a | ATL | 87 | 3.75 | 1.41 | 19.4 | 3.8 | 10.2 | 2.7 | 0.7 | 35 | 74 | 101 |
| | 18 | L | 22 | a/a | ATL | 60 | 5.76 | 1.42 | 19.7 | 2.6 | 7.5 | 2.9 | 1.5 | 33 | 62 | 58 |
| Gomber,Austin | 17 | L | 24 | aa | STL | 143 | 4.38 | 1.36 | 23 | 3.4 | 7.0 | 2.1 | 1.2 | 29 | 71 | 52 |
| | 18 | L | 25 | aaa | STL | 69 | 3.89 | 1.37 | 24.1 | 2.6 | 7.9 | 3.1 | 1.2 | 33 | 75 | 76 |
| Gonsalves,Stephe | 17 | L | 23 | a/a | MIN | 110 | 4.80 | 1.39 | 23.2 | 2.7 | 7.8 | 2.8 | 1.2 | 33 | 68 | 70 |
| | 18 | L | 24 | a/a | MIN | 122 | 3.67 | 1.33 | 22 | 5.1 | 7.1 | 1.4 | 0.7 | 25 | 74 | 62 |
| Gonsolin,Tony | 18 | R | 24 | aa | LA | 45 | 2.58 | 1.10 | 19.7 | 2.9 | 8.3 | 2.8 | 0.6 | 27 | 79 | 103 |
| Gonzales,Marco | 17 | L | 25 | aaa | SEA | 80 | 3.74 | 1.18 | 24.7 | 2.5 | 6.2 | 2.5 | 0.8 | 28 | 70 | 74 |
| Gonzalez,Brian | 18 | L | 23 | aa | BAL | 93 | 6.37 | 1.74 | 23.6 | 3.8 | 6.3 | 1.7 | 1.6 | 35 | 66 | 15 |
| Gonzalez,Derian | 18 | R | 23 | a/a | STL | 30 | 3.85 | 1.27 | 5.93 | 3.0 | 5.4 | 1.8 | 0.0 | 30 | 66 | 75 |
| Gonzalez,Harol | 18 | R | 23 | a/a | NYM | 58 | 7.28 | 1.81 | 26.9 | 2.8 | 4.2 | 1.5 | 1.4 | 36 | 60 | 1 |
| Gonzalez,Luis | 18 | L | 26 | a/a | BAL | 72 | 4.05 | 1.40 | 7.25 | 3.5 | 8.2 | 2.3 | 0.8 | 32 | 72 | 76 |
| Gonzalez,Merand | 18 | R | 23 | aa | MIA | 73 | 5.04 | 1.51 | 22.6 | 4.1 | 5.0 | 1.2 | 0.8 | 30 | 67 | 31 |
| Gonzalez,Rayan | 18 | R | 28 | aa | COL | 18 | 8.02 | 2.03 | 4.62 | 5.0 | 6.0 | 1.2 | 3.2 | 34 | 68 | -47 |
| Gonzalez,Severin | 17 | R | 25 | aa | MIA | 80 | 6.29 | 1.52 | 7.93 | 2.1 | 5.2 | 2.5 | 1.4 | 34 | 60 | 36 |
| | 18 | R | 26 | aaa | MIA | 35 | 6.44 | 1.58 | 7.39 | 2.4 | 4.3 | 1.8 | 1.8 | 32 | 63 | 1 |
| Gorman III,John | 18 | R | 26 | aa | OAK | 66 | 3.31 | 1.23 | 6.38 | 2.1 | 5.0 | 2.4 | 1.0 | 28 | 77 | 53 |
| Gorst,Matthew | 18 | R | 24 | a/a | BOS | 42 | 2.60 | 1.12 | 8.35 | 2.2 | 4.3 | 1.9 | 0.8 | 25 | 80 | 51 |
| Gossett,Daniel | 17 | R | 25 | aaa | OAK | 76 | 4.38 | 1.39 | 23 | 2.8 | 6.5 | 2.3 | 0.7 | 32 | 69 | 66 |
| | 18 | R | 26 | aaa | OAK | 40 | 1.96 | 1.20 | 23.1 | 3.7 | 7.3 | 2.0 | 0.2 | 27 | 84 | 90 |
| Gott,Trevor | 17 | R | 25 | aaa | WAS | 37 | 5.03 | 1.65 | 5.57 | 3.4 | 6.8 | 2.0 | 0.5 | 37 | 69 | 60 |
| | 18 | R | 26 | aaa | WAS | 30 | 4.97 | 1.27 | 4.4 | 2.6 | 8.9 | 3.4 | 0.4 | 34 | 58 | 117 |
| Goudeau,Ashton | 17 | R | 25 | aa | KC | 57 | 7.75 | 2.09 | 13.3 | 3.0 | 5.3 | 1.8 | 1.3 | 42 | 63 | 9 |
| | 18 | R | 26 | a/a | SEA | 90 | 7.15 | 1.84 | 14.5 | 3.5 | 5.5 | 1.6 | 1.2 | 37 | 61 | 16 |
| Graham,Josh | 18 | R | 25 | aa | ATL | 41 | 9.21 | 2.09 | 6.32 | 7.1 | 7.2 | 1.0 | 1.1 | 37 | 54 | 23 |
| Green,Chad | 17 | R | 26 | aaa | NYY | 27 | 6.76 | 2.02 | 25.8 | 4.2 | 9.0 | 2.1 | 0.5 | 45 | 65 | 68 |
| Green,Nick | 18 | R | 23 | aa | NYY | 18 | 4.64 | 1.22 | 24.4 | 3.7 | 3.9 | 1.0 | 1.4 | 21 | 66 | 14 |
| Greene,Conner | 17 | R | 22 | aa | TOR | 133 | 6.84 | 1.90 | 24.1 | 5.8 | 5.4 | 0.9 | 0.6 | 35 | 62 | 28 |
| | 18 | R | 23 | a/a | STL | 90 | 4.33 | 1.57 | 9.92 | 5.9 | 5.7 | 1.0 | 0.3 | 29 | 71 | 52 |
| Gregorio,Joan | 17 | R | 25 | aaa | SF | 74 | 3.72 | 1.51 | 24.6 | 4.5 | 6.1 | 1.4 | 1.0 | 29 | 78 | 37 |
| Griep,Nate | 18 | R | 25 | aa | MIL | 58 | 4.85 | 1.77 | 5.24 | 6.2 | 6.8 | 1.1 | 0.9 | 32 | 74 | 36 |
| Griffin,Foster | 17 | L | 22 | a/a | KC | 105 | 4.90 | 1.59 | 25.6 | 3.0 | 5.8 | 1.9 | 1.1 | 34 | 71 | 37 |
| | 18 | L | 23 | aa | KC | 154 | 6.42 | 1.77 | 25.3 | 2.4 | 5.6 | 2.3 | 1.2 | 38 | 65 | 32 |

| PITCHER | yr | t | age | lvl | org | ip | era | whip | bf/g | ctl | dom | cmd | hr/9 | h% | s% | bpv |
|---|---|---|---|---|---|---|---|---|---|---|---|---|---|---|---|---|
| Griggs,Scott | 18 | R | 27 | aa | COL | 57 | 5.48 | 1.73 | 5.29 | 4.3 | 7.3 | 1.7 | 1.5 | 35 | 72 | 28 |
| Grills,Evan | 18 | L | 26 | aa | COL | 86 | 5.97 | 1.61 | 23.9 | 2.0 | 6.3 | 3.1 | 1.3 | 37 | 65 | 55 |
| Grimes,Matthew | 17 | R | 26 | aa | BAL | 85 | 7.09 | 1.90 | 23.6 | 4.0 | 4.6 | 1.2 | 2.2 | 35 | 67 | -26 |
| | 18 | R | 27 | a/a | BAL | 88 | 4.87 | 1.67 | 11.3 | 3.9 | 5.0 | 1.3 | 1.1 | 33 | 73 | 19 |
| Griset,Ben | 17 | L | 25 | aa | NYM | 49 | 3.68 | 1.47 | 6.01 | 5.2 | 5.7 | 1.1 | 0.5 | 28 | 75 | 48 |
| Grover,Taylor | 17 | R | 26 | aa | BOS | 75 | 7.17 | 1.81 | 12 | 4.5 | 7.6 | 1.7 | 1.6 | 36 | 62 | 25 |
| Gsellman,Robert | 17 | R | 24 | a/a | NYM | 18 | 5.49 | 2.11 | 18.1 | 4.5 | 5.2 | 1.2 | 0.6 | 41 | 73 | 20 |
| Guduan,Reymin | 17 | L | 25 | aaa | HOU | 46 | 5.61 | 1.66 | 5.29 | 2.5 | 7.8 | 3.2 | 0.7 | 40 | 66 | 82 |
| | 18 | L | 26 | aaa | HOU | 56 | 3.77 | 1.43 | 5.55 | 4.8 | 10.7 | 2.2 | 0.8 | 33 | 75 | 94 |
| Guerrero,Jordan | 17 | L | 23 | aa | CHW | 146 | 5.88 | 1.62 | 26 | 3.1 | 7.4 | 2.4 | 0.7 | 38 | 62 | 67 |
| | 18 | L | 24 | a/a | CHW | 131 | 6.24 | 1.77 | 23.1 | 3.6 | 7.0 | 2.0 | 0.9 | 38 | 64 | 46 |
| Guerrero,Tayron | 17 | R | 26 | a/a | MIA | 31 | 6.13 | 1.96 | 4.99 | 8.3 | 7.8 | 0.9 | 1.6 | 30 | 72 | 19 |
| Guerrieri,Taylor | 18 | R | 26 | aaa | TOR | 58 | 7.25 | 1.94 | 12 | 3.8 | 5.0 | 1.3 | 1.6 | 37 | 64 | -5 |
| Guillon,Ismael | 17 | L | 25 | a/a | CIN | 70 | 6.65 | 2.17 | 8.69 | 7.0 | 8.3 | 1.2 | 1.1 | 40 | 70 | 29 |
| | 18 | L | 26 | aa | WAS | 31 | 3.80 | 1.40 | 4.87 | 4.4 | 7.3 | 1.7 | 1.0 | 28 | 76 | 53 |
| Gunkel,Joe | 17 | R | 26 | a/a | MIA | 124 | 6.47 | 1.62 | 20.4 | 1.7 | 4.4 | 2.6 | 1.5 | 35 | 62 | 26 |
| | 18 | R | 27 | aaa | MIA | 66 | 3.68 | 1.27 | 12.3 | 1.0 | 5.3 | 5.1 | 0.8 | 32 | 73 | 111 |
| Gutierrez,Alfred | 18 | R | 23 | a/a | DET | 35 | 10.45 | 2.33 | 22.5 | 4.0 | 6.7 | 1.7 | 1.9 | 45 | 55 | -6 |
| Gutierrez,Vladimi | 18 | R | 23 | aa | CIN | 147 | 5.78 | 1.41 | 23.1 | 2.5 | 7.7 | 3.1 | 1.4 | 33 | 61 | 66 |
| Hader,Joshua | 17 | L | 23 | aaa | MIL | 52 | 5.58 | 1.57 | 19 | 5.0 | 7.6 | 1.5 | 2.6 | 27 | 74 | 1 |
| Hagens,Bradin | 18 | R | 29 | aaa | ARI | 56 | 7.59 | 1.80 | 16.3 | 3.8 | 5.1 | 1.3 | 1.1 | 36 | 57 | 16 |
| Haley,Justin | 17 | R | 26 | aaa | BOS | 61 | 4.70 | 1.36 | 21.4 | 1.8 | 5.2 | 2.9 | 2.0 | 29 | 74 | 28 |
| | 18 | R | 27 | aaa | BOS | 115 | 5.86 | 1.81 | 24.2 | 3.0 | 6.3 | 2.1 | 1.1 | 39 | 68 | 36 |
| Hall,Brooks | 17 | R | 27 | a/a | ARI | 60 | 6.78 | 1.78 | 16.2 | 2.8 | 5.3 | 1.9 | 0.5 | 39 | 60 | 42 |
| Hall,Matt | 17 | L | 24 | aa | DET | 35 | 3.92 | 1.66 | 26.1 | 5.7 | 8.1 | 1.4 | 0.6 | 33 | 77 | 62 |
| | 18 | L | 25 | a/a | DET | 115 | 2.88 | 1.28 | 12.8 | 3.8 | 8.2 | 2.2 | 0.2 | 31 | 76 | 97 |
| Halstead,Ryan | 17 | R | 25 | aa | SF | 24 | 6.30 | 1.82 | 4.22 | 3.0 | 6.5 | 2.2 | 1.2 | 39 | 66 | 36 |
| | 18 | R | 26 | a/a | SF | 62 | 3.76 | 1.43 | 7.58 | 2.5 | 6.3 | 2.5 | 1.1 | 33 | 78 | 53 |
| Hamilton,Ian | 17 | R | 22 | aa | CHW | 19 | 7.18 | 2.15 | 6.74 | 4.3 | 9.4 | 2.2 | 0.0 | 48 | 63 | 82 |
| | 18 | R | 23 | a/a | CHW | 53 | 2.18 | 1.18 | 4.95 | 2.9 | 9.1 | 3.1 | 0.4 | 31 | 83 | 116 |
| Hanhold,Eric | 18 | R | 25 | a/a | NYM | 45 | 4.78 | 1.47 | 6.24 | 3.2 | 8.7 | 2.7 | 0.4 | 37 | 66 | 97 |
| Hansen,Alec | 18 | R | 24 | aa | CHW | 37 | 8.81 | 2.30 | 21.2 | 11.6 | 7.2 | 0.6 | 1.0 | 31 | 60 | 29 |
| Harber,Conor | 18 | R | 25 | aa | MIL | 21 | 5.73 | 1.63 | 23.5 | 2.9 | 6.4 | 2.2 | 1.3 | 35 | 67 | 37 |
| Harper,Bryan | 18 | L | 29 | aa | WAS | 47 | 5.11 | 1.90 | 5.05 | 6.2 | 5.3 | 0.9 | 0.7 | 34 | 73 | 23 |
| Harris,Greg | 17 | R | 23 | aa | TAM | 97 | 6.09 | 1.57 | 14.7 | 4.1 | 7.6 | 1.9 | 1.5 | 32 | 64 | 37 |
| Harris,Jon | 17 | R | 24 | aa | TOR | 143 | 7.28 | 1.81 | 25.4 | 3.2 | 6.0 | 1.9 | 1.6 | 37 | 61 | 13 |
| | 18 | R | 25 | a/a | TOR | 149 | 6.22 | 1.62 | 24.5 | 2.1 | 5.2 | 2.5 | 1.6 | 35 | 65 | 23 |
| Harrison,Jordan | 17 | L | 25 | aa | TAM | 58 | 4.25 | 1.72 | 4.94 | 7.3 | 6.5 | 0.9 | 0.4 | 29 | 74 | 53 |
| | 18 | L | 26 | a/a | TAM | 58 | 2.01 | 1.34 | 4.84 | 5.0 | 6.8 | 1.4 | 0.4 | 27 | 86 | 71 |
| Hart,Kyle | 18 | L | 26 | aa | BOS | 140 | 4.68 | 1.61 | 25.9 | 3.3 | 4.9 | 1.5 | 0.9 | 33 | 72 | 28 |
| Hartlieb,Geoff | 18 | R | 25 | aa | PIT | 59 | 3.91 | 1.56 | 5.51 | 3.9 | 6.7 | 1.7 | 0.5 | 34 | 75 | 59 |
| Hartman,Nick | 18 | R | 24 | aa | TOR | 29 | 6.83 | 2.08 | 7.92 | 5.2 | 5.3 | 1.0 | 1.1 | 38 | 67 | 6 |
| Hartman,Ryan | 18 | L | 24 | aa | HOU | 122 | 3.43 | 1.25 | 19.9 | 2.0 | 8.8 | 4.5 | 1.0 | 33 | 76 | 118 |
| Harvey,Hunter | 18 | R | 24 | aa | BAL | 33 | 6.31 | 1.51 | 15.9 | 2.4 | 6.6 | 2.7 | 0.9 | 35 | 58 | 61 |
| Harvey,Joe | 18 | R | 26 | a/a | NYY | 60 | 2.29 | 1.19 | 5.61 | 4.2 | 8.3 | 2.0 | 0.4 | 26 | 82 | 92 |
| Hatch,Thomas | 18 | R | 24 | aa | CHC | 145 | 4.89 | 1.51 | 24.2 | 4.1 | 6.0 | 1.4 | 1.2 | 30 | 70 | 32 |
| Hauschild,Mike | 17 | R | 27 | aaa | HOU | 90 | 4.57 | 1.58 | 22.1 | 5.0 | 6.4 | 1.3 | 0.7 | 31 | 71 | 45 |
| | 18 | R | 28 | aaa | TOR | 120 | 7.22 | 1.98 | 25.1 | 4.1 | 5.8 | 1.4 | 1.0 | 39 | 63 | 19 |
| Head,Louis | 17 | R | 27 | aaa | CLE | 61 | 4.71 | 1.62 | 5.45 | 4.9 | 6.7 | 1.4 | 0.4 | 33 | 70 | 56 |
| | 18 | R | 28 | aaa | CLE | 17 | 16.30 | 2.83 | 6.48 | 6.2 | 7.9 | 1.3 | 2.1 | 50 | 39 | -18 |
| Healy,Tucker | 17 | R | 27 | aaa | OAK | 43 | 5.80 | 1.86 | 5.71 | 4.9 | 5.4 | 1.1 | 0.7 | 36 | 68 | 27 |
| | 18 | R | 28 | a/a | SEA | 31 | 5.16 | 1.71 | 5.62 | 3.8 | 7.6 | 2.0 | 2.4 | 34 | 79 | 9 |
| Heaney,Andrew | 17 | L | 26 | aaa | LAA | 17 | 3.23 | 1.30 | 23.8 | 2.0 | 6.0 | 3.1 | 0.9 | 31 | 79 | 71 |
| Hearn,Taylor | 18 | L | 24 | aa | TEX | 129 | 4.67 | 1.40 | 22.7 | 3.7 | 7.9 | 2.1 | 1.0 | 31 | 68 | 66 |
| Hedges,Zach | 17 | R | 25 | a/a | CHC | 146 | 5.60 | 1.76 | 25.8 | 2.7 | 3.9 | 1.5 | 0.9 | 36 | 69 | 13 |
| | 18 | R | 26 | a/a | CHC | 90 | 4.13 | 1.36 | 10.5 | 2.0 | 4.6 | 2.3 | 0.9 | 31 | 72 | 46 |
| Heller,Ben | 17 | R | 26 | aaa | NYY | 56 | 4.11 | 1.20 | 5.53 | 3.8 | 10.6 | 2.8 | 1.5 | 27 | 72 | 90 |
| Helsley,Ryan | 17 | R | 23 | a/a | STL | 39 | 3.48 | 1.44 | 23.5 | 4.3 | 8.7 | 2.0 | 1.0 | 32 | 79 | 69 |
| | 18 | R | 24 | a/a | STL | 69 | 4.47 | 1.17 | 23 | 3.6 | 8.2 | 2.3 | 0.9 | 26 | 63 | 83 |
| Helton,Bret | 18 | R | 25 | aa | PIT | 61 | 7.76 | 1.89 | 8.23 | 5.9 | 5.2 | 0.9 | 1.3 | 33 | 59 | 4 |
| Herb,Tyler | 17 | R | 25 | aa | SF | 163 | 4.26 | 1.55 | 27.4 | 3.0 | 6.1 | 2.1 | 0.6 | 35 | 72 | 58 |
| | 18 | R | 26 | aaa | SF | 72 | 5.65 | 1.71 | 25.1 | 3.4 | 5.8 | 1.7 | 0.9 | 36 | 67 | 35 |
| Heredia,Luis | 17 | R | 23 | aa | PIT | 52 | 4.15 | 1.59 | 6.41 | 5.7 | 6.0 | 1.0 | 0.6 | 29 | 74 | 45 |
| Herget,Jimmy | 17 | R | 24 | a/a | CIN | 62 | 4.18 | 1.46 | 5.1 | 3.5 | 9.0 | 2.6 | 1.0 | 34 | 74 | 77 |
| | 18 | R | 25 | aaa | CIN | 61 | 4.42 | 1.56 | 5.36 | 3.4 | 8.0 | 2.4 | 1.0 | 36 | 73 | 65 |
| Herget,Kevin | 17 | R | 26 | a/a | STL | 82 | 5.27 | 1.62 | 10.4 | 2.9 | 6.8 | 2.4 | 1.0 | 36 | 69 | 52 |
| | 18 | R | 27 | aaa | STL | 140 | 5.47 | 1.56 | 21.9 | 2.2 | 5.9 | 2.6 | 1.4 | 35 | 68 | 40 |
| Hernandez,Ariel | 17 | R | 25 | a/a | CIN | 50 | 4.76 | 1.74 | 5.85 | 8.2 | 8.8 | 1.1 | 0.3 | 30 | 71 | 77 |
| | 18 | R | 26 | a/a | MIL | 58 | 3.47 | 1.58 | 6.12 | 6.5 | 6.7 | 1.0 | 0.2 | 29 | 77 | 65 |
| Hernandez,Arnalc | 18 | R | 22 | a/a | KC | 76 | 4.47 | 1.30 | 24.2 | 2.9 | 5.1 | 1.8 | 1.1 | 28 | 68 | 39 |
| Hernandez,Jonatl | 18 | R | 22 | aa | TEX | 64 | 6.33 | 1.68 | 24 | 5.5 | 6.7 | 1.2 | 1.0 | 32 | 62 | 35 |
| Herrera,Ronald | 17 | R | 22 | a/a | NYY | 66 | 2.21 | 0.97 | 22.9 | 2.2 | 5.7 | 2.7 | 0.8 | 23 | 82 | 80 |
| Herrmann,Spence | 18 | L | 25 | aa | SEA | 66 | 5.96 | 1.76 | 10.5 | 4.0 | 6.4 | 1.6 | 0.5 | 38 | 64 | 49 |
| Hess,David | 17 | R | 24 | aa | BAL | 154 | 4.85 | 1.44 | 24.4 | 3.5 | 6.2 | 1.8 | 1.1 | 30 | 68 | 43 |
| | 18 | R | 25 | aaa | BAL | 47 | 4.18 | 1.45 | 22.4 | 4.0 | 6.6 | 1.7 | 0.8 | 31 | 72 | 54 |
| Higgins,Tyler | 17 | R | 26 | aa | MIA | 60 | 4.92 | 1.66 | 7.94 | 2.9 | 5.7 | 2.0 | 1.3 | 35 | 73 | 29 |
| | 18 | R | 27 | aaa | SEA | 35 | 3.43 | 1.38 | 5.25 | 2.5 | 8.0 | 3.2 | 1.1 | 34 | 80 | 80 |
| Hightower,Scoote | 18 | R | 25 | aa | PIT | 38 | 3.03 | 1.21 | 14 | 2.3 | 5.8 | 2.6 | 0.3 | 30 | 74 | 85 |
| Hill,Cameron | 17 | R | 23 | a/a | CLE | 64 | 4.09 | 1.36 | 6.25 | 2.6 | 5.3 | 2.1 | 1.2 | 30 | 74 | 38 |
| | 18 | R | 24 | aaa | CLE | 15 | 7.68 | 1.76 | 4.36 | 5.1 | 6.4 | 1.2 | 3.6 | 27 | 66 | -47 |
| Hill,Kevin | 18 | R | 26 | aa | HOU | 19 | 2.54 | 1.62 | 8.48 | 5.1 | 5.3 | 1.0 | 0.6 | 31 | 86 | 36 |
| Hissong,Travis | 17 | R | 26 | aa | MIL | 50 | 7.29 | 1.96 | 8.91 | 6.3 | 8.0 | 1.3 | 1.5 | 36 | 64 | 22 |
| Hodson,Chase | 18 | R | 26 | aa | NYY | 17 | 5.93 | 1.86 | 7.33 | 6.0 | 5.9 | 1.0 | 0.8 | 34 | 68 | 28 |
| Hofacket,Adam | 17 | R | 23 | a/a | LAA | 53 | 4.41 | 1.40 | 6.08 | 1.6 | 6.8 | 4.2 | 0.8 | 35 | 70 | 99 |
| | 18 | R | 24 | a/a | LAA | 37 | 8.85 | 2.05 | 6.96 | 3.8 | 4.1 | 1.1 | 1.0 | 39 | 55 | 0 |
| Hoffman,Jeff | 17 | R | 24 | aaa | COL | 50 | 6.32 | 1.50 | 21.4 | 3.7 | 6.5 | 1.8 | 0.7 | 32 | 56 | 53 |
| | 18 | R | 25 | aaa | COL | 107 | 5.79 | 1.60 | 22.6 | 4.1 | 6.5 | 1.6 | 0.9 | 33 | 64 | 43 |

| PITCHER | yr | t | age | lvl | org | ip | era | whip | bf/g | ctl | dom | cmd | hr/9 | h% | s% | bpv |
|---|---|---|---|---|---|---|---|---|---|---|---|---|---|---|---|---|
| Holmberg,David | 18 | L | 27 | aaa | COL | 107 | 6.48 | 1.86 | 22.7 | 2.7 | 4.0 | 1.5 | 1.8 | 36 | 68 | -14 |
| Holmes,Ben | 18 | L | 27 | aa | LA | 46 | 3.59 | 1.19 | 16.8 | 2.5 | 5.4 | 2.2 | 0.8 | 27 | 72 | 60 |
| Holmes,Brian | 17 | L | 26 | aaa | HOU | 53 | 8.90 | 1.96 | 13.4 | 4.5 | 6.5 | 1.4 | 1.7 | 38 | 55 | 6 |
| Holmes,Clay | 17 | R | 24 | aaa | PIT | 113 | 4.54 | 1.62 | 20 | 5.1 | 6.3 | 1.2 | 0.4 | 32 | 71 | 53 |
| | 18 | R | 25 | aaa | PIT | 96 | 4.10 | 1.59 | 19.2 | 3.9 | 7.4 | 1.9 | 0.4 | 36 | 73 | 69 |
| Holmes,Grant | 17 | R | 21 | aa | OAK | 148 | 5.05 | 1.49 | 22 | 3.5 | 7.6 | 2.2 | 0.8 | 34 | 66 | 65 |
| Honeywell,Brent | 17 | R | 22 | a/a | TAM | 137 | 4.40 | 1.41 | 22.2 | 2.4 | 10.2 | 4.2 | 0.9 | 38 | 70 | 121 |
| Horacek,Mitch | 18 | L | 27 | aa | COL | 62 | 3.43 | 1.64 | 5.43 | 4.8 | 7.9 | 1.7 | 0.7 | 35 | 80 | 61 |
| House,Austin | 17 | R | 26 | aaa | COL | 68 | 2.59 | 1.43 | 5.9 | 3.4 | 5.1 | 1.5 | 0.4 | 31 | 82 | 52 |
| | 18 | R | 27 | aaa | COL | 41 | 10.34 | 2.06 | 5.91 | 5.5 | 4.5 | 0.8 | 2.2 | 34 | 50 | -34 |
| Houser,Adrian | 18 | R | 25 | a/a | MIL | 80 | 6.05 | 1.74 | 17.4 | 2.9 | 6.2 | 2.1 | 1.2 | 38 | 67 | 33 |
| Houston,Zac | 18 | R | 24 | a/a | DET | 56 | 2.15 | 1.09 | 4.76 | 4.3 | 10.2 | 2.4 | 0.6 | 24 | 83 | 113 |
| Hovis,Reilly | 18 | R | 25 | aa | MIA | 22 | 7.46 | 2.11 | 9.04 | 6.9 | 7.1 | 1.0 | 1.3 | 37 | 65 | 17 |
| Howard,Brian | 18 | R | 23 | aa | OAK | 68 | 3.93 | 1.40 | 23.9 | 2.9 | 6.9 | 2.4 | 0.9 | 32 | 74 | 64 |
| Howard,Nick | 18 | R | 25 | aa | CIN | 18 | 4.10 | 1.55 | 6.55 | 3.9 | 5.0 | 1.3 | 0.7 | 31 | 74 | 35 |
| Howard,Sam | 17 | L | 24 | a/a | COL | 127 | 4.84 | 1.51 | 23 | 3.4 | 5.6 | 1.6 | 1.1 | 31 | 70 | 32 |
| | 18 | L | 25 | aaa | COL | 96 | 6.02 | 1.66 | 20.5 | 3.3 | 5.7 | 1.7 | 1.4 | 34 | 66 | 20 |
| Hu,Chih-Wei | 17 | R | 24 | aaa | TAM | 62 | 4.17 | 1.40 | 8.39 | 1.9 | 7.2 | 3.7 | 1.6 | 33 | 76 | 70 |
| | 18 | R | 25 | aaa | TAM | 103 | 5.93 | 1.62 | 19.1 | 2.6 | 6.8 | 2.6 | 1.4 | 36 | 65 | 46 |
| Huang,Wei-Chieh | 18 | R | 25 | aa | TEX | 47 | 5.24 | 1.46 | 10.6 | 3.3 | 8.6 | 2.6 | 1.5 | 33 | 68 | 61 |
| Hudson,Dakota | 17 | R | 23 | a/a | STL | 153 | 3.75 | 1.45 | 26.1 | 2.9 | 4.6 | 1.6 | 0.4 | 32 | 74 | 45 |
| | 18 | R | 24 | aaa | STL | 113 | 2.77 | 1.39 | 25.1 | 2.9 | 5.6 | 1.9 | 0.1 | 32 | 78 | 72 |
| Huffman,Chris | 17 | R | 25 | a/a | SD | 102 | 3.86 | 1.48 | 24.3 | 2.1 | 6.1 | 2.8 | 1.1 | 34 | 77 | 57 |
| | 18 | R | 26 | a/a | SD | 100 | 6.47 | 1.81 | 17.2 | 4.0 | 4.4 | 1.1 | 1.2 | 35 | 65 | 5 |
| Hurlbut,David | 17 | L | 28 | aaa | MIN | 131 | 5.79 | 1.95 | 27.1 | 2.5 | 5.1 | 2.0 | 0.6 | 42 | 69 | 35 |
| | 18 | L | 29 | aaa | TEX | 85 | 8.04 | 2.16 | 23.5 | 3.1 | 4.7 | 1.5 | 1.8 | 41 | 65 | -18 |
| Hursh,Jason | 17 | R | 26 | a/a | ATL | 52 | 6.14 | 1.94 | 6.56 | 3.5 | 7.3 | 2.1 | 0.6 | 43 | 67 | 53 |
| | 18 | R | 27 | a/a | ATL | 68 | 5.13 | 1.89 | 6.04 | 5.4 | 5.9 | 1.1 | 0.0 | 37 | 70 | 51 |
| Irvin,Cole | 17 | L | 23 | aa | PHI | 84 | 4.92 | 1.27 | 26.6 | 2.6 | 6.2 | 2.4 | 1.5 | 28 | 66 | 45 |
| | 18 | L | 24 | aaa | PHI | 162 | 3.21 | 1.22 | 25.2 | 2.0 | 6.3 | 3.1 | 0.8 | 30 | 76 | 83 |
| Isaac,Sean | 18 | R | 26 | a/a | LAA | 41 | 7.38 | 1.67 | 10.2 | 5.8 | 8.9 | 1.5 | 1.1 | 33 | 55 | 53 |
| Isaacs,Dusty | 17 | R | 26 | aa | TOR | 62 | 5.33 | 1.49 | 6.48 | 4.6 | 8.9 | 1.9 | 1.4 | 31 | 67 | 57 |
| | 18 | R | 27 | a/a | TOR | 60 | 7.23 | 1.90 | 6.43 | 6.3 | 7.4 | 1.2 | 1.5 | 34 | 63 | 18 |
| Istler,Andrew | 18 | R | 26 | a/a | LA | 64 | 2.57 | 1.02 | 7.95 | 2.0 | 6.0 | 3.0 | 0.1 | 27 | 73 | 105 |
| Jackson,Luke | 17 | R | 26 | aaa | ATL | 24 | 8.42 | 2.10 | 13.3 | 6.8 | 7.1 | 1.0 | 0.8 | 38 | 58 | 30 |
| | 18 | R | 27 | aaa | ATL | 22 | 2.13 | 1.09 | 8.66 | 4.2 | 10.6 | 2.5 | 0.0 | 28 | 78 | 135 |
| Jackson,Tyler | 18 | R | 25 | a/a | SEA | 26 | 10.60 | 2.00 | 14 | 3.5 | 5.0 | 1.4 | 2.2 | 37 | 47 | -26 |
| Jackson,Zach | 18 | R | 24 | aa | TOR | 62 | 3.21 | 1.44 | 6.14 | 7.8 | 8.9 | 1.1 | 0.3 | 22 | 77 | 89 |
| James,Joshua | 17 | R | 24 | aa | HOU | 76 | 5.51 | 1.66 | 16.2 | 3.9 | 7.4 | 1.9 | 0.1 | 38 | 64 | 75 |
| | 18 | R | 25 | a/a | HOU | 117 | 3.58 | 1.18 | 20.4 | 3.7 | 10.7 | 2.9 | 0.7 | 30 | 71 | 115 |
| Jankins,Thomas | 18 | R | 23 | a/a | MIL | 136 | 4.98 | 1.38 | 23.8 | 2.5 | 5.7 | 2.3 | 1.0 | 31 | 65 | 50 |
| Jankowski,Jordan | 17 | R | 28 | aaa | LA | 43 | 6.99 | 1.81 | 4.9 | 5.8 | 8.9 | 1.5 | 1.0 | 37 | 61 | 52 |
| | 18 | R | 29 | aaa | LAA | 20 | 7.76 | 2.00 | 6.5 | 6.4 | 7.8 | 1.2 | 0.8 | 38 | 60 | 39 |
| Jay,Tyler | 18 | L | 24 | aa | MIN | 61 | 5.15 | 1.77 | 7.39 | 3.0 | 5.8 | 1.9 | 1.2 | 37 | 73 | 27 |
| Jaye,Myles | 17 | R | 26 | a/a | DET | 132 | 5.54 | 1.83 | 24.5 | 3.6 | 6.1 | 1.7 | 1.0 | 38 | 71 | 31 |
| | 18 | R | 27 | aaa | CLE | 72 | 8.82 | 1.99 | 20.4 | 3.6 | 3.4 | 0.9 | 2.2 | 35 | 58 | -44 |
| Jemiola,Zach | 17 | R | 23 | aaa | COL | 82 | 8.97 | 2.02 | 24.7 | 4.4 | 3.4 | 0.8 | 1.9 | 35 | 57 | -35 |
| Jenkins,Tyrell | 17 | R | 25 | aaa | SD | 82 | 8.08 | 2.06 | 23.6 | 5.3 | 4.9 | 0.9 | 1.6 | 36 | 62 | -12 |
| Jensen,Chris | 17 | R | 27 | aaa | OAK | 85 | 7.45 | 1.83 | 13.1 | 3.2 | 4.4 | 1.4 | 0.9 | 37 | 58 | 16 |
| | 18 | R | 28 | a/a | TEX | 91 | 8.67 | 2.33 | 16.8 | 5.4 | 4.3 | 0.8 | 1.7 | 40 | 64 | -30 |
| Jerez,Williams | 17 | L | 25 | a/a | BOS | 63 | 4.76 | 1.62 | 7.4 | 3.7 | 6.4 | 1.7 | 1.1 | 34 | 73 | 37 |
| | 18 | L | 26 | aaa | LAA | 57 | 4.22 | 1.45 | 6.42 | 3.7 | 9.4 | 2.6 | 0.8 | 35 | 72 | 87 |
| Jester,Jason | 17 | R | 26 | aaa | SD | 67 | 6.29 | 1.70 | 5.71 | 3.4 | 4.3 | 1.2 | 1.1 | 34 | 63 | 10 |
| | 18 | R | 27 | aa | SD | 61 | 5.60 | 1.65 | 6.83 | 2.1 | 6.5 | 3.1 | 0.3 | 40 | 64 | 83 |
| Jeter,Bud | 18 | R | 27 | aa | ARI | 47 | 3.48 | 1.45 | 5.91 | 4.4 | 7.0 | 1.6 | 0.6 | 30 | 77 | 61 |
| Jewell,Jake | 17 | R | 24 | aa | LAA | 125 | 6.73 | 1.72 | 23.6 | 3.2 | 5.0 | 1.6 | 1.2 | 35 | 61 | 16 |
| | 18 | R | 25 | a/a | LAA | 38 | 3.38 | 1.60 | 6.46 | 4.3 | 6.9 | 1.6 | 0.7 | 34 | 81 | 51 |
| Jimenez,Dedgar | 17 | L | 21 | aa | BOS | 46 | 3.69 | 1.53 | 25.2 | 3.6 | 4.1 | 1.1 | 0.9 | 30 | 78 | 21 |
| | 18 | L | 22 | a/a | BOS | 144 | 5.63 | 1.45 | 23.7 | 3.5 | 6.3 | 1.8 | 1.3 | 30 | 63 | 37 |
| Jimenez,Francisc | 18 | R | 24 | aaa | BAL | 22 | 6.00 | 1.55 | 8.79 | 3.5 | 4.9 | 1.4 | 0.5 | 33 | 59 | 39 |
| Jiminian,Johendi | 17 | R | 25 | a/a | COL | 63 | 8.04 | 2.25 | 8.91 | 6.7 | 4.4 | 0.7 | 2.1 | 35 | 67 | -39 |
| | 18 | R | 26 | aa | SEA | 71 | 4.24 | 1.60 | 19.7 | 4.2 | 5.5 | 1.3 | 1.2 | 31 | 77 | 23 |
| Johansen,Jake | 17 | R | 26 | aa | CHW | 38 | 6.38 | 1.80 | 6.51 | 5.9 | 6.3 | 1.1 | 1.0 | 33 | 65 | 26 |
| | 18 | R | 27 | aa | CHW | 49 | 6.02 | 1.95 | 7.57 | 3.6 | 5.1 | 1.4 | 0.5 | 40 | 68 | 29 |
| Johnson,Brian | 17 | L | 27 | aaa | BOS | 90 | 5.05 | 1.65 | 23.8 | 3.5 | 5.3 | 1.5 | 1.4 | 33 | 73 | 14 |
| Johnson,Chase | 18 | R | 26 | aa | SF | 59 | 5.00 | 1.48 | 14.1 | 3.5 | 4.5 | 1.3 | 0.4 | 31 | 65 | 40 |
| Johnson,D.J. | 17 | R | 28 | aa | COL | 64 | 4.87 | 1.68 | 6.73 | 4.3 | 5.0 | 1.2 | 1.0 | 33 | 72 | 20 |
| | 18 | R | 29 | aaa | COL | 56 | 5.01 | 1.58 | 4.94 | 2.7 | 9.4 | 3.4 | 1.0 | 40 | 70 | 90 |
| Johnson,Jordan | 17 | R | 24 | aa | SF | 92 | 6.06 | 1.63 | 19.6 | 4.0 | 5.3 | 1.3 | 1.2 | 32 | 64 | 20 |
| | 18 | R | 25 | a/a | SF | 138 | 4.69 | 1.60 | 23.5 | 4.2 | 6.0 | 1.4 | 0.3 | 34 | 69 | 54 |
| Johnson,Michael | 17 | L | 26 | aa | LA | 61 | 3.47 | 1.43 | 6.51 | 3.4 | 8.4 | 2.5 | 1.5 | 32 | 83 | 57 |
| | 18 | L | 27 | a/a | LA | 68 | 5.72 | 1.66 | 7.1 | 3.5 | 5.0 | 1.4 | 1.4 | 33 | 68 | 11 |
| Johnson,Pierce | 17 | R | 26 | aaa | CHC | 54 | 5.03 | 1.64 | 5.64 | 4.7 | 9.9 | 2.1 | 0.5 | 38 | 68 | 86 |
| | 18 | R | 27 | aaa | SF | 24 | 3.69 | 1.13 | 5.63 | 3.7 | 8.7 | 2.3 | 0.3 | 27 | 66 | 106 |
| Johnstone,Conno | 18 | R | 24 | a/a | ATL | 40 | 4.66 | 1.61 | 14.8 | 3.4 | 5.0 | 1.5 | 1.9 | 31 | 78 | -1 |
| Jokisch,Eric | 17 | L | 28 | a/a | ARI | 141 | 5.38 | 1.64 | 21.6 | 3.0 | 4.7 | 1.6 | 1.0 | 34 | 68 | 22 |
| | 18 | L | 29 | aaa | OAK | 150 | 5.36 | 1.76 | 26.5 | 3.1 | 5.3 | 1.7 | 0.8 | 37 | 70 | 32 |
| Jones,Connor | 18 | R | 24 | a/a | STL | 112 | 4.53 | 1.71 | 19.6 | 5.0 | 5.3 | 1.1 | 0.4 | 33 | 72 | 40 |
| Jones,Spencer | 18 | R | 24 | aa | TAM | 16 | 4.82 | 1.71 | 7.29 | 2.9 | 3.4 | 1.2 | 1.2 | 34 | 75 | -2 |
| Jorge,Felix | 17 | R | 23 | a/a | MIN | 149 | 5.40 | 1.66 | 26.7 | 2.6 | 5.2 | 2.0 | 1.1 | 36 | 69 | 30 |
| Junis,Jakob | 17 | R | 25 | aaa | KC | 71 | 3.80 | 1.27 | 24.2 | 2.0 | 8.6 | 4.3 | 0.8 | 34 | 72 | 118 |
| Jurado,Ariel | 17 | R | 21 | aa | TEX | 157 | 6.19 | 1.69 | 26.2 | 2.3 | 4.6 | 2.0 | 1.1 | 36 | 64 | 23 |
| | 18 | R | 22 | aa | TEX | 103 | 4.15 | 1.40 | 27.2 | 1.6 | 4.2 | 2.6 | 1.3 | 31 | 75 | 37 |
| Kalish,Jake | 17 | L | 26 | a/a | KC | 87 | 4.92 | 1.76 | 19 | 2.5 | 5.2 | 2.1 | 0.6 | 39 | 72 | 43 |
| | 18 | L | 27 | a/a | KC | 129 | 5.20 | 1.56 | 17.2 | 1.6 | 6.5 | 4.0 | 0.7 | 38 | 66 | 92 |
| Karalus,Reece | 18 | R | 24 | aa | TAM | 22 | 9.58 | 1.80 | 8.47 | 4.6 | 7.5 | 1.6 | 1.8 | 35 | 46 | 18 |
| Keel,Jerry | 17 | L | 24 | aa | SD | 18 | 1.45 | 1.30 | 24.3 | 2.7 | 5.8 | 2.1 | 0.0 | 32 | 88 | 82 |
| | 18 | L | 25 | a/a | SD | 150 | 5.10 | 1.49 | 23.1 | 2.4 | 5.4 | 2.2 | 0.9 | 33 | 67 | 45 |

| PITCHER | yr | t | age | lvl | org | ip | era | whip | bf/g | ctl | dom | cmd | hr/9 | h% | s% | bpv |
|---|---|---|---|---|---|---|---|---|---|---|---|---|---|---|---|---|
| Keller,Brad | 17 | R | 22 | aa | ARI | 131 | 6.27 | 1.76 | 23 | 4.1 | 6.6 | 1.6 | 0.6 | 37 | 63 | 47 |
| Keller,Brian | 18 | R | 24 | aa | NYY | 125 | 5.09 | 1.51 | 24.6 | 2.9 | 6.9 | 2.4 | 1.3 | 34 | 69 | 47 |
| Keller,Kyle | 18 | R | 25 | a/a | MIA | 37 | 4.34 | 1.38 | 5.39 | 5.1 | 11.2 | 2.2 | 0.5 | 33 | 68 | 109 |
| Keller,Mitch | 17 | R | 21 | aa | PIT | 35 | 4.05 | 1.18 | 23.1 | 3.0 | 9.8 | 3.3 | 0.6 | 31 | 65 | 119 |
| | 18 | R | 22 | a/a | PIT | 139 | 4.10 | 1.38 | 24.3 | 3.4 | 7.2 | 2.1 | 0.7 | 31 | 71 | 70 |
| Kelley,Trevor | 17 | R | 24 | aa | BOS | 27 | 4.82 | 1.53 | 7.43 | 2.5 | 4.5 | 1.8 | 0.4 | 34 | 67 | 47 |
| | 18 | R | 25 | a/a | BOS | 57 | 3.94 | 1.56 | 6.11 | 3.7 | 5.6 | 1.5 | 0.4 | 33 | 74 | 51 |
| Kelly,Michael | 17 | R | 25 | a/a | SD | 127 | 5.08 | 1.51 | 19.6 | 4.0 | 7.2 | 1.8 | 0.9 | 33 | 67 | 55 |
| | 18 | R | 26 | a/a | BAL | 68 | 10.98 | 2.47 | 11.6 | 11.0 | 6.3 | 0.6 | 1.4 | 34 | 54 | 3 |
| Kennedy,Brett | 17 | R | 23 | aa | SD | 141 | 5.15 | 1.45 | 23.2 | 2.5 | 7.1 | 2.8 | 1.2 | 34 | 67 | 61 |
| | 18 | R | 24 | aaa | SD | 90 | 2.67 | 1.13 | 22.2 | 2.0 | 6.8 | 3.3 | 0.5 | 29 | 78 | 102 |
| Kent,Matt | 18 | L | 26 | a/a | BOS | 150 | 5.19 | 1.55 | 23.5 | 2.4 | 6.0 | 2.5 | 1.0 | 35 | 67 | 52 |
| Keselica,Sean | 17 | L | 24 | aa | PIT | 74 | 4.85 | 1.71 | 7.94 | 5.2 | 7.0 | 1.3 | 0.3 | 35 | 70 | 59 |
| | 18 | L | 25 | aa | PIT | 59 | 6.26 | 1.57 | 6.49 | 7.0 | 5.9 | 0.8 | 0.7 | 25 | 59 | 43 |
| Kikuchi,Yusei | 18 | L | 27 | for | JPN | 164 | 3.82 | 1.15 | 28.3 | 3.1 | 8.0 | 2.6 | 1.5 | 25 | 73 | 69 |
| Kilome,Franklyn | 17 | R | 22 | aa | PHI | 30 | 4.33 | 1.46 | 25.4 | 4.5 | 5.4 | 1.2 | 0.7 | 28 | 71 | 41 |
| | 18 | R | 23 | aa | NYM | 140 | 4.71 | 1.45 | 23 | 4.0 | 7.0 | 1.8 | 0.6 | 31 | 67 | 62 |
| King,Michael | 18 | R | 23 | a/a | NYY | 121 | 2.33 | 1.01 | 25.7 | 1.5 | 6.9 | 4.6 | 0.7 | 27 | 81 | 125 |
| Kingham,Nick | 17 | R | 26 | aaa | PIT | 113 | 5.83 | 1.64 | 25.3 | 2.6 | 5.6 | 2.2 | 0.8 | 37 | 64 | 46 |
| | 18 | R | 27 | a/a | PIT | 68 | 5.00 | 1.45 | 22.4 | 2.5 | 6.2 | 2.5 | 0.8 | 34 | 65 | 63 |
| Kinley,Jeff | 17 | L | 25 | aa | MIA | 26 | 6.80 | 2.07 | 6.36 | 5.4 | 4.3 | 0.8 | 0.8 | 37 | 66 | 5 |
| | 18 | L | 26 | a/a | MIA | 61 | 3.77 | 1.22 | 6.03 | 4.1 | 6.3 | 1.5 | 0.8 | 24 | 70 | 60 |
| Kinley,Tyler | 17 | R | 26 | aa | MIA | 26 | 6.95 | 2.10 | 4.74 | 6.3 | 9.6 | 1.5 | 0.8 | 43 | 66 | 53 |
| | 18 | R | 27 | aaa | MIA | 40 | 3.59 | 1.57 | 4.39 | 5.4 | 10.0 | 1.9 | 0.5 | 35 | 77 | 89 |
| Kipper,Jordan | 17 | R | 25 | a/a | BAL | 132 | 4.99 | 1.79 | 23.5 | 2.9 | 3.8 | 1.3 | 0.9 | 36 | 73 | 9 |
| | 18 | R | 26 | aa | BAL | 20 | 2.70 | 1.11 | 26.5 | 0.9 | 4.5 | 4.8 | 1.1 | 28 | 82 | 98 |
| Kline,Branden | 18 | R | 27 | aa | BAL | 45 | 2.23 | 1.22 | 5.68 | 3.2 | 7.2 | 2.3 | 0.7 | 28 | 85 | 77 |
| Klonowski,Alex | 17 | R | 25 | a/a | LAA | 129 | 5.19 | 1.43 | 22 | 2.1 | 5.3 | 2.5 | 1.3 | 32 | 66 | 41 |
| | 18 | R | 26 | a/a | LAA | 108 | 5.32 | 1.56 | 22.5 | 2.6 | 6.1 | 2.4 | 0.9 | 35 | 66 | 54 |
| Knapp,Ricky | 17 | R | 25 | a/a | NYM | 172 | 6.79 | 1.73 | 26.9 | 2.3 | 4.4 | 1.9 | 1.1 | 37 | 61 | 20 |
| Koerner,Brody | 17 | R | 24 | aa | NYY | 71 | 5.97 | 1.84 | 27.5 | 2.9 | 4.8 | 1.7 | 1.4 | 38 | 70 | 7 |
| | 18 | R | 25 | a/a | NYY | 65 | 6.20 | 1.57 | 13.6 | 2.7 | 4.7 | 1.7 | 0.6 | 34 | 59 | 39 |
| Kopech,Michael | 17 | R | 21 | a/a | CHW | 134 | 3.57 | 1.31 | 22.2 | 4.7 | 10.5 | 2.2 | 0.5 | 31 | 73 | 107 |
| | 18 | R | 22 | aaa | CHW | 127 | 4.39 | 1.39 | 22.3 | 4.4 | 10.7 | 2.4 | 0.7 | 33 | 69 | 100 |
| Kowalczyk,Karch | 17 | R | 26 | aa | LA | 62 | 3.96 | 1.58 | 6.23 | 3.2 | 5.4 | 1.7 | 0.8 | 34 | 77 | 36 |
| | 18 | R | 27 | a/a | LA | 33 | 7.29 | 2.00 | 6.96 | 4.5 | 6.9 | 1.5 | 0.0 | 42 | 60 | 59 |
| Krehbiel,Joey | 17 | R | 25 | a/a | ARI | 57 | 3.90 | 1.43 | 5.24 | 4.4 | 9.8 | 2.2 | 0.6 | 34 | 73 | 94 |
| | 18 | R | 26 | aaa | ARI | 58 | 3.94 | 1.29 | 4.97 | 3.6 | 8.7 | 2.4 | 1.1 | 29 | 73 | 78 |
| Kremer,Dean | 18 | R | 22 | aa | BAL | 53 | 2.46 | 1.21 | 23.8 | 3.3 | 9.1 | 2.8 | 0.6 | 30 | 82 | 105 |
| Krol,Ian | 18 | L | 27 | aaa | NYM | 57 | 2.61 | 1.64 | 5.92 | 4.0 | 7.4 | 1.8 | 0.5 | 36 | 85 | 63 |
| Krook,Matt | 18 | L | 24 | aa | TAM | 74 | 5.25 | 1.60 | 8.85 | 6.3 | 10.1 | 1.6 | 0.4 | 34 | 65 | 89 |
| Kruczynski,Evan | 18 | L | 23 | aa | STL | 41 | 2.57 | 0.94 | 25.8 | 2.0 | 6.0 | 2.9 | 0.2 | 24 | 71 | 106 |
| Kuntz,Brad | 18 | L | 26 | aa | MIL | 55 | 5.22 | 1.91 | 7.25 | 5.0 | 8.1 | 1.6 | 1.2 | 39 | 75 | 35 |
| Kuzminsky,Scott | 18 | R | 27 | aa | SEA | 28 | 4.90 | 1.97 | 9.58 | 7.0 | 4.2 | 0.6 | 1.5 | 30 | 79 | -12 |
| Labourt,Jairo | 17 | L | 23 | a/a | DET | 53 | 3.36 | 1.40 | 6.01 | 5.4 | 8.0 | 1.5 | 0.8 | 27 | 78 | 65 |
| Ladwig,A.J. | 17 | R | 25 | a/a | DET | 116 | 7.20 | 1.86 | 23.7 | 1.9 | 4.9 | 2.6 | 1.5 | 39 | 63 | 20 |
| | 18 | R | 26 | a/a | DET | 135 | 6.60 | 1.67 | 24.3 | 1.8 | 5.0 | 2.7 | 1.5 | 36 | 63 | 27 |
| Lail,Brady | 17 | R | 24 | a/a | NYY | 145 | 6.95 | 1.66 | 23.2 | 3.2 | 5.2 | 1.7 | 1.8 | 33 | 61 | 4 |
| | 18 | R | 25 | a/a | NYY | 65 | 7.12 | 1.85 | 8.25 | 5.5 | 7.5 | 1.4 | 1.6 | 35 | 63 | 20 |
| Lakins,Travis | 17 | R | 23 | aa | BOS | 30 | 8.13 | 2.08 | 18.6 | 6.6 | 4.6 | 0.7 | 0.7 | 35 | 59 | 13 |
| | 18 | R | 24 | a/a | BOS | 55 | 3.11 | 1.20 | 6.15 | 3.1 | 7.5 | 2.4 | 0.6 | 28 | 75 | 87 |
| LaMarche,Will | 18 | R | 27 | a/a | SF | 33 | 6.89 | 1.96 | 9.92 | 4.6 | 6.3 | 1.4 | 1.7 | 37 | 67 | 3 |
| Lambert,Jimmy | 18 | R | 24 | aa | CHW | 25 | 4.04 | 1.28 | 20.5 | 2.5 | 9.2 | 3.7 | 1.0 | 33 | 71 | 107 |
| Lambert,Peter | 18 | R | 21 | a/a | COL | 150 | 4.01 | 1.35 | 24.1 | 1.7 | 5.2 | 3.1 | 0.8 | 32 | 72 | 69 |
| Lane,Trevor | 18 | L | 24 | aa | NYY | 21 | 5.22 | 1.83 | 8.93 | 2.8 | 7.6 | 2.7 | 0.6 | 42 | 71 | 69 |
| Lau,Adam | 18 | R | 24 | aa | BOS | 58 | 5.11 | 1.66 | 7.24 | 4.4 | 7.3 | 1.7 | 1.5 | 33 | 73 | 29 |
| Lauer,Eric | 17 | L | 22 | aa | SD | 55 | 5.36 | 1.46 | 23.6 | 2.9 | 6.6 | 2.3 | 1.2 | 33 | 65 | 51 |
| | 18 | L | 23 | aaa | SD | 22 | 2.37 | 0.98 | 21 | 3.3 | 7.7 | 2.3 | 0.3 | 22 | 76 | 105 |
| Law,Derek | 17 | R | 27 | aaa | SF | 33 | 3.17 | 1.62 | 5.8 | 3.7 | 5.6 | 1.5 | 0.3 | 35 | 80 | 53 |
| | 18 | R | 28 | aaa | SF | 42 | 4.57 | 1.17 | 5.1 | 2.0 | 7.0 | 3.5 | 0.4 | 31 | 58 | 110 |
| Lawson,Brandon | 18 | R | 24 | aa | TAM | 43 | 5.15 | 1.85 | 14.4 | 3.7 | 6.0 | 1.6 | 0.9 | 38 | 73 | 30 |
| LeBlanc,Randy | 17 | R | 25 | aa | MIN | 79 | 5.93 | 1.81 | 19.2 | 3.0 | 4.3 | 1.4 | 0.2 | 38 | 64 | 37 |
| | 18 | R | 26 | aa | MIN | 51 | 2.75 | 1.48 | 24.5 | 2.4 | 5.4 | 2.2 | 0.4 | 34 | 82 | 62 |
| Ledbetter,David | 17 | R | 25 | a/a | TEX | 110 | 6.47 | 1.75 | 17.4 | 4.9 | 5.5 | 1.1 | 1.7 | 31 | 66 | 0 |
| | 18 | R | 26 | a/a | TEX | 45 | 7.87 | 1.70 | 25.5 | 3.4 | 4.8 | 1.4 | 1.5 | 34 | 54 | 5 |
| Lee,Chris | 17 | L | 25 | aaa | BAL | 116 | 7.08 | 2.11 | 21.3 | 5.0 | 5.4 | 1.1 | 1.1 | 39 | 67 | 7 |
| | 18 | L | 26 | a/a | BAL | 29 | 8.06 | 2.68 | 10.6 | 5.7 | 5.3 | 0.9 | 0.0 | 48 | 67 | 22 |
| Lee,Dylan | 18 | L | 24 | a/a | MIA | 31 | 2.04 | 1.03 | 5.43 | 3.0 | 9.3 | 3.1 | 0.0 | 28 | 78 | 137 |
| Lee,Zach | 17 | R | 26 | aaa | SD | 67 | 7.57 | 1.96 | 20 | 4.3 | 4.5 | 1.0 | 1.4 | 36 | 62 | -6 |
| | 18 | R | 27 | a/a | TAM | 147 | 4.78 | 1.62 | 25.1 | 2.4 | 5.3 | 2.3 | 0.7 | 36 | 71 | 48 |
| Leftwich,Luke | 18 | R | 24 | aa | PHI | 64 | 4.20 | 1.37 | 6.11 | 3.5 | 8.8 | 2.5 | 0.5 | 33 | 69 | 94 |
| Leibrandt,Brandoı | 17 | L | 25 | a/a | PHI | 137 | 4.69 | 1.58 | 24.1 | 3.3 | 5.8 | 1.8 | 1.0 | 34 | 72 | 37 |
| | 18 | L | 26 | aaa | PHI | 52 | 1.81 | 1.02 | 10 | 1.9 | 4.6 | 2.4 | 0.2 | 25 | 82 | 82 |
| Leiter,Mark | 17 | R | 26 | aaa | PHI | 30 | 5.69 | 1.35 | 17.9 | 2.0 | 9.4 | 4.7 | 2.0 | 34 | 64 | 94 |
| | 18 | R | 27 | aaa | PHI | 29 | 4.98 | 1.72 | 6.61 | 4.5 | 7.6 | 1.7 | 1.3 | 35 | 74 | 38 |
| Lemond,Zech | 18 | R | 26 | aa | MIA | 20 | 5.59 | 1.46 | 6.58 | 3.9 | 6.9 | 1.8 | 1.4 | 30 | 64 | 38 |
| Lenik,Kevin | 17 | R | 26 | aaa | KC | 24 | 2.50 | 0.93 | 7.5 | 3.2 | 6.9 | 2.2 | 0.4 | 20 | 74 | 96 |
| | 18 | R | 27 | aaa | KC | 50 | 6.49 | 1.68 | 6.64 | 4.9 | 6.9 | 1.4 | 0.8 | 34 | 60 | 45 |
| Lewicki,Artie | 17 | R | 25 | a/a | DET | 141 | 4.63 | 1.44 | 24 | 2.2 | 6.2 | 2.8 | 0.6 | 35 | 67 | 75 |
| | 18 | R | 26 | aaa | DET | 63 | 6.62 | 1.61 | 23.3 | 2.6 | 6.0 | 2.3 | 1.0 | 36 | 58 | 47 |
| Lewis,Sam | 18 | R | 27 | aa | ARI | 46 | 7.61 | 1.68 | 14.8 | 3.7 | 6.1 | 1.7 | 0.8 | 35 | 53 | 39 |
| Leyer,Robinson | 17 | R | 24 | aa | CHW | 58 | 5.09 | 1.74 | 7 | 6.1 | 8.2 | 1.4 | 0.4 | 35 | 69 | 65 |
| | 18 | R | 25 | aa | CIN | 59 | 3.55 | 1.44 | 5.99 | 4.8 | 8.3 | 1.7 | 0.8 | 30 | 78 | 67 |
| Lietz,Daniel | 18 | L | 24 | aa | ATL | 17 | 5.75 | 1.76 | 8.76 | 5.4 | 6.0 | 1.1 | 0.7 | 33 | 66 | 36 |
| Light,Pat | 17 | R | 26 | aaa | SEA | 55 | 5.58 | 1.75 | 5.98 | 5.8 | 4.6 | 0.8 | 0.6 | 31 | 67 | 26 |
| Lillis-White,Conn | 17 | L | 25 | aa | LAA | 45 | 5.73 | 1.53 | 7.47 | 7.1 | 9.2 | 1.3 | 1.0 | 26 | 63 | 66 |
| | 18 | L | 26 | a/a | LAA | 74 | 3.80 | 1.37 | 6.78 | 3.8 | 9.6 | 2.6 | 0.8 | 33 | 74 | 93 |
| Linares,Leandro | 18 | R | 24 | aa | CLE | 20 | 8.10 | 2.08 | 7.04 | 7.0 | 4.8 | 0.7 | 0.6 | 35 | 59 | 18 |
| Liranzo,Jesus | 17 | R | 22 | aa | BAL | 65 | 5.86 | 1.66 | 9.4 | 6.4 | 9.3 | 1.5 | 1.8 | 29 | 69 | 36 |
| | 18 | R | 23 | a/a | PIT | 57 | 4.73 | 1.37 | 5.82 | 5.4 | 8.4 | 1.6 | 1.2 | 25 | 68 | 61 |
| Littell,Zack | 17 | R | 22 | aa | MIN | 86 | 3.38 | 1.32 | 25.3 | 2.8 | 7.3 | 2.6 | 0.5 | 32 | 75 | 85 |
| | 18 | R | 23 | a/a | MIN | 129 | 5.25 | 1.57 | 23.6 | 3.4 | 7.4 | 2.2 | 0.7 | 36 | 66 | 66 |
| Lively,Ben | 17 | R | 25 | aaa | PHI | 97 | 4.18 | 1.40 | 25.6 | 2.2 | 6.4 | 2.9 | 0.4 | 35 | 69 | 86 |
| | 18 | R | 26 | aaa | PHI | 52 | 3.18 | 1.20 | 19 | 2.8 | 6.8 | 2.4 | 0.7 | 28 | 75 | 77 |
| Lloyd,Kyle | 17 | R | 27 | a/a | SD | 147 | 6.34 | 1.67 | 24.5 | 3.3 | 6.7 | 2.1 | 0.7 | 37 | 61 | 55 |
| | 18 | R | 28 | aaa | SD | 48 | 5.84 | 1.61 | 14.3 | 3.6 | 6.1 | 1.7 | 0.9 | 34 | 64 | 41 |
| Loaisiga,Jonathar | 18 | R | 24 | aa | NYY | 35 | 5.23 | 1.49 | 16.8 | 1.7 | 8.7 | 5.2 | 2.2 | 36 | 73 | 86 |
| Lockett,Walker | 17 | R | 23 | aaa | SD | 55 | 4.39 | 1.48 | 23.8 | 1.9 | 4.5 | 2.4 | 1.3 | 33 | 74 | 31 |
| | 18 | R | 24 | aaa | SD | 134 | 4.65 | 1.37 | 24.4 | 2.0 | 6.7 | 3.3 | 1.0 | 33 | 68 | 77 |
| Long,Grayson | 17 | R | 23 | aa | DET | 126 | 3.57 | 1.33 | 21.7 | 2.9 | 6.7 | 2.3 | 0.7 | 31 | 75 | 69 |
| Long,Jaron | 17 | R | 26 | a/a | WAS | 164 | 4.80 | 1.48 | 26.2 | 1.9 | 5.0 | 2.6 | 1.3 | 33 | 71 | 38 |
| | 18 | R | 27 | a/a | WAS | 130 | 5.24 | 1.69 | 21.8 | 2.2 | 4.1 | 1.9 | 0.8 | 37 | 69 | 29 |
| Long,Lucas | 17 | R | 25 | a/a | BAL | 128 | 3.79 | 1.47 | 17.8 | 2.7 | 6.3 | 2.4 | 0.6 | 34 | 75 | 66 |
| | 18 | R | 26 | a/a | BAL | 112 | 7.39 | 1.79 | 15.7 | 2.3 | 4.4 | 1.9 | 1.3 | 37 | 59 | 11 |
| Long,Nolan | 18 | R | 24 | aa | LA | 37 | 5.20 | 1.19 | 6.21 | 3.8 | 8.2 | 2.2 | 0.5 | 27 | 54 | 93 |
| Lopez,Edua | 18 | R | 23 | aa | TAM | 59 | 5.15 | 1.53 | 21.4 | 4.5 | 5.1 | 1.2 | 0.5 | 30 | 65 | 42 |
| Lopez,Jorge | 17 | R | 24 | aa | MIL | 104 | 6.64 | 1.60 | 11.8 | 3.8 | 7.7 | 2.0 | 1.0 | 35 | 58 | 55 |
| | 18 | R | 25 | aaa | KC | 39 | 6.47 | 1.56 | 6.61 | 2.7 | 6.1 | 2.3 | 1.2 | 35 | 59 | 42 |
| Lopez,Jose | 17 | R | 24 | aa | CIN | 96 | 4.01 | 1.35 | 23.6 | 4.0 | 7.7 | 1.9 | 1.4 | 28 | 76 | 51 |
| | 18 | R | 25 | aaa | CIN | 141 | 5.85 | 1.55 | 23.7 | 2.9 | 6.2 | 2.2 | 1.6 | 33 | 66 | 30 |
| Lopez,Pablo | 18 | R | 22 | a/a | MIA | 65 | 1.55 | 0.95 | 20.6 | 1.6 | 8.0 | 4.9 | 0.8 | 26 | 90 | 140 |
| Lopez,Reynaldo | 17 | R | 23 | aaa | CHW | 121 | 4.43 | 1.38 | 23.1 | 3.9 | 8.6 | 2.2 | 1.3 | 30 | 72 | 63 |
| Lopez,Yoan | 18 | R | 25 | aa | ARI | 63 | 3.54 | 1.15 | 5.58 | 3.9 | 9.9 | 2.5 | 0.6 | 28 | 70 | 110 |
| Love,Reid | 18 | L | 26 | a/a | BAL | 39 | 8.34 | 1.72 | 9.89 | 2.7 | 6.7 | 2.5 | 1.5 | 38 | 51 | 36 |
| Lovegrove,Kieran | 18 | R | 24 | a/a | CLE | 42 | 4.32 | 1.55 | 5.93 | 6.3 | 7.3 | 1.1 | 0.5 | 28 | 72 | 61 |
| Lovelady,Richard | 17 | L | 22 | aa | KC | 33 | 2.93 | 1.42 | 6.73 | 3.6 | 8.1 | 2.2 | 0.3 | 34 | 79 | 89 |
| | 18 | L | 23 | aaa | KC | 73 | 3.03 | 1.13 | 6.28 | 2.6 | 7.2 | 2.8 | 0.4 | 28 | 73 | 99 |
| Lovvorn,Zach | 17 | R | 23 | aa | KC | 117 | 6.69 | 1.80 | 17.5 | 2.8 | 5.9 | 2.1 | 0.7 | 39 | 61 | 44 |
| | 18 | R | 24 | a/a | KC | 145 | 6.54 | 1.67 | 24.1 | 3.1 | 4.1 | 1.3 | 0.9 | 34 | 60 | 16 |
| Lowry,Thaddius | 17 | R | 23 | aa | CHW | 82 | 8.79 | 1.97 | 14 | 4.1 | 5.9 | 1.4 | 1.6 | 38 | 56 | 2 |
| Lucas,Josh | 17 | R | 27 | aaa | STL | 60 | 4.15 | 1.43 | 5.43 | 2.0 | 7.6 | 3.9 | 0.5 | 37 | 71 | 107 |
| | 18 | R | 28 | aaa | OAK | 40 | 3.21 | 1.29 | 5.33 | 3.6 | 5.3 | 1.5 | 0.5 | 27 | 75 | 55 |
| Lucchesi,Joey | 17 | L | 24 | aa | SD | 60 | 2.54 | 1.21 | 24.3 | 2.2 | 6.4 | 2.9 | 0.5 | 30 | 81 | 86 |
| Lugo,Luis | 17 | L | 23 | aa | CLE | 134 | 5.73 | 1.70 | 23.3 | 4.0 | 4.7 | 1.2 | 1.6 | 32 | 70 | -1 |
| | 18 | L | 24 | aa | KC | 25 | 5.06 | 1.65 | 14.1 | 4.1 | 6.0 | 1.5 | 1.1 | 33 | 71 | 29 |
| Luzardo,Jesus | 18 | L | 21 | a/a | OAK | 96 | 3.47 | 1.19 | 19.3 | 2.2 | 8.3 | 3.8 | 0.6 | 32 | 72 | 116 |
| Machado,Andres | 17 | R | 24 | a/a | KC | 38 | 4.81 | 1.57 | 20.7 | 4.8 | 7.5 | 1.6 | 1.6 | 30 | 74 | 31 |
| | 18 | R | 25 | a/a | KC | 83 | 7.18 | 1.97 | 10.7 | 4.4 | 6.1 | 1.4 | 1.0 | 39 | 63 | 21 |
| Maddox,Austin | 17 | R | 26 | a/a | BOS | 49 | 4.34 | 1.45 | 5.69 | 5.5 | 6.5 | 1.2 | 0.5 | 27 | 69 | 59 |
| Mader,Michael | 17 | L | 23 | aa | ATL | 65 | 5.99 | 1.84 | 8.61 | 6.6 | 7.0 | 1.1 | 0.8 | 33 | 67 | 38 |
| | 18 | L | 24 | a/a | ATL | 104 | 4.70 | 1.70 | 15.7 | 4.6 | 6.0 | 1.3 | 0.6 | 34 | 72 | 41 |
| Magliaro,Marc | 18 | R | 28 | aa | COL | 50 | 6.94 | 1.75 | 6.37 | 3.4 | 6.5 | 1.9 | 1.7 | 36 | 63 | 18 |
| Magnifico,Damien | 17 | R | 26 | a/a | LAA | 53 | 7.56 | 2.18 | 5.67 | 6.6 | 8.1 | 1.2 | 0.4 | 42 | 63 | 51 |
| | 18 | R | 27 | aaa | PIT | 72 | 4.43 | 1.68 | 7.74 | 5.9 | 6.0 | 1.0 | 0.1 | 32 | 71 | 55 |
| Mahle,Greg | 17 | L | 24 | a/a | LAA | 72 | 5.54 | 1.47 | 6.15 | 3.1 | 5.6 | 1.8 | 0.8 | 32 | 62 | 47 |
| | 18 | L | 25 | a/a | LAA | 63 | 4.99 | 1.34 | 6.11 | 3.3 | 6.7 | 2.1 | 0.9 | 30 | 63 | 61 |
| Mahle,Tyler | 17 | R | 23 | a/a | CIN | 144 | 2.90 | 1.17 | 24 | 2.1 | 7.6 | 3.6 | 0.8 | 30 | 78 | 102 |
| | 18 | R | 24 | aaa | CIN | 31 | 3.32 | 1.22 | 25.2 | 3.4 | 4.9 | 1.4 | 1.5 | 23 | 81 | 25 |
| Mahoney,Kolton | 18 | R | 26 | a/a | MIA | 95 | 5.55 | 1.74 | 14.4 | 2.7 | 5.5 | 2.0 | 1.1 | 37 | 69 | 31 |
| Mantiply,Joe | 17 | L | 26 | aaa | NYY | 70 | 4.05 | 1.62 | 8.89 | 2.6 | 6.5 | 2.5 | 0.6 | 38 | 75 | 64 |
| Mapes,Tyler | 18 | R | 27 | aa | WAS | 44 | 5.49 | 1.68 | 24.8 | 2.7 | 5.3 | 2.0 | 0.8 | 37 | 67 | 40 |
| Maples,Dillon | 17 | R | 25 | a/a | CHC | 32 | 3.16 | 1.60 | 4.56 | 6.7 | 13.0 | 2.0 | 0.3 | 38 | 80 | 118 |
| | 18 | R | 26 | aaa | CHC | 40 | 3.16 | 1.68 | 4.41 | 9.3 | 13.3 | 1.4 | 0.2 | 32 | 80 | 121 |
| Markey,Brad | 17 | R | 25 | a/a | CHC | 79 | 3.56 | 1.34 | 8.22 | 1.7 | 6.9 | 4.0 | 1.2 | 33 | 78 | 88 |
| | 18 | R | 26 | a/a | CHC | 58 | 5.44 | 1.52 | 7.65 | 2.4 | 5.8 | 2.4 | 2.1 | 32 | 71 | 15 |
| Marshall,Evan | 17 | R | 27 | a/a | SEA | 24 | 6.63 | 2.13 | 7.53 | 3.2 | 8.1 | 2.5 | 1.8 | 45 | 72 | 26 |
| | 18 | R | 28 | aaa | CLE | 24 | 1.60 | 1.14 | 4.75 | 1.3 | 6.0 | 4.5 | 0.5 | 30 | 89 | 119 |
| Marte,Yunior | 17 | R | 22 | aa | KC | 36 | 7.80 | 1.89 | 9.97 | 7.0 | 8.0 | 1.1 | 1.4 | 33 | 59 | 28 |
| | 18 | R | 23 | aa | KC | 81 | 3.65 | 1.37 | 7.9 | 3.3 | 7.3 | 2.2 | 0.8 | 31 | 75 | 69 |
| Martes,Francis | 17 | R | 22 | aaa | HOU | 32 | 4.75 | 1.95 | 19.3 | 6.6 | 9.6 | 1.5 | 1.1 | 38 | 78 | 48 |
| | 18 | R | 23 | aaa | HOU | 20 | 5.98 | 2.01 | 24.4 | 6.7 | 6.1 | 0.9 | 0.8 | 36 | 70 | 24 |
| Martin,Brett | 18 | L | 23 | aa | TEX | 89 | 9.55 | 2.22 | 15.5 | 3.2 | 8.0 | 2.5 | 0.9 | 48 | 55 | 49 |
| Martin,Cody | 17 | R | 28 | aaa | SEA | 57 | 5.26 | 1.57 | 12.4 | 2.4 | 8.4 | 3.5 | 1.3 | 38 | 69 | 76 |
| | 18 | R | 29 | aaa | NYM | 82 | 7.04 | 1.82 | 22.5 | 4.4 | 5.9 | 1.3 | 1.8 | 34 | 64 | 0 |
| Martin,Corbin | 18 | R | 23 | aa | HOU | 103 | 3.76 | 1.24 | 19.9 | 2.5 | 7.2 | 2.9 | 0.7 | 30 | 71 | 86 |
| Martin,Jarrett | 17 | L | 28 | aa | SF | 40 | 3.01 | 1.65 | 4.8 | 8.2 | 7.0 | 0.9 | 0.0 | 27 | 80 | 73 |
| | 18 | L | 29 | a/a | OAK | 51 | 5.10 | 1.86 | 5.99 | 6.8 | 7.4 | 1.1 | 0.4 | 35 | 71 | 54 |
| Martin,Kyle | 17 | R | 26 | aaa | BOS | 54 | 6.98 | 2.02 | 7.86 | 5.3 | 6.5 | 1.2 | 1.6 | 37 | 68 | 3 |
| | 18 | R | 27 | aaa | BOS | 52 | 5.13 | 1.65 | 7.76 | 5.6 | 7.4 | 1.3 | 0.5 | 33 | 68 | 60 |
| Martinez,Henry | 18 | R | 24 | aa | CLE | 45 | 6.15 | 1.62 | 4.78 | 2.8 | 7.6 | 2.7 | 0.2 | 39 | 59 | 86 |
| Martinez,Juan | 18 | L | 26 | a/a | CIN | 31 | 7.51 | 1.93 | 7.39 | 4.6 | 7.8 | 1.7 | 1.2 | 40 | 61 | 35 |
| Marvel,James | 18 | R | 25 | aa | PIT | 33 | 3.85 | 1.36 | 27.6 | 2.6 | 4.7 | 1.8 | 0.3 | 31 | 70 | 57 |
| Marzi,Anthony | 18 | L | 26 | aa | MIN | 82 | 7.17 | 1.85 | 17.4 | 3.5 | 5.5 | 1.6 | 1.1 | 38 | 61 | 21 |
| Maton,Phil | 17 | R | 24 | aaa | SD | 25 | 2.90 | 1.22 | 4.45 | 2.6 | 8.9 | 3.5 | 0.3 | 33 | 76 | 122 |
| May,Dustin | 18 | R | 21 | aa | LA | 35 | 3.67 | 1.10 | 22.9 | 2.7 | 6.4 | 2.4 | 0.0 | 28 | 63 | 99 |
| Mayers,Mike | 17 | R | 26 | aaa | STL | 110 | 4.23 | 1.62 | 15.7 | 2.8 | 6.1 | 2.2 | 1.1 | 36 | 77 | 40 |
| Mayza,Tim | 17 | L | 25 | a/a | TOR | 53 | 4.76 | 1.66 | 5.89 | 4.3 | 8.1 | 1.9 | 1.2 | 35 | 74 | 49 |
| | 18 | L | 26 | aaa | TOR | 27 | 6.09 | 1.69 | 6.14 | 4.1 | 9.4 | 2.3 | 0.9 | 39 | 63 | 73 |
| Mazza,Chris | 17 | R | 28 | aa | MIA | 147 | 4.51 | 1.60 | 23.2 | 2.9 | 4.5 | 1.5 | 0.5 | 34 | 71 | 35 |
| | 18 | R | 29 | a/a | SEA | 50 | 3.27 | 1.36 | 16.1 | 2.8 | 5.5 | 1.9 | 1.5 | 28 | 84 | 29 |
| McAvoy,Kevin | 17 | R | 24 | aa | BOS | 118 | 5.70 | 1.64 | 23.8 | 3.8 | 6.0 | 1.6 | 0.7 | 35 | 64 | 42 |
| | 18 | R | 25 | aa | BOS | 34 | 10.96 | 2.26 | 19.3 | 8.8 | 5.8 | 0.7 | 1.2 | 35 | 49 | 5 |
| McCain,Shane | 17 | L | 26 | aa | TEX | 51 | 8.16 | 1.80 | 6.5 | 1.7 | 5.2 | 3.1 | 2.4 | 37 | 58 | 6 |
| McCasland,Jake | 18 | R | 27 | aa | SF | 107 | 6.20 | 1.83 | 15.6 | 4.0 | 4.9 | 1.2 | 0.6 | 37 | 65 | 27 |
| McCreery,Adam | 18 | L | 25 | a/a | ATL | 112 | 4.67 | 1.79 | 6.18 | 6.1 | 9.1 | 1.5 | 0.2 | 38 | 72 | 79 |

| PITCHER | yr | t | age | lvl | org | ip | era | whip | bf/g | ctl | dom | cmd | hr/9 | h% | s% | bpv |
|---|---|---|---|---|---|---|---|---|---|---|---|---|---|---|---|---|
| McCullough,Masc | 17 | R | 24 | aa | ARI | 24 | 3.14 | 1.53 | 4.35 | 8.1 | 9.6 | 1.2 | 0.0 | 26 | 77 | 101 |
| | 18 | R | 25 | aa | ARI | 19 | 10.61 | 2.57 | 4.27 | 13.5 | 9.2 | 0.7 | 0.5 | 36 | 55 | 55 |
| McCurry,Brendan | 17 | R | 25 | aaa | HOU | 45 | 4.24 | 1.44 | 5.43 | 2.2 | 8.9 | 4.1 | 1.1 | 37 | 73 | 104 |
| | 18 | R | 26 | aaa | HOU | 64 | 3.73 | 1.34 | 5.8 | 2.2 | 8.2 | 3.7 | 0.7 | 35 | 73 | 105 |
| McGarry,Seth | 18 | R | 24 | aa | PHI | 69 | 4.50 | 1.55 | 6.72 | 5.4 | 7.4 | 1.4 | 0.9 | 30 | 72 | 50 |
| McGeorge,Austin | 18 | R | 24 | aa | NYM | 26 | 9.16 | 2.24 | 5.98 | 2.9 | 8.0 | 2.8 | 1.8 | 47 | 60 | 27 |
| McGowan,Kevin | 17 | R | 26 | aaa | NYM | 65 | 4.58 | 1.52 | 6.01 | 3.8 | 6.6 | 1.8 | 1.2 | 32 | 73 | 40 |
| | 18 | R | 27 | a/a | NYM | 84 | 4.99 | 1.63 | 11.3 | 3.8 | 6.6 | 1.7 | 1.2 | 34 | 72 | 34 |
| McGowin,Kyle | 17 | R | 26 | a/a | WAS | 88 | 8.53 | 1.99 | 25 | 4.0 | 5.3 | 1.3 | 1.8 | 38 | 58 | -9 |
| | 18 | R | 27 | a/a | WAS | 132 | 3.66 | 1.09 | 24.6 | 2.1 | 7.2 | 3.4 | 0.9 | 27 | 69 | 97 |
| McGrath,Daniel | 18 | L | 24 | aa | BOS | 90 | 4.57 | 1.58 | 12 | 3.8 | 6.3 | 1.7 | 0.4 | 35 | 70 | 57 |
| McGrath,Kyle | 17 | L | 25 | a/a | SD | 30 | 2.94 | 0.89 | 4.4 | 1.2 | 7.7 | 6.4 | 1.0 | 25 | 72 | 164 |
| | 18 | L | 26 | aaa | SD | 53 | 2.80 | 1.20 | 4.96 | 2.9 | 5.8 | 2.0 | 0.9 | 26 | 81 | 56 |
| McGuire,Deck | 17 | R | 28 | aa | CIN | 168 | 5.02 | 1.56 | 26.3 | 4.1 | 7.2 | 1.8 | 1.3 | 32 | 71 | 41 |
| | 18 | R | 29 | aaa | LAA | 58 | 4.29 | 1.38 | 16.3 | 4.2 | 5.9 | 1.4 | 0.9 | 27 | 70 | 44 |
| Mciver,Anthony | 18 | L | 26 | a/a | SEA | 29 | 7.16 | 2.04 | 7.05 | 3.9 | 7.2 | 1.8 | 0.7 | 43 | 63 | 44 |
| McKay,David | 18 | R | 23 | a/a | SEA | 53 | 2.70 | 1.15 | 5.87 | 3.5 | 10.7 | 3.0 | 0.5 | 30 | 78 | 124 |
| McKenzie,Triston | 18 | R | 21 | aa | CLE | 92 | 3.49 | 1.13 | 22.8 | 2.9 | 7.4 | 2.6 | 1.0 | 26 | 73 | 80 |
| McKinney,Ian | 17 | L | 23 | aa | STL | 23 | 6.63 | 1.97 | 7.75 | 4.5 | 3.2 | 0.7 | 1.3 | 35 | 68 | -19 |
| | 18 | L | 24 | aa | STL | 32 | 5.50 | 1.75 | 8.15 | 6.1 | 5.5 | 0.9 | 1.3 | 29 | 71 | 12 |
| McLaughlin,Sean | 18 | R | 24 | aa | ATL | 18 | 10.32 | 2.15 | 8.14 | 2.6 | 3.7 | 1.4 | 1.9 | 41 | 52 | -29 |
| McNamara,Dillon | 17 | R | 26 | aa | SF | 33 | 8.08 | 1.94 | 8.73 | 6.3 | 5.0 | 0.8 | 1.5 | 32 | 59 | -3 |
| | 18 | R | 27 | a/a | SF | 53 | 2.88 | 1.17 | 5.42 | 2.5 | 8.3 | 3.3 | 0.2 | 31 | 74 | 122 |
| McRae,Alex | 17 | R | 24 | aa | PIT | 150 | 4.94 | 1.67 | 24.9 | 2.4 | 4.3 | 1.8 | 0.6 | 36 | 70 | 33 |
| | 18 | R | 25 | aaa | PIT | 117 | 5.80 | 1.80 | 20.8 | 4.0 | 6.3 | 1.6 | 0.7 | 37 | 67 | 39 |
| McWilliams,Sam | 18 | R | 23 | aa | TAM | 101 | 6.02 | 1.67 | 23.9 | 3.6 | 7.4 | 2.1 | 1.2 | 36 | 65 | 44 |
| Means,John | 17 | L | 24 | aa | BAL | 142 | 5.17 | 1.60 | 24.2 | 2.6 | 6.8 | 2.6 | 1.2 | 37 | 70 | 52 |
| | 18 | L | 25 | a/a | BAL | 158 | 4.70 | 1.48 | 24.3 | 1.9 | 5.8 | 3.0 | 1.1 | 35 | 70 | 59 |
| Medeiros,Kodi | 18 | L | 22 | aa | CHW | 139 | 4.79 | 1.58 | 22.7 | 4.8 | 8.1 | 1.7 | 1.1 | 32 | 72 | 52 |
| Medina,Yeison | 18 | R | 26 | aa | STL | 26 | 6.70 | 2.09 | 5.56 | 4.5 | 5.1 | 1.1 | 0.7 | 40 | 67 | 17 |
| Megill,Trevor | 18 | R | 25 | aa | SD | 17 | 3.98 | 1.56 | 6.77 | 3.9 | 3.9 | 1.0 | 1.2 | 30 | 78 | 8 |
| Meisinger,Ryan | 17 | R | 23 | aa | BAL | 63 | 3.70 | 1.38 | 6.46 | 3.3 | 8.4 | 2.5 | 0.3 | 34 | 72 | 96 |
| | 18 | R | 24 | a/a | BAL | 48 | 3.71 | 1.37 | 6.33 | 2.9 | 8.2 | 2.8 | 1.1 | 33 | 77 | 75 |
| Meisner,Casey | 17 | R | 22 | aa | OAK | 59 | 4.68 | 1.47 | 21.1 | 3.9 | 4.7 | 1.2 | 0.6 | 30 | 67 | 37 |
| | 18 | R | 23 | aa | OAK | 40 | 3.85 | 1.17 | 22.8 | 2.9 | 6.2 | 2.1 | 0.6 | 27 | 67 | 71 |
| Mejia,Adalberto | 17 | L | 24 | aaa | MIN | 29 | 4.35 | 1.43 | 20.3 | 2.1 | 5.4 | 2.6 | 0.4 | 34 | 68 | 69 |
| | 18 | L | 25 | aaa | MIN | 64 | 4.82 | 1.47 | 18.4 | 3.2 | 6.9 | 2.2 | 0.6 | 34 | 67 | 67 |
| Mekkes,Dakota | 18 | R | 24 | a/a | CHC | 55 | 1.37 | 1.31 | 5.57 | 5.0 | 9.6 | 1.9 | 0.4 | 29 | 91 | 100 |
| Mella,Keury | 17 | R | 24 | aa | CIN | 134 | 7.09 | 1.77 | 22.8 | 3.5 | 6.3 | 1.8 | 1.6 | 36 | 61 | 18 |
| | 18 | R | 25 | a/a | CIN | 108 | 4.01 | 1.41 | 21.8 | 3.4 | 7.0 | 2.1 | 1.0 | 31 | 74 | 57 |
| Melotakis,Mason | 17 | L | 26 | a/a | MIN | 50 | 5.03 | 1.47 | 5.15 | 4.3 | 7.3 | 1.7 | 0.8 | 31 | 66 | 59 |
| | 18 | L | 27 | aaa | COL | 31 | 9.31 | 2.20 | 6.53 | 5.0 | 4.2 | 0.8 | 2.1 | 37 | 59 | -40 |
| Melville,Timothy | 17 | R | 28 | aaa | SD | 76 | 3.28 | 1.27 | 24 | 3.9 | 6.3 | 1.6 | 0.6 | 27 | 75 | 64 |
| | 18 | R | 29 | aaa | BAL | 106 | 7.86 | 1.96 | 12.7 | 4.3 | 5.0 | 1.2 | 1.9 | 36 | 62 | -16 |
| Mendez,Roman | 18 | R | 28 | aa | WAS | 54 | 5.04 | 1.52 | 5.33 | 3.7 | 7.4 | 2.0 | 1.7 | 32 | 72 | 34 |
| Mendez,Yohande | 17 | L | 22 | aa | TEX | 138 | 5.17 | 1.34 | 23.9 | 3.0 | 6.8 | 2.2 | 1.9 | 28 | 68 | 33 |
| | 18 | L | 23 | a/a | TEX | 92 | 6.46 | 1.66 | 22.9 | 3.6 | 6.6 | 1.8 | 2.2 | 33 | 67 | 4 |
| Mendoza,Hector | 18 | R | 24 | a/a | STL | 62 | 5.44 | 1.36 | 5.32 | 3.9 | 5.4 | 1.4 | 1.2 | 26 | 62 | 30 |
| Menez,Conner | 18 | L | 23 | a/a | SF | 85 | 4.71 | 1.47 | 21.5 | 4.0 | 9.1 | 2.3 | 0.1 | 36 | 65 | 101 |
| Mengden,Daniel | 17 | R | 24 | aaa | OAK | 41 | 4.89 | 1.55 | 19.9 | 3.9 | 7.0 | 1.8 | 1.1 | 33 | 70 | 46 |
| | 18 | R | 25 | aaa | OAK | 46 | 3.58 | 1.16 | 20.4 | 1.4 | 5.3 | 3.8 | 0.4 | 30 | 68 | 102 |
| Merritt,Ryan | 17 | L | 25 | aaa | CLE | 116 | 4.23 | 1.51 | 26.5 | 2.2 | 4.8 | 2.2 | 1.9 | 31 | 80 | 9 |
| | 18 | L | 26 | aaa | CLE | 72 | 5.08 | 1.47 | 20.6 | 0.3 | 5.2 | 18.3 | 1.6 | 36 | 70 | 357 |
| Merryweather,Juli | 17 | R | 26 | a/a | CLE | 129 | 7.52 | 1.74 | 23.5 | 2.8 | 6.4 | 2.3 | 1.5 | 37 | 57 | 29 |
| Mesa,Jose | 17 | R | 24 | aa | NYY | 34 | 1.15 | 1.12 | 16.9 | 5.0 | 8.6 | 1.7 | 0.0 | 23 | 89 | 110 |
| | 18 | R | 25 | aa | NYY | 18 | 6.90 | 1.72 | 9.13 | 6.7 | 8.6 | 1.3 | 2.9 | 26 | 68 | -5 |
| Meyer,Alex | 17 | R | 27 | aaa | LAA | 24 | 6.36 | 1.77 | 22 | 3.3 | 9.4 | 2.9 | 1.4 | 41 | 66 | 63 |
| Meyer,Ben | 18 | R | 25 | aaa | MIA | 65 | 4.86 | 1.49 | 18.8 | 2.7 | 5.6 | 2.1 | 0.5 | 34 | 67 | 56 |
| Milbrath,Jordan | 17 | R | 26 | aa | CLE | 30 | 5.47 | 1.71 | 9.05 | 3.8 | 6.2 | 1.6 | 2.0 | 33 | 74 | 4 |
| | 18 | R | 27 | a/a | CLE | 65 | 5.54 | 1.79 | 6.99 | 4.7 | 6.5 | 1.4 | 0.2 | 37 | 66 | 56 |
| Miller,Jared | 17 | L | 24 | a/a | ARI | 71 | 3.53 | 1.21 | 5.37 | 3.6 | 9.9 | 2.8 | 0.6 | 30 | 71 | 111 |
| | 18 | L | 25 | a/a | ARI | 48 | 7.35 | 2.49 | 5.79 | 12.2 | 9.0 | 0.7 | 1.0 | 36 | 70 | 37 |
| Mills,Alec | 18 | R | 27 | aaa | CHC | 126 | 5.74 | 1.51 | 23.7 | 3.2 | 6.0 | 1.9 | 0.8 | 33 | 61 | 49 |
| Mills,Jordan | 18 | L | 26 | aa | WAS | 21 | 2.79 | 1.12 | 5.57 | 3.2 | 6.7 | 2.1 | 0.0 | 27 | 72 | 96 |
| Mills,McKenzie | 18 | L | 23 | aa | MIA | 18 | 8.64 | 1.59 | 20.1 | 2.0 | 3.4 | 1.7 | 1.5 | 33 | 44 | 2 |
| Milner,Hoby | 17 | L | 26 | aaa | PHI | 28 | 3.52 | 1.25 | 5.12 | 1.4 | 7.3 | 5.1 | 0.4 | 34 | 71 | 136 |
| | 18 | L | 27 | aaa | TAM | 42 | 3.71 | 1.50 | 4.56 | 4.0 | 8.5 | 2.1 | 0.8 | 34 | 77 | 74 |
| Minch,Jordan | 18 | L | 25 | aa | CHC | 42 | 5.06 | 1.64 | 6.97 | 5.0 | 4.5 | 0.9 | 1.5 | 28 | 73 | -1 |
| Minter,A.J. | 17 | L | 24 | a/a | ATL | 18 | 5.37 | 1.83 | 4.26 | 6.7 | 8.5 | 1.3 | 0.6 | 35 | 70 | 61 |
| Misiewicz,Anthon | 17 | L | 23 | aa | TAM | 70 | 4.98 | 1.35 | 24.2 | 2.2 | 6.4 | 2.9 | 1.0 | 32 | 64 | 69 |
| | 18 | L | 24 | aa | SEA | 98 | 6.57 | 1.87 | 21.9 | 2.7 | 7.3 | 2.7 | 1.4 | 41 | 67 | 41 |
| Mitchell,Bryan | 17 | R | 26 | aaa | NYY | 64 | 4.65 | 1.43 | 19.3 | 2.1 | 7.6 | 3.6 | 0.2 | 37 | 65 | 110 |
| Mitchell,Evan | 17 | R | 25 | aaa | CIN | 39 | 6.32 | 2.16 | 7.77 | 3.1 | 5.5 | 1.8 | 0.3 | 45 | 69 | 38 |
| | 18 | R | 26 | a/a | CIN | 40 | 5.20 | 1.85 | 6.06 | 5.1 | 5.5 | 1.1 | 0.3 | 36 | 70 | 39 |
| Moats,Dalton | 18 | L | 23 | aa | TAM | 63 | 6.37 | 1.52 | 6.69 | 4.2 | 8.2 | 2.0 | 1.8 | 31 | 62 | 37 |
| Molina,Marcos | 17 | R | 22 | aa | NYM | 78 | 5.68 | 1.56 | 26.3 | 2.9 | 6.7 | 2.3 | 0.8 | 35 | 63 | 58 |
| | 18 | R | 23 | a/a | NYM | 83 | 6.80 | 1.81 | 24.1 | 3.5 | 6.0 | 1.7 | 1.4 | 37 | 64 | 17 |
| Moll,Sam | 17 | L | 25 | aaa | OAK | 54 | 4.36 | 1.67 | 4.88 | 3.2 | 6.1 | 1.9 | 0.7 | 37 | 74 | 48 |
| | 18 | L | 26 | aaa | TOR | 20 | 6.94 | 1.81 | 6.24 | 2.5 | 6.7 | 2.6 | 0.6 | 41 | 59 | 63 |
| Montas,Frankie | 17 | R | 24 | aaa | OAK | 29 | 6.12 | 1.21 | 13.1 | 2.1 | 9.0 | 4.3 | 1.2 | 32 | 49 | 112 |
| | 18 | R | 25 | aaa | OAK | 73 | 5.56 | 1.48 | 21 | 3.2 | 6.0 | 1.8 | 0.9 | 32 | 62 | 46 |
| Montgomery,Mark | 17 | R | 27 | aaa | STL | 67 | 3.20 | 1.11 | 5.7 | 2.2 | 7.4 | 3.3 | 0.6 | 28 | 73 | 104 |
| | 18 | R | 28 | aaa | BOS | 15 | 2.83 | 2.19 | 6.35 | 5.6 | 7.4 | 1.3 | 0.0 | 44 | 86 | 56 |
| Moore,Andrew | 17 | R | 23 | a/a | SEA | 110 | 3.57 | 1.19 | 21 | 1.8 | 7.2 | 4.0 | 1.2 | 30 | 75 | 95 |
| | 18 | R | 24 | a/a | TAM | 134 | 4.76 | 1.46 | 22.1 | 3.0 | 5.8 | 2.0 | 1.5 | 31 | 72 | 28 |
| Morales,Andrew | 17 | R | 24 | a/a | STL | 26 | 4.35 | 1.83 | 5.33 | 4.2 | 8.2 | 1.9 | 0.8 | 40 | 77 | 56 |
| | 18 | R | 25 | a/a | STL | 65 | 4.68 | 1.40 | 5.61 | 3.9 | 8.1 | 2.1 | 0.9 | 31 | 68 | 68 |
| Morales,Osmer | 18 | R | 26 | aaa | LAA | 102 | 6.17 | 1.80 | 19.6 | 4.5 | 6.7 | 1.5 | 1.2 | 36 | 67 | 25 |
| Moreno,Gerson | 17 | R | 22 | aa | DET | 28 | 7.84 | 1.56 | 6.13 | 5.5 | 9.7 | 1.7 | 1.4 | 31 | 49 | 57 |
| | 18 | R | 23 | aa | DET | 17 | 6.67 | 2.02 | 5.88 | 7.6 | 9.0 | 1.2 | 1.2 | 36 | 68 | 39 |
| Morimando,Shawi | 17 | L | 25 | aaa | CLE | 159 | 6.16 | 1.82 | 28.4 | 3.7 | 5.3 | 1.4 | 1.6 | 35 | 69 | 1 |
| | 18 | L | 26 | aaa | TOR | 45 | 8.20 | 2.16 | 25 | 2.7 | 3.5 | 1.3 | 1.5 | 41 | 63 | -23 |
| Morin,Michael | 17 | R | 26 | aaa | LAA | 39 | 3.32 | 1.12 | 7.05 | 1.5 | 4.7 | 3.1 | 1.0 | 27 | 75 | 67 |
| | 18 | R | 27 | aaa | SEA | 55 | 4.54 | 1.36 | 5.64 | 2.3 | 6.9 | 3.1 | 0.5 | 34 | 66 | 88 |
| Moronta,Reyes | 17 | R | 24 | a/a | SF | 35 | 3.92 | 1.57 | 4.8 | 5.5 | 9.3 | 1.7 | 0.5 | 33 | 75 | 81 |
| Morris,Akeel | 17 | R | 25 | a/a | ATL | 54 | 3.70 | 1.47 | 6.47 | 4.8 | 8.8 | 1.8 | 0.6 | 32 | 75 | 78 |
| | 18 | R | 26 | aaa | LAA | 46 | 6.75 | 1.65 | 5.14 | 4.9 | 7.1 | 1.4 | 0.7 | 34 | 57 | 51 |
| Morrison,Preston | 17 | R | 24 | aa | CHC | 119 | 7.41 | 1.68 | 19.2 | 3.2 | 5.5 | 1.7 | 1.3 | 35 | 56 | 21 |
| | 18 | R | 25 | a/a | CHC | 63 | 5.61 | 1.38 | 7.37 | 2.6 | 6.3 | 2.4 | 1.4 | 30 | 62 | 44 |
| Moss,Benton | 17 | R | 24 | aa | TAM | 70 | 4.55 | 1.50 | 23.3 | 2.5 | 6.2 | 2.5 | 1.4 | 33 | 74 | 42 |
| | 18 | R | 25 | aa | TAM | 102 | 3.44 | 1.23 | 23 | 2.0 | 5.6 | 2.8 | 1.3 | 28 | 78 | 56 |
| Moya,Gabriel | 17 | L | 22 | aa | MIN | 58 | 1.08 | 0.90 | 4.62 | 2.4 | 11.0 | 4.6 | 0.4 | 27 | 91 | 169 |
| | 18 | L | 23 | aaa | MIN | 44 | 2.62 | 1.37 | 7.13 | 2.6 | 8.4 | 3.2 | 0.5 | 35 | 82 | 100 |
| Muckenhirn,Zach | 18 | L | 23 | aa | BAL | 27 | 6.44 | 1.73 | 6.14 | 5.9 | 7.4 | 1.3 | 0.4 | 34 | 60 | 59 |
| Mujica,Jose | 17 | R | 21 | aa | TAM | 154 | 3.66 | 1.23 | 25 | 2.6 | 4.5 | 1.7 | 1.1 | 26 | 74 | 36 |
| | 18 | R | 22 | aaa | TAM | 38 | 3.12 | 1.19 | 21.9 | 2.3 | 7.3 | 3.1 | 0.2 | 31 | 72 | 107 |
| Muller,Kyle | 18 | L | 21 | aa | ATL | 29 | 4.06 | 1.10 | 22.7 | 1.8 | 7.2 | 4.0 | 1.1 | 28 | 67 | 100 |
| Munoz,Andres | 18 | R | 19 | aa | SD | 19 | 1.06 | 1.17 | 3.79 | 4.9 | 8.3 | 1.7 | 0.0 | 25 | 90 | 105 |
| Musgrave,Harriso | 17 | L | 25 | aaa | COL | 54 | 9.30 | 2.00 | 21.8 | 4.7 | 4.8 | 1.0 | 2.3 | 35 | 55 | -32 |
| | 18 | L | 26 | aaa | COL | 18 | 6.01 | 1.86 | 10.7 | 3.2 | 6.6 | 2.1 | 1.2 | 40 | 69 | 34 |
| Naile,James | 17 | R | 24 | aa | OAK | 62 | 3.80 | 1.30 | 18.2 | 2.5 | 4.9 | 2.0 | 0.7 | 29 | 72 | 51 |
| | 18 | R | 25 | a/a | OAK | 152 | 5.43 | 1.62 | 26 | 2.5 | 4.0 | 1.6 | 0.8 | 34 | 66 | 24 |
| Nakaushiro,Yuhei | 17 | L | 28 | a/a | ARI | 68 | 3.32 | 1.47 | 5.81 | 3.9 | 6.6 | 1.7 | 0.3 | 32 | 77 | 66 |
| | 18 | L | 29 | aaa | ARI | 34 | 7.20 | 2.08 | 6.94 | 4.9 | 7.1 | 1.4 | 0.6 | 42 | 64 | 39 |
| Nance,Tommy | 18 | R | 27 | aa | CHC | 22 | 4.47 | 1.39 | 6.24 | 5.2 | 6.3 | 1.2 | 0.5 | 26 | 67 | 58 |
| Navas,Carlos | 17 | R | 25 | aa | OAK | 53 | 3.93 | 1.38 | 6.71 | 2.6 | 6.4 | 2.5 | 0.7 | 33 | 72 | 69 |
| | 18 | R | 26 | aa | CIN | 74 | 4.41 | 1.42 | 8.06 | 2.2 | 8.8 | 4.0 | 1.0 | 37 | 71 | 102 |
| Navilhon,Joe | 18 | R | 25 | aa | DET | 37 | 5.12 | 1.55 | 6.74 | 2.3 | 8.7 | 3.7 | 1.8 | 37 | 73 | 70 |
| Neidert,Nick | 17 | R | 21 | aa | SEA | 23 | 7.70 | 1.79 | 17.9 | 1.9 | 4.5 | 2.4 | 1.7 | 38 | 58 | 11 |
| | 18 | R | 22 | aa | MIA | 154 | 3.67 | 1.22 | 24 | 1.8 | 7.9 | 4.4 | 1.0 | 32 | 73 | 113 |
| Neverauskas,Dov | 17 | R | 24 | aaa | PIT | 50 | 3.87 | 1.61 | 5.57 | 4.1 | 6.5 | 1.6 | 0.2 | 35 | 74 | 64 |
| | 18 | R | 25 | aaa | PIT | 47 | 3.02 | 1.44 | 6.08 | 5.9 | 8.7 | 1.5 | 0.4 | 28 | 79 | 83 |
| Newberry,Jake | 17 | R | 23 | a/a | KC | 62 | 3.43 | 1.50 | 6.23 | 3.9 | 5.2 | 1.3 | 0.6 | 31 | 78 | 41 |
| | 18 | R | 24 | a/a | KC | 51 | 2.01 | 1.26 | 5.1 | 2.5 | 7.5 | 2.9 | 0.6 | 32 | 87 | 94 |
| Newcomb,Sean | 17 | L | 24 | aaa | ATL | 58 | 3.81 | 1.57 | 23 | 5.7 | 10.1 | 1.8 | 0.5 | 34 | 76 | 87 |
| Nicolino,Justin | 17 | L | 26 | aaa | MIA | 79 | 3.98 | 1.47 | 24.2 | 2.9 | 4.8 | 1.6 | 1.2 | 31 | 77 | 24 |
| | 18 | L | 27 | aaa | CIN | 135 | 6.37 | 1.82 | 25.1 | 2.7 | 4.6 | 1.7 | 1.2 | 38 | 66 | 13 |
| Niebla,Luis | 17 | R | 26 | a/a | COL | 51 | 8.91 | 2.28 | 16.1 | 6.0 | 4.5 | 0.8 | 1.4 | 39 | 61 | -15 |
| Nix,Jacob | 17 | R | 21 | aa | SD | 28 | 7.47 | 1.72 | 20.9 | 3.0 | 6.1 | 2.0 | 0.0 | 39 | 52 | 69 |
| | 18 | R | 22 | a/a | SD | 60 | 1.89 | 0.92 | 22.5 | 1.3 | 5.8 | 4.6 | 0.4 | 25 | 81 | 131 |
| Nogosek,Stephen | 18 | R | 23 | aa | NYM | 20 | 9.13 | 1.96 | 5.97 | 9.6 | 8.2 | 0.9 | 1.4 | 28 | 52 | 34 |
| Norwood,James | 17 | R | 24 | aa | CHC | 19 | 7.14 | 1.98 | 6.41 | 4.8 | 7.7 | 1.6 | 0.6 | 41 | 62 | 50 |
| | 18 | R | 25 | a/a | CHC | 53 | 2.90 | 1.29 | 5.49 | 4.4 | 7.8 | 1.8 | 0.6 | 27 | 79 | 78 |
| Nunn,Chris | 17 | L | 27 | aa | CHC | 17 | 6.84 | 1.70 | 19.2 | 6.3 | 5.9 | 0.9 | 0.7 | 30 | 58 | 37 |
| | 18 | L | 28 | a/a | HOU | 28 | 5.84 | 1.74 | 8.54 | 4.7 | 7.9 | 1.7 | 1.5 | 35 | 69 | 33 |
| Oaks,Trevor | 17 | R | 24 | aaa | LA | 84 | 4.16 | 1.37 | 23.5 | 1.8 | 6.5 | 3.7 | 0.6 | 35 | 69 | 96 |
| | 18 | R | 25 | aaa | KC | 129 | 4.11 | 1.58 | 25.8 | 3.2 | 3.8 | 1.2 | 0.4 | 33 | 73 | 32 |
| Ogando,Emilio | 17 | L | 24 | a/a | KC | 138 | 4.55 | 1.49 | 24.8 | 2.7 | 4.5 | 1.7 | 1.1 | 32 | 72 | 25 |
| | 18 | L | 25 | aa | KC | 119 | 6.27 | 1.96 | 21.9 | 5.8 | 5.6 | 1.0 | 1.8 | 34 | 72 | -9 |
| Okert,Steven | 17 | L | 26 | aaa | SF | 25 | 4.00 | 1.06 | 4.09 | 3.1 | 6.0 | 1.9 | 1.3 | 21 | 68 | 51 |
| | 18 | L | 27 | aaa | SF | 33 | 4.79 | 1.52 | 4.37 | 2.2 | 9.1 | 4.1 | 0.7 | 40 | 68 | 114 |
| Olczak,Jon | 18 | R | 25 | aa | MIL | 57 | 2.12 | 1.19 | 5.45 | 3.3 | 7.8 | 2.4 | 0.2 | 29 | 82 | 100 |
| O'Reilly,Mike | 18 | R | 24 | a/a | STL | 79 | 5.92 | 1.52 | 18.1 | 3.0 | 4.4 | 1.5 | 1.4 | 31 | 63 | 11 |
| Orlan,R.C. | 17 | L | 27 | aa | WAS | 23 | 6.90 | 1.93 | 4.37 | 4.4 | 7.3 | 1.7 | 2.3 | 37 | 70 | -4 |
| | 18 | L | 28 | a/a | CLE | 20 | 0.00 | 0.89 | 6.32 | 2.1 | 5.7 | 2.7 | 0.0 | 23 | 100 | 108 |
| Ort,Kaleb | 18 | R | 26 | aa | NYY | 33 | 3.10 | 1.66 | 6.72 | 6.8 | 9.3 | 1.4 | 0.0 | 33 | 79 | 91 |
| Ortiz,Luis | 17 | R | 22 | aa | MIL | 94 | 6.01 | 1.50 | 18.5 | 3.9 | 6.6 | 1.7 | 1.8 | 29 | 64 | 21 |
| | 18 | R | 23 | a/a | BAL | 101 | 4.44 | 1.37 | 19.3 | 2.3 | 6.3 | 2.7 | 1.2 | 32 | 71 | 57 |
| Oswalt,Corey | 17 | R | 24 | aa | NYM | 134 | 3.43 | 1.52 | 24.3 | 3.4 | 7.0 | 2.1 | 0.9 | 34 | 80 | 57 |
| | 18 | R | 25 | aaa | NYM | 53 | 5.54 | 1.49 | 20.8 | 3.2 | 7.4 | 2.3 | 1.3 | 33 | 65 | 52 |
| Otani,Shohei | 17 | R | 23 | for | JPN | 16 | 6.17 | 1.79 | 18.8 | 9.6 | 10.0 | 1.0 | 1.8 | 23 | 70 | 41 |
| Ott,Travis | 18 | L | 23 | a/a | TAM | 72 | 4.26 | 1.38 | 6.89 | 4.0 | 10.1 | 2.5 | 0.8 | 33 | 70 | 94 |
| Overton,Connor | 18 | R | 25 | a/a | SF | 24 | 5.60 | 1.70 | 12.2 | 3.8 | 7.5 | 2.0 | 1.0 | 37 | 68 | 51 |
| Overton,Dillon | 17 | L | 26 | aaa | SD | 91 | 7.15 | 1.66 | 21.5 | 2.7 | 4.0 | 1.5 | 1.9 | 33 | 60 | -12 |
| | 18 | L | 27 | a/a | SD | 96 | 3.27 | 1.23 | 17 | 2.3 | 4.7 | 2.0 | 1.1 | 27 | 78 | 40 |
| Owens,Henry | 17 | L | 25 | a/a | BOS | 126 | 6.14 | 2.04 | 23.5 | 9.4 | 6.8 | 0.7 | 0.7 | 31 | 69 | 37 |
| Paddack,Chris | 18 | R | 22 | aa | SD | 39 | 2.16 | 0.76 | 20.1 | 0.9 | 7.5 | 8.3 | 0.2 | 24 | 71 | 228 |
| Pagan,Emilio | 17 | R | 26 | aaa | SEA | 32 | 3.11 | 0.98 | 5.23 | 2.4 | 8.5 | 3.6 | 0.0 | 28 | 65 | 141 |
| Palmquist,Cody | 17 | R | 23 | a/a | TEX | 53 | 5.25 | 1.25 | 6.34 | 2.3 | 5.2 | 2.2 | 1.6 | 26 | 62 | 32 |
| | 18 | R | 24 | a/a | TEX | 15 | 8.71 | 1.97 | 7.29 | 4.7 | 6.2 | 1.3 | 4.5 | 31 | 68 | -82 |
| Pannone,Thomas | 17 | L | 23 | aa | TOR | 117 | 3.85 | 1.27 | 23.9 | 2.4 | 7.2 | 3.1 | 1.4 | 30 | 75 | 70 |
| | 18 | L | 24 | a/a | TOR | 47 | 5.82 | 1.54 | 25.7 | 2.4 | 8.1 | 3.3 | 2.1 | 35 | 68 | 49 |
| Paredes,Eduardo | 17 | R | 22 | aa | LAA | 50 | 2.83 | 1.24 | 5.93 | 3.6 | 9.0 | 2.5 | 0.5 | 30 | 78 | 99 |
| | 18 | R | 23 | aaa | LAA | 43 | 4.13 | 1.39 | 4.77 | 3.4 | 6.3 | 1.9 | 0.9 | 30 | 72 | 53 |
| Parks,Adam | 18 | R | 26 | aa | TEX | 45 | 5.86 | 1.55 | 5.8 | 3.5 | 7.2 | 2.1 | 1.6 | 33 | 66 | 36 |
| Parsons,Wes | 17 | R | 25 | a/a | ATL | 111 | 4.40 | 1.56 | 16.2 | 3.7 | 7.4 | 2.0 | 0.5 | 35 | 71 | 70 |
| | 18 | R | 26 | a/a | ATL | 118 | 3.72 | 1.39 | 20.7 | 2.8 | 6.2 | 2.2 | 0.8 | 32 | 75 | 61 |
| Pasquale,Nick | 17 | R | 27 | a/a | CLE | 86 | 8.17 | 1.93 | 20.4 | 5.1 | 5.6 | 1.1 | 1.4 | 35 | 58 | 4 |
| | 18 | R | 28 | a/a | CLE | 37 | 4.94 | 1.55 | 7.11 | 4.9 | 4.6 | 0.9 | 0.7 | 29 | 68 | 30 |
| Paulino,Felix | 18 | R | 23 | aa | CHW | 40 | 8.30 | 1.93 | 23.9 | 5.0 | 4.5 | 0.9 | 1.5 | 34 | 57 | -10 |
| Paulson,Jake | 18 | R | 26 | aa | CLE | 116 | 4.39 | 1.49 | 25 | 2.9 | 5.6 | 1.9 | 1.0 | 32 | 73 | 39 |
| Payamps,Joel | 17 | R | 23 | a/a | ARI | 104 | 5.39 | 1.50 | 23.7 | 2.0 | 4.8 | 2.4 | 1.2 | 33 | 66 | 34 |
| | 18 | R | 24 | a/a | ARI | 117 | 3.99 | 1.19 | 15.1 | 2.0 | 7.8 | 3.9 | 0.7 | 31 | 67 | 113 |
| Payano,Pedro | 17 | R | 23 | aa | TEX | 84 | 5.05 | 1.67 | 22.3 | 5.0 | 6.7 | 1.4 | 0.5 | 34 | 69 | 51 |
| | 18 | R | 24 | aa | TEX | 120 | 7.32 | 1.67 | 21.6 | 4.1 | 5.2 | 1.3 | 1.4 | 32 | 57 | 11 |

| PITCHER | yr | t | age | lvl | org | ip | era | whip | bf/g | ctl | dom | cmd | hr/9 | h% | s% | bpv |
|---|---|---|---|---|---|---|---|---|---|---|---|---|---|---|---|---|
| Payano,Victor | 17 | L | 25 | a/a | MIA | 65 | 4.50 | 1.52 | 7.66 | 6.3 | 9.2 | 1.5 | 0.8 | 29 | 71 | 73 |
| | 18 | L | 26 | aa | CIN | 32 | 5.90 | 1.74 | 6.95 | 7.4 | 10.4 | 1.4 | 2.0 | 30 | 71 | 39 |
| Pearce,Matt | 17 | R | 23 | a/a | STL | 164 | 5.06 | 1.41 | 25.7 | 1.7 | 4.4 | 2.6 | 1.0 | 32 | 65 | 46 |
| | 18 | R | 24 | aa | STL | 54 | 5.81 | 1.54 | 23.6 | 1.7 | 6.2 | 3.6 | 1.3 | 36 | 64 | 65 |
| Pelham,C.D. | 18 | L | 23 | aa | TEX | 19 | 8.08 | 2.02 | 3.83 | 6.8 | 7.4 | 1.1 | 0.6 | 38 | 57 | 43 |
| Pena,Felix | 17 | R | 27 | aaa | CHC | 39 | 6.61 | 1.68 | 7.3 | 3.5 | 8.4 | 2.4 | 1.5 | 37 | 62 | 49 |
| | 18 | R | 28 | aaa | LAA | 34 | 3.44 | 1.42 | 14.4 | 4.0 | 7.8 | 2.0 | 0.5 | 32 | 76 | 77 |
| Pena,Jose | 18 | R | 27 | a/a | MIA | 47 | 5.71 | 1.65 | 6.03 | 6.7 | 6.8 | 1.0 | 1.0 | 28 | 66 | 39 |
| Pena,Luis | 17 | R | 22 | aa | LAA | 20 | 4.21 | 1.42 | 21.2 | 4.2 | 7.7 | 1.8 | 1.6 | 29 | 77 | 41 |
| | 18 | R | 23 | a/a | LAA | 107 | 5.03 | 1.42 | 19.8 | 4.4 | 7.3 | 1.7 | 1.2 | 28 | 67 | 48 |
| Pena,Richelson | 17 | R | 24 | aa | TEX | 33 | 4.60 | 1.49 | 28.7 | 1.8 | 5.0 | 2.7 | 1.1 | 34 | 71 | 48 |
| | 18 | R | 25 | a/a | TEX | 119 | 4.40 | 1.57 | 23.8 | 1.8 | 5.4 | 3.0 | 1.1 | 36 | 75 | 51 |
| Pena,Ronald | 18 | R | 27 | aa | WAS | 25 | 6.29 | 1.73 | 5.41 | 5.9 | 7.8 | 1.3 | 2.2 | 29 | 69 | 7 |
| Peoples,Michael | 17 | R | 26 | a/a | CLE | 89 | 8.87 | 2.17 | 26.1 | 3.8 | 3.5 | 0.9 | 1.5 | 39 | 59 | -26 |
| | 18 | R | 27 | a/a | CLE | 45 | 7.44 | 1.67 | 20.3 | 3.0 | 6.4 | 2.1 | 1.1 | 37 | 54 | 41 |
| Perakslis,Stepher | 17 | R | 26 | a/a | CHC | 73 | 4.07 | 1.43 | 9.17 | 3.1 | 7.7 | 2.5 | 0.4 | 34 | 71 | 84 |
| | 18 | R | 27 | aa | SEA | 43 | 7.41 | 1.65 | 6.9 | 2.5 | 4.6 | 1.8 | 1.5 | 34 | 55 | 12 |
| Peralta,Freddy | 17 | R | 21 | aa | MIL | 64 | 3.36 | 1.29 | 20.1 | 4.8 | 11.4 | 2.4 | 0.4 | 31 | 74 | 118 |
| | 18 | R | 22 | aaa | MIL | 61 | 3.03 | 1.24 | 19 | 3.7 | 11.3 | 3.0 | 0.1 | 34 | 74 | 137 |
| Perdomo,Luis | 18 | R | 25 | aaa | SD | 75 | 3.76 | 1.30 | 23.8 | 2.4 | 6.1 | 2.6 | 1.3 | 29 | 76 | 53 |
| Perez,Cionel | 18 | L | 22 | a/a | HOU | 75 | 2.18 | 1.19 | 15.1 | 3.1 | 9.3 | 3.0 | 0.4 | 31 | 82 | 117 |
| Perez,Williams | 17 | R | 26 | aaa | CHC | 120 | 5.85 | 1.63 | 23.3 | 4.0 | 6.2 | 1.5 | 0.6 | 34 | 63 | 46 |
| | 18 | R | 27 | a/a | SEA | 99 | 3.05 | 1.30 | 24 | 1.6 | 6.7 | 4.3 | 0.6 | 34 | 78 | 109 |
| Perrin,Jon | 17 | R | 24 | aa | MIL | 105 | 4.54 | 1.53 | 19.9 | 2.1 | 6.6 | 3.2 | 1.3 | 36 | 74 | 60 |
| | 18 | R | 25 | a/a | KC | 70 | 4.83 | 1.49 | 9.18 | 4.2 | 6.5 | 1.5 | 0.7 | 31 | 68 | 52 |
| Perry,Blake | 17 | R | 25 | aa | SEA | 62 | 7.14 | 1.84 | 7.22 | 5.0 | 8.2 | 1.6 | 0.9 | 38 | 60 | 51 |
| Peters,Dillon | 17 | L | 25 | aa | MIA | 46 | 2.77 | 1.19 | 20.3 | 2.4 | 6.6 | 2.7 | 0.2 | 30 | 76 | 95 |
| | 18 | L | 26 | aaa | MIA | 104 | 6.64 | 1.76 | 25.1 | 2.7 | 5.9 | 2.2 | 1.3 | 38 | 63 | 30 |
| Peterson,Tim | 17 | R | 26 | a/a | NYM | 58 | 2.41 | 1.05 | 5.22 | 2.2 | 7.2 | 3.3 | 0.4 | 27 | 78 | 110 |
| | 18 | R | 27 | aaa | NYM | 40 | 3.27 | 1.02 | 4.83 | 2.2 | 9.9 | 4.5 | 0.8 | 29 | 70 | 141 |
| Pfeifer,Philip | 17 | L | 25 | a/a | ATL | 59 | 4.87 | 1.83 | 6.72 | 7.4 | 10.0 | 1.3 | 0.4 | 36 | 72 | 80 |
| | 18 | L | 26 | a/a | ATL | 57 | 7.44 | 1.79 | 6.77 | 6.6 | 6.4 | 1.0 | 0.4 | 32 | 55 | 48 |
| Phillips,Evan | 17 | R | 23 | a/a | ATL | 51 | 8.22 | 1.97 | 6.15 | 6.7 | 8.3 | 1.2 | 1.2 | 37 | 57 | 34 |
| | 18 | R | 24 | aaa | BAL | 52 | 3.01 | 1.15 | 5.31 | 3.2 | 10.0 | 3.2 | 0.5 | 30 | 74 | 124 |
| Pierpont,Matt | 17 | R | 26 | aa | COL | 62 | 3.37 | 1.11 | 8.74 | 2.3 | 5.8 | 2.5 | 1.2 | 25 | 75 | 60 |
| | 18 | R | 27 | aa | COL | 60 | 3.08 | 1.44 | 4.65 | 3.9 | 8.4 | 2.2 | 0.7 | 33 | 81 | 78 |
| Pike,Tyler | 17 | L | 23 | aa | ATL | 75 | 6.57 | 2.02 | 24.1 | 8.8 | 9.2 | 1.1 | 0.4 | 36 | 65 | 65 |
| | 18 | L | 24 | aa | ATL | 32 | 7.69 | 2.09 | 7.92 | 11.6 | 7.8 | 0.7 | 0.4 | 28 | 60 | 61 |
| Pinales,Erasmo | 18 | R | 24 | aa | HOU | 57 | 6.50 | 1.61 | 6.68 | 5.0 | 9.5 | 1.9 | 1.0 | 35 | 59 | 68 |
| Pineyro,Ivan | 17 | R | 26 | a/a | ARI | 86 | 5.63 | 1.59 | 16.5 | 1.8 | 6.2 | 3.5 | 1.1 | 37 | 66 | 67 |
| | 18 | R | 27 | a/a | LAA | 124 | 7.55 | 1.71 | 21.6 | 2.3 | 6.3 | 2.7 | 1.2 | 38 | 55 | 46 |
| Pinto,Ricardo | 17 | R | 23 | aaa | PHI | 61 | 4.90 | 1.50 | 13.8 | 2.8 | 6.0 | 2.2 | 0.7 | 34 | 67 | 55 |
| | 18 | R | 24 | aaa | CHW | 55 | 7.10 | 1.89 | 9.61 | 3.9 | 5.3 | 1.4 | 1.4 | 37 | 63 | 6 |
| Pivetta,Nick | 17 | R | 24 | aaa | PHI | 32 | 1.82 | 1.01 | 24.5 | 0.6 | 9.0 | 15.1 | 0.4 | 33 | 83 | 365 |
| Plesac,Zach | 18 | R | 23 | aa | CLE | 22 | 3.35 | 1.26 | 22.4 | 1.8 | 7.3 | 4.1 | 0.5 | 33 | 74 | 114 |
| Plutko,Adam | 17 | R | 26 | aaa | CLE | 136 | 8.43 | 1.92 | 26.8 | 4.1 | 4.9 | 1.2 | 2.2 | 35 | 58 | -23 |
| | 18 | R | 27 | aaa | CLE | 86 | 2.32 | 0.92 | 23 | 1.9 | 6.6 | 3.4 | 0.7 | 23 | 78 | 106 |
| Poche,Colin | 18 | L | 24 | a/a | TAM | 66 | 1.02 | 0.89 | 6.12 | 2.7 | 13.1 | 4.9 | 0.3 | 29 | 91 | 192 |
| Ponce,Cody | 17 | R | 23 | aa | MIL | 18 | 2.34 | 1.06 | 22.8 | 2.9 | 4.0 | 1.4 | 0.0 | 24 | 75 | 66 |
| | 18 | R | 24 | aa | MIL | 95 | 6.37 | 1.59 | 14.4 | 3.6 | 7.1 | 2.0 | 1.4 | 34 | 61 | 37 |
| Poncedeleon,Dan | 17 | R | 25 | aaa | STL | 29 | 2.74 | 1.30 | 19.9 | 4.2 | 6.0 | 1.4 | 0.7 | 26 | 81 | 56 |
| | 18 | R | 26 | aaa | STL | 97 | 2.61 | 1.35 | 21.3 | 4.7 | 7.9 | 1.7 | 0.4 | 29 | 81 | 81 |
| Pop,Zach | 18 | R | 22 | aa | BAL | 22 | 2.72 | 0.95 | 5.96 | 2.3 | 5.8 | 2.5 | 0.0 | 24 | 68 | 102 |
| Poppen,Sean | 18 | R | 24 | aa | MIN | 94 | 4.79 | 1.41 | 22.1 | 2.7 | 6.1 | 2.2 | 1.2 | 31 | 69 | 45 |
| Poteet,Cody | 18 | R | 24 | aa | MIA | 121 | 6.19 | 1.64 | 24.6 | 3.4 | 6.2 | 1.8 | 1.1 | 35 | 63 | 35 |
| Povse,Max | 17 | R | 24 | a/a | SEA | 71 | 6.27 | 1.60 | 14.2 | 3.3 | 6.7 | 2.0 | 0.6 | 36 | 59 | 59 |
| | 18 | R | 25 | a/a | SEA | 100 | 6.28 | 1.67 | 25 | 4.3 | 8.0 | 1.8 | 0.8 | 36 | 61 | 59 |
| Powers,Alex | 17 | R | 25 | aa | CIN | 61 | 7.25 | 2.07 | 8.73 | 5.0 | 10.6 | 2.1 | 1.3 | 46 | 66 | 56 |
| | 18 | R | 26 | aa | CIN | 43 | 3.21 | 1.18 | 4.42 | 2.6 | 9.4 | 3.6 | 0.9 | 31 | 76 | 112 |
| Poyner,Bobby | 17 | L | 25 | aa | BOS | 38 | 1.28 | 0.94 | 5.33 | 2.9 | 9.6 | 3.4 | 0.6 | 24 | 91 | 131 |
| | 18 | L | 26 | a/a | BOS | 44 | 4.36 | 1.56 | 5.67 | 2.5 | 5.7 | 2.3 | 1.0 | 35 | 74 | 44 |
| Prevost,Josh | 18 | R | 26 | a/a | NYM | 18 | 5.78 | 1.68 | 27.3 | 3.5 | 3.2 | 0.9 | 0.9 | 32 | 66 | 3 |
| Procopio,Daniel | 18 | R | 23 | aa | LAA | 38 | 8.99 | 2.02 | 7.07 | 6.4 | 9.0 | 1.4 | 1.4 | 39 | 55 | 34 |
| Pugliese,James | 17 | R | 25 | aa | CHC | 78 | 2.53 | 1.38 | 8.22 | 4.3 | 4.6 | 1.1 | 0.7 | 26 | 84 | 35 |
| Puk,A.J. | 17 | L | 22 | a/a | OAK | 64 | 4.95 | 1.48 | 21.2 | 3.3 | 10.0 | 3.0 | 0.3 | 39 | 64 | 114 |
| Quantrill,Cal | 17 | R | 22 | aa | SD | 42 | 5.51 | 1.88 | 24.9 | 3.5 | 6.1 | 1.7 | 1.3 | 39 | 73 | 22 |
| | 18 | R | 23 | a/a | SD | 148 | 5.16 | 1.55 | 23.1 | 2.5 | 6.5 | 2.6 | 0.9 | 36 | 68 | 59 |
| Quiala,Yoanys | 17 | R | 23 | aa | HOU | 50 | 3.52 | 1.72 | 19 | 2.0 | 5.2 | 2.7 | 0.6 | 39 | 80 | 55 |
| | 18 | R | 24 | aa | HOU | 58 | 7.60 | 1.72 | 20.3 | 3.5 | 5.7 | 1.6 | 1.0 | 36 | 54 | 31 |
| Quijada,Jose | 18 | L | 23 | a/a | MIA | 65 | 3.32 | 1.08 | 5.79 | 4.0 | 9.6 | 2.4 | 0.4 | 25 | 69 | 115 |
| Radke,Travis | 18 | L | 25 | a/a | SD | 17 | 2.32 | 0.96 | 10.9 | 1.5 | 3.4 | 2.2 | 0.0 | 24 | 73 | 79 |
| Rainey,Tanner | 17 | R | 25 | aa | CIN | 17 | 2.68 | 1.47 | 5.2 | 7.3 | 12.1 | 1.7 | 1.8 | 24 | 92 | 71 |
| | 18 | R | 26 | aaa | CIN | 51 | 3.54 | 1.38 | 4.87 | 6.9 | 9.4 | 1.4 | 0.5 | 24 | 74 | 90 |
| Ramirez,Carlos | 17 | R | 26 | a/a | TOR | 38 | 0.00 | 0.87 | 5.56 | 2.8 | 8.6 | 3.1 | 0.0 | 23 | 100 | 139 |
| | 18 | R | 27 | aaa | OAK | 49 | 4.46 | 1.30 | 6.12 | 4.9 | 6.9 | 1.4 | 0.6 | 25 | 65 | 66 |
| Ramirez,Emmanu | 18 | R | 24 | a/a | SD | 28 | 2.82 | 1.23 | 22.7 | 2.5 | 8.7 | 3.5 | 0.6 | 32 | 79 | 111 |
| Ramirez,Roel | 18 | R | 23 | aa | STL | 52 | 3.88 | 1.33 | 6.01 | 3.5 | 8.0 | 2.3 | 0.8 | 31 | 72 | 77 |
| Ramirez,Williams | 18 | R | 26 | aa | MIN | 54 | 7.40 | 1.93 | 6.57 | 6.0 | 9.8 | 1.6 | 0.8 | 40 | 60 | 62 |
| Ramirez,Yefrey | 17 | R | 24 | aa | BAL | 124 | 4.37 | 1.45 | 22.1 | 4.0 | 7.3 | 1.8 | 1.3 | 30 | 74 | 47 |
| Ramirez,Yefry | 18 | R | 25 | aaa | BAL | 72 | 5.31 | 1.41 | 21.8 | 3.0 | 7.1 | 2.3 | 1.2 | 32 | 64 | 56 |
| Ravenelle,Adam | 17 | R | 25 | aa | DET | 52 | 6.69 | 1.81 | 5.77 | 3.9 | 6.6 | 1.7 | 1.6 | 36 | 65 | 16 |
| | 18 | R | 26 | aa | DET | 20 | 5.44 | 1.79 | 7.09 | 5.4 | 5.1 | 1.0 | 1.7 | 31 | 74 | -3 |
| Ray,Corey | 17 | R | 25 | aa | KC | 143 | 7.81 | 1.99 | 23.7 | 4.1 | 4.6 | 1.1 | 1.5 | 37 | 61 | -9 |
| Rea,Colin | 18 | R | 28 | a/a | SD | 76 | 6.79 | 1.93 | 20.1 | 4.5 | 6.4 | 1.4 | 1.7 | 37 | 68 | 4 |
| Reed,Cody | 17 | L | 24 | aaa | CIN | 106 | 4.54 | 1.80 | 23.4 | 5.6 | 7.4 | 1.3 | 0.8 | 36 | 76 | 46 |
| | 18 | L | 25 | aaa | CIN | 107 | 5.05 | 1.56 | 26.1 | 2.8 | 7.4 | 2.6 | 1.4 | 35 | 71 | 50 |
| Reed,Jake | 17 | R | 25 | a/a | MIN | 38 | 3.26 | 1.48 | 6.05 | 4.5 | 6.0 | 1.3 | 0.3 | 30 | 77 | 58 |
| | 18 | R | 26 | aaa | MIN | 49 | 2.79 | 1.41 | 6.95 | 4.4 | 7.0 | 1.6 | 0.3 | 31 | 80 | 74 |
| Reeves,James | 18 | L | 25 | a/a | NYY | 59 | 3.71 | 1.33 | 7.47 | 5.7 | 9.0 | 1.6 | 0.9 | 25 | 74 | 77 |
| Reid-Foley,Sean | 17 | R | 22 | aa | TOR | 133 | 6.49 | 1.70 | 22.2 | 3.7 | 7.2 | 1.9 | 1.8 | 35 | 66 | 21 |
| | 18 | R | 23 | a/a | TOR | 131 | 4.20 | 1.34 | 22.7 | 3.6 | 8.6 | 2.4 | 0.6 | 32 | 69 | 88 |
| Reininger,Zac | 17 | R | 24 | a/a | DET | 36 | 2.03 | 1.05 | 5.53 | 3.3 | 6.9 | 2.1 | 0.0 | 25 | 79 | 101 |
| | 18 | R | 25 | aaa | DET | 52 | 3.69 | 1.47 | 6.04 | 3.1 | 7.1 | 2.3 | 0.7 | 34 | 76 | 69 |
| Reyes,Alex | 18 | R | 24 | a/a | STL | 16 | 0.00 | 0.37 | 25.9 | 2.1 | 11.7 | 5.5 | 0.0 | 8 | 100 | 232 |
| Reyes,Arturo | 17 | R | 25 | aaa | STL | 63 | 5.56 | 1.48 | 12.4 | 2.5 | 4.5 | 1.8 | 0.8 | 32 | 62 | 37 |
| | 18 | R | 26 | aaa | STL | 35 | 7.51 | 2.05 | 7.46 | 4.4 | 7.0 | 1.6 | 1.3 | 41 | 64 | 20 |
| Reyes,Gerardo | 18 | R | 25 | aa | SD | 39 | 3.76 | 1.44 | 5.36 | 4.1 | 9.4 | 2.3 | 0.3 | 35 | 72 | 100 |
| Reyes,Jesus | 17 | R | 24 | aa | CIN | 52 | 5.46 | 1.92 | 24.5 | 4.3 | 6.6 | 1.5 | 0.9 | 39 | 72 | 33 |
| | 18 | R | 25 | a/a | CIN | 79 | 5.47 | 1.66 | 9.34 | 4.5 | 5.9 | 1.3 | 1.1 | 32 | 68 | 28 |
| Reyes,Luis | 18 | R | 24 | aa | WAS | 65 | 6.45 | 1.73 | 24.7 | 4.6 | 4.1 | 0.9 | 1.4 | 31 | 65 | -5 |
| Reynolds,Danny | 17 | R | 26 | a/a | ATL | 61 | 4.42 | 1.73 | 6.76 | 5.6 | 6.6 | 1.2 | 0.0 | 35 | 72 | 64 |
| | 18 | R | 27 | a/a | MIL | 33 | 5.22 | 1.73 | 6.54 | 4.4 | 5.4 | 1.2 | 1.4 | 33 | 73 | 10 |
| Rhame,Jacob | 17 | R | 24 | aaa | NYM | 54 | 4.23 | 1.28 | 4.92 | 1.7 | 9.7 | 5.5 | 1.0 | 36 | 70 | 143 |
| | 18 | R | 25 | aaa | NYM | 33 | 2.79 | 0.92 | 4.95 | 2.0 | 9.3 | 4.5 | 0.9 | 25 | 74 | 140 |
| Rhoades,Jeremy | 17 | R | 24 | aa | LAA | 27 | 8.46 | 1.92 | 6.32 | 5.1 | 6.7 | 1.3 | 1.6 | 36 | 57 | 8 |
| | 18 | R | 25 | a/a | LAA | 80 | 2.70 | 1.23 | 6.02 | 2.1 | 6.5 | 3.0 | 0.7 | 30 | 81 | 85 |
| Richards,Trevor | 17 | R | 24 | aa | MIA | 75 | 3.94 | 1.37 | 22.5 | 2.4 | 7.9 | 3.3 | 0.6 | 35 | 71 | 99 |
| | 18 | R | 25 | aaa | MIA | 40 | 2.37 | 1.00 | 25.5 | 0.9 | 6.9 | 7.4 | 0.9 | 28 | 82 | 177 |
| Richman,Jason | 18 | L | 25 | a/a | LA | 15 | 6.62 | 2.11 | 7.5 | 5.6 | 5.9 | 1.1 | 1.2 | 38 | 70 | 7 |
| Rios,Francisco | 17 | R | 22 | aa | TOR | 86 | 5.54 | 1.70 | 16.9 | 4.2 | 5.8 | 1.4 | 1.3 | 33 | 70 | 19 |
| | 18 | R | 23 | aa | TOR | 39 | 9.11 | 1.98 | 13.4 | 5.0 | 5.6 | 1.1 | 2.4 | 35 | 57 | -27 |
| Rios,Yacksel | 17 | R | 24 | a/a | PHI | 56 | 2.43 | 0.94 | 5.72 | 2.3 | 8.8 | 3.8 | 1.0 | 24 | 81 | 119 |
| | 18 | R | 25 | aaa | PHI | 24 | 4.78 | 1.66 | 4.93 | 6.8 | 8.2 | 1.2 | 1.0 | 29 | 73 | 52 |
| Rivero,Alexis | 17 | R | 23 | a/a | PHI | 66 | 5.56 | 1.63 | 6.87 | 3.7 | 6.2 | 1.7 | 1.5 | 33 | 69 | 22 |
| | 18 | R | 24 | a/a | PHI | 48 | 4.06 | 1.48 | 7.94 | 4.6 | 5.9 | 1.3 | 1.4 | 27 | 78 | 25 |
| Roach,Donn | 18 | R | 29 | aaa | CHW | 95 | 3.68 | 1.58 | 26.1 | 2.4 | 4.4 | 1.9 | 0.4 | 35 | 76 | 45 |
| Robinson,Duncan | 18 | R | 25 | a/a | CHC | 143 | 3.79 | 1.44 | 23.5 | 1.7 | 6.1 | 3.6 | 0.6 | 36 | 74 | 86 |
| Rodgers,Brady | 17 | R | 27 | aaa | HOU | 16 | 1.10 | 0.99 | 20.8 | 0.5 | 4.9 | 9.6 | 0.0 | 29 | 88 | 236 |
| | 18 | R | 28 | aaa | HOU | 41 | 5.87 | 1.58 | 22.5 | 2.2 | 5.1 | 2.3 | 0.9 | 35 | 63 | 43 |
| Rodriguez,Bryan | 17 | R | 26 | a/a | SD | 138 | 5.90 | 1.75 | 22.5 | 2.6 | 3.5 | 1.3 | 0.6 | 36 | 65 | 17 |
| Rodriguez,Dereck | 17 | R | 25 | aa | MIN | 75 | 5.86 | 1.68 | 22.6 | 3.6 | 5.7 | 1.6 | 1.4 | 34 | 68 | 17 |
| | 18 | R | 26 | aaa | SF | 51 | 3.61 | 1.29 | 23.3 | 1.9 | 7.4 | 3.9 | 1.6 | 31 | 80 | 79 |
| Rodriguez,Jefry | 18 | R | 25 | a/a | WAS | 102 | 4.42 | 1.50 | 23.2 | 4.0 | 7.2 | 1.8 | 0.6 | 33 | 71 | 62 |
| Rodriguez,Joely | 17 | L | 26 | aaa | TEX | 27 | 8.10 | 2.13 | 6.08 | 6.6 | 5.4 | 0.8 | 2.4 | 34 | 66 | -33 |
| | 18 | L | 27 | aaa | BAL | 50 | 6.42 | 1.69 | 6.85 | 3.7 | 7.0 | 1.9 | 0.3 | 38 | 59 | 67 |
| Rodriguez,Jose | 18 | R | 23 | aa | LAA | 116 | 7.64 | 1.82 | 23.4 | 3.2 | 7.0 | 2.2 | 0.9 | 40 | 56 | 48 |
| Rodriguez,Ricard | 17 | R | 25 | aa | TEX | 15 | 1.74 | 0.85 | 4.59 | 0.7 | 8.0 | 11.6 | 0.8 | 26 | 86 | 280 |
| | 18 | R | 26 | a/a | TEX | 30 | 3.23 | 1.07 | 4.7 | 1.4 | 6.4 | 4.7 | 0.8 | 28 | 72 | 119 |
| Rodriguez,Richar | 17 | R | 27 | aaa | BAL | 71 | 3.50 | 1.36 | 7.03 | 2.9 | 8.2 | 2.9 | 0.8 | 33 | 77 | 86 |
| Rodriguez,Wuilde | 18 | R | 25 | aa | MIL | 20 | 6.01 | 1.89 | 8.61 | 4.1 | 5.2 | 1.3 | 0.7 | 38 | 67 | 25 |
| Roegner,Cameror | 18 | L | 25 | a/a | MIL | 24 | 6.80 | 1.98 | 16.7 | 4.2 | 5.2 | 1.2 | 2.3 | 36 | 71 | -26 |
| Rogers,Josh | 17 | L | 23 | aa | NYY | 39 | 6.62 | 1.35 | 23.3 | 2.0 | 5.8 | 2.8 | 1.8 | 30 | 53 | 39 |
| | 18 | L | 24 | aaa | BAL | 141 | 4.70 | 1.53 | 25.6 | 2.5 | 5.2 | 2.1 | 1.4 | 33 | 73 | 28 |
| Romano,Jordan | 18 | R | 25 | a/a | TOR | 143 | 5.55 | 1.44 | 23.5 | 3.1 | 6.5 | 2.1 | 1.2 | 32 | 63 | 47 |
| Romero,Fernandc | 17 | R | 23 | aa | MIN | 125 | 5.03 | 1.63 | 23.2 | 3.4 | 6.9 | 2.0 | 0.4 | 37 | 67 | 67 |
| | 18 | R | 24 | aaa | MIN | 92 | 5.14 | 1.56 | 25.3 | 3.4 | 5.4 | 1.6 | 0.7 | 33 | 67 | 42 |
| Romero,JoJo | 18 | L | 22 | aa | PHI | 108 | 4.14 | 1.35 | 25 | 3.3 | 7.5 | 2.3 | 1.2 | 30 | 73 | 61 |
| Romero,Miguel | 18 | R | 24 | aa | OAK | 30 | 7.01 | 1.73 | 6.2 | 3.5 | 8.0 | 2.3 | 1.2 | 38 | 59 | 51 |
| Rosa,Adonis | 18 | R | 24 | a/a | NYY | 35 | 5.07 | 1.42 | 25.1 | 1.9 | 4.1 | 2.1 | 1.4 | 31 | 68 | 21 |
| Rosario,Randy | 17 | L | 23 | aa | MIN | 57 | 5.82 | 1.67 | 8.05 | 3.8 | 5.7 | 1.5 | 0.8 | 35 | 65 | 35 |
| | 18 | L | 24 | aaa | CHC | 24 | 0.84 | 0.86 | 5.94 | 2.3 | 4.6 | 2.0 | 0.4 | 20 | 94 | 78 |
| Roseboom,David | 17 | L | 25 | aaa | NYM | 17 | 8.97 | 1.97 | 4.61 | 5.6 | 5.4 | 1.0 | 1.1 | 36 | 53 | 10 |
| | 18 | L | 26 | a/a | NYM | 56 | 3.73 | 1.34 | 5.46 | 3.9 | 8.6 | 2.2 | 1.1 | 30 | 76 | 73 |
| Ross,Joe | 17 | R | 24 | aaa | WAS | 28 | 6.22 | 1.73 | 25.2 | 2.8 | 5.9 | 2.2 | 1.1 | 38 | 65 | 36 |
| | 18 | R | 25 | a/a | WAS | 18 | 4.57 | 1.32 | 25.1 | 2.1 | 4.0 | 1.9 | 0.6 | 30 | 65 | 45 |
| Rowley,Chris | 17 | R | 27 | a/a | TOR | 116 | 3.43 | 1.35 | 16.7 | 2.4 | 5.8 | 2.4 | 0.7 | 32 | 76 | 65 |
| | 18 | R | 28 | aaa | TEX | 144 | 4.55 | 1.72 | 27.3 | 4.3 | 4.4 | 1.0 | 1.0 | 33 | 76 | 10 |
| Rucker,Michael | 18 | R | 24 | aa | CHC | 134 | 4.77 | 1.31 | 21.3 | 2.8 | 6.6 | 2.3 | 1.3 | 29 | 67 | 51 |
| Ruiz,Jose | 18 | R | 24 | aa | CHW | 46 | 4.38 | 1.37 | 5.85 | 4.2 | 9.2 | 2.2 | 0.5 | 32 | 67 | 91 |
| Ruiz,Norge | 18 | R | 24 | aa | OAK | 135 | 5.75 | 1.62 | 25 | 2.5 | 4.7 | 1.9 | 1.0 | 35 | 65 | 28 |
| Rumbelow,Nick | 17 | R | 26 | a/a | NYY | 40 | 1.65 | 1.00 | 6.16 | 2.8 | 8.1 | 2.9 | 0.0 | 26 | 82 | 125 |
| | 18 | R | 27 | a/a | SEA | 21 | 2.11 | 1.27 | 5.78 | 3.7 | 9.0 | 2.5 | 0.5 | 31 | 85 | 99 |
| Ruotolo,Patrick | 18 | R | 23 | aa | SF | 26 | 2.99 | 1.20 | 4.54 | 3.5 | 10.5 | 3.0 | 1.6 | 28 | 85 | 89 |
| Ryan,Kyle | 17 | L | 26 | aaa | DET | 45 | 7.33 | 2.29 | 4.83 | 6.2 | 6.0 | 1.0 | 1.3 | 40 | 69 | -1 |
| | 18 | L | 27 | aaa | CHC | 66 | 3.44 | 1.17 | 12 | 2.7 | 6.5 | 2.4 | 1.3 | 26 | 77 | 57 |
| Ryan,Ryder | 18 | R | 23 | aa | NYM | 34 | 4.45 | 1.17 | 5.26 | 2.7 | 8.3 | 3.1 | 1.3 | 28 | 66 | 82 |
| Ryan,Zac | 18 | R | 24 | aa | LAA | 33 | 7.00 | 1.92 | 7.87 | 5.8 | 7.1 | 1.2 | 0.3 | 38 | 61 | 51 |
| Sadzeck,Connor | 17 | R | 26 | aa | TEX | 94 | 9.26 | 1.95 | 11.8 | 4.4 | 8.2 | 1.9 | 1.7 | 40 | 52 | 24 |
| | 18 | R | 27 | aaa | TEX | 38 | 5.41 | 1.69 | 5.36 | 4.4 | 7.7 | 1.7 | 0.6 | 37 | 67 | 60 |
| Sampson,Adrian | 18 | R | 27 | aaa | TEX | 128 | 5.00 | 1.57 | 17.1 | 2.0 | 4.5 | 2.3 | 1.1 | 35 | 70 | 33 |
| Sampson,Keyvius | 17 | R | 26 | aaa | MIA | 79 | 7.39 | 2.10 | 14.9 | 7.3 | 7.8 | 1.1 | 1.1 | 37 | 65 | 30 |
| Sanchez,Jake | 17 | R | 28 | a/a | OAK | 26 | 1.76 | 1.15 | 4.55 | 2.2 | 8.2 | 3.7 | 0.0 | 32 | 83 | 134 |
| | 18 | R | 29 | a/a | OAK | 43 | 5.25 | 1.74 | 5.77 | 2.8 | 6.1 | 2.2 | 0.9 | 38 | 71 | 42 |
| Sanchez,Mario | 17 | R | 23 | aa | PHI | 56 | 3.49 | 1.30 | 12.2 | 2.1 | 4.5 | 2.1 | 1.3 | 28 | 79 | 32 |
| Sanchez,Miguel | 18 | R | 24 | a/a | MIL | 43 | 3.02 | 1.27 | 7.33 | 3.4 | 11.5 | 3.4 | 0.8 | 34 | 79 | 124 |
| Sanchez,Ricardo | 18 | L | 21 | aa | ATL | 59 | 5.17 | 1.70 | 20.6 | 3.6 | 5.8 | 1.6 | 0.5 | 36 | 69 | 44 |
| Sandoval,Patrick | 18 | L | 22 | aa | LAA | 21 | 1.58 | 1.02 | 20.4 | 3.3 | 10.1 | 3.0 | 0.0 | 28 | 83 | 141 |
| Santana,Dennis | 17 | R | 21 | aa | LA | 33 | 6.25 | 1.70 | 21.1 | 5.6 | 9.1 | 1.6 | 0.6 | 36 | 62 | 70 |
| | 18 | R | 22 | a/a | LA | 51 | 2.59 | 1.03 | 19.7 | 2.5 | 10.1 | 4.0 | 0.5 | 29 | 76 | 143 |
| Santana,Edgar | 17 | R | 26 | aaa | PIT | 58 | 3.94 | 1.61 | 5.84 | 2.1 | 6.4 | 3.0 | 0.7 | 38 | 77 | 69 |
| Santiago,Andres | 17 | R | 28 | a/a | ATL | 28 | 5.82 | 2.25 | 15.6 | 4.4 | 4.2 | 0.9 | 0.4 | 42 | 73 | 10 |
| | 18 | R | 29 | a/a | ATL | 108 | 6.50 | 1.72 | 18.9 | 3.5 | 4.8 | 1.3 | 1.4 | 34 | 64 | 5 |
| Santillan,Tony | 18 | R | 21 | aa | CIN | 63 | 4.54 | 1.46 | 24.6 | 2.4 | 7.8 | 3.3 | 1.4 | 35 | 74 | 68 |
| Santos,Luis | 17 | R | 26 | a/a | TOR | 115 | 6.23 | 1.60 | 18.1 | 4.3 | 6.4 | 1.5 | 1.6 | 31 | 64 | 21 |
| | 18 | R | 27 | aaa | TOR | 44 | 3.83 | 1.56 | 9.69 | 3.1 | 6.3 | 2.1 | 0.5 | 35 | 76 | 59 |
| Santos,Ramon | 18 | R | 24 | aa | STL | 58 | 5.91 | 1.70 | 7.73 | 3.8 | 5.8 | 1.5 | 0.9 | 35 | 65 | 33 |

| PITCHER | yr | t | age | lvl | org | ip | era | whip | bf/g | ctl | dom | cmd | hr/9 | h% | s% | bpv |
|---|---|---|---|---|---|---|---|---|---|---|---|---|---|---|---|---|
| Saucedo,Tayler | 18 | L | 25 | aa | TOR | 64 | 6.70 | 1.78 | 26.9 | 2.7 | 4.3 | 1.6 | 1.5 | 36 | 64 | -1 |
| Saupold,Warwick | 17 | R | 27 | aaa | DET | 40 | 4.38 | 1.77 | 26.4 | 4.5 | 5.6 | 1.2 | 0.6 | 35 | 75 | 34 |
| | 18 | R | 28 | aaa | DET | 54 | 7.33 | 1.86 | 16.9 | 3.3 | 5.2 | 1.6 | 1.4 | 37 | 61 | 8 |
| Sborz,Josh | 17 | R | 24 | aa | LA | 117 | 4.61 | 1.50 | 21 | 4.0 | 5.3 | 1.3 | 0.7 | 30 | 69 | 39 |
| | 18 | R | 25 | a/a | LA | 54 | 4.29 | 1.38 | 4.93 | 3.1 | 9.8 | 3.1 | 0.2 | 37 | 66 | 121 |
| Scheetz,Kit | 18 | L | 24 | aa | HOU | 40 | 3.48 | 1.38 | 6.73 | 1.9 | 8.1 | 4.4 | 0.6 | 37 | 75 | 120 |
| Schiraldi,Lukas | 18 | R | 25 | aa | MIA | 19 | 9.68 | 2.42 | 7.2 | 11.9 | 7.0 | 0.6 | 1.0 | 33 | 58 | 24 |
| Scholtens,Jesse | 18 | R | 24 | a/a | SD | 137 | 4.54 | 1.33 | 21 | 2.2 | 6.6 | 3.0 | 0.6 | 33 | 65 | 86 |
| Schreiber,John | 18 | R | 24 | aa | DET | 58 | 3.20 | 1.32 | 4.9 | 3.1 | 7.3 | 2.4 | 0.4 | 32 | 75 | 86 |
| Schultz,Jaime | 18 | R | 27 | aaa | TAM | 36 | 7.69 | 2.26 | 5.71 | 6.4 | 11.8 | 1.9 | 1.5 | 48 | 67 | 50 |
| Schwaab,Andrew | 17 | R | 24 | aa | NYY | 21 | 3.77 | 1.71 | 7.32 | 3.9 | 7.6 | 2.0 | 0.0 | 39 | 76 | 80 |
| | 18 | R | 25 | aa | DET | 26 | 6.37 | 1.80 | 6.01 | 5.2 | 6.7 | 1.3 | 0.4 | 36 | 62 | 50 |
| Scioneaux,Tate | 17 | R | 25 | aa | PIT | 83 | 3.33 | 1.22 | 7.14 | 1.8 | 5.7 | 3.1 | 0.5 | 31 | 73 | 86 |
| | 18 | R | 26 | aa | PIT | 61 | 6.39 | 1.78 | 6.53 | 3.0 | 7.8 | 2.6 | 1.7 | 39 | 67 | 38 |
| Scott,Robby | 18 | L | 29 | aaa | BOS | 49 | 3.00 | 1.54 | 4.76 | 4.7 | 8.3 | 1.8 | 0.3 | 34 | 80 | 81 |
| Scott,Tanner | 17 | L | 23 | aa | BAL | 69 | 2.73 | 1.49 | 12.4 | 6.6 | 10.0 | 1.5 | 0.3 | 30 | 81 | 95 |
| Scott,Tayler | 17 | R | 25 | a/a | TEX | 75 | 4.37 | 1.82 | 6.42 | 5.3 | 7.2 | 1.3 | 0.9 | 36 | 78 | 39 |
| | 18 | R | 26 | aaa | TEX | 62 | 4.18 | 1.66 | 6.33 | 4.1 | 5.8 | 1.4 | 0.7 | 34 | 76 | 38 |
| Scribner,Troy | 17 | R | 26 | aaa | LAA | 103 | 4.52 | 1.42 | 21.9 | 3.1 | 7.4 | 2.4 | 1.0 | 32 | 70 | 63 |
| | 18 | R | 27 | aaa | ARI | 44 | 4.93 | 1.30 | 22.6 | 3.3 | 7.0 | 2.1 | 1.6 | 27 | 67 | 43 |
| Seabold,Connor | 18 | R | 22 | aa | PHI | 60 | 5.29 | 1.30 | 22.6 | 2.7 | 8.7 | 3.2 | 1.7 | 30 | 64 | 71 |
| Seddon,Joel | 17 | R | 25 | a/a | OAK | 98 | 5.88 | 1.70 | 13 | 3.2 | 5.4 | 1.7 | 0.7 | 36 | 65 | 37 |
| | 18 | R | 26 | aa | OAK | 118 | 5.86 | 1.66 | 18.9 | 3.0 | 4.8 | 1.6 | 1.5 | 34 | 67 | 9 |
| Self,Derek | 17 | R | 27 | a/a | WAS | 62 | 5.16 | 1.63 | 7.41 | 3.3 | 4.2 | 1.3 | 1.2 | 32 | 71 | 9 |
| | 18 | R | 28 | a/a | WAS | 60 | 4.01 | 1.34 | 5.68 | 1.2 | 4.8 | 4.1 | 1.0 | 32 | 72 | 80 |
| Selman,Sam | 17 | L | 27 | a/a | KC | 68 | 3.80 | 1.29 | 6.62 | 5.7 | 9.7 | 1.7 | 0.3 | 26 | 69 | 102 |
| | 18 | L | 28 | a/a | KC | 42 | 6.51 | 1.85 | 5.64 | 7.2 | 9.1 | 1.3 | 0.0 | 37 | 61 | 82 |
| Sendelbach,Loga | 18 | R | 24 | aa | PIT | 70 | 5.34 | 1.76 | 9.17 | 5.5 | 4.9 | 0.9 | 0.8 | 32 | 70 | 19 |
| Sexton,Austin | 18 | R | 24 | aa | STL | 22 | 5.80 | 1.60 | 6.94 | 3.5 | 7.3 | 2.1 | 0.4 | 37 | 61 | 71 |
| Shafer,Justin | 17 | R | 25 | a/a | TOR | 62 | 4.89 | 1.50 | 6.86 | 4.4 | 6.2 | 1.4 | 1.2 | 29 | 70 | 32 |
| | 18 | R | 26 | a/a | TOR | 57 | 1.53 | 1.28 | 4.99 | 3.7 | 6.1 | 1.6 | 0.2 | 28 | 88 | 73 |
| Sharp,Sterling | 18 | R | 23 | aa | WAS | 70 | 5.22 | 1.57 | 23.7 | 3.4 | 5.0 | 1.5 | 0.9 | 33 | 67 | 31 |
| Shaw,Joe | 18 | R | 25 | aa | NYM | 66 | 7.52 | 1.82 | 25.5 | 4.2 | 5.6 | 1.3 | 1.3 | 35 | 59 | 13 |
| Shawaryn,Michae | 18 | R | 24 | a/a | BOS | 152 | 4.58 | 1.32 | 24.3 | 2.4 | 6.3 | 2.7 | 0.9 | 31 | 66 | 67 |
| Sheffield,Justus | 17 | L | 21 | aa | NYY | 93 | 4.43 | 1.61 | 24.3 | 3.4 | 7.0 | 2.1 | 2.0 | 33 | 81 | 20 |
| | 18 | L | 22 | a/a | NYY | 116 | 3.18 | 1.28 | 19 | 4.0 | 8.4 | 2.1 | 0.4 | 29 | 75 | 91 |
| Sheller,Walker | 18 | R | 23 | aa | KC | 51 | 4.46 | 1.41 | 6.17 | 2.5 | 3.9 | 1.5 | 0.9 | 30 | 70 | 26 |
| Shepherd,Chandl | 17 | R | 25 | aaa | BOS | 60 | 6.38 | 1.68 | 7.9 | 3.2 | 8.1 | 2.5 | 1.0 | 39 | 62 | 61 |
| | 18 | R | 26 | aaa | BOS | 131 | 5.87 | 1.74 | 24 | 2.7 | 5.7 | 2.1 | 1.2 | 38 | 68 | 30 |
| Sherfy,Jimmie | 17 | R | 26 | aaa | ARI | 49 | 3.45 | 1.06 | 4.32 | 1.8 | 8.9 | 4.9 | 1.2 | 29 | 73 | 130 |
| | 18 | R | 27 | aaa | ARI | 45 | 1.54 | 1.16 | 4.72 | 3.8 | 9.0 | 2.4 | 0.2 | 28 | 87 | 113 |
| Shew,Anthony | 18 | R | 25 | aa | STL | 114 | 5.01 | 1.54 | 26.2 | 2.5 | 6.0 | 2.5 | 1.0 | 35 | 69 | 51 |
| Shipley,Braden | 17 | R | 25 | aaa | ARI | 105 | 6.12 | 1.75 | 25.3 | 3.5 | 4.8 | 1.4 | 1.6 | 34 | 68 | 0 |
| | 18 | R | 26 | aaa | ARI | 75 | 5.42 | 1.75 | 11.4 | 4.0 | 5.5 | 1.4 | 1.2 | 35 | 71 | 17 |
| Shore,Logan | 18 | R | 24 | aa | OAK | 70 | 6.29 | 1.65 | 24.2 | 2.4 | 5.1 | 2.1 | 0.9 | 36 | 61 | 38 |
| Short,Wyatt | 18 | L | 24 | aa | CHC | 30 | 4.26 | 1.46 | 5.83 | 2.6 | 7.0 | 2.6 | 1.4 | 33 | 76 | 51 |
| Sierra,Carlos | 18 | R | 24 | aa | HOU | 21 | 7.75 | 1.52 | 5.69 | 4.9 | 6.8 | 1.4 | 3.2 | 23 | 56 | -21 |
| Sierra,Yaisel | 17 | R | 26 | a/a | LA | 71 | 3.71 | 1.58 | 8.01 | 3.8 | 8.6 | 2.3 | 0.4 | 37 | 76 | 83 |
| Simms,John | 17 | R | 25 | a/a | WAS | 157 | 5.29 | 1.47 | 24.9 | 2.7 | 5.7 | 2.1 | 1.0 | 32 | 65 | 43 |
| | 18 | R | 26 | aaa | WAS | 64 | 5.06 | 1.72 | 12.1 | 4.3 | 6.3 | 1.4 | 1.4 | 34 | 74 | 19 |
| Simpson,William | 18 | R | 27 | aa | SF | 30 | 2.01 | 2.00 | 5 | 9.6 | 8.6 | 0.9 | 0.0 | 33 | 89 | 76 |
| Sims,Lucas | 17 | R | 23 | aaa | ATL | 115 | 4.71 | 1.31 | 23.8 | 3.0 | 9.2 | 3.0 | 1.6 | 31 | 69 | 75 |
| | 18 | R | 24 | aaa | CIN | 102 | 3.95 | 1.42 | 21.6 | 3.7 | 8.7 | 2.4 | 1.2 | 32 | 76 | 66 |
| Singer,Jeff | 18 | L | 25 | a/a | PHI | 39 | 5.06 | 1.37 | 5.31 | 5.5 | 7.4 | 1.3 | 0.6 | 26 | 62 | 68 |
| Skoglund,Eric | 17 | L | 25 | a/a | KC | 104 | 5.57 | 1.72 | 23.6 | 3.0 | 7.0 | 2.4 | 1.4 | 38 | 70 | 40 |
| | 18 | L | 26 | a/a | KC | 18 | 5.28 | 1.50 | 19.5 | 1.1 | 3.8 | 3.6 | 1.6 | 33 | 69 | 38 |
| Slack,Ryne | 17 | L | 25 | a/a | TEX | 44 | 5.46 | 1.91 | 6.55 | 5.9 | 6.9 | 1.2 | 1.0 | 36 | 73 | 29 |
| | 18 | L | 26 | aa | TEX | 50 | 9.27 | 2.04 | 7.17 | 5.5 | 5.4 | 1.0 | 1.9 | 35 | 55 | -16 |
| Slania,Dan | 17 | R | 25 | a/a | SF | 141 | 7.02 | 1.83 | 26.3 | 4.1 | 5.8 | 1.4 | 1.2 | 36 | 62 | 19 |
| | 18 | R | 26 | aa | SF | 71 | 3.16 | 1.21 | 6.1 | 2.9 | 6.9 | 2.4 | 0.9 | 28 | 77 | 73 |
| Slegers,Aaron | 17 | R | 25 | aaa | MIN | 148 | 5.35 | 1.62 | 27.4 | 2.0 | 5.6 | 2.8 | 0.9 | 37 | 68 | 52 |
| | 18 | R | 26 | aaa | MIN | 86 | 5.74 | 1.57 | 25.2 | 2.3 | 4.6 | 2.0 | 1.8 | 33 | 68 | 8 |
| Smeltzer,Devin | 18 | L | 23 | aa | MIN | 97 | 5.45 | 1.51 | 12.7 | 1.9 | 6.3 | 3.3 | 1.0 | 36 | 64 | 70 |
| Smith,Caleb | 17 | L | 26 | a/a | NYY | 101 | 3.57 | 1.35 | 22.1 | 3.2 | 7.4 | 2.3 | 1.1 | 30 | 78 | 62 |
| Smith,Drew | 17 | R | 24 | a/a | NYM | 20 | 1.71 | 0.89 | 4.86 | 2.6 | 6.8 | 2.6 | 0.5 | 21 | 84 | 100 |
| | 18 | R | 25 | a/a | NYM | 39 | 2.62 | 1.11 | 6.18 | 3.0 | 6.9 | 2.3 | 0.6 | 26 | 79 | 83 |
| Smith,Kyle | 17 | R | 25 | a/a | HOU | 76 | 4.65 | 1.46 | 17.2 | 2.0 | 6.0 | 3.0 | 0.5 | 35 | 67 | 78 |
| Snead,Kirby | 18 | L | 24 | aa | TOR | 44 | 5.56 | 1.83 | 5.71 | 5.4 | 6.7 | 1.2 | 0.7 | 36 | 69 | 39 |
| Sneed,Cy | 17 | R | 25 | a/a | HOU | 115 | 6.53 | 1.72 | 20 | 3.0 | 6.4 | 2.1 | 1.3 | 37 | 63 | 33 |
| | 18 | R | 26 | aaa | HOU | 127 | 3.91 | 1.43 | 20.7 | 3.5 | 6.5 | 1.8 | 0.4 | 32 | 72 | 66 |
| Snell,Blake | 17 | L | 25 | aaa | TAM | 44 | 3.69 | 1.62 | 27.9 | 3.5 | 10.5 | 3.0 | 1.2 | 40 | 82 | 84 |
| Snelten,D.J. | 17 | L | 25 | a/a | SF | 74 | 2.85 | 1.28 | 5.93 | 3.1 | 7.1 | 2.3 | 0.5 | 31 | 79 | 82 |
| | 18 | L | 26 | aaa | BAL | 47 | 6.96 | 2.09 | 6.6 | 5.6 | 6.6 | 1.2 | 0.5 | 40 | 65 | 35 |
| Sobotka,Chad | 17 | R | 24 | aa | ATL | 31 | 8.07 | 1.92 | 8.17 | 6.5 | 5.8 | 0.9 | 0.4 | 35 | 54 | 38 |
| | 18 | R | 25 | a/a | ATL | 38 | 2.51 | 1.27 | 5.03 | 5.3 | 9.3 | 1.7 | 0.3 | 27 | 80 | 100 |
| Sopko,Andrew | 17 | R | 23 | aa | LA | 105 | 4.83 | 1.52 | 19.8 | 3.5 | 5.5 | 1.6 | 1.0 | 31 | 70 | 32 |
| | 18 | R | 24 | aa | LA | 54 | 4.12 | 1.56 | 16.9 | 2.0 | 6.8 | 3.4 | 1.5 | 36 | 79 | 58 |
| Soroka,Michael | 17 | R | 20 | aa | ATL | 154 | 3.75 | 1.28 | 24.2 | 2.2 | 6.8 | 3.1 | 0.7 | 32 | 72 | 88 |
| | 18 | R | 21 | aaa | ATL | 27 | 2.34 | 1.03 | 20.8 | 1.9 | 8.9 | 4.8 | 0.0 | 31 | 75 | 164 |
| Sosebee,David | 18 | R | 25 | a/a | NYY | 39 | 4.37 | 1.72 | 7.43 | 4.1 | 8.6 | 2.1 | 1.7 | 37 | 80 | 39 |
| Soto,Giovanni | 17 | L | 26 | aaa | CHW | 25 | 6.63 | 1.64 | 7.06 | 4.4 | 9.4 | 2.1 | 1.7 | 35 | 62 | 47 |
| Sparkman,Glenn | 17 | R | 25 | a/a | KC | 27 | 3.65 | 1.47 | 12.9 | 3.2 | 3.7 | 1.1 | 1.1 | 29 | 79 | 11 |
| | 18 | R | 26 | a/a | KC | 103 | 4.74 | 1.47 | 24.6 | 1.1 | 5.0 | 4.4 | 1.0 | 35 | 69 | 84 |
| Speer,David | 17 | L | 25 | a/a | CLE | 59 | 6.93 | 2.01 | 6.83 | 3.8 | 5.4 | 1.4 | 0.4 | 41 | 63 | 34 |
| | 18 | L | 26 | aa | CLE | 62 | 5.06 | 1.59 | 5.95 | 2.2 | 5.7 | 2.6 | 0.2 | 38 | 66 | 72 |
| Speier, James | 17 | R | 22 | aa | ARI | 69 | 5.76 | 1.88 | 9 | 4.2 | 5.6 | 1.3 | 0.7 | 38 | 69 | 30 |
| | 18 | R | 23 | aa | KC | 61 | 4.47 | 1.75 | 6.06 | 2.9 | 5.8 | 2.0 | 0.5 | 39 | 74 | 51 |

| PITCHER | yr | t | age | lvl | org | ip | era | whip | bf/g | ctl | dom | cmd | hr/9 | h% | s% | bpv |
|---|---|---|---|---|---|---|---|---|---|---|---|---|---|---|---|---|
| Spitzbarth,Shea | 18 | R | 24 | a/a | LA | 68 | 4.63 | 1.26 | 6.96 | 3.2 | 9.6 | 3.0 | 1.5 | 30 | 68 | 84 |
| Springs,Jeffrey | 18 | L | 26 | a/a | TEX | 58 | 5.45 | 1.48 | 7.59 | 3.4 | 11.7 | 3.4 | 0.4 | 41 | 61 | 129 |
| Squier,Scott | 18 | L | 26 | a/a | MIA | 16 | 7.51 | 1.86 | 6.28 | 5.4 | 3.6 | 0.7 | 0.6 | 33 | 57 | 12 |
| St. John,Locke | 18 | L | 25 | aa | TEX | 17 | 5.79 | 1.72 | 7.02 | 4.9 | 7.1 | 1.5 | 2.0 | 32 | 72 | 8 |
| Stanek,Ryne | 17 | R | 26 | aaa | TAM | 45 | 1.72 | 1.16 | 4.81 | 3.7 | 10.0 | 2.7 | 0.0 | 31 | 84 | 129 |
| Stankiewicz,Tedd | 17 | R | 24 | aa | BOS | 140 | 6.69 | 1.76 | 25.6 | 2.5 | 5.5 | 2.2 | 1.0 | 38 | 61 | 37 |
| | 18 | R | 25 | a/a | BOS | 151 | 6.87 | 1.66 | 26 | 2.7 | 5.4 | 2.0 | 1.7 | 34 | 61 | 12 |
| Stashak,Cody | 18 | R | 24 | aa | MIN | 57 | 3.35 | 1.21 | 6.58 | 2.1 | 8.7 | 4.2 | 0.7 | 33 | 74 | 122 |
| Staumont,Josh | 17 | R | 24 | a/a | KC | 125 | 7.45 | 1.86 | 22.5 | 7.4 | 8.0 | 1.1 | 1.3 | 32 | 60 | 34 |
| | 18 | R | 25 | aaa | KC | 75 | 4.45 | 1.68 | 8.24 | 6.5 | 9.7 | 1.5 | 0.5 | 34 | 73 | 79 |
| Steckenrider,Drev | 17 | R | 26 | aaa | MIA | 33 | 2.02 | 0.91 | 4.78 | 2.3 | 9.7 | 4.2 | 0.9 | 24 | 84 | 139 |
| Stephan,Trevor | 18 | R | 23 | aa | NYY | 84 | 5.99 | 1.52 | 21.5 | 3.3 | 8.4 | 2.5 | 0.8 | 36 | 60 | 78 |
| Stephens,Jacksor | 17 | R | 23 | aaa | CIN | 139 | 6.15 | 1.70 | 24.2 | 3.5 | 6.3 | 1.8 | 1.3 | 36 | 65 | 28 |
| | 18 | R | 24 | aaa | CIN | 44 | 6.81 | 1.64 | 12.3 | 3.5 | 6.1 | 1.7 | 1.0 | 35 | 58 | 35 |
| Stephens,Jordan | 17 | R | 25 | aa | CHW | 92 | 4.60 | 1.65 | 25.6 | 4.2 | 6.9 | 1.6 | 0.6 | 35 | 72 | 55 |
| | 18 | R | 26 | a/a | CHW | 148 | 5.76 | 1.71 | 24 | 3.8 | 6.9 | 1.8 | 1.0 | 37 | 67 | 42 |
| Stephenson,Robe | 17 | R | 24 | aaa | CIN | 40 | 4.84 | 1.15 | 20 | 3.1 | 8.7 | 2.8 | 2.3 | 23 | 68 | 52 |
| | 18 | R | 25 | aaa | CIN | 113 | 3.75 | 1.35 | 23.6 | 5.0 | 9.0 | 1.8 | 1.2 | 27 | 77 | 65 |
| Stevens,Tyler | 18 | R | 22 | a/a | LAA | 49 | 6.97 | 1.80 | 6.89 | 3.3 | 10.6 | 3.2 | 1.0 | 45 | 61 | 88 |
| Stewart,Brock | 17 | R | 26 | aaa | LA | 17 | 3.72 | 1.46 | 14.8 | 1.5 | 10.5 | 7.1 | 1.2 | 41 | 79 | 169 |
| | 18 | R | 27 | aaa | LA | 97 | 3.54 | 1.32 | 21.2 | 2.7 | 5.9 | 2.2 | 0.7 | 30 | 75 | 62 |
| Stewart,Kohl | 17 | R | 23 | a/a | MIN | 82 | 6.28 | 1.83 | 22.4 | 5.4 | 5.0 | 0.9 | 0.7 | 34 | 65 | 22 |
| | 18 | R | 24 | a/a | MIN | 110 | 5.95 | 1.76 | 24 | 2.8 | 6.6 | 2.3 | 0.7 | 40 | 65 | 55 |
| Stinnett,Jake | 18 | R | 26 | aa | CHC | 52 | 6.52 | 1.76 | 5.69 | 4.3 | 7.8 | 1.8 | 1.7 | 36 | 66 | 26 |
| Stout,Eric | 17 | L | 24 | aaa | KC | 69 | 3.81 | 1.43 | 6.55 | 3.9 | 5.8 | 1.5 | 0.5 | 30 | 74 | 53 |
| | 18 | L | 25 | aaa | KC | 55 | 6.08 | 1.79 | 6.67 | 2.2 | 5.7 | 2.5 | 0.9 | 40 | 66 | 46 |
| Strahan,Wyatt | 18 | R | 25 | aa | CIN | 120 | 8.72 | 2.00 | 21.4 | 4.4 | 5.2 | 1.2 | 1.5 | 37 | 56 | -5 |
| Stratton,Chris | 17 | R | 27 | aaa | SF | 79 | 6.53 | 1.77 | 24.3 | 2.8 | 6.3 | 2.3 | 1.1 | 39 | 63 | 40 |
| | 18 | R | 28 | aaa | SF | 24 | 3.39 | 1.57 | 26.3 | 3.1 | 6.8 | 2.2 | 0.9 | 35 | 81 | 54 |
| Stull,Cody | 17 | L | 25 | aa | OAK | 43 | 6.38 | 2.00 | 7.92 | 5.1 | 4.3 | 0.8 | 0.8 | 36 | 68 | 6 |
| | 18 | L | 26 | aa | OAK | 43 | 6.38 | 1.96 | 7.34 | 3.6 | 6.5 | 1.8 | 0.2 | 42 | 65 | 54 |
| Stutzman,Sean | 17 | L | 24 | a/a | HOU | 34 | 3.65 | 1.44 | 8.6 | 3.5 | 7.5 | 2.2 | 1.0 | 32 | 78 | 61 |
| | 18 | L | 25 | a/a | HOU | 26 | 7.25 | 2.14 | 8.67 | 8.7 | 4.8 | 0.6 | 2.6 | 28 | 72 | -41 |
| Suarez,Albert | 18 | R | 29 | aaa | ARI | 64 | 4.96 | 1.81 | 9.58 | 4.6 | 5.3 | 1.2 | 0.9 | 35 | 74 | 20 |
| Suarez,Andrew | 17 | L | 25 | a/a | SF | 156 | 4.28 | 1.59 | 26.4 | 2.6 | 6.4 | 2.4 | 0.6 | 37 | 73 | 64 |
| | 18 | L | 26 | aaa | SF | 18 | 1.07 | 1.00 | 23.2 | 3.4 | 6.3 | 1.8 | 0.0 | 23 | 88 | 95 |
| Suarez,Jose | 18 | L | 20 | a/a | LAA | 110 | 4.00 | 1.41 | 19.4 | 3.0 | 9.2 | 3.0 | 0.4 | 36 | 70 | 107 |
| Suarez,Ranger | 18 | L | 23 | a/a | PHI | 125 | 3.22 | 1.30 | 24.6 | 2.5 | 5.4 | 2.1 | 0.3 | 31 | 75 | 69 |
| Suero,Wander | 17 | R | 26 | a/a | WAS | 65 | 2.38 | 1.30 | 4.98 | 2.9 | 7.1 | 2.5 | 0.5 | 31 | 83 | 84 |
| | 18 | R | 27 | aaa | WAS | 17 | 5.25 | 1.49 | 5.24 | 2.4 | 6.5 | 2.7 | 0.7 | 35 | 64 | 70 |
| Sulser,Cole | 17 | R | 27 | a/a | CLE | 63 | 3.91 | 1.79 | 6.49 | 5.1 | 7.0 | 1.4 | 1.0 | 35 | 81 | 36 |
| | 18 | R | 28 | a/a | CLE | 62 | 5.52 | 1.51 | 5.74 | 2.9 | 10.4 | 3.5 | 0.8 | 40 | 63 | 109 |
| Supak,Trey | 18 | R | 22 | aa | MIL | 88 | 3.87 | 1.36 | 23 | 3.1 | 6.7 | 2.2 | 0.6 | 32 | 72 | 71 |
| Swanson,Erik | 18 | R | 25 | a/a | NYY | 117 | 3.44 | 1.18 | 21.3 | 2.5 | 8.4 | 3.4 | 1.1 | 29 | 75 | 96 |
| Swarmer,Matt | 17 | R | 24 | a/a | CHC | 16 | 8.94 | 2.09 | 26.2 | 3.0 | 7.6 | 2.6 | 1.2 | 45 | 56 | 40 |
| | 18 | R | 25 | aa | CHC | 78 | 5.02 | 1.30 | 21.5 | 1.8 | 7.1 | 3.9 | 1.1 | 33 | 63 | 91 |
| Szkutnik,Trent | 18 | L | 25 | aa | DET | 46 | 4.35 | 1.58 | 5.99 | 3.7 | 7.7 | 2.1 | 0.9 | 35 | 74 | 58 |
| Takahashi,Rodrig | 18 | R | 21 | aa | ARI | 73 | 5.43 | 1.26 | 21.3 | 2.4 | 8.3 | 3.4 | 1.4 | 30 | 60 | 82 |
| Tapia,Domingo | 17 | R | 26 | a/a | CIN | 88 | 6.12 | 1.88 | 10.9 | 3.2 | 7.2 | 2.3 | 1.4 | 41 | 70 | 33 |
| | 18 | R | 27 | a/a | CIN | 65 | 5.03 | 1.69 | 6.11 | 4.6 | 5.0 | 1.1 | 0.8 | 32 | 71 | 26 |
| Tarpley,Stephen | 18 | L | 25 | a/a | NYY | 71 | 2.58 | 1.12 | 7.8 | 3.6 | 7.4 | 2.0 | 0.5 | 25 | 79 | 86 |
| Tate,Dillon | 17 | R | 23 | aa | NYY | 25 | 4.65 | 1.55 | 27.3 | 3.6 | 5.3 | 1.5 | 1.7 | 30 | 76 | 10 |
| | 18 | R | 24 | aa | BAL | 124 | 4.80 | 1.33 | 23.4 | 2.5 | 5.6 | 2.3 | 0.8 | 31 | 64 | 57 |
| Taveras,Jose | 17 | R | 24 | a/a | PHI | 52 | 2.40 | 1.14 | 23 | 2.9 | 7.1 | 2.5 | 1.5 | 24 | 90 | 60 |
| | 18 | R | 25 | aa | PHI | 21 | 6.49 | 1.80 | 16.3 | 4.4 | 6.1 | 1.4 | 2.0 | 34 | 68 | -3 |
| Taylor,Ben | 18 | R | 26 | aaa | CLE | 58 | 3.36 | 1.09 | 4.93 | 1.6 | 8.6 | 5.5 | 1.0 | 30 | 73 | 144 |
| Taylor,Corey | 17 | R | 24 | a/a | NYM | 62 | 5.44 | 1.72 | 6.74 | 2.5 | 6.0 | 2.4 | 0.6 | 39 | 68 | 54 |
| | 18 | R | 25 | a/a | NYM | 67 | 3.21 | 1.52 | 6.48 | 2.3 | 6.3 | 2.8 | 0.2 | 37 | 78 | 81 |
| Taylor,Cory | 17 | R | 24 | aa | SF | 128 | 5.81 | 1.71 | 23.1 | 4.5 | 5.9 | 1.3 | 0.6 | 34 | 65 | 39 |
| | 18 | R | 25 | aa | SF | 56 | 4.94 | 1.65 | 22.9 | 4.6 | 4.0 | 0.9 | 1.2 | 30 | 73 | 3 |
| Taylor,Curtis | 18 | R | 23 | aa | TAM | 62 | 2.80 | 1.05 | 8.03 | 3.8 | 9.5 | 2.5 | 0.9 | 23 | 78 | 100 |
| Taylor,Josh | 17 | L | 24 | aa | ARI | 97 | 6.98 | 2.00 | 14.2 | 4.6 | 7.0 | 1.5 | 0.9 | 40 | 64 | 34 |
| | 18 | L | 25 | a/a | BOS | 39 | 4.78 | 1.88 | 5.42 | 4.4 | 7.2 | 1.6 | 0.3 | 40 | 73 | 58 |
| Taylor,Logan | 17 | R | 26 | a/a | NYM | 47 | 6.46 | 1.84 | 7.82 | 5.0 | 5.5 | 1.1 | 1.7 | 33 | 68 | -2 |
| | 18 | R | 27 | aaa | NYM | 32 | 6.31 | 1.77 | 7.73 | 5.3 | 6.5 | 1.2 | 1.0 | 34 | 64 | 32 |
| Tenuta,Matt | 17 | L | 24 | aa | KC | 53 | 8.11 | 2.09 | 15.4 | 3.1 | 5.2 | 1.7 | 1.8 | 41 | 63 | -9 |
| | 18 | L | 25 | a/a | SEA | 60 | 3.56 | 1.54 | 6.9 | 3.6 | 7.9 | 2.2 | 0.2 | 37 | 75 | 87 |
| Terrero,Franco | 18 | R | 23 | aa | KC | 65 | 6.63 | 1.95 | 7.07 | 5.5 | 7.0 | 1.3 | 1.6 | 36 | 68 | 12 |
| Tewes,Sam | 18 | R | 23 | aa | STL | 32 | 5.11 | 1.67 | 20.5 | 3.4 | 4.2 | 1.2 | 1.3 | 33 | 72 | 4 |
| Therrien,Jesen | 17 | R | 24 | a/a | PHI | 57 | 1.79 | 0.98 | 5.58 | 1.5 | 8.8 | 6.0 | 0.6 | 29 | 85 | 171 |
| Thome,Andrew | 17 | R | 24 | a/a | HOU | 53 | 4.19 | 1.45 | 6.29 | 3.2 | 5.9 | 1.8 | 0.5 | 33 | 71 | 58 |
| | 18 | R | 25 | aaa | HOU | 38 | 4.71 | 1.43 | 6.49 | 3.2 | 3.5 | 1.1 | 1.1 | 28 | 69 | 10 |
| Thompson,Jake | 17 | R | 23 | aaa | PHI | 118 | 6.67 | 1.77 | 24.7 | 3.7 | 6.0 | 1.6 | 1.1 | 36 | 63 | 26 |
| | 18 | R | 24 | aaa | MIL | 53 | 4.32 | 1.46 | 6.89 | 4.6 | 7.9 | 1.7 | 0.9 | 30 | 72 | 62 |
| Thompson,Jeff | 18 | R | 27 | aa | DET | 17 | 7.27 | 2.66 | 6.66 | 7.6 | 6.7 | 0.9 | 2.0 | 43 | 76 | -25 |
| Thompson,Keega | 18 | R | 23 | aa | CHC | 62 | 5.15 | 1.62 | 21.2 | 3.3 | 6.6 | 2.0 | 0.5 | 37 | 67 | 61 |
| Thompson,Ryan | 17 | R | 25 | a/a | HOU | 67 | 4.44 | 1.48 | 7.75 | 1.7 | 7.0 | 4.2 | 0.7 | 37 | 70 | 101 |
| Thompson,Zach | 18 | R | 25 | aa | CHW | 40 | 1.93 | 1.42 | 8.08 | 4.7 | 7.5 | 1.6 | 0.9 | 29 | 92 | 57 |
| Thomson,Colton | 18 | L | 26 | aa | STL | 17 | 4.79 | 1.80 | 5.27 | 4.7 | 4.1 | 0.9 | 0.5 | 34 | 73 | 20 |
| Thornton,Trent | 17 | R | 24 | a/a | HOU | 131 | 5.59 | 1.52 | 22.8 | 1.5 | 6.0 | 4.1 | 0.9 | 37 | 64 | 83 |
| | 18 | R | 25 | aaa | HOU | 125 | 4.39 | 1.24 | 21.2 | 2.0 | 7.2 | 3.5 | 0.9 | 31 | 66 | 92 |
| Thorpe,Lewis | 18 | L | 23 | a/a | MIN | 131 | 4.62 | 1.43 | 21.5 | 2.6 | 8.8 | 3.5 | 1.4 | 35 | 72 | 82 |
| Tinoco,Jesus | 18 | R | 23 | aa | COL | 141 | 6.94 | 1.64 | 24.2 | 2.7 | 6.7 | 2.5 | 2.1 | 35 | 62 | 19 |
| Topa,Justin | 18 | R | 27 | aa | TEX | 41 | 8.15 | 2.07 | 22.3 | 3.4 | 5.6 | 1.6 | 1.2 | 42 | 60 | 13 |
| Torres,Joshua | 18 | R | 24 | a/a | NYM | 55 | 2.99 | 1.40 | 5.82 | 3.3 | 9.5 | 2.8 | 0.7 | 35 | 81 | 96 |
| Torres-Costa,Quii | 17 | L | 23 | aa | MIL | 21 | 8.00 | 2.25 | 5.82 | 8.4 | 9.4 | 1.1 | 0.7 | 41 | 63 | 50 |
| | 18 | L | 24 | a/a | MIL | 55 | 1.57 | 1.03 | 4.93 | 4.2 | 9.0 | 2.2 | 0.0 | 24 | 83 | 121 |

| PITCHER | yr | t | age | lvl | org | ip | era | whip | bf/g | ctl | dom | cmd | hr/9 | h% | s% | bpv |
|---|---|---|---|---|---|---|---|---|---|---|---|---|---|---|---|---|
| Torrez,Daury | 18 | R | 25 | a/a | CHC | 77 | 5.16 | 1.62 | 10.4 | 2.8 | 4.8 | 1.7 | 0.9 | 35 | 69 | 30 |
| Toussaint,Touki | 17 | R | 21 | aa | ATL | 40 | 4.42 | 1.54 | 24.7 | 5.6 | 9.1 | 1.6 | 0.8 | 32 | 72 | 71 |
| | 18 | R | 22 | a/a | ATL | 137 | 2.95 | 1.23 | 23.1 | 3.4 | 9.1 | 2.7 | 0.5 | 31 | 77 | 105 |
| Trivino,Lou | 17 | R | 24 | a/a | OAK | 68 | 3.57 | 1.38 | 5.98 | 2.7 | 6.8 | 2.5 | 0.0 | 34 | 71 | 93 |
| Tseng,Jen-Ho | 17 | R | 23 | a/a | CHC | 145 | 3.04 | 1.27 | 24.8 | 2.4 | 6.5 | 2.7 | 0.8 | 30 | 79 | 74 |
| | 18 | R | 24 | aaa | CHC | 137 | 7.03 | 1.63 | 23.5 | 3.0 | 6.3 | 2.1 | 1.4 | 35 | 57 | 33 |
| Turley,Josh | 17 | L | 27 | a/a | DET | 49 | 8.72 | 2.35 | 21 | 6.8 | 4.6 | 0.7 | 1.4 | 38 | 63 | -19 |
| | 18 | L | 28 | a/a | DET | 70 | 7.10 | 1.95 | 24 | 7.3 | 5.2 | 0.7 | 0.3 | 33 | 61 | 34 |
| Turley,Nik | 17 | L | 28 | a/a | MIN | 92 | 3.36 | 1.36 | 16.7 | 3.4 | 8.8 | 2.6 | 0.6 | 33 | 76 | 93 |
| Turnbull,Spencer | 17 | R | 25 | aa | DET | 20 | 8.04 | 1.74 | 23.2 | 3.8 | 7.7 | 2.0 | 0.5 | 39 | 50 | 64 |
| | 18 | R | 26 | a/a | DET | 114 | 5.72 | 1.54 | 23.7 | 3.8 | 7.4 | 2.0 | 0.4 | 35 | 60 | 72 |
| Turner,Colton | 17 | L | 26 | a/a | CHW | 55 | 5.75 | 1.64 | 7.05 | 3.1 | 7.5 | 2.4 | 1.3 | 37 | 67 | 50 |
| | 18 | L | 27 | a/a | CHW | 66 | 3.05 | 1.22 | 7.23 | 3.2 | 7.1 | 2.2 | 0.9 | 27 | 79 | 69 |
| Turner,Jacob | 17 | R | 26 | aaa | WAS | 66 | 6.93 | 1.92 | 22.3 | 5.0 | 5.8 | 1.2 | 0.8 | 37 | 63 | 25 |
| | 18 | R | 27 | aaa | DET | 104 | 5.92 | 1.76 | 18.3 | 3.7 | 4.8 | 1.3 | 1.2 | 35 | 68 | 11 |
| Uceta,Adonis | 18 | R | 24 | aa | NYM | 26 | 4.76 | 1.56 | 7.15 | 4.3 | 8.2 | 1.9 | 0.7 | 35 | 70 | 68 |
| Uhen,Josh | 17 | R | 25 | aa | MIL | 59 | 5.87 | 1.98 | 6.4 | 4.7 | 6.7 | 1.4 | 0.3 | 41 | 68 | 50 |
| | 18 | R | 26 | aa | MIL | 25 | 9.80 | 2.24 | 5.32 | 12.5 | 6.4 | 0.5 | 1.1 | 26 | 54 | 25 |
| Underwood Jr.,Du | 17 | R | 23 | aa | CHC | 138 | 5.85 | 1.53 | 24 | 3.5 | 5.5 | 1.6 | 1.0 | 32 | 62 | 33 |
| | 18 | R | 24 | aaa | CHC | 120 | 5.07 | 1.51 | 19.2 | 2.8 | 6.5 | 2.3 | 0.6 | 35 | 66 | 65 |
| Unsworth,Dylan | 17 | R | 25 | a/a | SEA | 128 | 4.04 | 1.30 | 24.1 | 1.6 | 5.3 | 3.4 | 0.7 | 32 | 70 | 79 |
| | 18 | R | 26 | a/a | LAA | 104 | 6.39 | 1.66 | 19.4 | 2.0 | 5.1 | 2.5 | 1.5 | 36 | 64 | 26 |
| Urias,Julio | 17 | L | 21 | aaa | LA | 31 | 2.81 | 1.10 | 20.5 | 3.7 | 8.2 | 2.2 | 0.3 | 26 | 74 | 102 |
| Valdez,Framber | 17 | L | 24 | aa | HOU | 49 | 7.38 | 1.93 | 19.4 | 4.3 | 8.5 | 2.0 | 0.8 | 42 | 61 | 54 |
| | 18 | L | 25 | a/a | HOU | 105 | 4.57 | 1.38 | 20.1 | 2.7 | 9.0 | 3.4 | 0.6 | 36 | 67 | 105 |
| Valdez,Jose | 17 | R | 27 | aaa | SD | 41 | 5.78 | 1.62 | 5.47 | 3.4 | 7.6 | 2.2 | 0.4 | 38 | 62 | 74 |
| | 18 | R | 28 | aaa | SF | 50 | 5.48 | 1.75 | 6.19 | 6.5 | 7.9 | 1.2 | 0.5 | 34 | 67 | 61 |
| Valdez,Phillips | 17 | R | 26 | a/a | WAS | 67 | 5.53 | 1.54 | 8.36 | 2.7 | 5.7 | 2.1 | 0.3 | 36 | 62 | 63 |
| | 18 | R | 27 | a/a | WAS | 137 | 3.71 | 1.50 | 19.1 | 3.4 | 5.2 | 1.6 | 0.8 | 32 | 77 | 37 |
| Van Steensel,Tod | 17 | R | 26 | aa | MIN | 59 | 2.10 | 1.44 | 6.94 | 4.3 | 6.8 | 1.6 | 0.0 | 32 | 84 | 78 |
| | 18 | R | 27 | aa | MIN | 44 | 4.10 | 1.31 | 7.28 | 5.1 | 7.6 | 1.5 | 0.3 | 27 | 67 | 82 |
| Vargas,Cesar | 17 | R | 26 | a/a | SD | 69 | 6.82 | 1.74 | 7.29 | 5.1 | 8.0 | 1.6 | 0.4 | 37 | 58 | 64 |
| | 18 | R | 27 | a/a | WAS | 99 | 7.39 | 2.06 | 24.2 | 4.6 | 5.0 | 1.1 | 1.5 | 38 | 65 | -8 |
| Vargas,Emilio | 18 | R | 22 | aa | ARI | 37 | 4.53 | 1.15 | 24.6 | 1.9 | 6.3 | 3.3 | 1.4 | 27 | 65 | 69 |
| Varner,Seth | 18 | L | 26 | aa | CIN | 120 | 4.71 | 1.40 | 20.3 | 2.7 | 6.1 | 2.3 | 2.0 | 29 | 74 | 24 |
| Vasquez,Andrew | 18 | L | 25 | a/a | MIN | 38 | 1.62 | 1.08 | 7.1 | 2.0 | 13.2 | 6.5 | 0.3 | 38 | 86 | 214 |
| Vasquez,Kelvin | 18 | R | 25 | a/a | ATL | 50 | 7.14 | 1.72 | 7.58 | 5.7 | 5.9 | 1.0 | 0.9 | 31 | 57 | 31 |
| Vasquez,Pedro | 18 | R | 23 | aa | PIT | 64 | 6.23 | 1.56 | 21.6 | 2.6 | 5.3 | 2.1 | 1.4 | 33 | 62 | 27 |
| Vasto,Jerry | 17 | L | 25 | aaa | COL | 54 | 9.41 | 2.03 | 6.35 | 4.4 | 7.8 | 1.8 | 1.8 | 41 | 54 | 12 |
| | 18 | L | 26 | aaa | KC | 38 | 4.03 | 1.62 | 4.44 | 4.6 | 8.2 | 1.8 | 0.8 | 35 | 76 | 63 |
| Ventura,Angel | 17 | R | 24 | a/a | MIL | 129 | 4.84 | 1.44 | 22.1 | 3.6 | 5.2 | 1.4 | 1.2 | 29 | 69 | 26 |
| | 18 | R | 25 | a/a | MIL | 30 | 8.03 | 1.96 | 13.1 | 4.9 | 8.1 | 1.6 | 2.6 | 37 | 64 | -5 |
| Vera,Eduardo | 18 | R | 24 | aa | PIT | 97 | 4.55 | 1.26 | 23.3 | 2.2 | 5.1 | 2.3 | 1.1 | 28 | 67 | 47 |
| VerHagen,Drew | 17 | R | 27 | aaa | DET | 97 | 7.40 | 2.02 | 24.8 | 4.7 | 4.8 | 1.0 | 0.9 | 38 | 62 | 9 |
| | 18 | R | 28 | aaa | DET | 34 | 2.40 | 1.06 | 13.3 | 3.1 | 9.8 | 3.1 | 0.0 | 29 | 75 | 139 |
| Vieaux,Cam | 18 | L | 25 | aa | PIT | 89 | 4.54 | 1.28 | 24.4 | 1.8 | 5.7 | 3.1 | 1.1 | 30 | 67 | 66 |
| Vieira,Thyago | 17 | R | 24 | a/a | SEA | 54 | 4.80 | 1.44 | 5.61 | 3.7 | 6.6 | 1.8 | 0.4 | 32 | 65 | 67 |
| | 18 | R | 25 | aaa | CHW | 41 | 6.40 | 1.82 | 5.28 | 5.8 | 9.2 | 1.6 | 0.5 | 38 | 63 | 68 |
| Vieitez,Ivan | 17 | R | 24 | aa | LA | 38 | 5.94 | 1.81 | 16 | 4.2 | 4.2 | 1.0 | 0.5 | 35 | 66 | 21 |
| Villegas,Kender | 17 | R | 24 | aa | TOR | 40 | 6.36 | 1.91 | 9.45 | 5.8 | 4.9 | 0.8 | 0.9 | 34 | 66 | 14 |
| Vines,Jace | 18 | R | 24 | aa | KC | 43 | 8.06 | 1.81 | 22.2 | 3.3 | 4.7 | 1.4 | 1.1 | 37 | 54 | 12 |
| Viza,Tyler | 17 | R | 23 | aa | PHI | 140 | 6.33 | 1.60 | 23.8 | 3.1 | 5.7 | 1.8 | 1.5 | 33 | 63 | 19 |
| | 18 | R | 24 | a/a | PHI | 85 | 3.56 | 1.39 | 15 | 2.8 | 7.1 | 2.5 | 0.6 | 33 | 75 | 76 |
| Voelker,Paul | 17 | R | 25 | a/a | DET | 32 | 3.08 | 1.37 | 4.47 | 2.5 | 7.5 | 3.0 | 1.0 | 33 | 82 | 76 |
| | 18 | R | 26 | aaa | DET | 68 | 4.62 | 1.47 | 6.79 | 3.6 | 5.9 | 1.6 | 1.2 | 30 | 72 | 32 |
| Voth,Austin | 17 | R | 25 | a/a | WAS | 121 | 7.57 | 1.92 | 24.9 | 3.8 | 5.2 | 1.4 | 1.7 | 37 | 62 | -5 |
| | 18 | R | 26 | aaa | WAS | 127 | 5.98 | 1.54 | 23.1 | 3.1 | 6.5 | 2.1 | 1.2 | 34 | 62 | 43 |
| Waddell,Brandon | 17 | L | 23 | aa | PIT | 66 | 4.75 | 1.54 | 19.2 | 4.0 | 6.2 | 1.6 | 0.5 | 33 | 68 | 55 |
| | 18 | L | 24 | a/a | PIT | 138 | 4.30 | 1.51 | 21.4 | 3.7 | 5.4 | 1.5 | 0.5 | 32 | 71 | 47 |
| Wade,Konner | 17 | R | 26 | aa | COL | 109 | 7.13 | 1.74 | 15.1 | 2.1 | 4.8 | 2.2 | 2.1 | 36 | 63 | -1 |
| Waguespack,Jac | 17 | R | 24 | aa | PHI | 37 | 4.52 | 1.63 | 23.5 | 4.0 | 7.3 | 1.8 | 0.6 | 36 | 72 | 61 |
| | 18 | R | 25 | a/a | TOR | 124 | 6.38 | 1.73 | 20.2 | 3.6 | 6.5 | 1.8 | 0.6 | 37 | 61 | 49 |
| Wahl,Bobby | 18 | R | 26 | aaa | NYM | 45 | 2.10 | 0.88 | 4.38 | 3.7 | 11.9 | 3.3 | 0.3 | 22 | 77 | 156 |
| Walker,Matt | 18 | R | 24 | aa | SEA | 62 | 4.33 | 1.46 | 6.81 | 3.3 | 7.1 | 2.2 | 0.8 | 33 | 71 | 63 |
| Walsh,Connor | 17 | R | 25 | a/a | CHW | 56 | 4.46 | 1.56 | 6.32 | 6.1 | 8.5 | 1.4 | 0.2 | 31 | 69 | 82 |
| | 18 | R | 26 | aa | CHW | 30 | 14.81 | 2.74 | 8.85 | 6.7 | 10.0 | 1.5 | 2.6 | 50 | 45 | -14 |
| Walter,Corey | 17 | R | 25 | a/a | OAK | 117 | 5.00 | 1.73 | 17.2 | 2.7 | 4.6 | 1.7 | 0.3 | 38 | 69 | 41 |
| | 18 | R | 26 | aa | OAK | 76 | 7.50 | 1.82 | 13.6 | 3.3 | 3.6 | 1.1 | 0.7 | 36 | 57 | 10 |
| Wang,Wei-Chung | 17 | L | 25 | aaa | MIL | 57 | 2.23 | 1.32 | 5.02 | 1.8 | 6.3 | 3.4 | 1.1 | 32 | 89 | 75 |
| Warmoth,Tyler | 17 | R | 25 | a/a | LAA | 52 | 3.87 | 1.39 | 6.48 | 3.3 | 7.4 | 2.3 | 1.1 | 31 | 75 | 62 |
| Warner,Austin | 18 | L | 24 | a/a | STL | 68 | 5.27 | 1.80 | 24.2 | 3.8 | 5.2 | 1.4 | 1.3 | 35 | 73 | 11 |
| Warren,Art | 18 | R | 25 | aa | SEA | 17 | 1.91 | 1.54 | 5.36 | 7.6 | 9.8 | 1.3 | 0.0 | 28 | 86 | 102 |
| Watkins,Spenser | 18 | R | 26 | a/a | DET | 26 | 6.71 | 1.68 | 23.6 | 4.6 | 6.3 | 1.4 | 1.3 | 33 | 61 | 23 |
| Watson,Shane | 17 | R | 24 | aa | PHI | 83 | 5.08 | 1.87 | 11.8 | 4.5 | 4.2 | 0.9 | 1.6 | 34 | 77 | -13 |
| Watts,Devan | 17 | R | 22 | aa | ATL | 32 | 3.16 | 1.50 | 6.91 | 4.1 | 7.9 | 1.9 | 0.3 | 34 | 78 | 79 |
| | 18 | R | 23 | aa | CHW | 15 | 4.06 | 1.42 | 6.45 | 3.3 | 3.6 | 1.1 | 0.8 | 28 | 73 | 21 |
| Weaver,Luke | 17 | R | 24 | aaa | STL | 78 | 3.15 | 1.21 | 20.8 | 2.2 | 7.0 | 3.1 | 0.4 | 31 | 74 | 101 |
| Webb,Braden | 18 | R | 23 | aa | MIL | 20 | 2.58 | 1.37 | 20.9 | 4.9 | 9.3 | 1.9 | 0.0 | 31 | 79 | 106 |
| Webb,Jacob | 17 | R | 24 | aa | ATL | 24 | 3.84 | 1.60 | 6.62 | 6.2 | 8.5 | 1.4 | 0.5 | 31 | 76 | 72 |
| | 18 | R | 25 | a/a | ATL | 57 | 3.95 | 1.18 | 4.51 | 3.7 | 8.7 | 2.4 | 1.3 | 25 | 72 | 73 |
| Webb,Logan | 18 | R | 22 | aa | SF | 32 | 4.39 | 1.40 | 22.7 | 3.1 | 6.3 | 2.0 | 1.0 | 31 | 71 | 51 |
| Weems,Jordan | 18 | R | 26 | a/a | BOS | 47 | 5.68 | 1.89 | 6.18 | 5.4 | 6.8 | 1.2 | 0.9 | 36 | 70 | 31 |
| Weigel,Patrick | 17 | R | 23 | a/a | ATL | 78 | 5.54 | 1.55 | 22.8 | 3.6 | 6.9 | 1.9 | 0.9 | 34 | 64 | 52 |
| Weir,T.J. | 17 | R | 26 | aa | SD | 58 | 3.22 | 1.38 | 6.77 | 2.6 | 6.9 | 2.6 | 0.8 | 33 | 79 | 72 |
| | 18 | R | 27 | a/a | SD | 73 | 3.30 | 1.29 | 6.84 | 3.4 | 6.2 | 1.8 | 0.5 | 29 | 75 | 67 |
| Weiss,Zack | 17 | R | 25 | aa | CIN | 28 | 4.88 | 1.59 | 5.14 | 4.4 | 10.0 | 2.3 | 1.1 | 36 | 71 | 74 |
| | 18 | R | 26 | a/a | CIN | 20 | 7.30 | 2.19 | 6.33 | 9.6 | 7.3 | 0.8 | 1.8 | 32 | 69 | 3 |
| Wells,Tyler | 18 | R | 24 | aa | MIN | 34 | 1.97 | 1.21 | 23 | 3.7 | 8.2 | 2.2 | 0.3 | 29 | 84 | 97 |
| Wendelken,Jeffre | 18 | R | 25 | a/a | OAK | 50 | 3.46 | 1.34 | 6.33 | 3.6 | 10.7 | 3.0 | 0.9 | 34 | 77 | 104 |
| Whalen,Rob | 17 | R | 23 | aaa | SEA | 53 | 7.52 | 1.65 | 23.8 | 3.3 | 6.4 | 1.9 | 1.6 | 34 | 55 | 23 |
| | 18 | R | 24 | a/a | SEA | 106 | 6.12 | 1.77 | 22.1 | 3.4 | 7.4 | 2.2 | 0.5 | 40 | 64 | 62 |
| White,Mitchell | 17 | R | 23 | aa | LA | 28 | 3.01 | 1.11 | 15.7 | 3.8 | 8.6 | 2.3 | 0.7 | 25 | 75 | 93 |
| | 18 | R | 24 | aa | LA | 106 | 4.84 | 1.47 | 20.7 | 2.6 | 6.3 | 2.4 | 1.0 | 34 | 69 | 54 |
| Whitehouse,Matt | 17 | L | 26 | a/a | CLE | 117 | 6.88 | 1.71 | 17.6 | 2.8 | 5.0 | 1.8 | 1.5 | 35 | 62 | 9 |
| | 18 | L | 27 | a/a | CLE | 86 | 5.69 | 1.89 | 11.6 | 5.6 | 6.2 | 1.1 | 1.0 | 35 | 71 | 25 |
| Whitley,Forrest | 18 | R | 21 | aa | HOU | 27 | 4.48 | 1.03 | 13.1 | 3.6 | 9.9 | 2.8 | 0.8 | 24 | 56 | 113 |
| Wick,Rowan | 17 | R | 25 | a/a | STL | 38 | 4.58 | 1.52 | 5.54 | 4.5 | 6.2 | 1.4 | 0.8 | 30 | 71 | 44 |
| | 18 | R | 26 | a/a | SD | 56 | 2.92 | 1.34 | 4.78 | 5.0 | 8.3 | 1.7 | 0.5 | 28 | 79 | 82 |
| Widener,Taylor | 18 | R | 24 | aa | ARI | 138 | 3.34 | 1.16 | 21.1 | 2.9 | 9.5 | 3.3 | 0.8 | 30 | 74 | 111 |
| Wieck,Brad | 18 | L | 27 | a/a | SD | 47 | 2.90 | 1.28 | 4.39 | 3.4 | 10.6 | 3.2 | 0.6 | 34 | 79 | 119 |
| Wiles,Collin | 17 | R | 23 | aa | TEX | 150 | 6.76 | 1.67 | 24 | 1.9 | 5.3 | 2.8 | 1.7 | 36 | 62 | 27 |
| | 18 | R | 24 | aa | TEX | 22 | 7.60 | 1.74 | 25.4 | 2.3 | 8.5 | 3.7 | 2.6 | 39 | 62 | 38 |
| Wilkerson,Aaron | 17 | R | 28 | aa | MIL | 142 | 5.39 | 1.51 | 25.7 | 2.9 | 7.0 | 2.4 | 1.4 | 34 | 67 | 48 |
| | 18 | R | 29 | aaa | MIL | 73 | 2.80 | 1.40 | 20.6 | 3.2 | 5.7 | 1.8 | 0.4 | 31 | 81 | 60 |
| Williams,Austen | 17 | R | 25 | aa | WAS | 46 | 8.89 | 2.04 | 22.3 | 2.3 | 5.4 | 2.3 | 1.3 | 42 | 55 | 19 |
| | 18 | R | 26 | a/a | WAS | 70 | 1.55 | 0.98 | 8.35 | 2.4 | 9.0 | 3.8 | 0.0 | 28 | 82 | 148 |
| Williams,Garrett | 18 | L | 24 | aa | SF | 83 | 7.48 | 2.13 | 12.5 | 6.9 | 6.5 | 1.0 | 0.6 | 38 | 63 | 31 |
| Williams,Taylor | 17 | R | 26 | aa | MIL | 47 | 5.03 | 1.79 | 9.78 | 4.9 | 8.9 | 1.8 | 0.7 | 39 | 72 | 66 |
| Wilson,Bryse | 18 | R | 21 | a/a | ATL | 99 | 5.27 | 1.40 | 20.9 | 2.5 | 9.2 | 3.6 | 0.9 | 36 | 63 | 102 |
| Windle,Tom | 17 | L | 25 | aa | PHI | 51 | 5.35 | 1.31 | 5.85 | 3.9 | 6.6 | 1.7 | 0.9 | 27 | 59 | 56 |
| | 18 | L | 26 | aaa | PHI | 54 | 5.47 | 1.67 | 4.85 | 5.1 | 7.2 | 1.4 | 1.3 | 32 | 70 | 32 |
| Wingenter,Trey | 18 | R | 24 | aaa | SD | 45 | 3.36 | 1.17 | 4.5 | 4.4 | 8.9 | 2.0 | 0.7 | 25 | 73 | 92 |
| Winkelman,Alex | 17 | L | 23 | aa | HOU | 71 | 4.97 | 1.79 | 18.3 | 3.7 | 7.2 | 2.0 | 0.9 | 39 | 73 | 48 |
| | 18 | L | 24 | aa | HOU | 79 | 3.96 | 1.73 | 11.3 | 6.8 | 7.7 | 1.1 | 0.4 | 32 | 77 | 61 |
| Wiper,Cole | 18 | R | 26 | aa | TEX | 23 | 8.71 | 2.55 | 7.3 | 5.5 | 5.7 | 1.0 | 1.5 | 45 | 66 | -17 |
| Wisler,Matthew | 17 | R | 25 | aaa | ATL | 94 | 4.66 | 1.56 | 22.8 | 2.2 | 5.2 | 2.4 | 0.7 | 36 | 71 | 51 |
| | 18 | R | 26 | aaa | CIN | 91 | 5.01 | 1.55 | 19 | 1.9 | 6.9 | 3.7 | 0.8 | 38 | 68 | 86 |
| Withrow,Matt | 17 | R | 24 | aa | ATL | 48 | 6.54 | 1.57 | 21.2 | 4.8 | 7.1 | 1.5 | 1.8 | 29 | 62 | 20 |
| Wivinis,Matt | 18 | R | 25 | aa | NYY | 18 | 6.18 | 1.27 | 6.21 | 3.3 | 7.8 | 2.3 | 1.5 | 27 | 53 | 59 |
| Wolff,Sam | 17 | R | 26 | a/a | TEX | 43 | 4.02 | 1.59 | 4.74 | 4.5 | 9.5 | 2.1 | 1.3 | 35 | 79 | 61 |
| | 18 | R | 27 | aa | SF | 28 | 9.02 | 2.26 | 6.49 | 5.7 | 9.5 | 1.7 | 0.3 | 47 | 56 | 64 |
| Wood,Hunter | 17 | R | 24 | a/a | TAM | 123 | 6.04 | 1.59 | 17.5 | 3.5 | 7.2 | 2.1 | 1.3 | 34 | 63 | 44 |
| | 18 | R | 25 | aaa | TAM | 42 | 3.84 | 1.00 | 6.69 | 2.3 | 11.5 | 5.1 | 1.0 | 29 | 64 | 159 |
| Woodford,Jake | 18 | R | 22 | a/a | STL | 145 | 5.22 | 1.56 | 22.7 | 3.5 | 5.3 | 1.5 | 1.0 | 32 | 68 | 29 |
| Woodruff,Brandor | 17 | R | 24 | aaa | MIL | 75 | 4.57 | 1.45 | 20.1 | 2.9 | 7.1 | 2.5 | 1.1 | 33 | 71 | 60 |
| | 18 | R | 25 | aaa | MIL | 72 | 4.15 | 1.44 | 18.1 | 3.8 | 7.0 | 1.8 | 1.0 | 31 | 74 | 52 |
| Wotherspoon,Mat | 17 | R | 26 | a/a | BAL | 68 | 2.72 | 1.41 | 7.54 | 4.0 | 8.7 | 2.2 | 0.8 | 32 | 84 | 77 |
| | 18 | R | 27 | aaa | BAL | 94 | 6.57 | 1.79 | 11.1 | 4.2 | 7.6 | 1.8 | 1.8 | 36 | 66 | 22 |
| Wright,Daniel | 17 | R | 26 | aaa | LAA | 93 | 7.26 | 1.69 | 22 | 3.2 | 4.9 | 1.5 | 1.5 | 34 | 58 | 7 |
| | 18 | R | 27 | aa | CIN | 152 | 5.92 | 1.55 | 23.7 | 2.5 | 5.0 | 2.0 | 2.1 | 31 | 68 | 2 |
| Wright,Kyle | 18 | R | 23 | a/a | ATL | 140 | 4.32 | 1.35 | 21.7 | 3.2 | 7.1 | 2.2 | 0.6 | 31 | 68 | 74 |
| Wynkoop,Jack | 17 | L | 24 | aa | COL | 150 | 7.09 | 1.69 | 28.2 | 1.5 | 3.7 | 2.4 | 1.6 | 36 | 60 | 8 |
| | 18 | L | 25 | aa | COL | 82 | 9.76 | 2.21 | 25.9 | 2.1 | 3.1 | 1.5 | 1.8 | 42 | 56 | -32 |
| Yacabonis,Jimmy | 17 | R | 25 | aaa | BAL | 61 | 1.83 | 1.16 | 5.96 | 4.9 | 5.9 | 1.2 | 0.0 | 22 | 82 | 80 |
| | 18 | R | 26 | aaa | BAL | 76 | 5.96 | 1.50 | 15.6 | 4.2 | 5.7 | 1.3 | 1.0 | 30 | 60 | 34 |
| Yamamoto,Jordar | 18 | R | 22 | aa | MIA | 17 | 2.42 | 1.02 | 21.7 | 2.1 | 10.7 | 5.1 | 0.5 | 31 | 78 | 168 |
| Yarbrough,Ryan | 17 | L | 26 | aaa | TAM | 157 | 4.87 | 1.47 | 25.9 | 2.6 | 7.5 | 2.9 | 1.4 | 34 | 71 | 60 |
| Ynoa,Gabriel | 17 | R | 24 | aaa | BAL | 106 | 7.12 | 1.76 | 23.2 | 2.4 | 5.3 | 2.2 | 0.8 | 39 | 58 | 38 |
| Young,Alex | 17 | L | 24 | aa | ARI | 137 | 5.13 | 1.60 | 22.4 | 4.1 | 5.6 | 1.4 | 1.0 | 32 | 69 | 28 |
| | 18 | L | 25 | a/a | ARI | 132 | 5.41 | 1.52 | 19.8 | 2.6 | 6.0 | 2.3 | 0.9 | 35 | 65 | 52 |
| Young,Danny | 17 | L | 23 | aa | TOR | 33 | 5.08 | 1.56 | 6.81 | 4.1 | 5.4 | 1.3 | 0.7 | 32 | 67 | 38 |
| | 18 | L | 24 | aa | TOR | 58 | 5.22 | 1.65 | 6.51 | 3.1 | 6.1 | 2.0 | 0.5 | 37 | 67 | 53 |
| Ysla,Luis | 17 | L | 25 | aa | LA | 58 | 6.43 | 1.86 | 7.55 | 5.8 | 6.7 | 1.2 | 0.5 | 36 | 64 | 43 |
| | 18 | L | 26 | a/a | BAL | 96 | 6.80 | 1.93 | 13.9 | 5.9 | 7.3 | 1.2 | 1.4 | 36 | 66 | 19 |
| Yuhl,Keegan | 17 | R | 25 | aaa | HOU | 20 | 14.87 | 2.71 | 15.5 | 6.2 | 5.1 | 0.8 | 1.6 | 45 | 42 | -29 |
| Zamora,Daniel | 18 | L | 25 | aa | NYM | 53 | 3.97 | 1.12 | 5.25 | 2.9 | 9.8 | 3.4 | 0.5 | 30 | 64 | 125 |
| Zanghi,Joseph | 18 | R | 24 | a/a | NYM | 31 | 5.58 | 1.41 | 6.94 | 3.1 | 6.4 | 2.1 | 0.5 | 32 | 58 | 66 |
| Zastryzny,Rob | 17 | L | 25 | aaa | CHC | 47 | 6.78 | 1.53 | 14.6 | 2.8 | 6.3 | 2.3 | 1.4 | 33 | 56 | 39 |
| | 18 | L | 26 | aaa | CHC | 56 | 4.54 | 1.52 | 7.36 | 4.8 | 6.4 | 1.3 | 0.9 | 30 | 71 | 43 |
| Zeuch,T.J. | 18 | R | 23 | aa | TOR | 120 | 3.92 | 1.45 | 24.4 | 2.4 | 5.1 | 2.1 | 0.6 | 33 | 73 | 53 |
| Zimmer,Kyle | 17 | R | 26 | a/a | KC | 37 | 7.55 | 1.91 | 8.26 | 4.3 | 7.6 | 1.8 | 1.1 | 40 | 60 | 36 |

# LEADERBOARDS

This section provides rankings of projected skills indicators for 2019. Rather than take shots in the dark predicting league leaders in the exact number of home runs, or stolen bases, or strikeouts, the Forecaster's Leaderboards focus on the component elements of each skill.

For batters, we've ranked the top players in terms of pure power, speed, and batting average skill, breaking each down in a number of different ways. For pitchers, we rank some of the key base skills, differentiating between starters and relievers, and provide a few interesting cuts that might uncover some late round sleepers. Plus, some potential gainers/faders lists in several categories.

These are clearly not exhaustive lists of sorts and filters—drop us a note if you see something we should consider for next year's book. Also, the database at BaseballHQ.com allows you to construct your own custom sorts and filters. Finally, remember that these are just tools. Some players will appear on multiple lists—even mutually exclusive lists—so you have to assess what makes most sense and make decisions for your specific application.

## Power

**Top PX, 400+ AB:** Top power skills among projected full-time players.

**Top PX, -300 AB:** Top power skills among projected part-time players; possible end-game options are here.

**Position Scarcity:** See which positions have deepest power options.

**Top PX, ct% over 80%:** Top power skills among the top contact hitters. Best pure power options here.

**Top PX, ct% under 70%:** Top power skills among the worst contact hitters; free-swingers who might be prone to streakiness and lower BAs.

**Top PX, FB% over 40%:** Top power skills among the most extreme fly ball hitters. Most likely to convert their power into home runs.

**Top PX, FB% under 35%:** Top power skills among those with lesser fly ball tendencies. There may be more downside to their home run potential.

## Speed

**Top Spd, 400+ AB:** Top speed skills among projected full-time players.

**Top Spd, -300 AB:** Top speed skills among projected part-time players; possible end-game options here.

**Position Scarcity:** See which positions have deepest speed options.

**Top Spd, OB% .330 and above:** Top speed skills among those who get on base most often. Best opportunities for stolen bases here.

**Top Spd, OB% under .300:** Top speed skills among those who have trouble getting on base; worth watching if they can improve OB%.

**Top Spd, SBO% over 20%:** Top speed skills among those who get the green light most often. Most likely to convert their speed into stolen bases.

**Top Spd, SBO% under 15%:** Top speed skills among those who are currently not running; sleeper SBs here if given more opportunities.

## Batting Average

**Top ct%, 400+ AB:** Top contact skills among projected full-time players. Contact is strongly correlated to higher BAs.

**Top ct%, -300 AB:** Top contact skills among projected part-time players; possible end-gamers here.

**Low ct%, 400+ AB:** The poorest contact skills among projected full-time players. Potential BA killers.

**Top ct%, bb% over 9%:** Top contact skills among the most patient hitters. Best batting average upside here.

**Top ct%, bb% under 6%:** Top contact skills among the least patient hitters; free-swingers who might be prone to streakiness or lower BAs.

**Top ct%, GB% over 50%:** Top contact skills among the most extreme ground ball hitters. A ground ball has a higher chance of becoming a hit than a non-HR fly ball so there may be some batting average upside here.

**Top ct%, GB% under 40%:** Top contact skills from those with lesser ground ball tendencies. These players make contact but hit more fly balls, which tend to convert to hits at a lower rate than GB.

## Potential Gainers and Faders

These charts look to identify upcoming changes in performance by highlighting 2018 results that were in conflict with their corresponding skill indicators. Use these as a check on recency bias, as players here could compile stats in the upcoming season that look every different than the one just completed. Additional details are provided on the page in which the charts appear.

## Pitching Skills

**Top Command:** Leaders in projected K/BB rates.

**Top Control:** Leaders in fewest projected walks allowed.

**Top Dominance:** Leaders in projected strikeout rate.

**Top Ground Ball Rate:** GB pitchers tend to have lower ERAs (and higher WHIP) than fly ball pitchers.

**Top Fly Ball Rate:** FB pitchers tend to have higher ERAs (and lower WHIP) than ground ball pitchers.

**High GB, Low Dom:** GB pitchers tend to have lower K rates, but these are the most extreme examples.

**High GB, High Dom:** The best at dominating hitters and keeping the ball down. These are the pitchers who keep runners off the bases and batted balls in the park, a skills combination that is the most valuable a pitcher can own.

**Lowest xERA:** Leaders in projected skills-based ERA.

**Top BPV:** Two lists of top skilled pitchers. For starters, those projected to be rotation regulars (180+ IP) and fringe starters with skill (<150 IP). For relievers, those projected to be frontline closers (10+ saves) and high-skilled bullpen fillers (<9 saves).

## Risk Management

These lists include players who've accumulated the most days on the disabled list over the past five years (Grade "F" in Health) and whose performance was the most consistent over the past three years. Also listed are the most reliable batters and pitchers overall, with a focus on positional and skills reliability. As a reminder, reliability in this context is not tied to skill level; it is a gauge of which players manage to accumulate playing time and post consistent output from year to year, whether that output is good or bad.

## Daily Fantasy Indicators

Players splits, teams and park factors designed to give you an edge in DFS.

## BATTER SKILLS RANKING - Power

### TOP PX, 400+ AB

| NAME | POS | PX |
|---|---|---|
| Gallo,Joey | 3 7 | 228 |
| Judge,Aaron | 9 | 184 |
| Martinez,J.D. | 0 7 9 | 182 |
| Davis,Khristopher | 0 | 179 |
| Stanton,Giancarlo | 0 7 9 | 176 |
| Story,Trevor | 6 | 175 |
| Trout,Mike | 8 | 173 |
| Ohtani,Shohei | 0 | 168 |
| Hoskins,Rhys | 7 | 161 |
| Grichuk,Randal | 8 9 | 158 |
| Sano,Miguel | 5 | 157 |
| O'Neill,Tyler | 9 | 155 |
| Aguilar,Jesus | 3 | 154 |
| Schwarber,Kyle | 7 | 154 |
| Harper,Bryce | 8 9 | 152 |
| Renfroe,Hunter | 7 9 | 151 |
| Carpenter,Matt | 3 5 | 150 |
| Olson,Matt | 3 | 149 |
| Goldschmidt,Paul | 3 | 149 |
| Hernandez,Teoscar | 7 9 | 148 |
| Chapman,Matt | 5 | 148 |
| Pederson,Joc | 7 8 | 147 |
| Arenado,Nolan | 5 | 147 |
| Happ,Ian | 7 8 9 | 147 |
| Grandal,Yasmani | 2 | 145 |
| Sanchez,Gary | 2 | 145 |
| Donaldson,Josh | 5 | 145 |
| Muncy,Max | 3 5 | 145 |
| Upton,Justin | 7 | 143 |
| Bryant,Kris | 5 | 143 |
| Acuna,Ronald | 7 | 143 |
| Conforto,Michael | 7 8 | 143 |
| Cespedes,Yoenis | 7 | 142 |
| Baez,Javier | 4 5 6 | 141 |
| Smoak,Justin | 3 | 141 |
| Dahl,David | 7 9 | 139 |
| Ramirez,Jose | 5 | 139 |
| DeJong,Paul | 6 | 138 |
| Voit,Luke | 3 | 137 |
| Bruce,Jay | 3 9 | 136 |

### TOP PX, 300 or fewer AB

| NAME | POS | PX |
|---|---|---|
| Austin,Tyler | 0 3 | 171 |
| Broxton,Keon | 8 9 | 141 |
| Marisnick,Jake | 8 | 141 |
| Reed,A.J. | 3 | 140 |
| Reynolds,Mark | 3 | 136 |
| Duda,Lucas | 0 3 | 134 |
| Duvall,Adam | 7 | 129 |
| Granderson,Curtis | 0 7 9 | 129 |
| Riley,Austin | 0 | 129 |
| Cooper,Garrett | 7 | 128 |
| Wisdom,Patrick | 5 | 128 |
| Tellez,Rowdy | 3 | 125 |
| Vogelbach,Daniel | 3 | 125 |
| Avila,Alex | 2 | 125 |
| Smith,Dominic | 3 | 124 |
| Altherr,Aaron | 9 | 123 |
| Dixon,Brandon | 3 | 122 |
| Pearce,Steve | 0 3 | 122 |
| Tatis Jr.,Fernando | 0 | 121 |
| Bichette,Bo | 6 | 120 |
| Field,Johnny | 7 9 | 118 |
| Williamson,Mac | 7 | 117 |
| Canha,Mark | 7 8 | 116 |

### POSITIONAL SCARCITY

| NAME | POS | PX |
|---|---|---|
| Martinez,J.D. | DH | 182 |
| Davis,Khristopher | 2 | 179 |
| Stanton,Giancarlo | 3 | 176 |
| Austin,Tyler | 4 | 171 |
| Ohtani,Shohei | 5 | 168 |
| Davidson,Matthew | 6 | 147 |
| Zunino,Mike | CA | 164 |
| Grandal,Yasmani | 2 | 145 |
| Sanchez,Gary | 3 | 145 |
| Chirinos,Robinson | 4 | 136 |
| Murphy,Tom | 5 | 130 |
| Avila,Alex | 6 | 125 |
| Hedges,Austin | 7 | 124 |
| Mejia,Francisco | 8 | 121 |
| Gallo,Joey | 1B | 228 |
| Austin,Tyler | 2 | 171 |
| Thames,Eric | 3 | 168 |
| Aguilar,Jesus | 4 | 154 |
| Carpenter,Matt | 5 | 150 |
| Olson,Matt | 6 | 149 |
| Goldschmidt,Paul | 7 | 149 |
| Davidson,Matthew | 8 | 147 |
| Muncy,Max | 9 | 145 |
| Smoak,Justin | 10 | 141 |
| Barreto,Franklin | 2B | 143 |
| Baez,Javier | 2 | 141 |
| Shaw,Travis | 3 | 134 |
| Lowe,Brandon | 4 | 129 |
| Torres,Gleyber | 5 | 123 |
| Dozier,Brian | 6 | 122 |
| Moncada,Yoan | 7 | 120 |
| Pinder,Chad | 8 | 117 |
| Sano,Miguel | 3B | 157 |
| Carpenter,Matt | 2 | 150 |
| Chapman,Matt | 3 | 148 |
| Arenado,Nolan | 4 | 147 |
| Donaldson,Josh | 5 | 145 |
| Muncy,Max | 6 | 145 |
| Bryant,Kris | 7 | 143 |
| Baez,Javier | 8 | 141 |
| Ramirez,Jose | 9 | 139 |
| Shaw,Travis | 10 | 134 |
| Story,Trevor | SS | 175 |
| Baez,Javier | 2 | 141 |
| DeJong,Paul | 3 | 138 |
| Bregman,Alex | 4 | 130 |
| Lindor,Francisco | 5 | 123 |
| Machado,Manny | 6 | 123 |
| Torres,Gleyber | 7 | 123 |
| Taylor,Chris | 8 | 121 |
| Gallo,Joey | OF | 228 |
| Judge,Aaron | 2 | 184 |
| Martinez,J.D. | 3 | 182 |
| Stanton,Giancarlo | 4 | 176 |
| Trout,Mike | 5 | 173 |
| Thames,Eric | 6 | 168 |
| Hoskins,Rhys | 7 | 161 |
| Grichuk,Randal | 8 | 158 |
| O'Neill,Tyler | 9 | 155 |
| Schwarber,Kyle | 10 | 154 |
| Harper,Bryce | 11 | 152 |
| Renfroe,Hunter | 12 | 151 |
| Hernandez,Teoscar | 13 | 148 |
| Pederson,Joc | 14 | 147 |
| Happ,Ian | 15 | 147 |
| Upton,Justin | 16 | 143 |

### TOP PX, ct% over 75%

| NAME | Ct% | PX |
|---|---|---|
| Arenado,Nolan | 81 | 147 |
| Donaldson,Josh | 76 | 145 |
| Ramirez,Jose | 87 | 139 |
| Bruce,Jay | 75 | 136 |
| Freeman,Freddie | 77 | 134 |
| Betts,Mookie | 85 | 134 |
| Encarnacion,Edwin | 76 | 134 |
| Shaw,Travis | 76 | 134 |
| Adams,Matt | 75 | 131 |
| Cruz,Nelson | 75 | 130 |
| Bregman,Alex | 84 | 130 |
| Castellanos,Nick | 75 | 129 |
| Braun,Ryan | 80 | 128 |
| Yelich,Christian | 77 | 127 |
| Hicks,Aaron | 78 | 126 |
| Andujar,Miguel | 84 | 126 |
| Soto,Juan | 76 | 126 |
| Turner,Justin | 85 | 126 |
| Pollock,A.J. | 80 | 125 |
| Gattis,Evan | 77 | 125 |
| Haniger,Mitch | 76 | 125 |
| Tellez,Rowdy | 78 | 125 |
| Puig,Yasiel | 79 | 125 |
| Blackmon,Charlie | 80 | 124 |
| Lindor,Francisco | 85 | 123 |
| Machado,Manny | 82 | 123 |
| Pearce,Steve | 80 | 122 |
| Dozier,Brian | 77 | 122 |
| Zimmerman,Ryan | 79 | 122 |
| Moreland,Mitch | 75 | 122 |
| Rendon,Anthony | 83 | 121 |
| Piscotty,Stephen | 78 | 121 |
| Gonzalez,Carlos | 76 | 121 |
| Abreu,Jose | 78 | 121 |
| Mejia,Francisco | 79 | 121 |
| Bichette,Bo | 80 | 120 |
| Senzel,Nick | 75 | 120 |
| Moustakas,Mike | 83 | 120 |
| Polanco,Gregory | 78 | 119 |
| Bogaerts,Xander | 80 | 118 |

### TOP PX, ct% under 70%

| NAME | Ct% | PX |
|---|---|---|
| Gallo,Joey | 57 | 228 |
| Judge,Aaron | 64 | 184 |
| Davis,Khristopher | 69 | 179 |
| Stanton,Giancarlo | 68 | 176 |
| Story,Trevor | 68 | 175 |
| Austin,Tyler | 64 | 171 |
| Thames,Eric | 66 | 168 |
| Ohtani,Shohei | 70 | 168 |
| Zunino,Mike | 62 | 164 |
| Grichuk,Randal | 70 | 158 |
| Sano,Miguel | 59 | 157 |
| O'Neill,Tyler | 60 | 155 |
| Schwarber,Kyle | 66 | 154 |
| Hernandez,Teoscar | 67 | 148 |
| Chapman,Matt | 69 | 148 |
| Davidson,Matthew | 62 | 147 |
| Happ,Ian | 63 | 147 |
| Muncy,Max | 69 | 145 |
| Upton,Justin | 68 | 143 |
| Barreto,Franklin | 65 | 143 |
| Broxton,Keon | 57 | 141 |
| Cordero,Franchy | 65 | 141 |
| Marisnick,Jake | 66 | 141 |

### Top PX, FB% over 40%

| NAME | FB% | PX |
|---|---|---|
| Gallo,Joey | 49 | 228 |
| Davis,Khristopher | 45 | 179 |
| Story,Trevor | 45 | 175 |
| Trout,Mike | 45 | 173 |
| Thames,Eric | 44 | 168 |
| Zunino,Mike | 46 | 164 |
| Hoskins,Rhys | 49 | 161 |
| Grichuk,Randal | 45 | 158 |
| Sano,Miguel | 41 | 157 |
| O'Neill,Tyler | 45 | 155 |
| Schwarber,Kyle | 41 | 154 |
| Carpenter,Matt | 46 | 150 |
| Olson,Matt | 44 | 149 |
| Hernandez,Teoscar | 46 | 148 |
| Chapman,Matt | 44 | 148 |
| Pederson,Joc | 40 | 147 |
| Arenado,Nolan | 42 | 147 |
| Davidson,Matthew | 43 | 147 |
| Grandal,Yasmani | 42 | 145 |
| Muncy,Max | 43 | 145 |
| Bryant,Kris | 43 | 143 |
| Barreto,Franklin | 47 | 143 |
| Cespedes,Yoenis | 47 | 142 |
| Smoak,Justin | 42 | 141 |
| Marisnick,Jake | 44 | 141 |
| Bird,Gregory | 50 | 140 |
| Reed,A.J. | 46 | 140 |
| Ramirez,Jose | 42 | 139 |
| DeJong,Paul | 43 | 138 |
| Bruce,Jay | 47 | 136 |
| Chirinos,Robinson | 47 | 136 |
| Bellinger,Cody | 42 | 136 |
| Duda,Lucas | 46 | 134 |
| Betts,Mookie | 43 | 134 |
| Encarnacion,Edwin | 43 | 134 |
| Shaw,Travis | 43 | 134 |
| Belt,Brandon | 46 | 132 |
| Cron,C.J. | 40 | 132 |
| Adams,Matt | 45 | 131 |

### Top PX, FB% under 35%

| NAME | FB% | PX |
|---|---|---|
| Ohtani,Shohei | 33 | 168 |
| Goldschmidt,Paul | 35 | 149 |
| Broxton,Keon | 30 | 141 |
| Baez,Javier | 34 | 141 |
| Cordero,Franchy | 31 | 141 |
| Santana,Domingo | 27 | 135 |
| Freeman,Freddie | 35 | 134 |
| Cave,Jake | 31 | 131 |
| Nimmo,Brandon | 33 | 131 |
| Lowe,Brandon | 35 | 129 |
| Lamb,Jake | 35 | 128 |
| Braun,Ryan | 29 | 128 |
| Myers,Wil | 34 | 128 |
| Reyes,Franmil | 30 | 128 |
| Yelich,Christian | 25 | 127 |
| Pham,Thomas | 28 | 126 |
| Soto,Juan | 30 | 126 |
| Avila,Alex | 30 | 125 |
| Blackmon,Charlie | 34 | 124 |
| Altherr,Aaron | 35 | 123 |
| Schebler,Scott | 33 | 123 |
| Dixon,Brandon | 33 | 122 |
| Zimmerman,Ryan | 34 | 122 |

## BATTER SKILLS RANKING - Speed

### TOP Spd, 400+ AB

| NAME | POS | Spd |
|---|---|---|
| Hamilton,Billy | 8 | 186 |
| Gordon,Dee | 4 8 | 183 |
| Rosario,Amed | 6 | 164 |
| Smith,Mallex | 7 8 9 | 164 |
| Hernandez,Cesar | 4 | 163 |
| Adames,Willy | 6 | 156 |
| Hernandez,Teoscar | 7 9 | 151 |
| Turner,Trea | 6 | 150 |
| Taylor,Chris | 6 7 8 | 147 |
| Margot,Manuel | 8 | 146 |
| Difo,Wilmer | 4 5 | 146 |
| McNeil,Jeff | 4 | 146 |
| Brinson,Lewis | 8 | 145 |
| Marte,Ketel | 4 6 | 145 |
| Mondesi,Adalberto | 6 | 144 |
| Eaton,Adam | 9 | 144 |
| Robles,Victor | 8 | 144 |
| Anderson,Tim | 6 | 143 |
| Duggar,Steven | 8 | 141 |
| Gardner,Brett | 7 8 | 141 |
| Marte,Starling | 8 | 140 |
| Cain,Lorenzo | 8 | 139 |
| Baez,Javier | 4 5 6 | 139 |
| Pham,Thomas | 7 8 | 137 |
| Albies,Ozzie | 4 | 137 |
| Arcia,Orlando | 6 | 137 |
| Bader,Harrison | 8 9 | 136 |
| Moncada,Yoan | 4 | 136 |
| Desmond,Ian | 3 | 133 |
| Acuna,Ronald | 7 | 132 |
| Peraza,Jose | 6 | 131 |
| Pollock,A.J. | 8 | 131 |
| Inciarte,Ender | 8 | 130 |
| Kingery,Scott | 6 | 130 |
| Betts,Mookie | 9 | 130 |
| Bellinger,Cody | 3 8 | 129 |
| O'Neill,Tyler | 9 | 129 |
| Segura,Jean | 6 | 129 |
| Blackmon,Charlie | 8 | 128 |
| Andrus,Elvis | 6 | 127 |

### TOP Spd, 300 or fewer AB

| NAME | POS | Spd |
|---|---|---|
| Quinn,Roman | 8 | 183 |
| Sierra,Magneuris | 8 | 158 |
| Andreoli,John | 7 | 154 |
| Engel,Adam | 8 | 146 |
| Jankowski,Travis | 7 8 9 | 145 |
| Broxton,Keon | 8 9 | 142 |
| Lagares,Juan | 8 | 142 |
| Spangenberg,Cory | 4 5 | 139 |
| Perez,Michael | 2 | 139 |
| Tapia,Raimel | 8 | 139 |
| Reyes,Victor | 0 7 8 | 138 |
| Mahtook,Mikie | 7 | 137 |
| Davis,Rajai | 7 8 | 131 |
| Cuevas,Noel | 9 | 130 |
| Marisnick,Jake | 8 | 128 |
| Dyson,Jarrod | 8 | 128 |
| Tatis Jr.,Fernando | 0 | 127 |
| Tilson,Charlie | 7 | 126 |
| Pence,Hunter | 7 | 125 |
| Perez,Hernan | 4 5 9 | 124 |
| Lugo,Dawel | 4 | 123 |
| Gonzalez,Erik | 4 5 | 123 |
| Taylor,Michael | 8 | 123 |

### POSITIONAL SCARCITY

| NAME | POS | Spd |
|---|---|---|
| Reyes,Victor | DH | 138 |
| Tatis Jr.,Fernando | 2 | 127 |
| Diaz,Yandy | 3 | 126 |
| Hiura,Keston | 4 | 118 |
| Ellsbury,Jacoby | 5 | 118 |
| Ohtani,Shohei | 6 | 117 |
| Perez,Michael | CA | 139 |
| Alfaro,Jorge | 2 | 124 |
| Joseph,Caleb | 3 | 121 |
| Knapp,Andrew | 4 | 119 |
| Barnes,Austin | 5 | 116 |
| Realmuto,Jacob | 6 | 115 |
| Jansen,Danny | 7 | 114 |
| Swihart,Blake | 8 | 108 |
| Desmond,Ian | 1B | 133 |
| Bellinger,Cody | 2 | 129 |
| Goodrum,Niko | 3 | 123 |
| Miller,Bradley | 4 | 113 |
| Dixon,Brandon | 5 | 110 |
| Profar,Jurickson | 6 | 108 |
| Goldschmidt,Paul | 7 | 108 |
| Slater,Austin | 8 | 106 |
| Gurriel,Yulieski | 9 | 105 |
| Voit,Luke | 10 | 105 |
| Gordon,Dee | 2B | 183 |
| Hernandez,Cesar | 2 | 163 |
| Hanson,Alen | 3 | 155 |
| Barreto,Franklin | 4 | 147 |
| Difo,Wilmer | 5 | 146 |
| McNeil,Jeff | 6 | 146 |
| Marte,Ketel | 7 | 145 |
| Spangenberg,Cory | 8 | 139 |
| Difo,Wilmer | 3B | 146 |
| Spangenberg,Cory | 2 | 139 |
| Baez,Javier | 3 | 139 |
| Duffy,Matt | 4 | 126 |
| Perez,Hernan | 5 | 124 |
| Gonzalez,Erik | 6 | 123 |
| Nunez,Eduardo | 7 | 122 |
| Beckham,Tim | 8 | 122 |
| Anderson,Brian | 9 | 121 |
| Sanchez,Yolmer | 10 | 120 |
| Rosario,Amed | SS | 164 |
| Adames,Willy | 2 | 156 |
| Hampson,Garrett | 3 | 155 |
| Turner,Trea | 4 | 150 |
| Taylor,Chris | 5 | 147 |
| Marte,Ketel | 6 | 145 |
| Mondesi,Adalberto | 7 | 144 |
| Anderson,Tim | 8 | 143 |
| Hamilton,Billy | OF | 186 |
| Gordon,Dee | 2 | 183 |
| Quinn,Roman | 3 | 183 |
| Smith,Mallex | 4 | 164 |
| Buxton,Byron | 5 | 160 |
| Sierra,Magneuris | 6 | 158 |
| Andreoli,John | 7 | 154 |
| Hernandez,Teoscar | 8 | 151 |
| Cordero,Franchy | 9 | 149 |
| Taylor,Chris | 10 | 147 |
| Engel,Adam | 11 | 146 |
| Phillips,Brett | 12 | 146 |
| Margot,Manuel | 13 | 146 |
| Brinson,Lewis | 14 | 145 |
| Jankowski,Travis | 15 | 145 |
| Eaton,Adam | 16 | 144 |

### TOP Spd, .330+ OBP

| NAME | OBP | Spd |
|---|---|---|
| Smith,Mallex | 351 | 164 |
| Hernandez,Cesar | 355 | 163 |
| Hampson,Garrett | 340 | 155 |
| Turner,Trea | 337 | 150 |
| McNeil,Jeff | 335 | 146 |
| Marte,Ketel | 336 | 145 |
| Eaton,Adam | 384 | 144 |
| Robles,Victor | 344 | 144 |
| Gardner,Brett | 340 | 141 |
| Marte,Starling | 336 | 140 |
| Cain,Lorenzo | 373 | 139 |
| Pham,Thomas | 366 | 137 |
| Moncada,Yoan | 332 | 136 |
| Acuna,Ronald | 345 | 132 |
| Inciarte,Ender | 336 | 130 |
| Betts,Mookie | 398 | 130 |
| Bellinger,Cody | 347 | 129 |
| Segura,Jean | 338 | 129 |
| Blackmon,Charlie | 367 | 128 |
| Frazier,Clint | 330 | 128 |
| Duffy,Matt | 338 | 126 |
| Altuve,Jose | 390 | 126 |
| Diaz,Yandy | 365 | 126 |
| Gamel,Benjamin | 336 | 123 |
| Nimmo,Brandon | 377 | 122 |
| Merrifield,Whit | 344 | 122 |
| Trout,Mike | 443 | 122 |
| Anderson,Brian | 337 | 121 |
| Yelich,Christian | 385 | 121 |
| Fowler,Dexter | 343 | 120 |
| Castellanos,Nick | 337 | 120 |
| Story,Trevor | 331 | 119 |
| Urias,Luis | 351 | 119 |
| LeMahieu,DJ | 341 | 118 |
| Ohtani,Shohei | 354 | 117 |
| Bryant,Kris | 381 | 117 |
| Chapman,Matt | 330 | 116 |
| Barnes,Austin | 343 | 116 |
| Benintendi,Andrew | 356 | 115 |
| Springer,George | 356 | 115 |

### TOP Spd, OBP under .300

| NAME | OBP | Spd |
|---|---|---|
| Hamilton,Billy | 297 | 186 |
| Buxton,Byron | 292 | 160 |
| Sierra,Magneuris | 266 | 158 |
| Hanson,Alen | 280 | 155 |
| Andreoli,John | 294 | 154 |
| Engel,Adam | 268 | 146 |
| Phillips,Brett | 297 | 146 |
| Margot,Manuel | 298 | 146 |
| Brinson,Lewis | 278 | 145 |
| Mondesi,Adalberto | 289 | 144 |
| Anderson,Tim | 282 | 143 |
| Broxton,Keon | 277 | 142 |
| Perez,Michael | 271 | 139 |
| Jones,JaCoby | 280 | 139 |
| Reyes,Victor | 263 | 138 |
| Arcia,Orlando | 296 | 137 |
| Mahtook,Mikie | 287 | 137 |
| Davis,Rajai | 275 | 131 |
| Kingery,Scott | 279 | 130 |
| Cuevas,Noel | 290 | 130 |
| Marisnick,Jake | 286 | 128 |
| Tilson,Charlie | 286 | 126 |
| Hechavarria,Adeiny | 285 | 126 |

### Top Spd, SBO% over 20%

| NAME | SBO% | Spd |
|---|---|---|
| Hamilton,Billy | 41% | 186 |
| Gordon,Dee | 38% | 183 |
| Quinn,Roman | 40% | 183 |
| Rosario,Amed | 27% | 164 |
| Smith,Mallex | 38% | 164 |
| Buxton,Byron | 21% | 160 |
| Sierra,Magneuris | 21% | 158 |
| Hampson,Garrett | 25% | 155 |
| Hanson,Alen | 29% | 155 |
| Andreoli,John | 25% | 154 |
| Turner,Trea | 35% | 150 |
| Cordero,Franchy | 24% | 149 |
| Engel,Adam | 28% | 146 |
| Margot,Manuel | 23% | 146 |
| Jankowski,Travis | 29% | 145 |
| Mondesi,Adalberto | 39% | 144 |
| Robles,Victor | 32% | 144 |
| Anderson,Tim | 26% | 143 |
| Broxton,Keon | 31% | 142 |
| Duggar,Steven | 21% | 141 |
| Marte,Starling | 35% | 140 |
| Kiermaier,Kevin | 22% | 140 |
| Tapia,Raimel | 20% | 139 |
| Jones,JaCoby | 24% | 139 |
| Reyes,Victor | 24% | 138 |
| Meadows,Austin | 20% | 134 |
| Acuna,Ronald | 20% | 132 |
| Davis,Rajai | 47% | 131 |
| Peraza,Jose | 25% | 131 |
| DeShields Jr.,Delino | 30% | 131 |
| Marisnick,Jake | 30% | 128 |
| Martin,Leonys | 25% | 128 |
| Dyson,Jarrod | 38% | 128 |
| Tilson,Charlie | 24% | 126 |
| Fowler,Dustin | 26% | 125 |
| Perez,Hernan | 21% | 124 |
| Taylor,Michael | 28% | 123 |
| Merrifield,Whit | 27% | 122 |
| Allen,Greg | 34% | 120 |
| Hiura,Keston | 22% | 118 |

### Top Spd, SBO% under 15%

| NAME | SBO% | Spd |
|---|---|---|
| Hernandez,Cesar | 13% | 163 |
| Adames,Willy | 11% | 156 |
| Hernandez,Teoscar | 14% | 151 |
| Taylor,Chris | 10% | 147 |
| Phillips,Brett | 12% | 146 |
| McNeil,Jeff | 9% | 146 |
| Brinson,Lewis | 13% | 145 |
| Marte,Ketel | 9% | 145 |
| Eaton,Adam | 10% | 144 |
| Gardner,Brett | 13% | 141 |
| Spangenberg,Cory | 14% | 139 |
| Perez,Michael | 3% | 139 |
| Arcia,Orlando | 14% | 137 |
| Mahtook,Mikie | 12% | 137 |
| Cuevas,Noel | 15% | 130 |
| Bellinger,Cody | 13% | 129 |
| O'Neill,Tyler | 9% | 129 |
| Blackmon,Charlie | 11% | 128 |
| Frazier,Clint | 11% | 128 |
| Duffy,Matt | 12% | 126 |
| Diaz,Yandy | 5% | 126 |
| Hechavarria,Adeiny | 4% | 126 |
| Pence,Hunter | 7% | 125 |

# BATTER SKILLS RANKING - Batting Average

### TOP ct%, 400+ AB

| NAME | Ct% | BA |
|---|---|---|
| Simmons,Andrelton | 91 | 281 |
| Panik,Joe | 90 | 276 |
| Brantley,Michael | 89 | 301 |
| Iglesias,Jose | 89 | 266 |
| Gurriel,Yulieski | 88 | 286 |
| Murphy,Daniel | 87 | 295 |
| Ramirez,Jose | 87 | 287 |
| Peraza,Jose | 87 | 279 |
| Segura,Jean | 87 | 294 |
| Nunez,Eduardo | 87 | 280 |
| McNeil,Jeff | 87 | 276 |
| Altuve,Jose | 86 | 326 |
| Molina,Yadier | 86 | 273 |
| Inciarte,Ender | 86 | 283 |
| Zobrist,Ben | 86 | 273 |
| Solarte,Yangervis | 86 | 250 |
| Markakis,Nick | 85 | 277 |
| Gordon,Dee | 85 | 284 |
| Cano,Robinson | 85 | 297 |
| Kinsler,Ian | 85 | 255 |
| Turner,Justin | 85 | 307 |
| Heyward,Jason | 85 | 260 |
| Betts,Mookie | 85 | 318 |
| Lucroy,Jonathan | 85 | 256 |
| Lindor,Francisco | 85 | 286 |
| LeMahieu,DJ | 85 | 286 |
| Frazier,Adam | 85 | 269 |
| Andrus,Elvis | 85 | 271 |
| Span,Denard | 84 | 269 |
| Escobar,Alcides | 84 | 253 |
| Franco,Maikel | 84 | 258 |
| Rizzo,Anthony | 84 | 284 |
| Marte,Ketel | 84 | 276 |
| Guerrero Jr.,Vladimir | 84 | 294 |
| Diaz,Aledmys | 84 | 269 |
| Bregman,Alex | 84 | 285 |
| Profar,Jurickson | 84 | 266 |
| Reddick,Josh | 84 | 266 |
| Andujar,Miguel | 84 | 294 |
| Winker,Jesse | 84 | 296 |
| Rendon,Anthony | 83 | 298 |
| Moustakas,Mike | 83 | 264 |
| Wendle,Joe | 83 | 270 |
| Santana,Carlos | 83 | 242 |
| Jones,Adam | 83 | 278 |
| Pillar,Kevin | 83 | 258 |
| Cozart,Zack | 82 | 251 |
| Machado,Manny | 82 | 285 |
| Merrifield,Whit | 82 | 293 |
| Duffy,Matt | 82 | 275 |
| Almora,Albert | 82 | 273 |
| Cain,Lorenzo | 82 | 304 |
| Margot,Manuel | 82 | 254 |
| Robles,Victor | 82 | 279 |
| Benintendi,Andrew | 82 | 284 |
| Polanco,Jorge | 82 | 272 |
| Arenado,Nolan | 81 | 297 |
| Ramos,Wilson | 81 | 269 |
| Dickerson,Corey | 81 | 292 |
| Mullins II,Cedric | 81 | 243 |
| Albies,Ozzie | 81 | 267 |
| Eaton,Adam | 81 | 296 |
| Barnhart,Tucker | 80 | 257 |
| Kepler,Max | 80 | 247 |
| Mercer,Jordy | 80 | 252 |
| Lowrie,Jed | 80 | 262 |

### LOW ct%, 400+ AB

| NAME | Ct% | BA |
|---|---|---|
| Gallo,Joey | 57 | 209 |
| Sano,Miguel | 59 | 227 |
| Davis,Chris | 59 | 207 |
| O'Neill,Tyler | 60 | 239 |
| Alfaro,Jorge | 62 | 243 |
| Moncada,Yoan | 62 | 243 |
| Happ,Ian | 63 | 239 |
| Dozier,Hunter | 64 | 221 |
| Judge,Aaron | 64 | 273 |
| Schwarber,Kyle | 66 | 235 |
| Souza,Steven | 66 | 241 |
| Hernandez,Teoscar | 67 | 238 |
| Upton,Justin | 68 | 260 |
| Stanton,Giancarlo | 68 | 267 |
| Story,Trevor | 68 | 271 |
| Soler,Jorge | 68 | 245 |
| Lamb,Jake | 69 | 247 |
| Bader,Harrison | 69 | 241 |
| Davis,Khristopher | 69 | 247 |
| Muncy,Max | 69 | 249 |
| Chapman,Matt | 69 | 251 |
| Nimmo,Brandon | 69 | 260 |
| Taylor,Chris | 70 | 250 |
| Adames,Willy | 70 | 253 |
| Villar,Jonathan | 70 | 256 |
| Ohtani,Shohei | 70 | 282 |
| Reyes,Franmil | 70 | 258 |
| Grichuk,Randal | 70 | 241 |
| Flowers,Tyler | 70 | 248 |
| Beckham,Tim | 70 | 248 |
| Duggar,Steven | 70 | 246 |
| Laureano,Ramon | 70 | 247 |
| Mondesi,Adalberto | 70 | 257 |
| Smoak,Justin | 70 | 244 |
| Olson,Matt | 71 | 253 |
| Pham,Thomas | 71 | 274 |

### TOP ct%, 300 or fewer AB

| NAME | Ct% | BA |
|---|---|---|
| Astudillo,Willians | 95 | 277 |
| Pedroia,Dustin | 87 | 295 |
| Fernandez,Jose M. | 87 | 264 |
| Suzuki,Kurt | 87 | 269 |
| Cabrera,Melky | 86 | 278 |
| Lugo,Dawel | 86 | 257 |
| Newman,Kevin | 86 | 247 |
| Kiner-Falefa,Isiah | 85 | 267 |
| Rivera,T.J. | 84 | 270 |
| Dyson,Jarrod | 84 | 239 |
| Heredia,Guillermo | 84 | 241 |
| Reyes,Jose | 83 | 221 |
| Smith,Kevan | 83 | 249 |
| Ellsbury,Jacoby | 83 | 262 |
| Diaz,Elias | 82 | 258 |
| Kelly,Carson | 82 | 229 |
| D'Arnaud,Travis | 82 | 252 |
| Kemp,Anthony | 82 | 250 |
| Parra,Gerardo | 81 | 280 |
| Cuevas,Noel | 81 | 257 |
| Lagares,Juan | 81 | 268 |
| Jay,Jon | 81 | 271 |
| Tapia,Raimel | 81 | 289 |
| Bichette,Bo | 80 | 287 |
| Osuna,Jose | 80 | 249 |
| Pirela,Jose | 80 | 239 |
| Tulowitzki,Troy | 80 | 255 |

### TOP ct%, bb% over 9%

| NAME | bb% | Ct% |
|---|---|---|
| Pedroia,Dustin | 9 | 87 |
| Ramirez,Jose | 12 | 87 |
| Posey,Buster | 10 | 87 |
| Zobrist,Ben | 11 | 86 |
| Markakis,Nick | 10 | 85 |
| Turner,Justin | 10 | 85 |
| Betts,Mookie | 11 | 85 |
| Lindor,Francisco | 9 | 85 |
| Rizzo,Anthony | 11 | 84 |
| Guerrero Jr.,Vladimir | 9 | 84 |
| Bregman,Alex | 12 | 84 |
| Profar,Jurickson | 10 | 84 |
| Reddick,Josh | 9 | 84 |
| Winker,Jesse | 13 | 84 |
| Rendon,Anthony | 11 | 83 |
| Santana,Carlos | 15 | 83 |
| Cain,Lorenzo | 9 | 82 |
| Benintendi,Andrew | 10 | 82 |
| Kelly,Carson | 9 | 82 |
| Arenado,Nolan | 10 | 81 |
| Jansen,Danny | 11 | 81 |
| Eaton,Adam | 11 | 81 |
| Barnhart,Tucker | 10 | 80 |
| Kepler,Max | 10 | 80 |
| Lowrie,Jed | 11 | 80 |
| Bell,Josh | 12 | 80 |
| Votto,Joey | 17 | 80 |
| Narvaez,Omar | 12 | 80 |
| McCann,Brian | 10 | 80 |
| Wieters,Matt | 10 | 80 |
| Cabrera,Miguel | 12 | 80 |
| Pearce,Steve | 10 | 80 |
| Gardner,Brett | 11 | 79 |
| Hernandez,Enrique | 11 | 79 |
| Holt,Brock | 10 | 79 |
| Kieboom,Spencer | 10 | 79 |
| Wolters,Tony | 11 | 79 |
| Diaz,Yandy | 12 | 79 |
| Kipnis,Jason | 9 | 78 |
| Polanco,Gregory | 9 | 78 |

### TOP ct%, bb% under 6%

| NAME | bb% | Ct% |
|---|---|---|
| Astudillo,Willians | 2 | 95 |
| Simmons,Andrelton | 6 | 91 |
| Iglesias,Jose | 4 | 89 |
| Fletcher,David | 5 | 88 |
| Gurriel,Yulieski | 5 | 88 |
| Peraza,Jose | 4 | 87 |
| Fernandez,Jose M. | 5 | 87 |
| Suzuki,Kurt | 6 | 87 |
| Flores,Wilmer | 6 | 87 |
| Segura,Jean | 6 | 87 |
| Nunez,Eduardo | 3 | 87 |
| Rojas,Miguel | 6 | 87 |
| Cabrera,Melky | 6 | 86 |
| Molina,Yadier | 6 | 86 |
| Lugo,Dawel | 3 | 86 |
| Newman,Kevin | 5 | 86 |
| Gordon,Dee | 3 | 85 |
| Escobar,Alcides | 5 | 84 |
| Diaz,Aledmys | 5 | 84 |
| Rivera,T.J. | 4 | 84 |
| Andujar,Miguel | 5 | 84 |
| Jones,Adam | 5 | 83 |
| Smith,Kevan | 6 | 83 |

### Top ct%, GB% over 50%

| NAME | GB% | Ct% |
|---|---|---|
| Simmons,Andrelton | 51 | 91 |
| Segura,Jean | 53 | 87 |
| Nunez,Eduardo | 51 | 87 |
| Lugo,Dawel | 66 | 86 |
| Newman,Kevin | 55 | 86 |
| Gordon,Dee | 57 | 85 |
| Kiner-Falefa,Isiah | 53 | 85 |
| LeMahieu,DJ | 52 | 85 |
| Dyson,Jarrod | 52 | 84 |
| Smith,Kevan | 60 | 83 |
| Duffy,Matt | 52 | 82 |
| Cain,Lorenzo | 50 | 82 |
| Kelly,Carson | 50 | 82 |
| Ramos,Wilson | 56 | 81 |
| Lagares,Juan | 50 | 81 |
| Mullins II,Cedric | 52 | 81 |
| Jay,Jon | 55 | 81 |
| Kendrick,Howie | 56 | 80 |
| Pirela,Jose | 51 | 80 |
| Marte,Starling | 50 | 80 |
| Reyes,Victor | 51 | 80 |
| Castro,Starlin | 51 | 79 |
| Hays,Austin | 56 | 79 |
| Riddle,J.T. | 51 | 79 |
| Tilson,Charlie | 55 | 79 |
| Hosmer,Eric | 58 | 79 |
| Peralta,David | 52 | 79 |
| Herrera,Rosell | 54 | 79 |
| Holt,Brock | 52 | 79 |
| Mejia,Francisco | 54 | 79 |
| Munoz,Yairo | 54 | 79 |
| Wolters,Tony | 55 | 79 |
| Diaz,Yandy | 56 | 79 |
| Arcia,Orlando | 51 | 78 |
| Caratini,Victor | 58 | 78 |
| Marte,Jefry | 51 | 78 |
| Maybin,Cameron | 53 | 78 |
| Sierra,Magneuris | 56 | 78 |
| Rosario,Amed | 50 | 78 |
| Urias,Luis | 50 | 78 |

### Top ct%, GB% under 40%

| NAME | GB% | Ct% |
|---|---|---|
| Fletcher,David | 38 | 88 |
| Murphy,Daniel | 35 | 87 |
| Ramirez,Jose | 37 | 87 |
| Peraza,Jose | 39 | 87 |
| Suzuki,Kurt | 37 | 87 |
| Flores,Wilmer | 36 | 87 |
| McNeil,Jeff | 39 | 87 |
| Gregorius,Didi | 39 | 86 |
| Calhoun,Willie | 39 | 86 |
| Kinsler,Ian | 35 | 85 |
| Turner,Justin | 32 | 85 |
| Betts,Mookie | 37 | 85 |
| Lindor,Francisco | 39 | 85 |
| Rizzo,Anthony | 39 | 84 |
| Rivera,T.J. | 38 | 84 |
| Bregman,Alex | 35 | 84 |
| Reddick,Josh | 37 | 84 |
| Rendon,Anthony | 34 | 83 |
| Moustakas,Mike | 36 | 83 |
| Pillar,Kevin | 39 | 83 |
| Cozart,Zack | 39 | 82 |
| Merrifield,Whit | 37 | 82 |
| Beltre,Adrian | 40 | 82 |

# POTENTIAL SKILLS GAINERS AND FADERS - Batters

## Power Gainers

Batters whose 2018 Power Index (PX) fell significantly short of their underlying power skill (xPX). If they show the same xPX skill in 2019, they are good candidates for more power output.

## Power Faders

Batters whose 2018 Power Index (PX) noticeably outpaced their underlying power skill (xPX). If they show the same xPX skill in 2019, they are good candidates for less power output.

## BA Gainers

Batters who had strong Hard Contact Index levels in 2018, but lower hit rates (h%). Since base hits come most often on hard contact, if these batters can make hard contact at the same strong rate again in 2019, they may get better results in terms of hit rate, resulting in a batting average improvement.

## BA Faders

Batters who had weak Hard Contact Index levels in 2018, but higher hit rates (h%). Since base hits come most often on hard contact, if these batters only make hard contact at the same weak rate again in 2019, they may get worse results in terms of hit rate, resulting in a batting average decline.

### PX GAINERS

| NAME | PX | xPX |
|------|----|----|
| Kratz,Erik | 68 | 139 |
| Wieters,Matt | 77 | 137 |
| Joyce,Matt | 92 | 134 |
| Flowers,Tyler | 88 | 132 |
| Calhoun,Kole | 99 | 132 |
| Molina,Yadier | 94 | 130 |
| Votto,Joey | 85 | 129 |
| Lamb,Jacob | 87 | 127 |
| Mathis,Jeff | 61 | 126 |
| Sisco,Chance | 82 | 126 |
| Bruce,Jay | 95 | 126 |
| Walker,Neil | 83 | 124 |
| Owings,Christopher | 71 | 123 |
| Pujols,Albert | 89 | 122 |
| Garver,Mitch | 97 | 122 |
| Davis,Chris | 96 | 121 |
| Kipnis,Jason | 97 | 120 |
| Galvis,Freddy | 86 | 118 |
| Harrison,Josh | 68 | 114 |
| Cozart,Zack | 87 | 113 |
| Knapp,Andrew | 90 | 113 |
| Hechavarria,Adeiny | 60 | 112 |
| Gordon,Alex | 82 | 112 |
| Ozuna,Marcell | 83 | 112 |
| Beltre,Adrian | 100 | 112 |
| Gonzalez,Adrian | 77 | 111 |
| Cano,Robinson | 100 | 110 |
| Flores,Wilmer | 86 | 109 |
| Brinson,Lewis | 87 | 108 |
| Winker,Jesse | 80 | 107 |
| Perez,Roberto | 83 | 106 |
| Margot,Manuel | 83 | 106 |
| Gyorko,Jedd | 96 | 105 |
| Suzuki,Kurt | 99 | 105 |
| Perez,Hernan | 78 | 104 |
| Diaz,Elias | 93 | 104 |

### PX FADERS

| NAME | PX | xPX |
|------|----|----|
| Ohtani,Shohei | 184 | 129 |
| Judge,Aaron | 177 | 126 |
| Austin,Tyler | 178 | 124 |
| Sano,Miguel | 163 | 121 |
| Choi,Ji-Man | 161 | 116 |
| Palka,Daniel | 165 | 115 |
| Stanton,Giancarlo | 167 | 113 |
| Baez,Javier | 165 | 110 |
| Soler,Jorge | 147 | 110 |
| White,Tyler | 150 | 101 |
| Bogaerts,Xander | 144 | 101 |
| Andujar,Miguel | 135 | 99 |
| Laureano,Ramon | 137 | 86 |
| Kendrick,Howie | 114 | 82 |
| Guzman,Ronald | 121 | 81 |
| Camargo,Johan | 115 | 81 |
| Mazara,Nomar | 109 | 80 |
| Schoop,Jonathan | 112 | 79 |
| Frazier,Adam | 107 | 79 |
| Nunez,Renato | 108 | 78 |
| Robertson,Daniel | 104 | 77 |
| Tucker,Preston | 117 | 76 |
| Culberson,Charlie | 130 | 72 |
| Hanson,Alen | 108 | 64 |

### BA GAINERS

| NAME | h% | HctX |
|------|----|----|
| Molina,Yadier | 27 | 140 |
| Kratz,Erik | 27 | 137 |
| Pujols,Albert | 25 | 134 |
| Perez,Salvador | 25 | 133 |
| Carpenter,Matt | 29 | 130 |
| Lindor,Francisco | 28 | 128 |
| Renfroe,Hunter | 28 | 127 |
| Flowers,Tyler | 29 | 126 |
| Olson,Matt | 29 | 125 |
| Braun,Ryan | 28 | 125 |
| Suzuki,Kurt | 28 | 125 |
| Pollock,A.J. | 29 | 124 |
| Moustakas,Mike | 26 | 124 |
| Piscotty,Stephen | 29 | 124 |
| Pederson,Joc | 26 | 122 |
| Martinez,Victor | 26 | 122 |
| Calhoun,Kole | 24 | 120 |
| Longoria,Evan | 28 | 120 |
| Cruz,Nelson | 27 | 119 |
| Zimmerman,Ryan | 29 | 118 |
| Gonzalez,Adrian | 26 | 118 |
| Margot,Manuel | 29 | 118 |
| Davis,Khristopher | 27 | 116 |
| Sandoval,Pablo | 28 | 116 |
| Encarnacion,Edwin | 27 | 115 |
| Morales,Kendrys | 28 | 115 |
| Shaw,Travis | 25 | 115 |
| Ramirez,Jose | 26 | 115 |
| Ahmed,Nick | 27 | 114 |
| Gregorius,Didi | 26 | 114 |
| Profar,Jurickson | 27 | 114 |
| Marte,Ketel | 28 | 113 |
| Hicks,Aaron | 27 | 112 |
| Bregman,Alex | 29 | 112 |
| Kepler,Max | 24 | 112 |
| Barnhart,Tucker | 29 | 112 |
| Puig,Yasiel | 29 | 111 |

### BA FADERS

| NAME | h% | HctX |
|------|----|----|
| Jackson,Austin | 39 | 70 |
| Gamel,Benjamin | 35 | 74 |
| Happ,Ian | 37 | 80 |
| Villar,Jonathan | 34 | 80 |
| Smith,Mallex | 37 | 80 |
| Garcia,Leury | 36 | 81 |
| Almora,Albert | 34 | 82 |
| Bryant,Kris | 35 | 83 |
| Alfaro,Jorge | 41 | 83 |
| Culberson,Charlie | 34 | 83 |
| Holt,Brock | 34 | 83 |
| Moncada,Yoan | 35 | 84 |
| Maile,Luke | 36 | 84 |
| Spangenberg,Cory | 34 | 84 |
| Adames,Willy | 38 | 86 |
| Cave,Jake | 38 | 89 |
| LaMarre,Ryan | 40 | 89 |
| Adduci,James | 34 | 90 |
| Slater,Austin | 38 | 90 |
| Nimmo,Brandon | 35 | 93 |
| Bader,Harrison | 36 | 93 |
| Duffy,Matt | 35 | 93 |
| Santana,Domingo | 40 | 94 |
| Polanco,Jorge | 35 | 94 |
| Taylor,Chris | 35 | 95 |
| Baez,Javier | 35 | 96 |
| Hicks,John | 34 | 96 |
| Dietrich,Derek | 34 | 96 |
| Eaton,Adam | 36 | 96 |
| Soto,Juan | 34 | 98 |
| Gonzalez,Carlos | 34 | 98 |
| Freese,David | 37 | 99 |
| Miller,Bradley | 35 | 100 |
| McNeil,Jeff | 36 | 100 |
| Laureano,Ramon | 40 | 100 |
| Parra,Gerardo | 34 | 102 |
| Stanton,Giancarlo | 34 | 103 |

# POTENTIAL SKILLS GAINERS AND FADERS - Pitchers

## Dom Gainers

From a pitcher's swinging-strike rate (SwK), we can establish a typical range in which we would expect to find their Dom (k/9). The pitchers on this list posted a 2018 Dom that was in the bottom of that expected range based on their SwK. The names above the break line are in the bottom 10% of that range, and are the strongest candidates for Dom gains. The names below the break line are in the bottom 25%, and are also good candidates for strikeout gains.

## Dom Faders

From a pitcher's swinging-strike rate (SwK), we can establish a typical range in which we would expect to find their Dom (k/9). The pitchers on this list posted a 2018 Dom that was in the top of that expected range based on their SwK. The names above the break line are in the top 10% of that range, and are the strongest candidates for a Dom fade. The names below the break line are in the top 25%, and are also good candidates for a Dom fade.

## Ctl Gainers

From a pitcher's first-pitch strike rate (FpK), we can establish a typical range in which we would expect to find their Ctl (bb/9). These pitchers posted a 2018 Ctl that was in the bottom of that expected range based on their FpK. The names above the break line are in the bottom 10% of that range, and are the strongest candidates for Ctl gains. The names below the break line are in the bottom 25%, and are also good candidates for Ctl gains.

## Ctl Faders

From a pitcher's first-pitch strike rate (FpK), we can establish a typical range in which we would expect to find their Ctl (bb/9). These pitchers posted a 2018 Ctl that was in the top 10% of that expected range based on their FpK, making them the strongest candidates for a Ctl fade.

### DOM GAINERS

| NAME | SwK | K/9 |
|---|---|---|
| Hughes,Jared | 12 | 6.8 |
| Musgrove,Joe | 12 | 7.8 |
| Tropeano,Nick | 12 | 7.6 |
| Gant,John | 12 | 7.5 |
| Gausman,Kevin | 12 | 7.3 |
| Dyson,Sam | 12 | 7.2 |
| Chirinos,Yonny | 11 | 7.6 |
| Barria,Jaime | 11 | 6.8 |
| Shields,James | 11 | 6.8 |
| Estrada,Marco | 11 | 6.5 |
| Ziegler,Brad | 10 | 6.1 |
| Straily,Dan | 10 | 7.3 |
| Manaea,Sean | 10 | 6.1 |
| Mikolas,Miles | 10 | 6.6 |
| Montgomery,Mike | 10 | 6.2 |
| Bailey,Homer | 9 | 6.4 |
| Nova,Ivan | 9 | 6.4 |
| Keller,Brad | 9 | 6.2 |
| Fillmyer,Heath | 9 | 6.2 |
| Castillo,Luis | 14 | 8.8 |
| Hildenberger,Trevor | 13 | 8.6 |
| Hamels,Cole | 12 | 8.9 |
| Anderson,Tyler | 12 | 8.4 |
| Fulmer,Michael | 11 | 7.5 |
| Hammel,Jason | 10 | 6.5 |
| Rodon,Carlos | 9 | 6.7 |
| Rodriguez,Dereck | 9 | 6.8 |
| Stroman,Marcus | 9 | 6.8 |
| Urena,Jose | 9 | 6.7 |
| Jackson,Edwin | 9 | 6.7 |
| Biagini,Joe | 9 | 6.6 |

### DOM FADERS

| NAME | SwK | K/9 |
|---|---|---|
| Pomeranz,Drew | 7 | 8.0 |
| Santiago,Hector | 9 | 9.1 |
| Porcello,Rick | 9 | 8.9 |
| Bradley,Archie | 9 | 9.5 |
| Foltynewicz,Mike | 11 | 9.9 |
| Happ,J.A. | 11 | 9.8 |
| Lucchesi,Joey | 11 | 10.0 |
| Hill,Rich | 11 | 10.2 |
| Peralta,Freddy | 12 | 11.1 |
| Glasnow,Tyler | 12 | 11.0 |
| Ottavino,Adam | 13 | 13.1 |
| Ray,Robbie | 13 | 12.1 |
| Green,Chad | 14 | 11.3 |
| Bauer,Trevor | 14 | 11.4 |
| Hand,Brad | 14 | 13.3 |
| McHugh,Collin | 14 | 11.7 |
| McCarthy,Brandon | 8 | 7.5 |
| Quintana,Jose | 8 | 8.2 |
| Wright,Mike | 8 | 7.9 |
| Kennedy,Ian | 9 | 7.9 |
| Lauer,Eric | 9 | 8.0 |
| Garcia,Jaime | 9 | 8.0 |
| Matz,Steven | 10 | 8.9 |
| Price,David | 10 | 9.1 |
| Lugo,Seth | 11 | 9.2 |
| Lynn,Lance | 11 | 9.3 |
| Rodriguez,Eduardo | 11 | 10.2 |
| Ramirez,Noe | 12 | 10.3 |
| Stripling,Ross | 12 | 10.0 |
| Buehler,Walker | 12 | 9.9 |
| Richards,Garrett | 12 | 10.3 |
| Morton,Charlie | 12 | 10.8 |
| Strasburg,Stephen | 12 | 10.8 |
| Marquez,German | 13 | 10.6 |

### CTL GAINERS

| NAME | FpK | BB/9 |
|---|---|---|
| Bradley,Archie | 68 | 2.5 |
| Lyles,Jordan | 67 | 2.9 |
| Biagini,Joe | 65 | 3.0 |
| Quintana,Jose | 65 | 3.5 |
| Moore,Matt | 65 | 3.6 |
| Guerra,Junior | 63 | 3.5 |
| Holland,Derek | 63 | 3.5 |
| Hernandez,Felix | 63 | 3.4 |
| Gallardo,Yovani | 63 | 4.5 |
| Mahle,Tyler | 62 | 4.3 |
| Richards,Trevor | 62 | 3.9 |
| Gant,John | 61 | 4.5 |
| Bettis,Chad | 61 | 3.5 |
| Teheran,Julio | 61 | 4.3 |
| Ottavino,Adam | 60 | 4.2 |
| Godley,Zack | 60 | 4.1 |
| Martinez,Carlos | 60 | 4.6 |
| Hughes,Jared | 66 | 2.6 |
| Sanchez,Anibal | 66 | 2.8 |
| Hammel,Jason | 66 | 2.8 |
| Hill,Rich | 65 | 2.8 |
| Anderson,Tyler | 65 | 3.0 |
| Berrios,Jose | 64 | 2.9 |
| Clevinger,Mike | 64 | 3.0 |
| Vargas,Jason | 64 | 2.9 |
| Bumgarner,Madison | 64 | 3.0 |
| Bauer,Trevor | 64 | 2.9 |
| Estrada,Marco | 63 | 3.1 |
| Maeda,Kenta | 63 | 3.1 |
| Chen,Wei-Yin | 63 | 3.2 |
| Ziegler,Brad | 63 | 3.1 |
| Anderson,Chase | 63 | 3.2 |
| Kennedy,Ian | 63 | 3.0 |
| Fulmer,Michael | 63 | 3.1 |
| Freeland,Kyle | 62 | 3.1 |
| Blach,Ty | 62 | 3.1 |
| German,Domingo | 62 | 3.5 |
| Stratton,Chris | 62 | 3.4 |
| Foltynewicz,Mike | 62 | 3.3 |
| Richard,Clayton | 61 | 3.4 |
| Weaver,Luke | 60 | 3.6 |

### CTL FADERS

| NAME | FpK | BB/9 |
|---|---|---|
| Borucki,Ryan | 53 | 3.1 |
| McFarland,T.J. | 54 | 2.8 |
| Treinen,Blake | 55 | 2.4 |
| Nova,Ivan | 57 | 2.0 |
| Minor,Mike | 58 | 2.2 |
| Anderson,Brett | 58 | 1.5 |
| Ryu,Hyun-Jin | 58 | 1.6 |
| Tomlin,Josh | 63 | 1.5 |
| Kluber,Corey | 63 | 1.4 |
| Eovaldi,Nathan | 64 | 1.6 |
| Colon,Bartolo | 64 | 1.5 |
| Erlin,Robbie | 64 | 1.0 |
| Manaea,Sean | 64 | 1.8 |
| Chavez,Jesse | 64 | 1.6 |
| Zimmermann,Jordan | 65 | 1.8 |
| Leake,Mike | 65 | 1.7 |
| Barria,Jaime | 55 | 3.3 |
| Gausman,Kevin | 57 | 2.5 |
| Rodriguez,Dereck | 57 | 2.7 |
| Boyd,Matthew | 58 | 2.7 |
| Syndergaard,Noah | 59 | 2.3 |
| Koch,Matt | 61 | 2.3 |
| Mengden,Daniel | 62 | 2.0 |
| Taillon,Jameson | 64 | 2.2 |
| Carrasco,Carlos | 65 | 2.0 |

## PITCHER SKILLS RANKINGS - Starting Pitchers

### Top Command (k/bb)

| NAME | Cmd |
|---|---|
| Sale,Chris | 6.8 |
| Kershaw,Clayton | 6.6 |
| Kluber,Corey | 5.8 |
| Bieber,Shane | 5.8 |
| Scherzer,Max | 5.4 |
| Verlander,Justin | 5.2 |
| Carrasco,Carlos | 5.1 |
| deGrom,Jacob | 4.9 |
| Syndergaard,Noah | 4.8 |
| Tanaka,Masahiro | 4.5 |
| Mikolas,Miles | 4.4 |
| Stripling,Ross | 4.4 |
| Ryu,Hyun-Jin | 4.4 |
| Greinke,Zack | 4.4 |
| Paxton,James | 4.4 |
| Musgrove,Joe | 4.3 |
| Corbin,Patrick | 4.3 |
| Severino,Luis | 4.1 |
| Strasburg,Stephen | 4.1 |
| Cole,Gerrit | 4.0 |
| Nola,Aaron | 3.9 |
| Price,David | 3.9 |
| Pineda,Michael | 3.8 |
| Porcello,Rick | 3.8 |
| Marquez,German | 3.7 |
| Junis,Jakob | 3.7 |
| Leake,Mike | 3.7 |
| Chirinos,Yonny | 3.6 |
| Heaney,Andrew | 3.6 |
| Hendricks,Kyle | 3.6 |
| Eovaldi,Nathan | 3.6 |

### Top Control (bb/9)

| NAME | Ctl |
|---|---|
| Bieber,Shane | 1.4 |
| Kershaw,Clayton | 1.5 |
| Mikolas,Miles | 1.6 |
| Leake,Mike | 1.6 |
| Kluber,Corey | 1.7 |
| Sampson,Adrian | 1.7 |
| Musgrove,Joe | 1.8 |
| Sale,Chris | 1.9 |
| Greinke,Zack | 2.0 |
| Colon,Bartolo | 2.0 |
| Tanaka,Masahiro | 2.0 |
| Chirinos,Yonny | 2.0 |
| Syndergaard,Noah | 2.0 |
| Zimmermann,Jordan | 2.0 |
| Nova,Ivan | 2.0 |
| Carrasco,Carlos | 2.0 |
| Ryu,Hyun-Jin | 2.1 |
| Stripling,Ross | 2.1 |
| Hendricks,Kyle | 2.1 |
| Verlander,Justin | 2.1 |
| deGrom,Jacob | 2.1 |
| Junis,Jakob | 2.1 |
| Soroka,Michael | 2.1 |
| Eovaldi,Nathan | 2.1 |
| Suter,Brent | 2.2 |
| Porcello,Rick | 2.2 |
| Scherzer,Max | 2.2 |
| Gonzales,Marco | 2.2 |
| Anderson,Brett | 2.2 |
| DeSclafani,Anthony | 2.3 |
| Hellickson,Jeremy | 2.3 |

### Top Dominance (k/9)

| NAME | Dom |
|---|---|
| Sale,Chris | 12.7 |
| Scherzer,Max | 11.8 |
| Ray,Robbie | 11.6 |
| Verlander,Justin | 10.9 |
| Darvish,Yu | 10.8 |
| Strasburg,Stephen | 10.8 |
| Peralta,Freddy | 10.8 |
| Cole,Gerrit | 10.7 |
| Salazar,Danny | 10.7 |
| deGrom,Jacob | 10.5 |
| Carrasco,Carlos | 10.4 |
| Paxton,James | 10.4 |
| Snell,Blake | 10.4 |
| Archer,Chris | 10.3 |
| Hill,Rich | 10.3 |
| Reyes,Alex | 10.3 |
| Glasnow,Tyler | 10.2 |
| Bauer,Trevor | 10.2 |
| Buehler,Walker | 10.2 |
| Flaherty,Jack | 10.2 |
| German,Domingo | 10.0 |
| Corbin,Patrick | 10.0 |
| Kluber,Corey | 9.9 |
| Loaisiga,Jonathan | 9.9 |
| Severino,Luis | 9.8 |
| Morton,Charlie | 9.8 |
| Kershaw,Clayton | 9.7 |
| Rodriguez,Eduardo | 9.6 |
| Pivetta,Nick | 9.6 |
| Syndergaard,Noah | 9.5 |
| Nola,Aaron | 9.5 |

### Top Ground Ball Rate

| NAME | GB |
|---|---|
| Stroman,Marcus | 61 |
| Reed,Cody | 60 |
| Anderson,Brett | 56 |
| Chatwood,Tyler | 56 |
| Richard,Clayton | 56 |
| Keuchel,Dallas | 55 |
| Keller,Brad | 55 |
| Fedde,Erick | 54 |
| Gray,Sonny | 53 |
| Covey,Dylan | 53 |
| Syndergaard,Noah | 51 |
| Castillo,Luis | 51 |
| Leake,Mike | 51 |
| Richards,Garrett | 51 |
| Nola,Aaron | 51 |
| Mitchell,Bryan | 51 |
| Perez,Martin | 51 |
| Godley,Zachary | 50 |
| Gibson,Kyle | 50 |
| Beeks,Jalen | 50 |
| Ross,Tyson | 50 |
| Suarez,Andrew | 50 |
| Morton,Charlie | 50 |
| Sanchez,Aaron | 50 |
| Corbin,Patrick | 50 |
| Buehler,Walker | 50 |
| Cobb,Alex | 50 |
| Senzatela,Antonio | 50 |
| Miley,Wade | 49 |
| Wood,Alex | 49 |
| Gaviglio,Sam | 49 |

### Top Fly Ball Rate

| NAME | FB |
|---|---|
| Gohara,Luiz | 57 |
| Plutko,Adam | 57 |
| Estrada,Marco | 53 |
| Peralta,Freddy | 51 |
| Smith,Caleb | 51 |
| Pannone,Thomas | 50 |
| Mendez,Yohander | 49 |
| Verlander,Justin | 47 |
| Odorizzi,Jake | 47 |
| Boyd,Matt | 47 |
| Scherzer,Max | 47 |
| Hess,David | 46 |
| Ramirez,Yefry | 46 |
| Bundy,Dylan | 46 |
| Smyly,Drew | 46 |
| Lopez,Reynaldo | 45 |
| Straily,Dan | 45 |
| German,Domingo | 45 |
| Kennedy,Ian | 45 |
| Santana,Ervin | 44 |
| Barria,Jaime | 43 |
| Anderson,Chase | 43 |
| Skoglund,Eric | 42 |
| Minor,Mike | 42 |
| Chen,Wei-Yin | 42 |
| Tropeano,Nicholas | 42 |
| Sampson,Adrian | 42 |
| Shields,James | 42 |
| Rodriguez,Eduardo | 42 |
| Zimmermann,Jordan | 42 |
| Hill,Rich | 42 |

### High GB, Low Dom

| NAME | GB | Dom |
|---|---|---|
| Anderson,Brett | 56 | 5.6 |
| Richard,Clayton | 56 | 6.0 |
| Keller,Brad | 55 | 6.3 |
| Covey,Dylan | 53 | 6.1 |
| Leake,Mike | 51 | 6.1 |
| Mitchell,Bryan | 51 | 5.8 |
| Perez,Martin | 51 | 5.4 |
| Suarez,Andrew | 50 | 6.5 |
| Cobb,Alex | 50 | 6.3 |
| Senzatela,Antonio | 50 | 6.8 |
| Miley,Wade | 49 | 6.7 |
| Gaviglio,Sam | 49 | 6.6 |
| Freeland,Kyle | 49 | 6.7 |
| Davies,Zachary | 49 | 6.6 |
| Alcantara,Sandy | 49 | 6.6 |
| Wright,Kyle | 48 | 7.0 |
| Borucki,Ryan | 48 | 6.3 |
| Fister,Doug | 47 | 6.0 |
| Urena,Jose | 47 | 6.2 |
| Nova,Ivan | 47 | 6.3 |
| Romano,Sal | 46 | 6.6 |
| Koch,Matt | 46 | 4.5 |
| Romero,Fernando | 45 | 6.4 |
| Bailey,Homer | 45 | 6.7 |
| Manaea,Sean | 44 | 6.9 |
| Fillmyer,Heath | 44 | 5.7 |
| Rodriguez,Jefry | 44 | 6.9 |
| Cashner,Andrew | 44 | 5.7 |
| Allard,Kolby | 44 | 6.3 |
| Stratton,Chris | 44 | 6.6 |
| De Los Santos,Enyel | 44 | 6.9 |

### High GB, High Dom

| NAME | GB | Dom |
|---|---|---|
| Syndergaard,Noah | 51 | 9.5 |
| Castillo,Luis | 51 | 8.8 |
| Richards,Garrett | 51 | 8.8 |
| Nola,Aaron | 51 | 9.5 |
| Godley,Zachary | 50 | 8.7 |
| Morton,Charlie | 50 | 9.8 |
| Corbin,Patrick | 50 | 10.0 |
| Buehler,Walker | 50 | 10.2 |
| Kershaw,Clayton | 48 | 9.7 |
| Matz,Steven | 48 | 8.7 |
| Tanaka,Masahiro | 48 | 9.0 |
| Fried,Max | 48 | 9.0 |
| Carrasco,Carlos | 48 | 10.4 |
| Glasnow,Tyler | 47 | 10.2 |
| Marquez,German | 47 | 9.2 |
| Gray,Jonathan | 47 | 9.0 |
| Stripling,Ross | 47 | 9.2 |
| Wheeler,Zack | 47 | 8.7 |
| Lynn,Lance | 47 | 8.6 |
| Ryu,Hyun-Jin | 47 | 9.0 |
| Greinke,Zack | 46 | 8.6 |
| Pivetta,Nick | 46 | 9.6 |
| deGrom,Jacob | 46 | 10.5 |
| Pineda,Michael | 45 | 8.8 |
| Honeywell,Brent | 45 | 8.8 |
| Archer,Chris | 45 | 10.3 |
| Severino,Luis | 45 | 9.8 |
| Lucchesi,Joey | 44 | 9.0 |
| Bauer,Trevor | 44 | 10.2 |
| Karns,Nathan | 44 | 9.2 |
| Kluber,Corey | 44 | 9.9 |

### Lowest xERA

| NAME | xERA |
|---|---|
| Sale,Chris | 2.40 |
| Kershaw,Clayton | 2.78 |
| deGrom,Jacob | 2.85 |
| Carrasco,Carlos | 2.86 |
| Kluber,Corey | 2.90 |
| Scherzer,Max | 2.91 |
| Syndergaard,Noah | 2.95 |
| Corbin,Patrick | 2.96 |
| Buehler,Walker | 3.04 |
| Nola,Aaron | 3.05 |
| Strasburg,Stephen | 3.07 |
| Paxton,James | 3.09 |
| Severino,Luis | 3.13 |
| Verlander,Justin | 3.17 |
| Morton,Charlie | 3.21 |
| Tanaka,Masahiro | 3.21 |
| Cole,Gerrit | 3.22 |
| Stripling,Ross | 3.23 |
| Archer,Chris | 3.24 |
| Ryu,Hyun-Jin | 3.25 |
| Bauer,Trevor | 3.25 |
| Greinke,Zack | 3.26 |
| Snell,Blake | 3.30 |
| Marquez,German | 3.31 |
| Castillo,Luis | 3.34 |
| Wood,Alex | 3.37 |
| Bieber,Shane | 3.38 |
| Flaherty,Jack | 3.39 |
| Salazar,Danny | 3.40 |
| Hill,Rich | 3.42 |
| Darvish,Yu | 3.44 |

### Top BPV, 180+ IP

| NAME | BPV |
|---|---|
| Sale,Chris | 198 |
| Scherzer,Max | 166 |
| Carrasco,Carlos | 159 |
| deGrom,Jacob | 155 |
| Kluber,Corey | 154 |
| Verlander,Justin | 150 |
| Corbin,Patrick | 144 |
| Cole,Gerrit | 137 |
| Severino,Luis | 135 |
| Nola,Aaron | 135 |
| Archer,Chris | 130 |
| Greinke,Zack | 126 |
| Bauer,Trevor | 126 |
| Marquez,German | 125 |
| Snell,Blake | 119 |
| Flaherty,Jack | 115 |
| Gray,Jonathan | 113 |
| Taillon,Jameson | 113 |
| Porcello,Rick | 110 |
| Mikolas,Miles | 109 |
| Hendricks,Kyle | 106 |
| Berrios,Jose | 100 |
| Keuchel,Dallas | 97 |
| Foltynewicz,Mike | 96 |
| Leake,Mike | 94 |
| Clevinger,Michael | 92 |
| Hamels,Cole | 90 |
| Quintana,Jose | 90 |
| Gausman,Kevin | 88 |
| Roark,Tanner | 85 |
| Arrieta,Jake | 84 |

### Top BPV, <150 IP

| NAME | BPV |
|---|---|
| Stripling,Ross | 135 |
| Ryu,Hyun-Jin | 131 |
| Salazar,Danny | 121 |
| Pineda,Michael | 120 |
| Hill,Rich | 118 |
| Darvish,Yu | 118 |
| Loaisiga,Jonathan | 114 |
| Honeywell,Brent | 114 |
| Musgrove,Joe | 112 |
| Paulino,David | 108 |
| Luzardo,Jesus | 106 |
| Reyes,Alex | 105 |
| Smyly,Drew | 101 |
| Rodriguez,Eduardo | 100 |
| Sanchez,Anibal | 100 |
| Soroka,Michael | 100 |
| German,Domingo | 99 |
| Chirinos,Yonny | 98 |
| Skaggs,Tyler | 96 |
| Karns,Nathan | 95 |
| Walker,Taijuan | 94 |
| Pena,Felix | 93 |
| Weaver,Luke | 92 |
| Shoemaker,Matthew | 92 |
| Richards,Garrett | 91 |
| Lopez,Pablo | 90 |
| Glasnow,Tyler | 90 |
| Ross,Joe | 88 |
| Richards,Trevor | 86 |
| Gray,Sonny | 86 |
| Whitley,Forrest | 86 |

# PITCHER SKILLS RANKINGS - Relief Pitchers

### Top Command (k/bb)

| NAME | Cmd |
|---|---|
| Doolittle,Sean | 8.0 |
| Jansen,Kenley | 7.2 |
| Osuna,Roberto | 7.2 |
| Otero,Dan | 6.1 |
| Diaz,Edwin | 5.2 |
| Giles,Ken | 4.9 |
| Martin,Christopher | 4.9 |
| Neshek,Pat | 4.7 |
| Green,Chad | 4.7 |
| Harris,Will | 4.6 |
| Tomlin,Josh | 4.5 |
| Petit,Yusmeiro | 4.5 |
| Oh,Seung-Hwan | 4.5 |
| Devenski,Chris | 4.4 |
| Ferguson,Caleb | 4.4 |
| Perez,Oliver | 4.4 |
| Reed,Addison | 4.3 |
| Yates,Kirby | 4.3 |
| McHugh,Collin | 4.2 |
| Erlin,Robert | 4.2 |
| Miller,Andrew | 4.2 |
| Castillo,Jose | 4.1 |
| Romo,Sergio | 3.9 |
| Rogers,Taylor | 3.9 |
| Pressly,Ryan | 3.9 |
| Chavez,Jesse | 3.9 |
| Vincent,Nick | 3.9 |
| Watson,Tony | 3.9 |
| Stammen,Craig | 3.8 |
| Hernandez,David | 3.8 |
| Pruitt,Austin | 3.7 |

### Top Control (bb/9)

| NAME | Ctl |
|---|---|
| Otero,Dan | 1.0 |
| Tomlin,Josh | 1.4 |
| Osuna,Roberto | 1.4 |
| Doolittle,Sean | 1.4 |
| Martin,Christopher | 1.7 |
| Erlin,Robert | 1.7 |
| Neshek,Pat | 1.7 |
| Jansen,Kenley | 1.7 |
| Claudio,Alexander | 1.8 |
| Petit,Yusmeiro | 1.8 |
| Reed,Addison | 1.9 |
| Pruitt,Austin | 2.0 |
| Brasier,Ryan | 2.0 |
| Hunter,Tommy | 2.1 |
| Harris,Will | 2.1 |
| Cimber,Adam | 2.2 |
| Wisler,Matthew | 2.2 |
| Chavez,Jesse | 2.2 |
| Herrera,Kelvin | 2.2 |
| Devenski,Chris | 2.2 |
| Ramirez,Erasmo | 2.2 |
| Oh,Seung-Hwan | 2.2 |
| Vincent,Nick | 2.2 |
| Green,Chad | 2.2 |
| Wilson,Alex | 2.2 |
| Watson,Tony | 2.3 |
| Giles,Ken | 2.3 |
| Lugo,Seth | 2.3 |
| Ferguson,Caleb | 2.3 |
| Bradford,Chase | 2.4 |
| Stammen,Craig | 2.4 |

### Top Dominance (k/9)

| NAME | Dom |
|---|---|
| Chapman,Aroldis | 15.4 |
| Betances,Dellin | 15.2 |
| Kimbrel,Craig | 14.6 |
| Diaz,Edwin | 13.7 |
| Knebel,Corey | 13.5 |
| Miller,Andrew | 13.1 |
| Yates,Kirby | 12.7 |
| Hader,Josh | 12.7 |
| Barnes,Matt | 12.5 |
| Black,Ray | 12.4 |
| Jansen,Kenley | 12.4 |
| Robertson,David | 12.1 |
| Castillo,Jose | 12.0 |
| Peacock,Brad | 12.0 |
| Leclerc,Jose | 12.0 |
| Ottavino,Adam | 11.9 |
| Hand,Brad | 11.9 |
| Boxberger,Brad | 11.9 |
| Neris,Hector | 11.8 |
| Smith,Will | 11.8 |
| Kela,Keone | 11.6 |
| Edwards,Carl | 11.4 |
| Perez,Oliver | 11.4 |
| Scott,Tanner | 11.4 |
| Allen,Cody | 11.4 |
| Cingrani,Tony | 11.3 |
| Doolittle,Sean | 11.3 |
| Ramirez,Neil | 11.1 |
| Giles,Ken | 11.1 |
| May,Trevor | 11.1 |
| Wilson,Justin | 11.0 |

### Top Ground Ball Rate

| NAME | GB |
|---|---|
| Britton,Zach | 77 |
| Alexander,Scott | 72 |
| Hughes,Jared | 63 |
| Dyson,Sam | 63 |
| Hill,Tim | 62 |
| Claudio,Alexander | 61 |
| Hicks,Jordan | 61 |
| Hudson,Dakota | 61 |
| McCarthy,Kevin | 60 |
| Cimber,Adam | 60 |
| Otero,Dan | 60 |
| Petricka,Jacob | 59 |
| Jeffress,Jeremy | 58 |
| Dominguez,Seranthony | 56 |
| Oberg,Scott | 56 |
| Treinen,Blake | 55 |
| Chafin,Andrew | 55 |
| Floro,Dylan | 55 |
| Cahill,Trevor | 55 |
| Buttrey,Ty | 54 |
| Kintzler,Brandon | 54 |
| Anderson,Justin | 54 |
| Alvarado,Jose | 54 |
| Montgomery,Mike | 54 |
| Strop,Pedro | 53 |
| Garcia,Luis | 53 |
| Bummer,Aaron | 53 |
| Familia,Jeurys | 53 |
| Lorenzen,Michael | 52 |
| Rosario,Randy | 52 |
| Flynn,Brian | 52 |

### Top Fly Ball Rate

| NAME | FB |
|---|---|
| Pagan,Emilio | 56 |
| Clippard,Tyler | 55 |
| Doolittle,Sean | 55 |
| Stanek,Ryne | 52 |
| Hernandez,Elieser | 52 |
| Brebbia,John | 51 |
| Santiago,Hector | 50 |
| Hader,Josh | 49 |
| Kelley,Shawn | 49 |
| Black,Ray | 49 |
| Vincent,Nick | 49 |
| Oh,Seung-Hwan | 48 |
| Goody,Nicholas | 48 |
| Leclerc,Jose | 48 |
| Ramirez,Neil | 48 |
| Rodriguez,Richard | 47 |
| Allen,Cody | 47 |
| Neshek,Pat | 47 |
| Miller,Justin | 46 |
| Holder,Jonathan | 46 |
| Petit,Yusmeiro | 46 |
| Jansen,Kenley | 46 |
| Kimbrel,Craig | 45 |
| Green,Chad | 45 |
| Jimenez,Joe | 45 |
| Romo,Sergio | 44 |
| Wisler,Matthew | 44 |
| Bracho,Silvino | 44 |
| Yates,Kirby | 44 |
| Strahm,Matt | 44 |
| Hernandez,David | 43 |

### High GB, Low Dom

| NAME | GB | Dom |
|---|---|---|
| Hughes,Jared | 63 | 6.5 |
| Dyson,Sam | 63 | 7.3 |
| Claudio,Alexander | 61 | 5.8 |
| Hudson,Dakota | 61 | 5.5 |
| McCarthy,Kevin | 60 | 5.5 |
| Cimber,Adam | 60 | 5.9 |
| Otero,Dan | 60 | 6.3 |
| Floro,Dylan | 55 | 6.0 |
| Kintzler,Brandon | 54 | 6.0 |
| Montgomery,Mike | 54 | 6.7 |
| Lorenzen,Michael | 52 | 6.9 |
| Rosario,Randy | 52 | 5.7 |
| Flynn,Brian | 52 | 6.1 |
| Grace,Matt | 51 | 6.4 |
| Biagini,Joe | 51 | 6.6 |
| Brice,Austin | 51 | 7.3 |
| Bradford,Chase | 50 | 6.1 |
| Blach,Ty | 50 | 5.5 |
| Velazquez,Hector | 50 | 5.5 |
| Gsellman,Robert | 50 | 6.7 |
| Castro,Miguel | 49 | 6.0 |
| Bettis,Chad | 49 | 5.6 |
| Stock,Robert | 49 | 7.5 |
| Wright,Steven | 47 | 6.5 |
| Wilson,Alex | 47 | 6.2 |
| Butler,Eddie | 46 | 4.6 |
| Erlin,Robert | 45 | 7.0 |
| Santana,Edgar | 45 | 7.2 |
| Brault,Steven | 45 | 7.5 |
| Lopez,Jorge | 43 | 6.9 |
| Font,Wilmer | 43 | 7.3 |

### High GB, High Dom

| NAME | GB | Dom |
|---|---|---|
| Britton,Zach | 77 | 8.5 |
| Jeffress,Jeremy | 58 | 8.9 |
| Dominguez,Seranthony | 56 | 11.0 |
| Treinen,Blake | 55 | 10.1 |
| Chafin,Andrew | 55 | 9.1 |
| Buttrey,Ty | 54 | 9.1 |
| Anderson,Justin | 54 | 9.4 |
| Alvarado,Jose | 54 | 10.9 |
| Strop,Pedro | 53 | 9.4 |
| Garcia,Luis | 53 | 9.6 |
| Familia,Jeurys | 53 | 10.0 |
| Barnes,Jacob | 51 | 8.7 |
| Harris,Will | 50 | 9.8 |
| Pressly,Ryan | 50 | 10.4 |
| Martinez,Carlos | 50 | 8.9 |
| Stammen,Craig | 50 | 8.9 |
| Barnes,Matt | 49 | 12.5 |
| Diekman,Jake | 49 | 10.9 |
| Morrow,Brandon | 49 | 8.8 |
| Roe,Chaz | 49 | 9.5 |
| Rodney,Fernando | 49 | 9.6 |
| Bradley,Archie | 48 | 9.4 |
| Kelly,Joe | 48 | 8.9 |
| Pazos,James | 48 | 9.2 |
| Cishek,Steve | 48 | 9.6 |
| Tuivailala,Sam | 48 | 8.7 |
| Miller,Andrew | 47 | 13.1 |
| Hildenberger,Trevor | 47 | 8.6 |
| Rondon,Hector | 47 | 10.1 |
| Vazquez,Felipe | 47 | 10.7 |
| Drake,Oliver | 47 | 9.8 |

### Lowest xERA

| NAME | xERA |
|---|---|
| Betances,Dellin | 2.23 |
| Chapman,Aroldis | 2.38 |
| Diaz,Edwin | 2.38 |
| Miller,Andrew | 2.40 |
| Britton,Zach | 2.51 |
| Kimbrel,Craig | 2.60 |
| Jansen,Kenley | 2.66 |
| Knebel,Corey | 2.73 |
| Dominguez,Seranthon | 2.76 |
| Treinen,Blake | 2.79 |
| Robertson,David | 2.81 |
| Harris,Will | 2.82 |
| Hand,Brad | 2.83 |
| Yates,Kirby | 2.84 |
| Osuna,Roberto | 2.87 |
| Castillo,Jose | 2.89 |
| Giles,Ken | 2.91 |
| Alvarado,Jose | 2.93 |
| Doolittle,Sean | 2.94 |
| Barnes,Matt | 2.95 |
| Perez,Oliver | 2.97 |
| Pressly,Ryan | 2.98 |
| Smith,Will | 3.00 |
| Vazquez,Felipe | 3.01 |
| Familia,Jeurys | 3.09 |
| Hader,Josh | 3.10 |
| Peacock,Brad | 3.10 |
| Ferguson,Caleb | 3.10 |
| Otero,Dan | 3.15 |
| Alexander,Scott | 3.16 |
| Ottavino,Adam | 3.16 |

### Top BPV, 10+ Saves

| NAME | BPV |
|---|---|
| Diaz,Edwin | 196 |
| Jansen,Kenley | 189 |
| Betances,Dellin | 185 |
| Doolittle,Sean | 170 |
| Kimbrel,Craig | 165 |
| Chapman,Aroldis | 165 |
| Yates,Kirby | 163 |
| Osuna,Roberto | 163 |
| Giles,Ken | 161 |
| Knebel,Corey | 152 |
| Hand,Brad | 152 |
| Robertson,David | 150 |
| Smith,Will | 145 |
| Hader,Josh | 143 |
| Vazquez,Felipe | 138 |
| Neris,Hector | 138 |
| Treinen,Blake | 137 |
| Dominguez,Seranthony | 131 |
| Rogers,Taylor | 129 |
| Romo,Sergio | 125 |
| Bradley,Archie | 123 |
| Britton,Zach | 122 |
| Familia,Jeurys | 120 |
| Alvarado,Jose | 120 |
| Iglesias,Raisel | 116 |
| Minter,A.J. | 115 |
| Steckenrider,Drew | 115 |
| Davis,Wade | 112 |
| Allen,Cody | 112 |
| Fry,Jace | 110 |
| Leclerc,Jose | 108 |

### Top BPV, <10 Saves

| NAME | BPV |
|---|---|
| Miller,Andrew | 177 |
| Castillo,Jose | 158 |
| Perez,Oliver | 152 |
| Harris,Will | 148 |
| Pressly,Ryan | 144 |
| Peacock,Brad | 144 |
| Ferguson,Caleb | 140 |
| McHugh,Collin | 140 |
| Green,Chad | 138 |
| Barnes,Matt | 137 |
| Black,Ray | 134 |
| Devenski,Chris | 132 |
| Cingrani,Tony | 131 |
| Castillo,Diego | 131 |
| Maeda,Kenta | 128 |
| Oh,Seung-Hwan | 127 |
| Ottavino,Adam | 126 |
| Stammen,Craig | 126 |
| Nicasio,Juan | 125 |
| May,Trevor | 125 |
| Rondon,Hector | 124 |
| Otero,Dan | 123 |
| Kela,Keone | 123 |
| Colome,Alexander | 122 |
| Rodriguez,Richard | 122 |
| Martin,Christopher | 119 |
| Watson,Tony | 118 |
| Parker,Blake | 116 |
| Strahm,Matt | 116 |
| Trivino,Lou | 115 |
| Chavez,Jesse | 114 |

# RISK MANAGEMENT

## GRADE "F" in HEALTH

| Pitchers | | Batters |
|---|---|---|
| Anderson,Brett | Morrow,Brandon | Adrianza,Ehire |
| Bailey,Homer | Morton,Charlie | Bird,Gregory |
| Bettis,Chad | Neshek,Pat | Brantley,Michael |
| Black,Ray | Norris,Daniel | Cabrera,Miguel |
| Boxberger,Brad | Ottavino,Adam | Castro,Jason |
| Britton,Zach | Paxton,James | Cervelli,Francisco |
| Buchholz,Clay | Perez,Martin | Cespedes,Yoenis |
| Bumgarner,Madison | Petricka,Jacob | Chisenhall,Lonnie |
| Butler,Eddie | Pineda,Michael | Cooper,Garrett |
| Cahill,Trevor | Pomeranz,Drew | Cordero,Franchy |
| Chen,Wei-Yin | Price,David | Cozart,Zack |
| Cingrani,Tony | Ramirez,Erasmo | D Arnaud,Travis |
| Claudio,Alexander | Ramos,A.J. | Dahl,David |
| Cobb,Alex | Reyes,Alex | Donaldson,Josh |
| Cueto,Johnny | Richards,Garrett | Duda,Lucas |
| Darvish,Yu | Rodon,Carlos | Duffy,Matt |
| Davies,Zachary | Rodriguez,Eduardo | Eaton,Adam |
| DeSclafani,Anthony | Roe,Chaz | Ellsbury,Jacoby |
| Doolittle,Sean | Ross,Joe | Frazier,Clint |
| Eickhoff,Jerad | Ross,Tyson | Garcia,Leury |
| Eovaldi,Nathan | Ryu,Hyun-Jin | Goodwin,Brian |
| Erlin,Robert | Sabathia,CC | Jackson,Austin |
| Familia,Jeurys | Salazar,Danny | Kendrick,Howie |
| Faria,Jake | Samardzija,Jeff | Kiermaier,Kevin |
| Fister,Doug | Sanchez,Aaron | Lagares,Juan |
| Flynn,Brian | Sanchez,Anibal | Lamb,Jake |
| Font,Wilmer | Santana,Ervin | Mesoraco,Devin |
| Glover,Koda | Santiago,Hector | Myers,Wil |
| Goody,Nicholas | Shoemaker,Matthew | Pearce,Steve |
| Harvey,Matt | Skaggs,Tyler | Pedroia,Dustin |
| Heaney,Andrew | Skoglund,Eric | Pence,Hunter |
| Hernandez,David | Smith,Caleb | Pollock,A.J. |
| Hernandez,Felix | Smith,Will | Rivera,T.J. |
| Hill,Rich | Smyly,Drew | Seager,Corey |
| Holland,Derek | Soroka,Michael | Soler,Jorge |
| Honeywell,Brent | Strahm,Matt | Souza,Steven |
| Jones,Nate | Strasburg,Stephen | Tilson,Charlie |
| Karns,Nathan | Stroman,Marcus | Travis,Devon |
| Kelley,Shawn | Suter,Brent | Tulowitzki,Troy |
| Kennedy,Ian | Swarzak,Anthony | Vazquez,Christian |
| Kershaw,Clayton | Syndergaard,Noah | Villanueva,Christian |
| Leone,Dominic | Tomlin,Josh | Vogt,Stephen |
| Lorenzen,Michael | Tropeano,Nicholas | Wieters,Matt |
| Lyles,Jordan | Urias,Julio | Zimmerman,Ryan |
| Lynn,Lance | Vargas,Jason | |
| Matz,Steven | Velasquez,Vincent | |
| May,Trevor | VerHagen,Drew | |
| McHugh,Collin | Vizcaino,Arodys | |
| Melancon,Mark | Wacha,Michael | |
| Middleton,Keynan | Wainwright,Adam | |
| Miley,Wade | Walker,Taijuan | |
| Miller,Andrew | Warren,Adam | |
| Miller,Shelby | Wheeler,Zack | |
| Minor,Mike | Winkler,Daniel | |
| Mitchell,Bryan | Wood,Alex | |
| Montgomery,Jordan | Wright,Steven | |

## Highest Reliability Grades-Health/Experience/Consistency (Min. Grade BBB)

| CA | POS | Rel |
|---|---|---|
| Grandal,Yasmani | 2 | ABB |
| Molina,Yadier | 2 | BBB |
| Realmuto,Jacob | 2 | ABA |

| 1B/DH | POS | Rel |
|---|---|---|
| Bauers,Jake | 3 | ABB |
| Bell,Josh | 3 | AAA |
| Carpenter,Matt | 35 | AAB |
| Cruz,Nelson | 0 | AAB |
| Davis,Khristopher | 0 | AAA |
| Dietrich,Derek | 37 | ABA |
| Encarnacion,Edwin | 03 | AAB |
| Freeman,Freddie | 3 | BAB |
| Goldschmidt,Paul | 3 | AAB |
| Granderson,Curtis | 079 | ABA |
| Guzman,Ronald | 3 | ABA |
| Morales,Kendrys | 0 | AAA |
| Moreland,Mitch | 3 | BBA |
| O'Hearn,Ryan | 3 | ABA |
| Pujols,Albert | 03 | BAB |
| Rizzo,Anthony | 3 | AAB |
| Santana,Carlos | 3 | AAB |

| 2B | POS | Rel |
|---|---|---|
| Albies,Ozzie | 4 | AAB |
| Baez,Javier | 456 | ABB |
| Cabrera,Asdrubal | 456 | BAA |
| Castro,Starlin | 4 | BBB |
| Gennett,Scooter | 4 | AAB |
| Hernandez,Cesar | 4 | BAB |
| Marte,Ketel | 46 | ABB |

| SS | POS | Rel |
|---|---|---|
| Adames,Willy | 6 | ABA |
| Anderson,Tim | 6 | AAA |
| Baez,Javier | 456 | ABB |
| Bregman,Alex | 56 | AAB |
| Cabrera,Asdrubal | 456 | BAA |
| Crawford,Brandon | 6 | AAB |
| Escobar,Alcides | 56 | AAA |
| Galvis,Freddy | 6 | AAA |
| Gregorius,Didi | 6 | BAA |
| Lindor,Francisco | 6 | AAA |
| Marte,Ketel | 46 | ABB |
| Mercer,Jordy | 6 | BBA |
| Russell,Addison | 6 | BBA |
| Segura,Jean | 6 | BAB |
| Simmons,Andrelton | 6 | BAA |
| Turner,Trea | 6 | BAB |

| 3B | POS | Rel |
|---|---|---|
| Anderson,Brian | 59 | ABB |
| Arenado,Nolan | 5 | AAB |
| Baez,Javier | 456 | ABB |
| Bregman,Alex | 56 | AAB |
| Cabrera,Asdrubal | 456 | BAA |
| Candelario,Jeimer | 5 | ABB |
| Carpenter,Matt | 35 | AAB |
| Escobar,Alcides | 56 | AAA |
| Franco,Maikel | 5 | AAB |
| Longoria,Evan | 5 | BAB |
| Sanchez,Yolmer | 5 | ABB |

| OF | POS | Rel |
|---|---|---|
| Anderson,Brian | 59 | ABB |
| Andreoli,John | 7 | ABA |
| Benintendi,Andrew | 78 | ABB |
| Bradley,Jackie | 8 | AAB |
| Cabrera,Melky | 9 | ABB |
| Cain,Lorenzo | 8 | BAB |
| Calhoun,Kole | 9 | BAB |
| Castellanos,Nick | 9 | BAB |
| Dickerson,Corey | 7 | BAB |
| Dietrich,Derek | 37 | ABA |
| Duvall,Adam | 7 | ABB |
| Gardner,Brett | 78 | AAB |
| Gonzalez,Carlos | 9 | BAB |
| Granderson,Curtis | 079 | ABA |
| Hamilton,Billy | 8 | BBA |
| Haniger,Mitch | 89 | BBA |
| Herrera,Odubel | 8 | AAB |
| Heyward,Jason | 89 | BBB |
| Inciarte,Ender | 8 | AAB |
| Jones,Adam | 89 | AAB |
| Kemp,Matt | 79 | BBB |
| Kepler,Max | 89 | ABA |
| Margot,Manuel | 8 | BBB |
| Markakis,Nick | 9 | AAB |
| Marte,Starling | 8 | ABB |
| Mazara,Nomar | 9 | AAA |
| Pillar,Kevin | 8 | AAA |
| Rosario,Eddie | 7 | ABB |
| Trout,Mike | 8 | BAB |
| Williams,Nick | 9 | ABB |

| SP | Rel |
|---|---|
| Arrieta,Jake | AAA |
| Berrios,Jose | ABB |
| Boyd,Matt | ABB |
| Bundy,Dylan | BAA |
| Clevinger,Michael | ABB |
| deGrom,Jacob | BAA |
| Fiers,Mike | BAA |
| Freeland,Kyle | ABB |
| Gonzalez,Gio | AAA |
| Leake,Mike | BAA |
| Lester,Jon | BAB |
| Lopez,Reynaldo | ABA |
| Marquez,German | AAB |
| Montgomery,Mike | ABA |
| Nola,Aaron | BAA |
| Porcello,Rick | AAB |
| Quintana,Jose | AAA |
| Roark,Tanner | AAA |
| Scherzer,Max | BAA |
| Severino,Luis | AAB |
| Snell,Blake | ABB |
| Teheran,Julio | BAB |
| Urena,Jose | BBB |
| Williams,Trevor | ABA |

| RP | Rel |
|---|---|
| Allen,Cody | ABB |
| Chavez,Jesse | BBB |
| Giles,Ken | ABA |
| Hammel,Jason | AAB |
| Hand,Brad | ABA |
| Osuna,Roberto | ABB |
| Robertson,David | ABB |
| Rodney,Fernando | BBA |
| Treinen,Blake | ABB |
| Vazquez,Felipe | ABA |

# RISK MANAGEMENT

## GRADE "A" in CONSISTENCY

| Pitchers (min 120 IP) | Batters (min 400 AB) |
|---|---|
| Anderson,Tyler | Adames,Willy |
| Archer,Chris | Alfaro,Jorge |
| Arrieta,Jake | Anderson,Tim |
| Barria,Jaime | Bell,Josh |
| Bauer,Trevor | Cabrera,Asdrubal |
| Bieber,Shane | Davis,Khristopher |
| Bumgarner,Madison | Delmonico,Nick |
| Bundy,Dylan | Dietrich,Derek |
| Carrasco,Carlos | Escobar,Alcides |
| Cashner,Andrew | Frazier,Adam |
| Castillo,Luis | Frazier,Todd |
| Chacin,Jhoulys | Galvis,Freddy |
| Chen,Wei-Yin | Grichuk,Randal |
| Darvish,Yu | Guzman,Ronald |
| Davies,Zachary | Hamilton,Billy |
| deGrom,Jacob | Haniger,Mitch |
| Fiers,Mike | Iglesias,Jose |
| Fulmer,Michael | Kepler,Max |
| Gausman,Kevin | Lindor,Francisco |
| Giolito,Lucas | Mazara,Nomar |
| Gonzalez,Gio | Mercer,Jordy |
| Gray,Jonathan | Moncada,Yoan |
| Gray,Sonny | Morales,Kendrys |
| Greinke,Zack | Moreland,Mitch |
| Happ,J.A. | Mullins II,Cedric |
| Hendricks,Kyle | Myers,Wil |
| Hernandez,Felix | Ohtani,Shohei |
| Hill,Rich | Pillar,Kevin |
| Kennedy,Ian | Polanco,Jorge |
| Kershaw,Clayton | Pollock,A.J. |
| Lauer,Eric | Realmuto,Jacob |
| Leake,Mike | Schebler,Scott |
| Lopez,Reynaldo | Semien,Marcus |
| Lucchesi,Joey | Simmons,Andrelton |
| Maeda,Kenta | Span,Denard |
| Martinez,Carlos | Torres,Gleyber |
| Morton,Charlie | |
| Musgrove,Joe | |
| Newcomb,Sean | |
| Nola,Aaron | |
| Nova,Ivan | |
| Odorizzi,Jake | |
| Paxton,James | |
| Peralta,Freddy | |
| Price,David | |
| Quintana,Jose | |
| Ray,Robbie | |
| Richard,Clayton | |
| Richards,Trevor | |
| Roark,Tanner | |
| Rodriguez,Eduardo | |
| Romano,Sal | |
| Romero,Fernando | |
| Sabathia,CC | |
| Scherzer,Max | |
| Shields,James | |
| Straily,Dan | |
| Strasburg,Stephen | |
| Stripling,Ross | |
| Stroman,Marcus | |
| Syndergaard,Noah | |
| Tanaka,Masahiro | |
| Wacha,Michael | |
| Williams,Trevor | |
| Wood,Alex | |

## TOP COMBINATION OF SKILLS AND RELIABILITY
### Maximum of one "C" in Reliability Grade

### BATTING POWER (Min. 400 AB)

| PX 100+ | PX | Rel |
|---|---|---|
| Gallo,Joey | 228 | ABC |
| Davis,Khristopher | 179 | AAA |
| Trout,Mike | 173 | BAB |
| Grichuk,Randal | 158 | BCA |
| Renfroe,Hunter | 151 | BCB |
| Carpenter,Matt | 150 | AAB |
| Goldschmidt,Paul | 149 | AAB |
| Hernandez,Teoscar | 148 | ACB |
| Chapman,Matt | 148 | ABC |
| Arenado,Nolan | 147 | AAB |
| Grandal,Yasmani | 145 | ABB |
| Bryant,Kris | 143 | BAC |
| Baez,Javier | 141 | ABB |
| Ramirez,Jose | 139 | AAC |
| Voit,Luke | 137 | ACB |
| Freeman,Freddie | 134 | BAB |
| Encarnacion,Edwin | 134 | AAB |
| Shaw,Travis | 134 | AAC |
| Cruz,Nelson | 130 | AAB |
| Bregman,Alex | 130 | AAB |
| Castellanos,Nick | 129 | BAB |
| Davis,Chris | 129 | BAC |
| Suarez,Eugenio | 127 | AAC |
| Haniger,Mitch | 125 | BBA |
| Lindor,Francisco | 123 | AAA |
| Dozier,Brian | 122 | AAC |
| Moreland,Mitch | 122 | BBA |
| Rendon,Anthony | 121 | BAC |
| Piscotty,Stephen | 121 | ABC |
| Gonzalez,Carlos | 121 | BAB |
| Abreu,Jose | 121 | BAC |
| Moncada,Yoan | 120 | ACA |
| Bogaerts,Xander | 118 | AAC |
| Candelario,Jeimer | 117 | ABB |
| Seager,Kyle | 116 | AAC |
| Frazier,Todd | 115 | CAA |
| Perez,Salvador | 115 | BBC |
| Rosario,Eddie | 115 | ABB |
| Bradley,Jackie | 115 | AAB |
| Kemp,Matt | 115 | BBB |
| Escobar,Eduardo | 115 | ABC |
| Kepler,Max | 114 | ABA |
| Guzman,Ronald | 114 | ABA |
| Williams,Nick | 114 | ABB |
| Rizzo,Anthony | 114 | AAB |
| McCutchen,Andrew | 113 | AAC |
| Dickerson,Corey | 111 | BAB |
| Bauers,Jake | 111 | ABB |
| Cabrera,Asdrubal | 111 | BAA |
| Realmuto,Jacob | 109 | ABA |
| Morales,Kendrys | 108 | AAA |
| Goodrum,Niko | 108 | ACB |
| Contreras,Willson | 107 | ACB |
| Mazara,Nomar | 107 | AAA |
| Gennett,Scooter | 107 | AAB |
| Santana,Carlos | 106 | AAB |
| Healy,Ryon | 106 | ABC |
| Calhoun,Kole | 105 | BAB |
| Gyorko,Jedd | 105 | BCB |
| Longoria,Evan | 101 | BAB |
| Bell,Josh | 101 | AAA |
| Choo,Shin-Soo | 101 | CBB |
| Cano,Robinson | 100 | AAC |
| Bader,Harrison | 100 | ACB |

### RUNNER SPEED (Min. 400 AB)

| Spd 100+ | SX | Rel |
|---|---|---|
| Hamilton,Billy | 186 | BBA |
| Gordon,Dee | 183 | BBC |
| Rosario,Amed | 164 | ACB |
| Hernandez,Cesar | 163 | BAB |
| Adames,Willy | 156 | ABA |
| Hernandez,Teoscar | 151 | ACB |
| Turner,Trea | 150 | BAB |
| Margot,Manuel | 146 | BBB |
| Difo,Wilmer | 146 | ACB |
| Marte,Ketel | 145 | ABB |
| Anderson,Tim | 143 | AAA |
| Gardner,Brett | 141 | AAB |
| Marte,Starling | 140 | ABB |
| Cain,Lorenzo | 139 | BAB |
| Baez,Javier | 139 | ABB |
| Albies,Ozzie | 137 | AAB |
| Bader,Harrison | 136 | ACB |
| Moncada,Yoan | 136 | ACA |
| Desmond,Ian | 133 | CBB |
| Peraza,Jose | 131 | ABC |
| Inciarte,Ender | 130 | AAB |
| Segura,Jean | 129 | BAB |
| Goodrum,Niko | 123 | ACB |
| Nunez,Eduardo | 122 | BBC |
| Merrifield,Whit | 122 | ABC |
| Trout,Mike | 122 | BAB |
| Anderson,Brian | 121 | ABB |
| Simmons,Andrelton | 121 | BAA |
| Swanson,Dansby | 120 | ACB |
| Dickerson,Corey | 120 | BAB |
| Sanchez,Yolmer | 120 | ABB |
| Castellanos,Nick | 120 | BAB |
| Williams,Nick | 119 | ABB |
| Escobar,Alcides | 117 | AAA |
| Bryant,Kris | 117 | BAC |
| Chapman,Matt | 116 | ABC |
| Benintendi,Andrew | 115 | ABB |
| Realmuto,Jacob | 115 | ABA |
| Wendle,Joe | 114 | ABC |
| Bregman,Alex | 114 | AAB |
| Rosario,Eddie | 114 | ABB |
| Frazier,Adam | 112 | ACA |
| Herrera,Odubel | 112 | AAB |
| Bogaerts,Xander | 112 | AAC |
| Semien,Marcus | 111 | CAA |
| Galvis,Freddy | 110 | AAA |
| Nunez,Renato | 109 | ACB |
| Goldschmidt,Paul | 108 | AAB |
| Span,Denard | 108 | CAA |
| Ramirez,Jose | 108 | AAC |
| Polanco,Jorge | 107 | ACA |
| Kepler,Max | 107 | ABA |
| Haniger,Mitch | 106 | BBA |
| Heyward,Jason | 105 | BBB |
| Voit,Luke | 105 | ACB |
| Grichuk,Randal | 104 | BCA |
| Lindor,Francisco | 104 | AAA |
| Contreras,Willson | 103 | ACB |
| Dietrich,Derek | 103 | ABA |
| Arenado,Nolan | 102 | AAB |
| Castro,Starlin | 102 | BBB |
| Freeman,Freddie | 101 | BAB |
| Longoria,Evan | 101 | BAB |
| Kinsler,Ian | 100 | BAC |
| Dozier,Brian | 100 | AAC |

### OVERALL PITCHING SKILL

| BPV over 80 | BPV | Rel |
|---|---|---|
| Diaz,Edwin | 196 | ABC |
| Jansen,Kenley | 189 | CAB |
| Scherzer,Max | 166 | BAA |
| Kimbrel,Craig | 165 | BAC |
| Osuna,Roberto | 163 | ABB |
| Giles,Ken | 161 | ABA |
| deGrom,Jacob | 155 | BAA |
| Kluber,Corey | 154 | CAB |
| Hand,Brad | 152 | ABA |
| Robertson,David | 150 | ABB |
| Verlander,Justin | 150 | CAB |
| Vazquez,Felipe | 138 | ABA |
| Neris,Hector | 138 | ACB |
| Treinen,Blake | 137 | ABB |
| Barnes,Matt | 137 | ACB |
| Severino,Luis | 135 | AAB |
| Nola,Aaron | 135 | BAA |
| Devenski,Chris | 132 | BCA |
| Archer,Chris | 130 | CAA |
| Maeda,Kenta | 128 | CAA |
| Greinke,Zack | 126 | CAA |
| Bauer,Trevor | 126 | CAA |
| Marquez,German | 125 | AAB |
| Rondon,Hector | 124 | BCA |
| Otero,Dan | 123 | ACA |
| Colome,Alexander | 122 | BAC |
| Castillo,Luis | 120 | ACA |
| Snell,Blake | 119 | ABB |
| Watson,Tony | 118 | ACB |
| Parker,Blake | 116 | ACB |
| Chavez,Jesse | 114 | BBB |
| Taillon,Jameson | 113 | CBB |
| Davis,Wade | 112 | CBA |
| Allen,Cody | 112 | ABB |
| Cishek,Steve | 112 | BCA |
| Petit,Yusmeiro | 112 | ACB |
| Porcello,Rick | 110 | AAB |
| Mikolas,Miles | 109 | AAC |
| Reed,Addison | 108 | BCB |
| Givens,Mychal | 106 | ACA |
| Hendricks,Kyle | 106 | CAA |
| Clippard,Tyler | 106 | ACA |
| Junis,Jakob | 105 | ACB |
| Hirano,Yoshihisa | 104 | ABC |
| Jeffress,Jeremy | 100 | BBC |
| Berrios,Jose | 100 | ABB |
| Bundy,Dylan | 100 | BAA |
| Foltynewicz,Mike | 96 | CBB |
| Leake,Mike | 94 | BAA |
| Wilson,Justin | 94 | ACA |
| Gonzales,Marco | 93 | BCB |
| Weaver,Luke | 92 | ACB |
| Clevinger,Michael | 92 | ABB |
| Quintana,Jose | 90 | AAA |
| Brach,Brad | 89 | ACB |
| Tepera,Ryan | 88 | BCA |
| Fiers,Mike | 88 | BAA |
| Gausman,Kevin | 88 | CAA |
| Roark,Tanner | 85 | AAA |
| Arrieta,Jake | 84 | AAA |
| LeBlanc,Wade | 83 | BCB |
| Boyd,Matt | 81 | ABB |

# DAILY FANTASY INDICATORS

## Top OPS v LHP, 2017-2018

| Hitter | OPS |
|---|---|
| Arenado, Nolan | 1250 |
| Martinez, J.D. | 1134 |
| Stanton, Giancarlo | 1119 |
| Turner, Justin | 1111 |
| Zimmerman, Ryan | 1077 |
| Betts, Mookie | 1071 |
| Story, Trevor | 1054 |
| Bryant, Kris | 1025 |
| Rendon, Anthony | 1022 |
| Flowers, Tyler | 993 |
| Donaldson, Josh | 990 |
| Goldschmidt, Paul | 987 |
| Abreu, Jose | 981 |
| Bregman, Alex | 971 |
| Suzuki, Kurt | 971 |
| Castellanos, Nick | 971 |
| Martinez, Jose | 963 |
| Suarez, Eugenio | 963 |
| Trout, Mike | 956 |
| Judge, Aaron | 950 |
| Gyorko, Jedd | 947 |
| McCutchen, Andrew | 943 |
| Lindor, Francisco | 943 |
| Baez, Javier | 933 |
| Garcia, Avisail | 932 |
| LeMahieu, DJ | 929 |
| Correa, Carlos | 929 |
| Posey, Buster | 927 |
| Renfroe, Hunter | 925 |
| Camargo, Johan | 917 |
| Pham, Thomas | 917 |
| Aguilar, Jesus | 912 |
| Freeman, Freddie | 907 |
| Albies, Ozzie | 906 |
| Cain, Lorenzo | 906 |
| Marte, Ketel | 905 |
| Chirinos, Robinson | 903 |
| Springer, George | 899 |
| Ramirez, Jose | 895 |
| Merrifield, Whit | 887 |
| Cabrera, Miguel | 886 |

*600+ PA, 2017-2018*

## Top OPS v RHP, 2017-2018

| Hitter | OPS |
|---|---|
| Trout, Mike | 1116 |
| Martinez, J.D. | 1028 |
| Judge, Aaron | 1007 |
| Harper, Bryce | 983 |
| Ramirez, Jose | 976 |
| Votto, Joey | 974 |
| Blackmon, Charlie | 959 |
| Freeman, Freddie | 946 |
| Hoskins, Rhys | 929 |
| Goldschmidt, Paul | 928 |
| Nimmo, Brandon | 925 |
| Murphy, Daniel | 925 |
| Yelich, Christian | 917 |
| Puig, Yasiel | 914 |
| Bellinger, Cody | 912 |
| Altuve, Jose | 909 |
| Carpenter, Matt | 906 |
| Gennett, Scooter | 904 |
| Rizzo, Anthony | 904 |
| Olson, Matt | 897 |
| Rendon, Anthony | 894 |
| Shaw, Travis | 893 |
| Davis, Khristopher | 891 |
| Betts, Mookie | 890 |
| Thames, Eric | 888 |
| Cruz, Nelson | 887 |
| Conforto, Michael | 887 |
| Peralta, David | 885 |
| Hosmer, Eric | 885 |
| Brantley, Michael | 878 |
| Andujar, Miguel | 877 |
| Donaldson, Josh | 873 |
| Lamb, Jacob | 873 |
| Bour, Justin | 872 |
| Rosario, Eddie | 872 |
| Stanton, Giancarlo | 871 |
| Pham, Thomas | 867 |
| Cano, Robinson | 867 |
| Bryant, Kris | 862 |
| Encarnacion, Edwin | 862 |
| Smoak, Justin | 861 |

## Top L-R Splits, 2017-2018

| Hitter | OPS vL-vR |
|---|---|
| Arenado, Nolan | 417 |
| Story, Trevor | 288 |
| Flowers, Tyler | 286 |
| Hundley, Nick | 262 |
| Turner, Justin | 259 |
| Stanton, Giancarlo | 248 |
| Zimmerman, Ryan | 245 |
| LeMahieu, DJ | 226 |
| Marte, Ketel | 222 |
| Renfroe, Hunter | 216 |
| Gyorko, Jedd | 211 |
| Ahmed, Nick | 196 |
| Suzuki, Kurt | 189 |
| Albies, Ozzie | 188 |
| Betts, Mookie | 180 |
| Castellanos, Nick | 179 |
| Candelario, Jeimer | 173 |
| Posey, Buster | 171 |
| McCutchen, Andrew | 170 |

## Top R-L Splits, 2017-2018

| Hitter | OPS vR-vL |
|---|---|
| Lamb, Jacob | 332 |
| Spangenberg, Cory | 312 |
| Puig, Yasiel | 299 |
| Pederson, Joc | 293 |
| Duda, Lucas | 256 |
| Adams, Matt | 255 |
| Hosmer, Eric | 251 |
| Walker, Neil | 238 |
| Nimmo, Brandon | 235 |
| Thames, Eric | 235 |
| Joyce, Matt | 228 |
| Bour, Justin | 207 |
| Murphy, Daniel | 203 |
| Alonso, Yonder | 199 |
| Shaw, Travis | 199 |
| Marte, Starling | 192 |
| Gonzalez, Carlos | 190 |
| Brantley, Michael | 189 |
| Schwarber, Kyle | 186 |

## Best Parks - RH HR

| Ballpark | Factor |
|---|---|
| PHI | 24% |
| NYY | 22% |
| COL | 22% |
| CIN | 17% |
| BAL | 15% |
| WAS | 14% |
| HOU | 10% |
| TEX | 9% |
| CHC | 9% |
| LAA | 7% |

## Worst Parks-RH HR

| Ballpark | Factor |
|---|---|
| MIA | -27% |
| SF | -26% |
| PIT | -26% |
| STL | -19% |
| OAK | -16% |
| ATL | -16% |
| KC | -15% |

## Best Parks - Ks

| Ballpark | Factor |
|---|---|
| PHI | 12% |
| SEA | 11% |
| CIN | 11% |
| NYM | 9% |
| TAM | 9% |

## Worst Parks - Ks

| Ballpark | Factor |
|---|---|
| COL | -10% |
| DET | -9% |
| TEX | -8% |
| KC | -7% |

## Worst Parks - BB

| Ballpark | Factor |
|---|---|
| LAA | -10% |
| BOS | -7% |
| STL | -7% |

## Best Parks - LH HR

| Ballpark | Factor |
|---|---|
| NYY | 38% |
| LAA | 34% |
| PHI | 25% |
| CIN | 24% |
| MIL | 24% |
| COL | 18% |
| TEX | 17% |
| CLE | 17% |
| CHW | 17% |
| LAA | 17% |

## Worst Parks - LH HR

| Ballpark | Factor |
|---|---|
| SF | -40% |
| KC | -22% |
| BOS | -21% |
| SD | -19% |
| CHC | -18% |
| MIA | -16% |
| OAK | -15% |

## Best Parks - Runs*

| Ballpark | Factor |
|---|---|
| COL | 33% |
| TEX | 24% |
| CLE | 10% |
| BOS | 10% |

## Worst Parks - Runs*

| Ballpark | Factor |
|---|---|
| MIA | -19% |
| NYM | -15% |
| LAA | -12% |
| HOU | -11% |
| SEA | -10% |

## Best Parks - BB

| Ballpark | Factor |
|---|---|
| TEX | 8% |
| CHC | 8% |
| CIN | 7% |

*Note: for Runs, the best parks for hitters are also the worst for pitchers and vice versa*

## Consistent High-PQS SP

| Pitcher | QC* |
|---|---|
| deGrom, Jacob | 150 |
| Verlander, Justin | 112 |
| Scherzer, Max | 110 |
| Cole, Gerrit | 100 |
| Sale, Chris | 82 |
| Kluber, Corey | 80 |
| Corbin, Patrick | 78 |
| Bauer, Trevor | 74 |
| Strasburg, Stephen | 52 |
| Severino, Luis | 46 |
| Nola, Aaron | 44 |
| Buehler, Walker | 42 |
| Kershaw, Clayton | 38 |
| Snell, Blake | 34 |
| Greinke, Zack | 30 |
| Carrasco, Carlos | 26 |
| Heaney, Andrew | 22 |
| Glasnow, Tyler | 18 |
| Clevinger, Michael | 10 |
| Syndergaard, Noah | 8 |

## Consistent Low-PQS SP

| Pitcher | QC* |
|---|---|
| Perez, Martin | (292) |
| Oswalt, Corey | (268) |
| Pomeranz, Drew | (256) |
| Moore, Matt | (252) |
| Blach, Ty | (248) |
| Colon, Bartolo | (242) |
| Koch, Matt | (242) |
| Mitchell, Bryan | (238) |
| Fedde, Erick | (238) |
| Gallardo, Yovani | (232) |
| Bailey, Homer | (230) |
| Hess, David | (222) |
| Cashner, Andrew | (214) |
| Romano, Sal | (208) |
| Sanchez, Aaron | (200) |
| Gaviglio, Sam | (200) |
| Johnson, Brian | (200) |
| Samardzija, Jeff | (200) |

*10+ Games Started, 2018*

*\*Quality-Consistency score*

## Most DOMinant SP

| Pitcher | DOM |
|---|---|
| deGrom, Jacob | 75% |
| Scherzer, Max | 67% |
| Sale, Chris | 63% |
| Verlander, Justin | 62% |
| Bauer, Trevor | 59% |
| Kluber, Corey | 58% |
| Snell, Blake | 55% |
| Nola, Aaron | 52% |
| Cole, Gerrit | 50% |
| Carrasco, Carlos | 47% |
| Wheeler, Zack | 45% |
| Greinke, Zack | 45% |
| Price, David | 43% |
| Bieber, Shane | 42% |
| Severino, Luis | 41% |
| Wacha, Michael | 40% |
| Ryu, Hyun-Jin | 40% |
| Foltynewicz, Mike | 39% |
| Buehler, Walker | 39% |
| Corbin, Patrick | 39% |

## Most DISastrous SP

| Pitcher | DIS |
|---|---|
| Perez, Martin | 73% |
| Colon, Bartolo | 67% |
| Moore, Matt | 67% |
| Oswalt, Corey | 67% |
| Bailey, Homer | 65% |
| Pomeranz, Drew | 64% |
| Mitchell, Bryan | 64% |
| Fedde, Erick | 64% |
| Koch, Matt | 64% |
| Blach, Ty | 62% |
| Gallardo, Yovani | 61% |
| Hess, David | 58% |
| Cashner, Andrew | 57% |
| Hammel, Jason | 56% |
| Romano, Sal | 56% |
| Vargas, Jason | 55% |
| Sanchez, Aaron | 55% |
| Romero, Fernando | 55% |

## Universal Draft Grid

Most publications and websites provide cheat sheets with ranked player lists for different fantasy draft formats. The biggest problem with these tools is that they perpetuate the myth that players can be ranked in a linear fashion.

Since rankings are based on highly variable projections, it is foolhardy to draw conclusions that a $24 player is better than a $23 player is better than a $22 player. Yes, a first round pick is better than a 10th round pick, but within most rounds, all players are pretty much interchangeable commodities.

But typical cheat sheets don't reflect that reality. Auction sheets rank players by dollar value. Snake draft sheets rank players within round, accounting for position and categorical scarcity. But just as ADPs have a ridiculously low success rate, these cheat sheets are similarly flawed.

We have a tool at BaseballHQ.com called the Rotisserie Grid. It is a chart—that can be customized to your league parameters—which organizes players into pockets of skill, by position. It is one of the most popular tools on the site. One of the best features of this grid is that its design provides immediate insight into position scarcity.

So in the *Forecaster*, we have transitioned to this format as a sort of Universal Draft Grid.

### How to use the chart

Across the top of the grid, players are sorted by position. First and third base, and second and shortstop are presented side-by-side for easy reference when considering corner and middle infielders, respectively.

The vertical axis separates each group of players into tiers based on potential fantasy impact. At the top are the Elite players; at the bottom are the Fringe players.

**Auction leagues:** The tiers in the grid represent rough breakpoints for dollar values. Elite players could be considered those that are purchased for $30 and up. Each subsequent tier is a step down of approximately $5.

**Snake drafters:** Tiers can be used to rank players similarly, though most tiers will encompass more than one round. Any focus on position scarcity will bump some players up a bit. For instance, with the dearth of Elite catchers and the wealth of Elite outfielders, one might opt to draft Jacob Realmuto (from the Stars tier) before the Elite level Starling Marte. The reason we target scarce positions early is that there will be plenty of solid outfielders and starting pitchers later on.

To build the best foundation, you should come out of the first 10 rounds with all your middle infielders, all your corner infielders, one outfielder, at least one catcher and two pitchers (at least one closer).

**The players** are listed at the position where they both qualify and provide the most fantasy value. Additional position eligibility (20 games) is listed in parentheses. Listings in bold are players with high reliability grades (minimum "B" across the board).

Each player is presented with his 7-character Mayberry score. The first four digits (all on a 0-5 scale) represent skill: power, speed, batting average and playing time for batters; ERA, dominance, saves potential and playing time for pitchers. The last three alpha characters are the reliability grade (A-F): health, experience and consistency.

Within each tier, players are sorted by the first character of their Mayberry score. This means that batters are sorted by power; pitchers by ERA potential. If you need to prospect for the best skill sets among players in a given tier, target those with 4s and 5s in whatever skill you need.

### CAVEATS and DISCLAIMERS

The placement of players in tiers does not represent average draft positions (ADP) or average auction values (AAV). It represents where each player's true value may lie. It is the variance between this true value and the ADP/AAV market values—or better, the value that your league-mates place on each player—where you will find your potential for profit or loss.

That means *you cannot take this chart right into your draft with you*. You have to compare these rankings with your ADPs and AAVs, and build your draft list from there. In other words, if we project Freddie Freeman as a "Elite" level pick but you know the other owners (or your ADPs) see him as a third-rounder, you can probably wait to pick him up in round two. If you are in an auction league with owners who overvalue players from the Pacific Northwest, and Jean Segura (projected at $27) gets bid past $30, you will likely take a loss should you decide to chase the bidding, especially given the depth of shortstops in 2019.

Finally, this chart is intended as a preliminary look based on current factors. For Draft Day, you will need to make your own adjustments based upon many different criteria that will impact the world between now and then. Daily updates appear online at BaseballHQ.com. A free projections update is available in March at **http://www.baseballhq.com/bf2019**

### Simulation League Cheat Sheet

Using Runs Above Replacement creates a more real-world ranking of player value, which serves simulation gamers well. Batters and pitchers are integrated, and value break-points are delineated.

## Universal Draft Grid

| TIER | FIRST BASE | | THIRD BASE | | SECOND BASE | | SHORTSTOP | |
|---|---|---|---|---|---|---|---|---|
| **Elite** | **Goldschmidt,Paul** | **(4345 AAB)** | Ramirez,Jose | (4455 AAC) | Altuve,Jose | (2555 AAD) | Story,Trevor | (5435 BBF) |
| | **Freeman,Freddie** | **(4255 BAB)** | **Arenado,Nolan** | **(4155 AAB)** | Merrifield,Whit (O) | (2545 ABC) | **Lindor,Francisco** | **(4355 AAA)** |
| | | | | | Gordon,Dee (O) | (0545 BBC) | **Bregman,Alex (3)** | **(4355 AAB)** |
| | | | | | | | Machado,Manny | (4345 AAD) |
| | | | | | | | **Turner,Trea** | **(2535 BAB)** |
| **Gold** | Bellinger,Cody (O) | (4525 ABD) | Rendon,Anthony | (4255 BAC) | Villar,Jonathan | (2415 BBD) | **Baez,Javier (23)** | **(4535 ABB)** |
| | **Rizzo,Anthony** | **(3155 AAB)** | Andujar,Miguel | (4255 ACC) | | | Bogaerts,Xander | (3455 AAC) |
| | Votto,Joey | (3255 BAF) | | | | | Mondesi,Adalberto | (3515 BDB) |
| | | | | | | | Rosario,Amed | (2535 ACB) |
| | | | | | | | Peraza,Jose | (1545 ABC) |
| | | | | | | | **Segura,Jean** | **(1445 BAB)** |
| **Stars** | Abreu,Jose | (4245 BAC) | Turner,Justin | (4255 DBC) | Dozier,Brian | (4325 AAC) | Torres,Gleyber (2) | (4325 AFA) |
| | Aguilar,Jesus | (4035 ACC) | Myers,Wil (O) | (4435 FBA) | Shaw,Travis (3) | (4235 AAC) | Correa,Carlos | (3335 CBF) |
| | **Encarnacion,Edwin** | **(4235 AAB)** | Bryant,Kris | (4235 BAC) | **Gennett,Scooter** | **(3235 AAB)** | **Anderson,Tim** | **(2525 AAA)** |
| | Desmond,Ian | (2535 CBB) | **Carpenter,Matt (1)** | **(4145 AAB)** | Murphy,Daniel | (3255 DBD) | Simmons,Andrelton | (1455 BAA) |
| | Hosmer,Eric | (2245 AAF) | Suarez,Eugenio | (4135 AAC) | Cano,Robinson | (2155 AAC) | Andrus,Elvis | (1445 CBC) |
| | | | Moustakas,Mike | (3045 CCB) | **Albies,Ozzie** | **(2525 AAB)** | | |
| | | | Gurriel,Yulieski (1) | (2345 ACD) | | | | |
| **Regulars** | Thames,Eric (O) | (5323 CCC) | Chapman,Matt | (4125 ABC) | Moncada,Yoan | (4405 ACA) | DeJong,Paul | (4125 BBD) |
| | Olson,Matt | (4225 ABD) | Donaldson,Josh | (4345 FBC) | Odor,Rougned | (3225 BAD) | Seager,Corey | (3255 FBC) |
| | Smoak,Justin | (4025 ABD) | Devers,Rafael | (4025 BDF) | Schoop,Jonathan | (3135 BAD) | Profar,Jurickson (31) | (3455 QCD) |
| | Cabrera,Miguel | (3055 FCF) | Seager,Kyle | (3135 AAC) | Wendle,Joe (3) | (2445 ABC) | Escobar,Eduardo (3) | (3145 ABC) |
| | Mancini,Trey (O) | (3135 AAD) | **Franco,Maikel** | **(2245 AAB)** | Kinsler,Ian | (2335 BAC) | **Cabrera,Asdrubal (23)** | **(3135 BAA)** |
| | **Bauers,Jake** | **(3125 ABB)** | Duffy,Matt | (1435 FDB) | **Castro,Starlin** | **(1235 BBB)** | **Marte,Ketel (2)** | **(2555 ABB)** |
| | Martinez,Jose (O) | (2045 ACF) | | | McNeil,Jeff | (1535 AFF) | Semien,Marcus | (2325 CAA) |
| | | | | | LeMahieu,DJ | (1255 BAD) | **Adames,Willy** | **(2405 ABA)** |
| | | | | | **Hernandez,Cesar** | **(1525 BAB)** | Polanco,Jorge | (2235 ACA) |
| | | | | | Nunez,Eduardo (3) | (1443 BBC) | Diaz,Aledmys (3) | (2235 BCF) |
| | | | | | Difo,Wilmer (3) | (1535 ACB) | Gurriel,Lourdes (2) | (2335 BFC) |
| | | | | | | | Iglesias,Jose | (1355 CBA) |
| **Mid-Level** | Gallo,Joey (O) | (5215 ABC) | Muncy,Max (1) | (4125 ADF) | Barreto,Franklin | (4403 ACA) | Taylor,Chris (O) | (4425 ACC) |
| | Bruce,Jay (O) | (4035 CBC) | Lamb,Jake | (4215 FBC) | Lowe,Brandon | (4323 AFF) | Gonzalez,Marwin (2O) | (3135 ABF) |
| | Voit,Luke | (4045 ACB) | Sano,Miguel | (4205 CCD) | Kipnis,Jason | (3235 CBC) | Ahmed,Nick | (3245 DDB) |
| | **Moreland,Mitch** | **(4135 BBA)** | Beltre,Adrian | (2243 CBD) | Goodrum,Niko (1) | (3425 ACB) | Hernandez,Enrique (2O) | (3335 BDC) |
| | Cron,C.J. | (4033 BCC) | Camargo,Johan | (3235 BCC) | Lowrie,Jed | (2035 DAC) | Beckham,Tim (3) | (3315 DCC) |
| | Belt,Brandon | (4225 DBB) | Gyorko,Jedd | (3225 BCB) | Frazier,Adam | (2253 ACA) | **Gregorius,Didi** | **(3343 BAA)** |
| | Adams,Matt | (4033 CDC) | Frazier,Todd | (3115 CAA) | Kendrick,Howie | (2523 ADB) | **Galvis,Freddy** | **(2325 AAA)** |
| | Zimmerman,Ryan | (4043 FCF) | Candelario,Jeimer | (3125 ABB) | Hanson,Alen | (2523 ADB) | **Crawford,Brandon** | **(2135 AAB)** |
| | **Santana,Carlos** | **(3235 AAB)** | Cozart,Zack | (2335 FCF) | Solarte,Yangervis | (2035 CBC) | Adrianza,Ehire (3) | (2323 FFB) |
| | **Bell,Josh** | **(3145 AAA)** | **Anderson,Brian (O)** | **(1135 ABB)** | Perez,Hernan (3O) | (2523 ACA) | Kingery,Scott | (2515 ACF) |
| | Alonso,Yonder | (3135 BBF) | Moran,Colin | (1035 BCC) | Zobrist,Ben (O) | (1145 BBF) | Hampson,Garrett | (1523 AFF) |
| | Healy,Ryon | (3025 ABC) | **Sanchez,Yolmer** | **(1325 ABB)** | Panik,Joe | (1345 DBC) | Swanson,Dansby | (1315 ACB) |
| | McMahon,Ryan | (3233 ACF) | | | Harrison,Josh | (1323 CBB) | | |
| | Bour,Justin | (3223 DCD) | | | Wong,Kolten | (1343 BCC) | | |
| | **Pujols,Albert** | **(2143 BAB)** | | | Pedroia,Dustin | (1143 FCF) | | |
| | **Dietrich,Derek (O)** | **(2225 ABA)** | | | Fletcher,David (3) | (1323 ADD) | | |
| | Flores,Wilmer | (2133 BCA) | | | | | | |
| | Slater,Austin (O) | (1313 BDA) | | | | | | |
| **Bench** | Austin,Tyler | (5123 CDB) | Villanueva,Christian | (3123 FFB) | Pinder,Chad (O) | (3213 BDB) | Bichette,Bo | (3441 AFF) |
| | Pearce,Steve | (4043 FDF) | Nunez,Renato | (2305 ACB) | Descalso,Daniel (3) | (3213 BCB) | **Mercer,Jordy** | **(2235 BBA)** |
| | Reynolds,Mark | (4111 ACB) | Bote,David | (2223 ADB) | Travis,Devon | (2243 FDC) | Munoz,Yairo (23) | (2241 ACB) |
| | Davis,Chris | (4105 BAC) | Ward,Taylor | (2211 AFA) | Walker,Neil (31) | (2123 CCC) | **Russell,Addison** | **(2323 BBA)** |
| | Vogelbach,Daniel | (4023 ACB) | Drury,Brandon | (2023 DCB) | Spangenberg,Cory (3) | (2513 DDB) | Rodriguez,Ronny | (2213 ACA) |
| | Duda,Lucas | (4123 FDB) | | | Urias,Luis | (1335 ADB) | Culberson,Charlie (3O) | (2223 ADF) |
| | Tellez,Rowdy | (4241 ABF) | | | | | Robertson,Daniel (2) | (2113 DDB) |
| | **O'Hearn,Ryan** | **(4113 ABA)** | | | | | Riddle,J.T. | (2133 DDA) |
| | Dixon,Brandon | (4311 ACB) | | | | | Crawford,J.P. | (2425 DCB) |
| | Reed,A.J. | (4001 ACA) | | | | | **Escobar,Alcides (3)** | **(1335 AAA)** |
| | **Guzman,Ronald** | **(3225 ABA)** | | | | | Arcia,Orlando | (1425 ABD) |
| | White,Tyler | (3023 ACB) | | | | | Hechavarria,Adeiny | (1423 CCB) |
| | Morrison,Logan | (3113 DCF) | | | | | Holt,Brock (2) | (1231 DDF) |
| | Osuna,Jose | (3151 ADA) | | | | | Newman,Kevin | (1441 ACA) |
| | | | | | | | Rojas,Miguel (31) | (1243 BDD) |
| **Fringe** | Bird,Gregory | (4023 FFB) | Dozier,Hunter (1) | (4205 BDC) | Miller,Bradley (1) | (3301 BCB) | Saladino,Tyler | (2411 CDF) |
| | Davidson,Matthew | (4003 CCA) | Wisdom,Patrick | (4201 ACB) | Gonzalez,Erik (3) | (2431 AFB) | Rodgers,Brendan | (2221 AFA) |
| | Smith,Dominic | (4221 ABC) | Davis,J.D. | (3221 ACA) | Forsythe,Logan | (1201 CBB) | Reyes,Jose (3) | (2431 ACB) |
| | Marte,Jefry | (2121 BDB) | Bautista,Jose (O) | (3101 BBC) | Pirela,Jose (O) | (1231 ADF) | | |
| | Jones,Ryder | (1201 ACC) | | | Lugo,Dawel | (1351 ACC) | | |
| | Fernandez,Jose M. | (0051 AFA) | | | Blandino,Alex | (1101 CDC) | | |
| | | | | | Asuaje,Carlos | (1211 ACA) | | |

## Universal Draft Grid

| TIER | CATCHER | | DH | | OUTFIELD | | | |
|------|---------|---|----|----|----------|---|---|---|
| **Elite** | | | | | Trout,Mike | **(5545 BAB)** | Acuna,Ronald | (4535 BDB) |
| | | | | | Martinez,J.D. | (5355 CBC) | Marte,Starling | (2545 ABB) |
| | | | | | Betts,Mookie | (4555 AAF) | Smith,Mallex | (1535 CCC) |
| | | | | | Yelich,Christian | (4455 AAD) | Cain,Lorenzo | **(1545 BAB)** |
| | | | | | Blackmon,Charlie | (4455 AAD) | | |
| **Gold** | | | | | Stanton,Giancarlo | (5235 BAF) | | |
| | | | | | Judge,Aaron | (5235 CBF) | | |
| | | | | | Soto,Juan | (4345 AFF) | | |
| | | | | | Pham,Thomas | (4535 CCF) | | |
| | | | | | Benintendi,Andrew | **(2445 ABB)** | | |
| | | | | | Brantley,Michael | (2355 FDF) | | |
| **Stars** | Realmuto,Jacob | (3345 ABA) | Davis,Khristopher | (5235 AAA) | Hoskins,Rhys | (5145 AAD) | Springer,George | (3235 CAC) |
| | | | Ohtani,Shohei | (5345 ADA) | Harper,Bryce | (4245 BAF) | Robles,Victor | (3535 AFC) |
| | | | | | **Castellanos,Nick** | **(4245 BAB)** | Ozuna,Marcell | (3235 AAF) |
| | | | | | **Haniger,Mitch** | **(4235 BBA)** | Dickerson,Corey | **(3345 BAB)** |
| | | | | | Upton,Justin | (4225 AAD) | Winker,Jesse | (3055 CCB) |
| | | | | | Pollock,A.J. | (4555 FDA) | McCutchen,Andrew | (3235 AAC) |
| | | | | | Dahl,David | (4445 FDF) | Garcia,Avisail | (3325 DCF) |
| | | | | | Puig,Yasiel | (4345 CCB) | **Gardner,Brett** | **(2535 AAB)** |
| | | | | | Hicks,Aaron | (4345 DCD) | Inciarte,Ender | **(1445 AAB)** |
| | | | | | **Rosario,Eddie** | **(3335 ABB)** | Hamilton,Billy | (1515 BBA) |
| **Regulars** | Contreras,Willson | (3235 ACB) | Cruz,Nelson | **(4135 AAB)** | Braun,Ryan | (4255 CBC) | **Bradley,Jackie** | **(3325 AAB)** |
| | **Molina,Yadier** | **(2145 BBB)** | Senzel,Nick | (3333 CFF) | Piscotty,Stephen | (4145 ABC) | **Pillar,Kevin** | **(2345 AAA)** |
| | | | Guerrero Jr.,Vladii | (3155 AFF) | Conforto,Michael | (4135 BBF) | Eaton,Adam | (2545 FCB) |
| | | | | | Nimmo,Brandon | (4225 CCC) | **Jones,Adam** | **(2235 AAB)** |
| | | | | | Renfroe,Hunter | (4235 BCB) | **Herrera,Odubel** | **(2325 AAB)** |
| | | | | | Pederson,Joc | (4135 BCF) | Reddick,Josh | (2335 CCF) |
| | | | | | Cespedes,Yoenis | (4233 FDB) | **Margot,Manuel** | **(2535 BBB)** |
| | | | | | Schebler,Scott | (4135 CCA) | Bader,Harrison | (2415 ACB) |
| | | | | | Peralta,David | (3355 CCC) | **Markakis,Nick** | **(1045 AAB)** |
| | | | | | **Kemp,Matt** | **(3135 BBB)** | | |
| | | | | | **Mazara,Nomar** | **(3135 AAA)** | | |
| | | | | | **Kepler,Max** | **(3235 ABA)** | | |
| | | | | | Choo,Shin-Soo | (3135 CBB) | | |
| **Mid-Level** | Sanchez,Gary | (4135 CCC) | Choi,Ji-Man | (4133 ADB) | Grichuk,Randal | (4225 BCA) | Laureano,Ramon | (2515 ADF) |
| | **Grandal,Yasmani** | **(4025 ABB)** | **Morales,Kendrys** | **(3025 AAA)** | Cordero,Franchy | (4523 FDA) | Fowler,Dustin | (2523 CCB) |
| | Hedges,Austin | (4213 BDB) | Trumbo,Mark | (3215 DBC) | **Gonzalez,Carlos** | **(4235 BAB)** | Tucker,Kyle | (2323 AFA) |
| | Perez,Salvador | (3035 BBC) | Jimenez,Eloy | (3053 AFB) | Souza,Steven | (4415 FCD) | Duggar,Steven | (2415 BFC) |
| | Garver,Mitch | (3223 ACC) | | | O'Neill,Tyler | (4505 ABD) | Ervin,Phillip | (2323 ACA) |
| | Alfaro,Jorge | (3405 ADA) | | | Happ,Ian | (4215 ACC) | Kiermaier,Kevin | (2523 FCC) |
| | Ramos,Wilson | (2035 DCF) | | | Reyes,Franmil | (4025 ADD) | Gordon,Alex | (2225 CBC) |
| | Posey,Buster | (1143 BBD) | | | Hernandez,Teoscar | (4315 ACB) | Span,Denard | (2345 CAA) |
| | | | | | Santana,Domingo | (4313 BCD) | Martin,Leonys | (2513 DCC) |
| | | | | | Schwarber,Kyle | (4115 DDF) | Owings,Christopher | (2323 CCC) |
| | | | | | Soler,Jorge | (4215 FDC) | Fowler,Dexter | (2415 DCD) |
| | | | | | Goodwin,Brian | (4313 FDB) | Brinson,Lewis | (2525 CDD) |
| | | | | | **Williams,Nick** | **(3235 ABB)** | Mullins II,Cedric | (1335 ADA) |
| | | | | | Meadows,Austin | (3543 ADF) | Allen,Greg | (1533 AFB) |
| | | | | | Polanco,Gregory | (3333 BBC) | **Heyward,Jason** | **(1235 BBB)** |
| | | | | | **Calhoun,Kole** | **(3225 BAB)** | DeShields Jr.,Delino | (1503 BCD) |
| | | | | | Buxton,Byron | (3503 CCC) | Almora,Albert | (1235 ACC) |
| | | | | | Chisenhall,Lonnie | (3433 FFB) | Quinn,Roman | (1513 AFB) |
| | | | | | Frazier,Clint | (3403 FDB) | Verdugo,Alex | (1233 ACA) |
| | | | | | Gomez,Carlos | (3413 CCD) | Gamel,Benjamin | (1423 ACA) |
| | | | | | Bonifacio,Jorge | (3123 ACB) | Garcia,Leury | (1423 FDA) |
| | | | | | Tapia,Raimel | (3543 ACC) | Jankowski,Travis | (0513 CDD) |
| **Bench** | Zunino,Mike | (5003 BCD) | Alonso,Peter | (4013 AFD) | Cave,Jake | (4223 ACC) | Calhoun,Willie | (2233 ABC) |
| | Chirinos,Robinson | (4203 CDD) | Gattis,Evan | (4033 BCB) | Palka,Daniel | (4113 ACA) | Rickard,Joey | (2423 BDC) |
| | Mejia,Francisco | (4243 AFD) | Riley,Austin | (4413 AFD) | McKinney,Billy | (4133 BCC) | Parra,Gerardo | (1233 CCD) |
| | Murphy,Tom | (4203 BFF) | Tatis Jr.,Fernando | (4421 AFD) | **Granderson,Curtis** | **(4231 ABA)** | Dyson,Jarrod | (1531 DDC) |
| | Gomes,Yan | (3023 CCC) | Hiura,Keston | (3433 AFF) | Broxton,Keon | (4501 ADC) | Maybin,Cameron | (1423 CCB) |
| | Jansen,Danny | (3433 AFB) | Tulowitzki,Troy | (2133 FDC) | **Duvall,Adam** | **(4111 ABB)** | Hernandez,Gorkys | (1313 ACA) |
| | Castillo,Welington | (3213 BDD) | Ellsbury,Jacoby | (1531 FDB) | Cooper,Garrett | (4031 FDF) | Kemp,Anthony | (1333 ACB) |
| | Hundley,Nick | (3123 BDB) | Hays,Austin | (1221 AFF) | Taylor,Michael | (3503 ADD) | Lagares,Juan | (1521 FFC) |
| | Flowers,Tyler | (2005 CDB) | Diaz,Yandy | (1233 ACB) | Canha,Mark | (3223 CDD) | Davis,Rajai | (1501 BCB) |
| | Cervelli,Francisco | (2113 FCB) | | | Stewart,Christin | (3003 ACB) | Reyes,Victor | (0533 AFD) |
| | Pina,Manny | (2223 ADB) | | | Jones,JaCoby | (3503 ACA) | | |
| | Suzuki,Kurt | (2043 ADD) | | | Williamson,Mac | (3223 CDB) | | |
| | Diaz,Elias | (2133 CFD) | | | Phillips,Brett | (3503 ACD) | | |
| | D'Arnaud,Travis | #N/A | | | Delmonico,Nick | (3225 CCA) | | |
| | Barnes,Austin | (2321 ADF) | | | Mahtook,Mikie | (3411 ADF) | | |
| | Lucroy,Jonathan | (1335 ABD) | | | **Cabrera,Melky** | **(2153 ABB)** | | |
| | Barnhart,Tucker | (1035 ACB) | | | Zimmer,Bradley | (2403 ADC) | | |
| | Kiner-Falefa,Isiah (23) | (1253 ABC) | | | Grossman,Robert | (2123 ACA) | | |
| | Astudillo,Willians | (1051 AFC) | | | Luplow,Jordan | (2213 AFC) | | |
| | Vazquez,Christian | (0223 FDD) | | | Naquin,Tyler | (2231 DDC) | | |
| **Fringe** | Avila,Alex | (4001 CDF) | Rondon,Jose | (3221 ADA) | Marisnick,Jake | (4511 BFD) | | |
| | Casali,Curtis | (3013 AFB) | Vogt,Stephen | (2021 FDA) | Altherr,Aaron | (4313 DDF) | | |
| | Iannetta,Chris | (3113 ADF) | Rivera,T.J. | (1241 FFB) | Shaw,Chris | (4303 ACC) | | |
| | Castro,Jason | (3103 FDD) | | | Fisher,Derek | (3301 ACB) | | |
| | McCann,James | (2013 ACD) | | | Field,Johnny | (3311 ACA) | | |
| | Hicks,John (1) | (2111 BDA) | | | Engel,Adam | (2503 ACB) | | |
| | Romine,Austin | (2221 AFC) | | | Dean,Austin | (2331 ACB) | | |
| | Mesoraco,Devin | (2111 FFC) | | | Alford,Anthony | (2301 BFF) | | |
| | Wieters,Matt | (2023 FCB) | | | Herrera,Rosell | (1331 ACB) | | |
| | Sisco,Chance | (2103 ADC) | | | **Andreoli,John** | **(1501 ABA)** | | |
| | McCann,Brian | (2013 DDB) | | | Jay,Jon | (1341 CCB) | | |
| | Martin,Russell (3) | (2011 BCB) | | | Pence,Hunter | (1321 FCD) | | |
| | Plawecki,Kevin | (2011 BDC) | | | Williams,Mason | (1221 DDB) | | |
| | Knapp,Andrew | (2401 ADD) | | | Martini,Nick | (1221 ACB) | | |
| | Stassi,Max | (2101 BFB) | | | Heredia,Guillermo | (1121 ADA) | | |
| | Ciuffo,Nick | (2301 AFA) | | | Jackson,Austin | (1301 FDF) | | |
| | Murphy,John | (2003 AFB) | | | Cuevas,Noel | (1311 ACB) | | |
| | Perez,Roberto | (2101 BFC) | | | Sierra,Magneuris | (0521 AFC) | | |
| | Caratini,Victor (1) | (1221 ADD) | | | Tilson,Charlie | (0511 FFC) | | |
| | Swihart,Blake | (1301 DFD) | | | | | | |

# Universal Draft Grid

| TIER | STARTING PITCHERS | | RELIEF PITCHERS | |
|---|---|---|---|---|
| **Elite** | deGrom,Jacob (5405 BAA) | Scherzer,Max (5505 BAA) | | |
| | Kluber,Corey (5405 CAB) | Verlander,Justin (4505 CAB) | | |
| | Sale,Chris (5505 DAB) | | | |
| **Gold** | Kershaw,Clayton (5403 FAA) | Cole,Gerrit (4505 DAB) | | |
| **Stars** | Carrasco,Carlos (5405 DAA) | Nola,Aaron (4305 BAA) | Diaz,Edwin (5530 ABC) | |
| | Syndergaard,Noah (5303 FBA) | Severino,Luis (4405 AAB) | Jansen,Kenley (5530 CAB) | |
| | Bauer,Trevor (4405 CAA) | Snell,Blake (4405 ABB) | Kimbrel,Craig (5530 BAC) | |
| | Buehler,Walker (4403 CDB) | Mikolas,Miles (3105 AAC) | Treinen,Blake (5431 ABB) | |
| | Greinke,Zack (4305 CAA) | | Vazquez,Felipe (5531 ABA) | |
| **Regulars** | Corbin,Patrick (5405 DAB) | Hendricks,Kyle (3105 CAA) | Chapman,Aroldis (5530 DBB) | Hader,Josh (4521 ACC) |
| | Paxton,James (4403 FBA) | Price,David (3303 FAA) | Doolittle,Sean (5530 FCB) | Iglesias,Raisel (4431 DBA) |
| | Strasburg,Stephen (4503 FAA) | Berrios,Jose (2305 ABB) | Hand,Brad (5530 ABA) | Davis,Wade (3530 CBA) |
| | Tanaka,Masahiro (4303 DAA) | Clevinger,Michael (2305 ABB) | Osuna,Roberto (5430 ABB) | Leclerc,Jose (3530 BDD) |
| | Flaherty,Jack (3405 ADB) | Foltynewicz,Mike (2305 CBB) | Yates,Kirby (5530 CDB) | |
| **Mid-Level** | Archer,Chris (4405 CAA) | Wheeler,Zack (3303 FCB) | Alvarado,Jose (5520 ABB) | Allen,Cody (3520 ABB) |
| | Morton,Charlie (4403 FBA) | Wood,Alex (3203 FBA) | Betances,Dellin (5520 ACC) | Maeda,Kenta (3403 CAA) |
| | Bieber,Shane (3203 ADA) | Arrieta,Jake (2205 AAA) | Dominguez,Seranthony (5520 AFF) | Minter,A.J. (3420 ADB) |
| | Castillo,Luis (3303 ACA) | Bumgarner,Madison (2203 FAA) | Giles,Ken (5530 ABA) | Morrow,Brandon (3320 FDF) |
| | Gray,Jonathan (3305 DAA) | Hamels,Cole (2205 DAB) | Robertson,David (5520 ABB) | Steckenrider,Drew (3521 ADC) |
| | Hill,Rich (3403 FBA) | Happ,J.A. (2303 DAA) | Smith,Will (5520 FDB) | |
| | Keuchel,Dallas (3105 DAB) | Lester,Jon (2205 BAB) | Bradley,Archie (4320 CCB) | |
| | Marquez,German (3305 AAB) | Porcello,Rick (2205 AAB) | Familia,Jeurys (4420 FBA) | |
| | Martinez,Carlos (3303 DAA) | Quintana,Jose (2205 AAA) | Jeffress,Jeremy (4320 BBC) | |
| | Taillon,Jameson (3205 CBB) | Rodriguez,Eduardo (2303 FBA) | Rogers,Taylor (4321 ADB) | |
| **Bench** | Ryu,Hyun-Jin (4301 FCC) | Junis,Jakob (2203 ACB) | Barnes,Matt (5510 ACB) | Givens,Mychal (3421 ACA) |
| | Stripling,Ross (4303 CAA) | Kikuchi,Yusei (2203 AAC) | Britton,Zach (5220 FBB) | Green,Chad (3411 BDC) |
| | Darvish,Yu (3503 FCA) | Lynn,Lance (2203 FBB) | Castillo,Jose (5510 BFF) | Hernandez,David (3310 FCA) |
| | Eovaldi,Nathan (3203 FCB) | Matz,Steven (2303 FBC) | Knebel,Corey (5520 DBB) | Herrera,Kelvin (3210 DBB) |
| | Glasnow,Tyler (3403 BCC) | Reyes,Alex (2401 FFF) | Miller,Andrew (5510 FCB) | Hunter,Tommy (3110 DDB) |
| | Lucchesi,Joey (3303 CDA) | Roark,Tanner (2105 AAA) | Pressly,Ryan (5411 CCB) | Lugo,Seth (3211 DCB) |
| | Musgrove,Joe (3203 DCA) | Ross,Joe (2103 FDD) | Cishek,Steve (4310 BCA) | Rodriguez,Richard (3411 ADC) |
| | Pivetta,Nick (3303 ACC) | Skaggs,Tyler (2301 FCB) | Colome,Alexander (4310 BAC) | Romo,Sergio (3420 DCA) |
| | Ray,Robbie (3503 DAA) | Anderson,Chase (1203 DAB) | Devenski,Chris (4400 BCA) | Strahm,Matt (3401 FDC) |
| | Anderson,Tyler (2203 DBA) | Boyd,Matt (1205 ABB) | Ferguson,Caleb (4401 AFF) | Trivino,Lou (3410 ADA) |
| | Bundy,Dylan (2303 BAA) | Chacin,Jhoulys (1105 CAA) | Kela,Keone (4510 DCA) | Burnes,Corbin (2201 ADB) |
| | Chirinos,Yonny (2103 CDC) | Freeland,Kyle (1103 ABB) | McHugh,Collin (4501 FCB) | Neshek,Pat (2210 FDC) |
| | Eflin,Zach (2203 DDF) | Hellickson,Jeremy (1003 DAC) | Neris,Hector (4520 ACB) | Petit,Yusmeiro (2201 ACB) |
| | Fiers,Mike (2203 BAA) | Mengden,Daniel (1003 DDB) | Peacock,Brad (4511 DCC) | Vizcaino,Arodys (2420 FCA) |
| | Gausman,Kevin (2205 CAA) | Minor,Mike (1203 FCF) | Stammen,Craig (4311 DDD) | |
| | Godley,Zachary (2303 ABF) | Samardzija,Jeff (1103 FAB) | Strop,Pedro (4310 CCB) | |
| | Gonzales,Marco (2103 BCB) | Urena,Jose (1003 BBB) | Boxberger,Brad (3520 FCC) | |
| | Heaney,Andrew (2203 FCF) | | Fry,Jace (3520 ADD) | |
| **Fringe** | Honeywell,Brent (3301 FFC) | Duffy,Danny (1203 DAB) | Harris,Will (5400 CCA) | Erlin,Robert (2101 FDA) |
| | Loaisiga,Jonathan (3401 AFF) | Faria,Jake (1201 FDB) | Perez,Oliver (5500 ADD) | Floro,Dylan (2100 ADD) |
| | Pineda,Michael (3301 FCA) | Gomber,Austin (1201 ADC) | Alexander,Scott (4210 BDC) | Greene,Shane (2320 CCA) |
| | Salazar,Danny (3501 FCA) | Gonsalves,Stephen (1101 ADD) | Black,Ray (4500 FFC) | Hicks,Jordan (2211 ADF) |
| | Soroka,Michael (3100 FDB) | Gonzalez,Gio (1203 AAA) | Castillo,Diego (4410 AFC) | Hildenberger,Trevor (2220 ADC) |
| | DeSclafani,Anthony (2203 FDB) | Holland,Derek (1203 FBC) | Oberg,Scott (4200 CDC) | Jimenez,Joe (2410 ADF) |
| | Fried,Max (2303 CDC) | Kennedy,Ian (1203 FAA) | Otero,Dan (4000 ACA) | Kelley,Shawn (2300 FDF) |
| | Fulmer,Michael (2103 DBA) | Lauer,Eric (1103 CDA) | Ottavino,Adam (4510 FCF) | Montgomery,Mike (2101 ABA) |
| | German,Domingo (2401 BDB) | LeBlanc,Wade (1101 BCB) | Buttrey,Ty (3320 ADC) | Moronta,Reyes (2500 ADA) |
| | Gibson,Kyle (2103 CBC) | Lopez,Reynaldo (1203 ABA) | Chavez,Jesse (3200 BBB) | Norris,Bud (2310 DBA) |
| | Gray,Sonny (2203 DBA) | Newcomb,Sean (1303 ACA) | Cimber,Adam (3001 ADB) | Ramirez,Noe (2301 ADC) |
| | Harvey,Matt (2203 FBC) | Odorizzi,Jake (1203 CAA) | Dyson,Sam (3110 ABD) | Reed,Addison (2211 BCB) |
| | Karns,Nathan (2301 FDB) | Peralta,Freddy (1503 ADA) | Edwards,Carl (3500 CDC) | Rodney,Fernando (2420 BBA) |
| | Leake,Mike (2005 BAA) | Rodon,Carlos (1203 FBB) | Hirano,Yoshihisa (3210 ABC) | Swarzak,Anthony (2210 FDD) |
| | Lopez,Pablo (2101 CFF) | Rodriguez,Dereck (1003 ADF) | Hughes,Jared (3010 BCB) | Tepera,Ryan (2310 BCA) |
| | Luzardo,Jesus (2203 AFF) | Santana,Ervin (1101 FBC) | Jones,Nate (3410 FDB) | VerHagen,Drew (2201 FDF) |
| | Miley,Wade (2103 FBB) | Smith,Caleb (1301 FDA) | Maton,Phil (3410 CDA) | Vincent,Nick (2300 DCB) |
| | Nova,Ivan (2005 DAA) | Straily,Dan (1205 CAA) | May,Trevor (3510 FDC) | Warren,Adam (2200 FDB) |
| | Paulino,David (2301 CDB) | Teheran,Julio (1203 BAB) | Melancon,Mark (3110 FCB) | Wilson,Justin (2500 ACA) |
| | Pena,Felix (2201 ADF) | Williams,Trevor (1003 ABA) | Nicasio,Juan (3410 DCA) | Wood,Hunter (2311 ADD) |
| | Richards,Trevor (2203 ADA) | Yarbrough,Ryan (1103 ACC) | Oh,Seung-Hwan (3400 ABD) | Woodruff,Brandon (2201 CDB) |
| | Sabathia,CC (2203 FAA) | Zimmermann,Jordan (1103 DBB) | Parker,Blake (3310 ACB) | Gsellman,Robert (1121 CCD) |
| | Sanchez,Anibal (2203 FBF) | | Roe,Chaz (3310 FDC) | Hardy,Blaine (1103 CDF) |
| | Senzatela,Antonio (2101 BCB) | | Rondon,Hector (3410 BCA) | Holder,Jonathan (1310 ADD) |
| | Shoemaker,Matthew (2201 FCB) | | Scott,Tanner (3510 ADD) | Miller,Justin (1210 ADF) |
| | Smyly,Drew (2301 FDF) | | Smith,Joe (3300 DDC) | Robles,Hansel (1310 BDB) |
| | Toussaint,Touki (2301 ADC) | | Soria,Joakim (3410 DCB) | Stanek,Ryne (1411 ADA) |
| | Urias,Julio (2201 FDC) | | Watson,Tony (3310 ACB) | Stock,Robert (1100 AFF) |
| | Velasquez,Vincent (2303 FBB) | | Winkler,Daniel (3410 FDD) | Glover,Koda (0110 FDC) |
| | Wacha,Michael (2203 FBA) | | Alvarez,Jose (2210 ADA) | |
| | Wainwright,Adam (2201 FBB) | | Arano,Victor (2310 BDD) | |
| | Walker,Taijuan (2201 FCA) | | Baez,Pedro (2300 DCC) | |
| | Weaver,Luke (2201 ACB) | | Bedrosian,Cam (2300 DDB) | |
| | Whitley,Forrest (2300 AFF) | | Brach,Brad (2310 ACB) | |
| | Barria,Jaime (1103 ADA) | | Bracho,Silvino (2310 ADB) | |
| | Borucki,Ryan (1003 ADC) | | Brasier,Ryan (2100 CDD) | |
| | Buchholz,Clay (1101 FCF) | | Cahill,Trevor (2201 FDB) | |
| | Chen,Wei-Yin (1103 FCA) | | Clippard,Tyler (2510 ACA) | |
| | Davies,Zachary (1103 FBA) | | Conley,Adam (2211 BCC) | |

## Universal Draft Grid

| TIER | STARTING PITCHERS | | | | RELIEF PITCHERS | | | |
|---|---|---|---|---|---|---|---|---|
| Below | McCullers,Lance | (4500 FBA) | Chatwood,Tyler | (0101 DBB) | Cingrani,Tony | (4500 FDC) | Hudson,Dakota | (1001 ADB) |
| Fringe | Richards,Garrett | (3300 FDA) | Colon,Bartolo | (0001 DAB) | Garcia,Luis | (4300 DDB) | Maurer,Brandon | (1200 BCD) |
| | Stroman,Marcus | (3103 FAA) | Covey,Dylan | (0001 DDC) | Hill,Tim | (4210 ADC) | Mayers,Mike | (1200 BDC) |
| | Anderson,Brett | (2000 FDB) | Estrada,Marco | (0103 CAB) | Bummer,Aaron | (3200 AFA) | McGee,Jake | (1200 DCB) |
| | Beeks,Jalen | (2201 ADB) | Fillmyer,Heath | (0001 ADC) | Chafin,Andrew | (3310 CDA) | Middleton,Keynan | (1310 FDB) |
| | Cueto,Johnny | (2100 FAB) | Gallardo,Yovani | (0001 CBA) | Claudio,Alexander | (3010 FCB) | Minaya,Juan | (1310 BDA) |
| | Fedde,Erick | (2101 DDB) | Giolito,Lucas | (0103 ACA) | Diekman,Jake | (3500 CDB) | Pagan,Emilio | (1300 ADD) |
| | Keller,Mitch | (2200 AFC) | Gohara,Luiz | (0200 DDC) | Drake,Oliver | (3400 ADA) | Ramirez,Erasmo | (1101 FCA) |
| | Manaea,Sean | (2100 DBA) | Hess,David | (0001 ADC) | Martin,Christopher | (3200 DDC) | Rosario,Randy | (1000 AFF) |
| | Reed,Cody | (2201 ADA) | Jackson,Edwin | (0001 CCB) | Petricka,Jacob | (3210 FDC) | Smith,Burch | (1300 DDD) |
| | Turnbull,Spencer | (2201 AFC) | Kingham,Nick | (0000 ADA) | Andriese,Matt | (2301 DCA) | Strickland,Hunter | (1210 DCB) |
| | Allard,Kolby | (1000 ADA) | Koch,Matt | (0000 ADF) | Barnes,Jacob | (2310 BDB) | Tomlin,Josh | (1001 FBB) |
| | Bailey,Homer | (1101 FDF) | Mejia,Adalberto | (0000 DDB) | Brebbia,John | (2300 ADF) | Velazquez,Hector | (1001 ADA) |
| | Cobb,Alex | (1003 FBF) | Mendez,Yohander | (0001 ADF) | Brice,Austin | (2100 DDB) | Williams,Taylor | (1300 CDC) |
| | De Los Santos,Enyel | (1100 ADA) | Mitchell,Bryan | (0001 FDB) | Feliz,Michael | (2400 CDB) | Wisler,Matthew | (1101 ADB) |
| | Eickhoff,Jerad | (1201 FBB) | Nix,Jacob | (0003 AFC) | Grace,Matt | (2000 DDB) | Wright,Steven | (1001 FCC) |
| | Fister,Doug | (1001 FCB) | Pannone,Thomas | (0101 ADC) | Hembree,Heath | (2400 ADA) | Brault,Steven | (0100 ACD) |
| | Gant,John | (1101 DDB) | Perez,Martin | (0001 FAA) | Holland,Greg | (2410 CCC) | Butler,Eddie | (0000 FDD) |
| | Gaviglio,Sam | (1101 ADA) | Plutko,Adam | (0001 ADF) | Kelly,Joe | (2310 DDA) | Castro,Miguel | (0001 BDF) |
| | Guerra,Junior | (1201 DCD) | Poncedeleon,Daniel | (0100 ADA) | Kintzler,Brandon | (2000 DCA) | Farmer,Buck | (0100 ACB) |
| | Hernandez,Felix | (1103 FBA) | Ramirez,Yefry | (0201 ADA) | Kittredge,Andrew | (2200 ADF) | Flynn,Brian | (0001 FDF) |
| | Keller,Brad | (2203 AFF) | Rodriguez,Jefry | (1200 FFF) | Leone,Dominic | (2300 FDC) | Guerrero,Tayron | (0210 BDF) |
| | Liriano,Francisco | (2201 DDB) | Romero,Fernando | (1101 ADB) | Lorenzen,Michael | (2101 FCB) | **Hammel,Jason** | **(0101 AAB)** |
| | Mahle,Tyler | (2203 AFF) | Sampson,Adrian | (1200 FFF) | Lyles,Jordan | (2200 FDC) | Hernandez,Elieser | (0000 DDF) |
| | Miller,Shelby | (2201 DDB) | Shields,James | (1101 ADB) | McAllister,Zach | (2300 BDA) | Johnson,Brian | (0101 BDC) |
| | Montas,Frankie | (1101 DDD) | Skoglund,Eric | (0001 FDD) | McCarthy,Kevin | (2000 ADB) | Lopez,Jorge | (0101 ADC) |
| | Montgomery,Jordan | (1200 FCA) | | | Olson,Tyler | (2300 CDF) | Magill,Matthew | (0200 ADC) |
| | Norris,Daniel | (1303 FCB) | | | Pazos,James | (2300 ADB) | Moore,Matt | (0201 DAA) |
| | Reid-Foley,Sean | (1201 ADF) | | | Pruitt,Austin | (2101 ADC) | Peralta,Wily | (0210 DDA) |
| | Richard,Clayton | (1003 DAA) | | | Ramirez,Neil | (2500 DDA) | Pomeranz,Drew | (0201 FBC) |
| | Romano,Sal | (1103 ACA) | | | Ramos,Edubray | (2300 CDB) | Ramos,A.J. | (0410 FBB) |
| | Ross,Tyson | (1100 FCF) | | | Santana,Edgar | (2100 ADB) | Santiago,Hector | (0201 FBB) |
| | Sanchez,Aaron | (1103 FBC) | | | Shreve,Chasen | (2400 ADA) | Wright,Mike | (0111 CCA) |
| | Sheffield,Justus | (1101 ADF) | | | Tuivailala,Sam | (2300 DDD) | | |
| | Sims,Lucas | (1301 ADA) | | | Wilson,Alex | (2000 DCB) | | |
| | Stratton,Chris | (1101 ADB) | | | Anderson,Justin | (1310 ADF) | | |
| | Suarez,Andrew | (1003 ADB) | | | Barraclough,Kyle | (1411 CCB) | | |
| | Suter,Brent | (1000 FCA) | | | Biagini,Joe | (1100 ADC) | | |
| | Tropeano,Nicholas | (1201 FDA) | | | Blach,Ty | (1001 ABC) | | |
| | Vargas,Jason | (1103 FCB) | | | Bradford,Chase | (1000 ADB) | | |
| | Volquez,Edinson | (1101 DCA) | | | Crick,Kyle | (1300 ADD) | | |
| | Wright,Kyle | (1100 AFF) | | | Font,Wilmer | (1101 FDB) | | |
| | Alcantara,Sandy | (0101 CDC) | | | Garcia,Jaime | (1201 DBB) | | |
| | Bettis,Chad | (0000 FBC) | | | Garrett,Amir | (1300 BDF) | | |
| | Cashner,Andrew | (0003 DAA) | | | Goody,Nicholas | (1400 FDC) | | |

# SIMULATION LEAGUE DRAFT  TOP 500+

| NAME | POS | RAR | NAME | POS | RAR | NAME | POS | RAR | NAME | POS | RAR |
|------|-----|-----|------|-----|-----|------|-----|-----|------|-----|-----|
| Trout,Mike | 8 | 80.0 | Gennett,Scooter | 4 | 21.4 | Bieber,Shane | P | 13.7 | Tapia,Raimel | 8 | 9.6 |
| Betts,Mookie | 9 | 62.2 | Sanchez,Gary | 2 | 21.3 | Keuchel,Dallas | P | 13.6 | Zobrist,Ben | 479 | 9.6 |
| Martinez,J.D. | 79 | 58.7 | Greinke,Zack | P | 21.3 | Dominguez,Seranthony | P | 13.6 | Godley,Zachary | P | 9.5 |
| Sale,Chris | P | 57.3 | Contreras,Willson | 2 | 21.2 | Treinen,Blake | P | 13.6 | Inciarte,Ender | 8 | 9.5 |
| Arenado,Nolan | 5 | 47.8 | Torres,Gleyber | 46 | 21.2 | Iglesias,Raisel | P | 13.5 | Berrios,Jose | P | 9.4 |
| Ramirez,Jose | 5 | 47.2 | Guerrero Jr.,Vladimir | 0 | 21.2 | Castillo,Jose | P | 13.5 | Schwarber,Kyle | 7 | 9.4 |
| Goldschmidt,Paul | 3 | 46.6 | Baez,Javier | 456 | 21.1 | Barnes,Matt | P | 13.4 | Clevinger,Michael | P | 9.4 |
| Altuve,Jose | 4 | 44.9 | Carrasco,Carlos | P | 20.9 | Hill,Rich | P | 13.4 | Colome,Alexander | P | 9.3 |
| Yelich,Christian | 789 | 44.8 | Mikolas,Miles | P | 20.8 | Martinez,Jose | 39 | 13.4 | Rogers,Taylor | P | 9.3 |
| Blackmon,Charlie | 8 | 44.5 | Encarnacion,Edwin | 3 | 20.5 | Robles,Victor | 8 | 13.1 | Chapman,Matt | 5 | 9.3 |
| Votto,Joey | 3 | 44.4 | Tanaka,Masahiro | P | 20.2 | Hader,Josh | P | 13.1 | Hedges,Austin | 2 | 9.2 |
| Lindor,Francisco | 6 | 41.6 | Davis,Khristopher | 0 | 20.2 | Hendricks,Kyle | P | 13.0 | Iannetta,Chris | 2 | 9.2 |
| Freeman,Freddie | 3 | 40.8 | Morton,Charlie | P | 20.1 | DeJong,Paul | 6 | 12.9 | Devenski,Chris | P | 9.1 |
| Scherzer,Max | P | 40.7 | Marquez,German | P | 20.0 | Jansen,Danny | 2 | 12.8 | Albies,Ozzie | 4 | 9.1 |
| Machado,Manny | 6 | 40.6 | Pollock,A.J. | 8 | 19.9 | Ozuna,Marcell | 7 | 12.8 | Hamels,Cole | P | 9.1 |
| Judge,Aaron | 9 | 40.1 | Profar,Jurickson | 356 | 19.7 | Diaz,Edwin | P | 12.7 | Chisenhall,Lonnie | 9 | 9.0 |
| Rendon,Anthony | 5 | 38.3 | Flaherty,Jack | P | 19.3 | Moustakas,Mike | 5 | 12.6 | Gallo,Joey | 37 | 8.8 |
| Soto,Juan | 7 | 37.8 | Shaw,Travis | 45 | 19.0 | Lucchesi,Joey | P | 12.6 | Strahm,Matt | P | 8.8 |
| Bregman,Alex | 56 | 37.3 | Suarez,Eugenio | 5 | 18.7 | Peacock,Brad | P | 12.5 | Narvaez,Omar | 2 | 8.7 |
| deGrom,Jacob | P | 36.6 | Peralta,David | 7 | 18.7 | Gregorius,Didi | 6 | 12.5 | Eovaldi,Nathan | P | 8.7 |
| Story,Trevor | 6 | 36.5 | Benintendi,Andrew | 78 | 18.5 | Martinez,Carlos | P | 12.3 | Neris,Hector | P | 8.7 |
| Harper,Bryce | 89 | 36.2 | Miller,Andrew | P | 18.3 | Pressly,Ryan | P | 12.2 | Turner,Trea | 6 | 8.7 |
| Turner,Justin | 5 | 35.0 | Kimbrel,Craig | P | 18.0 | Piscotty,Stephen | 9 | 12.2 | Kela,Keone | P | 8.6 |
| Stanton,Giancarlo | 79 | 34.7 | Bellinger,Cody | 38 | 17.9 | Vazquez,Felipe | P | 12.1 | Kendrick,Howie | 4 | 8.6 |
| Bogaerts,Xander | 6 | 34.3 | Conforto,Michael | 78 | 17.9 | Cabrera,Asdrubal | 456 | 12.0 | Watson,Tony | P | 8.6 |
| Kershaw,Clayton | P | 32.1 | Senzel,Nick | 0 | 17.2 | Perez,Salvador | 2 | 12.0 | Stroman,Marcus | P | 8.6 |
| Kluber,Corey | P | 31.2 | Eaton,Adam | 9 | 17.0 | Alvarado,Jose | P | 11.9 | Familia,Jeurys | P | 8.5 |
| Corbin,Patrick | P | 30.8 | Castillo,Luis | P | 17.0 | Cervelli,Francisco | 2 | 11.9 | Diaz,Aledmys | 56 | 8.5 |
| Cano,Robinson | 4 | 30.5 | Stripling,Ross | P | 16.9 | Muncy,Max | 35 | 11.6 | D'Arnaud,Travis | 2 | 8.4 |
| Winker,Jesse | 79 | 29.2 | Severino,Luis | P | 16.6 | Bumgarner,Madison | P | 11.6 | Happ,Ian | 789 | 8.4 |
| Seager,Corey | 6 | 28.5 | Jansen,Kenley | P | 16.5 | Mejia,Francisco | 2 | 11.6 | Musgrove,Joe | P | 8.3 |
| Verlander,Justin | P | 28.2 | Dahl,David | 79 | 16.5 | Glasnow,Tyler | P | 11.5 | Pina,Manny | 2 | 8.3 |
| Bryant,Kris | 5 | 27.8 | McCutchen,Andrew | 9 | 16.2 | LeMahieu,DJ | 4 | 11.2 | Beltre,Adrian | 5 | 8.3 |
| Nola,Aaron | P | 27.0 | Dozier,Brian | 4 | 16.1 | Wheeler,Zack | P | 11.2 | Ottavino,Adam | P | 8.3 |
| Ohtani,Shohei | 0 | 26.9 | Gray,Jonathan | P | 16.1 | Suzuki,Kurt | 2 | 11.1 | Voit,Luke | 3 | 8.2 |
| Andujar,Miguel | 5 | 26.8 | Marte,Ketel | 46 | 15.9 | Britton,Zach | P | 11.1 | Arrieta,Jake | P | 8.2 |
| Donaldson,Josh | 5 | 26.8 | Cruz,Nelson | 0 | 15.8 | Pederson,Joc | 78 | 11.0 | Castro,Starlin | 4 | 8.1 |
| Hicks,Aaron | 8 | 26.4 | Aguilar,Jesus | 3 | 15.7 | Braun,Ryan | 7 | 11.0 | Cishek,Steve | P | 8.1 |
| Rizzo,Anthony | 3 | 26.3 | Molina,Yadier | 2 | 15.7 | Simmons,Andrelton | 6 | 11.0 | Perez,Oliver | P | 8.1 |
| Pham,Thomas | 78 | 26.2 | Nimmo,Brandon | 789 | 15.6 | Smith,Mallex | 789 | 10.9 | Maeda,Kenta | P | 8.0 |
| Syndergaard,Noah | P | 26.2 | Posey,Buster | 2 | 15.4 | Doolittle,Sean | P | 10.8 | Reyes,Franmil | 9 | 7.9 |
| Betances,Dellin | P | 26.2 | Taillon,Jameson | P | 15.3 | Stammen,Craig | P | 10.8 | Rodriguez,Eduardo | P | 7.9 |
| Hoskins,Rhys | 7 | 26.1 | Knebel,Corey | P | 15.3 | Smith,Will | P | 10.8 | Polanco,Gregory | 9 | 7.9 |
| Bauer,Trevor | P | 25.5 | Abreu,Jose | 3 | 15.2 | Kemp,Matt | 79 | 10.7 | Taylor,Chris | 678 | 7.9 |
| Grandal,Yasmani | 2 | 25.2 | Cespedes,Yoenis | 7 | 15.1 | Escobar,Eduardo | 56 | 10.6 | Dyson,Sam | P | 7.7 |
| Murphy,Daniel | 4 | 25.0 | Dickerson,Corey | 7 | 15.1 | Leclerc,Jose | P | 10.6 | Zunino,Mike | 2 | 7.7 |
| Realmuto,Jacob | 2 | 24.9 | Puig,Yasiel | 9 | 15.1 | Ferguson,Caleb | P | 10.5 | Trivino,Lou | P | 7.6 |
| Cain,Lorenzo | 8 | 24.6 | Ramos,Wilson | 2 | 15.0 | Foltynewicz,Mike | P | 10.5 | Strop,Pedro | P | 7.6 |
| Archer,Chris | P | 24.3 | Yates,Kirby | P | 14.9 | Belt,Brandon | 3 | 10.4 | Pearce,Steve | 3 | 7.6 |
| Carpenter,Matt | 35 | 23.8 | Jimenez,Eloy | 0 | 14.6 | Harris,Will | P | 10.4 | Choo,Shin-Soo | 79 | 7.5 |
| Acuna,Ronald | 7 | 23.6 | Thames,Eric | 39 | 14.6 | Osuna,Roberto | P | 10.3 | Edwards,Carl | P | 7.5 |
| Correa,Carlos | 6 | 23.5 | Robertson,David | P | 14.6 | Happ,J.A. | P | 10.3 | Steckenrider,Drew | P | 7.5 |
| Castellanos,Nick | 9 | 23.4 | Rosario,Eddie | 7 | 14.5 | Jones,Adam | 89 | 10.3 | Mazara,Nomar | 9 | 7.5 |
| Cole,Gerrit | P | 23.1 | Wood,Alex | P | 14.4 | Ryu,Hyun-Jin | P | 10.1 | Gomes,Yan | 2 | 7.4 |
| Paxton,James | P | 23.0 | Segura,Jean | 6 | 14.4 | Green,Chad | P | 10.1 | Smoak,Justin | 3 | 7.4 |
| Snell,Blake | P | 22.8 | Olson,Matt | 3 | 14.2 | Porcello,Rick | P | 10.0 | Polanco,Jorge | 6 | 7.2 |
| Springer,George | 89 | 22.1 | Hernandez,Enrique | 468 | 14.2 | Bruce,Jay | 39 | 9.9 | Paulino,David | P | 7.2 |
| Buehler,Walker | P | 22.0 | Upton,Justin | 7 | 14.1 | Lowrie,Jed | 4 | 9.9 | Pivetta,Nick | P | 7.2 |
| Cabrera,Miguel | 3 | 21.9 | Hand,Brad | P | 14.1 | Flowers,Tyler | 2 | 9.9 | Luzardo,Jesus | P | 7.1 |
| Chapman,Aroldis | P | 21.7 | Garver,Mitch | 2 | 14.0 | McNeil,Jeff | 4 | 9.8 | Davis,Wade | P | 7.1 |
| Merrifield,Whit | 48 | 21.6 | Price,David | P | 13.8 | Chirinos,Robinson | 2 | 9.8 | May,Trevor | P | 7.1 |
| Brantley,Michael | 7 | 21.4 | Strasburg,Stephen | P | 13.8 | McHugh,Collin | P | 9.7 | Winkler,Daniel | P | 7.1 |
| Haniger,Mitch | 89 | 21.4 | Marte,Starling | 8 | 13.7 | Barnhart,Tucker | 2 | 9.7 | Loaisiga,Jonathan | P | 7.0 |

# SIMULATION LEAGUE DRAFT          TOP 500+

| NAME | POS | RAR | NAME | POS | RAR | NAME | POS | RAR | NAME | POS | RAR |
|------|-----|-----|------|-----|-----|------|-----|-----|------|-----|-----|
| Fry,Jace | P | 7.0 | Adames,Willy | 6 | 5.1 | Gurriel,Lourdes | 46 | 3.6 | Kipnis,Jason | 4 | 2.5 |
| Markakis,Nick | 9 | 6.9 | Wendle,Joe | 45 | 5.1 | Holland,Derek | P | 3.5 | Shoemaker,Matthew | P | 2.5 |
| Peraza,Jose | 6 | 6.9 | Otero,Dan | P | 5.1 | Morales,Kendrys | 0 | 3.5 | Floro,Dylan | P | 2.5 |
| Chirinos,Yonny | P | 6.9 | Andriese,Matt | P | 5.0 | Nunez,Eduardo | 45 | 3.5 | VerHagen,Drew | P | 2.5 |
| Castillo,Diego | P | 6.8 | Oh,Seung-Hwan | P | 5.0 | Chafin,Andrew | P | 3.5 | Tepera,Ryan | P | 2.5 |
| Kepler,Max | 89 | 6.8 | Givens,Mychal | P | 5.0 | Petit,Yusmeiro | P | 3.5 | Hiura,Keston | 0 | 2.4 |
| Gyorko,Jedd | 5 | 6.8 | Schoop,Jonathan | 4 | 5.0 | Avila,Alex | 2 | 3.4 | Adams,Matt | 3 | 2.4 |
| Rondon,Hector | P | 6.8 | Herrera,Odubel | 8 | 5.0 | Ramirez,Noe | P | 3.4 | Wilson,Alex | P | 2.4 |
| Gonzalez,Carlos | 9 | 6.7 | Eflin,Zach | P | 4.9 | Maton,Phil | P | 3.4 | Swarzak,Anthony | P | 2.3 |
| Lowe,Brandon | 4 | 6.7 | Warren,Adam | P | 4.9 | Bundy,Dylan | P | 3.4 | Vincent,Nick | P | 2.3 |
| Myers,Wil | 57 | 6.7 | Smith,Joe | P | 4.9 | Hildenberger,Trevor | P | 3.4 | Reynolds,Mark | 3 | 2.3 |
| Brasier,Ryan | P | 6.7 | Cimber,Adam | P | 4.9 | Vogelbach,Daniel | 3 | 3.4 | Granderson,Curtis | 79 | 2.3 |
| Bell,Josh | 3 | 6.6 | Urias,Julio | P | 4.8 | Claudio,Alexander | P | 3.4 | Montgomery,Mike | P | 2.3 |
| Freeland,Kyle | P | 6.6 | Salazar,Danny | P | 4.8 | Fowler,Dexter | 9 | 3.4 | Cabrera,Melky | 9 | 2.3 |
| Lucroy,Jonathan | 2 | 6.6 | Santana,Domingo | 9 | 4.8 | Sheffield,Justus | P | 3.4 | Chacin,Jhoulys | P | 2.2 |
| Santana,Carlos | 3 | 6.6 | Wong,Kolten | 4 | 4.8 | Hicks,Jordan | P | 3.3 | Sabathia,CC | P | 2.2 |
| Andrus,Elvis | 6 | 6.6 | Giles,Ken | P | 4.8 | Grossman,Robert | 79 | 3.3 | McCann,Brian | 2 | 2.2 |
| Lugo,Seth | P | 6.6 | Wieters,Matt | 2 | 4.7 | McMahon,Ryan | 3 | 3.3 | Fiers,Mike | P | 2.2 |
| Urias,Luis | 4 | 6.6 | Anderson,Tyler | P | 4.7 | McCarthy,Kevin | P | 3.3 | Murphy,Tom | 2 | 2.2 |
| Diaz,Elias | 2 | 6.6 | Pedroia,Dustin | 4 | 4.7 | Moronta,Reyes | P | 3.3 | Garcia,Luis | P | 2.2 |
| Jeffress,Jeremy | P | 6.4 | Wood,Hunter | P | 4.6 | Lorenzen,Michael | P | 3.3 | Gardner,Brett | 78 | 2.1 |
| Reyes,Alex | P | 6.3 | Buttrey,Ty | P | 4.6 | Drake,Oliver | P | 3.3 | Walker,Taijuan | P | 2.1 |
| Honeywell,Brent | P | 6.2 | Minter,A.J. | P | 4.5 | Bour,Justin | 3 | 3.3 | Woodruff,Brandon | P | 2.1 |
| Scott,Tanner | P | 6.2 | Hundley,Nick | 2 | 4.5 | Mesoraco,Devin | 2 | 3.3 | Bracho,Silvino | P | 2.1 |
| Hampson,Garrett | 6 | 6.2 | Martin,Christopher | P | 4.5 | Pazos,James | P | 3.3 | Feliz,Michael | P | 2.1 |
| Quintana,Jose | P | 6.1 | Hernandez,David | P | 4.5 | Smyly,Drew | P | 3.3 | Lyles,Jordan | P | 2.1 |
| Hernandez,Cesar | 4 | 6.1 | Weaver,Luke | P | 4.5 | Clippard,Tyler | P | 3.2 | Ramos,Edubray | P | 2.0 |
| Alexander,Scott | P | 6.1 | Darvish,Yu | P | 4.4 | Zimmerman,Ryan | 3 | 3.2 | O Neill,Tyler | 9 | 1.9 |
| Renfroe,Hunter | 79 | 6.0 | Hirano,Yoshihisa | P | 4.4 | Bonifacio,Jorge | 9 | 3.2 | Reed,Addison | P | 1.9 |
| Semien,Marcus | 6 | 6.0 | Reed,Cody | P | 4.3 | Gibson,Kyle | P | 3.1 | Goodwin,Brian | 8 | 1.9 |
| Reddick,Josh | 79 | 6.0 | Erlin,Robert | P | 4.3 | Frazier,Clint | 7 | 3.1 | Parker,Blake | P | 1.9 |
| Astudillo,Willians | 2 | 5.9 | Jimenez,Joe | P | 4.2 | Bummer,Aaron | P | 3.1 | Tatis Jr.,Fernando | 0 | 1.9 |
| Roe,Chaz | P | 5.9 | Gonzales,Marco | P | 4.2 | Santana,Edgar | P | 3.1 | Pineda,Michael | P | 1.8 |
| Choi,Ji-Man | 0 | 5.9 | Diekman,Jake | P | 4.2 | Ross,Joe | P | 3.1 | Beckham,Tim | 56 | 1.8 |
| Boxberger,Brad | P | 5.9 | Gausman,Kevin | P | 4.1 | Ahmed,Nick | 6 | 3.1 | Franco,Maikel | 5 | 1.8 |
| Gonzalez,Marwin | 467 | 5.9 | Riley,Austin | 0 | 4.1 | Norris,Bud | P | 3.0 | Keller,Mitch | P | 1.8 |
| Heaney,Andrew | P | 5.9 | Lester,Jon | P | 4.1 | Span,Denard | 7 | 3.0 | Crick,Kyle | P | 1.8 |
| Bradley,Archie | P | 5.9 | German,Domingo | P | 4.1 | Vizcaino,Arodys | P | 3.0 | Wainwright,Adam | P | 1.8 |
| Allen,Cody | P | 5.8 | Alfaro,Jorge | 2 | 4.0 | Canha,Mark | 78 | 2.9 | Panik,Joe | 4 | 1.8 |
| Jones,Nate | P | 5.8 | Cron,C.J. | 3 | 4.0 | Frazier,Adam | 4 | 2.9 | Diaz,Yandy | 0 | 1.8 |
| Leake,Mike | P | 5.7 | Chavez,Jesse | P | 3.9 | Cingrani,Tony | P | 2.9 | Romo,Sergio | P | 1.8 |
| Soroka,Michael | P | 5.7 | Rosario,Amed | 6 | 3.9 | Martin,Russell | 25 | 2.8 | McAllister,Zach | P | 1.7 |
| Skaggs,Tyler | P | 5.6 | Hembree,Heath | P | 3.9 | Lopez,Pablo | P | 2.8 | Shreve,Chasen | P | 1.7 |
| Casali,Curtis | 2 | 5.6 | Lamb,Jake | 5 | 3.9 | Melancon,Mark | P | 2.8 | Samardzija,Jeff | P | 1.6 |
| Baez,Pedro | P | 5.6 | Gurriel,Yulieski | 35 | 3.9 | Black,Ray | P | 2.7 | Gray,Sonny | P | 1.6 |
| Bradley,Jackie | 8 | 5.5 | Moncada,Yoan | 4 | 3.9 | Schebler,Scott | 9 | 2.7 | Senzatela,Antonio | P | 1.6 |
| Rodriguez,Richard | P | 5.5 | Herrera,Kelvin | P | 3.9 | Caratini,Victor | 23 | 2.7 | Mengden,Daniel | P | 1.6 |
| Matz,Steven | P | 5.5 | Barreto,Franklin | 4 | 3.9 | Arano,Victor | P | 2.7 | Fedde,Erick | P | 1.6 |
| Descalso,Daniel | 45 | 5.5 | Wacha,Michael | P | 3.8 | Whitley,Forrest | P | 2.7 | Conley,Adam | P | 1.5 |
| Morrow,Brandon | P | 5.5 | Roark,Tanner | P | 3.8 | Meadows,Austin | 9 | 2.7 | Tuivailala,Sam | P | 1.5 |
| Mondesi,Adalberto | 6 | 5.5 | Hughes,Jared | P | 3.7 | Pena,Felix | P | 2.7 | Miley,Wade | P | 1.5 |
| Hunter,Tommy | P | 5.5 | Toussaint,Touki | P | 3.7 | Holder,Jonathan | P | 2.6 | Urena,Jose | P | 1.4 |
| Nicasio,Juan | P | 5.5 | Kikuchi,Yusei | P | 3.7 | Barnes,Jacob | P | 2.6 | Knapp,Andrew | 2 | 1.4 |
| Hill,Tim | P | 5.4 | Barnes,Austin | 2 | 3.7 | Ramirez,Neil | P | 2.6 | Olson,Tyler | P | 1.4 |
| Oberg,Scott | P | 5.4 | Velasquez,Vincent | P | 3.6 | Nova,Ivan | P | 2.6 | Middleton,Keynan | P | 1.4 |
| Ray,Robbie | P | 5.4 | Verdugo,Alex | 9 | 3.6 | Soler,Jorge | 9 | 2.6 | LeBlanc,Wade | P | 1.4 |
| Camargo,Johan | 5 | 5.3 | Lynn,Lance | P | 3.6 | Brach,Brad | P | 2.6 | Kintzler,Brandon | P | 1.3 |
| Castillo,Welington | 2 | 5.3 | Garcia,Avisail | 9 | 3.6 | Kelley,Shawn | P | 2.6 | Brebbia,John | P | 1.3 |
| Bichette,Bo | 6 | 5.3 | Buchholz,Clay | P | 3.6 | Fulmer,Michael | P | 2.6 | Kinsler,Ian | 4 | 1.2 |
| Soria,Joakim | P | 5.3 | Petricka,Jacob | P | 3.6 | Alvarez,Jose | P | 2.5 | Tellez,Rowdy | 3 | 1.2 |
| Devers,Rafael | 5 | 5.2 | Munoz,Yairo | 456 | 3.6 | Souza,Steven | 9 | 2.5 | Grichuk,Randal | 89 | 1.1 |
| Anderson,Chase | P | 5.1 | Wilson,Justin | P | 3.6 | Neshek,Pat | P | 2.5 | Cave,Jake | 8 | 1.1 |
| Burnes,Corbin | P | 5.1 | Bedrosian,Cam | P | 3.6 | Rodney,Fernando | P | 2.5 | Crawford,Brandon | 6 | 1.1 |

# LIVE EVENTS — THIS SPRING!

## *"An unforgettable experience"*

Get a head start on the 2019 season with a unique opportunity to go one-on-one with some of the top writers and analysts in the fantasy baseball industry. First Pitch Forums are coming to top US cities for lively and informative draft prep seminars.

Winning strategies! Player pool insights! Sleepers! Mock draft exercises! You will come away with the tools you need to win in 2019!

BaseballHQ.com founder Ron Shandler, and GMs Brent Hershey and Ray Murphy bring a dynamic energy to each event.  They are joined by BaseballHQ analysts and experts from ESPN.com, MLB.com, RotoWire, The Athletic.com, FanGraphs, Baseball Prospectus, Mastersball, and more.

### *Dates and locations to be announced soon!*

### For complete details visit *www.firstpitchforums.com*

### and follow *@BaseballHQ* on Twitter

---

Plus, don't forget "the best weekend of the year":
First Pitch Arizona in Phoenix at the Arizona Fall League.
October 31-November 3, 2019. Save the date!

# Get Forecaster Insights
# Every Single Day.

The **Baseball Forecaster** provides the core concepts in player evaluation and gaming strategy. You can maintain that edge all season long.

From spring training to the season's last pitch, **BaseballHQ.com** covers all aspects of what's happening on and off the field—all with the most powerful fantasy slant on the Internet:

- Nationally-renowned baseball analysts.
- MLB news analysis; including anticipating the **next** move.
- Dedicated columns on starting pitching, relievers, batters, and our popular Fact or Fluke? player profiles.
- Minor-league coverage beyond just scouting and lists.
- FAAB targets, starting pitcher reports, strategy articles, daily game resources, call-up profiles and more!

Plus, **BaseballHQ.com** gets personal, with customizable tools and valuable resources:

- Team Stat Tracker and Power Search tools
- Custom Draft Guide for YOUR league's parameters
- Sortable and downloadable stats and projection files
- Subscriber forums, the friendliest on the baseball Internet

Visit **www.baseballhq.com/subscribe**
to lock down your path to a 2019 championship!

**Full Season** subscription **$89**
(prorated at the time of order; auto-renews each October)

**Draft Prep** subscription **$39**
(complete access from January through April 30, 2019)

Please read our Terms of service at  www.baseballhq.com/terms.html

# Baseball Forecaster & BaseballHQ.com:
# Your season-long championship lineup.